THE ENCYCLOPEDIA OF
WORLD FACTS AND DATES

Staff

Managing Editor

Dorcas H. Malott

Researchers and Writers

Hayden Carruth
Tom Crippen
Kate Dunham
Mary Kathleen Greiner
Stephen M. Halpern
Raymond V. Hand, Jr.
Michael Kronenwetter
Perry Morse

Keyboarders

Mary Bunch
Mary Egner

THE ENCYCLOPEDIA OF

WORLD FACTS AND DATES

GORTON CARRUTH

A Hudson Group Book

HarperCollinsPublishers

FIRST EDITION

Designed by C. Linda Dingler

Library of Congress Catalog Card Number 89-46521
ISBN 0-06-270012-X

93 94 95 96 97 CC/RRD 10 9 8 7 6 5 4 3 2 1

To Gisèle, Nicole, Gorton, Hayden, and Christopher with thanks for their forbearance during the years I worked on this book.

Preface

The historian Oswyn Murray has written "Chronology, the dating and ordering of human events, is the basic grammar of history. . . ." *The Encyclopedia of World Facts and Dates* has engaged this idea but has set for itself an even bolder path: In chronological order it traces global history *from before human events* to the latest happenings of 1992. Its first entry is dated 18,000,000,000 B.P. (Before the Present) and its last entry is dated December 31, 1992. The first entry covers the formation of the universe and discusses the Big Bang theory. The last entry tells about drought and famine in Africa and Asia. In between this long span the entries cover such major subjects as population shifts and growth; natural and human-caused disasters; national politics and the ever-present spectacle of war; trade and economy; world religion and philosophy; the development of science and technology; the ever-changing world of the arts, including literature, painting, and sculpture; and crime, sports, and social happenings. There are more than 10,000 entries about these kinds of events in the histories of nearly all the countries now seated in the United Nations.

As *World Facts and Dates* comes toward the present, its coverage is more detailed. To help orient the reader, the text is divided into the following time spans:

18,000,000,000 B.P.–7000 B.P.	one span, without subject categories
5000–3500 B.C.	one span, subject categories begin
3499–500 B.C.	in spans of 100 years
499 B.C.–A.D. 1499	in spans of 50 years
1500–1799	in spans of 10 years
1800–1899	in spans of 5 years
1900–1992	in spans of 1 year

Running heads at the top of each page show which time span is covered by the text.

Subject categories within these time spans (except the first) help readers find the information they want. These categories are numbered:

    I. Vital Statistics and Demographics
   II. Disasters
  III. Exploration and Colonization
  IV. Politics and War
   V. Economy and Trade
  VI. Religion and Philosophy
 VII. Science, Education, and Technology
VIII. Arts and Leisure
  IX. Sports, Games, and Society

When one of the categories is not included, the numbering system is revised. For example,

   I. Disasters
  II. Politics and War
 III. Economy and Trade
 IV. Science, Education, and Technology
  V. Sports, Games, and Society

Finally, there is a comprehensive index that points the way to individual entries. An explanatory note about how to use the index appears on page 1063.

No other chronology contains so many dates. In addition to the entry date, nearly every person has a complete birth and death date if it is available in standard sources. Events discussed within entries, such as treaties, battles, discoveries, and publications, are also dated. Beginning and end dates for reigns and dynasties help the reader place an event in the historical context. The dates within entries often serve as cross-references to other entries, so the reader can look up a series of entries without turning to the index.

Though arranged chronologically, instead of alphabetically, *The Encyclopedia of World Facts and Dates* is indeed an encyclopedia. It is much more than a listing of significant historical dates. The entries are enriched with detail, as are the entries of most short-entry encyclopedias, and the descriptions of events are placed in the context of other happenings of the same subject. It is possible to follow a theme from one entry to another. For example, there is ample coverage in a number of entries of the growth of the Roman Catholic Church, the exploration and settlement of the New World, or the progress of the American Civil War.

The Encyclopedia of World Facts and Dates is a companion volume to the ever-popular *Encyclopedia of American Facts and Dates,* now in its ninth edition. Together these two reference books provide a unique guide to history, easy-to-use and suitable for both student and general reader. They belong in the home as well as in the library.

The information contained in *World Facts and Dates* comes from both original research and scores of standard sources. Since the coverage is so broad no one source stands out. Special acknowledgment should go, however, to *The New York Times* for much of the recent detail. The Staff of the Mount Pleasant Public Library in Pleasantville, N.Y., has, during the more than 10 years in which this encyclopedia was developed, always given ready assistance.

Many people have helped. They all deserve thanks for their help and loyalty. Those who assumed special responsibility over an extended period of time are acknowledged on page ii. Four colleagues must be singled out, and warmly thanked, for their exceptional contribution in particular areas over the years: Fon W. Boardman, Jr., in government and politics, especially of the 20th century; Gérard Cochepin in modern European history; Edgar M. Reilly, Jr. in technology and science; and David H. Scott in religion and sports.

G.C.

May 13, 1993
Briarcliff Manor, N.Y.

Contents

THE ENCYCLOPEDIA OF
WORLD FACTS AND DATES

From the Beginning to 7000 Years Before the Present [B.P.]

Dating note: Dates calculated as Before the Present [B.P.] are approximate. In the earliest reaches of time the degree of their accuracy may be ± millions of years; in more recent times their accuracy may be measured in one or two thousand years. A "c." placed before an entry date means more precision has been attained, probably by means of modern radioactive carbon dating [carbon 14 dating]. The degree of accuracy obtained by radioactive **carbon** (C_{14}) can, for dates more than 5000 years ago, be ± 800 years.

18,000,000,000 B.P. Most scientists believe that the universe began about this time. The **Big Bang**, as it is called today by astronomers, most of whom believe in an ever-expanding universe, has been dated by using light-year measurements based on the physics and colors of light received from a distant galaxy. A few astronomers believe that the universe had no beginning and will have no end. According to their theory, electric and magnetic forces, along with gravity, are sufficient to form galaxies and other large elements of the universe from **plasma**.

4,550,000,000 B.P. The age of the earth, given here, was computed from the ratios of lead isotopes from **meteorites** with lead from the earth. The oldest known rocks on earth were dated by radioactive measurements made at Oxford University in England that yielded an age of 3,750,000,000 years. The rocks used in the measurements were **Amîtsok gneisses** found on the southwestern coast of Greenland near Godthaab [Godthåb]. **Apollo 15** found (1971) **moon rocks** believed to be 4,150,000,000 years old.

4,550,000,000–600,000,000 B.P. This span of years is known as the **Cryptozoic** eon [time of hidden life], referring to the fact that there were very few, and only hidden, signs of life. A few fossil forms, mainly microscopic or submicroscopic, are dated today as coming from the later period of the eon. On the basis of life in any time period as shown by fossils, geologists divide eons into eras. This is impracticable for the Cryptozoic eon, because there are still too few fossils to use as index fossils in establishing points of time division.

3,500,000,000 B.P. Fossil marine algae appeared on the earth. Apparently these blue-green algae began to thrive when free oxygen became available in the atmosphere. Fossils recovered today do not necessarily contain any of the original plant or animal, but may be natural casts or molds of the life form, or even burrows, worm holes, or structures formed by the plant or animal when it was alive. Hard parts, such as shells or skeletons, were most commonly preserved, but in fine-grained rocks even soft parts may have left their imprints. Presumably life existed before 3,5000,000,000 B.P.; indeed, chemical traces of **photosynthesis** were found in sediments dated to 3,770,000,000 B.P. Life from which present organisms evolved probably did not exist before 4,000,-000,000–3,800,000,000 B.P., when the earth was apparently bombarded by asteroids, killing any life forms present.

3,400,000,000 B.P. **Microfossils** found in rocks from **South Africa** formed at about this time, probably a type of plant life.

1,000,000,000 B.P. Rocks formed at this time were found to contain possible sponge **spicules**, tiny hard parts contained within the sponge's body, indicating that the first known animal life on earth started about 1,000 million years ago.

600,000,000 B.P.–Present This span of years was called the **Phanerozoic** eon [time of visible life]. At the beginning of this eon fossils of such life forms as sponges, algae, **brachiopods** [lamp shells], and mollusks appeared, became common, and evolved into similar related forms on earth today. The Phanerozoic was divided into the **Paleozoic**, **Mesozoic**, and **Cenozoic** eras.

600,000,000–225,000,000 B.P. The **Paleozoic** [old life] era was divided into six periods: the **Cambrian**, **Ordovician**, **Silurian**, **Devonian**, **Carboniferous**

[**Mississippian** and **Pennsylvanian** in the U.S.], and **Permian**. The Paleozoic was dominated at first by invertebrates and simple plants.

600,000,000–500,000,000 B.P. The **Cambrian** period was characterized by numerous, though not abundant, plant and animal fossils, becoming more abundant and varied toward the end of the period. From this evidence scientists today are able to hypothesize that the land masses were apparently devoid of life, except possibly in some large freshwater habitats, and that signs of life appeared along the marine coasts, where the tides tossed some of the dead and dying from the seas. Invertebrates existed during the Cambrian. Some lacked hard parts, but left imprints of their soft bodies on the finer-grained shales and limestones, which originally were mud and limy sea bottoms. Scientists know there were animals like jellyfishes in the Cambrian. There were also animals with external hard parts, such as mollusks; lamp shells [shelled like the mollusks but with different body arrangements and anatomy]; ancestral crustaceans; **echinoderms** [spiny-skinned, five-parted animals like starfish, sea urchins, and sea cucumbers]; and an extinct group of floating crustaceans known as **graptolites**, that left abundant fossils. Another extinct marine group, the insectlike **trilobites**, thrived in the seas. Fossil plants were relatively rare, but algae left their marks.

500,000,000–440,000,000 B.P. The **Ordovician** period, the second division of the Paleozoic era, contained the first known vertebrates. They were jawless fishes, probable ancestors of modern bony fishes, sharks, and rays, and more direct ancestors of the jawless lamprey eels and hagfishes. Among the invertebrates, the first corals appeared, as well as the mollusks known as the **nautiloids** and **ammonoids**, whose descendants survive today in the chambered nautilus, the paper nautilus, and the squids and octopuses. The plant fossils of the period were still mainly seaweeds. The land masses were barren, except for the jawless fishes found in freshwater habitats. The exposed rocks, by then eroding into soils, formed continents of ill-defined shapes and positions, bearing little resemblance to modern continents.

440,000,000–400,000,000 In the **Silurian** period, the third division of the Paleozoic era, the first known land plants appeared. Called **psilotids**, they had underground stems that served as roots, scale-like leaves, and resembled the **lycopodiums**, or club

mosses. Late in the period scorpion-like animals appeared as the first land animals, while earlier marine crustaceans known as **eurypterids** probably crawled up on the marine shores after tide-strewn animals upon which they fed. In the oceans there now appeared sharks and their relatives, the rays; and fishes, armor-plated and jawed, known as **placoderms**.

400,000,000–350,000,000 The **Devonian** period, fourth of the Paleozoic era, is commonly called the **Age of Fishes** because of the abundant fossils of bony fishes. But there appeared now the first **amphibians** (one, salamanderlike, was about 12 feet long), the first true insects, and the first ferns and club mosses, which grew as large as trees.

350,000,000–270,000,000 The **Carboniferous** period, fifth in the Paleozoic era, in America was divided by some geologists into the Mississippian and the Pennsylvanian periods, each about 40 million years long. The Carboniferous was referred to as the Great Coal Age since many of the present extensive coal beds of the world were deposited during this period. Many new ferns appeared; coniferous trees and other seed plants, known as **gymnosperms** [naked seeds], and mosses and liverworts also first appeared. Amphibians were more varied and ventured farther on land from freshwater. Spiders and winged insects first appeared.

300,000,000–200,000,000 The several continental land masses that existed prior to this time now drifted together, forming one large continent called **Pangaea**. Because the result was less marine shoreline and therefore fewer shallow seas for breeding, marine species experienced their first great dieback.

270,000,000–225,000,000 The **Permian**, sixth and final period of the Paleozoic era, saw the rise of the reptiles, land animals able to spread nearly everywhere because they were independent of fresh water, being able to lay eggs on dry land. The coniferous trees, gingkos, and others were spreading over the rapidly greening landscape.

225,000,000–70,000,000 The **Mesozoic** [Middle Life] era, the second in the Phanerozoic eon, was divided into the **Triassic**, **Jurassic**, and **Cretaceous** periods, and was generally referred to as the Age of Reptiles. At the beginning of the era the one large land mass, Pangaea, gave land animals the opportunity to reach all parts of the land world.

225,000,000–180,000,000 During the **Triassic** period, earliest major division of the Mesozoic era, land reptiles spread and diversified into, among others, the first lizards, snakes, and turtles. Before it ended the dinosaurs had evolved. In the seas reptiles called **ichthyosaurs**, fishlike in form but airbreathing, evolved from land-dwelling reptiles not at all related to dinosaurs. The **pterosaurs**, giant flying reptiles, also arose in the Triassic, and the first primitive mammals, tiny creatures, appeared.

180,000,000–70,000,000 **Pangaea** began to break up. **North America**, attached to **Europe** and **Asia**, drifted to the **Northern Hemisphere**. The subcontinent of **India** was isolated but drifting northward, while the rest of the land masses remained connected in the **Southern Hemisphere**. The northern land mass was called **Laurasia**; the southern, **Gondwana**. By the end of the **Jurassic period** Gondwana began to fracture: **Africa** and **South America** were still joined in the equatorial region, but Australia and Antarctica, connected, were drifting south. While land animals could move from one continental area to another, the marsupials and early placentals survived best in Gondwana. When Africa separated from South America and drifted northward, reestablishing contact with Laurasia, more advanced placental mammals entered from Laurasia.

180,000,000–135,000,000 The **Jurassic**, second period of the Mesozoic era, was marked by the appearance of truly large dinosaurs. The first **angiosperms** appeared, as did large marine reptiles, the **mosasaurs** and **plesiosaurs**, sharing the seas with the now varied and abundant **ichthyosaurs**. **Birds** first appeared c.150,000,000 B.P.. By the end of the Jurassic, the continents had drifted farther apart, with North America joined to Eurasia, with Africa and South America forming one southern land mass, with India being a small continent to its east; and Australia, joined to the continent of Antarctica, forming a more southerly mass to the south, but not covering the South Pole.

135,000,000–70,000,000 By the end of the **Cretaceous** period, the last division of the Mesozoic era, the continents had just about reached their present positions and shapes, and all the giant ruling reptiles had become extinct, including all dinosaurs, big and small; and all the **pleiosaurs**, **mosasaurs**, **plesiosaurs**, and **ichthyosaurs** disappeared from the marine waters, all without apparent cause beyond some climatic cooling. Left were smaller reptiles, such as

lizards, snakes, turtles, alligators, and a few others. Also remaining were the small mammals that had originated as early as the Triassic period and had evolved through primitive egg-laying stages, like the present duck-billed platypuses, to more advanced forms, such as the marsupials, and even to the more advanced placental mammals.

70,000,000–Present This time span, the latest era of the Phanerozoic eon, was called the **Cenozoic** era. It included the **Tertiary** and the beginning of the **Quaternary** periods. These periods are today subdivided into five epochs and two epochs respectively. In the Tertiary: **Paleocene** [Old Recent], **Eocene** [Early Recent], **Oligocene** [Newer Recent], **Miocene** [Mid-Recent], and **Pliocene** [More Recent] epochs. In the Quaternary: the **Pleistocene** [Most Recent] and the **Recent** epochs. The Tertiary is called the **Age of Mammals**; the Quaternary, the **Age of Mankind**.

70,000,000–60,000,000 The **Paleocene** epoch was the earliest in the Tertiary period. Plants, especially trees and flowering plants, were beginning to resemble those of today. The mammals, not very large, looked primitive—barely suggesting the creatures that would evolve into modern horses and elephants.

60,000,000–40,000,000 In the **Eocene** epoch, the second of the Tertiary period, a few of the mammals would look somewhat familiar to us today but many would look odd. Ancestral whales, up to 80 feet long, were already roaming marine waters; **creodonts**, archaic carnivores looking like hyenas, searched the fields and forests for food; **uintatheres**, colossal long-legged, rhinoceroslike mammals with strange, blunt nose horns, roamed the grassless fields. Marsupials ruled in South America, Australia, and Antarctica, isolated from areas where the placental mammals lived. A heavy flightless bird *Diatryma* lived in the fields and open areas of Europe and North America. In position and shape the continents were as they are today, except for the still-widening Atlantic Ocean.

40,000,000–25,000,000 In the **Oligocene** epoch, the third of the Tertiary period, the first true **opossums** [generalized marsupials], dogs, and weasels appeared amid **saber-toothed cats**, **three-toed horses**, and **mastodons**. The largest known land mammal, an 18-foot-tall member of the rhinoceros family, was also present in Asia. During the Oligocene, North America was at times almost connected with South America by volcanic islands over which various small placental mammals moved into South America. The small mammals able to cross the water barriers on floating vegetation included ancestors of the monkeys found today only in South America and many rodents that began to replace marsupials and more primitive placentals in many habitats. Late in the Oligocene, grasses made their appearance.

25,000,000–11,000,000 In the **Miocene** epoch, the fourth of the Tertiary period, the mammalian fauna took on a more familiar look. Grazing animals developed in variety and abundance, evolving **dentition** to cope with the abrasive quality of their new food, either by continual growth of teeth throughout life or by continual replacement of worn teeth. Development of harder tooth enamel was another evolutionary response. Animals whose dentition had these qualities survived, while others adapted to different foods or became extinct. A genus of manlike apes appeared in Africa.

11,000,000–Present The **Panamanian Isthmus** formed and became a bridge between North and South America over which many animals crossed. Many new mammal species reached South America: rabbits, squirrels, dogs, bears, cats, mastodons [elephants], horses, camels, deer, and others. Spreading rapidly and competing for shrinking food and living places, they eliminated many less adaptable species. Mammals that crossed from south to north included opossums, armadillos, porcupines, and sloths. Many South American mammals got no farther than northern Mexico, which marked also the point where some northerners stopped their southward movements. Other animals, such as birds, reptiles, and fishes, followed the same pattern.

11,000,000–2,000,000 The plants and animals of the **Pliocene** epoch, the final one of the Tertiary period, were very similar to those of today. They included one-toed horses, bison, various elephants, weasels, dogs, bears, and cats, as well as all major types of plants extant today. Some scientists hold that the Pliocene began 7 million years ago and lasted only 5 million years.

3,800,000 Definite evidence has shown that **continental glaciation** occurred, at least in North America, during the later part of the Pliocene epoch. Glaciation had occurred in various parts of the world

throughout much of its history, even before the Cambrian period. The continental glaciation that began in the Pliocene and continued to the Recent Epoch at times covered more than 50 percent of North America, Europe, and Asia north of the Himalaya mountains. The frigid climates associated with glaciation had great impact on the biota: plants and animals unable to survive the cold moved southward to warmer regions or died out; life inured to the Arctic weather or able to adapt to it survived and even flourished.

3,800,000 Fossil anthropoids dating to this time were found, along the **Rift Valley** of eastern Africa from northern Ethiopia south to northern Tanzania. They were discovered by various scientists, including **M. Leakey** and **D.C. Johanson**, during the period from A.D. 1965 to 1974. Johanson and **T.D. White** concluded, particularly from a careful examination of a skull nicknamed "Lucy," that these fossils represented a new species in the family of man, **Hominidae**, and named it *Australopithecus afarensis*, deciding that it was midway between the subfamily Australopithecinae [genus *Australopithecus*] and the subfamily of true men, Homininae [genus *Homo*]. Since *A. afarensis* had anatomical characteristics of both subfamilies, they concluded it was probably ancestral to the more recent *Australopithecus robustus*, which became extinct about 1 million years ago, and to modern man [*Homo sapiens*]. Not all authorities agreed.

2,800,000 A fragmented fossil skull thought to belong to a man of the genus *Homo*, found near Lake Rudolph in Kenya by Bernard Ngeneo, was dated to about this time. It was contemporaneous with species of *Australopithecus*, manlike animals placed in the family Hominidae. Skull "1470" had a brain capacity of 800 cc, compared with modern man's 1,400 cc. Some authorities believe it was another *Australopithecus*.

2,000,000–Present The **Quaternary** period started about this time and continues to the present. During this relatively brief period, thousands of human cultures existed, hundreds of civilizations rose and declined, intricate tools were developed, and industry produced products of astonishing variety.

2,000,000–12,000 The **Pleistocene** epoch of the Quaternary, usually referred to as the **Ice Age**, lasted nearly 2 million years, though continental glaciation actually began in the Pliocene. The biota resembled today's, but at the end of the epoch many species of plants and animals became extinct, including elephants in North America. Paleontologists agreed that the Pleistocene epoch should be defined as beginning when certain fossil-bearing strata, dated c.2,000,000 years ago, were formed.

2,000,000 The **Paleolithic** [Old Stone] Age began about this time in **Europe**, **Asia**, and **Africa** [Old World]. Early man learned that certain kinds of pebbles, bones, and wood could be split and shaped for use as tools. The Paleolithic was subdivided on the basis of tool assemblages into "cultures" or "industries," the earliest and crudest tools, split pebbles or shaped points, being assigned to the **Chellean** culture or Industry. Next, c.1,000,000 B.P., came the **Acheulean** culture, when the tools were more obviously shaped by man. Starting c.500,000 B.P., when *Homo erectus* appeared as the dominant Old World man, new cultures sprang up in various areas, each of which has been given its own name. Since **Australian aborigines** in the 20th century were using a Paleolithic culture or industry as primitive as Acheulean, it is clear that setting times to cultures is impossible.

1,500,000 Apparently in northeastern Africa *Australopithecus robustus* in the family Hominidae, the last known **Australopithecine**, coexistent relative of *Homo*, became extinct about this time.

1,000,000 **Acheulian** stone-tool cultures were apparently worldwide in distribution. This culture of the Paleolithic lasted in Africa and Eurasia for c.800,000 years and overlapped other cultures. Acheulian was a general category for more or less definitely man-made Paleolithic tools. Slightly different tools made in specific areas were given special subcultural names, such as **Oldowan** and **Abbevillian**. The most common tool of the Acheulian culture was the pointed hand ax.

600,000 Four major continental glaciations, practically contemporaneous in Eurasia and North America, began about this time. The first, known as the **Günz** glacial stage in Europe and the **Nebraskan** glacial stage in North America, erroneously considered the first such glaciers, lasted c.80,000 years. During these glaciations, Europe and Asia were never covered completely. Nevertheless, the much colder climate forced people to quickly adapt tools,

homes, and methods of hunting; new or different species of plants and animals appeared and others became extinct. *Homo erectus*, was first recorded in Europe after the Günz glaciation, during the Günz-Mindel Interglacial stage, and was probably the ancestor of **Heidelberg Man** [*Homo erectus heidelbergensis*]. The ice in some places was 10,000 feet thick or more, and the water withdrawn from the oceans lowered sea levels around the world. Lower sea levels exposed the continental shelves, and many areas, now separated, were joined together: for example, Indonesia became a single land connected as a peninsula to southeastern Asia, and New Guinea was joined to Australia. Animals, including early man, could walk from one area to another over these land bridges.

600,000 *Homo erectus*, apparently directly ancestral to *Homo sapiens*, first appeared about this time. All living people belong to the *Homo sapiens*, which is divided into many races [subspecies], all capable of interbreeding with all others. *H. erectus* in all parts of the world transformed or evolved (c.100,000) into *H. sapiens*. In order for *H. sapiens* to replace *H. erectus* so completely, there had to be enough time for the former to prove superior in survival capabilities. Early scientists gave Java Man [*Pithecanthropus erectus*], **Peking Man** [*Pithecanthropus pekinensis*], **Lantian Man** [*Sinanthropus lantianensis*], and others separate generic and specific names. Modern anthropologists now consider these to belong to *H. erectus*.

525,000 The first great interglacial stage, known in Europe as the **Günz-Mindel Interglacial** and in North America as the **Aftonian Interglacial**, lasted until c.475,000 B.P. The climate was probably warmer than today, since biota from warm southern areas penetrated much farther north than it did after the last glaciation.

500,000 **Peking Man** [*Homo erectus*] was somewhat apelike in appearance, knew the use of fire, and made primitive stone tools. At Choukoutien, a cave site formed in a dense loess deposit, southwest of Peking, was discovered in A.D. 1927. It was older than some believed possible and was taken as a link between ape men and man.

475,000 The second of the last four continental glaciations in the Northern Hemisphere, known as the **Mindel** in Europe and the **Kansan** in America, lasted c.50,000 years. Heidelberg Man, Lantian

Man, and Peking Man existed in Europe and Asia at this time.

425,000   A warm second interglacial stage, called the **Mindel-Riss** in Europe and the **Yarmouth** in America, began about this time. It was known as the "**Great Interglacial**" because of its long duration of c.175,000 years. Fossils of men found from deposits of this interglacial period were all considered to belong to *Homo erectus*, including **Steinheim Man**, **Swanscombe Man**, and **Vértesszöllös Man** from Europe, and Peking Man and Lantian Man from Asia. Fossil mammals in Europe about this time included many more species than are found in the tropics today, such as three or four different kinds of elephants, tapirs, rhinoceroses, hippopotamuses, monkeys, two-humped camels, and various deer, horses, and big cats.

225,000   The third of the last four major continental glaciations began about this time. It was known as the **Riss** in Europe and the **Illinoian** in America and lasted c.45,000 years. Fossil man at this stage was still *Homo erectus* and included types referred to as **Swancombe**, **Steinheim**, etc., but they were definitely trending toward Neanderthal Man [*Homo sapiens neanderthalensis*].

180,000   A warm interglacial period, lasting over 80,000 years, followed the Riss and Illinoian glaciers of Eurasia and North America. It was known as the **Riss-Würm** in Europe and the **Sangamon** in America.

160,000–40,000   During this period, the **Mousterian** culture of the Paleolithic Age followed the Acheulian culture. Now, stone artifacts were generally smaller, finer, and often flaked on both sides, creating sharper edges. The Mousterian also had a wider range of tools than the Acheulian, reflecting more complex human activities. In occupying a wider variety of habitats, people needed harpoons, fishhooks, awls, and engraving tools. **Neanderthal Man** [*Homo sapiens neanderthalensis*], a variety of modern man, was dominant during this period.

130,000–50,000   Excavation of **Tabun Cave** on Mount Carmel in Israel showed that this site was continuously occupied by Paleolithic people. A gradual evolution from Neanderthal Man to modern man occurred with no indication of combat between the two.

120,000   Among the **first known buildings** were a number of huts, excavated in Nice, France, during

A.D. Oct. 1965, believed by archaeologists to have been built about this time. The huts were sturdier than the crude skin-and-branch structures typically used at encampments.

100,000   The most recent continental glaciation, known as the **Würm** stage in Europe and the **Wisconsin** stage in America, began about this time, or perhaps a few thousand years earlier, lasting nearly 90,000 years.

43,000   The **earliest known mining operations**, in the Ngwenya Hills of Swaziland, were for iron ore, presumably to get a reddish dye, composed mainly of iron oxide, for body painting.

40,000   **Cro-Magnon man** appeared in numbers throughout Eurasia about this time. Until this date Neanderthal Man predominated. The steadily warming climate was probably a distinct disadvantage for the Neanderthals, who had adapted to a cooler climate and were generally hairier and of more compact build.

40,000   Art during the Paleolithic Age, manifested itself in beautifully designed and crafted stone tools and utensils, with animal carvings on bone and of ivory. Commonly found objects among the debris and abandoned possessions of early man were small carved figures of women, called generically "**Venuses**." These figures appeared as late as the Neolithic Age.

35,000   **Neanderthal Man**, relatively common about this time in Europe and the Near East, began to disappear. Neanderthals had a brain capacity somewhat larger than modern man's, walked erect with a striding gait, and are today believed to have been a variation or subspecies of modern man. Neanderthal's presence coincided with the Mousterian culture, a relatively high achievement of the Paleolithic.

30,000   The **Solutrean culture**, involving new techniques in the making of stone tools and projectile points, arose in present Spain and France. The points were artistically crafted. At this time the Würm glaciation was temporarily advancing again in Europe, and early man was adapting his tools and culture to cooling climatic conditions and to changing fauna and flora. The culture lasted until c.20,000 B.P., and encompassed the period of the great cave paintings.

25,000 The **aborigines** probably first arrived in Australia about this time, or somewhat earlier. Rising sea levels after the melting of the Würm glaciation cut off the humans of Australia from the rest of the world (12,000 B.P.).

25,000 Sometime after the Australian aborigines reached Australia and perhaps after a rise in sea level separated New Guinea from Australia (12,000 B.P.), the **Melanesians** settled in the archipelago from New Guinea east to the Fiji Islands. They are thought to have originated in India or Southeast Asia.

22,000 The **Gobi Desert** of Mongolia was once a fertile land that supported many humans during the Stone Age and the beginning of the Bronze Age. Gradual desiccation drove the population out, and by 6500 B.P. the Gobi was almost a desert.

22,000 The **earliest known representation of a human face** was dated from this time. A head carved in limestone was found at Aq Kupruk, Afghanistan, in A.D. 1965.

20,000 An early form of art was the impressing of hand prints on the soft, clay walls of the **Gargas cave**, often called the Cave of the Hand, in the French Pyrénées.

20,000 People of the Aterian culture in northwestern Africa may have invented the **bow and arrow** about this time. They were believed to have shared in the Solutrean culture, which arose in Spain and France c.40,000 B.P., but definitely lived in the Late or Upper Paleolithic Age.

20,000 The **Mesolithic** [Middle Stone] Age, a designation little used today, referred to the transition period from older, somewhat cruder stone tools to more finely made, polished stone artifacts of the **Neolithic** [New Stone] Age. In some areas, the Mesolithic lasted until c.6000, but the dates varied from one part of the world to another.

19,000–10,000 Paintings executed during this period on the ceilings and walls of a cave in **Altamira**, Spain, and more than 80 other caves in northern Spain and France depicted long-horned bison and other animals now extinct in the area, as well as other species hunted by the cavemen.

18,300–17,000 Neolithic people of Wadi Kubbaniya, west of the Nile Valley in Upper Egypt, were growing and harvesting **wheat, barley, lentils, chickpeas, dates, and capers** at this time, as discovered by a joint Polish-American archaeological expedition and reported in A.D. 1979. This was the first known farming of these plants.

17,250 The **Magdalenian culture** arose in Europe during a brief, colder, and drier interval in the Würm glaciation (100,000–10,000 B.P.). Although cave art seemed superior, the projectile points and other tools were not quite as advanced as those produced in the Solutrean culture. The Magdalenian culture merged into the **Azilian culture** (c.12,000 B.P.) as the last continental glaciers were melting back.

c.17,000 Painted Cave at **Lascaux**, France, was occupied for c.2,000 years. The cave was discovered on A.D. Sept. 12, 1940, by boys rescuing a dog that had fallen into an opening leading to the cave. The hunter society of the Paleolithic Age left paintings, etchings, and other art work on the ceilings and walls of the cave, some of which were probably done as early as 23,500 B.P. The paintings told scientists a great deal about Paleolithic animals and about how cavemen lived and how their culture evolved.

17,000 Based on artwork and on decoration on pottery, tools, etc., the **earliest music** was probably sung or chanted, using only two tones, and accompanied by the clapping of hands.

15,000 The **population of England, Scotland and Wales** at this time in the **Late or Upper Paleolithic Age** was estimated at 2,000. In the Mesolithic Age (c.10,000), it was probably 4,000. By 5500 B.P. or 3500 B.C., during the Neolithic Age, it had risen to c.20,000. By 2500 B.P., or 500 B.C., the Iron Age population of Great Britain was c.400,000; at about the same time (2400–2300 B.P., or 400–300 B.C.), **Egypt's population** was about 7 million.

c.14,000 At **Cerro Chivateros** in Peru, stone tools were found in strata dated to this time, earlier than most present archaeologists had believed possible. However, many archaeologists today believe Indians did not even reach the area of the present United States until after the ice of the last glaciation melted back c.12,000–10,000 B.P. They suspect that earlier dates were the result of faulty dating methods or other mistakes.

14,000 The **reindeer hunters** near what is now Hamburg, Germany, sheltered themselves in crude tents made of animal skins, mainly of the reindeer.

12,000 The **Recent [Holocene] epoch**, second of the Quaternary period, began after the most recent continental glacier melted back in the Northern Hemisphere. A few of the large animals that existed at the end of the Pleistocene survived into the Recent epoch, some being hunted by early man in North America and Eurasia c.6000 B.P.

12,000 As the glaciers receded, **nomadic reindeer hunters** arrived in **Scandinavia** equipped with bows and arrows, stone axes, and other tools. They traveled across waters in dugout canoes, and like the reindeer hunters of **Germany** c.14,000 B.P., they probably lived in tents. **Farming** and permanent dwellings did not become prevalent until after 6200 B.P.

12,000 By this time man was definitely established in Mexico, although there has been speculation he arrived earlier. The **first human migrations into North America** probably crossed from Siberia to Alaska as long ago as 75,000–45,000 B.P., but most archaeologists believe the crossing occurred 25,000–15,000 B.P. During both periods heavy glaciation lowered the sea level, exposing the **Bering Land Bridge**. By c.12,000 B.P. the New World's total population was possibly no more than 10,000 people.

12,000 **Africa's population** stood at an estimated 1,250,000, comprising Berbers and Egyptians 100,-000, Cushites 100,000, Nilo-Saharans 250,000, Negroes 250,000, Pygmies 200,000, and Bushmen 350,000.

12,000 The **Azilian culture** of Europe, which followed the **Magdalenian culture**, was found mainly in western Europe and exhibited poorer workmanship. This culture occurred during a colder interval of the **Würm glaciation**, when local advances of the ice sheets separated the people into large enough groups to create their own cultures. The Azilian culture was marked by harpoon heads, rather poorly made, using deer antlers. A series of cultures in Europe followed the Azilian, such as the **Sauveterrian**, mainly of France and Britain, which made and used microliths as projectile points; the **Tardenoisian** culture of Spain, France, and northern Germany, which made trapezoidal points; the **Ahrensburg** and others of northern Europe; and also of northern Europe the **Maglemose culture** that extended from Britain to the countries of the eastern Baltic, which introduced heavy stone axes, adzes, and picks with ground points.

12,000 Ground and polished **stone tools** began to appear in Asia and Europe, the time when the **Neolithic Age** began. The Neolithic reached its height at about the time farming and stock breeding replaced hunting and gathering (c.6000). The natives of New Guinea were in the Neolithic Age when first visited by Europeans. The Neolithic began in Egypt c.12,000 B.P. and between 10,000 and 9000 in the Near East. A Neolithic village, **Pan-P'o-Ts'un**, existed in the **Yellow River** [Huang Ho] valley of China 7000–6000 B.P. Other early starts of the Neolithic were Eastern Mediterranean—10,000 B.P.; southern Russia and the Balkans—9000; Baltic—9000; Italy—8500; Britain—8000; Indus Valley—8000; and the Far East—8000 B.P. (all dates approximate). In the Americas the Indians of Mexico and of Central and South America had a Neolithic culture, which started c.6500–6000 B.P., or c.4500–4000 B.C., and they were using copper, gold, and silver, a step toward Bronze Age technology.

12,000 A **reaping knife**, usually made of wood with flint blades inset along one side, was used in Palestine. It was probably used for cutting wild grains.

11,000 **Jericho**, in the present Israeli-occupied West Bank, was already a human settlement. It was occupied through the **Neolithic**, **Chalcolithic** [Copper], and **Bronze** ages until c.3000 B.P., or c.1000 B.C. It was the longest continually occupied site known (8,000 years) and had defensive walls.

11,000 The **first bronze artifacts** were made apparently in Turkestan, central Asia, but bronze itself was probably discovered elsewhere when tin and copper were mixed accidentally. A Bronze culture using some manufacturing controls appeared in Egypt c.7000 B.P. or c.5000 B.C. The **Bronze Age** began when ancient man learned which formulas to use for weapons and for other artifacts. The Bronze Age appeared fully developed in China between 6000 and 5500 B.P., or 4000 and 3500 B.C.

10,000 Cultivated **wheat**, planted and harvested earlier than this time, was bred through the millennia from about 225 wild species that grew in the temperate or even cooler regions of the world. By this time the kernels of wheat and other cultivated cereal plants were quite different from the wild species, showing the results of long-term selection by man. At the beginning **barley** was favored over wheat in cultivation, and two kinds of cultivated barley existed: one with two rows of seeds [*Hordeum distichum*] and the other with six [*Hordeum hexastichum*].

10,000 Domestication of the dog [*Canis lupus familiaris*] occurred about this time. A skeleton of a dog discovered at **Palegawra Cave** in northern Iraq was dated recently to c.14,000 B.P.

10,000 Native **copper**, found in its pure metallic state, was used for tools and ornaments at about this time in Switzerland and central Europe. It first appeared in **Mesopotamia** c.6500 B.P. and some 500 years later in Egypt.

9500 Settling land, rising sea levels, and forces of erosion completed the physical separation of **England** from the European continent. **Ireland** had been separated from both Europe and Britain at perhaps 12,000–10,000 B.P.. Recent excavations in Ireland show that people with a **Mesolithic Age** culture were present at this time. They built huts and were hunters and gatherers.

9000 **Ceramic pottery** made its appearance about this time in the Near East. **Potter's clay**, a natural material relatively free of impurities, was changed to a hard impermeable substance when heated to high temperatures. It held its shape when heated, so it was used to make variously shaped containers and vessels.

c.8690 At **Palli Aike** near the Strait of Magellan, a carbon $_{14}$ date of 8639 ±400 years B.P. (6689 ±400 B.C.) was obtained from charred bones found at an ancient Indian campfire. The nearby **Fell's Cave** archaeological site obtained readings of 10,000 ±300 B.P. (8050 ±300 B.C.).

c.8500 B.P. A Neolithic town called **Çatal Hüyük** near Konya in present southwestern Turkey flourished for about 700 years. The abutting houses of sun-dried brick were flat-topped with entrances from the roof like some of the **Pueblo Indian dwellings** of the American Southwest. Excavations begun in A.D. 1961 showed a town three times the size of Homer's Troy, with a population of about 3,000. The walls were decorated with mainly **animal murals** reminiscent of Paleolithic cave paintings. Research-

ers identified 14 food plants cultivated by the residents, including wheat, barley, peas, lentils, and **bitter vetch**. The inhabitants also wove the **first known carpets**.

8500 B.P. **Qalat Jarmo**, the ruins of an ancient Neolithic town east of present Kirkuk, Iraq, yielded evidence that the inhabitants were cultivating **pistachio nuts**, peas, and lentils, as well as wheat and barley.

8500 B.P. **Paleo-Indians**, early Indians in America using **distinctive stone points**, at a site southeast of Kit Carson in present Colorado, stampeded a herd of a now-extinct bison into what was then a deep arroyo and butchered them there. The Indians left behind many of their typical projectile points. Evidence showed how they butchered the animals and which cuts of meat they preferred.

8500 B.P. **Cultivated gourds, lima beans,** and **squashes**, identified by their seeds, were found with Indian remains dating to this period at **Ocampo**, Mexico, north of present Mexico City. Beans, squash, and corn were the main food staples grown by Indians throughout much of the Americas.

8000 B.P. People with a **Neolithic culture** occupied **Nabta**, a site about 100 kilometers west of the Nile in Upper Egypt, about 1,000 years before any dated Neolithic remains were recorded at the Nile itself.

8000 B.P. The earliest positive evidence of **domestication of sheep**, based on animal carvings and painted murals dating to this period, was found in **Iran**.

8000 B.P. The 250,000 **inhabitants of the Americas** subsisted mainly by **hunting and fishing**, which supplemented primitive agriculture. With most of the **big game**, such as mammoths and the giant bison, killed off, only a few thousand bison hunters on the North American plains still followed a hunting and gathering life.

c.7800 B.P. Evidence that **cattle** were domesticated this early was found at **Çatal Hüyük**, near Konya in present southwestern Turkey; there were also indications that they were domesticated 500 years earlier. Other animal remains from the dig included: Anatolian mouflon or **wild sheep, Asian wild goat, wild boar, onager,** and **domesticated dog**. The people at this time apparently were primarily raisers of cattle.

7598 B.P. The **ancient Greeks** believed that this was the date when the **Gods created the earth.**

7300 B.P. Evidence of the earliest known **domesti-** cation of pigs, dated to this time, was uncovered at **Belt Cave,** a site of the Neolithic Age in northern Iran.

5000–3500 B.C.

At this point the system of chronology shifts from **Before the Present** (B.P.) to **Before Christ** (B.C.). As events enter the period of recorded history, their dates will now correspond to the conventional chronology. Because the B.P. chronology is about 2,000 years (corresponding roughly to the period from A.D. 0 to 1990) longer than the B.C. chronology, this shift results in what appears to be a gap of 2,000 years. However, because 7000 B.P. = 5000 B.C. there is in fact no disruption of continuity.

I. VITAL STATISTICS AND DEMOGRAPHICS

5000 B.C. The **Halafian culture,** first uncovered at **Tell Halaf** in present Syria, was dominant over much of **Mesopotamia** from this time until c.4200. The people were excellent stone workers and potters and lived in small towns; about this time many small farming villages were also established through the Nile Valley of Egypt.

4500 B.C. No clues have yet been found to the **languages** spoken in the **Mesolithic** and **Neolithic** ages by the people occupying the area from central Europe eastward to the Caspian and Aral seas. The **written languages** of people who originated from this large area were definitely **Indo-European.**

4200 B.C. A much-advanced **Neolithic agricultural community** unearthed at **Tell al-Ubaid,** near **Ur** in **Sumer,** gave the name **Ubaidian** to the contemporary cultures of the area. The people were non-Semitic, probably from the Iranian highlands to the east, who began to settle in the lowlands and marshy areas between the mouths of the **Tigris and Euphrates** rivers, known later as Sumer, in present Iraq. They began to drain the swamps and construct buildings of mud and reeds, and soon were establishing towns and cities. These same people founded the settlement since discovered beneath the ruins of the Sumerian royal city of **Eridu.** They were the **first** to establish **farming based on extensive drainage and irrigation.** Near present **Mandali,** Iraq, the **earliest known canals,** used for transportation as well as for irrigation, were dated to c.4000. The Ubaidian culture spread northward and west- ward, reaching as far as the the Mediterranean Sea.

II. DISASTERS

3500 B.C. A flood that inundated the city of **Ur,** on the Euphrates River in Sumer, present southern Iraq, deposited eight to nine feet of clays and silts over parts, if not all, of the city. The idea of **worldwide flooding** became an element of the **folklore of the Mesopotamian people,** which then probably included the ancestral **Hebrews.** Scientists have found no signs of any but local or at most regional flooding anywhere at any time. Archaeologists studying the ruins of ancient civilizations in Mesopotamia uncovered many traces of fairly widespread, but still relatively local, catastrophic floods caused by the rising of the Euphrates and Tigris rivers.

III. POLITICS AND WAR

4500 B.C. **Uruk** [biblical: **Erech**; present: **Warka**] was founded about this time in Sumer, present Iraq. At first there were two communities; later c.3500 B.C., they merged into one, and c.2800 B.C. became the walled city called Uruk. A dynasty was established that intermittently ruled much of Sumer until c.2500 B.C., after which Uruk was maintained as one of Sumer's holy cities.

4400 B.C. The **Neolithic Age** began in southwestern Europe about this time. Even as it began in one area, it was being replaced in other areas by the **Chalcolithic** [Copper] **Age** as man learned to find and use native copper and later (c.4000) smelt copper from its ores.

3500 B.C. The country of **Elam** [Susiana], in the present Iranian province of Khuzistan, had its origin at this time. Its leading cities were **Susa** [biblical: **Shushan**], the capital of Elam, **Madaktu**, and **Khaidalu**. Its people were neither Semitic nor Sumerian, but they worshipped Sumerian gods and had a Sumerian culture.

IV. SCIENCE, EDUCATION, AND TECHNOLOGY

5000 B.C. The **weaving of flax threads** into fabrics occurred in Egypt, the Near East, and Europe at the start of or before the Neolithic Age. Flax was one of the first fibers regularly used. The **earliest textile** remains from Egypt came from sites on the Nile Delta c.5500 B.C.

5000 B.C. **Megalithic structures**, the first **menhirs**, tall, upright stones set in place with great effort by early men, and their **dolmens**, large, flat stones set atop smaller erect boulders, were being built through much of Europe during the Neolothic Age. The dolmens were originally crude rock burial chambers covered with soil to form barrows, which contained the remains of humans and a few of their possessions. When the covering earth eroded away, the structures looked like huge, flat-topped tables to which the name dolmen was given.

5000 **Maize** [*Zea mays*], called American or Indian corn, was identified in archaeological sites of about this date.

4400 The Neolithic Swiss **Lake Dwellers** of this time were the first known people to cultivate the **carrot**. They grew them along with garden **peas**.

4400 **Horse bones** found in an archaeological site of this date at **Tell Halaf**, in present Syria, suggest this date for the **domestication of the horse.**

4000 Agriculture began along the **Yellow River** [Huang Ho, Huang He] and **Yangtze River** [Chang Jiang], in present China. The **earliest known culture of the ancient Chinese**, called the **TangShao**, cultivated cereals, especially millet, and began the domestication of dogs, pigs, and horses.

4000 Evidence from graves in the **Nile Valley** indicated that **barley** was cultivated as a main crop in Egypt.

4000 The **sickle**, at first a straight piece of wood with flint blades inset on one side, was used at least this early by people of the Neolithic Age for harvesting wild grain. A Neolithic group from the Palestine area, known as the **Natufians**, used such a tool for harvesting grain that may have been at least semi-cultivated.

4000 The **thatched-roof, rectangular-shaped, long houses** of the **Danubian people** were among the best made houses in Europe at this time.

4000 **Agriculture** became relatively common in **Scandinavia** as the climate grew warmer and farming was introduced to the hunting culture by people from the more southerly areas.

4000 A domesticated animal—**half onager**, or ass, and **half horse**—was common at this time at the archaeological sites **Anau I and II** near Ashkhabad in present southern Turkmen.

3900 The **Almerians**, Neolithic tribes who occupied southeastern Spain about this time, were the first people known to have cultivated **olives** in the western Mediterranean.

3800 **Seals** were first used to imprint identifying symbols and designs on clay, which was then baked, and on other materials, such as cloth. These seals were possibly the **beginning of writing and printing.** The **Sumerians** used curved rocker seals, the **Harappans** cylindrical seals, and the **Egyptians** flat seals.

3760 **+ 3 months** The **Hebrew calendar** set this date as the time of creation, and Jews still reckon their chronology from this time on. The calendar was originally based on lunar months and divided into cycles of 235 lunations, about 19 years, with years of 12 months adding up to between 353 to 355 days with seven years of between 383 to 385 days interposed. Months vary between 29 to 30 days, the number being changed as needed to adjust to the actual length of the years and other factors.

3700 The **houses** built at Khirokitia on the island of Cyprus were **shaped like beehives**, with the main floor sunk below ground level.

3500–3000 The Sumerians developed a **phonetic alphabet** based on their ideographic writing symbols. About the same time they reduced the number of their earlier ideographic signs from about 2,000 to a few hundred.

3500 The **potter's wheel** was apparently brought into Sumer by semicivilized invaders from the north. Pottery was now produced more rapidly and was of finer texture and more symmetrical.

3500 **Molded and kiln-fired bricks** were being used in Sumer during the early Ubaidian period. Hand-molded, sun-dried bricks were used earlier, but their exact age is not known.

3500 **Copper** was almost certainly first smelted from ores in the area between the Black and Caspian seas and northern Mesopotamia.

V. ARTS AND LEISURE

4500 **Pigeons**, appearing commonly on **bas-reliefs**, **pottery**, and **seals** from this time, were probably domesticated.

4500 **Cattle motif designs** were found on pottery from **Arpachiyah**, an archaeological site near present Mosul [Al-Mawsil], Iraq.

4000 **Furniture** and other articles of everyday life, unwanted or too bulky for tomb robbers, were well preserved in the warm, dry climate of ancient Egypt. The custom of burying these articles in **tombs** has given a clear picture of the domestic arts of those days. Folding stools and a couch frame mounted atop four bull's hoofs were from at least 4,000 B.C. Richer pieces (c.3500) included chests, sarcophagi, tables, stands, chairs, and folding seats of excellent design and workmanship.

3800 The **oldest known pottery** in western South America was found near **Valdivia**, in present Ecuador, hence the culture named the **Valdivian Stage**. The culture extended to northern Peru.

3600 So old a musical instrument was the **harp** that the Sumerians, who used it in many religious and social functions, attributed its invention to their greatest god, **Enlil**. A bow-shaped harp was shown in the decoration on a ceramic vase from this time found at **Bismya**, in present Iraq.

3500–3000 In Egypt, male and female **temple singers** formed **guilds**, which concentrated on the extensive liturgical music.

3500–2300 Ruins of this date at **El Paraíso** near present Lima, Peru, indicated that early temples and government buildings were probably in existence in South America.

3500–2000 **Temple building** proceeded at a great pace in Mesopotamia. At the holy city of **Eridu** the Sumerians built (c.3500) **Temple III** as a home for their god of wisdom, **Enki**. This was the third in a series of temples built on the rubble, ruins, or foundations of an immediately preceding building. Temple III and an Assyrian temple built (c.2000) at **Tepe Gawra**, an archaeological site northeast of present Mosul [Al-Mawsil] in Iraq, were considered the finest examples of this period's temple architecture. The temples were built on mounds, usually artificial, called **ziggurats**, with a platform on the top; Enki's temple at Eridu was on a 20-by-80-foot platform.

3500 **Arched doorways** were found in the ancient city of **Ur** dating to about this time.

3500 **Figurines of ivory and terra cotta** were created in Egypt. They probably originated in **burial customs** wherein the statuettes, placed with the dead, were substituted for companions and slaves formerly buried alive or slain.

3499–3400 B.C.

I. SCIENCE, EDUCATION, AND TECHNOLOGY

3400 The **earliest known clay tablets** covered with early **pictographic cuneiform writing** were found at the archaeological sites of **Jamdat Nasr**, northeast of the site of ancient Babylon, and **Uruk** [Erech] of ancient Sumer, present southern Iraq. A cow or sheep head was drawn in the clay with a wedge-shaped tool, with dots, circles, etc. representing the actual number of animals. The tablets were commercial records, from which writing probably developed.

3400 **Sails** made of matting were shown on pottery paintings made in Egypt as early as the **Late**

Predynastic Period (the Neolithic period that preceded the first Dynasty).

3350 Truewriting appeared in Sumer about this time. Using wedge-shaped impressions in clay—then baked for permanence—communications of all sorts appeared.

3399–3300 B.C.

I. ECONOMY AND TRADE

3300 **Accounting** may have begun in Sumer, where temples kept detailed accounts of many kinds of economic and financial transactions, including loans and rent.

c.3300 **Agriculture** made its first known appearance in **Ireland** following the warming climate and its introduction by peoples from the south, possibly the first human arrivals. Small areas of the forests were cut down and burned before crops could be planted.

II. SCIENCE, EDUCATION, AND TECHNOLOGY

3300 The use of **copper**, obtained from mines in the Sinai, became relatively common in Egypt. **Smelting** was apparently done at the mines, but the copper may have been further refined in Egypt.

III. ARTS AND LEISURE

3300 **Glazed pottery** and earthenware were being made in ancient Egypt. It may have been discovered accidentally when some pottery became dusted or covered with **siliceous sand** before firing.

3299–3200 B.C.

I. POLITICS AND WAR

3200–2700 **Dynasties I and II** of ancient Egypt together formed the **Early Dynastic** or **Archaic period.** Menes [*Narmer* or his son *Hor-aha*?] was the first pharaoh. Dynasty I had eight pharaohs, Dynasty II also eight. The dynasties ruled from **Thinis** [This] near present Girga southwest of Abydos in southern Egypt and today are referred to as the **Thinitedynasties.**

3200 *Menes*, pharaoh of Upper [southern] Egypt, was credited with conquering the Lower [northern] Kingdom of the Nile Delta and thus unifying Egypt. Long believed to be legendary, Menes is now known to have been a real person although which person is uncertain. He was believed by some to be *Narmer*, and by others to be Narmer's son *Hor-aha.*

II. ECONOMY AND TRADE

3200 The **first cultivated wheat** in the Near East was a one-kernel species known as **einkorn.** It was cultivated to some extent prior to this date, but was soon replaced by a two-kernel variety. Barley and millet were probably cultivated there before wheat.

III. SCIENCE, EDUCATION, AND TECHNOLOGY

3250 **Paper** made of papyrus reed appeared about this time in Egypt, replacing stone and animal skins. The central pulp of the **papyrus reed** [*Cyperus papyrus*], which grew all around the Mediterranean Sea, was dried, split, and glued together in sheets running at right angles to each other, forming the first known paper.

3200–2900 The single-humped dromedary **camel** [*Camelus dromedarius*] was shown in carvings and pottery designs from Dynasty I of Egypt. At this time the animal may not have been domesticated in Egypt, though in Arabia they were probably tamed about this time. Like the bactrian camel [*Camelus ferus*], which has two humps, the one-humped dromedary was a true camel.

3200 **Hieroglyphic writing** developed in Egypt shortly after the Sumerians developed their **cuneiform writing.** The **Palette of Narmer** [Menes?] (c.3200), a small, flat stone with bas-relief scenes of a battle, told the story in pictographs. Pictographs were more like rebuses than actual writing.

3200 History's **earliest recorded dam**, a masonry structure 15 meters [49 feet] in height, was built to supply water to Menes's capital at ancient **Memphis**, Egypt.

3200–2180 During the **Early Dynastic** (Dynasties I and II) and the **Old Kingdom** (Dynasties III to VI) periods, Egyptians manufactured **bronze**, **brick**, ce-ment, **plaster** and **varnish**, and developed the techniques of **glass-blowing** and **enameling**.

IV. ARTS AND LEISURE

3200 The **Baboon of Narmer** [Menes], an alabaster representation of the god **Thoth** as a baboon, was called Egypt's first great piece of sculpture.

3199–3100 B.C.

I. SCIENCE, EDUCATION, AND TECHNOLOGY

3100 The **Lake Dwellers of Switzerland**, a Neolithic farming people, established communities built on pilings, extending over the surface of the lakes, which may have been intended to furnish protection against enemies.

3099–3000 B.C.

I. VITAL STATISTICS AND DEMOGRAPHICS

3000–400 **Asia's population** was about 36 million, of which 25 percent was located in the Near East, centered in present **Iraq**, **Syria**, and **Israel**. **India** and northern **China** probably accounted for about 15 to 20 percent each. After 400 B.C. the population of China and India grew rapidly and soon outnumbered that of the Near East. **Japan's population** was less than 5 million until after A.D. 1000. Supported by irrigation-based agriculture, ancient **Egypt's** population had risen (c.3000) to about 1 million, almost half the total for all of **Africa**.

3000 The **Aegean Civilization** (to c.1100) developed its roots about this time. As used by archaeologists, it included mainland **Greece** with its **Helladic culture**, the Aegean Islands with their **Cycladic culture**, and **Crete** with its **Minoan culture**. The origins of these populations are still uncertain.

3000 The **Sahara Desert** area, now mostly semiarid, was becoming even more desiccated. Previously the area was wet (c.40,000), but it grew progressively dryer, becoming eventually the largest tropical belt desert in the world, almost completely dry. Humans and animals adapted or emigrated south to the **Sahel**, the sub-Sahara dry grasslands, north to the **Maghrib**, and east to the **Nile River Valley**.

II. POLITICS AND WAR

3000 Tribes known to the later Greeks as **Maeotians** lived in the **valley of the Kuban** [Hypanis] **River**, on the northeast coast of the **Black Sea**. Their metal-based culture, which used objects made of copper, silver, and gold, existed at the same time as the **Stone Age tribes** of other parts of present **Russia**.

3000 The city of **Uruk** [Erech] dominated **Sumer**, and its culture spread over great areas of the Near East. Historical records were kept in pictographs plus symbols for numbers, and the buildings were made of baked brick (though the **oldest stonework** found in **Mesopotamia**, a small portion of pavement, was uncovered here). The **Bible** identified **Nimrod**, the great-grandson of **Noah**, as the founder (c.4500) of Uruk.

III. ECONOMY AND TRADE

3000 The **white potato**, native to the **Andes Mountains** of Peru, Bolivia, and Ecuador, was probably first cultivated about this time.

3000   The **tomato**, native to the **Andes Mountains** of Peru, Ecuador, and Bolivia, was cultivated by the Indians.

3000   The **grape** was introduced from **Anatolia** into much of the Near East.

3000   **Sailing ships**, with triangular lateen sails and broad sweeps [oars], were used on both the Tigris and Euphrates rivers. They carried such products as lumber and stone from the north, but they had to remain in the south since they could not return upriver, even with the help of sails. Most often these ships were broken up in the south, and their valuable timbers sold.

IV. SCIENCE, EDUCATION, AND TECHNOLOGY

3050   The **oldest extant medical treatises**, known as the **Edwin Smith Papyrus**, included works commonly attributed to Dynasty I, but certainly not later than Dynasty IV in Egypt (c.2600–2500). The medicine and surgery expounded in these treatises appear amazingly modern. The Egyptians produced the leading doctors and the most effective medicines for millennia.

3000   **Wheeled vehicles** and crude **chariots** had appeared in Sumer by this date. The wheels, made of solid wood, were heavy and cumbersome. The **first known wheels** were attached (c.3500) to children's toys at **Jamdat Nasr**, northeast of the site of ancient Babylon.

3000–1200   **Stonehenge**, north of Salisbury, England, and the associated barrow cemeteries were constructed and used from about 3000 to 1200 B.C. Stonehenge, although part of the **Megalithic culture** of Europe, was nearly unique. While other megalithic monuments, some even formed in circles as in Stonehenge, have been found in France, none match Stonehenge, or the similar megaliths at Amesbury,

England, in size or complexity. Stonehenge was certainly perfectly aligned with the midsummer sunrise and midwinter moonrise. The huge stones were quarried and cut some 40 to 50 miles away and transported to the site.

3000–2000   The **sundial** was probably developed during this time.

3000   The Egyptians began to use reeds and rushes, the **first crude pens**, for writing.

3000   In eastern **North America the Indians** of the **Archaic period**, a stage between crude hunting and gathering and agriculture, were producing polished stone tools for a number of sophisticated purposes, including working wood and preparing skins for clothes.

3000   The process of mixing copper and tin to make **bronze** was already in use in **Mesopotamia**, presaging the Bronze Age.

3000   The **plow** was in use in both **Sumer** and **Egypt**. The animal-drawn plow enabled farmers to cultivate much more land. A tomb mural from the Old Kingdom of Egypt (c.2700–2100) showed an oxen-drawn plow.

V. ARTS AND LEISURE

3000–1800   A **Stone Age culture** called **Comb-Ceramic** existed throughout Finland. The name referred to earthenware vessels with patterns that may have been drawn in the soft clay with the teeth of a comb. The people subsisted on hunting, fishing, and trade.

3000   **Neolithic paintings** on exposed rock formations or boulders in eastern Spain and northern Africa were probably made about this time. They usually show hunting and gathering activities, with the human figure dominating and done in monochromes, sometimes picked or incised into the stone.

2999–2900 B.C.

I. POLITICS AND WAR

2999–2000   The **Celts**, later the **Gauls**, a major branch of the **Indo-Europeans**, began to spread rap-

idly throughout Europe from western Asia somewhere north of the Caucasus. They may have been pushed by the **Scythians** into the plains west of the Carpathian Mountains of central Europe. From there they attacked the more highly civilized people of northern Italy and southeastern Europe, with some eventually settling in central Anatolia and elsewhere. One tribal group, many scholars believe, settled in southern Scandinavia and became known as the **Teutons**, later called the **Goths** and **Germans.**

2900 The **second dynasty** of the **Archaic Period,** ruling Egypt from Memphis, began. It was apparently a weak dynasty of eight pharaohs, including **Sekhemwy** [Sekhemury], **Peribsen** [Perabsen], and **Kha Sekhemwy** [Khasekhem].

2900 The **Indus River,** or **Harappan,** civilization began about this time, although some claim it began c.3300. The term Harappan is derived from the first discovered site in present Pakistan, ruins named **Harappa,** on the banks of the **Ravi River.** Though the oldest carbon 14 dating using radioactivity measurements from bones and wood was about 2195, there was positive evidence in the form of trade goods that marine trade existed between the **Harappans** and **Sumerians,** who flourished at this time. The Harappans used writing, as yet undeciphered, seemingly for business accounts and records.

2900 **Early Dynasty I** of **Ur** gained brief hegemony over **Sumer,** Mesopotamia. The **Sumerians** had developed an urban life centered in the **city-states** of **Eridu, Issin** [Isin], **Kish, Lagash** [Shirpurla], **Larsa** [Ellasar], **Nippur, Umma,** Ur, and **Uruk** [Erech].

2900 The city of **Kish** began to dominate in **Sumer.** The earliest settlement at Kish was dated to c.3500; it was situated about eight miles east of ancient Babylon.

II. ECONOMY AND TRADE

2900–2800 **Soy beans** were cultivated in **China** prior to this period, according to a Chinese medical book written during these years.

III. ARTS AND LEISURE

2900 **Tombs** from the period of **Ur's first dynasty** contained items of clothing and technology.

2900 **Arches and arched vaulting** were used in ancient **Sumer** during Early Dynasty I & II at **Ur** and elsewhere, especially in burial vaults. The arches were used only for spanning short distances.

2900 The Mesopotamian creation epic *Enuma elish* told about creation as a struggle between the gods and **Tiamut,** the monstrous earth mother, who was killed in the end and whose body was split in two to make heaven and earth. The story was revealed in tablets found A.D. 1854 in **Ashur-bani-pal's library** in the ruins of **Nineveh.**

2899–2800 B.C.

I. POLITICS AND WAR

2800 The Early **Minoan culture** began on the island of **Crete.** It continued as a mainly Neolithic culture for about 900 years, gradually entering the early **Copper-Bronze Age,** and was followed by the Middle Minoan (c.2000). **Knowledge of metalworking** may have entered Crete as early as c.3000. The first settlers on Crete were believed to have come from southwestern Anatolia during Neolithic times. **Egyptians** who had established themselves on the southern shores of the island were driven out during civil wars at the start of the Early Minoan culture.

II. ECONOMY AND TRADE

2800–2700 The **first domesticated swine** were probably developed in this century. Swine were known in **Hungary** (c.2500–2400 B.C.), and appeared somewhat later (c.2000 B.C.) in **China.**

2800 **Sumer** exported considerable amounts of **woolen cloth.** This textile was easy to produce in a sheep-raising nation and could be traded to other peoples for wood and stone.

III. ARTS AND LEISURE

2800 The **oldest known poem,** written on a clay tablet by a Sumerian named **Dingiraddamu,** lamented the sack of the city of **Lagash** [Shirpurla] and the destruction of its goddess idol. The Sumerian language has now been deciphered almost completely in its written form. The **Sumerians** used an agglutinative language with words and their roots strung together, resulting in very long words. Sumerians wrote from right to left; the **Babylonians**, using the same symbols as the Sumerians, wrote from left to right.

2799–2700 B.C.

I. VITAL STATISTICS AND DEMOGRAPHICS

2750 Various peoples speaking an **Indo-European group of related languages** apparently occupied a broad belt of land from north central and southeastern Europe east, north of the Black Sea, and farther east to the area of the northern Caspian Sea and the Aral Sea. By c.2250 B.C. all of Greece and the Aegean area had been occupied by people of this language group.

II. DISASTERS

2700 The "stele of famine," one of history's earliest authenticated records of a **famine**, was carved on a tomb on the Nile island of **Sehel** near Aswan, Egypt. Lamenting starvation caused by the seven-year failure of the Nile flood, the chronicler wrote: "Each man has become a thief to his neighbor. They desire to hasten and cannot walk. The child cries, the youth creeps along, and the old man; their souls are bowed down, their legs are bent together and drag along the ground, and their hands rest in their bosoms. The counsel of the great ones in the court is but emptiness. Torn open are the chests of provisions, but instead of contents there is air. Everything is exhausted."

III. POLITICS AND WAR

2760–1000 The **Helladic**, or **Bronze Age**, culture of mainland **Greece** started as a series of Neolithic communities, which developed gradually through infiltration of ideas and techniques, as well as through conquest by peoples from the north and along the coasts. For example, the **Dorians**, wielding bronze and perhaps some iron weapons, entered peninsular Greece c.1200 B.C.

2700–2180 This was the period of the **Old Kingdom, Dynasties III to VI of ancient Egypt**, with the capital still at **Memphis**. Most of the **great pyramids** at **Giza** were built during the Old Kingdom, including those of **Zoser** [Djoser], **Snefru, Khufu** [Cheops], **Khafre** [Chephren], and **Menkaure** [Mycernus]. Giza was a center of extensive necropoli and religious buildings. Burial goods and wall paintings showed high levels of civilized arts and techniques, costumes, and writing in a crude alphabet.

2700–2500 A group of **marble statues** of human figures, the largest 30 inches high, was made for the temple at **Tell Asmar** [Eshnunna], about 20 miles north of Baghdad.

2700 **Zoser** [Djoser], a pharaoh of **Dynasty III** in the Old Kingdom of Egypt, initiated the **tomb pyramids** by having his engineer and architect **Imhotep** build a step pyramid tomb at **Saqqara** [Saqqārah, Sakhara, Sakkara], about 12 miles south of Giza in Lower Egypt. The pyramid is today the **oldest extant, free-standing stone structure** in the world.

IV. ECONOMY AND TRADE

2700 Agriculture in China probably had at least small beginnings before this time, but by now the **Anyang Neolithic peoples** certainly raised barley, millet, and possibly rice. **Anyang**, in Honan [Henan] province of central northern China, was the capital of the **Shang** (Yin) **Dynasty** (c.1766–c.1027).

2700 According to legend, the **Si-Ling**, empress of China, was the first to discover that by unraveling the cocoons of certain worms [caterpillars], a fine **silk** thread could be obtained.

V. SCIENCE, EDUCATION, AND TECHNOLOGY

2781 The **Egyptian calendar** probably began about this time, though some have said as early as 4241 B.C. Their year began on about our January 1, with the flooding of the Nile River. On that date, the Egyptians noted, **Sirius**, the **Dog Star**, which they named **Sothis**, rose into the heavens just as the sun was setting. This coincidence did not occur again for 365 days, which they made the length of the year in their calendar.

2700–c.2650 The pharaohs of Dynasties III and IV conquered what later became known as **Nubia** and established **foundries** there for working **copper**. Nubia was located on the Upper Nile, in present southern Egypt and northern **Sudan**; later it was the northern area of ancient **Ethiopia** [Cush or Kush], situated mostly in the present Sudan.

2700 **Imhotep**, chief adviser to **Zoser** [Djoser], a pharaoh of Dynasty III, was the first person known who was widely described as a scientist. He de-

signed the first step pyramid and was a noted physician and artist. Late Egyptians ranked him with the gods, and the Greeks considered him a manifestation of **Asclepius**, their god of medicine and healing.

VI. SPORTS, GAMES, AND SOCIETY

2700–2180 **Costumes** worn by **Egyptians** were depicted on the walls of pyramids and other tombs. Men wore a loincloth of white linen wrapped about the waist and fastened with a looped belt. Women wore a garment of the same material, a long, rather tight costume covering the body from below the breasts to the calves, fastened with one or two shoulder straps.

2699–2600 B.C.

I. POLITICS AND WAR

2698–2205 According to legend dynasties of demigods ruled **China**. There is archaeological evidence supporting the existence of **Neolithic cultures** (c.4000), and later Bronze Age cultures and industries, which included this period.

2600–2500 **Dynasty IV in Egypt** lasted for more than 100 years and was prosperous, enabling its six pharaohs to erect their pyramids at and around **Giza**, near Cairo.

II. SCIENCE, EDUCATION, AND TECHNOLOGY

2650 The use of **papyrus-reed paper** had become common in Egypt for writing. One of the earliest known examples of writing on papyrus was the *Book of Wisdom* [or *Teaching*], a collection of proverbial instruction and occultism written by government officials to their sons and surviving in texts from c.2000.

2634 According to legend, the **compass** was invented in China, possibly at this time, or in the 11th century A.D.

2630 According to legend **silk** moth larvae fed with mulberry leaves grown in special gardens were producing silk for a widespread industry, which China preserved as a monopoly until sometime after A.D. 1200.

2600 **Stone beehives** were being used in Egypt about 2500 B.C., but there probably were earlier hives made of wood or other material.

2600 One of the **first great walled cities** of history was created when a wall was built around **Uruk** [Erech] in Mesopotamia [present southern Iraq]. Nine and one-half kilometers long, it was built of baked bricks and rubble, and had over 800 semicircular towers. According to *Gilgamesh*, an epical Babylonian work based in large part on Sumerian myths, the walls were built by Gilgamesh, king of Uruk c.2675 B.C.

2600 **Khufu** [Cheops], pharaoh and founder of **Dynasty IV**, built the greatest of the pyramids at **Giza** [Gizeh], near Cairo. It was the first of the **Seven Wonders of the Ancient World**, originally 481 feet high with a base covering 13 acres. According to the Greek historian **Herodotus**, it required the work of 100,000 people for 20 years. The huge stones used in building the pyramids were cut by hand at the quarries and hauled many miles to the building site using only manpower assisted by rollers, sleds, ropes, and barges. The construction and transportation techniques became known from carvings on the pyramid walls.

2600 The **Pyramid Texts**, inscribed on the walls of pyramid tombs of the pharaohs of Dynasties IV and V, were accounts of creation and of the Egyptian pantheon. They included instructions on the funerary rites for the dead pharaoh and for his heir.

III. ARTS AND LEISURE

2600 The Babylonian epic *Gilgamesh*, which apparently originated about this time in Sumerian myths, was probably the **first important work of literature** to deal with mankind's fear of death as a major theme. The story apparently involved an actual king Gilgamesh, who ruled Uruk (c.2675) in Sumer and about whom nothing else is now known. In it appeared the story of a great flood, a description of the underworld, and a search for the plant of life that gave immortality.

2600 The seated figure of **Khafre** [Chephren, Chefren], a pharoah of Dynasty IV in Egypt, was considered the **first great work of Egyptian sculpture** and one of the great works of portrait sculpture in history. At the time it was one of 24 figures of the king carved for his tomb.

2600 A number of somewhat **crude musical instruments** were in use in **Sumer**, particularly at Ur. Clappers, drums, cymbals, timbrels, and sistra in the percussion class; flutes, pipes, horns, and trumpets in the wind instruments; harps, lyres, and perhaps zithers in the strings.

2600 The **first large palaces** were built at **Kish** and **Eridu** in Sumer.

2599–2500 B.C.

I. POLITICS AND WAR

2599 The legendary **Yellow Emperor** [Luozu, Huang Ti, Huang Di] of China may have died at this time. His date of birth was reported as 2698. Though there was some evidence that such a person actually lived, several persons may have been intermingled as one through the ages.

2598–2205 This was the period before the so-called legendary dynasties of China. The descendants (dates often traditional but suspect) of the **Yellow Emperor** were named **Xuanxiao** [Qingyang, Shaohao] (ruled 2598–2515), **Gaoyang** [Zhuanxu] (ruled 2514–2437), **Gaoxin** [Ku] (ruled 2436–2367), **Zhi** (ruled 2366–2358), **Yao** (ruled 2357–2258), and **Shun** (ruled 2255–2208). In 2205 **Yü** (d.2198), the first legendary emperor of the **Hsia** [Xia] **Dynasty** (2205?–?1767), began his reign. These rulers were all legendary, with little information surviving to indicate their possible reality. **Ssuma Ch'ien** [Sima Qian] (145–87), the historian who reported these events, claimed he wrote nothing in his history that he considered suspect.

II. ECONOMY AND TRADE

2500 **Cotton** was grown in the **Chicama and Virú river valleys**, near Trujillo in present northern Peru, and woven into cloth. The Indians were also cultivating **squashes, gourds, beans, and chili peppers**. The cotton of the New World was very similar to that grown in the Old World.

2500 **Promissory notes** were in use in Akkad, a city-kingdom north of Sumer in central Mesopotamia, where inscribed clay tablets were used to promise payment of a debt in gold or silver.

2500 **Trading companies** operated in Mesopotamia for commercial dealings with distant lands.

III. SCIENCE, EDUCATION, AND TECHNOLOGY

2500 **Mari**, the largest of a chain of city-kingdoms in the mid-Tigris and Euphrates valleys, began to expand southward and increase its trade with Sumer. At the same time these Semitic people learned to use the Sumerian script. The **Sumerians** had by now begun to keep **written journals**.

2500 The **Bronze Age** began in central Europe, probably in **Bohemia**, in present Czechoslovakia, because both tin and copper ores occurred there in close juxtaposition.

2500 The **horse** was known and probably used in Macedonia at this time. **Horse-drawn chariots** were used in battle by c.2000 B.C. in western Asia and eastern Europe. Perhaps attempts were made to domesticate wild horses as early as 4000 B.C., but the accounts of **Fo-Hi**, a Chinese emperor, about bringing domestic horses into China were as unbacked by archaeological evidence as was the emperor himself. The domestic horse of c.2500 B.C. was often hybridized with the wild asses, with unsatisfactory results.

2500 Extremely **advanced weaving techniques** were practiced in Egypt, while similar looms were being developed separately in China. The production of textiles with as many as 540 warp threads to the inch became possible.

2500 **Pottery** appeared among the Woodland Indians of eastern North America. Coils of clay were pressed together and unevenly fired, with no glaze and only simple decorations imprinted before firing.

IV. ARTS AND LEISURE

2550 The **Great Sphinx** was built at **Giza**, near Cairo, Egypt. **Khafre** [Chephren, Chefren], whose pyramid was the second one constructed at Giza, probably was also responsible for erecting the Sphinx to guard his tomb. Khafre was the third pharaoh of Dynasty IV, which ruled from Memphis in Lower Egypt.

2500–2000 The **pentatonic** [five-tone] **scale** was developed in China, where it is still the basic scale in use. Tuned slabs were played in **Stone Age China** (2698–1766), superseded by tuned bells made of horn, shell, and other materials.

V. SPORTS, GAMES, AND SOCIETY

2500 **Egyptian tomb carvings** showed dogs strikingly similar to present Greyhounds, Afghans, and Salukis.

2500 A ski found in a bog at **Hoting** in the Ångermanälven River region in northern central Sweden is thought today to be 4,500 years old, the **oldest ski** so far to be found. Early skis were made from bones of large animals. A rock carving from **Rødøy**, Norway, provided the earliest known pictorial representation of skiing.

2499–2400 B.C.

I. POLITICS AND WAR

2494–2345 **Userkaf**, pharaoh of Egypt, founded the prosperous but weak **Dynasty V** (c.2494–c.2345). A priest of **Re** [Ra], the sun-god at **Heliopolis**, he initiated official worship of Re as his ancestor.

2470 A victorious battle fought by one of Sumer's kings, **Eanatum of Lagash**, was depicted and described on a stone stele, the **"Vulture Stele,"** without naming the location nor the identity of the foe. Still extant, it is one of the **earliest known written accounts of a battle**.

II. ECONOMY AND TRADE

2400 Cantaloupe, honeydew melon, and **muskmelon** first appeared in the records of an **Egyptian garden** of this date.

III. SCIENCE, EDUCATION, AND TECHNOLOGY

2400 The **Sumerian script** penetrated northern and northwestern Mesopotamia.

IV. ARTS AND LEISURE

2400 The **Minoan artists** of Crete produced murals painted on freshly limed walls, mainly using floral designs, and various statuettes that gave some indication of the dress of the period.

2399–2300 B.C.

I. POLITICS AND WAR

2340 **Sargon** [Sharrukin] **I**, king of Akkad (c.2340–c.2280), usurped the throne of that Semitic kingdom

north of Sumer; conquered the city-states of **Sumer**; subjugated **Elam**; and drove north around the **Syrian Desert** [Badiet esh Sham], lying mostly in present Iraq and Jordan, and then westward to the Mediterranean. He established his capital at **Agade**, near Sippar, 16 miles southwest of present Baghdad.

2350 **Dynasty VI** in Egypt lasted about 170 years, marked with considerable political and commercial expansion. Noted rulers of this period included **Pepi** [Piopi] **I** (ruled 2330–2300), **Pepi II** (ruled c.2300–2206), and **Queen Nitokerti** (ruled c.2180–?). The end of Dynasty VI (c.2180) marked the end of the Old Kingdom.

II. ARTS AND LEISURE

2332 The palace of **Sargon I** in **Akkad** was built using glazed bricks with designs baked into them.

2300 Relatively small **copper and bronze sculptures in Mesopotamia**, particularly in Akkad, were fully three-dimensional and more lifelike than those done earlier.

2299–2200 B.C.

I. DISASTERS

2297 The first recorded flood of the **Yellow River** [Huang Ho, Huang He] occurred in China.

II. POLITICS AND WAR

2206 **Pepi II**, pharaoh of Egyptian Dynasty VI, died after a rule of 94 years, the longest recorded reign of any monarch in history—or legend.

2205–1767 The **Hsia** [Xia] **Dynasty** ruled in China, according to written legend but without other verification. Sometimes called **China's First Dynasty**, it probably existed only as a small state. Hsia was supposedly founded by **Yü** [Ta Yü], to whom legend had granted the sobriquet "the Great," and had endowed him with much wisdom, kindness, and ability to rule well.

2200 A barbarian people known as the **Guti** [Kuti] swept down on Elam and Akkad from the Zagros

Mountains of southwestern Iran. They adopted the Akkadian language and the cuneiform writing for their official communiques but little else of civilization, although they occupied much of Mesopotamia for about one century. Except that the Guti were non-Semitic, no one seems to know anything about them or their origins.

III. ECONOMY AND TRADE

2200 **Domestic fowl** were known to the **Harappan Civilization** of the Indus River valley. They were shown as designs on pottery and seals.

IV. RELIGION AND PHILOSOPHY

2205 **Yü**, founder of the **Hsia Dynasty** (c.2205–c.1767) in China, may be taken today as representative of the ancient rulers and sages whom later Taoists and Confucians idealized.

2199–2100 B.C.

I. POLITICS AND WAR

2180–1990 This was the **First Intermediate period**, sometimes called the **Feudal Age, of Egypt**: a period of turmoil, no central rule, and no great building activity. **Dynasties VII and VIII**, the **Ephemeral Kings**, ruled from Memphis; **Dynasties IX and X**, the **Heracleopolitan**, ruled from **Heracleopolis Magna** [Ihnâsya el Madîna], both cities of Lower Egypt.

2150–1750 The Middle Kingdom, **Dynasties XI and XII**, ruled in Egypt. Its actual beginning was considered to date from the **reunification of Egypt** by rulers from Thebes, in Upper Egypt. This was the **classical age of Egypt** in literature, and arts and crafts flourished.

2150 **Gudea**, king of the Sumerian city-state of **Lagash** [Tello, Tellow], in present southeastern Iraq, was credited as a very successful ruler and was deified by his subjects after his death.

2150 Mentuhotep [Nibhapetre] **II**, second pharaoh of **Dynasty XI** (2150–1990), defeated the Heracleopolitan pharaoh of Dynasty IX, thus reunifying Egypt. Mentuhotep expelled the Asians and Libyans from the Nile Delta area, and began the reconquest of Nubia.

2113 The **Third Dynasty of Ur** (not to be confused with the third Early Dynasty of Sumer c.2600–2500) was founded by the Sumerian king **Ur-Nammu**. Ur-Nammu promulgated (c.2105) a **code of laws** for his people.

II. SCIENCE, EDUCATION, AND TECHNOLOGY

c.2180 A **tunnel** for the transportation of goods was constructed under the Euphrates River in **Mesopotamia.** The river was diverted from its bed into a temporary channel. Then, across the river bed a trench was dug in which a tube of bricks was constructed, and the river was then returned to its bed. The tunnel was about 3,000 feet long, 12 feet wide, and 15 feet high.

c.2150 In **Sumer**, at Lagash, **Gudea** filled a **library** with an estimated 30,000 clay tablets.

c.2100 Iron objects first appeared in Mesopotamia.

c.2100 Glass first appeared in Sumer, then in Egypt, as a glaze on pottery, produced when a siliceous paste was used to create the gloss. From this, small beads of glass formed and eventually larger glass beads, used for decoration and art work.

c.2100 The **Harappan culture** in the Indus River Valley was the **earliest known** to have invented a **method of printing.** Thousands of small block seals, cut intaglio into flat pieces of soapstone, have been found. Some were cut in copper. The blocks had raised portions, or bosses, on the back indicating that they may well have been held by hand like modern rubber stamps. The Harappans also made cylindrical seals, which produced imprints when rolled on soft clay and baked.

III. ARTS AND LEISURE

2150 The temples and enclosure at **Karnak** in Egypt were begun. Karnak occupied the northern part of the ancient capital of **Thebes**, in Upper Egypt, some 300 miles south of present Cairo. The great **temple of Amon** was commenced by **Sesostris I** (ruled c.1980–c.1935) of **Dynasty XII** (c.1990–1750), and was completed by **Ramses II** (ruled 1290–c.1224) of **Dynasty XIX** (c.1320–1200) in the New Kingdom.

2100 A remarkable diorite **statue of Gudea**, king of Lagash, was made about this time.

2100–1100 Egyptian murals and bas-reliefs flourished as never before or after. Skillful use of hundreds of colors yielded beautiful and realistic works, many preserved until today by the dry desert air.

2100 Jomon Ware, black pottery of Japan, was decorated with a twisted-rope design. Some authorities believe it was made by the ancestors of the Ainu, the hairy aborigines now living on Hokkaido.

IV. SPORTS, GAMES AND SOCIETY

2150–1750 Women playing ball were depicted in the **tombmurals** recovered at **Beni-Hasan**, Egypt, dated as belonging to the Middle Kingdom period.

2150–1750 During the **Egyptian Middle Kingdom**, men wore several skirts, one above the other. Underneath was a loincloth, with a longer one worn over it. Women still wore the long, close-fitting garment of the Old Kingdom.

2099–2000 B.C.

I. VITAL STATISTICS AND DEMOGRAPHICS

2000 The **population of the Indus River Valley**, with its great cities, **Mohenjo-daro and Harappa**, was approaching 5 million. Population of the rest of the Indian subcontinent may have numbered 1 million.

II. POLITICS AND WAR

2000 Horse-riding **Aryans**, who occupied the steppes north of the Caspian Sea and Transoxiana, moved south and west, perhaps because of population pressure.

2000 The **Third Dynasty of Ur**, weakened by Sumerian intercity warfare and invaded by **Amorites** from the north and by **Elamites** from the east, came to an end. **Ur**, the last king of the Third Dynasty **Ibbi-Sin**, was captured and carried away.

2000 The **Middle Minoan Civilization** began, with the Minoans now in the Early Bronze Age. Their culture soon spread into Greece at **Tiryns**, **Mycenae**, and **Argos**.

2000 The **Mayan Pre-Classic Age** began in Mexico along the Gulf Coast in Yucatan and in Guatemala. It was a time of significant agricultural progress and development of sophisticated pottery and a calendar.

2000 The **Yang-Shao Neolithic culture**, dated near the legendary **Hsia Dynasty** (2205–1767), occupied the area around the **mid-Yellow River** [Huang Ho, Huang He]. Millet and swine were raised, and excellent red pottery, decorated with painted designs, was produced.

III. ECONOMY AND TRADE

2000 **Aquatic rice**, which could produce larger amounts of food per acre than any previously cultivated crops, was introduced into China from India.

2000 Efficient **fishing methods**, including elaborate systems of **weirs**, had developed among the **Woodland Indians of North America**. Weirs were found in the tidewaters of the Charles River near present-day Boston, Massachusetts.

2000 The image of **elephants** appeared commonly on the seals of the Harappan Civilization at Mohenjo-Daro and elsewhere in the Indus River Valley, suggesting that they had been domesticated.

IV. RELIGION AND PHILOSOPHY

2050 The **Ziggurat of Ur**, a three-storied temple-tower to the moon god **Nanna**, was built by **Ur-Nammu**, the Sumerian king of the Third Dynasty of Ur. With a base of 200 by 150 feet, it was the finest building of the Sumerian revival.

V. SCIENCE, EDUCATION, AND TECHNOLOGY

2000 A system for calculating arithmetical problems had developed by this time among the **Babylonians**. The Babylonians invented and used a **sexagesimal system**, based on units of 60 which later evolved into the duodecimal method on the basis of twelves. They divided the circle into 360 units, never discovered 0, and their value for *pi* (the ratio of the diameter to the circumference of a circle) was 3.

2000 The great stone **palaces** of Crete at **Knossos** and **Mallia** were built. They were the first palaces designed with features to help cool the interiors—ventilation shafts and elaborate corridors—and they contained drains and systems for pumping water.

2000–1500 **Percussion instruments** were added to the Egyptian orchestra. In Africa tuned slabs evolved into ancestors of the xylophone.

2000–1700 Pottery from Crete, now produced on the potter's wheel, called the **Kamares** ware, spread to Egypt and elsewhere in the eastern Mediterranean.

2000 Ceramics and other artifacts, as well as architectural styles, found at the archaeological site of **Swasey**, near Cuello in present northern Belize, indicated a possible ancestry of the Mayan culture.

2000 **Fragments of hundreds of papyrus rolls** from about this time tell a tale much like that of Sinbad the Sailor and several shorter tales.

2000 The **basic house plan** in Mesopotamia had evolved by this time into a square with the rooms set around an open inner court.

VI. SPORTS, GAMES, AND SOCIETY

2000–1100 In the Middle Minoan Civilization the primary **masculine costume** of Crete was a short loincloth. Women wore a two-piece outfit consisting of a bell-shaped, tiered skirt and a small jacket.

1999–1900 B.C.

I. POLITICS AND WAR

1990–1750   **Dynasty XII of Egypt** was characterized by economic prosperity and the extension of Egyptian influence abroad. There were eight pharaohs: **Amenemhet** [Ammenemes] **I** (ruled 1990–1970), **Sesostris** [Senusret, Senworse] **I** (ruled 1970–1935), **Amenemhet II** (ruled 1938–1903), **Sesostris II** (ruled 1906–1887), **Sesostris III** (ruled 1887–1849), **Amenemhet III** (ruled 1849–1801), **Amenemhet IV** (ruled 1801–1792), and **Queen Sebekneferu** (dates unknown). Lower Nubia was completely conquered.

1900   The **Mycenaeans** arrived in mainland Greece through infiltration and conquest of the apparently Indo-European but non-Greek-speaking natives. Many authorities today consider that the Minoans were closely related to the Mycenaeans.

1900   Babylon became under **Sumuabum**, the king of the Amorites, the capital of the **First Dynasty of Babylonia** (c.1894–1630). Its ruins, about 55 miles south of Baghdad in present southern Iraq, still exist.

II. RELIGION AND PHILOSOPHY

1900–1700   According to Genesis, within this time the Hebrew patriarch **Abraham** moved his clan from Ur to Haran in northern Mesopotamia and then into Palestine.

III. SCIENCE, EDUCATION, AND TECHNOLOGY

1900   Cotton was grown and woven into cloth by the Harappan people at the cities of Mohenjo-Daro and Harappa in the Indus River Valley of present Pakistan. The Harappans were probably the **first to weave cotton** in the Old World.

1900   An apparently **alphabetic inscription**, as yet undeciphered and dating to this time, was found at the ancient ruins of **Serabit el Khadim** in the Sinai Peninsula.

IV. SPORTS, GAMES, AND SOCIETY

1900   Fishing with a rod and line and with a hand-line and net were depicted in an Egyptian angling scene in the tomb of Chnemhotep, administrator of the eastern desert during the reign of Sesostris III of Dynasty XII.

1899–1800 B.C.

I. POLITICS AND WAR

1850   People classified as belonging to the **Steppe Battle Ax culture** occupied an area that the Greeks later called Thracia, west of the Black Sea, north almost to present Russia, and then east to the Caspian Sea. These **Thraco-Cimmerians** may have been related to the Greeks and also the Aryans.

1850   **Amenemhet III** was the greatest Egyptian pharaoh (1849–1801) of the Middle Kingdom **Dynasty XII.** He created the artificial lake Moeris, near present El Faiyūm depression in Lower Egypt, to control the Nile flood, and he colonized Nubia. He also built the great funerary temple that the Greeks called the **Labyrinth at Hawara** [Hauwâret el Maqta'] near El Faiyūm.

1805   Hyksos, driven from Canaan at this time, probably by Indo-European invaders from the north, entered the Nile delta (c.1780). They were largely Semitic.

1800–1600   The **Battle Ax culture**, carried by people speaking an Indo-European language, replaced the Comb-Ceramic culture in southwestern Finland. It was also a Neolithic Age culture, but the people developed agriculture, mainly cattle raising. The culture's name came from the boat-shaped battle axes that the people used.

1800   **Aryan tribes** migrated from the Caspian Sea area into eastern Mesopotamia, Persia, and the Indian subcontinent. They developed a pastoral-agricultural economy, bringing with them the use of the horse, chariot, and **Sanskrit** language.

II. SCIENCE, EDUCATION, AND TECHNOLOGY

1800 The Bronze Age and its techniques reached central and then western Europe, carried by the **Celtic people.** The Celts never formed any cohesive kingdom or empire, but they dominated much of Europe until c.200 B.C.

1800 Bronze was introduced in Scandinavia as the basic material for weapons. The battle ax, its head now made of bronze, continued to be the main weapon, but spearheads and helmets were also made of bronze.

III. ARTS AND LEISURE

1850 The sculptures of **Sesostris** [Senusrit, Usertesen] **III** and of **Amenemhat III**, both pharaohs of **Dynasty XII**, were unique in Egyptian art. These Middle Kingdom sculptures, expressing emotion, stood apart from the youthful, idealized royal sculptures of the Old Kingdom.

1799–1700 B.C.

I. DISASTERS

1720–1580 During this period, as foretold to the pharaoh by the captive **Israelite Joseph**, Egypt was visited by **seven years of famine** after **seven years of abundant harvest.** Following Joseph's counsel, grain had been stored under royal control. The famine forced the peasants to sell their land to obtain the stored food, enabling the pharaohs to become vast landowners along the Nile. There was no Egyptian confirmation of the story of Joseph.

1700 An **earthquake** destroyed most of the palaces and other buildings built on **Crete** and elsewhere by the Minoans. The people recovered and rebuilt on an even grander scale.

II. POLITICS AND WAR

1792 **Hammurabi** [Hammurapi, Khammurabi] the Great succeeded to the **Amorite throne** of **Babylon** in Mesopotamia. The famous conqueror and lawgiver ruled a prosperous state that reached from the Persian Gulf to the Mediterranean. Hammurabi built many temples, dug two long canals, and was best remembered for his code of laws.

1780–1600 For almost two centuries Egypt, during the beginning of the **Second Intermediate Period,** wallowed in mediocrity, anarchy, and helplessness under weak and short-lived governments and rulers. **Dynasties XIII and XIV** encompassed many kings; they were listed, but none were really noteworthy. The later pharaohs of **Dynasty XIV** ruled only in

Upper Egypt. New powers, infiltrators, and invaders disrupted life throughout the Near East. The **Hyksos** began (c.1715) to infiltrate the Nile Delta region of Egypt.

1766 The partially legendary **Shang**, an agricultural people who knew the use of war chariots, defeated the legendary **Hsia** [Xia] **Dynasty**, which was probably only a petty state in the **Yellow River** [Huang Ho, Huang He] **Valley**, China. Although little archaeological evidence of the Hsia Dynasty exists today, bronze work and other artifacts and remains of the Shang [Yin] Dynasty provide evidence that this dynasty had actually existed.

1760 **Hammurabi**, king of Babylonia, promulgated his code, one of the earliest and most famous **codes of law.** It provided for civil, economic, family, and criminal laws, most remembered for its principle "an eye for an eye."

1752 **Hammurabi**, first king of the First Babylonian Empire (c.1792–c.1630), died and was succeeded by his son (?) **Samsu-Iluna** (ruled to c.1750).

1720–1570 During **Dynasties XV and XVI** the Semitic **Hyksos** ruled Egypt, at least in the north, though for short periods they may have ruled all of the country. The deeds of these 14 Hyksos pharaohs went unrecorded. Their capital was at **Avaris** [Tanis or Pelusium], known to be in the eastern part of the Nile Delta, and they probably also controlled Palestine and Syria. The Hyksos, whose last pharaoh was **Apophis III**, were driven out by **Khamos of Dynasty**

XVII and his brother **Ahmose** (ruled 1580–1557), founder of **XVIII Dynasty**.

1716–612 **Assyria**, one of the most violent kingdoms of Mesopotamia, first arose under **Shamsi-Adad II** (ruled 1716–1687). The kingdom had two declines and three rises in power. At times it ruled large parts of Mesopotamia and Egypt until its capital Nineveh was destroyed (612 B.C.).

1700 The **Celtic Battle Ax people** from the steppes of central Russia gradually settled among the people of Scandinavia north of the Teutons. They brought with them the **domesticated horse**, used for **pulling wagons**, and an **Indo-European language**.

III. ECONOMY AND TRADE

1750 **Hammurabi**, king of Babylonia, tried unsuccessfully to outlaw interest above 20 percent on loans in silver and grain.

1700 **Crete** developed and built **seaworthy vessels** propelled by oars and sails. The Syrians, Greeks, and Phoenicians used the same sort of vessels but soon improved on them and built them with higher bulwarks and two masts.

IV. SCIENCE, EDUCATION, AND TECHNOLOGY

1766–1122 Oracle bones excavated in Honan [Henan] province of China were dated to the **Shang** [Yin] **Dynasty** (c.1766–1027). They were the shoulder bones of domestic animals, such as sheep, cattle, and swine. The **earliest known form of Chinese writing** came from the early days of the Shang, and characters similar to these ideographs were put on the bones, which were then heated by fire; the way the bones cracked in relation to the characters foretold the future, particularly the weather.

1700 The first of two waves of construction began on the megalithic monuments at **Avebury** in central southern England. Similar to the monument at Stonehenge, Avebury contained stones as heavy as 40 tons.

1699–1600 B.C.

I. VITAL STATISTICS AND DEMOGRAPHICS

1600 The **Phoenicians**, whose origins are still unknown and who were probably Semites, first appeared. Phoenicia was never more than a rather loose confederation of seaport city-states occupying a narrow 150-mile-long stretch of the eastern Mediterranean coast from **Dor** [Tantura] north to **Ugarit**. The Phoenicians were merchants who established trading colonies, such as **Carthage** and **Gades** [Cadiz], along the Mediterranean coasts and elsewhere.

1600 The **Teutons** at this time occupied present Denmark and southern Scandinavia. They spoke an Indo-European language probably similar to present German, and they may have been a branch of the **Celto-Ligurians** (a Celtic people who lived then in most of present France, Germany, Switzerland, and Austria).

II. POLITICS AND WAR

1645–1580 A native **Dynasty XVII** ruled in Upper Egypt while the **Hyksos Dynasties XV and XVI** continued to rule in Lower Egypt. Seventeen kings—possibly some were rulers of very small areas—and an additional six who ruled all of Upper Egypt were listed for this dynasty, the last two being **Sekenenre** [Seqenenre, Sekenre] and **Khamose** [Kamose].

1680 The **Hittites** infiltrated Anatolia from the west and northeast about this time. They were Indo-European peoples who fought with battle axes from horses and horse-drawn chariots. By c.1650 B.C. they were in control of northern Syria and the trade routes to the Euphrates River. They invaded **Babylonia** and captured Babylon briefly (c.1590).

1630–1175 The **Kassite Dynasty** in Babylonia lasted about 455 years, ruling from **Dur-Kurigalzu** ['Agar Quf, Akerkuf], to the west of present Baghdad. After intermittent warfare with Assyria, Kassite Babylonia was conquered by the **Elamites**.

III. SCIENCE, EDUCATION, AND TECHNOLOGY

1600 The **Smith Papyrus** of this time described 48 clinical surgery cases.

1600 The **earliest known map** was inscribed on a clay tablet dating from 1600 B.C. It showed the Babylonian Province of Shat-Azalla, indicating the directions north and south on the margins.

IV. ARTS AND LEISURE

1600 Of the few faded and scorched examples extant of **Greek paintings**, one dated to Late Mycenaean times was a fresco of a boar hunt.

1600 The **pylon**, a gateway building looking like a truncated pyramid, came into use in Egyptian temple architecture.

1599–1500 B.C.

I. VITAL STATISTICS AND DEMOGRAPHICS

1500 The middle Bronze Age **population of Great Britain** has been estimated at 40,000. The **world's population** at 1500 B.C. has been estimated to exceed 28,000,000, with the greatest concentrations in southwestern Asia.

II. POLITICS & WAR

1595 The **Kassite Babylonian Empire** (1630–1175) was invaded by **Mursilis I**, king of the Hittites. Babylon was laid waste, and much booty was carried back to the Hittite capital **Hattusas** [Hattushash, Boğazkale], in present Turkey.

1580–1090 The New Kingdom of Egypt, which included **Dynasties XVIII, XIX, and XX**, began. During this time Egypt became an empire, annexing Syria, Palestine, Nubia, and the ancient kingdom of Mittani in present northwestern Iraq. Drained of wealth and willing soldiers, Egypt declined toward the end of **Dynasty XX** (c.1090).

c.1580 **Khamose** [Kamose] of the **Theban XVII Dynasty** in Egypt drove the last of the **Hyksos** out of Egypt, capturing their capital **Avaris**, and eventually annihilating them in a battle at Sharuhen in central western Palestine. His successor **Ahmose** firmly established **Dynasty XVIII** in Egypt.

1580–1320 Dynasty XVIII of the New Kingdom of Egypt lasted more than 230 years. It included the reigns of the empire builders **Ahmose** (ruled 1580–1557), **Amenhotep I** (ruled 1557–1501), and **Thutmose III** (1501–1481), who ruled jointly with his half-sister and wife **Queen Hatshupset** [Hatasu]

(c.1495–1475) from 1501 to 1496 and from 1493 to 1481 and alone from 1481 to 1447.

1540 **Thutmose** [Dhutmose, Thutmosis] **I** of **Dynasty XVIII** in Egypt (d.1501) conquered (c.1525 B.C.) the **Nubian** [Kushite] **territory** situated beyond the Third Cataract of the Nile. Nubia then became for almost five centuries a dependency of Egypt both politically and culturally, and under the control of the **high priests of Amon** [Amen].

1500 The **kingdom of Mitanni** arose in northwestern Mesopotamia, as a union of small Hurrian states centered at Washukkani on the Khabur River in the border region of present northern Iraq and southeastern Turkey. It was led by an Aryan warrior caste, using the horse-drawn war chariot, and became strong enough to control Assyria and to challenge the power of Egypt in ancient Syria.

III. ECONOMY & TRADE

1500–1200 The **cucumber**, a native plant of the lower Himalaya mountains, was evidently carried into India as a cultivated plant by the Aryans.

1500 **Murals** in a tomb in Egypt showed the casting of copper in molds.

IV. RELIGION & PHILOSOPHY

1500 Historians generally estimate this date as the start of the **Vedic age**, a cultural period consequent to the appearance in northern India of Aryan tribes from the northwest. In the Vedic period, approximately 1000 years, were composed the four chief *Vedas*, the *Brāhmanas* and the *Upanishads*. These comprised the **sacred scriptures of Hinduism**, a religion without a founder and without dogma.

V. SCIENCE, EDUCATION, AND TECHNOLOGY

1580–1320 The **cat was certainly domesticated** during **Dynasty XVIII** in Egypt.

1500 By this time many nations in Mesopotamia had adopted the **cuneiform writing** of the Sumerians. There was almost simultaneous development of **phonetic alphabets** in parts of Mesopotamia. For example, at Ras Shamra, in present Syria, the Sumerian alphabet of some hundreds of signs was reduced to 29 symbols, each of which stood for a sound in the language.

1500 The **Bronze Age** came to **China** some time prior to 1500 B.C. **Anyang**, capital of the early **Shang [Yin] Dynasty** (c.1766–1027), displayed very high craftsmenship in bronze tools and vessels by 1500.

c.1500 The **process of making hard iron** began in Anatolia. Iron had been known from at least the times of pre-dynastic Egypt, and pre-historic projectile points were made from meteorites long before. Now smiths learned that carbon beaten into iron yielded a much harder product, suitable for weapons.

VI. ARTS & LEISURE

1501–1481 The **Temple of Queen Hatshepsut** was built at **Deir el-Bahri**, across from Karnak in present Egypt. **Hatshepsut** was the first Egyptian monarch to build a tomb in the Valley of the Kings; about 60 pharaohs followed her example.

VII. SPORTS, GAMES, & SOCIETY

1500–1200 During the **Scandinavian Bronze Age**, men wore woolen caps, cloaks, and undergarments. Women wore two-piece garments, one piece falling from the shoulders, the other from the hips.

1499–1400 B.C.

I. DISASTERS

1450 A **violent earthquake on Thera** [Thira, Santorin], in the Cyclades [Kikládhes] of the southern Aegean Sea, ruined or destroyed many of the forts and palaces of the **Mycenaean Civilization** on mainland Greece. Radiocarbon dating suggests the date may have been c.1600 and ice cores extracted in Greenland indicate the date as 1645. Three-fourths of the island of Thera disappeared, the crater of the huge volcano filled with sea water, and now small islands ring the area. The earthquake damaged Crete extensively, marking the decline of the **Minoans**. After this cataclysm mainland Greece became the heart of the Aegean Civilization.

II. POLITICS AND WAR

1496–1493 **Thutmose II** ruled Egypt for three years after **Thutmose I**, coming out of retirement, ousted **Queen Hatshepsut** and Thutmose III from their joint rule; they resumed rule after the death of Thutmose II.

1480 In a **battle at Megiddo** in Palestine, Egyptian forces defeated an army of Palestinians commanded by forces from **Kadesh**. In 17 expeditions **Thutmose** conquered ancient Syria-Palestine, reduced the kingdoms of **Kadesh**, near Homs in present northwestern Syria, and **Mitanni**, between the Euphrates and Tigris rivers in present Syria and Turkey, and conquered **Nubia** to the south of Upper Egypt.

1447–1420 The reign of **Amenhotep II**, a pharaoh of **Dynasty XVIII**, was a long series of successful campaigns in Egypt's territories in the Near East. Revolts of the cities of ancient Palestine and Syria resulted in Egypt's draining much booty and more than 50,000 captives from those countries.

III. ECONOMY AND TRADE

1400 The **Iron Age** was firmly established by the development of ironworking in the area now known as Armenia, then inhabited by the **Chalybes**. The Chalybes were subject to the **Hittites**, who held a **monopoly on iron** for about 200 years because they kept secret the means of raising the temperature of iron in forges so it could be worked and hardened. When the Hittite Empire fell (c.1200), iron working spread rapidly.

IV. SCIENCE, EDUCATION, AND TECHNOLOGY

ante 1400 The **oldest known actual water clock**, made of alabaster and found in Egypt, was dated to 1400 B.C. Water clocks were used, according to records, in Mesopotamia earlier than this. Time was measured by the amount of water that flowed from one vessel to another.

V. ARTS AND LEISURE

1499–1400 The **first known linen tapestries** were produced at Thebes, Egypt, most notably those of **Thutmose IV** (1420–1411). The designs were appliquéd onto the linen rather than woven into the fabric itself.

1400 The **treasury of Atreus** was built at ancient Mycenae, Greece. It was the **most famous of the vaulted tombs** used for the kings and princes during the **Late Minoan III**, a Bronze Age culture. It also marked the **beginning of the building of fortified palaces** and monumental citadels, such as those of **Mycenae, Tiryns, Pylos, Thebes,** and **Athens.**

VI. SPORTS, GAMES, AND SOCIETY

1470 **Men's and women's clothing** during the later years of the New Kingdom (c.1580–1090) was influenced by the recent Egyptian conquest of Syria and Palestine. The seamed tunic, or **Kalasiris,** was introduced. Men wore the Kalasiris with one or more skirts, and for women it became the main garment, worn with a cape tied at the breast.

1399–1300 B.C.

I. POLITICS AND WAR

1375–1360 **Amenhotep IV,** pharaoh of **Dynasty XVIII** in Egypt, built a new capital, **Akhetaton,** at present Tell el'Amarna, south of present Mallawi, and later changed his name to **Ikhnaton** [Akhenaten, Akhenaton]. He initiated the almost monotheistic cult of the sun god **Aton** [Aten]. Amenhotep obliterated the names of the other gods in the belief that the destruction of the name meant the destruction of the person. His neglect of foreign affairs soon resulted in the downfall of his dynasty and almost of his nation.

1360 **Tutankhamen** (c.1371–c.1352) succeeded to the throne of Egypt, ending the religious and political reforms of his father, **Amenhotep IV.** He returned the capital to Thebes, and restored the traditional gods and the **priesthood of Amon.** Amenhotep's capital **Akhetaton** was razed. This work was completed by his general and successor **Harmhab** [Horemhab, Horemheb] (c.1350–1315), who restored the Egyptian Empire to its stability both internally and externally. Tutankhamen is the King "Tut" whose tomb, with its funerary furniture and artifacts almost intact after c.3280 years, was found in A.D. 1922 by **Howard Carter** (May 9, 1873– Mar. 2, 1939).

1340 Hittite forces led by **Suppiluliumas** [Shuppiluliumash] **I** (ruled c.1380–1339) invaded the kingdom of **Mitanni** and conquered its capital, **Washuk-** kani. The western territories of Mitanni were annexed by the **Hittites,** who at this time were the main power in Anatolia and northern Syria. The eastern part of the kingdom of Mitanni was soon taken over by the **Assyrians,** led by **Ashuruballit I.** Mitanni had been weakened by its wars against the Hittites and its dynastic rivalries. Its fall marked the rise in power of the Assyrian Empire in Mesopotamia.

1320 **Dynasty XIX** of Egypt was founded by **Harmhab** [Horemhab], a war minister in Tutankhamen's reign of Dynasty XVIII, and ended with the reign of **Queen Twosre** (ruled c.1202–1189). Pharaohs prominent in this dynasty were **Ramses I** (1315–1310), **Seti I** (ruled 1305–1290), **Ramses II** (ruled 1290–1224), and **Merneptah** (ruled 1224–1214).

II. ARTS AND LEISURE

1390 Construction began (completed c.1375) on the **Colossus of Memnon,** consisting of two seated figures, erected by **Amenhotep III,** pharaoh of Egypt, at Thebes. It stood 63 feet high.

1380 **"The Hymn to the Sun,"** ascribed to **Amenhotep IV,** was a hymn to monotheism and similar to Psalm 104 in the Bible, written hundreds of years later.

1360 **Amenhotep IV,** pharaoh of Egypt, had a sculpture made of the head of his wife **Nefertiti** that endures today.

1299–1200 B.C.

I. VITAL STATISTICS AND DEMOGRAPHICS

1200 The **Peoples of the Sea** were mainly maritime folk who, as a result of widespread barbarian migrations and of raids by nomads on civilized areas—which disrupted, among other areas, Greece, Italy, and Sicily—were displaced from their homelands in the eastern Mediterranean. No names of these people have survived.

II. POLITICS AND WAR

1288 Egyptian forces led by **Ramses II** (c.1292–1224), pharaoh of **Dynasty XIX**, were checked by **Muwatallis**, king of the Hittites (ruled c.1306–1282), at the **battle of Kadesh** on the Orontes River in present Syria.

1276 **Shalmaneser I** (died c.1257), king of **Assyria** [Assur, Ashur, Asshur], emerged as a powerful ruler after having conquered much of ancient Syria, then partially controlled by the Hittites and Egypt. Assyria captured (c.1249 B.C.) Babylon, then ruled by the **Kassites**, and carried off the idol of the god **Marduk**.

1256 **Ramses II**, pharaoh of Egypt, and **Hattusilis III**, king of the Hittite Empire (ruled 1275–1250), signed a treaty of peace and friendship, sealed by Ramses's marriage with Hattusilis's daughter.

1250 The **Philistines** [Pelesets] established themselves in the coastal plains of present Israel about the same time the Israelites were moving into the inland areas. Their exact origins are still unknown, but they were marine nomads driven from their eastern Mediterranean homelands by the widespread barbarian movements of the times. The Philistines created a military confederacy of five city-states: **Ashdod, Ashqelon, Ekron, Gath,** and **Gaza.** Their knowledge of iron tools and weapons gave them an initial advantage over the bronze-using Israelites in the struggle over the Canaanite lands.

1240 The Israelites established themselves firmly in **Canaan**, in what later came to be called Palestine. Their occupation of the land was supported by the turmoil in the Mediterranean region and especially by the struggle of Egypt to repulse the Libyans and the Peoples of the Sea. By 1200 B.C. the Israelites were organized into 12 tribes.

1230 It was more likely that **Troy fell** to the **Mycenaeans** from mainland Greece on this date than the one traditionally assigned (1184 B.C.).

1230 The king of a **Berber tribe** from Libya, with the help of five groups of the **Peoples of the Sea**, led a nearly successful attack against Egypt during the latter years of the reign of **Ramses II**. Although repulsed, many of the attackers remained in the Nile delta as mercenaries in the Egyptian armies. One group settled along the eastern shore of the Mediterranean and became known as the **Philistines.**

1200 **Suppiluliumas II**, king of the Hittites (1190–?), was the **last recorded ruler of the Hittite Empire** (from c.1450), finally destroyed by invading Greeks and Peoples of the Sea. The Hittite Empire was replaced in Anatolia by that of the **Phrygians** in Anatolia, while the Arameans moved into the former Hittite lands in Syria.

1200 The Greek-speaking **Dorians**, armed with iron weapons, first appeared in the **Peloponnesus**. They probably came through the mountains of northern and central Greece and captured and destroyed many of the Mycenaean strongholds, eventually entering Ionia and even Anatolia. Their invasions coincided with disruptive raids and invasions by the **Phrygians** and the **Peoples of the Sea.**

1200 The **Phrygians** were moving into Anatolia from the west. They eventually met and defeated or merged with the **Cimmerians** from the east. Knowledge of the sequences and movements of the various people through Greece, Anatolia, and northern Mesopotamia is still muddled.

1200–1100 Many Greeks, largely Mycenaean, driven from their homelands by the more barbaric **Dorian Greeks**, fled to the islands and coasts of western Anatolia, where they eventually became known as **Ionian Greeks.** They formed loose federations of prosperous, autonomous city-states, such as **Ephesus, Erythrae, Colophon, Clazomenae, Miletus,** and **Phoca.** They warred with their neighbors, Greek and non-Greek, and between periods of independence fell successively under the rule of Lydia, Persia, Macedonia, and Rome.

1200 The rule of **Ramses III**, either the first or the second pharaoh of **Dynasty XX** in Egypt, was marked by a long series of campaigns to repulse the invasions of the Libyans and Peoples of the Sea. Some authorities now list **Setnakht**, who ruled for only two years, as the first pharaoh of this dynasty. Ramses succeeded in holding his empire except for its Asian territories. By the end of his reign, however, Egyptian society, increasingly controlled by the wealthy priesthood, was more threatened internally than externally. The dynasty collapsed (c.1090 B.C.) under **Ramses XI**.

III. ECONOMY AND TRADE

1200 **Cotton** was said to have been **introduced into China**. It was probably grown first somewhere in the south.

IV. RELIGION AND PHILOSOPHY

1280 A group of Hebrews of indeterminate number were led from bondage in Egypt by **Moses**. No extrabiblical evidence of the **Exodus** itself exists today. The long reign of **Ramses II** (c.1292–1224) is regarded by scholars as the most likely period, and has provided archaeological evidence of Moses and of the Exodus itself.

1235 The **Bible**, a collection of books produced at various times in several places by diverse people, made what was probably its beginning with the formulation of part of the **Mosaic Law**, or **Torah**. When completed, the Torah [instruction], also referred to as the **Pentateuch**, or the first five books of the Old Testament, was believed to record the **ancient laws of Moses**.

1200 The Chinese attributed the discovery of the **Yang-Yin philosophy** to a legendary ruler of a legendary tribe, **Wen Wang** (c.1231–1135 B.C.). Wen Weng was said to have written *I Ching [Book of Changes]* while imprisoned by **Chou Hsin**, the legendary final ruler of the **Shang [Yin] Dynasty** (c.1766–1027). Legend further implied that **Fu Hsi** (c.2800) had already laid the basis for this philosophy. Yang-Yin represented opposites but together constituted the **T'ai-yi**, **Great Monad**: the Yang the positive, and the Yin the negative forces or things. Yang meant light, Yin darkness; Yang male to Yin female; Yang heaven, Yin earth, etc. Cosmic harmony existed when Yang and Yin acted together.

V. SCIENCE, EDUCATION, AND TECHNOLOGY

1200 The **Iron Age** began throughout the Near East. The **Hittites** had monopolized mining, smelting, and other production, perhaps for more than a century prior to 1200 B.C. Production and use of iron did not enter China until some time during the Warring States period (450–221) of the **Chou Dynasty** (c.1027–256 B.C.) The **Dorian Greeks** brought the Iron Age to Greece, and iron was also becoming common in Palestine. The **Philistines**, who had apparently learned how to work iron from the Hittites, monopolized the importation and use of iron in **Palestine**.

1200 An alphabetic script on clay tablets in an **ancient library at Zapouna**, in present Syria, was dated to this time by a French archaeological expedition. The script read from right to left and was in a Semitic language. It was not known how long before this date the alphabet existed, but Zapouna was sacked and burned shortly after the tablet was made. At **Ugarit**, in present Syria, archaeologists deciphered writing (reading from right to left) composed of a 30-character alphabet. This was the **earliest known true alphabet**. Ugarit, a Phoenician Semitic center, was destroyed (c.1195 B.C.) in an earthquake.

VI. ARTS AND LEISURE

1298 According to tradition, the **first draw loom**, an important invention for the development of **silk weaving**, was built in China during the **Shang [Yin] Dynasty** (c.1766–1027). The draw loom was used to create damask patterns in the fabric.

1292 **Ramses II** (died c.1224), the last of the great pharaohs, was Egypt's most prolific builder. He completed the hypostyle hall of the **temple at Karnak** and his father's funerary temple at Luxor. He built his own funerary temple, known as the **Ramasseum**, at Thebes, and he was the main builder of the **rock temples at Abu Simbel** [Abu Sunbul, Ip-sam-bul] on the west bank of the Nile River near the present border with the Sudan. The Great Temple there had four statues of Ramses, each 65 feet high.

1250 The **Lion Gate to the citadel of Mycenae** in Greek Peloponnesus was constructed of such large pieces of stone that it was later believed to have been built by a race of giants.

1200–300 **Ancient Greek furniture**, as depicted on vases and shown in sculpture, consisted of many varieties of couches, chairs, and tables. Tables were low, chairs well proportioned with curved legs and backs.

1200–500 **Persian sculpture** flourished, showing a variety of styles. Some of the finest sculpture came from Luristan [Loristan] and Azerbaijan, provinces in present Iran.

1199–1100 B.C.

I. POLITICS AND WAR

1184 According to tradition, this was the year in which the **Achaean Greeks** of Mycenaean culture captured the city of **Troy** after a ten-year siege. Achaea was a region of the northern Peloponnesus. The Trojans were probably a mixed population, including invaders from the Balkans, Phrygians, Minoans, and Mycenaeans. The Trojan War was probably caused by trade rivalries, because Troy controlled trade through the Hellespont [Dardanelles] between the Aegean and Black seas.

1175 The **Kassite kingdom of Babylonia** was conquered by the Elamites under **Shutruk-Nahunte**, king of Elam (c.1185–1155), the region of present Khuzistan, Iran. He took rich booty to his capital, **Susa**, notably the famous stele containing the laws of Hammurabi. The end had come for the Kassite Dynasty of Babylonia (from 1630).

1150 The **Mycenaean Civilization** (from c.1600) came to its end with the destruction of most of their mighty stone fortresses by the invading **Dorian Greeks**. As a result of the Mycenaean collapse, mainland Greece, the islands of the Aegean, and Crete suffered a decline in civilization.

1146–1103 The **Second Babylonian Dynasty**, known as the **Pashé**, was secured by **Nebuchadnezzar** [Nebuchadrezzar] **I** (died 1103), who defeated the Elamites and restored the wealth and power of Babylonia. His reign was marked by a period of peace and high artistic achievement. He later lost power to the Assyrians, and from then until 626 B.C. Babylonia's status fluctuated as the power of Assyria rose and fell. (This Nebuchadnezzar was not the biblical Nebuchadnezzar.)

1100–1000 The **Aramaeans**, a largely Semitic people, established several relatively small kingdoms, the largest of which was **Bit-Adini**, centered at Carchemish in Anatolia and Damascus in present Syria.

They controlled much of present Lebanon, southern Turkey, and Syria. The language of the Aramaeans became the common tongue of Palestinians at the time of Jesus.

1100 The **Hallstatt culture** developed. The name came from the town of Hallstatt in Austria where a large cemetery contained the remains of a Celtic people who occupied the area from about this time until c.500 B.C., when it was replaced by the **La Tène culture**. The earliest artifacts found with their remains were from the Bronze Age, which in this region of Europe soon evolved into the Iron Age. Their distinctive culture, marked by rectilinear designs on pottery and metal work, spread through most of Europe, from the British Isles and Scandinavia south to central southern Spain, northern Italy, and the Balkans.

1100 The **Dorian Greeks** drove many of the Mycenaeans out of mainland Greece and destroyed much of their culture and civilization. Remnants of the Mycenaeans began to settle on the offshore islands and along the Mediterranean coast of Anatolia, but some remained in fortresses in Greece. Athens, Thebes, and Pylos were among the cities, or city-states, that remained largely Mycenaean.

1100 An approximately 20-mile strip of the coast of western Anatolia and the islands off that coast were occupied by Greeks, later called **Ionian Greeks**. Mainly Mycenaeans and their Greek predecessors, they fled from the Dorians now subduing mainland Greece. These refugees mingled with other, mainly Greek, peoples who had already settled in western Anatolia, where they prospered.

1100 **Gadir** [Gades, Cadiz] was apparently first settled by Phoenicians from Tyre, who probably used it as a trading center to obtain raw materials, including the silver and tin of **Tartessus** (founded c.1200 B.C.), an ancient kingdom and port on the southwestern coast of Spain.

II. ECONOMY AND TRADE

1100 The **domestication of the dromedary camel** became an important political factor in the Near East. Using camels the Aramaeans gained mobility and power during their penetration of the Syrian desert. As successful desert-dwellers they were soon able to become a large part of the Mesopotamian population. Although they did form minor nations and merged with their neighbors, they never became a cohesive power.

III. RELIGION AND PHILOSOPHY

1125 **The Song of Deborah**, the most significant piece of early **Hebrew literature** before the reign of **David**, king of Judah and Israel (c.1010–961), celebrated the victory of several tribes, united by the **prophetess Deborah**, over the **Canaanite general Sisera** [Sisara] on the plain of Jezreel, near Megiddo.

IV. ARTS AND LEISURE

c.1199–700 The *Shu-ching* [*Shang-shu*], or *Book of History* [*Book of Documents*], which dealt with the period from the 12th to the 8th centuries, was considered the **first Chinese work of history**. The original work, a collection of ancient texts, was apparently written by many people. **Confucius** [K'ung Fu-Tzǔ] was said to have rewritten much of the work, adding his own interpretations and moralizing. The *Shu-ching*, as well as the *I-ching*, was one of the Chinese Five Classics.

1100 The **Dorian Greeks** brought the Iron Age to Greece and, with their iron weapons, a dark age when art almost disappeared. Greece became a disorganized group of walled city-states warring almost constantly on each other.

1099–1000 B.C.

I. VITAL STATISTICS AND DEMOGRAPHICS

1000 **Africa's population** of more than 6.5 million was largely concentrated in the north, with Egypt's 3 million people forming nearly 40 percent of the total. In Western Africa people began to practice agriculture, and the population increased. This was also true of the Nilo-Saharans living in the Sudan and the people of the Sahel, the dry grasslands south of the Sahara Desert. The rain-forest pygmies and the bushmen of eastern and southern Africa continued their pre-agricultural traditions and showed little population growth. The **population of Asia** at this time was estimated at 50 million, of which 25 percent was located in the Near East. China had less than 20 million people and Japan probably less than 30,000. **India** may have had a population as large as 20 million. At the same time the **European population** was about 8 million, and that of both **Americas** probably less than 5 million.

1000 **Polynesians** probably arrived in the region of the Tongan and Samoan islands in the central South Pacific. The Polynesians developed a variety of sea-going ships equipped with one, and sometimes two, masts, sails, and oars. Their navigation was based on the stars, sun, moon, and ocean currents as well as on an ancient knowledge of the seas. They frequently sailed, like the **Vikings** at this time, over long distances, from one south Pacific island group to another.

II. POLITICS AND WAR

1090 **Nubia** became independent of Egypt when **Dynasty XX** (c.1200–1090) of the New Kingdom disintegrated under its last pharaoh, **Ramses XI**. Nubia, with its capital at **Napata** (750) near the fourth cataract of the Nile, grew steadily in wealth and power. The southern portion of Nubia was a region known to the Egyptians and Hebrews as **Kush** [Cush], whose people apparently extended southward to occupy most of present northern Ethiopia and northern Somalia.

1090 **Ramses XI** died, ending **Dynasty XX** (c.1200–1090) and the New Kingdom, or Empire, (c.1580–1090) of Egypt. He had been preceded by seven other Ramses, IV through X, as ineffective as he was. With the kingdom split in two and no longer politically significant, the priesthood, led by Hrihor [Herihor], ruled Upper Egypt from Thebes [Thebae, Diospolis, No], near present Qena.

1087 **Smerdes** [Smendes] took control of Lower Egypt as the first pharaoh of **Dynasty XXI** (1087–945), called the **Tanite**, with its capital in Tanis in the eastern Nile delta near present Sân el Hagar. The priests, ruling in the south, were little disturbed.

1076 The **collapse of Assyria** c.27 years after the death of **Tiglath-pileser I** (ruled 1115–1102) resulted from almost unremitting attacks by invading peoples, including Midianites and Aramaeans.

1027 The vassal tribe of Chou, under **Wu Wang** [Wang = king], son of **Wen Wang**, defeated the **Shang** [Yin] **Dynasty** (from 1766) and established a new dynasty in China. This date has been determined from archaeological evidence; the classical date is 1122. The **Chou** [Chow, Zhou] **Dynasty** (to 256 B.C.), was the longest-reigning in Chinese history. There was a Western Chou Dynasty (c.1027–771), which held court at Hao in the Wei River valley in Kansu [Gansu] province, and an Eastern Chou (c.771–256), which subsequently ruled from Lo-yang in Honan [Henan] province.

1020 The Israelites—hard-pressed by the Philistines living west of them—turned to **Saul**, the military hero of the tribe of Benjamin, and made him the first king of Israel. The period of rule by the judges in Israel thereby ended, marking the transfer of power from clan chiefs and town elders to a monarchical organization.

1010 **Saul, first king of Israel**, slew himself with his sword after losing a battle and three of his four sons at Mount Gilboa, west of the Jordan River, to the Philistines. His fourth son, **Ishbosheth**, survived but was soon assassinated. In 1003 B.C. **David** was proclaimed king of all Israel (to 961), reuniting the states of Judah and Israel, and keeping his capital at Hebron, near present Jerusalem.

1000 Artifacts found near La Victoria, an archaeological site in present southwestern Guatemala, indicated that the **Mayan culture** may have originated at this time, possibly evolving from the presumed earlier **Olmec culture** of the Gulf Coast, in the present Mexican states of Vera Cruz and Tabasco. Other Mayan finds in the northwestern Yucatán Peninsula showed that the area of Dzibilchaltun, north of Mérida, may have been continuously occupied from 1000 B.C. to the present. The Mayas used an arithmetic system based on 20 and a hieroglyphic alphabet of more than 850 characters. The highly success-ful **Mayan agricultural system** provided the economic basis necessary for their civilization.

III. ECONOMY AND TRADE

1000–500 Pictures etched on bone and ivory by ancient man revealed that **reindeer were used in northern Europe as horses** and for food, milk, leather, and other purposes.

1000 The **horse was first ridden in central Asia.** The development resulted in more efficient management of the herds.

1000 By this time, the Indians of present Mexico were raising **corn**, **beans**, **squashes**, and a variety of other plants, including **chili peppers.**

IV. RELIGION AND PHILOSOPHY

1050 In a **battle at Aphek**, near Kefar 'Eqron [Ekron] in present Israel, the Philistines routed the Israelites and captured the **Ark of the Covenant.** The Ark had been brought from its shrine at Shiloh [Khirbat Saylūn], in the West Bank, in the hope that Yahweh's presence on the battlefield would turn the tide. The Philistines apparently then razed Shiloh, the religious center of the Hebrew tribal confederacy.

1003 Hebron [Al Khalil, Kirjath Arba], in the West Bank of Israel, was one of the holy cities of the **Talmud.** It contained the **Haram**, the structure enclosing the mosque built over the **Cave of Machpelah** where, according to Genesis, Abraham and Sarah were buried.

1000–500 The *Vedas*, literally books of knowledge, which included the **Rig-Veda, Sama-Veda, Yajur-Veda, Atharva-Veda**, the Hindu sacred learnings of their early days, were probably perfected in their oral form and arranged in sequence sometime in this period. They passed orally from generation to generation by the priests and were not written down until well into the Christian era. The Rig-Veda consisted of 1028 hymns of praise and petition to the many Aryan gods, and included such practical items as the names of medicinal herbs. The Sama-Veda included verses from the Rig-Veda arranged as a hymnal; the Yajur-Veda, composed 1000–800, was a collection in prose of prayers and magical spells; and the Artharva-Veda, composed somewhat later, consisted of rhythmic chants showing Dravidian influences.

1000   Shintoism, as a name, was first recorded in Japan, but it was practiced much earlier. Shinto in Japanese meant "the way of the gods"; it was initially pure animism, which endowed things in the environment with spirits to be placated if dangerous or rewarded if friendly. No regular pantheon or established rituals existed; these came in late sixth century A.D., by which time Shinto was firmly established, distinguishing it from Buddhism and Confucianism. In A.D. c.800 the Japanese Buddhist monks **Saicho** [Dengyo Daishi] (767–822) and **Kukai** [Kobo Daishi] (744–835) blended Buddhism with Shintoism, which developed into today's Shinto religion.

V. SCIENCE, EDUCATION, AND TECHNOLOGY

1027–250   Sometime during the **Chou Dynasty** of China, the much more efficient **breast-strap harness for horses** was invented. It enabled farmers to work larger farms, producing more food for larger populations.

1027   **Wu Wang** (ruled 1027–1020), first emperor of the **Chou** [Zhou] **Dynasty** in China, established the **first recorded zoo** in the world. Called a "park of intelligence," it was not known how long it survived nor whether it was open to the public.

1000   **The Hindus developed a calendar.** Following the Babylonian partitioning of the skies through zodiacal constellations, the year was divided into 12 months, each of thirty 30-hour days, with an extra month inserted every five years.

1000   **Parchment**, usually of sheep or goat skin, was developed as writing material in western Asia.

VI. ARTS AND LEISURE

1000–500   The *Vedas*, the Hindu sacred texts, were chanted using two tones. During this period musicians were portrayed in wall sculpture using the arched harp and drums, which were important also in secular music.

1000–900   The **Protogeometric style of design for ceramics**, based on primitive geometric designs, originated in Greece.

1000   Assyrian potters developed **tin-glaze ware.** It was used in the production of faience and, later, delftware.

1000   **Musical instruments** proliferated in the Near East. Harps, zithers, cymbals, and sistra were played in Israel; male and female professional musicians performed at David's court, and priests sang as part of the Temple liturgy.

999–900 B.C.

I. POLITICS AND WAR

997–995   **David**, king of Judah and Israel, and his small army of professional soldiers, twice defeated attacking Philistine armies in the hills near Jerusalem. David captured Jerusalem, a Jebusite enclave on the border between Judah and Benjamin, and made it both a royal holding, "the City of David," and a national capital. To it he brought the **Ark of the Covenant**, also making Jerusalem the religious capital of the kingdom.

961   **David**, king of Judah (from 1010) and Israel (from 1003), died. During his long reign he established his nation as a strong, independent state and extended its territory by defeating the **Moabites, Aramaeans, Edomites, Ammonites**, and others. David declared **Solomon**, his son by Bathsheba, his

heir, and Solomon succeeded to the throne peacefully on David's death.

945–730   **Dynasty XXII**, the **Libyan Bubastite Dynasty**—so-called because its capital was at ancient Bubastis, near present Zagizig in the eastern Nile Delta—ruled Egypt for c.150 years. Libyans had infiltrated the Nile Delta for generations and finally rose under **Sheshonk I** [Shoshonk, Shishak] (died 920), placing him on the throne as the first pharaoh of the new dynasty.

940   The **Queen of Sheba** [Saba] made a state visit to Judah and Israel bringing gifts of gold, incense, and precious stones. **Solomon** gave her many gifts in return. Sheba, an important Arabian nation in the southwestern corner of the Arabian Peninsula, controlled many trade routes.

934–783 **Assyria** began a renascence under **Assur-dan II** (ruled 934–911) during which all of Syria was conquered (911) and Palestine, Lebanon, and Babylon became virtual vassal states. Noted kings of this era were **Adadnirari II** (ruled 911–889); **Ashurnasir-pal II** (ruled 884–859); **Shalmaneser III** (ruled 859–825), **Shamsi-Adad V** (ruled 824–811); and **Adad-nirari III** (ruled 811–783), whose mother, **Sammu-ramat**, probably the legendary Semiramis, was the virtual ruler.

922 **Solomon** (ruled from 961), king of Judah and Israel, died, leaving his kingdom with serious internal problems. Solomon had rapidly transformed Israel from a tribal confederation with sacral institutions to a dynastic, structured, secular state regarding itself as divinely instituted. Solomon was succeeded by his arrogant son **Rehoboam** (d. 917). The northern tribes, dissatisfied with the royal policy of forced labor for construction projects, refused to recognize Rehoboam as king. They chose instead **Jeroboam** (died 912), an Ephraimite clan chief who years earlier had been forced to flee to Egypt for protesting the same policy. With his capital at Shechem [Samaria] in the central highlands of Manasseh, the kingdom was split into the southern kingdom of Judah and the northern kingdom of Israel.

920 **Sheshonk I**, pharaoh of Egypt, overran Palestine during the reign of Rehoboam. Many towns, including Jerusalem, were plundered in both Israel and Judah.

900–283 **Etruria**, the Etruscan nation, occupied most of present central Italy from the Tiber River to the Arno River. It ruled over Rome for short periods. According to the Greeks of the time, the Etruscans called themselves **Rasenna**. Their language and culture differed from those of the other peoples of Italy, and their origin is unknown. No Etruscan literature survives today, and there are only short inscriptions from tombs. Though the Estruscan language has not been deciphered, the **Roman alphabet** was derived from the **Etruscan alphabet**. The Etruscans were finally conquered by Rome and, except for their tombs and artifacts found over much of Italy, they disappeared from history.

II. ECONOMY AND TRADE

980 The **kingdom of Sheba** [Saba] occupied present Yemen. Its economic power arose from its control of trade routes for gold, precious stones, and spices, particularly frankincense and myrrh. Its capital, now in ruins, was **Marib**, about 90 miles east of present San'a.

III. RELIGION AND PHILOSOPHY

997 The sacred **Ark of the Covenant**, a chest of acacia wood ornamented with gold containing **Aaron's rod**, the Decalogue inscribed on stone, and a container of manna was brought to Jerusalem by David. The Ark was about 45 inches long and 27 inches high and wide.

957 **Solomon** began the building of the **Temple at Jerusalem**, at a site north of the area now occupied by a Muslim shrine. The rear of the long, rectangular building contained a windowless chamber, the "Holy of Holies," which housed the Ark of the Covenant. The Temple, completed in 950, was built of white limestone, cut and finished at the quarries, and the interior walls were paneled with cypress, ornamented with carved floral designs, and inlaid with gold and ivory.

950 Scholars believe that during the prosperity of Solomon's peaceful reign in Israel, an unknown writer wrote down for the first time the **historical traditions**, folk tales, and ballads of the Israelite tribes. This document, called *J* because of its author's use of "Jahweh" for "God," now more commonly spelled Yahweh, became the chief strand to which other writings were later inserted or added, forming the canonical history of the Hebrew people to the time of Solomon.

921 Israel's capital was placed by **Jeroboam** at Shechem [Samaria]. Lacking a religious center to rival Jerusalem's Temple, Jeroboam set up two national shrines, at Bethel and Dan. He supplied these shrines with golden bulls, intended to represent pedestals upon which the invisible Lord sat enthroned, but too easily regarded by some as Baal-worshiping symbols. The shrines and the bulls were "the sin of Jeroboam," decried in the **book of Kings**, written later in Judah. The southern kingdom of Judah, hence the name "the Jews," retained Jerusalem as its capital.

900–500 The **Upanishads** of the Hindu religion—preserved by the **Brahmins** or the priestly caste—were chanted or sung in the **Sanskrit language** from memory. They presented a view of the origin of the gods, philosophy, the cosmos, and the people.

IV. SCIENCE, EDUCATION, AND TECHNOLOGY

960 The **Phoenicians** were using an alphabet, probably developed from the Egyptian syllabary. Prior to this date, a bronze cup with alphabetic inscription was offered to the gods by **Hiram** [Huram], king of Tyre (970–936). Though the Phoenician alphabet was adopted by the Greeks, probably some time in the eighth century, the Greeks wrote from left to right and the Phoenicians from right to left, and the configurations of some letters were reversed.

900 **Pre-Incan society** in present Peru reached a highly developed stage, with the building of large structures, the advancement of pottery, and the introduction of metallurgy. Recent archaeological excavations indicate that the pre-Incan people of the Andes had been building step pyramids and monumental temples as long ago as 5000–3500 B.C., thousands of years before the **Aztec civilization** rose in Mexico.

V. SPORTS, GAMES, AND SOCIETY

900–283 As **underclothing of the men of Etruria** wore either a long tunic or a short, doubletlike garment, both of which were called *chitons* by the Greeks. Over the chiton they wore a cloak, somewhat like the later Roman *toga*. The women wore a beltless chiton and a large cloak.

899–800 B.C.

I. EXPLORATION AND COLONIZATION

899–800 As early as this time, **Phoenician sailors** were visiting the coast of present Portugal in search of new trading areas and sites for possible new colonies.

II. POLITICS AND WAR

889 **Omri**, king of Israel (876–869), regained most of Israel's former territory; made an ally of Judah; secured the Phoenician princess, **Jezebel**, as wife for his son Ahab; and chose a new capital, **Samaria** [Sabastye], the holy city of the Samaritans on the west bank of the Jordan River. With prosperity based on international trade came laxity in religious matters, official tolerance of the worship of foreign gods, oppression of the poor, and disaffection among the people of the land.

876 **Ashurnasirpal II**, king of Assyria (884–859), began a campaign of westward expansion. He captured Carchemish [Karkamis] on the Euphrates River in present Turkey, and subdued the Aramaeans in Mesopotamia and present Syria. He reached the Mediterranean coast and collected tribute from the Phoenician cities.

855 A **battle at Karkar** near or at the Orontes ['Asi] River, near Hama in present Syria, was fought between the Assyrians led by **Shalmaneser III** (ruled 859–825) and the combined armies of **Ahab**, king of Israel, and **Adad-idri** [Ben Hadad] of Syria. Both sides claimed victory, but Shalmaneser's advance toward the Mediterranean was halted for almost 12 years. Ahab (ruled from c.869) died fighting Adad-idri's Syrian army in 853 B.C.

c.842 **Jehu** (?–c.816), a general in the army of Israel, was caused by **Elisha the prophet** to be anointed king, and in a bloody coup wiped out Jehoram [Joram], king of Israel (ruled c.849) and all the house of Omri, including Jezebel and her priests. Though he ridded Israel of Baalism, he destroyed the relationship with Phoenicia and Judah on which Omri and Ahab had built Israel's strength and prosperity. Syria, another former ally, reduced Israel to a dependency in 836 B.C.

840 The **Vannic Kingdom**, in present Turkey, Russia, and Iran, arose under Sardur [**Sarduris**] I (ruled c.840–830). It united the former Hurrian principalities into a strong military state, centered at Tushpa near Lake Van. The kingdom was known as **Urartu** to the Assyrians and **Ararat** to the Hebrews. It was one of several moderate-sized kingdoms, including **Samaria**, **Aramaea**, **Israel**, **Phoenicia**, **Phrygia**, and **Syria** that proliferated during periods of weakness of Assyria, Babylon, and Egypt.

827–800 During the **Chou** [Zhou] **Dynasty** (c.1027–c.256 B.C.), the Chinese were able to expel many of the **Huns** [Hsiung nu] from China. Though driven westward in search of living space, the Huns did not fully leave China at this time.

820 **Dynasty XXIII** of Egypt arose from a split in the **Bubastite Dynasty** that divided the nation. Dynasty XXIII, still Libyan, ruled from Thebes, and lasted until c.730 B.C.

814 **Carthage**, near present Tunis, was founded by colonists from Tyre, the capital of Phoenicia. It developed into a great maritime empire, eventually challenging Rome for control of the western Mediterranean Sea.

800 **Corinth**—a Dorian Greek city situated on the isthmus between the Gulf of Corinth and the Saronic Gulf—began its western expansion and colonization of the island of Ithaca. A leading commercial city, Corinth reached its peak of prosperity under the **Bacchiadae Dynasty** (750–655); it was noted for its bronze work and pottery.

III. RELIGION AND PHILOSOPHY

877 **Ahab**, king of Israel, tolerated his wife Jezebel's promotion of the worship of **Melkart**, the Baal of Tyre. A sizable group of Baal cultists lived in Samaria, the capital of Israel. Religious backsliding from the traditional worship of God spread widely. A spokesman for conservative people was the **prophet Elijah**. On Mount Carmel Elijah and God won a notable victory over Baal and his priests, as told in Kings.

825–800 **Parshva** [Pershwanath], now regarded as a historical personage, opposed the Hindu caste system and the sacrificial killing of animals. His community was open to all persons without distinctions of any kind. He preached an ascetic way of life and the keeping of four vows, including tolerance of all forms of life [*ahimsa*].

800 B.C.–A.D. 1200 **Tiahuanaco**, near the southern shores of Lake Titicaca in Bolivia, now in ruins, was once one of the most important religious centers of the **Andean Indian cultures**. Its influence extended into Peru and as far as Argentina and Chile.

800–c.500 The sacrifices of developing **Hinduism** had become increasingly elaborate and the rites too complicated for the fathers of families to perform. Priests grew in numbers, with the highest class being called **Brahmins**.

IV. SCIENCE, EDUCATION, AND TECHNOLOGY

870 The **first known zoo** in western Asia was established by **Ashurnasirpal II**, king of Assyria, in present northern Iraq at Calah [Nimrud], his capital. He kept lynxes, wild oxen, elephants, lions, ostriches, wild asses, gazelles, antelopes, wild dogs, panthers, and two animals he called *pagu* and *sikurru*, which are unidentified today. The zoo was open to the public.

850 The **ram**, a pointed, reinforced projection, was added to the prows of fighting ships. The Greeks were credited with the invention, which revolutionized **naval warfare**.

800 A **pyramid**, probably constructed at this time, was found at La Venta, an island in the mangrove swamps of Tabasco, southeastern Mexico. It was built of clay, probably by the early **Olmecs**.

V. ARTS AND LEISURE

884 **Ashurnasirpal II**, king of Assyria, built a palace at the site of his new capital Calah [Nimrud] in present northern Iraq. The walls of the palace were decorated with carvings of scenes of hunts and wars. These were the first examples of the great **Assyrian bas-reliefs**, a form of art that attained its height in the ninth century B.C.

850 **Homer**, the Greek poet to whom the *Iliad* and the *Odyssey* are traditionally assigned, probably lived in the mid-ninth century B.C. Nothing certain of the man is known today, not even his birthplace. According to legend, Homer was an old, blind, and poor man who lived as an itinerant singer. Many scholars believe the two poems were composed by different men.

800 The **temple of Aphaea** on the island of Aegina in the Saronic Gulf of southeastern Greece was the **earliest known structure built in the Doric architectural order**. Twenty-two columns still stand. The order, first of the three developed by the Greeks, was based on the proportions of various elements of the building, and it was marked by sturdy, fluted columns, with rather simple capitals. Developed in Mycenaean Greece from Minoan beginnings, the order may have arisen prior to the Doric invasions (c.1200 B.C.). The **earliest known important temple in the Ionic order** was built (c.600) at Ephesus. The capitals of the Ionic order were like infolded scrolls, but the proportions of buildings and columns were similar to those of the Doric order. The **Corinthian order** probably arose about the same time, or slightly after the Ionic. The columns were more slender and were capped by a design of down-curling laurel leaves. The **temple of Olympian Zeus** at Athens, built (c.550) by **Peisistratus the Tyrant**, used both Doric and Corinthian columns; some of these Corinthian columns still stand along the road from Athens to Piraeus.

799–700 B.C.

I. POLITICS AND WAR

780–560 Colonies were established by the Greek city-states around the coasts of the Mediterranean, Aegean, and Black seas. **Miletus** founded more than 80 colonies around the Black Sea, including **Abydos** (560 B.C.); **Cyzicus** (757); **Dioscurias** (750); **Olbia** (650); **Sinope** (780); and **Trapezus** (757); as well as a colony in Egypt and several in Sicily. **Chalcis** founded **Cumae** (760), the first Greek colony in mainland Italy, and **Rhegion** (730) in southern Italy. **Corinth** founded **Syracuse** (734) in Sicily and **Corcyra** [present Corfu] (734). **Sparta** founded **Tarentum** [Taras, present Taranto] (708?) in southern Italy, and **Achaea** founded **Sybaris** (721) and **Crotona** (710), in southern Italy. **Megara** founded **Chalcedon** (685) and **Byzantium** (638) on the Bosporus, and **Thera** [present Thíra, Santorin] founded **Cyrene** (630 B.C.) in northern Africa.

771–c.256 The **Eastern Chou Dynasty of China**, with its capital at Lo-yang [Luoyang], in present Honan [Henan] province, survived feudal upheavals, but its kings were mere figureheads known as the "Kings of Heaven." China became a loose confederation of feudal states.

753 Apr. 22 According to legend, **Rome** was founded by **Romulus and Remus**, twin sons of the goddess **Rhea Silvia** but raised and suckled by a wolf after Rhea abandoned them. Romulus slew Remus in a quarrel and later became the legendary first king of Rome. He was later worshipped by the Romans as the god **Quirinus**. A Bronze Age culture occupied the site of Rome as early as 1500 B.C., and Iron Age cultures were present from the ninth to seventh centuries B.C.

745–608 **Tiglath-pileser III** [Pul] (ruled to 727) took over the throne of Assyria and began wars of conquest that established an Assyrian Empire, claiming suzerainty by 663 B.C. over Egypt, Palestine, Syria, portions of eastern Turkey, Babylonia, and Elam. Great kings of this era included **Sargon II** (ruled 722–705), **Sennacherib** (ruled 705–681), **Eserhaddon** (ruled 681–668), and **Assurbanipal** (ruled 668–626). After 626 a series of weak rulers were unable to cope with rebellions in Egypt, Babylon, and elsewhere, nor with invasions from the east by the **Medes** and other peoples. The Assyrian capital Nineveh, in present northern Iraq, fell in 612 to the Medes, Scythians, and Babylonians. Finally, under their last king, **Ashuruballit II** (ruled 612–609), the Assyrians failed to recapture their fortress city of Haran, and their kings vanished from history.

735–715 **Sparta**, master of Laconia in the southern Peloponnesus, conquered Messenia just to its west in the **First Messenian War**, conducted by the double kings **Alcmenes** (ruled 740–700) and **Theopompus** (ruled 720–675). Sparta favored expansion against its close neighbors as the means of accommodating its growing population and wealth. The First Messenian War resulted in the annexation of the Messenian plains, one of the most fertile areas of Greece, and the payment of massive annual tribute to Sparta.

730–715 The **XXIVth Dynasty** of ancient Egypt took control of Lower Egypt from the Bubastite pharaohs and moved the capital from Bubastis to Saïs, about 70 miles north of present Cairo. This dynasty of two pharaohs was often referred to as the **Saïte Kings**. Dynasty XXIV was conquered in 1715 by the Ethiopian [Nubian] rulers of **Dynasty XXV**.

730 Egyptian **Dynasty XXV**, the Ethiopian, began when **Piankhi**, king of Nubia [Kush], who ruled (747–716) from Meroë, in present Sudan, subdued Upper Egypt, defeated **Tefnakhte**, the Saïte pharaoh of Lower Egypt, and conquered Memphis with military and naval forces. Piankhi returned to his Nubian capital at Napata near the fourth cataract of the Nile, but his brother and successor, **Shabaka**, ruled (717–702) as pharaoh from Thebes in Upper Egypt.

The dynasty lasted until c.656 and offered strong resistance to the invading Assyrians, who never completely conquered them.

722 After a long holdout, Samaria, capital of Israel, fell to **Sargon II**, king of Assyria. **Shalmaneser V (or IV)**, Sargon's predecessor as king of Assyria (ruled 727–722), had occupied Israel and begun the siege of Samaria in 724 because **Hoshea** (ruled 733–722), last king of Israel, withheld tribute. Sargon claimed he deported 27,290 Israelites to upper Mesopotamia. These people became known as "**the Ten Lost Tribes of Israel**." The kingdom of Judah survived.

714 The **kingdom of Urartu** [Van, Ararat] (c.1270–612), was raided by **Sargon II**. Urartu could not resist the Assyrian attack and lost its political and military importance.

700–650 A people known as the **Cimmerians** occupied the northern and eastern Black Sea coasts. Between 700 and 652, driven by the **Scythians** from the east, they invaded the Near East. Defeated by the Assyrians, they retreated to an area north of the Black Sea, where they were absorbed by the Scythians. The Cimmerians were noted for having developed iron tools, swords, and plows, and for fighting from horseback using bows and arrows in the manner of the Scythians, their teachers.

700–c.200 The **Scythians**, invading the steppes of present southern Russia, took control of the region from the **Cimmerians** and set up a military kingdom. Their cavalry was swift and effective and used short bows and arrows.

II. ECONOMY AND TRADE

720 The **first known coinage** in the Near East probably appeared near the end of the eighth century B.C. in Lydia, a nation of western Anatolia. These coins were made of **electrum**, a mixture of gold and silver, and of other metals, such as copper and lead.

700 The oared, two-banked galley called the **bireme**, which permitted shorter, more compact and easily defended vessels, was an important advance in shipbuilding. The bireme was probably developed by either the Phoenicians or the Greeks.

III. RELIGION AND PHILOSOPHY

750 The **E Document of the Pentateuch**, so named today because the word for God prevalently used in it is *Elohim* [the deity], was written in the northern kingdom, Israel, perhaps at Bethel. Scholars are now able to differentiate the Pentateuch E strands from those of J.

750 **Amos** (fl. 765–750), a shepherd of Tekoa in Judah, answered a divine call to prophesy in the northern kingdom, Israel. For Amos, God was the God of justice, not the "God of Israel"; Amos was interested in the internally moral, not the externally correct. Until stopped, he preached Israel's doom. He was the first of the great Hebrew reforming prophets and the first to collect his messages in a book.

740–700 **Isaiah of Jerusalem**, author of Isaiah 1-39, put faith in the center of religion–faith in the holiness and righteous rule of God. He also introduced the idea of a righteous remnant who would be spared and of the **Messiah**, who would rule in an age of universal peace. With **Amos** and **Hosea** (fl. c.750), Isaiah reshaped the Hebrew idea of God into an uncompromising ethical monotheism.

IV. SCIENCE, EDUCATION, AND TECHNOLOGY

753 Apr. 22 B.C. This is the legendary date of the founding of **Rome**. Dates during the Republic and Empire were reckoned from this day and year, a chronology used throughout most of the western world until A.D. 533, when **Dionysius Exiguus**, a Christian monk and scholar, fixed the date of Christ's birth as Roman Year 754 and our year 0, with B.C. [Before Christ] and A.D. [*Anno Domini*] to designate dates prior to and after that point in time.

V. ARTS AND LEISURE

799–700 The Etruscans, in central Italy, developed the gray or polished black **Bucchero Ware pottery**.

725 **Hesiod**, who probably lived toward the end of the eighth century B.C., was called the **father of Greek didactic**—or instructional—**poetry**, and Greeks regarded him second only to **Homer**. Born at Cyme in Anatolia, he lived most of his life as a shepherd and farmer on the slopes of Mount Helicon in Boeotia, mainland Greece. His epic poem *Theogony* [genealogy of the gods], which described the origin of the world, excoriated the rich, maintained that Zeus would punish the oppressors of the poor, and declared that the righteous will be rewarded and the wicked punished. Only about 1000 lines are extant. Another of Hesiod's surviving poems, *Works and Days*, praised hard work and contained much detail about the everyday life of the farmer.

700   The **flute** and **lyre** were now played to accompany songs, and the seven-stringed lyre was introduced in Greece. **Arion**, a semi-legendary Greek lyric poet and musician, was reported to have originated strophe and antistrophe in music.

VI. SPORTS, GAMES, AND SOCIETY

776   This was the first year in which the victors of the **Olympian Games** (today called the Olympic Games) were recorded. The Olympian Games were held every four years and were used as a device to

mark chronology, known as an **Olympiad**, by which the Greeks noted important events. The Games had begun at an unknown prior date. Coroebus of Elis won the 200-yard foot race. The games honored the god **Zeus**, first at Olympia and then at the ancient city of Elis in the Peloponnesus of Greece. They were held regularly until A.D. 394.

700–475   Greek men wore either a close-fitting *chiton* [tunic] or a long, smooth ceremonial *chiton*, usually patterned. The women wore the *peplos*, a long woolen garment with a high, belted waist. The Greek *chiton* and *peplos* appeared in the wardrobes of Roman men and women as the *tunica*. Women wore the *tunica* as a housedress, over which was worn a *stola* [robe], then a *palla* [outer cloak]. The male *tunica* was belted. Over it men wore a cloak, or *toga*, which was an elegant draped garment requiring many yards of material. The *toga* was usually white, but officials wore it with a purple band on the border.

699–600 B.C.

I. EXPLORATION AND COLONIZATION

660   According to legend, Greeks from Argos and Megara, led by Byzas, built the city of **Byzantium**.

650   Greek immigrants from Thera [Santorin, present Thíra], an island of the Cyclades in the Aegean Sea, established **Cyrene** near present Shahhat in Libya. During the next century, four other important Greek cities were established on or near the coast: **Barca** [Barce, present Al Marj], **Berenice** [Euhesperides, present Benghazi], **Arsinoë** [Tauchira, Teuchira, present Tukrah], and **Apollonia** [present Marsa Susah]. Together the five cities became known as the **Pentapolis**.

640   The Ionian city of Miletus founded the colony of **Naucratis** on the Nile Delta with permission of **Psammetichus I** [Psamtik], pharaoh of Egypt (663–609). It flourished as the only Greek trading center in Egypt until the founding of **Alexandria** about 332 B.C.

ante 600   The **Dong Son culture**, named from an archaeological site south of Hanoi in present Vietnam, was carried into southeast Asia by Malays or Indonesians bringing tools, weapons, and decora-

tions made of bronze and iron. The most ancient writing of the region developed from the Dong Son culture. The Dong Son people, who had domesticated the ox and the buffalo, raised rice with the aid of irrigation. They made huge, elaborately decorated kettledrums of bronze and many stone monuments.

600   **Africa was circumnavigated**, according to Herodotus, Greek historian of the fifth century B.C., by a Phoenician fleet at the orders of **Necho II** (ruled 609–593), Saïte pharaoh of **Dynasty XXVI**.

II. POLITICS AND WAR

680–c.350   Many Greek city-states were ruled for long periods by **dictators or tyrants**, for example, **Pheidon** (from 680) of Argos, **Orthagoras** (from 676) at Sicyon, **Cypselus** (655–625) at Corinth, **Myron** (from 648) at Sicyon, **Periander** (625–c.585) at Corinth, **Polycrates** (535–513) at Sámos, **Hippias** (527–c.516) at Athens, and **Theron** (488–472) at Acragas. Many of the Greek city-states alternated between periods of democracy and rule by tyrants.

680   **Midas**, king of Phrygia, in Anatolia, was defeated by the **Cimmerians**, who proceeded to plunder the wealthy country. The Cimmerians were being driven ever westward by the **Scythians**, who this time were invading Armenia. The preeminence in the area then shifted to the kingdom of Lydia at the western end of Anatolia.

672–671 **Esarhaddon**, king of Assyria (680–669), won control of Media, a region of present Iran, and also conquered parts of Egypt.

668 **Ashurbanipal**, king of Assyria, defeated the Egyptians, thus completing the conquest begun by his son, **Esarhaddon**. Ashurbanipal appointed **Necho I** as pharaoh, who founded **Dynasty XXVI**. Necho was never recognized as pharaoh by the Egyptians. Necho's son **Psamtik** [Psammeticus] (ruled 664–609), recognized as first true pharaoh of the dynasty, expelled (656) the Assyrians and moved his capital to Saïs. Under the Saite XXVI Dynasty, Egypt entered a 140-year renascence.

660 According to tradition, **Jim-mu Ten-no** (ruled to 585) established the empire of Japan, based on Kyushu Island. He founded the **Yamato family**, today considered the direct ancestor of the present imperial dynasty in Japan.

660 A naval battle between **Corinth** and **Corcyra** [Corfu], its colony, was the first sea battle known to **Thucydides**, the Greek historian.

652 **Gyges** [Gugu], first king of the third, or Mermadae, dynasty of Lydia (687–547), was defeated and his capital sacked by the **Cimmerians**. His son **Ardys** (ruled 652–629), allied with Assyria, drove out the invaders and restored Lydia's wealth and power by raiding the Ionian cities. The first two dynasties of Lydia were legendary.

650 Assyrian forces under **Ashurbanipal** crushed a revolt led by Babylon in a **battle at Babsame**, north of Babylon. Babylon was destroyed (648), and Susa, capital of Elam, suffered (639) the same fate, resulting in the **destruction of the kingdom of Elam**.

640 The **Second Messenian War** broke out, a revolt led by **Aristomenes** of Arcadia against Spartan overlordship in the **Peloponnesus**. It was not crushed by Sparta until 631, and led to Sparta organizing itself as a garrison state where the military training of its male youths began at age seven. Messenia was formally incorporated into Spartan territory, and its people became helots.

632 **Cylon**, son-in-law of **Theagenes**, the **tyrant of Megara**, a city-state near Athens, encouraged by Athenian discontent with the ruling aristocracy, unsuccessfully attempted to seize control of Athens. Except for Sparta, no Greek city-state had a standing army or police force, so it was sometimes relatively easy for a discontented citizen to seize power.

626 **Nabopolassar** (ruled 626–605), the viceroy for Assyria at Chaldea, near the Persian Gulf, took advantage of Assyria's weakening power and seized the Babylonian crown. He founded the **Chaldean** [Neo-Babylonian] **Empire** (626–539) under which Babylonia enjoyed a golden age.

625 The **kingdom of Media**, in present Iran, was raised to power (550) under **Cyaxares** (ruled 625–585). Media declared its independence from the Assyrian Empire, and Cyaxares built a strong army.

621 The Greek lawgiver **Draco** promulgated the **first written Athenian laws**. Death was the penalty for nearly all crimes.

612 The **kingdom of Urartur** [Van, Ararat] collapsed following the fall of its Assyrian allies. It was taken over by the expanding Median Empire (c.625–550), and the Armenians gradually reestablished themselves in the region.

612 The **Assyrian capital Nineveh** was captured after a three-month siege by the Medes and Babylonians. **Sinsharishkun** (ruled 621–612) died during the subsequent massacre.

608 **Necho II**, pharaoh of Egypt, chose to support the Assyrian military as a buffer to rising Babylonia. **Josiah**, king of Judah (c.638–c.608), wanted Assyria destroyed. In an apparent attempt to intercept Necho at the pass of Megiddo [Tel Megiddo] in present Israel, Josiah was slain. His body was brought to Jerusalem in his chariot, and Judah's end as an independent state was imminent.

605 At **Carchemish** on the Euphrates River's western bank in present Turkey, the Babylonians under **Nebuchadnezzar II** defeated the Egyptians under **Necho II**, who were then forced to retreat to Egypt.

600 The Etruscans founded **Capua** as a colony in Italy, near present Naples. They were now a confederation of 12 cities that extended northeastward in the Po Valley of northern Italy and southward in the Latium and Campagna areas of central Italy.

III. ECONOMY AND TRADE

680   Pheidon, king of Argos, a city-state of the northeastern Peloponnesus, established a **mint** on Aegina producing coins marked with the island's symbol of a tortoise. These tortoises were the **first official coins of mainland Greece**.

c.610   The Egyptians under **Necho II**, pharaoh of the **XXVI Dynasty**, partially constructed a **canal** from Bubastis [Zagazig], former Egyptian capital, on a branch of the Nile in the Delta to Heroopolis on the then Gulf of Heroopolis, which connected to the Red Sea near present Suez. The canal was completed by **Darius I** (ruled 521–486) after the Persians conquered Egypt.

600   The **Celts** of Europe and Anatolia were known to cultivate **cabbages** about this time.

IV. RELIGION AND PHILOSOPHY

c.680–669   Esarhaddon, reigning over the Assyrian Empire, deported leading citizens and craftsmen of defeated nations to distant parts of his realm. He relocated many vanquished easterners into the region of Samaria, where they brought with them other religions, other traditions. Thereafter, the Jews of Judah increasingly looked down on Samaritans as perverters of the faith.

c.650   A reviser fused the roughly parallel narrative sources of the **Pentateuch, J and E**, into a single narrative. It was in this edition, known as **JE**, that later editors inserted the Deuteronomic and priestly sources.

c.626–c.586   Across four decades it was Jeremiah's dangerous mission to denounce the hypocrisy of the people of Judah and the foreign policy of its kings. **Jeremiah** achieved a faith in God so direct, so personal, that it operated independently of nation and ritual.

622   Josiah, king of Judah, brought to a climax his nationalistic and religious reforms. In addition to expressing political independence from Assyria and regaining parts of the former Northern Kingdom, Josiah had been purging his nation of Mesopotamian religious cults and practices. While repairing the Temple, workers found a manuscript, some form of the **canonical book of Deuteronomy** ("the second law"), attributed to **Moses**. When read to the people

by Josiah, it provided a basis for closing shrines of Yahweh throughout Judah and centralizing public and sacrificial worship in the Temple at Jerusalem.

c.604–c.531   Lao-Tzu [Lao-Tse], a Chinese philosopher and reputed founder of **Taoism**, lived during this time. Chinese scholars generally hold that there was a historical person named Lao-Tzu and that he contributed substantially to the most important Taoist book, the *Tao Té Ching*.

c.600   The appearance of the earliest of the *Upanishads*, philosophical discussions on the meaning of life and death, marked the beginning of the delivery of **Hinduism** from the control of the priesthood and ritualistic religion. With philosophical questioning came ultimately the ideas of transmigration, the desire for release from the bonds of existence, and asceticism as leading to ultimate truth and salvation.

c.600   The **book of Kings** reached its nearly final form—additions were made about fifty years later—probably just before Nebuchadnezzar's first deportation of Jewish leaders in 597. Kings supplied a history of the period from Solomon to Josiah, but it also sought to inculcate the religious lessons of **Deuteronomy**, particularly the notions of earthly rewards for fulfilling the law of Moses and of the public worship of God in Jerusalem's Temple.

V. ARTS AND LEISURE

699–600   Arion of Corinth, a semi-legendary poet of Greece traditionally assigned to this century, formalized the revelers who had led the processions at the Dionysian festivals into organized choral groups. Spoken words were added to the ceremonies.

c.650   Archilochus of Paros, a Greek lyric poet and singer, was credited with establishing escape from battle as a traditional subject for poets (he was eventually killed in battle) but at the ultimate disgrace of abandoning one's shield. Archilochus experimented with many metrical forms and was noted for his bitter lampoons, especially against the aristocracy.

c.615–c.590   The *Sounion* [Cape Colonna, Sunium Promentorium], statues found at the Sounion Akroterion southeast of Athens, were the **earliest known examples of kouros** [Greek *kóros* = boy] sculpture. These young nude male figures, made to be viewed from the front, along with the kore type, constituted the main sculptural form of the archaic period of

Greek sculpture. The complement of the kouros was the kore [*kóre* = girl], young females, also made to be viewed from the front but fully clothed.

c.610 Sappho, considered to be one of the greatest of the Greek lyric poets, was born on the island of Lesbos off the coast of Anatolia. Nearly four centuries later her extant verses were collected in nine volumes of about 12,000 lines, of which barely 600 lines remain today. She was banished from Lesbos to Sicily in c.590 for political activity and upon her return opened a school for young women, teaching and practicing with them poetry, music, and dancing. Many of Sappho's poems were addressed to these devotées. According to legend Sappho drowned herself after being rejected by a young man, Phaon.

c.600–300 The **Chavín culture** of present northern Peru developed distinctive art styles in pottery and architecture that were copied and traded freely with other cultures of western South America.

c.600 Alcaeus, a famous Greek lyric poet born in Mytilene, was exiled because of his politics. He wrote hymns, odes, and drinking songs as well as anti-tyrant odes in what is now called **Alcaic meter**. He also wrote martial songs until, in battle, he threw away his shield and ran.

c.600 The **Maya** of Guatemala and the Yucatán began to produce fine **pottery** for practical use and decoration.

c.600 The **Hanging Gardens of Babylon**, one of the **Seven Wonders of the Ancient World**, were built during the reign of **Nebuchadnezzar II**, king of Babylonia, for one of his wives, possibly Nitocris of Media, who missed the green hills of her native land. The gardens were a series of terraces covered with enough soil for large trees. Pumps brought water from the Euphrates River through conduits concealed in the pillars supporting the terraces.

c.600 Corinthian pottery was predominant in Greek trade; it was an incised ware painted with many colors and showing considerable innovation of form.

VI. SPORTS, GAMES, AND SOCIETY

684 Boxing was introduced into the **Olympian Games** at their 23rd meeting since 776. The entrants competed in one class regardless of weight, wearing bound soft-leather thongs around their fists and lower forearm for protection.

599–500 B.C.

I. VITAL STATISTICS AND DEMOGRAPHICS

c.500 The **Ganges Basin** became India's permanent population center. About 15,000,000 of the subcontinent's 25,000,000 inhabitants lived in an area that today comprises the provinces of Uttar Pradesh, Bihar, and Bengal.

II. DISASTERS

c.500 In Scandinavia, **glaciers** reappeared at high altitudes, and the tree line moved downhill. Oak forests began to be replaced by beech and coniferous trees. **Torrential rains** washed away the soil and its nutrients, and farmlands became bogs.

III. EXPLORATION AND COLONIZATION

c.525 Hanno the Carthaginian made a voyage of discovery along the west coast of Africa, probably to the area of present western Cameroon. His expedition had about 60 ships furnished by Carthage, and he returned only because he ran out of supplies.

IV. POLITICS AND WAR

c.595 The **First Sacred War** (c.595–c.585) for control of Delphi was initiated by Greeks from Thessaly and its allies, including Athens, in order to protect pilgrims visiting Apollo's shrine against the Phocians, in whose land Delphi was located. The Phocian city of Crisa, near Delphi, was destroyed because of the tolls it levied against pilgrims visiting the oracle.

594 Solon (c.640–558), a Greek statesman and one of **Greece's Seven Wise Men**, was elected archon [chief magistrate] at Athens. With unlimited powers he stimulated the economy and reformed social conditions, thus saving the city-state from revolution. He changed the government from an oligarchy to a democracy, annulled mortgages and debts, outlawed enslavement for debt, gave even the lowest class access to the assembly and appeal to the law court, banned the export of agricultural products except olive oil, and granted citizenship to immigrant artisans.

588 Jan. Nebuchadnezzar's army arrived in Judah from Babylon, blockaded Jerusalem, and began to take the outlying fortress cities because the nobles of Jerusalem had persuaded **Zedekiah**, king of Judah, to rebel in league with Egypt and Tyre. The siege was lifted briefly in the late spring to enable the Babylonians to drive back an Egyptian force, but it was resumed, and **Jerusalem fell** in the next year. Babylonian assault troops breached (July 587) the walls of Jerusalem. Zedekiah, with his family and a small troop, fled in the dark of evening but were caught near Jericho. Zedekiah's sons were executed in his sight, his eyes were then put out, and he was led in chains to Babylon. It was the **end of the kingdom of Judah**.

585 Periander, tyrant of Corinth (from 625), died. He was one of **Greece's Seven Wise Men**, a patron of science and letters, who made Corinth one of the foremost cities of Greece. He was also cruel.

585 May 28 A battle outside Sardis in western Turkey between **Medes**, under **Cyaxares** (ruled from 625), who died there, and **Lydians** was interrupted by a solar eclipse, allegedly foretold by Thales. The battle was a draw, but with Babylonia acting as a mediator, peace was agreed upon, and a royal marriage arranged between the Medes and Lydians. The Halys [Kizil Irmak] River in present Turkey was agreed upon as the boundary between the Lydian and Median empires. The eclipse enabled modern astronomers to set an accurate date for the battle and the death of Cyaxares.

c.570 Pittacus (born c.650), tyrant of Mytilene (589–579) on Lesbos and one of the **Seven Wise Men of Greece**, died. He was a moderate ruler, who voluntarily resigned in 579.

c.560 Croesus became the last king of the **Lydian Empire** (c.685–546) which, under his rule (to 546), reached the height of its prosperity. Lydia's expansion in Anatolia, however, was soon halted (546) by the Medes and Persians under **Cyrus the Great**, king of Persia.

c.560 The Ionian Greeks of Phocaea on the Mediterranean coast of Anatolia founded the colony of **Aleria** [Alalia] in Corsica.

559 Cyrus the Great (c.600–529), founder and king of the Persian Empire (559–330), rebelled against **Astyages**, king of Media (from 585), held him captive, and seized the throne in 550, thus destroying the **Median Empire** (from c.625). Cyrus, a member of the **Achaemenid Dynasty** (c.700–329), then became king of Media and Persia and had to meet the threat of the powerful Lydian Empire allied with Egypt, Babylonia, and Sparta. **Persis** [present Fars, Iran], a small kingdom to the north of the Persian Gulf, became the ruler of Persia.

546 Cyrus the Great, avenging his indecisive battle at the Halys River with the Lydians under **Croesus**, stormed the Lydian capital Sardis. Croesus, last of the Lydian Mermnadaen Dynasty (from c.685), was captured, and his territories were annexed to the Persian Empire.

c.540–c.430 The **kingdom of Magadha** (?–321), in the Ganges basin, was ruled by the **Saisunaga Dynasty**. It was derived from the Kshatriya caste and was probably related to the Tibetans. One king, **Bimbisara** (ruled c.540–c.490), was a Jain; he was murdered by his son **Ajatasatru** (ruled c.490–c.460), who moved the capital to Pataliputra [Patna]. No other rulers are known with certainty.

540 The Phocaean colony of **Aleria** in Corsica was defeated by the allied naval forces of the Carthaginians and Etruscans. The Etruscans occupied the island, and the Carthaginians became the leading power in the western Mediterranean. Their subsequent control of the **Strait of Gibraltar** also brought an end to the **kingdom of Tartessus** (from c.1200) and enabled the Carthaginians to take the colonies of Mainake [Malaga, Maenaca, Malaca] and Hemeroscopium [Dianium, present Denia] in southern Spain from the Phocaeans.

539 Cyrus the Great took Babylon in October from **Nabonidus**, the last of the Babylonian [Chaldean] kings, signaling the end of the renaissance (from c.626) of the **Second Babylonian Empire** (c.1146–539). At its greatest extent (c.500), the Persian Empire extended from the Indus River of India to parts of Greece, the Anatolian and African shores of the Mediterranean including the Pentopolis, and all of Egypt.

527 Pisistratus [Peisistratus], tyrant of Athens (ruled from 554), died and was succeeded by his sons **Hippias** (to 510) and **Hipparchus** (to 514). Athens prospered under his agrarian and economic reforms. His building of a middle class at the expense of the aristocracy helped secure an opening for Athenian democracy.

525 Dynasty XXVII, the first of two Persian dynasties, began when Egypt was conquered by **Cambyses II**, king (530–522) of the Persian Empire, in a **battle at Pelusium**, where he defeated **Psamtik III**, the **last pharaoh of the XXVI Saite Dynasty**. The other pharaohs of the XXVII Dynasty were **Darius I the Great** (521–486), **Xerxes I** (486–465), **Artaxerxes I** (464–424), **Xerxes II** (424), and **Darius II** (423–404), with whom the dynasty ended.

521 Darius I Hystaspis (ruled 521–486) succeeded **Cambyses II** as king of Persia and pharaoh of Egypt. Known as Darius the Great, his first years of rule were highly successful. He suppressed the rebellions developed by his succession and organized the administration and communications of the empire.

516 Darius I the Great invaded India, annexing a province in the **Indus River Valley** to the Persian Empire.

514 Hipparchus, co-tyrant of Athens with his brother **Hippias**, was assassinated. Following this event, Hippias's rule became much more severe, leading to his overthrow in 510. He was driven into exile by the Athenian citizens with the help of Sparta and the oracle of Delphi. **Cleisthenes**, recalled from exile by the Athenians, replaced Hippias in 507.

c.509 This was the traditional date of the **founding of the Roman Republic**, which followed the expulsion of **Tarquinius Superbus** [Tarquin the Proud] (ruled c.534–510), and the last of the legendary Etruscan kings.

c.507 Latin [from Latium, south of Rome] cities, helped by **Aristodemus of Cumae**, defeated the **Etruscans** in a **battle at Aricia** [Ariccia], at about the same time the Romans were throwing out their Etruscan ruler Tarquinius Superbus.

c.504 Vijaya, a Hindu prince supposedly from northeastern India, settled in **Ceylon** [present Sri Lanka], where he imposed his rule over the aboriginal **Veddas**. According to the **Mahavamsa chronicle** dating from 6th century A.D., Vijaya was the first Singhalese king; he married a Vedda princess and ruled northern Ceylon. From the following waves of Hindu migration emerged the **Singhalese Kingdom**, with Anuradhapura as its capital.

c.500 The **Iron Age La Tène culture**, which evolved from the **Hallstatt culture**, was marked mainly by a change in pottery styles and burial customs. The name was derived from the La Tène area of Lake Neuchâtel in Switzerland, where the distinctive remains were first unearthed. **La Tène art**, apparently of Celtic origin, was known by its cursive designs on pottery and other artifacts, unlike the realistic animal motifs of the Hallstatt culture.

c.500 This period marked the end of the Bronze Age and the **beginning of the Iron Age in Scandinavia**. The years from 1800 B.C. had been relatively prosperous for Scandinavia. Craftsmanship in gold and bronze surpassed other European work. At this time also the **Iron Age began in China**. A great variety of agricultural tools, including the plow, were developed there.

V. ECONOMY AND TRADE

c.578–534 Servius Tullius, the sixth legendary king of Rome, was the **first to put an impress on copper bars**, or ingots, which served as the primary medium of exchange in Rome. The one-pound bar was the basic unit of exchange.

c.560 The **first state-authorized coinage** in the western world was traditionally thought to have been produced by order of **Croesus**, king of Lydia. All the coins were to be made of pure silver or pure gold.

c.550 The **trireme** was developed in Greece. With its triple layers of oarsmen, it was the greatest fighting ship of the period.

c.500 Darius I, king of Persia and pharaoh of Egypt (521–486) built a **royal highway** from the Persian capital Susa [Shushan, Shush], former capital of

Elam, in present Iran, across northern Mesopotamia, west through Anatolia to Sardis. The road was important for the Persian Empire's commerce.

c.500 Probably around this time **foremasts and foresails began to be used on Etruscan cargo vessels**. The addition of the masts allowed more sails and thus greater speed.

VI. RELIGION AND PHILOSOPHY

c.599–500 The spreading **Aryan culture** in India encountered people who argued against the Brahman view of Hinduism. Materialists challenged the entire Vedic apparatus of ritual and thought. Less heretical but more significant were two initiators of protest movements that became separate religions: **Vardhamana** (died c.527) or **"Mahavira,"** the founder of **Jainism**, and **Siddhartha Gautama** [Gotama] (c.563–c.483), who founded **Buddhism**. Both Buddhism and Jainism rejected the religious authority of the Vedas, preached salvation, and openly disregarded caste.

597 Mar. **Jehoiachin of Judah** (ruled c.608–c.597), after a three-month siege, **surrendered Jerusalem** to troops of **Nebuchadnezzar II**, king of Babylonia. King and court, high officials, leading landowners and artisans, plus much Temple booty, were carried off in captivity. Jeremiah stated that 3,023 men were exiled.

c.588 (576) At age 42 **Zoroaster** converted **Vishtaspa**, a local monarch in northeast Persia. Under Vishtaspa's patronage Zoroaster's monotheistic faith became regional in scope, and in the sixth to the fourth centuries B.C. spread steadily south and west.

587 Aug. **Zedekiah**, the last king of Judah (ruled 597–586), rebelling against Babylonia, mistakenly relied on Egypt and found Jerusalem besieged again by **Nebuchadnezzar**. **Jerusalem fell** and after a month of plundering by Babylonian troops, Jerusalem and its Temple and palace buildings were burned to the ground. It was recorded that 832 men, plus their families, were led off in the **second deportation to Babylon**. Judah became a Babylonian province.

587–538 The **Exile in Babylonia** profoundly affected the Jewish religion. Separated from their land and with their community shattered, Jews in exile fashioned a new community centered on the reading of their sacred scrolls. The places where a few could gather together for this purpose saw the beginning of the **institution of the synagogue**. Observance of the Sabbath increased; **circumcision** and **ritual cleanliness** became marks of a loyal Jew. Prophets taught that God had not deserted His people.

c.586 After the Babylonians under **Nebuchadnezzar II** destroyed the **First Temple in Jerusalem**, the Jews initiated *Tishah B'Ab*, a fast day to mourn the destruction of their First Temple and, later, the **destruction of the Second Temple** by the Romans in A.D. 70.

585 **Gedaliah**, a Jew of noble birth, appointed governor of Judah by the Babylonians, was murdered at Mizpah by one **Ishmael**, who regarded him as a collaborationist. Friends of Gedaliah, fearing a reprisal and another deportation by Nebuchadnezzar, fled to Egypt, taking the prophet **Jeremiah** with them.

582 The **third and final deportation of Jews** from Jerusalem to Babylon saw another 745 persons deported, bringing to 4,600 the number of exiles from Judah, according to the most reliable figures, found near the end of the **book of Jeremiah**. Men only were represented in these figures, although their wives and children accompanied them into exile.

c.571 The prophet **Ezekiel** regarded the exiled Jews of Babylon as the nucleus of a restored nation. His later messages (c.571) marked the turn of Hebrew prophecy from oral delivery of a divine message for the present times into written prediction of the future, usually in apocalyptic form.

c.570–c.480 **Xenophanes** of Colophon, on the Mediterranean coast of Anatolia, argued that the primary substance must be a constant controlling thing—a God. He believed in a philosophic monotheism. Only small parts of his writings are extant.

c.553 **Zoroaster** [Old Persian: *Zarathustra*] (b. c.630), a religious teacher who founded **Zoroastrianism**, the religion of ancient Persia and the Magi, died. The portion of the **Avesta**, the Zoroastrian sacred writings, long hymns known as the **Gathas**, were generally ascribed to Zoroaster himself. The religion was monotheistic, with believers worshipping the **Lord of Light and Heaven**, **Ahura-Mazda**, and with evil represented by **Ahriman**.

547 **Anaximander** of Miletus (born c.610), a Greek philosopher, died. Considered the **founder of astron-**

omy and the **inventor of cartography** (his map of the world showed it as a flat disc), Anaximander developed the first known cosmology, based on what he called unlimited matter, the *apeiron.*

c.540 An unknown author, today called the **Second Isaiah**, probably in Babylon began composing religious rhapsodies (Isaiah 40–55) that dispelled the pessimism of Jews about their national and religious rebirth. Second Isaiah fused three notions of God: the national God of Israel, the prophetic God of justice and love, and God the creator of all that exists. He denounced the existence of all other gods but Yahweh. "I am the first, and I am the last; and beside me there is no God."

c.540–c.480 The Greek **Heraclitus** [Heracleitus], known as the **Weeping Philosopher of Ephesus**, on the Mediterranean coast of Anatolia, believed there was a significant connection between all things, especially important being the connections between opposites. It was the duty of humankind to learn about these connections, but most people did not make the effort and therefore lived in a state of delusion.

538 Having captured (Oct. 539) Babylon, **Cyrus II** ruled the largest empire yet seen in world history. The policy of Cyrus toward defeated peoples was much more lenient than that of any predecessor. He authorized the Jews of Babylon to return to Jerusalem and rebuild the Temple.

c.531 **Lao-Tzu** [Lao-Tse, Lao-Tsze, Li Erh] (born c.604), the Chinese philosopher known as **"the Old Philosopher,"** died. He was reputed to be the author of *Tao Tê Ching* and the founder of **Taoism** (from *Tao* "the way," or "the eternal essence"), a philosophy of mysticism and metaphysics in which personal tranquility could be achieved by renouncing human institutions, ambition, and striving.

c.530/c.510 *Tao Tê Ching*, the chief classic of Taoism, appeared. The book, only about 5,250 words long, was concerned first with Tao as the first and all-embracing principle whereby all things were produced, and secondly with right living in accord with Tao.

c.530 **Zerubbabel** (fl. sixth century B.C.), a grandson of **Jehoiachin**, the exiled king of Judah, headed a major **return of Jewish exiles from Babylon**, with his appointment as governor of the Persian province of Judaea, formerly the kingdom of Judah. Apparently Joshua ben Jehozadek came with him to assume the post of high priest in charge of spiritual affairs.

527 **Mahavira**, born Vardhamana Jnatiputra in c.599, a seeker for salvation through release from the rigidity of the doctrine of *karma*, died. He was the founder of *Jainism*, which began as a protest against the sacrificial system of the *Brahmanas* and the philosophical speculation of the *Upanishads*. Ultimately, Mahavira came to teach especially that *karma* could be overcome and salvation (*nirvana*) attained by following an ascetic path to secure mastery over material existence.

c.520 **Zerubbabel** apparently aroused Messianic hopes of a restoration of David's throne in Jerusalem. While **Darius I**, king of Persia, was engaged elsewhere, Zerubbabel's clique crowned him king. Almost at once he disappeared, probably removed from Judaea by the Persian authorities. From this time on, the house of David disappeared, the high priest became the head of state, and the onetime monarchy became a hierocracy.

c.520 The Jews of Jerusalem were persuaded by the **prophet Haggai** to **rebuild the Temple**, barely begun c.538. Four years in the building and smaller than its predecessor, the Second Temple, completed (c.516), developed an elaborate sacrificial worship and a priestly hierarchy, the origins of which later writers of Scripture traced back to divine revelations to Moses. The community life of the Jews again had a focus.

c.500 B.C.–c.A.D. 300 This was the cultural era in India that produced the body of Hindu writings known as the *smriti* [that which is remembered]. These works set out to extend, comment upon, and make more accessible the **Vedic classics**. The *smriti* varied widely in content and form. They were instrumental in the development of the principal forms of **Hinduism**, **Vaishnavism**, the worship of **Vishnu**, and **Shaivism** [Shivaism], the worship of Shiva.

c.500 The concept of *bhakti*, single-minded devotion to God, began to appear in Hindu thought. It has been traced to a group of tribes near Delhi. Its thrust was monotheistic, and its benevolent God was **Krishna**. Hindus have termed this religion *Bhagavata*. It would ultimately be caught up and developed in the work known as the *Bhagavad-Gita* [Song of God].

c.500 Pythagoras (born c.580) of Sámos, an island off the Mediterranean coast of Anatolia, who had lived for about 20 years in Crotona, a Greek city in southern Italy where he had gone to avoid the tyrant Polycrates, died. At Crotona he had established a school that lasted for more than a century. The Pythagoreans believed that ultimate knowledge of the universe and the release of the soul could be achieved through rigorous study of science, as well as through dietary and ritual observances. Among their many mathematical discoveries was proof that the square of the hypotenuse of a right-angled triangle was equal to the sum of the squares of the other two sides. They taught that the relationships of heavenly bodies could be understood and expressed through **mathematics**. Especially influential on later Platonic thought was their belief in the duality of body and soul and in mathematics as the way of discovering the ultimate truths.

VII. SCIENCE, EDUCATION, AND TECHNOLOGY

c.550 The **first quill pens** were used about this time in Egypt.

c.546? **Thales** (born c.640?), an Ionian Greek mathematician, died. It was said he used relationships of geometric figures, such as triangles, rectangles, pyramids, and spheres to measure cubic contents. He developed the method of **triangulation** to measure distances of ships at sea from shore and to determine the height of pyramids. He was reputed to have forecast the solar eclipse of May 28, 585, which occurred during a battle in Anatolia between the Lydians and the Medes.

c.525 **Polycrates**, the tyrant of Sámos, had Eupaulinus construct a tunnel 3,400 feet long, 6 feet high, and 6 feet wide through Mount Castro, north of Sámos, to carry water to the city in the case of siege. Eupaulinus dug at both ends simultaneously, meeting in the middle with little horizontal or vertical error. He also constructed an underground conduit c.2,800 feet long to bring water from its source to the northern end of the tunnel. The location of the tunnel was kept secret for many years, then used in Roman times, and lost again until A.D. 1853.

VIII. ARTS AND LEISURE

c.560 **Aesop** (born c.620), author of the *Fables*, died. These fables have been repeated for thousands of years. Aesop was probably a Phrygian Greek born in Anatolia and enslaved in Greece, then freed.

c.560 A new black-figure style of pottery, which originated at Athens, became more popular in Greece and the eastern Mediterranean region than the customary Corinthian pottery. It consisted of black silhouettes of men and animals on orange-red ground. *Hercules Strangling the Nemean Lion* by Psiax was perhaps the high point of the **Attic Black-Figure style**. It was replaced later by red figures on a black background. These pottery designs established Athens as the ceramic center of the civilized world for centuries.

c.550–200 The period of the **Paracas culture** in Peru is noted today for extremely fine and varied textiles preserved over the centuries by the dry airs of the deserts. Its pottery showed some trading association with the **Chavin culture** from north of Lima in Peru.

c.550 The **first building to employ a caryatid column** was the treasury building at Cnidus, an ancient Greek city near the tip of the Caria peninsula. A caryatid was a column carved in the shape of a draped female figure, such as those of the famous **Porch of the Maidens** carved by Greek sculptors on the **Acropolis** of Athens.

c.550 **Pythagoras** of Sámos introduced the numerical relationships of musical tones, using an instrument called a monochord. He discovered that ratios between the dimensions of the instruments produced certain basic harmonies.

c.550 The **vina**, a stringed musical instrument, appeared in India. The strings, stretched from a parchment-covered drum to a hollow gourd soundbox over a thin metal plate, were plucked with a plectrum.

c.550 Recent scholarly opinion has tended to date the biblical **Book of Job** at about this time, though various dates between 700 and 250 are still argued for.

c.534 The **first of the famous competitions for tragedy** was held at Athens. Victory went to **Thespis** of Icaria, a town northeast of Athens. He was the first playwright known to have used an actor, along with the standard chorus and leader. Thespis's plays have not survived.

c.500   The **first great epic of Indian literature** was the *Mahabharata* which, along with the much later *Ramayana*, served as the source for many of the plots and themes of later Hindu drama. Episodes were added throughout the years, and in its present form contains about 107,000 octameter couplets, making it the longest poem in the world. By tradition the author's name is "Vyasa," which means "The Arranger." The story unfolded in violence, gambling, and war, with many couplets drenched in gore. It concerned conflicts between the Kuru and Pandavas tribes; one battle lasting eighteen days was told in five books. Enclosed within the great epic was the *Bhagavad-Gita* [Song of God].

c.500   **Confucius** considered as vulgar music that varied in loudness, although he felt that knowledge of music was essential to a cultivated person. The single tone and the subtleties of color and timbre with which it was played were more important than groups or successions of tones in **Chinese music.**

IX. SPORTS, GAMES, AND SOCIETY

582   The **Pythian Games**, one of four great Greek festivals held in honor of Apollo, probably began this year at Delphi. They began as a celebration of Apollo's destruction of the giant reptile Python. Later they developed into contests in art, athletics, and music. A laurel wreath was awarded to the victors of each contest. The last Pythian games were held near the end of the fourth century A.D.

581   The **Isthmian games**, the third of the four Greek national festivals, were held on the Isthmus near Corinth in honor of Poseidon, Greek god of the sea, and were founded, according to tradition, by the god or by the legendary Greek hero Theseus. These contests in music, athletics, and equestrianism were held biennially during the spring. The games ended (A.D. c.400), when the Roman Empire, then Christianized, decreed the end of all pagan events.

573   The **Nemean games** were held biennially in the valley of Nemea in the Peloponnesus, Greece. They included contests in athletics, horse racing, and music. The Nemean games were held in honor of Zeus.

c.550   The **stoa**, a roofed colonnade running the length of store fronts in the agora, the Greek marketplace, to give shoppers protection from the sun or rain, appeared about this time in Athens. The idea spread throughout the Hellenistic world and into the Orient. Zeno's disciples used to gather under the stoas in Athens and elsewhere for lessons or discourses, which gave members of Zeno's philosophic school the name of **Stoics.**

499–450 B.C.

I. DISASTERS

480 Oct. 2   A **solar eclipse** frightened the Greek navies into abandoning any attempt to follow the Persians after defeating them at **Salamis**. However, in 479 the **Persian fleet was destroyed** by the Greeks off the coast of Anatolia at Mycale, enabling the Ionian Greek cities to become independent of Persia.

464   A severe **earthquake at Sparta** did much damage. During the aftermath, the helots rebelled, and fighting lasted about two years before the uprising was quashed.

II. POLITICS AND WAR

499   **Aristagoras**, governor of Miletus (511–c.497) in the absence of his brother-in-law the tyrant Histiaeus, led a revolt of the Greek cities of Ionia against the Persian occupation. With support from Athens and from Eretria, the army razed Sardis (498), former capital of Lydia, thereby antagonizing the remaining Lydians, then retreated toward the coast. Because Athens and Eretria supported Ionia, the **Ionic Revolt** (to 493) involved most of the Greek settlements of western Anatolia from Byzantium to Rhodes and precipitated Darius's assault on mainland Greece.

497   **Aristagoras**, retreating from Sardis, was met by a Persian army, which **defeated the Ionian**

Greeks. Aristagoras fled from the battlefield to Thrace, where he died in 497. His brother-in-law Histiaeus, who had returned to Ionia, was captured by the Persians in Byzantium, and taken to Sardis, where he was crucified (494).

494 Forces of **Darius I**, king of Persia, **defeated the Ionian Greeks in a naval battle** off Lade, an island near Miletus. After the battle the Persians captured and sacked Miletus (494), then one of the greatest commercial cities of Ionia. By 493, all other Ionian cities and centers of revolt were subdued, **ending the Ionian Revolt** (from 499).

490 Sept. 12 The Persian army, led by **Datis**, a Median commander, and **Artaphernes** [Artaphrenes], a Persian general, on its naval invasion of Greece to punish Athens and Eretria for their support of the Ionians in the Ionic Revolt, after destroying Eretria, was badly defeated by the Athenians and Plataeans under **Miltiades** (c.554–c.589) and 10,000 Greeks in a **battle at Marathon**, in the plains of Attica. The Persian army departed after a vain attempt to capture Athens.

c.490 **Bimbisara**, king of Magadha (from c.540) in western Bengal, India, was assassinated, probably by his son **Ajatasatru** (died c.460). The **Saisunaga Dynasty** (c.540–c.430) under Bimbisara built a new capital at Pataliputra [present Patna] and was religiously tolerant, espousing **Jainism** but supporting Hinduism and Buddhism. Ajatasatru extended his domain to the west and strengthened his armies, which carried efficient siege engines and armored carts.

483 **Themistocles** (c.527–c.460) persuaded Athens to build a navy using the wealth from the silver mines at Mount Laurium [Laurion], at the southern tip of Attica. His judgment was proved correct when the Greeks won a naval victory over the Persians at **Salamis** in Sept. 480.

480 **Gelon** [Gelo], tyrant of Syracuse (485–478), the principal city of Sicily, defeated a Carthaginian army led by **Hamilcar**, in a battle just outside Himera, an ancient Greek city of northern Sicily. **Theron**, tyrant of Acragas [Agrigentum] (488–472), Gelon's ally, was able to take control of Himera after the victory, which resulted for a time in Sicily's independence from Carthage.

480 Aug. In the **second invasion of Greece** the Persian army under **Xerxes I the Great**, king of Persia

(486–465) and successor to Darius I, won control of the strategic pass of Thermopylae, near Lamia in present Greece. Most of the Greeks defending the pass withdrew, but about 500 men under **Leonidas**, king of Sparta (from c.480), fought to their deaths but checked the Persians. In September Xerxes plundered Attica and sacked Athens, razing the Acropolis. The Greek army retreated to the Isthmus of Corinth, while the Greek fleet patrolled the Saronic Gulf, unable to stop the marauding Persians. Most of Greece north of Attica went over to the Persian side.

480 Sept. The **Persian fleet of Xerxes the Great was routed** by the Greeks under the Athenian Themistocles in a **naval battle in the narrow strait off Salamis**, an island in the Saronic Gulf, near Athens, while Xerxes watched from land. Xerxes returned to Asia, leaving his army to winter in Thessaly.

479 The Persian army under Mardonius was defeated in a **battle at Plataea**, southwest of Thebes, by combined Greek forces under the Spartan Pausanias. Mardonius probably died in the battle. It was followed by the **naval battle of Mycale** off the shore of the Mediterranean coast of Anatolia near Sámos where the Greeks won again.

478 The Spartan general **Pausanias**, commander of the combined forces of the Greek army and admiral of the Greek fleet, pursued the Persian army and captured Byzantium and most of Cyprus. When success went to his head, he plotted to conquer all Greece with help from the common enemy, Persia.

478 **Gelon**, tyrant of Syracuse (from 485), died. He was a soldier and statesman who extended the power of Syracuse over much of Sicily, and was noted for his benevolent and wise administration. He was succeeded as tyrant at Syracuse by his brother **Hiero** [Hieron] I (ruled c.478–c.467).

477 The **League of Delos** [Delian League] (to 404) was established as a federation of Greek states to defend themselves against the Persian Empire. Its uncontested leader was Athens, which marked the beginning of her hegemony in Greece at the expense of Sparta.

476 The Athenian **Cimon** (c.507–c.449) gained power there and was able to oust **Pausanias** and his Spartans from Byzantium and the Bosporus region. Sparta recalled Pausanias who, on his return to the

Peloponnesus, began to plot against Sparta. Discovered, Pausanias sought sanctuary in the temple of Athena, where he was walled in and died of starvation between 470 and 465. Before dying, he was removed from the temple so as not to pollute it.

474 **Hiero** [Hieron] I, tyrant of Syracuse, **destroyed the Etruscan naval fleet** off Cumae, near present Naples. Syracuse then became the leading Greek power in the western Mediterranean, and increased its dominance of Sicily.

470 The Greeks of the island of **Naxos** attempted to secede from the **League of Delos** but were forcefully prevented from doing so.

467–c.466 The Greek fleet led by **Cimon** of Athens **destroyed the Persian fleet** at the mouth of the Eurymedon River off southern Anatolia. It secured the supremacy of Athens and the **League of Delos** in the eastern Mediterranean.

466 **Syracuse**, on the death of its tyrant **Hiero I** [Hieron I], established a limited democracy after expelling **Thrasybullus**, Hiero's brother and successor. The democracy, based on wealth and commerce, lasted about 60 years.

465 The island of **Thasos**, in the Aegean Sea, a member of the **League of Delos**, rebelled against Athens. The quarrel was over the control of parts of inland Thrace and of a gold mine discovered there. It took Athens two years to subdue the Thaseans. This subjugation marked the beginning of Athenian overlordship of the Aegean maritime powers. By c.450 Athens controlled the League itself and had established an **Athenian Empire** (to 404).

c.463–461 The Athenian statesman and supporter of the democratic faction, **Ephialtes**, with the assistance of **Pericles**, the leader of the faction, was able to curtail the political powers of the **Council of Areopagus**, which was composed mainly of ex-archons, and increase the powers of the more democratic institutions of Athens, such as the **Council of Five Hundred**, the **Assembly**, and the **courts of law**.

462 The pro-Spartan **Cimon** of Athens sent a relief force to Sparta to aid it in suppressing the revolt of the helots. In the following year, after Sparta rebuffed help, Athens ostracized Cimon in favor of **Ephialtes**, who was almost immediately murdered (c.461), probably at the instigation of the more con-

servative members of the oligarchy, and **Pericles** began to take control.

459 Led by the Libyan **Inaros**, a **revolt against Persian** rule broke out in Egypt.

458 **Lucius Quinctius Cincinnatus** (c.519–439), appointed dictator by the Roman Senate, left his farm just long enough to save the Republic by crushing an invasion by the **Aequians** and **Volscians** of the mountainous regions of central Italy.

454 An Athenian expedition to relieve Egypt from Persian rule was routed at Memphis and its fleet defeated in the Nile. The Persians captured and executed the Libyan rebel **Inaros**. After a last abortive campaign to help Cyprus and Egypt in 450, the **League of Delos** under Athens signed (449) the **peace of Callias** with Persia, which had reestablished its hegemony in the eastern Mediterranean. At times called by historians the **Athenian Empire** (c.477–404), the League of Delos extended as far west as Sicily because of its alliance with Segasta [Egestu] and Halicyae, cities of Sicily, and included most of the states fronting on all sides of the Aegean Sea as well as the Aegean islands.

451 Athens passed a law proposed by **Pericles** that restricted **Athenian citizenship** to those whose parents were Athenians. This policy increased the animosity with which Athens was regarded throughout Greece, especially among cities held by force in the **League of Delos**, which was now a confederation of tributary states.

451 In Rome the **Twelve Tables of the Law** were enacted by the **Decemviri**, a special ten-member commission. It was the **first written codification of Roman laws**, and constituted an important step in the struggle of the plebeians against the patrician magistrates for political equality. Five of the Decemviri were plebeians.

III. RELIGION AND PHILOSOPHY

c.490–c.435 According to tradition, **Empedocles**, a Greek Pythagorean philosopher, committed suicide by leaping into the crater of Mount Etna, thinking his sudden disappearance would prove him a god. Actually he died in the Peloponnesus to which he had fled to avoid persecution for his leadership of the democratic faction in Acragas, Sicily. Empedocles thought that all matter was composed of irreducible particles of fire, water, earth, and air, and that all change was the result of change in the motion of these elements.

483 Gautama [Gotama] **Buddha** (born c.563), founder of a great religion, died. His birthplace was in northeastern India near the border with Nepal in **Kapilavastu**, an ancient city no longer existing. Traditionally believed to be the son of Suddhodana, a king of the Sakya warrior caste, his name was originally Prince Siddhartha. Gautama was his family name, and Buddha meant the "**Enlightened One.**"

c.479 Confucius [Kung Fu-Tse, K'ung Fu-Tzǔ, K'ung Ch'iu] (born c.551), China's greatest sage, died at Ch'ü-fu [Ch'ufu, Kufow, Qufu] in the ancient kingdom of Lu in western Shantung [Shandong] province of northeastern China. He spent most of his adult life training young men for political office and inculcating disciples with the virtues of ancient sages. His own teachings are found with certainty today only in the *Analects [Lun-yül] of Confucius*, one of The Chinese Four Classics in the Confucian Canon. Words attributed to him, most uncertainly, were collected and written down (c.470) by his disciples. Confucius was the founder of a school of thought that emphasized social harmony, filial piety, reverence for the emperor, acceptance of a fixed social hierarchy, and ethical and moral development. His philosophy was probably best expressed in the second *Shu*, known as *Ta Hsüch* or *The Great Learning*, in the fourth and fifth paragraphs.

fl.c.450–c.200 An early and popular branch of philosophy competitive mostly with Confucianism was **Moism**, named for **Mo Tzu** [Mo Ti] (c.468–c.376), called the Chinese philosopher of love. Mo challenged **Confucianism** at almost every point, irreconcilably with his doctrine of universal love (for example, of all parents) against the Confucian love with distinctions (for example, special affection reserved for one's own parents). Moism opposed ceremonial rites and musical festivals as wasteful and found a religious basis for ethics. Mo Tzu was openly scorned by the rulers of his day. After Confucianism was adopted as official teaching for China's governing class, Moism died out c.150.

c.450 The **Priestly Code** (**P Document**), based on the current practices of the Second Temple, was composed by priests and inserted into the forming **Pentateuch**, the last revision. Setting forth a religion of observance, its effect was to advance a policy of separation, to set off Jews from Gentiles.

IV. SCIENCE, EDUCATION, AND TECHNOLOGY

fl. 5th century Hippodamus, a Greek architect of Miletus, laid out the street plans of **Piraeus, Thurii, and Rhodes**.

c.499–c.400 Work began during the Eastern Chou Dynasty (771–256) on the **Grand Canal**, which would be added to periodically over the next 2,000 years. It provided one of the major commercial routes in China, from Peking [Beijing] to Ningpo [Ningbo], connecting the Yellow River [Huang Ho, Huang He] with the Yangtse River (Chang Jiang).

V. ARTS AND LEISURE

499 The wooden seats of the Theater of Athens, the **first theater in Greece**, collapsed. Later, a stone auditorium was built in its place.

early 5th century Simonides of Keos [Ceos], an island in the Cyclades, who was an ancient Greek lyric poet and epigrammist, died. He apparently originated the literary form of the **epinician ode**, an ode in honor of victors in the games at Olympia.

c.484–c.468 Aeschylus (c.525–456), the author of perhaps 80 tragedies and the earliest of the three great Greek tragedians (with Sophocles and Euripides), was active during this period. Only seven of his plays are extant, but he won first prize in tragedy 13 times in the annual competitions. *Persai [The Persians]* (472) and *Seven Against Thebes* (467) are the earliest of his still extant dramas; the other five are *Prometheus Bound* (c.466), *The Suppliants* (c.463), *Agamemnon*, *Choephoroi [The Libation Bearers]*, and *Eumenides*; the last three form the trilogy *Oresteia* (produced c.458).

480 The **Persians** sacked the Acropolis of Athens, destroying most of the structures that existed there, including a Parthenon that was in construction and the **Temple of Athena Polias** (540–520), only the foundations of which still exist. The structures still standing date from after 480–the **Parthenon** (c.448–438), the **Erechtheum** (421–407), the **Propylea** (437–432), and the **Ionic Temple of Athena Nike** (c.425).

c.480–430 The **Temple of Zeus**, which contained Phidias's famous statue of Zeus, was built sometime within this period at Olympia, on the western side of the Peloponnesus. It was built as a symbol of Greek pride and unity, following that country's repelling of the Persian invaders. None of the temples built at Olympia still stands, but archaeologists have uncovered the ruins of many temples and buildings on the site.

c.477 The bronze statues of Harmodius and Aristogeiton (both died 514), by the sculptors Critius and Nesiotes (both fl. 5th century), installed in Athens, constituted an important step in **Greek sculpture** from the archaic to the early classical period. The statues were made to replace those of Antenor (fl. 6th century), carried off to Persia by **Xerxes I**. When **Alexander the Great** captured the Persian capital of Susa (c.331) Antenor's originals were found and returned to Athens. There is no record of what happened to the replacements.

c.470 **Myron** (fl. 5th century) of Attica, a region in eastern Greece, sculpted *The Discus Thrower* [*Diskobolos*], a figure in bronze. Copies exist today in the Vatican and the British Museum.

c.468 **Sophocles** won a victory over **Aeschylus** in the yearly dramatic competition at Athens. It was the first of 20 first prizes he was to win. The festival of 468 was regarded as a symbolic passing of the torch between the two giants of Greek tragedy.

454 The treasury of the **League of Delos** in Greece was moved from Delos, where it had been kept for about 25 years, to Athens to protect it from Persia's reviving power in the Mediterranean. **Pericles**

used it to fund his extensive building program in Athens.

c.450 **Aristotle** (384–322) and his pupil **Aristoxenus** (born c.370) stated the relationships of the modes and pitches to each other and to the emotions. Music was thought to cure illness by catharsis. Aristoxenus was considered the greatest musical theoretician of antiquity. Only fragments of two of his works survive, and one only on music, *The Elements of Harmony*.

c.450–c.408 **Euripides** (c.485–c.406), ranked with Sophocles and Aeschylus as one of the great Greek tragedians, lived in Athens during this period, then lived in Pella, at the court of Archelaus, king of Macedonia (413–399), where presumably he died. His plays won five first prizes at the annual festivals in Athens. Eighteen of his many plays are still extant, including *Medea* (431), *Andromache* (c.426), *Electra* (c.413), *Iphigenia* (c.412) and *Orestes* (408).

VI. SPORTS, GAMES, AND SOCIETY

490 Sept. A Greek soldier ran 26 miles from the **battlefield of Marathon** to Athens to announce the great victory over the Persians. According to tradition, he proclaimed "Rejoice, we conquer," before dying of exhaustion.

c.480–c.325 During the classical period of ancient Greece, the masculine costume was still the *chiton*, often shortened by a belt. The long *chiton* was worn to denote the wearer's occupation or function, such as musician or actor. Women now wore the *Doric peplos*, full and graceful compared with the close-fitting *peplos*.

449–400 B.C.

I. VITAL STATISTICS AND DEMOGRAPHICS

c.410 Some Celtic tribes, known to the Romans as **Gauls**, crossed the Alps from central Europe into Italy, pressed by the Germans, who were also Celtic. They conquered the Etruscans and, before c.350, occupied all the land between the Ticinus River and Lake Maggiore southeast to the Adriatic.

c.400 The **population of ancient Greece** peaked at 3,000,000, having tripled since 1000, a period during which the total **European population** doubled, reaching 10,000,000.

c.400 **Asia's population**, reflecting the link between food production and real growth, was clustered in three agricultural areas: the Near East (12,000,000); China (30,000,000); and India (30,000,000). The population of Siberia, Korea, and Japan, where food was obtained through hunting and fishing, numbered no more than 200,000. In these twilight years of the Persian Empire (559–330), the Near East, with only 12,000,000 people, was no longer Asia's population center, having about 17 percent of the Asian total of about 100,000,000.

II. DISASTERS

430 Plague broke out in Athens. The overpopulated city lost a third of its inhabitants in four years.

415 When statues of the god Hermes were mutilated in Athens on the day before the departure of the fleet to campaign in Sicily, the incident was seen as a bad omen. **Alcibiades** (c.450–404) was charged with the sacrilege and recalled from his command, leaving the expedition without a competent leader.

III. POLITICS AND WAR

449 The Greek city-states led by Athens made peace with the Persian Empire, called the **Peace of Callias** after the wealthy Athenian aristocrat who negotiated the treaty.

447 Boeotia and Megaris, states on the border of Attica, rebelled and won their independence from Athens by a victory over the Athenian Tolmides at Coronea in western Boeotia. Euboea, the large island off Attica's coast, followed suit with Spartan support, and Athens sued for peace. By the **Peace of Thirty Years**, signed (446) with Sparta, Athens lost Achaea [Achaia] in northern Peloponnesus but recovered Euboea.

443 The **first election of censors** was held in Rome. The censors' primary function was to take the census; they gradually became more and more the inspectors of public morals.

440 Sámos, as a semi-independent member of the **League of Delos**, appealed to Athens during an argument with Miletus. **Pericles** took Miletus's side, and sailed to Sámos to enforce this decision. The Persians helped Sámos, and the Spartans threatened to aid it too. But the Samians surrendered after a siege lasting nine months and became a dependency of Athens.

431 The invasion of Attica by Sparta sparked the **Peloponnesian War** (to 404), a struggle for the control of Greece between Athens and Sparta. It was a war of destruction without major battles as the Spartan army plundered the countryside of Attica while Athens, protected by its walls, sent its fleet to raid the Peloponnesian coast.

c.430 The **Saisunaga Dynasty** (from c.540) of Magadha (?–321) was overthrown by the Nandas, a low-caste group whose first king was of the sudra [shudra] caste, lowest of the main castes. The **Nanda Dynasty** ended when **Chandragupta Maurya**, a general for the Nanda king, rebelled in 322 and established the **Maurya Dynasty** (c.321–c.185).

429 Pericles, who controlled Athens for 31 years, died of the plague that had struck besieged Athens in 430. He made Athens a city of beauty and the center of art and learning. He also attracted noted philosophers to the city-state. He successfully fought off attacks on Athens by Persians, Sparta, and other Greeks, and died while **Athens** was still at the height of its power.

427 The **first Athenian military expedition to Sicily**, commanded by Laches (d.418), was initiated by a plea from the city of Leontini [Lentini] for military help, and was bolstered by Athens's desire to blockade Sicilian grain from Sparta. The expedition was too small for the task.

425 A **second Athenian expedition to Sicily**, under the command of Eurymedon (d.413) and Sophocles [not the dramatist], the son of Sostradides, was forced by a storm into the Spartan waters between Pylos [Pylus, Navarino] and the island of Sphacteria [Sphagia], on the southwestern coast of the Peloponnesus. A small force was left under command of the general Demosthenes, causing the Spartans to immediately send hoplites to blockade the invaders. Athens sent a larger force to which the Spartans, cut off on the island of Sphacteria, surrendered.

424 Under the leadership of **Syracuse** the Sicilians forced the inadequate Athenian expeditions to depart, and after they had left, Syracuse captured **Leontini** and razed it.

424 A Spartan expedition under Brasidas (d.422) to Thrace resulted in the capture of the Athenian city of Amphipolis, on the Strymon [Struma] River in eastern Macedonia. The Athenians were also defeated at Delium in Boeotia by their ancient enemy Thebes. **Thucydides**, the Athenian commander in Thrace, was held responsible and exiled by Cleon from Athens. During his exile Thucydides wrote his famous history of the Peloponnesian War (431–404).

422 Sent to recapture Amphipolis the Athenians, led by Cleon, were again defeated by the Spartans under Brasidas. Both commanders were killed in battle, and the **peace of Nicias** (d.413), an Athenian general who opposed Cleon's policies, temporarily ended the Peloponnesian War in 421.

418 Spartan forces defeated a pro-Athenian army led by Argos in a **battle at Mantinea**, in the central Peloponnesus. After the battle Argos switched sides, and fought alongside Sparta. Thus this Athenian attempt to carry the war into Sparta's territory ended in failure.

414 An Athenian expedition to Sicily under Nicias and Alcibiades **laid siege to Syracuse**, an ally of Sparta in the Peloponnesian War. When the expedition was leaving Athens, charges of impiety were lodged against **Alcibiades**, and a trireme was sent to arrest him and return him to the city. Alcibiades escaped to the Spartans where he traitorously advised the Spartans in their war against Athens. The Athenians were repulsed by troops under the Syracusan general Hermocrates (died c.407) and the Spartan general Gylippus. The **Athenian fleet was destroyed** (c.413) in the harbor of Syracuse and its army routed. The Athenian commanders, Demosthenes and Nicias, were executed in 413 at the Assinarus River by command of the Syracusans, who then interned the remnants of the Athenian army and its allies in stone quarries for six months.

411–410 A briefly successful oligarchic revolution at Athens resulted in the Assembly being reduced to 5000 men, the abolition of pay for public office, and the establishment of a **Council of Four Hundred**—all intended to make the government more efficient and less democratic. These efforts failed, and Athens reverted to the old system.

411 **Alcibiades**, back in command of the Athenian fleet, **defeated the Spartan navy** in a **battle at Cynossema**, on the northern shore of the Hellespont, in the Peloponnesian War. He won another naval victory at Cyzicus, on the southern coast of the Propontis [Sea of Marmara] in present Turkey, in 410.

409 The Carthaginians under **Hannibal** (d.406) invaded Sicily, taking advantage of the fratricidal wars

among the Greeks. Selinus was sacked and Himera was destroyed; Acragas and Gela fell to the Carthaginian Himilco during a second invasion in 406; Syracuse was directly threatened the following year. The Carthaginian general Hannibal, not to be confused with the great Carthaginian general during the **Second Punic War** (218–201) with Rome, died of the plague during the seige of Acragas [Agrigento].

406 The Athenian fleet under Conon defeated the Spartans at Arginusae Island off the Mediterranean coast of Anatolia, near Lesbos. Athens executed some of its generals for failing to rescue the crews of ships wrecked during the battle and along the shores. This was the **last Athenian victory in the Peloponnesian War**.

405 **Dionysius I the Elder** (405–365), tyrant at Syracuse, made peace with Carthage, and began to fortify Syracuse. Carthage retained the western half of Sicily. Dionysius began to unite the eastern cities under his rule and build his forces in order to eventually oust the Carthaginians.

405 The Spartan Lysander, with Persia's help, annihilated the Athenian fleet in a **battle at Aegospotami**, on the northern shore of the Hellespont. This was the **last naval battle of the Peloponnesian War**, and Athens was subsequently besieged by sea as well as by land.

404 **Dynasty XXVIII** of Egypt began with a rebellion after the death of the Persian king **Darius II**, last pharaoh of the first Persian Dynasty. Pharaoh Amyrtaeus, who ruled for only five years (404–399), regained Egypt's independence from Persia with the aid of the Greeks.

404 **Athens capitulated to Sparta**, ending the Peloponnesian War. The **Council of the Thirty**, which under the leadership of Critias (d.403) soon degenerated into the Thirty Tyrants, was established as a puppet government of Sparta, now the leading power in Greece. Democracy in Athens was restored in 403, when **Thrasybulus** (d.388) led the Athenians against the Thirty Tyrants, whose leader **Critias** was slain and the Council dissolved.

c.402 The 180-year **Period of the Warring States** began in China while the Eastern Chou [Zhou] Dynasty (791–256) were nominal kings with their capital in Luoyang [Lo-yang] in northern Honan [Henan] province. The major state of Chin broke up into three small states: Chao, Wei, and Han. The major contending states for control of China were Ch'i, Ch'u, Yen, the three successor states to the Chin, and Ch'in.

401 In a **battle at Cunaxa**, north of Babylon, the attempt of Cyrus the Younger to overthrow his brother Artaxerxes II from the Persian throne, was defeated. **Cyrus** (born c.424) was killed in the battle. His Greek mercenaries, known as the **Ten Thousand**, retreated in good order to Cotyora, on the Euxine [Black Sea]. The exploit was immortalized by one of the Greek leaders, the Athenian historian **Xenophon**, in his book *Anabasis*.

c.400 The **Mound-builders** occupied much of the U.S. from Minnesota, Wisconsin, southern Michigan, and western New York south to Louisiana, Mississippi, Alabama, Georgia, and northern Florida, where they left their distinctive earthen mounds and artifacts. At the height of their activity, especially in southern Ohio and in places along the Mississippi River system, the mounds were very large and of various shapes. The mound-building culture apparently died out by A.D. c.850.

c.400 The **Lapps**, a Ural-Altaic people closely related to the Finns, Mongols, and others, settled in northern Finland and northern Scandinavia about this time. The Lapp culture was nomadic, based on reindeer herding, and differed greatly from the more settled peoples to the south.

00–c.350 **Celts** from France and Spain, carrying the **Iron Age** culture, probably reached and entered Ireland. **Ireland** had been sparsely populated with much more primitive people, possibly just entering the **Bronze Age**.

IV. RELIGION AND PHILOSOPHY

c.444 **Nehemiah**, a Jewish leader at the Persian court of **Artaxerxes I**, was given permission to return to Jerusalem and authority to rebuild its walls. This he accomplished quickly. He also improved the lot of the poor, raised morale, ended mixed marriages, and generally readied the community to become a religious group impervious to assimilation.

c.440 **Tzu Ssu** (483–402), grandson of Confucius, was the probable contributor to Chinese philosophy of the *Doctrine of the Mean* [*Chung Yung*]. This was one of the Four Books [*Shu*], Chinese classics of the

Confucian Canon, which during the **Sung Dynasty** (A.D. 960–A.D. 1279) were rated second to China's Five Classics. It taught conduct based on uprighteousness, accord with the universe, and the golden mean, viewed as the central harmony.

c.400 The **Pentateuch**, the five books of the Hebrew law [Torah], attributed to Moses, had been canonized [considered holy] and hence closed to additions. The effect was to reconstitute the stateless Jewish community on the basis of written law, and to define a Jew as one who accepts the law's obligations.

V. SCIENCE, EDUCATION, AND TECHNOLOGY

c.430 **Hippocrates** (fl. c.460) of Chios [Khios], an island off the Mediterranean coast of Anatolia, was the first to compose, before Euclid, a book on the elements of mathematics. None of his works is extant.

c.400 The Greek mathematician **Archytas** (born c.450), living in Tarentum, in southern Italy, died. He solved the problem of doubling the cube, advanced the study of acoustics and music, and invented the pulley. He was also credited with building the first flying machine heavier than air, made of wood and designed like a pigeon. It was said to have actually flown.

c.400 **Philolaus** of Thebes [also called "of Tarentum"] (born c.480) died. He was of the Pythagorean school of philosophy and mathematics and was among the first to declare that the earth was not the center of the universe.

VI. ARTS AND LEISURE

c.448 **Construction began on the Parthenon in Athens**; it was completed in 438. It was built by the greatest Greek architect of the age, **Ictinus**, who also built the **Hall of Mysteries** at Eleusis, and the **temple of Apollo Epicurius** at Bassae, near Phigalia, in the central Peloponnesus.

c.442 The Theban poet **Pindar** (born c.522) died. His extant works are chiefly his odes of victory, written to celebrate victories in athletic festivals, such as the Olympian Games. These odes, intended to be sung by a chorus, were set down in irregular verse, a freedom of style which was sometimes called "Pindaric" and which permitted the development of powerful rhythms and striking images.

c.430 The Greek historian **Herodotus** wrote, "Neither snow, nor rain, nor heat, nor gloom of night stays these couriers from the swift completion of their appointed rounds." referring to the couriers of the Persian Empire. This has become the unofficial motto of the U.S. Postal Service.

c.430 **Phidias** [Pheidias] (born c.490), one of the greatest sculptors of ancient Greece, died at a time or place unknown today. He began as a painter but switched to sculpture, using marble, ivory, gold, silver, bronze, and other materials on a grand scale. He and his pupils worked in Athens from 447 to 438 carving statues and reliefs for the Parthenon. His *Athene Parthenos* was 38 feet tall, the exposed body parts were made from ivory and about 2,545 lbs. of gold were used for Athena's robe. His **statue of Zeus**, made for the city of Olympia c.435, was considered his finest sculpture. Made of ivory and gold, the seated figure of the god stood about 60 feet high and was considered one of the **Seven Wonders of the Ancient World**. Many of his notable works have disappeared completely, and only fragments or copies remain of others. He made three statues of Athena for the Acropolis.

425 **Herodotus** (born c.484) of Halicarnassus [Bodrum] in Anatolia, died. The first writer of antiquity to research the past and to write about it rationally, Herodotus was famous for his narrative of the Persian invasion of Greece.

c.416 The Greek dramatist **Agathon** of Athens (c.448–c.400) won his first victory in the dramatic competitions at Athens. Agathon, none of whose works has survived, was credited as the first western dramatist to develop his own characters, rather than

basing his plot on myth or history. He was remembered chiefly for his role in Plato's dialogue *Symposium*.

c.411 autumn **Aristophanes'** (c.450–380) anti-war play *Lysistrata* was first performed. It is considered the most modern of the plays of antiquity. Aristophanes was generally considered the finest Athenian writer of comedy. His other works included *The Clouds* (423), *The Wasps* (422), *The Birds* (414), and *The Frogs* (405).

406? **Sophocles** (born c.496), the great Greek tragedian, died in Athens. Born in Colonus, a suburb of Athens, he wrote at least 123 plays, of which only seven are extant in their entirety along with fragments of about 60 others. He won prizes for wrestling and music, and was, for a while, a general (c.440) in the Athenian army. Beginning in 468, when he was 28, Sophocles won first prize for tragedy at the annual Athenian dramatic contest and repeated at least 20 times for first, never winning less than second prize. His seven existing plays, possibly in order of their writing are *Antigone, Oedipus Tyrannus [Oedipus Rex], Electra, Ajax, Trachinioe, Philoctetes, and Oedipus Coloneus*. It is now known that the last tragedy was produced in 401, after Sophocles' death. He was the first to use three, rather than two, actors; his plays were independent of each other rather than trilogies; and he focused on psychological aspects of drama.

c.400 **Thucydides** (born c.471), ranked as the greatest historian of western antiquity, died. He was an Athenian who had fought in the Peloponnesian War as a commander of forces in Thrace. Suffering defeat he was forced into exile, during which he wrote his famous *History of the Peloponnesian War*, a well-written, factual, and critical account of the war to 411.

399–350 B.C.

I. VITAL STATISTICS AND DEMOGRAPHICS

c.399–c.300 **Korea** was inhabited by a Neolithic Age, pre-agricultural, Mongolian people apparently ruled, or influenced, by shamans. But the **Tungusic tribes**, also Mongolian, from Manchuria, driven by the Hsiung-nu [Huns] originating in the area of present Mongolia, entered and soon controlled much of northern Korea. The Tungusic people used both bronze and iron.

II. POLITICS AND WAR

c.399–c.200 The tribes of the **Hsiung-Nu [Huns]** in the area of present Mongolia began to dominate the other Mongolian peoples, and by 221 had become an effective military and political force along the northern borders of China. After the death (210) of the Ch'in emperor, Shih Huang-Ti, the Hsiung-Nu king Mao Tun ruled an empire that ran from present Manchuria west through Mongolia and the trade routes through Chinese Turkestan to western Siberia.

c.398–c.378 Egyptian **Dynasty XXIX** lasted a mere 20 years and ruled mostly from Upper Egypt, leaving little memorable behind and surviving only so long as Persia was occupied by troubles at home concerning the succession to the throne.

c.396 The Etruscan city of Veii, about 15 miles north of Rome in Etruria, was captured by the Romans under Furius Camillus (died c.365) after a possibly mythical 10-year siege. Rome annexed the territory, becoming the leading power of the **Latin Military League**. It was a common defense pact in which leadership was based on pragmatic strength: the strongest city with the best equipped army automatically became the leader. The Latin League was finally dissolved in 336 B.C.

395 Thebes, in a **battle at Haliartos** in Boeotia, defeated the Spartan commander **Lysander**, who was killed. In a reversal of Persian financial support and intrigue, an anti-Spartan coalition, fomented by Artaxerxes II, king of Persia, was organized in Greece by Thebes, Athens, Corinth, and Argos, and later the **Corinthian War** (395–387) began. Sparta, led by Agesilaus II (ruled c.400–c.360), won battles at Nemea in Argolis of the northeastern Peloponnesus and at Coronea in western Boeotia.

394 The **Spartan fleet** under Peisander [Pisander] was routed by the Athenian Conon and the Persian Pharnabazus, commanding the Persian fleet off southwestern Anatolia. Persia granted autonomy to the **Ionian cities**, thus forcing its former ally Sparta to reverse its governing policy in Anatolia. These cities then revolted from Spartan control, setting up democracies, which soon felt the imperialistic designs of Athens.

392 Sparta, with Agesilaus II in command, was victorious in a **battle at Lechaeum** outside Corinth.

Even after several victories the Spartans were unable to cross the Corinthian Isthmus to reach home, demonstrating the declining power of Sparta and the resurgence of Athens.

c.390 Roman forces were routed by the Celtic tribe of the Senones led by Brennus in a **battle at Allia**, a river just north of Rome. The city was sacked, except for its capitol, and the invaders ransomed the city for 1,000 pounds of gold before departing northward to their lands in the Po River valley of northeastern Italy.

390 **Iphicrates** (died c.351), an Athenian general, destroyed Spartan morale at a battle near Corinth when his new tactic of using lightly armed troops called *peltasts* to supplement his regular troops wiped out one of Sparta's six divisions of hoplites.

387 The treaty negotiated by the Spartan statesman Antalcidas, known as the **King's Peace, ending the Corinthian War** (from 395) in Greece, was accepted by Artaxerxes II. Athens and Thebes were forced by Sparta's threats to agree to its terms. Persia regained control of the Greek cities of Anatolia, while the mainland Greek cities retained their autonomy.

383 The **citadel of Thebes** was seized by Sparta with the help of pro-Spartan Thebans, but later the Spartan garrison was massacred (c.379) in a revolt led by Pelopidas (d.364) and Epaminondas (c.418–362).

c.378 **Dynasty XXX**, Egypt's last native dynasty, was established under Nectanbeo I (ruled to 364). He repulsed attempts by Artaxerxes II to reassert Persian rule in 378 and in 373. Nectanbeo II (ruled 361–340), the last pharaoh of the dynasty, fled to Nubia when the Persians under Artaxerxes III reconquered Egypt in 343.

371 July The Thebans under Epaminondas won a decisive victory in a **battle at Leuctra**, a Boeotian city of present Greece, over a Spartan army led by Cleombrotus I, king of Sparta (ruled jointly with Agesilaus II from 380), who was killed in battle. The Spartan army outnumbered the Thebans by 10,000 to 6,000. Theban hegemony (c.371–c.362) in Greece ended Spartan control of the Peloponnesus, and the **Arcadian League**, formed in 370 against Sparta, was firmly established with Megalopolis in the Peloponnesus as its capital. Sparta never again regained its power.

370 Jason of Pherae, an ancient town in Thessaly, was murdered by an unknown assassin. A political and military genius who had united the squabbling city-states of Thessaly under his rule, he was planning to dominate Greece.

367 The **laws of G. Licinius and L. Sextius** were promulgated in Rome, an important step in the plebeian struggle for political equality with the patricians. Debtors were relieved, the size of land-holding was limited, and one of the two consulates was opened to men of plebeian birth.

367 Dionysius (born c.430) the Elder, who ruled Syracuse as tyrant from 405, died. He had cemented his power in Sicily through astute diplomacy and political marriage. But his last war with the Carthaginians was disastrous. Carthage retained most of Sicily, and Syracuse lost its preeminence. He won first prize in 367 at the annual **Lenaea Festival** in honor of Dionysus in Athens with a tragedy he had written; while celebrating, Dionysius drank too much wine and died of a resultant fever. He was succeeded by his son Dionysius II the Younger.

362 Epaminondas (born c.418), the great Theban general, died in a battle at Mantineia, in the central Peloponnesus. The Thebans defeated a coalition led by Sparta and Athens, but lost Epaminondas, the last of their able commanders. The final word of Epaminondas was to make peace with the enemy. He was obeyed, and it marked the end of Theban hegemony in Greece.

359 Philip II became regent of Macedonia following the death this year of his brother Perdiccas III, and he organized the state into a strong military power. He defeated the Illyrians to the west in 358, retook control of Amphipolis in the east from Athens in 357, captured the nearby Thracian gold mines of Mt. Pangaion and began to expand in Thessaly and Chalcidice in 356. In this same year he seized the Macedonian crown from his nephew Amyntas IV (d. 336; ruled from 360).

356 Menaced by Boeotia, the Phocians under **Philomelus**, supported by Athens and Sparta, seized the **temple of Delphi** and its treasure, which had been protected by Thebes and other Greeks from Thessaly. It precipitated the **Second Sacred War**

(c.356–c.346), and led to the intervention of Philip II of Macedonia on the side of Boeotia and Thessaly.

c.354 Demosthenes, the great Greek orator, made his first public speech. An Athenian statesman of the anti-Macedonian party, he stirred the Greeks to resistance against the encroaching power of Philip II, king of Macedonia, in speeches called the Philippics.

III. RELIGION AND PHILOSOPHY

399 Socrates (born c.470), the great Athenian philosopher, died. His method of inquiry—the Socratic dialogue—created a new force in Greek philosophy and, because it questioned, among other things, the Greek Pantheon, led to public outrage and his execution, as a suicide, by drinking the juice of the poisonous hemlock plant [*Conium maculatum*]. His most famous pupils were **Plato**, whose recreations of Socrates' symposiums made his teacher immortal, and **Xenophon**, the historian. Socrates' searching dialectic required clear, logical responses that opened philosophic challenges. Yet, what remains for history is the idealized figure created by Plato. Socrates left no written works.

385 Plato founded his **Academy**, open to both men and women, at Athens. According to one biographical version, he had been sold into slavery in Sicily by the dictator Dionysius I the Elder, was ransomed and, on his return to Athens, raised money to repay his benefactor Anniceris of Cyrene. The repayment was refused, and the money was then used to purchase a recreational grove in a suburb near Athens, which was named Academus after the local god. Aristotle was one of its pupils.

c.370 Democritus (born c.460), a great Greek metaphysical philosopher of Abdera, an ancient city of Thrace, died. Known as the "**Abderite,**" Democritus, following the proposals of Leucippus of Miletus (fl. fifth century B.C.), further developed the **atomic theory**. Leucippus had envisioned a universe containing nothing but space and tumbling atoms always in constant motion from which all things were constructed. Democritus reasoned that all sensations were due to atoms, differing in figure, size, and weight, that composed all matter, including the planets and stars. The number of atoms remained constant. He gave an explanation of the creation of the world and made the first attempt to explain the phenomenon of color.

IV. SCIENCE, EDUCATION, AND TECHNOLOGY

c.350–c.322 The extant major works of **Aristotle** of Stageirus, who wrote during this period, treated of logic, physics, meteorology, mechanics, biology, metaphysics, rhetoric, poetry, ethics, and politics. These works, more lecture notes than polished writings, and revised or added to over Aristotle's lifetime, were generally lost to the European world during the barbarian invasions; fortunately, they had been preserved by the Arabs and were introduced into western Europe (c.A.D. 950–1300), where they had a profound effect on late medieval science and theology.

c.377 **Hippocrates** of Cos (born c.460), the physician, died (possibly in 359). He placed medicine on a firm, logical basis founded on meticulous observations and careful clinical records. He believed diseases had natural causes. The famous **Hippocratic Oath** as well as many Hippocratic documents, came from the **Coan school of medicine**, rather than from "the father of medicine" himself. Cos [Kos] was an island off the southwestern coast of Turkey.

c.370 The **first of the Roman roads** was the *via Latina*, from Rome to the Alban hills. It served the military, but was probably the only Roman road built mainly for communications and commerce. At least parts of these roads still carry traffic.

c.350 Indian grammarian **Panini** (probably from the northern Punjab) compiled his *Astadhyayi*, "the work in eight chapters," a study of classical **Sanskrit** language. He recorded it by inventing a system of algebraic symbols, and his descriptions of the phonemes, morphology and syntax, as well as his studies of social, historical, and geographical aspects of language foreshadowed modern linguistics. His grammar, still used, is considered the **first work of descriptive linguistics**.

V. ARTS AND LEISURE

364 The *Saturae*, brief dramas of ordinary life, were first performed in Rome about this date. They were relatively crude and short but led into later comedy, particularly satire.

c.355 **Isocrates**, a Greek oratorical writer, appealed in his *Areopagiticus*, for a return to the old Athenian custom of public meeting and debate. This work formed a model for the *Areopagitica* (A.D. 1644) of John Milton. In 392 B.C. Isocrates had established a school of rhetoric in Athens that made him wealthy and famous.

c.354 **Xenophon** (born c.430), an Athenian historian, philosopher, soldier, and essayist, died in Corinth. He had joined **Cyrus the Younger** as a mercenary in the Persian war of succession; when Cyrus was slain in a battle at Cunaxa (c.401), he became the leader of about 10,000 Greek soldiers who succeeded in fighting their way through hostile country to safety on the shores of the Black Sea, a feat that formed the basis of his *Anabasis*. He also wrote an account of the life of Socrates, a history of Greece from about 411, and other pieces, including essays on hunting and horsemanship.

c.353 The Greek architect **Pythius** and sculptors **Scopas** and **Leochares** (all fl. fourth century) built a great shrine at Halicarnassus [Budrum], capital of the Persian satrapy of Caria on the mainland of Anatolia. Erected as a tomb and in the memory of the satrap Mausoleus (377–353) by his widow Artemisia (fl. 350), it was considered one of the **Seven Wonders of the Ancient World**.

c.350–322 In *The Poetics*, perhaps the **most influential work of dramatic theory** ever written, **Aristotle** set down his principles of dramatic unity, his definition of tragedy, and his concept of catharsis as a justification for tragedy. His theories have formed the major basis for discussions of dramatic theory ever since.

c.350 The **Temple of Diana** [Artemis], one of the **Seven Wonders of the Ancient World**, in Ionic style, was built at Ephesus, an Ionian city of Anatolia. One of the largest Greek temples, it was designed by Dinocrates with sculptures in part by Scopas (both fl. fourth century). It was destroyed by Goths in A.D. 262.

349–300 B.C.

I. VITAL STATISTICS AND DEMOGRAPHICS

323 When **Alexander the Great** died, his **Macedonian Empire** (334–323) included 12,000,000 subjects in Mesopotamia, the Near East, excluding Arabia, and 1,500,000 in Persia, Central Asia, and India. The remainder were 3,000,000 Greeks and 3,500,000 Egyptians.

c.300 The **Polynesians** who had colonized the Tonga Islands around 3000 B.C. numbered c.10,000 at this time.

II. EXPLORATION AND COLONIZATION

332 The city of **Alexandria**, Egypt, was founded by Alexander the Great at the western mouth of the Nile River. It became a leading trading center between Europe and Asia, and under the later Greek Ptolemy Dynasty (323–30), the **largest library of the ancient world**, a museum, and numerous schools were established there. It was the intellectual, religious, and commercial center of the Hellenistic world.

320 Mar.–Oct. **Pythias** of Massilia [present Marseille, France] sailed from Massilia to explore northward from the Strait of Gibraltar. He fixed the latitude of Massilia quite accurately and compiled an accurate itinerary of his voyage. This log enabled scientists to arrive at the date for his voyage. He went as far north as Cape Ortegal in Spain, then to Ile d'Ouessant [Ushant] off France, then around Great Britain to Kent on the English Channel, and on to Europe. He then followed the coast northeast to the mouth of the Elbe River in present Germany, then north to the vicinity of Trondheim in present Norway, then west along the 63rd parallel into the open sea before retracing his route around Great Britain to Massila about Oct. 320. He used the sun to determine his latitude and correctly determined the cause and timing of the tides.

III. POLITICS AND WAR

c.346 The **Peace of Philocrates** (fl. c.350), an Athenian statesman who headed the negotiators, between Athens and Macedonia ended the **Second Sacred War** (c.356–c.346), leaving Athens at a disadvantage. Philip II kept control of Chalcidice and soon took Phocis and most of northern and central Greece, including the strategic pass of Thermopylae.

c.344 **Syracuse**, Sicily, called on Corinth for assistance in overthrowing its tyrant **Dionysius II the Younger** (ruled 367–356; and from 347). He was ousted by a Corinthian force led by Timoleon (died c.337), and a **democracy was established in Syracuse** as well as in the other Greek cities of the island.

c.343 **Artaxerxes III**, king of Persia, conquered Egypt and established there the second Persian domination with **Dynasty XXXI**. There were two rulers after Artaxerxes III (ruled 343–338): **Arses** (ruled 338–336) and **Darius III** (ruled 335–330).

343 Capua asked Rome for military aid against Samnium, a rival power in central Italy, initiating the **Samnite Wars**. Rome was defeated in the **First Samnite War** (to 341). Thereupon, the Latin League rebelled against Rome (340–338), which won this conflict with the aid of the Samnites, who changed sides briefly. The Samnite Wars with Rome occurred in three phases: 343–341, 324–304, and 298–290.

340 Rome defeated the **Latin League** in a series of battles on the Campanian coast near Mt. Vesuvius, then dissolved (336) the League, annexed or organized the cities as allies, and took complete control in Latium.

338 Early Fall **Philip II**, king of Macedonia, defeated Athens and Thebes in a **battle at Chaeronea** in western Boeotia. Athens and Thebes had no highly trained armies in spite of the impassioned pleas of the Athenian orator Demosthenes, who called on the Greek allies to arm against the growing menace from the north. Demosthenes fought as a citizen-soldier in this decisive battle. It marked the end of Greek independence; in the following year the Greek city-states, except Sparta, were organized by Philip into the panhellenic **League of Corinth**, which was dominated by Macedonia. It was said that Isocrates (born c.436), the Athenian oratorical writer famous for his speeches on Greek unity, killed himself in despair five days after Philip's victory over Athens. Philip II's army of c.10,000 men was highly trained and more flexible on the battlefield. Powerful and wealthy Macedonians formed an elite cavalry numbering c.800 and called the "King's Companions." The Macedonian phalanxes were modeled after those of the Thebans under Epaminondas, but they were trained so that ranks could open on command and close again in flank attacks. Their lances were 21 feet long; shorter ones could be thrown as spears. The soldiers of the phalanx were also armed with short swords and were capable of fighting other than as a phalanx. Infantrymen and the cavalry wore brass helmets and carried a small light shield.

336 Philip II (b. 382), king of Macedonia, was murdered by a young Macedonian named Pausanias at Aegae [Edessa], the ancient capital of Macedonia, and his son **Alexander III the Great** took over the throne. Alexander crushed internal Macedonian opposition, put down (359–336) a rebellion of the Thracians and Illyrians, then rushed to Thebes, the leader of a Greek rebellion. He razed Thebes and enslaved its surviving inhabitants in Oct. 335. Alexander was soon able to begin his conquest of the Persian Empire.

334 May Alexander, leading an army of c.35,000 soldiers, won his first victory over the Persian army under Darius III, king of Persia and pharaoh of Egypt, in a **battle at Granicus** [Kocabaş] River in present Turkey. Most of Anatolia then fell into his hands as few cities offered resistance. The Greek city-states of the Mediterranean shore of Anatolia cast off Persian rule.

c.333 Alexander again defeated the Persian army of Darius in a **battle at Issus** in Cilicia, now a region of Turkey. Syria and Phoenicia were then conquered without much opposition except for Tyre in central Palestine, which Alexander sacked in July 332, after a 7-month siege. The fall of Gaza, Syria, after a 2-month siege left Egypt open to Alexander.

c.332 Alexander entered Egypt without opposition, and was welcomed as the liberator of the Egyptians from Persian tyranny. He was proclaimed pharaoh in Memphis, and the following year, in the temple of Amon in Lower Egypt, near present Libya, he was recognized by the oracle as son of Amon, the Egyptian god of the sun.

331 Oct. 1 Alexander defeated Darius in a battle at **Arbela** [Erbil], a city in present Iraq. He thus gained the treasures of Babylon, in present Iraq, and of Susa and Persepolis in present Iran. Persepolis resisted

and was partially destroyed. These Macedonian advances marked the **end of the Persian Empire** (559–330) and of the **Achaemenid Dynasty** (c.700–329). Darius, who had fled eastward to Bactria, present Afghanistan, was murdered in 330 by his Bactrian governor, Bessus (d. 329), who unsuccessfully tried to organize resistance to Alexander.

c.329 Alexander moved eastward into Bactria, then northward into Sogdiana, a region around present Bukhara and Samarkand, pursuing the Scythians to the Jaxartes [Syr Darya] River in 328. He was wounded in Sogdania and spent some time in its capital Maracanda [Samarkand], where he married (c.327) Roxana, the daughter of a Bactrian chief. He then entered India [present Pakistan], where he defeated (c.326) Porus, who ruled a kingdom in the Indus River Valley, in a **battle at Hydaspes** [Jhelum] River. Alexander led his army farther east and reached (c.326) the Hyphastes [Bea] River just inside the boundary of present India where his Macedonian troops refused to go farther eastward. Alexander and his army followed the upper Hydaspes River downstream to the Indus River and then by c.325 all the way to the Arabian Sea [Indian Ocean] by land and by sail. Along the present Makran coast and desert, he lost more troops to thirst and heat prostration than he had in all the previous journeys and battles, but reached Persepolis, in southwestern Iran, in Dec. 325. A small part of his army sailed westward under the command of Nearchus along the coast into the Persian Gulf and reached Susa [Shush], near present Dezful in western Iran, also in December.

324 May Alexander resumed control of his empire at Susa, punishing those who had not done their duties properly during his absence. While here he married Darius's eldest daughter Strateira to seal the union of the Greek and Persian cultures. He summered at Ecbatana, capital city of the Median kingdom, in Iran, and then marched toward Babylon.

323 Athens and other northern Greek city-states rebelled in the **Lamian War** (323–322) against Macedonia, then ruled, in Alexander's absence, by Antipater, a Macedonian general. They were reconquered and incorporated (c.322) into Antipater's realm of Macedonia.

323 June 13? Alexander the Great (b. 356; ruled from 336) died at the palace of Nebuchadnezzar in

Babylon of a sudden fever. His death marked the **end of the Macedonian Empire** (from 334). Alexander was thought of as an all-conquering general, but his other accomplishments showed his real genius: along the route of his conquests he kept careful records and sent much knowledge and many specimens back to Greece and **Aristotle**, his teacher; he established many cities; he tried to bring the peoples and cultures of both east and west together, even marrying some of his officers and men to women of the eastern cultures; at his death he had laid plans for various explorations; and his conquests affected the arts and cultures of the entire area and beyond. When Alexander left his crown "to the strongest," there began the **Wars of the Diadochi** ["the successors"] (323–281). Alexander's generals, who fought for all or parts of his empire, battled each other throughout most of this period. They included the regent **Perdiccas** (c.365–321), supported by **Eumenes** (c.362–316); the regent **Antipater** (c.397–319), supported by **Antigonus** (382–301); **Ptolemy** (c.367–284); and **Craterus** (c.370–321). The others were **Seleucus** (?358–280) and **Lysimachus** (361?–281). Ptolemy, possibly a half-brother of Alexander, and a general in his army, moved Alexander's body to Memphis in Egypt for burial in a gold coffin. There he married Thais, formerly a Greek hetaera [courtesan] with Alexander's army and one of Alexander's mistresses, and took control of Egypt, founding (323) as Ptolemy I Soter ["the preserver"] the **Ptolemy Dynasty** (to 30 B.C.).

322 **Roxana**, Alexander's Bactrian wife, bore his son Alexander Aegus who, with Alexander's half-brother Arrhidaeus, were considered the rulers of the splintered Macedonian Empire, with Alexander's general Perdiccas striving to maintain control as regent.

322 Cyrenaica in present Libya was seized and annexed by **Ptolemy I Soter**, king of Egypt.

322 Oct. 12 **Demosthenes** (b. 384), the greatest of the Greek orators, died by taking poison, following the unsuccessful revolt of the Greeks against Macedonian rule.

321 **Perdiccas**, a former general in Alexander's army and regent controlling Macedonian Babylonia, was murdered by his army after an unsuccessful attempt to crush **Ptolemy** in Egypt. At the same time Perdiccas's general Eumenes defeated and killed Craterus in Cappadocia, in central Anatolia. An-

tipater and Ptolemy, meeting at Triparadisus, Syria, agreed that Antipater should replace Perdiccas as regent of the Macedonian Empire. Ptolemy was recognized as satrap of Egypt, and Seleucus as satrap of Babylonia. Antigonus, commander-in-chief of the Macedonian army, was assigned to crush Eumenes.

c.321 **Chandragupta Maurya** (c.321–297) overthrew the Nanda ruler of the **Magadha kingdom** of the Ganges River Valley in northeastern India, and founded the **Hindu Mauryan Dynasty** (to c.185) with Pataliputra [Patna] as its capital.

321 Near Cadium, an ancient town in southern Italy, a Roman army was defeated and captured in a **battle at the Caudine Forks** during the **Second Samnite War** (326–304). The Caudine Forks were mountain passes in which the Romans were trapped and forced to surrender.

319 **Antipater** (b. c. 397), regent of the **Macedonian Empire**, died. He was succeeded by Polysperchon, who appointed Eumenes as ruler of the Asian territories. But Antipater's son Cassander (c.350–297) ousted (317) Polysperchon, and Antigonus defeated and slew Eumenes (b. 360?) at Gabiene in Persis [Fars], a province of southwestern Iran, in 316. He was thus able to conquer most of the Asian territories, including Babylonia, which had been allotted to Seleucus. Antigonus was well on his way to assuming control of Alexander's empire. Fearing Antigonus's power, Ptolemy, Cassander, Lysimachus, and Seleucus allied against him in the **First Coalition War** in 315.

c.312 The *Lex Ovinia* empowered the censors of Rome to remove from the Senate any senator who was guilty of breaking the law or offending the public morality of Rome.

c.312 Antigonus's son Demetrius I Poliorcestes [= besieger] was defeated at **Gaza**, Syria, by Ptolemy and Seleucus. **Seleucus** was then able to reconquer Babylonia. A truce signed in 311 recognized Cassander as regent in Macedonia, Lysimachus as governor of Thrace, and Ptolemy as ruler of Egypt. Antigonus, as ruler of the western regions of the Near East, was left free to continue fighting against Seleucus.

311 **Cassander** had Roxana, the wife of Alexander the Great, and her 11-year-old son Alexander Aegus, put to death in order to protect himself from future claimants. He had previously, in 316, murdered Olympias, the widow of Philip II and mother of Alexander the Great.

306 Ptolemy, satrap of Egypt, was defeated by Antigonus's son Demetrius in a naval battle off Salamis, Cyprus. **Antigonus** was now in control of most of Greece, the Aegean Sea, and the Near East, and he assumed the title of king of Macedonia for himself and his son. By 305 Cassander was recognized as king of Macedonia in Macedonia itself, Lysimachus as king of Thrace, Ptolemy as king of Egypt, and Seleucus as king of Babylonia, marking the formal partition of Alexander's empire.

c.305 **Bovanium**, one of the capitals of the Samnites, was captured by the Romans under the consuls Fulvius and Postumius. This victory **ended the Second Samnite War** (326–304). The peace treaty recognized Rome's rule over Campania.

301 The **battle of Ipsus** in Phrygia, called the battle of kings because most of the surviving Diadochi, successors to Alexander, were engaged one way or another, resulted in a victory for Lysimachus of Thrace and Seleucus of Babylonia (Ptolemy was an ally, but not present at the battle) over Antigonus I Monophthalmos [the one-eyed] (b. 382), who was killed, and his son Demetrius I Poliorcetes, who fled to Greece. Antigonus's ambition of reuniting Alexander's empire was ended. Seleucus secured his rule of most of the Asian regions of the former Macedonian Empire, except for Palestine and southern Syria.

III. ECONOMY AND TRADE

312 The **Appian Way**, between Rome and Capua, was initiated by Caecus "the Blind" [caecus = blind] (fl. 312–290), a Roman censor. Roman roads were 10 to 25 feet wide, 4 feet deep, and paved with either concrete (made from limestone), squared stone, or pounded gravel. The Appian Way was built to enable the Roman army to control the Campania.

c.325 Because of Alexander the Great's campaigns in India, Greece was brought into closer contact with the East. **Cotton and silk** were imported, and gold and silver threads began to be sewn into women's garments.

c.300 The **first clear mention of coal** in history was by **Theophrastus of Lesbos,** an Athenian philosopher and Aristotle's successor as head of the Peripatetic school, in Athens.

IV. RELIGION AND PHILOSOPHY

c.347 **Plato** [Platon] (born c.427), a Greek philosopher, died. His original name was Aristocles, but he was nicknamed Plato [= broad] for his wide brow and broad shoulders. Born of the aristocracy in Athens he traveled extensively, became a disciple of Socrates, leaving Athens upon Socrates' execution (399). When he finally returned (387) to Athens, he founded his famous Academy. His extant writings, almost always cast in dialogue form, often had Socrates as the chief character. His republic, or city-state, described in the *Republic* and named Callipolis, is the first surviving description of Utopia. His philosophy was based on the belief that ideas, or ideal forms, exist always outside the mind.

331 Oct. 1 Alexander the Great's victory at Arbela and the Greek occupation of the Persian Empire had the effect of introducing **Zoroastrianism** into western thinking.

c.328 The Samaritans, rebuffed by the Jews in the time of Nehemiah, built themselves a temple on Mount Gerizim near Shechem. The **schism between Samaritans and Jews** now became irreparable.

V. SCIENCE, EDUCATION, AND TECHNOLOGY

c.338 The **earliest fragments extant of an encyclopedia**, *On Pythagorean Numbers*, are attributed to **Speusippus** (fl. 365–338), a nephew of Plato, who died at this time.

338 **Isocrates** (b. 436) died. He was a famous oratorical writer and educator who founded (c.392) a school of rhetoric in Athens at which **Ephorus** (fl. fourth century), **Isaeus** (fl. fourth century), **Lycurgus** (c.396–c.323), and other famous Greeks—including all the orators—were pupils. The school, founded shortly before Plato's Academy, was the most famous in Greece. His extant works are 9 letters and 21 speeches. His most famous discourse was *Panegyricus* (c.380), urging Sparta and Athens to unite against Persia. In *Areopagiticus* (c.355) Isocrates took a stand against the Athenian democracy of his day, urging a return to the old virtues of Solon's time. According to tradition, he died a suicide by starvation in despair over the loss of Greek independence after the **battle of Chaeronea** (338), in which Philip was victorious. Isocrates was 98 years old at his death.

'322 **Aristotle** of Stageirus [Stagirus], in Macedonia, where he was born (384), died. The philosopher had been a student of Plato and was tutor (342–338) to **Alexander the Great**. He taught philosophy in Athens while walking in the Lyceum—hence his school was known as the Peripatetic school. Aristotle believed in constant observations as the basis of knowledge. A great deal of his writing is still extant, under the following divisions: Logic, Science (divided into Natural Science, Biology, and Psychology), Metaphysics, Esthetics (including Rhetoric and Poetics), Ethics, and Politics. Arab scholars preserved his writings and passed them on to the Christian world.

c.312 The Roman censor Appius Claudius Caecus had the **first Roman aqueduct** built. It was called *Aqua Appia* and brought fresh water to Rome.

VI. ARTS AND LEISURE

c.332 The great architect **Dinocrates** [Deinocrates] designed the city of Alexandria on the Nile Delta for Alexander the Great. Dinocrates also designed the **Temple of Artemis** at Ephesus, one of the **Seven Wonders of the Ancient World**.

c.330 *Hermes and the Infant Dionysus* was one of the best known and is the only extant work (now at the Olympia Museum in Olympia, Greece) of the great master of early Greek sculpture **Praxiteles** (fl. c.360–c.330). Among the ancients he was celebrated for his graceful statue of *Aphrodite*. Only copies exist, one in the Vatican.

c.325 A theater was built by **Polyclitus** [Polycleitus] the Younger (fl. fourth century), a Greek architect, at Epidaurus, a city on the northeastern coast of the Peloponnesus. With its rows of seats fanning out in semi-circles before a rectangular stage [scenebuilding], it became the prototype for theaters ever since.

c.313 The **temple of Apollo Didymaeus** [Didyma], in Caria, near Miletus, in its time one of the greatest of Greek temples, was designed by Paeonius (fl. 313) and Daphnis (fl. 313), although it would not be completed until A.D. 41. Little of this huge building remains today.

c.307 Ptolemy I Soter, helped by Demetrius Phalereus, established the great **library at Alexandria**. It was said to have contained as many as 700,-000 volumes at one time. After suffering severe damage from fire in 48 b.c. during Caesar's invasion of Egypt, and again in A.D. 391, it was finally destroyed in A.D. 642 at the command of Omar I, the second caliph.

c.300 b.c.–a.d. 700 The **Nazca culture** of southwestern Peru made exceptionally fine pottery decorated with brightly colored designs of religious motifs and demons. They also made the mysterious lines and other cleared areas in the high plateau areas between Lima and Cuzco. Careful plotting of these lines and designs suggests now that they had astro-religious significance.

299–250 B.C.

I. POLITICS AND WAR

295 In the **Third Samnite War** (298–290) Roman forces under the consuls F. Rullianus [Quintus Fabius Maximus] (died c.290) and P. Decius Mus won a victory against the combined forces of the Gauls and Samnites at **Sentinum** [Sassoferrato], c.37 miles southwest of the Adriatic port of Ancona. Both Decius Mus, who ritually sacrificed himself [*devotio*], probably by exposing himself to the onslaught of the enemy, in order to ensure victory to the Romans, and the Samnite general Gellius Equatius lost their lives in the battle. The Samnites and their allies lost 25,000 men. The Samnites capitulated in 294,

and a peace treaty ended the Third Samnite War in 290.

287 **Lysimachus**, king of Thrace, and Pyrrhus, king of Epirus, a kingdom in northwestern Greece, defeated Demetrius I Poliorcetes, who had taken over the Macedonian throne from Pyrrhus in 294 after the death of Cassander in 297. Lysimachus now controlled Macedonia. Demetrius (born c.337), captured by Seleucus I Nicator in 285, died in captivity two years later.

281 **Seleucus I** Nicator killed Lysimachus (born c.361) in a **battle at Corupedium**, in Lydia, the last

battle of the **Wars of the Diadochi** (from 323). Seleucus (born c.358), then in position to reunite Alexander's empire, was murdered in 280 by a son of Ptolemy I Soter and a brother of the current king of Egypt, Ptolemy II Philadelphus (ruled from 285), Ptolemy Ceraunos [Keraunos], who thereupon became king of Macedonia and Thrace (280–279).

c.280 The Greek city-state of Tarentum [Taras, Taranto] in southern Italy asked Pyrrhus, king of Epirus, in northwestern Greece, for help against Roman territorial expansion. **Pyrrhus** defeated the Romans at Heraclea and, in 279, at Asculum [Ascoli Satriano], in east central Italy. So great were his losses in victory that they gave name to "**pyrrhic victory.**"

c.279 **Celtic tribes**, called **Gauls** by the Romans, migrated southward to Thrace, Macedonia, and Greece, ravaging the area and defeating and killing Ptolemy Keraunos [Ceraunus], king of Macedonia (280–279). Some of the Celts were defeated by the **Aetolian League** near Delphi, others settled in Thrace, and a third group entered Asia by crossing into northwestern Anatolia at the invitation of Nicomedes I (ruled 278–250), the Thracian king of Bithynia.

c.277 **Antigonus II Gonatas** (c.320–239) regained the Macedonian throne of his father Demetrius I Poliorcetes when he defeated and ousted the Celts at Lysimacheia in Thrace. Founder of the **Antigonid Dynasty** of Macedonia (276–168), Antigonus was able to keep control of most of Greece.

275 The Roman army decisively defeated Pyrrhus, king of Epirus, in a **battle at Beneventum**, northeast of present Naples. Tarentum surrendered in 272, and the Greek city-states of southern Italy were occupied, completing the **Roman conquest of most of the Italian peninsula.** Pyrrhus (b. 319) was killed in 272 in Argos during a campaign to reduce Sparta.

c.275 **Antiochus I Soter** (324–261), king (280–261) of the **Seleucid** [Syrian] **Empire** (305–64), defeated the Celtic tribes, known there as Galatians, who had ravaged Anatolia for four years. The Celts, or Gauls, retired to eastern Phrygia to found the **kingdom of Galatia**, in central Anatolia. They built fortified villages from where they ruled as a military aristocracy, living from plunder or as mercenaries.

265 The Etruscan city of Volsinii was captured by the Romans, completing the **conquest of Etruria by Rome**.

265 The **First Punic War** (264–241) between Rome and Carthage began when Hiero [Hieron], the tyrant of Syracuse, attempted at this time to oust the Mamertini, Samnite mercenary soldiers from the Campagna area around Rome, who had seized the Sicilian city of Messana after leaving Syracuse's service. The Mamertini appealed for aid to Carthage and Rome. Rome sent two legions under Appius Claudius, who drove off both the Syracusans and the Carthaginians. Carthage sent larger forces to the island, and the First Punic War began.

261 **Asoka**, king (c.273–232) of the **Mauryan Empire** (c.321–c.185) in India, conquered the state of Kalinga, which completed the **unification of most of present northern and central India**. Asoka's famous stone pillars with their engraved epigraphs marked the beginning of India's recorded history.

260 **Antiochus II Theos** (286–247), king of the **Seleucid** [Syrian] **Empire**, launched the war with Egypt under Ptolemy II Philadelphus known as the **Second Syrian War** (260–253).

260 Rome won her first naval victory over Carthage in a **battle at Mylae** [Milazzo], off Sicily. The Romans employed the technique of using grappling hooks to draw the Carthaginian ships to their own vessels, where the Roman infantry could board and capture them. They also used gangplanks pivoted to the decks of the Roman vessel with an iron spike on the far underside that pinned into the decks of the enemy vessels, making a secure walkway for the soldiers. The victory enabled Rome to capture Corsica and attack Sardinia.

256 **Rome won a second naval victory over Carthage** at Ecnomus off the southern coast of Sicily. Emboldened by the success, Rome transferred the war to Africa and was defeated (255) near Tunis. The Roman general M. Atilius Regulus was captured. According to legend, Regulus, after giving his promise to return to Carthage, was freed and sent to Rome to negotiate an exchange of prisoners and peace. After urging the Roman Senate not to agree, Regulus returned to Carthage, where he was tortured and executed c.250.

II. ECONOMY AND TRADE

269 Rome began to mint silver coins for the first time. The new coins, called *denarius* (pl.: *denarii*), weighed ⅙ of a Roman ounce.

III. RELIGION AND PHILOSOPHY

299–200 The *Ramayana*, second after the *Mahabharata* (c.500) of India's greatest poems, appeared. The 24,000 verses [slokas] in seven books were traditionally accredited to the poet Valmiki, but were probably the work of many bards. The verses chronicled the life of its hero Ramachandra and his wife Sita.

c.298–230 Another seminal Confucian teacher, **Hsün Tzu** [Hsün K'uang], was active. Hsün held that man's nature was originally evil and could not be relied on to become virtuous. Discipline through strictly controlled education was required to tame natural, selfish, and societally dangerous human desires.

c.289 Mencius [Mèng-Tzǔ, Meng-Tse] (born c.372), one of the greatest Confucians, died. He held that man's nature was originally good and virtue was not only important but natural, for he has in him "four beginnings"—love, righteousness, propriety, and wisdom—which gave him native knowledge of the good and native ability to do good.

c.287 Theophrastus of Lesbos (born c.372), philosopher and scientist, died. He was born on the island of Lesbos, went to Athens, where he studied under Aristotle, then moved to Alexandria in Egypt. While in Athens he became the head of the Peripatetic school after Aristotle. He specialized in botany, developing in his *History of Plants* and *Theoretical Botany* a classification that was not improved on for more than 1,200 years. He was noted also for character sketches, such as *The Flatterer*, *The Grumbler*, and *The Man of Petty Ambition*.

284 Chuang-Tzu [Chuang Chou] (b. 369), a famous Chinese philosopher, died. He taught the positive value of naturalism, the goal being spiritual freedom and peace achieved through knowing one's nature and seeking always a more perfect accord with the *Tao*. This accord was brought about by deep meditation, resulting in the realization of perfect happiness and the prolongation of life.

c.270 Epicurus, a Greek philosopher, born in Sámos c.342, died. Epicurus taught that, since we have but one life to live, we should seek pleasure (or freedom from pain); hence, an epicurean today is misconstrued as one who thinks only of pleasure. Actually Epicurus taught that such pleasure must not ignore consideration for others, prudence, honor, and justice. Serenity was to be achieved only through a virtuous and simple life.

c.264 Zeno of Citium, a town on Cyprus, died. He studied and then taught for c.50 years in Athens, where he founded the **Stoic school** of philosophy. Stoics embraced a stern simplicity. They were the antithesis of the epicureans of the day, and Zeno believed young people wasted their time in the study of philosophy.

c.250 A writer called the **Chronicler** by scholars set down a history of the Jews, often fanciful, from Joshua to Nehemiah, known as the *Chronicles*. The history traced Jewish sacred institutions back to Moses and Aaron or to an idealized King David. The Chronicler extolled the Temple, its ritual and its clergy, as the earthly abode of the one true God.

c.250 Asoka, king of the **Mauryan Empire** (c.321–c.185) in India, was converted to Buddhism. He sent out missionaries who spread Buddhism throughout India and Ceylon.

c.250 In Alexandria, Egypt, 70 Jewish scholars finished a translation from Hebrew into Greek of the Law of Moses [the **Pentateuch**]. This translation, later called the Septuagint [*septuaginta* = seventy], was intended for Jews outside Judaea who had forgotten their Hebrew, Greek now being the language of culture and business in the eastern Mediterranean world. The *Septuagint*, in expanded form, became the Bible of the early Christian churches.

IV. SCIENCE, EDUCATION, AND TECHNOLOGY

289 Ptolemy II Philadelphus, king of Egypt, completed a **lighthouse on the island of Pharos** at the mouth of the Nile near Alexandria. The light, from a fire of resinous wood, was made visible for c.40 miles by using convex metal mirrors. Designed by Sostratus of Cnidus and considered one of the **Seven Wonders of the Ancient World**, the lighthouse was a terraced building of white marble 400 feet high. At its top a pillared cupola, crowned by a 21-foot statue of Poseidon, held the fire.

c.280 The Egyptian high priest **Manetho** (c.300–250) produced in Greek for the Ptolemies a history of Egypt, *Aegyptiaca*. The fragments preserved have proven a major source for today's knowledge of the country's ancient history. His table of the rulers of Egypt, a king list, arranged into 31 dynasties, is still used. The original book was burnt with the library of Alexandria in A.D. 392 or 642.

260 Euclid of Alexandria (born c.330), a Greek mathematician and philosopher, died. Euclid moved to Alexandria, where he wrote **Elements of Geometry** in 13 volumes, which for more than 2,200 years was practically the only text on geometry. It also dealt with other mathematical subjects. Euclid also wrote on optics, astronomy, and music.

256 Arabic numerals using the **decimal system** were found on the **Rock Edicts of Asoka**, king of the **Mauryan Empire** (c.321–c.185) in India, a thousand years before their appearance in Arabic literature and records. Asoka had the remarkable Rock Edicts carved on rocks and erected throughout India. Ten are extant, and the former locations of 20 more have been determined. They presented the most humane and tolerant set of rules to live by ever promulgated by any earthly ruler.

V. ARTS AND LEISURE

299–200 The **earliest mention in India of musical scales** was in the *Ramayana*, the second great Sanskrit religious epic poem. Indian scales were and are today divided into 22 tones to the octave.

291? Menander (born c.342), an Athenian dramatist, regarded in his own time as the second leading writer of the New Comedy after Philemon, died. Now he is regarded as the first. He wrote over 100 plays of which only one, *Dyskolos* [*The Bad-tempered Man*] (317), and fragments of adaptations by other authors have survived.

c.280 The **Seven Tragic Poets** of Alexandria in Egypt called themselves the **Pleiad** after the Greek mythological seven daughters of Atlas. They were led by Ptolemy II Philadelphus, who was noted for encouraging the arts and literature.

c.280 The **Colossus of Rhodes**, a port on the island of Rhodes, commemorating the city's successful resistance to the siege (306–304) by Demetrius I Poliorcetes of Macedonia, was completed. The bronze statue of Apollo as Helios [the Sun], created by Chares of Lindas and rising more than 100 feet next to the harbor, was considered one of the **Seven Wonders of the Ancient World**. It was destroyed by an earthquake in 225 B.C.

c.275–215 This period was the zenith of **Alexandria as center of the new Hellenistic culture**. It attracted brilliant men: **Theocritus**, in literature; **Eratosthenes**, in geography, who calculated the circumference of the earth with an error of less than 1 percent; **Aristarchus**, in astronomy, who propounded the heliocentric theory of the solar system; **Theophrastus**, in botany; and **Euclid** and **Archimedes**, in mathematics.

c.262 The Greek comic playwright **Philemon** (born c.360) died. Although only fragments of his plays have survived, Philemon was credited with being one of the inventors of comedy. Philemon was the great rival of Menander, defeating him several times in the dramatic festivals.

249–200 B.C.

I. VITAL STATISTICS AND DEMOGRAPHICS

c.200 B.C.–A.D. c.200 The **Sarmatians**, an Indo-European folk, gradually replaced the **Scythians** as the dominant people in southern Russia. The Sarmatians were excellent soldiers as well as traders, developing trade routes from China, from the Baltic Sea, and from Germany into the Black Sea areas and then beyond to Greek markets.

II. POLITICS AND WAR

248 A Scythian chief, **Arsaces I**, founder of the kingdom of Parthia, died. He was the ruler (from 250) of a nomad tribe of the Parni, in present Iran, which had gained independence from the **Seleucid** [Syrian] **Empire**. He founded the **Arsacid Dynasty** (c.250 B.C.–A.D. 226), in present Iran, which lasted until overthrown by the Sassanids.

c.245 Diodotus I, governor of Bactria (ruled c.250–230), won independence from Antiochus II Theos of the **Seleucid [Syrian] Empire**. Bactria had been a province of the Persian Empire (559–330) at the time of Alexander's conquest and was a province of the Seleucid [Syrian] Empire from 302. The kingdom was destroyed by the Sakas [Scythians] after 135 B.C.

245 The **Third Syrian War** (to 241) started after Laodice of Seleucia murdered (246) her former husband **Antiochus II Theos** (b. 286) and his wife Berenice, sister of Ptolemy III Euergetes (c.282–c.222), ruler of Egypt (from 246), who invaded the **Seleucid** [Syrian] **Empire** to avenge Berenice. Ptolemy's army penetrated all the way to Bactria, captured Susa and Babylon, and brought back much booty to Egypt when he was forced to return there by a sudden revolt, which he quelled.

241   Rome won a decisive victory over Carthage by destroying the Carthaginian fleet at the Aegates [Eqadi] Islands off Lilybaeum [Marsala] in western Sicily. It marked the end of the **First Punic War** (from 264). Carthage agreed to pay an indemnity of 3,200 talents [about $17.5 million] in ten years and to abandon Sicily, which became the first Roman province.

238   Rome annexed Sardinia and then Corsica, without Carthaginian opposition, though the island's inhabitants resisted Roman rule. The two Mediterranean islands were organized into a single Roman province in 227 B.C.

237   Hamilcar Barca, a Carthaginian general and father of Hannibal, began the **occupation of the Iberian Peninsula**. Carthage had taken control of some of the Phoenician colonies on the coast of Spain, such as Gades [Gadir, Cadiz], the Straits of Gibraltar, and the native state of Tartessus. Hamilcar (born c.270) was drowned during the siege of an unnamed Spanish town in 228 and was succeeded by his son-in-law Hasdrubal (d. 221) as commander in Spain.

232   Asoka (ruled from 273), third king of the **Mauryan Dynasty** (c.321–c.185) in India, died. Before his conversion to Buddhism (c.250), Asoka had expanded by bloody conquest the Mauryan Empire to include Afghanistan and Baluchistan in the west, and in the east the region extending nearly to present Burma [Myanmar], and from the Himalaya Mountains in the north to a line running roughly from Coondapoor to Nellore in present southern India.

c.230   Attalus, ruler of Pergamum [Pergamus] (241–197) in western Anatolia, defeated the Celts, or Gauls, of Galatia and for two more years successfully resisted counterattacks by Antiochus II's son, Antiochus Hierax. Attalus thus secured his independence from the **Seleucid** [Syrian] **Empire** and was known as Attalus I Soter [Greek: *sōter* = preserver]. During Attalus's reign, Pergamum became one of the centers of the Hellenistic world, with a library at its capital second only to that of Alexandria in Egypt.

229   Rome sent a naval expedition across the Adriatic Sea that succeeded in subduing the Illyrian tribes of the northwestern Balkan Peninsula. The Roman success won the gratitude of the Greeks but the resentment of the Macedonians, who were allies of the Illyrians and controlled the Greek state of Epirus and the region just south of Illyria in present southern Albania and Yugoslavia. The Roman presence initiated a series of four Macedonian Wars (216–148).

c.225   The kingdom of Andhra (to A.D. c.235) along the east coast of India, was founded. Andhra became the leading power of the Indian subcontinent. The Andhras were Hindus but tolerant of, even supporting, the Buddhists. They spoke a non-Sanskrit language known as **Prakit**, were dark-skinned, possibly Dravidian, and exercised loose governmental control, leading often to internal struggles.

225   Roman forces defeated the invading Gallic [Celtic] tribes, including the transalpine Gaesati and the Boii of the eastern Po valley, in a battle at **Telamon**, Etruria, in western Italy. Roman rule of northern Italy was secured by a victory of the consul **Marcus Claudius Marcellus** (c.268–208) over the Insubres, cisalpine Gallic tribes settled around present Milan in northern Italy, in a **battle at Clastidium** [Casteggio] in 222. Roman colonies were established in northern Italy, and trade, as well as military movement, was facilitated in 220 by the building across Italy of the **Via Flaminia**, from Rome to Ariminum [Rimini].

221   The Ch'in [Ts'in] Dynasty (c.246–206) was now firmly established in China. It was the **first truly imperial dynasty of China**.

219   Hannibal, a Carthaginian general, destroyed the Greek colony of Saguntum [Sagunto] in eastern

Spain near the Mediterranean coast with which Rome had made an alliance. This precipitated the **Second Punic War** (218–201), often called the **Hannibalic War**, when Rome decided to avenge its allies and to check Carthage's expansion in the Iberian Peninsula.

218 A Roman army was sent to Spain under Gn. Cornelius **Scipio** (d. 211), who won a foothold north of the Ebro River. He then was joined (217) by a second army under his brother P. Cornelius Scipio (d. 211). Both armies invaded Carthaginian territory south of the Ebro, recaptured Saguntum and prevailed on many Spanish tribes to desert the Carthaginians. The Carthaginian general **Hasdrubal**, brother of Hannibal, crushed the two Roman armies separately with both Scipios dead on the field of battle in 211. In the meantime **Hannibal** marched (218) his army of c.40,000 men, 6,000 cavalry, and 50 elephants from Carthago Nova [Cartagena] on Spain's Mediterranean coast through southern France and across the Alps (Nov. 218) probably by the Col de la Traversette, a mountain pass on the border between present France and Italy, and into Italy. Hannibal reached northern Italy with only 20,-000 infantry and 4,000 cavalry and only about 20 elephants. While he wintered in northern Italy (Dec. 218–Mar. 217), his army grew to c.50,000 with the addition of Celts [Gauls]. He defeated three Roman armies, one at the Trebia River (218) in northern Italy, another at Lake Trasimenus [Trasimeno] (217) in central Italy, and the third at Cannae (216) in southern Italy. Despite these victories, his forces were always threatened because most of Rome's allies remained loyal. Hannibal's elephants died in Italy from the cold during the winter of 218–217.

218 Dec. The **battle of Trebia** [Trebbia] **River**, south of the Po River, was the first major battle of the **Second Punic War** fought in Italy. **Hannibal**, the Carthaginian general, first won a skirmish on the Tincino River, southwest of present Milan, against forces of P. Cornelius Scipio, a Roman consul, who then retreated south of the Po River. In a few days the Romans attacked again, at Trebia, and were defeated, losing at least 20,000 men. Encouraged by this defeat, 10,000 Gallic warriors joined the Carthaginian army. Hannibal now controlled northern Italy.

217 June 21 Carthaginian forces led by **Hannibal** destroyed a Roman army under the consul Gaius Flaminius in a **battle at Lake Trasimenus** [Trasimeno], near Perugia in central Italy. Flaminius, who with most of his troops was killed in this battle, was noted especially for the construction of the Circus Flaminius and the Via Flaminia.

217 **Ptolemy IV Philopater**, king of Egypt (221–203) defeated the Seleucids under **Antiochus III the Great** (242–187; ruled from 223) in a **battle at Raphia** [Rafah], in the Gaza strip. It ended the **Fourth Syrian War** with no territorial changes, and the Ptolemies recovered their Syrian territories lost early in the war.

216 The **First Macedonian War** with Rome began when Philip V, king of Macedonia (221–179) invaded Illyria. In numerous engagements along the coast, Philip was thwarted by the Roman navy, which was able to reinforce or supply his opponents or shift them from one place to another. Rome's Greek allies halted Philip's armies with no great battles. Philip was forced to sign the **Peace of Phoenice** (in northwestern Epirus) in 205.

216 Aug. 2 Roman forces 85,000 strong led by the consuls L. Paullus Aemilius and G. Terentius Varro were routed by the Carthaginian army under **Hannibal** in a **battle at Cannae**, near Naples, in the **worst defeat ever for Roman arms.** The Romans lost perhaps 80 percent of their soldiers, and L. Paulus Aemilius was killed. The cities of southern Italy, including Capua, began to rally around Hannibal, who soon abandoned the offensive for lack of reinforcements. **Q. Fabius Maximus** (d. 203), called **Cunctator** [the Delayer], became famous for his strategy of avoiding head-on conflict with the Carthaginian army. The term "**Fabian**" today means attaining victory by harassment or delay, or gradual achievement, as in Fabian Society, or Fabian policy. Reappointed dictator after Cannae, Fabius prevented Hannibal from securing supplies and reinforcements and from settling into a permanent Italian base.

212 Roman forces under **M. Claudius Marcellus** (c.268–208), a Roman consul, conquered Syracuse, which had allied itself with Carthage during the **Second Punic War** (218–201). The whole of Sicily was gradually returned to Roman rule. Capua in southern Italy surrendered to Rome the same year, and Tarentum in Sicily was recovered (209) by Q. Fabius Maximus after three years of Carthaginian occupation.

210 Shih Huang-Ti (b. 259), the first emperor of the Ch'in Dynasty (221–206), died while on a trip to the eastern provinces. His oldest son Fu-su, who was to succeed him, was tricked into committing suicide by the chief eunuch Chao Kao, who then, in collaboration with the Prime Minister Li Ssu, placed Huang-Ti's youngest, weak, and corrupt son Hu-Hai on the throne. **Shih Huang-Ti** drove the **Hsiung-Nu [Huns]** out of China and then built the first part of the Great Wall of China. He had rebuilt the army into an efficient fighting force equipped with many weapons of iron and replaced the chariots with cavalry. He also established a centralized nation, codified laws, standardized weights and measures, and attempted to standardize the writing ideograms.

210 Rome sent another army to Spain under another **P. Cornelius Scipio** (237–183), later called **Africanus** and **Scipio the Elder**. Scipio captured (209) the chief Carthaginian base New Carthage, which contained a large amount of military stores and many Spanish hostages. Scipio defeated Hasdrubal in Spain, but **Hasdrubal** extricated his army and crossed the Pyrenees (208) on his way to join **Hannibal** in Italy.

207 Hannibal's brother **Hasdrubal** was defeated and killed in a **battle at the Metaurus [Metauro] River**, in central eastern Italy, by a Roman army led by the consuls M. Livius Salinator and G. Claudius Nero. The Carthaginian army was annihilated.

206 In a **civil war in China** Liu Pang defeated the **last Ch'in emperor** and, as emperor Kao-Tsu, he founded the **Western [Early] Han Dynasty** (206 B.C.–A.D. 9). The Han emperors mitigated some of the excesses of the Ch'in by promulgating less severe laws. Under the fifth Han emperor **Wu-Ti** (157–87), a major canal to facilitate the transport of grain was dug between the capital Changan and the Yellow River [Huang Ho, Huang He].

206 Roman forces in Spain, led by **P. Cornelius Scipio the Elder**, decisively defeated the Carthaginians in a **battle at Ilipa**, near present Sevilla [Seville]. The fall of Gades [Cadiz] followed in the same year, **ending Carthaginian occupation of Spain**. The entire campaign took about two years after Hasdrubal's departure.

204 A Roman army led by **P. Cornelius Scipio the Elder** landed in North Africa near Utica, an ancient city c.15 miles from ancient Carthage [Tunis], to carry the war to the Carthaginian homeland. The Carthaginians and their Numidian allies, led by **Syphax** (died c.201), king of Numdia, were defeated in 203, and **Hannibal** was ordered to come back from southern Italy.

c.203 Ptolemy IV (born c.244), king of Egypt (from 221), died. He was succeeded by his 7-year-old son **Ptolemy V Epiphanes** (c.210–181). **Antiochus III the Great**, king of the **Seleucid [Syrian] Empire**, made an alliance with **Philip V**, king of Macedonia, and launched the **Fifth Syrian War** (202–198) between the Seleucids and Ptolemies. He quickly occupied southern Syria and Palestine.

202, Oct. The **Roman army led by Scipio** and reinforced by the Numidians under Masinissa [Massinissa] (283?–c.148), a Numidian chief who was the political opponent of Syphax, king of Numidia, won a decisive victory over the Carthaginians led by **Hannibal** at **Zama [Zoz]**, then 50 miles southwest of Carthage. This was the **last battle of the Second Punic War** (219–201) and marked the complete triumph of Rome. **Scipio**, Rome's greatest general, was awarded the surname **Africanus** for his exploits in Africa.

201 A peace treaty between Rome and Carthage officially ended the **Second Punic War**. Carthage lost Spain, parts of which it had held for c.300 years; its Mediterranean islands; and all of its fleet except about 10 triremes. Spain agreed to pay an indemnity of 200 talents a year for 50 years [about a million dollars each year at today's rate]. Masinissa was recognized as king of Numidia (ruled to c.148).

c.200 The **Greeks ruling in Bactria**, pressed by the Scythians from the north, moved into northern India following the decline of the **Mauryan Empire** (c.321–c.185). The Greeks took the region of Gandhara, in present Pakistan and Afghanistan, and parts of the Sind along the southern Indus River Valley, including the city of Taxila. Menander [Milinda of the Buddhists], the Greek who ruled from Kabul in present Afghanistan, nearly succeeded (c.150) in capturing the old Mauryan capital of **Pataliputra [Patna]** far to the east.

200 The **Second Macedonian War** (200–197) broke out between Rome and Philip V, king of Macedonia. Philip's policy of territorial expansion against the Greek city-states and the kingdoms of Rhodes and Pergamum forced them to seek Roman help. Rome feared that Philip would soon attack Italy. In 201/200 the Romans sent an ultimatum to Philip to submit his differences with Attalus I Soter (269–19?), king of Pergamum, to Roman arbitration. When Philip refused, a Roman army crossed the Adriatic Sea to Illyricum, then moved toward Macedonia.

III. ECONOMY AND TRADE

241 The **Aurelian Way** from Rome to Antibes by way of Pisa and Genoa was begun.

c.221–c.206 During the **Ch'in Dynasty** in China **copper coins** were introduced, the first such coins known in China.

c.220 **Shih Huang Ti**, emperor of China, had a **network of roads** built throughout much of China. The roads were built to facilitate the movement of troops, but they greatly aided commerce.

IV. RELIGION AND PHILOSOPHY

c.246 **Mahinda** [Mahendra], brother of Asoka, with missionaries, took **Buddhism** to Ceylon [Sri Lanka], where it soon flourished, and today survives strongly as the **Theravadin branch**. Nowadays, two-thirds of Sri Lanka's population are Buddhists.

c.240 The **first schism within Buddhism** occurred when the **Mahasanghikas** [Great Assemblists], based in the state of Magadha in the **Mauryan Empire** (c.321–c.185), broke from the conservative **Old Wisdom School**, determined to broaden Buddhism's order of monks by relaxing the restrictive rules laid down in the *Vinaya*.

c.206 The incoming **Han Dynasty** of China (206 B.C.–A.D. 220) elevated the reputation of **Confucius**. His ethical teachings were now linked with familial ancestor worship, the worship of Heaven, and various imperial ceremonies. **Confucianism** soon became the official cult of the scholar class.

c.200 By this date the *Bhagavad-Gita* [Sanskrit: **the Song of God**] appeared as an independent Indian epic. It profoundly affected post-Vedic Hinduism with its tangle of ritualism on the one side and arid philosophical speculation on the other. In narratives of wide popular appeal, the *Gita* taught instead the way of loving devotion to a gracious God who is a living Presence.

V. SCIENCE, EDUCATION AND TECHNOLOGY

c.240 **Archimedes** gave the **first value of π [pi]** accurate to two decimal places but expressed as "between $3\frac{1}{7}$ and $3\frac{10}{71}$" as the Greeks were not familiar with the decimal system. Archimedes discovered that the area of a circle was exactly equal to the area of a triangle whose base was equal to the circumference of the circle and whose altitude was equal to the radius of the circle. Therefore, pi was equal to the ratio of the diameter of the circle to its circumference. One could determine the circumference merely by pi × diameter or the area by pi × r^2.

230 **Aristarchus** of Sámos (b. 310) died. He had calculated the sizes of the earth, sun, and moon, and showed that the earth orbited the sun; the moon, the earth. He also determined the inclination of the earth's axis. Aristarchus determined that the relative distances between the earth, the moon, and the sun could be measured using the right-angled triangle formed by the three bodies when the moon was exactly at half, as then the sun would be at a right angle to the moon and an observer on the earth then only had to measure the angle formed between himself, the sun, and the moon. Aristarchus estimated the angle as 87°; modern instruments give it as 89° 52'.

c.221 The **different forms of ideograph script then in use in China were standardized** and something much like the system of writing still being used there was adopted. **Shih Huang Ti**, the emperor of China, promulgated the use of but one written form, and he made attempts to unify the many spoken dialects in use. The divergence between the spoken languages of China and the written language, which persists today, dated from this time.

c.221 **Shih Huang Ti** ordered a great defensive wall [**the Great Wall of China**] to be built along some 1,200 miles of China's northern border. The completed wall (c.206), 200 miles longer, protected the settled Chinese from nomads and ushered in a period of peace along the northern border. The wall was 20–50 feet or more high; the top, 18–30 feet wide, enclosed between crenellated walls a passageway c.10 feet wide. There were large tower/fortresses at intervals of 100–150 yards.

c.221 **Shih Huang Ti**, ordered all **books burned** except for works on agriculture and a few others to be kept in the imperial library. Thus, the large majority of works ascribed to the time before 221 were reconstructions made by scholars. During the **Civil War** (c.206), the imperial library was burned accidentally, with much historical data lost forever.

c.215 **Archimedes** discovered the principle of **specific gravity**, which states that a body submersed in any liquid loses weight by the same amount as the weight of the liquid displaced. The principle was used to determine whether gold was pure or mixed with baser metals, which produced a substance of lower specific gravity.

212 **Archimedes** (born c.287) of **Syracuse** in Sicily, the Greek mathematician, was killed in the massacre of Syracusans after the capture of the city by Roman forces under Marcellus. He was one of the greatest mathematicians of his day. He invented a device for raising water to higher levels for irrigation; discovered the principle of specific gravity; devised the mathematical ratios of the lever and other mechanical devices; and discovered how to find the area of a circle, setting a reasonable early value for pi.

c.200 A **blowpipe** for **glassblowing** in Syria was dated to c.200. The blowpipe allowed the glass makers more freedom of design and greater control over the amount of material the finished product could hold.

c.200 Mediterranean maritime powers were building large, oared **galleys**. The Romans built ships with a broad beam, which helped stabilize the platforms from which catapults were aimed and fired, and which also enabled a large number of soldiers to be transported. Some vessels with five, or even seven, banks of oars required as many as 500 rowers; there was even a huge vessel with room for 4,000 oarsmen built (c.210) by Ptolemy IV Philopater at Alexandria.

c.200 **Paper**, made from bark, hemp, or rags, was introduced in China sometime during the early **Han Dynasty** (206 B.C.–A.D. 220). Since the wooden and bamboo strips formerly used in Chinese books did not lend themselves well to rolling into scrolls, it was likely that the books printed on paper invented in China were flat, folded products like our modern books.

VI. ARTS AND LEISURE

c.240 **Livius Andronicus** (c.284–204), a former Greek slave and translator into Latin of Greek drama and epic, brought to Rome the **first translations of the great Greek plays**. Until this time, the theater in Rome consisted only of a kind of local burlesque.

c.237 **Ptolemy III Euergetes**, king of Egypt (ruled 246–221), began to build at Idfu south of Luxor a temple dedicated to the falcon-god **Horus**. Completed (57 B.C.) under **Ptolemy IV Philopater**, its walls showed details of the religious ceremonies and accounts of the Egyptian gods.

c.221–c.206 The short period of the **Ch'in Empire** in China constituted one of the great flowerings of Chinese prose, particularly in the fields of philosophy and history. **Shih Huang Ti**, the emperor of China, was buried in a massive tomb near his capital of Hsien-yang in present Shensi [Shaanxi] Province near Sian [Xi'an]. Probably begun in 246, when he became king of the Ch'in, the tomb was covered with a dirt mound almost 150 feet high. Chinese archaeologists in A.D. 1974 uncovered an army of more than 6,000 life-sized terra-cotta warriors with which the emperor had surrounded himself, complete with arms, armor, and horses, and ready to defend his remains as guards in after life. Each figure was a good portrait of a distinct individual. Other models in the vast tomb show houses of that remote day, gardens, palaces, women, horses, etc.

c.215 **Apollonius** of Rhodes (born c.295), the last great epic poet of Alexandrian Greece, when Alexander and his immediate successors ruled, died. His most famous work the **Argonautica** was an account of the legend of **Jason and the Golden Fleece**.

c.206 B.C.–A.D. 220 The period of the **Han Dynasty** in China was the first highly important period of **Chinese pottery**. Some of its pottery exhibited a western influence, using a fine glaze in the same techniques of an earlier day in Mesopotamia. From this beginning the beautiful ceramic works of art blossoming during the **Sung** (A.D. 960–1279) and the **Ming** (A.D. 1368–1644) periods developed.

c.200   The **Nike**, or **Winged Victory**, by an unknown artist, of Samothrace, a damaged example of superb **Greek sculpture**, was probably made about this time.

It was found in the 19th century A.D. on the island of Samothrace in the northeastern Aegean Sea. The statue is now in the Louvre Museum of Paris.

199–150 B.C.

I. VITAL STATISTICS AND DEMOGRAPHICS

c.175   The **Yüeh-chi**, nomadic barbarians along the western border of China, present Kansu [Gansu] province, were driven away from the vicinity of the Great Wall by the rulers of the **Han Dynasty**. An estimated 500,000 Yüeh-chi migrated across central Asia through the Tarim Basin in present western China to the Syr Darya and Amu Darya [Oxus] rivers east of the Aral and Caspian seas.

II. POLITICS AND WAR

198   **Antiochus III the Great**, king of the **Seleucid [Syrian] Empire**, defeated the Egyptian forces of **Ptolemy V Epiphanes** (c.210–181; ruled from 203) in a battle at **Paneas** [Baniyas] a present Syrian village of Baniyas near the border with Lebanon. It secured Seleucid annexation of all Egyptian territories in the Near East, excepting the Sinai, which was confirmed in 195 by a peace treaty and sealed by the betrothal of Antiochus' daughter, who became **Cleopatra I**, to the 15-year-old Ptolemy V.

197   The **Second Macedonian War** (200–197) ended in a **battle at Cynoscephalae** in southeastern Thessaly with a victory by the Roman legions, led by the consul T. Quinctus Flaminius (c.227–174), over Philip V, king of Macedonia. During the course of the war the **Achaean League** changed sides and joined Rome. The **Aetolian League**, already allied with Rome, fought well at Cynoscephalae. Rome recognized the independence of the Greeks at the **Isthmian Games** at Corinth in 196 B.C.

c.195   **Kao-Tsu** [Liu Pang, Liu Chi] (born c.247), first Western [Early] Han emperor of China (ruled from c.206), died. He initiated the first expansion of China's territory during the **Han Dynasty** (206 B.C.– A.D. 220) by driving the **Hsiung-nu** [Huns] out of China and as far west as Turkestan. He added Inner Mongolia to his realm. He introduced a system of civil service, opened the silk route from China to Syria (then to Rome), and encouraged the printing of books.

192   Greece was invaded by **Antiochus III the Great**, king of the **Seleucid [Syrian] Empire**, at the invitation of the **Aetolian League** during its rebellion against Roman rule. The **Achaean League**, Macedonia, and the kingdoms of Rhodes and Pergamum allied with Rome. In the same year the Seleucids were defeated and driven from Greece by a Roman victory in a **battle at Thermopylae**. Antiochus retreated into Anatolia while his fleet was destroyed off Myonnesus, near present Doğanbey on the western coast of Anatolia in 190.

189   Led by the consul **L. Cornelius Scipio Asiaticus** and his brother **P. Cornelius Scipio Africanus**, Roman forces, allied with Eumenes, king of Pergamum, decisively defeated **Antiochus III the Great**, king of the **Seleucid [Syrian] Empire**, in a **battle at Magnesia** and Sipylum [Manisa] in present Turkey. In 188, by terms of the **Treaty of Apamea**, Antiochus lost Anatolia west of the Taurus Mountains, which was divided between the kingdoms of Rhodes and Pergamum.

188   **Hannibal**, the famous Carthaginian general, sought refuge from Rome at the court of Prusias I, king of Bithynia, a small non-Greek country bordering the southwestern coast of the Black Sea. He had been ruler (202–196) of Carthage until the Romans accused him of plotting to start the war again. Despite efforts on his behalf by **Scipio Africanus**, he had to flee to the court of **Antiochus III** the Great in Syria for safety. The Romans asked Antiochus to surrender him at Apamea, but he avoided capture by fleeing to Bithynia. Hannibal (b. 247) committed suicide there in 183.

187   **Antiochus III the Great** (b. 242), king of the **Seleucid [Syrian] Empire**, was killed while plundering a temple in Elymaïs [Elam] in the Khuzestan province of Iran. Under his rule the Seleucid Empire (305–64) reached its greatest size, extending from the Indus River on the east to include northern Palestine and Anatolia on the west, and from the Caspian Sea on the north to the Persian Gulf and the Arabian Sea [Indian Ocean] on the south. He was

succeeded by his son **Seleucus IV** (born c.217), who was murdered (175) and his throne seized by **Antiochus IV** [Epiphanes = the illustrious] (d. 163).

c.185 The **Mauryan Empire** (from c.321) in India collapsed, perhaps under the pressure of invasions by the **Sakas** [Scythians] and others from the northwest; the new powers that arose among the **Dravidians** in the Deccan; and Pushyamitra's murder of the **last Mauryan king. Pushymitra** took power as the **first of the Sunga Dynasty** (to c.75). The Sungas were anti-Buddhist, espoused the return of **Brahmanism**, and saw the reduction of their realm on all sides.

184 M. Porcius Cato (234–149) became a Roman censor. Cato the Elder (so-called to distinguish him from his grandson) became one of the leading orators of Rome, a conservative power urging Rome to follow the virtues of an earlier time. He upheld strictly all laws, placed heavy taxes on luxuries, and forced tax collectors to deliver the taxes they collected. An inveterate enemy of **Carthage**, he was said to have been principally responsible for starting the **Third Punic War** (149–146) by his ringing call for Carthage's destruction.

172 The **Third Macedonian War** (172–168) broke out between Rome and Philip V's son, Perseus, king of Macedonia (179–168). Macedonia's revival threatened Roman interests in the eastern Mediterranean. Perseus, on the death of Philip in 179, inherited an army of 30,000–40,000 men, a treasury of 6,000 talents (c.20 million dollars), and a hatred of Rome. When he was found to be plotting against Rome, the Romans immediately declared war.

168 Roman legions led by the consul L. Aemilius Paulus Macedonicus (c.229–160) destroyed the Macedonian forces under Perseus, king of Macedonia, in a **battle at Pydna**, in Macedonia. Macedonia and its ally, the city-state of Epirus, were devastated; the power of Rhodes was curtailed by the establishment of a free port at Delos; a thousand leading citizens of Greece were deported to Rome; and **Perseus** (born c.212), the **last king of Macedonia**, died in captivity c.166.

167 Mattathias [Mattathiah] **Maccabee** (d. 166?), an aged Jewish priest, fled from Modi'in, a community c.20 miles northwest of Jerusalem, with his five sons after refusing to obey an edict by Antiochus IV Epiphanes to set up altars to Greek gods in his town. From the mountains to which he had fled with his

followers he proclaimed and led a rebellion, the **War of the Maccabees** (167–160), against the Seleucid [Syrian] Empire (305–64).

160 Judas [Judah] **Maccabeus** [the hammerer], who established (166) the **Hasmonean Dynasty** (to 37), died in a **battle with a Syrian army at Elasa** [Eleasa]. He had succeeded his father Mattathias as leader of the rebellion against Antiochus IV Epiphanes. He successively defeated (166–165) four Syrian [Seleucid] armies, and in Dec. 165, led his army into Jerusalem. Later in the same year he defeated a Syrian army numbering over 100,000 men.

154–133 Revolts broke out in both Hither and Farther Spain [Portugal] against harsh Roman rule. The people of **Hither Spain** were called **Celtiberians** and those from **Farther Spain Lusitanians**; other tribes of Spain also rebelled. The Roman consuls were incapable, cruel, and faithless. The drain on Rome for more troops was such that the tribunes in 151 and 138 tried unsuccessfully to protect the Italian peasants by murdering thousands of Lusitanians after a treaty had been negotiated.

III. ECONOMY AND TRADE

167 Roman citizens were freed of direct taxation on their property. The aggressive expansion of the Republic enabled the government to live off the plunder of war and conquest.

IV. RELIGION AND PHILOSOPHY

c.191 Through the **Phrygians**, the **cult of Cybele**, the Great Mother Goddess, was introduced into Rome. **Cybele** was a Greek nature goddess, the mother and source of life. Initiation into the mystery cult was considered a rite of purification, sacrifice, revelation, and regeneration built about the death and resurrection of the goddess.

175 The accession in the **Seleucid** [Syrian] **Empire** of **Antiochus IV Epiphanes** was followed by the successful contriving of the Hellenizing Jew, **Jason**, to get himself appointed high priest in Jerusalem. In horrified reaction to the steady encroachment of Hellenization, the Hasidim ["the pious ones"] banded together in opposition to foreign practices, even in the face of death.

169 Dec. 15 Antiochus IV Epiphanes determined to proscribe Judaism throughout his Palestinian province. He profaned the Temple and transformed it into a sanctuary of the Olympian Zeus. He forbade the observance of the **Law of Moses**, most especially circumcision, observance of the Sabbath, and the celebration of festivals. Possession of a scroll of the Law became a capital offense.

167 At Modi'in [Modin], a village 20 miles northwest of Jerusalem, an aged Jewish priest named **Mattathias** refused to sacrifice on an altar to a heathen god, as ordered by a Seleucid [Syrian] officer. Instead he killed the Jew who agreed to perform the ceremony and the officer too. Then he and his five sons fled to the mountains, urging others to take up arms and follow. Thus began the **War of the Maccabees** (167–160) against the **Seleucid** [Syrian] **Empire**.

165 Dec. The Temple was cleansed and rededicated by **Judas Maccabeus** and his men, after several successful engagements in the region with Syrian troops. The 25th day of Chislev has since been celebrated by Jews as the **Hanakkuh** [Rededication]. Religious liberty for Jews was regained by a treaty.

160 **Judas Maccabeus** [the hammerer] (ruled from c.166), third son of Mattathias, died in **battle at Eleasa** [Elasa], after leading the Jewish revolt for over six years. One of his last diplomatic acts had been to strike up an alliance with the rising western power, Rome.

c.160 The **Original Prajnaparamita Sutras**, Buddhist teachings on perfect Wisdom, began to take written form. The *Prajnaparamita* urged attention to the extinction of self-interest, while also recommending such wisdom as conferring practical and tangible advantages in this life.

V. SCIENCE, EDUCATION, AND TECHNOLOGY

c.194 The Greek **Eratosthenes** (born c.276) of Alexandria in Egypt, died. He measured the circumference of the earth as 24,662 miles and computed the sun's distance from the earth as 92,000,000 miles, amazingly close to present day computations. Eratosthenes established a system of prime numbers and historical chronology, reckoning subsequent dates from the fall of Troy, and drew one of the **first maps of the then known world**.

153 Jan. 1 The **Roman Republican calendar** was declared officially to begin each new year on Jan. 1 rather than Mar. 1. The consuls took office on this date instead of Mar. 15, due to a revolt of the Lusitanians in the Roman provinces of Spain. This change established the present New Year's Day as the beginning of the civil year. The period of intercalation, when adjustments between the civil calendar and the solar year were made simply by adding the necessary number of days as needed, began on Feb. 23, the month that today carries the extra day of Leap Year.

VI. ARTS AND LEISURE

c.199 B.C.–A.D. c.599 The **wall paintings of the Ajanta caves** in northwestern Maharashtra state of central India were executed during this period. The 30 caves, carved out in a ravine, consisted of meeting halls, monasteries, and sanctuaries whose frescoes and sculptures provided an incomparable record of **Buddhist art**.

c.184 **Titus Macius Plautus** (born c.251), the great Roman comic dramatist, died. A very popular writer, who depended on the farcical elements of Greek New Comedy, Plautus's most popular work was **The Pot of Gold** (194). As late as A.D. 1427 twelve new comedies were discovered, making 20 plays, or nearly all he probably wrote, extant today. Among his other popular plays were **The Rope** (189), **The Captives** (188), **Amphitryon** (186), and **The Twin Menaechmi** (186).

c.169 The Roman poet **Quintus Ennius** (b. 239) died. The **first Roman epic poet**, he introduced the **Greek dactylic hexameter in Latin**. His major work was **Annales** in 18 volumes.

161 The Roman comic dramatist **Terence** [Publius Terentius Afer] (c.195–c.159) received 8,000 sesterces, perhaps $8,000 in today's American currency, for his play *The Eunuch* (161), an enormous price. Terence, who was born in Carthage, was most popular among intellectuals. Six of his plays are extant; all were translations, or close adaptations, from the Greek New Comedy. Among them were *The Woman of Andros* (166), *The Mother-in-law* (165), and *Phormio* (161).

c.150 The great **Buddhist temple gateway** was erected at Sanchi, in central northern India. The elaborately carved stone gateway, still standing, was the most outstanding example of the opulent style of sculpture that was developing in India.

149–100 B.C.

I. VITAL STATISTICS AND DEMOGRAPHICS

c.125 The **Yüeh-chi** dominated Bactria, driving the Scythians [Sakas, Shakas] to the south and east. At this time the Yüeh-chi controlled much of the area between the Caspian Sea and Chinese Turkestan, present western Sinkiang [Xinjiang] Uygur Autonomous Region of western China.

II. EXPLORATION AND COLONIZATION

c.128 **Chang Ch'ien** (d. 128), envoy of Wu-Ti, emperor (141–86) of the **Western [Early] Han Dynasty** of China, visited the central Asian countries of Sogdiana and Bactria. He sought unsuccessfully for help against the **Hsiung-nu** [Huns] from the **Yüeh-chi** tribes. But he opened the way to new trade relations and introduced to China new plants and a breed of Sogdian horses that impressed the Chinese.

III. POLITICS AND WAR

149 The **Fourth Macedonian War** (149–148) broke out in Macedonia against Roman strictures. The Macedonians were aided by the Thracians. The rebellion, led by **Andriscus**, who claimed to be the son of Perseus, the last king of Macedonia, and who assumed (148) the title of king, was crushed the following year by the consul Q. Caecilius Metellus (d. 115) and Macedonia was annexed (146) as a Roman province. Andriscus was taken captive to Rome and there executed.

149 The **Third Punic War** (to 146), instigated by Rome, broke out between Carthage and Rome. The Romans feared a Carthaginian revival because of the remarkable commercial recovery of its capital city Carthage. The Carthaginians decided to resist when Rome announced harsh conditions, which required the Carthaginians to leave their city and resettle at least ten miles from the sea. The Carthaginians manned their walls using improvised weapons and held out for two years.

c.148 **Masinissa** (born c.240), king of Numidia, died. He changed the **Berbers of Numidia** from a nomadic life to that of an agricultural society, disciplined them, and ruled them well for 60 years. Masi-

nissa's tomb, a large pyramid, still stands near Constantine in Tunisia.

146 A revolt of the Greek **Achaean League** against Rome was led by Corinth. Crushed by Roman forces under the consul L. Mummius Achaicus, Corinth was sacked and its inhabitants massacred or enslaved, its treasure and art removed to Rome. The League was disbanded, and Greece became a Roman province called **Achaia** and administered by the Roman governor of Macedonia.

146 The **Third Punic War** (149–146) between Rome and Carthage ended. The Romans, under **P. Cornelius Scipio Aemilianus**, the adopted grandson of Scipio Africanus, razed Carthage and organized the area into the Roman province of Africa, whose capital was Utica, c.15 miles from Carthage.

143 **Jonathan Maccabee** was kidnapped and murdered by **Tryphon**, a pretender to the Seleucid throne, whom Jonathan was aiding at the time. Jonathan was the youngest son of Mattathias and the successor (160) to Judas. He rallied and reorganized the Jewish army after the **battle at Elasa**. He was so successful that the Seleucids recognized him as the Jewish leader (157), after which he was able to reunite the Jews and become a strong political force in the **Seleucid [Syrian] Empire**.

135 The **First Servile [Slave] War** broke out in Sicily, where agricultural slaves, led by the Syrian **Eunus**, rose up against the owners of the big estates. The revolt was crushed by Roman troops in 132.

134 **Simon Maccabee [Maccabaeus]** and his two older sons were assassinated by Ptolemy [not of Egypt], his son-in-law. Simon, Jonathan's elder brother and successor (143), had negotiated a treaty by which the Seleucids recognized Judaea, no longer to be called Palestine, as politically independent. He was the hereditary ethnarch [civil ruler] of the **Hasmonaean Dynasty** (166–37) and was succeeded by John Hyrcanus (ruled 134–104).

133 **Attalus III**, king of Pergamum (ruled 138–133), in order to protect his subjects from the Seleucids, bequeathed his entire kingdom to Rome. The territory was organized (129) into the Roman province of Asia.

133 **Numantia**, on the Duero River in northeastern Spain, the main city of the rebelling **Celtiberians**, was captured by the Romans under **P. Cornelius Scipio Aemilianus**. The Lusitanian rebel leader Viriathus (fl. 149–139) had been assassinated (139) by Lusitanians in the pay of Rome, and Roman rule was thus reestablished in most of the Iberian Peninsula.

129–102 The **Roman Republic was continually expanding** by the capture of states around the Mediterranean basin: Asia, formerly the kingdom of Pergamum, in 129; the Balearic Islands off Spain, in 123; Gallia Narbonensis, the part of present France along the Mediterranean coast, in 121; Tripolitania, in present Libya, in 105; and western Cilicia, south of the Taurus Mountains in southern Anatolia, in 102.

129 **Antiochus VII Euergetes** (b. 159) king of the **Seleucid** [Syrian] **Empire** (from c.138), was defeated and killed by the Parthians under Phraates II, Arsacid king of the **Parthian Empire** (c.250 B.C.–A.D. 226), which controlled the region of present northeastern Iran. The Greco-Macedonian Seleucids were ousted from all the territories east of the Euphrates River, including all of present Iran. The Seleucid Empire (305–64 B.C.) was reduced to Greater Syria, from Egypt on the south to the Taurus Mountains and the Euphrates River on the north and east.

c.128 **Phraates II**, Arsacid king (from c.138) of the **Parthian Empire** (c.250 B.C.–A.D. 224), was defeated and killed in battle during an attempt to halt the southward and westward penetration of the Scythians [Sakas, Shakas], themselves pushed by the Yüeh-chi tribes from Sogdiana and Bactria. The eastern territories of the Parthian Empire were ravaged by these nomadic tribes, which then turned their drive into northern India. Phraates II was succeeded by **Artabanus II** (ruled c.128–c.123).

123 **G. Sempronius Gracchus**, elected tribune of the plebeians, continued the struggle of his brother Tiberius (163–133), to **reduce the privileges of the Roman aristocracy** and improve the lot of the plebeians. The two were known as "the Gracchi." G. Gracchus (b. 153), himself also a plebeian, died in 121 with many of his supporters in the aftermath of a riot in the Forum. His abortive reforms initiated a period of unrest and social wars.

121 The Roman army under the consul Fabius Maximus and proconsul Gn. Domitius Ahenobarbus defeated the **Celtic tribes** of the Allobroges and the Averni, **giving Rome complete control of southern Gaul from the Pyrenees to the Alps** except for Massilia, which was at this time still a Roman ally. Later, in 118, the area became the Roman province **Gallia Narbonensis**.

c.111 Rome declared **war on Jugurtha** (c.160–104), king of Numidia (118–105), after he had caused a massacre of Romans at Cirta [Constantine]. When Micipsa, king of Numidia and the successor of Massinissa, died in c.118, he left his kingdom to be ruled jointly by his sons Adherbal and Hiempsal and their cousin Jugurtha. But Jugurtha had Hiempsal murdered (112), and he ousted (117) Adherbal, who sought help from Rome. Though Rome decided in Jugurtha's favor by dividing Numidia between the cousins, Jugurtha laid siege to Cirta, where Adherbal and so many Roman settlers were slain that the Senate was forced by popular reaction to declare war.

109–108 **Chinese forces invaded Korea** to forestall the **Hsiung-nu** [Huns], who were expanding their empire in that direction. The Chinese soon dominated the entire peninsula, which by A.D. 50 had a uniform culture throughout.

107 The **Jugurthine War** had gone badly for Rome because of widespread bribery and treason until the consul G. Marius was made general of the Roman forces in Africa. Marius seized all the towns and strongpoints that served as bases for the Numidians, now joined by the Mauretanians. Through treachery by the Mauretanian king, however, Jugurtha was delivered (c.105) to L. Cornelius Sulla (138–78), Roman quaestor in Africa, paraded in chains in a triumphal procession in Rome, and executed there (104). Numidia was served by docile kings appointed by Rome until Juba I (c.85–46) asserted independence c.49 B.C., but was defeated by **Julius Caesar** Apr. 4, 46 B.C., whereupon Numidia was annexed by the Roman province of Africa.

104 **John Hyrcanus** [Maccabee], son of Simon and king of Judaea (from 134), died. He freed Judaea completely from Seleucid [now only Greater Syria] control in an alliance with Rome and in military campaigns conquered Samaria, Idumanaea, and areas east of the Jordan River.

103–101   The **Second Servile** [Slave] **War** in Sicily began when the Roman Senate, needing troops to quell rebels in Italy, freed all males enslaved for unpaid taxes. When some slaves in Sicily heard this they demanded their liberty but were refused. Led by a slave named **Salvius**, they rebelled and defeated armies sent against them by the Roman praetor. In the western part of Sicily the slaves were led by a man named **Athenion**. The rebel groups joined forces and repeatedly defeated the Roman armies sent against them. In 102, Salvius was slain in battle and, when Athenion was slain in single combat with the Roman consul Manius Aquilius, the leaderless slaves were defeated and cruelly punished.

102   Improved and disciplined **Roman legions**, led by **G. Marius**, defeated the **Teutoni** [Teutons] in a **battle at Aquae Sextiae** [Aix-en-Provence] near Massilia [Marseille] in present France. This victory liberated Transalpine Gaul from this Germanic invasion.

101   Roman legions led by **G. Marius** annihilated the **Cimbri**, a German tribe, in a **battle at Vercellae** [Vercelli], north of the Po River in northern Italy. Marius, having lifted Italy from the barbarian threat, returned to Rome a national hero.

IV. ECONOMY AND TRADE

149–146   **Carthaginian books on agriculture** were translated from the Punic [from Greek **Phoînix** = Phoenician] into Latin by order of the Roman Senate, and became authoritative works on farming in Italy for generations.

146   **Corinth and Carthage were destroyed by Roman armies.** This resulted in a substantial reduction in free trade in the Mediterranean and in the power and prestige of the traders.

140   **Paper, or parchment, money** was used for the first time during the reign of **Wu-Ti**, emperor (141–86) of the Western [Early] **Han Dynasty** in China. Pasteboard notes circulated, along with p'i pi, or skin notes, which were made from white stag skin.

133–123   The Gracchi brothers in Rome provided grain at nominal prices for the poor, pending their resettlement on public land. The granting of cheap (eventually, free) grain to the citizenry became the **first in a long series of Roman "relief" measures**. In 133 Tiberius Sempronius Gracchus, elected tribune of the plebeians, tried to enforce his own agrarian law designed to limit the amount of public landholding by one person. Tiberius was killed in a riot while seeking reelection in 132.

c.100   During the reign of **Wu-Ti**, emperor of China, a route to the West, the **Old Silk Route**, was opened. It stretched from the edge of the empire to Anatolia and the Mediterranean coast. The Old Silk Route made possible the **first regular commercial contacts between East and West**. The Old Silk Route was not a paved road, but a caravan route made relatively safe from brigandage. When the Hans drove the Yüeh-chi away from their borders, the eastern end of the route became safe. In the orient the route began and ended at such Chinese capitals as Loyang, Changan, and Pekin; it moved west through Tun-huang, then either north of the Tarim Basin or the Takla Makan Desert, through Lou-lan, Karashahr, Kucha, Kashgar, or south of the desert through Miran, Cherchen and Niya to Ferghana, and Tashkent to Maracanda [Samarkand]. Both routes then converged to Merv, Bactra, Seleucia, Hatra, and Antioch in Syria where goods were transferred to ships.

V. RELIGION AND PHILOSOPHY

141 Sept.   By popular vote a grateful people conferred upon **Simon**, last of the sons of Mattathias, and upon his descendants, the office and authority of **ruling High Priest**. Thus the **Hasmonean Dynasty** (166–37) (named for an ancestor of Mattathias) was given recognition at home and abroad.

136   **Confucianism** was proclaimed the state doctrine by **Liu Pang**, first emperor of the Western [Early] **Han Dynasty** in China. In 124 an imperial university for Confucian studies was founded. Shortly thereafter the government singled out five Confucian works for educational purposes as required texts, known later as the **Five Classics**: **The Book of Odes, The Book of Changes, The Book of Rites, The Book of History**, and **The Book of Spring and Autumn Annals**.

c.130   The **Huai-nan-tzu**, a compilation of treatises attributed to Liu An [Huai-nan Tzu] (d. 122), grandson of the first Han emperor Liu Pang and prince of the community of Huai-nan in Anhwei [Anhui] province, along with writings by his scholar-retainers, was prepared. It set forth ancient Chinese cosmological ideas and the developing concept of **Tao**.

c.125 In the **first mention of the Pharisees and Sadducees** in a historical source, Josephus, a Jewish historian, indicated that by now both were established parties in the Jewish state. The Pharisees (those who are separated, i.e., from impurity) represented the educated lay element in Judaism. Pharisees emphasized the Law, both oral and written, and believed in a resurrection and a future world. The interests of the opposing Sadducees, the priestly party, centered in the Temple.

c.100 The **Essenes**, an ascetic community of Jews, with origins among the Hasidim of the Maccabean revolt, broke with the Hasmonean rulers of Judaea, and established their headquarters at Qumran on the west bank of the Dead Sea. The Essenes practiced communal ownership of property, went to extremes in the avoidance of ceremonial uncleanness, and practiced celibacy.

VI. SCIENCE, EDUCATION, AND TECHNOLOGY

144 At this time the **aqueducts** that brought fresh water to Rome were improved with the construction of the first high-level aqueduct for bringing water into the city at higher pressure. The introduction of **hydraulic cement**, which hardened under water and was not dissolved in it, enabled larger and more efficient aqueducts to be built.

142 The **Pons Aemilius**, the **first bridge to use stone arches**, was built across the Tiber River in Rome.

124 **Wu-Ti**, emperor of China, created an **imperial university** to further the study of the Confucian classics. After passing examinations, scholars were given official positions in the Han government. **Confucianism** was thus promoted as a state doctrine.

120 **Hipparchus** (b. 190) of Nicaea, in northwestern Anatolia, died. Hipparchus was undoubtedly the **greatest astronomer of ancient times**. Working in Rhodes, he prepared the first still extant catalogue of the stars, listing (c.850) their heavenly latitudes and longitudes and positions in the constellations. He made a map and a globe of the heavens showing the stars. Timochares (fl. 300) had made a chart of the heavens in 295, and a comparison of the two charts enabled Hipparchus to calculate that the stars had apparently shifted their positions 2° in the 166-year interval and from this to determine the precession of the equinoxes (the slight daily advance of the precise time the equinoctial points reached meridian). He also developed a hypothesis explaining the movements of the sun and the moon as well as the planets in terms of a moving eccentric. After Hipparchus, eclipses of the moon could be forecast quite accurately.

c.118 **Polybius** (born c. 200), a Greek historian, died. Taken (168) to Rome as a political prisoner, he became an important figure in the Roman literary world. Polybius was present (146) at the destruction of Carthage at the end of the **Third Punic War**. He devoted much of his life to writing **Histories**, an account (220–146) of the rise of Rome. His history was not only factual but also included discussions of the reasons for writing history, which he thought of as giving guidance to the conduct of politics. Only the first 5 of his 40 books survive today, but large parts of others are extant.

107 The consul **G. Marius** initiated the **Roman professional army** by recruiting and training his own forces instead of using the traditional conscription.

VII. ARTS AND LEISURE

140 **Mei Shèng**, who has been regarded as a chief founder of Chinese **fu**, a prose-poem, died. His best-known work was *Ch'i-fa*. The *fu*, elaborate and lengthy, became very popular before being dismissed much later as hollow and artificial.

c.100 The **Imperial Office of Music**, the **Yüeh Fu**, was established in China, to supervise ceremonial— as well as foreign, aristocratic, and folk—music and to found an archive of national melodies. Because it was mainly concerned with the preservation of correct pitch, it was part of the Office of Weights and Measures.

99–50 B.C.

I. POLITICS AND WAR

c.94 **Tigranes** [Tigran] **II the Great** (c.140–55) succeeded Artaverdes [Artavazd] I (ruled from 123) as king of Greater Armenia. He embarked on a policy of territorial expansion, beginning with the conquest of Sophene, a neighboring Armenian kingdom to the southwest, which thus reunited all Armenia under one rule.

92 **Mithridates II**, king of Parthia (c.123–88), concluded a **peace treaty** with Rome. His restoration of Parthian power in present Iran and his western drive against the Seleucids of Greater Syria had brought him in contact with the Roman province of Asia in western Anatolia.

91 A civil war, called the **Social War** (90–88), broke out against Rome, following the assassination of the tribune M. Livius Drusus. Some of Rome's allies (**socii**) formed an army, which after initial successes was defeated, and Asculum, where the rebellion began, was captured in 89. Rome's eventual concession, to grant citizenship to all Italians, as demanded by the rebels, brought the war to an end in 88. Italy was finally united into a single political framework.

89 The **Mithridatic War** (c.89–84) broke out between Rome and the Anatolian kingdom of Pontus, along the southern coastland of the Black Sea, when Mithridates VI Eupator (ruled 120–63) seized the kingdoms of Cappadocia, Paphlagonia, and Bithynia, Roman protectorates, and occupied the Roman province Asia. His army, which had been invited to Greece by Athens, landed there in December, and his fleet won control of the Aegean Sea. The Romans gave command to L. Cornelius Sulla, who had first to subdue Athens, then march to meet Mithridates in Boeotia, in central Greece.

87 **Wu-Ti** [Kuang Wu-ti] (b. 157), emperor (from 141) of the Western [Early] Han (206 B.C.–A.D. 9) of China, died. He accomplished great territorial expansion of China during the Han Dynasty (206 B.C.–A.D. 220).

87 Roman forces under Sulla invaded Greece and captured Athens from the Pontines in 86, but spared it from destruction. In 85 Roman legions defeated the superior forces of Mithridates, first in a **battle at Chaerona**, then at Orchomenus, both in Boeotia in central Greece. Sulla, unable to cross the Aegean Sea while the Pontine navy was in control, wintered in Greece. The quaestor Lucius Lucullus arrived with a Roman fleet, which defeated the Mithridates navy. Sulla crossed into Anatolia where, by the **Treaty of Dardanus** in 84 B.C., Mithridates abandoned his conquests, lost his fleet, and paid an indemnity to Rome.

86 **Gaius Marius** (born c.155) died. A popular Roman general, he had been elected consul seven times. He had led Roman troops against Jugurtha and against the Cimbri and Teutons. During the **Social War** (90–88) he was the plebeian rival of the patrician Sulla, who drove him out of Rome in 88. While Sulla was in Greece fighting Mithridates, Marius and L. Cornelius Cinna (d. 84) recaptured Rome in 86 and took revenge by massacring thousands of citizens, especially the aristocrats, a bloodbath stopped only by Marius's death.

82 The consul **Sulla** entered Rome after a successful campaign against the supporters of the regime of Cinna, who had been killed by his own troops in 84. Elected dictator, Sulla repressed his opponents, restored the power of the aristocracy and the Senate, and destroyed the power of the tribunes before retiring from public life in 79.

76 **Alexander Jannaeus** [Maccabee] (b. 126), king of Judaea (from 103), died after a rule of war and internal strife. He was succeeded (to 67) by his wife Salome Alexandra.

c.75 **Maues** (fl. c.75), king of the Sakas [Shakas, Scythians], captured Gandhara to control all of the Punjab south to the Jumna [Yamuna] River. The **Sunga Dynasty** (from c.185) collapsed at this time, probably from Saka pressure. Under Azes I (fl. c.50) the Sakas gained control of all of northern India east to the Ganges Plains and south to the Narmada River.

74 To protect his people from Pontus, Nicomedes III, king (81–74) of Bithynia, bequeathed his kingdom to Rome, an action that precipitated another **Mithridatic War** (74–64) between Rome and Mithridates VI, king of Pontus (120–63), who promptly invaded Bithynia. The Pontines were driven from Bithynia in 73 by the Roman consul L. Licinius

Lucullus (c.117–?57), and Mithridates fled to Armenia in 72.

73 A revolt led by the Thracian gladiator **Spartacus** (d. 71) developed into a slave war, known as the **Third Servile War** (73–71), against Rome. Roman legions under L. Crassus (115–53) defeated the rebels, who had overrun and held much of southern Italy. Crassus crushed them in 71 with help from G. Pompeius [Pompey], and thousands of the slaves were crucified along the Appian Way.

72 The Roman governor of Spain, **Q. Sertorius** (born c.123), who had led the faction of Marius in Spain and had continued the popular cause against Sulla after Marius's death, was assassinated. His death allowed **Pompey** to pacify the Iberian peninsula and to return to Italy in time to help Crassus in the Third Servile War. For the victories Pompey became known as **Pompeius Magnus** [Pompey the Great]. Crassus and Pompey were elected consuls in 70.

69 **Tigranocerta**, capital of Greater Armenia, was captured by Roman legions under L. Licinius Lucullus. Lucullus then returned those areas of Syria occupied by Armenia to Antiochus XIII, king (69–64) of the much reduced **Seleucid** [Syrian] **Empire**. Tigranes, king of Armenia, recovered much of his power in northern Armenia after Lucullus was recalled by the Roman Senate in 67. **Pompey the Great** was appointed commander in Asia to replace Lucullus.

67 With orders to clear the eastern Mediterranean of pirates, **Pompey** completed in three months the task begun by Q. Caecilius Metellus Pius (died c.63), and won tremendous prestige by thus securing the trade and grain routes to Rome. **Crete was captured** and joined as a Roman province to Cyrenaica in present Libya.

67 **Salome Alexandra**, Hasmodean queen of Judaea from 76, died after a peaceful and prosperous reign.

65 Roman forces under **Pompey** defeated Mithridates VI Eupator, king of Pontus, and Tigranes, king of Armenia, in a swift campaign. Fleeing to the Crimean peninsula, Mithridates (born c.132) committed suicide in 63, after his army had revolted. Tigranes was allowed to retain his kingdom east of Anatolia as a buffer state between Rome and Parthia.

64 Roman forces under **Pompey** deposed Antiochus XIII Asiaticus, the last of the Seleucid kings (69–64) of Greater Syria, who disappeared completely from history. **Palestine was occupied** in 63, and the Roman territories of the Near East were organized into four provinces: the former province of Asia, Bithynia (with part of Pontus), Cilicia, and Syria, which included Palestine as a protectorate.

63 The **conspiracy of** [L. Sergius] **Catiline** (c.108–62), an attempt to seize power in Rome, was denounced by the consul **Cicero** (106–43). Through a series of orations, called the **Catilinares**, in the Roman Senate, Cicero foiled the conspiracy. Catiline fled and was slain in battle.

60 The **first triumvirate**—**Pompey**, **Crassus**, and **G. Julius Caesar**—was formed in Rome. Caesar had been quaestor in Spain, where he earned honor and wealth. The short-sighted Roman Senate in effect forced Pompey, Crassus, and Caesar into the triumvirate by their treatment of Pompey and Crassus, who felt their service to Rome had not been sufficiently rewarded. Caesar, after serving as consul from 59, was given the coveted five-year governorship of Cisalpine Gaul and Illyria with a garrison of three legions. Later Transalpine Gaul and another legion were added to his command.

58 **Julius Caesar** defeated the **Celtic Helvetii tribes**, of the region of present Switzerland, in a **battle at Bibracte**, near Autun in present France. Pushing northward, he repulsed a Germanic tribal army, led by the Suevian Ariovistus (fl. 71–58) at Vesoretio [Besançon] in eastern France to complete his **occupation of eastern Gaul**. The **Rhine** became a frontier between Gaul [France] and Germania Magna. The tribes to the east of the Rhine, probably Celtic in origin centuries before, were now called by the Romans **Germans**.

57 **Julius Caesar** defeated the Celtic Belgae tribes in the region of present northern France and the Celtic Nervii of present Belgium and the southern Netherlands. Most of western Gaul was occupied the following year, and the Roman conqueror was given five more years of command through a conference with Pompey and Crassus, the other two members of the triumvirate, at Luca in Italy c.38 miles north of Florence in Apr. 56.

55 In the **first invasion of Britain** by Julius Caesar, his Roman legions crossed the Straits of Dover with a small reconnaissance force, but returned quickly. In 54 the legions again crossed into Britain, where they defeated the **Catuvellauni**, a tribe of Britons [Celts] led by Cassivellaunus (fl. 54), who had established a kingdom in an area north and west of present London. Caesar then withdrew to Gaul.

53 June 9   The Roman army, during an **invasion of Parthia** to settle a dispute in the succession, was defeated by **Orodes II**, Arsacid king (57–37) of the **Parthian Empire** in a **battle at Carrhae** [Haran, Harran, Altinbasak] in present Turkey near the Syrian border. M. Licinius Crassus (b. ?115), the Roman consul, was captured and executed. The Parthians then plundered Syria for two years.

52   **Vercingetorix**, chief of the Celtic Averni, united all Gaul in a last-ditch effort to oust the Roman invaders. Julius Caesar had been defeated in south central Gaul at Gergovia in 53, but he now won a decisive victory at the **siege of Alesia** [Alise Ste. Reine] near present Dijon, where he had surrounded Vercingetorix and his army and, with great losses, beat off relieving Celtic forces. It was the greatest and last battle of Caesar's conquest of Gaul. Vercingetorix was taken to Rome for display in Caesar's triumph and there beheaded c.46.

c.51   Peace developed between the **Western Han Dynasty** (206 B.C.–A.D. 9) and the Mongolian **Hsiung-nu** [Huns]. The Hsiung-nu Empire had begun to fade in power after the death of their great leader **Mao Tun** c.174, and because the Hans had gained control of the border areas and of the silk route to the west. Other Mongolian tribes and leaders were beginning to rise.

c.50   The **Three Kingdoms of Korea** made their first appearances: **Koguryo** to the north in the area of present Manchuria and Korea; **Silla** in southeastern Korea; and **Pakche** [Paekshe] in southwestern Korea. They each declared their independence of China, then in turmoil, but maintained cultural ties. The Chinese still controlled Lo-lang and its surrounding areas.

II. ECONOMY AND TRADE

54   Consul **Julius Caesar** built a new forum on the north side of the old Forum Romanum, which was overcrowded. Caesar's forum was a large square with a temple at one end.

III. RELIGION AND PHILOSOPHY

63   At the end of a three-month siege **Pompey the Great** entered the holy of holies of the **Temple in Jerusalem** after breaking down the massive walls surrounding it. He had been invited to settle a Jewish dynastic dispute between Hyrcanus II and his brother Aristobulus II (d. 48), and had found an excuse to lead troops into Judaea and to attack Jewish forces holed up within the Temple. Twelve thousand Jews were killed by Roman soldiers.

55   **T. Lucretius** [Carus] (b. 96), a Roman epicurean poet-philosopher, died a suicide. His greatest work, **De Rerum Natura**, in six volumes, has survived nearly intact. Based on the beliefs of Democritus and Epicurus, Lucretius demonstrated that man acted according to his own, rather than divine or supernatural, law. *De Rerum Natura* provided the first systematic account of the atomic, or particle, theory operating in the natural world. In language the work often rose to great heights, and next to Vergil's *Aeneid*, was the greatest long poem in Latin.

IV. SCIENCE, EDUCATION, AND TECHNOLOGY

86   Ssŭ-Ma Ch'ien [Sze-Ma Ts'ien] (b. 145), author of the **first complete history of China** up to his day, died. His *Shih Chi* [*Records of the Grand Historian*] was researched in the imperial library, but it incorporated also much of China's oral tradition. Aside from its value as history, the *Shih Chi* was of immense literary importance, highly prized for its innovatively natural, living language. It contained a revision of the Chinese calendar and determined the chronology still in use. The Pan family carried on Ssŭ-Ma Ch'ien's historical work, and one of them, **Pan Chao** (A.D. c.45–115), was **China's earliest female scholar**.

c.63   **M. Tullius Tiro** (fl. 1st century B.C.), a Roman freedman [former slave], invented a kind of shorthand called the **Tironian system**. He was a private secretary of Cicero.

V. ARTS AND LEISURE

ante 80   The city of **Pompeii**, near Naples, founded (c.530) by the Greeks and destroyed during the eruption of Mount Vesuvius on Aug. 24, A.D. 79, was occupied mainly by Romans at this time. The ejecta of the volcano covered and protected many Greek and Roman frecoes on the walls of the houses and other works of art and artifacts.

c.75 The **last of Greek military power** and influence disappeared from India when the region was conquered by the **Sakas** [Scythians], but Hellenism left a marked influence on Indian art, particularly that of the Buddhists. Sculptures of the human figure especially became more lifelike and were draped in graceful flowing garments.

61 **Pompey the Great** brought Chinese silk back to Rome after his campaigns in the Near East, starting a vogue for the cloth among the wealthy. Silk cloth was the main commodity carried over the "**silk route**" from China to India to Rome.

c.57 **L. Licinius Lucullus**, patron of the arts, epicure, and the period's **famous gourmet**, died. He had been a successful general, defeating Mithridates in Anatolia. Only a mutiny by his troops against his harsh discipline barred additional victories. Yet he is remembered today most for the Lucullan banquets

he gave in Rome, using wealth he gathered in Asia.

55 The **first theater of stone in Rome** was built by **Pompey** the Great. Rome now proceeded over the next centuries to build magnificent theaters throughout the empire.

c.54 **G. Valerius Catullus** (born c.84) died. He was acclaimed as the **greatest lyric poet of Latin literature**. He had arrived c.62 in Rome where he met Clodia, a beautiful but treacherous Roman matron who became his mistress and the Lesbia of Catullus's poetry. They were the first in Latin to utilize fully the Greek [Alexandrian] meters of lyric and elegiac poetry. About 116 of his poems are extant today.

c.50 The **Corinthian Order of architecture**, first introduced in Greece during the fourth century B.C., became a major influence in Rome, thanks to a great influx of Hellenistic stone carvers and masons into the city.

49–0 B.C.

I. POLITICS AND WAR

49 Jan. 10 or 11 **Julius Caesar** and his army crossed the **Rubicon** [**Rubicone**] **River** just north of Arminium [Rimini] on Italy's northeastern coast, which marked the legal boundary of his province of Cisalpine Gaul, initiating a civil war against **Pompey the Great**. The Roman Senate had outlawed Caesar since he had not abandoned his army command on July 1, 48, as ordered. Pompey fled to Greece before Caesar's rapidly growing army. Caesar then pacified Italy, marched to Spain where he defeated forces loyal to Pompey at Ilerda [Lérida, Lareda] in northeastern Spain, and finally subdued Massilia [Marseille] on his way back to Rome. Some of Caesar's forces under his lieutenants seized Sicily, Sardinia, and Africa which, with his victories in Spain, gave him complete control of the central and western Mediterranean.

48 **Julius Caesar** won a stunning victory against **Pompey** in a **battle at Pharsalus** [Pharsala, Farsala; Phthia] in Thessaly, Greece. Pompey (b. 106), abandoned by most of his troops, sought refuge in Egypt, where he was assassinated later this year.

48 **Julius Caesar** put down a rebellion of **Ptolemy XIII**, king of Egypt (from 51), and reinstalled Ptolemy's sister **Cleopatra VII** on the throne. Ptolemy (b. 61) was drowned while fleeing. Caesar's successful eastern campaign was completed in a battle (47) at **Zela** [Zile] in Anatolia, where he defeated **Pharnaces II**, king of Pontus (63–47). *Veni, Vidi, Vici* (*I came, I saw, I conquered*) was his famous dispatch to Rome.

46 Apr. 4 **Julius Caesar** defeated forces loyal to the Pompeian faction that was led by S. Pompey the Younger, son of Pompey the Great, and Juba I, king of Numidia, at Thapsus, near Cap Afrique [Ras Kerkenna] on the coast of present Tunisia. Part of Numidia, in present Algeria, was added to the Roman province of Africa. The region became a prosperous center of Roman culture where **Christianity,** as well as agriculture and commerce, flourished.

45 Mar. 17 **Caesar** defeated Pompey's sons, Gnaeus and Sextus, in a **battle at Munda** in southern Spain. Though Caesar had previously subdued Spain, Pompeian adherents had been fomenting rebellion there. It was said that more than 20,000 Pompeians were slain while only about 1,000 of Caesar's legionnaires were lost. Gnaeus (born c.75) was captured and executed; Sextus escaped to the mountains of northern Spain. It was the final battle of the civil war, and Caesar returned to Rome, where he was made dictator for life; he had been made dictator in 49, again in 47, and in 46 for a term of ten years. He was consul from 48 and from 45 sole consul.

44 Mar. 15 **Julius Caesar** (b. 100) was assassinated at the Senate, in a conspiracy led by **M. Junius Brutus** and **G. Cassius Longinus**. It initiated a struggle for the succession between **Marcus Antonius** [Mark Antony], the surviving consul; **G. Julius Caesar Octavius** [Octavian], the adopted son and heir of Caesar; and the conspirators at the assassination, who fled to the eastern provinces to raise armies.

43 Nov. The **Second Triumvirate** was formed in Rome as **Mark Antony, Octavian,** and **M. Aemilius Lepidus** (d. 13 B.C.), a former consul and now governor of Gaul and allied with Antony, agreed to share power. A reign of terror broke out as the triumvirs ordered massive proscriptions to crush the senatorial opposition and raise money to finance their armies.

43 Dec. 7 **M. Tullius Cicero** (b. 106), a Roman orator and statesman, was assassinated near Caieta [Gaeta], on the Gulf of Gaeta south of Rome. The **greatest of the Roman orators**, he was famous for his Verrines, a denunciation of the exactions and cruelty of the Sicilian governor Verres in 70; his *In Catilinam*, a series of four orations against a plot led by Catiline in 63; his brilliant fourteen *Philippics* (Sept. 44–Apr. 43) against Mark Antony for his role in Caesar's assassination, which resulted in his death when Antony came to power in November and ordered his murder. He was also noted for his correspondence, and for his philosophical and rhetorical treatises, such as *De Natura Deorum* (45?) and *De Oratore* (55).

42 Oct. 27 **Mark Antony** defeated the forces of G. Cassius Longinus at Philippi near the Aegean coast in Macedonia in his war against Caesar's murderers. **Cassius** committed suicide, as did **Brutus** (born c.85), whose forces were defeated by the combined army of Antony and Octavian also at Philippi 20 days later (Nov. 16). The last hopes of the republican party in Rome were dashed. Antony, who remained to govern in the east, then met **Cleopatra VII**, the Ptolemy

queen of Egypt, at Tarsus, in present Turkey, and wintered in Egypt while Antony's wife and brother, leading Italian landowners, rebelled against Octavian in Italy, who finally defeated them at Perusia [Perugia], north of Rome, in 41.

40 The **pact of Brundisium** [Brindisi], an Adriatic seaport in southern Italy, sealed the reconciliation of the Roman triumvirs. **Antony**, whose wife had just died, married Octavian's sister Octavia (69–11), and ruled over the eastern provinces; **Octavian** appropriated the western provinces and Italy; and **Lepidus** was limited to the rule of the province of Africa.

38 June 9 In a **battle at Mt. Gindarus** in northern Syria, forces of Mark Antony under the Roman general P. Ventidius (died c.38) defeated the **Parthians** under their general Pacorus, son of Orodes I, Arsacid king of Parthia, and the Roman Q. Labenius, who had allied themselves with Crassius and Brutus. Pacorus, who had been king for less than a year, was killed. Anatolia and Syria, which had been invaded by the Parthians, were regained by Antony, while Antigonus II (born c.80) [Maccabee], high priest of Jerusalem and last ruler (from 40) of the **Hasmonaean Dynasty**, who had allied himself to Parthia, was executed (37) by the Romans. **Herod** was then recognized by the Roman Senate as king of Judaea (37–4).

36 The Roman fleet under M. Vipsanius Agrippa (63–12) defeated Pompey the Younger, Pompey the Great's surviving son, in a **battle at Naulochus**, off the northern coast of Sicily, securing Rome's grain supply. Pompey (b. 75) fled to Anatolia, where he was executed by troops of Mark Antony in 35. Lepidus, who had attempted to seize Sicily, was betrayed by his own troops and forced into retirement, leaving **Octavian** in control of Italy, the western provinces, and Africa.

33 **Bocchus II**, king of Mauretania (49–33), in northwestern Africa, died and his kingdom was taken over by Rome. Juba II (d. 19 A.D.), formerly king of Numidia, who had married Cleopatra Selene, daughter of Mark Antony and Cleopatra VII, was established by the Romans as king of Mauretania, most of which Bocchus had previously seized. Numidia and Mauretania were annexed as the Roman province of Africa Nova in 27 B.C.

32 The second five-year term of the Roman triumvirate came to an end, precipitating a crisis between the two remaining rivals, **Octavian** and **Mark An-**

tony. Octavian succeeded in discrediting Antony, who had married Cleopatra, the Ptolemy queen of Egypt, and bequeathed the eastern provinces to the Ptolemies. Rome, fearing an oriental domination, declared Octavian its champion in the inescapable civil war to come.

31 Sept. 2 Forces of **Mark Antony** and **Cleopatra** were defeated by **Octavian's** fleet in a **battle at Actium**, off Epirus in western Greece. The two returned to Alexandria, where Antony (born c.82) committed suicide on Aug. 1, 30, on the arrival of the Roman army. At about the same time Cleopatra (b. 69) also committed suicide after failing to sway Octavian, who had annexed Egypt to Rome on Aug. 3, 30. Thus ended the **Ptolemy Dynasty** (from 323) in Egypt and with it the last chance of Hellenism exercising a major influence on western Europe. Ptolemy XIV Caesarion (b. 47), Cleopatra's son by Julius Caesar, who was co-regent with his mother (from c.44), was killed by Octavian in 30.

30 Hyrcanus II [Maccabee], king of Judaea and high priest (72–40), was killed. Hyrcanus's brother Aristobulus II had seized power and taken the crown from Hyrcanus in 67 after Hyracanus had been in office only three months. In 63, when **Palestine** became a Roman protectorate, **Pompey the Great** deposed Aristobulus and restored Hyrcanus to the high priesthood but not to effective civil power. Antipater, Hyrcanus's prime minister, became procurator (47) for Rome as a reward for helping **Julius Caesar** in Egypt. Antigonus II, the son of Aristobulus II and last of the Hasmonaean [Maccabean] Dynasty, became king of Judaea (40-37) with the help of Parthia. He seized Hyrcanus and, after having his ears clipped so he could never again be high priest, shipped him to Babylon. **Herod** the Great, son of Antipater and king of Judaea from 37, had Hyrcanus returned from Babylon to Jerusalem and then, seven years later, had him killed on suspicion of plotting.

27 Jan. 16 It was on this date that the **Roman Empire** (to A.D. 395) was traditionally said to have begun. **Octavian** was given the title of **Augustus** [exalted] and virtually full power by the Roman Senate following an offer to resign. Augustus was also given the title Imperator for life, which meant he was commander of all Roman armies. Thus he became the **first Roman emperor**.

25 Augustus strengthened the Roman territories of Anatolia [Asia, Bithynia] by creating the province of Galatia in present Turkey. He also signed (20) a **treaty with Parthia** that confirmed Roman control of Armenia. This treaty secured the empire's eastern frontier, which permitted Augustus to turn his attention to the north where he began strengthening Roman defenses against barbarian invasions from across the Danube and Rhine rivers.

c.25 At this time the **Sakas** [Shakas, Scythians] in India were at the height of their power, ruling south to Gujarat, the region north of Bombay, and east to the Malwa area of northern central India, with their capital at Ujjain. The **Andhra Empire** in eastern and central India also reached its greatest extent c.25.

25 G. Aelius Gallus (d. 26), the Roman prefect of Egypt (from 30), was sent by **Augustus** on a military expedition to southern Arabia. A treaty was signed the following year with the **kingdom of Saba** [Sheba] that secured for Rome a trade route to eastern Africa, India, and the Far East.

19 Roman forces under **Agrippa** completed the pacification of Spain. The Iberian Peninsula was divided into the three provinces of **Lusitania** [roughly present Portugal]; **Baetica** [present western Andalusia]; and **Tarraconensis** [present northern, central, and southeastern Spain].

16 Roman legions under **Tiberius**, the future Roman emperor and the present governor of Gaul, and his brother [Nero Claudius] **Drusus**, began a campaign against the Germanic tribes. The empire was extended to the upper Danube by the annexation of **Rhaetia**, **Noricum**, and **Pannonia** [roughly present Switzerland, southern West Germany, Austria, and western Hungary].

4 Mar.–Apr. Herod the Great (b. 73), king of Judaea (from 37), who established the **Herodian Dynasty** (37 B.C.–A.D. c.100), died. Strongly favored by Rome for bringing order in a troubled spot of the empire, he was disliked by the Jews for his lack of religious zeal. He was remembered chiefly for his program of reconstruction and building, among them the **Temple at Jerusalem**, magnificent forts, and cities, including Caesarea.

II. RELIGION AND PHILOSOPHY

47 Antipater [Antipas] the Idumean, son of the ruler of Idumea [Edom] in southern Judaea, probably saved **Julius Caesar** from disaster by breaking up an Egyptian siege of Alexandria, where Caesar was trapped with a small force. As a reward Antipater was appointed procurator of Judaea (47–43). Antipater's ability to change sides smoothly during the Roman civil wars led to Rome's election (37) of his son **Herod** as king of the Jews (to 4 B.C.)

c.40 The reforms of the **Mahasanghita Buddhist monks** across two centuries had by now brought great changes in Buddhism. Popular interest in it had grown with the intended downplaying of monastic life; the new stress on **karma** and rebirth, at the expense of less graspable concepts; the new adoration of the **Buddha**, including human-form reproductions; and the development of popular literature and art.

37–4 B.C. In Judaea the reign of **Herod**, called "the Great" by Roman historians and intensely disliked by most Jews, was marked by much bloodshed as he consolidated his power and vented his suspicions toward members of his family.

c.30 **Hillel**, a young rabbinical student, arrived in Jerusalem from Babylon and soon became the most influential Jewish teacher-scholar of the Augustan Age. Liberal in his interpretation of **Torah**, Hillel determined the direction taken by rabbinical Judaism in the difficult centuries to follow.

c.25 *The Lotus of the Good Law*, [Saddharma-Pundarika] one of Buddhism's **most sacred sutras**, made its appearance in the last half of the first century B.C.

20 **Herod** the Great began rebuilding the **Temple at Jerusalem** on a Hellenistic-Roman style, but he retained the arrangement of rooms within the sanctuary given to Solomon's Temple. Within two years the basic structure of this **third Temple** had been completed, but work on subsidiary buildings was still incomplete by the time of **Jesus**, 50 years later.

c.6 or 5 B.C. **Jesus** was born in Nazareth, a town in southern Galilee. A Jew and probably a carpenter by trade, he was, according to Gospel accounts, baptized at about age 30 by the prophet **John the Baptist**, after which he began an itinerant ministry in the vicinity of the Sea of Galilee.

III. SCIENCE, EDUCATION, AND TECHNOLOGY

46 The **Julian calendar** was established in Rome by **Julius Caesar**. Devised by **Sosigenes** of Alexandria, it divided the 365-1/4–day year into 12 months of 30 or 31 days, except for February with 29 days and in a leap year 30 days. The length of the months was altered, but otherwise the general divisions have since remained the same. The first year, which began on Jan. 1, was lengthened so that the calendar year and the solar year, now three months different at the equinox, were in agreement. In 8 B.C. the month of Sextilis was renamed August in honor of the Roman emperor Augustus. It was given an extra day, taken from February, to be equal to the 31-day month of July named in 46 B.C. to honor Julius Caesar.

31 The fragment of a stone monument on which the **Olmec Indians** had carved their date equivalent to this date was found at Tres Zapotes in present eastern Vera Cruz state of Mexico.

27 **M. Terentius Varro** (b. 116), who wrote a nine-volume work called *Disciplinae* on the arts and sciences, died. Portions of his *Rerum Humanorum et Divinarum Antiquitates* are extant. It was an attempt to consolidate Roman learning and compare it with the Greek. He recognized nine disciplines in the liberal arts: grammar, dialectic, rhetoric, geometry, arithmetic, astronomy, music, medicine, and architecture.

c.25–c.23 *De Architectura*, compiled about this time by the Roman **M. Vitruvius Pollio** (fl. first century B.C.), was the only surviving work on architecture written before the Christian era and was considered the authority for many centuries. Vitruvius described machinery, water clocks, aqueducts, town planning, and sanitation. He warned the Italians that water in some areas caused goiters and that lead was a poison; he also recognized in discussing architectural acoustics that sound was caused by vibrations in air.

10 **Herod** completed an extensive rebuilding of a Mediterranean coastal town, naming it **Caesarea** and dedicating it to Augustus. In the absence of a natural harbor Herod constructed a concrete breakwater 200 feet wide to provide shelter for vessels. It was said to have been the **first harbor built in the open sea**. Caesarea, with its palace, temple to the divine Augustus, theater, hippodrome, and other typical Greek-city buildings, became the provincial capital of the Roman governors of Judaea. By the time Herod died (4 B.C.) he had provided Jerusalem and Caesarea with aqueducts that assured them an ample flow of good water; had rebuilt and enlarged several fortresses, including Machaerus and Masada, and had constructed new ones; and had built in Jerusalem a magnificent royal palace and the Tower Antonia to house the Roman cohorts assigned there.

IV. ARTS AND LEISURE

48 B.C. The magnificent **library at Alexandria**, Egypt, the greatest in the ancient world, was partially destroyed when Julius Caesar was besieged there in the winter of 48–47 B.C.

44 Mar. 15 B.C. **Julius Caesar**, assassinated this day, is also remembered for his prose writings. *De Bello Gallica* [*Gallic Wars*] and *De Bello Civili* [*Commentaries*] are admired by scholars today for their clear, strong, and concise Latin prose as well as their excellent history.

c.27 B.C. The **Pantheon in Rome** was built by M. Vipsanius Agrippa (63?–12), the Roman statesman and general. The circular building, of poured concrete made of lime, volcanic ash [pozzolana], water, and rubble of bricks, marble, and stone, supported a dome that was one of the largest constructed up to this time.

c.25 B.C. The **basilica** built by the Roman architect M. Vitruvius Pollio at Fano, central Italy, with its short rectangular form, two-storied aisle and central hall set the style for the European imperial basilicas.

20 B.C. M. Vipsanius Agrippa inaugurated the first of the huge **baths in Rome**, the distinctive recreational buildings built throughout the empire, around which much of the social life of the times would revolve over the next centuries.

19 Sept. 21 B.C. The great Latin poet **P. Vergilius Maro** (b. Oct. 15, 70), known as **Vergil** [**Virgil**], died, leaving his epic, the **Aeneid**, unfinished. Vergil requested that it be destroyed on his death, but **Augustus** ordered that it be edited without additions. The 12 books of the *Aeneid* recorded the adventures of the Trojan hero Aeneas, from whom Vergil traced Augustus's lineage. Before composing the *Aeneid*, Vergil had already become famous for the *Bucolics* [*Bucolica*] (37) and the *Georgics* [*Georgica*] (37–30), both of which praised the virtues of the Roman farmer but also strongly endorsed the rejuvenation under Augustus of the Roman world that had been demoralized by civil wars.

16 B.C. The Roman temple now called *Maison Carrée* was built at Nemausus, present Nîmes in southern France. Surrounded by Corinthian columns, its dimensions were 40 ft. by 82 ft.

13 July 4 B.C. The **Ara Pacis**, or **Altar of Peace**, was dedicated by the Roman Senate to Augustus. This magnificent raised altar, elaborately decorated by an unknown artist, was the first Roman monument to be decorated with a representation of an historical event, Augustus's triumphal procession into Rome.

8 B.C. The Roman poet and satirist **Q. Horatius Flaccus** (b. 65), known as **Horace**, died. One of his prose works still extant is **Ars Poetica**. There are also four books of odes, two of letters, two of satires, and one of epodes. Horace's ambition, and signal success, was to adapt the meters of Greek lyrics to Latin. Because of their refined, sometimes exalted, sentiment; polished verses; and yet conversational, sometimes slangy, language, Horace's **Odes** (19) became world famous.

V. SPORTS, GAMES, AND SOCIETY

44 B.C. **Julius Caesar** rebuilt the **Circus Maximus**, situated between the Aventine and Palatine hills of Rome. The Circus was first built, according to legend, by Tarquinus Priscus, an Etruscan king, in the 6th century.

0–49

0 B.C. ended and **a.d. began** precisely at midnight on December 31 of 1 B.C., which was also the start of January 1 A.D. 1. The Christians fixed this as the start of counting "**the years of our Lord**," or **Anno Domini**, who was thought to have been born on Dec. 25, A.D. 1. All the years prior to year one were "before Christ," or B.C. The months, days, minutes, and seconds in B.C. were listed in their chronological order, the same as in the years *Anno Domini;* however, the years, centuries, and millennia in B.C. were counted backwards from 0.

I. VITAL STATISTICS AND DEMOGRAPHICS

A.D. c.1–400 **Ugric peoples** from the region along the Ob River in western Siberia migrated across the Ural Mountains to present Estonia on the Gulf of Finland, forcing the nomadic **Lapps** and their herds of reindeer northward.

1st century A.D. The **first catacombs** were built under the basilica of San Sebastiano on the Appian Way near Rome, Italy.

A.D. 1 The **world's population** was an estimated 170 million. The population of the **British Isles** was an estimated 800,000. In the **Americas**, where c.4.5 million people lived, growth occurred primarily in the tropical-temperate zone. The population of **China** was estimated at c.45 million.

II. POLITICS AND WAR

A.D. 6 **Herod Archelaus** (22. B.C.–c.18 A.D.), ethnarch of Judaea (from 4 B.C.), was deposed and exiled by Augustus, the Roman emperor, because of his brutal treatment of Jews and Samaritans.

A.D. 9 **German tribes** led by Arminius (17? B.C.–A.D. 21) destroyed three Roman legions under P. Quinctilius Varus in the Teutoburg Forest in central Germany, causing Varus to commit suicide. The victory secured German independence of Rome.

A.D. 9 **Wang Mang** (45 B.C.–A.D. 23), regent of the Chinese empire since 8 B.C., took over the throne and founded the short-lived **Hsin Dynasty** (9–23) at the Han capital of Ch'ang-an [Sian, Xi'an] on the Wei River. His radical reforms alienated influential families, and the Han Dynasty (206 B.C.–A.D. 220) was restored as the **Eastern [Later] Han Dynasty** (25–220) following Mang's murder in 23 by Prince Liu Hsiu (6 B.C.–A.D. 57), who as emperor took the title Kuang Wu-Ti [Kuang-wu] in 25.

A.D. 14 Aug. 19 **Augustus** [G. Julius Caesar Octavianus] (b. Sept. 23, 63 B.C.), the first Roman emperor, died. **Tiberius** [Tiberius Claudius Nero Caesar] succeeded him unopposed as the Senate abandoned any attempt to restore the republic.

A.D. 17 **Tiberius**, the Roman emperor, annexed the client states of Cappadocia and Commagene, in present Turkey.

A.D. 25 The **Eastern [Later] Han Dynasty** (25–220) of China was founded with its capital at Lo-yang [Honan, Henan], in central eastern China south of the Yellow River [Huang Ho, Huang He), after the unsuccessful interregnum of Wang Mang.

A.D. 26 **Pontius Pilate**, who delivered Jesus for crucifixion in 30, was appointed governor of Judaea by Tiberius, the Roman emperor. During his ten years in office, Pilate had recurring difficulties with the Jews because of his insensitivity to their aversion to images of the emperor, and his reliance on force to break up public demonstrations. He was dismissed in 36, but charges against him were dropped and he retired from public life.

41 Jan. 24 **Caligula** [Gaius Caesar] (b. Aug. 31, 12), the Roman emperor who had succeeded (37) Tiberius, was assassinated by the Praetorian Guards led by G. Cassius Chaerea, who himself was executed the next day for his deed. Caligula was succeeded by **Claudius** (to 54), Tiberius's nephew, after an abortive attempt by the Senate to restore the republic.

43 Roman legions under Aulus Plautius defeated the **Catuvellauni** under Caractacus [Caratacus, Caradoc] (20?–?75) on the Medway River, in southeastern England, initiating the Roman invasion of Britain. **Camulodunum** [Colchester], the first Roman settlement in Britain, was founded as a colony for veterans by **Claudius**, the Roman emperor. The Romans also founded **Londinium** [London] in this year.

47 The Romans under P. Ostorius Scapula established a frontier across Britain, the **Fosse Way**, a defensive road from the Exe River, in southwestern England, to Lindum [Lincoln] near the Humber Estuary, in northeastern England.

c.48 **Kujula Kadphises** [Kozulokadphises] united the **Yueh-chi tribes** of Bactria, the former Greek kingdom in present Afghanistan, and founded the **Kushan Empire** (to c.225). The Kushans created a powerful empire that extended across present Afghanistan, Pakistan, and northern India, achieving its greatest influence under Kanishka I (ruled c.78–96).

A.D. c.50   The **Kingdom of Funan** (to c.600) was the first important Hindu state to rise in southeastern Asia. It was centered on the plains of the Mekong Delta, in present Cambodia [Kampuchea].

III. RELIGION AND PHILOSOPHY

A.D. 1   The **Vedanta school of Hindu philosophy** was probably in existence by the start of the Christian era, or shortly thereafter. After the *Upanishads* themselves, the basic text of this school was a collection of aphorisms called the *Brahma Sutras* or *Vedanta Sutras*, by Badarayana. This work summarized the teachings of the *Upanishads*.

c.6   **Judas** of Galilee, in opposition to Rome on religious grounds, stirred followers to a futile rebellion in Galilee against Roman authority.

c.27   **Jesus** of Nazareth was baptized by **John the Baptist** in the Jordan River and shortly thereafter began his public ministry.

c.29   **John the Baptist** (born c.5 B.C.), an ascetic Judaean prophet, was put to death at the Machaerus fortress, east of the Dead Sea, in present Jordan, by **Herod Antipas** (d. after 40). This Herod, a son of Herod the Great, ruled Galilee and Peraea as a tetrarch (4 B.C.–A.D. 39). Josephus, the Jewish historian, later wrote (c.93) that John's death was due to the fear of Antipas that the prophet's influence was lighting a fire of insurrection. The Gospels attributed John's death to his criticism of the marriage of Antipas to his brother's wife Herodias. Two Gospels add that Herodias instructed her daughter [**Salome**] to ask her stepfather Antipas to give her on a platter, as a promised reward for her dancing for him, the head of John the Baptist, then imprisoned in the castle's dungeon.

30 Apr. 7   **Jesus Christ** (born c.6 or 5 B.C.) was crucified on the eve of a Passover, that is, on the 14th of Nisan, in Jerusalem by the Romans at the instigation of the Jewish Sanhedrin. Of the two possible years in Jesus's ministry in which the 14th of Nisan fell on a Friday, the year 30 best fits the slim evidence provided by the Gospels. The 14th of Nisan in 30 translates to Apr. 7 on a modern calendar.

c.35   The **Pharisee Paul** [Saul] of Tarsus (3?–?68), a prosecutor of the followers of **Jesus** of Nazareth, had a vision of Christ while journeying to Damascus. This experience caused Paul to turn away from the legalism of the Pharisees, the predominant Jewish party, and to devote himself to Christ.

41–44   **Herod Agrippa I** (10 B.C.–A.D. 44), vassal-king of Rome's reassembled Palestinian province and friend of Claudius, the Roman emperor, instigated persecution of the Christian community in Jerusalem. The **Apostle James** was beheaded, Peter was imprisoned but escaped, and the Apostles were scattered.

47–48   Barnabas and Paul of Tarsus, with John Mark [Mark], traditionally identified with the author of the second Gospel, as assistant, undertook the **first missionary expedition in the history of Christianity.**

IV. SCIENCE, EDUCATION, AND TECHNOLOGY

c.25   An **elementary reaping machine**, powered by an OX, was used by the Gauls.

43   The **Roman invasion of Britain** was soon followed by the **systematic building of roads**. One such road was **Watling Street**, running northwest from London for more than 100 miles.

V. ARTS AND LEISURE

17   **Livy** [Titus Livius] (b. 58 B.C.), a Roman historian, died. His *History of Rome* was a rich source of information for the early Roman Republic. Only 35 books are now extant of the original 142 that covered Roman history from the city's founding to A.D. 9.

17   **Ovid** [P. Ovidius Naso] (b. 43 B.C.), a Roman poet, died in the village of Tomis [Constanta] on the Black Sea, in present Romania, where he had been banished (A.D. 8) by Augustus, the Roman emperor, for the moral laxity of his work. He was famous for *Art of Love* (1 B.C.), three books of verse in which he gave prescriptions for dalliance, and for *Metamorphoses* (A.D. 1), a retelling of Greek and Roman myths and legends.

VI. SPORTS, GAMES, AND SOCIETY

c.40 Under the Roman emperor **Caligula**, **boxing** had become a battle to the death between **gladia-** tors, each equipped with a **cestus**—leather straps and pads wrapped around the fists and studded with iron and brass.

50–99

I. DISASTERS

64 July The city of Rome was nearly destroyed by a **great fire** attributed by the ancients to **Nero**, the Roman emperor. Nero blamed the Christians, and many were executed as arsonists. He rebuilt the city lavishly, including for himself a magnificent palace, the **Golden House**, which extended from the Palatine Hill to the slopes of the Esquiline Hill.

79 Aug. 24 **Mount Vesuvius**, near Naples, erupted, destroying the ancient cities of **Pompeii** and **Herculaneum**. Most inhabitants were able to flee, but c.20,000 died, including the Roman naturalist **Pliny the Elder** (b. 23 A.D.), who was killed at Pompeii.

II. POLITICS AND WAR

51 **Caractacus**, who led the resistance of the Silures and Ordovices in Wales, was defeated and captured by the Romans under P. Ostorius Scapula. The **conquest of Wales** was completed (74–78) by Sextus Julius Frontinus (c.35–103), the Roman governor of Britain.

54 Oct. 13 **Claudius** [Tiberius Claudius Drusus Nero Germanicus] (b. Aug. 1, 10 B.C.), the Roman emperor, was murdered by order of his wife **Agrippina**, who had her son **Nero** proclaimed emperor (to 68). Later Nero ordered (59) his mother's assassination.

60 **G. Suetonius Paulinus**, a Roman goverher of Britain (59–61), led a campaign to conquer the island of Mona [Anglesey], off the coast of Wales. Mona was the center and last stronghold of the **Druids**, who led the British resistance against Rome, and Druidism waned in Britain after the island's capture.

61 A widespread **revolt against Roman rule** broke out in Britain, led by **Boadicea** [Boudicca] (d. 61), queen of the Iceni. Camulodonum [Colchester], Londinium [London], and Verulamium [St. Albans] were sacked and their inhabitants massacred before G. Suetonius Paulinus crushed the rebellion.

66 **Rebellion against Rome** broke out in Judaea. The fortress Antonia in Jerusalem was seized and its garrison slaughtered. Romans taking refuge in the governor's palace surrendered and were killed. A Roman army from Syria was massacred in the pass of Beth-horon.

67 **Nero**, the Roman emperor, sent his general Vespasian [T. Flavius Sabinus Vespasianus] (9–June 23, 79), to Judaea, supported by a powerful army. Vespasian put **Jerusalem under siege** and spent two years regaining control of the countryside.

68 Mar. G. Julius Vindex, a Roman governor in Gaul, led the first of a series of revolts against the **despotic rule of Nero** that soon spread throughout the Roman provinces. Vindex, failing to control his Gallic troops, committed suicide in May, but the Senate condemned **Nero** [Lucius Domitius Ahenobarbus] (b. Dec. 15, 37), the Roman emperor, who committed suicide on June 9. A period of anarchy and **civil war** ended with **Vespasian's** return (Oct. 70) from Palestine, after he had been proclaimed (July 1, 69) emperor (to June 23, 79) by his troops.

70 July–Aug. On the ninth or tenth day of Ab [July–August] **Jerusalem fell** to Vespasian's son **Titus** [T. Flavius Sabinus Vespasianus] (Dec. 30, 39–Sept. 13, 81) emperor of Rome (from 79). The city was burned and virtually leveled, and tens of thousands of Jews died or were sold into slavery.

73 Apr. **Masada**, last of the Judaean fortresses held by Jewish insurrectionists against Rome, fell after a lengthy siege. The fortress, once a palace of Herod the Great, stood atop a hill 1,300 feet above the western shore of the Dead Sea. The Jews put one another to death when the collapse of their defenses became certain. Only two women and five children were captured.

74 The **Edict of Vespasian** was promulgated in Rome, giving rights, including Roman citizenship, to the inhabitants of the Roman province of Spain.

c.78–c.102 The reign of **Kanishka I**, sometimes placed as late as 162, brought great prosperity to the **Kushan Empire** (c.48–c.225) which consisted of parts of present Afghanistan and India. The Kushans maintained diplomatic relations with Rome and supported the Buddhist missionaries who were more and more frequently dispatched to China.

79 **Gn. Julius Agricola** (37–93), a Roman governor of Britain (78–84), **invaded Caledonia** [Scotland]. At Mons Graupius, west of the Firth of Tay, he won (83) a victory over the Caledonians, led by Galgacus [Calgacus].

86 The **Dacians**, a German tribe led by Decebalus (died c.107), crossed the Danube River from Romania to invade the Roman province of Moesia in present Bulgaria. **Domitian**, the Roman emperor, made peace by agreeing to pay an annual tribute to Decebalus.

89 Jan. 1 **Domitian**, the Roman emperor, following an abortive revolt led by Antoninus Saturninus (fl. first century) in Germany, launched a reign of terror against his opponents, which reached its peak in 93. Domitian levied heavy taxes on the provinces and confiscated property to support his army and to finance his extensive building program. As a result of a conspiracy which included the emperor's wife, the period of hardship ended with the murder of Domitian [T. Flavius Domitianus Augustus] (b. Oct. 24, 51) on Sept. 18, 96, by a freedman. He was succeeded by **Nerva** [M. Cocceius Nerva] (born c.35–Jan. 25, 98).

III. RELIGION AND PHILOSOPHY

c.50 The **Mahayana sect of Buddhism**, known as the **Greater Vehicle**, was dominant in India. These Buddhists believed in saints and demons, and placed **Buddha** and 17 of his incarnations in Heaven as a demigod. The Greater Vehicle was the sect accepted by Kanishka I, ruler of the **Kushan Empire**, and was the form of Buddhism that Kushan missionaries took to Tibet and China.

c.50 The **first New Testament book** to be written was probably **Paul's First Epistle** to the Thessalonians. In it the apostle met charges that enemies in

Thessalonica [Salonika], Greece, had circulated about him, and dealt with several problems that had arisen in the young Church.

64 July **Nero**, the Roman emperor, initiated a **persecution of Christians** in Rome following the city's great fire. A large number of Christians suffered death by various forms of torture in public spectacles. According to the writer Dionysius (fl. late second century), **Peter the Apostle** died in Rome during the persecution. Tradition maintains that Peter's remains now rest under the basilica that bears his name. During the period c.60–62, Paul had lived in Rome under police custody.

65 **L. Annaeus Seneca** [Seneca the Younger] (b. 4 B.C.), a Roman dramatist, philosopher, and statesman, died. He was forced to commit suicide as a result of political charges Nero brought against him. Seneca's plays included *Agamemnon*, *Medea*, *Oedipus*, and *Troades*. His letters on moral problems to his friend Lucilius, and his moral treatises, such as *De Clementia* and *De Providentia*, were important among his philosophical works.

68 The **Gospel of Mark** was set down in Greek. It is today widely believed to be the work of **John Mark**, the companion of Paul, Barnabus, and Peter, and to have originated in Rome. Some scholars have preferred a later date, perhaps 75, for its composition, which was based on oral traditions.

69 **Rabbi Johanon ben Zakkai** reportedly slipped out of besieged Jerusalem and obtained an audience with the Roman general Vespasian just before he was proclaimed emperor by his troops (July 1). Johanon obtained permission for Jews to establish an **academy at Jabneh** [Jamnia] for the unhindered study of the Torah. The academy laid the foundations for the **reconstruction of Judaism** and the refocusing of Jewish worship in local synagogues rather than in the ancient capital.

c.80 **Jainism** split into two sects, chiefly over the question of whether Jain monks should wear clothes. The **Shvetambara**, or white-robed sect, held that nudity was no longer permissible. The **Digambara**, or skyclad [nude] sect, continued to embrace the original tenet.

c.95 **Domitian**, the Roman emperor, initiated a **persecution of Christians**. He executed (85), his cousin Flavius Clemens and exiled his niece for being attracted to Christian teaching and refusing to worship the imperial gods.

IV. SCIENCE, EDUCATION, AND TECHNOLOGY

c.50 **Water wheels**, used by the Romans in grinding corn, were first moved to a vertical position, greatly improving their efficiency.

c.50 The **Pont du Gard aqueduct** was constructed by the Romans at Nîmes, France, where it spanned a large valley. It was the essential feature of an otherwise underground conduit system that brought water 25 miles from the mountains to the city.

79 **G. Plinius Secundus [Pliny the Elder]** (b. 23), Roman naturalist and scholar, died while witnessing an eruption of Vesuvius. His 37-volume *Historia Naturalis*, preserved by his nephew G. Plinius Ca-

ecilius Secundus [**Pliny the Younger**] (62–113), covered zoology, botany, forestry, agriculture, metallurgy, and painting.

80 The **Colosseum in Rome**, built during the reign of Vespasian, was dedicated by his son Titus. It was used for gladitorial combat until 404.

V. SPORTS, GAMES, AND SOCIETY

52 A **naumachia**, an imitation of a sea battle, was organized by **Claudius**, the Roman emperor. It was performed on Fucinus [Fucino, Celano] Lake, now drained, c.60 miles east of Rome, by 20,000 gladiators and criminals, many of whom died during the spectacle.

86 The **Capitoline Games** were instituted by Domitian, the Roman emperor. They were contests in poetry, literature, and music.

100–149

I. VITAL STATISTICS AND DEMOGRAPHICS

100 The **world's population** was an estimated 180 million people, of whom c.33 million lived in **Europe**, 120 million in **Asia**, and 4.6 million in the **Americas**. The Asian population included c.60 million in **China** and 38 million in India.

II. POLITICS AND WAR

106 Roman forces under Aula Cornelius Palma (?–108) conquered the **Nabataean Kingdom**, on the east coast of the Red Sea in present Jordan. It was annexed and organized as the Roman province of Arabia Petraea, which included the Sinai Peninsula.

107 Decebalus, king of Dacia, in present Romania, was defeated by Trajan, the Roman emperor. **Dacia** became a prosperous Roman province after the extermination or expulsion of a large number of its inhabitants. The Romanian language evolved from the language spoken by the Roman colonists.

117 July 9 **Trajan** [Marcus Ulpius Trajanus] (b. Sept. 15, 53), the Roman emperor (ruled from 98), died. In 114 he had deposed Parthamasiris, king of

Armenia (from 113), and Armenia was organized as a Roman province. Trajan's invasion of Parthia (115–116) and annexation of Assyria (114) and Mesopotamia (115) proved to be brief successes, when his death prevented consolidation of these conquests. His successor, **Hadrian** [P. Aelius Hadrianus] (Jan. 24, 76–July 10, 138), abandoned (117) the territories east of the Euphrates River, which he restored (118) as the frontier with Parthia.

122 **Hadrian**, on an inspection tour of Britain, ordered a wall built "to divide the barbarians from the Romans." The emperor traveled extensively, in Gaul, Spain, Africa, and elsewhere. In western Anatolia, where he visited, he had a **temple built at Cyzicus** that was soon ranked as one of the **seven wonders of the world**. He sailed (125) to Rhodes and returned to Rome via Athens and Sicily, where he climbed Mt. Etna. When he died (138) he left the empire better governed, healthier, and wealthier than it had ever been before or was to be later.

III. RELIGION AND PHILOSOPHY

c.100–300 The *Manu Dharma Shastras* [*Sastras*], the essence of the **Hindu code of law**, was written down at this time. Traditionally attributed to the mythological figure **Manu the Lawgiver**, it enforced a rigid social hierarchy in India, while promising promotion to a high caste in the next life to those who followed the rules.

c.100 At **Jabneh**, the Jewish academy in western Judaea, a synod of Palestinian Jewish scriptural experts determined which of the many books then circulating were to be regarded as Holy Writ. The synod also established a standard Hebrew text, known as the **Masora**, for the approved books.

c.111 **Pliny the Younger**, governor of the Roman province of Bithynia, on the Black Sea, advised Trajan, the Roman emperor, that the spread of Christianity and the Christians' refusal to join in emperor worship were affecting the temple worship of the older gods. **Trajan** directed Pliny to persecute Christians if they would not renounce their faith. Adherence to Christianity was now a crime.

c.115 **Gamaliel II** of Jabneh, also called the Younger, grandson of Gamaliel I, died. After a distinguished career as *nasi*, or president, of the Sanhedrin of Jerusalem and head of the academy at Jabneh, Gamaliel healed the division within Palestinian Judaism caused by the conflicting views of Hillel and Shammai.

115 A **Jewish revolt** against Roman rule broke out in Cyrenaica [Cirenaica], in present Libya, and in Cyprus, Egypt, and Mesopotamia. It was suppressed so harshly that Judaism was virtually erased from these provinces.

130 **Hadrian** ordered Jerusalem to be rebuilt as a Roman colony and named Aelia Capitolina. He forbade the reading of the Law [the **Pentateuch**], the rite of circumcision, and the observance of the Sabbath. He also built a temple to Jupiter on the site of the destroyed Jewish Temple.

131 **Simon Bar Cocheba**, whose origins and earlier history are now unknown, put forward claims to be the Jewish Messiah. Many Jews, in addition to members of the violent **Zealot party**, believed him and prepared for a final effort to throw off the Roman yoke.

132 **Rabbi Akiba ben Joseph** (born c.50), influential in the development of the **Mishnah**, the oral traditions that form the first part of the **Talmud**, died.

Akiba sponsored the claim of the revolutionary leader Bar Cocheba to be the Jewish Messiah. For his support of the rebellion that followed, Akiba was taken prisoner by Roman soldiers, and was reportedly flayed alive.

132 The **Jews**, led by **Simon Bar Cocheba**, began a last effort to free themselves from Rome. Surprising early successes included the expulsion of the Roman presence from Jerusalem and the seizure of many strongholds in the countryside.

c.135 The Gnostic theologian **Valentinus** (fl. 135–160) left Alexandria for Rome, where for about 30 years he taught a syncretistic religion based on mystical knowledge. When Valentinian Gnosticism adopted the person of Christ as the revealer to men of the hitherto unknown God, Christianity was imperiled. In meeting the challenges of **Gnoticism** and **Montanism**, the **Catholic Church** developed (by c.190) an organization, creeds, and approved canon of Scriptures.

c.135 **Epictetus** (born c.55), a Greek philosopher who had created his own school of **Stoicism**, died. Banished (c.89) from Rome he established himself thereafter in Greece, where he taught until his death. The religious tone of his teachings, and his emphasis on the brotherhood of man, made him popular with early Christian thinkers.

135 After a bitter struggle, **Jerusalem** and the outlying fortress of Bethar fell; their defenders, including **Simon Bar Cocheba** [Bar Kokhba, Bar Coziba], were slaughtered. The ancient capital of the Jews was once more devastated, and was now prohibited to them. It was not barred to the Christians, who had refused to join Bar Cocheba's rebellion.

c.145 **Marcion** (d. 160), a wealthy Christian shipowner who aspired to reform the Church at Rome with his Gnostic views, created a separate church after being excommunicated for heresy. He compiled a canon of New Testament writings, ten epistles of Paul and the Gospel of Luke—all expurgated—which was the **first actual New Testament**. He spent the rest of his life organizing converts into competitive churches throughout the Roman Empire.

147–167 In this period the Taoist scholar **Wei Po-Yang** wrote his *Ts'an-T'ung-Chi* [The Three Ways Unified and Harmonized]. Wei provided a foundation for the branch of **Taoism** that sought immortality through such techniques as meditation, breathing exercises, sexual arts, medicine, and chemistry, to which he added teachings from the Confucian occult classic *I Ching* [Book of Changes].

c.180   Arrian [Flavius Arrianus] (b. 96?), a Greek historian and philosopher, died. Arrian is now remembered primarily for his *Anabasis*, a seven-volume history of Alexander the Great.

IV. SCIENCE, EDUCATION, AND TECHNOLOGY

c.100   Thamugadi [Timgad], in present Algeria, was founded by Trajan, the Roman emperor. Excavations begun here in 1881 have uncovered the most extensive and best-preserved **Roman ruins in Africa**.

c.100 By this time the **Roman colony at Bath**, Britain, was established. The surface springs provided hot water for the bath. The Romans called the spa **Aquae Solis** [Waters of the Sun].

c.100   Flavius Josephus [Joseph ben Matthias] (born c.37), a Jewish general and historian, died. At the start (66) of the Jewish revolt against Rome, he became governor of Galilee but was forced to surrender in the next year. Josephus wrote *The Jewish War; Antiquities of the Jews*, a history from creation to A.D. 66; *Against Apion*, a fervent defense of the Jews; and an autobiography.

c.105 A new kind of **paper** was invented by **Ts'ai Lun** (c.50–118), a Chinese bureaucrat. It was a combination of tree fibers, fish nets, hemp waste, and rags, all pressed or matted together.

113   Trajan's Column to commemorate the subjugation (107) of Dacia was completed in Rome. The 140-foot high column still stands today in a courtyard near the Forum of Trajan.

122   Hadrian, the Roman emperor, on his visit to Britain, ordered the building of a great wall to protect the Roman-occupied territories from the **Caledonians. Hadrian's Wall**, completed in 127, stretched 70 miles between the Solway Firth and the Tyne River.

c.124   Plutarch (b. 46?), a Greek biographer and philosopher, died. He was chiefly known for his *Par-*

allel Lives [*Bioi paraleloi*], comparative Greek and Roman biographies. The *Lives* has since proven to be a key source of historical information.

c.127–c.151   Ptolemy [Claudius Ptolemaeus], a great astronomer, geographer, and mathematician, flourished in Alexandria, Egypt. His famous work, the *Almagest*, was preserved and translated by the Arabs from the original Greek; the Greek title was *Megale Syntaxis* [**Great Composition**]. In the *Almagest*, Ptolemy provided the bases for trigonometry, described the astrolabe, and reckoned the distance to the moon from the earth (he computed it to be 236,000 miles—modern calculations show an average distance of 238,860 miles). In another important work *Guide to Geography* he developed a method of map projection far more accurate for showing distances than any previous projection.

138 The Romans completed the **Carthage Aqueduct**. It carried water more than 88 miles from the Zaghouan Springs to Djebe Djougar, in present Tunisia.

139   Chang Heng (b. 78), a Chinese poet, astronomer, and inventor of the **seismograph**, died. Chang Heng's water-powered **orrery** was an ancestor of the modern clock.

142 The **Antonine Wall** was erected by the Roman governor of Britain, Q. Lollius Urbicus, following an uprising of the **Brigantes** in Scotland. It was named for the reigning Roman emperor Antonius Pius [T. Aurelius Fulvus Boionius Arrius] (Sept. 19, 86–Mar. 7, 161; ruled from 138). The 33-mile-long wall followed the temporary fortifications constructed between the firths of Forth and Clyde by the Roman governor of Britain, Gn. Julius Agricola, in 78.

c.150 The Chinese were reproducing the classics by holding a sheet of paper flat against a stone in which hieroglyphics had been carved in **Chinese ideographs**, even decades before, and rubbing over the paper with some dark material, such as soot.

V. ARTS AND LEISURE

c.100   Aśvaghosa (80?–150), an Indian Buddhist poet, wrote the **earliest Sanskrit dramas**, of which only parts are extant. They were nearly all propaganda pieces for the Mahayana sect of Buddhism, and were written for Kanishka I, king of the Kushan Empire (c.48–c.225).

c.105 Martial [M. Valerius Martialis] (b. Mar. 1, 40?), a gifted Latin epigrammatist, died. Martial recorded observations of daily life in his couplets. *Liber Spectaculorum* [On the Spectacles] was written in honor of the Roman emperor Titus's dedication (80) of the Colosseum. Among the epigrams in the approximately 15 volumes of his work was *Fortuna multis dat nimis, satis nulli* [Fortune gives too much to many, enough to none].

c.117 Cornelius Tacitus (born c.55), a Roman historian, died. His major works were the *Annales* and *Historiae*, covering Roman history from the death of Augustus (14 A.D. to the beginning of Vespasian's rule in 69), and *Germania*, a detailed account of the German tribes. Only 15 of the original 30 books of the *Annales* and *Historiae* have survived.

c.140 Juvenal [D. Junius Juvenalis] (born c.60), a Roman satirist, died. He attacked the lax morality of imperial Roman society in the five-volume *Satires* (100–130).

140 Suetonius [G. Suetonius Tranquillus] (b. 72?), a Roman historian, died. Suetonius was famous for *Lives of the Caesars* (119–121), a lively account of the Caesars from Augustus to Domitian.

150–199

I. VITAL STATISTICS AND DEMOGRAPHICS

c.150 The **Mochica** [Moche] **culture**, centered about present **Trujillo** in northern Peru, began to develop. The Mochica Indians were credited with building the **first true cities in South America**, and it is believed they achieved an organized political state.

c.150 The **Goths** [Teutons], a Germanic people probably related to the Celts, began to move from their settlements along the Baltic Coast and the Vistula and Oder rivers to the area north of the Black Sea. According to Gothic legend, they had originated in southern Scandinavia. The Goths came to dominate the region along the Dnieper [Dnepre] River, extending east to the Don River by the early fourth century, west to the Dniester [Dnestr] River, and north to the Pripet Marshes before **Huns** overwhelmed them in 376.

II. DISASTERS

166 The Roman army carried **infectious disease** back from its campaign against Vologesus III, king of Parthia (148–191), after having captured the Parthian capital of **Ctesiphon**, in present Iraq. The disease was probably **smallpox**, although some authorities believed it was the **bubonic plague**. It did not seriously reduce the population.

III. POLITICS AND WAR

167 The **Germanic tribes** of the Marcomanni and Quadi crossed the Danube River and penetrated the Roman Empire as far south as Aquileia in northern Italy. They were finally repulsed (169) by the Roman co-emperors **Marcus Aurelius** and **Lucius Verus** [L. Ceionius Commodus] (b. Dec. 15, 130), who died in battle in February. Marcus Aurelius became sole emperor.

180 Mar. 17 Marcus Aurelius [M. Annius Verus Antoninus] (b. Apr. 26, 121), the Roman emperor, died in Vindobona [Vienna]. His reign was marked by a series of campaigns against the German tribes, pushing them back beyond the Danube River. He was succeeded as emperor by his son **Commodus** [L. Aelius Aurelius Commodus] (Aug. 31, 161–Dec. 31, 192).

183 The **Antonine Wall** was attacked by the Caledonians [Highlanders] of Scotland. They were repulsed by Ulpius Marcellus, the Roman governor of Britain, but the wall was finally abandoned (185) for the more defensible **Hadrian's Wall** to the south.

184 The **Revolt of the Yellow Turbans**, an uprising by the peasantry, broke out in China. The corrupt ministers were finally massacred, and the two-year old **Hsien-Ti** was set up (190) as a puppet emperor. He was the **last emperor of the Eastern [Later] Han Dynasty** (25–220).

193 Mar. 28 Following its mutiny and the assassination in Rome of **P. Helvius Pertinax** (b. Aug. 1, 126), the Roman emperor, who had ruled only three months, the Praetorian Guard auctioned off the imperial throne. **Didius Julianus**, the highest bidder, was declared emperor. He was challenged by **Septimius Severus**, who led the armies in Pannonia; by **Septimius Albinus**, who led those in Britain; and by **Pescennius Niger**, who led those in Syria. All three were proclaimed emperor by their legions in 193.

193 June 1 **Septimius Severus** entered Rome at the head of an army from Pannonia [in present Hungary and former Yugoslavia] and arranged the murder of Didius Julianus [M. Didius Severus Julianus] (b. 133?), the Roman emperor, who had ruled for only about two weeks. The next year, at Issus, at the head of the Gulf of Alexandretta [Iskenderun Körfezi] of present Turkey, Severus defeated and killed (194) Pescennius Niger, the governor of Syria, a rival for power. He completed his victory by sacking Byzantium [Constantinople, İstanbul] in 196.

197 Feb. 19 **Septimius Severus** defeated and killed his rival, Septimius Albinus [Septimius Decimus Clodius Albinus] (born c.145), the governor of Britain, at **Lugdunum** [Lyon], France, which was sacked. Severus was now the undisputed ruler (to 211) of the Roman Empire.

III. RELIGION AND PHILOSOPHY

c.150 **Chang Tao-Ling** [Chang Ling] (died between 157 and 178), called the **Celestial Master**, founded the important Taoist sect of **Right Unity** in China. Chang was featured in many legends as master alchemist, creator of a pill of immortality, or great healer. Thousands of peasants in the area of present Szechwan [Sichuan] province joined his movement, the dues for which were five pecks of rice annually.

c.150 Two Buddhists of the Mahayana branch, **Nagarjuna** and **Aryadeva**, founded in southern India a school that taught the doctrine of the now-flowering **Mahayana sutrus** and the *Prajnaparami*. Scholars of this school were called **Madhyamikas**, those of the Middle Way.

c.155 **Montanus**, a Christian of Ardabau in Phrygia, in present Turkey, proclaimed himself a vessel of the Holy Spirit promised by Christ. Montanus also held that the end of the world was at hand and that the heavenly Jerusalem would shortly descend. The spread of **Montanism** led to the calling of the Church's first synods, intended to condemn this heresy.

c.165 **Justin the Martyr** (born c.100) went to his death in Rome under the prefect Rusticus for refusing to recant his faith. Justin, a converted Hellenist, had written (153) a strong defense of Christianity, which he addressed to Antoninus Pius, the Roman emperor. His *Dialogue with Trypho* argued the Christian case for attacks against Jews.

177 **Irenaeus** (c.130–c.200), a presbyter in the recently created see of Lugdunum [Lyon], France, escaped the persecution of the Gallic Church directed by Marcus Aurelius, the Roman emperor, by being on a mission to Rome for his bishop Pothinus, who suffered martyrdom. On his return to Lyon, Irenaeus was chosen bishop and, until his death, was a distinguished theologian of salvation, writing in defense of traditional Christianity.

184 **Chang Chio**, a charismatic leader of the **Taoist T'ai-Ping** [Universal Peace] sect, died during an armed struggle with government forces. Normally a peaceful sect that protested against maladministration, oppressive taxation, neglect of the poor after national disasters, and even the low status of women, its innumerable members took up arms after being attacked in 183. The rebellion dragged on for years.

c.185 **Irenaeus**, bishop of Lyon, in *Against Heresies* argued that the Church itself was the repository of true teaching; that the Apostles had full and perfect knowledge of the Gospel; and that in the churches founded by the Apostles, the apostolic teaching had been faithfully preserved and transmitted through the succession of bishops, at Rome above all others.

c.190 By this time, a **consolidated Roman Church** had emerged. It was widely described as "catholic," which meant "universal" but soon came to be taken as "orthodox." Independent congregations had been knit into a single entity; the authority of the bishops had been strengthened, even to the extent of being granted power to excommunicate dissidents; and a New Testament canon and an official baptismal creed had been formulated.

c.190 The controversy between the bishops of Rome and the Eastern churches over the proper time to observe **Easter**, first raised c.154, was referred to synods held in Rome, Palestine, and elsewhere. Polycrates, bishop of Ephesus, in western Anatolia, refused to conform to the decision in favor of Rome's practice, so Victor I (d. July 28, 199), bishop of Rome (from 189?), excommunicated nonconforming churches. By 200 Rome was the **preeminent church in Christendom.**

197 In Carthage **Tertullian** [Q. Septimius Florens Tertullianus] (c.160–222), the "**father of Latin theology,**" and the first prominent ecclesiastic to use Latin, began a series of writings that provided Christianity with the underpinnings of theological concepts in a clear format. In c.202 Tertullian, repelled by the persecutions of the Roman emperor Septimius Severus in North Africa and attracted by the ascetic demands of **Montanism**, broke with the Catholic Church and became the most eminent Montanist.

IV. ARTS AND LEISURE

c.150 *Metamorphoses*, popularly known as *The Golden Ass*, was written by **Lucius Apuleius** (124–c.170) of Hippo [Bône], in present Algeria. *Metamorphoses* was particularly influential during the Renaissance, when its humorous, bawdy stories and episodic plot influenced such writers as Giovanni Boccaccio and François Rabelais.

c.175 *Meditations* was written by **Marcus Aurelius**, the Roman emperor. This collection of philosophical thoughts, composed in Greek, was an outstanding presentation of Stoic principles.

After 180 Lucian (born c.120), a Greek satirist, died. His best-known works included *Dialogues of the Gods* and *Dialogues of the Dead*.

V. SPORTS, GAMES, AND SOCIETY

c.150 **Horseshoe pitching** was enjoyed by Roman soldiers as a pastime. From the Parthians, the Romans had learned to shoe their military horses, and horseshoes were plentiful.

200–249

I. VITAL STATISTICS AND DEMOGRAPHICS

200 **World population** was c.190 million: **Europe**, c.35 million; **Africa**, c.20 million; **Asia**, c.130 million; the **Americas**, c.5 million. Fewer than 1 million people lived in the rest of the world.

220 At the **end of the Eastern [Later] Han Dynasty** (25–220), **China's population** was more than 50 million.

II. POLITICS AND WAR

208 **Septimius Severus**, the Roman emperor, launched a campaign against the **Caledonians** [Highlanders] in Britain. He had Hadrian's Wall rebuilt and raided Scotland to make the frontier secure.

c.208 After the death of his father **Papak** [Babek] and having murdered his brothers, **Ardashir I** [Artaxerxes] (died c.240) was crowned shah [king] of Persis [Fars], a vassal kingdom of Parthia. He established his capital at **Gur**, renamed **Ardashir Kwarrah** [Khurra], now Firuzabad in present Iran, and began a series of campaigns of territorial expansion at the expense of the declining Parthian Empire (c.250 B.C.–A.D. 224).

211 Feb 4 **Septimius Severus** [Lucius Septimius Severus] (b. Apr. 11, 146), the Roman emperor, died at Eboracum [York], which ended his three-year campaign in Britain. He was succeeded by his sons, **Caracalla** [M. Aurelius Antoninus Bassianus] (Apr. 4, 188–Apr. 8, 217) and **Geta** [P. Septimius Geta] (b. May 27, 189), who was murdered by Caracalla on Feb. 26, 212.

212 The *Constitutio Antoniniana* was promulgated by **Caracalla**, extending Roman citizenship to most of the free inhabitants of the empire.

220 **Hsien-Ti** [Liu Hsieh] (b. 182), the **last emperor of the Eastern [Later] Han Dynasty** (25–220) in China, was deposed by **Tsao Pei** [Tsao Pi], a Han military leader, who founded the **Wei Dynasty** (220–265) at the former Han capital Lo-yang, Honan [Luoyang, Henan], in northern China. This marked the end of the Han Dynasty (from 206 B.C.) There now began in China an era of division known as the **Six Dynasties** (220–618), which started with a period of rivalry between the **Three Kingdoms** (220–265). The suzerainty of the Wei Dynasty was contested by the **Shu Han Kingdom** (221–264), with its capital at Ch'eng-tu in southwestern China in present Szechwan [Suchuan] province, and the **Wu Dynasty** (222–280). The Wu Dynasty was considered the first legitimate dynasty of the Six Dynasties, despite the fact that most of China paid homage to other rulers at this time.

224 Artabanus V, king of the **Parthian Empire** (c.250 B.C.–A.D. 224), was defeated and killed by Ardashir I, shah of Persia, in a **battle at Hormizdagan** [Hormozia, Hormuz], bringing about the end (228) of the **Arsacid Dynasty** of Parthia. Ardashir was crowned (c.226) King of Kings, founding the **Sassanid** [Persian] **Empire** (c.226–642).

c.225 The **Kushan Empire** of northern India had been reduced to petty states in the Punjab by this time. With only scarce records surviving, Indian history entered a period of obscurity lasting until the founding of the Gupta Dynasty in 320.

c.235 The **Andhra Empire** (from c.225 B.C.) of the Deccan in central India collapsed, partly because of invasions by the **Sakas** [Shakas, Scythians] to its west. Tribal states warred with one another throughout India, but the Tamil kingdoms maintained their cultural heritage.

235 Mar. 19 The Roman army stationed along the Rhine River revolted and had **Alexander Severus** [M. Aurelius Alexander Severus] (b. Oct. 1, 208), the Roman emperor, murdered, following his indecisive campaign against the Germanic tribes of the Alemanni and Marcomanni. He was replaced by the Thracian general **Maximinus** [Thrax] (173–June 17, 238), beginning nearly 50 years of anarchy and barbarian invasions of the empire.

241 The first of several wars broke out between the Roman and **Sassanid** [Persian] **empires**. Shapur I, shah of Persia (240–271), began invading the Roman provinces of Mesopotamia and Syria.

243 The Roman army under **Timesitheus**, regent for the boy-emperor Gordian III, defeated the Persians at Resaina [Ras el 'Ain], in present northeastern Syria on the border with Turkey. Timesitheus [G. Furius Sabinus Aquila Timesitheus; Misitheus] was killed in battle and was succeeded as regent by Philip the Arabian [M. Julius Phillipus] (c.204–249), who subsequently murdered his charge, Gordian III [M. Antonius Gordianus III Pius] (b. 224?) in Jan. 244. **Philip the Arabian** made peace with **Shapur I**, shah of Persia, and returned to Rome to rule as emperor until 249.

247 **Rome**, under Philip the Arabian, celebrated the **1,000th anniversary of its founding**.

III. RELIGION AND PHILOSOPHY

c.200 The god **Shiva** rose from association with Rudra, in the Vedas, who personified the dangerous elements in nature, to join **Brahma** and **Vishnu** in the Hindu threefold godhead, all equally divine. Their consorts were respectively **Parvati**, **Saraswati**, and **Lakshmi**.

c.200 The **four Gospels**, and the 13 letters then ascribed to the **apostle Paul**, were by this year almost everywhere recognized by Christians as canonical.

c.200 **Rabbi Judah Hanasi** (135–217), head of the **Jabneh Academy**, completed the sorting and codifying of the **Mishnah**—the literature consisting of the oral tradition, customs and usages, interpretations, parables, and commentary that supplement the Torah.

230 **Origen**, head of the Catechetical school in Alexandria since 203, left for Caesarea in Palestine when the Roman emperor **Caracalla** drove all teachers of philosophy from the Egyptian city. A noted theologian of the Greek church, he prepared (c.250) the Old Testament in the *Hexapla*, or sixfold version, in which the Hebrew text, the Hebrew text in Greek letters, and the translations of Aquila of Pontus, of Symmachus, of the Septuagint, and of Theodotion appeared in six columns side by side. Only fragments of it are extant. Origen (born c.185) died about 254 as a consequence of torture during the persecution of the Christians begun (250) by Decius, the Roman emperor.

c.240 The Persian prophet **Mani** experienced a vision of an angel, his "Twin," who dictated to him the chief doctrines of **Manichaeism**. Manichaeism contained elements of Judaism, Christianity, and Buddhism, but it emphasized Zoroastrian dualism: light-dark, God-Satan, soul-body, all of which are separate in the beginning and again at the end.

IV. SCIENCE, EDUCATION, AND TECHNOLOGY

c.201 **Galen of Pergamum** (b. 131), a Greek physician, died, having spent much of his life in Rome. Galen was the first to demonstrate that the correct **function of the arteries** was to carry blood, not air, as had been generally believed.

c.200 The **first Christian church to be built in the Roman Empire** was constructed at **Dura-Europa**, in the province of Mesopotamia, in present Syria.

216 The **Roman basilica** was completed in Leptis Magna, one of the three chief cities of the Roman colony Tripolitania on the North African coast. The long central aisle was capped with a ceiling 100 feet high, supported by columns of red Egyptian granite and green marble that today are no longer standing. Scenes of Hercules and Dionysus, the city's patron gods, decorated the walls.

V. ARTS AND LEISURE

c.200 The *Kamasutra* [Aphorisms on Love] was written by the Hindu **Vatsyayana**.

226 The growth of the **Sassanid** [Persian] **Empire** (c.226–642) brought a revival of the arts, particularly sculpture, in Persia. The only extant remains of **Sassanid architecture** are the ruins of royal palaces. One, possibly the palace of Ardashir I, southeast of Shiraz in present Iran, had a dome 100 feet high and 50 feet wide covering a former hall and a portal arch 89 feet high spanning 42 feet. The circular dome was supported by a rectangular structure with squinch arches, a double wall, and exterior flying buttresses.

VI. SPORTS AND GAMES

c.220 **Aelian** (170–235), a Roman poet and teacher of rhetoric, was the first to write on **fly-casting**. In his work on natural history, Aelian described how the Macedonians caught trout with artificial flies.

250–299

I. POLITICS AND WAR

259 **Marcus Postumus** [M. Cassianius Latinius Postumus] (d. 268?), a Roman general, successfully defended Gaul against the invasions of the **Alamanni** and **Franks**. In 260 he challenged the succession of Gallienus [Publius Licinius Valerianus Egnatius Gallienus] (c.218–268), the Roman emperor, by organizing the **Gallic Empire** (260–274), which had the capacity to resist the barbarian invasions.

260 **Valerian**, the Roman emperor, was captured by **Shapur I**, the Sassanid shah of Persia, at Edessa [Urfa] in the Roman province of Mesopotamia, in present Turkey. Valerian [P. Licinius Valerianus] (b. 193?) died in a Persian prison, while his son **Gallienus**, co-ruler of the empire with his father (from 254), met challenges as emperor (to 268) from several pretenders.

261 Acting on behalf of Rome, **Odenathus**, king of Palmyra [Tadmor, Tamar], in present Syria, drove the Persians under Shapur I back across the Euphrates River. He was named Chief of the East by Gallienus, the Roman emperor, and was able to recover the province of Mesopotamia for Rome before his death.

266 **Odenathus**, king of Palmyra, was assassinated, and his wife **Zenobia** (d. after 274) succeeded him (to 272). She declared the **kingdom of Palmyra** independent of Rome and began to build an empire by invading Anatolia and Egypt.

269 **Claudius II** [M. Aurelius Claudius], the Roman emperor (268–270), crushed the **Goths** in a **battle at Naissus** [Nish, Niš] in Upper Moesia, in present Serbia. His success relieved Greece and the Balkans and earned him the honorific Gothicus.

271 **Aurelian** [Lucius Domitius Aurelianus] (c.200–Apr. 13, 276), the Roman emperor, repulsed Germanic tribes of the **Alamanni** in northern Italy, defeating them in a **battle at Pavia** [Ticinum]. He then drove the invaders back across the Danube River.

271 The **Goths** formed the first wave of the barbarian invasions to enter Dacia, in present Romania, as Aurelian evacuated the area. The Romans retreated into Lower Moesia, in present Bulgaria, forming their northern frontier along the right bank of the Danube River.

272 Roman forces, led by **M. Aurelius Probus** (d. 282), defeated the army of **Zenobia**, queen of Palmyra. In 273 **Aurelian**, the Roman emperor, succeeded in destroying Palmyra; in the same year he reconquered Egypt, retaking Alexandria with much destruction. Zenobia was taken to Rome as prisoner, putting an end to her independent empire.

274 In a **battle at Châlons**, in present France, Roman forces under Aurelian defeated G. Pius Esuvius Tetricus (d. 276?), successor to the Gallic general Marcus Postumus. Thus ended the short-lived **Gallic Empire** (260–274), the most successful attempt by the provinces of Gaul to break from Roman rule.

280 The **Western Chin** [T'sin] **Dynasty** (265–317) reunited China, but only for two decades. Nomadic tribes from the north, including the **Hsiung-nu** [Huns], poured into the disintegrating country.

284 Nov. 20 The Illyrian general **Diocletian** [G. Aurelius Valerius Diocletianus Jovius] (245–313) was proclaimed emperor (to 305) by the eastern army on the death of **Numerianus** [Marcus Aurelius Numerianus] (b. 245; ruled from 283), who had succeeded his murdered father, **Carus** [Marcus Aurelius Carus] (b. 223?), in Aug. 283. In 285 Diocletian secured his imperial title through the death of **Carinus**, the last of Carus's sons, in a **battle at the Margus** [Morava] River in present Serbia.

286 The city of **Rome** lost its political supremacy under **Diocletian**, who transferred his capital to **Nicomedia** [İzmit], near Byzantium [Constantinople, İstanbul], and **Maximian** [Marcus Aurelius Valerius Maximianus Herculius] (c.250–310) founded his capital at **Milan** [Mediolanum], Italy. Maximian had been raised to the rank of Caesar and Son of Augustus by Diocletian, then to the rank of Augustus (286) after his successes against the German Bagaudae in Gaul. Thus, Diocletian was the eastern, and Maximian the western emperor.

287 M. Aurelius Carausius (245?–293), commander of the Roman fleet in the English Channel, revolted against Rome to establish an **independent kingdom in Britain**. He repelled the Saxon pirates and built forts along the southeastern coast of Britain to guard against the pirates.

293 Mar. 1 Diocletian, the Roman emperor, established the **Tetrarchy**, in which two augusti and two caesars ruled together. Diocletian ruled in the east, and Maximian governed Italy and Africa. The two caesars, **Galerius** [G. Galerius Valerius Maximianus] (died c. May 311) and **Constantius I Chlorus** (c.250–July 25, 306) received, respectively, the Danubian provinces, and Gaul and Britain.

296 Narses, Sassanid shah of Persia (293–301), routed Roman forces in a **battle at Carrhae** [Altinbasak, Haran] in Mesopotamia, in present Turkey. However, he was defeated the following year by the Roman caesar Galerius, and the **treaty of Nisibis** [Nusaybin] in 298 halted the Persian expansion westward. The Tigris River became the common frontier of Rome and the Sassanid [Persian] empires.

296 Constantius I Chlorus, a Roman caesar, invaded **Britain** and defeated the prefect **Allectus**, who had murdered and then succeeded Marcus Aurelius Carausius. The independent empire in Britain, established by Carausius in 287, was pacified, reunited with the Roman Empire, and reorganized into four provinces: Britannia Prima, Britannia Secunda, Flavia Caesariensis, and Maxima Caesariensis.

II. ECONOMY AND TRADE

c.268 The **first clad coin**, the *antoninianus*, was issued during the reign of Gallienus, the Roman emperor. It was made of a base metal with a precious metal covering.

273 The **province of Dacia**, in present Romania, was abandoned by Aurelian, the Roman emperor, as a source of **gold** for the empire in face of the barbarian invasions that began in 271.

III. RELIGION AND PHILOSOPHY

c.250 Wang Pi (b. 226?), a neo-Taoist philosopher of China, died. Wang Pi and other Taoists of the period were combining Taoist and Confucian thought. His commentaries on the *Tao te Ching* [Lao-Tzu] and the *I Ching* [Book of Changes] were popular in Taoist-Confucian scholarly circles. **Kuo Hsiang** (d. 312) was known for a similar commentary on the works of the Taoist philosopher, **Chuang-Tzu**, who flourished at the close of the third century B.C.

c.250 The revival of **Taoist philosophy** in the second and third centuries produced a new fatalistic movement. This school was represented in the *Book of Lieh Tzu*, purportedly written by a Taoist philosopher of the fourth century B.C. Its main argument was that life was mechanistically determined, without ultimate meaning, futile, and ended by death, but nevertheless preserved and enjoyed.

c.250 **Himiku**, a female shaman-ruler, who had devoted herself to magic, reigned over one of the two chief kingdoms within **Japan**. In addition to divination, the characteristics of Japanese religion of this era were polytheism and nature worship, conducted with simple rites in simple shrines. The central features of the ancient **Shinto** religion were beginning to coalesce.

c.250 **Cyprian**, converted to Christianity by 246 and elected bishop of Carthage in 248, gave the fullest early expression to the ideas that underlie the development of the **Catholic Church** as the one orthodox community of Christians. The fundamental concept was that the Church was based on the unity of bishops, with **Rome** as the "chief church whence priestly unity takes its source."

250 **Decius** [G. Messius Quintus Trajanus Decius] (c.200–June 251), the Roman emperor (from 249), initiated the **first systematic persecution of Christians** throughout the empire. His aim was to force Christians to return to offering sacrifices to the old gods of Rome.

251 A **synod of the Church** meeting in Rome decreed that **all sins were forgivable**, a decision that ultimately became regulative in Christendom. **Novatian** [Novatianus] (c.200–?258), a Roman theologian, who argued the rigorous position that certain cardinal, or deadly, sins were unforgivable, founded schismatic churches over the issue. This sect, the Novatians, lasted until the seventh century.

258 Sept. 14 **Cyprian** [Thascius Caecilius Cyprianus] (born c.200), bishop of Carthage (from 248) in present Tunisia, was beheaded during the Chris-

tian persecution carried out by Valerian, the Roman emperor. His support for the bishop of Rome, Cornelius, against the Novatians had prevented a dangerous schism.

270 **Plotinus** (born c.205), an Egyptian-born Roman philosopher, died. His study of Aristotle and Plato formed the basis of his philosophical system, **Neoplatonism**, which has profoundly affected philosophic and religious thought in both the Christian and Islamic worlds. In its rejection of dualistic thought, Neoplatonism assumed a hierarchy of reality at the center of which lay the mystical concept of the One. The *Enneads*, published posthumously, was a collection of his writings.

274 **Aurelian**, the Roman emperor, having restored the unity of the Roman Empire, was given a triumphal celebration in the imperial capital. He took the title "**Dominus et Deus**" and reintroduced the cult of the sun god, **Sol Invictus**. Worship of the sun god became the dominant state religion of Rome until the acceptance of Christianity.

c.276 **Mani** [Manichaeus] (b. 216?), a Persian prophet, died after 26 days in prison. He was persecuted by **Varahran I** [Bahram], the Sassanid shah of Persia (c.273–c.276), who fell under the influence of fanatical Zoroastrian priests. **Manichaeism** existed for some time in **Baghdad**, but it flourished especially in Chinese Turkestan, east of the Oxus River, now part of present Sinkiang Uighur Autonomous Region of western China.

IV. SCIENCE, EDUCATION, AND TECHNOLOGY

c.250 **Diophantus of Alexandria**, a Greek mathematician, wrote his *Arithmetica*. Only about half of the original work has survived. It was a treatment of determinate and indeterminate algebraic equations.

271 The **Aurelian Wall**, c.12 miles in circumference, was built to fortify Rome against attack by barbarian invaders.

V. ARTS AND LEISURE

c.250 The **Sanskrit theater** in India was the first among eastern cultures to develop plays. The extant treatise *Natyasastra*, written at this time by the Hindu priest **Bharata**, described the structure and performance of these early plays.

300–349

I. VITAL STATISTICS AND DEMOGRAPHICS

300 The **world population** of 190 million and its distribution among the various continents remained unchanged since A.D. 200.

II. POLITICS AND WAR

305 May 1 The two Roman augusti, Diocletian and Maximian, abdicated and were succeeded by Galerius and Constantius I, the two caesars. The **second Tetrarchy** was completed, without regard for the **principle of heredity**, by two caesars, **Flavius Valerius Severus** (d. 307) and **Maximinus Daia** [Galerius Valerius Maximinus] (d. 314). Maximian's son Maxentius, whose pride was wounded when he was not appointed caesar, led (306) a revolt in Rome. Subsequently named caesar by the praetorians, Maxentius ousted Flavius Valerius Severus and drove Galerius from Italy.

306 July 25 **Constantius I Chlorus** [Fl. Valerius Constantius Chlorus] (born c.250), the Roman augustus, died at Eboracum [York], after a successful campaign against the Picts in Britain. His son **Constantine I**, who became known as "the Great," was proclaimed augustus by the Roman troops in Britain. He subsequently occupied Gaul, initiating a civil war of succession (307–324) against five rival claimants to the Roman throne.

311 May Galerius, the Roman augustus, who as caesar to Diocletian had persuaded him to persecute (303) the Christians, died. He had become convinced of the failure of the persecution of the Christians and promulgated Apr. 30, 311, an **edict of toleration** recognizing Christianity as a lawful religion and begged their prayers for "our most gentle clemency."

312 Oct. 28 **Constantine I the Great,** recognized as the Roman emperor in Britain and Gaul, defeated and killed **Maxentius** [Marcus Aurelius Valerius Maxentius] (born c.280), the Roman emperor and augustus of Italy and North Africa, in a **battle at Saxa Rubra**, north of Rome.

317 Tatar [Turkish-Mongolian] warriors, the **Hsien-Pi** from central Asia, broke through the **Great Wall** protecting northern China and drove out the **Western Chin** [Tsin] **Dynasty** (265–317), which moved the remnants of its capital to Nanking [Nanjing], farther south. There, safer from attack by warmongering tribes, the **Eastern Chin** [Tsin] **Dynasty** (317–420), one of the six "Legitimate" Dynasties, was founded.

320 Feb. 26 Chandragupta I, emperor of India (320–335), founded the **Gupta Dynasty** (320–c.550) with his marriage to a princess from Bihar. The Guptas came to power in the same region as the earlier Andhra and Mauryan dynasties, and they succeeded in uniting India north of the Narmada [Nerbudda] River for 160 years.

324 July 3 In a **battle at Adrianople** [Edirne], in present Turkey, **Constantine the Great** defeated his last rival for the throne of the Roman Empire, **Licinius**, who had ruled (from 308) in the eastern part of the empire with limited success. Constantine consolidated (Sept. 18) his victory at Chrysopolis [Scutari, Üsküdar], near present İstanbul. Licinius [Valerius Licinianus] (born c.270) and his son were executed in 325 to secure reunification of the Roman Empire.

c.325 The **Pallava Dynasty** (c.315–897) began to dominate in southern India. Its capital was at Kanchipuram, inland from Madras. The Hindu Pallavas, who spoke Sanskrit, prospered in their trade with Burma [Myanmar], Siam [Thailand], and the Malay Peninsula.

c.325 The Persians under **Shapur II** the Great (309–379), the Sassanid shah, repelled an Arab invasion and then launched a campaign of retaliation in the Arabian Peninsula. **Imir al-Qays** [Imru'l-Quis], later the founder of the Kingdom of the Lakhmids and king (?–405) of Hira [al-Hirah], near Kufah in present Iraq, one of the most important centers of pre-Islamic Arab culture, submitted to the Sassanids, and was named by Shapur "King of all Arabs."

330 May 11 Constantine the Great established his capital at **Byzantium** [İstanbul], ending Rome's supremacy in Western history. The city was renamed **Constantinople** and dedicated to the Blessed Virgin on this day.

337 May 22 Constantine the Great [Flavius Valerius Aurelius Constantinus] (b. Feb. 17, 288?), the Roman emperor, died, and the Roman Empire was divided among his three sons. In 340 Constantine II [Flavius Claudius Constantinus] (b. 317?) was killed at Aquileia, on the shore of the Adriatic Sea, by his brother Constans, who was defending his territory against Constantine's attempted invasion of northern Italy. The Roman Empire was thereafter divided between Constans and Constantius II, who ruled, respectively, the West Roman Empire from Rome and the East Roman Empire from Constantinople.

III. ECONOMY AND TRADE

c.300–600 "Living money" was the most common medium of exchange in the British Isles. Slaves, cattle, hawks, falcons, greyhounds—with specific values defined by law—were used to purchase goods and pay debts. In buying penance, however, slaves were not permitted as payment by the Roman Catholic Church.

c.300 Ghana [Ghanata] was the earliest known Sudanese kingdom of West Africa to achieve preeminence. Its capital, Ghana, was in the western Sahara, and is sometimes identified today with Oualata in present Mauretania. Situated between the gold mines of Wangara, in present Guinea, and the Saharan salt mines of Taghaza, it controlled the trans-Siberian caravan roads and derived its wealth from duties imposed on trade.

301 The Edict of Prices of Diocletian was issued by the Roman emperor. Prices were fixed in an effort to stabilize the currency of the empire. The Edict was generally disregarded, and barter became more common. Diocletian also ordered a census of the population, land, and animals, so that resources of the empire could be estimated and needed goods distributed.

IV. RELIGION AND PHILOSOPHY

301 The Armenian Church was born out of the missionary labors of Gregory the Illuminator (257?–332), which culminated in the conversion of Tiridates III the Great (238?–314), king (259–314) of Armenia and a Roman ally. Armenia became the first Christian nation with Tiridates' adoption of Christianity as the state religion. Gregory, honored with the title of "Catholicos," became the first bishop of the national Armenian Church.

303 Feb. 23 Persecution of the Christians began under Diocletian, the Roman emperor, whose edicts were issued in an effort to halt the Church's growth in numbers and strength. Christian churches were destroyed, books seized, clergymen imprisoned and, in 304, all Christians were required to offer sacrifices to the pagan gods. Persecutions in the West Roman Empire ebbed in 305 with Diocletian's abdication; in the East Roman Empire they continued until his death in 313.

305 Anthony (251?–356), a pioneer of monasticism, was said to have struggled with the devil through rigorous fasting and prayer as a hermit at Pispir, on the right bank of the Nile River. Gathering disciples about him, he moved near the Red Sea. There, he established a pattern of conduct that was developed further by Pachomius, who founded (c.320) the first cenobitic monastery near Thebes.

312 Jan. 7 Lucian (born c.240), a martyr of the Church, was tortured to death for refusing to recant during the persecution of the Christians by Maximinus Daia, the Roman emperor. Lucian had founded the theological school of Antioch and, as a biblical scholar, provided the Church with an edition of the Greek Old Testament that he corrected by comparison with the Hebrew text. This version was used for over 12 centuries.

313 The Edict of Milan was agreed upon in Milan in February by the Roman co-emperors, Constantine I the Great and Licinius, who issued it first, on June 13. The Edict granted absolute freedom of conscience, so Christianity achieved legal status. Judaism, on the other hand, lost its standing as a licit religion, and was declared a "nefarious sect." Jews were prohibited from marrying Christians, from proselytizing, and from entering certain honorable professions.

314 The synod of Arles, a meeting of Christian leaders in southern Gaul, was called by Constantine the Great, who desired a disciplined, orthodox Church. The principal issue considered at the synod was the validity of the ordination of the bishop of Carthage by an unworthy cleric. Donatus and other Christians of North Africa challenged the appointment, supported by Rome, and the Donatists were condemned by the bishops.

c.317 The *Pao-P'u Tzu* [The Master Who Embraces Simplicity], a Taoist treatise on alchemy, magic, and diet, was written by **Ko Hung** (254?–?334), a Chinese philosopher. In his work, he formulated a merit system for acquiring immortality on earth: the number of days of one's life was increased by good deeds, decreased by evil ones.

319 **Constantine the Great** initiated a series of edicts and actions advantageous to the Church. For three years the clergy were exempted from civil burdens and public obligations, Sunday work was forbidden, the Church was given the right to receive legacies, private heathen sacrifices were forbidden, and public funds were devoted to building great churches in Rome and on holy sites in Palestine.

c.320 **Arius** (d.336), the aging presbyter of the church in Alexandria known as Baucalis, entered into dispute with his bishop, Alexander (born c.250–Apr. 18, 328), the patriarch (from 312). The bishop held the orthodox view that there was unity of substance between Christ and God, and that the Son was eternal. Arius, following Origen, contended that Christ was a created being and not of the substance of God. The controversy over the Arian contention spread through the Eastern churches and led to the calling of the **Council of Nicaea** in 325.

c.320 **Pachomius** (c.290–346) established the **first Christian monastery** at Telennisi, in Upper Egypt. An organizational innovator, Pachomius provided the model for cenobitic life: a community that offered a disciplined, Christian society as an alternative to a corrupt secular society.

c.325 **Frumeniut** [Frumentius] of Tyre (died c.380), taken as a slave to the court of the **Kingdom of Aksum** [Axum] in present Ethiopia, converted **Ezana**, the king (ruled 325–?356), to Christianity and began to evangelize the country. He was consecrated the first bishop of Aksum by Athanasius (c.295–May 2, 373), patriarch (from 328) of Alexandria, and Christianity became the official religion.

325 May The **First General Council of Nicaea** [İznik, Nice], in present Turkey, was called by Constantine the Great to settle the Arian controversy. It rejected the proposed Arian creed, and adopted one affirming that Christ was "begotten, not made," and "of one essence with the Father." This formula, approved by the entire West but opposed by most of the East, was brought to a virtually unanimous vote of approval by pressure from Constantine. Arius and two dissenting bishops were banished.

326 **Constantine the Great** ordered that only those "of small fortune" should be ordained in the Christian Church in an effort to halt the loss of tax revenues from the well-to-do who entered tax-free clerical office.

328 **Athanasius** was chosen patriarch of Alexandria to succeed Alexander. Until his death, Athanasius was the preeminent exponent of **Nicene theology** and defender of the Creed's key phrase, "of one essence with the Father," the doctrine of consubstantiality. The Nicene Creed was not acceptable to most Eastern churchmen, who renewed the dispute almost immediately after the Council of Nicaea. They spread Arianism from Constantinople by missionaries, among them Ulfilas [Ulfila, Wulfila] (c.311–381), to the Ostrogoths and Visigoths in southern Russia and in regions north of the Danube River.

339 **Eusebius of Caesarea** [Eusebius Pamphili] (born c.260), a Palestinian theologian and historian of the Christian church, died. He became (c.313) bishop of Caesarea and was active in church affairs at the First General Council of Nicaea (325) and other similar sessions. As a historian his most important work was *Historia ecclesiastica* [*Ecclesiastical History*], an account of the Christian church to 324. Eusebius also wrote *Chronicon*, a short universal history to 303; and *Life of Constantine* (c.338).

341 A new clerical hierarchy rapidly developed in Eastern churches; it grew more slowly in the West. A **synod at Antioch** [Antakya] in this year gave precedence in rank to the metropolitans, stipulating that "other bishops do nothing extraordinary without him."

343 Guidelines for widening the authority of the bishops of Rome were laid down by the **Council of Serdica** [Sofia], capital of present Bulgaria. Under them, a deposed bishop could appeal to Julius I, bishop of Rome, for a new trial. Eastern bishops withdrew from the council, widening the split between the eastern and western churches.

V. SCIENCE, EDUCATION, AND TECHNOLOGY

c.300   **Bound books** with pages stitched together and enclosed in wooden covers had become familiar items in the Roman Empire.

c.300   Remarkable structures built at this time mark the beginning of the classical period of **Mayan civilization** in the Yucatán Peninsula, in Mexico. The edifices were large, pyramidal in shape, and had corbeled vaults supported by brackets. By this time the Mayan Indians had developed a **hieroglyphic alphabet** and an advanced mathematics, which used the base 20 and included the zero. Their calendar system was based on astronomical observation and lengthy calculations. Elaborate sculpture and painting decorated the great ceremonial centers located at Tikal, Uaxactún, Palenque, and Copán.

305   Construction was completed on the **Palace of Diocletian** at the Roman town of Salona, in present Croatia. After the town was destroyed by invading Avars, its inhabitants built (639) the town of Spalato [Split] within the walls of the palace. Four gates and 16 towers guarded the rectangular structure, which covered nearly ten acres.

315   The **Arch of Constantine** was constructed in Rome by order of Constantine the Great to commemorate his victory in the battle at **Saxa Rubra** in 312.

c.324   The **Constantinian Basilica**, the **Basilica of St. John Lateran**, as it is now known, was built in Rome.

VI. ARTS AND LEISURE

c.300   The **peak of Sanskrit literature**, the great Indian epics the *Mahabharata* and the *Ramayana*, had by now been written down. For several previous centuries they had been preserved orally by court bards and wandering poets.

350–399

I. POLITICS AND WAR

350   **Constans** [Fl. Julius Constans] (b. 323?), West Roman emperor (from 337), was murdered by Fl. Popilius Magnentius, who usurped the throne. On Sept. 28, 351, Magnentius was defeated in a **battle at Mursa** [Osijek], in present Croatia, by **Constantius II**, East Roman emperor. Constantius II thus **reunited the Roman Empire** (27 B.C.–A.D. 395). Magnentius escaped to Gaul, and there committed suicide on Aug. 11, 353.

350   **Ezana**, king of Aksum [Axum], in present Ethiopia, led a successful campaign against the **Noba people**, who had migrated from the drying Sahara. He then conquered Meroë [Merowe], the capital of Nubia [Cush, Kush].

357   The **battle of Argentoratum** [Strasbourg], on the Rhine River, climaxed a successful campaign by Julian, a Roman general and caesar in Gaul, to drive the **Franks** and the **Alamanni** from Gaul. With the Rhine frontier restored and his popularity ensured, Julian was now a threat to the rule of Constantius II.

361 Nov. 3   **Constantius II** [Flavius Julius Constantius] (b. Aug. 7, 317), the Roman emperor, died, and his rival **Julian the Apostate** was proclaimed emperor by his troops at **Lutetia** [Paris] on Dec. 11, 361. During his 18-month reign Julian tried to restore paganism.

363 June 26   **Julian the Apostate** [Flavius Claudius Julianus] (b. 331), the Roman emperor, died near the Persian capital of **Ctesiphon**, where he was campaigning against the Persians. **Jovian** accepted the title of emperor from his troops, and concluded a disadvantageous peace with **Shapur II**, the Sassanid shah of Persia, losing Roman districts east of the Tigris River, eastern Mesopotamia, and the kingdom of Armenia.

364 Feb. 17   **Jovian** [Flavius Claudius Jovanianus] (b. 331?), the Roman emperor, died and was succeeded by **Valentinian I** (d. Nov. 17, 375), who was chosen from among Jovian's army stationed at Ancyra [Ankara], in present Turkey. On Feb. 26 Valentinian I was crowned emperor (to 375) and on Mar.

28 he placed his brother **Valens** as emperor in charge of the East. Valentinian proclaimed (Aug. 24, 367) his son **Gratian** co-emperor in the west.

c.370 The **Huns** [Hunni] dominated the Russian steppes as they moved westward, driving the **Goths** before them.

376 The **Ostrogoths** [East Goths], under the semi-legendary **Ermanaric** [Eormenric, Jormunrek], were subjected by the **Huns**, who were pressing westward into Europe from the Russian steppes. This brought an end to a kingdom that had dominated eastern Europe from c.150.

378 Aug. 9 The East Roman emperor, **Valens** (b. 328), was routed and killed by the **Visigoths** [West Goths] in a **battle at Adrianople** [Edirne], present Turkey. Valens was succeeded as East Roman emperor by **Theodosius the Great**, who was temporarily successful in settling the Visigoths as federated allies in the Balkan peninsula. For the first time in western history, **cavalry** had played a decisive role in the battle and contributed to one of the worst defeats the Romans had ever suffered.

c.380 Chandragupta II [Vikramaditya] of the **Gupta Empire** (320–c.550), whose empire controlled most of northern India, became king. His reign was marked by great territorial expansion.

383 Maximus led a revolt in Britain against the unjust rule of **Gratian**, West Roman emperor. His Roman legions advanced into Gaul, where they were welcomed by Gratian's own army, and killed Gratian [Fl. Gratianus] (b. 359) at Lyon on Aug. 25, 383. Maximus [Magnus Clemens Maximus] was joined by forces from Spain in his invasion of northern Italy, where he was finally defeated and killed on Aug. 28, 388, in a **battle at Aquileia**, near present Trieste, by the East Roman emperor **Theodosius the Great**.

395 Jan. 17 Theodosius I the Great [Fl. Theodosius] (b. Jan. 11, 347), the **last emperor to rule both the East and the West Roman empires**, died. His death resulted in the final division of the Roman Empire. After the death of Theodosius, the Roman Empire was partitioned between his sons. **Arcadius** (c.378–May 1, 408) ruled as emperor of the East in Constantinople, and **Honorius** [Fl. Honorius] (Sept. 9, 384–Aug. 15, 423) ruled as emperor of the West from Milan and later from Ravenna.

II. RELIGION AND PHILOSOPHY

353 A **synod at Arles**, France, convoked to settle the **Arian controversy**, began its six-year session. **Constantius II** forced the Church to abandon Athanasius, the upholder of Christian orthodoxy, and to set aside the **Nicene Creed**, formulated in 325. The only resisting bishop was banished. The new doctrine with regard to Christ and God was: **The Son is** *like* **the Father.**

361 Dec. 11 Julian, the Roman emperor, promptly disavowed Christianity on his accession, and earned by his public profession of Hellenistic paganism the epithet "Apostate." Julian removed Christians from office, but did issue a proclamation of universal toleration, which briefly ameliorated the lot of the Jews. During Julian's two-year reign, Athanasius succeeded in winning to the anti-Arian position many church conservatives.

367 Athanasius, bishop of Alexandria, in a festal letter to his churches, listed as canonical 27 **New Testament books**. This is the first extant list that conforms exactly to the New Testament canon accepted today.

372 Buddhism spread to Korea from China. Though Confucianism had arrived in Korea earlier, and the native shamanism was still a powerful influence, Buddhism was enthusiastically embraced by many.

374 Ambrose [Ambrosius] (340?–397), the son of a Roman provincial prefect and himself a consular prefect, was elected bishop of Milan on popular demand. He devoted his wealth to the poor and his lands to the Church. Ambrose became a preeminent ecclesiastic in the West and one of the **four Latin fathers of the Roman Catholic Church**, ranking with **Jerome**, **Pope Gregory the Great**, and **Augustine**, whose own conversion to Christianity was influenced by Ambrose.

c.379 Basil (born c.330) of **Caesarea Mazaca** [Kayseri] in Cappadocia, in present Turkey, who was an ardent opponent of Arianism, died. Known as "Basil the Great," he had propagated monasticism throughout Anatolia. Basil's Rule, perhaps written later by disciples, emphasized a communal life devoted to charitable works, prayer, and the reading of Scripture.

380 **Theodosius the Great**, the East Roman emperor, in concert with **Gratian**, the West Roman emperor, issued an edict decreeing that all beliefs that differed from "the faith clearly taught by the pontiff Damasus [of Rome] and by Peter, bishop of Alexandria, were heresies and [were] to be suppressed accordingly." In effect, there was to be one religion, **Christianity**, and only in the form that taught the consubstantiality of the Trinity.

381 The **Nicene Creed** was restated at the **Second General Council**, held in Constantinople, where Theodosius the Great, the East Roman emperor, had called together a synod of Eastern churches. The Arian forces had already been routed by the views of the **three great Cappadocian churchmen**: **Basil of Caesarea Mazaca**, his brother **Gregory of Nyssa** (331?–?396), and their friend **Gregory of Nazianzus** [Theologus] (329?–?389). Henceforward, the Church would proclaim a Trinity of Father, Son, and Holy Spirit, one substance in three persons.

386 **John Chrysostom** began a 12-year pastorate in Antioch [Antakya], where his preaching attracted a wide following. He preached charity and the responsible use of wealth, decrying luxury and laziness among his clerics. In so doing he angered the empress Eudoxia (d.404), wife of Arcadius, the East Roman emperor. John was also an early anti-Semite within the Church.

386 Dec 20 John Chrysostom, in this year or in 388, stated that the birth of **Jesus Christ** had from the beginning been celebrated in parts of the West on Dec. 25, a date long associated with the pagan winter solstice festival, **Sol Invictus**. John's pronouncement began the process of moving the date from Jan. 6, a date still celebrated as Christ's birth and baptism in some Eastern churches.

390–404 In this period **Jerome** translated nearly all of the **Old Testament** from the original Hebrew into Latin. Jerome had already revised an existing Latin version of the **New Testament**. Though his work was bitterly attacked by the conservatives of his day, it gradually became the authoritative Bible of western Christendom. Known as the **Vulgate**, meaning "in common speech," Jerome's Bible was unrivaled for over 1,100 years.

390 **Christianity** became the official religion in Egypt, and in 391 Theophilus, bishop of Alexandria, began to destroy everything that celebrated pagan deities. Thousands of statues were smashed, the temples were closed or sacked, and the great **library of Alexandria** was burned.

III. SCIENCE, EDUCATION, AND TECHNOLOGY

c.382 **Ulfilas** (b. 311?), bishop of the Goths, died in Constantinople. He had devised the **Gothic alphabet** of 27 symbols, providing the Germanic world with a tool for written language and the first Bible in that language.

IV. ARTS AND LEISURE

c.350 **Bhasa**, one of the Sanskrit dramatists of India, wrote his epic plays at this time. *Svapna-Vasavadatta* [Dream of Vasavadatta] is one of the extant plays attributed to Bhasa.

c.355 **Theater**-loving Romans were devoting over 100 days a year to various performances. During the Empire the most popular theatric forms were farces, which usually centered on country or small town life and utilized a number of stock characters in masks; and mimes, short, dramatic farces, acted without words or masks.

379 **Wang Hsi-Chih** (b. 321), a great calligrapher, died. He invented the technique of one-brush calligraphy and wrote the preface to the *Orchid Pavilion*, a collection of poems.

c.380 An early form of **plainsong**, or plain chant, credited to Ambrose, bishop of Milan, developed. The plainsong was unaccompanied and followed the rhythm of the Latin text. In an effort to counter Arianism, which Ambrose suggested was the source of the current general uneasiness, he promoted **hymnody**.

395–450 Long sleeves on **tunics** first appeared during the period of the division between the East and West Roman empires, and during the later Byzantine Empire. The **cloak**, worn over the long-sleeved tunic, was much the same as before. However, **sandals** took second place to shoes with closed toes. Gold thread and embroidery, as well as pearls and other **precious stones**, decorated Byzantine women's dress.

c.395 **Tai Kuei**, a Chinese painter and sculptor known mainly for his lacquer statuary, died. He portrayed Buddhist and Taoist subjects and was sometimes considered the **originator of lacquer ware**, in which the fine wood grain of a carving was highlighted.

V. SPORTS, GAMES, AND SOCIETY

393 As the Roman Empire entered its period of decline, the emperor Theodosius the Great discontinued the **Olympic Games**, which had been held in Athens since 776 B.C., because they had originated as a pagan festival.

400–449

I. VITAL STATISTICS AND DEMOGRAPHICS

400 For over two centuries the **world's population** remained at c.190 million. A notable change in population distribution at the beginning of the fifth century was **Europe's** loss of c.4 million people, and the gain of the same number by **Africa**. This was thought to have occurred because of Europe's continuing battles with barbarian hordes, while in Africa a more settled life based on more extensive agriculture promoted a larger population.

II. POLITICS AND WAR

406 **Germanic tribes**, the **Vandals**, **Alans**, and **Suevi**, pushed westward by the **Ostrogoths**, crossed the Rhine River into Roman Gaul. By 409 they reached the Iberian Peninsula, settling in present Portugal and southern Spain. The Alans and the Vandals later went to North Africa (429), and the Vandals eventually crossed from North Africa to Italy (455).

407 **Constantine**, a Roman soldier in Britain, was granted imperial powers by his troops. He invaded and subdued Gaul and Spain, established his capital at Arles, and forced **Honorius**, the West Roman emperor, to recognize him as co-emperor. However, Honorius's troops succeeded in killing Constantine [Fl. Claudius Constantinus] in Sept. 411.

410 Aug. 24 **Rome** was sacked by the **Visigoths**, led by **Alaric**. Alaric (born c.370) died on a subsequent invasion of Africa in the same year, and his successor Ataulf [Ataulphus, Atawulf] (d. 415) led the Visigoths into southern Gaul in 412. The sack of Rome, precipitated by discontented peasants and slaves who opened its gates, was a disaster to the empire.

414 At the death of **Chandragupta II** (ruled from c.380), his son **Kumaragupta** assumed power (to c.455) in the **Gupta Empire** (c.320–c.550). The realm stretched from the area of present Karachi and Baroda east to present eastern Bengal province and from the Ravi River in the Punjab south to the Narmada River and the latitude of Cuttack. The capital, established by Chandragupta II, was Ayodhya in present Uttar Pradesh state. In this period an **iron memorial pillar**, which has never rusted, was cast and erected in Delhi.

419 The **Visigoths** under Wallia (ruled 415–419) settled in southwestern Gaul and northern Spain, where they founded the **Kingdom of Toulouse** [Tolosa] (to 508).

c.425 According to tradition the **Angles**, **Saxons**, and **Jutes** began to settle in eastern and southeastern **England** at the invitation of **Vortigern**, king of the Britons, who desired their aid in subduing the **Picts** and the **Scots**. Britain, visited earlier by bands of Saxon pirates, now received a large migration from the region of present northern Germany, especially Schleswig, and from the Jutland peninsula in present Denmark. The **Frisians**, who joined in this migration, came from the North Sea coast of the present Netherlands.

429 The **Vandals**, led by **Genseric** (d. 477), crossed from Spain to North Africa. They defeated (431) **Boniface** [Bonifacius] (d. 432), a Roman general, after a two-year **siege of the city of Hippo**, near Bône [Anaba] in present Algeria. **Constantine** [Cirta], in present Algeria, and **Carthage** are today the only

cities of the Roman province of Africa where extensive Roman fortifications exist.

437 The **Burgundian Kingdom of Worms**, now a city of Germany, was destroyed by the **Huns**, who acted on behalf of the Roman general **Aëtius**. Burgundians, forced southward, finally settled (443) in the region of Savoy. There they established the **Kingdom of Burgundy**, covering areas of present southeastern France, northwestern Italy, and southern Switzerland, with its capital at Geneva.

439 Oct. 19 The Roman city of **Carthage** was captured by **Genseric**, king of the Vandals. He made Carthage his capital and the chief naval base of the **Vandal Kingdom** (439–533) in North Africa.

441 In Britain the **first Saxon revolt** against native Britons was led by two legendary soldiers, the brothers **Hengest** (d. 488?) and **Horsa**. According to tradition, they were Jutes who had settled peacefully in Kent at the invitation of Vortigern. The invitation proved a mistake, since the Saxons began an uprising that lasted until c.500. This revolt was said to have initiated the **first migration of Britons to Britanny**.

c.448 The **Merovingian Dynasty** (to 751) of the Salian Franks [from the region of the lower Rhine] was established according to tradition by Merovich [Mérovée, Merovaeus] (ruled to 458), grandfather of Clovis I. His capital was Tournai, in present Belgium.

III. RELIGION AND PHILOSOPHY

c.400 **Japan**, through trade, was being brought into close relations with the kingdoms of the Korean peninsula. Immigrants from **Korea** brought to the islands of Japan elements of Chinese civilization, notably **Confucianism** and **Taoism**; **Buddhism** arrived later in a similar fashion.

c.400 The **Yogacara school** of Buddhist teaching was founded in northwestern India by **Asanga** (fl. fourth century A.D.), who was said to have converted his brother Vasabandhu. The **Mayahana Buddhist school** of thought reflected the influence of the recent **Samkya-Yoga philosophy** of Hinduism, which stated that salvation was to be sought through introspective meditation, or **Yoga**, leading to an understanding that the reality people perceive is ephemeral, and that the soul can transcend the material world, which is mere illusion.

c.400 **Augustine of Hippo** published his *Confessions*, an account of his mental and spiritual development to the moment of his conversion. This was the **first spiritual autobiography** written by a Christian.

401 Elevated to bishop of Rome, **Innocent I** (d. Mar 12, 417) claimed universal jurisdiction for the Roman see as custodian of the apostolic tradition. He buttressed his claim for the authority of Rome as the ultimate resort of all disputes on Canons 3–5 of the **Council of Serdica** [Sofia] in 343.

407 Sept. 14 **John Chrysostom** [the Golden-mouthed] (born c.345), bishop of Antioch [Antakya] and patriarch of Constantinople, died in exile. His frequent attacks on the luxury and frivolity of the court of Arcadius (c.378–May 1, 408), East Roman emperor (from 395), and of his wife, Eudoxia, had been taken by the empress as directed at her. In John's absence from the city in 403, Theophilus, patriarch of Alexandria (385–428), jealous of the new preeminence in the Eastern Church of the patriarchate in the capital city, and probably with the connivance of Eudoxia, traveled to Constantinople and convened an illegal synod that deposed John on trumped-up charges, including treason. Eudoxia arranged for John's exile to Armenia in 404.

411 The **Pelagian controversy** within the Christian Church began with the efforts of Coelestius, a disciple of Pelagius, to obtain ordination from Aurelius, bishop of Carthage. A deacon in Milan intervened with a list of "errors" in Coelestius's views, and Augustine of Hippo joined the attack on this friend of Pelagius. Augustine challenged **Pelagianism** by his writings on sin and grace, by convening regional synods to condemn it, and by appealing to the Roman bishops, Innocent I and Zosimus. The controversy continued for a decade after the death of Pelagius (b. 360?) in 420. Pelagianism was finally rejected (431) at the **General Council of Ephesus**, and from this date Coelestius disappeared from history.

c.420 The organization of the Palestinian or "Western" **Talmud** was completed by Jewish scholars at the academy in Tiberius [Teverya], near the port of Haifa. The Talmud soon came to be regarded as a single entity, but today it is better regarded as a structured presentation of the **Mishnah**, the oral laws set down about two centuries earlier, and the **Gemara** [Completion], a commentary on the Mishnah dating from c.200.

420 Jerome [Sophronius Eusebius Hieronymus] (born c.345), one of the early fathers of the Church, and probably the most learned man of his day, died. Jerome had (from 386) lived in Bethlehem, where he helped to establish and lived in the monastery at which he died. Here he conducted a wide correspondence with church leaders, wrote books dealing with monastic life, and completed (390–404) his Latin translation of all the books of the Hebrew Bible.

c.425 The **Abhi-dharma**, or philosophical treatment of the **Pitaka** [Three Baskets] underlying **Buddhist doctrine**, had been codified at this time. Two versions have come down to us: the earlier (c.25 B.C.) and more orthodox interpretation held by the Theravadins in Ceylon, written by **Buddha-ghosa** in the Pali language; and the more liberal interpretation held by the Sarvastivadins in northern India, written by **Vasabandhu**, brother of Asanga, in Sanskrit. The Theravadin view of the prescribed Eightfold Path to salvation as demonstrated by the life of the Buddha was to persist in Burma [Myanmar], Thailand, Laos, and Cambodia. The **Mahayana sect** of Buddhism, whose influence spread to Tibet and China, had developed from the Sarvastivadin belief that **Gautama Buddha** himself was only one of many possible manifestions of the Buddha.

c.425 The **monastery at Whithorn** in Galloway, Scotland, was founded by Ninian (died c.432), an Irish monk of the Celtic Church, according to a tradition recorded by Bede. Its church is said to be the **first stone church in Scotland**. From Whithorn, Ninian and his companions converted the southern **Picts**.

425 The prestigious office of **patriarch**, president of the Jewish **Sanhedrin** [Legislative Council] at Jabneh, was abolished by Valentinian III, the West Roman emperor. Rabbinical academies in Palestine withered thereafter, and the center of Jewish intellectual life moved east to Babylonia.

430 Aug. 28 Augustine (b. Nov. 13, 354), bishop of Hippo, died during the two-year siege of that city by the Vandals. He remained the preeminent influence on European thought until **Thomas Aquinas** (the 13th century). In addition to his *Confessions* (c.400), his *On the Trinity* became determinative for western theology, and his *City of God* (c.426) provided medieval thinkers with a storehouse of socio-political, as well as religious, ideas.

431 The **Third General Council of the Church**, at Ephesus in western Anatolia, ended acrimoniously. The council had been called by Theodosius II, East Roman emperor, and Valentinian III, West Roman emperor, to resolve long-standing disputes over the relationship of the divine and the human in Jesus Christ and the designation of Mary as the "Mother of God." **Nestorius**, patriarch of Constantinople, believed that Jesus had two distinct natures, one divine, the other human, and that Mary gave birth to only the human aspect. Nestorius preferred the term "Mother of Christ," saying that which "is born of flesh is flesh." However, the cult of the Virgin Mary was fast spreading, and Nestorius was banished by **Theodosius** to The Great Oasis in Upper Egypt, where he died in 451.

432 K'ou Ch'ien-Chih, who organized religious **Taoism** after his revelation (c.415), died. K'ou regulated Taoist ceremonies with borrowings from Buddhism, fixed the names of the many deities, and formulated a theology.

432? According to Irish tradition, **Patrick** [Patricius] (389?–?461), a Roman citizen of Welsh birth and Christian parentage, was ordained a missionary bishop at Auxerre, eastern France, following his education at a monastery at Lens (?), and sent to Ireland. He brought the Latin language and Roman Christianity and civilization to **Ireland**. The scattered Christianity there was organized, but Patrick's diocesan episcopate became tribally regulated after his death, and Christianity became basically monastic. There is today little certain knowledge about the dates and events of Patrick's life. Some scholars now believe he lived somewhat later (c.415-c.493), that he was ordained (c.460) in Britain, and that he was sent by the British to Ireland, where Christianity had already been introduced. Patrick was certainly the most successful evangelist during the period of Ireland's conversion.

c.434 Tao-Sheng (born c.360), a Chinese monk who had brought together Taoist and Buddhist thought, died. Tao-Sheng, who identified the Buddha with the Tao [The Way], was regarded by some as the founder of **Zen** [Ch'an] **Buddhism**. His own original contribution was the doctrine of sudden enlightenment: "The Absolute is absolute; the way is not the goal; when the mountain is climbed, the landscape of the goal appears all at once."

c.435 Ibas, a bishop of **Edessa**, Syria, in present Turkey, and Barsumas, bishop of Nisibis, Persia, taught Nestorian views about the human and divine in Christ that led ultimately to a separate sect, whose followers are now called **Nestorians**, owing much less to Nestorius than to Theodore (c.350–428) of Mopsuestia [Misis], in present Turkey, who had been Nestorius's teacher. The Nestorians would later suffer crushingly at the hands of Mongol invaders.

438 The **Code of Theodosius** was issued by Theodosius II, the East Roman emperor. The code, containing far-reaching **anti-Semitic legislation**, impressed upon later western law the notion of Jewish inferiority.

c.440 The **Zen** [Ch'an] **sect** of Mahayana Buddhism in China began its formative period. Its scholars studied Gunabhadra's Chinese translation of the Sanskrit work *Lankavatara Sutra*, which argued the limited nature of what was perceived only by the mind.

440 Sept. 29 **Pope Leo I** (c.400–Nov. 5, 461), later called "the Great," and the **first bishop of Rome** whose right to be designated as pope is now unchallenged, was consecrated. The notion of the primacy of the see of Rome found its master exponent in this able prelate. Leo maintained that Christ had entrusted the power of the keys to St. Peter; that Peter had then passed this jurisdiction on to the other Apostles; and, thereby, Peter's authority had passed to the popes of Rome, Peter's successors.

449 June Pope Leo I addressed to Flavian, patriarch of Constantinople (446–449), a letter now called the *Tome to Flavian*, which supported him and set forth the traditional western view of the **nature of Christ**. Both Flavian and Eutyches (378?–c.450), an abbot of a monastery in Constantinople, had appealed to Leo after the former had condemned the monk, a Monophysite, for heresy in 448.

449 Aug. 8 A **Council of the Church**, urged upon Theodosius II, the East Roman emperor, by Dioscorus (d.454), bishop (from 444) of Alexandria, Egypt, opened at Ephesus, with Dioscorus presiding. Dioscorus wanted to review the sentence of Eutyches by Flavian, patriarch of Constantinople, and to extend his own power. With high-handed

use of the chair and the threat of force by the emperor's police, he managed to restore Eutyches and depose (Aug. 8, 449) Flavian, who died shortly thereafter, and to have the earlier **Twelve Propositions of Cyril** (d. 444), Dioscorus's predecessor as bishop of Alexandria, adopted as a definition of faith in the East.

IV. SCIENCE, EDUCATION, AND TECHNOLOGY

412 **Theodosius II**, the East Roman emperor, called for construction of a wall, over 15 feet thick and four miles in length, to protect his capital at **Constantinople**.

V. ARTS AND LEISURE

c.400 **Kalidasa**, a Hindu dramatist and poet, was writing his master works. He probably lived at the court of Chandragupta II, the king of northern India, and there wrote his greatest play *Shakuntala*, renowned for its sensitive treatment of the emotions.

c.400 With techniques borrowed from Korea and China, **Japanese sculptors** were making simple figures of men and horses, usually in or ready for battle, as well as women, for their great, circular tombs.

405 **Ku K'ai Chih** (born c.345), one of the early masters of **Chinese painting**, died. He had lived in Nanking [Nanjing], the capital of the Eastern Chin [Tsin] Dynasty (317–420) in southeastern China, where art continued to be produced despite the lack of a unified government. *Admonitions of the Instructress to the Court Ladies* was attributed to Ku K'ai Chih, but his work has been confused with that of other scroll decorators, especially Lu T'an Wei, who flourished later in the fifth century. No works have been definitely ascribed to either artist.

427 **T'ao Ch'ien** [T'ao Yuan-Ming] (b. 365), a great Chinese Taoist poet, died. In his poems he treated the subjects of country life in a format called "t'ienyüan" [fields and gardens]. He had retired from an official post to return to farming, which he preferred to the rigors of serving the faltering Eastern Chin Dynasty (317–420).

450–499

I. POLITICS AND WAR

451 June 20 Attila the Hun, in **one of the momentous battles of history**, suffered a stunning defeat in a **battle on the Catalaunian Plains**, fought north of Troyes on the Seine River, or at an unidentified place called Maurica, in eastern France. **Aëtius**, the Roman general, had secured the aid of the **Visigoths** under **Theodoric I** [Thierry] (ruled from 419), who died in battle, as well as that of the **Alamanni** and the **Franks**. Together, they forced Attila's retreat to the east, beyond the Rhine River. According to legend, Attila had been requested by Honoria, sister of Valentinian III, the West Roman emperor, to save her from a prearranged marriage. More probably, Honoria, who was ambitious, had made a bid for power by forming an alliance with the **Huns**, which Attila regarded as a marriage proposal. He had then claimed the **Visigothic Kingdom of Toulouse** [Tolosa] (419–508) for a dowry, and was refused.

453 Attila [Etzel, Atli] the Hun (b.406?; ruled from 434), died on the eve of a planned invasion of Italy. The power of the **Huns** subsequently declined. Attila's burial place was hidden, and it remains a mystery because participants in the ceremony were put to death.

455 The Britons were crushed by the encroaching Saxons under the legendary Hengest and Horsa in a **battle at Aylesford** [Aegelsthrep?] in Kent, England. Horsa was said by the chronicler Bede to have lost his life in this battle. The victory, followed by a merciless slaughter, was an important step in the **Saxon conquest of Britain**. Bede wrote 225 years after the event.

455 Mar. 16 **Valentinian III** (b. July 2, 419; ruled from 425), the West Roman emperor, was murdered by two men avenging Valentinian's assassination of Aëtius [Flavius Aëtius] (b. 396?), an important Roman general, on Sept. 21, 454. The **Vandals** under Genseric took this opportunity to capture **Rome**, which was sacked (455).

474 Feb. 3 **Leo I** (born c.400), the East Roman emperor (from 457), died. His daughter Ariadne had a seven-year-old son who had been designated successor as **Leo II** in Oct. 473. However, Ariadne's husband, **Zeno** [Tarasicodissa] **the Isaurian** (426–

Apr. 9, 491), took the throne because Leo (b. 467?) died in this same year. Historians have called Leo II the **last East Roman emperor**. The realm of Zeno the Isaurian, the East Roman Empire (from 395), came to be known as the **Byzantine Empire**, and Zeno the **first Byzantine emperor** (ruled 474–491).

476 Sept. 4 The **West Roman Empire** (from 395) came to an end as its last ruler, the boy-emperor **Romulus Augustulus** (ruled 475–476), was deposed at **Ravenna** by Germanic mercenaries under the leadership of **Odoacer**, who declared himself king over an area approximately that of present Italy. In the East, **Basiliscus**, brother-in-law of Leo I, the East Roman emperor, temporarily occupied the throne in Constantinople from Jan. 475 to Aug. 476, while Zeno was absent to put down revolts. Basiliscus was first banished by Zeno, then beheaded in 478.

480 The **Britons** were defeated and driven back by the invading **Saxons** in a **battle at Portsmouth Harbor** in southern Britain. The flow of Saxon immigrants greatly increased as the fifth century ended, making it virtually impossible for the Britons to reconquer their former territories.

483 **Firuz II**, the Sassanid shah of Persia (from 459), was defeated and killed while defending his realm against an invasion of the **Ephthalites** [White Huns], who came from Bactria, a former region of present Afghanistan. He was succeeded by his brother Balas (ruled 484–487).

484 Following their victory over the Persians, the **Ephthalites** raided northern India. By c.500, under **Toramana**, they established a kingdom in central India.

486 The **Roman occupation of Gaul** came to an end with the defeat and death of its last Roman governor, Syagrius (b.430?; ruled from 464), at Soissons, France, by **Clovis I**, king of the **Salian Franks**. Clovis had succeeded (486) his father Childeric I, who had ruled from Tournai, in present Belgium, and died in 481 or 482. Childeric's father was Merovech, of whom nothing is known today but that the **Merovingian Dynasty** (c.448–751) was named for him. With this victory Clovis established the **Kingdom of the Franks**. Clovis gained control of all Gaul south to the Loire River. He established his rule over the Salian and **Ripuarian Franks**, and the **Alamanni**, and also defeated the Arian **Visigoths**, forcing them beyond the Pyrénées.

488 **Theodoric I the Great** (454–526), the leader of the **Ostrogoths**, invaded northern Italy at the instigation of Zeno, the Byzantine emperor, who feared Theodoric's ambitions in the East. Theodoric murdered Oadacer (b.434?) at Ravenna in 493, and founded the **Ostrogothic Kingdom of Italy** (to 553) and, with the exception of Clovis, became the most powerful Germanic ruler. Without further support from the Byzantine Empire, Theodoric could not extend his influence beyond Italy.

II. RELIGION AND PHILOSOPHY

c.450 The **Mahayana** [Greater Vehicle] **branch of Buddhism** was introduced into **Burma** [Myanmar] from India. But Theravadin Buddhists from southern India and Ceylon became dominant (c.1050). A similar pattern prevailed in **Siam** [Thailand].

451 Oct. At **Chalcedon**, a Greek city on the Bosporus, the **Fourth General Council of the Church** deposed Dioscorus, who was exiled by Marcian [Marcianus] (c.392–457), the East Roman emperor (from 450). A revision of the **Nicene Creed** was adopted that for the Latin and Greek churches established an orthodox Christological statement. In **Christ** were two full and complete natures which, without detracting from the properties of either nature, or of substance, came together in one person. **Monophysitism**, the belief that in Christ there was only one divine nature, persisted in the East, leading eventually to the establishment of the **Coptic Church**, among others.

452 **Valentinian III**, the West Roman emperor, forbade the Church hierarchy to engage in any secular or gainful occupation. The Church retained its right to receive gifts from the faithful and bequests from wealthy Church members. Control of this income and property lay in the hands of the bishops.

459 **Simeon Stylites** (b. 390), foremost of the **pillar hermits**, died after living for 30 years atop a 60-foot pillar he erected near Antioch [Antakya], in present Turkey. In this period Simeon preached and taught disciples without ever descending.

c.460 The **Jewish community of Isfahan** [Esfahan] in **Persia** [Iran] was wiped out by the ruling Sassa-

nids, who had adopted **Zoroastrianism** as their state religion.

476 **Basiliscus** (d. 478), a usurping Byzantine emperor, attempting to gain Monophysite support, issued his *Encyclion*. It anathematized the "so-called *Tome to Flavian* of Pope Leo and all things done at Chalcedon." Basiliscus required all Eastern bishops to sign the declaration.

476 Sept. 4 With the official **end of the West Roman Empire**, the prestige of the pope at Rome increased in the absence of secular authority. **Pope Simplicius** (d. Mar. 2, 483; ruled from 468) initiated a division of church income into quarters: one each for the bishop, the other clergy, the upkeep of edifices and services, and charity.

c.480 Egyptian Coptic monks, who were Monophysites, spread Christianity through **Ethiopia** [Abyssinia] at this time, although the first Christian missionary there (c.325) was probably Frumeniut [Frumentius]. The **Abyssinian Church** today remains Monophysite and dependent on the mother Coptic Church in Egypt.

482 **Zeno the Isaurian**, the Byzantine emperor, at the urging of Acacius (fl. fifth century), patriarch of Constantinople, issued a religious formulary, the *Henoticon*, in an attempt to heal the schism opened by the usurping Monophysite emperor Basiliscus in 476. It failed to please the Eastern Catholics and the Monophysites. It approved **Cyril's Twelve Propositions**, omitted Leo's *Tome*, and avoided comment on the **Council of Chalcedon**. But the Eastern Church remained divided: half Catholic, half Monophysite. In 484 Pope Felix III (d. Feb. 26, 492; ruled from 483) excommunicated Acacius because the *Henoticon's* effect was to undercut the Christological statement of Chalcedon. Acacius responded by excommunicating Felix. A 35-year schism between Rome and Constantinople began.

491 An **Armenian Church** council held in the monastery Etchmiadzin [Ejmiadzin], in present Armenia, condemned the pronouncements of the **Council of Chalcedon** and the *Tome* of Pope Leo I.

494 **Pope Gleasius I** (d. Nov. 19, 496; ruled from 492), in a letter lectured **Anastasius I** (c.430–July 9, 518), the Byzantine emperor (from 491), a Monophysite, on the authority of the pontiffs and secular rulers. In his long reign Anastasius carried out an anti-

Chalcedon policy, aided by the Syrian monk-theologian Severus (c.465–538), later patriarch of Antioch (512–518), who laid the theological foundations of Monophysitism.

496 Dec. 25 **Clovis I**, king of the Franks, was baptized, along with several thousand of his followers, at Reims [Rheims] on Christmas Day. The ceremony, performed by Remigius (died c.530), archbishop of Reims, followed Clovis's defeat of the **Alamanni** in a **battle at Tolbiac** [Tolbiacum, Zülpich], near Cologne, Germany. Clovis gained the support of the Church over German Arians, strengthening both the papacy and his own **Kingdom of the Franks** (486–887). Remigius [Remi or Remy, also early names for Reims] was called the Apostle of the Franks.

499 **Rabbina**, chief compiler of the **Babylonian Talmud**, died amid the persecution of Jews in the **Sassanid** [Persian] **Empire**. The Babylonian Talmud, begun under Rabbi Ashi (352–427) and notably advanced under Rabbi Tosepha'a (d. 470), was finally complete.

III. SCIENCE, EDUCATION, AND TECHNOLOGY

c.450 The **first known use of block printing** was by Chinese government officials, who stamped their seals in ink onto scrolled documents.

c.480 The **cruciform**, or barrel-vaulted cross, was introduced in the design of Byzantine churches. The square central area of the church was topped with a dome, supported by arches. The form was adapted to carry any number of domes and vaults, but the most common number was four, one extending from each side of the central square.

IV. ARTS AND LEISURE

c.499 Some of the **first Buddhist sculpture in China** was made for a **cave shrine at Lung-Men**, near the **Northern Wei Dynasty** (386–534) capital of Lo-yang [Honan; Luoyang, Henan], in central China. The lines made by the folds of the skirt on the Buddha and the female Bodhisattva were emphasized, forming a design of their own.

500–549

I. VITAL STATISTICS AND DEMOGRAPHICS

500 The **world's population** reached 195 million. **Europe** and **China** each lost c.2 million people as barbarian tribes wreaked havoc along their borders.

II. DISASTERS

526 May 20 An **earthquake at Antioch** [Antakya] in present Turkey, claimed 250,000 lives. On Nov. 29, 521, 4,870 persons had died in a previous Antioch earthquake.

c.541 A **bubonic plague** began in Egypt and spread eastward and throughout Europe. After sweeping through the remains of the fallen Roman Empire, it reached (543) **Constantinople**, killing about 60 percent of the city's inhabitants. Cases of the plague were recorded (544) in **Ireland**; from there it traveled to **Britain**.

543 July 9 Thousands died in an **earthquake** affecting the Syrian cities of Tyre, Sidon, Beirut, Tripoli [Tarabulus esh Sham], and Byblos [Jubayl, Jubaïl], in present Lebanon.

III. POLITICS AND WAR

c.500 The **Britons**, under the legendary **Arthur**, won a victory over the **Saxons** in a **battle at Mons Badonicus** [Mount Badon], in Dorset, southern England, which slowed the Saxon conquest of Britain. The legends of Arthur were begun by Welsh-speaking Celts.

c.500 **Svealand**, the **first Swedish state**, began to emerge around Lake Mälaren in the central lowlands, known as Uppland. The **Goths** inhabited Götaland, the southern part of the Swedish peninsula. The epic *Beowulf*, set down (c.700) in **Old English** but based on Norse legends of the early sixth century, provided clues to the development of the Swedish people and early Swedish state, and contained the earliest written version of *sve-*, which was the root of the name, Sweden.

507 Clovis I, the **Merovingian king of the Franks**, with the help of the **Burgundians**, defeated the **Visigoths** under **Alaric II** in a **battle at Vouillé**, near Poitiers, France. The **Visigothic Kingdom of Toulouse** [Tolosa] (from 419) was annexed (508) by the **Kingdom of the Franks**, and the Visigoths retreated into their territory on the Iberian Peninsula. Clovis, having achieved supremacy in the Gallo-Roman world, established (507) his capital at Paris.

c.510 The **Salic Law**, named for the Salian Franks it was intended to govern, was promulgated by Clovis I. This code of penal and civil laws, notable for forbidding the inheritance of land by daughters, was falsely interpreted much later by lawyers as the basis for the **Salic Law of Succession**, which excluded women from succession to the throne.

511 Nov. 27 **Clovis I** [Chlodwig] (b. 466?), king of the Franks, died. Clovis succeeded in creating the **Kingdom of the Franks**, a Catholic kingdom and antecedent of present France. He secured the power of the **Merovingian Dynasty** (c.448–751). Clovis divided his kingdom among four sons: **Thierry I** [Theuderic] (486?–534), who ruled from Reims; **Clodomir** [Chlodomer] (495?–June 25, 524), who ruled from Orléans; **Childebert I** (495?–Dec. 23, 558), who ruled from Paris; and **Clotaire I**, who ruled from Soissons.

c.525 The **migration of Britons** to Europe began in earnest as a result of their inability to win new lands from the Saxon kings for the settlement of their growing population.

529 The **first codification of Roman imperial law**, the *Codex Constitutionum*, was promulgated by **Justinian I the Great**, the Byzantine emperor. Roman law was reduced to a manageable size and systematized. The *Codex* became law immediately and replaced all previous law that contradicted it. It was quickly followed by digests and student manuals, which also had the force of law. Together, they formed the body of what was soon called the **Justinian Code**.

532 The factions of the Blues and the Greens united in the **Nika revolt**, which attempted the overthrow of Justinian I the Great. The revolt was ended by the slaughter of thousands of the rebels by troops under **Belisarius** (505?–565), the great Byzantine general, and the destruction of much of **Constantinople**.

533 Sept. 13 **Gelimer** [Gelimir], the king of the Vandals (530–534), was defeated at Tricamarum, near Carthage, by a Byzantine army under Belisarius, and the **Vandal Kingdom** (from 439) came to an end. **Carthage** was captured, and Justinian reorganized North Africa into seven provinces.

540 Belisarius completed his conquest of Italy by the capture of **Ravenna**, the Ostrogothic capital. By 548, however, the **last king of the Ostrogoths, Totila** [Baduila] (d. 552), had recaptured most of Italy following Belisarius's recall to Constantinople by Justinian.

IV. ECONOMY AND TRADE

c.500–1500 During the Middle Ages the prices of manufactured goods came to be determined, in theory at least, according to the principle of the "**just price.**" This was a set amount arrived at by adding up the cost of the materials used in its production, the wage of the laborer who fashioned it, and a small fee or wage for the seller.

V. RELIGION AND PHILOSOPHY

c.500–600 Sanskrit works known as **Tantras** [warp, essence], celebrating the **Shakti cult**, appeared within **Hinduism**. Shakti was the personification of the female principle in the creation of the universe. The central object of the cult's worship was Parvati, wife of Shiva. Shaktas, the cult members, also called Tantrists, while retaining such basic Hindu concepts as karma and samsara, added practices of an occult and sexual nature to achieve practical ends. The path of ascent to the spiritual world lay through the material world.

c.500 After 1,000 years of maintaining **celibacy** almost everywhere throughout Buddhist regions, monks in the Kashmir were allowed to marry. Nevertheless, the majority of Buddhist monks have always been celibate.

519 Mar. Legates from Rome brought the *Formula of Pope Hormisdas* to **Justin I** (c.450–Aug. 1, 527), the new Byzantine emperor (from 518) and a Roman Catholic. The conditions of reconciliation were harsh, requiring Eastern bishops to condemn past and present Monophysite leaders, to accept the decisions of the Councils of Ephesus and Chalcedon, and to acknowledge that the faith of the Roman Church had never failed. The patriarch of Constantinople quickly capitulated, and **Severus**, bishop of Antioch [Antayka], was deposed and exiled.

c.520   Finnian (470?–548), an Irish Celtic Christian, founded a **monastery on the Boyne River at Clonard** in eastern Ireland. Here, for two centuries, the light of learning was kept burning and was even carried back to Britain and Europe. Clonard was so successful, its missionary urge so strong, that it formed a dozen other monasteries in Ireland, especially in the north and in present Northern Ireland, and in western Scotland through its most famous son Columba (c.521–June 9, 597).

c.525   Buddhism, now colored by the native Taoism, began to achieve popularity in China. Buddhist missionaries from India came in numbers, Chinese Buddhists went on pilgrimages to sacred sites in India, monarchs converted, and Buddhist art thrived.

529   Benedict of Nursia (480–c.545) founded the mother monastery of the Benedictine order on **Monte Cassino**, between Rome and Naples. The **Benedictine Rule**, composed (c.530–540) here by Benedict, became the most celebrated monastic rule in the Roman Church. A monk's day was spent in roughly equal portions of worship, reading, and labor, including teaching boys. At the head of each monastery was an abbot, Benedict's innovation in monastic governance. It was largely thanks to the work of Benedict's monks in copying and preserving the **classic manuscripts** in the library he had established at the monastery that Western literature was kept alive through the Dark Ages (c.450–1000).

529   The Second Council of Orange was convoked by **Caesarius** (c.470–542), bishop of Arles, in France, to modify Augustinian thought to appease the **Pelagians**. While the council approved the views of Augustine in general, it ignored his emphasis on the irresistibility of God's grace and condemned his concept of man's predestination to evil.

529   The Platonic Academy (from c.387 B.C.), in Athens, was shut down by Justinian I the Great, the Byzantine emperor, who ordered the closing of all pagan institutions and the conversion of their lecturers to Christianity. Those refusing to comply were exiled, and their property was confiscated.

538   A king of Korea presented to the court of the Japanese emperor a Buddhist image, copies of Buddhist scriptures, and various liturgical objects. This event (sometimes dated 552) is today usually used for the **beginning of Buddhism in Japan**, where it expanded rapidly with the support of the court.

c.541   Jacob [Baradaeus, James Baradai] (d. July 30, 578), a Syrian monk, was ordained bishop of Edessa, Syria, in present Turkey. Jacob spent his 37 years as a bishop in missionary work, establishing churches and ordaining thousands of clergy.

544   The Byzantine emperor **Justinian I the Great** ceased the persecution of the **Monophysites**. Instead, he condemned in due course the person and writings of Theodore of Mopsuestia in criticism of Cyril of Alexandria, as well as a letter of Ibas of Edessa containing an account of the Council of Ephesus. In condemning these dead Nestorians Justinian hoped to exclude Nestorian interpretations of the Creed of Chalcedon and to establish as orthodox the non-abrasive Cyrillac interpretation of that creed, and thereby win over the Monophysites.

VI. SCIENCE, EDUCATION, AND TECHNOLOGY

c.500   The **dromon**, built with two banks of 100 oars each and two or three masts, became the standard oared fighting ship of the Mediterranean.

533   The **present dating system** in the Christian world was initiated by **Dionysius Exiguus** (c.550–c.560), a Scythian monk and scholar, who fixed the date of Christ's birth in the Roman year 754 (making a 4- to 7-year error in the process), which he then designated as our year 0. He used the notations B.C. and A.D. to designate dates before and after Christ's birth. The first second of the first minute of the first hour A.D. is the start of A.D. The exact moment of 0 is both B.C. and A.D.

537   The **Hagia Sophia** [Holy Wisdom] **Cathedral** in Constantinople [İstanbul] was completed under the direction of Justinian I the Great. The cathedral represented the culmination of the **Byzantine style of architecture**. Its central structure was like the typical domed basilica, but greatly elaborated by aisles and side galleries that arched upward to join the central dome. After the Turkish conquest (1453) the cathedral became a mosque and four slender minarets were added singly in later times.

VII. ARTS AND LEISURE

510 Shanfarā, the Arab poet, died. While his poetry was some of the finest ever written in Arabic, his life had been that of a reclusive desert outlaw. His experiences in the desert were conveyed in the poem *Lāmiyah* [Poem Rhyming in One].

524 Anicius Manlius Severinus Boëthius (born c.480), a Roman mathematician and philospher, was executed. He had been arrested (522) for treason when he was serving Rome as consul, and condemned (524) by Theodoric I the Great, the Ostrogothic king who ruled Italy. While in prison, Boëthius had written *De Consolatione Philosophiae* [*On the Consolation of Philosophy*]. It was influential during the Middle Ages (c.500–1500) when it was thought, probably falsely, that Boëthius was a Christian. He had written, prior to his arrest, the five-volume *De Institutione Musica* [Principles of Music], the first theory of music to be published in Europe during the Christian era. This served as the chief source book for music theorists of the Middle Ages.

c.540 Imir al-Qays [Imru'l-Quis], an almost legendary Arab poet, died, perhaps as a result of betrayal at the Byzantine court. The son of the king of Hira, himself murdered by tribal enemies, Imir al-Qays was noted for his romantic life, and for being one of the poets represented in the famous *Mu'allaqat*, a collection of Arabic poetry written before the advent of Islam.

VIII. SPORTS, GAMES, AND SOCIETY

532 The Blues and the Greens of the **Nika revolt** against Justinian I the Great, the Byzantine emperor, were factions divided by their support of favorite chariot drivers as well as by their political and social differences. They were charged with keeping order, and with presenting the complaints of the people to the emperor at the **horse races**.

549 The **last recorded games were held at the Circus Maximus**. Rome's grandest arena, built during the time of Julius Caesar, was a tiered, oval enclosure open to the sky. It was nearly 2,000 feet long and may have held as many as 350,000 spectators.

550–599

I. VITAL STATISTICS AND DEMOGRAPHICS

c.550 The **Turks**, a Ural-Altaic people, from the steppes and plateaus of central Asia, sometimes called Turko-Tatars, descended on the Persians and Byzantines. First they conquered and probably absorbed the Ephthalites [White Huns]; then, for nearly 500 years, until interrupted (c.1200–1260) by the Mongolian conquest, they raided the civilizations to their south.

II. DISASTERS

551 July 9 The city of Beirut, in present Lebanon, was leveled by an **earthquake**.

III. EXPLORATION AND COLONIZATION

568 Refugees from the wars and various invasions in northeastern Italy founded the city of **Venice** on the marshy islands at the head of the Adriatic Sea.

IV. POLITICS AND WAR

552 July The **Byzantine army**, led by the aged Narses (478?–?573), defeated the **Ostrogoths** under Totila [Baduila], who was killed in a **battle at Taginae** [Tadinum] near Gubbio, central Italy. The Byzantines used a combined **pike and bow offensive**, the earliest recorded instance of this military development. The Ostrogothic Kingdom of Italy (493–553) collapsed, and the decimated Goths retreated to the mountains around Naples.

558–650 The **Avars**, who were Turkic Mongolian tribes, crossed the Russian steppes and drove westward the **Bulgars**, also apparently Turkic-speaking people, from the area of the Volga River, northwest of the Caspian Sea. The **Avar Empire** eventually extended from the Volga to the Hungarian Plains. The **Byzantine Empire** considered the Avars a threat; in 626 the Avars laid siege to Constantinople, but an epidemic forced them to withdraw. The Avars introduced the **stirrup** into Europe, which gave their horsemen an advantage over their enemies because it enabled them to shoot arrows more easily to the side and rear.

560 Eormenric, king of the Jutes in Kent, died and was succeeded by his son **Ethelbert I** [Aethelberht] (c.552–616), under whose reign Kent enjoyed a period of expansion. Ethelbert married Berhta [Bertha], daughter of the Frankish king Charibert (c.520–567) of Neustria and a Christian. Ethelbert was converted (597) by Augustine, becoming the **first Christian Saxon king** in England and making Canterbury, his capital, a center of Christianity.

561 Clotaire I [Clothaire, Chlotar, Lothaire] (b. 497?), the Merovingian king of the Franks (ruled from 511) and the only surviving son of Clovis I, died. The **Kingdom of the Franks**, briefly reunited (from 558), under Clotaire was divided among his four sons. Three predominant kingdoms began to emerge: **Austrasia** [east], including the territory between the Meuse and the Moselle rivers, with its capital at Metz; **Neustria** [west], including the region surrounding the Loire River, with its capital at Paris; and **Burgundy**, situated along the Rhône River and extending north as far as the Seine River, with its capital at Orléans.

565 Nov. 14 **Justinian I the Great** [Flavius Petrus Sabbatius Justinianus] (b. 483), the Byzantine emperor (from 527), who had established a unified code of law, died. His wife Theodora (c.500–June 29, 548) had a moderating influence on Justinian's reign, especially in religious matters as Theodora sympathized with the Monophysites and other heretics. Justinian was succeeded by **Justin II** (d. Oct. 5, 578), his nephew, who at first ruled with promise, but suffered increasingly from attacks of insanity by 575.

568 The Germanic tribe of the **Lombards**, driven out of Pannonia in present Hungary by the Avars, invaded Italy under the leadership of Alboin (d. 573). By 573 they had ousted the Byzantine forces from the north of Italy.

572 **Leovigild** (?–586), king of the Visigoths (from c.565), became sole ruler of the **Kingdom of the West Goths** (507–711) in Spain. He began a program of conquest that revitalized the kingdom. Before he died in 586 he not only controlled nearly all of the Iberian Peninsula, but also held a court that rivaled the emperor's in Constantinople.

575 The **Himyarites**, with Persian help, ousted the Abyssinians [Ethiopians], who had occupied their lands of South Arabia since 525. The southern part of the Arabian Peninsula became a Persian province, and the pro-Byzantine **Kingdom of the Ghassanids** (c.529–636) and the pro-Persian **Kingdom of the Lakhmids** (380—602) declined in power.

577 The **Saxon conquest of Britain** was virtually completed by a victory over the Welsh in a **battle at Deorham** [Dyrham], north of the Avon River in southwestern England. The period of the Heptarchy, which traditionally referred to the period beginning with the arrival of the Saxons (c.425) to Egbert, king of Wessex, who became overlord (c.828) of all England, took shape with the founding of seven kingdoms: the **kingdom of the Jutes** in Kent (c.450); the **Saxon kingdoms** in Essex (c.600), **Sussex** (c.490), and **Wessex** (c.519); and the **kingdoms of the Angles** in **East Anglia** (c.600), **Mercia** (c.606), and **Northumbria** (c.547).

589 **China** was reunited after 400 years of disunion by the founding of the **Sui Dynasty**, which ruled until 618. Its empire extended from the Great Wall to Annam, in present Vietnam. The dynasty, whose capital was at Ch'ang-an [Sian, Xi'an] on the Wei River in central northern China, was founded by **Yang Chien** (541–604), of the Northern Chou [Chow] Dynasty (556–581), who seized the throne and took the name Wen as emperor.

593 **Ethelfirth** [Aethelferth] (d. 617) united the two Anglian kingdoms of Bernicia and Deira to found the **Kingdom of Northumbria** (to 954), in northeastern England. The defeat (603) of the Scots in a **battle at Degsastan** [Dawston], an unknown site south of the Firth of Forth, and victory (c.615) over the Welsh at Chester on the Dee River near the border of Wales marked the supremacy of the Northumbrians over the other six English kingdoms.

593 **Taishi Shotoku** (574–622), a nephew of Suiko (d. 628), the empress of Japan, was named crown prince and regent of Japan. He instituted a constitution creating a **centralized bureaucracy** in the Chinese style.

598 **Pope Gregory I the Great** secured a 30-year truce with the Lombards, the last of the Germanic tribes to invade Italy. Gregory's efforts saved Rome and Ravenna from being taken over by the Arian Lombards.

V. ECONOMY AND TRADE

552 Silkworms were smuggled into the Byzantine Empire, making **silk production** possible for the first time outside China. Justinian I the Great established a state monopoly in silk production centered at Constantinople.

VI. RELIGION AND PHILOSOPHY

553 May The **Fifth General Council of Constantinople** was convoked by the Byzantine emperor Justinian I the Great. The Council upheld Justinian's condemnation (543) of Origen as a heretic, his condemnation (544) of the three Nestorians, and his approval of the Theopaschite formula of Scythian monks which stated that in Christ's passion, God suffered.

c.560 **David** (c.520–589), the patron saint of Wales, began his missionary work in Wales during the golden age of Welsh monasticism. Known for his asceticism, David "the Water Drinker" established many monastic foundations in Wales.

c.563 **Columba**, an Irish Celtic monk and warrior-abbot, with a few companions, established a **monastery at Iona**, an island off northwestern Scotland, from which missionary monks set out to convert the northern Picts and gird the coastline of northern England and Scotland with churches. Columba had already organized monasteries in Derry, Durrow, Kells, and other locations in Ireland.

570 **Muhammad**, the founder of the Islamic religion, was born in Mecca. His father died before he was born, his mother before he was six. The boy grew up under the guardianship of a grandfather, then of an uncle. As an adult Muhammad entered the service of a rich merchant's widow, whom he later married. Four daughters, but no sons, lived to maturity.

c.585 **Columbanus** [Columba the Younger] (543?–Nov. 23, 615), with 12 companions, undertook missionary work on the continent of Europe. These Irish monks, perhaps the best educated people of their time in the West, made their mark at the court of the Frankish kings, founded monasteries, converted thousands, and began the revival of nearly forgotten knowledge of classical secular literature.

587 **Reccared**, the Arian king of the **Visigoths** in Spain, converted to Roman Catholicism, which became (589) the state religion.

589 At the **Third Council of Toledo**, Reccared, king of the Visigoths in Spain, renounced Arianism, leaving only the German **Kingdom of the Lombards** (584–774) as an Arian center. The Council then went on to adopt the word *filioque* [and son] in a statement on the source of the Holy Spirit, adopting the thought expressed by Augustine in **On the Trinity**.

589 After more than a century of proscription Jewish academies for the study of the **Torah** were reopened in Babylonia in the area between the lower Euphrates and Tigris rivers in present Iraq. A new office, the **Gaon**, was created and filled by a succession of individuals of distinction. The Gaons, supported by a council, provided dispersed Jewry with authoritative answers to questions not treated in the Talmud. Babylon became the preeminent Jewish center.

590–604 During his pontificate **Pope Gregory I the Great** profoundly affected the **papal approach to Jewish relations**. At the same time that he limited the rights and denigrated the religion of Jews, he also enjoined bishops and princes not to curtail the rights granted to Jews. The second prong of this policy proved unenforceable on occasions when anti-Semitic feelings were generated locally.

597 Spring **Augustine** [Austin] of Rome (d. 604), a Benedictine monk, landed with monastic companions at Thanet, an island off the northeastern end of Kent, in England, with a commission given (596) by Pope Gregory I the Great to begin the conversion of the Saxons. Augustine was received at court in Canterbury by Ethelbert I, king of Kent, whose wife was a Christian. Ethelbert became an early convert, and Kent the base for later missionary endeavors in England.

VII. SCIENCE, EDUCATION, AND TECHNOLOGY

c.550 *Aryabhata* (b. 476), the greatest of the Hindu astronomers and mathematicians, died. He treated quadratic equations in his **Aryabhta-Tantra**, one of the first known uses of algebra; developed plane and spherical trigonometry; and composed a table of sines. He deduced that the earth was a sphere and that it rotated on an axis. From this he explained the eclipses, solstices, and equinoxes. His most noted contribution was assigning a value to o of 3.1416, an accuracy not reached in Europe until c.1440.

550 Byzantine engineers constructed the **first dam to curve upstream** at **Dara** in northern Mesopotamia. At this time Dara was a Byzantine fortress confronting the Sassanid [Persian] fortress of Nisibis [Nusaybin], in present Turkey on Syria's northeastern frontier.

570? **Gildas**, a British monk and historian, died at the monastery he founded on Houat Island off the southern coast of Brittany. Gildas "the Wise" was the only Briton to write an extant British account of the period of the Saxon conquest of Britain, the *De excidio et conquestu Britanniae* [On the Ruin and Conquest of Britain], which was described by the Venerable Bede, the early eighth-century English historian, as the "tearful discourse concerning the ruin of Britain."

594 **Gregory of Tours** [Georgius Florentius] (b. 538), a Frankish clergyman and historian, died. He was bishop of Tours (from 573). As a historian his most important work was *Historia Francorum* [*History of the Franks*], an account in ten volumes of the Merovingian kingdom to 591. Gregory also wrote on the lives of the saints, on miracles, and a commentary on the Psalms.

VIII. ARTS AND LEISURE

c.570 The **cathedral of Sante Apollinare Nuovo** in Ravenna, Italy, built by Theodoric the Great (454–526), king (from 488) of the Ostrogothic Kingdom of Italy (488–553), came under the jurisdiction of the Catholic Church. It was renowned for its mosaics, which were among the earliest examples of this religious art form, completed while the cathedral was serving its original Arian community.

600–649

I. VITAL STATISTICS AND DEMOGRAPHICS

600 **World population** in the sixth century gained only c.5 million people, for a total of approximately 200 million. The populations of **China** and **Europe** declined slightly, as the other continents showed a gain. **North Africa's** population dropped to c.6 million from its peak of 9 million in A.D. 200. The **sub-Saharan** population increased during the same period, from c.9 million to c.13 million, reflecting the southward migration, since the fourth century B.C., of the Negro and Bantu-speaking tribes from their traditional West African homelands.

II. POLITICS AND WAR

c.600 The declining Hindu **Kingdom of Funan** (from c.50), present Cambodia [Kampuchea], was taken over by its northern neighbor, the Hindu **Kingdom of Chenla** (from c.150) under Bhavavarman.

602 **Maurice** [Mauricius Flavius Tiberius] (b. 539?), the Byzantine emperor (ruled from 582), was

murdered and **Phocas**, a commander of imperial forces defending the Danubian frontier, was elevated to the throne by mutinous soldiers, who objected to the unpopular economic measures forced on Maurice by the expense of defending the empire's borders. During the reign (to 610) of Phocas, the **Byzantine Empire** was invaded from the east by the Persians under **Khosrau II**, shah of the Sassanid [Persian] Empire (c.226–642), and from the north by the **Slavs**, who were beginning to spread out from central western Europe.

603–620 Khosrau II, in a war of retaliation against the **Byzantine Empire**, reached Edessa [Urfa], in present Turkey, and the shores of the Bosphorus at Scutari [Üsküdar]; captured Antioch [Antakya], Damascus, and Jerusalem; and then entered Egypt. These wars and internal struggles over who would rule weakened the **Persians**, making them easy prey for the Muslim Arabs.

c.606–647 Another golden age comparable to that of the **Gupta Empire** (320–c.550), arose briefly in India with the coming to power of Harsha [Harshavardhana], the king of Thanesar [Kurukshetra], a city in Haryana state, and the last ruler of the **Pushpabhuti Dynasty** (590?–647). Buddhism enjoyed a return to royal favor under Harsha, a Hindu who converted to Buddhism. Harsha (born 590?) was assassinated by Brahmins in 647, and his empire collapsed rapidly.

610 Oct. 3 **Phocas**, the cruel and inept Byzantine emperor (ruled from 602), was murdered by forces of **Heraclius** (fl. 586–610), governor of North Africa, who had refused to accept the authority of the emperor. Heraclius's son Heraclius was elevated to the imperial throne.

614 **Clotaire II** [Clothaire, Chlotar, Lothaire] (584–Jan. 4, 629), the Merovingian king of the Franks, issued an edict that explained the role of the Mayors of the Palace, who governed the divisions of the kingdom: Burgundy, Neustria, and Austrasia. They were semi-independent of the king, holding great powers over their designated territories, and royal power was weakened.

618 The Chinese **T'ang Dynasty** (to 907) was established by Li Yüan (565–635), originally the duke of T'ang, who took the name **Kao-Tsu** as emperor. He had gained control during the civil wars that followed the murder in 618 of **Yang Kuang**, the **last emperor of the Sui Dynasty** (589–618). Kao-Tsu revived and strengthened the civil service and extended China's border through warfare to bring the peoples of present Mongolia, Tibet (temporarily), Manchuria, and Vietnam under China's suzerainty.

623 **Dagobert I** (600?–Jan. 19, 639) was given part of Austrasia to rule by his father Clotaire II, king of the Franks. Later, (625 or 626) he received Reims, Toul, and Verdun, which earlier had been part of Austrasia. To this he added (629) Soissons and Neustria. When Dagobert's half-brother Charibert II (b. 602?) died in 631, Aquitaine, with its capital at Toulouse, came nominally to Dagobert.

627 Dec. 12 In a **battle at Nineveh** on the Tigris River near present Mosul [Al-Mawsil], in present Iraq, the forces of Khosrau II, the Sassanid shah of Persia, were defeated by the forces of Heraclius, the Byzantine emperor. The victory saved the Byzantine Empire from assault by the Persians and capped a series of victories that recovered for the empire lost outposts in Armenia and Mesopotamia. During Khosrau's reign (from 590) the Sassanid [Persian]

Empire (c.226–642) had reached its peak, but it fell into a period of anarchy following the murder of **Khosrau** [Khusrau, Khosrau] in 628.

629 **Tibet** entered a period of expansion under **Srong-tsan Gam-po** (d. 650), who united the country, annexed Nepal, and invaded China in 632. He introduced writing and developed the Tibetan culture. He founded (639) his capital at Lhasa, in southeastern Tibet, which became one of the leading Buddhist centers of the world.

632 The **first Islamic caliphate** was formed after the death of **Muhammad the Prophet**. **Abu-Bakr** [Abu Bekr] (576–July, 634), the Prophet's close friend and advisor, was chosen by Muhammad's followers as their leader in Medina. His title, *khalifat rasul-Allah* [one who follows the Messenger of God], was the origin of the term caliphate [caliph = successor]. Abu-Bakr's mission was to consolidate all tribes of the Arabian Peninsula under the Islamic faith.

634 **Omar I** succeeded Abu-Bakr as caliph, and took the title *emir al-mu'minin* [leader of the faithful]. During the period of the second caliphate (to 644), he brought under Islamic control the western half of the **Sassanid** [Persian] **Empire**. He developed a judicial system for all of Islam and ordered the sayings of Muhammad to be collected.

634 **Khalid ibn-al-Walid** (d. 642), known as "the Sword of God," led the Muslim military expedition to take Syria, the western region of the **Sassanid** [Persian] **Empire**. He captured (Sept. 635) Damascus after a six-month siege. By the terms of the peace treaty, security was assured for the conquered, and land taxes and a poll tax were to be paid to the victors by non-Muslims. The Muslim forces defeated (636) a Byzantine army twice their size on the banks of the Yarmuk River, in present Jordan.

635 **Muslim armies**, chiefly under **Sa'ad ibn-Abi-Waqqas** [Wakkas] defeated the **Persian army** under Rustam, regent for the child Yazdegerd III, at Kadisiya [al-Qadisiyah], near present Kufah, Iraq. The fall of the Sassanid capital at Ctesiphon followed in 637. As the court of **Yazdegerd III** (d. 651), the **last Sassanid shah** of Persia, withdrew eastward, Muslim armies followed, and won another major **battle at Jalula**, southwest of Khanaqin, Iraq, near the Iranian border. In 642, at Nihawend [Nahavand, Nehavend], about 40 miles south of present Hamadan,

Iran, the Muslims shattered resistance in the center of the once mighty empire, and the **Sassanid** [Persian] **Empire** (from c.226) came to an end.

637 Jerusalem surrendered after a four-month siege to attacking Muslim troops, who treated the inhabitants with moderation and left the Christian churches unmolested. Omar I, the second caliph, journeyed from Medina to Jerusalem to cleanse and consecrate the rock in the temple area sacred to Jews, Christians, and Muslims.

639 Jan. 19 Dagobert I (born c.600), the Merovingian king of the Franks (from 623), died. The period of the *rois fainéants* [idle or lazy kings] began as the **Mayors of the Palace** actually administered the Kingdom of the Franks. Austrasia and Neustria became rival kingdoms as the **Merovingian Dynasty** (448–751) weakened. Burgundy, which had overthrown (627) its Mayor of the Palace, was ruled by Neustria.

641 Feb. 11 Heraclius (born c.575), the Byzantine emperor, died. Heraclius achieved a tighter control of the empire by reorganizing the loose provincial system of government into "themes," a unit based on the military *thema*, in which the military commander was supreme and soldiers were rewarded with land grants within the empire. After his victory (627) over the Persians at Nineveh, Heraclius was to see much of the empire disintegrate under the invading Muslim Arabs. Heraclius was succeeded briefly by his eldest son, Constantine III.

641 Apr. 9 The Byzantine province of **Egypt** surrendered to Muslim Arabs led by **Amr ibn-al-As** [Amru] (594?–664). On Sept. 17, 642, **Cyrus**, the patriarch of **Alexandria**, capitulated to the Muslims.

641 May 25 After reigning for only three months, **Constantine III** (b. May 3, 612), the Byzantine emperor, died. His half-brother, **Heracleonas** (b. 615), seized the throne, but he was banished to Rhodes in September for complicity in the suspected murder of Constantine and never seen again. **Constans II Pogonatus**, son of Constantine III, was elevated and ruled the **Byzantine Empire** to 668.

642 Oswald, the Christian king of Northumbria (from 634), England, was defeated and killed by **Penda**, the pagan king of Mercia (from 626), in a **battle at Mansfield**.

642 Muslim forces led by Amr ibn-al-As took the coastal portions of **Cirenaica** and **Tripolitania** and drove out the Byzantines.

642 Al-Fustât [Cairo], the **earliest Arab settlement in Egypt**, was founded when Amr ibn-al-As built a military encampment near the captured Roman city of Babylon.

644 Nov. 23 Omar I ['Umar ibn-al Khat-tab] (b. 581?), the second caliph, was assassinated in the mosque at Medina by a disgruntled Persian slave of a provincial governor. **Othman**, from the Omayyad clan in Mecca, a Muslim convert, was elected the third caliph. Othman turned over power to his kinsmen, who made the government independent of the armies stationed in the colonies.

645 The **Taika** [Great Change] began in Japan, following a revolt led by Naketomi no Kamatari (614–669) that ousted the Soga clan from power. **Kotoku**, the emperor of Japan (596–654, ruled from 645), strengthened his power by annexing land and by organizing a highly centralized government run by officials who constituted the nobility.

649 Summer Cyprus was overrun by Islamic troops. **Muawiya**, the Arab governor of Syria, had begun his attacks on Cyprus in 647. Temporarily regained by the Byzantines, Cyprus fell again to Islam in 653.

III. RELIGION AND PHILOSOPHY

600 Isidore of Sevilla [Isidorus Hispalensis] (c.560–636) became archbishop of Sevilla [Seville] and head of the Spanish church, a position he held until his death. Theologian, historian, and encyclopedist, Isidore wrote *Etymologiarum libri XX* [Etymologies], an encyclopedia of all the secular and religious knowledge of western scholars of the time, which had an enormous influence on subsequent encyclopedias. It contained what was probably the **first printed map of the world**. His *Sententiarum libri tres* [Three Books of Sentences] was useful to students of Church doctrine for over 500 years.

601 Augustine was made bishop of all England by Pope Gregory I the Great, with authority to create additional bishops as the Roman Catholic Church expanded there. Augustine consecrated (603) Christ Church, Canterbury, as his see, thus becoming the **first archbishop of Canterbury**.

604 Mar. 12 **Gregory I the Great** (born c.540; ruled from 590), the **first monarchical pope** and the founder of the **medieval papacy**, died. He had developed an impoverished bishopric into an ecclesiastical monarchy accepted as the center of moral authority in the chaotic western world.

608 The **Kaaba** [Caaba] was built in **Mecca**. At first a pagan sanctuary, it became the holiest of Islam's shrines. The Kaaba is still a small building within which the sacred **Black Stone** is kept; the building itself is within the Great Mosque, the **Haram**, of Mecca.

610–641 **Heraclius**, the Byzantine emperor deported or enslaved much of the diminished **Jewish population of Palestine**.

610 **Muhammad** heard an angelic voice urging him to "recite in the name of the Lord." Thus began a 22-year period of revelations received and recorded by Muhammad, who believed he had been charged to be God's messenger to the polytheistic Arab tribes.

615 About 100 of **Muhammad's earliest converts** migrated to Christian Ethiopia [Abyssinia] to escape increasing persecution by the commercial establishment in Mecca.

619 **Muhammad's** wife and patron uncle died. He now sought relief from persecution by removing to the mountain town of Taif, about 40 miles from Mecca. The inhabitants of the town soon drove him out, and he returned to Mecca after receiving assurances of protection from one of his kinsmen.

622 July 16 The **basal point of the Islamic calendar**, a date fixed by the second caliph Omar I in 639 as the start of Muhammad's *hirjah* [Hegira; flight, departure, migration] from Mecca to Yathrib, later renamed Medina, the "City of the Prophet." The abbreviation A.H. came from the Latin *anno Hejirae* [in the year of the Hegira] and is still used before Islamic dates.

622 Sept. 24 **Muhammad** arrived in Medina [Yathrib] from Mecca, where the hostility of commercial interests had made life increasingly dangerous. Two hundred of his followers had preceded him, on assurances of security from Medina's leading tribes. In Medina, Muhammad was eventually acknowledged as the Prophet.

623 **Muhammad** ended the strife between two Arab tribes of Medina, and the many clans involved agreed to form one community under Allah's rule and protection. This put the Muslims into a position of local ascendancy. Muhammad's ensuing attempts to bind Jewish groups to his community and to establish his religion within the framework of Judaism failed. His **Koranic writings** began now to treat economic and social matters more than spiritual matters.

624 **Muhammad**, to support his followers, began raiding Meccan caravans. In March at Badr, in present Saudi Arabia, he and some 300 followers captured a heavily defended caravan. The victory, attributed to divine support, brought the cause much booty and many converts, and the Prophet's prestige increased throughout the region. Muhammad began a succession of **harassing acts** against the Jews of Medina by stripping a tribe of goldsmiths of their possessions.

625 **Muslims** and **Meccan soldiers** fought another **battle near Mt. Uhud**, near Medina. Apparently defeated and with Muhammad injured, the Muslims were spared disaster by the failure of the Meccan soldiers to follow up their advantage. Muhammad attacked a second Jewish group within Medina, forcing them to flee to the Khaybar [Khaibar] oasis, a fertile area 100 miles north of Medina.

627 Mar. **Muhammad** and the populace of Medina held off an attacking **Meccan army**, spearheaded by cavalry and camel contingents. They defended the only easy approach to Medina with a vast trench. In bad weather the frustrated Meccans withdrew. This was the final challenge from Mecca. Muhammad thereafter liquidated a Jewish tribe within Medina that had treated with the enemy.

628 **Muhammad** captured and despoiled the oasis of **Khaybar**, where Jews from Medina had settled. An annual tribute of one-half of the produce of its fields was imposed. Muhammad led an army to **Mecca,** but ultimately signed a pact of nonaggression with that city.

629–639 During the last ten years of his reign, **Dagobert I**, king of the Franks, expelled from his realm all **Jews** who refused to convert to Christianity.

629 **Muhammad** sent out successful expeditionary forces against tribes and towns to the northwest of Medina, reopening the disrupted caravan trade route as far as Mutah in southern Palestine.

630 Jan. **Muhammad** and 1,000 of his followers returned in triumph to Mecca, which gave up its opposition to him.

632 June 8 **Muhammad**, complaining of a severe headache, died in his home in Medina. The elders of the community declared **Abu-Bakr**, longtime companion of the Prophet, caliph.

634 The abbot **Aidan** (d. 651) from Iona established a center for Celtic Christianity on the island of Lindisfarne off the northeastern coast of England. He had brought about (635) the **conversion of Northumbria.**

641 By now the **Gospels** could be read in ten languages, and Christian missions had reached China.

649 **Pope Martin I** (d. Sept. 16, 655; ruled from 649) assembled a synod in Rome that decreed that in Christ there were "two natural wills, the human and the divine." Constans II had Martin arrested for defiance of an imperial edict forbidding discussion of this topic. He was brought (653) to Constantinople, tried for treason, and condemned to death. His sentence was commuted to exile in the Crimea, where he died at Cherson.

IV. SCIENCE, EDUCATION, AND TECHNOLOGY

c.600 The **first known text employing the English vernacular**, a code of laws promulgated by **Ethelbert** [Aethelbert], king of Kent, was issued. Modeled after Roman laws, the code was titled *This Syndon tha Domas, the Aethelbirht Cyning assette on Augustinus daege*, or "These are the Laws that King Aethelbert fixed in Augustine's Days."

c.600 One of the **oldest hospitals of Europe**, the Hôtel-Dieu in Paris, was founded as part of a monastery connected to the Cathedral of Notre Dame (first built c.400).

c.600 **Windmills** were used to grind grain in Persia. The sails revolved horizontally around a vertical post that was attached directly to the millstone.

607 The **oldest extant wooden structure**, the monastery of the Buddhist **temple of Horiuja** [Horyuji] near Nara, Japan, was dedicated.

610 The first part of the **Grand Canal** (begun in 605), was completed in China. Utilizing streams, rivers, and lakes, it stretched 500 miles to connect the second Sui capital, Lo-yang [Luoyang], with the Yellow River [Huang Ho Huang He] and Hangchou [Hangzhow].

c.620 **Damascus steel**, one of the strongest and hardest types of steel known, was produced. It was so called because medieval armorers first encountered it in the Near East, especially from the markets of Damascus, although its use extended back into antiquity.

629–790 Ruins uncovered, beginning in 1956, at the Mayan city of **Tikal** in present Guatemala are now dated to this time. Slabs of stone, erected to mark a calendar, revealed a highly developed astronomy. The **Mayan ceremonial calendar** [*tzolkin*] consisted of a year of 260 days in 13 months of 20 days each.

642 Upon capturing **Alexandria**, Egypt, Muslim Arabs destroyed what remained of its **library**, which had been the largest library of the ancient world, said to have once contained 500,000–700,000 volumes.

ARTS AND LEISURE

c.600 **Pope Gregory I the Great** was said to have had published a collection of chants *Antiphonar missarum* [Antiphonarius cento], which were written in a pentatonic scale (D, E, G, A, C) that was used at the time only in China and in Scotland.

c.600 The *Schola Cantorum*, for church song, was said to have been established in Rome by Pope Gregory I the Great. Originally a "school of singers," it was the foundation of the trained choirs, which in Roman Catholic or Anglican churches still sing the parts of the liturgy not sung by the priest or laity.

612 A Korean named **Mimashi** brought the **Gigaku**, sacred plays of Buddhism, from China to Japan, where they became a staple of the Japanese theater. The Gigaku orchestra, the **oldest functioning orchestra** in the world, was begun by Mimashi, who also founded the **first school of music and dance** in Japan.

623 The **Mosque of Medina**, the **first Islamic mosque**, was constructed. It served as a model for future mosques. The earliest mosques had an open rectangular courtyard, usually containing fountains, with porticoes on three sides. The fourth side, oriented toward Mecca, opened into a prayer hall in which the many parallel arcades supported a flat roof.

650–699

I. POLITICS AND WAR

650–737 The **Khazars** [Chazars], a nomadic Turkic people who had established an independent state north of the Caucasus, began to expand west and north of the Caspian Sea, eventually establishing a powerful empire (c.750–965). They were primarily interested in trading with the Scandinavians, Arabs, Persians, and Chinese. The Khazar nobility were converted (c.740) to Judaism, but their empire tolerated Arab and Christian worship. Toward the end of this period the Khazars were fighting a Muslim penetration of the Transcaucasian area of the lower Don River and the Kuban River valleys.

651 **Yazdegerd III** [Yezdegerd] (ruled 632–642), **last of the Sassanid shahs** of Persia, was assassinated at the instigation of a treacherous satrap while hiding from advancing Muslims in Tabaristan, south of the Caspian Sea.

651 A Muslim expedition from Egypt invaded the Nubian Christian **kingdom of Dongola** in the present Sudan. In return for gold and slaves, and freedom of trade and worship, Dongola's independence was granted by the Muslims.

655 **Cynddylan**, a legendary ruler of the **Welsh kingdom Scrobesbyrig** along the Severn River, was killed in battle by an Anglo-Saxon chief to whom Cynddylan refused tribute. His people, who were Britons, withdrew into present Wales.

655 The **last pagan king of Mercia**, **Penda** (born c.575), was killed in a **battle at Winwaed River**, near Leeds, in England, by Bernicians under Oswy [Oswiu] (612?–670), the Christian king of Northumbria (from 651). Oswy became overlord of Mercia, and married his daughter to an East Anglian king on the condition he accept Christianity.

656 June 17 **Othman** ['Uthman ibn-'Affan] (b. 574?), the third caliph (from 644), was assassinated in his palace by rebelling Arab troops from Egypt. In the mosque at Medina later on this day, **Ali**, a son-in-law of Muhammad, accepted the public oath of allegiance to him as the fourth caliph.

656 Dec. 4 In the **Battle of the Camels**, **Ali** defeated the Omayyad clan, led by Muawiyah and Muhammad's widow, Aisha ['Aishah] (611–678), who rode camelback from the fortress at Basra. Ali moved the capital of the caliphate from Medina to Kufah [Al-Kufah], in present Iraq. Medina and Mecca gradually grew as centers of Islamic culture.

658 July 17 **Ali** defeated the troops of Abdallah-ar-Rasibi, a claimant to the caliphate, in a **battle at Nahrawan** in present Iraq. Those who shared Abdallah's views on the caliphate, that the caliph should be elected democratically by the whole Islamic community, were known as **Kharijites** [kharji = outgoer or dissenter].

660 The **Kingdom of Silla** (57 B.C.–A.D. 935) in the Korean Peninsula conquered the neighboring state of **Paekche** with Chinese help. The unification was completed (668) by the annexation of **Koguryu**, which ended the period of the Three Kingdoms.

660 May In **Jerusalem**, Muawiyah's Syrian followers swore allegiance to him as caliph. His troops began to prepare for a decisive encounter with Ali.

661 Jan. 24 **Ali** ['Ali ibn-abi-Talib] (born c.600) was assassinated in a mosque in **Kufah**, ostensibly as an act of vengeance by the **Kharijites** for his victory in a **battle at Nahrawan** in July 658. His death brought a close to the **four orthodox caliphates**. From Ali, his sons, and their followers evolved the **Shiite** branch of Islam. **Hasan**, the first son of Ali and grandson of Muhammad, claimed the caliphate but abdicated under threat from Muawiyah I. Hasan [al-Hasan] (b. 625) died in 669, perhaps of poisoning.

661 Apr.? **Muawiyah I** founded the **Ommiad** [Umayyad, Omayyad] **Caliphate** (to 750), named for his clan, the Omayyads, at Damascus following the death of Ali. The Ommiads regarded the caliphate as a secular office only. In Damascus the Islamic religion for the most part tolerated Greek-Christian philosophy.

662–675 **Ziyad ibn-Abihi**, who served Muawiyah as provincial governor at **Basra** and Kufah, both in present Iraq, established the authority of Muawiyah's regime and brought a new security to the region of the old Sassanid [Persian] Empire.

668 Sept. 15 **Constans II Pogonatus** (b. 530), the Byzantine emperor (ruled from 641), was assassinated. His reign was riddled by attacks by Muslim Arabs, who expanded at Byzantine expense. Constans lost (646) Alexandria and soon thereafter Egypt, to Muslim Arabs, who were firmly established in North Africa. Constantinople was saved from attack only by the disputed succession among the Muslim leaders. In 662 Constans, hoping to establish his capital at Rome, campaigned unsuccessfully against the **Lombards** in Italy. **Slavs** migrating into the Balkans fell under Constans's attack in 658. Constans was succeeded (668) by his son **Constantine IV** (652–July 10, 685).

670 The **first effective Muslim penetration into the Tunisian** area was made by the Arab general **Okba**, governor of the province of Egypt under the Ommiad Caliphate. With Berber allies, he was able to end Byzantine control in Libya and Tunisia. Near the site of ancient Carthage, he built (670) **al'Qayrawan** [Sidi 'Uqbah], now Kairouan [Qairwan], the **fourth-ranking holy city of Islam** after **Mecca, Medina,** and **Jerusalem.**

673–678 Arab forces failed to capture Constantinople, the Byzantine capital, after five years of siege. The new invention of "Greek fire," a jet of burning liquid forced from tubes mounted on galleys, was effective against the Muslim fleet. Constantine IV secured a peace treaty with the Ommiad Caliphate in 678.

674 Muslim Arab troops crossed the Oxus River [Amu Darya] into the Turkish-speaking region of Transoxiana. This brought the **Islamic faith into contact with the Turks**, who were then Buddhists.

680 **Asparukh** [Isperikh] (ruled 680–701), khan of the **Danube** [Western] **Bulgars**, crossed the Danube, defeated the Byzantine army of Constantine IV, and

settled his people in Moesia, in present Bulgaria, after agreeing to accept tribute in exchange for withdrawing from the gates of Constantinople. This marked the establishment of the **First Bulgarian Empire** (681–1018) in the Balkans.

680 Apr. 18 **Muawiyah** [Mu'awiyah ibn-abi-Sufyan], the founder of the **Ommiad Caliphate** (661–750), died and was succeeded by his son **Yazid** (d. Nov. 10, 683). The hereditary succession incited the rebellious Shiites of Persia to turn to Husain, the second surviving son of Ali.

680 Oct. 10 **Husain** [al-Husayn] (born c.625), leader of the Shiites, was killed in **battle at Karbala** [Kerbala] in Persia by the troops of Yazid, whose caliphate was contested by the Shiites. Husain's death, which was perceived by his followers as a martyrdom, became the emotional **root of Shiism.** Husain's grave in Karbala, south of Baghdad, Iraq, is still a sacred site for Shiite pilgrims.

682 **Okba**, a Muslim Arab general, extended Ommiad suzerainty across North Africa, seizing land from Byzantine vassals.

683 **Okba** ['Uqbah ibn-Nafi], was killed at Biskra, Algeria, by Berbers. His tomb, a mosque in al-Qayrawan [Kairouan], which he founded in 670, is one of the **oldest surviving examples of Muslim architecture** in Africa.

685 **Malik I** [Abd-al-Malik ibn Marwan] (646–705) succeeded to the **Ommiad Caliphate** (661–750) and by a series of victories over his rivals ended the period of factional dissent that began with Muawiyah's death in 680. During his reign Malik instituted a postal service and substituted Arabian coins for the Greek and Persian coins in use.

685 **Ecgfrith**, king (670–685) of Northumbria, while invading northern Scotland, was defeated by the **Picts** at Nechtansmere, north of the Firth of Tay, in present Scotland.

687 **Pepin II** of Herstal, the Mayor (ruled 686–714) of the Palace of Austrasia, won a decisive victory over the Neustrians at Tertry in present northern France, asserting the dominance of Austrasia. The **Kingdom of the Franks** was once again reunited.

695 **Justinian II**, the Byzantine emperor, gained the epithet **Rhinotmetus** [with the cut-off nose] when his nose was cut off during a revolt inflamed by Justinian's favoritism and his corrupt ministers.

II. ECONOMY AND TRADE

c.692 The **gold dinar** minted by Malik I, the Ommiad caliph, became part of one of the **most stable monetary systems** known. For over 450 years it was not once devalued.

III. RELIGION AND PHILOSOPHY

c.650 One of the **great figures of Chinese Buddhism**, **Hiuen Tsiang** [Hsuan Tsang, Huan Chwang, Yuan Chwang] (c.600–664), carried the Buddhist **Yogacara school** to China, where it was known as **Weih-shih**. His textbook is still used by Yogacara centers in the Far East.

c.650 Suffering from ties to a decadent state, its priests killed, and its adherents forced into mass conversions by zealous Muslims, **Zoroastrianism** was nearly eliminated from Persia.

653 **Othman**, the third caliph, decided to establish an official version of all the **Koranic writings** of Muhammad, using materials gathered by his predecessor and by Muhammad's scribe, **Zayd** [Zaid] **ibn-Thabit**. The version produced subsequently achieved veneration throughout Islam.

656 The struggle between Ali and Muawiyah over the caliphate caused a lasting **rift within Islam**. Shiites, partisans of Ali, held he was the only legitimate successor to **Muhammad** and should have been the first caliph. Ali was held to be a divinely designated **Imam** [Arabic: leader, guide]. **Shiites** denied the validity of the **Sunna** [Arabic: path, way, guide], based on the sayings and doings of Muhammad, which became the foundation of orthodox, or **Sunnite**, jurisprudence.

663 **Cuthbert of Lindisfarne** (635?–687), the last outstanding monk-missionary of the Celtic Church, submitted to Rome after the **synod of Whitby** in Northumbria, on the coast of northeastern England. The synod, supported by the Christian Oswy, king of Northumbria and overlord of all Saxon kingdoms, upheld Rome's claim as the inheritor of Peter's commission and its diocesan system. Celtic monks thereafter retreated from England, and Roman Catholicism became part of the dominant western European tradition of the Church in England.

668 **Theodore of Tarsus** (c.600–690), a Greek scholar and clergyman, was consecrated in Rome **archbishop of Canterbury** by Pope Vitalian (d. Jan. 27, 672; ruled from 657). Over 20 years Theodore reorganized the Church in England, arranging the various sees with mutually exclusive territories, all subordinate to Canterbury, and subjecting monasteries to the Roman ecclesiastical system. One of Theodore's associates, Hadrian, founded a school at Canterbury; another, Benedict Biscop (c.618–690), established monasteries in Jarrow and Wearmouth [Sunderland].

c.670 **Caedmon** (died c.680), a cowherd at Whitby Abbey and probably the **first English poet**, made the first known attempts to render biblical materials into English. Only nine lines from his work, a portion of his *Creation Hymn*, have survived.

680–681 The **Sixth General Council of the Church**, held in Constantinople, ended the argument over monothelitism, begun in 638. Constantine IV, the Byzantine emperor, withdrew imperial support for monothelitism, and the Council, acting on a definition issued by Pope Agatho (d. June 10, 681; ruled from 678), declared that Christ had "*two* natural wills . . . not contrary one to the other."

685 The **Japanese government** issued a decree ordering all households to install Buddhist altars.

688 Construction of the **Dome of the Rock mosque** was begun in Jerusalem during the reign of Malik I, the Ommiad caliph, to commemorate Muhammad. The octagonal structure still stands atop a rock held to be sacred.

692 Justinian II Rhinotmetus (669–Dec. 710), the Byzantine emperor (from 705), convoked a **council of the Eastern churches** to provide new canons of ecclesiastical discipline. The council claimed to legislate for the whole empire and hence for the Roman Catholic Church. The new canons bristled with an anti-Roman spirit, and failed to gain Roman confirmation.

700–749

I. VITAL STATISTICS AND DEMOGRAPHICS

700   The **world's population** jumped to c.210 million in the preceding century. **Europe** gained c.1 million people, **Asia** c.6 million, and **China** c.2 million.

II. POLITICS AND WAR

c.700   The **Srivijaya** [Shrivijaya] **Empire** (c.100–c.1250), originating in southern Sumatra, became a leading power in **Indonesia**, controlling most of the trade routes throughout the islands, especially the Strait of Malacca between the Malay Peninsula and the island of Sumatra.

702   The port of Adulis [Adovlis] on the Red Sea, near present Zula in northern Ethiopia [Abyssinia], was destroyed by Muslim forces from Egypt. It was the last maritime outlet of the **Kingdom of Aksum** [Axum, first to eighth century A.D.], which had controlled much of the Red Sea trade before the Persian conquest of Arabia (572) and the Muslim conquest of Egypt (642). Now isolated from the outer world, Aksum fell into decline.

705   **Wu Hou** (b. 625), empress of China (from 690), died. She became ruler after she (683) deposed her son Chung Tsung. Wu Hou, the **first woman to rule China**, consolidated the empire and strengthened the **T'ang Dynasty** (618–907).

705   **Malik I** [Abd-al-Malik] (b. 646?), the Ommiad caliph (from 685), died and was succeeded by his son **Walid I** [al-Walid] (675?–715). The **Ommiad Caliphate** (661–750) under Walid achieved its greatest expansion, both eastward into India and Pakistan and westward into Spain. Walid finished the **Dome of the Rock Mosque** in Jerusalem and re-fashioned a Christian church in Damascus into the **Mosque of the Ommiads**.

707   Muslim armies under **Musa ibn-Nusayr** (660?–?714), the Ommiad governor of North Africa, captured **Tangier**, intending to use it as a base from which to attack Spain. Musa then subdued the Moroccan Berbers.

710   **Gemmei**, empress of Japan (707–715), made Nara, east of Osaka, the **first fixed Japanese capital** and a center of Buddhism.

711 July 19   The **Islamic conquest of Spain** began under Tariq (died c.720), a Muslim general and former Berber slave, when he crossed the Strait of Gibraltar from Tangier into Spain under orders from **Musa ibn-Nusayr**, the Ommiad governor of North Africa. On July 26 his Moorish [combined Arab and Berber] army of 7,000 defeated **Roderick** (d. 711; ruled from 710), **last king of the Visigoths**, in a **battle at Wadi Bekka** on the Barbate River in southwestern Spain. Toledo and Sevilla [Seville] fell to the Muslims in 712, Merida and Saragossa in 713. The Muslim army reached the Pyrénées by 718, completing the downfall of the **Kingdom of West Goths** (from c.475).

712   **Liutprand** [Liudprand, Luidprand] (690–744) was crowned king in northern Italy, and in the next 30 years brought his **Kingdom of the Lombards** (584–774) to the height of its power. He subdued the duchies of Benevento and Spoleto, extended his territory into Bavaria, and attacked Ravenna and Rome. He subdued the bishops, and brought order to his domain.

712   Muslim troops under **Hajjaj** [al-Hajjaj] (661?–716) penetrated the **Sind region** in India and Pakistan. Sind has remained Muslim ever since.

714 Dec. 16   **Pepin** [Pippin] **II** of Herstal [Pépin d'Héristal], Mayor of the Palace in Austrasia (from 686) and, in effect, ruler of all the Franks, died, and was succeeded by his illegitimate son, **Charles Martel** [*martel* = hammer]. Charles gradually wrested complete control of the Frankish dominions from various contending factions.

717   **Leo III the Isaurian** (c.680–June 18, 741), from an area of central Anatolia, was elected Byzantine emperor on the overthrow of Theodosius III. Leo maintained friendly relations with the Bulgars and strengthened the empire by subdividing its larger regions into more governable smaller units.

718   **Pelayo**, a Visigothic chieftain (718–737) and a Christian, defeated the Muslims at Covadonga in northwestern Spain, founding there the **Kingdom of Asturias**, which became the base for the Christian reconquest.

732 Oct. 11   One of the momentous battles in history, the **Battle of Tours**, France, brought defeat to a Muslim expedition that had crossed the Pyrénées from Spain. The **Franks** under **Charles Martel**, the Frankish Mayor of Austrasia, killed Abd-er-Rahman, the fanatical Arabic emir of Spain, and halted what was the deepest penetration ever made by Islamic forces into western Europe.

741   The **Berbers** rebelled against the Arab Muslim armies occupying North Africa, hastening the disintegration of the **Ommiad Caliphate**. The Berbers fell easy prey to Kharijite agitators from Iraq. Persians and Turks also proved fertile ground for rebellious schemes. Worst of all, the quarrels among the leading tribes of Syria and western Persia became almost unmanageable.

741 Oct. 22   **Charles Martel** (b. 689?), virtual ruler (from 714) of the **Kingdom of the Franks** as Mayor of the Palace in Austrasia, died. He was succeeded by his two sons, Carloman [Karlmann] (d. 754) and Pepin the Short who, as joint Mayors of the Palace, ruled a divided kingdom.

744 Apr. 17   **Walid II** (b. 707), who had succeeded Hisham as caliph only a year earlier, was assassinated in his castle at Bakhra', south of Palmyra, Syria. In that short time Walid had alienated even his kinsmen because of his cruelty and dissolute life. Walid was succeeded by **Marwan II, last of the Ommiad caliphs**.

749 Nov. 28   **Abu-al-Abbas**, the great grandson of Muhammad's uncle, accepted a public oath of allegiance as first ruler of the **Abbaside Caliphate** (750–1258) in the mosque at Kufah, later Baghdad. After the defeat of Marwan II in 750, the Abbasides proceeded to murder all members of the Ommiad clan. Few escaped, but Abd-er-Rahman I, grandson of Hisham, fled to Africa and later established the **Western Emirate of Córdoba** in Spain. The reign (to 754) of Abu-al-Abbas, who chose as his title al-Saffah [The Blood-Pourer], was marked by a settling of scores. The Abbasides had succeeded in toppling the **Ommiad Caliphate** (661–750) by creating a fusion of disparate parties and interests who shared a common hatred of the Ommiads. The Abbaside profession of religiosity was but a pretense as the **Shiites** soon discovered, but the close blood relationship of Abu-al-Abbas to Muhammad strengthened the Abbaside legitimacy against the Ommiads.

III. ECONOMY AND TRADE

717   **Omar II** (d. 720; ruled 717–720), the Ommiad caliph, freed all Muslims, whether by birth or conversion, from the poll and land taxes payable by non-Muslims. The large numbers of conversions seriously upset the finances of the **Ommiad Empire**.

IV. RELIGION AND PHILOSOPHY

701   **En-no-Gyoja**, the Japanese religious innovator, died. He had synthesized the folk traditions of the Shinto religion, Buddhism, and Taoism, and built the order of **Mountain People** [Shugen-do].

712–755   During his long reign **Hsüan Tsung**, emperor of China's **T'ang Dynasty** (618–907), an ardent Taoist, ordered a Taoist temple built in every city and every noble family to acquire a copy of the *Tao Te Ching*.

713   **Hui-Heng** (b. 638), one of the earliest Buddhist teachers to whom modern **Zen** can be traced, died. Hui-Heng and his disciple Shen-Hui founded a school that emphasized the awakening of the **prajna** [pure knowledge] from its ordinarily dormant state, and deemphasized the slavish following of the Buddha's instructions.

722 Nov. 30   **Boniface** [Winfred] (c.675–755), an English monk from Devon, was consecrated missionary bishop to **Germany** by Pope Gregory II (d. Feb. 10, 731; ruled from 715). Enjoying also the protection of the Frankish ruler Charles Martel, Boniface evangelized Hesse and Thuringia, founded monasteries, revived ancient sees, and established new ones. Before his death Boniface had largely reformed the Catholic Church of the Franks, stiffening its organization and discipline, and increasing the authority of the papacy.

725   **Leo III the Isaurian**, the Byzantine emperor, banned the veneration of images of the saints, and ordered them removed from churches. Leo III was attempting to purify the Church from superstition as well as mastering the Church, ending its immunities from taxes and service, and centralizing his empire. A religious revolt followed, the **"Iconoclastic Controversy"** in 726. The campaign to destroy sculpture and other religious images in the Byzantine Empire continued for over a century and destroyed many invaluable works of art.

728   Hasan al-Basri (b. 642) of Iraq, whose teachings later formed the basis of **Sufism**, died. His asceticism and piety set an example for Muslims who found unsatisfying the theological and juridical paths to knowledge of God offered by traditional Islam.

c.740   The **Khazars**, a trading people north of the Caucasus Mountains, were converted to **Judaism** by Jews of the Dispersion. With their capital at Itil, in the Volga Delta, they enjoyed about four centuries of relative peace and prosperity until they were defeated in battle by Kievan Russia (965).

V. SCIENCE, EDUCATION, AND TECHNOLOGY

c.700   The Chinese invented **gun powder**, a combination of saltpeter, sulphur, and carbon, using it chiefly for fireworks.

731   The **first work of English history**, *Historia Ecclesiastica Gentis Anglorum* [*The Ecclesiastical History of the English Nation*], was written in Latin by the Venerable **Bede** [Beda, Baeda] (c.673–735). It would later serve as the basis for much of *The Anglo-Saxon Chronicle*, which was written down from c.891 to 924, with fragmentary entries to 1154.

VI. ARTS AND LEISURE

c.700–800   **Punctuation symbols** began to be used with some frequency in western Europe. Manuscripts traditionally contained no punctuation, and no division between words.

c.700   Work on the **Buddhist shrines at Ajanta**, India, came to an end. The shrines, in the form of 30 caves cut into a large cliff, contained many sculptures, carvings, and paintings.

c.700   **Japanese furniture** at this time was characterized by various types of containers, such as stands, boxes, and chests. These were usually laquered to a brilliant finish, which was sometimes flecked with gold. There are only a few surviving examples from this period.

c.700   *Beowulf*, an Old English epic poem with a Scandinavian background, was developed orally about this time, probably by an Anglian Christian poet of Northumbria.

c.700   **Muslim music notation** began to become mensurable: the notes showed duration as well as pitch.

712   **Omar Abi Rabia** ['Umar ibn'abnabi Rabi'ah al-Makhzui] (b. Nov. 644), one of the greatest **Arabic love poets**, died. His works provided a detailed account of Meccan life by one who was carefully observant of human emotion. His poetry was largely concerned with sensual pleasures.

712   The *Kojicki* [Records of Ancient Events], the **oldest extant history of Japan**, compiled from oral traditions by scholars working under imperial order, was completed. It opened with creation myths and closed with the death of the Empress Suiko in 628.

720   The *Nihongi* [Chronicles of Japan] was completed. Its 30 books were written almost entirely in the classical Chinese style. Attributed to the Buddhist prince Taishi Shotoku, but probably compiled by many, the work is today a primary source for knowledge of ancient Shinto, and of great importance to an understanding of Japanese antiquity. The work covered Japanese history up to c.697.

720   The **first dramatic school in China**, the **Pear Garden**, was founded by Hsüan Tsung, the T'ang emperor.

750–799

I. VITAL STATISTICS AND DEMOGRAPHICS

c.750   The **Morioris**, who originated in the Polynesian Marquesas several thousand miles east of Australia, were probably the **first humans to** populate present New Zealand. They migrated in several waves, starting at about this time, and they traversed the great distance in outrigger canoes.

II. POLITICS AND WAR

c.750 The **Pala Dynasty** (to c.1197) began its rise to power in present India under the leadership of Gopala, who probably ruled from Monghyr [Mongeer], on the Ganges River. The dynasty reigned over the regions of Bengal, Assam, and Orissa.

750 Aug. **Marwan II**, the last Ommiad caliph (ruled from 744), fled to Egypt, having lost his army in a nine-day battle (January) on the Great Zab River, in present Iraq. He was caught and decapitated. A blood bath followed in which the **Ommiad clan** was destroyed.

751 In a momentous five-day **battle at the Talas River** in Ferghana, western Turkestan, the Arabs under Ziyad ibn Salih, formerly Ommiad governor of Kufah in present Iraq, routed a Chinese army under the Korean general Kao Hsien-Chih. After this battle, **Islam** took control of central Asia west of Sinkiang [Xinjiang] Uygur Autonomous Region, and the **T'ang Empire** lost prestige and some of its western provinces because their governors defected. The Chinese army had been sent to Turkestan to protect their westernmost allies from invading Arabs.

751 **Childeric III** (c.730–755), the **last Merovingian king** of the Franks (ruled from 743), was deposed by **Pepin the Short**, Mayor of the Palace in Austrasia. Pope Zacharias [Zachary] (d. Mar. 14, 752; ruled from 741) approved the transfer of royal power to Pepin, and he was probably crowned (or anointed) at Soissons by Boniface in Nov. 751, establishing the **Carolingian Dynasty**.

754 June 5 **Abu-al-Abbas al-Saffah** [The Blood-Pourer] (b. 721?), the founder of the **Abbaside Caliphate** (750–1258), died. He was succeeded by his brother **Al-Mansur** [= the divinely guided; abu-Ja'far 'Abdullah al-Mansur] (712–775), who quickly disposed of all threats to his power from friends and former allies, as well as from Ommiad sympathizers. The Abbaside court and the administration steadily became more Persian, less Arab or Syrian.

754 July 28 **Pepin the Short**, king of the Franks, was officially anointed and crowned by Pope Stephen II (d. Apr. 25, 757; ruled from 752), thus becoming sanctified both as king and as head of the Frankish Church. His sons, Carloman I and Charlemagne, were also consecrated. This established the aristocratic lineage of the Frankish rulers who followed Pepin, founder of the **Carolingian Dynasty** (751–987). Pepin launched a campaign (754–756) against the Lombards in northern Italy, defeating and killing their king Aistulf [Astolf] in 756, and regaining Ravenna.

756 **Hsüan Tsung**, emperor of China (from 713), was forced to abdicate as a result of the defeat of Chinese forces in a **battle at the Talas River** in 751, with the subsequent loss of Central Asia to the Muslims, and because of a revolt by the military commander of China's northeastern region in 755.

756 **Abd-er-Rahman I** ['Abd-al-Rahman ibn-Mu'awiyah] (731–788), sole survivor of the slaughter (750) of the Ommiad princes, established a regime at **Córdoba** [Cordova] in Spain, independent of the **Abbaside Caliphate** at Baghdad. By 800 Córdoba was the most prosperous city and the largest center of learning west of Constantinople.

756 **Pepin the Short**, the Carolingian king of the Franks, placed Desiderius (d. 774?) on the throne as puppet-king of the Lombards in Italy, and donated the exarchate [province, bishopric] of Ravenna to Pope Stephen II. This famous "Donation" initiated establishment of the **Papal States**, beginning an era of temporal rule for the papacy.

757 **Offa the Great** (d. 796) succeeded to the throne of the Anglian **kingdom of Mercia** in England following the murder of his cousin Ethelbald [Aethelbald] (ruled from 716). He brought the kingdom of Mercia to the height of its power and fortified the western border against raids from Celtic Wales. In his relations with the Kingdom of the Franks (486–887) and the papacy, Offa was the first to be referred to as king of England.

768 Sept. 24 **Pepin the Short** [Pépin le Bref] (b. 714), the Carolingian king of the Franks and, as Pepin III, king of Germany (from 754), died. The eastern part of Pepin's kingdom, primarily Austrasia and Burgundy, passed to his son **Carloman I**; his other son **Charlemagne** held the remainder of the kingdom, primarily Neustria and Aquitaine.

771 Dec. 4 **Carloman I** (b. 751), the Carolingian Frankish ruler, died, and the Frankish realm in the east passed to his brother, **Charlemagne**, who united and further extended the Kingdom of the Franks.

777 **Charlemagne**, the Carolingian king of the Franks, completed two campaigns in northern Italy, during which the **Kingdom of the Lombards** (584–774) was extinguished, and he renewed the "Donations" to the papacy made by his father, Pepin the Short.

778 Returning from a campaign in Moorish Spain, **Roland**, Charlemagne's nephew, was killed by the Basques at Roncesvalles, a defile of the Pyrénées. The story was told in the *Chanson de Roland* [*Song of Roland*], first written down in the early 12th century.

780 Sept. 8 **Leo IV the Khazar** (b. Jan. 25, 749), the Byzantine emperor, died. His wife **Irene** (752?–803) acted as co-emperor and regent for their ten-year-old son **Constantine VI** until 790, when he took power and banished Irene. She returned (792) as co-ruler and arrested and imprisoned (797) Constantine. Irene was sole ruler (797–802) until she was dethroned and banished.

782 An Abbaside army under **Harun-al-Rashid** reached **Constantinople**, but turned back after a short siege.

786 **Harun-al-Rashid** began his rule (ruled to 809) of the **Abbaside Caliphate**, centered at Baghdad. The fifth of the Abbaside caliphs, he was portrayed as the character Harun in the *Arabian Nights' Entertainments*. His caliphate marked the peak of Abbaside power, wealth, trade, and cultural achievements. Harun's court at Baghdad attracted poets, artists, dancers, and musicians.

787 **Raiders from the Scandinavian peninsula** were first recorded to have appeared in Britain at this time, in the Saxon **Kingdom of Wessex**. The monastery of Lindisfarne, off the northeastern coast of England, was raided in 793; the monastery of Iona off the western coast of Scotland in 795; and, in the same year, the Irish coast was plundered.

787 **Egfrith** [Ecgfrith] (d. 796), son of Offa the Great, king of Mercia, was approved as successor to the throne by the pope in Rome. Egfrith began to share the royal power with Offa in this year, but did not become king of Mercia until Offa's death in 796, when he reigned for only a few months. A distant relative, Coenwulf, then assumed the throne (to 821).

788 **Idris ibn-Abdullah** (d. 793) founded the **Idrisid Dynasty** (to 974), the **first Islamic Shiite Dynasty**, after being accepted as imam by a Moroccan Berber tribe.

794 **Kammu**, emperor of Japan (781–806), founded the nation's capital (to 1868), **Heian-kyo** [The Capital of Tranquil Peace], at present Kyoto, to escape the power of the Buddhists, whose monasteries threatened the authority of the imperial rulers. Kammu initiated important reforms, among them restrictions on Buddhist influence.

797 Aug. 15 **Constantine VI** (b. Jan. 14, 770), the **last of the Isaurian Byzantine emperors**, was blinded (and probably killed) by order of his mother **Irene**, who was opposed to Constantine's divorce in order to marry his mistress. Irene then ruled as "emperor, not empress," until 802, when she was replaced by the minister of finance, Nicephorus I (d. July 26, 811).

III. ECONOMY AND TRADE

c.750 The great **agricultural innovation** of the Middle Ages in Europe was the **three-field system of crop rotation**: one section for spring planting, one for autumn planting, and one left fallow. Each year the fields were shifted. Cattle were placed in the fallow fields, especially in England, where beef became over the centuries a staple.

755 **Pepin the Short**, king of the Franks, issued a new **system of coinage** based on the silver denarius.

c.770 **Charlemagne**, king of the Franks, established **cloth fairs** throughout his domain in order to facilitate the buying and selling of textiles.

779 The **first clear reference to permanent guilds** in Europe occurred in one of **Charlemagne's Capitularies**, or legislative and administrative acts, in which guild members were forbidden to bind themselves by oaths. At that time, European guilds were protective associations formed to defend the lives and properties of members.

780 The **Double Tax** was initiated in China. It was based solely on the amount of land one owned and was paid twice yearly. Feudal landlords were now permitted to acquire large tracts of land.

IV. RELIGION AND PHILOSOPHY

c.750–770 During the reign of **Gopala**, who founded the **Pala Dynasty**, which ruled northeastern India, Buddhism flourished. Gopala supported the building of Buddhist temples and monasteries, as well as the Buddhist center of learning known later as the University of Nalanda, near Patna in present Bihar state.

760 **Ismail** [Isma'l], son of the sixth imam Jafar al-Sadiq [Ja'far al-Sadiq] (699–765), in direct descent from Ali, died. He had been designated by Jafar as his successor. In 765 a sect within Shiism with apocalyptic doctrines came to regard Ismail as the seventh, and final, imam until the appearance of a messianic Mahdi.

c.770 **Padmasambhava** [= born of the lotus], probably an Indian prince who was a Buddhist monk active in Tibet and considered by some a **second Buddha**, introduced a fast-spreading form of **Tantra**, which included the freeing of monks from the ban on marriage and sexual intercourse.

781 **Alcuin** [Albinus] (735–May 19, 804), from the English Christian school at York, England, became the principal figure in the efforts of Charlemagne, king of the Franks, to revive the intellectual life of France and Italy, especially classical and biblical learning. Charlemagne made (796) Alcuin head of the monastery of St. Martin in Tours where, with other scholars brought together by Charlemagne, a center of learning was created.

c.787 The **Seventh General Council of the Church**, at Nicaea [İznik], in present Turkey, was called by **Irene**, co-emperor and regent for Constantine VI, the Byzantine emperor. The council reversed the policy of Leo III the Isaurian against icons, accepting instead the traditional Catholic teaching on the veneration of pictures, the Cross, and the Gospels, as set forth at the Council by legates of Pope Adrian I (d. Dec. 25, 795; ruled from 772).

V. ARTS AND LEISURE

c.750 In China the essays and stories of the great third-century B.C. Taoist philosopher **Chuang-Tzu** began to be written down. The stories emphasized plot and character development.

c.750 Construction was completed on the Buddhist temple, the **Todaiji**, at Nara, Japan. Its Great Hall remains today, even in its present incomplete state, the **largest wooden structure in the world**. The Hall was built to contain the Great Buddha [Dai Butsu], a statue 53 feet high.

752 The **temple of Sok-kul-am** was built in the **Kingdom of Silla**, near the present city of Kyongju, South Korea. It was part of the Pulguk-sa complex of cave temples constructed on Mount T'oham. Some of the finest examples of **Korean Buddhist sculpture** are found within the temple.

757 **Ibn al-Muqaffa'** (b. 721?), the greatest stylist of early Arabic prose writers, was executed for heresy. Ibn al-Muqaffa' was important for his translation into Persian of the collection of Indian fables and parables, *Kalila va Dimna*, composed (c.300) originally in Sanskrit.

c.760 *Man-yoshu*, the first great anthology of Japanese poetry, appeared. About 4,500 poems were included in this collection.

c.762 **Li Po** [Li Tai Po, Li Tai Peh] (b. 701?), perhaps the most famous **Chinese poet**, died. After traveling the country he came to Hsüan Tsung's court, but he soon tired of the intrigue and left in 744. Li Po became involved in the revolts of c.755, and was banished in 758. His poetry was romantic and lyrical, his themes traditional, and his images, especially of nature, delicate and imaginative. He wrote thousands of verses, of which some 2,000 have survived.

770 **Tu Fu** (b. 712), a **Chinese poet** who ranked in popularity with Li Po, died. His life was one of wandering and privation; though he craved imperial favor, he never succeeded in holding an official position for long. His poetry was noted for its adherence to Chinese classical form, rather than for its originality. Tu Fu's themes were traditional, but tinged with bitterness.

c.772 **Hammad al-Rawiyah** [Hammad al-Rawiyah] (born c.713), whose collections of poems, legends, genealogies, and dialects preserved much of Arabic literature, died. He collected qasidas, poems in which all the lines rhyme. These he published in the *Mu'ualla-gat*, one of the finest collections of early Arabic poetry.

784? **Bashshar ibn Burd** (b. 714?), an Arab poet, died. He was a Zoroastrian of Persian ancestry and lived at a time when Arab culture was quickly assimilating Persian culture. The traditional Arab poetic form, the **qasida**, became less formal as non-Arabic poets became established. Burd excelled in panegyrics and also in scornful addresses that may have produced enmity at the court.

794 Heian-kyo [Kyoto] was constructed by Kammu, emperor of Japan, to serve as a well-organized government center. Each craft guild or service had its own section, and all met at one of two central marketplaces to exchange their wares.

796 Work began on the **Palatine Cathedral** in Aix-la-Chapelle [Aachen], in present Germany. The cathedral, ordered built by **Charlemagne** and designed by **Odo of Metz**, the **first architect** of northern Europe who today is known by name, was consecrated in 805 by Pope Leo III. Charlemagne was probably buried here.

800–849

I. VITAL STATISTICS AND DEMOGRAPHICS

800 The estimated **population of the world** reached 220 million. **Europe** now had c.29 million people; **Asia**, c.155 million, of whom about 20 million lived in the Near East. Altogether, the Islamic world numbered c.30 million subjects.

II. EXPLORATION AND COLONIZATION

c.800 Leaders of the **Irish Church** fled their homeland for **Iceland** with their adherents to escape the formularies of the Roman Catholic Church, which threatened to destroy the Irish form of Christianity.

808 Idris II (d. 828; ruled from 791) founded the city of Fez [Fès] as the capital of the **Idrisid Dynasty** (788–974), established in Morocco by his father, Idris ibn-Abdullah.

834 Danish **Vikings** made a successful raid on Friesland of the northern Netherlands, at Dorestad [Wijk-bij-Duurstede), near the mouth of the Rhine River. Within ten years the Viking raids became more and more common along the coasts of Germany, the Netherlands, France, and Spain.

III. POLITICS AND WAR

c.800–900 The great **Mayan cities** of the Yucatán Peninsula, Mexico, declined. It was hypothesized that their agricultural system, based on extensive irrigation and drainage systems, failed. The Maya did not disappear altogether, but fragmented into enclaves centered in the northern tip of the peninsula and around Lake Petén in present northern Guatemala.

c.800 East of Lake Chad in central Africa, the **Kingdom of Kanem** emerged with **Dugu**, the founder of the **Sefawa** [Saifawa] **Dynasty** (to 1846), as mai [king]. Nomadic Saharan tribes, attracted by the well-watered Lake Chad basin, had progressively settled and gained influence over the native agriculturists, called the **So people**. Kanem and its capital, Njimi, became a wealthy and powerful trade center.

800 Dec. 25 Charlemagne, the Carolingian king of the Franks (from 768), was crowned **Emperor of the West** by Pope Leo III (d. June 12, 816; ruled from 795). This event planted the seed for the birth, nearly two centuries later, of the **Holy Roman Empire**, when **Otto the Great** was crowned (962) the **first Holy Roman emperor**. Leo V (d. Dec. 25, 820), the Byzantine emperor (from 813), acknowledged (817) Charlemagne as Emperor of the West and, in return, Charlemagne ceded to the Byzantine Empire Dalmatia and Istria, both in present Croatia, and Venetia, in Italy.

801 Ibrahim ibn Aghlab [Ibrahim ibn-al-Aghlab] (756–812), appointed governor by Harun-al-Rashid, founded the **Aghlabite Dynasty** (801–909) of Ifriqiya [Africa] in present Tunisia. The Aghlabites captured Malta, Sardinia, and Sicily, and developed a brilliant civilization with al-Qayrawan [Kairouan] as its center.

c.802 The **Angkor Period** (to 1434) of the **Khmer Empire** began with the reign of **Jayavarman II** (c.802–850), who established his capital near Angkor, in present Cambodia. He united the Khmer territories of Chenla, which had succeeded (c.600) the **Kingdom of Funan**; achieved independence from the **kingdom of Java**; and initiated a unified state bound by the new religion of the god-king.

809 Mar. Harun-al-Rashid [Harun al-Rashid, Aaron the Upright] (born c.764), the **fifth Abbaside caliph** and the most famous of all caliphs, died. It was during his reign that the caliphate reached its zenith, and Harun made his capital, Baghdad, the most powerful and prosperous city of Islam, and perhaps the most populous city of the world. Harun is famous today as the caliph of the *Arabian Nights' Entertainments* [*A Thousand and One Nights*]. After Harun's death a civil war between two of his sons **Amin** and **Mamun** raged until Mamun [al-Mamoun] (736–833) succeeded in capturing and killing al-Amin, the sixth caliph (809–813), and became (813) the seventh caliph of the **Abbaside Dynasty** (750–1258).

811 July 26 Krum [Crummus, Crumn] (d. 814), khan of the Bulgars (from 802), defeated and killed **Nicephorus I** (ruled from 802), the Byzantine emperor, in a **battle at Virbitza**, a Balkan mountain pass. Bulgaria's territorial expansion of the **First Bulgarian Empire** (681–1018) was finally checked (817) at Mesembria [Mesambria], on the Black Sea north of Adrianople [Edirne] and a truce was signed.

811 The Eider River in present Germany was established (to 1864) as the southern border of **Denmark** by **Charlemagne** and **Hemming** (d. 812), king of the Danes. His brother and predecessor Godfred [Godefridus, Gudfred] (d. 810) had earlier defeated the advancing Franks.

813 Michael I Rhangabe (died c.845; ruled from 811) the Byzantine emperor, was defeated by **Krum**, khan of the Bulgars, near Andrianople [Edirne]. The Byzantine troops deserted under the leadership of Leo V the Armenian (d. Dec. 25, 820), who declared himself emperor (to 820). Michael fled to a monastery, where he spent the remainder of his life.

814 Jan. 26 Charlemagne [Carolus Magnus, Charles the Great] (b. Apr. 2, 742), the Carolingian king of the Franks (from 768) and Emperor of the West (from 800), died. He was succeeded by his son **Louis I the Pious**, who was crowned Emperor of the West at Reims in Oct. 816 by Pope Stephen IV (d. Jan. 24, 817; ruled from 816). There followed a period of nearly two centuries in which the **popes**

conveyed legitimacy on claimants to the throne of what later became the Holy Roman Empire (962–1806).

825 Egbert [Ecgbert] (775?–839), king of Wessex (from 802), decisively defeated **Beornwulf**, king of Mercia (823–825), in a **battle at Ellandun**, present Wroughton, near Swindon, England. This marked the beginning of the hegemony of Wessex [West Saxons] in England. Egbert was recognized (828) as the first overlord of all the English.

827 A Muslim army, mostly **Saracens** originally from Arabia, landed in **Sicily**, answering the appeal of Euphemius of Syracuse, who had revolted against the Byzantine Empire. This marked the beginning of the conquest of the island by the **Aghlabite Dynasty** (801–909).

c.833 Mutasim [al-Mu'tasim] (794–842), the eighth Abbaside caliph (from 833), began to rely heavily on mercenary troops loyal to him personally, chiefly Turks from beyond the Oxus River, which helped lead to the dissolution of the **Abbaside Dynasty** (749–1258). These troops in Baghdad became so unruly that Mutasim built a new city, Samarra, in Iraq, comprising his palace and their quarters.

840 The Uighurs [Uigurs], Turkic-speaking semi-nomadic tribes who controlled Mongolia, were defeated by the Kirghiz and forced to migrate to T'fan [Tu-Lu-Fan, Tufan], then part of northern Tibet. Centered around the Tarim River basin, in Chinese Turkestan, the Uighurs established another empire, which prospered and grew powerful because it controlled trade along the **Silk Route**, from China to eastern Europe.

840 June 20 Louis I the Pious [le Débonnaire] (b. 778), son of Charlemagne and Emperor of the West (from 814), died. He was succeeded as emperor by his eldest son **Lothair I** (795–Sept. 29, 855), who had already been crowned in 823 as Emperor of the West, a title he held jointly with his father. Civil war ensued, and Lothair's brothers **Louis II the German** (805?–Aug. 28, 876) and **Charles II the Bald** (June 13, 823–Oct. 6, 877) joined to defeat him in a **battle at Fontenoy** [Fontanet], in northern France, on June 25, 841.

842 Jan. 20 Theophilus, the Byzantine emperor (from 829), died and was succeeded by his infant son, **Michael III**, for whom his mother, empress **Theodora** (c.810–862) and her brother **Bardas** (d. 865) acted as regents. In 856, with the murder of Theodora's minister Theoctistus, and her banishment to a convent, Bardas came to exert a great influence over Byzantine affairs.

843 Aug. The Carolingian Kingdom of the Franks was divided into three kingdoms by the **Treaty of Verdun**. Louis II the German ruled the Frankish kingdom east of the Rhine River, founding the political entity known as Germany. The Emperor of the West, Lothair I, ruled northern Italy, including most of the territory of the Burgundians, and Lorraine in present France, all of Belgium, and part of the Netherlands. Charles II the Bald ruled the western Frankish kingdom, the nucleus of present France.

848 A union of Picts and Scots, traditionally considered the **first kingdom of Scotland**, was established by **Kenneth I MacAlpine** (d. 858?), the son of Alpin (d. 834?), of the western Scottish **Kingdom of Dal Riata** [Dalriada], which had subdued the Picts.

IV. ECONOMY AND TRADE

827 **Looms** were first used in Palermo, Sicily, probably introduced by the invading Arabs.

839 **Amalfi**, in southern Italy, began to display its independence from Naples. Amalfi's naval strength in the Mediterranean had developed along with its trade routes to Constantinople [İstanbul] and Antioch [Antakya], both in present Turkey, and Durazzo [Durrës], in present Albania. The standard Mediterranean code of maritime conduct was the *Tavole Amalfitane* [Table of Amalfi].

V. RELIGION AND PHILOSOPHY

c.800 Four centuries of competition among the many cults of **Hinduism** ended with two survivors: **Vaishnavism** and **Shaivism**, their respective gods being Vishnu and Shiva.

c.800 **Shankara** (780–820), a Brahmin from Malabar, on the southwestern coast of India, and one of India's greatest religious philosophers, wrote commentaries on the *Upanishads*, the *Vedanta Sutras*, and the *Bhagavad-Gita*. He composed poems,

hymns, and prayers to the gods, primarily to Shiva, and he established monastic centers of learning.

c.800 **Pachácamac**, a religious center for most of the **pre-Inca Andean Indians**, was thought to have been built at this time, just south of present Lima, Peru. During religious festivals c.100,000 Indians participated in rites here.

801 **Rabiah al-'Adawiyah** [Rabe'a bint Esma 'il al-Adawiya], a celebrated **female saint of Islam**, died. A Sufi, Rabiah was influential in the development of the doctrine of divine love within Islamic mysticism.

c.813 **Mamun**, the seventh Abbaside caliph, espoused a school of philosophic-theologic thought first developed in Islam nearly a century earlier by the **Qadarites** [from *qadar*, meaning "power"], whose Baghdad school now became known as **Mutazilah**. Their rational ideas reflected the penetration of **Islamic theology** by Greek-Christian philosophic speculation. Its members denied divine predestination and asserted human freedom of will. They also held that the **Koran** was a created work of **Allah**, co-eternal with him.

820 Jan. 20 **Al-Shafi'i** [Abu 'Abd Allah Muhammad ibn-Idris al-Shafi'i] (b. 768), perhaps the greatest figure in the creation of a **system of jurisprudence for Islam**, died. His system, which predominates today in eastern Africa and in parts of Indonesia, flourished among Sunnite Muslims along with systems founded by **Malik-ibn-Anas** (718–796), **abu-Hanifah** [al-Nu'man ibn-Thabit] (699–767), and **ibn-Hanbal** [abu-'Abdullah Ahmad ibn-Hanbal] (780–855).

822 **Saicho** [Dengyo Daishi] (b. 767), a Japanese Buddhist master and founder of a Buddhist monastic center at Mount Hiei, on Honshu, died. **Kukai** [Kobo Daishi] (b. 774), the head of another influential Japanese Buddhist center at Mt. Koya, south of Kyoto, died in 835. Both had blended **Buddhism** with **Shintoism**, Saicho relying on Zen, Kukai on more esoteric Buddhist teachings.

829 The **first Christian missionary to Sweden, Ansgar** (c. 801–Feb. 3, 865), was sent by Louis the Pious, king of the Franks. A church was built at Birka, but Christianity did not take hold in Sweden until Olaf Skötkonung (died c.1022), king of Sweden, was baptized (1008).

c.831 **Paschasius Radbertus** (c.785–860), a French abbot, wrote the first major *De corpore et sanguine Christi* [Concerning the Body and Blood of Christ], a treatise on the Lord's Supper. He stated that, by divine miracle, the substance of the bread and wine is transformed into the body and blood of Christ. Paschasius was promptly challenged by **Ratramnus** (d. 868?) in *De corpore et sanguine Domini* [Concerning the Body and Blood of the Lord]. Ratramnus contended that the elements became the body and blood of Christ only in a symbolic sense, remaining bread and wine to the senses. The issue at this time was not drawn, but gradually the view of Paschasius became orthodox doctrine.

845 **Wu-Tsung** (ruled 840–846), emperor of the T'ang Dynasty (618–907), turned on the **Buddhists**, causing the worst **religious persecution** in China's history. According to imperial pronouncements, 4,600 Buddhist temples and 40,000 shrines were destroyed, and 260,500 monks and nuns killed. **Zoroastrians** and **Manichaeans** were also obliterated; Christian **Nestorians**, whose mission in the T'ang capital of Chang-an [Sian, Xian] had been established (c.635) by the monk Alopen [Olopen], were scattered.

c.847–852 An **ecclesiastical forgery**, now called the **Pseudo-Isidor** [or False] **Decretals**, appeared in France. Purportedly compiled by one Isidor Mercator [Isidor "the merchant"], who called himself a "servant of Christ," the work consisted of conciliar and papal pronouncements, some genuine, some forged, dating from 90–730. The Decretals tended to justify contemporary papal claims of supreme jurisdiction and freedom from secular control.

VI. SCIENCE, EDUCATION, AND TECHNOLOGY

c.820 The branch of mathematics now known as **algebra** [from Arabic: *al jabr*] was set forth by the Arabic scholar **al-Khwarizmi** [Muhammad ibn-Musa al Khwarizmi or al-Khowarizmi] (780–?850) in his treatise *Kitab al jabr wa'l muqabala*. It was not original material. Al-Khwarizmi borrowed from Hindu works, most probably the Hindu poem *Brahmasiddhanta* by Brahmagupta (588–?660), an Indian astronomer. This work, in turn, reflected Greek influence. In fact, the rules for solution of both linear and quadratic equations and the principles of simple geometry can be traced to Hebrew studies, and may have originated with the Babylonians. Nevertheless, Al-Khwarizmi's work survived, because his exposition was clear and well organized.

c.842 A pledge of mutual support between two grandsons of Charlemagne, Louis II the German and Charles II the Bald, was drawn up in the languages spoken by their troops. It was the **first surviving written document in the West European vernaculars**.

VII. ARTS AND LEISURE

800–1200 The **Eight Great Masters of Prose, Han Yü** [Han Wên-Kung] (768–824), **Liu Tsung-yuan** (773–819), **Ou-yang Hsiu** (1007–1072), **Su Hsun** (birth and death dates unknown), **Su Shih** [Su Tung-p'o] (1036–1101), **Su Ch'e** (birth and death dates unknown), **Wang An-Shih** (1021–1086), and **Tseng Kung** (birth and death dates unknown) led a reform movement calling for a return to an older prose style, which was, in fact, closer to ordinary speech than the conventional prose style.

804 **Ibrahim al-Mausili** [Mawsili = Mosul or Al-Mawsil, a city in present Iraq] (b. 742), considered the greatest musician of his day, died. His son **Ishaq al-Mausili** was equally famous as the composer of the *Great Book of Songs*.

813 **Abu-Nuwas** [al-Hasan ibn-Hani'] (b. 747), an Arabic poet of Persian and Arabic descent, died. His work extolled the pleasures of sexual love and strong drink.

819 Construction on the abbey church at Fulda, in present Germany, introduced the plan of the **two-ended church** with an altar at each end.

826 **Abu-al-Atahiyah** (b. 748), the first important writer of religious poetry in Arabic, died. He had begun his writing career as a somewhat dissolute love poet who had gained distinction for breaking with the tradition of non-Muslim Arab poets in using a less formal language more appropriate to the villages.

850–899

I. DISASTERS

856 Dec. A strong **earthquake** shook **Corinth**, Greece, killing at least 45,000.

893 In the region of **Armenia**, in the Caucusus, a strong **earthquake** killed c.20,000 people.

II. EXPLORATION AND COLONIZATION

870 The **first Viking settlements in Iceland** were established following the accidental discovery of the island by Norwegian (861) and Swedish (864) seafarers.

III. POLITICS AND WAR

851 Danish **Vikings** entered the Thames Estuary in England and sacked Canterbury and London. They were finally defeated and repulsed by **Ethelwulf** [Aethelwulf] (839–858), a king of the West Saxons, in a **battle at Ockley** [Oakley], just south of London.

c.862 Rurik [Ryurik] (d. 879), a Scandinavian chieftain who had led **Viking** raids to western Europe, became the ruler of the trading settlement of Novgorod, south of present St. Petersburg, Russia. According to legend, Rurik and his Viking band, called **Varangians**, were invited to Novgorod. The native **Slavs** in the area and the Varangians became known as **Rus**, later as **Russians**.

867 Sept. 24 Michael III the Drunkard (born c.840), the Byzantine emperor (from 842), was murdered by the co-emperor **Basil I the Macedonian** (812?–Aug. 29, 886). Basil founded the **Macedonian Dynasty** (867–1056), a **golden age for the Byzantine Empire**. The **Basilica**, a system of jurisprudence based on the **Justinian Code**, was instituted.

872 Harold I [Harald Fairhair; Harald Haarfager] (850?–933), king of Norway (860–930), became the **first king of a united Norway**. Harold expelled the petty nobles, forcing them and their Viking bands to resettle elsewhere. They went to the British Isles, Iceland, and the north of France.

c.873 Oleg (died c.912), a Scandinavian chieftain, entered northern Russia with his followers and gained control of the **Slavs** and Scandinavian traders living there, succeeding his kinsman Rurik, who had returned to Scandinavia. As head of the **Varangians**, Oleg moved into southern Russia (c.880) to establish the **first important Russian state**, centered around **Kiev**.

c.875 According to legend, **Irish sailors** reached the shores of **North America**, establishing settlements in present Nova Scotia. If so, they were the first whites to see the continent.

877 June 14 Charles II the Bald, king of the West Franks, promulgated the **Capitulary of Kiersy** [Quierzy], on the Oise River in present France, which made hereditary the revenues and honors, but not the land, of the petty nobility. This legislation strengthened the position of the local counts [*comtes*] in France, which had by this time been divided into counties [*comtés*].

878 Syracuse, Sicily, was sacked by Muslim Aghlabite forces from Tunisia after a nine-month siege, completing the capture of the island from the Byzantine Empire. The Muslims had now become masters of the western Mediterranean.

878 Alfred the Great, king of Wessex, won a victory over Danes led by **Guthrum** [Guthorm, Guttorm] (d. 890) in a **battle at Edington** in southern England. Guthrum, by the **Treaty of Wedmore**, accepted Christianity and settled in the Danelaw—the former kingdoms of East Anglia, Essex, and northeastern Mercia. **Wessex**, the **last important Saxon kingdom**, was saved and remained unmolested by the Danes for nearly the remainder of Alfred's reign. In 885 Alfred reoccupied London, which he rebuilt and fortified.

884 The **Empire of the Franks** was reunited by **Charles III the Fat** (839–Jan. 13, 888), king of Germany (from 876) and emperor (crowned in 881), who was elected king of the West Franks following the death of Carloman II (866?–Dec. 12, 884), who had ruled Aquitaine and Burgundy and, jointly with his brother Louis III (863?–Aug. 5, 882), northern France. Charles was deposed (887) as king and emperor by the nobility at Tribur [Trebur], in present Germany, for having failed to help Count Odo of Paris against the Norse invaders.

886 A period of Muslim weakness in Spain followed the death of **Muhammad I**, Ommiad emir of Córdoba (ruled from 852). It enabled the Christian **Kingdom of Asturias** (718–910) to expand in northeastern Spain under **Alfonso III** (866–911), and the **Basque Kingdom of Navarre** to assert its independence.

887 **Arnulf of Carinthia** (850?–Dec. 8, 899) was elected ruler of Germany by the East Frank, German, and Italian nobles. **Odo** [Eudes] (860?–Jan. 1, 898), count of Paris, was elected king of the West Franks in 888. The **Empire of the Franks** was once again thus divided.

899 Oct. 26 **Alfred the Great** (b. 849), king of Wessex, died. In the years following the final major Scandinavian [Danish] invasion of West Saxon lands (876–878), Alfred turned to the restoration of the scholarly and religious life of Wessex. In concert with the scholars he invited to England, Alfred produced a series of translations from Latin into the English of his day of notable works, including *Pastoral Care* by Pope Gregory I the Great, Bede's *Ecclesiastical History*, and a handbook of philosophy by Boethius.

IV. ECONOMY AND TRADE

887 Importation of silk into western Europe was cut off by military conflicts in China and along trade routes in the Near East, resulting in greater emphasis on **silk production** within the Byzantine Empire.

V. RELIGION AND PHILOSOPHY

c.850 The word "sufism" first appeared in Arabic writings. It was derived from an Arabic root meaning "wool," which referred to the woolen garment worn by its adherents, probably in imitation of Christian ascetics. As a literary and philosophical movement among Shiite Muslims, Sufism emerged in the late 10th and early 11th centuries and was strongest in Persia. Though it took in various ideas and practices, Sufism emphasized the personal union of one's soul with God.

855 **Ahmad ibn-Hanbal** (b. 780), head of the **Hanbali**, the most conservative of the four orthodox Sunni schools of Islamic law, died. The Hanbali rejected the use of analogy in Islamic law, preferring to base rules on tradition as to what the Prophet did, said, or permitted, no matter how flimsily supported.

858 **Photius** (c.820–891), a learned Greek layman, was appointed patriarch of Constantinople by Michael III the Drunkard, the Byzantine emperor, to succeed Ignatius (c.798–877), deposed for refusing the sacraments to the emperor's unsavory guardian-uncle Bardas. Ignatius appealed to Pope Nicholas I (d. Nov. 13, 867; ruled from 858) in Rome, who declared (863) Photius deposed. Photius responded by charging Rome with various heresies. Thus began the so-called **schism of Photius**.

863 **Pope Nicholas I** (d. Nov. 13, 867; ruled from 858) declared void the divorce of Lothair II (826?–869), king of Lorraine (from 855), sanctioned by a synod of local bishops so that he might marry his mistress. Despite political and military threats, Nicholas excommunicated two archbishops who had supported Lothair, reasserted the queen's rights, and proclaimed that the Church was superior to secular powers and that the pope was ruler of the Church.

864 **Cyril** [Constantine] (827–869) was sent by Michael III the Drunkard to proselytize the Slavs of Moravia, in the present Czech Republic. With his brother Methodius (825–885) Cyril converted Moravia, formed a seminary for priests, and provided lessons in Scripture. Cyril invented a modified Greek, or **Cyrillic, alphabet** that replaced Slavonic characters and formed the basis of the modern Russian alphabet.

870 **Boris I** (d. May 15, 907), king of Bulgaria (ruled 852–889), finally consented to the introduction of the Eastern Orthodox Church into his empire. He had been baptized (865) in Constantinople, with Michael III, the Byzantine emperor, acting as his godfather; but he feared domination by the emperor, and had sought missionaries from Rome as a counterbalance. Byzantine influence was mitigated by Boris's acceptance of the Slavic clergy who were expelled from Moravia in 884. The **First Bulgarian Empire** (681–1018) thus acquired an independent archbishopric.

875 **Al-Kindi** [abu-Yusuf Ya'qub ibn Ishaq al-Kindi] (born c.800), an Arab philosopher, died. He served as court physician to the Abbaside caliph in **Baghdad** and became known as the "**philosopher of the Arabs**." Al-Kindi's prolific writings covered virtually every field of study.

878 **Muhammed al-Muntazar**, called "the expected," died. The majority of **Shiites** today regard him as the twelfth and final imam, tracing his line down from Husain [al-Husayn], grandson of Muhammad, and then through a brother of Ismail (d. 760). These Shiites are today called "**Twelvers.**" They expect **Muhammad** to reappear as **Mahdi** and bring victory to the faithful, and peace and justice to the world.

c.880 The people of present Yemen became attracted to the heretical teachings of **Hamdan Qarmat**, a missionary of the **Ismaili branch of the Shiite sect.** By 903 the **Karmathians** [Carmathians, Qarmatians] had gained control of most of Yemen, and had captured Hajar, capital of Bahrain.

VI. SCIENCE, EDUCATION, AND TECHNOLOGY

c.850 The main hall of **Fu-Kuang-ssu**, built at this time, is the only surviving wooden building from the **T'ang Dynasty** (618–907) in China.

VII. ARTS AND LEISURE

c.850 At this time in Europe nearly all **writing** was done in monasteries, where illustrated manuscripts were copied out by hand.

868 May 11 A scroll called the *Diamond Sutra*, containing Buddhist writings with this date, was the **earliest known example of a printed book**.

869 Jahiz (born c.776), an Iraqi Arab of black ancestry, who was renowned as one of the finest essayists in the Arabic language, died. His works included *Kitab al-Bayan we al-Tabyin* [Elegance of Expression and Clarity of Exposition], a scholarly treatise on style and usage, and *Kitab al-bukhala'* [Book of Misers], a collection of stories.

873 Hunayn ibn Ishaq (b. 809), a Nestorian who had headed the Baghdad school of translation and the library called the **House of Wisdom**, died. Founded by Mamun, the Abbaside caliph, it centered its interests on Greek literature.

900–949

I. VITAL STATISTICS AND DEMOGRAPHICS

900 The **world's population** at this time was an estimated 240 million people, a gain of c.20 million during the preceding century. In **Europe** and **China**, despite barbarian harassment and internal strife, a gain was made, although less than in other areas of the world.

II. EXPLORATION AND COLONIZATION

900 By this time the Norse and Danish **Vikings** had landed in England, Ireland, Iceland, and Friesland. They also had made settlements at Rouen and Nantes, in France, from which they raided far inland. Skirting the coast of Spain, they sailed their longships into the Mediterranean Sea, where they raided Arles, in southern France, and reached the northwestern coast of Italy.

III. POLITICS AND WAR

c.900 The **Toltecs** gained supremacy in central Mexico. They were centered around Tula [Tollán] and Teotihuacán, both near present Mexico City, but they had also spread into the Yucatán Peninsula, where their appearance coincided with the decline of the **Mayan civilization**. The Toltec legend of their origin told of their god **Quetzalcoatl** [Feathered Serpent], who had been driven from Tula by the deception of the evil god **Tezcatlipoca**, and had wandered for over 100 years before returning to his home along the eastern coast of Mexico.

c.900 The **Mixtec Indians**, of the Mexican central plateau, began to raid the **Zapotecs** of the Oaxaca valley in southern Mexico. Here the Mixtecs settled, seizing Monte Albán and other cities.

c.900 The **Chimu Indians** began to grow into a powerful nation along the northern coast of Peru. Their capital Chan Chan, near present Trujillo, was estimated to have a population of between 100,000 and 200,000. The strength of the Chimu came from their highly developed irrigation system that enabled cultivation of Peru's coastal desert.

906 Leo VI (Sept. 866–May 12, 912; ruled from 886), the Byzantine emperor, married his fourth wife to legitimize the birth of an heir in Sept. 905. Leo's son, **Constantine VII Porphyrogenitus** [= Born to the Purple] (Sept. 905–Nov. 9, 959), was emperor only in name until his uncle and regent **Alexander** (b.870; ruled from 912), died on June 6, 913. However, Constantine VII's stepfather, **Romanus I Lecapenus** (c.870–June 15, 948; ruled from 919), seized (919) the throne and held it until Constantine finally succeeded in deposing him in 944.

907 Árpád, chief of the seven **Magyar tribes** that had migrated (c.875) to the region of the Danube River, died. He was the founder of the **Árpád Dynasty** (896–1301), which established Hungary.

907 The period of the **Five Dynasties** (907–960) began in China when Kao **Tsung-Ti** [Chao-Hsuan-Ti], the **last emperor of the T'ang Dynasty** (618–907), and about 15 years old, was forced to abdicate by a warlord who had murdered the previous emperor Chao-Tsung (ruled 888–904). The capital of the Five Dynasties was Kaifeng in northern central China.

909 Said ibn-Husayn [Ubaidallah] (d. 933), a leader in Syria of the **Ismaili movement** of the Shiite sect, seized Kairouan [Qairwan], in present Tunisia, and ousted the Sunni **Aghlabite Dynasty** (801–909). Said founded the **Fatimid** [Fatimite] **Caliphate** (909–1171) with the aim of gaining control of all the Muslim world.

911 The **Treaty of St. Clair-sur-Epte**, near Gisors in northern France, was signed between Charles III the Simple (Sept. 17, 879–Oct. 7, 929; ruled from 893), king of the West Franks, and the Vikings, who had been settled (from 896) in northwestern France. The treaty created the duchy of Normandy under **Rollo** [Rolf or Hrolf] (d. 931), who became the **first duke of Normandy** and was a direct ancestor of William the Conquerer. Fulfilling a condition of the treaty, Rollo was baptized (912).

911 A treaty signed by the Varangian rulers of **Kievan Russia** (c.880–1240) and representatives of the **Byzantine Empire** called for Russian mercenaries to be recruited into the imperial army. Later these and other Vikings formed the powerful **Var-**angian Guards**, powerful personal units of the emperor.

911 Sept. 24 Louis III the Child (b. 893), the **last ruler** (from 899) **of the Carolingian Dynasty** in Germany (from 843), died. He was succeeded by **Conrad I** (d. Sept. 23, 918) of Franconia, who vainly attempted to restore some unity, but after whom began a century of Saxon rule (from 919), starting with Henry I the Fowler (876–July 2, 936).

919 Niall [O'Neill] **Glundub** [Niall of the Black Knee], the high king of Ireland (from 915), was defeated and killed at Kilmashogue [Cell Mosamhog], near Dublin, in his attempt to destroy the Norse **Kingdom of Dublin**, where the **Vikings** had settled in 840.

925 Symeon I the Great (863?–927) took the title of czar of the Romans and Bulgars. By appointing a patriarch, he made the Bulgarian Church independent of Constantinople, strengthening the primacy of Rome.

929 Abd er-Rahman III ['Abdul-Rahman] (891–961), the emir of Spain (from 912), declared himself caliph [= successor] and founded the **Ommiad Caliphate of Spain** (to 1031), which in the next 30 years became the greatest cultural center in Europe. With the Abbasides established in the East and the Fatimids in North Africa, Islam was now divided into three rival caliphates.

930 Iceland established itself as a republic when the aristocrats convened the **Álthing**, the **oldest legislative assembly** in Europe. It was consultative in nature, with one of its members serving as the law speaker, or chairman. The Álthing met every summer until 1262, when Haakon IV Haakonsson (1204–Dec., 1263), also called Haakon the Old, king of Norway (1217–1263), joined Iceland and Greenland to Norway. The Álthing was reestablished in 1843 and survives today.

c.935 The **Koryo Dynasty** (to 1392), in western central Korea, was founded by **Wang Kon**, after having annexed the **Kingdom of Silla** (57 B.C.–A.D. 935). The **Wang Dynasty** (918–1392) now began a period of dominance in the Korean Peninsula, establishing a central government and a civil service based on Confucian precepts.

936 The **Abbaside Caliphate** (749–1258) was rendered nominal when power was taken from al-Radi

(d. Dec., 940; ruled from 934) by Muhammad Ibn Raiq, who took the title of chief emir.

936 July 2   Henry I the Fowler (b. 876), the **first German king** (from 919) **of the Saxon Dynasty** (919–1024), died, and was succeeded by his son **Otto I the Great** (Oct. 23, 912–May 7, 973) when he was elected king on Aug. 7. Otto's reign began with a reassertion of authority over the German lords (939) and over the duchy of Lorraine (942). He secured control (950) of Bavaria and, through marriage, reduced to vassalage (952) both the **Kingdom of Burgundy**, centered at Arles, France, and the **Kingdom of Italy**.

937   Athelstan (895–Oct. 17, 940), king of the West Saxons and of England (from c.924), defeated a combined force of Danes, Welsh, and Scots in a **battle at Brunanburh**, near the English-Scottish border. This victory secured Athelstan's control of most of present England and was the subject of a poem in the *Anglo-Saxon Chronicle.*

940   Harold Bluetooth [Harald Blaatand] (d. 985) became king of Denmark, beginning a reign that lasted almost 50 years. Harold was converted (960) to Christianity, and Denmark became the first Scandinavian country to officially adopt that religion.

c.945   Wales achieved a period of relative unity under **Howel [Hywel] Dda** the Good (d. 950), king of Wales (ruled from 942), whose codification of Welsh law provided the basic elements of governance for the Welsh people.

945   Ahmad ibn-Buwayh, a member of a Persian clan from the mountainous region of northwestern Iran, entered Baghdad unopposed, captured the caliph, and began the Persian **Buwayhid** [Buyid] **Dynasty** (to 1055). Ahmad ruled to 967.

IV. ECONOMY AND TRADE

907   Oleg, the Varangian ruler of Kievan Russia, led a fleet that attacked **Constantinople**. Fearing defeat, the Byzantine emperor signed a trade treaty with Oleg.

c.928   Athelstan, king of the West Saxons and king of England, established **rules for his country's coinage.**

V. RELIGION AND PHILOSOPHY

c.900   A poetical book of major importance for the Vaishnavite cult of **Hinduism**, the *Bhagavata Purana*, was written in Sanskrit. Of the many *Puranas*, collections of Hindu legends and precepts written across ten centuries, this one included accounts of the exploits of **Krishna**, who now became immensely popular as an avatar [incarnation] of Vishnu.

c.900   Soon after this time, the **Masoretes**, scholars and preservers of the text of the **Hebrew Bible**, in Tiberias in Palestine, with the help of Masoretes located in other centers of learning, completed work on a Hebrew Bible begun three centuries earlier. The Masoretes had now completed and stabilized a system of vowel signs and had provided accent marks that indicated places to pause in reading aloud and served as musical notes for cantillation. This edition has been regarded as authoritative ever since.

910   William the Pious (d. 918), duke of Aquitaine, founded the **monastery of Cluny** in Burgundy, France, under the rule of Benedict. Cluny was independent of the local bishop; the sole superior of its abbot was the pope. **Berno** (910–927) was its first abbot.

922 Mar. 26   Al-Hallaj [al-Husayn ibn-Mansur al-Hallaj, The Wool Carder] (b. 858), a Persian ascetic and wandering preacher, was hanged and gibbeted in Baghdad as a heretic and blasphemer. Al-Hallaj preached constant suffering as the method of immersing the self in God, and taught that, once achieving ecstatic intimacy and union with divine truth, the ascetic became above religious law. Al-Hallaj's followers fled to Khorasan [Khurasan], an Abbaside province of Persia.

930 Jan. 12   Abu Tahir, a Karmathian general, startled the Muslim world by capturing Mecca and carrying off to Bahrain the sacred **Black Stone**. It was not returned for 30 years.

935   Ali al-Ashari [Abu-al-Hasan 'Ali al-Ashari] (b. 873), who reestablished as normative for Islam the orthodox **Sunnite creed**, died. The creed included four major doctrines: Allah is unique; Muhammad is Allah's messenger; the Koran is the eternal, infallible word of Allah; and there will be a resurrection and final judgment.

942   Saadia ben Joseph al-Fayouni (b. 882), known as Saadia Gaon, that is, head of the Jewish academy at Sura, Babylonia, died. His basic contribution was to provide religion with a rational foundation. Saadia had translated nearly all **Hebrew Scriptures** into Arabic and written extensively on Talmudic and philosophical subjects.

VI. SCIENCE, EDUCATION, AND TECHNOLOGY

901   **Thabit ibn-Qurrah** [Tobit ben Korra] (b. 836), an Arab astronomer, mathematician, and translator, died. Thabit had organized a school of translators around an observatory built (c.830) in Baghdad by al-Mamun, the Abbaside caliph. **Euclid's** *Elements*, Ptolemy's *Almagest*, and many other Greek works of science were made available to Arabic scholars.

VII. ARTS AND LEISURE

c.900   **Polyphony** began to replace the Gregorian chant in churches. **Organum**, the simultaneous singing of two melodies, usually a fifth or an octave apart, was an early form of polyphony.

c.900   The **Mixtec culture** began to flourish west of the Oaxaca valley of southern Mexico. Artifacts suggested the possible influence of the earlier Olmec culture of Mexico's central plateau. Their codices, written in hieroglyphics, are the largest such collection extant from the Americas.

c.918   Two centers of **ceramic production, Kangjin** and **Puan,** flourished in the **Kingdom of Koryu** (935–1392) in present Korea. Korean potters began to produce (from c.1250) their own distinctive **Mishima technique** of inlaid decoration.

c.940   The *Waltharius*, a Germanic saga, was probably composed as a Latin exercise by **Ekkehart I** [Ekkehard], the Elder (c.900–973), a monk of St. Gall, a Benedictine monastery near Lake Constance in present Switzerland. The saga told of the great migration of peoples; one of its characters was Attila the Hun.

945   **Rudagi** [Rudaki] (born c.870), an early Persian poet, died. Only fragments of Rudagi's work are extant, but it is clear he was a master of many poetic forms, from the epic to lyric.

950–999

I. POLITICS AND WAR

955 Aug. 10   **Otto I the Great,** king of Germany, defeated the **Magyars** [Hungarians] on the Lechfeld River near Augsburg, Bavaria, finally freeing western Europe from devastating Magyar raids.

960   **Kao Tsu** [T'ai-Tsu, Chao Kuang-Yin] (d. 976) founded the **Northern Sung Dynasty** (960–1127) in China, and ruled from the capital at Kaifeng. Kao had been a general for the later **Chou** [Chow] **Dynasty** (951–960); he usurped the throne and, by the time of his death, had reunited most of China. The Sung era was known for assistance to the needy, loans to farmers, a progressive income tax, and the use of a budget.

961   **Nicephorus II Phocas** (912?–Dec. 11, 969), a Byzantine general, began a remarkable series of victories by reconquering Crete from the Saracen pirates. Co-emperor (963–969) with the infant **Basil II**

(958–December 15, 1025; ruled from 976) after the death of Romanus II (938?–Mar. 15, 963; ruled from 959), he retook Cyprus and Cilicia from the Arabs (965), and reoccupied northern Syria by the conquest (969) of Aleppo and Antioch.

c.962   **Svyatoslav** [Sviatoslav] became grand prince of **Kievan Russia** (c.880–1240) when his mother Olga (d. 969), the regent, allowed him to rule. During his ten years on the throne, he led armies to fight against the **Khazars** (965), the **Volga Bulgars** on the Kama River (966), the Bulgarians on the Danube River (971), and the Pechenegs. The **Khazar Empire** (c.750–965) had shrunk to a trading state around the northern coast of the Black Sea. Svyatozlav destroyed (965) the Khazar army, and the Khazar Empire collapsed.

962   **Otto I the Great,** king of Germany, was crowned emperor in Rome by the pope. Otto extended his power by deposing (963) the Roman

prince-pope John XII (d. May 14, 964; ruled from 955).

969   The **Fatimid** [Fatimite] **Caliphate** (909–1171) centered in the area of present Tunisia, led by Moizz [al Muizz] (ruled 953–975), the fourth caliph, invaded Egypt, and the Fatimid general Jawhar al-Sigilli (d. 991 or 992) captured al Fustat [Old Cairo], capital of the **Ikhshidid Dynasty** (935–969). Moizz founded al-Quahira [New Cairo], and Egypt once again became a center of Islamic culture. Moizz's **Mosque of Al-Azhar**, completed June 22, 972, became and remains today a famous university.

c.970   The **Seljuk Turks**, a nomadic tribe from the steppes of central Asia, began to move from the Syr Darya River Valley east of the Aral Sea, into eastern Persia, where they became Sunnite Muslims and were used by the Buwayhid masters of the Abbaside caliphs as mercenaries.

973 May 11   **Edgar the Peaceful** (944?–July 8, 975; ruled from Oct. 959), a Saxon king, was officially crowned king of England by **Dunstan** (c.925–988), **archbishop of Canterbury** (from 961).

976 Jan. 10   **John I Zimisces** [Tsimisces], the Byzantine emperor (from 969), died and was succeeded by **Basil II Bulgaroctonus** [Bulgar Slayer] (958?–1025). Basil's succession had been delayed during his minority by the acting regents, the generals Nicephorus II Phocas and John. Basil continued the Byzantine warfare against the Bulgars.

977   The Muslim **Ghaznivids** [Ghaznavides, Chaznavids], Turkic-speaking people with their capital at Ghazni, in present Afghanistan, established the **Ghaznavid Dynasty** (to c.1175). The dynasty was founded by **Subuktigin** [Sabuktagin], a Turkish slave who gained control of Ghazni.

980   The **Danes** recommended raiding the English coasts in search of spoils. At first the raids were infrequent, but by 991 **Ethelred II the Unready**, king of England, facing a large invasion, bought peace by paying tribute. He enacted a regular tax, called the **Danegeld**, to raise money for future tribute.

982   **Eric** [Eirik] **the Red** sailed from Iceland to Greenland, and explored the southwestern coasts (982–985). He returned (986) there from Iceland with settlers; there were probably 10,000 Scandinavians living there (c.1200) along the coasts.

985   The **Karmathians** were defeated in the area that is present Iraq, and before the end of the century their strongholds in Arabia fell to local sheiks. After 1050 there was no mention of them in writings of the time.

c.987   The **Itza**, a Mayan tribe, probably reoccupied the city of Chichén Itzá, in the Yucatán Peninsula. They arrived there possibly by invitation of the **Toltecs**. The Toltec mythical leader, **Kulkulcán** [Kukulcán], a personification of their god **Quetzalcoatl**, was credited with having led his people earlier into the Mayan city.

987 July 3   **Hugh Capet** (941–Oct. 24, 996), duke of Francia, a *comté* that included Paris, was elected king of France by the West Frankish lords and crowned at Noyon to succeed **Louis V the Sluggard** (967?–May 21, 987; ruled from 986), the **last ruler of the Carolingian Dynasty** (from 751). The Capetian Dynasty ruled to 1328.

989 June 1   The **Peace of God** was initiated at the **Council of Charroux**, supported by Hugh Capet, king of France. The Church, using the threat of excommunication, began its attempt to reduce feudal warfare and protect noncombatants by limiting private wars to certain periods of the year.

c.990   The **Kingdom of Ghana** (fl. first century A.D.–c.1076), now at the height of its power, defeated the Saharan Berber tribes of the Lemtuna. It captured their capital, Audaghost, in present Mauritania, which had been challenging Ghana's trade monopoly.

II. ECONOMY AND TRADE

979   Teutonic **guilds** were established in London by German merchants.

III. RELIGION AND PHILOSOPHY

c.950   In Japan **Buddhism** as taught by the **Mayahana school of Amidism** [Amida = Buddha], began to spread. Amidists believed in a Pure Land presided over by Buddha, who strove to bring all beings into this paradise.

955   The **first Russian ruler to convert to Christianity** was **Olga** (c.890–969), wife of Igor (c.877–945; ruled from 912). After his death she ruled Kievan Russia until her son Sryatoslav (d. 972) came of age.

Her conversion improved the relations of **Kiev** with **Constantinople**. It did not lead to widespread growth of Christianity in Russia: even her son refused to accept the new religion. **Svyatoslav** proved to be the last non-Christian Russian ruler for many centuries.

961   Dunstan, abbot of Glastonbury, became **archbishop of Canterbury**, and was chosen by **Edgar the Peaceful** as his chief adviser. Dunstan promoted the revival of ascetic ideals and reestablished monastic discipline throughout England. Edgar rebuilt monasteries destroyed by the Danish Vikings in East Anglia and granted the Church feudal jurisdictional powers.

967   Mieszko I [Mieczyslaw], prince of **Poland** (963–992), accepted Christianity for himself and his people. He also acknowledged himself a vassal of Otto I, the Holy Roman emperor. Mieszko had married (965) a Catholic Czech princess, who may also have influenced his conversion.

976   Hakam II [al-Hakam, al-Hakim] (b. 913?), the scholarly caliph of the **Ommiad Caliphate of Spain** (929–1031), died. Hakam had enjoyed a relatively peaceful reign (961–976).

988   Vladimir I, grand prince of all **Russia** (from 980), received baptism in the Orthodox Church. He turned from riotous living to good works for the rest of his reign, establishing Christianity on a firmly organized basis with a patriarch in Kiev, and bringing about public recognition of the Orthodox faith.

992   Boleslav I [Boleslaw] **the Mighty** (d. 1025), on succeeding his father Mieszko as prince of **Poland**, set about reorganizing and strengthening the young Roman Catholic Church in his country. Boleslav gave the Church new missionary opportunities in Prussia and the territories of the expanding principality of Poland.

994   Odilo (962–Jan. 1, 1049), the **fifth abbot of Cluny**, began his long control (to 1048) of the increasingly vast organization of monasteries and priories dependent on the mother house at Cluny and responsible to him.

995   Olaf I [Olaf Tryggvesson] (969–1000), a marauding Norwegian who had been converted to Christianity by a hermit in the Scilly Islands and confirmed later by the bishop of Winchester, England, returned to **Norway** to be acclaimed king (to 1000). He immediately began the conversion of Norway, by persuasion, negotiation, and sometimes force. Olaf imported priests from England to advance the missionary work.

996   Otto III (980–Jan. 27, 1002), the Holy Roman emperor (from 996), obtained the papacy for his cousin **Gregory V** [Bruno of Carinthia] (d. Feb. 4, 999), the **first German pope**. On May 3, 996, Gregory in return crowned Otto emperor. When Gregory died, Otto gave the papacy to **Sylvester II** [Gerbert] (d. May 12, 1003; ruled from 999), the **first French pope**.

998   Strongest of the Turkish sultans of Persia was **Mahmud** [Mohammed] of Ghanzi (ruled to 1030). The **Ghaznavid**, as well as the succeeding **Ghorite** and **Seljuk** sultans, found the **Sunni** version of Islam congenial, and strongly opposed the **Shiite** sect. They suppressed the remaining remnant of the **Zoroastrians**, which led several thousand of them to migrate to Gujarat, in northwest India. Ultimately these immigrants clustered in Bombay, where they became known as Parsees, or "Persians."

998   Stephen I (977–1038), the Árpád overlord of Hungary, routed rebel pagan princes at Veszprém, in present Hungary, and concentrated during the remainder of his rule on the consolidation. Stephen was canonized in 1083.

IV. ARTS AND LEISURE

c.950   Al-Farabi (c.870–950) wrote *Kitab al-musiqi al-Kabir* [The Grand Book of Music], the most important treatise on the theory of **Arabic music**. Al-Farabi, who lived in Aleppo [Haleb], northwestern Syria, attempted to introduce the Greek musical system into his country, and was the first writer to mention an instrument that was bowed, the rabab.

955   Al-Mutanabbi (b. 915), the most highly regarded of all Arabic poets, was killed by Bedouins. Court poet to the **Hamdanids** [Hamdanites] (945–1004), the ruling dynasty at Aleppo [Haleb] in Syria, al-Mutanabbi was close to both the Bedouin and the town Arabs, and his poetry was influenced by the attitudes and beliefs of both.

c.960   The **Northern Sung Dynasty** in China encouraged the development of the arts. The **pottery** produced was nearly as fine as the Ming porcelain that appeared later. Painting, sculpture, and literature also flourished.

c.960   The **practice of binding the feet of young girls** spread throughout the middle classes in China during the **Northern Sung Dynasty**. It had been inflicted on aristocratic girls at court during the late **T'ang Dynasty** (618–907). The "lily foot" ["golden lotus," "golden lily"; *chin-lien*] that resulted from restricting normal foot growth for years was considered elegant and sexually appealing.

969–1171   Under the **Fatamid Caliphate** (909–1171), **Fustat pottery** was produced at al-Fustat [Old Cairo], Egypt. After the fall of the Fatamids, many of the Fustat potters went to Persia, where they helped make the pottery of that country famous.

c.969   The **earliest known playing cards** were printed in China. They were used for recreation and probably for gambling.

970–990   The *Kagero-nikki* [*Gossamer Diary*], written in these years by a Japanese woman, the wife of the chief minister, was a revealing document about the mind and feelings of the medieval Japanese.

980   The largest **organ** of its time, with 400 pipes, was built in **Winchester Monastery**, England. It required two people to operate its slides and 26 bellows. The slides were pulled to allow air to enter the pipes, as do the keys of present organs.

981   The second Benedictine abbey of Cluny, France, called **Cluny II**, which replaced the first church Cluny I (begun 910), was dedicated.

c.990   The *Anglo-Saxon Chronicle* (c.891), was expanded into a more complete history of the people of England. The resulting work, eventually extended to cover the years to 1154, was a major source for the history of the Britons and English from the beginning of the Christian era.

1000–1049

I. VITAL STATISTICS AND DEMOGRAPHICS

1000   **World population** reached 265 million. **Europe's** population was c.36 million, **Asia's** c.185 million, **Africa's** c.33 million, the **Americas'** c.9 million. **China's** population was c.60 million.

1000   **Population** of present Morocco, Libya, and Egypt, invigorated by Islamic culture brought by the Arab conquest in the seventh century, rose above 9 million.

II. EXPLORATION AND COLONIZATION

1001   **Leif Ericson** [Ericsson, Eriksen], known as Leif the Lucky, the son of Eric the Red, who had discovered Greenland, sailed in search of **Vinland** [Wineland *or* Vineland]. According to the sagas, new lands to the west of Greenland had been accidentally sighted by **Bjarni Herjolfsson**, who had been blown off his course (c.985) southwest of Greenland. Leif and his crew landed on Baffin Island; Labrador, which they called Markland; and

Belle Isle. They wintered at Vinland, now thought to be Anse aux Meadows, Newfoundland. Later, Norsemen settled here as colonizers; but Indians and internal dissension drove away (c.1013) the survivors.

1007   **Snorro**, the **first white child in America**, was born in Vinland to Thorfinn and Gudrid Karlsefni, Norse colonizers who returned to Greenland three years later. Eventually they settled and prospered in Iceland, and Snorro's descendents were said to have included three bishops.

III. POLITICS AND WAR

c.1000   **Stephen I** (977–1038; ruled from 997) of the **Árpád Dynasty** (896–1301) was sent a crown and given the title the Apostolic King by **Pope Sylvester II** and so became the first crowned monarch of the dynasty.

1001   **Mahmud** (971–1030), the Turkish sultan (from 998), of the **kingdom of Ghasni**, added to his empire present Pakistan and the Punjab region of India.

1002 The **Norman and the West Saxon dynasties were united** by the **marriage of Emma** [Elfgifu] (d. 1052), sister of Richard II the Good (d. 1027), duke of Normandy, to Ethelred II the Unready, king of England. The English, suffering from Danish raids for 20 years, hoped to gain an ally in the Normans.

1002 Nov. 3 On St. Brice Day, **Ethelred II**, king of England, ordered a massacre of the Danes who had invaded England. The Danes, under **Sweyn I** [Svein], Forkedbeard, Viking king of Denmark, embarked on a series of retaliatory raids until Sweyn was acknowledged king of England in 1013, and Ethelred fled to Normandy.

1014 **Basil II**, the Byzantine emperor, defeated the **Bulgarians** at Cimbalugu near Ochrida [Ohrid], the Bulgar capital, and had the remnant army of nearly 24,000 men blinded. Basil II earned his honorific "Bulgaractonus" [Bulgar Slayer] from this action. The Khagan [Khan] of the Bulgars reportedly fainted and died two days after hearing the news. The crushed **First Bulgarian Empire** (from 681) was annexed by the Byzantine Empire in 1018.

1014 Feb. 3 **Sweyn I** Forkedbeard (born c.960), the Viking king of Denmark and part of Norway (ruled from 987), died suddenly at Gainsborough, England, before his coronation as king of England. **Ethelred II** the Unready was restored as king of England, only to face renewed Danish attacks led by Sweyn's son, **Canute II the Great.**

1014 Apr. 23 **Brian Boru** [Brian Boramha, Boraimhe, Boroimhe, Borumha] of Munster (b. 926), high king of Ireland (from 1002), defeated the **Danes** in a **battle at Clontarf**, near Dublin, although he died in the effort. A period of anarchy followed Brian's death.

1016 Apr. 23 **Ethelred II** the Unready (b. 968?), king of England, died, and his son **Edmund II** Ironside was chosen in **London** to succeed him. The **Witan**, the advisory council to the king, elected the Danish king, **Canute II** [Cnut] the Great, as king of England. The defeat of Edmund (b. 993) at Ashington in Northumberland on Oct. 18 and his death at Oxford on Nov. 30 freed Canute from further opposition to his rule over all of England.

1017 July The **Norman Viking Dynasty** was united with the **Scandinavian Viking Dynasty** by the **marriage of Emma** [Elfgifu] (d. 1052), widow of King Ethelred II of England and sister of Richard II, duke of Normandy, to **Canute II**, king of England.

1025 The **Srivajyia Kingdom** (100–1250), once the most powerful state in the region of present **Indonesia**, was invaded by forces of the **Chola Kingdom** of southern India, which sacked its capital at Palembang in Sumatra. Trade was so disrupted that Srivajyia never fully recovered.

1025 June 17 **Boleslav I** the Mighty, son of Mieszko I, was crowned the **first king of Poland** at Gniezno. Boleslav died in the same year and was succeeded by **Mieszko II** Lambert (990–1034).

1027 **Canute II**, king of England (from 1016) and Denmark since the death of his brother Harold in 1018, extended his control over Scotland. Then Canute conquered (1028) Norway with the aid of Norwegian chieftains, who rebelled against the enforced Christianity under Olaf II, king of Norway.

1030 July 29 **Olaf II** [Olaf Haraldsson] (b. 995?), king of Norway, was killed in a **battle at Sticklestad.**

1031 The **Ommiad Caliphate** of Spain (from 929) finally dissolved after nearly 30 years of anarchy, conspiracies, and dethronements of incompetents. A score of small Muslim states arose on the Iberian Peninsula, of which **Sevilla** [Seville] became the most important. **Ferdinand I** the Great (c.1016–Dec. 27, 1065) became king of Castile (from 1033), and acquired (1037) the Christian **Kingdom of León** by defeating and killing his brother-in-law, Bermudo III (b. 1016).

1035 Nov. 12 **Canute II the Great** (born c.995), king of England (from 1016), of Denmark (from 1018), and of Norway (from 1028), died. Canute became ruler of all of England by conquest (1016–1018). He was succeeded by his illegitimate son **Harold I** Harefoot (1017?–Mar. 17, 1040), then by Harold's brother Hardecanute.

1040 **Abdallah** ['Abdallah ibn Yasin] (d. 1058), a leader of **Saharan Berbers**, initiated a holy war in Morocco. His successor, **Yusuf ibn Tashfin** (d. 1106), united the Moroccan territories and, with the conquest of Algeria, founded the **Almoravid Dynasty** (1056–1147), with Marrakech as its capital.

1040 Aug. 16 **Duncan I** [Canmore], king of Scotland (from 1034), was murdered by **Macbeth** [Maelbaethe], who usurped the throne and ruled until 1057 when he was killed by Duncan's son, Malcolm. Malcolm was crowned the following year as **Malcolm III MacDuncan** [Canmore] (ruled 1058–1093).

1042 June 8 Hardecanute [Harthacnut] (born 1018?), king of Denmark (from 1035) and of England (from 1040), died suddenly. Hardecanute, the son of Emma and Canute II the Great, was succeeded (1043) by **Edward** [Eadward] **the Confessor**, son of Emma and her first husband, Ethelred II the Unready.

1047 Oct. 25 Magnus I the Good (b. 1024), king of Norway (from 1035) and Denmark (from 1042), died. This halted the planned invasion of England to restore the Danish Dynasty to the English throne.

IV. ECONOMY AND TRADE

c.1000 Venice became the textile center of Europe, thanks largely to her position as a major hub of Asian-European trade.

1020 The **first known merchant guild** in Europe was formed by traders of Tiel in Gelderland [Gelre], now a province of the Netherlands. Local merchant guilds flourished over the next two centuries, controlling much of the economic life of the cities by preventing competition by tradesmen of other cities.

1024 Inflation occurred during the latter days of the **Northern Sung Dynasty** (960–1127) in China, when too much paper currency was printed by the national government.

V. RELIGION AND PHILOSOPHY

c.1000 The **Jews of Europe** flourished during most of the 11th century. Talmudic academies opened in Germany, notably at Worms and Mainz [French: Mayance], and at Troyes, at this time an important commercial center of northeastern France. Early in this century, there came into use the terms "**Sephardim,**" to designate Jews of Spain and Portugal, and "**Ashkenazim,**" to designate Jews of northern or transalpine Europe.

c.1000 Collections of the poems and hymns of the greatest of the Shaivite singer-teachers, known as **Adiyars,** or "ode singers," appeared in India.

c.1000 Buddhists in northwestern India, influenced now by Islamic notions of the origin of the universe,

developed the concept of a primordial and omnipotent Buddha, known as **Adi-Buddha**. It did not persist, except among sects in the Himalaya mountains.

c.1000 Two schools of **Buddhism** in China had now become preeminent: the meditational **Ch'an [Zen] sect** and **Amidism,** or the "**Buddhism of Faith.**" Amidism, later to become the most important in China and Japan, offered the easier path to salvation.

1000 The **Ålthing,** Iceland's consultative assembly, proclaimed that all men should be baptized as Christians.

1008 Olaf Sköttkonung (?–?1022), king of Sweden (from 994), was baptized. Under his strong rule Christianity was established, though heathenism persisted for another century.

1009 Simeon [Symeon] (d. 1022), called the New Theologian, was exiled from the monastery of St. Mamas, where he was abbot, by the patriarch of Constantinople. Simeon had built up the monastery along lines of strict discipline, and produced numerous mystical writings that were of lasting influence in the Greek Church.

1010 The roof and much of the walls of the **Church of the Holy Sepulcher** in **Jerusalem** were destroyed by **al-Hakim,** the Fatimid known as the Mad Caliph because of his fanatical rages. Al-Hakim also terminated the Frankish protectorate in Palestine. This was one of many actions that led to the **Crusades.**

1010 Dia Kossoi, ruler of the West African **Songhai Kingdom,** was converted with his court to Islam at Gao, in present Mali. The act brought political unity to his kingdom and intensified Gao's trading and cultural contacts with Muslim North Africa, leading to the establishment of the Songhai Empire (c.1050–1591).

1016 Chen Tsung, the Northern Sung emperor (997–1022) of China, recognized the claim of Chang Cheng-Sui to be the direct descendant of Chang Tao-Ling [Chang Ling], who had founded (c.150) the **Taoist sect of Right Unity**. He gave Chang the title Celestial Master and established him as the titular head of the Taoist faith.

c.1017–c.1150 These are the traditional dates of **Ramanuja,** the Tamil Brahmin who opposed Shankaracharya's [Shankara] (fl. 788–820) monistic interpretation of the *Upanishads*, the holy scriptures of Hinduism. Ramanuja founded a school near Srirangam, in Tamil Nadu, India, where he taught a modified non-dualism. In popular terms, Ramanuja, a Vaishnivite, opposed Shankara's "way of knowledge" with a "way of devotion."

1019 The Taoist religious canon *Tao Tsang*, a collection spanning over a millennium, was catalogued and published. The two chief branches of Taoism were now established. One followed an eremitic and monastic path. The other, based on beliefs and practices, appealed to the masses, who worshiped in hereditary temples served by married priests who performed ceremonies and sold charms.

1021 Feb. 23 **Al-Hakim** [abu-'Ali Mansur al-Hakim] (b. 985), the sixth Fatimid caliph (ruled from 996), was assassinated. The Mad Caliph believed he had direct intercourse with the deity and had publicly claimed (1016) divine honors. The Muslim Shiite sect called the Druses [Druzes] took its name from **al-Darazi** [Muhammad ibn-Isma'il al-Darazi], a Persian mystic who gave substance to Hakim's creed. Al-Darazi and Aamza al-Zuzani, Hakim's vizier, attracted adherents by preaching Hakim's ultimate return as the reincarnation of the deity.

1037 **Avicenna** [ibn-Sina; *in full:* abu-'Ali al-Husayn ibn-Sina] (b. 980), an Arab scholar of immense capabilities, died. Having studied all the philosophic and religious systems within the known world at the time, he had attempted a comprehensive system of his own, the first in Islam. His view of God and man was rational. When he was declared an atheist, his books were burned.

1037 The patriarch of the Orthodox Church in Constantinople named **Theopemptus** as the first metropolitan to head the Russian Orthodox Church, in Kiev. The **Russian church** thus gained semiautonomy. In honor of the event, the grand prince of Kiev, Yaroslav the Wise (ruled 1019–1054), son of Vladimir I, began the construction of the cathedral of St. Sophia, modeled after churches in Constantinople.

1049 **Henry III the Black** (Oct. 29, 1017–Oct. 5, 1056), the Holy Roman emperor (from 1046), placed in the papacy his cousin Bruno, bishop of Toul, who took the name **Leo IX** (d. Apr. 19, 1054). Leo, a member of the Church's reform party, began the slow process of freeing the papacy from imperial control and bishops from local secular investiture.

VI. SCIENCE, EDUCATION, AND TECHNOLOGY

c.1000–1500 **Copper** was smelted from ores on an industrial scale in northern **Peru** at this time.

c.1000 The **production of gold-leafed thread** was begun in Cyprus. It gained great popularity in the weaving of luxurious brocade and damask.

c.1045 **Movable type**, using clay type pieces, was developed in China.

VII. ARTS AND LEISURE

c.1000–1500 The **Chibcha culture** of central and southern Colombia flourished. The Chibchas' ornate gold ornaments were the probable source of the legend of the **Gold Man** [El Dorado], the magnet that drew adventurers and explorers to South America.

c.1000 **Goldfish** were commonly bred in China under the **Northern Sung Dynasty**. They were kept primarily for decoration, and several varieties were already known.

c.1000 The *Edda*, a collection of 34 epic poems in the Old Icelandic language recounting the legends of Norse gods and heroes, was probaby first written down. The poems originated in heroic ballads sung as early as the fourth century.

c.1000 Bone **ice skates** were used in Sweden prior to this time, perhaps as early as 800.

c.1000 The manuscript printing of the *Gospel Book of Otto III* was produced in honor of Otto III (980–Jan. 27, 1002), the Holy Roman emperor (from 996).

c.1000 **Roswitha** [Hrosvitha] (born c.935), a German Benedictine nun, poet, and dramatist, died. She wrote six short prose comedies modeled after the satires of Terence but designed as Christian substitutes. Although they were about the lives of saints, they were noteworthy for their touches of comedy.

c.1000 The **Lingaraja Temple** was built. It is today one of the finest of the 7,000 Hindu shrines claimed by tradition to have been erected in the Orissa state on the eastern coast of India. The **Shiva** [Saiva] **Temple** was also built about this time in the Orissa capital at Bhubaneshwar [Bhuvaneshwar].

c.1001 The *Tale of Genji* [Genji Monogatari] was begun by Lady **Murasaki no-Shikibu** (978?–?1031). This 54-volume tale of a Japanese prince was perhaps the **first novel to be written by a woman**, and it is now considered a masterpiece of Japanese literature.

1008 **Al-Hamadhani** (b. 968), a Muslim poet whose Arabic name Badi' al-Zaman means "Wonder of the Age," died. He originated the *maqamat* [discourses], anecdotal sketches designed to amuse and instruct, which became popular in Arabic literature.

1010 The *Shah-Nameh* [Shahname, Shahnamah, Book of Kings] was written by **Abul Qasim** [Kasim] **Mansur** (c.940–1020), whose pen name **Firdausi** [Ferdowsi, Firdousi, Firdusi] meant "garden." A priceless source of Persian language and history, it contained 60,000 couplets.

c.1020 The **earliest forms of Romanesque architecture** began to appear in France. The Romanesque style came (c.1100) to its height when the Crusaders were influenced by the designs of Muslim mosques. The monumental strength of Romanesque form rested on the Roman arch.

1020 The Benedictine **Abbey of Bury-St.-Edmunds**, Suffolk, England, was founded by Canute II, king of Denmark and England, at the shrine of **St. Edmund the Martyr** (died c.870), king of East Anglia.

c.1023 **Ibn-Hazm** ['Ali ibn-Ahmad ibn-Hazm] (994–1064), an Arab writer and theologian, completed *Tawq al-Hamama* [The Ring of the Dove], an anthology of love poems.

c.1030 The *Ar'junawiwaha*, one of the earliest extant examples of Javanese poetry, was composed. It is a metrical tale of Arjuna, the disciple of Krishna, his loves and adventures, and of Krishna, the great Hindu God from the Mahabharata.

1050–1099

I. EXPLORATION AND COLONIZATION

1052 The Beni [Banu] Hilal, Beni Sulaim, and Beni Maquil, all **Karmathian Arabian tribes**, invaded and ravaged Tunisia. The invading Arab Bedouins took over much of the cultivated land for pasture and eventually pushed the **Berbers** into the mountains.

II. POLITICS AND WAR

1051 Spring **Edward the Confessor**, childless king of England, designated **William II** [William the Conqueror], duke of Normandy, as his heir, after having repudiated his wife, Edith [Eadgyth], and exiled her father, Godwin [Godwine] (d. 1053), earl of Wessex. William II was the illegitimate grandson of Richard II. In the following year, Godwin forced Edward to reinstate him and his daughter Edith as heirs to the throne.

1054 **Yaroslav** (born c.980), grand prince of Kiev and ruler (from 1019) of Kievan Russia, died, and the decline of his empire set in. Yaroslav's testament divided the state among his sons, which gave increased prominence to such principalities as Novgorod and Smolensk.

1055 **Seljuk Turks** under Togrul [Toghril, Tughril] Beg (1038–1063), grandson of the tribal leader Seljuk, ousted the Persian **Buwayhid Dynasty** (from 945) from Baghdad, where the Abbaside caliph welcomed Togrul. Togrul ruled the **Seljuk Empire** (c.1080–1243) from Baghdad, where the Abbasides considered him a liberator, and his Turkish followers soon became staunch Sunnites.

1057 **Anawratha** [Anawrata], the Burmese king of Pagan (1044–1077), conquered the Mon **Kingdom of Thaton** in lower Burma and Pegu in central Burma. The country was for the first time united under a single authority.

1066 Jan. 5 **Edward the Confessor** (born c.1005), king of England (from 1042), died and was succeeded (Jan. 6) by **Harold II** of Wessex, the last

Anglo-Saxon king of England. Harold, son of Godwin, earl of Wessex, secured his power by defeating his exiled brother, Tostig of Northumbria, and Harold III Hardruler [Hardrader, Haardraade] (b. 1015), king of Norway, at Stamford Bridge, on Sept. 25, killing both in battle.

1066 Oct. 14   Harold II, king of England, was decisively defeated and killed in a **battle at Hastings** by the invading forces of **William II**, duke of Normandy. On Dec. 25, at Westminster Abbey, William, known today as "the Conqueror," was crowned William I, king of England.

1067   Malcolm III MacDuncan (d. 1093), king of Scotland (from 1058), married Margaret (1046–1093), a Saxon princess, who bore him six sons.

1069   Wang An-Shih (1021–1086), a noted Chinese poet and author, was named second privy councilor to Shen Tsung, the Sung emperor (1067–1085). His liberal ideas and goals angered many people, and he was forced to resign in 1076.

1071   The capture of Bari, Byzantine's chief Italian seaport, by the Normans under Robert Guiscard (1015?–1085), duke of Apulia and Calabria, signaled the **end of Byzantine rule in southern Italy**. With the help of his brother Roger I (1031–1101) of Sicily, the duke captured Sicily from the Arabs.

1071   The **Seljuk Turks** under Alp Arslan, son of Togrul Beg, defeated the Byzantines under Romanus IV Diogenes (ruled from 1067), who was captured and then murdered later this year, in a **battle at Manzikert** [Malazkirt], eastern Turkey.

1072   Alp Arslan (b. 1029), sultan of the Seljuk Turks (from 1063), died. He had conquered Georgia and Armenia, and defeated the Byzantine army in a battle at Manzikert [Malazkirt]. He was succeeded by **Malik Shah**, his son.

1076   The **Berber Almoravids**, a reformed Islamic sect, expanded south from their base in the western Sahara and conquered the Sudanese **Kingdom of Ghana** and sacked its capital at Kumbi Saleh, in present Mauritania. The kingdom broke apart as its agriculture was ruined and the trans-Saharan trade was disrupted. Yusuf ibn-Tashfin (d. 1106), the Almoravid emir (from 1061), conquered northern Morocco and western Algeria (1063–1082).

1085   Houme [Umme ibn 'Abdul-Jalil], a sultan (1085–1098) of the **Sefawa** [Saifawa] **Dynasty** (c.800–1846), was the **first sultan of Kanem**, a region of present **Chad**, to take the Islamic faith.

1085   Alfonso VI (c.1042–June 30, 1109), king of León (from 1065) and Castile (from 1072), conquered Toledo from the **Almoravids** and made it his capital.

1086 Oct. 23   In a **battle at Zallaca** in southwestern Spain, Yusef ibn-Tashfin, emir (from 1061) of the **Almoravid Dynasty** (1056–1147) of Morocco (from 1061), responded vigorously to the threat posed by the Christian reconquest of Toledo. Invited to enter Spain by the weak Spanish emirates, he defeated Alphonso VI, king of Castile and León, and established his empire as far north as the Tagus River.

1092   Malik Shah [Jalal-al-Din], sultan of the **Seljuk Turks** (from 1072), died. The Seljuks reached the peak of their power during his reign.

1094   Rodrigo [Ruy] **Díaz de Vivar** (c.1043–July 10, 1099), famous as **el Cid** [Arabic *Sid* = lord] captured the Moorish **kingdom of Valencia** in eastern Spain from the **Almoravids**. The Spanish national hero ruled the kingdom until his death.

III. ECONOMY AND TRADE

1050–1200   The *veche*, a form of popular government, became established in various Russian towns. It was an assembly of merchants, traders, artisans, and other free males who could be convened by either the ruling prince or by citizens.

1060   Leather money was first issued in Europe by Philip I (1052–July 29, 1108; ruled from 1060), king of France.

1082   Alexius I Comnenus (1048–1118), the Byzantine emperor (from 1081), was aided by **Venice** against the Normans led by Robert Guiscard. Alexius gave his allies exclusive trading privileges, which was a decisive step for the Venetian commercial empire.

1086   The *Domesday* [Doomsday] *Book*, a two-volume record of William the Conqueror's survey of England, was the first tenurial and economic assessment of that country. *Domesday* included the names of all landholders, descriptions of their fiefs and manors, with holders named for the time of Edward the Confessor, of William's redistribution of land after the conquest, and of the period 1085–1086. It included the number of agricultural workers, as well as the mills, ponds, and other holdings, and their pound value. Greatly resented by the English populace, *Domesday* was called "the record from which there is no appeal."

1095–1267 The need to raise money for the **Crusades** to the Holy Land provided the feudal kings of Europe with their first opportunity to levy direct **taxes.**

IV. RELIGION AND PHILOSOPHY

1054 July 16 Pope Leo IX, through his legate in Constantinople, excommunicated **Michael Caerularius** (c.1000–Jan. 21, 1059), the patriarch (from 1043) of Constantinople, who had begun a campaign against the Roman church in the previous year. The patriarch closed all Latin churches in his see in defense of the independence of the Greek Church. From this time on, the **Eastern and Western Churches drifted apart.**

1059 Apr. The **Papal Election Decree** was announced by **Pope Nicholas II** (d. Aug. 27, 1061; ruled from 1059), who summoned the ecclesiastics of Rome to a synod at the Lateran Palace. He obtained their approval of a constitution regulating the election of popes under purely canonical rules.

1059 Aug. 23 Pope Nicholas II entered into an alliance with the Normans of southern Italy in the **treaty of Melfi**, recognizing Robert Guiscard as duke of Apulia and Calabria, and of Sicily, and Richard of Aversa (d. 1078) as prince of Capua.

1061 Honorius II (d. 1072) was elected pope (to 1064) by the Lombard bishops at an assembly in Basel. This elevation was in protest against the election earlier in 1061 of Anselm of Lucca as **Alexander II** (d. Apr. 21, 1073). The forces behind the election of Honorius were hostile German and disaffected Lombard prelates, and Roman nobles who had lost control of the **papacy**. The schism, under the antipope Honorius II, lasted three years.

1066 Pope Alexander II, on the advice of the influential Cardinal Archdeacon **Hildebrand** (d. May 25, 1085), sanctioned the **invasion of England** by **William II**, duke of Normandy. This provided Wil-

liam with the appearance of conducting a crusade, enabling him to assemble an army committed to a much longer campaign than the usual 40-day limit under feudal law.

1070 Aug. 29 William the Conquerer installed **Lanfranc** (1005?–May 24, 1089) as archbishop of Canterbury to succeed the deposed Stigand (d. 1072), who was out of favor in Rome. Lanfranc immediately began the reorganization of the English church along French-Roman lines.

1073 Hildebrand, for nearly 40 years the astute adviser of popes, was acclaimed **pope** by the crowd attending the funeral of Alexander II, and was enthroned promptly at the Church of St. Peter in Chains. As **Gregory VII** he pushed the claims of the papacy to their ultimate: a universal sovereignty, founded by God, to which all earthly rulers are responsible.

1075 Pope Gregory VII precipitated the contest over lay investiture with Henry IV, king of Germany and Holy Roman emperor. His prohibitions of married clergy and simony, issued in 1074, having been resisted by kings and ecclesiastics in France and Germany, Gregory issued his *Dictatus Papae*, 27 propositions exalting the primacy of the Roman see by divine right. He supported this policy by suspending several German bishops.

1076 Jan. 24 Twenty-four German bishops and the archbishops of Mainz and Trier [Trèves], summoned to Worms by Henry IV, the Holy Roman emperor, declared **Pope Gregory VII** deposed. The emperor urged the Roman ecclesiastics to choose a successor. Henry was supported by anti-reformatory bishops in Lombard. The **battle** for domination had finally been joined **between Church and State.**

1076 Feb. 22 Pope Gregory VII excommunicated **Henry IV** and released all his vassals from their oaths of allegiance. A month earlier, many of Henry's German bishops had denounced Gregory and rejected his authority. Also, Henry had trafficked in bishoprics and abbeys. Henry replied with a vituperative letter of defiance.

1078 Anselm (c.1033–Apr. 21, 1109) finished his *Proslogion*, containing his ontological argument for the existence of God.

1079 May 8 Stanislas (b. 1030), the bishop of Kracòw [Cracow] (from 1071), was executed by dismemberment on his own altar by **Boleslav II** [Boleslaus, Boleslaw] the Bold (1039?–?1083), king of Poland (1058–1079), who had accused the bishop of treason. Boleslav, as a result, lost all support and fled to Hungary, where he spent the remainder of his life in a monastery as a penitent.

1080 Mar. Pope **Gregory VII**, in an effort to support Rudolf, duke of Swabia (from 1057), as counterking in Germany (from Mar. 13, 1077), excommunicated and deposed **Henry IV** for a second time. Rudolf died on Oct. 16, 1080, in a civil war battle.

1080 June 25 At Brixen in northern Italy, **Henry IV**, king of Germany and the Holy Roman emperor, through a council of 30 imperial bishops, **deposed Gregory VII**. The council then elected as antipope Guibert (c.1025–Sept. 8, 1100), archbishop of Ravenna and long-time supporter of the emperor against the papacy. After Henry captured (Mar. 24, 1084) Rome, Guibert was installed in the Lateran as **Clement III**.

1090 Hasan ibn-al-Sabbah [al-Hasan ibn-al-Sabbah] (d. 1124), founder of the secret order of the Ismailian branch of the Shiite sect known as the **Assassins**, with a few fanatical followers, seized the mountain fortress of Alamut near the Caspian Sea and transformed it into a seat for training recruits. The Assassins eliminated Hassan ibn-Ali Nizam-al-Mulk (1018–1092), vizier to Malik Shah, sultan of the Seljuk Turks, who recognized their threat to stability.

1093 Dec. 4 Anselm, abbot of the Benedictine monastery at Bec, near Rouen, France, was consecrated archbishop of Canterbury. A champion of the reform policies of Hildebrand [later **Pope Gregory VII**], Anselm had refused investiture by William II and Henry I, kings of England. A compromise solution retained for the king only the right to investiture with temporal powers upon reception of an oath of fealty.

1095 Mar. The **First Crusade** arose out of a proposal made by **Pope Urban II** (d. July 29, 1099; ruled from 1088), in a synod held at Piacenza, Italy, for a crusade to aid the Byzantine emperor, who was fighting **Seljuk Turks**. On Nov. 26, at another synod at Clermont, France, Urban brought the First Crusade into being and promised plenary indulgence to all participants.

1095 Nov. 26 Pope Urban II forbade clergy to perform fealty to kings or other laymen. Urban's statement proved unenforceable, but succeeding bishops worked successfully toward a **division of temporal and spiritual powers**.

1096 Apr. Five companies of **pilgrim-crusaders**, composed largely of peasants, began their treks to the Holy Land from France via **Constantinople**. Only the groups led by **Peter the Hermit** (1050?–?1115) and **Walter the Penniless** (d. 1097), known later as the **Peasant's Crusade**, reached the Byzantine capital. In Bulgaria these foraging hordes were nearly destroyed by the inhabitants. Ultimately, the remnants were slaughtered or dispersed by Turkish forces.

1096 Aug. 15 On this date, set by Pope Urban II, three divisions raised by the feudal nobility of France and Norman Italy set out for Constantinople on the **First Crusade**. Godfrey of Bouillon (1061?–1100) and his brother Baldwin (1058?–Apr. 2, 1118) led crusaders of Lorraine, via Hungary; Raymond IV of Toulouse [Raymond de Saint-Gilles] (d. 1105) led Provençals via the Balkans; and Bohemund (1056?–1111), eldest son of Robert Guiscard, duke of Apulia and Calabria, with his nephew Tancred (1078?–1112), led those of southern Italy via sea to Albania and thence overland.

1097 July 1 The **Crusaders**, having captured Nicaea in Anatolia on June 18 after a month's siege, now defeated the **Seljuk Turks** at nearby Dorylaeum [Eskişehir], opening their way to Antioch [Antakya], Syria, in present Turkey. The **siege of Antioch** began in October.

1098 Robert de Molesmes (1029?–1111), a French monk, founded a monastery at **Citeaux**, near Dijon, to practice a self-denying life, rejecting all current softening of the rule of Benedict. The monks lived in austerity and supported themselves by manual agricultural labor. This was the **beginning of the Cistercian order**.

1098 June 3 Antioch [Antakya] fell to the Christian knights of the **First Crusade** under Godfrey of Bouillon and other French and Norman princes. Islamic power in Syria was momentarily in disarray. Three days later Turks under Kerbogha of Mosul [Al-Mawsil], in present Iraq, laid siege to the Crusaders. When a Crusader found the lance said to have pierced the side of Jesus Christ, the Crusaders broke out of the city and routed Kerbogha's forces.

1099   Anselm in his *Cur Deus Homo*? offered a fully developed theory of the atonement of Christ. The work was written near Capua, Italy, where Anselm retreated to seek respite from arguments with William II, king of England.

1099   The Knights of the Order of the Hospital of St. John of Jerusalem [Hospitalers] began to play an enlarged charitable role in the new **Latin Kingdom of Jerusalem** (1099–1187), under its director, Gerard (died c.1120). The order had historical roots in Charlemagne's hospital for pilgrims, served by Benedictines for some decades before the First Crusade.

1099 July 15   The Crusaders captured **Jerusalem**, and later again defeated the Egyptian Fatimids under Afdal ibn Badr on Aug. 12 at Ascaelon [Asc], near Ashquelon, Israel. Godfrey of Bouillon was then named Protector of the Holy Sepulcher, and the **Latin Kingdom of Jerusalem** (to 1187) was established.

VI. SCIENCE, EDUCATION, AND TECHNOLOGY

1054   A **supernova**, which remained visible in the skies for months, was observed from China and Japan, but not noticed by the rest of the world. China and Japan had established organized sky watches that recorded in detail such heavenly events, but there were no observatories in Christian or Muslim nations. According to Chinese and Japanese records, it was visible for 22 months and was about as bright as Venus, which meant the casual observer might not have noticed it.

1066 Apr. 24   The appearance of **Halley's Comet** was considered in Europe to be an omen of the events surrounding the disputed succession to the English throne. It impressed witnesses greatly, and its appearance was pictured in the **Bayeux Tapestry** (c.1090) that recorded William the Conqueror's conquest of England later that year.

1066 Dec.   William the Conqueror began construction of what became the **Tower of London**, on the north bank of the Thames River. In 1078 construction was started on what became its main feature, the White Tower.

1096   Beginning this year, the viscounts of Carcassone built walls and other fortifications **enclosing the medieval city of Carcassone**, on top of a hill on the Aude River in southern France.

VII. ARTS AND LEISURE

c.1050   **Guido d'Arezzo** (born c.997), a Benedictine monk and music teacher and theorist, died. He wrote *Micrologus de Disciplina Artis Musicae* (c.1040), which contained a complete theory of music. He originated the system of hexachords, applying *ut, re, mi, fa, so, la* to the first six notes of the diatonic scale, which may start at any pitch. The syllables were from a hymn in which the first word of each measure formed the scale CDEFGA.

c.1050   The *Konjaku-monogatari*, or *Tales of Long Ago*, was a Japanese collection of over 700 stories about Japan, China, and India traditionally ascribed to **Minamoto no Takakuni** (1004–1077).

1052   The **Hoodo of the Byodoin**, one of the few buildings that remain today in Japan to give a clue to the shinden-zukuri style of residential architecture, was built in Uji, near Kyoto.

1057   **Abu-al-Ala al-Maarri** (b. 973), an influential Arabian poet, died. Born at al-Ma'arratu near Aleppo in northern Syria he was, at the age of four, blinded by smallpox. He memorized his favorite manuscripts in various libraries. His major extant work, *Luzumiyyat* [*Obligations*], is a collection of short poems.

1057   **Jocho** (d. 1057), a Japanese sculptor, died. He was a leading master of the **yosegi method of wood sculpture** in which several wood blocks are joined together. His extant *Amida Buddha of the Western Paradise* (1053) in the *Hoodo of the Byodoin* in Uji, near Kyoto, marked the beginning of the cult of the Buddha, during which many Amida Buddhas were modeled after Jocho's.

1072   **Kuo Hsi**, an important painter of the Northern Sung (960–1127) period in China, produced his finest extant work, a large landscape entitled *Early Spring*.

1078   Construction began on the **cathedral of Santiago de Compestela**, in northern Spain. It was finished in 1211. The cathedral was built over a marble coffin containing remains believed to be those of the Apostle James, brother of Christ.

c.1090 The **Bayeux Tapestry**, telling the story of William the Conqueror's invasion (1066) of England, was embroidered at this time. It was 231 ft. long and 20 in. wide, made of wool threads woven into canvas linen web cloth. It was commissioned by Odo [Eucles] (1036?–1097), the bishop of Bayeux and half brother to William the Conqueror.

1094 The **Cathedral of St. Mark's** in Venice (completed 1071), under the direction of Domenico Contarini (doge 1043–1071), was consecrated. It was built in the Byzantine style and was noted for the rich colors and designs of its interior.

1099 The Romanesque **Cathedral of Modena**, Italy, was begun. It was noted especially for its

paintings and inlaid work and for the reliefs on its facade, depicting bibical scenes, and attributed to Viligelmo da Modena. Still standing next to the cathedral is a magnificent campanile, called La Ghirlandina, which is 289 feet high and built of white marble.

VI. SPORTS, GAMES, AND SOCIETY

c.1075 **Malcolm III Canmore**, king of Scotland, seeking a fleet-footed courier to carry his messages, was said to have arranged a race up Craig Choinnich in the mountains near the royal residence at Braemar, in northeastern Scotland, the winner to earn employment. The Royal Braemar Gathering considers Malcolm's race the inauguration of today's annual spectacle.

1100–1149

I. VITAL STATISTICS AND DEMOGRAPHICS

1100 During the 11th century the **world's population** rose by c.5.5 million. **Europe's** population rose by c.8 million, **Asia's** by c.45 million, with **China** alone accounting for 40 million.

1143 **Lübeck**, a German seaport on the Baltic, was founded by the count of Holstein and soon became the leading trading city of the *Hanse* in the Baltic region.

II. DISASTERS

1104 Iceland's **Hekla volcano erupted**, leveling the Viking village of Pjórsárdalur, settled toward the end of the ninth century. Since then, Hekla, called the "mountain of hell," has erupted more than 20 times.

III. POLITICS AND WAR

1105 Dec. 31 **Henry IV**, the Holy Roman emperor (from 1084), was forced to abdicate as king of Germany by his son **Henry V**, who believed that Henry IV was alienating his subjects and endangering his son's succession. Imprisoned by his son, Henry IV (b. Nov. 11, 1050) escaped, but soon died, on Aug. 7, 1106.

1106 Sept. 28 In a **battle at Tinchebray**, in Normandy, a fraternal war of succession ended. It had begun with the death of William II Rufus (born c.1056), king of England (from 1087), on Aug. 2, 1100. His brother **Henry I Beauclerc**, who seized the crown and crushed opposition in England, defeated his older brother Robert II Curt-hose (c.1054–Feb. 3?, 1134), duke of Normandy. Robert spent the rest of his life in custody in England, and Normandy was reunited with England.

1113 The **Khmer Empire** (c.600–c.1434), centered in present Cambodia [Kampuchea], reached the peak of its power under **Suryavarman II** (ruled 1113–1150). He subjugated Amman, a region of present Vietnam, and took over part of the **Champa Kingdom** (c.270–1492), also in present Vietnam. His territories extended to the borders of China in the north and to the **Srivijaya** [Shrivijaya] **Empire** (c.100–c.1250) in the south.

1120 Nov. 25? **William Athling** (b. 1103), the only son of Henry I, king of England, drowned off Harfleur, France. The succession in England and Normandy was left unsettled; Henry tried to secure it for his daughter, Empress Matilda [Maud] (1102–1167), wife of Henry V, the Holy Roman emperor and, later, wife of Geoffrey Plantagenet (1113–1151) of Anjou (ruled 1129–1149).

1125 The **Juchen tribes** of Manchuria destroyed the **Liao Dynasty** of the Khitans (from 947) and then turned against their former allies, the **Northern Sung Dynasty** (960–1127) of China. They captured (1126) the Sung capital, Kaifeng, and established the **Chin Dynasty** (to 1274) in northeastern China. The Chinese, under the emperor Kao Tsung (ruled 1127–1162), moved their capital to Hangchow to begin the **Southern Sung Dynasty** (1127–1280).

1125 May 23 **Henry V** (b. 1081), king of Germany (from 1106) and the Holy Roman emperor (from 1111), died. Henry's widow, Matilda, returned to England where her father, Henry I, forced the English barons to recognize her as his successor. Frederick II of Hohenstaufen (1090–1147), duke of Swabia (from 1105), was turned down by the Papacy, which supported Lothair III, duke of Saxony (from 1106), who was elected king on Aug. 30, 1125, and crowned emperor on June 4, 1133. It was the beginning of a **great rivalry in the Holy Roman Empire** and, in Italy, between the pro-papal and pro-imperial factions, respectively known as the **Guelphs** [**Welfs**] and **Ghibellines**.

1126 The capital of the **Northern Sung Dynasty**, Kaifeng [Pien-ching] fell to invading Chin tribes. Most of the imperial family was exiled except for one son, Kao Tsung, who was absent when the city was invaded. He withdrew to Hangchow [Hangzhou] and founded what became known as the **Southern Sung Dynasty** (1127–1280).

1127 **Imael-al-Din Zangi** [Sengi, Zengi] (1084–Sept. 14, 1146), founder of the **Zangid Dynasty** (to 1250), was appointed governor of Mosul [Al-Mawsil], in present Iraq, by the Seljuk sultan Mahmud II (ruled 1118–1131) as a reward for his support against rebels. He was given the task of repulsing the Crusaders.

1130 Dec. 25 **Roger II** (1095–Feb. 26, 1154), count of Sicily (from 1112), and duke of Apulia and Calabria (from 1128), was crowned as king of Sicily by the antipope **Anacletus II** (ruled 1130–1138) at **Palermo**. The kingdom was secured in July 1139, when Pope Innocent II (d. Sept. 24, 1143; ruled from 1130), defeated and captured by Roger, was forced to recognize it.

1135 The **republic of Amalfi**, in Italy, was **sacked** by a fleet of rival **Pisans** from northern Italy. A sec-

ond Pisan raid (1137) marked the end of the flourishing southern trade, benefiting Pisa and Genoa.

1135 Dec. 1 **Henry I** (b. 1068), king of England, died in Normandy, bringing an end to the relative stability and peace of his reign. Civil war broke out when **Stephen of Blois**, son of William the Conquerer's daughter Adele and Stephen, Count of Blois, refused to recognize Matilda, Henry's daughter, as the designated heir, and seized the English throne (to 1154) for himself. War ended in 1148, when Matilda retired to Normandy.

1138 Mar. 7 **Conrad III** (1093–Feb. 15, 1152), duke of Swabia, was elected king of Germany at Coblenz, following the death of Lothair III (born c.1070) on Dec. 4, 1137. Although Conrad was never crowned emperor by the pope, his reign marked the beginning of the **Hohenstaufen Dynasty** (1138–1268) of the Holy Roman emperors.

1143 Oct. 4–5 **Alfonso I** [Affonso or Afonso Henriques] (c.1110–1185) was recognized as the **first king of Portugal** by his cousin Alfonso VII (c.1104–Aug. 1157), king of Castile and León at the **Treaty of Zamora**, in present Spain. Alfonso had already claimed the crown (c.1140), and at his death Portugal was a firmly established country.

1147 **Abd-al-Mumin** ['Abd-al-Mu'min ibn-'Ali] (1094–1163), leader of the Berber Muslim **Almohad Dynasty** (1130–1269), defeated the Almoravids at Marrakech after an 11-month siege ending the **Almoravid Dynasty** (from 1056), and conquered Morocco. By 1152 the Almohads had brought Algeria under their control.

c.1147 **Moscow** was first mentioned by Russian chroniclers as a village. Its site had been almost continuously occupied since Neolithic times. Sacked and burned several times by neighboring principalities, Northmen [Swedes], and Mongols, Moscow always recovered because its location on the Moskva River made it a great trade city between the Near East and Scandinavia.

IV. ECONOMY AND TRADE

c.1100 The use of the **collar harness for draft horses** had become fairly widespread in Europe by this time. The collar harness enabled a horse to pull a much greater load because the harness did not constrict the animal's windpipe and jugular vein.

c.1100   The city of Timbuktu [Tombouctou], in present Mali, was founded as a camp for nomads. It soon became a prosperous market for farming and fishing industries on the banks of the Niger River.

1111   The Scottish woolen industry was begun under Henry I, king of England, along the mouth of the Tweed River. Wool had long been a product of agricultural England, and soon the manufacture of woolen cloth became a major industry.

1137   Les Halles, the great food market for all of France, opened in Paris.

1147   Manufacture of silk began in Italy. Though the silk industry may have reached Italy from Sicily earlier, it was not mentioned prior to this time.

V. RELIGION AND PHILOSOPHY

1100 Dec. 25   Baldwin I, brother of Godfrey of Bouillon, who had captured (1098) Edessa [Urfa], in present Turkey, during the First Crusade and declared himself its prince, was elected king of the Latin Kingdom of Jerusalem (1099–1187).

1105 July 13   Rashi [Solomon ben Isaac] (born c.1040), a preeminent French-Jewish scholar of the 11th century, died. He had revived the interest in and influence of Torah and Talmud by his modern translations and commentaries, which are still studied. The last decade of Rashi's life was darkened by the increasing violence of antisemitic Christians inflamed by the rhetoric that surrounded the First Crusade to the Holy Land.

1107   A compromise on the issue of investitures was reached at a synod held at Westminster, England. Henry I, king of England, ended the confrontation of the crown with Anselm, archbishop of Canterbury, by giving up the right of investiture of bishops and abbots with spiritual authority, while retaining the requirement of homage to him in secular affairs.

1112   Bernard of Clairvaux joined the Cistercians at Citeaux. His arrival and the direction of the order by its third abbot (from 1109), the Englishman Stephen Harding (c.1060–1134), marked the beginning of the vast development of Cistercian monasteries and membership. By 1115 there were four affiliated monasteries; by 1168, nearly 300, all under the authority of the abbot of Citeaux. Bernard (b. 1090) founded

(1115) the affiliated Cistercian monastery of Clairvaux, where he remained abbot until his death on Aug. 20, 1153.

1115   Pierre Abélard, a canon of Notre Dame, a theologian, and a popular lecturer in Paris, fell in love with Héloïse (c.1098–1164), and married her secretly. Her uncle, a canon named Fulbert, had entrusted her education to Abélard. Regarding him as a seducer, Fulbert arranged to have Abelard emasculated. As a monk he continued his brilliant teaching and criticism, winning more enemies, including Bernard of Clairvaux. He and Héloïse, who became a nun, continued to love each other from afar and were buried side by side in Paris.

1119   In Jerusalem Hugh de Payens founded a military order, the Knights of the Temple [Templars], for the protection of Christian pilgrims and the Church of the Holy Sepulcher. This lay order took the usual monastic vows. Baldwin II (d. Aug. 31, 1131), king of the Latin Kingdom of Jerusalem (from 1118), granted them quarters near the site of the Temple.

1120 Sept. 3   Raymond du Puy [de Podio] succeeded Gerard as grand master of the Knights of the Order of the Hospital of St. John of Jerusalem. Without diminishing the work of caring for Jerusalem's sick, du Puy transformed the order into a potent military force by enlisting western European laymen, and ultimately, along with the Templars, became the chief military support of the Latin states in the East.

1122   The Concordat of Worms ended for a time the issue of lay investiture of ecclesiastics. The compromise arranged between the Holy Roman emperor Henry V and Pope Calixtus II (d. Dec. 13, 1124; ruled from 1119) lifted Henry's excommunication and granted him the investiture of bishops with the secular authority of office, but without demand of payment by the candidate. The pope retained the conferral of the spiritual title and authority.

c.1130   Pierre de Bruys, a radical critic of the worldly aspects of the Church and its clergy, and founder of a small sect, the Petrobrusians, at Embrun, in France, was burned to death by an incensed mob at Saint-Gilles in southern France. Pierre had denied reverence to the cross, and he repudiated all

Church ceremonies, including the Lord's Supper in any form and infant baptism.

1130 Ibn-Tumart [abu-'Abdullah Muhammad ibn-Tumart] (born c.1078), founder of the Berber Muslim sect of the Almohads, died. He had initiated the new Islamic reform movement, stirring up the Masmuda and Zenata Berber tribes centered in the Atlas Mountains, to purify Islam and supplant the Almoravids. Ibn-Tumart was succeeded by **Abd-al-Mumin**, who unified the local tribes and established the **Almohad Dynasty** (1130–1269).

c.1140 Judah Ha-Levy [*Arab:* Abu'l Hasan; *also:* Judah ben Samuel Halevi] (born c.1086), who had originally trained to be a physician but instead became a philosopher, died. He was famous as a poet for his liturgical hymns, used today in the Sephardic liturgy. As a philosopher, he believed that knowledge and truth were arrived at by intuition and not by Aristotelian logic.

1140 Pressed by Bernard of Clairvaux, the **synod of Sens** condemned **Abélard** for heresy. Abélard had raised questions challenging the Augustinian tradition and had irritated the ecclesiastical and intellectual world for a generation. His appeal to the pope was unavailing. He now made submission, and spent the last two years of his life in a Cluniac monastery. Abélard (b. 1079) died on Apr. 12, 1142.

c.1141 The **Koran** for the first time was translated into a foreign language, Latin, under the sponsorship of Peter the Venerable (1092?–Dec. 25, 1156), abbot of Cluny.

1145 Dec. 25 Louis VII (1120–Sept. 18, 1180), king of France (from 1137), took the crusading vow. In Dec. 1146, Conrad III, king of Germany, was persuaded to join the **Second Crusade** by Bernard of Clairvaux. Lack of unified leadership and intentions brought about a disastrous failure with the collapse of the **siege of Damascus** on July 28, 1148.

1148 The arrival in **Spain** of the **Almohads** initiated a period of persecution of Jews and Christians in the Muslim areas of the Iberian Peninsula. The practice of Judaism was proscribed, backed by forced conversions, slavery, or martyrdom. Many Jews fled to northwestern Europe. A coalition of the Christian states of Spain ended the oppression in 1212.

VI. SCIENCE, EDUCATION, AND TECHNOLOGY

c.1100 The **process of alcohol distillation** was said to have been rediscovered at the Salerno school of medicine at this time. Distillation was known by the Chinese at least as early as 800 B.C. but apparently not distillation of alcohol.

c.1100 The **University of Bologna** (founded c.1088), gained renown for the study of civil and canon law. Frederick I Barbarossa (1122–June 10, 1190), the Holy Roman emperor (from 1155), granted (1158) the university students the right to be judged by their masters.

1111 Al-Ghazzali [al-Ghazali; Abu-Hamid Muhammad al-Ghazzali] (b. 1058), an Arabic philosopher who wedded Greek mathematics and Aristotelian logic with Islamic theology, died. His work influenced **Maimonides** and **Thomas Aquinas**.

1119 This date marked the first mention in Chinese texts of the use of the **compass** in maritime navigation. The Vikings, Polynesians, Arabians, and others used some forms of navigation by stars and constellations for centuries before the compass became available.

1131 Construction began on the **Krak des Chevaliers** [Castle of the Knights] near Kerak [Krak], in present Jordan. It was built by the **Knights Hospitalers**, whose successes had resulted (1099) in the capture of Jerusalem. Krak des Chevaliers had a double line of walls around it, with great towers, underground passages, and a beautiful chapel. Surrounded by steep banks, it was considered impregnable. Nevertheless, Saladin, sultan (1174–1193) of Egypt, Syria, and other areas in the Near East, captured it in 1188.

1148? Anna Comnena (b. 1083), a Byzantine princess, daughter of Alexius I Comnenus, and generally regarded as the **first female historian**, died. She plotted against her brother John II Comnenus (1088–Apr. 8, 1143), the Byzantine emperor (from 1118), in order to secure the throne for her husband Nicephorus Bryennius (1062–1137). When she failed, Anna retired to a convent where she wrote *Alexiad*, an account of her father's reign with much praise for his achievements. It remains today a valuable historical source.

VII. ARTS AND LEISURE

c.1100–c.1300 The **troubadours** were medieval poet-musicians originating in southern France. Their language was the southern dialect, *langue d'oc* [Provençal]. About 250 poems with music survive today. The main genres were the **chansons de geste** [songs of deeds, like *Roland*], **alba** [dawn songs, as when lovers part], and pastoral songs [as a romance]. Famous troubadours were **Bertran de Born** (c.1170–c.1200), **Arnaud Daniel** (c.1180–c.1210), **Peire Vidal** (fl.c.1175–c.1215), **Bernard de Ventadour** (c.1150–c.1195), and **Marcabru** (fl.c.1130–1148).

c.1100 The title of "**Mother of Japanese Drama**" was bestowed upon **Iso-no-Zenji**, whose dances entertained the Fujiwara Court (850–1160).

1101 **Hui Tsung** (1082–1135), emperor (1101–1125) of the **Northern Sung Dynasty** (960–1127) in China, issued an edict declaring that his painters be truthful in color and form. Very soon (1102) the "scholar-gentleman" school of painting arose in China in opposition to the imperial academy style of representational accuracy. The new school centered around the poet-calligrapher, Su Tung-Po [Su Shih] (1036–1101), who held that the feelings and intellect of the artist should be expressed in the artist's work.

c.1110 The **first Russian historical work**, *The Chronicle*, was reportedly written by the **Russian monk Nestor** (c.1056–Oct. 27, 1113) in Kiev.

1113–1150 The **temple of Ankgor Wat** [Wat or Vat-temple], a three-story structure covered with miles of bas-reliefs, was built near Ankgor, the Khmer [Cambodia] capital.

1122 **Al-Hariri** [Abu Muhammad al-Qasim al-Hariri] (b. 1054), an Arab scholar and poet from Basra, in present Iraq, died. His *Maqamat* [discourses] brought this form of anecdotal sketch, originated by Al-Hamadhani, to its peak. The *Maqamat* concerned the adventures of the witty scoundrel Abu Zaid, whose tricks and character appeared in many tales by other authors all over the world.

c.1130 The sculptor **Gislebertus** did much of the sculpture for the **Cathedral of St. Lazare** at Autun, France. His work, particularly the tympanum of the doorway, was typically Romanesque, depicting majestic scenes of Christ and Hell.

1132 **Omar Khayyam** (b. 1050), often called the "tentmaker," a Persian astronomer, mathematician, and poet, died. His astronomical tables, an algebra treatise, and revision of the Muslim calendar (c.1075) were all surpassed in popular history by his *Rubáiyát* [quatrains].

1137 *Historia Regum Britanniae* [*History of the Kings of Britain*] by **Geoffrey of Monmouth** (1100?–1154), contained the first major historical account of **Arthur**, the legendary sixth-century king of the Britons. A Norman French version of Geoffrey's tale was written (c.1154) by Wace (fl. 12th century), an Anglo-Norman poet. Five French verse romances (1165–1181) by Chrétien de Troyes, introduced Lancelot du Lac and the legend of the Holy Grail.

c.1140–1144 The **earliest example of the Gothic style of architecture** (c.1100–1500) was the unified geometric design and structure of the **abbey church of Saint Denis**, near Paris. The original church (751–987) was rebuilt in the Gothic style. Its primary distinctive features were pointed arches of entryways and windows, ribbed vaulting, and flying buttresses.

1145 *Samguk Sagi* [*Historical Records of the Three Kingdoms*] was compiled by **Kim Pusik** (1075–1151), a Korean writer. A related work, *Samguk Yusa* [*Anecdotes of the Three Kingdoms*], written by **Ilyŏn** (d. 1288), contained poems that are the earliest surviving works in the Korean language.

c.1147 *Mystère d'Adam* [Representation of Adam] marked the gradual separation of mystery plays from the formal liturgy. It was one of the **earliest extant plays written in the French vernacular**. During the regular church services, an event from the Bible was often presented to the congregation as a small drama or dialogue, with parts taken by members of the choir. These plays soon were separated from the regular services and performed outside the church. They were called mystery plays when dealing with Biblical persons, miracle plays when dealing with saints.

1150–1199

I. POLITICS AND WAR

1152 Mar. 21   The 15-year marriage of **Louis VII**, king of France, and **Eleanor of Aquitaine** (1122?–Apr. 1, 1204), which had not produced a male heir, was annulled. Two months later, Eleanor married Henry, duke of Normandy and count of Anjou, Maine, and Touraine. Henry, later (1154) king of England, was the son of Geoffrey IV Plantagenet (1113–1151), count of Anjou (1129–1149), and Matilda, daughter of Henry I, king of England.

1154 Oct. 25   Stephen of Blois (born c.1097), king of England (ruled from 1035), died, and was succeeded by **Henry II Plantagenet** (Mar. 5, 1133–July 6, 1189) on Dec. 19. It was the beginning of the powerful Anglo-French Anjou [Angevin] house of the **Plantagenet Dynasty** (1154–1499), which ruled England and about half of France.

1156   Frederick I Barbarossa, the Holy Roman emperor, established Austria as a hereditary duchy under Henry II (1114–Jan. 13, 1177) Jasomirgott of the **Babenberg Dynasty** (976–1246). Henry chose Vienna as capital of his territories.

1157   **Eric IX Jedvardsson** (d. 1160), king of Sweden (from 1150), called "the Saint" for his crusade to convert the Finnish people, defeated the Finns. The Englishman Henry, bishop of Uppsala, Sweden, remained to convert the Finns, but was slain within a year.

1159   **Abd-al-Mumin**, the Almohad caliph, conquered Tunis in order to halt the destruction of Berberdom by the advancing Bedouins. The whole Maghrib [northwestern Africa] and Spain, was thus brought under one government, and the area became a major force in the Islamic and Mediterranean worlds.

1162   **Magnus V Erlingsson** (1156–1184) succeeded to the Norwegian throne. For the first time in **Norway** succession was determined by the rule of primogeniture whereby inheritance goes to the oldest son.

1164 Jan.   The **Constitutions of Clarendon**, a series of papers issued by **Henry II**, king of England, defined the relations between Church and State in England and restricted the role of ecclesiastical courts.

1166   At the **Assize of Clarendon**, in Wiltshire, England, Henry II initiated what later became the **grand jury system** when he reformed the existing legal system by appointing small groups of men in each community to identify under oath those suspected of crimes to royal officers. Itinerant royal judges were given prerogative over local feudal courts in these and other cases.

1169   **Waldemar I** [Valdemar] (1131–1182), king of Denmark (from 1157), with the help of his foster brother, Bishop Absalon (1128–1201), waged war against the pagan **Wends**. The Wends were Slavs who had overrun part of Denmark and menaced shipping. The Danes forcibly Christianized the Wends. With the aid of Henry the Lion (1129–1195), duke of Saxony, the Danes and Germans subdued the Wends of Mecklenburg, in present Germany.

1169   **Andrei Bogolyubsky** (1111?–July, 1174), a Russian prince of Rostov-Suzdal, a region of the upper Volga River, invaded and sacked the city of **Kiev**. Bogolyubsky removed many works of art and religious items from the city.

1171   **Saladin** [Salah-al-Din Yusuf ibn-Ayyub] (1138–1193), vizier of Egypt (from 1169), pushed the **last Fatimid caliph al-Adid** (ruled from 1160), out of office, marking the end of the **Fatimid** [Fatimide] **Dynasty** (from 909). Saladin, a brilliant general, declared himself sultan and established the **Ayyubid Dynasty** (to 1250), named for his father, Ayyub ibn-Shadhi (d. 1173).

1171   **Henry II**, king of England, launched an **invasion of Ireland** to assert his authority over the island. His rule was recognized by most of the Irish kings at the **Synod of Cashel**, in southern Ireland, and **Roderic O'Connor** (1116?–1198), the **last high king of Connaught** (from 1156), acknowledged Henry's suzerainty by the **Treaty of Windsor** (1175).

1174 July 13   **William I the Lion** (1143–Dec.4, 1214), the king of Scotland (from 1165), was defeated and captured during a **siege of Alnwick Castle**, in northern England, by Henry II, king of England. William officially accepted (1175) the suzerainty of the English crown by the **Treaty of Falaise**, in northwestern France.

1176 May 29 Frederick I Barbarossa, the Holy Roman emperor, was decisively defeated at Legnano by the **Lombard League** (founded 1167), in his attempt to reassert his authority over northern Italy.

1180 Sept. 24 Manuel I Comnenus (born c.1121), the Byzantine emperor (from 1143), died. His rule was marked by the attention he gave to West European politics in an effort to restore the Roman Empire (c.250 B.C.–A.D. 395).

1185 The **Taira clan** in Japan was decisively defeated by the **Minamoto clan** in a sea **battle off Dannoura**, now a suburb of Shimonoseki, Honshu. Antoku (b. 1178), the child emperor of Japan (from 1181), was killed in the battle.

1186 Two Bulgarian leaders, Asen (d. 1196) and Peter (d. 1197), led a successful revolt against Byzantine rule. The establishment of the **Asen Dynasty** (1187–1280) marked the beginning of the **Second Bulgarian Empire** (to 1396), which soon regained its supremacy in the Balkans.

1189 Nov. 18 The Norman **kingdom of Sicily** was claimed by Henry VI (1165–Sept. 28, 1197), the Holy Roman emperor (from 1191) at the death of William II the Good (b. 1154) in Palermo. His rival, Tancred of Lecce, king of Sicily (ruled from 1190), died in 1194, and Henry easily conquered the realm.

1192 Mohammed of Ghor, sultan of Ghazni (1173–1206), a principality in Afghanistan, defeated and killed **Prithiraj** [Prithvi Raja], the **last Hindu ruler** (from 1170) **of Dilli** [Delhi] and Ajmer, in a **battle at Tarain** [Tirawari, Tirauri], near Thenesar.

1192 Yoritomo (1147–1199) of the **Minamoto clan**, based at Kamakura, was given the title of **Shogun** [General] by the Japanese emperor. It marked the beginning of the **Kamakura Period** (1192–1333).

1199 Apr. 6 Richard I (b. Sept. 8, 1157), **the Lion-Hearted** [Coeur de Lion], king of England, died from an arrow wound while besieging Châlus, in western France. Richard spent most of his reign on the continent, defending Normandy and Aquitaine from French incursions. Richard was succeeded by his brother John.

II. ECONOMY AND TRADE

c.1150 The **Champagne Fairs**, originating in the Champagne district of France, became so popular during the next 150 years that they ran consecutively from town to town from January to October.

1152 The *grosso*, or groat, was coined in Genoa. This **coin** was the first of the larger coins necessitated by the trade generated by the Crusades.

1159 In England the **practice of scutage** was established. It enabled the vassals of the king to substitute money payments for the aid in arms they owed their sovereign.

1163 The **first** *Hanse*, a local protection association, was formed by a settlement of German traders in Gotland, a large island off the Swedish coast.

III. RELIGION AND PHILOSOPHY

1155 June Arnold of Brescia (born c.1100), an Italian clergyman and political reformer, was hanged and his body burned by the prefect of Rome at the order of Frederick I Barbarossa, the Holy Roman emperor. Arnold had long preached apostolic poverty and clerical abandonment of wealth and temporal power.

1160 Aug. 21/22 Peter Lombard [Latin: Petrus Lombardus] (born c.1095), an Italian theologian, died. He compiled *Sententiarum libra quator* [*Four Books of the Sentences*] (1148–1151). This work, a collection of quotations on doctrinal matters from Church fathers and other authorities, became the official textbook of theological schools.

1166 Al-Jilani ['Abd-al-Qadir al-Jili] (b. 1077), the founder of the **first Sufi order** [al-Qadiri], died. Suleiman the Magnificent, the Turkish sultan of the Ottoman Empire, erected a shrine in al-Jilani's honor just outside Baghdad.

1167 The **Albigenses**, one of the Cathar sects [from *Cathari*, "the Pure"], came into prominence with a council held at St. Felix de Caraman, near Toulouse, France. The movement's criticism of current Church practices and aversion to anything sexually begotten led the movement deep into heresy.

1170 Dec. 29 The **assassination of Thomas à Becket** (b. 1118?), **archbishop of Canterbury** (from 1162), by four knights of **Henry II**, king of England, climaxed the power struggle between Henry and the Church of England. Henry was forced to recognize Church authority and made penance in 1174. Henry had opposed any increase in the powers of the church. Becket fought for increasing ecclesiastical powers.

1176 A wealthy French merchant of Lyon, **Peter** (?) **Waldo** [Valdes, or Valdez] accepted literally the advice that Jesus Christ gave to the rich young man who asked how to gain life eternal. Waldo provided for his family, sold the rest of his property, gave the proceeds to the poor, and lived in apostolic poverty, preaching repentance. Within a year he had gathered a band of followers called the **Poor Men of Lyon**. As the movement spread, they became known as the **Waldensians**. They appealed to the **Third Lateran Council** (Mar. 1179) for permission to carry on their itinerant preaching ministry. **Pope Alexander III** (d. Aug. 30, 1181; ruled from 1159) and the Council, regarding them as ignorant laymen, rejected their request. They persisted nevertheless, spreading their doctrines into Spain and northern Italy.

1184 At a synod held in Verona Pope **Lucius III** (d. Nov. 25, 1185; ruled from 1181) excommunicated the **Waldensians,** not for heresy, but for disobeying a previous rejection of their request for permission to preach. Another group forbidden similar permission, the **Humiliati** of the Milan region, joined the Waldensians in itinerant preaching of the Bible, especially the New Testament.

1187 July 4 **Saladin**, the sultan of Egypt and Syria, defeated an army of **Crusaders** in a **battle at Hittin** near Tiberias, along the Sea of Galilee. Saladin undertook the reduction of the Crusader fortresses. Acre surrendered on Aug. 9, and Jerusalem on Oct. 2, bringing an end to the **Latin Kingdom of Jerusalem** (from 1099). Saladin destroyed all Christian places of worship in Jerusalem. As a result, the **Third Crusade** was initiated.

1187 Oct. 2 Saladin's capture of Jerusalem terminated the activities there of the **Sovereign Military Order of the Hospital of St. John of Jerusalem**, of Rhodes, and of Malta, and the Templars, many of whom were massacred.

1189 May Frederick I Barbarossa of Germany, Philip II Augustus of France (Aug. 21, 1165–July

14, 1223; ruled from 1180), and Richard I the Lion-Hearted of England raised armies to free the Holy Land of infidels. The **Third Crusade** (1189–1192), conducted by secular states for their own purposes, was made ineffective by internal dissensions.

1190 The **Order of Teutonic Knights** was founded at **Acre** in Palestine, where they served a hospital. On Mar. 5, 1198, they became a crusading military order.

1190 A book by a Córdoban Jew, **Maimonides** [Moses ben Maimon] (Mar. 30, 1135–Dec.13, 1204), who had fled to **Cairo** to escape the Almohadic persecution of Jews in Spain, profoundly influenced Judaism, Islam, and Christianity. *The Guide to the Perplexed* mediated between Aristotelian rationality and the reliance on revelation of the great monotheistic faiths. This work made Maimonides the preeminent Jew of his era and became a textbook for Catholic scholastics.

1191 **Richard I the Lion-Hearted**, king of England, conquered the island of **Cyprus** from the Byzantine Empire in the Third Crusade (1189–1192).

1191 **Al-Suhrawardi** [as-Suhrawardi] (born c.1150), a Persian immigrant who had taught a Sufi gnostic doctrine of illumination derived from Neoplatonism, was executed for heresy in Aleppo, Syria, after a trial by orthodox doctors of jurisprudence.

1192 July 12 The **Crusaders**, under Kings Richard I the Lion-Hearted of England and Philip II Augustus of France, retook **Acre** after a long siege. Saladin refused to pay ransom for the release of his captured troops, who were then massacred by the Crusaders.

1192 Sept. 2 A three-year truce was signed between Saladin and the Frankish army of the **Third Crusade**. The Franks kept their coastal possessions from Antioch to Jaffa, and Jerusalem, in Muslim hands, was opened to the Christians.

1197 **Peter II** [Pedro] (1174–Sept. 12, 1213), king of Aragon (from 1196), in Spain, decreed that **heretics** remaining within his kingdom after a stated period would be put to death by burning.

1198 Dec. 10 **Averroës** [abu-al-Walid Muhammad ibn-Ahmad-Rushd; *commonly:* ibn-Rushd] (b.

1126), a Spanish-Arabian philosopher, died. As with al-Kindi and Avicenna, he had difficulties with the Muslim doctrines of predestination and corporeal resurrection, preferring Greek rationalism. His writings played a significant role in bringing Greek and Arab philosophy to the Christian West.

1198 Jan. 8   Innocent III (1161?–July 16, 1216), theologian and canonist, was unanimously elected pope by assembled cardinals on the day Pope Celestine III died (b. 1106; ruled from 1191). During his pontificate (1198–1216), **papal supremacy,** first proclaimed by Pope Gregory VII, became a reality.

1199   Yoritomo (b. 1147), Japan's first shogun of the **Minamoto Dynasty,** died. Under him, the **Buddhist Zen sect** flourished. Zen masters introduced into Japanese life Neo-Confucian principles, **Sung period** art, and the **tea ceremony.**

IV. SCIENCE, EDUCATION, AND TECHNOLOGY

c.1166   Al-Idrisi [abu-'Abdullah Muhammad ibn-Muhammad al-Idrisi] (born c.1099), an Arab geographer, died. He lived in Sicily at the court of Roger II, where he completed (1154) his main work, the *Kitab Rujjar* [Book of Roger].

1184   The **custom of paving streets,** uncommon outside of Italy, was begun in Paris, where the first paved street was in front of the Louvre, the royal palace.

V. ARTS AND LEISURE

1150   The *Gitagovina* [*Gita-Govinda*] ("Song of the Cowherd"), an idyll concerning Krishna, was written by the Hindu poet **Jayadeva.** Hindus consider it a reference to the soul's longing for God.

1163   Work began on the **Notre-Dame Cathedral** in Paris. Conceived by Maurice de Sully, bishop of Paris, who laid the first stone, Notre-Dame served as a model for many Gothic churches.

c.1170   Heinrich von Veldeke (fl. 1170–1190), who also wrote lyrics in the style of the minnesingers [German troubadours] at this time, was called the **father of German epic poetry** for his *Eneida,* a re-

telling of the history of Aeneas as a courtly romance.

c.1175–1178   The **Gothic style of architecture** was introduced into England by William of Sens, a Frenchman who reconstructed much of the cathedral at Canterbury. The building had been built from 1070 to 1077.

1181   The **Khmer Empire** (c.600–c.1434) in Cambodia enjoyed a revival under **Jayavarman VII** (ruled 1181–c.1218). He rebuilt the capital, thereafter known as Angkor Thom [Great Angkor], and was responsible for the tower temple of Bayon.

1187   The **first work of Russian literature** was the *Lay of Igor's Campaign,* of unknown authorship. It commemorated the death of the grand prince of Kiev when he was putting down an uprising in 945.

1188   The **bridge of St. Bénezet,** completed after ten years of work, was the first in history **to cross the Rhône River,** at Avignon, France.

c.1192   Chand [Chund] **Bardai** (fl. c.1200) was the first major Indian poet to write in Hindi rather than Sanskrit. His epic *Prithiraj Rasau,* composed of more than 50,000 verses, praised Prithiraj [Prithvi Raja], last of the Rajput kings of Delli [Delhi], who died fighting the invading Muslims in a battle (1192) at Tarain.

1195   Construction of **Chartres Cathedral** began on the site of an earlier Romanesque church that had burned. The cathedral initiated the transitional **High Gothic style.** Chartres was noted for its magnificent stained glass windows separated by **flying buttresses.**

1196   Benedetto Antelami (1150–c.1233) began work on the baptistry at Parma, for which he was both architect and sculptor.

VI. SPORTS, GAMES, AND SOCIETY

c.1174   At Smithfield, now a part of London, the **first recorded horse races** held for the public were conducted at weekly horse fairs, where gentlemen came to inspect and buy horses. The races were on turf over a four-mile course, a distance selected in imitation of the chariot races of the ancient Greek Olympiads.

1200–1249

I. VITAL STATISTICS AND DEMOGRAPHICS

1200 Medieval **Asia's population** peaked at c.250 million and then declined for two centuries before beginning to rise again. There were population losses after 1200 in the Near East, China, and Korea, and India's population grew slowly.

II. POLITICS AND WAR

c.1200 **Manco Capac**, the legendary **first ruler of the Incas**, was said to have entered the Cuzco Valley of southeastern Peru and shortly after to have founded the city of Cuzco [Navel of the Earth, City of the Sun]. With the aid of his three brothers and four sister/wives, Manco subdued the local tribes, and Cuzco became the capital of a budding empire.

c.1200 About this time the Hindu **Srivijaya** [Shrivijaya] **Empire** (c.100–c.1250), with its capital in Palembang, Sumatra, went into final decline. The island kingdom had held control of Sumatra, Java, the southern Malay Peninsula, and Cambodia. The **Tais** moving down the Malay Peninsula and the **Javanese** under their ruler Kertanagara invading from the south put an end (c.1250) to the Srivijaya Empire.

c.1200 The **Chichimecs** [Dog People], nomadic tribes of the Valley of Mexico, a large basin in the central plateau, broke the power of the **Toltec Empire** (from c.900) and captured their capital at Tula, north of Mexico City.

1202 Nov. 12 **Valdemar II** [Waldemar] (1170–1241) succeeded to the Danish throne on the death of his brother, **Canute VI** [Cnut, Knut] (b. 1163; ruled from 1182). During Valdemar's rule, the **Danes** expanded their empire to include **Holstein**, then part of Saxony, and the ports of Hamburg, on the North Sea, and Lübeck, on the Baltic Sea, all in present Germany, thus giving them **control of the North Sea** and Baltic littoral.

1203 The **Sossos** [Susus] under their king, Sumanguru Keita (ruled c.1200–1235), completed the destruction of the Ghana Kingdom of Western Africa by conquering its capital and enslaving the inhabi-

tants. The **Kingdom of Sosso** was the **last state to resist the spread of Islam in North Africa**.

1204 May 6 **Philip II**, king of France, captured Château Gaillard, built (1197) by Richard I, king of England. Normandy, Anjou, Maine, Poitou, and Touraine came under French rule, while Aquitaine and Gascony remained under the Anglo-Norman **Plantagenet Dynasty** (1154–1499). Philip starved the defenders into surrender.

1204 May 9 One month after the sack of **Constantinople** by forces of the **Fourth Crusade** (1201–1204), Baldwin IX (1171?–1205), count of Flanders, was elevated as **Baldwin I**, the **first emperor** (1204–1205) **of the Latin Empire** (1204–1261). Outlying regions of the old Byzantine Empire refused to submit, and three Byzantine dynasties were established. The **Dynasty of the Great Comneni** (1204–1461) ruled at Trebizond on the Black Sea; the **Despotate of Epirus** (1204–1337) was established in Greece with Arta as its capital; and Theodore I Lascaris (c.1171–1222) founded the **Nicaean Empire** (1204–1261) in Bithynia in Anatolia.

1206 Temujin, a Mongol leader, was proclaimed **Genghis** [Jenghiz] **Khan** [Universal Ruler] at Karakorum, the capital he established in Mongolia. It marked the beginning of the **Mongol Empire** (to 1294) that Genghis began to expand by a campaign into north China (1211–1216) and Korea (1217) before invading Persia in 1220.

1208 **Theodore I Lascaris** was officially crowned Nicaean emperor (to 1222) at Nicaea, in Anatolia. The **Nicaean Empire** was the main center of resistance to the Latin Empire, whose forces they expelled from Anatolia in 1224.

1212 **Frederick II** (Dec. 26, 1194–Dec. 13, 1250), king of Sicily as Frederick I, king of Germany (from 1212), and the Holy Roman emperor (from 1220), this year granted an hereditary crown to **Ottokar I** [Otakar] (d. Dec. 15, 1230), king of Bohemia, and made his state autonomous within the **Holy Roman Empire** (962–1806).

1212 July 16 **Alfonso VIII** [Alfonso III of Castile] (d. 1214), the Spanish king of León and Castile (from 1158), gained a great Christian victory over the

Moors in a battle at **Las Navas de Tolosa**, in Spain. The united North African Islamic Berber empire began to disintegrate.

1214 July 27 Philip II, king of France, defeated the allied forces of John, king of England; of Otto IV (1174–May 19, 1218), the Holy Roman emperor (from 1209); and of the princes of Flanders in a **battle at Bouvines**, in France. It brought Flanders under French rule and secured France's conquests from England north of the Loire River. The crown of Germany and later of the **Holy Roman Empire** went to Philip's ally, Frederick II.

1215 June 15 John, king of England, was forced by the English lords, the English Church, and the communes to sign **Magna Charta** at **Runnymede** near London. It asserted the supremacy of the law over the king and protected the freedom of the barons and the Church.

1216 Oct. 19 John (b. Dec. 24, 1167), **king of England** (from 1199), died. The country was divided by civil war and partially occupied by French forces under Prince Louis of France (later **Louis VIII**) (Sept. 5, 1187–Nov. 8, 1226; ruled from 1223), who was offered the crown by the Francophile faction of the English baronage. But John's son, **Henry III** (Oct. 1, 1207–Nov. 16, 1272), was crowned (ruled from 1216), and the French retreated from English soil after their **defeat at Lincoln** on May 20, 1217, and the loss of their fleet in a **naval battle off Sandwich** on Aug. 24, 1217.

1218 Denmark adopted the **Danneborg**, a red flag with a white cross, as emblem. It is the **oldest national flag in the world**.

1227 Aug. 18 Genghis Khan (born c.1162), the Mongol emperor, died. In his last six years, he had devastated the Turkish Muslim **Khwarizm** [Khwarezm, Khuwarizm, Khwarazm] **Empire** in Persia, raided the Russian plains, and annihilated the rebelling Tanguts of the **Hsi Hsia Kingdom** in northwestern China and Tibet, annexing (1227) this former kingdom into the Mongol Empire. He was succeeded by his third son, Ogadai (1185–1241), as Great Khan (from 1229).

1228 The **Hafsid Dynasty** (to 1574) of western Libya and Tunisia came to power under **Abu Zakaria Yahya** (1228–1249), previously appointed viceroy by the Almohades. The region enjoyed a period of stability and prosperity.

1231 Frederick I, king of Sicily and, as Frederick II, king of Germany and the Holy Roman emperor, promulgated a new comprehensive **code of laws for Sicily**. This code, sometimes called the **Golden Bull of Sicily** by later historians, was a secular pronouncement of laws by a ruler.

c.1235 Sundiata Keita [Mari Jata I], king of Mali (ruled 1230–1255), defeated the **Sosso** [Susu] people led by Sumanguru Keita. The gold-bearing areas and trade routes of the Mandingo [Wangara] centered around Bamako, in present Mali, were captured, giving supremacy in West Africa to the **Mali Empire** (fl. c.1230–c.1400).

1235 The Zenata Berber Yaghmurasan, emir of Tlemcen (1235–1283), gained independence from the declining **Almohade Dynasty** and founded the **Zayyanid** [Zyanid, Abd al-Wadid] **Dynasty** (1235–1550), in present Algeria.

1236 A Mongol army under **Batu Khan** (d. 1255) swept across Russia, taking Moscow and Kiev (1240), then Silesia and Hungary (1241). **Kievan Russia** (from c.880) was destroyed (1240). The **Khanate of the Golden Horde** (1241–1480) established their capital at Sarai, on the lower Volga River, where Batu ruled as khan (1241–1255).

1236 Ferdinand III (c.1200–1252), king of Castile and Léon (from 1217 and 1230 respectively), captured Córdoba from the **Moors**. The conquest of Murcia (1243), Jaén (1246), and Sevilla [Seville] (1248) followed, leaving Granada as the last Moorish stronghold in Spain. Nearly all of Spain was under Christian control.

1240 Alexander Nevsky [from the Neva] (1220?–1263), a Russian prince of Novgorod (from 1238), defeated invading Swedes near present **St. Petersburg**. The Swedes had been urged by Pope Gregory IX (c.1145–Aug. 21, 1241; ruled from 1227) to take Novgorod and its territories as punishment of the Orthodox Russians for helping the Finns resist conversion to Latin Christianity.

1241 Dec. 11 Ogadai, the Great Khan (from 1229) of the **Mongol Empire**, died, after a reign that saw the fall of the **Chin Dynasty** in northern China (1234), the conquest of Korea (1236), and the plunder of eastern Europe. He was succeeded briefly by his son Kuyuk as Great Khan (1246–1248), who subjugated Tibet in 1247.

1242 Apr. Russian forces under **Alexander Nevsky** defeated a German army led by the crusading **Teutonic Knights** in a **battle at Lake Peipus** [Chudskoye Ozero].

1243 The **Mongols** defeated Kay-Khusraw II (d. 1245) of the Seljuk Sultanate of Rum in Anatolia in a **battle at Kösedagh** [Kös Dag], a mountain in Turkey. It marked the **end of the [Turkish] Seljuk Empire** (from c.1080), which was absorbed into the **Il-Khanate Empire** (1256–1335).

III. ECONOMY AND TRADE

c.1200 A variety of **rice** had been developed that permitted a second rice harvest throughout much of China. This important agricultural advance allowed for three grain harvests in all, the third probably of millet or barley.

1231 Frederick II, the Holy Roman emperor, began to issue **gold coins** to supplement the *bezant*, minted for the Byzantine Empire and in general use for trade.

1236 The **Statute of Merton** required the lords of manors in England to provide land for the free use of their tenants. It was the first legal enforcement of the concept of common lands.

IV. RELIGION AND PHILOSOPHY

c.1200 **Chu Hsi** [Chu Hi] (b. 1130), the preeminent Chinese rationalist philosopher of the **Southern Sung Dynasty** (1127–1280), died. He left behind a body of commentaries on the Confucian classics and a systematized, all-embracing Confucian philosophy that held the field until the early 20th century.

1200 By this date, the **Aztec pyramid of Quetzalcoatl** at Cholula, c.70 miles southeast of present **Mexico City**, had been built. Its base covered 42 acres, and it stood 180 feet high.

1204 Apr. 12 The **Fourth Crusade** (1201–1204) ended with the sack of **Constantinople**. Church relics were looted and carried to the West. **Alexius IV**, who had been installed (Aug. 1203) as co-emperor with his father **Ksdaac II**, had been deposed and killed in Jan. 1203, by a palace revolution supported by the Greek population, which detested the Latin Crusaders and their puppet emperor. **Isaac II** (born c.1155; emperor 1185–1195, 1203–1204) died at the same time. In revenge, the Crusaders were merciless in their pillage of the city.

1204 Oct. 12 **Pope Innocent III** confirmed the German order of the **Knights of the Sword** (formed 1202). He declared that Crusader vows might be fulfilled within the order in the conquest and conversion of heathen Estonians and Livonians. The Christianization of Livonia, a region in present Estonia and Latvia, was completed before the death of Innocent, and the new bishoprics were placed in direct dependence on Rome.

1208 **Pope Innocent III** approved a lay organization under ecclesiastical oversight known as "**Catholic paupers**," which embodied some of the anti-worldly practices of the **Waldensians** and kept or won back for the Church significant numbers of laymen. This organization gradually reduced the Waldensian movement to a small sect in the Piedmont northwestern Italy.

1208 **Pope Innocent III** named **Stephen Langton** (d. 1228) as **archbishop of Canterbury**, refusing the choice made by **John, king of England**. Innocent laid England under an interdict and, when John punished English clerics opposing him, the pope **excommunicated the king** and declared his throne forfeited.

1208 Feb. 24 **Giovanni Bernadone**, the future **Francis of Assisi**, received his call to a life in imitation of Christ and the preaching of repentance and the kingdom of God. A few months later, Francis and a dozen associates received a papal blessing for their work, and dispersed through central Italy to live among the poor and the outcasts.

1209 The **Albigensian Crusade** (to 1229), conducted against the heretic sect of Cathars of southern France, was proclaimed by Pope Innocent III. The murder (1208) of a papal legate with the complicity of Raymond VI (1156–1222), count of Toulouse, and the failure of Bernard of Clairvaux and other Cistercian missionaries sent to preach against the Cathars, provided the justification. France's monarchs joined, eager to bring the independent nobles of southern France under their suzerainty. The political drive for the crusade ended in Apr. 1229 with the **Treaty of Paris** by which France acquired the county of Toulouse.

1210 The study of **Aristotle**, except for his works on logic, was forbidden by **Pope Innocent III**. In 1230 the prohibition was renewed, with modifications, by Pope Gregory IX. But "correction" of inaccurate translations of Aristotle was underway by scholars, and his *Physics* and *Metaphysics* soon became required studies in all universities.

1212 In an outburst of revivalist emotion, perhaps 30,000 children were recruited for the **Children's Crusade** by two boys, Stephen, a French tender of sheep, and Nicholas of **Cologne**, Germany. Stephen's followers were lured by slave dealers into slavery in Egypt. Nicholas's contingent straggled in diminishing numbers into Italy, after which their fate is unknown.

1213 Sept. 12 Pedro II (b. 1174), king of Aragon (from 1196), a Roman Catholic who had fought as a Crusader against the Muslim Almohades, died fighting in defense of heretic **Albigensians** and his own property interests in France, against forces backed by **Pope Innocent III** and the king of France.

1213 John, king of England, acknowledged his kingdom to be a fief of the papacy, thus ending the interdict of England and the threat of deposition laid on him by Pope Innocent III in 1208. This act of submission saved John from an invasion by French forces.

1215 Nov. The **Fourth Lateran Council**, attended by 412 bishops and 800 abbots and priors, met in the papal cathedral of the Church of St. John Lateran, in Rome. Among the canons adopted were a confession of faith mentioning a transubstantiation of the elements in the Lord's Supper, provisions for the organized suppression of heresy, and requirements for at least annual confession and for receiving the Eucharist at Easter.

1216 Dec. 22 The **Dominican order** was confirmed by **Pope Honorius III** (d. Mar. 18, 1227; ruled from 1216). It had grown out of the activities of the self-denying missionaries of **Diego of Acevedo** [Didacus of Acebes] (d. 1207), bishop of Osma [Old Castile], Spain, and Dominic (1170?–Aug. 6, 1221), a canon of its cathedral. Dedicated to winning adherents by preaching, the order was committed to study and apostolic poverty.

1218 The **Fifth Crusade** (1218–1221), proclaimed by **Pope Innocent III** at the Fourth Lateran Council (1215), arrived in the East ostensibly to recover Jerusalem. The Crusaders battled only in Egypt, with some initial success, and then met disastrous defeat after they had refused to accept the sultan's generous terms for peace. The European troops returned home with virtually nothing accomplished.

1226 Oct. 3 Francis of Assisi (b. 1182) died in the church of Portiuncula outside Assisi, his birthplace in central Italy. While Francis was preaching in Egypt and Syria (1219–1220), the **Franciscans** were organized by others into a true monastic order along Dominican lines of governance. Francis's last years were spent in contemplation, prayer, singing, and enjoyment of nature. He experienced the **miracle of the stigmata**, according to legend, in 1224.

1228 The **Sixth Crusade** (1228–1229) was led by Frederick II, the Holy Roman emperor, even though excommunicated by Pope Gregory IX because he had delayed so long after taking the Crusader's vow in 1215. Frederick had talks with al-Kamil, the Egyptian Sultan's general, and (1229) signed a treaty that gave the Christians access to Jerusalem and other places in the Holy Land for ten years. Pope Gregory refused to confirm the pact, and the Christian leaders in Jerusalem took the city by force and renewed the fighting in Palestine. Jerusalem was held for ten years before it once again fell to Muslim forces.

1229 Acting to suppress the Scripture-oriented **Cathars** and **Waldensians**, the **synod of Toulouse** forbade the laity of the region to possess the Scriptures except the Psalter and such portions as were contained in the breviary.

1233 To end the use of the charge of heresy for political purposes, **Pope Gregory IX** instituted the **Papal Inquisition**. Preaching friars, predominantly Dominicans, were employed for the discovery and repression of heresy in southern France.

1236 After having studied in China, **Dogen** [Joyo Daishi; Kigen Dogen] (1200–1253) established his monastery in Japan at Koshohorinji, where he **introduced Zen Buddhism to Japan**. Dogen, an advocate of *Zazen*, a posture for meditation, taught the purification of the ego, the elimination of selfish desires, and the surrender of the self.

1240 Ibn-Arabi [Muhyi-al-Din ibn-'Arabi] (b. 1165), the Arab mystic and distinguished poet, died. Ibn-Arabi wrote an encyclopedic work on **Sufism**, centered on the thesis that all that now is is substantially of one sort and a manifestation of the divine substance.

1244 Jerusalem, reoccupied by local Christian troops in the previous year, was sacked by **Khwarizm** [Khwarezm, Khuwarizm, Khwarazm] **Turks**, who had been driven from Persia c.20 years earlier by the advancing Mongols, and were at this time vassals of **Ayyub**, the Ayyubid sultan of Egypt (1240–1249).

1245 Apr. 16 Giovanni da Pian del Carpini (1200?–?1252), an Italian Franciscan monk, was sent by Pope Innocent IV (c.1190–Dec. 7, 1254; ruled from 1243) on a journey throughout the Mongol Empire (1206–1294) with the intention of converting the Mongols to Christianity. Unable to carry out his mission, he returned (June 9, 1247). He recorded his observations in *Liber Tartarorum* (1839), not published in its entirety until 1839.

1248 Louis IX, king of France, who had vowed a crusade after the fall of Jerusalem in 1244, started for the East with a small force on the **Seventh Crusade**. The capture of Damietta (June 1249) in Egypt was followed by the capture of Louis (Apr. 1250), who later was ransomed at a heavy price. The Seventh Crusade ended with the king's return (Apr. 1254) to France, after he had ransomed as many Christians as his purse would allow.

V. SCIENCE, EDUCATION, AND TECHNOLOGY

c.1200 The **school at Oxford** (founded c.1168), England, an offshoot of one in Paris, developed into a university. A dispute with the townspeople led (1209) to a temporary closing of the university and transfer of students and faculty to **Cambridge**.

c.1200 Stern rudders began to be used on northern sailing ships.

1200 Philip II, king of France, issued a charter marking the official foundation of the **University of Paris**. It had moved from the *Île de la Cité* to the left bank of the Seine, thereafter known as the Latin Quarter.

c.1232 The **first known rockets**, powered by gunpowder, were used by the Chinese to frighten their enemies.

c.1235 Mechanical saws, turned by water power, were first used. The new water-powered saws also marked the introduction of circular saws.

c.1236 Lead piping was first used in England for the distribution of water. The Romans were known to have earlier employed lead pipe for this purpose.

1239 The **first royal charter** was granted to the men of Newcastle, England, to mine and sell coal, initiating the development of the great Newcastle coal fields.

1243 The **earliest known example of linen paper** was dated to this year.

VI. ARTS AND LEISURE

c.1200–1450 Russian icon painting, which flourished at this time, was centered at Novgorod. Icons, representing events or persons sacred to the **Orthodox Church**, were important in the religious training of worshipers.

c.1200–1480 During the late Middle Ages many people in Europe wore a **costume** which the Crusaders brought back from the Byzantines. It consisted of a long tunic worn with a hooded cloak and pointed shoes. Women wore sleeveless robes over an undertunic with tight sleeves. Men wore multicolored hose, and flamboyant colors were the rule for both sexes.

c.1200–c.1220 *Aucassin et Nicolete*, a romance, was written by an anonymous French poet in alternating prose and verse. It was based on the tale of *Floire et Blancheflor* (before 1170).

1200–1210 *Parzival*, based on the French courtly romance *Perceval* (before 1191) by Chrétien de Troyes, was rendered in German by **Wolfram von Eschenbach** (1170?–?1220), a German poet.

c.1200 The 12th and 13th centuries saw a renascence of nearly all forms of **art in western Europe**. Painting, sculpture, architecture, stain glass work, and other arts improved and flourished. Huge castles, communities in themselves, surrounded by great moats and by walls up to 25-feet thick, were built throughout Europe. Floral and other ornamental forms typical of Romanesque sculpture began to appear in French cathedrals, and soon spread to cathedrals throughout Europe.

c.1200 According to Inca tradition, **weaving** was begun by the wife of the first Inca emperor, **Manco Capac**, who ruled at this time. The **Incas** developed sophisticated weaving techniques and produced beautifully colored fabrics.

c.1200 **Ife**, the holy city of the **Yoruba States**, in present Nigeria, began to produce its famous naturalistic terracotta heads, and bronze and brass castings by using the lost wax process.

c.1200 Under the patronage of the Minamoto shogun Yoritomo, the Japanese sculptor **Unkei** (1148–1223) and his sons flourished at this time. Unkei, directing more than 200 craftsmen, completed a set of six 32-foot high figures for the **Daibutsu**, or giant statue of Buddha, whose temple at Nara had been damaged by fire. These figures were lost in the 15th century by another fire.

c.1213–1215 The *Heike Monogatari* [Tales of the Taira clan] was a prose epic, revised and retold often, popular during the **Kamakura period** in Japan. The stories were about the rivalry between the Taira and Minamoto clans.

c.1200 The *Nibelungenlied* was written in Middle High German by an anonymous Austrian in southern Germany. Its essential themes of revenge and loyalty were borrowed from the Scandinavian *Edda*, collected and written down (c.1100 or c.1200). The *Nibelungenlied* also contained plot elements of the Merovingian conquest of the Burgundians (c.500) and the death of Attila (453).

1203 The three-terraced **Mont-Saint-Michel**, with its church, abbey, cloister, knight's hall, and hospice, began to rise on its small rock island off the northwestern coast of France.

c.1205 **Layamon** (fl. c.1190–c.1207), an English priest, paraphrased into Middle English the Norman French *Roman de Brut* (c.1154), which was based on **Geoffrey of Monmouth's** work and retold the Arthurian legends.

1205 **Yusof Nezami** (b. 1140), a leading Persian romantic poet, died. Nezami was best remembered for his collection of five poems entitled *Khamseh* [The Quintuplet].

1206 The *Shinkokinshu* (the new *Kokinshu*) was compiled by **Fujiwara no Sadaie** (1162–1241) by command of the emperor of Japan. It was one of 20 volumes of anthologies of poetry, beginning with *Kokin waka shu* [Anthology of Japanese poems, old and new] in 905. The project was an attempt by the emperor to preserve the best Japanese poetry for future generations.

c.1208 The *Gesta Danorum* (or *Historia Danica*) was completed by **Saxo Grammaticus** (1150?–?1220). Written in Latin, it told the history of the Danes through 1185.

c.1210 *Gudrun* [*Kudrun*], of unknown authorship, was written in Middle High German. A Viking saga, it was similar to the *Nibelungenlied*, but dwelt more on romance and borrowed more from sea lore.

c.1210 **Jehan Bodel** (born c.1167), a troubadour, died in Arras, in present France. His miracle play *Le Jeu de Saint Nicolas* (c.1205) was the first French miracle play and was performed on the saint's vigil night. *Le Jeu de Saint Nicolas* was marked by wit and fine characterization.

1211 Construction of the **cathedral at Reims** began on the traditional site for the coronation of French kings. It was noted especially for its sculpture, done mostly by a man now known only as Joseph Master. The original plan was probably the work of Jean d'Orbais, but a number of architects worked on the building before it was completed in 1430.

1216 **Kamo no Chomei** [Kamo no Nagaakira] (b. 1153), Japanese poet-essayist, died. His *Hojoki* [Account of My Hut] (1212) was a collection of meditations contrasting city life with his hermit existence.

1220 Work began on the English Gothic **cathedral at Salisbury**, England. Its 404-foot, spired tower designed by Master Richard of Farleigh was constructed between c.1334 and c.1380.

1220 Work began on the Gothic **cathedral at Burgos**, Spain, borrowing design elements from Moorish structures but tending toward French Gothic in its massive vertical lines. The cornerstone was laid by Fernando III of Castile in 1221. Additions were made until as late as 1736. In the cathedral are buried the Spanish heros of the Moorish wars Fernán Gonzaléz and Rodrigo Díaz de Bivar, known as el Cid.

1225 The **Outb Minar tower**, 238-feet high and of fluted red sandstone and white marble, was erected near present New Delhi.

1228 Work began on the **basilica of Saint Francis at Assisi**, Italy. In the church are frescoes by Giotto (1266?–1337) depicting the lives of Christ and St. Francis.

c.1229 **Attar** [*Pers:* Farid ud-din Attar; *real name:* Mohammed ibn-Ibrahim] (b. 1119), the Sufi poet, died. His best-known work, *The Bird Parliament*, was an allegorical account of Sufi doctrine.

c.1230 **Walther von der Vogelweide** (born c.1170), a celebrated German lyric poet, or minnesinger [troubadour], died. Among his love songs is the still famous *Unter den Linden*.

c.1235 The first part of the *Roman de la Rose*, an allegorical idyll that was to influence **Chaucer**, was written by **Guillaume de Lorris** [William of the Loire] (died c.1235). The second part was written (c.1280) by **Jean** [Clopinel] **de Meung** (fl. c.1280). The work has endured as one of the great romantic poems. Except for the narrator, all human characters in the poem represent human qualities and the rose, representing women, was beautiful, pursued by various characters, and surrounded by thorns.

c.1240 *The Secret History of the Mongols*, the earliest extant work in the Mongol language, represented the beginning of Mongolian [Tatar] literature. It was recited by bards and told about the lives of **Genghis Khan** and his successors.

1247 **Sarangadeva** (b. 1210), a Hindu musician at the Yadava court in Deogiri [Daulatabad] in the Deccan of central India, died. His *Sangeet-rat-nakara*, a compilation of earlier Indian music theories, lists 264 ragas with their appropriate seasons and times of day.

1248 Construction of the **Alhambra Palace** near Granada, Spain, was begun by order of **Mohammed I** [Mohammed ibn al-Ahmar], the Nasrid sultan of Granada (1230–1272), and was almost completed by **Mohammed V** (1334–1391; ruled from 1354) in c.1354. Planned as both a palace and fort, it represented the culmination of 600 years of **Moorish architecture**.

VII. SPORTS, GAMES, AND SOCIETY

1200 **Ski-equipped military troops** were first employed by **Sverre** [Sverre Sigurdsson or Swerro] (c.1552–1202), king of Norway, in a **battle at Oslo**. Skis first appeared in Neolithic times in northern Europe, where they were used mainly for hunting.

1250–1299

I. DISASTERS

1268 An **earthquake** in the **Cilicia** region of present southeastern Turkey, claimed the lives of c.60,000 people.

1290 Sept. 27 Deaths numbered c.100,000 in an **earthquake** at **Chihli**, in the present region of Hopeh [Hopei, Hebei], in northeastern China.

1293 May 20 An **earthquake** in **Kamakura**, Honshu, Japan, claimed c.30,000 lives.

II. EXPLORATION AND COLONIZATION

1253–1255 **Louis IX**, king of France, sent the Franciscan monk **Guillaume Rubruquis** [William of Ruys-

broeck, Wilhelm van Ruysbroek] (1220?–?1293) on a mission to Mongolia in the hope of extracting sympathy from the **Mongols** warring in eastern Europe and the Near East. William returned with the Great Khan's suggestion that France submit to Mongolia. He also brought back an excellent account of Mongolian life and history.

1271–1295 Venetian **Marco Polo** (1254?–Jan. 8, 1324), accompanying his father Nicolo and his uncle Maffeo, set out for China [Cathay], traveling through the Holy Land, Turkey, Persia, present southern Siberia, Turkestan, and the Gobi Desert to the court of **Kublai** [Kubilai] **Khan** (1216–1294; ruled from 1260), the Mongolian ruler of China at Cambaluc [Khanbalik], present Beijing. After reaching (1275) Cambaluc the Polos remained in Cathay until 1292 in the Khan's service. They returned to Venice mostly by sea, via Sumatra, southern India, Sri Lanka, and the Persian Gulf, then overland to the Mediterranean Sea, then to Venice, where Marco was captured during a naval battle and jailed in **Genoa**. There he dictated *The Book of Marco Polo* (c.1298). This **first western work on the Far East** greatly influenced trade explorations for centuries, and indirectly led to the discovery of America by Europeans who hoped to find a new trade route to China.

III. POLITICS AND WAR

c.1250   Dounama II, the Saifawa sultan (c.1221–1259) of the **Sultanate** [Kingdom] **of Kanem** (from c.800), gained control of the whole **Lake Chad basin in central Africa** to become king of Kanem and Bornu. After an agreement with the sultan of Tunis, he expanded his territories northward to Marzuq [Murzuk] in the Fezzan [Fazzen] region of present southwestern Libya to secure the trans-Saharan routes.

1250 Dec. 13   **Frederick II** (b. Dec. 26, 1194), the Holy Roman emperor, died. As Frederick I, he was king of Sicily (1198–1250), and king of Germany after the **battle of Bouvines** (1215). He was excommunicated three times but, in spite of this, led the **Sixth Crusade** (1228–1229), which regained access to Jerusalem and other places in the Holy Land. Frederick was succeeded by his son Conrad IV (Apr. 26, 1228–May 21, 1254) who, though he ruled as emperor, was never crowned.

1250   The **first of the two Mameluke** [Arabic: mamluk = slave] **Dynasties** of Egypt began after the death of **al-Salih**, the Ayyubid sultan (from 1240), in 1249. A disputed succession was initiated when his widow, **Shajar-al-Durr**, murdered Salih's stepson and declared herself queen. She married the slave **Aybak** [al-Din Aibak], who took control as the first ruler of the **Bahri** [= River] **Mameluke Dynasty** (to c.1382). Aybak was murdered by Shajar-al-Darr in 1257.

1253   **Ottokar II** [Otakar] (c.1230–Aug. 26, 1278), duke of Austria (from 1251), succeeded his father **Wenceslas I** as king of Bohemia and Moravia.

1256   **Hulagu** [Hülegü] (1216–1265), a grandson of Genghis Khan, was sent by his brother, the Great Khan, **Mangu** [Möngke] **Khan** (1207?–1259; ruled from 1251) of the **Mongol Empire**, to put down a rebellion in Persia [Iran]. Hulagu soon suppressed the rebels and extended Mongolian rule farther west and north. He captured and burned Baghdad on Feb. 28, 1258, killing hundreds of thousands and ending the **Abbaside Caliphate** (from 750). **Il-Khanate**, with its capital in Tabriz, in present Iran, was established (1256–1335). Meanwhile, Mangu had captured and annexed the kingdoms of **Nan-Chao** [Thailand], **Annam** [Vietnam], and **Korea**.

1258 Jan. 17   During Hulagu's siege of Baghdad, **al-Mustasim** (ruled from 1242), 37th and **last of the Abbaside caliphs** (from 750), was put to the sword after delivering himself and his family to the Mongols. One of the dynasty escaped to Cairo to continue the line (until 1517) under the rule of the Mamelukes.

1258 June 11   A crisis caused by the levy of new taxes by **Henry III**, king of England, led to the **Provisions of Oxford**. Forced by rebellious barons, led by **Simon de Montfort**, Henry accepted the program of reforms enacted by the so-called **Mad Parliament**. Among several reforms agreed to by Henry was the intention to convoke Parliament at least three times a year.

1259   **Alexander Nevsky**, the Russian prince of Novgorod (from 1230) and grand duke of Kiev and Novgorod (from 1246), agreed to pay tribute to the Mongols of the **Khanate of the Golden Horde** (1241–1480) in order to secure protection from the south.

1260 Sept. 3   **Baybars I** [al-Malik al-Zahir Rukn-al-Din Baybars] (1233–1277), the Mameluke sultan of Egypt (from 1260), defeated the Mongol forces of **Hulagu** in Syria in a **battle at Ain Jalut**, near Nazareth in present Israel. It preserved the independence of Egypt, brought Syria under Egyptian rule, and checked the westward expansion of Il Khanate.

1261 July 25   **Michael VIII** (c.1225–Dec. 11, 1282), co-emperor of the **Nicaean Empire** (1204–1261), captured Constantinople and ousted **Baldwin II** (1217–1273; ruled from 1228), the **last Latin emperor of Constantinople**. Michael founded the **Palaeologus Dynasty** (to 1453) of the Byzantine Empire.

1262   **Haakon IV Haakonsson**, king of Norway (from 1217), intervening in a civil war in Iceland, annexed Iceland and Greenland. Norway imposed a monopoly of trade with the two islands.

1263 May 14 Simon de Montfort, earl of Leicester, defeated and captured **Henry III**, king of England, at Lewes, in southern England, in a revolt called the **Barons' War** (1263–1267) precipitated by Henry's renunciation of the **Provisions of Oxford**. The new Parliament summoned on June 20, 1265, by Montfort, leader of the reform faction, for the first time included representatives of the towns [**the Commons**] as well as of the knighthood, baronage, and church. The Barons' War subsided with the defection of the barons after the defeat of Montfort (born c.1208), who was killed at Evesham on Aug. 4, 1265, by **Edward Longshanks**, later Edward I.

1266 Jan. 6 Charles I (1226–Jan. 7, 1285), count of Anjou and Provence (from 1246) and brother of Louis IX, king of France, accepted the kingdom of Naples and Sicily [the Two Sicilies] from Pope Clement IV (d. Nov. 29, 1268; ruled from 1265) in return for ousting the German Hohenstaufens from Italy. Charles killed his rival Manfred (b. 1232?), the excommunicated king of Naples and Sicily, in a **battle** (Feb. 26) **at Benevento. Conradin** (b. 1252), the **last of the Hohenstaufen Dynasty**, was beheaded at **Naples** on Oct. 29, 1268.

1269 Sept. 8 Some of the **Zenata Berbers** of Morocco, led by Abu Yusuf Yaqub (1258–1286) captured Marrakech and overthrew the **Almohade Dynasty** (from 1130). He established the **Marinid Dynasty** (1269–1420), which at its peak controlled Algeria and Tunisia.

1270 Yekuno Amlak (d. 1285), king of Ethiopia, overthrew the **Zagwe Dynasty** (from 1137) with the help of the monastic clergy, and restored the traditional Solomonian line, descended from **King Solomon** of the Hebrews.

1270 Aug. 25 Louis IX (b. Apr. 25, 1214), king of France (from 1226), died of plague at Carthage in Tunisia, bringing an end to the **Eighth Crusade**. As a symbol of the Christian king, Louis IX was the **most celebrated monarch of the Middle Ages** (c.500–1500). He was succeeded by his son Philip III (Apr. 30, 1245–Oct. 5, 1285).

1273 Oct. 1 Count **Rudolf I** of Hapsburg [Habsburg] (May 1, 1218–July 15, 1291) was elected king of Germany and the Holy Roman emperor (though he was never crowned by the pope), ending the **Great Interregnum** (1254–1273) in the **Holy Roman Empire**. Thus, the **Hapsburg Dynasty** (1273–1740)

was established in Germany and Austria. A war broke out with the powerful Ottokar II, king of Bohemia, who finally recognized Rudolf on Nov. 21, 1276.

1275 Magnus III Ladulås [Barn Lock] (1240–1290) deposed his brother Valdemar I [Waldemar] (1238?–?1302; ruled from 1250) during a civil war and seized the Swedish crown. Valdemar was the **first ruler of the Folkung** [Folkungar] **Dynasty** (1250–1387), which occupied several Scandinavian thrones during the 13th and 14th centuries.

1277 The pro-papal **Guelf party**, led by the **Della Torre family** (from 1237), lost its power to the pro-imperial **Ghibelline party** in Milan. Thus began the supremacy of the **Visconti family** (1277–1447) in **Milan**.

1278 The territory of **Andorra**, located between France and Spain, was made an autonomous principality. It was ruled jointly by the Spanish bishops of Urgel, and by the French counts of Foix.

1278 Aug. 26 Ottokar II [Otakar] (born c.1230), king of Bohemia (from 1253), was defeated and killed by the allied forces of **Rudolf I of Hapsburg**, the Holy Roman emperor, and of the Hungarians at **Dürnkrut on the Marchfeld** near Vienna.

1280 Kublai [Kubilai] **Khan**, grandson of Genghis Khan and brother of Mangu Khan and Hulagu of Persia [Il-Khanate Empire] (1256–1335), founded the **Yuan** [Mongol] **Dynasty** (1280–1368) in China with Khanbalik [City of the Great Khan], Marco Polo's Cambaluc, and present Beijing, as capital. His conquest of China was completed in 1279 with the defeat of the **Southern Sung Dynasty** (1127–1280). Kublai thus established the **first non-Chinese dynasty to control China**. Kublai's empire stretched from Korea to Arabia and eastern Europe.

1282 The nobility forced **Eric V** [VII] **Klipping** (1249?–1286), king of **Denmark** (from 1259) to sign a constitution limiting his powers. It established a *Danehof* [parliament], required to meet once a year.

1282 Mar. 30 An uprising broke out on Easter Monday in Palermo, **Sicily**, against the French occupation forces of Charles I, king of Naples and Sicily. **Peter** [Pedro] **III the Great** (1239–1285), king of Aragon (from 1276) and Manfred's son-in-law, who claimed the Hohenstaufen inheritance, was offered the Sicilian crown, and a 20-year war began. It was known as the **War of the Sicilian Vespers** because it was ignited by a French soldier who mistreated a young woman on her way to vesper services.

1282 Dec. 11 Llewelyn II [Llywelyn] ab Gruffydd, prince of **Wales** (from 1258), was killed near Builth by the English forces of **Edward I**. Llewelyn's brother **David III [Dafydd]** was executed on Oct. 3, 1283, and his territories in northwestern Wales were annexed in 1284.

1284 The republic of **Genoa** defeated its rival **Pisa** in a **naval battle off Meloria**, a small island near Leghorn. Genoa enjoyed a golden age, while Pisa was successively occupied by the city states of Lucca, Milan, and Florence.

1287 The **Pagan Dynasty** (from 1044), the ruling dynasty of **Burma [Myanmar]**, was destroyed by **Kublai Khan**, Mongol emperor of China. The country was divided between lower Burma, where the Mon Kingdom recovered its independence, and upper Burma, which was occupied by tribes from Thailand and Laos, the Shan, who sacked Pagan in 1299.

1291 The **first recorded use of Swiss mercenaries** occurred when the Swiss sent **Henry VII of Luxemburg** (1275–Aug. 24, 1313; ruled from 1308), the Holy Roman emperor (from 1312), 300 soldiers for an expedition against Italy.

1291 Aug. 1 The three cantons of Uri, Nidwald, and Schwyz signed the **Perpetual Pact** to defend one another against the growth of the **Hapsburg** power. This pact marked the **founding of the Swiss Confederation**.

1292 Nov. 17 Edward I, king of England, was called upon to choose the successor to the **Scottish throne** after Margaret [Maid of Norway] (b. 1283), queen of Scotland (from 1286), died in 1290. Edward gave the throne to **John de Baliol** (1250–1314) in preference to **Robert de Bruce VI** (1210–1295). John refused to help England against France in 1295, and Edward forced John to resign his crown to him at **Dunbar**, in Scotland, on Apr. 27, 1296. The Bruces, who eventually secured (1306) Scotland's independence from the English crown, never accepted John's submission.

1293 Prince **Vijaya [Kertarajasa Jayavardhana]** (d. 1309) of Singhasari [Singosari], in present **Indonesia**, drove out a Mongol expedition, and founded the **Empire of Majapahit** (to c.1465).

1293 Finland was completely conquered by **Sweden**, under **Torgils Knutsson** (d. 1306), who was acting as regent for **Birger II** (1280–1321), king of Sweden (1290–1318). The Swedes built a fortress in Karelia, near present St. Petersburg, and battled the Russians for 30 more years.

1295 The **Model Parliament** was summoned by Edward I, king of England, the **first Parliament in English history** where every estate, including the merchant class of the towns and cities, was represented. The dictum "Let that which touches all be approved by all" originated here.

1298 July 22 A **Scottish rebellion** against English rule, led by **William Wallace**, the Scottish national hero, was quelled by Edward I in a **battle at Falkirk**. Wallace had succeeded in driving the English from all of Scotland, and had commenced raiding northern England. **Robert the Bruce VIII** assumed the rebel leadership in Scotland.

IV. ECONOMY AND TRADE

1250–1450 Novgorod in northern Russia became a leading center of the **fur trade**. Fur dealers from Novgorod obtained pelts from villagers along the Russian frontier and sold them to merchants from the Hanseatic cities in the Baltic.

c.1250 The **Consolat de Mar**, one of the **earliest attempts at a written code of maritime conduct**, was compiled at Barcelona.

c.1250 The price of **silver** began a long rise that continued until c.1550.

c.1260 Kublai Khan issued paper notes to circulate as **currency** in the areas of China his armies controlled.

1278 Nearly 280 **Jews** were hanged in the city of London for **clipping coin**, that is, shaving or nicking bits of the precious metal off the coins before paying them out. In 1290 England expelled all Jews.

1279 The first **Statute of Mortmain**, which forbade the conveyance of land to a corporation, was passed in England. Mortmain, "dead hand," was the common practice of naming a corporation as owner of a piece of land, which then became exempt from feudal obligations. Monasteries, especially, had benefited from this practice.

V. RELIGION AND PHILOSOPHY

1252   Pope Innocent IV (c.1190–Dec. 7, 1254; ruled from 1243) issued the bull *Ad extirpanda*, approving the use of torture and confiscation of property in the discovery of heresy. His continuation of the policy of **Gregory IX** of expanding the **Inquisition** resulted in the elimination of the **Cathari** and the repression of the **Waldensians**.

1252   Peter of Verona (b. 1205), a Dominican inquisitor at Milan who became **St. Peter Martyr** when canonized in 1253, was waylaid by members of a Catharist sect and murdered near Como. The murderers were tried and executed as heretics and adversaries of the **Inquisition**, not as murderers.

1256   The Persian strongholds of the Assassins were destroyed by **Hulagu** and his Mongol army.

1259   Thomas Aquinas began the first of his two major works, *Summa contra Gentiles*, a reasoned account of Christianity, addressed to nonbelievers. In 1266 he began his *Summa Theologiae*, a valuable and influential synthesis of faith and reason.

1269   By this date, **Kublai Khan** had been converted to **Buddhism** by the high priest of the Sakya Gompa monastery in Tibet. Buddhism in Tibet gradually compromised with the local animistic religion, Bon, to emerge as Tibetan Buddhism [Lamaism].

1271 May   Edward, soon to be **Edward I**, king of England, landed at Acre, where he eased the plight of the Crusaders in what was sometimes called the **Ninth Crusade**. Edward left Acre in Sept. 1272, after some success—he had gained the nearby port of Haifa—and was in Sicily when his father Henry III (b. Oct. 1, 1207), king of England (from 1216), died on Nov. 16. On Nov. 20 Edward was named Henry's successor.

1273   Jalal-ad-Din Rumi (b. 1207 in Persia), the greatest mystic poet of Islam, died. He founded the influential order of Mawlawis, or **Dancing Dervishes**. His masterwork *Mathnavi*, though cast in poetical language, was a systematic presentation of the basic concepts and theories of **Sufism**.

1274 Mar. 7   Thomas Aquinas (b. 1225?) died en route to the second council of Lyons, having devoted his adult life to the proposition that Aristotelian and neo-Platonic naturalism and rationalism could be wedded to Christian truth. Aquinas was canonized in 1323.

1280 Nov. 15   Albertus Magnus [Albrecht von Bollstädt, Albert of Cologne] (b. 1206), a German-born Dominican scholar, died. He was noted for his compilation of Greek and Arabic writings for western students of theology. His commentaries on the works of Aristotle helped to bring an understanding of the natural world to the medieval mind.

1282 Oct. 13   Nichiren [Zenshobo Rencho] (b. 1222), a fanatic Japanese religious reformer, died, leaving behind the militant Buddhist sect he founded, the **Hokkes** or **Nichiren Shoshu**. Nichiren taught that only his beliefs were right and that, if official support continued to be given to other sects, great calamities would occur.

1291   The exhaustion of the crusading spirit in western Europe was symbolized by the **capture and destruction of Acre** by Muslim forces. Despite a long and brave defense by the Franks, the **Templars**, and the **Knights Hospitaller**, Acre fell to the Mameluke sultan Khalil [al-Ashraf Khalil] (ruled 1280–1293).

VI. SCIENCE, EDUCATION, AND TECHNOLOGY

1270   Gunpowder, possibly discovered first by the Chinese, was first positively recorded in a book written in Italy by M. Graecus. He gave a correct formula for its manufacture in the *Book of Fires for Burning Enemies*.

1281   In one of the largest military deployments in early history, c.150,000 **Mongols** were transported in Chinese and Korean ships from the Asian mainland to invade **Japan**. The ships were all destroyed enroute by a *Kamikaze* [divine wind], a typhoon.

VII. ARTS AND LEISURE

c.1250   The great **chariot-temple was begun at Konarak** by Narashimadeva (d. 1264), ruler of Orissa in India. It was never completed.

1252 A bronze image of **Amida**, nearly 50 feet high, symbolizing the faith of most Japanese Buddhists, was erected at Kamakura, headquarters of the shogunate.

1253 The **Kenchoji**, the **first building in the Kara-yo style** borrowed from China, was built in Kamakura, Japan.

1257 The Persian poet **Sa'di** [Mushariff-ud-Din] (c.1184–1291) published his classic **Bustan** [Orchard], followed the next year by **Gulistan** [Rose Garden]. *Bustan*, written almost entirely in verse, contained many stories in an epic style, usually illustrating Islamic virtues. *Gulistan*, of mingled verse and prose, contained reflections on the human condition, often of a moralizing nature.

c.1260–1270 The sculptor known only as the **Naumburg Master** completed the group of ten figures representing the founders of the **Naumburg Cathedral** at Naumburg, in present Germany.

c.1260 **Vincent of Beauvais** (c.1190–?1264) produced *Speculum Majus* [The Bigger Mirror] in three volumes: *Speculum Historiale*, *Speculum Naturale*, and *Speculum Doctrinal*. This was the best-known encyclopedia of its age. It was a leading work in the burgeoning of science in the 13th century.

c.1260 **Emir Khusro** (b. 1234) was the **first great Muslim musicologist of India**, reflecting the spread of Islamic culture eastward. He introduced Persian and Arabic elements into Indian music.

1260 **Nicola Pisano** (c.1220–1284) produced his finest work, the hexagonal pulpit with bas-reliefs of Christ in the baptistry at Pisa.

c.1283 **James of St. George**, a medieval military architect, began work on the castles at Caernarvon and Harlech, the last of the group of castles he built in **Wales** for **Edward I**, king of England. Edward had six other castles constructed in Wales to keep the conquered Welsh under control.

c.1287 **Adam de la Halle** [Adam le Bossu] (born c.1238), a French troubadour, died. He is credited with writing the **first French comedy**, *Le Jeu de la feuillée* (c.1260), and the **first comic opera**, *Le Jeu de Robin et Marion* (c.1283).

c.1291 **Crusaders** returning home by way of Cyprus introduced the use of **sugar** as a sweetener.

1294 **Safi al-Din 'Abd al-Mu'min**, chief court minstrel to al-Mustasim, the last Abbaside Caliph, died. *Kitab al-Adwar* [Book of Musical Modes] and *Risalat al-Sharafiya*, a treatise on harmonic relations, are among his extant works on music theory.

c.1297 **Thomas the Rhymer** [Thomas of Erceldoune] (born c.1220), a legendary Scottish poet and prophet, died. He was reputed to have foreseen the death of Alexander III, king of Scotland (1249–1286), and the battle of Bannockburn (1314), and to have composed the poetical romance *Sir Tristrem*.

VIII. SPORTS, GAMES, AND SOCIETY

c.1250 Extant depictions show an elementary form of **club ball**, the precursor of English **cricket**, existed at this time.

1299 The Southhampton [England] Town Bowling Club was formed, the **oldest lawn bowling organization** still in existence. Members today play on the green laid out at the club's inception.

1300–1349

I. VITAL STATISTICS AND DEMOGRAPHICS

1300 Europe's population reached c.80 million by the end of the 13th century. **Asia's population** fell from c.250 million to c.230 million. This decline was attributed to the zeal of the Mongols in exterminating the Asian peasantry.

II. DISASTERS

1314–1317 The **Great European Famine** struck England, Ireland, Poland, and the Baltic region. There were eyewitness reports that in **London**, the poor ate cats, dogs, even their own children.

1333–1337 **Famine** and **pestilence** in China followed a series of earthquakes, excessive rainfall, floods, and drought. In Kiangsi province, c.4 million deaths from starvation were recorded. The pestilence may have been the same **Black Death** that reached Europe in 1347.

1347–1353 The **Black Death** [called at the time "The Great Dying"], a **bubonic plague**, reached Mediterranean ports. The spread of this plague was attributed to the siege of a Genoese post in the Crimea by a Turkic Kipchak [Cuman] army from the Black Sea area. The Kipchaks were said to have catapulted the dead bodies of their plague victims over the fortifications into the town, where the disease spread. By c.1350 the plague had reached Scandinavia when, it was said, rats carrying the disease went ashore from a ship at the port of Bergen, Norway. By 1351, nearly one-third of the population of Europe had been killed by the Black Death. It has been estimated that 75 percent of the world's population died.

III. EXPLORATION AND COLONIZATION

1318–1330 **Oderico** [Odoric of Pordenone, a city in northeastern Italy] (c.1280–1331), a Franciscan missionary, traveled throughout Asia. Oderico crossed India and the Malay Peninsula before sailing to Canton, China. He became the **first European to visit** (1325) **Tibet**.

1324 **Mansa Musa**, king of Mali (1312–1337), a kingdom of West Africa, made a pilgrimage to **Mecca**. Among the many scholars and artists he brought back with him was the Andalusian poet and architect **As-Saheli**, who introduced the Arabian style and the technique of building with brick.

1325–1349 The Arabian **Ibn-Batuta** [Muhammad ibn-'Abdullah ibn-Battutahl] (1304–1377), born in Tangiers, explored the Near East, Turkestan, and India, and later the East Indies and China for **Muhammed Tughlak**, the Muslim sultan of Delhi (1332–1349). His journals, which also covered his extensive travels in Africa and Spain, enlightened the Muslim world. He described (1331) the city-state of Kilwa, in present Tanzania, as the leading center of Islamic civilization on the east African coast. He gave accounts of the Swahili civilization there, a mixed culture of Arab and Bantu people who lived in a town

of palaces, mosques, and fine houses constructed from stone and mortar.

IV. POLITICS AND WAR

c.1300–1499 The Muslim **kingdom of Arakan** flourished in present southwestern **Myanmar** as an independent state, bordering the Buddhist Burmese and Siamese states to Arakan's east.

1301 Jan. 14 The **Árpád Dynasty** (from 896) ended with the death of Andrew III the Venetian, king of Hungary (from 1290), and a war of succession broke out. It ended (1310) with the coronation of **Carobert** [Charles Robert of Anjou] (1288–1342), who founded (1308) the **Angevin Dynasty** (to 1387) in **Hungary**, and initiated a period of prosperity for Hungarians.

1302 Apr. **Philip IV**, king of France, called the **first meeting of the Estates-General**, a gathering of nobility, clergy, and townsmen, in order to gain their support against Pope Boniface VIII.

1306 Mar 25 **Robert the Bruce** [Robert de Bruce VIII] was crowned Robert I, king of Scotland, after the resistance leader William Wallace (b. 1272?), had been executed in London on Aug. 23, 1305. The tide turned in favor of **Scotland** as Edward I (b. June 17, 1239), king of England (from 1272), died on July 7, 1307, and was succeeded by his less competent son Edward II.

1314 June 24 Scottish forces, c.10,000 strong, led by **Robert I the Bruce**, king of Scotland, won an overwhelming victory over c.23,000 men led by Edward II, king of England, in a **battle at Bannockburn**, on the Bannock River, central Scotland. The battle secured Robert's throne and an independence that **Scotland** maintained for the next three centuries.

1314 Nov. 29 **Philip IV the Fair** (b. 1268), king of France (from 1285), died. A crisis of succession ensued as his three sons died without male heirs: **Louis X** (Oct. 4, 1289–June 5, 1316; ruled from 1314), **Philip V** (1294–Jan. 3, 1322; ruled from 1316), and **Charles IV** (1294–Feb. 1, 1328; ruled from 1322). Thus ended the direct line of the **Capetian Dynasty** (987–1328). Under the Salic Law the collateral **House of Valois** (1328–1589) gained the throne under Philip VI (1293–Aug. 22, 1350; ruled from 1328).

1315 The Nubian Christian **Kingdom of Maqurrah**, in present Sudan, was invaded by the Mamelukes of Egypt. The kingdom was gradually assimilated by the Arabs. **Alwa**, its southern neighbor, remained as the **last Nubian Christian kingdom**.

1315 Nov. 15 Forces of the canton of **Schwyz** destroyed the larger force of Leopold I (1290?–1326), Hapsburg duke of Austria, in a **battle at Morgarten**, a mountain in Switzerland. It strengthened Schwyz's alliance with the cantons of Underwald and Uri and, by 1353, Lucerne, Zurich, Glarus, Zug, and Bern had joined the confederation, named **Switzerland** from the victory of the Schwyz canton.

1316 The death of **Ala-ud-Din Mohammad Shah** (b. 1296), second king of the **Khilji Dynasty** (1290–c.1321) in India, ended a golden age for the Delhi Sultanate (1206–1526). He had subdued the Rajput principalities, the Pandyas of Madura, the Yadavas of Devagiri, and the Vaghelas of Gujarat to rule most of India. The ensuing war of succession ended in victory (c.1321) for Ghazi Malik [Ghiyas-ud-din] (d. 1325), who founded the **Tughlak** [Taghlak, Tughlug] **Dynasty** (1320–1414).

1316 Gedimin [Gedymin, Gediminas] (c.1275–1341), duke of **Lithuania**, succeeded his brother Vitenis (ruled from 1297) and went on to establish his country as a major power in eastern Europe. He founded (1323) Vilna [Vilnus] as his capital, doubled his territories by conquest and diplomacy, and succeeded in maintaining his pagan religion.

1316 May 1 Edward de Bruce, brother of Robert I the Bruce, king of Scotland, was crowned king of **Ireland** with the approval of the native chieftains. He had helped the Irish expel the English. Edward was defeated and killed at Faughart, near Dundalk, on Oct. 14, 1318, and English rule was restored.

1326 The **Ottoman** [from 'Uthman-Osman] **Empire** (to 1920) was founded when the Byzantine fortress of Bursa in Bithynia in northwestern Anatolia fell after a nine-year siege to the **Osmanli Turks** under Osman I [al-Ghazi, meaning "The Warrior"] (1258–1326), who had established an emirate in 1299.

1327 Jan. 7 Edward II, king of England (from 1307), was forced to abdicate. Edward (b. Apr. 25, 1284), imprisoned and finally murdered, at Berkeley Castle, on Sept. 21, was succeeded by his son Edward III (Nov. 13, 1312–June 21, 1377), under the co-regency of his mother Isabella of France (1292?–1358) and Roger Mortimer, earl of March.

1329 June 7 Robert I the Bruce (b. July 11, 1274), king of Scotland, died of what was thought to be leprosy. The Scottish crown, whose independence he had gained, had finally been recognized by the papacy and by England in the **Treaty of Northampton** (May 4, 1328). He was succeeded by his five-year old son David II (Mar. 5, 1324–Feb. 22, 1371).

1330 Oct. Edward III, king of England (to 1377), forced an end to the regency with aid from the barons. Roger Mortimer (b. 1287), earl of March, was executed on Nov. 29, and Queen Isabella retired, as Edward assumed full powers. In support of **Edward de Baliol** [Balliol] (d. 1364), aspirant to the crown of Scotland, he defeated a Scottish army at **Halidon Hill** on July 19, 1333. **David II de Bruce**, king of Scotland, fled to France in 1334. Edward de Baliol, who had been crowned king of Scotland in 1332, was now confirmed in his royal prerogatives by Edward III.

1333 The **Hojo Shogunate** (c.1200–1333), which controlled the Japanese puppet emperor at Kyoto from their seat in Kamakura, was ousted by **Ashikaga Takauji** (1305–1358). Though Takauji acted in support of the emperor **Daigo II** [Go-Daigo] (1287–1339; ruled from 1318), he assumed the military power of the Hojo clan and overthrew (1338) the emperor, forcing Daigo II to move his court to the south. From Shikoku, Daigo conducted a war against Takauji, now established at Kyoto as the first shogun of the **Ashikaga Shogunate** (1338–1573) [Muromachi Period].

1337 Mansa Musa, ruler of the West African Kingdom of Mali, died, and **Mali** began to decline, plagued by a dynastic struggle.

1337 The **Hundred Years' War** (to 1453) between France and England broke out as Edward III, king of England, claimed the French crown of Philip VI on the ground that Edward's mother, Queen Isabella of England, was the daughter of Philip IV, king of France.

1340 June 23 The French fleet, assembled for an invasion of England, was annihilated by the English in a **battle off the coast of Flanders at Sluis** [Sluys or l'Ecluse]. England gained naval supremacy, ending any threat of a French invasion during the Hundred Years' War.

1345   The capital of the **Aztec Empire**, **Tenochtitlán** [the Place of the High Priest or the Place of the Prickly Pear], was founded near the present site of **Mexico City** on an island in the great Lake Texcoco that then covered much of the central valley of Mexico.

1346 Aug. 26   The **battle of Crécy**, in Picardy, France, brought defeat to the French army under **Philip VI** by a smaller English force under Edward III. The battle marked one of the **first uses of small firearms and cannons** on a limited scale. These weapons lacked the effectiveness of the English longbow, but the French commander **Villoni** said that their noise was their greatest effect. The English bowmen destroyed about a third of the French army, with small losses to themselves.

V. ECONOMY AND TRADE

c.1300   By this time **European fishermen** were working the waters off Iceland. They brought their catches of herring, cod, flatfishes, pilchards, and other species to the British Isles and other regions of northern Europe for sale and processing.

c.1300   The two-banked **dromon**, a Mediterranean ship with two levels of oars, was replaced by the *zenzile*, galleys with a single bank of oars. Each oar in the *zenzile* required two or three men, seated side by side, for its handling.

1317   The **first merchant fleet** sailed between Venice and Flanders. The Venetian galleys also sailed annually to France, Alexandria, Beirut, the Holy Lands, and the Black Sea area, and gained for Venice its position as the center of Mediterranean trade during the 14th and 15th centuries.

1335   **Serfdom** was formally abolished in **Sweden**.

VI. RELIGION AND PHILOSOPHY

1302   **Pope Boniface VIII**, near the end of his church-state quarrels with Philip IV, king of France, issued the bull *Unam sanctam*, declaring: "It is altogether necessary to salvation for every human being to be subject to the Roman pontiff." Philip responded by sending troops into Italy to force a retraction.

1303 Sept. 7   A French expeditionary force, under orders of **Philip IV**, king of France, broke into the papal palace at Anagni, central Italy, where **Pope Boniface VIII** was about to issue a bull of excommunication against Philip. The pope refused to repeal his decrees against the king. The commanding officer was slow to take a further step, the people of Anagni rose up, and the French retreated. Boniface (c.1275–Oct. 11, 1303; ruled from 1294), who had collapsed after the confrontation, died one month later.

1305   **Moses de Leon** (born c.1250), the author-compiler of the **Zohar**, the most important book of the Kabbalistic system of Jewish mystical thought, died. The *Zohar*, a commentary on the Pentateuch, was in effect a medieval system of theosophy claiming to be coeval with the Torah of Moses and offering a revelation reserved for the few.

1307 Oct. 13   **Philip IV**, king of France, brutally suppressed the **Templars**, sweeping up overnight all known members in France, seizing properties, and then employing paid informers and the apparatus of the **Inquisition**, including torture, to obtain confessions to offensive acts and heresies. **Pope Clement V** (1264?–Apr. 20, 1314; ruled from 1305), a French ecclesiastic who owed his office to Philip, acquiesced.

1308 Nov. 8   **John Duns Scotus** [from Duns, Scotland] (born c.1265), the most respected Franciscan teacher and dialectician of his day, died. Duns Scotus led the attack on Thomistic thought, including the contention of Thomas that there was no basic disagreement between philosophy and theology.

1309   The **Avignonese Papacy** (1309–1378) began when Pope Clement V, strongly influenced by Philip IV, king of France, took up residence at **Avignon**. During Clement's tenure, Philip attempted to put on trial his enemy, the late Pope Boniface VIII. Though Clement revoked or emasculated Boniface's pronouncements against Philip, he thwarted the king's efforts to have Boniface condemned as a heretic.

1312 Mar. 22   Pope Clement V abolished the order of the **Knights of the Temple**, already destroyed in France by Philip IV and elsewhere by other monarchs throughout Europe. The **Council of Vienna**, held later in 1312, completed the order's suppression on the basis of alleged heresies and offenses against morality.

1314 Mar. 18 **Jacques de Molay** (b. 1243?), the **last grand master of the Templars**, after a series of trials, appeals, confessions, and recantations under the Inquisition in France, ceased further confession upon hearing his sentence of life imprisonment. Thereupon, Philip IV had him burned as a relapsed heretic.

1317 Feb. 17 **Pope John XXII** (1245–Dec. 4, 1334; ruled from 1316) condemned a Franciscan group nicknamed "the Spirituals," who sought a return to absolute poverty and a literal observance of Francis's Rule. John set (1318) the **Inquisition** against the Spirituals in Languedoc [southern France]; four were burned at **Marseille**.

1320 The **Pastoureaux** were two outbreaks of religious and political passions in France, a minor event in 1251 and a major eruption in 1320. The outbreak of 1320 was originally directed against **Philip V**, king of France, whom the people blamed for not undertaking a crusade. Ill-led by a preacher who called himself "the Master of Hungary," the mass of people, estimated at one time to number c.100,000, first sacked **Paris**, then marched into the Garonne Valley waging pogroms against Jews and lepers along the way. At **Orléans** the Pastoureaux massacred clergy and students, but at Bordeaux they were overcome by police, and their leaders were captured and executed.

1324 A treatise, **Defensor Pacis**, whose principal author was **Marsilio [Marsilins] of Padua** (c.1280–1343), a teacher in Paris, attacked the authority of the pope. It held that the only final authority in the Church was the New Testament, that the Church was the whole body of believers, and that the pope had no authority beyond that of their executive.

c.1327 **Meister Eckhart [Johannes Eckhardt]** (b. 1260?), a German Dominican, first of the great speculative mystics of the west and **father of German philosophy**, died while awaiting scrutiny for heresy. He brought into Christianity an emphasis on the divine dwelling within each soul.

1347 Apr. 10 **William of Ockham [Occam]** (b. 1285?), an English philosopher, died. **Occam's Razor**, the corollary stating that "entities must not be unnecessarily multiplied," sums up his nominalistic doctrine that the universal can be real only in individual terms. He had attacked (1339) the temporal power of the papacy in a treatise **Octo ques-**

tiones de potestate papae. Occam's defense of the state from ecclesiastical authority awoke interest in theories of government. Occam contended that no theological doctrines could be philosophically provable, all ultimately having to be accepted on authority.

1348 With the outbreak of the **Black Death**, **Jews of Europe** were charged with causing it by poisoning water supplies out of hatred of Christians and, again, with killing Christian children to use their blood in the Passover ritual. Jews were murdered by the tens of thousands in a vast arc from Spain to Poland. Rhineland Jewish communities were especially hard hit.

VII. SCIENCE, EDUCATION, AND TECHNOLOGY

c.1300–1400 The **pistol** appeared during this century. Its advantage lay in the fact that it left a hand free to hold another weapon or to hold the reins of a horse.

1300 The burning of **coal** in **London** was forbidden by **Edward I**, who objected to the dirty air it caused. The charter (1239) to mine coal at Newcastle was nullified.

1304 The **earliest recorded use of gunpowder** was by the Arabs as a propellant in a gun constructed of bamboo and iron to shoot arrows.

1340 The **first paper mill in Europe** was built at Fabriano, Italy.

1348 **Universita Karlova [Charles University]** was founded in Prague by Charles IV (May 14, 1316–Nov. 29, 1378), the Holy Roman emperor (from 1347). The university, the **first institution of higher learning in central Europe**, at the beginning taught arts, divinity, law, and medicine.

VIII. ARTS AND LEISURE

c.1300–1700 The **Renaissance**, which began in Italy in the 14th century, and moved into northern Europe during the early part of the 16th century, was characterized by a rejection of traditional medieval values and by an increased interest in and imitation of the literature and art of ancient Greece and Rome.

c.1300 **Household furniture** of this period borrowed from Gothic motifs, especially in its decoration. Unpolished oak with floral forms as well as grotesque human and animal forms, often humorously portrayed, were common expression of the Gothic sentiment.

c.1300 **Kao Ming's** [Giao Ming] *P'i-p'a chi* [The Story of the Lute] was considered the best of five surviving examples of the Yüan drama of southern China.

c.1300 The **Miracle and Mystery plays** began to come under the control of the local trade guilds, resulting during the next 250 years in the gradual secularization of **English drama**.

c.1302 **Giovanni Cimabue** [Cenni di Pepo] (born c.1240), a Florentine artist whose work broke with the Byzantine tradition by moving toward realism and portrayal of life, died. Mosaics, frescoes, and paintings appeared in the Pisa Cathedral and the church of St. Francis of Assisi but none positively his alone are extant.

c.1307 Work began on the great Imperial Palace known as the **Forbidden City** in Peking [Beijing], China. Built on the site of Kublai Khan's capital and possibly containing some buildings from that time, the Palace, comprising several buildings, had over 900 rooms.

1309 The present **Doges' Palace** [Palazzo Ducale] was begun in Venice, Italy.

1311 **June 9** **Duccio di Buoninsegna's** (1255?–?1319) great work, the **altarpiece for the Cathedral of Siena**, was installed. The leading painter of the **Sienese school**, he symbolized the Byzantine-Gothic tradition, which was characterized by a stilted religious expression now made more lifelike and real.

1314 The golden age of the **Ge'ez literature** began with the rule of **Amda Seyon I** (d. 1344), king of Ethiopia. Although the literature mainly comprised translations of Arabic works, it produced the great historical tale of the *Kebra Negast* [Glory of Kings]. Its central theme was the legend of Solomon and the Queen of Sheba, the traditional founders of the Ethiopian [Solomonic] Dynasty (1268–1974).

1319 The *Fugashu*, another of the *Kokinshu* anthologies, was compiled by **Hanazono II**, emperor of Japan (1308–1319) during a "dark age" of Japanese literature, disrupted by civil wars and revolts.

c.1320 **Walter of Evesham** [Walter Odington] described the medieval knowledge of music in **De Speculatione Musices**. It covered late 13th century rhythmic practice: mensural music, intervals, notation, and musical forms.

1321 The **first French guild of minstrels** was formed. The many amateur theatrical guilds springing up throughout Europe played an important part in the development of the performing arts as membership was regulated and fees standardized.

1321 Sept. 13? **Dante** [Dante Alighieri] (b. 1265), the great Italian poet, died. He was noted especially for the *Divina commedia* [*Divine Comedy*] (1307–1321), an elaborate tale of his journey through Hell, Purgatory, and Paradise. Dante was led through the first two by Virgil, and the last by his love Beatrice Portinari (1266–1290), whom he had idealized in *La Vita Nuova* [The New Life] (1295) as the Muse of poetry. Both works were written in Tuscan and helped establish Tuscan as the forerunner of modern Italian.

1329 May 5 **Albertino Mussato** (b. May 23, 1261), the author of *Ecerninus* (1315), the first Italian tragedy borrowing from the classical style, died. His other works included histories in the style of Livy and poems in Latin.

1337 **Giotto di Bondone** (b. 1266?), a pupil of Cimabue and friend of Dante, died. Giotto ushered in the Italian Renaissance with his allegorical frescoes at the church of St. Francis at Assisi, the Peruzzi chapel in Florence, and the Duomo in Florence.

1338–1568 The **tea ceremony**, one of the Zen arts borrowed from China, grew in importance in Japan under the **Ashikaga Shogunate** (1338–1573). Japanese ceramics of this period, increasingly patterned after Korean wares, reflect the new emphasis on the tea ceremony.

IX. SPORTS, GAMES, AND SOCIETY

c.1300 **Bowling**, with wooden pins and stone balls, was played in Germany, the number of pins varying with the locality.

1314 To celebrate the return of 600 Fife County bowmen under **Robert I the Bruce**, king of Scotland, victorious over English troops at Bannockburn, the villagers of Ceres held what has traditionally been regarded as the **first Scottish "gathering,"** held annually ever since.

1314 **Apr. 13** **Edward II**, king of England, banned the playing of **football** in London as conducive to public disturbances.

1349 Edward III, king of England, established the **Order of the Garter**, an order of knighthood having as members the English sovereign and 25 knights.

1350–1399

I. EXPLORATION AND COLONIZATION

c.1350 The **population of New Zealand** at this time was c.15,000. The **Maori culture**, which included agriculture and weaving, was more advanced than that of their distant cousins, the **Morioris**. Maori warriors, who were said to have eaten their captured enemies, dominated the Morioris and eventually drove them from New Zealand. The Morioris are thought to survive today, if at all, only in the Chatham Islands, c.500 miles east of New Zealand.

II. POLITICS AND WAR

1350 The **Thai states** were unified by **Rama Thibodi** (ruled from 1350 to 1369), founder of present Thailand [Siam]. The kingdom, centered at Ayutthaya, on the Chao Phraya River north of Bangkok, soon became one of the leading powers of Southeast Asia, extending into Myanmar [Burma], Cambodia, and the Malay Peninsula.

1356 **Chu Yüan-chang** [T'ai-tsu] (1328–1398), a Chinese Buddhist monk, gained leadership of a peasant revolt against the ruling Mongols of China's **Yüan Dynasty** (1280–1368). By 1368 Chu had driven the **Mongols** from the Yangtze River [Chang Jiang] Valley in southern China, captured the Yüan capital of Khanbalik [Beijing], and established his capital at Nanking as **Hung Wu**, the **first emperor of the Ming Dynasty** (1368–1644).

1356 **Sept. 19** English forces under the **Black Prince Edward** [Edward of Woodstock], prince of Wales (1330–1376), defeated and took prisoner John II (Apr. 26, 1319–Apr. 8, 1364), king of France (from 1350), in a **battle at Poitiers**. As an indirect result, the Estates-General tried to affirm its right to approve any new tax, and demanded the removal of some of the royal advisers.

1358 **May 21** The **Jacquerie**, a revolt by the peasantry against depressed conditions caused by the havoc of the Hundred Years' War (1337–1453), broke out in northwestern France. It was supported by the Parisian movement of the Estates-General, led by **Étienne Marcel**. Most of the rebels were massacred. Marcel (born c.1316) was murdered in Paris on July 31; and the dauphin, later Charles V the Wise (Jan. 21, 1338–Sept. 16, 1380; ruled as king from 1364), reentered the capital.

1360 **May 8** England and France, exhausted by war and facing unrest at home, signed the **Treaty of Brétigny**, followed by the **Treaty of Calais**, on Oct. 24. John II, king of France, was ransomed, and Edward III, king of England, was recognized as sovereign in Aquitaine and abandoned his claim to the French throne. It was only a short break in the Hundred Years' War (1337–1453).

1361 **Philippe I de Rouvres** (b. 1346), duke of Burgundy and last Capetian of his line, died, and his duchy was attached to the French crown. **John II**, king of France, granted (1363) it to his fourth son **Philip II the Bold** (Jan. 17, 1342–Apr. 27, 1404), who later married (1369) Margaret (1350–1405), daughter and heiress of the count of Flanders.

1361 Denmark's capture of the major commercial center of Visby, in present Sweden, precipitated a war with the Hanseatic League (1241–1669). The war ended with the defeat of the Danes and the **Peace of Stralsund** (1370).

1361 The Byzantine fortress of Adrianople [Edirne], in present Turkey, was conquered by

Turkish forces of **Murad** [Amurath] **I** (1319–1389), the Ottoman sultan (from 1359), who made it his capital. A crusade in 1366 under **Amadeus IV**, count of Savoy (1346–1383), temporarily relieved John V (Apr. 18, 1332–Feb. 16, 1391), the Byzantine emperor (from 1341), but Murad extended his rule northward into Bulgaria, Macedonia, and Serbia.

1362 Olgierd [Algirdas], the grand duke of Lithuania (1345–1377), conquered vast areas of Russian territory reaching to the Black Sea and made his duchy one of the largest European states at the time.

1364 May 16 Charles II the Bad (1332–1387; ruled from 1349), king of Navarre and a pretender to the French throne, was defeated by the French under **Bertrand Du Guesclin** (1320–July 13, 1380) at Cocherel, northwest of Paris in Normandy where Charles II held lands. Charles was forced to retreat to Navarre, and Charles V, king of France, consolidated his hold on Normandy. Du Guesclin then entered Spain to support **Henry of Trastamara** (1333–1379) in the war of succession in Castile. Henry finally won the crown by defeating and killing his rival **Peter the Cruel** [Pedro el Cruel] (b. 1334), king of Castile and León (from 1350), on Mar. 23, 1369 and ruled (1369–1379) as Henry II.

1364 Sept. 29 Jean de Montfort (1341–1399), supported by England, defeated and killed Charles de Blois [Châtillon] (b. 1319) in a **battle at Auray**, France. He was recognized as duke of Brittany by the **Treaty of Guérande** (1365), which ended the war of succession to the duchy of Brittany (1341–1365).

1365 Tamerlane [Timur Lenk or "Timur the Lame"; also Tambourlane], the Mongol conqueror, took over Transoxania to initiate his plan of restoring the Mongol Empire. With Turkish and Mongol troops he conquered (1369) Turkestan and made **Samarkand** his capital, establishing the **Timurid Dynasty** of Turkestan (1370–1501).

1372 June 23 In a revival of the **Hundred Years' War**, the English fleet was defeated off La Rochelle by France, helped by the powerful fleet of Castile. By the **Truce of Bruges** on June 27, 1375, only Bayonne, Bordeaux, Brest, Calais (captured in 1347), and Cherbourg remained under England's rule.

1380 In a **battle at Chioggia**, a seaport near **Venice**, the Venetian fleet under Vittorio [Vettore] Pisano struck a decisive blow against the maritime power of

its rival, **Genoa**. The dispute ended with the **Peace of Turin** (May 20, 1381). Venice entered its golden age, and Genoa declined.

1381 June 14 The **Peasants' Revolt**, which had begun in Essex and Kent, came to a climax when the rebels, led by [Walter] **Wat Tyler,** marched on London. After they had plundered and burned many houses, they captured the Tower of London and put the archbishop of Canterbury to death. Although Richard II, king of England, granted some of their demands, a fight broke out in which Tyler was killed (June 15) and troops dispersed the mob, ending the revolt. The revolt had its background in the Statute of Labourers (1351) which was intended to hold down wages in the light of a shortage of labor. Also, the poll tax was increased in 1380.

1382 The **Burji** [Tower] **Dynasty** (to 1517), the second **Mameluke** [Arabic: mamluk = slave] **Dynasty**, began in Egypt, succeeding the **Mameluke Bahri** [River] **Dynasty** (from 1250). No Burji sultan was particularly noteworthy or able, and the Burjis were overthrown by the Turks.

1385 Aug. 14 John I of Aviz [Avis], known as John the Bastard or the Great (1357–Aug. 14, 1433), king of Portugal (from 1385), defeated John I (1358–Oct. 9, 1390), king of Castile (from 1379), in a **battle at Aljubarrota**, in western Portugal, which secured Portuguese independence from Spain. John of Portugal founded the ruling **Aviz Dynasty** (1385–1580), and Portugal entered an age of territorial expansion.

1386 Mar. 4 Jagello (1350–1434), grand duke of Lithuania (from 1377), was crowned king of **Poland** as **Ladislas** [Wladyslaw] **II** [V] following his baptism and marriage to the Polish Queen **Jadwiga** [Hedwig] (1370–1399).

1389 June 20 Muslim Turks under Murad I, the Ottoman sultan, defeated a combined Christian force from the Balkan states led by Lazar I, prince of Serbia (1371–1389), in a **battle at Kosovo** [Kossovo], present Serbia. Both leaders were killed, and Murad was succeeded by his son Bajazet [Bayazid] I. The **Serbian Empire** in the Balkans became a vassal of the Ottoman Empire (1326–1920).

1390 Abu Faris (d. 1433) repulsed a Franco-Genoese expedition against Bougie [Bejaïa], in present Algeria, which had become the center of organized piracy. The leader of the **Hafsid Dynasty**, Abu Faris, restored the power of the Hafsid Berber Sultanate (1228–1574), centered in Tunisia, at the expense of the Marinids of Morocco and brought renewed prosperity to North Africa.

1392   The **Koryo Dynasty** (from 935), of present Korea, which had been dominated by the Mongols since 1217, came to an end when General Yi Songgye overthrew its last king. He established the **Yi Dynasty** (to 1910), which ruled the Korean Peninsula from its capital at Hanyang [Hansung], present Seoul. The kingdom was renamed Chosŏn, an early name used by the native Koreans.

1392   Rent by civil war for decades, Japan was reunited under the **Ashikaga Shogunate** (1338–1573), which ruled from Kyoto, where the imperial temple, Kinkakuji [Ginkakuji, meaning "Golden"] was soon erected. The shogunate, especially under Yoshimitsu (1358–1395; ruled from 1367), reestablished Japan as an economic and military power in the Far East.

c.1395   Mai [= ruler] **Omar I** ['Umar] **ibn Idris**, king of Kanem (1393–1397), was expelled to the west of Lake Chad, in present Nigeria, after a rebellion of the Bulala tribes. He organized his new country into the **kingdom of Bornu.**

1393   Trnovo [Veliko Turnovo], the capital of **Bulgaria**, was captured by the Turkish forces of **Bajazet I**, the Ottoman sultan.

1396 Sept. 25   A European army of **Crusaders**, called by **Pope Boniface IX** (c.1345–Oct. 1, 1404; ruled from 1389), led by **Sigismund**, king of Hungary (from 1387), was defeated by the Ottoman Turks under Bajazet I in a **battle at Nicopolis** [Nikopol]. About 10,000 prisoners were executed by the Turks.

1397   Margaret [Margrete] (1353–1412), queen of Sweden (1389) and regent of Denmark (1387) and Norway (1388), established the **Union of Kalmar** (1397–1523) in which Sweden, Denmark, and Norway were united as one nation, and had her grandnephew **Eric VII of Pomerania** (1382–1459) crowned king.

1398 Dec. 12   Tamerlane [Timur], the Mongol conqueror, defeated the sultan of Delhi at nearby Panipat on his invasion of India. Delhi was plundered for 15 days, and c.100,000 Hindus were massacred.

1399 Sept. 30   The struggle of **Richard II**, king of England, to gain absolute power failed. He submitted to Parliament, and this led to his capture and forced abdication by the Lancastrians led by Henry. Parliament then elected **Henry IV Bolingbroke** (Apr. 3, 1367–Mar. 20, 1413), son of John of Gaunt (1340–1399), duke of Lancaster, as king of England (to 1413). Thus ended the direct line of succession of the **Plantagenet Dynasty** (1154-1499) and began the rule of the **House of Lancaster** (1399–1461).

III. ECONOMY AND TRADE

c.1350   The *Mesta*, an association of Spanish sheep ranchers, was organized to protect their stock. Spain at this time had a monopoly on Merino sheep, whose export was banned.

1351   The **English Parliament**, alarmed by the scarcity of farm laborers after the **Black Death**, and consequent rise in wages, passed the **Statute of Laborers**, which set lower wages and contributed to the **Peasants' Revolt** of 1381.

1358   **Lübeck**, on the Baltic coast of present Germany, was chosen as headquarters of the **Hanseatic League** (1241–1669).

1369   The financial decline of Constantinople reached its nadir with the arrest of **John V Palaeologus** (Apr. 18, 1332–Feb. 16, 1391), the Byzantine emperor (from 1341), for debt while he was in **Venice** to borrow money.

1381 June 14   Wat Tyler led the unsuccessful attack on London in the **Peasants' Revolt**, which had spread from Essex and Kent in southeastern England. The peasants were protesting the poll tax and the use of its revenues for French wars and the **Statute of Laborers** (1351), which placed severe restrictions on their chances of improving their lot or income.

IV. RELIGION AND PHILOSOPHY

1356   Charles IV of Luxemburg (May 14, 1316–Nov. 29, 1378), the Holy Roman emperor (from 1355) and king of Bohemia, issued the **Golden Bull**, setting forth procedures for electing emperors and for administering the imperium during a vacancy. No reference to the pope was made.

1366   **Edward III** and Parliament repudiated the **feudal supremacy of the papacy over England**, declaring that, in making over (1213) his kingdom as a fief to Pope Innocent III, John had acted without the consent of the nation.

1367 Oct. 16 The Benedictine **Pope Urban V** (c.1310–Dec. 19, 1370; ruled from 1362) briefly returned the papacy to Rome from **Avignon**, over obstacles raised by the king of France and the numerous cardinals created by a succession of French popes. On Sept. 27, 1370, unrest in Rome forced Urban's return to Avignon.

1377 May 22 John Wycliffe [Wyclif, Wiclif] (1320?–Dec. 31, 1384), the rector of Lutterworth, in central England, was condemned in five papal bulls issued by Pope Gregory XI (1331–Mar. 27, 1378; ruled from 1370). Wycliffe had, in *De civilo dominio*, denounced the entire church establishment. His campaign for ecclesiastical reform became known as **Lollardry.** He argued for the limitation of Church supremacy in temporal affairs and held that the only law of the Church was the Scriptures. Christ was the sole head of the Church. A pope eager for power and money, he held, was antichrist.

1378 The **Western Schism** (1378–1417) in the Roman Catholic Church began upon the death of Pope Gregory XI. The cardinals, in Rome, elected (Apr. 8) an Italian bishop, Urban VI (1318?–Oct. 15, 1389; ruled from 1378), who soon alienated his electors. Four months later, in Avignon, France, many of the same cardinals voided their choice, charging pressure by the Roman mob, and elected Clement VII (1342–Sept. 16, 1394; ruled from 1378) as pope, who settled in Avignon. **Rival popes,** at Avignon and Rome, were elected until 1417.

c.1380 The third great commentator on the *Upanishads*, **Madhava** [Madhavacharya] (1296?–?1386), extended Ramanuja's thought that God was not an impersonal Absolute and urged a complete dualism. Grace was all-important in Madhava's teaching, but grace was bestowed only on those who live righteously, with faith and devotion.

1380 Apr. 29 Catherine of Siena [Caterina Benincase] (b. Mar. 29, 1347), died in Rome, where for two years she had defended **Pope Urban VI** against the anti-pope, **Clement VII.** Catherine, with her self-sacrificial service, intelligence, and will power, had labored to end the political and papal chaos. She was canonized in 1461.

1382 John Wycliffe left teaching at Oxford to translate the **Latin Bible** [the Vulgate] for the first time into English with the help of **Nicholas of Hereford** (d. after 1417). **John Purvey** completed the editing (c.1388). The order of preachers he then founded, known as **Lollards,** spread this Bible widely.

1392 **Buddhism,** which had dominated the Korean peninsula under the **Koryo Dynasty** (c.935–1392), was curbed by General Yi upon taking the throne. Buddhist monasteries were seized and their lands distributed among the people.

V. SCIENCE, EDUCATION, AND TECHNOLOGY

c.1350 **Chimneys** were not in common use until about this date, judging from written sources.

1362 **English** was made the official language, replacing French, for arguing cases in the **courts of England.**

1364 The **University of Kraców** [Cracow] was founded by **Casimir III** (1309–Nov. 5, 1370) **the Great,** king of Poland (from 1333).

c.1375 William Benkelsoor, a Dutch fisherman, was credited with finding a way to **salt and store gutted herring** on board ship.

1379 **Ibn-Khaldun** ['Abd-al-Rahman ibn-Khaldun] (May 27, 1332–Mar. 19, 1406), perhaps the greatest Arab historian, completed his universal history of Arabs, Berbers, and Muslims in North Africa, *Kitab al'Ibar* [Instructive Examples].

VI. ARTS AND LEISURE

c.1350 The *Story of the Three Kingdoms* [*San-kuo-chih-t'ung-su-yen-i*] by **Lo Kuan-Chung** [Lo Pen] (c.1330–c.1400) was the **first major Chinese historical novel**. It was almost certainly based on oral traditions.

1350 **Yoshida Kenko** [*real name:* Yoshida Kaneyoshi; *also:* Urabe Kaneyoshi] (b. 1283), a Japanese writer on religious topics, died. *Grasses of Idleness* was probably his most important work.

1351–1388 **Firoz Shah Tughlak,** sultan of Delhi in India, was said to have overseen the building of 200 towns, 30 colleges, and 150 bridges during his reign.

1368–1644 During the **Ming Dynasty** (1368–1644), a **porcelain** factory renowned for its blue underglaze was built at Ching-t'ou-chiang [Ching-te-chen, Jing-toujlang; Fowliang].

1374 July 18 Francesco Petrarch [Petrarco] (b. July 20, 1304), an Italian poet, died. *Rime* [*Canzoniere*], a collection of poems in the Italian vernacular, idealized his love for Laura [Laure de Noves?], a woman he first saw on the night of Holy Friday in 1327. Petrarch, with Boccaccio, laid the basis for Italian Humanism.

1375–1379 Jehan of Bruges designed the famed tapestry of the *Apocalypse*, ordered by the duke of Anjou.

1375 Dec. 21 Giovanni Boccaccio (b. 1313), the father of Italian prose, died. His works, especially *Decameron* [Ten Days' Entertainment] (1353), were a model for Geoffrey Chaucer, William Shakespeare, and Gabriele D'Annunzio. The *Decameron*, a collection of 100 stories, drew in turn on many sources.

1377 Guillaume de Machaut [Machault] (born c.1300), a French poet and musician, died. Machaut's *Mass for Four Voices* was composed for the coronation of Charles V, king of France, at Reims [Rheims]. He wrote both monodic and polyphonic works, including lays, ballades, rondeaus, virelais, and motets.

c.1383 *The Play of the Lord's Prayer*, an antecedent to the **Morality plays** that became popular in the 15th century, was performed at York in England. The Morality plays relied on allegory and named characters for their prominent traits.

1384 Motokiyo Se'ami [*real name:* Yusaki Saemondayu Motokiyo; *also:* Kanze Motokiyo] (1363–1443), took over the direction of the acting troupe of his father, Kan'ami Kiyotsugu [Kanze Kanami] (1333–1384). He turned the **No drama of Japan** into the standard entertainment of the samurai, the aristocratic warrior class. Almost half of the 240 surviving No plays are now attributed to him, of which **Takasago** [Aioi] is today the best known.

1389 Hafiz [Shams ud-din Mohammed] (b. 1324), a lyric poet, Persian dervish, and mystic philosopher, died. *Divan* was a collection of his odes.

1390 The **first** *emaki*, or narrative scrolls illustrated by printed pictures, were produced in Japan.

1397 Sept. 2 Francesco Landino [degli Organi] (b. 1325), a composer of *ars nova*, died. More than one-third of the extant Italian works of the 14th century were by Landino.

c.1390 Kalidasa, a Sanskrit poet, presented his plays at the courts of Ujjain, capital of the former Indian **Kingdom of Malwa**.

1400–1449

I. VITAL STATISTICS AND DEMOGRAPHICS

1400 Europe's population was only c.60 million compared with its medieval high of c.80 million. **World population** had dropped during the 14th century from c.360 to c.350 million. **Asia** increased from c.230 to c.235 million, **Africa** from c.38 to c.43 million, and the **Americas** from c.12.5 to c.13.5 million.

1400 The **Hawaiian Islands**, colonized by Polynesians who came there (400–900) in canoes, was home to half of Polynesia's population of c.200,000.

II. EXPLORATION AND COLONIZATION

1405 Cheng Ho (d. 1433), a Chinese admiral, began the first of his voyages, under the Ming emperors **Yung Lo** [Chu Ti, Ch'eng Tsu] (1359–1424; ruled from 1403) and **Hsuan-Te** [Chu Chan-Chi, Hsuan-Tsung] (1398–1435; ruled from 1426). Cheng Ho's **seven expeditions of exploration**, diplomacy, and trade brought him in contact with states in Southeast Asia, India, Ceylon, Arabia, Egypt, and East Africa.

1420 João Gonçalves Zarco [Zargo] discovered **Madeira**, an island in the Atlantic Ocean off the Moroccan coast, and founded (1421) its capital city of **Funchal**. It was the first step by the Portuguese prince, **Henry the Navigator** (Mar. 4, 1394–Nov. 13, 1460), in his aim to dominate Indian Ocean trade by rounding Africa.

1432 The uninhabited islands of the **Azores**, in the North Atlantic, visited (c.1427) by **Diogo de Sevilla**, a Portuguese explorer, were first settled by **Gonçalo Velho Cabral** (1460?–?1526) at Santa Maria.

1441 Antão Gonçalves and Nuño Tristão, **Portuguese explorers** sailing for Prince Henry, discovered Cape Blanc and Rio de Oro, a bay on the western Saharan coast. They returned to Lisbon with Berber captives, who provided information about caravan trade routes in West Africa.

1443 Gilianes [Gil Eanes] and Nūno Tristão, **Portuguese explorers** sent forth by Prince Henry the Navigator, discovered Arguin Island off the West African coast, in present Mauritania. **Arguin Fort** (1445) was the **first European trading settlement established in West Africa.**

III. POLITICS AND WAR

c.1400 The **Kingdom of Malacca** (to 1511), on the Malay peninsula, was founded by **Paramesvara** (d. 1424) of the Hindu **Srivijaya Kingdom** [Shrivijaya] (100–1250) in Sumatra, in present Indonesia. with the decline of the neighboring Hindu Empire of **Majapahit** (1293–c.1465), and Malacca became the leading maritime power in southeastern Asia.

1400 **Tamerlane** [Timur], the Mongol conqueror, invaded **Syria** after a devastating campaign in Georgian Russia and Anatolia. Aleppo and Damascus were laid to waste in 1401, along with Baghdad, also in 1401.

1402 July 28 **Tamerlane** defeated the forces of Bajazet I, the Ottoman sultan, who was taken prisoner, in a **battle at Angora** [Ankara], in Anatolia. Bajazet [Bayazid, Bayezid] (b. 1347) died in captivity in 1403.

1403 July 21 **Henry IV**, king of England, defeated the Percy family of Northumberland in a **battle at Shrewsbury**, in which Henry Percy (b. May 20, 1364) was killed. Percy, called Hotspur, had conspired

with the Welsh and others to dethrone the king. The powerful Welsh barons, unable to reach Shrewsbury in time for the battle, united under Owen Glendower [Owain ab Gruffydd] (1359?–c.1416), who had proclaimed himself prince of Wales in 1401. Glendower fought until 1415, but Henry IV's further victories virtually put an end to the Welsh rebellion.

1405 **Tamerlane** [Timur, Timur Lenk, Tambourlaine] (b. 1336) died during a projected invasion of Ming China. He was buried at Samarkand in Turkestan, the capital of his short-lived **Mongol Empire**, which was divided between his two sons, the Timurids, under Miran Shah (most of whose legacy died with him in 1407), and Shah Rokh [Rukh] (d. 1447), under whom Persia enjoyed a revival.

1407 Nov. 23 The brother of the French king, Louis (b. Mar. 13, 1372), duke of Orléans (from 1392), was murdered in Paris by **John the Fearless**, duke of Burgundy (from 1404), in a struggle for control of the mad **Charles VI**. Bernard VII (d. 1418), count of Armagnac, took over the **Orléanist** [Armagnac] **party**, in opposition to the Burgundians. A civil war broke out between the two factions.

1410 May 8 **Rupert III** (b. 1352), king of Germany (from 1400), died. **Sigismund of Luxemburg**, king of Hungary (from 1387), was elected (July 21, 1411) to succeed him. Sigismund was elected the Holy Roman emperor in 1411, but was not crowned by the pope until May 31, 1433.

1414 **Khizr Khan** (d. 1422), governor of the Punjab since Tamerlane's invasion into India (1398), overthrew the **Tughlak** [Taghlak, Tughlug] **Dynasty** (from 1320) of Delhi.

1415 June 13 **Henry the Navigator**, prince of Portugal, started from Lisbon on an expedition that took Ceuta, in present Morocco, from the **Marinid Dynasty** (1269–1420) on Aug. 24. It marked the **beginning of Portuguese dominance of West Africa.**

1415 Oct. 25 Having invaded France at the invitation of the **Burgundians**, the English forces of **Henry V**, king of England, and their allies destroyed the French army of the **Orléanist party** at Agincourt in Picardy, northern France. The Burgundians gained control of the mad **Charles VI**, king of France, whose heir, the dauphin **Charles VII**, organized (1418) a rival government in Bourges, c.125 miles south of Paris.

1419 Jan. 19 Henry V, king of England, completed his conquest of Normandy and, with the capture of Rouen, threatened Paris, now occupied by the Burgundians, sometime allies of the English. An attempt by the French dauphin **Charles VII** and John (b. May 28, 1371), duke of Burgundy, to reconcile in order to meet the English threat to Paris ended with John's murder on Sept. 10. His successor, **Philip the Good** (July 31, 1396–June 15, 1467), continued the Burgundian pro-English policy.

1419 Aug. 16 Wenceslaus IV (b. 1361), king of Bohemia, died and was succeeded by his half brother Sigismund, the Holy Roman emperor (1411–1437) and king of Hungary by marriage (from 1387). The **Hussite Wars** (1419–1434) broke out in Bohemia, where the followers of John Huss, an anti-Rome religious leader and reformer, opposed the new ruler.

1420 In China **Yung Lo** [Chu Ti, Ch'eng Tsu], the second Ming emperor, moved the capital from **Nanking** to **Peking** [Peiping, Beijing].

1420 June 2 The mad Charles VI, king of France, under Burgundian influence, married his daughter, Catherine of Valois (Oct. 27, 1401–Jan. 3, 1437), to Henry V, king of England, after naming him the French heir by the **Treaty of Troyes** (May 21). Both kings, Henry (b. Sept. 16?, 1387; ruled from Mar. 21, 1413) and Charles (b. Dec. 3, 1368; ruled from Nov. 4, 1380) died in 1422, on Aug. 22 and Oct. 21, respectively, and the infant Henry VI of England (born Dec. 6, 1421) was proclaimed king of France, a title already assumed by the French dauphin Charles VII.

1423 Aug. 1 The allied forces of France and Scotland were decisively defeated at Cravant, south of Paris, by English and Burgundian forces under **John Plantagenet**, duke of Bedford (1389–1435), regent for the infant **Henry VI**. Bedford won another striking victory over the French and Scots at Verneuil, west of Paris, on Aug. 17, 1424, gaining control of France north of the Loire. On Oct. 23, 1428, the English and Burgundians began their siege of Orléans, whose fall would lead to the **conquest of Bourges**.

1424 May 21 James I (1394–Feb. 20, 1437), king of Scotland, but held captive in England since 1406, was finally released and crowned at Scone, Scotland. He attempted to reassert royal authority over the nobility with the execution (1425) of **Murdoch** [Mur-

dac], duke of Albany, regent (from 1420), and his sons.

1428 **Tenochitlán** formed an alliance with Texcoco and Tlacopán, neighboring Aztec cities in the central valley of Mexico, creating the **Aztec Empire** (c.1428–1520). In 1440, when **Montezuma I** [Moctezuma; Nahuatl: Motecuhzoma] (1390?–?1464) came to the throne, he ruled an empire that extended from the Atlantic to the Pacific oceans.

1428 The **Kingdom of Annam** under Le Loi, in present Vietnam, rebelled against Chinese suzerainty and reestablished its independence (to 1883) from China. Le Loi established the later **Le Dynasty** (1428–1787). In 1431, Hsuan-Te [Chu Chan-Chi, Hsuan-Tsung], the Chinese emperor (1426–1435), recognized the independent kingdom.

1429 May 8 Joan of Arc freed Orléans, besieged by the English forces, and induced Charles VII, king of France, to go to Reims, where he was crowned on July 17. It was another turning point in the **Hundred Years' War** (1337–1453) between England and France.

1429 The **Order of the Golden Fleece**, the knightly order prominent in Spain and Portugal, was established by **Philip the Good**, duke of Burgundy, in Bruges.

1431 The Khmer capital of Angkor, in present **Cambodia** [Kampuchea], was sacked by a **Thai** [Siamese] **invasion**. The territorial expansion of the Thai Kingdom [Thailand], centered at Ayutthaya, nearly destroyed the **Khmer Empire**, which abandoned (1434) Angkor for the more southern site of present Phnom Penh.

1435 Feb. 2 Joanna II (b. 1414), queen of Naples (from 1415), died without issue. Thus ended the rule in Italy of the French **House of Anjou**. **René I of Anjou** (1409–1480) was defeated by his rival **Alfonso V** [el Magnánimo] (1385–1458), king of Aragon and Sicily (from 1416), who was finally recognized as king of Naples as well as already being king of Sicily by **Pope Eugenius IV** (1383?–Feb. 23, 1447; ruled from 1431) in 1442.

1435 Sept. 21 Philip the Good, duke of Burgundy, signed the **Peace Treaty of Arras** with Charles VII, king of France. The French regained Île de France, captured by England earlier during the Hundred

Years' War, and Paris was freed from English occupation on Apr. 13, 1436.

1437 Dec. 9 Sigismund (b. Feb. 15, 1368), the Holy Roman emperor (from 1411), died, ending the **House of Luxemburg's** contribution to the line of emperors. He was succeeded (1438) by his son-in-law **Albert V** (Aug. 10, 1397–Oct. 27, 1439), duke of Austria, who was crowned as Albert II, king of Hungary (Jan. 1, 1438), of Germany (Mar. 18), and of Bohemia (June 29, 1438).

1438 Pachacutec [Pachacuti] Yupanqui (ruled 1438–1471) began the expansion of the **Incas** centered in the Cuzco Valley of southeastern Peru by conquering the neighboring **Chancas**. Within 35 years the Inca realm was almost three-quarters the size of the empire of Alexander the Great (c.1,600,000 to 2,000,000 sq. mi.).

1439 **Eric VII [Erik] of Pomerania** (c.1381–May 3, 1459), king over the **Union of Kalmar** (since 1397), was deposed from the thrones of Denmark and Sweden due to the unpopularity of his foreign wars and his favoritism toward Danes. He was deposed from the throne of Norway in 1442, thus essentially ending the Union of Kalmar.

1443 **Scanderbeg** [Turkish: Iskender Bey; real name: George Castriota] (1405–1468), prince of **Albania**, organized resistance against Ottoman rule. Until his death, Albania successfully repulsed every Ottoman invasion, and Scanderbeg became a national hero.

1444 May 28 William de la Pole (Oct. 16, 1396–May 2?, 1450), earl of Suffolk, negotiated the **Treaty of Tours** with France, which arranged a two-year truce in the Hundred Years' War and led to the marriage of Henry VI, king of England, and Margaret of Anjou (1430–1482) on Apr. 22, 1445.

1444 Nov. 10 Ladislas III (b. 1424), king of Poland (from 1433) and of Hungary (from 1440), was defeated and killed by the Turkish forces of Murad II, the Ottoman sultan (1404–Feb., 1451; ruled from 1421), in a **battle at Varna** [Stalin] on the Black Sea. The Balkans fell to the Ottoman Empire.

1447 Shah Rukh [Rokh], ruler of Khorasan [Khurasan], a province in present Iran, and Persia [Iran], died. He ruled a large area, including Samarkand from 1404, and subjugated the **Turkoman**

Black Sheep Dynasty, which had originated in northwestern Persia [Azerbaijan].

1448 The Hanseatic town of Berlin was captured by **Frederick II** [the Iron], a member of the **Hohenzollern Dynasty** (1415–1918), who was the elector of Brandenburg (from 1440), a state in the **Holy Roman Empire**. Berlin became capital of the Hohenzollern who, in control of Brandenburg since 1415, were building a strong centralized state.

1448 Oct. 20 The Turkish forces of Murad II, the Ottoman sultan, defeated a Crusader army under the Hungarian regent John Hunyadi (c.1387–1456) at the **second battle of Kosovo**.

IV. ECONOMY AND TRADE

c.1400–1450 **Bankers of Florence**, notably the houses of Bardi, Frescobaldi, and Peruzzi, were the most important financiers in Europe. When **Edward III**, king of England, defaulted on his loans during the Hundred Years' War, both the Bardi and Peruzzi failed.

1401 The **Bank of Barcelona**, in the **Kingdom of Aragon** in Spain, was established. It minted coins, handled the accounts of military orders, and made loans to the city of Barcelona.

1410 The **first known endorsement of a bill of exchange** in Europe was made. It had been used earlier in the Near East, but had become popular in Europe only since the crusades.

1420 **High interest rates** charged by the moneylenders of **Florence**, as much as 266 percent, caused the Florentine government to set a maximum rate of 20 percent. The measure failed because moneylenders were unwilling to take bad risks at lower rates, and prospective borrowers were willing to pay the high rates.

1439 A change was made in the **method of pricing bread** in **Paris**. Previously, the price charged for a loaf of bread had been fixed, and bakers varied the size of a loaf according to economic fluctuations. Now the weight of a loaf was set, and the prices were allowed to vary.

1439 Nov. 2 Under the guidance of **Jacques Coeur** (1395?–Nov. 25, 1456), financial adviser to **Charles VII**, king of France, all taxes previously paid by tenants to their feudal lords, known as the *taille*, were assigned to the French crown; later this included a yearly tax based on estimated farm income. This change in taxes made the crown independent of any parliament, giving the king almost absolute power.

1443 Jan. 22   Jacques Coeur, now a shipping owner, was granted the right by Charles VII, king of France, to **impress vagrants** to fill out his crews.

V. RELIGION AND PHILOSOPHY

1401   As **Tamerlane** captured **Baghdad** by storm, an estimated 20,000 persons were massacred, among them the Christian Nestorians. Surviving **Nestorians** fled to the mountains of Kurdistan and the region west of Lake Urmia in northwestern Iran.

1401   The law *De Heritico Comburendo* was passed in England. England's first statute to condemn heretics to death by burning, it initiated a persecution of the **Lollards**.

1409 Mar. 25   The **Council of Pisa**, called by the cardinals of both popes, **Gregory XII** and **Benedict XIII** [the antipope], met to attempt to heal the **Western Schism** (1378–1417). Neither pope attended. Both were deposed on June 5, and neither accepted the decision. The council then elected (June 26) Alexander V (born c.1340), who died the following year (May 3). The Church now had three popes, Benedict XIII having support in Spain, Portugal, and Scotland; and Gregory XII, in parts of Germany and Italy.

1410   **John Huss**, rector of the University of Prague and popular as a preacher, was excommunicated by Prague's archbishop for his Wycliffe-like doctrines and criticisms of the clergy. Huss became a national hero. In 1412 Huss attacked a promise of indulgence from the antipope **John XXIII** (d. Nov. 22, 1419; ruled 1410–1415 deposed) to Crusaders against the pope's enemy, **Ladislas** (1379?–1414), king of Naples (1386–1414), and publicly burned John's bull.

1412 Jan. 6   **Joan of Arc** was born at Domremy on the Meuse River in France to devout farming folk. Before her 13th birthday she had heard for the first time a heavenly voice; in the years following they spoke to her two or three times weekly.

1414 Nov.   The **Council of Constance** convened. It was called by antipope John XXIII, under pressure

from Sigismund, the Holy Roman emperor. Some 100,000 persons attended. In Mar. 1415, John, perceiving that he would be tried, fled the city but was seized by Sigismund, and the council proceeded.

1415 May 29   **Pope John XXIII** was deposed by the Council of Constance. Since the Council had been called by John, it implicitly recognized him as pope, but he is generally listed today as an anti-pope. The aging **Gregory XII** abdicated in mid-June. **Benedict XIII**, his authority reduced to his estate in Spain, hung on until his death in 1424.

1415 July 6   **John Huss** [Jan Hus] (b. 1372 or 1373) was burned to death, condemned by the **Council of Constance** for having refused to recant or modify positions he had taken on the ultimate authority in Christianity. Hussites in Prague thereupon confiscated Church property, administered the cup to the laity in defiance of the Council's dictum, and demanded free preaching of the Gospel.

1417 Nov.   At the Council of Constance, a Roman cardinal, Ottone Colonna, was elected **Pope Martin V** (1368–Feb. 20, 1431), ending the **Western Schism** (from 1378). Yet, when the council adjourned in Apr. 1418, its reform intentions were unrealized. It insisted on Martin's calling another council for 1423.

1419   **Tsong-Kha-Pa** (b. 1357), a Tibetan Buddhist reformer, died. He had founded a **Mahayana** [Greater Vehicle] **Buddhist sect** called the Yellow Bonnets [Yellow Sect; Yellow Hats], which differed from the established Red Bonnets [Red Sect; Red Hats] and soon came to be the more powerful of the two. The title of **Dalai Lama** [all-embracing monk] was bestowed upon the successors of Tsong-Kha-Pa, who ruled Tibet.

1420 Nov. 1   A crusade, summoned by **Pope Martin V** and led by **Sigismund**, the Holy Roman emperor, was defeated in a **battle at Vysehrad**, near Prague, by the Hussite forces under **Count Jan Zizka** (1376–1424). The military innovations introduced by Zizka, such as mobile cannons and armored peasant chariots, proved effective throughout the **Hussite Wars** (1420–1434).

c.1425   The *Tao-tsang*, or canon of **Taoist writings**, was published with imperial patronage but begun under Chu Ti [Yung-Lo] (1360–1424), of the **Ming Dynasty**. It consisted of 1464 works, arranged in three sections.

c.1430–1490 Islam spread steadily to the port cities of Java and eastward to the Molucca Islands by means of the conversion of their rulers.

1431 The **last of the crusades**, sent by Pope Martin V during the **Hussite Wars**, was routed by Procop the Great at Damazlice in Bohemia. The pope died on Feb. 20 and his successor, Eugenius IV (1383?–Feb. 23, 1447; ruled from 1431), could not deter the **Council of Basel** from negotiating with the moderate Hussites.

1431 The **Council of Basel**, which had been called by Pope Martin but was opposed by Pope Eugenius, opened. It proceeded to discuss the ecclesiastical and spiritual reforms that the Council of Constance had failed to accomplish. Two years later the Council's initial successes, including an accommodation with moderate dissenting Hussites in Bohemia, forced the reluctant pope to recognize it. Thereafter animosity toward Eugenius spoiled the Council's judgments and gradually brought about its collapse (c.1439).

1431 Jan. 3 **Joan of Arc** was turned over by English commanders in France to **Pierre Cauchon** (d. 1442), bishop of Beauvais, for trial by a French ecclesiastical tribunal hostile to the charismatic military leader and the interests of **Charles VII**, king of France. She had been sold into English hands by Burgundian allies who had accidentally captured her at Compiègne on May 23, 1430. The English forced Cauchon to try her on religious charges.

1431 May 30 **Joan of Arc**, found guilty by a packed French tribunal presided over by Bishop Cauchon, of 12 assorted offenses, such as wearing masculine dress, sinful pride, disobedience to parents, making worthless claims of visions, and false claims of prophecy, and her claim that she was responsible not to the Church or its tribunal but to God only, was excommunicated, returned to the English forces, and **burned alive at Rouen**.

1434 May 30 The radical **Hussites** [Taborites], led by Procop the Great, were defeated and Procop [Andrew Prokop] (b. 1380?) was killed by the allied Catholics and moderate Hussites [Utraquists Calixtins] in a **battle at Český-Brod** [Böhmisch-Brod, Lipan], ending the **Hussite Wars** (from 1420) in Bohemia. An agreement, known as the **Compact of Iglau** [Jihlava], was promulgated on July 5, 1436; it was so worded that each faction could safely interpret the Four Articles of Prague as they chose.

1438 The **Pragmatic Sanction of Bourges** was promulgated by Charles VII, king of France, with the support of clergy and nobles in conclave. It asserted France's national rights by limiting papal jurisdiction and tax collections as well as establishing the liberty of the Gallican Church. In 1439 the German princes at Mainz also enacted into law some of the reforms first proposed at the Council of Basel in 1431.

1439 July The reunion of the Greek and Latin churches was proclaimed at Florence, to which the **Council of Ferrara** had moved earlier in the year. But the reconciliation was attacked by large elements in the Greek communion, no significant military assistance to beleaguered Constantinople was given, and the reunion was nullified when the Turks captured the eastern capital in 1453.

1442 A papal bull of **Pope Nicholas V** (1398–Mar. 24, 1455; ruled from 1445) encouraged Portuguese engagement in the slave trade along the West African coast. The **first black slaves** were imported from Africa in 1444 by captains of the ships of Henry the Navigator.

VI. SCIENCE, EDUCATION, AND TECHNOLOGY

c.1400 The **Chimu Indians** of northern Peru built their capital, **Chan Chan**, the **largest known adobe city** in the world prior to this date, and attempted to furnish it with water from the Chicama River c.50 miles to the north. The Chimus built La Cumbre canal, but it was never used because the canal sloped in the wrong direction.

1406 Mar. 19 **Ibn-Khaldun** [Abd-al-Kahman ibn-Khaldun] (b. May 27, 1332), an Arab historian, died. His most important work was the *Kitab-al-Ibar* [*Universal History*] (1377), in which he developed a philosophy of history.

1410 **Scotland** established its first university, at **St. Andrews**, by Scottish teachers and students driven out of Paris during the **Western Schism**. Glasgow followed in 1451, and **Aberdeen**, Scotland's third university, was founded in 1495.

1418 **Henry the Navigator**, prince of Portugal, established a **school of navigation at Sagres** on Cape Saint Vincent, Portugal. The school studied all possible means of improving navigation, observations of skies and seas, and design of ships; maps and instruments for marine navigation were made, preserved, and improved.

c.1420 In China **Chu Ti** [Yung-Lo], the Ming emperor, created a **palace school to educate imperial eunuchs**, who performed administrative duties essential to the functioning of the government. Training in the Chinese classics became mandatory for these civil service positions.

1423 **Venice** opened the **first lazaretto**, or quarantine station, on a nearby island, at first declaring a 30-day [trentina], then later a 40-day [quarantina], period of isolation for persons infected with contagious diseases. The lazaretto grew out of an ancient concept of isolation as a means of disease control.

1445 The newly devised **Korean alphabet**, *ŏnmum*, was used to explain Chinese texts. Although China's great culture overshadowed Korea's own literary development, the Korean alphabet was more advantageous for international communication than the Chinese picture alphabet.

VII. ARTS AND LEISURE

1400–1499 **Ballet** had its origins at Italian Renaissance courts. Between courses at important banquets, nobles offered their guests dramatic entertainments that included dance, poetry, mime, and songs, often centered on a single theme, such as a classical myth.

c.1400 **William Langland** [Langley] (born c.1332), author of the allegorical poem *The Vision of William concerning Piers the Plowman* (c.1370), died.

c.1400 The *Rederijkers* [referring to rhetoric] of Holland began to form. These groups wrote poetry and allegorical dramas, and organized festive functions. The English morality play *Everyman* was thought to have originated with *Elckerijk* [Everyman] (c.1495), in which the main character Everyman has as his only friend Good Deeds.

c.1400 **Jean Froissart** (born c.1337), a French poet and chronicler, died. His *Chronicles* covered the history of his time from 1325 to 1400. He had traveled throughout Europe, notably to Milan (1368) with Chaucer and Petrarch.

1400 Oct. 25 **Geoffrey Chaucer** (born c.1340), a medieval English poet, died. His *Troilus and Criseyde* (c.1384), a tale of chivalric love based on classical mythology and other sources, remains today one of the great narrative poems in English. He acknowledged that c.2,700 lines were translations from Boccaccio's *Filostrato*, to which he added c.5700 lines of his own, an accepted practice in those days. His other works: *Canterbury Tales* (c.1387–1400), his most famous; *The Duchess* (1369); *Boece* (1373–1385); *The Legend of Good Women* (c.1386); and *The Complaint of Chaucer to His Empty Purse* (1399–1400), a humorous attempt to win a pension from Henry IV.

1402 The *Confrérie de la Passion*, the most celebrated association for the production of Mystery plays was formed in Paris.

1404 **Claus Sluter** (c.1350–1406), a Dutch-born sculptor, completed his restoration (begun 1380), of six figures for the **Well of Moses** in the Carthusian monastery at Dijon, France. There, after the death of Jean de Marville (d. 1389), who began the work on the mausoleum of Philip the Bold, he worked until his own death; it was completed by Clause [or Nicolas] de Werve [Klass van de Werve] (c.1380–1439), a nephew of Sluter.

1404 Jan. **Lorenzo Ghiberti** (1378–1455) began work on the **bronze doors for the baptistry of San Giovanni** in Florence.

1408 **John Gower** (born c.1325), an English poet and contemporary of Chaucer, died. His extant works include *Speculum Meditantis* (in French, 1376); *Miroir de l'Omme* (c.1375), a French allegory; *Confessio Amantis* (1390), a collection of stories similiar to Chaucer's *Canterbury Tales*; and *Vox Clamantis* (in Latin, 1382). *Chaucer* dedicated *Troilus and Cresyde* to "moral Gower."

c.1417 The three Belgian minature painters, Pol, Hermann, and Jehannequin **Malouel** of Limburg [Limbourg], died. Their collaborative work produced a book of daily prayers *Les très riches heures* and other illuminated manuscripts typical of the finest gothic painting. They are now in the Condé Museum at Chantilly.

1420 **Filippo Brunelleschi** [Brunellesco] (1379–Apr. 16, 1446) designed the **grand dome of the Santa**

Maria del Fiore cathedral in Florence. Said to be the first to use scientific principle to determine perspective, he was considered the **founder of Renaissance architecture**.

1422 Jan van Eyck (c.1390–1441) and his brother Hubert [Huybrecht van] (1370?–?1440) **pioneered in the use of oil paints** in *The Adoration of the Lamb* for the cathedral of St. Baron at Ghent. The Adoration was called a supreme masterpiece of art; it was a polyptych of six panels of wood, eleven feet high and fourteen wide.

1428 Masaccio [Tommaso Guidi] (b. 1401) **of Florence**, Italy, died. His few extant works include **frescoes** in the Brancacci Chapel of the church of Santa Maria del Carmine in Florence. He used landscapes for backgrounds and gave depth and realism to his paintings.

c.1430 Engraving developed in the Rhine River Valley at this time.

1434 Fernão Lopes (c.1380–c.1460) received a commission from John I, king of Portugal, to write a history of the Portuguese kings. He wrote for twenty years, producing his voluminous *Cronicas*. Today, only three of the chronicles exist, covering the establishment of the **Aviz** [Avis] **Dynasty** (1385–1580) in 1385.

c.1435 Leone Battista Alberti (Feb. 14, 1404–Apr. 25, 1472), an Italian painter and architect, wrote *De pictura*, which formulated a critical standard for Renaissance painting and presented for the first time the idea that a flat canvas must create a scene by means of perspective.

1435 Abd el-Kadir [al-Qadir], a Persian music historian, died. *Jami 'al-Alhan* (1405), a treatise on Per-

sian music, and *Kanz al-Alhan* (*Treasury of melodies*) (1418) were among his works.

1436 Fra Angelico [*orig*.: Guido di Pietro or Giovanni da Fiesole] (1387–1455), a Dominican friar, decorated the cells of the monks at the convent of San Marco in Florence, which was taken over by the Dominican order in this year. Fra Angelico executed c.50 frescoes as aids to the monks' devotions.

1438 Oct. 20 Jacopo della Quercia (born c.1374), an early Renaissance sculptor in Siena, Italy, died. His work on the center portal of **San Petronio in Bologna** was considered his masterpiece.

c.1440–1550 *The Book of the Thousand and One Nights* was written down in Arabic.

1441 Iacopo Bellini (c.1400–c.1470) won a competition over Antonio Pisano (1395–1455) with a portrait of Lionello d'Este, which helped establish him as the **founder of the Venetian school of painting**.

1444 Konrad Witz (c.1400–1447), a Swiss painter, exhibited *The Miraculous Draught of Fishes*, a wide landscape of Lake Geneva, considered to be the **first landscape painting in Europe**.

1448 Andrea Mantegna (Sept. 13, 1431–1506), an Italian painter in Padua, was certified an independent master when he was only 17. His engravings especially were characterized by a combination of intellectual strength, classicism, and realism.

VIII. SPORTS AND GAMES

1410 Fencing in Germany was described in a manuscript, with the suggestion that the sport first appeared in the 14th century. The double-edged sword was used, a clumsy weapon for dueling.

1450–1499

I. VITAL STATISTICS AND DEMOGRAPHICS

1450 The **Itzá Maya** moved from southeastern Mexico into present northern Guatemala, at Lake Petén.

1492 The **Americas** were inhabited by c.14 million people. The Aztecs and Incans of Mexico and Peru

numbered from 3 to 4 million each. Tribes along the North American eastern seaboard, in the Caribbean, southern Mexico, and Central America accounted for c.5 or c.6 million more. Peoples of the western U.S. and Canada, the Brazilian jungles, and southern Argentina contributed c.1 million to the continental total.

1492 Oct. 12 Christopher Columbus's expedition was the first to bring Europeans information about the people of the Western Hemisphere whom he called Indians and who today are known as Amerinds or Native Americans. Their origin is thought today to have been in eastern Asia, and they probably entered America over the **Bering Land Bridge** between 35,000 and 12,000 years ago.

II. DISASTERS

1492 A second **Coming of Christ and the Last Judgment** was predicted for this year, thought to be the 7000th from Creation by many Orthodox Christians, especially in Russia.

III. EXPLORATION AND COLONIZATION

1456 **Alvise da Cadamosto** (1432?–?1511), a Venetian navigator in the service of Henry the Navigator, discovered the **Cape Verde Islands** in the Atlantic Ocean west of Dakar, in present Senegal. Portuguese colonists began to settle (1462) the islands, which became a collecting point for the **West African slave trade**.

1472 **Fernão do Pó**, a Portuguese explorer, discovered the island of **Fernando Póo** [Bioko], in present Equatorial Guinea, **West Africa**. He entered the Bight of Biafra and visited the Wouri estuary, in present Cameroon, whose river he named Rio dos Camarões, [Portuguese: prawns].

c.1484 **Diogo Cam** [Diego Cano or Cão] (fl. 1480–1486), a Portuguese explorer, discovered the mouth of the **Congo** [Zaire] **River**.

1485 **Joao d'Aveiro**, a Portuguese explorer, initiated trade and diplomatic relations with Ozolua (d. 1504), king of Benin. **Benin** was a wealthy and well organized state, linked with North Africa by the trans-Saharan trade routes. The Portuguese developed a flourishing trade in pepper, ivory, cloth, and slaves.

1488 Feb. **Bartholomeu Dias** (?1450–May 29, 1500), a Portuguese explorer, was the **first to sail around the Cape of Good Hope** [Cabo da Bõa Esperanca].

1492 **Pero da Covilhão** (c.1460–after 1526), the Portuguese explorer, reached **Abyssinia** [Ethiopia], where he was entertained at the court of the emperor, who was pleased to end the isolation of his Christian kingdom surrounded by the Islamic world.

1492 Apr. 17 **Ferdinand and Isabella**, king and queen of a united Aragon and Castile, agreed to sponsor Christopher Columbus's "Enterprise of the Indies" to find a new route to the Far East by traveling west and to acquire "islands and mainlands" for Spain. **Columbus** [Italian: Cristoforo Colombo, Spanish: Cristóbal Colón] (1451–May 20, 1506) was made an admiral, and promised one-tenth of all spice, precious stones, and gold found in the lands discovered.

1492 Aug. 3 Christopher **Columbus** began his first voyage, sailing from Palos, Spain, with three caravels. He commanded the *Santa María*; the Pinzón brothers, Martín Alonso (1440?–1493) and Vicente Yáñez (1460?–1524), commanded the *Pinta* and *Nina*.

1492 Oct. 12 Christopher Columbus's fleet first sighted land in the New World, probably Watlings Island of later days, one of the Bahama Islands, which he named San Salvador. On Oct. 15 he discovered and named Santa María de la Concepción [Rum Cay], and on Oct. 28 he sighted Cuba, naming it Juana. On Dec. 4 he discovered Hispaniola [Haiti and the Dominican Republic], where the *Santa Maria* was wrecked on the night of Dec. 24. Columbus then left for Spain on the *Nina,* arriving on Mar. 15, 1493.

1493 Christopher **Columbus** began his second voyage to the New World, sailing from Cadiz, Spain, with a fleet of 17 ships and 1,500 colonists. The expedition crossed in 21 days and discovered **Puerto Rico**, which he named San Juan Bautista, and Jamaica, as well as a number of smaller islands. On Jan. 2, 1494, he founded **Isabela**, the **first European colony in America**, on the northern coast of Hispaniola. Columbus returned to Spain on June 11, 1496.

1494 June 7 The **Treaty of Tordesillas** established the areas of control by Portugal and Spain in the New World, Africa, and the Far East. The New World went to Spain, while Africa and India went to Portugal. Brazil went to Portugal, possibly as a result of inaccurate geographical knowledge.

1496 Santo Domingo, oldest surviving European city in the New World, was founded by Christopher Columbus's brother Bartholomew (1445?–?1514), who named it Nueva Isabella.

1497–1498 Amerigo Vespucci [Americus Vespucius] (1454–1512), an Italian navigator and explorer, left an account of a voyage he took at this time during which he claimed to have reached the mainland of South America and North America, which would have been before either Columbus or Cabot. Most experts today believe Vespucci sailed on three other voyages, along the coasts of South America.

1497 June 24 John Cabot [Giovanni Caboto] (c.1450–c.1498), a Venetian navigator sailing for England, discovered Newfoundland, which he called Prima Vista. His ship *Mathew* was about the size of Columbus's *Nina*, the voyage lasted 35 days, and the discovery gave England a claim to North America against the claims of Spain and the Netherlands.

1498 May Vasco de Gama (1469?–Dec. 24, 1524), a Portuguese navigator, landed in Calicut, India, thus opening a direct sea route from Europe around the **Cape of Good Hope**. In July 1499, one of Gama's ships returned to Portugal with the news that India had at last been reached by sea. This voyage of 4,500 miles opened western Europe to India's riches and **initiated Portugal's commercial empire**.

1498 May 30 Christopher **Columbus** began his third voyage to the **New World**, taking a more southerly route and discovering (July 31) **Trinidad**. He put ashore (Aug. 5) at Ensenada Yacua, the Paria Peninsula, Venezuela, probably becoming the first European since the Norsemen to set foot on the American mainland.

IV. POLITICS AND WAR

1450 Apr. 15 The French were victorious at **Formigny**, in northwestern France, which enabled them to recover most of Normandy from England during the **Hundred Years' War**. It strengthened the faction of the **House of York** (1461–1499) in England as **William de la Pole**, duke of Suffolk, the main counselor of **Henry VI**, was held responsible for the English setbacks, impeached by Parliament, and exiled.

1453 Shin Sawbu (d. 1472?) gained the throne of **Lower Burma's Mon Kingdom** with its capital at

Pegu, inland from present Rangoon [Yangon]. She was the **first woman to rule in Burma** [Myanmar], where the status of women was generally well-regarded. Shin Sawbu built Shwe Dagon, the holy Buddhist pagoda at Dagon, which is the basis for present Rangoon.

1453 Richard Plantagenet (1411–1460), duke of York and England's heir apparent, was appointed regent while Henry VI suffered from insanity. However, the birth (Oct. 13) of Henry's heir Edward was followed by the king's mental recovery and the reappointment in 1455 of Edmund Beaufort, duke of Somerset, as head of the Royal Council. Beaufort had been excluded from the succession, which would pass to the **House of York** (1461–1499) if Henry VI died without issue. The Yorkists nevertheless did not relinquish their claim to the throne.

1453 May 29 Constantinople [İstanbul] fell to the Turkish forces of Muhammad II (Mar. 30, 1430–May 3, 1481), the young Ottoman sultan. On the same day **Constantine XI Palaeologus** (b. Feb. 7, 1404), the last Byzantine emperor (from 1449), was killed. It marked the end of the **Byzantine Empire** (from 474) and the **firm establishment of the Ottoman Empire** (1326–1920), and Constantinople became the seat of the Ottoman sultans.

1453 July 17 The English forces were defeated, and John Talbot (b. 1388), earl of Shrewsbury, was killed in a **battle at Castillon** on the Dordogne River, in France. It marked the **end of the Hundred Years' War** (from 1337) as France recovered Bordeaux in October, freeing herself from English occupation with the exception of Calais (recovered in 1558).

1454 Apr. 9 The **Treaty of Lodi** was signed in Italy between Milan and Venice. Venice recognized Francesco Sforza (1401–1466), duke of Milan, who had seized power in 1450. In return, Venice recovered its northern Italian territories. The Italian states of Florence, Milan, Naples, the Papal States, and Venice began an uneasy 40-year peace and set up a defensive league on Mar. 2, 1455.

1455 May 22 The Yorkists defeated the English royal forces, and Edmund Beaufort (c.1406), duke of Somerset, was killed at **St. Albans**, near London, in the **first battle of the Wars of the Roses** (to 1485). Richard Plantagenet, duke of York, was reinstated as protector of the Lancastrian crown held by Henry VI.

1457 The city of **Edo** [Yedo] was founded on Honshu, Japan.

1459 The Turkish army of **Muhammad II**, the Ottoman sultan, captured Smederevo [Semendria], in present Yugoslavia, the Serbian capital of **Stephen Tomashevich** (1458–1459), a local reigning prince, thus reducing **Serbia** to a province of the Ottoman Empire and destroying the independence of Serbia.

1460 The Byzantine vassal state of **Morea** [the Peloponnesus, in present Greece] was conquered by Turkish forces. **Trebizond**, the last independent Byzantine territory on the southeastern Black Sea, was annexed by the Ottoman Empire in 1461.

1460 July 10 In England **Yorkists** led by Richard Neville, earl of Warwick, defeated the **Lancastrians** at Northampton, in central England, and captured Henry VI in the **Wars of the Roses**. Parliament was summoned (Oct. 7) to recognize Richard Plantagenet, duke of York, as heir to the crown, but Richard was killed at Wakefield, in northern England, in a Lancastrian victory on Dec. 30.

1461 Feb. 2 Edward, duke of York since the death of his father, Richard Plantagenet, defeated the **Lancastrians** at Mortimer's Cross, in western England, in the **Wars of the Roses**.

1461 Mar. 29 Edward, duke of York, secured the throne as **Edward IV**, king of England, with the help of Richard Neville, earl of Warwick, in a victory over the Lancastrians at **Towton Moor**, in northern England, the bloodiest battle in the **Wars of the Roses**. The deposed Henry VI and Queen Margaret [of Anjou] (1430–1482) fled to Scotland, and Edward was formally crowned (June 28) at Westminster.

1464 The accession of Sunni Ali (1464–1492) to the throne of the **Songhai Empire** (c.1050–1591) began its period of hegemony in West Africa at the expense of the **Mali Empire** (fl. c.1230–c.1400). Sunni 'Ali repulsed the Mossi to the south and, by the capture of Timbuktu (1468) and Jenne (1473), annexed the eastern Mali territories.

1465 The **Zenata Berbers** of the Bani Wattas took control of Fez, ending the **Marinid Dynasty** (from c.1200) of Morocco.

1467 Jehan Shah (1437–1467) of the Turkoman **Black Sheep** [Kara Koyunlu] **Dynasty** was defeated and killed by Uzun Hasan (1453–1478) of the **White Sheep** [Ak Koyunlu] **Dynasty** at Diyarbakir [ancient Amida] in southeastern Turkey. Hasan now controlled Mesopotamia [Iraq] and western Persia [Iran].

1469 **Abu Said** (1447–1469), sultan of the **Timurid Dynasty** (1370–1501) of western Turkestan in northeastern Persia, was defeated and killed by **Uzun Hasan** of the **White Sheep Dynasty**. Hazan now ruled Azerbaijan, Kurdistan, Mesopotamia, and most of Persia.

1469 Oct. 19 **John II** (1398–1479), king of Aragon (from 1458) and Navarre (from 1425), married his son **Ferdinand II of Aragon** to the future Queen **Isabella of Castile**.

1470 The **Incas**, under Pachacuti (ruled 1438–1471), conquered the **kingdom of Quito**, in present Ecuador. From his capital at Cuzco, he ruled an empire that extended from northern Ecuador southward into Chile and eastward to Bolivia.

1470 Oct. 9 **Richard Neville**, earl of Warwick, called the kingmaker, deposed **Edward IV**, the Yorkist king of England, and reinstated **Henry VI**, the Lancastrian king, to the English throne (to 1471). Warwick, with French aid, thus exercised the real power in England, while Edward fled, searching for help from his brother-in-law, **Charles the Bold**, duke of Burgundy.

1471 The **Kingdom of Annam** (1428–1883) under Le Thanh-Ton (1460–1497) defeated the Cham [Champa] forces and captured their capital Vijaya, in present Vietnam. The **Champa Kingdom** (c.270–1492) became a vassal and was thereafter progressively annexed by Annam.

1471 Apr. 14 **Edward IV**, the Yorkist king of England, with the aid of forces from Burgundy, defeated and killed **Richard Neville** (b. Nov. 22, 1428), earl of Warwick, at **Barnet**, now in London. The Lancastrians were again defeated on May 4 at **Tewkesbury**, in southern England, where Edward (b. 1453), prince of Wales and the only son of Henry VI, was killed. **Henry VI** (b. Dec. 6, 1421; ruled from Sept. 1, 1422) was murdered (May 21) in the Tower of London, securing **Edward IV's** restoration to the English throne.

1472 Nezahualcoyotl (born c.1418), poet king of Texcoco, a city-state allied with the Aztecs, died. He had ruled 41 years during a period of exceptional peace. A noted lawmaker and engineer, he founded (c.1430) a zoo and botanical garden with animals and plants from all over the Aztec domains and neighboring countries.

1472 Nov. 12   Ivan III the Great (Jan. 22, 1440–Oct. 27, 1505; ruled from 1462), the grand prince of Moscow, married **Sophia [Zoë] Palaeologus**, niece of **Constantine XI Palaeologus**, who had been the last Byzantine emperor (to 1453). Ivan's reign saw the consolidation of Russian principalities under one rule, and the marriage gave the Russian throne the prestige of the former empire.

1474 Mar. 30   The **Perpetual Peace** was signed between Switzerland and Frederick III, archduke of Austria and Hapsburg Holy Roman emperor.

1474 Dec. 11   Henry IV (b. Jan. 25, 1425), king of Castile (from 1454), died and was succeeded by his sister **Isabella**. Henry IV's step-daughter, **Juana la Beltraneja** (1462–1530), and her husband, **Alfonso V** (1432–1481), king of Portugal (from 1438), challenged the succession until their defeat (1476) in a **battle at Toro** in northwestern Spain. After failing to secure French aid, they recognized Isabella as queen of Castile in 1479.

1475 Aug. 29   Edward IV, king of England, who had invaded France in support of the Burgundians, signed the **Treaty of Picquigny**, in northern France, with **Louis XI** (July 3, 1423–Aug. 30, 1483), king of France (from 1461). Edward withdrew his help to Charles the Bold, duke of Burgundy, in return for a large payment and an annual pension.

1476 Mar. 2   Swiss forces defeated **Charles the Bold**, duke of Burgundy, in a **battle at Grandson**, in present Switzerland. Charles, who had seized the duchy of Lorraine in 1475, was defeated again at Morat, Switzerland, on June 22.

1477 Jan. 5   Charles the Bold (b. Nov. 10, 1433), the **last duke of Burgundy**, was defeated and killed in a **battle at Nancy**. Burgundy, with Artois and Picardy, was annexed by Louis XI, king of France, and Lorraine was restored to René II (1473–1508), duke of Lorraine and a member of the Angevin family.

1477 Aug. 19   Frederick III, the Holy Roman emperor, married his son **Maximilian of Hapsburg** to Mary, daughter of Charles the Bold of Burgundy. War broke out between France and the empire for possession of the Burgundian territories.

1478   Ivan III the Great, grand prince of Moscow (from 1462), captured the city-state of **Novgorod**. Ivan had been defeated by **Tatars** [Mongols] of the **Golden Horde** (1240–1480), but from 1478 Russia was free of Mongolian rule.

1479   The **Treaty of Alcaçovas**, in southern Portugal, was signed by Portugal and the Spanish kingdom of Castile. Portugal abandoned its claims to the Castilian throne and to the Canary Islands, while Castile recognized Portuguese suzerainty in the islands of the Azores, Cape Verde, and Madeira, and on the northern and western African coast.

1479 Jan. 20   John II (b. 1398), king of Aragon, died and was succeeded by his son Ferdinand II of Aragon. As **Ferdinand V**, king of Castile, he was able to unite the Spanish kingdoms and enlarge his domain.

1480   Changa (d. 1494), governor of the southern provinces of the **Monomotapa Empire**, in present Zimbabwe and Mozambique, founded the **Changamire Kingdom** at the death of Matope Nyanhehwe Nebedza, king (from c.1450) of the Monomotapa [Motapa, Mutapa] Empire (c.1440–c.1629). Thus began a long civil war that vitiated the Central African empire.

1480 July 10   René I the Good, duke of Anjou (from 1434) and Lorraine (1434–1453), died. Anjou, Maine, and Provence, bequeathed to **Louis XI**, king of France, were thus united to the French crown, which was also given the Angevin rights to the **Kingdom of Naples**.

1482 Mar. 27   Mary (b. Feb. 13, 1457), duchess of Burgundy (ruled from 1477) died at Bruges and was succeeded, as regent, by her husband, the Hapsburg Maximilian, who later was king of Germany (1486–1519) and the Holy Roman emperor (1493–1519). He ended the war with France over the Burgundian territories by the **Treaty of Arras** on Dec. 23. Hapsburg rule was recognized in the Netherlands, Belgium, Luxembourg, Artois in northern France, and Franche-Comté in eastern France.

1483 Apr. 9   Edward IV (b. Apr., 1442), king of England (from 1461), died and was succeeded by his teenage son Edward V, with Edward IV's brother

Richard, duke of Gloucester, as regent. Richard usurped (June 26) the throne as **Richard III**, and was probably responsible for the murder (August) in the Tower of London of Edward V (b. Nov. 1?, 1470) and his brother Richard (b. 1473), duke of York.

1485 Aug. 22 Henry Tudor, earl of Richmond, won a decisive victory at **Bosworth Field**, killing **Richard III** (b. Oct. 2, 1452), king of England (from 1483) and **last of the Planatagenet Dynasty** (1154–1499), in the **last battle of the Wars of the Roses. Henry VII** who, through marriage, united the houses of Lancaster and York, was crowned on Oct. 30 at Westminster, beginning the **Tudor Dynasty** (1485–1603).

1486 Minkyinyo (1486–1531), king of the **Burmese Toungoo Dynasty** (1347–1752) in Burma [Myanmar], began to expand his territory.

1490 Shogun **Yoshimasa** (b. 1435) died. Trade between China and Japan, disrupted by pirates, worsened as the local Japanese rulers fought among themselves.

1490 The **Nizam Shahi Dynasty** was established by **Ahmad Nizam Shah** at Ahmadnagar in western India, which had been a province of the Bahmani Sultanate before Ahmad's revolt. It was a Muslim sultanate, one of five eventually established in the Deccan, replacing the **Bahmani Sultanate** (1347–1527).

1490 Apr. 4 Matthias Corvinus (b. 1440), king of Hungary (from 1458), died, having established the most powerful kingdom in central Europe. He was succeeded by Ladislas II [Vladislav Jagiellon] **Jagello** (1456–1516), king of Bohemia (from 1471), who was so weak that at the **Treaty of Pressburg** on Nov. 7, 1491, in order to secure his throne, he recognized Maximilian of Hapsburg as his successor should he die without a male heir.

1491 Nzinga Nkuwu (d. 1506), king of Kongo, welcomed a Portuguese embassy at Mbanza [São Salvador], capital of his Bantu state, in present Angola. The **Kongo** ruler willingly accepted the Portuguese penetration. The same year he was converted to Catholicism under the name of João I.

1491 Dec. 6 The **marriage of Charles VIII**, king of France, to Anne (Jan. 25, 1477–Jan. 9, 1514), duchess of Brittany (from 1488), led to the union of Brittany and France.

1492 Jan. 2 King Ferdinand and Queen Isabella drove the **Moors** out of **Granada**, the **last independent Moorish kingdom in Spain**, establishing a Castilian governor but allowing the Moors to keep their religion, laws, judges, language, and dress.

1492 Apr. 9 Lorenzo de' Medici [Lorenzo the Magnificent] (b. 1449), the ruler of Florence, died. Under his patronage **Florence** achieved its greatest renown as a center of intellectual and artistic life. In 1494 his son Pietro (1471–1503), who succeeded Lorenzo, was expelled from the city, and its republican government was restored briefly under Girolamo Savonarola.

1492 June Casimir IV (b. 1427), king of Poland and grand prince of Lithuania, died. He was succeeded in Poland by his son John I (1459–1501), and in Lithuania by his son Alexander (1461–1506). Upon the death of John, Alexander became king of Poland also. Casimir had raised **Poland** to the status of a European power.

1492 Oct. England invaded France to prevent annexation of Brittany by Charles VIII, king of France. In Nov. 1492, the **Treaty of Étaples** ended the invasion, with Brittany remaining French and Charles agreeing to withdraw his support of Perkin Warbeck, pretender to the English throne.

1493 Husain Shah became sultan (to 1519) of **Bengal**, in northeastern India. He had been chief minister of the tyrannical **Sultan Shams-ud-din**, who was overthrown and killed.

1493 Aug. 19 Frederick III (b. 1415), the Holy Roman emperor (from 1440), died and was succeeded by his son **Maximilian I**, king of Germany.

1494 Sept.–1495 Dec. Poynings' Law, a series of 49 statutes called the **Drogheda Statutes**, were enacted by the Irish Parliament under Edward Poynings (1459–Oct. 1521), who served as lord deputy of **Ireland** under Henry VII, king of England. Poynings had been appointed to draft legislation to prevent Irish separatism and home rule. Ireland became subject to English law, and Ireland's Parliament was rendered ineffective by the provision that it could not convene without prior approval of the English Privy Council.

1494 Sept. 1 Charles VIII, king of France, invaded Italy, initiating the devastating **Italian Wars** (1494–

1559). Charles entered (Nov. 17) Florence, forcing the state to yield Pisa and other Italian towns. Then he entered (Feb. 22, 1495) Naples, where he was crowned king on May 12, 1495. An alliance initiated by the Hapsburgs and Spain soon forced Charles to withdraw from Italy.

1495 At the **Diet of Worms**, Maximilian I, the Holy Roman emperor agreed to an edict forbidding private wars and establishing a **Court of Justice** to judge between warring princes and act as the highest court of appeals for common citizens. A "common penny," or general poll and property tax, was to be imposed by the emperor to fund and maintain this Court of Justice. These reforms represented a step in the recognition of common rights and the maintenance of internal peace.

1496 Sept. 29 The defeat of the native **Guanches** in Teneriffe completed the Spanish conquest of the **Canary Islands**. Grand Canary had fallen in 1483 and Palma in 1490.

1497 **John I** [Hans] (1455–1513), king of Denmark and Norway, defeated Swedish forces in a **battle at Brunkebeberg** and became **John II**, king of the joint kingdoms of Denmark, Norway, and Sweden (to 1501).

1497 **Ladislas II**, king of Bohemia and Hungary, virtually enslaved the peasants of **Bohemia** with new laws binding them to the land and greatly increasing the power of the nobles. These laws, however, eventually reduced the power of the king, who was deprived of the loyalty of his people.

1497 **Enslavement of the Russian peasantry** was accelerated by the first Code of Laws, or **Sudebnik** [Book of Justice], promulgated by **Ivan III the Great**, grand prince of Moscow. The code vested immense power in the hands of local governors, and confirmed the ancient right of the creditor to enslave the debtor.

1497 The bestowal of the title "**Most Catholic Majesties**" on **King Ferdinand and Queen Isabella** of Spain by Pope Alexander VI recognized their total control of both Church and State. They exercised unparalleled power over the lives of their subjects, determining not only traditional matters of policy, taxation, and religious belief, but also how artisans shaped their products, farmers tilled their soil, and merchants shipped their goods.

1497 Oct. **Perkin Warbeck**, pretender to the English throne as Richard, duke of York, believed slain in the Tower of London in 1483, was captured at Taunton after an invasion of Cornwall. Warbeck's claim had been recognized by the kings of France and Scotland and by Maximilian I. Warbeck (b. 1474) was executed on Nov. 23, 1499, after he and the earl of Warwick, in a plot against Henry VII, tried to escape from the Tower of London. **Edward Plantagenet** (b. Feb. 21, 1475), the earl of Warwick, beheaded on Nov. 28, 1499, was the **last Planatagenet in direct line of succession in England**.

1498 Apr. 8 **Charles VIII** (b. June 30, 1470), king of France (from 1483), died. His successor **Louis XII** continued the **Italian Wars** (1494–1559), expelling Lodovico Sforza [Il Moro, the Moor] (1451–1508) from the duchy of Milan in 1499. To maintain the union of Brittany and France, Louis had his first marriage annulled and married Charles's widow, Anne of Brittany, in 1499.

1499 Sept. 22 The **Peace of Basel** recognized **Switzerland** as an independent republic, though in name it remained part of the Holy Roman Empire until the **Treaty of Westphalia** in 1648. Maximilian I, the Holy Roman emperor, was furious when the Swiss refused to pay the common penny tax decreed by the **Diet of Worms** in 1495. In the war that followed, the Swiss defeated the imperial forces at **Calven** in May and at Dornach in July 1499.

1499 Oct. 6 In a continuation of the **Italian Wars**, French forces of Louis XII recaptured Milan from Lodovico Sforza (b. 1452). The continuing warfare of this period resulted from the French policy of trying to keep the Hapsburgs and the Spanish out of northern Italy and to keep the prosperous Italian city-states under French hegemony. When Genoa also submitted, Louis signed the **Treaty of Granada** on Nov. 11, 1500, with Ferdinand, king of Spain, settling the conquest and partition of Naples.

V. ECONOMY AND TRADE

1450–1550 Economic prosperity prevailed throughout Europe. Trading fairs prospered, and land was cleared and developed.

1463–1499 Forerunners of **pawnshops**, the *montes pietatis*, first established in Italy at Orvieto (1463) and at Perugia (1467), were flourishing by the end of the century. These credit organizations lent money at low interest rates. The Franciscans of northern Italy, especially Bernardino de Feltre (1439–1494), the future patron of pawnbrokers, promoted establishment of these charitable organizations, and they soon spread throughout Europe—the first German pawnshop opening in Nürnberg [Nuremburg] (1498)—where they often were established as official departments of municipal governments.

c.1470 France established what was perhaps the **first modern postal system** in Europe. Over 230 mounted couriers carried official mail throughout the country.

1480 Perhaps the **first advertising flyer** was printed on the press of **William Caxton** (1422?–1491) in London to promote his book of Church law, *The Pyes of Salisbury Use*. It was printed on small pieces of scrap paper and displayed on church doors.

1490–1499 **Book publishing** as a profession began to develop. In Europe the printer at first was also the bookseller and frequently the author. But soon these functions began to separate and, as the bookseller went to different printers to meet the heavy demand of rich patrons, publishing emerged.

1490 **Aldine Press** was established in Venice by **Aldo Manuzio** [Aldus Manutius] (1450–1515), the **first to use italic type**. Between 1493 and 1515, Manuzio produced 27 editions of Greek and Latin classics at moderate prices, making available to western scholars for the first time the philosophy of ancient Greece and Rome. Manuzio's colophon was the dolphin and anchor.

1492 Nov. 2 **Christopher Columbus**, who observed the inhabitants of **Cuba** smoking **tobacco**, introduced his discovery to Europe.

1493 Mar. The famous "**Columbus Letter**" arrived at the Spanish Court. It was written aboard ship and forwarded from Lisbon, where Columbus had put in to escape foul weather. This report painted the so-called **New World** as a beautiful and fertile paradise of unlimited gold, and had an immense impact on the life of Europe.

1499 At least 1,000 **black slaves** a year were entering **Lisbon** by the end of the 15th century as a result of the exploration of the West African coast by the Portuguese during the century.

VI. RELIGION AND PHILOSOPHY

1453 A treatise entitled *De pace seu concordantia fidei* was written by **Nicholas of Cusa** (1401–1464), bishop of Brixen in Germany, in which Christianity was compared with Judaism and Islam. It reached the conclusion that there was a unity of faith in the diversity of religion.

1453 May 29 **Muhammad II**, the Ottoman sultan, after his capture of the city, invited the patriarchs of the Greek and Armenian churches and the Jewish chief rabbi to reside at **Constantinople**, now the center of the Ottoman Empire (1326–1920).

1456 June 16 The judgment (1431) of witchcraft and heresy against **Joan of Arc** was annulled posthumously by a tribunal of three French bishops, a decision affirmed by Jean Brehal, grand inquisitor of France. Joan's family had previously obtained permission from Pope Calixtus III (Dec. 31, 1378–Aug. 8, 1458; ruled from 1455) to proceed with the presentation of their case. Brehal then published a document setting forth Joan's orthodoxy.

c.1470 **Ramananda** (born c.1400), successor to **Ramanuja** (d. 1150) as leader of the **Vaishnivite sect of Hinduism**, died. He taught at Benares [Varanasi], on the Ganges River in northern India, and founded a new order of ascetic monks, the **Ramanandi**, which still exists.

1471 **Sixtus IV** (July 21, 1414–Aug. 12, 1484) began his tenure as pope, inaugurating a 60-year period in papal history marked by involvement in Italian power politics, venality, and unscrupulous appointment of relatives to high office. The successors to Sixtus IV, **Innocent VIII** and **Alexander VI** (Jan. 1, 1431–Aug. 18, 1503; ruled from 1492), brought the **spiritual level of the papacy to its lowest point**.

1471 Aug. 8 **Thomas à Kempis** [Thomas Hammerken] (b. 1380), a German-born monk, died. He had spent his adult life at the Augustinian convent of Mount St. Agnes near Zwolle, the Netherlands. His numerous and varied writings included the *Imitation of Christ*, an enormously influential text within Christendom.

1480 The **Spanish Inquisition** was established as a royal instrument by Ferdinand II and Isabella I of Castile and Aragon, the "Catholic Majesties." By 1482 they had pressed Pope Sixtus IV into issuing a concordat that gave them control over nomination to the higher Spanish ecclesiastical positions and assumed the right of approval of papal bulls before their promulgation in Spain.

1480   The **Parsis of Sanjan**, in northwestern India, were forced to flee into the mountains, taking their sacred fire with them, to escape Muslim soldiers overrunning the region. **Zoroastrianism** survives today in isolated areas of India, where adherents are called Parsis [Parsees], and in present Iran.

1482   Girolamo Savonarola, who had joined the Dominican order in 1472, began to preach in **Florence**. Savonarola converted thousands to a penitential life and became the actual ruler of Florence at a time when Italian independence had collapsed.

1484   **Pope Innocent VIII** issued a bull against German witches. **Thomas Aquinas** earlier had accepted witchcraft as a reality. *Malleus Maleficarum* [*Witches' Hammer*] (1486), a book popular in three languages, was written by two German inquisitors, **Heinrich Kraemer** and **Johann Sprenger**. By c.1485, perhaps as many as 2 million people in Europe had been executed as **witches**.

1487   Tomás de Torquemada (1420?–Sept. 16, 1498) was named grand inquisitor by Pope Innocent VIII. As the **first inquisitor general** (c.1483) of the Inquisition in Spain, he had urged expulsion of all Jews. Under Torquemada c.2000 people were burned at the stake.

1492 Mar. 31   The **expulsion of Spanish Jews**, who were given three months to accept Christianity or leave Spain, was ordered. Many of the c.400,000 Spanish Jews fled to North Africa and the Netherlands. The measure was promoted by Tomás de Torquemada, ostensibly in order to prevent unconverted Jews from seducing the New Christians or Conversos, Jews who had been recently baptized as Christians. This edict was supported by **Ferdinand II and Isabella I**, whose treasury was replenished by the Jews' confiscated property. By 1496 when **Portugal expelled its Jews**, most openly practicing Jews had left the Iberian peninsula.

1492 July 25   **Pope Innocent VIII** (b. 1432; ruled from 1484) died. He had constantly been embroiled in the conflicts between the Italinate states, gotten the papacy heavily into debt, and sold newly created church posts to the highest bidder. On Aug. 10 Ro-

drigo Borgia was elected **Pope Alexander VI**. Of the leading candidates for the Holy See, Borgia had bought the largest number of votes. Rodrigo Borgia fathered a number of children, among them Cesare (1475) and Lucrezia (1480).

1495   Askia Muhammad, ruler (1493–1528) of the **Songhai Empire** (c.1050–1591) in western Africa, made a **pilgrimage to Mecca,** said to rival in magnificence that of Mansa Musa.

1496   John Colet (1467?–1519), a lecturer at Oxford University in England, opened a **new era in biblical exegesis** by his approach to Paul's epistles through the apostle's personality and the life of first century Hellenistic cities.

1498 May 23   **Girolamo Savonarola** (b. Sept. 21, 1452) was hanged and his body burned by the civil authorities of Florence. With his followers, the **Piagnoni** [democratic party], he had driven Pietro de' Medici (1471–1503) out of Florence and incurred the wrath of Pope Alexander VI. Until shortly before his death he had ruled **Florence** with ecclesiastical fervor.

1499   Francisco Jiménez [Ximenes] **de Cisneros** (1436–Nov. 8, 1517), confessor to Queen Isabella I and inquisitor general of Castile and León, mandated **baptism of all Muslims in Spain**. Protesters were given the choice of conversion to Christianity or expulsion from the country. Jiménez, as bishop of Alcalá de Henares and later cardinal of Toledo, founded (1508) a great **university at Alcalá**, and raised the standards of the priesthood in Spain.

1499 Oct. 1   **Marsilio Ficino** (b. Oct. 19, 1433), an Italian philosopher and classicist, died. His translations into Latin of Plato and other Greek writers helped promote Renaissance humanism. His most important work was *Theologica Platonica* (1482).

1499   Rennyo (b. 1415), Japan's outstanding defender of pure **Buddhism**, died.

VII. SCIENCE, EDUCATION, AND TECHNOLOGY

c.1450   **Pope Nicholas V** (1398–Mar. 24, 1455; ruled from 1445) founded the **Vatican Library**, adding his own collection to works already owned by the Church. He actively acquired many more works during his papacy so that, at the time of his death, the library was the largest in Europe.

c.1450   By this time, **Johann Gutenberg** (1398?–Jan., 1468) in Mainz had completed the **invention of his printing press**, which used **movable metallic type**. By 1456, the famous *Gutenberg Bible*, also known as the Mazarin or 42-line Bible, was printed.

1463   **Flavio Biondo** [Flavius Blondus] (b. 1392), an Italian humanist and historian, died. He was the first person to suggest the idea of the 1000-year period ending in his era as the Middle Ages (c.500–1500). His substantial histories of Rome and of the Christian church included *De Roma instaurata* (1444–1446) and *De Roma triumphante* (1459).

c.1470   Topa [Tupac] Inca, who ruled the **Inca Empire** (1471–1493), began a period of **road construction** that, ironically, **facilitated the later Spanish conquest of the Incas**. The Inca roads wound through mountains where they were often very narrow with steps cut into the rock and bridges made of rope crossing river gorges, ravines, and deep chasms. Some of these rope bridges, kept in repair by the area natives, are still in use today.

1474   **Paolo dal Pozzo Toscanelli** (1397–1482), an astronomer, geographer, and physician, of Florence, Italy, wrote a letter to **Alfonso V**, king of Portugal, accompanied by a map that explained how one could reach Asia from Europe by sailing west.

1477   The **University of Uppsala**, the first in northern Europe, was founded in **Sweden** by Sten Sture the Elder (1440?–1503), regent of Sweden (1470–1503).

1491   The **teaching of Greek** was begun at **Oxford University** by **William Grocyn** (c.1446–1519) who, with **Erasmus**, helped introduce **humanism** in England.

1492   The **first modern globe** was constructed by **Martin Behaim** (c.1436–c.1506) at Nürnberg [Nuremburg]. Based on contemporary Portuguese maps that derive from Ptolemy, it shows the Atlantic 100° too narrow, a misconception shared by **Columbus**, reinforcing his belief that the West Indies were in Asia.

1492   The city of **Ferrara**, Italy, was enlarged under the direction of the architect Biagia Rossetti (1465–

1516), in one of the **first overall city-planning endeavors** of the Renaissance (c.1300–1700).

1492   The **first modern grammar**, *Arte de la Lengua castellana*, by **Elio Antonio de Legrija** (1444–1522), was published. The author was a tutor of Queen Isabella I of Castile.

1493   The *Nuremburg Chronicle* by **Hartmann Schedel** was published at Nürnberg [Nuremburg]. Illustrated with woodcuts based on classical legend, such as bearded women, horned men and bird men, this book, like many others then printed, helped fuel the appetite for wondrous stories already being stimulated by tales told by explorers.

1495   According to the *Apologetica Historica* (1530), **syphilis**, also known as French pox or Neapolitan disease, erupted throughout Europe. Modern historians speculate that the upheavals of the Renaissance, with its traveling armies and laxity of morals, caused the outbreaks. **Mercury**, known as a cure for the disease for centuries, became widely used by 1495 for this purpose.

VIII. ARTS AND LEISURE

1450–1499   Colorful **Renaissance dress**, for both men and women, began to replace the costumes of the Middle Ages. Men, clean shaven and with short hair, wore doublets, sometimes with puffed shoulders and sleeves. Hats, worn increasingly after 1450, were typically circular and padded. Women concealed their hair under high hats, such as the French *hennin*, a steeple-shaped headdress with long kerchiefs sometimes reaching the floor. Their gowns were often cut low in front and had long skirts, sometimes with trains.

1454   The **first known poster** was designed by **Saint-Flour** (?), a French artist.

1463 Jan. 6   **Francois Villon** [*orig.*: de Montcorbier] (b. 1431), a French poet, thief, and murderer, received a commutation of his sentence to hang. He was banished instead and disappeared completely. His major works included *Le petit testament* [or *Le Lais* (c.1456)] and *Le grand testament* (1461), in which appear many of his most famous *ballades*.

1464   **Rogier van der Weyden** [French: Roger de la Pasture] (b. 1399?), a Flemish master painter, died. He studied in Brussels and traveled from his native

Flanders to northern Italy where he introduced the art and techniques of oil painting.

1466 Enguerrand Quarton [Charonton] (born c.1410), a French painter, died. He was commissioned to do *le Triomphe de la Vierge* (1453) and also possibly painted the *Avignon Pietà* (1457).

1466 Dec. 13 Donatello [Donato di Niccolo di Betto Bardi] (b. 1386?), an Italian Renaissance sculptor, considered the founder of modern sculpture, died. His statue of **Mary Magdalene** (c.1455) in Florence substituted realism for classical perfection.

1468 The **first known performances of the Coventry Cycle** [Ludus Coventriae] of 42 mystery plays took place in England. Although they did not all necessarily originate at Coventry, they were performed there until c.1591.

1469 Oct. 8 or 10 Fra Filippo Lippi [Filippo del Carmine] (born c.1406), a Florentine master painter, died. His *Coronation of the Virgin* (1441), painted for Sant' Ambrogio in Florence, was one of his most important works, which also included *Annunciation* in San Lorenzo, *Madonna and Child* in the Medici Palace, and a Madonna in the Uffizi.

c.1470 *The White Book of Sarnen* contained the **earliest written version of the William Tell legend**. It set the story in the time of the founding of the **first Swiss Confederation** (1291), which opposed the effort by Rudolph I of Hapsburg, the Holy Roman emperor, to assert his feudal claims over the Swiss.

1473 Joannes de Tinctoris (1435–Oct., 1511), an early Flemish music theorist and lexicographer, completed his *Terminorum Musicae Diffinitorium*, the **earliest dictionary of music**.

1474 Nov. 27 Guillaume Dufay (born c.1399), a Flemish composer and canon at Cambrai, in France, died. He was famous as an innovator of three- and four-part harmony.

1475 Dec. 10 Paolo Uccello [Paolo di Dono] (b. 1397), a Florentine painter who experimented with foreshortening, died. He was known especially for *Battle of San Romano* (1456?) and portraits.

c.1480 Politian [Angelo Poliziano] (July 14, 1454–Sept. 24, 1491), wrote *Favola d' Urfeo*, considered one of the best examples of *sacra reppresentazione*,

Italian theatrical performances based on the Bible. It was written in the Italian vernacular.

c.1481 A group of painters from Tuscany and Umbria, perhaps under the guidance of Botticelli, began work on the frescoes of the **Sistine Chapel**. The most noted work of these was *Christ Giving the Keys to Peter* by **Perugino** [Pietro Vannucci, Pier della Pieve] (1446–Feb. 1523).

1482 Majolica [maiolica], the technique of using a low-temperature, tin-enamel glaze to produce an opaque white background on terra cotta, was first introduced to **Italian sculpture** by Luca della Robbia (c.1400–Feb. 20, 1482), who completed decoration for a cathedral near his native Florence in this year.

c.1485 *The Birth of Venus*, perhaps the most famous painting by **Botticelli**, was painted for Lorenzo and Juliano Medici about this time. It represented the change from religious subjects to pagan motifs, beginning about this time and not fully appreciated by many Florentines.

1485 William Caxton printed *Le Morte d'Arthur*, completed by **Thomas Malory** (d. ?1471) in Mar. 1470. It is now considered the definitive version of the French romances treating of Arthur and the adventures of the Knights of the Round Table.

1488 Andrea Verrocchio (b. 1435), a Florentine sculptor considered second only to Donatello, died. He worked with Leonardo da Vinci and possibly instructed him. His best-known works included a statue of David with the head of Goliath at his feet (c.1475).

1491 Feb. 2 Martin Schongauer (born c.1445), a German artist known best for his engravings, died. He established a **school for etching and painting at Colmar** [Kolmar], now in northeastern France, which greatly influenced Holbein and Dürer.

c.1490 The **classical form of Spanish dance** began to develop as Christianity became dominant throughout Spain. Muslim dance forms had to adapt to changing social and religious customs, resulting in this distinctive kind of dancing. The theme was either of courtship or bull fighting, and the dance was usually performed by a single person or, rarely, by a couple. It emphasized rhythm, which was marked by castanets, tambourines, and elaborate footwork.

1492 *Tiunfo de la fama* by **Juan del Encina** (1469?–?1534), sometimes called the **father of Spanish drama**, was characteristic of the current transition from religious to secular subjects in the theater.

1492 **Jami** [Mulla Nuru'd-Din Abd-er-Rhaman Jami] (b. 1414), a classical Persian poet, died. Two of his better-known poems were *Salaman wa Absal* and *Laila wa Majnun*, written in Persian.

1492 **Bramante** [Donato d'Angelo] (1444–Mar. 11, 1514) designed the gallery of the Santa Maria delle Grazie church in Milan, imparting an illusion of depth to its shallow interior.

1492 **Piero della Francesca** [Piero dei Franceschi] (b. c.1420), a leading painter of the Italian school of realism, died. Francesca painted the fresco *The Story of the True Cross* (1452–1459) in the presbytery of San Francesco in Arezzo.

1494 **Sebastian Brant** (1457?–May 10, 1521), a German poet, wrote the satire *Narrenschiff*, which **Alexander Barclay** (1475?–June 8, 1552) rewrote as *The Shyp of Folys* (1508). It depicted, by Brant's count, the 114 varieties of fools, and foreshadowed a larger attack on clericalism and narrow-mindedness to come in the 16th century.

1494 Jan. 11 **Domenico Ghirlandaio** [Domenico di Tommaso Bigordi] (b. 1449), a Florentine painter noted for his realistic frescoes depicting details of 15th-century life, died. He had completed (1491) his cycle of the life of Mary and St. John the Baptist in Santa Maria Novella, in Florence. A famous surviving painting depicts an old man with a large reddened nose posing with his son.

1496 Feb. 6 **Jean d'Okegham** [Johannes Ockenheim] (born c.1425), a Flemish contrapuntist and pupil of Guillaume Dufay, died. In 1465, under Louis XI, king of France, he became "Maitre de la Chapelle du Roi" or royal "Kapellmeister."

1497 Oct. 4 **Benozzo Gozzoli** [di Lese di Sandro] (b. 1420), died. An important member of the Florentine school, he produced many works of art noted for realism, bright colors, and dramatic action, one of the most notable being the *Procession of the Wise Men* (1459–1460) for the Palazzo Medici in Florence. Many members of Cosimo de' Medici's family and court appear in the fresco.

1497 **Bajazet II** [Beyazid] (1447–May, 1512), the Ottoman sultan (1481–Apr. 1512), began building the **Bajazet mosque** in Constantinople. Completed in 1503, the mosque gave its name to the surrounding city quarter.

1497 *Fulgens and Lucres* by **Henry Medwall** (fl. 1486–1500), considered the **first purely secular drama written in English**, was a translation, with Medwall's own additions, of a medieval script in Latin.

1498 **Felipe Bignary** (c.1470–1543), a French artisan, was commissioned to do a transaltar for the noted Gothic cathedral (1221) at Burgos, northern Spain. This was one of the **first documented instances of the introduction of the Renaissance style into Spain.**

1498 **Michelangelo** completed his sculpture *Piéta*, now in the Basilica of St. Peter, Rome. Michelangelo lived (1490–1492) at the court of Lorenzo de' Medici in Florence, where he became knowledgeable about early Roman antiquities. In Rome, where he stayed from 1496 until 1501, he executed his *Bacchus* (1496) and *Cupid* (1497).

1498 **Albrecht Dürer** issued his celebrated series of 15 large woodcuts of *The Apocalypse*, which reflected a late Gothic influence rather than the Renaissance spirit of his later work.

1498 *The Last Supper*, **Leonardo da Vinci's** most famous mural, was completed.

1499 *La Celestina*, a popular Spanish work often called the **first European novel**, was first printed. **Fernando de Rojas** (1475?–?1538), a lawyer in Toledo, is now believed to be the author of most of it. The book's chief interest was its portrayal of the low-life of 15th-century Spain.

IX. SPORTS, GAMES, AND SOCIETY

1457 A decree of **Scotland's** Parliament under James II (Oct. 16, 1430–Aug. 3, 1460; ruled from 1437) ordered "fute-ball and golfe" to be "utterly cryde down and not used," because they were supplanting the militarily useful practice of **archery**.

1477 Edward IV, king of England, banned the playing of **cricket** as an interference with the compulsory practice of archery, on which the English army relied heavily. The king fixed a fine and a jail sentence not only for players, but for those who allowed the game to be played on their property.

1496 The **first handbook on the art of angling** in any language was printed in the London shop of **Wynken de Worde** (c.1534), successor to William Caxton, as part of a larger work, the reprinted *Book*

of St. Albans, first printed (c. 1486) English sporting book. *The treatise of Fishing with an Angle* was written c.1420 but the earliest surviving manuscript dates to c.1450. The author was, according to tradition, **Juliana Berners** [Barnes, Bernes], a nun and sportswoman. Twelve artificial flies are listed, along with methods for their making. Six of these flies are still used today.

1500–1509

I. VITAL STATISTICS AND DEMOGRAPHICS

1500 **World population** was c.400 million: **India**, c.100 million; **England**, c.3 million; and Florence, c.70,000. Although the **Black Death** had shattered the growth of Europe's population and prosperity in the mid-14th century, by 1500 these losses had been regained, and population growth in the west had been reestablished.

II. EXPLORATION AND COLONIZATION

c.1500 **Fishing** on the **Grand Banks** off Newfoundland was common long before permanent settlements were made in North America. French and Portuguese sailors were probably the first to make landings on the island in order to salt their cod.

1500 **Diego Diaz** [Diogo Dias], a Portuguese navigator, was the **first European to visit Madagascar**, which he named St. Lawrence. His ship had been blown off its course to India. The island was inhabited by Indonesians and Africans. The Muslims had arrived in the 13th century, and subsequently their trading settlements were often raided by the Portuguese.

1500 **Vicente Yáñez Pinzón** (1460?–?1524), who had sailed with Christopher Columbus in command of the *Niña*, discovered the mouth of the **Amazon River**. On the same voyage, he explored for Spain the coasts of northern South America and sailed as far north as present Costa Rica.

c.1500 The coast of **Guiana**, which included present French Guiana, Surinam, and Guyana, was explored by the Spanish.

1500 Apr. 22 **Pedro Alvares Cabral** (1467?–c.1520), commissioned by **Emanual I** [Manuel I] (May 31, 1469–Dec. 1521), king of Portugal (from 1495), to lead an expedition to India, sailed farther west than planned and landed on the coast of **Brazil**, which he claimed for his nation. Without exploring Brazil, he continued his voyage to the East, where he established a Portuguese trading post near Calicut, southwestern India.

1501 May 13 **Amerigo Vespucci** [Americus Vespucius] (1454–1512), an Italian navigator in the service of Portugal, sailed from Lisbon on his second expedition (there is doubt about his first, 1497–1498) to the **New World**, to explore the Brazilian coast. He concluded that it was not part of Asia.

1502 **Vasco da Gama**, a Portuguese explorer on his second voyage to India, built a factory and buildings for traders in Cochin, the capital of a princely state in southwestern India. A fort was built there the following year by Affonso de Albuquerque (1453–Dec. 15, 1515), to defend the strategic harbor. This was the **first European settlement in India**.

1504 The **earliest report of French activity in North America** was the record of a French fishing expedition to the coast of Newfoundland led by **Jean Denys** [Denyn] of Honfleur, near Le Havre, France.

1505–1509 **Francisco de Almeida** (c.1450–Mar. 1, 1510), the **first viceroy of Portuguese India**, conquered the wealthy city-states of the East African coast. Mombasa, in present Kenya, was taken; Kilwa, in present Tanzania, was sacked; and Sofala, in present Mozambique, was taken.

1505 A Spanish expedition under **Pedro Navarro** (1460–1528) took the port of Mers-el-Kébir, in present Algeria, from the **Zyanid** [Abd al-Wadid] **Dynasty** (1235–1550). The Algerian ports of Oran and Bougie [Bejaïa] were taken in 1509 and 1510. Tunis and Tripoli, also taken in 1510, were held only briefly.

1507 Francisco de Almeida, a Portuguese viceroy of India, established the **first European settlement in the Singhalese Kingdom of Kotte** (?–1598), a capital city near present Colombo, the capital of Sri Lanka [Ceylon].

1508 The Spanish ship **Ocampo** made the **first circumnavigation of Cuba**. **Fernandina**, as the island was called in Spain, was thus proven not to be a part of the mainland, which was still thought by most Europeans to be China.

1508 **Muscat** [Masqat] a port of southeastern Arabia was conquered by the Portuguese. It became their Arabian headquarters.

1509 The island of **Jamaica** was conquered for Spain by **Juan de Esquivel**, who became its first governor.

1509 **António Fernandes**, a Portuguese explorer, was the **first European to penetrate the Sofala** hinterland, in present Mozambique. He visited most of the **Monomotapa** [Motapa, Mutapa] **Empire** (c.1440–c.1629), whose **gold** mines were the main attraction for the Portuguese trade.

1509 Feb. 2 **Francisco de Almeida** won for Portugal complete **mastery of the African and Indian trade** when he destroyed the combined Egyptian and Indian fleet in a **battle off Diu**, a small island in the Arabian Sea near the coast of the Kathiawar Peninsula, India.

III. POLITICS AND WAR

c.1500 New upheavals in central Africa began with the **spread of firearms**, introduced originally through the Ottoman Empire (1326–1920). Powerful kingdoms developed, such as **Ashanti**, **Yoruba**, **Dahomey**, and **Kanem-Bornu**, whose capitals were the main slave centers for Arab markets.

1501 In a **battle at Shurer**, Persia, Ismail [Esmail] I of Ardabil (July 17, 1487–1524), shah of Persia, defeated Alwand, the Sunni Turkoman leader of the **White Sheep** [Ak Koyunlu] **Dynasty** that had ruled

eastern Anatolia, present Iraq, and northwestern Iran since 1378. Tabriz, the capital, was captured, and Ismail founded (July) the **Safawid** [Safavid] **Dynasty** of the **Shiite** Islamic sect, which ruled Persia until 1736.

1501 **Cesare Borgia**, duke of Valentinois [Valence] (from 1499), in southeastern France, was made duke of the Romagna, a region of northern Italy on the Adriatic Sea, by his father **Pope Alexander VI**. Borgia lost power with the accession of **Pope Julius II** (Dec. 5, 1443–Feb. 21, 1513; ruled from 1503) of the rival **della Rovere family**. Imprisoned in Spain, Borgia (b. 1475) died on Mar. 12, 1507.

1501 **Schaffausen** and **Basel** were admitted to the **Swiss Confederation**. In 1513, **Appenzell** was admitted, increasing the number of cantons to 13.

1503 Aug. 8 **James IV**, king of Scotland (from 1488), married **Margaret Tudor** (Nov. 29, 1489–Oct. 18, 1541), eldest daughter of **Henry VII**, king of England. The marriage failed to improve Anglo-Scottish relations.

1503 Dec. 27 French forces were defeated at the Garigliano River north of Naples by the Spanish under Gonzalo Fernández de Córdoba [El Gran Capitán] (1453–Dec. 1, 1515), and surrendered at nearby Gaeta on Jan. 1, 1504. By the **Treaty of Lyon** (Mar. 31), Louis XII, king of France, abandoned **Naples**, which remained a Spanish possession until 1713.

1504 Nov. 26 **Isabella** (b. Apr. 22, 1451), queen of Castile, died, bequeathing her kingdom to her daughter **Juana la Loca** [Joan the Mad] (1479–1555). Juana's husband was **Philip I the Handsome**, duke of Burgundy and now the disputed regent for his mad wife.

c.1505 The **Tuluva Dynasty** (1491–c.1570) came to power in the **Vijayanagar** [Bijanagar] **Empire** (1336–c.1670), whose capital was Vijayanagar [Hampi] on the Tungabhadra River in southern India. Under the rule of **Krishna Deva Raya**, the Hindu kingdom gained the status of an empire.

1506 June 27 The Hapsburg **Philip I**, duke of Burgundy and heir to the Spanish throne since his marriage to Juana in 1496, received Castile from **Ferdinand II of Aragon** [V of Castile] by the **Treaty of Villafavila**. Philip's eldest son Charles was recognized as heir to Aragon as well as to Castile. On Philip's death (b. July 22, 1478) on Sept. 25, Ferdinand became king of Castile.

1508 Dec. 10   Pope Julius II; Maximilian I, the Holy Roman emperor; Louis XII, king of France; and Ferdinand II, king of Spain, organized the **League of Cambrai** to reduce the republic of Venice. **Venice** was defeated (May 14, 1509) in a **battle at Agnadello** in northern Italy, and surrendered Ravenna and the Romagna to the Papal States. When Venice refused to surrender, the League disbanded.

1509 Apr. 21   Henry VII (b. Jan. 28, 1457), king of England (from 1485), died. His son **Henry VIII** succeeded to the throne, and married **Catherine of Aragon**, a daughter of Ferdinand and Isabella of Spain, on June 11. The marriage provided him the opportunity to ally with the Spanish as well as with the Papacy in the **Holy League**, formed (1511) against France.

IV. ECONOMY AND TRADE

c.1500–1680   The influx of **gold** and **silver** from Spanish America was thought to have caused the **inflation** that occurred in Europe at this time by adding to the money supply of the world.

c.1500   An element of **competition** began to develop in Europe, partly as a result of the European discovery of the New World, which generated vast wealth and a sense of enterprise in people.

c.1500   **Brazilwood**, prized in Europe because from it came a valuable red and purple dye, was discovered in **Brazil**, and it became the first important export from this Portuguese territory. The discovery spurred exploration and settlement of Brazil.

1509   A Portuguese factory [trading fort] was built at Malindi, in present **Kenya**, the main East African center of iron mining and export. The town weakened when the Portuguese later diverted the trade routes southward to reach the **Mozambique Coast**.

V. RELIGION AND PHILOSOPHY

1502   **Ismail of Ardabil**, shah of Persia and founder of the **Safawid** [Safavid] **Dynasty** (1501–1736), made the **Shiite** sect of Islam the state religion despite the fact that only one-third of his subjects were Shiites. Ismail's father was a fanatical Shiite who died in battle with the Sunnites.

1502   **Ferdinand and Isabella**, king and queen of Spain, required the inspection by the bishops of all books on sale or available in Spain. A penalty of death or confiscation of property was decreed (1558) for anyone convicted of selling or possessing condemned **books**.

1502   **Desiderius Erasmus** [Gerhard Gerhards or Geert Geerts] (Oct. 26?, 1466–July 12, 1536), a Dutch scholar, published the first of his criticisms of the Church, *Handbook of the Christian Soldier*, a plea for a return to the sources of Christianity. In *Praise of Folly* (1509) Erasmus satirized the evils in both Church and State, and in *Familiar Colloquies* (1518), the externalities of the Christian life.

1506   **Johannes Reuchlin** [Capnio] (Feb. 22, 1455–June 6, 1522), a German humanist and Hebraist, published the **first Hebrew grammar** and lexicon *De Rudimentis Hebraicia*, which promoted the study of that language and of the Old Testament. A long, bitter controversy between humanists and church conservatives over the publication of Jewish books ensued, helping to unite the humanists.

1509   **Jacques Lefèvre d'Étaples** (1455–Mar., 1536), a French Christian humanist and publisher of the works of Nicholas of Cusa, issued his *Psalterium Quincuplex*, an exposition of the Psalms based on five Latin versions. In this and in later works on Paul's epistles and the Gospels, Lefèvre departed entirely from the spiritual-allegorical approach to Scripture of the medieval schoolmen.

1509   **Chaitanya** (1485–1533), a scholarly Brahmin, took the vow of a *sannyasi* [mendicant monk] and became a devotee of **Krishna**. In six years of missionary wanderings and a final 16 years spent in devotions at Puri [Bombay], India, he created a movement based on a revived Radha-Krishna theme: **Radha** in her love for Krishna represented to Chaitanya the love of man for God. After Chaitanya's death this theme generated many sexual and **Tantric cults**.

VI. SCIENCE, EDUCATION, AND TECHNOLOGY

16th Cent.   **Maize** [*Zea mays*], or American Corn, spread rapidly through suitable areas of the world as a grain crop. The Portuguese introduced it from Brazil to North Africa, and it was soon planted in parts of Europe.

c.1500   The **galleon**, a three-masted, square-rigged ship, usually with two decks, became the standard sailing vessel for both merchants and the navy, especially in Spain. Its great stability made it possible to carry more merchandise or firepower than its predecessors, though it was cumbersome.

c.1500   The **musket** was developed in Spain about this time. It was more accurate and could penetrate armor much better than the smaller gun, the **harquebus**, it replaced.

1500   **Juan de la Cosa** (1460?–1510), who had accompanied Christopher Columbus on his second voyage, drew a world map containing the **first formal rendering of the New World**. On ox hide, more than three feet wide and six feet long, the map shows Brazil as an island and a "Cape of England," probably Newfoundland or Nova Scotia. La Cosa drew Cuba accurately as an island. La Cosa made a number of voyages to the New World, where he died, in present Venezuela.

1507   **Martin Waldseemüller** (1470?–?1518), a German geographer, praised **Amerigo Vespucci's** accounts of the New World and suggested it should be called "America." He placed the name next to South America on the world map that accompanied his *Introduction of Cosmography.*

1509   The **first watch** was said to have been made by a Nürnberg [Nuremberg] locksmith, **Peter Henlein** (1480–1542), who constructed "portable timepieces."

VII. ARTS AND LEISURE

c.1500–1550   During the High Renaissance in Germany, **puffed sleeves and breeches** were in style as were wide-brimmed hats worn by men and women. "Slashing," slits cut in an outer garment to display the lining, was an innovation.

c.1500   The **English Tudor style of architectural design** may best be distinguished by its Gothic elements, while the Continent was enjoying a classical renaissance in design. Great, high windows and doors, gabled roofs, wood-paneled walls, and molded plaster decoration were popular. Hampton Court Palace, the residence of **Henry VIII**, was an example of this style.

c.1500   **White glass**, instead of oiled paper, was first used by the French in their windows.

c.1500   The *Mona Lisa* was completed by **Leonardo da Vinci** in Florence before he departed for Milan in 1506.

1501   The **first book of music printed with movable type**, *Harmonice Musices Odhécaton*, was published by **Ottaviano dei Petrucci** (June 18, 1466–May 7, 1539). His invention of casting each note with its staff line, a great innovation, had been granted exclusive privileges in Venice in 1498.

1501 Jan. 3   **Ali Şir Nevar** (b. Jan. 9, 1441), who perfected the Turkish literary language of *chagatai*, died. He was considered one of the greatest Turkish scholars of his day.

1501 Sept. 13   **Michelangelo**, commissioned by Florence's Operai del Duomo, began work on his marble statue of *David*. Completed Jan. 1504, it stood about 13½ feet high. It stands at the Academy of Fine Arts in Florence.

1501 Sept. 26   **Djordje Drážíc** (b. Feb. 6, 1461), an early poet of Dalmatia, a coastal region of Croatia, died. His poetical style, perhaps influenced by Petrarch, may be seen in his adaptation of the play *Alulularia.*

1504   **Fra Bartolommeo** [Bartolommeo di Pogolo del Fattorino; *also*: Baccio della Porta] (Mar. 28, 1474–Oct. 31, 1517) became head of the monastery of San Marco in Florence where, influenced by **Raphael and Mariotto Albertinelli** (1474–1515), he dominated the development of the high Renaissance style in painting.

1504   *L'Arcadia*, the first of the pastoral dramas set in an imaginary and ideal Arcadia, was composed by **Jacopa Sannazzaro** [Actius Sincerus] (July 28, 1458–Apr. 24, 1530), an Italian poet.

1504 Apr. 18   **Filippino Lippi** (born c. 1457), a Florentine painter and son of Fra Filippo Lippi, died. He was a student of Botticelli. His most famous painting was *The Madonna Appearing to St. Barnard* (c.1486); among his frescoes was a notable series (completed 1502) in S. Maria Novella, Florence.

1505   **Jakob Obrecht** (b. Nov. 22, 1450), a Flemish composer, died of the plague. He was a prolific composer of a blend of polyphony and folk traditions. His *St. Matthew Passion* (1471) is known today as perhaps the earliest four-part setting of this text.

1506 Sesshu (b. 1419), a Zen priest and one of Japan's greatest painters, died. His masterpiece is now generally considered to be the 50-foot long landscape scroll *Sansui Chokan*, which was probably completed in 1486.

1507 Gentile Bellini (born c.1430), a Venetian painter, died. Known especially for his large, ceremonial canvasses, Bellini went to **Constantinople** in 1479 under the patronage of **Muhammad II**, the Ottoman sultan. There he painted the sultan's portrait (1480). On his return to Venice he painted a series of large public scenes containing numerous contemporary portraits.

1508 Mar. 10   A contract was signed commissioning **Michelangelo** to paint frescoes on the ceiling of the **Sistine Chapel** in the papal palace in Rome. Completed without assistance in Sept. 1512, the ceiling was unveiled prematurely on the Feast of the Assumption on Aug. 14, 1511.

1509 Mar. 17 Necati [Isa Çelebi], one of the founders of the classical school of **Turkish poetry** and a leading writer of *gazel* **poetry**, died in İstanbul.

1510–1519

I. EXPLORATION AND COLONIZATION

1510   The first "stable settlement of continental America" was founded by **Vasco Núñez de Balboa** and **Francisco Pizarro** (d. 1541), Spanish explorers, at **Darién** [Santa María la Antigua del Darién], in present Colombia on the Isthmus of Darién [Isthmus of Panama]. The colony of Darién was also called Nueva Andalucía.

1511   António d'Abreu, a Portuguese explorer, discovered the **Sunda Islands**, an island group of the Malay Archipelago. The Portuguese explored large areas of the East Indies, Australasia, and western Oceania.

1511   The city of **San Juan**, the **first permanent European settlement on the island of Puerto Rico**, was founded by **Juan Ponce de Léon**, who was then appointed its first governor.

1513 Mar. 27   Juan Ponce de Léon, in search of the great mythical island of **Bimini**, discovered the mainland of **Florida** on Easter Sunday, landing near the present site of **St. Augustine** on the eastern coast. Claiming the area for Spain, he named it *Pascua Florida* [Flowery Easter]. Believing it was Bimini, the land of the **Fountain of Youth**, the explorer attempted unsuccessfully to establish a colony on the western coast of Florida during a second expedition in 1521. Ponce de Léon (born c.1460) was severely wounded in a fight with Indians there and died upon returning to Cuba in the same year.

1513 Sept. 25 or 27   Vasco Núñez de Balboa, guided across the **Isthmus of Panama** by natives, was the **first European to view the Pacific Ocean**, at least from its eastern edge.

1514   A Portuguese ship reached Lintin Island near Canton, one of the **first direct contacts between China and the West** during the Age of Exploration. In 1517 the Portuguese sent an embassy to the emperor of China, Wu Tsung (ruled 1505–1521), of the **Ming Dynasty** (1368–1644).

1514 July   Pedro Arias de Ávila [Pedrarias Dávila] (c.1440–?1530) arrived at Darién and founded the colony of Castilla del Oro, on the present Isthmus of Panama. In 1519 Pedrarias found **Panama City** near its present site.

1515   Fernández de Oviedo, a Spanish navigator, sailed near the **Bermuda Islands** in the North Atlantic Ocean. He attributed their discovery to Juan de Bermúdez, who made a voyage at an earlier date, perhaps before 1511, when an Italian map was published, showing the approximate location of the islands.

1516   Diaz de Solís, a Spanish explorer, was the first European known to enter the **Río de la Plata**, which marks the present boundary of Argentina and Uruguay. Solis (born c.1470), after landing in present Uruguay, was killed and reported to have been eaten by the Charrúa Indians.

1518 The Spanish captain **Alonso Álvarez de Piñeda** sailed along the shores of the **Gulf of Mexico**, 23 years before Hernando de Soto explored the region. Piñeda sailed c.20 miles up the **Mississippi River**, which he named Río Espiritu Sancto [Holy Ghost River]. He reentered the Gulf of Mexico and mapped the coast of present Texas.

1519 Jan. **Vasco Núñez de Balboa** (born c.1475) was beheaded for treason by Pedro Arias de Ávila, Balboa's jealous rival in the Spanish colony of Darién, on the Isthmus of Panama. Balboa had been named governor of the South Sea and Panama by the king of Spain, in honor of his explorations across the isthmus to the Pacific Ocean. Because the area was thought to be so rich, Arias de Ávila had been sent to Darién to head a new colony.

1519 The city of **Havana** was founded on the island of Cuba as a port for Spanish galleons plying the Atlantic between Spain and the New World.

1519 Aug. 10 **Ferdinand Magellan** [Fernando de Magalhães], a Portuguese sailing for Spain, left Sevilla [Seville] with five ships to find a westward route to the Spice Islands [the Moluccas]. In Nov. 1520, he passed from the Atlantic to the Pacific Ocean through the strait named after him, at the southernmost tip of the South American mainland. Magellan (b. 1480) reached the **Philippine Islands** (which he claimed for Spain), where he was killed on Apr. 27, 1521, by natives. On Nov. 6, 1521, the remainder of Magellan's crew reached the Spice Islands [Moluccas]. **Juan Sebastian del Cano** (1476–Aug. 4, 1526), in command of the *Victoria*, the only ship of the five to complete the **first circumnavigation of the globe,** returned to Spain on Sept. 6, 1522.

II. POLITICS AND WAR

1510 Nov. Affonso de Albuquerque [Alboquerque] (1453–Dec. 13, 1515), known as Affonso the Great, viceroy of Portuguese territory in India and Asia, conquered **Goa** in southwestern India from Yusuf Adil Shah, the sultan of Bijapur (1498–1510).

1511 Aug. Portuguese soldiers under Affonso de Albuquerque conquered **Malacca**, a port on the

coast of Malaya, from Mahmud (d. 1528), the sultan of Malay (1488–1511), destroying the **Kingdom of Malacca** (from c.1400). Control of the **Strait of Malacca** gave the Portuguese a monopoly on trade in the Far East.

1511 Oct. 5 The **Holy League** was organized by Pope Julius II, who was joined by Ferdinand II, king of Aragon; Henry VIII, king of England; Maximilian I, the Holy Roman emperor; the Swiss; and the Venetians.

1512 Apr. 11 The French under **Gaston de Foix** (1489–1512), king of Navarre (1505–1512), won their **last victory over the Holy League** at **Ravenna**, capital of the Romagna. While Spain invaded Navarre, annexing the present Spanish region, the French were driven in May from Milan, which was restored (to 1515) to **Massimiliano Sforza** (1493–1530), and Florence was restored to **Cardinal Giovanni de' Medici**, the future Pope Leo X (Dec. 11, 1475–Dec. 1, 1521; ruled from 1513). Louis XII, king of France, finally abandoned Italy after the Swiss victory at Novara, west of Milan, on June 6, 1513.

1513 Aug. 17 Pursuing the mandate of the **Holy League, Henry VIII**, king of England, defeated the French in a **battle at Guinegatte** [Enguinegatte], in northern France, called the "Battle of the Spurs" because the French quickly retreated. Then **Thomas Howard II** (1473–1554), earl of Surrey, defeated and killed **James IV** (b. Mar. 17, 1473), king of Scotland, at **Flodden Field** in northern England on Sept. 9. Hostilities between England and France and her Scottish allies were ended by the **Peace of London**, signed on Aug. 6, 1514, and the marriage of Henry's sister Mary (?Mar. 1496–June 24, 1533) to **Louis XII**, king of France, on Oct. 9.

1514 May **Claude de France** (1499–1524), daughter of Louis XII and Anne of Brittany, and heiress to the duchy of Brittany, married Francis, count of Angoulême, the future **Francis I**, king of France, and **Brittany passed formally to the French crown.**

1514 Aug. 23 Turkish forces under Selim I [the Grim] (1467–1520; ruled from 1512), the Ottoman sultan and a persecutor of **Shiites** in his empire, defeated Shah Ismail of Persia at Chaldiran [Çaldiran], in present Turkey. Anatolia and Kurdistan were annexed to the **Ottoman Empire**, initiating a series of wars between the **Sunni Ottomans** and the **Shiite Safawid** [Safavid] **Dynasty** of Persia.

1515 Sept. 14   Francis I, king of France after **Louis XII** (b. June 27, 1462; ruled from 1498) died on Jan. 1, defeated Massimiliano Sforza's Swiss mercenaries at Marignano [Melegnano] near Milan and recovered the duchy of Milan. Peace followed in 1516: with Spain by the **Treaty of Noyon** on Aug. 13; with the papacy by the **Concordat of Bologna** on Aug. 18; with Switzerland by the **Perpetual Peace** signed at Fribourg on Nov. 29; and with the Holy Roman Empire by the **Treaty of Brussels** on Dec. 13.

1516 Jan. 23   **Ferdinand the Catholic**, king of Spain [Ferdinand II of Aragon; Ferdinand V of Castile] (b. Mar. 10, 1452), died. Spain passed to his grandson Charles I (Feb. 24, 1500–Sept. 21, 1558) of the **Hapsburg Dynasty** (1273–1740). Charles arrived from Flanders to end the regency of Cardinal Jiménez [Ximénez] de Cisneros (1436–Nov. 8 1517) on Sept. 17, 1517.

1516 Aug. 24   In a **battle at Marj Dabiq** near Aleppo, in present Syria, the Turkish forces of **Selim I**, the Ottoman sultan, defeated the combined Syrian and Egyptian forces of **al-Ghawri**, the Mameluke sultan of Egypt (from 1501), who was killed during the battle.

1517 Jan. 22   In a **battle at Ridanya** near Cairo, Selim I completed his conquest of **Egypt** by defeating Tuman Bey, the new sultan (from 1517), of the **Mameluke Burji** [Tower] **Dynasty** (from 1382). The Turks sacked Cairo and hanged Tuman Bey on Apr. 14. The sharif of Mecca, Barakat II (ruled 1512–1566), recognized Ottoman suzerainty, as did the whole of Arabia.

1519 Jan. 12   **Maximilian I** (b. Mar. 22, 1459) the Holy Roman emperor (from 1493), died. The Hapsburg Charles I of Spain was elected emperor June 28 as **Charles V** to begin the supremacy of the **Hapsburg Dynasty** (1273–1740). Charles's dream of reuniting Christendom was opposed mainly by the **Valois of France**.

1519 Nov. 8   Hernando [Hernán] **Cortés** (1485–Dec. 2, 1547), a Spanish conquistador, entered the **Aztec capital of Tenochtitlán**, near present Mexico City, and took its emperor **Montezuma II** hostage. Cortés departed to attack **Pánfilo de Narváez** (1480?–1528), who had been sent from Spain to arrest Cortés. At first the **Aztecs** confused the Spanish arrival with the legendary return of **Quetzalcoatl** [Feathered Serpent], the Aztec god of creation.

Horses, never before seen by the Aztecs, were thought for a while to be the same creatures as the men riding them, and muskets were powerful weapons.

III. ECONOMY AND TRADE

1516   The **oldest social settlement in the world** still in existence, the **Fuggerei**, low rent housing for poor Catholics, was built in Augsburg, Bavaria, with profits earned by the **Fugger banking family**.

1516   **Henry VIII**, king of England, introduced experienced Flemish **weavers** to Coventry, already known for its fine woolen caps.

1519   The coin called a **Joachimsthaler** was first minted in Bohemia.

IV. RELIGION AND PHILOSOPHY

1514 Aug. 18   Upon payment of 10,000 ducats, **Pope Leo X** appointed **Albert of Brandenburg** (June 28, 1490–Sept. 24, 1545), 26-year-old brother of **Elector Joachim I Nestor** of Brandenburg (Feb. 24, 1484–July 11, 1535), as archbishop of Mainz. Albert, who already held two sees, borrowed the money from moneylenders, expecting to recover it by the **sale of indulgences**, which then took the place of temporal punishment for sins repented before God.

1515 Mar. 31   Pope Leo X published the bull announcing the **indulgence plan for Germany**. The drive for funds for the rebuilding of Saint Peter's in Rome was headed in Germany by the Dominican preacher **John Tetzel** (1470–July 4, 1519), who shortly thereafter became the focal point of **Martin Luther's** attacks for misleading beliefs, and for overzealous preaching about indulgences.

1516   The **Concordat of 1516**, signed by **Francis I**, king of France, and the Medici **Pope Leo X**, partially reestablished the independence of the Gallican Church after the **Pragmatic Sanction** (1438) of Bourges had been revoked in 1461. The pope secured the right to collect *annates* [the first year's revenue] from each new papal appointment, and Francis was granted the right to nominate all high French ecclesiastics and to tax the clergy.

1516   **Desiderius Erasmus**, a Dutch scholar, completed his edition of the **New Testament in Greek**. Published in parallel columns with the **Vulgate** and

Erasmus's translation, this text quickly became the cornerstone of biblical scholarship and of the era of Bible translation from the original tongues.

1517 Oct. 31 **Martin Luther** nailed his **Ninety-five Theses** to the door of the castle church in Wittenberg, Saxony, a university community in present Germany. The door was a kind of bulletin board, and the Theses were propositions Luther was prepared to argue in academic debate. They centered primarily on abuses of the sale of indulgences and related church views about purgatory, repentance, and grace. This date is often cited today as the beginning of the **Protestant Reformation**.

c.1518 **Bartolomé de las Casas** (1474–July 17, 1566), a Dominican friar, came to the region of present **Venezuela** to establish a colony where the Indians could be free from slavery and domination by the Spanish military. Las Casas had become appalled by Spanish cruelty and by the slaughter of thousands of Indians. Though his experiment failed, he remained the staunchest Spanish advocate of the native Indians.

1518 **Kabir** (b. 1440), a Hindu mystic poet, died. Kabir wished to bring together Hindus and Muslims as children of one God, but was unsuited for the role as his poems and hymns condemned the sacred rituals of Hinduism and Islam for dividing men. His message of the pure heart, trust in God, and love of brother appealed to many Hindus, Muslims, and Christians.

1518 Oct. 20 **Martin Luther** appeared at Augsburg, Bavaria, before **Cardinal Cajetan** [Gaietanus] (Feb. 20, 1469–Aug. 10, 1534), legate of **Pope Leo X**. Luther's protector, the Elector of Saxony, had negotiated this examination as a substitute for a summons to Rome made earlier in 1518. Luther, finding Cajetan unwilling to hear arguments in his defense, left Augsburg to write a defiant appeal from Leo X's judgment. Leo was inclined to give full pardon to Luther if he would recant and submit.

1519 Jan. 2 **Huldreich** [Ulrich] **Zwingli** (Jan. 1, 1484–Oct. 11, 1531), much influenced by Luther and now a priest at the Great Minster of Zürich, initiated a series of sermons that marked the beginning of the **Swiss Reformation**.

1519 June Martin Luther and a supporter, **Andreas Rudolf Bodenstein von Karlstadt** [Carlstadt] (1477?–

Dec. 24, 1541), began a heavily attended, two-part debate with the Dominican **Johannes Meyer** [Maier] of Eck (Nov. 13, 1486–Feb. 10, 1543). Forced into a declaration that a general council was not infallible, and having previously declared popes fallible, Luther now stood squarely on scriptural authority alone. The debate terminated the efforts of a papal nuncio, **Karl von Miltitz** (1490?–1529), to placate Luther.

V. SCIENCE, EDUCATION, AND TECHNOLOGY

c.1510 **Nicolaus Copernicus**, a Polish astronomer, in his *Commentariolus*, first laid out the premises of the Copernican system of the universe holding that the planets, including earth, orbited around the sun and that the earth rotated on its axis.

1514 The warship *Henry Grâce à Dieu*, carrying 180 guns (some records claimed it carried 385 guns) was launched by England. Built by order of Henry VIII, it had four large masts and two smaller mizzenmasts, eight decks in the stern, could carry 700 men, and could be boarded only at the waist, which was covered by many swivel guns to rake any attackers who boarded.

1519 May 2 **Leonardo da Vinci** (b. Apr. 15, 1452), the genius painter, sculptor, architect, and scientist, died. Among his works were intricate studies in anatomy and technological problems.

VI. ARTS AND LEISURE

1510 **Giorgione** [Giorgio Barbarelli, Zorzi da Castelfranco] (born c.1477), a seminal Venetian painter, died of the plague. A *Madonna* in the cathedral at Castelfranco and *Venus Asleep* (c.1509) are two of the half-dozen or so works definitely established at present as Giorgione's. His naturalistic use of color without formal line greatly influenced Titian.

1510 May 17 **Sandro Botticelli** [Alessandro di Mariano dei Filipepi] (born c.1445), a Florentine painter, died. A pupil of **Fra Filippo Lippi** and protégé of the Medici, he had worked on the Sistine Chapel (c.1485) and illustrated Dante's *Divina Commedia* (c.1490) in addition to painting his own canvases. Some of his more noted works were *Primavera* (c.1477), *Adoration of the Magi* (1477), *Mars and Venus* (1485), and the *Birth of Venus* (1486).

1515 **Giovanni Giorgio Trissino** (July 8, 1478–Dec. 8, 1550), an Italian playwright, published *Sophonisba*, the first drama of the Renaissance to adhere to the rules of classical Greek tragedy.

1516 **Hieronymus Bosch** [Hieronymus van Aeken Bosch] (born c.1450), a Dutch allegorical painter of religious subjects, died. His works included *The Temptation of St. Anthony* (c.1500) and *The Ship of Fools* (after 1500), which illustrated through the use of grotesque symbols his preoccupation with temptation. Bosch's technique influenced subsequent painters, especially Pieter Brueghel the Elder.

1516? **Nov. 29** **Giovanni Bellini** (born c.1430), a Venetian painter whose students included most of that city's artists of the 15th century, died. Many of his works survive today, including *The Madonna with Sleeping Child* (c.1465), *The Agony in the Garden* (1465), *Pietà* (c.1470), and *St. Dominic* (1515).

1517 Mar. 26 **Heinrich Isaak** (born c.1450), a Flemish composer who developed the use of melody in the soprano part, died.

VII. SPORTS, GAMES, AND SOCIETY

1511 Henry VIII, king of England, banned the "game of bowles" [lawn bowling] as an evil because it had become a form of "vicious gambling." Henry also felt it kept the men from practicing archery.

1519 **Marina** [Malintzin] (1501?–?1550), an Aztec Indian princess, was offered to the Spanish conquistadors to buy peace. She became mistress and guide to **Hernando Cortés**, translating the **Maya** and **Nahuatl** languages for him and his men. After the death of Cortés, Marina married another Spanish soldier, who brought her to Spain where she was welcomed at the court.

1520–1529

I. EXPLORATION AND COLONIZATION

1524 **Giovanni da Verrazano** (1485?–?1528), a Florentine navigator, explored the coast of North America from the Carolinas to Maine, and was probably the **first European to enter New York Bay**.

1524 **León and Granada**, on the northwestern shore of Lake **Nicaragua**, both in present Nicaragua, were founded by **Francisco Fernández** [Hernández] de Córdoba [Córdova], for **Pedro Arias de Ávila** [Pedrarias], the Spanish governor of Panama. Pedrarias, noted for his ruthlessness, arrived at León, had Córdoba (born c.1475) executed in 1526, and assumed the governorship of Nicaragua (1526–1530). During this time he exported Indian slaves to Panama.

1525 **Rodrigo de Bastidas** (1460–1526) established the **first permanent European settlement in present Colombia** at Santa Marta, on the northern coast.

1526–1530 Serving Spain, **Sebastian Cabot** (1476?–1557), son of the Italian explorer John Cabot, sailed along the eastern coast of South America. He had been told that silver and gold could be found in the region of the Río de la Plata. He found no great store of precious metals but his explorations allowed Spain to claim successfully what are now **Argentina** and **Uruguay**.

1526 June or July **Lucas Vazques de Ayllón** landed with c.550 settlers at the mouth of a river located at 33° 40′ north latitude, possibly the Peedee River, South Carolina. The area was unhealthy, and many soon died of fever. Ayllón (born c.1475) died on Oct. 18, and the remaining settlers headed back to Hispaniola, towing Ayllón's body in a small boat. It capsized, and the body was lost at sea.

1528–1536 **Álvar Núñez Cabeza de Vaca** (c.1490–1560) sailed with the expedition of Pánfilo de Narváez to explore, conquer, and colonize Florida for Spain. The expedition was a complete failure and their ships wrecked near **Pensacola Bay** in April of 1528. Cabeza de Vaca built crude vessels and set sail for Mexico. Their boats were wrecked off the coast of Texas and Narváez (born c.1470) was lost. The survivors were captured by the Indians, but Cabeza de Vaca and two others escaped and made their way to the Gulf of California in 1536, where they were rescued by Spanish soldiers.

1529–1536 Nuño de Guzmán (d. 1542), a Spanish conquistador and former president of Mexico City, conquered the Pacific coast of northwestern Mexico. This area became known as **Nueva Galicia**, comprising the present Mexican states of **Jalisco**, **Nayarit**, and southern **Sinaloa**.

II. POLITICS AND WAR

1520 Suleiman the Magnificent succeeded his father, Selim I, as sultan of the **Ottoman Empire** (1326–1920). His reign saw the expansion of the empire further into eastern Europe; it extended north and south from Hungary to Mesopotamia and west to include Egypt. In 1521 Suleiman took Belgrade and in 1522 the island of Rhodes.

1520 June 4 Kings **Henry VIII**, of England, and **Francis I**, of France, met at the **Field of the Cloth of Gold**, near English-held Calais, to begin a three-week conference. The meeting failed to secure an alliance with England. Instead, on July 10, Henry, at the meeting of **Gravelines** on the border with Flanders, promised aid to the Hapsburg Charles V, king of Spain and the Holy Roman emperor.

1520 June 30 Known in Spanish and Mexican history as *"la noche triste"* [the night of sorrow], this day found the Spanish, under **Hernando Cortés**, retreating from their conquest of the Aztec capital at Tenochtitlán. **Montezuma II** (b. 1480?), during a speech to his people, was mortally wounded and in the ensuing riot Cortés lost half his men. **Pedro de Alvarado** made his famous *salta de Alvarado*, using his spear to vault across a broad opening in one of the city's causeways.

1520 July 29 The **Comuneros**, a revolt of the Spanish cities, began at **Toledo** against the Hapsburg rule in Spain of **Charles V**, the Holy Roman emperor, who had just departed for Germany to pursue his imperial aims. The rebellion was crushed at Villalar on Apr. 23, 1521, and Charles had the leaders executed.

1521 The Arab sultanate of **Bahrain**, an island in the Persian Gulf, was captured by the Portuguese.

1521 Apr. A combined Spanish and Indian force, sent to aid Hernando Cortés, resumed the **siege of Tenochtitlán**. On Aug. 21 they razed the city and captured the Aztec ruler, **Guatemotzin** [Cuauhtémoc] (1495?–1525), successor to Montezuma II. It was the end of the **Aztec Empire** (from c.1428).

1521 Apr. 28 **Ferdinand**, the younger brother of Charles V, the Holy Roman emperor, was granted the Hapsburg Austrian possessions and the regency of Germany. He was elected king of Germany in 1531. In May he married Anne, sister of Louis II, king of Hungary and Bohemia, enabling him to claim both kingdoms at Louis's death in 1526.

1522 Apr. 27 The French were defeated in a **battle at Bicocca**, now a suburb of Milan, by the imperial forces of Charles V in the **first Valois-Hapsburg War** (1521–1526), and were ousted from most of Italy. Meanwhile, the English, under Charles Brandon (1484–Aug. 24, 1545), duke of Suffolk and Henry VIII's brother-in-law, campaigned unsuccessfully in France in support of Charles, plundering Normandy and Picardy.

1523 June 6 **Gustavus I Vasa** [Gustavus Eriksson] (1496–Sept. 29, 1560) was proclaimed king of **Sweden**. With the support of the peasantry and merchants, he drove Christian II the Cruel from Sweden. Christian was responsible for the Massacre at Stockholm in Nov. 1520, when nearly all rival claimants to Sweden's throne had been murdered.

1525 Huayna Capac, the **greatest ruler of the Incas**, died, leaving the empire to his two sons, the true Inca Huáscar (1495?–1532) and the usurper Atahualpa [Atabalipa]. A quarrel between them led to civil war, which left the **Incas** demoralized and unready to defend themselves against the Spanish soldiers.

1525 Feb. 24 **Francis I**, king of France, was defeated and captured in a **battle at Pavia**, near Milan, during the **first Valois-Hapsburg War** (1521–1526) by the imperial forces of the Holy Roman Empire, commanded by Fernando Francisco de Ávalos, marqués of Pescara (1490–1525). Francis was imprisoned in Spain until he signed the **Treaty of Madrid** on Jan. 14, 1526.

1526 Francisco de Montejo tried to conquer the **Mayan tribes** of the Yucatán Peninsula but, by 1545, only the northern coast had been subdued.

1526 Apr. 21 The **first battle of Panipat**, near Delhi, India, brought defeat and death to Ibrahim Lodi, sultan of Delhi (from 1517). The victorious **Baber** [Babur, Babar; Zahir ud-Din Mohammed Babur] (Feb. 14, 1483–Dec. 26, 1530) the Muslim ruler of Kabul in Afghanistan, founded the **Mogul**

[Mughal] **Empire of Hindustan** (to 1857) in India, becoming its first emperor.

1526 May 23   Pope Clement VII (May 26, 1478–Sept. 25, 1534; ruled from 1523) organized the **League of Cognac** between Florence, Milan, Venice, and France in an attempt to curb the Hapsburg hegemony in Italy. This led to the sack of Rome (1527) by Spanish imperial forces of Charles V, the Holy Roman emperor, and to the capture and imprisonment of Clement.

1526 Aug. 29   A Turkish army under **Suleiman the Magnificent**, the Ottoman sultan, defeated **Louis II**, king of Hungary and Bohemia (from 1516), in a **battle at Mohács** on the Danube River, in present Hungary. Louis (b. July 1, 1506), the **last of the Jagiello Dynasty** (founded c. 1350), died without male heir after the battle by drowning in flight, and his kingdom collapsed. **Ferdinand I** of Austria was elected king of Bohemia on Oct. 23, but **John Zápolya** of Transylvania [now central Romania], contested the succession of the Hungarian crown. Crowned as John I, king of Hungary, in 1526, Zápolya was forced by Ferdinand to retreat to Transylvania; but the Ottomans entered (1529) central Hungary, and restored Zápolya as a puppet king of Hungary. Ferdinand retained western Hungary.

1527   King Henry VIII, of England, anxious because his wife, **Catherine of Aragon**, bore no children after the birth of **Princess Mary**, began alleging religious scruples to invalidate his 1509 marriage. He commissioned his lord chancellor **Cardinal Thomas Wolsey** to obtain a decree of nullity from Pope Clement VII.

1527   The **Shans**, still migrating from China's Yünnan province, conquered the city of Ava on the Irrawaddy River, in present **Burma** [Myanmar].

1527   With the founding of **Guatemala City**, the Spanish **captaincy general of Guatemala** was organized, comprising present Guatemala, El Salvador, Honduras, Nicaragua, and Costa Rica. Its capital was at Santiago de los Caballeros de Guatemala [Guatemala City].

1528   The coastal **city-state of Mombasa**, in present Kenya, led an uprising against **Portuguese rule in East Africa**. Nunho da Cunha (1487–1539) easily suppressed the revolt, and the Portuguese sacked Mombasa.

1529   Imam Ahmad ibn Ibrahim the Grañ, the Somalian Muslim leader, launched a holy war against Christian **Ethiopia** [Abyssinia]. With firearms brought by the Ottomans into the Red Sea area, he was able to conquer most of Ethiopia. Ahmad established the **Emirate of Harar** (1525–1887), in eastern Ethiopia.

1529 May 27   Algeria became a vassal state of the Ottoman Empire and the main stronghold of the Barbary States after the expulsion of the Spanish by the Muslims, aided by the Turkish pirate Barbarossa II [Khair ed-Din] (c.1480–1546), who became pasha under Suleiman I. The **Barbary States** were the string of Islamic nations of the northern coast of Africa that arose as the Mohammedans spread into the area after the defeat (from 642) of the Byzantine Empire in North Africa.

1529 June 29   Pope Clement VII and Charles V, the Holy Roman emperor, signed the **Treaty of Barcelona**, which restored the Papal States to the pope, and Florence to the Medici family, in return for Charles's official coronation as the Holy Roman emperor, on Feb. 24, 1530. France renounced its claims in Italy by the **Treaty of Cambrai** on Aug. 5, 1529, and Milan was restored to Francesco Sforza II.

1529 July 23   Cardinal Lorenzo Campeggio (1474–July 25, 1539), Pope Clement VII's legate in the matter of the annulment of Henry VIII's marriage to Catherine of Aragon, broke off discussions with Cardinal Thomas Wolsey in England. The pope refused to sanction the annulment. On Oct. 17 Wolsey was dismissed by **Henry VIII** as lord chancellor and was replaced by **Thomas More** on Oct. 25.

1529 Nov. 3   The **Reformation Parliament**, summoned by Henry VIII, convened for what would prove to be more than six years. It enacted statues that would strip the **authority of the pope in England** and invest it in the crown.

III. ECONOMY AND TRADE

c.1520   Chocolate was introduced into Spain from the New World, where the Aztecs had prized the cacao tree for its rich oil as well as its chocolate.

1520   Sugar cane was first introduced to the island of Puerto Rico, then (1526) to Brazil. Throughout the 15th and 16th centuries, Spanish and Portuguese explorers brought sugar cane from Asia, where it had been grown from antiquity, to the Old and New Worlds.

1520   Francis I, king of France, introduced Italian **silk** into his country, bringing growers and weavers into **Lyon**.

1521   **Hernando Cortés** introduced into New Spain [Mexico] the **system** of *encomiendas*, under which the Aztec towns and villages were parceled among his men to be governed as fiefs, with the Indians virtual slaves of the Spaniards.

1522   The **Single-Whip tax law** initiated a century-long process of tax reform in China. Tax and labor payments were combined into a single "whip." Payment in silver, rather than in kind, simplified the complex tax system begun early in the **Ming Dynasty** (1369–1644).

1526   Spain, whose treasure ships were harassed by privateers, began to send its vessels out in protective fleets. These *flotas*, which included warships, were generally successful in protecting Spain's trade.

1528   The Bavarian Welser banking firm in Augsburg, whose most prominent member was **Bartholomäus Welser** (1488–1561), was granted the territory of present **Venezuela** by Charles V, the Holy Roman emperor who was also king of Spain as Charles I, in return for a large loan earlier extended to him.

1529 June   The **Höchstetter banking house**, with offices in Bavaria, the Netherlands, and Portugal, went bankrupt and was taken over by its creditors. Höchstetter had attempted to monopolize Europe's supply of **mercury**, which was the most effective remedy for **syphilis**. To raise enough capital to secure the monopoly, large sums of money were raised, often by issuing shares to ordinary people. Thus, when a firm like Höchstetter went bankrupt, many from the middle and lower classes lost their savings.

IV. RELIGION AND PHILOSOPHY

1520 June 15   Pope Leo X excommunicated **Martin Luther** in the papal bull, named for its opening words, *Exsurge domine*. In it Leo set forth c.41 erroneous propositions that he maintained were the cause of trouble in the Church in Germany. He then charged Luther with these and other errors, ordered

his books burned, and gave him and his followers 60 days to recant. Not until Oct. 10 did Luther receive a copy, which he burned on Dec. 10, risking little as most of the German bishops were opposed to Rome's position of ecclesiastical supremacy.

1521   **Henry VIII**, king of England, published his treatise *Assertio Septem Sacramentorum* [Assertion of the Seven Sacraments], which earned him from the pope the solemn title, "**Fidei Defensor**," Defender of the Faith.

1521 Apr. 17   **Martin Luther** appeared before the Diet of Worms, a special meeting of the assembly called by Charles V, to consider the request made by Pope Leo X for formal condemnation of the reformer as stated in the papal bull of Jan. 2, 1521, called *Decet Romanum pontificem*. When Luther was asked to recant the views expressed in his exhibited books, he requested time to prepare a reply. Luther was given one day.

1521 Apr. 18   **Martin Luther**, in refusing to retract the substance of his written positions, demanded to be proved wrong on the basis of the Scriptures and not solely on the authority of the Church. No immediate action was taken against him. When in May Luther was put under an imperial ban, **Frederick III** (1463–1525), elector of Saxony, gave him protection in the castle at Wartburg, in present Germany.

1521 Apr. 19   **Charles V** now read his own profession of faith, a belief in the authority of councils. He charged Luther with opposing his private judgment against 1,000 years of Church authority. Charles called for action against Luther: No one was to harbor Luther, his followers were to be condemned, and his books were to be burned.

1521 Dec.   **Melanchthon** [Philipp Schwarzert] (Feb. 15, 1497–Apr. 19, 1560), a lifetime associate of Luther and professor of Greek at Wittenberg, in present Germany, published his *Loci Communes Rerum Theologicarum* [Cardinal Points of Theology], the first systematic account of Luther's theology.

1522   Martin Luther's translation of the Greek New Testament into German, followed in 1534 by the Old Testament, not only abetted the **Protestant Reformation** but helped shape the modern German language.

1522 Charles V instituted the **Inquisition** against the Swiss-Rhineland type of Reformation in **the Netherlands.** Later, as the **Anabaptist movement** spread in this region, adherents received severe treatment, perhaps because of their view that in religion there is no authority aside from the individual conscience.

1522 Mar. 6 Martin Luther returned to Wittenberg from the security of the castle of Frederick III, elector of Saxony, at Wartburg. Luther now undertook the creation of a **revised rite of the Mass,** which on Christmas 1524, with the elector consenting, replaced the traditional Mass at Wittenberg. One year later the German language was substituted for the Latin.

1523 Frankfurt Am Main [Hesse] and Magdeburg in present Germany [Saxony] adopted the **Lutheran form of Christian worship.** In 1524 Nürnberg [Nuremberg] in central Germany, Strasbourg in the southwest, and Bremen in the north followed, and Philip II the Magnanimous (Nov. 13, 1504–Mar. 31, 1567), the landgrave of Hesse (from 1519), adjacent to Lutheran Saxony, joined the Lutheran movement.

1523 Jan. Huldreich Zwingli successfully engaged the orthodox ecclesiastics in Zürich of the **Swiss Confederation** in a public debate. Zwingli upheld salvation by faith and denied the validity of several Roman Catholic doctrines.

1524 Desiderius Erasmus challenged Luther's denial of free will in *De Libero arbitrio* [Concerning Free Will]. Luther then replied (1525) in *De Servo arbitrio* [On the Bondage of the Will]. A breach between humanists and Lutherans was opened.

1524 The **divergence between Huldreich Zwingli and Martin Luther** concerning the Lord's Supper, with Zwingli denying any physical presence therein, broke into controversy. Zwingli and **Johannes Oecolampadius** [Heussgen, Hussgen] (1482–Nov. 23, 1531), on the one side, and Luther and **Johannes Bugenhagen** (June 24, 1485–Apr. 19, 1558) on the other, with their respective followers, issued a flood of pamphlets, often uncharitable, defending and attacking.

1524 Dec. 27 Gustavus I Vasa, king of **Sweden,** looking toward disendowment of the Church as a means of filling the royal coffers, held a public disputation on the subject at his palace. Olaf Petersson

was the chief spokesman for the Lutheran party, Peter Galle for the Roman. The Diet decided (1527) in favor of **Lutheranism** and disendowment.

1525 William Tyndale (c.1494–Oct. 6?, 1536) printed his **English translation of the New Testament in Germany.** Copies were smuggled into England. Tyndale worked from the original Greek text edited (1516) by Erasmus, not from the Latin, as did John Wycliff (c.1388).

1525 Jan. 17 Conrad Grebel (c.1498–c.1526) and other religious reformers in Zürich publicly debated infant baptism with Huldreich Zwingli. Zwingli, urging infant baptism, used the term "Anabaptists" [rebaptizers] for those like Grebel, Felix Manz, Balthasar Hübmaier, and others who regarded infant baptism as invalid and urged instead adult "believer's baptism."

1525 Jan. 21 The Anabaptist **Conrad Grebel** baptized the priest **Georg Blaurock,** who in turn baptized the others present, in demonstration of "believer's baptism." Swiss Anabaptists [Swiss Brethren] opposed the use of force in matters of faith and opposed state churches of the kind developing in Reformation centers.

1525 May 15 Philip II the Magnanimous, landgrave of Hesse, put down the **Peasants' Revolt** at [Bad] Frankenhausen in Thuringia, in present Germany. Thomas Munzer, now an Anabaptist minister at Allstedt, had inflamed the revolt with his radical views of bringing about a new social order of justice and love through revolution, bloody if necessary. Captured, Munzer (born c.1490) was executed on May 30. Although the peasants were inspired by Martin Luther's teachings and hopeful of gaining rights from the nobility, **Luther** himself denounced their actions in the pamphlet *Against the Rapacious, Murdering Hordes of Peasants* (1525).

1525 June 13 Martin Luther married Katharina von Bora (1499–1552), a former Cistercian nun. Luther had long attacked celibacy in his pamphlets and sermons, holding that it was something opposed to the will of God.

1526 Mar. 7 The Zürich government, a democratically elected council, ordered **Anabaptists** drowned. Their crime was not heresy, but nonconformity; their sectarianism was regarded as evidence of hostility to ordered society. **Felix Manz** was martyred;

Conrad Grebel had died previously in a plague; **Balthasar Hübmaier** fled to Moravia, where he propagated Anabaptist beliefs with great success. The movement spread throughout Switzerland, the Netherlands, and Germany.

1526 Spring Balthasar Hübmaier led a group of Swiss Anabaptists [Swiss Brethren] to Moravia, in present **Czechoslovakia**. They were given refuge on estates of the counts of Liechtenstein at Nicholsburg. Taken by Austrian authorities, Hübmaier (b. 1485) was burned at the stake in Vienna on Mar. 10, 1528, and his wife forcibly drowned in the Danube.

1527 May 21 Michael Sattler, a monk converted to Anabaptist views, was burned at Rottenburg by Austrian authorities, his wife forcibly drowned. The **Seven Articles of Faith**, drawn up by Sattler for the council (Feb. 24) at Schlatt of Swiss and Swabian Anabaptists, foreshadowed the modern concept of a free church in a free state.

1528 Zumárraga (1468–1548) was named the **first bishop of Mexico**. He organized the Roman Catholic Church and systematized the Indian conversions to Christianity. He brought (1539) the **first printing press to the New World** in order to print religious manuals in both the native Indian languages and Spanish.

1528 Matteo di Bassi [Bascio] (c.1495–Aug. 6, 1552), a Franciscan, obtained the sanction of Pope Clement VII to live as a hermit, preach to the poor, and persuade others to join him in the literal observance of St. Francis' rule. Matteo's pyramided hood, the *capuche*, provided the name of the **Capuchin order**, which by century's end was active throughout Catholic regions of Europe.

1528 Feb. 29 Patrick Hamilton (b. 1504), a youthful abbot of Ferne, became **Scotland's first native Protestant martyr**, by burning. Hamilton had studied in Germany and was a friend of Martin Luther and William Tyndale.

1529 Jakob Hutter began to reorganize the **Anabaptist groups** in Moravia, split after the death of Hübmaier by the apocalyptic views of Hans Hut, who preached the imminence of the Second Coming of Jesus Christ. In the community at Austerlitz [Slavko], in present Czechoslovakia, Hutter provided Moravian Anabaptists with a structured life within communes and a viable economy.

Jakob Hutter was burned to death on Feb. 25, 1536.

1529 Apr. 19 Lutheran members of the German Reichstag meeting at Speyer [Spires], in present Germany, issued a document called *Protestatio*. From this response of a legislative minority came the name given to their party: **"Protestant."**

V. SCIENCE, EDUCATION, AND TECHNOLOGY

1525 *Prose della volgar lingua* by **Pietro Bembo** (May 1470–Jan. 1547) defended the use of the Italian language, then considered unworthy of serious writing.

1527 The **University of Marburg**, in present Germany, was founded by the German prince, Philip the Magnanimous, landgrave of Hesse.

1527 June 22 Niccolò Machiavelli (b. May 3, 1459), an Italian political figure and philosopher, died. *Il Principe* [*The Prince*] (1513) set forth rules for governing a state. *Discorsi* (1513–1521) was a fuller representation of Machiavelli's republican theory.

VI. ARTS AND LEISURE

1520 Apr. 6 Raphael [Raffaello Santi] (b. Apr. 6, 1483), one of the great Italian painters and architects, died. In Rome he designed part of Saint Peter's cathedral and tapestries for the Sistine Chapel.

1521 Aug. 27 Josquin Deprès [Jodocus Pratensis] (born c.1450), a Flemish composer, died. His three books of masses (1502, 1512, 1516), and numerous motets and chansons were highly regarded by his contemporaries.

c.1525 The distinctive **Japanese pottery** called **raku-ware** originated near Kyoto with the potter Tanaka Chojiro.

1526 A masterpiece of **Burmese literature**, the *Kogan Pyo*, by **Shin Rat-hta-tha-ra** (1468–1530), a Burmese poet, appeared.

1528 Baldassare Castiglione (Dec. 6, 1478–Feb. 2, 1529) published *Il Libro del Cortegiano* [The Courtier], a revealing document of life in the Italian court in Urbino, treating issues of the day in dialogue.

1528 Apr. 6   Albrecht Dürer (b. May 21, 1471), the great German engraver and painter, died. The woodcut *The Apocalypse* is often considered his masterpiece. Continuing Dürer's tradition were the "Little Masters," who included Hans Sebald Beham (1500–1550) and his brother Barthel (1502–1540),

Georg Pencz [Jörg Penz] (1500?–1550), and Jakob Binck (1500?–1569).

1528 Aug.   Matthias Grünewald [Mathis Gothart Nithart] (born c.1475), died. His masterpiece was *The Isenheim Altarpiece* (1515), a huge folding altar for the Antonite monastery in Bavaria, near Munich.

1530–1539

I. DISASTERS

1531 Jan. 26   An **earthquake** in **Lisbon**, Portugal, claimed the lives of 30,000.

II. EXPLORATION AND COLONIZATION

1534–1542   Jacques Cartier (1491–Sept. 1, 1557) a French explorer, made three expeditions to the New World, intending to find a Northwest Passage to China. Instead, he discovered **Prince Edward Island** and the **Saint Lawrence River**. He claimed the region of eastern **Canada** for Francis I, king of France, on July 24, 1534.

1535   Francisco Pizarro founded the city of **Lima** as headquarters for the Spanish of Peru.

1535   Diego de Almagro, who accompanied Pizarro in his conquest of Peru, led an expedition into **Chile**, where he discovered and crossed the **Atacama Desert**.

1536   Hernando Cortés, the Spanish conqueror of Mexico, discovered what is now **Lower California** [Baja California].

1536   Estavanico [Esteban, Little Stephen] (c.1500–1539), a Moroccan scout on the expedition (1528–1536) to Florida led by Pánfilo de Narváez and Álvar Núñez Cabeza da Vaca, was the **first European to enter present New Mexico and Arizona**. He purportedly saw the fabled wealthy Indian Empire, the **Seven Cities of Cibola**.

1536 Feb.   Pedro de Mendoza (1487–June 23, 1537) established a fort in the name of Spain, near the Río

de la Plata, which he named Nuestra Señora de Buen Aire. One day it would be **Buenos Aires**, Argentina's capital.

1538 Aug. 6   Gonzalez Jiménez de Quesada (1500?–?1579) founded the city of **Santa Fé de Bogotá** [now Bogotá, the capital of Colombia].

1539 May 30   Hernando de Soto (1499–May 21, 1542), a Spanish explorer, landed in **Florida** and claimed the region for Spain. For three years his search for gold took him northward through Georgia and South Carolina, across Alabama into Mississippi, where he crossed the **Mississippi River**. He continued into Arkansas and turned back through Louisiana to return to the Mississippi River, where he died.

III. POLITICS AND WAR

1530 Nov. 29   Cardinal **Thomas Wolsey** (b. 1473?), en route from York to face trial for heresy and treason, died in London. The cardinal's strategy for obtaining a marriage annulment for **Henry VIII** had gone awry. The king was now listening to **Thomas Cromwell**.

1531 Feb.   Henry VIII invoked the 1353 **Praemunire Statute**, which provided for royal control over legal and financial matters, previously the jurisdiction of the pope, in order to intimidate Church officers unfriendly to his proposed divorce from Catherine of Aragon. Eight bishops were indicted for recognizing Cardinal Thomas Wolsey as papal legate in England.

1531 Oct. 11   A battle at **Kappel** ended a short civil war in **Switzerland** between the Catholic Forest

Cantons and Protestant Zürich. The Protestants lost, and their leader, Huldreich Zwingli (b. Jan. 1, 1484), was killed. A subsequent treaty (Nov. 23) restored an uneasy religious truce.

1532 Feb. **Thomas Cromwell**, privy councilor to Henry VIII, secured passage of the **Act of Annates** by the English Parliament. Henry apparently regarded suspension of annual payments to the papacy as a means of forcing Pope Clement VII to issue a writ of annulment of his marriage to Catherine of Aragon.

1532 May **Suleiman the Magnificent**, the Ottoman sultan, invaded Hungary in support of John I [John Zápolya], and marched toward Vienna, while his fleet, led by Barbarossa II and supported by Francis I, king of France, raided the Italian and Spanish coasts. Already alarmed by the Ottoman siege of Vienna, Charles V, the Holy Roman emperor, and the Protestant Schmalkaldic League agreed to a truce by the **Peace of Nürnberg** [Nuremberg] on July 23.

1532 May 16 The **Submission of the Clergy** was passed by the Convocation of the English clerics after being enacted by Parliament. Passed under pressure from Henry VIII, it reflected a growing sense of national loyalty. It was legal custom that any legislation affecting the Church in England must also be confirmed by the **Convocation of Clergy** under the archbishops of Canterbury and York. After the Submission, ecclesiastical orders were no longer promulgated without the approval of the crown nor were there to be any more payments and fees to Rome.

1532 May 17 **Thomas More**, lord chancellor to Henry VIII, resigned his office. More had refused to accept the Submission of the Clergy and to swear to sovereign primacy.

1532 Nov. 16 **Francisco Pizarro**, the Spanish conquistador, took Cuzco, Peru, the capital of the **Inca Empire**. When the Inca ruler **Atahualpa** came to dinner, Pizarro and his men took him prisoner and slaughtered many of his c.5,000 unarmed retinue. The Incas had a force of c.40,000 men nearby but did not attack, in the belief that Atahualpa would be ransomed. A ransom was collected; nevertheless, Pizarro had him executed on Aug. 29, 1533.

1533 Jan. 25? **Henry VIII**, king of England, secretly married the pregnant **Anne Boleyn**, former maid [Lady in Waiting] to the court of Claude (1499–1524), Queen of France. Henry's act openly denied the pope's authority in England.

1533 Apr. 7 The English Parliament adopted the **Statute of Appeals**. All matrimonial cases were to be decided by English bishops with no appeal to Rome. **Thomas Cromwell** was made Secretary of State on Apr. 12.

1533 May 23 **Thomas Cranmer**, archbishop of Canterbury, annulled Henry VIII's marriage to Catherine of Aragon, declared the marriage to Anne Boleyn good and lawful on May 28, and crowned her queen on June 1. On Sept. 7 a daughter Elizabeth Tudor, a future queen of England, was born to the new queen.

1533 June 2 **Peace was reached between Suleiman the Magnificent, and Ferdinand I**, the Hapsburg ruler of Austria. Ferdinand received northern Hungary in return for an annual tribute and recognition of the Hungarian king, John I [John Zápolya], as vassal to the Ottomans.

1533 Sept. **Pope Clement VII** excommunicated **Henry VIII** along with the participants in Archbishop Thomas Cranmer's inquiry into the marriage annulment.

1533 Dec. 3 **Basil** [Vasili] **III Ivanovich** (b. 1479), prince of Moscow and ruler of Russia (from 1505), died, leaving his three-year-old son Ivan as his heir under the regency of his mother Helena Glinski (d. 1538).

1534 Mar. 30 The **Act of Succession** was enacted by the English Parliament, at the urging of Thomas Cromwell. All subjects of the king were to swear an oath accepting Henry VIII's marriage to Anne Boleyn. Thomas More, former lord chancellor, refused to take the oath on Apr. 13.

1534 Nov. 3 The English Parliament passed the **Act of Supremacy**, completing England's constitutional revolution against Rome and establishing the **Church of England**. Under law the king was now the Supreme Head of the Church of England.

1535 **New Spain**, including Mexico and parts of present U.S., Central America to present Panama, the West Indies, Venezuela, and the Philippines, was organized as a Vice-Royalty (1535–1821) under **Antonia de Mendoza** (c.1490–July 21, 1552), the first viceroy. The viceroy was assisted by *audiencias*, or administrative and judicial courts, and by city councils, which possessed little power and were filled later mostly by Creoles, persons born in the New World of Spanish parents.

1535 Jan. 21 **Thomas Cromwell** was appointed vicar-general of the Church of England by Henry VIII, to undertake a survey of the country's monasteries in the name of financial efficiency.

1535 June **Christian III** (Aug. 12, 1503–Jan. 1, 1559), king of Denmark and Norway (from 1534), assaulted the Hanseatic port of Lübeck in a **battle at Svendborg** on the Baltic Sea.

1535 June 22 **John Fisher** (b. 1469), the bishop of Rochester, was beheaded and his head displayed on London Bridge for denying the **Act of Supremacy** and the national church it instituted. While imprisoned in the Tower, Fisher was made a cardinal by Pope Paul III (Feb. 29, 1468–Nov. 10, 1549; ruled from 1534). He was canonized in 1935.

1535 June 24 Charles V, the Holy Roman emperor, with a fleet led by **Andrea Doria** (c.1468–Nov. 25, 1560), a Genoese admiral, took **Tunis** from the Turkish pirate Barbarossa II. The Hafsid Berber Muhammad Hassan (ruled 1526–1543), sultan of Tunis, was restored, and thousands of Christian slaves were liberated.

1535 July 6 **Thomas More** (b. Feb. 7, 1477?) was beheaded on Tower Hill and his head displayed on London Bridge for his refusal to take the oath of Supremacy. He was canonized in 1935.

1535 Nov. 1 Francesco Sforza II (b. 1495), duke of Milan, died without a male heir, and the subsequent **annexation of the duchy of Milan** by Charles V, the Holy Roman emperor, led to the **second Valois-Hapsburg War** (1535–1538).

1536 **Manco Capac** (1500?–1544), brother of the last Inca emperor Atahualpa, laid siege to the Spanish at Cuzco, the former Inca capital in Peru, nearly destroying the city. After abandoning the siege for lack of resources, he conducted small attacks on the Spanish.

1536 The English Parliament passed an **Act of Union**, joining the principality of **Wales** with England. English was designated the official tongue of the Welsh people.

1536 May 19 **Anne Boleyn** [Bullen] (b. 1507?), second wife of **Henry VIII**, was beheaded after being found guilty of adultery and incest. The Parliament proclaimed illegitimate her daughter Elizabeth, as well as Mary, daughter of Henry's first wife, Catherine of Aragon. The death of Catherine (b. Dec. 5, 1485) on Jan. 7, 1536, and the execution of Anne enabled Henry to marry **Jane Seymour** on May 30.

1537 Apr. 8 An uneasy **truce at Cuzco**, between Francisco Pizarro and Diego de Almagro was broken by Almagro, who suspected Pizarro and his brothers of duplicity. Almagro captured the city and the brothers, Hernando (1475?–?1578) and Gonzalo (1506?–1548), but soon released them.

1537 Oct. 12 Henry VIII, king of England, finally had a legitimate male heir, by Jane Seymour. The birth of the future **Edward VI** was followed by the death of Jane (b. 1509?) twelve days later.

1538 Apr. 26 **Hernando Pizarro** captured Diego de Almagro in fighting near Cuzco, Peru, and regained the Inca capital for his brother Francisco. Almagro (born c. 1475) was executed in June.

1538 Sept. 28 The Venetian-Spanish fleet, commanded by Andrea Doria, a Genoese admiral, was defeated off Préveza, Greece, by the Ottoman fleet, under **Barbarossa II**. The subsequent **supremacy of the Ottoman fleet in the Mediterranean** facilitated recovery of Tunis for the **Barbary States** and expulsion of the Venetians from Nauplia, their last stronghold in Morea [Peloponnesus], in the same year.

1539 **Tabinshwehti**, the Burmese king (1531–1550) of the **Toungoo Dynasty** (1347–1752), conquered the **Mon Kingdom** of Pegu and began to subjugate the Shan states. The powerful Toungoo Empire (1531–1752) was now firmly established.

1539 Oct. 6 **Thomas Cromwell**, lord great chamberlain of England, initiated the **Treaty of Hampton Court** by which Anne (Sept. 22, 1515–July 16, 1557), sister of the German Protestant leader, William of Cleves, a duchy in present Germany, was betrothed to Henry VIII. Cromwell's policy proved a political failure, and the marriage lasted only from Jan. 6 to

July 9, 1540. The Catholic alliance did not come about, and Cromwell's influence rapidly declined. Thomas Cromwell (born c. 1485) was accused of treason by his political enemies and executed on July 28, 1540.

IV. ECONOMY AND TRADE

1531 The **Bourse** was built in **Antwerp**, becoming probably the **first international stock exchange**.

1534 **Peter's Pence** was abolished. It was an annual tax of one penny on each household in England to be paid to the pope.

1535 Feb. 13 The **treasures stolen from the Incas** during the Spanish conquest of Peru were ordered melted down and made into coin by Charles V, the Holy Roman emperor.

1536 The Spanish established a **mint at Mexico City**, using the gold of their spoils for coinage.

V. RELIGION AND PHILOSOPHY

1530 June 25 **Melanchthon** read before the Diet of Augsburg the **Augsburg [Protestant] Confession**, a statement demanded by Charles V, the Holy Roman emperor. It was approved by seven German princes and representatives of two cities. Moderate in tone, Lutheran in doctrine, this Confession became the chief creed of the **Lutheran Church**.

1531 Dec. 9 The Holy Virgin was said to have appeared to an Indian peasant and ordered construction of a church on the spot, a hill in the present district of Mexico City. This was the **Virgin of Guadalupe**.

1532 Mar. Death by burning at the stake was the desired fate of the ascetic **Solomon Molcho** (born c.1500). After predicting the flood that ravaged Rome on Oct. 8, 1530, Molcho, who was born a Christian, had been protected from the Inquisition by Pope Clement VII. When he left his haven to try to reach Charles V, he was seized in Mantua and burned as a renegade.

1534 Feb. 10 The **Anabaptists** drove their opposition, including the 2,000 troops under Bishop Franz von Waldeck, out of Münster, in present Germany. After they were besieged in the city by the Bishop and his army, the 1200 Anabaptist survivors were massacred on June 24, 1535.

1534 Apr. 20 **Elizabeth Barton** (b. 1506?), called "**the Nun of Kent**," was put to death with four priests at Tyburn, a place of execution, in London. Barton, a Benedictine nun, had attracted a following over several years for the visions she claimed to have seen. She was convicted by means of a Parliamentary bill of attainder because of her denunciation of Henry VIII's divorce; her companions were guilty by association.

1534 Aug. 15 The Roman Catholic order of the **Jesuits** [Society of Jesus] developed from vows taken by **Ignatius Loyola** (1491–July 31, 1556) and six friends, including **Francis Xavier** [Francisco de Yasu y Xavier] (Apr. 7, 1506–Dec. 3, 1552), at Montmartre near Paris to observe poverty and chastity and to offer their lives to the pope for God's service.

1534 Oct. A young Lutheran reformer placed placards on the walls of Paris and other French towns, attacking the Mass. As an outcome of the incident, Francis I, king of France, issued an edict on Jan. 29, 1535, ordering the **extermination of heretics**.

1534 Dec. **John [Jean] Calvin**, trained in philosophy, dialectics, and the law, left his native France for the security of Protestant Basel. Calvin had experienced, in his words, a "sudden conversion," and in this period had been close to French humanist and Lutheran reformers.

1535 **Miles Coverdale** (1488–Jan. 20, 1569), a friend of **William Tyndale**, **edited the first complete printed Bible in English**. His New Testament was basically Tyndale's, and so also probably was his Pentateuch. Coverdale himself, with anonymous scholars, translated the remainder, using as sources the Vulgate and the German translations by Luther and Zwingli.

1535 Aug. 8 **Guillaume Farel** (1489–Sept. 13, 1565), a radical Protestant, and his followers seized the Cathedral of Saint Pierre at **Geneva**. On Aug. 27, 1535, the Mass was suppressed and the reformed religion established. On May 21, 1536, the general assembly declared Geneva Protestant.

1536 **Christian III**, king of Denmark and Norway, confiscated Catholic Church property and had many ecclesiastics arrested. The state took over the religious functions of the clergy, and new Lutheran bishops were appointed.

1536 Jan.   Menno Simons (c.1496–Jan. 31?, 1561) joined one of the Anabaptist groups remaining in the Netherlands after the tragedy at Münster on June 24, 1535. In 1537 Menno became the preacher of the Anabaptist community at Groningen in the Netherlands and traveled widely through the Netherlands and Germany, organizing churches, strengthening established communities, and building a unified denomination: the **Mennonites**.

1536 Mar.   John Calvin published his *Institution Chrétienne* [*Institutes of the Christian Religion*]. The preface, addressed to Francis I, king of France, presented the Protestant position. The book provided the Reformation a clear synthesis of Protestant thought.

1536 July 12   The **Ten Articles of Religion**, an effort by **Henry VIII** to mandate religious doctrine in England, were accepted by Convocation of the Clergy. Henry remained a staunch Catholic in all views except papal supremacy.

1536 Aug.   The **First Act of Dissolution of the Monasteries**, passed by the English Parliament, closed monasteries and transferred their property to the Crown. It also resulted in the redistribution of land from the Church to secular ownership, primarily nobles, when the Crown sold this land to fill its coffers.

1536 Oct. 6   William Tyndale (b. 1484) was brought to trial as a heretic for his determination to give the Bible to the common people in their native tongues. Tied to a stake, he was strangled and then burned at Vilvorde, near Brussels. Tyndale's work was the basis for perhaps 75 percent of the Authorized **King James Version of the Bible** (1611).

1536 Oct. 23   The **Revolt of the Pilgrimage of Grace** occurred when 30,000 to 40,000 armed protesters against the dissolution of the monasteries, under the leadership of **Robert Aske**, achieved control of Lincolnshire and, later, Yorkshire, England. Diverted by the parleys of the duke of Norfolk and his small royal army, the insurrection force accepted the offer of a great conference. Two hundred and sixteen "Pilgrims" would be executed by July 12, 1537.

1538   Nanak (b. 1469), venerated today by six million Sikhs [disciples] as their founding *guru* [teacher], died. Born in the Punjab and influenced by Kabir as well as Muslim Sufis, Nanak sought to syncretize the Islamic conception of one god and the Hindu teaching of an internalized devotional response to God. He compiled the **Granth**, the sacred scriptures of the **Sikh religion**, which preserved the teachings of Kabir.

1538 Apr. 23   John Calvin and **Guillaume Farel** were banished from Geneva. They refused to comply with a City Council order that ministers adopt the liturgy of Bern, in league with Geneva, and were continuing to reject unworthy communicants at the Lord's Supper.

1539 Apr.   Miles Coverdale published a revised Bible in English. Called the **Great Bible** by reason of its size, 9 by 11 inches, it was based on Tyndale's translations, supplemented by Coverdale's own translations and the work of anonymous scholars. For 30 years thereafter the Great Bible was the authoritative Bible of the English people.

1539 Apr.   The **Second Act of Dissolution** of the Monasteries closed larger monasteries in England and furthered the secular gain obtained by the First Act of Dissolution in 1536.

1539 June 28   The **Six Articles Act**, inspired by Stephen Gardiner (1482?–Nov. 12, 1555), the bishop of Winchester, was an attempt by Henry VIII to establish a consistent religious policy in England by reverting to the Roman Catholic position on clerical celibacy, the Real Presence, monastic vows, masses for the dead, oral confessions to a priest, and communion of one kind.

VI. SCIENCE, EDUCATION, AND TECHNOLOGY

1530   Girolamo Fracastoro (1478?–Aug. 8, 1553), a Veronese philosopher and poet, gave a name to the disease that had afflicted 10 million Europeans since 1495. In his poem *Syphilis sive Morbus Gallicus* [Syphilis or the French Disease], Fracastoro described the curse of the ailment on a young shepherd, named Syphilis, by the angered god Apollo.

1531   Work began on building the **alcázar** [Arabic: *al-qasr* = castle] at **Toledo**, Spain. The building built on the site centuries earlier by the **Moors** had been restored in the 13th century but was transformed into a fortress and a lavish residence for the kings of Spain.

1537 Pedro Nunes (1502–Aug. 11, 1578), a Portuguese mathematician and navigator, observed that on long voyages the existing navigational charts were inaccurate. The problem was that ships attempting to sail across the meridians in a series of constant angles were actually moving in a spiral rather than in a circle. The navigational problem would be solved by **Gerhardus Mercator's map** projection in 1569, in which the lines of latitude and longitude were constructed at right angles to each other. A navigator from then on had only to draw a straight line to his destination and follow the compass direction subtended by that line.

VII. ARTS AND LEISURE

c.1530 **Rosso** [Il Rosso Fiorentino; Giovanni Battista de Rossi] (Mar. 8, 1495–Nov. 14, 1540), a student of Andrea del Sarto, was appointed court painter by Francis I, king of France. With Francesco Primaticcio (1504–1570), he decorated the **château at Fontainebleau**.

1530 Sept. 29 **Andrea del Sarto** [Andrea Domenico d'Agnolo di Francesco, born Vannucchi] (b. July 16, 1486), an influential Florentine painter, died. His style, as in *Madonna of the Harpies* (1517), tended toward mannerism.

1532 *Orlando Furioso*, a masterpiece of Italian epic poetry, was published. Ludovico Ariosto (Sept. 8, 1474–July 6, 1533) had further developed Matteo Maria Boiardo's (1441–1494) *Orlando Innamorato* (1487), which fused the Arthurian legends with traditional Carolingian tales.

1532 Nov. *Pantagruel*, by **François Rabelais** (c.1490–Aug. 19, 1553), a French satirist and humanist, was published under the pseudonym of Alcofribas Nasier. It was followed by *Gargantua* (1534), *Tiers Livre* (1546), *Quart Livre* (1552), and *Cinquième Livre* (1564), completed the series known in English as *The Histories of Gargantua and Pantagruel*.

c.1533 *Ralph Roister Doister* by **Nicholas Udall** [Uvedale] (1505–Dec. 23, 1556), headmaster at **Eton** (1534–1541), appeared. It is considered the **first English comedy**.

1533 The **first book of madrigals**, including works by **Philippe Jacques Verdelot** and **Jakob Arcadelt** [Archadelt, Archadet] (c.1500–1570), was printed in Rome.

1534 Mar. 5 **Correggio** [Antonio Allegri] (born c.1490), an Italian painter, died. His use of foreshortening, and bold use of light and shadow, in the *Assumption of the Virgin* (1526–1530) lent a dramatic quality to this fresco in the cupola of the Romanesque cathedral in Parma.

c.1535 **Gil Vicente** (b. 1465), the Portuguese writer who laid the foundation for Portuguese drama, died. His plays included much social satire as well as music. There are extant 44 plays. Some were banned by the **Inquisition** for their criticism of Church practices.

1538 **Albrecht Altdorfer** (born c.1480), a German painter and engraver, died. The painting *Battle of Alexander* (1529) showed Altdorfer's skill in creating extensive canvases.

1538 June 24 The **first plays** known to have been **produced in Mexico** were religious dramas performed at Tlaxcala.

1539 **Sinan** (1489?–1587) was appointed court architect to Suleiman I the Magnificent, the Ottoman sultan. The mosque constructed (1550–1557) in Suleiman's honor in **Constantinople**, and especially the mosque constructed (1568–1574) for his son, Selim II, in Adrianople [Edirne], are considered the finest of Sinan's works.

VIII. SPORTS, GAMES, AND SOCIETY

1534–1542 **Jacques Cartier**, while exploring the Saint Lawrence River Valley, observed Iroquois Indians playing a game called "Baggataway." This **forerunner of lacrosse** was played with a stick bent at the top and resembling a bishop's crozier [French: *la crosse*]. A rawhide bag or sack was attached for catching the deerskin ball stuffed with feathers.

1536 **Fencing** began to come of age with the publication of the first practical book on the art, by the Italian Achille Marozzo. The faster one-handed rapier, with its deadly point, had replaced the two-edged sword.

1538 **Henry VIII**, king of England, created by royal patent the **Fraternity of Saint George** for expert archers. The **Honorable Artillery Company** grew out (1585) of this organization and continued to meet for competitions until 1780.

1540–1549

I. EXPLORATION AND COLONIZATION

1540–1542 Tales of a wealthy Indian Empire, the **Seven Cities of Cibola**, inspired **Francisco Vásquez de Coronado** (c.1510–Sept. 22, 1554), a Spanish explorer, to lead a well-organized expedition into the present states of New Mexico, Texas, Oklahoma, and Kansas. He saw the **Zuñi Indian pueblos** and was the first European to describe the bison [*Bison bison*, American buffalo]. A side party discovered the **Grand Canyon**, probably in May 1540.

1540 **Hernando de Alarcón**, a Spanish explorer who commanded the marine division of the expedition of Francisco Vásquez de Coronado, sailed up the Gulf of California and explored the mouth of the Colorado River.

1541–1542 **Francisco de Orellana** (c.1490–1546), in command of an expedition embarking from the Spanish colony at Quito, Ecuador, became separated from the main group. He continued down the Napo River to the **Amazon River** which eventually brought him to the Atlantic Ocean. He was the first to travel the entire length of the Amazon River from its source in the Andes mountains. Accounts of his travels mention the female Indian warriors after whom the river was named.

1541 Feb. 12 **Pedro de Valdivia**, who had been with Francisco Pizarro during his conquest of Peru, established a settlement at **Santiago**, the present capital of Chile. Valdivia (b. 1500?) may have met his death at the hands of the native Araucanian Indians early in 1554.

c.1542 Portuguese traders, led by **Antonio da Mota** and blown off their course, landed on **Tanegashima Island**, near Kyushu, Japan, where they soon established a trading port.

1542 **Juan Rodriguez Cabrillo** (d. Jan. 3, 1543?), a Spanish explorer, landed on the coast of present **California**. He was probably the **first European to visit** the area.

II. POLITICS AND WAR

1540 July 23 John I [John Zápolya] (b. 1487), king of central and eastern **Hungary** (from 1526), died and was succeeded by his infant son, John II [John Zápolya] (1540–1571). Ferdinand I, the Hapsburg ruler of Austria, Bohemia, and Germany, who had controlled western Hungary since 1526, invaded central Hungary to enforce his claim by marriage to the throne. The Ottoman Turks intervened, taking **Buda** [Budapest] on Aug. 26, 1541.

1540 July 28 **Henry VIII**, king of England, married **Catherine Howard**, niece of Thomas Howard (1473–1554), duke of Norfolk.

1541 The **Mixtón War** broke out in Mexico after Francisco Vásquez de Coronado had taken a large number of Spanish soldiers on an expedition northward in 1540 to find the fabled city of wealth Quivira. Fighting was severe around Mixtón, Guadalajara, and Nochistlán. **Pedro de Alvarado** (born c.1485/1495), one of the Spanish conquerors of Mexico famed for his *salta de Alvarado* on *la noche triste* (1520), died June 4 in a fall from his horse at either Guadalajara or Nochistlán. Spanish troops, aided by Tlaxcaltec and Aztec Indians, finally put down the uprising.

1541 June 25 **Francisco Pizarro** (born c. 1475), Spanish conqueror of the Inca capital at Cuzco, Peru, was murdered by the son of **Diego de Almagro**. In 1538 de Almagro had been executed by Hernando Pizarro, Francisco's brother.

1541 Nov. 9 **Catherine Howard**, fifth wife of Henry VIII, was imprisoned in the Tower of London on the charge of unchaste conduct. Catherine (b. 1520?) was beheaded on Feb. 13, 1542.

1542 Jan. 23 **Henry VIII**, king of England and lord of Ireland, took the title, **king of Ireland**. His recognition by the Irish Parliament was secured by Anthony St. Leger (c.1496–1559), lord deputy of Ireland.

1542 Nov. 25 English forces, under Thomas Howard, duke of Norfolk, defeated the Scottish in a **battle at Solway Moss**, near the Scottish border in England. **James V** (b. Apr. 10, 1512), king of Scotland (from 1513), wounded in the battle, died on Dec. 14, and was succeeded by his week-old daughter, Mary (b. Dec. 8), as queen of Scots. Scotland, under James V, had invaded England. Scotland's pro-English party secured peace, and the betrothal of Queen Mary, an heir to the English throne through her grandmother Margaret Tudor, to the future Edward VI, the future king of England by the **Treaty of Greenwich** on July 1, 1543.

1544 At the age of thirteen **Ivan IV** (the Terrible) had **Andrei Shuiski**, leader of the boyars, the Russian nobility, thrown to his dogs and Ivan assumed control of Moscow and Russia.

1544 Sept. 18 The **Treaty of Crépy** ended a two-year war between Francis I, king of France, and Charles V, the Holy Roman emperor, initiated by Charles's gift (1540) of the duchy of Milan to his son Philip II, king of Spain. Francis was bankrupt.

1546 June 7 The **Peace of Ardres** concluded the war between England and France. England was to receive an indemnity from France and retained for eight years the French port of Boulogne, which it had captured Sept. 14, 1544.

1547 Jan. 16 Ivan IV (the Terrible) was crowned "**Czar of all the Russias,**" the first Russian ruler to take this title. Ivan soon undertook the task of reorganizing Russia's ruling class. Foremost of Ivan's policies was creation of support among the landed gentry, whose loyalties he cultivated by granting estates.

1547 Jan. 28 **Henry VIII** (b. June 28, 1491), king of England (from 1509), died and was succeeded by his nine-year-old son **Edward VI**. The uncle of the young king, Edward Seymour, earl of Hertford, was created duke of Somerset and named Lord Protector on Feb. 16. His initiation of Protestant reforms was received unfavorably.

1547 Mar. 31 Francis I (b. Sept. 12, 1494), king of France (from 1515), died. Like Henry and Charles V, the Holy Roman emperor, Francis was a temporal ruler in every sense, allying himself to either the Protestant reformers and the Roman Catholics as policy demanded. He was succeeded by his son Henry II (Mar. 19, 1519–July 10, 1559).

1547 Apr. 24 The **Schmalkaldic League** (from 1531), organized to protect independent Protestant states, was defeated at Mühlberg by the Catholic forces of Charles V, the Holy Roman emperor, commanded by Fernando Álvarez de Toledo (Oct. 29, 1507–Dec. 11, 1582), duke of Alva [Alba]. The Protestant leader John Frederick I (June 30, 1503–Mar. 3, 1554), elector of Saxony (1542–1547), was captured, and the Ernestine Saxon line lost the electorate as well as much of its territory to the Albertine Saxon line (to 1806) of electors, beginning with Maurice (Mar. 21, 1521–July 9, 1553), duke of Saxony.

1547 Sept. 10 The Scottish party favorable to union with England was weakened by the victory of the English under Edward Seymour, duke of Somerset, in a **battle at Pinkie**, near Edinburgh.

1548 The **Sufi sect** of the Saadi in Morocco captured Fez and ousted the **Wattasid Dynasty** (from 1472), which had been unable to resist Portuguese penetration. The **Saadi Dynasty** (1548–1666), the first of the **Sharifian dynasties**, was established and successfully ousted the Portuguese from some of their coastal bases.

1548 June 3 The **Interim of Augsburg** was accepted by the German Diet, meeting at Augsburg, Bavaria, in present Germany. It was an attempt by Charles V to unite Germany by making concessions to German Protestants until the **Council of Trent** could come to a decision that might heal divided Germany. The Interim instead increased the division among German Protestant leaders and was rejected by German Catholic princes. It was expressed as *caius regio eius religio* ["his realm his religion"], that is, the ruler may decide which way his realm will go.

1549 **Edward Seymour**, duke of Somerset and Lord Protector, announced his plan to marry the young Edward VI, king of England, to the young Mary, queen of Scots; it was a pretext for invading Scotland. Mary had been betrothed, in 1548, to the French dauphin Francis II, and had left for France.

1549 Mar. **Thomé de Souza** (?–1579), a new royal governor-general, arrived in the Portuguese colony of **Brazil** with c.1,000 men to reorganize the government. The near independence granted (1534) to the hereditary rulers of the 13 Capitanias was abolished, and the region was brought firmly under the control of the Portuguese monarch.

1549 Oct. 10 **John Dudley**, earl of Warwick, imprisoned **Edward Seymour**, duke of Somerset and Lord Protector. Warwick, now virtual ruler of England, was made duke of Northumberland on Oct. 11, 1551; Seymour (born c.1500) was beheaded on Jan. 22, 1552.

III. ECONOMY AND TRADE

c.1540   Horses were introduced to the American continents by the Spanish explorers and conquistadors. As they escaped from the expeditions, they soon populated both continents.

1542 Nov. 20   The first of the New Laws, urged by the Spanish Dominican, **Bartolomé de las Casas,** called for an end to the *encomiendas* and the freeing of Indians enslaved in **New Spain** under this system of land distribution. Although legally abolished, the system of *encomiendas* was replaced by the ***repartimiento*** [assessment], in which a fixed amount of labor or goods was exacted from the otherwise "free" Indian.

1545   Silver was discovered at Potosí in Upper Peru [present Bolivia], c.50 miles south of Sucre. The first great silver lode in Mexico was discovered (1546) at Zacatecas, and others were found at Guanajuato and San Luis Potosí.

IV. RELIGION AND PHILOSOPHY

1541 Sept. 13   John Calvin returned to Geneva to stay. As a model city ordered by religious discipline, **Geneva,** under Calvin, became the European center for the defense of Protestantism.

1542 May 6   Francis Xavier (Apr. 7, 1506–Dec. 3, 1552), a Spanish Jesuit, arrived in Goa, India, to undertake missionary work for the Roman Catholic Church.

1542 July 21   Pope Paul III, on the urgent recommendation of Cardinal Gian Pietro Caraffa [later to be Pope Paul IV (June 28, 1476–Aug. 18, 1559; ruled from 1555)] introduced the **Spanish Inquisition into Italy.** It had the effect of extinguishing several small groups of reformers and evangelicals in Italy.

1545   Francis I, king of France, ordered an army into the mountain villages along the Durance River in southeastern France to put down the **Waldensians,** who had grown from a medieval sect into a Lutheran-oriented Protestant denomination. Twenty-two villages were burned and 3,000 persons massacred.

1545 Dec. 13   The Council of Trent, in Italy, first convened (to 1563). Charles V, the Holy Roman emperor, hopeful of reconciling Protestants to his imperial policies, urged Pope Paul III to undertake ecclesiastical reform, but Paul was interested only in new doctrinal statements of the Roman Catholic Church and a condemnation of **Protestantism.** No Protestants attended.

1546   The final action of Francis I, king of France, against **Protestants** was the arrest of 60 who were celebrating the Lord's Supper in the Protestant manner. There followed at Meaux a judicial *auto-da-fé,* in which 50 were tortured, and 14 of them were put to death by burning.

1546 Feb. 18   Martin Luther (b. Nov. 10, 1483) died in Eisleben, Saxony, and was buried in the Castle Church [Schlosskirche] where on Oct. 31, 1517, he had posted his Ninety-five Theses. Shortly before his death he had preached a sermon urging the expulsion of Jews from the German Protestant states. Luther had more than once condemned the persecution of Jews, but his tract *On Jews and Their Lies* (c.1541) described them in virulent terms.

1547   At the behest of the Lord Protector, the duke of Somerset, and of the **council of Edward VI,** the young king of England, Parliament ordered the dissolution of the chantries. This was the **final confiscation of church lands** begun in Henry VIII's reign. The Six Articles (1539) were repealed.

1549   The first Jesuits arrived in Brazil with the new governor general, Thomé de Souza. Charged with converting the natives, the Jesuits became strong defenders of the Indians' rights and established many native schools.

1549 Jan. 21   The English Parliament passed the Act of Uniformity, requiring the use throughout England of the *Book of Common Prayer* in English. Almost single-handedly, Archbishop **Thomas Cranmer** produced this official book of services and prayers. Cranmer selected what seemed best from the multiplicity of service books available for public worship to create, in his words, "a single, convenient guide for priest and people."

1549 Aug. 15   Francis Xavier, Spanish Jesuit missionary, arrived from India at Kagoshima, Kyushu, Japan, where he established a Jesuit mission.

V. SCIENCE, EDUCATION, AND TECHNOLOGY

1543 A **cannon weighing 5,000 pounds** was produced by **Corneille Wagevens** at Antwerp.

1543 **Andreas Vesalius** (Dec. 31, 1514–Oct. 15, 1564), a Flemish physician, called the "**father of human anatomy**," published *De corporis humani fabrica*, an eight-volume work on the human body. The **Inquisition** mandated the death sentence for dissection of a cadaver, and Vesalius had a near escape from death at its hands.

1543 May 24 **Nicolaus Copernicus** [Mikolaj Kopernik, Niklas Koppernigk] (b. Feb. 14, 1473), a Polish astronomer, died. *De revolutionibus orbium coelestium* (finally printed in this year) set forth his epochal theory that the earth and planets turn on their axes and revolve around the sun.

1545 **Girolamo Cardano** [Jerome Cardan] (Sept. 24, 1501–Sept. 21, 1576), an Italian mathematician, astronomer, and gambler, published *Ars magna*, a treatise on algebra in which he claimed the solution of the cubic equation. His teacher Niccolò Tartaglia [Nicola Fontana, tartaglia = the stutterer] (1500?–Dec. 13, 1557), claimed he himself had developed (1535) the solution.

VI. ARTS AND LEISURE

1541 **Jean Goujon** (c.1510–1568) journeyed to Paris to work under **Pierre Lescot** (1510–1578) in decorating Saint Germain l'Auxerrois and Chateau d'Ecouen and in working on the **Louvre** (1547–1550, 1550–1562), which Francis I, king of France, ordered built as a new palace for himself.

1543 **Hans Holbein** the Younger (born c.1497), a German portrait painter famous in his own time,

died of the plague in London. His many portraits included *The French Ambassadors* (1533), *Erasmus* (1523), *Edward VI* of England at age six, and *Henry VIII* of England (1537).

1543 **Mikolaj Rej** [Nicholas Rey] (Feb. 4, 1505–1569), the **father of Polish literature**, became the first to use his native language rather than Latin in his writing. His works included *Żywot Józefa* (1545), a biblical drama.

1546 What one day would become the **Musée National de Louvre** got its start when **Francis I**, king of France, had a building constructed on the present site in Paris. Francis was an art collector and during his reign he acquired Leonardo's *Mona Lisa*, still the single most popular attraction of the Louvre.

1548 Nov. 17 The *Confrérie de la Passion*, the guild in control of Parisian theater, was forbidden to perform other than secular drama in an effort to halt the blending of secular events with traditional religious themes. Also in this year, the **Hôtel de Bourgogne**, the **first building specifically designed as a theater**, was built in Paris.

1549 **Joachim du Bellay** (1522–Jan. 1, 1560), a friend of Pierre de Ronsard, published his *Défense et Illustration de la Langue Française*, which set forth the principles of the **Pléiade**, a group of French poets who turned to classical Greek and Latin literature for inspiration but insisted on cultivation of the French language.

VII. SPORTS AND GAMES

1545 **Roger Ascham** (1515–1568), a Cambridge scholar, wrote *Toxophilus*, the **first book on archery in English**. Ascham was later engaged by Henry VIII to tutor his daughter Elizabeth, the future queen of England.

1550–1559

I. DISASTERS

1556 Jan. 24 A devastating **earthquake** killed more than 830,000 in northern China, in the present province of **Shensi** [Shaanxi].

II. EXPLORATION AND COLONIZATION

1554 **Hugh Willoughby**, an English explorer, in search of a Northeast Passage to China and India, was shipwrecked and lost in the White Sea off the coast of the **Kola Peninsula** [Kolski Poluosfrov], USSR.

1554 The present city of **São Paulo**, Brazil, was founded by Jesuit missionaries, who established a school in the village of Piratininga.

1555 Aug. 14 Under Nicolas de Villegaignon [Villegagnon] (c.1510–1571), a French Huguenot settlement *La France Antartique* was established on Governador Island, north of present **Rio de Janeiro**.

1556 Stephen Borough (1525–1584), an English explorer, in search of the Northeast Passage, sailed part way up the **Ob**, a **river** in Russia.

1557 The Portuguese colonized the island of **Macao** at the mouth of the **Pearl River** in southeastern China.

III. POLITICS AND WAR

1550 Ivan the Terrible, czar of Russia, summoned the first national assembly (the **Zemski Sobor**). The assembly passed acts requiring that all lands free from liens that had been deeded to the church be returned to the former owners or the state, that gifts made to the church in Ivan's minority be restored, and that monasteries could no longer accept certain properties without the czar's consent.

1550 Mar. 24 The **Peace of Boulogne** ended the war between England and the allies, France and Scotland. France regained Boulogne in return for an indemnity.

1551 Sinan Pasha (died c.1553), a Turkish admiral, captured Tripoli, in present Libya, from the **Knights Hospitallers**. Once a rich grain producing region, it had been overgrazed and deforested, and piracy became the major occupation of the coastal region.

1552 Apr. Henry II, king of France, occupied the imperial bishoprics of Metz, Toul, and Verdun, while the German Protestant princes, led by Maurice, duke and elector of Saxony, defeated Charles V, the Holy Roman emperor, at Innsbruck, in present Austria. On Aug. 2 Charles was forced to leave Germany and to sign the **Treaty of Passau**, granting **religious liberty to the Protestants in Germany**.

1553 May 21 John Dudley, duke of Northumberland, married his son Guildford to Lady **Jane Grey**, great-granddaughter of Henry VII. Northumberland then conspired to have her recognized as heir to the throne by the dying king **Edward VI**, at the expense of Henry VIII's daughters, Mary Tudor and Elizabeth.

1553 July 6 Edward VI (b. Oct. 12, 1537), king of England (from 1547), died. Lady Jane Grey was proclaimed queen by John Dudley, duke of Northumberland. His scheme quickly collapsed as the Catholic **Mary Tudor** [Bloody Mary], who had been declared the heir by Henry VIII, with popular support, was crowned queen of England on July 19. Northumberland (b. 1502) was beheaded on Aug. 22, and Lady Jane Grey (b. 1537) and Guildford Dudley were beheaded on Feb. 12, 1554.

1554 Jan. 26 Thomas Wyatt (b. 1521) led a rebellion against the impending marriage of Mary, queen of England, to Philip of Spain and against efforts by Mary to restore Roman Catholicism as the state religion. His army was defeated in London on Feb. 9, and Wyatt (b. 1521), a son of the English poet of the same name, surrendered and was executed on Apr. 11.

1554 Mar. 6 Mary I, queen of England, was married by proxy to Philip, son of Charles V, the Holy Roman emperor and, as Charles I, king of Spain. Philip came to England on July 20 and remained 13 months. The reign of the devoutly Catholic Mary and Philip, who was crowned Philip II, king of Spain in 1556, caused many of England's well-known Protestants to emigrate to the continent, especially to Geneva.

1555 The **Treaty of Amasya**, in present Turkey, was signed by the **Ottoman Empire** and **Persia**. Persia recognized Ottoman rule of Mesopotamia, in present Iraq, where Baghdad recovered under the Ottomans some of its former prosperity as a trading center.

1555 Oct. 25 At Brussels **Charles V**, the Holy Roman emperor (from 1519), announced his resignation and intention to retire to a Spanish monastery. Charles (b. Feb. 24, 1500) died there on Sept. 21, 1558. On Jan. 16, 1556, his son, Philip, was crowned **Philip II**, king of Spain.

1556 Nov. 5 Akbar I the Great (Oct. 1542–Oct. 16, 1605) fought and won the **second battle of Panipat**. Then, he reestablished his dynasty in Hindustan [northern India] and re-created the **Mogul** [Mughal] **Empire** (to 1857).

1557 **Ivan the Terrible** sent a Russian army commanded by Shah-Ali, formerly ruler of the Khanate of Kazan, to invade Livonia [later most of Latvia and Estonia], which had been established by the **Livonian Brothers of the Sword** allied with the **Teutonic Knights** during the 14th and 15th centuries. Ivan hoped to gain the seaport city of Riga.

1557 Aug. 10 England, allied with Spain, contributed to a Spanish victory against the French in a **battle at Saint Quentin**, France. As Paris was threatened, the French forces under François de Lorraine (Feb. 17, 1519–Feb. 18, 1563), duke of Guise, were recalled from Italy, where they had unsuccessfully attempted to recover the Spanish-held **Kingdom of Naples**.

1558 Jan. 7 The port of **Calais** was captured by a French force led by François de Lorraine, duke of Guise. On July 13, however, the French were defeated nearby at **Gravelines**, by a Spanish army with English naval support. The **Valois-Hapsburg wars** came to an end as peace negotiations opened at Cambrai in October.

1558 Nov. 17 **Mary I** (b. Feb. 18, 1516), queen of England (from 1553), daughter of Henry VIII and his first wife, Catherine of Aragon, died. Her half-sister Elizabeth I, daughter of Henry VIII and **Anne Boleyn**, was crowned queen of England on Jan. 1, 1559.

1559 Apr. 3 The **Treaty of Cateau-Cambrésis**, signed by England, France, and Spain, put an end to 60 years of conflict between France, the Holy Roman Empire, Spain, and often England. France annexed the three bishoprics of Metz, Toul, and Verdun, and retained Calais, in return for payment of an indemnity to England. France restored Savoy and Piedmont to Spain's ally, Emmanuel-Philibert (July 8, 1528–Aug. 30, 1580), duke of Savoy (from 1553). Corsica was returned to Genoa, and France abandoned its claims to Italy.

1559 Apr. 29 The English Parliament reversed its reconciliation with Rome, again denying papal authority in England, by a new **Act of Supremacy**. The authority of the crown over the Church, instituted in 1534 by Henry VIII, was reinstated, but the title Supreme Head, obnoxious to Catholics, was changed to **Supreme Governor**, at **Queen Elizabeth's** request.

IV. ECONOMY AND TRADE

c.1550 The price of **gold** began a general rise, due to an overabundance of silver.

1555 The **roads of England** were placed under the jurisdiction of the local parishes, with every householder to work four days a year to repair them.

1555 In London the **Muscovy Company** was established to conduct England's trade with Russia at the urging of Richard Chancellor (d. Nov. 10, 1556), who had met with the czar in 1553. Special monopoly privileges, including freedom from taxation, were granted the company.

1556 The **Stationers' Company**, a guild of printers and booksellers, was chartered in England. The guild required payment of a fee and registration of all books with the Company, intended to prevent heretical and libelous works from being printed.

1558 **Tobacco** began to be cultivated in Europe.

V. RELIGION AND PHILOSOPHY

1552 The *Book of Common Prayer* was revised and reissued under a new **Act of Uniformity** enacted by the English Parliament. Prayers for the dead, exorcism, and anointing were dropped, and the Eucharist was given a more Calvinist slant.

1552 **Angad** (b. 1504), chosen by Nanak in 1538 to succeed him as *guru*, died. His leadership kept **Sikhism** distinct from **Hinduism** or **Islam**. From contemporary speech, he formulated the language **Gurmukhi**, in which the sacred writings of Sikhism could be expressed.

1553 June 12 The **Forty-Two Articles**, drawn up by Thomas Cranmer, the archbishop of Canterbury, were authorized by the young Edward VI, king of England. The Articles carried the Church of England further toward Protestantism.

1553 Oct. 27 **Miguel Servet** [Michael Servetus] (b. 1511?), a brilliant Spaniard of heretical unitarian beliefs, was put to death by fire in Geneva. His continual attacks on the traditional notions of the Trinity, Christology, and infant baptism, as well as his disparagement of Calvin's *Institutes*, led to his arrest in Geneva in Aug. 1553. This month-long trial before civil authorities made it clear that the Calvinists were masters of Geneva.

1554   Theresa [Teresa] **of Ávila** (Mar. 28, 1515–Oct. 4, 1582), a Carmelite nun and mystic, experienced her conversion. Thereafter, she experienced frequent visions of Christ and the Devil. On Aug. 24, 1562, Theresa dedicated an **Order of Discalced** [Barefoot] **Carmelites**, whose discipline returned to earlier, more ascetic Carmelite rules.

1554 Feb. 4   The first of the Protestants to be martyred during the reign of England's Queen Mary I, was **John Rogers** (born c.1500), a divinity lecturer at Saint Paul's cathedral in London. Under the five years of **Bloody Mary's reign**, there would be death by burning of more than 300 Protestants.

1554 Nov. 30   Cardinal Reginald Pole (Mar. 3, 1500–Nov. 17, 1558), the papal legate, was admitted to England, signaling **England's reconciliation with Rome**. During Mary's reign, the English Parliament voted restoration of papal authority but without return of confiscated church properties. Pole absolved the nation of heresy.

1555 July 12   **Pope Paul IV**, in his bull *Cum nimis absurdam*, directed that Jews in cities be restricted to their own quarter, surrounded by a high wall with gates to be locked at night. Venice already had such a ghetto, in its *Getto Nuova* [New Foundry] quarter. The bull prohibited Jews from owning real estate and practicing medicine among Christians.

1555 Sept. 25   The **Peace of Augsburg** stated that within the German lands of Charles V, the Holy Roman emperor, each prince must choose the religion of his territory. Germany thus became permanently divided along religious lines.

1555 Oct. 16   Former Protestant bishops **Hugh Latimer** (born c.1485) and **Nicholas Ridley** (born c.1503) were burned to death at Oxford, England. Also meeting death by burning at the hands of **Queen Mary's persecution** in 1555 were Bishops **Robert Ferrar** (born c.1500–Mar. 30, 1555) and **John Hooper** (born c.1500–Feb. 9, 1555). All refused to disown the doctrines of the *Book of Common Prayer*.

1556 Mar. 21   **Thomas Cranmer** (b. July 2, 1489), former archbishop of Canterbury, creator of the Protestant *Book of Common Prayer*, was burned at the stake in Oxford at Queen Mary's order. Cranmer

had recanted his Protestantism, but just before his execution, he repudiated his retractions and died for his faith.

1557   William Whittingham (c.1524–June 10, 1579) and numerous other English scholars and reformists, living in exile during the aggressively Catholic reign of Mary, queen of England, produced the *Genevan New Testament*, with an introduction by **John Calvin**, Whittingham's brother-in-law. Although only a minor revision of William Tyndale's translation, this Testament for the first time in English divided chapters into verses. It also carried marginal notes strongly Protestant in nature.

1557 Dec. 3   Certain Scottish nobles of Calvinist persuasion bound themselves by covenant to "establish the most blessed word of God and His congregation." Nicknamed "**the Lords of the Congregation**," they had been aroused by the preaching of **John Knox** during his six-month stay in **Scotland** in 1555. With this act the nobility of Scotland became divided on the Reformation issues.

1559   At Valladolid, Spain, two *autos-da-fé* were held, in which 27 men and women perished. Two more *autos-da-fé* were held at Sevilla [Seville] in 1559 and 1560, in which 24 others were burned.

1559 May   The **First General Synod of the Huguenots** [French Calvinists] was held in Paris. At the time Huguenots numbered about 400,000, under the leadership of **Louis I de Bourbon**, prince of Condé, and Admiral **Gaspard II de Coligny**. Another leader of the Protestants was Antoine de Bourbon, king consort of Navarre (from 1548).

1559 May 2   **John Knox** returned permanently to Scotland from Geneva, where he had ministered to English-speaking exiles. On May 11 he preached at Perth, after which a mob destroyed the local monastic establishments.

1559 June 24   A new **Act of Uniformity**, by which all Christian worship in England was to be conducted, was adopted by Parliament. Anti-Roman features of the *Second Prayer Book of Edward VI* had been deleted, and by this Act the new version was firmly established as the liturgy of the Church of England.

1559 Dec. 17   **Matthew Parker** (Aug. 6, 1504–May 17, 1575), the choice of Elizabeth, queen of England, for **archbishop of Canterbury**, was consecrated by four bishops who had received their ordinations to the bishopric under either Henry VIII or Edward VI.

VI. SCIENCE, EDUCATION AND TECHNOLOGY

c.1550 **Indians in Central America**, trained by the Jesuit missionaries to transcribe their native hieroglyphics into the Spanish alphabet, produced such works as the *Popol Vuh* and the *Cakchiquel Annals*, both chronicles of Mayan mythology and history.

c.1550 The **table fork** appeared in Europe, probably first in either Italy or Spain. Europe was reluctant to adopt the implement in place of spearing food with a knife and using it to convey the food to the mouth.

c.1550 **Indoor lighting** from **candles** came to be used throughout Europe due to the availability of tallow from animal fats.

1551 **Konrad von Gesner** (Mar. 26, 1516–Dec. 13, 1565), a Swiss naturalist, published the first volume of *Historia Animalium*. The five-volume work was the most detailed since Pliny the Elder's *Historia Naturalis* (c.A.D. 77).

c.1552 **Leo Africanus** (born c.1483), a Moorish traveler and geographer, died in Tunis. He had been captured by pirates while crossing North Africa, and was taken as a slave to Pope Leo X, who baptized and freed him. In 1526 he completed his *Description of Africa*, translated into English in 1600 and still a basic source of knowledge of the Sudan prior to 19th-century explorations.

1556 *De Re Metallica* by **Georgius Agricola** [Georg Bauer] (Mar. 24, 1494–Nov. 21, 1555), a German scholar, was published. It firmly established the science of metallurgy.

1557 **Bartolmé de Medina** (1528–1580), while working at the mining center of Pachuca, Mexico, developed a method for separating **silver** from silver ore by using mercury.

VII. ARTS AND LEISURE

c.1550 The **K'un-ch'ü school**, which dominated **Chinese drama** for 300 years, was founded in Kiangsu by Liang Chên-Yü [Liang Po-Lung] (1520?–?1580) and Wei Liang-Fu, who provided the musical arrangement for this type of opera.

1550 *Le Vite de' Più eccellenti architetti, pittori, e scultori, italiani* [*Lives of the Artists*] (1912-1914), by **Giorgio Vasari** (July 30, 1511–June 27, 1574), a classic source for the lives of Italian Renaissance artists, was published. Vasari was a successful painter and architect, best-known for the gallery of the Uffizi, Florence.

1550 **John Marbeck** [Merbeck] (c.1510–c.1585), an English organist and theologian, published the first musical setting of the English liturgy, *The Boke of Common Praier Noted*.

1552 The *Accademia della Crusca*, the **oldest literary academy in Italy**, was founded in Florence for the purpose of purifying the Italian language. The Cruscani published the **first Italian dictionary** *Vocabolario* (1612)

1552 *Cléopâtre captive* [*Captive Cleopatra*], the **first classical French tragedy**, was performed before the court of Henry II, king of France. Its author was **Étienne Jodelle** (1532–July, 1573), sieur de Lymodin.

1553 **Cristóbal de Morales** (born c.1500), a Spanish composer, died. He was the first Spanish musician to achieve international reputation. In 1538 his cantatas were performed in Nice to celebrate peace negotiations held between Francis I, king of France, and Charles V, the Holy Roman emperor.

1554 *Lazarillo de Tormes*, the **first Spanish novel**, attributed to **Diego Hurtado de Mendoza** (1503?–1575), was published. A picaresque novel, its satire was directed against greed and hypocrisy.

c.1555 **Fuzulî** [Mehmed, son of Suleiman] (born c.1495), a celebrated Turkish poet of the classical school, died of the plague. *Leylâ ve Mecnun*, an unhappy love story popular in Muslim literature, was the best of his works, which were written in Azeri Turkish.

1556 **Suleiman the Magnificent**, the Ottoman sultan of Turkey, built the **mosque** bearing his name **in İstanbul** [Constantinople]. Sinan (1489?–1587) was the architect. The earlier Byzantine style is still visible, but the massing of domes and half-domes was carried further later. More strikingly, the decoration, both exterior and interior, and the use of tile and paint rather than marble and gold mosaic, was Persian in style.

1557 The first miscellany of English lyrics *Songs and Sonnets*, printed by Richard Tottel (c.1530–July, 1593), introduced the **sonnet** form to the language. Written by **Thomas Wyatt** [Wyat] (1503?–Oct. 11, 1542), an English poet, they were modeled after the Petrarchan sonnet popular in Italy.

1558 **Gioseffo Zarlino** (Mar. 22, 1517–Feb. 14, 1590), an Italian music theorist and composer, published *Institutioni Harmoniche*. Zarlino emphasized the Ionian as the preponderant mode, renumbering the other modes after this, and suggested equal temperament for tuning the lute. His ideas anticipated musical developments in the 17th and 18th centuries, especially in the work of Jean Philippe Rameau.

1558 **Francisco de Sá de Miranda** (b. Aug. 28, 1481), the Portuguese poet who introduced the Italian Renaissance to Portugal, died. His *Os Estrangeiros* (1527) was among the first classical comedies.

1558–1603 The **Elizabethan style of architecture**, considered to coincide with the reign of Elizabeth I, queen of England, was noted for the introduction of classical elements that distinguished it from the earlier **Tudor style** (c.1500), which displayed more Gothic features. Wollaton Hall in Nottinghamshire, built in 1588 by Robert Smythson (1536?–1614), an early English architect, remains today a good example. The term **Jacobean**, referring to the reign of James I (ruled 1603–1625), was sometimes used to indicate a similar style. Holland House in Kensington, London, is an example today of the elements of the Jacobean style.

c.1559 **Clement Janequin** (born c.1485), the French musician who was the chief representative of 16th century French polyphony, died. His many chansons, generally written in celebration of events

at the French court, included *La Guerre*, *Le Chant des Oiseaux*, and *Au Joly Moys de May*.

1559 The **Uffizi Gallery**, containing one of the finest collections anywhere, traced its origin to the construction of a building by Cosimo I de' Medici, duke of Florence. The structure, which became known as the Uffizi Palace and was later enlarged, was intended originally to house government offices. But eventually the de' Medici family's art collection was moved there. Now it is known especially for its art of the Italian Renaissance. But the single best known object in its collection is the Greek statue *Venus de' Medici*.

VIII. SPORTS, GAMES, AND SOCIETY

c.1550 That **cricket** was being played by English schoolboys as early as the mid-16th century was reported by one John Derrick in a 1598 trial. Derrick, then 59, in the course of his testimony, stated that he and his schoolmates in the free grammar school of Guildford, Surrey, played cricket when he was a student there.

1551 That **curling** existed as an organized sport in **Scotland** at this time was supported by the finding in the 1880s of a curling stone with the date "1551" etched into it. The stone was discovered at the bottom of a pond near Dunblane in southern Perthshire, central Scotland. The Dutch artist Pieter Brueghel the Elder showed a game of curling in a winter scene. Regardless of its place of origin, the development of the game is generally conceded now to Scotland.

1559 June 20 Henry II, king of France (from 1547), was mortally wounded in a tournament held during the festivities following the **Treaty of Cateau-Cambrésis**. Henry (b. Mar. 19, 1519) died on July 10, and was succeeded by his son, Francis II. This struck a heavy blow to the day, already declining, of tournaments in western Europe.

1560–1569

I. EXPLORATION AND COLONIZATION

1562 May 1 French **Huguenots**, under **Jean Ribaut** [Ribault], arrived at St. Johns River near St. Augus-

tine, Florida; but they soon moved to Parris Island in Port Royal Sound, South Carolina, where they became the **first French colonizers of the New World**. Not having been supplied in time by a second expedition from France, the starving colonists abandoned the colony. In the meantime a second haven for French Protestants, Fort Caroline, was established in 1564 at St. Johns River; but most of the colonists, including Ribaut (born c.1520), were massacred and the colony destroyed in 1565 by the Spanish under **Pedro Menéndez de Avilés** (1519–1574).

1563 Cartago, in **Costa Rica** near the present capital of San José, was founded by **Juan Vázquez de Coronado**, the Spanish explorer of Guatemala and Central America. Cartago served as capital of Spanish Costa Rica until 1825.

1565 Apr. 27 **Miguel López de Legazpe** (1510–1572) arrived at the island of Cebu in the Philippines near Mactan, where Ferdinand Magellan had been slain. There, López de Legazpe built a chapel, in the **first Spanish Catholic settlement in the Philippines**. In 1565 Spain took possession of the Philippines, which it held until 1898.

1565 Sept. 8 **Pedro Menéndez de Avilés**, a Spanish explorer, established the **first permanent European settlement in Florida** at St. Augustine, where Ponce de León had landed in 1513. Menéndez de Avilés had been made Adelantado [governor] of Florida in 1565 to explore, colonize, and defend the province.

1567 **Rio de Janeiro** in Brazil was founded by the Portuguese Mem de Sá [Men de Sá] (1500?–1572) and his nephew Estacio de Sá after expelling a French Huguenot colony which had been established nearby in 1555 by Nicolas de Villegaignon.

1568 **Álvaro de Mendaña de Neyra** [Neira] (1541–1595), a Spanish navigator and explorer, discovered the **Solomon Islands**, which are located east of New Guinea in the Pacific Ocean.

II. POLITICS AND WAR

1560 Mar. The **Conspiracy of Amboise** was organized by the Huguenot **Louis I de Bourbon**, prince of Condé. The goal of the **Huguenots**, which was to end control over the French throne by the Catholic house of Guise, collapsed when the conspirators failed in their attempt to capture Francis II, king of France. Under orders from the Guises the participants in the plot were horribly tortured and then executed, though Louis de Bourbon, under sentence of death, was spared by the death of Francis.

This marked the beginning of the use of political violence in France by both parties, Catholic and Protestant.

1560 July 6 The **Treaty of Edinburgh** or Leith was signed by France and England. It called for the withdrawal of French soldiers from Scotland. England's successful effort to come to peace with France halted the Catholic **French-Scottish alliance** and resulted in a victory for the revolutionary Protestant party of Scotland when **Elizabeth I** was confirmed the rightful ruler of Protestant England. **Mary Stuart**, queen of Scotland and great-granddaughter of England's Henry VII, was never affirmed as heir to the English throne, though over the following years she tried to press her right on the claim of Elizabeth's illegitimate birth.

1560 Dec. 5 **Francis II** (b. Jan. 19, 1544), king of France for about 18 months (from July 10, 1559), who had married Mary Stuart, queen of Scotland, in 1558, died. Sickly and weak-minded Francis was controlled by his uncles by marriage, François de Lorraine, duc de Guise, and Charles, cardinal of Lorraine, the real rulers of France and strongly anti-Protestant. He was succeeded by his brother Charles IX, then only 10 years old and completely dominated by his mother Catherine de Médicis (Apr. 13, 1519–Jan. 5, 1589), who attempted to establish a political counterforce to the **Guises** by at first welcoming Huguenot influence at the French court.

1561 **Nogomo Mupunzagutu**, king of the **Monomotapa** [Motapa, Mutapa] **Empire** (c.1440–c.1629), in present **Zimbabwe**, was converted, along with some of his subjects, to Roman Catholicism by Gonçalo da Silveira (c.1523–Mar. 11, 1561), a Portuguese Jesuit. A few weeks later, the pro-Muslim faction, perceiving a threat from Christianity, murdered the king and the priest.

1561 Aug. 19 **Mary, queen of Scots**, landed at Leith, returning to her native Scotland from France without crossing England, which she was forbidden to enter by Elizabeth I for not signing the **Treaty of Edinburgh** in 1560. After the death of her first husband, Francis II, king of France, on Dec. 5, 1560, Mary's mother-in-law, Catherine de Médicis, left Mary no opening for her ambitious nature. For the next several years Mary, who ruled a largely Protestant Scotland, won friends for Catholicism. The Protestant nobles were divided and the Roman Mass was increasingly used despite its ban. During this time she held many fiery debates with the Protestant reformer **John Knox**.

1562 Jan.   Catherine de Médicis, regent for her son Charles IX, king of France, in an effort to avoid a religious war with the Huguenots, authorized their assemblies to meet outside of the towns. On Mar. 1 French Catholics led by François de Lorraine, duke of Guise, unwilling to accept this edict, set upon a Huguenot congregation worshipping at Vassy, northeast of Troyes, in northeastern France, killing several Huguenots. The **French Wars of Religion** followed: the **First** from 1562 to 1563, the **Second** from 1567 to 1568, the **Third** from 1568 to 1570, the **Fourth** from 1572 to 1573, the **Fifth** from 1574 to 1576, the **Sixth** in 1577, the **Seventh** in 1580, and the **Eighth** [**War of the Three Henrys**] from 1585 to 1598.

1562 Sept. 22 A treaty of alliance was signed at Hampton Court between England and the Huguenot leader Louis I de Bourbon, prince of Condé. As the reigning **House of Valois** (1328–1589) weakened, the struggle for power between the Catholic **Guise family** and the Huguenot **Bourbons** intensified. In support of the Bourbons, an English force invaded France and occupied Le Havre on Oct. 4.

1563 Mar. 19 The **Peace of Amboise** ended the **First War of Religion** (1562–1563) in France. The Catholics were victorious at Dreux over the allied Huguenots and German Protestant princes on Dec. 19, 1562. The Huguenots lost Antoine de Bourbon (b. 1518), duke of Vendôme and king consort of Navarre, who had died in **battle at Rouen** in Oct., 1562, and the Catholic forces lost François de Lorraine (b. Feb. 17, 1519), duke of Guise, who was murdered at Orléans on Feb. 24, 1563. The Huguenots were granted limited freedom of worship and, in return, aided their country in ousting the English force from Le Havre on July 27, 1563. The **Peace of Troyes** was signed by England and France on Apr. 11, 1564.

1564 July 25 Ferdinand I (b. Mar. 10, 1503), the Holy Roman emperor (from 1558), died in Vienna. His reign was marked by an **end to the religious wars in Germany** and the annexation of the kingdoms of Bohemia and Hungary as hereditary Hapsburg possessions. He was succeeded by his eldest son Maximilian II (July 31, 1527–Oct. 12, 1576), whose sympathy for the Reformation helped him pursue a conciliatory religious policy.

1565 Jan. 23   Rama Raya (fl. 1542–1565), emperor of Vijayanagar, the great empire and the last important Hindu state of southern India, was defeated in a **battle at Talikota** [Rankasa-Tangadi], in present northern Karnataka state of western India, by the allied Muslim sultans of Ahmadnagar, Bidar, Bijapur, and Golconda. The great days of the **Vijayanagar Empire** (from 1336), under which Hindu culture thrived, were over; the empire came to a final end in 1614.

1565   Ivan IV, czar of Russia, withdrew from Moscow and threatened to retire because the **boyars** [nobles] were fighting his policies in Livonia and elsewhere. The people in Moscow threatened rebellion against the boyars, and both sides persuaded him to return. He then divided Russia in two: the **Zemstchina** to be ruled locally by the old boyars and the **Oprichnina** to be directly under Ivan. The oprichniki, who became the new boyars, were chosen from the younger sons of the old nobles because they could inherit no titles or lands and their elevation made them loyal to Ivan. The Oprichnina included nearly half of Russia, most of Moscow, and the main trade routes. This act centralized the government in Ivan's hands.

1566 Mar. 9   David Rizzio (b. 1540), secretary to **Mary, queen of Scotland**, was stabbed to death at the royal palace in Edinburgh, Scotland. He was the chief target of a plot devised by Henry Stewart [Stuart], lord Darnley, second husband (1565) of Mary, who regarded Mary's attention to Rizzio jealously. The Protestant Scots supported Darnley because they feared the Roman Catholicism of the Italian, who was charged with Mary's papal correspondence. During the melodramatic episodes, which included the murder of Darnley at Kirk o'Field in Edinburgh (1567), following close on the heels of Rizzio's murder, Mary not only lost the support of Catholics in Scotland, England, and on the Continent, but **Scotland** became even more Protestant.

1566 Apr. 5 The **Compromise of Breda** organized the Protestant nobles of the **Netherlands** [present Belgium and the Netherlands] into the **Confederacy of the Beggars** [les Gueux]. Its aim was to repeal the Inquisition there, initiated in the Netherlands by Margaret of Parma (1522–1586), sister and regent (1559–1567) of Philip II, king of Spain.

1566 July   Philip II, king of Spain, consented to withdraw the **Inquisition** from the Netherlands, an act of strategy which in no way turned the king from his intent to root out heresy brutally. The **Iconoclastic Riots** ensued in August and were harshly repressed.

1566 Sept. 5 **Suleiman the Magnificent** (b. 1495?), sultan (from 1520) of the Ottoman Empire (1326–1920), died at Szigeth, Hungary, in battle against the Holy Roman Empire. Suleiman's reign marked the golden age of the **Ottoman Empire** (1326–1920) when it ruled northward to present Yugoslavia, Hungary, Romania, southern Russia, and the Caucasus and southward to Algiers, Tunis, Libya, Egypt, Palestine, Syria, and Iraq. He was succeeded by a son, Selim II (1524–Dec., 1574).

1567 Feb. 9 **Henry Stewart** [Stuart], Lord Darnley (b. Dec. 7, 1545), second husband to Mary, queen of Scots, died when his lodgings outside Edinburgh were blown up, probably at the instigation of Mary. On May 15 Mary wed her intimate James Hepburn, earl of Bothwell (1536?–Apr. 14, 1578), in a Protestant ceremony insisted upon by Bothwell. With this act, more so than the murder of Henry, Mary effectively divorced herself from Scottish Catholics. Forced to abdicate (July 24), but not driven from **Scotland** until defeated near Glasgow on May 13, 1568, Mary finally sought refuge in England. **Elizabeth I**, queen of England, arranged a hearing on her behalf. Mary was declared "not proved guilty" of Darnley's murder, but she was nonetheless placed under stringent guard in a form of house arrest for 19 years.

1567 July 9 **James VI**, the infant son of Mary, former queen of Scotland, and **Henry Stewart**, Lord Darnley, was crowned king of Scotland. **John Knox**, the Protestant reformer, preached the sermon at the coronation ceremony. In Dec., 1567, the Scottish Parliament passed provisions that fully established Protestantism. James Stewart [Stuart], earl of Moray (1531?–Jan. 21, 1570), natural son of James V, and half-brother to Mary, was to act as regent.

1567 Aug. **Fernando Álvarez de Toledo**, duke of Alva [Alba], a Spanish general, was sent to the Spanish Netherlands by Philip II, king of Spain, to punish the northern inhabitants, rebellious Dutch, and to root out heresy. He established an institution of terror, the **Council of Troubles**, soon called the **Blood Council**, which superseded all local laws. It momentarily united religious and secular dissidents.

1567 Sept. 29 The **Second French War of Religion** (1567–1568) followed upon the **Huguenot Conspiracy of Meaux** to capture the young king Charles IX and his regent-mother Catherine de Médicis. The war ended with the signing of the **Peace of Longjumeau**, on Mar. 23, 1568. Peace was short-lived, however, as the **Third French War of Religion** (1568–1570) broke out the following September.

1569 Mar. 13 Henry, duke of Anjou and the future Henry III, king of France, defeated the Huguenots in a **battle at Jarnac**, central western France. Louis I de Bourbon (b. May 7, 1530), prince of Condé, was slain during the battle, and succeeded as leader of the Huguenots by Admiral Gaspard de Coligny. Coligny was defeated by Henry at Moncontour, also in central western France, on Oct. 3, but he raised a new army in the south and marched toward Paris.

1569 Aug. **Cosimo 1 de' Medici** (June 12, 1519–Apr. 21, 1574; ruled from 1537) was granted the title of grand duke by **Pope Pius V** (Jan. 17, 1504–May 1, 1572; ruled from 1566). The Italian city-states under his rule were formally united as the grand duchy of Tuscany, with Florence as capital. The title was confirmed by the Holy Roman Empire in 1576.

1569 Nov. 9 The **Northern Rebellion** was initiated by Thomas Percy, duke of Northumberland, and Charles Neville (1542?–1601), earl of Westmoreland, whose goal was to restore **Catholicism in England**. The plan was to free **Mary, queen of Scots**, prisoner of **Elizabeth**, queen of England, and, by wedding her to Thomas Howard, duke of Norfolk, establish Mary as Elizabeth's heir. Elizabeth was unwed and childless; furthermore, Mary was legitimately next in the line of succession. Popular support for the Catholics failed to materialize. Norfolk, forced to surrender by Elizabeth, was pardoned and released from the Tower of London the following August. Elizabeth's troops routed the forces of the rebellion and c.3000, including troops, local supporters, and their immediate leaders, were ruthlessly slain. For his part in the uprising and the pro-Catholic plot of 1571, Northumberland (b. 1528) was beheaded in 1572; Westmoreland escaped to the Continent where he led an English force that supported the duke of Alva in his suppression of religious dissidents in the Netherlands.

III. ECONOMY AND TRADE

1563   An apprenticeship of seven years prior to working at a trade was mandated in England by the **Statute of Apprentices**.

1566   Elizabeth I attempted to stabilize **English currency** by ordering a fixed silver and gold content of coins and establishing the value of gold at fifteen and one-half times that of silver.

1569   The government in **Spain declared bankruptcy**. During the next century, Spain went bankrupt in 1607, 1627, and 1647.

IV. RELIGION AND PHILOSOPHY

1560   The *Geneva Bible* was completed by English Bible scholars in Geneva under **William Whittingham** (1524?–1579). The New Testament had been produced in 1557. Their work of translation and revision resulted in a Bible popular with English-speaking Protestants, especially with the Pilgrim Fathers.

1560 Aug. 17   Through the work of **John Knox**, the Scottish Parliament adopted a Calvinistic confession of faith following the withdrawal of French troops under terms of the **Treaty of Edinburgh** (July 6). Soon afterward, papal jurisdiction in Scotland was denied, the celebration of the Mass was forbidden, and statutes establishing Catholic tenets were repealed.

1560 Dec.   The **General Assembly of the Kirk**, the **first Scottish General Assembly**, was held under the leadership of John Knox and his Reformist associates. In Jan. 1561, they introduced into the Scottish Parliament the *First Book of Discipline*, a scheme for applying John Calvin's principles of church governance to a whole kingdom. Parliament adopted only the ecclesiastical sections.

1561   The **Belgic Confession** of the Dutch Reformed Church was printed. It was a statement of the principles of the faith composed of 37 articles written by Guido de Brès (1522–1567).

1562   The **Heidelberg Confession** [Catechism] was prepared by the two young theologians Kaspar Olevianus (1536–1587) and Zacharias Ursinus (1534–1583) for use in the Calvinist churches within the territories ruled by Frederick III the Pious (1515–1576), elector of the Palatinate, who had re-

cently been persuaded to adopt the Calvinist position.

1563   The **Thirty-Nine Articles of Religion** were adopted by the **Church of England**. A revision of the Forty-Two Articles of 1553 and designed to embrace a wider spectrum of belief, they did maintain the Church's original doctrinal position.

1563 Dec. 4   As the **Council of Trent** (from 1545) adjourned under the leadership of Pope Pius IV, it provided the Roman Catholic Church with fresh statements on faith and practice. In matters of reform the Council swung entirely away from the position of the **Council of Constance** that a general council spoke for a universal church.

1564   The revised *Book of Common Order* was approved for the conduct of public worship by the General Assembly of Scottish Calvinists. Often called *Knox's Liturgy*, it was a revision of a book John Knox published (1556) in Geneva that reflected the practices of English Protestants living in Europe and was modeled on John Calvin's precepts. By order of the General Assembly, the *Book of Common Order* replaced the English *Second Book of Common Prayer* [Edward VI's Book], which was widely used in **Scotland** at this time.

1564 May 27   John [Jean] **Calvin** (b. 1509), a French Protestant reformer, died in Geneva. Calvin's influence, through his books, his vast correspondence with religious and educational leaders, and students from his Genevan Academy (1559), spread throughout France, the Netherlands, Scotland, and among English Puritans.

1564 Nov. 24   The Roman Catholic Church published its *Index expurgatorius* [Index of Prohibited Books], a list of books that Catholics were forbidden to read.

c.1565   In **India**, Sri Chand, a son of Nanak, formed a schismatic ascetic sect known later as the **Udasis**, the mendicants, or "those who have renounced the world." The Udasis served as missionaries.

1567   **Theresa of Ávila** [Teresa de Cepeda], who had founded the Discalced Carmelites, made the acquaintance of the Carmelite priest Juan de Yepes [Yepis] y Álvarez, known today as **St. John of the Cross**. In 1568 he opened the first monastery for men under the "Primitive Rule of Carmel," and, with Theresa, battled Carmelite forces opposing their return to an austere, contemplative life. John's poems were among the classics of mystical experience. Theresa also wrote mystical works, the remarkable *El castillo interior* [*The Interior Castle*] (c.1583) and *Camino de perfección* [*Way of Perfection*] (c.1583).

1568 The *Bishops' Bible* was published in England. A revision of the Great Bible undertaken by ecclesiastics who were displeased by the popularity of the Protestant Geneva Bible, it earned its name from the fact that at least nine of the revisers were bishops.

1568 William Allen (1532–Oct. 16, 1594), an Oxford man and a Lancashire Roman Catholic priest, founded an **English college at Douai** [Douay] in northern France for Roman Catholics fleeing the Protestant reign of Elizabeth I.

V. SCIENCE, EDUCATION, AND TECHNOLOGY

1564 Graphite for early pencils was mined in a pure state near Borrowdale Valley in northwestern England. Pencils were made by wrapping sticks of graphite with string.

1565 Dec. 13 Konrad von Gesner (b. Mar. 26, 1516), a dedicated Swiss physician, scholar, and zoologist, died. He became known for his careful descriptions of animals, which provided a basis for modern zoology.

1569 Gerhardus Mercator [Gerhard Kremer] (Mar. 5, 1512–Dec. 2, 1594), a Flemish geographer, applied the **Mercator projection** of drawing maps to a world chart, which could be used by navigators to accurately plot their course. His projection was the first to be useful to navigators sailing to faraway places.

VI. ARTS AND LEISURE

1561 Louis Bourgeois (b. 1510), a French musician and follower of John Calvin, died. His musical settings of the *Genevan Psalter* were sung by French Calvinists. In *Le Droict Chemin de Musique* (1550), Bourgeois suggested a revised nomenclature for tone syllables that was subsequently adopted generally throughout France.

1562 Jan. 1 The tragedy *Gorboduc or Ferrex and Porrey* was performed for Elizabeth I in London by the actors of the Inner Temple. The drama, the earliest extant English play in blank verse, was written by **Thomas Norton** (1532–Mar. 10, 1584) and **Thomas Sackville** (1536–Apr. 19, 1608).

1562 Dec. 8 Adrian Willaert (born c.1490), a Flemish composer who founded the **Venetian school of composition**, died. A master of the madrigal, Willaert's chief contribution was to introduce composition for two antiphonal choirs.

1563 Sur Das (b. 1483), a famous poet of the Krishna tradition in northern India, died. He was said to have written more than 75,000 verses in Hindi. His best-known work was *Sur Sagar*, a collection of hymns devoted to Krishna.

1563 The *Accademia del Disegno*, perhaps the first academy of fine arts in Europe, was founded in Florence by **Giorgio Vasari**, an Italian artist and biographer, as well as architect.

1563 Oct. 22 Diego de Siloé (born c.1495), a Spanish architect and sculptor, died. The San Salvador chapel at Ubeda (1559) and the Granada cathedral (1528) are the best examples of his ornate style, a highlight of the Spanish Renaissance.

1564 Feb. 17 Michelangelo [Buonarotti] (b. Mar. 6, 1475), the great Italian sculptor and architect, died. Many of his drawings preserve designs never used. Among the extant works of Michaelangelo in sculpture: **"The Battle of the Centaurs"** (c.1490) in the Casa Buonaroti at Florence; **"Bacchus"** (1501) in the Bargello, Florence; **"Madonna"** (c.1503) in the Church of Notre Dame, Bruges, Belgium; **"Madonna"** (in bas relief) (c.1507) also at the Bargello; **"Moses"** (1513–1516) in the church of San Pietro in Rome; and two **"Slaves"** now in the Louvre, Paris. From 1516 to 1534 he sculpted in Florence the facade of San Lorenzo, the Laurentian Library, and the sepulchre chapel of the Medici. In 1534 in Rome he produced **"Deposition from the Cross"** (now in the Duomo, Florence). He also painted the ceiling of the Sistine Chapel in the Vatican (1508–1512) and the **"Last Judgment"** on the rear wall of the Sistine Chapel sometime after 1534.

1565 Lope de Rueda (born c.1505), a Spanish dramatist, died. Many of his plays were written in prose, a sharp departure from custom. His best-known play today, a farcial comedy, is *Eufemia* (c.1545).

1569   The *Araucana*, the most famous Spanish Renaissance epic, was written by **Alonso de Ercilla y Zúñiga** (1533–1594). Published in three parts (1569, 1578, 1589), it was based on Ercilla's experiences as a volunteer soldier in Chile during Spain's conquest of the Araucanian Indians.

1569 Sept. 9?   Pieter Breughel the Elder (born c.1525), a Flemish painter of minutely detailed landscapes and peasant life, died. The best known of his works today are *Children's Games* and *Peasant Wedding*. So detailed were his paintings, that historians have been able to see just how things were built and done in those days and also to discover what games or sports were engaged in by the people.

1570–1579

I. EXPLORATION AND COLONIZATION

1571   A Spanish force under **Miguel López de Legazpe** (c.1510–1572) founded the city of **Manila** after the conquest of its Muslim settlement.

1576–1578   Martin Frobisher (c.1535–Nov. 22, 1594), an English admiral, in search of the Northwest Passage, explored part of the **Arctic archipelago**, passing through the Hudson Strait between Baffin Island and Canada. Frobisher brought back lumps of black earth falsely rumored to be gold.

1576   Paulo Dias de Novais (d. 1589), the Portuguese governor, founded **Saõ Paulo de Luanda**, the present capital of Angola, and constructed the fortress of Saõ Miguel, built to protect the flourishing commercial and slave-trading center.

1577 Dec. 13   Francis Drake (1540–Jan. 28, 1596) sailed from Plymouth, England, with five vessels on a voyage of plunder and exploration, which carried him around the world.

II. POLITICS AND WAR

1570 Aug. 8   The **Peace of Saint Germain-en-Laye** ended the French **Third War of Religion** (1568–1570). The four cities of La Charité-sur-Loire, Cognac, Montauban, and La Rochelle, all in central western France, were granted to the Huguenots as places of refuge.

1571   The Crimean **Tatars** [Tartars], a mixture of Turks and Mongols, who swept north into Russia on periodic raids, advanced to **Moscow**, setting fire to much of the city. Of Moscow's c.200,000 inhabitants,

only c.30,000 survived death or capture. The Kremlin escaped the fire.

c.1571   Idris Alooma (died c.1603) of the **Sefawa** [Saifawa] **Dynasty** (c.800–1846), became king of Bornu, in present Chad, and then brought his empire to its apogee. Alooma instituted diplomatic relations with the North African states, then vassals of the Ottomans.

1571 Sept. 7   Thomas Howard, duke of Norfolk, was again taken into custody on the discovery of a conspiracy against **Elizabeth I. Roberto Ridolfi** (Nov. 18, 1513–Feb. 18, 1612), a Florentine living in London, had masterminded a plot to murder Elizabeth and to place the imprisoned Mary, former queen of Scotland, on the English throne under the cover of a Spanish invasion. Norfolk (b. 1536) was beheaded on June 22, 1572. Ridolfi, on the Continent when the plot was discovered, returned to Florence.

1571 Oct. 7   The Turkish fleet of **Selim II**, the Ottoman sultan, was destroyed in a **battle off Lepanto** [Návpaktos] by ships of a **Holy League** composed of the Papal States, Spain, and Venice, led by **Don John** of Austria. Not only was this the biggest naval engagement since the battle of Actium (32 B.C.), it was also the **last major battle fought between galleys**. The Turkish fleet was rowed by c.15,000 chained Christian slaves, who were freed by the victorious western allies.

1572 Apr. 1   The capture of the stronghold of Brielle [Brill], near Rotterdam, in the present Netherlands, by the **Dutch Sea Beggars** marked the first important victory for the Dutch rebels in the **Eighty Years' War** (1568–1648), the war of independence of the Low Countries against Spain. When the **Duke of Alva** [Alba] was sent (1567) to the Spanish Netherlands by Philip II, king of Spain, to punish the rebellious Protestant Dutch, who lived mostly in the northern provinces of the Low Countries, his harsh repressive measures and military successes, which marked the beginning of the Eighty Years' War, drove the armed Dutch merchant vessels out to sea. They continued their depredations on Spanish shipping, and the uprising spread from the north under the leadership of **William I the Silent**, prince of Orange, who was elected the **first stadtholder** [chief of state] of the northern provinces on July 18, 1572.

1572 Aug. 22 Catherine de Médicis arranged an attempt on the life of the Huguenot political leader, Admiral **Gaspard de Coligny**, at the time of the marriage between her daughter Margaret of Valois, sister of Charles IX, the young king of France, to Henry III of Bourbon, the Huguenot king of Navarre. Catherine was afraid that Charles, under the strong influence of Coligny, would upset the balance of power between Catholics and Protestants and would promote war with Spain. Though Coligny was only wounded, the Catholics persuaded Charles, with the consent of Catherine, to order a general **massacre of the Huguenots**.

1572 Aug. 24 The **Saint Bartholomew's Day Massacre**, begun in the early hours, lasted several days in Paris, claiming the lives of several thousand **Huguenots** there, including Admiral Gaspard de Coligny (b. 1519). Perhaps as many as 20,000 Huguenots were killed throughout France. La Rochelle, the principal Huguenot city of France, withstood a siege of six and one-half months by a Catholic army, which lost c.20,000 men.

1574 Tunis, from which the Turks had been driven the year before by Don John of Austria, was retaken for the **Ottoman Empire** (1326–1920) by **Sinan Pasha** (1515–Apr. 3, 1596), a Turkish general. Tunis was annexed to the Ottoman Empire under the authority of a pasha, or Turkish governor.

1574 May 30 Charles IX (b. June 27, 1550), king of France (ruled from 1560), died and was succeeded by his brother Henry, duke of Anjou, who was crowned **Henry III** on Feb. 13, 1575. Catherine de Médicis, the wife of Henry II, a former king of France, had successfully brought three of her four sons (Francis II, Charles IX, and Henry III) to the French throne.

1576 Sept. 4 The **bankruptcy of Spain** led to a mutiny in the Netherlands by unpaid Spanish soldiers. Beginning at Alost [Aalst], in present Belgium, the mutiny climaxed on Nov. 4 at Antwerp, also in present Belgium where, in the so-called **Spanish Fury**, thousands of civilians were massacred during the sack of the city. This bloodshed led to the signing of the **Pacification of Ghent** on Nov. 8 by which all 17 Dutch provinces agreed to unite against Spanish rule.

1577 Ralamba, emperor of **Ethiopia** (1575–1610), captured Harar, capital of the Emirate of Harar (1525–1887) [former Sultanate of Adal [Adel, Ifat, Awfat]], in present Ethiopia, and drove its remaining inhabitants northward to the salt plains around Lake Aussa [Lake Abbe]. There they were threatened by an invasion of the Galla, a tribe that had probably migrated to the area from Arabia via present Somalia.

1577 Aug. 17 The **Peace of Bergerac** ended the brief **Sixth War of Religion** in France (Mar.–Sept. 1577). Henri I de Lorraine, duke of Guise, had organized the Catholic Holy League in protest against the liberal settlement granted to the Huguenots in 1576. On Nov. 26, 1580, the **Peace of le Fleix**, near Bergerac, which suppressed briefly both the Protestant and Catholic leagues, ended the short **Seventh War of Religion** (Apr.–Nov. 1580), small skirmishes in southwestern France.

1578 Aug. 4 The troops of Sebastian [Sebastião] (b. 1554), king of Portugal from 1557, were annihilated by the Moroccans in a **battle at Alcazarquivir** [Al Kasr al-Kabir], near Fez, in their attempt to restore the deposed sultan of Morocco. Two rival sultans and Sebastian were killed during this **Battle of the Three Kings**, which secured **Morocco's independence** from Portugal. Under Ahmad II al-Mansur the new sultan (1578–1603), the **Saadi Dynasty** (1548–1666) continued its rule of Morocco.

1578 Oct. 1 Don John of Austria [Gerónimo] (b. Feb. 24, 1547), the Spanish governor of the Netherlands (from 1576), died. He was succeeded by **Alessandro Farnese** (Aug. 27, 1545–Dec. 2, 1592), the future duke of Parma. A skillful soldier and diplomat, Farnese exploited the cultural differences between the Spanish Netherlands's southern and northern provinces to secure reconciliation among the predominantly Catholic southern provinces by the **Treaties of Arras** signed on Jan. 6 and May 17, 1579.

1579 Jan. 23   The **Union of Utrecht** (to 1591) was organized by the northern, predominantly Protestant, Dutch provinces of the Spanish Netherlands and by the few southern territories that had wearied of Spanish rule. This was the foundation of the **United Provinces of the Netherlands** [the Dutch Republic].

III. ECONOMY AND TRADE

1575   A treaty of trade cooperation was signed by the Portuguese and the **Monomotapa** [Motapa, Mutapa] **Empire** (c.1440–c.1629), in present **Zimbabwe**.

1575   Spain levied the *alcabala*, a controversial sales tax, in her territory of **New Spain**.

1577 Mar. 1   **Portugal ended her monopoly of trade** with her colonial possessions, permitting them to trade more lucratively with other nations.

IV. RELIGION AND PHILOSOPHY

1570   Pope Pius V issued the bull *Regnans in excelsis*, in which he excommunicated **Elizabeth I**. In 1569 Pius had provided papal financial support to rebellious Catholics in northern England.

1572   **Remā** [Moses ben Israel Isserles] (born c.1525), one of Poland's most renowned Jewish scholars, died. Often compared with Spain's Maimonides, his intellect ranged from the Talmud to metaphysics to secular sciences.

1572   Unable to persuade Elizabeth I to reform the Anglican Church along Presbyterian lines, English **Puritans** turned to pamphleteering. In *An Admonition to Parliamanet*, two London ministers instructed members and the public on the marks of a truly Christian church, not surprisingly those that characterized Anglican churches following Puritan practices.

1572 Nov. 24   **John Knox** (b. 1514?), the spokesman of the Scottish Reformation, died. Knox strongly promoted the 1560 confession of faith that, with other measures passed at that time by the Scottish Parliament, crystalized the Protestant movement. The personal life of Mary Stuart, queen of Scotland, had done much to marshal public opinion against Catholicism and to support Knox as the religious leader of Protestant Scotland.

1577   **Ram Das** (1534–1581), **Sikhism's** fourth guru, founded the city of **Amritsar**, in the Punjab, India. The city, built around a holy pool called the *amrit-sar* [Pool of Nectar], became the center of Sikh worship. Ram Das was known for introducing hereditary succession to the Sikh guruship.

V. SCIENCE, EDUCATION, AND TECHNOLOGY

1570   **Abraham Ortelius** [Oertel, Wortels] (Apr. 14, 1527–1598), a Flemish cartographer, completed the **first modern world atlas**, the *Theatrum orbis terrarum*.

1570   The **earliest known music festival** was held in Normandy, France, in honor of St. Cecilia, the patroness of music.

1572   **Rafael Bombelli**, an Italian mathematician, published *L'Algebra parte maggiore dell'aritmetica*, the first systematic examination of the question of imaginary numbers. The work introduced an improved algebraic notation and helped in the ongoing attempts to solve the cubic equation.

VI. ARTS AND LEISURE

1570   **Akbar the Great**, ruler of the **Mogul** [Mughal] **Empire** of Hindustan (1526–1857), began construction of his new capital Fatehpur Sikri. The magnificent palace-city was inhabited for less than 15 years, when its water supply ran out.

1571 Feb. 13   **Benvenuto Cellini** (b. Nov. 3, 1500), an Italian sculptor and goldsmith, died. He worked under Michelangelo in Rome; Francis I, king of France, for whom he made a celebrated gold saltcellar (1540); and the Médici in Florence. The bronze relief "**Nymph of Fontainbleau**" (c.1543) was one of his best-known works. His *Autobiography* (begun 1558) was a self-centered account of Renaissance life in Italy and France.

1572   **Luíz Vaz de Camões** [Camoëns] (1524?–1580), a Portuguese poet, published the great

Renaissance epic *Os Lusíadas* [The Lusiads *or* the Portuguese], celebrating the voyage by Vasco da Gama to India and the triumph of humanism.

1573 The **Myoki-an**, a *chaseki* or tea house, the first of this characteristic Japanese architectural form, was built in Kyoto.

1575 Jan. 21 **Thomas Tallis** [Talys] (1505–Nov. 23, 1585) and **William Byrd** [Bird] were granted a 21-year license by Elizabeth I to print music. Together they collaborated on *Cantiones Sacrae*, printed the same year.

1576 Jan. 19 **Hans Sachs** (b. Nov. 5, 1494), a prolific writer of German meisterlieder, died. As many as 6,000 works altogether may be attributed to the character romanticized later by **Richard Wagner** in *Die Meistersinger von Nürnberg* (1868).

1576 Apr. 13 **James Burbage** (c.1531–1597), an English actor, obtained a lease to a site in Shoreditch where he built **The Theatre**, London's first. Torn down in 1597, the timber and materials were used in 1599 to build the **Globe Theatre**, home of **William Shakespeare**'s plays.

1576 Aug. 27 **Titian** [Tiziano Vecellio] **Pieve di Cadore** (born c.1490), the famous Italian painter, died of the plague in Venice. Throughout his long career he painted for royalty, perhaps the largest work being the mythological and religious series

begun in 1553 for Philip II, king of Spain, which included *The Last Supper* (1564), *The Adoration of the Magi*, and *Saint Jerome*.

c.1577 *The Chronicles of England, Scotland, and Ireland*, compiled by **Raphael Holinshed** [Hollingshead] (died c.1580) and others from various historical sources, provided material for many Elizabethan plays, among them William Shakespeare's *Macbeth* and *King Lear*.

1577 Jan. 25 The **Gelosi Troupe**, important performers of *commedia dell'arte*, arrived at Blois to perform for Henry III, king of France. On their way they had been captured by the Huguenots and had to be ransomed. Led by **Franscesco Andreini** (1548–1624) and his wife, Isabella (1562–1604), one of the leading actresses of the time, the Gelosi Troupe greatly influenced French theater.

1578 **Andrea Amati** (born c.1530), the **first of an Italian family of violin makers**, died. He was credited with the design of the modern violin, introducing the shape and the characteristic amber-colored varnish. The earliest surviving violin known to be an Amati has been dated to 1564.

VII. SPORTS, GAMES, AND SOCIETY

1575 Angelo Viggiani, an Italian **fencing** master, published a book describing his method of the lunge, which soon replaced the previous reliance upon passes in swordplay attack.

1580–1589

I. EXPLORATION AND COLONIZATION

1583 Aug. 3 **Humphrey Gilbert**, half-brother of the English explorer and colonizer **Walter Raleigh**, staked England's claim to **Newfoundland**, Canada, when he established at St. John's the **first English settlement**. Gilbert (born c.1539) died Sept. 15 when the small frigate in which he was returning to England sank with all hands.

1585–1587 **John Davys** [Davis] (c.1550–Dec. 30, 1605), an English explorer in search of the **Northwest Passage**, pushed through the strait between Baffin Island and Greenland [Davis Strait] to discover un-

wittingly the key to this northern route. The Northwest Passage was not actually traversed until 1903–1906 by the Norwegian explorer **Roald Amundsen**.

1585 Aug. **English colonists landed at Roanoke Island** in the Croatan Sound along the coast of present North Carolina. The colony, sponsored by **Walter Raleigh**, had disappeared by 1591.

II. POLITICS AND WAR

c.1580–1589 A warlike **Bantu tribe**, the Zimba, from an area around Lake Rukwa, in present **Tanzania**, plundered the Portuguese settlements at Sena and Tete, in present Mozambique, and then began to raid the East African coast, loosely held by Portugal. They decimated Kilwa, in present Tanzania, which lost (1587) nearly one-half of its c.6,000 inhabitants and sacked the coastal city of Mombassa in present Kenya, thus enabling the Portuguese to occupy (1588) the city. They were finally annihilated (1589) at Malindi in present Kenya by the Portuguese, aided by Segeju tribesmen.

c.1580   **Idris Aloma**, king of Bornu (ruled 1571–1603), reconquered Kanem and established the strongest state the central **Sudan** had ever known. Idris Aloma introduced legal and administrative reforms based on Islamic law, which unified his country, and built a powerful army, equipped with firearms, noted for its cavalry of armored horses and men.

1580 Jan. 31   **Henry** (b. 1512), a cardinal of the Church and the last king of Portugal in the direct line of the ruling **house of Aviz**, died. On Aug. 25 an invading Spanish army, led by Fernando Álvarez de Toledo, duke of Alva, defeated the Portuguese under Dom Antonio (1531–1595), prior of Crato, to assert the claim of Philip II, king of Spain. Philip was recognized as Philip I of Portugal on Apr. 1, 1581, and the country remained under Spanish Hapsburg rule until 1640.

1581   The **Tatar** [Tartar] **Khanate of Siberia** came under Russian control, doubling the size of Russia. The khanate had existed from the 13th century following the death of Genghis Khan in 1227. Ermak Timofeev (d. 1584), a Russian national folk hero, and his Cossacks, semiautonomous peasant-soldiers, were hired by **Ivan the Terrible**, czar of Russia, to subdue the tribes east of the Ural Mountains.

1581   The Poles under **Stephen Báthory** [István Báthory or Báthoril] (Sept. 27, 1533–Dec. 12, 1586), king of Transylvania (from 1571) and Poland (from 1575), defeated the Russian army in a **battle at Polotsk** [Pskov], in present Belarus [Byelorusse], forcing Ivan the Terrible to yield (Jan. 15, 1582) Livonia to Poland [**Peace of Zapoli**] and end the **Livonian War** (1557–1582).

1584 Mar. 18   **Ivan IV the Terrible** (b. Aug. 25, 1530), czar of Russia (from 1547), died. He was succeeded by his youngest son **Fëdor I Ivanovich** (ruled to 1598).

1584 June 15   The last son of Catherine de Médicis, Francois (b. 1554), brother of Henry III, king of France, and duke of Anjou, who was the closest heir to the French throne, died. Henry of Bourbon, king of Navarre, was heir to the throne by marriage (in 1572), but as a Protestant, he was opposed by the Catholic League under **Henri I de Lorraine**, duke of Guise. The **War of the Three Henrys** [**Eighth War of Religion**] (1585–1598) ensued over the future succession.

1584 July 10   **William I the Silent** (b. Apr. 24, 1553), prince of Orange and count of Nassau, was murdered at Delft, the United Provinces [the Netherlands], by **Balthasar Gérard** (1558–1584), a Catholic from a region of France controlled by the Spanish Hapsburgs. In 1578 Philip II, king of Spain, had offered a reward for the life of William, the **father of Dutch independence** from Spain. William's son, Maurice of Nassau (Nov. 13, 1567–Apr. 23, 1625), succeeded him as stadholder (to 1625) of the Dutch Republic (1581–1795) and of the **Union of Utrecht** (1579–1591).

1585 Aug. 17   **Antwerp**, in present Belgium, was sacked by **Alessandro Farnese**, governor of the Spanish Netherlands, and later duke of Parma (1586) in the **Dutch War of Independence**. Farnese drove all the remaining Protestants into exile.

1586 Sept. 20   The **Babington Plot** to murder **Elizabeth I** and install **Mary, queen of Scots**, failed with the execution of Anthony Babington (b. Oct., 1561); a priest, John Ballard (birth date unknown), the alleged instigator; and others. Mary's role in the plot was discovered by Francis Walsingham (1530?–Apr. 6, 1590), and she was tried and convicted on Oct. 25. Mary (b. Dec. 7, 1542) was beheaded on Feb. 4, 1587, at Fotheringhay Castle.

1587   Mohammed Khudabanda, Persian shah (from 1578) of the **Safawid** [Safavid] **Dynasty** (1501–1736) was deposed and succeeded by his son **Abbas I the Great** (1571–1629). Abbas was forced to make peace (1590) with the Ottomans to the west in order to meet the threat of the **Uzbeks**, who had moved southwest from Khwarizm [Khwarezm, Khuwarizm, Khwarazen], in present Uzbekistan, to overrun most of Khorasan [Khurasan], in northeastern Persia. With a standing army organized and trained by an English soldier-of-fortune, Robert Shirley [Sherley] (c.1581–July 13, 1628), Abbas defeated (1597) the Uzbeks near Herat in

Afghanistan, and transferred his capital to Isfahan [Eşan], Persia [Iran].

1587 Apr. 19 A fleet led by **Francis Drake** plundered the Spanish port of Cadiz, taking much booty and preventing, for a year, an invasion of England by the **Spanish Armada.**

1588 May 12 The populace of Paris rose against **Henry III**, king of France, forcing him to flee to Chartres. Henry had **Henri I de Lorraine**, duke of Guise (b. 1550) and his brother, Cardinal **Louis II de Lorraine** (b. 1555), assassinated at a meeting of the **États Généraux** [States General] at Blois on Dec. 23, and signed an alliance with the Protestant Henry of Bourbon, king of Navarre, on Apr. 3, 1589.

1588 Aug. 8 The **Armada of Spain** proved vincible when it met the English fleet off the coast of England at Gravelines, near Dunkerque [Dunkirk], both ports then in the Spanish Netherlands but now in France. The English victory owed much to the leadership of **Charles Howard** (1536–Dec. 14, 1624), baron of Effingham and lord high admiral of England, **Francis Drake**, and **John Hawkins** (1532–Nov. 12, 1595), but it was helped by storms at sea.

1589 Aug. 2 **Henry III** (b. Sept. 19, 1551), king of France and **last of the House of Valois** (from 1328), was fatally stabbed at Saint-Cloud, now a suburb of Paris, by the Jacobin monk **Jacques Clément** (1567–1589). His designated successor, Henry of Bourbon, the Protestant king of Navarre, established his headquarters at Tours in France as Henry IV to meet the combined challenge of the Catholic League and Philip II, king of Spain.

III. ECONOMY AND TRADE

1587 The **Banco di Rialto in Venice**, a public bank, was established by the government of Venice. It was forbidden to lend money.

1589 The **first patent for the use of coal** in the manufacture of iron was issued in Great Britain.

IV. RELIGION AND PHILOSOPHY

1582 **Matteo Ricci** (Oct. 6, 1552–May 11, 1610), an Italian Jesuit missionary, won the confidence of **Wan Li** [Shên Tsung] (1563–1620) the Chinese Ming emperor (from 1573), who allowed him to **introduce Christianity to China.**

1582 *A* ***Treatise of Reformation***, a radical Congregational view of the true church, was published by **Robert Browne** (1550–1633), a Separatist preacher in England who had recently fled with members of his Norwich congregation to the United Provinces [the Netherlands] to escape persecution.

1582 The **English-language Rheims New Testament** was published by Roman Catholic scholars at Rheims, France. The Englishman **Gregory Martin** (c.1540–Oct. 28, 1582), who was chiefly responsible for the translation, completed his work in the four years between 1578 and his death.

1582 A report to Rome of **Jesuit missionaries in Japan** claimed 150,000 converts. The feudal lord in Nagasaki burned Buddhist temples and welcomed the Jesuits, who usually engaged in trade themselves.

1587 **Toyotomi Hideyoshi**, Japan's most powerful warlord, ordered the **Jesuits to leave Japan.** Competition between various orders, especially Franciscans and Jesuits, had soured Hideyoshi's initial acceptance of the foreign missionaries.

V. SCIENCE, EDUCATION, AND TECHNOLOGY

1582 Mar. The **Gregorian Calendar** was promulgated by **Pope Gregory XIII** (June 7, 1502–Apr. 10, 1585; ruled from 1572). When it went into effect in the Holy Roman Empire on Oct. 5, the date became Oct. 15, correcting the ten-day discrepancy between the astronomical equinox and the calendar date for spring, Mar. 21.

1585 **Simon Stevin** [Stevinus] (1548–1620), a Flemish mathematician and engineer, published *De thiende* [The Tenth], a plea for the use of systematic decimal fractions for both engineering and mathematics.

VI. ARTS AND LEISURE

c.1580 **Wu Ch'êng-ên** (born c.1510), a Chinese author, died. His *Hsi-yu chi* [Monkey], a tale of the pilgrimage made by Hsüan-Tsang (600?–664) to India (c.630), was based on previous versions of the tale, incorporating Indian legend, that had appeared during the Sung and Yüan dynasties.

1580 Aug. Andrea Palladio [Andrea di Pietro] (b. Nov. 30, 1508), an Italian architect, died. The *Villa Rotunda*, symmetrical on both axes, and the *Teatro Olimpico* (built 1580–1584), employing perspective in its stage set, were examples of his style, which Inigo Jones brought to England. There, during the Georgian period, it came to be called Palladian.

1581 The *Geuzenlied Boek*, an anthology of Dutch marching, military, and historical songs, was published. Included was the national anthem "*Wilhelmus van Nassauwe*," composed in 1568 by **Marnix de Ste. Aldegonde** (1540–Dec. 15, 1598) in honor of William the Silent, leader of the Dutch provinces in revolt against Spain.

1581 Juan de la Cueva de la Garoza (1550?–?1610), a Spanish dramatist, wrote *El infamador* [*The Scoundrel*], a comedy that anticipated the work of Lope de Vega.

1585 Dec. 27 Pierre de Ronsard (b. Sept. 11, 1525), who was instrumental in developing French lyric poetry, died. He was known for *Odes* (1550, 1552), *Amours* (1552, 1555–1556), and *Sonnets Pour Hélène* (1578), a celebrated collection of love poetry.

1586 Oct. 17 Philip Sidney [Sydney] (b. Nov. 30, 1554), an English poet influential at Queen Elizabeth's court, died in the battle of Zutphen, an unsuccessful attempt to liberate the Dutch city from the Spanish. Sidney is now remembered chiefly for the sonnet sequence *Astrophel and Stella* (1591).

c.1587 *The Spanish Tragedy*, the most popular English drama of the time, was written by **Thomas Kyd** [Kid] (Nov. 6, 1558–Dec., 1594). Its plot was based on bloody revenge, a common theme in Elizabethan drama.

1587 Christopher Marlowe, in his first play, *Tamburlaine the Great*, established himself as one of the great Elizabethan playwrights.

1588 *Rakuware*, perhaps the most renowned of **Japanese pottery** styles, was so dubbed when a prize engraved with the word, "raku," meaning felicity, was given by a state official to **Tanaka Chojiro**, whose family was instrumental in developing the low-temperature lead glaze used in decorating the simple forms of rakuware.

1588 Paolo Veronese [Pado Cagliari] (born c.1528), a Venetian decorative painter, died. His *Feast in the House of Levi* (1573) was criticized by the **Inquisition** for its secular approach to religious subject matter.

1589 Richard Hakluyt (c.1553–Nov. 23, 1616), an English clergyman and scholar, completed *The Principall Navigations, Voiages, Traffiques and Discoveries of the English Nation*. This and Hakluyt's other works provided documentation of numerous voyages, especially to the New World, and helped to generate more exploration by the English.

1590–1599

I. EXPLORATION AND COLONIZATION

1592 The **Falkland Islands** [Islas Malvinas], off the coast of South America c.300 miles east of Cape Horn, were discovered by John Davys, an English navigator.

1593 The Portuguese built and garrisoned Fort Jesus at Mombasa, a coastal city of present **Kenya**, in order to protect their East African trade, which had been disrupted during their conquest of the coastal towns and diverted by the Muslims still holding the hinterland.

1595 The Spanish settlement on **Trinidad**, off the coast of present Venezuela, was destroyed by **Walter Raleigh's** fleet. They had set sail for the Orinoco River of Venezuela to search for gold and scout the possibility of establishing a British settlement in Spanish America.

1595 Alvaro de Mendaña de Neyra (1541–1595), a Spanish navigator, discovered the **Marquesas Islands**, the first inhabited Polynesian islands visited by Europeans.

1596 **Willem Barents**, a Dutch navigator, discovered the **Spitsbergen** [Svalbard] **Archipelago** in the Arctic Ocean, north of Norway. Sailing in search of the Northeast Passage, Barents and his crew were frozen in near the Russian island of Novaya Zemlya [New Land]. Barents (born c.1550) died on June 20, 1597, when he and his crew abandoned their ship and made their way to the mainland in two small boats.

II. POLITICS AND WAR

1590 **Ahmad II al-Mansur**, the Saadi sultan of Morocco, sent an army of 3,000 men, equipped with firearms, to conquer the salt mines and gold possessions of the **Songhai Empire**. They took (1591) Gao and Tombouctou [Timbuktu], where Judar Pasha, the Moroccan commander, was enthroned as the first Moroccan sultan of Timbuktu.

1590 **Toyotomi Hideyoshi**, virtual head of government of **Japan**, gained control of most of the country by a series of military campaigns. His most powerful vassal **Tokugawa Iyeyasu** (1542–1616) governed eastern Japan from Edo [Tokyo]. Hideyoshi, son of a woodcutter, following **Oda Nobunaga** (1534–1582), the shogun of Japan (from 1568), in the struggle to reunify Japan, had been appointed (1585) regent-dictator by the emperor.

1590 Mar. 14 **Henry IV**, Protestant king of France, defeated the **Catholic League** led by Charles de Lorraine (Mar. 26, 1554–Oct. 3, 1611), duke of Mayenne, at Ivry-la-Bataille, c.40 miles west of Paris, and then marched on Paris. They established a siege there, lasting until September, when Paris was relieved by a Spanish army under Alessandro Farnese, duke of Parma.

1592 **Toyotomi Hideyoshi**, regent-dictator of Japan, **invaded Korea** to establish a military base for the conquest of China. China aided Korea in repulsing (1593) the Japanese.

1592 Nov. 17 **John III** (b. Dec. 21, 1537), king of **Sweden** (from 1568), died and was succeeded (1594) by his son **Sigismund III Vasa** (June 20, 1566–Apr. 30, 1632), already king of Poland from 1587, having inherited the throne from his uncle **Sigismund II Augustus** (Aug. 1, 1520–July 7, 1572), king of Poland (from 1548). As a Catholic, Sigismund III Vasa was unpopular in Lutheran Sweden and was deposed in 1599.

1594 Feb. 27 The **French House of Bourbon** (1589–1792; 1814–1848) was firmly established with the official and Roman Catholic coronation of Henry of Bourbon, king of Navarre, as Henry IV, king of France, at Chartres. Henry freely entered (Mar. 22) Paris, abandoned by the Catholic League and relieved of Spanish occupation.

1595 Jan. 17 Henry IV, king of France, formally declared war on Spain, and won an important victory in a **battle at Fontaine-Française**, near Dijon, on June 5. Philip II, king of Spain, was abandoned by the **Catholic League** when its leader, Charles de Lorraine, duke of Mayenne, submitted to Henry IV on Jan. 31, 1596, by the **Articles of Folembray**.

1597 **Dom Joao Dharmapala**, the Christian king of Kotte (origin obscure) in Ceylon [Sri Lanka], died, and left his **Singhalese kingdom** to the Portuguese.

1598 The British captured the city of **San Juan on Puerto Rico**, held by the Spanish, but an attack of plague drove the British from the island five months later.

1598 Jan. 7 **Fëdor I Ivanovich** (b. 1557), czar of Russia (from 1584) and **last of the Rurik Dynasty** (879–1598) to hold the throne, died without a male heir. **Boris Fëdorovich Godunov**, brother-in-law of Fëdor I and a powerful boyar, was elected (Feb. 21) czar of Russia by the *zemsky sobor*.

1598 Mar. 20 Phillipe Emmanuel de Lorraine (Sept. 9, 1558–Feb. 19, 1602), duke of Mercoeur, governor of Brittany and the last opponent of **Henry IV**, king of France, submitted by the **Treaty of Ponts-de-Cé**. Philip II, king of Spain, abandoned his claim to the French crown by the **Treaty of Vervins** (May 2), which also restored all Spanish conquests (except Cambrai [Cambray], which protruded into the Spanish Netherlands), to France. Henry now ruled a reunited France.

1598 Aug. 14 **Hugh O'Neill** (1540–1616), earl of Tyrone, defeated an English force at the Yellow Ford, on the Blackwater River, in Munster, a former province of southern Ireland. **Revolt against the English** swept through **Ireland**. Elizabeth I appointed Robert Devereux, earl of Essex, lord lieutenant of Ireland, and English forces landed in Dublin on Apr. 15, 1599, to restore order.

1598 Sept. 13 Philip II (May 21, 1527–Sept. 13, 1598), the Hapsburg king of Spain (from 1556), died and was succeeded by his son, **Philip III** (Apr. 14, 1578–Mar. 31, 1621). On Nov. 13, Philip III married his cousin, a Hapsburg, Margaret of Austria (1584–1611), and Margaret's brother Albert (1559–1621), archduke of Austria, married the Spanish **Infanta Isabella** [Isabel Clara Eugenia] (1566–1633). The Spanish Netherlands were granted to Albert as a dowry.

1598 Sept. 25 Charles, regent for the Swedish crown, defeated Sigismund III Vasa, king of Poland and of Sweden (from 1594) in a **battle at Linkoping** [Stangbro], southwest of Stockholm. By 1599 Charles was acting as king of Sweden as **Charles IX**.

1599 Sept. 7 **Robert Devereux**, earl of Essex and lord lieutenant of Ireland, was defeated by **rebel Irish forces** near Dublin and signed a truce with their leader Hugh O'Neill, earl of Tyrone. He was retired in shame from his command by Elizabeth I. **Charles Blount** (c.1562–Apr. 3, 1606), earl of Devonshire, succeeded Devereux as lord lieutenant of Ireland, and the war was resumed in Jan. 1600.

III. ECONOMY AND TRADE

1590 **Coal mining** first began in Germany's Ruhr Valley region.

1591 Spain issued a royal decree requiring that sufficient land in the **New World** be set aside to protect the native peoples. The decree was largely ignored by the Spanish colonists.

1592 The **Levant Company** was chartered to conduct England's trade in the Near East.

1595 A **Protestant Dutch expedition sailed in search of spices** that could no longer be imported from Portugal, ruled by Catholic Spain since 1580. In 1597 the expedition returned from the East Indies with a load of spices.

IV. RELIGION AND PHILOSOPHY

1593 Apr. 6 **Henry Barrow** (born c.1550), a London lawyer of Separatist views, and John Greenwood (birth date unknown), a London Separatist clergyman, were hanged for **denying the crown's supremacy in ecclesiastical matters**. Later in 1593, the En-glish Parliament adopted more stringent laws prohibiting religious assemblies at any private place. Great numbers of Separatists emigrated to the United Provinces [the Netherlands].

1593 July 25 **Henry IV**, king of France, who had been brought up a Huguenot, converted to Catholicism, which he declared the state religion of France. By this politically motivated act he was able to end the civil hostilities between Protestants and Catholics that had badly torn France for more than 60 years.

1598 Apr. 13 By the **Edict of Nantes**, Henry IV, king of France, provided Protestants with the right to live in equality of citizenship anywhere in France, the right to bipartisan hearings on political or religious charges, and the right to assemble and worship in a number of specified places.

V. SCIENCE, EDUCATION, AND TECHNOLOGY

1590 **Bernard Palissy** (born c.1510), a French potter and scientist, died in the Bastille where he had been imprisoned for his Huguenot beliefs. Concerned with the qualities of various earths, he became interested in hydrology and the study of fossils. His *Discours admirables* (1580) proposed the reconstruction of ancient shorelines by studying fossil records.

1590 The **first compound microscope**, using a second lens with which to magnify the image further, was invented by **Zacharias Janssen** (fl.1570–1630), a Dutch eyeglasses maker.

1590 Dec. 20 **Ambroise Paré** (b. 1510), a great French surgeon, died. His skill as a physician was sought by four monarchs. More importantly, he reformed surgery by introducing the **technique of ligature**, tying wounds closed after an operation.

1596 **John Harington** (1562–Nov. 20, 1612), an English courtier, designed an early **flush toilet**.

1598 A forerunner of the **armored ship**, called the **"turtle boat"** because it was a shell of four-inch thick wood with a hole for a mast, was built by a Korean admiral, Yi Sunsin. These vessels were instrumental in winning for Korea a major naval **battle in Chinhae Bay** over the invading Japanese.

VI. ARTS AND LEISURE

c.1590 Robert Greene (July, 1558–Sept. 3, 1592), an English poet and playwright, began to publish his "conycatching" pamphlets, vivid descriptions of the criminal underworld of London. Among his tracts was *A Groatsworth of Wit Bought with a Million of Repentence* (1592), which contained an attack on **William Shakespeare**, one of the first contemporary references to him.

1590 Aug. 15 Robert Garnier (born c.1545), a French dramatic poet, died. His *Bradamante* (1582), based on *Orlando furioso* (1532) was the **first French tragicomedy**. *Sédécie, ou les Juives* [*The Jewesses*] (1583) was the best known of his tragedies.

1591 Juan Suárez de Peralta (b. 1537), the **first notable Spanish prose writer born in the New World**, died. He wrote on the Spanish conquest of Mexico.

1591 June Vincenzo Galilei (born c.1520), an Italian music critic and composer, died. An admirer of classical Greek simplicity, his *Dialogo della Musica Antica e Moderna* (1581) attacked the contrapuntal theories of Gioseffo Zarlino (1517–1590), an Italian composer.

1592 Sept. 13 Michel Eyquem de Montaigne (b. Feb. 28, 1533), a French essayist, died. His three volumes of *Essais* (1571–1590, 1588) were inspired by a classical education, which included study of Plutarch, and by the numerous houseguests he entertained. Montaigne was the epitome of a skeptical and tolerant humanistic intelligence in an age of sectarian brutality and intolerance.

c.1593 The bunraku, a **Japanese theater** form which combined marionettes with storytelling and singing, was first performed when the narrator Menukiya Chozaburo invited the puppet players of his town to act out the story he was telling.

1593 May 30 Christopher Marlowe (b. Feb. 26, 1564), an English dramatist, was stabbed to death in a brawl, alleged to have been over a tavern bill, but thought now to have had some official sanction. Among Marlowe's plays were *Tamburlaine* (1587), *The Tragical History of Dr. Faustus* (1588), and *The Jew of Malta* (1589).

1594 May 31 Tintoretto [Jacopo Robusti] (b. 1518?), one of the greatest Venetian painters, died.

He painted (1564–1587) scenes of Christ, the Virgin, and the Passion, filling three rooms of the Scuola di San Rocco. Among his best-known works were *Susannah and the Elders* (1555–1560) and *The Last Supper* (1592–1594).

1594 Feb. 2 Giovanni Pierluigi da Palestrina (b. 1525), the foremost Italian composer of the 16th century Renaissance, died. As a master of counterpoint, he influenced generations of musicians. The hymn *Stabat Mater* and the mass *Missa Papae Marcelli* were particularly good examples of his work.

1594 June 14 Orlando di Lasso [Roland de Lattre] (b. 1532), a Flemish composer, died. He was a versatile and prolific writer, producing works in every musical form used in his day. His love songs set Petrarchan verse to music. *Penitential Psalms of David* (1584) was considered the best of his works.

1595 Apr. 25 Torquato Tasso (b. Mar. 11, 1544), an Italian poet subject to episodes of insanity, died. *Gerusalemme Liberata* [*Jerusalem Delivered*] (1575), a masterpiece of the Counter Reformation, was an epic detailing Jerusalem's capture during the First Crusade.

1596 Ju Tzayyuh, a Chinese prince of the **Ming Dynasty** (1368–1644), published the *Book of Songs*, a treatise covering music from the earliest times through the 16th century. In his 19-volume *Handbook of Music*, an encyclopedic work covering music, dance, and ritual in ancient China, he attempted to reconstruct the music of the **Chou Dynasty** (c.1027–c.256 B.C.).

1597 *Sacrae symphoniae* was published, containing "Sonata pian'e forte," the **first piece of music to specify the use of dynamics and instrumentation**. It was written by **Giovanni Gabrieli** (1557?–Aug. 12, 1612). Giovanni's experimentation with choral orchestration at St. Mark's Cathedral in Venice prepared the way for development of the concerto.

1597 *Dafne*, considered the **first opera**, was performed at the carnival in Florence. The pastoral play was written by **Ottavio Rinuccini** (1562–1621) and set to music by **Jacopo Peri**.

1597 Dec.? *Love's Labour's Lost* was the first play published under **William Shakespeare's** own name.

1598   George Chapman (c.1559–May 12, 1634), an English dramatist, completed the first part of his translation of Homer's *Iliad.*

1598 Sept.   Ben Jonson, an English playwright, achieved his first great success with *Every Man in His Humour*, which opened in London.

1599   The Spanish novel *Guzmán de Alfarache* by Mateo Alemán (1547–?1614), was the first to use the word *picaro* (the origin of the word picaresque) to describe its hero.

1599 Aug. 22   Luca Marenzio [Marencio] (b. 1553), an Italian composer who brought the madrigal to the height of its development during the Renaissance, died. His complex interlude *Il Combattimento d'Appoline col Serpente* was a fine example of the new

baroque style in which harmony formed the basis of composition.

1599 Jan. 13   Edmund Spenser (b. 1552?) died and was buried in Westminster Abbey. *Shepheardes Calendar* (1579), dedicated to his friend Philip Sidney, established Spenser as a poet of moral vision. His masterpiece was *The Faerie Queene* (1589; 1596).

VII. SPORTS, GAMES, AND SOCIETY

1592   The first rules for court, or royal, tennis were written by a Frenchman, Forbet. Henry VIII, king of England, had a court built (1529–1530) at Hampton Court, still in use today.

1600–1609

I. VITAL STATISTICS AND DEMOGRAPHICS

1600   World population at this time was estimated at c.545 million. In the area of the present U.S. and Canada, there were c.1 million Indians comprising over 230 tribal groups. By 1620 there were only c.210 Europeans in colonial North America; by 1630, c.2,500; by 1640, almost 6,000; and by 1650, c.30,000. By 1600, the c.100,000 original Spanish colonists in the Americas had swelled to c.250,000, and they controlled the c.9 million Indians centered in present Peru and Mexico. The population of Indians in the Americas, an estimated 14 to 50 million before Columbus, had dropped by 20 percent as a result of smallpox and measles, against which the Indians had no resistance. For example, during an epidemic (1545) c.800,000 Indians of Central America died.

1609 Sept. 22   Spain undertook to expel its remaining Morisco population, which numbered c.300,000 descendants of the original Muslim invaders. Some Moriscos had accepted Christianity, but most were Muslim. The Spanish economy was disrupted by this great deportation. In North Africa the refugees contributed to the strengthening of the Barbary states.

II. DISASTERS

1601–1604   Drought, crop failure, and an outbreak of the plague characterized the reign of Boris Fedorovich Godunov, czar of Russia. Chronicles of the time tell of people eating grass, mice, and carrion, and of human flesh sold in pies in marketplaces.

III. EXPLORATION AND COLONIZATION

c.1600   *The Paulistas* [men from São Paulo] of Brazil began a century and a half of expeditions, called *bandeiras*, into the Brazilian hinterlands to take Indians as slaves.

1600 May 16   Will Adams (1564–1620), a member of a Dutch expedition, was the first Englishman to reach Japan. Out of five ships in the fleet, only one, *Charity*, reached Japan. Scurvy had reduced the *Charity*'s crew from over 100 to 27. Adams accepted an invitation by Tokugawa Iyeyasu [Ieyasu], the shogun of Japan, to organize Japan's shipbuilding. He married a Japanese woman and remained in Japan for the rest of his life.

1602   Sebastián Vizcaíno (1550?–1615), a Spanish explorer, charted the coast of California. Vizcaíno entered Monterey Bay, where he discovered the ruins of an Indian city noted by **Juan Rodríguez Cabrillo** in 1542.

1603   Martin Pring (c.1580–1626), the **first European to explore present New Hampshire**, sailed into the mouth of the Piscataqua River. Pring had been on his way to Virginia. John Smith (c.1580–June, 1631) explored the coast of New England and landed on the Isles of Shoals, near present Portsmouth, New Hampshire, in 1614.

1604   Samuel de Champlain (c.1567–Dec. 25, 1635), commissioned by Henry IV, king of France, sailed to what came to be called New France to colonize Acadia [present Nova Scotia, Prince Edward Island, New Brunswick and part of present Maine]. The expedition was financed by **Pierre du Guast** (c.1560–1630), sieur de Monts, a wealthy Huguenot. They founded (1605) **Port Royal** [Annapolis Royal], Nova Scotia, one of the oldest settlements in North America.

1604   Cayenne, now the capital, was founded in French Guiana, on the northeastern coast of South America.

1606   The Spanish explorers **Don Diego de Prado y Tovar** and **Luis Vaez de Torres** (both fl. early 17th century), sailed through what is now known as **Torres Strait**, which separates New Guinea and Australia. While attempting to sail north of New Guinea, they established that it was an island, separate from the vaguely known region of **Terra Australis Incognita**.

1606   The Dutch ship **Duyfken**, commanded by **Willem Jansz** [Janszoon], was the **first European vessel to make a recorded landing on the continent of Australia**, which he called New Holland. He came ashore on the York Peninsula, in present Queensland, thinking it was a part of New Guinea.

1606   The **New Hebrides Islands** in Melanesia in the Pacific Ocean were discovered by the Portuguese explorer **Pedro Fernandes de Queirós** (1560?–1614).

1607 May 13   The **first permanent English settlement in the U.S.** was founded at **Jamestown**, Virginia, by the London Company. Captain **John Smith** and more than 100 colonists had sailed to the New World aboard the *Sarah Constant, Godspeed,* and

Discovery. During their first year nearly half of them died. The successful planting of tobacco was an important factor in permanently establishing the colony.

1607 Aug. 22   Bartholomew Gosnold died of swamp fever in Jamestown, Virginia, where he had gone in command of the *Godspeed.* In 1602, in command of the ship **Concord**, he had explored the North American coast from Maine to **Narragansett Bay**. He named Cape Cod, Martha's Vineyard, and other islands in **Nantucket Sound**.

1608 July 3   The site of present **Québec**, where the Indian village Stadacona once stood, was founded as a trading post by **Samuel de Champlain** and by colonists from the earlier settlement of Port Royal, which they had been forced to leave after Pierre du Guast, sieur de Monts, had lost his trade monopoly in Acadia.

1609   New Amsterdam was founded as a trading post on the present site of New York City by **Henry Hudson**, an English navigator in the service of the **Dutch East India Company**. Aboard the *Half Moon*, he had sailed to find the Northeast Passage and, near Spitsbergen in the Arctic Ocean, his crew had threatened mutiny. Hudson changed course and explored the coast of North America from **Chesapeake Bay** to the **Hudson River,** which he ascended to the areas of **Albany**, establishing the Dutch claim to New York state.

IV. POLITICS AND WAR

1600 July 2   Spanish Hapsburg forces under Albert [Albrecht], archduke of Austria, were decisively defeated in a **battle at Nieuwpoort**, near Oostend [Ostend], Belgium, by a combined force of Dutch and English under Maurice of Nassau, the Dutch Protestant leader. The **independence of the United Provinces** [the Netherlands] was secured against the Hapsburg claim to the northern provinces. The Hapsburgs remained in control of present Belgium, Luxembourg, and part of France.

1600 Sept.   Tokugawa Iyeyasu [Ieyasu] defeated his rivals in a **battle at Sekigahara**, Honshu, to secure his control of Japan. Iyeyasu was appointed (1603) shogun (to 1605) and founded the **Tokugawa Shogunate** (1603–1867) from his capital at Edo [Tokyo].

1601 Jan. 17 The **Treaty of Lyon** ended a war between France and the duchy of Savoy. France gained Bresse, Bugey, Gex, and Valromey, extending her territories to the Swiss border. **Charles Emmanuel I the Great** (Jan. 12, 1562–July 26, 1630), duke of Savoy (ruled from 1580), retained the margraviate of Saluzzo, Italy.

1601 Feb. 7 The deposed English governor general of Ireland, **Robert Devereux**, earl of Essex, attempted a revolt in London against **Elizabeth I**. Essex (b. Nov. 10, 1566?) was arrested, brought to trial, and executed on Feb. 25.

1601 Oct. 26 The **Irish chieftains**, led by the absent **Hugh O'Neill**, earl of Tyrone, submitted when Catholic Spanish troops, allied in O'Neill's cause against Protestant England, were surrounded at Kinsale on the southern Irish coast by English troops under Charles Blount, earl of Montjoy. O'Neill, marching south to aid the Irish and Spanish forces, was unable to stop an attack (Dec. 24) against the English, who won the day and accepted the Spanish surrender. The Spaniards evacuated Ireland, and Philip II, king of Spain, abandoned support of the Irish.

1603 Mar. 24 **Elizabeth I** (b. Sept. 7, 1533), **last of the Tudor Dynasty**, died and was succeeded by **James VI**, king of Scotland and a descendant of Margaret Tudor, sister to Henry VIII, king of England. He was crowned **James I**, king of England, on July 25, initiating the **Stuart Dynasty** (1603–1714). As James VI he had restored order in Scotland, forcing the Presbyterian baronage to recognize the authority of the crown.

1603 Mar. 30 **Hugh O'Neill**, earl of Tyrone, submitted to the English lord lieutenant of Ireland, Charles Blount, earl of Mountjoy. The Irish rebel leader, his country devastated, hoped for more tolerance with the succession of James I to the English throne.

1603 July 11 The **Treaty of Saint-Julien-en-Genevois** was signed by **Geneva** and Charles Emmanuel, duke of Savoy. After a last attempt (Dec. 12, 1602) to capture the city, on the northern border of the duchy, Charles Emmanuel, who had just won Saluzzo (1601) on the duchy's eastern border, was forced to recognize the independence of Geneva, which had proclaimed itself a republic in 1536.

1603 Oct. 21 **Abbas I the Great**, the Persian shah of the **Safawid** [Safavid] **Dynasty** (1501–1736), representing the Shiite Muslim sect, took the offensive and recaptured the former Persian capital of Tabriz, near Lake Urmia in present Iran, to check the territorial expansion of the **Ottoman Empire** (1326–1920) to the west.

1605 Apr. 23 **Boris Fëdorovich Godunov** (born c.1551), czar of **Russia** (ruled from 1598), died suddenly. His son **Fëdor II** (b. 1589), who succeeded him briefly, was murdered on order of the boyars in June. From Poland and with some Polish help **Pseudo-Demetrius** [Demetrius, Dimitry, Dmitry], who claimed to be the youngest son of Ivan IV the Terrible, entered (June 30) Moscow with a small army to claim the throne. Supported, at least at first, by the populace, Demetrius was crowned czar (Aug. 9) as **Demetrius II**, but his foreign wife, retainers, and manners quickly alienated the boyars, led by **Prince Basil IV Shuiski** [Vasily Shuiski] (1552–Sept. 12, 1612). Basil held the throne for four years (to 1610).

1605 Nov. 5 The **Gunpowder Plot**, a Catholic conspiracy aimed at murdering James I, king of England, and blowing up Parliament, was discovered. **Guy Fawkes** (1570–1606), **Thomas Percy** (1560–1605), **Thomas Winter** (1572–1606), and others were either killed while resisting arrest, or executed with their leader, **Robert Catesby** (b. 1573), on Jan. 31, 1606. November 5th is celebrated each year in England as **Guy Fawkes' Day**.

1606 June 23 The **Treaty of Vienna**, followed by the **Treaty of Zsivatorok** on Nov. 11, ended a revolt by the Protestants in the western part of **Hungary** controlled by the Austrian Hapsburgs. The Hungarians had been supported by **István Bocskay** (1557–Dec. 29, 1606), who had arrived with an army from Transylvania, and by the **Ottoman Empire** (1326–1920). The Hapsburgs recognized Bocskay as prince of Transylvania (1605–1607) and restored constitutional rights and religious liberties to Imperial Hungary, which agreed to cease paying tribute to the Ottomans.

1608 The **Peace of Liben** ended an insurrection in Hungary which had been led by István Bocskay against the anti-Protestant policies of the Catholic Rudolf II, the Holy Roman emperor. Matthias, brother to Rudolf II, was crowned king of Hungary in November.

1609 July 9 *The Majestätsbrief* [*Letter of Majesty*] was issued by **Rudolf II**, the Holy Roman emperor. The charter granted the Protestant majority of **Bohemia** a degree of toleration unknown in other Catholic states. However, the statement of their rights was so obscure that they were nearly impossible to defend. **Matthias** was crowned (1611) king of Bohemia, in present Czechoslovakia.

V. ECONOMY AND TRADE

c.1600 Spain instituted the **sale of** *pulque*, an alcoholic drink made from the agave plant, to Mexicans.

1600 The **slave trade** now brought c.5,000 Africans to the Americas each year, mostly to the Spanish possessions of Central and South America.

1600 Dec. 31 The **British East India Company** was chartered by **Elizabeth I** to meet the challenge of the Dutch and Portuguese in the growing spice trade with the East Indies. The first fleet, commanded by **James Lancaster** (c.1550–June 6, 1618), sailed from London on Feb. 13, 1601; it reached (1602) Achin [Atjeh] in Sumatra and Bantam in Java, where it was loaded with pepper.

1601 England instituted the **Poor Laws**, which guaranteed government aid to the poor in order to maintain order and reduce social unrest.

1602 The **oldest stock exchange in the world** opened in Amsterdam, the United Provinces [the Netherlands].

1602 Mar. 20 The **Dutch East India Company** was chartered by the States-General of the United Provinces [the Netherlands] to expand and regulate trade in the Indian Ocean. **Pieter Both**, its first governor general (1609–1614), was instructed to gain complete monopoly of trade in the East Indies, Ceylon, India, and along the Persian Gulf and the Red Sea.

1604 **Henry IV**, king of France, issued a decree known as *La Paulette*, which permitted government officials to pass their offices on to their sons in the same way as the hereditary law of succession was applied to kings. This policy established a new hereditary class in France, based for the most part on families with wealth derived from business.

1605 The **Briare Canal**, one of the first to use locks, was begun. Completed in 1642, it connected the Loire and Seine rivers in central France.

1606 The **Virginia Company** was formed in England for the purpose of trading along the North American coast. Its most promising enterprise was the establishment of trade in **tobacco**.

1607 **Cotton** was first introduced to Jamestown, Virginia, where its successful cultivation later formed the basis of the agricultural economy of the southern U.S.

1607 Aug. **English settlers established the Popham Colony** on the lower Sagadahoc [Kennebec] River in Maine, and there **built the first ship in North America**. Weighing 30 tons, it was used for transatlantic travel. The Popham Colony folded the following year, but shipbuilding was revived by the **Massachusetts Company**.

1608 **Jamestown** shipped the first cargo from the English colonies. Pitch, tar, and soap were sent to England. The Jamestown export was the **first of American manufactured goods**.

1609 The **Bank of Amsterdam** was founded to act as a clearinghouse for the rapidly expanding international trade that followed the colonization and conquest of the New World.

1609 **Tea** was first imported by the Dutch East India Company to Amsterdam, the first European port to engage in the soon-to-be profitable tea trade.

VI. RELIGION AND PHILOSOPHY

1601 Jan. 25 **Matteo Ricci**, an Italian **Jesuit missionary in China** for more than 25 years, was granted permission by Wan Li [Shên Tsung], the Ming emperor of China, to enter Peking with two associates and to offer presents.

1603 As **Tokugawa Iyeyasu** [Ieyasu] began his rule as Japan's shogun at Edo [Tokyo], he greatly encouraged **Confucian studies**, which became again part of the training of loyal, honest bureaucrats. Confucian schools flourished, notably the Chinese Sung Neo-Confucianism developed during the 12th century by Chu Hsi, who had introduced elements of Buddhism and Taoism. Most warrior households had their own

Confucian tutor, to instruct themselves and their sons in history and ethical behavior.

1604   **Arjun** [Arjan], the fifth guru of the **Sikhs** in the Punjab, compiled the *Adi Granth* [the original book]. These sacred scriptures of the Sikhs were called in their later, enlarged form, the *Granth Sahib* or the *Guru Granth*. Arjun (b. 1581), accused by Jahangir [Jehangir, Prince Selim] (Aug. 31, 1569–Oct. 28, 1627) of having given financial aid to an unsuccessful claimant to the Mogul throne, was tortured to death on May 30, 1606.

1604 Jan. 16   **James I**, king of England, called together a conference of high churchmen at Hampton Court, near London, to hear complaints voiced by a delegation of **Puritans** against the practices of the Anglican Church. **Dr. John Reynolds** [Rainolds] (1549–May 21, 1607) spoke for the Puritans when he cited corrupt translations of Bible passages used in the *Book of Common Prayer*. He urged a new translation that would be acceptable to all English Protestants. A few months later James directed **Richard Bancroft** (1544–Nov. 2, 1610), the anti-Puritan bishop of London, to assemble qualified scholars for the project.

1604 Mar. 4   **Socinus** [Faustus Sozzini] (b. Dec. 5, 1539), a lay Italian theologian who had lived for many years in **Poland**, died. He had greatly influenced the Reformed [Anabaptist] churches of Poland and Transylvania. Socinus denied many doctrines of Calvinism and the Roman Catholic Church, substituting a strict supernaturalism for their rational reason. Elements of Socinianism survived in Holland and England and became a source of Unitarianism.

1604 July 22   **Richard Bancroft**, bishop of London, announced to his fellow bishops that James I had appointed "certain learned men for the translation of the Bible." He also described how the 54 scholars would be assigned to translation teams located at **Oxford** and **Cambridge** universities and Westminster Cathedral. This date served to mark the **official start of work on the King James Bible** by all participants.

1606   The sixth **Sikh** guru, **Har Govind** [Hargobind] (1595–1645), son of Arjun, was heavily guarded against attacks by the Mogul emperors, and the guruship grew to become a militant sacred dynasty. Har Govind taxed the Sikhs of the Punjab for

the purchase of weapons, the creation of a cavalry troop, and the construction of a stronghold. He made the sword the symbol of his leadership.

1608   A congregation of **Separatists at Gainsborough**, in Lincolnshire, England, under the pastor **John Smyth** [Smith] (1570–Aug. 1612), exiled themselves to Amsterdam. In 1609 the Separatist congregation at nearby Scrooby, in England, which included **William Brewster** (1567–Apr., 1644), **William Bradford** (Mar., 1590–May 9, 1657), and **John Robinson** (c.1545–Mar. 1, 1625), followed their Gainsborough friends, settling finally at Leiden in the United Provinces [the Netherlands]. It was a minority group within the Leiden church that founded (1620) the colony of **Plymouth**, Massachusetts.

1608   **Claudio Aquaviva** [Acquaviva] (Sept. 14, 1543–Jan. 31, 1615), the Italian fifth general of the **Society of Jesus** (from 1581), allowed the Jesuits to establish missions among the Indians of Old Paraguay, in present Argentina and Paraguay.

1608 May 4   The **Protestant Union** [Union of Evangelical Estates] was formed by German Protestant princes to gain protection against the increasing Catholic demands for the restitution of church property confiscated by the Protestants since 1555. The Calvinist **Frederick IV** (Mar. 5, 1574–Sept. 19, 1610), elector of the Palatinate (from 1592), organized the union. Catholic princes, led by **Maximilian I** (Apr. 17, 1573–Sept. 27, 1651), duke of Bavaria (from 1597), formed the **Catholic League** on July 10, 1609.

1609 Oct. 19   **Jacobus Arminius** (b. Oct. 10, 1560), a professor of theology at the **University of Leiden** in the United Provinces [the Netherlands], died. This peace-loving teacher paved the way for a doctrinal split within Dutch Calvinism by expressing doubts, in classroom and pulpit, over John Calvin's doctrine of unconditional predestination. He held that election and reprobation (rejection by God leading to eternal misery) was conditional. He left a place for free will and the efficacy of "good works."

VII. SCIENCE, EDUCATION, AND TECHNOLOGY

1601 Oct. 24   **Tycho Brahe** (b. Dec. 14, 1546), a Danish astronomer, died. Brahe's studies greatly contributed to astronomical knowledge. He proposed that five planets orbited the sun, as Copernicus believed, but he thought that the sun, with its five planets, then circled the earth. Working with an assistant named **Johannes Kepler**, Brahe made detailed observations of the heavens, noting (1572) Tycho's star, a supernova in the constellation Cassiopeia, and charting the location and movements of the planets and other heavenly bodies.

1603 Nov. 30 **William Gilbert** (b. 1544), an English physicist, died. His *De magnete* (1600) formed a basis for the further study of magnetism and electricity, as well as meteorology and cosmology.

1603 Dec. 13 **François Viete** [Vieta] (b. 1540), a French mathematician, died. He introduced the practice of substituting letters for numerical quantities in algebraic equations. His *Canon mathematicus* (1579) applied algebraic principles to trigonometry.

1604 **Galileo Galilei**, an Italian astronomer, demonstrated the law of falling bodies, the effects of gravity, it was said, at the leaning tower of Pisa, from which he dropped objects of varying weights that all fell to the ground in the same length of time. Galileo's discovery of the isochronism of the pendulum also occurred in Pisa.

1605 May **Ulisse Aldrovandi** (b. Sept. 11, 1522), an Italian naturalist, died. Aldrovandi's work encompassed botany, embryology, and pharmacology in addition to other areas. He designed (1568) the first botanical garden in his **Bologna**.

1608 Oct. 2 **Hans Lippershey** (c.1570–1619), a Dutch spectacle maker of Middleburg, invented one of the **first telescopes**. Leppershey's telescope, called "kijker," or "looker," came into use at the court of Henry IV, king of France, by Dec. 1608.

VIII. ARTS AND LEISURE

c.1600 **Miyán Tansen** [Ata Mohammad Khan], who wrote **Hindu ragas** and composed Muslim music as well, died. Tansen was renowned as a singer, and furthermore, exerted great political influence. He was invited to join the court of Akbar the Great, the Mogul emperor of Hindustan, and was named one of the "Nine Gems of the Empire," the highest rank below the emperor himself.

c.1600 **Delft** in the United Provinces [the Netherlands] became one of Europe's great centers of **pottery making**. The major factories, often located in old

breweries, were especially noted for their production of tin-enameled earthenware, which came to be known as **Delftware**.

1600 **Mahmud Abdülbaki Baki** (b. 1526), the leading Turkish poet of the 16th century, died. He was a master of *divan* **poetry**, the Turkish classical form which had by now assimilated earlier Persian forms and was no longer imitative.

1600 *Euridice*, the first opera whose score is extant, was completed by the Italian composers **Jacopo Peri** (Aug. 20, 1561–Aug. 12, 1633) and **Ottavio Rinuccini** (1562–1621) for the wedding of Henry IV, king of France, to **Marie de Médicis** [Maria de' Medici] (Apr. 26, 1573–July 3, 1642).

1602 Mar. 11 **Emilio del Cavalieri** (born c.1550), an Italian composer, died. His masterpiece was *La Rappresentazione di Anima e di Corpo* (1600), a morality play set to music. His works stressed monophony, or a single melody line, rather than the more usual counterpoint or polyphony of his time.

1602 July 26 The play *Hamlet*, by **William Shakespeare**, was noted on the Stationer's Register in London, an early form of copyrighting. The actor **Richard Burbage** (1567?–Mar. 13, 1619) probably played the title role in its first performance.

1602 Oct. **Thomas Morley** (b. 1557), an English composer, died. His *A Plaine and Easie Introduction to Practicall Musick* (1597) demonstrated modal practices of the late 16th century. He excelled as a madrigalist. His surviving compositions include balletts [dance airs] and solo songs with lute and bass viol accompaniment.

1603 It is thought that the **Kabuki form of theater** in Japan began when a woman named Okuni danced some popular dramas at a Buddhist shrine. Kabuki, which means song, dance, and skill, was enjoyed for its fresh portrayal of incidents not obscured by legend and tradition.

1605 Feb. 19 **Orazio Vecchi** (b. 1550), an Italian composer in the madrigal style, died. He was most famous for his *L'Amfiparnasso*, a farce that employed several voices in madrigal form.

1606 Nov. 30 **John Lyly** [Lilly] (born c.1554), an English writer, died. His two-part novel *Euphues* (c.1580) used ornate phrases and obscure allusion, and gave birth to "euphuism," meaning an artificial and overly fancy style.

1607 The **first of the de la Planche family of tapestry makers** in France, **François de la Planche** of Flanders, began work in Paris.

1608 The **Himeji Castle** in Hyogo [Kobe], Honshu, Japan, which had originally been built in the 16th century, or perhaps even as early as the 14th century, was reconstructed and essentially completed in its present form. It is today considered the finest and best-preserved example of Japanese castle architecture.

1608 The **first book written in the U.S.** was printed in London. *A True Relation of Such Occurrences and Accidents of Noate as Hath Hapned in Virginia Since the First Planting of that Collony* was written by John Smith after he had helped found the Jamestown colony.

IX. SPORTS, GAMES, AND SOCIETY

1608 Soon after the golf-playing Scotsman James VI succeeded to the throne of England as **James I,** a society of golfers was formed at Blackheath, London. The **Royal Blackheath Golf Club of London** is today widely regarded as the oldest existing golf club.

1610–1619

I. DISASTERS

1616 **Smallpox** swept through Indian tribes in New England from the Penobscot River in Maine to Narragansett Bay in Rhode Island.

II. EXPLORATION AND COLONIZATION

1610 **Sante Fe,** in present New Mexico, was founded as the capital of Nuevo Méjico [New Mexico] by New Spain. It is today the second oldest city, after St. Augustine in Florida, and the oldest capital city, in the U.S.

1610 An attempt to form a colony in **Newfoundland** was made by **John Guy** (died c.1628), on behalf of English businessmen. This, and a number of other colonizing attempts there, were unsuccessful because of the climate and the opposition of the French.

1610 Aug. 3 **Henry Hudson,** an English navigator, commissioned by the English to lead a new expedition, entered Hudson's Bay in his bark *Discovery* in an attempt to find the Northwest Passage. Hudson and his crew endured a harsh winter on the bay. In the spring he was still determined to search for the elusive **Northwest Passage.** His mutinous crew cast Henry Hudson (birth and death dates unknown) adrift in June 1611, with his son, six followers, and no food or water. Hudson and his loyal men were not heard of again.

1614 A trading post, later called **Fort Orange,** the first permanent settlement in New York state, was established at the site of present Albany by Dutch fur traders. Fort Orange's name was changed (1652) to Beverwyck village; after its capture by the English, it was renamed (1664) **Albany.**

1614 **Adrian Block** explored the area of present Connecticut for the Dutch, who failed to colonize it. In May **Cornelis Jacobsen** sailed up the Delaware River in New Jersey, establishing the Dutch claim to the region, which Henry Hudson may have briefly explored for the English in 1609 when he sailed into Newark Bay.

1615 Sept. **Thomas Roe** (1581?–Nov., 1644) became the first **British representative to Jahangir** [Jehangir, Prince Selim] (Aug. 31, 1569–Oct. 28, 1627), the Mogul [Mughal] emperor of Hindustan, at his court in Agra, in central India.

1616 Jan. 29 **Willem Cornelison Schouten** (c.1567–1625) and **Jacob Le Maire** (1585–1616), Dutch explorers, discovered **Cape Horn** at the tip of South America, separated from the **Strait of Magellan** by **Tierra del Fuego.** The Strait of Magellan, as well as Africa's **Cape of Good Hope,** were claimed by the Dutch East India Company, which tried to monopolize trade with the East Indies.

1617 Dec. 23 The first penal colony in the present U.S. was established by a royal proclamation that provided for the exile of habitual criminals to the English colony of **Virginia**.

1618 Étienne Brulé (1592?–1633), a French explorer, was perhaps the first European to venture into the Michigan region, when he explored the **Great Lakes**.

1618 Pedro Paez (1564–May 20, 1622), a Spaniard employed by the Portuguese government, discovered the **source of the Blue Nile River** in the mountains of Ethiopia. At **Khartoum**, the capital of the present Sudan, the Blue Nile joins the White Nile.

1618 Oct. 29 Walter Raleigh [Ralegh] (b. 1552?), out of favor at the court of Elizabeth I, was beheaded by order of her successor James I, king of England, because the expedition he was with as a guide attacked the Spanish fort of San Tomás in Guiana (now in Venezuela). He had hoped to find and conquer a legendary, gold rich Indian city Manoa, supposedly on the Orinoco River, which would bring him back to favor. Raleigh earlier had been imprisoned in the Tower of London by James, and his execution had been scheduled. He was granted a reprieve and lived in the tower until he was released on condition that he lead the expedition to Guiana. When he returned empty-handed to England, he was executed at the insistence of the Spanish ambassador. Raleigh wrote *The Discoverie of Guiana* (1596) about his exploration of northern South America.

III. POLITICS AND WAR

1610 May 14 Henry IV (b. Dec. 13, 1553), king of France (from 1589), was mortally stabbed in Paris by a religious fanatic, **François Ravaillac** (1578–1610). He was succeeded by his nine-year-old son Louis XIII under the regency of his mother Marie de Médici.

1610 July 3 Polish troops were defeated at **Klushino**, not far from Moscow, by allied Russian and Swedish forces, who had already put the second Psuedo-Demetrius to flight. **Basil IV Shuiski**, czar of Russia (from 1606), was taken prisoner, and the power of the boyars was restored by a treaty signed on Sept. 30. Though **Sigismund III Vasa**, king of Poland, pressed his advantage, dissension among the Cossacks, landed gentry, and boyars precluded election of a candidate to the **Russian** throne before 1613.

1611 Oct. 30 Charles IX (b. Oct. 4, 1550), king of Sweden (from 1604), died and was succeeded by his son **Gustav II Adolf**, who was officially crowned in 1617.

1612 Jan. 20 Rudolf II (b. July 18, 1552), the Holy Roman emperor (from 1576), died and was succeeded by his brother Matthias. Matthias was moderate in his views, but his weak policies further antagonized the religious division created by the **Protestant Union** (1508) and the **Catholic League** (1609).

1612 Dec. 7 Polish troops withdrew from **Russia** as Swedish intervention and Russian opposition had made impossible the Polish king **Sigismund III Vasa's** goal of gaining the Russian crown.

1613 Feb. Elizabeth (Aug. 19, 1596–Feb. 13, 1662), daughter of James I, king of England, married Frederick V (Aug. 26, 1596–Nov. 29, 1632), a leading Calvinist and elector of the **Palatinate** (1610–1623). Their marriage established the **Hanover/Windsor line of English rulers**.

1613 Under the nominal rule of the **Le Dynasty** (1428–1787) **of Annam** [Vietnam], rivalry between the northern **Kingdom of Tongking**, ruled by the Trinh family, and the southern **Kingdom of Cochin** China, ruled by the Nguyen family at Hue, reached its height with the Nguyen constructing two walls across present Vietnam at the 18th parallel near Dong Hai.

1613 Jan. The **Treaty of Knaerod** [Knäred] ended the **Kalmar War** (1611–1613) between Denmark and Sweden. Danish troops had taken the Swedish southern frontier fortresses of Kalmar in the summer of 1611, and Älvsborg in May 1612.

1613 Mar. 3 The 17-year-old **Michael Romanov** [Mikhail Fëdorovich Romanov] (July 22, 1596–July 23, 1645), hiding in a monastery in Poland, was elected czar of Russia (to 1645) by the *zemsky sobor*, establishing the **Romanov Dynasty** (to 1917) of Russian rulers and ending Russia's Time of Troubles (1610–1613). Michael's father Philaret [Filaret; Fëdor Nikitich Romanov] (1553?–1633), patriarch of Moscow and cousin to the last Rurik czar **Fëdor I Ivanovich**, acted as regent.

1614 Nov. 12   The **Treaty of Xanten** ended a war of succession fought by the German duchies of Cleves and Jülich, both located along the Rhine River, east of the United Provinces [the Netherlands]. Hostilities had begun on Mar. 25, 1609, with the death of John William, duke of Cleves, who had no heir. The elector of Brandenburg, backed by the Holy Roman Empire, gained the duchy of Cleves and the elector of the Palatinate-Neuburg, supported by England, France, and the United Provinces, received the duchy of Jülich.

1616   A Manchu named **Nurhachi** [Nurhachu] established a new **Manchu Dynasty**, independent of the Mings, in Manchuria. The Manchus, related more closely to their allies the Mongols than the Chinese, were from eastern Manchuria. The Manchus under Nurhachi (ruled to 1626) controlled the territories north of the Great Wall and had made Mukden [Moukden, Chinese: Shenyang], in Liaoning Province, present northeastern China, their capital.

1617   The **Peace of Stolbova** was concluded by Sweden and Russia. Russia ceded Estonia to Sweden and relinquished its claims to Polish Livonia, a region of southern Estonia and northern Latvia.

1618   Fighting broke out between the **Manchus** and **Chinese** outside the Great Wall in northeastern China. The Chinese Ming forces were defeated (1619), and the Manchus occupied (1621) the Liao He basin in southern Manchuria.

1618 May 23   The beginning of the **Thirty Years' War** (1618–1648) dated from the **Defenestration of Prague**, in which a group of Bohemian Protestants, dissatisfied with the Catholic rejection of their requests to honor the *Majestätsbrief*, threw two Catholic members of the Diet, who represented the interests of Matthias, the Holy Roman emperor, from the window of the Chancelry in Prague.

1619 Mar. 20   **Matthias** (b. Feb. 24, 1557), the Holy Roman emperor (from 1612), died, and Ferdinand II (July 9, 1578–Feb. 15, 1637), king of Bohemia (from 1617) and Hungary (from 1621), was elected to succeed him on Aug. 28. In the meantime the **revolt of the Bohemian Protestants** had gathered strength since the Defenestration of Prague, and the Bohemian Diet deposed (Aug., 1619) the Catholic Ferdinand as their king. In his place they elected as king of Bohemia the Calvinist **Frederick V**, elector of the

Palatinate and leader of the **Protestant Union**. He was crowned in Prague in November.

1619 July 30   The **General Assembly**, the first representative governing body to convene in the present U.S., was elected in Jamestown, Virginia. The next day the Assembly passed its first law, which set the price of tobacco and facilitated the use of tobacco as a medium of exchange. Tobacco became the primary currency in the colony as reflected in an act that was enforced from 1632 to 1656 that forbade the use of money to settle contracts.

IV. ECONOMY AND TRADE

1611   The **first British trading post in India** was founded by the British East India Company at Machilipatnam [Masulipatam, or Bandar] on the southeastern coast of India, in present Andhra Pradesh. In 1612 the **East India Company** was granted the right to trade at the port of Surat on the northwestern coast of India, in present Gujarat state, by Jahangir, the Mogul emperor. Surat, the most important port in the **Mogul** [Mughal] **Empire of Hindustan** (1526–1857), was the first British settlement to be established along India's western coast.

1619   **Batavia** [Djakarta], present capital of Indonesia, was founded and fortified by **Jan Pieterszoon Coen** (Jan. 8, 1587–Sept. 21, 1629) as headquarters for the Dutch East India Company.

1619   The **Banco del Giro** was founded in Venice. The bank was permitted to lend money according to the amount of credit extended to it by the government. This practice enabled it to make more and larger loans than before.

1619 Aug. 1   The **first black slaves were brought to the U.S.** by a Dutch privateer, to Jamestown, Virginia. Although chattel slavery was not then legally recognized in America, they were sold as indentured servants who could earn their freedom after a specified number of years of service.

V. RELIGION AND PHILOSOPHY

1611   The **King James Version of the Bible** was printed in the London shop of Robert Barker. It was more of a revision of previous English Bibles than the entirely new translation originally contemplated. This new version leaned on the Bishop's Bible, the Geneva Bible, the translations of William Tyndale, and the Rheims New Testament. Its Old Testament clearly surpassed all predecessors in its faithfulness to the Hebrew text. The purity, beauty, and simplicity of style remain notable to this day.

1614 Hidetada (1579–1632), the Tokugawa shogun (1605–1623), ordered all **Christian missionaries to leave Japan.** The Jesuits and Franciscans, and more recently the Dominicans, had quarreled periodically. Now the arrival of Dutch traders (from c.1600) generated quarrels with their Spanish and Portuguese rivals. Suspicion about the loyalty of converts to the **Tokugawa Shogunate** (1603–1867) arose, and Hidetada ordered all Japanese to register as members of a Buddhist sect.

1616 Feb. 26 Galileo Galilei, an Italian mathematician and astronomer, was advised by Cardinal Robert Bellarmine (Oct. 4, 1542–Sept. 17, 1621), a papal theologian, that he might no longer hold or defend the doctrine that the earth revolves around the sun, as set forth by Copernicus, but might discuss it as a mere "mathematical supposition." Galileo's work in question, *Letters on the Solar Spots* (1613), which had also included efforts to find support for the Copernican system in the Bible, was placed on the **Inquisition's Index of Forbidden Books** on Mar. 5, 1616.

1617 Several **foreign Christian priests in Japan were executed** in a determined move to eradicate Christian influence. Most remaining missionaries left Japan, as did many converts.

1618 Nov. 13 The **Synod of Dort** [Dordrecht], in the United Provinces [the Netherlands], convened. A national convention of Dutch Calvinists, it excluded Arminians and "Remonstrants." The Arminians had adopted a more liberal view about predestination, holding that God's sovereignty and man's free will were not in conflict, and in 1610 some of them had "remonstrated" to the States General by announcing their points of difference with strict Calvinism. Maurice of Nassau, stadholder of the United Provinces [the Netherlands], had determined upon a synod to end the controversy. Before it opened he imprisoned two Remonstrant spokesmen, the jurist **Hugo Grotius** [Huig de Groot] (Apr. 10, 1583–Aug. 28, 1645) and **Jan van Oldenbarneveldt** (Sept. 14, 1547–May 13, 1619).

1619 May 9 The **Synod of Dort** closed, having condemned Arminianism and the Remonstrants, and

having adopted bristly statements of orthodox Calvinist doctrines. Soon after the synod's close, Remonstrants were banished, allowed to return only after the Stadholder Maurice's death in 1625.

VI. SCIENCE, EDUCATION, AND TECHNOLOGY

1614 Logarithms, the exponential notation used to indicate by what power a base number must be raised to equal a given number, were developed by **John Napier** [Neper] (1550–Apr. 4, 1617), an amateur mathematician, and described in the brochure *Mirifici logarithmorum cononis descriptio*.

VII. ARTS AND LEISURE

1610 *Mariane* was perhaps the most highly regarded of the nearly 1,200 plays attributed to **Alexandre Hardy** (c.1565–?1631), a French playwright. Hardy's work dispensed with the unities of time and place and with the ever-present chorus.

1610 *The Philaster* was the first important play to be produced by the collaborative efforts of **Francis Beaumont** (c.1584–Mar. 6, 1616) and **John Fletcher** (Dec. 20, 1579–Aug. 29, 1625), one of the most notable teams of the English theater. As a team they are credited today with c.15 plays; separately they are credited with c.50 plays.

1610 July Michelangelo da Caravaggio [Michelangelo Merisi] (b. Sept. 28, 1573), the great Italian artist, died. Though not greatly influential within his native Italy, his work was known elsewhere, notably by Rembrandt. Caravaggio offended his contemporaries by using street people as models for religious works. His works included *The Supper at Emmaus* (1598), *Death of the Virgin* (1666), and several portraits of St. Matthew.

1611 Aug. 27 Tomás Luis de Victoria [Tommaso Lodovico da Vittoria] (born c.1549), a Spanish church composer of the Renaissance, died. He probably studied under Palestrina. His works included, in addition to many church pieces, *Liber Primus* (1576), which contained masses and canticles, and his masterpiece *Officio Defunctorum* (1605), a requiem mass.

1614 Apr. 7 El Greco [orig.: Domenikos Theotokopoulos] (b. 1514), a Crete-born Spanish painter, died. He gained the appellation "El Greco" [the Greek] when he settled in Toledo, Spain, in 1577. His paintings included *Laocoön* (1610–1614), *The Resurrection* (1608–1610), and *The Vision of the Apocalypse* (c.1610).

1615 Nov. 24 Sethus Calvisius [Seth Kallwitz] (b. Feb. 21, 1556), a German musician, died. His *Compendium Musicae Practicae pro Incipientibus* was considered the first western history of music.

1616 Apr. 19 Cervantes [Miguel de Cervantes Saavedra] (b. Oct. 5, 1547), a Spanish novelist, died. His masterpiece *Don Quixote de la Mancha* (two parts: 1605, 1615), was a farce of the chivalric romances, popular at the time, taken to an extreme. Cervantes also wrote the pastoral novel *Galatea* (1585). He had been a soldier at the battle of Lepanto and was enslaved by the Barbary pirates until he was ransomed after five years.

1616 Apr. 23 William Shakespeare died in his hometown of **Stratford-upon-Avon**. The date of his birth was traditionally given as Apr. 26, 1564, the same date as his christening, recorded according to the Old Style calendar; May 3 is the New Style date. His plays form the greatest single body of work in the English language theater. Among them dated by their earliest known production, are *Henry VI*, parts 2 and 3 (1591); *Henry VI*, part 1 (1593); *Richard III* (1593); *Comedy of Errors* (1593); *Taming of the Shrew* (1594); *Two Gentlemen of Verona* (1595); *Love's Labour's Lost* (1595); *Romeo and Juliet* (1595); *Richard II* (1596), *A Midsummer Night's Dream* (1596), *Merchant of Venice* (1597); *Henry IV*, parts 1 and 2 (1598); *Much Ado About Nothing* (1598); *Henry V* (1599); *Julius Caesar* (1599); *As You Like It* (1600); *Twelfth Night* (1601); *Hamlet* (1601); *All's Well That Ends Well* (1603); *Measure for Measure* (1604); *The Merry Wives of Windsor* (1604); *Othello* (1605); *King Lear* (1605); *Macbeth* (1606); *Antony and Cleopatra* (1606); *Winter's Tale* (1611); and *The Tempest* (1612). His sonnets (1609)—154 in all—were probably written 1593–1601. They fall into two groups, one addressed to an intimate friend, a handsome young man, and the other to the famous "Dark Lady," a false lover.

VIII. SPORTS, GAMES, AND SOCIETY

1613 In *Travels to Persia*, **Anthony Shirley** [Sherley] (1565?–c.1635), brother of the English soldier-of-fortune Robert Shirley, described to British readers **polo** as he had seen it played by Persians.

1617 **James I**, king of England, issued a **Declaration of Sports** granting permission for Sunday participation in dancing, archery, leaping, vaulting, and for having May games, Whitsun ales, and morris dances, provided they did not interfere with attendance at divine services. At the same time he forbade bear- and bull-baiting and bowling on the Sabbath.

1620–1629

I. DISASTERS

1624 **Oslo**, completely destroyed by **fire**, was rebuilt and named **Christiania**, in honor of Christian IV (Apr. 12, 1577–Feb. 28, 1648), king of Denmark and Norway (from 1588). It was renamed Oslo in 1925.

II. EXPLORATION AND COLONIZATION

1620 Nov. 11 The **Mayflower Compact**, inspired by religious as well as civil aims, was signed by the **Pilgrims**, emigrant English Separatists from England and the United Provinces [the Netherlands], aboard the *Mayflower*, at anchor near present Provincetown, Massachusetts. The Pilgrims solemnly agreed to create a "civil body politic" for the enactment of "just and equal laws mete and convenient for the general good of the colony."

1620 Dec. 21 The **Pilgrims** landed at Plymouth, Massachusetts, after having set out (Sept. 16) from England with the expectation they would arrive in Virginia. **Plymouth** was the **first permanent European settlement in New England**, and it retained its separate identity until 1691.

1622 Territory between the Merrimack River, in present New Hampshire, and the Kennebec River, in present Maine, was granted by royal charter to the Englishmen **Ferdinando Gorges** (1566?–1647) and Captain **John Mason** (1586–1635). They divided (1629) the land along the Piscataqua River, so

Gorges received the equivalent of **Maine**, and Mason called his share **New Hampshire**.

1623 David Thompson established the **first permanent settlement in present New Hampshire** near Portsmouth.

1624 Cornelis J. Mey, as first governor, arrived in the Dutch colony of **New Netherland** with 30 ships. As early as 1612 two Dutch ships, *Tiger* and *Fortune*, had traded with the Indians from huts built on **Manhattan Island** and in 1613 they built a more permanent trading post. The Dutch had built by 1614 a stockaded trading post at Albany. In 1623 the Dutch West India Company had brought in families who were settled along the shores of the Hudson River and who now fell under the jurisdiction of Mey.

1625 Saint Christopher [Saint Kitts] was the **first island of the West Indies to be settled by English colonists**. It was followed by Barbados (1626), Nevis (1628), and Antigua and Montserrat (1632).

1626 May 6 Peter Minuit (c.1580–June, 1638), the Dutch director general of New Netherland, bought **Manhattan Island** from the **Canarsie Indians**, paying them with trinkets worth at that time 60 guilders [gulden], approximately $24. **Fort Amsterdam** was erected at a site already chosen by the early Dutch traders on the southern tip of Manhattan Island for the purpose of conducting transatlantic trade.

1627 The first British settlement was established on **Barbados**, West Indies.

1627 Cardinal Richelieu, France's chief minister of foreign affairs, created the **Company of New France** to conduct the fur trade in the colony of New France, in present Canada, and to secure and develop France's possessions in the New World.

1629 Mar. The **Massachusetts Bay Colony** was established by royal charter, addressed to the "Governor and Company of the Massachusetts Bay," John Endicott [Endecott] (1588–Mar. 15, 1665). The charter provided the colony with an unintended degree of independence: Massachusetts prospered and colonists from the original settlements [Salem and Boston] later founded Windsor (1633), Wethersfield (1634), and Hartford (1635), all in the present state of **Connecticut**.

1629 June 27 John Endicott of Massachusetts Bay Colony landed with c.100 settlers at Naumkeag [Salem], set up a community, and acted as governor until the arrival of John Winthrop (Jan. 12, 1588–Mar. 26, 1649) in 1630.

1629 June 7 The Dutch West India Company issued the **Charter of Freedoms and Exemptions for New Netherland**, which provided estates, called patroonships, for members who established substantial settlements in the colony. One of the more successful patroonships, Rensselaerswyck, was founded by **Kiliaen Van Rensselaer** (1595–1644) in 1630. It extended 24 miles along both sides of the Hudson River from near the present city of Albany southward, and included several thousand tenants. Van Rensselaer managed the settlement from his home in Amsterdam, the United Provinces [the Netherlands], without ever seeing it.

1629 July 20 Reflecting the enmity in Europe between France and England caused by the **Thirty Years' War** (1618–1648), the **British Canada Company**, represented by the **Kirke brothers**, David (1596?–?1654), Ewin Lewis (1599?–?1683), and Thomas, raided and seized New France, which had been explored, claimed for France, and now surrendered by **Samuel de Champlain**, governor of the colony.

III. POLITICS AND WAR

1620 Nov. 8 The **Catholic League** (1609) under **Johan Tserciaes** (Feb. 1559–Apr. 30, 1632), count of Tilly, crushed the **Bohemian Revolt** led by **Frederick V**, elector of the Palatinate and newly elected king of Bohemia, in the **Battle of White Mountain** [Weisser Berg], fought near Prague. Frederick fled to the United Provinces [the Netherlands] where he was supported by the English as well as the Dutch.

1621 Gustavf II Adolphus, king of Sweden, invaded Polish Livonia to complete Swedish control of the Baltic Sea.

1621 May 31 Philip III (b. Apr. 14, 1578), king of Spain (from 1598), died and was succeeded by his son Philip IV. This coincided with the end of the **Twelve Years' Truce** signed at Antwerp on Apr. 9, 1609, with the **United Provinces** [the Netherlands], still formally a part of the **Hapsburg Spanish Netherlands**. The harsh terms offered at the treaty's expiration by **Gaspar de Guzmán** (Jan. 6, 1587–July 22,

1645), duke of Olivares and counselor to Philip IV, were unacceptable to the Dutch, and war was resumed by the United Provinces against Spain.

1621 Sept. Forces of **Sigismund III Vasa**, king of Poland, routed the Turks under **Osman II**, the Ottoman sultan (from 1618), in a **battle at Khotin** [Hotin] on the Dneister [Dnestr] River on the border of Poland and the Ottoman vassal state of Moldavia, now in Ukraine. Osman was forced to return to Constantinople, where he announced his intention to reorganize his army. Osman (b. Nov. 16, 1603) was captured by the Janissaries, who had fled at Khotin, and murdered on May 20, 1622.

1622 Mar. 22 Settlements outside Jamestown, Virginia, were almost destroyed in the **first Indian massacre of Americans**, led by Opechancanough, a brother of Powhatan (d.1618), who led the **Powhatan Confederacy** (c.1607–c.1705) in Virginia. Jamestown itself was heavily fortified and escaped destruction.

1624 Aug. 13 Louis XIII, king of France, appointed **Cardinal Richelieu** as his prime minister. Richelieu, however, quickly abandoned the prevailing pro-Hapsburg policy as he feared the more powerful Hapsburgs as neighbors. He gave his support to the United Provinces [the Netherlands] and Denmark. Denmark, a Protestant country, was engaged in the Thirty Years' War against the Hapsburgs in Germany.

c.1625 The **Kingdom of Abomey**, in present Benin, gained its independence from the **Kingdom of Allada**, leader of the Aja states, in West Africa. Abomey, the predecessor of the present state of Dahomey, rose in power, taking advantage of the arrival of the Europeans and the subsequent turmoil brought by the slave trade.

1625 Mar. 27 **James I** (b. June 19, 1566), king of England (from 1603), Ireland (1603), and Scotland as James VI (from 1657), died and was succeeded by his son **Charles I**. On June 13 Charles married **Henrietta Maria** (Nov. 25, 1609–Sept. 10, 1669), sister of Louis XIII, king of France. Charles, who believed in absolute monarchy, soon came into conflict with Parliament.

1625 Apr. 23 **Maurice of Nassau** (b. Nov. 13, 1567), stadtholder [chief magistrate] (1584–1625) of the **United Provinces** [the Netherlands], died. He made

the Dutch army a modern force able to hold its own against the armies of the Spanish, but was unable to drive the Spanish out of the southern provinces of the Netherlands.

1625 Dec. 29 By the **Treaty of The Hague**, Christian IV, king of Denmark and Norway, secured the financial aid of England and the United Provinces [the Netherlands] to invade Germany as leader of the **Protestant Union** against the **Catholic League** of the Holy Roman Empire. He was supported by the forces of the German general, Count Peter Ernst II Mansfeld (1580–1626), and Gábor Bethlen [Gabriel Bethlen von Iktár] (1580–1629), prince of Transylvania (from 1613).

1626 Apr. 25 Imperial forces under **Albrecht Wenzel Eusebius von Waldstein** [Waldenstein, Wallenstein] (Sept. 15, 1583–Feb. 25, 1634) defeated **Count Peter Ernst II Mansfeld** (1580–Nov. 29, 1626) at Dessau, on the Mulde River, in present Germany. It was a major battle of the **Thirty Years' War** (1618–1648). Count Mansfeld retreated to Hungary to join Gábor Bethlen. Another Protestant defeat followed (Aug. 27) in a **battle at Lutter am Barenberge**, near Braunschweig [Brunswick] in present Germany, in which Christian IV, king of Denmark and Norway, was routed by the imperial forces of the Catholic Johan Tserclaes, count of Tilly.

1627 The **Manchus**, who were already threatening the **Ming Dynasty** (1368–1644) of China, invaded Korea. By 1644, when the **Ch'ing** [Manchu] **Dynasty** (1644–1911) was established by the Manchus in China, Korea was a vassal of the Manchus.

1627 Dec. 26 **Vincenzo II Gonzaga**, duke of Mantua (from 1612), died without direct heir. In the ensuing war of succession, **Charles Gonzaga** (1580–1637), duke of Nevers, who had been designated successor by Vincenzo, was supported by France, the Papacy, and Venice. The opposing forces of the Holy Roman Empire captured Mantua on July 18, 1630.

1628 June 7 **Charles I**, king of England, reluctantly accepted the **Petition of Rights** drafted by the predominantly Puritan House of Commons, which refused to legislate taxes for the foreign wars conducted by their king. On Mar. 2, 1629, Charles I dissolved Parliament, and ruled without one until 1640.

1628 Oct. 28 Following the policy of Cardinal Richelieu, prime minister of France, who sought to eliminate dissent at home, French royal forces captured **La Rochelle**, the Huguenot stronghold in western France. The fall of the city, besieged since Aug. 10, 1627, despite several English expeditions, led to the **Peace of Alais** (June 28, 1629), which eliminated the military strength of the French Protestants.

c.1629   Mavura, king of **Monomotapa** [Motapa, Mutapa] **Empire** (from c.1440), in present Zimbabwe, placed his territory under the protection of the Portuguese, who controlled the coast of East Africa. His kingdom then began to disintegrate under the *prazo* **system**, which established large private concessions worked by slaves and whose powerful rulers became virtually independent of Portuguese control.

1629 May 22   The **Peace Treaty of Lübeck** ended the **Danish War**, begun (1625) when the Protestant coalition led by Christian IV, king of Denmark and Norway, opened hostilities against the imperial **Catholic League** (1609). The Hapsburg victory marked the decline of Denmark and its vassal state Norway.

IV. ECONOMY AND TRADE

1621 June 3   The **Dutch West India Company** was formed to conduct trade with Africa and the New World. The **United Provinces** [the Netherlands] became the leading trading country of Europe, conducting nearly half of the shipping of the continent.

1622   The **island of Hormuz**, in the Persian Gulf, occupied by the Portuguese (from 1514), was reconquered by the Persians with the aid of the British East India Company.

1622 May   The *Weekly News*, the **first regularly appearing English newspaper**, was founded by the English printer **Nicholas Bourne**.

1623 Feb. 17   The Dutch sacked a British settlement at **Ambon in the Spice Islands** [the Moluccas] and massacred its inhabitants. The Dutch now consolidated their trade monopoly as the British East India Company concentrated its efforts in India.

1623 Sept. 10   The **Plymouth colony** in Massachusetts exported its first cargo. The *Anne*, commanded by William Pierce, carried lumber and furs to England.

1628   The **port of Le Havre**, on the English Channel, at the mouth of the Seine, was greatly improved by the construction of **sluices**, which controlled the flow of the river. Since more and larger ships could anchor at the entrance to the Seine, Le Havre became one of the country's most important ports.

1628   **Piet Heyn** [Pieter Pieterszoon Heijn] (Nov. 15, 1577–June 18, 1629), a Dutch privateer, seized an entire fleet of Spanish ships, returning from the New World laden with silver.

V. RELIGION AND PHILOSOPHY

1620 Dec.   The **first Separatist Church in America** was established in Plymouth, Massachusetts. In England Separatists were called Independents; later, in the U.S., and to a lesser degree in England, they were called Congregationalists. The Pilgrim congregation was at first led by **William Brewster** (1567–Apr. 1644), **William Bradford** (Mar. 1590–May 9, 1657), and **Edward Winslow** (Oct. 18, 1593–May 8, 1655).

1621   **William Bradford**, governor of the Plymouth colony in Massachusetts proclaimed a "day of **thanksgiving** and prayer" when the colonists gathered in their first harvest in the New World.

1622   **Pope Gregory XV** (Jan. 15, 1554–July 8, 1623; ruled from 1621) organized the **Sacra Congregatio de Propaganda Fide** as a permanent department of the government of the Roman Catholic Church. Its function was to reduce rivalries between the different orders and to supervise missionary labors from Rome.

1622 Dec. 28   **Francis of** [François de] **Sales** (b. Aug. 21, 1567) died in Lyon, France. As a missionary, as bishop of Geneva from 1602 to his death, and as a writer, Francis was one of the most effective adversaries of Calvinism in French-speaking Europe. His classic *The Introduction of the Devout Life* (1609) has perennially appealed to Protestants and Catholics.

1624   **Edward Herbert** of Cherbury (Mar. 3, 1582–Aug. 5, 1648), an English soldier, diplomat, and philosopher, wrote in Latin and published in France a book known as *De Veritate.* In it he outlined the articles of belief he held were found in all religions and were also in accordance with reason. Translated (1637) into English, this anti-ecclesiastical work has won Herbert the epithet "**Father of Deism**."

1625 Vincent de Paul (Apr. 24, 1581–Sept. 27, 1660), a French Roman Catholic, founded the **Congregation of the Mission** [Lazarists or Vincentians] to evangelize the rural districts of France and to train clergy for such service. Vincent also established the **Confraternities of Charity**, associations of laywomen who served the sick poor in their homes; the **Foundling Hospital**; and, with Louise de Marillac (Aug. 12, 1591–Mar. 15, 1660), the **Daughters of Charity**. He was canonized in 1737.

1627 Ferdinand II, the Holy Roman emperor, issued a decree banning Protestantism in Bohemia and Moravia, where the Bohemian revolt had been quelled in 1620. Leading Protestant nobles were beheaded, the **Fellowship of the Brethren** [*Unitas Fratrum*] shattered, its churches destroyed, and its members converted to Catholicism or driven into exile.

1628 The **first Dutch Reformed church in the U.S.**, and the first of the Presbyterian polity, was established by the Dutch in New Amsterdam, the future New York City. **Jonas Michaeleus** was its first pastor. This church is the oldest church in the U.S. with an uninterrupted ministry.

1629 Mar. 6 Ferdinand II, the Holy Roman emperor, close on the heels of the victories won by Albrecht Wenzel Eusebius von Waldstein [Waldenstein, Wallenstein] over the Protestant forces, issued the imperial **Edict of Restitution**, which not only gave back c.150 ecclesiastical foundations to the Catholics but also reestablished the principle *cuius regio, eius religio*–only one religion in a country, that of the ruler.

VI. SCIENCE, EDUCATION, AND TECHNOLOGY

c.1620 The **first submarine** was piloted on the Thames River for the benefit of James I, king of England, by **Cornelis Drebbel** [Cornelius van Drebel] (1572–1634), a Dutch physicist who remained underwater, according to reports, for about two hours in his enclosed boat constructed of leather stretched over a wooden frame. The craft carried 12 rowers whose oars projected through watertight openings. A witness related that "liquid air," possibly oxygen, was used to restore the air in the sealed submarine.

1620 Edmund Gunter (1581–Dec. 10, 1626), an English mathematician, published his **Canon triangulorum**, which included a seven-place table of common logarithms. He developed the logarithmic Gunter scale for determining distance with a compass, and was the first to use the terms "cosine" and "cotangent."

1621 Willebrord von Roijen Snell (1580–Oct. 30, 1626), a Dutch mathematician and astronomer, discovered the law of the refraction of light, occurring when light moved from one transparent medium to another in an oblique manner so that there was a difference in speed between some waves and others. What became known as **Snell's Law** related the angle of incidence to the angle of refraction.

1622 The **Bibliothèque Nationale**, the national library of France, was opened to the public. Its beginnings were traced to Charles V, king of France, who established a collection of c.1,200 manuscripts in the **Louvre** in Paris. The library now contains more than nine million volumes.

1625 Hugo Grotius [Huig de Groot], a Dutch jurist and statesman, published **De Jure Belli et Pacis** [On the Laws of War and Peace], a fundamental work in international law. His **Mare Liberum** (1609) was a plea for the free use of the seas by all nations.

1626 Apr. 9 Francis Bacon (b. Jan. 22, 1561), an English essayist, statesman, and philosopher, died. He was known particularly for his advocacy of inductive reasoning based on objective observation, which was contrary to the prevailing scholastic philosophy, based on authority and syllogistic reasoning. His works included **The Advancement of Learning** (1605), **Novum Organum** [New Instrument] (1620), **De Augumentis** (1623), and **Essays** (1597–1625).

1628 The **circulation of blood** was explained for the first time by **William Harvey** (Apr. 1, 1578–June 3, 1657), an English physician, in **Exercitatio Anatomica de Motu Cordis et Sanguinis in Animalibus** [Anatomical Essay on the Motion of the Heart and the Blood in Animals].

VII. ARTS AND LEISURE

1620 Mar. 1 Thomas Campion (b. Feb. 12, 1567), an English poet and musician, died. His lyrics, written for music, were included in **Two Bookes of Ayres** (1613) and **The Third and Fourth Booke of Ayres** (1617).

1621 *The Anatomy of Melancholy* was published by **Robert Burton** (Feb. 8, 1577–Jan. 25, 1640), an English clergyman. Organized as a medical treatise, it explored "melancholy [madness] and its causes, love and religion," but its subject was life and mortality, richly and wittily observed.

1621 Feb. 15 **Michael Praetorius** (b. Feb. 15, 1571), a German composer, died. He produced more than 40 volumes of works, mostly of church music. His treatise on music theory, *Syntagma Musicum*, still regarded as an important work, supplied information about the ancient secular music of Asia and Egypt, the Greek and Latin liturgies, and Hebrew music, as well as information on individual musicians and musical instruments.

1621 Oct. 16 **Jan Pieters[zoon] Sweelinck** (b. Apr., 1562), a Dutch baroque organist, died. During his lifetime he was known for his vocal works, primarily psalms, motets, and chansons. However, today he is remembered chiefly for his organ works, published as recently as 1895 and 1903.

1624 **Tulsi Das** (b. 1532), a Hindu poet during Akbar I the Great's reign in Hindustan, died. *Ramacharita Manasa* (**The Lake of Rama's Exploits**), a Hindi version of the Ramayana tale, was regarded by many in northern India as a bible. In his work Tulsi Das built a monotheism about Rama, saying "There is one God, it is Rama, creator of heaven and earth, and redeemer of mankind."

1623 July 4 **William Byrd** [Bird] (born c.1540), an English composer and organist, second in his time only to his teacher Thomas Tallis, died. His music for the virginal, perhaps the oldest keyboard instrument of the harpsichord family, included *My Ladye Nevells Booke* and the *Fitzwilliam Virginal Book*.

1625 June 5 **Orlando Gibbons** (b. Dec., 1583), an English composer of church music, died. An organist at **Westminster Abbey**, he became famous for his Anglican church music, in which a solo voice with independent instrumental accompaniment was interspersed with the chorus.

1626 Jan. 21 **John Dowland** (b. Dec., 1562), an English composer and virtuoso lute player, died. His many works included three books of *Songs or Ayres* and *Lachrymae* (1604). Dowland's innovative compositions added elaborate chromatic elements to the harmonic role of the accompaniment.

1627 The noted French romance *L'Astrée* by **Honoré d'Urfé** (Feb. 11, 1568–June 1, 1625) was published posthumously. This love story of a shepherd and shepherdess became a prime model for popular pastoral romances, dealing with the art of courtship.

1627 Mar. 23 **Lodovico Zacconi** (b. June 11, 1555), an Italian composer and theorist, died. He was a tenor at the court chapel at Graz (1585) and at Munich (1591–1595). His *Prattica di Musica* (1592, 1619) included treatises on the use of musical notation, especially to indicate the length of a note; counterpoint; and descriptions of musical instruments.

1627 May 23 **Luis de Góngora y Argote** (b. July 11, 1561), a Spanish poet, died. His influence was seen in the use of the term "Gongorism" to mean a complex and elaborate, often obscure, poetical style. Gongorism was compared to Euphuism (from *Euphues, the Anatomy of Wit* by John Lyly) in English literature. One of Spain's great baroque poets, Góngora was known best for *Fábula de Polifemo y Galatea* (1613) and the *Solidades* (1613).

c.1628 **Thomas Morton** (1590?–1646) began to lose favor with the Puritan founders of Mount Wollaston, present Quincy, Massachusetts, where Morton had settled in 1625. Since his arrival the village became known as "Merrymount" for the revelry Morton introduced. Among his antics was to erect a Maypole, as was customary in England for May Day celebrations. He was repeatedly arrested and twice deported to England (1628, 1630) for his activities. **Nathaniel Hawthorne** embellished Morton's life in the story *The Maypole of Merry-Mount* (1836).

1628 Mar. 12 **John Bull** (b. May, 1562), an English organist and composer, died. He was influential in the development of counterpoint for the keyboard, and wrote an early version of *God Save the King*.

1629 **Kabuki theater** performances were banned because its female performers were considered immoral. Boys replaced the women on stage, and Kabuki performances continued.

1629 Oct. 3 **Paolo Agostini** (b. 1583?), an Italian musician, died. Most of his compositions, published as well as unpublished, are extant and include masses, magnificats, and psalms. Agostini employed the developing form of counterpoint with great finesse.

1630–1639

I. DISASTERS

1631 Dec. 16   Mount Vesuvius, on the eastern side of the Bay of Naples, erupted, destroying six villages on its slope and sending mud flows over nine others. The lava flowed into the bay, and the sky was darkened for several days by smoke and ashes.

II. EXPLORATION AND COLONIZATION

1630   Hoboken, in New Jersey, was purchased by the Dutch from the Indians.

1630   French pirates established a base on Spanish-held **Hispaniola**, called Saint Domingue by the French, who thus began their encroachment of the Caribbean island.

1630 July 7   John Winthrop, elected governor of the **Massachusetts Bay Colony** by the board of directors and the members, landed at Salem. The following day a formal thanksgiving was held celebrating their safe arrival. He came with 11 ships and carried the colony's charter; estimates of the number of colonists who came with him vary from c.900 to c.2,000. Some of these went south of Salem to found Charlestown, then moved (Sept. 17) to a hilly peninsula they had named Trimontaine and changed the name to Boston.

1632 June 20   The charter of Maryland was granted by Charles I, king of England, to **Cecil Calvert** (1606–Nov. 30, 1675), Lord Baltimore, whose father **George Calvert** (born c.1580) had first applied for the concession but had died on Apr. 15, 1632, before it was issued. The Baltimores had long wanted to establish a haven for English Roman Catholics in the New World. On Mar. 25, 1634, more than 200 colonists landed at St. Clement's Island, present Blakiston Island, at the mouth of the Potomac River. They built Fort St. George, which became **Saint Marys** [Saint Marys City], the first and oldest colonial settlement in Maryland.

1634   Jean Nicolet (1598–1642) landed at **Green Bay, Wisconsin**, on the shore of Lake Michigan during an exploring trip to find a waterway to the Pacific Ocean. Green Bay became important as part of an inland westward route from the Great Lakes, along the Fox and Wisconsin rivers to the as yet undiscovered northern reaches of the **Mississippi River**.

1635 Sept. 17   Martinique, West Indies, was occupied by French settlers led by **Pierre Belain d'Esnambuc** (1585–1637). **Guadeloupe** was also settled at this time, and flourishing colonies developed from the export of sugar cane.

1635 Oct.   Roger Williams (1603?–c.Mar. 1683), a nonconforming Puritan clergyman of Salem, Massachusetts, was banished by the magistrates of the **Massachusetts Bay Colony**, whose use of power to enforce religious principles Williams had protested. In Jan. 1636, he fled with a group of followers and founded (June) a colony at **Providence**, the first permanent settlement in Rhode Island. The government established by Williams was characterized by religious toleration, democratic institutions, separation of church and state, and friendly relations with the Narragansett Indians.

1638   Fort Christina was built near the present site of **Wilmington, Delaware**, by Peter Minuit, the former governor of the Dutch colony of New Netherland, and by Finnish and Swedish settlers he had brought from Sweden. He purchased from the Minquas Indians the region extending indefinitely westward between **Trenton**, New Jersey, on the Delaware River, and the Schuylkill River in Pennsylvania. The colony became known as **New Sweden**.

III. POLITICS AND WAR

1630 July 6   During the Thirty Years' War (1618–1648) Gustav II Adolf, king of Sweden, landed in Pomerania, a Protestant duchy on the Baltic shore of Germany, to begin his invasion of the Holy Roman Empire (962–1806) on behalf of the Protestant princes. On Jan. 23, 1631, by the **Treaty of Bärwalde**, he secured the aid of France, which paid the Swedes for their warfare against Ferdinand II, the Holy Roman emperor. Gustav then secured the alliance of most of the German Protestant princes at the **Convention of Leipzig** on Feb. 20.

1630 Nov. 10   On the Day of the Dupes, Louis XIII finally supported his prime minister **Cardinal Richelieu** in a pro-national, anti-Hapsburg policy against his mother Marie de Médicis and his wife Anne of

Austria (Sept. 22, 1610–Jan. 20, 1666), sister of Philip IV, the Hapsburg king of Spain. Marie, banished (Feb. 1631) to Compiègne in northern France, fled to Brussels and never again returned to France.

1631 May 20 Imperial Catholic forces led by Johan Iserclaes, count of Tilly, destroyed the strategic fortress of **Magdeburg**, in present Germany. The massacre of the Protestant population, followed by Tilly's invasion of Saxony, brought the electorates of Brandenburg and Saxony into the Swedish-led Protestant coalition on, respectively, June 20 and Sept. 11. Imperial forces seized (Sept. 15) Leipzig, and the Protestant forces, commanded by Gustav II Adolf, king of Sweden, moved southward across the Elbe. On Sept. 18 the two armies met at Breitenfeld, just north of Leipzig, and the Saxons and Swedes overwhelmed the imperial troops in the **first major Protestant victory of the Thirty Years' War** (1618–1648).

1631 June 19 The **Treaty of Cherasco** ended the war of succession in Mantua, Italy, which was the first direct confrontation between France and the Holy Roman Empire in the **Thirty Years' War**. The empire abandoned its claim to Mantua, which passed to the Frenchman Charles Gonzaga, duke of Nevers.

1632 The **Treaty of St. Germain-en-Laye**, a suburb of Paris, restored to France the territory of New France that stretched along the St. Lawrence River and included the coastal region of present eastern Canada.

1632 **Susenyos**, emperor (from 1607) of the **Ethiopian** [Solomonic] **Dynasty** (1268–1974), abdicated in favor of his son Fasilidas (to 1667). The Portuguese and Spanish Jesuit missionaries were expelled, and the native **Coptic religion** and customs were restored.

1632 Nov. 16 In a **battle at Lützen**, near Leipzig, in present Germany, Protestant forces again defeated troops of the Holy Roman Empire, commanded by Albrecht Wenzel Eusebius von Waldstein [Waldenstein, Wallenstein]. But the Protestant commander Gustav II Adolf (b. Dec. 9, 1594), king of Sweden (from 1611), now at the height of his power, was killed. His daughter Christina (Dec. 8, 1626–Apr. 19, 1689), succeeded him, and ruled under the regency (until 1644) of Count Axel Oxenstierna [Oxenstjerna] (June 16, 1583–Aug. 28, 1654).

1634 Sept. 6 Imperial troops, led by Matthias Gallas (Sept. 16, 1584–Apr. 25, 1647) and the archduke Ferdinand, son of Ferdinand II, the Holy Roman emperor, routed the Protestant army under Bernhard of Saxe-Weimar, in a **battle at Nördlingen** in Bavaria. Most of the German princes now abandoned the Protestant coalition led by Sweden. The **Peace of Prague**, signed by Ferdinand II on May 30, 1635, rendered null and void the **Edict of Restitution** (1629).

1635 The **Arabian tribes** of the Zaydis [Zaidi] sect, in present Yemen, regained their independence from the **Ottoman Empire** (1326–1920). Under the Qasimid Imam Muhammad al-Mu'ayyad (ruled 1620–1654), they recaptured most of the southeastern Arabian Peninsula, including the port of Mocha, noted for the export of Arabian coffee.

1635 May 19 Fearing encirclement by Hapsburg domains, **Cardinal Richelieu** led Catholic France into war with Catholic Hapsburg Spain, following the recent defeat suffered by Sweden and the Protestant German princes in the **Thirty Years' War** (1618–1648). French armies invaded the Spanish Netherlands and Hapsburg-controlled Franche-Comté, situated north of Savoy on the eastern border of France. On July 11 France formed the anti-Hapsburg **League of Rivoli** with Savoy and Parma.

1636 The **Pequot War** (to 1637), the **first war between Indians and New England colonists**, broke out when a Pequot Indian was held responsible for the murder of an English trader, John Oldham, on Block Island, in Long Island Sound. The Narragansett Indians of Rhode Island, under the influence of Roger Williams, came to the aid of the English settlers.

1636 Oct. 4 In a **battle at Wittstock**, Swedish troops led by Johan Banér (July 3, 1596–May 20, 1641), commander-in-chief of Swedish forces in Germany, routed allied imperial and Saxon forces. The victory reestablished Swedish and Protestant supremacy in northern and central Germany during the Thirty Years' War.

1637 The West African fort of Elmina, on the Gold Coast of present **Ghana**, was seized from Portugal by a Dutch force. The **Portuguese expulsion from West Africa** was completed in 1642, when the Dutch conquered the fort of Axim, securing their commercial hegemony along Cape Verde and the Gold Coast.

1637 May 26 Captains **John Underhill** (1597?–1672) of Fort Saybrook and **John Mason** (1600?–1672) of Windsor, both on the Connecticut River, led colonial troops supported by the Narragansett Indians in an assault of the main Pequot fort at Mystic, Connecticut. Remaining Pequot tribesmen were slaughtered by Massachusetts troops, commanded by **Israel Stoughton** (d. 1645?), at Fairfield, Connecticut, on July 13, 1637.

1638 Murad IV (July 27, 1612–Feb. 8, 1640), the Ottoman sultan (ruled from 1623), recaptured Baghdad from Persia, forcing Safi, shah (1629–1642) of the **Safawid** [Safavid] **Dynasty** (1501–1736), to sue for peace. The **Treaty of Sehab** [Zohab, Sarab, Kasr-i Shirim] (1639) stabilized the Turko-Persian frontier after more than a century of intermittent warfare.

1639 May 24 The minor military engagement of Turrif, Scotland, opened and closed the **First Bishops' War** between Charles I, king of England and of Scotland, and the Scottish Presbyterians. Charles signed the **Peace of Berwick-upon-Tweed** (June 18), granting the right of the Scottish Parliament and the Presbyterians to assemble freely but failing to secure establishment of the episcopacy in Scotland.

IV. ECONOMY AND TRADE

1630 A partially successful attempt to **drain large swampy areas** was directed by a Dutch engineer **Cornelius Vermuyden** (1595–?Apr. 1683), in c.400,000 acres of England's southeastern counties.

1631 May The **first weekly French newspaper**, *Gazette de France*, was published. It covered local news as well as foreign events.

1633 The **first sawmills in North America**, wind driven and inefficient, were built on Manhattan Island. The first water-driven sawmill in North America was probably built (c.1633) on Salmon Falls River, near Portsmouth, New Hampshire.

1634 Oct. 20 Charles I, king of England, issued the **first writ of ship money**, a tax levied on the tonnage handled by the port of London.

1637 The *Sovereign of the Seas*, a great warship of the 17th century, was launched by England. It was 232 feet long and carried 100 guns.

1638 The **first textile factory in the present U.S.** was established in the newly settled town of Rowley, near present Ipswich, Massachusetts.

1639 Oct. The **first apple crop in North America** was harvested on an island near Boston Harbor.

V. RELIGION AND PHILOSOPHY

1632 The **first Roman Catholic Church in colonial America** was erected at Saint Marys City, Maryland, where Lord Baltimore established his colony in this year.

1633 June 21 Galileo Galilei, the Italian astronomer, was found guilty by the Inquisition at Rome of "vehement suspicion of heresy" for having "held and taught" the Copernican view of the universe in his *Dialogo dei due Massimi Sistemi del Mondo* [*Dialogue of the Two Chief World Systems*] (1632), in defiance of the injunction issued by Cardinal Robert Bellarmine in 1616. The decision ignored the fact that Galileo's book had been cleared by papal censors before publication. Galileo was sentenced to indefinite house arrest at Arcetri, near Florence, where he had a professorship at the university.

1637 The **Shimabara Revolt**, a peasants' uprising, said to have been instigated by **Iyemitsu** (1604–1651), the Tokugawa shogun (from 1623) of Japan, broke out in the area of Nagasaki. The peasants carried many banners bearing Christian crosses, which the shogunate interpreted as a sign that the Christians in Japan fomented and were supporting the action. About 37,000 Christians were massacred. After this the Dutch and Portuguese, the last European traders in Japan, were forcibly expelled.

1637 England's Star Chamber ordered that all books imported for the purpose of sale had to be approved by representatives of either the archbishop of Canterbury or the bishop of London.

1637 July 23 Scottish Presbyterians in Edinburgh rioted in protest against the order of Charles I, king of England, requiring the use of the Anglican liturgy in the churches of Scotland. William Laud, archbishop of Canterbury (from 1633), had promoted this decree.

1639 The **first Baptist church in the present U.S.** was established in Providence, Rhode Island, the colony founded (1636) by **Roger Williams**. Williams's assertion of freedom in religious belief and his own declaration (1639) of being a "Seeker" brought large numbers of dissenting Anabaptists and Quakers to the colony.

VI. SCIENCE, EDUCATION, AND TECHNOLOGY

1630 **William Bradford**, governor of the Plymouth Colony, began an early account of life in Puritan New England. His *History of Plymouth Plantation* took more than 20 years to complete and was not published until 1856.

1630 Nov. 15 **Johannes Kepler** (b. Dec. 27, 1571), a German astronomer, died. Kepler formulated laws of planetary motion that supported and explained the Copernican system by mathematical elaborations of the premise that the path of orbit is an ellipse.

1631 Jan. 26 **Henry Briggs** (b. Feb., 1556), an English mathematician, died. With John Napier, considered the inventor of the logarithm, Briggs developed the logarithms in the base ten system that are used today. His *Arithmaetica logarithma* (1624) contained a table of all the common logarithms from one to 20,000 and from 90,000 to 100,000, carrying the decimal to 14 places.

1632 **Shah Jahan** [Jehan] (Jan. 5, 1592–Jan. 22, 1666), the Mogul [Mughal] emperor of Hindustan (ruled 1628–1658), brought **Mogul architecture** to its height with the construction at Agra of the **Taj Mahal**, the tomb of his favorite wife, Mumtaz Mahal [Arjumand Banu] (d. 1631). It was designed by **Ustad Isa**, a Persian; **Austin de Bordeaux**, a Frenchman; and **Gieronimo Veroneo**, an Italian. It was completed in 1648.

1634 **Boston Common**, 45 acres of land in downtown Boston, was designed town, or "common," property.

1634 Sept. 3 **Edward Coke** (b. Feb. 1, 1552), an English jurist, died. As chief justice (1606) of the Court of Common Pleas and as chief justice (1613) of the King's Bench, he supported application of the common law against attempts by the crown to rule by royal prerogative. Coke's judicial writings included *Reports* (1600–1615), compilations of the records of law cases, and his four *Institutes* (1628–1644).

c.1635 An **early map of the moon's surface** was attributed to **Nicolas Claude Fabri de Peiresc** (Dec. 1, 1580–June 24, 1637), born in France, who had a reputation for scholarship in broad fields of knowledge.

1635 The **oldest public school in the U.S.**, the **Boston Latin School**, opened. Its classical curriculum followed that of the English schools.

1636 Oct. 28 **Harvard College** was founded, the **oldest such institution in the U.S.**, in New Towne [present Cambridge], Massachusetts, as decreed by the general court of the Massachusetts Bay Colony. It was endowed by **John Harvard**, a nonconformist minister, to provide for "education such as offered by the best such institutions in Europe for the progeny of well-placed colonial families."

1638 The **log cabin** was first introduced in America by Swedish settlers along the Delaware River in Pennsylvania.

1638 The American printer **Stephen Daye** [Day] (1594?–Dec. 22, 1668) introduced the **first press into Protestant North America**, at Cambridge, Massachusetts. It was a Dutch press with a platen that rose automatically. Invented (c.1620) by **Willem Janszoon Blaeu** (1571–1638), in Amsterdam, the automatic platen, which pressed the paper against the type, greatly increased the efficiency of the press. Daye had brought with him a case of type from England, which he used in printing the first document in colonial America, **Oath of a Free-Man (1639)**.

1639 **Gérard Desargue** (1593–?1662), a French mathematician, published a treatise on conic sections, which are projections of circles and ellipses.

VII. ARTS AND LEISURE

1630 The stock character of **Don Juan** first appeared in a literary work *El Burlador de Sevilla* [*The Trickster of Seville*], by **Tirso de Molina** (1581?–Mar. 12, 1648), a Spanish friar and playwright, said to have written c.400 plays. The tale of Don Juan incorporated the key elements of folklore: the heartless seducer, who shamed a girl and killed her father, was haunted by the father's ghost, and suffered eternal punishment for his deed.

1631 **Michael Drayton** (b. 1563), an English poet, died. *Idea, The Shepherd's Garland* (1593) was a pastoral in the common style of the day, celebrating a young woman. *Polyalbion* (1622), a poetic description of the physical beauty of the British Isles, was his most ambitious effort.

1631 Mar. 31 John Donne (b. 1572), the most celebrated English metaphysical poet, died. Donne was ordained (1615) as an Anglican minister after a deep struggle with his Roman Catholic upbringing. Before his ordination, Donne wrote *Elegies, Songs and Sonnets*, and *Divine Poems*. His later work included many sermons; especially famous was the last sermon he preached, *Death's Duel*. The first collection of Donne's poems appeared in 1633.

1633 The **Oberammergau Passion Play**, a renowned pageant based on the Passion of Christ, began its cycle of performances, which is said to have been repeated every ten years to the present. The custom was initiated by the townspeople of Oberammergau in Bavaria, Germany, who were spared from the Black Death.

1633 Mar. 1 George Herbert (b. Apr. 3, 1593), an English metaphysical poet and church rector, died. All his poetry was religious in nature. His main work, *The Temple; Sacred Poems and Private Ejaculations*, was published in this year shortly after his death.

c.1635 The **Urdu language**, a form of Hindi written in the Persian script, gained new prominence with its first major literary work, *Sab Ras*, by **Mulla Vajhi**.

c.1635 Thomas Dekker [Decker] (born c.1570), an English writer, died. A play, *The Shoemaker's Holi-*

day (1600), his best-known work, satirized London's aristocrats.

1635 The **Académie Française**, the arbiter of French literary standards and guardian of the French language, was founded by **Cardinal Richelieu** in Paris.

1635 Aug. 27 Lope de Vega [Lope Félix de Vega Carpio] (b. Nov. 25, 1595), a Spanish dramatist, died. Known as the most prolific dramatist in world literature, Lope was said to have written more than 2500 *comedias* and shorter pieces. Though his plays were well constructed and many of them are performed today, no single play has emerged as a world masterpiece.

1637 Aug. 6 Ben Jonson (b. June 11, 1572), an English actor, playwright, and poet, died. Jonson was famous for his comedies, among them: *Volpone, or the Fox* (c.1605); *Epicene, or the Silent Woman* (1609); *The Alchemist* (1610); *Bartholomew Fair* (1614); and *The Devil Is an Ass* (1616). In his day Jonson was generally considered the greatest figure of the English stage, but with the passage of time his plays, which were filled with topical allusion and turned character into caricature, have passed into relative obscurity.

1639 Aug. 4 Juan Ruiz de Alarcón y Mendoza (born c.1580), a Mexican-born Spanish dramatist, died. A leading playwright in the style of Lope de Vega, he usually wrote the so-called "comedy of ethics," poking fun at the despicable among us. *La verdad sospechosa* [*The Truth Suspected*] (c.1619) was his best-known play.

1640–1649

I. VITAL STATISTICS AND DEMOGRAPHICS

1642 Abel Janszoon Tasman (c.1603–c.1659), a Dutch navigator, explored eastern Australia and **Tasmania**, becoming probably the first European to encounter the aborigines there.

II. DISASTERS

1642 Severe **flooding** occurred in central northeastern **China** when the course of the Yellow River [Hwang Ho, Huang He] was diverted by rebel forces opposing the **Ming Dynasty** (1368–1644). K'aifeng, in present Honan [Henan] province, was destroyed and c.300,000 people lost their lives.

1642 Plague broke out in Egypt, killing c.2 million people.

III. EXPLORATION AND COLONIZATION

c.1640 French **Jesuits** founded a mission at the present site of **Sault Ste. Marie**, Michigan, where Lake Superior joins Lake Huron.

1642 Aug. **Abel Janszoon Tasman**, commissioned by the **Dutch East India Company**, sailed south of Australia to discover Tasmania, which he called Van Diemen's Land after the governor general of the company. He reached New Zealand [Nieu Zealande], which Tasman called Staaten Land and believed it to be part of a continent, on Dec. 13, 1642.

1642 The French established the **first European settlement on Madagascar** at Fort-Dauphin. In 1648 Étienne de Flacourt (1607–1660) was appointed governor general of the colony, which was situated on the southeastern shore of the island.

1642 The town of **Ville-Marie de Montréal** was founded by Paul de Chomedey (1612–1676), sieur de Maisonneuve, a French explorer, on the present site of Montreal.

1643 Johan Björnsson Printz (1592–1663), governor of New Sweden, founded the **first permanent settlement in present Pennsylvania** south of Philadelphia, on Tinicum Island, in the Delaware River.

1644 **Roger Williams**, the founder of Providence, Rhode Island, received a formal charter for his settlement from Charles I, king of England. On May 29, 1647, the **Rhode Island General Assembly** convened at Portsmouth, where representatives from the towns of Providence, Newport, and Warwick drafted a constitution.

IV. POLITICS AND WAR

1640 Apr. After 11 years during which no Parliament met, the **Short Parliament** was convened by **Charles I**, king of England, in order to request financial subsidies and to offer, in return, the withdrawal of the writs of ship money issued from 1634. The House of Commons under the leadership of John Pym (1584–Dec. 8, 1643) ignored the king's request and, instead, presented a list of grievances, which included opposition to the impending **war with Scotland**. After the shortest tenure in British history the Parliament was dissolved on May 5 by Charles, who would tolerate no interference with his Scottish policy.

1640 Aug. 20 The **Second Bishops' War** began as a Scottish force invaded England. The Scots, supported by Presbyterian elements of Parliament, won (Aug. 28) a skirmish at Newburn-on-Tyne and occupied Durham and Northumberland, compelling Charles to compromise at the **Treaty of Ripon** (Oct. 26), which called for the end of hostilities and required Charles to support the Scottish army in England.

1640 Nov. 3 The **Long Parliament** (to 1644) was summoned by Charles under pressure from his advisors. Charles agreed to sign the **Triennial Act**, which mandated the meeting of Parliament at least once every three years; signed legislation abolishing prerogative courts, such as the Star Chamber; and agreed to provisions that prevented the dissolution of Parliament without its own consent. He was coerced into signing an order for the execution of his favorite counselor Thomas Wentworth, earl of Strafford (b. Apr. 13, 1593), who was beheaded on May 12, 1641, on a charge of treason initiated and passed by Parliament for supporting Charles's anti-Presbyterian policies in Scotland.

1640 Dec. 1 **Portugal** seized its independence from Spain, taking advantage of Spain's involvement in the Thirty Years' War and its preoccupation with quelling a revolt in Catalonia. John (Mar. 18, 1604–Nov. 6, 1656), duke of Braganza and a descendant of John III, king of Portugal (ruled 1521–1557), was crowned **John IV** [the Fortunate] on Dec. 15, beginning the **Braganza Dynasty** (to 1910).

1641 Nov. 23 The **Grand Remonstrance**, a long list of royal errors, was recited to Charles I, king of England, by **John Pym**, leader of church reform and anti-Royalist sentiment in Parliament. The Parliamentary faction demanded the right of Parliament to appoint the royal ministers, administer the church, and to raise an army.

1642 Aug. 22 **Charles I** raised the Royal Standard at Nottingham and began his march to London, beginning the **English Civil War** (to 1648). The first major battles, including the one fought at Edgehill on Oct. 23, were indecisive. Success, however, generally favored the Parliamentary forces, due to the military skill of Thomas Fairfax (Jan. 17, 1612–Nov. 12, 1671) and Oliver Cromwell.

1643 May 14 Louis XIII (b. Sept. 27, 1601), king of France (from 1610), died and was succeeded by his son, **Louis XIV**, under the regency of the queen mother Anne of Austria. Anne appointed (May 18) **Cardinal Mazarin** as prime minister to replace Cardinal Richelieu (b. Sept. 9, 1585), who had died on Dec. 4, 1642. Mazarin followed the nationalistic policies of Richelieu, strengthening the crown and avoiding encirclement of France by the Hapsburgs.

1644 Apr. **Li Tzu-Ch'eng**, a Chinese rebel, took Peking, capital of China under the **Ming Dynasty**. Chu Yu-Chien [Ch'ung-Chen, Chuang-Lieh-Ti, Ssu-Tsung, Huai-Tsung, I-Tsung] (b. 1611), the Ming emperor (ruled from 1627), committed suicide on Apr. 25, bringing an end to the Ming Dynasty (from 1368). On Oct. 30 the Manchu, Fu-lin [Shun-chih, Chang Huang-ti, Shih-tsu] (d. 1661), established the **Ch'ing** [Manchu] **Dynasty** (1644–1911) at Peking.

1644 July 2 In the **English Civil War Oliver Cromwell**, leading the Parliamentary army of **Roundheads** and Scots, in a **battle at Marston Moor** in northern England dealt a major blow to the Royalist troops led by Prince Rupert (1619–Nov. 29, 1682), the German nephew of Charles I, king of England. Cromwell won another victory, at Naseby in central England on June 14, 1645. Later in the year the Royalists were again defeated (Sept. 13) at Philiphaugh in southern Scotland. In the spring of 1646 Charles slipped through the Royalist lines to surrender (May 5, 1646) to the Scots. The English Civil War was effectively ended. The Scots agreed to sell Charles to Parliament for their back pay (£400,000) and he was delivered to the English Parliament on Feb. 3, 1647. He escaped from London and found refuge on the Isle of Wight, off southern England.

1647 Dec. 26 **Charles I** sought alliance with Scotland in return for certain favors to Presbyterians if they aided him in regaining the throne of England. Oliver Cromwell and his **New Model army** brought swift defeat to the invading Scottish army in a **battle at Preston** below the Scottish border from Aug. 17 to 20, 1648, ending the so-called **second phase of the English Civil War** (1642–1648). On Jan. 20, 1649, the **Rump Parliament**, the last remnant of the **Long Parliament** (1640), brought Charles I to trial. He was sentenced to death for his treasonable alliance with Presbyterian Scotland.

1648 Jan. 30 The **Peace of Westphalia** between Spain and the United Provinces [the Netherlands] was signed at Münster, in present Germany. Spain recognized the independence of the Netherlands, first declared (1579) by the **Union of Utrecht**.

1648 May Cossack troops, seeking **Ukrainian independence**, under Bogdan Chmielnicki [Chmielnitzki, Khmelnitski] (1593?–Aug. 25, 1657) defeated a Polish army in the Ukraine in eastern Poland. The Cossacks' slaughter of Poles, especially Jews, was unremitting. The Cossacks carried their campaign into Lithuania until, on July 1, 1651, they suffered a stunning defeat by the Polish army under **John II Casimir** (Mar. 22, 1609–Dec. 16, 1672) in a **battle at Berestechko** [Beresteczko] in the northwestern Ukraine.

1648 May 17 French forces under Turenne [Henri de La Tour d'Auvergne, vicomte de Turenne], allied with Swedish forces under Karl Gustav Wrangel (Dec. 13, 1613–June 25, 1676), routed the army of the Holy Roman Empire at Zusmarshausen in Bavaria, Germany, and gained control of **Bavaria**.

1648 Oct. 24 The **Treaty of Westphalia** [Peace of Westphalia], signed at Münster, in present Germany, ended the **Thirty Years' War** (from 1618) between the Holy Roman Empire, allied with the German Catholic princes, and the German Protestant princes, allied with France and Sweden. The empire recognized the sovereignty and religious freedom of the Protestant northern German states, as well as of Saxony and Bavaria. The Palatinate gained an additional elector in compensation for ceding the Upper Palatinate to Bavaria. The Hapsburg hereditary possessions, which included Austria, Bohemia, Hungary, Silesia, and Milan, remained Catholic. Sweden obtained Pomerania and Bremen; control over the Elbe, Oder, and Weser estuaries; a seat in the imperial Diet; and an indemnity. France, the main beneficiary of the broken empire, gained full control of the towns of Metz, Toul, and Verdun, in Lorraine; many of the imperial rights in Alsace; and a military outpost along the Rhine River in southern Germany. The treaty officially recognized the independence of the Swiss cantons. Spain made separate settlements following the Treaty of Westphalia, but the French-Spanish War continued.

1649 Jan. 30 **Charles I** (b. Nov. 19, 1600), king of England, of Scotland, and of Ireland (from 1625), was beheaded at Whitehall Palace, London. His son, **Charles II**, was proclaimed king by Scotland on Feb. 5 and, soon afterwards, by Ireland. However, he was exiled to the Hague and the English Parliament abolished the monarchy on Mar. 17, replacing it with a Commonwealth on May 29. **Oliver Cromwell** became its first Lord Protector.

1649 Mar. 11 The **Peace of Rueil** ended the conspiracy of the **Old Fronde** in the French parliament, an attempt by the nobles to curb the expanding power of the kings. The Old Fronde failed, but it was was followed immediately by the conspiracy of the **New Fronde**, organized by the princes in which, at first, the Great Condé, Louis II de Bourbon, duke of Enghein, took a major part, as he was frustrated in his hopes for political power. He was arrested on Jan. 18, 1650, for plotting against the government and released on Feb. 6, 1651. The **Fronde rebellion**, begun in 1648, replete with many battles, ended in 1653, with Louis XIV exercising absolute power.

1649 Spring The **Iroquois Indians** allied with the English in driving the **Huron Indians**, allied with the French, from their lands in the present province of Ontario, Canada.

1649 Aug. 15 Oliver Cromwell's **New Model army** landed at Dublin to subdue the Irish who supported the Royalists and Charles II. Cromwell led the **storming of the garrison at Drogheda** (Sept. 12) and Wexford (Oct. 11), and the campaign resulted in a general massacre of Royalists in Ireland. On May 26, 1650, after a last victory at Kilkenny (1650), Cromwell departed from Ireland, leaving it in the hands of **Henry Ireton** (1611–Nov. 28, 1651), a general in the New Model army and Cromwell's son-in-law.

V. ECONOMY AND TRADE

1641 The Dutch traders remaining in **Japan** since the persecution of the Christians (1623) were transported to the three-acre artificial island of **Deshima** in the harbor of Nagasaki, where a Jesuit mission had been established (1582). There, the handful of traders formed the **only tie between Japan and the western world**.

1646 The **first major iron forge in the New World** was built at Saugus, Massachusetts, which is now Lynn, a suburb of Boston.

1648 England began a nine-year experiment with **tin money**. The experiment failed when it was discovered that tin rusted too easily.

1649 The *Ulozhenie*, a new legal code, institutionalized the practice of **serfdom in Russia**. Although most of the peasantry were already tied to the land, the new law bound them and their descendants to individual landowners for life. Serfs had no legal rights and were at the mercy of their landlord, who administered justice as he saw fit, and who was not allowed to free them. Other repressive measures date from this time. They had grown out of rioting in Moscow during the summer of 1648 in protest against the policies of the regent to Alexis I Mikhailovich [Aleksei] (Mar. 20, 1629–Feb. 8, 1676), czar of Russia (from 1645), who consequently dismissed the regent and called for a meeting of the *zemsky sobor* [Assembly of the Land Committee], which represented all the landed gentry and merchants and was responsible for composing the *Ulozhenie* to present to the czar.

VI. RELIGION AND PHILOSOPHY

1640 **Jansenism**, a Roman Catholic reform movement, was said to have begun with the publication of *Augustinus*, a posthumous work based on the works of St. Augustine, by **Cornelis Jansen** (Nov. 3, 1585–May 6, 1638), bishop of Ypres. Jansen maintained that theology had been diverted from an understanding of real religious devotion. He believed in the need for greater personal holiness, downgraded frequent communion, and held extreme predestinarian views. *Augustinus* was condemned (1642) by Pope Urban VIII (Apr., 1568–July 29, 1644; ruled from 1623).

1642 By this year at least, the **Parsis** [Parsees] of western and central India had adopted the **Hindu system** of *panchayat* for the internal government of their highly restricted community. Of Zoroastrian faith, the Parsis modified the local community council, which decided virtually all cases, from commercial suits to those involving immorality. Excommunication was the direst penalty.

1643 The **Puritan Long Parliament** abolished episcopacy, the practice of church government by bishops. It named 121 clergymen and 30 laymen, overwhelmingly Presbyterian, to the Westminster Assembly, which acted as advisory council on religious matters.

1645 Jan. 10 The archbishop of Canterbury, **William Laud** (b. Oct. 7, 1573), an opponent of English Puritans and Scottish Presbyterians, was executed on Tower Hill in London. He had been impeached by the Puritan Long Parliament on Dec. 18, 1640, and imprisoned in Mar. 1641. His trial for treason proving lengthy and the charges difficult to substantiate, a Parliamentary bill of attainder was substituted, the House of Lords consenting on Jan. 4, 1645.

1646 The Englishman **George Fox** (July, 1624–Jan. 13, 1691), a Leicestershire shoemaker, underwent a transforming experience convincing him that individuals have the capacity to know the divine leader in their lives and that the following of this "Inner Light" leads to the "Light of Life." He became an itinerant preacher, a career that was interrupted eight times for prison sentences as a blasphemer for his protests against the Presbyterians. His followers called themselves the "Children of Light" or "Friends of Truth"; they formed the **Society of Friends**, popularly known as **Quakers**.

1646 John Eliot (1604–May 21, 1690), who as a young minister arrived in the Massachusetts Bay Colony in 1631, began his missionary work among the Indians of Massachusetts, preaching in their Algonqian tongue. Eliot's work led to the formation (1649) in England of the **Society for the Propagation of the Gospel in New England**, the first English missionary society. His translation of the Bible into Indian language (1661–1663) was the **first Bible printed in America**. His success in Christianizing Indians was almost totally erased by the Indian uprisings in 1675, but Eliot continued his labors until his death.

1646 Sept. 1 The **Cambridge Platform**, the constitution of Congregational churches in the colonies of Massachusetts and Connecticut, including Plymouth and New Haven, was drafted by the **Cambridge Synod of Congregational Churches** under the direction of the General Court of Massachusetts. They agreed on a form of church government in which each congregation was self-contained and led by elders or clergymen, of equal rank.

1648 Oct. 27 Ferdinand III (July 16, 1608–Apr. 2, 1657), the Holy Roman emperor (from 1637), abandoned the **Edict of Restitution**, and declared the year 1624 as the basis for determining whether a given ecclesiastical property should be in Catholic or Protestant hands.

1648 **Margaret Jones** of Charlestown, part of present Boston, was the **first person executed as a witch in America**. She was accused of possessing a "malignant touch" that caused deafness or violent illness.

1649 The **Toleration Act**, or Act Concerning Religion, was passed by the Maryland assembly. The act was the first by a colonial governing body to recognize freedom of conscience to be effected by the separation of Church and State.

VII. SCIENCE, EDUCATION AND TECHNOLOGY

1640 The *Bay Psalm Book* [*The Whole Booke of Psalmes Faithfully Translated into English Meter*] was printed in Cambridge, Massachusetts, by Stephen Daye. It was the **first book printed in Colonial America**.

1641 Jan. 3 **Jeremiah Horrocks** (born c.1617), an English astronomer, died. Horrocks described the elliptical path of the moon's orbit, which was first suggested by Johannes Kepler. He also was the first to record (1639) the transit of Venus across the face of the sun.

1642 Jan. 8 **Galileo Galilei** (b. Feb. 15, 1564), an Italian astronomer, mathematician, and physicist, died. In 1604 he noted the effect of gravity and in 1610 he made his first observations of the universe with a refracting telescope of his own design. He found that the moon's light was reflected, there appeared to be mountains on the moon, the Milky Way was made of many stars, Jupiter had four moons, and sunspots moved across the sun's surface. He was condemned (1633) by the **Inquisition**, for public expression of the heretical heliocentric explanation of the movement of heavenly bodies.

1643 **Evangelista Torricelli** (Oct. 15, 1608–Oct. 25, 1647), an Italian physicist and mathematician, discovered the principles on which **mercury barometers** operate to measure air pressure and to measure altitudes and predict weather.

1644 The **Ming Dynasty** (1368–1644) was the last to add to and repair the **Great Wall of China**. Work had begun c.210 B.C. on the c.1,400 miles of defensive walls joining forts around the northern and northwestern frontiers of China.

1647 Nov. 30 Francesco Bonaventura Cavalieri (b. 1598), an Italian mathematician, died. In *Exercitationes geometricae* (1635), he developed the method of calculating indivisible numbers that made possible the solution of problems posed by Johannes Kepler.

VIII. ARTS AND LEISURE

c.1640 Francesca Caccini (Sept. 18, 1587), an Italian musician, died. She may have been the first woman composer of opera. She played several instruments and wrote one of the most extensive collections of solo songs, *Primo Libro* (1618).

1640 The **settle**, a piece of furniture that resembled a chest, appeared in colonial American households. It could be used as a seat, bed, chest, or table. The high back blocked out drafts, and the narrow seat allowed it to be placed in a narrow hallway or corner.

1640 May 30 Peter Paul Rubens (b. June 24, 1577), a Flemish baroque painter, died. He had brought the works of the Italian painters, Michelangelo da Caravaggio, Raphael, and Titian, from Italy to his native Flanders. Rubens excelled in enormous scenes of biblical events or mythical battles as well as in portraiture and landscape. His works included *The Raising of the Cross* (c.1609), *Helen Fourment and Her Children* (c.1635), and *Peasant Dance* (c.1637).

1641 Dec. 9 Anthony Vandyke [Van Dyke] (b. Mar. 22, 1599), a Flemish painter, died. Vandyke's best works included portraits of Charles I, king of England, where he lived for many years, and such religious works as *Crucifixion*, *Elevation of the Cross*, and *St. Augustine* (c.1627–c.1632).

1642 John Suckling (b. 1609), an English wit, poet, and courtier, died, perhaps a suicide. At his own expense Suckling raised a troop of horses for Charles I's projected invasion of Scotland in 1640, and like the rest of the Royalist army, performed poorly. Though Suckling wrote four plays, he was known best for his lyrics and love songs.

1643–1715 The reign of Louis XIV, king of France, lent its name to the **Louis XIV style of furniture**, which was characterized by the luxurious use of wood and veneers, elaborate surface textures, gilt edges, and the generally baroque quality of large curves and extravagant decoration.

1643 Mar. 1 Girolamo Frescobaldi (b. Sept., 1583), an Italian baroque composer, died. His collection of five-part madrigals (1608) was influential, but it was his organ works that displayed an unusual originality in their emotional exuberance. His works are thought to have influenced Johann Sebastian Bach.

1643 Nov. 29 Claudio Monteverdi (b. May, 1567), an Italian opera and madrigal composer, died. *Orfeo*, first performed on Feb. 22, 1607, is the earliest opera still performed. Monteverdi published eight books of five-part madrigals, which by now had supplanted the two-part madrigals prevalent during the 14th century.

1645 Feng Meng-Lung, a Chinese story teller, died. He had collected in written form the many tales that were recited by story tellers in the cities. The *hua-pen*, as they were called, were thus preserved in a vernacular tongue.

1646 Richard Crashaw (born c.1610), an English metaphysical poet, died. A Puritan who converted to the Roman Catholic faith, Crashaw was known best for his religious poetry, especially the collection *Steps to the Temple* (1646).

1648 Jan. 23 Francisco de Rojas Zorrilla (b. Oct. 4, 1607), a popular Spanish playwright, died. Rojas was especially known for his *comedias de pundonar*, plays that treated seriously the Spanish code of honor. His play *Del rey abajo, ninguno, o el labrador más honrado, o García del Castañar* [**None But the King, or The Most Honored Peasant, or García del Castañar**] (1650), set in the 14th century, used an elaborate plot of disguised king, courtier, and peasant to explore seduction and the role of the avenger.

1648 Alexis I Mikhailovich, czar of Russia, decreed a **ban on all amusements** and ordered all theaters and musical instruments destroyed.

1648 May 23 Louis Le Nain (b. 1593), a French painter, died. He painted peasant scenes and poor people in everyday situations, such as *The Peasants' Meal* (1642), in collaboration with his brothers, Antoine (1588?–May 25, 1648) and Mathieu (1607–Apr. 20, 1677). Their subject matter departed from the allegorical scenes characteristic of baroque French art.

1648 Sept. 1 Marin Mersenne (b. Sept. 8, 1588), a French music writer, died. His two-volume *Harmo-*

nie Universelle (1636) described the musical techniques of his day, and compared French music with Italian music. *Traité des Instruments* was an encyclopedia of musical instruments.

1649 **Tukaram** (b. 1608?), generally regarded as the **greatest of Hindu poets** who flourished in the Deccan of central India from the 13th to the 17th centuries, died. Over 4,000 of his poems, written in the Mahrathi language and mostly short and very lyrical, survive today.

IX. SPORTS, GAMES, AND SOCIETY

1642 The **Skating Club of Edinburgh**, Scotland, was formed, giving impetus to the formation of skating clubs across northern Europe.

1650–1659

I. VITAL STATISTICS AND DEMOGRAPHICS

1650 The 300,000 Indians estimated to have lived on the Caribbean Islands in 1492 were extinct by this time. European diseases, such as **smallpox** and **measles**, were much more to blame than the harsh treatment meted out by the Spaniards.

1650 The **population of the Netherlands** reached nearly two million, having increased by two-thirds since 1550.

II. EXPLORATION AND COLONIZATION

1650 **Grenada**, in the West Indies, was purchased from the British by **Dyel Duparquet** (d. 1658), the French governor of Martinique. Duparquet had previously bought Martinique from the French trading company that originally settled it, so the two islands were private domains.

1651 The first settlement in present **Surinam**, on the northeastern coast of South America, was founded by the English under **Francis Willoughby** of Parham, an English nobleman.

1652 Apr. 6 **Capetown** [Kaapstad], Republic of South Africa, was founded by **Jan van Riebeeck** (Apr. 21, 1619–Jan. 18, 1677) of the **Dutch East India Company**. He remained there for about ten years in charge of turning the port into a harbor of refuge and a resupply station for ships enroute between Europe and the Far East.

1659 The French trading post of **Saint-Louis**, Senegal, was founded at the mouth of the Senegal River. It was the first European city on the northern coast of West Africa.

III. POLITICS AND WAR

1650 Sept. 3 The Commonwealth army, led by **Oliver Cromwell**, routed the Scottish army under **David Leslie** (1601–1682), Lord Newark (1661) at **Dunbar**, Scotland. The Scots crowned (Jan. 1, 1651) **Charles**, later Charles II, king of Great Britain and Ireland (from 1660), as king of Scotland at Scone, near Perth. Charles was the last Scottish king to be crowned at this ancient coronation site. An army under Charles marched south into England to Worcester, where Charles was decisively defeated (Sept. 3) by the forces of the Commonwealth. Charles escaped by hiding in a hollow oak tree afterward called the "Royal Oak" at nearby Boscobel, then fled to France, arriving on Oct. 17.

1651 Feb. 6 The French Parlement voted for release of the **Great Condé**, **Louis II de Bourbon**, duke of Enghein, and the dismissal of Cardinal Mazarin as prime minister, thus supporting the alliance of the Old and New Frondes in their conspiracies against the royal government. Condé fled to the Spanish Netherlands, and **Louis XIV**, then thirteen years old, reentered Paris on Oct. 21.

1651 Oct. 9 The **First Navigation Act** was enacted by the British Parliament. It limited the trade of the British colonies in the New World to English or colonial vessels.

1651 Oct. 27 The Royalist stronghold of Limerick, Ireland, was captured by Henry Ireton, completing the **Commonwealth's pacification of Ireland**. To pay the officers who fought in Ireland, Oliver Cromwell granted large tracts of Irish land to his major supporters by an **Act of Settlement**. Protestant English soon started to colonize especially the northern part of Ireland.

1652 June 30 The **First Anglo-Dutch War** (1652–1654) was formally declared. By a series of naval battles, England forced the Netherlands to recognize the **Navigation Act** (1651) in the **Treaty of Westminster** (Apr. 5, 1654).

1653 Apr. 20 **Oliver Cromwell** dissolved the **Rump Parliament**. On July 4 it was replaced with the **Barebones Parliament**, named after a member, Praisegod Barbon [Barebone] (c.1596–1679). It was also known as the **Nominated Parliament**, because it was composed of radicals proposed by Cromwell and the **New Model army**. Cromwell took the oath as Lord Protector and ruled under the **first written English Constitution** (1653–1657), called the **Instrument of Government**, which established a balance of power between the lord protector and Parliament.

1654 In the **Thirteen Years' War** (1654–1667) between Russia and Poland, the Zaporozhian Cossacks, under the leadership of Bogdan Chmielnicki [Khmelnitsky], accepted Russian suzerainty by the **Union of Pereyaslav** (1654), a town near the Dnieper River and Chmielnicki's headquarters.

1655 May **Jamaica** was seized by the British under **William Penn** (Apr. 23, 1621–Sept. 16, 1670), the British admiral and father of William Penn (Oct. 14, 1644–July 30, 1718), founder of Pennsylvania, as part of the expedition to the Spanish West Indies sent by Oliver Cromwell.

1655 Aug. 30 The **First Northern War** (1655–1660) began as Charles X, king of Sweden, invaded Poland and occupied **Warsaw** (Oct. 8, 1655), and Kraków [Cracow] (Oct. 19, 1655). **Frederick William** [Friedrich Wilhelm] (Feb. 16, 1620–May 9, 1688), the Great Elector of Brandenburg (from 1640), allied himself with Sweden at the start of the First Northern War, but in the following year took Poland's side when that country promised to recognize his right to the duchy of Prussia.

1658 June 14 An Anglo-French army under the command of the French **Marshall Turenne**, who was beseiging the Spanish-held city of Dunkerque [Dunkirk] in the Spanish Netherlands, defeated a Spanish army in the **Battle of the Dunes**. The Spaniards, who had been sent to relieve the city, were commanded by **Don John** of Austria; the Great Condé, **Louis II de Bourbon**, duke of Enghein; and **James Stuart**, the duke of York [the future James II, king of England], who led a corps of English Royalists. **Dunkerque** [Dunkirk] fell June 25, and **Gravelines** fell two months later (Aug. 24).

1658 Sept. 3 **Oliver Cromwell** (b. Apr. 25, 1599), the lord protector of England, died and was succeeded by his son **Richard** (Oct. 4, 1626–July 12, 1712). Unable to arbitrate the struggle for power between Parliament and the army, Richard dissolved (Apr. 22, 1659) Parliament, but the Protectorate came to an end with his dismissal (May 25). England now lapsed into a **military tyranny**.

1659 May 25 **George Monck** (Dec. 6, 1608–Jan. 3, 1670), a general in the Commonwealth army and governor of Scotland, reached London (Feb. 3, 1660) with his troops and freed the Rump Parliament, which then voted its own adjournment. Monck then forced new, free parliamentary elections, forming the **Convention Parliament** (Apr. 25), which passed some acts designed to make for a peaceful transition to royal rule and invited Charles II back to England. He arrived in London on May 29, 1660.

1659 Nov. 7 The Franco-Spanish **Peace of the Pyrénées** confirmed the end of the Hapsburg hegemony in Europe, to the benefit of France. By gaining Roussillon and Cerdagne, France established its southern frontier along the Pyrénées. From the Spanish Netherlands, France also acquired Artois and some fortresses in present Belgium and Luxembourg. **Louis XIV**, king of France, married the Spanish infanta **Marie Thérèse** [Maria Theresa] (1638–1683) in June 1660.

IV. ECONOMY AND TRADE

c.1650 The Portuguese gained control of the waters off the coast of present **Angola** near **Šao Paulo de Loanda** [Luanda], where **zimbos**, a species of sea shell, is still found. The zimbo [*Cypraea moneta*], a relatively rare cowry shell, small and greenish yellow, was used throughout primitive areas from West Africa to the southwestern Pacific as a unit of exchange.

1651 Oct. 9 The first of what are called the **Navigation Acts** was passed by the British Parliament. It required a special license of anyone wishing to conduct trade with British colonies. Other acts included: the **Staple Act** (1663), the **Wool Act** (1699), the **Hat Act** (1732), and the **Iron Act** (1750). Each act specified trade restrictions for certain items to benefit England's own industry.

1652 The **colony of Rhode Island** passed legislation stating that no man could be sold or held in the service of another for more than ten years.

1652 May 27 The **pine tree shilling** was the **first coin minted in colonial America**. Boston, Massachusetts, was able to issue its own currency as it had been given a measure of political and financial independence from England.

1657 The **Dutch East India Company** granted land near its base at **Cape Town**, in present South Africa, to some of its employees so that the land could be farmed to provide the naval station with fresh products, which were used to resupply ships rounding the cape.

1659 Feb. 16 The **earliest surviving example of a check** was drawn on this day in London for the sum of £400. Its payment was guaranteed by a firm that handled banking, real estate, and law cases.

V. RELIGION AND PHILOSOPHY

1650 The epithet "Quakers" was used by an English judge, **Gervase Bennet** of Derby, as a taunt while sentencing **George Fox**, founder of the **Society of Friends**, to prison for blasphemy. The legend was that Fox, hailed into court, told the judge to "tremble at the word of the Lord."

1650 Feb. 11 **René Descartes** (b. Mar. 31, 1596), a French philosopher and mathematician, died. Descartes' contributions to algebra included developing Cartesian [from his name] coordinates, which helped locate a point in space; making use of the convention of exponential notation; and developing a method for treating negative roots. As a philosopher, he tried to introduce the discipline of reasoning, intrinsic to mathematics, into philosophical argument. "Cogito, ergo sum" [I think, therefore I am] was the conclusion Descartes reached when he proceeded from the supposition of universal doubt. His works included *Discours de la méthode* [*Discourse on Method*] (1637), *Meditationes de prima philosophia* [*Méditations métaphysiques, Metaphysical Meditations*] (1641), and *Principia philosophiae* [*Principes de la philosophie, Principles of Philosophy*] (1644).

1651 The social contract theory was proposed by **Thomas Hobbes**, an English political philosopher, in *Leviathan, or The Matter, Form, and Power of a Commonwealth, Ecclesiastical and Civil*. The social contract was an agreement for providing the individual security necessary when people live together in a group. For self-preservation, the foremost law of nature, to be effectively secured, Hobbes believed, it was necessary to invest power in a single individual, the monarch, who was able to maintain order by the awe with which he was regarded.

1652 Aug. 1 **Nikon** [Nikita Minin or Minov] (1605–Aug. 17, 1681) was elected patriarch of Moscow, and head of the **Russian Orthodox Church**. His reforms of church ritual and a new translation of the Russian Orthodox liturgical books caused a deep split in the church. But with the liturgy and ikons brought more in line with the **Greek Orthodox Church**, Russia's assimilation of the Ukraine became easier.

1654 July 8 **Jacob Barsimson**, believed to be the **first Jewish settler in New Amsterdam** [New York City], arrived on a ship from the Netherlands. In September of the same year 23 Jews from the Dutch colony of Recife, Brazil, which had just fallen to the Portuguese, fearing the Inquisition, arrived at New Amsterdam. They received permission from the Dutch West India Company to settle here, despite the objection of Peter Stuyvesant, the Dutch colony's director general, and organized their first congregation, **Shearith Israel**.

1655 **Menasseh ben Israel** (1604–Nov. 20, 1657), a distinguished rabbi at Amsterdam, the Netherlands, negotiated with **Oliver Cromwell**, lord protector of England, for authorization for Jews to return to England, from which they had been banned 350 years earlier. The talks broke down when Cromwell's theological advisers urged restrictive conditions, but permission was granted (1656) to establish a synagogue and cemetery, and resettlement soon followed.

1655 Dec. The **Miracle of Częstochowa**, a turning point in the **First Northern War** (1655–1660), between Protestant Sweden and Catholic Poland, occurred in southern Poland as Polish monks and soldiers took refuge in the town's monastery. There they beat back the Swedes. The shrine at Częstochowa, long a goal of religious pilgrimage, also became a symbol of Polish nationalism.

1656 July The **first Quaker missionaries to North America**, Mary Fisher and Ann Austin, arrived at Boston from the West Indies. They were arrested and deported to Rhode Island, the only state that did not bar Quakers. Strict laws were passed (Oct. 14) in Massachusetts forbidding the presence of the sect, and soon the first trespassers were hanged (Oct. 27, 1659) under this legislation.

1656 July 27   **Baruch Spinoza**, a celebrated Dutch-born Jewish philosopher, was excommunicated and anathematized by the rabbis of Amsterdam, the Netherlands, for his challenge of the Mosaic authorship of the Pentateuch, his notion of salvation, and especially his pantheistic concept of God as substance. Spinoza from then on neither remained a Jew nor became a Christian.

1658   Within the previous ten years, an estimated 100,000 Jews had been killed in the **Ukraine** by the followers of **Bogdan Chmielnicki** [Khmelnitski], whose uprising (1648) against the Polish inhabitants was also directed, with special vengeance, against the Jews that Poland had allowed to settle east of the Dnieper [Dnepr] River.

1658 Sept.   **English Congregationalists** at "a meeting of Elders and Messengers," held at the Savoy, London, produced their first doctrinal statement as a denomination. Their **"Declaration of the Faith and Order owned and practiced in the Congregational Churches in England"** severed ties to Presbyterianism, and set the growing numbers of Congregational churches on their own course, confident of their separatist principles.

1659 June 16   The **first bishop of New France**, François Xavier de Laval-Montmorency (Apr. 30, 1623–May 6, 1708), a Jesuit missionary, landed at Quebec to begin his work as vicar apostolic. Laval strongly promoted the establishment of mission schools, churches, and seminaries.

VI. SCIENCE, EDUCATION, AND TECHNOLOGY

c.1650   European missionaries to present Vietnam completed a dictionary, published in Rome, that **romanized the Vietnamese** [Annamese] **language**, which had been written in adapted Chinese characters since the era when China dominated Vietnam (to A.D. 938).

1657 Sept. 17   **Joachim Jung** [Jungius] (b. Oct. 22, 1587), a German mathematician and philosopher, died. His work on a systematic approach to naming plants foreshadowed that of Carolus Linnaeus. He was the author of **Logica Hamburgensis**, attacking scholastic philosophy and stressing orderly approaches to problems.

VII. ARTS AND LEISURE

c.1650   **Sakaida Kakiemon I** (1596–1666) was said to have perfected a special multi-colored enamel glaze process at his kiln in Arita, Kyushu, Japan. This marked an improvement over an earlier blue underglaze and was perhaps the **first innovation of Japanese pottery**.

1650   *Silex Scintillans*, the major collection of the works of the Welsh metaphysical poet **Henry Vaughan** (Apr. 17, 1622–Apr. 23, 1695) was published.

1650   The **first work in English by an American poet**, *The Tenth Muse Lately Sprung Up in America* by English-born **Anne Dudley Bradstreet** (1612–Sept. 16, 1672), was published in London.

1652 Feb. 17   **Gregorio Allegri** (born c.1582), an Italian musician, died. His *Miserere* is still sung in the Sistine Chapel during Passion Week.

1652 June 21   **Inigo Jones** (b. July 15, 1573), an influential English architect, died. He had studied in Italy and introduced to England the architectural style formulated by **Andrea Palladio**. His work on the Queen's House (1616), Greenwich, near London, was perhaps the earliest expression in England of the **Palladian style**, which exercised a dominating influence there for more than 150 years.

1654 Oct. 12   **Carel Fabritius** (b. 1622), a Dutch painter, was killed in a gunpowder explosion at Delft. Fabritius was one of Rembrandt's students. About ten works by Fabritius have survived, among them *Goldfinch* (1654) and *View of Delft* (1652).

1656   The tragedy *The Siege of Rhodes* by **William D'Avenant** [Davenant] (Feb., 1605–Apr. 7, 1668), an English dramatist, was first performed at Rutland House, where Davenant was able to avoid the Protestant ban (1642) on public performances. This play, which had a musical recitative, was the **first English opera**. D'Avenant became (1638) the **first poet laureate of England**.

1656 Sept. 8   Joseph Hall (b. July 1, 1574), an English author and Catholic bishop, died. His most notable works were the two volumes of verse *Toothless Satires* (1597) and *Biting Satires* (1598), which were patterned after Juvenal.

1657?   Richard Lovelace (b. 1618), one of the Cavalier poets of England, died. Most of Lovelace's poems appeared in two collections of 1649 and 1660.

VIII. SPORTS, GAMES, AND SOCIETY

1653   *The Compleat Angler, or the Contemplative Man's Recreation* by **Izaak Walton** (Aug. 9, 1593–Dec. 15, 1683), an English biographer, first appeared. The work has been reissued in more than 300 editions since its first printing.

1655   Charles Kirby, a London angler and hookmaker, invented a hook with an offset bend of the point. This style of hook, named for him, is still used.

1660–1669

I. VITAL STATISTICS AND DEMOGRAPHICS

1662   Isaac Vossius [Voss] (1618–Feb. 21, 1689), a Dutch scholar, suggested a **world population** figure of 545 million. A year earlier **Giovanni Batista Riccioli** (Apr. 17, 1598–June 25, 1671), an Italian Jesuit professor, had estimated the world population at 900 million.

II. DISASTERS

1660   Quito, present capital of Ecuador, was destroyed by the **eruption of the nearby Pichincha volcano**.

1664–1665   The **Great Plague of London** caused more than 70,000 deaths in a population of c.460,000. This outbreak of **bubonic plague** in England actually claimed fewer lives than the plagues of 1603 and 1625, two in the series of recorded plagues afflicting Europe since 1347. A famous account of life in London during 1665 appeared in *A Journal of the Plague Year* (1722) by **Daniel Defoe**, only five years old at the time of the outbreak.

1666 Sept. 2   The **Great Fire of London** began on Pudding Lane near the Tower of London, started, it was said, by the king's baker. Over three-fourths of the city was destroyed by the time the fire had burned itself out three days later, sparing only the northwestern part of the city. **St. Paul's Cathedral** was destroyed, as were c.13,200 houses, leaving more than 80,000 people homeless. The English architect **Christopher Wren** was commissioned to design a plan for the rebuilding of London.

1667 Nov.   An **earthquake in Caucasia**, between the Black and Caspian seas, claimed the lives of c.80,000 people.

1669 Mar. 25   An **eruption of Mount Etna**, in Sicily, preceded by an earthquake, caused lava to flow over about a dozen villages and towns, killing c.20,000 people. Residents of the area dug trenches to try to direct the flow of lava away from their homes.

III. EXPLORATION AND COLONIZATION

1661   An English force captured a West African Dutch trading fort at the mouth of the Gambia River, in present The Gambia. As **Fort James** it became the **first permanent British settlement in Africa**.

1662   John Winthrop the Younger (Feb. 12, 1606–Apr. 5, 1676), son of the governor of Massachusetts Bay Colony, obtained from Charles II the charter for **Connecticut**, a parcel of land 73 miles wide, but stretching all the way to the Pacific Ocean. The colony of **New Haven** [Quinnipiac], founded in 1638, united with **Hartford**, settled in 1635 by members of the Massachusetts Bay Colony, and other towns to establish the new colony of Connecticut, and to be governed under the Fundamental Orders of self-government drawn up (1639) at New Haven.

1663   Charles II granted to eight Lord Proprietors all lands between the 31st and 36th parallels from the Atlantic to the Pacific. It was called **Carolina**.

1663 Feb. 24 The **colony of New France**, formed for the most part by the present province of Quebec, was returned to the French crown by the financially distressed **Company of New France**, which had done its best to develop the colony for profit since 1628. Louis XIV, king of France, named the region a province of France.

1664 An English force captured the Cape Coast Castle, now Cape Coast in present **Ghana**, from the Swedes, who had built it in 1652.

IV. POLITICS AND WAR

1660 Apr. 14 **Charles II**, exiled king of England, issued the **Declaration of Breda**, a city in the Netherlands, in which he announced a policy of reconciliation toward Parliament. The **Convention Parliament** agreed to the proposals, and Charles II entered London on May 29, to be restored to the throne.

1660 May 3 The **Treaty of Oliwa** [Oliva], a town on the Baltic Sea near Gadansk, Poland, ended the **First Northern War** (1655–1660). **John II Casimir**, king of Poland, abandoned his claim to the Swedish crown and recognized the suzerainty of **Frederick William**, the Great Elector of Brandenburg, over Prussia. Sweden's foothold in the eastern Baltic area was secured by the treaty's acceptance of her occupation of Livonia, a region of southern Estonia and northern Latvia.

1660 June 6 The **Treaty of Copenhagen** ended the war begun in June 1657 by Sweden and Denmark over the Baltic sea ports. It established the present boundaries between Sweden, Denmark, and Norway. It appeared that all Europe was at peace.

1661 Mar. 9 Cardinal Giulio Mazarin (b. July 14, 1602), chief minister of France, died, and **Louis XIV**, king of France, assumed full control of the government. Thus began the personal rule (to 1715) of the **Sun King**, the archetype of absolute monarchy, who said of himself, "L'état, c'est moi" [I am the State].

1661 Apr. 23 The monarchy, and Stuart rule, was formally reestablished in England with the coronation of **Charles II** as king of England and Ireland. He had been crowned king of Scotland in 1651. On May 8, 1661, Charles gained the support of the new Anglican and Royalist "Cavalier" Parliament just elected, which included men who had earlier supported his father, Charles I. On May 21, 1662,

Charles II married Catholic **Catherine de Braganza** (1638– Dec. 31, 1705), daughter of John IV, late king of Portugal. Her large dowry included the Portuguese possessions of Bombay in India and Tangier in Africa.

1662 British forces under the command of **Henry Morgan** (c.1635–Aug. 25, 1688), a Welsh-born buccaneer, sacked the seaport of **Santiago** [de Cuba] on the southern coast of Cuba, the Spanish-held island.

1664 Aug. 29 **Peter Stuyvesant** (1610–Feb., 1672), governor (from 1645) of the Dutch possessions in colonial America, surrendered **New Netherland** to **Richard Nicolls** (1624–May 28, 1672) in the **Second Anglo-Dutch War** (1664–1667). The region comprising present New York state and eastern New Jersey was granted by Charles II to his brother **James Stuart**, duke of York [James II, later king of England]. New Amsterdam was renamed New York and Fort Orange, captured on Sept. 24, with the neighboring Beverwyck village, was renamed Albany.

1666 The sharifian [sherifian] **Saadi Dynasty** (from 1548) was ousted from **Fès**, the capital of Morocco, by the sharif **Mulay al-Rashid** II (ruled 1666–1672). He was a member of the **Filali** [Alawid, Alaouite, Alawite] **Dynasty** (1631–to the present), the second dynasty of sharifs (rulers descended from Muhammad through his daughter Fatima) to rule Morocco.

1666, Jan. 22 **Shah Jahan** [Shahjahan, Shah Jehan, or in youth: Prince Khurram] (b. Jan. 5, 1592) of the **Mogul** [Mughal] **Empire of Hindustan** (1526–1857) died in captivity in the fort at Agra, the empire's capital, where he had been placed when deposed (1658) by his son **Aurangzeb**. Under him and Aurangzeb, Mogul power in India was at its height.

1667 The **Peace of Andrusova**, in present Russia, ended the **Thirteen Years' War** (1654–1667), fought by Russia and Poland over the Ukraine. Russia gained land lying east of the Dnieper [Dnepr] River and including Kiev.

1667 May The **War of Devolution** broke out between France and Spain as the troops of Louis XIV, king of France, seized the Spanish Netherlands. **Devolution** was a form of succession occasionally practiced in the Netherlands, in which the preference for the oldest heir was given to the female offspring of the first marriage. Thus, with the death of Philip IV (b. Apr. 8, 1605), king of Spain (from 1621), on Sept. 17, 1665, Louis claimed the Spanish dominion through his wife Marie Thérèse [Maria Theresa], the daughter of Philip. However, their marriage in 1660 had been preceded in 1659 by the **Treaty of the Pyrénées**, in which Marie had renounced her right of succession, and the four-year-old Charles II was rightfully named king of Spain.

1667 July 31   The **Treaty of Breda** ended the **Second Anglo-Dutch War** (1664–1667). England returned Dutch Guiana [present Surinam] to the Netherlands and loosened the trade controls established by the Navigation Acts. France returned the West Indies islands of Antigua, Montserrat, and St. Christopher to England in return for French Guiana, in South America, and Acadia [Nova Scotia], in Canada. The Dutch colony of New Netherland remained in British hands.

1668 Jan. 23   The [Protestant] **Triple Alliance** was formed by England, Sweden, and the Netherlands, much to the dismay of France, which had signed an agreement with the Holy Roman Empire to take possession of Spanish territory on the death of Charles II, the sickly child-king of Spain. **Louis XIV**, king of France, was forced by the Triple Alliance to rescind his claims.

1668 May 2   The **Treaty of Aix-la-Chapelle** [Aachen], in present Germany, ending the **War of Devolution** (1667–1668) fought by France and Spain, was signed by Louis XIV. Spain regained the Franche-Comté and the Spanish Netherlands from France, which retained 12 fortified sites in Flanders, including Lille, and Tournai and Charleroi, in present Belgium.

1669 Sept. 6   The **Ottoman Turks** captured Candia [Heracleum], the besieged Venetian capital of **Crete**, whose walls had been under Turkish fire from 1648.

V. ECONOMY AND TRADE

1660 July 4   **Charles II**, king of England, established the **Committee for Trade and Plantations of the Privy Council** to oversee the administration of British colonies. Its name was later changed to the **Lords of Trade**.

1662   The **Law of Settlement and Removal**, limiting the responsibility of each parish for its poor to only

what it could support, was enacted in England. Only the poor who were settled were eligible to receive relief, but to be settled a laborer or craftsman had to pay rent at a rate generally above the wages he could earn. The practice of removing the unsettled poor to the last place where they had been settled was now legal.

1663   The **Turnpike Tax** was first levied in England, setting tolls for the use of major roads.

1663   The **export of gold bullion and foreign coins from England** was made legal in order to raise revenues for the government of Charles II without direct parliamentary controls.

1666   **Seigniorage**, the fee collected by the government for the privilege of minting privately owned gold and silver bullion into coins, was abolished in England.

1668   The **Shell-St. Gobain Company**, a glass-making firm, was founded in France.

1669   The once powerful **Hanseatic League** (from 1241) held its last assembly at Lübeck.

VI. RELIGION AND PHILOSOPHY

1662 May 19   The **Act of Uniformity** was passed by **Parliament**. The act required all public religious services to use the ***Book of Common Prayer***, newly revised and including services memorializing the martyrdom of Charles I, king of England, and the Restoration. About 2,000 Puritan clergymen resigned their livings or were forced out during this time of anti-Puritan sentiment.

1663   The **first Bible printed in the Americas**, at Cambridge, Massachusetts, by **Samuel Green** and **Marmaduke Johnson**, was a translation by **John Eliot**, called "the Apostle to the Indians," into the Algonquian language. The Old Testament appeared in this year; the New Testament had been completed in 1661.

1666   **Sabbatai Zebi** [Shabbetai Tzevi] (1626–1676), the messianic Jewish mystic, born in Smyrna [İzmir] on Turkey's Aegean coast, returned there, with growing public affirmation of his claim to being the messiah. The year 1666, chosen by more than one cabalistic cult as the year of the **Apocalypse**, found Sabbatai under arrest in Constantinople where, however, he continued to hold court with his followers. Sabbatai, accused of riding on the surge of popular sentiment, converted to Islam when called to face his captor **Mohammed IV** (Jan. 2, 1642–Jan. 7, 1693), the Ottoman sultan (1648–1687), and many adherents fell away.

VII. SCIENCE, EDUCATION, AND TECHNOLOGY

1660 June 30 **William Oughtred** (b. Mar. 5, 1574), an English mathematician, died. *Clavis mathematicae* (1631) introduced the signs used in multiplication. *The Circles of Proportion and the Horizontal Instrument* (1632) described the use of the predecessor of the logarithmic slide rule.

1660 Dec. 5 The **Royal Society of London for Improving Natural Knowledge** made a formal agreement to meet regularly once a week and to charge dues; a week later the members approved a formal written constitution. They had been meeting irregularly since 1645. It has published, since 1665, *Philosophical Transactions* and, later, *Proceedings of the Royal Society*, which have furnished a survey and resume of scientific endeavors and advancements to the present day.

1662 Aug. 19 **Blaise Pascal** (b. June 19, 1623), a French mathematician and philosopher, died. He designed (1642) a mechanical calculator to be used in the computation of taxes in Normandy, where his father was a tax collector. With his brother, Pascal conducted experiments proving the effects of altitude on barometric pressure in 1646. Pascal defended **Jansenism**, the Roman Catholic reform sect, in *Provinciales* [*Lettres écrites par Louis de Montalte à un provincial*] (1656). In *Les Pensées*, a posthumously published (in complete form, 1844) collection of Pascal's notes and letters, he not only defended Jansenism but revealed the depth of his religious beliefs.

1663 **François Xavier de Laval**, vicar apostolic to **New France** and, later, the first bishop of Quebec, founded a Jesuit seminary in the present city of **Quebec**. The **first college in Canada**, it has since been named **Laval University** in honor of its founder.

1663 The **first turnpike in Great Britain**, along the **Great North Road**, was authorized by the government.

1663 Dec. 28 **Francesco Maria Grimaldi** (b. Apr. 2, 1613), an Italian Jesuit physicist, died. He was noted for his discovery of the refraction of light, revealed in a posthumous publication, *Physico-Mathesis de lumine coloribus et iride* [*Mathematical Physics concerning Light, Color, and the Rainbow*] (1665). Grimaldi drew maps of the surface of the moon, establishing names for features that are in use today.

1665 Jan. 12 **Pierre de Fermat** (b. 1601), a French mathematician credited with invention of differential calculus, died. With Blaise Pascal, Fermat developed the theory of probability. Fermat's crowning achievement was work in the theory of numbers; **Fermat's Last Theorem** (1637?) is still an unsolved problem of number theory.

1665 Nov. 16 The **London *Gazette*, the oldest English newspaper still in publication**, first appeared . . . at Oxford! The official biweekly newspaper was called the Oxford Gazette until the displaced English government returned to London in 1666, when the city was free of the plague.

1666 Construction of the **Canal du Midi** [Languedoc Canal] was begun in France. Completed in 1681, it ran c.150 miles east from Toulouse in southern France where the canal joins the Garonne River to the Étang de Thau, a lagoon that was connected by another canal to the Mediterranean Sea. The canal and the Garonne River together made it possible for shipping to go from the **Bay of Biscay**, on the Atlantic Ocean, to the Mediterranean without going around by way of the **Strait of Gibraltar**.

VIII. ARTS AND LEISURE

1660 The *Chaturdandi-prakashika* (1660), collected by **Venkatamakhi**, a musicologist of southern India, regrouped all ragas, the traditional form of Hindu music, under 72 scales, called **melakartas**. This system is still followed by Hindu musicians.

1660 Aug. 6 **Diego Rodríguez de Silva y Velázquez** [Velásques] (b. June 6, 1599), a Spanish painter whose naturalistic style greatly influenced subsequent Spanish painters, died. Although famous as a portraitist, Velázquez was also known for a style of still lifes he adopted from German predecessors. His use of lighting and composition, especially in his late paintings, as exemplified by *Las Meninas* [The Maids of Honor] (1656), greatly influenced European painters of the 19th century.

1660 Nov. 15 **William D'Avenant** [Davenant], an English dramatist, was granted the authority to form the Duke of York's Players, who performed at Lincoln's Inn Fields, London, producing many of Shakespeare's plays.

1661 The great palace at **Versailles** was begun according to a design of **Louis Le Vau** (1612–1670), who had been commissioned by Louis XIV, king of France. Completed (1708) by **Jules Hardouin-Mansart** (Apr. 16, 1646?–May 11, 1708), the palace was used as a seat of government until the outbreak of the French Revolution.

1661 Jan. 3 The **Drury Lane Company** was the first of London's theatrical companies to use **women actors** to play female roles. The play performed on this day was *The Beggar's Bush* (1622?) by **John Fletcher**.

1662–1722 **Kingtehchen porcelain** was produced in China during the peaceful reign of K'ang-Hsi [Shêng-Tsu] (1654–1722), the Ch'ing [Manchu] emperor (from 1622). The porcelain, noted for its varied colors, came to be known in Europe as Famille Jaune [Yellow group], Famille Verte [Green group], Famille Noire [Black group], and Famille Rose [Pink group]. The pigments were imported from Europe, and the completed pieces often returned there.

1662 *The Day of Doom* or *A poetical description of the great and last Judgement*, a gloomy poem written by the New England Puritan clergyman **Michael Wigglesworth** (Oct. 18, 1631–May 22, 1705), was the first best seller in colonial America.

1665 Aug. 27 *Ye Beare and Ye Cub*, by **Philip Alexander Bruce**, was the **first play** known to have been **performed in colonial America**, at Accomac, Virginia.

1665 Nov. 19 **Nicolas Poussin** (b. 1593?), a French painter, died. For most of his life he worked in Italy, where he executed *The Arcadian Shepherds* (1620). Poussin's works included two series of *Seven Sacraments*, both inspired by the work of Raphael, and the *Four Seasons* (1661), perhaps the most characteristic example of classicism.

1666 Aug. 29 **Frans Hals** (born c.1580), a Dutch painter, died. His paintings included *Gypsy Girl* (1628), an early piece with a festive mood, and a

more somber example, *Man Holding a Skull*. The group portrait *Lady Governors of the Old Men's Home at Haarlem* (1664) and *The Laughing Cavalier* (1624) are his most popular works today.

1666 Sept. 23 **François Mansart** [Nicolas François Mansard] (b. Jan. 23, 1598), a French classical architect, died. In 1636 he had been appointed royal architect by Louis XIII, king of France. His primary contribution was the **Mansard roof**, a two-sloped roof usually separated by dormer windows. The upper roof was nearly flat, and the lower roof nearly vertical.

1667, May 7 **Johann Jakob Froberger** (b. May 18, 1616), a Viennese composer, died. His works for the harpsichord and organ, most of them published posthumously, were among the first to bring keyboard composition to full development.

1668 The first of the 12-volume *Fables choisies, mises en vers* [*Fables*] by **Jean de La Fontaine** (July, 1621–Apr. 13, 1695), a French writer, was published. Although drawn heavily from Aesop's *Fables*, La Fontaine's tales commented more on human nature and social behavior than strictly on a moral point, as did Aesop's.

1669 Oct. 4 **Rembrandt** [Rembrandt Harmenszoon van Rijn] (b. July 15, 1606), a Dutch painter and engraver, died. He mastered the technique of handling light and shadow, the hallmark of the Dutch school of painting. His many paintings include *Night Watch* [*The Sortie of the Banning Cocq Company*] (1642) and *Simeon in the Temple* (1669). His etchings include *Christ Healing the Sick* [also called the "Hundred-Guilder Print"] (c.1645) and *Christ Preaching* (1652).

IX. SPORTS, GAMES, AND SOCIETY

1660 The sport of **yachting** was introduced to England by Charles II, who had been an enthusiast in exile on the Continent.

1668 A **horse race** was held near Hempstead, Long Island, New York, at the so-called "Newmarket Course," named after a race track in England. The winner was awarded a silver porringer, a shallow cup with handles, now in the collection of early colonial silver at Yale University.

1670–1679

I. EXPLORATION AND COLONIZATION

1670   The **Bahamas** were granted to the proprietors of the Carolinas, but the islands were left to pirates until 1717, when **Woodes Rogers** (d.1732) obtained the lease and was appointed governor by the British king.

1670   The **first permanent British settlement in South Carolina** was established at Albermarle Point, near Charleston. The Carolina Charter (1663) set as boundaries of the Carolinas the Atlantic and Pacific oceans between the 31st and the 36th parallels.

1670 May 7   The **Hudson's Bay Company** was established with a charter from Charles II, king of England, granting to British adventurers the right to trap and sell furs in the region of northern Canada draining into Hudson Bay, called Prince Rupert's Land after the nephew of Charles I, king of England. Prince Rupert's Land covered a vast area of what is now Canada. It also included small portions of North Dakota and Minnesota.

1673 June 17   **Louis Jolliet** [Joliet] (Sept. 21, 1645–1700), a Canadian-born explorer, and **Père Jacques Marquette**, entered the **Mississippi River**, proving the existence of a great river of which the Indians had told. They had departed in early spring from Michilimackinac [St. Ignace] on the Straits of Mackinac, and canoed across Lake Michigan to Green Bay, where they entered the Fox River and portaged to the Wisconsin River.

1674   The **first permanent trading settlement of the French East India Company** was established at Pondicherry [Pondichery] on the southeastern coast of **India** in the present state of Tamil Nada.

1677   **Burlington**, near Trenton on the Delaware River, was founded by c.270 **Quakers**, who made this their **first colony in the New World**.

1678   **Bluefields**, on the southeastern coast of Nicaragua, was named capital by the British of their protectorate on the **Mosquito [Miskito] Coast**, in present Nicaragua and Honduras. Bluefields served primarily as a rendezvous port for pirates in the Caribbean Ocean.

1678   A French force took over the trading fort of Arguin, on the cape of Arguin, Mauritania, which the Dutch formally abandoned by the **Treaty of Nijmegen** (Aug. 10).

II. POLITICS AND WAR

1670 June 1   The secret **Treaty of Dover** was signed by Charles II, king of England, at the urging of Louis XIV, king of France, providing for a joint attack on the Netherlands. There was also an open treaty designed to hide the secret treaty. Louis gained the support of Sweden, some German principalities, and finally secured a declaration of neutrality by the Holy Roman Empire in 1671. Then England and France publicly declared war on the Netherlands, respectively on Mar. 17 and on Apr. 6, 1672, beginning the **Third Anglo-Dutch War** (1672–1674).

1671 Jan. 28   **Panama City** was destroyed when **Henry Morgan**, a Welsh-born buccaneer, leading more than 1,000 pirates, sacked this Spanish colonial capital. Ensuing riots damaged whatever remained. Morgan's force also attacked Porto Bello [Portobelo, Puerto Bello], on the Caribbean coast of the isthmus directly across from Panama City.

1672 June 12   The **Third Anglo-Dutch War** began as the French army crossed the Rhine River and overran the Netherlands, whose fleet was engaged at the time by the English. The Dutch resisted the French invasion by opening the dykes to flood their country. On July 4 William III, prince of Orange, who opposed the French, was proclaimed stadtholder. The De Witt brothers, Jan (b. 1625) and Cornelis (b. 1623), Dutch statesmen opposing William's election, were murdered on Aug. 20 by an Orangist mob.

1673 Aug. 8   The Dutch, anchored off Sandy Hook near Manhattan Island, forced the **surrender of New York** during the **Third Anglo-Dutch War** (1672–1674). They held the region until the **Treaty of Westminster**, signed on Feb. 9, 1674, returned it to England.

1674 Feb. 9   The Treaty of Westminster was signed by Charles II, king of England, who shifted from his alliance with France in the **Third Anglo-Dutch War** to a neutral stance toward the Netherlands. His primary reason was that trade with the Netherlands would benefit the battered British economy. Spain, the Holy Roman Empire, Brandenburg, and the Palatinate continued the war against France, allied with Sweden.

1674 Dec. 9   Edward Hyde (b. Feb. 18, 1609), first earl of Clarendon, an English historian and statesman, died. A supporter of Charles I during the **English Civil War** (1642–1648), Hyde was made chancellor of the exchequer and, with the war lost, went into exile. At the Restoration (1660), Charles II, king of England, made him (1659) lord chancellor, but he was dismissed (1667) and went again to France where he wrote the still important *History of the Rebellion* (published 1702–1704).

1675 Jan. 9   Turenne saved Alsace for France against the allied forces of Brandenburg and the Holy Roman Empire in a **battle at Türkheim** [Turckheim] near the Rhine River. The death of Turenne [Henri de La Tour d'Auvergne] (b. Sept. 11, 1611) in battle on July 27, 1675, produced a French retreat and loss of morale. His ability to strike when the opposition was at a disadvantage had maintained France's position of military strength against the greater forces of her opponents.

1675 June 24   King Philip's War began with a **massacre of Plymouth colonists** at Swansea, Massachusetts. **Metacomet**, also called King Philip, the Wampanoag Indian leader, had been angered by the encroachment of colonists on Indian land and by the recent deaths of three of his men at their hands. He headed a coalition of Five Indian Nations in the New England area that included the **Wampanoags**, **Narragansetts**, **Podunks**, **Nipmucks**, and **Mohegans**.

1676 Aug. 12   Metacomet died from a bullet, said to have been shot by another Indian in the service of the Plymouth colonists. **King Philip's War** thus came to an end. The colonists of New England, who had lost many men, were considered the victors because they retained their settlements.

1676 Sept. 19   Bacon's Rebellion broke out in Jamestown, Virginia, under the colonist **Nathaniel Bacon**, who advocated a harsh policy toward the Indians of the region. He had initially raised troops against the Indians but, with growing popular support, turned instead on **William Berkeley** (1606–July 9, 1677), the governor of Virginia (from 1642). Bacon (b. 1647) died in this same year, and the insurrection came to an end.

1677   A French force captured the Dutch naval base of **Gorée**, in present **Senegal**. Ceded formally by the Netherlands in 1678, it was made the **first capital of French West Africa**.

1678 Mar.   Ghent [Gent] and Ypres [Ieper] in the Spanish Netherlands [Belgium] were taken by the French, thereby compelling the **United Provinces of the Netherlands** to sue for peace. France was eager to discontinue the war since, without adequate funds, it was unlikely that France could continue to wage war against all of Europe.

1678 Aug. 10   By the Franco-Dutch **Treaty of Nijmegan** [Nimwegen], in the Netherlands, France abolished its harsh trading measures against the Netherlands, and returned all conquered territory except for the West African forts of Gorée and Arguin. The Spanish Netherlands remained under French occupation. By the Franco-Spanish Treaty of Nijmegen, signed on Sept. 17, 1678, Spain abandoned the Franche-Comté, in present eastern France, and 12 more fortifications in the Spanish Netherlands. France continued to occupy Lorraine, just to the north of Franche-Comté.

1679 May 27   The **Habeas Corpus Act** was passed in England, establishing the supremacy of the court over the monarch in treating criminal offenses. To safeguard the personal liberties of those arrested, penalties were imposed on judges who failed to determine the legality of a person's detention before commencing a trial.

III. ECONOMY AND TRADE

1670   England and France signed an agreement to provide twice-weekly **postal service between London and Calais**. The service had been operating informally since the 1500s.

1672   The **first regular postal service in colonial America** was established by Francis Lovelace (1618?–1675), governor of New York, between New York City and Boston along what came to be known as the **Boston Post Road** and, later, as **U.S. Highway 1**. Mail was carried between the two cities monthly.

1672   With the founding of the **Royal Africa Company**, the English slave trade, monopolized by the company, was centered at Jamaica.

1672 Jan. 2   The **Exchequer of England suspended payment of debts** for one year in order to finance the **Third Anglo-Dutch War** (1672–1674). The economic upheaval in England caused by the war resulted in the bankruptcies of many businesses, and the over-spending by the government of Charles II brought on severe financial difficulties.

IV. RELIGION AND PHILOSOPHY

1672   **Margaret Mary Alacoque** (July 22, 1647–Oct. 17, 1690) made her profession of vows as a **Visitandine**, the Roman Catholic visitation order of nuns founded in France in the early part of the 17th century. She was soon testifying to visitations by Jesus Christ, which led her with a priest, **Claude de la Colombière**, to initiate a cult of devotion to the **Sacred Heart of Jesus**.

1672 Mar. 15   The **Declaration of Indulgence** was issued by **Charles II**, king of England. It provided that religious dissenters be given the right of public worship. Parliament, strongly Anglican and holding the purse strings, forced Charles II to cancel the declaration.

1673 Mar. 22   The **Test Act** was pressed on Charles II by Parliament. It barred Catholics from serving in public office by requiring an oath of allegiance to the Anglican Church. **James II**, duke of York and successor to the English throne, was exempted from this act as were other individuals able to obtain an act of indemnity releasing them from this requirement.

1675   **Philipp Jakob Spener** (Jan. 23, 1635–Feb. 5, 1705), a Lutheran pastor at Frankfurt-am-Main, published *Pia desideria*, proposing reforms for **Lutheranism** which, he held, was smothering Christian life. He began to hold meetings at his home for laymen to discuss his sermons, New Testament passages, and religious questions. Other ministers followed his lead. Those who emphasized this kind of intense, personal devotion over the usual religious orthodoxy were dubbed "**Pietists**."

1675 Nov. 11   **Teg Bahadur** (b. 1621), the ninth guru of the **Sikh religion** in India, was executed for his refusal to accept Islam, and his mutilated body was publicly displayed. He had been elevated into martyrdom by **Aurangzeb**, the Mogul emperor of Hindustan (from 1658) and a fanatic Muslim.

1677 Feb. 20   **Baruch Spinoza** [Benedict] (b. Nov. 24, 1632), a Dutch philosopher, died. Spinoza, born in Amsterdam to a family of Jewish heritage that had fled the Spanish **Inquisition**, was excommunicated from the Jewish community in 1656. Unlike Descartes, Spinoza perceived no split between mind and body, nor any division between intellect and will. Similarly God and Nature cannot be distinguished. Spinoza held that a true idea was arrived at by clear thinking, a process like induction, rather than by reliance on deduction or the senses, both of which produced an inferior level of knowledge.

1678 Feb. 18   *Pilgrim's Progress* was published by **John Bunyan** (Nov. 1628–Aug. 31, 1688), an English Puritan, who told the allegorical story of his own conversion, effected in 1655. *Pilgrim's Progress* described Christian's journey to the Heavenly City and the lessons he learned along the way from such companions as Hopeful and Ignorance.

1678 Aug. 28   The so-called **Popish Plot** was revealed to advisers of **Charles II**, king of England. **Titus Oates** (Sept. 15, 1648–July 13, 1705), a renegade son of an Anabaptist preacher, had devised the details of a plot against the life of Charles II in order to enthrone his brother and heir, James II, duke of York, who had converted to Catholicism.

1679   **Aurangzeb**, the Mogul emperor of Hindustan, destroyed 232 Hindu temples in three provinces of **India** this year in his effort to force Hindus to accept Islam.

1679 Dec. 4   **Thomas Hobbes** (b. Apr. 5, 1588), an English political philosopher, died. In addition to *Leviathan* (1651), in which Hobbes set forth his social contract theory, he wrote many other books, especially on mathematics.

V. SCIENCE, EDUCATION, AND TECHNOLOGY

1675   Charles II founded the **Royal Greenwich Observatory** in a suburb of London for the study of celestial bodies to aid navigation. The **prime meridian** was established (1884) at Greenwich, and longitude was calculated from it in order to provide a basis for establishing standard time and a standard reference as to east–west distances around the world.

1679 The **bomb ketch,** or mortar ketch [galiote à bombe], a ship specially designed to carry a mortar large enough to fire a 200-pound or larger bomb, was first constructed by **Bernard Renau de Eliçagay** in France.

VI. ARTS AND LEISURE

1672 Nov. 6 Heinrich Schütz (b. Oct. 8, 1585), a German composer, died. Schütz, who had studied in Venice, introduced to German music the innovations of Italian composers, especially those of **Claudio Monteverdi.** The complete edition of his works, finished in 1894, comprised 16 volumes of choral music, motets, and madrigals.

1672 Dec. 30 John Banister (1630–Oct. 3, 1679), an English violinist and composer, held what may have been the **first public concert for which admission was charged,** at his home in London. Concerts were customarily given only in private homes.

1673 Feb. 17 Molière [Jean Baptiste Poquelin] (b. Jan. 15, 1622), a French playwright, died. He was perhaps the greatest classical dramatist of France. Molière first came to royal attention with a performance of *Le Docteur amoureux* in 1658. Among his better known plays were *Les Précieuses ridicules* (1659), *Le Misanthrope* (1666), *Le Bourgeois gentilhomme* (1670), and *Les Femmes savantes* (1672). Molière was performing in *Le Malade imaginaire* (1673), his play about a hypochondriac, when he fell mortally ill.

1674 Feb. 22 John Wilson (b. Apr. 5, 1595), an English composer and lutenist, died. Wilson's work included *Psalterum Carolinum* (1657) and *Cheerfull Ayres or Ballads* (1660).

1674 Oct. Robert Herrick (b. Aug. 24, 1591), an English lyric poet, died. His collected works, *Hesperides, or the Works both Human and Divine of Robert Herrick, Esq.* (1648), expressed his delight in nature, religious sentiment, and the pleasures of daily life.

1674 Nov. 8 John Milton (b. Dec. 9, 1608), one of the great figures of English literature, died. Milton had lost his eyesight at age 44. *Areopaqitica* (1644), the most famous of Milton's pamphlets, was a protest against the control of publication, repeatedly exercised by England's Star Chamber, put in the context of an examination of the meaning of liberty.

His great epics *Paradise Lost* (1667) and *Paradise Regained* (1671), as well as his play *Samson Agonistes* (1671), formed a trilogy that treated the themes of good and evil, and heroic virtue. A vigorous defender of the Commonwealth and the anti-Episcopal party, as a result of the Restoration he was fined and subsequently lost most of his fortune.

1675 Dec. 15 Jan Vermeer [Jan van der Meer van Delft] (b. Oct. 31, 1632), a Dutch painter, died. His careful study of light and its optical effects was not fully appreciated until photography provided an understanding of the painter's mechanics. Of the relatively few works he produced, *Servant Pouring Milk* (c.1660) and *View of Delft* (c.1660) show Vermeer's technique at its best.

1677 *La Princesse de Clèves* by the **Comtesse de La Fayette** [Marie Madeleine Piache de La Vergne] (1634–May 25, 1693), a French writer, introduced psychological realism to the French novel. La Fayette explored deeply the characters involved in this story of a chaste woman who, though in love with a man, turns down his offer of a love affair.

1677 Aug. Matthew Locke (born c.1630), an English composer of theater music, died. He wrote the musical accompaniment to many theatrical pieces of the time, including *The Siege of Rhodes* (1656), usually considered the first English opera, by William D'Avenant and *The Tempest, or The Enchanted Island* (1674) by Thomas Shadwell.

1678 Aug. 18 Andrew Marvell (b. Mar. 31, 1621), an English metaphysical poet, died. He had been a friend of **John Milton** and served in Parliament, where he became known for his defense of individual liberty. A collection of his works was published posthumously as *Miscellaneous Poems* (1681), which included the lyrics "The Garden," "To His Coy Mistress," and "The Definition of Love."

1679 Feb. 5 Joost van den Vondel (b. Nov. 17, 1587), the national poet and greatest dramatist of the Netherlands, died. The historical tragedy *Gijsbrecht van Aemstel* (1637) celebrated Dutch independence, and *Palamedes* (1625), a political tragedy, was an attack on Calvinist doctrine. *Gijsbrecht van Aemstel,* considered the Dutch national drama, is produced every year on New Year's Day in Amsterdam.

VII. SPORTS, GAMES, AND SOCIETY

1675 Charles II, king of England, attempted to suppress the **coffee houses** because he believed they were hotbeds of sedition.

1676 The **Royal Company of Archers of Edinburgh**, the King's Bodyguard for Scotland, existed as early as this year, though possibly the company was informally organized at an earlier time before records of their activities were kept.

1679 The **Affair of the Poisons** was unmasked in France. At the time it was common practice, for nobility especially, to consult fortunetellers to obtain love powders and poisons for less than honorable reasons. An investigation headed by **Nicolas de La Reynie** led to the execution of 34 people, mostly the purveyors of such potions. Two notables involved in this affair were the fortuneteller **La Voisin** [Catherine Deshayes, Madame Monvoisin], who was burned on Feb. 22, 1680 after implicating **Madame de Montespan** [Françoise Anténaïs de Rochechouart, marquise de Montespan] (1641–May 27, 1707), mistress of Louis XIV.

1680–1689

I. EXPLORATION AND COLONIZATION

1680 Jan. Fort Crèvecoeur was erected on the **Illinois River**, south of present Peoria, Illinois, by **La Salle** [René Robert Cavalier, sieur de la Salle] and **Louis Hennepin** (1626–?1701), French explorers who had sailed the Great Lakes aboard the *Griffon*. They had explored the western shore of Lake Michigan, where at the mouth of St. Joseph River they had constructed Fort Miami, near St. Joseph in southwestern Michigan. In the spring of 1682 La Salle with c.50 men portaged to the Illinois River, descended it to the **Mississippi River**, and explored the Mississippi all the way to its mouth, reaching there on April 9, 1682.

1680 July Louis Hennepin, a French explorer, captured by Sioux Indians while ascending the Mississippi River, was rescued by **Daniel Greysolon** (1636–1710), sieur de Lhut.

1680 Aug. The **Pueblo Revolt** against the Spanish at their capital **Santa Fe** was begun by **Popé**, a respected medicine man of the **Pueblo Indians** in **Taos**, New Mexico. After the deaths of c.380 settlers and 31 missionaries, surviving Spanish colonists retreated down the **Rio Grande** to a site near **El Paso**, where they founded the **Ysleta** [Isleta] **mission** in 1682, the **first European settlement in Texas**. The revolt was possibly the only instance when Native Americans successfully recovered and retained extensive territory taken from them by white men.

1681 Mar. 4 The Quaker **William Penn** obtained from Charles II, king of England, the grant of **Pennsylvania**, which included West Jersey and a large section of present western New York state and, by grants made in 1682, the Lower Counties [Delaware]. Penn intended it to be a refuge, an ideal commonwealth, for **Quakers** and other persecuted people. "There may be room there, though not here [in England] for such a Holy Experiment." From 1682 to 1684 Penn stayed in Pennsylvania and helped to plan the city of **Philadelphia**. In 1682 Penn acquired East New Jersey from **George Carteret**.

1682 The **first European settlement in the present state of Texas** was established at Isleta, near El Paso, by Spaniards retreating from Santa Fe.

1682 Apr. 9 The entire region of the Mississippi River and its tributaries was claimed for **Louis XIV** and named **Louisiana** in his honor by the French *voyageur* la Salle. French Louisiana included all or parts of the present states of Arkansas, Iowa, Missouri, Nebraska, Louisiana, Minnesota, Oklahoma, Kansas, Colorado, Wyoming, Montana, and North and South Dakota. Later, in December, **La Salle** and his companion **Henri de Tonti** [Tonty] (1650–1704) constructed Fort St. Louis, the first permanent white settlement in present Illinois, at Starved Rock on the Illinois River.

1683 **K'ang-Hsi** [Sheng Tsu] (1652–1722), the emperor of China (from 1662), of China's **Ch'ing** [Manchu] **Dynasty** (1644–1911), conquered the island of Taiwan from the rebel remnants of the **Ming Dy-**

nasty (1368–1644). Koxinga [Cheng Ch'eng Kung] (1623–1663) had led deposed Ming supporters to Taiwan after their overthrow in 1644.

1683 Oct. 6 Germantown, a district of Philadelphia, was founded by the **first German settlers in the New World**. **Mennonites** came to the "city of brotherly love" from the Rhineland and Frankfurt under the leadership of Francis Daniel Pastorius.

1685 **French Huguenots** made their appearance in large numbers in the American colonies after the **Edict of Nantes** was revoked. They primarily settled in Massachusetts, New York, Rhode Island, Virginia, and South Carolina.

1686 **Arkansas Post**, the **oldest white settlement in Arkansas**, was established as a trading post on the Arkansas River by **Henri de Tonti**, the French explorer and companion of la Salle.

II. POLITICS AND WAR

1680 Charles II, king of Great Britain, met with Parliament but found his opponents, called **Whigs**, strong enough to introduce a bill of Exclusion designed to bar Charles's brother James, the duke of York, from the throne. The bill failed to pass the **House of Lords**. Parliament was again called into session (Feb. 1681) but dissolved by Charles (Mar. 28) and he began to persecute the leading Whigs, charging them with treasonable acts.

1682 May 7 **Fëdor III** [Feodor, Fyodor] **Alekseevich** (b. June 9, 1661), czar of Russia (from 1676), died without an heir. Both his retarded brother **Ivan V Alekseevich** (Sept. 6, 1666–Feb. 8, 1696) and his half-brother **Peter I** [Pëtr Alekseevich], later "the Great," were placed on the throne as co-czars, but the **Miloslavskaya family**, to which the first wife of **Alexis I Mikhailovich**, czar of Russia and Ivan and Peter's father, belonged, gained dominance and forced Peter, still a boy, to a Moscow suburb where he was brought up in isolation. Sophia Alekseevana (1657–1704), a sister of Fedor and Ivan, was named regent. She excluded her half-brother Peter from crown affairs until Aug. 1689, when the streltsy, the royal guard, revolted, and Peter's maternal family, the **Naryshkina**, assumed power. Ivan (b. 1666) died on Jan. 29, 1696, and Peter became sole czar.

1683 **John III Sobieski**, king of Poland (from 1674), brought reinforcements to relieve the **Turkish siege** of **Vienna**, ably defended by Count **Ernst Rüdiger von Starhemberg** (1635–1701). The Polish attack drove the Turks back to the Rába [Raab] River.

1684 The **charter of the Massachusetts Bay Company was revoked** by England's strongly Anglican Restoration Parliament.

1685 Feb. 6 **Charles II** (b. May 29, 1630), king of England (from 1660), died suddenly after a stroke, without legitimate issue. He made a deathbed profession of his Roman Catholic faith. **James II**, brother of Charles, acceded to the throne (to 1689) with little opposition although he was publicly known as a Roman Catholic.

1685 July 15 **James Scott** [James Fitzroy; James Croft] (b. Apr. 9, 1649), duke of Monmouth, was hanged for treason. He was the natural son of Charles II. In 1684, on the insistence of James, duke of York and the legitimate heir to the throne, Monmouth had been banished from England for the second time. On the death of Charles, he returned to England to claim the throne. He raised followers in western England, capturing Axminster and Taunton; but the earl of Argyll, who supported Monmouth, was defeated in the western Highlands. Monmouth, coming to Argyll's aid, was routed and captured. There now followed in the west of England the so-called **Bloody Assizes**, trials conducted by **George Jeffreys** (May 15, 1645–Apr. 18, 1689), baron of Wem, to quell the uprisings that supported Monmouth. Between 150 and 700 were executed for treason, and others were transported to the colonies. Jeffreys, whose conduct was entirely legal, was condoned by the king, who named him lord chancellor in this same year.

1686 July 9 The **League of Augsburg** was formed by **Leopold I** (June 9, 1640–May 5, 1705), the Holy Roman emperor (from 1658), and the German states over which he exerted influence. Leopold hoped to contain French aggression.

1687 Aug. 12 In the **second battle of Mohács**, along the Danube River in present Hungary, the **Ottoman Turks** were routed by imperial forces under Charles V [Charles Leopold] (Apr., 1643–Apr. 18, 1690), duke of Lorraine. Then Venetian forces captured (Sept. 28) Athens, gaining control of Morea [Peloponnesus], the southern peninsula of Greece. Count **Imre Thököly** (Sept. 25, 1657–Sept. 13, 1705), the Hungarian Protestant revolutionary renewed his insurrectionist efforts against the repressive Leopold I, the Holy Roman emperor.

1687 Oct. 31? The **Charter Oak incident** began after **Edmund Andros**, former governor of New York, assumed control (1686) of the New England colonies by appointment from the **Restoration government** in England. His goal was to consolidate Massachusetts, Plymouth, New Hampshire, and Maine, which formed the New England Confederation, with Rhode Island and Connecticut, forming the **Dominion of New England**. However, Andros needed first to obtain the surrender of the Connecticut and Rhode Island charters. When meeting with Connecticut officials one evening at the end of October in Hartford, all candles in the room were suddenly extinguished and, it was said, the Connecticut charter was whisked away to be hidden in a large white oak in town. The "Charter Oak," as it came to be known, stood until 1856.

1687 Nov. 2 The Turks revolted against **Mohammed IV** (1641–1691), the Ottoman sultan (from 1648). He was deposed and was succeeded by his brother **Suleiman II** (1641–1691).

1688 Sept. 25 France precipitated a general state of warfare, known as the **War of the Grand Alliance** (1689–1697), throughout Europe with the invasion of the Palatinate, one of the German states under the Holy Roman Empire. **Louis XIV** wanted to assert the claim of his sister-in-law **Elizabeth Charlott**, the duchess of Orléans, to the Palatinate and at the same time establish Cardinal **Wilhelm Egon von Furstenburg** as the elector of **Cologne**. On May 12, 1689, the Grand Alliance (to 1697) against France was formed with the signing of the **Treaty of Vienna** by the Netherlands and the Holy Roman Empire, as well as Spain, England, Savoy, and several German states.

1688 Nov. 5 In the so-called **Glorious Revolution** in England, the Protestant **William III**, stadtholder of the Netherlands and count of Nassau [prince of Orange], entered London, having landed (Nov. 5) in England at the invitation of both the **Whigs and Tories**, who disliked **James II**, the Roman Catholic king of England. James, having fled to France, was deposed by Parliament on Jan. 28, 1689, which then offered the throne to William and to Mary (Apr. 30, 1662–Dec. 28, 1694), his wife and the daughter of James II.

1689–1697 King William's War, the **first of the French and Indian Wars**, was fought in North Amer-

ica as an extension of the **First War of the Grand Alliance** in Europe. The French, supported by mostly Huron Indians, raided British settlements in New York, Massachusetts, and Maine, in an effort to expand the territory held by New France. On May 11, 1690, Massachusetts troops under the governor, **William Phips** [Phipps] (Feb. 2, 1651–Feb. 18, 1695), captured Port Royal [Annapolis Royal] in Acadia, present Nova Scotia. Phips attempted to take **Quebec** but, despite 34 ships under his command, failed.

1689 England took control of the **colony of Maryland** when the colony's proprietor **Charles Calvert**, Lord Baltimore, was unable to stem the tide of Protestant uprisings. Baltimore at the time was in England to settle a boundary dispute with **William Penn** of Pennsylvania.

1689 The **Treaty of Nerchinsk**, a town east of Lake Baikal in Russia, near the Chinese border, settled the long-disputed border between China and Russia. China regained control of the Amur River, and both countries had equal authority in maintaining the boundary.

1689 Feb. 13 William, stadtholder of the Netherlands and count of Nassau, and his wife Mary were crowned king and queen of England, to serve jointly as **William III and Mary II**. Their power was tempered by a **Bill of Rights**, which secured a constitutional monarchy, free of Catholic succession, over which the Parliament presided as the supreme lawmaking body of England.

1689 Mar. 12 James II, deposed king of England, landed in Ireland, where he gained the support of Roman Catholic loyalists, called **Jacobites**. They laid siege (Apr. 17) to the Protestant-occupied town of **Londonderry**, whose small garrison held out for 105 days before a naval expedition brought (July 30) relief. James was forced to abandon the siege.

III. ECONOMY AND TRADE

1680 The **first fire insurance company** in the world opened in London, following the disastrous fire of 1666. The premium rates established were five percent of one year's rent for wooden houses and half that for brick houses.

1683 Sept. 6 Jean Baptiste Colbert (b. Aug. 26, 1619), a French statesman, died. Under **Louis XIV**,

Colbert served as controller general of finance, and was responsible for raising revenues to meet Louis's expenses. He also strengthened the navy, built roads, and helped to consolidate the royal government. As a patron of the arts and sciences, Colbert founded several academies, among them the **Académie des Sciences** (1666), established to promote scientific discovery as a benefit to the monarchy. To a great extent as a result of Colbert's energy and his loyalty to Louis, **France became the strongest country in Europe**.

1684   The **British East India Company** was granted the right to establish a trading station at **Canton**, China.

1685   **Cadiz** gained precedence over Sevilla [Seville] as the leading Spanish port conducting trade with India and the Far East.

1685 Oct. 18   **Revocation of the Edict of Nantes** damaged the economy of France by forcing many skilled Huguenot artisans and tradespeople to leave the country. The depression caused by this and other factors, such as the First War of the Grand Alliance (1689–1697), lasted for more than 30 years.

IV. RELIGION AND PHILOSOPHY

1685 Oct. 18   The **Edict of Nantes** (1598) was revoked by Louis XIV in the **Edict of Fontainebleau**, culminating a growing judicial war waged by Catholic ecclesiastics against Huguenot rights to freedom of worship. Though promised freedom to worship in private, the Huguenots were mercilessly persecuted; c.400,000 of France's ablest citizens went into exile, principally to England and Prussia.

1687 Mar.   The **first Anglican service in Boston** was held on Good Friday at the South Meeting House.

1687 Apr. 4   The royal **Declaration of Indulgence** suspended the laws against Catholics and Protestant dissenters in England. James II had already recreated the dreaded High Commission, which had been used to repress Dissenters and Roman Catholics but which also had control over the Anglican clergy.

1688 Apr. 27   James II reissued his **Declaration of Indulgence**. On May 4 he ordered it read twice in every English church. Many Protestant ecclesiastics, alarmed by the king's attempts to reestablish Catholicism in England, refused to comply. On June 30 seven Anglican bishops charged with seditious libel were acquitted.

1689 May 24   The **Toleration Act** was passed by the English Parliament and approved by **William and Mary**, king and queen of England. The act terminated efforts by church parties, the Crown, and Parliament to force religious conformity on all Englishmen. Nonconforming Protestants and Catholics won essential religious freedom, though Catholics would not achieve full relief for another century.

V. SCIENCE, EDUCATION, AND TECHNOLOGY

c.1680   The **dodo**, a large flightless bird of Mauritius Island in the Indian Ocean, was exterminated at about this time. Two close relatives, known as solitaires, from Rodriguez and Réunion Islands, also of the Mascarene Island group in the Indian Ocean, survived somewhat longer.

1680   **Thomas Bartholin** (b. 1616), second son of the Danish physician **Kaspar [Caspar] Bartholin** (1585–1629), died. Thomas was the first to describe the function of the **human lymphatic system**.

1683   The **Ashmolean Museum**, the **first public museum in Great Britain**, was opened to the public in Oxford. The institution was the result of a gift to Oxford University of the collection of Elias Ashmole (May 23, 1617–May 18, 1692), an antiquarian and archaeologist.

1686 May 11   **Otto von Guericke** (b. Nov. 20, 1602), the German physicist responsible for the air pump, died. He was a rich man and the mayor of Magdeburg, Germany, where he constructed (1654) the **first air pump** for a celebrated experiment demonstrating the effect of a vacuum so strong that two joined hemispheres could be pulled apart only by using 32 horses to do the job.

1687   *Principia Philosophiae Naturalis Principia Mathematica* [*Mathematical Principles of Natural Philosophy*] was published by **Isaac Newton**, an English scientist. He was said to have been directed to these mathematical studies chiefly by consideration of a question posed by the Copernican system: What force held the planets in an elliptical orbit around the sun? Working with **Kepler's Laws** of planetary motion and his own observations of the reasons for and the effects of gravity, he developed the three laws of motion that today still form one of the bases for the study of physics.

1687 Jan. 28   Johannes Hevelius [Hewel, Höwelcke] (b. Jan. 28, 1611), a Polish astronomer, died. In *Selenographia* (1647) Hevelius provided one of the first detailed descriptions of the moon's surface, based on observations he and his wife Elizabeth made in Danzig. His other achievements included the cataloguing of more than 1,000 stars and observations of sunspots, the transit of Mercury, and the phases of Saturn. He discovered four comets and suggested that the path of their movement around the sun was parabolic.

1689   The Friend's Public School, now the William Penn Charter School, was established in Philadelphia. No fee was charged, and only practical subjects were taught: the rudiments of reading, writing, and arithmetic, as well as some science.

1689   The *New England Primer* was published by **Benjamin Harris** (1673?–1716), a colonial printer in Boston. Each letter of the alphabet was illustrated with a separate woodcut and a catchy couplet with a moral lesson. The children's textbook was liberally endowed with Puritan theology and, revised many times, was a standard text for more than a century.

VI. ARTS AND LEISURE

1680 Mar. 16/17   La Rochefoucault [François, duc de la Rochefoucauld] (b. Sept. 15, 1613) died. A friend and intimate of many notable French men and women, La Rochefoucault was a prominent French author who was also active in court life, diplomacy, and politics. His works included *Les Mémoires sur la Régence d'Anne d'Autriche* (1662) and *Réflexions ou Sentences et Maximes Morales* (1665), whose insight and wit made this work one of the classics of French literature.

1680 Sept. 25   Samuel Butler (b. Feb. 8, 1612), an English poet, died. He was known especially for his three-part satirical poem *Hudibras* (1663–1678), which made fun of the Presbyterians and Independents [Congregationalists] in a plot styled after that of *Don Quixote*. Its wit and mock heroism easily pricked the alleged self-importance and casuistry of Puritan religious fervor so successfully that Charles

II granted Butler an annual pension. He died, however, forgotten and in poverty.

1680 Nov. 28   Giovanni Lorenzo Bernini (b. Dec. 7, 1598), a leading Italian baroque sculptor and architect, died. He was most noted for having designed the square of St. Peter's Cathedral in Rome. Bernini's sculptures, such as *David* (1623) and *Ecstasy of St. Theresa* (1652), were seen as dramatically real moments in life, a breakaway from the grotesque forms of the pre-baroque period. Bernini, once invited by Louis XIV to work on the Louvre, was famous for his design of churches and fountains in Italy.

1681 May 25   Pedro Calderón de la Barca (b. Jan. 17, 1600), a great Spanish baroque playwright, died. Calderon followed in, and kept alive, the tradition of Lope de Vega, writing plays based upon Spanish concepts of honor that, by this time, had begun to be questioned. He was credited with more than 200 plays. In addition to *comedias de pundonor* [honor plays], Calderon wrote many *comedia de capa y espado* (cloak and dagger plays] and *comedia de santos* [religious plays]. Calderón, deeply religious from c.1650, began to write *autos sacramentales*, the Spanish religious dramas generally performed on the feast of Corpus Christi. He was thought to have written more than 70 that treated of the Fall and Redemption, among them *La Viña del Señor* [*The Vineyard of the Lord*] (1673) and *La Nave del Mercader* [*The Merchant's Ship*] (1674).

1682   *The Sovereignty and Goodness of God, Together With the Faithfulness of His Promises Displayed; Being a Narrative of the Captivity and Restoration of Mrs. Mary Rowlandson,* the first of many colonial "captivity narratives," was published. It was an account of her and her child's abduction by American Indians. The book was very popular in colonial America, reflecting the generally hostile attitude of the settlers toward the Indians; it went through more than 30 editions, and was the **first American best-seller written by a woman.**

1682 Mar. 14   Jacob van Ruisdael [Ruijsdael, Ruysdael] (b. 1628?), a Dutch landscape painter, died. He was noted for the spacious landscapes typical of Dutch painters, who were masters of lighting, sky and clouds. Ruisdael often painted forest scenes, as in *Pool in the Wood*. His other works included *Waterfalls* (c.1670), as a number of his canvases are entitled; *Wheatfields, The Burst of Sunshine* (c.1670); and *Mill at Wijk near Duurstede* (c.1670).

1682 Oct. 19   Thomas Browne (b. Oct. 19, 1605), an English writer and physician, died. His chief work was *Religio Medici* (1643), a religious confession colored by skepticism and written with great erudition and lore. His *Urn Burial* (1658), a meditation on death, remains still a classic of English prose. His other works included an encyclopedia of non-traditional knowledge *Pseudodoxia Epidemica* (1646), often called "Vulgar Errors."

1682 Nov. 23   Claude Lorrain [Claude Gelée, Le Lorraine] (born c.1600), a French landscape painter, died. He worked in Rome for most of his life, but his style belonged to the French landscape school: a large dark object in the foreground, such as a tree, frames the play of light on a central theme. *La Vue d'un Port au Soleil Levant* [*View of a Seaport with the Rising Sun*] (1639) was typical of Lorrain's work, which often treated of biblical or mythical scenes. In order to preserve his works against copyists, who were legion in his day, Lorrain produced shaded outlines of each work, publishing these as *Libro de Verità*.

1684 Aug. 12   Nicolò Amati (b. Sept. 3, 1596), the grandson of the Italian violin-maker Andrea Amati, died. The **Amati violins**, renowned for their beauty, power of tone, and shallow, practical design, were enhanced by the grand Amati, an enlarged violin, by Nicolò. In their turn, Nicolò's sons inherited the instrument business and increased the family fame. Two other noted instrument makers received their early training in the Amati shop—**Antonio Stradivari** and **Andrea Guarnieri** (1626–1698), whose nephew **Giuseppe Antonio** (c.1685–1745) became the most noted member of the Guarnieri family. It was said that the favorite violin of **Nicolò Paganini** was one made by Giuseppe.

1684 Oct. 1   Pierre Corneille (b. June 6, 1606), a great French dramatist, died. In Jan., 1637, his *Le Cid* inaugurated the great age of French drama; the techniques developed by Corneille were perfected by his contemporary Jean Baptiste Racine. Corneille's comedies *Melite* (1629) and *Le Menteur* (1643) were generally considered surpassed by his tragedies *Horace* (1640), praised by Voltaire; *Cinna* (1641); *Polyeucte* (1642); *Rodogune* (1644); and *Nicomède* (1651).

c.1685   Pieter de Hooch [Hoogh] (b. 1629?), a Dutch painter, died. Little is known today of de Hooch's life. He lived in Delft, where he painted many interior scenes, usually lighted with the full sun of daylight. Characteristic of these was *The Courtyard of a House in Delft* (1658).

1685 Apr. 10   Thomas Otway (b. Mar. 3, 1651 or 1652), a noted English dramatist, died, probably of starvation in a garret on Tower Hill in London. Otway was best-known for two tragedies, *The Orphan, or the Unhappy Marriage* (1680), a tremendous success, and *Venus Preserved, or A Plot Discovered* (1682), sometimes considered the best tragedy of its period. Otway, a chronic alcoholic, had incurred many debts; he died while in hiding from his creditors.

1687 Mar. 22   Jean Baptiste Lully (b. Nov. 28, 1632), a French composer and one of the founders of French opera, died. At the French court (from 1653), he wrote ballets and other lively pieces, to which Louis XIV danced. Lully developed a form for the overture that began with a slow movement, jumped into a fast section, and returned to the slower, earlier theme for its conclusion. He was apt at court theater productions, presiding over all roles of direction and composition. Molière requested Lully's musical accompaniment for some of his comedies. Lully's operas included *Alceste* (1674), *Proserpine* (1680), and *Armide et Renaud* (1686).

1687 Sept. 28?   During the bombardment of Athens by the Venetians, the famed **Parthenon**, the temple of Athena on the Acropolis, was badly damaged when a shell ignited the Turkish munitions stored in the building. Considered the epitome of the Doric style of architecture, the Parthenon had been erected from c.448 to c.438 B.C.

VII. SPORTS, GAMES, AND SOCIETY

1685   The stallion **Byerly Turk** was brought to England. He was one of three studs listed in the 1793 edition of *Stud Book* that, of almost 200 sires listed, have survived in the records. The other two are **Darley Arabian**, imported in 1704, and **Godolphin Barb**, imported in 1724. All three names are composed of the owner's name and the geographical breed-name, e.g., Barb stands for Barbary. All horses descended from these three are classified "thoroughbreds"; a horse that cannot be traced back to them cannot be listed.

1688 The professional class of the **geisha** came into prominence in Japan with the **Genroku period** (c.1675–c.1725), a time of preoccupation with the luxury and sensual delight of every day life. At the age of about seven years, the future geisha was sold by her parents to an organization that trained her in the social entertainments, such as dance, music, poetry, song, and theater. Her contract could be ended only by marriage. The selling of young girls as geishas was outlawed in 1946.

1690–1699

I. DISASTERS

1693 Jan. 11 More than 60,000 people died in an earthquake and volcanic **eruption of Mount Etna** on Sicily, where c.40 towns, including the coastal city of Catania, were partially or completely destroyed. Eruptions of Mount Etna have continued to the present; today it is the most active volcano in Europe.

1697 An epidemic of **smallpox** struck the colony of Charleston, in present South Carolina. Yellow fever raged through the area the following year, killing c.150 people in six days. Charleston, a busy Atlantic port, was an easy point of entry for diseases from the West Indies, with which colonial ships did much trade.

1697 The worst **famine in Finland**, the result of a crop failure, brought death to nearly one-third, or c.100,000, of the population.

II. EXPLORATION AND COLONIZATION

1691 A royal charter established **Maine** as a colony separate from Massachusetts. First granted to **Ferdinando Gorges** as early as 1622, the region had joined (1660) with Massachusetts to gain protection against the French, who occupied the eastern part of the region. Although Maine was restored to Gorges's grandson, the state of Massachusetts had bought the rights to govern Maine in 1677.

1696 Fort William was constructed at **Calcutta**, where the **British East India Company** had established (1690) a trading post. From this time Calcutta grew in importance as the chief city of Bengal and as the capital (1773–1912) of British-occupied India.

1697 In northeastern U.S.S.R. the Kamchatka Peninsula in **Siberia** was explored by the Russian Vladimir Atlasov (d.1711). Soon fur traders came to the region to exploit the sea otter for their pelts, popular in western Europe. The region still provides the bulk of **furs** for Soviet Russia.

1698 **New Caledonia**, a colony in Darién on the present Isthmus of Panama, was founded by a group of Scottish settlers headed by **William Paterson**. The expectation was to establish an easy land route to the Pacific Ocean. However, the colony succumbed to disease and, by Apr., 1700, all had returned to Great Britain or died.

1698 Dec. 12 The Portuguese stronghold of Fort Jesus on the island of Mombasa, part of present **Kenya**, fell to the sultan of Oman. By 1700 the Omani controlled **Zanzibar**, an island governed now by Tanzania, and most of the cities of the central eastern African coast, including Malindi, Tanzania; Pate [Patta] Island, Kenya; and Pemba Island, just north of Zanzibar, and governed now by Tanzania. Portuguese influence was confined to the southeastern African coast of present **Mozambique**.

1699 **Willem A. van der Stel** (1699–1707) was appointed administrator of the **Dutch East India Company's** settlement of **Cape Town**, in present South Africa. He encouraged immigration from the Netherlands, and allowed the colonists to concentrate on stock farming, which produced good provision for trading ships, and to occupy vast land areas by paying a small annual redemption to the company. This opened South Africa to the pastoral **Boers** [Dutch: peasant, countryman], who began to spread inland, clearing their way through the scattered bands of Hottentots [Khoikhoi] and Bushmen [San].

1699 The **first permanent settlement in present Mississippi** was established on the coast of the Gulf of Mexico at Old Biloxi, present Ocean Springs, near the present site of **Biloxi**, by **Pierre le Moyne** (June 16, 1661–July 9, 1706), **Sieur d'Iberville**, a French explorer. The town was named for the Biloxi Indians [biloxi = broken pot], a gulf enclave of the more northern Sioux.

1699 Jan. 14 **William Dampier** (c.May, 1652–Mar., 1715), an English buccaneer, departed from England, aboard the *Roebuck*, on a voyage to Australia. On Dec. 3 to the east of New Guinea he found an island that he named **New Britain**. It was the largest island in the **Bismarck Archipelago**, part of present **Papua New Guinea**, in the Coral Sea. Dampier kept careful, readable accounts of his voyages to the East Indies, the western coast of South America, and throughout the Pacific Ocean, some of which he made as a pirate.

III. POLITICS AND WAR

1690 July 1 **William III**, king of England, defeated the Catholic Irish forces [Jacobites] of James II, the deposed king of England, who was supported by French troops, in a **battle at the Boyne River**, near Drogheda, in northeastern Ireland. James returned to France while another victory at Aughrim [Aghrim], in East Galway, on July 12, 1691, and the surrender of Limerick, on Oct. 3, completed William's **pacification of the Irish**. James himself was never again involved in any serious attempt to overthrow **William and Mary**. After this definitive defeat, the Irish were subjected to numerous penal laws which limited Catholic authority and privilege. These included: Catholics, and Presbyterians in present Northern Ireland, were prohibited from buying land in 1704; their leases, rents, and inheritances were strictly regulated. The British Parliament was authorized to legislate for the Irish Parliament in 1719 and, in 1727, Catholics lost the vote altogether. Only one-sixth of Irish holdings remained in Catholic hands.

1690 July 1 A **battle at Fleurus**, in present Belgium, was a victory for France in the Spanish Netherlands during the **First War of the Grand Alliance** (1689–1697). English troops, engaged in Ireland, were unable to provide support to the Alliance. By 1692, however, the combined Anglo-Dutch fleet had regained mastery of the sea, offsetting France's early victories.

1690 Oct. 8 The **Ottoman Empire** (1326–1920), prevented from a collapse by the **First War of the Grand Alliance** (1689–1697), which drew imperial armies from its borders, reconquered Belgrade from the Holy Roman Empire. By the end of the year the Turks had recovered their Bulgarian territories, Moldavia and Walachia in Romania, and Serbia, Croatia, and Slavonia near present Yugoslavia.

1692 **Diego de Vargas Zapata**, the Spanish governor of New Mexico, regained the region of present southwestern U.S. for New Spain. He was successful in driving out the Pueblo leader **Popé** after Apache raids and Popé's own bloody rule had splintered the Indian community.

1692 May 29 The Anglo-Dutch fleet defeated the French in a **naval battle at La Hogue** [La Hougue] off the Contentin Peninsula in northwestern France. English supremacy at sea was restored, preventing an opportunity for a French invasion of England to reinstate James II. The position of France was weak against the rest of Europe, and her hopes for Spanish dominions were dashed by the birth of a male heir to the granddaughter of **Philip IV**, king of Spain (1621–1665), on Oct. 28. **Charles II**, king of Spain (to 1700) was childless.

1693 The ruler of the **Monomotapa** [Motapa, Mutapa] **Empire** (c.1440–c.1629) in southeastern Africa appealed to his rival Dombo, king of Changamire, to unite and expel the Portuguese from the southeastern African coast. By 1695 the **Changamire Kingdom** (c.1480–?) had defeated the Portuguese and was able to annex most of the Rhodesian plateau. The Monomotapa territory, however, was also reduced by Dombo to the small region around Sena and Tete, the Portuguese strongholds of the Zambezi River Valley, in present Mozambique.

1696 The fortress of Azov, guarding the outlet of the Don River into the Sea of Azov, was taken by **Peter the Great**, czar of Russia. This secured Russian access to the Black Sea and was a first step in stemming border raids by the **Crimean Tatars** [Tartars], vassals of the **Ottoman Empire** (1326–1920).

1697 **Peter the Great** embarked on a two-fold diplomatic mission to western Europe, traveling incognito under the name Sergeant Pëtr Mikhailov, in order to observe more closely the people and places he visited. The primary object of the "**Grand Embassy**," (more than 200 Russian ministers having been sent abroad at this time), was to gain alliances against the **Ottoman Empire** (1326–1920) and to learn more of the international situation. Peter himself studied shipbuilding, in order to gain knowledge about constructing a better navy, and he wanted to understand western customs. On his return he introduced shorter sleeve lengths at the Russian court and the shaving of beards. The **Raskolniki** [Old Believers] who refused to part with their beards were taxed. Peter continued to send Russian representatives abroad to maintain contact with Europe, and he invited many western European dignitaries to visit his court.

1697 Apr. 5 Charles XI (b. Nov. 24, 1655), king of Sweden (from 1660), died and was succeeded by his 15-year-old son **Charles XII**. Charles XI worked to strengthen the Swedish kingdom and to integrate its vassal Denmark into Swedish affairs. As the young Charles XII took the throne, however, the victims of Swedish expansion eagerly sought redress.

1697 Sept. 11 Prince Eugene of Savoy (Oct. 18, 1663–Apr. 20, 1736), the Austrian general and statesman, at this time commander-in-chief of the imperial forces in Hungary, routed the Ottoman Turks at a **battle at Zenta** [Senta], in present northeastern Yugoslavia. At the **peace of Karlowitz** which ended the **war of the Holy League** (Austria, Poland, and Venice) against Turkey, Austria gained Croatia, Hungary, Transylvania, and Slavonia; much later the Austro-Hungarian Empire (1867–1918), or the dual Kingdom of Austria-Hungary, was formed.

1697 Sept. 15 Frederick Augustus I, elector of Saxony (from 1694), was elected king of Poland as **Augustus II** [the Strong] to take the throne vacated by the death of **John III Sobieski** (b. June 2, 1624) on June 17, 1696. John had ruled from 1674. In 1699 he concluded alliances with Russia and Denmark against Sweden.

1697 Sept. 20 The **Treaty of Rijswijk** [Ryswick] ended the **First War of the Grand Alliance** (from 1689) between France and the Netherlands, the Holy Roman Empire, Spain, Savoy and (sometimes) England. France evacuated the Spanish Netherlands and the duchy of Lorraine, and recognized William III as king of England. France was allowed to keep Alsace and regained the settlement at Pondicherry, India, from the Dutch. In the West Indies, Spain lost to France the western part of Hispaniola.

1698 The **streltsy**, the privileged army regiments of Russia that served as royal units, attempted a coup in Moscow in favor of the former regent, **Sophia Alekseevana**, while the czar **Peter the Great** was in Vienna to negotiate an alliance against the Turks. The revolt was put down before Peter's return in the summer. Peter himself conducted the trials and attended the brutal executions, which forever reduced the power of the streltsy.

1698 Oct. The **First Partition Treaty** of the Spanish dominions, drawn up by Louis XIV, king of France, and William III, king of England and stadtholder of the Netherlands, was signed at the Hague. The treaty recognized **Joseph Ferdinand**, great-grandson of Philip IV, king of Spain, as rightful heir to Spain, the Spanish Netherlands, and the West Indies, while Milan and Spanish Italy were to pass to the Hapsburgs who ruled Austria.

1699 Jan. 26 The **Ottoman Empire** (1326–1920) signed the **Treaty of Karlowitz** [Sremski Karlovci], following a disastrous defeat by the Holy Roman Empire in the **battle at Senta**, Serbia, on Sept. 11, 1697. Austria gained much of present Hungary and Yugoslavia. Poland gained Podolia [Podolsk], a region to the north of the Dniester [Dnestr] River, and the Polish Ukraine.

IV. ECONOMY AND TRADE

1690 The **Massachusetts Bay Colony**, unable to pay its militia, gave its soldiers promissory notes, which were declared legal tender for the payment of taxes. In 1692, when Massachusetts offered a five percent bonus for the redemption of this paper money, the flood of counterfeit notes surfacing amounted to nearly four times the original number of notes issued.

1694 July 27 The **Bank of England** was granted its charter in London. The bank was authorized to accept deposits and to borrow, lend, and issue notes of legal tender. As chief financial agent of the English government, it presided over the management of the national debt.

1695 The **Window Tax** was established in England. The wealth of a taxpayer was determined by the number of windows on his buildings, and he was taxed accordingly.

1696 The **first workhouse in England** was founded at Bristol. A **Corporation of the Poor** was established to provide employment for the poor, but little work was available within the parish.

1696   The discovery of **gold in Brazil** near the city of Ouro Preto, north of Rio de Janeiro, launched a gold rush to the Portuguese colony.

1699   The **Woolen Act**, one of the **Navigation Acts**, passed by the British Parliament, forbade the export of all wool and wool products produced in British colonies. Wool produced in England could be traded, but the colonies were denied a means of trade.

V. RELIGION AND PHILOSOPHY

1690   **John Locke** (Aug. 29, 1632–Oct. 28, 1704), one of the most influential philosophers of his age, published in England the *Essay Concerning Human Understanding* and *Two Treatises on Civil Government,* which held untenable the doctrine of the divine right of kings, thus vindicating the Glorious Revolution of 1688 and greatly influencing English, French, and American political philosophers. Locke's philosophy assumed an original state of nature that was happy and tolerant, but since every person then was a judge of his own actions, man developed a social contract to protect him from those who lived outside law. He also believed that man was born without innate ideas and that he developed science, philosophy, and political ideas by means of rational thought acting upon impressions derived from experience and upon the relationships between ideas derived from experience. Thus, Locke laid the groundwork for nearly all of modern philosophy.

1692 Mar. 1   The **Salem Witch Trials** in the Massachusetts Bay Colony opened. At the preliminary hearings, testimony given by hysterical young females aged 9 to 19, presumably suffering from "demonic possession," accused three defenseless older women. Before the trials were halted in September, 20 persons had been put to death. The Salem episode marked the end of witch trials in the U.S.

1693   **Jean Le Clerc** (Mar. 19, 1657–Jan. 8, 1736), a French Protestant preacher-theologian who had settled (1684) in **Amsterdam**, began his series of Bible commentaries. Le Clerc insisted that dogmatic suppositions be set aside when approaching the teaching of Scriptures. Le Clerc, editor of journals of biblical studies, exercised considerable influence.

1695   **John Locke**, the English philosopher, published *Reasonableness of Christianity,* expounding his thesis that "religion must be essentially reasonable," and joining the irreconcilable opposites, rea-

son and faith. In his earlier *Letter concerning Toleration* (1689), Locke had maintained that the doctrines that divided Christianity were matters upon which knowledge is not possible, and that their acceptance was an improper test of character or condition for the exercise of civil rights.

1695   **Madame Guyon** [Jeanne Marie de la Motte-Guyon; née Bouvier] (Apr. 13, 1648–June 9, 1717), a French mystic and advocate of **Quietism**, was imprisoned for her beliefs.

1696   *Christianity Not Mysterious* by the Irish Protestant **John Toland** [Junius Janus] (Nov. 30, 1670–Mar. 11, 1722) offended English religious orthodoxy. Tracts by divines accusing Toland of being "anti-Trinitarian" soon followed, and in 1697 Toland was prosecuted for his deistic views by the grand jury of Middlesex, England. Fleeing to Dublin, Toland was denounced there from pulpits, and his book condemned by the Irish Parliament.

1697 Jan. 14   Judge **Samuel Sewall** (Mar. 28, 1652–Jan. 1, 1730) of Boston's Old South Church, who had held court during some of the Salem witchcraft trials that had begun in 1692, confessed to his guilt in condemning the alleged witches.

1699 Mar. 12   The volume *Maximes* by **François Fénelon**, archbishop of Cambrai and a mystical theologian, was condemned by Pope Innocent XII (Mar. 13, 1615–Sept. 27, 1700; ruled from 1691). His humanistic of pure love based on simplicity of heart and the substitution of God's activity for the will of the individual, had drawn the fire of the French controversialist Jacques Bénigne Bossuet (Sept. 27, 1627–Apr. 12, 1704), bishop of Meaux.

VI. SCIENCE, EDUCATION, AND TECHNOLOGY

1690 Sept. 25   *Publick Occurences Both Forreign and Domestick*, the first American colonial newspaper, was printed in Boston by Benjamin Harris, a bookseller and coffee house proprietor from England. It was quickly suppressed by royal authority and did not last beyond its first issue.

1691 Dec. 30   **Robert Boyle** (b. Jan. 25, 1627), an Irish philosopher and one of the principal **founders of modern chemistry**, died. Boyle practiced science as an act of homage to God; he regarded his work as an instrument of revelation. Boyle's Law, treating of the properties of gases, stated that the volume of a mixture of gases or of any one gas at a constant temperature is in inverse proportion to the amount of pressure applied. He published *The Skeptical Chymist* (1661), in which he redefined the concept of an element, introducing the modern science of chemistry. He also published the *Origin of Forms and Qualities According to the Corpuscular Philosophy* (1666), *Discourse of Things Above Reason* (1681), *Memoirs for the Natural History of Human Blood* (1684).

1693   William and Mary College was chartered this year at Williamsburg, Virginia, with funds provided by William and Mary, king and queen of England.

1694   The first edition of *Dictionnaire de l'Académie française* was published under the auspices of the Académie française. It took the academy nearly 60 years to prepare this first edition. It was intended to give the approved and proper usage of the always zealously guarded French language.

1694 Nov. 30   Marcello Malpighi (b. Mar. 10, 1628), an Italian physiologist, died. He was among the first to rely on the microscope to study animal and vegetable structure. He was the first scientist to observe the completion of the circulation of blood. He also described (1665) **red blood corpuscles** and demonstrated the structure of **secreting glands**.

1695 June 8   Christian Huygens [Huyghens] (b. Apr. 14, 1629), a Dutch astronomer and physicist, died. His first notable achievement was the discovery (1655) of a superior method for **grinding and polishing lenses**. He soon constructed a telescope with which he discovered the rings of Saturn and Titan, a moon of Saturn. Huygens developed (1656) a pendulum, which swung in a periodical and regular arc, that made possible the accurate measurement of time.

VII. ARTS AND LEISURE

1690 Feb. 12   Charles le Brun (b. Feb. 24, 1619), a French painter and architect, died. As painter to Louis XIV, king of France, he set the style that soon became identified with that monarch. Le Brun designed the richly decorated state rooms of the palace at **Versailles**, and executed many of the paintings there.

1692 Nov. 19   Thomas Shadwell (b. 1642?), an English playwright and poet, died. Shadwell, a Whig, was named to supersede John Dryden, a Tory, as poet laureate after the accession of William and Mary. Immensely popular was Shadwell's first play, *The Sullen Lovers, or the Impertinents* (1668), a comedy based on Molière's *Les fâcheux* [The Bores].

1694   Matsuo Basho [Matsuo Munefusa] (b. 1644), the Japanese poet most responsible for the development of **haiku** [hokku], died. In 1666, on the death of his master, the samurai Basho turned his attention to the construction of perfect verse. His elegant allusions brought the previously conversational tone of haiku to its height of compression.

1694 Dec. 2   Pierre Puget (b. Oct. 16, 1620), a French baroque sculptor and painter, died. He studied the baroque in Italy, under Giovanni Lorenzo Bernini, but he transformed it to a French style. His most famous works were the sculpture *Milo of Crotona* (1671–1683) and the relief *Alexander and Diogenes* (1671–1693).

1695 Nov. 21   Henry Purcell (born c.1659), an English composer, died. His versatile style of composition won Purcell the distinction of being the greatest musical genius of the English Restoration. His church music included fine melodies and mastery of form, especially of harmony and counterpoint. In all of Purcell's work, the preeminent quality was his ability to evoke emotion with music.

1696   *Love's Last Shift*, considered the first sentimental comedy, was produced at Drury Lane Theatre and brought instant success to its author, **Colley Cibber** (Nov. 6, 1671–Dec. 11, 1757), an English actor, dramatist, and poet. His other plays included *She Would and She Would Not* (1702), *The Careless Husband* (1704), and many adaptations, one of William Shakespeare's *King John* (1745), in which he performed. Some say of Cibber that he lived his life just in order to write *The Apology for the Life of Colley Cibber, Comedian* (1740), a captivating account of the theater of his day.

1696 Apr. 17   Madame de Sévigné [nee Marie de Rabutin-Chantal] (b. Feb. 5, 1626), a famous French letter writer, died. She wrote primarily to her daughter: published as *Lettres de Mme de Sévigné* (1697), the letters chronicled the life of country, city, and court in lively fashion.

1699 Apr. 21 Jean Baptiste Racine (b. Dec. 22, 1639), a great French playwright, died. Racine, the master of the rhymed Alexandrine couplet, could express subtle and delicate emotions as well as violent passion. Racine's tragedies included *Andromaque* (1667); *Bajazet* (1672), whose characters are taken from the Ottomans; *Iphigenie* (1674); *Bérénice* (1670; *Phèdre* (1677); and *Athalie* (1691), which form even today a substantial part of the tragic repertory of the Comédie Française.

VIII. SPORTS, GAMES, AND SOCIETY

1697 The word "**American**" was used for the first time to describe a European colonist in the New World, rather than its native inhabitant, by **Cotton Mather**, the Congregational clergyman in Boston.

1697 The **first recorded cricket match** of a formal sort, played with 11 men to a side, was held in Sussex, England.

1699 Captain Kidd, born William Kidd in Scotland, purportedly buried some treasure upon visiting an old friend of his in **Narragansett**, Rhode Island, before surrendering to New York authorities on a charge of piracy. According to legend, Kidd's treasure may have been buried somewhere along the northeastern Atlantic coast, perhaps even along the Hudson River. He was said to have murdered his assistant in this task and buried the body with the treasure to guard against treasure seekers. Kidd surrendered to the governor of New York in hope of being cleared of piracy charges. Instead, Kidd (b. 1645?) was sent to England, tried, and executed on May 23, 1701.

1700–1709

I. VITAL STATISTICS AND DEMOGRAPHICS

1700 Europe's population stood at c.120 million. England's estimated population was 6,045,000. The estimate took into account the numbers of recorded baptisms, burials, and marriages.

1700 There were c.275,000 **European settlers in the American colonies**, nearly ten times the number 50 years earlier. Of noteworthy size were the settlements of Albany, Providence, New Haven, Hartford, and Richmond. The most populous cities were Newport, c.2,000 citizens; Charleston, c.2,500; New York, c.5,000; Philadelphia, c.6,000; and Boston, c.7,000.

1700 The **slave trade** was bringing c.30,000 Africans each year to the Americas. A total of c.300,000 African slaves had been carried to the islands of the West Indies by this time. Since 1590, when Philip II, king of Spain, had forbade his governors from importing slaves without a special license, most of the slaves were carried by British, Dutch, and French vessels. The Spanish colonists ignored the forbidden trade edicts by not counting the slaves they carried to the Indies. The Spaniards of this time constituted at least half of the **European population** of c.200,000 **in the West Indies**. In 1700 the total **population of Mexico** was c.4,000,000;

Central America, c.700,000; and **South America**, c.6,000,000.

1700 By practicing **infanticide** and delaying marriage, Japan kept its population at c.30 million people for the next 125 years, even though their material wealth increased. **China's population** at this time was c.150,000,000 and **India's** c.165,000,000.

1700 New Zealand's semi-agricultural **Maoris** now numbered c.250,000.

II. DISASTERS

1703 The so-called **Great Storm in England** took the lives of c.1,500 seamen, destroying 15 warships and many merchant ships.

1703 Dec. 30 An **earthquake** struck Edo [Tokyo], capital of Japan's Tokugawa Shogunate (1603–1867), causing c.200,000 deaths.

1707–1709 A **smallpox epidemic in Iceland** took the lives of more than one-third of the population of c.50,000.

III. EXPLORATION AND COLONIZATION

1701 July 24 Sieur Antoine de la Mothe Cadillac (Mar. 5, 1658–Oct. 15, 1730), a French colonial proprietor, built Fort Ponchartrain near present **Detroit**, Michigan, named after the French word for narrows [détroit], which here connects Lake Huron and Lake Erie.

1702 French Canadians founded **Fort Louis de la Mobile**, the **first permanent settlement in present Alabama**, as one of the forts located along the Mississippi River Valley from the Gulf of Mexico northward into Canada to provide protection against the British.

1702 Apr. Since 1682 both East and West New Jersey belonged to **William Penn** as the proprietor, and other adjacent areas had other proprietors, when all ceded their rights to the king (then William III), except for ownership of the land. This combined entity, called **New Jersey**, was placed politically under the governor of New York.

1703 May 27 Construction began on the city of **St. Petersburg** on the site of the earlier fortress of St. Peter and St. Paul where the Neva River flows into the Gulf of Finland.

1709 Feb. **William Dampier**, an English buccaneer, rescued Alexander Selkirk (1676–Dec. 12, 1721) from one of the Juan Fernández islets c.400 miles west of the Chilean coast. Selkirk, who was left there in Oct. 1704 by an irate ship captain, and his rescuers gave accounts of this adventure, which provided **Daniel Defoe** with material for *Robinson Crusoe* (1719).

IV. POLITICS AND WAR

c.1700 **Osei Tutu** (died c.1715) united the **Akan forest tribes** surrounding **Kumasi**, present capital of Ghana, to form the **Ashanti Kingdom** (to 1901) in West Africa. Osei Tutu, according to legend, was aided by the **Golden Stool**, which fell at his feet from the sky. With the power bestowed by the Golden Stool, Osei Tutu led the Ashanti in becoming predominant on the **Gold Coast**.

1700 Feb. The **Great Northern War** (1700–1721) began as Augustus II, king of Poland (1697–1704,

1709–1733), invaded Riga, a port of Swedish Livonia, using a military force from his native Saxony because the Polish army refused its support. In March Frederick IV (Oct. 11, 1671–Oct. 12, 1730), king of Denmark and Norway (from 1699), invaded Schleswig-Holstein, in present Germany. In August Peter the Great, czar of Russia, occupied the Estonian city of Narva, which Sweden had earlier annexed.

1700 Mar. 25 The **Second Partition Treaty** of the Spanish Hapsburg dominions was ratified by France, England, and the Netherlands. Spain, the Spanish Netherlands, and the West Indies were granted to the son of Leopold I, the archduke Charles, the future Holy Roman emperor (1711–1740). Spanish Italy and Lorraine were to go to the French dauphin Louis (1661–1711), son of Louis XIV of France and another claimant to the Spanish throne. This was an attempt to create a balance of power in Europe as a means of avoiding a general war. Charles II, king of Spain, rejected the treaty, preferring to announce (Oct. 3) in a new will that he was to be succeeded by the Bourbon prince Philip, duke of Anjou and grandson of Louis XIV. The ascendancy of France's **Bourbon Dynasty** (1589–1792; 1814–1848), as signaled by these events, was unacceptable to the remaining European powers.

1700 Nov. 1 Charles II (b. Nov. 6, 1661), king of Spain (from 1665), died. The following month, **Louis XIV**, king of France, recognized at Fontainebleau his own grandson, the duke of Anjou, as named in Charles II's will, as **Philip V**, king of Spain. Louis XIV decided to risk war rather than allow the imperial **Hapsburgs** to acquire the extensive Spanish dominions. Philip V, also acclaimed king at Madrid in December, established the **Bourbon Dynasty** (1700–to the present) in Spain.

1700 Nov. 30 **Charles XII**, king of Sweden, in the first major battle of the **Great Northern War** (1700–1721), decisively defeated **Peter the Great**, czar of Russia, at Narva, in Swedish Estonia. Charles XII then invaded Poland, which he devastated for the next six years, taking Warsaw (May 8, 1702) and Torun [Thorn] early in 1704.

1701 Jan. 18 Frederick III (July 11, 1657–Feb. 25, 1713), elector of Brandenburg (from 1688), was named **Frederick I**, first king of Prussia, as reward for the courage with which Frederick and his armies served Leopold I, the Holy Roman emperor, in the

War of the Grand Alliance (1688–1697). Leopold thus gained an ally in the **War of the Spanish Succession** (1701–1713).

1701 June 12   The English Parliament passed the **Act of Settlement**, which secured the royal succession of the **House of Hanover** (1714–1901), united to the English throne by the marriage (1658) of Elizabeth, sister of Charles I, to Frederick V, elector of the Palatinate and king of Bohemia. Their daughter Sophia, who married the elector of Hanover, was the mother of **George I, first Hanoverian king of England**. Anne, sister of Mary, queen of England, and Mary's successor (1702), had no heir, so the Act of Settlement was deemed essential by Parliament to ensure a Protestant ruler for England.

1701 Sept. 7   The Holy Roman Empire, Great Britain, and the Netherlands signed the **Treaty of the Hague**, forming the **Second Grand Alliance** (to 1711) against the succession of France's **Bourbon Dynasty** to the throne of Spain.

1701 Sept. 5   **James II** (Oct. 14, 1633), deposed king of England (1685–1688), died at St. Germain, France.

1702 Mar. 8   **William III** (b. Nov. 14, 1650), king of England (from 1689), stadtholder of the Netherlands, count of Nassau, and prince of Orange, died. On Apr. 23, 1702, the Protestant **Anne Stuart**, second daughter of James II, was crowned queen of England. Her reign was marked by the domination of John Churchill, duke of Marlborough (May 26, 1650–June 17, 1722), who served as commander of Anglo-Dutch armies in the **War of the Spanish Succession** (1701–1713).

1702 July   The **revolt of the Camisards** began in France in the Cévennes, in southern France, west of the Rhône River. There, the Protestant peasants who had found refuge since the **Revocation of the Edict of Nantes** (1685), rose up against the policy of extermination pursued by **Villars** [Claude Louis Hector, duke of Villars] (May 8, 1653–June 17, 1734), marshal of France. The promise of concessions made to Protestant leaders finally brought a halt to the main part of the insurrection by 1705.

1703   **Francis II** [Ferenc] Rákóczy (Mar. 27, 1676–Apr. 8, 1735), prince of Transylvania, headed a **Hungarian revolt against the Hapsburg rule** of Leopold I, the Holy Roman emperor. At first successful, the

upheaval continued until 1711, when concessions were granted to Hungary.

1703 Sept. 12   The Hapsburg **Charles III**, archduke of Austria and the future Holy Roman emperor as Charles VI (ruled 1711–1740), was proclaimed Charles III, king of Spain, in Vienna. His title was disputed by the Bourbon Philip V, king of Spain, supported by Louis XIV, Bourbon king of France.

1704 Aug. 4   **Gibraltar** was seized from Spain by forces under **George Rooke** (1650–Jan. 24, 1709), an English admiral, in the **War of the Spanish Succession** (1701–1713).

1704 Aug. 13   In a great **battle** the armies of the **Second Grand Alliance** (1701–1711) saved **Vienna** from French capture **at Blenheim**, on the Danube River in Bavaria, in present Germany. Though outnumbered, **John Churchill**, duke of Marlborough, leader of the Anglo-Dutch forces, and Prince **Eugene of Savoy**, leader of the imperial army, forced the French armies commanded by **Camille d'Hostun** (1652–1728), comte de Tallart, to withdraw west of the Rhine River, and removed Bavaria from the war.

1705   The **Husain Dynasty** of Tunis was established by **Moriscos** [Spanish Muslims] driven from Spain.

1705 Oct. 15   The British fleet led by **Charles Mordaunt** (1658–Oct. 25, 1735) earl of Peterborough, **captured Barcelona** on the Spanish Mediterranean coast in the **War of the Spanish Succession** (1701–1713). His victory forced the recognition of Charles, archduke of Austria, as king of Spain by the provinces of Catalonia, Aragon, and Valencia.

1706 May 23   French armies commanded by François de Neufville (Apr. 7, 1644–July 18, 1730), duke of Villeroi, were expelled from the Spanish Netherlands by combined Anglo-Dutch forces under John Churchill, duke of Marlborough, in a **battle at Ramillies**, in present Belgium.

1706 Sept. 7   French forces under **Philippe II** (Aug. 2, 1647–December 2, 1723), duc d'Orléans, were defeated by imperial troops under Prince **Eugene of Savoy** in a **battle at Turin**, Savoy, which had long been under French siege in the **War of the Spanish Succession** (1701–1713). With this defeat, the French army was forced to withdraw from northwestern Italy.

1706 Sept. 24 **Augustus II**, elector of Saxony and the unpopular king of Poland, signed the **Treaty of Altranstädt**, in present Germany, which recognized Sweden's success in the **Great Northern War** (1700–1721). Augustus then officially abdicated the Polish crown in favor of Stanislas I Leszczynski.

1707 Mar. 3 **Aurangzeb** [Aurungzeb] (b. Nov. 6?, 1618), the last great Mogul emperor of India (from 1658), died. Under Aurangzeb, the **Mogul Empire** had attained its **greatest extent**. It stretched from the Hindu Kush mountain range in the north to the Coromandel Coast in the southeast.

1707 Apr. 25 The British, under Henri de Massue (1648–1720), earl of Galway, were routed by the French, under Maréchal James Fitzjames (Aug. 21, 1670–June 12, 1734), duke of Berwick and son of the exiled King James II of England, at Almansa, Spain, in the **War of the Spanish Succession** (1701–1713). The French victory safeguarded the right of the Bourbon **Philip V**, king of Spain, to remain on his throne.

1707 May 1 The **Act of Union**, ratified by the English Parliament, joined Scotland to England and Wales to constitute the nation of Great Britain. The sole British Parliament, meeting at Westminster, represented all three countries.

1708 Feb. 13 In England the Tory secretary of state **Robert Harley** (Dec. 5, 1661–May 21, 1724), earl of Oxford, was dismissed at the instigation of John Churchill, duke of Marlborough, hoping to placate **Whig** opposition to involvement in the **War of the Spanish Succession** (1701–1713). **Robert Walpole** (Aug. 26, 1676–Mar. 18, 1745), earl of Orford, was named secretary of war, and Lord **John Somers** (Mar. 4, 1651–Apr. 26, 1716), president of council.

1708 Mar. 23 **James Francis Edward Stuart**, the "Old Pretender," son of James II, king of England, by his second wife, arrived in Scottish waters as James III, king of England, and James VIII, king of Scotland. The attempted **Jacobite insurrection** was aborted when the accompanying French fleet was defeated by **George Byng** (Jan. 27, 1663–Jan. 17, 1733), a British admiral. The Pretender returned to France without landing in Scotland.

1708 July 11 **Second Grand Alliance** forces under John Churchill and Prince Eugene of Savoy defeated French forces in a **battle at Audenaarde** [Oudenaarde], near Brussels, in the War of the Spanish Succession (1701–1713). The French, under **Louis Joseph** (July 1, 1654–June 15, 1712), duke of Vendôme, were attempting to regain the Spanish Netherlands.

1709 July 8 **Charles XII**, king of Sweden, was defeated by **Peter the Great**, czar of Russia, in a **battle at Poltava**, east of the Dnieper [Dnepr] River in the Ukraine, during the **Great Northern War** (1700–1721). **Russia thus became dominant in northern Europe** and made it possible for **Augustus II**, elector of Saxony, to renounce his abdication of the Polish crown by the **Treaty of Altranstädt** (1706). After the battle Charles XII fled to the Turks to seek the support of **Ahmed III** (1673–1736), the Ottoman sultan (1703–1730), against Russia, which had already seized some of Sweden's Baltic territory and now threatened Finland.

1709 Sept. 11 The **battle at Malplaquet**, France, was a costly victory for the armies of the **Second Grand Alliance** in the War of the Spanish Succession (1701–1713). The French casualties amounted to little more than half the c.20,000 suffered by the Alliance, whose costly victory was due to the Allies' hesitation while peace negotiations were going on.

1709 Oct. 29 The first **Barrier Treaty** was signed between Great Britain and the Netherlands, providing the latter with fortresses in the Spanish Netherlands to prevent a French invasion. The British government, criticized by the **Tories** for overt favoritism for Holland, set aside the treaty, and its chief negotiator Charles Townshend (Apr. 18, 1675–June 21, 1738) was denounced in 1712.

V. ECONOMY AND TRADE

c.1700 **Cocoa** became during the 18th century the favorite nonalcoholic beverage of the North American colonists. Cacao beans, discovered by the Spanish in Mexico, were made into the beverage cocoa, with the addition of vanilla and sugar. **Coffee**, which had come to Europe via Turkey and was popular there, was drunk infrequently in the colonies. **Tea** was first introduced to Europe and North America at the beginning of this century. The consumption of these drinks, however, was small in comparison to the consumption of **rum** at this time in New England, a consequence of the thriving rum and **slave trade**.

c.1700   The new **Ashanti Kingdom** (to 1901) on the Gold Coast grew in power by trading slaves with the Dutch in return for firearms.

1700   **Newport**, Rhode Island, grew rapidly when the North **American slaves and rum** trade became centered on this shipbuilding port. Generally, rum was shipped out of New England, where it was distilled, to the Gold Coast, where it was exchanged for slaves. The slaves were taken to the West Indies, where some were traded for molasses, the essential ingredient of rum. Slaves and molasses were brought to Newport, where 22 distilleries were located.

1702 Mar. 11   **England's first daily newspaper**, the *Daily Courant*, was first printed. The *Courant* was published until 1735.

1703   The Moscow *Vedomosti* [News], **Russia's first newspaper**, appeared irregularly in editions of from 100 to 2,500 copies. Beginning in 1710 *Vedomosti* used the new simplified form of the Old Church Slavonic alphabet, required by **Peter the Great** for standard use.

1703 Dec. 27   The **Methuen Treaty** was signed by Great Britain and Portugal. It was a commercial agreement under which British textiles were exported to Portugal, and wines from Portugal were imported by England at two-thirds the duty levied on French wines.

1704 Apr. 24   The first issue of the *Boston News-Letter* appeared. In May the *News-Letter* carried the first of what came to be known as classified ads.

1705   The **Amicable Society for a Perpetual Assurance**, perhaps the earliest life insurance company, was founded in England. In 1866 it merged with the Norwich Union Life Insurance.

1707 May 1   The **Act of Union** joining Scotland to England and Wales also established **free trade** among these countries, increasing the profitability of trade within Great Britain. Most countries in Europe had internal systems of tariffs and trade restrictions that hampered trade within nations.

1708 Sept. 29   The **British East India Company** and the **New East India Company** were joined as the **United Company of Merchants of England Trading to the East Indies**, which was granted a trade monopoly to the East Indies and India at the ports of Madras, Bombay, and Calcutta. The new company, still, but erroneously, called the British East India Company after its predecessor, greatly influenced East Indian affairs.

1709 Apr. 12   *The Tatler*, the political journal edited by **Richard Steele** (Mar. 12, 1672–Sept. 1, 1729), first appeared and, despite its failure on Jan. 2, 1711, inaugurated an era of essay periodicals. **The Spectator**, edited by **Joseph Addison** (May 1, 1672–June 17, 1719), succeeded *The Tatler* on Mar. 1, 1711, and was published until Dec. 6, 1712. Addison and Steele collaborated on both of these publications.

VI. RELIGION AND PHILOSOPHY

c.1700   The **Age of Enlightenment**, or **Age of Reason**, was said to have begun with **John Locke** and coincided generally with the 18th century. Although his philosophy grew out of the prevailing intellectual climate of the late 17th century, Locke formulated the basic premise of the Enlightenment, the optimistic belief in the goodness of human nature which, when rationally engaged in the pursuit of happiness, arrived at social justice. Enlightenment philosophers disagreed on methods and often despaired of man's ever reaching rational pursuit, especially after they were forced to confront the bloody upheavals of the **French Revolution** (1789–1799), whose basic premises were founded on Enlightenment principles.

1700 Oct. 14   **Judah Hasid** (b. 1660?), a wandering Polish preacher, who had gathered adherents to the order of **Hasidim** [the Pious], dedicated to hastening the "end," now led c.800 followers into Jerusalem, where he expected the Messiah to appear. Hasid died suddenly a few days later, and his followers scattered. (These Hasidim should not be confused with the followers of **Baal Shem-Tov** [Rabbi Israel] (c.1700–1760), Hasidim who exist today.)

1702   **Samuel Wesley** (1662–Apr. 1735), an Anglican minister in Epworth, Lincolnshire, England, formed a "religious society" which met weekdays to pursue a more earnest cultivation of the religious life. Stressing prayer, Scripture reading, lay preaching, and charity to the unfortunate, such groups paved the way for **Methodism**, founded by Samuel's son, John Wesley (June 17, 1703–Mar. 2, 1791), later in the century.

1707 Isaac Watts (July 17, 1674–Nov. 25, 1748), the English theologian who was generally regarded as the founder of modern hymnody, published *Hymns*, several of which are still sung throughout the English-speaking world. Watts's hymns favored original verse based on biblical themes.

1707 June 9 John Mill (1645–June 23, 1707), an English scholar, published an edition of the **New Testament in Greek**, based on his own collation of early manuscripts over more than 30 years, with the encouragement of Dr. **John Fell** (June 23, 1625–July 10, 1686), bishop of Oxford. Mill demonstrated the extent of the variations among these manuscripts.

1708 The **German Baptist Brethren** organized their first church from a nucleus of eight persons of Pietist backgrounds at Schwarzenau in the Prussian province of Westfalen [Westphalia]. Under the leadership of Alexander Mack, the Brethren took the New Testament as their Rule of Faith and Practice. Two more churches sprang up at Marienborn and Krefelt. Persecution at the hands of Catholics, Lutherans, and Calvinists ensued.

1708 Oct. 7 Govind Singh [Govind Rai, Gobind] (b. 1666), the tenth and **last Sikh guru**, was assassinated. He was responsible for transforming the Sikh organization, originally one of the most pacific and democratic of faiths, into a militant order. His four sons having been killed by Muslims, Govind had determined that the guruship end with him and that temporal authority would be vested in the **Khalsa** [the Pure], an elite corps open to all who met the requirements and partook of the initiatory rites. All members would be able to add "Singh" [Lion] to their names.

1709 Oct. 23 The **convent of Port-Royal**, south of Versailles, was closed by Louis XIV, and the buildings were razed the following year. It was the **final blow to the great center of Jansenism**, the Catholic reform movement begun in 1640.

VII. SCIENCE, EDUCATION, AND TECHNOLOGY

1700 Sept. 15 André Lenôtre (b. Mar. 12, 1613), a French landscape architect, died. At Versailles Lenôtre developed the **formal garden** to perfect expression, setting a standard that influenced garden design long after his death. He also planned the gardens of Chantilly, St. Cloud, Fontainebleau and, in England, those at Chatsworth, Greenwich, and Hampton Court.

1701 The **Russian Naval Academy** was founded in Moscow by **Peter the Great** as the institution to train Russia's naval officers.

1701 Oct. 16 Yale College was chartered at New Haven, Connecticut, by Congregationalists who were dissatisfied with the flourishing climate of liberalism at Harvard College. **Elihu Yale** (Apr. 5, 1649–July 8, 1721), benefactor of Yale, was the son of one of the founders of the New Haven colony. He had gained his wealth in India as a governor of the East India Company.

1703 Mar. 3 Robert Hooke (b. July 18, 1635), an English experimental physicist and philosopher, died. He made important contributions in the realm of optics and in the observation of the effects of gravity. **Hooke's Law of Elasticity** of gases was formulated in 1660. *Micrographica* (1665) explained the process of combustion. *Attempt to Prove the Motion of the Earth* (1674) described the elliptical path the earth's orbit around the sun as affected by the gravitational pull of the moon.

1703 Oct. 28 John Wallis (b. Nov. 23, 1616), an English mathematician, died. His work in arithmetic developed ideas which led to the binomial theorem and then to differential and integral calculus, greatly influencing **Isaac Newton** in the development of his calculus. He systematized the use of negative and fractional exponents; and introduced the symbol ∞ for infinity.

1705 Aug. 16 Jacob [Jacques] **Bernoulli** (b. Dec. 27, 1654), a Swiss mathematician, died. He was credited with the discovery of the infinitesimal calculus. *Ars conjectandi* (1713), a pioneer work in the theory of probability, was Bernoulli's major publication. His brother **Johann** [Jean] pioneered in differential calculus.

1705 Jan. 17   John Ray [Wray] (b. Nov. 29, 1627), an English naturalist, died. Ray noted (1682) the distinction between monocotyledons and dicotyledons, which became basic in the systematic **classification of plants**.

1704   Lexicon technicum, or **Dictionary of the Arts and Sciences**, was compiled by the English editor **John Harris** (1666–1719).

1707 Mar. 30   Sébastien Le Prestre de Vauban (b. May 15, 1633), a French military engineer who was his era's leading expert both in besieging fortresses and building fortifications, died. He played an important role in the wars of **Louis XIV**, in which the tactics he devised resulted in the capture (1667–1703) of a dozen cities and fortresses. Vauban also invented the **socket bayonet**, which could be fastened to a rifle without interfering with its firing.

VIII. ARTS AND LEISURE

c.1700   In marked difference to the elaborately decorated **French baroque style of furniture** that prevailed during the reign of Louis XIV, there began to appear in England a simpler, less ornamated style, based on the cabriole or reverse-curve leg, which became known as the **Queen Anne style**. This style of furniture began to appear (c.1725) in the American colonies where it was dominant until the American Revolution.

c.1700   Men throughout much of the western world wore the three-cornered hat, and the noble, wealthy, or powerful among them powdered their hair or wigs. Their waistcoats began to shrink until, in the 19th century, they became the typical vests of today. Women wore hoop skirts, invented in 1711, and low-cut bodices served as corsets. Whale bone [baleen] was commonly used in women's clothing as support for the basket-like hoop, which was worn around the hips, and as strengtheners for stiff hoods and collars. In the American colonies, the sturdy clothes of the early settlers began to be replaced by garments more closely resembling **European fashions**, especially those of France.

1700 May 1   John Dryden (b. Aug. 19, 1631), an English writer, died. As a playwright he produced *The Rival Ladies* (1663), *Marriage à la Mode* (1673), and his masterpiece *All for Love* (1677).

Absalom and Achitophel (1681) established his reputation as a great political satirist. Dryden as a critic is noted especially for *Essay of Dramatic Poesy* (1668). When he refused to take the oath at the accession of William and Mary, he was replaced as Poet Laureate.

1703 May 16   Charles Perrault (b. Jan. 12, 1628), a French writer, died. He is known primarily today for his collection of fairy tales *Les histoires ou contes du temps passé* (1697) also called *Les contes de ma mère l'Oye* [Tales of Mother Goose]. Based on oral tradition, they included "Sleeping Beauty," "Beauty and the Beast," and "Little Red Riding Hood."

1703 May 26   Samuel Pepys (b. Feb. 23, 1633), **chronicler of Charles II's England**, died. He began writing his famous diary on Jan. 1, 1660. His gift as a writer was an ability to select the episode, little or big, that conveyed a sense of the life and times of the **Restoration**. His eyesight failing, he ceased his diary on May 31, 1669. It was published first in a partial edition in 1825; the full edition of 1893–1896 contained more than a million words.

1704 Oct.   Sarah Kemble Knight (Apr. 19, 1666–Sept. 27, 1727), a schoolmistress, embarked on her travels, recorded in *Private Journal of a Journey from Boston to New York in the Year 1704* (posthumously published, 1825). Among her notes were comments on the conditions at inns where she lodged and observations of local people and their customs.

1706 Mar. 3   Johann Pachelbel (b. Aug., 1653), a German composer and organist, died. Influenced by Italian music, he was an outstanding composer of **cantatas and chorales**.

1707 Apr. 29   George Farquhar (born c.1677), an Irish-born English late Restoration dramatist, died. He was known particularly for two highly successful comedies, *The Recruiting Officer* (1706) and *The Beaux' Stratagem* (1707), often revived today.

1707 May 9   Dietrich Buxtehude (born c.1637), a Danish-German organist and composer, died. In 1673 he first performed the *Abendmusiken*, services of organ music and instrumental pieces for chorus and orchestra given on the five Sundays preceding Christmas.

1710–1719

I. DISASTERS

1711 An outbreak of **plague** became the first of a series of natural catastrophes that would burden the Kingdom of **Denmark**. In 1717 floods caused widespread damage along the western coast of Denmark and, in 1728, the capital at Copenhagen was nearly destroyed by fire.

II. EXPLORATION AND COLONIZATION

1713 France established colonies near **Charlottetown**, the present capital of **Prince Edward Island**, Canada, one of France's colonial possessions not ceded to Great Britain by the **Treaty of Utrecht** (Apr. 11, 1713).

1715 The island of **Mauritius**, off the coast of Madagascar, occupied (1598–1710) by the Dutch, was settled by French colonists and renamed **Île de France**.

1718 The city of **New Orleans** was founded by French and Canadian settlers at the mouth of the Mississippi River. It was the **first permanent settlement in the present state of Louisiana** and was named (1722) capital of Louisiane [the Louisiana Territory], which included the extent of the Mississippi River and its tributaries.

1718 May 1 **San Antonio**, in present Texas, was founded as a Franciscan mission [San Antonio de Valero, **the Alamo**] by the Spanish on the site of an earlier Indian village, Yanaguana.

III. POLITICS AND WAR

1710 Nov. 13 The Ottoman Empire (1326–1920) officially declared war on Russia, joining the **Great Northern War** (1700–1721).

1710 Nov. 25 The fourth Parliament under **Anne, queen of Great Britain**, convened with a Tory majority. The Tory victory was helped, in part, by the sermons of **Henry Sacheverell** (1674–June 5, 1724), a high Anglican priest who had violently attacked **Sidney Godolphin** (c.June 15, 1645–Sept. 15, 1712), Earl Godolphin, the pro-Whig lord treasurer. Godolphin had him impeached and suspended from his pulpit,

but this act created much sympathetic support for the Tories. As a result, the Queen dismissed Godolphin.

1711 Apr. 17 **Joseph I** (b. July 26, 1678), the Holy Roman emperor (from 1705), king of Hungary (from 1687), and king of Germany (from 1690), died without a male heir. The Austrian Hapsburg lands passed to his brother, the archduke Charles, who also was automatically elected as **Charles VI**, the Holy Roman emperor, and who now became through inheritance Charles III, king of Hungary.

1711 May 1 By the **Treaty of Szatmár** [Satu-Mare], Hungarian rebels agreed to cease hostilities (from 1703) against Austrian Hapsburg rule, begun in 1703. General amnesty was granted the insurrectionists, and the **Hungarian Diet** was allowed regular convocation.

1711 Sept. 22 The **Tuscarora Indian War** (1711–1713), sparked by encroachment on Indian land, began with a massacre of settlers along the Chowan and Roanoke rivers in North Carolina. The settlement of New Bern was abandoned. On Mar. 23, 1713, the Indian-built Fort Nohucke in South Carolina was captured, bringing an end to the important Indian stronghold. Surviving Indians left their land in the Carolinas and went north, where they joined the Iroquois League of Six Nations.

1711 Dec. 31 **John Churchill**, duke of Marlborough, was dismissed by the Tory government as commander of the English forces in the **War of the Spanish Succession** (1701–1713). A brilliant military commander, he was labeled a warmongering Whig. His dismissal removed the last barrier to England's negotiating a peace with France.

1712 May **Philip V**, king of Spain and grandson of Louis XIV, king of France, renounced his right to succeed to the French throne following the deaths of his father, the dauphin **Louis de France** in Apr. 1711; his elder brother, Louis, duke of Bourgogne, in Feb. 1712; and his nephew, Louis, duke of Bretagne, in Mar. 1712.

1712 July 24 The French, under Marshall Villars, defeated combined Austrian and Dutch forces under Prince Eugene of Savoy in a **battle at Denain** in northern France. The Dutch now eagerly joined Great Britain in negotiating for peace.

1712 July 25   The Protestant Swiss cantons led by Bern [Berne] defeated the Catholics in a **battle at Villmergen**, in Aargan canton. On Aug. 11 the ensuing **Treaty of Aargau** confirmed Protestant domination of the confederacy, but established true religious equality between Catholics and Protestants.

1713 Apr. 11   The **Peace of Utrecht**, bringing the **War of the Spanish Succession** (from 1701) to a close, was effected by a number of separate treaties signed by France and powers of the Second Grand Alliance: France and the Holy Roman Empire settled their claims by the **Treaty of Rastatt** (1714). The Bourbons, France's royal house, were officially installed in Spain in the person of Philip V. However, the French and Spanish thrones were to remain separate. France recognized the Protestant royal succession in England and agreed not to aid the Stuarts or their supporters, the Jacobites. The Spanish Netherlands became a possession of the Austrian Hapsburgs. Gibraltar and the island of Minorca were ceded to England, and Sicily to Savoy, while France gained the principality of Orange, in present France. Portuguese dominions along Brazil's Amazon River were officially recognized.

1713 Apr. 11   **Queen Anne's War** (1701–1713) ended. By the **Peace of Utrecht**, the French lost **Nova Scotia** (except for Cape Breton Island), Newfoundland, and Prince Rupert's Land [Hudson's Bay Company's territory] to Britain.

1713 Apr. 19   The **Pragmatic Sanction** was issued by Charles VI, the Holy Roman emperor. It was intended to settle the question of his succession by naming his eldest daughter Maria Theresa as heir in the absence of a son.

1714   **Ahmed Bey**, governor of **Tripoli**, in present Libya, was recognized as pasha by Ahmed III of the **Ottoman Empire** (1326–1920). He was the founder of the **Karamanli Dynasty** (1711–1835), which succeeded in maintaining Tripoli's independence from Constantinople.

1714 Mar. 7   The **Treaty of Rastatt** [Rastadt], in present Germany, was signed by France and the Holy Roman Empire, assigning Milan, Naples, and Sardinia to the empire. Charles VI, the Hapsburg Holy Roman emperor, withdrew his claim to the Spanish throne and accepted the Spanish Netherlands as a Hapsburg possession of Austria. In return, France received Strasbourg and Alsace, and her allies, Bavaria and Cologne, were restored to their prewar boundaries.

1714 Mar. 13   The Russians completed the **occupation of Finland** with a victory at Storkyro, Finland, over the Swedes in the **Great Northern War** (1700–1721). They had already seized most of Livonia. In September the Aland Islands [Ahvenanmaa], in the Baltic Sea, were also captured by Russia.

1714 Aug. 1   **Anne** (b. Feb. 16, 1665), **queen of England** (from 1702), died. She was the **last of the Stuart Dynasty** (from 1603) to rule in Great Britain. She was succeeded by **George I** of the Hanoverian line established by the **Act of Settlement** (1701).

1715 Sept. 1   **Louis XIV** (b. Sept. 5, 1638), king of France, died and was succeeded by his great-grandson, **Louis XV**, then four years old. **Philippe II** (b. Aug. 2, 1674–Dec. 2, 1723), duke of Orléans, served as regent until Louis XV gained his majority (Feb., 1723). Louis XIV had ruled for 73 years.

1715 Nov. 13   The **Jacobites** were again defeated in an uprising in Scotland in a **battle at Sheriffmuir** in the Highlands. The revolt had been organized by John Erskine (1675–1732), earl of Mar. James Francis Edward Stuart, the Old Pretender, nevertheless landed (Dec. 25) in Scotland, but soon went back to France as the revolt disintegrated.

1715 Nov. 15   The **Third Barrier Treaty** was signed by Great Britain, the Holy Roman Empire, and the Netherlands [Holland]. The Dutch were permitted to occupy seven fortresses in the Austrian Netherlands [Belgium], along the French border.

1715   The Whig **Robert Walpole**, later earl of Orford (1742), became **England's prime minister**, the first minister to bear this title. Traditionally, the cabinet's first lord of the treasury had been the first minister.

1716 Apr. 13   **Austria** declared war on the **Ottoman Empire**, and imperial troops under Prince Eugene [Eugène] of Savoy defeated (Aug. 5) the Turks in a **battle at Peterwardein** [Petrovaradin], in present Yugoslavia. By November the Banat of Temesvár, the present Yugoslavian district of Vojvoidina, had fallen to the Austrians, completing their conquest of Hungary.

1717 The **viceroyalty of New Granada** was created. It comprised present Venezuela, Ecuador, Colombia, and Panama, and was established as separate from the viceroyalty of Peru. **Bogotá** [Santa Fé de Bogotá], founded in 1538, was the capital.

1717 Jan. 4 The **Triple Alliance** was signed at **The Hague** between Great Britain, France, and the Netherlands. It was aimed at preserving peace in western Europe by securing the French throne of the sickly Louis XV against the claim of his uncle, Philip V, king of Spain, and at securing the French promise to end aid to the Jacobites.

1717 Aug. 17 The **Convention of Amsterdam** was signed by France, Prussia, and Russia, to enforce the terms of the treaties ending the War of the Spanish Succession (1701–1713).

1717 Aug. 22 **Philip V**, king of Spain, sent a Spanish military force to seize Sardinia from the Hapsburgs. In July 1718, Spain occupied Sicily, and on Aug. 2 the Austrian Hapsburg Charles VI, the Holy Roman emperor, joined the Triple Alliance, which now became the **Quadruple Alliance** against Spain.

1718 July 7 **Alexis Petrovich** (b. Feb. 28, 1690), the eldest son of **Peter the Great**, czar of Russia, was put to death by his father. The dissolute behavior of the son had led to his expulsion from Russia. Despite the able performance of Alexis during the **Great Northern War** (1700–1721), estrangement between father and son continued, and Alexis was treacherously recalled from his refuge in Vienna, to be tried for treason. After sending his first wife and mother of Alexis, Eudoxia [Evdokiya Fëderovna Lopukhina] (Feb. 6, 1699–Sept. 7, 1731), to a convent, Peter had married (1712) **Catherine I** [Ekaterina Alekseevna, Marfa Skavronskaya] (1684–May 17, 1727), who bore him a son in 1715.

1718 July 21 The **Treaty of Passarowitz** was signed by Austria and the Ottoman Empire, formalizing the exchange of territories seized in border hostilities. The Turks retained Morea [the Peloponnese of Greece], recaptured from Venice in 1715, but it lost **Belgrade**, northern Serbia, Little Valachia, and the Banat of Temesvár. This important expansion of Austria established the Sava and Danube rivers as the **frontier between Islam and Christianity in East Europe.**

1718 Dec. 11 **Charles XII** (b. June 17, 1682), king of Sweden (from 1697), died of a bullet wound in the **siege of Frederikshald**, while on an invasion of Norway during the **Great Northern War** (1700–1721). In Jan. 1719, the Swedish Diet convened to approve the succession of Charles XII's sister **Ulrika Eleonora** (Jan. 23, 1688–Nov. 24, 1741). Ratification of a new constitution in the same year brought the end of the absolute monarchy instituted in Sweden by Charles XI.

1719 June 10 A **battle at Glenshiels** in the Highlands ended a futile **Spanish invasion of Scotland** in support of the Jacobites. The Spanish and Jacobite troops were decisively defeated in the poorly planned battle, which was supported by Philip V, king of Spain.

1719 Sept. 23 **Liechtenstein** was created an independent principality of the Holy Roman Empire by the emperor Charles VI. It was formed by the unification of the lordships of **Vaduz** and **Schellenberg** on the upper Rhine River.

1719 Nov. 20 The **Peace of Stockholm** was signed by Hanover and Sweden. George I, king of Great Britain, as elector of Hanover, received Bremen and Verden, both adjacent to Hanover, in present Germany, for the promise of British naval support in future Swedish efforts to regain her Baltic possessions, lost in the Great Northern War.

IV. ECONOMY AND TRADE

1711 The **South Sea Company** was founded in Great Britain, with a charter providing a monopoly of trade with the Spanish colonies in the Americas.

1712 **Christopher Hussey**, an American whaler whose ship had been blown off course, made the **first capture of a sperm whale** [*Physeter catodon*], up to 60 feet in length. Although whaling had been practiced by New Englanders since before 1645, with the advent of sperm whaling the industry boomed.

1712 A **Stamp Act** was imposed in Great Britain to curtail publication of the popular essay periodicals that discussed government policy. Circulation of the popular *Spectator* dropped by 60 percent, and other papers folded.

1713 Mar. 26 By the **Asiento Treaty** [Asiento de Negros] Spain granted to Great Britain the right to sell slaves to the Spanish colonies under the aegis of the South Sea Company.

1716 May 2 **John Law**, a Scottish financier, was granted a royal charter to found the **Royal Bank of France** in Paris. The bank issued notes, convertible into coin, which Law then lent to the French government. In 1717 Law gained the right to exclusive trade in Louisiane [the Louisiana territory], and by Dec. 1719, the stock of Law's banking venture was worth 40 times its original value. But Law's scheme failed in 1720, and thousands of investors were ruined.

V. RELIGION AND PHILOSOPHY

1715 **Pope Clement XI** (July 21, 1649–Mar. 19, 1721; ruled from 1700) decided the famous **Rites Controversy** between Franciscans and Jesuits by ordering the Jesuits to cease accommodating to local customs and ritual observances of the Chinese in their mission work. The emperor of China, as a result, now forbade any Christian missionary to enter China.

1715 Oct. 13 **Nicolas Malebranche** (b. Aug. 6, 1638), a French metaphysician, died. Malebranche expanded on the theory of Occasionalism, which held physical events and mental states to be dependent on the contemplation of God. Malebranche's works included the four-volume *De la Recherche de la Vérité* [**The Search for Truth**] (1674) and *Traité de l'Amour de Dieu.*

1717 June 24 Four workmen's guilds in London, England, combined into the **Grand Lodge of England**, the **first major Freemason organization**. The Freemasons believed that religious belief was the sole concern of the individual.

1719 The **German Baptist Brethren community** of Krefeld in Prussia, led by Pastor **Peter Becher**, migrated to North America to settle on lands offered by William Penn. In this year another Brethren group fled persecution to the Netherlands, then went to Pennsylvania in 1729.

VI. SCIENCE, EDUCATION, AND TECHNOLOGY

1712 **Denis Papin** (b. Aug. 22, 1647), a French physicist, died in London. He had worked with **Christian Huygens** and **Robert Boyle** and, in 1690, was credited with having been the **first to use steam to power a piston.**

1712 The **first practical atmospheric steam engine** began to operate in England. Fully developed in 1705 by the engineer **Thomas Newcomen** (1663–Aug. 15, 1729), in collaboration with **Thomas Savery** (1650–May, 1715), it was used primarily to pump water out of coal mines.

1712 Sept. 11 **Jean Dominique** [Giovanni Domenico] **Cassini** (b. June 8, 1625), a French astronomer, died at the Paris Observatory he founded and which his family directed until 1845. He observed (1666) the polar ice caps of Mars and calculated the earth's orbit in 1672 and the parallax of the sun in 1680. He discovered (1661–1684) several of Saturn's moons and confirmed (1675) the belief that Saturn's rings were not joined.

1715 **Brook Taylor** (Aug. 18, 1685–Dec. 29, 1731), an English mathematician, published his **Methodus incrementorum directa et inversa**, containing Taylor's Theorem on expansion, basic in the treatment of calculus functions.

1716 Nov. 14 **Gottfried Wilhelm von Leibnitz** [Leibniz] (b. July 1, 1646), a German philosopher and mathematician, died. *Nouveaux essais* (1765), his most important philosophical work, greatly influenced the Enlightenment in Germany. Leibnitz strove to develop a system of mathematical logic that could encompass all knowledge. His pioneer efforts made him the founder of symbolic logic and yielded a theory of determinants, a perfected binary system, and the invention (1676) of the calculus, independently of Isaac Newton. Leibnitz held that, according to logic, there were many possible worlds, that God knew them all *a priori,* and that, being good, He created "the best of all possible worlds."

VII. ARTS AND LEISURE

1710 The **Meissen porcelain factory**, the oldest of its kind still in operation, was founded near Dresden, Germany, where large deposits of china clay and potter's earth were discovered. **Johann Friedrich Böttger**, a German alchemist, developed (1709) the first hard paste porcelain in Europe, and it was this white porcelain that became famous as **Dresden china.**

1712 Yusuf Nabi (born c.1630), a Turkish poet at the court in Istanbul, died. Popular and influential with other poets, Nabi introduced Persian themes and style to Turkish poetry.

1713 *Mérope*, by the Italian dramatist **Francesco Scipione di Maffei** (June 1, 1675–Feb. 11, 1755), was first presented on stage. It was highly regarded as the first Italian tragedy written in the style of the great French classical tragedists. Voltaire's *Mérope* (1743) was an adaptation.

1713 Jan. 8 **Arcangelo Corelli** (b. Feb. 17, 1653), an Italian composer, died. He introduced an early form of the concerto called the **concerto grosso**, in which the parts played by instrumental groups were in contrast to the orchestra.

1715 P'u Sung-Ling (b. 1640), a Chinese story writer, died. His *Liao-chai chih-i*, completed in 1679, was a collection of supernatural tales.

1715 Dec. 31 **William Wycherley** (b. 1640), an English playwright, died. One of the chief comedy writers of the Restoration, he was known especially for *The Country Wife* (1675). His other works included his first comedy *Love in a Wood, or St. James's Park* (1671) and *The Plain Dealer* (1676).

1716 The **first theater in colonial America** was constructed this year in **Williamsburg**, Virginia. It did not last.

1716 **Korin Ogata** (b. 1653), a Japanese painter, died. He was the best known of the Ogata family of artists, and was a major painter of the Tokugawa era. He produced such masterpieces as the screens entitled *God of Thunder and God of Wind; Red and White Plum Trees;* and *Waves.*

1718 Feb. 14 **K'ung Shang-Jèn** (b. Nov. 1, 1648), a Chinese writer, died. *T'ao-hua shan* [The Peach Blossom Fan] (1699), his chief work, was a romance set at the end of the Ming Dynasty (c.1640).

1718 Dec. 6 **Nicholas Rowe** (b. June 20, 1674), an English dramatist and poet, died. He was the first to produce a critical edition of William Shakespeare's works (1709). An ardent Whig, he succeeded Nahum Tate as poet laureate in 1715. His best-known plays were *Tamerlane* (1701), *The Fair Penitent* (1703), and *The Tragedy of Jane Shore* (1714).

VIII. SPORTS, GAMES, AND SOCIETY

1714 **Anne, queen of England**, a **horse racing** enthusiast, originated cash prizes at the big annual race at Doncaster. Owners of all starters were required to put up an entry fee of ten guineas, winner take all. The queen's horse Star won the first running of this sweepstakes event.

1718 Nov. 22 **Blackbeard** [Edward Teach, Thatch], a notorious English pirate, was shot to death aboard his ship *Queen Anne's Revenge*, in the James River of Virginia. Blackbeard's raids on colonists along the Atlantic coast had prompted **Alexander Spotswood** (1676–June 7, 1740), governor of Virginia, to offer a bounty for his head.

1719 English county **cricket** was introduced in a match between "the Londoners," from Middlesex, and "the Kentish men."

1719 **James Figg** (c.1695–Dec. 7, 1734) was acclaimed England's champion at **bareknuckle fighting**, after winning 15 successive bouts. At the time, the sport permitted wrestling holds, tossing an opponent to the ground, kicking, kneeing, and other ungentlemanly acts.

1720–1729

I. DISASTERS

1720 The last notable **plague** [Black Death] epidemic in western Europe occurred in Provence, France. The outbreak never extended beyond Provence.

II. EXPLORATION AND COLONIZATION

1721 July **Hans Egede** (Jan. 31, 1686–Nov. 5, 1758), a Norwegian missionary, established the **first European settlement on Greenland** still existing, at **Godthåb** [Godthaab] on the southwestern coast.

1721 Dec. 29 The French annexed **Mauritius**, abandoned by the Dutch in 1710, and renamed it Île de France.

1722 Jacob Roggeveen (1659–1729), a Dutch explorer, discovered the **Samoa Islands** [Navigators Islands], in the southwestern Pacific. On the same exploratory trip Roggeveen discovered **Easter Island** on Easter Sunday, April 5, 1722.

1724 Fort Drummer, near present Brattleboro, was the **first permanent settlement in Vermont**, founded by colonists from Massachusetts.

1726 Montevideo, present capital of Uruguay, was founded by **Bruno Mauricio de Zabala**, the governor of Buenos Aires, in order to provide a garrison against Portuguese encroachment from present Brazil.

1729 Gaspard Joseph Chaussegros de Léry was sent by the French to **fortify the length of the Ohio River** against **westward expansion by English colonists**, who felt justified in moving west since the charters granted by the English crown to the seaboard colonies specified either no western bounderies or the Pacific Ocean as the western limits.

1729 Feb. Henry Osborne was appointed the first royal governor of the British colony of **Newfoundland**. The province had been acquired from France by the **Treaty of Utrecht** (1713).

III. POLITICS AND WAR

1720 K'ang-Hsi, the Chinese emperor, launched a military campaign in **Tibet** to drive out the **Dzungars**, destroying the last remnants of Mongol influence in the country. A pro-Chinese **Dalai Lama**, as well as Chinese representatives and a small garrison, were installed in the capital at **Lhasa**.

1720 Feb. 1 The **Treaty of Stockholm** ended hostilities between Sweden and Prussia toward the close of the **Great Northern War** (1700–1721). **Frederick William I**, king of Prussia, gained Swedish Pomerania, a region along the Baltic coast of present Germany, including the coveted port of Stettin [Szczecin], in present Poland. Prussia promised in return to support Sweden against Russia.

1720 Feb. 17 The **Treaty of The Hague** ended the war between Spain and the **Quadruple Alliance**,

begun in 1717. Philip V, the Bourbon king of Spain, renounced his claims to the Spanish Hapsburg territories in northern Italy, but secured the succession of his son Charles, the future Charles III, king of Spain, to Parma, Piacenza, and Tuscany. **Victor Amadeus II** (May 14, 1666–Oct. 31, 1732), duke of Savoy, obtained Sardinia in return for Sicily. He ruled as Victor Amadeus I, the first king of Sardinia, Savoy, and Piedmont (abdicated 1730).

1720 Feb. 29 **Ulrika Eleonora**, queen of Sweden (from 1719), abdicated in favor of her husband, **Frederick I** (Apr. 28, 1676–Mar. 25, 1751) of Hesse. His 31-year reign was marked by the increasing power of the parliamentary system.

1721 José de Antequera, a lawyer from the audiencia of Charcas, was called to **Asunción, in present Paraguay**, to investigate charges against the governor of the city, **Diego de los Reyes Balmaseda**. In Asunción Antequera led the comuneros, the city leaders, in an uprising, supported by the belief that "the authority of the people is superior to that of the king." Antequera (b. 1690) ruled Asunción until he was beheaded in 1731.

1721 Apr. 3 **Robert Walpole**, earl of Orford, took office as the **first prime minister of Great Britain**. As head of the executive branch, Walpole achieved transfer of the center of Parliamentary power to the House of Commons.

1721 Sept. 10 Russia and Sweden signed the **Treaty of Nystad** [Uusikaupunki], on the southwestern coast of Finland, bringing the **Great Northern War** (1700–1721) to a close. Russia gained Sweden's Baltic territories of Estonia, Livonia, and Finnish Karelia.

1722 The territory of the **League of Six Nations**, a confederation of Iroquois tribes, was recognized by American colonists in a **treaty signed in Albany**, New York, the center for the fur trade. The agreement, concluded with **Alexander Spotswood** (1676–June 7, 1740), governor of Virginia, established the Potomac River and the Blue Ridge Mountains as a western border of the colonies, which left present western New York, Pennsylvania, and the Ohio River Valley open to the League.

1722 Peter the Great, czar of Russia, conducted a military campaign into northern **Persia** to establish Russian supremacy on the **Caspian Sea**. In 1723 he captured the Persian ports of Baku and Derbent, said to have been built by the Persians in the sixth century for the defense of the **Caspian Gates**, a narrow pass long used by traders bypassing the Caucasus Mountains.

1722 Mar. 8 **Mir Mahmud** [Mahmud Kahn], emir of Kandahar (1722–1725), in present Afghanistan, leading an uprising against Persian rule, won an overwhelming victory in a **battle at Gulnabad**, c.10 miles from the Persian capital of Isfahan [Ẹsfahān], which he then captured (Oct. 23). He ousted Husein I (1675?–1729; ruled 1694–1722), the Safawid shah of Persia, nearly ending the power of the **Safawid** [Safavid] **Dynasty** (1501–1736).

1722 Sept. 24 **Francis Atterbury** (Mar. 6, 1662–Feb. 22, 1732), bishop of Rochester, was convicted of treason for corresponding with the Old Pretender, **James Francis Edward Stuart** [James III]. Atterbury's plot resulted in the suspension (Oct. 17) of the **Habeas Corpus Act** of 1679, and Atterbury was banished in 1723.

1722 Dec. 20 **K'ang-Hsi** [Shêng-Tsu] (b. May 4, 1654), the Manchu emperor (from 1662) of the **Ch'ing Dynasty** (1644–1911), died in Peking. One of the greatest Chinese emperors, he had strengthened imperial power, eliminated any danger of a foreign invasion, and brought the empire to its greatest extent.

1723 Feb. 16 **Louis XV**, the Bourbon king of France, reached his majority. Following the deaths of his prime minister, Cardinal **Guillaume Dubois** (b. Sept. 6, 1656), on Aug. 10, and his regent, Philippe II (b. Aug. 2, 1674), duke of Orléans, on Dec. 2, the administration was taken over by **Louis Henri** (Aug. 18, 1692–Jan. 27, 1740), duke of Bourbon and prince of Condé.

1723 Oct. 12 The **Treaty of Charlottenburg**, now a suburb of Berlin, was signed by Prussia and Great Britain. It provided for a military alliance to be sealed by the marriage of the grandson of George I, king of Great Britain, with a Prussian princess and by the marriage of a Prussian prince with the daughter of the prince of Wales.

1724 Jan. 10 **Philip V**, king of Spain, abdicated in favor of his son Louis I. However, Louis (b. Aug. 25, 1707) died on Aug. 31, and Philip V agreed to return to the throne, controlled largely by his wife **Eliza-**

beth **Farnese**, since Philip suffered increasingly from melancholy and paranoia.

1724 Apr. 3 The British secretary of state, **John Carteret** (Apr. 22, 1690–Jan. 2, 1763), earl Granville (from 1744), was dismissed by **Robert Walpole**, earl of Orford, the British prime minister, when he opposed Walpole's pro-French policy. Lord Carteret, who was appointed lord lieutenant of Ireland, was replaced as secretary of state by **Thomas Pelham-Holles** (1693–Nov. 17, 1768), duke of Newcastle, who held the post for 18 years when he was replaced briefly (1742–1744) by Carteret but then resumed his position (1744–1754).

1724 June 23 The **Treaty of Constantinople** provided for the partition of **Persia** between **Russia** and the **Ottoman Empire** (1326–1920). Persia was on the verge of disintegration after the Afghan invasion (1722). In 1723 the Persian nobility and most of the populace of Isfahan [Ẹsfahān] had been slaughtered by **Mir Mahmud**, the Afghan shah. Russians and Turks occupied the north and west of Persia while **Tahmasp II** (d. 1739), the Safawid [Safavid] shah, tried to organize forces to oust the invaders.

1725 Feb. 8 **Peter I** [Pëtr Alekseevich] **the Great** (b. June 9, 1672), czar of Russia (from 1682), died. Peter's second wife **Catherine I**, whom he had married in 1712, kept the Russian throne as czarina, despite the rightful claim of Peter II, grandson of Peter the Great by his first marriage to **Eudoxia** (1669?–Sept. 7, 1731). On the death of Catherine (b. Apr. 15, 1684) on May 17, 1727, Peter II was placed on the throne.

1725 May 1 The **Treaty of Vienna** was signed by the Spanish Bourbons and the Austrian Hapsburgs. The emperor gave up his claim to the Spanish throne and agreed to help Spain regain Gibralter and Minorca. The alliance resulted from the revocation by France of the betrothal of Louis XV, king of France, to the **Infanta Mariana**, daughter of Philip V, king of Spain. In the interest of mutual aid, Great Britain, France, and Prussia signed the **Treaty of Hanover** [Herrenhausen] (Sept. 23) in answer to the Spanish Bourbon-Austrian Hapsburg threat.

1726 Oct. 12 The **Treaty of Wusterhausen**, in present Germany, was signed by Charles VI, the Holy Roman emperor, and Frederick William I, king of Prussia. The treaty was formalized by the **Treaty of Berlin** (1728). In the meantime Spain, allied with

Hapsburg Austria, now had gained an opportunity to enforce its claims for Gibraltar and trade concessions against Great Britain as Prussia withdrew from the alliance [Treaty of Hanover] between France and Great Britain.

1727 **Agadja**, king of Dahomey (c.1708–1732), whose centralized state was founded on conquest, subdued the West African kingdoms of **Allada** and **Quidah** in present Benin. He thus established contact with the European coastal trade, which increased his access to firearms.

1727 Feb. **Gibraltar** was besieged by Philip V, king of Spain, beginning a war with Great Britain over territorial rights and trade rivalries. The effort soon was brought to a conclusion with the status quo settlement decided at the **Convention of Prado** (a royal palace of Spain), on Mar. 6, 1728.

1727 June 11 **George I** (b. May 28, 1660), king of Great Britain (from 1714), died. He was succeeded by his son **George II**, who reappointed Robert Walpole, earl of Orford, as prime minister at the insistence of his wife **Caroline of Anspach** [Wilhelmina Carolina] (Mar. 1, 1683–Nov. 20, 1737).

1728 Dec. 23 The **Treaty of Berlin** was signed by Charles VI, the Holy Roman emperor, and Frederick William I, king of Prussia. Charles recognized Prussia's claim to the German duchies of Berg and Jülich, on the northern frontiers of Austrian Netherlands, in return for Frederick William's acceptance of the **Pragmatic Sanction** (1713).

1729 **North and South Carolina became separate royal provinces** and were governed under British administration until the Revolutionary War.

1729 Nov. 9 The **Treaty of Sevilla** [Seville] was signed by Spain, Great Britain, and France, ending the Austro-Spanish alliance established in 1725. Great Britain retained **Gibraltar**.

IV. ECONOMY AND TRADE

1720 Sept. The **South Sea Bubble burst** as stocks in the British financial scheme worth £1,060 in June fell to £150 in late September. The overvalued stocks had been offered to holders of state-backed bonds in order to relieve the national debt. The **Bank of England** had been outbid. Many similar spurious ventures were launched with the hopes of cashing in on the profits offered by the **South Sea Company**, founded in 1711 in Great Britain. All speculators but a lucky few were disappointed, though the South Sea Company itself did not collapse.

1720 Nov. 1 The **bankruptcy of the Royal Bank of France**, founded in 1716, signaled the end of John Law's financial schemes. The so-called **Mississippi Bubble**, caused by an excessive issue of paper money and a wave of speculation, discredited the banking system in France.

1721 In the wake of the financial ruin brought on by the South Sea Bubble and the Mississippi Bubble, Great Britain passed the **Bubble Act** for its regulation of joint-stock companies. These were now required to obtain a charter.

1721 The Russian government decreed industrial workers constituted a new type of laboring class. The decree permitted the assigning of **serfs to particular industries**, from which they could not leave for the rest of their working lives.

1723 **William Wood** (1671–1730), a British ironmaster, was granted a patent to mint a new **copper coinage** for Ireland, which suffered a shortage of metal currency. The lack of consultation by the British government with leaders in Ireland bound the Irish Protestants and Catholics together against England. **Lord Carteret** was sent to Ireland as lord lieutenant to resolve the turmoil.

1727 **Paper currency**, backed by tobacco rather than silver or gold, was issued in **Virginia** as legal tender.

1728 The *Real Compañía Guipuzcoana*, or Caracas Company, was founded in Spain by Basque merchants to conduct trade in cocoa and tobacco from present Venezuela, part of the viceroyalty of **New Granada**. **Venezuela** prospered as the company defended the colony from pirates and foreign aggression.

1729 In a pamphlet *A Modest Inquiry into the Nature and Necessity of a Paper Currency* Benjamin Franklin argued for the circulation of paper money in the American colonies, prohibited by the British government.

1729 Mar. 21 **John Law** (b. Apr. 21, 1671), a pioneering Scottish economist, banker, and financier, died in obscurity and poverty in Venice. Once enormously rich and powerful Law saw his speculative enterprises, notably the **Mississippi scheme** collapse when the French government would no longer stand behind him. Law published *Money and Trade Considered, with a Proposal for Supplying the Nation* [Scotland] *with Money* in 1705.

V. RELIGION AND PHILOSOPHY

1721 The **Russian Orthodox Church** was no longer presided over by a patriarch. Instead, a **Holy Synod**, a college of clerics, administered church affairs. The synod was supervised by a government appointee, bringing the Russian Orthodox Church under the authority of the state.

1722 Descendants of the Protestant survivors of the hardships of the **Counter Reformation** in Bohemia and Moravia settled on the estate of Count **Nicolaus Ludwig von Zinzendorf** (May 26, 1700–May 9, 1760) at Berthelsdorf, in Saxony. Under Zinzendorf's benign direction the **Lutheran community**, called **Herrnhut**, grew steadily.

1723 Aug. 23 Increase Mather (b. June 21, 1639), the first son of **Richard Mather** (1596–Apr. 22, 1669) and also a Congregational clergyman, died. Increase wrote many theological works, but he was noted also for his efforts (1683–1686) to keep the original theocratic Massachusetts charter from the liberalizing influence of **Charles II**, king of England. When these failed, he represented the interests of the colony in the drawing up (1691) of a new charter under **William III**, king of England. Mather had become (1685) president of **Harvard College**, but he lost (1701) this post because of his opposition to the new charter. Mather wrote *An Essay for the Recording of Illustrious Providences* (1684) and *Case of Conscience Concerning Evil Spirits Personating Men* (1693), which helped to calm the public hysteria over witches.

1727 A communion service held by **Moravian Protestants** at their center Herrnhut provided the fellowship with so unifying an experience that this date has been regarded as the rebirth of the Moravian Church, so nearly obliterated in the **Thirty Years' War** (1618–1648).

1728 The influential *Serious Call to a Devout and Holy Life* was published by **William Law** (1686–Apr. 9, 1761), an English mystic and spiritual writer. In

1729 John Wesley, with his brother Charles (Dec. 18, 1707–Mar. 29, 1788) and the members of a small club of religiously serious students at Oxford began to practice Law's counsels for consecrated living. Other Oxford students nicknamed them the "Holy Club" and later **"Methodists,"** meaning, then, devotees of a specific method.

1728 Feb. 13 The third member of a family of preachers, **Cotton Mather** (b. Feb. 12, 1663), died. Mather was criticized for his vehement support of the **Salem witchcraft trials**, which he attended and which he condoned particularly in his fanatical sermons from the pulpit and in *Memorial Providences Relating to Witchcraft and Possessions* (1689), a collection of instances of the diabolical presence in man and woman. Though he was passed over for the presidency of Harvard College, he established an intellectual home at **Yale**, which he helped found and where he was offered but refused the presidency (1721). He strongly promoted the education of children and blacks and believed firmly in a very personal parish ministry. Among his more than 400 books, he wrote the best account of Massachusetts in the *Magnalia Christi Americana*; or *the Ecclesiastical History of New England* (1702), in which he demonstrated that the history of Massachusetts showed the exercise of God's will. Paradoxically, perhaps, for a Puritan clergyman, Mather strongly supported scientific pursuits.

VI. SCIENCE, EDUCATION, AND TECHNOLOGY

c.1720 Gabriel Daniel Fahrenheit (May 14, 1686–Sept. 16, 1736), a German physicist living in Amsterdam, developed the modern **thermometer** using mercury in place of alcohol and, indoors, water.

1721 June 26 Zabdiel Boylston (1679–1766), a prominent Boston surgeon, gave the **first vaccinations in the U.S.** when he inoculated his son Thomas and two black slaves against smallpox, using smallpox vaccine. Onesimus, Cotton Mather's slave, had described similar inoculations performed by African tribesmen, so it was at Mather's urging that Boylston performed the experiment.

1723 Aug. 26 Anton van Leeuwenhoek (b. Oct. 24, 1632), a Dutch biologist, died. A master lens grinder, Leeuwenhoek became famous for his improved **microscope**. He gave (1674) the **first complete descrip-**

tion of the red blood corpuscle. He also observed spermatozoa and described (1677) protozoa. Leeuwenhoek's greatest discovery, however, was his observation of **bacteria**, of which he drew the first representation in 1683.

1724 The **Royal Society of London** began to keep regular records of **weather data** of Great Britain, Europe, India, and North America.

1725 *The Astronomical Diary and Almanack* was first published by **Nathaniel Ames** (July 22, 1708–July 11, 1764) of Massachusetts. Although an almanac was usually a calendar of astronomical phenomena pertinent to the planting season, Ames's almanac quickly became popular for its verse, interspersed with factual content.

1727 Mar. 31 **Isaac Newton** (b. Jan. 4, 1643), an English scientist and metaphysician, died. His experiments in optics, conducted from c.1665, and his investigations in calculus were capped by his *Principia* (1687), which set forth his three laws of motion and formed the bases for the development of modern **physics**.

1728 The *Ku-chin t'u-shu chi-ch'ĕng* [*Synthesis of Books and Illustrations of Ancient and Modern Times*], a 5,000-volume Chinese encyclopedia, was published. It had been compiled under the direction of **K'ang-Hsi** [**Shĕng-Tsu**], the Ch'ing emperor, and was perhaps largely the work of the scholar **Mĕng-Lei Ch'ĕng**.

1728 **Ephraim Chambers** (1680–May 15, 1740), an English encyclopedist, published his *Cyclopaedia*, or *An Universal Dictionary of Arts and Sciences*. The two-volume work was the first to employ a system of **cross references**.

VII. ARTS AND LEISURE

c.1720–1770 The **rococo style of decoration** began to appear in France. For furniture the curved leg became important. In Italy, especially in Venice, late baroque features were bedecked with the forms of flowing ribbons and leaves. Light blue was frequently used on painted furniture, and cut mirrors further ornamented the pieces.

1720 Apr. **Rosalba Carriera** (Oct. 7, 1675–Apr. 15, 1757) of Venice came to Paris for a year to paint **miniature portraits** of the French royalty. Her spe-

cialty was working in pastels, and she decorated many **snuffboxes** with her miniatures.

1721 July 18 **Antoine Watteau** (b. Oct. 10, 1684), a French painter, died. A leading artist of the rococo period, he became known as a painter of *fêtes galantes* [gay parties of the demimonde] upon his election to the Royal Academy in 1712. His works included *La Conversation* (1712–1715), *Le Bal Champetre* (c.1715), and *Gilles* (1720–1721).

1723 Feb. 23 **Christopher Wren** (b. Oct. 20, 1632), an English architect, died. Though early in his career Wren was a noted mathematician and astronomer, it was as an architect that he achieved fame. The new **St. Paul's Cathedral** was completed (1716) under Wren's direction, and 52 parish churches were constructed from his designs. He also designed many public and private buildings.

1723 Apr. The cornerstone of **Boston's Christ Church** was laid. Designed by **William Price**, who had studied the work of Christopher Wren, it was better known as the **Old North Church**, where lanterns strategically placed on the night of Apr. 18, 1775, warned patriots across the Charles River in **Charlestown** of approaching British troops on the eve of the **American Revolution**.

1725 Jan. 6 **Chikamatsu Monzaemon** [Sugimori Nobumori] (b. 1653), a Japanese playwright, died. His *Kokusenya Kassen* [The Battle of Kokusinya] (1715), an historical drama, was one of the first of the *joruri*, or puppet plays, popular as part of Japan's Kabuki theater.

1725 Oct. 24 **Alessandro Scarlatti** (b. May 2, 1660), an Italian composer, died. He wrote in all forms, but was most famous for his operas; his most celebrated was *Il Tigrane* (1715). Scarlatti also wrote many cantatas and much keyboard music.

1727 Mar. 22 **Francesco Gasparini** (b. Mar. 5, 1688), an Italian opera composer, died. A pupil of Corelli, he was director of music at the **Conservatore della Pietà**, Venice, and became (1725) maestro di cappella at the **Lateran**, Rome. His approximately 50 operas were very successful, as were his masses, motets, and oratorios.

c.1728 The **first history of Burma** [Myanmar], the *Ya-zawin-gyi Chronicle*, was published by **U Kala** (1638?–?1678). The chronicle was later expanded in the *Glass Palace Chronicle*, which carried the history to 1886.

1729 Jan. 19 **William Congreve** (b. Jan. 24, 1670), an English dramatist of Restoration comedy, died. Congreve wrote one tragedy, *The Mourning Bride* (1697), which contained the famous line "Music hath charms to soothe a savage breast." But it was as a writer of comedies of manners that Congreve became noted: *The Double Dealer* (1693), with the line, "She lays it on with a trowel"; *Love for Love* (1695); and *The Way of the World* (1700), his masterpiece.

1729 June 27 **Elisabeth Jacquet de la Guerre** (born c.1664), a French musician, died. Her **cantatas** were among the first published in France. She also wrote theater music, harpsichord works, and sonatas.

VIII. SPORTS, GAMES, AND SOCIETY

1720 The **Water Club of Cork Harbor**, Ireland, regarded as the **first organized yacht club**, was certainly in existence at this time; its date of formation is unknown.

1730–1739

I. DISASTERS

1730 Dec. 30 An **earthquake** struck Hokkaido, the northernmost island of Japan, killing c.137,000 people.

1733 The first serious **epidemics of influenza in the American colonies** broke out in **New York City** and **Philadelphia**.

1737 Oct. 7 Disaster struck the **Bay of Bengal** area when an **earthquake** struck the port of **Calcutta**. A subsequent tidal wave of 40 feet in height claimed many lives and c.20,000 sailing craft. Violent tornados also ravaged the countryside coincidentally at the same time, and the final death toll was set at c.300,000.

II. EXPLORATION AND COLONIZATION

c.1730 **Pierre Gautier de Varennes** (Nov. 17, 1685– Dec. 5, 1749), and Sieur de La Vérendrye, a French fur trapper, began to explore the Canadian West, reaching **Lake Manitoba** and **Lake Winnipeg** by c.1740.

1733 Feb. 12 **James Oglethorpe** (Dec. 22, 1696– June 30/July 1, 1785) arrived in **Georgia**, the last of the original 13 American colonies to be settled, with a charter granted to him by George II. He founded the port city of **Savannah**.

c.1735 **Vincennes**, on the Wabash River, became the **first permanent settlement of present Indiana**. **François Marie Bissot** (Jan., 1688–1736), Sieur de Vincennes, the French fur trapper, had organized and fortified an earlier French mission at the same site.

1735 **Sainte Genevieve** on the Mississippi River was the **first permanent settlement in present Missouri**. Great lead deposits there, mined by John Law's **Companie de la Louisiane ou d'Occident**, led to the success of the town.

1739 The town of **Campbellton** was founded on the present site of **Fayetteville, North Carolina**, by Scottish Highlanders fleeing Scotland in the face of an impending Jacobite defeat. When Campbellton merged with nearby Cross Creek in 1783, the residents named the new town "Fayetteville" in honor of the marquis de Lafayette, the French general who fought with the Americans in the American Revolution (1775–1783).

III. POLITICS AND WAR

c.1730 The **Bambara state of Ségou** [Segu], on the Niger River in present Mali, reached its greatest extent, occupying lands of the Bambara **Kingdom of Kong**, in present Ivory Coast.

c.1730 Various **legislative bodies in the colonies**, able to discuss and pass laws (subject to veto by the royal governors) without interference from London provided they were within the framework of British law, were found a necessary adjunct to the rule of far away Great Britain. Difficulties arose when Parliament attempted to raise monies from taxes on activities in the colonies for programs in Britain or for wars in Europe, especially when the colonists thought they were paying for their own suppression because of taxation of their local industries and trade.

1730 **Persia** was freed from **Afghan** occupation by **Nadir**, the leader of the Afshar, a Persian tribe, on behalf of **Tahmasp II**, Persian shah of the **Safawid** [Safavid] **Dynasty** (1502–1736). Persia was, in fact, in the hands of Nadir himself, who deposed (1732) Tahmasp (d. 1739) and replaced him on the throne with Tahmasp's infant son **Abbas III** (to 1736).

1730 Jan. 30 **Peter II** (b. Oct. 23, 1715), czar of Russia (from 1727), died on the day before his marriage to **Princess Dolgoruki** of a noble Russian family. He was succeeded by Ivan V's younger daughter **Anna Ivanovna**, who quickly abolished (Mar. 8) the **Supreme Privy Council**. Established in its place was a cabinet of ministers, dominated by a small group of Germans headed by her favorite, **Ernst Johann Biron** [Bühren] (Nov. 23, 1690–Dec. 29, 1772).

1731 Jan. 10 **Antonio Farnese** (b. 1679), duke of the Italian duchies of Parma and Piacenza, died without direct heir. **Charles VI**, the Holy Roman emperor, challenged the treaty of 1729 that gave the throne to **Don Carlos** [Don Carlos of Bourbon], future Charles III of Spain, and heir to the Spanish throne.

1731 July 22 The **Treaty of Vienna** was signed by Austria, Great Britain, the Netherlands, and Spain. The Italian duchies of Parma and Piacenza, which were the inheritance of the Farnese, were given to Charles III, future king of Spain.

1733 Feb. 1 **Augustus II the Strong** (b. May 12, 1670), king of Poland (from 1697–1704; 1709–1733) and elector of Saxony as **Frederick Augustus I** (from 1694), died, bringing on the **War of the Polish Succession** (1733–1738). Austria and Russia preferred Augustus II's son, **Frederick Augustus II**, elector of Saxony, over the Polish candidate **Stanislas I Leszczynski**, who was supported by France and Spain. On Oct. 10, 1733, France declared war on Austria.

1733 Nov. 7 The **Treaty of the Escorial** [Escurial], also known as the **First Family Compact**, was signed

by the Bourbons of Spain and the Bourbons of France, and was directed against Austria and Great Britain. This was one of several French-Spanish alliances made by the Bourbons; it was renewed [**Second Family Compact**] in 1743. These military alliances were directed mainly at England as a rival colonizing power and Austria, which had allied with Britain since the two Bourbon powers had become united.

1734 May 25 Spanish forces under Don Carlos of Bourbon, duke of Parma, defeated the Austrians in a **battle at Bitonto**, Italy. Victorious throughout Italy, Don Carlos assumed the crown of the **Two Sicilies** [Naples and Sicily].

1734 June 30 Russian forces took **Danzig** [Gdansk], where **Stanislas I Leszczynski** of Poland had sought refuge during the **War of the Polish Succession** (1733–1738). In the meantime the French were ready for peace. Austria desired peace as well, as Charles VI, the Holy Roman emperor, was preoccupied with his uncertain succession.

1735 Oct. 3 The preliminary peace of Vienna was signed by Austria and France to bring an end to the **War of the Polish Succession** (1733–1738). They were joined by Spain on Dec. 1, and Stanislas I Leszczynski officially renounced the Polish crown on Jan. 26, 1736.

1736 The **Safawid** [Safavid] **Dynasty** (1502–1736) of Persia disappeared with the death of Abbas III (b. 1732), the infant shah (from 1732). **Nadir**, a Khorasan [Khurasan] Turk, Persia's strongman, took the title of shah as founder of the **Afsharid Dynasty** (1736–1749) with the agreement that the Muslim Sunnite sect be honored to the exclusion of the Shiites. He completed the expulsion of the Afghans by conquering lost Persian territory and signed a treaty with Russia that recognized the Persian Empire.

1737 July 9 **Gian Gastone** (b. 1671), duke of Tuscany, the last of the grand dukes of the **Medici family**, died. He was succeeded by **Francis Stephen**, duke of Lorraine, who had married **Maria Theresa**, daughter of Charles VI, the Holy Roman emperor, on Feb. 12, 1736. It was agreed in the preliminary **peace of Vienna** (1735) that Francis Stephen's duchy of Lorraine should go to the deposed Stanislas I Leszczynski of Poland.

1738 Nov. 18 The **Treaty of Vienna** formally ended the **War of the Polish Succession** (1733–1738). Frederick Augustus II, elector of Saxony, was confirmed king of Poland as **Augustus III**, and Stanislas I Leszczynski received the duchy of Lorraine and the neighboring county of Bar, to revert to France on his death. The Bourbon Don Carlos of Spain retained Naples and Sicily, but ceded Parma and Piacenza to Austria. Russia received Courland [Kurland], a duchy in Latvia, from Augustus III. France guaranteed the **Pragmatic Sanction** (1713).

1739 The Persian army under **Nadir Shah** invaded India and defeated **Muhammad Shah** (1702–1748), the Mogul [Mughal] emperor of Hindustan (from 1719), in a **battle at Karnal**, near Delhi, which was subsequently sacked. The Persians retired from the invasion with invaluable booty that included the legendary **Peacock Throne**, built (1630) for **Shah Jahan**, the former emperor of Hindustan, and the **Koh-i-noor** [Mountain of Light] **diamond**, which later became part of the collection of the **British Royal Crown Jewels**.

1739 Sept. 18 The **Peace of Belgrade** was signed by Austria, Russia, and the Ottoman Empire. The Turks had already recaptured the Crimea; Niš [Nish], a Serbian city in eastern Yugoslavia; and Vidin, a Serbian city on the Danube River, and were now besieging **Belgrade**. Austria returned Belgrade to the Turks and rescinded further claims in the Balkan Peninsula. Russia agreed to withdraw from her posts along the Sea of Azov and lost her right to navigation in the Black Sea.

1739 Oct. 19 The **War of Jenkins' Ear** (1739–c.1744) began as Great Britain declared war on Spain over Spanish attacks on British shipping in general and, in particular, the reputed loss of an ear by Robert Jenkins, a British sea captain aboard the *Rebecca,* which had been plundered by the Spanish in the West Indies near Havana, Cuba, in 1731. Warfare continued until c.1744, when Spain and France, Spain's ally, were no longer able to endure heavy naval losses inflicted by the British fleet. The War of Jenkins' Ear merged with the **War of the Austrian Succession** (1740–1748).

IV. ECONOMY AND TRADE

c.1730 **Pepper**, for centuries a prime commodity of the spice trade in the **Far East**, slipped in importance as the discovery of new sea routes to the East made it easier to acquire and it was no longer regarded a luxury.

1733 May 17 The **Molasses Act** placed heavy duties on molasses, sugar, and rum that the New England colonies imported from the West Indies. Colonial merchants carrying shiploads of American commodities, including fish, lumber, and barrel staves, generally succeeded in eluding customs officials.

V. RELIGION AND PHILOSOPHY

1730 **Matthew Tindal** (1657–Aug. 16, 1733), an English Roman Catholic and professor of divinity, published his major work *Christianity as Old as the Creation* near the end of his life, spent teaching at Oxford and writing on deistic principles. This book became known as "the Bible of deism."

1734 **Jonathan Edwards** delivered a sermon on **Justification by Faith Alone**, at his influential Congregational church in Northampton, Massachusetts, producing a remarkable revival in that city. Thereafter, Edwards's writings and the evangelistic preaching of the American **Gilbert Tennent** (Feb. 5, 1703–July 23, 1764), helped spread the **Great Awakening** (1734–c.1750) throughout southern New England, New York, and New Jersey.

1734 Nov. The **first English translation of the Koran** made directly from an original version was done by **George Sale** (1697?–Nov. 13, 1736), an English orientalist.

1738 May 24 **John Wesley** (June 28, 1703–Mar. 2, 1791), at a prayer meeting in Aldersgate, near St. Paul's Cathedral in London, "felt his heart strangely warmed" and came to "trust in Christ, Christ alone, for salvation." This experience of salvation by faith alone, so central to evangelicals, prepared him to start what became **Methodism**, one of the largest branches of Protestantism. From then on, Wesley gave himself wholeheartedly to evangelism, with an emphasis on conversion and holiness.

1739 Apr. 2 **John Wesley** began a ministry in Bristol, England, and founded there his first truly **Methodist "society."** In association now with the powerful preacher **George Whitefield** (Dec. 16, 1714–Sept. 30, 1770), an English Calvinistic Methodist, **John and his brother Charles Wesley** (Dec. 18, 1707–Mar. 29, 1788) began preaching in the open-air wherever an opportunity to proclaim the Gospel presented itself, especially among the working class.

1739 Fall   George Whitefield began his successful evangelistic preaching mission in the Mid-Atlantic region of the American colonies, bringing it to New England in 1740. Accompanied by **Gilbert Tennent**, the eloquent Whitefield stirred crowds to emotional fervor. Conversions were by the hundreds, and many communities were transformed spiritually. The **Great Awakening** (1734–c.1750) was at its peak.

VI. SCIENCE, EDUCATION, AND TECHNOLOGY

1731   *New Horse Hoeing Husbandry*, by the English agrarian **Jethro Tull** (1674–Feb. 21, 1741), introduced the concept of scientific crop cultivation. Tull introduced a systematic method of sowing seeds that made use of his **seed drill**, invented in 1701, which planted three parallel rows at once. At about the same time, **Charles Townshend** (Apr. 18, 1675–June 21, 1738) turned to the pursuit of improved methods of crop cultivation.

1733 May 26   The flying, or **mechanical, shuttle** was patented by **John Kay** (July 16, 1704–?1764), an English inventor. No longer was it necessary for weavers to manually return the shuttles on their looms.

1735   **Abraham Darby** (1677–1717) of Shropshire, England, was the **first to use coke successfully in a blast furnace to smelt iron**, a process which required high temperatures to burn off the impurities found in iron ore.

1735 Aug. 4   John Peter Zenger (1697–July 28, 1746), a German-born printer and editor of the New York **Weekly Journal**, went on trial in New York City on charges of libel for his attacks on the governor of New York. Zenger was acquitted in a celebrated case in defense of the **freedom of the press**.

1738   Daniel Bernoulli (Jan. 29, 1700–Mar. 17, 1782), a Swiss mathematician and the son of Johann [Jean] Bernoulli, published his only work, the *Hydrodynamica*, which set forth the Bernoulli principle of hydrodynamics.

VII. ARTS AND LEISURE

1731   The **first known public concert of secular music in the American colonies** was held in Boston at the house of Peter Pelham.

1731 Jan. 27   Bartolommeo Cristofori (b. May 4, 1655), an Italian manufacturer of harpsichords, died. By 1711 he had constructed what was often considered the **first modern pianoforte**, or piano.

1731 Apr. 24   Daniel Defoe (b. 1660), an English writer, died. Renowned as the author of *Robinson Crusoe* (1719), he was also a noted satirist, as in *The True-born Englishman* (1701) and *The Shortest Way with the Dissenters* (1702). His works included *Moll Flanders* (1722), one of England's earliest novels of social realism; *The Journal of the Plague Year* (1722), a semi-fictional account of the devastation of the plague in London (1665); and *Roxana* (1724).

1732   The **first recorded public performance of a play in New York City** was a production of *The Recruiting Officer* (1706) by **George Farquhar**, a Restoration dramatist.

1732 Dec. 4   John Gay (b. June 30?, 1685), an English playwright, died. The work for which Gay became famous, *The Beggar's Opera* (1728), was considered the first of a genre called the ballad opera and was often said to be the **first modern musical comedy**. A sequel was *Polly* (1728), which was published but prohibited from performance (not performed until 1777) by **Robert Walpole**, the prime minister, who had been satirized in **The Beggar's Opera**.

1732 Dec. 7   The **Theatre Royal** opened in London's **Covent Garden** with a performance of William Congreve's *The Way of the World* (1700).

1733 Sept. 12   François Couperin (b. Nov. 10, 1688), a French composer, organist, and harpsichordist, died. His treatise on keyboard technique *L'Art de Toucher le Clavecin* (1716) may have influenced **Johann Sebastian Bach**. Couperin's work also included the four-volume *Pièces de Clavecin* (1713–1730) and *Le Parnasse, ou l'Apothéose de Corelli* (1724).

1736–1796   During the reign of **Ch'ien Lung** [Kao Tsung], the Manchu emperor of China, the **Chinese export trade in porcelain** and ceramics reached its height.

1737 Dec. 18   Antonio Stradivari [Stradivarius] (born c.1645), the celebrated Italian violin maker, died. He studied and worked under Nicolò Amati until c.1680, when he opened his own instrument shop. **Stradivari's instruments** were considered the finest, especially those made between 1700 and 1725. About half of the more than 1,000 instruments made by Stradivari are still extant, some in performance condition.

1738 **Domenico Scarlatti** (Oct. 26, 1685–July 23, 1757), son of the Italian composer Alessandro Scarlatti, published in London his *Essercizi per Gravicembalo* [Harpsichord Exercises].

1739 **Samuel Richardson** (1689–July 4, 1761), an English printer, asked to write a guide to letter writing, began the popular novel *Pamela: or Virtue Rewarded* (1740). In a series of letters, Richardson told about a young woman who fended off the advances of a young man who had taken a fancy to her. With virtue still intact, in the end she happily married him. His equally famous other novels were *Clarissa Harlowe,* or *the History of a Young Lady* (1748) and *Sir Charles Grandison* (1753).

VIII. SPORTS AND GAMES

1730 The British stallion **Bulle Rock**, of Darley Arabian lineage, was sent to the American colonies for breeding purposes. Nearly a decade later a British race mare, Bay Bolton, was bred to the stallion. The foal, some claim, was the **first thoroughbred born in the U.S.**

1740–1749

I. EXPLORATION AND COLONIZATION

1740 **War between the French and the Fox**, a tribe of Algonquian-speaking Indians in the area of present **Wisconsin**, came to an end with a general Indian defeat. Hostilities had begun (1712) with the massacre of a band of Fox near Detroit by combined French and Indian forces.

1741 Aug. 20 **Vitus Bering**, a Dane sailing for Russia, entered the **Gulf of Alaska** and made a landing on one of the western Aleutian Islands. He had been exploring Kamchatka Peninsula and the Bering Sea since 1725 to determine whether Asia and America were connected. Bering (b. 1681) died of hunger, scurvy, and exposure on Dec. 19, 1741, on Beringa [Bering] Island, one of the Russian Komandorskie [Commander] Islands lying just west of the Aleutian Islands.

1741 Dec. 24 **Bethlehem**, in Pennsylvania, was founded by Count **Nikolaus Ludwig von Zinzendorf** as a haven for persecuted Moravians. The count, who had arrived in Pennsylvania early in 1741, subsequently established several other **Moravian communities** in the colony before (1743) returning to England.

1744 The **Iroquois League** ceded territory in the **Ohio Valley** north of the Ohio River to Great Britain in a treaty signed at **Lancaster**, Pennsylvania.

1749 The **Ohio Land Company** was granted land around the area where the Allegheny and Monongahela rivers meet to form the Ohio River, at present **Pittsburgh**, Pennsylvania. The company's purpose was to develop an English presence in the Ohio River Valley, thus far dominated by French trappers, but the French soon drove out the English.

1749 The port of **Halifax** was founded by the British in Nova Scotia.

II. POLITICS AND WAR

1740 May 31 Frederick William I (b. Aug. 15, 1688), king of Prussia (from 1713), died and was succeeded by his son **Frederick II the Great**. Frederick the Great gained a position of leadership over Germany, bringing Prussia to the rank of world power.

1740 Oct. 20 Charles VI (b. Oct. 1, 1685), the Holy Roman emperor (from 1711), archduke of Austria and king of Hungary and of Bohemia, died. He was succeeded by his daughter **Maria Theresa**, who had married (1736) **Stephen Francis**, duke of Lorraine; thus, the **Hapsburg-Lorraine Dynasty** (1736–1918) was established firmly in Europe.

1740 Oct. 28 Anna Ivanovna (b. Feb. 7, 1693), czarina [empress] of Russia (from 1730) and daughter of Ivan V, died. On her deathbed, Anna appointed her minister **Ernst Johann Biron** [Bühren], regent for her niece's two-month son, who was to rule as Ivan VI. **Anna Leopoldovna** (Dec. 18, 1718–Mar. 18, 1746), the boy's mother, stole the throne on Nov. 20, 1740, and exiled Biron. Russia, however, did not wish to be ruled by Germans. On Dec. 6, 1741, Anna Leopoldovna was ousted by **Elizabeth, younger daughter of Peter the Great** and **Catherine I**. Ivan VI and Anna Leopoldovna were imprisoned at Dünamünde [Daugavgriva, Ust Dvinsk], near Riga, in present Latvia, and, under Elizabeth, Russia regained some of the distinction it had enjoyed during the reign of Peter the Great.

1740 Dec. 16 The **First Silesian War** (1740–1741) broke out between Prussia and Austria. Frederick the Great, king of Prussia, invaded the province of Silesia, in present Poland, following Maria Theresa's refusal to cede the territory in return for Prussia's support. On Apr. 10, 1741, Austrian troops were defeated in a **battle at Mollwitz** [Matujowice], in present Poland.

1741 June 5 By the **Treaty of Breslau** [Wroclaw], on the Oder River in Silesia, France joined Prussia and Bavaria against Austria in the **War of the Austrian Succession** (1740–1748). On Oct. 9 Austria ended the **First Silesian War** (1740–1741) by ceding Silesia to Frederick the Great, king of Prussia, in the more-or-less secret **Treaty of Klein-Schnellendorf**, in Silesia, freeing troops to meet better the challenge of France.

1741 Aug. Sweden declared war on Russia. Frederick I, king of Sweden, acted under the influence of the party of nobles known as the **Hats** (opposed to the Caps who favored conciliatory foreign policy), who wished to regain Swedish dominance in the area. The war went badly for the Swedes and at its end (1743) they were forced to give up parts of **Finland** to the Russians.

1742 Jan. 24 **Charles Albert**, elector of Bavaria, with the backing of France was elected the Holy Roman emperor (to 1745) as **Charles VII**. However, on this day Munich fell to Austrian troops supporting Maria Theresa's claim to the Hapsburg inheritance, including the imperial title. Prussia remained neutral, observing the truce of Klein-Schnellendorf, and further assured her Silesian conquest by the **Treaty of Berlin**, signed on July 28 with Austria.

1742 Feb. 13 **Robert Walpole**, prime minister of England, resigned. After 20 years in power, Walpole had lost influence as public opinion began to favor an aggressive foreign policy. Walpole once boasted to **Queen Caroline** (Mar. 1, 1683–Nov. 20, 1737), wife of **George II**: "There are 50,000 men slain in Europe this year and not one Englishman."

1743 June 27 **George II**, king of England, commanded English, Hanoverian, Hessian, Austrian, and Dutch troops in a **battle at Dettingen**, Bavaria, in present Germany. The French were defeated in this battle, the last in which a British king actively participated. It was part of the War of the Austrian Succession.

1743 Aug. The **Treaty of Åbo** [Turku], in present Finland, was signed by Russia and Sweden. The Hats, by agreeing to the Russian candidate to the Swedish throne, **Adolphus Frederick** (May 14, 1710–Feb. 12, 1771), duke of Holstein, Sweden was able to keep part of Finland, rather than ceding everything to Russia. This treaty resulted in removing both powers from the War of the Austrian Succession (1740–1748).

1743 Oct. By the **Treaty of Fontainebleau**, Louis XV, king of France, agreed to intercede in Italy on behalf of Spain, which wanted to assert its rights to the Hapsburg possessions there. Forced by superior British naval power to attempt an overland invasion, French troops nearly succeeded in autumn 1745, despite the opposition of **Charles Emmanual III** (1701–1773), king of Sardinia (from 1730), who held Savoy and Piedmont. The French were ultimately defeated in their invasion by Spanish disagreement with the French commander over military strategy.

1744 Mar. 15 France declared war on Great Britain in the **War of the Austrian Succession** (1740–1748). Great Britain was already at war with France's ally Spain since the **War of Jenkins' Ear** (1739–c.1744). On Apr. 26 France declared war on Austria. Since Frederick the Great, king of Prussia, feared that he could not retain Silesia in face of the mounting successes of Austria and her allies, he invaded Bohemia in August to start the **Second Silesian War** (1744).

1745 May 11 In a **battle at Fontenoy**, near Tournai, in present Belgium, France won a victory under Count Hermann Maurice de Saxe (Oct. 28, 1696–Nov. 30, 1750), taking over part of Flanders. The subsequent victory of Frederick the Great, king of Prussia and ally of France, in a **battle** (June 4) **at**

Hohenfriedeberg [Dabromierz] in Silesia, persuaded Great Britain to accept the **Treaty of Hanover** offered by Prussia on Aug. 15. On Sept. 13, with the support of Austrian troops, Francis, archduke of Austria and co-regent with Maria Theresa, was elected as Francis I to succeed Charles VII (b. Aug. 6, 1697), the Holy Roman emperor (from 1742), who had died on Jan. 20, 1745.

1745 June 17 Louisburg, key port of Isle Royale [Cape Breton Island], Nova Scotia, was wrested from French control by **William Pepperell** (June 27, 1696–July 6, 1759) of Massachusetts, acting as an agent for the British crown. The port was returned to France in 1748 by the **Treaty of Aix-la-Chapelle,** which ended **King George's War.**

1745 Sept. 16 Charles Edward Stuart (Dec. 31, 1720–Jan. 31, 1788), called the Young Pretender, son of James III, the Old Pretender, took **Edinburgh,** Scotland, in the **Second Jacobite Rebellion.** With the support chiefly of the Macdonald clan, Charles reached the Trent River in England by Dec. 4 but soon was forced to retreat.

1745 Dec. 25 Frederick the Great, king of Prussia, signed the **Treaty of Dresden** with Austria and again was assured of his conquest of Silesia, in return for his support of Maria Theresa's claim to the Austrian throne and of her husband Francis's imperial title.

1746 Joseph François Dupleix (Dec., 1697–Nov. 10, 1763), governor general of all **French possessions in India,** consolidated the defenses of Pondicherry and captured (Sept. 10–26) Madras.

1746 Apr. 16 English forces under **William Augustus** (Apr. 15, 1721–Oct. 31, 1765), duke of Cumberland and second surviving son of George II, defeated a much smaller force of **Jacobites** led by **Charles, the Young Pretender,** in a **battle at Culloden Moor** [Drummossie Moor], near Iverness, Scotland. The fleeing Highlanders were mercilessly slaughtered by the duke's cavalry, earning him the epithet, the "Butcher." "**Bonnie Prince Charlie,**" as Charles was known, escaped to the Hebrides where, in June, **Flora Macdonald** (1722–Mar. 5, 1790) aided him in his escape by procuring a false passport, issued to Betty Burke, an "Irish spinning maid." The prince sailed for Skye and remained there until a French ship took him to France on Sept. 29.

1747 June 19 Nadir Shah [Tahmasp Kuli Khan, Nadir Quli Beg] (b. Oct. 22, 1688), shah of Persia (from 1736), was assassinated. During the turmoil that followed, **Shahrukh,** the **last of the Afsharid Dynasty** (1736–1749) ruled briefly; in 1750 the turbulence ended with the victory of **Karim Khan** (c.1700–Mar., 1779), who founded the **Zand Dynasty** (1750–1794).

1747 July? Ahmad Shah Durrani (1723?–Oct. 16?, 1773), an Afghan chief of the Abdali tribe, was proclaimed emir of **Afghanistan** following the assassination of Nadir Shah of Persia. Ahmad took the name **Durrani,** meaning "Pearl of Pearls." Ahmad's rule marked the beginning of Afghanistan as a political unit.

1747 July 2 French forces under Count **Hermann Maurice de Saxe** defeated an Anglo-Dutch force under William Augustus, duke of Cumberland, at Lauffeldt, in present Belgium. This victory completed the **French conquest of the Austrian Netherlands.**

1748 Oct. 18 The **Treaty of Aix-la-Chapelle** ended the **War of the Austrian Succession** (1740–1748). Nearly all conquered territory was restored. The major exception was Silesia, which the Austrian Hapsburgs lost to Prussia. The Italian duchies of Parma, Piacenza, and Guastalla were ceded to Spain. The right of the House of Hanover (1714–1901) to succeed to both the crowns of Great Britain and Hanover was approved.

1749 A dispute arose between New Hampshire and New York colonies over the territory lying between the Connecticut River and Lake Champlain when Benning Wentworth (1696–1770), royal governor of New Hampshire, started issuing large grants of land in that area. New York declared these grants illegal. London ruled that the New York-New Hampshire boundary was the Connecticut River (1765) but later ruled that the territory belonged to neither colony.

III. ECONOMY AND TRADE

1740 Manchester, England, was the site of the establishment of one of the **first great cotton mills.** With the adoption of the **powerloom,** the city began its rise to leading cotton manufacturing center of England.

1740 Sept. A **food shortage in France** brought on by continual warfare was alleviated, in part, by the prohibition against baking white bread and rolls in Paris, making available more flour for baking bread.

1741 **Bakers in New York City** refused to work, in protest over city control of bread prices.

1745 By this year more than 22 **newspapers** had been founded in **colonial America**.

1747 **George Anson** (Apr. 23, 1697–June 6, 1762), an admiral, reorganized the British warfleet with the primary objective of severely disrupting French trade in the West Indies and India. Attacks on French shipping this year brought ruin to the French economy.

1749 Oct. 26 The proprietors of Georgia voted to allow slavery and the importation of rum, repealing an act of 1735 that had prohibited both. This act enabled the **inauguration of the plantation system in Georgia**.

IV. RELIGION AND PHILOSOPHY

1740 **Mohammed ibn-Abd-al-Wahab** (c.1695/1703–1790/1792), convinced by his own studies that contemporary Islam was permeated with abuses, found a patron in Dariyah, in Saudi Arabia. At Dariyah he created a Muslim sect promoting a return to purity of doctrine, worship, and behavior. The Wahabi movement ultimately gained power with the rise of Abdul-Aziz ibn-Saud as king of Saudi Arabia in the 20th century.

1741 **Jonathan Edwards**, an American Congregationalist minister, delivered the sermon *Sinners in the Hands of an Angry God*, at Northhampton, Massachusetts. His vivid account of the fate of those who failed to repent was instrumental in sustaining New England's **Great Awakening** (1734–c.1750).

1743 **John Woolman** (Oct. 19, 1720–Oct. 7, 1772), "the Tailor of Mount Holly," in present New Jersey, began his travels through the American colonies to spread the principles of the **Society of Friends** [Quakers], to inspire their various meetings and to promote the abolition of slavery.

1747 The **Shaker sect**, so-called for its emphasis on "shaking" produced by religious ecstasy in which the gift of prophecy may be received, originated at a Quaker meeting in England.

1748 **Henry Melchior Muhlenberg** (Sept. 6, 1711–Oct. 1, 1807), a leader of German Lutherans, rapidly growing in numbers in the American colonies, especially in Pennsylvania, organized the **first Lutheran synod in the U.S.** that has had permanent existence.

V. SCIENCE, EDUCATION, AND TECHNOLOGY

c.1740 **Benjamin Huntsman** (1704–1776), a British inventor, developed the **crucible process of steelmaking**. Taking advantage of coke as a fuel in his furnace, Huntsman raised the temperature of the crucible to 2,900° F for the first time, completely melting the impure steel scrap he began with and causing all its impurities to rise to the surface to be skimmed off.

1742 The **celsius**, or centigrade, **thermometer** was first described by **Anders Celsius** (Nov. 27, 1701–Apr. 25, 1744), a Swedish astronomer.

1742 Jan. 14 **Edmund Halley** (b. Nov. 8, 1656), an English astronomer, died. Halley correctly predicted (1705) the return of the comet that was named in his honor after its reappearance in 1758. He also observed a transit of Mercury on Nov. 7, 1677, and produced a catalogue of the southern sky in 1679.

1743 The **American Philosophical Society**, the **first American scientific association**, was founded in Philadelphia by **Benjamin Franklin**. It was similar to the century-old Royal Society of London, but emphasized the exchange of information pertaining to agriculture.

1743 *L'École des Ponts et Chaussées* [The School of Bridges and Roads], perhaps the **first school of engineering** in the world, was founded in Paris.

1745 **Pieter van Mus[s]chenbroek** (Mar. 14, 1692–Sept. 9, 1761), a Dutch philosopher and mathematician at the University of **Leiden** [Leyden], began experimenting with a jar filled with water that acted as a capacitor, or condenser, holding static electricity. It became known as the **Leyden jar**, eventually refined by the addition of tin foil to both sides of the glass.

1746 Oct. 22 **Princeton University** was granted a charter as the College of New Jersey, and classes opened at Elizabeth, New Jersey, in May 1747.

From 1756, with the completion of Nassau Hall, the college made its home at Princeton.

1748 **Pompeii**, at the foot of Mount Vesuvius, near Naples, Italy, which had been quickly covered to a depth of 12 feet by pebbles and ash during the massive **volcanic eruption** of Aug. 24, 79 A.D., began to be excavated.

1748 Jan. 1 **Johann** [Jean] **Bernoulli** (b. July 27, 1667), brother of the Swiss mathematician Jakob and father of Daniel Bernoulli, also a noted mathematician, died. Johann introduced the concept of imaginary numbers into trigonometry.

VI. ARTS AND LEISURE

1740 The song *Rule Britannia* was composed by **Thomas Augustine Arne** (Mar. 12, 1710–Mar. 5, 1778), an English composer, for the opera **The Masque of Alfred**, written by the Scottish poets **James Thomson** and **David Mallet** (1705?–Apr. 21, 1765).

1741 Feb. 13 **Johann Joseph Fux** (b. 1660), an Austrian composer and theorist, died. He was best known for *Gradus ad Parnassum* (1725), a treatise on counterpoint, although he was a prolific composer, with 405 works extant. These include masses, sonatas, and operas.

1741 July 28 **Antonio Vivaldi** (b. Mar. 4, 1678), an Italian composer and violinist, died. Vivaldi brought the concerto to its highest form before the advent of Johann Sebastian Bach by providing a firm contrast between ensemble and soloist. *The Four Seasons* [*Le quattro stagioni*] was from a set of program music and illustrated four accompanying sonnets. Over half of Vivaldi's compositions were concertos. He also wrote church music and opera.

1744 May 30 **Alexander Pope** (b. May 21, 1688), a great English classical poet, died. *The Rape of the Lock* (1714), perhaps his best-known work, was written with the encouragement of Pope's influential Catholic friend **John Caryll**, who provided Pope with the outline of an incident that had actually taken place and involved some of his family. The long poem satirized the customs of Pope's time. His early descriptive poems included *The Pastorals* (1709) and *Windsor Forest* (1713). Pope wrote only two poems treating the subject of love: *Eloisa to Abelard* and *Verses to the Memory of an Unfortunate Lady*. His

translation of Homer's *Iliad* (1720) and *Odyssey* (1726) earned him a fortune, despite criticism of their lack of accuracy. *The Dunciads* (1728–1743) attacked Pope's critics; *Imitations of Horace* (1733–1738) satirized social inequity and political corruption. *Essay on Criticism* (1711) outlined standards of criticism. *Essay on Man* (1734) described the current philosophical speculations about God and human nature.

1745 Oct. 19 **Jonathan Swift** (b. Nov. 30, 1667), an English satirist, died. He was best known for *Gulliver's Travels* (1726), in which Lemuel Gulliver related his observations of the strange inhabitants of the mythical lands he visited. *The Tale of the Tub* (1704) satirized religious excesses, and *The Battle of the Books* (1704) argued that nothing of modern literature can be compared to that of the ancients. Swift's *Modest Proposal* (1729) suggested that children of the poor be sold to provide food for the rich.

1747 The first neo-classical tragedy written in Russian, *Khorev* by **Aleksandr Petrovich Sumarokov** (July 4, 1718–Sept. 1, 1777), was performed.

1747 Nov. 17 **Alain René Lesage** [Le Sage] (b. Dec. 13, 1668), a French novelist and dramatist, died. His four-volume comic novel *L'Histoire de Gil Blas de Santillane* (1735) is thought to be the first novel of manners. Lesage wrote a number of plays, among them *Crispin, rival de son maître* (1707) and *Turcaret ou le financier* (1709), and a great many farces.

1748 The **Royal Danish Ballet** was founded in Copenhagen.

c.1748 *Chushinqura* [Treasury of Royal Retainers], a long Japanese **kabuki play**, was first performed. Written primarily by **Takeda Izumo** (1688–1756), it told of a double suicide.

1748 Mar. 23 **Johann Gottfried Walther** (b. Sept. 18, 1684), a German composer and music historian, died. His *Musikalisches Lexicon oder Musikalisches Bibliotheck* (1732) was the first music encyclopedia that included information arranged alphabetically and covering biography, bibliography, and musical terms.

1748 Aug. 27 **James Thomson** (b. Sept., 1700), a Scottish poet, died. He won a reputation with a poetical series entitled *The Seasons* (1726–1730), which introduced an emotional, realistic view of nature. *Castle of Indolence* (1748) expressed concern about the absence of industriousness.

1748 Nov. 25 Isaac Watts (b. July 17, 1674), an English theologian and hymnist, died. He was considered one of the founders of modern hymnody, which grew out of the Congregational revival of evangelism. "O God, Our Help in Ages Past" was in *The Psalms of David Imitated in the Language of the New Testament* (1719).

1749 Dec. 4 Claudine Alexandrine Guérin de Tencin (b. Apr. 27, 1682), a French writer and member of the demi-monde, died. She was a leading court figure during the reign of Louis XV. Her most notable work was the *Mémoires du Comte de Comminges* (1735), an autobiographical novel. The son she abandoned, Jean le Rond d'Alembert (Nov., 1717–Oct. 29, 1783), became a famous mathematician.

VII. SPORTS, GAMES, AND SOCIETY

1743 Aug. 10 Jack Broughton, a **British boxing** champion from c.1735 to 1750, introduced new boxing rules. Broughton's rules, which prevailed until 1838, outlawed hitting a man when down and established the authority of the referee to control the fighting without interference from seconds or spectators.

1744 June 18 The "Kent vs. All-England" **cricket match** was the first game to be fully recorded in the bible of cricket, *Scores and Biographies*. Kent dominated cricket for the first half of the 18th century.

c.1745 **Whist**, similar to bridge, had become extremely popular, both in England and in the American colonies. Rules for playing whist were first published by **Edmond Hoyle** (1671?–Aug. 29, 1769) in *A Short Treatise on the Game of Whist* (1742).

1745 The earliest known rules of **golf** were adopted by the **Company of Gentlemen Golfers** (1744), later renamed the **Honourable Company of Edinburgh Golfers**. The club at first played on a five-hole course at Leith, later at Musselburgh, and finally at Muirfield. In April of this year, the club sponsored a tournament.

1747 Aug. 1 The **Act of Proscription**, the sequel of the crushing (1746) of the **Second Jacobite Rebellion** by the English, took effect. It banned the carrying of arms, public gatherings of persons, and such Highland customs as **wearing the kilt and bagpiping**.

1750–1759

I. DISASTERS

1752 A **fire** leveled c.18,000 houses **in Moscow**. Although the loss was great, it enabled the Russians in rebuilding to enlarge the streets and squares.

1755 Nov. 1 An **earthquake** on All Saints' Day, in Lisbon, Portugal, caused the deaths of c.60,000 people, partly from fires and partly from a tidal wave set off by the quake. Portugal, Spain, and northern Morocco were affected by the tremors, estimated to have been more than 8.0 on the Richter scale. On June 7 northern Persia had been rocked by an earthquake that killed 40,000.

II. POLITICS AND WAR

1751 Sept. 12 **Arcot**, in southeastern India, was taken by **Robert Clive** (Sept. 29, 1725–Nov. 22, 1774), an agent of the British East India Company, thus lifting the French-supported **siege of Trichinopoly** [Tiruchchirappalli], on the Cauvery [Kaveri] River.

1752 The **Toungoo Dynasty** (from 1347) collapsed when the **Mons** captured **Ava**, the capital, in present **Myanmar** [Burma]. The Mons were aided by the French stationed in India.

1754 May 28 The **French and Indian War** (1754–1763) broke out when British troops commanded by the 21-year old **George Washington** wiped out a French scouting party at Grand Meadows near **Fort Necessity**, in present Pennsylvania. The immediate cause of the war was the claim of British colonists from Virginia and Pennsylvania, represented by the **Ohio Land Company**, to land west of the Allegheny Mountains. The French claim to the same area was based on the explorations of La Salle, who had begun a system of fortifications that eventually extended along the length of the Mississippi River basin and reached up some of its tributaries, including the Ohio River Valley.

1754 June 19 The **Albany Congress**, composed of representatives of the New England colonies, convened at Albany, New York, to address the issue of mutual defense against France during the **French and Indian War.**

1755 An Italian, **Pasquale Paoli** (Apr. 26, 1725– Feb. 5, 1807), became the leader of a **nationalist revolt against Genoese rule** in **Corsica.** On the defeat of the Genoese, Paoli established a democratic government that ruled most of the island until 1768.

1755 Mar. **Fort Beauséjour**, on the spit of land connecting Nova Scotia to the mainland of Canada, was overwhelmed by British troops in the **French and Indian War.** The English were now in control of New Brunswick. The **Acadians**, descendants of the original French settlers, were expelled and forcibly relocated in new homes from Maine to Louisiana.

1755 July 9 **Edward Braddock**, leading British troops ["redcoats"] and Virginia militia in another attack on the French at Fort Duquesne in the French and Indian War, was mortally wounded in an ambush near the fork of the Ohio River. Braddock (b. 1695), commanding general of British forces in the colonies, died on July 13. Settlers from central New York state to western Virginia were forced to flee as the French and their allied Indian tribes conducted murderous raids.

1756 **Three clans of the ’Anaiza [Anaiza] tribe,** including the Utbi, settled in present **Kuwait** and founded the **Sabah Dynasty** (1759–to the present) at Al-Kut [= fortress], which was the origin of the word "Kuwait."

1756 Jan. 16 The so-called **Diplomatic Revolution**, a series of alliances preceding the **Seven Years’ War** (1756–1763) in Europe, began with the signing of the **Treaty of Westminster** by Great Britain and Prussia. They agreed, in the event of an Austrian invasion, to join together in Prussia’s defense. On May 1 the **First Treaty of Versailles** was signed by France and Austria. Austria was not bound to honor the alliance if it involved war against Great Britain. On May 17 France and Britain were again officially at war. On July 12 France concluded a

treaty with Sweden, and on the same day Sweden and Denmark made an alliance directed at Great Britain. These diplomatic treaties and alliances created new alignments of the European powers for the Seven Years’ War.

1756 June 20 **Siraj-ud-Daula** [Surajah Dowlah], the nawab of Bengal, whose goal was to drive all Europeans out of Bengal, led an attack on Calcutta and locked up 146 Europeans and non-Europeans in the tiny, windowless guardroom—the "**Black Hole of Calcutta**"–of Fort William. In the heat at least two-thirds of the imprisoned succumbed overnight.

1756 Aug. 14 **Fort Oswego** on Lake Ontario surrendered to the French under the **marquis de Montcalm** in the French and Indian War.

1756 Aug. 29 The **Seven Years’ War** (1756–1763) began with the invasion of Saxony, in present Germany, by Frederick the Great, king of Prussia. Fearing that Maria Theresa, archduchess of Austria, was trying to regain Silesia, Frederick struck first at her territory. Saxony fell to Frederick on Oct. 14. By Jan. 1757, Austria, France, Russia, and Sweden had declared war on Prussia. Britain had declared war against France in May.

1757 June 18 The Prussian forces of Frederick the Great were badly defeated by the Austrians under **Count Leopold [Joseph Graf] von Daun** [Dhaun] (Sept. 24, 1705–Feb. 5, 1766), at Kolín, causing the Prussians to lift their siege, begun May 6, of nearby Prague. With the French defeat (July 26) of Hanoverian and British troops under **William Augustus**, duke of Cumberland (1721–1765), at Hastenbeck in lower Saxony near Hanover, the **Capitulation of Kloster-Zeven**, a preliminary to final peace negotiations, was concluded on Sept. 8, 1757. Hanover and Brunswick were given to France.

1757 June 23 **Robert Clive** of the British East India Company defeated the numerically superior forces of **Siraj-ud-Daula**, the nawab of Bengal, in a **battle at Plassey**, north of Calcutta. Much of the nawab’s army was commanded by **Mir Jafar** (1691–1765), who had secretly allied with the British cause in return for his appointment as nawab after the capture of Siraj-ud-Daula [Surajah Dowlah] (b. 1732?), who was executed on July 2. Clive went on to capture the French port and city of **Chandanagar** [Chandernagor] 21 miles north of **Calcutta.**

1757 Aug. 9 The British **Fort William Henry**, on the southern tip of Lake George, in New York state, fell to the French under Montcalm, in the French and Indian War.

1757 Nov. 5 Prussia's victory over combined Austrian and French armies at Rossbach, Saxony, in present Germany, was a **turning point in the Seven Years' War**. Encouraged by another Prussian victory (Dec. 5) at Leuthen [Lutynia], in present Poland, over Austrian forces, Great Britain renounced the **Capitulation of Kloster-Zeven** and again took up arms.

1758 July 26 In the French and Indian War, the British seized the French colony and **fort of Louisbourg** [Louisburg], on Cape Breton Island at the mouth of the Gulf of St. Lawrence, after a seven-week siege. The siege forces were led by **Jeffrey Amherst** (Jan. 29, 1717–Aug. 3, 1797), **James Wolfe**, and **Edward Boscawen** (Aug. 19, 1711–Jan. 10, 1761). **Fort Frontenac** on Lake Ontario near its juncture with the St. Lawrence River, fell (Aug. 27) to the British under **John Bradstreet**.

1758 Oct. 2 The **first representative assembly to convene in Canada** met at **Halifax**, Nova Scotia, where many New England colonists, especially from Massachusetts, had settled after the Acadian deportation (1755).

1758 Nov. 25 The French-built **Fort Duquesne** in western Pennsylvania was overcome by British forces under **John Forbes** (1710–1759). It was renamed **Fort Pitt**, for William Pitt the Elder, the British prime minister. Because of its strategic location at the fork where the Allegheny and Monongahela rivers join to form the Ohio River, the city of **Pittsburgh** began to develop.

1759 July 26 **Jeffrey Amherst**, leading British troops in the French and Indian War, routed the French from **Fort Carillon** at Point Ticonderoga, on the southern tip of Lake Champlain. The French fled to their **Fort St. Frédéric** at present Crown Point, farther north on Lake Champlain, where Amherst again drove them off on July 31.

1759 Aug. 12 Prussia suffered a stunning defeat in the **Seven Years' War** inflicted by combined Russian and Austrian forces at Kunersdorf [Kunowice], in present Poland, near the German border. **Pëtr Semënovich Saltykov** (1698?–1772), the Russian

commander, lacking supplies, did not press the advantage and returned to Russia. To the southwest **Leopold von Daun**, a commander of Austrian forces, captured (Sept. 4) Dresden, in Saxony. Then **Friedrich August von Finck** (1718–1766) surrendered (Nov. 21) his Prussian troops at Maxen, south of Dresden. Meanwhile, on the western front at Minden on the Weser River west of Hanover, in present Germany, British and Hanoverian troops commanded by Ferdinand (Jan. 12, 1721–July 3, 1792), duke of Brunswick, had defeated (Aug. 1) a superior French army, thus ending any further major threat from France against Hanover and Prussia in the war.

1759 Sept. 13 British forces under **James Wolfe** stormed the French city of **Quebec**, commanded by Montcalm, in the French and Indian War. On the night of Sept. 12 he and his forces succeeded in climbing the cliffs to the Plains of Abraham, where they surprised the French. Both commanders were mortally wounded this day: James Wolfe (b. Jan. 2, 1727) died on the 13th, and **Louis Joseph de Montcalm de Saint-Veran** (b. Feb. 28, 1712), the marquis of Montcalm, died the next day, on the 14th.

1759 Nov. 20 The French fleet was destroyed in a **battle in Quiberon Bay**, in northwestern France, ending French hopes for an invasion of England. **Edward Hawke** (1705–Oct. 17, 1781), a British admiral, defeated **Hubert de Brienne**, comte de Conflans (c.1690–1777), marshal of France, in a day of close fighting. Another French fleet, harbored at Toulon on the Mediterranean, had been wrecked by **Edward Boscawen** in a **battle at Lagos** off southern Portugal on Aug. 18.

III. ECONOMY AND TRADE

1750 **Brazil** began its exportation of **coffee**.

1750 The **Royal Africa Company**, founded on Sept. 27, 1672, gave up its charter to conduct Great Britain's slave trade to the Caribbean area. The company was financially drained by the cost of defense against rival European interests and Africans hostile to the slave trade.

1750 Commercial **coal mining** began in North America.

1750 Great Britain forbade the establishment of certain kinds of **forges and mills in its New World colonies**. This control over manufacturing in the colonies was designed to foster the growth of industry in Great Britain itself.

1752 May 11 The first mutual fire insurance company in the U.S., the **Philadelphia Contributorship for the Insurance of Homes**, was founded by **Benjamin Franklin.**

1759 The **first life insurance company in the U.S.**, "A Corporation for the Relief of Poor and Distressed by Presbyterian Ministers and of Poor and Distressed Widows and Children of Presbyterian Ministers," was established by Presbyterian Synods in New York and Philadelphia.

IV. RELIGION AND PHILOSOPHY

1753 **Jean Astruc** (Mar. 19, 1684–May 5, 1766), a French Roman Catholic professor of medicine, propounded the view in his anonymously published *Conjectures* that the biblical book of Genesis was composed of different documents, the chief ones being distinguished by their use, in the Hebrew, of different names for God.

1753 Jan. 14 **George Berkeley** (b. Mar. 12, 1685), an Anglo-Irish philosopher and bishop, died. Berkeley held that everything perceived about an object was known only in the mind. Only God perceived all objects and, in doing so, made possible our perception of some of them. The thought was expressed in Berkeley's phrase *esse est percipi* [to be is to be perceived]. Berkeley's works included *Essay Towards a New Theory of Vision* (1709); *A Treatise Concerning the Principles of Human Knowledge* (1710); and *Three Dialogues Between Hylas and Philonous* (1713).

1754 Nov. Western knowledge of the **Avesta**, the sacred scriptures of Zoroastrianism, began with the trip of Frenchman **Abraham Hyacinthe Anquetil du Perron** [A. H. Anquetil Duperron] (Dec. 7, 1731–Jan. 17, 1805) to India to study the then-indecipherable language Avestan, in which they were written. He returned in 1761 with *Avesta* manuscripts, whose authenticity was much debated at first.

1755 The publication of **David Hume's** *Natural History of Religion,* along with his earlier essay "On Miracles," included in *Enquiry Concerning Human Understanding* (1748), introduced into the prevailing religious climate a deep-seated skepticism. Hume's rejection of the miraculous helped force theologians to a more critical study of religion and the Bible.

1759 Sept. 3 The **Jesuits** [Society of Jesus] were expelled from **Portugal** and her possessions by **Sebastião José de Carvalho e Mello** (May 16, 1699–May 8, 1782), marquês de Pombal, the Portuguese prime minister. In **Brazil** the Jesuits were trying to gain political rights for the Indians, which aroused opposition from the Portuguese governors.

V. SCIENCE, EDUCATION, AND TECHNOLOGY

1752 Sept. 14 The British Parliament adopted the **Gregorian calendar** for Great Britain and its colonies, abandoning the Julian calendar, which most Catholic countries had abandoned in 1582.

1754 Nov. 27 **Abraham Demoivre** (b. May 26, 1667), a French-born mathematician, died. He was an important figure in the early fields of probability and analytical geometry. His *Doctrine of Chances, or Method of Calculating the Probability of Events in Play* (1718) was followed by a related work on life annuities in 1725.

1755 The **University of Moscow**, the **first Russian university**, was founded by the Empress Elizabeth.

1757 Oct. 17 **René Antoine Ferchault de Réaumur** (b. Feb. 28, 1683), a versatile French scientist, died. He conducted a ten-year study of **steel production** that resulted in the production of a much stronger metal. Réaumur investigated other metals and minerals, gastric juices, and the artificial incubation of eggs, produced a thermometer and a new type of porcelain, and studied the process of limb regeneration in crustaceans.

1759 **James Brindley** (1716–Sept. 30, 1772), an English engineer, began construction of the **Bridgewater Canal**, so-called because it was used to haul coal from the collieries of **Francis Egerton**, duke of Bridgewater (1736–1803). This was the first canal built without benefit of a preexisting stream bed, and the achievement initiated the age of canal building, crucial to the **Industrial Revolution** in Great Britain.

1759 Jan. 15 The **British Museum** opened in London's Montague House. Its collection was formed mostly from the bequest of **Hans Sloane** (Apr. 16, 1660–Jan. 11, 1753), an English physician and naturalist. Sloane's library included more than 50,000 volumes.

VI. ARTS AND LEISURE

1750 *The Life of Harriet Stuart* was the first successful novel by **Charlotte Ramsay Lennox** (1720–Jan. 4, 1804), who was born in New York City, but lived nearly all her life in England. It was also notable for being the **first novel set in North America**.

1750 July 28 **Johann Sebastian Bach** (b. Mar. 21, 1685), the great German composer, died. Bach's early works included Passacaglia and Fugue in C Minor and *Das Orgelbüchlein* [The Little Organ Book] (1717), a collection of choral preludes. His instrumental compositions included the Well-Tempered Clavier (1722), the Chromatic Fantasy and Fugue, the English and French Suites, Two- and Three-Part Inventions, violin sonatas, and cello suites. Especially well known were the **Brandenburg Concertos** (1721), the **Goldberg Variations** [Aria with 30 Variations] (1732), **Partita in B Minor** (1735), **Prelude and Fugue in E Flat** [St. Anne] (1739), *Musical Offering* (1747), and the **Art of the Fugue** (1749). Much of Bach's work was religious, including **St. John Passion** (1723), **Magnificat** (1724?), **St. Matthew Passion** (1729), **The Christmas Oratorio, Mass in B Minor** (1738), motets, cantatas (some of which were secular), and chorales.

1750 Aug. 17 **John Tufts** (b. Feb. 26, 1689), a Congregational clergyman in the American colonies, died. He compiled church music and wrote the **Very Plain and Easy Introduction to the Art of Singing Psalm Tunes** (c.1720), a collection of 37 songs in which the music was written with letters instead of notes on the staff.

1750 Dec. The **Tiepolos**, an Italian family of painters, arrived at Würzburg, on the Main River in Bavaria. There Giovanni Battista (Mar. 5, 1696–Mar. 27, 1770) and his two sons, Giovanni Domenico (Aug. 30, 1727–Mar. 3, 1804) and Lorenzo (1736–1776), collaborated on a series of frescoes, including *The Marriage of Frederick Barbarossa and Beatrice of Burgundy* (c.1754), for the archbishop's palace. **Giovanni Battista Tiepolo**, who painted in the rich Venetian style, also completed the canvases *The Meeting of Antony and Cleopatra* (1745–1750) and *The Adoration of the Kings.*

1752 Sept. 15 The **first production in the American colonies by a professional acting troupe** was a performance of *The Merchant of Venice*, given at Williamsburg, Virginia, under the direction of Lewis

Hallam (1714–1756) of London, where his brother operated a theater.

1753 **Thomas Chippendale** (June 15, 1718–Nov. 13, 1779) began producing **furniture** at his workshop on St. Martin's Lane in the cabinetmaking district of London. The Chippendale style of household furnishings was characterized by the use of mahogany and other fine woods, and the blend of French rococo effects with Gothic and Chinese motifs. A distinctive feature of the **Chippendale style** was the lattice that decorated the backs of Chippendale chairs.

1754 Jan. 28 **Ludvig Holberg** (b. Dec. 3, 1684), a Danish literary figure, died. Holberg's *Peder Paars* (1719), a lighthearted heroic poem, was the first major work written in Danish. His notable comedies included *Den politiske Kandestöber* [*The Political Tinker*] (1722), *Den Vgelsindede* [*The Weather Cock*] (1722), and *Den Stundeslöse* [*The Fussy Man*] (1726).

1754 Oct. 8 **Henry Fielding** (b. Apr. 22, 1707), an English novelist, died. His *Tom Jones* (1749) was one of the first fully developed English novels, with sharply delineated characters, lively dialogue, and dramatic plot structure. His other novels included *Joseph Andrews* (1742), *Jonathan Wild* (1743), and *Amelia* (1751).

1755 Feb. 10 **Montesquieu** [Charles Louis de Secondat, baron de la Brède et de Montesquieu] (b. Jan. 18, 1689), a French political philosopher, died. In his most important work, *De L'Esprit des lois* [*The Spirit of Laws*] (1748), Montesquieu set forth his theory of the separation of power within government and his classification of different kinds of governments. He analyzed the history of law and he discussed the relationship between man-made and natural laws. This book had a profound effect on western political thinking, and either directly or indirectly influenced the constitutions of nearly every modern country.

1757 Mar. 27 **Johann Stamitz** (b. June 19, 1717), a Bohemian composer, died. He helped develop the **classical sonata** and symphonic forms. In addition to symphonies and concertos, Stamitz wrote chamber and church music.

1759 Apr. 14 **George Frederich Handel** [Georg Friedrich Händel] (b. Feb. 23, 1685), a German-born English composer, died. The greatest part of his compositions were English oratorios and operas, in the Italian style. Handel came (1711) to London, where he produced Italian operas, beginning with *Rinaldo* (1711). The orchestral piece *Water Music* (1717) was written for George I. Handel's processional *Zador, the Priest* (1727) was composed for the coronation of George II and has since been played at British royal coronations. His oratorios, especially the *Messiah* (1742), were considered his masterpieces.

VII. SPORTS AND GAMES

c.1750   The evolution of **fencing** as sport was completed with the appearance of a work by **D. Angelo [Domenico Angelo Malevolti] Tremamondo** (1716–

July 11, 1802) and **G. Danet**, who set down accepted rules for the game. This code of fencing established measures for the safety of the contestants. Likewise, its equipment served to protect the players.

1751   The **Jockey Club** was formed in London by a small group of aristocratic turfmen, although it was not so named until a meeting in 1752 at which the members also drew up rules to govern thoroughbred racing in England.

1754 May 14   The **Society of St. Andrews**, known later as the **Royal and Ancient Golf Club of St. Andrews**, was formed by a group of 22 Scottish golfers. The rules they adopted closely followed those of the Edinburgh Golfers.

1760–1769

I. DISASTERS

1766   **Mount Hekla** [Hecla], in **Iceland**, **erupted** in the volcano's most violent known episode. The earliest recorded eruption was in A.D. 1300.

II. EXPLORATION AND COLONIZATION

1763   **Rio de Janeiro** replaced Bahia [Salvador] as capital of the Portuguese colony of Brazil. Rio was nearer the gold fields and its natural harbor on the Atlantic was an easy point for export.

1763   Great Britain issued the **Proclamation of 1763**, ordering American colonists to halt settlement west of the Allegheny Mountains. They were to return any land purchased from the Indians, and colonists already settled in the Ohio River Valley were to return. The colonists largely ignored the proclamation.

1763 Sept. 1   **Prince Edward Island**, won by Great Britain in the French and Indian War and officially ceded by France in this year in the **Treaty of Paris**, was joined politically to Nova Scotia and named **St. John's Island**.

1764 Feb. 15   **St. Louis** was founded by the fur trader **Pierre Laclède** [Liguest] (1724?–1778) and **René Auguste Chouteau** (Sept. 7, 1749–Feb. 24,

1829), who was only 14 years old and acted as Laclède's guide and secretary. The strategic site was destined to become an important trading center, located on a major waterway between the port of New Orleans and the Great Lakes.

1765 Jan.   The **Falkland Islands** [Islas Malvinas], located in the South Atlantic near Cape Horn, were occupied by **John Byron** (Nov. 8, 1723–Apr. 10, 1786), an English navigator, also known as "Foulweather Jack" for the terrible gales he encountered while retrieving British troops from the U.S. on a later expedition. The Falklands had been abandoned by the French after **Louis Antoine de Bougainville** (Nov. 11, 1729–Aug. 31, 1811) had attempted a settlement there in 1764. Pressure from the Spanish and bad weather drove Bougainville's settlers away.

1766 Dec.   **Louis Antoine de Bougainville** embarked on the **first French circumnavigation of the world**. He passed through the Strait of Magellan, continued northwest to **Tahiti**, **Samoa**, and the **New Hebrides**, in the South Pacific Ocean, and sailed waters off the coast of Australia uncharted by Europeans. De Bougainville stopped in the Moluccas [Spice Islands] near New Guinea to allow his crew to recover from scurvy. Bougainville's ship *La Boudeuse* returned to St. Malo, France, in Mar. 1769.

1767   The French crown took control of Île de France and Île de Bourbon, off the coast of southeastern Africa, which had been managed by the **French East India Company**. The former became (1810) the British island of **Mauritius**, while Bourbon, renamed **Réunion** in 1793, became (1946) a French Overseas Territory.

1768   The archipelago of the **Seychelles**, in the Indian Ocean, was first settled by French colonists from nearby Île de France [Mauritius].

1768 Apr. 25–July 12, 1771   **James Cook**, an English navigator, began his first exploration voyage to the South Pacific in the bark *Endeavor* to observe from Tahiti the transit (June, 1769) of the planet Venus. He then probed the southern waters in search of the Antarctic continent. During these trips he explored and surveyed the **New Zealand** coast and the east coast of **Australia**, laying claim to both places for Great Britain.

1769   **Daniel Boone** (Nov. 2, 1734–Sept. 26, 1820) continued his exploration of the region west of present North Carolina. In 1750 **Thomas Walker** and a scouting party had explored the region of eastern Kentucky, and it was being entered by frontiersmen, especially hunters, from Virginia and North Carolina. Boone opened the territory further west between Mar. and Aug. 1775, when he blazed the **Wilderness Road** across the Appalachian Mountains in eastern Tennessee at the **Cumberland Gap**, through northern Tennessee and Kentucky to Boonesborough [Boonesboro], a fort he founded (1775) on the Kentucky River for **Richard Henderson's** Transylvania Company.

1769   **San Diego**, in California, was settled by **Gaspar de Portolá** (1723?–1784), Spanish governor (1767–1770) of the Californias. A member of the same expedition, Father **Junípero Serra** (Nov. 24, 1713–Aug. 28, 1784), established a Franciscan mission at San Diego before continuing through the Southwest to found many others.

1769 Oct. 7   The British ship *Endeavour*, commanded by **James Cook**, arrived at New Zealand. He circumnavigated the two islands, establishing that they were not connected to any continent, and laid the basis for British claims to New Zealand.

III. POLITICS AND WAR

1760   The **British East India Company** withdrew from **Burma** [Myanmar] after **Alaungpaya**, the Burmese king (1752–1760), attacked the British settlement of Negrais on the Bay of Bengal.

1760 Sept. 8   Canadian-born **Pierre François de Rigaud** (1698–1778), marquis de Vaudreuil-Cavagnal, the **last French governor of Canada**, surrendered **Montreal** to the British **Jeffrey Amherst**, as the **French and Indian War** moved to its close. The British divided Canada into three parts, administered from three centers: Quebec, Montreal, and Trois-Rivières.

1760 Oct. 9   **Berlin**, the Prussian capital, was occupied by Russian troops in the **Seven Years' War**. As Frederick the Great, king of Prussia, returned from defending Silesia to save his capital, the Russians withdrew after burning the city.

1760 Oct. 25   **George II** (b. 1683), king of Great Britain and Ireland (from 1727) and elector of Hanover, died. During his reign England saw the beginnings of the establishment of an overseas empire in North America, Africa, and India, but he aroused popular discontent at home by often promoting Hanoverian policies in Europe over British interests. He was succeeded by his 12-year old grandson, **George III**.

1760 Nov. 29   **Detroit**, nearly the last French fortification to surrender in the French and Indian War, fell to British troops under the American frontiersman **Robert Rogers** (1731–1795).

1761 Jan. 14   **Ahmad Shah**, the **Afghan** ruler of the **Durrani Dynasty** (1747–1818), defeated the Hindu **Marathas** [Mahrattas] at Panipat, a stronghold of the Punjab near the Yamuna River north of Delhi. By turning back the Marathas to the Deccan in southern India, Durrani unwittingly opened the door in Bihar and Bengal in the northeast to British control, which had been repeatedly threatened by the local Maratha rulers.

1761 Aug. 3   **Étienne Francois de Choisul** (June 28, 1719–May 8, 1785), the French foreign minister, arranged the so-called **Third Family Compact** between members of the Bourbon family ruling in France, Spain, Parma, and Piacenza. The treaty guaranteed to the Bourbons their possessions and made commercial provisions against the possibility of a British victory interrupting the balance of colonial trade.

1762 Following the capture of **Martinique**, in the West Indies, by **George Brydges Rodney** (Feb., 1718–May 24, 1792), a British admiral, the nearby islands of St. Lucia, St. Vincent, and Grenada surrendered. British possession of St. Vincent, Dominica, and Tobago was confirmed by the **Treaty of Paris** (1763). Martinique, Gaudeloupe, and St. Lucia were returned to France.

1762 Jan. 5 **Elizabeth** [Elizaveta Petrovna] (b. Dec. 18, 1709), czarina of Russia (from 1741), died. For the succession she had favored **Peter III**, the son of her sister Anna, choosing for his wife **Sophia Augusta Frederica**, princess of Anhalt-Zerbst, the future **Catherine II the Great**. Peter's mean disposition, childish moods, and irresponsible favoritism toward Prussia and Austria in the Seven Years' War resulted in his overthrow (July 9) by Catherine. Peter III [Pëtr Feodorovich] (b. Feb. 21, 1728), was murdered on July 17 by his guards led by Count **Aleksei Grigorievich Orlov** (Oct. 5, 1737–Jan. 5, 1808), whose brother, Count **Grigori Grigorievich Orlov** (Oct. 17, 1734–Apr. 24, 1783), a paramour of Catherine's, had planned the coup.

1762 May 5 The **Treaty of St. Petersburg** was signed by Russia and Prussia, bringing a switch in alliance during the **Seven Years' War**. The new Russian czar **Peter III** restored hard-won territory to Prussia and offered Russian aid. Prussian troops drove the Austrians from Silesia in a series of victories: Burkersdorf [Burkatów] on July 21, Reichenbach on Aug. 16, and Schweidnitz [Świdnica] on Oct. 9. Peter's plans to carry the campaign into Denmark were cut short in July by the coup mounted in favor of his wife **Catherine II the Great.**

1762 Aug. Havana, the chief Spanish naval base in the New World, was captured by the British under **George Keppel** (1724–1772), earl of Albemarle. It was a severe blow to the viceroyalty of New Spain. The city of **Manila** on Luzon, in the Spanish-held Philippines, was also occupied by the British.

1763 May 7 In an **American Indian revolt** Pontiac (1720?–1769), an Ottawa chief, began the siege of Fort Detroit. But Pontiac, unskilled at conducting a long siege, abandoned it. Then his forces were defeated (Aug. 5–6) by **Henry Bouquet** (1719–1765), a

British officer, at Bushy Run, Pennsylvania. Indians, however, continued their raiding for two years. **Pontiac's Rebellion** (1763–1764) was a unified effort by Indian tribes to coordinate their attacks on English forts, and in May and June they had destroyed eight forts in the region of the Great Lakes.

1763 Feb. 10 The **Treaty of Paris** [Peace of Paris] was signed by France, Spain, and Great Britain, concluding the **French and Indian War** in North America and the **Seven Years' War** in Europe, Africa, and Asia. In the West Indies France regained the islands of Guadeloupe and Martinique; Grenada was ceded to Great Britain, and St. Vincent, Dominica, and Tobago remained in British hands. France ceded to Great Britain all of present Canada, including Cape Breton Island, Nova Scotia, and her fortifications east of the Mississippi River. Spain received the Louisiana Territory and all French possessions lying west of the Mississippi River. Only the port of **New Orleans**, at the mouth of the Mississippi River, and the islands of St. Pierre and Miquelon, off the coast of Newfoundland, remained in French hands. Spain ceded present Florida to Great Britain in return for Havana [Cuba], and Manila, in the Philippines. Thus, **Great Britain acquired claim to most of North America.** In India, France was permitted to keep trading posts in Bengal but was not allowed to fortify them, in effect giving **control of India to England.** In Africa, Great Britain retained the French posts captured in Senegal, and established along the Gambia River the British colony of Senegambia.

1763 Feb. 15 The **Treaty of Hubertusburg**, in present Germany, was signed by Austria, Prussia, and Saxony, settling the status of Silesia, the uncertainty of which had directly led to the outbreak of the Seven Years' War. **Frederick the Great**, king of Prussia, kept Silesia, and prewar boundaries were restored.

1763 Oct. 5 **Augustus III** (b. Oct. 17, 1696), king of Poland (from 1734) and as **Frederick Augustus II**, elector of Saxony (from 1733), died. On Apr. 11, 1764, a treaty was signed by Russia and Prussia agreeing to Russian support of **Stanislas II Poniatowski** [Augustus] (Jan. 17, 1732–Feb. 12, 1798), who was subsequently elected (Sept. 7) king of Poland (1764–1795).

1764 July 15 **Ivan VI Antonovich** (b. Aug. 13, 1740), the son of Anna Leopoldovna and heir to the Russian throne, was murdered by his jailers at the fortress of

Schlüsselburg [Petrokrepost], on an island in Lake Ladoga. Here Ivan had spent the last eight years of his life-long imprisonment, mostly in solitary confinement. One of the guards at the fortress, **Vasili Yakovlevich Mirovich**, had plotted unsuccessfully to escape with Ivan and proclaim him czar of Russia.

1764 Oct. 23 In a **battle at Buxar** [Baxar], on the Ganges River in western Bihar, the British under **Hector Munro** (1726–Dec. 27, 1805) smashed the final attempt by the Mogul **Mir Kasim** (d. 1777) to rule an independent **Bengal**. He fled to Oudh, further west, and the **British East India Company** set up **Shah Alam** (1728–1806) to rule from Calcutta as nawab of Bengal.

1767 A Burmese force invaded **Siam** [Thailand] and sacked **Ayuthia** [Phra Nakhon Si Ayutthaya], which had been the capital of Siam since 1350. The **Ch'ing** [Manchu] **Dynasty** (1644–1911) in China attacked **Burma** [Myanmar] in Siam's defense, and by 1769 had made it a vassal state.

1768 The **boundary between Pennsylvania and Maryland** was established by the Englishmen **Charles Mason** (1730–1787) and **Jeremiah Dixon** (fl. 1760–1770). The two astronomers surveyed along the parallel 39°43′ from the Delaware River c.244 miles westward, marking the line with milestones. The project cost $75,000. Later this boundary plus the Ohio River from the Pennsylvania boundary west to the Mississippi River and the eastern, northern, and western boundaries of Missouri, then westward on 36°30′ was called loosely the **Mason and Dixon Line**, separating slave states from free.

1768 May 15 The Italian republic of **Genoa** sold the island of **Corsica**, which was seeking independence under the Corsican patriot **Pasquale Paoli**, to France. By Aug. 1769, the French were in control of the island, following the defeat and the flight to England of Paoli.

1768 Aug. The **Confederation of Bar** convened in the village of Bar in Podolia [Podolsk] in the Ukraine. **Casimir Pulaski** [Kazimierz Pulawski] and **Adam Krasinski** (d. 1800), bishop of Kamenets [Kamieniec] (1759–1795), led a union representing the patriotic Catholic nobility of Poland, who wished to assert Poland's right to govern its own internal affairs. In Oct. 1767, **Nikolai Vasilievich Repnin** (Mar. 22, 1734–May 24, 1801), a Russian general, had obtained by force the Sejm's approval of certain

fundamental rights for "dissidents," who were non-Catholic and constituted about a tenth of Poland's population. Of these, about half were Protestant, residing in Polish Prussia, and the other half lived in Lithuania.

1769 Apr. The **Mysore** [Carnatic] **War** (1767–1769) ended when the winner **Haidar Ali** (1722–1782), a Muslim adventurer who had recently reduced the Hindu **Wadiyar Dynasty** (1399–1949) of Mysore to puppets and installed himself as ruler of Mysore, a Hindu state, signed a treaty with the British enclave at Madras, on the Carnatic coast, where the growth of French trade and influence along the whole coast threatened Britain's supremacy. By the terms of the treaty, the British, who had been abandoned by the Hindu Maratha confederacy and the Muslim Nizam Ali of Hyderabad, agreed to an alliance with Haidar.

IV. ECONOMY AND TRADE

c.1760 The **Conestoga wagon**, first made (c.1750) in Conestoga, Lancaster county, Pennsylvania, became important in wagon trains. Carrying up to eight tons, they were drawn by six horses.

1761 **José Gálvez** (1729–1787), marqués de la Sonora, was sent to **Mexico** by Charles III, king of Spain, as inspector general [*visitador general*] (to 1774). Gálvez instituted (1765) a series of reforms that resulted in more efficient administration of the colony.

1761 The art of gathering **maple sap** and converting it to syrup and sugar, long known by the Indians, was introduced to the colonists of North America.

1764 **George Grenville** (Oct. 14, 1712–Nov. 13, 1770), prime minister of Great Britain (1763–1765), began to enforce strictly the **Navigation Acts**, including the Molasses and Sugar Acts passed (1733) by Parliament to increase revenue, particularly from the colonies. Molasses and sugar were cheaper in the islands of the French and Dutch West Indies, so the Navigation Acts stipulated that these commodities had to be bought from the British islands and shipped by British or colonial vessels.

1764 The **Currency Act**, passed by the British Parliament, banned paper money in the American colonies. In the early 1700s most of the currency circulated in the American colonies was Spanish, received in trade with the West Indies. German silver *dalers* (*thalers*), which gave us the name dollar, were also in circulation.

1764 Apr. 19 The **British Company of Merchants Trading to Africa** was given the right to govern **Senegambia**.

1765 Mar. 23 The **Stamp Act**, another of the **Navigation Acts,** passed by the British Parliament, required stamps, indicating the payment of a tax, on all legal and commercial documents, newspapers, and pamphlets issued in the American colonies. The revenue thus gained was to be used to finance British troops in North America.

1765 May 29 **Patrick Henry** (May 29, 1736–June 6, 1799), speaking before the Virginia legislature, the **House of Burgesses**, on the Stamp Act, ended his speech with, "Caesar had his Brutus—Charles the First, his Cromwell—and George the Third—('Treason,' cried the Speaker)—*may profit by their example*. If *this* be treason, make the most of it." On Oct. 7, 1765, the **Stamp Act Congress** convened in New York City to organize resistance to the Stamp Act. It adopted 13 resolutions against the importation of any goods that required a payment of duty to British officials.

1767 June 29 The **Townshend Acts** were passed by the British Parliament. Duties were levied on paper, lead, glass, color for paint, and tea imported by the American colonies. **Charles Townshend** (Apr. 27, 1725–Sept. 4, 1767), chancellor of the exchequer, who engineered these acts, intended to establish a source of revenue to finance colonial administration.

V. RELIGION AND PHILOSOPHY

1760 **Israel ben Eliezer** [Rabbi Israel], known as the Baal Shem Tov [Tob, Tobh] (born c.1700), known also as Besht (from the initials B-SH-T), **founder of the modern sect of Hasidism** [Chassidism], died in Medzhibozh [Miedzyborz] in the Little Ukraine, Poland, where he had taught hundreds attracted by his wisdom and personality. The message he taught was simple and non-philosophical, couched frequently in anecdote or parable.

1769 **John Wesley**, apprised of the growth of uncoordinated **Methodist "societies"** between New York and Virginia, sent two preacher-missionaries to assist in the orderly development of the societies. In

1771 two more were sent, one of them Francis Asbury (Aug. 20, 1745–Mar. 31, 1816). Asbury was responsible for developing the system of **"circuit riders,"** Methodist preachers who covered their circuit of approximately 30 appointments by horseback about once every month.

VI. SCIENCE, EDUCATION, AND TECHNOLOGY

1760 The **Industrial Revolution**, a period of wide-ranging economic and social change, was said to have begun at about this time in England, where Lancashire [Lancaster] and Yorkshire developed as textile centers, and where the Midlands near the Welsh border assumed importance as a coal-producing region. The growth of international trade, a more mobile labor force, and the discovery of cheaper, more efficient energy sources were based on the invention of the **steam engine** in 1769, the **spinning jenny** in 1770, and the **Bessemer process** in 1856. In Europe the Industrial Revolution came early to Belgium. In the U.S. it was said to have begun with the invention of the **cotton gin** by Eli Whitney in 1793, although it did not reach its peak until from 1860 to 1890, after the Civil War. France, whose industrial development was steady from 1830, did not expand its industrial capacity as rapidly as did Great Britain. In Germany the Industrial Revolution did not gain momentum until as late as 1850.

1760 The **blast furnace** was invented by **John Smeaton** (June 8, 1724–Oct. 28, 1792), an English engineer. The furnace was named for the "blast," or current, of air forced into the combustion chamber where iron ore was melted to form pig iron. Impurities were converted in the presence of limestone and carbon into slag. Coke, a high temperature fuel, furnished the carbon.

1762 July 13 **James Bradley** (b. Mar., 1693), an English astronomer, died. Among other achievements, he described (1728) the relativity of movements of the earth, stars, and sun, and explained the aberration of starlight as the angle of the path of light from a star refracted by the atmosphere.

1763 **Nevil Maskelyne** (Oct. 6, 1732–Feb. 9, 1811), an English astronomer, published *The British Mariner's Guide*, which introduced his method of determining longitude from calculations based on astronomical units called "lunars." Maskelyne observed

(1761) the transit of Venus from St. Helena and published (1766) the first edition of the *Nautical Almanac* covering the year 1767.

c.1765   The **spinning jenny** was first developed by an English mechanic **James Hargreaves** (d. Apr. 22, 1778). This hand-operated machine for twisting and winding cotton fibers into thread on a spindle increased the speed of conventional spinning eight times.

1765   **John Metcalf** (1717–1810) began his career **building roads** in northern Great Britain. Roads between Holyhead, Chester, and Shrewsbury were improved by Metcalf, who carefully had the roadbed graded and a foundation set.

1765 May 3   The **first medical school in the American colonies** opened in Philadelphia. Founded by **Dr. John Morgan** (June 10, 1735–Oct. 15, 1789) and Dr. **William Shippen** (1736–1808), the school later became the **University of Pennsylvania School of Medicine.**

1768 June 8   Johann Joachim Winckelmann (b. Dec. 9, 1717), a German archaeologist and art critic, died. His *Thoughts on the Imitation of Greek Works in Painting and Sculpture* (1755) influenced neoclassicism in the art of Europe. In *Geschichte der Kunst des Altertums* [*The History of Ancient Art*] (1764), Winckelmann discussed the superior quality of ancient Greek art over ancient Roman.

1768 Dec.   The first two six-penny parts–there were to be 100 parts–of the *Encyclopaedia Britannica* were published in Edinburgh, Scotland. The parts were collected into three volumes in 1771. The second edition (1777–1784), published in 10 volumes, was the first summary in English of all knowledge.

1769   The **waterframe** was patented by an English inventor, **Richard Arkwright** (Dec. 23, 1732–Aug. 3, 1792). Like the spinning jenny, it produced a twisted thread of cotton fibers, but it was powered by water.

1769   Nicolas Joseph Cugnot (Sept. 25, 1725–Oct. 2, 1804), a French officer, built a **steam-powered carriage.** It carried four people for 20 minutes at 2.5 miles per hour and, after a 20-minute rest, could resume operation.

1769 Jan. 5   **James Watt** (Jan. 19, 1736–Aug. 19, 1819), an English inventor, patented the **first effi-** cient **steam engine.** A separate condensing chamber greatly increased the power of the engine. Watt established the "**horsepower**" as a unit of measurement in order to arrive at the amount and rate of work produced by his engine.

VII. ARTS AND LEISURE

c.1760–1870   **Romanticism,** a set of concepts that arose in reaction to classicism and rationalism, came to dominate European art, literature, and music. Romanticism emphasized individualism; revolt against authority; the love of nature; an interest in medieval, instead of ancient, art and literature; a fascination with orientalism; and a preoccupation with subjective values and the inner life. The movement was said to have originated with **Jean Jacques Rousseau's** image of the "noble savage."

c.1760   Many wealthy women in the American colonies again adopted the **tower style of hairdress,** in which the hair was frizzed and piled over pads to form a mountain of curls that was then greased and powdered to maintain its shape.

1760 Mar. 1   The first "**toile de Jouy**" **fabric** was printed at the Jouy works in Jouy-en-Josas, near Versailles, France, by **Christophe Philippe Oberkampf** (June, 1738–Oct. 14, 1815), a German-born textile manufacturer.

1761   The **glass harmonica,** or vérillon, was improved by **Benjamin Franklin,** who added a treadle to rotate the tuned glasses, each of which held a different amount of water and produced a note when its rim was rubbed with the fingers. The vérillon was a popular instrument of the time; Ludwig van Beethoven and Wolfgang Amadeus Mozart composed for it.

1762 June 17   **Crébillon** [Prosper Jolyot, sieur de Crais-Billon] (b. Feb. 13, 1647), a French tragic playwright and rival of Voltaire, died. His career began with *Idoménée* (1705) and reached its peak with *Atrée et Thyeste* (1707), *Electre* (1708), and *Rhadamiste et Zénobie* (1711).

1763   **Wu Ching-Tzu** (born c.1715), a Chinese author, died. He wrote *The Unofficial History of Men and Letters,* printed between 1768 and 1779. It was considered a masterpiece of social satire.

1763 Feb. 12 Ts'ao Chan [Ts'ao Hsüeh-Ch'in] (born c.1715), a Chinese writer, died. His great work *The Dream of the Red Chamber* remained unfinished at his death. A tragic romance, it was inspired by Ts'ao Chan's experience of poverty.

1763 Nov. 25 Abbé Prévost [Antoine François Prévost d'Exiles] (b. Apr. 1, 1697), a French Benedictine monk and novelist, died. Prévost's seven-volume *Mémoires d'un Homme de Qualité* (1732) was well-known, but especially its seventh volume, *L'Histoire du Chevalier Des Grieux et de Manon Lescaut* (1731), which introduced Manon Lescaut to the world.

1764 What is now the great **Hermitage Museum** in St. Petersburg, traces its beginnings to **Catherine the Great**, czarina of Russia, who had a building erected adjoining the Winter Palace to be used as a court museum.

1764 Apr. 17 Johann Mattheson (b. Sept. 28, 1681), a German composer and writer on music theory, died. Mattheson was best known for his *Critica Musica* (1722); *Grundlage einer Ehrenpforte* (1740), a biographical dictionary of nearly 150 composers; and other theoretical and encyclopedic works.

1764 Sept. 12 Jean Philippe Rameau (b. Sept. 25, 1683), a French organist and music theorist, died. Rameau composed his first opera *Hippolyte et Aricie* (1733) when he was 50 years old. Among Rameau's approximately 30 stage works, *Les Indes Gallantes* (1735), a dramatic ballet, and Rameau's best-known opera *Castor et Pollux* (1737), rivaled the works of Jean Baptiste Lully. Rameau also composed harpsichord music and chamber music in the rococo style.

1764 Oct. 26 William Hogarth (b. Nov. 10, 1697), an English painter and engraver, died. His first success was *A Harlot's Progress* (1732), a series of six plates treating moral issues. This was followed by *The Rake's Progress* (1735) and *Marriage à la Mode* (1745). *Beer Street, Gin Lane,* and *Four Stages of Cruelty* (all 1751) strike at the brutality of society.

c.1765 *Mother Goose's Melody: or Sonnets for the Cradle* was first published in London. An edition dated 1791 is the earliest surviving volume of these nursery rhymes.

1765 The three-volume *Reliques of Ancient English Poetry* [*Percy's Reliques*], a collection of Scottish and English songs, ballads, and poems, was published by **Thomas Percy** (Apr. 13, 1729–Sept. 30, 1811), an English bishop and antiquarian. This work sparked an interest in earlier literary forms and provided material for the romantic poets in England and abroad.

1765 Apr. 11 Mikhail Vasilievich Lomonosov (b. Nov. 19, 1711), died. Most important of Lomonosov's linguistic studies was a Russian grammar, *Rossiskaya grammatika* (1755), which provided a classification of literary styles. His development of a theory of verse became the standard basis for Russian poetry.

1766 Nov. 12 The **Southwark Theater** [South Street Theater], opened in Philadelphia with productions of Colley Cibber's **The Provok'd Husband** (**1728**) and **Thomas and Sally**. Despite Puritan sentiment, the theater began to prosper in the American colonies.

1767 The unique comic novel *The Life and Opinions of Tristam Shandy, Gentleman* by **Laurence Sterne** (Nov. 24, 1713–Mar. 18, 1768) was completed. It was among the first works of literature to use the stream of consciousness technique.

1767 June 25 Georg Philipp Telemann (b. Mar. 14, 1681), a German composer, died. Nearly 650 suites, overtures, concertos, pieces of chamber music, and operas by Telemann have been listed. Perhaps the best-known of his works is the oratorio *Der Tag des Gerichts* [*The Day of Judgment*] (1762).

1768 The **Royal Academy of Arts** was founded in London under the patronage of George III, king of Great Britain. Joshua Reynolds (July 16, 1723–Feb. 23, 1792), the day's leading portrait painter, was appointed the first president of the academy.

1768 June 20 Antonio Canaletto [Giovanni Antonio Canale] (b. Oct. 18, 1697), an Italian painter, died. Canaletto worked chiefly in Venice and produced notable scenes of that city. He took his realistic style to Rome and London, where he remained for ten years. His best works included *View on the Grand Canal, Palace of the Doges, The Square of St. Mark's, Regatta on the Grand Canal* (c.1735), and *The Piazza on the Grand Canal.*

1768 July 6 Johann Conrad Beissel (b. Apr., 1690), a musician and clergyman of the Palatinate, Germany, who immigrated (1720) to the American colonies, died. Beissel established (1732) a community, called "Economy," of **Seventh-Day Baptists** [Dunkers] at Ephrata, Pennsylvania, that gained renown for its choral singing. There, Beissel composed the many hymns and sacred scores that so much influenced American hymnody.

1769 *The History of Emily Montague,* written by **Frances Brooke** (1724–Jan. 23, 1789), was the first novel published by a French Canadian.

1769 Ground was broken for construction of **Monticello,** near Charlottesville, Virginia. Monticello, "little mountain," referred to the hill upon which **Thomas Jefferson** built his home. One of the earliest examples of the classic revival in the U.S., it reflected Jefferson's interest in classical architecture.

1769 Josiah Wedgwood (1730–Jan. 3, 1795), an English potter, perfected a cream-colored earthenware, called "**Queen's ware**" because it was admired by the British queen, that soon gained worldwide renown for its combined beauty and durability. Wedgwood's special ability rested in his scientific approach to glazes. A black ware, known as basalt, when used with red decoration enabled Wedgwood to imitate Greek vases, then very much in vogue in England.

VIII. SPORTS, GAMES, AND SOCIETY

1763 Francisco Romero (born c.1700), the **first famous Spanish matador**, died. It was said that in 1726 he was the first to use the **muleta**, the red cape with which the matador enticed the bull. He was active for 30 years.

1763 June 2 Accounts vary about the details of a game of *baggataway* [lacrosse] played by visiting Chippewas and Sacs, at **Fort Michilimackinac** [Mackinac], Michigan, to lure British soldiers and residents out of their compound during **Pontiac's Rebellion**. With most spectators absorbed in the game, the Indians suddenly removed tomahawks that had been concealed under blankets by their squaws and murdered the spectators. The Indians then seized the fort and massacred most of those who had remained inside.

1770–1779

I. VITAL STATISTICS AND DEMOGRAPHICS

1775 The **population of the 13 American colonies** was c.2,418,000. The smallest colony, Delaware, had c.30,000, and the largest, Virginia, had c.400,000.

1776 Serving in the American Revolution were **c.5,000 blacks,** both free and slave. A black, **Crispus Attucks** (b. 1723?), a leader of a Boston crowd, was one of three persons killed in the **Boston Massacre** on Mar. 5, 1770. The colonial population included c.700,000 blacks.

II. DISASTERS

1770 May 30 During a fireworks display held in Paris to celebrate the marriage of **Marie Antoinette**, archduchess of Austria, to the French dauphin, later **Louis XVI,** a small **fire** broke out and a water cart being taken to extinguish it overturned. In the ensuing panic, more than 200 people died and hundreds were injured.

1776 During the British occupation of **New York City, a fire,** cause undetermined, broke out. Much of New York City's Dutch architecture was destroyed.

1779 An epidemic, thought to be **smallpox,** claimed the lives of nearly a fifth of the population of **Mexico City**.

III. EXPLORATION AND COLONIZATION

1770 Apr. 20 James Cook, aboard the bark *Endeavour,* sighted the eastern coast of **Australia**. He landed at **Botany Bay** and claimed the land for England. **Joseph Banks** (Feb. 2, 1743–June 19, 1820), a British naturalist with Cook, collected samples of Australian plants to take back to England.

1770 Nov. 14 James Bruce (Dec. 14, 1730–Apr. 27, 1794), a Scottish explorer, reached the **source of the Blue Nile** [Bahr al-Azraq] at Lake Tana [Tsana], in present Ethiopia. Bruce had arrived at the court at

Gonder [Gondar], capital of Ethiopia [Abyssinia], in February as a welcome guest.

1770 Dec. 6 Samuel Hearne (1754–Nov., 1792) set out from Churchill on Hudson Bay, to search for copper as an agent and surveyor for the Hudson's Bay Company. In May 1771, Hearne began his crossing of the Barren Lands of the Northwest Territories; on July 6, 1771, he discovered the **Coppermine River** and traced it to its mouth on the **Coronation Gulf**, becoming the **first white person to travel overland to the Arctic Ocean** and the first white person to view that ocean from Baffin Island to the eastern tip of Siberia.

1772 The **Kerguelen** [Desolation] **Islands** in the southern Indian Ocean were discovered by **Yves Joseph de Kerguélen-Trémarec** (1734?–1797), a French navigator.

1772 July 13 Back in England after his voyage to the South Pacific, **James Cook** prepared to return to the South Seas in the barks *Resolution* and *Adventure*, his mission to explore Antarctic waters.

1774 The **coast of the present state of Washington** was probably first explored by **Juan Pérez** for Spain. Russia, with an interest in the fur trade, had already claimed the area south of Alaska, although it had not yet explored the region. An expedition under **Bruno Heceta** was believed to have been first to set foot (1775) in Washington.

1774 Jan. 30 James Cook reached 71° 10′ South at longitude 106° 54′ West, the most southern latitude yet sailed. Although Cook searched for Antarctica with the barks *Resolution* and *Adventure*, he did not find the southern continent. He did discover **New Caledonia** east of Australia in 1774.

1775 Mar. 17 The **Transylvania Purchase** was made by **Richard Henderson** (1735–1785), who founded the Transylvania Company for this purpose. By the **Treaty of Sycamore Shoals**, on the Watauga River in Tennessee, **Dragging Canoe**, the Cherokee chief, agreed to sell Henderson 20 million acres of Cherokee lands bounded by the Ohio, Tennessee, and Kentucky rivers for £10,000. The area was named Transylvania and comprised parts of the present states of North Carolina, Virginia, Kentucky, and Tennessee. At this time (March) Daniel Boone was blazing the Wilderness Trail from the Cumberland Gap to Boonesborough [Boo-nesboro], in present Kentucky, where he founded a fort.

1776 The Spanish friars **Silvestre Vélez de Escalante** and **Francisco Atanasio Dominguez**, embarked from **Santa Fe**, in present New Mexico, to find a route to California. They did not achieve their goal of establishing new settlements in California, but they did open the way for the **Old Spanish Trail**.

1779 Feb. 14 James Cook (b. Oct. 27, 1728), on his third voyage to the Pacific Ocean, was killed by natives in an argument over the theft of a cutter on the beach at Kealakekua, **Hawaii**, the largest of the **Sandwich Islands** [Hawaiian Islands], which Cook discovered on Jan. 18, 1778. On his three Pacific voyages, he eliminated scurvy on his ships by enforcing a rigorous diet using vegetables, fresh fruits, and sauerkraut, an accomplishment for which he was awarded the Copley gold medal. He made an art of navigation and cartography. His work was so valued by mariners that nations at war with Great Britain during Cook's voyages were ordered not to molest or fire upon him.

IV. POLITICS AND WAR

1770 In the **continuing dispute** (since c.1749) **between New York and New Hampshire** over the territory now known as **Vermont**, a grand jury at Albany attempted to oust the settlers by indicting some of them as rioters. **Ethan Allen** (Jan. 21, 1738–Feb. 11, 1789), who had argued for the legal defense of these grants, formed the **Green Mountain Boys** to defend the western border and resist New York's claim.

1770 Mar. 5 The **Boston Massacre** occurred as a crowd of Boston citizens, who had been harassing the British soldiers stationed in the city to enforce the **Townshend Acts**, were fired upon by several soldiers. Three people were killed and seven wounded, of whom two died later. All nine soldiers and their commander were relieved of their duty and tried for murder, with **Robert Treat Paine** (Mar. 11, 1731–May 11, 1814) the prosecutor and **John Adams** the defending attorney. The commander and six of his men were acquitted; two soldiers were convicted of manslaughter. As a result of the so-called massacre, **Lord North** [Frederick North] (Apr. 13, 1732–Aug. 5, 1792), earl of Guilford, the British prime minister, rescinded the Townshend Acts (1767), except on tea. The American colonies then ended their embargo on British imports, except for tea.

1770 July 5 In a **battle at Çesme** [Chesme], near Álzmir [Smyrna] on the Aegean coast of Anatolia, the Russian fleet under **Aleksei Grigorievich Orlov** destroyed the Turkish fleet of the Ottoman Empire in the **Russo-Turkish War** (1768–1774). This naval victory brought European attention to the Russian fleet as a force to reckon with.

1770 Oct. 22 **Stanislas II Poniatowski** [Augustus], king of Poland, unsympathetic toward the demands of the anti-Russian **Confederation of the Bar** that represented Poland's Catholic majority, was accused by the confederation's French military consultant, **Charles François Dumouriez** (1739–1823), of being a tyrant. Stanislas, who urged more rights for Protestant and Eastern Orthodox churches, then allied himself more strongly with Russia. From this point international support of the confederation declined.

1770 Dec. 5 **Johann Friedrich von Struensee**, a German-Danish philosopher and statesman, was named minister of **Denmark** by **Christian VII** (Jan. 29, 1749–Mar. 13, 1808), king of Denmark and Norway (from 1766). Between Mar. 1771 and Jan. 1772, Struensee introduced reforms, often at the rate of three per day. Most of his reforms conflicted with the customs of the Danes, but many were improvements and beneficial. Because of his insistence on the use of his native German and his affair with the queen, **Caroline Matilda** (1751–May 10, 1775), Struensee (b. Aug. 5, 1737) was arrested on Jan. 17, 1772, and beheaded and quartered on Apr. 28. The marriage of Christian and Matilda was dissolved.

1772 **Warren Hastings** (Dec. 6, 1732–Aug. 22, 1818) was appointed British governor of Bengal, India. In the same year an act of Parliament granted the governor of Bengal sovereignty over the British possessions of Bombay and Madras. Hastings became (1773) the **first governor-general** (to 1785) **of India.**

1772 Feb. 17 **Russia** and **Prussia** agreed to the **First Partition of Poland** in a treaty signed at **St. Petersburg**, capital of Russia (1712–1917). Later **Austria** joined (Aug. 5) in the partition. Russia agreed not to annex the **Danubian Principalities** from the **Ottoman Empire** in return for part of White Russia. Austria received Galicia south of the Vistula River. Prussia received West Prussia and Ermeland, which joined

Prussian Pomerania with eastern Prussia. About a third of Poland was thus taken over. Poland's **Sejm** [parliament] agreed to the partition, under threat, on Sept. 18.

1772 Aug. 19 **Gustavus III**, king of Sweden, arrested the members of the Council and menaced the **Riksdag**. On Aug. 21 he presented a new constitution to the Riksdag, which was dissolved upon its acceptance. Gustavus instituted liberal reforms, strengthened the royal power, and tried to unify Sweden. The liberal reforms reduced the power of the nobles and gave more to the merchants and middle class.

1772 Nov. 2 The **first Committee of Correspondence** was formed in Boston by **Samuel Adams** (Sept. 27, 1722–Oct. 2, 1803). Its purpose was to communicate with other towns in Massachusetts about the causes for discontent generated by British rule over the American colonies and to help unify colonial opposition. The first intercolonial Committee of Correspondence was appointed by the Virginia House of Burgesses on Mar. 12, 1773.

1773 A rebellion broke out against the weak **Le Dynasty** (1428–1788) of **Annam** [Vietnam], which was really controlled by the **Nguyen Dynasty** (1558–1776) of Hue [Húe] in the south and by the **Trinh Dynasty** (1539–1787) of Tonkin in the north. Annam was divided between these two bitterly opposed ruling families.

1773 May A **Regulating Act** passed by the British Parliament established dual control of Indian affairs by the British East India Company and the British government. A court governed by British law was founded for the trial of **British citizens living in India.** At this time Indians could bring suit against British citizens only in British courts.

1773 Sept. **Emelyan Ivanovich Pugachev** proclaimed himself **Peter III**, czar of Russia, whom many peasants believed to still be alive. He announced the **end of serfdom** and gathered an army of followers discontented with the repressive policies of **Catherine the Great**, and dissidents, composed of Cossacks, Old Believers, Tatars, and runaway serfs. They succeeded in capturing most of the Russian strongholds along the Volga and Ural rivers, north of the Caspian Sea, where they razed many churches and slaughtered all opponents. On Oct. 16 they laid siege to Oldenburg [Chkalov] on the Ural River, and by December the insurgents numbered c.30,000. On

Apr. 3, 1774, Pugachev's army abandoned the siege. His defeat, with c.10,000 of his followers slain or taken prisoner, near Tsaritsyn [Volgograd] on the Volga River on Sept. 3, 1774, marked the decline of the uprising. Pugachev (b. 1742?) was captured about Sept. 25 and executed in Moscow on Jan. 22, 1775. **Pugachev's Rebellion** led to further repression of the serfs.

1773 Dec. 16 In the **Boston Tea Party**, a band of colonists disguised as Indians and led by **Samuel Adams** looted three ships in Boston Harbor, the *Dartmouth, Eleanor,* and *Polly,* carrying tea of the East India Company. These ships had been detained by the Boston governor Thomas Hutchinson (Sept. 9, 1711–June 3, 1780) until they could pay their duty for entering the harbor, even though the tea would not be unloaded.

1774 Mar.–June The **Coercive Acts**, known in the American colonies as the **Intolerable Acts**, were issued by the British Parliament to reassert British royal authority after the Boston Tea Party. The first of these acts was the **Boston Port Bill**, passed on Mar. 31. It closed Boston harbor, effective June 1, until the East India Company could be reimbursed for its loss of tea. The **Massachusetts Government Act** banned public meetings without prior consent of British colonial authorities. The **Administration of Justice Act** provided for transfer of accused British officials to England for trial. The **Quartering Act** required colonists to provide room and board for British soldiers stationed in the colonies and to supply the British troops upon demand.

1774 May 10 **Louis XV** (b. Feb. 15, 1710), king of France (from 1715), died and was succeeded by his grandson Louis, duc de Berry, who was crowned king of France as **Louis XVI**. Louis XVI was the third son of Louis XV's only son. On Aug. 12, 1774, Louis appointed **Anne Robert Jacques Turgot** (May 10, 1727–Mar. 18, 1781), baron de l'Aulne, as comptroller general of finance. Turgot, an economist, attempted without much success to reform the tax system, which exempted many elements of French society. He proposed the abolition of privilege and promoted the right to work for all men. But the nobility and the queen, **Marie Antoinette**, opposed Turgot's reforms, which were stringently applied, and he was dismissed from office on May 12, 1776.

1774 June 22 The **Quebec Act**, one of the Coercive Acts, was passed by the British Parliament in an effort to effect a compromise between British interests in Quebec and its majority French Canadian population. **More rights were granted to French Canadians.** Roman Catholics were allowed to become citizens and hold office, and the legal system was reorganized. The boundaries of Quebec were extended beyond the Ottawa River, south to the Ohio River, and west to the Mississippi River. The Quebec Act was considered by American colonists to infringe on their western territories.

1774 July 21 The **Treaty of Kuchuk Kainarji** [Kaynardzha], in present Bulgaria, was signed by the **Ottoman Empire** and **Russia**, ending the **Russo-Turkish War. Mustafa III** (Jan. 28, 1717–Jan. 21, 1774), the Ottoman sultan (from 1757), who had begun the war to halt Russian encroachment, died before it was ended. Russia was granted the right to intervene in the affairs of the Danubian Principalities of Moldavia [including Bessarabia] and Wallachia, which were governed by Ottoman officials. In 1775 Austria gained Bukovina, part of Moldavia, in a separate agreement. The khanate of Crimea was declared independent, and Russia acquired several ports on the Black Sea. Russia was named protector of the Orthodox Christians living within the Islamic Ottoman Empire.

1774 Sept. 5–Oct. 26 The **First Continental Congress** convened at Carpenter's Hall in Philadelphia with **Peyton Randolph** (1723–Oct. 22, 1775) of Virginia serving as its first president. He presided over representatives from all the colonies except Georgia. **John Dickinson** (Nov. 8, 1732–Feb. 14, 1808) of Pennsylvania drafted a petition to the king that was adopted on Oct. 14. It listed colonial grievances against the crown, stated colonial rights, and urged repeal of the oppressive acts of Parliament. The document made mention of the right to "life, liberty, and property." An **Association of the Colonies** was created to establish rules for non-importation, non-exportation, and non-consumption. It ordered a boycott of British imports, including slaves, to begin Dec. 1, 1774, but it delayed implementing non-exportation until Sept. 11, 1775.

1774 Oct. 10 **Andrew Lewis** (1720–1781), commanding British troops in **Lord Dunmore's War** (1774), defeated the Indian nations under **Chief Cornstalk** in a **battle at Point Pleasant** on the Ohio River, in present West Virginia. The victory sufficiently quelled the Indians to permit the opening of Transylvania after Daniel Boone had blazed the Wilderness Trail there (1775), to keep the western frontier relatively quiet during the first years of the **American Revolution** (1775–1783), and to permit **George Rogers Clark** (Nov. 19, 1752–Feb. 13, 1818) to wrest control (1778–1779) of the west from the British. **John Murray** (1732–1809), earl of Dunmore, was governor of New York (1770), then of Virginia (1771–June 1, 1775). He was said to have incited the Indians to attack the settlers, thus starting Lord Dunmore's War.

1774 Dec. 14 **Fort William and Mary**, at Portsmouth Harbor, New Hampshire, was seized from the British by **John Langdon** (June 26, 1741–Sept. 18, 1819) in a military encounter just prior to the outbreak of the American Revolution. With several hundred men he stole 100 barrels of powder from the fort. There were no casualties.

1775 Indian **slavery was outlawed in the Portuguese colony of Brazil** by **Sebastião José de Carvalho e Mello**, marquês de Pombal, the Portuguese prime minister, who mandated that Indians and whites have the same legal rights.

c.1775 The Muslim **Fulani** of the western **Sudan** completed a 50-year holy war against the pagan **Susu** and **Mande**. The Fulani subsequently founded an imamate in the Futa Jallon [Fouta-Djallon] plateau, West Africa, in present Guinea.

1775 Mar. 23 "I know not what course others may take; but as for me, give me liberty, or give me death!" rang out in a speech by **Patrick Henry** against arbitrary British rule and for the organization of a militia for Virginia. The **Virginia Convention** had convened at St. John's Church, in Richmond.

1775 Apr. 18 **Paul Revere** (Jan. 1, 1735–May 10, 1818) made his **Midnight Ride** to warn the Massachusetts town of Concord, where munitions were stored, of the route a detachment of British soldiers were taking to seize the depot. He was met at Lexington, several miles northwest of Boston, by **William Dawes** (1745–1799), who had ridden from South Boston a few hours earlier, while Revere had left North Boston by canoe across the Charles River to Charlestown. A set of lights, earlier agreed upon and set in the tower of Christ [The Old North] Church, had in the meantime warned patriots in Charlestown that the British were to embark from Boston by water to the mainland, and would march to Concord via Lexington. Revere and Dawes were

joined by **Samuel Prescott** (c.1750–1777), a young Concord doctor, on their ride toward Concord. Revere was captured outside Lexington, Dawes escaped on foot, and Prescott rode on to Concord with news of the Regulars march. With the countryside thus aroused, a major incident was inevitable.

1775 Apr. 19 The **first battle of the American Revolution** occurred when British soldiers at Lexington, Massachusetts, were surprised and shot at by a group of **Minutemen**, the local militia. Eight of the patriots died, and nine were wounded. **Ralph Waldo Emerson** referred to this event as "... **the shot heard round the world**" in a hymn written for a monument at Concord. The British continued to Concord to destroy the arms depot said to be there, and to arrest Samuel Adams and John Hancock (Jan. 12, 1737–Oct. 8, 1793), the patriot leaders. At North Bridge the British were engaged by the Concord militia, which forced them to turn back to Boston. On their return, the British Regulars were repeatedly fired upon by Minutemen collected from around the countryside. The British suffered c.275 casualties, including c.75 dead; the Americans c.90 casualties, with c.50 dead.

1775 May 10 The **British garrison at Fort Ticonderoga** on Lake Champlain, New York, was seized by the **Green Mountain Boys**, under **Benedict Arnold** and **Ethan Allen**. Not a shot was fired, and ammunition, including cannon, lead shot, and musket flints, was taken for the seige of Boston.

1775 May 10 The **Second Continental Congress** (1775–1789) convened at Philadelphia. It founded the Revolutionary army, appointed **George Washington** as commander-in-chief, opened colonial ports, established diplomatic relations with foreign countries, issued the **Declaration of Independence** (1776), formed new territories in the West, established the Confederation (1781–1789) and, in many respects, was the prime force in creating the American nation.

1775 June The **Second Continental Congress** authorized the printing of $2 million in **paper currency**. The value of this continental money was to be redeemed by gold and silver and by the Spanish milled dollar [peso], which was thus thought likely to remain stable. Known as "**Continentals**," these dollars, too often printed, actually became greatly inflated, and the phrase "Not worth a continental!" passed into the American language.

1775 June 15 George Washington was chosen by the Second Continental Congress, at the instigation of John Adams, a Boston patriot, to command the **Continental Army** in the American Revolution. On July 3 Washington arrived at Cambridge, Massachusetts, to take command of the **siege of Boston.**

1775 June 17 The **battle of Bunker Hill,** across the Charles River from Boston, commenced. Colonial militia, commanded by **William Prescott** (1726–1795), successfully defended Breed's Hill, slightly nearer Boston than Bunker Hill, which had been fortified by **Israel Putnam** (Jan. 7, 1718–May 19, 1790), a Continental general. The colonial militiamen repulsed two British assaults. Short of ammunition, Prescott was said to have ordered, "Don't fire until you see the whites of their eyes." With the third assault by the Redcoats, the militia retreated toward Bunker Hill and Charlestown Neck, the narrow road to safety on the mainland, but the tired British did not pursue immediately. Soon the British renewed the attack, driving the last militiamen from Bunker Hill. But the retreating Americans stopped to fortify Winter Hill, which blocked further pursuit by the Redcoats and contained them on the Charlestown peninsula. The British casualties were 266 killed and 828 wounded; the American casualties were c.450.

1775 Oct. 10 Thomas Gage, commander of British troops in North America, and governor of Massachusetts, resigned his office and left for England, having failed to dislodge the Continental militia from its positions around Boston. Gage was the **last royal governor of Massachusetts.** He was replaced by **William Howe** (Aug. 10, 1729–July 12, 1814), who was appointed commander-in-chief (to 1778) of the British army in the American colonies. **Guy Carleton** (Sept. 23, 1724–Nov. 10, 1808) was appointed commander of British forces in Canada (to 1777).

1775 Nov. 13 Montreal, where Ethan Allen had been captured on Sept. 25, fell to colonial troops under **Richard Montgomery** in the **American Revolution.** Colonial forces held Montreal until June 17, 1776. Montgomery joined with **Benedict Arnold** in an attack on Quebec on Dec. 30. Guy Carleton, the British commander, escaped, it was said, disguised as a fisherman. Montgomery (b. Dec. 2, 1738), was killed in battle on Dec. 31, and Arnold, failing to take Quebec, retreated May 7, 1776, chased by Carleton.

1776 The **viceroyalty of Río de la Plata** [viceroyalty of Buenos Aires] was organized by Spain with its capital at **Buenos Aires.** The viceroyalty included most of present Argentina, Bolivia, Paraguay, and Uruguay, which was called *Banda Oriental* by the Spanish. The audiencia of Charcas [Upper Peru, Chuquisaca], formed (1559) of areas in present Chile and Peru, in addition to Bolivia, Argentina, and Paraguay, was now joined to the viceroyalty of Río de la Plata.

1776 The **Boers,** trekking eastward from the Cape Colony, began to encounter the Xhosa branch of the **Bantu tribes** along the Great Fish River. A series of the so-called **Kaffir Wars** (1779–1878) began in 1779 as the Xhosa, like the Boers, were pastoralists and owned great herds of cattle that required large amounts of land to sustain.

1776 Serving in the **American Revolution** (1775–1783) were c.5,000 blacks, both free and slave. The colonial population of c.2.5 million included c.700,000 blacks.

1776 Jan. 1 The **British fleet** of **John Murray,** earl of Dunmore, governor of Virginia, **bombarded Norfolk,** Virginia, the chief port at the mouth of Chesapeake Bay. The governor had been driven to his ship by colonial militia on June 1, 1775. Later in 1776 colonial forces completed the destruction of Norfolk to prevent its use as a headquarters by the British.

1776 Jan. 10 Thomas Paine (Jan. 29, 1737–June 8, 1809) issued his political pamphlet *Common Sense,* advocating independence. Encouraged by Benjamin Rush (1745–Apr. 19, 1813), the leading young doctor in Philadelphia, Paine wrote passionately about the evils of kingship and the necessity for securing the natural rights due to free men. It was a radical tract that struck a deep sympathy in most patriots and, reportedly, was read by at least half of all Americans within months after publication.

1776 Feb. 27 At the **battle of Moore's Creek Bridge** near Wilmington, North Carolina, a large force of loyalists led by Donald Macdonald, a British officer, and raised by Josiah Martin (1737–1786), the royal governor of North Carolina, were met by James Moore (1737–1777), a patriot officer, and his militia regiment and diverted northward, where he was defeated at the bridge by militia regiments under Richard Caswell (1729–1789) and Alexander Lillington of North Carolina. Macdonald was captured by Caswell.

1776 Mar. 3 Almost the entire **Continental Navy**, established (Dec. 22, 1775) by the Continental Congress, won its **first victory in the American Revolution** under **Esek Hopkins** (Apr. 26, 1718–Feb. 26, 1802), the navy's first commodore, commanding the *Alfred*, the *Columbus*, the *Andrea Doria*, the *Cabot*, the *Providence*, the *Hornet*, the *Fly*, and the *Wasp*, by capturing New Providence Island in the Bahamas, which was held for the two weeks necessary to load the booty into the ships. Hopkins was dismissed (1777) for disobeying orders although, as it turned out, his was the only victory for the Continental Navy in the entire Revolution.

1776 Mar. 17 Boston was **evacuated** by **William Howe**, commander-in-chief of British troops in the American colonies. By tacit agreement Washington let the British troops and loyalist civilians leave unmolested in exchange for Howe's decision not to burn the city. Howe and c.7,500 soldiers, half of the British army in the American colonies, sailed for **Halifax**, Nova Scotia, where Boston loyalists were disembarked and fresh supplies taken aboard ship. Washington and his army marched to **New York City**.

1776 June 10 A committee was appointed by the **Continental Congress** to draft a formal **declaration of independence from Great Britain**. The five committee members were **John Adams, Benjamin Franklin, Roger Sherman** (Apr. 19, 1721–July 23, 1793), **Robert R. Livingston** (Nov. 27, 1746–Feb. 26, 1813), and chairman **Thomas Jefferson**.

1776 June 28 Charlestown [now Charleston], South Carolina, was **attacked by a British fleet** commanded by **Peter Parker** (1721–1811) and an army led by **Henry Clinton**, the overall British commander in the South. Congress had appointed **Charles Lee** (1731–1782) as commander of the American forces there. Lee did not reach Charlestown until June 4; he tried to rearrange defensive positions, especially by ordering **William Moultrie** (Dec. 4, 1730–Sept. 27, 1805), a South Carolina militia commander, who had built a fort on Sullivan Island, to abandon his position. Lee managed to withdraw some troops and gunpowder from the fort. Clinton landed c.2,500 soldiers and seamen on an island near the fort and then found the men could not cross over the water as he had hoped. Moultrie's fort [later renamed **Fort Moultrie**, in honor of its gallant commander] withstood bombardment by eight warships while doing tremendous damage to the British ships and personnel.

1776 July 1 The **Second Continental Congress**, sitting in **Philadelphia**, began debate on the motion that the colonies by right ought to be free and independent. Most of the colonies favored it; but South Carolina remained reluctant; New York had not instructed its delegates to vote for independence, and Delaware's delegation was evenly split on the issue. **Caesar Rodney** (Oct. 7, 1728–June 26, 1784), of Delaware, ill with cancer, rode 90 miles to the convention to cast his vote in favor of independence. South Carolina fell into line, and on July 2 the first clause of the **Declaration of Independence**, which actually proclaimed independence, was adopted unanimously by the Continental Congress; only New York abstained.

1776 July 2 The **first granting of female suffrage in the present U.S.** was made by the colony of New Jersey, which repealed the legislation in 1807.

1776 July 4 The **Declaration of Independence**, drafted by **Thomas Jefferson** and amended chiefly by **John Adams** and **Benjamin Franklin**, was adopted by the Second Continental Congress, except for the abstaining vote cast by delegates from New York, who were not given permission by the state assembly until July 19 to vote for independence. On July 5 **John Hancock**, president of the Continental Congress, was the first to sign the Declaration of Independence when he signed the draft copies circulated to the colonial assemblies for their approval. Formal signing of the Declaration took place on Aug. 2.

1776 July 6 The **Declaration of Independence** was first published in the *Pennsylvania Evening Post* with the title *A Declaration by the Representatives of the United States of America*, in General Congress Assembled. On July 8, **John Nixon** (1733–Dec. 31, 1808), commander of the Philadelphia guard, read the document aloud to a cheering populace in Philadelphia. On July 9 it was read to the Continental Army in New York City.

1776 Aug. 27 Continental forces under **Israel Putnam** were defeated and driven back to Brooklyn Heights by British troops under **Henry Clinton** in a **battle fought in Gravesend and Flatbush**, in present Brooklyn, a borough of New York City. The British, who had arrived from Halifax during July, occupied Staten Island, where they were reinforced by troops under Clinton. In addition, **New York Harbor was controlled by the British fleet. William Howe**, the

British commander-in-chief, had c.32,000 men, among them c.8,000 German mercenaries, who soon came to be called **Hessians** by Americans. About 15,000 Redcoats and Hessians, commanded by Clinton, had landed (Aug. 22) at Gravesend Bay, on the southwestern shore of Brooklyn, to confront the Continental Army of c.9,000 men. After their defeat Putnam and his troops withdrew from Brooklyn on the night of Aug. 29, under cover of rain and fog, across the East River to Manhattan Island, where they secured themselves at Harlem Heights, on the island's northern end.

1776 Sept. 9 The term **"United States"** was adopted by the Continental Congress to be used instead of the "United Colonies."

1776 Sept. 15 After **bombarding the lines of the Americans at Kip's Bay** on the southeastern shore of **Manhattan Island** with the guns of four frigates in the East River, **William Howe**, the British commander, landed his troops and drove the defenders away. Israel Putnam and his troops escaped northward along a route up western Manhattan Island, leaving much cannon and equipment behind. On Sept. 16 the American army was safely behind lines at Harlem. **Thomas Knowlton** with c.150 rangers, on a scouting mission, encountered British troops and opened fire on them. When **Washington** sent reinforcements, they drove the British back in a near rout until he called off the attack. The British had lost c.100 men, and the Americans regained confidence lost at Kip's Bay.

1776 Sept. 22 **Nathan Hale** (b. June 6, 1755) was hanged at Artillery Park in New York City by the British as a spy during the American Revolution. A Connecticut officer, Captain Hale had volunteered to infiltrate British positions on Long Island. He was known for the remark: **"I only regret that I have but one life to lose for my country."**

1776 Oct. 12 **William Howe**, the British commander, began to move his troops on frigates to Throgs Neck, in the present Bronx, New York City, to try to flank Washington's lines on Manhattan Island to the south. When he arrived at Throgs Neck he found it too well-defended and difficult to cross. He moved the troops farther north to Pell's Point (Oct. 18). **John Glover** (1732–1797), with only c.750 men, moved against Howe in Mamaroneck, in present Westchester County, in delaying actions, causing c.200 British casualties while losing only 8 dead

and 13 wounded. However, **Washington** was forced to abandon his position on Harlem Heights and retreat northward into Westchester, where he established his headquarters at White Plains, upon which the British were now advancing.

1776 Oct. 18 **Thaddeus** [Tadeusz] **Kosciusko** [Andrzej Bonawentura Kósciuszko] (Feb. 4, 1746–Oct. 15, 1817), a Polish military commander, was appointed colonel of engineers in the Continental Army during the American Revolution (1775–1783). He was put in charge of building and maintaining fortifications at **West Point**, the key defense point along the Hudson River.

1776 Oct. 28 The **Continental Army was defeated by British troops in a battle at White Plains**, c.20 miles north of New York City. On Nov. 1 the troops under **George Washington** were forced to retreat northward to nearby North Castle, which Howe did not attack. Instead, he struck at the two strategic forts guarding the lower Hudson River, and thus the approach to West Point, farther up the Hudson. Howe took (Nov. 16) Fort Washington on the northern end of Manhattan Island and he captured (Nov. 20) Fort Lee, across the Hudson, in New Jersey. Washington led his men slowly across the Hudson at Peekskill, New York, then south, through New Jersey, and across the Delaware River at New Brunswick, New Jersey, into Pennsylvania on Dec. 11. Howe retired to New York City, after placing a garrison at Trenton and other sites in New Jersey. Washington and his army camped west of the Delaware River.

1776 Dec. 25 **George Washington** and the Continental army, decimated by cold and defections, crossed the Delaware River to launch (Dec. 26) a **dawn attack at Trenton**, New Jersey, held mainly by Hessian mercenaries. The **Hessians** were completely overwhelmed by the Continentals, whose victory there and subsequently (Jan. 3, 1777) at Princeton proved to the overly confident British that the American army could inflict damage on the more disciplined troops of Europe. Washington retired across the Delaware River, but returned (Dec. 30–31) to occupy Trenton.

1777 Jan. 3 In a surprise **attack at Princeton**, New Jersey, the American army under George Washington defeated part of the British army under **Charles Cornwallis** (Dec. 31, 1739–Oct. 5, 1805). Cornwallis had set out from New Brunswick for Trenton by way of Princeton to drive the American army out of New Jersey. Arriving at Trenton after dark, Cornwallis decided that the forts south of the town were too strong to attack until morning. Washington stealthily abandoned the forts, circled to the rear of Cornwallis, and was at Stony Brook outside of Princeton before the British knew their trap was empty. After the attack the Americans, loaded with loot, marched 15 miles to Somerset Courthouse, then crossed the Delaware to safety, then recrossed again to Morristown, New Jersey, to spend the winter.

1777 Feb. 24 **Joseph Emanuel** [José Manuel] (b. June 6, 1714), king of Portugal (from 1750), died and was succeeded by his eldest daughter **Maria I** [Maria Francisca] (Dec. 17, 1734–Mar. 20, 1816). Her husband **Pedro III** [Peter] (July 5, 1717–May 25, 1786), brother of **Joseph Emanual**, became king in name only. Maria's mother, **Marianna Victoria**, was the power behind the throne, as both Maria and Pedro exhibited weakness of character.

1777 June 14 The **Second Continental Congress** chose the design of the **Stars and Stripes for the flag of the American states**. On Feb. 14, 1778, the flag received its first international recognition when **La-Motte-Picquet** [Toussaint Guillaume, comte Picquet de La Motte] (1720–1791), a French admiral, fired a salute to the flag flown aboard the *Ranger,* commanded by **John Paul Jones** (July 6, 1747–July 18, 1792), a colonial naval commander, in Quiberon Bay in northwestern France.

1777 July **Vermont**, pressing for recognition as an independent state, adopted a **constitution** in a convention held at Windsor. The constitution provided for complete male suffrage and was the first in the United States to forbid slavery. Earlier Vermont had issued (Jan. 16, 1777) a declaration of independence from both New York on its west and New Hampshire on its east, and chose the name **New Connecticut**, which was changed to Vermont in June. **Thomas Chittenden** (1730–1797) was elected the first governor of Vermont on Mar. 3, 1778.

1777 July 5 British troops under **John Burgoyne** (1722–Aug. 4, 1792), in an **invasion of New York state** through the Champlain Valley, took Fort Ticonderoga, on the southern end of Lake Champlain, and was now poised for a drive on Albany from the north. At nearly the same time (July 25) British forces, which included Tories and Indians as well as Regulars, took Oswego on Lake Ontario in western New York state, to attack Albany from the west.

1777 July 31 **Lafayette** [Marie Joseph Paul Yves Roch Gilbert du Motier, marquis de Lafayette] (Sept. 6, 1757–May 20, 1834), a young French reformer and revolutionary, was commissioned a major general in the Continental Army and assigned to Washington's staff.

1777 Aug. 6 The **battle of Oriskany**, fought on the Mohawk River, near present Utica, New York, brought great losses to the colonial force led by **Nicholas Herkimer** (b. 1728), who died on Aug. 6, but was considered an American victory because it halted the British advance from the west toward Albany. Herkimer was ambushed by a band of Indians and British Regulars.

1777 Aug. 16 **John Burgoyne**, the British commander leading a force south through the Lake Champlain Valley, detached c.500 men to **Bennington** in Vermont to seize food and other supplies from the Americans. Led by **Frederick Baum**, a British officer, the troops suddenly found themselves deserted by their Indian allies and set up a camp about four miles west of Bennington. The Americans, led by **John Stark** (Aug. 28, 1728–May 8, 1822), a Vermont militia general, attacked; the loyalists and remaining Indians fled, and eventually the **Hessians** surrendered. The Americans captured more than 600 prisoners and accounted for 207 casualties. Relief columns hurrying to the aid of Baum were driven back. Burgoyne, with supplies running low, troops exhausted, and Canada too far away, was forced to continue toward Albany, New York, with the remainder of his army.

1777 Aug. 22 The **siege of Fort Schuyler** [Stanwix], in central New York, begun on Aug. 3, was abandoned by the British, who were threatened by the approach of Continental troops under **Benedict Arnold**. The British retreated to Oswego, New York.

1777 Sept. 11 **George Washington** failed to check a **British advance on Philadelphia**, led by William Howe, in a **battle at Brandywine Creek**. Outmaneuvered by a flank attack, Washington fell back in some disarray, and Howe secured Wilmington, Delaware.

1777 Sept. 19 **John Burgoyne**, the British commander, was defeated in a **battle at Freeman's**

Farm, near Saratoga, on his march to Albany, New York. On Oct. 7 Burgoyne was again defeated, in a battle at Bemis Heights, south of Freeman's Farm. Henry Clinton, the British commander, moving north from New York City, had captured Forts Clinton and Montgomery (Oct. 6), near Bear Mountain. His troops cleared away the chain across the Hudson that had stopped the British flotilla from advancing toward Albany, and forced Israel Putnam to abandon Forts Independence and Constitution, near Peekskill, New York. Clinton sent warships as far north as Livingston Manor, north of Kingston, which he burned (Oct. 16). Thinking Clinton had completed his task by clearing the Hudson, Burgoyne fell back to Saratoga, north of Albany.

1777 Sept. 27 The British occupied Philadelphia, capital of the American Colonies. The colonial government left Philadelphia for York, Pennsylvania, which served as the capital from Sept. 30, 1777, to June 27, 1778.

1777 Oct. 4 In a battle at Germantown, outside Philadelphia, George Washington failed to drive the British from their position guarding Philadelphia. The two armies suffered about the same number of casualties, but the British remained comfortably settled in Philadelphia while the Continental Army retired to nearby Valley Forge, where it would spend a harsh winter of deprivation.

1777 Oct. 17 The British under John Burgoyne surrendered at Saratoga, New York, to Horatio Gates (1727?–Apr. 10, 1806), the Continental commander.

1777 Nov. 20 With the British capture of Fort Mercer, the Delaware River all the way to Philadelphia was held by the British. Fort Mifflin, near Philadelphia, had fallen on Nov. 15.

1777 Dec. 30 Maximilian III Joseph (b. 1727), the elector of Bavaria, died. Bavaria then passed to Charles Theodore (1724–1799), elector of the Palatinate, cut in two by Bavaria. At this time the Upper Palatinate was part of Bavaria, lying to the east. The Lower Palatinate, lying along the Rhine River to the west of Bavaria, was at this time independent of Bavaria. Contestants for the Palatine electorate included Joseph II, king of Germany (from 1764), the Holy Roman emperor (from 1765), and co-regent with his mother Maria Theresa of Austria. Frederick the Great announced he would not allow Austria to acquire any land of Bavaria and espoused the claim

of Charles, duke of Zweibrücken. The stage was set for the so-called War of the Bavarian Sucession (1778-1779).

1778–1782 Some of the Roman Catholic disabilities enacted in Ireland after the battle of the Boyne (July 1, 1690) were repealed. Among the leaders of the campaign for Irish rights were Henry Flood (1732–Dec. 2, 1791), who urged formation of an Irish Volunteer Army to oppose France if that country invaded Ireland in its war against Great Britain; and Henry Grattan (July 3, 1746–June 6, 1820), who introduced a Declaration of Rights into the Irish Parliament that led to the partial repeal (Apr. 16, 1782) of Poynings Law.

1778 The West African islands of Annobón and Fernando Po [Macias Nguema Biyogo], in present Equatorial Guinea, were ceded by Portugal to Spain.

1778 Feb. 6 France signed a treaty of alliance with the American states, approved by the Continental Congress on May 4. France recognized the independence of the "United States of America" and promised further aid in the American Revolution. Benjamin Franklin and Silas Deane (Dec. 24, 1737–Sept. 23, 1789) had departed for France in Mar. 1776 to negotiate the treaty.

1778 May 11 William Pitt the Elder (b. Nov. 15, 1708), earl of Chatham, died. He served as the prime minister (1766–1768) of Great Britain. From 1756 he had been the virtual prime minister in his capacity as both the secretary of state and an outspoken member of the House of Commons. He supported efforts to win India from the French and opposed taxing the American Colonies.

1778 June 18 The British began to evacuate Philadelphia, fearing that the arrival of French aid would subject them to a siege. William Howe resigned (May 1) his position as chief commander of the British army in North America and was replaced the same day by Henry Clinton.

1778 June 28 In a battle at Monmouth Courthouse [Freehold], New Jersey, Charles Lee, an American general, led the Continental Army against British troops retreating from Philadelphia to New York City. He lost his advantage near the end of the battle by retreating instead of advancing and was later court-martialed for this. George Washington arrived during the battle with reinforcements. The outcome was inconclusive, and casualties were about the same for each side. **Molly MacCauley** [nee Ludwig] (c.1750–1832) gained the name Molly Pitcher in this battle for carrying water to the wounded in the stifling heat. She was said to have taken up her husband's gun after he was mortally wounded. Henry Clinton and the British army reached Sandy Hook, New Jersey, across the Lower New York Bay from New York City, on June 30. George Washington reached White Plains, north of New York City, with his army on July 20, to fortify the Hudson River Valley, especially, West Point, which became a major American stronghold.

1778 July 3 Butler's Rangers, a band of **Iroquois Indians** and loyalists led by the Mohawk Indian **Joseph Brant** [Thayendanegea] (1742–Nov. 24, 1807) and the American loyalist **John Butler** (1728–1794) massacred and scalped the citizens and burned the houses at Wyoming Valley, near present Wilkes-Barre in Pennsylvania, in what became known as the **Wyoming Massacre**. Cherry Valley, west of Albany, New York, was ravaged in a similar manner by Brant on Nov. 11.

1778 July 3 Frederick the Great, king of Prussia, declared war on Austria on behalf of Charles, duke of Zweibrücken, second in line to **Charles Theodore**, elector of the Palatinate, initiating the **War of the Bavarian Succession** (1778–1779). It was sometimes also called the **Potato War** [Kartoffelkrieg], because when opposing troops met in Bohemia, they concentrated on cutting off supply lines rather than on fighting.

1778 July 4 On the western frontier in what later became **Indiana Territory**, Kaskaskia, the chief fortification, near the Mississippi River in present Illinois, fell to **George Rogers Clark**. The area was claimed by Virginia, which had commissioned Clark to drive out the British during the American Revolution.

1778 Aug. 11 The **French fleet** commanded by **Jean Baptiste Charles Henry Hector d'Estaing** (Nov. 24, 1729–Apr. 28, 1794) **failed to aid the American siege at Newport**, Rhode Island, the port held by the British since Dec. 1776. The Continental Army under **John Sullivan** had launched (Aug. 5) a land assault, but it had to abandon (Aug. 30) the effort.

1778 Sept. 4 The **Netherlands** [Holland] **signed a treaty of friendship with the American states**, trad-

ing freely with American ports and providing safe harbor for American ships, but as a neutral.

1778 Sept. 25 Benjamin Lincoln (Jan. 24, 1733–Sept., 1810) was placed in charge of the southern Continental army, succeeding **Robert Howe** (1732–Dec. 14, 1786).

1778 Dec. 29 Savannah, Georgia, commanded ineptly by Benjamin Lincoln, **fell to the British** under **Archibald Campbell** (Aug. 21, 1739–Mar. 31, 1791). The loss of Savannah opened the way for the British to move into the southern states. Troops lost in the capture and military supplies had to be replaced. The guerrillas performed heroically in slowing down the British, but lacked supplies and manpower that Lincoln could have saved by leaving the fort with his men, supplies, and equipment.

1779 Muhammad Karim Khan Zand (b. 1699?), the Persian shah (from 1757) and founder of the **Zand Dynasty** (1757–1794), died. Agha Mohammed Khan, a court eunuch, gathered (c.1779) a force of his native Kajar tribe, from northeastern Persia, and succeeded (1794) in establishing there the **Kajar** [Qajar] **Dynasty** (to 1925).

1779 Feb. 14 Andrew Pickens (1739–1817), leading a patriot militia, defeated loyalist forces at Kettle Creek, near Augusta, Georgia. Later, a patriot militia under **John Ashe** (1720?–1781) was defeated in a **battle at Briar Creek** (Mar. 3), near Savannah.

1779 Feb. 25 Vincennes, a strategic post in what later became the Indiana Territory, fell to patriot forces led by **George Rogers Clark**.

1779 May Benedict Arnold, in command of American forces in Philadelphia since June 1778, made an offer to British headquarters in New York City to act on their behalf, although he did not specifically mention spying. In April Arnold had married a loyalist, **Margaret Shippen** (1760–1804). The British response indicated a preference that Arnold remain in American service. **John André**, a British officer who knew Mrs. Arnold, acted as go-between. When the British failed to make exact a definite financial offer, Arnold in October gave up the scheme. In December **Arnold was reprimanded by George Washington** for military irregularities, for the most part involving financial schemes.

1779 June 20 Benjamin Lincoln and his American forces were defeated in a **battle at Stony Creek** near Charlestown [now Charleston] South Carolina, by British troops under the command of **Augustine Prevost**. Though Moultrie and Lincoln had been driven from Georgia, their strong defense of Charlestown forced Prevost to abandon plans to take South Carolina.

1779 July 15 **Stony Point**, on the Hudson River, was recaptured from the British by **Anthony** ["Mad Anthony"] **Wayne** (Jan. 1, 1745–Dec. 15, 1796). Stony Point was a major American fort, and Washington was determined to hold it at all costs. Anthony's victory relieved British pressure on West Point and the Hudson River Valley.

1779 Aug. 29 **Butler's Rangers**, the combined Indian and loyalist band, was routed at Newtown, near Elmira, New York, by **John Sullivan**. The defeat brought an end to the Rangers' raids on the western frontier and seriously weakened the **Six Nations of Iroquois tribes**.

1779 July 25 In the **Penobscot Expedition**, British-occupied Bagaduce [present Castine], Maine, near Bangor, was attacked by an American force supplied with three ships of the Continental navy. Massachusetts, Maine, and New Hampshire furnished c.2,000 militia, 19 armed vessels, and 20 frigates. The militia was commanded by **Solomon Lovell** with **Peleg Wadsworth** (1748–1829) second, and **Paul Revere** third. The fleet was under the command of **Dudley Saltonstall**. Saltonstall refused to bring his ships close to the fort as they might be damaged or destroyed. British naval reinforcements arrived (Aug. 13), and the American forces fled up the river and destroyed the ships to prevent their capture.

1779 Sept. 13 **D'Estaing**, the French admiral, and his fleet **landed 3,000 French soldiers at Beaulieu** near Savannah, Georgia, which were joined (Sept. 15) by Pulaski and his legion and the following day by Benjamin Lincoln and his troops. **Prevost**, the British general at Savannah, was asked to surrender. He requested 24 hours in which to arrange his terms, but used the time to call in all troops from outlying areas and then told d'Estaing that he would fight to the last man. A siege commenced with d'Estaing urging an assault as quickly as possible, because he feared entrapment by a British fleet rumored to be in the West Indies. The allies were beaten off (Oct. 9) with severe losses, including **Count Casimir Pulaski** [Kazimierz Pulaski] (b. Mar. 4, 1747), who was wounded, and died on Oct. 11. Pulaski had distinguished himself in the American Revolution.

1779 Sept. 23 **John Paul Jones** (July 6, 1747–July 18, 1792), a Scottish sea captain who had accepted a U.S. naval command, while sailing for France aboard the **Bon Homme Richard**, carrying 137 French soldiers as marines, encountered the British ship **Serapis** in the North Sea, near Scarborough, England. **"I have not yet begun to fight!"** Jones warned the British commander. In a night battle lasting less than four hours, with firing at point-blank range, the **Bon Homme Richard** was sunk and the **Serapis** set fire. The British surrendered and Jones boarded the **Serapis**, put out the fire, and sailed it and his captives to Texel, the Netherlands, a neutral country. In Texel the **Serapis** was rebuilt while British ships waited offshore insisting that the Dutch turn the "pirates" over to them. Jones escaped.

V. ECONOMY AND TRADE

1771 The **Regulator insurrection**, under the leadership of **Harmon Husband** (1724–1795), erupted in back-country North Carolina against excessive taxes, which were imposed by the slave-holding estate owners of the tidewater region. The Regulators, chiefly Scotch-Irish frontiersmen holding small parcels of land in western North and South Carolina, wanted to reform unjust tax laws, alleviate the conditions of slaves, and bring law and order to the neglected frontier region. The revolt, which consisted mostly of refusing to pay taxes and to let courts sit, was brutally put down by colonial troops led by the royal governor, notably at the pitched **battle of Alamance Creek**, near Hillsboro, May 16, 1771.

c.1775 The **first building society** was founded in Birmingham, England. By paying a regular fee to the society, members could secure money for constructing houses.

1776 *Inquiry into the Nature and Causes of the Wealth of Nations* was published by **Adam Smith** (June 5?, 1723–July 17, 1790), a Scottish economist and moral philosopher. Smith argued that a nation's wealth resided in its labor force, which grew as a country's capital grew, and that the way to increase a nation's wealth was to make labor more productive instead of restricting trade or industry, as was commonly practiced by the mercantilists dominant at this time in European nations. Smith believed that enlightened self-interest motivated the accumulation of capital and that therefore self-interest was good for all.

1776 Jan. The **Second Continental Congress** (1775–1789) passed a resolution declaring that anyone who "shall be so lost to all virtue and regard for his country" as to refuse payment for goods in Continental paper currency should be "treated as an enemy in this country."

1776 Apr. The **Second Continental Congress** voted to **halt the importation of slaves by the American states.** Some delegates from the South and New England had protested a proposal by **Thomas Jefferson** to abolish slavery. **Rhode Island**, which had early called for political and religious freedom for all its citizens, was the **first of the colonies to prohibit (1774) slave importation.**

1779 Nov. The **Second Continental Congress** had by this time issued a total of $241,600,000 in **paper currency** called "Continentals." The states had issued another $209,500,000, but these efforts failed to offset depreciation as the paper money was not backed by gold or silver. One silver dollar cost 40 paper dollars. Shoes in Virginia cost $5,000 at one point. By 1780 the Continental currency was worthless and it was retired.

VI. RELIGION AND PHILOSOPHY

1770 At a conference of Methodists, **John Wesley** took a strongly Arminian position. In this controversy he split with **George Whitefield** and **Selina Hastings** (1707–1791), countess of Huntingdon, whose "Calvinistic Methodists" otherwise ran on a parallel course. Wesley's position marked his final break with orthodox Calvinism. Thereafter, Wesleyan **Methodism** retained its Arminian character.

1772–1795 As a result of the **three Partitions of Poland**, a large Jewish population came under Russian control for the first time. **Jews**, and Christians who were not of the Eastern Orthodox Church, soon found they were **persecuted by Russian authorities.**

1772 Mar. 29 **Emanuel Swedenborg** [Svedberg] (b. Jan. 29, 1688), a Swedish theologian and scientist, died. Swedenborg wrote *Arcana Coelestia* (1756), *Heaven and Hell* (1758), *Divine Love and Wisdom* (1763), *True Christian Religion* (1771), and *Apoca-*

lypse Revealed (1785–1789). After Swedenborg's death, his followers founded (1784) the New Jerusalem Church.

1773 July 21 The **Jesuit order was dissolved** by **Pope Clement XIV** (Oct. 31, 1705–Sept. 22, 1774; ruled from 1769), under pressure from the Bourbon courts of France and Spain. This action was a sign of the papacy's domination by secular rulers.

1774 **Gotthold Ephraim Lessing**, a German critic and advocate of religious tolerance, began publishing the *Wolfenbüttel Fragments* of the Hamburg Deist, **Hermann Samuel Reimarus** (Dec. 22, 1694–Mar. 1, 1768). Reimarus for the first time applied to the life of Jesus Christ the methods of secular history.

1774 Aug. 6 The **Shaker sect**, or The United Society of the Believers in Christ's Second Coming [Millennial Church], was introduced to the American colonies when **Ann Lee** arrived from England, where she had recently begun to preach the dual nature of God as both male and female. "Mother" Ann represented the incarnation of the female principle, as Jesus Christ was the incarnation of the male principle. She founded the Shaker settlement at New Lebanon, New York, which was the principal location of the Shakers.

1776 Aug. 25 **David Hume** (b. May 7, 1711), a Scottish philosopher, died. Hume's concepts became important philosophic underpinnings of modern scientific method. His works included the three-volume *A Treatise of Human Nature* (1739–1740), of which book one was revised in *An Enquiry Concerning Human Understanding* (1748); *An Enquiry Concerning the Principles of Morals* (1751), a revision of book three of *A Treatise; Political Discourses* (1752); *The Natural History of Religion* (1755); and *Dialogues Concerning Natural Religion* (1779).

VII. SCIENCE, EDUCATION, AND TECHNOLOGY

1772 The 28-volume *Encyclopédie, ou Dictionnaire raisonné des Sciences, des Arts et des Métiers*, edited by **Jean le Rond d'Alembert** and **Denis Diderot**, was completed (first volume published 1751). The work included among its authors such figures as Voltaire, Montesquieu, Anne Robert Jacques Turgot, and Jean Jacques Rousseau. Its contributors, usually specialists in their fields, discarded authority and tradition in order to promote progress. This revolutionary attitude influenced late-18th-century social and political thought in France and elsewhere.

1773 John Harrison (1693–Mar. 4, 1776), a Yorkshire carpenter, was awarded a prize of £2,000 by the British government for his **chronometer**, a major development for navigational accuracy as well as in clockmaking. It was successfully tested at sea in 1762. On its arrival at Jamaica the chronometer was only five seconds from true time, a deviation that would produce a longitudinal error of only one and one-quarter minutes.

1774 Aug. 1 Oxygen was discovered by **Joseph Priestly** (Mar. 13, 1733–Feb. 6, 1804), an English clergyman and chemist. He burned the calyx [the slag resulting from burning metals at high heat] of mercury to collect the gas emitted over liquid mercury and observed that the gas sped the process of burning: Candles burned clearer and brighter in the gas. **Karl Wilhelm Scheele** (Dec. 9, 1742–May 21, 1786), a Swedish chemist, coincidentally discovered oxygen in about the same way about the same time.

1775 The *American Turtle,* a precursor of today's submarine, was built by **David Bushnell** (1742?–1824) of Connecticut. It was driven by a hand-operated screw propeller. On Sept. 7, 1776, the *Turtle* entered the New York City harbor to mine the *Eagle,* commanded by Richard Howe (Mar. 8, 1726–Aug. 5, 1799), a British admiral. The mine failed to stay attached to the ship's hull, and no damage resulted.

1776 Dec. 5 Phi Beta Kappa, the first American college fraternity, was organized as a social group by five students at **William and Mary College** in Williamsburg, Virginia. In 1831 it became an academic honor society.

1777 Sept. 22 John Bartram (b. Mar. 23, 1699), the first American botanist, died. Self-taught, he became internationally known, exchanging plants with European scientists, notably **Linnaeus.** He established a famous garden, now part of Philadelphia's park system. John Bartram wrote two widely read travel books, *Observations* (1751), about his trips in Pennsylvania and New York, and *Description of East Florida* (1769). His son **William**

(1739–1823) was also a noted botanist and travel writer.

1777 Sept. 25 Johann Heinrich Lambert (b. Aug. 26, 1728), a German physicist, died. Known for his work on the properties of light and in mathematics, he was the first to treat systematically the **trigonometric theory of hyperbolic functions.** In 1768 he demonstrated that π could not be measured.

1777 Dec. 17 Albrecht von Haller (b. Oct. 16, 1708), a Swiss physiologist, died. In his eight-volume *Elementa physiologiae corporis humani* (1757–1766), Haller developed a **theory of muscle contraction** by discovering that under stimulation muscle fibers contracted and with the removal of the stimulation the fibers returned to their original shape. He also noted that the senses were not in the receptors but traveled via nerves to the brain. In 1766 he suggested that the thyroid, thymus, and spleen secreted substances into the blood.

1778 Jan. 10 Carolus Linnaeus [Carl von Linné] (b. May 23, 1707), a Swedish botanist and physician, died. He established the binomial system of nomenclature used in modern plant and animal taxonomy. *System naturae* (1735) provided a system for identifying flowering plants based on anatomical similarities—particularly in the reproductive system. *Genera plantarum* (1737) and *Species plantarum* (1753) provided a complete list of plant names. The tenth edition of *Systema naturae* (1758) gave binomial nomenclature for the animal kingdom. Linnaeus also classified minerals and diseases.

1778 July 2 Jean Jacques Rousseau (b. June 28, 1712), a Swiss-born French romantic writer, died. He wrote **Le Contrat Social** [*The Social Contract*] (1762) and *Émile, ou Traité de l'Éducation* (1762). These contained far-reaching proposals for the improvement of society that had great impact on European intellectual life. His books were burned, but *Émile* has since formed a basis for some contemporary concepts about education. *Julie: Ou La Nouvelle Héloïse* [*Julie, or the New Heloise*] (1760) was a novel and *Confessions* (1781–1788) was autobiographical.

1779 The **first cast-iron bridge** was completed by **Thomas Farnolls Pritchard.** Spanning the Severn River at Coalbrookdale in western England, it carried a road still in use.

1779 Samuel Crompton (Dec. 3, 1753–June 26, 1827), an English inventor, greatly improved spinning efficiency with his "mule," which capitalized on the combined improvements of the waterframe (1770) and the spinning jenny (c.1765).

1779 Jan Ingenhousz (Dec. 8, 1730–Sept. 7, 1799), a Dutch physician, published *Experiments upon Vegetables, Discovering Their Great Power of Purifying the Common Air in the Sunshine and of Injuring it in the Shade.* In this work Ingenhousz was the first to describe the process of photosynthesis.

VIII. ARTS AND LEISURE

c.1770–1795 Men's clothes were much as they are today. Pantaloons replaced breeches; coats were often double breasted. Riding boots replaced silk stockings and shoes. Women wore their hair in loose curls rather than in the extravagant coiffures seen earlier.

1770 The Spode ceramics factory was founded in Stoke-on-Trent in the Potteries district [present Stoke-on-Trent] of Staffordshire, England, by Josiah Spode (1733–1797). He developed a more durable bone china that is still produced at the factory.

1770 May 30 François Boucher (b. Sept. 29, 1703), a French rococo painter, died. Madame de Pompadour, his patroness, commissioned many of his works. His output, which included tapestry designs, stage scenery, and interior decorations, especially boudoirs, was large. He painted portraits, nudes, and pastoral scenes. Boucher's best paintings included *Diana Resting after the Bath* (1742), *Birth and Triumph of Venus* (1740), and several portraits, including a number of Madame de Pompadour.

1771 July 30 Thomas Gray (b. Dec. 26, 1716), an English poet, died. His best-known work was *Elegy Written in a Country Churchyard* (1751), to the present a favorite of students and their teachers. His other works included *Ode on a Distant Prospect of Eton College* (1742), *Progress of Poesy* (1758), and *The Bard* (1758).

1771 Sept. 17 Tobias Smollett (b. Mar., 1721), a Scottish-born English novelist, died. He was known particularly for *The Expedition of Humphrey Clinker* (1771). His other works included *The Adventures of Roderick Random* (1748), *The Adventures of Peregrine Pickle* (1751), *The Adventures of an Atom* (1769), and *Ferdinand Count Fathom* (1753).

1773 Phillis [Phyllis] Wheatley (1753?–Dec. 5, 1784), the first black poet in the New World, published in London, *Poems on Various Subjects, Religious and Moral.* Born in Africa she was sold (1761) to John Wheatley of Boston, who encouraged her writing and helped her gain freedom.

c.1774–1792 The Louis XVI style of decoration, sometimes called classicism, was marked by a return to straight lines and angles, from the fancy curves and gilding of the rococo period. The secretaire, made popular by Marie Antoinette, was a small writing desk with a rectangular shape.

1774 *Die Lieden des Jungen Werthers* [*The Sorrows of Young Werther*] by Johann Wolfgang von Goethe, a German poet, initiated the Sturm und Drang [Storm and Stress] school of German literature. *Werther* was a love story inspired by Goethe's affair with Charlotte Buff (1753–1828), and perhaps others as well. It appealed especially to a discontented longing among young people throughout Europe.

1774 John Singleton Copley (July 3, 1738–Sept. 9, 1815), an American portrait painter, left the American colonies for London, where he was received with critical acclaim. A native of Boston, Copley had painted portraits of many of the American patriots, including Samuel Adams and John Hancock (1772).

1774 Apr. 4 Oliver Goldsmith (b. Nov. 10, 1730?), an Irish-born English writer, died. His comedy *She Stoops to Conquer; or, The Mistakes of a Night* was produced (1773) at the Convent Garden Theater in London the year before he died. Goldsmith's other works included *Enquiry into the Present State of Polite Learning in Europe* (1759); *The Citizen of the World* (1762), a series of essays known earlier as *Chinese Letters* and his first successful work; the classic novel *The Vicar of Wakefield* (1766); the poem *The Deserted Village* (1770); and *A History of England* (1771).

1775 Feb. 23 *Le Barbier de Séville* [*The Barber of Seville*] by **Pierre-Augustin Caron** [Pierre de Beaumarchais] (Jan. 24, 1732–May 18, 1799), a French clockmaker and playwright, was first produced.

1777 *The School for Scandal*, a comedy of manners by **Richard Brinsley Sheridan** (Oct. 30, 1751–July 7, 1816), was produced at the **Drury Lane Theatre** in London, where Sheridan had become manager in 1776. Sheridan's other plays included *The Rivals* (1775) and *The Critic* (1779).

1778 The **La Scala Opera House** in Milan, Italy, was completed. It was designed by Giuseppe Piermarini (1734–1808), an Italian architect.

1778 May 30 **Voltaire** (Jean François Marie Arouet] (b. 1694), a French writer, philosopher, and poet, died. Voltaire's satire, directed against religious intolerance and political and economic injustice, had made him famous. He wrote articles for the Diderot *Encyclopedie* (1772) and carried on a correspondence (more than 12,000 letters) with nearly all the leading men of science and letters in Europe. Among his correspondents was Frederick the Great, at whose Prussian court Voltaire for a time resided. And it was **Madame de Pompadour** who was his first notable patroness, helping to get him elected to the Académie. His best-known work came to be *Candide, ou L'Optimisme* (1759), a satire on the foolish and eternal optimist. Voltaire wrote the tragedies *Brutus* (1730), *Mahomet* (1741), and *Mérope* (1743); and the poem *Discours sur l'Homme* (1738).

1779 Jan. 20 **David Garrick** (b. Feb. 19, 1717), considered one of England's greatest actors, died. Garrick made his debut at Ipswich (1741) in *Oroonoko, or the Royal Slave* (1696) by the Irish dramatist **Thomas Southerne** (1660–May 26, 1746); his success brought him to London in the same year as Richard III in Shakespeare's play. He appeared in 18 different roles during a six-months period, bringing him recognition as one of the best actors of the day.

1779 Feb. 7 **William Boyce** (b. 1711), an English composer, died. During his lifetime, Boyce was, next to George Frederick Handel, the most important English composer. He composed symphonies, vocal music, and incidental music for the stage.

His three-volume *Cathedral Music* (1778), was a compilation of two centuries of English church music.

1779 Dec. 6 **Jean Baptiste Siméon Chardin** (b. Nov. 2, 1699), a French still-life painter, died. Chardin was the greatest painter of still-lifes of the 18th century. His works included *La Toilette du Matin*, *Le Jeune Violiniste*, and *Le Bénédicité* (c.1740).

IX. SPORTS, GAMES, AND SOCIETY

1770 The **first modern circus ring** was devised by **Philip Astley** (1742–1814), an English trick rider who used an amphitheater for his stunts.

1774 At the instigation of **John Howard** (Sept. 2, 1726–Jan. 20, 1790), a propertied gentleman, philanthropist, and high sheriff of Bedfordshire, England, Parliament passed the first national act regulating prison operations and abolishing discharge fees. A second act was aimed at the health of prisoners. Howard broadened his investigations and became **"the father of prison reform"** in western Europe.

1775 The **first recorded rowing regatta** was conducted on the Thames River as a pastime and competitive sport.

1776 The **first coursing organization**, the **Swaffham Coursing Club**, was formed in Norfolk, England, by Lord Orford and his sporting friends. Their coursing—the pursuit of running game with dogs that follow by sight instead of scent—was done at the Norfolk village of Swaffham, which gave its name to the club.

1776 Sept. The **St. Leger race for three-year-olds** was initiated by **Arthur St. Leger**, an English horse breeder, at the Doncaster racetrack in Yorkshire. It was a one-heat, two-mile race and was named the "St. Leger" in 1778. The St. Leger was the oldest of the stake races for three-year-old thoroughbreds known among British racing fans as "the Classics," now five in number.

1777 June The **cricket club of Hambledon**, a small village in Hampshire, England, whose team possessed nearly mythical talents, routed a representative "England XI."

1780–1789

I. VITAL STATISTICS AND DEMOGRAPHICS

1788 Jan. 26   Australia had c.250,000 aborigines on the date of the founding of the British penal colony at **Sydney**. The total number of **convicts deported** (1788–1839) **to Australia** was estimated at 160,000.

II. DISASTERS

1780 Oct. 3–18   Three severe hurricanes ravaged the **West Indies**. The first, on Oct. 3, destroyed the port of Savannah-la-Mar, on the southwestern coast of Jamaica. The second, called the "Great Hurricane," started near Barbados on Oct. 10, wrecking a British fleet anchored at St. Lucia, to the west. At Martinique, more than 40 French transports were sunk, with a loss of c.4,200 men. The Great Hurricane also ravaged Antigua, Dominica, Tobago, Grenada, St. Vincent, and Santo Domingo before it ended on Oct. 18. On Oct. 16 and 17, the Great Hurricane was accompanied by **Solano's Storm**, a hurricane that struck Cuba and crippled the Spanish fleet as it sailed through the Gulf of Mexico from Havana to attack Pensacola, Florida.

1783 Feb. 4   An earthquake struck southern **Italy** and Sicily. From c.60,000 to c.100,000 persons died, including c.30,000 in Calabria, the southern tip of Italy.

1783 June 8   The greatest volume of liquid lava released in recorded history came from **Iceland's Laki Volcano**, or Fissure, after it was opened by a week of earthquakes. The 14-mile-long opening, just off Iceland's great snowfield, the **Vatnajökull**, poured 2.8 cubic miles of lava into central southern Iceland before volcanic activity ceased months later. The dust, ash, and gases scorched the land, destroying livestock and causing c.10,000 deaths from starvation.

1788   Spanish New Orleans, characterized by French and Spanish architecture, was largely destroyed by **fire**.

III. EXPLORATION AND COLONIZATION

1784 Aug. 14   The first permanent settlement in Alaska was established on **Kodiak Island**, in the Gulf of Alaska, by **Grigori Ivanovich Shelekhov** (1747–1795), a Russian trader.

1786   The Ohio Company of Associates was founded to exploit the development of the Ohio River Valley, earlier attempted (1749) by the Ohio Land Company but interrupted by the **French and Indian War** (1754–1763). Under the leadership of **Manasseh Cutler** (May 13, 1742–July 28, 1823) and **Rufus Putnam** (Apr. 19, 1738–May 14, 1824), the company bought land at the present site of Marietta, on the Ohio River, from the U.S. Congress. **Marietta** became (Apr. 1788) the **first permanent settlement in Ohio**.

1786 Aug. 11   George Town [Pulau Pinang] was founded on Penang Island, in present **Malaysia**, by **Francis Light**, an English trader, after an agreement made with the sultan of Kedah, one of the present Malaysian states. The settlement challenged the Dutch monopoly of the spice trade.

1787   Alexander Mackenzie (1764–Mar. 11, 1820), a Scot, entered the employ of the **Northwest Company** (founded in 1783). He constructed (1788) Fort Chippewyan near the oil-rich lands of Lake Athabasca, in Canada, and the next year departed (1789) from there to follow the **Mackenzie River** to its outlet on the Arctic Ocean.

1787 May   An expedition of c.400 former slaves led by **Granville Sharp** (1735–1813) landed in St. George's Bay, in present **Sierra Leone**, bought a piece of land from the Temne [Timne] tribe, and founded **Granville Town**. The enterprise failed because of disease and the hostility of the natives.

1788   Julien Dubuque (1762–1810), a French-Canadian trader, became the **first settler of present Iowa**. He was granted lead mining rights along the Mississippi River, at the site of present **Dubuque**, by the Fox Indians. He made friends with the local Indians, learned their language, and traded with them. Upon his death, they gave him a chief's funeral.

1788 Jan. 26   The first British settlement in Australia was founded at **Port Jackson** [Sidney] in New South Wales. **Arthur Phillip** (Oct. 11, 1738–Aug. 31, 1814) commanded the ships of the expedition and was designated governor of the colony. About 750 convicts and about 275 others reached Botany Bay, just south of Port Jackson, on Jan. 20, but they landed at Port Jackson. The first convicts had generally been convicted of property-related crimes, such as theft. The loss of life among the colonists was not as high as it could have been due to the intelligent and humane treatment accorded en route by Phillip whenever he found it possible, but on some of the ships the convicts were treated with great cruelty.

IV. POLITICS AND WAR

1780–1781 The **Comunero Rebellion** broke out in New Granada, the Spanish viceroyalty in northwestern South America. The *Comuneros*, who were citizens of the cities, usually Creole, opposed the introduction of taxes and reforms by newly appointed Spanish royal governors. Because of this uprising, the *intendencia* system, under which provinces were ruled by governors responsible directly to the Spanish king, was not established in New Granada.

1780 **Túpac Amaru II** led an **uprising of the enslaved Indians** against the Spanish in the viceroyalty of Upper Peru [present Bolivia]. **La Paz**, the capital of Bolivia, was placed under siege by the Indians, who suffered in the mines and textile mills. In Mar. 1781, Túpac Amaru [José Gabriel Condorcanqui] (b. 1742?) was captured and he was executed on May 18, 1781. The rebellion continued until 1783, by which time all its leaders had been killed.

1780 Mar. 1 **Pennsylvania became the first American state to abolish slavery**, passing a law stipulating that no person born after this date could be forced into slavery. Vermont was not a state when it abolished slavery in its constitution of July 1777.

1780 May 12 In the **American Revolution** (1775–1783), **Charlestown**, South Carolina, defended by Benjamin Lincoln, **surrendered**, after a relentless bombardment, to **Henry Clinton**, the British general. The British had mounted a combined land and sea assault by forces that had sailed (Dec. 26, 1779) from New York City. Lincoln had to surrender his whole force. **Charles Cornwallis** remained in Charlestown to conduct a British campaign in the southern colonies. The British, victors at Savannah and Augusta, Georgia, and now at Charlestown, believed the South was in their hands. Clinton, with his aide, **John Andre**, returned to New York City where, confident

of ultimate victory, he and his forces remained inactive.

1780 June **John André** in New York City was informed by **Benedict Arnold**, the American commander of Philadelphia, that he was to be given the command of West Point, on the Hudson River. On Aug. 3 Arnold received his orders to assume his command. On Sept. 21 **André and Arnold met along the Hudson**, about two miles below Haverstraw. Arnold gave his terms for the surrender of West Point: £20,000 and the supplies stored there, half that amount if the plot failed. To make his way back to New York City, André had to disguise himself and travel by horse through the Continental lines, because the British boat *Vulture*, which was to return him to the safety of the British lines, drew fire and had to retreat down river without him.

1780 June 2 The **No-Popery**, or **Gordon**, **Riots** began in London when Anglican **George Gordon** (Dec. 26, 1751–Nov. 1, 1793) led a crowd of supporters to the steps of the British Parliament to present a petition seeking repeal of the **Catholic Relief Act of 1778**, which freed Roman Catholic priests from the threat of imprisonment and allowed Roman Catholics to swear loyalty to the British crown. Rioting and looting continued for about a week, spurred by fear of a Catholic conspiracy in government. More than 800 persons died; Roman Catholic chapels were damaged and prisons opened. Gordon was acquitted of a charge of treason.

1780 Aug. 16 In a **battle at Camden**, South Carolina, the Continental Army under **Horatio Gates** was defeated by British forces commanded by **Charles Cornwallis**. Johann, baron de Kalb (b. June 29, 1721), a German officer commissioned by the Continental Army, died on Aug. 19 of wounds received in this battle. Gates was replaced (Oct. 7, 1780) as commander of the Continental Army in the South by **Nathanael Greene**.

1780 Sept. 23 **John André**, in a civilian disguise, was stopped and questioned near Tarrytown, New York, by three colonial militiamen. **Papers concerning the betrayal of West Point by Benedict Arnold** were found in his boot, and André was arrested. Arnold, in command of West Point, received word of this and escaped to join the British. Henry Clinton, the British commander in chief headquartered in New York City, refused to exchange Arnold for André and, after being tried by a council appointed by **George Washington**, John André (b. May 2, 1750) was hanged as a spy on Oct. 2 at Tappan, New York.

1780 Oct. 7   A **battle at Kings Mountain**, on the border of North and South Carolina, was a major American victory in the southern colonies. The patriots, under the nominal command of **William Campbell** and **James Williams**, were frontier militia led by their local officers; the British were under the command of **Patrick Ferguson**. Ferguson was killed in action and Williams by a stray shot as prisoners were rounded up, resulting in some indiscriminate shooting of captive British and loyalist troops.

1780 Nov. 29   **Maria Theresa** (b. May 13, 1717), archduchess of Austria, queen of Hungary and Bohemia, and ruler of the Hapsburg lands (from 1740), died. She was succeeded by her son **Joseph II**, the Holy Roman emperor (1765–1790), king of the Romans (from 1764), and sole ruler of Austria (1780–1790).

1781 Jan. 17   In a **battle at Cowpens**, in the Piedmont region of South Carolina, the British suffered a major defeat. At Cowpens **Daniel Morgan** (1736–July 6, 1802) planned his defensive lines and tactics to take advantage of **Banastre Tarleton's** (Aug. 21, 1754–Jan. 25, 1833) impulsiveness in battle and to use his untrained militia to the best advantage. The British losses were estimated at 100 killed, 229 wounded, 600 captured; American losses were 12 killed and 60 wounded.

1781 Mar. 1   The **Articles of Confederation** were finally ratified by all the states when Maryland at last agreed to accept them. **Maryland** held out until the rest of the states agreed to cede to the U.S. all conflicting claims to lands west of the Allegheny Mountains. Under the Articles it was up to the states, not Congress, to clarify the rights of Congress and the individual states in voting procedures, taxation, and the rights of citizens. Indeed, under the Articles, the **Congress** was almost powerless.

1781 Mar. 15   A **battle at Guilford courthouse**, near Greensboro, North Carolina, resulted in great losses to both British and patriot forces. Though **Nathanael Greene**, who became (Oct. 7, 1780) commander of the American Army of the South and assumed command in the field on Dec. 2, 1780, retreated, he had succeeded in forcing **Charles Cornwallis**, the British commander, to abandon his campaign plans in the South.

1781 Apr. 25   A **skirmish at Hobkirk's Hill**, near Camden, South Carolina, was led by **Nathaniel Greene** against British troops remaining in South Carolina. Although Greene retreated first, the British under **Francis Rawdon** (1754–1826), marquis of Hastings, suffered more casualties. Their supply lines were further disrupted by raids conducted by **Francis Marion** [the "**Swamp Fox**"] (1732–Feb. 27, 1795). Seldom in command of as many as 1000 men, Marion attacked larger forces of British and loyalists, successfully bagging captives and supplies, then disappearing into the swamps to avoid chase and capture. Among his raids were Singleton's Mills, Camden, and Fort Balfour at Pocataligo (all in 1781).

1781 Apr. 25   **Charles Cornwallis**, the British commander, retreated from Wilmington, North Carolina, north to Petersburg, Virginia, where he arrived on May 20, to join reinforcements sent by Henry Clinton, commander in chief of British forces in the U.S.

1781 June   **Augusta, Georgia,** was liberated from British control by **Henry "Light-Horse Harry" Lee** (Jan. 29, 1756–Mar. 25, 1818) during the American Revolution (1775–1783). British forces did not evacuate Savannah, Georgia, until July 1782, long after the surrender (Oct. 19, 1781) of **Yorktown**, Virginia.

1781 July 1   In a **battle at Porto Novo** on the Coromandel Coast of India, during the **First Mysore War** (1780–1784), the sultan of Mysore, **Haidar Ali** [Hyder Ali Khan, Haidar Naik] was defeated by the British forces of the East India Company, led by **Warren Hastings**. The sudden death of Haidar (born c.1730) on Dec. 7, 1782, left his son **Tipu Sahib** [Tippoo Sultan], who immediately became sultan, to continue the war.

1781 Aug.   **Charles Cornwallis**, the commander of British forces in Virginia, **retired to Yorktown**, Virginia, on Chesapeake Bay to await arrival of the British navy to carry him to New York City. Meanwhile **George Washington** and de Rochambeau [Jean Baptiste Donatien de Vimeur, comte de Rochambeau] (July 1, 1725–May 10, 1807), marched southward from New York toward Yorktown to meet the French fleet of de Grasse [François Joseph Paul, comte de Grasse] (1722–Jan. 11, 1788), sailing from the West Indies. On Aug. 30 de Grasse anchored at the mouth of Chesapeake Bay, where he engaged (Sept. 5) in battle with **Thomas Graves** (1725?–Feb. 1802), the British naval commander. De Grasse pushed Graves southward from the mouth of the bay, allowing a Continental fleet to enter the bay. Graves turned back to New York City.

1781 Sept. 8 In a **battle at Eutaw Springs**, north of Charlestown [Charleston in 1783], South Carolina, Nathanael Greene leading Continental troops, militia, and Henry Lee's special legion of mounted militia forced the British to retreat to Charlestown.

1781 Oct. 9 Continental troops under **George Washington**, reinforced by a French contingent under de Rochambeau, began to **shell Yorktown**, at the mouth of Chesapeake Bay, where **Charles Cornwallis** was trapped, waiting in vain for the British fleet to relieve him.

1781 Oct. 19 Charles Cornwallis surrendered his British troops to George Washington at Yorktown. The American forces under Washington and Lafayette numbered c.13,000, with c.3,000 French troops under de Rochambeau and the French fleet under de Grasse. At Yorktown and Gloucester, the Americans and French captured c.7,170 British, Hessian, and loyalist troops, c.5,000 pounds sterling, 191 guns, four frigates, 39 troop transports, and c.1,140 sailors and marines. Benjamin Lincoln, the American general who had been captured at Savannah and exchanged, arranged the formal surrender.

1782 **St. Kitts** [St. Christopher], in the West Indies, was lost by William Cornwallis (Feb. 25, 1744–July 5, 1819), the British admiral, to the French during the American Revolution. It had been held jointly by the French and British from the expulsion (1629) of the native **Caribs** to the **Treaty of Utrecht** (1713), when Great Britain took over the island. By the **Treaty of Paris** (1783) St. Kitts was returned to British control.

1782 **Phraya Tak Sin** [Phaya Takh Sin, P'ya Taksin], king of Siam [Thailand] (from 1767), became insane and was succeeded by his general, **Chao Phraya Chakkri** [P'ra P'utt'a Yot Fa Chulalok] (1737–1809) who, as **Rama I**, founded the **Chakkri Dynasty** (1782 to the present) and made his new capital at the village of **Bangkok** [Krung Thep], in present Thailand. Phraya Tak Sin, a half-Chinese general, had reunited Siam and had reasserted Siamese control of the states of Laos, including Chiang Mai, in present Thailand. Rama I added the Cambodian provinces of Battambang and Siem Reap to Siam.

1782 Mar. 20 Lord North, earl of Guilford, resigned as prime minister of Great Britain as a result of Great Britain's losses during the **American Revolution** (1775–1783). His Tory ministry was replaced by the Whig ministries of, at first, **Charles Watson-Wentworth** (May 13, 1730–July 1, 1782), marquis of Rockingham, and, later in 1782, that of **William Petty** (May 20, 1737–May 7, 1805), earl of Shelburne.

1782 Apr. 12 In the so-called **Battle of the Saints**, fought near Les Saintes islands, off Dominica in the Caribbean Sea, the French fleet, commanded by de Grasse, was defeated by **George Brydges Rodney** (b. Feb., 1718), a British admiral, who was mortally wounded in battle. By their victory the **British won virtual control of the Caribbean** area over both the Spanish and French.

1782 June 20 The **Second Continental Congress** adopted the design for the **Great Seal of the U.S.**, which was to be imprinted on documents of state. The seal was designed in the spring of 1782 principally by a Congressional Committee composed of **John Rutledge** (1739–July 23, 1800), and **Arthur Middleton** (June 26, 1742–Jan. 1, 1787) of South Carolina and **Elias Boudinot** (May 2, 1740–Oct. 24, 1821) of New Jersey.

1782 Aug. 19 A battle at Blue Licks near Lexington, Kentucky, was fought when a band of pioneers, attempting to retaliate for an Indian raid (Aug. 15) on Bryan's Station, a fort near Lexington, fell into an ambush led by **Simon Girty** (1741–1818), a renegade American who conducted British and Indian raids against the American frontier settlements. Girty and his Indians imposed the worst defeat ever on the Kentuckians; 70 of the 210 settlers were killed and 20 were captured.

1782 Nov. 30 An agreement preliminary to the final **Treaty of Paris** was signed by Great Britain and the U.S. John Jay (Dec. 12, 1745–May 17, 1829), **John Adams**, and **Benjamin Franklin** played a key role in the negotiations with the British. Final formal signing did not occur until Sept. 3, 1783.

1782 Dec. **Russian armies** under the orders of **Grigori Aleksandrovich Potëmkin** (Sept. 24, 1739–Oct. 16, 1791) **invaded the Crimea**. The Tatar rulers were quarreling among themselves and were open to bribery, so the Russian armies had little difficulty conquering them.

1783 The sheikdom of **Bahrain**, an archipelago in the Persian Gulf, gained independence from Persia under the Arab **Ahmad al-Khalifah** (d. 1796), establishing the **al-Khalifah Dynasty** (to the present).

1783 Sept. 3 The **Treaty of Paris** was signed by the U.S., Great Britain, France, and Spain, bringing an end to the **American Revolution** (from 1775) and related hostilities in the West Indies and Africa. The boundaries for the U.S. were clarified and American fishing rights off Newfoundland confirmed. The Mississippi River was to remain open to British and American explorers. The northern boundaries of the U.S. were to be much as they are today. The western boundary was set at the Mississippi River. The southern boundary was the 31° parallel from the Mississippi east to the northern boundary of Florida; the land south of this belonged to Spain as part of Florida. Franklin insisted that the source of the Mississippi River be part of the United States. The final boundary between Canada and Maine was not settled for several years. On Jan. 20, 1783, Great Britain had made separate arrangements with France and Spain, making only minor exchanges in colonial possessions in the West Indies and Africa.

1783 Dec. 23 **George Washington** resigned as commander-in-chief of the Continental Army. Although he submitted a bill to the Congress for his expenses of £24,700, he refused to accept payment of any salary for eight years of service.

1784 Jan. 6 The **Crimea**, recognized as independent by the **Treaty of Kuchuk Kainarji** [in Romania] on July 21, 1774, had been annexed by Russia in 1783; the **Ottoman Empire** now acknowledged this act by the **Treaty of Constantinople**. Russia also abrogated the **Treaty of Ainali-Kavak**, an agreement made by Russia and the Ottoman Empire (Mar. 10, 1779) to establish a Tatar khan to rule the Crimea. **Russia thus gained control of the Black Sea.**

1784 Mar. 1 The **Second Continental Congress** passed the **Northwest Ordinance**, which established the Old Northwest Territory, a region comprising present Ohio, Illinois, Indiana, Michigan, Wisconsin, and the eastern part of Minnesota. The Ordinance set up a government for the territory and stipulated that no more than five nor fewer than three states be formed in the area. Slavery was banned, religious freedom guaranteed, and a population of 60,000 was required of each of the areas designated before they could apply for statehood.

1784 May **Andreas Peter von Bernstorff** (Aug. 28, 1735–June 21, 1797), a nephew of the Danish statesman **Johann Hartwig Ernst von Bernstorff** (May 13, 1712–Feb. 18, 1772), was appointed **Denmark's** foreign minister. At home, he supported the liberal reforms begun (1770) by **Johann Friedrich von Struensee**.

1784 Aug. The province of **New Brunswick**, in Canada, was created from part of the British province of Nova Scotia for the many **loyalists emigrating from the U.S. after the American Revolution**.

1784 Aug. 13 The **India Act**, which superseded the Regulating Act of 1773, was passed by the British Parliament. It established a policy of nonintervention in the domestic affairs of India and enforced control by the British government of the actions of the East India Company. **Warren Hastings**, the first governor-general of British India, returned (1785) to England, satisfied that the new regulations prevented him from advancing his career in India. Under pressure from the Whigs, he was impeached (1787) by the Tory government of **William Pitt the Younger** (May 28, 1759–Jan. 23, 1806) for extortion, judicial corruption, and misuse of British troops; in his seven-year trial, begun in Feb. 1788, Hastings was acquitted of all charges, but he was not allowed to hold public office again.

1785 July 23 The **League of the Princes** [Fürstenbund] was formed by **Frederick the Great**, king of Prussia, against **Joseph II**, the Holy Roman emperor and ruler of Austria, who had offered to **Charles Theodore**, elector of the Palatinate, an exchange of part of the Austrian Netherlands for Bavaria. The league succeeded in curbing the emperor's plans.

1786 The *intendencia*, a new local unit of Spanish colonial administration, was established in Spanish America, which consisted of four viceroyalties: New Spain, which included parts of present southwestern U.S., Mexico, Central America [except for Panama], and the Caribbean; New Granada, which included present Panama, Columbia, Venezuela, and Ecuador; Peru, which included present western Bolivia, Peru, and northern Chile; and La Plata, which included present eastern Bolivia, southern Chile, Argentina, Paraguay, and Uruguay. The *intendencias*, with combined legislative, executive, and judicial powers, replaced local administrative units.

1786 Aug. 17 Frederick II, the Great (b. Jan. 24, 1712), king of Prussia (from 1740), died and was succeeded by his nephew **Frederick William II.**

1787 Nguyen Anh (d. 1820) of southern **Annam** [Vietnam] secured French aid in the civil war he was waging against the **Tay Son Dynasty** (1788–1802), which had led a rebellion (beginning 1773) deposing first the ruling **Nguyen Dynasty** of Hue [Hué] (1558–1776) in the south and then the ruling **Trinh Dynasty** of Tonkin (1539–1787) in the north. With French support Nguyen Anh founded the **Nguyen Dynasty** (1788–1955) and was able to gain control of the whole country in 1801, becoming in 1802 its first emperor as **Gia-Long.** The French were now firmly established in Indochina.

1787 Feb. 22 In France the **Assembly of Notables,** called by the minister of finance **Charles Alexandre de Calonne** (Jan. 20, 1734–Oct. 29, 1802), rejected his plan to tax the clergy and nobility more equitably in order to relieve the public debt, which had increased with France's aid to the patriots during the American Revolution. On July 6 the parlement demanded the summoning of the **Estates General** [États généraux], which were not convened until May 5, 1789. Calonne was dismissed (Apr. 17, 1787); he was replaced briefly by **Étienne Charles Loménie de Brienne** (Oct. 9, 1727–Feb. 19, 1794). In 1788 **Jacques Necker** (Sept. 30, 1732–Apr. 9, 1804) was recalled as minister of finance. This **financial crisis indicated the social and political discontent that precipitated the French Revolution.**

1787 May 25 The **Federal Constitutional Convention** first met at Philadelphia to draft a document to replace the **Articles of Confederation.** A growing awareness of the need for a more effective national government had developed in most of the states as they tried to create a unified commercial policy. All states except Rhode Island sent delegates to the Federal Constitutional Convention.

1787 June 28 Morocco and the U.S. signed the **Treaty of Marrakech,** then the capital of Morocco, which settled a dispute arising from the seizure of American ships by Moroccan pirates. The treaty established commercial relations favorable to the U.S. which, in return, agreed to pay Morocco an annual tribute of $10,000.

1787 Aug. 10 A **Russo-Turkish War** (1787–1792) opened when the Ottoman Empire declared war on Russia in an effort to regain lands seized by Russia in 1784. Turkey was joined by Sweden (1788), but **Alexander Suvorov** (Nov. 24, 1730–May 18, 1800), a brilliant Russian general, won victories over both nations. Sweden made peace in 1790 and, through the **Treaty of Jassy** [Iasi] (1792), Romania, Russia's control of the Black Sea steppes and Crimea was recognized.

1787 Aug. 17 Riots over taxes, food, and other matters in France broke out in Paris. In 1788 similar riots occurred in Rennes (May 9–10), Dijon (June 11), and Pau (June 19).

1787 Sept. 17 The **Federal Constitutional Convention adopted the U.S. Constitution** and subsequently submitted the document to the states for ratification. **Roger Sherman** (Apr. 19, 1721–July 23, 1793) and **Oliver Ellsworth** (Apr. 29, 1745–Nov. 26, 1807), delegates from Connecticut, had proposed the vital **"Connecticut Compromise,"** which established two bodies for the U.S. Congress. The number of representatives in the House of Representatives was to reflect differences in the population of each state. But acceptance of this principle depended on the so-called **Three-Fifths Compromise,** which counted each slave as three-fifths of a man. When the Constitution went into effect in 1788, it contained a clause providing for the end of the importation of slaves within 20 years. The number of representatives in the Senate were to be the same from each state. Thus, the small states and the large states were satisfied.

1787 Oct. 27 The first in a series of 77 essays for *The Federalist,* also called *The Federalist Papers,* was printed in a New York newspaper under the pseudonym **Publius. Alexander Hamilton** wrote the majority of them, which were published with an additional eight essays in two volumes on Apr. 4, 1788. **James Madison** and **John Jay** also wrote some, but the question of actual authorship of each has fired many debates. Hamilton, in his essays, discussed the role of a republican government in protecting individual freedom within a strong, centrally governed state, and defined the roles of many of the organs of government familiar in America today.

1787 Dec. 7 Delaware was the first state to ratify the U.S. Constitution. The other 12 states ratified the Constitution in the following order: Pennsylvania, December 12, 1787; New Jersey, December 18, 1787; Georgia, January 2, 1788; Connecticut, January 9, 1788; Massachusetts, February 6, 1788; Maryland, April 28, 1788; South Carolina, May 23, 1788; New Hampshire, June 21, 1788; Virginia, June 25, 1788; New York, July 26, 1788; North Carolina, November 21, 1789; Rhode Island, May 29, 1790. Washington chose (1789) his cabinet from among both of the developing major factions. Those favoring a strong federal government became known as the **Federalists** and their opponents as either **Democrats** or **Republicans**.

1788 Feb. 9   Austria declared war on the Ottoman Empire in support of Russia in the **Russo-Turkish War** (1787–1792). Austria captured (Oct. 6) **Belgrade**, but did not press the advantage. Austria withdrew from the war by the **Treaty of Sistova** [Svishtov] (Aug. 11, 1791), in present Bulgaria, which established the boundaries between Hungary and the Ottoman Empire.

1788 June 21   **Sweden** declared war on Russia to regain the provinces of Karelia and **Finland** while Russia was at war with the Ottoman Empire during the Russo-Turkish War. Hostilities came to an end in 1790 with Sweden in control of Finland but not Karelia.

1788 June 21   **New Hampshire**, the ninth state to ratify the U.S. Constitution, was the last needed to adopt it.

1789 Feb. 4   The **first electoral college** met in **New York City**, serving as the U.S. capital, to vote for the **first president of the U.S.** The college unanimously elected **George Washington** and chose **John Adams** as vice president, both of the Federalist party. On Apr. 30 Washington was inaugurated. Washington selected advisers, who came to be known as "**cabinet members**" in 1793, when **Thomas Jefferson** used the term first.

1789 Feb. 20   The **Riksdag**, the Swedish parliament, passed the **Unity and Security Act**, which strengthened the monarchy over the nobles and other classes. The Riksdag gained greater authority in financial affairs, but Gustavus III gained the upper hand in legislative matters.

1789 Mar. 4   The **first session of the U.S. Congress** met in New York City and proposed 12 amendments to the U.S. Constitution. They were designed to protect individuals and states from the encroaching power of a strong national government. Ten were

adopted; they became known as the **Bill of Rights**, which was ratified by the necessary number of states on Dec. 15, 1791.

1789 Apr.   **Honoré Gabriel Victor Riqueti** (Mar. 9, 1749–Apr. 2, 1791), comte de Mirabeau, was elected by the Third Estate in Aix-en-Provence as a representative to the Estates General, where he soon became known for oratory and debating. Mirabeau supported a limited monarchy, ably defending his position against the radical revolutionaries, called the **Jacobins**.

1789 May 5   The French **Estates General**, which had not been called since 1614, convened at Versailles, near Paris, to consider tax reform. It included representatives from the clergy, nobility, and the Third Estate [le Tiers-État], or middle class [bourgeoisie]. Over the opposition of **Marie Antoinette**, queen of France, **Louis XVI** granted a majority of seats to the Third Estate at the urging of **Jacques Necker**, minister of finance.

1789 May 6   Noota, a British settlement on Nootka Island off the western coast of **Vancouver Island**, founded in 1788 by **John Meares** (c.1756–1809), was seized by the Spanish. Spain and Great Britain nearly went to war over this incident. In 1790, however, negotiations led to the **Nootka Convention** (Oct. 28, 1790), in which Spain returned the island, paid an indemnity for the seized ships, and Great Britain and Spain recognized their mutual rights in the Pacific Northwest.

1789 June 17   The majority of the Third Estate delegation to the Estates General, joined by most of the lower clergy and some of the nobles, declared themselves the **National** [Constituent] **Assembly**, spokesmen for the whole of **France**. When they were turned out of their meeting place by the king, they gathered at a nearby indoor tennis court [Jeu de Paume]. On June 20 they took the **Tennis Court Oath**, pledging not to disband until they could draft a French constitution.

1789 July 14   A mob of French citizens stormed the **Bastille**, the fortress in Paris where political prisoners were held, in protest against dismissal (July 11) of Jacques Necker as minister of finance by Marie Antoinette, queen of France. The fall of the Bastille signaled the beginning of the **French Revolution** (1789–1799) to the French peasantry and to the world.

1789 Aug. 4 The **National Assembly of France**, in an all-night session, voted to abolish the feudal system in an effort to end the **Grande Peur** [Great Fear], a series of bloody riots that erupted between July 2 and Aug 6 throughout France. These were peasant uprisings triggered by famine, unemployment, and debt. The nobility, fearing the rioting and loss of income and privilege, accepted this compromise measure. For the peasants, the benefits were illusory, as the representatives of the nobility had exacted a stipulation that an equitable payment be made to the feudal lords for the loss of their lands. This was a requirement most peasants could not meet.

1789 Aug. 27 The French National Assembly approved the **Declaration of Rights of Man and of the Citizen**. The Declaration was largely the work of **Lafayette**, who consulted **Thomas Jefferson**, then in Paris as the U.S. minister; the American Declaration of Independence; and the U.S. state constitutions.

1789 Sept. **Alexander Hamilton** was appointed the **first American secretary of the treasury** by **George Washington**, president of the U.S. Hamilton, to establish national credit, urged that the national debt be accepted at its full value, that debts incurred by the states during the American Revolution be assumed by the federal government, and that taxes to finance the debt be established. Hamilton's fiscal proposals were adopted on July 1790, by the U.S. Congress after Hamilton made an agreement with **Thomas Jefferson** that secured the southern vote in exchange for his help in locating the new capital on the Potomac River. In order to fund the debt Congress passed (Mar. 3, 1791) a law that led to an excise tax on distilled spirits.

1789 Oct. 5 A mob of Parisian women, upon receiving rumors of a large banquet planned by the royal family, rushed the palace at Versailles. On Oct. 6 **Lafayette**, who had been chosen on July 15 to head the **National Guard** [Paris militia] rescued the king, and carried him with his court to the Tuileries palace in Paris.

1789 Dec. 12 Austrian troops were driven from Brussels, in the Austrian Netherlands, and the states of the Brabant, in present Belgium, declared (Dec. 27) independence. On Jan. 11, 1790, the whole of the **Austrian Netherlands declared independence as the republic of the United States of Belgium**. The revolution had been led by **Henri van der Noot** (Jan. 7,

1731–Jan. 12, 1827) and **Jean François Vonck** (Nov. 29, 1743–Dec. 1, 1792).

V. ECONOMY AND TRADE

1780 Mar. 10 Russia, declaring it would protect its shipping against British interference, established the **League of Armed Neutrality**. France, Spain, Austria, Prussia, Denmark, and Sweden joined Russia's efforts to reduce the power of Great Britain, which had aroused hostility by its enforcement of the trade blockade of the American states during the American Revolution.

1781 **Serfdom was abolished in Austria** by a number of decrees issued in this and the following year. Peasants were permitted to buy the land they had worked, to change their residence at will, and to marry as they chose.

1783 **Massachusetts banned slavery** according to a reinterpretation of the state constitution, which declared that all men were "born free and equal." **Maryland banned the slave trade** in this year and, in 1784, **Connecticut and Rhode Island declared slavery illegal**.

1784 **Ch'ien Lung**, the Chinese emperor (1736–1796) of the **Ch'ing** [Manchu] **Dynasty** (1644–1911), **opened trade relations with the U.S.** at the port of **Canton**.

1784 Feb. 22 The **first American sailing ship to open the way to trade with China** and elsewhere in the Orient sailed from New York. The *Empress of China*, 360 tons and 100 feet long, had just been built in Boston by the Peck family shipbuilders and purchased by **Robert Morris** (Jan. 20, 1734–May 8, 1806), the Philadelphian financier and American statesman, specifically for the trading trip to China. The ship sailed around the Cape of Good Hope and through the Indian Ocean and the East Indies with a cargo of c.3,000 fur pelts and tons of ginseng roots. They reached China on Aug. 23 and returned to New York on May 11, 1785, with a cargo of tea, porcelain, silks, and other products of China.

1785 Jan. 1 The predecessor to the **London** *Times*, the *Daily Universal Register*, was first published in London to advertise a print shop and the books it published. On Jan. 1, 1788, the name and format were changed.

1786 Aug. 8 The **U.S. Congress adopted the decimal system for its system of coinage**. The system had been proposed (July 6, 1785) to Congress by **Thomas Jefferson**. Silver was set at a ratio of 15 to 1 to gold. The first coins were minted in 1792.

1787 Jan. 25 **Shays' Rebellion** (1786–1787) broke out as **Daniel Shays** (1747?–Sept. 29, 1825) led the seizure of a U.S. government arsenal in Springfield, Massachusetts. Shays and his followers were protesting high land taxes that forced foreclosure on their mortgages. They were caught (Feb. 2) at Petersham, near Worcester, Massachusetts; Shays, sentenced to death, was pardoned on June 13, 1788.

1788 **Serfdom was abolished in Denmark** by Crown Prince Frederick (Jan. 28, 1768–Dec. 3, 1839), later **Frederick VII** (1808–1839), who ruled as regent (from 1784) for his father, **Christian VII**, the unstable king of Denmark (1766–1808). Frederick established a credit bank to help peasants buy the land they worked. He also instituted Europe's first **pauper law**, which prohibited owning and trading slaves.

1789 July 4 The **first American protectionist tariff**, enacted by the U.S. Congress, went into effect. Tariffs between 5 and 15 percent were placed on more than 30 commodities.

1789 Dec. 19 *Assignats* [treasury notes] were issued in France by the National Assembly to finance the **French Revolution**. These *Assignats* were backed by land confiscated from the Church or the Crown by the revolutionary government. By 1796 inflation reduced them to one percent of their value at issuance.

VI. RELIGION AND PHILOSOPHY

1780 July **Robert Raikes** (Sept. 4, 1736–Apr. 5, 1811), an English newspaper publisher, aided by a clergyman and a woman teacher, opened a **Sunday school** on Sooty Alley in Gloucester, England. It was intended to educate slum children, many of whom worked six days a week. By 1786 c.200,000 English children attended Sunday schools.

1781 **Joseph II**, the Holy Roman emperor, issued the **Patent of Tolerance**, providing nearly complete freedom of worship. It was designed in part to prevent emigration of Jews, Protestants, and those of the Eastern Orthodox faith.

1783 **Moses Mendelssohn** [Moses Dessau] (Sept. 26, 1729–Jan. 4, 1786), a German Jewish philosopher, educator, and defender of Judaism, completed his **translation of the Pentateuch into German**. This work served as the means whereby many German and eastern European Jews began to break out of their Yiddish-ghetto intellectual isolation.

1784 Feb. 28 **John Wesley**, previously reluctant to separate his movement from the established Anglican church, took the first of two steps to make separation inevitable. His "Deed of Declaration" provided for the future of the movement by naming a "conference" of 100 persons to hold property and direct the movement. On Sept. 1 he and Methodist Anglican presbyters ordained presbyters and a superintendent for his movement in the U.S.

1784 Nov. 14 **Samuel Seabury** (Nov. 30, 1729–Feb. 25, 1796) was consecrated as the **first American bishop** by three Scottish bishops. Seabury had been elected (1783) bishop by Episcopal clergymen of Connecticut.

1784 Dec. 24 The **Methodist Episcopal Church in the U.S.** was organized by American Methodist ministers, called into conference at Baltimore, Maryland, by **John Wesley's** emissary, **Thomas Coke** (Sept. 9, 1747–May 3, 1814), at the urging of **Francis Asbury** (Aug. 20, 1745–Mar. 31, 1816). Asbury and Coke were chosen joint superintendents. A discipline was adopted, along with a Sunday service and articles of religion, adapted by Wesley from the Anglican *Book of Common Prayer* and Articles of Religion.

1787 May 22 A **committee for the abolition of slavery** was formed by **William Wilberforce** (Aug. 24, 1759–July 29, 1833), a member of the British Parliament, with **Granville Sharp** (Nov. 10, 1735–July 6, 1813), **Thomas Clarkson** (Mar. 28, 1760–Sept. 26, 1846), and other well-placed humanitarians.

1788 June 21 **Johann Georg Hamann** (b. Aug. 27, 1730), a German Protestant writer, died. His philosophy, opposed to the prevailing rationalism of the Enlightenment, influenced Johann Gottfried von Herder. Hamann's works included *Sokratische Denkwürdigkeiten* (1759), *Kreuzzüge eines Philologen* (1762), and *Golgatha und Scheblimini* (1784).

1789 **Pope Pius VI** (Dec. 25, 1717–Aug. 29, 1799; ruled from 1775), acting on the petition of American priests for the right to elect their own bishop, confirmed the election of **John Carroll** (Jan. 8, 1735–Dec. 3, 1815) as bishop of Baltimore. He was consecrated on Aug. 15, 1790. Carroll, born in Upper Marlboro, Maryland, was the **first native-born American bishop of the Roman Catholic Church**. Later Carroll helped found (1789) **Georgetown University** in Washington, D.C.

1789   The **first Prayer Book in the U.S.** appeared. It did not depart noticeably from England's *Book of Common Prayer* in doctrine or discipline, but changes were made to meet the requirements of "local circumstances." For example, prayers for the president of the U.S. replaced prayers for the royal family.

1789 Nov. 2   The **French National Assembly voted to confiscate ecclesiastical lands** and nationalize church property in order to restore the treasury. The Roman Catholic Church subsequently withheld its support of the French Revolution.

VII. SCIENCE, EDUCATION, AND TECHNOLOGY

1781 Mar. 13   **William Herschel**, an English astronomer, **discovered the planet Uranus**, which he named "Georgium Sidus" after George III, king of England. It was not until August, however, that its path of orbit was determined, thus establishing that the observed body was not a comet.

1783 June 5   **Joseph Michel Montgolfier** (1740–June 6, 1810) and his brother **Jacques Étienne** (Jan. 7, 1745–Aug. 2, 1799) succeeded in keeping a **hot-air balloon in flight**, without passengers, for ten minutes, at Annonay, France.

1783 July 15   The **first boat powered by a steam engine**, the *Pyroscaphe*, was demonstrated on the Saône River, near Lyon, France, by **Claude François Dorothée** (1751–1832), marquis de Jouffroy d'Abbans. The gearing from the engine to the sidewheels was after a sketch by **Leonardo da Vinci**.

1783 Aug. 27   **Hydrogen was first used to inflate a balloon** and send it aloft by **Jacques Alexandre César** (Nov. 12, 1746–Apr. 7, 1823), a French physicist. With hydrogen, balloons could carry more weight for longer distances per cubic foot of balloon size in their

ascent. Hot-air balloons required dangerous open flames and cooled quickly, losing lift.

1783 Sept. 18   **Leonhard Euler** (b. Apr. 15, 1707), a Swiss mathematician who had taught in St. Petersburg and in Berlin, died. Euler introduced (1734) the concept of partial derivatives, and developed (1737) the **modern theory of continual fractions**.

1783 Oct. 15   **Jean François Pilâtre de Rozier** made the **first hot-air balloon ascent**, in Paris. On Nov. 21, he traveled more than five miles by balloon within 25 minutes near Paris. De Rozier (b. 1756) was killed on June 15, 1785, when his double balloon, one filled with hydrogen and one with hot air, exploded before he could attempt a crossing of the English Channel.

1783 Oct. 29   **Jean le Rond d'Alembert** (b. Nov. 17, 1717), a French physicist and mathematician, died. His *Traité de dynamique* (1743) set forth his principle of kinetics, which he applied to the equilibrium and motion of fluids in 1744, and of air, as wind, in 1746.

1784   **Jean Pierre [François] Blanchard** (July 4, 1753–Mar. 7, 1809), a French aeronaut, was credited with the **invention of the parachute**, which he tested by using animals. On Jan. 7, 1785, he was joined by an American physician and balloonist, **John Jeffries** (Feb. 5, 1774 or 1775–Sept. 16, 1819), to make **the first crossing of the English Channel**, from Dover to Calais, **in a balloon**.

1784   **Edmund Cartwright** (Apr. 24, 1743–Oct. 30, 1823), an English inventor, produced the **first power-driven machine** that could weave a full width of fabric. A great advance in the automation of weaving, it was protested by workers who set fire (1790) to a mill containing c.400 of Cartwright's machines.

1786   The **first threshing machine** was invented by the Scotsman **Andrew Meikle** (1719–Nov. 27, 1811). Its basic principle combined flailing, by a series of beaters, with toothed combs to separate the wheat from the chaff.

1787 Jan. 11   **William Herschel** discovered the first two moons of Uranus, Titania and Oberon.

1787 Aug. 22   **John Fitch** (Jan. 21, 1743–July 2, 1798), an American inventor, demonstrated the **first steamboat in the U.S.**, along the Delaware River. He later launched three more but abandoned his plans to establish a steamboat company when he lost his financial backing after the fourth boat was lost in a storm.

VIII. ARTS AND LEISURE

c.1780 Urdu literature reached its height at this time with the poets **Sauda** (1713–1781), **Mir Hasan** (1727–1786), and [Mohammed Taqi] **Mir** (1729?–1810). Mir was noted for writing for the populace while the two older poets explored subtle aspects of poetic style.

1780 The **Bolshoi** [Great, Big] **Theater of Opera and Ballet** was founded in Moscow.

1781 Feb. 15 **Gotthold Ephraim Lessing** (b. Jan. 22, 1729), a German critic and chief promoter of the Enlightenment in Germany, died. His prose drama *Miss Sarah Sampson* (1755) was called the first German tragedy treating German middle-class themes. *Minna von Barnhelm* (1767), a comedy, was another play that helped to establish German classicism. Lessing's most famous work of aesthetic criticism was *Laocoön* (1766), in which he advanced the theory that art criticism should be based on different principles than literary criticism. His play *Nathan the Wise* (1779) explored the conflicts and unities of Christianity, Islam, and Judaism.

1781 Mar. 17 **Johannes Ewald** [Evald] (b. Nov. 18, 1743), the Danish national poet, died. Ewald borrowed from Danish legend for *Rolf Krage* (1770) and *Balder's Dod* [Balder's Death] (1774), which stimulated Danish interest in Scandinavian mythology.

1782 *Theseus and the Minotaur,* one of the first works of the classic revival style, by an Italian sculptor **Antonio Canova** (Nov. 1, 1757–Oct. 13, 1822), was completed.

1782 *Letters from an American Farmer* by **St. John de Crèvecoeur** [Michel Guillaume Jean de Crèvecoeur] (Jan. 31, 1735–1813) was published in London. Known in America as **J. Hector St. John**, de Crèvecoeur, who was caught up in the conflicting loyalties produced by the American Revolution, left his farm in western New York and headed for Europe in 1780. His letters, optimistic in spirit, gave one of the first accounts of the American character and were avidly read in Europe as well as in America.

1782 Jan. 1 **Johann Christian Bach** (b. Sept. 5, 1735), the eleventh and youngest son of the German composer Johann Sebastian Bach, died. Bach's works included 13 operas, among them *Artaserse* [with Pietro Metastasio] (1761), *Alessandro nell'Indie* (1762), *Orione* (1763), and *Lucio Silla* (1776), as well as numerous symphonies, concertos, sonatas, chamber works, and songs.

1782 Apr. 12 **Pietro Metastasio** [Pietro Antonio Domenico Bonaventura Trapassi] (b. Jan. 3, 1698), an Italian poet and dramatist, died. He was noted for his musical dramas [melodramas], to which a number of composers provided musical accompaniment, including *Didone abbandonata* [*Dido Abandoned*] (1724), *La Clemenza di Tito* [*The Mercy of Titus*] (1734), and *Achille in Sciro* [*Achilles in Scyros*] (1736). Metastasio wrote 34 major musical dramas, all of which were set to music by noted composers of the day, including Vivaldi, Beethoven, Scarlatti, J.C. Bach, and Mozart.

1782 Sept. 16 **Carlo Broschi Farinelli** [Il Ragazzo] (b. Jan. 24, 1705), a renowned castrato, or male soprano, died. In 1737 he was appointed court singer by **Philip V**, king of Spain, who was said to have been cured of melancholia by Broschi's singing.

1783 **John Broadwood** (1732–1812) patented his improved piano pedals. This and his other modifications to the keyboard became the basis of the **modern piano**.

1784 July 1 **Wilhelm Friedemann Bach** (b. Nov., 1710), the eldest son of the German composer Johann Sebastian Bach, died. He was organist at Dresden from 1733 to 1747 and at Halle from 1746 to 1764. His works included compositions for the keyboard, symphonies, concertos, and church music.

1784 July 30 **Denis Diderot** [Pantophile] (b. Oct. 5, 1713), a renowned French encyclopedist, died. His other works included *Pensées Philosophiques* (1746), *Lettre sur les aveugles* (1749), *Lettre sur les sourdes et muets* (1751), *Pensées sur l'interpretation de la nature* (1754), and *Elements de physiologie* (1774–1780).

1784 Dec. 13 **Samuel Johnson** (b. Sept. 18, 1709), an English lexicographer, also called **Dr. Johnson**, died. In 1747 he began work on his *Dictionary of the English Language,* which was published in 1755. Johnson established his reputation as a moralist and stylist in two series of essays, *The Rambler* (1750–1752) and *The Idler* (1758–1760). He also wrote a philosophical romance *Rasselas* (1759). In 1764, with the painter Joshua Reynolds, Johnson founded a literary club ("The Club"), which included as members David Garrick, James Boswell, and Oliver Goldsmith. Boswell's *Life of Samuel Johnson, LL.D.* (1791) captured brilliantly the conversation of the great doctor.

1785 Jan. 3   Baldassare Galuppi (b. Oct. 18, 1706), an Italian composer, died. Of his 20 oratorios and 112 operas, the most popular were his comic operas, among them *Il Filosofo di Campagna* [*The Guardian Trick'd*] (1754) and *Il Re Pastore* (1762).

1785 Apr. 14   William Whitehead (b. 1715), an English dramatist and poet, died. His works included a comedy *The School for Lovers* (1762), and the poems *The Sweepers* and *The Goat's Beard.* He was appointed poet laureate in 1757.

1785 May 21   Thomas Warton (b. Jan. 9, 1728), an English literary historian and poet, died. The poems *The Pleasures of Melancholy* (1747) and *The Triumph of Isis* (1749), established his reputation. Warton was appointed poet laureate in 1785.

1787 Apr. 16   *The Contrast*, the first comedy written in the U.S., was first produced in New York City. The play was written by **Royall Tyler** (July 18, 1757–Aug. 26, 1826), who later became chief justice of the state supreme court in Vermont. He also wrote satirical verse and the novel *The Algerine Captive* (1797).

1787 May 28 [Johann Georg] **Leopold Mozart** (b. Nov. 14, 1719), the father of the German composer **Wolfgang Amadeus Mozart**, died. He taught his children, including his daughter **Maria Anna Nannerl** (1751–1829), who toured as a teacher and performer before her marriage and after her husband's death in 1801. Leopold wrote *Versuch einer Gründlichen Violinschule* [**Violin School**] (1756), an early attempt to establish a uniform method for playing the violin. Leopold composed oratorios, chamber music, symphonies, and operas.

1787 Nov. 15   Christoph Willibald Gluck (b. July 2, 1714), a Bavarian opera composer, died. With *Orfeo ed Euridice* (1762), the earliest classic opera still regularly performed, Gluck revolutionized operatic style. He simplified the musical format to heighten the dramatic impact, an innovation that greatly influenced operatic form. Gluck's other operas included *Alceste* (1767), *Iphigénie en Aulide* (1774), and *Iphigénie en Tauride* (1779).

1788   The final three volumes of *The History of the Decline and Fall of the Roman Empire* were completed by **Edward Gibbon** (Apr. 27, 1737–Jan. 16, 1794), an English historian. The six-volume work covered the history of Rome from A.D. 180 to 1453.

1788 Aug. 2   Thomas Gainsborough (b. May, 1727), an English painter of portraits and landscapes, died. Among his works were *Mrs. Portman* (1763), *The Blue Boy* (1770), and *The Harvest Wagon* (1767).

1788 Dec. 14   Carl [Karl] **Philipp Emanuel** [C.P.E.] **Bach** (b. Mar. 8, 1714), the third son of the German composer Johann Sebastian Bach, died. C.P.E. was important in developing the sonatic form in three movements, which was further refined by Franz Joseph Haydn. C.P.E.'s many works included piano sonatas, for which he was best known, concertos, symphonies, and vocal and instrumental pieces.

IX. SPORTS, GAMES, AND SOCIETY

1780   The **Epsom Downs**, a 1-½ mile race open to horses of both sexes, was established by **Edward Stanley** (1752–1834), the 12th earl of Derby, who had founded the **Epsom Oaks** race for fillies in 1779 to parallel the St. Leger race for colts at Doncaster.

1785 Aug. 15   Louis René Édouard (1734–1803), cardinal de Rohan (from 1778), archbishop of Strasbourg (from 1779), and a member of one of France's most noble families, was arrested in the **Affair of the Diamond Necklace** (*Affaire du Collier*) when he could not pay the jewelry firm of Boehmer and Bassenge the first installment due on a diamond necklace the cardinal had been led to believe he had purchased for **Marie Antoinette**, queen of France. The hoax, with the cardinal as scapegoat, had been contrived by the comte **Marc Antoine Nicholas** (1754–1831) and **comtesse de La Motte** [Jeanne de Saint-Rémy but known as Jeanne de Valois] (1756–1791), who played on the cardinal's wish to regain favor at the French court. On May 31, 1786, though acquitted of a crime, he was removed from office and banished to an abbey. The comtesse, the only one convicted of a crime, was sentenced to flogging, branding, and life in prison, but she escaped from Salpêtrière, a prison for women in Paris, to London, where the jewelry turned up in pieces.

1786 Aug. 7–8 The **top of Mont Blanc**, the highest mountain of the Alps, was reached for the first time, by **Michel Gabriel Paccard** (1757–1827) and his guide Jacques Balmat (1762–1834).

1787 The prince of Wales, the future George IV, king of England, became patron of the **Toxophilic** [= bow-lover (1545)] **Society**, founded (1781) by Ashton Lever, thus justifying its change of name to the Royal Toxophilic Society. The prince also fixed the distances, called **"the Prince's lengths,"** and the point-scoring values for the target rings, both still used in archery contests.

1788 The **Marylebone Cricket Club**, a reorganization of the White Conduit Cricket Club, which was in turn the successor to the Artillery Ground Club, was formed in London and was quickly recognized as the paramount authority for the rules of cricket. The MCC to this day retains total control of the game.

1788 The publication of an excerpt of *Histoire de ma Fuite* [*History of My Flight*] by the Italian adventurer and rake **Giacomo Girolamo Casanova** [de Seingalt] (Apr. 5, 1725–June 4, 1798) made the name "Casanova" a household word. The story was based on his escape from the Leads [les Plombs], the prison under the roof of the Doge Palace, in Venice, on Oct. 31, 1756. He wrote a series of famous *Mémoires*, which were not published until 1826 to 1838, recounting his adventures, especially with women, throughout Europe.

1789 Apr. 28 The famous **Mutiny on the *Bounty*** occurred when **William Bligh** (Sept. 9, 1754–Dec. 7, 1817), captain of a British naval vessel, was cast adrift near the Tonga [Friendly] Islands, in the Pacific Ocean, with 18 men in an open boat by members of his crew led by **Fletcher Christian**. On June 12, after sailing westward for c.4,000 miles, Bligh and his crew reached Timor Island, between the Malay Archipelago and Australia. Some of the mutineers established a colony on Pitcairn Island (discovered 1808) east of **Tahiti**, where their descendants still live.

1790–1799

I. VITAL STATISTICS AND DEMOGRAPHICS

1790 The **first official census in the U.S.** showed a population of 3,929,214, almost evenly divided between North and South. The racial distribution was: North—1,900,616 whites and 67,424 blacks; South—1,271,390 whites and 689,784 blacks. About 3,728,000 people lived in rural areas, c.202,000 in cities.

II. DISASTERS

1793 Nov. 4 **Benjamin Rush**, a signer of the Declaration of Independence and a controversial Philadelphia physician, was advised of the day's only death from yellow fever, signaling the end of the city's **yellow fever epidemic**. Brought to **Philadelphia** that summer by c.2,000 refugees from the slave revolts on the island of Santo Domingo, yellow fever killed c.5,000 people, nearly 10 percent of Philadelphia's population, since its beginning on Aug. 24.

1797 Feb. 4 More than 40,000 people lost their lives when an **earthquake** destroyed Cuzco, **Peru**, and Quito, **Ecuador**.

III. EXPLORATION AND COLONIZATION

1790 Aug. 10 **Robert Gray** (1755–1806) returned to Boston, completing the **first voyage around the world made by a U.S. citizen**. He had sailed westward to Canton on the *Columbia Rediviva*.

1792 Apr. 17 **George Vancouver** (June 22, 1757–May 10, 1798), an English navigator, sailing eastward across the Pacific, sighted the Pacific Coast of North America, near present San Diego. During the summers of 1792, 1793, and 1794, Vancouver charted the coastline of the **Pacific Northwest**, not only laying claim to that region for Great Britain but also proving there was no passage from the Pacific Ocean to Hudson Bay.

1793 Feb. **John Macarthur** became the leader of the **first group of free settlers** (not convicts) in **Australia**.

1793 June 22 **Alexander Mackenzie**, a Scottish explorer, led a party on the **first overland crossing of**

the North American continent. They went from Fort Chippewyan on Lake Athabasca, Canada, to the outlet of the Dean River on Queen Charlotte Sound, in present British Columbia. They made the journey in a canoe 25 feet long. They returned to Fort Chippewyan on Aug. 23.

1794 Aug. 20 Anthony Wayne (Jan. 1, 1745–Dec. 15, 1796), a commander of U.S. army forces, defeated Indians of the Old Northwest Territory in a **battle at Fallen Timbers**, near present **Toledo**, Ohio. This victory secured the old Northwest frontier and cleared the mouth of the Chicago River on Lake Michigan for settlement, where **Fort Dearborn** was built (1803). Peace terms were concluded with the Indians in the **Treaty of Fort Greenville** (1795), in present Ohio.

1795 Sept. 16 The **British occupied the Dutch settlement of Cape Town**, in present South Africa, on behalf of the prince of Orange, who was exiled in England during the **War of the First Coalition** (1792–1797), when the French invaded the Netherlands.

1796 The **first permanent settlement in the area of Chicago** was established by **John Kinzie** (1763–1828), a Canadian-born fur trader. He acquired the trading business established at Chicago by **Jean Baptiste Point de Sable** [de Saible].

1798 Van Diemen's Land [Tasmania] was first circumnavigated by **Matthew Flinders** (Mar. 16, 1774–July 19, 1814) and **George Bass** (d. 1812?), English navigators, establishing that it was an island.

1798 Sept. 10 Great Britain established its claim to British Honduras [present **Belize**], in Central America, when British settlers, engaged in the region's mahogany trade, drove the Spanish from their coastal foothold in a **battle at St. George's Cay**, an island off the northeastern coast.

1799 Mammoth Cave, in Kentucky, was discovered, although it had been known by Indians before this time. It was said that a hunter named **Peter Houchins** followed a wounded bear into the mouth of the cave, either in this year or in 1809. Remains of a mummified body found there were thought to be pre-Columbian.

IV. POLITICS AND WAR

1790 Feb. 1 The **Supreme Court of the U.S. convened for its first session**. Established (Sept. 24, 1789) by an act of Congress, according to Article Three of the U.S. Constitution, the members of the court were appointed by the U.S. president with the advice and consent of the Senate. **John Jay** was the **first chief justice** (1789–1795); but it was not until **John Marshall** (Sept. 24, 1755–July 6, 1835) served as chief justice (1801–1835) that the court established its power as a separate but equal branch, with the Presidency and Congress, of the U.S. government. Originally there were six members of the court; in 1807 there were seven; in 1837 there were nine; in 1863 there were ten; in 1866 the court was reduced to eight members, and in 1869 it was increased to nine, the present number.

1790 Feb. 20 Joseph II (b. Mar. 13, 1741), the Holy Roman emperor and ruler of the Hapsburg lands, died and was succeeded by his brother **Leopold II**. At Pillnitz, a castle on the Elbe River southeast of Dresden, he signed (Aug., 1791) an agreement with **Frederick William II**, king of Prussia, allying the two powers against France.

1790 May 29 Rhode Island was the 13th state to ratify the U.S. Constitution, and the last of the original 13 colonies to do so. Rhode Island agreed to ratify the Constitution when the other 12 states threatened to halt trade with the state.

1790 Aug. 14 In the **Russo-Turkish War** (1787–1792) the **Treaty of Värälä** [Verala] ended the hostilities between Sweden and Russia. Despite a stunning **Swedish naval victory at Svenskund**, on the Gulf of Finland, on July 10, 1790, Sweden failed to gain any territory. Boundaries were restored, and Sweden and Russia concluded (Oct. 1791) a defensive alliance.

1790 Oct The **Society of United Irishmen** was founded in Ireland under the leadership of Wolfe Tone, the most prominent of those trying to unite Catholics and dissenters to join in the cause for an independent Ireland.

1790 Dec. 2 The **imperial forces of the Austrian ruler Leopold II**, the Holy Roman emperor, **recaptured Brussels**, capital of the new republic of the United States of **Belgium**, ending the revolt begun in 1789.

1791 The U.S. guaranteed independence to the Cherokee Nation by a treaty.

1791 Spain withdrew from the port of Oran, Algeria, after being besieged by the governor of Mascara, a city to the southeast. Oran then became a provincial capital of the Ottoman Empire.

1791 Mar. 4 Vermont, after ratifying the U.S. Constitution in January, was the 14th state to enter the union. Vermont had established itself as a state by convention on July 2 to 8, 1777; but it had not been recognized as independent by other states.

1791 May 3 A Polish diet [national constituent assembly], called the Four Years' Diet because it was in session from 1788 to 1792, approved a new constitution that strengthened the monarchy by abolishing the liberum veto, or veto power, formerly held by each member of the Sejm [parliament] and serving primarily to disrupt policy-making. The Third Estate, the burghers, were given the right to hold office and sit on the Sejm. Peasants were placed under the protection of the state. In order to prevent the monarchy, previously elective, from falling into the hands of an aristocratic faction, the constitution arranged for the House of Saxony to occupy the throne on a hereditary basis upon the death of the Stanislas II Poniatowski, the king of Poland.

1791 June 10 The Canadian Constitutional Act was passed by the British Parliament to provide a new constitution and government patterned more closely after that of Great Britain. The act divided the province of Quebec into Upper and Lower Canada, which later formed the provinces of Ontario, predominantly English, and Quebec, mostly French.

1791 June 20 Louis XVI, king of France, escaped with his family from the Tuileries Palace in Paris to Varennes, in northeastern France, where they were captured. The National Assembly maintained control by asserting that the king had been kidnapped. Because a compromise between the monarchy and more radical factions could not be achieved, efforts to establish a constitutional monarchy were unsuccessful.

1791 Aug. 4 The Treaty of Sistova [Svishtov], on the Danube River in present Bulgaria, was signed by Austria and the Ottoman Empire (1326–1920) to clarify their common boundary.

1791 Aug. 22 Rebellion broke out in the French territory of Saint Dominique [Haiti] on the island of Hispaniola [Dominican Republic and Haiti] under Pierre Dominique L'Ouverture, the Haitian general, and the Haitian ex-slaves Jean Jacques Dessalines (1748/1758–Oct. 17, 1806) and Henri Christophe (1767–Oct. 8, 1820). Slaves formed the majority of Haiti's population.

1791 Aug. 27 The Declaration of Pillnitz was issued by Austria and Prussia, in response to a fear of a general uprising against the nobility as was signaled throughout Europe by the French Revolution. They pledged to intervene in French domestic affairs if the French king were harmed.

1791 Sept. 3 In France the National Assembly [*Assemblée nationale constituante*] (July 9, 1789–Sept. 20, 1791) adopted a constitution that established a constitutional monarchy with an elected legislative body. The new Legislative Assembly [*Assemblée législative*] (Oct. 1, 1791–Sept. 20, 1792) convened (Oct. 1) for its first session to discuss the question of a continental war.

1791 Oct. 1 The French Jacobin party [Society of Friends of the Constitution], so-called because it first met at a Dominican convent in Paris (Dominicans were often called Jacobins in France because their hospice housed pilgrims on their way to Santiago de Compostela, Spain, to visit the shrine of St. James), was split by the question of waging a continental war. The Girondists [Brissotins], under Jacques Pierre Brissot de Warville, mostly of the upper-middle class, hoped to gain international support by extending the revolution across Europe. Maximilien Robespierre, speaking for the Jacobins who supported internal reform to improve the condition of the lower classes, argued that unless the old order was entirely crushed, France could not wage war successfully on privilege and aristocracy elsewhere.

1792 Jan. 9 The Treaty of Jassy [Iași], in present Romania, was signed, ending the Russo-Turkish War (1787–1792). Due to the victories of Aleksandr Vasilievich Suvorov, the Russian general, Russia established her southwestern frontier at the Dniester [Dnestr] River and gained the port of Ochakov on the Black Sea. Catherine the Great, czarina of Russia, had hoped to take Constantinople and establish there her grandson Constantine in a resurrection of the Byzantine Empire.

1792 Mar. 1 Leopold II (b. May 5, 1747), the Holy Roman emperor and ruler of the Hapsburg lands (from 1790), died and was succeeded by his son **Francis II** (Feb. 12, 1768–Mar. 2, 1835), the last Holy Roman Emperor (1792–1806).

1792 Mar. 16 Gustavus III (b. Jan. 24, 1746), king of Sweden (from 1771), was shot at the Stockholm opera house by **Johan Jacob Anckarström** [Ankarström] (1762–1792), an officer in the Swedish army acting on behalf of a conspiracy by the Swedish nobility. On Mar. 29 Gustavus died. He was succeeded by his son **Gustavus IV** [Gustavus Adolphus] (Nov. 1, 1778–Feb. 7, 1837), whose uncle Charles (Oct. 7, 1748–Feb. 5, 1818), duke of Södermanland and the future Charles XIII, king of Sweden (1809–1818), acted as regent.

1792 Mar. 19 In the **Second Mysore War** (1790–1792) Tipu Sahib, sultan of Mysore, was defeated by the British and their allies, the Hindu Marathas [Mahrattas] in a **battle at Seringapatam**, India, where Tipu had established his capital.

1792 Apr. 20 France declared war on Austria, with the intention of invading the Austrian Netherlands to reestablish the United States of Belgium, thus initiating the **War of the First Coalition** (1792–1797). Prussia, called upon by an earlier treaty, supported Austria, and dispatched **Charles William Ferdinand** (Oct. 9, 1735–Nov. 10, 1806), duke of Brunswick, to attack France's borders. On Feb. 1, 1793, Great Britain declared war against France and, soon thereafter, signed treaties with Spain, the Italian States, Sardinia, Naples, Denmark, Sweden, and the Ottoman Empire.

1792 May 19 Russia invaded Poland to prevent the strengthening of the Polish monarchy by the reforms established by the **Constitution of 1791**. The **Confederation of Targowica** was formed (May 14) in the Polish Ukraine to force restoration of the old constitution, with Russian aid. **Thaddeus Kosciusko** [Tadeusz Andrzej Bonawentura Kościuszko], a former brigadier general in the American army, led a valiant but futile defense of Poland.

1792 June 1 Kentucky, a county of Virginia, was the **15th state admitted to the U.S.** Settlers came through the Cumberland Gap and over the Wilderness Road and increased the population sufficiently to make Kentucky eligible for statehood.

1792 Aug. 9 A **Jacobin insurrection was launched in Paris** to overthrow the constitutional monarchy established in 1791. **George Jacques Danton** and his followers, the Jacobins, stormed the Tuileries, which was protected by the National Guard and the Swiss Guard. The Jacobin-dominated Legislative Assembly called for the suspension of Louis XVI from office and made arrangements to elect a **National Convention** to draft a new constitution.

1792 Sept. 2 In the "September Massacres" rioters in Paris broke into the prisons, killing more than 1,000 imprisoned nobles and clergy in their cells. Although the **Girondists** were accused of instigating the riots, the actual causes were more complex. Fear of the Prussian army advancing on Paris and the threat of starvation may have contributed most to the chaos. Rioting eased by Sept. 7.

1792 Sept. 20 In a **battle at Valmy**, France, **Charles François Dumouriez** (Jan. 25, 1739–Mar. 14, 1823) led the French to a victory that halted the invading Prussian advance on Paris. France's first victory, after several reverses, in the **War of the First Coalition** (1792–1797) marked the beginning of a prolonged Prussian retreat as a three-pronged French offensive occupied Nice and Savoy before the end of the month, the middle Rhine near Strasbourg in October, and the Austrian Netherlands in November. The new French Republic annexed Savoy and Nice on Nov. 27.

1792 Sept. 20 The **National Convention** (1792–1795), elected by universal manhood suffrage, convened with 749 members. The Convention, which replaced the Legislative Assembly (from Oct. 1791), was often separated into three distinct periods characterized by the factions that dominated: *La convention girondine* (Sept. 1792–June 2, 1793), *La convention montagnarde* (June 2, 1793–July 27, 1794), and *La convention thermidorienne* (July 28, 1794–Oct. 26, 1795, when the Directory was established). On Sept. 21, 1792, the Convention established the **First French Republic** (to May 18, 1804), and appointed a committee to draft an appropriate constitution. **Robespierre**, perhaps the strongest member of the Jacobins, called for the execution of the king on charges of treason, without a trial, on the basis of the discovery of an iron chest full of letters indicating court intrigues. The National Convention, composed entirely of republicans, was divided by two major factions: the Brissotins or Girondists [la Gironde], numbered c.180; the Montagnards, who were controlled by the Jacobins, c.100; and the remainder, c.470.

1792 Nov. 6 In a **battle at Jemappes**, in present Belgium, during the **War of the First Coalition** (1792–1797), the Austrian Netherlands [Belgium] fell to the French under **Charles François Dumouriez**, who defeated the Austrian forces of Albert [Albrecht Kasimir] (1738–1822), duke of Saxe-Teschen. French troops under **Adam Philippe** (Feb. 4, 1740–Aug. 28, 1793), comte de Custine, had crossed the Rhine River on Oct. 19 and advanced toward Frankfurt am Main, in present Germany.

1792 Dec. 15 The **Bill of Rights** went into effect with ratification by Virginia, providing the necessary approval of two-thirds of the states. The Bill of Rights, which ensured the protection of personal liberties and the limitation of federal powers, had been drafted by **James Madison**, and was similar to the Virginia constitution and its bill of rights drafted by George Mason (1725-Oct. 7, 1792) in 1776.

1792 Dec. 26 The trial of **Louis XVI** began, the charges having been read (Dec. 11). On Jan. 15, 1793, the National Convention found him guilty of treason by a nearly unanimous vote. The death sentence was approved by 387 to 334 on Jan. 16. Reprieve was denied by a vote of 380 to 310 on Jan. 19.

1793 The **first British diplomatic representative to China**, George Macartney (1737–1806), earl of Macartney, arrived at Peking. **Kao Tsung** [Ch'ien Lung], the Ch'ing [Manchu] emperor (1736–1796), was receptive, but he responded to George III, king of Great Britain, that China could not profit by trade with the British.

1793 **Bodawpaya**, king of **Burma** (1781–1819), signed a treaty with **Rama I** acknowledging the legitimacy of the powerful Siamese state [Thailand] by ending a long series of Burmese invasions.

1793 Jan. 21 **Louis XVI** (b. Aug. 23, 1754), king of France (from 1774), was **guillotined** for treason in Paris at the Place de la Révolution [Place de la Concorde].

1793 Jan. 23 The **Second Partition of Poland** divided Polish territory between Russia and Prussia. The parts of White Russia, Lithuania, and the Ukraine lying west of the Dnieper [Dnepr] River went to Russia. Prussia received the district of Poz-

nań [Posen], west of Warsaw, and surrounding territories, together called Greater Poland, including Częstochowa [Czenstochau; German: Tschenstochau], and Toruń [German: Thorn]. Prussia also gained the port of Gdańsk [German: Danzig]. The Polish **Constitution of 1791 was annulled**, and Poland was virtually a protectorate of Russia.

1793 Mar. 4 **George Washington** was inaugurated for his second term as president of the U.S. **John Adams** served again as vice president.

1793 Mar. 13 By this date the Vendée, a region in western France, was in a state of open royalist rebellion against the French Republic. On Mar. 4 Cholet, on the Maine River, had been ravaged by peasants protesting enactment of conscription and statutes restricting the clergy. During the following months in the **Wars of the Vendée** (1793–1796), insurgents under **Jacques Cathelineau** joined with the Chouans to capture Fontenay-le-Comte, the capital of the Vendée department, and Saumur, the Protestant center on the Loire River. Their initial successes turned after the capture of Angers, near Nantes, on June 18. Jacques Cathelineau (b. Jan. 5, 1759) died of wounds received in the attack on Nantes on July 14.

1793 Apr. 6 The **Jacobin faction came to power in France** as the National Convention created the **Committee of Public Safety** (to 1795) and appointed as its head **George Jacques Danton**, a former Montagnard who had just defected to the Jacobins. When Danton vacillated in following the radical revolutionaries, he was dropped from the committee in July.

1793 Apr. 22 George Washington issued the **Neutrality Proclamation** in the face of hostilities between Great Britain and France. Despite the military defense treaty signed with France in 1778 and popular support in the U.S. for the French Revolution, Washington asked for the recall of **Edmond Charles Édouard Genèt** (Jan. 8, 1763–July 14, 1834), the French minister to the U.S., who had tried to organize an invasion of Spanish Florida and piracy of British ships.

1793 June 2 The **Reign of Terror** was initiated in France by **Maximilien Robespierre**, a leader of the Jacobins and a member of the Committee of Public Safety, as he began a purge of those suspected of treason against the French Republic. He ordered the arrest of 31 Girondist deputies in the National Convention, initiating the period of *La convention mon-*

tagnarde (to July 27, 1794). Nearly 50,000 throughout France were executed on charges of treason before the Reign of Terror came to an end on July 28, 1794. The Girondist faction was crushed.

1793 July 13 Jean Paul Marat (b. May 24, 1743), president of the Jacobins, was stabbed to death in his bath, necessitated by a painful skin disease, by **Charlotte Corday** (b. July 27, 1768), a royal sympathizing Girondist from Normandy, who was arrested and executed on July 17, 1793. Marat, with support from a strongly organized Parisian mob, had succeeded in gaining control of the National Convention, to which he had been elected on Sept. 9, 1792. Marat had succeeded in having a bill passed calling for the arrest of all Girondist leaders on June 2. Charlotte's action initiated a flurry of anti-counterrevolutionary activity which had the effect of unifying the new republic.

1793 Aug. 1 The **Committee of Public Safety** authorized organization of an army to march on the insurgents in western France in the **Wars of the Vendée** (1793–1796). On Oct. 17 at Cholet, near Angers, the rebels were defeated, and later they failed to take Granville on Nov. 13 due to lack of support promised by the British. On Dec. 23, upon another defeat at Savenay, near Nantes, the insurgents retreated.

1793 Aug. 23 The **National Convention** in France ordered a draft of all able-bodied men and women of all ages. **Lazare [Nicolas Marguerite] Carnot** (May 13, 1753–Aug. 2, 1823), a member of the Committee of Public Safety, devoted himself to organizing the French armies for the **War of the First Coalition** (1792–1797).

1793 Oct. 16 Marie Antoinette [Josèphe Jeanne Marie Antoinette] (b. Nov. 2, 1755), widow of Louis XVI, was **guillotined** in the Place de la Révolution [Place de la Concorde] in Paris.

1793 Oct. 31 **Jacques Pierre Brissot de Warville** (b. Jan. 15, 1754), the Girondist leader and outspoken member of the National Assembly, was executed during the **Reign of Terror** (June 1793–July 1794) in France. Brissot had lost favor with Maximilien Robespierre, the Jacobin leader, by opposing the execution of the king.

1794 Agha Mohammed Khan founded the **Kajar** [Qajar] **Dynasty** (1794–1925) of Persian rulers with the murder of the last of the **Zand Dynasty** (1757–1794), Lutfr Ali Khan (ruled from 1789). In 1796 Agha Mohammed Khan was crowned shah at Tehran, which he made the capital of Persia.

1794 Mar. 24 Invited to lead a popular uprising against Russian hegemony during the period of the **Second Partition of Poland, Thaddeus Kosciusko,** the military commander, had Polish arms consecrated at the church of the Capuchins in order to gain religious sanction for the revolt. After an initial victory (Apr. 4, 1794) at Raclawice, northeast of Kraców, the Poles met repeated defeats, especially at the hands of **Aleksandr Vasilievich Suvorov,** the Russian general. Kosciusko engineered a brilliant defense of Warsaw, besieged (July 13–Sept. 6) by the Russians, but the Poles had already lost (June 15) Kraców. Kosciusko was wounded and captured (Oct. 10) at Maciejowice, near Warsaw. He was imprisoned at the fort of Peter and Paul in St. Petersburg, Russia, from Dec. 10, 1794, to Nov. 26, 1796, when Paul I, czar of Russia, released him and permitted him to travel to London.

1794 Mar. 24 Jacques René Hébert (b. 1757), the leader of the worker-supported **Club of the Cordeliers** [Society of the Friends of the Rights of Man and of the Citizen], with some of its other members, was **guillotined** during the **Reign of Terror** in France. The Cordeliers represented radical popular sentiment [the Parisian mob: *sans-culottes*] and had helped Robespierre and his Jacobins to power, especially through Hébert's journal *Le Père Duchesne,* (founded 1790). But the great popularity of the Hébertists threatened Robespierre's position. After Hébert's death, the Cordeliers disappeared.

1794 Apr. 5 Georges Jacques Danton (b. Oct. 26, 1759), a chief leader of the Jacobins, was **executed** during the Reign of Terror. Danton and the Indulgents had urged relaxation of emergency measures when France had repulsed the threat of foreign invasion.

1794 June 1 The **Battle of the Glorious First of June** was fought in the **War of the First Coalition. Richard Howe,** the British admiral, attacked an American grain convoy to Brest escorted by **Louis Thomas** (1747–1812), comte de Villaret de Joyeuse. The battle was fought c.430 miles off Ushant [Île d'Ouessant], in Brittany. Though the French fleet was dispersed, neither side gained a clear advantage.

1794 July 28 Maximilien [François Marie Isidorede] **Robespierre** (b. May 6, 1758), leader of the Jacobins during the French Revolution, was executed in Thermidor (the 11th month of the republican calendar: July 19–Aug. 17), bringing an end to the **Reign of Terror**. The period of *La convention thermidorienne* (to Oct., 1795) began. The Convention began to draft a new Constitution (1795) to establish a bicameral legislature, the **Council of Elders** [Ancients] and the **Council of Five Hundred**, to be headed by a five-man committee, the Directory [*le Directoire*].

1794 Aug. 7 On orders from **George Washington**, the **Whiskey Rebellion** (1794) was put down by militia. Especially on the western frontier, grain was converted to whiskey by farmers because it was easier and cheaper to transport than the grain itself. The settlers in Pennsylvania west of the Allegheny Mountains, who relied on whisky production, were protesting against an excise tax initiated (1791) by **Alexander Hamilton** on every gallon of liquor distilled in the U.S.

1794 Nov. 19 The **Jay Treaty**, engineered by John Jay, was signed by the U.S. and Great Britain in an attempt to settle the dispute arising from Great Britain's seizure of U.S. ships in the French West Indies and her impressment of American seamen, despite assurances given in the **Treaty of Paris** (1783). The British agreed to withdraw from their forts in the Old Northwest Territory by June 1, 1796.

1795 The **Yazoo Land Fraud** was the name given to the sale (Jan. 7) by the Georgia legislature of territory drained by the Yazoo River, including parts of present Mississippi and Alabama. Not only did the land not belong to Georgia, but all but one of the legislators were shareholders of the land companies speculators had established. The sale was retracted (1796), but a full settlement between the state of Georgia and the speculators was not reached until 1810, when the federal government paid them $4,282,151.

1795 Rama I, king of **Siam** [Thailand], annexed the western territories of Cambodia, including **Battambang** and **Angkor Thom**, the ruined Khmer capital.

1795 Antonio Nariño (1765–1823), a South American revolutionary, was found guilty of conspiracy and sentenced to prison. He had translated *The Declaration of the Rights of Man*, the French document of independence, and was circulating copies in **New Granada**. He escaped to France, then England, before returning (1797) to New Granada to continue his revolutionary activities.

1795 Feb. 17 The **Convention of La Jaunaye** [Jaunaie] was signed by the Vendée leaders and France's revolutionary government, permitting open and free religious worship and ending conscription, the chief grievances of the peasants of the Vendée.

1795 Apr. 5 Prussia and France signed the **Treaty of Basel**, Switzerland. Prussia wanted to conserve military forces for the conquest of Poland, now at the brink of collapse. France ceded her conquests of Prussian territories except for those along the western bank of the Rhine River. On July 22, by the **Second Treaty of Basel**, negotiated by **Manuel de Godoy** [y Álvarez de Faria] (May 12, 1767–Oct. 4, 1851), Spain made peace with France, ceding the eastern two-thirds of the island of Haiti [Hispaniola]. Fighting continued in northern Italy between France and the allies—Great Britain, Austria, and Sardinia.

1795 May 16 The **Netherlands** was seized by France, which established the **Batavian Republic**, the first of a series of satellite republics created by France during the French Revolutionary (1792–1802) and Napoleonic (1803–1815) wars. On Oct. 1 France annexed the Austrian Netherlands [Belgium and Luxembourg].

1795 Oct. 5 In Paris **Napoléon Bonaparte** won his **first distinction** by crushing the royalist insurrection of Vendémiaire (the first month of the republican calendar: Sept. 22–Oct. 21), in which Parisian citizens rebelled against decrees that would establish the **Directory**. He was appointed commander of the Army of the Interior.

1795 Oct. 24 The **Third Partition of Poland was completed**; Poland as an independent kingdom did not exist for the next 125 years. Russia received what remained of Lithuania, including the city of Vilna [Polish: Wilno], White Russia, and the Ukraine, and Courland [Kurland], a duchy in Latvia. Austria gained Kraków [Cracow] and Lublin, Poland. Prussia gained Warsaw and surrounding territories. **Stanislas II Poniatowski**, last king of an independent Poland, abdicated on Nov. 25.

1795 Oct. 27 The **Pinckney** [San Lorenzo de Real] **Treaty** negotiated by **Thomas Pinckney** (Oct. 23,

1750–Nov. 2, 1828) of the U.S. and **Manuel de Godoy** of Spain established trade relations between the U.S. and Spain, granting to the U.S. the right of shipping through New Orleans and establishing boundaries for Louisiana and the Floridas. All territory east of the Mississippi River was ceded by Spain to the U.S., and the **31st parallel was accepted as the boundary** between the U.S. and the Spanish colony of West Florida.

1795 Nov. **William Pitt** the Younger, prime minister of Great Britain, introduced in Parliament the **Treasonable Practices and Seditious Meetings Acts**. These redefined treason to include publication of seditious material. Public gatherings could only be held with government approval.

1795 Nov. 3 The **Directory** [*le Directoire*] (1795–1799), established in October by France's new Constitution, took office. The **National Convention had been dissolved** (Oct. 26), and the Committee of Public Safety came to an end. The Directory, a five-member committee and the executive head of the republican government, was dominated by members of the middle class, both the established and the newly rich, who had profited from the war inflated economy. With corruption and rivalries rampant, the Directory and its supporters relied on the generals, such as Bonaparte, to maintain power and control.

1796 Apr. 13 **Napoléon Bonaparte**, commander of the Army of the Interior, **assumed direction of French forces in Italy**, where he captured Piedmont and Lombardy in an attack planned by **Lazare Carnot**, now supreme commander of French troops. After crossing the Alps Bonaparte was joined by **Jean Victor Marie Moreau** (Feb. 14, 1763–Sept. 2, 1813). They marched across southern Germany and met **Jean Baptiste Jourdan** (Apr. 29, 1762–Nov. 23, 1833), driving southeast from the newly captured Austrian Netherlands.

1796 June **François Athanase Charette de la Contrie** landed with French émigrés at Quiberon Bay in Brittany and led a new army to retake the Vendée. In the following month they were defeated by republican forces, and Charette was captured, bringing an end to the **Wars of the Vendée** (1793–1796). Charette (b. 1763) was hanged on Mar. 29, 1797.

1796 June 1 **Tennessee** was the 16th state admitted to the U.S.

1796 June 1 The British evacuated the Old Northwest Territory under the terms of the **Jay Treaty** (1794). Settlers were permitted to choose whether they were to be British or American citizens, and compensation was arranged for those who withdrew to Canada.

1796 Sept. 17 **George Washington**, after declining a third term, delivered his **Farewell Address**, in which he outlined a basis for future U.S. policy. He urged an isolationist policy, warning against forming permanent alliances with foreign nations. He also warned of the pitfalls of overextending the public debt, and noted that power wielded by the smallest of political groups could interfere with just government.

1796 Nov. 15–17 In a **battle at Arcole**, Italy, near Verona, **Napoléon Bonaparte** defeated Austrian forces led by **Josef Alvinczy** (1735–1810), baron von Borberek [Barberek], in the **War of the First Coalition** (1792–1797). In Feb. 1797, Napoléon took Mantua, Lombardy, thus securing French control from Sardinia on the west to Venice on the east.

1796 Nov. 17 **Catherine II the Great** [Ekaterina Alekseevna, Yekaterina Alekseyevna; Sophia Augusta Frederica of Anhalt-Zerbst] (b. May 2, 1729), czarina of Russia (from 1762), died and was succeeded by her son **Paul I**. Russia's borders and international influence expanded greatly during her reign.

1797 Paul I, czar of Russia, decreed that the **succession of Russian rulers be based on heredity**, the line passing to the eldest male child. Since 1722 Russian rulers had been able to choose their successors, a procedure that led to uncertainty since reigning monarchs often waited to announce their decisions until near death.

1797 Mar. 4 **John Adams**, the second and last president of the Federalist party, was inaugurated as the second president of the U.S. **Thomas Jefferson**, of the Republican party, served as vice president. George Washington retired from public life to his estate Mount Vernon, in Virginia.

1797 Spring **Agha Mohammed Khan**, shah of Persia (from 1794) and founder of the **Kajar** [Qajar] **Dynasty** (1794–1925), was murdered in his tent by two attendants. He was enroute to Georgia to subdue **Erekle II** [Irakli, Heraclius], the Georgian ruler.

Agha Mohammed Khan was succeeded by his nephew **Fath Ali** (1762?–1835).

1797 July   Charles de Talleyrand [Charles Maurice de Talleyrand-Périgord] (Feb. 2, 1754–May 17, 1838), became France's foreign minister. He was credited with restoring France's prestige after the chaos of the revolutionary period.

1797 Sept. 4   In Paris the **Coup d'État of 18 Fructidor** (the 12th and last month on the republican calendar: Aug. 18–Sept. 21) by minority and republican members of the Directory and Council was against the recently elected (Apr. 1797) majority of moderates and reactionaries, some of whom were accused of trying to reestablish a constitutional monarchy. Two of the Directory's members were ousted; the elections were determined invalid, and many deputies were deported to French Guiana. The republicans were supported by the generals.

1797 Oct. 17   Austria and France signed the **Treaty of Campo Formio**, ending the **War of the First Coalition** (1792–1797). Austria ceded the Austrian Netherlands [Belgium and Luxembourg] to France. The Republic of Venice [Venetia] was partitioned, with the eastern part going to Austria in exchange for the Austrian Netherlands, and the Ionian Islands to France.

1797 Nov. 16   Frederick William II (b. Sept. 25, 1744), king of Prussia (from 1786), died and was succeeded by his son **Frederick William III** (Aug. 3, 1770–June 7, 1840).

1798   The **British were driven out of Saint Dominique, Haiti,** by Pierre Dominique Toussaint L'Ouverture, the Haitian black patriot, who was professedly acting in the interest of France.

1798   The **Mississippi Territory** was organized by the U.S. government; its capital was established at **Natchez,** on the Mississippi River. It included parts of present Mississippi and Alabama. The territory was bounded on the north by the Yazoo River and on the south by the 31st parallel. The Chattahoochee River marked the eastern, and the Mississippi River the western boundaries.

1798 Feb.   France established the **Roman Republic in central Italy** after occupying Rome. **Pope Pius VI** (b. Dec. 25, 1717; from 1775) was taken to France, where he died in captivity at Valence on Aug. 29, 1799.

1798 Feb. 9   The **Helvetic Republic** (1778–1814) was established by France to control Switzerland, following the French invasion of the country. After Bonaparte's approval, a **French army**, supported by revolutionaries in the Swiss republic, **invaded Switzerland** and soon controlled the entire nation.

1798 Apr. 3   The **XYZ Affair** was disclosed by **John Adams**, president of the U.S. Discussions with France to ease tensions created by the U.S. refusal to honor its 1778 military agreement with France, had proceeded poorly, and Adams had sent (1797) new representatives to negotiate with Talleyrand, the French foreign minister. Before he would deal officially with the U.S. envoys, Talleyrand asked through intermediaries called X, Y, and Z in correspondence with the U.S. government, for a payment of $250,000. Paying tribute outraged many in the U.S., and the negotiations broke off, much to the delight of the pro-British faction. Relations between the U.S. and France worsened.

1798 June 10   Napoléon Bonaparte, on his way to Egypt, captured Malta with the loss of only three men. The French Directory had previously bribed the grandmaster and other leaders of the **Knights of Malta** [formerly the order of the Hospital of St. John of Jerusalem] to make only token resistance. **Paul I**, czar of Russia, enraged by Bonaparte's seizure of Malta, obtained permission from **Francis II**, the Holy Roman emperor to march a Russian army of c.18,000 men through parts of Austria into northern Italy and permission from the Turks to move a fleet with transports through the Dardanelles. Under **Suvorov**, the able Russian marshal, the allied army (Italian, Austrians, and Russians) drove (1799) the **French out of nearly all the lands Bonaparte had won in Italy**.

1798 June 18   The **first of the Alien and Sedition Acts** was passed by the Federalist-dominated U.S. Congress. An amendment to the Naturalization Act of 1795, it required a residence period of 14 years to gain eligibility for U.S. citizenship, and was aimed at the supporters of the Republican party, who were often recent arrivals from Europe and sympathetic to the French Revolution.

1798 June 21   Irish insurrectionists were defeated at Vinegar Hill, in southeastern Ireland. The rebellion had broken out despite efforts by William Pitt the Younger, the British prime minister, to suppress radical activity in Ireland. In light of the rebellion's strength, he suggested a **union of Ireland with Great Britain**, which was effected in 1800.

1798 June 25 The **Alien Act**, the second of the Alien and Sedition Acts, was passed by the U.S. Congress. It granted to the president of the U.S. for two years the authority to deport any alien considered a risk to the nation.

1798 July 6 The **Alien Enemies Act**, third of the Alien and Sedition Acts, was passed by the U.S. Congress. It provided for apprehension and deportation of male citizens of a "hostile" country.

1798 July 14 The **Sedition Act**, the fourth and last of the Alien and Sedition Acts, aimed directly at supporters of the Republican party, was passed by the U.S. Congress. In providing for the arrest and imprisonment of any person, either U.S. citizen or alien resident, who attempted to impede the lawful processes of the U.S. government by writing, publishing, or speaking any statement against the U.S. government, the act **curtailed** the freedoms of speech and the press guaranteed by the **First Amendment to the U.S. Constitution**.

1798 July 21 In the **Battle of the Pyramids**, the only striking success in **Napoléon Bonaparte's plan to block Great Britain's Near Eastern trade routes** by invading Egypt during the **French Revolutionary Wars** (1792–1802), the French defeated the Egyptian Mamelukes under **Murad Bey** (d. 1801). Napoléon hoped to win the Ottoman Empire's support. On July 22, Bonaparte entered Cairo.

1798 Aug. 1 The **French fleet in Egypt was destroyed by British naval forces** under **Horatio Nelson** in the **Battle of the Nile at Abukir** [Aboukir, Abu Qir] Bay in the Nile Delta during the French Revolutionary Wars. Though without land forces able to drive the French army from Egypt, British power was restored in the Mediterranean, while Napoléon's army was now cut off from France. Naples under Austrian leadership attacked the newly formed Roman Republic, occupying the city on Nov. 29. On Aug. 22, 1799, Bonaparte returned to France to assume power there. In September the Ottoman Empire (1326–1920) declared war on France during the **War of the Second Coalition** (1798–1802).

1798 Nov. The **Kentucky Resolution**, drafted by **Thomas Jefferson**, was adopted by the Kentucky leg-

islature. In December the **Virginia Resolution**, drafted by **James Madison**, was adopted by the Virginia legislature. These resolutions declared that states had the right to decide the constitutionality of federal laws. In Feb. 1799, the Kentucky legislature declared further that the state could enforce its rights by nullifying objectionable laws.

1798 Nov. 19 **Wolfe Tone** [Theobald Wolfe Tone] (b. June 20, 1763), a leader of the **Irish Rebellion**, died after slitting his throat (Nov. 12) on Nov. 19. He had been sentenced to death by hanging after his capture (Oct. 12) by British forces, when the small French naval force he was leading to liberate Ireland was intercepted off Lough Swilly, on the northern coast of Ireland in County Donegal.

1798 Dec. 29 Great Britain and Russia signed a treaty of alliance against France, beginning the **War of the Second Coalition** (1798–1802), under the leadership of **Paul I**, czar of Russia. In Jan. 1799, after the French had driven the Austrians and Neapolitans from Rome and Naples, Naples was reorganized as the **Parthenopean Republic** (it existed for only a few months). The exiled Neapolitan government, the Ottoman Empire, and Portugal soon joined the Coalition against France.

1799 Feb. 7 **Ch'ien Lung** [Kien Lung, Hung Li, Kao Tsung] (b. Sept. 25, 1711), emperor of China (1736–1796) during the Ch'ing [Manchu] Dynasty (1644–1911), died. He had abdicated (1796) in favor of his son **Chia Ch'ing** (1760–1820). During his reign Ch'ien Lung established control over Tibet, invaded Burma [Myanmar], and took Nepal. A great patron of the arts he issued (1789) the massive **catalogue of the Imperial Library**, Ssu-k' u ch'üan-shu. Ch'ien-Lung's reign was one of the longest and most beneficial in Chinese history.

1799 Mar. 18 In the last stage of the **French Revolutionary Wars**, French forces under **Napoléon Bonaparte** began a **siege of Acre**, Syria, in an effort to defeat the Ottoman Empire. **Djezzar** [Ahmed Pasha] (1735?–1804) commanded the Ottoman Turks, supported by a small British naval force. Though the French, under **Jean Baptiste Kléber** (Mar. 9, 1753–June 14, 1800), held out against the Turks at nearby Mount Tabor [Har Tavor], in present Israel, on Apr. 16 **plague** struck Bonaparte's troops, forcing him to break siege on May 20 and withdraw from Syria to Egypt.

1799 Mar. 25 At Stockach, in present Baden-Württemberg, Germany, the **French advance toward Vienna**, led by Comte **Jean Baptiste Jourdan**, was halted by the Austrians under **Charles Louis** [Karl Ludwig] (Sept. 5, 1771–Apr. 30, 1847), archduke of Austria and duke of Teschen.

1799 May 4 **Tipu Sahib** [Tippoo Sultan] (b. 1749), the military ruler of Mysore, died fighting during a British drive on his capital of **Seringapatam** in the **Fourth Mysore War** (1799). The British thus gained direct control of the coastal Carnatic region when **Richard Colley** (June 20, 1760–Sept. 26, 1842), **Lord Wellesley**, the governor general of British India (1797–1805), decided to administer the area directly from Calcutta.

1799 Aug. 15 The **French**, encamped at Novi Ligure in Piedmont, in present Italy, were **routed by the allied Russian and Austrian forces** led by Suvorov, the Russian marshal. The French commander **Barthélemy Catherine Joubert** (b. Apr. 14, 1769) was killed in the battle. Suvorov then crossed the Alps into Switzerland to rescue the Russian troops of **Aleksandr Korsakov** (1753–1840) from the French. The Russian Black Sea fleet and the Turkish navy captured the French-occupied Ionian Islands and Corfu.

1799 Oct. 22 **Russia withdrew from the Second Coalition** (1798–1802), because Austria showed a reluctance to cooperate with Russian goals. Deprived of Russian support, Great Britain and Austria were unable to force a surrender from France, and the Second Coalition weakened.

1799 Nov. 9 In the **coup d'état of 18 Brumaire** (the second month in the revolutionary calendar: Sept. 22–Nov. 21) **Napoléon Bonaparte** overthrew the failing **Directory** [*le Directoire*] and established the **Consulate** (1799–1804), aided by the politician **Emmanuel Joseph Sieyès** (May 3, 1748–June 20, 1836); Napoléon's brother **Lucien Bonaparte**, president of the Council of Five Hundred; and popular discontent with the Directory's corruption. Bonaparte was put in charge of the troops stationed in Paris. On the next day the Council of Five Hundred was broken up. The **French Revolution was now effectively ended**.

1799 Dec. 14 **George Washington** (b. Feb. 22, 1732), the first president of the U.S. and the Commander-in-chief of American forces during the American Revolution, died. **Henry Lee**, called "Light-Horse Harry," drafted these words summarizing Washington's contribution to his country: "First in war, first in peace, and first in the hearts of his countrymen," which were spoken by Lee at a memorial service on Dec. 18, 1799.

Dec. 24 **Napoléon Bonaparte was selected as the first consul** under the Consulate. Although he was aided by two other consuls, whom he selected himself, Bonaparte became virtual dictator of France. His term of office was set at ten years. A Senate of 80 members, appointed for life, was established; a consultative tribunate of 100 members, who did not vote, and a legislature of 300 members, who approved or rejected proposals, were also established.

V. ECONOMY AND TRADE

1790–1800 **Rum** became the principal medium of exchange in **Australia**, where at this time most of the white population were convicts serving sentences of forced labor. The unlawful distillation of rum became an easy way to turn a profit. A few of the colony were "emancipists," who had completed their sentences and remained. Officers administering the colony were forbidden to reap a profit from convict labor, and the British government maintained control over importation of goods by the Australian colony.

1790 Mar. The *gabelle*, a tax on salt production that kept smugglers in business, was abolished in France. Salt, which was produced primarily in western France, was distributed throughout the country in a manner that encouraged high prices. Soon after this, the **Chouans** [Owls], whose name came from the call of the owl they used to warn one another, organized resistance to the conscription and high tax of the French government. Under **Jean Cottereau** (1757–1794), who styled himself **Jean Chouan**, marquis de la Rouerie [John the Owl, marquess of Mischief], the resistance dissolved into brigandage.

1790 Dec. 21 The **first successful textile mill in the U.S.** opened in Pawtucket, Rhode Island, under the direction of **Samuel Slater** (1768–1835). He had arrived in the U.S. in the previous year. To avoid being caught carrying secret blueprints, he had memorized the design of the best British mills. Ultimately Slater built 12 mills in New England.

1791 The **farming of taxes**, practiced in France since 1681, was abolished. Collection of taxes had been assigned to financiers, called farmers general, who guaranteed delivery of an agreed-upon sum, but could make a profit by collecting more. Many former farmers general were guillotined during the **Reign of Terror** (June 1793–July 1794).

1791 The **first American stock exchange** was founded in **Philadelphia**, the U.S. capital (1790–1800), although informal stock traders had existed for a long time. On May 17, 1792, stock brokers on New York City's **Wall Street** were organized. They were the first to charge commissions as agents in buying and selling stocks.

1791 The **First Bank of the U.S.** was granted a charter by the U.S. Congress following a proposal made by **Alexander Hamilton**, the **first secretary of the treasury**, to establish a bank to act as the fiscal agent of the government. The government was the largest stockholder in the enterprise, owning one-fifth of the shares, worth $10 million.

1791 Mar. 2 The **Allarde Law** was enacted in France. It forbade secret societies and abolished guilds and journeymen's associations. In order to enter a trade, business, or profession, it now was necessary to obtain a license from the government, instead of approval from a guild.

1791 June 14 The **Chapelier Law** was passed in France. Its primary effect was to prohibit labor organizations.

1791 Aug. 26 **John Fitch**, a U.S. inventor, received a **patent for his paddle wheel steamboat**, which he had launched on the Delaware River on July 26, 1790, to provide service from Burlington, New Jersey, to Philadelphia.

1792 The **first union in the U.S.** was formed by a group of Philadelphia shoemakers. It lasted less than a year. The first permanent union, the **Federal Society of Cordwainers**, or shoemakers who use cordovan leather, was founded in 1794.

1792 Apr. 2 The **First Coinage Act** authorized a mint to be established at Philadelphia to mint coins for the U.S. Anyone with gold or silver could bring it to the mint and have it pressed into coins free of charge.

1793 May 4 The **first Law of the Maximum** was passed in France, setting a ceiling on the price of grain. On Sept. 29 a more general Law of the Maximum was enacted, which set a ceiling on the prices of all basic commodities. The Hébertists had pressed for these controls.

1794 Stretching 62 miles from Philadelphia to Lancaster, Pennsylvania, the **Lancaster Turnpike**, the **first road in the U.S. with a macadam surface**, was completed. It led to a boom in roadbuilding.

1796 May Because of the worthlessness of the **Assignats** [treasury notes], first issued by the French government in 1789, *Mandats Territoriaux* [land notes] were issued, but they suffered from inflation as had the *Assignats*. Inflation in France was slowed in May when the value of currency was set: 100 francs in *Mandats Territoriaux*, or 3,000 livres in *Assignats*, equaled one franc in gold.

1797 **Merino sheep** were introduced into **Australia**, soon providing the British colony with a firm economic basis.

1797 The **drain on the Bank of England's resources** caused by the war with France was so great that the Bank found itself with only £1.5 million to meet liabilities of £16.5 million. To meet the crisis, the government authorized the Bank to stop specie payments temporarily. Payments were not resumed for 22 years.

1797 The **first beet sugar factory** was built by **Franz Karl Achard** (1753–1821) in Silesia, at this time a Prussian province. By 1806 he was successfully producing beet sugar.

1797 Feb. 4 The **French government repudiated all paper money**, which had already become virtually worthless because of inflation. On Sept. 30 the **Law of the Consolidated Third** repudiated two-thirds of France's internal debt. The peasants and workers almost certainly suffered severely.

1798 The assets of the **bankrupt Dutch East India Company** were taken over by the Dutch government. The company had maintained high dividend payments even after financial losses had become burdensome, adding to its downfall. In general, the company foundered because of the high cost of staffing and defending trade ports in the Far East.

1798 *An Essay on the Principle of Population as it Affects the Future Improvement of Society* was published by **Thomas Robert Malthus** (Feb. 14, 1766–Dec. 23, 1834), an English economist and social philosopher. The work maintained that population growth, unless checked by disease, war, and famine, increased geometrically, but food crops increased only arithmetically. Malthus concluded that poverty and misery were an inevitable condition for the largest part of mankind.

1799 Great Britain imposed a tax on incomes exceeding £200 at the rate of two shillings per pound. Exemptions were permitted, and the tax was levied in progressive amounts; overall, the rate was ten percent. This was the **first successful major income tax.**

1799 The **Act to Prevent Unlawful Combinations of Workingmen,** passed by the British Parliament, established penalties for forming unions of workingmen.

VI. RELIGION AND PHILOSOPHY

1790 Jan. 27 France's revolutionary National Assembly granted **citizenship rights to Sephardic Jews** in the Bordeaux region, reflecting the same sentiment expressed in the *Declaration of the Rights of Man* (1789). This action was followed, after extensive debate, by political equality for all Jews (1790), which brought in **Ashkenazic Jews,** chiefly in the region of Alsace-Lorraine.

1790 July 12 The **Civil Constitution of the Clergy,** enacted in France, brought Catholic priests under governmental control by naming them civil functionaries.

1791 With the adoption of the **First Amendment to the Constitution,** declaring that "Congress shall make no law respecting an establishment of religion, or prohibiting the free exercise thereof," the U.S. government turned its back on European patterns of establishment and uniformity. All churches were now voluntary associations and equal before the law.

1791 Mar. Published in London, the first part of **Thomas Paine's** *The Rights of Man* was a defense against an attack made by Edmund Burke on the French Revolution. Paine's argument limited democracy to providing only the least amount of government. Monarchy, he stated, could permissibly be overthrown, because it violated the natural rights of man by assuming too much power, which by right

belonged to the citizens. Paine was forced to flee to France after publishing this attack on the British crown; he was tried (Dec. 18) *in absentia* for treason and outlawed from England. The **Jacobins** imprisoned Paine because he was a British citizen, in 1793; he returned to the U.S. in 1802.

1791 July 14 For his defense of the cause of the French Revolution and the new regime there, **Joseph Priestley,** a dissenting English clergyman better known today for his **discovery of oxygen,** had to flee his home city of Birmingham in disguise on this second anniversary of the fall of the Bastille. Priestley's home, church, and laboratory were burned by a mob.

1792 Mohammed Abd al Wahab (born c.1704), religious leader and founder of the **Wahabis,** a Muslim sect, died. He taught that strict adherence to the *Koran* was the way to salvation; he abjured all innovations made after Muhammad's death, the Muslim saints, and luxuries such as tobacco, dancing, music, and gambling.

1792 Oct. 2 The **Baptist Missionary Society,** the first of English Protestants, was organized in Kettering, England, by a dozen ministers under the leadership of **William Carey** (Aug. 17, 1761–June 9, 1834), a shoemaker, school teacher, and Baptist minister in Moulton. Carey had provided motivation for the society's founding with his tract on the obligations of Christians to convert the heathen. Carey and John Thomas, a medic, the first missionaries dispatched by the Baptist Missionary Society, arrived in Calcutta, India, in Nov. 1793.

1793 Oct. 5 The **Committee of Public Safety** (1793–1795) **abolished Christianity in France,** and priests were forbidden to exercise their office outside the churches. On Nov. 10 the new **Cult of Reason** was ceremonially installed at the cathedral of Notre Dame in Paris by **Pierre Gaspard Chaumette,** and all Paris churches were named Temples of Reason on Nov. 23. However, freedom of worship was granted on Nov. 25. The Cult of Reason, with its associated cults, generally disappeared by 1795, after Chaumette (b. May 24, 1763) was guillotined on Apr. 13, 1794.

1794 The publication of the first part of **Thomas Paine's** *Age of Reason* marked the literary high point of aggressive, anti-sectarian deism. Paine was ostracized as an atheist in England and the U.S. Paine believed reason was the means of rescuing religion from superstition and effecting a return to rational simplicity and purity.

1795 The **London Missionary Society** was formed by English Congregationalists, with other nonconforming denominations represented. Their first missionaries arrived in **Tahiti** on Mar. 5, 1797. Following a dispute with the Tahitians over a trade encounter, all but five fled the island.

VII. SCIENCE, EDUCATION, AND TECHNOLOGY

1790 **John Frere** (Aug. 10, 1740–July 12, 1807) discovered flint implements dating to the Stone Age at Hoxne, a village in eastern England. His careful notes of the remains, made as they were uncovered, anticipated the methodology of later archaeologists.

1790 The **first wristwatch** was made by **Jaquet-Droz and Leschot**, a Swiss firm, whose books record a watch attached to a bracelet.

1790 The **first canal in the U.S.** built for general commercial use was completed. Known as the **James River and Kanawha Canal**, it ran for seven miles from Richmond to Westham, Virginia, along the James River.

1790 Apr. 10 The U.S. Congress enacted its **first patent law**, through the efforts of **John Stevens** (1749–Mar. 6, 1838). He was concerned about protecting his own invention, a boiler and engine with two underwater screw propellers.

1790 Apr. 17 **Benjamin Franklin** (b. Jan. 17, 1706), scholar, scientist, statesman, newspaperman, and inventor, died. About 20,000 mourners attended his funeral in Philadelphia. Franklin discovered the **law of conservation of charge** in 1747, and invented the **lightning rod** in 1752. He made the first chart of the Gulf Stream and invented the **Franklin stove** (1740) and **bifocals** (1752). Franklin was given the prestigious Copley Medal by the Royal Society of London for his work in electricity. His practical philosophy became known chiefly through *Poor Richard's Almanac* (1732–1757). Franklin founded (1727) in Philadelphia "Junto," a group that later became the American Philosophical Society. He established (1743) an academy that became the **University of Pennsylvania**. He was elected (1750–1764) to the Pennsylvania Assembly and was chosen a member of the Second Continental Congress. Franklin was one of a five-member committee to draft (1776) the **Declaration of Independence** and was one of its signers. On Feb. 6, 1778, he arranged a treaty of commerce and a defensive alliance with France; with John Adams and John Jay he concluded a peace treaty with England. At age 81 he was (1787) a delegate to the Constitutional Convention. When he was president of the Pennsylvania Abolition Society, he introduced (Feb. 12, 1790) a petition urging the abolition of slavery and the suppression of slave trade.

1793 Apr. **Eli Whitney** (Dec. 8, 1765–Jan. 8, 1825), a U.S. manufacturer and inventor, developed the **first hand-operated cotton gin**. Patented on Mar. 14, 1794, Whitney's gin increased fivefold the production of cotton in the U.S.

1793 June 20 **Charles Bonnet** (b. Mar. 13, 1720), a Swiss naturalist, died. His most important work was the discovery of parthenogenesis in aphids. In *Contemplation de la nature* (1764–1765), Bonnet suggested that all living creatures, from lowest to highest, represented a continuum in development.

1794 The **first lathe** for turning metal was produced, greatly increasing the usefulness of this early machine tool.

1794 May 8 **Antoine Laurent Lavoisier** (b. Aug. 26, 1743), a French chemist who laid the groundwork for the development of modern chemistry, was guillotined during the **Reign of Terror**. On Nov. 1, 1772, Lavoisier had announced observations that anticipated the existence of oxygen. Lavoisier measured specific heats and suggested that the state of solids, liquids, and gases depended on the amount of heat, or energy, they held. Lavoisier's *Traité Élémentaire de la Chimie* (1789) contained a list of the elements, which he called simple substances, organized by their properties.

1794 June 13 **James Lind** (b. 1716), a Scottish physician, died. His work to improve hygiene aboard ship resulted (1795) in an order by the British admiralty to give lemon juice to sailors for the prevention of **scurvy**. Lind was credited with inventing a practical wind gauge (1775).

1796 May 14 **Edward Jenner**, an English physician, performed the **first inoculation against smallpox** on

James Phipps, an eight-year-old boy, using cowpox virus. The cowpox virus produced a safer vaccine than the potent smallpox virus. Jenner's *Inquiry into the Causes and Effects of the Variolae Vaccinae* (1798) described the discovery.

1797 June 26 The **cast-iron plow** was first patented by **Charles Newbold** of New Jersey.

1798 Dec. 4 Luigi [Alisio] **Galvani** (b. Sept. 9, 1737), an Italian physicist, died. Galvani was the discoverer of galvanism, which he called animal electricity.

1799 The **manufacture of paper became an industrial process** with the invention in France of the **Fourdrinier machine** by **Louis Robert** (1794–1835), which was then developed (c.1803) by **Henry Fourdrinier** (1766–1854) in England.

1799 Feb. 12 Lazzaro Spallanzani (b. Jan. 10, 1729), an Italian biologist, died. In 1777 Spallanzani succeeded in an experiment with **artificial insemination**, discovering the nature of spermatic fluid and sperm. He also studied oxidation, digestion, and circulation.

1799 Aug. The **Rosetta Stone** was found by **Pierre Bouchard** [Boussart], an officer in Napoléon's army, at the town of Rosetta [Rashid], Egypt. It was inscribed in two languages and three scripts: Greek, Egyptian hieroglyphics, and a script called Egyptian demotic. It was a commemorative record of the succession of Ptolemy V Epiphanes [illustrious] (210?–181 B.C.) to the Egyptian throne in c.195 B.C. **Jean-François Champollion** (Dec. 23, 1790–Mar. 4, 1832), a French archaeologist, worked more than 20 years with the inscriptions, knowing Greek but not the other two languages, before fully deciphering the writings. He found the entire Egyptian alphabet and much history covering 2,000 years in the hieroglyphic writings on tombs and papyrus.

1799 Nov. 10 Joseph Black (b. Apr. 16, 1728), a Scottish chemist, died. In *Experiments Upon Magnesia Alba, Quicklime, and Some Other Alcaline* [sic] *Substances* (1756), Black described the properties of **carbon dioxide**, then called fixed air. Although he published no study on it, Black described the concepts of latent heat and specific heat.

VIII. ARTS AND LEISURE

1790 The *Journal of New England* by **John Winthrop**, the first governor of the Massachusetts Bay Colony, was published in two volumes. Winthrop gave a detailed account of many aspects of daily life, and his work is today a primary historical source for the early American colonial period.

1790 The publication of *Puteshestvie iz Peterburga v Moskvu* [*A Journey from St. Petersburg to Moscow*] established the radical element in Russian literature. In this work, **Aleksandr Nikolaevich Radishchev** [Radischev] (Aug. 31, 1749–Sept. 24, 1802) portrayed social conditions in Russia and criticized serfdom, religion, and the government. He was exiled to Siberia by **Catherine the Great**, the czarina of Russia.

1790 May 30 The **first copyright law in the U.S.** was enacted. Modeled on an earlier British law, it granted protection for a published work during a period of 14 years, with a renewable period.

1791 *Charlotte Temple*, one of the first romance novels with an American scene, was published in England by English-born **Susannah Rowson** [*nee* Haswell] (1762–Mar. 2, 1824), an Anglo-American writer and actress, who had lived in Massachusetts as a girl. It was published in the U.S. in 1794.

1791 May 9 Francis Hopkinson (b. Sept. 21, 1737), a signer of the Declaration of Independence, composer, lawyer, and poet, died. His *Ode to Music* (1754) may have been the first musical composition written by an American. His work also included *My Days Have Been So Wondrous Free* (1759), harpsichord and vocal music, and *A Collection of Psalm Tunes With a Few Anthems* (1762).

1791 Dec. 5 Wolfgang Amadeus Mozart [Johannes Chrysostomus Wolfgangus Theophilus Mozart] (b. Jan. 27, 1756), an Austrian classical composer, died. His operatic works included *Die Entführung aus dem Serail* [*The Abduction from the Seraglio*] (1782), *Le Nozze di Figaro* [*The Marriage of Figaro*] (1785), *Don Giovanni* (1787), *Cosi fan Tutte* (1790), and *Die Zauberflöte* [*The Magic Flute*] (1791). Mozart's more than 500 works included The Symphony in D [**Paris Symphony**] (1778), the symphonies No. 39 in E Flat, No. 4 in G Minor, and No. 41 in C [**Jupiter Symphony**], written in 1788. His chamber works included three string quartets written (1789–1790) for

Frederick William II, king of Prussia, and a clarinet quintet (1789). Mozart's nearly 30 concertos included the Piano Concerto in B Flat (1791).

1792 Feb. 23   Joshua Reynolds (b. July 16, 1723), an English portrait painter, died. His more than 2,000 paintings included **portraits** of David Garrick, Edward Gibbon, Edmund Burke, Oliver Goldsmith, and Samuel Johnson.

1793   Francesco Guardi (b. Oct. 15, 1712), a Venetian painter, died. He was best known for panoramic scenes around and in Venice, which he began to paint c.1760, when his brother, Giovanni Antonio [Gianantonio] (1699–1760), died. Among Guardi's paintings were *Piazza San Marco* (c.1735), *The Doge's Procession to S. Zaccaria* (c.1763), and *Punta della Dogana with S. Maria della Salute*.

1793 Feb. 6?   Carlo Goldoni (b. Feb. 25, 1707), an Italian comic playwright, died. He was famous for the "sixteen comedies" he wrote in one year (1750), including *Il padre de famiglia* [**The Father of a Family**] and *Il teatro comico* [**The Comic Theater**]. His last successful comedy was *Le bourru bienfaisant* [*The Beneficent Bear*], performed by the Comédie-Française in 1771. Altogether he wrote c.130 comedies.

1791–1793   In Philadelphia, the U.S. capital, the *National Gazette*, established and edited by **Philip Morin Freneau**, came to prominence for its Republican views and its attacks on such Federalists as Alexander Hamilton and John Adams. Thomas Jefferson and James Madison supported Freneau, approving especially his criticism of Federalist policies. Because of competition of the *Gazette of the United States*, supported by Hamilton, and because of the yellow fever epidemic in Philadelphia (1793), Freneau closed his paper in 1793.

1794 Mar. 5   Ramón de la Cruz [Ramón Francisco de la Cruz Cano y Olmedilla] (b. Mar. 28, 1731), a Spanish playwright, died. He wrote more than 500 plays, of which many were in one act, a form called **sainetes**, depicting everyday situations. De la Cruz was the first to translate Shakespeare's *Hamlet* into Spanish.

c.1795–1799   The **transitional Directoire style** appeared in French furniture and decoration. Named for the short-lived Directory [*le Directoire*] (1795–1799), it showed Greek and Roman forms and, later,

Egyptian motifs, which influenced the subsequent **Empire Style** (c.1800). In dress the dandies (*incroyables*) of France began to wear tight breeches and coats with wide lapels. But for others, **fashion** took a second seat. Beaver hats, covering ear-length hair, presented a sober appearance. Women abandoned the corset, preferring the chemise, a loose-fitting dress that hung straight from the shoulders and was gathered somewhat at waist or hips.

1795 May 19   James Boswell [Bozzy] (b. Oct. 29, 1740), a Scottish-born English writer and lawyer, died. He was best known for his *Life of Samuel Johnson* (1791). Boswell first met Johnson on May 16, 1763, in London. Boswell also wrote *An Account of Corsica* (1768) and *Journal of a Tour to the Hebrides* (1786).

1796 Feb. 2   Vortigern and Rowena, said to be a newly discovered play by **William Shakespeare**, was performed at the Drury Lane Theatre in London under the direction of **Richard Brinsley Sheridan**. The production was not successful, and it was discovered the same year that the script was an imitation produced by **William Henry Ireland** (1777–Apr. 17, 1835), who had written a number of false Shakespearean documents, including forgeries of fragments from another play supposed to have been **William the Conqueror**, fragments from *Hamlet*, and a transcript of **King Lear**.

1796 July 21   Robert Burns (b. Jan. 25, 1759), a Scottish poet, died. His first collection was *Poems, Chiefly in the Scottish Dialect* (1786), which brought him renown and some money. His songs were included in the collections *Scots Musical Museum* and **Scottish Airs with Poetry**. These included *Comin' Thro' the Rye*, *The Cotter's Saturday Night*, *Flow Gently Sweet Afton*, and *Auld Lang Syne* (c.1789).

1797 Mar. 2   Horace Walpole (b. Sept. 24, 1717), an English writer, died. His *The Castle of Otranto* (1764), called the first Gothic novel, was very popular. Walpole also wrote *Mysterious Mother* (1768), a verse tragedy, compiled the *Catalogue of Engravers in England* (1763), and researched *Historic Doubts on Richard III* (1768), but he was most famous for his correspondence (c.7,000 sent and received), much of which was saved.

1797 July 9   Edmund Burke (b. Jan. 12?, 1729), an Irish-born British statesman, died. For most of his political career he opposed the policies of the British government, notably in its relations with the American colonies. He argued against royal favoritism and the influence of monarchy on parliamentary affairs. In two famous speeches, *American Taxation* (1774) and *Conciliation with America* (1775), he advocated against British policy. Best known for his violent hostility to the French Revolution, which he carried to the end of his life, he wrote the tract *Reflections on the Revolution in France* (1790), which occasioned Thomas Paine's equally famous reply *The Rights of Man* (1791–1792). Burke was an impassioned orator, and his speeches were widely circulated in England and America.

1798 *Lyrical Ballads*, on which **William Wordsworth** and **Samuel Taylor Coleridge** collaborated, was published, marking the beginning of the Romantic movement in English poetry.

1799 Oct. 24 **Karl Ditters von Dittersdorf** (b. Nov. 2, 1739), an Austrian composer and violinist, died. His best-known opera was *Doktor und Apotheker* (1786). He also wrote concertos and piano works.

IX. SPORTS, GAMES, AND SOCIETY

1790 **Oliver Booth**, on the **first recorded iceboat in North America**, raced on the Hudson River at Poughkeepsie in a box-like craft set on three runners.

1791 **James Weatherby** initiated the **General Stud Book**, which by 1808 gained recognition as the authoritative collection of race horse pedigrees.

1793 Sept. 18 Construction began on the **U.S. Capitol building** at Washington, D.C. The site was chosen in consultation with the city's chief planner, **Pierre Charles L'Enfant** (Aug. 2, 1754–June 14, 1825). **William Thornton** (May 20, 1759–Mar. 28, 1828) won approval for his plans, submitted separately. **Charles Bulfinch** and **Benjamin Henry Latrobe** (1764–Sept. 3, 1820), among others, were later to work on the Capitol. The U.S. Congress first met in its new quarters in Nov. 1800.

1795 The **Dudingston Curling Society**, the oldest curling club extant, was founded this year in Edinburgh, Scotland.

1796 Mar. 9 **Napoléon Bonaparte** married **Joséphine de Beauharnais** [Marie Joséphine Rose Tascher de la Pagerie] (June 23, 1763–May 29, 1814).

1796 July 8 The **first recorded American passport** was signed personally by **Timothy Pickering** (July 17, 1745–Jan. 29, 1829), secretary of state in George Washington's administration.

1800–1804

I. VITAL STATISTICS AND DEMOGRAPHICS

1800–1839 By 1815 the **Native American lands** in the Southeast were restricted to Georgia, the Carolinas, and parts of Alabama, Mississippi, and Tennessee. By 1835 entire tribes and nations had been moved to present Oklahoma, Florida, Kansas, and elsewhere.

1800 **World population** was c.900 million—Europe 180 million, **Asia** 625 million, **North America** 13 million, **South America** 11 million, **Africa** 70 million, and **Oceania** [including Australia and New Zealand] 2.5 million. London had c.864,000 people, Paris c.545,000, Vienna c.230,000, and Berlin c.180,000. New York City had c.60,000 people.

1800 The **Industrial Revolution** stimulated a growth in Europe's population. In 1800 the combined population of Belgium and Luxembourg was c.3,200,000. The population of the Netherlands had dwindled to c.2,100,000. Its prosperity suffered because the nation had overextended itself by fighting in the European wars. In 1801, when the first general census of England, Wales, and Scotland was conducted, a total population of 10,500,956 was reported.

1800 Although c.10 million black **Africans** had been sent across the Atlantic to slavery in the Americas since the end of the 15th century, there were c.70 million people in all of Africa.

1800 The **second U.S. census** reported a population of 5,308,483, a ten-year gain of 1,379,269. Included in the count were 896,849 slaves, a gain of 199,168 over the previous 10 years. Virginia had the largest state population at 880,200. Canada at this time had c.0.5 million, Mexico c.5.3 million.

II. EXPLORATION AND COLONIZATION

1803 June 9 The continent of **Australia was first circumnavigated** by **Matthew Flinders**, a British mariner, establishing that Australia did not consist of a number of small islands, as previously thought.

1804 May 14 **Meriwether Lewis** (Aug. 18, 1774– Oct. 11, 1809) and **William Clark** (Aug. 1, 1770–Sept. 1, 1838) left St. Louis, Missouri, to explore the wilderness of the **Louisiana Purchase** and the northwest Oregon country. Commissioned by **Thomas Jefferson**, president of the U.S., the group of c.50 men went up the Missouri River; crossed the Rocky Mountains at Lemhi Pass, in eastern Idaho, and at Lolo Pass, in the Bitterroot Range along the Montana–Idaho border; then traveled along the Snake and Columbia rivers to the Pacific Coast. On Nov. 15, 1805, they reached the mouth of the Columbia River, where they built Fort Clatsop. They had been joined by the Indian woman **Sacajawea** [Sacagawea, Sakajawea; meaning Bird Woman] (1787?–Dec. 12, 1812), who served as a guide and translator. The expedition left Fort Clatsop on Mar. 23, 1806, and returned to St. Louis. The expedition brought back voluminous notes on the fauna and flora, the tribes they encountered, the geology, the trails, and natural resources. The exploration cost $2,500, and the leaders were rewarded later with 1,600 acres of land each.

III. POLITICS AND WAR

1800 May 1 The U.S. Congress created the **Indiana and Ohio territories** by dividing the Old Northwest Territory. The Indiana Territory comprised the present states of Indiana, Illinois, Wisconsin, and parts of Michigan and Minnesota.

1800 May 5 Ireland was joined to Great Britain by an **Act of Union**, forming the United Kingdom of Great Britain and Ireland. On Aug. 1 the Irish Parliament was dissolved, and the British Parliament accepted Irish representation. The plans of William Pitt the Younger, prime minister of Great Britain, to ease the Irish political problem by granting **Catholic emancipation** were blocked by George III, king of Great Britain.

1800 June 14 **Napoléon Bonaparte**, first consul of France, was victorious against the Austrians in a **battle at Marengo**, near Allessandria, Italy, during the **War of the Second Coalition** (1798–1802). After a long siege, Austria had finally taken (June 4) the French-held Kingdom of Genoa, but now they were forced to retreat to northeastern Italy. Bonaparte returned to Paris to begin consolidation of his military and civilian control.

1800 Aug. 30 In America, the slave revolt known as **Gabriel's Insurrection** was crushed in Virginia. Gabriel Prosser (b. 1775) ["General Gabriel"] and the other ringleaders were soon executed. Slave revolts had never been common in America; by 1804 all northern U.S. states had abolished slavery.

1800 Sept. 30 The **Treaty of Mortefontaine**, also called the **Convention of 1800**, was signed by France and the U.S., restoring commercial relations between the two countries.

1800 Oct. 1 By the secret **treaty of San Ildefonso**, Spain ceded the **Louisiana Territory** to France. The U.S. was not informed for nearly two years of the change of ownership of the Louisiana Territory, which had been a Spanish possession since 1763.

1800 Dec. 3 The Austrians were defeated in a **battle at Hohenlinden**, Bavaria, in present Germany, by the French under Jean Victor Moreau (Feb. 14, 1763–Sept. 2, 1813). By now the **Second Coalition** (1798–1802) was completely demoralized. Though the seas were controlled by Great Britain, much of Europe was dominated by France.

1801 **John Marshall** (Sept. 24, 1755–July 6, 1835) began his **34-year term as chief justice** of the U.S. Supreme Court (to 1835). A Federalist, he upheld the power of the government to enact legislation against those advocating states' rights. However, Marshall also upheld the right of states to refuse to enforce unconstitutional laws passed by Congress.

1801 Feb. 9 Austria signed the **Treaty of Lunéville**, a city of northeastern France, capitulating to the French as Bonaparte advanced on Vienna, the Austrian capital. **Austria surrendered** all its territory west of the Rhine to France, including the Austrian Netherlands [present Belgium and Luxembourg]. Venice remained an Austrian possession, but the Adige River divided French and Austrian territories in northern Italy.

1801 Feb. 17 The U.S. House of Representatives elected **Thomas Jefferson** third president of the U.S. and **Aaron Burr** as the vice president. On Feb. 11 the vote of the electoral college had been tied between these two candidates, requiring the House of Representatives to decide the election. Jefferson, the first Republican to become president, was the first to be inaugurated in the capital at Washington, D.C. In his inaugural address he introduced the term "entangling alliances" to describe factions among nations and to assert the American need to cooperate peacefully and honestly with all nations.

1801 Mar. 21 A British army led by **Ralph Abercromby** defeated French forces under **Jacques François 'de Menou** (1750?–Aug. 13, 1810) near Alexandria in Egypt. Abercromby (b. Oct. 7, 1734) died March 28 of wounds received in the battle. **Cairo** was captured on June 27, leading to the French evacuation of Egypt in September. Earlier, in a **battle off Copenhagen**, the British under Horatio Nelson destroyed (Apr. 2) the fleet of a coalition of Russia, Sweden, Denmark, and Prussia, neutral countries sympathetic to the French.

1801 Mar. 23 **Paul I** [Pavel Petrovich] (b. Oct. 1, 1734), czar of Russia (from 1796), was assassinated in a plot by noblemen and palace guards dissatisfied with his curtailment of the power of the nobility. Paul's son **Alexander I** succeeded to the throne. At the beginning of his reign (to 1825) Alexander enacted sweeping reforms. In 1801 a Senate, or supreme high court, was established. In 1802, a Council of Ministers was created to advise the czar.

1801 May 14 **Tripoli**, one of the Barbary States along the coast of North Africa, in present Libya, declared war on the U.S. Piracy had always been a source of income for the **Barbary States**, which were governed by semi-independent Turkish governors. Nations could buy immunity for their ships by paying tribute to the corsairs. The U.S. naval officer **William Bainbridge** (May 7, 1774–July 27, 1833) refused to pay extra tribute to **Yusuf**, pasha (1795–1832) of the **Qaramanid Dynasty** (1795–1835) of Tripoli. Yusuf then ordered that the flagpole at the U.S. consulate in Tripoli be cut down.

1802 The **Treaty of Bassein** between the British in India and the Hindu Maratha peshwa, or overlord, **Baji Rao II** (ruled 1796–1818), led to the **Second Maratha War** (1803–1805), when a dispute erupted among the different branches of the Maratha [Mah-

ratta] Confederacy. **Arthur Wellesley** (May 1, 1769–Sept. 14, 1852), later the Duke of Wellington, defeated branches of the Marathas at Assaye in Hyderabad, India, on Sept. 23, 1803. On Nov. 29 Wellesley was again victorious, at Argaon [Argaum], in Berar, ending Maratha control of the Deccan, in India.

1802 Mar. 27 Great Britain and France signed the **Treaty of Amiens**, France, ending the **War of the Second Coalition** (from 1798). Great Britain abandoned her claims to the French throne, returned territorial gains to France, agreed to withdraw from Malta, but retained Trinidad and Ceylon [Sri Lanka]. France agreed to abandon Naples. In October a separate treaty restored Egypt to the Ottoman Empire.

1802 Aug. 2 A plebiscite in France approved **Bonaparte as first consul for life**. In this year he also became president of the Cisalpine Republic in Italy, while Piedmont was annexed by France.

1803 Mar. 1 **Ohio** was the 17th state admitted to the U.S. By the **Northwest Ordinance of 1787** slavery in the territory had been outlawed, and when Ohio adopted its state constitution it became the first state to prohibit slavery before it entered statehood.

1803 Apr. 30 The **Louisiana Purchase** was made by the U.S. after delicate negotiations by the U.S. and French foreign ministers, **Robert R. Livingston** (Nov. 27, 1746–Feb. 26, 1813) and **Charles Maurice de Talleyrand**. The U.S. paid about $15 million, plus interest, for territory that nearly doubled the size of the U.S. The territory extended west from the Mississippi River to the Rocky Mountains and north from the Gulf of Mexico to Canada; the area included the present states of Louisiana, Arkansas, Missouri, Iowa, Minnesota, Kansas, Nebraska, Oklahoma, Montana, Wyoming, South Dakota, and parts of the states of North Dakota, Idaho, Colorado, New Mexico, and Texas.

1803 May 18 Great Britain declared war on France, suspecting Napoléon of breaching the **Treaty of Amiens** (1802). Great Britain feared France's ambition of regaining its world empire: France had recently acquired Louisiana from Spain and had invaded Haiti and Martinique. In Dec. 1804, Sweden allied with Great Britain and, in Apr. 1805, Russia signed a formal agreement with Great Britain against France. They were joined by Austria in August to complete the **Third Coalition**. Spain was allied with France. The **War of the Third Coalition** (1803–1805) was waged at sea for the first year. While Napoléon made preparations to invade Great Britain by gathering c.100,000 men at Boulogne, French privateers interfered with British trade. Great Britain maintained a blockade of French and Spanish ports.

1803 Nov. 18 **French forces on Hispaniola** prepared to return to France, where the French fleet was needed. British intervention and the loss of the French commander, **Charles Victor Emmanual Leclerc** (Mar. 17, 1772–Nov. 2, 1802), and nearly 18,-000 men to yellow fever had foiled efforts to maintain Hispaniola.

1804 **Uthman** [Usaman] **dan Fodio** (1754–1817), sultan of the Muslim **Fulah Dynasty** (1804–1938), launched a holy war against the pagan **Hausa states**, in present Nigeria. His conquest was completed (1808) with the capture of **Alkalawa**, capital of Gobir, and he began (1809) to organize the Fulah [Fulani] Empire (to 1906).

1804 Jan. 4 The **Republic of Haiti**, occupying the entire island of Hispaniola, declared independence under **Jean Jacques Dessalines**, who proclaimed himself emperor. Haiti was the second colony in the Americas, after the U.S., to gain independence from European rule.

1804 Feb. 14 The Serbs rose up against the **Ottoman Empire** under the leadership of **Karageorge** [Karadjordje, orig.: George Petrovich] (Nov. 14, 1762–July 25, 1817), hospodar of **Serbia**. He had gained his reputation as a ruthless military commander against the Turks in Italy. The Serbian insurrection followed the assassination (1801) of the Ottoman governor of Belgrade by the **Janizaries**, a fanatical and oppressive Turkish military faction. In May the Serbian uprising spread to **Bosnia**. Either the **Karageorgevichi family** or their mortal rivals, the Obrenovichi family, held the crown of Serbia and, later, of **Yugoslavia** until 1945.

1804 Feb. 16 **Stephen Decatur**, a U.S. naval officer, won distinction when he led a band of men into the harbor of **Tripoli** and set fire to the *Philadelphia*, a U.S. frigate captured by the pasha of the Barbary State of Tripoli. Decatur and his band escaped with their lives in this daring escapade under the guns of the enemy.

1804 Mar. 21 The **Code Napoléon** was promulgated. It incorporated elements from the Justinian Code, set down in 528, and served as a basis for the legal systems of many European nations and former dependencies. In the U.S. only Louisiana borrowed directly from Napoléonic law. The Code Napoléon was the **first completely rewritten code of laws, revised and modernized, since Roman days**, containing new concepts of a nation's people as people and concern for average citizens and their rights. Napoléon and leading French jurists read and commented upon the preliminary draft before it was reviewed by a committee of the Council of State. The Code became the law of France, surviving with some changes until today.

1804 May 18 The **French Empire** (to 1814) under Napoléon was approved by plebiscite (3,572,000 yes; 2,579 no), and on Dec. 2 **Napoléon I was crowned its first hereditary emperor** by Pope Pius VII (Aug. 14, 1742–Aug. 22, 1823; ruled from 1800) in the Cathedral of Notre Dame. The declaration strengthened the authority of the government, especially against the royalist faction.

1804 July 11 **Alexander Hamilton**, the American statesman, was mortally wounded in a pistol duel with **Aaron Burr**, vice president of the U.S. Hamilton (b. Jan. 11, 1755?) died the following day. In the duel, Hamilton deliberately misfired; Burr aimed to kill. Among other reasons for their enmity, Hamilton had played a key role in persuading (1801) the House of Representatives to elect Thomas Jefferson, instead of Burr, as president of the U.S.

1804 Sept. 25 Adoption of the **Twelfth Amendment to the Constitution of the U.S.**, requiring separate ballots for the election of president and vice president, eliminated the problem of deciding a tie, such as the tie in the election of 1801. Previously the candidate with the most electoral votes was chosen president and the one with the second greatest number of votes became vice president. The state legislatures chose the state electors, who were equal in number to the number of senators and representatives of each state. When the movement for popular suffrage gained momentum (1820–1840), the electors began to be chosen directly by the people.

1804 Nov. 14 At Farrukhabad on the Ganges River, **Jaswant Rao Holkar**, the Maratha ruler (1797–1811) of Indore, in central India, was defeated by **Gerard Lake** (July 27, 1744–Feb. 20, 1808), commander-in-chief of British forces in India. The **Second Maratha War** (1803–1805) came to a close in the following year without further pursuit by the British.

IV. ECONOMY AND TRADE

1800 Jan. 1 **Robert Owen** (May 14, 1771–Nov. 17, 1858), a Welsh economist and social reformer, took over cotton mills in New Lanark, Scotland, from **David Dale** (1739–1806), who had built them. With **Jeremy Bentham** (Feb. 15, 1748–June 6, 1832) as a partner, Owen **established a model factory**, improving the conditions of the workers and increasing the mill's profits. He introduced recreational facilities, insurance for sickness and old age, and stores with low prices for the workers. The workers' children were not allowed to work in the factory, and schools were built for them. When an embargo closed (1806) the factory for four months, Owen paid his workers their full wages.

1800 Jan. 18 The **Bank of France** was established to finance Napoléon's costly wars. On Apr. 14, 1803, the banks of Paris were permitted to issue bank notes.

1802 **Textile workers in Great Britain** challenged their employers, requesting court action to set minimum standards for wages and working conditions. Parliament passed the **Factory Act of 1802**, establishing a twelve-hour day for working children but then refused to finance enforcement of the act.

V. RELIGION AND PHILOSOPHY

1801 July 15 The **Concordat** signed by Pope Pius VII and Napoléon established Catholicism as the predominant religion of France but endorsed religious tolerance. By the agreement, the pope was to confer the office of bishop and archbishop on nominees chosen by the French government. The Gallican Church was organized under the auspices of the French government.

1803 Dec. 18 **Johann Gottfried von Herder** (b. Aug. 25, 1744), a German poet and essayist of the **Sturm und Drang** movement and a leading theorist of German romanticism, died. His *Abhandlung Uber den Ursprung der Sprache* (1772) treated of the origin of language and discussed poetry as a way for human nature to come to terms with reality. Herder's greatest work was *Ideen zur Philosophie der Geschichte der Menschheit* [Outlines of the Philosophy of Man]

(1784–1791), in which he developed an evolutionary theory of history.

1804 The **British and Foreign Bible Society** was founded by leading Evangelical laymen in England as urged by the **Religious Tract Society** (1799). Its function was to "encourage the wider circulation of Holy Scriptures, without note or comment." Ever since, the Society has distributed inexpensive editions of the Bible at prices below cost.

1804 Feb. 12 **Immanuel Kant** (b. Apr. 22, 1724), a German philosopher, died. Kant asserted that certain ideas and things can be believed in because they can be shown to conform to categories of rational thought. Kant laid out these categories and provided an organization for empirical knowledge. The existence of ultimate realities, however, in which German idealists believed, could not be demonstrated, among them the existence of God. Thus, Kant pointed out a middle way for philosophy between skepticism and idealism. His principal works were *Critique of Pure Reason* (1781), *Critique of Practical Reason* (1788), and *Critique of Judgment* (1790).

VI. SCIENCE, EDUCATION AND TECHNOLOGY

1800 **Alessandro Guiseppe Volta** (Feb. 18, 1745–Mar. 5, 1827), an Italian physicist, invented the voltaic pile [electric battery], the **first source of continuous electric current**.

1800 **Benjamin Waterhouse** (1754–1846), an American physician, **introduced to the U.S. the method of using cowpox vaccine against smallpox**, first used (1796) in England by **Edward Jenner**. In 1801 the first Native Americans were vaccinated against smallpox through the efforts of **Thomas Jefferson**, president of the U.S., who had immunized his own children the same year with cowpox vaccine received from England. There were c.14 million Native Americans in 1492 and no smallpox or other European diseases. By 1600, there were only c.9.5 million. Smallpox and measles accounted for most of this drop.

1800 Apr. 24 The **Library of Congress** in Washington, D.C., was established by an act of Congress, which intended that the library should serve the legislative branch of the government.

1800 Sept. 12 The American inventor **Robert Fulton** (1765–Feb. 24, 1815), with a crew of two French sailors, successfully demonstrated in France his submarine *Nautilus*. Later, in the harbor of Brest, France, he blew up (1802) a small boat with a torpedo. It was the **first undersea craft accommodating more than one person** to be successfully tested.

1801 **Jean Baptiste Pierre Antoine de Monet**, (Aug. 1, 1744–Dec. 18, 1829), chevalier de Lamarck, a French naturalist, set forth his theory of evolution in *Système des animaux sans vertèbres*. Lamarck asserted that acquired characteristics, such as bodily changes resulting from disease, special diet, training, accident, etc., could be inherited by offspring, a belief that was disproved by the now accepted genetic explanation for heredity.

1801 **Robert Trevithick** (Apr. 13, 1771–Apr. 22, 1883), an English engineer and inventor, began adapting the steam engine to four-wheeled carts. By 1824, he had demonstrated the usefulness of **steam-driven vehicles** by carrying passengers and hauling loaded carts from Gloucester to Cheltenham and back.

1801 The first nearly complete skeleton of the American **Mastodon** [*Mastodon americanus*], a hairy elephant-like mammal, was dug up in Orange County, New York, by laborers hired and directed by **Charles Willson Peale**, a noted portrait painter and staunch proponent of scientific study. The bones were brought to Peale's museum in Philadelphia and assembled there for exhibition. It was necessary to model a few bones, missing from the skeleton, from the bones of other mastodons found near the original site.

1802 *The New American Practical Navigator*, by the American mathematician and astronomer **Nathaniel Bowditch** (Mar. 26, 1773–Mar. 16, 1838), was published. He provided an accurate method of figuring longitudes by using a sextant to measure angular distances between fixed stars and the moon.

1802 Mar. 16 The **Military Academy at West Point**, New York, was established by an act of the U.S. Congress. At first the academy was a major source of civil engineers in the U.S., reflecting the influence of the Corps of Engineers stationed there initially.

1802 July **Eleuthère Irénée du Pont** (1771–1834), with expertise learned in his father's factory in France, began construction of a gunpowder plant on Brandywine Creek in Delaware. He had been forced to leave France under the **Jacobins** during the French Revolution (1789–1799).

1802 Sept. 21 **André Jacques Garnerin** (Jan. 31, 1769–Aug. 18, 1831), a French aeronaut, made a spectacular **parachute jump**, descending 8,000 feet from a balloon. He had made the first jump, in Paris on Oct. 22, 1797, from a height of 3,000 feet.

1804 May 18 **Frederick Albert Winsor** (1763–1830), a German businessman, received the first **patent for the production of coal and wood gas**. Winsor saw the potential of gas to be used for heating and cooking in addition to providing light.

VII. ARTS AND LEISURE

1800–1816 **George Bryan "Beau" Brummell** (June 7, 1778–Mar. 30, 1840), an English dandy and friend of the prince of Wales, the future George IV, dominated the world of **fashion**. The custom of wearing **trousers**, instead of breeches, was credited to him. Deploring ostentatious clothes, he wore simple-cut suits of a dark color, which subsequently became popular.

c.1800–1815 Under the influence of the architects **Charles Percier** (Aug. 22, 1764–Sept. 5, 1838) and **Pierre François Leonard Fontaine** (Sept. 20, 1762–Oct. 10, 1853), the **Empire Style of design** was introduced to France. It had elements borrowed from Greek and Roman design. The bee, a symbol of royalty, was commonly used, and later, when French troops were campaigning in Egypt, Egyptian motifs were adopted. Empire furniture, massive and often resting upon claw feet, was usually made of ebony, mahogany, and rosewood. Ormolu, a gold or imitation gold finish, was used to decorate the furniture mountings.

1800 By this time the **use of underwear** had become common. It was considered a health measure, as underwear promoted cleanliness in a period when baths were infrequent. Hands, feet, and faces were often washed, but perfumes, pomanders, and other scents covered the lack of more extensive bathing.

1800 Apr. 25 **William Cowper** (b. Nov. 15, 1731), an English poet, died. Cowper was one of the great, quiet innovators in English poetry, freeing verse from the artificiality that characterized much of the classical work of the 18th century. He wrote a humorous ballad *The Diverting History of John Gilpin* (1782); *The Task* (1785), in blank verse and his most famous poem; many nature and religious poems; and several well-known hymns. At his death Cowper left many letters, which are still admired for their sensitivity and self-insight.

1800 May 8   Niccolo Piccini [Nicola Piccinni] (b. Jan. 16, 1728), a leading Neapolitan composer of French and Italian operas, died. His more than 60 operas showed a melodic and dramatic sense unusual for the time. *La Buona Figliuola* (1760) and *Didon* (1783) were his most enduring works.

1800 Sept. 26   William Billings (b. Oct. 7, 1746), the first professional American composer, died. *The New-England Psalm-Singer* (1770), the first book of his six-volume collection of church music, represented many styles by Billings and others. *The Singing Master's Assistant* (1778), *Music in Miniature* (1779), *The Psalm Singer's Amusement* (1781), *The Suffolk Harmony* (1786), and *The Continental Harmony* (1791) completed the series.

1801   Publication of **How Gertrude Teaches Her Children** brought international renown to the Swiss educational reformer **Johann Heinrich Pestalozzi** (Jan. 12, 1746–Feb. 17, 1827). Pestalozzi's theories influenced curriculum development in Europe and the U.S.

1801 Mar. 25   Novalis [Friedrich von Hardenberg] (b. May 2, 1772), a leading German romantic poet, died. He held the belief that the highest state of the human soul was rest, in which it could achieve unity with all natural things. Novalis's most important works were a volume of poems *Hymnen an die Nacht* [**Hymns to the Night**] (1800), and the unfinished novel *Heinrich von Ofterdingen*, in which he idealized the religious unity of the Catholic Middle Ages.

1802–1812   The French architects **Charles Percier** and **Pierre François Leonard Fontaine**, the leading exponents of the Empire Style, collaborated on the **reconstruction and decoration of the Louvre museum** and the **Tuileries**, in Paris.

1802 Oct. 22   Samuel Arnold (b. Aug. 10, 1740), an English composer, organist, and music scholar, died. He had edited the music of **George Frederick Handel**, which he published in 36 volumes. He was noted for several oratorios, vocal music, nine plays set to music, and the four-volume *Cathedral Music* (1790), his principal work.

1804   Jacques Louis David (Aug. 30, 1748–Dec. 29, 1825) was appointed court painter by Napoléon. David, who established the **Classic Revival in French art**, reflected **Napoléon's drive to reconstruct the Roman Empire** (127 B.C.–A.D. 395). He based his work on the designs of ancient Greece and Rome, where he had studied, and expressed his vision of what he thought the classical essence to be.

1805–1809

I. EXPLORATION AND COLONIZATION

1805   The **Michigan Territory** was created from part of the Old Northwest Territory. **Detroit** was named its capital. Fur trade was profitable in Michigan's wilderness, its only business until settlement became safe.

1805 Aug. 9   Zebulon Montgomery Pike (Jan. 5, 1779–Apr. 27, 1813), a U.S. army officer, with 20 companions, was sent on an unsuccessful expedition to find the source of the Mississippi River. They reached as far as Leech Lake, in northern Minnesota, which drained into the Mississippi River.

1806 Nov. 15   Zebulon Pike, while on an expedition to explore the headwaters of the Arkansas and Red rivers, spotted **Pike's Peak** at the edge of the Great Plains, just to the west of present Colorado Springs.

1807   David Thompson (Apr. 30, 1770–Feb. 10, 1857) was the **first white man to cross Howse Pass**, in present Banff National Park, in Alberta, Canada, to reach the source of the Columbia River at Columbia Lake on the western side of the Rocky Mountains in Canada.

1807–1808   John Colter (c.1775–Nov., 1813) crossed on foot the **Wind River Mountains** and the Teton

Range in Wyoming. He was believed to be the **first white man to enter Wyoming and the first to report on Yellowstone.** Colter had been a member of the Lewis and Clark expedition.

II. POLITICS AND WAR

1805 Mar. 5 **Thomas Jefferson** was inaugurated for his second term as president of the U.S., having defeated the Federalist candidate **Charles Cotesworth Pinckney** (Feb. 25, 1746–Aug. 16, 1825), who had made an unsuccessful bid for the vice presidency in 1800. **George Clinton** replaced **Aaron Burr** as vice president. The electors had met on Dec. 5, 1804, and for the first time voted separately for president and vice president.

1805 Apr. 27 In an unsuccessful effort to depose **Yusuf,** pasha (1795–1832) of the **Qaramanid Dynasty** (1795–1835) of the Barbary State of Tripoli, **William Eaton** (Feb. 23, 1764–June 1, 1811), U.S. consul to Tunis, **captured the seaport of Derna,** in present Libya. A peace treaty was signed (June 4) by Tripoli and the U.S., but piracy on U.S. trade ships in the Mediterranean continued. Eaton was accompanied by Lt. **Presley N. O'Bannon** (c.1776–Sept. 12, 1850) and seven marines. The action is commemorated in the Marine anthem by the line "To the shores of Tripoli."

1805 May 26 Napoléon I of France was crowned at Milan as king of North Italy, to legitimize the French claim to northern Italy. The kingdom consisted of the former French established Cisalpine Republic. Also, within a month the Ligurian Republic was incorporated into France. This growth of the **French Empire** so alarmed Austria and Russia that they joined Great Britain and Sweden in the **Third Coalition** (1803–1805).

1805 Oct. 21 Combined French and Spanish fleets were destroyed by the British under Nelson in a **battle off Trafalgar,** a cape near the Straits of Gibraltar. **Horatio Nelson** (b. Sept. 29, 1758) was killed by a sharpshooter's bullet in the battle. This **last sea battle of the Napoléonic Wars** (1803–1815) ended the threat of an invasion of Great Britain.

1805 Dec. 2 The **battle of Austerlitz** [Slavkov], near Vienna, marked the **collapse of the Third Coalition** (from 1803) as Napoléon's army defeated the combined Russian and Austrian troops commanded

by **Mikhail Ilarionovich Kutuzov** (Sept. 16, 1745–Apr. 28, 1813).

1805 Dec. 26 By the **Peace of Pressburg** [Bratislava in present Czechoslovakia], Austria ceded the Tyrol to Bavaria, was forced to recognize Bavaria and Württemberg as independent kingdoms, and surrendered Venice, its last Italian possession, to France. Austria now recognized Napoléon as king of North Italy, and the **War of the Third Coalition** (from 1803) was formally concluded.

1806 **Jean Jacques Dessalines** (born c.1748), emperor of **Haiti** (1804), who had antagonized many of his followers, was assassinated by **Henri Christophe,** and Christophe took control of the northern part of the island.

1806 Jan. Great Britain seized the **Cape of Good Hope** from the Kingdom of Holland, as Napoléon I had renamed the Netherlands.

1806 Jan. 1 **Maximilian IV Joseph** (May 27, 1756–Oct. 13, 1825), elector of Bavaria, was proclaimed king of Bavaria as Maximilian I. He soon joined the **Confederation of the Rhine** as Napoléon's ally.

1806 Mar. 30 **Joseph Bonaparte** (Jan. 7, 1786–July 28, 1844) was appointed king of Naples by his brother, Napoléon I. On June 5 another brother, **Louis Bonaparte** (Sept. 2, 1788–July 25, 1846), was named king of Holland.

1806 June 27 **Home Popham** (Oct. 12, 1762–Sept. 10, 1820), a British commodore, captured **Buenos Aires** and sent $1,000,000 in prize money to Great Britain. The British were soon expelled by the inhabitants with the aid of a Spanish fleet commanded by a French-born officer, **Santiago [Antonio María Jacques] de Liniers** (1756-1810).

1806 Summer Russia and Turkey became embroiled in war when **Alexander I,** czar of Russia, without warning invaded Moldavia and Wallachia, Danubian territories of Turkey. **Selim III,** the Ottoman sultan, declared war (Dec. 30) on Russia. There were no major battles in the fight and Alexander signed, with Turkey, at the **Peace of Bucharest** on May 28, 1812, an agreement by which he abandoned his claims to the Danubian principalities.

1806 July 12 Napoléon created the **Confederation of the Rhine**, which eventually included the German kingdoms of Bavaria, Saxony, Westphalia, and Württemberg; and the grand duchies of Baden, Hesse-Darmstadt, Frankfurt, Wurzburg, Berg; the duchies of Anhalt, Arenberg, Mecklenberg-Schwerin, Nassau, Oldenburg, Saxe-Coburg, Saxe-Gotha, Saxe-Weimar; and other small states constituting the geographical entity of Germany, which once formed the core of the Holy Roman Empire. The French Empire controlled most of Germany as well as North Italy, the Kingdom of Naples, and the Kingdom of Holland.

1806 Aug. 6 The **Holy Roman Empire**, founded in 962 by Otto I the Great, was formally dissolved by **Francis II**, who surrendered his crown as the Holy Roman emperor. He retained his title of Francis I, emperor of Austria, which he had established on Aug. 1, 1804, when he raised Austria to an empire, and he retained the hereditary Hapsburg lands.

1806 Oct. 14 The **battles of Jena and Auerstedt** [Auerstädt], both southwest of Berlin, resulted in a double defeat for the Saxons and Prussians as **Napoléon** overwhelmed retreating Prussian troops under **Friedrich Ludwig Hohenlohe-Ingelfingen** (Jan. 31, 1746–Feb. 15, 1818) at Jena. **Louis Nicolas Davout** (May 10, 1770–June 1, 1823), a French general, commanded a separate flank, which routed a second Prussian force at Auerstedt, where the Prussian general **Karl Wilhelm Ferdinand** (b. 1735), duke of Brunswick, died in battle. On Oct. 27 Napoléon occupied Berlin, and the remaining Prussian troops, under **Leberecht von Blücher** [Marschall Vorwärts, Marshall Forward] (Dec. 16, 1742–Sept. 12, 1819) surrendered near Lübeck on Nov. 4.

1806 Oct. 25 **Henry Knox** (b. July 25, 1750), an American military leader who began his career as a volunteer in the **battle of Bunker Hill** (1775), died. The owner of a bookstore in Boston, Knox was put in charge of the men sent to Fort Ticonderoga after its capture (1775) by Ethan Allen to bring its cannon to the siege of the British in Boston. Knox was at the **battles of Princeton and Monmouth** and at the **siege of Yorktown**. He commanded (1782–1784) the fortress at West Point. He was U.S. Secretary of War (1785–1789) and was the first Secretary of War (1789–1794) under the Constitution.

1806 Nov. 21 **Napoléon** issued his **Berlin Decree** declaring that no vessel coming from Britain or its colonies would be able to enter any port of the French Empire or of any of its allies and barred Britons from entering any part of the empire or its allied lands. This Continental System or Blockade, the so-called **Paper Blockade**, was the decree under which the ships of the U.S. and other neutral nations were seized by the French.

1807 Feb. 8 Russian forces under **Levin August Theophil Bennigsen** (Feb. 10, 1745–Dec. 3, 1826) **attacked the French at Eylau** [Bagrationovsk] near the Vistula River in eastern Prussia. A blinding snowstorm and the arrival of Prussian reinforcements prevented a decisive French victory, and Bennigsen withdrew.

1807 Mar. 17 A **British force invaded Egypt** following the Ottoman withdrawal from the Anglo-Russian alliance against France. The expedition was defeated at Rosetta [Rashid], near the Mediterranean coast. British troops in nearby Alexandria were evacuated on Sept. 25.

1807 May 29 **Selim III**, the Ottoman sultan (from 1789), was deposed and imprisoned by the reactionary **Janizaries**, who opposed Selim's efforts to modernize the **Ottoman Empire** (1326–1920). Selim (b. Dec. 24, 1761) was killed on July 28, 1808. On the same day **Mustafa IV**, who had usurped (May, 1807) the throne with the aid of the Janizaries, was overthrown by **Mustafa Bairakdar** [Bayraktar] (1775–1808), the grand vizier, who had supported Selim. Mustafa IV's brother **Mahmud II** (July 20, 1785–July 1, 1839) succeeded to the throne to continue Selim's reforms.

1807 June 14 In a **battle at Friedland** [Pravdinsk], c.30 miles southeast of Königsberg, **Napoléon** turned to advantage a chance encounter between **Levin Bennigsen**, in command of a major Russian force, and a small French detachment, who held off the Russians for nine hours. Napoléon, with reinforcements of Poles, Dutch, Saxons, and others, drove the Russians back to the Niemen [Neman, Nemunas] River with heavy losses.

1807 July 7 The **First Treaty of Tilsit** established a Franco-Russian alliance. **Napoléon** promised aid to Russia in regaining the Swedish possession of Finland, which Russia thereupon invaded (1808). In return, Russia agreed to abandon Walachia and Moldavia and, if settlement with the Ottoman Empire failed, not to resume fighting before Apr. 1808.

1807 July 9 The **Second Treaty of Tilsit** dealt a heavy blow to Prussia: its territory was reduced by half and its army to slightly more than 40,000 men. All Prussian lands west of the Elbe River, in present Germany, were ceded to France, which created from them the **Kingdom of Westphalia**. France, with its **Grande Armée** now internationalized, controlled nearly all of Europe.

1807 July 10 **Serbia** concluded an agreement with Russia following the renewal of hostilities in the **Russo-Turkish War** (1806–1812). That war had ground to a halt as **Alexander**, czar of Russia, had become enmeshed in confrontations with French troops in northern Poland and elsewhere, and **Selim III**, the Ottoman sultan, faced a rebellion at home and was deposed. The Serbs of Bosnia, Montenegro, and Austria, had already joined in denying aid (Mar. 31) to the Ottoman Empire.

1807 Oct. 18 A French army under **Andoche Junot** (Oct. 23, 1771–July 29, 1813), duke of Abrantès, crossed into Spain with the aim of conquering Portugal. Junot was joined by Spanish infantry and cavalry in the **invasion of Portugal**. With the Portuguese unable to oppose such a force, the royal family sailed to Brazil and set up a government in exile. This was the start of the first phase of the **Peninsular War** (to Aug. 21, 1808). By the secret **Treaty of Fontainebleau** (Oct. 27, 1807), France and Spain agreed to conquer and divide Portugal between them. In November Junot occupied Portugal.

1807 Oct. 31 **Denmark** announced an alliance with France following the bombardment of **Copenhagen** harbor by British forces under **James Gambier** (Oct. 13, 1756–Apr. 19, 1833) on Sept. 22. The purpose was to prevent the Danish navy from being taken over by the French; instead, the fleet surrendered to the British.

1807 Nov. 7 Russia broke relations with Great Britain, as provided by the **First Treaty of Tilsit** (July 7). It was tantamount to a declaration of war. Though Russia did not engage in battle with Great Britain, its ports were closed to British ships until 1810.

1808 Feb. 16 French armies under **Joachim de Murat** (Mar. 25, 1767–Oct. 13, 1815), a French marshal and **Napoléon**'s brother-in-law, entered **Spain**, on the pretext of joining Junot, stationed in Portugal. On Mar. 17 a popular uprising near the royal palace in Aranjuz, near Madrid, against the sympathetic

policy toward France taken by **Charles IV** (Nov. 11, 1748–Jan. 20, 1819; ruled 1788–1808), king of Spain, and his minister, Manuel de Godoy [Manuel de Godoy y Álvarez de Faria] (May 12, 1767–Oct. 4, 1851), forced Charles to abdicate (Mar. 19) in favor of his son **Ferdinand VII** (Oct. 14, 1784–Sept. 29, 1833), who led the faction against his father. Ferdinand was forced by Napoléon to restore the crown to his father Charles, who then immediately abdicated (May 8) in favor of Napoléon. On May 10, 1808, Ferdinand renounced his rights, and Napoléon appointed (June 10) his brother **Joseph Bonaparte** king of Spain. When civil strife spread through Spain, Joseph fled Madrid on Aug. 1.

1808 Aug. 21 In a **battle at Vimeiro**, northwest of Lisbon, in the **Peninsular War** (1807–1814), the French were defeated by a British expeditionary force under **Arthur Wellesley** [later duke of Wellington]. Junot surrendered Lisbon (Aug. 30), and all of Portugal now fell into British hands.

1808 Oct. Napoléon I and Alexander I, czar of Russia, met at the **Congress of Erfurt** to renew the Franco-Russian alliance. Napoléon agreed to support a Russian invasion of Moldavia and Wallachia.

1808 Dec. 26 **Karageorge** was named the ruler of **Serbia**, a hereditary position, with the adoption of Serbia's first constitution. Law was to be formulated by the Serbian State Council.

1809 In May, an uprising at Chuquisaca [Sucre] in central Bolivia, called for the **independence of all Spain's colonies** in the New World. In July the revolt was joined by La Paz in Argentina. Both revolts were soon quelled. Similar revolts took place in Ecuador in 1809 and 1811, but they were suppressed by royalists from Peru.

1809 Feb. 8 Austria declared war on France, while French armies were preoccupied in the **Peninsular War** against Spain and Great Britain.

1809 Mar. **Gustavus IV** [Gustavus Adolphus], king of **Sweden** (from 1800), was deposed by military leaders who blamed the king for the loss of Finland to Russian troops. **Charles XIII**, uncle to Gustavus, gained the throne (to 1818), restored the aristocracy to power, and established a constitutional monarchy.

1809 Mar. 4 **James Madison** of the Republican [Democratic-Republican] party was inaugurated president of the U.S., having defeated the Federalist **Charles Cotesworth Pinckney** (Feb. 25, 1746–Aug. 16, 1825). **George Clinton** served as vice president.

1809 May 12   Arthur Wellesley, named duke of Wellington in September, led the British victory at Oporto, a Portuguese port, against the French under **Nicolas Jean de Dieu Soult** (Mar. 29, 1769–Nov. 26, 1851), in the second phase of the **Peninsular War**. Wellesley advanced into Spain and defeated (July 27–28) French forces commanded by **Joseph Bonaparte** in a battle at Talavera [Talavera de la Reina], southwest of Madrid. But another French army, under Soult, forced Wellesley to retreat to Portugal. In the next year, the French reinvaded Portugal.

1809 May 22   In a battle at Aspern-Essling, outside Vienna, though losses on both sides were heavy, **Charles Louis**, archduke of Austria, failed to turn away the French advance on Vienna. Napoléon withdrew to muster his troops for another attack on the imperial capital.

1809 May 27   Napoléon ordered annexation of the Papal States and, excommunicated (June 10) by **Pope Pius VII**, ordered his arrest. Pius remained Napoléon's prisoner at Savonna, near Genoa, Italy, and at Fontainbleau, near Paris, France, from July 6, 1809, to Jan. 21, 1814.

1809 July 6   In a battle at Wagram, northeast of Vienna, French troops defeated the Austrian forces of Charles Louis, archduke of Austria, who surrendered to Napoléon. The French once again occupied Vienna. With this final victory against the Austrians, Napoléon was free to divert his troops to the Peninsular War in Spain and Portugal.

1809 Sept. 17   The **Treaty of Frederikshamn** [Hamina], on the Gulf of Finland, concluded Russia's invasion of **Sweden** begun in 1808. The Swedish territory of Finland was annexed by Russia and organized as an autonomous grand duchy under the czar.

1809 Oct. 14   The **Peace of Schönbrunn** ended France's invasion of Austria. Austria was forced to cede the Illyrian Provinces, south and west of the Sava River [most of former Yugoslavia], to France; and western Galicia to the grand duchy of Warsaw. Russia received portions of eastern Galicia. Upper Austria [the area around Salzburg] was ceded to Bavaria.

III. ECONOMY AND TRADE

1806   Fur trade between America and China exceeded $5,000,000 annually. Ginseng and furs went to China; returning vessels brought tea, spices, china, and other goods. American vessels were also active in the West Indies, the East Indies, the Philippines, and India. In 1805, more than 7,000,000 pounds of pepper entered the U.S.

1806   The British colony of **New South Wales** in eastern Australia made its first export of nearly 250 pounds of wool to Great Britain.

1806 Nov. 21   Napoléon I issued the **Berlin Decree**, initiating the Continental System or Blockade, a series of laws banning trade with Great Britain by any French ally or dependency. England had already begun a blockade of French ports by an **Order in Council** (Nov. 11), after Napoléon's victory at Jena (Oct. 14), in present Germany, had secured French control of the Hanseatic ports along the Baltic coast.

1807 June 22   The American frigate *Chesapeake* was fired on by the British ship *Leopard* just outside U.S. territorial waters off the coast of Norfolk, Virginia. The U.S. crew was forced to submit to search, and **four members of the crew were impressed into the British Royal navy**. Britain ignored the U.S. government's official protests.

1807 Oct. 9   The **Edict of 1807**, largely the work of **Heinrich Friedrich [Freiherr] Karl vom und zum Stein** (Oct. 26, 1757–June 29, 1831), the Prussian minister of foreign affairs, **abolished serfdom and the estate system throughout Prussia**. All trades and professions were open to nobles, citizens, and peasants. Furthermore, restrictions against the sale of land owned by nobles to burghers were lifted.

1807 Dec.   Great Britain issued an **Order in Council** that established a British blockade of all European ports and levied a duty on the cargoes of all neutral ships engaged in trade with France.

1807 Dec.   The **Milan Decree** was issued by **Napoléon** authorizing seizure of neutral vessels engaged in trade with Great Britain or that submitted to search by the British.

1807 Dec. 22   The **Embargo Act**, passed by the U.S. Congress, banned all international trade to and from American ports. **Thomas Jefferson**, president of the

U.S., believed the act would impress on Great Britain and France the value of this trade so they would suspend their own trade restrictions.

1808   The **U.S. government forbade the importation of slaves.** The policy was largely ignored.

1808 Jan. 1   **Sierra Leone** was made a British crown colony and Freetown, its capital and main seaport, became the primary anti-slave trade harbor of West Africa. A naval patrol was established and, by 1815, 6,000 slaves captured at sea had been released in the colony.

1808 Jan. 26   The **Rum Rebellion**, led by officers and men of the New South Wales military corps, occurred in Sydney, Australia. **John Macarthur** was a prominent leader and benefactor of the unsuccessful rebellion; his wealth and social position saved him from grave consequences. **William Bligh**, the severe British admiral and equally severe governor of New South Wales, was briefly imprisoned by the rebels as a result of his interference in the lucrative liquor traffic.

1808 Apr. 17   The **Bayonne Decree**, issued by Napoléon I, authorized the seizure of any U.S. ships entering French, Italian, or Hanseatic ports. Napoléon's spoils from these seizures brought about $10,-000,000 to the depleted French treasury.

IV. RELIGION AND PHILOSOPHY

1806   At the so-called **Haystack Conference**, students at **Williams College**, in Massachusetts, pledged to devote themselves to conversion of heathens. Their efforts led to the formation (1810) of the **American Board of Commissioners for Foreign Missions.**

1806 July 29   At the **Assembly of Notables**, a group of 112 prominent Jews met with a representative of Napoléon I in Paris. He confronted them with 12 questions designed to discover the reliability of their commitment to the French nation. Napoléon received assurances that French civil law would have supremacy over Jewish law. A Sanhedrin convoked (1807) by the emperor ratified the assembly's statements.

1807   **Robert Morrison** (Jan. 5, 1782–Aug. 1, 1834), a Scotsman and the **first Protestant missionary to China**, began his work in Canton under the auspices of the London Missionary Society. He established (1807) an Anglo-Chinese college at Malacca, on the Malay Peninsula.

1808   The **bishopric of Baltimore**, under **John Carroll**, was **raised to an archbishopric**, the first in the U.S., by Pope Pius VII. New bishoprics were created in New York, Boston, Philadelphia, and Bardstown, Kentucky.

1809   Members of the **Bible Christian Church** of Salford, England, pledged themselves to eat no flesh. This marked the **start of the vegetarian movement in Great Britain.**

V. SCIENCE, EDUCATION, AND TECHNOLOGY

1805   **Joseph Marie Jacquard** (July 7, 1752–Aug. 7, 1834), a French inventor, introduced a new attachment to weaving looms that automatically raised and lowered the warp threads. The device revolutionized the **weaving industry**.

1806   **David Melville** of Newport, Rhode Island, demonstrating the **first practical use of gas in the U.S.**, used coal gas to light his home and the street in front of his house. In 1816 **Baltimore** became the first city to light its streets with gas lights.

1807 Aug. 17   **Robert Fulton's steamboat**, the *Clermont*, made its maiden voyage up the Hudson River from New York City to Albany in 32 hours. It made the return trip in a bit more than 30 hours.

1808   *A New System of Chemical Philosophy* by **John Dalton**, an English chemist and physicist, set forth the first concrete **atomic theory:** 1) All matter was composed of indivisible units called atoms. 2) All atoms of a given element were the same average weight and possessed the exact same properties. 3) A compound was formed from different elements in an unchanging ratio by weight.

1808 July 14   **John Wilkinson** (b. 1728), an English inventor and ironmaster, died. Among his major achievements were the design and construction of the **first iron bridge** (1779) and the **first iron ship** (1787) in England.

1809   The *Phoenix*, built by **John Stevens** (1749?–Mar. 6, 1838), an American inventor, made the **first**

successful sea voyage by a steamboat, going from New York City to Philadelphia in 13 days. It had been launched the previous year at Hoboken, New Jersey.

VI. ARTS AND LEISURE

1805 May 9 Friedrich [Johann Christoph] von Schiller (b. Nov. 10, 1759), a German dramatist, poet, and historian, died. Among his dramatic works were *Wallenstein* (1799), *Maria Stuart* (1800), *Die Jungfrau von Orleans* [*The Maid of Orleans*] (1801), *Die Braut von Messina* [*The Bride of Messina*] (1803), and *Wilhelm Tell* [*William Tell*] (1804). Schiller, with Goethe, raised German theater to a dominant European position. Schiller's *Ode to Joy* (1785) was used by Beethoven in the finale of his Ninth Symphony (1823). His most notable history was *Die Geschichte des dreissigjährigen Krieges* [*History of the Thirty Years' War*] (1791).

1805 May 28 Luigi Boccherini (b. Feb. 19, 1743), an Italian composer, died. He was an important composer of instrumental music, primarily chamber music. In all he wrote nearly 500 works.

1806 Work began on the Arc de Triomphe de l'Étoile at the Place de l'Étoile, in Paris. Ordered by Napoléon, who wished to commemorate his victories, the triumphal arch was designed by Jean François Thérèse Chalgrin (1739–1811).

1806 Apr. 4 Carlo Gozzi (b. Dec. 13, 1720), an Italian playwright and poet, died. In all Gozzi wrote ten major *fiabe*, or fable plays. His first, *L'amore delle tre melarance* (1761), was set (1921) to music as *The Love of Three Oranges* by Prokofiev. Gozzi's *Turandot* (1762) was used by Puccini in the opera *Turandot* (1926).

1806 Aug. 10 Johann Michael Haydn (b. Sept. 14, 1737), brother of the Austrian composer Franz Joseph Haydn, died. His remarkable three-octave voice made him famous as a boy soprano (1745–1755) at St. Stephen's cathedral in Vienna. His *Partitur-Fundamente* was a collection of exercises in harmonic composition.

1806 Aug. 22 Jean Honoré Fragonard (b. 1732), a highly successful French court painter, died. He won (1752) the Prix de Rome for his *Jeroboam Sacrificing to the Idols*. The series *Progress of Love in the Hearts of Young Girls* (1771) included *The Swing*

and *The Furtive Kiss*. Fragonard's landscape technique, which usually included gardens and monuments, was exemplified by *La Fête à Saint-Cloud* (c.1770).

1806 Oct. 22 Thomas Sheraton (b. 1751), an English furniture maker, died. The chief characteristic of his design was the simple line of rectangular chair backs with square legs. Sheraton furniture is well regarded for its utilitarian appearance.

1807 The term "Gotham City" was first used in reference to New York City in the whimsical essay series *Salmagundi* (1807–1808), written by Washington Irving and inspired by Joseph Addison and Richard Steele, the 18th century English essayists. The epithet was used to poke fun at the overly pretentious tastes of New Yorkers.

1809 May 31 Franz Joseph Haydn (b. Mar. 31, 1732), the great Austrian composer, died. His development of the symphony, especially as heard in his later works, gave it the full orchestral effect, greatly influencing his student, Ludwig van Beethoven. Haydn's greatest achievements were string quartets and his more than 100 symphonies. *The Creation* (1798) and *The Seasons* (1801) were the most popular of his oratorios.

VII. SPORTS, GAMES, AND SOCIETY

1805 Eton and Harrow, prestigious English boys' schools founded in the 16th century, played their first cricket match. George Gordon Byron, the future poet, played on the Harrow side.

1805 Tom Cribb, an English boxer, defeated an American-born slave, Bill Richmond, in a bout lasting 90 minutes. Cribb, as champion from 1807 to 1822, twice defeated another former American slave, Tom Molineaux, on Dec. 10, 1810, at Clopthall Common in 40 rounds, and again on Sept. 28, 1811, at Wymondham, Norfolk.

1806 The first cricket match took place between the "Gentlemen" [amateurs] and the "Players" [professionals], which ultimately became an annual feature of the English cricket season. Not until 1853 did the Gentlemen win.

1807 The Royal Montreal Curling Club was founded in Canada.

1808 The **first temperance society**, dedicated to ending the consumption of alcoholic beverages and soon followed by many similar groups, was organized at Saratoga, New York.

1809 Sept. 18 The **Old Prices Riot** broke out in London when **John Philip Kemble** (Feb. 1, 1757–Feb. 26, 1823), actor and manager of the Covent

Garden Theatre, stepped forward to speak his first lines on the night of the theater's reopening. The mob cried out, "Old prices! Old prices!" The price of admission had been raised to finance reconstruction of the theater after fire had damaged it. The disturbance continued for 61 nights, until Kemble lowered the price.

1810–1814

I. VITAL STATISTICS AND DEMOGRAPHICS

c.1813 The **Zulus** [Amazulus], a Nguni-speaking people of Natal, in the present republic of South Africa, were beginning to gather in stronger tribal groups.

II. DISASTERS

1811 Dec. 16 **Tremors shook the Ohio and Mississippi river valleys**, and the earth's surface rose or sank between 5 and 25 feet throughout an area of 30,000 square miles. Reelfoot Lake in western Tennessee was formed during this cataclysm.

1812 Mar. 26 The northern part of South America was struck by an **earthquake**, heavily damaging Caracas, the capital of present Venezuela where c.20,000 people died. The quake struck during the revolt against Spain, strengthening support for the royalists, who retook Caracas on July 31.

III. EXPLORATION AND COLONIZATION

1810 The **first settlement in present Washington state** built by Europeans was Spokane House, constructed near present **Spokane**. The fur trading post was established by **David Thompson**, an English fur trader and explorer working for the Canadian North West Company.

1810 June 23 The **first permanent U.S. settlement on the Pacific Coast** was established by **Wilson Price Hunt** (1782?–Apr. 1842) and a band of fur traders at Fort Astoria, in present Oregon. They were known as **Astorians** because they worked for **John Jacob Astor**, who had just established (1810) the **Pacific**

Fur Company. Astor strengthened his monopoly of the American fur trade by chartering (Jan. 28, 1811) the **Southwest Company** to operate in the area of the Great Lakes.

1811 The **Red River Settlement**, centered at present Selkirk in the province of Manitoba, Canada, was founded at the mouth of the Red River by the Scottish colonizer **Thomas Douglas** (June 20, 1771–Apr. 8, 1820), earl of Selkirk.

1812 **Fort Ross** [Rossiya] was built on the Pacific coast just north of Bodega Bay, in present California, where **Ivan Kuskof** of the **Russian-American Fur Company** had established a temporary settlement in 1809. The Russian interest lay in the rich sea otter [*Enhydra lutris*] fur trade.

1813 May The **Blue Mountains**, in southeastern Australia, were first crossed by **William Charles Wentworth** (Oct. 26, 1793–Mar. 20, 1872), a journalist. His discovery of the grasslands plateau to the west initiated the exploration of Australia's interior. In *Description of New South Wales* (1817), he gave an account of his travels.

IV. POLITICS AND WAR

1810 A British force captured the French islands of **Mauritius** and **Réunion** off the coast of southeastern Africa. The nearby **Seychelles** islands, which the French had first occupied in 1768, were made (1814) a dependency of Mauritius.

1810 Apr. 19 **Francisco** [Antonio Gabriel] **Miranda** succeeded in overthrowing the Spanish captain general of **Venezuela** at Caracas and formed a republic (1811–1812), governed by a junta, independent from Spain. On July 25, 1812, he was forced to capitulate to royalists, headed by **Juan Domingo Monteverde** (c.1772–?1823).

1810 May 25 **Insurgents in Argentina**, acting in the name of Ferdinand VII, overthrew the viceroy. Shortly after, the revolutionaries broke with Ferdinand's representatives, but the campaign to win complete independence from Spain failed from the beginning, though the revolutionaries maintained some control over areas in present Bolivia, Paraguay, and Uruguay. Argentina now celebrates this day as its date of independence, but independence was not achieved until July 19, 1816, when the **first congress of the Argentine Republic** convened at San Miguel de Tucumán.

1810 July 9 The **Kingdom of Holland** was annexed by France, when Napoléon deposed the king, his brother **Louis Bonaparte**, who had refused to end the mostly secret trade with Great Britain or turn over to the French Empire the vast Dutch naval resources. Napoléon annexed (Dec. 10) the north German coast adjacent to Holland and the Hanseatic cities of the Prussian Baltic coast for the same reasons. Enforcement of the **Continental System**, intended to threaten Great Britain, was causing hardship and resentment that were in part responsible for convincing French allies to change sides, leading to Napoléon's downfall.

1810 July 20 **Antonio Nariño** (1765–Dec. 13, 1823) led a **revolt against Spanish rule at Bogotá** in New Granada [Colombia] and succeeded in establishing a junta government.

1810 Aug. 21 **Jean Baptiste Jules Bernadotte** (Jan. 26, 1763–Mar. 2, 1844) was chosen by the Swedish Diet as crown prince and successor to **Charles XIII**. Bernadotte had been a conspirator against Bonaparte during the Directorate and did not wholeheartedly favor the emperor's policies. Nevertheless, Napoléon did not oppose Bernadotte's move to **Sweden**.

1810 Sept. 16 **Miguel Hidalgo y Costilla**, a Creole priest, launched the **Mexican War of Independence** (1810–1821) as he sounded the bells of his parish church at Dolores Hidalgo, issuing the *Grito de Dolores* [cry of independence]: "Viva religion, viva America, death to bad government!" Today Mexico celebrates Sept. 16 as Independence Day. After an initial victory the rebel armies were turned away (Nov. 6) from an attack on Mexico City by Spanish

troops commanded by **Félix María Calleja del Rey** (1750–1820), a Spanish general, who pushed them nearly 300 miles northwest to Guadalajara.

1810 Sept. 18 **Garcia Carrasco**, the captain general of **Chile**, was overthrown by revolutionaries who announced Chile's independence from Spain. A year later **José Miguel de Carrera** (Oct. 15, 1785–Sept. 4, 1821) overthrew (Sept. 1811) the combined moderate and royalist government to establish a junta under his dictatorship.

1810 Oct. 27 **James Madison**, president of the U.S., ordered the occupation of the disputed territory of **West Florida**, then claimed by Spain. The territory, which lay between the Perido River and the Mississippi, was seized and annexed to the U.S.

1811 The term **"gerrymander,"** meaning reapportion voting districts to the benefit of the dominant political party, originated in the effort by **Elbridge Gerry** (July 17, 1744–Nov. 23, 1814), in his second term as governor of Massachusetts, to maintain Republican [Democratic-Republican] control of the state. An odd salamander-shaped district was formed, providing the "mander" in gerrymander.

1811 By this year the **Wahabis**, headed by the **Saud Dynasty** (c.1720–to the present), ruled all **Arabia**, except present Yemen, from their capital at Riyadh [Riah], the present capital of Saudi Arabia.

1811 Jan. **Paraguay** refused the aid offered by independent Buenos Aires, capital of the former viceroyalty of La Plata (which nominally ruled Paraguay, Bolivia, and Uruguay), when it proclaimed **independence from Spanish rule**. The bloodless overthrow of the Spanish administrators of Paraguay was followed (1813) by independence from Buenos Aires.

1811 Jan. 17 The **battle at Calderón Bridge**, on a branch of the Santiago River, east of Guadalajara, during the **Mexican War of Independence**, was a defeat for the troops of **Hidalgo y Costilla** (b. May 8, 1753), who was captured by Calleja del Rey, a Spanish general, and executed on July 31, 1811. José María Morelos y Pavón became leader of the independence movement.

1811 Mar. 1 **Mohammed** [Mehemet] **Ali, pasha of Egypt**, eliminated most of the remaining Mamelukes. He invited the beys to Cairo as guests and massacred them inside the citadel, signaling a general slaughter of Mamelukes throughout the country. The survivors fled south to Dongola [Dungulah], in present northern Sudan.

1811 May 5 French forces under **André Masséna** (May 6, 1758–Apr. 4, 1817) failed to defeat British forces under the duke of Wellington at Fuentes de Oñoro, near Almeida, Portugal. Masséna withdrew and **Portugal was finally liberated** as the French suffered the first in a series of defeats leading to the end of the **Peninsular War** (1807–1814).

1811 July 5 The **United Provinces of Venezuela** [Estados Unidos de Venezuela] declared their independence, initiating a decade of civil war by the followers of **Francisco de Miranda** and **Simón Bolívar** against Pablo Morillo (1777–1838), a Spanish general.

1811 Nov. 7 **William Henry Harrison** led the U.S. defense against a surprise Native American attack in a **battle at Tippecanoe River**, in present Indiana, and succeeded in razing the Indian village there.

1811 Nov. 11 The province of **Cartagena**, in present Colombia, declared independence from Spain as the Republic of Cartagena.

1812–1813 **José María Morelos y Pavón**, fighting Spanish royalist forces in the **Mexican War of Independence**, defeated **Félix María Calleja del Rey** at Cuautla, 45 miles southeast of Mexico City, and took Orizaba and Oaxaca, in southeastern Mexico. In 1813 Acapulco fell to Morelos, enabling him to call the **congress of Chilpancingo**, in southern Mexico, which named Morelos generalissimo and again declared Mexican independence on Nov. 6, 1813.

1812 Mar. 5 **Sweden** signed the **Treaty of Abo** [Turku], in present Finland, with Russia, pledging support against France. In April Russia demanded the withdrawal of French troops from Prussia and an end to the Continental System, the French embargo of British goods. In July Great Britain joined this new alliance against France.

1812 Mar. 18 **John Horne Tooke** (b. June 25, 1736), an English politician and philologist, died. In 1771 he founded the **Constitutional Society** to encourage reform of Parliament and to offer support to the American colonists. He was fined and jailed (1778) for fund raising efforts on behalf of Americans killed at the battle of Lexington and Concord, saying the British government had murdered them. Tooke won (1801) election to Parliament only to have the government prevent him from taking his seat. As a philologist he wrote two of three planned volumes entitled *Epea Pteroenta, or The Diversions of Purley* (1786–1805).

1812 Apr. 8 **Louisiana** was the 18th state to be admitted to the U.S. Congress then organized the **Missouri Territory** from the remainder of the former Louisiana Territory.

1812 May 14 The U.S. Congress agreed to annex **West Florida** to the Mississippi Territory, officially joining the region to the U.S.

1812 May 28 The **Treaty of Bucharest** ended the **Russo-Turkish War** (from 1806) and resolved the century-long struggle between Russia and the Ottoman Empire over the Danuban Principalities, located along the western coast of the Black Sea. Bessarabia, the northeastern part of the province of Moldavia, was ceded to Russia, and the Prut River formed the new Russo-Turkish boundary. The Serbs were promised amnesty and local autonomy under Turkish rule, but the Serbs refused the Ottoman call for surrender, and their capital Belgrade fell to Turkish forces on Oct. 7, 1813. For two weeks every male above 15 was hunted to be killed, and thousands of women and children were sold into slavery.

1812 June 18 The **U.S. declared war on Great Britain**, in what is known as the **War of 1812**. It developed chiefly from the dispute over the shipping rights of neutral nations, which had been violated during the numerous trade embargoes imposed throughout Europe. On the American side, frontiersmen wanted more land and hoped to expand westward and even take British Canada.

1812 June 24 Napoléon I and his troops, called the Grande Armée, crossed from Poland into Russia at Kovno [Kaunas] on the Nemen [Niemen] River. As **Napoléon advanced into Russia**, the Russians retreated toward Moscow, outmaneuvering Napoléon's attempts to engage them in decisive battle. **Mikhail Barclay de Tolly** (Dec. 27, 1761–May 26, 1818), the Russian commander, encircled the French at Vilna [Vilnius] on June 28, clashed with them at Vitebsk in late July, and again at Smolensk in mid-August, a major defeat for the Russians.

Smolensk was burned (Aug. 17–18) by the French, and Barclay was replaced by Kutuzov. The French faced starvation as the Russians burned crops and villages in the path of the Grande Armée's advance.

1812 July 22 In a **battle at Salamanca**, northwest of Madrid, French troops under Auguste Marmont [Frederic Louis Viesse de Marmont] (July 20, 1774–July 22, 1852), duke of Raguse, were defeated by British forces commanded by **Arthur Wellesley [Duke of Wellington]**, who had forced a wedge from Portugal into Spain.

1812 Aug. 16 William Hull (June 24, 1753–Nov. 25, 1825), governor of the Michigan Territory (1805), surrendered U.S. troops at **Detroit** to a small Canadian force under **Isaac Brock** (Oct. 6, 1769–Oct. 13, 1812), a British officer, in the **War of 1812**. On the previous day Fort Dearborn [Chicago] was evacuated because of confused orders issued by Hull. In 1814 he was court-martialed for neglect of duty, but the death sentence was not carried out in honor of his valorous service during the American Revolution (1775–1783).

1812 Aug. 19 The American frigate *Constitution* defeated the British *Guerrière* off the coast of Nova Scotia in a battle in the **War of 1812**. It was in this engagement that the Constitution earned the nickname **"Old Ironsides."**

1812 Sept. 7 Mikhail Kutuzov made a stand against advancing French troops at **Borodino**, c.70 miles from Moscow, in a bloody battle of the Napoléonic Wars. Defeated, the Russian troops withdrew to Moscow. The French lost c.30,000 men; the Russians c.45,000.

1812 Sept. 14 Napoléon entered Moscow, already evacuated by the Russians, who had taken food and supplies with them and set fire to the city. Three-fourths of the city was destroyed from Sept. 15 to 18. Napoléon remained in Moscow for little over a month while cold and hunger decimated the **Grande Armée**.

1812 Oct. 9 Jesse Duncan Elliott (July 14, 1782–Dec. 10, 1845), a U.S. naval lieutenant, captured the British ships *Detroit* and *Caledonia* on Lake Erie in a surprise dawn attack, the **first major U.S. success during the War of 1812**.

1812 Oct. 13 In a **battle at Queenston Heights**, Canada, near Niagara Falls, during the War of 1812 (1812–1815), U.S. forces under **Stephen Van Rensselaer** (Nov. 1, 1764–Jan. 26, 1839) failed to maintain their position in an attack launched across the Niagara River into Ontario. The New York militia refused to follow, and the other Americans were driven back. **Isaac Brock** (b. Oct. 6, 1769), the British commander, was killed in this battle.

1812 Oct. 19 Faced with starvation and the onset of the Russian winter, Napoléon ordered the **withdrawal of French forces from Moscow**. Attacked along their route from Moscow by the Russian army, peasants, and **Cossacks**, the French retreat took them through countryside which had already been looted. Sporadic forays were fought, but there were no major battles between the armies. On Dec. 13 the French armies crossed the Neman [Nieman] River into the grand duchy of Warsaw. Only c.30,000 of the c.600,000 troops of the **Grande Armée** had survived.

1813 Bernardo O'Higgins (Aug. 20, 1776–Oct. 24, 1842) became general of the revolutionary army of **Chile**. He was defeated at Rancagua (1814) and fled to Argentina with most of his followers.

1813 Mar. 4 James Madison of the Democratic-Republican party was inaugurated for his second term as president of the U.S., having defeated **De Witt Clinton** (Mar. 2, 1769–Feb. 11, 1828), candidate of the Federalists and the Peace party. **Elbridge Gerry** served as vice president.

1813 Mar. 17 Frederick William III, king of Prussia, with Russia as ally, declared war against France while **Napoléon** was retreating from Russia. Driven westward through Prussia, the Grande Armée reached the Elbe River on Apr. 28. Victory was necessary to Napoléon if he was to keep the **Confederation of the Rhine** from dissolving. After French victories at Lützen [**Battle of Grossgörschen**] on May 2 and Bautzen on May 21, Russia and Prussia signed (June 4) a temporary armistice with France. In the meantime, Austria, nominally an ally of France, presented demands to Napoléon: withdrawal from northwest Germany and the Hanseatic cities and the dissolution of the grand duchy of Warsaw; the return of the Illyrian Provinces to Austria; and the dissolution of the Confederation of the Rhine. Napoléon refused, and Austria joined (Aug. 12) the allies, who were heavily subsidized by Great

Britain. The armistice ended (Aug. 20), and allied forces converged at Dresden, in present Germany, which had been occupied by Napoléon.

1813 June 21 In a **battle at Vitoria**, in northern Spain, French forces were decisively defeated. **Joseph Bonaparte**, king of Spain, had evacuated his government northward from Madrid to seek protection by **Jean Baptiste Jourdan**, commander of the French forces. Bonaparte fled through the Pyrénées to France, followed by the French army, driven by **Arthur Wellesley [Duke of Wellington]**, who crossed (Oct. 8) the French border and began a siege of Bayonne. The Spanish city **San Sebastián**, near the French border, was captured on Sept. 9, and **Pamplona** on Oct. 31. Spain was now controlled by the British, Portuguese, and free Spanish forces.

1813 Aug. 30 **Creek Indians** under leadership of **William Weatherford** [Red Eagle] (1780?–1824), massacred settlers hiding in Fort Mims, near Mobile, Alabama, initiating the **Creek Indian War** (1813–1814). The Creeks had sided with the British in the **War of 1812** .

1813 Sept. 10 **Oliver Hazard Perry** (Aug. 23, 1785–Aug. 23, 1819), an American naval officer, won an important **battle at the southwestern end of Lake Erie**. The British fleet under **Robert H. Barclay** (d. 1837) was captured, forcing a British retreat into Canada. Sending word of his victory, Perry wrote, "We have met the enemy and they are ours."

1813 Oct. 5 In a **battle at a bridge over the Thames River at Moraviantown** [Schoenfeldt, Fairfield] in southeastern Ontario, U.S. forces commanded by **William Henry Harrison** defeated combined British and Indian forces commanded by **Henry Procter** (1787–1859) and the Shawnee chief **Tecumseh** [Tecumtha, Tecumthe, Tikamthi] (b. 1768?), who was slain in the battle. The battle **secured the Old Northwest Territory for the U.S.** Fairfield, an Indian mission village, was burned by the Americans.

1813 Oct. 12 **José Gaspar Rodríguez Francia** [Dr. Francia, El Supremo] (1761?–Sept. 20, 1840) was named consul of **Paraguay** by the legislature. The following year he became dictator, ruling until his death.

1813 Oct. 12 The **Treaty of Gulistan** [Gyulistan, Golestan], a town in present Azerbaijan, was signed by **Russia** and **Persia,** which ceded to Russia the region of Georgia, between the Black and Caspian seas. A border war between the two powers had been conducted since 1801, when Russia annexed the area as a buffer against Persian raids.

1813 Oct. 16–19 The **Battle of the Nations** [Volkerschlacht] was fought at **Leipzig**, in present Germany. Austrian, Prussian, and Russian armies converged upon Leipzig, where **Napoléon** had gathered his troops after failing in his second attempt to take **Berlin**. Though the battle was inconclusive (c.35,000 killed or wounded plus 15,000 taken prisoner for the French; c.50,000 killed or wounded for the allies), it was a defeat for Napoléon, and he was forced to withdraw toward Frankfurt am Main to the southwest. The **Confederation of the Rhine** began to disintegrate, its main cities capitulating to the advancing allies.

1813 Nov. 9 An unofficial, unsigned offer of peace was sent by the allies to **Napoléon** from **Frankfurt**. France was to withdraw behind the natural frontiers of the Rhine, the Alps, and the Pyrénées. Napoléon sent his consent by his minister for foreign affairs, but the **rebellion of Holland** meant that France no longer controlled the mouths of the Rhine, causing the allies to change their tactics. They promulgated (Dec. 5) the more formal **Declaration of Frankfurt**, which withdrew their offer in regard to the frontiers, then aided the revolt of Holland and pursued a policy of alienating Napoléon's friends and allies in France and abroad. Allied armies crossed the Rhine into France on Dec. 21, and the main allied army invaded from Switzerland through Lorraine about the same time.

1814 Jan. 14 By the terms of the **Treaty of Kiel**, **Denmark**, which had been an ally of France, was forced to **cede Norway**, united with Denmark for 400 years, to Sweden. The **Congress of Vienna** (1814–1815) approved the terms, but granted Swedish Pomerania to Prussia and gave the Duchy of Lauenburg, in present Germany, to Denmark. The Norwegians refused to accept the terms of the Treaty of Kiel, declared themselves independent, established a liberal constitution, and offered the Norwegian throne to the Danish crown prince **Christian Frederick** (Sept. 18, 1786–Jan. 20, 1848), future king of Denmark (1839–1848), who held it only from May 17 to Aug. 14, 1814.

1814 Mar. Shortly after the defeats of French armies in the Iberian Peninsula by the British under

Wellington, **Napoléon** released **Ferdinand VII** from house arrest at the chateau of Valençay in France near Bayonne. Ferdinand again became (1814) king of Spain with the blessings of the allies. He immediately abrogated the liberal Spanish constitution of 1812 and reinstated the **Inquisition**.

1814 Mar. 9   The **Quadruple Alliance** [Alliance of Chaumont] was signed by Great Britain, Russia, Prussia, and Austria to strengthen the allied offensive against France. The combined allied armies dealt (Mar. 9–10) Napoléon a decisive defeat at Laon, northeast of Paris.

1814 Mar. 29   In a **battle at Horseshoe Bend** on the Tallapoosa River, Alabama, the Americans defeated the **Creek Indians**. The American militia was led by **Andrew Jackson**, who was soon appointed to the regular U.S. army, taking command of the Mobile-New Orleans region. The Creeks ceded to the U.S. two-thirds of their land, forming a large part of the present state of Alabama.

1814 Mar. 30   Austrian, Prussian, and Russian troops entered Paris. On Apr. 1 **Charles Maurice de Talleyrand** convoked the Senate, till then the tool of **Napoléon**; on Apr. 2 it demanded Napoléon's abdication. The emperor continued to resist until he could no longer hold out.

1814 Apr. 10   The French troops under Soult were defeated by Wellington at Toulouse, France, in the **last battle of the Peninsular War** (1808–1814). On Apr. 11 Napoléon signed the **Treaty of Fontainebleau** and abdicated as emperor of France. The allies granted Napoléon sovereignty over the island of **Elba**, off the coast of Italy.

1814 May 30   The **First Treaty of Paris** between France and Austria, Prussia, Russia, and Great Britain [the Quadruple Alliance] established a preliminary peace in Europe. **Charles Maurice de Talleyrand**, the French minister of foreign affairs, won extraordinary leniency for France. French boundaries were kept to those of 1792, and France did not have to pay any reparations. She also kept the colonial possessions taken by Great Britain, except for Mauritius, the Seychelles islands in the Indian Ocean, and the West Indian islands of St. Lucia and Tobago. The treaty confirmed Great Britain's possession of Malta. Russia, Prussia, Austria, and Great Britain convened representatives of all the former countries at an international conference, the **Congress of Vienna**, to restore the balance of power in Europe.

1814 June 4   **Louis XVIII**, the brother of Louis XVI and king of France in exile since 1795, was restored to the French throne as a result of the negotiations of Talleyrand and the acquiescence of the allies. The boy king Louis XVII (b. Mar. 27 1785), who became (Jan. 21, 1793) king in name when his father Louis XVI was guillotined, was said to have died on June 8, 1795 in a revolutionary prison from mistreatment.

1814 Aug. 24–25   British troops set fire to Washington, D.C., destroying parts of the White House, Capitol Building, Navy Yard, Treasury Building, and some private homes, in retaliation for the U.S. burning of York [Toronto], Canada, on Apr. 27, 1813, in the **War of 1812**. This attack was one part of a three-pronged British offensive, another being in the north along Lake Champlain in an attempt to drive on New York City, and the other in the south along the coast of the Gulf of Mexico in an attempt to take New Orleans. The British entered Washington unopposed: **Pres. Madison and his government had fled across the Potomac**, taking essential documents with them. After failing in an attempt to take Baltimore, the British fleet sailed for Jamaica in the West Indies.

1814 Oct. 1–2   Garcia Carrasco, former captain general of Chile, regained **Chile** for Spain, defeating at Rancagua, c.50 miles south of Santiago, the revolutionary forces of **Bernardo O'Higgins**.

1814 Nov. 1   The **Congress of Vienna** convened. Representatives from all European states in existence prior to the Napoléonic Wars gathered to settle territorial disputes and establish a perpetual **balance of power** in Europe to be overseen by Russia, Prussia, Austria, and Great Britain [**Quadruple Alliance**]. The congress remained in session until June 9, 1815, when the Final Act of the Congress of Vienna was signed. During the conference Great Britain returned to the Netherlands all the overseas territories she had seized in 1806 except for Ceylon [Sri Lanka], the Cape Colony in Africa, and part of the Guyana coast of South America east of Venezuela. The various settlements on the coast, including the colonies of the Essequibo River, Berbice, and Demerara were united in 1831 to form the **British Crown Colony of British Guiana**, the only British colony in South America.

1814 Sept. 11 A British fleet commanded by **George Downie** was defeated by an American fleet commanded by **Thomas MacDonough** (Dec. 31, 1783–Nov. 10, 1825) in a **battle on Lake Champlain** in New York state. MacDonough had anchored his ships and gunboats opposite Plattsburg, which had been occupied by a British army commanded by **George Prevost** (May 19, 1767–Jan. 5, 1816), who had marched south from Canada with c.11,000 men, with the intention of capturing New York City and dividing the U.S. MacDonough in the *Saratoga* captured Downie in the *Confiance*, and the remaining British ships were soon destroyed. Downie was killed in the battle, and Prevost retreated to Canada. This was the **last battle in the north during the War of 1812**, though the British still controlled Lake Michigan and the northern Mississippi River.

1814 Dec. 24 The **Treaty of Ghent** [Gent], in present Belgium, ended the **War of 1812** between Great Britain and the U.S. All territory was returned to its prewar status, and boundaries in the northeastern U.S. were settled. **John Quincy Adams** and **Henry Clay** (Apr. 12, 1777–June 29, 1852) were among the U.S. statesmen negotiating in Ghent. The **battle of New Orleans**, the biggest of the war, took place two weeks (Jan. 8, 1815) after the treaty was signed.

V. ECONOMY AND TRADE

1810 Mar. 23 Napoléon issued the **Rambouillet Decree**, ordering seizure of any American vessel that had violated French trade embargoes that was found in a French port.

1810 Oct. 10 Napoléon issued the **Fontainebleau Decree**, to curtail the illegal trade between France and Great Britain, including that conducted by her allies and neutrals, and established stiff penalties for smugglers who were caught. Napoléon's hope to break the Bank of England was countered by Great Britain's **Order in Council**, forbidding trade with any nation submitting to the Fontainebleau Decree.

1811 The 20-year charter of the **First Bank of the U.S.** lapsed without renewal. The bank's officers obtained a charter in New York from the state government and continued operations without interruption. Many sections of the country remained deeply suspicious of a central bank, believing it would concentrate too much power in the hands of government and become a source of regulation curtailing speculation and growth.

1811 Sept. 14 **Karl August von Hardenberg** (May 31, 1750–Nov. 26, 1822), chancellor of Prussia (1810–1817), issued two decrees **altering the feudal land system**. Peasants could become proprietors of the land they had been working for nobles, restrictions on the buying and bequeathing of land were lifted, and a property tax was levied on nobility.

1812 The **first life insurance company in the U.S.**, the Pennsylvania Company for Insurance on Lives and Granting Annuities, was incorporated.

1812 Sept. 19 **Mayer Amschel Rothschild** (b. Feb. 23, 1744), a German banker who established at Frankfurt what became one of the most successful banking dynasties in history, died. As financial agent for the landgrave of Hesse-Cassel [German: Hessen-Kassel], a state centering around Kassel, a city of present Germany, Rothschild established the basis of the family fortune. The Rothschilds were particularly successful in their dealings with governments and reigning monarchs. The senior Rothschild was succeeded at Frankfurt by his eldest son **Amschel Mayer** (June 12, 1773–Dec. 6, 1855). Other sons established branches of the business elsewhere: **Salomon Mayer** (Sept. 9, 1774–July 28, 1855), Vienna (1804); **Nathan Mayer** (Sept. 16, 1777–July 28, 1836), London (1804); **Karl Mayer** (Apr. 24, 1778–Mar. 10, 1855), Naples ; and **Jakob** (May 15, 1792–Nov. 15, 1868), Paris (1811).

1814 The **first factory in the U.S. to use power machinery** enclosed within a single building was constructed in Waltham, Massachusetts. The Boston Manufacturing Company produced cotton cloth there under the direction of **Francis Cabot Lowell** (Apr. 7, 1775–Aug. 10, 1817).

VI. RELIGION AND PHILOSOPHY

1810 The **American Board of Commissioners for Foreign Missions**, the first foreign missionary society in the U.S., was organized by Congregationalists in cooperation with the Presbyterians and two Reformed Church denominations.

1813 **Adoniram Judson** (Aug. 9, 1788–Apr. 12, 1850), pioneer missionary to **Burma** [Myanmar], began his life work there. Having little success with Burmese Buddhists, he found the Karens and Kachins receptive, and the Karen Baptist Church soon flourished and became self-supporting. Located at Rangoon [Yangon], Judson prepared a Burmese dictionary (1826) and translated a complete Burmese Bible (1834).

1814 Jan. 27   Johann Gottlieb Fichte (b. May 19, 1762), a German philosopher, died. His most important work was **Über den Begriff der Wissenschaftslere** [*On the Science of Knowledge*] (1794), in which he maintained that the ultimate essence was the ego, which created the idea of material and spiritual reality, and that a person's mind learned the truth, not by reason applied to what was acquired through the senses, but by belonging to the universal mind. Fichte greatly influenced the development of German romanticism, but he became equally famous as a German liberal nationalist, especially for **Reden an die Deutsche Nation** [*Addresses to the German People*] (1807), in which he retracted his earlier admiration for Napoléon and called on the Germans to unite against him.

1814 Dec. 25   The Christian gospel was preached to **Maoris** of New Zealand for the first time by **Samuel Marsden**, an Anglican missionary from Sydney, Australia. He returned to New Zealand six times during the next 23 years, spreading the Christian faith and giving presents of nails, axes, and hoes.

VII. SCIENCE, EDUCATION AND TECHNOLOGY

1810   The **first silk mill in the U.S.** was built in Connecticut.

1810   *De la défense des places fortes*, a study of military fortifications, was published by **Lazare Nicolas Marguerite Carnot** (May 13, 1753–Aug. 2, 1823), a famous military leader during the French Revolution known as **le Grand Carnot**, and one of the leaders of the provisional government formed after Napoléon's abdication. It was the standard for 50 years.

1810 Jan. 30   Nicolas [François] **Appert** (Oct. 23, 1752–June 3, 1841) was awarded a prize by the French navy for his perfection of the **art of canning**, or sealing a glass container of food to prevent spoiling. Appert began his investigation in 1795, when the French government offered a prize to anyone discovering such a method.

1811   Steamboats began to appear on the Mississippi River. The first steamboat to travel down the

Mississippi arrived in New Orleans on Jan. 12, 1812, and initiated a regular New Orleans-Natchez run, costing $18 for the trip downstream and $25 for returning upstream.

1811   Charles Bell (Nov., 1774–Apr. 28, 1842), a Scottish anatomist, determined that the posterior and the anterior nerves of the spinal column were specialized to serve different functions. He described them in the **Anatomy of the Brain** (1811) and **The Nervous System of the Human Body** (1830).

1811   The **Great National**, or **Cumberland Road** opened from Cumberland, Maryland, to Wheeling, West Virginia. It was the **first national road built with federal funding**. Eventually extending to St. Louis, Missouri, it was the major road leading westward for settlers prior to the growth of the railroads.

1811 May 11   Chang and Eng Bunker (d. Jan. 17, 1874), the **original Siamese twins**, were born at Maklong in Siam [Thailand]. They toured in Barnum and Bailey's circus and, during their 63 years of life, married and fathered 22 children.

1813   Jethro Wood received the 19th patent issued in the U.S., for a plow. His plow was made of iron and worked well in the stony soil of the East, but not in the stickier soil of the Midwest.

1813 Apr. 10   Joseph Louis Lagrange (b. Jan. 25, 1736), a French mathematician, died. His most important works were **Mécanique analytique** (1788) and **Théorie des fonctions analytiques contenant les principes du calcul differentiel** (1797).

1814 Aug. 21   Benjamin Thompson [Count Rumford] (b. Mar. 26, 1753), a British-American scientist, died. In 1798 he presented to the Royal Society of London an **Enquiry Concerning the Source of Heat Which is Excited by Friction**, in which he introduced the concept of heat as a form of motion.

1814   Robert Fulton designed the **first steam-powered warship**, the **Demologus**. The twin-hulled vessel, 167 feet long, was powered by a paddle-wheel secured between the hulls, the walls of which were five feet thick. The **Demologus** blew up in the Brooklyn Navy Yard in 1829.

VIII. ARTS AND LEISURE

1810 **Heinrich von Kleist** (Oct. 18, 1777–Nov. 21, 1811), a German dramatist, novelist, and poet, completed his masterpiece, the romantic drama *Der Prinz von Homburg*, which was not produced until 1821 because the Prussian princess, Miriame, thought the work portrayed her ancestor in an unwelcome light. Nearly all of Kleist's work explored the insecurity, instability, and erratic behavior of modern man. Kleist is often said to have been Germany's greatest dramatist and its greatest writer of novellas, among them his famous novelette *Michael Kolhass; Die Marquise von O* [*The Marchioness of O*]; and *Das Erbeben in Chile* [*The Earthquake in Chile*], contained in the first volume of *Erzählungen* [**Narratives**] (1810).

1810 *The Scottish Chiefs* by **Jane Porter** (1776–May 24, 1850), a Scottish novelist, was published. It was one of the most popular historical novels of the early 19th century.

1812–1815 *Kinder-und Hausmärchen* [Children's and Household Stories], better known as *Grimm's Fairy Tales*, was published. It was collected over 13 years by **Jacob** (Jan. 4, 1785–Sept. 20, 1863) and **Wilhelm** (Feb. 24, 1788–Dec. 16, 1859) **Grimm** from townspeople throughout Germany.

1813 *Swiss Family Robinson*, compiled and edited by the Swiss writer and philosopher **Johann Rudolf Wyss** (Mar. 13, 1781–Mar. 21, 1830), was published. It was based on stories told by his father **Johann David Wyss** (1743–1818). Wyss was also author of the Swiss national anthem *Rufst Du, Mein Vaterland?* (1811).

1813 *Pride and Prejudice* by **Jane Austen** (Dec., 1775–July 18, 1817), an English writer, was published. Her quiet genius, comic irony, and all but perfect style made her one of the greatest English novelists. *Sense and Sensibility* (1811), *Mansfield Park* (1814), and *Emma* (1815) were published before her death; *Northanger Abbey* and *Persuasion* were published in 1818. *Pride and Prejudice* was written when Austen was only twenty-one.

1813 Jan. 30 **Christoph Martin Wieland** (b. Sept. 5, 1733), a German writer, died. He was called the "German Voltaire" because of his satirical and didactic style and political bent. His best known work was the romantic epic *Oberon* (1780). In 1766 he completed the first German translations of some of William Shakespeare's plays.

1814 **Aleijadinho** [Little Cripple; Antônio Francisco Lisbôa] (b. 1730), perhaps the foremost sculptor of Latin America, died. He carved in wood and soapstone in the baroque style. The best example of his work is found today in the **Church of St. Francis of Assisi** in his native Ouro Preto [Vila Rica], then a center of gold mining in eastern Brazil.

1814 **Walter Scott**, a Scottish romantic writer, completed **Waverly**, the first of a series of historical novels, called the Waverly novels: *Rob Roy* (1818), *Ivanhoe* (1820), *Kenilworth* (1821), and *The Talisman* (1825) followed. Scott had been known previously as a poet, especially for ballads and long narrative poems, and as a translator. His first important original work was *The Lay of the Last Minstrel* (1805), a romantic narrative poem. *The Lady of the Lake* (1810) was probably Scott's best-known long narrative poem.

1814 Jan. 26 **Edmund Kean** (Mar. 17, 1787–May 15, 1833), an English tragic actor, first played Shylock in Shakespeare's *Merchant of Venice*. His performances at the Drury Lane Theater in London saved the theater from financial ruin.

1814 Apr. 12 **Charles Burney** (b. Apr. 12, 1726), an English composer and music historian, died. His first success was music for the pantomime *Queen Mab*, produced by **David Garrick** at the Drury Lane Theatre in London. Burney's travels throughout Europe resulted in *The Present State of Music in Germany, the Netherlands and the United Provinces* (1773). He wrote the four-volume *History of Music* (1776–1789), and composed sonatas, concertos, and cantatas.

1814 May 6 **Abbé** [Georg Joseph] **Vogler** (b. June 15, 1749), a German composer, teacher, and priest, died. He founded music schools at Mannheim, Darmstadt, and Stockholm, and taught **Karl Maria Friedrich Ernst von Weber** and **Giacomo Meyerbeer**. The subject of Robert Browning's poem *Abt Vogler*, he was the **inventor of a portable organ** as well as a composer of operas and of keyboard and chamber music.

1814 Sept. 14 **Francis Scott Key** (Aug. 1, 1779–Jan. 11, 1843) wrote the words to the *Star-Spangled Banner* aboard a British launch in Chesapeake Bay while awaiting the outcome of the British assault on Fort McHenry, guarding the approach to Baltimore, in the War of 1812. Key had arrived at the British fleet with a letter from the U.S. president requesting the release of Dr. **William Beanes**, an elderly, prominent physician being held by the British for his insults to British soldiers in the Baltimore area. Escorted out of firing range on the bay to wait out the nighttime bombing, Key could see at "dawn's early light" that the "star-spangled banner" was still flying over Fort McHenry, indicating a U.S. victory. Key and Beanes were escorted ashore. On Sept. 20 Key's poem was published with great acclaim in the **Baltimore Patriot** as the *Defence of Fort M'Henry*. The poem was easily set to the tune *To Anacreon in Heaven*, by **John Stafford Smith** (1750–1836).

1814 Oct. 19 Mercy Otis Warren (b. Sept. 12, 1728), an American author and patriot, died. A strong supporter of the American Revolution, she wrote two plays satirizing the Tories, *The Adulateur* (1773) and *The Group* (1775). Later Warren wrote *History of the Rise, Progress, and Termination of the American Revolution* (1805), still of interest as a contemporary record. As a poet she wrote *Poems Dramatic and Miscellaneous* (1790).

IX. SPORTS, GAMES, AND SOCIETY

1810 Dec. 10 The **first unofficial heavyweight champion** of the U.S., **Tom Molineaux** (Mar. 23, 1784–Aug. 4, 1818), was finally beaten after 40 rounds in a fight with **Tom Cribb** (July 8, 1781–May 11, 1848) held at Copthall Common in England. Molineaux was a freed slave from Virginia.

1810 Dec. 14 The **Musselburgh Golf Club** near Edinburgh, Scotland, offered a prize in the first women's tournament.

1811 The "Ferrymen of Whitehall" defeated rival **rowing** crews from Long Island and Staten Island in a race on the Hudson River at New York City.

1812 Yacht racing in England began with the founding of the Yacht Club at Cowes on the Isle of Wight. The sport and the club were enthusiastically patronized by the royal family for three decades, a period in which the club's name became the Royal Yacht Squadron.

1813 Thomas Lord moved the turf of his **cricket** grounds, used by the prestigious Marylebone Cricket Club, to its present site in the St. John's Wood section of London. He enclosed his new grounds with a high fence and built a pavilion and a tavern on it. Lord's is now famed to cricket lovers everywhere as the mecca of the sport.

1813 June 1 James Lawrence (b. 1781), captain of the *Chesapeake*, mortally wounded, was carried below deck during an attack by the British ship *Shannon*, blockading the Boston harbor. He cried out, "**Don't give up the ship.**" The *Chesapeake* was defeated.

1814 The **first recorded speed skating competition** in England was held. The contestants wore skates made of iron.

1815–1819

I. DISASTERS

1815 Apr. 5 The **Tambora volcano**, on Sumbawa [Soembawa] Island, Indonesia, experienced one of the worst eruptions witnessed by humans. The violent explosions, heard c.1,000 miles away, continued for 7 days. Nearly 24 cubic miles of debris were thrown into the air, causing complete darkness for 300 miles around the volcano. Ultimately, c.10,000 people perished, and famine took the lives of c.82,000 more.

II. EXPLORATION AND COLONIZATION

1815 Paul Cuffé (Jan. 17, 1759–Sept. 7, 1817), an African-American sailor and merchant, made the **first effort at establishing a colony of freed American slaves in Africa**. At his own expense, he brought 38 former slaves from the U.S. to Sierra Leone in his merchant vessel *Traveller*.

1816   Great Britain founded Bathurst [Banjul], the present capital of **The Gambia**, after returning Senegal to France by the **First Treaty of Paris** (1814).

1819 May 23–1822 Oct.   John Franklin (Apr. 16, 1786–June 11, 1847), an English explorer, set out from England to explore the northern coast of the North American mainland. With a party of 20 men, he arrived at York Factory, on the southwestern coast of Hudson Bay, where he set out for Cumberland House. Traveling along the northern branch of the Saskatchewan River, then striking north past Fort Chipewyan on Lake Athabasca and Old Fort Providence, on Great Slave Lake, he pushed north up the Yellowknife River to the Coppermine River. He and a small party reached its mouth on Coronation Gulf on July 19, 1821, and in two canoes he explored the coast eastward 600 miles to Bathhurst Inlet. The party turned south along Hood River and, after extreme hardship, which included starvation, murder, and cannibalism, 9 men straggled into **Fort Providence** on Nov. 21, 1821. Franklin returned to England 42 months after he had set out. He had succeeded in exploring an isolated coast of the Arctic Ocean and in establishing part of the route of the **Northwest Passage**.

1819 Feb. 6   Singapore was founded as a trading settlement by **Thomas Stamford Raffles** (July 6, 1781–July 5, 1826), for the British East India Company.

III. POLITICS AND WAR

1815 Jan. 8   The **battle of New Orleans** was fought. **Alexander Cochrane** (Apr. 22, 1758–Jan. 26, 1832) entered (Dec. 13) Lake Borgne near New Orleans with a fleet of 50 ships. Under the command of Pakenham, a British general, he landed c.7,500 seasoned British troops, who advanced on the city. **Andrew Jackson**, a U.S. general, hastened from Baton Rouge and checked (Dec. 23–24) successfully the British advance. He then fell back to fortify a position between the Mississippi River and a cypress swamp. Packenham launched a frontal attack, using c.5,200 of his best regulars, against c.4,500 Americans, many of them sharpshooters from Kentucky and Tennessee. The result was devastating: In half an hour the British lost in killed and wounded more than 2,000 men, while the Americans lost only 13 killed, c.50 wounded. **Edward Michael Pakenham** (b. Mar. 19, 1778) and two other generals lost their lives in the battle. The battle restored American military pride, and Jackson ["Old Hickory"] became a national hero. This was the **last battle between the U.S. and Great Britain**.

1815 Feb.   The **Congress of Vienna** reached a compromise on the Polish question, which had almost threatened war between Austria and Russia. A major portion of Poland was granted to Russia, and remaining Polish territories to Prussia and Austria. The Russian parcel, known as "Congress Poland," was nominally independent as the **Kingdom of Poland**. Kraków [Cracow], Poland, was named a republic [free city] under the protection of Russia, Prussia, and Austria. Austria received Italian territories. Prussia received Westphalia, the Rhine Province, and parts of Saxony, in present Germany. Great Britain retained Ceylon [Sri Lanka], Cape Colony, and Malta, and received some of the West Indies and the protectorate of the Ionian Islands. The Austrian Netherlands and the United Provinces were joined as the United Kingdom of the Netherlands [present Belgium and the Netherlands] (to 1830), under the rule of the House of Orange. The Grand Duchy of Luxembourg was formed and became a vassal of the Netherlands. The kingdoms of Bavaria and Württemberg, and the Grand Duchy of Baden were granted nearly their present boundaries as states [Bavaria and Baden-Württemburg] in present Germany.

1815 Mar.   The **Congress of Vienna** enlarged the boundaries of **Switzerland** and established its principle of **perpetual neutrality**.

1815 Mar. 3   The **U.S. declared war on Algeria**, citing harassment of American ships off the Barbary Coast and the demand from the bey [dey] of Algiers for tribute. **Stephen Decatur**, a U.S. commodore, captured (June 17) the *Mashouda [Mashuda]*, an Algerian ship whose admiral Hammida was killed during the battle. The *Estido* fell (June 19) to Decatur in a **battle off Cape Palos**, near Cartagena, Spain.

1815 Mar. 20   Napoléon entered Paris, after escaping (Mar. 1) from the island of Elba and marching from Cannes, gathering loyal troops on the way. During his period of rule, called **"The Hundred Days"** (Mar. 20–June 22), Napoléon played upon the popular resentment against the reactionary Bourbon rule that had been imposed upon France by foreign armies.

1815 Mar. 25   Austria, Great Britain, Prussia, and Russia signed a pact against Napoléon and invited the other European nations to join them in the **Allied Coalition**. A concerted attack on Paris was planned.

1815 June 8   The **German Confederation** (to 1866) adopted a constitution. Established by the **Congress of Vienna** to replace the Holy Roman Empire and to unite the numerous German states, it served primarily as a union for mutual defense. It consisted of 39 members. **Metternich** [Klemens Wenzel Nepomuk Lothar von Metternich] (May 15, 1773–June 11, 1859), the Austrian statesman, came to dominate the governing diet at Frankfurt until its disruption in 1848. He was largely responsible for a policy of stability achieved by suppression of social and political reform.

1815 June 9   The **Congress of Vienna** (convened Nov. 1, 1814) came to an end with the signing of the Final Act, which confirmed all previous agreements. During its sessions it provided for an international condemnation of the slave trade. It also improved the status of religious minorities, including Jews, who won at this time their first international recognition of equal rights.

1815 June 18   British and Prussian forces completely defeated the French at the **Battle of Waterloo**. **Napoléon** had planned an offensive strategy, concentrating on the greatest threat, from the north by **Arthur Wellesley** [**Duke of Wellington**] and Blücher, who had gathered their forces in the Netherlands near Brussels. **Jean Rapp** (Apr. 27, 1772–Nov. 8, 1821), a French general, was to hold the Rhine River against von Schwarzenberg. On June 16 Napoléon attacked Blücher at Ligny, near Waterloo, to drive him away from Wellington's encampment; but **Michel Ney**, in command of Napoléon's left flank at Quatre Bras, failed to support the main engagement. Twice during the battle, Ney flouted Napoléon's orders, which could have meant victory for the French. Blücher's troops retreated, not away but toward Wellington's position. On the day of the Battle of Waterloo, Wellington was well prepared for Napoléon's attack, and Blücher arrived in time with crucial support. During the final phase of the battle, troops under Grouchy [**Emmanuel de Grouchy**] (Oct. 23, 1766–May 29, 1847), a French marshal, failed to arrive in time to prevent rout of the French forces. Napoléon fled to Paris. Total casualties, killed, wounded, and taken prisoner on June 18: 40,000 French,

15,000 British and Dutch, and 7,000 Prussians. It is estimated today that c.1 million French soldiers lost their lives during the **Napoléonic Wars** (1803–1815).

1815 June 22   **Napoléon** abdicated before armies of the Allied Coalition could reach Paris, ending The Hundred Days. **Louis XVIII** was reinstalled (June 28) on the throne. Napoléon was taken (Aug. 2) to St. Helena, a British island in the South Atlantic, to remain in exile under close guard. Napoléon I [Napoléon Bonaparte] (b. Aug. 15, 1769), known also as le Petit Caporal [the Little Corporal] and as the Corsican, died there of various diseases on May 5, 1821.

1815 July 3   A treaty signed by the bey of Algiers and the U.S. **ended the piracy inflicted on American ships by Barbary corsairs**. All American prisoners were released without ransom, and the policy of paying tribute was ended.

1815 July 8   **Louis XVIII** entered Paris and again became king of France, as a constitutional monarch. Much of France was in turmoil as, in many areas, royalists killed, looted, and searched down those who had wielded power under the Revolution as well as under Napoléon. This revenge, spontaneous and violent, centered in southeastern France and became known as the **"White Terror"** (August–September). Louis did not aid in these acts, but **Ney** was arrested and tried for treason because Ney joined in Napoléon's campaign. Ney (b. Dec. 10, 1769), a marshall of France, was shot by a firing squad on Dec. 7.

1815 Sept. 26   **Alexander I**, czar of Russia, announced the establishment of the **Holy Alliance** of Russia, Austria, and Prussia for the purpose of ending wars and conducting diplomatic negotiations on Christian principles. Little direct action was taken on the basis of this alliance, but its reactionary policy, like that of Metternich, antagonized Great Britain and the U.S., both countries refusing to join. The Holy Alliance became almost at once an instrument to suppress liberalism and revolution all over Europe.

1815 Nov. 20   The **Allied Coalition** and **Louis XVIII** concluded the **Second Treaty of Paris**. France was to pay an indemnity of 700 million francs for Napoléon's Hundred Days, cede the Saar and Savoy and the towns of Philippeville, Marienburg, and two others, return all looted art works, and be subjected to occupation by foreign troops for three to five years and pay for the troops' maintenance. On the same day, Great Britain, Russia, Austria, and Prussia signed a secret treaty agreeing to act in concert against France and to keep Louis XVIII on the throne of France. They also agreed to suppress any revolutions in France. With France becoming (1818) a member, it became known as the **Concert of Europe**, its chief aim being to suppress revolutions and maintain the balance of power.

1815 Dec. 22 **José María Morelos y Pavón** (b. Sept. 30, 1765), who had led the **Mexican War for Independence** (1810–1821), was executed in Mexico, after his capture by **Agustín de Iturbide**, the royalist leader.

1816 With the death of **Senzangakhona** (b. 1757), chief (from c.1781) of one of several small **Zulu tribes** of Bantu people centered along the Tugelo River, near Durban in southeastern Africa, **Chaka** [Shaka, Tshaka] became chief and began to gain control of the other tribes.

1816 In accordance with agreements made at the **Congress of Vienna**, several of France's former colonies were returned to France, including her ports in India.

1816 July **Edmund Pendleton Gaines** (Mar. 20, 1777–June 6, 1849), a U.S. general, was sent into Florida by **Andrew Jackson**, his military district commander, where he attacked and blew up Negro Fort, thus initiating the **first full-scale war with the Seminole Indians** (1816–1818). Negro Fort had been built by **Edward Nichols**, a colonel in the British army during the War of 1812, and stocked with considerable gunpowder when it was abandoned. The fort had been taken over by escaped slaves from the U.S. and various Indians who raided into Georgia, stealing cattle and sheep and terrorizing white settlers. Gaines burned a Seminole village in retaliation.

1816 Dec. 11 **Indiana** was the 19th state admitted to the U.S.

1817 **Radama I**, the Merina king of **Madagascar** (1810–1828), whose rule was confined to a tiny mountainous area, secured the aid of the British governor of nearby Mauritius and took control of the island's main port. He then expelled the French from Madagascar, leaving them only the island of Sainte-Marie.

1817 Mar. 4 **James Monroe** of the Democrat-Republican party was inaugurated as the fifth president of the U.S., having defeated **Rufus King** (Mar. 24, 1755–Apr. 29, 1827) of the Federalist party by an electoral vote of 183 to 34. **Daniel D. Tompkins** (June 21, 1774–June 11, 1825) served as vice president.

1817 Apr. 28 The **Rush-Bagot Treaty**, between the U.S. and Great Britain, limited the number of warships on the Great Lakes to four for each nation, with none weighing more than 100 tons. Formulated by **Richard Rush** (Aug. 29, 1780–July 30, 1859), acting U.S. secretary of state, and **Charles Bagot** (Sept. 23, 1781–May 18, 1843), the British minister to Washington, D.C., and later a governor general (1841–1843) of Canada, it set a precedent for peaceful relations between the U.S. and Great Britain.

1817 Dec. 10 **Mississippi** was the 20th state admitted to the U.S.

1818 Feb. 5 **Charles XIII** (b. Oct. 7, 1748), king of **Sweden** (from 1809) and king of Sweden and Norway (from 1814), died and was succeeded by **Charles XIV** [Carl Johan; Jean Baptiste Jules Bernadotte], who had been elected (Aug., 1810) heir to the Swedish throne by the **Riksdag** [Swedish Parliament] with the acquiesence of Napoléon.

1818 Feb. 12 The **Republic of Chile** was proclaimed under the benevolent dictatorship of **Bernardo O'Higgins** as director-general on the anniversary of the defeat (Feb. 12, 1817) of the Spanish royalists in the **battle at Chacabuco**, near Santiago. On Apr. 5, 1818, the Spanish made their last and unsuccessful attempt to regain Chile in a **battle at Maipo**, south of Santiago, in which the governor of Peru aided the royalists against republican forces led by San Martín.

1818 Apr. 4 The U.S. Congress adopted the design of the **U.S. flag** that is used today.

1818 Oct. 20 The **Canadian-U.S. boundary** was extended westward along the 49th parallel from Lake of the Woods, where the present boundaries of Manitoba, Ontario, and Minnesota meet, to the Rocky Mountains. Beyond the Rocky Mountains, the Oregon Territory north of the 42nd parallel was to be shared by the U.S. and Canada for ten years, an arrangement that was extended in 1827.

1818 Nov. 15 The **Congress of Aix-la-Chapelle** [Aachen] in the Rhine Province of Prussia, in present Germany where the borders of Belgium and the Netherlands meet, convened to discuss the policy of the **Quadruple Alliance** (1814) against France and to strengthen the **Holy Alliance** (1815). The chief result of the congress was to establish a precedent for holding future congresses when trouble threatened to destabilize the European system. Great Britain, whose strength was mainly maritime, never joined the Holy Alliance, and thus became increasingly isolated from continental affairs.

1818 Dec. 3 **Illinois** was the 21st state admitted to the U.S.

1819 The **Arkansas Territory**, comprising the present states of Arkansas and Oklahoma, was organized from areas of the Missouri Territory.

1819 Feb. 22 By terms of the **Transcontinental Treaty**, negotiated with Spain by **John Quincy Adams**, Spanish claims to land east of the Mississippi River were rescinded in return for Texas. Spain did not ratify the treaty until 1820. After the Transcontinental Treaty it was said that, for the first time, the **U.S. stretched from sea to sea**, though the Oregon country was jointly held at this time with Great Britain.

1819 Aug. 7 **Simón Bolívar**, the South American revolutionary leader, won a decisive victory over Spanish royalists in a **battle at Boyacá**, New Grenada [present Colombia]. In December the **Congress of Angostura** [Ciudad Bolívar], in present Venezuela, convened to form the **Republic of Colombia**, later called Great Colombia [Gran Colombia]. It comprised the present countries of Colombia, Panama, and Venezuela.

1819 Sept. 20 The **German Diet** ratified the **Carlsbad Decrees**, which placed universities under government censorship and broke up secret student societies. Metternich, the Austrian minister of foreign affairs, had pressed for the decrees in order to control social disorder and radical reforms, and especially to keep the balance of power established by the **Congress of Vienna**. The murder by a radical student of the German reactionary journalist **August Friedrich Ferdinand von Kotzebue** (b. May 3, 1761) on Mar. 28, 1819, had accelerated ratification of the Carlsbad Decrees.

1819 Aug. 16 England's **Peterloo "massacre"** resulted in the deaths of 11 people. Agitation for broader Parliamentary representation had culminated in a large rally at St. Peter's Field in Manchester. The government, fearing an uprising, sent cavalry to break up the disturbance. The incident turned public opinion against the Tory government.

1819 Dec. The British Parliament passed the **Six Acts**, restricting the press and curbing political gatherings. The Tory prime minister **Robert Banks Jenkinson** (June 7, 1770–Dec. 4, 1828), earl of Liverpool, feared a rebellion of the working class during a time of economic difficulties, as had happened in the French Revolution (1789–1799). His efforts were diluted by declining public support, and the Six Acts were never enforced.

1819 Dec. 14 **Alabama** was the 22nd state admitted to the U.S. There were now the same number of states permitting slavery and states forbidding slavery.

III. ECONOMY AND TRADE

1816 Mar. 14 The **Second Bank of the U.S.** was chartered. Because its legality was questioned on constitutional grounds and because many state banks were hampered by the more conservative regulation of capitalization demanded by the federal bank, opposition to a U.S. bank still remained.

1817 *The Principles of Political Economy and Taxation*, by **David Ricardo** (Apr. 19, 1772–Sept. 11, 1823), an English banker and classical economist, was published. Ricardo held that an increase in wages does not necessitate an increase in prices, that profits were inversely affected by rising or falling wages, and that profits throughout society were dictated by the cost of production of its most expensive item, food.

1817 June 23 Articles of association were drawn up for the **Bank of Montreal**, the **first bank to be established in Canada**. The charter was officially granted in 1822.

1817 July 4 Construction began on the **Erie Canal**. When it eventually opened on Oct. 26, 1825, it provided the U.S. with a convenient water route between states in the northern Midwest and the Atlantic Ocean.

1819 The **Panic of 1819** was precipitated in the U.S. when many state banks, speculating in western lands, lost credit with the **Second Bank of the U.S.** These lands became the property of the Second Bank. It was not until 1822 that the value of currency evened out again.

1819 Mar. 6 **John Marshall**, the chief justice of the U.S. Supreme Court, delivered a decision in the case of *McCulloch vs. Maryland* that defined the powers of the federal government in establishing a federal bank. Marshall found that the state of Maryland had interfered with federal constitutional laws by taxing the Baltimore branch office of the **Second Bank of the U.S.** Marshall, relying on the constitutional federal authority to conduct fiscal operations, declared that the Second Bank was "within the scope of the Constitution," and was "consistent with the letter and spirit of the Constitution," and was therefore constitutional.

1819 May 26 The **first steamship to cross the ocean**, mostly under sail, was the American *Savannah*, which departed from Savannah, Georgia, and arrived at Liverpool, England, on June 20. The crossing took 28 days and 11 hours.

IV. RELIGION AND PHILOSOPHY

1815 The end of the Napoleonic domination of Europe brought a return of **repressions for Jews**, especially in Germany, but also in Spain and Italy. Gains made during the Napoleonic era were either reduced or eliminated.

1816 The **African Methodist Episcopal Church** was founded as a separate Protestant denomination by **Richard Allen** (Feb. 14, 1760–Mar. 26, 1831), in protest against segregation in Philadelphia.

1816 The use of **torture** in the investigation of heresy by those tribunals of the **Inquisition** still in practice was abolished in a bull issued by **Pope Pius VII**.

1816 **Robert Moffat** (Dec. 21, 1795–Aug. 9, 1883), a Scottish Congregationalist, became the **first Protestant missionary to Africa**, sent by the London Missionary Society to Namaqualand in South Africa.

1816 May 8 The founding convention of the **American Bible Society** convened in the Garden Street Reformed Church, New York City. Present were 56 delegates from 34 state and city Bible societies, as-

sembled to form a needed national society to "encourage a wider circulation of the Holy Scripture without note or comment."

1817 **Jainism** suffered a split when Swami **Bhikkanaji Maharaja** and his followers in India separated from the Sthanakavasis, who still are a majority among Jains, to form the Jain sect known as the **Terapanthis**. Their chief characteristics were a systematized body of doctrine, organization under one religious head, discipline, and severe penances for its sinners.

1817 **Elias Hicks** (Mar. 19, 1748–Feb. 27, 1830) of Jericho, New York, who during the American Revolution had begun a lifelong itinerant ministry of preaching, successfully urged rejection of the adoption of a creed by the yearly meeting of Friends at Baltimore. When a schism among Friends developed in 1827, the liberal branch was dubbed "Hicksite."

1817 Apr. **Elizabeth Fry** (May 21, 1780–Oct. 12, 1845), a Friend in England, with the help of prominent Friends, founded the **Society for the Reformation of Prison Discipline**. Her immediate targets were London's Newgate prison and the treatment of female prisoners everywhere. Her labors led eventually to prison reforms in England and western Europe.

1819 **John Philip** (Apr. 14, 1775–Aug. 27, 1851) became superintendent for the London Missionary Society in the British Cape Colony [Cape Province], in present South Africa. Through his speeches and writings, published as *Researches in South Africa* (1828), Philip did much to defend the rights of the **Khoikhoi** [Hottentots], natives of present Namibia [South-West Africa], and was instrumental in the passage (1829) of an ordinance by the British Parliament abolishing color discrimination.

1819 **William Ellery Channing** (Apr. 7, 1780–Oct. 2, 1842), pastor of Boston's liberal Federal Street Congregational Church, delivered a sermon in Baltimore entitled "**Unitarian Christianity**." In the sermon, the Unitarians found their platform: the oneness of God (in opposition to Trinitarianism), the humanity of Jesus, the perfectability of human character, the natural [not divinely written] character of the Bible, and the ultimate salvation of all souls.

1819 The **Jewish Synagogue Reform movement** began in Germany at the Hamburg Temple [Hamburger Tempel]. A revised prayer book was issued that dropped some of the traditional liturgy for the coming of a Messiah and the restored Jewish state of Zion, replacing them with prayers of a more universalist nature.

V. SCIENCE, EDUCATION, AND TECHNOLOGY

1815 The first natural gas deposit in the U.S. was accidentally discovered by **James Wilson** when he drilled for water near Charleston, West Virginia.

1815 John Loudon McAdam (Sept. 21, 1756–Nov. 26, 1836), a Scottish engineer and surveyor of roads in Bristol, was the first to recognize the necessity of dry road surfaces to support traffic adequately. For this purpose, he developed a surface of crushed rock packed in thin layers, called "**macadam**" after him.

1817 Nov. 7 Jean André Deluc (b. Feb. 8, 1727), a Swiss-born geologist and meteorologist, died. His best-known invention was the **dry pile**, a kind of voltaic battery, used by physicists in electrical experiments. Deluc also discovered that the density of water was greatest at 40°F [4°C].

1818 July 28 Gaspard Monge (b. May 10, 1746), a French mathematician considered the founder of descriptive geometry, died. His major work on differential geometry was *Application de l'analyse à la géométrie*, which he revised continually to his death (4th. edition, 1819). Monge's theory of curves and the properties of a curved surface were included in *Sur la théorie de deblais et des reblais* (1781). *Feuilles d'analyse appliquée à la géometrie* (1795) was a discussion of the development of infinitesimal geometry.

1819 René Théophile Hyacinthe Laënnec (Feb. 17, 1781–Aug. 13, 1826), a French physician, published *Traité d'auscultation médiate*, in which he described auscultation, a method of medical diagnosis through listening, which he had made more accurate with his invention of the stethoscope.

1819 The **Prado Museum** [Museo del Prado], the Spanish national art gallery, opened in Madrid as the Royal Museum of Painting. Construction began in 1785 but was delayed by the Napoleonic Wars.

1819 The **Dartmouth College Case** was decided by the U.S. Supreme Court. **Daniel Webster** had argued that the state of New Hampshire, in making the private Dartmouth College a state university, breached the contract established by the original charter of the university. The inviolability of a contract, even against interference by the state, was upheld by Chief Justice **John Marshall**.

1819 Christian Jürgensen Thomsen (Dec. 29, 1788–May 21, 1865), curator of the newly created **Royal Museum of Nordic Antiquities** [National Museum of Copenhagen], was the first to formulate the concept of a Stone Age, Bronze Age, and Iron Age in classifying ancient objects. His study of prehistoric tools, weapons, and other relics was published as *A Guide to Northern Antiquities* (1836), which served as a catalog of the museum.

VI. ARTS AND LEISURE

c.1815–1848 The **Biedermeier Style** in Germany was an adaptation of the French Empire Style. Named for a humorous character created by **Ludwig Eichrodt** (1827–1892), "Papa Biedermeier," who appeared as political satire in the German magazine *Fliegende Blätter*, the style was more suited than the opulent Empire Style to a Europe drained of wealth by the Napoleonic Wars. Although chairs and sofas sometimes had exaggerated curves along their arms and backs, larger pieces were more severe in line. Black lacquer replaced ebony, and decorations often were only painted on wooden furniture. Color played an important role.

1815 Augustin-Eugène Scribe (Dec. 24, 1791–Feb. 20, 1861), a French playwright, achieved his first success with the play *Encore une nuit de la Garde Nationale* [*Another Night in the National Guard*].

1817 *Thanatopsis*, the first poem by **William Cullen Bryant**, was published, and instantly became famous. While pursuing a career as a lawyer, Bryant began to establish himself as one of America's foremost poets.

1817 July 14 Madame de Staël [*née* Anne Louise Germaine Necker] (b. Apr. 22, 1766), a French writer, died. Daughter of Jacques Necker, minister of finance during the French Revolution (1789–1799), she married a Swedish diplomat, Baron **Eric de Staël-Holstein**, but separated from him to enjoy a retinue of lovers and admirers. Her salon attracted the brightest dignitaries of the day. Two novels *Delphine* (1802) and *Corinne* (1807) were surpassed in influence by *De la littérature considérée dans ses rapports avec les institutions sociales* [*The Influence of Literature on Society*] (1800) and her treatise extolling the virtues of German romanticism *De l'Allemagne* [On Germany] (1813). Madam de Staël was considered the most influential woman in Europe.

1818 Nikolai Mikhailovich Karamzin (Dec. 12, 1766–June 3, 1826), Russia's first major historian, published *The History of the Russian Empire*. Incomplete, its 12 volumes end with the Romanov succession in 1613.

1818 *Frankenstein, or the Modern Prometheus* by **Mary Wollstonecraft Shelley** [*née* Godwin] (Aug. 30, 1797–Feb. 1, 1851), wife of Percy Bysshe Shelley, was published.

1818 May 11 The **Coburg Theatre** opened on Waterloo Road in London. In 1833 it was renamed the Victoria and soon was called the **Old Vic**.

1818 May 14 Matthew Gregory Lewis (b. July 9, 1775), an English novelist, died. *The Monk* (1795), a shocking Gothic horror novel, earned for him the nickname "Monk." **Walter Scott** contributed to a collection *Tales of Wonder* (1801), edited by Lewis.

1819 *Ivanhoe* by **Walter Scott**, the Scottish novelist, was published in the U.S.

1819 Apr. 18 *A Tatárok Magyarországon* [Tatars in Hungary], by **Károly Kisfaludy** (Feb. 5, 1788–Nov. 21, 1830), was produced. The manuscript, completed eight years earlier, was produced by a repertory company in the ancient Hungarian city of Székesfehérvár, where Károly instantly became a celebrity. In the same year four more of his plays were produced in Pest.

VII. SPORTS, GAMES, AND SOCIETY

1816 Stephen Decatur, U.S. naval captain and hero of the war against the Barbary pirates, spoke the words "Our Country! In her intercourse with foreign governments, may she always be in the right; but our country, right or wrong" at a banquet given in his honor.

1818 The **White House** got its name this year, when it was repainted to cover smoke and scorch marks incurred in 1814 when the British burned Washington, D.C., during the War of 1812.

1820–1824

I. VITAL STATISTICS AND DEMOGRAPHICS

1821 Ireland's first official census reported a **population** of 6,801,827, nearly half the combined population of 14,091,757 reported for **England, Wales, and Scotland**, which had been counted at ten-year intervals since 1801.

II. DISASTERS

1822 Oct. 8 & 12 Galunggung, a volcano in western Java, Indonesia, erupted, giving forth mud, steam, and hot water. Four days later there was an explosion of rock and ash. About 4,000 people were killed and c.100 villages destroyed.

III. EXPLORATION AND COLONIZATION

1820 Jan. 27 Fabian Gottlieb von Bellingshausen [Faddei Faddeevich Bellingsgausen] (Aug. 18, 1779–Jan. 13, 1852), a Russian naval officer, while **sailing completely around the Antarctic continent** (1819–1821), was probably the first to sight the mainland of Antarctica, which he described as an icefield extending beyond the limits of sight. Great Britain claimed the first honors for **Edward Bransfield** (1795?–1852), a naval officer and explorer, who sailed south from the South Shetland Islands in Jan. 1820, and may have sighted the Palmer Peninsula, on the Antarctic continent directly south of the tip of South America, before Bellingshausen. Bransfield's charts he made of the area indicate he saw Mts. Jacquinot and Bransfield, on Jan. 30, 1820.

1821 Dec. 15 The **American Colonization Society** (1816) signed a treaty with West African coastal chiefs and bought a territory at Cape Mesurado on the western coast of Liberia. Monrovia was founded, the first effective colonization in Liberia of freed African slaves repatriated from the U.S.

1821 Feb. 7 **John Davis**, an American sealer, was the **first person to come ashore on the Antarctic continent** when his ship *Cecilia* landed on Hughes Bay, near the tip of the Palmer Peninsula. During the winter of the same year, 11 British sailors involuntarily spent a long, cold season waiting for rescue from the continent after their vessel *Lord Mellville* was shipwrecked.

1821 Nov. **William Becknell** (1790?–?1832), a Missouri trader, returned to Independence, Missouri, from Santa Fe, having mapped the extent of the **Santa Fe Trail**. In this year **Mexico won independence from Spain**, which had previously forbidden trade to Santa Fe, so the trail soon became a major trade route.

1823 Feb. 5 **James Weddell** (1787–1834), a Scottish-born English explorer, aboard the *Jane*, reached the record southern latitude of 74° 15′ while searching for fur seals. The area was named **Weddell Sea** and became the goal of later Antarctic explorers.

1824 **David Thompson**, an English fur trader, working for the North West Company, prepared a map of the northern U.S. and Canada, based on his own surveys.

1824 **Jedediah Strong Smith** (Jan. 6, 1799–May 27, 1831), an American explorer and mountain man, and **Thomas Fitzpatrick** (1799?–1854), a fur trapper, crossed the Rocky Mountains through the South Pass, in present central western Wyoming. Smith and Fitzpatrick's crossing initiated regular use of the **Oregon Trail** through this pass to Fort Vancouver, in the present state of Washington.

IV. POLITICS AND WAR

1820 **José Gervasio Artigas** (June 19, 1764–Sept. 23, 1850), the patriot leader of the Banda Oriental [= Eastern Shore] region [present **Uruguay**], across the Rio de la Plata from the newly independent Spanish settlement of Buenos Aires, fled to Paraguay following an invasion from Brazil, which then annexed Uruguay as the Cisplatine Province (to 1830).

1820 Jan. 1 An **uprising by army officers in Cadiz, Spain**, protesting orders for an expedition to South America to regain Spain's lost colonies there, was joined by a popular revolution against the rule of **Ferdinand VII**. On Mar. 7 the **liberal constitution of 1812** was reinstated by Ferdinand, who had been captured by the rebels.

1820 Jan. 29 **George III** [George William Frederick] (b. June 4, 1738), king of Great Britain and Ireland (from 1760), died. He was succeeded by **George IV** [George Augustus Frederick]. The **Regency Act** (Feb. 5, 1811) had established George IV as regent (1811–1820) because of his father's insanity.

1820 Feb. 13 In Paris **revolutionaries assassinated Charles Ferdinand de Bourbon**, duke of Berry (b. Jan. 24, 1778), third in line of succession after his father, the future Charles X [brother of Louis XVIII] and his brother Louis Antoine de Bourbon (Aug. 6, 1775–June 3, 1844), duke of Angoulême, and presumed to be the last of the Bourbons because Angoulême had no children. A similar revolutionary plot in England, the **Cato Street Conspiracy**, directed against the Cabinet, was uncovered on Feb. 23. Angoulême was the last dauphin in French history.

1820 Mar. 15 **Maine** was the 23rd state admitted to the U.S.

1820 Mar. 22 **Stephen Decatur** (b. Jan. 5, 1779), an American naval officer, died. As one of three naval commissioners, he opposed a move to return Commodore James Barron (1769?–Apr. 21, 1851) to active duty. Barron had surrendered (1807) the U.S. frigate *Chesapeake* to a British search party and been courtmartialed. Barron killed Decatur in a duel.

1820 July 2 Riots broke out in the **Kingdom of the Two Sicilies** [Kingdom of Naples] at Nola, Italy, against the Bourbon ruler **Ferdinand I** (Jan. 12, 1751–Jan. 4, 1825), king of Naples (1759–1806, 1815–1825), who had joined Sicily to Naples in Dec. 1816. The Sicilians forced Ferdinand to grant them a charter on July 7. The Sicilians and their charter were later suppressed with aid from Austria.

1820 Aug. 24 A rebellion by the **Portuguese army** against the Spanish-supported regency began in Oporto, Portugal. Gradually gaining popular support, the revolution promulgated a liberal constitutional monarchy and invited **John VI**, living in exile in Brazil, to return to Portugal. John landed there in 1822 and swore to uphold the new constitution.

1820 Oct. 8   **Henri Christophe** (b. Oct. 6, 1767), the cruel king of northern Hispaniola [**Haiti**], shot himself with a silver bullet. **Jean Pierre Boyer** (1776–July 9, 1850), who had succeeded **Alexandre Sabès Pétion** (1770–1818) as ruler of southern Hispaniola, took control of the entire island and ruled to 1843.

1820 Oct. 27–Dec. 17   The **Congress of Troppau** [Opava] in Austrian Silesia [present northeastern Czechoslovakia] convened to discuss the uprising in the **Kingdom of the Two Sicilies**. On Nov. 19 the representatives of Austria, Prussia, and Russia signed a protocol declaring their responsibility to intervene militarily in any revolutionary activities threatening the stability of Europe.

1821   The **Missouri Compromise** resolved the question of whether Missouri should be admitted to the U.S. as a slave state or a free state. Missouri was to be admitted as a slave state, but all territory north of 36° 30' latitude, Missouri's southern border, was to be free. Arkansas Territory, south of this parallel, was allowed slaves. Maine, admitted the previous year, was not a slave state. The Senate thus preserved its equal representation of slave and free states.

1821 Jan. 26–May 12   At the **Congress of Laibach** [Ljubljana, Lyublyana] in Austrian Slovenia [present northern Yugoslavia] Austria, Russia, and Prussia discussed the situation in the **Kingdom of the Two Sicilies** and affirmed the decision made at the **Congress of Troppau** (1820). These powers decided it was in their own best interests to suppress the rebels, thus preventing the spread of rebellion into their own territories. Austrian armies, acting with the approval of the Concert of Europe, defeated (Mar. 7) the rebels at Rieti, Italy. Austrian armies then entered (Mar. 23) Naples and successfully restored the Bourbon Ferdinand I, king of Naples. Austria also invaded the Piedmont in northern Italy, where a revolt had arisen against Austria. In a **battle at Novara**, near Milan, Austria defeated (Mar. 10) the Piedmontese.

1821 Feb. 24   The **Plan of Iguala** was announced by **Agustín de Iturbide**, leader of the royalist forces in the **Mexican War of Independence**, and the revolutionary **Vicente Guerrero** (Aug. 10, 1783–Feb. 14,

1831), who had continued to conduct guerrilla warfare from his last strongholds. The plan would guarantee an independent Mexico, Roman Catholicism, and equality between those of Spanish descent born in the New World and those born in Spain. On Aug. 24 the **Treaty of Córdoba**, ending the revolution and granting Mexican independence, was signed by **Juan O'Donojú** (1775?–1821), the **last viceroy of New Spain**.

1821 Mar. 5   **James Monroe** of the Democratic-Republican party was inaugurated for his second term as president of the U.S., having defeated **John Quincy Adams** by an electoral vote of 231 to 1. The one vote for Adams was cast symbolically by New Hampshire to preserve Washington's distinction of being the only president elected unanimously. **Daniel D. Tompkins** was also reelected as vice president.

1821 Mar. 6   The **Greek War of Independence** (1821–1829) began as the Phanariot [a Greek of Constantinople] **Alexander Ypsilanti** [Hypselantes, Hypsilantis] (Dec. 12, 1792–Jan. 31, 1828) initiated an uprising at Jassy [Iasi] in Moldavia [present northeastern Romania] against the Ottoman rule of Greece. Later the same year Alexander's brother, **Demetrius** (Dec. 28, 1793–Aug. 16, 1832) aided patriots from Morea [Peloponnesus] in taking the Turkish fortress at Tripolitza [Tripolis].

1821 June 14   Sennar, in the eastern **Sudan** on the Blue Nile River, the capital of the **Funj** [Fung] **Sultanate** [roughly ancient Nubia], fell to Egyptian soldiers augmented by a Turkish and Albanian force. **Badi VI**, the last sultan (from 1790–1796; 1803–1821) of the Funj Dynasty (from c.1504), was deposed. **Mohammed Ali,** the Ottoman pasha of Egypt, extended his hegemony throughout the eastern Sudan, establishing an empire that rivaled the biggest of the ancient Egyptian empires.

1821 June 24   The **battle at Carabobo**, near Valencia, Venezuela, was the final battle of **Venezuela's War for Independence** (1811–1821) from Spain as **Simón Bolívar** defeated Spanish royalist forces.

1821 July 21   The **U.S. officially occupied Florida**. **Andrew Jackson** was appointed military governor.

1821 July 28   The **independence of Peru** was declared by **José de San Martín** after driving the Spanish out of the capital at Lima with a fleet from Chile.

1821 Aug. 10   Missouri was the 24th state admitted to the U.S.

1821 Sept. 15   The **Central American states** governed by the captaincy general of Guatemala declared independence from Spain and joined the Mexican Empire of **Agustín de Iturbide**.

1822 Jan.   Stephen Fuller Austin (Nov. 3, 1793–Dec. 27, 1836) completed the efforts of his father **Moses** (1761–1821) to establish a legal American community in the **Texas** area through purchase of land. The Spanish agreed, and the Americans bought land situated between the Brazos and Colorado rivers for twelve and one half cents an acre.

1822 May 19   **Agustín de Iturbide** was declared emperor **Agustín I** of **Mexico** at the Congress of Mexico City. His policies soon led to revolts under Vicente Guerrero and Santa Ana [Antonio López de Santa Ana] (Feb. 21, 1794–June 21, 1876), causing Iturbide's abdication and flight on Mar. 19, 1823. Upon his return to Mexico, Iturbide (b. Sept. 27, 1783) was shot as a traitor on July 19, 1824.

1822 May 24   **Antonio José de Sucre** (June 13, 1795–June 4, 1830), the chief lieutenant of Bolívar, won **Ecuador's liberation** from Spain by defeating Spanish forces in a **battle at Mount Pichincha**, near Quito. After Sucre's victory Ecuador became the Department of the South in the **Republic of Great Colombia** [Gran Colombia].

1822 Sept. 7   **Brazil** was proclaimed independent of Portugal by **Dom Pedro** [Antonio Pedro de Alcantara Bourbon] (Oct. 12, 1798–Sept. 24, 1834), the Portugese regent in Brazil for his father John VI, king of Portugal. On Oct. 22 he styled himself the first emperor of Brazil (until 1831) as Dom Pedro I.

1822 Sept. 16   **George Canning** took office for the second time as British foreign secretary (to 1827) after the suicide of **Robert Stewart** (June 18, 1769–Aug. 12, 1822), viscount Castlereagh. Canning continued Castlereagh's policy of nonintervention in continental alliances and turned to the expansion of British trade.

1822 Oct. 20   The **Congress of Verona**, the last council held under the provisions of the **Quadruple Alliance** (1814), agreed to a French invasion of Spain.

1823 Apr. 7   French forces under **Louis Antoine de Bourbon**, duke of Angoulême, entered Spain as ordered by the **Congress of Verona** to end the threat of the Spanish uprising. On Oct. 1 **Ferdinand VII** was restored as king of Spain.

1823 Dec. 2   The **Monroe Doctrine**, issued by **James Monroe**, president of the U.S., stated the U.S. position in foreign affairs. It warned against European intervention in the Western Hemisphere, specifically against interference in the increasingly independent South American colonies. Furthermore, the U.S. was to remain neutral in any European power struggles.

1824   New political ideals were beginning to crystalize in the U.S. The Federalists had lost unity, and their causes had merged with the opposing Democratic-Republicans after the days of Jefferson. The **National Republican party**, which only lasted about ten years, arose mainly as opposition to Jackson. The **Whigs** (1824–c.1855) were a collection of conservatives filling a void and composed of remnants of splintered parties of previous times.

1824   The **U.S. Bureau of Indian Affairs** was created in order to negotiate treaties with the Indian population. The bureau also provided health services to the Indians.

1824 Mar. 5   The **First Anglo-Burmese War** (to 1826) was declared, provoked by the expansionist policy of **Bagyidaw**, king of Burma [Myanmar] (1819–1838), whose armies had entered the Chittagong region, in present Bangladesh, in 1823. On May 11 **Archibald Campbell** (1769–1843), a British officer, entered Rangoon [Yangon]. After a number of costly defeats, the Burmese accepted British conditions by the **Treaty of Yandabu** on Feb. 24, 1826.

1824 Mar. 17   The **Treaty of London** was signed by the United Kingdom of the Netherlands and Great Britain, whereby the Dutch ceded Malacca [Melaka], on the southwestern tip of the Malay Peninsula, and abandoned their claims to Singapore and the Malay Peninsula in return for Benkulen [Bencoolen, Bengkuli] in Sumatra.

1824 Apr. 17   Russia signed a treaty with the U.S. permitting Great Britain and the U.S. to trade in the area of present **Alaska**. The 54° 40′ parallel was established as the southern limit of Russian land on the North American continent.

1824 June 21   The British Parliament repealed 35 so-called **Combination Acts**, which had prohibited the formation of associations by workingmen. At the same time Parliament specifically legalized trade societies.

1824 Aug. 6   In a **battle at Junín**, northeast of Lima, **Simón Bolívar** defeated a superior Spanish loyalist force. On Dec. 9 in a **battle at Ayacucho** [Guamanga, Huamango], Bolívar's general Antonio José de Sucre defeated the Spanish royalist forces commanded by José de La Serna y Hinojosa (1770–1832), who was captured. **Independence was won for Peru**, and Bolívar was elected president-dictator (Feb. 1825–1827).

1824 Sept. 16   **Louis XVIII** [Louis Xavier Stanislas, also Louis le Désiré] (b. Nov. 17, 1755), king of France (1814–1815, 1815–1824), died and was succeeded by his brother **Charles X**, a leader of the conservative *Ultras*.

1824 Oct. 4   **Mexico** adopted a constitution modeled after the U.S. Constitution, and **Guadalupe Victoria** [Manuel Félix Fernández] (1789–Mar. 21, 1843) was elected the **first constitutional president** (1824–1829) **of the Republic of Mexico**.

V. ECONOMY AND TRADE

1820   A major advance in the **ventilation of mines** began when coal mines were partitioned so that air could flow from the downdraft shaft at one end to the updraft shaft on the other. Adding a furnace at the foot of the updraft shaft promoted the circulation, because the heated air rose more rapidly, pulling fresh air into the downdraft shaft and through the mine.

1821 July 2   The **Hudson's Bay Company** was recognized by the British government. The company controlled (to 1869) Prince Rupert's Land, the Yukon Territory, British Columbia, Alberta, and western parts of present Saskatchewan and the Northwest Territories.

1822   **Mohammed Ali**, the Ottoman pasha of **Egypt**, launched a program of **economic development** that gave his country the foundations of a modern state. With the help of **Louis Alexis Jumel** (1785–1823), a French engineer, who had discovered and first grown **long-fiber cotton**, Ali had already begun exporting (1821) **Jumel cotton** to the European markets.

1822   The *Société Genéral pour Favoriser L'Industrie Nationale* was founded in Brussels to act as the national bank of Belgium. By issuing notes and supplying capital for industrial and commercial enterprises, it boosted Belgium's booming industrialization.

1823   The **Baltic Club** was formally established in meetings of merchants and sea captains at the Baltic Tavern in London. Its purpose was to expedite shipping by matching cargoes ready to be shipped with vessels available for transport. Eventually, the club became the **Baltic Mercantile and Shipping Exchange, Ltd**.

VI. RELIGION AND PHILOSOPHY

1820 May 3   The **Roman Catholic Church was established in Australia**. Its rapid growth and acceptance was due mostly to its stand against convict transportation, or the policy of settling British criminals in Australian penal colonies, and to its support of representative government for the Australian provinces.

1821   **Charles Grandison Finney** (Aug. 29, 1792–Aug. 16, 1875), an American law student who was to become the most expert revivalist preacher of the **"Second" Great Awakening**, experienced a sudden conversion. He raised revival methods to a fine art by introducing new techniques designed to produce results.

1824   In Charleston, South Carolina, 47 members of the orthodox congregation Jewish Beth Elohim (1750), requested changes in the synagogue ritual, calling especially for a shorter service and wider use of English. The request was denied. Twelve dissidents seceded to found the **Reform Society of Israelites**. By 1840 the reformers gained control of Beth Elohim.

VII. SCIENCE, EDUCATION, AND TECHNOLOGY

1820   **Wood began to be used as paving material for streets and roads**. In St. Petersburg, Russia, two streets were paved with blocks held together with wooden pegs. Wood blocks were also tried (1835) in New York City. The **first plank road in North America** was constructed (1835–1836) in **Toronto**, Canada; the first plank road in the U.S. opened (1846) from **Syracuse**, New York, to Oneida Lake, a distance of 16 miles.

1820 **Quinine** was isolated by the French chemists **Pierre Joseph Pelletier** (Mar. 22, 1788–July 19, 1842) and **Joseph Bienaimé Caventou** (June 30, 1795–May 5, 1877). In 1818 Caventou had isolated **strychnine**.

1820 **Nineveh**, the ruined Assyrian city on the eastern bank of the Tigris River, was first extensively surveyed. Since then numerous excavations at the mound of **Kuyunjik** [Quyunjik], covering most of Nineveh, have revealed artifacts dating to the sixth millennium B.C.

1820 Apr. The science of **electromagnetism** began with the discovery by **Hans Christian Oersted** [Örsted, Ǿrsted] (Aug. 14, 1777–Mar. 9, 1851), a Danish physicist, that an electric current deflected the magnetic pull of a needle.

1821 The **first public high school in the U.S.**, the Boston English High School, held its opening classes this year.

1821 **Troy Female Seminary**, the first women's college in the U.S., was founded by **Emma Hart Willard** (Feb. 23, 1787–Apr. 15, 1870), at Troy, New York. Its curriculum became a model of higher education for women in the U.S. and Europe.

1822 **François Magendie** (Oct. 15, 1783–Oct. 7, 1855), a French physiologist, demonstrated in experiments on dogs the theory of the specialized function of anterior and posterior spinal nerves, first stated by the Englishman Charles Bell in 1811.

1822 **Jean Baptiste Joseph Fourier** (Mar. 21, 1768–May 16, 1830), a French mathematician and physicist, published his *Théorie Analytique de la Chaleur*, on the properties of heat.

1822 Projective geometry began with the publication of *Traité des propriétés des figures* by **Jean Victor Poncelet** (July 1, 1788–Dec. 22, 1867), a French mathematician. Poncelet's work outlined the chief properties of geometric figures—lines, points, planes, and their angles of relationship—that do not change.

1822 Aug. 25 **William Herschel** [Friedrich Wilhelm] (b. Nov. 15, 1738) who, with the aid of his sister **Caroline Lucretia** (Mar. 16, 1750–Jan. 9, 1848),

was credited with the **establishment of astronomy** as a science, died. He had migrated from his native Hanover to England where, as a master lens grinder, he built a telescope enabling him to discover (1781) Uranus, two of its moons (1787), and the sixth (Aug. 28, 1787) and seventh (Sept. 17, 1789) moons of Saturn. His further contributions included discovery of binary stars and description of their motion, the length of Saturn's day, and the composition of nebulae and the Milky Way.

1822 Sept. **Jean François Champollion** (Dec. 23, 1790–Mar. 4, 1832), a French archaeologist, discovered the **key to decipherment of Egyptian hieroglyphics** made possible by the finding (Aug. 1799) of the **Rosetta stone**.

1823 **Michel Eugène Chevreul** (Aug. 31, 1786–Apr. 9, 1899), a French chemist, published *Recherches chimiques sur les corps gras*. A definitive work on the chemical nature of fats, it was also the first description of the chemical constitution of an organic substance.

1824 **William Sturgeon** (1783–1850), an English inventor, developed the **first electromagnet**.

VIII. ARTS AND LEISURE

c.1820–1870 The **hourglass silhouette**—a large bust, tiny waist, and billowing skirt—became popular for women. It required the use of a corset to create the unnaturally slender waistline. **Crinolines**, adorned with bows, fringe, and lace, increased in popularity as its already bulky width also increased. Men's trousers were long and narrow, secured by a strap under the foot. Colors became more uniform and the phrase, "**suit of clothes**," was first used to refer to men's apparel.

1820 The *Venus de Milo* was discovered in the ruins of the city of Melos [Mílos], on Melos, an island in the Cyclades, by **Jules Sébastien César Dumont d'Urville** (May 23, 1790–May 8, 1842), a French naval commander, while on a hydrographic survey of the Mediterranean. His report to the French ambassador at Constantinople urged its protection. The statue was thought to have been sculpted (c.150 B.C.) by an artist from Antioch [Pisidian Antioch], and to be based on a 4th-century B.C. Venus from Corinth.

1820 Mar. 11   Benjamin West (b. Oct. 10, 1738), an American artist, died. West, who had lived in England for more than 50 years, painted historic, religious, and mythological subjects in a neoclassical style, often infused with forward-looking social and political ideals, which anticipated romantic ideals. One of West's best-known paintings, *The Death of General Wolfe on the Plains of Abraham* (c.1771), was a departure from the mode of his contemporary artists in that the historical characters were depicted in clothing styles of their days. Among his other paintings were *Christ Healing the Sick* (c.1803), *Death on a Pale Horse* (1817), and *Penn's Treaty with the Indians* (1771).

1820 Sept. 3   Benjamin Henry Latrobe (b. May 1, 1764), considered the **first professional architect in the U.S.**, died. He introduced the Greek classic revival to the U.S. and aided in rebuilding the **U.S. capitol** (1815–1817). An engineer by training, Latrobe designed city water and sewage systems and worked with Robert Fulton on the steamboat.

1821 Feb. 23   John Keats (b. Oct. 31, 1795), an English romantic poet, died. His first volume *Poems* (1817) included "On First Looking into Chapman's Homer." *Endymion* (1818) attracted strong criticism at first. Many of his most famous poems were included in the better-received volume *Lamia, Isabella, The Eve of St. Agnes, and Other Poems* (1820). Famous poems, written mostly from 1818 to 1819 were the odes "On a Grecian Urn," " To a Nightingale," and "To Autumn"; such sonnets as "Bright star! Would I were as steadfast as thou art"; and the narrative poems "The Eve of St. Agnes" and "La Belle Dame sans Merci."

1821 July 13   Andrew Law (b. Mar., 1789), a U.S. composer and singing teacher, died. He pioneered the practice of setting the melody of his songs in the soprano voice rather than the tenor, as was then customary. Law compiled several books of hymns as well as *The Art of Playing the Organ and Pianoforte* (1809) and *Essays on Music* (1814).

1821 Oct. 5   Junius Brutus Booth (May 1, 1796–Nov. 30, 1852), an English actor, made his **New York debut**. He continued to perform in the U.S. with his three sons, among them **John Wilkes Booth**.

1822 July 8   Percy Bysshe Shelley (b. Aug. 4, 1792), an English romantic poet, drowned when a storm swamped the boat he and a companion were sailing off the coast of Italy, near Viareggio. Shelley was a passionate supporter of English reform movements, and when reaction set in, he exiled (1818) himself to Italy. His *annus mirabilis* was 1819 in which he produced such lyrics as "Ode to Heaven," "The Indian Serenade," and "Ode to the West Wind"; his finest long poem *Prometheus Unbound*; and the poetic tragedy *The Cenci*. In the two years before his death, Shelley wrote "Adonais," mourning the death of Keats; "To a Skylark"; and a prose work, *The Defence of Poetry*, in which he warned against the progress of science at the expense of creative imagination and joy.

1822 July 24   Ernst Theodor Wilhelm [Amadeus] **Hoffmann** [E.T.A. Hoffmann] (b. Jan. 24, 1776), a German composer and writer, died. He was a master of short stories on supernatural themes. *Fantastic Pieces in Collot's Manner* (1814–1815) was a multivolume collection. His other works included the influential *Die Elixiere des Teufels* [*The Devil's Elixir*] (1815) and *Die Serapionsbrüder* [*The Brothers of Serapion*] (1819–1821). He set to music the novel *Undine* by **Friederich Heinrich Karl La Motte-Fouqué** (Feb. 12, 1777–Jan. 23, 1843), which was the basis for **Jacques Offenbach's** opera *Les Contes d'Hoffmann* [*The Tales of Hoffmann*].

1822 Oct. 13   Antonio Canova (b. Nov. 1, 1757), an Italian sculptor, died. He sculpted a number of heroic statues of **Napoléon** as a Greek god and a particularly famous statue of Napoléon's sister, **Pauline Bonaparte Borghese**, as a reclining Venus (c.1808). Canova executed a statue of **George Washington in Roman costume**, which was placed in the state capitol at Raleigh, North Carolina, but was destroyed by fire there on June 21, 1831.

1824   *Slávy dcera* [The Daughter of Slava], written in Czech, the principal work of the Slovak poet **Jan Kollár** (July 29, 1793–Jan. 24, 1852), was published. This first edition contained 151 sonnets and a prologue, but Kollár added to the original sonnet cycle throughout his life. The posthumous version of 1858 had more than 600 sonnets.

1824   The Paris Salon of 1824 featured the first breath of French romanticism, the exhibition of **Eugene Delacroix's** *Massacre of Chios* (1824), and the last gasp of French classicism, the *Vow of Louis XIII* (1824) by **Jean Auguste Dominique Ingres**. **John Constable** exhibited *The Hay-Wain* (1821).

1824 Feb. 1   Maria Thérèsia von Paradis (b. May 15, 1759), an Austrian composer and pianist, died.

Although blind from her fifth year, she was an accomplished and popular pianist and organist. She wrote many works, including the opera *Rinaldo und Alcina*.

1824 Mar. 3 Giovanni Battista Viotti (b. May 12, 1755), an Italian violinist and composer, died. He was one of the first to compose concertos for the violin in true sonata form, exploiting the full capabilities of the violin and accompanying orchestra. Viotti composed many chamber works and concertos for violin and for piano.

1824 Apr. 19 George Gordon [Noel] **Byron,** Lord Byron (b. Jan. 22, 1788), an English romantic poet, died of fever at Missolonghi [Mesolóngion], in present Greece, where he had gone to aid the Greek struggle for independence from the Ottoman Empire. In 1818 Byron had left England because of his political liberalism, leaving behind his wife and daughter. Most ambitious of his works was the unfinished *Don Juan* (1819–1824), but he was noted for *Childe Harold* (1812–1818), *The Siege of Corinth* (1816), *Beppo* (1818); *The Vision of Judgment* (1822), and the dramas *Manfred* (1817) and *Cain* (1821). In his poem *English Bards and Scotch Reviewers* (1809), Byron wrote a satirical response to criticism in the *Edinburgh Review* of his volume of poems **Hours of Idleness** (1807).

IX. SPORTS, GAMES, AND SOCIETY

1820 Football, different from the English game of football [soccer], first appeared on U.S. college campuses as a form of hazing. Especially at Yale and Harvard, sophomores would kick freshmen instead of the ball.

1820 Robert Mackey won the **racquets championship** of England to become the first professional champion of the game. Mackey had learned to play while in Debtor's Prison in London, where the game was played against a single wall in a courtyard. After students at Harrow took up racquets c.1822, it eventually became a sport of the wealthy, played on four-walled indoor courts.

1822 July 2 Denmark Vesey (b. 1767?) and 34 others were hanged for their roles in the **Vesey Slave Plot.** Vesey, who had bought (1800) his freedom from slavery with $600 of $1,500 he had won in a lottery, had formed a conspiracy to take over **Charleston,** South Carolina. He used church meetings as a cover for the planned insurrection. In June an informer gave the plot away.

1823 The game of **rugby** was initiated by a Rugby schoolboy, **William Webb Ellis,** who, in a football [soccer] game, took the ball in his arms and ran with it. This innovation was neither forgotten nor formalized into a new game. However, in 1839, students at Cambridge University experimented with "Rugby's game," and rugby began to be played as an intramural sport at many boys' schools.

1823 May In the **first great horse race in the U.S.,** at the Union Course on Long Island in New York, American Eclipse represented the North and Sir Henry, the South. With c.100,000 in attendance, American Eclipse won the race.

1825–1829

I. DISASTERS

1828 Dec. 28 An **earthquake** caused the deaths of c.30,000 people on Honshu, Japan.

II. EXPLORATION AND COLONIZATION

1825–1827 An expedition under **John Franklin,** an English explorer, mapped c.800 miles of the **Canadian Arctic coast** in an attempt to search out the Northwest Passage. He arrived at Great Bear Lake in northwestern Canada on Aug 7, 1825, and there built Fort Franklin, where he spent the winter. On June 28, 1826, he and his party descended the Mackenzie River and at its mouth split into two groups. Franklin mapped the coast westward to Return Reef [149° west] in about six weeks, but was forced by bad weather to return to Fort Franklin before reaching Point Barrow, where he was to rendezvous with British ships sailing east from the Bering Sea. The second party, under **John Richardson** (Nov. 5, 1787–June 5, 1865), a Scottish naturalist, mapped eastward from the Mackenzie to the Coppermine rivers in about five weeks, returning overland to Fort

Franklin. The rescue vessels meanwhile had charted the coast to Point Barrow.

1825   James Bridger (Mar. 17, 1804–June 17, 1881), an American fur trader and trapper, with his partner **William Henry Ashley** (1778?–Mar. 26, 1838), also American, was credited with the discovery and exploration of **Great Salt Lake** in present Utah. **Peter Skene Ogden** (1794–Sept. 27, 1854), a Canadian fur trader and agent of the Hudson's Bay Company, also visited Great Salt Lake in 1825.

1826 Sept. 26   Alexander Gordon Laing (b. Dec. 27, 1793), a Scottish explorer, was murdered two days after he departed from **Tombouctou** [Timbuktu], on the Niger River, in present Mali. He was the first European to reach this city from the north, after crossing the Sahara. **Mungo Park** (Sept. 10, 1771–?1806) was probably the first European to reach the city (1805) by way of the Niger River.

1827   Henry Leavenworth (Dec. 10, 1783–July 21, 1834) built **Fort Leavenworth** along the Missouri River in Kansas to protect travelers on the Santa Fe Trail.

1827 Apr. 27   Hugh Clapperton (b. May 18, 1788), a Scottish explorer, died at Sokoto, in present Nigeria, the capital of the **Fulah** [Fulani] **Empire** (c.1809–1906) of West Africa. Clapperton was the first European to describe the Hausa tribes. His companion, **Richard Lemon Lander** (1807–Feb. 6, 1834), an English explorer, returned to London with Clapperton's journals for publication.

1828–1830   One of the **first successful crossings of the Australian continent** was led by **Peter Egerton Warburton** (Aug. 15, 1813–Dec. 16, 1889), an English explorer, who discovered the **Darling River**, in southeastern Australia.

III. POLITICS AND WAR

1825   The **War of the Thirty-Three Immortals** [Treinta y Tres, Band of 33] (1825–1828) began as **Uruguay** [Banda Oriental], aided by Argentina, declared war on Brazil in order to gain independence.

1825   The **Central American Federation** was founded by Costa Rica, Guatemala, Honduras, Nicaragua, and El Salvador. **Manuel José Arce** (1783?–1847) was appointed president of the federa-

tion for a four-year term as provided by its constitution.

1825 Feb. 9   Antonio José de Sucre, supported by **Simón Bolívar**, triumphantly entered **La Paz**, the present capital of **Bolivia**, declaring independence from Spain for Upper Peru [Bolivia]. In 1826 Bolívar had a constitution drafted, and the name of the republic changed to Bolivia in his honor. La Paz [Pueblo Nuevo de Nuesta Senora de la Paz] was renamed La Paz de Ayacucho, in commemoration of the victorious **battle fought at Ayacucho** on Dec. 9, 1824.

1825 Mar. 4   John Quincy Adams of the Democratic-Republican party was inaugurated as the sixth president of the U.S. On Dec. 1, 1824, no candidate received a majority of electoral votes, but **Andrew Jackson** received a plurality in the electoral vote. All four candidates—Adams, Jackson, Clay, and William Harris Crawford (Feb. 24, 1772–Sep. 15, 1834)—were of the Democratic-Republican party. On Feb. 25, 1825, the House of Representatives chose Adams over Jackson. **John C. Calhoun** (Mar. 18, 1782–Mar. 31, 1850) served as vice-president.

1825 Dec. 26   The **Decembrist** [Dekabrist] **uprising** broke out in St. Petersburg over the question of who was to succeed **Alexander I** [Aleksandr Pavlovich] (b. Dec. 23, 1777), czar of Russia (from 1801), who had died on Dec. 1. Alexander's testament named Nicholas, his younger brother. **Constantine** [Konstantin Pavlovich] (May 8, 1779–June 27, 1831), another brother of Alexander and older than Nicholas, had already renounced his right to succession. The Decembrists, demonstrating in support of Constantine, refused to swear fealty to Nicholas and were fired at by troops loyal to Nicholas. Liberal-minded members of the ruling class made up most of the Decembrists. In an inquisition that followed, some leaders were executed. **Nicholas I** ruled for the next 30 years.

1826   Russia occupied the **Caucasus** [Persian Armenia], as promised in the ambiguous Treaty of Gulistan (1813). **Persia declared war on Russia.**

1826   **Davy** [David] **Crockett**, a U.S. frontiersman, ran for a seat in the **U.S. House of Representatives**. He served two terms (1827–1831, 1833–1835). As a staunch conservative, he became a leader in the Whig party, in opposition to Andrew Jackson.

1826 Apr. **Missolonghi** [Mesolóngion], the city guarding the opening to the Gulf of Corinth, fell to Ottoman forces in the **Greek War of Independence** (1821–1829). But in a battle on Oct. 20, 1827, at **Navarino** [Pylos], in the Peloponnesus, the fleet of the Ottoman sultan, supported by **Mohammad Ali**, pasha of Egypt, was defeated by a combined British, French, and Russian fleet sympathetic to the Greek fight for independence. In four hours, approximately 60 ships and 8,000 men were lost by the Turkish-Egyptian fleet. No allied ships were lost, and fewer than 200 men were killed. This battle was said to have been the **last major engagement between wooden sailing ships**.

1826 Apr. 4 The **St. Petersburg Protocol**, signed by Great Britain and Russia, demanded Greek independence but stipulated that Greece become an autonomous province of Turkey.

1826 June 15–16 The **Janissaries** [Janizaries], the regular standing army of the Turks, were massacred in their barracks by order of **Mahmud II**, the Ottoman sultan. The **Spahis** who attacked the Janissaries were a special mounted army corps loyal to the sultan who rewarded them with grants of royal fiefdoms. The Spahis were disbanded after the massacre, and Mahmud II continued his reform of the **Ottoman Empire** (1326–1920).

1826 July 4 **John Adams** (b. Oct. 30, 1735) and **Thomas Jefferson** (b. Apr. 13, 1743), though often estranged in their politics but friends since their meeting in the U.S. Congress in 1775, died on this day. Adams was nearly 91. Jefferson was 84.

1827 Feb. 20 A battle at Ituzaingó, Argentina, brought final defeat to Brazilian forces under **Feliberto Caldeira Brant Pontes** (Sept. 19, 1772–June 13, 1841), marquis de Barbacena, by the allied revolutionary Argentinian and Uruguayan forces under the Argentine **Carlos María de Alvear** (c.1789–c.1853) in the **War of the Thirty-Three Immortals** (1825–1828).

1827 Apr. **Ioannes Antonios Kapodistrias** [Johannes Antonius Capodistrias, Capo d'Istria] (Feb. 11, 1776–Oct. 9, 1831), was elected ruler of Greece. Born in Corfu, Kapodistrias had served in the Russian foreign service until 1822, when he devoted himself to the Greek cause from Geneva, the meeting place for volunteers in the **Greek War of Independence** .

1827 Nov. 15 The **Creek Indians** of the southeastern U.S. ceded the remaining portion of their territory to the U.S. government. Most of their lands had already become (1814) U.S. property.

1828 The **National Republican party** (to 1836) had been formed during the administration of John Quincy Adams in opposition to the **Democratic party** and Andrew Jackson, who now won this year's presidential election.

1828 **Radama I** (b. 1792), king of **Madagascar**, died and was succeeded by his wife **Ranavalona I**, queen of Madagascar (to 1861). She instituted a policy forbidding foreign influence, causing Great Britain and France to launch joint naval and military campaigns, which were unsuccessful.

1828 Apr. 26 **Nicholas I**, czar of Russia, declared war on the Turkish **Ottoman Empire**. Nicholas I fought the Turks not only to aid the Greek patriots, but also to serve Russian interests. The war ended in 1829, with Greece becoming an autonomous region in the Ottoman Empire and with the Concert of Europe disrupted.

1828 May 9 The **Test Act of 1673**, which forbade Roman Catholics and nonconforming Protestants to hold public office, was repealed by the British Parliament, under pressure from the duke of Wellington, the prime minister. It was an attempt to curb the growing restlessness of the Irish, who were threatening civil strife in Ireland. In the following year the **Emancipation Act** was passed, granting suffrage to Catholics and permitting them to hold seats in Parliament and locally.

1828 Aug. 28 The **War of the Thirty-Three Immortals** (1825–1828) ended as Brazil and Argentina recognized the independent state of **Uruguay** [Republica Oriental del Uruguay]. Great Britain stipulated in the treaty negotiations that Uruguay's constitution (1830) be acceptable to Argentina and Brazil.

1828 Sept. In the **second presidential election in Mexico**, supporters of the incumbent liberal vice president **Vicente Guerrero** (Aug. 10, 1783–Feb. 14, 1831), who was defeated, were led by **Santa Ana**, who forced the withdrawal of the elected conservative president **Manuel Gomez Pedraza** (1788?–1851) on charges of corrupt election procedures. Guerrero thus became Mexico's second president. In 1829 Anastasio Bustamante (Aug. 27, 1780–Mar. 6, 1853), a conservative, emerged as the strongman and overthrew Guerrero.

1829 Mar. 4   Andrew Jackson of the Democratic party was inaugurated as the seventh president of the U.S., having defeated John Quincy Adams of the National Republican party. As Jackson was the first president elected from the Democratic party [formerly the Democratic-Republican party], a great celebration was held in his honor at the White House in which, it was said, the guests had to be lured out again with buckets of punch set out on the lawn. **John Caldwell Calhoun** served again as vice president until he resigned in 1831.

1829 Sept. 14   The **Treaty of Adrianople** [Edirne], Turkey, concluded the **Russo-Turkish War** (1828–1829) to Russia's advantage, and marked the decline of Ottoman influence in the Balkans. The Turks promised autonomy for Serbia and Greece, thus formally ending the **Greek War of Independence**. Russia gained important outposts at the mouth of the Danube River and along the eastern shore of the Black Sea.

1829 Dec. 8   After a period of virtual anarchy in the **United Provinces of La Plata** [Argentina], the Federal party, under **Juan Manuel de Rosas** (Mar. 30, 1793–Mar. 14, 1877), gained power when he was elected governor (to 1832; 1835–1852) of Buenos Aires Province. Though nominally a provincial governor, he assumed dictatorial powers, subsequently winning control over most of the provinces, which he administered as a federation.

IV. ECONOMY AND TRADE

1825 Oct. 26   The **Erie Canal**, in New York state, opened. It was then the **longest canal in the world**. At the same time that the West thus became more accessible to development, **New York City's** position as the major port on the American East Coast was ensured.

1825 Nov.   In Europe, **prices of stocks and bonds dropped**, and bankruptcies occurred at an unprecedented rate. In December, within a single week, six banks closed in London alone. The crisis was precipitated by bad harvests in 1824 and 1825, in addition to the numerous poor harvests during the French Revolution and Napoleonic Wars. Farmers were forced to abandon land held by their families for generations.

1827   Rubber was first exported by Brazil.

1827   The **first French railway opened**, running c.15 miles between Saint-Etienne and Andrézieux, in central France. The carriages were drawn by horses.

1828 Aug. 11   The **first statewide labor party in the U.S.** was the Working Men's party, organized in Philadelphia. Its goals included a ten-hour workday, free public education for all children, and an end to imprisonment for debt.

1829   The **Rocket**, built by **George Stephenson** (June 9, 1781–Aug. 12, 1848), an English engineer and inventor, first demonstrated the potential for using a **steam locomotive to transport commercial goods**. Stephenson won £500 for his engine, which was tested on the Liverpool and Manchester Railroad.

1829   The **omnibus**, a horse-drawn bus that carried passengers on the roof as well as inside, was introduced in London, where it became an accepted mode of transportation.

V. RELIGION AND PHILOSOPHY

1825 May 19   Saint-Simon [Claude Henri de Rouvroy, comte de Saint-Simon] (b. Oct. 17, 1760), a French economist and social philosopher, died. In *L'Industrie ou Discussions politiques, morales et philosophiques* (1817) and *Système Industriel* (1820–1823), Saint-Simon developed a plan for the reorganization of society by a scientific division of labor. In *Le Nouveau Christianisme* [*The New Christianity*] (1825), he argued that the Christian concept of brotherhood must permeate this new society.

1826 Feb. 5   The **Utopian socialist community at New Harmony**, Indiana, drew up a constitution. In Apr. 1825, **Robert Owen**, a Welsh social reformer, had purchased the town of Harmonie from [Johann] George Rapp (Nov. 1, 1757–Aug. 7, 1847), a German separatist whose group [Rappites] were relocating. Owen's hope was to prove that a society based on cooperation could benefit all.

1827   Nicholas I, czar of Russia, issued an **anti-Jewish conscription ukase**, in which compulsory military service was used to force conversion. Jews were inducted for 25-year periods. The czar tried similar harsh tactics in education.

1828 Bennet Tyler (July 10, 1783–May 14, 1858), an American theologian of Congregational ministry, became leader of a conservatively orthodox group of clergymen preaching **Tylerism**, in contrast to Taylorism [New Haven theology] after **Nathaniel W. Taylor** (July 23, 1786–Mar. 10, 1858).

1828 Aug. 20 Rammohan Roy [Ram Mohan Roy] (1772?–1833) founded the **Brahmo Samaj** [One God Society] in Calcutta. The church offended orthodox Hindus, and the society did not survive Rammohan Roy. It was monotheistic and "open to men of all categories and condition," reflecting Rammohan Roy's studies of Islamic culture and Christianity.

1829 Dec. 4 The British colonial government in India outlawed suttee. In 1811 Rammohan Roy had begun protesting against the practice of suttee to the British administrators in India when he witnessed his sister-in-law perform the ancient Hindu rite of self-immolation on the funeral pyre of her husband.

VI. SCIENCE, EDUCATION, AND TECHNOLOGY

1825 Work began on the construction of the **first tunnel under the Thames River**, London, England. It was to run from the Rotherhithe district on the northern bank to Wapping on the southern side. The project was the work of two engineers, **Marc Isambard Brunel** (Apr. 25, 1769–Dec. 12, 1849), and his son, **Isambard Kingdom Brunel** (Apr. 9, 1806–Sept. 15, 1859). The elder Brunel's invention of a shield for use in tunneling made this project the first example of modern tunnel building technique. The shield consisted of a large rectangular framework with 36 cubbyholes. A workman stood in each of these, digging out a few inches of earth in front of him at a time. The shield was then moved forward and the process repeated.

1826 Nikolai Ivanovich Lobachevski (Nov. 20, 1792–Feb. 12, 1856) proposed the **hyperbolic form of non-Euclidean geometry** based on the postulate that two lines may pass through a given point parallel to a given line.

1826 Sept. 3 By the time of the crowning of Nicholas I, there were c.50 secondary **schools**, c.300 primary schools, six universities, and a teacher's training college in Russia.

1827 Fourah Bay College was founded at Leicester, in the British colony of Sierra Leone, by the Church Missionary Society. It was the **first institution of higher education in West Africa**.

1827 John James Audubon (Apr. 26, 1785–Jan. 27, 1851), an American naturalist and nature artist, published the first volume of his comprehensive *Birds of America*. The four illustrated volumes were completed (1838) with 435 color plates, portraying more than 1,000 birds in natural settings. The *Ornithological Guide* (1838), a fifth volume, provided the text for *Birds of America*, and *A Synopsis of the Birds of North America* (1839) served as an index.

1827 Georg Simon Ohm (Mar. 16, 1787–July 7, 1854), a German physicist, **formulated Ohm's law** in which the ohm, the unit of electrical resistance, was calculated for any circuit as inversely proportional to the strength of the electric current or electromotive force.

1827 Mar. 5 Alessandro [Giuseppe Antonio Anastasio] **Volta** (b. Feb. 18, 1745), an Italian physicist, died. His development of the voltaic pile (1800), which was based on chemical reactions, led him to disagree with Luigi Galvani's theory of the source of animal electricity.

1827 Mar. 5 Pierre Simon de Laplace (b. Mar. 28, 1749), the French mathematician and astronomer largely responsible for describing movements within the solar system, died. His five volume *Traité de mécanique céleste* [*Celestial Mechanics*] (1799–1825) applied to planetary movement the laws of gravitation first developed by Isaac Newton. In 1780, with **Antoine Laurent Lavoisier**, Laplace was influential in founding the science of thermochemistry. In 1796 he hypothesized the nebular explanation of the formation of the solar system. His *Théorie analytique des probabilités* (1812) established the modern form of the study of probabilities.

1827 Mar. 16 *Freedom's Journal*, the **first newspaper written for black readers**, was published in New York City. It was founded by **Samuel E. Cornish** (1790–1859) and **John B. Russworm** (Oct. 1, 1799–June 17, 1851), born in Jamaica and said to be the **first black college graduate** [Bowdoin College, 1826].

1827 July 14 Augustin Jean Fresnel (b. May 10, 1788), a French physicist, died. In 1819 he developed the mathematical basis for the wave theory of light, confirming earlier formulations by **Christian Huygens** made in the 17th century. The wave theory explained how light waves of different lengths interfered with each other. He also explained the diffraction of light while trying to describe the nature of ether. In 1821 he made improvements in the lenses of lighthouses.

1828 *An American Dictionary of the English Language* by **Noah Webster** (Oct. 11, 1758–May 31, 1843), an American orthographer and lexicographer, was published. Its 70,000-odd entries were excellent, although there were no illustrative quotations. It became the standard dictionary in the U.S., but after 1830 it faced competition from **Joseph Emerson Worcester**'s *Comprehensive Pronouncing and Explanatory Dictionary of the English Language* (1830).

1828 James Beaumont Neilson (June 22, 1792–Jan. 18, 1865), a Scottish inventor, developed an improved method for the **manufacture of iron**. Efficiency was increased by a blast of hot air to the furnace, cutting fuel consumption by about half.

1829 David Walker (Sept. 28, 1785–June 28, 1830) made an appeal to other blacks to rise up against slavery in *Walker's Appeal . . . with a Preamble to the Coloured Citizens of the World, but in Particular and Very Expressly to Those of the United States of America*. It was widely read despite attempts to prevent its printing and sale in the South, where a price was put on Walker's head.

1829–1833 The **first encyclopedia written and published in the U.S.**, the 13-volume *Encyclopaedia Americana*, was edited by **Francis Lieber** (Mar. 18, 1800–Oct. 2, 1872) and published in Philadelphia. Lieber's American work was based on the seventh edition of the German encyclopedia **Konversations Lexikon**, first published (1808) by the Brockhaus firm.

1829 Louis Braille (1809–1852), a French inventor and teacher, published his **alphabet for the blind**, which he had developed for his students at the *Institution National des Jeunes Aveugles* in Paris, where Braille was also taught. The Braille alphabet was formed by a maximum of six dots, whose positions in an oblong were embossed on heavy paper and varied to make 63 possible combinations. Braille himself

was blind as the result of an accident when he was three.

1829 Apr. 6 Niels Henrik Abel (b. Aug. 5, 1802), a Norwegian mathematician and **founder of the theory of elliptical functions**, died. **Karl Gustav Jakob Jacobi** (Dec. 10, 1804–Feb. 18, 1851), a German mathematician, had independently come to the same theory of elliptical functions in 1823.

1829 May 10 Thomas Young (b. June 13, 1773), an English physicist and physician, died. His most important work was with light and vision. He developed (1801) an **explanation for astigmatism** and was the first to suggest that color vision was achieved by different structures of the retina that respond separately to the colors red, green, and violet.

1829 May 29 Humphry Davy (b. Dec. 17, 1778), an English chemist, died. A pioneer in **electrochemical research**, Davy isolated potassium on Oct. 6, 1807; one week later, he isolated sodium. A year later he isolated (1808) barium, strontium, calcium, and magnesium. A lamp he designed (1815) for coal miners was a great advance in mine safety.

1829 Nov. 14 Louis Vauquelin (b. May 16, 1763), a French chemist, died. In 1797 Vauquelin **discovered the element chromium**. In 1806 he **isolated the amino acid asparagine**.

VII. ARTS AND LEISURE

1825 May 7 Antonio Salieri (b. Aug. 18, 1750), an Italian composer and teacher, died. Salieri taught Beethoven, Schubert, and Liszt. *La Grotto di Trionfonio* (1785) and *Tarare* (1787) were the best of his nearly 40 operas.

1825 Nov. 14 Jean [Johann] Paul Friedrich Richter (b. Mar. 21, 1763), a German novelist, died. A prolific writer, he was known best for the prose idyll *Leben der Quintus Fixleins* [The Life of Quintus Fixleins] (1796) and the six-volume novel **Titan** (1800–1803).

1826 Benjamin Disraeli, an English conservative political leader, published his first novel, *Vivian Grey*. His later works included *Coningsby* (1844), *Sybil* (1845), and *Tancred* (1847).

1826 Heinrich Heine (Dec. 13, 1797–Feb. 17, 1856), a German lyric poet, published his first success, *Reisebilder*, part of the *Nordsee* cycle of travel sketches (1826–1831). Heine is considered one of the finest lyric poets of any language.

1826 June 5   Karl Maria Friedrich Ernst von Weber (b. Nov. 18, 1786), a German composer, died. His operas, which combined German folklore with a strong nationalistic spirit, challenged the Italian and French domination of opera. His major works, *Der Freischutz* [*The Marksman*] (1821) and *Oberon* (1826), are still performed.

1827 Feb. 22   Charles Willson Peale (b. Apr. 15, 1741), an American portrait painter, died. He painted seven full-size portraits of George Washington between 1772 and 1795. Peale decided to paint most of the notable men of his time, and he constructed (c.1781) a gallery in Philadelphia to present his canvases. By 1784 he had painted 44 of these portraits.

1827 Mar. 26   Ludwig van Beethoven (b. Dec. 16, 1770), a German composer whose works reflected a transition from the eras of classical to romantic music, died. He began to lose his hearing gradually and was profoundly deaf by 1817. Beethoven's famous nine symphonies (1800–1823) included the third, or *Eroica* (1804); the fifth symphony (1808); the sixth, or *Pastorale* (1808); and the ninth, or *Choral* (1817–1823). His only opera, *Fidelio* (1805–1814), was at first a failure but after revision a success. His sonatas included the *Pathétique* (1798), *Moonlight* (1801), *Appassionata* (1804), and the *Kreutzer* (1803). Perhaps Beethoven's best-known piano concerto was No. 5, the *Emperor Concerto* (1809). His other works included the *Missa Solemnis in D* (1818–1823), the violin concerto in D (1806), piano variations, quartets, quintets, cantatas, canons, oratorios, and songs.

1827 Aug. 12   William Blake (b. Nov. 28, 1757), an English poet, artist, and mystic, died. The collections *Songs of Innocence* (1789) and *Songs of Experience* (1794) contained illustrations reproduced by the new method of copper etching, which he executed himself. He produced many religious designs for his *Inventions to the Book of Job* (1820–1826). *The Marriage of Heaven and Hell* (1790) and *The Gates of Paradise* (1793) were prophetic books. At the time of his death, Blake was involved in engraving illustrations for an edition of Dante's *Divina Commedia*.

1827 Sept. 10   Ugo Foscolo [*orig.:* Niccolo] (b. Feb. 6, 1778), an Italian poet, died. His most highly regarded poem was *De' Sepolcri* [**The Sepulchers**] (1807), an ode reaffirming faith in mankind, a message of special importance during the Napoleonic Wars.

1828   Issa (b. 1763), who had revived Japan's interest in the haiku form of poetry, died. **Haiku** had been introduced by Basho in the late 17th century.

1828   Elf Hill, an epic play by the Danish writer **Johan Ludvig Heiberg** (Dec. 14, 1791–Aug. 25, 1860), won him the position of stage poet for the Theater Royal in Copenhagen.

1828 Apr. 16   Francisco José de Goya y Lucientes (b. Mar. 31, 1746), a Spanish painter and engraver, died. An illness, considered to be lead poisoning, left Goya deaf in 1793. He created (1798) a series of religious frescoes for the Church of San Antonio de la Florida in Madrid. His most highly regarded paintings included *Maja Nude* and *Maja Clothed* (1800) and *May 2* and *May 3, 1808*. His series of satirical etchings included Caprichos (1799), Desastres de la Guerra [Disasters of War] (1810–1813), and Tauromaquia [The Bullfighter].

1828 July 9   Gilbert Stuart (b. Dec. 3, 1755), an American portrait painter known best for his portraits of George Washington, died. Among his other works were *Mr. Grant Skating* (1782) and *Mrs. Richard Yates* (1793–1794). His portraits made him the most famous American painter of his time.

1828 July 15   Jean Antoine Houdon (b. Mar. 20, 1741), a highly regarded French classical sculptor, died. *Voltaire Assis* [*Voltaire Seated*] (1781), exhibited at the Comédie Française, and *Diana* (c.1776) were among the best of his works.

1828 Oct. 13   Vincenzo Monti (b. Feb. 19, 1754), an Italian neoclassical poet who lived in France, died. His *Bassvilliana* (1793) depicted the French Revolution and Louis XVI, king of France, as its victim; in *le Fanaticisme* (1797) he was a democrat; and in *La Mascheroniana* (1800) he was a dedicated admirer of Napoléon.

1828 Nov. 19   Franz Peter Schubert (b. Jan. 31, 1797), an Austrian composer, died. He brought the German lieder to its highest form, especially with "*Who Is Sylvia?*"; "*The Erl King*"; and "*Hark,*

Hark, the Lark", the most familiar of his more than 600 songs. Schubert also wrote sonatas, chamber and piano music, and symphonies, including one in C major.

1829 **Zygmunt Krasiński** (Feb. 19, 1812–Feb. 23, 1859), a leading Polish romantic poet, left for Switzerland to remain abroad as an exile for the rest of his life. His work *Nieboska Komedia* [**Undivine Comedy**] (1834) depicted social revolution in an apocalyptic fashion.

1829 The mouth, or reed, organ, known today as a **harmonica**, was patented by **Charles Wheatstone**, the English physicist responsible for the Wheatstone Bridge. In Berlin, **C.F.L. Buschmann** had produced a harmonica using a wooden box with metal reeds in 1821.

1829 July 23 **Wojciech Bogusawski** (b. Apr. 9, 1757 or 1760), considered the **founder of Polish theater**, died. His chief play was **Cud mniemany**. Bogusawski translated many plays into Polish, and was active in establishing theaters throughout the country.

VIII. SPORTS, GAMES, AND SOCIETY

1829 Oxford and Cambridge participated in their **first crew race** along a two-mile course on the Thames River at Henley, England.

1829 The athletic event of **weight throwing** appeared at least this early as a contest at the Tailtean [Teltown] games, held near Dublin, Ireland.

1829 Oct. 16 The **Tremont Hotel** opened in Boston, boasting eight bathrooms.

1830–1834

I. VITAL STATISTICS AND DEMOGRAPHICS

1830 June 30 The **Indian Removal Act of 1830** authorized the president of the U.S. to relocate American Indian populations west of the Mississippi River. The unorganized **Indian Territory**, which comprised the present states of Kansas, Nebraska, and northeastern Oklahoma, was approved by the **Indian Intercourse Act** of June 30, 1834. Over the next ten years, c.60,000 American Indians were forced to move westward, mainly to present Oklahoma and Kansas.

II. DISASTERS

1832 An **Asiatic cholera epidemic** struck northeastern North America. On June 28 in New York City, 2,251 were reported dead. From Oct. 25 to Nov. 6 in New Orleans, c.6,000 died. In Canada, as many as c.7,000 people died in Quebec, Montreal, and surrounding regions. The disease spread westward, decimating the Indian tribes inhabiting the Great Plains.

III. EXPLORATION AND COLONIZATION

1831 May–June The position of the **North Magnetic Pole** was plotted from instruments by **James Clark Ross** (Apr. 15, 1800–Apr. 3, 1862), a Scottish explorer. Ross placed the pole on Boothia Peninsula, Northwest Territories, Canada. The North and South Magnetic poles drift in a northwesterly direction, moving c.8 miles a year. The North Magnetic Pole is now just southwest of Ellef Ringnes Island, part of the Queen Elizabeth Islands, c.500 miles from where Ross found it.

1832 **Benjamin Louis Eulalie de Bonneville** (Apr. 14, 1796–June 12, 1878), an American army officer and explorer, led 100 men attracted by the fur trade to the region of present **Wyoming**.

1834 **William Lewis Sublette** (c.1799–July 23, 1845) and **Robert Campbell** (Mar., 1804–Oct. 16, 1879) established **Fort William [Fort Laramie]**, on the eastern side of the Rocky Mountains, in the present state of Wyoming. Here wagon trains would gather for the trek west. Sublette, a fur trader, was one of the first regularly to guide wagons across the Rocky Mountains.

1834   The **South Australia Act**, passed by the British Parliament, provided for settlement of that Australian state. Land prices were set, and it was agreed that convicts would not be used to settle the colony.

IV. POLITICS AND WAR

1830   **Salic Law**, first enacted (c.510) in Spain, was repealed by the Cortes by means of a sanction issued by **Ferdinand VII**, permitting women to be included in the royal succession. This act secured the throne for **Isabella**, Ferdinand's only heir, who had just been born. Ferdinand's brother, who had been heir to the throne, was cut off. Conservatives and clericals rallied to the cause of **Don Carlos de Bourbon** (Mar. 29, 1788–Mar. 20, 1855), while Liberals sided with Isabella, leading to three Carlist [from Carlos] revolutions. The outbreak (1833) of the **First Carlist War** was a direct consequence of this ruling.

1830 Feb. 3   The **London Protocol**, issued jointly by England, France, and Russia, recognized Greek independence as a kingdom under their joint protection.

1830 May 13   **Juan José Flores** (July 19, 1800–Oct. 1, 1864) declared the **independence of Ecuador** from the federation of Great Colombia [Gran Colombia]. Ecuador's constitution established a republic with Flores as its first president (1830–1835), and named Roman Catholicism the state religion.

1830 June 26   **George IV** (b. Aug. 12, 1762), king of Great Britain and Ireland (from 1820), died. Since George's only child, **Princess Charlotte**, who had married Leopold of Saxe-Coburg (Dec. 16, 1790–Dec. 10, 1865), later **Leopold I**, first king (1831–1865) of Belgium, had died (1817) in childbirth, George's brother succeeded as **William IV**.

1830 July 18   **Uruguay** accepted a constitution, and **José Fructuoso Rivera** (1790?–Jan. 13, 1854) became the first president (1830–1835) of the new republic. A rift developed, however, when **Manuel Oribe** (Aug. 27, 1792–Nov. 12, 1857) became president in 1835. The **Colorados** [Reds] supported Rivera and the **Blancos** [Whites] followed Oribe. The fierce rivalry of the Colorados and the Blancos, which led to the **Great War** (1843–1852), shaped Uruguayan history.

1830 July 25   The city of **Algiers capitulated to the French**. In Apr., 1827, the French consul in Algiers had been insulted by **Husain III** (ruled from 1818), the dey, who had threatened to withdraw an agreement that allowed the French to maintain a trading post at Bastion, near Bona [Bone; Annaba]. When a French expedition under **Louis Auguste Victor de Bourmont** (1773–Oct. 27, 1846) took Algiers, the rule of the nominally Ottoman but actually independent deys (1671–1830) ended.

1830 July 27   The **July Revolution** began as rioting instigated by radicals broke out in Paris against the **Five Ordinances** enacted by **Charles X**, king of France, on July 25. He had hoped to suspend the constitution in order to abrogate the recent Parliamentary elections, which had resulted in an increase in the opposition. With Paris controlled by the opposition, Charles abdicated on Aug. 2 in favor of his grandson **Henri Charles** (Sept. 29, 1820–Aug. 24, 1883), **ending the Bourbon line of French rulers**. On July 31, the legislature selected **Louis-Philippe** [**Louis XIX**], of the junior Bourbon-Orléans line, as lieutenant-general of France. On Aug. 9 Louis-Philippe, known as the **Citizen King** [Roi Citoyen], was crowned king of France (to 1848).

1830 Sept. 22   **Venezuela** seceded from the federation of Great Colombia [Gran Colombia], leading to the demise of the federation.

1830 Nov. 18   **Belgium**, having gained independence from the United Kingdom of the Netherlands, adopted a constitution. It provided for civil liberties and a parliamentary government under a constitutional monarchy. **Leopold I** [Georges Chrétien Frédéric] was elected the first king (to 1865) of Belgium on June 4, 1831.

1830 Nov. 29   The **Polish Insurrection** against Russian rule began as Russian troops were forced to withdraw from Warsaw and a Polish Republic was declared, but the revolt was put down by Oct. 1831, when some insurrection leaders were deported to Siberia. In Feb. 1832, the Polish constitution of 1815 was abrogated, and eastern Poland was annexed by Russia.

1830 Dec. 17   **Simón Bolívar** [El Libertador] (b. July 24, 1783), the liberator of much of South America, died. Born in Venezuela, he was directly instrumental in the liberation from Spanish rule of Venezuela, Colombia, Peru, and Bolivia as well as aiding other countries in their battles to secure independence.

1831 In **India**, **Mysore**, a major state in the southern Deccan, came under British administration. It had been a center of resistance and rebellion against the British.

1832 The **Galápagos Islands**, west of Ecuador, in the Pacific Ocean, were seized by Ecuador.

1832 **Sayyid** [Sa'id] (1806–1856), the sultan of Oman and Muscat [Masqat] on the Arabian Peninsula, of the **Al-Busayyid** [Busa'id] **Dynasty** (1741-to the present), moved his capital to the island of Zanzibar, off the eastern coast of Africa, and now part of present Tanzania. He made the new capital the leading trade center of Arabia and East Africa and, by using slave labor, the largest producer of cloves in the world.

1832 A decision of the U.S. Supreme Court in the case of **Worcester vs. Georgia** was handed down by Chief Justice **John Marshall**, striking down a Georgia law that required all whites living in Cherokee territory to obtain a license and swear allegiance to the state, or leave the territory. Marshall held that the Cherokee nation had never given up its right to control its own territory and that Georgia (and, by extension, other states) had no right to infringe upon Indian sovereignty.

1832 The South Carolina state legislature passed the **Ordinance of Nullification**, which declared federal tariff laws null and void. Policies based on an agrarian economy dominated the politics of South Carolina, whose plantations were threatened by Eli Whitney's cotton gin and by cotton produced in western states. The Ordinance was repealed the following year.

1832 During the first party nominating convention held to choose a candidate for the U.S. Presidency, the "Jacksonians," supporters of **Andrew Jackson**, began to call themselves "Democrats." Jacksonians nation-wide had organized as the **Democratic party** and convened delegates at Baltimore; a two-thirds majority was declared necessary for nomination. **Martin Van Buren** (Dec. 5, 1782–July 24, 1862) was the organizational force behind Jackson's second presidential campaign, which promoted Jackson as the plainspoken military hero who stood up for the rights of the common man.

1832 June 4 The **Reform Bill of 1832** extended the voting franchise in England to the middle class, and in parliamentary representation favored larger communities over rural constituencies.

1832 June 28 The **Six Acts** passed by the **Diet of the German Confederation** deprived the parliaments of the petty German states of their authority, censored the press, and imposed limitations on the German monarchs to deal with petitions of reform in order to preserve the confederation's stability against revolutionary tendencies generated by the July Revolution (1830) in France.

1832 July By the **Treaty of Constantinople**, the Ottoman Empire (1326–1920) recognized the independence of Greece. Greek citizens were granted full constitutional rights.

1832 Aug. 2 Despite the display of a white flag **Black Hawk** (1767–Oct. 3, 1838), leader of the **Fox and Sac** [Sauk] **Indians**, was defeated and most of his men were killed or captured at the Mississippi River near the mouth of the Bad Axe River, in southwestern Wisconsin. This was the final defeat for the American Indians in the **Black Hawk War** (1832), which was a protest against the involuntary removal of these tribes from the region of northern Illinois by forcing them westward into the Mississippi area.

1833 **Santa Ana** [Anna] became president of **Mexico**, leading liberals to power after the conservative administration of **Anastasio Bustamante**. Santa Ana permitted anti-clerical measures to be enacted, which nearly caused civil war. In Apr., 1834, Santa Ana abrogated the measures and declared himself dictator, betraying the liberals.

1833 **Stephen Fuller Austin** was sent to Mexico City to represent American settlers in Texas who wanted to petition for a separate Mexican state from the Mexican state of Coahuila. Accused of treason, Austin was thrown into prison for 18 months. When he returned (1835) to Texas he took a leading role in opposing Santa Ana's repressive policies toward the Americans.

1833 Mar. 4 The Democrat **Andrew Jackson** was inaugurated for his second term as president of the U.S., having defeated **Henry Clay** of the National Republican party. **Martin Van Buren** served as vice president.

1833 May 25 Chile, under the leadership of **Joaquín Prieto** (Aug. 20, 1786–Nov. 22, 1854), president of Chile (1831–1841), and **Diego José Victor Portales** (June 26, 1793–June 6, 1837), Chile's minister of war, adopted a constitution that mandated a legislature composed of landholders.

1833 July 8   The **Treaty of Unkiar** [Hunkiar] **Skelessi** [now Hunkyar Iskelesi], on the eastern bank of the Bosporus near the Black Sea, was signed by Russia and the Ottoman Empire. It was agreed that each country would come to the aid of the other.

1833 Sept. 29   The **First Carlist War** (1833–1839) in Spain broke out when **Ferdinand VII** (b. Oct. 13, 1784), king of Spain (1808 and from 1814), died. He was succeeded by his infant daughter **Isabella II** [Maria Isabella Louisa] (Oct. 10, 1830–Apr. 9, 1904), queen of Spain (1833–1868) with her mother **María Cristina** as regent. Ferdinand's brother **Don Carlos** led a revolt to maintain the Bourbon succession through his claim to the throne. He was supported by political reactionaries who wanted to restore **Salic Law**. Carlos had the support also of the Catalans and Basques, disaffected by the effort in 1833 to centralize Spanish administration by forming 49 provinces from the traditional kingdoms.

1834–1835   The **Sixth Kaffir War** was fought in southeastern Cape of Good Hope Colony [Cape Province], in the present republic of **South Africa**, between the British and the Xhosa, a pastoral Bantu tribe, who had extended their territory after a particularly severe drought had affected their grazing lands. The Bantu were driven back, and land between the Kei and Keiskama rivers was annexed by the colony as Queen Adelaide province.

1834   The **Ninety-Two Resolutions** were adopted by the elected *Assemblée Législative* [Legislative Assembly], or Lower House, in Quebec, **Canada**. This list of French-Canadian grievances against the anti-democratic colonial government in Lower Canada [Quebec], was drawn up under the direction of the Reform leader **Louis Joseph Papineau** (Oct. 7, 1786–Sept. 24, 1871), who recommended establishment of an elected Conseil Législatif [Legislative Council], or Upper House.

V. ECONOMY AND TRADE

1830 May 24   The **B.&O.** [Baltimore and Ohio] **Railroad** began with service on 13 miles of track between Baltimore and Ellicott's Mills [Ellicott City], Maryland. It was the **first American railroad** chartered for passengers and freight. At first horses pulled the carriages, but in Aug., 1830, the *Tom Thumb* inaugurated the use of steam power on the line.

1830 May 29   The **Preemption Act** authorized purchase of public land in the U.S. on terms favorable to individuals who had cultivated it within the previous year.

1830 Aug.   Near Baltimore, Maryland, the New York ironmaster **Peter Cooper** (Feb. 12, 1791–Apr. 14, 1883) accepted a challenge from a stagecoach operator to race one of his best horses. Cooper's little engine, about the size of a modern hand car and aptly named the *Tom Thumb*, was the **first steam locomotive built in the U.S.** It pulled ahead of the horse only to fall behind with a broken belt.

1830 Sept. 15   The **Manchester and Liverpool Railway** in England was the **first public railroad to offer regular service with a steam-powered locomotive**. The Stockton and Darlington Railway had opened in 1825, but its passenger service remained horse-drawn until 1833.

1831   The **greatest recorded haul by sealers** took place this year in the North Atlantic Ocean as c.300 ships brought in more than 687,000 seals, mostly Harp, or Greenland, Seals [*Phoca groenlandica*]. The greatest activity was off the coast of Newfoundland and around the Gulf of St. Lawrence.

1832   The **Göta Canal**, connecting Stockholm with Göteborg via natural lake channels, opened. It helped **develop commerce and communication in Sweden**.

1832 Sept. 2   The **Equitable Labor Exchange** opened on Gray's Inn Road in London, an experiment in exchanging "labor notes," rather than money, for goods. The difficulty of determining the relative value of a specific product in terms of labor led to failure of such experiments, whose purpose was to win for the workers a fair share of the value of their labor.

1833 Aug. 29   The **Antislavery Society of Great Britain**, founded (1828) by **Thomas Fowell Buxton** (Apr. 1, 1786–Feb. 19, 1845), an English philanthropist, succeeded in having legislation passed mandating the abolition of slavery in all British possessions, to be achieved at the end of six years of apprenticeship to condition slaves, and their masters, to freedom. This **Emancipation Bill** went into effect on Jan. 1, 1834.

1833 Aug. 17 The Canadian steamship *Royal William*, the **first to cross the Atlantic Ocean entirely under power**, left Pictou, Nova Scotia, carrying eight passengers. She arrived at the Isle of Wight on Sept. 4.

1833 Sept. 3 Benjamin Henry Day (1810–1889), an American entrepreneur, founded the daily **New York *Sun*, the first of the popular newspapers to sell for a penny a copy.**

1834 Jan. 1 The **Zollverein** [= customs union] joined 17 German states and Prussia in a customs union, which removed trade barriers between the states by adopting a uniform policy of taxing commerce. It provided **free trade within Germany**, protected trade with foreign nations, and weakened Austrian control over the German Confederation.

VI. RELIGION AND PHILOSOPHY

1830 Joseph Smith of Palmyra, New York, having been subject to visions, in his own account, since 1820, published the *Book of Mormon*, purporting to be a translation of sacred records of American Indians descended from ancient Hebrews, which were inscribed on golden plates and found with the guidance of the Angel Moroni. He immediately began to win converts, and founded the **Church of the Latter-Day Saints** [*in full:* Church of Jesus Christ of the Latter-Day Saints, Mormon Church] on Apr. 6.

1831 In **India** the British government declared war on the **Thugs** [Hindu: *Thaga*], members of a cult that had existed since the 12th century. This organization of professional assassins preyed on travelers, strangling them with a noose. Captain **William Sleeman** (Aug. 8, 1788–Feb. 10, 1856), as agent for the British governor general, destroyed the Thug cult in four years through the hanging, life imprisonment, or deportation of more than 3,000 individuals.

1831 Nov. 14 George Friedrich Wilhelm Hegel (b. Aug. 27, 1770), a German philosopher, died. According to Hegel, reality was not static but an active historical process that took a dialectical form: A thesis brought forth an antithesis, from which developed a synthesis, and so on. Among Hegel's works were *Die Phänomenologie des Geistes* [*The*

Phenomenology of the Spirit] (1807) and *Grundlinien der Philosophie des Rechts* [*The Philosophy of Right*] (1821).

1832 June 6 Jeremy Bentham (b. Feb. 15, 1748), an English philosopher and political theorist, died. He was the founder of **utilitarianism**, a theory which held that whether an act or a policy was good or bad depended entirely on the consequences. Thus the basic principle of morality was to seek the greatest happiness for the greatest number. He wrote *Introduction to the Principles of Morals and Legislation* (1789).

1833 July 14 John Keble (Apr. 25, 1792–Mar. 29, 1866), an Oxford don of High Church persuasion, preached a sermon entitled *National Apostasy* from the University pulpit at St. Mary's, initiating the Oxford, or Tractarian, Movement, as it was later called by **John Henry Newman**. He hoped the Church of England would regain the "high-church ideals" which prevailed during the late 1600s. Soon Keble and Newman were joined in the writing of systematically planned High Church tracts by **Edward Bouverie Pusey** (Aug. 22, 1800–Sept. 16, 1882), **Henry Edward Manning**, and other Oxford luminaries.

1834 July 15 After nearly 350 years of operation the **Spanish Inquisition**, last and most national of its kind, was brought to a close by **Maria Cristina de Borbon**, the fourth wife of Frederick VII, and queen regent of Spain for the Infanta Queen Isabella II.

VII. SCIENCE, EDUCATION, AND TECHNOLOGY

1830 Joseph Emerson Worcester, an American lexicographer who published *A Comprehensive Pronouncing and Explanatory Dictionary of the English Language* (1830), died. **Noah Webster**, whose *American Dictionary of the English Language* appeared two years earlier, charged plagiarism and steady competition between the two dictionaries followed. Worcester's most important work was *A Universal and Critical Dictionary of the English Language* (1846), which was strong on neologisms.

1830 Robert Livingston Stevens (Oct. 8, 1787–Apr. 20, 1856), son of the American inventor John Stevens, invented the **T-rail**, named for the shape of a vertical cross section of the rail. It was to become the standard rail in the U.S.

1831 Prussia began the **first systematic attempt at reforestation** known in modern Europe. Between 1831 and 1840 schools of forestry were established by the Prussians in Berlin, Leipzig, and Jena, a course followed soon by other European nations and by the U.S.

1831 The Virginian **Cyrus Hall McCormick** (Feb. 15, 1809–May 13, 1884) invented a **reaper for harvesting grain**. Although 20 patents had already been issued for reapers when McCormick applied (1834) for a patent, his reaper was to change agricultural life.

1831 **Joseph Henry** (Dec. 17, 1797–May 13, 1878), an American inventor, devised the first of his many contributions to the physical sciences by inventing the **electric bell**. The invention came about through Henry's effort to demonstrate the possibility of magnetizing iron from a distance.

1832 A **hydraulic turbine** capable of producing 50 horsepower was developed by **Benoît Fourneyron** (1802–1867) of France. In 1855 his design was modified by **James Bichenou Francis** (May 18, 1815–Sept. 18, 1892), an English-born American engineer, whose Francis turbine was capable of operating with variable flows of water.

1832 May 13 **Georges Léopold Chrétien Frédéric Dagobert Cuvier** (b. Aug. 23, 1769), a French naturalist and **founder of the sciences of comparative anatomy and paleontology**, died. Cuvier had developed a natural system of classification of the animal kingdom, which he divided into four phyla, or major branches, based on an organism's structure.

1832 Aug. 24 **Nicolas Léonard Sadi Carnot** (b. June 1, 1796), a French physicist, died. His essay on heat *Réflexions sur la Puissance Motrice du Feu* (1824) formed the basis of the science of thermodynamics. Carnot's principle was essentially the second law of thermodynamics: Heat cannot pass of its own accord from a cold to a warmer body.

1833 The **first tax-supported library in the U.S.** opened in Peterborough, New Hampshire.

1833 **John Deere** (Feb. 7, 1804–May 17, 1886), a blacksmith in Illinois, invented the **first steel plow in**

America. Deere had noticed that after being drawn through soil, steel became polished and shiny so that the soil would clean off easily. The self-cleaning concept was the long-sought solution for the sticky soil of the Midwest and heavy prairie sod.

1833 **Oberlin Collegiate Institute** [present Oberlin College], in Ohio, opened. It was one of the first colleges in the U.S. to hold **coeducational classes**.

1833 *Principles of Geology* by **Charles Lyell** (Nov. 14, 1797–Feb. 22, 1875), an English geologist, was completed and Lyell thus became the **founder of modern geology**. His basic principle was that geologic forces at work on earth today, such as erosion, accounted also for all prehistoric geological activity: The key to the past lay in the present. His other works included *Elements of Geology*, a standard work on stratigraphical and paleontological geology, and *The Antiquity of Man* (1863), in which Lyell argued for the early appearance of man on earth, supporting Charles Darwin's theory of the origin of the species, and discussed in particular the deposits laid down during the glacial age epoch.

1834 **Thomas Davenport** (July 9, 1802–July 6, 1851), a Brandon, Vermont, blacksmith, improving upon Joseph Henry's observations (1831) of the properties of the electromagnet, constructed the **first electric motor** by setting four electromagnets on a wheel which spun when the battery they were hooked to was turned on. On Feb. 25, 1837, Davenport patented the first electric motor for practical use, for drilling holes and for turning wood. By 1839 he had developed a motor large enough to drive a rotary printing press.

1834 The **Pennsylvania Canal**, a combination of waterway and railway, was completed. The opening (1825) of the Erie Canal in New York State had drawn traffic that formerly traveled across Pennsylvania. To regain lost business the Pennsylvania Canal was constructed across difficult terrain. From Philadelphia west to Columbia canal boats were carried in sections on rail cars. At Columbia they were assembled and launched on the canal. They then sailed west 172 miles to Hollidaysburg, where they were again loaded onto cars of the Portage Railroad and hauled over the crest of the Allegheny Mountains. At Johnstown the boats again entered the canal for the rest of the trip to Pittsburgh. The total distance was 394 miles and the journey took 4 days.

1834 Jacob Perkins (July 9, 1766–July 30, 1849), an American inventor in England, received the **first patent on a refrigeration machine**. Refrigeration was based on the principle derived from chemistry that a fluid changing from a liquid state to a gaseous state absorbs heat from the surrounding air, cooling it down.

1834 Sept. 2 Thomas Telford (b. Aug. 9, 1757), a Scottish engineer, died. He had developed the **gravel road surface**, an achievement of increasing importance since the beginning of the Industrial Revolution in 1760. In all Telford built c.1,000 miles of roads and c.1,200 bridges. His most famous road was the one that ran from London to Holyhead, the island off the northwestern coast of Wales.

VIII. ARTS AND LEISURE

1830 *Godey's Lady's Book*, the monthly women's magazine, first appeared. Printed in Philadelphia, it was popular, especially for its stenciled color plates of fashion designs.

1830 Michel Bibaud (Jan. 19, 1782–Aug. 3, 1857), a French-Canadian writer, published the first volume of poetry in Canada. His *Histoire du Canada*, in three volumes, was the first substantial treatment of Canada's history. Most of Bibaud's work was included in his newspaper *L'Aurore*, founded in 1817.

1830 *Abén Humeya, o La rebelión de los moriscos* [**Abén Humeya**], an historical drama by the Spanish writer **Francisco Martínez de la Rosa** (Mar. 10, 1787–Feb. 7, 1862), was published. Originally written in French, in its Spanish translation (1836) it greatly influenced the development of Spanish romantic drama.

1830 Sept. 18 William Hazlitt (Apr. 10, 1778–Sept. 18, 1830), an English lecturer and essayist, died. He was one of the great stylists in the English language. His works included *Lectures on the English Poets* (1818), *Lectures on the Dramatic Literature of the Age of Elizabeth* (1820), and *Table Talk* (1821–1822).

1831 *Le Rouge et le Noir* [*The Red and the Black*] by **Stendhal** [Marie Henri Beyle] (Jan. 23, 1783–Mar. 23, 1842), a French novelist, introduced to literature a new psychological type, a hero who, because of his spirit, passion, and honesty, was at odds with, and therefore had to be duplicitous in order to

get along in, the world. *La Chartreuse de Parma* [*The Charterhouse of Parma*] (1839) developed a similar theme.

1831 Feb. 25 Victor Marie Hugo's play *Hernani* opened in Paris at the Théâtre Français, where the classicists arrived in force to boo and hiss while the romantics came to cheer the playwright's success. For 100 nights they continued their din, making the play an unparalleled romantic *cause célèbre*.

1831 July 4 *My Country 'Tis of Thee*, also known as *America*, was first sung to the tune of *God Save the King*. Samuel Francis Smith (Oct. 21, 1808–Nov. 16, 1895) was said to have composed the words in one-half hour.

1831 Nov. 14 Ignaz [Joseph] Pleyel (b. June 1, 1757), an Austrian composer, died. His best-known opera was *Ifigenia in Aulide* (1780). In 1807 he established in Paris a pianoforte factory which still makes keyboard instruments under the Pleyel name.

1832 Honoré Daumier (Feb. 20, 1808–Feb. 10, 1879), a French caricaturist, was sentenced to prison for one of his political drawings. Released after six months, he was forbidden to portray political subject matter for the next 38 years. Instead, he created thousands of lithographs, generally depicting bourgeois society, and did some painting as well.

1832 Mar. 10 Muzio Clementi (b. Jan. 23, 1752), an Italian musician residing in London, and called the **father of pianoforte technique**, died. He played in a public contest in Vienna with Amadeus Wolfgang Mozart in 1781. Among his students were Ignaz Moscheles, a Bohemian composer; John Field, an English composer; and Giacomo Meyerbeer, a German composer.

1832 Mar. 22 Johann Wolfgang von Goethe (b. Aug. 28, 1749), a German poet, dramatist, and critic, died. He was also a lawyer, scientist, and statesman, as well as an actor, director, novelist, and essayist. His verse drama *Faust*, (Part I written 1791–1806) but completed the year of his death (Part II written 1832), was often considered the most important work of German literature. Among his other dramatic works were *Götz von Berlichingen with the Iron Hand* [*Götz von Berlichingen mit der eisernen Hand*] (1774), a prose drama that inaugerated the Sturm und Drang movement in German literature and greatly influenced the romantic movement throughout Europe; *Iphigenia in Tauris* (1779); *Egmont* (1789); and *The Natural Daughter* [*Die natürliche Tochter*] (1803). Among his other works were a short novel *The Sorrows of Young Werther* [*Die Leiden des jungen Werthers*] (1774; 1787); and the novels *The Elective Affinities* [*Die Wahlverwandtschaften*] (1809) and *Wilhelm Meister* (1795–1796; 1829).

1832 Sept. 21   Walter Scott (b. Aug. 15, 1771), a Scottish poet and novelist, died. A prolific writer, Scott was perhaps the most successful novelist of his times and wrote two biographical works, a 9-volume *Life of Napoléon* (1827), and a 19-volume *Life and Works of Swift* (1814) in addition to more than 30 historical novels, the first published in 1814 and the last in 1831, all published anonymously. Among the better-known today are *Waverley* (1814), *Guy Mannering* (1815), *Rob Roy* (1817), *Ivanhoe* (1819), *Kenilworth* (1821), *Peveril of the Peak* (1823), and *Quentin Durward* (1823).

1832 Dec. 19   Philip [Morin] **Freneau** (b. Jan. 2, 1752), an American poet and newspaper editor, died. He became known as the "**Poet of the Revolution**" because of *The British Prison Ship* (1781), which recounted his capture and harsh imprisonment by the British. Because of his strong anti-British and radical democratic stance **Thomas Jefferson** employed him as the anti-Federalist editor (1791–1793) of the *National Gazette*, published in Philadelphia, then the U.S. Capital. Freneau was the first poet to utilize purely native American character and natural themes, as exemplified by two well-known poems, "The Wild Honey Suckle" (1786) and "The Indian Burying Ground" (1788).

1834 July 25   Samuel Taylor Coleridge (b. Oct. 21, 1772), an English romantic poet and critic, died at the house of Dr. James Gillman, who allowed him to reside there for treatment of opium addiction. Coleridge's best-known poems were *The Rime of the Ancient Mariner*, included in *Lyrical Ballads* (1798), and the fragment "Kubla Khan" (1797), which he said came to him in a dream. *Biographia Litteraria* (1817), a volume of criticism and of critical theory, introduced to England the new criticism already practiced in Germany.

1834 Dec. 29   Charles Lamb (b. Feb. 10, 1775), an English essayist, died. With his sister **Mary Anne** (Dec. 3, 1764–May 20, 1847), Lamb wrote *Tales of Shakespeare* (1807) for Godwin's juvenile library. They also wrote a version of *Ulysses* (1808) for children. An early work of Lamb's was *A Tale of Rosamund Gray* (1797). Lamb's most noted works were the charming, familiar essays he contributed to the *London Magazine* (1820–1825), collected as *Essays of Elia* (1823) and *Last Essays of Elia* (1833).

IX. SPORTS, GAMES, AND SOCIETY

1831 Nov. 11 In the U.S., **Nat Turner** (b. 1800) was executed for leading the **Southampton Insurrection**, in which he and other slaves murdered nearly 60 whites during August in Virginia. The insurrection actually impeded abolition efforts and resulted in stricter slave laws.

1834 Cartoons of "**Uncle Sam**" began to portray him in his familiar stars and stripes costume but as a young man, without a beard.

1834 The first recorded **lacrosse** contest, as far as can be ascertained now, played as a spectator sport, was between teams representing Iroquois and Algonquin Indians at the Pierre racetrack in Montreal, Canada.

1835–1839

I. VITAL STATISTICS AND DEMOGRAPHICS

1837 *A True Account of America for the Information and Help of Peasants and Commoners* by **Ole Rynning** (Apr. 4, 1809–Sept., 1838), a Scandinavian emigrant to the U.S., was published and soon helped stimulate the large influx of Scandinavians to the U.S. Between 1865 and 1914, c.674,000 Norwegian immigrants and, between 1851 and 1910, c.950,000 Swedish immigrants arrived in the U.S.

1838 Oct. 1 In the U.S. c.15,000 **Cherokee Indians** began their forced march on the **Trail of Tears** [Nuna-da-ut-sun'y] from their southeastern mountain homelands to exile on the plains west of Arkansas. By Jan. 4, 1839, when the first group had reached their destination, nearly 4,000 had died. In all, more than 20 Indian nations were exiled to the west.

II. DISASTERS

1835 Dec. 16   In **New York City** fire destroyed c.700 buildings and caused $20 million worth of property damage.

1836 Feb. 14   In **St. Petersburg**, Russia, fire killed c.700 theatergoers.

III. EXPLORATION AND COLONIZATION

1838–1842   **Charles Wilkes** (Apr. 3, 1798–Feb. 8, 1877), an officer in the U.S. navy, was placed in command of the **first scientific expedition ever organized by the U.S.** The purpose was to explore the South Seas. The members reached Antarctica from Sydney, Australia, and made extensive maps of its coast (1840). They also explored the North American Coastal Range from Puget Sound to San Francisco (1841). They collected thousands of bird, mammal, fish, coral, and plant specimens. The expedition circumnavigated the globe, covering 87,000 miles. Some of the members later became famous in their fields, including zoologist and painter **Titian Ramsay Peale**, botanist **William Brackenridge**, minerologist **James Dwight Dana**, and anthropologist **Horatio Hale**.

1839   **John Lloyd Stephens** (Nov. 28, 1805–Oct. 12, 1852), an explorer, author, and archaeologist, accompanied by **Frederick Catherwood**, an artist and draftsman known for his drawings of Egyptian ruins, entered the jungles of the Guatemala-Honduras border. After much hardship the two finally found ancient ruins on the banks of the Rio Copán near the village of Santa Rita de Copán in Honduras. Stephens was able to buy the city for $50. The site had many buildings and 14 or more stelae covered with carvings and **Mayan hieroglyphs**. Stephens' book *Incidents of Travel in Central America, Chiapas, and Yucatan* (1842) and Catherwood's drawings *Views of Ancient Monuments in Central America, Chiapas, and Yucatan* (1844) created a sensation.

1839   The **New Zealand Company**, organized in London by **Edward Gibbon Wakefield** (Mar. 20, 1796–May 16, 1862), sent its first group of settlers to New Zealand on the *Tory*. The colony was intended to prevent French possession of New Zealand, and the settlers moved in with little regard for the native **Maori**.

1835–1836   The **Great Trek** began in southern Africa by the **Boers**, Dutch settlers who spoke Afrikaans and called themselves **Voortrekkers**. Nearly 12,000 left the Cape [of Good Hope] Colony [present Cape Province, South Africa] to escape British domination and to found the republics of **Natal**, **Transvaal** [South African Republic], and the **Orange Free State**.

IV. POLITICS AND WAR

1835 Jan. 30   The **first attempt on the life of a U.S. president** ended without harm when the pistol misfired. **Richard Lawrence** fired twice at **Andrew Jackson**, president of the U.S., during the funeral in Washington, D.C., of **Warren Ransom Davis** (May 8, 1793–Jan. 29, 1835), a South Carolina congressman. Lawrence was found to be insane.

1835 Dec.   **Texas revolutionary forces took San Antonio**, among other Mexican command posts, by surprise, initiating the Texan fight for independence from Mexico.

1836   The **Confederation of Peru and Bolivia** was formed and **Andres Santa Cruz** (1794?–Sept. 25, 1865), president of Bolivia (1829–1839), was declared (1837) the Confederation's Protector.

1836   The **Territory of Wisconsin** was organized, comprising the present U.S. states of Wisconsin, Minnesota, Iowa, and the Dakotas.

1836 Feb. 24   The **siege of the Alamo**, a mission turned fort near San Antonio, in present southern Texas, began as 150 Texans refused to surrender to Santa Ana, dictator of Mexico, leading several thousand Mexican troops in the recapture of San Antonio and other American-held towns.

1836 Mar. 2   At Washington, a settlement on the Brazos River, Texas declared its independence from Mexico and adopted a constitution which established the **Republic of Texas**. Similar to the U.S. Constitution, its chief difference was the explicit permission to hold slaves. The U.S. government refused to recognize the new republic.

1836 Mar. 6   Santa Ana succeeded finally in capturing the **Alamo** as the last of its stubborn defenders were slaughtered in hand-to-hand combat. The American frontiersman **Davy Crockett** (b. Aug. 17, 1786), among c.180 others, died as the siege came to an end.

1836 Mar. 27   About **300 Texan prisoners** held near Goliad in southern Texas by Santa Ana and his Mexican troops were shot in cold blood.

1836 Apr. 21   In a **battle at the San Jacinto River**, near Galveston Bay, the **Texan fight for independence** was won. **Sam Houston** (Mar. 2, 1793–July 26, 1863), in charge of Texan troops retreating to Louisiana from Santa Ana's sweep across Texas, maneuvered his men to great advantage. As Santa Ana's men enjoyed their afternoon siesta near the mouth of the San Jacinto River, Houston attacked and routed the c.1,200 Mexicans, and captured Santa Ana, who was forced to acknowledge the **independence of Texas**.

1836 June 15   **Arkansas** was the 25th state admitted to the U.S. It was a slave state.

1836 Sept. 14   **Aaron Burr** (b. Feb. 6, 1756), a U.S. political leader and former vice president (1801–1805), died. After the duel he had fought (1804) with **Alexander Hamilton**, which destroyed his political career, Burr conspired (1805) with **James Wilkinson** (1757–Dec. 28, 1825), a U.S. general, to invade Mexico to organize an independent empire, with the added possibility of gaining, through secession, the western states. Wilkinson betrayed Burr, who was acquitted (1807) of charges of treason by **John Marshall**, chief justice of the U.S., for lack of evidence.

1836 Oct. 22   **Sam Houston** became the **first president of the Republic of Texas**. Although Texas was recognized as an independent republic by the U.S. and foreign nations (but not formally by Mexico), her petition for annexation to the U.S. was not granted for nearly ten years.

1837 Oct.   Without regard for the flag of truce he carried, **Osceola** (1804?–Jan. 30, 1838), leader of the **Seminole Indians** in the southeastern U.S., was captured as he arrived at St. Augustine for a conference during the **Second Seminole Indian War** (1835–1842). The rest of his tribe remained in hiding in the Everglades in southern Florida, where they vowed to fight until the last Seminole died. The war had

begun (1835) when the Seminoles, especially the younger men, resisted orders to move to Indian territories west of the Mississippi River.

1837   In an attempt to gain liberal support for the monarchy against **Don Carlos,** a constitution was adopted in Spain during the **First Carlist War** (1833–1839). It established a bicameral parliament, called the **Cortes,** over which the crown had veto power.

1837 Jan. 26   **Michigan** was the 26th state admitted to the U.S. It was a free state with slavery forbidden.

1837 Mar. 3   The U.S. Congress enacted legislation increasing the number of seats in the **U.S. Supreme Court** from seven to nine.

1837 Mar. 4   **Martin Van Buren** (Dec. 5, 1782–July 24, 1862) of the Democratic party was inaugurated as the eighth president of the U.S., having defeated **William Henry Harrison** of the Whig party, newly organized from the remnants of the National Republican party in 1832. **Richard Mentor Johnson** (Oct. 17, 1781–Nov. 19, 1850) was chosen vice president, the only vice president to be elected in this manner, by the Senate alone, as none of the four candidates for this office had gained a majority electoral vote. (Johnson, Democrat from Kentucky, was defeated in his bid for the Presidency in 1840.)

1837 May 30   The **Treaty of Tafna**, a river in northwestern Algeria, defined the boundaries between the Algerian territories held by Abd-el-Kader [Abd-al-Kadir] (c.1807–1883), emir of Mascara (from 1832), a city in northwestern Algeria, and the localities, mostly port cities at this time, under French control. The **Berber revolt** against French penetration in Algeria had begun under **Abd-el-Kader** in May 1832, and resulted in a series of French defeats.

1837 June 20   **William IV** [called the Sailor-King or Silly Billy] (b. Aug. 21, 1765), king of Great Britain and Ireland (from 1830), died and was succeeded by his niece **Victoria** [Alexandrina Victoria].

1837 Nov.   The Afghan city of **Herat** was put under siege by **Mohammed**, shah (1834–1848) of Persia [Iran], who had been promised Russian support.

1837 Nov. 22–23   **Louis Joseph Papineau**, a Reform leader of Lower Canada [Quebec], led an insurrection at St. Denis, near Montreal, in the **Canadian Rebellion of 1837**. The rebellion was put down and, because troops were diverted to quell this uprising, an opportunity existed for another similar rebellion to break out in Upper Canada. Papineau escaped to the U.S., then Paris until 1845, when he returned to Canada under a general amnesty (1844).

1837 Dec. 5   William Lyon Mackenzie (1795–Aug. 28, 1861), the radical Candianian reformer, led a force of c.750 farmers and laborers in an attack on Toronto in the **Canadian Rebellion of 1837.** They were easily driven back by British forces under the command of **John Colborne** (1778–1863), former lieutenant-governor (1828–1836) of Upper Canada. Mackenzie fled to Buffalo, New York, where he established a base from which he led raids into Canada during 1838.

1838–1848   Chartism, a British national working-class movement, gained its name from the **People's Charter,** a petition which was drafted by the **London Working Men's Association** and set forth six points regarding electoral equality, as universal suffrage, abolishing property requirements, payment of Parliament members, and vote by ballot. The climactic moment for the Chartists came on Apr. 10, 1848, when a third petition was to be presented to the House of Commons by a large group marching from Kensington; but, to prevent disturbance, the government barred them. The Chartist movement subsided, remaining active only in the provinces.

1838   Iowa, earlier a part of the Michigan or Wisconsin territories, was organized as a separate territory.

1838 Oct. 1   The First Anglo-Afghan War (1838–1842) was instigated by **George Eden** (Aug. 25, 1784–Jan. 1, 1849), earl of Auckland and British governor general of India (1836–1842), in an attempt to forestall Persian or Russian control of Afghanistan and to establish a boundary between Russia and British India.

1839   The Durham Report [*Report on the Affairs of British North America*] was published by **John George Lambton** (Apr. 12, 1792–July 28, 1840), earl of Durham. In 1838 Durham had been governor general of Canada, where he had been sent to investigate the **Rebellion of 1837,** and had resigned in the same year. He suggested reuniting the two Canadas and instituting self-government on a local level. His suggestion that the French population of Lower Canada would be assimilated eventually by a careful

plan of immigration was proven wrong with the passage of time.

1839   Mississippi was the **first state in the U.S. to recognize property rights of its married female citizens.**

1839 Jan. 20   The Confederation of Peru and Bolivia was defeated in a **battle at Yungay,** in northwestern Peru, by Chilean forces under Manuel Bulnes (Dec. 25, 1799–Oct. 18, 1866). As the Confederation dissolved, **Andres Santa Cruz,** president of Bolivia, went into exile in Europe.

1839 Apr. 19   A treaty was signed by Great Britain, Germany, and France, stating that in the event of a dispute between any of these three nations, **Belgium** would be permitted to remain neutral.

1839 June 27   [Maharaja] Ranjit Singh (b. Nov., 1780), a Sikh ruler who had brought most of the Punjab under his control, died. Appointed (1799) governor of Lahore, the capital of the Punjab by **Zaman Shah,** the Afghan emir (1793–1800), Ranjit Singh expanded his kingdom, annexing Amritsar in 1802. The British, threatened by his power, signed a treaty with him in 1809, establishing a boundary at the Sutlej River. With Ranjit Singh's death, the Punjab grew lawless, rebelled against the British, and by 1849 the area was no longer ruled by the **Sikhs,** but by Great Britain.

1839 Aug. 31   Following a military defeat of a Carlist army, the **First Carlist War** (from 1833) in Spain was ended by the **Convention of Vergara,** a city in northern Spain. **Don Carlos** left Spain for France.

1839 Sept. 25   France was the first European power to recognize the Republic of Texas. The following year, The Netherlands, Belgium, Great Britain, and the U.S. would also recognize the new republic.

1839 Nov. 4   The First Anglo-Chinese War (to 1842), known as the **Opium War,** between China and Great Britain, began. The Ch'ing [Manchu] government (1644–1912) prohibited the opium trade as early as 1729, but it did not seriously enforce the ban until c.1830. The East India Company lost its monopoly, but the Chinese demand for the drug resulted in large-scale smuggling by independent merchants at great profit.

V. ECONOMY AND TRADE

1835 Failure of the wheat crop in the western U.S. brought financial distress to the rural population there and added to the **Panic of 1837**. Loan facilities were drained of their reserves. Another crop failure occurred in 1837, draining reserves even more.

1835 June City workers in Philadelphia gained shorter working hours in the **first general strike organized in the U.S. to succeed** in its purpose.

1836 **Massachusetts** passed the **first child labor law in the U.S.** It required that those under 15 years of age be allowed to attend school for one-fourth of the year.

1836 **Nassau William Senior** (Sept. 26, 1790–June 4, 1864), a professor of political economy at Oxford, argued in *An Outline of the Science of Political Economy*, a classical view of economics, that the true cost of goods included not only the labor used to produce it, but also the "abstinence," or lack of spending, needed to accumulate the necessary capital for investment in the means of production.

1836 June 23 The **Surplus Revenue Act** required all U.S. federal revenue exceeding $5 million to be distributed among the states. At least one bank in each state was to be designated as a repository for federal funds. The Act caused, in part, the **Panic of 1837**, by placing with local banks funds used in wild speculation, such as land mortgages and get-rich-quick business schemes.

1836 July 11 The **Specie Circular**, proposed by **Thomas Hart Benton** (Mar. 14, 1782–Apr. 10, 1858), a U.S. senator, was issued to restore diminished specie reserves in the U.S. After Aug. 15, the U.S. government would accept payment for the sale of public land only in specie, gold or silver, a restriction considered necessary due to the increasing speculation in western land.

1837 Mar. The **Panic of 1837** in the U.S. began as American stock and commodity prices began to drop, acting in concert with the demand made on banks by the provisions of the **Surplus Revenue Act** of 1836. The Panic of 1837 swept the financial world in May, after the Bank of England, frightened by the failure of several British financial institutions that had invested heavily in U.S. speculative schemes, cashed in its U.S. securities, further

depleting the specie reserves of U.S. banks. On May 1 New York banks suspended specie payments altogether, and banks across the U.S. closed. The laboring classes, whose money had been deposited in the failing savings banks, suffered from not only loss of jobs but also rapidly rising prices. Farmers recovered the quickest since their produce fetched good prices in city markets. More than 600 banks failed in the U.S., and the resulting depression lasted about seven years.

1838 The **first state railroad in the German Confederation** was built in Brunswick [Braunschweig], in present northeastern Germany.

1838 Apr. 23 The steamships *Sirius*, a ferryboat and the **first British steamboat to cross the Atlantic** solely under power, and the British *Great Western* both reached New York City, demonstrating the practicality of transatlantic travel. They were the first of ten steamships to make the voyage from Europe in 1838, the *Great Western* achieving the record time of 15 days in crossing the Atlantic and the distinction of inaugurating regular transatlantic steamship service.

VI. RELIGION AND PHILOSOPHY

1835 The publication of *Das Leben Jesu* [*Life of Jesus*] by **David Friedrich Strauss** (Jan. 27, 1808–Feb. 8, 1874), a young German theologian, aroused controversy when he held that none of the Gospels had been written by an eyewitness and that the Christian belief of Jesus as the promised Messiah had led New Testament writers to overlay the facts of his life with mythology. Translated into several languages [English: 1846], it was widely circulated and, with **Ernest Renan's** *Life of Jesus* (1863), became the most influential 19th-century work on Jesus.

1838 **Ralph Waldo Emerson**, a onetime Congregational minister, delivered an address to the graduating class of Harvard [Cambridge] Divinity School that attacked formal religion and encouraged intuitive and spiritual experiences and self-reliance. Emerson brought his transcendental ideas to bear on the reform of the ministry for a new age.

1839 Nov. 20 **John Williams** (b. 1796), an English missionary, was murdered by cannibals while visiting Eromanga, an island of the New Hebrides group in the South Pacific. Williams had arrived (1816) in the Society Islands, where he made Raiatéa his permanent headquarters.

VII. SCIENCE, EDUCATION, AND TECHNOLOGY

1835 Apr. 8   Wilhelm von [Freiherr von] **Humboldt** (b. June 22, 1767), a German philologist, died. Humboldt's chief work, unfinished at the time of his death, was a study of Kawi, an ancient language of Java. In 1836 his brother **Alexander**, a famous German naturalist and explorer, published an edited version of part of the work which included the landmark essay *On the Difference in the Construction of Language, and its Influence upon the Intellectual Development of the Human Race.*

1835 June 18   William Cobbett (b. Mar. 19, 1762), an English reformer and author, died. Cobbett was active on behalf of rural laborers, who were at this time being dispossessed, and of the urban working class. He was also involved in political reform, especially the expansion of the franchise. He wrote *Grammar of the English Language* (1818) to help students from working class backgrounds, and *Rural Rides* (1830), which portrayed the hard times of rural laborers.

1836   The first two of six **McGuffey Eclectic Readers** were published this year. The Sixth Reader was published in 1857. **William Holmes McGuffey** (Sept. 23, 1800–May 4, 1873) compiled these books for children, which contained extracts from English literature and were immensely popular for their moral lessons. They were revised for nearly two generations of school children, selling c.122,000,000 copies, and were instrumental in shaping American moral and cultural attitudes in the 19th century.

1836   Samuel Colt (July 19, 1814–Jan. 10, 1862), an American inventor, obtained a **patent for his revolver** in England. The following year, it was patented in the U.S. The Colt revolver gained renown because of the effectiveness of its revolving breech. Colt was a pioneer in the development of modern production lines and the use of standard, interchangeable parts.

1836 May   Francis Pettit Smith (Feb. 9, 1808–Feb. 12, 1874), an English inventor, obtained the **first patent on a practical screw propeller**. Six weeks later, **John Ericsson** (July 31, 1803–Mar. 8, 1889), a Swed-

ish engineer, also patented a screw propeller. In 1839 Smith constructed the **Archimedes**, the first screw steamer.

1836 June 10   André Marie Ampère (b. Jan. 20, 1775), a French mathematician and physicist, died. He established the **mathematical basis of electricity**, from which the ampere, a unit for measuring electric current, was formulated.

1837   The Englishman **Isaac Pitman** (Jan. 4, 1813–Jan. 12, 1897), published *Stenographic Soundhand*, a new system of shorthand based on phonetic spelling. **Benn** [Benjamin] **Pitman** (July 24, 1822–Dec. 28, 1910), Isaac's brother, taught Pitman shorthand in the U.S.

1837   Horace Mann (May 4, 1796–Aug. 2, 1859), called the "**father of American public education**," officiated as secretary on the first state board of education in the U.S., organized in Massachusetts.

1837   Charles Wheatstone, an English physicist, received a patent for an early version of the **electric telegraph**. **William Fothergill Cooke** (May 4, 1806–June 25, 1879) collaborated with Wheatstone, but later they disputed credit.

1838 Sept. 27   Bernard Courtois (b. Feb. 8, 1777), a French pharmacist and chemist, died. He was famous for his accidental **isolation of iodine** in 1811, essential in an extremely small quantity to human health. Courtois was also noted for his **discovery of morphine** in opium.

1837 Oct. 8   [François Marie] **Charles Fourier** (b. Apr. 7, 1772), a French social theorist, died. He devised a model for a utopian community that he called a **phalanstery**, a social and economic unit of c.1,600 people in which all would work and share the results. Fourier's ideas had more effect in the U.S. than in France.

1839   Samuel Finley Breese Morse came to the U.S. from France, where he had studied with **Louis Jacques Mandé Daguerre**, a French painter, and brought with him the skill and equipment to make the **first daguerreotype portraits of American citizens**.

1839   Charles Goodyear (Dec. 29, 1800–July 1, 1860) accidentally discovered the **vulcanization process**, a momentous event that made possible the development of the commercial rubber industry. The process was patented on June 15, 1844, but Goodyear did not profit from his discovery. He was arrested for debt in Dec. 1855, and died in poverty.

1839 The **first practical bicycle** was invented by **Kirkpatrick Macmillan** in Scotland. Macmillan devised foot treadles and cranks for pedaling and built handlebars for steering.

1839 The **cell theory** was described by **Theodor Schwann**, a German biologist, and **Matthias Jakob Schleiden** (Apr. 5, 1804–June 23, 1881), a German botanist. It stated that all living things were composed of cells or products of cells, and it was based on the premise that the units, or cells, in plants and animals were essentially similar.

1839 Mar. *Light Reading for the Danish People*, a Danish journal, told of the discovery of a prehistoric woman's body at the bottom of a peat bog. Scientists have since noted that the body was one of many Iron Age "bog people" whose remains have been found in Scandinavia. The article surmised that the body had been punctured by stakes and suggested that the woman had been killed for being a witch.

1839 Aug. 19 The **photographic process of daguerreotype** was made public at the Academy of Sciences in Paris. It had been conceived and developed by **Louis Daguerre**, a French painter, at first in collaboration with [Joseph] **Nicéphore Niepce** (Mar.7, 1765–July 5, 1833), a French physicist, from 1829. The calotype process developed by **William Henry Fox Talbot** (Feb. 11, 1800–Sept. 17, 1877), an English photographer, was patented at about the same time. Despite its greater possibilities, the calotype process required a long time for printing and failed to reproduce detail.

VIII. ARTS AND LEISURE

1835 **Elias Lönnrot** [Lönnrott] (Apr. 9, 1802–Mar. 19, 1884), a Finnish scholar, completed the *Kalevala*, the national epic of Finland, which he had collected and edited from the mythic traditional tales, passed down orally for generations.

1835 The production of *Don Àlvaro ò la fuerza del sino* [*Don Alvaro, or the Force of Destiny*] in Madrid established its author, the Spanish politician **Angel de Saavedra** (Mar. 10, 1791–June 22, 1865), duke of Rivas, as a leader of the romantic movement in Spanish literature.

1835 The play *Dantons Tod* [*Danton's Death*], by **Georg Büchner**, a young German writer, told the story of the French revolutionary Georges Jacques Danton, as both victim and cause of the French Revolution (1789–1799). Büchner (b. Oct. 17, 1813) died on Feb. 19, 1837 at age 23, but his influence as an important dramatist was not recognized until c.50 years later.

1835 The first volume of tales, *Eventyr*, by **Hans Christian Anderson** (Apr. 2, 1805–Aug. 4, 1875), was published. The Danish writer produced more than 150 tales, which are read throughout the world.

1835 May 13 **John Nash** (b. 1752), an English architect, died. He had designed Regent's Park (1811) and Regent Street (1813–1820) in London, and redesigned **Buckingham Palace**.

1835 Sept. 23 **Vincenzo Bellini** (b. Nov. 3, 1801), an Italian opera composer, died. Bellini's best work was *Norma*, first performed at La Scala Opera House on Dec. 26, 1831. Very influential even outside the world of opera, he was known for the simplicity of his melodic line.

1836 Apr. 7 **William Godwin** (b. Mar. 3, 1756), an English writer, died. *The Adventures of Caleb Williams* (1794) was his best known novel, and *Enquiry Concerning Political Justice* (1793) was a noted essay.

1836 Apr. 19 *Revizor* [*The Inspector General*] by **Nikolai Vasilievich Gogol**, a Russian writer, was performed at the Court Theater in St. Petersburg, with the permission of Nicholas I, czar of Russia. The satire-comedy of corruption and petty qualities symbolized by the Russian bureaucracy was highly controversial.

1836 Sept. 19 The first meeting of the **Transcendentalists**, an American literary-philosophical group, was held in Boston at the home of **George Ripley** (Oct. 3, 1802–July 4, 1880), a preacher and literary critic. The influential group included **Ralph Waldo Emerson**, **Nathaniel Hawthorne**, **Henry David Thoreau**, and [Sarah] **Margaret Fuller** (May 23, 1810–July 19, 1850), who edited the *Dial* (1840–1842), a Transcendental journal.

1836 Nov. 5 **Karel Hynek Macha** (b. Nov. 16, 1810), a leading Czech romantic poet, died. His great work *Máj*, modeled after George Gordon Byron's romantic intrigues, was published the same year.

1836 Dec. 9 *Ivan Suganin* [*A Life for the Czar*], Russia's first national opera, composed by **Mikhail** [Michael] **Ivanovich Glinka** (June 1, 1804–Feb. 15, 1857), was produced.

1837 Jan. 29 **Aleksander Sergeevich Pushkin** [Alexander Sergeyevich Pushkin] (b. May 25, 1799), a Russian poet, died in a duel with Baron Heckerend'Anthès, who had begun to court Natalia Goncharova, Pushkin's wife. The poem *Ruslan and Ludmila* (1820), which established Pushkin as a major poet, was adapted by **Mikhail Ivanovich Glinka** as an opera in 1842. His tragedy *Boris Godunov* (1826) was later adapted by **Modest Petrovich Musorgski** [Moussorgsky], a Russian composer, for an opera of the same name. Perhaps Pushkin's greatest work was *Eugene Onegin* (1831), a novel in verse. Pushkin was also remembered for *The Queen of Spades* (1833), a short story about a gambler.

1837 Mar. 31 **John Constable** (b. June 11, 1776), an English landscape painter, died. In this year he received a gold medal for his exhibition at the Paris Salon. Constable's best works included *Boat-building* (1815), *The White Horse* (1819), *The Hay-Wain* (1821?), and *Salisbury Cathedral From the Bishop's Grounds* (1823).

1838 June 12 **Rachel** [real name: Elisa Félix] (Feb. 28, 1820–Jan. 3, 1858), a French actress, made her debut at the Comédie Française. She brilliantly portrayed the tragic roles of Phèdre, Cléopâtre, Lucrèce, Camille, and Roxane.

1838 Aug. 21 **Adelbert von Chamisso** [Louis Charles Adélaïde de Chamisso] (b. Jan. 30, 1781), a French-born German writer of the romantic school, died. *Peter Schlemihls Wunderbare Geschichte* (1814) told the story of a man who sold his shadow to the devil. As a lyric poet, he was highly regarded for his *Frauenliebe und-leben* (1831), later set to music by **Robert Schumann.**

1839 Sept. 28 **William Dunlap** (b. Feb. 19, 1766), an American playwright, died. His first success was the comedy of manners *The Father; or, American Shandyism*, performed at the John Street Theater in New York City on Sept. 7, 1789. It was later published as *The Father of an Only Child* (1806). He also wrote romance tragedies in verse, one of which was *André* (1798), based on the capture and execution of Major John André, a British spy, during the American Revolution (1775–1783).

IX. SPORTS, GAMES, AND SOCIETY

1838 The Grand Caledonian **Curling** Club was organized in Scotland. Upon receiving royal approval in 1842, its name became the Royal Caledonian Curling Club.

1839 Feb. 12 In the **first championship boxing match** fought under London Prize Ring laws, **Jim Burke** [James "Deaf" Burke] lost his title to **William Thompson**, called "Bendigo." The new laws, an expansion of Broughton's and revised again in 1853, declared low blows, kicking, gouging, butting, and biting to be fouls. A round ended when a fighter fell to the floor.

1839 June 14 The **Henley Regatta** was first rowed at Henley-on-Thames in Oxfordshire, England.

1840–1844

I. DISASTERS

1842 May 5 A fire swept through **Hamburg**, a free city of the German Confederation, in present Germany. It destroyed c.4,000 buildings and killed c.100 people.

1842 May 8 The **first railroad disaster** occurred as a heavily loaded train derailed on its return to Paris following a public birthday celebration for Louis-Philippe, king of France, held at Versailles. The wooden coaches caught fire, and locked doors made escape difficult. Fifty-three passengers died.

II. EXPLORATION AND COLONIZATION

1841 **Edward John Eyre** (Aug. 5, 1815–Nov. 3, 1901), an English colonist in **Australia**, crossed the continent, proceeding east to west from Adelaide to

Albany. His most important explorations were of the interior deserts.

1841 **Copper beds** were discovered on the Keweenaw Peninsula, jutting into Lake Superior from the Upper Peninsula of Michigan.

1841 Jan. 22 **Jules Sébastien César Dumont d'Urville** (May 23, 1790–May 8, 1842), a French navigator, in command of the ships *Astrolabe* and *Zeleé*, landed on the **Antarctic continent**, after sighting Adélie Coast late in 1840. He made the first accurate assessment of the continent as a base of rocks covered with a crust of ice.

1842–1846 **John Charles Frémont** (Jan. 21, 1813–July 13, 1890), an American frontiersman and officer in the U.S. army, led three trips during these years into the **Oregon Territory**, where, searching for suitable trails to the west, he mapped a great part of the **Oregon Trail**, explored the Great Basin, and reached the Pacific Coast (1843) at the mouth of the Columbia River. **Kit** [Christopher] **Carson** (Dec. 24, 1809–May 23, 1868), an American scout, accompanied Frémont.

1844 **George Bush** (1791?–?1867), formerly a servant for a French family in Missouri, led a group of settlers into the Oregon Territory to make Puget Sound area, in present Washington state, their new home. Bush's colony formed the basis for the **U.S. claim to all land south of the 49th parallel.**

1844 **William A. Burt** (June 13, 1792–Aug. 18, 1858) discovered **iron ore** near Lake Superior in southeastern Minnesota, while surveying in the region.

III. POLITICS AND WAR

1841 Jan. 1 **Francisco Ferrera** (fl.1820–1860) was named the **first constitutional president of Honduras.**

1840 Feb. 10 The **colonies of Lower [Quebec] and Upper [Ontario] Canada** were united as provinces of Canada, called respectively, Canada East and Canada West, by an act of the British Parliament.

1841 Mar. 4 **William Henry Harrison** of the Whig party was inaugurated as the ninth president of the U.S., having defeated Martin Van Buren of the Democratic party. **John Tyler** served as vice president. Harrison had gained national reputation for his victory in a **battle at Tippecanoe Creek** (1811), which earned him the nickname of "Tippecanoe" and was the basis for the famous campaign slogan, "Tippecanoe and Tyler too!" Harrison (b. Feb. 9, 1773) died on Apr. 4, after one month in office. Tyler was inaugurated the same day as president, the **first time in U.S. history that the vice president was called on to replace a president who had died in office.**

1841 Nov. 20 **Augustín Gamarra** (b. Aug. 27, 1785), president of Peru (1829–1833) and president-dictator of Peru (from 1839), was killed in a **battle at Ingaví** [Yngaví], south of La Paz, when he attempted an **invasion of Bolivia**. **Manuel Menéndez** (1790?–?1845) became acting president of Peru.

1842 The British Parliament passed the **Constitution Act**, granting limited self-government to the Australian colony of **New South Wales**.

1842 Jan. 6 The British [Anglo-Indian] forces evacuated **Kabul** in **Afghanistan** under pressure of a revolt against **Shah Shuja** led by a son of **Dost Mohammed Khan**; the Anglo-Indians, who were given **a safe conduct from Kabul to India, were massacred en route**. About 4,500 soliders and 12,000 civilians were lost. This marked the end of the **First Afghan War** (1838–1842).

1842 May **Thomas Wilson Dorr** (Nov. 5, 1805–Dec. 21, 1854) led an attack, known as **Dorr's Rebellion**, on the arsenal at Providence, Rhode Island, after the state and the federal government refused to recognize the **People's Constitution**, which had been drafted by a convention in session from Oct. 4 to Nov. 18, 1841. This constitution, which had been approved (Dec., 1841) by popular vote provided for universal manhood suffrage.

1842 Aug. 9 The **Webster-Ashburton Treaty**, signed by Great Britain and the U.S., established the border between northeastern Canada and the U.S. The local inhabitants had become involved (1831) in a dispute called the **Aroostook War**. **Alexander Baning Ashburton** (Oct. 27, 1774–May 11, 1848) was sent to Washington by Great Britain. In his talks with **Daniel Webster**, Great Britain won the highlands south of Quebec city. The U.S. obtained slightly more than half of the disputed land and the right to ship timber down the St. John River, still part of the boundary between Maine and New Brunswick, to the Bay of Fundy.

1842 Aug. 29   The **Treaty of Nanking** ended the **Opium War** (1839–1842), which was precipitated by China's attempt to block the British and others from bringing opium into China. China ceded **Hong Kong** to Great Britain and agreed to allow **British trade at the ports of Canton and Shanghai.**

1843–1848   In the **Treaty of Waitangi** (1840) the British in New Zealand agreed to respect the **Maoris** rights of land ownership, but disputes broke out leading to Maori uprisings. In the so-called **First Maori War** fighting between the settlers and the Maori lasted five years.

1843 Feb.   The **Great War** (1843–1852) began when **Manuel Oribe**, president of Uruguay, and **Juan Manuel de Rosas**, Argentina's dictator, laid **siege to Montevideo**, the capital of Uruguay. The siege lasted for nine years.

1843 Feb. 12   The **Sind**, a region of present southeastern Pakistan, was annexed by the British in a treaty signed by the local emirs. **Charles James Napier** (Aug. 10, 1782–Aug. 29, 1853), a British military commander, defeated the Sind rulers who opposed the **treaty at Miani** [Meeanee], near Hyderabad [Haidarabad], then its capital on Feb. 17, and then Hyderabad surrendered in March.

1843 Apr. 11   The West Africa territory of **Gambia** was separated from Sierra Leone and made a British Crown Colony.

1843 Oct.   The **Young Ireland movement** culminated in plans for a rally of nearly one million at Clontarf, near Dublin. Troops, mobilized by **Robert Peel** (Feb. 5, 1788–July 2, 1850), the British prime minister (1834–1835; 1841–1846), halted the operation and arrested its leaders, including **Daniel O'-Connell** (Aug. 6, 1775–May 15, 1847), the Liberator, who was released in 1844.

1843 Dec. 13   **Moshesh I** [Moshoeshoe] (c.1790–1870), king of **Basutoland** [present Lesotho] (from 1823), achieved British recognition and protection against encroachment by white settlers.

1844   **Nicholas I**, czar of Russia, met in London with **George Hamilton Gordon** (Jan. 28, 1784–Dec. 14, 1860), earl of Aberdeen and British foreign secretary (1841–1846) (later prime minister 1852–1855), to discuss how to maintain their respective roles of influence in the **Ottoman Empire** (1326–1920).

If the empire were to dissolve, Russia and Great Britain were to agree on the division and rule of Turkey and the future cooperation of Russia and Britain.

1844 Mar. 2   **Charles XIV** [Carl Johan; Jean Baptiste Jules Bernadotte], king of **Sweden** and Norway (from 1818), died. He had fought in the French Revolution (1789–1799) and had been promoted to marshall during the **Napoleonic Wars** (1803–1815). Charles XIV was succeeded by his son **Oscar I** (July 4, 1799–July 8, 1859; ruled to 1859).

1844 Mar. 6   The treaties known as the **Bond of 1844** were signed by Great Britain and the **Fante** [Fanti] **Confederacy** in the Gold Coast, in present **Ghana**. They provided a legal justification in the region for British sovereignty, which had been established peaceably by the outstanding civil administration (1830–1843) of **George Maclean** (Feb. 24, 1801–May 22, 1847), who had been hired by British merchants after Great Britain withdrew its military presence there.

1844 Aug. 6   The **Franco-Moroccan War** (1844) began as the French bombarded Tangier, near the Strait of Gibraltar, and occupied Mogador [Essaouira], on the coast of southwestern Morocco. On Aug. 14, in a **battle at Isly** in northeastern Morocco, **Thomas Robert Bugeaud de la Piconnerie** (Oct. 15, 1784–June 10, 1849), marshal of France, defeated the Moroccans and **Abd-el-Kader** [Abd-al-Kadir] (Sept. 6, 1808–May 26, 1883), the Algerian rebel leader who had sought aid and refuge in Morocco. On Sept. 10, by the **Treaty of Tangier**, the Algerian ally **Abd-er-Rahman II** [Abd-ur-Rahman; Abd ar-Rahman; 'Abdul-Rahman] (1778–1859), the sultan of Fez and Morocco (from 1822), was forced to recognize the **French occupation of Algeria.**

IV. ECONOMY AND TRADE

1840   [Jean Joseph Charles] **Louis Blanc** (Oct. 29, 1811–Dec. 6, 1882), a French socialist critic of capitalism, published *Organisation du Travail* [*The Organization of Labor*], which contained the proposition, "from each according to his abilities; to each according to his needs." He proposed a system of "national workshops" [ateliers nationaux] founded (briefly in 1848) by the state which guaranteed employment and united the efforts of all laborers for the common good.

1840   *Qu'est-ce que la Propriété?* [*What is Property?*] was published by **Pierre Joseph Proudhon** (July 15, 1809–Jan. 26, 1865), a French moralist and anarchist philosopher, who stated that *"La propriété c'est le vol"* [*Property is theft*]. Proudhon's definition of property referred to the concentrated assets of large businesses, or middle-class [bourgeois] wealth, and unearned profit by smaller businesses.

1840 Mar. 31   Legislation was enacted by the U.S. government that established a **maximum ten-hour work day** for all federal employees engaged in public works.

1840 May 6   The **first postage stamp** was issued in Great Britain. **Jacob Perkins**, an American inventor in England, had been granted the contract for printing **Penny Blacks**, the first adhesive postage stamp generally used.

1840 July 4   The **Independent Treasury Act** established a system in the U.S. whereby seven subtreasuries would receive the deposit of federal funds and gradually make government disbursements in specie payments.

1841   British companies in the Niger Delta, in present Nigeria, began production of **palm oil**, for which there was a heavy demand in Great Britain.

1842   In the case of **Commonwealth of Massachusetts vs. Hunt** the Massachusetts supreme court established for the first time in the U.S. that unions could not be prosecuted as criminal conspiracies merely because their activities resulted in economic loss to employers. **Lemuel Shaw** (Jan. 9, 1781–Mar. 30, 1861), the chief justice, ruled that union activity "far from being criminal . . . may be highly meritorious and public spirited."

1842   The **Mines Act** was passed by the British Parliament, prohibiting women and children from working underground. Anthony Ashley Cooper (Apr. 28, 1801–Oct. 1, 1885), earl of Shaftesbury, led efforts by Tories, Anglican clergymen, and working class radicals to ameliorate working conditions in textile factories and other unsafe places.

1844   The **Bank Charter Act of 1844** was issued by the British Parliament in an effort to ensure that the Bank of England would not again overextend its credit. The act fixed the amount of money issued by

the Bank at 14 million pounds, which was to be secured by government bonds.

1844 Dec. 21   The **Rochdale Pioneers**, followers of **Robert Owen**, the Welsh socialist philanthropist and manufacturer, founded a consumers' cooperative at Rochdale in Lancashire, England. It was the **first cooperative consumer group** to pay its members dividends earned from purchases.

V. RELIGION AND PHILOSOPHY

1840 Dec. 8   **David Livingstone**, a Scottish missionary, sailed for southern Africa. From Kuruman, the mission of **Robert Moffat** in Bechuanaland, in present northern South Africa, and from his own station at Mabotsa, a valley c.200 miles to the northeast, Livingstone made journeys into little known country, where he allowed native agents to continue his work.

1841   **George Ripley** (Oct. 3, 1802–July 4, 1880), an American social reformer, organized the **Brook Farm experimental community** in West Roxbury, Massachusetts. Those living there hoped to prove that reason could be profitably applied to the daily affairs of living.

1843 Oct. 13   **B'nai B'rith** [Sons of the Covenant], a fraternal order for U.S. Jews, was established by 12 laymen at a cafe on New York City's Lower East Side.

1844   Two German missionary-explorers, **Johann Ludwig Krapf** (1810–1811) and **Johann Rebmann** (Jan. 16, 1820–Oct. 4, 1876), of the Church Missionary Society, established the **first Christian mission near Mombasa**, in present Kenya. They may have been the first modern Europeans to visit **Mount Kilimanjaro**, Africa's highest mountain (19,340 feet), in 1848 and **Mount Kenya** (17,058 feet) in 1849.

1844   **Abraham Geiger** (May 24, 1810–Oct. 23, 1874), theoretician of the **Jewish Reform movement** in Germany and senior rabbi at Breslau, Germany, was the guiding spirit of three conferences of reform-minded rabbis held annually in Germany beginning in this year. The conferences focused on reform of liturgy, prayer in the vernacular, and marriage and divorce laws.

1844 Mar. 21   The Second Coming of Christ did not occur during the year ending this day, disappointing followers of **William Miller** (Feb. 5, 1782–Dec. 20,

1849) of Low Hampton, New York. He and his followers formed (1845) at Albany, New York, the first loose **Adventist organization**, formerly known as Millerites, in the U.S.

1844 May 23 The **Bab** [Babel-Din-Gateway to Religion], or **Ali Muhammad** of Shiraz, made public pronouncements in Shiraz, Persia [Iran], that soon led to formation of a modern Muslim sect, **Babism**, and later to development of **Bahaism**. The Bab held that revelation was progressive and no revelation was final. His inflammatory action of revealing a new holy book, the **Bayan** [the Manifestation], which superseded the laws of the Koran, brought him into conflict with the Persian shah and his troops in 1850.

1844 June 6 **George Williams** (Oct. 11, 1821–Nov. 6, 1905), a clerk in a dry-goods store in London, founded the **Young Men's Christian Association** [YMCA] with financial help from concerned Evangelicals. The purpose was to provide workers with greater recreational opportunities in a wholesome environment.

1844 June 27 **Joseph Smith** (b. Dec. 23, 1805), leader of the **Church of the Latter-Day Saints**, was dragged from jail in Carthage, Illinois, and **shot**, with his brother Hiram [Hyrum], by a mob of non-Mormons. In 1838 Smith and followers had journeyed to Missouri, then relocated at Nauvoo, Illinois, despite local hostility. On July 12, 1843, Smith had announced a divine revelation sanctioning the practice of polygamy, which further antagonized community relations.

VI. SCIENCE, EDUCATION, AND TECHNOLOGY

1840 The final two volumes of the four-volume *La Démocratie en Amérique* [*Democracy in America*] by **Alexis de Tocqueville** [Charles Henri Maurice Clérel] (July 29, 1805–Apr. 16, 1859), appeared. This sociological study of American life was based on Tocqueville's visit to the U.S. in 1831 to study its prisons. As a result of this book Tocqueville was elected to the Académie Française.

1840 The **first public arboretum** was opened at Derby, England. It reflected the Victorian enthusiasm for study of horticulture and the natural sciences.

1840 **John William Draper** (May 5, 1811–Jan. 4, 1882) made the **first photograph of the moon**. Draper, a scientist and author, was an Englishman who had moved (1831) to the U.S. He was noted for research in photography, radiant energy, and the electric telegraph.

1842 **Justus von Liebig** (May 12, 1803–Apr. 18, 1873), a German chemist who developed methods of **organic analysis**, divided the major organic constituents of living tissues into fats, carbohydrates, and proteins, and determined that these substances were the source of energy for the human body.

1842 **Julius Robert von Mayer** (Nov. 24, 1814–Mar. 20, 1878), a German scientist, propounded the **first law of thermodynamics**, which stated that during transformation or transfer of energy from one form to another there was no gain or loss in the total energy involved. Mayer's claim to have discovered this principle was contested by many scientists. Actually, various scientists contributed to the understanding of this law of the conservation of energy, among them **Hermann von Helmholtz** (Aug. 31, 1821–Sept. 8, 1894), **Humphry Davy**, **Gustave Adolphe Hirn** (1815–1890), **James Prescott Joule**, and **Benjamin Thompson** [Count Rumford].

1843 Mar. The appearance of a comet so bright that it could be seen during the daytime prompted purchase of the largest telescope available by the **Harvard Astronomical Observatory**.

1844 May 24 The message "What hath God wrought" was relayed by the American inventor **Samuel Finley Breese Morse** over the **first telegraph line**, which connected Washington, D.C., and Baltimore, Maryland.

1844 July 27 **John Dalton** (b. Sept. 6, 1766), an English chemist and physicist, died. He wrote *Absorption of Gases by Water and other liquids* (1805), in which he developed the law of partial pressures: "The total pressure of a mixture of gases is equal to the sum of the partial pressures of the individual constituent gases."

VII. ARTS AND LEISURE

1840 Construction began on the **Houses of Parliament** in London under direction of the architects, **Charles Barry** (May 23, 1795–May 12, 1860) and **Augustus Welby Northmore** Pugin (Mar. 1, 1812–Sept. 14, 1852).

1840 Jan. 6 **Fanny Burney** [Frances d'Arblay] (b. June 13, 1752), an English writer, died. She wrote the novels *Evelina* (1778) and *Cecilia* (1782) and a great body of letters and journals. Fanny Burney was one of the more outspoken members of the Bluestockings, a group of women in England who conducted literary and social gatherings.

1840 Mar. 24 **Bertel Thorvaldsen** (Nov. 13, 1768), a Danish sculptor, died. Thorvaldsen had assumed preeminence in the international revival of classicism in sculpture, especially with his figures from mythology and such bas-reliefs as *Triumphal Entry of Alexander into Babylon* and *Christ and the Twelve Apostles*. An especially famous piece was the *Lion of Lucerne* (1819), a monument carved in the local rock at Lucerne, on Lake Lucerne, Switzerland.

1840 May 27 **Nicolò Paganini** (b. Oct. 27, 1782), an Italian violinist and composer, renowned for his flamboyant individualism, died. He combined a romantic style with brilliant technical mastery to become the premier virtuoso performer throughout Europe.

1841 Mar. 4 **Dion Boucicault** [Dionysus Lardner Boursiquot] (Dec. 26, 1820 or 1822–Jan. 18, 1890), an Irish playwright, achieved his first success with the opening of *London Assurance* at Covent Garden in London. In Sept., 1853, he went to the U.S., where his play *The Octoroon* (Dec. 6, 1859) was an early and successful serious portrayal of a black character on the American stage.

1841 June 15 **Mikhail Yurievich Lermontov** (b. Oct. 2, 1814), a Russian poet, was killed at the age of 27 in a duel. He was considered a worthy successor to **Aleksander Pushkin**.

1841 July 5 **Thomas Cook** (Nov. 22, 1808–July 18, 1892), an English entrepreneur and founder of the **Thomas Cook and Sons travel agency**, conducted his first tour, an excursion of 570 people 15 miles by railroad to a temperance meeting.

1842 **St. Mary Magdalene** [La Madeleine] in Paris was finally completed, 36 years after it was originally designed (1806) as a military monument by **Pierre Vignon** (1763–1828). It was intended as a secular Temple de la Gloire, but Napoléon I turned it into a church.

1842 Mar. 13 [Maria] **Luigi** [Carlo Zenobio Salvatore] **Cherubini** (b. Sept. 14, 1760), an Italian composer who had settled in Paris, died. He composed primarily church music and operas, especially *Les Deux Journées* (1800), which employed full orchestration, harmonics, and a strong rhythm.

1843 The **Theater Act** in England authorized the closing of theaters that had violated their license. Since the 16th century, the lord chamberlain, senior officer of the royal household, had powers enabling him to censor plays. With this act his powers to institute a ban became statutory.

1843 Mar. 21 **Robert Southey** (b. Aug. 13, 1774), an English poet, died. He wrote biographies, including one of **William Cowper**, and histories as well as long narrative poems but is now remembered for shorter lyrics, such as "Battle of Blenheim." In 1813 he was chosen poet laureate.

1843 July 9 **Washington Allston** (b. Nov. 5, 1779), an Anglo-American painter, died. Allston touched on supernatural subject matter in *Dead Man Revived by Touching the Bones of Elisha* (1813) and *Moonlit Landscape* (1819). Light and atmosphere were his hallmarks, as exemplified in *The Flight of Florimell* (1819).

1843 Aug. **Sequoya** [Sequoyah, Sequoia] (1770?), a Cherokee tribesman who took the name **George Guess** [Gist], died. He studied the **Cherokee language** and devised for it an alphabet of 85 characters. He helped the tribe establish a republican form of government based on that of the U.S.

1843 Nov. 10 **John Trumbull** (b. June 6, 1756), an Anglo-American painter and architect, died. The only one of his architectural designs still standing is the Congregational house in Lebanon, Connecticut. In 1789 Trumbull began a series of historical paintings and engravings that are now housed in the Yale Museum. The rotunda of the Capitol building in Washington, D.C., contains The Declaration of Independence and other scenes of the American Revolution that Trumbull executed between 1815 and 1837.

1844 Mar. 14 The first installment of *Les Trois Mousquetaires* [*The Three Musketeers*], by **Alexandre Dumas** [Dumas père] (July 24, 1802–Dec. 5, 1870), a French writer, appeared in *Le Siècle*. *Vingt Ans Après* [*Twenty Years Later*] was a sequel (1845). Dumas' many works—he is said to have written more than 300—included *Le Comte de Monte Cristo* [*The Count of Monte Cristo*] (1844).

1844 Apr. 4   Charles Bulfinch (b. Aug. 8, 1763), a New England architect who developed the design subsequently used in many capitol buildings throughout the U.S., died.

1844 Nov. 21   Ivan Andreevich Krylov (b. Feb. 13, 1769), an important Russian fabulist, died. He began by translating the fables of **Jean de La Fontaine** into Russian and later came to write his own fables. The first of his classic tales was published in 1809.

VIII. SPORTS, GAMES AND SOCIETY

1840–1860   Norwegians, emigrating to the U.S. in significant numbers during these two decades, introduced **skiing** to the regions where they settled, especially Minnesota, Wisconsin, northern Michigan, and Plumas County in the Sierra Nevadas of California.

1840   The U.S. participated in its first international **cricket** match, held in Toronto, Canada. The New York team won by a single run.

1842   The **Olympic Club of Montreal**, in Canada, was established with the purpose of holding athletic contests at its annual meeting.

1844   The **New York Yacht Club** [NYYC] was formed, with eight yachts enrolled in the club's fleet. In the same year, the **Royal Bermuda Yacht Club** was also established.

1845–1849

I. VITAL STATISTICS AND DEMOGRAPHICS

1845   Europe's **population** rose in less than 100 years from c.140 million in 1750 to c.250 million in 1845. Mortality rates were decreasing, and famines and disease were increasingly controlled.

II. DISASTERS

1845 Apr. 10   Pittsburgh, Pennsylvania, lost c.1,000 buildings in a major **fire**. Property damage was set at $6 million.

1845 May 25   The **greatest death toll caused by fire** in a single building occurred at a theater in **Canton**, China, where 1,670 people died.

1846 Fall   A blight destroyed Ireland's potato crop, the mainstay of the Irish diet. By 1851 nearly one-third of Ireland's population had starved to death, died in the typhoid fever epidemic following the famine, or emigrated. The combined figure for death and emigration stood at about two million.

1846 Oct.   The **Donner Tragedy** developed when a party of 87 made camp, and became snowbound, at Donner Lake in the Sierra Nevada mountains in California on a journey that had originated at Fort Bridger, Wyoming. When the spring thaw came, the nearly 40 survivors returned with stories of cannibalism.

1847 Nov. 21   The steamboat *Phoenix*, on its regular run between Buffalo, New York, and Chicago, Illinois, caught fire and burned on Lake Michigan off Sheboygan, Wisconsin. Of c.200 passengers, c.160 died.

1849 May 17   More than 400 buildings and 27 steamships were destroyed by **fire in St. Louis**, Missouri.

III. EXPLORATION AND COLONIZATION

1848 Jan. 24   On the South Fork of the American River, in California, **gold was discovered at Sutter's Mill**, near Coloma, c.45 miles northeast of Sacramento, by **James Wilson Marshall** (Oct. 8, 1810–Aug. 10, 1885), while he was constructing the mill in partnership with **John Augustus Sutter** [Johann August Suter] (Feb. 15, 1803–June 18, 1880). Nine days later, California became (Feb. 2) a U.S. territory. By Mar., 1849, c.80,000 prospectors were journeying to California to search for gold. The so-called "forty-niners" arrived in California from many countries of the world but especially from the American East Coast, traveling by boat (c.18,000 miles) around Cape Horn or, to shorten the trip, by crossing the isthmus of Panama. In 1848 the population of California was c.20,000; by 1852 it was c.225,000.

IV. POLITICS AND WAR

1845 The **Know-Nothing party** [American party], also called the Order of the Star Spangled Banner, reached its height in U.S. politics. In this year elections in New York City and Boston showed strong Know-Nothing support, especially in combination with Whig backing which, however, was withdrawn within two years. The party gained its name by a supposed resemblance to the secrecy of the Masons; any party member, asked what he knew or believed, was reputed to respond that he "knew nothing." In general the party grew out of the Federalist opposition to Thomas Jefferson and to the influx of Irish immigrants, who were Roman Catholic. In 1854 the party's name officially became the **American party**; the anti-slavery issue was a rallying point, though in the South the issue was evaded. By 1860 the party had nearly disappeared.

1845 **Ramón Castilla** (Aug. 30, 1796–May 30, 1867) was elected president of **Peru**. Succeeding acting president **Manuel Menéndez**, he established a strong government. Peru's finances were improved by the government's exploitation of the rich guano deposits discovered on the coastal islands. Castilla ended slavery, abolished forced tribute by the Indians to the landed proprietors, and built **Peru's first railroad**. José Rufino Echenique (1808–1887), who succeeded Castilla as president (1851–1855), became very unpopular and was deposed by Castilla in a coup d'état. Castilla was elected president again in 1858.

1845 **Don Carlos**, leader of the Carlists in Spain, transferred his claim to the Spanish throne, which had resulted in the **First Carlist War** (1833–1839), to his son **Don Carlos II** [Carlos Luis Fernando de Borbón (Jan. 31, 1818–Jan. 13, 1861), conde de Montemolín].

1845 Mar. 3 **Florida** was the 27th state to join the U.S. Under the terms of the **Missouri Compromise** (1820) it was a slave state.

1845 Mar. 4 **James Knox Polk** (Nov. 2, 1795–June 15, 1849) of the Democratic party was inaugurated as the 11th president of the U.S., having defeated **Henry Clay** of the Whig party. **George Mifflin Dallas** (July 10, 1792–Dec. 31, 1864) served as vice president.

1845 Mar. 18 France and Morocco negotiated the **Convention of Lalla Marhnia** [Marnia, Maghnia], a town in northwestern Algeria, which fixed the boundary between Algeria and Morocco from the Mediterranean to Teniet al Sassi, a mountain pass c.80 miles south of the coast.

1845 Dec. 29 **Texas** was the 28th state to join the U.S. It was admitted as a slave state.

1846 Great Britain and the U.S. signed a treaty that set the northern extent of U.S. territory west of the Rocky Mountains at the **49th parallel**. Territory north of this line became part of Canada. Pressing for a more northern limit, Pres. James Polk's election campaign of 1844 had coined the slogan "**Fifty-four Forty or Fight.**"

1846 **James Bruce** (July 20, 1811–Nov. 20, 1863), earl of Elgin, was appointed governor general of **Canada** (to 1854), where he successfully introduced "**responsible government**," which meant that the executive cabinet had to keep the confidence of the legislature to stay in office.

1846 Feb. **Galicia**, a region in present southern Poland, rebelled unsuccessfully against Austria, which had occupied the area since the **Third Partition of Poland** in 1795.

1846 Feb. 10 The **First Sikh** [Anglo-Sikh] **War** (1845–1846) in India ended with victory for British forces under **Hugh Gough** (Nov. 3, 1779–Mar. 2, 1869) in a **battle at Sobraon**, in the Punjab of northwestern India. Under terms of the subsequent **Treaty of Lahore** (Mar. 9) **Henry Hardinge** (Mar. 30, 1785–Sept. 24, 1856), governor general of British India (1844–1848), **annexed Kashmir**.

1846 Apr. 24 Hostilities between the U.S. and Mexico began when a troop of U.S. dragoons was ambushed by Mexican cavalry. A message carrying this information reached James Polk, president of the U.S., on May 9, and **Congress declared war against Mexico** on May 13. On the same day the president, a Democrat, appointed general **Winfield**

Scott, a prominent Whig and aspirant to the Presidency himself, to command the U.S. forces being raised to fight in Mexico. In the meantime a Mexican army, ordered to invade by **Mariano Arista** (July 2, 1802–Aug. 7, 1855), the Mexican commander-in-chief, crossed (Apr. 30–May 1) the Rio Grande into Texas. Polk, committed to acquiring California and possibly New Mexico and Arizona, from Mexico, now had an excuse for declaring war on Mexico. Many Americans thought the **Mexican War** (1846–1848) a national disgrace.

1846 May 8   The U.S. army, commanded by **Zachary Taylor**, defeated the numerically superior Mexican army led by **Mariano Arista** in a **battle at Palo Alto** in southeastern Texas. Taylor had correctly guessed that Arista would head for Point Isabel, the American supply base in Texas, so he left a force of c.500 men at Fort Texas [later Fort Brown, now Brownsville], which held the fort until relieved by Taylor after the battles of Palo Alto and nearby Resaca de la Palma (May 9). The **battle at Resaca de la Palma** drove the Mexican army from the field, and on May 18 Taylor crossed the river and entered Matamoros, Mexico, unopposed.

1846 June 14   The **Bear Flag Revolt** in California drove from power the area's last Mexican governor. A group of American settlers under **John Charles Frémont** raised the new standard of the **Republic of California**, the Bear Flag, at Sonomo, near San Francisco. Since 1824 when California had become a province of Mexico, there had been frequent disturbances for separation, secularization of church lands, and general discontent with the Mexican government. In the period from 1835 to 1840 the missions had been secularized, but three Mexican governors were driven from the state. On July 7 **John Drake Sloat** (July 26, 1781–Nov. 28, 1867), commander of the U.S. Pacific naval squadron, who had occupied Monterey and Yerba Buena [San Francisco], declared California a territory of the U.S.

1846 Aug. 13   **Antonio López de Santa Ana** [Anna] returned to Mexico from exile in Cuba. Prior to his return Santa Ana had agreed with American agents of Polk that he would end the war and negotiate with the U.S., but the temper of the Mexican people barred such an action. Santa Ana went immediately to San Luis Potosí in central Mexico to raise an army.

1846 Sept. 25   After a three-day **battle Monterrey** [Monterey], in the Mexican State of Nuevo Leon,

was captured during the **Mexican War** by a U.S. army led by **Zachary Taylor**. The Mexicans, under **Pedro de Ampudia**, fought well but was forced to surrender to superior arms, particularly artillery.

1846 Oct. 11–1847 May 21   Alexander W. Doniphan (July 9, 1808–Aug. 8, 1887), in command of the **Missouri Mounted Volunteers**, led his troops from Santa Fe, in present New Mexico, which had just been taken by U.S. forces, through El Paso del Norte, Chihuahua City, Parras, and Saltillo, a distance of more than 3,500 miles. His army successfully fought Mexican armies along the way. The largest battle was fought at **Hacienda Sacramento** on Feb. 28, 1847, against a numerically superior force of entrenched troops, which were defeated.

1846 Dec. 6   Stephen Watts Kearny (Aug. 30, 1794–Oct. 31, 1848), leading a U.S. army, which had marched from Independence, Missouri, by way of Santa Fe, was halted and suffered heavy losses in a **battle at San Pasqual** [Pascual], near San Diego, in present southern California. Kearny held the field with his exhausted and depleted army, but when a relief force sent by **Robert Field Stockton** (Aug. 20, 1795–Oct. 7, 1866) from San Diego arrived, he resumed his march to that city. On Dec. 12 Kearny, led by the American scout and frontiersman **Kit Carson**, who had joined Kearny just before the battle, reached San Diego, where they gave what help they could to Stockton on his march to Los Angeles. On Jan. 8, 1847, Kearny and Stockton defeated Mexican forces at **San Gabriel**, near present Los Angeles, in the last major battle in California during the Mexican War (1846–1848).

1846 Dec. 28   Iowa was the 29th state to join the U.S. It was admitted as a free state.

1847   Faustin Élie Soulouque (c.1785–Aug. 6, 1867), a black military leader, was named president of **Haiti**. He had been chosen by mulattos who expected he would be an easy candidate for the figurehead position. However, in 1849 he declared himself **Emperor Faustin I**. Until his overthrow in 1859 Faustin ordered the executions of many mulattos, and tried unsuccessfully to invade the Dominican Republic.

1847 Mar. 9   Winfield Scott led an American army of c.10,000 onto the beaches south of Vera Cruz, Mexico. It was the **first large-scale amphibious operation in U.S. military history**. Two weeks later Scott began the siege of the city, which surrendered on Mar. 27. He then started (Apr. 8) with his army toward Mexico City. He defeated a Mexican army under **Santa Ana** at Cerro Gordo (Apr. 17–18), at Churubusco (Aug. 20), and at Chapultepec (Sept. 13). Scott entered **Mexico City** on Sept. 13 and 14.

1847 Aug. 26 **Liberia** was proclaimed an independent republic under a constitution resembling that of the U.S. and drafted at Harvard University. **Joseph Jenkins Roberts** (Mar. 15, 1809–Feb. 24, 1876), since 1841 governor of the American Colonization Society in Liberia, was named president (1848–1856) of the **first republic of black Africa**.

1847 Oct. 2 The **Sonderbund War** broke out in Switzerland as a result of political and religious differences between the Liberal cantons and the Sonderbund League, formed by seven conservative Catholic cantons in 1845. On Nov. 29 the war ended with the victory of the federal forces under the Liberal **Guillaume Henri Dufour** (1787–1875).

1848 **Algeria**, invaded by the French in 1830 but not completely conquered until 1847, was **declared part of France** and organized into the French departments of Algiers, Oran, and Constantine.

1848 Jan. 1 British forces occupied Greytown [San Juan del Norte] at the mouth of the San Juan River on Nicaragua's Mosquito Coast to forestall the tentative U.S. plan to construct a transisthmian canal at this point. On Oct. 16, 1849, British forces occupied Tigre Island on the Pacific coast of Honduras for the same reason. The island, a possession of Honduras, had been temporarily ceded to the U.S. for a base against British designs in the region. The **Clayton-Bulwer Treaty** in 1850 settled the transisthmian dispute.

1848 Feb. 2 By the **Treaty of Guadelupe Hidalgo**, a city in central Mexico, which ended the **Mexican War** (1846–1848), the U.S. was ceded Mexican territory that constitute the states of California, Nevada, Colorado, New Mexico, Utah, and Arizona. The southern border of Texas was set at the Rio Grande. Mexico was granted $15 million as compensation.

1848 Feb. 3 **Harry George Wakelyn Smith** (June 28, 1787–Oct. 12, 1860), the British governor (1847–1852) of the Cape of Good Hope Colony [Cape Province], proclaimed the **Orange River Sovereignty** a

British territory, following the annexation of British Kaffraria in 1847. Bringing these areas under British control was an attempt to force peace upon the Boers and the natives in South Africa's hinterland. In an attempt to create independent states, a **Boer uprising** against the British led by **Andries Wilhelmus Jacobus Pretorius** (Nov. 27, 1798–July 23, 1853) was crushed by Smith at Boomplaats, in the Orange River region, on Aug. 29.

1848 Feb. 24 As the **February Revolution [Revolution of 1848]** broke out in France, **Louis-Philippe**, king of France, **abdicated**. Louis-Philippe had refused to consider such reforms as an extension of suffrage and laws against corrupt practices during elections. He made it illegal to hold any political meetings without permits; many took to holding banquets after which they discussed politics. When the government tried to ban a banquet in Paris in February, one of the most violent riots ever seen broke out. The **Second Republic** (1848–1852) was created by radical students and workers, and the middle class, who demanded liberal reform.

1848 Mar. 4 **Charles Albert** [Carlo Alberta] (Oct. 2, 1748–July 28, 1849), king of Sardinia [including Piedmont and Savoy] (from 1831), granted a constitution for limited parliamentary government to his people. On Mar. 23 he declared war on the Austrian forces occupying the richest and most populous regions of Italy. After the Piedmontese defeat by the Austrians at Novara, a Sardinian city west of Milan in northern Italy, on Mar. 23, 1849, Charles Albert abdicated (Mar. 26) in favor of his son **Victor Emmanuel II** (Mar. 14, 1820–Jan. 9, 1878; ruled 1849–1861), the future king of Italy (Mar. 17, 1861), who retained the liberal constitution. The defeat at Novara signaled the defeat of the revolutionary reform movement in northern Italy and the reimposition of dictatorial Austrian rule there.

1848 May 29 **Wisconsin** was the 30th state to join the U.S. It was admitted as a free state.

1848 June 3 A treaty with New Grenada [now Colombia] allowing **travel rights across the isthmus of Panama** [then part of New Grenada] in exchange for a guarantee that the area's neutrality would be upheld, was approved by the U.S. Senate.

1848 June 23–26 The **June Insurrection** in Paris by mostly unemployed workers was brutally suppressed by **Louis Eugène Cavaignac** (Sept. 15, 1802–Sept. 23, 1857), the minister of war in the **Second Republic** (1848–1852). It was decreed that single unemployed men from 17 to 25 be conscripted into the army while other unemployed or striking workers be transported to labor in the countryside. The loss of life was heavy on both sides, and the repression perhaps the worst Paris had ever seen.

1848 July 19 At the **first women's rights convention**, held in Seneca Falls, New York, **Elizabeth Cady Stanton** (Nov. 12, 1815–Oct. 26, 1902), **Lucretia Mott** (Jan. 3, 1793–Nov. 11, 1880), and others drew up the first declaration of the rights of women in the U.S., proposing that women be allowed to vote.

1848 Aug. 12 The **Viennese Revolution** was suppressed by Austrian troops. Inspired by events of the February Revolution in Paris, students and workers had begun (Mar. 12) to demonstrate in Vienna. Metternich immediately resigned (Mar. 13) as minister of foreign affairs, and the ineffectual **Ferdinand I** (Apr. 19, 1793–June 29, 1875) who, trying to preempt liberal reform and deflate the radical elements dominating events in Vienna, had promulgated (Apr. 25) a reform constitution guaranteeing responsible government, was **forced to abdicate as emperor** (from 1835) on Dec. 2 after the forces of reaction had regained control toward the end of the year. His nephew, **Francis Joseph I** [Franz Josef], succeeded as the Hapsburg emperor of Austria. The new Austrian constitution was now repudiated. **Lajos** [Louis] **Kossuth** (Sept. 19, 1802–Mar. 20, 1894), the Hungarian nationalist leader, continued to resist Austria's efforts to join all Hapsburg principalities under its own monarch.

1848 Aug. 26 The **Peace of Malmö** concluded a war between Germany and Denmark. Fighting had broken out in April over the duchies of Schleswig-Holstein [south of Denmark proper], which Denmark wanted to annex. The Danish army moved into the two duchies when they rebelled. The Prussians drove out the Danes, who tried again in 1849, upon which the Germans abandoned the area to the Danes.

1848 Sept. 11 **Josip Jelačić od Bužima** (1801–1859), a Croatian general, led an **invasion into Hungary** on behalf of Austria against the separatist Magyar revolutionary movement, whose goals were to declare independence from Austrian rule and to withdraw from union with Croatia. **Lajos Kossuth** led the Hun-

garian uprising. Jelačić took Buda on Jan. 5, 1849, but Pest, across the Danube River, remained the capital of the insurrectionists.

1848 Dec. 10 France elected as president of the **Second Republic** (1848–1852) **Louis-Napoléon Bonaparte** [Charles Louis Napoléon Bonaparte; also: Carbonaro or Napoléon le Petit], nephew of Napoléon Bonaparte. His election was the result of the magic of the Napoléon name, and of his campaign promises to support the working man and to work for law and order and financial prosperity.

1849 The U.S. Congress granted territorial status to **Minnesota**. Under terms of the **Missouri Compromise** (1820) it was organized as free territory: Slavery was not permitted there.

1849 **Harriet Tubman** (1821?–Mar. 10, 1913), a field hand on a plantation in eastern Maryland, escaped from her master to freedom in Philadelphia. She soon became a hero in the **Underground Railroad**, a network of abolitionists who took escaping slaves from one hiding place to the next. Approximately 75,000 slaves found their freedom in the northern U.S. or Canada in this way.

1849 Apr. The Parliament buildings at Montreal, capital of Canada (1844–1849), were destroyed by fire in riots conducted by Tories in Montreal against passage of the **Rebellion Losses Bill**, which they considered to be outright payment and reward to insurrectionists. The bill, meant to reimburse losses incurred during the **Rebellion of 1837**, had been passed by the Canadian legislature and, though petitioned by its opponents, **James Bruce**, earl Elgin, the governor general of Canada, signed the bill.

1849 Jan. 14 British forces won a **battle at Chilianwala**, near the Jhelum River in the Punjab of present Pakistan, during the **Second Sikh War** (1848–1849), but they suffered such heavy casualties that they had to wait for reinforcements before at last defeating the Sikhs in a **battle at Gujrat**, also in the present Pakistani Punjab, on Feb. 22.

1849 Mar. 5 **Zachary Taylor** of the Whig party was inaugurated as the 12th president of the U.S., having defeated **Lewis Cass** (Oct. 9, 1782–June 17, 1866) of the Democratic party. **Millard Fillmore** served as vice president.

1849 Mar. 27 The **German National Assembly** [Frankfurt National Assembly] adopted a German constitution, having convened at Frankfurt on May 18, 1848, to draft the document. On Mar. 19, 1848, troops had been recalled from Berlin where they were sent to suppress revolutionary demonstrations, which had begun six days earlier. On Mar. 21 **Frederick William IV**, king of Prussia, had declared his support for a unified German state, into which, he declared, he would merge Prussia. The **German Confederation** (1815–1866) at this time consisted of more than 30 kingdoms, four republics, and many duchies and principalities. Most Germans appeared to want to combine into one nation, and the national assembly at Frankfurt was one of several attempts to accomplish this. The anti-democratic rulers of Prussia, Austria, and others supported counter-revolutionary activities throughout the confederation and caused the failure of the assembly.

1849 Apr. 14 The **Hungarian diet** declared an independent state and called for the removal of the Hapsburg emperor of Austria, who was also king of Hungary. **Lajos Kossuth** was chosen governor. This national development was Hungary's response to a **new Austrian constitution**, which had replaced the liberal constitution of Apr. 25, 1848, and was signed at Olomouc [Olmütz] on Mar. 4, 1849. It established a strong, centralized Austrian government, and made Transylvania and Croatia separate Austrian provinces; granted special status to Hungarian Serbs; and denied all independent Hungarian institutions.

1849 June 5 The **national assembly of Denmark** adopted its constitution. **Frederick VII** (Oct. 6, 1808– Nov. 15, 1863), king of Denmark (from 1848), had announced (Mar. 21, 1848) plans for a representative government. The **Rigsdag** was bicameral, one chamber was elected directly and the other by indirect vote.

1849 Aug. 11 The **Hungarian revolution** against Austria failed with **Lajos Kossuth's** resignation as its leader after the defeat (Aug. 9) of the insurgents at Temesvár [Timişoara], in present western Romania, by the Russians under **Ivan Feodorovich Paskevich** (May 19, 1782–Feb. 1, 1856). **Arthur von Görgey** [Görgei] (Jan. 30, 1818–May 20, 1916) succeeded Kossuth, who fled to the Ottoman Empire (1326– 1920) and later to the U.S. and England. Görgey surrendered (Aug. 13) to the Russians at Világos, in present eastern Hungary, and was interned by the Austrians for nearly 20 years.

V. ECONOMY AND TRADE

1846 **Wheat and potato crops failed in France**, leading to a general economic slump and in 1847 and helping to cause the political upheavals of 1848.

1847 The **Ten Hours Act** was passed by the British Parliament at the urging of **Anthony Ashley Cooper** (Apr. 28, 1801–Oct. 1, 1885), earl of Shaftesbury. The Act limited to ten hours the amount of time an industrial worker could spend at his machine each day.

1847 June 8 The **Factory Act** in the U.S. limited the workday to ten hours for women and children between the ages of 13 and 18.

1848 *The Communist Manifesto* [*Workers' Declaration of Independence*], written by the German socialist economist and philosopher **Karl** [Heinrich] **Marx** and his colleague **Friedrich Engels** (Sept. 28, 1820–1895), in German, was published in London on the eve of the **Revolutions of 1848**. A French translation appeared in Paris in June, just before the savage street fighting there. In 1850, in London, there appeared the first English translation. It stated that history was a record of a class struggle between the exploited [proletariat] and the exploiters [bourgeoisie], and that the time had been reached in the evolution of history when the proletariat would destroy class distinctions and private property. *Das Kapital* (1867–1885), by Marx and Engels, formed with the *Manifesto* the ideological and intellectual basis for numerous socialist and communist movements.

1848 **France ended slavery** in all her possessions.

1848 Several New York newspapers banded together to form the **New York Associated Press**, the **first news wire service**, in order to exchange information between newspapers in different cities.

1848 **William Haldane** opened the first **U.S. furniture factory** at Grand Rapids, Michigan, called the "furniture capital of the world." Designers from the Netherlands, Sweden, and Switzerland helped to establish the reputation of the factory.

1848 June 23 During the **June Insurrection**, the unemployed in Paris rioted in the streets. They had grown to more than 100,000 workers, but they frightened the bourgeoisie, who now controlled the parliament, and so gave impetus to the growing split between workers and the middle class in France.

1849 Harrods, Limited, the famous department store, opened in London.

1849 Aug. 12 Albert [Abraham Alphonse] **Gallatin** (b. Jan. 29, 1761) died. Swiss-born, Gallatin emigrated (1780) to the U.S. and was successively a merchant, professor of French at Harvard, land speculator, and U.S. Senator. He was unseated from the Senate because he lacked the required nine years as a U.S. citizen. Elected (1795) to the House of Representatives, he soon established the Finance Committee, predecessor of the Ways and Means Committee, and was appointed (1801) secretary of the treasury by Jefferson. His report (Apr. 4, 1808) on the condition of transportation in the U.S. led to great improvements in canals, roads, and water systems. After retirement from politics he became president of the National Bank [Gallatin Bank], founded the American Ethnological Society, and was president of the New York Historical Society. He wrote *Considerations on the Currency and Banking System of the United States (1831)* and other works.

VI. RELIGION AND PHILOSOPHY

1845 May Representatives of all the southern conferences of the **Methodist Episcopal Church** met in Louisville, Kentucky, to organize the separate Methodist Episcopal Church, South. The schism was the result of a vote at the **General Conference of 1844** in which a motion to suspend a slaveholding bishop **James O. Andrews** (1794–1871) was passed by a clear majority.

1845 May The **General Baptist Convention** became divided over the issue of slavery. The southerners "seceded" to form their own Southern Baptist Convention. From this point onward there was to be a Northern [now American] and a Southern Baptist convention.

1845 Oct. 9 John Henry Newman (Feb. 21, 1801–Aug. 11, 1890), a prominent English High Churchman, was received into the Roman Catholic Church at Rome. As an Anglican he had preached his last sermon in England in Sept., 1843. In Oct., 1846, he was ordained a priest in Rome. He returned (1847) to England as an **Oratorian** and established that order's chief home in England at Edgbaston near Birmingham, where he settled. On Mar. 12, 1879, he

was made a cardinal at age 78 by **Pope Leo XIII** (Mar. 2, 1810–July 20, 1903; ruled from 1878).

c.1847 Qurrat al-'Aynin Qazwin, a poet and gifted follower of the charismatic founder of a Persian sect known as the **Bab** [Ali Muhammad of Shiraz], put into effect his liberalization of the restrictive Islamic rules concerning women by removing her veil and preaching in public. She was one of the most successful Babi missionaries. In 1852 she was strangled in a persecution of the Babis that followed an accusation that the heretical sect planned to assassinate the shah.

1847 The publication of *Christian Nurture* by **Horace Bushnell** (Apr. 14, 1802–Feb. 17, 1876), a Hartford [Connecticut] Congregational minister, marked the beginning of the modern interest in methods of religious education for children. Bushnell attacked the revivalistic approach to conversion and urged instead the fostering of religious development under appropriate influences.

1847 At Oneida, New York, **John Humphrey Noyes** (Sept. 8, 1811–Apr. 13, 1886) founded a utopian religious community called **Bible Communists** or Perfectionists. The Oneida Community shared the income brought in by the manufacture of items, including silver plate. The community's marriage arrangements, which its members denied were free love, caused suspicion in the surrounding neighborhood, and Noyes fled (1879) to Canada. The community nevertheless thrived, especially after it abandoned its social principles, becoming (1881) a joint-stock enterprise.

1847 The **first secular vegetarian organization** was formed at Manchester, England. Today the **International Vegetarian Union** (1908), has more than 30 affiliated national societies.

1847 The **dispute between Greek Orthodox and Roman Catholic ecclesiastics in Palestine** broke out afresh at the Church of the Nativity in Bethlehem. The rival churches were competing over the right to mark the birthplace of Jesus Christ with a star.

1847 Brigham Young and more than 5,000 Mormons who had migrated with him to the area along the shores of the Great Salt Lake founded **Salt Lake City**, in present Utah, which still is the Mormon headquarters. They had left hostile Nauvoo, Illinois, in 1846, and had spent most of 1847 in choosing a place with irrigable land to settle.

1848 The failure of the liberal revolutions in Europe during this year persuaded many of the best-educated **Jews**, especially of the Reform branch, to **migrate to the U.S.** In 1842 Congregation Har Sinai of Baltimore had been founded. In 1845 Congregation Emanu-el had been established in New York City, and in 1860 Temple Sinai of Chicago was founded.

VII. SCIENCE, EDUCATION AND TECHNOLOGY

1845 **George Bancroft** (Oct. 3, 1800–Jan. 17, 1891), secretary of the navy, opened the **U.S. Naval School at Annapolis**, Maryland, for the training of young men as navy and marine officers.

1846 **Henry Creswicke Rawlinson** (Apr., 1810–Mar. 5, 1895) completed **decipherment of cuneiform inscriptions** found on the monument of Darius I Hystaspis the Great (558?–486 B.C.), king of Persia (521–486 B.C.), found at Behistun [Bisitun], in present western Iran, while he was the British consul at Baghdad. He was aided by the English photographic pioneer **William Henry Fox Talbot** (Feb. 11, 1800–Sept. 17, 1877).

1846 The planet **Neptune** was first observed by **Johann Gottfried Galle** (June 9, 1812–July 10, 1910), a German astronomer. The planet's location had been estimated by others, among them **Urbain Jean Joseph Le Verrier** (Mar. 11, 1811–Sept. 23, 1877), a French astronomer, who had noted the erratic orbit of Uranus and predicted it was caused by another planet still farther from the sun.

1846 **Ascanio Sobrero** (Oct. 12, 1812–May 26, 1888), an Italian chemist, discovered **nitroglycerine**, the colorless liquid that exploded when heated or jarred.

1846 **Walter Hunt** (1796–1859) of New York City was the first to patent a design for the **safety pin**.

1846 **Norbert Rillieux** (1806–1894), a freed slave in New Orleans, invented the **vacuum pan** for use in the refining process, which revolutionized the world's sugar industry.

1846 The **rotary printing press** was invented by **Richard March Hoe** (Sept. 12, 1812–June 7, 1886), brother of **Robert Hoe** (1784–1833), who founded R. Hoe and Company. in the U.S. to manufacture printing presses. Capable of printing 8,000 newspapers in an hour, the first of these machines was installed (1847) in the offices of the Philadelphia *Public Ledger*.

1846 Mar. 17 **Friedrich Wilhelm Bessel** (b. July 22, 1784), a German astronomer, died. By 1818 he had catalogued the positions of more than 50,000 stars, which led to the **first accurate determination of the distances between stars**. He described (1824) the Bessel functions, used in physics and astronomy, and he was the first to determine (1838) the parallax of a star other than the sun.

1846 Aug. 10 The **Smithsonian Institution** was established by an act of the U.S. Congress according to a bequest of **James** [Lewis Macie] **Smithson** (1765–June 27, 1829), an English minerologist, who donated his fortune for the purpose of bettering knowledge and to exchange information among people.

1846 Sept. 10 **Elias Howe** (July 9, 1819–Oct. 3, 1867), an American inventor, received a patent for his practical **sewing machine**. The first workable sewing machine was invented and patented by **Thomas Saint** in England during 1790.

1846 Oct. 16 **William Thomas Green Morton** (Aug. 9, 1819–June 15, 1868), an American dentist and physician, demonstrated the use of ether as a **general anesthetic** at Massachusetts General Hospital. An earlier demonstration (1842) by **Crawford Williamson Long** (June 16, 1815–Nov. 1, 1878), an American physician, had shown its usefulness during an operation. **Ether** was soon replaced by **chloroform**, after its discovery (Nov., 1847) in Edinburgh by **James Young Simpson** (June 7, 1811–May 1, 1870), a Scottish obstetrician.

1847 The **Portland Vase**, apparently produced in the first century B.C., was irreparably broken by an apparently deranged man in the **British Museum** in London, where it had been loaned by the duke of Portland. It had been found in a marble sarcophagus at Monte de Grano near Rome in the early 1600s.

1847 **Frederick Douglass** [Frederick Augustus Washington Bailey] (Feb., 1817–Feb. 20, 1895) founded the abolitionist journal *The North Star* in Rochester, New York, nine years after his escape from slavery. It lasted until 1864. Douglass advocated **peaceful political means of ending slavery.** Douglass later went to Washington, D.C., where he worked on various government agencies and later became the U.S. minister to Haiti (1889–1891).

1847 Feb. 4 René Joachim Henri Dutrochet (b. Nov. 14, 1776), a French physiologist and physician, died. In 1824 he had formulated an **elementary version of the cell theory.** In 1826 he gave his first explanation of osmosis, which he fully described in 1831. But perhaps his most important discovery was made (1837) when he demonstrated that the assimilation of carbon dioxide in plants could only occur in cells containing chlorophyll.

1847 July 23 Hermann von Helmholtz, a German scientist, before the Physical Society of Berlin, set forth the **theory of the conservation of energy,** or the first law of thermodynamics, which had already been advanced, at least in part, by others.

1848 Passage of the **Public Health Act** in England empowered local administrations to create "public walks," or open spaces for public recreational use, to provide a means of exercise for the common people.

1848 Aug. 7 Jons Jakob Berzelius (b. Aug. 30, 1779), a Swedish chemist and one of the founders of modern chemistry, died. He was noted especially for the **development** (1813) **of the symbols used in chemical notation.** His calculation of atomic weights and proportions were published in a table in 1818 (revised 1826). He isolated the elements cerium (1803), selenium (1817), silicon (1823), zirconium (1824), titanium (1825), and thorium (1828).

1849 The **speed of light** was measured for the first time with reasonable accuracy by **Armand Hippolyte Louis Frizeau** (Sept. 23, 1819–Sept. 18, 1896), a French physicist, by using the interruption of light beams several miles long traveling to and from a mirror. Frizeau had also observed the characteristics of light originating from a moving source, known as the Doppler-Frizeau effect, now just the **Doppler effect.**

1849 John Snow (Mar. 15, 1813–June 16, 1858), an English physician, **traced a London cholera outbreak** to its source at a Broad Street well that had been contaminated by nearby privies. When the pump's handle was removed, the epidemic began to subside.

1849 Austen Henry Layard (Mar. 5, 1817–July 5, 1894), an English archaeologist, **found at the ruined city of Nineveh** the palace of **Sennacherib,** king of Assyria (c.705–c.680 B.C.). Layard also found the library of **Ashurbanipal,** king of Assyria (c.668–c.639 B.C.), and brought back to England some cuneiform tablets from Ashurbanipal's collection of more than 20,000 tablets on all subjects, including letters, gathered from throughout Mesopotamia and copied by scribes.

1849 Mar. 24 Johann Wolfgang Döbereiner (b. Dec. 13, 1780), a German chemist, died. Before 1829 he had recognized the relationship between properties of elements and their atomic weights, the basis for establishing the **periodic table and the periodic law.**

VIII. ARTS AND LEISURE

1845 The first volume of *Histoire du Canada* by **François Xavier Garneau** (June 15, 1809–Feb. 3, 1866) was published. It was the first major work of French-Canadian literature.

1845 Eugène Emmanuel Viollet-le-Duc (Jan. 27, 1814–Sept. 17, 1879), a leading architect of the French gothic revival, began an extensive restoration (completed in 1864) of the **Notre Dame Cathedral** in Paris.

1845 May 3 Thomas Hood (b. May 23, 1799), an English poet, died. He wrote both humorous and serious poetry. *Song of the Shirt* (1843), about factory conditions, and *Bridge of Sighs* (1844) were his two best-known serious poems.

1845 May 12 August Wilhelm von Schlegel (b. Sept. 8, 1767), a German critic and translator, died. With his younger brother Friedrich (Mar. 10, 1772–Jan. 12, 1879), he founded the *Athenaeum,* a journal for romantic writers in Germany. August Wilhelm worked with **Madame de Staël,** whose *Corinne* was translated by Friedrich's wife Dorothea [nee Mendelssohn] (1763–1839) in 1807.

1845 July 12 Henrik Arnold Wergeland (b. June 17, 1808), a Norwegian romantic poet and prose writer, died. Wergeland was an important spokesman for a national Norwegian literature, in opposition to the strong cultural influence of Denmark. His best-known work was the dramatic poem *Skabelsen,*

Mennesket og Messias [*The Creation, Man and Messiah*] (1830).

1847 Emily Jane Brontë (July 30, 1818–Dec. 19, 1848), an English writer, completed her only novel *Wuthering Heights,* the dramatic tale of embittered love. In the same year her sister **Charlotte** (Apr. 21, 1816–Mar. 31, 1855), published the equally famous *Jane Eyre.*

1847 May 14 Fanny Cäcilia Hensel [nee Mendelssohn-Bartholdy] (b. Nov. 14, 1805), sister of Felix Mendelssohn and composer in her own right, died. Four books of songs and a collection of part-songs were attributed to her.

1847 Nov. 4 Felix Mendelssohn [Jakob Ludwig Felix Mendelssohn-Bartholdy] (b. Feb. 3, 1809), a German composer, died. *Midsummer Night's Dream* (1826) was Mendelssohn's first important work. His symphonies included the *Reformation* (1830–1832), the *Scottish* (1830–1842), and the *Italian* (1833). A famous overture was the *Hebrides Overture* [Fingal's Cave] (1830–1832). *St. Paul* (1836) and *Elijah* (1846) were oratorios. Mendelssohn also wrote the Violin Concerto in E Minor (1844), organ sonatas, chamber music, choral music, and songs.

1848 The Pre-Raphaelite Brotherhood was founded by **Dante Gabriel Rossetti** [Gabriel Charles Dante] (May 12, 1828–Apr. 10, 1882), an English painter and poet. The motto of the Pre-Raphaelites was "True to Nature," and their chief aim was to reproduce nature as observed for the first time, a reaction against what they considered to be a "derivative" element in art and poetry since Raphael, an early 16th century painter. The painting *Ecce Ancilla Domini* (1850) by Rossetti was a well-known example of the Pre-Raphaelite style. Others associated with the movement included **William Morris**, **John Everett Millais**, and **John Ruskin**.

1848 Thyagaraja (b. 1760), an ascetic and religious mystic in India, died. He composed c.2,000 religious songs, which have preserved much folksong material. He also wrote three **operas in the Telugu language**, a Dravidian language of southern India. Other composers of the time were **Ksetrayya**, **Mutthuswamy Dikshitar** (1775–1835), and **Shyama Sastri** (1763–1827) who, together with Thyagaraja, made Telugu a language noted for its literary capabilities.

1848 Khachatur Abovian (b. 1810?), by some considered the "father of the modern Armenian intelligentsia," died. His most important work *The Wounds of Armenia* was published posthumously.

1848 Feb. 11 Thomas Cole (b. Feb. 1, 1801), a romantic landscape painter and founder of the Hudson River School in the U.S., died. **Asher B. Durand** (Aug. 21, 1796–Sept. 17, 1886) and **John Trumbull** (June 6, 1756–Nov. 10, 1843) discovered Cole's work in a New York City shop, and the three became lifelong friends, painting the lush scenery of the Hudson River Valley.

1848 Apr. 8 Gaetano Donizetti (b. Nov. 29, 1797), an Italian operatic composer, died. Donizetti's more than 60 operas included *L'Elisir d'Amore* (1832), *Lucrezia Borgia* (1833), *Lucia di Lammermoor* (1835), *La Fille du Regiment* (1840), and *La Favorita* (1840).

1848 Nov. 2 Esaias Tegnér (b. Nov. 13, 1782), a Swedish poet and churchman, died. He was noted especially for *Frithiofs Saga* (1825), a modern version of a traditional Swedish tale. **Henry Wadsworth Longfellow** translated Tegnér's *Nattuardsbarnen* (1820) as *The Children of the Lord's Supper* (1842).

1849 Hokusai [Hokusai Katsushika] (b. 1760), a Japanese artist, painter, and wood engraver, died. He illustrated books and taught drawing. His technical skill was unrivaled. His best-known works included *Ducks in a Stream; Mangwa, or Ten Thousand Sketches* (15 vols., 1836); and *Hundred Views of Mount Fuji* (1835), considered his finest work.

1849 The Petrashevsky circle, a group of revolutionary Russian thinkers and writers, were arrested by the reactionary government of **Nicholas I**, tried, and sent to Siberia. **Fëdor Mikhailovich Dostoevski**, the Russian novelist, was arrested on Apr. 29 and sentenced to death for participating in this circle, but his sentence was changed to penal servitude in Siberia at Omsk, from which he was released in 1854.

1849 Sept. 25 Johann Strauss (b. Mar. 14, 1804), an Austrian composer, died. He was known for his waltzes, of which he composed c.150. He organized (1826) his own orchestra, which toured the world and which his son Johann Strauss continued to lead after his death.

1849 Oct. 7 **Edgar Allan Poe** (b. Jan. 18, 1809), an American poet and short story writer, died. Enormously influential, he is credited now with **inventing the detective story.** Among his best-known stories were "**The Gold Bug**" (1843) and "**Fall of the House of Usher**" (1840). His best-known poems were "**The Raven**" (1845), "**The Bells**" (1847–1849), and "**Annabel Lee**" (1849).

1849 Oct. 17 **Frédéric François Chopin** (b. Mar. 1, 1810), a French-Polish composer and piano virtuoso, died of tuberculosis. Chopin advanced the use of the piano as a solo instrument. For the piano Chopin wrote the concertos in E Minor (1830) and F Minor (1829) and the sonatas in B Flat Minor (1840) and B Minor, Opus 35 [**Funeral March**]. He also wrote many etudes, preludes, nocturnes, impromptus, scherzos, and songs.

IX. SPORTS, GAMES, AND SOCIETY

1845 **Alexander Cartwright,** a New York sportsman, wrote a set of rules for the evolving game of **baseball.** Each team had nine men and the bases were set 90 feet apart. The Knickerbocker Base Ball Club of New York formed this year and adopted Cartwright's rules.

1846 June 19 In the **first baseball game of record** played under Alexander Cartwright's rules, the "New Yorks" defeated the Knickerbockers by 23 to 1. They played on the Elysian Fields, a recreational park in Hoboken, New Jersey.

1848 The introduction of the longer-driving gutta-percha **golf ball ended the feather-ball era** in golf. This ball was made solid of a single lump of gutta-percha and hand-molded by rolling the material on a flat board.

1849 May 5 **Hambletonian,** a colt destined to become the peerless sire of American harness horses, was foaled at Chester, New York. Bought cheaply by a hired hand **William Rysdyk** from the farm's owner **Jonas Seeley,** Hambletonian never raced, yet sired 1,331 foals in the period from 1851 to 1875. Virtually every American harness horse today traces directly back to this stallion.

1849 May 10 The **Astor Place Riot** occurred outside the Astor Opera House in New York City where an English actor, **William Charles Macready** (Sept. 3, 1793–Apr. 27, 1873), was performing. The feud between Macready and **Edwin Forrest** (Mar. 9, 1808–Dec. 12, 1872), an American actor who had recently performed in London, achieved riot proportions when the crowd of Forrest's supporters began to throw stones. Twenty people were killed when troops fired to disperse the mob.

1850–1854

I. VITAL STATISTICS AND DEMOGRAPHICS

1850 The **world population** was an estimated 1,200,000,000. **Europe** had c.265 million, **Asia** c.795 million, **Africa** c.81 million, the **Americas** c.59 million, **Australia** c.600,000, and the rest of the world less than a million.

1850 An Asiatic **cholera epidemic** moved through the Midwest of the U.S. after having struck the South the previous year. It appeared first in Marseille, France, then progessed through Europe, thence to New Orleans. There were no reliable estimates of fatalities.

1851 The official **population of the United Kingdom** was 27,511,862: England and Wales, 17,927,-609; Scotland, 2,888,742; and Ireland, 6,552,385.

II. DISASTERS

1850 June 2 Property worth several million dollars was destroyed in San Francisco, California, by a series of **fires.**

1850 June 17 On Lake Erie the ship *Griffith* caught **fire** and burned, killing c.300.

1852 The course of the **Yellow River** [Huang Ho, Huang He] in China was altered by catastrophic flooding. The river now entered the Yellow Sea at the Gulf of Chihli [Pohai] instead of hundreds of miles to the south.

1853 A **yellow fever epidemic** in New Orleans, Louisiana, killed more than 5,000 persons during the next two years. A sixth of the population of nearby Vicksburg also succumbed.

1854 Sept. 27 The Collins liner **Arctic**, a U.S. mail steamer, **collided with** the French steamer **Vesta** in a heavy fog c.50 miles east of Newfoundland. The loss of more than 350 people led to establishment of separate eastbound and westbound steamer lanes across the Atlantic Ocean.

III. EXPLORATION AND COLONIZATION

1850–1854 Robert John Le Mesurier McClure (Jan. 28, 1807–Oct. 17, 1873), a British naval officer searching for the **John Franklin** expedition to the Arctic, found the long sought **Northwest Passage**. He came from the west along the northern coast of Canada, penetrated Prince of Wales Strait, and discovered, going overland by sledge, **Viscount Melville Sound**, which had been entered (1819–1829) from the east by Parry. McClure did not, however, sail through the sound, enter Barrow Strait, and reach Baffin Bay, thus losing the chance that he would be the first to traverse the entire Northwest Passage, a feat that would not be accomplished until 1903 to 1906 by **Roald Amundsen**.

1851 Edward Hammond Hargraves (Sept. 7, 1816–Dec. 1, 1891), a sheep rancher, found **gold** at Bathurst in New South Wales, and Sandhurst [Bendigo] in Victoria was founded as a gold mining town. The resulting gold rush spurred settlement, and over the next ten years, **Australia's population** nearly tripled as British, Germans, and Americans came in search of gold.

1853 Russia formally claimed **Sakhalin Island** [Saghalien; Karafuto], near the Russian mainland north of Japan in the Okhotsk Sea.

IV. POLITICS AND WAR

1850–1864 The **Taiping Rebellion** was led by **Hung Hsiu-ch'üan** [T'ien Wang = Heavenly Prince; T'ai Ping = Great Peace], who believed he was God's second son. He organized a revolt of native Chinese against the Ch'ing [Manchu] emperor and overlords after failing a civil service exam for the third time. Hung espoused Christianity in his ideology and many followed him because of his system of communal land ownership, emphasis on equality of the sexes, and the aura of social revolution (the Chinese Communists claim him as a precursor to their movement). Twenty million peasants lost their lives before the rebellion was quelled by, among others, **Frederick Townsend Ward** (Nov. 29, 1831–Oct. 21, 1862), an American general and soldier of fortune leading a Manchu army, and was halted finally (1864) by **Charles George Gordon** [Chinese Gordon], a British general. Hung Hsiu-ch'üan (b. 1812) swallowed poison on July 19, 1864, upon hearing of the defeat.

1850–1853 The **Eighth Kaffir War** was fought in southeastern Cape of Good Hope Colony [Cape Province], in present South Africa, by the **Xhosa**, a Bantu tribe, and the British. The Xhosa, whose pastoral way of life was disturbed by British and Boer settlements and by continual (from 1776) warfare with British forces, committed (1857) a kind of mass suicide by destroying their corn and cattle.

1850 Apr. 19 The **Clayton-Bulwer Treaty** was signed by the U.S. and Great Britain. Negotiated by **John Middleton Clayton** (July 24, 1796–Nov. 9, 1856), the U.S. secretary of state, and **William Henry Lytton Earle Bulwer** (May 25, 1801–Jan. 18, 1872), a British statesman, the treaty affirmed that no nation was to control a proposed transisthmian canal in Central America or to dominate political affairs in Central American states.

1850 July 9 Zachary Taylor (b. Nov. 24, 1784), president of the U.S., died in office of cholera morbus, not a true cholera, but a form of gastroenteritis also called sporadic cholera. **Millard Fillmore** succeeded him (July 10) as president of the U.S., and no one held the office of vice president until 1853.

1850 Sept. The **Compromise of 1850**, a series of bills proposed by senators **Henry Clay** and **Stephen Arnold Douglas** (Apr. 23, 1813–June 3, 1861) to defuse public unrest about **slavery**, was passed by the Congress. California was to be admitted as a free state, the District of Columbia was given the option to prohibit slavery, and in the territories of New Mexico and Utah the question of slavery was to be settled by their inhabitants.

1850 Sept. 18 The **Fugitive Slave Law** was enacted by the U.S. Congress, requiring return to their owners of escaped slaves, without trial or personal testimony about their status.

1852 The **Oregon Territory** was organized to help protect the region's settlers from warring Indians. In 1853 the territory was divided to create the **Washington Territory**. In 1863 the **Idaho Territory** was organized from part of the Washington Territory.

1852 In present **Botswana**, the **Boers** of the Transvaal raided **Dimawe**, capital of the **Kwena tribe** that was ruled by **Sechele**, a Christian king. The Boers then sacked the nearby Livingstone mission at Kolobeng.

1852 **Al-Hajj Umar** [Omar] (1797–1864), the Tukulor [Toucouleur] leader of the **Muslim Tijaniyya brotherhood**, launched a holy war from Dinguiraye, in present Guinea, against the pagan Mandingo and Bambara kingdoms of the western Sudan.

1852 Jan. Provisional government in **Hungary**, enacted in 1848, was made permanent. Autonomy of local governments were cancelled under the reinstitution of Austrian rule. Croatia-Slavonia, which included the port of Fiume [Rijeka], was enlarged, while Transylvania and Serbian Voivodina were severed from Hungary.

1852 Jan. 17 Under the terms of the **Sand River Convention**, the British government recognized the independence of the **Boer Republic of the Transvaal**, in present northeastern South Africa. It was reorganized (Dec. 16, 1856) as the **South African Republic**, in order to unite its different factions under **Marthinus Wessels Pretorious** (Sept. 17, 1819–May 19, 1901), president (1857–1871).

1852 Feb. 3 During the **Great War** (1843–1852) the **siege of Montevideo**, the present capital of Uruguay, was lifted by a victory of the Argentine general **Justo José de Urquiza** (Mar. 19, 1800–Apr. 11, 1870) over **Juan Manuel de Rosas**, dictator of Argentina [from his power base of Buenos Aires province] allied with Manuel Oribe, exiled president of Uruguay. Rosas fled to England and never returned to Argentina.

1852 Apr. 1 The **Second Anglo-Burmese War** (1852) led to annexation of the province of Pegu by **James Andrew Broun Ramsay** (Apr. 22, 1812–Dec. 19, 1860), Lord Dalhousie, British governor general

of India. **Pagan Min**, king of Burma [Myanmar] (from 1846) was deposed (1853) and succeeded by his brother **Mindon Min** (1853–1878), who was supported by the British.

1852 Nov. 4 **Camillo Benso** (Aug. 10, 1810–June 6, 1861), **conte di Cavour**, was appointed prime minister of **Piedmont** by **Victor Emmanuel II**, king of Sardinia [including Piedmont and Savoy]. Cavour led a drive toward the unification of Italy, which meant wresting the northern Italian states from the military dictatorship of Austria.

1852 Dec. 2 Louis Napoléon, president of the French Republic, was crowned emperor as **Napoléon III** (deposed 1871). On Dec. 2, 1851, Louis Napoléon had proclaimed himself dictator after securing absolute power by a coup d'état.

1853 Mar. 4 **Franklin Pierce** (Nov. 23, 1804–Oct. 8, 1869) of the Democratic party was inaugurated as the 14th president of the U.S., having defeated **Winfield Scott** of the Whig party. **William Rufus DeVane** [Devane] **King** (b. Apr. 7, 1786) was sworn in as vice president, also on this day, but he died on Apr. 18 before actually taking office. There was no vice president of the U.S. until 1857.

1853 Oct. 23 A **Russo-Turkish War** broke out as Omer [Omar] Pasha [Michael Lattas] (1806–1871), a Croatian-born general, led a Turkish attack on Russian forces that had occupied (June 27) the Ottoman-controlled Danubian Principalities of Walachia, in present southern Romania, and Moldavia, in present eastern Romania and southwestern U.S.S.R. On Nov. 1, in return, Russia declared war on the Ottoman Empire (1326–1920).

1853 Dec. 30 The **Gadsden Purchase**, land that now is part of southern Arizona and New Mexico, was acquired by the U.S. from Mexico, completing the present boundary of the continental U.S. The purchase also allowed the U.S. to avoid paying damages to Mexico for the ravages of the border Indians whom the U.S. had agreed to control.

1854 Feb. 17 Under the terms of the **Bloemfontein Convention**, Great Britain granted independence to the **Boer Republic of the Orange Free State**, which drafted a constitution in April and elected **J.P. Hoffman** as its first president (1854–1855). Great Britain then completed withdrawal of troops from present inland South Africa and abandoned the treaties made with the natives north of the Orange River.

1854 Mar. 27   The **Crimean War** (1854–1856) broke out as France, in support of the Ottoman Empire in the Russo-Turkish conflict, declared war on Russia. Great Britain joined France on Mar. 28, and Sardinia [including Piedmont and Savoy] declared war on Russia on Jan. 26, 1855. In the meantime, Austria, in an ultimatum (June 3, 1854) to Russia secured Russia's withdrawal from the Danubian Principalities, which Austrian troops now occupied. Earlier, on Jan. 3, 1854, French and British fleets had entered the Black Sea to enforce an allied ultimatum (Feb. 27) demanding Russian withdrawal from Moldavia and Walachia. On Sept. 14 allied troops landed in the Crimea. In October the allied forces, having defeated (Sept. 20) the Russians in a **battle at the Alma River** in the central Crimea, began their siege of the Russian port of Sevastopol.

1854 Mar. 31   The **Treaty of Kanagawa** was signed by Japan and the U.S. after four American warships were sent in Aug. 1853 to Tokyo Bay under **Matthew Galbraith Perry** (Apr. 10, 1794–Mar. 4, 1858), a U.S. commodore. The treaty, which provided for diplomatic and trade relations, ended the Japanese policy of isolation from the outside world. Treaties soon followed with other major powers.

1854 May 24   On the birthday of Victoria, queen of the United Kingdom of Great Britain and Ireland, the first colonial Parliament of New Zealand convened. This day is now celebrated as **Empire Day**.

1854 May 30   The **Kansas-Nebraska Act** became law, establishing the territories of Kansas and Nebraska and invalidating the **Missouri Compromise of 1820**, which had prohibited slavery in any new territories organized in the U.S. The act allowed local citizens to choose whether the territories were to become slave or free states. In the aftermath there was in Kansas a race between proslavery and antislavery settlers, with people entering the territory just to be counted on one side or the other. Minor battles, murder, rapine, arson, and other crimes were so commonplace that what law existed was helpless; armed bands entered the fracas from neighboring slave and free states. It was known as "**Bloody Kansas.**"

1854 July 6   The **present Republican party** held its first convention in Jackson, Michigan. The added

support of abolitionists in opposition to the establishment of slavery in the territory of Kansas gained enough popular support to elect Republican **Abraham Lincoln** as president in 1860.

1854 Oct. 25   In a **battle at Balaklava** [Balaclava], near Sevastopol in the Crimea, during the **Crimean War** (1854–1856), there took place the event memorialized by **Alfred Tennyson** in the poem "**The Charge of the Light Brigade.**" During this Russian attack on the British supply depot at Balaklava, **James Thomas Brudenell** (Oct. 16, 1797–Mar. 28, 1868), earl of Cardigan, commanded a brigade numbering c.600 light cavalry against a well-defended Russian position. Orders from **Fitzroy James Henry Somerset** (Sept. 30, 1788–June 28, 1855), baron Raglan, the chief British commander, were confused, and Cardigan made a disastrous frontal attack on the Russians, who were withdrawing with captured British guns. Though Cardigan's men made a valiant stand, more than two-thirds were killed or wounded. Raglan's action was criticized; but he, in turn, held responsible **George Charles Bingham** (Apr. 16, 1800–Nov. 10, 1888), earl of Lucan, who led the heavy support brigade of cavalry that backed the light brigade's assault. Cardigan returned to England a hero.

1854 Nov. 5   The **battle at Inkerman**, near Sevastopol in the Crimea, was a decisive victory for Anglo-French forces during the **Crimean War** (1854–1856). To try to break the **siege of Sevastopol** the Russians launched a surprise dawn attack in the fog. Pierre Jean François Bosquet (Nov. 8, 1810–Feb. 6?, 1861), the French commander, arrived with reinforcements. After a loss of c.12,000 men the Russians were forced to withdraw into Sevastopol. The allies lost c.3,500 men.

V. ECONOMY AND TRADE

1850–1873   **Great Britain led world industrial production** by means of an advanced technology and a laissez-faire economy. Liberal politics and the middle classes dominated society. The abrupt change from a feudal-agricultural world to an industrial one had resulted in a population of exploited and socially disoriented laborers. Their plight was instrumental in the growth of trade unions and in the origins of socialism as a political and intellectual force. The U.S. and Germany soon rivaled Great Britain's abrupt transformation to an industrial economy. The economic results of the turmoil in Europe, famine in

India, and other disturbances, such as the American Civil War, caused a slump in production beginning in 1873.

c.1850 **James Young** (1811–1883), a Scottish chemist, found a method of **producing oil from cannel coal and shale**. This discovery created a Scottish shale oil industry that lasted until the mid-20th century.

c.1850 **Modern consumer credit** was initiated in Paris, where a photographer and clothes store owner named **Crépin** allowed his customers to pay in installments. In 1871 **G. Dufayel** bought the store from Crépin and expanded the establishment into a complete department store whose customers could make a down payment of one-fifth to one-half of their purchase and then pay off the balance in monthly installments.

1850 **Arab caravans** from the eastern coast of Africa had **established regular trade routes** into the interior. For the most part, this trade was controlled by the Indian moneylenders on the island of **Zanzibar**, who acquired large numbers of slaves and much ivory, as well as some copper.

1850 Mar. 2 **Rent banks** were established in Prussia, enabling peasants to buy the land they had been renting from their landlords. Peasants paid their rents into the rent banks, which then issued bonds in payment to the landlords. The interest generated from the money paid in this way was used for the purchase of a parcel of land.

1851 **The New York Times** began publication under **Henry Jarvis Raymond** (Jan. 24, 1820–June 18, 1869).

1851 The **Landlord and Tenant Act in Great Britain** was the first reform in land leasing practices which spelled out, if not tenant rights specifically, their right to ownership of improvements they had made themselves.

1851 **Cornelius Vanderbilt** (May 27, 1794–Jan. 4, 1877), an American financier, established a **route by steamship from New York City to California** via Nicaragua. At Nicaragua, the ship ascended the San Juan River to Lake Nicaragua, where a stage coach conveyed passengers to the Pacific. There they could travel again by steamship to California. This passage was much quicker than the transcontinental routes.

1851 The **Great Eastern**, an enormous iron steamship designed by **Isambard Kingdom Brunel**, became stuck on the Thames River during launching. It had paddle and screw engines as well as sails. Nearly 700 feet long and able to carry 4,000 passengers, the **Great Eastern** became famous by laying the **transatlantic cable**.

1851 The French established a trading port at Cotonou, in present **Benin**, as agreed in a treaty signed by France and **Gezo**, king of Dahomey (1818–1858).

1851 The St. Petersburg-Moscow railway line, the **first major railway link in Russia**, was opened.

1851 May 15 The **New York and Erie Railroad** opened its c.400 miles of track for service. At this time, it was the longest length of track in service, and later it became one of the first lines to reach into the American West.

1852 The **Bon Marché**, France's first department store, opened in Paris. A wide variety of goods were offered at a fixed price.

1852 France established a **convict settlement at Saint Laurent du Maroni**, at the mouth of the Maroni River in French Guiana. Slavery had been abolished in 1848, and it was hoped that the settlement would provide the labor necessary to exploit the timber of the region. However, most Europeans sent to French Guiana as prisoners died from tropical diseases and from the neglect of corrupt prison officials. **Devil's Island**, one of the *Îles du Salut*, which have the only deep water harbor near the capital city of **Cayenne**, was the most notorious of the prison settlements in French Guiana. They were phased out from 1938 to 1951.

1852 The highly speculative **Crédit Mobilier**, an investment bank, was founded in France to finance industrial enterprises. Over the next 15 years it provided funds for railroads in France, Hungary, Spain, and other countries and financed other ventures. The Crédit Mobilier was dissolved in 1867.

1853 Feb. 21 The **Coinage Act of 1853** decreased the amount of silver used in minting all U.S. silver coins except the dollar.

1854 Nov. 30 **Said Pasha** (1822–Jan. 18, 1863), viceroy of Egypt (from 1854), granted the concession for construction of the **Suez Canal** to **Ferdinand Marie de Lesseps** (Nov. 19, 1805–Dec. 7, 1894), a French engineer. Work began on Apr. 25, 1859, and the canal opened to traffic on Nov. 16, 1869.

VI. RELIGION AND PHILOSOPHY

1850 July 9   The **Bab** [Bab-el-Din = Gateway to Religion; Mirza 'Ali Mohammed ibn-Radhik] (b. 1819?), the leader of the controversial Muslim sect of Babism, was executed in the public square of Tabriz, Persia, by order of the vizier after a judgment of heresy pronounced by religious authorities. A rebellion by his followers resulted in as many as 20,000 deaths when they attempted to assassinate **Nasr-ed-Din** [Nasir-ad-Din] (July 17, 1831–May 1, 1896), the shah of Persia.

1850 Nov. 11   **Nicholas Patrick Stephen Wiseman**, an English Catholic bishop, educator, and papal diplomat, was named a cardinal by **Pope Pius IX** (May 13, 1792–Feb. 7, 1878; ruled from 1846). Wiseman returned to England to reestablish the Roman Catholic diocesan hierarchy there. He arrived in London amid a storm of public protest over "papal aggression," instigated by the pope's pronouncement renewing the system of hierarchy and hereditary titles. Wiseman's tactful *Appeal to the English People* (1850), calling on the accepted principle of religious toleration, helped to enable reason to prevail over the renewed old passions.

1851   **Samson Raphael Hirsch** (June 20, 1808–Dec. 31, 1888), the Jewish theologian regarded as the founder of the **New Orthodoxy**, became rabbi of the orthodox congregation in Frankfurt, after having been chief rabbi of Moravia and Austrian Silesia. He steered the New Orthodoxy away from both Reform and Positive-Historical Judaism.

1853   **Isaac Leeser** (Dec. 12, 1806–Feb. 1, 1868), a rabbi (from 1829) at several synagogues in Philadelphia, **published a translation of the Hebrew Bible**. Leeser's work remained the commonly approved English version in U.S. synagogues until the appearance of the Jewish Publication Society's new translation in 1917.

1854   **Isaac Mayer Wise** (Mar. 29, 1819–Mar. 26, 1900) became rabbi of the congregation Bnai Yeshurun of Cincinnati, which he served for 46 years. An immigrant in 1846, he came from Bohemia, where he had been a Reform activist.

1854   **Abraham Geiger** (May 24, 1810–Oct. 23, 1874) was instrumental in founding the *Judisch Theologisches Seminar* of Breslau, where he was rabbi of the community and leader of the Jewish Reform movement. Geiger and his intellectually rigorous fellow reformers aspired to deliver Judaism from what they saw as a lifeless orthodoxy.

1854 Dec. 8   **Pope Pius IX**, in his **Ineffabilis Deus**, defined the dogma of the **Immaculate Conception** thus: Mary, mother of Jesus Christ, "by a singular privilege and grace granted by God, was preserved free from all stain of original sin." Since then, the Immaculate Conception has been a necessary dogma of faith.

VII. SCIENCE, EDUCATION, AND TECHNOLOGY

1850   **Samuel Kier** (1813–1874) of Tarentum, Pennsylvania, became the **first oil refiner in the U.S.** when he and a chemist **J.C. Booth** (July 28, 1810–Mar. 21, 1888) developed a method for purifying the oil that had seeped into Kier's salt wells. Refined into kerosene, it was used in lamps.

1850   **Rudolf Julius Emanuel Clausius** (Jan. 2, 1822–Aug. 24, 1888), a German scientist, stated the **Second Law of Thermodynamics** as "Heat cannot flow from a colder to a hotter body." He introduced the concept of entropy in 1865, and later developed a kinetic theory of gases for which he developed a mathematical formula.

1850 May 9   **Joseph Louis Gay-Lussac** (b. Dec. 6, 1778), a French chemist and physicist, died. He began (1802) his career with studies of the thermal expansion of gases, and made measurements of the earth's magnetic density and the chemical composition of the atmosphere. On Dec. 31, 1808, he propounded **Gay-Lussac's law**, which fixed, or determined, the volume of gases in combination.

1850 July 16   The **Loi** [Law] **Tinguy** was passed by the French Assembly. It provided that the author of a news article was required to sign his name to his story. False signatures were penalized by fines, and both the reporter and his editor were held responsible. Intended to enforce accountability in news reporting, the regulation made it possible for reporters and writers to come to prominence.

1851 Work began on the **Hoosac Tunnel, the first important railroad tunnel in the U.S.** It was to go through the Hoosac Mountains of western Massachusetts for a distance of 4.75 miles. Nitroglycerine, a powerful new explosive, and the compressed air drill had their first practical use in America in this tunnel. The project was not completed until 1875. A shaft that was sunk down at about the mid-point of the tunnel was 1208 feet deep. The tunnel required use of 20 million bricks.

1851 **Elias Howe, inventor of the sewing machine**, received a patent for an "automatic, continuous clothing closure," forerunner of the modern **zipper**. In 1891 **Whitcomb L. Judson** was given two U.S. patents for "Clasp Locker or Unlocker for Shoes," which was an improvement of Howe's invention, but the marketing of it failed. In 1917 **Gideon Sundback** (Apr. 24, 1880–June 21, 1954) was granted a U.S. patent for a metal zipper, which proved successful on the market, especially after B.F. Goodrich Company, which originated the name "zipper," began marketing the zipper on galoshes in 1923.

1851 **Frederick Scott Archer** (1813–May 2, 1857), an English photographer and sculptor, invented the collodion, or wet plate, method of **photography**. A glass plate was coated with a silver iodide solution, exposed while still wet, and developed immediately. Archer's process dominated photography for 20 years.

1851 **Isaac Merrit Singer** (Oct. 27, 1811–July 23, 1875) patented a **sewing machine** and opened **I.M. Singer and Company**. A suit by **Elias Howe**, who had invented and patented the sewing machine, failed to deter Singer, whose commercial success facilitated payment of a judgment against him. By 1860 American plants were producing each year more than 100,-000 sewing machines, which were soon found throughout the world.

1851 **Alexander William Williamson** (May 1, 1824–May 6, 1904), an English chemist, set forth an early version of the **theory of valence**, which was later perfected by **Edward Frankland** (Jan. 18, 1825–Aug. 9, 1899), an English chemist, in 1852. Valence theory stated that the atoms of any element may combine with only a fixed number of other atoms of different elements; the number varies from element to element.

1851 **Jean Bernard Léon Foucault** (Sept. 18, 1819–Feb. 11, 1869), a French physicist, conducted his **pendulum experiments** which demonstrated that the earth rotates on its axis and led to the development of the gyroscope in 1852.

1851 July 10 **Louis Jacques Mandé Daguerre** (b. Nov. 18, 1789), a French inventor and painter, died. He began working with **Joseph Nicephore Niepce**, a French physicist, then experimenting with photography. Together they developed (1839) the **daguerretype**, in which a picture was imprinted on a metal plate, leading eventually to modern photography.

1852 The first part of **Deutsches Wörterbuch** was published in Germany. Its compilers were the brothers **Jacob** and **Wilhelm Grimm**, known best for **Grimm's Fairy Tales**. They were both philologists as well as folklorists and in this dictionary they prepared the most important German lexicographical work ever undertaken. Wilhelm lived only long enough to see the work completed through "D"; Jacob through "F." The 16th and final volume did not appear until 1960.

1852 **Elisha Graves Otis** (Aug. 3, 1811–Apr. 8, 1861), an American engineer, invented the **elevator**.

1853 **Nicholas Pike** introduced to the U.S. the **House Sparrow** [*Passer domésticus*, English Sparrow] in New York City. Brought originally to control canker worms, it was introduced in a number of American cities, and is now found throughout most of North America.

1852 Sept. 24 The **first sustained, engine-powered flight** was achieved by **Henri Giffard** (Feb. 8, 1825–Apr. 14, 1882), a French balloonist, who piloted his balloon, powered by a steam engine, for a 17-mile trip over Paris.

1853–1854 In Switzerland a drought, which lowered the level of many lakes, revealed evidence of **lake villages c.5,000 years old**. In Neolithic Switzerland lakeside villages had been supported on piles.

1853 Oct. 2 **Dominique François Jean Arago** (b. Feb. 26, 1786), a French physicist, died. Arago investigated **electromagnetism** and the wave theory of light. He discovered the principle of creating magnetism by rotation and was one of those who proved (1820) that iron could be magnetized by an electrical current. In 1806 he was joined by **Jean-Baptiste Biot**

(Apr. 21, 1774–Feb. 3, 1862), a French physicist and geodesist for whom the mica biotite was named, in measuring an arc of the meridian in Spain. Biot summarized the values of magnetic force engendered by direct current in a law which carried his name.

1854   Georg Friedrich Bernhard Riemann (Sept. 17, 1826–July 19, 1866), a German mathematician, in a contest for appointment to Göttingen University, delivered a lecture *On the Hypotheses Which Form the Foundation of Geometry*, in which he set forth a new concept of geometry, more wide-ranging than the work (1826) in non-Euclidean geometry by **Nikolai Ivanovich Lobachevski**. Many theorems and methods have been named for Riemann, whose studies of physics combined with an understanding of analytical geometry helped **Albert Einstein** in his work on the theory of relativity.

1854   A major reference library, established by a $400,000 bequest (1848) from **John Jacob Astor**, opened in New York City. It was the first part of what became the **New York Public Library**, primarily an institution for scholarly research. **John Lenox** (Aug. 10, 1800–Feb. 17, 1880), a philanthropist and book collector, funded the Lenox Library (1876), which was followed by a free reading room established by a grant of $2 million from the Tilden Trust Fund, established for the purpose of supporting the library by the will of **Samuel J. Tilden** (Feb. 9, 1814–Aug. 4, 1886), a lawyer and important political figure. These three libraries were consolidated (1895) to form the New York Public Library, housed (from 1911) on Fifth Avenue, New York City.

1854   Henri Étienne Sainte-Clair-Deville (Feb. 11, 1818–July 1, 1881), a French chemist, developed the first successful **process for producing solid aluminum**. Sainte-Clair-Deville's improvements resulted eventually in the commercial production of aluminum.

1854 Aug. 20   Friedrich Wilhelm Joseph von Schelling (b. Jan. 27, 1775), a German philosopher, died. Schelling had helped initiate a romantic movement in German philosophy. His *Ideen zu einer Philosphie der Natur* (1797), although similar to Johann Gottlieb Fichte's work, departed from it with his assertion that the mind cannot be more powerful than nature.

1854 Oct. 21   Florence Nightingale, the daughter of a well-to-do English family, sailed for the Crimea, where her work formed the **foundation of both modern nursing and public health**. When she arrived at Sevastopol, she found that sanitary conditions in the so-called hospitals engendered disease in even the healthy. She organized a barracks hospital where she introduced sanitary measures to curb the incidence of dysentery, cholera, and typhus, and became known to the soldiers there as the "**Lady with the Lamp**."

VIII. ARTS AND LEISURE

1850   *David Copperfield* by **Charles Dickens**, appeared. His novel was autobiographical. Dickens was born into a lower middle class family and as a child had worked at a blacking factory. His father was imprisoned for debt at about the same time. The novel, which described lower middle class life in London and the countryside, was a powerful indictment of child labor in 19th century England.

1850 Apr. 23   William Wordsworth (b. Apr. 7, 1770), an English poet, died. A member of the **Lake Poets**, which included **Percy Bysshe Shelley** and **Samuel Taylor Coleridge**, Wordsworth attracted attention first by a collection of poems *Lyrical Ballads* (1798), to which Coleridge contributed. The Wordsworth poems included "Lines Composed a few miles above Tintern Abbey". Among his poems were "Resolution and Independence" (1807), "Nuns Fret Not at Their Convent's Narrow Room" (1807), and "Ode: Intimations of Immortality from Recollections of Early Childhood" (1807). His two long works "The Excursion" (1814) and "The Prelude" (published posthumously, 1850) contained autobiographical elements. Wordsworth became poet laureate in 1843.

1850 Aug. 18   Honoré de Balzac [orig.: Balssa] (b. May 20, 1799), one of France's greatest novelists, died. Balzac produced a prodigious number of books. By bringing together most of his important stories and novels within one grand scheme, which Balzac called *La Comédie Humaine* [*The Human Comedy*] (1842), his major work, he gave a nearly complete portrayal of the life and society of France. Among his 92 novels were *Eugénie Grandet* (1833), *Le Père Goriot* (1834), and *Le Cousin Pons* (1847).

1851 Sept. 14   James Fenimore Cooper (b. Sept. 15, 1789), an American writer of romantic adventure novels, died. *The Spy* (1821) set romance against a backdrop of the American Revolution. *The Pioneers*

(1823) was the first of the Leatherstocking Tales. Other works included *The Last of the Mohicans* (1826) and *The Deerslayer* (1841).

1851 Dec. 2 **Edmont Louis Antoine de Goncourt** (May 26, 1822–July 16, 1896) and his brother, **Jules Alfred Huot** (Dec. 17, 1830–June 20, 1870), began their *Journals*, in which they introduced the major French literary figures of the age, as well as many foreign writers. Edmond established the **Prix Goncourt**, France's most prestigious literary prize, awarded each year to an author of fiction.

1851 Dec. 19 **Joseph Mallord William Turner** (b. Apr. 23, 1775), an English romantic landscape painter, died. His works included *Calais Pier* (1802); *The Battle of Trafalgar* [*The Death of Nelson*] (1806–1808); *Sun Rising Through Vapor* (1807); the watercolor *The Lake of Lucerne, Frosty Morning* (1813); *The Bay of Baial* (1823); *Hero and Leander* (1837); *The Fighting Téméraire Towed to Her Last Berth* (1839), a tribute to the great age of sailing ships; and *Rain, Steam, and Speed* (1844).

1852–1870 The **Second Empire Style** in France was similar to the design of furniture and architecture constructed (c.1800–c.1815) during the First Empire (1804–1814), but may be distinguished by its somewhat showy, even gaudy, decoration.

1852 What became the **Victoria and Albert Museum** opened in London as the **Museum of Manufacturers** to house articles of the applied and decorative arts that had been exhibited at the **Great Exhibition of 1851**. It now houses one of the world's greatest collections of the decorative arts, including ceramics, glass, textiles, as well as miniatures and women's fashions, among an almost countless variety of items.

1852 *Uncle Tom's Cabin, or, Life Among the Lowly* was published by **Harriet Beecher Stowe** (June 14, 1811–July 1, 1896). The book exposed the conditions of slavery in the U.S. It had first appeared (1851) as a serial in the *National Era*, an abolitionist newspaper in Washington, D.C. Mrs. Stowe soon wrote *Key to Uncle Tom's Cabin* to refute charges of inaccuracy and to demonstrate the factual basis for her portrayal of slave life.

1852 Mar. 4 **Nikolai Vasilievich Gogol** [Nikolay Vasilyevich Gogol] (b. Mar. 31, 1809), a Russian novelist, died. His historical novel *Taras Bulba* (1839) depicted the struggle that took place during the 16th century of Cossacks against the Poles and Tatars. His most famous novel, *Dead Souls* [*Myortvye Dushi*] (1842), was a powerful satire involving the buying and selling of dead serfs.

1852 Dec. 18 **Horatio Greenough** (b. Sept. 6, 1805), an American sculptor best known for a huge figure of **George Washington**, now in the Smithsonian Institution, died.

1853–1869 **Georges Eugène Haussmann** (Mar. 27, 1809–Jan. 11, 1891) laid out a new **street plan for central Paris**. His system of wide, straight boulevards and circumferential avenues gave Paris its beauty and practicality, copied in Washington, D.C., and other cities.

1853 **Pon Nya** [U Ponnya] (c.1812/1817–1866), a Burmese writer, was named poet to the court of **Kanaung**, the crown prince of Burma [Myanmar]. Pon Nya excelled in writing **Myit-ta-za**, a form of classical verse with four syllables to the line.

1853 Apr. 28 **Ludwig Tieck** (b. May 31, 1773), a German romantic novelist and playwright, died. In the theater he was probably best known for the satiric fairy tale play *Der Gestiefelte Kater* [*Puss in Boots*] (1796, produced 1844). Tieck's other works included one of the first German romantic novels, *Franz Sternbalds Wanderungen* (1798); the heroic poem *Kaiser Octavianus* (1804), in form a medieval romantic play; and the historical novel *Der Aufruhr in den Cevennen* (1826).

1854 Aug. 16 **Duncan Phyfe** (b. 1768?), the greatest of U.S. cabinetmakers, died. From his New York factory, he introduced the **European classical revival** to the U.S. The more than 100 cabinetmakers employed by Phyfe were able to manufacture, as well, items in the Sheraton, Regency, French Directoire, or Empire modes.

IX. SPORTS, GAMES AND SOCIETY

1850 **Amelia Jenks Bloomer** (May 27, 1818–Dec. 30, 1894), an American suffragette, proposed a new "rational" **mode of dress for women**. "Bloomers," named for their originator, were baggy pants gathered at the ankles similar to the baggy pants worn by Turks. Amelia Bloomer also campaigned for temperance and female suffrage.

1850 The first court known to have been built for the game of **racquets** in the U.S. was constructed for the Broadway Racquet Club of New York.

1850 The invention of a **steel-bladed skate** by E.W. **Bushnell** of Philadelphia revolutionized the sport of ice-skating and gave impetus to **ice hockey.**

1851 May 1–Oct. 15 The **Great Exhibition of the Works of Industry of All Nations** opened at the magnificent **Crystal Palace** in Hyde Park, London. The palace, employing much glass, was specially built for the occasion.

1851 July **William Decker,** representing "the East River, New York," outrowed **James Lee** "of the North River" [Hudson River], in a five-mile **sculling** race. Decker won by an estimated one-fifth of a mile, winning a side bet of $900.

1851 Aug. 22 The American schooner-yacht *America* outsailed a fleet of 17 of the best yachts in the Royal Yacht Squadron in a race of 53 miles around the Isle of Wight, off Southampton, England. The *America,* designed by George Steers of New York, was 101 feet at the waterline and weighed 170 tons. The winner's cup, called the "**Hundred Guineas Cup,**" was donated to the New York Yacht Club in 1857 as a perpetual trophy for international sailing. Since then, the races have been called the "**America's Cup Races.**"

1852 Aug. 3 Harvard and Yale rowed the **first formal intercollegiate boat race** in the U.S. with six-oared crews, on Lake Winnepesaukee in New Hampshire; Harvard won the race.

1853 The Irish national sport of **hurling** made its first appearance in the U.S. in an organized way when a club was formed in San Francisco, California.

1853 **George Cayley** (Dec. 27, 1773–Dec. 15, 1857), called by Englishmen "**father of the aeroplane,**" designed a man-carrying glider that carried his coachman over one-quarter of a mile in a valley near his estate in Brompton, Yorkshire. Cayley's exploit was the first recorded glider flight.

1855–1859

I. DISASTERS

1856 Lightning struck the Church of St. John on Rhodes, an island off the southwestern coast of Turkey, ruled by the Ottoman Turks. **Gunpowder in the church vault exploded,** killing c.4,000 persons.

1859 **Rabbits were introduced into Australia** by **Thomas Austin** (fl. 1850–1860). Their rapid takeover of grazing lands resulted in the loss of vital sheep grazing areas.

1859 The **Colorado Potato Beetle** [*Leptinotarsa decemlineata*], native to the plateau area of the eastern **Rocky Mountains,** where it fed mostly on the Buffalo Bur [*Solanum rostratum*], began to become a serious pest. By 1859 it had spread to eastern Nebraska and it reached the Atlantic Coast in 1874. The Colorado Potato Beetle is now a worldwide pest.

II. EXPLORATION AND COLONIZATION

1855 Nov. 17 **David Livingstone,** the Scottish medical missionary and explorer, discovered **Victoria** Falls, in present Zambia and Zimbabwe. He had begun at Capetown in 1852, and had traveled north to the Zambezi at Sesheka, then west to Loanda [Luanda] on the Atlantic Ocean, from where he retraced his journey to Sesheke and from there followed the Zambezi to its mouth. By the time he sailed to England (1856), he had crossed southern Africa from the Atlantic to the Indian Ocean.

1857 **James Bridger** joined the Mormon expedition of **Albert Sidney Johnston** (Feb. 2, 1803–Apr. 6, 1862), a U.S. military commander, as a guide. The expedition explored the region of present **Yellowstone National Park.**

1857 The discovery of **gold** near Melbourne, Australia, drew colonists from Great Britain. The population of the province of Victoria doubled in one year.

1857 The discovery of **silver** in western Nevada led to a wild search for more. California gold-rushers **Ethan Allen Grosh** and **Hosea Ballou Grosh** were said to have been first to find the famous **Comstock**

Lode, but they died mysteriously before officially confirming their claim. Instead, **Henry Tompkins Paige Comstock** (1820–1870), called "Old Pancake," laid a claim (1859) to the lode, the largest deposit of silver known in the U.S. He sold out when it produced only a small quantity. The real boom did not begin until the sand, of a bluish hue, was found to bear silver. **Virginia City** was founded (1859) and became a boom town. The lode was exhausted by 1898, and today Virginia City is a ghost town.

1858 Spring Gold discoveries along the Fraser River in present western **Canada** resulted in a gold rush that drew c.25,000 people into the region. Further gold discoveries were made in the Carizboo Mountains near the Fraser River in 1860.

III. POLITICS AND WAR

1855 John Mercer Langston (Dec. 14, 1829–Nov. 15, 1897) was the **first black American to be elected to office** when he became a member of the Brownhelm City Council in Ohio.

1855 The provincial Parliaments of Australia adopted the policy of **"White Australia"** by excluding Chinese immigrants.

1855 Santa Ana was again unseated and exiled when the Plan of Ayutla (Mar. 1, 1854) quickly became the **Revolt of Ayutla** in Mexico. The plan, which called for Santa Ana's deposition and the establishment of a provisional government, was also a series of reforms urged by **Benito Pablo Juárez** (Mar. 21, 1806–July 18, 1872) and Juan Álvarez (1790–Aug. 21, 1867), who began the liberal revolution at Ayutla, east of Acapulco in southwestern Mexico. The liberal constitution adopted on Feb. 5, 1857 was followed by the **War of Reform** (1858–1861); Juárez headed the Republican [provisional] government, which was seated at Veracruz, on the Gulf of Mexico, and a series of reactionary generals headed a rival government at Mexico City. The Republican government was recognized by the U.S. on Apr. 6, 1859 and, after the liberal victory in a **battle at Calpulálpum** on Dec. 22, 1860, Juárez entered Mexico City on Jan 11, 1861. A period of liberal reform, known as *La Reforma* (1854–1876), was established.

1855 Mar. 2 Nicholas I [Nikolai, Nikolai Pavlovich] (b. July 6, 1796), czar of Russia (from 1825), died, and was succeeded by his eldest son **Alexander II.** Nicholas's rule was noted for protecting the Orthodox Christians of eastern Europe and for fostering Russian alliance with European powers. The **Crimean War** in 1854 was a severe blow to his policies.

1855 Sept. 11 Sevastopol, the chief Russian port on the Black Sea, was taken by British and French forces during the **Crimean War** (1854–1856). The long siege of Sevastopol, begun on Sept. 20, 1854, had weakened Russian resistance. Peace negotiations began on Feb. 25, 1856.

1856 Mar. 30 The **Treaty of Paris** was signed by Great Britain, France, the Ottoman Empire, Sardinia, and Russia, bringing an end to the **Crimean War**. The Danube River was opened to free navigation. A period of diplomatic disunity began in Europe as Great Britain withdrew from continental affairs, Russia preferred to concentrate on social reform, and Austria remained isolated, viewed as a betrayer by both sides of the conflict.

1856 May 24 John Brown, in retaliation for a raid by pro-slavery marauders on Lawrence, Kansas, raided Pottawatomie, Kansas territory, with his five sons and killed five pro-slavery men. In August Brown and his followers successfully defended Osawatomie, in present eastern Kansas, against a large force of slavery men from Missouri.

1856 June 17–19 The **first national convention of the Republican party**, held in Philadelphia, forced by recent [May] bloody events in Kansas between pro-slavery and anti-slavery elements, adopted a militant, anti-Democratic, anti-slavery platform characterized by its slogan "Free Speech, Free Soil, and Frémont." The Republicans nominated **John C. Frémont** of California for the presidency and **William L. Dayton** of New Jersey for the vice-presidency, neither of whom had the national stature to win the election.

1856 Oct. 8 The **Second Anglo-Chinese War** (to 1860), the so-called **Arrow War**, broke out between China and Great Britain when Chinese officers searched the Arrow, a Chinese-owned, but British-registered craft, and lowered its British flag. In 1858 French and British troops reached Tientsin [Tianjin], a port city in northeastern China, threatening the capital at **Peking** [Beijing]. China agreed, in the **Treaties of Tientsin** (1858), to establish a residence in Peking for foreign diplomats, open more treaty ports, grant sanctions to Christians, and to legalize the importation of opium by establishing a fixed importation rate.

1856 Oct. 19   Sayyid II [Sa'id ibn Sultan] (b. 1791?), the greatest sultan (from 1806) of the **Al-Busayyid** [Busa'id] **Dynasty** (1741–to the present), which ruled Oman and surrounding territories, died. He had reigned over Oman, Muscat [Masquat], and Zanzibar, as well as established control over the coastal portion of Baluchistan, on the Arabian Sea, in present southwestern Pakistan. Altogether Sayyid commanded nearly 700 miles of East Africa's coastline.

1857   Victoria, queen of the United Kingdom of Great Britain and Ireland, chose the city of **Ottawa** to be the capital of British North America [Canada].

1857   Alexander Herzen [Aleksandr Ivanovich Gertsen; orig.: Yakovlev; pseud.: Iskander] (Apr. 6, 1812–Jan. 21, 1870), a Russian writer, began publication in London of the journal *Kolokol* [*The Bell*], which was smuggled into Russia to be widely read by intellectuals. Herzen called for the freeing of the serfs, supported the Polish insurrection of 1863, and urged Russian revolutionaries to appeal for support from the peasantry of Russia.

1857 Mar. 4   James Buchanan (Apr. 23, 1791–June 1, 1868) of the Democratic party was inaugurated as the 15th president of the U.S., having defeated **John Charles Frémont** of the Republican party. **John Cabell Breckinridge** (Jan. 21, 1821–May 17, 1875) served as the vice president.

1857 Mar. 6   Roger Brooke Taney (Mar. 17, 1777–Oct. 12, 1864), chief justice of the U.S. Supreme Court, handed down the final decision in the **Dred Scott case**. In declaring that the U.S. Congress had no power to prohibit **slavery** in U.S. territories, the court nullified the **Missouri Compromise** (1820). The court's opinion struck an even stronger blow against the abolitionist cause by stating that blacks were not citizens—they were property—and thus the federal court had no jurisdiction over their affairs and that merely by living any period of time in a free state did not free a slave. Dred Scott (1795?–Sept. 17, 1858) had sued for freedom based on his temporary residence in a free territory.

1857 May 10   The **Sepoy Mutiny** broke out in India at Meerut, on the Ganges River northeast of Delhi, when the Sepoy, or native, Indian troops in the service of Great Britain murdered their British officers. The Sepoys captured Delhi on the following day and proclaimed **Siraj-ud-Din Bahadur Shah II** (Oct. 24, 1775–Nov. 7, 1862), the **last Mogul emperor** (1837–1858) **of Hindustan**, a region of northern India, as emperor of all India (deposed by British 1858). The mutiny then evolved into a popular uprising against British influence but was put down by the British with the help of the **Sikhs** of the Punjab. **Charles John Canning**, (Dec. 14, 1812–Aug. 8, 1862), earl Canning, governor general (from 1856) of India, declared the end of the mutiny on July 8, 1858. He was nominated viceroy of British India when the governmental roles of the East India Company were assumed by the British crown, under the **Parliamentary Act for the Better Government of India** (Aug. 2).

1858   Abraham Lincoln won national prominence through the so-called **Lincoln-Douglas debates** during the Illinois senatorial race. Lincoln made the question of **slavery** a moral issue and part of the Republican platform. During these debates **Stephen Arnold Douglas** (Apr. 23, 1813–June 3, 1861), senator from Illinois (1847–1861), lost Southern support for his presidential race as a Democrat when he was unable to support adequately his position that the Dred Scott decision would not have guaranteed the spread of slavery.

1858 May 11   Minnesota was the 32nd state admitted to the U.S. It entered as a free state.

1859   Guatemala signed a trade agreement with Great Britain in which the two nations were to cooperate in constructing a road in British Honduras [Belize]. When it was found that the cost of building the proposed road would exceed the original estimate, Guatemala withdrew from the agreement.

1859 Feb. 14   Oregon was the 33rd state admitted to the U.S. By the Oregon Act of 1848 it was admitted as a free state.

1859 Feb. 17   Saigon was captured by the French, who occupied eastern Cochin China [Cochinchine] in the southern region of the **Annam Empire**, present Vietnam. Between 1827 and 1858 the Annamese policy of religious persecution had resulted in the deaths of nearly 150,000 Christians; it was ostensibly for this reason that France interceded. In 1867 an expedition under **Pierre Paul Moril de La Grandière** (1807–1876) extended French control to the whole of

Cochin China [southern Vietnam], which was made a French colony.

1859 Apr. 19 The **Italian War** (1859) broke out when Austria demanded that Piedmont, a section of northwestern Italy that formed the largest portion of the **Kingdom of Sardinia**, be disarmed. Austria controlled most of Italy, and even the Papal States tended to be friendly with Austria. Revolts broke out in Tuscany (Apr. 28) and in Modena (Apr. 29). Austria invaded Piedmont (May 1). France went to the aid of Sardinia, and the French and Sardinian armies defeated the Austrians at Montebello (May 21) and Palestro (May 20). The allies won again at Magenta (June 4), entered Milan (June 8), and defeated the Austrians again at Solferino (June 24). At an armistice in Villefranca de Verona, the French and Austrians agreed to peace terms, signed reluctantly by Sardinia. The basic terms of the peace were confirmed in a formal treaty at Zürich on Nov. 10, attended by the two emperors, **Napoléon III** and **Francis Joseph**.

1859 Oct. 16 **John Brown** and 21 other abolitionists took the U.S. arsenal at **Harper's Ferry** along the Potomac River in Virginia [now West Virginia]. His plan to establish headquarters there for freeing slaves was thwarted by **Robert Edward Lee** (Jan. 19, 1807–Oct. 12, 1870), who recaptured Harper's Ferry and wounded Brown. Convicted of treason, John Brown [Old Brown of Osawatomie] (b. May 9, 1800) was hanged on Dec. 2, 1859.

IV. ECONOMY AND TRADE

1856 The **Joint Stock Company Act** passed by Parliament established Great Britain as the first major European country to permit the "limited liability," or incorporated, company. Limited liability encouraged the growth of capital endeavors because investors had their risks reduced.

1856 Apr. 4 The **Western Union Telegraph Company** was founded with capital of $500,000. On Oct. 26, 1861, the first direct line between California and New York was established by the **Pacific Telegraph Company** and the **Overland Telegraph Company**. The three companies eventually merged. By 1867 the company had lines extending from Maine to California.

1856 July 17 The present **Swiss banking system** was initiated by **Johann Heinrich Alfred Escher**

(1819–1882) when he and his partners offered for public sale in Zürich 9,000 shares in their new enterprise, the **Swiss Credit Bank** [Kreditanstalt], the largest bank in Switzerland today.

1857 The U.S. Congress declared that **foreign coinage** was not legal payment for debt in America.

1857 Aug. The **Panic of 1857** was initiated by the failure in the U.S. of the **Ohio Life Insurance and Trust Company**. Its underlying causes were primarily overspeculation in railroads and real estate. The economy started to recover at the end of 1858, when a period of economic prosperity set in. During the panic, more than 12,000 American businesses went bankrupt.

1857 Nov. 12 The **Bank of England**, faced with the Panic of 1857 originating in the U.S., had only £581,-000 in reserves against £13,000,000 in liabilities to its depositors. The British government authorized issue of £2,000,000 in unsecured notes to prevent closing of the Bank.

1858 Oct. 28 **Macy's** opened in New York City, establishing the traditional American department store.

1859 *La Gloire*, the **first seagoing iron-clad ship**, was built. Iron plates, between 10 and 12 centimeters thick on the *Gloire*, were attached to a wooden or iron hull for further protection.

1859 Aug. 17 **Edwin Laurentine Drake** (Mar. 29, 1819–Nov. 8, 1880) was the first person to succeed in **drilling**, rather than digging, **an oil well**, at Titusville, Pennsylvania.

V. RELIGION AND PHILOSOPHY

1855 **Alexander II**, czar of Russia, did away with some of his father's special regulations respecting the **harsh treatment of Jews**, but hopes for fundamental improvements proved illusory.

1855 The YWCA [**Young Women's Christian Association**] originated in London as a **Prayer Union**, organized by **Emma Robarts**, and as the **General Female Training Institute**, begun by **Mrs. Arthur Kinnaird** (Mar. 14, 1816–Dec. 1, 1888). They merged (1877) as the Young Women's Christian Association. The first American YWCA was founded as the Ladies' Christian Association of New York City in 1858.

The first bearing the name of YWCA began in Boston in 1866.

1855 June 30 For the first time since the Crusades, the cross was borne aloft through the streets of **Jerusalem** in a ceremony, occasioned by the visit of a German prince.

1855 Nov. 11 Søren [Sören Aabye] **Kierkegaard** (b. May 5, 1813), a Danish philosopher and theologian, died. His main tenet was that "truth is subjectivity." Most important, Kierkegaard maintained, was the individual's relationship to objective fact, rather than the fact itself. His works included *Either/Or* (1843); *The Concept of Dread* (1844); *The Concluding Unscientific Postscript* (1846), his principal philosophic work; *Works of Love* (1847); and *The Sickness unto Death* (1849). Some modern philosophers have seen Kierkegaard as an early existentialist.

1857 The **Dutch Reformed Church**, the principal Christian church in South Africa, held a synod during which it was decided to separate the white and non-white believers.

1857 Sept. 5 Auguste Comte [Isidore Auguste Marie François Xavier Comte] (b. Jan. 19, 1798), a French philosopher, died. Comte was credited with founding the discipline of sociology and the philosophy of positivism. Comte outlined his concept of the perfect society, based on the tenets of positivism, in *Cours de philosophie positive* [*The Course of Positive Philosophy*] (1830–1842).

1858 The cornerstone for **St. Patrick's Cathedral** in New York City was laid. It was consecrated on May 25, 1879. The architect was **James Renwick** (Nov. 1, 1818–June 23, 1895), whose work included Grace Church in New York City and the **Smithsonian Institution** in Washington, D.C.

1859 Aug. 4 Jean Baptiste Marie Vianney (b. May 8, 1786), a French Roman Catholic priest, died. He was known as "**Curé d'Ars,**" for the tiny parish at Ars-les-Favets in Puy-de-Dôme department, central southern France, that he had revitalized and made famous almost from his arrival in 1818. An estimated 20,000 persons visited Ars annually to see the ascetic priest and to make confession to him.

VI. SCIENCE, EDUCATION, AND TECHNOLOGY

1855 The **Bunsen burner** was developed by **Robert Wilhelm Bunsen** (Mar. 31, 1811–Aug. 16, 1899), a German chemist. Bunsen also developed (1870) the **calorimeter** to measure heat, and found (1834) an **antidote to arsenic poisoning**.

1855 Feb. 23 [Johann] **Karl Friedrich Gauss** (b. Apr. 30, 1777), a German mathematician and astronomer, died. Most of his seminal work in mathematics was accomplished between the ages of 14 and 17. He wrote *Disquisitiones arithmeticae* (1801), on the theory of numbers. Gauss developed a method for figuring least squares, and a solution to binomial equations. In the 1830s he began the study of magnetism and electricity, and the gauss, a magnetic unit, was named for him.

1856 Henry Bessemer (Jan. 19, 1813–Mar. 15, 1898), an English engineer, developed what became known as the **Bessemer process** for refining steel. The Bessemer converter burned oxygen from the air to refine pig iron, greatly reducing the cost of production and producing a stronger steel. Bessemer opened a steel mill in England in 1860. The first mill in the U.S. to use the Bessemer process began operation in Feb. 1865.

1856 Workers found 14 fossils, including a skull, of what later came to be called **Neanderthal man** [*Homo sapiens neanderthalensis*] in **Feldhofer Cave**, located in the Neanderthal Valley east of Düsseldorf, in present Germany. The discovery (1886) of two more similar skeletons in Belgium associated with stone implements and bones from extinct animals confirmed that Neanderthal man was a precursor of modern man.

1856 William Henry Perkin (Mar. 12, 1838–July 14, 1907), an English chemist, produced the **first synthetic dye**, aniline purple [mauve]. By isolating this bluish dye Perkin founded the aniline dye industry. Later, Perkin also isolated alizarin red, which replaced the organic matter root red. In 1858 Perkin and a colleague first synthesized the amino acid **glycine**.

1856 Gail Borden (Nov. 9, 1801–Jan. 11, 1874), an American inventor, received a patent on a process for **condensing milk**. Borden also developed ways to condense fruit juices, coffee, tea, and cocoa.

1857 Construction of the **Mont Cenis Tunnel**, the first of the long tunnels under the Alps, began. Digging was speeded up by the invention by **Germain Sommeillier** (Mar. 15, 1815–July 11, 1871), a French engineer, of a **compressed air drill**. The tunnel, completed in 1871, was 8 miles long and 12 miles below the summit of the mountain it pierces, with one end in France, the other in Italy.

1857 May 23 **Augustin Louis** (b. Aug. 21, 1789), baron Cauchy, a French mathematician, died. His contributions to mathematics were included in the 27-volume *Oeuvres complètes d'Augustin Cauchy*. The concepts of limit and continuity in calculus as well as the theory of functions of a complex variable and the wave theory in optics, were defined by Cauchy.

1858 June 10 **Robert Brown** (b. Dec. 21, 1773), a Scottish botanist, died. In 1831 Brown recognized that the **nucleus was an essential element of living cells**. His observation, in 1827, of "Brownian motion," the vibratory movement of microscopic particles, went unexplained until the development of kinetic theory.

1859 Jan. 29 **William Cranch Bond** (b. Sept. 9, 1789), an American astronomer, died. In 1848 Bond discovered **Hyperion**, the eighth satellite of Saturn, and in 1850 he discovered Saturn's "crepe ring," the dim ring surrounded by two bright ones encircling the planet.

1859 Nov. 24 *On the Origin of the Species by Means of Natural Selection; or, the Preservation of Favoured Races in the Struggle for Life*, by **Charles Robert Darwin**, was published. Darwin had already proposed (1844) in an essay that natural selection within species was the principal explanation for the evolution of new species. **Alfred Russel Wallace**, an English naturalist, had independently arrived at a similar theory while making observations in the Malay Archipelago. In 1858 they shared authorship of a paper setting forth the premises of the theory. Aboard the *Beagle* from Dec. 1831 to Oct. 1836, Darwin had gathered information on species and fossils during the voyage, particularly in the **Galapagos Archipelago** off the coast of northwestern South America. There were individual outcries against Wallace and Darwin, but science prevailed over these protests in most educated societies and communities.

VI. ARTS AND LEISURE

1855 Nov. 3 **François Rude** (b. Jan. 4, 1784), a French romantic sculptor and an admirer of Napoléon, died. His best works included the relief on the **Arc de Triomphe** *Départ des Volontaires en 1792* [popularly known as *La Marseillaise*] (1835–1836); and his **monument to Ney**, marshal of France, called by **François Rodin** the most beautiful statue in Paris.

1855 Nov. 26 **Adam Mickiewicz** (b. Dec. 24, 1798), a Polish patriot and poet, died. He is known for his poem *Pan Tadeusz* [*Sir Thaddeus*] (1834), which told of his life in his native Lithuania before Napoléon's invasion (1812). *Grażna* (1851) was a historical epic poem stressing patriotic themes. An active leader of the Polish patriots, he died in Turkey while organizing Polish forces under a mission supported by Napoléon III.

1856 The celebrated novel *Madame Bovary* by **Gustave Flaubert** (Dec. 12, 1821–May 8, 1880) was published. Flaubert described the mediocrity of French provincial life and analyzed the character of Emma Bovary, the discontented wife of a country doctor.

1856 Feb. 17 **Heinrich** [**Harry**] **Heine** (b. Dec. 13, 1797), a German romantic poet, died. An ardent reformer and liberal, Heine was attracted to France after the July Revolution and lived (from 1831) in Paris the rest of his life. *Buch der Lieder* [*Book of Songs*] (1827), a collection of lyric poems, made Heine famous. The ballad cycles *Die Lorelei* also became very popular. His first literary success was *Die Harzreise* [*Trip in the Harz Mountains*] (1826), included in *Reisebuilder* [*Travel Sketches*] (1831).

1856 July 29 **Robert** [**Alexander**] **Schumann** (b. June 8, 1810), a German romantic composer, died. His lieder, written in 1840, included *Frauenliebe und-leben* [*Woman's Love and Life*] and *Dichterliebe* [*Poet's Love*]. His orchestral works included the Spring Symphony (1841); Piano Concerto in A Minor (1841–1845); and Symphony No. 4 in D Minor (1851).

1857 Work began on New York City's **Central Park**, the first large, landscaped park in the U.S. **Frederick Law Olmstead** (Apr. 27, 1822–Aug. 28, 1903) and **Calvert Vaux** (Dec. 23, 1824–Nov. 19, 1895), famous landscape architects, designed the park, which **Andrew Haswell Green** (Oct. 6, 1820–

Nov. 13, 1903), an American lawyer, carried to completion in 1876. The 843-acre park has ponds, bridle paths, walks, playgrounds, a formal garden, zoo, and open air theater.

1857 *Synnöve Solbakken*, the first novel by **Bjørnstjerne Martinius Bjørnson**, published in this year, has been called the start of modern Norwegian literature. In 1903 Bjørnson received the **Nobel prize** for literature.

1857 The **Obscene Publications Act**, also called **Lord Campbell's Act**, was passed in England. It provided a definition of obscenity as that which was meant to "deprave and corrupt those whose minds are open to such immoral influence."

1857 The political and literary magazines, *Harper's Weekly* in New York City and the *Atlantic Monthly* in Boston, began publication in the U.S.

1857 Mar. 11 **Manuel José Quintana** (b. Apr. 11, 1772), a Spanish writer and patriot, died. Much of his work, notably the play *El Pelayo* (1805) and the three-volume *Vidas de Españoles Célebres* [*Lives of Celebrated Spaniards*] (1807), was written in opposition to foreign intervention in Spain.

1857 May 2 **Louis Charles Alfred de Musset** (Dec. 11, 1810), a French romantic poet and playwright, died. His poetry included *les Nuit* (1837–1838), and his main prose work was the autobiographical *Confession d'une Enfant du Siècle* (1836).

1857 July 15 **Karl Czerny** (b. Feb. 20, 1791), an Austrian pianist, died. Though he wrote much music, he was best known for his **exercise books**, still used by students.

1857 Oct. 10 **Thomas Crawford** (b. Mar. 22, 1814), an American sculptor known best for *Freedom*, a large figure atop the U.S. Capitol dome, died.

1858 *The Autocrat of the Breakfast Table* by **Oliver Wendell Holmes** (Aug. 29, 1809–Oct. 7, 1894), an American physician noted for his wit and humor, was published. Holmes was the father of Oliver Wendell Holmes, Jr. (Mar. 8, 1841–Mar. 6, 1935), justice (1902–1932) of the Supreme Court.

1859 The satiric novel *Oblomov* by **Ivan Aleksandrovich Goncharov** (June 18, 1812–Sept. 27, 1891), a Russian writer, was descriptive of the inertia en-

demic in the Russian nobility. *Oblomov* has become a classic of Russian literature, usually admired for its realistic social analysis though it was also recognized as one of the first Russian literary works to advance psychological reasons for anti-social behavior.

1859 Jan. 27 **William Hickling Prescott** (b. May 4, 1796), a famous American historian, died. In 1843 his masterpiece, *History of the Conquest of Mexico*, achieved great popularity and is still read today.

1859 Aug. 28 [James Henry] **Leigh Hunt** (b. Oct. 19, 1784), an English poet and critic, died. His best-known works were the narrative poem *The Story of Rimini* (1816) and the novel *Sir Ralph Esher* (1834).

1859 Nov. 28 **Washington Irving** (b. Apr. 3, 1783), an American writer, died. The satirical *History of New York by Diedrich Knickerbocker* (1809) brought him to the attention of the public. He completed *The Alhambra* in 1812 and a five-volume *Life of Washington* between 1855 and 1859. He was best known for the collection of folk tales, travelogues, and stories in his *The Sketch Book* (1820), which included the classic American tales, "The Legend of Sleepy Hollow" and "Rip Van Winckle."

1859 Dec. 28 **Thomas Babington Macaulay** (b. Oct. 25, 1800), an English poet, historian, and statesman, died. A volume of poetry *Lays of Ancient Rome* (1842) and a volume of *Essays* (1843) were followed by his chief work *History of England from the Accession of James the Second* (1849–1861), which established his reputation as a historian.

VII. SPORTS, GAMES AND SOCIETY

1855 The first game of **ice hockey** was played in the city of Kingston, Ontario, Canada. The Royal Canadian Rifles, a military unit with barracks in Kingston, formed the first team.

1856 The **Montreal Lacrosse Club** was formed in Canada, the first organization devoted to the sport.

1857 Oct. 6 **Paul Charles Morphy** (June 22, 1837–July 10, 1884) became the **first American international chess master** at the American Chess Congress held in New York City.

1858 The **National Association of Baseball Players**, later known as the National League, was formed in the U.S. Henry Chadwick (Oct. 5, 1824–Apr. 20,

1908) wrote the first rule book for baseball, standardizing bat and ball size.

1859 June 28–29 The **first dog show** deserving the name was held at Newcastle-upon-Tyne, England.

1859 July 1 In the **first intercollegiate baseball game** held in the U.S., Amherst defeated Williams with a score of 66 to 32.

1859 July 26 In the **first intercollegiate regatta**, Harvard defeated Yale and Brown.

1860–1864

I. VITAL STATISTICS AND DEMOGRAPHICS

1860 **Australia's European population** reached one million. Only c.25 percent of the population growth that occurred since the first settlers had arrived (1788) was due to the birth and survival rate. The great majority had immigrated. About 150,000 British convicts had been forced migrants, and there had been a doubling of population from voluntary immigration, primarily British, during the 1850s Gold Rush.

II. DISASTERS

1860 Sept. 8 The *Lady Elgin*, a steam-driven, wooden sidewheeler, was struck by the schooner *Augusta* on Lake Michigan near Waukegan, Illinois. Almost 400 people lost their lives in the collision.

1863 Dec. 8 The **Church of Campania**, in **Santiago**, Chile, burned down, killing more than 2,000 people.

1864 Oct. 5 Along the shores of the Bay of Bengal, from 50,000 to 70,000 people died when a **cyclone** and a storm wave struck. Most of **Calcutta** was destroyed.

III. EXPLORATION AND COLONIZATION

1860 Aug. **Robert O'Hara Burke** (1820–June 28, 1861), an Irish explorer, and **William John Wills** (Jan. 5, 1834–June 29, 1861), a British explorer, with a party of nearly 20, set out from Melbourne to make the **first crossing of the Australian desert from south to north**. They reached the Gulf of Carpentaria in Feb. 1861. On the return trip, starvation killed all but one man.

1861 May In New Zealand **gold** was discovered on the Otago Peninsula, South Island.

IV. POLITICS AND WAR

1860–1872 The **Second Maori War** was fought on the North Island of New Zealand. Several native Maori tribes were involved in skirmishes with British colonists, who had considerable difficulty in dealing with guerrilla warfare. At war's end the Maoris were granted half the island.

1860 Mar. 24 The **Treaty of Turin**, signed by **Napoléon III** and **Camillo Benso**, conte di Cavour, prime minister of the Kingdom of Sardinia, forced Sardinia to transfer Savoy and Nice, provinces of Sardinia on the French side of the Alps, to France. In return France agreed to allow Sardinia to annex the central Italian duchies.

1860 Sept. 11 **Victor Emmanuel II**, king of Sardinia [including Piedmont] led a Piedmontese army into the Papal States of Umbria and the Marches. On Oct. 1 and 2 **Garibaldi** defeated the Bourbon troops of **Francis II**, king of the Two Sicilies in a **battle at the Volturna River** at Capua, north of Naples and a stronghold of the Two Sicilies. Victor Emmanuel and Garibaldi joined forces, essentially **reuniting Italy**. Italy was officially declared the **Kingdom of Italy** on Mar. 17, 1861, under Victor Emmanuel II.

1860 Nov. 2 Republican **Abraham Lincoln** was elected president of the U.S. with a popular vote of 1,866,352 and 180 electoral votes. Democrat **Stephen Arnold Douglas** received 1,375,152 popular votes but only 12 electoral votes, while Democrat **John Cabell Breckinridge** got 845,703 popular votes and 72 electoral votes. **John Bell** (Feb. 15, 1797–Sept. 10, 1869), nominated by the splinter Constitutional Union party won 589,581 popular votes and 39 electoral votes.

1860 Dec. 20 **South Carolina** was the **first state to secede from the Union**, citing as justification the nullification by northern states of the **Fugitive Slave**

Law (1850), and other actions disregarding southern political sentiment. **During 1861, 10 other states seceded from the Union**: Mississippi on Jan. 9; Florida on Jan. 10; Alabama on Jan. 11; Georgia on Jan. 19; Louisiana on Jan. 26; Texas on Feb. 23; Virginia on Apr. 17; Arkansas on May 6; North Carolina on May 20; and Tennessee on June 8, 1861.

1861 Great Britain made **Bahrain** [Bahrein], a group of islands in the Persian Gulf, an Arab sultanate, into a protectorate (to 1971). Bahrain renounced her previous policies of war, piracy, and slavery, in return for military protection.

1861 **Al-Hajj Umar** [Omar] of the Tijaniyya brotherhood and caliph of the **Tukulor Empire** (c.1857–c.1864) of the western Sudan, in the region of present eastern Senegal, attacked the **Fulani Kingdom of Massina** [Masina], a rival Muslim state of the Qadiriyya brotherhood, in present southern Senegal, and briefly occupied its capital at **Hamdallahi**. In the ensuing struggle for power, Al-Hajj Umar was killed in 1864 and the Tukulor Empire (from c.1857), extending from French-held western Senegal to **Timbuktu** [Tombouctou] on the Niger River in central southern Mali, soon disintegrated.

1861 Six new territories were organized as part of the U.S. The **Dakota Territory** was the largest, comprising present Montana, Wyoming, and North and South Dakota. The territories of Nebraska, Colorado, New Mexico, Utah, and Nevada roughly held their present boundaries as states. The present state of Oklahoma remained the unorganized Indian Territory.

1861 Jan. 8 The **first shots fired in the Civil War** (1861–1865) were directed against Confederates attempting to storm Fort Pickens, on Santa Rosa Island south of Pensacola in western Florida, to capture military supplies. The fort was held by Union forces throughout the war. On the next day, Confederate shots were fired on the *Star of the West* while it was trying to bring supplies to Fort Sumter in South Carolina.

1861 Jan. 29 **Kansas**, called "**Bleeding or Bloody Kansas**" for the skirmishes fought there over the slavery question, entered the Union as the 34th state. After first adopting a pro-slavery constitution in a vote boycotted by the anti-slavery forces, Kansas adopted the **Wyandotte Constitution** in 1859 in a vote boycotted by the pro-slavery forces. Congress

accepted this constitution, which prohibited slavery, and Kansas entered the Union as a free state.

1861 Feb. 4 The **Confederate States of America** was created by a committee meeting at **Montgomery**, Alabama, to which all seceding southern states sent delegates. **Richmond**, Virginia, officially became the capital of the Confederate states on May 21, with **Jefferson Davis** (June 8, 1808–Dec. 6, 1889), a U.S. senator from Mississippi until that state seceded, presiding as president.

1861 Mar. **Spain regained control of the Dominican Republic**, which had won its independence from Spain in 1844. However, the Dominicans revolted and Spanish forces, threatened by yellow fever and the U.S., abandoned the Dominican Republic for the last time on July 11, 1865.

1861 Mar. 4 **Abraham Lincoln** of the Republican party was inaugurated as the 16th president of the U.S., having defeated **Stephen Arnold Douglas** and **John C. Breckinridge** of the Democratic party and **John Bell** of the Constitutional Union party. **Hannibal Hamlin** (Aug. 27, 1809–July 4, 1891) served as vice president.

1861 Apr. 13 The **fall of Fort Sumter**, Charleston, South Carolina, closed the **first major action of the American Civil War** (1861–1865). On Apr. 12 **Pierre Gustave Toutant de Beauregard** (May 28, 1818–Feb. 20, 1893), an officer in the Confederate army, had opened fire on Union [Federal] troops holding Fort Sumter. **Robert Anderson** (June 14, 1805–Oct. 26, 1871), in command of the fort, was unable to obtain needed supplies or reinforcements and surrendered the fort.

1861 Apr. 19 **Abraham Lincoln**, president of the U.S., ordered a **trade blockade against the South**, initiating a military strategy based on blockading the southern agricultural economy from goods produced in the North and capturing communication centers of the Confederacy, especially its capital at Richmond.

1861 June 17 Union troops led by **Nathaniel Lyon** defeated a Confederate army at Boonville, central Missouri, after driving the pro-Confederate state government from Jefferson City, the state capital. Later, on August 10, Lyon (b. July 14, 1818) was killed leading his c.4,500 troops against c.11,600 Confederates under **Ben McCulloch** in a **battle at Wilson's Creek** near Springfield in southwestern

Missouri. Each side lost c.1,200 men. The Union forces withdrew northward, abandoning Springfield.

1861 July 21 The **first battle of Bull Run** [called First Manassas by the Confederates], a small creek near Manassas Junction in northeastern Virginia, 30 miles southwest of Washington, D.C., was the **first major battle of the American Civil War** (1861–1865). The Union army of c.35,000 troops under **Irvin McDowell** (Oct. 15, 1818–May 5, 1885) launched an offensive against **Pierre Gustave Toutant de Beauregard** (May 28, 1818–Feb. 20, 1893), whose troops numbered c.28,000 men. Confederate reinforcements under **Joseph Eggleston Johnston** (Feb. 3, 1807–Mar. 21, 1891) reached Beauregard by railroad in time to defend the key railroad junction at Manassas. Union forces retreated in a rout to Washington. There were c.2,800 Union casualties and c.2,000 Confederate casualties.

1861 July **George Brinton McClellan** (Dec. 3, 1826–Oct. 29, 1885) was put in command of the Union's Army of the Potomac by Lincoln after its defeat at Bull Run. McClellan had won battles against the Confederates in present West Virginia at Philippi, Rich Mountain, and Carrick's Ford involving only c.6,000 troops, Union and Confederate.

1861 Aug. 28–29 **Forts Hatteras and Clark** at Hatteras Inlet, North Carolina, were **captured by Union ships** and troops commanded by **Benjamin Franklin Butler** (Nov. 5, 1818–Jan. 11, 1893). This success closed one entrance to Pamlico Sound used by Confederate blockade runners and led to the closing of most of Pamlico and Albemarle sounds to the blockade runners.

1861 Dec. 17 **France, Great Britain, and Spain occupied Veracruz**, the Mexican port on the Gulf of Mexico, after **Benito Pablo Juárez**, president of Mexico, suspended payments on foreign debts because his country's treasury was empty. On May 17, 1863, the French under **Élie Frédéric Forey** (Jan. 10, 1804–June 20, 1874) captured Puebla, and the French and their Conservative Mexican allies entered Mexico City on June 7.

1862 **British Honduras** [now Belize] was formally declared a British colony, to be governed from Jamaica, the island in the West Indies.

1862 Feb. 6 **Andrew Hull Foote** (Sept. 12, 1806–June 26, 1863), commanding Union gunboats, and

U[lysses] S[impson] Grant [orig.: Hiram Ulysses] (Apr. 27, 1822–July 23, 1885), commanding a Union army, **captured Fort Henry** on the Tennessee River and then moved east to nearby Fort Donelson on the Cumberland River [both forts in central northern Tennessee], which they forced to capitulate on Feb. 16. Grant took from 12,000 to 15,000 Confederate prisoners. Grant was ordered by **Henry Wager Halleck** (Jan. 16, 1815–Jan. 9, 1872), commander of Union forces in the Missouri department, to move his army from Donelson south across Tennessee to Pittsburg Landing on the Tennessee River and await the arrival of troops under **Don Carlos Buell** (Mar. 23, 1818–Nov. 19, 1898), a Union general of volunteer troops; the landing was just north of Shiloh, Mississippi.

1862 Feb. 8 A Union army under **Ambrose E. Burnside** (May 23, 1824–Sept. 13, 1881), supported by a naval force under **L.M. Goldsborough** (Feb. 18, 1805–Feb. 20, 1877) entered Pamlico Sound and captured Roanoke Island, off North Carolina, commanding the southern entrance to Albemarle Sound. Then he took Elizabeth City (Feb. 10), New Bern (Mar. 14), and soon after Washington on the Pamlico River and Plymouth just north of Washington, near Albemarle Sound. Burnside captured (Apr. 26) Fort Macon near Cape Lookout, completing the **blockade of North Carolina's sounds**. Lincoln's reinforcements under Don Carlos Buell arrived from nearby Pittsburg Landing, to make possible a narrow Union victory when the Confederates withdrew to Corinth the following day. Union casualties were c.13,000, Confederate c.10,000 men.

1862 Apr. 25 **New Orleans** was captured by a Union fleet under **David Glasgow Farragut** (July 5, 1801–Aug. 14, 1870). Union troops under **Benjamin Franklin Butler** (Nov. 5, 1818–Jan. 11, 1893) occupied the city on May 1.

1862 May 13 **Robert Smalls** (Apr. 5, 1839–Feb. 22, 1915), born a slave, won renown during the American Civil War when he and his black crew commandeered *The Planter*, a Confederate gunboat, and sailed it into the hands of the Union navy as a prize of war.

1862 May 31–June 1 The **battle at Seven Pines**, northeast of Richmond, capital of the Confederate States, during the Union army's Peninsular Campaign between the York and James rivers in Virginia, under McClellan was a defeat for the Confederates, who were repulsed after the arrival of Union reinforcements under **Edwin Vose Sumner** (Jan. 30, 1797–Mar. 21, 1863). **Joseph Eggleston Johnston,** the Confederate commander, severely wounded, was replaced (June 1) by **Robert E. Lee,** who designated his forces the **Army of Northern Virginia.**

1862 June 25–July 1 The **Seven Days Battle** opened at Oak Grove when Lee attacked McClellan and maintained the pressure in the subsequent battles of Ellerson's Mill, Gaines Mill, Golding Farm, Trent Farm, Savage Station, Glendale, Frayser's Farm, and finally Malvern Hill, where the Union army at last repulsed Lee. The Union army retreated on July 2 to Harrison's Landing on the James River, where they were protected by guns of the Union navy. Union casualties were over 15,000 out of c.150,000 men; Confederate losses were more than 20,000 out of c.95,000. But the Union drive of the **Peninsular Campaign on Richmond had failed,** and the Confederate army could now turn its attention to Washington, D.C.

1862 Aug. 29–30 The **second battle at Bull Run** [called Second Manassas by the Confederates] resulted in a major defeat for the Union army. After McClellan's defeat in the Peninsular Campaign, Lee marched north toward Washington. Union leaders brought **John Pope** (Mar. 16, 1822—Sept. 23, 1892) from the western theater and placed him at the head of c.55,000 Union troops. He positioned them between where he thought Lee's army was and Washington, in the vicinity of Bull Run creek. Outmaneuvered by Confederate generals Lee, Jackson, and **James Longstreet** (Jan. 8, 1821–Jan. 2, 1904), Pope was driven back across the Potomac River with the loss of c.14,500 men to a Confederate loss of c.9,000. Meanwhile, McClellan's army was ferried off the peninsula for a march toward Washington to reinforce Pope. The troops who arrived near the battlefield were too late to save Pope from defeat. Lee was now positioned to take Washington.

1862 Sept. 17 The **battle at Antietam Creek** [called Sharpsburg by the Confederates], fought at Sharpsburg, Maryland, northwest of Washington, was a stand-off. Confederate troops under Lee withdrew, but Union forces under McClellan could not pursue despite having c.13,000 fresh troops and two corps that had hardly seen any fighting. In the **bloodiest single day of the war,** c.24,000 men fell during the battle. The **Confederate drive on Washington had**

failed. McClellan, perceived as indecisive, was replaced in October by **Ambrose Everett Burnside** (May 23, 1824–Sept. 13, 1881) as commander of the Army of the Potomac.

1862 Sept. 22 **Otto von Bismarck** [Otto Eduard Leopold von Bismarck-Schönhausen] (Apr. 1, 1815–July 30, 1898) was appointed prime minister of Prussia by **William I**, king of Prussia. In his first speech (Sept. 29) he said German unification could be brought about only by "blood and iron."

1862 Oct. 8 A Confederate army commanded by **Braxton Bragg** (Mar. 22, 1817–Sept. 27, 1876) was defeated by a Union army commanded by **Buell** at **Perryville** in central Kentucky. The Confederates had launched a two-prong attack from Tennessee into Kentucky, the first into central Kentucky under Bragg and the second into eastern Kentucky under **Edmund Kirby-Smith** (May 16, 1824–Mar. 28, 1893), who succeeded in capturing Richmond and Lexington, both in central eastern Kentucky. Kirby-Smith's drive on Cincinnati, Ohio, was thwarted by the defeat at Perryville, and both Confederate armies retreated south to Murfreesboro, Tennessee. Bragg suffered c.3,100 casualties, Buell c.4,000. Buell was replaced by **William Starke Rosecrans** (Sept. 6, 1819–Mar. 11, 1898), who spent nearly four months re-equipping his army.

1862 Oct. 23 **Otto I, first king of modern Greece** (from 1832), was deposed in a military and popular uprising. Otto had been unpopular throughout his rule due to his Roman Catholicism, his German advisors and officials, his high taxes, and his interfering wife **Princess Amalie** of Oldenburg (1818–1875). Great Britain rejected the election of **Prince Alfred** [Ernest Albert] (1844–1900), son of Victoria, queen of Great Britain, by the Greek National Assembly. On Mar. 30, 1863, the Assembly made **Prince William,** son of **Christian IX** (Apr. 8, 1818–Jan. 29, 1906), king of Denmark (from 1863).

1862 Dec. 13 A Union drive toward Richmond, Virginia, was halted by a **battle at Fredericksburg,** Virginia. **Lee** had assembled his Confederate troops along the Rappahannock River and held it against a superior number of Union soldiers under **Burnside.** Though the Union supply service had failed to deliver the pontoons required for crossing the river, which delayed the attack and gave Lee two extra weeks to prepare his defenses, Burnside insisted on advancing as planned. The Union forces lost c.13,000 killed, wounded, and missing; Lee about half that number.

1862 Dec. 31–1863, Jan. 2 A Union army commanded by **Rosecrans** defeated a Confederate army commanded by **Bragg** at **Stone's River** near Murfreesboro, Tennessee. On Dec. 29 Confederate cavalry under **Joseph Wheeler** (Sept. 10, 1836–Jan. 25, 1906) had attacked the rear of the Union column, capturing c.1,000 prisoners and the army's meat supply. On Dec. 31 the Confederates struck first and nearly won the battle except for the actions of **Philip Henry Sheridan** (Mar. 6, 1831–Aug. 5, 1888) and **George Henry Thomas** (July 31, 1816–Mar. 28, 1870). Both armies rested on Jan. 1 but renewed fighting the next day. Union forces drove the Confederates into retreat and captured Murfreeboro. Rosecrans lost c.13,000 casualties; Bragg c.12,000, or 30 percent of his army.

1863 **Norodom** [Ang Vody] (1834?–Apr. 24, 1904), king of **Cambodia** (from 1859), a vassal state of Siam [Thailand] on the west and Annam [Vietnam] on the east, accepted the French protection offered by **Pierre de La Grandière.**

1863 Four new territories were organized in the U.S. from parts of larger existing territories: **Wyoming**, **Nebraska**, **New Mexico**, and **Arizona**. Montana was made a separate territory in 1864.

1863 Jan. 1 **Abraham Lincoln** issued the formal version of the **Emancipation Proclamation**. It ordered an end to slavery in the Confederate States of America. It did not apply to slaves in areas occupied by Union forces or in the four slave states, Delaware, Kentucky, Maryland, and Missouri, which remained in the Union. The Proclamation had little direct effect in freeing slaves. It was, rather, a statement of policy designed to improve the Union image in the North and abroad.

1863 Jan. 22 A **Polish insurrection against Russian rule** broke out despite reforms instituted during the previous 30 years. The revolutionaries called for an independent Poland with borders restored to the pre-1772 extent. With the support of Prussia, Russian troops quelled the insurrection, but Polish partisan groups continued guerrilla fighting until May of 1864.

1863 Feb. 25 The king of Porto Novo, capital of present **Benin**, accepted French protection in order to free his kingdom from the nearby Kingdom of Dahomey, in West Africa.

1863 Mar. 3 In response to the need for troops in the Civil War, the U.S. Congress passed a **national conscription act**, requiring all male citizens between 20 and 45 to register for the army. The alternative of substitution or payment of $300 was accepted from those choosing not to accept duty. This was a cause for the **draft riots in New York City**, where c.1,000 people were killed in July.

1863 May 1–4 The **battle at Chancellorsville**, Virginia, in the Civil War (1861–1865) was a victory for Confederate forces under **Lee**, although **Thomas Jonathan "Stonewall" Jackson** (b. Jan. 21, 1824) died on May 10 of wounds accidentally received from his own troops. Union forces were commanded by **Joseph Hooker** (Nov. 13, 1814–Oct.31, 1879). During the battle the Union suffered c.17,000 casualties and the Confederates c.13,000. On June 28 **George Gordon Meade** (Dec. 31, 1815–Nov. 6, 1872) replaced Hooker as commander of the Army of the Potomac.

1863 June 20 **West Virginia** was the 35th state admitted to the U.S. The northwestern counties of Virginia had strongly opposed Virginia's secession from the Union. Protected by Union troops, these counties adopted their own constitution in May 1862 and entered the Union as a free state.

1863 June 23–Sept. 9 **Rosecrans** at Murfreesboro, Tennessee, finally began his advance southward to Chattanooga, the important rail center near the border with Georgia, defended by Bragg's army. He outflanked Confederate troops from successive defensive positions at Shelbyville, Tullahoma, and elsewhere in Tennessee and finally maneuvered **Bragg** out of Chattanooga (Sept. 9) with hardly a loss.

1863 July 1–4 The **Battle of Gettysburg**, Pennsylvania, ended Lee's last invasion into northern territory. Union troops under Meade gathered to protect the nation's capital at Washington, D.C., as Lee advanced north of the Potomac River. They met north of Washington a few miles from the Pennsylvania-Maryland border. On the first day of battle, Lee failed to press on to take Culp's Hill, the key to capturing the Union position along **Cemetery Ridge**. On July 3 **George Edward Pickett** (Jan. 25, 1825–July 30, 1875), a Confederate commander, made what was known as **"Pickett's Charge,"** an assault turned back by Union troops at Highwater Mark. It was the turning point in the battle. On July 4, more shells had been fired than throughout all the battles fought by Napoléon. The Union still held Cemetery Ridge, at the cost of 19 regiments. Victory was uncertain as **Lee** organized against an expected counterattack by the exhausted Union soldiers. It never came, and the remaining Confederate troops began to retreat across the Potomac and back down the Shenandoah Valley through the pouring rain on July 4. In this battle, the Confederates had lost 28,063 of c.75,000 men. The Union loss stood at 23,049 of c.88,000 men.

1863 July 4 **U.S. Grant took Vicksburg**, the Confederate port on the Mississippi River. After several unsuccessful assaults he began siege operations May 22, and by July 4 half of the Confederate forces had died or were disabled. The Confederate commander **John Clifford Pemberton** (Aug. 10, 1814–July 13, 1881) surrendered. Union troops had **cut the Confederacy in half.**

1863 Sept. 19–20 **Bragg's Confederate army**, reinforced by a corps from the Army of Northern Virginia commanded by Longstreet, turned on Rosecrans at **Chickamauga**, southeast of Chattanooga. Rosecrans, thinking Bragg's army was beaten, divided his own army as he began an advance toward Atlanta, Georgia. But the battlefield stand of a corps commanded by Thomas allowed most of the Union soldiers to retreat to Chattanooga, where they were besieged by the Confederate army. Union supply lines to Chattanooga were weak, and Rosecrans's position was precarious. Exasperated, Lincoln gave **Grant command of Rosecrans's army and of all Union troops in the west.** In the battle the Union lost c.11,000 men, the Confederates c.17,000.

1863 Nov. 19 **Abraham Lincoln** delivered the **Gettysburg Address** in the dedication ceremony of a national cemetery at the battle site. It began and ended with these words: "Fourscore and seven years ago our fathers brought forth upon this continent a new nation, conceived in liberty, and dedicated to the proposition that all men are created equal and that government of the people, by the people, and for the people, shall not perish from the earth."

1863 Nov. 23–25 Union troops under **Grant**, who had arrived (Oct. 23) in **Chattanooga**, Tennessee, defeated Confederate forces commanded by Bragg, ending the siege of Chattanooga. Union troops commanded by Hooker placed themselves at the foot of Lookout Mountain, the southern anchor of the Confederate line, which they stormed successfully the next morning. The turning point in the battle was the capture (Nov. 25) of **Missionary Ridge**. Union troops commanded by Thomas scaled the heights on their own initiative, and the Confederate artillery was unable to depress the muzzles of its guns enough to fire at them. Union losses were c.5,800; Confederate losses c.8,700. **Bragg** began his retreat to Atlanta, Georgia.

1864 **Spain took the Chincha Islands**, off the coast of Peru, valuable for the guano, used as fertilizer, found there.

1864 Jan. 13 Under **Alexander II**, czar of Russia, the **Zemstvo Law** [Zemstvo = local board or assembly] established institutions of self-government on the county and provincial levels in Russia. They included representatives of the nobility, townspeople, and peasants.

1864 Feb. 17 The Confederate submarine *H.L. Hunley*, hand-powered and screw-driven, blew up in Charleston harbor along with the Union ship *Housatonic*, which was the target for a *Hunley*-launched ram torpedo during the American Civil War. The force of the explosion was so great it sank the attacker as well as the target.

1864 Mar. 9 U[lysses] S[impson] **Grant** was made **commander of all Union armies and lieutenant general**, a rank in the U.S. army last held by George Washington.

1864 Mar. 14–May 18 A Union army under **Nathaniel Prentiss Banks** (Jan. 30, 1816–Sept. 1, 1894) was sent up the Red River to take Fort de Russy, guarding Alexandria in central Louisiana. The expedition was accompanied by a Union fleet commanded by **David Dixon Porter** (June 8, 1813–Feb. 13, 1891). The Confederate troops in Louisiana were led by **Richard Taylor** (Jan. 27, 1826–Apr. 12, 1879), a son of former president Zachary Taylor, and by **Kirby-Smith**. A Union army under **Frederick Steele** (Jan. 14, 1819–Jan. 12, 1868) marching south into Louisiana from Arkansas was met and defeated by Kirby-Smith, who then sent a part of his troops to reinforce Taylor, who had successfully attacked (Apr. 8) Banks at **Sabine Crossroads**, in northwestern Louisiana, and driven him back to Pleasant Hill the next day. The gunboats were almost stranded on the Red River by exceptionally low water, but they were saved by a series of dams built by **Joseph Bailey** (May 6, 1825–Mar. 21, 1867). The Union army continued its retreat toward the Mississippi River. On May 18 a final brush with the Confederates at **Yellow Bayou** ended the **Red River Fiasco**.

1864 May 5–June 15 Grant began to move Meade's **Army of the Potomac** south toward Richmond, engaging on the way Lee's **Army of Northern Virginia** in a series of bloody battles. The battles of **The Wilderness** (May 5–6), **Spotsylvania** (May 8–19), and **Cold Harbor** (June 3) were not decisive victories for either side, but Grant drove ahead, and on June 14 crossed the James River and began the **siege of Petersburg-Richmond** (to Apr. 1865). It cost the Union army c.50,000 casualties to reach Petersburg, an important rail junction c.25 miles south of Richmond.

1864 May 11 Sheridan, placed in command of c.13,000 Union cavalrymen to make a raid against Richmond, caught up with J.E.B. Stuart's Confederate cavalry, only c.2,500 strong, at a crossroads named **Yellow Tavern**, six miles north of Richmond. In the action **James Ewell Broun Stuart** (b. Feb. 6, 1833), a daring and effective Confederate general, was wounded and died the next day.

1864 June 10 Archduke **Maximilian**, brother of Francis Joseph I, emperor of Austria, and his wife Carlota [Carlotta, Charlotte] (June 7, 1840–Jan. 19, 1927) were crowned emperor and empress of **Mexico** in Mexico City.

1864 June 15 Grant laid **siege to Petersburg-Richmond**, Virginia. **Lee**, at the head of the Confederate Army of Northern Virginia, endured for ten months. On Mar. 25, 1865, he launched a final, unsuccessful offensive to break through Grant's lines. On Apr. 1 **Pickett** was defeated in a **battle at Five Forks**, near Petersburg by **Sheridan**, and Lee was forced to evacuate Petersburg and Richmond, retreating west toward Appomattox, Virginia.

1864 July 11 In a final push c.30,000 Confederate troops under **Jubal Anderson Early** (Nov. 3, 1815–Mar. 2, 1894), sent by Lee, who was trapped in Richmond, in a spectacular march through the Shenandoah Valley, reached the suburbs of Washington, which was defended by a makeshift army. While Early was reconnoitering, Union troops arrived by sea from New Orleans and took their places in the ring of defending forts. Early retreated (July 12) back

to the Shenandoah Valley, where he was defeated (Sept. 19) by Union troops under **Sheridan** at **Winchester**. Retreating up the valley with vastly outnumbered forces, Early was defeated again (Sept. 22) at **Fisher's Hill**, and finally (Oct. 19) at **Cedar's Creek**, near Winchester. Lee's Army of Northern Virginia was now doomed.

1864 Sept. 2 Sherman, at the head of a Union army, destroyed supplies at Atlanta, Georgia, after taking the city, and prepared for a march across Georgia to the seaport town of Savannah, which he took on Dec. 20 and 21.

1864 Sept. 5 A combined **American, British, Dutch, and French fleet attacked the Choshu and Satsuma daimyos**, the leading anti-westerners in the **Tokugawa Shogunate** (1603–1867) of Japan. They bombarded Kagoshima, on Kyushu Island, and Shimonoseki, on Honshu Island. The shogun was more pro-western, so the attack was launched strictly at the daimyos. In June 1863, the Choshu had attacked an American vessel and western establishments. A peace treaty was signed on Oct. 22 that alienated the Japanese more from the foreign policy of the shogun **Yoshinobu** [Hitotsubashi] (ruled 1866–1867). The Shogunate fell in 1867, and the emperor was restored to power in 1868.

1864 Oct. 30 The **Treaty of Vienna** settled the Schleswig-Holstein question by ceding the duchies to joint administration by Austria and Prussia. The duchies, on the southern tip of the Jutland Peninsula, had long had ties to one another. On Aug. 14, 1865, by the **Convention of Gastein**, Holstein was given to Austria, and Schleswig to Prussia.

1864 Oct. 31 Nevada was the 36th state admitted to the U.S.

1864 Nov. 16 Sherman and his Union army completed their "**March to the Sea**" when they reached Savannah, Georgia, after ravaging the countryside along his route to destroy Confederate supplies. With the aid of a Union fleet Sherman surrounded the Confederates, but the Confederate commander William Joseph Hardee (Oct. 12, 1815–Nov. 6, 1873) escaped with his troops into South Carolina by means of a pontoon bridge. **Sherman occupied Savannah** on Dec. 21.

1864 Dec. 15–16 Thomas and his Union troops, hemmed into **Nashville**, Tennessee, by a Confederate force under **John Bell Hood** (June 1, 1831–Aug. 30, 1879), routed Hood's army, which never formed again to menace the Union. Hood, after his defeat by Sherman at Atlanta, Georgia, had begun to raid northward into Tennessee, thinking to destroy Sherman's non-existent supply lines. Thomas had been sent to Nashville to gather his troops and guard against Hood. Hood had already lost c.6,000 soldiers in an attack on a Union army of c.32,000 under **John McAllister Schofield** (Sept. 29, 1831–Mar. 4, 1906) at **Franklin**, Tennessee, on Nov. 30. Hood was weakened by these losses, while Schofield was able to pull his troops back to Nashville to join Thomas. This Union victory essentially ended the Civil War in the west.

V. ECONOMY AND TRADE

1860 *History of the Railroad and the Canals of the United States*, a volume of financial research on American business, was published by **Henry Varnum Poor** (Dec. 8, 1812–Jan. 4, 1905). It was made (1868) an annual publication entitled *Poor's Manual on Railroads*, and it became a precedessor of the modern *Standard and Poor's Index.*

1860 Jan. 23 A treaty, signed by Great Britain and France, removed trade prohibitions and reduced import duties between the countries. The treaty with France, which moved it toward a general policy of free trade, became a **model for ending the mercantilist tradition in Europe**. It was the result of secret negotiations between **Michel Chevalier** (Jan. 13, 1806–Nov. 28, 1879), a French economist and statesman, and **Richard Cobden** (June 3, 1804–Apr. 2, 1865), a British statesman known as the "Apostle of Free Trade," and it became known as the "**Cobden-Chevalier Treaty.**"

1860 Apr. 3 **Buffalo Bill** [William Frederick] **Cody** (Feb. 26, 1846–Jan. 10, 1917) set out from St. Joseph, Missouri, to Sacramento, California, carrying mail on the **Pony Express. William Hepburn Russell** (Jan. 31, 1812–Sept. 10, 1872) had been instrumental in establishing the mail route. Capable of relaying mail in ten days under favorable conditions, the Pony Express could not compete with the transcontinental telegraph line and went bankrupt on Oct. 24, 1861.

1860 Nov. The election of **Abraham Lincoln** as president of the U.S. initiated a period of **deflation** as southern interests began to withdraw their assets from northern banks and businesses.

1861 Mar. 2 The U.S. Congress enacted the **Morrill Tariff Bill**, raising import duties to ten percent and promoting a policy of protectionism. The bill was advanced by **Justin Smith Morrill** (Apr. 14, 1810–Dec. 28, 1898), a member of the House of Representatives.

1861 Mar. 3 **Alexander II**, czar of Russia, **freed the serfs** of personal bondage to their owners. Peasants could now own property, marry at will, and use the country's court system.

1861 Aug. 5 The **first federal income tax in the U.S.** was instituted to help finance the **Civil War** (1861–1865). Initially, yearly incomes of $600–$10,000 were taxed at a rate of three percent. When it was discontinued in 1873, the income tax provided about one-fifth of government revenues.

1861 Oct. 24 **Telegraph lines** were joined at Salt Lake City, Utah, enabling Abraham Lincoln, to receive the first coast-to-coast telegram on this day.

1862 Feb. 25 To help finance the Civil War, the Congress authorized for the **first time the printing of legal-tender banknotes**, known as "**greenbacks.**" These demand notes were not backed by gold or silver on deposit but were issued against the credit of the U.S. government. At war's end a $1 greenback was worth 39 cents.

1862 May 20 The **Homestead Act** encouraged settlement of unoccupied lands in the U.S. For a nominal fee, any U.S. citizen or suitable alien could file for as much as 160 acres of surveyed land in the public domain. After living on or cultivating the land for five years, the homesteader received title upon payment of another small fee.

1863 Feb. 25 The **National Bank Act** provided for the federal chartering of banks in the U.S. and established the first uniform security in the form of bank notes issued against investment in federal securities.

1863 June 20 **Jay Cooke** (Aug. 10, 1821–Feb. 18, 1905), an American financier, opened the first National Bank in Philadelphia and, soon afterward, one in Washington, D.C. From 1862 he had been employed by the Treasury Department and helped enormously to finance the Civil War.

1864 The **U.S. North was booming**. There were almost 800,000 immigrants (1861–1865); petroleum production increased from 84,000 gallons in 1859 to 128,000,000 gallons in 1862; and 40,000,000 bushels of grain and flour were exported in 1865. Labor's wages from 1860 to 1865 rose 43 percent compared with a 117 percent rise in prices.

1864 Feb. 17 The **Congress of the Confederate States** of America passed an act repudiating its earlier bank notes. It required the exchange of three old notes for two new bonds. Confederate bank notes were known as "bluebacks" or "graybacks," issued without any backing in gold or silver. By war's end a Confederate dollar was worth about 1.7 cents.

1864 Sept. 28 The **First International** convened at St. Martin's Hall in London as the **International Workingmen's Association. Karl Marx**, a delegate to this meeting, soon came to act as the organization's leader.

VI. RELIGION AND PHILOSOPHY

1860 Sept. 21 Arthur Schopenauer (b. Feb. 22, 1788), a German philosopher, died. Pessimistic by nature, he believed everything stemmed from the will to live and that struggle could only cause pain and dissatisfaction. Relief came only from renunciation of desire. Schopenauer's works included *Die Welt als Wille und Vorstellung* [*The World as Will and Idea*] (1819), *Uber den Willen in der Natur* [*On the Will in Nature*] (1836), and *Die beiden Grundprobleme der Ethik* [*The Basis of Morality*] (1841).

1864 John Henry Newman, later English cardinal (1879) of the Roman Catholic Church, published *Apologia Pro Vita Sua*, on his personal spiritual growth.

VII. SCIENCE, EDUCATION, AND TECHNOLOGY

c.1860 The first use of **wood pulp**, instead of rag fibers, in making paper was said to have been developed by a German named **Voelter**. Americans **I. Augustus Stanwood** (Dec. 7, 1839–Mar. 4, 1914) and **William Tower** of Maine were said to be the first to employ wood pulp in their paper mill.

1860 William Siemens (Apr. 4, 1824–Nov. 19, 1883), an English electrical engineer, introduced an improved regenerative **open hearth furnace**, which improved the efficiency of furnaces used in making steel.

1860 June 29 Thomas Addison (b. 1793), an English physician, died. Serving at Guy's Hospital in London, he conducted experiments that enabled him to recognize (1855) what came to be called **Addison's disease**, caused by the atrophy of the outer layer of the adrenal gland. He also discovered (1849) that the cause of pernicious anemia was the body's inability to absorb vitamin B-12.

1861 A fossil animal showing feathers was discovered in a quarry of fine-grained lithographic limestone at Solnhofen, near Munich, in present West Germany. *Archaeopteryx lithographica* lived c.200 million years ago.

1862 Feb. 3 Jean Baptiste Biot (b. Apr. 21, 1774), a French physicist, died. In 1803 he announced that meteorites came from a celestial origin. On Aug. 23, 1804, he made an ascension in a balloon to prove terrestrial magnetism existed even at great heights. Biot was best known for studying, in collaboration with **Félix Savart** (June 30, 1791–Mar. 16, 1841), the **forces of a magnetic field generated by a direct current**, and together they gave their names to the law (1820) that described the relationship.

1862 May The **first practical internal combustion engine** was produced in Paris by **Jean Étienne Lenoir** (Jan. 12, 1822–Aug. 4, 1900), a Belgian engineer and inventor. He mounted the engine on a carriage. It ran on a mixture of air and illuminating gas and traveled at a speed of 4 miles per hour.

1862 July 7 Under terms of the **Morrill Land Grant Act**, introduced by **Justin Smith Morrill** in the House of Representatives, a widespread **system of four-year agricultural and technical colleges** was organized across the U.S., financed by sales of public land.

1862 Nov. 4 Richard Jordan Gatling (Sept. 12, 1818–Feb. 26, 1903), an American inventor, received a patent on the **first machine gun**. He demonstrated it (Dec. 1862) successfully during the Civil War, but the U.S. army did not adopt it until 1866.

1863 An atlas of the heavens *Bonner Durchmusterung* was completed by **Friedrich Wilhelm August Argelander** (Mar. 22, 1799–Feb. 17, 1875), a German astronomer. It catalogued more than 324,000 stars.

1863 Louis Pasteur, the French chemist and bacteriologist, introduced **pasteurization**, a method for preserving food products by heat treatments, or sterilization.

1863 Jan. 10 The **first subway opened**, in London. Steam locomotives were used to carry 9.5 million passengers in the first year of operation.

1863 Oct. 26 The **International Red Cross** was founded as delegates from 14 countries met in Geneva under the leadership of **Jean Henry Dunant** (May 8, 1828–Oct. 30, 1910), a Swiss philanthropist, to formulate the principles of the humanitarian organization.

VIII. ARTS AND LEISURE

1865 Oct. 6 **Charles Richardson** (b. July, 1775), an English philologist, died, He began compiling a dictionary of the English language, and it first appeared scattered through the *Encyclopedia Metropolitana* (1817). It was later (1836–1837) published separately in two volumes.

c.1860 The **first Beadle dime novel** was published in the U.S. by **Erastus Flavel Beadle** (Sept. 11, 1821–Dec. 21, 1894). In 1858 he had established the publishing firm Beadle and Adams, whose slogan was "a dollar book for a dime." These books were said to be significant in the increasing literacy of the U.S.

1860 **Benoît Constant Coquelin** [Coquelin Aîné] (Jan. 23, 1841–Jan. 27, 1909), a French actor, debuted at the Comédie Française. His most successful role was Cyrano in 1897 at the Théâtre de la Porte-Saint-Martin, Paris.

1860 **Multatuli** [Eduard Douwes Dekker] (Feb. 3, 1820–Feb. 19, 1881), a Dutch author who served in the Dutch East Indies, published his best-known work *Max Havelaar*, a romantic novel.

1860 May 15 *Les Pattes de Mouche* [*A Scrap of Paper*] was the first success of **Victorien Sardou** (Sept. 5, 1831-Nov. 8, 1908), a French playwright, who soon became the leading author of French popular theater.

1861 **William Morris**, an English poet and artist, who had studied painting and architecture, founded **Morris, Marshall, Faulkner, and Company**, the furniture and decorating firm out of which the Arts and Crafts Movement grew in the 1880s.

1861 Palgrave's *Golden Treasury of the Best Songs and Lyrical Poems* in the English Language was the first anthology of English verse since Richard Tottel's printing of **Thomas Wyatt's *Songs and Sonnets*** (1557). It was edited by **Francis Turner Palgrave** (Sept. 28, 1824–Oct. 24, 1897), an English writer and critic.

1861 *Kalevipoeg*, the national epic of Estonia, was compiled by **Friedrich Reinhold Kreutzwald** (Dec. 26, 1803–June 25, 1882). He translated many works into Estonian from the German, and his own works, such as *Lembitu* (1885), were often based on German works.

1861 Feb. 20 **Augustin-Eugène Scribe** (b. Dec. 24, 1791), a prolific French dramatist, died. Alone or in collaboration, he wrote and produced more than 300 plays. Today his best-known work survives in the books for several operas, among them Halévy's *La Juive* (1835), Meyerbeer's *Les Huguenots* (1836), and Verdi's *Les vêpres siciliennes* (1855).

1861 June 29 **Elizabeth Barrett Browning** [nee Elizabeth Moulton; later: Barrett] (b. Mar. 6, 1806), an English poet, died. Her works included *Sonnets from the Portuguese* (1850) and *Aurora Leigh* (1857), a very popular novel in verse.

1862 May 6 **Henry David Thoreau** (b. July 12, 1817), a transcendentalist American writer, died. *Walden, or Life in the Woods* (1854) was the most notable of his books. Thoreau's other books included *A Week on the Concord and Merrimack Rivers* (1849) and two posthumous books, *The Maine Woods* (1864) and *Cape Code* (1865).

1863 **Eleanora Duse**, an Italian actress, began her career in a production of *Les Misérables*. She performed in many plays by Gabriele D'Annunzio and Henrik Ibsen.

1863 Aug. 13 **Ferdinand Victor Eugène Delacroix** (b. Apr. 26, 1798), a leader of the French romantic school of painting, died. His works included *Greece Expiring on the Ruins of Missolonghi* (1827), *Women of Algiers* (1834), *The Jewish Wedding* (1839), and *The Lion Hunt* (1861). He also painted portraits of leading figures of the day and created a series of lithographs for *Faust* by **Johann Wolfgang von Goethe,** and designed murals for the Palais Bourbon and the royal palace in Luxembourg.

1863 Sept. 16   Alfred Victor de Vigny (b. Mar. 27, 1797), a poet, playwright, and a leader of the French romantic school, died. His first work *Poèmes Antiques et Modernes* [*Poems Ancient and Modern*] (1822) was followed by the historical novel *Cinq-Mars* (1826) and the romantic play *Chatterton* (1835).

1863 Dec. 13   Friedrich Hebbel (b. Mar. 18, 1813), a German poet and playwright, died. The play *Judith* (July 6, 1840) was the first of his powerful portraits of women.

1863 Dec. 24   William Makepeace Thackeray [pseud.: Michael Angelo Titmarsh, Charles James Yellowplush, George Savage Fitzboodle, Jeames, Mr. Brown, Théophile Wagstaff] (b. July 18, 1811), one of the greatest of English novelists, died. His most notable work was the novel *Vanity Fair*, the first major work under his own name and published as a serial (Jan., 1847–July, 1848). It became very popular, and Thackeray began to be compared to Dickens. *The History of Pendennis* (1848–1850) and *The History of Henry Esmond, Esq.* (1852) were historical novels.

1864   *Shto Delat?* [*What Is to Be Done?*], a novel popular with Russian revolutionaries, was completed by the Russian political writer, economist, and critic **Nikolai Gavrilovich Chernyshevski (July 1, 1828–Oct. 29, 1889) while he was in prison in St. Petersburg.

1864 Jan. 13   Stephen Collins Foster (b. July 24, 1826), a self-taught American musician and folksong writer, died penniless in New York City. Foster's works included "Oh, Susanna," "Old Folks at Home," "My Old Kentucky Home," and "Old Black Joe."

1864 May 2   Giacomo Meyerbeer [orig.: Jakob Liebmann Beer] (b. Sept. 5, 1791), a German composer, died. His operas, which included *Robert le Diable* (1831) and *Les Huguenots* (1836), were great stage spectacles, the prototypes of so-called grand opera.

1864 May 19   Nathaniel Hawthorne (b. July 4, 1804), an American author known for Puritan themes of secret guilt, spiritual arrogance, and search for perfection, all "unpardonable sins," died. *Twice Told Tales* (1837) established his career. His most popular novel *The Scarlet Letter* (1850) was

followed by *The House of the Seven Gables* (1851), *Tanglewood Tales* (1853), and *The Marble Faun* (1860).

1864 Sept. 17   Walter Savage Landor (b. Jan. 30, 1775), an English writer, died. His most memorable work was the multi-volume *Imaginary Conversations* (1824–1853), a collection of essays written in the words of famous personalities.

IX. SPORTS, GAMES, AND SOCIETY

1860   The **bowler hat** first appeared as the tie and its accompanying collar began to replace the popular standing collars and cravats.

1860 Sept. 14   Charles Blondin [Jean François Gravelet] (Feb. 28, 1824–Feb. 19, 1897), a French **tightrope walker**, crossed Niagara Falls on stilts along an 1100-foot cable suspended 160 feet above the falls.

1861   In England "Jem" [James] **Mace** (Apr. 8, 1851–Nov. 30, 1910) won the **heavyweight boxing championship**, defeating **Sam Hurst** (1832?–May 22, 1882) in eight rounds. Mace eventually claimed the world championship of bare-knuckle boxing by beating **Tom Allen** of England in a match that took place in Louisiana, May 10, 1870.

1861   The publication of *Routledge's Handbook of Croquet*, by **Edmund Routledge** of England, stabilized the rapidly growing lawn game that was spreading through the British Isles and the U.S. and was played by both sexes.

1861   The **world's first ski club**, the Trysil, was formed in Norway. In 1862 the first officially recorded ski competition was held near Christiana, renamed Oslo in 1924.

1862   Christmas cards were printed by the London printing house of Goodall and Sons, launching the Christmas-card industry. The first cards simply contained the words "A Happy Christmas" or "A Happy New Year."

1862   In the Punjab in northern India, horsemen from Manipur put on an exhibition of riding for British army officers that included a demonstration of skill in using a stick to hit a ball made of willow wood, called "**pulu**." Shortly thereafter, **polo** began to be played by British cavalry officers in the Punjab.

1863 Oct. 3 **Abraham Lincoln**, president of the U.S, proclaimed **Thanksgiving Day** a national holiday.

1864 **Alfred James Reach** (May 25, 1840–Jan. 14, 1928) of Philadelphia was the **first baseball player** to become an avowed professional and to make a career of it.

1864 **William Gilbert Grace** (July 18, 1848–Oct. 23, 1915) burst upon the **cricket** scene, scoring 170 and 56, not out, against the Gentlemen of Surrey. For two decades Grace dominated the sport as have few athletes. When he retired (1900) Grace in all had made 54,904 runs, with 126 centuries, and took 2,876 wickets.

1864 Aug. 21 At **Saratoga Springs**, New York, **John Morrissey** (Feb. 12, 1831–May 1, 1878), with the aid of others, opened a regular horse meeting. Morrissey named his first stakes race for a prominent New York sporting family, the **Travers**. The race is still run today.

1865–1869

I. VITAL STATISTICS AND DEMOGRAPHICS

1867 During the **Indian Wars** (1860–1890) in the American Northwest, the **Dakota Indians** [Sioux], by treaty with the U.S. government, gave up a large portion of their land in the northern Great Plains and agreed to depart for a reservation in the southwestern Dakota Territory by 1876.

II. DISASTERS

1865 Apr. 27 The steamship *Sultana* **exploded** and burned on the Mississippi River above Memphis, Tennessee, claiming a record death toll for an American ship disaster of 1,547 lives. When it exploded, the *Sultana* was carrying nearly 2,300 passengers, among them more than 2,000 Union soldiers returning from Confederate prisons.

1866 An Asiatic **cholera epidemic** raged throughout U.S. cities, claiming c.200 lives per day in St. Louis, Missouri, at its peak.

1866 July 4 **Fire in Portland**, Maine, destroyed 1500 buildings, but spared the birthplace of Henry Wadsworth Longfellow, the American poet. Property loss was set at $10 million.

1868 Apr. 9 In Lake Michigan the lake steamer *Seaborg* **caught fire** and sank, killing 99 passengers.

1868 Aug. 16 A three-day series of **earthquakes** ended, having destroyed many towns and leaving $300 million of property damage in southern Peru and northern Ecuador. A conservative estimate was 25,000 deaths.

III. POLITICS AND WAR

1865 **Carpetbaggers** and **scalawags** appeared on the scene almost before the last Confederate army surrendered. Carpetbaggers were generally northerners who entered the former slave states carrying their luggage in bags made from carpeting. Some truly wanted to help the blacks and did; many expected only to help themselves. Scalawags were southerners who joined the Republican party for the same reasons and with the same general aims and results.

1865 Jan. 13 **Fort Fisher**, North Carolina, the last Confederate port, fell to Union forces under **Alfred Howe Terry** (Nov. 10, 1827–Dec. 16, 1890), providing a base for **William Tecumseh Sherman**, who was proceeding northward through the Carolinas, routing Confederate troops. He took Columbia, South Carolina on Feb. 17; Fayetteville, North Carolina, on Mar. 11; and signed an armistice with **Johnston** at Raleigh, North Carolina, on Apr. 11.

1865 Mar. The **War of the Triple Alliance** [Great Paraguayan War] (1865–1870) began as **Francisco Solano López** (July 24, 1826 or 1827–Mar. 1, 1870), dictator of Paraguay, attempted to conquer Argentina. On May 1 Brazil signed an alliance with Argentina. Uruguay soon joined the alliance against Paraguay.

1865 Mar. 3 Congress established the **Freedmen's Bureau** to plan and provide education and assistance to free blacks. It was authorized for only one year but was later extended by Congress until 1872. The Bureau, headed by **Oliver Otis Howard** (Nov. 8,

1830–Oct. 26, 1909), issued emergency rations, set up more than 40 hospitals, urged blacks to work for their former masters at agreed wages, established courts to adjust disputes between the blacks and their employers, set up schools, and supported four colleges for blacks: Howard, Hampton, Atlanta, and Fisk. It also helped restore displaced whites to their homes.

1865 Mar. 4 **Abraham Lincoln** of the Republican party was inaugurated for his second term as president of the U.S., having defeated **George Brinton McClellan**, a Union general, of the Democratic party. **Andrew Johnson** (Dec. 29, 1808–July 31, 1875) served as vice president.

1865 Apr. 1 The **U.S. delivered an ultimatum to France** to remove its forces from Mexico. At the end of the Civil War (1861–1865), a U.S. army under **William Tecumseh Sherman** was sent to the Mexican border in Texas. This, coupled with a threat from the Prussians, forced a French withdrawal by Mar. 12, 1867.

1865 Apr. 1 In a **battle at Five Forks**, in eastern Virginia, Confederate troops under **Pickett** suffered a major defeat by Union forces under **Sheridan**. Nearby Petersburg, after a siege of nearly a year, had fallen to Union troops commanded by **Grant** on the previous day, which resulted in the **evacuation** (Apr. 3) **of Richmond**, after most of the city had been burned by its citizens.

1865 Apr. 2 **Robert E. Lee**, leading the **Army of Northern Virginia**, began a westward retreat across Virginia after the Confederate defeat (Apr. 1) at Five Forks. **Grant** maneuvered Union troops to block Lee from joining **Johnston**, whose Confederate forces were being mauled in North Carolina by Union forces under **Sherman**.

1865 Apr. 9 Lee's **Army of Northern Virginia** was attacked by Union troops at **Sayler's Creek**, in central southern Virginia. Six Confederate generals were taken prisoner. On the following day, the Confederate army escaped across the Appomattox River to its northern bank at Farmville, near Lynchburg, only to find retreat blocked by Union troops at Appomattox Station. On Apr. 9 the final attempt to break through Union lines to get to Lynchburg was made by **John Brown Gordon** (Feb. 6, 1832–Jan. 9, 1904), who drove back Sheridan's dismounted cavalry a short distance until lines of Union infantry brought the Confederates to a halt.

1865 Apr. 9 **Lee surrendered** his Army of Northern Virginia to Grant at **Appomattox Courthouse**, a **de facto ending of the Civil War**. On Apr. 18 **Joseph Eggleston Johnston** surrendered his Confederate troops in North Carolina to **William Tecumseh Sherman**. On May 26 **Simon Bolivar Buckner** (Apr. 1, 1823–Jan. 8, 1914), chief of staff of **Edmund Kirby-Smith** surrendered at New Orleans the remaining Confederate troops west of the Mississippi River. About 360,000 Confederate soldiers and 260,000 Union soldiers had died in the war. The number of wounded was about 100,000 Confederate soldiers and 275,000 Union soldiers.

1865 Apr. 15 **Abraham Lincoln** (b. Feb. 12, 1809) died after being shot the night before at the Ford Theater in Washington, D.C., by **John Wilkes Booth**. **Andrew Johnson**, the vice president, was sworn in as president of the U.S. Booth (b. 1838) escaped, but he was discovered hiding in a barn near Bowling Green, Virginia, where he was shot and killed on Apr. 26.

1865 Dec. 6 With Alabama becoming the 27th state to ratify it, the **Thirteenth Amendment to the U.S. Constitution** was adopted, prohibiting **slavery** or involuntary servitude in the U.S. and authorizing the Congress to enact legislation necessary to enforce this. The declaration of ratification was issued on Dec. 18.

1865 Dec. 24 The **Ku Klux Klan** was formed in Pulaski, Tennessee. The name derived from the Greek *Kyklos* [circle] and Klan was added later. In 1868 it adopted a revised constitution that stated the Klan was to be guided by the principles of chivalry, humanity, mercy, and patriotism. Its actions intimidated blacks and carpetbaggers in the South.

1866 **Edward** [Edwin] **Garrison Walker** (c.1830–Jan. 13, 1901), son of abolitionist **David Walker**, became one of the first two black men to be elected to a state legislature, the Massachusetts House of Representatives.

1866 **Sweden's present parliamentary system** was established. Members of the upper house were elected for nine-year terms by communal councils. General elections were held to choose members of the lower house. Citizens owning property were allowed to vote.

1866 Jan. Peru, experiencing economic crisis, declared war on Spain when the 1864 conflict over the **Chincha Islands** was not resolved satisfactorily. Chile, Ecuador, and Bolivia sided with Peru against Spain. On May 2 Spanish ships were driven from Peru's coast at the port of Callao, near Lima, in an unsuccessful attempt by Spain to regain its former colony.

1866 Apr. 2 **Andrew Johnson**, president of the U.S., issued a proclamation in the states of Alabama, Arkansas, Florida, Georgia, Louisiana, Mississippi, North Carolina, South Carolina, Tennessee, and Virginia declaring the end of the insurrection and, on Aug. 2, he added Texas to the list. The **American Civil War was officially over.**

1866 Apr. 9 Congress passed, over Johnson's veto, a **Civil Rights Act**, which granted citizenship rights to all persons born in the U.S., except Indians, and provided punishment of those persons who prevented free exercise of these rights. When the constitutionality of the act was questioned, the **Fourteenth Amendment to the Constitution** was passed by Congress on June 13 and ratified by the States on July 9, 1868.

1866 June 15 The **Seven Weeks' War** [Austro-Prussian War] began as Prussia invaded Saxony, an Austrian ally. **Otto von Bismarck**, chancellor of Prussia, had initiated the war in order to quell Austria's opposition to German nationalism.

1866 July 3 In a **battle at Sadowa** [Sadova, also Königgrätz, Hradec Kralové], in present Czechoslovakia, during the Seven Weeks' War, the Prussians under **Helmuth** [Karl Bernhard] von Moltke (Oct. 26, 1800–Apr. 24, 1891), defeated the Austrians under **Ludwig von Benedek** (July 14, 1804–Apr. 27, 1881).

1866 July 26 **Tennessee** was the first of the 11 states that had seceded to be **readmitted to the U.S.** Arkansas was readmitted on June 22, 1868. On June 25, 1868, South Carolina, the first to have seceded, was readmitted, as were Florida, Alabama, Louisiana, and North Carolina. In 1870 Virginia (Jan. 26), Mississippi (Feb. 23), Texas (Mar. 30), and Georgia (July 15) were readmitted.

1866 July 28 **Denmark** enacted a new constitution to replace the liberal constitution drafted in 1849.

1866 Aug. 23 The **Austro-Prussian Peace of Prague** settled the issues leading to the outbreak of the **Seven Weeks' War**. Schleswig-Holstein was ceded to Prussia, which also gained Frankfurt, Hanover, Hesse-Kassel, and Nassau to connect the eastern and western portions of the Prussian state. Austria was forced to accept the formation of the **North German Confederation**, which was to replace the **Zollverein**, the German customs union, destroyed by the war. On Oct. 3, by the **Peace of Vienna**, Venetia (a region of northeastern Italy whose capital was Venice) was ceded to the Kingdom of Italy.

1867 Mar. As a result of the growing discontent of the Hungarian nationalists, who were emboldened by Austria's defeat in the **Seven Weeks' War** (1866), the **Austro-Hungarian Empire** (to 1918) was created after the Hungarian parliament agreed to a compromise solution [Ausgleich] that granted limited autonomy to Hungary under the protection of the emperor of Austria. The empire included two states: Cisleithania, comprising present Austria, Bohemia, Moravia, Austrian Silesia, Slovenia, and Austrian Poland; and Transleithania, comprising Hungary—representing the empire's largest region—Bukovina, Romanian Transylvania, Polish Galicia, and areas [the Tyroland and Istria] of present northeastern Italy. Cisleithania was ruled by the Hapsburgs as emperors of Austria, and Transleithania was ruled by the Hapsburgs as kings of Hungary. Croatia enjoyed some autonomy under a government appointed by Transylvania.

1867 Mar. 1 **Nebraska** was the 37th state to join the U.S.

1867 Mar. 2 The first of four **Reconstruction Acts** was passed by the U.S. Congress over the veto of **Andrew Johnson**, president of the U.S. It imposed martial law over the southern states, which were organized into five military districts, each under the authority of a local army commander; and it provided for the restoration of civil government after the states were readmitted to the Union and had passed the **Fourteenth Amendment** (adopted on July 28, 1868). The **second Reconstruction Act** of Mar. 23 provided for the registration of voters who would decide the state's readmittance into the Union. The **third Reconstruction Act** of July 13 added the requirement that the terms of the **Fifteenth Amendment** (passed by Congress on Feb. 26, 1869, and ratified by the states on Feb. 3, 1870) must also be ratified. On Mar. 11, 1868, the **fourth Reconstruction**

Act, the only one not vetoed by Johnson, required only a majority of votes actually cast instead of a majority of votes by registered voters to adopt new state constitutions. It was an attempt to alleviate intimidation of black voters by the **Ku Klux Klan** and disenfranchised whites.

1867 Mar. 2   Congress, in its quest for power over the executive branch, passed the **Tenure of Office Act**, which denied the president the power to dismiss from office any officials appointed by and with the consent of the Senate. Cabinet officers, once appointed, could not be dismissed without the expressed consent of Congress. Johnson wished to dismiss **Edwin M. Stanton** (Dec. 19, 1814–Dec. 24, 1869), the secretary of war, who was known to be passing information about the president's cabinet meetings to the radicals in Congress. This was the primary cause for impeachment proceedings moved against the president. The Tenure of Office Act was declared unconstitutional by the U.S. Supreme Court in 1926.

1867 Mar. 30   Russia agreed to the U.S. purchase of the territory of **Alaska** for $7.2 million in gold, an equivalent of about 2 cents an acre. Americans called the deal, negotiated by **William Henry Seward** (May 16, 1801–Oct. 10, 1872), U.S. secretary of state (1861–1869), "Seward's Folly," as Russia was only too willing to sell territory that was too far away to colonize and defend adequately.

1867 Apr. 16   The **North German Federation** was formed by Prussia and states which had supported Prussian aims in the **Seven Weeks' War** (1866). The bicameral parliament of the North German Federation adopted (July) a constitution, which remained in effect until 1918. Representatives of each German state formed the Bundesrat council, in which Prussian representatives formed a majority vote. The Reichstag representatives were elected by popular vote. The Federation replaced the **German Confederation**, the alliance of German states created in 1815 after the demise of the Holy Roman Empire. By 1870, just before the establishment of the **German Empire** (1871), the southern kingdoms of Bavaria and Würtemberg and the duchies of Hess-Darmstadt and Baden had joined the Federation.

1867 July 1   **British North America**, comprising the four provinces of Quebec, Ontario, Nova Scotia, and New Brunswick, were joined under official Dominion status to become **Canada**. This day is now cele-

brated as Canada's national holiday. **John Alexander Macdonald** (Jan. 11, 1815–June 6, 1891), a Scottish-born Canadian statesman, became the **first prime minister** (to 1873; 1878–1891) **of the Dominion of Canada**. He was to oversee the political unification of British North America.

1867 Aug. 15   The **Second Reform Bill** was passed by the British Parliament through the efforts, in part, of **Benjamin Disraeli**, later earl of Beaconsfield (1876), chancellor of the exchequer. The extension of the voting franchise to those who met the new requirements roughly doubled the number of voters in Great Britain. In Feb., 1868, due to the resignation of **Edward Stanley** (Mar. 29, 1799–Oct. 23, 1869), earl of Derby, Disraeli became the Conservative prime minister; but, in spite of the Conservative-initiated reform, they failed to win the elections (Fall, 1868), which chose the Liberal **William Ewart Gladstone** (Dec. 29, 1809–May 19, 1898) as prime minister.

1868 Jan. 3   The **Meiji restoration** was initiated when **Mutsuhito**, the newly installed emperor of Japan (1867–1912), who had ousted the declining shogunate (1603–1867) of the Tokugawa clan, proclaimed the reestablishment of imperial rule, thus ending the traditional rule of Japan since the 12th century by shoguns or military leaders. Japan was not united under one ruler during the many shogunates until 1392. Mutsuhito reestablished the traditional powers of the emperor, moved his capital to Edo, which he renamed Tokyo, and began the westernization of his country. The **Meiji Dynasty**, which presently holds the throne in Japan, was in direct line of descent from the first Japanese emperors, who established themselves as rulers c.40 B.C. (by tradition c.660 B.C.).

1868 Feb.   The **Burlingame Treaty** between China and the U.S. was negotiated by **Anson Burlingame** (Nov. 14, 1820–Feb. 23, 1870), the U.S. ambassador to China, who was sympathetic to the Chinese in their problems with the western nations. The treaty was a reciprocal agreement giving the nationals of both nations rights of travel, commerce, and immigration in the other nation. It was abrogated (1882) by the U.S. because so many Chinese laborers entered the U.S. to work in the west on the railroads.

1868 Feb. 24   Impeachment charges were brought against **Andrew Johnson**, president of the U.S., by the House of Representatives, though the bill of impeachment failed by one vote in the Senate (May 16–26). Congressional members, especially the radical wing of the Republican party, had objected to Johnson's dismissal (Feb. 21) from office of **Edwin McMasters Stanton**, the secretary of war, who had worked against the president's temperate reconstruction efforts following the American Civil War (1861–1865).

1868 Mar. 12   Basutoland [present Lesotho] was annexed as a British protectorate by **Philip E. Wodehouse,** the British high commissioner of the **Cape Colony,** at the request of **Moshesh** (c.1790–1870), king of the Basutos [Sothos] (from 1823). It was the king's sole alternative to avoiding the annihilation of his nation by the **Orange Free State,** the neighboring Boer republic, which had defeated (1865) him and had taken a fertile strip of his land by the **Treaty of Thaba Bosiu** (1866). Despite the opposition of **Johannes Henricus** [Jan Henrik] **Brand** (Dec. 6, 1823–July 14, 1888), president of the Orange Free State (from 1864), part of the conquered territories were returned to Moshesh and a definitive frontier line between the Cape Colony and the Orange Free State was established (1869).

1868 Apr. 10   A British expeditionary force led by **Robert Napier** (Dec. 6, 1810–Jan. 14, 1890), later Lord Napier of Magdala, defeated the Ethiopians at Aroge and captured their capital Magdala three days later. **Theodore** [Tewoderos] **II** (b. 1820), the Ethiopian king (from 1855), who had imprisoned the British consul with c.60 other Europeans since 1863, committed suicide on Apr. 13, and the hostages were released. **John** [Yohannes] **IV** (d. Mar., 1888), later king of **Ethiopia** (1871–1889), a chieftain from Tigre, a northern province of present Ethiopia, now began the conquest of Ethiopia with firearms he had obtained by aiding the British in their punitive rescue expedition.

1868 May 16   Andrew Johnson, president of the U.S., was acquitted of the charges against him at his impeachment trial by the narrow margin of one vote in the U.S. Senate. The main charge against Johnson was that he had violated the **Tenure of Office Act** in dismissing Edwin M. Stanton, secretary of war, from his cabinet. Most of the charges were trumped up by the radicals in Congress and none had validity.

1868 July 28   The **Fourteenth Amendment** to the Constitution was adopted by means of a proclamation by **William H. Seward,** secretary of state. It had been proposed by the Congress to the legislatures of the states on June 13, 1866; a sufficient number of states had ratified it by July 9. It granted state and national citizenship to all persons born or naturalized in the U.S., barred all states from abrogating this right in any way, and stated that debts incurred in support of insurrection or rebellion against the U.S. were invalid though all debts incurred in suppression of insurrection or rebellion were "not to be questioned."

1868 Aug. 8   Paris signed a treaty of friendship with the **Kingdom of Merina** in **Madagascar,** recognizing the sovereignty of the **Merina Dynasty** (1810–1896) over the whole island in return for the establishment of a French consular jurisdiction at Tananarive [Antananarivo], the capital of present Madagascar. However, it did not mark the end of the Anglo-French competition for preeminence on the island. **Ranavalona II** (d. July 13, 1883), queen of Madagascar (1868–1883), was baptized by British missionaries and declared (1869) Protestantism the state religion. Until this time the Merinia Dynasty had been strongly xenophopic, and had killed or enslaved nearly all of the previously converted Christians.

1868 Sept. 23   El Grito de Lares, a revolt in **Puerto Rico** by radical liberals seeking independence from Spain, broke out. Spain had tried to suppress a report made by a local commission on the need for government reform and the abolition of slavery. Spain quickly subdued the rebellion. Most political prisoners were eventually freed by the republican government that followed the conservative government in Spain after the deposition of **Isabella II.**

1868 Sept. 18   Officers of the Spanish fleet at Cadiz proclaimed a revolution. Army rebels marched on Madrid and defeated (Sept. 28) government forces there, forcing **Isabella,** queen of Spain, to flee to France. The military thereupon declared Isabella deposed and announced a provisional government, which promulgated (1869) a liberal constitutional monarchy, though many Spaniards were in favor of a republican form of government. The provisional government headed by **Francisco Serrano y Dominguez** (Oct. 17, 1810–Nov. 26, 1885), duke de la Torre, sought a democratic king to appoint as king of Spain. In 1870 **Amadeo** (May 30, 1845–Jan. 18, 1890), duke of Aosta, son of **Victor Emmanuel II,** king of Italy, accepted the throne. Amadeo abdicated in 1873.

1868 Oct. 10 The **Ten Years' War** broke out in Cuba when **Carlos Manuel de Céspedes** [y Borja del Castillo] (Apr. 18, 1819–Mar. 22, 1874) demanded independence from Spain, universal suffrage, and the emancipation of the slaves. Céspedes was a wealthy plantation owner. Some factions desired simply reform; others annexation to the U.S. Fighting ended in 1878 with the **Convention of El Zanjón**, which granted reforms, the direct representation of Cuba in the Spanish Cortes, amnesty to the insurgents, and the complete abolition of slavery by 1886. Spain demanded in return the payment of damages by Cuba and continued to appoint local officials sympathetic to the royalist cause.

1868 Dec. 2 **William Ewart Gladstone** became prime minister of Great Britain after general elections returned a substantial majority of Liberal members to Parliament. He supported reform in Ireland despite Conservative opposition. Each year of Gladstone's tenure, due to his economic programs, there was a fiscal surplus followed by a tax reduction and, announcing plans to abolish the income tax, in Jan., 1874, Gladstone dissolved Parliament. But, in the following elections, he was after all soundly defeated. In 1880 Gladstone staged a political comeback.

1868 Dec. 25 As his last official act **Andrew Johnson**, president of the U.S., issued a **proclamation giving complete pardon to all those directly or indirectly involved in secession.**

1869 A constitutional amendment adopted by the Finnish Diet confirmed **Alexander II**, the czar of Russia, as Finland's constitutional monarch. The constitution was derived from Swedish law and could not be changed without the consent of the Diet. The Russian czar was also grand duke of Finland. **Finland** had its own parliament which, with the czar's consent, made its own laws. It also maintained its own customs tariff and its own religion [Lutheranism].

1869 Mar. 4 U[lysses] S[impson] **Grant** of the Republican party was inaugurated as the 18th president of the U.S., having defeated Horatio Seymour (May 31, 1810–Feb. 12, 1886) of the Democratic party. **Schuyler Colfax** (Mar. 23, 1823–Jan. 13, 1885) served as vice president. Although Grant won the election by an electoral landslide, the popular vote was close, and the southern black vote provided the margin of victory for Grant.

IV. ECONOMY AND TRADE

1865 The **Union Stockyards** opened in Chicago. They became perhaps the largest beef stockyards in the U.S., and established **Chicago** as the commercial center of the Midwest. In 1867 **Abilene**, Kansas, also became one of the first cattle towns of the region when cattle pens and loading chutes were constructed there.

1865 **John Wanamaker** (July 11, 1838–Dec. 12, 1922) of Philadelphia, who had opened the first Wanamaker retail men's clothing store in 1861, became the first merchant to advertise a money-back guarantee.

1865 Mar. 3 The U.S. Congress placed a **ten percent annual tax on notes** issued by all state banks, in an effort to control their excessive note issue. This effectively established a monopoly for national banks on the issuing of bank notes.

1866 The Bessemer Steel Company, Ltd., of Pennsylvania won three sets of patents representing the technological basis for the **modern production of steel**. By 1870 the U.S. was producing 77,000 tons of steel. By 1900 it was producing 10,000,000 tons.

1866 Mar. 17 The **Reciprocity Treaty**, signed by the U.S. and Canada on June 5, 1854, was allowed to lapse by the U.S. due to a rising tide of protectionism in the Republican party. The treaty had provided for mutual offshore fishing rights in certain waters, and for duty-free trade of agricultural commodities.

1866 May 11 **Black Friday of 1866**, a financial panic in London, England, began when the banking firm of Overend, Gurney, and Company suspended payments. The bank's partners were acquitted of the charge of conspiracy to defraud in Dec., 1869.

1866 Aug. 20 The **National Labor Union** [National Labor and Reform party or NLRP] was founded in Baltimore, Maryland. Although it failed in its objective, it was notable as an early attempt to organize American workers on a national basis across trade lines. When **David Davis** (Mar. 9, 1815–June 26, 1886), associate justice on the U.S. Supreme Court (1862–1877), declined nomination as its president on Feb. 21, 1872, the organization soon dissolved.

1866 Dec. 4 The **National Grange of the Patrons of Husbandry** was founded in Washington, D.C. Farmers organized in local "granges" to purchase jointly farm machinery and partake in agricultural education. It grew to become a highly effective political instrument when the "patrons" helped to bring about the **Granger Laws**, which established state regulation of the railroads and grain operators in their dealings with farmers. The U.S. Supreme Court affirmed (1876) that states had the power to regulate businesses operating in the public interest. Today the Grange, which was the first important American farmers' organization, works primarily at the local level, promoting better farming methods and education.

1867 The first volume of *Das Kapital* by the German political philosophers, **Karl Marx** and **Friedrich Engels**, was published. Marx maintained that labor itself had value, that all value was created by labor, and that in the direct confrontation between worker and capitalist, the latter becomes rich from the surplus value (the difference between the value of the product and the wages paid to the worker for producing it) created by the former. The injustices and social inequities inevitable under a capitalist system make socialism, in turn, inevitable. The remaining two volumes, which did not deal very successfully with how the system of surplus value worked when middlemen, such as bankers and merchants, intervened between the capitalist and the worker, were completed in 1885 and 1895 by Engels after Marx's death.

1867 May 7 The **Knights of St. Crispin**, a society of shoemakers, was founded in Milwaukee, Wisconsin, to protest new machines, such as the MacKay pegging machine, patented in 1862, and the use of semiskilled labor in shoe shops. By 1870 it had become the largest trade union in the country, but the shoe manufacturers formed their own association that soon broke the union. By the end of the 19th century, about six of every seven shoeworkers had been replaced by machines, greatly reducing the cost of shoes.

1868–1878 Japan's foreign trade more than doubled during the first decade of the **Meiji restoration**, heralding the start of Japan's growth in international trade.

1868 Children playing near the Orange River in South Africa discovered **diamonds**, which soon formed the basis of the economy of South Africa.

1868 June 25 The U.S. Congress issued a directive mandating an **eight-hour day for all laborers**. The Supreme Court found the directive not binding despite the personal support of U.S. Grant, president of the U.S.

1869 Having failed to pay off his creditors, **Mohammed III** as-Sadiq [es-Sadok] of the **Husain Dynasty** (1705–1957), the bey of **Tunis** (1859–1882), was forced to agree to tripartite financial control by Great Britain, France, and Italy as intense competition to take control of Tunisia followed the bey's bankruptcy.

1869 The **Trades Code** adopted by the **North German Federation** granted the right to organize to industrial laborers in the states belonging to the federation. Saxony had already developed a similar code in 1861.

1869 Mar. 18 The **Public Credit Act of the U.S.** declared that the federal government pay its debts in gold.

1869 Sept. 24 The **panic of Black Friday** occurred in the U.S. when it was discovered that the American financiers, **Jay** [Jason] **Gould** (May 27, 1836–Dec. 2, 1896) and **James Fisk** (Apr. 1, 1834–Jan. 6, 1872), had tried to corner the gold market. **U.S. Grant**, president of the U.S., arranged for the release of $4 million in government gold holdings, which caused not only the price of gold to collapse, ruining speculators in gold, but also a general financial **depression**.

1869 Dec. 28 The **Knights of Labor** [Noble Order of the], the **first effective labor union** with more than regional influence, was founded by a small group of garment cutters in Philadelphia led by **Uriah Smith Stephens** (May 3, 1821–Feb. 13, 1882). Soon they enlisted laborers and producers of all kinds in a cooperative effort to better working conditions by education and political means rather than strictly economic threats. This was the largest and most important of the early labor organizations.

V. RELIGION AND PHILOSOPHY

1865 **J. Hudson Taylor** (1832–1905), an English Protestant missionary, founded the **China Inland Mission** to carry the Gospel into interior regions of China as yet unreached by older missions. Taylor adopted Chinese dress and the queue. The China Inland Mission drew its funds from across denominational lines and was the first "faith mission," whose workers were unsalaried and without assured allowances, depending instead upon the response of donors.

1865 Nov. 6   Henry Edward Manning was consecrated archbishop in London, succeeding Cardinal **Nicholas Patrick Stephen Wiseman** (b. Aug. 2, 1802), who had died on Feb. 15. Manning was named by Pope Pius IX, who had passed over the three names the Westminster chapter had submitted to him. On Mar. 15, 1875, Pius elevated Manning to the cardinalate.

1866   The American who later founded the **Church of Christ, Scientist, Mary Baker Eddy** (July 16, 1821–Dec. 3, 1910) was a chronically ill person until she regained her health suddenly after reading Matthew's account of Jesus' healing of a man with palsy (Matt. 9:1–8). Previously a student of **Phineas Parkhurst Quimby** (Feb. 6, 1802–Jan. 16, 1866), a practitioner of healing, Mrs. Eddy published *Science and Health with Key to the Scriptures* (1875), which with the Bible became the twofold textbook of Christian Science.

1867   The **Bahai faith** was founded by **Baha'u'llah** [Mirza Husain 'ali Nuri], the surviving leader of **Babism**, who announced himself to be "him whom God should manifest," a figure foretold by the Bab. In his enforced exile at Akka [Acre], Baha'u'llah softened the strident apocalyptic accents of Babism and his gentler doctrines moved the Bahai sect toward a general religion of humanitarianism.

1868 May 30   Memorial Day [Decoration Day] was celebrated for the first time in the U.S., in honor of the Civil War dead. John Alexander Logan (Feb. 9, 1826–Dec. 26, 1886), a member of the U.S. House of Representatives and National Commander of the Grand Army of the Republic, chose this date. Memorial Day, now observed on the last Monday in May, now commemorates military women and men who died during all American wars.

1869 Dec. 8   The **Vatican Council** [Vatican Council I], called by Pope Pius IX, formally convened. The summons to the Council had been issued on June 29, 1868. Of 1,055 Fathers eligible to vote, 774 were in attendance. The Orthodox and Protestant churches declined invitations to appear as observers. On Dec. 23 two bishops, **Victor Auguste Dechamps** (Dec. 6, 1810–Sept. 29, 1883), bishop of Malines, Belgium, and **Henry Edward Manning**, archbishop of Westminster, England, launched a petition calling upon the Council to define papal infallibility. Over 500 Fathers responded affirmatively, 138 negatively. Later the dogma of **papal infallibility** was adopted (July 18, 1870), with only two bishops casting negative votes.

VI. SCIENCE, EDUCATION, AND TECHNOLOGY

1865   **Père Jean Pierre Armand David** (Sept. 7, 1826–Nov. 10, 1900), a French missionary, climbed the wall surrounding the Imperial Hunting Park outside Peking, where he discovered a large deer previously unknown to zoologists. In 1866 he obtained two specimens of the species, now known as **Père David's Deer** (*Elaphurus davidianus*), found only in this park, for the French Academy of Sciences in Paris. The English duke of Bedford obtained (1900–1901) a number of living deer for his estate at Woburn Abbey, and many zoos were supplied from his successful herd after World War II (1939–1945). The original Chinese herd was wiped out in a flood during 1895. In various zoos throughout the world there are now more than 400 individuals all descended from the Woburn Abbey herd.

1865   **Joseph Lister** (Apr. 5, 1827–Feb. 10, 1912), an English surgeon, developed **antiseptic surgery** by using carbolic acid to prevent septic infection, a practice which brought a spectacular decrease in postoperative mortality. It followed the work of **Louis Pasteur**, who had disproved the theory of the spontaneous generation of germs in 1862 and had shown that putrefaction could be attributed to organisms in the air, or bacteria.

1865   The first volume of the *Grand dictionnaire universal du XIXième siècle, français, historique, géographique, mythologique, bibliographique, littéraire, scientifique* was published in Paris by its editor **Pierre** [Anthannse] **Larousse** (Oct. 23, 1817–Jan. 3, 1875), who founded (1852) a publishing house bearing his name. In all 15 volumes of the dictionary were published, the last appearing in 1876. Other supplementary volumes were added later. The first edition of the popular one-volume *Nouveau Petit Larousse illustré* appeared in 1924. Larousse began his career in this field in 1849 when he published a vocabulary textbook.

1866 The Syrian Protestant College, renamed (1920) the **American University of Beirut**, was founded. Today the university is noted for its medical teaching curriculum.

1866 **Mendel's Law**, which established the principle of heredity, was published. **Gregor Johann Mendel** (July 22, 1822–Jan. 6, 1884), an Austrian monk and botanist, had conducted his experiments with peas at the monastery of Brünn [Brno], in present central Czechoslovakia, from 1856. The importance of his work was not recognized until 1900, when the principles were independently rediscovered by the botanists **Karl Erich Correns** (Sept. 19, 1864–Feb. 14, 1933) and **Erich Tschermak von Seysenegg** (1871–1952).

1866 **Oliver Fisher Winchester** (Nov. 30, 1810–Dec. 11, 1880), an American entrepreneur, developed the **repeating rifle**. He had made improvements upon existing inventions at the arms manufacturing plant he bought in New Haven, Connecticut.

1866 July 27 The **first successful transatlantic telegraph cable**, which made possible for the first time regular instantaneous communication between the U.S. and Europe, was completed by the Anglo-American Telegraph Company using the *Great Eastern*, an iron hulled vessel built in 1858, after three major unsuccessful attempts in 1857, 1858, and 1865. The cable laid in 1858, which was completed on Aug. 5, transmitted the first transatlantic cable, on Aug. 16, from Queen Victoria to Pres. Buchanan. However, it ceased functioning in a short time.

1867 Aug. 25 **Michael Faraday** (b. Sept. 22, 1791), an English physicist, died. He studied the behavior of electricity which enabled him to induce electrical current with a magnet in the **first electromagnetic generator** (1831). He developed a process for liquifying gases (1823) and discovered benzene (1825). The molecular structure of benzene, the benzene ring or nucleus, whose modern formula was suggested by the German chemist Friedrich August Kekulé in 1867, is a ring of six carbon and six hydrogen atoms which can react with various atoms of other chemicals, resulting in many important aromatic based compounds, like alcohols, vitamins (except C), alkaloids, phenols, naphthalenes, and analine.

1868 The **air brake**, invented by **George Westinghouse**, an American manufacturer, was an important development for the railroad industry. It permitted all the brakes on a train to be applied simultaneously, greatly increasing the safety of trains.

1868 The first edition of the annual *World Almanac and Book of Facts* was published in the U.S. It has, by its number of sales—c.50,000,000 copies in more than 120 years—become the world's most popular reference book.

1868 Feb. 10 **David Brewster** (b. Dec. 11, 1781), a Scottish physicist, died. Brewster's most popular invention was a **kaleidoscope** (1816). His more serious scientific studies, however, resulted in **Brewster's Law** (1815), or the law of polarization of light by reflection.

1868 Aug. 5 **Jacques Boucher de Crèvecouer de Perthes** (b. Sept. 10, 1788), a French archaeologist, died. In 1838 Boucher had discovered near Abbeville, France, crude axes, which he estimated to be several thousands of years old. In 1846 he published his findings, in which he stated that prehistoric man had existed during the Pleistocene epoch (2,000,000–12,000 B.P.), in contrast to the belief generally held then among archaeologists that man had only existed for c.6,000 years.

1868 Sept. 26 **August Ferdinand Möbius** (b. Nov. 17, 1790), a German mathematician, died. Well known in his day as an astronomer, Möbius is today celebrated for the **Möbius strip**, by which he demonstrated some of the properties of one-sided surfaces, a feature in the mathematical field of topology which Möbius pioneered. His discussion of the Möbius strip was discovered posthumously.

1869 **Johann Wilhelm Hittorf** (Mar. 24, 1827–Nov. 28, 1914), a German scientist, demonstrated the properties of **cathode rays**, the flow of electrons from the negative pole of a battery.

1869 The **American Museum of Natural History** was founded in New York City and in 1877 opened its first building on its present site. The **Hayden Planetarium** (1935) is today one of its most popular attractions. A vast storehouse of materials comprising all branches of natural history, it is especially noted for its exhibits of dinosaur skeletons.

1869 The **Periodic Table** of chemical elements was developed by **Dmitri Ivanovich Mendeleev** [Mendeléyev] (Feb. 7, 1834–Feb. 2, 1907), a Russian chemist. He had arranged all known elements by their atomic weights and declared that the properties of each element were a function of its weight. Using the **Periodic Law**, he was able to predict the properties of some elements as yet undiscovered.

1869 Mar. 11 The skin of a Chinese **Giant Panda** ["white bear"] (*Ailuropoda melanoleuca*), actually closely related to the raccoon, was obtained by **Père Jean Pierre Armand David**, a French missionary exploring Szechwan province in China. It was the first specimen brought to the attention of occidentals.

1869 May 10 A golden spike was driven into the last section of the **Transcontinental Railroad** to mark its completion near Promontory Point, Utah, where the track laid by the Union Pacific and the Central Pacific Railroad companies finally met.

VII. ARTS AND LEISURE

c.1865 **Burlesque** was introduced to the American stage by **Michael Bennett Leavitt** (1843–1935). At first a variety show featuring comedy and slapstick, burlesque came to be called the "leg show," and was designed chiefly to entertain male audiences. By 1920 the strip tease had evolved as a part of burlesque. Many entertainers got their start in burlesque, notably **W. C. Fields** [William Claude Dukenfield] (Jan. 29, 1880–Dec. 25, 1946), **Fannie Brice** [Fannie Borach] (Oct. 29, 1891–May 29, 1951), **Mae West** (Aug. 17, 1892–Nov. 22, 1980), and **Bert Lahr** [Irving Lahrheim] (Aug. 13, 1895–Dec. 4, 1967).

1865 The play *Society* was performed at the Prince of Wales Theater in London, bringing success to English playwright **Thomas William Robertson** (Jan. 9, 1829–Feb. 3, 1871), in his first "cup and saucer" comedy. It was followed by *Caste* (1867), *Play* (1868), and *School* (1869).

1865 *Alice's Adventures in Wonderland* was published by **Lewis Carroll** [Charles Lutwidge Dodgson] (Jan. 27, 1832–Jan. 14, 1898), a lecturer in mathematics at Christ Church, Oxford. It was originally hand-written by Carroll for Alice Liddell, the daughter of the dean of Christ Church, as *Alice's Adventures Under Ground*. It was followed by *Through the Looking-Glass* (1872). **John Tenniel** (Feb. 28, 1820–Feb. 26, 1914), a famous political cartoonist for

London's satirical weekly *Punch* (from 1851), drew the illustrations for both books. Carroll also wrote the nonsense poem *The Hunting of the Snark* (1876); *Phantasmagoria and Other Poems* (1869) and *Rhyme? and Reason?* (1883), both volumes of verse; an unsuccessful two-volume novel *Sylvie and Bruno* (1889, 1893); and several mathematical treatises.

1866 **Nikolai Rubinstein** (1835–1881), brother of **Anton Rubinstein**, founded the **Moscow Conservatory of Music**. Anton had founded the **Russian Musical Society** (1859) and the **St. Petersburg Conservatory of Music** (1862). These organizations were very influential in Russian music and still are today.

1866 *Crime and Punishment*, the first novel by **Fëdor Mikhailovich Dostoevski**, a Russian writer, was published. Dostoevski's subtle portrayal of the duality of good and evil, which showed the influence of **Nikolai Vasilievich Gogol**, was an early example of psychological realism in writing.

1866 The first edition of *Le Parnasse contemporain*, a famous anthology of poetry, was published in France. It gave the name **Parnassian** to a school of French poets that included **Charles Marie René Leconte de Lisle** (Oct. 22, 1818–July 17, 1894), **François Édouard Joachim Coppée** (Jan. 26, 1842–May 23, 1908), **José María de Heredia** (Nov. 22, 1842–Oct. 3, 1905), and to an extent, **René François Armand Sully Prudhomme**. Believers in "art for art's sake," the Parnassians experimented with verse forms but, in contrast to the romantics, emphasized technical perfection, especially in the sonnet, and as a result their work sometimes suffered from emotional detachment. The Parnassians were succeeded by the symbolists.

1866 Sept. 12 *The Black Crook*, one of the great hits of the American musical stage and possibly the first American musical comedy, opened in New York City at Niblo's Garden to play for a record-shattering run of 475 performances. It was an extravagant production, richly staged and costumed, which lasted for nearly six hours on opening night. Two of its well-known musical numbers were "March of the Amazons" and "You Naughty, Naughty Men."

1866 Sept. 26 **Karl Jonas Ludvig Almquist** [Carl Jonas Love Almqvist] (b. Nov. 28, 1793), a Swedish writer, died. His stormy life included being forced to flee from his native Sweden after an accusation of murder in 1851. *Törnrosens bok* [*The Book of the*

Wild Rose] (1832–1835) was a seven-volume series which included verse dramas and historical fiction. After this work, Almquist turned away from romanticism toward realism to write *Det går an* (1839), a long short story, a style and form which demonstrated the best of his talents.

1867 Jan. 14   Jean Auguste Dominique Ingres (b. Aug. 29, 1780), a leading painter of the French classical school, died. Jacques Louis David was his teacher and Raphael his inspiration. He painted primarily historical subjects. His somewhat stiff academic style was seen in *Apotheosis of Homer* (1827), but Ingres became better known for sensual nudes, such as *Bather of Valpinçon* (1808) and *The Turkish Bath* (1852–1863).

1867 Aug. 31   Charles Pierre Baudelaire (b. Apr. 9, 1821), a French symbolic poet and *poète maudit* ["poet damned"], died. On the basis of *Les Fleurs de Mal* [*The Flowers of Evil*] (1859), a volume of dark, satanic, sensual poetry written in a pure, classical style, Baudelaire was elevated to a status rivaling that of **Paul Verlaine**, a leader of the symbolists and founder of the decadents. In its description of evil and moral decay, Baudelaire's poetry foreshadowed the work of some of the greatest modern writers. Baudelaire was also a critic and translator, notably of **Edgar Allen Poe**, an American writer of horror tales. *Petits Poèmes en Prose* [*Poems in Prose*] (1868) was published posthumously.

1868   Alexander James Edmund Cockburn (Dec. 24, 1802–Nov. 21, 1880), lord chief justice of England, ruled in the case of Regina vs. Hicklin that, "to the minds of the young . . . thoughts of a most impure and libidinous character" was sufficient grounds for censoring literature in England. This formed the basis for **censorship of obscenity in England** and in the U.S. for many years.

1868 Nov. 13   Gioacchino Antonio Rossini (b. Feb. 29, 1792), an Italian opera composer, died. He was one of the last masters of opera buffa, as exemplified by his light and frivolous early works. His later, more serious works, established him as a leader of the bel canto style. His best known operas included *L'Italiana in Algeri* (1813), *Il Barbiere di Siviglia* (1814), *Armida* (1817), *Il Califfo di Baghdad* (1818), and especially his last opera *Guillaume Tell* (1829). He was also remembered for *Petite Messe Solenelle* (1864), and *Sins of My Old Age*, a collection of piano, vocal, and instrumental works.

1869   Lettres de Mon Moulin [*Letters From My Windmill*], a collection of short stories, was the first success of **Alphonse Daudet** (May 13, 1840–Dec. 17, 1897), a French novelist and short story writer of the naturalistic school. His most famous collection was the trilogy of *Tartarin de Tarascon* (1872, 1885, 1890), in whose title character he invented one of the great comic characters of French literature.

1869   Asadullah Khan Ghalib (b. 1797?), an Urdu writer, died. Ghalib, at the Mogul court in Delhi, India, developed **Urdu** not only as a literary language, but also for daily use to replace Persian. He helped develop the curriculum in Urdu prose at the College of Fort William in Calcutta.

1869   War and Peace by a Russian writer **Leo Tolstoi**, was published. One of the greatest novels of all time, it described events during the Napoleonic Wars and the French invasion of Russia.

1869 Feb. 28   Alphonse Marie Louis de Prat de Lamartine (b. Oct. 21, 1790), a French romantic poet and critic, died. His *Méditations Poétiques* (1820) helped define the French romantic movement. His other works included *Chute d'un ange* (1838), *Les Recueillements* (1839), *Raphael* (1849), *Le Tailleur de pierres de Saint-Point* (1851), the 28-volume work *Cours familier de littérature* (1856–1869), and the poem *Le désert, ou l'Immatérialité de Dieu*.

1869 Mar. 8   Louis Hector Berlioz (b. Dec. 11, 1803), a French romantic composer, died. In 1830 Berlioz composed his first big work, the *Symphonie Fantastique*, and was awarded the Prix de Rome. He then composed the symphonies *Lélio* [Le Retour à la Vie] (1832), *Harold en Italie* (1834), and *Roméo and Juliette* (1839). *Benvenuto Cellini* (1838), *The Damnation of Faust* (1846), and *Les Troyens* (1855–1858) were operas. *Le Corsaire* (1855) was an overture, and *L'Enfance du Christ* [*The Childhood of Christ*] (1854) was an oratorio.

1869 Oct. 13   Charles Augustin Sainte-Beuve (b. Dec. 23, 1804), a French writer and literary critic, died. His *Causeries du lundi* [*Monday Talks*], which appeared regularly in French newspapers, helped to develop literary criticism into a disciplined evaluation of a work utilizing psychological insight as well as the historical context. The *Causeries* and *Nouveaux Lundi* were published in 28 volumes. His best novel was *Volupté* (1835). His most important work

Port-Royal (1840–1859) used historical methods to analyze literary and social movements.

1869 Dec. 18 Louis Moreau Gottschalk (b. May 8, 1829), an American pianist and composer, died. The **first U.S. musician to win international renown**, Gottschalk held his formal U.S. debut at the Niblo Theater in New York City on Feb. 11, 1852. He used Latin American and Creole rhythms and folk tunes in his works, among which his piano pieces, such as "La Bamboula," based on black folk music, were probably his best.

VIII. SPORTS, GAMES, AND SOCIETY

1865 The **Goteborg System of temperance** was introduced in Sweden and Norway. All public houses and taverns were closed. Drinking was allowed only with meals in restaurants. Widespread alcoholism and the high consumption of alcohol decreased markedly after these measures had been taken.

1865 July 26 The **Royal Canoe Club** [RCC] was formed at a meeting of enthusiasts led by **John Mac-Gregor** (June 24, 1825–July 16, 1892), a London barrister and canoe designer. By 1868 there were clubs and fleets for paddling or sailing at the RCC's main facility at Kingston-on-Thames, on the Humber and Mersey Rivers, and at Oxford. MacGregor's canoe, the "Rob Roy," designed with sails and paddles, had aroused interest in the canoe for sporting and recreational purposes. In 1871 the New York Canoe Club on Staten Island became the first U.S. canoe club.

1866 Walking became an organized competitive athletic sport in England with the introduction of a seven-mile walking event in the championships of the Amateur Athletic Club. The time of the winner **John Graham Chambers** (1843–1883) was 59 minutes, 32 seconds. A vase named for him was awarded to each year's winner.

1866 May 1 The **first recorded competition of dog field trials** was held on an estate on Cannock Chase, an unenclosed hunting ground that once extended from Stafford to Lichfield, England. Pointers and setters were judged in this trial.

1866 Dec. The *Henrietta*, captained by the American adventurer, philanthropist, and newspaper publisher **James Gordon Bennett** (May 10, 1841–May 14, 1918), won the **first transatlantic yacht race**, defeating *Fleetwing* and *Vesta*. He sailed the course from Sandy Hook, New Jersey, to the Isle of Wight in the elapsed time of 13 days, 21 hours, and 45 minutes.

1867 The **Queensberry Rules for boxing** were drafted by John Graham Chambers (Feb. 12, 1843–Mar. 4, 1883) of England's Amateur Athletic Club under the sponsorship of John Sholto Douglas, the eighth marquis of Queensberry. For the first time, padded gloves were required. The length of a round was fixed at three minutes, and was followed by a one-minute rest period. A fighter who went down had to arise unaided within ten seconds; if he did not do so, he lost the fight. The Queensberry Rules were only gradually accepted for championship engagements.

1867 The first all-comers tournament for **croquet** players was held in the Cotswold town of Moreton-in-the-Marsh, in Gloucestershire, England.

1867 The **Montreal Lacrosse Club**, instrumental in founding the National Lacrosse Association, established the first widely accepted rules of lacrosse. The number of players on a side was fixed at 12, which remained unchanged in the U.S. until 1933 when it became 10.

1867 June 26 The **Grand National Curling Club of America**, an association of seven member clubs, was founded in New York. It was affiliated with the original Royal Caledonian Curling Club. Of the founding clubs, only the Caledonian Curling Club of New York survives today. However, the sport still thrives at other, smaller clubs, such as the St. Andrews Curling Club in Hastings, New York, and there are today a number of American leagues.

1868 The Mohawk Club of Troy, New York, the pioneering U.S. organization for the game of **lacrosse**, was founded.

1868 May 31 James Moore of Great Britain won the **first recorded bicycle race**, a two-kilometer event held at the Parc St. Cloud in Paris.

1869 British cavalry officers of the tenth Hussars introduced **polo** to England at a hunt club known as Hurlingham, just outside London. In 1871 the first recorded polo match was played by the Tenth Hussars against the Ninth Lancers, on Honslow Heath. Eight players were on each side.

1869   The Cincinnati Red Stockings toured the U.S. as the **first all-professional baseball team**. They won 56 out of 57 games, and tied the other. Their success stimulated entrepreneurs in other cities in the East and Midwest to assemble teams of professional players.

1869 June 15   In what was probably the **first international bare knuckles boxing match**, held at St. Louis, Missouri, the U.S. boxing champion Mike McCoole defeated Tom Allen of England on a foul in the ninth round.

1869 Nov. 6   The **first football game** played between two American colleges took place at New Brunswick, New Jersey. Rutgers was victorious over Princeton, with a score of six to four. Until the late 1870s, when elements of rugby were incorporated, the game played in the eastern colleges more closely resembled soccer than the football of the 20th century.

1870–1874

I. VITAL STATISTICS AND DEMOGRAPHICS

1872   New Zealand's **Maori population**, steadily declining because of warfare and exposure to European diseases, by the 1840s, dropped to c.100,000 Maoris; there had been c.250,000 in the 18th century. By 1895 the Maori population sank to its lowest point, c.42,000.

II. DISASTERS

1871 Oct. 8   In the great **Chicago Fire**, reputedly caused by Mrs. O'Leary's cow, which kicked over a lantern while being milked, nearly 100,000 people were left homeless and property damage was set at about $200 million in a three-day blaze that destroyed nearly a third of the city.

1871 Oct. 8   The lesser known **Peshtigo fire** raged through Wisconsin and Upper Michigan, killing 1182 and destroying more than a million acres of forest.

1873 Apr. 1   The British luxury steamer *Atlantic* **was wrecked** on Meagher Rock on the Nova Scotia coast while bound for New York City from Liverpool, England. The accident resulted in 481 deaths, more than half of those aboard.

III. EXPLORATION AND COLONIZATION

1871 Nov. 10   **Henry Morton Stanley** [John Rowlands] (Jan. 28, 1841–May 10, 1904), a newspaperman and explorer, greeted **David Livingstone** with "Dr. Livingstone, I presume?" as he found the missing Scottish missionary and explorer near the northern end of Lake Tanganyika in Africa.

1873 Mar. 1   **David Livingstone** (b. Mar. 19, 1813), world famous Scottish African explorer and medical missionary, died. He was ordained on completion of his medical courses and sent (1840) to Kuruman, in northern Cape Province of South Africa. He and his wife began explorations, in 1849 discovering Lake Ngami and, in 1850, the Zambezi [Zambesi] River. Searching for routes into the interior from both the east or west coasts (1852–1856) of Africa he crossed the continent from Luanda [Loanda], in present Angola, to the mouth of the Zambesi, in present Mozambique, and discovered Victoria Falls. He returned to England and wrote *Missionary Travels and Researches in South Africa* (1857). He returned to Africa as British consul at Quelimane and led an expedition up the Shire River and discovered Lake Nyasa (1858) and, in 1859, discovered Lake Chilwa and explored the area around Lake Nyasa. In 1866 he attempted unsuccessfully to discover the source of the Nile. It was during this trip that Henry Stanley, a Welsh-born American newspaper correspondent for the New York *Herald,* was sent to find Livingstone. Livingstone died in a native village. His heart was buried where he died, but his body was carried to Zanzibar and later transferred to Westminster Abbey.

IV. WAR AND POLITICS

1870   **Tomás Guardia** (Dec. 17, 1832–July 7, 1882) was elected president of **Costa Rica**. Under his guidance, albeit as a dictator from 1876 to his death, Costa Rica prospered.

1870   **Alexander II**, czar of Russia, organized a new system of self-government for cities and towns that allowed them elected assemblies [**dumas**] which could, within prescribed limits, impose taxes.

1870 Mar. 30 The **Fifteenth Amendment to the U.S. Constitution**, passed by Congress on Feb. 26, 1869, and ratified by the states on Feb. 3, 1870, was adopted, guaranteeing suffrage to citizens regardless of race, color, or previous condition of servitude. The Amendment was intended to grant the vote to former slaves, but not to women.

1870 June The **War of the Triple Alliance** [Great Paraguayan War] (1865–1870) ended with a treaty between Argentina, Brazil, and Uruguay, and Paraguay. During the war Paraguay, completely devastated, lost about a million people, primarily men, and a large part of its territory.

1870 June 21 The **Tientsin Massacre** occurred at that port city near Peking when Chinese, thinking that French nuns were kidnapping and killing their children, mobbed an orphanage there. The French consul fired on the mob, but he and 20 other foreigners were killed.

1870 July 19 The **Franco-German War** [Franco-Prussian War] (1870–1871) broke out as France declared war on Prussia. The precipitating event had been **Otto von Bismarck's** push for the candidacy of Prince Leopold von Hohenzollern-Sigmaringen (1885–1905) for the Spanish throne, vacated (1868) by the deposed Isabella II. Bismarck advocated war with France because he felt it would **unify the German people** behind Prussia and into a German nation. On July 12, Leopold had withdrawn his candidacy. On the following day, at Ems, in the Rhineland-Palatinate of present West Germany, William I, king of Prussia and head of the Hohenzollern family, received a telegram asking that he guarantee to Vincent Benedetti (Apr. 29, 1817–Mar. 28, 1900), the French ambassador, that Leopold would never again be named a candidate for the Spanish throne. Bismarck, in Berlin, edited and published the message with the aim of pushing the French to aggressive action and to arouse the anger of the German people. Bismarck used the revised telegram to whip up hatred between the two nations and force Napoléon to attack first.

1870 Aug. 24 The **Red River Rebellion** was put down by Canadian troops as they captured Fort Garry, near the original Red River Settlement, at the junction of the Red and Assiniboine rivers in Manitoba. **Louis Riel** (Oct. 23, 1844–Nov. 16, 1885) had led the métis [French: half-caste] of mixed French, Scotch, and Indian descent in the capture (Nov., 1869) of Fort Garry, to protest the acquisition of the Hudson's Bay Company by the Dominion of Canada. The *métis* feared the loss of their lands, which they had been occupying without formal ownership.

1870 Sept. 2 In a **battle at Sedan**, on the Meuse River in northeastern France, during the **Franco-German War** (1870–1871) the French were badly defeated by German forces, which took prisoner the French commander Marie Edmé Patrice Maurice (July 13, 1808–Oct. 17, 1893), comte de MacMahon, and Napoléon III. German armies then advanced on Paris. French resistance was fierce, and François Achille Bazaine (Feb. 13, 1811–Sept. 28, 1888), the commander-in-chief of French forces, did not surrender at Metz until Oct. 28, for which he was later court-martialed. The forts surrounding Paris were placed under siege on Dec. 27. On Jan. 28, 1871, **Paris fell** and an armistice was signed.

1870 Sept. 4 The **Third Republic of France** was declared two days after the defeat of **Napoléon III** in the **battle at Sedan** sealed French defeat in the **Franco-German War** (1870–1871). On Feb. 13, 1871, a new assembly, requested by Bismarck to conclude the peace treaty, convened at Bordeaux. On Feb. 17 **Louis Adolphe Thiers** (Apr. 18, 1797–Sept. 3, 1877) was elected president of the Third Republic; the overthrow of Napoléon III was complete.

1870 Sept. 20 **Italian patriots occupied Rome.** Pope Pius IX, imprisoned in the Vatican, was stripped of all temporal powers in Italy (and in the world), chiefly because he had withdrawn his support of republican governments following acts of terrorism and violence. The pope's new status was confirmed (Oct. 2) when Rome became the official capital of Italy, ending the **Italian drive** (from 1860) **for unification**.

1870 Nov. 16 **Amadeo**, second son of Victor Emmanuel II, king of Italy, was elected king of Spain by the Cortes. On Dec. 30 Amadeo arrived in Spain, where he served until his abdication in 1873.

1871 Jan. 18 **William I**, king of Prussia, was formally proclaimed German emperor in the Hall of Mirrors in the royal palace at Versailles, near Paris, at the insistence of Bismarck.

1871   The **Law of Free Birth** was enacted in **Brazil**, providing for the gradual emancipation of slaves, accomplished in 1888.

1871 Mar. 18   In Paris an insurrection broke out in protest against the possible reinstitution of a monarchy by the conservative dominated assembly, which had chosen to move to Versailles. Elections on Mar. 26 resulted in the formation of the radical **Commune of Paris**, which held power until May 28, when **Mac-Mahon**, marshal of France, entered Paris with an army and reestablished control. During the fierce fighting, c.20,000 lost their lives, and after MacMahon regained the city, almost another 40,000 were arrested.

1871 Apr. 14   The **German Empire**, or **Second Reich**, was formed when the German **Reichstag**, or parliament, accepted with some modification the constitution drafted in 1867 for the North German Federation. **Otto von Bismarck** was named the first chancellor. **William I** was designated king of Prussia and emperor of Germany. Belonging to the empire were 4 kingdoms; 18 duchies, grand duchies, and principalities; the free cities of Hamburg, Lübeck, and Bremen; and the former French territory of Alsace-Lorraine. It stretched from France on the west, Switzerland and Austria on the south, to Denmark on the north and Russia on the east.

1871 May 23   The **Treaty of Frankfurt** ended the **Franco-German War** (1870–1871) to the advantage of the German Empire, which gained Alsace and Lorraine, including Metz.

1871 July 20   The British Crown colony of **British Columbia** became a province of the Dominion of Canada.

1871 Oct. 27   In South Africa the **Kimberley diamond fields**, in northern Cape Province on the border with the Orange Free State, were granted by Great Britain to the state of **Griqualand West**, which was subsequently annexed to Cape Colony.

1872 Feb. 2   The Dutch sold their trading forts along the **Gold Coast** [present Ghana] to Great Britain. The Dutch departure from the region was forced by the British prohibition against the slave trade, which Great Britain policed by attempting to control the entire coast.

1872 Feb. 14   **Richard Worsam Meade** (Oct. 9, 1837–May 4, 1897), a U.S. navy officer, signed an agreement with the native residents of **Samoa** to establish a naval station at **Pago Pago** [Pango Pango].

1872 Spring   The **Second Carlist War** (to 1876), an attempt to restore the "legitimate" Bourbon rulers of Spain, who had been ousted when Ferdinand VII had abrogated the Spanish Salic law in order to place his daughter Isabella on the throne at his death, broke out in northern Spain. It was led by Don Carlos III [Don Carlos María de los Dolores de Borbón] (Mar. 30, 1848–July 18, 1909), nephew of Don Carlos II, against Amadeo, who had been chosen king of Spain by the Cortes. Isabella, in exile in France, abdicated her throne in favor of her son Alfonso (Nov. 28, 1857–Nov. 25, 1888), the future king of Spain (1874–1885), which meant that there were **two separate Bourbon claimants to the Spanish throne**.

1873   **Japan enacted a nationwide conscription** to replace the **samurai**, the privileged class of warriors.

1873 Jan. 9   **Napoléon III** [Louis Napoléon; Charles Louis Napoléon Bonaparte] (b. Apr. 20, 1808), president of France (1848–1852) and emperor of France (1852–1871) died in England. He was the second and **last of the Napoléons** (Napoléon II never assumed power) to rule France.

1873 Feb. 11   Confronted with the growing success of the **Carlist revolt** in northern Spain **Amadeo**, king of Spain, abdicated. The **First Republic** was declared on Feb. 12, and in May new elections were held for the Cortes.

1873 Mar. 4   U[lysses] S[impson] **Grant** of the Republican party was inaugurated for his second term as president of the U.S., having defeated **Horace Greeley** of the Democratic party. **Henry Wilson** (Feb. 10, 1812–Nov. 22, 1875) served as vice president.

1873 Mar. 22   **Slavery** was abolished in **Puerto Rico**.

1873 Summer   The **Populists** [Narodniks], thousands of university-age Russians, went into the countryside to spread the idea of revolution among the peasants, especially in the areas of the Volga, Don, and Dnieper [Dnepr] rivers. The Populists had thought peasants would naturally support socialist reforms, but the peasants often informed the police of the presence of these agents, who were then arrested.

1873 July 1 **Prince Edward Island** elected to become a province of the Dominion of Canada.

1873 July 16 **Don Carlos III**, leader of the Carlists in Spain, established his court in Navarra [Navarre], a province of northern Spain, after the abdication of Amadeo from the Spanish throne.

1873 Oct. 22 The **Three Emperors' Alliance** [Dreikaiserbund] was concluded among representatives of Austria, Germany, and Russia against the event of a war in the Balkans. Russia had already begun to construct a fleet in the Black Sea, having considered the **Franco-German War** (1870–1871) cause for disregarding the obligations of the **Paris Treaty** of 1856 forbidding such a fleet in peacetime.

1874 **Russia enacted a new law regulating conscription.** The term of active service was reduced from 25 years to 6 years, after which a soldier had to spend 9 more years at a reserve summer camp. The law was later changed so that a soldier spent 5 years in the local militia, an organization called to active service only in emergencies.

1874 Jan. 3 In Spain **Manuel Pavía y** [Rodriguez de] **Albuquerque** (Aug. 2, 1827–Jan. 4, 1895), a Spanish general, used his troops to gain control of Madrid. The **Cortes** was dissolved, and a coalition government was formed that declared **Alfonso XII** [Francisco de Asís Fernando Pío Juan María Gregorio Pelayo], son of Isabella II, as king.

1874 Jan. 31 A British force under Garnet Joseph Wolseley (June 4, 1833–Mar. 25, 1913), Viscount Wolseley, defeated forces of the **Ashanti Kingdom** (c.1700–1901) at Amoaful, in present **Ghana**. **Kumasi**, the capital, was captured and burnt (Feb. 4), whereupon the British retired. The Ashanti king accepted a treaty of peace, and Great Britain made the Gold Coast a Crown colony.

1874 Apr. 19 **Switzerland** adopted a revised constitution that provided the federal government with greater powers while introducing the principle of **referendum** for national legislation.

V. ECONOMY AND TRADE

1870–1888 This was the time of the **Long Drives**, in which large herds of Texas cattle were brought north to the better grazing lands of Kansas, Nebraska, and Montana. During this time, the **cattle industry** domi-

nated the western states and territories of the U.S. as cattle were allowed to graze freely on large tracts of land owned by the government.

1870 The **first post cards** were issued, in Austria.

1870 **Julius Vogel** (Feb. 24, 1835–Mar. 12, 1899) set forth a scheme for the economic development of the British colony of **New Zealand** based on £10 million to be borrowed over the next ten years.

1870 Jan. 10 **John Davison Rockefeller** and four partners incorporated the **Standard Oil Company**, with capital of $1,000,000. Standard Oil soon gained a monopoly on 95 percent of the oil refining industry in the U.S. by controlling oil pipelines and signing a special rate agreement with the railroad companies.

1870 Nov. 4 The **first official U.S. weather bulletins** were issued from Washington, D.C., by the newly established United States Weather Service.

1871 The **mark** was made the standard unit of currency of the **German Empire**, replacing the silver coins that had been circulating. In 1873 Germany went on the gold standard and used silver for small coins only.

1871 June 29 The **Trade Union Act** legalized trade organizations in Great Britain on the grounds that their prohibition constituted a restraint of free trade.

1871 Aug. The **Meiji restoration** in Japan undertook the economic modernization of Japan by abolishing fiefs. The **daimyo**, or landowning nobles, were appointed governors and, as a further step in ending feudalism, the governorships were later abolished.

1872 **Montgomery Ward and Company** opened in Chicago. The mail order service, operating out of a one-room office, proved successful in reaching a large rural market with the offer of low prices and a variety of goods.

1872 **Japan's first railroad** connected Tokyo and Yokohama on Honshu Island.

1873 The **Timber Culture Act** was passed by the U.S. Congress. It was the first federal regulation of the national forests.

1873 Feb. 12 The **silver dollar** was discontinued, and gold was made the single monetary standard of the U.S. by the passage of the **Fourth Coinage Act**.

1873 July   Japan, in an effort to raise a stable revenue, set a **tax** of three percent on the value of land to be paid yearly by the farmer in cash regardless of the quality of the harvest.

1873 Sept. 18   The **Panic of 1873** was set off in the U.S. by the bankruptcy of **Jay Cooke**, an American financier, whose financial firm had backed the **Northern Pacific Railroad**. On Sept. 20 the **New York Stock Exchange closed**; over the next five years more than 100 banks failed in the U.S.

1874   The **Universal Postal Union** was formed to facilitate international mail exchange. The set rate to send a letter between participating countries was five cents in U.S. money.

1874 Aug. 30   France **banned child labor** [children under 14] as well as other work practices considered cruel or unfair.

VI. RELIGION AND PHILOSOPHY

1870 Apr. 24   The **Vatican Council** adopted the important constitution *Dei Filius*, which treated the relation between reason and faith in an effort to free Roman Catholicism from errors stemming from rationalism.

1870 June 22   The **New Testament Company**, comprising 27 scholars, began its work on a revised version of the authorized version of the New Testament. The **Old Testament Company**, also of 27 scholars, began its work eight days later. Scholars of all Christian denominations were invited to participate by the Church of England's organizing committee. No Roman Catholics accepted.

1870 July 18   The **Vatican Council I** (1869–1870) reached a final vote on the question of **Papal Infallibility**. It was overwhelmingly affirmative. The Catholic Church had gained true primacy of jurisdiction with the doctrine of Papal Infallibility, which capped the triumph of Ultramontism, banished the notion of the supremacy of a General Council over a pope, and established the papacy as an absolute monarchy over religious affairs.

1871 Mar. 28   Johann Joseph [Josef] **Ignaz von Döllinger** (Feb. 28, 1799–Jan. 10, 1890), a German Catholic theologian, responded to his archbishop's request for his position on the new dogma of **Papal Infallibility** that he could not accept it as a Christian

theologian, a historian, or as a citizen. On Apr. 17 Döllinger was excommunicated.

1871 July 31   The **Kulturkampf**, or cultural struggle, in Germany began with orders by **Otto von Bismarck**, the German chancellor, to suppress the Roman Catholic Department for Spiritual Affairs. The Old Catholics, as many Catholics of Germany were called, were excommunicated by the pope, and Bismarck expelled the **Jesuits** from Germany.

1872 Oct. 4   The **American Revision Committee** began its work of cooperation with the British committee of Bible translators on a revision of the Authorized **King James Version** of 1611. At the completion of its work the American Committee did not disband, for it saw a probable need for a thoroughly American revision of the British Revised Version.

1873   The **Union of American Hebrew Congregations**, the first national federation of Jewish congregations in the U.S., was established by Rabbi **Isaac Mayer Wise**. Representatives of 34 synagogues met at Cincinnati and elected Wise their first president.

1873   **Christianity was declared a licit religion in Japan** under the **Meiji restoration** (1867–1912) based on the recommendation of a mission to Europe and the U.S. headed by Iwakura Tomomi (1825–July 20, 1883) to study what of western knowledge and technology would be beneficial to Japan's development.

1873 May 8   **John Stuart Mill** (b. May 20, 1806), an English economist and philosopher, died. His best-known work was probably *On Liberty* (1859), but Mill was also noted for *Utilitarianism* (1863) and *Auguste Comte and Positivism* (1865).

VII. SCIENCE, EDUCATION, AND TECHNOLOGY

1870   The **Elementary Education Act** was passed in **Great Britain**, instituting the first uniform and comprehensive legislation regarding the **education of children**. Under this act every school board was required to ensure that parents sent their children to school. At this time most of western Europe enacted education legislation that provided for free compulsory education.

1870 John Wesley Hyatt (Nov. 28, 1837–May 10, 1920), an American inventor, received a patent for the **manufacture of celluloid**, the **first synthesized plastic** invented as a substitute for ivory, bone, coral, and the like.

1870 Apr. The **ruins of Troy** [Ilion; Greek: Troia; Latin: Ilium], the ancient Greek city, were discovered by **Heinrich Schliemann** (Jan. 6, 1822–Dec. 25, 1890), a German archaeologist who had earlier acquired his wealth in business. Schliemann continued excavations at the hill of Hissarlik, where he accurately located Troy, until his death. The oldest finds were dated to between c.2600 and c.2300 B.C. The seventh city on the site was identified as Homer's Troy (c.1200 B.C.).

1871 Oct. 18 **Charles Babbage** (b. Dec. 26, 1792), an English mathematician and inventor, died. He designed (1834) a **calculating device**, a forerunner of the modern computer, as well as such other devices as the **speedometer**, the cowcatcher for use on locomotives, skeleton keys, and an **ophthalmoscope** (1847).

1872 **Eadweard Muybridge** [orig.: Edward James Muggeridge] (Apr. 9, 1830–May 8, 1904), an English photographer, captured **motion in photography** by stretching across the path of a running horse a series of threads that successively tripped the shutters of a series of cameras alongside the track. Muybridge had been asked to prove that a horse, when running, brings all four feet off the ground at one time.

1872 Mar. 1 **Yellowstone National Park** in Wyoming, the **first of the U.S. national parks**, was created when president **U.S. Grant** signed a bill of authorization.

1872 Apr. 2 **Samuel Finley Breese Morse** (b. Apr. 27, 1791), an American painter and inventor, died. He founded (1825) the **National Academy of Design** in the U.S. after studying in England with Washington Allston. Morse was best known, however, for his **invention** (1844) **of the telegraph**.

1873 **Barbed wire** was developed independently by two American farmers, **Joseph Farwell Glidden** (Jan. 18, 1813–Oct. 9, 1906) and **Jacob Haish** (Mar. 9, 1826–Feb. 19, 1926). The barbed wire fence transformed the West, enabling effective fencing of the previously open range and much reducing the need for cowboys.

1873 **Hermite's theorem**, stating that the base of natural logarithms, *e*, was a transcendental rather than an algebraic function, was first described by **Charles Hermite** (Dec. 24, 1822–Jan. 14, 1901), a French mathematician.

1873 Dec. 12 **Louis Jean Rodolphe Agassiz** (b. May 28, 1807), a Swiss-American naturalist and geologist, died. He attracted attention by the publication of *Études sur les Glaciers* [*Studies of Glaciers*] (1840), an explanation of the glacial movements and deposits that established the existence of ice ages. In 1846 he went to the U.S. where he emphasized the importance of studying directly from nature. Noted for his works on living and fossil fishes, including *Recherches Sur les Poissons Fossiles* (1833–1844), which established his authority, he published *Contributions to the Natural History of the U.S.* (1857–1863), which included "Essay on Classification," an argument opposing Charles Darwin's theory of evolution.

1874 The **Model I Remington**, the **first practical typewriter**, was produced by E. Remington and Sons, the American arms manufacturing company. **Christopher Latham Sholes** (Feb. 14, 1819–Feb. 17, 1890) had sold his patented rights in the machine for $12,000.

1874 The **triple arch bridge** over the Mississippi River at St. Louis was completed under the direction of **James Buchanan Eads** (May 23, 1820–Mar. 8, 1887), an engineer who had built iron hulled boats for the Union during the Civil War (1861–1865).

1874 Construction began on the **first underwater railway tunnel** in the U.S. Known as the **Hudson Tubes**, it was to run under the Hudson River from New York City west to Jersey City. There were to be two tubes, each 18 feet high and 16 feet wide. Compressed air was used to keep the river water out, but the river broke through (1880) and drowned 20 workmen. Though construction began again (1890) in earnest, the sponsor ran out of money and the tunnels lay flooded for 11 years. Finally another group of entrepreneurs took over the project, completing it in 1904.

VIII. ARTS AND LEISURE

1870 Mar. The first installment of *For the Term of His Natural Life*, about the convict system in Australia, appeared in the *Australian Journal*. It was written by **Marcus Andrew Hislop Clarke** (Apr. 24,

1846–Aug. 2, 1881), and was published in book form in 1874.

1870 Mar. 10 Ignaz [Isack] **Moscheles** (b. May 23, 1794), a Bohemian pianist, composer, and teacher, died in Leipzig, present Germany. His students included Felix Mendelssohn, and Moscheles influenced the later composers, Franz Liszt and Robert Schumann, with his explorations of tone color. In 1832 Moscheles conducted England's first performance of the *Missa Solemnis* by Ludwig van Beethoven.

1870 June 9 Charles [John Huffam] **Dickens** (b. Feb. 7, 1812), an enormously popular English novelist, died. His first book was *Sketches* (1836), written under the pen name Boz. It was soon followed by *The Pickwick Papers* (1837), *Oliver Twist* (1838), and *Nicholas Nickleby* (1839). His other works included *A Christmas Carol* (1843); *David Copperfield* (1850), part autobiographical; *Bleak House* (1853); *Little Dorrit* (1855–1857); the historical novel *A Tale of Two Cities* (1859); and the posthumous *Mystery of Edwin Drood* (1870).

1870 June 11 William Gilmore Simms (b. Apr. 17, 1806), an American novelist and poet of the pre-Civil War South, died. His Border Romances depicting frontier life among the woodsmen and Indians of Carolina and the Old Southwest included *Guy Rivers* (1834), *The Yamassee* (1835), *The Partisan* (1835), and *Katherine Walton* (1851).

1870 Sept. 23 Prosper Mérimée (b. Sept. 28, 1803), a French romantic author and companion of Madame de Staël, died. As a translator, he introduced Russian literature to France. His long story *Carmen* (1845) was adapted by Bizet for the opera of the same name. He wrote many short stories and the historical novel *La Chronique du Temps de Charles IX* [*The Chronicle of the Reign of Charles IX*] (1829).

1871 May 13 Daniel François Esprit Auber (b. Jan. 29, 1782), a French composer often said to be the founder of French grand opera, died. His first successful work, the comic opera *Le Bergère Châtelaine* (1820), was followed by the serious opera *La Muette de Portici* (1828), his greatest work, considered the first French grand opera. Most of Auber's 45 operas were produced at L'Opéra Comique in Paris.

1872 *Impression: Sunrise* by **Claude Monet** (Nov. 14, 1840–Dec. 5, 1926) was completed. It initiated the era of impressionist painters, named in derision of this canvas, executed in a soft, misty style. The impressionist leaders included **Paul Cézanne** (Jan. 19, 1839–Oct. 22, 1906), **Édouard Manet** (Jan. 23, 1932–Apr. 30, 1883), **Claude Monet, Camille Pissarro** (July 10, 1830–Nov. 13, 1903), and **Edgar Degas** (July 19, 1834–Sept. 27, 1917).

1872 Aug. 11 Lowell Mason (b. Jan. 8, 1792), an American composer of church music, died. He published the *Manual of Instructions* (1834), based on Pestalozzian methods, and *Handel and Haydn Society's Collection of Church Music* (1822). "Nearer my God, to Thee" was perhaps the best-known hymn for which he composed the music.

1872 Oct. 23 Théophile Gautier (b. Aug. 31, 1811), a French novelist and poet, died. His works included the novels *Mademoiselle de Maupin* (1835) and *Le Capitaine Fracasse* (1863), and the collection of poetry *Enamels and Cameos* (1856).

1872 Nov. 29 Horace Greeley (b. Feb. 23, 1811), an American journalist and abolitionist, died. He was founder and editor of the *New York Tribune*, which he used to broadcast his liberal political views. The phrase "Go West, young man, go West" was attributed to Greeley, who made it well known, though it was actually coined (1851) by an editorial writer **John B.L. Soule** of the *Terre Haute Express*.

1873 Jan. 18 Edward George Earle Lytton Bulwer-Lytton (b. May 25, 1803), an English writer, died. His work included the historical and romantic novels *Devereux* (1829), *Paul Clifford* (1830), *Eugene Aram* (1832), *The Last Days of Pompeii* (1834), *The Last of the Barons* (1843), *The Caxtons* (1848), and *Kenelm Chillingly* (1873).

1873 May 22 Alessandro [Francesco Tommaso Antonio] **Manzoni** (b. May 7, 1785), an influential romantic Italian playwright and novelist, died. His plays were more noted for their poetry than for drama. From 1840 to 1842 Manzoni republished a revision of his novel *I Promesi Sposi* [*The Betrothed*] (1825–1827), which he had labored over to achieve the purity of the Tuscan idiom. Manzoni also wrote the tragedy *Il Conte di Carmagnola* [*The Count of Carmagnola*] (1820) and the drama *Adelchi* (1822).

1873 June 27   Hiram Powers (b. June 29, 1805), an American sculptor working in the classical revival style, died. He executed many **busts** of American political leaders, including Andrew Jackson, John Caldwell Calhoun, Benjamin Franklin, and Thomas Jefferson (all between 1834 and 1837).

1873 Oct. 1   Émile Gaboriau (b. Nov. 9, 1832), a French writer of detective stories, died. Credited by some with developing the **detective story**, he was the creator of the characters Monsieur Le Coq and Père Tabaret.

1874 Feb. 9   Jules Michelet (b. Aug. 21, 1798), the most famous 19th-century French historian, died. Michelet was a passionate republican and a hater of both **Napoléons** and of the conservative right. Although his stature as a rigorous historian was debatable, there was no questioning his success as a man of letters, and his work brilliantly recreated the life and passions of the past. His most important works were the 17-volume *Histoire de France* (1833–1867) and *Histoire de la Révolution Française* (1852).

IX. SPORTS, GAMES, AND SOCIETY

1870   The **All-England Croquet Club** was formed and an annual contest for the championship was held on the club's grounds at Wimbledon, soon to become the Mecca of tennis. The popularity of croquet was at its height in England, the U.S., Australia, and New Zealand.

1870   Donald Dinnie (1837–Apr. 5, 1916), reigning champion of **Scottish Highland Games**, toured the U.S. with great success. He gave exhibitions of strength in the "heavy events," such as hammer throwing, putting the stone, weight-lifting and throwing, and caber tossing, as well as demonstrating Highland dancing and wrestling all comers.

1870   A Gaelic Athletic Association to sponsor Irish sports in America was organized in Chicago. Within three years their association had 15 clubs with a membership of c.2,000 and was sponsoring ten Gaelic football teams and five hurling teams.

1870   The Football Association determined that **soccer** should be played thenceforth between sides of 11 men. With the exception of a significant change in the offside rule adopted in 1928, the rules of soccer have remained uniform around the world.

1871   Jean Eugène Robert-Houdin (b. 1805), a French conjurer and **father of the modern stage profession of magician**, died. He was noted for his optical illusions and was the first to use electricity to achieve his effects. His successor as the best of his profession, the American **Erich Weiss**, took as his stage name **Harry Houdini** in tribute to Robert-Houdin.

1871 Jan. 26   The **Rugby Union** was created by 17 clubs and three schools in England. Rules were formulated specifically for rugby, chosen as the official name for the "rushing game." The number of players was fixed at 15 on each team.

1872 Jan.   The **first ski club in the U.S.** was formed in Berlin, New Hampshire, by Scandinavian Americans. It sponsored both jumping and cross country skiing.

1873   At "Badminton," the Gloucestershire estate of the duke of Beaufort, British officers on leave from India introduced into English society the game called "**poona**" they had brought back with them. It was this event that gave "poona" its new name of badminton and launched its development.

1873   The ceremony of **seppuku**, better known as **hara-kiri**, was abolished by **Mutsuhito**, the emperor of Japan. It had been performed primarily by order of an authority and used as a formal method of capital punishment for disgraced **samurai** [heriditary warrior class] or **daimyo** [hereditary feudal lords].

1873   The Hurlingham Club was formed for **polo** in the London area. In 1874 the **Hurlingham Polo Association**, an umbrella organization of polo associations, quickly became the authority for the game.

1873   Lawn tennis, an adaptation of court tennis widely played in England under local or family rules, was standardized by **Walter Wingfield** (1833–Apr. 18, 1912) when he compiled a rule book for the game.

1874   Mary E. Outerbridge of Staten Island, New York, brought tennis equipment home from Bermuda, where she had seen British military officers playing the new game. She and her brother set up a court on the grounds of the Staten Island Cricket and Baseball Club. In two or three years, the game of **tennis** had gained popularity in the suburban clubs of the northeastern cities and **New Orleans**.

1874 Oct. 7   The **first dog show in the U.S.** was held at Mineola, New York. Entries were limited to pointers and Irish and Gordon setters. The first all-breed dog show was held in Detroit in Jan. 1875.

1874 Oct. 8   The first combined bench and field-trial **dog competitions for sporting breeds** only was sponsored by the Tennessee Sportsmen's Association.

1875–1879

I. VITAL STATISTICS AND DEMOGRAPHICS

1876   The **last of the aboriginal Tasmanians**, who lived on Tasmania [Van Diemen's Land], an island off the southern coast of Australia, died. Originally a tribe numbering c.4,000 members, the Tasmanians succumbed to European diseases, against which they had no resistance, and to their slaughter, which accompanied British colonization.

II. DISASTERS

1875 May 16   An **earthquake** struck the South American republics of **Venezuela and Colombia**, killing c.16,000 people.

1876 Oct. 31   A large **tropical storm** combined with high winds, tides, and waves struck **Bakarganj**, India [present Barisa, Bangladesh], a key port city of the southern Ganges Delta, claiming more than 200,000 lives.

1876 Dec. 5   New York City's worst **theater fire** killed 289 of an audience of c.1200 at Brooklyn's Conway Theater.

1876 Dec. 29   A structurally **defective railroad bridge** at Ashtabula, Ohio, **collapsed** beneath the 13-car *Pacific Express*, plunging most of the wooden passenger cars into an abyss where they caught fire. Death estimates varied from 80 to 92.

1877–1878   Following a severe **drought** famine in China's northern provinces of Shansi [Shanxi], Shensi [Shaanxi], and Honan [Henan] claimed c.9,500,000 deaths. Mass graves, known as "**10,000-man holes**," were dug in an effort to bury the corpses.

1878   The worst **yellow fever epidemic** in U.S. history killed c.5,000 in **Memphis**, Tennessee; c.4,000 in **New Orleans**; and countless other deaths elsewhere.

1879 Dec. 28   **Tay Bridge** at **Dundee**, Scotland, which crossed the firth of Tay, **collapsed** during a storm, catapulting the 75 passengers and crewmen aboard the Edinburgh-Dundee train to their deaths.

III. EXPLORATION AND COLONIZATION

1878 July 21   Nils **Adolf Eric Nordenskjöld** (Nov. 18, 1832–Aug. 12, 1901), a Swedish explorer, sailed the Northeast Passage from Troms [Tromsö], in northeastern Norway, aboard the *Vega*, a steam-powered ship. He was the **first person to negotiate the Arctic passage**, which skirts the northern coast of Europe and Asia between the Atlantic and Pacific oceans.

IV. POLITICS AND WAR

1875 Mar. 1   The **Civil Rights Act of 1875** mandated that accommodations for blacks in public places must be equal to those for whites. An earlier act had established penalties for proprietors of public institutions who maintained segregated facilities, but as soon as whites regained control of local and state governments, the earlier Civil Rights Acts were virtually ignored, and local "**Jim Crow**" laws were enacted, establishing separate facilities for blacks and whites.

1875   **Sakhalin Island**, jointly administered by Russia and Japan since 1855, was ceded to Russia. In return, Russia recognized Japan's claim to the Kurile Islands [Russian: Kuril'skiye Ostrova; Japanese: Chishima Retto], between the Pacific Ocean and Okhotsk Sea.

1875 Aug. 6   **Gabriel Garciá Moreno** (b. Dec. 24, 1821), president of **Ecuador**, was assassinated in Quito as he was beginning his third term. He restored public order and established a theocratic government by making the **Roman Catholic Church the state religion** and signing (1863) a concordat with Pope Pius IX. Only practicing Catholics could vote. He was succeeded by two presidents, both Moreno's puppets, but took office again himself (1869).

1876 Feb. 26 **Korea** reentered world political affairs when the Korean "**Hermit Kingdom**" and Japan signed a treaty providing for diplomatic and trade relations.

1876 Feb 28 **Don Carlos III**, claimant to the Spanish throne, having lost the support of the army, which controlled the country, and of the Church, fled into exile, ending the **Second Carlist War** (from 1872).

1876 Mar. 7 **John** [Johannes] **IV**, king of **Ethiopia** (ruled 1872–1889), decisively defeated the Egyptians at **Gura**, near Asmera, in present northern Ethiopia. It marked the **end of Egyptian attempts to expand in East Africa**.

1876 June 25 During the **Indian Wars** (1860–1890) of the American Northwest, the **battle at Little Bighorn**, on the Little Bighorn River, in present southern Montana, resulted in the massacre of forces of **George Armstrong Custer** (b. 1839), an officer of the U.S. army, who died in the battle with all 264 of his men. Custer, grossly underestimating the number of warriors, had attacked the camp of **Sitting Bull** (1831?–Dec. 15, 1890) in southern Montana. The only survivor of Custer's forces was reported to have been Comanche, a horse.

1876 July 1 **Serbia** declared war on the **Ottoman Empire** (1326–1920) to protest the Muslim massacres during the Bulgarian uprising, which had occurred in Mar. 1876 in support of the uprising by Christian Slavs in **Bosnia-Herzegovina** in April and May 1875.

1876 Aug. 1 **Colorado** was the 38th state to join the U.S.

1876 Aug. 31 **Murad V** (Sept. 21, 1840–Aug. 29, 1904), sultan of **Turkey** (May 21, 1876), having been declared insane by European doctors, was replaced as sultan by the reactionary **Abdul-Hamid II** (Sept. 21, 1842–Feb. 10, 1918; ruled to 1909). Murad had announced his intention of reforming the constitution, and it was said he was deposed actually because of his liberal program.

1876 Nov. 16 In a **battle at Tecoac, Mexico**, Porfirio Díaz (Sept. 15, 1830–July 2, 1915) defeated the forces of **Sebastián Lerdo de Tejada**, president of Mexico, who had succeeded **Benito Juárez** at his death and whose reelection Díaz opposed. On May 2, 1877, Díaz was officially elected president (1876–1880; 1884–1911).

1877–1878 The **Ninth Kaffir War**, and the last of the Kaffir Wars (the first began 1779) between the Xhosa tribe, a Bantu people, and the British in **Cape of Good Hope Colony** [Cape Province], in the present Republic of South Africa, was fought. It resulted in the disarming of the Xhosa, who had begun to use European guns.

1877 The **Satsuma Rebellion**, on Kyushu Island, **Japan**, was led by **Saigo Takamori** (b. Dec. 7, 1827), who ordered an aide to put him to death on Sept. 14, 1877, with his sword when his uprising failed. This was the **last rebellion by the outlawed class of samurai**.

1877 Jan. 2 With the inauguration of a Democrat as governor, **carpetbag government ended in Florida**. It ended in **South Carolina** on Apr. 10 when federal troops were withdrawn from its capital, Columbia. The last southern state to regain control of its internal affairs was Louisiana, on Apr. 24.

1877 Mar. 4 **Rutherford Birchard Hayes** (Oct. 4, 1822–Jan. 17, 1893) of the Republican party was inaugurated as the 19th president of the U.S., having defeated **Samuel Jones Tilden** (Feb. 9, 1814–Aug. 4, 1886) of the Democratic party in a disputed election. Electoral votes from the states of Oregon, Louisiana, South Carolina, and Florida were disputed; together, they represented 22 electoral votes. The Republicans insisted that the black voters in the southern states had been intimidated at the polls, but the contention that all these popular votes would have gone for the Republicans could not be upheld. Democrats in Oregon ousted a Hayes elector, placing the entire electoral vote of that state under dispute. An **Electoral Commission of 1877** was created by an act of Congress (Jan. 29, 1877) with equal numbers of Republicans and Democrats plus one neutral (the neutral turned out to be pro-Republican). The commission awarded 184 electoral votes to Hayes and 183 to Tilden, although Tilden had won the popular vote by more than 250,000 ballots. Tilden conceded the election to avoid armed conflict, maintaining, however, that he had originally won the election. **William Almon Wheeler** (June 30, 1819–June 4, 1887) served as vice president.

1877 Apr. 24 Russia, claiming legal guardianship of Orthodox Christians in the Ottoman Empire, declared war on Turkey, which was massacring thousands of Bulgarians and Yugoslavians [South Slavs]. **Alexander II**, czar of Russia, tore up the **Paris Treaty of 1857**, which forbade Russia from maintaining a war fleet in the Black Sea and from invading the Balkans. The European powers remained neutral until the war's end, though the secret **Reichstadt Convention** of July 13, 1876, between Austria and Russia, agreed on a partition of Turkish territory following the war between Turkey and Serbia. At Berlin on June 13, 1878, the European powers acted in concert to protect Turkey after Russia won the war.

1877 Oct. 5 The **Nez Percés Indians**, led by **Chief Joseph** (1840–Sept. 21, 1904) [Hinmaton-Yalaktit; Hinmahtooyahlatkekht = Thunder Rolling in the Mountains] fled more than 1,500 miles from U.S. army troops before surrendering at Bear Paw, south of Chinook in central northern Montana, during the **Indian Wars** (1860–1890) of the American Northwest. By treaty the Nez Percés had been settled on a reservation along the borders of Oregon and Idaho, but the discovery of gold in the area caused the U.S. to break the treaty. Many of the Indians refused to leave Oregon after an ultimatum (May, 1877), and the troops sent to drive them out were defeated at White Bird, Idaho, while the Indians were on their way to what they thought would be safety in that part of their reservation in Idaho. During their 115-day trek seven battles were fought with the pursuing U.S. troops. The Indians had only c.250 warriors, and were escorting c.500 women, children, and more than 2,000 horses. After the 5-day battle at Bear Paw c.200 Indians managed to flee to Canada and join Sitting Bull.

1878 Mar. 3 The **Treaty of San Stefano** officially resolved the **Russo-Turkish War of 1877**. The Turkish principality of Bulgaria was granted autonomy under Russian suzerainty. The boundaries of Serbia and Montenegro were extended, but these areas remained under Russian control. Austria-Hungary occupied Bosnia-Herzegovina. Russia received southern Bessarabia, and Romania [the former Danubian principalities] received part of Dobruja.

1878 June 4 The Ottoman Empire and Great Britain agreed that **Cyprus** was to be administered by the British. The Turkish sultan acceded to Great Britain, which wanted to establish a naval base in the Mediterranean, in return for the promise of British naval support against future Russian attack.

1878 June 13 The **Congress of Berlin** was convened by Austria-Hungary, Prussia, and Great Britain to redress the provisions of the **Treaty of San Stefano**. The **Treaty of Berlin**, signed on July 13, reduced Russian Bulgaria, although the territories of Kars, Batum [Batumi], and Bessarabia remained in Russia's possession. Bosnia and Herzegovina were placed under Austro-Hungarian occupation, and Montenegro, Serbia, and Romania were recognized as independent.

1878 Oct. 18 The **Anti-Socialist Act** was legislated in Germany at the instigation of **Otto von Bismarck**, chancellor of the German Empire (1871–1918), following two assassination attempts on the kaiser, despite the fact that the attackers were not connected with the Socialist party. Union activities were curtailed, socialist associations were dissolved, and their funds seized.

1879 Oct. 7 **Bismarck** created the **Dual Alliance** in a secret treaty between the German and Austro-Hungarian empires, providing that each party would come to the aid of the other if it were attacked by Russia but would remain neutral should they be attacked by another nation unless Russia came to the aid of that nation.

1879 Jan. 12 The **Zulu War** was initiated by Great Britain when troops led from Natal by **Frederic Augustus Thesiger** [Lord Chelmsford] (May 3, 1827–Apr. 9, 1905) tried to capture Zululand, a Bantu kingdom on the southeastern coast of southern Africa. The British suffered a massacre at Isandhlwand on Jan. 22, but won a decisive **battle at Ulundi** on July 4, capturing and deposing Cetewayo [Cetshwayo] (1834–Feb. 8, 1884), the king of the Zulus (from 1772) on Aug. 28.

1879 Feb. 14 A dispute over mineral rights in the Bolivian province of Atacama led to the **War of the Pacific** (1879–1884), in which Peru allied itself with Bolivia against Chile. The **first battle between ironclad warships** took place during this war when the Chilean *Cochrane* defeated the Peruvian *Huáscar*. Chile, victorious in the war, was ceded Atacama and the port city of Antofagasta, at the **Treaty of Valparaiso** (Apr. 4, 1884), thereby **depriving Bolivia of all its coastal territory.**

1879 June 29   Isma'il I Pasha, khedive of **Egypt** (from 1863), was forced to abdicate by Great Britain, France, and Germany in favor of his son **Mohammed Tewfik** [Tawfiq] **Pasha** (Nov. 15, 1852–Jan. 7, 1892; ruled to 1892). Isma'il had grossly mismanaged Egypt's finances, but had made remarkable achievements in modernizing and rebuilding his country. Tewfik yielded to pressure from France and Britain, who had taken over (1876) Egypt's finances.

V. ECONOMY AND TRADE

1875 Jan. 14   The **Specie Resumption Act** provided for the revaluation of depreciated banknotes issued in the U.S. during the Civil War. On Jan. 1, 1879, payment resumed on these notes, which were redeemed in gold at face value.

1875 Mar.   The Bank of Prussia (1846) was reorganized as the **Reichsbank**, the central bank of Germany. It was privately owned but publicly administered.

1875 May 20   The **metric system** was made the system of standard measurement by 17 European nations.

1875 Aug. 13   The **Conspiracy and Protection of Property Act** legalized collective bargaining and picketing in England.

1875 Nov. 25   Isma'il, khedive of Egypt, facing bankruptcy, sold his country's 44 percent share of the **Suez Canal** to **Benjamin Disraeli**, acting as agent for the British government. Egyptian finances were placed in British and French custody on Nov. 18, 1876.

1876   A **transoceanic cable** was opened between New Zealand and Australia.

1876   The **first Chinese railroad** was built in Shanghai.

1876   The **Homestake Gold Mine**, largest producer of gold in the Western Hemisphere, was found during the Black Hills, South Dakota, gold rush.

1876–1877   In a series of trials, many members of the secret society of Irish-American coal miners, called the **Molly Maguires**, were convicted of violent crimes, including murder. Nineteen were hanged (1880), others went to jail. The Molly Maguires operated in the anthracite coal regions of Pennsylvania and adjacent states, and they executed a campaign of violence against those they considered their oppressors, including mine owners, mine superintendents, and local police departments under virtual control of the mine owners. The Molly Maguires disbanded shortly after the trials.

1877 July 17   Laborers on the Baltimore and Ohio Railroad struck to protest a reduction in their wages. Workers on other lines soon joined the strike, and Rutherford Hayes, president of the U.S., called out federal troops. The resulting strife in Baltimore, Pittsburgh, Chicago, and St. Louis left more than 30 people dead and millions of dollars of railroad equipment damaged.

1878 Feb. 28   The **Bland-Allison Act** restored a limited coinage of silver dollars in the U.S. A compromise between advocates of the gold standard and free silver, it was replaced (1890) by the more liberal **Sherman Silver Purchase Act.**

1879   The **earliest recorded cartel** [German: *kartell*] was formed by a group of German potash producers. Very quickly they expanded (1881) to form a sales syndicate. **Germany's world monopoly of potash** enabled the cartel to set its own pricing policy; they charged high prices for export and low prices inside Germany.

1879   In Russia the steamship *Zoroaster* was put into service on the Caspian Sea to transport oil from the Baku oil fields to the Volga River. Earlier attempts (1863) at placing **oil tanks on sailing ships** had been unsuccessful.

1879 June 21   Frank Winfield Woolworth (Apr. 13, 1852–Apr. 8, 1919), an American entrepreneur, who had opened the first **"5 cent" store** in **Utica**, New York, moved the store to Lancaster, Pennsylvania. Woolworth's sold merchandise that retailed for a nickle or less. It soon added a ten cent table, and the dimestore tradition began its growth toward a chain of nearly 500 stores.

VI. RELIGION AND PHILOSOPHY

1875 Dayananda Saraswati [orig.: Mula Sankara] (1824–Oct. 30, 1883), a Brahmin, organized in **Bombay**, India, the **Arya Samaj**, also called the **Society of Aryas**, a "reform" sect of **Hinduism** opposed to westernization and Christianization, and holding that the Vedas contained all knowledge. The Arya Samaj reconverted many former Hindus from Islam and Christianity.

1875 Rabbi **Isaac Mayer Wise**, with the support of the **Union of American Hebrew Congregations** [UAHC], opened **Hebrew Union College**, the **first seminary for the training of rabbis and teachers in the U.S.**

1876 Joseph Hardy Niishima [Niijima], the first native Japanese Christian minister, founded the **Doshisha School**, which is still an influential Christian university.

1876 The **Ethical Culture Society** was founded by **Felix Adler** (Aug. 13, 1851–Apr. 24, 1933), after abandoning what he considered the too constrictive tenets of Reform Judaism. Members of the movement accepted the supreme ethical aim in all relations of life. Formal creeds and ritual were avoided.

1878 Julius Wellhausen (May 17, 1844–Jan. 7, 1918), a German biblical scholar and professor at Greifswald, on the Baltic coast, in present Germany, published *Geschichte Israels*, in which he made a significant contribution to the evolving documentary theory of the composition of the Pentateuch, the first five books of the Old Testament.

1878 June The **Salvation Army** was founded in London as a mission organized along military lines by **William Booth** (Apr. 10, 1829–Aug. 20, 1912), who had begun preaching there in 1865.

1879 The Muslim sect known as **Ahmadiyya** was started by **Mirza Ghulam Ahmed** (1839?–May 26, 1908), who preached in the Punjab in India. Ahmed claimed (from 1891) to be both the promised Mahdi and the promised Masih [messiah], two distinct personages in orthodox Muslim theology, as well as to have come in the spirit and power of Jesus.

1879 The **Church of Christ, Scientist**, was founded and chartered in **Boston** under the direction of **Mary Baker Eddy**.

VII. SCIENCE, EDUCATION, AND TECHNOLOGY

1875–1881 The **Sacred Grove of Zeus**, or Altis, was cleared at Olympia, in the western Peloponnesus of Greece, by German archaeologists. The great **temple of Olympian Zeus** (c.450 B.C.), the most majestic in all Greece, was unearthed during this excavation. Within it was found one of the **Seven Wonders of the Ancient World**, a gold and ivory **statue of Zeus**, sculpted by **Phidias** [Pheidias] (c.490–c.430 B.C.), whose workshop was located here. Olympia was the site of the original **Olympic Games**, beginning 776 B.C. historically but certainly held for a very long time before this date.

1875 Kheireddine Pasha [Khaireddin = "Joy of Religion"] (birth date unknown–Jan. 30, 1890), chief advisor to **Muhammad III as-Sadiq** [es Sadok], bey of Tunis, founded the **Sadiki College** to offer free instruction to young Tunisians in modern subjects in French and Italian as well as traditional subjects in Arabic.

1875 Oct. 19 Charles Wheatstone (b. Feb., 1802), an English inventor, died. He was best known for the **Wheatstone Bridge**, a device for measuring electric resistance.

1876 The **Centennial Exhibition** was held in **Philadelphia**, with exhibits from 39 countries.

1876 Mar. 10 Alexander Graham Bell delivered the first **telephone** message when he said "**Mr. Watson, come here. I want you,**" to his assistant **Thomas** [Augustus] **Watson** (1854–1934), who heard him over the instrument on which Bell had been working in a **Boston** [Massachusetts] boardinghouse.

1876 Nov. 28 Karl Ernst von Baer (b. Feb. 29, 1792), an Estonian scientist considered the **founder of embryology**, died. He proved that mammalian development was similar to the development of other animals through his studies of the mammalian egg. Those advocating the theory of evolution welcomed von Baer's work.

1877 The design for an improved **refrigerator railroad car** was patented by **Joel Tiffany**, an American inventor. The refrigerator car, by making it safer to bring dressed meat from the stockyards of the Midwest to the East, was instrumental in the development of **Chicago** and other cities into national meat packing centers.

1877 Asaph Hall (Oct. 15, 1829–Nov. 22, 1907), an American astronomer at the **Naval Observatory** in Washington, D.C., discovered two **satellites of Mars**, which he named Deimos and Phobos.

1877 May 29 John Lothrop Motley (b. Apr. 15, 1814), an American historian, died. Motley's nearly lifelong project was the writing (from 1847) of the history of The Netherlands. Motley wrote two dramatic histories, *The Rise of the Dutch Republic* (1856) and *History of the United Netherlands* (1860–1867).

1877 Dec. 7 Thomas Alva Edison demonstrated his **phonograph** at his workshop in Menlo Park, New Jersey. He received a patent for this invention on Feb. 19, 1878.

1878 The treatise *On the Equilibrium of Heterogeneous Substances* was published by **Josiah Willard Gibbs**, an American physicist. This work is considered today one of the greatest on physical sciences of the 19th century. It was first published in an obscure journal *The Transactions of the Connecticut Academy*.

1878 The **praxinoscope**, an early device to produce animation, was patented by the Frenchman **Emile Reynaud** (Dec. 8, 1844–1918). The praxinoscope projected a series of drawings onto a screen in rapid succession.

1878 Feb. 10 Claude Bernard (b. July 12, 1813), a French physiologist, died. His *Introduction à l'étude de la médicine expérimentale* [*Introduction to the Study of Experimental Medicine*] (1851) established Bernard's reputation as a leading figure in physiological science. He was known for his work on the **pancreas**, and discovered the glycogenic functions of the **liver**. He discovered, while studying the vasomotor nerves, that the dilation of blood vessels was controlled by the nervous system, enabling the **body to regulate its own temperature**.

1879 Wilhelm Wundt (Aug. 16, 1832–Aug. 31, 1920), a German physiologist, founded the first laboratory of physiological psychology, at Leipzig, in present Germany. There he founded (1881) the first journal of psychology, *Philosophische Studien*. Wundt's output included *Lehre von den Muskel-*

bewegungen [*Study of Muscular Movements*] (1858); *System der Philosophie* (1889); *Grundiss der Psychologie* [*Outlines of Psychology*] (1896); *Völkerpsychologie* [*Ethnic Psychology*] (1900–1920), a ten-volume work; and *Einführung in die Psychologie* [*Introduction to Psychology*] (1911). Wundt's introduction of the experimental method to psychological study was important in helping to establish psychology as a scientific discipline.

1879 Johannes Diderik van der Waals (Nov. 23, 1837–Mar. 8, 1923), a Dutch physicist, announced his theory accounting for deviations from Boyle's Law of gases. Van der Waals explained that the deviations were caused by the action of slight attractant or repellent forces ["**Van der Waals' forces**"] that govern the behavior of molecules. Van der Waals received the **Nobel Prize for physics** in 1910.

1879 Summer The **wall paintings in a cave at Altamira**, near Santander in northern Spain, were discovered by the daughter of **Marcelino de Sautuola** (d. 1888), who had first visited the cave in 1875, when he found prehistoric tools there. The daughter, carried on her father's shoulders, caught sight of the paintings and called them to his attention. Most of the ceiling of the chamber was covered with red, black, and violet depictions of bison, some using the rough rock face to highlight anatomical areas. Other animals, generally hooved, were seen on the walls of adjacent galleries in black, or engraved. Tools and carved bone were found in the cave as well. The paintings and tools were dated to c.30,000 B.P. at the earliest.

1879 Mar. 3 Belva Ann Lockwood (Oct. 24, 1830–May 19, 1917) became the **first woman to practice as a lawyer before the U.S. Supreme Court**. She had drafted the law allowing this, which Congress passed. Lockwood was the **National Equal Rights party** candidate for the presidential elections of 1884 and 1888.

1879 May 8 George [Baldwin] **Selden** (Sept. 14, 1846–Jan. 17, 1922), an American inventor, applied for the first patent on a **carriage to be driven by an internal combustion engine**. The patent was not awarded until 1895, since Selden kept filing for revisions on his original design.

1879 Oct. 19 Thomas Alva Edison produced the first commercially practical **incandescent lamp**. Edison had developed a carbon filament for the light bulb as well as designing an electrical system to carry current to the lamp.

1879 Nov. 5   James Clerk Maxwell (b. Nov. 13, 1831), a Scottish mathematician and physicist, died. Between 1856 and 1865, he had formulated the electromagnetic theory of light, which stated that electrical impulses traveled at the speed of light and were similar in nature. He studied the kinetic theory of gases through experiments and mathematical studies. He also experimented with color perception and blindness. The unit measure of magnetic flux, the maxwell, was named after him. His publications included *Electricity and Magnetism* (1873), *Theory of Heat* (1871), and *Matter and Motion* (1876).

VIII. ARTS AND LEISURE

c.1875   The **straw hat** and **summer suit** began to appear. **Bustles** again began to be worn by women. They produce the illusion of large, ample hips.

1875   Gilbert and Sullivan found a successful agent to produce their comic operas when **Rupert D'Oyly Carte** (May 3, 1844–Apr. 3, 1901) formed the **D'Oyly Carte Company** in London to manage the partnership. Over the next two decades, **William Schwenck Gilbert** wrote scripts and **Arthur Seymour Sullivan** composed the music for such notable operettas as *H.M.S. Pinafore* (1878), *The Pirates of Penzance* (1879), *The Mikado* (1885), and *The Gondoliers* (1889).

1875   **L'Opéra** [Théâtre de l'Opéra], the home of 19th-century grand opera in **Paris**, was completed after 14 years of construction under the direction of **Jean Louis Charles Garnier** (Nov. 6, 1825–Aug. 3, 1898), a French architect.

1875 Jan. 23   Charles Kingsley (b. June 12, 1819), an English author and clergyman, died. A Christian and social reformer, he was noted for his historical novels *Hypatia* (1853) and *Westward Ho!* (1855). It was Kingsley who provoked Cardinal **John Henry Newman**'s *Apologia pro Vita Sua.*

1875 Feb. 22   Jean Baptiste Camille Corot (b. July 16, 1796), a French painter, died. In his attention to the nuances of light, Corot was a precursor of the impressionists. Greatly admired by the younger generation of painters, he was sympathetic to painters who broke with the academic tradition. His works included *Chartres Cathedral* (1830), *Hagar in the*

Desert (1835), *Diana Surprised by Actaeon* (1836), and *Belfry at Douai* (1871).

1875 June 3   Georges [Alexandre César Leopold] **Bizet** (b. Oct. 25, 1838), a French composer, died. His works included *Symphony in C Major* (1855), and the operas *Les Pêcheurs de Perles* [**The Pearl-fishers**] (1863), *Djamileh* (1872), and *L'Arlesienne* (1872). Bizet died three months after the disheartening opening of *Carmen* (Mar. 1, 1875, at the L'Opéra Comique in Paris), which became one of the most famous operas ever produced.

1875 Sept. 15   Louise Dumont Farrenc (b. May 31, 1804), a French pianist and composer, died. She was the only women in the 19th century to be granted a permanent position as instructor at the **Paris Conservatoire**. She wrote a piano concerto, 30 etudes, 8 chamber works, symphonies, and other works. With her husband Aristide, a flutist and music printer, she edited the 23-volume collection *Le Tresor des Pianistes* (1865).

1875 Sept. 28   Aleksei Konstantinovich Tolstoi [Tolstoy] (b. Aug. 24, 1817), a Russian writer, died. His trilogy of plays, comprising *The Death of Ivan the Terrible* (1866), *Czar Fëdor Ivanovich* (1868), and *Czar Boris* (1870), were not produced during Tolstoi's lifetime.

1876   The **founding of Yiddish theater**, reflecting a long Jewish tradition of folktales, proverbs, and Hasidic allegories, was attributed to **Abraham Goldfaden** (July 12, 1840–Jan. 19, 1908), who opened a performing group in **Jassy** [Iaşi], in present northeastern Romania. In October of this year he brought his troupe to **Munich**, where he successfully staged a two-act musical. Among his many plays were *Shulamit* (1880) and *Bar Kochba* (1882). In the U.S., he worked with Romanian and Yiddish groups.

1876 June 8   George Sand [Armantine Lucille Aurore; nee Dupin, later: Dudevant] (b. July 1, 1804), a French romantic novelist, died. Her works included *Lélia* (1833) and *Elle et Lui* (1859). George Sand's early novels treated women's issues and expounded the virtues of sexual freedom. Her later novels, written when she lived in retirement at her family estate in the French countryside, were studies of nature and rustic manners, among them *La Mare au Diable* [*The Haunted Pool*] (1846), *La Petite Fadette* [*Fanchon the Cricket*] (1848), and *François the Champi* [*Francis the Waif*] (1850).

1876 Aug. *Festspielhaus*, a theater built under the direction of **Richard Wagner**, a German composer, opened in **Munich**. The architects, **Wölfel and Karl Brandt**, used plans drawn up by **Gotfried Semper** (Nov. 29, 1803–May 15, 1879).

1877 May 6 **Johan Ludvig Runeberg** (b. Feb. 5, 1804), the national poet of Finland, died. A collection of prose and verse stories *The Tales of Ensign Stål* (1848, 1860), written in Swedish and centered on a Russo-Finnish conflict (1808–1809), helped crystalize Finnish national identity. The Finnish national anthem *Vårt Land* [*Our Land*] appeared in this work.

1877 Dec. 31 **Gustave Courbet** (b. June 10, 1819), an early French realist painter, died. His works included *After Dinner at Ornans* (1849), *Funeral at Ornans* (1850), *Stonebreakers* (c.1850), and *The Painter's Studio* (1855). Courbet was acknowledged as the founder of the school of realism in the late 1850s when he established his gallery **Pavilion of Realism**, after the Exposition in Paris refused to accept several of his works in 1855.

1878 June 12 **William Cullen Bryant** (b. Nov. 3, 1794), an American romantic poet and editor of the *New York Evening Post*, died. His poem *"Thanatopsis"* (1817), written when he was 16 years old, brought Bryant recognition. *"To a Waterfowl"* (1818) consolidated his reputation, and with the publication of his collected *Poems* (1832) Bryant was considered the leading American poet. Among his poems were *"The Death of Flowers," "To the Fringed Gentian,"* and *"The Song of Marion's Men."* While editor of the *Evening Post*, Bryant became a strong anti-slavery advocate.

1878 Nov. 30 **George Henry Lewes** (b. Apr. 18, 1817), an English philosopher and literary critic, died. His works, which popularized philosophy and science, included the four-volume *Biographical History of Philosophy* (1845–1846), *Comte's Philosophy of the Sciences* (1853), *Life of Goethe* (1855), and *The Problems of Life and Mind* (1873–1879), an important philosophical work.

1879 *Progress and Poverty*, a program for economic reform by **Henry George** (Sept. 2, 1839–Oct. 29, 1897), an American economist and social reformer, was published. George's declaration that land should provide the basis for a tax—the "single tax"—to support government was immensely popular in the U.S. and abroad. The book went through more than 100 editions, and today there exist Henry George schools and institutes that apply his economic principles to contemporary conditions.

1879 **Recâi-Zade Mahmud Ekrem** (1847–1914), a Turkish writer, established a new direction for Turkish literature with the publication of a collection of lectures *Talim-i-edebiyat* [*The Teaching of Literature*].

1879 Feb. 10? **Honoré Daumier** (b. Feb. 20 or 26, 1808), a French painter, engraver, sculptor, and caricaturist, died. He drew caricatures for the publication *Charivari*, which advanced his reputation as a social satirist. His lithographs included *Le ventre législatif* [*The Legislative Paunch*] (1834). His paintings included *The Third Class Carriage* (1862) and several on the theme of Don Quixote, especially *Don Quixote* (c.1865).

IX. SPORTS, GAMES, AND SOCIETY

1875 **Ice hockey** was first played in a form recognizable today by students at McGill University in **Montreal**, Canada. The number of players on a side varied and slowly settled on a standard seven. In 1926 the number was reduced to six.

1875 May 17 The horse **Aristides** won the **first Kentucky Derby** held at the **Churchill Downs** race track in **Louisville**, Kentucky. **Horse racing** as a "big time" sport in the U.S. dates from this year.

1875 Aug. 24 **Matthew Webb**, known as "Captain Webb," a captain in the British merchant marine and professional swimmer, was the **first person to swim the English Channel** without benefit of a life preserver. Webb swam the more difficult England-to-France route, from Dover to Calais, in 21 hours and 45 minutes, using the breast stroke. Webb (b. Jan. 19, 1848) drowned on July 24, 1883, when he tried to swim the rapids below Niagara Falls.

1876 The **first college football organization** was formed by five northeastern universities when their representatives met in Springfield, Massachusetts. The universities were Rutgers, Princeton, Columbia, Yale, and Harvard.

1876 **James Gordon Bennett** (May 10, 1841–May 14, 1918), an American newspaper publisher, interested his friends in the game of **polo**, which he had seen played in England. At Dickel's Riding Academy, an indoor facility on Fifth Avenue at 39th Street in **New York City**, Bennett and friends practiced the new game, using Texas cow ponies. In the summer of 1876 activities were transferred to the Jerome Park Race Track in the Bronx.

1876   The **safety bicycle** with rear-driven gears was invented by the Englishman **H.J. Lawson**. The rear wheel was powered by the rider through pedals attached to a large sprocket that, in turn, turned a small sprocket on the rear wheel by a connecting chain.

1876 Feb. 2   The **National League of Professional Baseball Clubs**, the parent organization of today's National League, was formed in the U.S. The original members were Philadelphia, New York, Hartford, Boston, Chicago, St. Louis, Louisville, and Cincinnati.

1876 Sept. 2   **Greyhound racing** was attempted with a mechanical rabbit for the first time at Hendon, then a rural section of northern London. The

hare ran on a straight-line rail and was propelled by a windlass.

1877   The All-England Croquet Club sponsored the **first lawn tennis championship** at its grounds in **Wimbledon**, a suburb of London. The winner of the only event, men's singles, was **Spencer W. Gore** (1850–1906).

1877   The **first Westminster Kennel Club show** was held at Gilmore's Gardens in New York City. Nearly 1,200 dogs were entered, representing c.20 breeds.

1879   **Karate** was introduced to Japan after the Japanese had annexed Okinawa. This form of unarmed combat had been developed on Okinawa in the 17th century when the Japanese landlords forbade possession of weapons by the islanders.

1879   The **first big ski jumping contest** in Norway was held at Huseby Hill near Oslo. It attracted c.10,000 spectators, including the Norwegian king, who donated the trophy.

1880–1884

I. VITAL STATISTICS AND DEMOGRAPHY

1880   The **world's population** reached c.1,250,000,000; that of the U.S., c.50,000,000.

II. DISASTERS

1881 June 24   A **bridge collapsed** under a troop train near **Cuantla** in Morelos state, central northern Mexico. The train then caught fire and more than 200 died.

1881 Dec. 8   The **Ring Theater in Vienna burned**, leaving c.850 dead.

1883 Aug. 26–27   Krakatau [Krakatoa, Malay: Rakata], an Indonesian volcanic island between Java and Sumatra, began a two-day eruption, including (May 27) a tremendous explosion in which an estimated cubic mile of rock was blown away, leaving a hole 600 to 900 feet deep in Sundra Strait where the island was located. The island was reduced from c.18 to c.6 square miles. The sound was heard 3,000

miles away, as far as Turkey and Japan. Ashes exploded to a height of 17 miles. The dust in the atmosphere caused the famous red sunsets of 1883 and 1884. Nearly 36,000 people were killed in the villages on the island or on nearby shores by tidal waves 60 to 130 feet high caused by the eruption.

1884 Aug. 10   An **earthquake** occurred in southwestern **Long Island** near New York City. Tremors were felt from Maine south to Virginia and inland throughout most of New York State, Pennsylvania, and West Virginia. Big buildings were shaken in New York City, but no injuries or deaths were reported.

III. EXPLORATION AND COLONIZATION

1884 Nov. 15   A **conference on African affairs** opened in **Berlin**. Thirteen European nations and the U.S. attended in an attempt to solve the problems posed by the European penetration into Africa. They resolved on free trade in the Congo Basin, freedom of navigation along the Congo and Niger rivers, and the abolition of slavery. Notwithstanding, the main result of the conference was to accelerate the European scramble for African territory.

IV. POLITICS AND WAR

1880 Rafael Núñez (Sept. 28, 1825–Sept. 12, 1894) became president of **Colombia**. A moderate liberal, he served from 1880 to 1882 and again from 1884 to 1894.

1881 Mar. 4 James Abram Garfield (b. Nov. 19, 1831) of the Republican party was inaugurated as the 20th president of the U.S., having narrowly defeated **Winfield Scott Hancock** (Feb. 14, 1824–Feb. 9, 1886) of the Democratic party. **Chester Alan Arthur** (Oct. 5, 1830–Nov. 18, 1886) served as vice president.

1881 Mar. 13 Alexander II [Aleksandr Nikolaevich] (b. Apr. 29, 1818), czar of Russia (from 1855), was killed (Mar. 1, Old Style) by a bomb explosion in St. Petersburg, after many previous assassination attempts had failed. A Russian secret society, the **People's Will**, claimed responsibility. Alexander was succeeded by his son **Alexander III** [Aleksandr Aleksandrovich].

1881 May 12 Following a **French invasion of Tunisia**, the **Treaty of Bardo** [Le Bardo, a suburb of Tunis] was signed by Muhammad III as-Sadiq, bey of Tunis. It gave France control of Tunisia's defense and foreign affairs. In Mar. 1881, Tunisian tribesmen had raided Algeria, giving France a pretext for invading Tunisia and blocking Italy's growing influence there.

1881 July Muhammad Ahmad, a Dongolese dervish of the Samaniyeh order, was summoned to explain his anti-Egyptian political activities in the Sudan to the Egyptian governor general at Khartoum. Instead of responding to the summons, Muhammad publicly proclaimed himself Mahdi [guided one, last iman] to his followers, the **Sudanese Mahdists**, and preached a holy war against infidels. By May 1882, he had defeated government troops and soon gained control (1883) of the **Sudan**.

1881 July 2 James Abram Garfield, president of the U.S., was shot in a railroad station in Washington, D.C., by **Charles Guiteau**, a lawyer and disappointed federal office seeker. Though mortally wounded, Garfield (b. Nov. 19, 1831) survived until Sept. 19, raising the question of presidential succession. Since an ambiguity in the U.S. Constitution made it unclear that the vice president should succeed an incapacitated president, **Chester Alan Arthur**, vice president of the U.S., acted informally as president according to the precedent set (1841) when Vice President **John Tyler** was sworn in to replace **William Henry Harrison**. On Sept. 20 Arthur was sworn in officially as president of the U.S. Guiteau (born c.1840) was hanged in Washington, D.C., on June 30, 1882.

1882 Ulises Heureaux (b. 1845) was proclaimed president of the **Dominican Republic**. His ruthless rule resulted in a period of relative peace for the country, but left it nearly bankrupt by his assassination on July 26, 1899. He had embarked, in partnership with the **San Domingo Improvement Company** of New York, on shady financial ventures, which ended with the loss of most of the foreign capital.

1882 May The **Triple Alliance** (to 1915) was formed when Italy joined in a treaty with the German and Austro-Hungarian empires. Serbia, through a treaty with Austria-Hungary, joined the alliance in 1882, and Romania joined in 1883. In 1884, Russia, fearing this powerful alliance, agreed to a proposal (1881) by **Bismarck** that Austria-Hungary, Germany, and Russia renew the **Three Emperors' Alliance** [Dreikaiserbund] (1873), which required neutrality of the third country in the event any one power were to war with another.

1882 May 6 The first of the **Chinese Exclusion Acts** in the U.S. restricted Chinese labor immigration for ten years. The politically potent western states, particularly California, objected to the Chinese laborers because their willingness to work for wages lower than those of American workers.

1882 Sept. 13 A British expeditionary force led by **Garnet Joseph Wolseley**, which had invaded Egypt in reprisal for anti-foreign riots (June 12) in **Alexandria**, defeated the army of **Arabi Pasha** [Ahmed Arabi, Ahmed Urabi Pasha Al-Misri] (1841?–Sept. 21, 1911), an Egyptian nationalist leader, at **Al-Tell al-Kabir** [Tell al Kabir]. **Cairo was taken by British forces** on Sept. 15. The nationalistic uprisings (1881–1882) were directed against British and French officials who occupied government posts under Tewfik [Tawfiq], khedive of Egypt. Arabi Pasha surrendered and was deported to Ceylon.

1883 The French sent an expedition under **Joseph Simon Gallieni** (Apr. 24, 1849–May 27, 1916) to conquer the upper Niger region in West Africa. They established a fort at Bamako on the Niger River, near the border with present Guinea. Thus, though the French had lost influence in East Africa with the British in full control of Egypt, they had firmly established themselves in North Africa in Algeria and Tunisia and in West Africa in Senegal and along the Niger River, resulting eventually in the establishment (1895) of the huge **federation of French West Africa**.

1883 **Liberation of Labor, Russia's first Marxist group**, was organized in Geneva, Switzerland, by Russian émigrés under **Georgi Valentinovich Plekhanov** (Dec. 11, 1857–May 30, 1918). The organization worked for a constitutional government with guaranteed freedoms.

1883 May 19 The **Sino-French War** (1883–1885) broke out as Chinese troops in contested areas of present northern Vietnam fought with French forces, then in control of most of Annam, under the command of **Amédée Anatole Prosper Courbet** (June 26, 1827–June 11, 1885), a French admiral. Since 1880 the **Black Flag Society**, or bands of Chinese outlaws operating in Tonkin, the northern region of Vietnam, and probably clandestinely supported by the Chinese government, disrupted French trade to the interior of southwestern China. Annam appealed to China to drive out the French. On Aug. 23, 1884, the Chinese navy was virtually destroyed by French naval forces as it lay at anchor near Foochow [Fuzhou; Fuchau; Minchow], in southeastern China on the Min Chiang [chiang = stream; Min Jiang].

1883 Aug. 25 The **Treaty of Hue** was signed by the Annamese Kingdom and France. It established a protectorate over Annam and Tonkin, thus completing **French hegemony in Vietnam**.

1883 Nov. 5 **Muhammad Ahmad**, leading the Mahdists of **Sudan** in their holy war, defeated an Anglo-Egyptian punitive expedition at **El Ubbayid** [Obeid, Ubayd'], in the central Sudan. The British then sent **Charles George Gordon** [Chinese Gordon, Gordon Pasha] to supervise withdrawal of Egyptian and British troops from the Sudan. In May 1884, Gordon was cut off from his base and surrounded in Khartoum. A relief force, on reaching Khartoum (Jan. 28, 1885), found that Gordon

(b. Jan. 28, 1833) had been executed on Jan. 26, 1885.

1884 Jan. The **Fabian Society**, a reorganization of the Fellowship for a New Life established the year before, was founded in England. Publication of *Fabian Essays* (1889), written by **George Bernard Shaw**, **Sidney Webb**, and others, brought national attention. Fabians believed in the gradual change of existing political institutions, rather than the revolution advocated by Marxism.

1884 Apr. 4 The government of Queensland, Australia, annexed eastern **New Guinea**. In response **Otto von Bismarck**, chancellor of Germany, promised to protect German interests in the Pacific, and Great Britain established a temporary protectorate over southern New Guinea on Nov. 6, 1884.

V. ECONOMY AND TRADE

1880–1917 The **Russian oil fields at Baku**, the capital of Azerbaijan, on the west coast of the Caspian Sea, were developed with the financial assistance of the Rothschilds and **Alfred Bernhard Nobel**, the Swedish philanthropist, who gained some of his great wealth by this investment. In 1883, completion of a rail line between the fields at Baku and Tbilisi [Tiflis] enabled export of the oil to Europe via the Black Sea.

1880 **Bon Marché**, the Paris department store (1852), was made an "**Employee's Republic**," when ownership was transferred to the employees as a joint stock company. The store's profits more than doubled over the next 30 years.

1880 The **Strathlever**, the **first refrigerated ship**, brought frozen meat from Australia to Great Britain. Soon New Zealand was sending meat, cheese, and butter to Great Britain.

1880 The **Canadian Pacific Railroad Company** received a grant of $25 million and 25 million acres of land as well as a monopoly on trade in order to build a transcontinental railroad line across Canada. On June 28, 1886, the first passenger train embarked on Canada's transcontinental run.

1880 Jan. Work began on a **canal across Panama** [at this time part of Colombia] under the supervision of **Ferdinand Marie de Lesseps**, the Frenchman who had directed construction of the Suez Canal. Between 20,000 and 40,000 of the laborers died, mostly of yellow fever and malaria, over the next eight years. The project was abandoned and de Lesseps, with his son, was sentenced to prison for fraud.

1881 The opening of the **first railroad in Nicaragua** completed a combined boat and train route, which took passengers from the Atlantic Ocean to the Pacific Ocean by boat up the San Juan River to Lake Nicaragua, where they boarded a train for the final leg of the journey.

1881 Sept. The **Knights of Labor**, the first labor organization to accept women as members, formed a woman's local at Philadelphia.

1882 The **Bank of Japan** (1872) was reorganized along the lines of western monetary systems.

1882 The **first commercial hydroelectric plant** in the world was established at Appleton, in central southern Wisconsin.

1882 Russia's **first factory law** prohibited children under 12 from working in factories and those from 12 to 15 from working more than eight hours a day.

1882 Jan. A speculative boom, centered on the French company **Union Générale**, collapsed, causing financial problems in England and on the Continent. The company, which had the blessing of the pope, was promoted as a means of breaking the purported monopoly of Jews and Protestants over French finances: In five years its shares had gone from 125 to 3,200 francs per share.

1882 May 20 The **St. Gothard Railway**, the **first of the great railroad tunnels through the Alps**, opened.

1882 Sept. 4 Lower Manhattan was lighted by the **Edison Electric Illuminating Company** of New York, which provided service to 59 business establishments there.

1883 **Terence Vincent Powderly** (Jan. 22, 1849–June 24, 1924) became head of the **Knights of Labor** [Noble Order of the], a labor organization founded (1869) in Philadelphia by Uriah Smith Stephens. Secret at first, it opened up during the economic depression (1870–1879) to function as a militant labor group against management, and by 1878 was the leading labor group in the U.S. It openly pressed for an eight-hour work day, no convict labor, no hiring of

children under 15 years of age in industry, opportunity and wages for women in industry equal to those of men, and the institution of a Bureau of Labor Statistics in the U.S. government. They were successful in the use of strikes in many instances (1878–1883) and accomplished much to improve working conditions for American labor.

1883 The **Peasants' Land Bank** was established in Russia to aid peasants and village cooperatives in buying more land. The bank helped primarily the *kulaks*, or wealthier peasants.

1883 **Sydney and Melbourne**, Australia, were connected by railroad.

1883 **Rickshaw drivers in Tokyo protested the introduction of streetcars** in the first strike in Japan. The strike leader was jailed, quickly ending the protest.

1883 May 1 Legislation was introduced in Germany, at the urging of **Otto von Bismarck**, chancellor of the German Empire (1871–1918), for **compulsory national health insurance**. It was to be financed both by employers and employees. In June 1884, employee-paid accident insurance was introduced.

1883 May 24 The **Brooklyn Bridge**, originally designed by **John Augustus Roebling** (June 12, 1806–July 22, 1869), an American engineer, opened to traffic. It was completed under Roebling's son, **Washington August Roebling** (May 26, 1837–July 21, 1926).

1884 The **National Cash Register Company** was formed in the U.S. by **John H. Patterson** (Dec. 13, 1844–May 7, 1922), who had paid $6500 to acquire the rights to the cash register invented by James J. Rity in 1879.

1884 The **world's largest copper-nickel deposit** was discovered near **Sudbury**, in southeastern Ontario, Canada, by the Canadian Pacific Railroad, which was laying track for its transcontinental line.

VI. RELIGION AND PHILOSOPHY

1880 Mar. 10 The **Salvation Army** came to the U.S. from London, England, under Commander **George Scott Railton** and seven "Hallelujah Lassies." **Evangeline Cory Booth** (Dec. 25, 1865–July 14, 1950), daughter of the founder **William Booth**, became commander (1904) of the Army in the U.S.

1881–1882 Pogroms against Russian Jews were initiated in Russia. A series of planned attacks on Jewish communities continued until 1917. New laws designed to be harsh on Jews both physically and economically, combined with anti-Jewish propaganda, helped to divert the working class from Russia's fundamental economic and social problems.

1881 A petition signed by c.255,000 Germans was submitted to **Otto von Bismarck**, chancellor of the German Empire (1871–1918), calling for **disenfranchisement of Jews** and declaring Jews "a menace not only to the economic welfare of the German people but to their culture and religion." The petition had been engineered by Bismarck, who was able to gain an electoral majority by creating false alarms and dividing public opinion. His objective was the demise of the National Liberal party, which held the majority.

1881 May 17 The **Revised Version of the New Testament** was published in England. The Oxford University Press had on hand orders of more than a million copies, and Cambridge University Press was not far behind. Within 12 months an estimated 3 million copies were sold in the British Empire and the U.S.

1882 Leo Pinsker (1821–1891), a Russian Jewish doctor once decorated by the czar and previously an advocate of Russification, published *Self-Emancipation*, urging Jews to cease looking to their governments for help. Jews, he held, comprise a nation and an ethnic group that cannot be assimilated; emancipation can come only by the creation of an independent nation.

1882 Eliezer Ben Yehudah [Elieser Ben-Yahuda] (1858–Dec. 16, 1922), a Hebrew scholar and lexicographer, began the task of making **Hebrew once again a living tongue**. Hebrew had become more and more a written language, so Ben Yehudah and his family, resettled in Palestine, began speaking it as work progressed on a modern Hebrew dictionary. It caught on among other Jewish immigrants.

1884 The **Watch Tower Bible and Tract Society** was founded by **Charles Taze "Pastor" Russell** (Feb. 16, 1852–Oct. 31, 1916), the American Congregationalist who had organized the International Bible Students' Association (IBSA) in 1872 and published books and journals on the Millennial Age, concerning Christ's Second Coming.

VII. SCIENCE, EDUCATION, AND TECHNOLOGY

1880 The **speed of light** was measured by **Albert Abraham Michelson**, an American physicist. In 1887, in experiments with **Edward Williams Morley** (Jan. 29, 1838–Feb. 24, 1923), Michelson showed that the absolute motion of the earth was not measurable, thus laying the groundwork for **Albert Einstein's relativity theory**. In 1907 Michelson received the **Nobel prize for physics**.

1880 Johann Friederich Wilhelm Adolph von Baeyer (Oct. 31, 1835–Aug. 20, 1917), a German chemist, **first synthesized the organic dye indigo**. He later formulated its molecular structure using the Structure Theory of Friedrich Auguste Kekulé [von Stradonitz]. Baeyer received the **Nobel prize for chemistry** for his work.

1881 The **first birth-control clinic** opened in Amsterdam under the direction of **Dr. Aletta Jacobs** (1849–Aug. 12, 1929), a Dutch suffragette. Her example was followed in other countries.

1881 May 21 Clara [Clarissa Harlowe] **Barton** (Dec. 25, 1821–Apr. 12, 1912), a U.S. nurse, organized the **first American chapter of the International Red Cross** after her experiences during the **Franco-Prussian War** (1870–1871), when she had worked under the International Red Cross. During the **American Civil War** (1861–1865) Barton had organized an agency to collect and distribute supplies for the wounded and, at the request of **Abraham Lincoln**, had compiled records for the identification of war dead.

1882 Jan. 11 Theodor Schwann (b. Dec. 7, 1810), a German biologist, died. Noted for his development of the **cell theory** in 1839, he also discovered **pepsin** when investigating the functioning of digestion and other mechanisms.

1882 Mar. 24 The discovery of the **tubercule bacteria** was announced by **Robert Koch** (Dec. 11, 1843–May 27, 1910), a German bacteriologist, who was the first to find a way to isolate a pure culture of bacteria. This discovery was essential to his identification of the Asiatic cholera bacillus in 1883 and the **tuberculin test** in 1890 to diagnose tuberculosis. After Koch isolated the comma bacterium (**Vibrio comma**), the cause of **Asiatic cholera**, a serum was developed which protected people for a relatively short time (five months in 1958).

1883 **Percy Everitt** set up the **first successful automatic vending machine**, which dispensed postcards, in London. On Dec. 13, 1884, he patented a **coin-operated scale**.

1883 The **Maxim machine gun** was developed by **Hiram Stevens Maxim** (Feb. 5, 1840–Nov. 24, 1916), an American-born inventor who moved to England. It could fire ten shots per second.

1883 Mar. 14 **Karl** [Heinrich] **Marx** (b. May 5, 1818), a German philosopher, economist, and foremost developer of socialist theory, died. After the suppressions of the revolutions of 1848 Marx settled in London, where he lived for the rest of his life, mostly in extreme poverty, frequently alleviated by generous help from his friend and collaborator **Friedrich Engels**.

1883 Nov. 18 At noon on this date the **U.S. converted from local to standard time**. The change was made at the request of the railroads, which needed it in order to set reasonable schedules, especially for transcontinental runs.

1884 The ten-story **Home Life Insurance Building** in Chicago was the **first skyscraper** to be erected, designed by **William Le Baron Jenney** (Sept. 25, 1832–June 15, 1907), an American architect.

1884 The **system of standard time calibrated to the prime meridian at Greenwich, England**, was informally adopted at an International Conference held in Washington, D.C. The world was divided into 24 zones, each 15° apart in longitude, starting at the meridian in Greenwich, England.

1884 Aug. 26 **Ottmar Mergenthaler** (May 11, 1854–Oct. 28, 1899), a German-born watchmaker, received a U.S. patent on the **first linotype machine**. By quickly producing a column-width of type at once, Mergenthaler's machine revolutionized the printing industry.

VIII. ARTS AND LEISURE

c.1880–1899 The **Arts and Crafts movement** influenced the arts in England. Handicrafts were revived and individual expression was stressed. Among the leaders of this movement were **William Morris** and **Walter Crane** (Aug. 15, 1845–Mar. 14, 1915), who was known primarily for his illustrations of children's books.

1880 *Uncle Remus, His Songs and Sayings*, a series of 34 black folk tales, was published by **Joel Chandler Harris** (Dec. 9, 1848–July 3, 1908), an American author. In it appeared the animal characters Brer Rabbit, Brer Fox, and others.

1880 Oct. 5 **Jacques** [Jacob Levy] **Offenbach** (b. June 20, 1819), a German-born French composer, died. He was the most successful and one of the most prolific composers of French operetta. These included *Orphée aux enfers* (1858) and *Les Contes d'Hoffmann* [*Tales of Hoffman*] (1881), finished and first produced after Offenbach's death.

1880 Dec. 2 **George Eliot** [real name: Mary Anne Evans] (b. Nov. 22, 1819), an English author, died. An early feminist, her best-known works included **Adam Bede** (1859), **The Mill on the Floss** (1860), **Silas Marner** (1861), and **Middlemarch** (1872).

1881 The satiric *El gran Galeoto* [adapted as **The World and His Wife**], one of the popular plays by **José Echegaray y Eizaguirre** (Apr. 19, 1832–Sept. 14, 1916), the Spanish writer and mathematician, appeared. Echegaray was the most popular Spanish playwright of the late 19th century. Among his other plays was *El libro talonario* [*The Checkbook*] (1874), his first popular play; *O locura o santidad* [*Madman or Saint*] (1877); and *El hijo de Don Juan* [*The Son of Don Juan*] (1892). In 1904 Echegaray became the first Spaniard to win the **Nobel prize for literature**, which he shared with **Frédéric Mistral**, a Provençal poet.

1881 Feb. 5 **Thomas Carlyle** (b. Dec. 4, 1795), a Scottish writer, died. *The French Revolution* (1837) and *Heroes and Hero-Worship* (1841) were his best-known works. Carlyle also wrote many essays, dealing with sociology, politics, and literary criticism.

1881 Feb. 9 **Fëdor Mikhailovich Dostoevski** (b. Nov. 11, 1821), a great Russian novelist, died. His works were noted for their studies of the dark, even murderous, regions of the human soul. He wrote about his experiences in *Memoirs from the House of the Dead*, which appeared in his own literary journal *Vremya* [*The Time*] (1861). The journal was subsequently suppressed. He also produced the novels *Crime and Punishment* (1866), *The Idiot* (1868), and

The Possessed (1869–1872). *The Brothers Karamazov* (1879–1880) appeared shortly before his death and reflected Dostoevski's deep concern with the conflicts between religion, guilt, and the forces of evil.

1881 Mar. 28   Modest Petrovich Mussorgsky [Musorgski; Moussorgsky] (b. Mar. 21, 1839), a Russian composer, died. His operas included *Boris Godunov* (1868–1869), based on the play by **Aleksander Sergeevich Pushkin**. Also well-known was *Pictures at an Exhibition* (1874).

1881 Apr. 19   Benjamin Disraeli (b. Dec. 21, 1804), an English statesman and writer, died. As a member of Parliament for a good part of his life and as prime minister (1867–1868, 1874–1880), Disraeli observed at first hand the workings of British society and politics. He achieved his first recognition as an author with the novel *Vivian Grey* (1826–1827), but his best novels were *Coningsby* (1844), *Sybil* (1845), and *Lothair* (1870). Disraeli was also known for his letters, political pamphlets, and *Lord George Bentinck: a Political Biography* (1852).

1881 May 11   Henri Frédéric Amiel (b. Sept. 27, 1821), a Swiss writer, died. His diary *Fragments d'un Journal intime* (1884) was a masterpiece of self-analysis.

1881 Sept. 7   Sidney Lanier (b. Feb. 3, 1843), an American critic, musician, and poet from the South, died. He wrote the novel *Tiger-Lilies* (1867), *The Science of English Verse* (1880), and *The English Novel and the Principle of Its Development* (1883). Lanier's best-known poem was "The Song of the Chattahoochee" (1883).

1882 Mar. 24   Henry Wadsworth Longfellow (b. Feb. 27, 1807), an American poet, died. His reputation as a poet was established with his second collection of verse, *Ballads and other Poems* (1842), in which appeared "The Wreck of the Hesperus" and "The Village Blacksmith." Other notable volumes included *Evangeline* (1847), *The Song of Hiawatha* (1855), *The Courtship of Miles Standish* (1858), *Paul Revere's Ride* (1860), and *Tales of a Wayside Inn* (1863). He was the **first American to be commemorated** [with a bust] **in the Poet's Corner of Westminster Abbey**, London.

1882 Apr. 27   Ralph Waldo Emerson (b. May 25, 1803), an American moral philosopher, essayist, and lecturer, died. Emerson was one of the chief American expounders of the semi-religious, semi-philosophic movement called **Transcendentalism**. He published a series of *Essays* (1841, 1844), in which he described his concept of Nature as equated with God and of the Over-Soul as the link of Man's soul with God's soul. His essays also discussed the American character, individualism, and moral idealism. His books included *Representative Men* (1850), *English Traits* (1856), and *The Conduct of Life* (1860).

1882 Dec. 6   Anthony Trollope (b. Apr. 24, 1815), a popular English writer, died. He was especially noted for two series of novels, the Barsetshire Chronicles, which included *The Warden* (1855) and *Barchester Towers* (1857), and the Palliser novels [Parliamentary Series], which began with *Can You Forgive Her?* (1864–1865) and concluded with *The Duke's Children* (1880). Trollope produced 46 novels, as well as travel sketches, and an *Autobiography* (1883).

1883 Apr. 30   Édouard Manet (b. Jan. 23, 1832), a French impressionist painter, died. Perhaps best-known of Manet's work was *Déjeuner sur l'herbe* [Picnic on the Grass] exhibited in Paris in 1863 at the Salon de Refusés. Manet's other works included *Buveur d'absinthe* [Absinthe Drinker] (1859), *La Musique aux Tuileries* [Concert in the Tuileries] (1862), *Olympia* (1863), *Le Fifre* [The Fife-Player] (1866), and *Bar at the Folies-Bergère* (1882).

1883 June 14   Edward FitzGerald (b. Mar. 31, 1809), an English writer, died. He was known best for his translation of the *Rubáiyát of Omar Khayyám* (1859).

1884   The **Ringling Brothers held their first circus** at Baraboo, Wisconsin. The five brothers were Albert C. (1852–Jan. 1, 1916), Otto (c. 1858–Mar. 31, 1911), Alfred T. (c. 1861–Oct. 21, 1919), Charles (Dec. 2, 1863–Dec. 3, 1926), and John Nicholas (c. 1866–Dec. 3, 1936).

1883 Aug. 22   Ivan Sergeyevich Turgenev (b. Nov. 9, 1818), a Russian novelist, short-story writer, and playwright, died. He was best known especially for *Fathers and Sons* (1861), one of the first Russian novels to be read in the West. Turgenev wrote ten plays, which were notable for initiating the transition between Russian romantic theater and the realistic theater of Chekhov. His best-known play, widely produced in the West, was *A Month in the Country* (produced 1872).

1884 Apr. 11   Charles Reade (b. June 8, 1814), an English writer, died. His most important novel, a medieval romance, *The Cloister and the Hearth* (1861), treated the life of Erasmus's father.

1884 May 12   Bedřich Smetana (b. Mar. 2, 1824), a Czechoslovakian composer, died. Smetana was noted for developing Czech national music, and for founding a national opera house in Prague, the Czech capital, as part of the National Theater, which he directed from 1866 to 1874, when he was overcome by deafness. His works included the operas *Braniboři v Čechách* [**The Brandenburgers in Bohemia**] (1866), *Prodaná nevěsta* [*The Bartered Bride*] (1866), and *Hubička* [*The Kiss*] (1876); the symphonic poem cycle *Má vlast* [*My Fatherland*] (1879); and the string quartets *Zmého zivota* [*From My Life*] (1876, 1882).

IX. SPORTS, GAMES AND SOCIETY

1880 May 30   The **world heavyweight boxing title** was taken by **Paddy Ryan** (Mar. 15, 1853–1901), an Irish-American who knocked out **Joe Goss** of England, the reigning heavyweight champion, in the 87th round at a ring near Colliers Station, West Virginia.

1880 Aug. 3   The **American Canoe Association** [ACA] was formed by prominent canoeists at a meeting held at Lake George, New York. William L. Alden (Oct. 9, 1837–Jan. 14, 1908), a founder of the New York Canoe Club, was elected commodore.

1881   The **Ice Yacht Challenge Pennant**, the top award of iceboating, was first offered in competition by the New Hamburgh [New York] Ice Yacht Club.

1881 Aug. 31   The **first U.S. national tennis championship** was held in Newport, Rhode Island. The winner was Richard D. Sears (Oct. 26, 1861–Apr. 8, 1943), who retained the championship through 1887 with a record seven straight victories.

1881 Oct. 24   **American vaudeville**, introduced (1842) to New York City at the Franklin theater, entered a new phase in its development when Tony [Antonio] Pastor (May 28, 1837–Aug. 26, 1908) produced a family style variety show at the 14th Street Theater in New York City.

c.1882   Handball was introduced to the U.S. in Brooklyn by Philip Casey (d. July 12, 1904), an Irish immigrant. The game was invented in Ireland in the 10th century. Casey built a four-wall court and later built or promoted other courts, successfully taking on all comers until his retirement in 1900.

1882   Jigoro Kano (c.1860–May 4, 1938), a Japanese sportsman, devised from an ancient Japanese method of unarmed combat known as **jujitsu** [jujutsu] a sport he called **judo** [the gentle way].

1882   The **U.S. Intercollegiate Lacrosse Association** was formed by Harvard, Princeton, and Columbia. In 1883 they were joined by Yale and by New York University, which had fielded the first American college lacrosse team some years previously.

1882   The **American Association of Baseball Players** formed to compete against the National League.

1882 Apr. 3   Jesse Woodson James (b. Sept. 5, 1847), an American bandit, was shot and killed by a fellow member of the notorious **James Gang** who, it was said, wanted to collect the $10,000 bounty declared by the governor of Missouri for the capture of James, dead or alive.

1882 Feb. 7   John Lawrence Sullivan knocked out Paddy Ryan in nine rounds, in Ryan's attempt to regain the world title he had lost to Sullivan. Sullivan, the **last bare-knuckle champion** and the first under the marquis of Queensberry Rules, had a ten-year reign as world heavyweight boxing champion.

1882 Aug. 29   England played so poorly in a **cricket** Test Match against Australia that the *Sporting Times* of London the next day ran an epitaph with a black border lamenting the death of English cricket, ending: "The body will be cremated and the ashes taken to Australia." The next year Australians presented the captain of the English team with a small pottery urn filled with ashes, which became the trophy, **"the Ashes,"** for the World Series of cricket.

1883 Oct. 22   The **first indoor horse show** in the U.S. opened at Gilmore Gardens in New York City. For four days, 299 horses of all breeds and purposes competed for the many prizes under the sponsorship of the **National Horse Show Association of America**.

1884 The **first known toboggan run** was laid out near St. Moritz, Switzerland, by winter vacationers there. One year later, the Cresta Run was built for one-man tobogganing and a Tobogganing Club was formed at St. Moritz. The **bobsled** [bobsleigh] was soon developed by providing a toboggan with sled-like runners, and the St. Moritz Bobsleigh Club came next.

1884 **Hurling**, an ancient game said to date back to days before St. Patrick, became an organized sport in Ireland when the **Gaelic Athletic Association** was founded and rules were laid down.

1884 The **first national women's singles tennis tournament** was held when the championship was added to the schedule of tennis events at Wimbledon, England. Maud Watson (1865–June 6, 1946) of England was the winner. The first American to win this championship was **May Sutton** (1887–Oct. 5?, 1975) of California, in 1904.

1885–1889

I. DISASTERS

1886 Aug. 31 An **earthquake**, reported throughout an area of c.1,000 square miles, damaged nearly all of the city of **Charleston**, South Carolina.

1887 The **Yellow River** [Hwang Ho, Huang He], in China, **flooded** its banks, causing c.900,000 deaths.

1887 Aug. 10 A **train** carrying vacationers bound for Niagara Falls, New York, **plunged through a burning bridge** near **Chatsworth**, central eastern Illinois. Of the c.800 passengers, 81 were killed outright; 372 were injured, with subsequent deaths from injuries.

1888 Mar. 11–13 The **Great Blizzard of '88** covered America's eastern seaboard states in snow, causing c.400 deaths and damage to property worth millions. Two storms, one from the Great Lakes and one from Georgia, converged at **New York City**, which was especially hard hit. Winds reached 84 miles per hour, and nearly 200 city residents lost their lives.

1889 May 31 After heavy rains an **earthen dam broke** above **Johnstown**, in central southern Pennsylvania, engulfing the city and killing 2,209 people. It is still the worst such disaster in U.S. history.

1889 June 12 Eighty schoolchildren were killed and 80 injured in a **train wreck at Armagh**, in present southern Northern Ireland. The brakes of the special children's excursion train, carrying 940 passengers, failed and cars rolled backward, with all doors locked, and crashed into an oncoming train.

II. EXPLORATION AND COLONIZATION

1888 Sept. 26 **Greenland** was first crossed on skis by **Fridtjof Nansen**, a Norwegian Arctic explorer. On this day he arrived with his party of six at Ameralik Fjord, near Godthåb, on the western coast of Greenland, having come across the ice cap of mountainous Greenland from its eastern shore.

III. POLITICS AND WAR

1885 Feb. 12 The **German East Africa Company** was chartered to administer the territories in present **Tanzania. Carl** [Karl] **Peters** (Sept. 27, 1856–Sept. 10, 1918) first explored the area for Germany, which secured its presence in East Africa by treaties signed with the native rulers since 1884. **Sayyid Barghash**, the sultan of Zanzibar [an island off the coast of Tanzania], nominal ruler (1870–1888) of the region, abandoned his claims when a German squadron entered the port of **Zanzibar**, the sultan's capital, in August 1885.

1885 Feb. 26 The **Conference of Berlin** recognized the **African International Association** (1876), a European organization for the exploration and civilization of Africa established by Leopold II, king of Belgium (from 1865), acting as the sovereign power of the just established **Congo Free State** [present Zaire] (already recognized by the U.S. in April 1884). Congo was proclaimed open to trade of all nations and the Congo River declared open to navigation of all nations; steps were taken to suppress the slave trade. The Congo Free State (1885–1908) was under the personal rule of Leopold, who did little to uphold the original high aims of the International Association. Excessive exploitation and oppressive administration eventually caused much unrest, raising international protests as well as protests from the Belgian people.

1885 Mar. 4 [Stephen] **Grover Cleveland** (March 18, 1837–June 24, 1908) of the Democratic party was inaugurated as the 22nd president of the U.S., having defeated **James Gillespie Blaine** (January 31, 1830–January 27, 1893) of the Republican party. **Thomas Andrews Hendricks** (b. September 7, 1819) served as vice president until his death from a stroke on November 25.

1885 Mar. 26 **Louis Riel** led a second rebellion, the **North West Rebellion**, against Canadian rule when white settlers threatened the livelihood of the *métis* of Indian and French ancestry in the present province of Saskatchewan. Riel (b. Oct. 22, 1844) was captured, tried, and executed on November 16, 1885.

1885 Apr. 2 **Justo Rufino Barrios** (b. 1835), ruler of **Guatemala** (from 1873), was killed at **Chalchuapa**, in western El Salvador, while invading the country in an effort to bring the restoration of the **Central American Federation**, which had dissolved in 1838.

1885 Sept. 18 Eastern Rumelia, in present southern Bulgaria, was reunited with Bulgaria, separated since the **Treaty of Berlin** (1878), when Eastern Rumelia was placed under Turkish administration, and Bulgaria under Russian, as autonomous principalities. Fearing Bulgarian supremacy in the Balkans, Serbia declared war (Nov. 14) on Bulgaria. The **Peace of Belgrade** (Mar. 3, 1886) resolved the **Serbian War** (1885–1886), and Bulgaria and Eastern Rumelia remained united.

1885 Sept. 30 Great Britain proclaimed the northern part of **Bechuanaland** [present Botswana] a protectorate and annexed the southern part as a British colony in order to prevent the German colony of South-West Africa from joining with the **Boer Republic of the Transvaal.**

1885 Dec. 17 A treaty signed by France and **Ranavalona III**, queen (1883–1896) of the **Merina Dynasty** (1818–1896), gave France control of foreign relations in **Madagascar.**

1885 Dec. 27 The **Indian National Congress**, founded by **Allan Octavian Hume** (June 6, 1829–July 31, 1912), held its first session in Bombay with **Surendranath Banerjea** (Nov. 10, 1848–Aug. 6, 1925) as president.

1886 The **American party** (to c.1890), whose major platform was anti-Chinese, came to temporary power in California, where its candidates were elected to local and state positions. It arose in response to economic difficulties, which were blamed widely on the Chinese laborers who were admitted to the U.S. (mainly into the West Coast states) on the basis of a reciprocal immigration treaty with China. Widespread unemployment was a big issue, especially in San Francisco, where cheap Chinese labor was used extensively.

1886 June Although the **Home Rule Bill** proposed by **William Ewart Gladstone**, prime minister of Great Britain, was defeated in the House of Commons, its chief supporter, **Charles Stewart Parnell** (June 27, 1846–Oct. 6, 1891), an Irish Nationalist leader, was encouraged by the formation of a coalition of the Irish members of Parliament and the Liberal party. The support of the Irish Home Rule party, secured by a promise of Liberal support for the Home Rule Bill, had made it possible for Gladstone, leader of the Liberal party, to take his seat as prime minister on Feb. 1, 1886. Parnell soon fell (1890) from public favor because of the divorce case brought by **William Henry O'Shea** (1840–Apr. 22, 1905) against his wife **Katharine** (1841–1921), who had been Parnell's mistress. Their subsequent marriage (June, 1891) cost Parnell much Roman Catholic support.

1886 Sept. 4 Geronimo (Goyathlay = He who Yawns), a Chiricahua Apache Indian warrior, surrendered for the last time to U.S. troops under **Nelson Appleton Miles** (Aug. 8, 1839–May 15, 1925) at Camp Bowie, in present southern Arizona. Geronimo went on many raids against the whites, but the enforced removal of the Apaches from Arizona precipitated even greater and more violent raids in 1876. Geronimo's last raid began on May 17, 1885; he was again captured by Crook on Mar. 27, 1886, escaped two days later, and finally surrendered to Miles on Sept. 4. Geronimo (b. June, 1829), who became a Christian, died of pneumonia at Fort Sill, Oklahoma, on Feb. 17, 1909.

1886 Oct. 27 The Senegalese national hero, **Lat Dior** (b. 1862), the Muslim **Wolof king of the Cayor** [the countryside surrounding the city of St. Louis], in present **Senegal**, was killed at Dekhle by French forces. His death marked the last important rebellion against French rule in Senegal.

1886 Nov. 1 An Anglo-German accord recognized **Sayyid Barghash**, sultan of Zanzibar (1870–1888), as ruler of the coasts of present **Somalia**, Tanzania, and Kenya. Germany annexed the hinterland of **Tanzania** while Great Britain annexed that of **Kenya**. In 1890 Great Britain established a protectorate over Zanzibar and in 1891 German East Africa [present Tanzania], was officially declared a German protectorate.

1887 France organized its southeastern Asian territories into the **Union of Indochina**, which included Cambodia and the Vietnamese territories of Annam, Cochinchina, and Tonkin. In 1893 the union was joined by Laos and in 1899 by the town of Chanchiang [Tsam Kong], in present southern China, which was leased from China for 99 years.

1887 Mar. 1 A plot to assassinate **Alexander III**, czar of Russia, by **Alexander Ulyánov** [Ulianov], an older brother of Lenin [Vladimir Ulyánov, Nikolai(?) Lenin], and 14 other university students was uncovered. Ulyánov and four others received the death penalty and were executed in May.

1887 Apr. The **Reinsurance Treaty** (to 1890) was concluded by Russia and Germany, after Austria-Hungary withdrew from the **Three Emperors Alliance** (1873). By its terms Germany and Russia agreed to remain neutral in the event of war with a third power, unless Russia attacked the Ottoman Empire or Germany attacked France.

1888 **Easter Island** [Isla de Pascua; Rapa Nui], c.2,000 miles west of **Chile** in the South Pacific Ocean, was annexed by Chile, which still holds it today. The island is remarkable for the **megalithic statues**, most carved from volcanic tuff and placed on bluffs overlooking the sea and for bas-reliefs cut in stone. Some experts consider that the statues were made as long as 1,000 years ago.

1888 Mar. 9 **William I** [Wilhelm Friedrich Ludwig] (b. Mar. 3, 1797), king of Prussia (from 1861) and emperor of Germany (from 1871), died. He was succeeded by **Frederick III**, a liberal in politics. He had led German armies against Austria during the **Seven Weeks' War** (1866) and he commanded the armies of the southern states of Germany against

France in the **Franco-Prussian War** (1870–1871). Frederick III (b. Oct. 18, 1831) died of throat cancer on June 15 after a reign of only 99 days.

1888 June 16 **William II** [Friedrich Wilhelm Viktor Albert] (Jan. 27, 1859–June 4, 1941), son of Frederick III, ascended to the throne as emperor of Germany and as king of **Prussia** (to 1918). **Bismarck** had frequent arguments with William leading to his dismissal (Mar. 18, 1890), when he was granted the title duke of Lauenberg.

1889 The **Social-Democratic party was formed in Sweden**. In 1917 the party was joined by the **Liberal party** and succeeded in electing their first government. Constitutional reforms were subsequently enacted that included female suffrage and universal and equal franchise in elections.

1889 The **First Congress of the Second** [Socialist] **International** opened in Paris. The Second International was established by national socialist parties, such as the Social Democratic party of Germany (1875), the French Socialist party (1879), the Social Democratic leagues of Denmark and the Netherlands (1879), the British Social Democratic federation (1880), and the Socialist Labor party of North America (1877). It held eight congresses in all, the last in **Basel**, Switzerland, in 1912.

1889 Jan. 27 **Georges Ernest Jean Marie Boulanger** [called: "Man on Horseback"] (Apr. 29, 1837–Sept. 30, 1891), a French general and popular reactionary who was thought to be planning a coup d'état in order to place himself in power as a military dictator, was accused of treason by prime minister **Pierre Emmanuel Tirard** (Sept. 27, 1827–Nov. 4, 1893). Boulanger fled to Brussels, and his movement collapsed in the general elections held in July. Boulanger committed suicide at the grave of his mistress.

1889 Feb. 11 **Mutsuhito**, emperor of Japan, promulgated **Japan's first constitution**, which provided for a constitutional monarchy with the emperor retaining almost absolute power.

1889 Mar. 4 **Benjamin Harrison** (Aug. 20, 1833–Mar. 13, 1901) of the Republican party was inaugurated as the 23rd president of the U.S., having defeated incumbent Democrat **Grover Cleveland**. The decisive electoral vote superseded Cleveland's victory by the popular vote. The combined popular vote for the remaining three candidates was more than four times the difference between that of Harrison and Cleveland. **Levi Parsons Morton** (May 16, 1824–May 16, 1920) served as vice president.

1889 Apr. 22 The **Oklahoma Territory**, part of the unorganized **Indian Territory**, was officially opened for settlement. "Sooners," land hungry pioneers, made camp along the border to the territory in hope of being first to claim the best land. At high noon a gun was fired to signal the start of the land rush. Much to everyone's dismay, it was found that some eager settlers, who were fortunate enough to know one of the border guards, had already entered the territory (thereby the nickname "Sooner") and claimed their stake.

1889 Nov. 2 **North** and **South Dakota** were the 39th and 40th states, respectively, to be admitted to the U.S.

1889 Nov. 8 **Montana** was the 41st state to be admitted to the U.S.

1889 Nov. 11 **Washington** was the 42nd state admitted to the U.S.

1889 Nov. 15 **Brazil** was proclaimed a republic after a coup d'état engineered by **Manuel Deodoro da Fonseca** (Aug. 5, 1827–Aug. 23, 1892). **Dom Pedro II** [Dom Pedro de Alcántara] (Dec. 2, 1825–Dec. 5, 1891), emperor of Brazil (from 1831), abdicated on Nov. 16 and was put aboard a ship for Portugal. On Feb. 24, 1891, a constitution, drafted by **Ruy Barbosa** (Nov. 5, 1849–Mar. 1, 1923) and patterned after those of the U.S., France, and Argentina, was adopted. Fonseca served as the provisional president, and in February was elected Brazil's first president.

IV. ECONOMY AND TRADE

1885 The **American Telephone and Telegraph Company** [AT&T] was incorporated in New York State to handle long distance telephone operations for the **American Bell Telephone Company**, which had been incorporated in 1881 in the state of Massachusetts where a capitalization limit prohibited the company from entering into long distance telephone service.

1885 Feb. 26 The **Contract Labor Act**, passed by the U.S. Congress, forbade the immigration of foreign laborers who were to work under contract for

their passage. Exempted were some professional and domestic workers, many of whom arrived from southern and eastern Europe.

1886 The U.S. Supreme Court handed down a decision in the case of **Santa Clara County vs. the Southern Pacific Company** that benefited American businesses. The Court decided that the definition of "persons" in the U.S. Constitution included corporations and, therefore, that corporations were entitled to the protection of their rights by the government of the U.S. as was any other citizen.

1886 May 4 In the U.S. the **Haymarket Riot** occurred when a bomb exploded in Chicago's Haymarket Square, killing nine policemen. On May 1 trade unions had begun a nationwide strike, demanding an eight-hour workday, and strike supporters, led by left-wing labor organizers, staged this demonstration. The identity of the bomb-thrower was never established, but seven so-called anarchists were sentenced to die; four were subsequently hanged and three sentenced to prison.

1886 June 10 The **Royal Niger Company** under **George Taubman Goldie** (May 20, 1846–Aug. 20, 1925) was given a royal charter to administer the **British Lower Niger Protectorate**, in present Nigeria. **Jaja**, king of Opobo (1869–1887), who controlled the palm oil trade in the Niger Delta and was reluctant to give up his monopoly, was deported to the West Indies in 1887.

1886 July 30 The 2,307-ton *Gluckaüff*, the **first oil tanker built for transoceanic travel**, by **W.G. Armstrong, Whithworth and Company, Ltd.**, and launched (1885) at Newcastle upon Tyne, in northern England, arrived at New York City on its maiden voyage.

1886 Dec. 8 The **American Federation of Labor** (AFL, A.F. of L.) was formed by representatives of 25 trade unions at a meeting held in Columbus, Ohio. **Samuel Gompers** (Jan. 27, 1850–Dec. 13, 1924) was chosen its first president and held this post until his death.

1887 **Bauxite**, from which aluminum is extracted commercially, was discovered near Little Rock, **Arkansas**. Arkansas still produces more than 90 percent of the aluminum ore used in the U.S.

1887   Japan levied its first income tax. The maximum rate was three percent.

1887 Feb. 4   The **Interstate Commerce Commission** [ICC], the **first federal regulatory agency**, was created by the U.S. Congress in order to regulate the railroads. The ICC grew out of a Supreme Court ruling (1886) that no individual state had the authority to regulate commerce between states.

1888   **John D. Rockefeller** formed the **first U.S. trust** in 1882 when he and his business partners merged various oil refineries and producers into the **Standard Oil Trust**, which was then able to drive out almost all competition and adjust prices to suit themselves. The success of Standard Oil led to the formation of many other trusts in other industries. Strong public protests arose, and Congress enacted the **Sherman Anti-Trust Law** (1890).

1888   The **De Beers Mining Corporation**, founded (1880) to mine diamonds in South Africa, took over the **Barnato Diamond Mining Company**, creating a monopoly over the chief source of the world's diamonds.

1888 May 13   The **Golden Law** was enacted in **Brazil** finally abolishing **slavery**. Conservative landholders, whose income depended on slaves, acting with the military and conservative prelates forced Dom Pedro II, emperor of Brazil, to abdicate in 1889.

V. RELIGION AND PHILOSOPHY

1885   Moderate Reform rabbis, led by **Isaac Mayer Wise**, and the more radical wing of the movement, led by **David Einhorn** (Nov. 10, 1809–Nov. 2, 1879) and **Emil G. Hirsch** (May 22, 1852–Jan. 8, 1923), 19 in all, met in Pittsburgh to compromise their differences and present a united front against attacks by Jewish Conservative spokesmen. The "**Pittsburgh Platform**" they produced, though it successfully served Reform rabbis for decades, convinced Conservatives that further cooperation was impossible.

1885   *History of Dogma*, still a basic work for Protestant and Catholic historical theologians, was published by **Adolf von Harnack** (May 7, 1851–June 10, 1930), the German Protestant who established the discipline of church history. Harnack traced the rise of the Church's authoritative doctrinal system and its development through the Reformation.

1885   The *Methodist Times*, which rapidly became a leading organ of Nonconformist opinion, was founded by **Hugh Price Hughes** (Feb. 8, 1847–Nov. 17, 1902), an English Methodist preacher, journalist, and political liberal. Hughes reawakened the conscience of **Methodism** and contributed significantly to the development of social concern within the Nonconformist denominations in England and Wales.

1885 Feb. 1   **Perez** [Peretz] **Smolenskin** (b. Feb. 25, 1842), a Russian Jew who had formulated a philosophy of Jewish nationalism, died of tuberculosis. Smolenskin, as a leader of the **Jewish National Progressive Movement**, contributed greatly to the birth of Zionism. Smolenskin was also known as a novelist. Among his works were *Hatohe Bedarke Hachayim* [*A Wanderer on the Path of Life*] (1868–1870) and *Kheburath Khmor* [*Burial of an Ass*] (1874), considered his masterpiece.

1886 Aug. 16   **Ramakrisha** [orig.: Gadadhar Chatterji or Chattopadhyaya] (b. Feb. 20, 1836), the **best known Hindu saint of modern times**, died. Born a Brahmin he had lived as a Muslim and as a Christian in Calcutta. A mystic, he had taught a universalist view of one God with varying names, and that the worship of Him was a service to man. The Ramakrishna order of Hindu monks was founded by one of Ramakrishna's chief followers, **Vivekenanda** [Vivekananda, Marendranath, Narendranath Datta, Narendra Nath Datta] (Jan. 12, 1863–July 4, 1902).

1887 Jan. 2   The **Jewish Theological Seminary** was opened in New York City by Conservative Jews under the leadership of **Sabato Morais** (Apr. 29, 1824–Nov. 11, 1897) of Mikveh Israel, Philadelphia's Sephardic congregation. The intent of the founders was to provide training that would preserve Judaism from the perceived dangers of Reform, especially that of assimilation. Conservatives specifically wished to preserve the Sabbath and dietary laws.

1889   **Jews in Russia** were prohibited by law from entering the legal profession. An 1887 law had instituted a quota system for the number of Jews allowed in secondary schools and in schools of higher learning. In 1890 and 1892 Jews were barred from voting in *zemstvo* (county and provincial councils) and city elections.

1889   The **Central Conference of American Rabbis**, its members largely from the alumni of Hebrew Union College, was created by **Isaac Mayer Wise**.

The conference, which was a result of the **Pittsburgh Platform** (1885), grew from an initial 50 members to more than 1,000 in 85 years. In 1894 the conference adopted a **Union Prayer Book**, based largely on the *Olat Tamid* (= daily sacrifice) of **David Einhorn**. The wide usage of the Union Prayer Book, often revised, maintained uniform worship throughout Reform Judaism's synagogues.

1889 Apr. 15 Joseph Damien [orig.: Joseph Veuster] (b. Jan. 3, 1840), a Belgian Roman Catholic priest and missionary, died of leprosy. In 1873 he had volunteered to go to the neglected leper colony on the Hawaiian island of Molokai, where he obtained and dispensed medicine and dressed wounds, built houses and water systems, in addition to preaching and building churches.

VI. SCIENCE, EDUCATION, AND TECHNOLOGY

1885 The **first high-speed internal combustion engine** was patented by **Gottlieb Wilhelm Daimler** (Mar. 17, 1834–Mar. 6, 1900), a German engineer. His design of a carburetor, which used a float and needle to maintain a continual supply of fuel, made practical the use of gasoline. The following year, with **Wilhelm Maybach** (Feb. 9, 1846–Dec. 30, 1929), Daimler constructed the first motorcycle by mounting his engine on a bicycle. In 1886 they mounted the engine on a carriage body and in 1887 on a boat. Maybach built the first Mercedes automobile in 1899.

1885 Karl [Carl] **Benz** (Nov. 26, 1844–Apr. 3, 1929), a German engineer, drove his automobile, the **first successful gasoline-driven automobile**, and the first with a four-stroke internal combustion engine, in Mannheim, on the Rhine River in Germany. Providing ¾ horsepower, Benz's engine could drive the three-wheel vehicle at ten miles per hour. He established (1888) in Mannheim the Rheinische Gasmotoren-fabrik Karl Benz to produce his three-wheeler. Five years later he began (1893) to produce four-wheel models.

1885 Feb. 21 The **Washington Monument** in Washington, D.C., was finally dedicated. Work on it had begun in 1834; its cornerstone was laid on July 4, 1848. It had been designed (1833–1834) by **Robert Mills** (Aug. 12, 1781–Mar. 3, 1855), an American architect.

1885 July Louis Pasteur, a French chemist, treated the first human with a series of **inoculations against rabies** [hydrophobia], one of the most dreaded diseases of the time. It was successful. The death rate of those known to have been bitten by a rabid animal dropped by c.1910 to less than 1 percent.

1885 Nov. 26 Thomas Andrews (b. Dec. 19, 1813), an Irish physical chemist, died. In experiments on the liquefaction of gases, Andrews developed (1869) the concept known today as the **Continuous State Law**: Gases at certain pressures and temperatures become liquids, and vice versa.

1886 Feb. 23 The **electrolytic process** for the recovery of pure aluminum was discovered by **Charles Martin Hall** (Dec. 6, 1863–Dec. 27, 1914), an American student. The metal became practical to use as the cost of aluminum dropped from about $5.00 to $0.50 per pound. Paul Louis Toussaint Héroult (Apr. 10, 1863–May 19, 1914), a French metal worker, developed the same process at about this time.

1886 May 23 Leopold von Ranke (b. Dec. 21, 1795), a German historian who pioneered the objective method of historical studies, died. The **objective method**, which required the assembling of a vast amount of data from original sources, was "to show how things actually were" without recourse to materials or ideas of later periods. Among a number of other more specific studies, he wrote *Weltgeschicht* [= universal history] (1881–1888), his greatest work.

1887 Construction began on the **Nord-Ostsee Kanal** [Kiel Canal, Kaiser Wilhelm Canal], which was completed in 1895. Sixty-one miles long, running northeast to southwest, from the city of Kiel to the mouth of the Elbe River, the canal was 388 feet wide and 37 feet deep. There were locks at each end. The original canal was enlarged (1907–1914) because of the amount of shipping it carried and to accommodate the growing Imperial German Fleet.

1887 Émile Levassor (d. 1897), a French auto builder, designed and built an automobile body into which he placed an **internal combustion engine**. In effect Levassor was the creator of the progenitor of the modern automobile. The date of its first appearance in public was probably in 1888. With **René Panhard** (1841–1908), Levassor had formed (1886) a manufacturing company called *Panhard et Lavassor*, in 1965 absorbed by **Citroën**. By 1900 France probably had more private automobiles (c.5,000) than any other country in the world.

1887 *Blitzlichtpulver* [flashlight powder] was invented in Germany. Made of magnesium, potassium chlorate, and antimony sulfide, the ignited powder gave off a very bright white light.

1887 Nikola Tesla (July 9, 1857–Jan. 7, 1943), an American electrician employed by the Edison Company for several years, invented the **induction motor**. The induction generator had been developed (1831) by **Michael Faraday**.

1888 Heinrich Rudolph Hertz, a German physicist, discovered the existence of **electromagnetic waves**, after his studies of the electromagnetic theory of light developed by **James Clerk Maxwell**.

1888 George Eastman (July 12, 1854–Mar. 14, 1932), an American inventor, produced the **Kodak hand camera** using rolls of flexible photosensitive film.

1888 Jan. 30 Asa Gray (b. Nov. 18, 1810), an American botanist, died. While he was professor (1842–1873) of natural history at Harvard University, he developed a systematic classification of American plants. His books included *Elements of Botany* (1836), the two-volume *Flora of North America* (1838–1843), and *How Plants Behave (1872).*

1888 Oct. 31 John Boyd Dunlop (Feb. 5, 1840–Oct. 23, 1921), a veterinary surgeon of Belfast, in present northern Ireland, was the first to patent the **pneumatic rubber tire**, or so he thought. More than 40 years earlier, the principle had been patented by Robert William Thompson, an English inventor, for use on carriages. But Thompson's inflatable rubber tires were expensive and clumsy, so they were quickly forgotten. Dunlop's tire improved the comfort, speed, and pleasure of bicycling.

1889 The **Eiffel Tower** was the central attraction of the Paris Exhibition. The tower, begun in 1887, was designed by **Gustave Alexandre Eiffel** (Dec. 15, 1832–Dec. 23, 1923). It was 1,001 feet in height, and now has an additional 55-foot TV antenna atop the tower. Eiffel, an engineer, also designed the **locks for the Panama Canal** in 1893.

1889 Sept. Jane Addams (Sept. 6, 1860–May 21, 1935), a social reformer and supporter of woman suffrage in the U.S., founded **Hull House** in Chicago with **Ellen Gates Starr** (Mar. 19, 1859–Feb. 10, 1940). Hull House was a place where people gathered to study the problems of poverty, women's rights, labor, and education. In 1931 Addams was awarded the **Nobel Peace Prize** with **Nicholas Murray Butler** (Apr. 2, 1862–Dec. 7, 1947), an American educator.

1889 Oct. 11 James Prescott Joule (b. Dec. 24, 1818), an English physicist, died. **Joule's law** (1840) stated the rate at which heat was produced by an electrical circuit.

VII. ARTS AND LEISURE

1885 May 22 Victor Marie Hugo (b. Feb. 26, 1802), a celebrated French romantic writer, died. His novels included *Le Dernier Jour d'un Condamné* (1829), *Notre Dame de Paris* [*The Hunchback of Notre Dame*] (1830), *Lucrèce Borgia* (1833), *Les Misérables* (1862), and *L'Homme qui Rit* (1869). His volumes of poetry included *Feuilles d'Automne* (1831) and *Voix Interieures* (1837). Known for his political activism in republican causes, he was exiled (1851) because of his opposition to Louis Napoleon, and lived for 20 years (until 1870) on Guernsey, one of the English Channel Islands. He returned to Paris in triumph and at his death was given a state funeral and burial in the Panthéon.

1886 At a convention held at Bern, Switzerland, an **international copyright code** was drafted providing authors, citizens of signatory nations, with copyright protection in all those nations. The U.S. did not participate, but has since signed reciprocal agreements with most of the nations concerned.

1886 Apr. 27 Henry Hobson Richardson (b. Sept. 29, 1838), a pioneering American architect, died. Richardson designed several churches in and near Boston, especially **Trinity Church** (1872), the Marshall Field Building in Chicago, and many private residences.

1886 May 15 Emily Dickinson (b. Dec. 10, 1830), an American poet, died. She had begun writing poetry in 1861, but would not allow it to be printed during her lifetime. It was published posthumously in six volumes (1890–1936).

1886 June 14 Aleksandr Nikolaevich Ostrovski (b. Apr. 12, 1823), a Russian playwright, died. His best-known play was a tragedy *The Thunderstorm* [**Groza**] (1860). He produced (from 1853) a new play each year in Russia—more than 50 altogether. These included *Enough Stupidity in Every Wise Man* (1868) and *The Snow Maiden* (1873). Ostrovski was noted for his plays about the banality, rapacity, and cruelty of the merchant class, which during this period began to emerge as a social and economic force in Russia. He also wrote often about the plight of women, powerless among the new bourgeoisie.

1886 July 31   Franz Liszt (b. Oct. 22, 1811), a Hungarian composer and piano virtuoso, died. His orchestral works included *Faust* (1854–1857), *Dante* (1855–1856), and *Les Préludes* (1856). These works were called symphonic poems, a style of composition which Liszt was said to have originated. His piano works included *Paganini Etudes* (1851), *Etudes d'Exécution Transcendantes* (1852), and c.20 Hungarian rhapsodies.

1886 Sept. 18   Jean Moréas (Apr. 15, 1856–Mar. 31, 1910), a French poet, writing in a newspaper, dubbed the recent movement (from c.1860) in French literature as "symbolism." The movement, which later spread to painting and the other arts, was a reaction against naturalism and realism and, instead of relying on the direct, detailed statement of fact, created an impression by suggestion, metaphor, or symbol.

1886   The **Statue of Liberty** was presented to the U.S. by France in celebration of 100 years of American independence and friendship between the two nations. **Grover Cleveland**, president of the U.S., presided over the dedication ceremony. The statue, designed by **Frédéric Auguste Bartholdi** (Apr. 2, 1834–Oct. 4, 1904), a French sculptor, still stands on Liberty [Bedloe's] Island in New York harbor.

1887–1889   *Drifting Clouds*, written by **Futabatei Shimei** (Apr. 4, 1864–May 10, 1909), was the **first modern Japanese novel**.

1887   **Victoria, queen of England**, celebrated her Golden Jubilee as sovereign. She was to remain on England's throne for another 14 years. In the arts the **Victorian Age** (1837–1901) brought a distinctive style based on the revival of, especially, Gothic architecture, which Prince Albert, the prince consort, promoted. In literature the period was at first characterized by an optimistic belief in progress, supported by industrialization and the growing middle class, but

later overpopulation, poverty, failed moral ideas, political corruption, and class favoritism brought forward bleak themes of cynicism and bitterness.

1887   The detective Sherlock Holmes and his assistant Dr. John Watson made their first appearance in the story *A Study in Scarlet* by **Arthur Conan Doyle** (May 22, 1859–July 7, 1930), appearing in the 28th issue of *Beeton's Christmas Annual* in late November or early December.

1887 Feb. 27   Aleksandr Porfirevich Borodin (b. Nov. 12, 1833), a Russian musician, died. In addition to two symphonies and several songs, Borodin composed the orchestral tone poem *In the Steppes of Central Asia* (1880). Borodin left incomplete the opera *Prince Igor*, which Nikolai Andreevich Rimski-Korsakov and Aleksandr Konstantinovich Glazunov completed for a performance in St. Petersburg in 1890.

1888   **Raffi** [Hakob Meliq-Hakobian; Akop Melik-Akopian] (born c.1835), an Armenian writer, died. Concerned with the plight of Armenians in Persia [Iran], Turkey, and Russia, he became popular among proponents of Armenian nationalism. His works included *Khent* [**The Fool**] (1880) and *Samuel* (1885).

1888 Apr. 15   Matthew Arnold (b. Dec. 24, 1822), an English poet and critic, died. His works included: poetry, *The Strayed Reveler and other Poems* (1849), *Poems* [included *Sohrab and Rustum]* (1853), *New Poems* (1867), *Poems* (two volumes, 1869); critical essays, *Culture and Anarchy* (1869) and *Literature and Dogma* (1873). Arnold was known as an important advocate of improved education in England.

1888 Dec. 2   Namik Kemal [orig.: Mehmed Namik] (b. Dec. 21, 1840), a Turkish revolutionary, romantic poet, translator, and playwright, died. Kemal, who wrote in Arabic, Persian, and Turkish, helped lay the foundation for the modernist movement in Turkish literature. He was also notable as the first writer of serious political poetry in the language. He translated Francis Bacon, Jean Jacques Rousseau, and others. Among his works were *Vatan* [*Fatherland*] (1872), a patriotic drama; *Akif Bey* (1874), a play; *History of Turkey*; and historical novels.

1889 June 8   Gerard Manley Hopkins (b. July 28, 1844), an English Jesuit priest and religious poet, died. His poetry, unpublished prior to his death, was edited and sponsored by a friend **Robert** [Seymour] Bridges, the poet laureate [from 1913]. Hopkins's poetry, noted for its use of innovative rhythms and for the dropping of words to achieve intensity of language, greatly influenced modern English and American poetry.

1889 Sept. 23 [William] **Wilkie Collins** (b. Jan. 8, 1824), an English author, died. He was best known for two mystery novels, *The Woman in White* (1860), perhaps the first true English mystery novel, and *The Moonstone* (1868).

1889 Dec. 10 Ludwig Anzengruber [Ludwig Gruber] (b. Nov. 29, 1839), an Austrian playwright, died. He won renown with the liberal, anti-clerical *Der Pfarrer von Kirchfeld* [*The Parson of Kirchfeld*] (1870), but also popular was *Das vierte Gebot* [*The Fourth Commandment*] (1877), to which *A Doll's House* (1879) by Henrik Ibsen was compared.

1889 Dec. 12 Robert Browning (b. May 7, 1812), an English poet, died. His works included *Pauline* (1833); *Sordello* (1840); *Bells and Pomegranates* (1841–1846), a series of pamphlets containing his poems; the two-volume *Men and Women* (1855); the four-volume *The Ring and the Book* (1868–1869), which brought him his first widespread recognition; and *Asolando* (1889). His best-known poems included "How They Brought the Good News from Ghent to Aix," "Fra Lippo Lippi," "Andrea del Sarto," and "Pippa Passes."

VIII. SPORTS, GAMES, AND SOCIETY

1886 The Westchester **Polo** Club of Newport, Rhode Island, presented a challenge cup to be played for by British and American teams. The **Westchester Cup** was for more than half a century the most important trophy in international polo and was contested this year for the first time. At Newport the British team defeated the U.S. team. Great Britain also won in 1902, the next time it was played for. There were ten more matches between 1909 and the last in 1939, the U.S. winning all but that of 1914.

1887 The **first U.S. tennis tournament for women**, the National Outdoor Championship, was held in Newport, Rhode Island. The winner was **Ellen F. Hansell.**

1887 The Foxburg **Golf** Club of Foxburg, in western Pennsylvania, was organized by **Joseph Mickle Fox** of Philadelphia. It has since successfully defended its claim to be the oldest golf club in the U.S. and to have the oldest golf course.

1887 The Bath **Badminton** Club was formed in Bath, southwestern England. It was largely composed of army officers who had played badminton in India.

1887 Charlotte [Lottie] **Dod** (1871–June 2, 1960) of England won the women's singles title at Wimbledon, England. At age 15 years, 9 months, she was the **youngest player ever to win a title at Wimbledon.** Dod won again in 1888 and from 1891 to 1893.

1887 Feb. 8 The **first well-organized ski event** in the U.S. was a jumping contest held at Red Wing, Minnesota. The winner was Mikkel Hemmestvedt, who had previously won the Norwegian jumping championship.

1888 William McGregor, later to be known as "father of the league," stimulated the founding of the **first league in England** for football [**soccer**]. Twelve clubs, playing each other on a home-and-away basis, constituted the original league.

1888 Feb. 22 Robert Lockhart, a Scottish resident of New York, and two American friends used a pasture in Yonkers, New York, to play **golf**. Later the **St. Andrews Golf Club of Yonkers** was organized (1888) and was mistakenly long regarded as the oldest U.S. golf club. The club established (1897) its permanent home at Hastings-on-Hudson, New York state.

1888 Aug. 7–Nov. 10 A murderer who was never caught and who became known as **Jack the Ripper** killed at least seven prostitutes in London, mostly in the Whitechapel district. In every case the victim's throat was cut and the body eviscerated, indicating that the perpetrator had some knowledge of human anatomy. The murderer, or someone posing as such, wrote taunting letters to the police, who were much criticized by the public for not catching the killer. The case has inspired movies and several books, most notably *The Lodger* (1913) by **Mrs. Belloc Lowndes** (1868–Nov. 14, 1947).

1889 Walter Chauncey Camp (Apr. 17, 1859–Mar. 14, 1925), Yale player, coach, and architect of the game of **football** in its developmental stage, picked his **first All-America football team**, a practice he was said to have originated. Camp continued this custom annually until his death in 1925. His immediate successor as selector was sportswriter **Grantland Rice** (Nov. 1, 1880–July 13, 1954), but ultimately the press syndicates took over the selection of the players.

1889 July 8   **John Lawrence Sullivan**, the American heavyweight **boxing** champion, in the **last important bare-knuckle fight** under the old **London Prize Ring rules**, stopped **Jake** [Joseph John] **Kilrain** (Feb. 9, 1859–Dec. 23, 1937) in 75 rounds at Richburg, Mis-

sissippi. Prize fighting under London rules was now illegal in every state.

1889 Nov. 14   **Nellie Bly** [née Elizabeth Cochrane; later Seaman], an American journalist, embarked from New York City on a famous 72-day journey around the world in an attempt to better the time of the record set by **Jules Verne's** fictional Phileas Fogg of *Around the World in Eighty Days* (1873), who made his trip from Oct. 2 to Dec. 20, 1872. Her exact time: 72 days, 6 hours, 10 minutes, and 58 seconds. She told of her adventures in *Nellie Bly's Book: Around the World in 72 Days* (1890).

1890–1894

I. VITAL STATISTICS AND DEMOGRAPHY

1890   The **world population** was c.1,600,000,000 with c.63,000,000 in the U.S., c.145 million in the Americas, and c.300 million in Europe.

1892 Jan. 1   **Ellis Island**, a small piece of land in New York Bay south of Manhattan Island, New York City, **opened** as a processing station for the immigrants from Europe arriving in the U.S. Ellis Island could deal with 1 million immigrants a year and by the time it closed (1943) c.20 million persons had passed through. Ellis Island was made (1965) part of the Statue of Liberty National Monument, and it was opened (1976) to the public as part of the observance of the 200th anniversary of the Declaration of Independence. The Great Hall, which had been the main registration area for immigrants, was restored and opened (1986) as a museum, recalling the experiences of the people of many lands whose descendants are today American citizens.

II. DISASTERS

1891–1892   Russia was struck with the double catastrophes of **famine and Asiatic cholera**. Caused primarily by crop failures, famine in the region of the Volga River was relieved in part by aid from the U.S., which contributed $700,000 of the $75 million appropriated to aid the suffering 15 to 30 million Russian subjects.

1891   An **explosion in a coal mine at Spring Hill**, Nova Scotia, in eastern Canada, killed 125 men.

There were at least two other major mine disasters at Spring Hill, one in 1956 and another in 1962, which killed 74 men.

c.1892   The **boll weevil** [*Anthonomus grandis*], called "the most costly insect in the history of American agriculture," was said to have entered the U.S. at Brownsville, Texas, having come from Central America. It devastated cotton crops throughout the southern U.S., causing about $200 million worth of damage each year before any good controls were developed. Research (begun 1894) for effective control of the boll weevil still continues.

1894   History's third pandemic **bubonic plague** originated in **China**, where it claimed c.100,000 lives before spreading to India, the Near East, Hawaii, and eastern **South America**. A million deaths were recorded throughout the world by 1914, when the plague reached the U.S. Gulf Coast. The disease claimed only c.250 lives, but it did continue to appear intermittently before running its course in the mid-20th century (1949).

1894 Aug. 1   **Fire swept again through Chicago**, Illinois, causing an estimated $3 million worth of property damage.

1894 Sept. 1   **Fire**, driven by tornado-like winds, razed c.160,000 acres of forest in eastern **Minnesota**, killing 418 people in the region around Hinckley. Nearly 700 fled from Hinckley aboard two trains before intense heat melted the tracks.

III. EXPLORATION
AND COLONIZATION

1893 June   Gold was found at Kalgoorlie, in southwestern Western **Australia** state. It was the most productive goldfield in Australia, and prospectors from eastern Australia gave the name "**Golden Mile**" to the region around Kalgoorlie.

IV. POLITICS AND WAR

1890 Mar. 18   Otto von Bismarck, first chancellor (from 1871) of the German Empire (1871–1918), was dismissed by **William II**, emperor of Germany. Though Bismarck's statecraft had unified Germany under Prussian leadership, the two had quarreled increasingly, and relations between Great Britain and Germany grew more strained.

1890 July 1   Great Britain ceded to Germany its strategic North Sea island of **Heligoland** [Helgoland], a ¼-square mile fort 28 miles off the western coast of Schleswig-Holstein, in present Germany, in return for German recognition of the British protectorate in Zanzibar and of British rights over the Buganda Kingdom, in present Uganda.

1890 July 3   Idaho was the 43rd state admitted to the U.S.

1890 July 10   Wyoming was the 44th state admitted to the U.S. Its territorial legislature had granted voting privileges to women in 1869, making Wyoming the **first state to provide woman suffrage**.

1890 Nov. 23   William III (b. Feb. 19, 1817), king of the **Netherlands** (from 1849), died. He was succeeded by his daughter **Wilhelmina** (Aug. 31, 1880–Nov. 28, 1962), who abdicated in favor of her daugher **Juliana** (b. Apr. 30, 1909) on Sept. 4, 1948.

1890 Dec. 18   Frederick [John] Dealtry Lugard (Jan. 22, 1858–Apr. 11, 1945), baron Lugard, the British commander in East Africa, **occupied Uganda for the British East Africa Company**, and forced **Mwanga**, king of Buganda (1884–1899), a region in southeastern Uganda, to sign a treaty permitting British occupation. Uganda was declared a British protectorate on Apr. 11, 1894.

1890 Dec. 29   A massacre at Wounded Knee, a creek in South Dakota, completed the defeat of the Indians in the **Indian Wars** (from 1860) of the American Northwest. While surrendering their arms to U.S. troops, c.200 Sioux men, women, and children became agitated by the actions of one of their medicine men, in the course of which an American guard was wounded by a shot from an Indian warrior. Immediately, the troops fired upon and killed c.145 Indians. About 30 soldiers were killed. It was the **last major battle in the U.S. between the white colonizers and the native Indians**.

1891 Apr. 15   The Belgian Katanga Company was created to exploit the mineral-rich province of Katanga [present Shaba in southern Zaire]. Leopold II, king of Belgium, annexed the Katanga region to the Congo Free State, which he ruled directly, and began extensive copper mining operations there.

1891 May 21   The Populist party [People's Party of the United States of America] was founded in Cincinnati, Ohio, by farmers from southern and northwestern U.S. Its basic platform was the free, unlimited coinage of silver. In the 1892 presidential elections the Populist candidate **James Baird Weaver** (June 12, 1833–Feb. 6, 1912) received 22 electoral votes and 1 million popular votes. On the local level, especially in the Northwest, the Populists gained many minor offices. After this time the Populists formed a coalition with the Democrats, who absorbed them after the defeat of William Jennings Bryan.

1891 June 11   An Anglo-Portuguese agreement ended rivalry in East Africa and gave the **British a free hand over** the territories of the broken **Malawi** Kingdom, in present Malawi. The British had proclaimed (1889) the Shire Highlands Protectorate, in present southern Malawi, and **Harry Hamilton Johnston** (June 12, 1858–Aug. 31, 1927), as British consul, had begun the pacification of the area. In 1893 the region became part of the British Central African Protectorate and in 1907 the protectorate became **Nyasaland** [present Malawi].

1891 Sept. 19   José Manuel Balmaceda (b. July 19, 1840), the Liberal president of **Chile** (from 1886), committed suicide, **ending the Civil War** (1890–1891) brought on by his decision to overrule the constitution and to assume dictatorial power in an effort to promote social reform. The Chilean Congress, dominated by Conservatives, assumed power and adopted a parliamentary system.

1891 Oct. 16 The *Baltimore* incident occurred at Valparaíso, Chile, after the Civil War (1890–1891) between the government and the congress had effectively ended. Congressional forces had driven the president from office; but, thinking the U.S. had supported him, a mob attacked and killed two sailors from the *Baltimore*. When the U.S. demanded an apology, Chile finally offered compensation of $75,000.

1892 Aug. 9 Béhanzin (1844–1900), last independent king of Dahomey [present **Benin**] (1888–1894), attacked a French exploratory mission moving through his kingdom. With the aid of a military force led by **Alfred Dodds** (Feb. 6, 1842–July 18, 1922), France captured Abomey, the native capital, and placed Béhanzin's brother on the throne under a French protectorate (Dec. 3). Dahomey was formally made a French colony on June 22, 1894.

1893 The **Labor party of Belgium called a general strike** of all workers to force the parliament to adopt universal male suffrage. As a result, suffrage was added to Belgium's constitution.

1893 Jan. 17 Liliuokalani (Dec. 2, 1838–Nov. 11, 1917), queen of **Hawaii** (from 1891), was deposed by a constitutional movement led mainly by those favoring annexation by the U.S. Grover Cleveland, president of the U.S., refused to approve annexation and on July 4, 1894, **Sanford Ballard Dole** (Apr. 23, 1844–June 9, 1926), an American lawyer and justice serving in Hawaii, proclaimed the **Republic of Hawaii**, which he served as president (to 1898). On July 6, 1898, Congress approved legislation and on June 14, 1900, Hawaii officially became a U.S. territory. Dole served (1900–1903) as the first territorial governor.

1893 Mar. 4 [Stephen] **Grover Cleveland** of the Democratic party was inaugurated as the 24th president of the U.S., his second term. He defeated incumbent **Benjamin Harrison** of the Republican party. **Adlai Stevenson** (Oct. 23, 1835–June 14, 1914) served as vice president.

1893 Sept. 19 **New Zealand granted woman suffrage**. Male suffrage had been granted in 1879.

1894 Apr. 28 **Jacob Sechler Coxey** (1854–1951) and c.500 followers, who formed the so-called **Coxey's Army**, arrived at Washington, D.C., to demonstrate in support of the Populist party's proposals for public works to help the unemployed during this period of widespread unemployment. The demonstration, on May 1, ended with Coxey's arrest.

1894 Nov. 1 **Alexander III** [Aleksandr Aleksandrovich] (b. Mar. 10, 1845), czar of Russia (from 1881), died. He was succeeded by **Nicholas II**, his eldest son. Nicholas, who ruled until the Russian Revolution, forced his abdication (Mar. 15, 1917). Nicholas, under the influence of advisors such as **Grigori Efimovidi Rasputin**, a reputed holy man, had resisted changes taking place in his country and refused to enact reforms that might have preserved the Russian monarchy.

V. ECONOMY AND TRADE

1890–1903 A series of measures passed during these years provided **New Zealand** with a comprehensive and progressive social welfare system. They included three sets of **Factory Acts** designed to aid workers (1891, 1894, 1901), a **Family Housing Protection Act** (1894), the introduction of a mandatory eight-hour day and old-age pensions (1898), and various government insurance plans (1899, 1903).

1890 **Civil disorder broke out in Persia** [present Iran] in protest against the sale of the previously state-owned tobacco monopoly to European investors. Nasr-ed-Din, shah of Persia, ended the troubles by buying the concession back in order to placate his subjects.

1890 **Labor unrest was prevalent throughout Russia**. In response to disorders the Russian government passed a law on June 2, 1897, that called for an 11½ hour working day (10 hours if the work was between 9 P.M. and 5 A.M.). Previously the work day had been 16 or more hours.

1890 The **Commercial Bureau of the American Republics**, an organization of the nations of North, Central, and South America, was formed at a conference in Washington, D.C. All the nations except the Dominican Republic were represented. The purpose of the bureau was to promote cooperation among the lands of the Western Hemisphere. The scope of its activities increased to include social welfare and political affairs, and treaties were signed to ensure cooperation and provide against conflicts. In 1910 the bureau became the **Pan American Union** and in 1948 the **Organization of American States**.

1890 July 2   The U.S. Congress passed the **Sherman Anti-Trust Act** in response to growing public demand for the regulation of large business combinations and monopolies.

1890 July 14   The **Sherman Silver Purchase Act** was passed by the U.S. Congress. It required the government to buy nearly twice as much silver as previously. Since the silver was purchased with notes redeemable in gold, the result was an increase in the amount of money in circulation and a drain on U.S. gold reserves.

1890 Nov.   The banking firm of **Baring Brothers and Company**, a respected and important financial institution in Great Britain, nearly collapsed when **Argentina defaulted on bond payments** to the Barings. The firm was saved by the intervention of the Bank of England and the Rothschilds.

1892   Great Britain and Germany each passed laws permitting small private companies the privilege of **limited liability**, which publicly owned joint-stock companies had already been granted.

1892   The first iron ore was shipped from the great **Mesabi Range** of northeastern Minnesota.

1892 July 12   The **Amalgamated Association of Iron, Steel, and Tin Workers** was broken when the governor of Pennsylvania called out state troops to control strikers at a Carnegie steel mill in **Homestead**, Pennsylvania. The strike had begun on July 2 over wage cuts, and four days later violence broke out with the arrival of c.300 strikebreakers from the Pinkerton Agency, summoned to break the strike. Seven workers and at least three Pinkertons were killed, and many others were wounded. The union's defeat left the steel workers largely unorganized for the next 40 years.

1892 Dec. 5   **Forced labor was imposed on the natives of the Congo Free State**, ruled directly by Leopold II, king of Belgium. Forced labor was later introduced in the French Congo in 1899.

1893 Apr. 21   The **Panic of 1893** began when U.S. gold reserves fell below the $100 million level, which had been considered a safe backing for U.S. currency. About 600 banks and more than 15,000 businesses failed. The resulting depression lasted until 1897.

1893 May 15   The **Western Federation of Miners** [WFM] was formed in Butte, Montana. The WFM practiced violence more often than most U.S. unions to pursue its aims, and confrontations with the equally violent western mine owners were often bloody.

1894   For the first time, **Mexico** achieved a national budget without a deficit, due to the efforts of **Porfirio Díaz**, president of Mexico. Díaz encouraged the investment of foreign capital in Mexico, especially in oil. Textile mills were constructed and the **first railroad**, between Mexico City and the port of Veracruz on the Gulf of Mexico, was built. Nevertheless, Díaz's land policy, which supported the large landowners but left Indians landless, failed to produce enough food for Mexico's population.

1894 May 11   The **Pullman strike** began at the company town near Chicago, Illinois, when workers protested a 25 percent cut in wages without a cut in rents or other fees. The **American Railway Union** joined (June 21) the Pullman workers, and sympathy strikes occurred throughout the U.S. After a Federal court issued (July 2) an injunction, Federal troops were summoned to end the strike. By Aug. 3 the walkout was officially over, the strike crushed.

VI. RELIGION AND PHILOSOPHY

1890   Japan's imperial government set forth the moral principles to be followed in state education. They were a mixture of practical, ethical Confucianism and Shinto ideology, combining the traits of loyalty from Confucianism and reverence from Shinto.

1890 Aug. 11   **John Henry Newman** (b. Feb. 21, 1801), an Anglican clergyman and convert to Roman Catholicism, died. He had been the most influential leader of the **Oxford [Tractarian] Movement**; but, distressed by the denunciations made against him when he tried to reconcile the tenets of the Church of England with statements of the 16th century Council of Trent, he converted on Oct. 9, 1845, went to Rome to become a priest, and was eventually made a cardinal (1879). Among his books were *University Sermons* (1843), *Idea of a University* (1852), and the famous *Apologia pro vita sua* (1864).

1892 Jan. 14   **Henry Edward Manning** (b. July 15, 1808), a former Anglican clergyman, prominent in the Oxford [Tractarian] Movement, and convert to Roman Catholicism, died. A strong supporter of the separation of church and state, Manning eventually found governmental interference intolerable, and entered the Roman Catholic church on Apr. 6, 1851. He argued forcefully for **papal infallibility** at the Vatican Council (1869). In 1865 he became archbishop of Winchester, where he was effective in establishing schools for Catholic children. He was made a cardinal in 1875.

1893 The **Bahai faith** was introduced to the U.S. from its stronghold in Persia.

1893 Sept. 19 Vivekenanda, the Hindu saint and religious leader, speaking impassionedly at the Parliament of Religions held in connection with the Chicago World's Fair, attracted wide attention in U.S. religious circles unfamiliar with the modern **Vedanta form of Hinduism**. In 1894 he founded the **Vedanta Society** in New York City.

1894 Oct. 15 The **Dreyfus Affair** began in France as **Alfred Dreyfus** (Oct. 19, 1859–July 12, 1935), a Jewish officer in the French army, was falsely accused of selling military secrets to Germany and court-martialed. On Jan. 5, 1895, he was condemned to solitary confinement for life on **Devil's Island** [Île du Diable], off the northern coast of French Guiana. Early in July 1906, after he had been found guilty (though with extenuating circumstances) a second time, Dreyfus was finally acquitted due to the influence on public opinion of Radical and Socialist intellectuals. In 1899 **Marie Charles Ferdinand Walsin Esterhazy** (1847–May 21, 1923), a French army officer, confessed to forging one of the documents on which Dreyfus's guilt had been determined.

VII. SCIENCE, EDUCATION, AND TECHNOLOGY

1890 Emil Adolph von Behring (Mar. 3, 1854–Mar. 31, 1917), a German bacteriologist, developed an **antitoxin for tetanus** that provided immunity to the disease. In 1892 he developed an antitoxin for diphtheria and in 1901 received the first **Nobel prize for medicine and physiology**.

1891 [Marie] **Eugene** [François Thomas] **Dubois** (Jan. 28, 1858–Dec. 16, 1940), a Dutch paleontologist serving as medical officer in Java, unearthed the remains of an early progenitor of man, which he named **Pithecanthropus erectus**, now **Homo erectus**. The bones of **Java Man** were dated as being possibly

600,000 years B.P., and are thought now to be a direct ancestor of modern man.

1891 The **first American correspondence school** opened in Scranton, Pennsylvania, for the purpose of instructing coal miners on safety procedures. It later became the **International Correspondence School**.

1891 The **first automobile with an internal combustion engine mounted in the front and rear-wheel drive** was built by **René Panhard** and **Émile Levassor**, who had acquired the French rights to the automobile patents of Daimler. The Panhard-Levassor performed well in competitions and was sold from 1892.

1891 Jan. 17 George Bancroft (b. Oct. 3, 1800), an American historian and government official, died. His major work was *A History of the United States* (1834–1874). He is remembered also for establishing (1845), while he was secretary of the navy (1845–1846), the U.S. Naval Academy at Annapolis, Maryland.

1891 July 31 The **kinetoscope**, for viewing continuous film, was patented in the U.S. by **Thomas Alva Edison**. It used 35 millimeter film in a continuous roll produced by **George Eastman** for the Eastman Kodak box camera. On Apr. 14, 1894, in New York City were displayed the first kinetoscopes to be viewed by the paying public, which numbered close to 500 the first day. A single viewer looked through the "peep-hole" on top of the machine to watch the 13-second show. This invention was copied overseas, where it had not been patented, and led to the development by the **Lumière** brothers, **Louis Jean** (Oct. 5, 1864–June 6, 1948) and **Auguste** (Oct. 19, 1862–Apr. 10, 1954), of the **cinématographe**, patented in Mar., 1895, which was the first machine capable of projecting film. The Lumière brothers made (1896–1900) more than 2,000 films, each lasting less than a minute. As early as 1888 Edison had secured (Oct. 8) preliminary patents for the **kinetograph**, which showed tiny images on a revolving cylinder and probably represented the **birth of motion pictures**.

1892 The **Yerkes Observatory** was founded at Williams Bay, in southern Wisconsin, in order to study comets and galaxies, and measure stars. Its 40-inch refracting **telescope** is still the largest of its kind in the world.

1892   The **diesel engine** was patented by **Rudolph Christian Karl Diesel** (Mar. 18, 1858–Sept. 29, 1913), a German inventor. It ran on low grade fuel, originally coal dust, and did not require a boiler, as did a steam engine.

1892 Apr. 19   **Charles Robert Darwin** (b. Feb. 12, 1809), the pioneering English evolutionist, died. Darwin expounded his theory of natural selection in *The Origin of Species by Means of Natural Selection* (1859), *The Descent of Man* (1871), and *Selection in Relation to Sex* (1871). Other publications of Darwin included: *Zoology of the Voyage of H. M. S. Beagle* (1840–1843), *Fertilization of Orchids* (1862), *Climbing Plants* (1875), *Formation of Vegetable Mold through the Action of Worms* (1881), and many other works.

1893   **Daniel Hale Williams** (Jan. 18, 1858–Aug. 4, 1931), a black American surgeon, performed the **first successful closure of a heart wound**.

1893   The development of a new **four-color printing process** made possible the printing of the first colored newspaper supplements.

1893 Sept. 22   The **first successful gasoline-powered automobile in the U.S.** was demonstrated by **Charles Edgar Duryea** (Dec. 15, 1862–Sept. 28, 1938) and his brother **J. Frank Duryea** (Oct. 8, 1869–Feb. 15, 1967), in Springfield, Massachusetts.

1893 Aug. 16   **Jean Martin Charcot** (b. Nov. 29, 1825), a French neurologist, died. From 1862 Charcot was at the clinic of Salpêtrière in Paris, where he established a neurological clinic. His studies of the **effects of hypnosis on hysteria** led **Sigmund Freud** to investigate further hysteria and hypnosis, but with an aim to study the psyche.

1893 Nov. 8   **Francis Parkman** (b. Sept. 16, 1823), an American historian, died. He wrote accurate accounts of the conflict (1512–1763) between the English and French for control of North America in a series of books that began with *Pioneers of France in the New World* (1865) and ended with *A Half-Century of Conflict* (1892).

1894   The ship *Turbinia* was the **first to be outfitted with a steam turbine engine**, invented by **Charles Algernon Parsons** (June 13, 1854–Feb. 11, 1931), an English engineer, about ten years earlier. It reached a speed of nearly 33 knots.

1894 June 7   **William Dwight Moody** (b. Feb. 9, 1827), an American lexicographer and Sanskrit scholar, died. He was a leading Orientalist of his generation and wrote several Sanskrit texts, including *Sanskrit Grammar* (1879). He became editor-in-chief of *The Century Dictionary* (1889–1891), a multi-volume work with considerable encyclopedic material.

1894 Sept. 8   **Hermann von Helmholtz** (b. Aug. 31, 1821), a German scientist, died. In 1847 he produced a mathematical statement for the law of the conservation of energy in his greatest work *Über die Erhaltung der Kraft* (1847). Helmholtz described the perception of tone quality in *On the Sensations of Tone* (1863). He further developed the theory of color vision and explained the phenomenon of lens accommodation in the eye in *Treatise on Physiological Optics* (1867).

1894 Oct. 20   **James Anthony Froude** (b. Apr. 23, 1818), the foremost English historian of the Victorian Age (1837–1901), died. He contributed to **John Henry Newman's** *Lives of the Saints*, but broke with him when Newman became a Roman Catholic. Among his major works were the 12-volume *History of England From the Fall of Wolsey to the Defeat of the Spanish Armada* (1856–1870) and *The English in Ireland* (1871–1874).

VIII. ARTS AND LEISURE

c.1890–1910   **Art Nouveau**, an architectural and decorative style, came to its height throughout Europe and the U.S. In Germany it was called **Jugendstil** and in Spain, **Modernismo**. The works of **Aubrey Beardsley** (Aug. 24, 1872–Mar. 16, 1898), an English artist, and **Louis Comfort Tiffany**, an American glass designer, were especially popular examples of Art Nouveau.

c.1890–1910   The **Gibson girl**, originated by **Charles Dana Gibson** (Sept. 14, 1867–Dec. 23, 1944), an American artist, was popular in the U.S. The Gibson girl, the epitome of current American femininity, was the model for clothing and hair styles. Gibson's drawings were published regularly in *Collier's Weekly*.

c.1890–1910   **Western literary works**, especially those by Dickens and Walter Scott, were **translated into Chinese** and enjoyed some popularity.

1890 July 29   Vincent [Willem] **van Gogh** (b. Mar. 30, 1853), a Dutch painter, died two days after shooting himself. Van Gogh did not begin painting until he was 27, and during his lifetime sold only one painting. His early works, usually depicting peasants in heavy, greenish-brown hues, included *The Potato Eaters* (1885). In 1888 van Gogh moved to Arles, in southeastern France, and there developed the bold, colorful, postimpressionistic style for which he was noted. His works at this time included a series of sunflowers and *The Public Gardens in Arles* (1888). In 1889 in the asylum at Saint-Rémy-de-Provence, near Arles, van Gogh painted *Starry Night* (1889). *Wheat Field with Crows* (1890) was one of his last paintings.

1890 Oct. 20   Richard Francis Burton (b. Mar. 19, 1821), an English explorer and author, died. In 1885 he completed an English translation of the *Arabian Nights* [*The Thousand Nights and a Night*] in 16 volumes. He had gone (1842) to India with the East India Company, where he studied Indian languages and native customs. With the support of the Royal Geographic Society, he participated (1853) in a pilgrimage to the Islamic holy city Mecca, becoming **one of the first Englishmen to explore Arabia.**

1890 Nov. 8   César Auguste [Jean Guillaume Hubert] **Franck** (b. Dec. 10, 1822), a Belgian-born French composer, pianist, and organist, died. Franck's best-known works are the *Symphony in D Minor* (1886–1888) and the Sonata for Violin and Piano in A Major (1886).

1891 Jan. 16   Léo [Clément Philidor] **Delibes** (b. Feb. 21, 1836), a French composer, pianist, and organist, died. His best-known works were the ballets *Coppélia* (1870) and *Sylvia* (1876), and the opera Lakmé (1883).

1891 Mar. 29   Georges [Pierre] **Seurat** (b. Dec. 2, 1859), a French painter, died. He developed **pointillism,** a style of painting in which pure colors are applied to the canvas as dots. Different shades and colors were achieved by the positioning of primary colors close together. Seurat's best-known work is *Un Dimanche à la Grande Jatte* [*An Afternoon at la Grande Jatte*] (1886).

1891 July 10   Pedro Antonio de Alarcón (b. Mar. 10, 1833), a Spanish poet, statesman, and journalist, died. *Diario de un testigo de la guerra de Africa* (1859) was written after he was wounded in the Moroccan campaign. His best-known work was the short novel *El Sombrero de Tres Picos* [*The Three-Cornered Hat*] (1874), which was a retelling of a traditional Spanish ballad.

1891 Aug. 12   James Russell Lowell (b. Feb. 22, 1819), a New England poet, died. *The Biglow Papers* (1848), poems and prose passages written in Yankee dialect, denounced the Mexican War (1846–1848). Lowell took a firm stand against slavery, publishing scores of abolitionist articles. He was the first editor of the *Atlantic Monthly* (1857–1861). His *Commemoration Ode*, given July 21, 1865, in honor of the Harvard dead in the Civil War, became widely known, especially because it was one of the first literary works to recognize Lincoln's greatness.

1891 Sept. 28   Herman Melville (b. Aug. 1, 1819), an American writer, died. He was best known for *Moby-Dick, or the Whale* (1851), one of the greatest American novels. Like his other works, it reflected his own experiences at sea. Melville's other works included *Typee* (1846) and *Omoo* (1847), both set in Polynesia, and *Billy Budd* (1924), which was used by Benjamin Britten for an opera in 1950.

1891 Nov. 10   Arthur Rimbaud [Jean Nicolas Arthur Rimbaud] (b. Oct. 20, 1854), a French symbolist poet, died. His works, all written before he was 20 years old, included **"Une Saison en Enfer"** [*A Season in Hell*] (written and published 1873), nine prose poems; and *Les Illuminations* [*Illuminations*] (written c.1872), 40 prose poems which were published by the symbolist poet **Paul Verlaine** in 1886. An earlier poem "Le bateau ivre" [*The Drunken Boat*] (1871) became widely known.

1892 Mar. 26   Walt Whitman (b. May 31, 1819), one of the most famous American poets, died. *Leaves of Grass* (1855), often revised and republished—its final edition appeared in 1892—was a glorification of the American spirit: exuberant love of people, democracy, individualism, fertility, and sex. Among Whitman's best known poems were "Song of Myself," the first, and longest, poem in *Leaves of Grass*, and two works memorializing Abraham Lincoln, "O Captain! My Captain!" (1865) and "When Lilacs Last in the Dooryard Bloom'd" (1866), both collected in the 1867 edition of *Leaves of Grass*.

1892 Sept. 7   John Greenleaf Whittier (b. Dec. 17, 1807), an American poet, died. He was known as **"the Quaker poet,"** not only because he was a

Quaker but for his strong abolitionist views. A well-known poem "Ichabod" (1850) was a denunciation of Daniel Webster, who had spoken in support of the **Compromise of 1850** and the **Fugitive Slave Law** (1850). His best-known poems were "The Barefoot Boy" (1855) and "Barbara Frietchie" (1864).

1892 Oct. 2 Joseph Ernest Renan (b. Feb. 27, 1823), a French religious historian, died. Christianity formed the main subject of his work. His best-known book was *La Vie de Jésus* [*Life of Jesus*] (1863), appearing first in the series *Histoire des Origines du Christianisme* [*Origins of Christianity*]. It depicted Jesus as a great man but knowable not as an unreachable religious figure but as an historical person. The series ended with *L'Église Chrétienne* [*The Christian Church*] (1879).

1892 Oct. 6 Alfred Tennyson (b. Aug. 6, 1809), an English poet, died. After *Poems* (1842), he was named (Nov., 1850) poet laureate. His other poetical works included *In Memoriam* (1850), *Charge of the Light Brigade* (1854), the drama *Maud* (1855), and *Idylls of the King* (1859).

1892 Dec. 9 The first play by **George Bernard Shaw** to be performed in London, *Widowers' House*, was staged by **Jack Grein** [Jacob Thomas Grein] (Oct. 11, 1862–June 23, 1935) at his Independent Theatre.

1893 *Heimat*, the most successful play by the German writer [Magda] **Hermann Sudermann** (Sept. 30, 1857–Nov. 22, 1928), was performed. The role was tailor-made for Sarah Bernhardt. Sudermann also wrote the novel *Frau Sorge* [*Dame Care*] (1887) and the play *Die Ehre* [*Honor*] (1889).

1893 Feb. 2 The **first moving close-up sequence**, *Fred Ott's Sneeze*, was filmed in West Orange, New Jersey, at the "**Black Maria**," the Edison movie studio.

1893 Mar. 5 Hippolyte Adolphe Taine (b. Apr. 21, 1828), a French critic and historian, died. He applied the rigorous determinism of the 18th-century English philosophers John Locke and David Hume to his view of history, which he called naturalistic objectivity. His works included *Histoire de la Littérature Anglaise* [*History of English Literature*] (1863) and the three-part *Origines de la France Contemporaine* [*Origins of Contemporary France*] (1875–1891)

1893 Apr. 19 John Addington Symonds (b. Oct. 5, 1840), an English historian, literary critic, and poet, died. He wrote biographies and translated the *Autobiography of Benvenuto Cellini* (1887), but his most important work was the seven-volume *History of the Renaissance in Italy* (1875–1886).

1893 May *The Second Mrs. Tanqueray* by **Arthur Wing Pinero**, an English playwright, was first performed in London. Its theme, involving a woman with a past, marked a new realistic trend in English drama, initiating the so-called modern theater.

1893 July 6 Guy de Maupassant [Henri René Albert Guy de Maupassant] (b. Aug. 5, 1850), a French writer, died. His first published story was "Boule de Suif" ["Tallow Ball"] (1880), one of his best. Writing in the naturalistic style, his subjects included peasant life in Normandy; scenes of the Franco-Prussian War (1870–1871); shopkeepers, clerks, and working girls; and episodes of love and madness.

1893 Oct. 6 Ford Madox Brown (b. Apr. 16, 1821), an English painter influenced by the Pre-Raphaelite Brotherhood, died. His best-known paintings were *The Last of England* (1855) and *Work* (1852–1865).

1893 Oct. 18 Charles François Gounod (b. June 18, 1818), a French musician, died. Best-known of his works were his operas *Faust* (1859), *Mireille* (1864), and *Roméo and Juliette* (1867).

1893 Oct. 30 The **World's Columbian Exposition** was held on the Midway in **Chicago** to mark the 400th anniversary of the historic voyage by Christopher Columbus. Many of the fair buildings were destroyed by a fire on Jan. 8, 1894.

1893 Nov. 6 Peter Ilyich [Pëtr Ilich] **Tchaikovsky** [Tschaikovsky, Chaikovsky] (b. May 7, 1840), a Russian composer, died. His musical style borrowed from western European idioms, but his work was considered characteristic of the Russian temperament. Tchaikovsky wrote the music for the ballets *Swan Lake* (1876), *The Sleeping Beauty* (1889), and *The Nutcracker* (1892). His operas included *Eugene Onegin* (1877), based on a story by Pushkin. Tchaikovsky also wrote the Piano Concerto in B Flat Minor (1875), the Violin Concerto in D (1878), the *Manfred Symphony* (1885), and the *Pathétique* [Sixth] *Symphony* (1893).

1894 *Salomé*, the play by the Irish writer **Oscar Wilde**, was published with illustrations by **Aubrey Beardsley** that shocked readers.

1894 Mar. 8 Bankim Chandra Chatterji (b. June 27, 1838), an Indian writer from Bengal, died. His *Durges Nandini* [*The Chieftain's Daughter*] (1865) was an international success. Chatterji also wrote *Bisha Brikka* [*The Poison Tree*] (1884) and other historical romances treating the popular theme of Hindu struggle against Muslim invasion.

1894 July 30 Walter Horatio Pater (b. Aug. 4, 1839), an English critic, died. In his conclusion to *Studies in the History of the Renaissance* (1873), Pater wrote, "To burn always with this hard, gem-like flame, to maintain this ecstasy, is success in life." His work directed the growing aesthetic sentiment in England, which had followed the efforts of the Pre-Raphaelites and was aimed at reintroducing Renaissance humanism to the arts. Pater's other works included *Marius the Epicurean* (1885), *Imaginary Portraits* (1887), *Appreciations* (1890), and *Plato and Platonism* (1893).

1894 Aug. 3 George Innes (b. May 1, 1825), an American painter of the Hudson River School, died. Romantic in style, he searched for the mystical in nature. Typical of his work were *Peace and Plenty* (1865) and *Autumn Oaks* (1875).

1894 Nov. 20 Anton [Grigorievich] Rubinstein (b. Nov. 28, 1829), a Russian composer and **founder of the St. Petersburg Conservatory**, died. His works included the opera *The Maccabees* (1875); the oratorio *The Tower of Babel* (1872); and symphonies, among them *The Ocean* [Second] *Symphony* (c.1855).

1894 Dec. 4 Robert Louis Balfour Stevenson [R.L.S.] (b. Nov. 13, 1850), a Scottish writer, died in Samoa, in the southwestern Pacific Ocean. A volume of poetry *A Child's Garden of Verses* (1885) was among Stevenson's best known work. His novels included *Treasure Island* (1883), *The Strange Case of Dr. Jekyll and Mr. Hyde* (1886), *Kidnapped* (1886), and the uncompleted *Weir of Hermiston* (1896). *Travels with a Donkey in the Cevennes* (1879), among the famous travel books in English, was a description of a trip through one of the wildest parts of France.

1894 Dec. 29 Christina [Georgina] Rossetti (b. Dec. 5, 1830), the sister of Dante Gabriel Rossetti, founder of the Pre-Raphaelite Brotherhood, died. Christina's best-known work was *Goblin Market and Other Poems* (1862).

IX. SPORTS, GAMES AND SOCIETY

c.1890–1900 Though **women's clothes** resisted change, feminists were popularizing emancipated clothing because long, tightly waisted skirts were difficult to move about in. For sports, especially bicycling and tennis, **bloomers** were beginning to become popular. The invention of the sewing machine and the growth of department stores led to increased sales of ready-made clothes.

1890 Nov. 29 In the U.S. the **first annual Army-Navy football game** was played at West Point, New York. Navy won, 24 to 0.

1891 Dec. The game of **basketball** was developed by **James A. Naismith** (Nov. 6, 1861–Nov. 28, 1939), the Canadian-born instructor at the International YMCA Training School in Springfield, Massachusetts, in response to demands of YMCA instructors for a healthful indoor game that could be played in a restricted area. One year later Naismith published the game's first rules book and the first public game was played on Mar. 11, 1892.

1892 Sept. 7 In the **first U.S. heavyweight boxing championship** fought under the Marquis of Queensberry rules, in New Orleans, [James J.] "Gentleman Jim" Corbett (Sept. 1, 1866–Feb. 18, 1933), 26 years old, knocked out the 34-year-old **John L. Sullivan** in the 21st round.

1893 The **first U.S. national fly-casting tournament** was staged by the **Chicago Fly-Casting Club** as an adjunct to the Chicago World's Fair. More than 20 years earlier, the **American Rod and Reel Association**, composed of members who pledged to fish by fly-casting only, had been formed.

1893 Frederick Arthur Stanley (Jan. 15, 1841–June 14, 1908) [Lord Stanley], governor general (1888–1893) of the Dominion of Canada, donated a trophy for the ice hockey championship of Canada. The **Stanley Cup** is now the **oldest trophy for professional athletes in North America**. The first winner was the Montreal A.A.A. team. In 1926 the cup's significance became associated entirely with the championship of the National Hockey League.

1894 **Emanuel Lasker** (Dec. 24, 1868–Jan. 11, 1941), a German **chess** player, won the world championship by defeating **Wilhelm Steinitz** (May 14, 1836–Aug. 12, 1900), the first person to hold the title. He defeated Steinitz again (1896), holding the title until 1921 when he lost it to **José Raúl Capablanca**.

1894 **June 22** The **first recorded automobile race** was run 78 miles between Paris and Rouen, France.

The announced purpose of the race was to settle conflicting claims as to which French automobile manufacturer was producing the fastest and most durable car. Apparently 21 cars started and 11 finished, the winner's speed averaging c.15 miles per hour.

1894 **Sept. 3** **Labor Day was first celebrated** as a holiday in the U.S.

1895–1899

I. DISASTERS

1895–1904 The worst recorded **drought in Australia** devastated large areas of the continent, causing many inland farmers to move to the coastal cities. The wool industry was decimated as the number of sheep raised was less than half of those in 1891.

1896 **June 15** An **earthquake and accompanying tsunami**, caused by earthquake disturbances of the sea bottom, at Sanriku on Honshu Island, Japan, killed 27,100 people and left more than 60,000 homeless.

1899 **Aug. 8** **San Ciriaco**, one of Puerto Rico's most destructive hurricanes, killed more than 3,000 islanders and caused property damage of about $20 million.

II. EXPLORATION AND COLONIZATION

1895 **Jan. 25** The **first landing on the Antarctic mainland** was made. **Carstens Egeberg Borchgrevink** (Dec. 1, 1864–Apr. 21, 1934), a Norwegian-Australian explorer, and **Leonard Kristensen**, Norwegian captain of the *Antarctic*, were in a group that went ashore at Cape Adare, on the tip of Victoria Land. According to the ship's log Cape Adare was sighted at midnight on Jan. 24 and a landing was made at 1 A.M. (Jan. 25) in light from the southern "Midnight Sun." They remained for two hours, collecting rock and wildlife samples and capturing several penguins.

1895 **Apr. 8** **Fridtjof Nansen**, a Norwegian Arctic explorer, reached the northernmost point yet achieved by man, 86° 13.6′ latitude. After his ship, the *Fram* [= forward], constructed to withstand ice

during the Arctic winter, was prevented from traveling any further north, Nansen and one companion set out on dogsleds.

1896 **Aug. 12** **Gold** discovered along the Klondike River in Canada's Yukon Territory initiated the **Klondike Stampede** (1897–1898). Rich glacier deposits were found (Aug. 17) in Bonanza [Rabbit] Creek, a tributary of the Klondike River. The news did not reach the U.S. until July 1897. Over the next seven years nearly 300,000 people rushed to find gold.

1897? **Salomon August Andreé** (b. 1854), a Swedish engineer, disappeared with two companions in the **first attempted aerial exploration of the Arctic**, a balloon flight. They lifted off from Danskøya, an island near Spitsbergen island, but traveled only a short distance to Kvitøya, another island of the archipelago, before crashing. The expedition's remains were found in Aug., 1930.

1898 **June 27** **Joshua Slocum** (Feb. 20, 1844–c.1910) of Martha's Vineyard, Massachusetts, age 51, on his return to Newport, Rhode Island, became the **first to complete a solo circumnavigation of the world**, which he accomplished in the 37-foot, 9-ton sloop *Spray*.

III. POLITICS AND WAR

1895 **Sun Yat-Sen**, the Chinese revolutionary and future statesman, who had been forbidden to practice medicine in his hometown of Macao [Macau], a Portuguese possession near Hong Kong, because he lacked a Portuguese degree, became involved in revolutionary activities in Canton [Kuang-chou; Guangzhou], in Kuangtung [Guangdong] province in southeastern China. The revolution failed, but Sun escaped abroad to begin a long exile (to 1911).

1895 Feb. 24 José Julián Martí, a Cuban writer, patriot, and revolutionary, joined **Máximo Gómex y Báez** (Nov. 18, 1826–June 17, 1905) in the **second Cuban rebellion against Spain**. This rebellion drew the U.S. to the support of Cuba and resulted in the **Spanish-American War** (1898). Martí was slain (1895) during a skirmish with Spanish troops at Dos Rios.

1895 Apr. 17 The **Treaty of Shimonoseki**, Honshú Island, Japan, concluded the **First Sino-Japanese War** (1894–1895), fought between China and Japan over **Korea**, which, though semi-independent, had been more or less a tributary of China for centuries. China recognized the independence of Korea, ceded the island of **Taiwan** [Portuguese.: Formosa] to Japan (to Oct. 25, 1945), and paid a large indemnity.

1895 June 15 France organized its West African colonies into **French West Africa** [Afrique Occidentale Française], a federation of the French protectorates of French Guinea [present Guinea], French Sudan [present Mali], the Ivory Coast, and Senegal, where the governor general made his headquarters at Dakar.

1895 Sept. 30 A French protectorate was established over the island of **Madagascar**, following the French occupation of the capital of the Merina Kingdom at Tananarive.

1896 Great Britain established a protectorate over **Sierra Leone**, naming it a crown colony within its present boundaries, following an Anglo-French territorial agreement (1895) to settle disputed territory in West Africa.

1896 Jan. 4 Utah was the 45th state admitted to the U.S.

1896 Jan. 20 Kumasi, the inland capital of the **Ashanti Kingdom** (c.1700–1901), in present **Ghana**, was conquered by an expeditionary force sent by **William Maxwell** (1846–Dec. 10, 1897), the British governor (1895–1897) of the Gold Coast. On Aug. 16 the region was made a British protectorate to prevent French or German claims to the area.

1896 Mar. 1 A **battle at Adwa** [Adowa, Aduwa, Italian: Adua] ended an **Italian invasion of Ethiopia** [Abyssinia] begun on Mar. 25, 1895. Ethiopian independence was recognized by the **Treaty of Addis**

Ababa on Oct. 26, 1896, and Ethiopia became a symbol of freedom for colonized Africans.

1896 May 18 The U.S. Supreme Court handed down a decision in the case of **Plessy v. Ferguson** that separate public facilities for different races were constitutional under the Fourteenth Amendment if they were **"separate but equal."** Thus, local **Jim Crow laws**, enacted by various southern states to circumvent the Civil Rights Act of 1875, were encouraged.

1896 May 20 **French Somaliland** [Côte française de Somalis; Afars and Issas], present Djibouti in northeastern Africa at the Gulf of Aden, was formally established as a French protectorate.

1896 July 8 **William Jennings Bryan** delivered his **Cross of Gold Speech** to the Democratic national convention held in Chicago, winning the nomination as Democratic presidential candidate. Twenty thousand listened to Bryan urge that the U.S. adopt free coinage of silver rather than be crucified on a "cross of gold."

1896 July 11 **Wilfrid Laurier** (Nov. 20, 1841–Feb. 17, 1919), Canada's Liberal party leader, became prime minister (to 1911). He was the **first French-Canadian prime minister**. During his term he promoted favorable relations with the U.S. and Great Britain, promoted immigration, and stressed the internal development of Canada, especially in the western provinces. He supported the union of all Canadian peoples and paved the way for Canada's later independence within the British Commonwealth of Nations.

1896 Sept. 1 Ouagadougou [Wagadugu], capital of the **Mossi Kingdom** (from the 14th century), present **Upper Volta**, was conquered by a French military force led by Paul Voulet (1866–1899). Kouka-Koutou, king of the Mossi [Moshi], was placed on the throne, and a French protectorate was established over the territory on Jan. 27, 1897.

1896 Dec. 30 José Rizal [y Mercado] (b. June 19, 1861), the national hero of the Filipinos, was executed by Spain for fomenting revolt. Though Rizal did not take part in the insurrection begun by the **Young Philippines** on Aug. 26, he was tried and convicted of being implicated. The uprising came to an end with promises of concessions by Spain in return for the departure of their revolutionary leader,

Emilio Aguinaldo (Mar. 23, 1869–Feb. 6, 1964), on Dec. 27, 1897.

1897 Feb. 4 After having failed in an insurrection during the previous year **Crete**, with Greek support, resumed its revolt against the **Ottoman Empire** (1326–1920). On Feb. 6 Crete was united, by Greek proclamation, to Greece, and on Mar. 10 Greek forces landed on the northern coast near Canea, the capital of Crete. But the European powers, fearing instability in the region, had landed their own troops on Feb. 15, thus probably saving the Greeks from almost certain defeat by the Turks. On Mar. 20 Crete was proclaimed autonomous by the powers which, excluding Austria and Germany, organized an international commission to rule the island.

1897 Mar. 4 **William McKinley** of the Republican party was inaugurated as the 25th president of the U.S., having defeated **William Jennings Bryan** of the Democratic party. **Garrett Augustus Hobart** (b. June 3, 1844) served as vice president until his death on Nov. 21, 1899.

1898 Feb. 15 The *Maine*, an American battleship in Cuba to protect American citizens there, was blown up in the harbor of Havana, Cuba. The incident inflamed American public opinion against Spain's presence in Cuba and provided an opportunity for the U.S. to enter openly the Cuban conflict with the cry "Remember the Maine!"

1898 Mar. 15 The **Russian Social Democratic Labor party** [RS-DRP] was formed in Minsk, central western Russia, by nine delegates of various Marxist organizations. The **Bolshevik party** that came to power in 1917 grew out of the RS-DRP, which had members both in Russia and abroad.

1898 Mar. 28 A **U.S. naval court** of enquiry reported that the battleship *Maine* had been blown up by an external bomb or mine. This was confirmed by examination of the wreck in 1911. William McKinley, president of the U.S., demanded from Spain an immediate armistice, release of prisoners, and American mediation between Spain and Cuba.

1898 Apr. 11 McKinley proposed to the U.S. Congress that he be authorized to use military force to cause Spain to evacuate Cuba. Congress recognized (Apr. 19) **Cuba's independence** and empowered the president to use the army and navy to secure it. On Apr. 20 McKinley issued an ultimatum to Spain and on Apr. 22 began a blockade of all Cuban ports. Also on the 22nd a **Volunteer Army Act** was passed and signed, and the following day McKinley called for 125,000 volunteers to fight in the **Spanish-American War** (1898).

1898 May 1 **George Dewey** (Dec. 26, 1837–Jan. 16, 1917), commander of the U.S. Pacific fleet, sailed into Manila Bay, the Philippines, where the **Spanish Pacific fleet** was at anchor and **destroyed** it. The Spaniards lost 381 killed and the Americans sustained only 8 wounded. On Aug. 13 **American troops occupied Manila**.

1898 June 11 **Kuang Hsü**, emperor of China, introduced the **Hundred Days of Reform**, during which he attempted to modernize China along western lines. On Sept. 21 a conservative faction led by his aunt **Tzu Hsi**, the **empress dowager**, overthrew the emperor and imprisoned him. The empress dowager ruled, with Kuang Hsü being only a figurehead, until 1908.

1898 June 11 About 600 **U.S. marines landed at Guantánamo Bay**, Cuba, and on June 15 repulsed a Spanish force.

1898 June 13 The **Yukon Territory**, the most northwestern region of Canada, separated from the Northwest Territories as a provisional district in 1895, was officially organized following the discovery of large gold deposits on Bonanza Creek and the subsequent influx of miners and other opportunists to the remote region. A detachment of the **Royal North West Mounted Police** was stationed in the Yukon to help keep order.

1898 June 20 The island of **Guam** in the western Pacific Ocean surrendered to the *Charleston*, a U.S. warship. The Spanish commander, not aware of the war, apologized for not returning the U.S. "salute" because he had no ammunition.

1898 June 24 In a **battle at Las Guásimas**, in eastern Cuba, U.S. troops under **Joseph Wheeler**, a former officer of the Confederate army, defeated the Spanish.

1898 July 1–3 The **battle at Santiago**, on the southern coast of Cuba, began with successful assaults on **San Juan Hill**, in which **Theodore Roosevelt** led his **Rough Riders**, and on nearby El Caney, both fortified positions on the outskirts of Santiago. The U.S.

victory led to the total **destruction of the Spanish fleet** as it fled from Santiago harbor on July 3.

1898 July 10 The **Fashoda Incident** began when **Jean Baptiste Marchand** (Nov. 22, 1863–Jan. 13, 1934), leading a French military and exploring expedition from the Atlantic coast, reached Fashoda, near present Kodok on the White Nile in the Sudan, c.400 miles south of Khartoum, in an effort to link France's territories of West Africa with Djibouti, a small French enclave on the Gulf of Aden in East Africa and capital of **French Somaliland** [Côte française de Somalis; Afars and Issas], present Djibouti. On Sept. 19 Anglo-Egyptian forces under **Horatio Herbert Kitchener** (June 24, 1850–June 5, 1916) arrived, precipitating a warlike crisis between England and France. The French, facing superior forces, evacuated the area and signed a convention with the British on Mar. 21, 1899, by which France renounced claim to the Nile basin and recognized British control over the area in return for recognition of French occupation of the Sahara and the western Sudan. But this agreement did not settle British control of the **Sudan** and Egypt. On Sept 2, 1899, at Omdurman, Kitchener annihilated the army of Khalifa ['Abdullah ibn Mohammed, Abdullah et Taaisha] (born c. 1846), the Arab leader of the **Mahdists**, who was killed in the battle. The British now reoccupied the Sudan capital of **Khartoum**, across the White Nile from the battle site.

1898 July 17 The **Spanish surrendered Santiago** and c.24,000 Spanish troops to the American army under Shafter.

1898 Aug. 7 **Theodore Roosevelt** and his **Rough Riders** left Santiago, Cuba, for Montauk Point, Long Island, New York, to escape sickness. On Aug. 1, there were c.4,200 sick American soldiers in Cuba, more than 3,000 of yellow fever.

1898 Aug. 9 Spain formally accepted peace terms, ending the **Spanish-American War** (1898). The treaty was signed (Dec. 10) in Paris. The U.S. acquired Guam and Puerto Rico; Cuba became a free republic. The U.S. paid $20 million for the Philippines.

1899–1902 The **One-thousand Days of Civil War** ravaged **Colombia**, where almost 100,000 died in fighting between political factions and between conservatives battling Panamanian separatists. The war began (Oct., 1899) as a liberal revolt against the government; in the end (Nov., 1902), the conservatives had retained power. France had begun to construct (1880, 1894) a canal in Panama, still a part of Colombia, and during the fighting British, French, and American forces were dispatched to Panama several times to keep the railroad open and to protect the canal builders. In 1903 the U.S. helped Panama to win independence from Colombia, and was quick to grant recognition.

1899 The **Hague Tribunal**, also known as the **Permanent Court of Arbitration**, was established to arbitrate international disputes. One of its most important cases was the arbitration of the **Venezuela Claims in 1904**.

1899 The **Open Door Policy** was issued by the U.S. in the form of circular notes addressed to the major European powers, Japan, and Russia. It was a unilateral statement of principle designed to protect the privilege of foreign nations to maintain trade without disrupting the integrity of China's own culture and rule.

1899 Oct. 12 The **South African Republic** and the **Orange Free State**, both Boer [Dutch] territories, declared war against the British in the **Cape of Good Hope Colony** [Cape Colony], initiating the **Boer War** [South African War] (to 1902).

1899 Dec. 2 The **Samoan Islands** in the southwestern Pacific Ocean were divided between Germany and the U.S. in an agreement also made with Great Britain. The islands east of 171° longitude, including Pago Pago, went to the U.S. and the islands west of this line went to Germany.

IV. ECONOMY AND TRADE

c.1895–1917 **Syndicalism** became prominent in France. Essentially syndicalism involved the ownership and management of the means of production and distribution by the workers in an industry. Syndicalism was widespread in France and developed to a lesser degree in Italy, Spain, and Latin America. It also influenced the labor movement in Great Britain.

1895 Feb. 8 **Grover Cleveland**, president of the U.S., arranged with a syndicate organized by **John Pierpont Morgan** and **August Belmont** (Feb. 18, 1853–Dec. 10, 1924) for the U.S. treasury to purchase $62,317,500 worth of gold to replenish dwindled gold reserves. The purchase failed to halt the drain on the gold reserves, but enabled the **U.S. to continue on a partial gold standard** through the monetary crisis brought on by the **Panic of 1893**.

1896 The **Tabulating Machine Company**, the **predecessor of International Business Machines [IBM]**, was formed in the U.S. by **Herman Hollerith** (Feb. 29, 1860–Nov. 17, 1929), who had developed (1884) an efficient method for sorting and analyzing data with punch cards. His system had been used effectively in the U.S. census of 1890.

1896 The success of mail order companies in the U.S. was established with the **free rural delivery** now offered by the Postal Service. Notably **Montgomery Ward**, founded in 1872, and **Sears, Roebuck Company**, founded in 1895, benefited from this development.

1896 Nov. 16 The city of **Buffalo** used power generated by the **Niagara Falls Power Company** (1886) from the Niagara Falls to run its street railway. Niagara Falls, site of one of the great hydroelectric projects of the 19th century, soon supplied all of Buffalo's demand for electricity.

1897 The **first subway in the U.S.** was completed in Boston. Begun in 1895, it was 1.5 miles long and used trolley streetcars.

1897 Mar. 1 Japan adopted the **gold standard** which, combined with recent economic progress, enabled Japan to borrow in the international financial markets.

1897 Aug. 6 A **Workmen's Compensation Act**, passed in Great Britain, ruled that employers were liable for injuries received by their employees in the course of their work.

1898 The U.S. Supreme Court handed down a decision in the case of **Holden vs. Hardy**, upholding the right of Utah to set maximum working hours for miners.

1899 **Sugar**, its production promoted by U.S. government, became the chief source of revenue for **Puerto Rico**. While the nearly complete dependence on sugar provided a tremendous boost to the island's economy for the next 40 years, it also proved disastrous when sugar prices fell.

1899 In *The Theory of the Leisure Class*, Thorstein Bunde Veblen, an American social scientist, argued that the consumer in a capitalistic society spent without judicious economic sense, but rather in an attempt to establish "invidious distinctions based on wealth and the power wantonly to consume." This produced, he declared, the phenomenon of "conspicuous consumption."

1899 Mar. The **United Fruit Company** was created when the **Boston Fruit Company** joined Minor Cooper Smith's steamship and plantation interests in Central America. It had its own fleet of ships, railroad lines, and communications systems, and sold fruit raised in the tropics to the U.S. and England.

V. RELIGION AND PHILOSOPHY

1895 June 29 **Thomas Henry Huxley** (b. May 4, 1825), an English biologist and writer, died. In 1869 Huxley introduced the term "agnosticism," which generally meant "one who repudiated traditional Judaeo-Christian theism and yet disclaimed doctrinaire atheism." Huxley used the term within the context of the theological debate engendered by the development of the theory of evolution. In *Lay Sermons, Addresses, and Reviews* (1870) Huxley discussed agnosticism. His other works included *Man's Place in Nature* (1863), *Evolution and Ethics* (1893), and the four-volume *Scientific Memoirs* (1898–1902).

1897 Aug. 29 The **Zionist movement** was founded by **Theodor Herzl**, a Hungarian Jewish journalist, when he opened the **First Zionist Congress** in Basel, Switzerland, with 200 delegates present from all nations having a significant Jewish population. Zionist organizations soon began to appear everywhere Jews lived.

1898 The **Union of Orthodox Jewish Congregations** was established for the achievement of greater unity among the Orthodox Jewish community in the growing competition with Reform Judaism in the U.S., represented by the **Union of American Hebrew Congregations** (1873). In 1902 a Union of Orthodox Rabbis of the U.S. and Canada was established. Both groups espoused preservation of the Sabbath, exemption for Jews from Sunday closing laws, kosher food regulation, and higher quality Orthodox Jewish education.

VI. SCIENCE, EDUCATION, AND TECHNOLOGY

1895 The **removable pneumatic tire** was first used for automobiles. This invention, by **André Michelin** (Jan. 16, 1853–Apr. 4, 1931) and his brother **Édouard** (June 23, 1859–Aug. 25, 1940) in 1891 for the bicycle, made possible the high-speed automobile.

1895 Sept. 28 Louis Pasteur (b. Dec. 27, 1822), a French chemist who demonstrated the **germ theory of disease**, died. In 1863 he developed the process of pasteurization. His other major contributions included the first vaccinations against chicken cholera (1879), anthrax in sheep (1881), and **rabies** [hydrophobia] (1885). On Nov. 14, 1888, he established the famous **Institut Pasteur** primarily for the purpose of treating persons who had been bitten by a rabid animal.

1895 Nov. 5 X-rays were discovered by **Wilhelm Conrad Roentgen** [Röntgen] (Mar. 27, 1845–Feb. 10, 1923), a German physicist. Roentgen announced his discovery on Dec. 28 and gave the first public demonstration of them on Jan. 23, 1896. X-rays, waves of electromagnetic radiation, have shorter wavelengths than light and are invisible.

1896 Mar. 1 Henri Becquerel (Dec. 15, 1852–Aug. 23, 1908), a French physicist, while studying phosphorescence, discovered naturally occurring **radioactivity** while working with uranium salts. He found that uranium at room temperature gave off radiation, which resembled X-rays because it was invisible. **Marie** and **Pierre Curie**, now working on radioactivity, announced (1898) they had discovered polonium and radium in the mineral pitchblende, still the chief natural source for uranium and radium today. Becquerel was awarded the **Nobel prize for physics** with the Curies in 1903.

1896 June Guglielmo [Marchese] **Marconi**, an Italian physicist, filed for a patent in England for his **wireless telegraph**. Marconi's cousin, Jameson Davis, financed the **Wireless Telegraph and Signal Company**, incorporated in London in July, 1897, which became (1900) Marconi's Wireless Telegraph Company. On Dec. 12, 1901, the first transatlantic wireless communication—the Morse code letter "S"—was received by Marconi in Cabot Tower at Signal Hill, St. John's, Newfoundland, from Poldhu in Cornwall, southwestern England.

1896 Dec. 10 Alfred Bernhard Nobel (b. Oct. 21, 1833), the Swedish inventor for whom the Nobel prizes were named, died. In 1867 Nobel received a patent for **dynamite**, an explosive which he planned to use in the construction of roads and canals. Nobel endowed his fortune for awards recognizing remarkable achievement in the five categories of physics, chemistry, medicine or physiology, literature, and the promotion of peace.

1897 Apr. 30 Joseph John Thomson (Dec. 18, 1856–Sept. 2, 1940), an English physicist, announced the existence of the **negative charge of the electron** at the Royal Institution in London, where he later became lecturer. He had discovered the electron by sending electricity through gases and afterwards measuring the charge. In 1906 he received the **Nobel prize for physics**.

1897 Oct. 19 George Mortimer Pullman (b. Mar. 3, 1831), an American inventor and industrialist, died. As a cabinet maker Pullman became interested in making railroad cars more comfortable and luxurious for long distance travel. He patented (1864, 1865) the folding upper berth and seats convertible into a lower berth. He organized (1867) the **Pullman Palace Car Company** and then designed the **first railroad dining car** (1868) and the chair car (1875).

VIII. ARTS AND LEISURE

1895 Mar. 10 Charles Frederick Worth (b. Oct. 13, 1825), an English fashion designer who was the founder of Parisian haute couture, died. He moved (1858) to Paris where his designs brought him the patronage of Eugénie (May 5, 1826–July 11, 1920), empress and sometime regent of France, and thus made him the dictator of **women's high fashion** for a generation.

1895 Mar. 22 The **Lumière** brothers **Auguste** and **Louis Jean**, expanding on Thomas Alva Edison's kinetoscope (1891), projected the film *La Sortie des Ouvriers de l'Usine Lumière* [*Workers Leaving the Lumière Factory*] before the Société d'Encouragement à l'Industrie Nationale in Paris.

1895 May 19 José Julián Martí (b. Jan. 28, 1853), a Cuban poet, essayist, and revolutionary leader, was killed in **battle on the plains of Dos Ríos**, in eastern Cuba, during the revolt in Cuba that led to the **Spanish-American War** (1898). Martí had joined (Mar., 1895) Máximo Gómez y Báez, who began the revolution which the Cubans continued until, with the aid of American armed intervention, they gained their freedom.

1895 Nov. 27 Alexandre Dumas [Dumas fils] (b. July 27, 1824), a French playwright, died. His best-known work was the play *La Dame aux Camélias* [*Camille*] (1852), which he first wrote as a novel in 1848 and which was the model for the opera *La Traviata* (1853) by Giuseppe Verdi.

1896 *Quo Vadis?*, a popular historical novel by **Henryk Sienkiewicz**, the Polish writer, appeared. This tale of Christian life under Nero was followed by *Knights of the Cross* (1900), which told about the downfall instigated by Polish and Lithuanian rulers of the Order of the Teutonic Knights. In 1905 Sienkiewicz received the **Nobel prize for literature**.

1896 Jan. 8 Paul [Marie] **Verlaine** (b. Mar. 30, 1844), a French poet, died. He was early identified with the Parnassians, and associated with the symbolists, but was also considered a leader of the decadents, a group of late 19th-century writers whose works centered on bizarre subjects and employed great subtlety of style. Verlaine's works included *Poèmes saturniens* (1866), *Romances sans Paroles* (1874), the prose work *Les Poètes Maudits* (1884), *Jadis et Naguère* (1885), and *Confessions* (1895).

1896 May 20 Clara Josephine Schumann [nee Wieck] (b. Sept. 13, 1819), wife of the German composer Robert Schumann and a celebrated pianist in her own right, died. She composed piano music and edited the music of **Karl Czerny** and **Robert Schumann**.

1896 May 22 Edward Bellamy (b. Mar. 26, 1850), an American author, died. He was best known for his Utopian novel *Looking Backward, 2000–1887* (1888), which presented life in Boston in the year 2000 as seen from the perspective of 19th-century man. The future society was based on state socialism. The book sold c.200,000 copies in less than two years.

1896 Aug. 13 John Everett Millais (b. June 8, 1829), an English Pre-Raphaelite painter, died. His best works included *The Return of the Dove to the Ark* (1851), *The Order of Release* (1853), and *The Blind Girl. Chill October* (1870) was Millais's first landscape.

1896 Oct. 3 William Morris (b. Mar. 24, 1834), an English writer, medievalist, and leader of the **Arts and Crafts movement**, died. In 1861 he established a firm to create interior design in the modern style, and eventually to make furniture, stain glass, textiles, etc. Morris also founded (1891) Kelmscott Press, which printed illustrated volumes of English classics as well as his own works. Morris translated Norse and Anglo-Saxon literary works which he then used as material for his own writing.

1896 Oct. 6 George [Louis Palmella Busson] **du Maurier** (b. Mar. 6, 1834), an English novelist, died. His works included *Peter Ibbetson* (1891) and *Trilby* (1895), first published in *Harper's Monthly* (1894), which was the story of a tragic love affair between Svengali, a musician with sinister, hypnotic powers, and Trilby, a young model.

1896 Oct. 11 Anton [Josef] **Bruckner** (b. Sept. 4, 1824), an Austrian composer, died. In addition to chamber music, motets, cantatas, piano and organ pieces, Bruckner wrote masses in D Minor (1864), E Minor (1866), and F Minor (1867–1871).

1897 The **Grand Guignol type of theatrical performance** made its first appearance in Paris at the **Théâtre Salon**, later renamed the **Théâtre du Grand Guignol**. The productions in such a theater were meant to shock and consisted of short plays whose subjects were horrible and haunting, with large doses of murder, suicide, rape, and sadism. Grand Guignol took its name from that of a popular French puppet called Guignol. Like Punch, this puppet was rough and heartless.

1897 *Cyrano de Bergerac*, the romantic classic by the French playwright **Edmond Rostand**, was published. His other popular plays included *La Samaritaine* (1897) and *Chantecler* (1910).

1897 Apr. 3 Johannes Brahms (b. May 7, 1833), the great German composer, one of the leaders of the romantic period in music, died. Brahms produced work in all forms except opera. Among them were the First Piano Concerto in D Minor (1861); *Variations and Fugue on a Theme by Handel in B Flat Major* (1862); the choral work *Ein Deutsches Requiem* [*A German Requiem*] (1868); *Variations on a Theme by Haydn in B Flat Major* (1874); four symphonies; the Violin Concerto in D Major (1879); the *Academic* (1880) and *Tragic* (1880–1881) overtures.

1897 Aug. 16   The **Tate Gallery** in London, devoted to British art, opened. It was founded as the result of a gift of 65 paintings and the cost of the building from **Henry Tate** (Mar. 11, 1819–Dec. 5, 1899), a businessman who made a fortune in sugar refining.

1898 Sept. 9   **Stéphane Mallarmé** (b. Mar. 18, 1842), a leading figure of the French symbolists, died. His best-known work was *L'Après-Midi d'un Faune* [*The Afternoon of a Faun*] (1876), which inspired **Claude Debussy's** piece of music by the same name and was illustrated by **Édouard Manet**. Mallarmé's other works included *Toast funèbre* (1873), and *Prose pour des Esseintes* (1885). In 1887 he published his *Poésies Complètes*, which secured his reputation as one of the greatest of French poets.

1898 Oct. 14   The **Moscow Art Theater** opened as the Moscow Art and Popular Theater with a performance of **Aleksei Konstantinovich Tolstoi's** *Fëdor Ivanovich*.

1899 June 3   **Johann Strauss** [the Younger] (b. Oct. 25, 1825), known as "the Waltz King," died. His best-known works were *Blue Danube* (1866), *Tales from the Vienna Woods* (1868), the operas *Die Fledermaus* [*The Bat*] (1873) and *Zigeunerbaron* [*The Gypsy Baron*] (1885).

VIII. SPORTS, GAMES, AND SOCIETY

1895   In the **first public U.S. auto race**, held on a course from Chicago to Evanston, Illinois, and back, **J. Frank Duryea**, an American inventor of an automobile, drove an improved Duryea model to victory against a German Benz. The race was sponsored by the Chicago *Times-Herald*.

1895   The **National Badminton Association of England was formed**, superseding the **Bath Badminton Club** (1887), as the game's ultimate authority. Standardization of the rules followed shortly thereafter.

1895   The game of **volleyball** was originated by **William G. Morgan** (Jan. 24, 1870–Dec. 28, 1942), a YMCA physical education director at Holyoke, Massachusetts. Morgan published a rules book in 1897 that gave the game its permanent shape.

1895   American universities with a **rowing** program formed an association for holding an **annual regatta**. Columbia University won the first meet.

1895 Aug. 31   The recognized **birthdate of professional football in the U.S.** was a game played by two teams representing industrial towns in Pennsylvania, Latrobe and Jeannette. Latrobe won, 12 to 0. The Latrobe team had hired John Brallier for $10 as a substitute quarterback, making him the first professional football player.

1896   The **first known intercollegiate basketball game** in the U.S. was played by girls' teams representing the universities of California and Stanford. This preceded by nearly a year the game recognized as the first between men's colleges, played at New Haven, Connecticut, on Mar. 20, 1897, when Yale beat the University of Pennsylvania, 32 to 10.

1896 Apr. 6   The **Olympic Games** were held in Athens, Greece, based on the model of their ancient counterpart, which had been discontinued in 393 A.D. by Theodosius I the Great, who tried to eliminate all remnants of paganism. The prime mover in the revival was **Pierre de Frédy** (Jan. 1, 1862–Sept. 2, 1937), baron de Coubertin, a Frenchman.

1897 Mar. 17   [Robert Prometheus] **"Bob" Fitzsimmons** (June 4, 1862–Oct. 22, 1917) beat **"Gentleman Jim" Corbett** in 14 rounds in Carson City, Nevada, in the **first formal boxing match recorded on film**.

1898 Jan. 19   The **first game of intercollegiate ice hockey** was played at Franklin Park, Boston. Brown beat Harvard 6 to 0. Previously American collegians had preferred to play an ice game called ice polo, which was played with a ball instead of a puck.

1899   **Bicycle racing** evolved from the dangerously exhausting one-man, six-day races begun in 1891 to a six-day race in which two-man teams shared more than 142 (later 144) hours of continuous racing at the original Madison Square Garden in New York City.

1899 Sept. 17   The **American League of baseball teams** was organized by **Byron** [Ban] **Bancroft Johnson** (Jan. 8, 1864–Mar. 18, 1931) and **Charles A. Comiskey** (Aug. 15, 1859–Oct. 26, 1931), both of Chicago. The initial franchises were awarded to Philadelphia, Boston, Baltimore, and Washington in the East; to Cleveland, Detroit, Chicago, and Milwaukee in the west.

1900

I. VITAL STATISTICS AND DEMOGRAPHICS

1900 The **population** of the **world** was c.1,550,000,000: **Europe**, 380 million; **Asia**, 970 million; **Africa**, 110 million; **North America**, 110 million; **South America**, 40 million; **Australia**, 3.75 million. (China, c.450 million; India, 290 million; Japan, 45 million; U.S., 76 million; Mexico, 13.5 million; British Isles, 42 million; France, 41 million; German Empire, 43 million; European Russia, 100 million; Austria-Hungary Empire, 46 million; Ottoman Empire, 25 million; Egypt, 10 million; Canada, 5.5 million; Brazil, 18 million; the Caribbean, 6.5 million.) The largest cities in the world: London, 4,536,063; New York, 3,444,675; Paris, 2,511,629; Berlin, 1,864,203; Chicago, 1,750,000; Vienna, 1,656,662; Philadelphia, 1,293,697; St. Petersburg, 1,248,643; Moscow, 1,023,817; Bombay, 821,764.

1900 **Iceland** again achieved its 12th-century population of c.80,000. Most of the loss had been due to the **Black Death** that raged throughout the 14th century.

II. DISASTERS

1900 Apr. 26 The Canadian cities of Hull and Ottawa were largely destroyed by **fire**. In less than 12 hours damage estimated at $15 million was caused and 12,000 people made homeless. Five square miles of buildings were leveled.

1900 Apr. 30 **Casey Jones** (b. Mar. 14, 1864), folk hero of American railroad engineers, was killed in a dawn train wreck on the Illinois Central line near Vaughn, Mississippi. Jones, overlooking warning signals, slammed into a freight stopped in a fog as he raced his train to make up time lost on a previous run by another engineer.

1900 June 30 A **fire** that destroyed piers and three steamships at **Hoboken, New Jersey**, claimed 326 lives of passengers and crew members.

1900 Sept. 8 The Gulf of Mexico, driven by **hurricane** winds reaching 135 miles per hour, rose about 15 feet, inundating Galveston, Texas. Of the city's c.38,000 inhabitants, c.6,000 were killed; c.3,000 homes were destroyed.

III. POLITICS AND WAR

1900–1905 After the founding in 1899 of the weekly newspaper *United Irishman* by **Arthur Griffith**, the **Sinn Fein** [Féin] **party** was established (1905) in Ireland under Griffith's leadership. At first, Sinn Fein [= Ourselves Alone] advocated passive resistance and obstructionist tactics in the British Parliament to gain privileges for Ireland. By 1905, the party had become basically a political movement.

1900 Jan. 10 The **Boer War** (1899–1902) turned against the Dutch when British reinforcements under **Frederick Sleigh Roberts** (Sept. 30, 1832–Nov. 14, 1904), with **Horatio Kitchener** as chief-of-staff, arrived in South Africa. The British regained (Feb. 28) the important rail junction of Ladysmith, and the territories of the Orange Free State were quickly overrun and then annexed (May 24) as a British Crown Colony, the Orange River Colony. Johannesburg having fallen (May 31) and Pretoria (June 5), the Transvaal was annexed (Oct. 25) as the Transvaal Colony.

1900 Feb. 28 What became **Great Britain's Labour party** was founded at a meeting of the Trade Unions Council which set up the Labour Representation Committee. Urban workers had had the vote since the Reform Acts of 1867 and 1884 and had first elected representatives to Parliament in 1869, but these men were mostly absorbed into the Liberal party.

1900 Apr. 22 A French military expedition defeated Rabah Zubayr (born c.1846), the conqueror of Sudan, in a **battle at Kusseri** [Kousseri], in present **Chad**. The French were now in full control of the **Baguirmi Kingdom**. They had succeeded in their long-sought goal of joining their African possessions: Algeria in the north, West Africa [western Sudan], and the French Congo [with Chad, Equatorial Africa].

1900 June 13 In China, the **Boxer Rebellion** erupted into widespread attacks against Christians, other foreigners, and their influence. The Boxers began calling themselves I Ho Ch'uan [Righteous and Harmonious Fists], which was a confusion of their true name I Ho T'uan [Righteous and Harmonious Bands or Militia]: hence the English name "Boxer." About this time the Boxers entered Peking [Beijing]. On June 17 foreign troops captured the Chinese forts at Taku [Dagu] along the Hai River in order to secure commerce from the coast to nearby Tientsin [Tianjin] and Peking. On June 20 the Manchu government under the reactionary Tzu Hsi, the dowager empress, merged the Boxers into the Imperial army and on the following day declared war against the intervening powers, England, Germany, Japan, Russia, and the U.S., and ordered the execution of all foreigners. On Aug. 14, 1900, an eight-week **siege by the Boxers of the foreigners and Chinese Christians in Peking** was lifted by a force of American, British, French, German, Japanese, and Russian troops which had fought its way from Tientsin. On Sept. 7, 1901, an agreement was signed with the international force, bringing an end to the uprising. Among the terms: The Taku forts were destroyed; foreign troops were stationed on the Hai River to maintain open trade; earlier trade treaties were reworded to establish more firmly commercial rights; and China was forced to pay an indemnity of $330 million.

1900 June 14 The **territory of Hawaii** was established.

1900 Summer The **Socialist Revolutionary party** of Russia was organized as an underground political group in Kharkov, near the Donets River in the Ukraine. It called for the overthrow of the czarist government and the freeing of land for the peasants. The Socialist Revolutionaries believed in political terror and were responsible for the assassination of a number of government officials.

1900 July 9 By an act of the British Parliament the **Commonwealth of Australia**, was established (effective Jan. 1, 1901). The act united the separate colonies (which already enjoyed a large measure of self-government) of New South Wales, Queensland, South Australia, Tasmania, Victoria, and Western Australia under a federal government. The Northern Territory was added to the federation in 1911.

1900 July 29 **Humbert I** [Umberto] (b. Mar. 18, 1844), king of Italy (from 1878), was assassinated by an anarchist at Monza in northern Italy. He was succeeded by his son **Victor Emmanuel III**.

1900 Oct. 18 **Bernhard** [Heinrich Martin Karl] **von Bülow** (May 3, 1849–Oct.. 28, 1929), a Prussian poli-

tician and diplomat, became chancellor of Germany, succeeding **Chlodwig Karl Hohenlohe**, who had resigned two days earlier. Bülow's aggressive foreign policy alienated France, Great Britain, and Russia, and thereby strengthened the ties between them.

IV. ECONOMY AND TRADE

1900 The **Police Regulations** of 1900 in Japan banned virtually any effort to bargain collectively, as well as any attempt to strike.

1900 The **first credit union in North America** was established in Quebec, Canada, by **Alphonse Desjardins** (Nov., 1859–Oct. 31, 1920). In 1909 he founded the first credit union in the U.S., at Manchester, New Hampshire, and in the same year Massachusetts was the first state to pass a Credit Union Act.

1900 The **International Ladies' Garment Workers' Union** [ILGWU] was founded in New York City. The main grievances of its members were a 70-hour work week and a work-at-home system that limited a woman's earnings to 30¢ a day.

1900 Mar. 14 Passage of the **Currency Act** [Gold Standard Act] in the U.S. set the value of the dollar at 25.8 grains of gold. The act placed the **U.S. firmly on the gold standard** and was a distinct setback for the silver mining interests.

V. SCIENCE, EDUCATION, AND TECHNOLOGY

1900 The **Chemin de Fer Métropolitain**, better known as the **Métro**, opened in Paris, with 6.25 miles completed. Work had begun two years earlier; today it has 157 route miles.

1900 **Sigmund Freud**, an Austrian psychiatrist and the **founder of psychoanalysis**, published one of his early works expounding his technique of "free association," *The Interpretation of Dreams* (tr. 1913). Freud's emphasis on the sexual nature of many human problems aroused antagonism among other scientists so that such works as *The Psychopathology of Everyday Life* (1904) and *Three Contributions to the Sexual Theory* (1905), were not well received.

1900 The *Holland submarine* was accepted for service by the U.S. navy after three years of trials. **John Holland** (Feb. 24, 1841–Aug. 12, 1914), who had built other submarines, developed a design for a submarine lighter than water.

1900 Max [Karl Ernst Ludwig] **Planck**, a German physicist, developed the **quantum theory** from his studies of the spectrum of electromagnetic radiation emitted by black bodies (black coated bodies which absorb all or nearly all radiations). He found that atoms gave off energy in waves, but only in discrete units, called quanta, not, as had been thought, in a continuous emission. Planck received the **Nobel prize for physics** in 1918.

1900 Karl **Landsteiner** (June 14, 1868–June 26, 1943), an Austrian-born American pathologist and immunologist, discovered the **A, B, and C types of human blood** and a system of blood typing that was necessary to make blood transfusions practicable. He was awarded the **Nobel prize for physiology** or medicine in 1930.

1900 At the **Paris Exposition of 1900** the **escalator** was introduced to the public for the first time. In 1901 it was installed at **Gimbel's Department Store** in Philadelphia, where it continued in use to 1939. In the meantime, in New York City, a similar escalator was installed in **Bloomingdale's Department Store** in 1900. It had been invented by the American **Charles A. Wheeler**, who patented it in 1892; but it was not built until the **Otis Elevator Company**, Yonkers, New York, constructed an improved model.

1900 July 2 The **first dirigible** constructed by **Ferdinand von Zeppelin**, the German aeronaut, made its maiden voyage. Inside the aluminum hull were 16 cells filled with hydrogen to give buoyancy. Powered by two 16-horsepower motors the Zeppelin had a speed of 14 miles per hour. On June 22, 1910, Zeppelin instituted regular passenger service, carrying an average of more than 11,000 passengers per year between German cities.

VI. ARTS AND LEISURE

1900 Jan. 20 John **Ruskin** (b. Feb. 8, 1819), an English Victorian art critic and social reformer, died. Ruskin believed that improved conditions for workingmen depended on labor organizations and national education for workers. With *Modern Painters* (1843–1860) Ruskin established himself as a leading critic. His other works included the well known architectural studies *The Seven Lamps of Architecture* (1849) and *The Stones of Venice* (1851–1853).

1900 Mar. 10 The decorative art style known as **Art Nouveau**, prominent from the 1880s until World War I (1914–1918), gained considerable public attention with the opening of the Paris Métro, begun in 1898, for which **Hector Guimard** (1867–1942), French architect, designed and decorated a number of its entrance ways. Cast iron railings, dominated by curved lines, were ornamented with tendril forms. The peacock became a key motif in Art Nouveau decoration. London, England, was one of the earliest centers of Art Nouveau: A leader there was **Aubrey Beardsley**, art editor of *The Yellow Book* (1894–1895), a periodical that epitomized the new movement, a reaction against mid-19th-century art. In its art, erotic elements, daring for the period, made their appearance. In Germany the style was known as *Jugendstil* and its leading exponents were **Otto Eckmann** (1865–1902), best known as an illustrator for periodicals, and **Henry Clemens van de Velde** (Apr. 3, 1863–1957), a Belgian architect. In France Art Nouveau appeared in the jewelry and glassware of **René Lalique** (1860–1945). Called Modernista in Spain, Art Nouveau was represented mainly by the architect **Antoni Gaudi** (1852–1926), who produced perhaps the most striking expressions of the period. Italy was little affected by the trend but in Austria, where it was called *Sezessionstil*, it developed an almost geometrical style. The artist **Gustav Klimt** (1862–1918) and the architect **Otto Wagner** (1841–1918) were leading figures in Vienna. In the U.S. the architect **Louis Sullivan** used Art Nouveau motifs in the decoration of his buildings but not in the structures themselves. The style in America was most clearly expressed in the glassware designs, especially lamps, of **Louis C. Tiffany**.

1900 Apr. 2 Frederick E[dwin] **Church** (b. May 4, 1826), an American painter of the Hudson River School, died. Although he painted nature in the romantic and grand style of the school, his subjects were found more often in South America than in the U.S. His panoramic scenes were striking in their grandeur and their pure rendering of light. Among his works were *The Heart of the Andes* (1855), *Niagara Falls* (1857), and *Icebergs* (1861).

1900 June 5 Stephen **Crane** (b. Nov. 1, 1871), an American author, died. He was best known for his realistic novels *The Red Badge of Courage* (1895) and *Maggie: A Child of the Streets* (1893).

1900 Aug. 25 Friedrich Wilhelm **Nietzsche** (b. Oct. 15, 1844), a German philosopher and poet, died. His works, highly critical of middle-class values and the so-called western slave mentality, expounded the concept of a superman with a creative "will to power" that would enable him to reach higher moral and creative levels. Nietzsche's works included *The Birth of Tragedy* (1872); *Thus Spake Zarathustra* (1883–1884; 1892), in four parts; *Beyond Good and Evil* (1886); *The Genealogy of Morals* (1887); and *Ecce Homo* (1908), his autobiography.

1900 Nov. 30 Oscar [Fingal O'Flahertie Wills] **Wilde** (b. Oct. 16, 1856), an English writer born in Ireland, died. On May 25, 1895, Wilde had been sentenced under the **Criminal Law Amendment Act of 1885** to two years' imprisonment at hard labor in Reading Gaol for homosexual offenses. Wilde wrote one novel, *The Picture of Dorian Gray* (1891); and eight plays, among them *Lady Windermere's Fan* (1892); *Salomé* (1893), in French; *An Ideal Husband* (1895); and *The Importance of Being Earnest* (1895), his most popular play. *The Ballad of Reading Gaol* (1898), and *De Profundis* (in part, 1905; in full, 1962), a book-length letter written in prison, were considered Wilde's most successful serious works.

1900 Nov. 22 Arthur [Seymour] **Sullivan** (May 13, 1842), an English composer noted especially for his collaboration with **W. S. Gilbert** on comic operas, died. Their partnership included such favorites as *H.M.S. Pinafore* (1878), *The Pirates of Penzance* (1879), and *The Mikado* (1885). Sullivan also composed the well-known songs "The Lost Chord" and "Onward, Christian Soldiers."

VII. SPORTS, GAMES, AND SOCIETY

1900 Jan. 31 John Sholto Douglas, 8th marquess of Queensbury (b. July 20, 1844), who gave his name to the **Queensbury Rules** governing **boxing**, died. The rules were actually formulated by **John Graham Chambers**, an English sportsman and journalist, and were issued in 1867 under the sponsorship of Queensbury.

1900 Spring Carry Amelia Nation [nee Moore] (Nov. 25, 1846–June 9, 1911) embarked on her own **temperance crusade** when she led a group of women into saloons across Kansas to wreak destruction with her hatchet, while her companions accompanied her with the singing of hymns. The intimidating six-foot-tall woman opposed other immoralities, such as tobacco, skirts of improper length, and pornographic art.

1900 May 20–Oct. 28 The second modern **Olympic games** were held in Paris with 1,330 athletes from 22 nations competing. France won 29 gold medals and 102 medals overall; the U.S. 20 and 53; and Great Britain 17 and 35.

1900 Aug. 8–10 The **Davis Cup**, the trophy for men's international team tennis, was first contested, between England and the U.S. **Dwight F. Davis** (July 5, 1879–Nov. 28, 1945), a tennis-playing Harvard student, had donated the trophy. The U.S. won, 3 to 0.

1900 Aug. 12 Wilhelm Steinitz (b. May 17, 1836), the first person acknowledged as the chess champion of the world, died.

1901

I. VITAL STATISTICS AND DEMOGRAPHICS

1901 The **Commonwealth of Australia**, formed on Jan. 1, had a population of c.3,772,000, of which 80 percent had been born there. This figure did not include most of the aborigines.

II. POLITICS AND WAR

1901 The annexation of **Baluchistan**, in present southwestern Pakistan and eastern Iran, was completed by Great Britain, which joined the region to its holdings in India.

1901 Jan. 1 By virtue of an act (July, 1900) of the British Parliament, the **Commonwealth of Australia**, uniting six formerly separate colonies, came into existence. The British monarch remained head of state and appointed a governor general. The first Australian Parliament, convened on May 9, passed three laws that established a "White Australia" policy intended to keep immigration from non-European countries to a minimum. It also passed a law granting voting rights to women.

1901 Jan. 22   **Victoria** (b. May 24, 1819), queen of the United Kingdom of Great Britain and Ireland (from 1837) and empress of India (from 1876), died. On Feb. 22, 1840, she had married her cousin **Prince Albert** of Saxe-Coburg-Gotha (Aug. 26, 1819–Dec. 14, 1861), who was made prince consort in 1857. Victoria was succeeded by her son **Edward VII.**

1901 Feb. 11   **Milan IV** [Obrenovich] (b. Aug. 22, 1854), a former king (1882–1889) of Serbia, died in exile in Vienna. A leader, as prince, of Serbia's struggle for independence from the Ottoman Empire (1326–1920), he led the country into war (1876) with Turkey. Not successful in war, he succeeded at the Congress of Berlin (1878) in getting the European powers to recognize Serbia's independence.

1901 Mar. 4   **William McKinley** of the Republican party was inaugurated for his second term as president of the U.S., having defeated **William Jennings Bryan** of the Democratic party. **Theodore Roosevelt** served as vice president. McKinley received 255 electoral college votes to 155 for Bryan. In the popular vote McKinley received 7,219,530 and Bryan 6,358,071. On Sept. 6 McKinley (b. Jan. 29, 1843) was shot by **Leon F. Czolgosz**, a self-proclaimed anarchist, while speaking at the Pan-American Exposition in Buffalo, New York, in favor of commercial reciprocity between nations. On Sept. 14 McKinley died, and Theodore Roosevelt was sworn in as the 26th president of the U.S.

1901 Mar. 23   **Emilio Aguinaldo**, leader of the native forces resisting the takeover of the **Philippines** by the U.S. as a result of the **Spanish-American War** (1898), was captured by army troops. On Apr. 19 Aguinaldo issued a proclamation in which he acknowledged American sovereignty.

1901 July 4   **William Howard Taft**, appointed (Mar., 1900) by William McKinley, president of the U.S., to head the Philippine Commission, was installed as the **first governor of the Philippines**. He engineered, through a visit to the Vatican, a peaceful transfer of ownership of the Church lands in the islands, by which c.400,000 acres of agricultural land was sold to c.50,000 new Filipino landowners.

1901 Sept. 26   The **Ashanti Kingdom** (from c.1700) in West Africa was annexed to the British Gold Coast colony of present **Ghana**. **Prempeh II**, king of the Ashanti (1886–1896; 1926–1935), was exiled to the Seychelles.

1901 Nov. 18   The **Hay-Pauncefote Treaty** between the U.S. and Great Britain was signed by **John Hay**, U.S. secretary of state, and **Julian Pauncefote** (Sept. 13, 1828–May 29, 1902), the British ambassador to the U.S. The treaty superseded the **Clayton-Bulwer Treaty** concerning a proposed transisthmian canal enacted in 1850. The U.S. was granted full control of the canal and was to guarantee the neutrality of the canal zone.

1901 Dec. 10   The **first Nobel Peace Prize** was jointly awarded to **Jean Henri Dunant**, the Swiss founder of the **International Red Cross** in 1863, and **Frédéric Passy** (May 20, 1822–June 12, 1912), the French founder of the **International League of Peace** in 1868.

III. ECONOMY AND TRADE

1901   Russia completed the **Trans-Siberian railroad** from Moscow to Port Arthur [present Lüshan], a warm-water port. The railroad opened Siberia for Russia, whose Siberian population in 1861 was c.630,000 people but reached 4.5 million by 1939.

1901 Jan. 10   **Oil** was discovered in the great **Spindletop** area of southeastern **Texas**, near Beaumont, initiating the Texas oil industry and signaling an end to control of the state by cattle and railroad interests. The well was estimated to be producing 75,000 barrels a day.

1901 Feb. 25   The **U.S. Steel Corporation** was created in the largest business deal to date in U.S. history. **John Pierpont Morgan** and **Elbert Henry Gary** (Oct. 8, 1846–Aug. 15, 1927), heading a group of investors, had bought out the industrial empire of **Andrew Carnegie**, which they joined with several other major firms. The new corporation, capitalized at $1,404,000,000, controlled 78 blast furnaces with a capacity of about 7.7 million tons of finished steel per year.

IV. RELIGION AND PHILOSOPHY

1901 The first of 12 volumes of the *Jewish Encyclopedia* was published in the U.S. **Isidore Singer** (Nov. 10, 1859–Feb. 22, 1939), an Austrian-born author, was perhaps the prime organizer, in which scores of Jewish scholars in the U.S. and abroad ultimately labored.

V. SCIENCE, EDUCATION, AND TECHNOLOGY

1901 The hormone **adrenalin** was first isolated by **Jokichi Takamine** (Nov. 3, 1854–July 22, 1922), a Japanese-born biochemist who came to the U.S. He extracted the hormone, also called epinephrine, from the suprarenal glands of slaughtered animals.

1901 **Gerrit Grijns**, a Dutch physiologist, determined the cause of **beriberi**, a deficiency disease of the human body characterized by neurological and gastrointestinal symptoms. Earlier with his colleague **Christiaan Eijkman** (Aug. 11, 1858–Nov. 5, 1930), a Dutch medical researcher, Grigns had discovered (1897) that people who ate unhulled rice did not contract the disease, while those who ate polished rice did. Now he found that thiamine [vitamin B_1] was removed when rice was polished and that this substance was needed by the body.

1901 A U.S. **Yellow Fever** Commission made its report at the Pan-American Medical Congress held at Havana, Cuba, where proof was presented that the carrier of the dread disease was a mosquito *Aedes* [*Stegomyia*] *aegypti* of nearly worldwide distribution, particularly in the tropics. A vaccine was developed (1930) which protected those exposed to the sickness.

1901 Dec. 10 The first **Nobel prizes** for the sciences were awarded. **William** [Conrad] **Roentgen**, a German physicist, received the **physics** prize for his discovery of X-rays; **Jacobus Henricus van't Hoff** (Aug. 30, 1852–Mar. 1, 1911), a Dutch chemist, the **chemistry** prize for his work on the laws of chemical dynamics and osmotic pressure; and **Emil** [Adolph] **von Behring** (Mar. 15, 1854–Mar. 31, 1917), a German bacteriologist, the prize in **physiology or medicine** for his work on serum therapy.

VI. ARTS AND LEISURE

1901 *The Octopus*, the first novel in a series by **Frank Norris** [Benjamin Franklin Norris] (Mar. 5, 1870–Oct. 25, 1902), an American naturalistic writer, was published. The trilogy, uncompleted, aimed to expose the manipulation of midwestern wheat farming by monopolies. This volume depicted the struggle between the farmers and the railroad. *The Pit* (1903) portrayed the speculation on the Chicago grain market.

1901 Jan. 27 **Giuseppe** [Fortunino Francesco] **Verdi** (b. Oct. 10, 1813), an Italian opera composer, died. His best-known works included *Rigoletto* (1851); *Il Trovatore* [*The Troubador*] (1853); and *La Traviata* [**The Frail One**] (1853). His other works included *Oberto, conte di San Bonifacio* (1841), his first opera, performed at the La Scala opera house in Milan on Nov. 17, 1839; *Nabucco* (1842), based on the story of Nebuchadnezzar, the Chaldean king of Babylon; *I Lombardi* (1843), on the First Crusade; *Ernani* (1844), based on *Hernani* (1830) by **Victor Hugo**; *Macbeth* (1847, revised 1865); *Luisa Miller* (1849); *I Vespri Siciliani* [*The Sicilian Vespers*] (1855); *Un Ballo in Maschera* [*A Masked Ball*] (1859); *La Forza del Destino* [*The Force of Destiny*] (1862); *Don Carlos* (1867); *Aïda* (1871), performed in Cairo to celebrate the opening of the Suez Canal; *Requiem Mass* (1874), written to honor the Italian writer Alessandro Manzoni; *Otello* (1887); and *Falstaff* (1893), based on **William Shakespeare's** *The Merry Wives of Windsor*, and *Henry IV*. Verdi also wrote a string quartet (1873), and his last composition was *Quattro Pezzi Sacri* (1898), four sacred choral pieces which included *Stabat Mater* and *Te Deum*.

1901 Sept. 9 **Henri** [Marie Raymond] **de Toulouse-Lautrec** [Monfa] (b. Nov. 24, 1864), a French lithographer and famous for poster art, died. His best-known poster was *La Goulue at the Moulin Rouge* (1891). Toulouse-Lautrec's posters, paintings, and more than 300 lithographs presented a study of the night world of entertainment in the Paris of the 1890s.

1901 Dec. 10 The **first Nobel prize for literature** was awarded to **René** [François Armand] **Sully-Prudhomme**, a French poet and writer, for his body of work, mostly poetry.

VII. SPORTS, GAMES, AND SOCIETY

1901 Aug. 1 The game of **field hockey** was introduced to the U.S. by **Constance M.K. Applebee** of the British College of Physical Education. Applebee later joined the Bryn Mawr athletics department, where she coached field hockey for more than 50 years.

1902

I. DISASTERS

1902 May 7 The **Soufrière volcano erupted**, severely damaging the Windward Island of St. Vincent in the British West Indies. The death toll was set at c.2,000.

1902 May 8 A cloud of red-hot ash, gas, and steam erupted from Mount Pelée on the island of Martinique in the Windward Islands and fell on the nearby city of St. Pierre. The Pelean death toll, the greatest ever caused directly by a **volcanic eruption**, stood at c.30,000, nearly the entire population of the city of St. Pierre.

II. POLITICS AND WAR

1902 A boundary dispute in Patagonia between Argentina and Chile was submitted to Great Britain for arbitration and settled peaceably. In commemoration a great statue *Christ of the Andes* was erected (Mar. 13, 1904) by the two nations in Uspallata Pass [La Cumbre], the major pass between Santiago, Chile, and Mendoza, Argentina, high in the Andes [10,469 ft.].

1902 Mar. 26 **Cecil John Rhodes** (b. July 5, 1853), foremost advocate and architect of Great Britain's African empire, died. As a young man he staked out successful diamond claims in South Africa and founded (1880) the **De Beers Mining Company** which became one of the richest businesses in the world. He was in effect dictator of Cape Colony, and Rhodesia [present Zimbabwe] was named for him. Rhodes is best remembered today for the fortune he left to finance the Rhodes Scholarships, which annually enable c.170 students from the former British colonies, the U.S., and Germany to study at Oxford University.

1902 May 20 **Tomás Estrada Palma** (July 9, 1835–Nov. 14, 1908), a Cuban soldier during the Cuban revolution launched in 1895, was elected the **first president** (to 1906) **of the independent Republic of Cuba**, as U.S. occupation came to an end.

1902 May 31 The **Peace of Vereeniging**, a town in the southern Transvaal, ended the **Boer War** [South African War] (from Oct. 12, 1899) as the Boers accepted British sovereignty.

1902 June 28 The U.S. Congress passed the **Isthmian Canal Act** which authorized the building of a canal across the Isthmus of Panama. It also authorized an alternate route across Nicaragua in the event that the Panama Canal Company of France would not sell its route to the U.S. Eventually (Apr. 23, 1904) it did so for $40 million.

1902 July 12 **Arthur** [James] **Balfour** (July 25, 1848–Mar. 19, 1930) became prime minister of Great Britain, succeeding his uncle Lord Salisbury. Balfour is remembered chiefly for the **Balfour Declaration** of 1917, which pledged British support for a Jewish national homeland in Palestine after World War I (1914–1918), with the proviso that the rights of non-Jews in Palestine be respected.

1902 Oct. 26 **Elizabeth Cady Stanton** (b. Nov. 12, 1815), a leading American advocate of women's rights, especially suffrage, died. Stanton attended (1840) the international convention on slavery in London and when women delegates were excluded from the floor her indignation was aroused to such an extent that she devoted the rest of her life to reform. With **Lucretia Mott** and others she organized (1848) the **first women's rights convention in the U.S.** at Seneca Falls, N.Y.

1902 Dec. 7 In an ultimatum Great Britain and Germany demanded that **Venezuela** pay them for damage done during a violent takeover (1899) of the government. When Venezuela did not act, the two nations blockaded the coast and began (Dec. 13) bombarding Venezuelan forts. The matter was referred (Feb. 13, 1903) to the **Permanent Court of Arbitration** [Hague Tribunal], which agreed (Feb. 22, 1904) that compensation was due and set the amounts to be paid.

III. ECONOMY AND TRADE

1902 Apr. 14 **James Cash Penny** (Sept. 16, 1875–Feb. 12, 1971), with two partners, opened the Golden Rule store in Kemmerer, Wyoming, to compete with the company stores of the mining area. Penny's successful venture grew into the **J.C. Penny department store chain**.

1902 June 17 The U.S. Congress passed the **Reclamation Act**, which enabled the president to establish the **National Park System** and add to the forest preserves. It also permitted the federal government to organize irrigation projects by selling some public lands which, after irrigation, produced more money-making crops, enabling the purchasers to pay off mortgages into a circulating fund. Irrigation and dam building led to the production and sale of hydroelectric power, flood control, and improved navigation. This act rendered millions of acres of land agriculturally productive, and formed the basis for national forests in the U.S.

1902 Oct. 16 When mine owners refused arbitration in a strike (from May 12) led by the **United Mine Workers of America**, **Theodore Roosevelt**, president of the U.S., appointed a commission to settle the strike. Because the price of coal had begun to rise, Roosevelt had earlier threatened (Oct. 13) to use U.S. troops to run the mines, thus forcing the mine owners to accept an arbitrated settlement, which proved to be generally favorable to the miners.

IV. SCIENCE, EDUCATION, AND TECHNOLOGY

1902 Working independently, **Oliver Heaviside** (May 18, 1850–Feb. 3, 1925), an English physicist, and **Arthur E[dwin] Kennelly** (Dec. 17, 1861–June 18, 1939), a British-American electrical engineer, discovered the existence of an electrified layer in the atmosphere that reflected radio waves and so made possible the long distance transmission of signals. The layer became known as the **Kennelly-Heaviside** or **Heaviside layer**.

1902 A practical system for **air conditioning** an enclosed area was devised by **Willis H. Carrier** (Nov. 26, 1876–Oct. 7, 1950), an engineer, for use in a printing plant in Brooklyn, New York.

1902 Feb. **Charles Wardell Stiles** (1867–1941), an American zoologist, announced his discovery of the *Hookworm* [*Necator Americanus*], which debilitated many poor people in the South. The larvae developed in the soil and penetrated the body usually through the feet. A cure was found in 1910 for what was called the "germ of laziness," which at the time affected 43 percent of the population of North Carolina.

1902 Nov. 23 **Walter Reed** (b. Sept. 15, 1851), surgeon in the U.S. army, died. As a major in 1893 he was curator of the **Army Medical Museum** in Washington, D.C., and professor of microscopy and bacteriology of the new **Army Medical College**. For seven years he conducted research on the etiology, control, and transmission of epidemic diseases, such as yellow and typhoid fevers. He was appointed (1898) by the U.S. War Department to head a committee of bacteriologists to study the typhoid epidemic among U.S. troops in Chickamauga, Georgia, which led to subsequent prevention and control of such epidemics. In 1900 he headed a similar committee to study yellow fever which, with the help of members of the committee, especially **Jesse William Lazear**, was equally successful.

V. ARTS AND LEISURE

1902 Mar. 5 [Francis] **Bret Harte** (b. Aug. 25, 1836), an American writer of western tales, died. His first success was the poem *Plain Language from Truthful James* [*The Heathen Chinee*] (1870), but he soon turned to writing western short stories, such as *The Outcasts of Poker Flat* (1869) and *The Luck of Roaring Camp* (1870), many of which first appeared in the *Overland Monthly*, a journal Harte established in 1868.

1902 June 18 **Samuel Butler** (b. Dec. 4, 1835), an English writer, died. *Erewhon* [an anagram of "nowhere"] (1872) and *Erewhon Revisited* (1901) were satirical romances written in a vein similar to *Gulliver's Travels* by **Jonathan Swift**. *The Way of All Flesh* (1903), considered Butler's masterpiece, was popular among those reacting against Victorian sentiment.

1902 Sept. 28 **Émile** [Édouard Charles Antoine] **Zola** (b. Apr. 2, 1840), a French writer, died. Zola was most noted for a series of 20 novels *Les Rougon-Macquart* (1871–1893), which he described as the "social and natural history of a family under the second empire." This series included *L'Assommoir* [*The Dram Shop*] (1877), a study of alcoholism; *Nana* (1880); *Germinal* (1883); *L'Argent* [*Money*] (1891); and *Débâcle* (1892), a description of war based on the French defeat in the Franco-Prussian War (1870). During the Dreyfus Affair (1894) Zola wrote the *J'accuse* letter, published in *L'Aurore* on Jan. 13, 1898, passionately criticizing the French system of justice.

1902 Dec. 18 Albert Bierstadt (b. Jan. 7, 1830), a German-born American painter, died. In 1831 he came to the U.S. and in 1859 accompanied an exploring expedition to the Rocky Mountains and the Yosemite area. The large-scale paintings that resulted from this experience captured the beauty and grandeur of the American Far West. Among them were *Laramie Peak* (1861), *The Rocky Mountains* (1863), and *Mt. Corcoran* (c.1875). Because he also painted scenes from nature in the New York region, Bierstadt was considered a member of the Hudson River School.

1903

I. DISASTERS

1903 Dec. 30 At Chicago's Iroquois Theater, **fire** broke out before a performance of the play *Mr. Bluebeard*. The audience stampeded for exit doors, many of which were locked. Other doors were jammed shut by the crush of screaming theatergoers. The final death count was 602.

II. EXPLORATION AND COLONIZATION

1903–1906 Roald Amundsen, a Norwegian explorer, piloted the *Gjöa* through the Northwest Passage, the **first successful voyage along the narrow sea connecting the Atlantic and Pacific oceans**. Amundsen described his voyage in *North West Passage* (1908).

III. POLITICS AND WAR

1903 Mar. 1 José Batlle y Ordóñez (May 21, 1856–Oct. 20, 1929) was elected president of **Uruguay** for his first term (1903–1907). He harshly repressed an uprising by the Blanco [White] party, but he granted amnesty to the rebels and took measures to improve conditions in the country.

1903 June 11 Alexander [Aleksandar] **I Obrenovich** [Obrenović] (b. Aug. 14, 1876), king of **Serbia** since the abdication of his father Milan on Mar. 6, 1889, and his wife **Draga Mashin** [Mašin; née Lunjevica] were assassinated in the royal palace at Belgrade by dissident army officers. Although Alexander had promoted Serbian nationalism, he

had become more and more reactionary and had offended his people by his marriage (Aug. 5, 1900), to Draga, who had once been his mother's lady-in-waiting. **Peter I Karageorgevich** (July 11, 1844–Aug. 16, 1921) was recalled from exile on June 15, 1903, and was crowned king of Serbia at Belgrade on Sept. 21, 1904.

1903 July 21 The **Irish Land Purchase Act** was passed in the British Parliament under the sponsorship of George Wyndham (Aug. 29, 1863–June 8, 1913), a British Tory who served as chief secretary for Ireland. The Act established a Land Commission to which landlords could sell their estates. The Land Commission then collected annuity payments, instead of rent, toward the purchase of the land by the tenants.

1903 July 30–Aug. 23 At the Socialist Congress held in London, the **Russian Social Democratic Labor party** was permanently divided into the **Bolsheviks** [majority party] and Mensheviks [minority party]. Actually it was the "**Mensheviks**" who were in the majority, but they walked out of the congress and the Bolsheviks declared themselves the majority in a rump session. The Bolsheviks chose **Vladimir Ilyich Lenin** as a leader in their call for revolution and dictatorship of the proletariat.

1903 Oct. 20 An American-British-Canadian commission established (Jan. 24) to arbitrate an **Alaskan boundary** dispute decided in favor of the U.S. With the finding (1896) of gold in the Klondike, the dispute was important to Canada, but the British representatives on the commission voted for the U.S. and against Canada, giving the Americans most of what they wanted.

1903 Nov. 3 Panama declared its independence from Colombia. Philippe Jean Bunau-Varilla, the French engineer instrumental in forming a canal company and selling it to the U.S., had organized the revolution. The arrival of a U.S. naval force prevented Colombia from regaining Panama. On Nov. 17 the **Hay-Bunau-Varilla Treaty** was signed by Panama, and the U.S., which granted the U.S. exclusive rights to control the **Panama Canal Zone**, a ten-mile wide strip of land connecting the Atlantic and Pacific oceans, for the purposes of constructing and maintaining a transisthmian canal.

IV. ECONOMY AND TRADE

1903 June 16 The **Ford Motor Company** was incorporated by **Henry Ford**. In 1908 Ford introduced the **Model T**, and by 1913 it became the best-selling car in the world. Ford introduced assembly-line production methods, developed elsewhere by others, into his factories in 1913 and 1914, which by 1926 enabled the Model T to be priced at $310 compared to $850, the price in 1908.

1903 July 4 **Theodore Roosevelt**, president of the U.S., sent the **first message over a Pacific cable** connecting San Francisco and Manila. The message was returned to him in 12 minutes.

V. RELIGION AND PHILOSOPHY

1903 Apr. For three days a **pogrom was conducted against the ghetto in Kishinev** [Chişinău], near Odessa, in the Ukraine. During the pillaging and violence, c.45 Jews died and c.1500 Jewish homes were destroyed. The pogrom occurred with the sanction, if not outright participation, of the Russian government. Those participating were never punished.

1903 July 20 **Pope Leo XIII** (b. Mar. 2, 1810; ruled from 1878) died. Leo was noted for his scholarship and for his effort to shape Roman Catholic attitudes to meet the realities of modern life. His most famous encyclical *Rerum novarum* (1891) pointed out the deficiencies of both capitalism and Marxist socialism. He was succeeded by **Pius X**.

VI. SCIENCE, EDUCATION, AND TECHNOLOGY

1903 Willem Einthoven (May 21, 1860–Sept. 28, 1927), a Dutch physiologist, developed a string galvanometer, from which evolved his invention (1924) of the **electrocardiogram** [EKG]. In 1924 he was awarded the **Nobel prize for physiology** or medicine.

1903 Ivan [Petrovich] **Pavlov**, a Russian physiologist, revealed for the first time his work on what he called "conditioned reflexes." In his experiments Pavlov found that physical actions can be stimulated by conditioning.

1903 Helium, a very rare gaseous element, was first discovered in a deposit of natural gases at Dexter, Kansas.

1903 Apr. 28 **Josiah** [Willard] **Gibbs** (b. Feb. 11, 1839), an American mathematical physicist and chemist, died. Gibbs brought the studies of thermodynamics and chemistry together. In 1901 he was awarded the **Copley medal** by the Royal Society of London for his application of the **second law of thermodynamics** to the relation between electrical, thermal, and mechanical energy.

1903 Dec. 8 **Herbert Spencer** (b. Apr. 27, 1820), an English philosopher, died. He was largely responsible for the popular acceptance of Charles Darwin's work. His ten-volume *Synthetic Philosophy* (1862–1893) attempted to account systematically for all phenomena, including social as well as organic, according to Darwin's theory of evolution. *Principles of Psychology* (1855) set forth a similar evolutionary theory that organic development was a progression from a homogeneous to a heterogeneous state. His three-volume *Principles of Sociology* (1876–1896), in which he traced the progression of an individual's differentiation from a group, helped establish sociology as a discipline.

1903 Dec. 17 The **Wright** brothers, **Orville** (Aug. 19, 1871–Jan. 30, 1948) and **Wilbur** (Apr. 6, 1867–May 30, 1912), made the **first airplane flight** at Kitty Hawk, North Carolina. Propelled by a 12-horsepower gasoline engine, the first of four flights that day lasted only 12 seconds. The longest flight, taking them 850 feet, lasted 59 seconds.

VII. ARTS AND LEISURE

1903   The **first movie** with a complete plot and running for ten minutes, *The Great Train Robbery*, was produced by the Edison Company and directed by **Edwin S. Porter** (1870–Apr. 30, 1941), an American inventor born in Scotland. The star was [**Gilbert M.**] **Bronco Billy Anderson** [orig.: Max Aronson] (Mar. 21, 1882–Jan. 20, 1971), who played both a passenger on the train and the bandit who shot him.

1903 May 8   **Paul** [Eugène Henri] **Gauguin** (b. June 7, 1848), a French painter, died. Gauguin broke with the Impressionists after a trip to Martinique in 1887, when he began to seek the emotional release of living a primitive, or "natural," life among natives of the tropics. As Gauguin's work developed it became increasingly symbolic. In 1891 Gauguin went to Tahiti and, except for a trip to Paris in 1893, remained there and in the Marquesas Islands the rest of his life. Gauguin's best-known works included *The Yellow Christ* (1889), *Nave, Nave Mahana* (1896), and an enormous multi-scene canvas, *Where Do We Come From? What Are We? Where Are We Going?* (1897).

1903 July 11   **William Ernest Henley** (b. Aug. 23, 1849), an English poet, died. He was best known for his poem "Invictus," which ended, "I am the master of my fate: I am the captain of my soul."

1903 July 17   **James Abbott McNeill Whistler** (b. July 10, 1834), an American painter and etcher who lived mostly in France and England, died. *The White Girl* (1862) and *Arrangement in Grey and Black* [*Whistler's Mother*] (1872) were among his best-known canvases.

1903 Nov.   **Camille Pissarro** (b. July 10, 1830), a pioneer impressionist, died. Pissarro's work went largely unrecognized by the general public during his lifetime. Among his best-known paintings were *Louveciennes Road* (1870); *Street in Pontoise, Winter* (1873); *Orchard in Flower, Pontoise* (1877); *Landscape at Chaponval* (1880); and *The Bridge at Bruges* (1903).

1903 Nov. 1 [Christian Matthias] **Theodor Mommsen** (b. Nov. 30, 1817), a German historian and classical scholar, died. His research and writings on ancient Rome were important contributions to classical history. Outstanding was *Römische Geschichte* [*History of Rome*] (1854–1856), popular with readers in spite of its length. An even more extensive project which he organized and helped edit was *Corpus inscriptionum Latinum* (1863 ff.), which was intended to collect all known Latin inscriptions from Roman buildings, monuments, and elsewhere. He was awarded the **Nobel prize for literature** in 1902.

1903 Dec. 28   **George Robert Gissing** (b. Nov. 22, 1857), an English novelist of the later Victorian era, died. His works included *New Grub Street* (1891) and the semi-autobiographical *The Private Papers of Henry Ryecroft* (1903).

VIII. SPORTS, GAMES, AND SOCIETY

1903   Alfred Charles William Harmsworth (July 15, 1865–Aug. 14, 1922), a British newspaper magnate and later Lord Northcliffe, donated a trophy for a major British motorboating event. The **Harmsworth Trophy** was first won later this year by an English boat *Napier I* with a speed of 19.53 miles per hour.

1903   The **first Tour de France bicycle race**, over a course of 1,500 miles, was won by M. Garin of France. Now a grueling event of c.2,500 miles lasting about four weeks, the course varies somewhat from year to year, but always includes climbs through mountain passes and over innumerable hills, and runs through hundreds of communities in France and bordering nations.

1903 Jan.   A peace pact between the American and National leagues paved the way for a **World Series** between the winning teams of each league.

1903 Aug. 22–Sept. 2   The American yacht *Reliance* successfully defended the **America's Cup** by winning three straight races from the British yacht *Shamrock III* 30 miles off New York harbor.

1903 Oct. 13   In the **first World Series** the Boston Red Sox, champions of the American League, defeated the Pittsburgh Pirates, champions of the National League, 5 games to 3.

1904

I. DISASTERS

1904 Feb. 7–8 The business center of Baltimore, Maryland's largest city, was destroyed by fire. Seventy-five city blocks, covering 140 acres, were razed, resulting in property losses estimated at $85 million.

1904 June 15 The excursion steamer *General Slocum* caught fire near Hell's Gate in New York City's East River, killing c.1,020 of 1,380 passengers aboard. All but 57 of the passengers were women and children. **William H. Van Schaick**, the ship's captain, was sentenced to ten years in jail following the disaster.

II. POLITICS AND WAR

1904 Jan. Negotiations between Russia and Japan over the Manchuria-Korea problem (Japan claimed Korea in exchange for Russia's claim on Manchuria; Russia claimed both) broke down when ultimatums were issued by both parties. **Japan severed relations with Russia** on Feb. 6, and on Feb. 8 **Nicholas II**, czar of Russia, ordered his navy to attack any Japanese vessel north of latitude 39° north. The two countries declared war on each other on Feb. 10.

1904 Feb. 8–Oct. 25 Fighting in the **Russo-Japanese War** (1904–1905) began when the Japanese navy made a surprise night attack with torpedo boats on the Russian fleet in Russian-held **Port Arthur** [Lüshan] in Manchuria, present Liaoning province of northeastern China, effectively bottling up the fleet. Trying to break the blockade the Russian fleet met with disaster (Apr. 13) when it left Port Arthur only to find the Japanese fleet reinforced and waiting. The battleship *Petropavlosk* hit a mine, sinking with the loss of c.700 men. The rest of the fleet returned to port. Meanwhile Russian forces occupied the city of Liaoyang north of Port Arthur in Liaoning province. From here they advanced to the Yalu River, on the border of present North Korea and China, where they were overwhelmed on May 1, 1904, by a Japanese army. From Aug. 25 to 31 Japanese forces battled the Russian army at Liaoyang and forced the Russians to withdraw to the north. The Japanese began (Oct. 25) to bombard Port Arthur from the land

side after capturing the forts overlooking the port, thus cutting off the port by land.

1904 Apr. 8 The **Entente Cordiale** between Great Britain and France came into existence. In part it was simply an understanding between the two nations, alarmed by the threatening power of Germany and Austria-Hungary, and in part a formal treaty concerning relations in colonial areas, especially Africa. France accepted Britain's position in Egypt while England allowed France and Spain to move on Morocco.

1904 Oct. The **U.S. took charge of the finances of the Dominican Republic**, which was in virtual bankruptcy. By agreeing to finance the debts of the Dominican Republic, the U.S. opened the door to her own interference in the internal affairs of such nations. The later use of U.S. military forces in the Dominican Republic led to much ill will in the Caribbean countries toward the U.S.

1904 July 14 **Paul** [Stephanus Johannes Paulus] **Kruger** (b. Oct. 10, 1825), a South African Transvaal statesman and foe of Great Britain, died. After Great Britain annexed the Dutch-speaking republic of Transvaal in 1877, Kruger at first cooperated with the British and in 1881 he was a leader in the negotiations by which the Boers were granted independence. Kruger was elected president in 1883 and then reelected three times. He continued to oppose British imperialists who wanted to reacquire the Transvaal because of its rich gold fields. Kruger fought the British in the early part of the **Boer War** (1899–1902), but in 1900 he went to Europe in a vain attempt to secure aid for his country. He died in Switzerland.

1904 Sept. 7 A British military expedition forced the **Dalai Lhama**, spiritual and governmental leader of **Tibet**, to sign a treaty granting Britain trading posts in three cities. By the treaty Tibet also guaranteed it would not cede territory to a foreign power, although in 1906 and 1907 England recognized China's suzerainty over Tibet. The British expedition had set out from India in July, 1903, and defeated Tibetan forces several times before capturing **Lhasa**, the Tibetan capital and sacred city in Aug. 1904.

1904 Dec. 6 What became known as the **Roosevelt Corollary to the Monroe Doctrine** was given formal statement by **Theodore Roosevelt**, president of the U.S., in his annual message to Congress. His position was that, since by the original Monroe Doctrine the U.S. would not allow foreign nations to intervene in the Western Hemisphere, it was the duty of the country to see to it that any wrongs inflicted by the protected nations on foreign powers were redressed.

III. ECONOMY AND TRADE

1904 The **German Steel Union**, an industrial union, was formed from several cartels that controlled the steel, rail, railroad tie, and girder industries. The Steel Union sold its goods at high prices within Germany, where it had a monopoly, and at lower prices to foreign nations. This system proved useful in Germany's drive for greater military strength.

1904 *The History of the Standard Oil Company*, a two-volume muckraking work by **Ida Minerva Tarbell** (Nov. 5, 1857–Jan. 6, 1944), disclosed rampant corruption in the largest U.S. oil company.

1904 Mar. 14 The U.S. Supreme Court dissolved **Northern Securities**, a large railroad holding company, under provision of the **Sherman Antitrust Act** of 1890. The act, little used previously, resolved the first suit brought by the Roosevelt administration in its "trust-busting" campaign.

IV. RELIGION AND PHILOSOPHY

1904 July 3 **Theodor Herzl** (b. May 2, 1860), a Zionist leader, died of a heart attack. Just prior to Herzl's death there had been a bitter dispute among delegates at the **Sixth Zionist Congress** in 1903 over the proposal by **Joseph Chamberlain**, colonial secretary of Great Britain, to provide territory in Uganda for a Jewish nation. Herzl was buried in Vienna, but his remains were removed (1949) to Israel and buried near Jerusalem on a hill renamed Mount Herzl.

V. SCIENCE, EDUCATION, AND TECHNOLOGY

1904 The **first tractor**, a gasoline powered farm vehicle, was constructed by **Benjamin Holt**, a blacksmith from Iowa.

1904 Oct. 27 The **first section of the New York City subway** system began operation. The line, on which work had begun in 1900, ran from City Hall to 145th Street and Broadway in Manhattan. In 1908 it began operations between Manhattan and Brooklyn when the first tunnel under the East River was completed.

VI. ARTS AND LEISURE

1904 May 1 **Anton** [Antonín] **Dvořák** (b. Sept. 8, 1841), a Czech composer, died. Dvořák's nine symphonies included *From the New World* (1893). The themes for many of Dvořák's works originated in the folk music he had heard at his father's village inn near Prague.

1904 July 2 **Anton** [Pavlovich] **Chekhov** [Chekov, Tchekhov] (b. Jan. 17, 1860), a Russian playwright, died. *Ivanov* (1887) was his first important play. *The Sea Gull* (1896) was produced by the Moscow Art Theater on July 2, 1898, after which this theater produced Chekhov's major plays, including *Uncle Vanya* (1897), *The Three Sisters* (1901), and *The Cherry Orchard* (1904). Chekhov also wrote short stories, which appeared in three collections, *Motley Stories* (1886), *At Twilight* (1887), and *Stories* (1888).

VII. SPORTS, GAMES, AND SOCIETY

1904 **Judo** was first publicly demonstrated and taught to individuals in the U.S. by Mr. **Yamashita** of the Kodokan school of judo from Japan. Among Yamashita's pupils was **Theodore Roosevelt**, president of the U.S.

1904 July 1–Nov. 23 The third Summer **Olympic Games** were held in St. Louis, Missouri, with 687 athletes from 12 countries, about half the number participating in Paris four years earlier. Because most European countries did not send athletes, U.S. athletes won 80 gold medals and 238 overall. Their nearest competitors were Germany with 5 and 15, Cuba with 5 and 11. The Americans won 21 of the 22 track events.

1905

I. POLITICS AND WAR

1905 Jan. 22 The **Russian Revolution of 1905** [First Russian Revolution] broke out on **Bloody Sunday** [Red Sunday] when almost 200,000 Russian workers marching to the Winter Palace in St. Petersburg [present Leningrad] with a petition for **Nicholas II,** czar of Russia, were fired upon. They had been requesting better pay and working conditions as well as democratic reforms in government. About 70 workers were killed; hundreds were injured. A wave of labor unrest and strikes swept the country.

1905 Mar. 4 **Theodore Roosevelt** of the Republican party was inaugurated for his second term as president of the U.S., having defeated **Alton Brooks Parker** (May 14, 1852–May 10, 1926) of the Democratic party. In the Nov. 8, 1904, election the Republican ticket had received 336 electoral college votes to 140 for the Democrats. The popular vote was 7,628,834 for Roosevelt to 5,884,401 for Parker. **Charles Warren Fairbanks** (May 11, 1852–June 4, 1918) served as vice-president.

1905 May 27 **A battle in the Straits of Tsushima** during the **Russo-Japanese War** (1904–1905), was a crushing defeat for the Russians. **Zenovi Petrovich Rozhdestvenski** (1848–1909), a Russian admiral, was captured by the Japanese led by **Heihachiro Togo** (1847–May 30, 1934), a Japanese admiral. Earlier the Japanese had also defeated (Feb. 21–Mar. 10) the Russians on land, at Mukden [Moukden, Fengtien, Shenyang], Liaoning province, a major city of eastern Manchuria, which was Russia's last major stronghold there.

1905 June 7 The Storting, Norway's parliament, voted to declare the **dissolution of the union of Norway and Sweden** under **Oscar II,** king of Sweden (from 1872). Sweden was forced to agree when Norway approved (Nov. 12) the dissolution in a plebescite. **Haakon VII** [Charles, Carl] (Aug. 3, 1872–Sept. 21, 1957), the second son of **Frederick VIII,** future king of Denmark, was chosen to be Norway's king, establishing the **Danish Oldenburg Dynasty** (1905 to the present) there. On Sept. 23 Sweden and Norway reached agreement to maintain a neutral frontier.

1905 June 27–28 **Mutiny broke out on the Russian battleship *Potemkin*** docked at the Russian port of Odessa, on the Black Sea. It was a workers' outbreak led by sailors on board. On June 30 the crew of the battleship *Pobiedonosets* also mutinied and in a short time the entire Russian Black Sea fleet was immobile. The crew of the *Pobiedonosets* surrendered (July 3), and the *Potemkin* surrendered (July 8) to Romanian authorities at Constanta, who turned it over to the Russians the next day. The mutiny reflected general unrest throughout Russia, resulting in part from the Russian defeat in the Russo-Japanese War (1904–1905) and in part from widespread political agitation and indignation stemming from the repression of workers in St. Petersburg.

1905 Aug. 20 **Sun Yat-Sen,** the Chinese Nationalist leader, issued the **San Min Chu I** [Three People's Principles], the principles being nationalism, democracy, and livelihood for the people, his first statement of political philosophy. His secret society the **Hsing Chung Hui** [Revive China Society] (founded by 1894) organized protests, published a newspaper that was smuggled into China, and hatched revolutionary plots. Its most important accomplishment, however, was to enlist the support of shareholders in Chinese companies against plans made by the Manchu court to nationalize the railroads and allow foreign investment in them.

1905 Sept. 1 **Alberta and Saskatchewan were made provinces of Canada.** In December Saskatchewan held its first provincial elections in which Walter Scott (Oct. 27, 1867–Mar. 23, 1938) led the Liberal party to victory.

1905 Sept. 5 The **Treaty of Portsmouth,** New Hampshire, in the U.S., mediated by **Theodore Roosevelt,** president of the U.S., ended the **Russo-Japanese War** (from 1904). Liaotung Peninsula, part of Manchuria, was transferred to Japan and the rest of Manchuria was returned to Chinese rule. Japan's interests in Korea were recognized: the Korean emperor was forced to abdicate on July 19, 1907, to be replaced by a figurehead as Japan proclaimed a protectorate over Korea on July 25.

1905 Oct. 30 The **October Manifesto** was issued by **Nicholas II,** czar of Russia, placing the czar's powers under a constitutional monarchy with an elected **Duma** [Parliament]. The manifesto was the work of

Sergei Yulievich Witte (July 29, 1849–Mar. 12, 1915), one of the czar's advisers, who soon became the first freely elected premier. The reform was welcomed by moderate elements, led by the Constitutional Democrat party, or **Cadets**, which won a majority of seats in elections held for the first Duma. The **Octobrists**, as the moderates were soon called, were pleased that the freedoms of the press, religion, assembly, and speech were guaranteed, at least on paper. The Octobrists were a new political group, loosely allied, which took the name of "Union of October Seventeenth" [Oct. 30 = Oct. 17 in the old Russian calendar]. The more radical Marxists, Populists, and Social Democrats boycotted Nicholas's offer of less than a full constituent assembly, by which they meant one elected by universal, direct, equal, and secret suffrage. The czar was not happy with the liberal composition of the Duma, which wanted to turn over the large estates to the peasants working them, and to grant equal civil rights to the Jews, who had suffered because they were the target of the czar's efforts to rechannel revolutionary fervor. Nicholas soon began to undermine and curtail the guarantees of the Manifesto. A general strike had already been declared (October) for all of Russia by the Social Democrat party. Delegates from striking industries formed (October–December) the St. Petersburg Soviet [Council] of Workers' Deputies. Soviets were soon formed in many other Russian cities and towns, and it appeared that a radical change in government could be achieved. **Leon Trotsky**, who had already begun to split from **Lenin**, came from Munich to direct the activities of the St. Petersburg Soviet. But on Dec. 16, 1905, this Soviet was dispersed and its members arrested by the czar's troops.

1905 Nov. 28   The **Sinn Fein** [Irish for "We, Ourselves"] was organized as an Irish nationalistic political party. It had its origins in the work of **Arthur Griffith**, who had founded (1899) the *United Irishman*. As a statesman Griffith urged that Irish members of the British Parliament withdraw and form their own assembly.

1905 Dec. 4–5   As a consequence of the Russian Revolution (Jan. 22), a **congress convened in Vilna** [Wilno, Wilna, Vilnius], capital of Lithuania, a vassal state of Russia, **and declared independence**. In Estonia, where workers rioted and pillaged the manor houses, owned mostly by Germans, martial law had to be declared.

1905 Dec. 4   **Arthur Balfour**, a Conservative prime minister (from 1902) of Great Britain, resigned. A split in the Conservative party between those advocating free trade and those in favor of protectionism led to his government's downfall. There was also dissatisfaction with the **Education Act of 1902**, sponsored by the Balfour ministry, because it provided financial support to schools sponsored by religious denominations. Balfour was succeeded (Dec. 5) by **Henry Campbell-Bannerman** (Sept. 2, 1836–Apr. 22, 1908), a member of Parliament (from 1868) and the leader of the Liberal party, which won the election (1906) by a large margin. He served until Apr. 5, 1908.

II. ECONOMY AND TRADE

1905   The **Trans-Siberian Railroad**, begun in 1881, was completed between Moscow and the Pacific coast, terminating at Vladivostok on the Sea of Japan. It was Russia's longest railroad line.

1905   The **Mining Act** was passed in Japan, where it was the first effective law to improve working conditions. The **Factory Act of 1911** supplemented the Mining Act. Their regulations affected only those enterprises with 15 or more employees. The work day was limited to 12 hours for women and children. One hour was set aside for rest. The minimum age for working children was set at ten and, for heavy work, twelve. Strong opposition by employers, however, kept these regulations from being fully enforced until 1916.

1905 June 27   The **Industrial Workers of the World** [IWW] was formed in Chicago under the leadership of **William Dudley Haywood** (Feb. 4, 1869–May 18, 1928), president of the Western Federation of Miners, by delegates representing 40 different trades. Their members became known as Wobblies. Its immediate goal became the organization of unskilled, itinerant labor, which was rejected by the **American Federation of Labor** [AFL]. The IWW earned a reputation as a radical organization because of its use of direct economic action, especially strikes and boycotts.

1905 Oct.–Dec.   A **general strike spread throughout Russia** in support of the **October Manifesto**. Workers called for an eight-hour day and a constitutional convention. In Kharkov and Odessa, in the Ukraine, police fought across barricades erected by civilians. In the countryside peasants initiated their own revolt by attacking the estates of nobles, burning manor houses and seizing land. Russia came to a standstill.

III. RELIGION AND PHILOSOPHY

1905 The first Buddhist church in the U.S. was consecrated in San Francisco, California.

1905 July 3 Both houses of the **French legislature passed a law for the complete separation of church and state.** The measure ended the terms of the Concordat of 1801, an agreement between **Napoleon I** and **Pope Pius VII** that reestablished the Roman Catholic Church in France. The new law, officially promulgated on Dec. 4, 1905, guaranteed all Frenchmen freedom of conscience and religion and withdrew government financial support for all religious institutions.

IV. SCIENCE, EDUCATION, AND TECHNOLOGY

1905 The **Cullinan Diamond** was discovered near Pretoria in Premier Mine, the largest diamond vein of South Africa. It was the largest known diamond in the world with a weight, uncut, of 3,106 carats [more than a pound]. The diamond was given to **Edward VII**, king of Great Britain, and 105 gems were cut from it, including the **Star of Africa**, which remains still the **largest existing cut diamond** [530.2 carats].

1905 June 30 **Albert Einstein**, a German physicist living in Switzerland, announced the **Theory of Relativity** in a restricted form [the Special Theory of Relativity]. He submitted (Sept. 27) a second paper on the subject in which was stated for the first time the now famous relationship between mass and energy: $E = mc^2$. Einstein's theory was published in a more extended form [the General Theory of Relativity] in 1915. No one has been able yet to disprove the theory or to advance another theory that explains better the physics of the universe.

V. ARTS AND LEISURE

1905 **Fauvism**, a short-lived school of painting characterized by its use of bright splashes of color, began with an exhibition at the Salon d'Automne in Paris. There the epithet "fauves" [wild beasts] was attached to the artists. By 1908 fauvism had subsided, to be overtaken by the **Cubist movement**.

Fauvists included **Henri Matisse, Georges Braque, Raoul Dufy,** and **Kees van Dongen** [Cornélius Théodorus Marie van Dongen] (July 26, 1877–May 28, 1968), **Albert Marquet** (Mar. 27, 1875–June 14, 1947), **Georges Rouault,** and **André Derain.**

1905 *Die Brücke* [*The Bridge*], the first coherent expressionist group to emerge in the postimpressionistic period, was formed in Dresden, in eastern Germany, by an association of German artists. The participants included **Ernst Ludwig Kirchner** (May 6, 1880–June 15, 1938), **Erich Heckel** (July 31, 1883–Jan. 27, 1970), **Karl Schmidt-Rottluff** (Dec. 1, 1884–Aug. 9, 1976), and **Max Pechstein** (Dec. 31, 1881–June 29, 1955). The group disbanded in 1913. **Expressionism** directly opposed impressionism in that the latter concentrated on depicting the object itself while the expressionists were concerned with portraying their own emotional response to the object.

1905 Mar. 24 **Jules Verne** (b. Feb. 8, 1828), a French writer and an **originator of present science fiction**, died. Verne was talented as a storyteller, but was also noted for accurately predicting several major technological advances made since his own time, including television, the submarine, the airplane, and space travel. Verne's novels included *Voyage au Centre de la Terre* [*Voyage to the Center of the Earth*] (1864), *Vingt Mille Lieues sous les Mers* [*Twenty Thousand Leagues Under the Sea*] (1869), and *Le Tour du Mond en Quatre-Vingts Jours* [*Around the World in Eighty Days*] (1873).

1905 Mar. 26 **Maurice Barrymore** [nee Herbert Blythe] (b. 1847), a famous English actor and founder of an Anglo-American acting family of renown, died. He made his professional debut in England in 1875 and the same year went to America where he had great success, beginning with *Under the Gaslight*. Barrymore performed with many of the leading ladies of the day in such plays as *The Heart of Maryland*. In 1876 he married Georgiana Drew (1856–July 2, 1893), daughter of the well-known stage personalities John and Luisa Lane Drew. The Barrymores had three children, all of whom became noted stage and movie performers: Lionel (1878–1954), Ethel (1879–1959), and John (1882–1942).

1905 June The **first nickelodeon theater** opened in Pittsburgh, Pennsylvania, where **John P. Harris** and **Harry Davis** (1861–Jan. 2, 1940) had rebuilt the inside of an old storeroom, with the showing of *The Great Train Robbery*, the first film to have a strong story line.

1905 Oct. 13 **Henry Irving** [orig.: John Henry Brodribb] (b. Feb. 6, 1838), who as actor and manager (1878–1903) of the Lyceum Theater in London, dominated the stage there, died. Irving made his professional debut on Sept. 29, 1856, and achieved stardom in 1871 with his performance in *The Bells*. With **Ellen Terry** as his leading lady he became a champion of the star system. His production (1881) of

Othello was one of his triumphs. In it he alternated with **Edwin Booth** in the roles of Iago and Othello. His troupe was very popular when it toured the U.S.

VI. SPORTS, GAMES, AND SOCIETY

1905 The **Intercollegiate Association Football League** was formed in the U.S. by five universities: Columbia, Cornell, Harvard, Haverford, and Pennsylvania. The first league competition (1906) was won by Haverford. Yale joined the league in May 1907.

1906

I. DISASTERS

1906 Mar. 10 An **explosion in a coal mine** at **Courrières**, near Lille in northern France, buried and killed 1,060 miners.

1906 Apr. 6 **Mount Vesuvius**, near Naples in southern Italy, erupted, destroying several towns. The mountain lost more than 600 feet in height.

1906 Apr. 18 A severe **earthquake struck San Francisco**, California, in the early morning hours, immediately destroying many buildings. The worst damage, however, came from the many fires that broke out after gas lines were ruptured. Fire destroyed nearly 500 blocks, about 500 people died, c.25,000 buildings were demolished, and c.225,000 people were left homeless.

1906 Aug. 16 Valparaiso and Santiago in Chile were hit hard by an **earthquake**. The death toll reached 20,000, and property damage was estimated at $300 million.

II. POLITICS AND WAR

1906 Jan. 12 A **British general election gave a landslide victory to the Liberal government**, headed by **Henry Campbell-Bannerman**, the prime minister, who initiated an era of unprecedented reform. The Liberals abandoned *laissez-faire* and strove to regulate the new society for the benefit of all.

1906 Jan 29 **Christian IX** (b. Apr. 8, 1818), king of Denmark (from 1863), died. Early in his reign (1864) war with Prussia and Austria resulted in the loss of

the duchies of Schleswig, Holstein, and Lauenburg to Prussia. His reign was marked by agitation for a more liberal constitution. Christian was succeeded (to 1912) by his son **Frederick VIII**.

1906 Mar. 7 **Finland** became the **first nation to grant women suffrage** when it gave the vote to all citizens more than 24 years old. On March 15 women won their first seats in the Finnish Parliament. Most of them belonged to the majority Social Democratic party.

1906 Apr. 7 The **Act of Algeciras** resolved the **First Moroccan Crisis** by reaffirming the independence and sovereignty of Morocco and announcing the principle of Morocco's commercial equality with the rival great powers. The act provided for a Franco-Spanish police force in Morocco and substantial control of Moroccan policy by the two countries.

1906 May 6 The **Fundamental Laws**, clarifying the **October Manifesto of 1905**, were issued by **Nicholas II**, czar of Russia, who at the same time reinstated most of his former imperial powers. These laws could not be changed without the czar's consent. He established a State Council, which was to act as the upper house of Russia's parliament; he appointed one-half of its members, the other half was elected by special groups favoring the imperial policy. On July 22 Nicholas dissolved the **Duma** and then ruthlessly repressed dissent throughout the country. However, he permitted a second Duma to meet on Mar. 5, 1907; but it too was dismissed quickly, on June 16. Later in the same year a third Duma, entirely controlled by the government was established; it lasted until 1912.

1906 May 19 **Carlos I**, king of **Portugal**, appointed as prime minister **Jõao Franco** (Feb. 14, 1855–Apr. 4, 1929), an unequivocal monarchist who established a virtual dictatorship. Parliamentary government was suspended, the press censored, and opposition republicans suppressed.

1906 July 12 The **Dreyfus Affair**, which had kept France in an uproar for more than a dozen years, ended when the supreme court of appeals [Cour de cassation] exonerated Alfred Dreyfus, who had been the central figure in the affair. After the court's action, Dreyfus was promoted to major and awarded the Legion of Honor. An immediate result of the affair was to bring the French left to power in government. Of more permanent importance was the decline of the influence of the military, clerical, and anti-Semitic forces. Church and state had been officially separated (July 3, 1905) the year before Dreyfus's final vindication.

1906 Sept. **China's imperial court agreed to adopt a constitution.** In Aug., 1908, the government set forth an outline of principles to be addressed by the constitution, which was to be completed and adopted in nine years. In Oct., 1907, popularly-elected provincial assemblies, designed to be consultative only, convened. In Oct., 1910, a national assembly, half-elected (some groups were barred from voting) and half-appointed, convened.

1906 Sept. 29 In the face of a liberal rebellion against the government of Tomás Estrada Palma, president of **Cuba**, **U.S. forces occupied** the country at the request of Estrada and organized a provisional government, headed by **William Howard Taft**, who became president of the U.S. in 1909. The intervention secured massive investments made by American firms in Cuba.

1906 Oct. 1 The **boundary of the Sinai Peninsula**, which had never been fixed, was agreed upon by Egypt, Turkey, and Great Britain. The peninsula remained in Turkish hands and its eastern boundary was a straight line drawn from Rafa, on the Mediterranean coast, to Aqaba, at the head of the Gulf of Aqaba.

1906 Oct. 18 **George Clemenceau**, a leading French politician and statesman, became premier

for the first time. During his term in office the alliance with Great Britain was strengthened but on July 20, 1909, the harsh measures he used against striking miners, including the use of troops, brought about his downfall. He was succeeded by **Aristide Briand** (Mar. 28, 1862–Mar. 7, 1932).

1906 Dec. 30 **Persia** [present Iran] was granted its first constitution by **Muzaffar-ed-Din** (Mar. 25, 1853–Jan. 8, 1907), shah of Persia (from 1896). The shah, recalling the assassination of his father **Nasir-ud-Din** (ruled 1848–1896), acted when rebels in Teheran who, in large numbers, took refuge in various buildings, including the British embassy, demanded reforms. The Persian assembly, the **Majli**, became a parliament.

III. ECONOMY AND TRADE

1906 In **Algeria a railroad was completed** between Oran and Colomb-Béchar in the northwestern Sahara. The route provided a base for the future French occupation of Morocco.

1906 Sept. **China** issued an imperial order **designed to end the opium trade.** In 1907 Great Britain agreed to reduce its importation into China from India while **China restricted its poppy cultivation.** The program was clearly a success by 1911, and Great Britain agreed to keep opium from India out of the provinces no longer growing poppies.

1906 Dec. 21 The **Trade Disputes Act** exempted unions in Great Britain from liability when sued for damages caused by its agents during a strike. The new Trade Disputes Act also legalized picketing.

IV. RELIGION AND PHILOSOPHY

1906 The **Muslim League** was founded in India by **Aga Khan III** [Aga Sultan Sir Mahomed Shah] (Nov. 2, 1877–July 11, 1957), leader of the Nizari Ismaili Muslims, to protect the rights of Muslims in India. Through these actions this minority group gained political representation and a role in political affairs.

V. SCIENCE, EDUCATION, AND TECHNOLOGY

1906 The **Wassermann test** for diagnosing **syphilis** was developed by **August von Wassermann** (Feb. 21, 1866–Mar. 15, 1925), a German bacteriologist, and

Albert [Ludwig Siegmund] **Neisser** (Jan. 22, 1885–July 30, 1916), a German dermatologist, who had discovered (1879) the syphilis bacterium.

1906 Walther Hermann Nernst (June 25, 1864–Nov. 18, 1941), a German chemist and physicist, formulated the **third law of thermodynamics**. His studies of thermodynamics, the science of the nature of heat and its conversion to chemical, mechanical, and electrical energy, resulted in his postulating that if absolute zero could be reached, all bodies would have the same energy and could exist in only one state.

1906 Feb. 10   Great Britain launched *HMS Dreadnought* which became the prototype of a new warship, more powerful than any ever previously built. It could travel at a speed of 21 knots and had 10 12-inch guns placed in turrets.

1906 Apr. 19   Pierre Curie (b. May 15, 1859), a French chemist, died after being struck by a horse-drawn streetcar in Paris. One of his most significant contributions to physics was the discovery of the **Curie point**, the temperature at which magnetic properties of substances change.

1906 May 19   The Simplon Tunnel, the longest railway tunnel in the world, 12.3 miles in length under the Lepontine Alps, was opened. It connects Brig, Switzerland, with Isella, Italy, and passes 7,000 feet under the top of Mt. Leone at a maximum elevation of 2,313 feet.

1906 June 30   The Pure Food and Drug Act was passed by the U.S. Congress. It was the first comprehensive legislation to regulate the adulteration and fraudulent labeling of food.

VI. ARTS AND LEISURE

1906   *Tears of Blood* by **Yi Injik** (1862–1916), the **first modern novel in Korean**, was serialized in a newspaper in that country. Yi has been called Korea's most important modern writer.

1906   *Jayatissa and Roslin* by **Piyádasa Sirisena** (1875–1946), the first by Ceylon's first major novelist, was published in that country.

1906 Mar. 1   José Mariá de Pereda (b. Feb. 6, 1833), a Spanish novelist, died. His *Men of Property* (1874) was considered the first realistic Spanish novel. Among his other works were ***Don Gonzalo Gonzalez*** (1878) and ***Ascent to the Heights*** (1895).

1906 May 23   Henrik Johan Ibsen (b. Mar. 20, 1828), a Norwegian playwright, died. His influential plays, marked by social criticism, included ***Peer Gynt*** (1867), ***The League of Youth*** (1869), ***A Doll's House*** (1879), ***Ghosts*** (1881), ***An Enemy of the People*** (1882), ***The Wild Duck*** (1884), and ***Hedda Gabler*** (1890).

1906 Oct. 22   Paul Cézanne (b. Jan. 19, 1839), a French postimpressionist painter, died. Cézanne developed a style based on the use of planes, defined by variations in coloring, which lent an open, airy quality to his works. A 1907 posthumous retrospective exhibition at the Autumn Salon made Cézanne famous. His works included ***Maison du Pendu á Auvers-sur-Oise*** (1873), ***Still Life With a Fruit Basket*** (1890), ***The Bathers*** (1898–1905), ***Mont Sainte-Victoire*** (c.1906), and many notable landscapes of the region around Aix-en-Provence, southern France, where he lived most of his life.

VII. SPORTS, GAMES AND SOCIETY

1906   The first French Grand Prix auto race was run at Le Mans, France. Hitherto the Gordon Bennet Trophy Race had been the leading such event, but French manufacturers decided to boycott it because no more than three cars per manufacturer were allowed to compete. The Le Mans race was run again in 1907 and 1908 and then not until 1912. Today the "**24 hours of Le Mans**," as it is often called, and the Indianapolis 500 in the U.S. are the best-known auto racing events.

1906   Rugby became popular at colleges on the U.S. Pacific coast, following the example of Stanford University in California, during the two-year period in which mass formation football was in bad repute for the injuries incurred.

1906 Jan. 12   The American Intercollegiate Football Rules committee was created at the insistence of **Theodore Roosevelt**, president of the U.S., and others disturbed by the fatalities and permanent injuries caused by the "flying wedge" type of football. The rules were revised to limit "mass momentum" plays and to permit the forward pass, hitherto proscribed.

1906 Feb. 23   The **heavyweight boxing champion-ship of the world** was won at Los Angeles by **Tommy Burns** [Noah Brusso] (June 17, 1881–May 10, 1955),

a Canadian, who defeated **Marvin Hart** (Sept. 16, 1876–Sept. 17, 1931), an American, in a match that went 20 rounds.

1907

I. DISASTERS

1907 Jan. 14   Kingston, Jamaica, in the West Indies, was struck by an **earthquake** and nearly destroyed. The death toll was c.1,400.

1907 Dec. 6   An **explosion in a coal mine in Monongah, West Virginia**, killed 361 persons. Thirteen days later, an explosion in a mine at Jacobs Creek, Pennsylvania, took 239 lives.

II. POLITICS AND WAR

1907   In an informal **Gentlemen's Agreement between Japan and the U.S.**, Japan agreed to curtail emigration to the U.S. rather than have its people sent back to Japan.

1907 Feb. 26   In the British colony of the **Transvaal**, southern Africa, the **Het Volk party** won an election and **Louis Botha** (Sept. 27, 1862–Aug. 27, 1919) became the prime minister (to 1910). Thus the **Boers**, defeated in the Boer War (1899–1902), regained some power. The new government passed (Mar. 22) an **Asiatic Registration Bill** restricting immigration from India, and it decided (June 14) to repatriate c.50,000 Chinese who had earlier been brought in as laborers.

1907 June 15–Oct. 18   The **Second International Peace Conference** failed in its main purpose of reducing world armaments, but did make some progress on other matters. The 46 participating nations adopted some new rules of war: the prohibition of aerial bombardment and the use of submarine mines and poison gas. The rights of neutral shipping were stated as were the rights of noncombatants.

1907 Aug. 31   An **Anglo-Russian Entente** was signed to settle the difference of interests between Great Britain and Russia in the countries of Persia [present Iran], Afghanistan, and Tibet, where they wished to block German influence. The two powers

withdrew from Tibet, which remained under Chinese control, and Russia recognized the British predominance in Afghanistan. Persia was divided into a Russian in the north, and British in the south, spheres of influence. Thus, Russia aligned itself with England and France against Germany, Austria, and Italy.

1907 Sept. 26   **New Zealand was granted dominion status**, joining Canada and Australia.

1907 Nov. 16   **Oklahoma** was the 46th state admitted to the U.S., complete with Indian territories but with no vote for the Indians.

1907 Dec. 8   **Oscar II** (b. Jan. 21, 1829), king of Sweden (from 1872), died. Though he had hoped it would continue, the **union of Sweden and Norway ended** (1905) during his reign. Oscar II was succeeded by his son **Gustav V**.

1907 Dec. 16   Sixteen American battleships—"**The Great White Fleet**"—left Hampton Roads, Virginia, on a round-the-world cruise ordered by **Theodore Roosevelt**, president of the U.S. The fleet and its sailors were greeted enthusiastically in many ports, including those in Japan, Australia, and Gibraltar. The ships arrived back in Hampton Roads on Feb. 22, 1909, having demonstrated that the U.S. was a major naval power.

III. ECONOMY AND TRADE

1907 Oct. 22   The **Panic of 1907** was set off when the **Knickerbocker Trust Company** in New York City closed its doors, fearing a run. Other banks also failed and there was unease in the stock market. The panic ended only after **J. Pierpont Morgan**, the leading banker and capitalist of the period, on Nov. 14 convinced other important bankers and financiers to pledge enough money to restore confidence in the banks.

IV. RELIGION AND PHILOSOPHY

1907 The **Free Synagogue of New York City**, a Jewish Reform synagogue, was founded by **Stephen Samuel Wise** (Mar. 17, 1874–Apr. 19, 1949), a Hungarian-born rabbi from Portland, Oregon. Wise energetically promoted **Zionism**, world peace efforts, the labor movement, civic reform, and broader education for the rabbinate.

1907 July 4 **Pope Pius X** issued a decree *Lamentabili* and this year also issued an encyclical *Pascendi*, both of which condemned religious "modernism," which he declared to be the "synthesis of all heresies." A very conservative man, Pius believed secular movements were threatening the authority and influence of the Roman Catholic Church.

V. SCIENCE, EDUCATION, AND TECHNOLOGY

1907 The British luxury liner the *Mauretania* was launched, initiating the era of the great trans-Atlantic cruise ships. Able to attain a speed of 25 knots, she was the fastest liner of her time.

1907 **Bakelite**, a synthetic resin that could be used as a substitute for hard rubber or celluloid, was developed by **Leo Hendrick [Hendrik] Baekeland** (Nov. 14, 1863–Feb. 23, 1944), a Belgian-born American inventor.

1907 **Maria Montessori** (Aug. 31, 1870–May 6, 1952), an Italian educator and physician, opened her first school in Rome for normal children. Here she developed teaching methods that spread to many parts of the world. The **first woman in Italy to earn a medical degree** (1894), she had first worked with subnormal children and had tried her ideas on them. Basically, she believed in self-motivation, encouraging children to use the materials which were provided in order to achieve a favorable educational environment.

1907 Mar. 18 **Eugène Marcelin Berthelot** (b. Oct. 25, 1827), a French chemist, died. Berthelot developed techniques for synthesizing organic substances that did not occur in nature and for producing organic compounds which were not a part of any organism. He synthesized alcohol in 1855, methane in 1858, and acetylene and benzene in 1866.

1907 Dec. 17 **William Thomson** (b. June 26, 1924), 1st Baron Kelvin, a British mathematician and physicist, died. He was best known for his work on heat and electricity. By coordinating the theories of other scientists Lord Kelvin established for good the **law of the conservation of energy**. He also inaugurated the Kelvin scale, or absolute scale of temperature, in which the lowest mark, zero, is absolute zero.

VI. ARTS AND LEISURE

1907 *The Quilt*, by **Tayama Katai** [orig.: Tayama Rokuya] (Dec. 13, 1871–May 13, 1930), was published, marking a turning point in the development of **naturalistic fiction in Japan**. Before Katai, Japanese novels were highly stylized and unrealistic; Katai's work, modeled on the French novel, introduced realism to Japanese literature.

1907 The unique haiku-influenced novel *Kusamakura* by **Natsume Soseki** [orig.: Natsume Kinosuke] (Feb. 9, 1867–Dec. 9, 1916) was published in Japan. Soseki was the author of eight important novels dealing with the plight of the early 20th-century modern Japanese in a drastically changing culture.

1907 Jan. 26 The opening performance of *The Playboy of the Western World* by **John Millington Synge** at Dublin's Abbey Theater caused an uproar which was repeated over the next several performances.

1907 Feb. 16 **Giosuè Carducci** (b. July 27, 1835), an Italian anti-romantic poet who returned to the classical tradition, died. Carducci first came into prominence as a result of his anti-papal work *Inno a Satana* [*Hymn to Satan*] (1865). Other works by Carducci included *Odi Barbare* [*Barbaric Odes*] (1877–1887) and *Rime Nuovo* (1897). He was awarded the **Nobel prize for literature** in 1906.

1907 May 12 **Joris Karl Huysmans** [Charles Marie Georges Huysmans] (b. Feb. 5, 1848), a French writer, died. His most famous work was a novel *A Rebours* [*Against the Grain, Against Nature*] (1884) about fin-de-siècle aesthetic decadence. His other works included *Là-Bas* (1891), about his spiritual world.

1907 Aug. 3 **Augustus Saint-Gaudens** (b. Mar. 1, 1848), one of the foremost American sculptors of the late 19th century, died. Among his works were *Farragut*, Madison Square, New York City; *Shaw Me-*

morial, Boston Common, Boston, Massachusetts; *Amor Caritas*, Luxembourg Gardens, Paris; *Lincoln* in Lincoln Park, Chicago, Illinois; and a memorial to Mrs. Henry Adams [*Grief*], Rock Creek Cemetery, Washington, D.C.

1907 Aug. 30   Richard Mansfield (b. May 24, 1854), an English and American actor, died. He appeared on the English stage (1877–1882), then went to the U.S. Mansfield staged the first American production (1895) of **Shaw's** *Arms and the Man* (1894) and the first English production (1906) of **Ibsen's** *Peer Gynt* (1867).

1907 Sept. 4   Edvard [Hagerup] **Grieg** (b. June 15, 1843), generally viewed as the Norwegian national composer, died. He wrote more than 100 Norwegian folk songs and lieder [with German text]. His first successful composition was the Concerto in A Minor (1869), for which he was the solo pianist in its first production. Grieg wrote the incidental music for *Peer Gynt* in 1876, which became an instant success and made him famous.

1907 Sept. 7   Sully Prudhomme [René François Armand Prudhomme] (b. Mar. 16, 1830), a French poet and member of the **Parnassians**, who were in revolt against what they saw as the excesses of romanticism, died. Prudhomme was awarded the first **Nobel prize for literature** in 1901.

1907 Nov. 13   Francis Thompson (b. Dec. 18, 1859), an English poet, died. His best-known poem was "The Hound of Heaven," published in *Poems* (1893). His other collections included *Sister Songs* (1895) and *New Poems* (1897).

VII. SPORTS, GAMES, AND SOCIETY

1907 Aug. 10   The longest and most difficult automobile race to date ended in Paris when Prince Borghese of Italy arrived from Peking. The race had begun on June 10, and the winner drove the c.8000-mile route in 62 days. The drivers had to cross such obstacles as the Gobi Desert.

1908

I. VITAL STATISTICS AND DEMOGRAPHICS

1908   Since the first c.2,000 whites settled (1840) in **New Zealand**, the population had expanded greatly. For some time the increase was due mainly to immigration, the population reaching c.100,000 as early as 1861. In mid-1908 an official estimate put the population at 950,000.

II. DISASTERS

1908 Mar. 4   A fire at the Lake View School in Collingwood, Ohio, a suburb of Cleveland, killed 161 children and teachers, the highest death toll in a school fire in U.S. history.

1908 June 30   An explosion in Siberia knocked down trees in a pattern radiating out for over a 30-mile radius. Forty miles away people were struck unconscious. Some scientists believed that this explosion was caused by a falling fragment of a meteorite.

1908 Sept.   An epidemic of **Asiatic cholera** was in full swing in Russia with 7102 deaths already reported. In St. Petersburg alone nearly 5,000 cases were recorded and c.1,875 deaths.

1908 Sept. 17   The first fatal military aircraft accident occurred at Fort Meyer, Virginia, when a plane piloted by **Orville Wright** crashed during an exhibition flight, killing the passenger, Lieutenant **Thomas Selfridge**. Wright escaped with injuries.

1908 Dec. 28   An earthquake rocked Messina in Sicily, killing more than 83,000 people and destroying 90 percent of its buildings.

III. EXPLORATION AND COLONIZATION

1908 Apr. 21   Frederick Albert Cook (June 10, 1865–Aug. 5, 1940), an American physician and explorer, claimed he reached the **North Pole** on this date. Cook said he had reached the pole before **Robert Edwin Peary**. Although his assertions were not then believed, recent research indicates he may have been the first to reach the North Pole.

IV. POLITICS AND WAR

1908 Feb 1   Carlos I (b. Sept. 28, 1863), king of **Portugal** (from 1869), and his eldest son **Luís Filipe**, the crown prince, were assassinated by rifle fire in Lisbon. The ringleader of the assassins, a sergeant in the Portuguese army, was shot dead. Carlos was succeeded (to 1910) by his second son **Manuel II** (Nov. 15, 1889–July 2, 1932).

1908 Apr. 8   Herbert [Henry] **Asquith** became prime minister (to 1916) of Great Britain following the resignation (Apr. 5) for reasons of health of **Henry Campbell-Bannerman**. Asquith had been chancellor of the exchequer.

1908 June 24   [Stephen] **Grover Cleveland** (b. June 18, 1837), president of the U.S. (1885–1889 and 1893–1897), died. As president, he devoted himself largely to a fight for lower tariff rates but was not successful. Renominated in 1888, Cleveland made this the major issue, but he lost the election to the Republican candidate, **Benjamin Harrison**. Nominated for the third time in 1892, he won and became the **only person elected president for non-consecutive terms**.

1908 July 24   Abdul-Hamid II, the Ottoman sultan, acceded to the demands made by the **Young Turks**, and restored the constitution of 1876. The Young Turks had begun as the Secret Society of Union and Progress in the 1880s for the purpose of restoring the constitution, which Abdul-Hamid had increasingly undermined by curtailing free speech. Abdul-Hamid was deposed in 1909, and **Mohammed V** [Rashad] (Nov. 3, 1844–July 2, 1918), his brother, replaced him as sultan on Apr. 27.

1908 Oct. 5   The **Bulgarian principality**, supported by Austria, declared its full independence from the Ottoman Empire (1326–1920). Prince Ferdinand (Feb. 26, 1861–Sept. 10, 1948) established a monarchy and as **Ferdinand I** became the first king (1908–1918) of present Bulgaria.

1908 Oct. 6   The **Bosnian Crisis** was precipitated by Austria-Hungary's foreign minister, **Alois Lexa von Aehrenthal** (Sept. 27, 1854–Feb. 17, 1912), when he annexed Bosnia and Herzegovina [Hercegovina], Turkish provinces in the Balkans that Austria-Hungary had occupied since the **Treaty of Berlin** (1878), without first gaining Russia's consent. Serbia protested this action and prepared for war against Austria-Hungary but lost the support of Russia. As a result, the Serbs accepted the annexations.

1908 Oct. 12   The former Boer states [the Transvaal and the Orange Free State], defeated in the **Boer War** (1899–1902), met with Cape Colony and Natal and drafted a constitution creating the **Union of South Africa**, which went into effect May 31, 1910.

1908 Oct. 18   By action of the Belgian parliament, the **Congo Free State** [present Zaire] was annexed as the **Belgian Congo**. Prior to this the Congo had been the personal possession of **Leopold II**, king of the Belgians. Leopold's personal rule of the region became so scandalous that he had no choice but to turn the region over to his country.

1908 Nov. 14   The deaths of **Kuang Hsü** [Kwang Hsu, Tsai T'ien, or Glorious Succession] (b. Aug. 14, 1871), the Chinese emperor (from 1875), and **Tzu Hsi** [Tz'u-Hsi, Tze-Hsi, Yehonala, "Old Buddha"] (b. Nov. 29, 1835), the dowager empress, were announced. **Hsüan T'ung** [Hsüan-Te, P'u-I, P'u-U, P'u-Yi] (Feb. 7, 1906–Oct. 17, 1967), infant nephew of Kuang Hsü, was named the emperor (abdicated Feb. 12, 1912). Hsüan T'ung was the **last Manchu emperor**.

1908 Nov. 30   The **Root-Takahira Agreement** averted the possibility of war between the U.S. and Japan by declaring mutual respect for their possessions in the Pacific and acknowledging the integrity of China.

V. ECONOMY AND TRADE

1908 Feb. 3   In the so-called **Danbury Hatters' Case**, the U.S. Supreme Court ruled that a **secondary boycott by a labor union was restraint of trade** and thus that the **Sherman Antitrust Act** (1890) applied to labor as well as to capital. The court also held (Feb. 24) that an Oregon law limiting the number of hours women could work did not violate the liberty of contract provision of the Fourteenth Amendment.

1908 May 26   Oil was discovered in large deposits in southwestern Persia [Iran]. The oil boom began in southwestern Asia as oil was subsequently discovered in many of the Arabian countries.

1908 May 30   The U.S. Congress enacted the **Aldrich-Vreeland Act** to attempt to correct inadequacies in the nation's banking system that were disclosed by the **Panic of 1907**, which had been brought on by excessive speculation. The new law permitted banks to issue notes based on securities other than federal bonds, but levied a ten percent tax on such notes.

1908 The **Hejaz railroad** connecting Damascus, in present Syria, and Medina, in present Saudi Arabia, was completed. The railroad had been planned and financed by the Ottoman Turks, who held nominal suzerainty over the region.

1908 Sept. 16 The **General Motors Corporation** was established. Its chief founder was **William C[rapo] Durant** (Dec. 8, 1861–Mar. 18, 1947), who had organized a carriage manufacturing company in 1886 and had bought the **Buick Motor Car Company** in 1905. Within a few years General Motors acquired 11 other automobile companies, including Buick, Cadillac, Oakland, and Oldsmobile. In Nov. 1911, with **Louis Chevrolet** (Dec. 25, 1879–June 6, 1941), a racing car driver and auto designer, Durant founded the **Chevrolet Motor Company** which became part of General Motors in 1915.

VI. RELIGION AND PHILOSOPHY

1908 The **South India United Church** was formed by Christian congregations associated with the American Board of Commissioners for Foreign Missions, Church of Scotland, Dutch Reformed Church in America, London Missionary Society, and United Free Church of Scotland. In 1947 this Church joined with the Methodist Church and several dioceses of the [Anglican] Church of India, Burma, and Ceylon to form the **Church of South India**.

VII. SCIENCE, EDUCATION, AND TECHNOLOGY

1908 The **age of the true skyscraper** arrived with the completion in lower Manhattan, New York City, of the **Singer Building**. With its 47 stories it was 612 feet high, the tallest building in the world. Later in 1908 the **Metropolitan Life Tower**, also in New York City, of 50 stories topped off at 700 feet. The first generation of skyscrapers reached its climax in 1913 with the completion of the **Woolworth Building**, in New York City, which had 55 stories and a height of 760 feet.

1908 **Fritz Haber** (Dec. 9, 1868–Jan. 29, 1934), a German chemist, invented the Haber process for producing ammonia synthetically by mixing hydrogen and nitrogen gases under heat and pressure. It was the first high-pressure chemical process to have commercial importance, and it won for Haber the **Nobel prize for chemistry** in 1918. During World War I (1914–1918) Haber directed Germany's chemical warfare program, including the introduction of poison gas. After the Nazis attained power in Germany, Haber went (1933) into voluntary exile in England.

VIII. ARTS AND LEISURE

1908 Jan. 23 **Alexander Edward MacDowell** (b. Dec. 18, 1861), an American composer, died. His best-known longer work was the Piano Concerto in D minor (1889). After his death his widow established the **MacDowell Colony**, a retreat for composers and writers, at their home in Peterborough, New Hampshire.

1908 Feb. *The Eight*, a new realistic trend in American painting, opened an exhibit at the Macbeth Gallery in New York City. The artists showing in this exhibit were **Robert Henri**, their leader; **John French Sloan** (Aug. 2, 1871–Sept. 7, 1951); **George Benjamin Luks** (Aug. 13, 1867–Oct. 29, 1933); **Maurice Brazil Prendergast** (Oct. 10, 1859–Feb. 1, 1924); **Arthur Bowen Davies** (Sept. 26, 1862–Oct. 24, 1928); **William James Glackens** (Mar. 13, 1870–May 22, 1938); **Everett Shinn** (Nov. 7, 1876–May 1, 1953); and **Ernest Lawson** (1873–Dec. 18, 1939). The exhibition, which toured several American cities, was a one time affair, and the artists did not exhibit together again. This new movement in American art, which later included such artists as **George Bellows, Glen Coleman** (July 18, 1887–May 8, 1932), **Eugene Higgins** (Feb. 1874–Feb. 18, 1958), **Jerome Myers** (Mar. 20, 1867–June 19, 1940), and **Edward Hopper**, came to be called loosely the Ashcan School because of its realistic portrayal of urban life.

1908 June 21 **Nikolai Andreevich Rimski-Korsakov** [Rimsky-Korsakov] (b. Mar. 18, 1844), a Russian composer, died. His symphony [unnamed] (1865) and symphonic poem *Sadko* (1867) were the first symphonic works produced by a Russian. His operas included *Ivan the Terrible* (1873, revised in 1892), *The Snow Maiden* (1881), and *The Golden Cockerel* (1909). Rimski-Korsakov's orchestral piece

Scheherezade (1888) is perhaps still his best-known work.

1908 Dec. 28 **Henri Matisse**, a French painter, sculptor, and illustrator, published *Notes d'un peintre*, one of the seminal documents of modern art, in *La Grande Révieu*. In it Matisse set forth his own credo: to express in his work not only the emotion evoked in him by a subject, but also to express an attitude toward life.

IX. SPORTS, GAMES, AND SOCIETY

1908 Jan. 24 The **first Boy Scout Troop** was formed by **Robert Stephenson Smyth Baden-Powell** (Feb. 22, 1857–Jan. 8, 1941), inspector general for the British cavalry, whose *Scouting for Boys* (1908), based on his earlier *Aids to Scouting* (1899), had sparked the scouting movement. The code of ethics included the popular "daily good turn" and the motto "Be Prepared." On Feb. 8, 1910, the Boy Scouts of America was incorporated. In 1912 the **Girl Scouts** were formed in the U.S. by **Juliette**

Gordon Low (Oct. 31, 1860–Jan. 18, 1927), in Savannah, Georgia.

1908 Apr. 27–Oct. 31 The fourth Summer **Olympic Games** were held in London with 2,035 athletes from 23 nations competing. British athletes won 56 gold medals and 145 medals in all; the U.S. 23 and 47; Sweden 8 and 25. The games were well organized but there were many disputes over the way they were run because the British alone were in charge and others disliked the rules they established.

1908 Dec. 26 [John Arthur] **Jack Johnson** (Mar. 31, 1878–June 10, 1946) of Galveston, Texas, became the **first black to win the heavyweight boxing championship of the world** when he defeated **Tommy Burns** [born Noah Brusso] (June 7, 1881–May 10, 1955) of Canada. The fight took place in Sydney, Australia, and Johnson won by a technical knockout in the 14th round. Johnson held the title until Apr. 5, 1915, when he was knocked out in the 26th round at Havana, Cuba, by **Jess Willard** (Dec. 29, 1881–Dec. 15, 1968).

1909

I. DISASTERS

1909 Aug. 26 The **first wireless report of a tropical storm from a ship at sea** was received in New Orleans, Louisiana, in time to forecast its route. The *Cartago* in the Yucatan Channel near the Gulf of Mexico, had ridden out 100 mile-per-hour winds on Aug. 25. The crew reported the violent **hurricane**, which had already ravaged Puerto Rico and Haiti and was approaching Mexico and Texas. By Aug. 27 the storm had caused an estimated 1,500 deaths, mostly from floods.

II. EXPLORATION AND COLONIZATION

1909 Apr. 6 **Robert Edwin Peary** (May 6, 1856–Feb. 20, 1920), an American explorer, was the first man generally credited with reaching the **North Pole**. Recent analyses of Peary's log indicate that, because he may not have made adequate corrections for detours and his chronometer was ten minutes fast, he probably missed the Pole by 30 to 60 miles. Amid continuing controversy the **National Geographic Society** concluded (Dec. 11, 1989) that Peary

did indeed reach the pole. It was Peary's third attempt between 1898 and 1909.

1909 Jan. 9 **Ernest Henry Shackleton** (Feb. 15, 1874–Jan. 5, 1922) came within 100 miles of reaching the **South Pole**. In the meantime another member of Shackleton's British Antarctic expedition (1907–1909), T[annatt] W[illiam] **Edgeworth David** (Jan. 28, 1958–Aug. 28, 1934) led a party that located the South Magnetic Pole on Jan. 16, 1909, c.1,500 miles from the South Pole.

III. POLITICS AND WAR

1909 **Rafael Reyes** (Oct. 19, 1852–Feb. 19, 1921), president of **Colombia** (from 1904), was forced to resign his office and flee the country. Reyes had done much to improve the economic condition of the country but his signing of a treaty with the U.S. recognizing the independence of Panama resulted in his ouster.

1909 Mar. 2 **War between Austria and Serbia** over the annexation of **Bosnia-Herzegovina** by Austria on

Oct. 6, 1908, was averted by the intervention of other European powers.

1909 Mar. 4 **William Howard Taft** of the Republican party was inaugurated as the 27th president of the U.S., having defeated **William Jennings Bryan** of the Democratic party. In the election Nov. 3, 1908, Taft received 7,679,006 popular votes and 321 in the electoral college to 6,409,106 and 162 for Bryan. **James Schoolcraft Sherman** (Oct. 24, 1855–Oct. 3, 1912) served as vice president.

1909 Mar. 10 After negotiating a treaty with Siam [present Thailand], Great Britain established the **Unfederated Malay States** [now part of Malaysia].

1909 Apr. 13 **Armenians revolted against Ottoman rule** after the sultan's forces had massacred demonstrating Armenians in Adana [Seyhan] in southern Turkey. The reactionary measures taken by Abdul-Hamid II, the Ottoman sultan, resulted in his overthrow (Apr. 27) by the nationalist **Young Turks**. He was succeeded by a younger brother Mohammad V.

1909 Oct. 26 **Hirobumi Ito** (b. Oct. 14, 1841), by far the most important figure in the late-19th-century **modernization of Japan**, was assassinated by a Korean nationalist bitter over Japan's attempts to control his country. Ito's experiences in Europe convinced him that his country must adopt western ways. Ito was prime minister three times (1892–1896, 1898, 1900–1901). In 1905 Ito forced an agreement on Korea that made the country a virtual protectorate. His assassination provided a pretext for Japan to annex Korea outright.

1909 Dec. 17 **Leopold II** (b. Apr. 9, 1835), king of the Belgians (from 1865), died. He was succeeded (to 1934) by his nephew **Albert I**.

IV. ECONOMY AND TRADE

1909 Aug. 6 The **Payne Bill**, passed by the U.S. Congress, introduced trade privileges to the **Philippines**. In 1913 the **Underwood Act** provided for free trade between the U.S. and the islands. This remained in effect until Jan. 1, 1941.

V. SCIENCE, EDUCATION, AND TECHNOLOGY

1909 **Igor Ivan Sikorsky** (May 25, 1889–Oct. 26, 1972), a Russian-born aeronautical engineer, in 1919 came to the U.S. where he became a naturalized citizen and founded (1923) the **Sikorsky Aeroengineering Corporation** to manufacture planes of his design. In 1929 Sikorsky's company became part of the **United Aircraft Corporation**.

1909 **Paul Ehrlich** (Mar. 14, 1854–Aug. 20, 1915), a German bacteriologist, who was one of the **first to treat disease with chemicals**, discovered **salvarsan**, a chemical compound that can treat **syphilis**. It became known as "606," because it was the 606th compound he tried, and also as **"the magic bullet."** Ehrlich made valuable contributions in hematology and cellular pathology as well. For his work in general he shared the **Nobel prize for physiology** or medicine in 1908 with **Elie Metchnikoff** (May 15, 1845–July 16, 1916), a Ukrainian biologist, director of the Pasteur Institute in Paris, who also worked on problems of immunology.

1909 **Andrija Mohorovičić** (Jan. 23, 1857–Dec. 18, 1936), a Croation geophysicist, discovered the change that occurred in earthquakes c.18 miles below the earth's surface at the boundary between the earth's crust and mantle. At this point there was a sudden change in the velocity of earthquake waves. It became known as the Mohorovičić discontinuity, or simply "**Moho.**"

1909 July 25 The **first flight in a heavier-than-air craft** to cross the English Channel was made by the French pilot **Louis Blériot** (July 1, 1872–Aug. 2, 1936). He crossed the Channel from Calais, France, to Dover, England, in a 25-horsepower monoplane of his own design.

VI. ARTS AND LEISURE

1909 **Charles Pathé** (1864?–Dec. 25, 1957) exhibited the **first newsreel** in a Paris theater. In the following year he introduced the newsreel to the U.S., where it became popular accompanying feature-length films.

1909 Jan. 1 The **Motion Picture Patents Company** was formed by leading figures in the industry. They included the inventors **Thomas Alva Edison** and **Charles Pathé**, and representatives of such studios as Biograph. The Patents Company tried to prevent production of films by firms or individuals not holding a license with them.

1909 Feb. 20 The **Futurist Manifesto**, written by the Italian novelist **Emilio Filippo Tommaso Mari-**

netti (Dec. 28, 1876–Dec. 2, 1944), appeared in the Paris newspaper *Le Figaro*. The manifesto identified the futurists, chiefly an Italian school of artists, as possessing a love of recklessness; they glorified war and destruction of the past for their dynamic effects. The foremost futurist painting was *Dog on Leash* (1912), by **Giacomo Balla** (July 18, 1871–Mar. 1, 1958), which showed movement with a series of overlapping forms in different positions. Futurism waned in influence after World War I (1914–1918), but it was later identified with fascism when **Benito Mussolini** declared futurism the national art of Italy.

1909 Mar. 24 [Edmund] **John Millington Synge** (b. Apr. 26, 1871), a poet and dramatist and one of the leading figures of the Irish literary renaissance, died. Synge was best known for *The Playboy of the Western World*, which was first performed in 1907 by the Abbey Theater players. It received a riotous reception and caused much resentment on the part of Synge's fellow Irishmen, who reacted badly to his bitter humor. *Deirdre of the Sorrows*, a tragedy not quite finished when he died, was produced in 1910.

1909 Apr. 10 **Algernon Charles Swinburne** (b. Apr. 5, 1837), an English poet, died. He achieved his first fame with a verse drama *Atalanta in Calydon* (1865) and *Poems and Ballads* (1866). He was associated with the pre-Raphaelites William Morris and Dante Gabriel Rossetti.

1909 May 18 **Isaac** [Manuel Francisco] **Albéniz** (b. May 29, 1860), a Spanish composer, died. His piano works included *Iberia* (1906–1909). He also wrote operas and songs.

1909 May 18 **George Meredith** (b. Feb. 12, 1828), an English novelist and poet, died. His first novel *The Ordeal of Richard Feverel* (1859), admired by fellow writers, was not popular. Meredith became better known with the success of his novels *Beauchamp's Career* (1876), *The Egoist* (1879), and *Diana of the Crossways* (1885).

1909 July 22 [Friedrich Adolf Axel] **Detlev Freiherr von Liliencron** (b. June 3, 1844), a German writer, died. He was considered one of the early founders of impressionism.

1909 Oct. 8 **Naphtali Herz Imber** (b. Dec. 27, 1856), a Hebrew poet and scholar, died. Born in Poland, Imber lived in the U.S. after 1892. He was remembered for his hymn "ha-Tiqwa" ["The Hope," "Hatikvah"], which became (1933) the hymn of the Zionist movement and after 1948 the unofficial national anthem of Israel.

VII. SPORTS, GAMES, AND SOCIETY

1909 Great Britain's polo team was defeated by the U.S. team, led by **Harry Payne Whitney** (Oct. 29, 1872–Oct. 26, 1930), at Hurlingham, near Buenos Aires, Argentina. It was the first time the U.S. polo team had captured the **American Polo Cup** since it was given in 1886, when a British team visited America.

1909 Aug. 23 The first race for the **Gordon Bennett Cup** for speed in powered flight was won by a plane flown by an American **Glenn H. Curtiss**, at Rheims, France. He flew the 20-km. course at an average speed of 47 mph.

1910

I. VITAL STATISTICS AND DEMOGRAPHICS

1910 The population of the **world** was c.1,522,200,000. The populations, in round figures, of the major regions of the world were: **Africa,** 127,000,000; **Asia,** 850,000,000; **Australasia,** 5,200,000; **Europe,** 380,000,000; **North America,** 115,000,000; and **South and Central America,** 45,000,000. The population of the U.S. was 92,228,496. Fourteen of the world's cities had populations (in descending order) of more than one million: New York, London, Paris, Chicago, Tokyo, Berlin, Vienna, St. Petersburg, Philadelphia, Moscow, Osaka, Canton, Buenos Aires, and Calcutta.

II. DISASTERS

1910–1911 In Manchuria c.60,000 people perished from **pneumonic plague**, the greatest known epidemic of this type of plague, usually transmitted by airborne droplets, as when a victim coughs.

1910 Jan. 26 In **France**, after a week of hard, steady rain, many Paris streets were flooded, rail lines were shut down, and food and drinking water were becoming scarce.

1910 Mar. 1 At Wellington, Washington state, an avalanche swept two trains into a canyon, killing 96 persons.

1910 Aug. 10 After a severe typhoon, parts of Japan were suffering widespread flood conditions. It was estimated that 500 people had been killed and c.400,000 made homeless.

III. POLITICS AND WAR

1910 Jan. 15 The French colonies of Chad, Gabon, the Middle Congo, and Ubangui-Shari were administratively joined as **French Equatorial Africa** with Brazzaville as capital.

1910 May 1 The National Association for the Advancement of Colored People [**NAACP**] was founded by eight prominent Americans, of whom one was black. He was **W**[illiam] **E**[dward] **B**[urghardt] **Du Bois** (Feb. 23, 1868–Aug. 27, 1963), a college professor and writer. The NAACP grew rapidly in size and influence, with both whites and blacks participating in its activities.

1910 May 6 **Edward VII** (b. Nov. 9, 1841), king of Great Britain and Ireland and emperor of India (from 1901), died. Nearly 60 before he succeeded to the throne, he was known chiefly as a sportsman, a leader of British high society, and an avid pursuer of love affairs. Although Edward's reign was a short one, this era of hedonistic elegance became known as the Edwardian Age. He was succeeded by his second son, **George V**.

1910 May 31 The **Union of South Africa**, with dominion status in the British Empire, came into being by act of the British Parliament. The new dominion consisted of the provinces of Cape Colony, Natal, the Orange Free State, and the Transvaal. In the first election (Sept. 15), the South African party, nationalistic and led by Boers, defeated the Union party, which represented British imperialist interests. The South African party was led by **Louis Botha**, who became the first prime minister (to 1919) when the Parliament first met on Dec. 17.

1910 Aug. 22 **Japan officially annexed Korea** as the puppet Korean emperor signed the final treaty recognizing this act. Korea was renamed **Chosen** [Korean: Choson] and was occupied for 35 years by Japan.

1910 Aug. 28 **Nicholas I** [Petrovic Njeges] (Oct. 7, 1841–Mar. 1, 1921), who had succeeded (Aug. 14, 1860) his uncle Danilo I as prince of Montenegro, proclaimed himself **king of Montenegro**. The independence of the country from the Ottoman Empire (1326–1920) had been recognized by the Congress of Berlin (1878).

1910 Oct. The Mexican Revolution (1910–1915), also called the Mexican Civil War, began with the **Plan of San Luis Potosí**, drafted by **Francisco** [Indalecio] **Madero**. Madero called for an armed uprising against the regime of **Porfirio Díaz**, president of Mexico (from 1877; as dictator from 1884), on Nov. 20. The uprising was successful and Díaz resigned on May 25, 1911; Madero was elected president (to 1913) and assumed office on Nov. 6, 1911.

1910 Oct. 5 After a successful revolt led by the army and navy, a republic was declared in **Portugal**, and [Joaquim] **Teófilo** [Fernandes] **Braga**, a noted author, poet, and scholar, was proclaimed interim president. Carlos I, king of Portugal (1889–1908), had aroused republican sentiment by suspending Portugal's constitution in 1907. **Manuel II**, who succeeded Carlos, had fled the previous day (Oct. 4) to England. A new liberal constitution was promulgated in 1911.

1910 Nov. 25 On his 75th birthday, the American multimillionaire industrialist and philanthropist, **Andrew Carnegie**, announced the founding of the **Carnegie Endowment for International Peace** with a fund of $10,000,000. The charter stated that once universal peace was established the endowment was to be "devoted to the banishment of the next most degrading evil or evils."

IV. ECONOMY AND TRADE

1910 **Elizabeth Arden** [orig.: Florence Nightingale Graham] (1887–Oct. 18, 1966), a Canadian-born entrepreneur, opened her first beauty salon on Fifth Avenue in New York City. She was the first major figure in the American cosmetics industry.

1910 Apr. 28 The **People's Budget** was passed by the British Parliament. David Lloyd George (Jan. 17,

1863–Mar. 26, 1945), chancellor of the exchequer (1908–1915), had introduced the budget, a decisive step toward the **Welfare State** in Great Britain. It called for a progressive increase in taxes to finance the Liberal government's growing system of social programs. Approved by the Commons on Nov. 4, 1909, the budget was rejected by the House of Lords on Nov. 30. After an election (Jan., 1910) based primarily on this issue, in which the Liberals again won a majority, the Commons again approved the budget, unopposed this time by the Lords.

1910 June 18   The **Mann-Elkins Act**, passed by the U.S. Congress, gave the Interstate Commerce Commission [**ICC**] authority over the telephone, telegraph, cable, and wireless companies. The **Esch-Cummins Act** [Transportation Act] of 1920 extended this authority to include the railroads.

1910 July 1   The U.S. **Bureau of Mines** was established under the Department of the Interior with full investigative powers to study and regulate mining safety. American mining fatalities, increasing steadily since 1890, had peaked in 1907 with c.920 deaths.

V. RELIGION AND PHILOSOPHY

1910 Dec. 4   **Mary Baker Eddy** [nee Mary Morse Baker] (b. July 16, 1821), an American religious leader and founder of Christian Science, died. Mrs. Eddy in 1875 published *Science and Health,* the textbook of the Church of Christ, Scientist, which she founded in 1879. The basis of Christian Science is faith healing, and illness is called an illusion that the mind can overcome.

VI. SCIENCE, EDUCATION, AND TECHNOLOGY

1910   The first volume of *Principia Mathematica* by **Bertrand Russell** and **Alfred North Whitehead** appeared in England and was at once recognized as a classic in mathematical logic, although it was not suitable reading for the casual layman. The third volume appeared in 1913.

1910   For the first time a scientist demonstrated that a cancerous tumor was caused by a virus. The scientist was **Francis Peyton Rous** (Oct. 5, 1879–Feb. 16, 1970), an American bacteriologist. Rous's investigation was carried out using a tumor found in a chicken. Rous was the joint winner of the **Nobel prize for physiology or medicine** in 1966.

1910   The *Casa Milá* apartment building was completed in Barcelona, Spain, toward the end of the Art Nouveau period. Designed by the Spanish architect **Antoni Gaudí** [y Cornet] (June 26, 1852–June 7, 1926), this extraordinary building took the form of a series of undulating curves; within the overall shape, each apartment was constructed in a different shape and size.

1910 May 18   **Halley's Comet** made its closest approach to the earth. It caused widespread fear in the U.S. and other parts of the world when it began to appear in the sky, as it does approximately every three-quarters of a century. This time it was closer to the earth than on other appearances and there were those who believed its fiery tail would destroy the earth. "Comet pills" that would supposedly protect one from the comet's otherwise fatal effects were sold.

1910 May 27   [Heinrich Hermann] **Robert Koch** (b. Dec. 11, 1843), a German pioneer in bacteriology, died. In 1876 he was the first scientist to isolate a pure culture of the anthrax bacillus. Koch also later isolated the tubercle and cholera bacilli. Koch was awarded the **Nobel prize for physiology or medicine** in 1905 for his work in developing tuberculin as a treatment for tuberculosis.

1910 Aug. 13   **Florence Nightingale** (b. May 15, 1820), best-remembered for her services in caring for British wounded and ill soldiers during the Crimean War (1853–1856), died. After that war the Nightingale School and Home for training nurses was founded in London. In 1907 she became the first woman awarded the **British Order of Merit**.

1910 Aug. 26   **William James** (b. Jan. 11, 1842), an American psychologist and philosopher, and brother of the writer Henry James, died. From 1872 he was a lecturer in anatomy and physiology at Harvard, where he introduced experimental psychology for the first time in the U.S. *The Principles of Psychology* (1890) expressed James's views on scientific methodology in the study of psychology. James turned to religion and philosophy to address such questions as free will, determinism, freedom, and the existence of God, which resulted in *The Varieties of Religious Experience* (1902), *Pragmatism* (1907), *The Meaning of Truth* (1909), and *Some Problems in Philosophy* (1911).

1910 Nov. 14   The first flight of an airplane from the deck of a ship took place in Chesapeake Bay, an inlet of the Atlantic Ocean, with a takeoff from the U.S. Navy's scout cruiser **Birmingham.** On Jan. 8, 1911, in San Francisco Bay, California, a plane landed successfully on the deck of a ship, the **Pennsylvania.**

VII. ARTS AND LEISURE

1910 *Der Blaue Reiter* [*The Blue Rider*], a book by **Franz Marc**, a German painter written in collaboration with **Wassily** [Vasili] **Kandinsky**, a Russian painter, appeared in Munich, Germany. It gave its name to one of the many post-impressionist schools of painting. The **Blaue Reiter school** promoted many seminal artists, among them Kandinsky and Paul Klee.

1910 An exhibition of modern art at gallery "291" [291 Fifth Avenue], the **Alfred Stieglitz** (Jan. 1, 1864–July 13, 1946) **Photo-Secession Gallery** in New York City, opened. Works were first displayed in the U.S. by **Gaston Lachaise** (Mar. 1, 1882–Oct. 18, 1935), **John Marin** (Dec. 23, 1870–Oct. 1, 1953), **Joseph Stella** (May 13, 1877–Nov. 5, 1946), **Max Weber** (Apr. 18, 1881–Oct. 4, 1961), and **William Zorach** (Feb. 28, 1887–Nov. 16, 1966).

1910 Apr. 21 Mark Twain [Samuel Langhorne Clemens] (b. Nov. 30, 1835), America's great humorist and writer, died. Known best for *The Adventures of Tom Sawyer* (1876) and *The Adventures of Huckleberry Finn* (1885), Twain also wrote *The Prince and the Pauper* (1882), *A Connecticut Yankee in King Arthur's Court* (1889), and the semi-autobiographical *Life on the Mississippi* (1883). Twain's fame as a humorist had been established earlier by a short story, "The Celebrated Jumping Frog of Calaveras County" (1865), and by *Innocents Abroad* (1869), a collection of hilarious letters describing a trip to Europe.

1910 Apr. 26 Bjørnstjerne Martinius Bjørson (b. Dec. 8, 1832), a Norwegian poet, author, orator, and political leader, died. His plays were considered among the earliest important native Norwegian dramas. Among his plays were *Between the Battles* (1857), *A Bankruptcy* (1875), *Beyond Human Power* (1883), and *When the New Wine Blooms* (1909); among his novels, *Arne* (1858), *Magnhild* (1877), and *In God's Way* (1889); and a cycle of epic poems *Arnljot Gelline* (1870). He won the **Nobel prize for literature** in 1903.

1910 Sept. 4 Henri [Julien Félix] **Rousseau** (b. May 20, 1844), a French painter, died. Before 1885, when he retired to paint, he served as a customs official [= "Le Douanier"] and he was sometimes called **Le Douanier** Rousseau. Among his best-known works, usually of jungle and animal scenes in bold colors, were *Sleeping Gypsy* (1897), *Jungle With a Lion* (1904–1906), *The Snake Charmer* (1907), *The Cart of Père Juniet* (1908), and *The Dream* (1910).

1910 Sept. 7 [William] **Holman Hunt** (b. Apr. 2, 1827), one of the founders of the English Pre-Raphaelite Brotherhood (1848) and a distinguished painter of that school, died. Hunt was a reformer by temperament and this was reflected in the symbolism, moral and social, in his work, such as *The Light of the World* (1854). His other important paintings included *The Triumph of the Innocents* (1884) and *The Hireling Shepherd* (1851).

1910 Sept. 11 O. Henry [William Sydney Porter] (b. Sept. 11, 1862), an American short-story writer, died. His first volume of short stories was *Cabbages and Kings* (1904). O. Henry began his writing career while serving a prison sentence in Columbus, Ohio, for embezzling bank funds in Austin, Texas. His most famous story, *The Gift of the Magi*, appeared in a collection, *The Four Million* (1906), which referred to the four million ordinary inhabitants of New York City (instead of the 400 of high society) from which he drew inspiration.

1910 Sept. 29 Winslow Homer (b. Feb. 24, 1836), an American painter of the realist school, died. His powerful seascapes included *Northeaster* (1895), *All's Well* (1896), and *The Gulf Stream* (1899). He gained fame and experience as a combat artist during the Civil War for *Harper's Weekly.*

1910 Nov. 20 Leo Tolstoi [Lev Nikolaevich Tolstoi] (b. Sept. 9, 1828), a Russian novelist, died. His works included *War and Peace* (completed in 1869), *Anna Karenina* (1876), *The Death of Ivan Ilyich* (1884), and *Resurrection* (1899). In the autobiographical *A Confession* (1874) and *What I Believe* (1884), Tolstoi defined and reaffirmed his deeply held Christian beliefs.

VIII. SPORTS, GAMES, AND SOCIETY

1910   In the U.S. the sport of rowing was revived at Princeton [New Jersey] University when **Andrew Carnegie**, steel manufacturer and philanthropist, provided money to create a lake on the edge of the campus by damming two streams. This afforded a 3½-mile sweep of water for rowing. Princeton soon inaugurated short-distance intercollegiate races. Intercollegiate racing gained in popularity, especially in the East, on the Cayuga and Onondaga lakes, in New York state, and on the Charles [Massachusetts], Housatonic [Connecticut], Severn [Maryland], Schuylkill [Pennsylvania], and Seekonk [Rhode Island] rivers.

1910 Mar. 8   Baronne de la Roche [Elise Deroche; Baronne Raymonde de Laroche] of France was the first woman to receive a license as an airplane pilot.

1910 July 4   [George Lewis] **Tex Rickard** (Jan. 2, 1871–Jan. 6, 1929) promoted the first U.S. championship boxing match with a purse of more than $100,000 at Reno, Nevada. The winner was the defending champion [John A.] **Jack Johnson**, who knocked out a former heavyweight champion [James J.] **Jim Jeffries** (Apr. 15, 1875–Mar. 3, 1953) in 15 rounds. Johnson was the first black to win this title and Jeffries came out of retirement in response to calls from certain quarters for a "white hope" to regain the championship. After the match, fights between groups of whites and blacks broke out in various parts of the country. An imaginative publicist, Rickard innovated the practice he followed nearly the rest of his career, of guaranteeing certain sums to each fighter in important bouts, and of sharing on a percentage basis the income from subsidiary rights.

1911

I. DISASTERS

1911 Sept.   Flooding of the Yangtze River [Chang Jiang], devastated its region and c.100,000 persons died.

1911 Mar. 25   Fire broke out in **New York City's garment district** at the **Triangle Shirtwaist Company**, a sweatshop employing mostly young women in a factory occupying the eighth to tenth floors of the Asch Building. The building's single elevator became clogged with bodies and stopped functioning. With escape routes blocked, 50 women leapt to their deaths. The final death toll was 145.

1911 Mar. 29   A fire in the old State Capitol building in Albany, New York, destroyed c.500,000 books and 300,000 manuscripts in the State Library, many dating from the Dutch colonial period. A portrait of George Washington by Gilbert Stuart was lost.

II. EXPLORATION AND COLONIZATION

1911   The ancient fortress city of the Incas, **Machu Picchu**, in the Andes Mountains of Peru, was discovered by **Hiram Bingham** (Nov. 19, 1875–June 6, 1956), an American archeologist, explorer, and statesman. The city covers five square miles of structures made of very large stones and with c.3,000 steps giving access to its various levels on a mountainside 2,000 feet above the Urubama River.

1911 Dec. 14   Roald [Raol] **Amundsen**, a Norwegian explorer, reached the **South Pole**, five weeks before **Robert Falcon Scott** (June 6, 1868–?Mar. 29, 1912), a British naval captain, and his ill-fated expedition reached the Pole (Jan. 18, 1912). Scott's entire party perished on the return journey.

III. POLITICS AND WAR

1911 Apr. 5   The **Szechwan uprising**, marking the start of the **Chinese Revolution** (1911–1912), began with the signing of the Hukwang Railway loan agreement in Wu-ch'ang, then capital of Hukwang province, between China and four foreign powers, which were to fund the construction of roads in central China. When the imperial government used foreign money to buy out a local company that had just begun work in Szechwan Province, anti-Manchu sentiment, which had run high for some time already, surged into open revolt. Prince Chun, regent for the five-year-old emperor Hsüan T'ung, last of the Ch'ing [Manchu] Dynasty (1644–1911), recalled as his advisor Yüan Shih-K'ai, who formed an imperial cabinet on Nov. 16. By December, 14 provinces had sided with Szechwan against the Manchu government.

1911 May 15 The **Parliament Act** was passed by the British House of Commons. It limited the influence of the House of Lords by removing its power to veto legislation.

1911 July 1 The **Moroccan crisis** erupted as the German gunboat *Panther* arrived in Agadir on the Moroccan Atlantic coast to protect German interests in the country, threatened by French expansion. The tension ended on Nov. 4 with an agreement that Germany was to cede its claims to Morocco in return for 100,000 square miles of French territory in the Congo.

1911 Sept. 14 **Pëtr Arkadevich** [Arkadievich] **Stolypin** (b. Apr. 14, 1862), the prime minister of Russia (from 1906), was shot by **Dmitri Bogrov**, a revolutionary, at the Kiev opera house and died four days later. Stolypin had initiated some social reforms, but his methods angered conservatives, liberals, and socialists.

1911 Oct. 5 An Italian force bombarded and captured **Tripoli** from the **Ottoman Empire** (1326–1920) in the first major Italian success during the **Italo-Turkish War** [Tripolitan War] (1911–1912), which Italy had initiated on Sept. 28. The conquest of the Libyan coast quickly followed and Italy annexed Tripolitania and Cyrenaica on Nov. 5.

1911 Oct. 10 A mutiny of troops occurred at **Wu-ch'ang**, the capital of what was then Hukwang province, China. The arsenal and mint at Wu-ch'ang were captured by revolutionaries on Oct. 11, and the **Chinese Republic** was declared on Oct. 26, marking the end of the **Ch'ing** [Manchu] **Dynasty** (from 1644). Yüan Shih-K'ai returned from exile in the north to lead his army against the uprising. He was named Yüan premier in November, and on Dec. 4 an armistice was concluded.

1911 Nov. 18 **Mongolia declared independence from China.** A government was established by **Jebstun Damba Khutukhtu** (d. May 20, 1924), the Living Buddha [Badgo Khan, or Gegen] of Urga [Ulan Bator], the capital in central northern Mongolia. Russia, which had sent arms and military officers to aid the rebellion, signed a treaty with Mongolia on Nov. 3, 1912, turning Mongolia into a protectorate of Russia.

IV. ECONOMY AND TRADE

1911 An International Convention was signed by Japan, Russia, the U.S., and Great Britain for Canada to regulate **sealing in the North Pacific Ocean.** Land sealing was also regulated by this act. By 1911 only c.125,000 fur seals remained on the Pribilof [Fur Seal] Islands and the Komandorskiye [Commander] Islands in the Bering Sea, where the seal population had been estimated to be more than 3.5 million in the early 1800s.

1911 The British Crown Colony of **Trinidad and Tobago** [now an independent republic] began to export oil at a rate of less than one-half million barrels a year.

1911 May 15 The U.S. Supreme Court found the **Standard Oil Company** guilty of restraint of trade under the **Sherman Anti-Trust Act** (1890). The company, which had an almost complete monopoly, was ordered to dissolve itself into smaller units.

1911 June 16 The organization that became **International Business Machines** [IBM] in 1924, and grew into the largest computer manufacturing company in the world, was organized as the Computing-Tabulating-Recording Company, a merger of three firms.

1911 Dec. The **National Insurance Act** was passed in Great Britain, providing unemployment insurance and health insurance for workers.

V. SCIENCE, EDUCATION, AND TECHNOLOGY

1911 The **Hertzsprung-Russell** [H-R] **diagram**, a scheme for showing the luminosity of a star as a function of the temperature at its surface, was devised by **Henry Norris Russell** (Oct. 25, 1877–Feb. 18, 1957), an American astronomer, and **Ejnar Hertzsprung** (Oct. 8, 1873–Oct. 21, 1967), a Danish astronomer.

1911 Oct. 18 **Alfred Binet** (b. July 8, 1857), a French psychologist, died. In 1905 Binet developed an intelligence scale, called the **Binet-Simon test**, at the **Sorbonne** in Paris with **Théodore Simon** (July 10, 1873–Sept. 4, 1961), a French doctor. In 1916 the test was introduced to the U.S. by **Lewis Madison Terman** (Jan. 15, 1877–Dec. 21, 1956) of **Stanford University**.

1911 Oct. 29 **Joseph Pulitzer** (b. Apr. 10, 1847), Hungarian-born U.S. newspaper publisher, died. In 1878 he acquired the **St. Louis** *Dispatch* and merged it with the *Post,* making it a highly successful newspaper. In 1883 he bought the **New York** *World* and in 1887 started the *Evening World.* Pulitzer built up circulation with crusades against corruption and with cartoons and numerous illustrations. Pulitzer left funds for the endowment of a school of journalism at **Columbia University**, which opened in 1912, and for the **Pulitzer prizes** in journalism, letters, and music, which have been awarded annually by Columbia since 1917.

VI. ARTS AND LEISURE

1911 May 18 **Gustav Mahler** (b. July 7, 1860), a Bohemian [Austria-Hungary] musician, died. His works included nine symphonies, songs, and orchestral song cycles. Among his best-known works were *Lieder eines fahrenden Gesellen* [*Songs of the Wayfarer*] (1883–1885), *Kinder toten Lieder* [*Songs on the Death of Children*] (1901–1904), and *Das Lied von der Erde* [*The Song of the Earth*] (1907–1910). His Eighth, Ninth, and unfinished Tenth symphonies marked the height of Mahler's exploration of the absence of tonality.

1911 May 29 **William Schwenck Gilbert** (b. Nov. 18, 1836), an English librettist, died. With the composer **Arthur Sullivan**, he collaborated on *H.M.S. Pinafore* and *The Pirates of Penzance*, performed at the Opéra Comique. These works brought Gilbert and Sullivan to the attention of **Richard D'Oyly Carte**, who built for them the Savoy, in London, where they put on such favorites as *Patience*, *The Mikado Ruddigore*, and *The Gondoliers* (Dec. 7, 1889).

1911 Oct. 1 **Wilhelm Dilthey** (b. Nov. 19, 1833), a German philosopher, died. He undertook to develop methodology that would separate the humanities from the natural sciences, believing the latter had too much influence on the former. Dilthey's most important work was *Einleitung in die Geisteswissenschaften* (1883).

VII. SPORTS, GAMES, AND SOCIETY

1911 May 30 The first Indianapolis 500-mile race was held at the Indianapolis Motor Speedway, in Indiana. **Ray Harroun** (Jan. 12, 1879–Jan. 19, 1968) driving a Marmon, won with a 74.59 mile per hour average.

1911 Aug. 22 The *Mona Lisa*, a painting by **Leonardo da Vinci** of **Lisa del Giocondo**, and probably the most famous painting in the world, was stolen overnight from the Louvre, in Paris, where it had hung for more than a century. The painting was not recovered until Dec. 13, 1913, when it was found in Florence, Italy, in the possession of a painter named **Vincenzo Perugia**.

1912

I. DISASTERS

1912 Apr. 14–15 The British ship *Titanic* struck an iceberg in the North Atlantic and sank. About 2,200 were aboard, and c.1,500 drowned. The White Star liner was on its maiden voyage from Southampton, England, to New York City. The iceberg cut a gash along the side of the hull, opening several of the watertight compartments. The sinking *Titanic* sent out an SOS, but only the Cunard liner *Carpathia* responded, ultimately carrying c.700 survivors to New York City.

1912 July 12 A troop train was deliberately exploded near Bachimba Pass in **Chihuahua** state during the **Mexican Revolution** (1910–1915) following the overthrow of **Porfirio Díaz**, president of Mexico (from 1884). Nearly everyone on the 22-car train, loaded with 50 soldiers in each car, was killed or injured.

II. POLITICS AND WAR

1912 Jan. 1 **Sun Yat-Sen** was inaugurated in Nanking [Nanjing] by his supporters in southern China as provisional president of the **Republic of China**.

1912 Jan. 6 **New Mexico** was the 47th state admitted to the U.S.

1912 Feb. 12 Yüan Shih-K'ai persuaded the Ch'ing [Manchu] **Dynasty** (1644–1911) in China to relinquish claims to power, and the boy-emperor **Hsuan T'ung** abdicated. Two days later **Sun Yat-Sen** resigned his presidency and Yüan succeeded him on Mar. 10. **Li Yüan-Hung** (1864–June 3, 1928), an early opponent of Sun's but a supporter of the anti-Manchu rebellion, was named vice president. A provisional constitution went into effect, and the government moved to Peking in April.

1912 Feb. 14 **Arizona** was the 48th state admitted to the U.S.

1912 Mar. 13 **Serbia** and **Bulgaria** concluded a **treaty of alliance against the Ottoman Empire** (1326–1920), perceiving in the **Italo-Turkish War** (1911–1912) the Turkish weakness that had been long apparent to most countries. On May 29, a treaty of alliance was signed by Bulgaria and Greece, which hoped to annex Crete from Turkey. On Oct. 3 Bulgaria, Greece, Montenegro, and Serbia made demands on Turkey. On Oct. 8 **Montenegro** declared war on the Turks and was joined by Bulgaria and Serbia nine days later.

1912 Mar. 30 By the **Treaty of Fez**, most of **Morocco** was named a French protectorate with its capital at Rabat, in northwestern Morocco on the Atlantic coast. **Abd-al-Hafiz**, sultan of Morocco (1908–1912), was obliged to sign the treaty before he abdicated on Aug. 11. He was succeeded by **Abd al-Yusuf** (ruled 1912–1927).

1912 Apr. The **first elections were held in Argentina** under the provisions of the **Sáenz Peña electoral reform law**, enacted earlier this year by the government of **Roque Sáenz Peña** (Mar. 19, 1851–Aug. 9, 1914), president of Argentina (1910–1914).

1912 May 14 **Frederick VIII** (b. June 3, 1843), king of **Denmark** (from 1906), died. He was succeeded (to 1947) by his eldest son **Christian X**. Another son, **Haakon VII**, was king of Norway (1905–1957).

1912 July 30 **Mutsuhito** (b. Nov. 3, 1852), the Meiji [enlightened peace] emperor of **Japan**, died. He was succeeded by his son **Yoshihito** (to 1926).

1912 Aug. **U.S. marines landed in Nicaragua** to suppress a revolt against **Adolfo Díaz** (1874–1964), effective president of Nicaragua (1911–1917). **Marines were also sent to Cuba**, on June 5, to protect American interests threatened by an insurrection.

1912 Aug. The **Kuomintang** [national people's party] was organized in China when the Revolutionary Alliance absorbed other parliamentary parties. Although the nominal head of the new organization was **Sun Yat-Sen**, Sung Chiao-Jen (1882–1913), who had been a revolutionary activist since 1905, was the de facto head. The Kuomintang urged parliamentary democracy and a moderate kind of socialism. In elections of 1912 to 1913 it won a majority in the national assembly, but in 1913 Yüan Shihkai, president of China, suppressed the Kuomintang and Sung was assassinated, allegedly on Yüan's orders.

1912 Sept. 28 The **Ulster Covenant of Resistance to Home Rule** was signed in Belfast, Ulster province, part of present Northern Ireland, by **Andrew Bonar Law** (Sept. 16, 1858–Oct. 30, 1923), leader of the British Conservative party, and **Edward Henry Carson** (Feb. 9, 1854–Oct. 22, 1935), Irish politician and Conservative member of the British Parliament. The covenant was a protest against a **Home Rule Bill for Ireland**, which had been passed by the Liberal party majority in the House of Commons, but was not yet law.

1912 Nov. 28 **Albanian independence** was declared at Vlorë [Vlona, Valona, Avlona, Aulon], the port city in present southwestern Albania. On the same day Durrës [Durazzo], the Turkish-held seaport on the Adriatic, was occupied by Serbia, but by the **Treaty of London** in 1913 it was given to Albania. The London Conference declared Albania an independent neutral state on July 29, 1913, and settled its borders. **Durrës** was made the Albanian capital by the appointed king, **William of Wied** [Wilhelm Friedrich Heinrich] (1876–1945), cousin of both the German emperor and the Russian czar as well as nephew to Queen Elizabeth of Romania.

III. ECONOMY AND TRADE

1912 The **Panama Canal Act** permitted toll-free passage for U.S. ships traveling from coast to coast. Great Britain and other European nations protested that this act violated the **Hay-Pauncefote Treaty** of 1901. The act was repealed in 1914.

1912 May 5 The newspaper *Pravda* [Truth] made its first appearance in St. Petersburg, Russia. One of its editors was **Joseph Stalin**.

IV. SCIENCE, EDUCATION, AND TECHNOLOGY

1912 The **automobile selfstarter** made its first appearance this year in the Cadillac motor car. It was the invention of **Charles F[ranklin] Kettering** (Aug. 29, 1876–Nov. 25, 1958), who also devised other practical improvements for motor vehicles, chiefly while with General Motors.

1912 Alfred Lothar Wegener (Nov. 1, 1880–Nov., 1930), a German meteorologist, first proposed the **theory of continental drift**. He postulated that at one time the land mass of the earth constituted one supercontinent, which he named **Pangaea**, and which over millions of years split and drifted to the present continental formations. His theory was not widely accepted until the 1960s because there was no creditable explanation for such events.

1912 Jan. 10 The **first practical seaplane**, called a "flying boat" at the time, was flown by its inventor, **Glenn H[ammond] Curtiss** (Mar. 21, 1878–July 23, 1930). The craft had a 60-horse-power engine and carried two people.

1912 Apr. 4 Isaac Kauffman Funk (b. Sept. 10, 1893), An American publisher and lexicographer, died. He established (1877) the publishing house of I.K. Funk Company, which became (1891) the **Funk & Wagnalls Company**. Funk founded and edited the magazine **Literary Digest** (1890). He was also the editor of **A Standard Dictionary of the English Language** (1890–1893), and assisted in the publication of **The Jewish Encyclopedia** (1901–1906).

1912 July 17 Jules-Henri Poincaré (b. Apr. 29, 1854), French mathematician and physicist, died. His work greatly enlarged the field of mathematical physics. Some of his scientific contributions are summed up in *Les Méthodes nouvelles de la mécanique céleste* (1892–1899).

V. ARTS AND LEISURE

1912 Marcel Duchamp, a French painter, completed *Nude Descending a Staircase*, a cubist painting. Employing a technique called simultaneity, Duchamp showed the figure in motion.

1912 The **blues** joined the mainstream of American popular music with the publication of *Memphis Blues* by **W[illiam] C[hristopher] Handy** (Nov. 16, 1873–Mar. 28, 1958). The song had originally been written in 1909 as **Mr. Crump** to aid the political fortunes of the Democratic leader of Memphis, Tennessee, Edward H. "Boss" Crump (Oct. 2, 1875–Oct. 16, 1954). Handy rose to fame with *Memphis Blues* and other similar pieces, such as **St. Louis Blues** (1914) and **Beale Street Blues** (1917).

1912 The **Castles**, idols of the English dance floor during World War I, made their American debut in *The Sunshine Girl*. **Vernon Blythe** (1887–Feb. 15, 1918) and **Irene Vernon** [*nee*: Foote] (1893?–Jan. 25, 1969) adopted "Castle" as their stage name.

1912 May 14 August Strindberg (b. Jan. 22, 1849), a Swedish playwright and novelist, died. His plays included *The Father* (1887), *Miss Julie* (1888), *The Dream Play* (1902), and *Great Highway* (1909). Among his novels were *The Red Room* (1879) and *Black Banners* (1907). His social and political ideas and religious beliefs were radical, which denied him official Swedish recognition, but by the end of his life he was widely recognized as Sweden's greatest writer.

1912 June 1 Daniel H[udson] Burnham (b. Sept. 4, 1846), an American architect, died. After he formed a partnership in 1873 with **John W[ellborn] Root** (Jan 10, 1850–Jan 15, 1891), their firm grew into one of the pioneers of modern building design. Working chiefly in Chicago, Illinois, they were responsible for such landmarks as the **Monadnock Building** (1891) and the 20-story **Masonic Temple Building** (1892), the **first important steel skeleton structure**. Burnham was also the architect for the **Flatiron Building** (1904) in New York City and the **Union Railroad Station** in Washington, D.C.

1912 June 10 Ion Luca Caragiale (b. Jan. 30, 1853), a Romanian writer, died. His plays included *O Noaple Furtunoasa* [*A Stormy Night*] (1879) and *O Scrisoare Pierdută* [*A Lost Letter*] (1884).

1912 Aug. 13 Jules [Émile Frédéric] **Massenet** (b. May 12, 1842), a French opera composer, died. He composed choral works and more than 20 operas. The best-known operas included **Manon** (1884), **Werther** (1892), **Thaïs** (1894), and **Le Jongleur de Notre Dame** (1902).

1912 Dec. 7 A limestone **bust of Nefertiti** [Nofretete] (fl. c.1375–1358 B.C.), queen of Egypt, was discovered at Amarna, Egypt, by **Ludwig Borchardt** (Oct. 5, 1863–Sept. 8, 1938), a German Egyptologist. Nefertiti was the wife of Akhenaton [Ikhnaton], pharaoh of Egypt (1375–1358 B.C.).

VI. SPORTS, GAMES, AND SOCIETY

1912 **Jim Thorpe** (May 28, 1886–Mar. 28, 1953), a great American athlete, was disqualified as a gold medal winner in the Olympic decathlon and pentathlon held this year. It was claimed he lacked amateur status, having played professional baseball the summer before. He had also been an early star of football. On Oct. 13, 1982, Thorpe's Olympic medals were posthumously restored to him.

1912 May 5–July 22 The fifth Summer **Olympic Games** were held in Stockholm, Sweden, with 2,547 athletes from 28 countries competing. Swedish athletes won 24 gold medals and 65 in all; the U.S. 23 and 61; and Great Britain 10 and 41. For the first time, swimming events for women were part of the games.

1912 Oct. 14 Just before giving a speech in Milwaukee, Wisconsin, ex-president **Theodore Roosevelt** was shot by John Schrank from a distance of only 6 feet. The bulky manuscript of his speech blocked the effect of the bullet, and Roosevelt prevented the crowd from attacking Schrank and then gave his speech before having his wound treated at a hospital. Schrank was a disappointed job-seeker from New York.

1913

I. DISASTERS

1913 Mar. 21–26 A flood in the **Miami River Valley** in Ohio, called the **Dayton flood,** killed more than 400 people and property damage was estimated at $200,000,000. Floods along the Indiana River and elsewhere in the west and south took about another 200 lives.

1913 Oct. 14 A fire in a coal mine in Mid Glamorgan, southern Wales, took the lives of 439 miners.

1913 Oct. 22 At Dawson, northeastern New Mexico, a **coal mine explosion** killed 259 persons.

II. POLITICS AND WAR

1913 **Francis Burton Harrison** (Dec. 18, 1873–Mar. 26, 1957) was appointed governor general of the Philippines (to 1921). During Harrison's term the **Philippines** received from the U.S. its first definite pledge for independence, although no date was set.

1913 **Women in Norway were granted universal suffrage.** Norway's action was the first permanent universal woman suffrage legislation in Europe.

1913 Jan. 23 A Turkish military officer, **Enver Pasha** (Nov. 23, 1881–Aug. 4, 1922), headed a coup by the **Young Turks** which ousted **Kiamil Pasha** (1832?–Nov. 14, 1913), the grand vizier, who was

willing to cede Edirne [Adrianople], in present Turkey on the border with Greece, to Bulgaria, which had captured it during the Balkan Wars (1912–1913). The Young Turks, who also opposed any concessions to the Christians of Macedonia, seated Mahmud Shevket Pasha (b. 1855 or 1858) as grand vizier, but he was assassinated on June 11. This led to a purge of government officials not sympathetic to the extreme nationalism of the Young Turks.

1913 Feb. 18 **Francisco I. Madero**, president of **Mexico**, an advocate of democracy and land reform, was ousted in a military coup by **Victoriano Huerta** (Dec. 23, 1854–Jan. 13, 1916). On Feb. 23, while under arrest, Madero (b. Oct. 30, 1873) was murdered, allegedly while trying to escape, but almost certainly on Huerta's orders. Huerta, formerly an associate of Madero, assumed the presidency.

1913 Feb. 25 The **Sixteenth Amendment to the U.S. Constitution,** providing a legal basis for imposing federal income taxes on individuals and corporations, became law. On May 31 the **Seventeenth Amendment**, providing for direct election of U.S. senators, went into effect.

1913 Mar. 4 **Woodrow Wilson** of the Democratic party was inaugurated as the 28th president of the U.S. The **Progressive**, or **Bull Moose**, party, a faction of Theodore Roosevelt's followers, who opposed **William Howard Taft's** conservatism, had split the Republican vote and enabled a Democrat to win the election on Nov. 5, 1912. Wilson received 6,293,454 popular votes and 435 in the electoral college. Roosevelt received 4,119,538 and 88; Taft, 3,484,980 and 8. **Thomas Riley Marshall** (Mar. 14, 1854–June 7, 1925) served as vice president.

1913 Mar. 18 George I [Christian William Ferdinand Adolphus George; Prince William of Denmark] (b. Dec. 24, 1845), king of **Greece** (from 1862), was assassinated in Salonika. George was succeeded by his son **Constantine I** (Aug. 2, 1868–Jan. 11, 1923), who continued his father's foreign policy.

1913 Apr. 3 Emmeline G. Pankhurst (July 14, 1858–June 14, 1928), a militant leader of Great Britain's suffragettes, was sentenced to three years in prison after she took responsibility for placing a bomb in the home of **David Lloyd George**, the chancellor of the Exchequer. Mrs. Pankhurst at once went on a hunger strike, refusing to sleep as well. Released, she was arrested again as soon as she recovered on the basis of the "Cat and Mouse Act," officially the "**Prisoners, Temporary Discharge for Health, Act**" of 1913. She was imprisoned 12 times in as many months. On May 6 the House of Commons voted down a bill to give women the vote, 266 to 219.

1913 Apr. 8 The **Chinese National Assembly** convened but **Yüan Shih-K'ai**, as president of China, attempted to rule without it. In general he did not keep his promises regarding a democratic leadership, made when he took over the presidency from Sun Yat-Sen. Sun and other opposition leaders led revolts, but with the military power behind him, Yüan put them down with great harshness. Sun fled to Japan on Aug. 6.

1913 May 30 The **Treaty of London**, the peace settlement following the first phase of the **Balkan Wars** (1912–1913), was concluded by the Great Powers: Austria-Hungary, supported by Germany and Italy; Russia, which was sympathetic to the cause of the South Slavs; and Great Britain, which had taken the role of mediator.

1913 June 20 The **Native Land Act** was approved in the **Union of South Africa**. One million whites were to possess 82.7 percent of the land in the Union, while four million Africans were to share the 7.3 percent remaining. Africans who were not driven away stayed on as squatters or labored as tenants, providing a cheap labor force for the white farmers.

1913 June 29 The second phase of the **Balkan Wars** (1912–1913) began when Bulgaria attacked Serbia and Greece. Serbia was dissatisfied with the May 30 settlement, had demanded a larger share of Macedonia from Bulgaria, and on June 1 had formed an alliance with Greece. On July 10 Romania declared war on Bulgaria and when Turkey on July 12 also entered the fray, Bulgaria admitted defeat on July 31 and agreed to an armistice. The war was ended on Aug. 10 by the **Treaty of Bucharest**. By its terms Bulgaria lost territory to three of its enemies, Romania, Serbia, and Greece. On July 20 the Turks had taken back the city of Adrianople [Edirne] from Bulgaria. By the **Treaty of Constantinople** (Sept. 29), between Turkey and Bulgaria, the former retained Adrianople as well as the line of the Maritza River. Neither the Balkan nations nor the great European powers were fully satisfied with these settlements. With the powers split in their support of the nations that constituted the Balkan "powder keg," the necessary ingredients were in place for igniting World War I.

1913 Oct. 6 Yüan Shih-K'ai was reelected president of China by a parliament cowed by Yüan's military power, threats of charges of treason, and the flight of their strongest leaders to Japan. His regime was granted international recognition by the great powers on condition that he grant autonomy to Russian-dominated **Outer Mongolia** and British-influenced Tibet. Earlier the National Assembly had promulgated a new constitution that greatly curtailed presidential powers. Thereupon Yüan expelled (Nov. 4) its majority **Kuomintang** members. Lacking a quorum the assembly became defunct. On May 1, 1914, Yüan promulgated a new constitution, which gave him complete power and a ten-year tenure. He was now virtually dictator of China.

1913 Dec. 18 Catalonia, in northeastern Spain, comprising Barcelona, Gerona, Lérida, and Tarragona, was granted the first step in autonomy by royal decree. The four provinces were to be joined together in a form of *Mancomunidad* [Commonwealth].

III. ECONOMY AND TRADE

1913 The **world's first moving assembly line** came into practical use at the **Ford Motor Company** plant in Highland Park, Michigan. In this system mechanical means moved the product while workers stationed along the line each performed one task over and over. The Ford line assembled the **Model T cars** and by 1914 was able to produce twice as many with no increase in the number of workmen. On Jan. 5, 1914, **Henry Ford** further astounded the industrial world by announcing that his employees would be paid $5 for an eight-hour day, about double the previous rate. Furthermore, Ford workers would share a $10,000,000 bonus from the previous year's profits.

1913 Mar. 31 J[ohn] P[ierpont] Morgan (b. Apr. 17, 1837), the most powerful financier in the U.S., died. When he formed J.P. Morgan & Company in 1895, he had already broken the monopoly on government financing long held by Jay Cooke. Morgan's most extensive dealings were in railroad consolidation and reorganization, involving such lines as the Northern Pacific and the New York, New Haven & Hartford. In 1901 he masterminded formation of the **first billion dollar corporation in the world**, the **U.S. Steel Corporation**. His power became such that in the **Panic of 1907** he saved the day by forcing other bankers to provide rescue funds for banks. In 1912 he was investigated by a Congressional committee looking into the "money trust," which was presumably controlled by him. After his death his New York City mansion became a museum of many of his art and book treasures.

1913 Oct. 4 **Woodrow Wilson**, president of the U.S., signed the **Underwood-Simmons Tariff Act** which for the first time since the Civil War (1861–1865) reduced duties on goods imported into the U.S. The law reduced duties on 958 articles, raised them on 86, and left 307 unchanged. The outbreak of war in 1914, with its disruption of trade, made the act of far less practical importance than its supporters had hoped. The revenue lost from tariff reduction was replaced by federal personal and corporate income taxes.

1913 Dec. 23 The **Federal Reserve Act** was signed by Woodrow Wilson, president of the U.S. It replaced the Independent Treasury system, established in 1840, by authorizing the formation of up to 12 Federal Reserve Banks around the country to be overseen by a Federal Reserve Board.

IV. RELIGION AND PHILOSOPHY

1913 The **United Synagogue of America** was formed by Conservative rabbis led by **Solomon Schechter**, whose Jewish Theological Seminary provided the guidelines for the U.S. organization.

1913 **B'nai B'rith** created its **Anti-Defamation League**, designed to counter the rise of anti-Semitism in the U.S. prior to World War I.

1913 **Franz Rosenzweig** (Dec. 26, 1886–Dec. 10, 1929), born to an assimilated German-Jewish family, decided against converting to Christianity and turned instead to the study and reinterpretation of Judaism. In 1920, already famed as a religious philosopher, he established the successful adult student center Freies Judisches Lehrhaus, in Frankfurt-am-Main, Germany.

V. SCIENCE, EDUCATION, AND TECHNOLOGY

1913 The **first electric refrigerator** for home use was put on the market. Called Domelre, it was made in Chicago, and sold for about $900, a very high price in that era for a home appliance.

1913 **Robert Andrews Millikan**, an American physicist, completed studies that enabled him to **measure the value of the charge of the electron**. In this period Millikan also studied the photo-electric effect, the emission of electrons by certain substances when light strikes their surfaces.

1913 May 14 **John D. Rockefeller, Sr.**, U.S. oil multimillionaire, established the **Rockefeller Foundation** with a donation of $100,000,000. During the next 14 years, he added another $83,000,000. Most of the foundation's work for many years was in the fields of medical research, public health, and education.

1913 Nov. 7 **Alfred Russel Wallace** (b. Jan. 8, 1823), an English naturalist who developed a **theory of evolution** independently of Charles Darwin, died. He conceived his theory while on an expedition to the Malay Archipelago (1854–1862) and in 1858 he wrote down his thoughts and sent a copy to Darwin. The statements of both men were published as a joint paper that year. Wallace's field work is now recognized in the term "Wallace's line," an imaginary line marking the division between Australian and Asian fauna in the Malay Archipelago.

VI. ARTS AND LEISURE

1913   In England **D.H. Lawrence** brought out *Sons and Lovers*, a work attacked because its frankness in treating sexual matters. In France **Marcel Proust** published *Du Coté de chez Swann* [*Swann's Way*], a detailed account of the narrator's childhood. It was the first part of what turned out to be a seven-part novel, the last part of which did not appear until 1927, after Proust's death. The overall title of the work was *A la recherche du temps perdu* [*Remembrance of Things Past*].

1913 Feb. 17   The Armory Show opened at the 69th Regiment Armory in New York. Officially entitled the **International Exhibition** [of] **Modern Art**, it was the first major showing of avant-garde art in the U.S. Exhibited were more than 1,000 works by European and American artists. Extremely controversial, the exhibition marked a change in American appreciation of Modern Art. It closed in New York on Mar. 15, but a smaller version was mounted in Chicago (Mar. 24–Apr. 16) and Boston (Apr. 28–May 19).

VII. SPORTS, GAMES, AND SOCIETY

1913   **One-wall handball**, an American version of the European four-wall game, began its tremendous popularity in large U.S. cities with the first appearance about this time of courts at the public beaches in Brooklyn, New York.

1913   The earl of Jersey, one of the stewards of the Jockey Club of London, sponsored a successful move to have the club declare those **horses** whose ancestors had not been registered in previous editions of the *Stud Book* ineligible for registering. This in effect declared American thoroughbreds ineligible for listing or racing in England.

1913 Apr. 5   The **United States Football Association** [USFA], so-called until 1945 when it changed its name to the United States Soccer Football Association, was formed.

1913 June 7   The **first ascent of Mt. McKinley**, Alaska, at 20,320 feet the highest mountain in North America, was accomplished by Episcopal clergyman **Hudson Stuck** (Nov. 11, 1863–Oct. 10, 1920) and three companions.

1913 Sept. 20   **Francis D. Ouimet** (May 8, 1893–Sept. 2, 1967), an American amateur golfer, defeated the famed British golf professionals **Harry Vardon** (1870–Mar. 20, 1937) and **Ted Ray** (1877–Aug. 27, 1943) in an 18-hole playoff at the Country Club in Brookline, Massachusetts, to win the **U.S. Open championship**.

1913 Dec. 21   The **first crossword puzzle** for adults appeared in the *New York World*. Its author was **Arthur Wynne**, an Englishman. Simple crosswords for children had appeared in England since the late 19th century.

1914

I. VITAL STATISTICS AND DEMOGRAPHICS

1914   On the verge of World War I (1914–1918) **Europe's** 19th century **population** explosion continued, with population rising 80 percent since 1845. The addition of c.200 million people brought the total figure to c.450 million. But for emigration, the total figure would have increased another c.50 million, the number of people leaving Europe between 1845 and 1914. By 1914, however, the "Great Migration" from Europe to the Americas had ended. Since 1845, c.41 million immigrants had come to the Americas. Of these, c.35 million came to North America, and of these c.33 million settled in the U.S. The remainder went to Africa, Australia, and many other places outside Europe. The first-generation European population nearly tripled in Central and South America, rising from c.30 million in 1845 to c.80 million in 1914, but it quintupled in the U.S., exploding from c.20 million in 1845 to c.100 million in 1914.

II. DISASTERS

1914 May 29   The Canadian passenger steamship *Empress of Ireland* **was struck by the collier** *Storstad* in the St. Lawrence River, northeastern North America, and sank in less than 15 minutes; 1,024 persons aboard were lost.

1914 May 30   Lassen Peak, in the Cascade Range in northern California, began a series of violent, spectacular **eruptions** that lasted for nearly two years. On May 19, 1915, hot lava flowed 1,000 feet down its slopes. Activity ceased in Feb., 1921.

III. POLITICS AND WAR

1914   A French force occupied the Tibesti Mountains in northern Chad, central northern Africa, inhabited by the **Islamized Teda** [Toubou] nomads. This followed the annexation in 1912 of the sultanate of Ouadaï [Wadai] in eastern **Chad** and completed the French occupation of Chad.

1914 May 25   Home Rule for Ireland was finally enacted by the British Parliament. Provision was made for Ulster, with a large Protestant population, to remain six more years in union with Great Britain. However, no part of the bill ever went into effect, being suspended (Sept. 15) for the duration of World War I (1914–1918).

1914 Apr. 21   Veracruz, the Mexican port on the Gulf of Mexico, was **occupied by U.S. marines** after a heavy bombardment in which hundreds of civilians in the city were killed or wounded. U.S. naval forces had been stationed off Veracruz in order to enforce an arms embargo against the government of **Victoriano Huerta**, the reactionary dictator of Mexico, whom the U.S. wanted to see removed from office. The incident had been provoked by a Mexican official's refusal to honor the American flag with a 21-gun salute ashore. In order to remove U.S. troops from Mexican soil, Huerta resigned on July 15, to be replaced by **Venustiano Carranza**. Troops were withdrawn (Nov. 23), but Carranza was opposed by the allied factions of **Pancho Villa** and **Emiliano Zapata**, who marched into Mexico City on Jan. 1, 1915, to place their candidate in the presidency. Carranza gained control by the end of 1915, ending the most violent part of the **Mexican Revolution** (1910–1915), although Pancho Villa continued to lead raids in northern Mexico.

1914 June 28   Franz Ferdinand (b. Dec. 18, 1863), the heir to the Austro-Hungarian throne, and his wife were assassinated by **Gavrilo Princip** (1893?–1918), a Serbian nationalist, at Sarejevo in the Austro-Hungarian province of Bosnia, in central Yugoslavia. Using the assassination as an excuse, Austria-Hungary issued an ultimatum to Serbia with terms impossible to accept if Serbia were to retain its sovereignty. As the crisis deepened, **Edward Grey** (later Viscount Grey of Fallodon) (Apr. 25, 1862–Sept. 7, 1933), the British foreign secretary (1905–1916), attempted to organize a conference of the powers to settle matters peacefully. Austria-Hungary, supported by Germany, rejected the plan.

1914 July 2   Joseph Chamberlain (b. July 8, 1836), an English businessman, politician, and reformer, died. After a successful business career in Manchester, he became (1876–1906) a member of Parliament and a leader of the Liberal party. His most important work was his vigorous efforts for reform in such fields as taxes, education, and workmen's compensation.

1914 July 28   World War I (to 1918) began when Austria-Hungary declared war on Serbia. In reply to an ultimatum (July 23) Serbia had accepted some of Austria-Hungary's demands but rejected others. Russia mobilized its armies in support of its fellow Slavs. In turn Germany issued an ulitmatum to Russia demanding it call off its mobilization. When there was no answer, Germany declared war on Russia on Aug. 1. Austria officially declared war on Russia on Aug. 6.

1914 Aug. 1   The Swiss Confederation [Switzerland] mobilized its forces as war appeared imminent, and announced its neutrality during World War I.

1914 Aug. 1   The Scandinavian countries of Denmark, Norway, and Sweden declared their neutrality in World War I. Trade restrictions later imposed by the Allies against Germany hurt Denmark and Sweden. But Norway prospered by trading with Great Britain, despite the great number of ships sunk by the Germans.

1914 Aug. 2   After occupying Luxembourg, Germany demanded passage for troops through **Belgium**, allowing 12 hours for a response to its ultimatum. Belgium called on the **Treaty of 1839** that guaranteed neutrality in the event of a dispute between Germany, Great Britain, and France. The Netherlands maintained its policy of neutrality, but as the example of Belgium showed, neutrality was no safeguard against invasion. Yet The Netherlands was protected, because it conducted a great deal of trade for Germany and did not lie in the path of the **German invasion of France**.

1914 Aug. 3   The German Empire declared war on France. Even though faced with a two-front war,

Germany went on the offensive in accordance with its military doctrine.

1914 Aug. 4   Great Britain declared war on Germany, using the German invasion of neutral Belgium as an excuse to join the battle. On Aug. 12 Britain and France declared war on Austria-Hungary. All the major powers of Europe, except Italy, were now arrayed on one side or the other.

1914 Aug. 5   Montenegro declared war on Austria-Hungary. The Austro-Hungarian province of Bosnia and Herzegovina bordered on Montenegro, and its annexation by Austria-Hungary in 1908 had deprived Montenegro of the chance to form a united Slav state.

1914 Aug. 5   The Bryan-Chamorro Treaty was signed by the U.S. and Nicaragua, providing the U.S. with a permanent concession to build a canal across Nicaragua. The treaty was negotiated by **William Jennings Bryan,** U.S. secretary of state, and **Emiliano Chamorro Vargas** (May 11, 1871–Feb. 26, 1966), a Nicaraguan general. It was ratified by the U.S. Senate in 1916.

1914 Aug. 8   A French offensive against Germany in World War I was launched in Lorraine with the support of the British Expeditionary Force. On Aug. 20 the French movement was checked along the border of Lorraine, in German hands since 1871, as well as in Belgium.

1914 Aug. 8   Great Britain and France attacked the German protectorate of Togo along Africa's Gold Coast. The small German forces capitulated on Aug. 26. German Togoland was divided into British and French territories by the **Convention of Lomé** on Sept. 2.

1914   Aug.   11   The   Ottoman   Empire (1326–1920), which had on Aug. 4 allied itself with Germany, allowed two German ships to pass unhindered through the Dardanelles to the Bosporus strait at the entrance to the Black Sea. There they joined the Turkish fleet. **Russia, thereupon, declared war on Turkey** on Nov. 3. **Great Britain declared war on Turkey** on Nov. 5 and on the same day **annexed Cyprus,** which had been occupied by the British since June 1878.

1914 Aug. 12   An expeditionary force from Wellington, New Zealand, set out in support of Great Britain. On Aug. 29 it took **German Samoa** and on Sept. 21 it occupied **German New Guinea.**

1914 Aug. 16   A Polish council formed in Galicia, which had been Austrian territory since the **First Partition of Poland** in 1772, to organize Polish troops to fight against Russia in World War I (1914–1918). This group desired to unite Austrian and Russian Poland under the aegis of the Austrian Hapsburg monarchy.

1914 Aug. 18   Nicholas [Nikolai Nikolaevich] (Nov. 18, 1856–Jan. 6, 1929), grand duke of Russia and chief commander of Russian troops, led an attack into the Austrian province of Galicia, in present Poland. On Sept. 12 the Russians were victorious in a **battle at Lemberg** [Lvov], the capital of Galicia. They were able to penetrate westward into the Carpathian Mountains before they were halted by the Germans in a **battle at Przeḿysl** on Mar. 22, 1915.

1914 Aug. 19   Woodrow Wilson, president of the U.S., urged the American people to be "neutral in fact as well as in name." The **U.S.** government had officially **declared its neutrality** on Aug. 4 and the next day offered mediation, an offer ignored by the belligerents.

1914 Aug. 20   The Germans took Brussels, capital of Belgium. Liège, near the German border, endured the German siege, which began on Aug. 4, holding out until Aug. 15, thus delaying for 11 days the German advance across Belgium. Namur, where the Meuse and Sambre rivers meet, was the last fortified city between the advancing Germans and France. It fell on Aug. 20, and the Belgian troops withdrew to the coastal city of Antwerp.

1914 Aug. 20   Radomir Putnik (Jan. 24, 1847–May 17, 1917) led the Serbian defense at the Jadar River against an invasion by Austria along Serbia's northern border. He again repulsed the Austrians at the nearby Drina [Drinus] River on Sept. 19 and in a **battle at the Rudnik Ridges** on Dec. 7. The Serbs reoccupied their capital of Belgrade and forced a complete Austrian retreat.

1914 Aug. 23   Japan declared war on Germany and, with British armed support, laid siege to Tsingtao, which protected Germany's leasehold to the Kiaochow [Chiao Hsien] region of China.

1914 Aug. 26–29 The **battle of Tannenberg** [Stebark, in present northeastern Poland], in East Prussia resulted in a tremendous victory for the Germans under **Paul** [Ludwig Hans Anton von Beckendorff und] **von Hindenburg** (Oct. 2, 1847–Aug. 2, 1935). The Russian armies were completely swamped: c.92,000 Russians were taken prisoner, c.30,000 were killed or missing, and large numbers of guns were captured. The Germans lost c.13,000 men. The Russians had invaded East Prussia on Aug. 18, and had enjoyed an initial victory under Pavel Karlovich Rennenkampf (1854–1918), general of Russia's First Army, in a **battle at Gumbinnen** [Gusev] on Aug. 20. **Aleksandr Vasilievich Samsonov** (b. 1859), commander in charge of the Russian attack at Tannenberg, committed suicide on Aug. 29 while in flight. Hindenburg instantly became the greatest German hero of World War I.

1914 Aug. 28 The **battle of Heligoland** [Helgoland] **Bight** was the **first naval battle of World War I** (1914–1918). The British sank four German vessels without injury to their own near the island of Heligoland in the North Sea, off Germany.

1914 Sept. 5 Great Britain, France, and Russia concluded a formal **treaty of alliance against Austria-Hungary and Germany**. The Allies, which already included Serbia, Belgium, Montenegro, and Japan, were joined in 1915 by Italy and Romania, in 1916 by Portugal, and in 1917 by the U.S. and Greece.

1914 Sept. 6–9 In the first **battle at the Marne River**, just east of Paris, German troops were decisively beaten by an Allied force under **Joseph Jacques Césaire Joffre** (Jan. 12, 1852–Jan. 3, 1931), the commander-in-chief of French forces. Since Aug. 21 the British and French had been falling back in the face of the superior military ability of the German army. The French were beaten (Aug. 22) at Charleroi on the Meuse River in Belgium, while the British Expeditionary Forces, led by **John** [Denton Pinkstone] **French** (Sept. 28, 1852–May 22, 1925), the commander-in-chief of British forces, were forced (Aug. 23) to fall back from Mons in southwestern Belgium in their first encounter with German troops. Then the Germans took Amiens, northern France, on the Somme River, and the French government moved (Sept. 3) from Paris to Bordeaux. After the Marne battle French troops advanced only to the Aisne River, just north of the Marne, to regroup. Because the Allied forces did not break the German line and the Germans were unable to advance on Paris, this battle determined the more or less stationary character of the Western Front during World War I.

1914 Sept. 7–14 German forces defeated the Russian armies in the first **battle at the Masurian lakes**, in present northeastern Poland. The Russians in previous battles with the Germans, especially at Tannenberg, had lost so many troops and so much military materiel that they were unable to contribute much to the Allied side during the remainder of the war.

1914 Sept. 18 Fierce fighting at the Aisne River resulted in a German retreat under **Alexander von Kluck** (May 20, 1846–Oct. 19, 1934) and **Helmuth** [Johannes Ludwig] **von Moltke** (May 25, 1848–June 18, 1916), who was replaced in his command by **Erich von Falkenhayn** (Nov. 11, 1861–Apr. 8, 1922). This meant that the **Schlieffen Plan**, developed by the German chief commander **Alfred Graf von Schlieffen** (Feb. 28, 1833–Jan. 4, 1913), had failed. This plan assumed Germany would have to fight both France and Russia at the same time. While holding Russia at bay with comparatively weak forces, the bulk of the German army would move to the north and west through Belgium and the Netherlands. It would come down upon the French army from the north where the frontier was less well defended. Meantime, smaller German forces would hold the French to the south. The failure of the plan to bring quick French defeat meant that the war along the Western Front was now a "race to the sea," in which the westernmost flank of both sides tried to sweep around its opponent to control the French coast on the English Channel. The Germans reached as far west as Ostende on the Belgium coast in northern Belgium but were stopped from moving south into northern France at Ypres [Ieper] near Belgium's French border.

1914 Oct. 1 The **first contingent**—c.30,000 strong—**of Canadian troops sailed for England**. When Great Britain declared war on Germany on Aug. 4 this action automatically brought the entire empire into the conflict. Canada's quick response was typical. Australia at once offered an expeditionary force of c.20,000 troops and, like Canada, supplied far more than that before the war was over. Australian and New Zealand soldiers combined to form the **Australia New Zealand Army Corps** [**ANZAC**]. The Indian army also took part in the conflict, fighting like the others in Asia, Africa, and

Europe. On Nov. 22 Indian troops captured Basra in Mesopotamia [present Iraq].

1914 Oct. 10 Antwerp, Belgium, fell to German artillery bombardment, and England faced the threat of German invasion across the English Channel.

1914 Oct. 13 A Boer rebellion broke out in the Transvaal under **Christiaan [Rudolf] De Wet** (Oct. 7, 1854–Feb. 3, 1922) and **Christiaan Frederik Beyers**, who opposed a South African offensive against German troops in South-West Africa [present Namibia]. Revolt was quelled by **Louis Botha** (Sept. 27, 1862–Aug. 27, 1919), prime minister of the Union (from May 31, 1910), who defeated Beyers on Oct. 27 and De Wet on Nov. 12.

1914 Oct. 21 The first **battle at Ypres [Ieper]** in Flanders, Belgium, began between British troops under John French and German troops led by Erich von Falkenhayn. By Nov. 17 the German advance was halted, but there was no victory. Fighting continued in the form of trench warfare as the strategy on the Western Front shifted from attack to defense for both sides. German casualties were c.130,000, and the nearly 60,000 British casualties reduced by more than half the original British Expeditionary Force. With French dead and wounded added, total casualties were nearly 250,000 in less than a month.

1914 Oct. 30 The **Ottoman Empire** (1326–1920) **declared war on Great Britain and Russia** as the Turkish fleet bombarded (Oct. 29) Odessa, as well as other Russian ports in the Black Sea.

1914 Nov. 2 Great Britain declared all of the North Sea a military area, meaning that neutral ships sailed it at their own risk. British ships were stopping merchant vessels from neutral countries on the high seas and seizing goods they considered contraband. The British paid for the goods they seized.

1914 Nov. 9 The Australian ship *Sydney* sank the German cruiser *Emden* near the Cocos [Keeling] Islands in the Indian Ocean. The *Emden* had bombarded Madras (Sept. 10–22) and sunk several Allied ships in the Far East.

1914 Nov. 15–Dec. 5 The **German army under Ludendorff captured Lódz**, in central Poland, by driving a wedge parallel to the Vistula River through the Russian army. This ended the Russian threat to

German Silesia, and the Germans now threatened Warsaw, capital of Congress [Russian] Poland, c.70 miles to the east northeast.

1914 Dec. Enver Pasha, leader of the Young Turk movement in the Ottoman Empire, was **defeated by Russian troops at Sarikanus [Sarikamis]** in Russian Armenia, in present eastern Turkey.

1914 Dec. 2 The **Austrian army captured Belgrade**, capital of Serbia, but the Serbs fought back. By Dec. 14 they retook their capital.

1914 Dec. 8 A naval **battle at the Falkland Islands**, in the South Atlantic Ocean, was a major defeat for the German fleet, whose commander **Maximilian von Spee** (b. June 22, 1861), a German admiral, and his two sons sank with his ship. The Germans lost four of five warships. The British fleet, under the command of **Frederick Charles Doveton Sturdee** (June 9, 1859–May 7, 1925), aboard the *Invincible*, more than evened the score after the **battle at Coronel**, fought (Nov. 1) off the coast of Chile near Concepción, when Spee defeated a much smaller British fleet commanded by **Christopher George Francis Maurice Cradock** (b. July 2, 1862), a British admiral, who went down with the *Good Hope*.

1914 Dec. 18 Great Britain announced the establishment of a **protectorate over Egypt**, declaring the Ottoman Empire's previous suzerainty null. **Hussein Kamil [Husain Kemal]** (1854?–Oct. 9, 1917), son of Ismail Pasha, was named **sultan of Egypt**, and the reigning Ottoman khedive, **Abbas II [Abbas Hilmi Pasha]** (July 14, 1874–Dec. 20, 1944), son of Hussein's brother, was deposed. **Arthur Henry McMahon** (Nov. 28, 1862–Dec. 29, 1949) was named the first British high commissioner of Egypt.

IV. ECONOMY AND TRADE

1914–1918 Chile prospered during World War I when its nitrates were used for making saltpeter for explosives. **Cuba's sugar industry also prospered** because of the destruction of European sugar-beet crops.

1914 The **first commercially important oil field in Venezuela** was developed by a subsidiary of **Royal Dutch/Shell** at Mene Grande on the east coast of Lake Maracaibo, in northwestern Venezuela.

1914 Aug. The **Russian government introduced prohibition** for the duration of World War I. Russians continued to drink homebrew and bootlegged liquor. The government lost a major source of revenue, the liquor tax.

1914 Aug. 2 **German labor** and management declared a *Burgfrieden* [truce], agreeing to cooperate in the war effort.

1914 Aug. 4 The German Reichstag passed a series of measures, which included continuing the suspension, begun on July 31, of **specie payments for banknotes** and issuing instead huge amounts of paper currency. The government was authorized to borrow large sums of money.

1914 Aug. 15 The **Panama Canal** opened for regular traffic, the first ship to traverse it being the *Ancon*, carrying government officials. Actually, the first passage through the length of the canal had been made on Jan. 7, 1914, by a small ship *Alexander la Valley*.

1914 Sept. 26 The **Federal Trade Commission** [FTC] was created in the U.S. to maintain properly competitive conditions in interstate business by the enforcement of antitrust laws.

1914 Oct. 15 The **Clayton Antitrust Act** was signed into law by **Woodrow Wilson**, president of the U.S. It supplemented and strengthened the Sherman Antitrust Act of 1890. Rebates and price cutting to eliminate competition were forbidden. The new law was especially favorable to unions. It excluded them from provisions concerning combinations in restraint of trade; made strikes, boycotts, and picketing legal; and restricted the use of court injunctions against labor. **Samuel Gompers**, a labor leader, called the act "Labor's Magna Carta."

V. RELIGION AND PHILOSOPHY

1914 The **American Jewish Committee**, established in 1906 to defend and aid suffering Jews around the world, collaborated with the **Zionist Organization of America** in establishing the **American Joint Distribution Committee** [JDC] as an instrument for relief and rehabilitation work overseas.

1914 Apr. 19 **Charles Sanders Peirce** (b. Sept. 10, 1839), an American philosopher and scientist, the **founder of pragmatism**, died. Pragmatism, as developed by Peirce, held that the truth of any proposition could be measured by its results. Peirce first expressed the precept in an article in *Popular Science Monthly* (1878). *Chance, Love, and Logic* (1923) was a collection of his essays published posthumously.

1914 Aug. 20 **Pope Pius X** (b. June 2, 1835; pope from 1903) died. He tried to make the church more efficient and services more attractive, appointing a commission to recodify the canon law and encouraging the use of plainsong. He was noted for his interest in the poor. Pius X was canonized in 1954. He was succeeded by **Benedict XV**.

VI. SCIENCE, EDUCATION, AND TECHNOLOGY

1914 The **first official training school for airplane pilots** was established by the U.S. navy at Pensacola, Florida.

1914 Feb. 13 **Alphonse Bertillon** (b. Apr. 23, 1853), a French criminologist, died. He was the **first to develop a scientific system for identifying criminals**. This system was based on body measurements, including skeletal and other characteristics. Bertillon was chief of criminal identification for the Paris police and his system was officially adopted by France in 1888, and later by other countries.

1914 Mar. 12 **George Westinghouse** (b. Oct. 6, 1846), an American inventor and manufacturer, died. He earned more than 400 patents during his career, most of which were for the practical advancement of the industrial age. In 1869 he invented the **air brake** and organized a company to produce it. He set up another company in 1882 to make his **automatic railroad signal devices**. Westinghouse also introduced in America the high tension **alternating current system for the transmisison of electricity**.

1914 Aug. 7 The **siege of Liège**, Belgium, during World War I, ended with a German victory facilitated by use of **Big Bertha** howitzers. The gun was named for the head of the Krupp family, **Bertha Krupp von Bohlen** (1886–Sept. 21, 1957). The firearms were produced by an arms works founded in 1899 at a factory in Plzeň [Pilsen], in Austria-Hungary near Prague, by the Czech engineer **Emil von Škoda** (Nov. 19, 1839–Aug. 8, 1900). Big Bertha had a bore diameter of 17 inches and fired a projectile weighing a ton.

1914 Sept. 1 The **last wild Passenger Pigeon** [*Ectopistes migratorius*] died in captivity at the Cincinnati Zoo. In 1810 Alexander Wilson, an American ornithologist, estimated that one flock contained 2,230,272,000 birds. The disappearance of the species, caused mainly by man, shocked the U.S. into conservation activity to save other species. The **last Carolina Parakeet** [*Conuropsis carolinenis*] also died in captivity in the same Cincinnati Zoo. It was the only parrot native to the U.S.

1914 Oct. **Ernest Dunlop Swinton** (Oct. 21, 1868–Jan. 16, 1951), a British military leader, proposed development of a mobile armed vehicle able to withstand the German howitzer. Based on the American Holt tractor, which had already been used without armor to carry heavy artillery behind military lines, the experimental model of the tank was kept a secret, its parts being produced in different places. The **first tank** was the **British Mark I**, [called "Big Willie"], weighing c.30 tons, with plate armor 0.2 to 0.4 inches thick. It attained a speed of 4.5 miles per hour, was powered by a Daimler gasoline engine, and was limited by its fuel supply to 24 miles. Eleven were available for the Somme offensive on Sept. 15, 1916, when their deployment spurred the morale of Allied troops.

1914 Dec. 1 **Arthur Thayer Mahan** (b. Sept. 27, 1840), an American naval officer and historian of naval warfare, died. His lectures, published as *The Influence of Seapower upon History, 1660–1783* (1890), argued that navies large enough to control the seas were necessary if a nation hoped to be a great power. The book was widely used in Germany, Great Britain, Japan, and the U.S. by advocates of big navies.

VII. ARTS AND LEISURE

1914 *Tarzan of the Apes*, the first of the Tarzan series of books, which have sold millions of copies worldwide, was published. The American author, **Edgar Rice Burroughs** (Sept. 1, 1875–Mar. 19, 1950), also wrote science fiction.

1914 Mar. 25 **Frédéric Mistral** (b. Sept. 8, 1830), a French poet who devoted his career to further the language and literature of his native Provence, died. He was one of the founders (1854) and the leading figure of Le Félibrige, an organization devoted to the promotion of Provençal as a literary language. Mistral's poetry included a pastoral *Mireio* [French: *Mireille*] (1859) and a narrative poem *Lou Pouème de Rose* (1897). A major work was his Provençal dictionary *Trésor du Felibrige* (1897–1886). He shared the **Nobel prize for literature** in 1904.

1914 June 21 **Bertha Felice Sophie von Suttner** [nee Kinsky von Chinic und Tettau] (b. June 9, 1843), an Austrian novelist and pacifist, died. She founded in 1891 the **Austrian Society of Friends of Peace**. In 1889 she had published a pacifist novel, *Die Waffen nieder* [*Lay Down Your Arms*] (1892). Her friendship with Alfred Nobel was said to have influenced him in establishing the **Nobel Peace Prize**. In 1905 Suttner became the fifth person and the first woman to be awarded this honor.

1914 Sept. 29 **August Macke** (b. Jan. 3, 1887), a German painter, died in battle. He was a leader of **Der Blaue Reiter** [the Blue Movement] of German expressionists. Centered in Munich, such artists in the group as Macke, Wassily Kandinsky, and Paul Klee tried to express more spiritual feeling in their work than they thought the impressionists had achieved. Among his works were *The Promenade* (1913) and *Landscape with Cows and Camel* (1914).

VIII. SPORTS, GAMES, AND SOCIETY

1914 July 4 An American crew for the first time won the main event at the **Henley Royal Regatta** in England when the Harvard University eight won the Grand Challenge Cup.

1914 Mar. 21 The **first U.S. figure skating championships** for men and women, open to all, were held in New Haven, Connecticut. The winners were **Norman N. Scott** of Montreal and **Theresa Weld** of Boston.

1915

I. VITAL STATISTICS AND DEMOGRAPHICS

1915 Spring The **Armenian population** of eastern **Turkey** was decimated when Turkey began to deport (to 1923) the entire population of 1.75 million Armenians to Ottoman outposts in Syria and Mesopotamia. On Apr. 20 the Armenians had revolted at Van, on the eastern shore of Lake Van, but Turkish forces recaptured the city from Russian and Armenian forces on Aug. 5. About 580,000 of the Armenian population escaped, but about another 600,000 lost their lives.

II. DISASTERS

1915 Jan. 13 An **earthquake rocked Avezzano**, central Italy, causing the deaths of c.29,980 people.

1915 May 22 **Great Britain's worst train wreck** was the result of a double collision at Quintinshill [near Gretna], in southwestern Scotland, in which 227 people died and 245 were injured. A troop train entered a track already occupied by another train, causing the first collision. Seconds later, an express, running at top speed, plowed into the wreckage. Two other trains became involved in the disaster as gas cylinders used to light the troop train exploded, enveloping the area in fire.

1915 July 24 The U.S. excursion steamer *Eastland* capsized as it left dock in the Chicago River. In the accident 812 people drowned, including 22 entire families. An engineer had failed to fill the ballast tanks properly.

III. POLITICS AND WAR

1915 Jan. 13 A disastrous **Dardanelles Campaign** was decided upon by the Allied War Council. Russia had requested that the strategic passageway between the Mediterranean Sea and Russia's Black Sea be captured from the Ottoman Empire (1326–1920) so that vital supplies could be shipped to her.

1915 Jan. 14 **Louis Botha**, prime minister of the Union of South Africa, who supported the Allies, sent forces to German South West Africa, taking Windhoek, its capital, on May 11. German troops surrendered at Otawi [Otavi] on July 9.

1915 Jan. 18 **Japan made Twenty-One Demands on the Chinese government** that would in effect establish a Japanese protectorate of China. The demands had five major divisions: (1) German extraterritorial rights in Shantung enlarged and transferred to Japan; (2) extension of Japan's leases and railroad rights in Manchuria and acquisition of additional rights in eastern Inner Mongolia; (3) joint control with China of iron and coal in the valley of the Yangtse River [Chang Jiang]; (4) China not allowed to grant new leaseholds to other powers; (5) and a miscellany of demands for joint control of police in trouble areas, joint control of arsenals, the right of Japan to proselytize throughout China, and many others. On May 25 **Yüan Shih-K'ai**, president of China, was forced to accept the conditions when Japan threatened to invade and the southern provinces indicated their unwillingness to support China's new central government.

1915 Jan. 24 In the **battle of Dogger Bank**, 60 miles off the east coast of England, a British battle cruiser force routed an outgunned German squadron, sinking the armored crusier *Blucher.* Of her crew, 1,951 died. Other German ships were damaged but escaped, while British casualties were only 14 killed and 6 wounded.

1915 Feb. 18 **Germany began its blockade of England and France**, using mainly U-boats [submarines] and, at first, sinking ships without warning. The sinking of such passenger ships as the *Lusitania* (May 7), which carried many American passengers, caused intense ill-feeling between the U.S. and Germany, leading to an order (May, 1916) to U-boat captains not to sink passenger or merchant ships without warning or providing for the security of passengers unless a ship resisted or attempted to flee.

1915 Feb. 19 French and British ships launched a preliminary **naval attack along the Dardanelles** to drive Turkish forces from the coastline for a landing by British troops.

1915 Feb. 21 The Germans, having won the second **battle at the Masurian Lakes** against the Russians, began a push eastward. In April Austrian forces, augmented by German troops, launched an offensive against the Russians in western Galicia. In May the Germans advanced into Poland and in August Warsaw, the capital of Congress [Russian] Poland, fell to German troops. In September Vilna [Vilnius], capital of Russian Lithuania, fell. By November, the Russians had been driven behind the borders they held prior to 1800.

1915 Mar. 1 Great Britain declared a blockade against Germany. This step was taken in retaliation for Germany's announcement on Jan. 25 that grain and flour would now be considered contraband of war and subject to seizure. Until this time neutral vessels with foodstuffs had been allowed by Great Britain to sail to Germany. England at once turned the tables on Germany by seizing an American freighter that was in an English port with a cargo of food destined for Germany.

1915 Apr. 22 In the **second battle at Ypres**, the Germans attacked the entrenched British Expeditionary Force, using **poison gas** for the first time. Unfortunately for the Germans, the wind had reversed itself and blown the gas back on the Germans. Canadian troops, who replaced Britons stricken by gas, held firm through another gas attack on Apr. 24. By May 25 the battle ended indecisively. The number of casualties, usually higher for the attacking side, was reversed in this battle; the defending Allies sustained losses nearly double those of the Germans.

1915 Apr. 25 Allied troops landed on Gallipoli [Turkish: Gelibolu] Peninsula, which forms the northwestern coast of the Dardanelles Straits. British and French troops were joined by the Australian and New Zealand Army Corps for a massive invasion. But Turkish forces under Kemal Mustafa had fortified their positions since the initial bombardment by the British in January, and the Allies could make little headway. Nearly nine months later, on Jan. 9, 1916, after heavy casualties—Allies c.50,000 killed, Turks c.250,000 killed—the Allies abandoned their attack, and the Dardanelles [Çanakkale Boğazi] remained in Turkish hands.

1915 Apr. 26 France, Great Britain, and Russia signed secret treaties in London. They were kept secret because the participants did not wish to antagonize Woodrow Wilson, president of the U.S., especially since the treaties showed the Allies were not fighting solely for defense but also for conquest. The treaties agreed that Russia would gain Constantinople and all of Poland; France would have the Rhine as its eastern boundary, and England would take

control of most of the German colonies. The Allies also signed a treaty with Italy in which Italy promised to enter the war on their side in return for gaining from Austria-Hungary some largely Italian-speaking areas in the South Tyrol and the city of Trieste. Italy accordingly declared war (May 23) on Austria-Hungary but did not declare war on Germany until Aug. 27, 1916.

1915 May 7 The *Lusitania*, the British Cunard Line's luxury transatlantic passenger ship, was torpedoed and sunk without warning off the Irish coast by the U-20, a German submarine [U-boat] while en route from New York to Liverpool. Of the 1,806 passengers and crew aboard, 1,198 perished, including 128 Americans. Although Germany asserted that the *Lusitania* was armed and loaded with war explosives, there appeared actually to be only a small amount of rifle ammunition aboard. The U.S. protested strongly to Germany in two notes (May 13, June 9). Reparations were demanded and a promise was expected that such an event would not recur.

1915 May 25 In **Great Britain the Liberal party government** entered into a war-time coalition government with the Conservative party. **Herbert Asquith** remained as prime minister and **Andrew Bonar Law**, the leader of the Conservatives, joined the cabinet. **Arthur Balfour**, another conservative, replaced as first lord of the admiralty **Winston Churchill**, in disgrace as the chief advocate of the ill-fated Gallipoli campaign.

1915 June 1 The **first air raid** by German Zeppelins over England was made. Zeppelin raids were principally made on London and eastern England; they were not very effective and proved quite costly because the Germans had to rely on highly flammable hydrogen gas to lift into the air, making them vulnerable to fire from British aircraft.

1915 June 23 The **Italian army launched an offensive against Austria-Hungary** along the Isonzo [Soca] River line, in present northwestern Yugoslavia, with Trieste as its objective. In all there were four **battles of the Isonzo** in 1915, the last ending on Dec. 2. The Italians failed to achieve their objective and suffered c.250,000 casualties.

1915 July 27 Guillaume Sam (birth date unknown), **Haiti's** dictator, was assassinated by a mob that stormed his refuge in the French embassy. On the following day **U.S. marines occupied Port-au-Prince,**

capital of Haiti, to protect American investments and to prevent German intervention. On Aug. 12 the Haitian congress elected **Phillipe Sudre Darteguenave** (b.?, d.?) president of Haiti (1915–1922). Darteguenave governed Haiti under an interim constitution backed by a treaty with the U.S. in which the Americans agreed to render political and economic aid for ten years (later extended for an additional ten years).

1915 Sept. 18 **Vilna** [Wilno, Wilna, Vilnius], the capital of Lithuania, governed by Russia, was **occupied by the Germans** during World War I. The Germans permitted a congress to assemble in Vilna, which under Antanas Smetona (Aug. 10, 1874–Jan. 9, 1944) declared (Sept. 18–22, 1917) Lithuanian independence. On Mar. 24 Germany recognized the independent state and forced on **Lithuania** a treaty of perpetual alliance.

1915 Sept. 22 **French and British forces launched a major offensive in the Artois** and Champagne regions of northern France. The French attack began with a three-day bombardment by c.2,500 cannon that before the battle was over fired almost 5,000,000 rounds. The French took c.25,000 German prisoners but suffered c.145,000 casualties. The British attack captured the mining town of Loos, but at a cost of c.60,000 casualties.

1915 Oct. 6 **Austrian and German troops invaded Serbia**. On Nov. 25 the Serbian army was forced to retreat across Albania to a refuge on the Greek island of Corfu, carrying their wounded king, Peter I Karageorgevich (July 11, 1844–Aug. 16, 1921) on a litter.

1915 Oct. 12 **Edith** [Louisa] **Cavell** (b. Dec. 4, 1865), an English nurse, was executed in Belgium by the Germans for helping Allied soldiers escape imprisonment. When war began in 1914 Cavell was the head of the nursing staff of a medical institute in Brussels. This became a Red Cross hospital that ministered to wounded soldiers of both sides. Cavell, arrested on Oct. 3 and tried by court-martial, admitted she had assisted more than 100 men to get across the Dutch border.

1915 Oct. 14 **Bulgaria joined the Central Powers and declared war on Serbia** after receiving a promise of Turkish territory in the **Treaty of Pless** [Pszczyna], in southwestern Poland, signed on Oct. 6, the same day that Austria and Germany had

launched their attack on Serbia. Twelve countries were now fighting in World War I: Italy, which had become a belligerent May 23, 1915, and Bulgaria as of this date joined the ten countries that had become belligerents by Oct. 30, 1914.

1915 Nov. 21 The Turks halted the advance of British troops into the Ottoman Empire from India in a **battle at Ctesiphon**, ruins of an ancient city near the Arab city of Baghdad [now in Iraq]. The British retreated to Kut al-Amara [Kut-al-Imara, Al-Kut, Kut], where they were forced to surrender on Apr. 29, 1916, temporarily halting the **British Mesopotamian Campaign** in World War I (1914–1918).

1915 Dec. 4 **Henry Ford** and a group of pacifists and others sailed on the liner *Oscar II* from Hoboken, N.J., in what the auto manufacturer said was an expedition "to get the boys out of the trenches by Christmas." Just how the warring nations were to be convinced they should end the war was not clear. Soon after the ship docked at Oslo, Norway, on Dec. 18, the **hairbrained scheme collapsed**. Ford started for home on Dec. 24.

IV. ECONOMY AND TRADE

1915 Nov. 18 **German textile workers were granted a dole**, following a decision by the Federal Council on Aug. 12 that had reduced the industry's work week.

V. SCIENCE, EDUCATION, AND TECHNOLOGY

1915 Jan. 25 The **first transcontinental telephone conversation** was held between New York and San Francisco. **Alexander Graham Bell**, repeating the conversation he held with his assistant in 1876, said, "Mr. Watson, come here, I want you."

1915 Mar. 21 **Frederick W**[inslow] **Taylor** (b. Mar. 20, 1856), an American industrial engineer, called the father of scientific management, died. In 1881, while chief engineer of a steel company, he began time and motion studies to determine how workmen could perform their tasks more efficiently and thus reduce manufacturing costs. His methods became widely practiced and were introduced in a number of industries. Taylor wrote *The Principles of Scientific Management* (1911).

1915 Apr. 22 & 24 The **Germans were the first nation to use poison gas** in World War I (1914–1918), spreading it against the French army at Ypres [Ieper] in Flanders, Belgium, by means of mortar shells filled with chlorine gas. Later in the war phosgene, a more deadly gas, was used.

1915 Oct. 21 The **first transatlantic radiotelephone call** was made between Arlington, Virginia, and the Eiffel Tower in Paris.

1915 Nov. 14 **Booker T**[aliaferro] **Washington** (b. Apr. 5, 1856), an American educator, died. Born into slavery, by hard work he secured an education and became a teacher. In 1881 he was selected to organize Tuskegee [Alabama] Institute, which he built into a leading institution for the education of blacks. Washington's autobiography *Up From Slavery* (1901) became a classic.

1915 Nov. 25 **Albert Einstein** completed his **General Theory of Relativity**, which extended his Special Theory of Relativity (1905). The work was published in its finished form in *Annalen der Physik* on Mar. 20, 1916.

VI. ARTS AND LEISURE

1915 The **dada art and literary movement** was founded by **Jean** [Hans] **Arp** (Sept. 16, 1887–June 7, 1966), an Alsatian poet and sculptor. The word "dada" [French: "wooden horse"], was chosen at random from the dictionary to name the movement. The objective of the dadaists, as stated in their manifesto, was to overturn all commonly practiced ethical and artistic standards.

1915 **Lillian Gish** (Oct. 14, 1896–Feb. 27, 1993), an American actress, became one of the first movie stars when she played a leading role in **D.W. Griffith's** *The Birth of a Nation* (1915), the first epic of the new medium.

1915 Feb. 8 The world premiere of ***The Birth of a Nation***, an epic film produced and directed by **David Wark Griffith** (Jan 23, 1875–July 23, 1948), took place at Clune's Auditorium in Los Angeles. Its first New York City showing was on Mar. 3 at the Liberty Theater. The film **established cinematography as a serious art form** but was attacked by liberals and blacks for showing the Ku Klux Klan in a favorable light in the post-Civil War South and for its downgrading of blacks in general. Other films by Griffith included *Intolerance* (1916), *Broken Blossoms* (1919), and *Orphans of the Storm* (1921).

1915 Apr. 23 **Rupert Brooke** (b. Aug. 3, 1887), an English poet, died in service with the British Mediterranean Expeditionary Force. He was probably best known for *1914 and Other Poems* (1915). *Collected Poems* (1918) appeared posthumously.

1915 Apr. 27 **Alexander Scriabin** [Aleksandr Nikolaevich Scriabine; Nikolayevich Skryabin, Skriabin] (b. Jan. 6, 1872), a Russian musician, died. Scriabin introduced the use of chords built on fourths instead of the major and minor triads common to classical music. Scriabin's works included *Le Divin Poème* [*The Divine Poem*] or Third Symphony (1903), *Satanic Poem* and other sonatas, and *Prometheus: A Poem of Fire* (1909–1910).

VII. SPORTS, GAMES, AND SOCIETY

1915 Apr. 5 **Jess Willard** (Dec. 29, 1881–Dec. 15, 1968) won the **heavyweight boxing championship of the world** when he knocked out the defending titleholder Jack Johnson in the 26th round. The fight took place in Havana, Cuba, with the temperature standing at 110° F.

1916

I. DISASTERS

1916 July 30 German saboteurs were held responsible for a **fire** originating on a barge at Black Tom Island pier near Jersey City, New Jersey. As the fire spread, stores of munitions and dynamite were ignited, causing explosions that continued for days. Property losses totalled $22 million. The **Statue of Liberty** was hit by flying debris, and the explosions were felt 90 miles to the south in Camden, New Jersey.

II. POLITICS AND WAR

1916–1928 This period, known as the **Warlord Era in China**, began with the disappearance of the last vestige of imperial power, when the Manchu-appointed **Yüan Shih-K'ai** sought (1915) to become a hereditary king but died (1916), and ended with **Chiang Kai-Shek's** defeat of warlord-held Peking in 1928. During this period of unrest the Chinese, always more loyal to clan allegiances than to the central government, fell back on blood, language, and geographic alliances.

1916 Jan. 24 The British House of Commons passed a bill establishing **compulsory military service**, to be effective on Feb. 9. The bill provided alternative service for conscientious objectors. By this time c.1,000,000 British males had volunteered for the army or navy.

1916 Feb. 21 The **Battle of Verdun**, on the Meuse River in northeastern France, began as the German chief commander **Erich von Falkenhayn** concentrated forces for a major assault on the eastern end of the Western Front. **Henri Philippe Pétain** led the French resistance. The nearby Fort Douaumont fell to the Germans on Feb. 25 and Fort Vaux on June 7, but they were regained by the French in November. The battle lasted until Dec. 18, 1916. After the last German attack on July 11, the battleground remained relatively quiet until the French began a counter-attack on Oct. 24. In the **longest battle of World War I** (1914–1918), the Germans suffered c.435,000 casualties, the French c.542,000.

1916 Feb. 26 A German U-boat torpedoed and sank the French transport *Provence* in the Mediterranean Sea as it was carrying c.3,500 troops to Salonika, Greece. About 3,100 lives were lost.

1916 Mar. 5 **Allied forces**, consisting of British, South African, Belgian, and Portuguese troops, **invaded German East Africa** [present Tanzania]. The British took the port of Dar es Salaam on Sept. 3, but the Allies were unable to capture the small German force defending the colony.

1916 Mar. 8 **Pancho Villa**, the Mexican rebel leader, led a band of c.500 men across the border into the U.S. and raided the small town of Columbus, New Mexico, where 17 residents died in the fray. Pancho Villa was protesting U.S. support of **Venustiano Carranza**, president of Mexico (from 1914).

U.S. cavalry under **John Joseph Pershing** (Sept. 13, 1860–July 15, 1948) pursued Villa and his band throughout the state of Chihuahua for 11 months, finally withdrawing on Feb. 5, 1917.

1916 Mar. 9 **Portugal joined the Allies** in World War I (1914–1918). Germany declared war on Portugal.

1916 Mar. 24 The unarmed French ship *Sussex* was sunk in the English Channel by a German submarine. Several Americans were aboard and three died. This event occasioned a strong note from **Robert Lansing** (Oct. 17, 1864–Oct. 30, 1928), U.S. secretary of state, in which he threatened that America would break off diplomatic relations with Germany unless such attacks ceased. Relations between the two countries were becoming more and more strained, and **American public opinion was becoming hardened against Germany.**

1916 Apr. 24 The **Easter Monday uprising** broke out in Dublin, where the post office and other vital services were seized by **Irish Nationalists** [Sinn Fein]. On Apr. 24 the **Irish Republic** was proclaimed by **Padhraic [Patrick] Pearse**, one of the leaders. Plans for the insurrection, organized by the **Irish Republican Brotherhood** [IRB], had been kept secret—even the IRB leader Eoin [John] MacNeill (May 15, 1867–Oct. 15, 1945) was uninformed. The revolt was undermined, however, on the same day (Apr. 24) when Roger David Casement was arrested in County Kerry after his return (Apr. 21) from Germany. Though Germany had refused to invade Ireland on the Nationalists' behalf, it had supplied some arms and escorted Casement aboard a submarine. The British sent reinforcements to Dublin, and the fighting ceased there on May 1 after Pearse's surrender (Apr. 29). Pearse (b. Nov. 10, 1879) was executed by a firing squad in Dublin on May 3. Casement (b. Sept. 1, 1864), an Ulster Protestant, was hanged on Aug. 3 in London for treason for his role in the uprising.

1916 May 15 **Austria-Hungary began an offensive against the Italian army** in the Trentino, the Austrian province bordering on northeastern Italy. The Austrians forced the Italians back to the town of Asiago but there the drive ended on June 17.

1916 May 31–June 1 The **largest naval engagement of World War I**, the **Battle of Jutland**, was fought off the west coast of Denmark by the British

Grand Fleet and the German High Seas Fleet. The British force consisted of 149 warships, including 28 battleships, while the Germans had 99 ships, of which 22 were battleships. Eventually the German fleet retreated to the safety of its bases, but the British suffered far heavier losses, 117,025 tons of warships compared with the Germans' 61,180. The German main fleet never ventured out again, so Britain retained command of the seas. ·

1916 June 4   Aleksei Alekseevich Brusilov (Aug. 19, 1853–Mar. 17, 1926) began a **Russian offensive into the Austrian province of Galicia** with the goal of taking its capital, Lemberg [Lvov], in present western Ukraine. The Austrian armies were easily defeated, but the arrival of German reinforcements on Sept. 16 prevented the Russians from reaching Lemberg.

1916 June 7   Husein ibn-Ali [Husain ibn Ali, Husayn ibn-'Ali] (c.1855–?1931), grand sherif of Mecca, led a **revolt of Hejaz** [Hijaz, Mecca] province, on the eastern shore of the Red Sea, against Ottoman rule. In November the British were able to advance from Egypt into the Sinai Peninsula. Husein ibn-Ali, founder of the **Hashimite Dynasty of Mecca** (1908–1925) was recognized as the first king of Hejaz (to 1924) by Great Britain, France, and Italy on Jan. 1, 1917.

1916 July 1   The first **battle at the Somme**, a river in northern France on a line with the Aisne River in northeastern France, began as British and French forces launched a counteroffensive along the Western Front. By Nov. 18, when the offensive was halted, the Allies had gained several miles but failed to break through the German line. Casualties totaled more than 1,265,000 men: c.650,000 German troops, c.420,000 British, and c.195,000 French.

1916 Aug. 9   Fighting along the Isonzo River in Austrian-controlled territory of northeastern Italy reached a peak as Italian and Allied troops won Gorizia [Görz] just north of Trieste on the present border with Yugoslavia, from Austria-Hungary, the only important victory along the Italian front in 1916.

1916 Aug. 27   Romania, heartened by the successful Russian campaign in Galicia, **declared war on Austria-Hungary** in World War I (1914–1918), but by Jan. 1917, the country was occupied by Austrian and German forces invading from Austria-Hungary and German and Bulgarian troops invading from Bulgaria.

1916 Sept. 30   The Central American Court, ruling on the **Bryan-Chamorro Treaty** (1914) concluded by the U.S. and Nicaragua, decided that the rights of **Costa Rica** had been violated by Nicaragua. The treaty allowed the U.S. to use the San Juan River, which forms part of the Costa Rica-Nicaragua boundary, for part of the route of the transisthmian canal without consulting Costa Rica. The U.S. had also been granted the right to construct a naval base in the Gulf of Fonseca, a sheltered inlet on the Pacific Ocean bordered by Nicaragua, Honduras, and El Salvador. Because the decision of the **Central American Court**, which had been established in 1908, went unrecognized, especially by Nicaragua, its charter was not renewed.

1916 Nov. 3   Eleutherios Venizelos (Aug. 23, 1864–Mar. 18, 1936), leading the provisional Greek government, declared war on Bulgaria and Germany. Venizelos joined the Greek admiral Pavolos Koundouriotes (Apr. 9, 1855–Aug. 22, 1935) in forming a pro-Allied provisional government of national defense at Salonika. On Dec. 19 Great Britain granted official recognition to the government. **Greece officially declared war on the Central Powers** on June 27, 1917.

1916 Nov. 5   Congress [Russian] **Poland** was declared independent by Austria-Hungary and Germany in order to create a buffer state to defend the Eastern Front against Russia during World War I (1914–1918). When **Józef Klemens Plisudski**, leader of the Polish army in Russian Poland, refused to swear allegiance to the two powers, he was arrested and imprisoned in Germany in July, 1917.

1916 Nov. 7   Jeannette Rankin (July 11, 1880–May 18, 1973), a Montana suffragist and pacifist, became the **first woman ever elected to the U.S. Congress**, serving in the House of Representatives (1917–1919, 1941–1943). A Republican, she voted against declaring war on Germany in 1917 and was in 1941 the only member of the House to vote against war with Germany.

1916 Nov. 21   Francis Joseph I (b. Aug. 18, 1830), emperor of Austria (from 1848) and king of Hungary (from 1867), died. He had come to the throne at the time of the turmoil of the liberal revolutions of 1848 and died in the midst of a war that threatened catastrophe to his **Austro-Hungarian Empire** (1867–1918). Under his rule Austria-Hungary was involved in a number of wars, mostly unsuccessfully. In 1867 Francis Joseph divided the empire into the **Dual Monarchy** with Austria and Hungary as equal partners and he took the title of king of Hungary. The emperor was generally popular with his subjects in Austria, but the many ethnic minorities in the conglomerate empire were often restless. Francis Joseph was succeeded by a great nephew who became Charles I [Karl] (Aug. 17, 1887–Apr. 1, 1922; ruled 1916–1918).

1916 Dec. 7   [David] **Lloyd George**, a member of the Liberal party, replaced Herbert Henry Asquith as prime minister of Great Britain. Lloyd George, a brilliant debater, strengthened popular confidence in Britain's role during World War I.

1916 Dec. 18   In identical **notes to all the nations at war in Europe**, **Woodrow Wilson**, president of the U.S., asked them to state their war aims. Germany replied on Dec. 26, not giving its terms as requested, but calling for a conference. The Allies on Dec. 30 answered by calling Germany's reply a "sham." Nothing further came of this peace move.

1916 Dec. 31   Members of the Russian royal family and the Duma murdered **Grigori Efimovich Rasputin** (b. 1871?), confidant to the Russian czarina **Alexandra Feodorovna** [orig.: Alix Victoria Helene Luise Beatrix] (June 6, 1872–July 28–29, 1918). Rasputin, who claimed to be a monk, had gained great influence over the czarina by apparently sustaining life in the hemophilic heir to the throne. He abused his power greedily. Undoubtedly he passed secret information to the Central Powers for gold and was a virulent influence on the weak czar.

III. ECONOMY AND TRADE

1916   **Marcus Garvey**, a Jamaican-born leader of black nationalism, brought his **Universal Negro Improvement Association** [UNIA] to New York City's Harlem. Garvey's "back to Africa" movement gained popularity during the 1920s, advocating establishment of an autonomous black state in Africa.

1916 July 3   **Hetty Green** [nee Henrietta Howland Robinson] (b. Nov. 21, 1834), generally conceded to be the **most successful female financier** in the world, and perhaps also the richest woman in America, died. She inherited fortunes from both her father

and an aunt and increased them to such an extent that when she died her estate was worth about $100,000,000.

IV. RELIGION AND PHILOSOPHY

1916 Dec. 10   **Modern Parsees** convened at Sanjan, India, in celebration of the first Zoroastrian emigrés from Persia who landed there 1,200 years ago.

V. SCIENCE, EDUCATION, AND TECHNOLOGY

1916 Feb. 19   **Ernst Mach** (b. Feb. 18, 1838), an Austrian physicist and philosopher, died. He was best remembered because his researches gave his name to the Mach number, the ratio of the speed of an object to the local speed of sound. Mach's major work, however, was in the philosophy of science. He tried to divest science of any metaphysical or religious assumptions and was one of the founders of *Empiriokritizismus*, devoted to this point of view.

1916 July 15   **Élie Metchnikoff** [Ilya Ilich Mechnikov] (b. May 15, 1845), a Russian bacteriologist, died. He studied blood diseases and formulated the **theory of phagocytosis**, in which certain blood cells protect the body against disease by ingesting harmful bacteria. In 1908 he received the **Nobel prize for physiology or medicine** with **Paul Ehrlich**.

1916 July 23   **William Ramsay** (b. Oct. 2, 1852), a Scottish chemist and winner of the **Nobel prize for chemistry** in 1904, died. Ramsay was the **first to isolate helium** and show that it was the result of disintegration of the atoms of radium (1895). With **John William Strutt** (Nov. 12, 1842–June 30, 1919) he discovered argon; and with **Morris William Travers** (Jan. 24, 1872–Aug. 25, 1961) neon, krypton, and xenon.

1916 Sept. 15   In fighting near Courcelette in the **battle at the Somme**, **armored tanks** were used by the British, who had hoped to develop a weapon impenetrable to German machine gun fire and thereby break the stalemate in the trench warfare.

1916 Nov. 12   **Percival Lowell** (b. Mar. 13, 1855), an American astronomer in Boston, died in Flagstaff, Arizona, where he had had an observatory constructed. He is primarily remembered today for predicting the existence of a planet beyond Neptune. The planet Pluto was discovered in 1930 by **Clyde**

William Tombaugh (b. Feb. 4, 1906) who was an astronomer at the Flagstaff observatory.

VI. ARTS AND LEISURE

1916 Feb. 28   Henry James (b. Apr. 15, 1843), an American-born novelist and pioneer of psychological realism, died. He lived most of his life in England and became a British subject in 1915. *Portrait of a Lady* (1881), considered one of the finest novels in English literature, explored the confrontation of simple American innocence and European culture, often corrupt. Among his other notable works were *The American* (1877), *The Europeans* (1878), *Daisy Miller* (1878), *The Bostonians* (1886), *The Wings of the Dove* (1902), *The Ambassadors* (1903), and *The Golden Bowl* (1904).

1916 Mar. 4   Franz Marc (b. Feb. 8, 1880), a German painter and one of the founders of Der Blaue Reiter, was killed in action near Verdun during World War I. Marc's best-known works included *The Tower of Blue Horses*, *The Fate of the Beasts* (1911), and *The Unhappy Tyrol* (1913–1914).

1916 June 25   Thomas Eakins (b. July 15, 1844), an American artist noted for his penetrating realism, died. His very large painting *The Surgical Clinic of Professor Gross* (1875) is now considered a masterpiece but when it was first shown it caused a scandal because of its realistic portrayal of blood and bones. Eakins was also a sculptor and a photographer. He was much interested in athletes and did compelling paintings of them in action, such as *Max Schmitt in a Single Scull* (1871). Eakins is recognized as one of the foremost painters of the 19th century.

1916 Nov. 15   Henryk [Adam Aleksandr Pius] **Sienkiewicz** (b. May 5, 1846), a Polish novelist and patriot, died. His work became well known abroad after publication of *Quo Vadis?* (1895), a tale of Christianity in the time of Nero's Rome. He agitated for Polish independence during World War I and earlier stimulated interest in the Polish struggle for nationhood in a trilogy, translated as *With Fire and Sword* (1890), *The Deluge* (1891), and *Pan Michael* (1893). He was awarded the **Nobel prize for literature** in 1905.

1916 Nov. 22   Jack London (b. Jan. 12, 1876), an American author of adventure tales romanticizing the struggle for survival against the elements, died. *Call of the Wild* (1903), one of several Alaskan stories; *The Sea-Wolf* (1904); and *White Fang* (1906) were among the 50 or more books London produced. *Martin Eden* (1909) chronicled London's own search for adventure and his struggle to become a writer.

1916 Nov. 27   Emile Verhaeren (b. May 21, 1855), a Belgian poet, died. His early work, such as *Les Flamandes* (1883) expressed faith in social reform and universal brotherhood. The poetic trilogy *Les Soirs* (1888), *Les Débacles* (1888), and *Les Flambeaux Noirs* (1891), in contrast, were dark works about the human condition.

VII. SPORTS, GAMES, AND SOCIETY

1916 Jan. 1   Washington State University defeated Brown University, 14 to 0, in the **first annual Rose Bowl football game** in Pasadena, California. The first post-season football game in the U.S. was a Tournament of Roses Association game played on Jan. 1, 1902, also at Pasadena. Michigan defeated Stanford, 49 to 0.

1917

I. DISASTERS

1917 May 26   A tornado, originating at noon near the town of Louisiana, Missouri, ended over seven hours later near the eastern boundary of Jennings County, Indiana, 293 miles away. Deaths in Mattoon and Charleston, both in Illinois, totaled 139, with personal and property damage set at $1,981,000.

1917 Dec. 6   The *Imo*, a Belgian relief ship, **collided** with the *Mont Blanc*, a French munitions ship, in the harbor at Halifax, Nova Scotia, Canada. The ensuing explosion destroyed a large section of the city and killed more than 1,630 persons.

1917 Dec. 12   A train carrying nearly 1,200 allied troops from the front lines **derailed near the Mt.**

Cenis tunnel at Modane, in Savoy, France, killing 543 and injuring 243. The wreck went unreported due to wartime censorship.

II. POLITICS AND WAR

1917 Jan. 17 The U.S. Senate ratified a treaty for the **purchase of the Virgin Islands** [St. John, St. Croix, St. Thomas, and c.50 islets, hitherto known as the Danish West Indies] from Denmark for $25,000,-000.

1917 Jan. 27 **Alfredo González Flores,** president of **Costa Rica** (from 1914), was ousted in a military coup staged by **Federico Tinoco Granados** (1870–1931). This was the first serious disruption in Costa Rica's peaceful and democratic transfer of power since the late 1800s.

1917 Feb. 1 **Germany announced unrestricted submarine warfare** against international shipping.

1917 Feb. 3 The **U.S. severed diplomatic relations with Germany.** In making the announcement, Woodrow Wilson, president of the U.S., cited Germany's policy of unrestricted submarine warfare. This same day a German U-boat sank the American liner *Housatonic* without warning. Bolivia, Brazil, and Peru followed the U.S. lead and broke off relations also. Wilson then asked (Feb. 28) Congress to authorize the arming of American merchant ships, but a filibuster by isolationist senators prevented passage of the measure. After the U.S. attorney general ruled (Mar. 9) that the power to arm the ships was inherent in the presidency, Wilson issued the necessary orders.

1917 Feb. 5 A new **constitution was adopted in Mexico** under Venustiano Carranza, president of Mexico (from 1914), and Álvaro Obregón, chief military advisor to Carranza. To the constitution of 1857 many reforms were added, which, if truly implemented, would have overturned Mexican feudalism.

1917 Feb. 23 **Frederick Stanley Maude** (June 24, 1864–Nov. 18, 1917) led the British rout of Turks from Kut al-Amara in Mesopotamia and marched to **Baghdad,** which **fell to the British** on Mar. 11. They continued northward in their Mesopotamian campaign to capture the cities of Ramadi and Tikrit, located respectively on the Euphrates and Tigris rivers.

1917 Mar. 1 The **Zimmerman Telegram** was made public by Woodrow Wilson, causing a sensation and an outburst of anger at Germany. On Jan. 16, **Arthur Zimmerman** (Oct. 5, 1864-June 6, 1940), the German foreign minister, sent a telegram to **Johann Heinrich von Bernstorff** (Nov. 14, 1862–Oct. 6, 1939), the German ambassador to the U.S., in which he proposed that if the U.S. entered the war against Germany, Mexico be urged to make war on the U.S. In return, Mexico would be promised the return of Texas, Arizona, and New Mexico, former Mexican territories. The telegram was intercepted and decoded by British intelligence which gave it to the U.S.

1917 Mar. 2 The **Jones Act** was passed by the U.S. Congress. It established **Puerto Rico as a territory of the U.S.** and granted U.S. citizenship to Puerto Ricans.

1917 Mar. 5 **Woodrow Wilson** of the Democratic party was inaugurated for his second term as president of the U.S., having defeated **Charles Evans Hughes** (Apr. 11, 1862–Aug. 27, 1948). In a close election on Nov. 7, 1916, Wilson received 277 electoral college votes to 254 for Hughes, the Republican candidate. The popular vote was 9,128,837 to 8,536,-380. **Thomas Riley Marshall** served again as vice president.

1917 Mar. 8–15 The **Russian Revolution** of 1917 began with strikes and riots in Petrograd [present St. Petersburg], the capital of Russia, protesting continuation of the war and food shortages. These events signaled the start of what became known as the **February Revolution,** because Russia still used the Old Style calendar by which the date was Feb. 23. Troops were sent to put down the riots but many of them joined the strikers. On Mar. 11 Nicholas II, czar of Russia, dissolved the Duma, the Russian legislative body of very limited powers. With the government crumbling, some liberal members of the Duma and representatives of the more radical elements who were now in power in the **Petrograd Soviet** [Soviet = council] agreed to form a provisional government. It was headed by Georgi Evgenievich [Georgy Yevgenyevich] Lvov (Nov. 2, 1861–Mar. 6, 1925), but Alexander **Fyodorovich** Kerensky, minister of justice, was the most influential member of it. This regime proposed to continue the war against the Central Powers. On Mar. 15, with his regime repudiated and powerless, **Nicholas II abdicated as czar,** bringing to an end the **Romanov Dynasty** (from 1613).

1917 Apr. 6 The **U.S. declared war against Germany**. On Apr. 2 **Woodrow Wilson**, president of the U.S., appeared before a special session of Congress to ask for a formal declaration. In the course of his remarks he declared: "The world must be made safe for democracy." The Senate voted for war on Apr. 4 and the House two days later. Wilson signed the war resolution the same day.

1917 Apr. 9–May 3 The third **battle at Arras** (the first Sept.–Oct., 1914; second June–July, 1915), in northern France, was fought by mostly British troops to draw German forces northward along the fortified **Hindenburg Line** and away from the Aisne River sector where a large French offensive was planned. Canadian troops successfully stormed Vimy Ridge, near Arras, on this day, but when fighting eased (May 3) there were great casualties and little gain for the Allied position.

1917 Apr. 16–May 9 The second **battle at the Aisne River** (first Sept. 13–17, 1914) was fought by the French army under **Robert Georges Nivelle** (Oct. 15, 1856–Mar. 22, 1924), the commander-in-chief of French forces in the northern and northeastern sector. The French suffered great casualties while gaining very little ground.

1917 Apr. 16–17 **Vladimir Ilich Lenin** [nee Ulyanov], a leader of the radical wing of the Russian Revolution, returned to Russia, arriving in Petrograd [present St. Petersburg], the center of revolutionary activity, after having been in exile in Switzerland since 1914. The German government allowed him, with a small number of followers, to cross Germany by train because it was in its interest to encourage discontent and unsettled conditions in Russia, with which it was still at war. Lenin's faction was against continuing the struggle. On Apr. 17 Lenin appeared before the revolutionary assemblage and demanded that power be turned over to the radical Bolshevik councils, with land and banks to be nationalized.

1917 May 18 The U.S. Congress passed the **Selective Service Act** to begin conscription of all men from 21 through 30 years of age.

1917 June 3 **Albania declared its independence**, and Italy established a protectorate over Albania.

1917 June 7 **British troops** under Douglas Haig (June 19, 1861–Jan. 29, 1928), **attempted to take Messines Ridge**, south of Ypres, but German resistance halted their advance by June 14.

1917 June 12 **Constantine I,** king of Greece, abdicated under pressure from an Allied invasion launched earlier in June and the popular pro-war faction led by **Eleutherios Venizelos,** who now headed the interim government. Constantine was succeeded by his second son Alexander (b. Aug. 1, 1893), who held the throne until his premature death from blood poisoning on Oct. 25, 1920. On June 27, 1917, **Greece officially declared war against the Central Powers**.

1917 June 17 George V (ruled 1910–1936) and the British royal family renounced their various German ties, establishing the **House of Windsor** (to the present). The British monarchy's close German relations began with George I (ruled 1714–1721), who was the first British sovereign of the **House of Hanover** (to 1901). Albert, husband and prince consort to Victoria (ruled 1837–1901), was the son of the German duke of Saxe-Coburg-Gotha, and his son Edward VII (ruled 1901–1910) established the House of Saxe-Coburg-Gotha (1901–1917).

1917 June 26 The first troops of the **American Expeditionary Force** [AEF] arrived in France. **John J[oseph] Pershing**, who had been named to command America's army in Europe, arrived in Paris on June 13. U.S. troops first saw combat on Nov. 3 near the Rhine-Marne Canal, when German forces attacked the infantrymen.

1917 July A **union of Serbia and Montenegro** as a South Slav state was proposed by Slav representatives on the Allied-held Greek island of Corfu, to which the Serbian army had retreated from advancing armies on the Central Powers occupying the Balkan area.

1917 July 1–20 **Alexander Kerensky**, Russian minister of war in the provisional government, ordered an offensive against Austrian forces in Galicia. While temporarily successful, it was halted amidst many desertions by Russian soldiers. In Ukraine there were demands for autonomy and in Petrograd there was rioting on July 17 and 18 by workers and soldiers opposed to the provisional government. On July 20 Kerensky succeeded Lvov as prime minister. His government was attempting to introduce such democratic measure as trial by jury and freedom of speech and of the press. Kerensky succeeded in forming a coalition of Socialist Revolutionaries and Mensheviks. Rioting failed to unseat Kerensky, and **Lenin**, who was involved, fled to Finland and did not return until Oct. 21.

1917 July 6 A British commander **Thomas Edward Lawrence** [Lawrence of Arabia], took from the Turks the city of Aquaba, at the head of the Gulf of Aquaba in present Jordan. Lawrence's bold seizure of the city was the first of a number of successful **attacks on Turkish strongholds that electrified the Arab world**.

1917 July 14 **Theobald von Bethmann Hollweg**, chancellor (from 1909) of Germany, was forced to resign by the military, led by Ludendorff and Hindenburg. Bethmann Hollweg was somewhat liberal in domestic matters, and in foreign affairs was dominated by the military. He failed in efforts to restrict submarine warfare and his attempt to end the war in 1916 through conciliation led to his ouster. He was succeeded by **Georg Michaelis** (Sept. 8, 1857–July 24, 1936), food minister since 1915. Michealis lost office in November in a dispute with the Reichstag over peace terms.

1917 July 31 The third **battle at Ypres** [Ieper] began with a British offensive at the nearby village of Passchendaele in West Flanders, northwestern Belgium. **Douglas Haig,** the British commander in charge of the attack, had hoped to surprise the Germans commanded by **Rupert** [Rupprecht] (May 18, 1869–Aug. 2, 1955), the crown prince of Bavaria, and break though their lines. With pressure thus taken off the French army to the south in the Aisne sector, the French succeeded in capturing Chemin des Dames, a vital highway along the Aisne River. Fighting in Flanders eased early in November. Both the Germans and the British suffered c.240,000 casualties, with little gain for either side.

1917 July 31 The Russian commander, Lavr Georgievich Kornilov (July 30, 1870–Apr. 13, 1918), launched another attack into Galicia, the **last Russian offensive on the Eastern Front**. By Aug. 9 German troops had driven the Russians back across their border, severely damaging the authority of the Russian provisional government. On Sept. 3 the Germans occupied Riga in Latvia and in October captured Russian islands in the Baltic Sea.

1917 Aug. 9 The **Conscription Act** [Military Service Act] was **passed in Canada** to offset declining enlistments in the armed forces, whose strength had been depleted by heavy casualties in Europe.

1917 Aug. 13 The **Socialist General Union of Labor** [UGT], based in Madrid, organized a **general strike throughout Spain**. This threat to Spain's economy brought a declaration of a state of war by the government.

1917 Sept. 8–15 **Laurus Georgievich Kornilov**, the Russian army commander, ordered troops to Petrograd to unseat the Soviets who were in power there. **Alexander Kerensky** ordered a halt to this move and dismissed (Sept. 9) Kornilov, who refused the order and attempted to make himself dictator of Russia. Kornilov (b. Apr. 30, 1870?) was arrested, escaped, and led a counter-revolutionary movement in the Caucasus where he was killed in action on Mar. 18, 1918. Kerensky declared Russia a republic on Sept. 15.

1917 Oct. 24–Nov. 12 The **battle at Caporetto** on the Italian Front was a major disaster for Italy. The Austro-German offensive under Otto von Below (Jan. 18, 1857–Mar. 9, 1944), after the **rout of the Italian army**, was finally halted along the Piave River with the help of British and French reinforcements. About 320,000 Italian troops were killed, wounded, or captured, but the Central Powers were unable to follow up their victories by crossing the Piave. Paolo Boselli (June 8, 1838–Mar. 10, 1932) prime minister of Italy, resigned his position, and was succeeded by Vittorio Emanuele Orlando (May 19, 1860–Dec. 1, 1952) on Oct. 29.

1917 Oct. 26 **Brazil declared war** as it entered the world conflict on the Allied side, prompted by the attacks made on her merchant shipping by German U-boats in commercial lanes. Other countries joined the Allies: Cuba, on Apr. 8; Panama, on Apr. 9; Siam [present Thailand], on July 22; Liberia, on Aug. 4; and China, on Aug. 14. There were now 17 Allies aligned against the four Central Powers.

1917 Nov. 2 The **Balfour Declaration** was issued by **Arthur James Balfour**, Great Britain's foreign secretary, in a letter to Baron Rothschild, who had financially supported many of the Jewish settlements in Palestine. It announced **British support for the establishment of a Jewish homeland in Palestine**, where many Jewish immigrants had already settled.

1917 Nov. 7 The **Bolshevik Revolution**, also known as the **October Revolution** because it took place on

Oct. 26 [Old Style], brought the **communists in Russia to power**. Now back in Petrograd, **Lenin** led workers and soldiers in the seizure of key points in the city, including the Winter Palace, seat of the Kerensky government. By this time the Bolsheviks were clearly dominant, with **Leon Trotsky** as chairman in Petrograd. The Soviet delegates chose a Council of Commissars to lead their revolutionary Marxist government with Lenin as head and Trotsky as minister of foreign affairs. The latter became commander of the **Red Guard**, organized to defend the city against the Germans and the Kerensky regime.

1917 Nov. 20   The **battle at Cambrai**, in northern France, opened with a bombardment of the German Hindenburg Line by British tanks, the **first massed use of tanks** in warfare. Haig, the British commander, lacked enough reserves to follow up on the initial breakthrough, and the German counterattack under Ludendorff drove the British back again by Dec. 3. Both the British and Germans suffered c.42,000 casualties.

1917 Nov. 28   **Estonia declared its independence** from Russia, which then appointed (Dec. 8) the communist Jaan Anvelt (d. 1937) to attempt to regain control of what it considered a vassal state. Anvelt never truly gained control of Estonia.

1917 Dec. 5   Russia and Germany agreed on an **armistice at Brest-Litovsk** [Brzesc and Bugiem], now in southwestern Belarus. Negotiations for a peace treaty began here on Dec. 21 but were not concluded until Mar. 3, 1918, when the **Treaty of Brest-Litovsk** was signed.

1917 Dec. 9   **Jerusalem**, long under Ottoman suzerainty, **fell to the British** under Edmund Henry Hynman Allenby (Apr. 23, 1861–May 14, 1936). On Nov. 7 he had captured Gaza, on the Mediterranean coast east of the Suez Canal, after unsuccessful attempts on Mar. 26 and Apr. 19.

1917 Dec. 19   The **Union party** won a landslide victory in the Canadian general elections and returned Robert Laird Borden (June 26, 1854–June 10, 1937) to office as prime minister (1911–1920).

1917 Dec. 19   The **Cheka** [later, Ogpu], Russia's secret police under the Bolsheviks, was organized and headed by **Feliks Edmundovich Dzerzhinski** (Sept. 11, 1877–July 20, 1926), to put down counterrevolutionary movements.

III. ECONOMY AND TRADE

1917   The **United States Steel Corporation** became the first corporation to surpass $1,000,000,000 in annual sales.

1917 Apr.   The **Emergency Fleet Corporation** was established as a subsidiary of the United States Shipping Board (Sept. 7, 1916) to construct merchant ships for war transport. By the end of World War I, 875 ships were built.

1917 Apr. 24   The U.S. Congress authorized the **first Liberty Bond Bill**, creating $5 billion in war bonds to finance the U.S. effort in World War I. The interest rate was 3½ percent per annum, and was exempt from taxation. On Oct. 1 a second Liberty Bond issue was offered to the public. It generated $2 billion at 4 per cent interest, and was oversubscribed by Nov. 15.

1917 July 28   The **U.S. War Industries Board** was organized under **Bernard Baruch** to coordinate industrial production for World War I.

1917 Dec. 26   **Woodrow Wilson**, president of the U.S., ordered the **government to take over operation of the railroads**. As it turned out, the railroads were run for the most part by the same people who had been running them before, but under government supervision.

IV. RELIGION AND PHILOSOPHY

1917   Friends of nearly all branches in the U.S. united to form the **American Friends Service Committee** [AFSC] for relief and rehabilitation work abroad.

1917 Jan. 30   Seven Jewish scholars in the United States, representing **Jewish Theological Seminary**, **Hebrew Union College**, and the **Dropsie College**, published a modern translation of Hebrew Scriptures for use by American Jews, under the sponsorship of the **Jewish Publication Society of America**. The translators' work on *The Holy Scriptures* had been finished in Nov. 1915.

1917 Dec. 22   **Frances Xavier Cabrini** [nee Maria Francesca] (b. July 15, 1850), an Italian-American nun who became the **first American citizen to be canonized**, died. She founded the **Missionary Sisters of the Sacred Heart of Jesus** in 1880. Sent by the pope to the U.S. in 1889 to aid Italian immigrants, Sister Cabrini established schools, nurseries, orphanages, and hospitals in Latin America as well as the U.S. She was canonized by Pope Pius XII in 1946.

V. SCIENCE, EDUCATION, AND TECHNOLOGY

1917 The **forerunner to the modern helicopter** was a machine built by **Louis Charles Bréguet** (Jan. 2, 1880–May 4, 1955). Its lift was obtained by powered rotary wings mounted horizontally; its forward power was obtained by a propeller mounted vertically. It had no fixed wings.

1917 Nov. 15 **Émile Durkheim** (b. Oct. 15, 1858), a French sociologist and a chief founder of that discipline, died. He believed that the methods of natural science could be used in the study of society. Among Durkheim's writings were *De la division du travail social* [*The Division of Labor in Society*] (1893) and *Règles de la méthode sociologique* [*The Rules of Sociological Method*] (1895).

1917 Mar. 8 **Ferdinand** [Adolf August Heinrich] **von Zeppelin** (b. July 8, 1838) died. An officer in the Prussian army, he was an observer with the Union army in the U.S. Civil War (1861–1865) and fought in the Franco-Prussian War of 1870. Zeppelin in 1900 constructed the **first airship** of the kind to which his name was soon attached. During World War I, Zeppelins were used to carry out air raids on England, but with insignificant results.

1917 Aug. 13 **Eduard Buchner** (b. May 20, 1860), a German chemist, died in Romania in service with German troops. In 1896 he found that it was the action in enzymes contained in yeast that caused alcoholic fermentation of sugars. In 1907 Buchner received the **Nobel prize for chemistry**.

VI. ARTS AND LEISURE

1917 The **Lenin State Library** in Moscow was founded under the auspices of **V.I. Lenin**, leader of the Russian Revolution (1917). It contains important collections of early printed books and manuscripts of ancient Slovanic codices, as well as once-private libraries seized at the time of the revolution.

1917 Apr. 1 **Scott Joplin** (b. Nov. 24, 1868), an American pianist and composer, died. His compositions changed **ragtime** from a honky-tonk form to a recog-

nized type of popular music. Joplin's first hit was the popular "Maple Leaf Rag" (1899). Others included the "Entertainer" (1902) and "Sugar Can Rag" (1908). He also wrote a ragtime opera *Treemonisha* (1911), which was not staged until 1972.

1917 Sept. 27 [Hilaire Germain] **Edgar Degas** (b. July 19, 1834), a French impressionist painter and sculptor, died. Degas was noted especially for his studies of ballet dancers and race horses. Among his works were *The Cotton Exchange* (1872), in New Orleans, where he was visiting relatives; *The Dancing Class* (1874); *The Absinthe Drinker* (1876); and *After the Bath: Woman Drying Herself* (1890). Degas produced a number of statues and statuettes of ballet dancers.

1917 Nov. 17 **François Auguste René Rodin** (b. Nov. 12, 1840), a noted French sculptor, died. His *L'Âge de Airain* [*Age of Bronze*], exhibited at the Paris Salon in 1877, sparked a heated controversy over what was true sculpture. By 1890 he was firmly established as a major figure in the world of art. He produced many busts and individual pieces, including *Le Penseur* [*The Thinker*] (1880), *Le Baiser* [*The Kiss*] (1886), and *The Burghers of Calais* (begun 1884).

VI. SPORTS, GAMES, AND SOCIETY

1917 Jan. 10 **William Frederick Cody** (b. Feb. 26, 1846), better known as "Buffalo Bill," who put the American wild west on the road as a tent show, died. Before becoming a performer, Cody rode for the Pony Express, scouted for the U.S. army against Indians, and hunted buffalo to provide food for railroad construction gangs on the western plains. In 1883 he organized **Buffalo Bill's Wild West Show**, with Indians, sharpshooters, stagecoaches, and much noise, smoke, and firing of guns.

1917 Feb. 13 **Mata Hari** [orig.: Gertrudida Margarethe Macleod; nee Zelle] (Aug. 7, 1876–Oct. 15, 1917) was arrested in Paris on charges of betraying Allied military secrets to the German Secret Service. On July 24 she was found guilty and sentenced to death. She died before a firing squad on Oct. 14.

1917 Nov. 22 The **National Hockey League** of Canada was organized in Montreal, succeeding the National Hockey Association, first formed in 1909. The first league games among the six Canadian professional clubs were played on Dec. 19.

1918

I. DISASTERS

1918   A forest **fire** destroyed most of the small city of **Cloquet** in northeastern Minnesota, killing 560 people.

1918 Apr.   Spanish Influenza spread from Asia throughout the world. When it was over, in May 1919, an estimated 22 to 30 million people were dead, more than all the deaths caused world-wide by World War I. In the U.S. the flu killed c.550,000 people.

1918 June 22   An empty troop **train crashed** into the rear of a circus train stopped near Ivanhoe, Indiana. Sixty-eight performers in the Hagenbeck-Wallace Circus were killed and 127 others hospitalized.

1918 July 9   Two passenger **trains** on the Nashville-Chattanooga-St. Louis line **collided** head-on at Nashville, Tennessee, causing 101 deaths.

1918 Nov. 2   Derailment of a New York City subway train at the Malbone Street Station, Brooklyn, killed 97 people.

II. POLITICS AND WAR

1918   Universal suffrage was granted in Great Britain with the passage of the **Representation of the People Act**. The act removed the limitation of property requirements and permitted women over 30 years of age to vote.

1918 Jan. 8   The **Fourteen Points** believed necessary to an effective peace settlement in World War I were proposed by **Woodrow Wilson**, president of the U.S., to the U.S. Congress. Wilson's Fourteen Points were: (1) No secret diplomacy; (2) Freedom of the seas, except by international agreement; (3) No international barriers and equal trade conditions; (4) Reduction of armaments; (5) Adjustment of colonial disputes; (6) Evacuation of Russian territory with self-determination; (7) Evacuation and restoration of Belgium and (8) of France; (9) Readjustment of Italian frontiers; (10) Autonomy for populations in Austria-Hungary; (11) Evacuation and restoration of Balkan nations and peoples; (12) Dardanelles internationalized; (13) Poland indepen-

dent, with access to the sea; (14) Creation of a league of nations.

1918 Jan. 18   The **Russian Constituent Assembly was forced to dissolve** by **Vladimir Ilyich Lenin**, who then proclaimed a dictatorship of the proletariat. Red Guard troops loyal to Lenin barred deputies from their chamber.

1918 Mar. 3   The **Treaty of Brest-Litovsk** was signed by the Central Powers (Germany, Austria-Hungary, Turkey, and Bulgaria) with the Soviet government. A similar treaty had been signed between the Central Powers and representatives of Ukraine on Feb. 9. Negotiations had begun on Dec. 1, 1917, at the instigation of the Soviet Union, but on Feb. 18, 1918, German troops occupied Estonia, Latvia, Ukraine, and most of Belorussia [present Belarus]. **Trotsky** allied his delegates with Lenin's to create a slim majority in favor of peace with the Central Powers. By the settlement the Soviet Union lost Estonia, Latvia, Lithuania, Russian Poland, Ukraine, and most of Belorussia. To Turkey were ceded Ardahan [Ardagan] and Kars, in present northeastern Turkey, and Batum [Batumi], on the Black Sea, which had all been seized by Russia in 1878. Finland and the Ukraine were recognized as independent. The Treaty of Brest-Litovsk was annulled (Nov. 11) by the Armistice between France, Great Britain, the U.S., and other Allies, and the Central Powers.

1918 Mar. 3   British, French, and American **troops landed in Murmansk** on the Kola Gulf of northwestern Russia, ostensibly to protect against the Germans the Allied war supplies gathered here. The troops occupied Arkhangelsk [Archangel], a port near the White Sea on Aug. 3. Allied troops remained in northwestern Russia until 1920. Other Allied troops, mostly Japanese, occupied the port of Vladivostok in the Far East on the Sea of Japan on Apr. 5–6. The Japanese did not withdraw until 1922.

1918 Mar. 10   The **Russian capital was moved from Petrograd to Moscow**, in the fear that Petrograd might be taken by foreign armies or by counterrevolutionaries.

1918 Mar. 21   The second **battle of the Somme** began. Germany intended to split the French and British armies and achieve a breakthrough on the

Western Front before fresh American troops were able to intervene. The Germans, who outnumbered the Allies, by Mar. 23 had advanced 14 miles to the Somme River. The Kaiser's troops fought on to capture Montdidier and Albert, a total advance of c.40 miles, but by Apr. 5 the attack ran out of steam and failed to take Amiens or Arras.

1918 Mar. 26   Ferdinand Foch was appointed to the **supreme command** of all the Allied armies. Foch was one of the French commanders who had halted the German advance at the Marne River. In 1917 he was named chief of the general staff of the French army and in Aug. 1918 was named a marshal of France.

1918 Apr. 21   Manfred von Richthofen (b. May 2, 1892), a German ace who had shot down 80 Allied airplanes in less than two years, was himself shot down and killed while participating in the **battle at the Somme**.

1918 May 7   Romania, defeated by German troops, signed the **Treaty of Bucharest**, pledging support to the Central Powers, returning the Dobruja region to Bulgaria, and ceding the passes through the Carpathian Mountains to Austria-Hungary.

1918 May 24   The **Women's Franchise Bill** granted suffrage to women in federal elections in Canada.

1918 May 27   The third **battle at the Aisne River** began as German forces took the bridges over the river, near Chemin des Dames, in a swift advance. On the same day to the north, U.S. troops won victory in a **battle at Cantigny**. They added to their victories when they cleared the Germans from **Belleau Wood**, to the northwest, by July 1. The Allies had gained the initiative.

1918 May 29   Robert Lansing (Oct. 17, 1864–Oct. 30, 1928), the U.S. secretary of state, declared U.S. support for the formation of **independent Czechoslovak and Yugoslav states**. On June 3 the other Allied nations also stated their support.

1918 May 30   Georgy Valentinovich Plekhanov (b. Nov. 26, 1857), a Russian political philosopher and revolutionary, died. He was one of the **first to introduce Marxist theory into Russia**. In 1883 he helped found the League for the Emancipation of Labor which in 1898 became the Russian Social Democratic Workers' party. After the February Revolution of

1917 broke out, Plekhanov supported continuing the war against Germany and opposed the Bolsheviks. Following the October Revolution, he retired from political life.

1918 July 16   The second **battle of the Marne**, the last important German offensive of the war, began. The Germans' first objective was Reims, but they failed to take it. By July 18 the Allies took the offensive at Soissons. In this battle c.250,000 Americans took part, the **first large-scale engagement for the doughboys**. This battle marked the beginning of the end of the long war.

1918 July 29–30   Nicholas II [Nikolai Aleksandrovich] (b. May 18, 1868), czar of Russia, was executed during the night on orders of Bolshevik authorities at Ekaterinburg [Yekaterinburg, Sverdlovsk] in the Ural Mountains. Killed with him were his wife, **Czarina Alexandra**, the **Crown Prince Alexis**, four daughters, and four servants. Their bodies were then destroyed by fire and acid.

1918 Aug.   The **Germans were driven from Serbia** by Allied troops under the French commander **Louis Félix Marie François Franchet d'Esperey** (May 25, 1856–July 8, 1942). On Sept. 26 the Bulgarians were defeated at the Vardar River, in Macedonia. They signed an armistice on Sept. 29 with the Allies, and Romania abrogated the treaty signed in May with the Central Powers. On Nov. 1 the Serbian army occupied Belgrade as Albania fell to Italian troops.

1918 Aug. 8   The second **battle at Amiens** began when British forces, including Australian and Canadian troops, attacked German troops holding the Amiens-Paris rail line. The Allies massed more than 500 tanks for the initial attack and also outnumbered the German infantry. Montdidier was regained on Aug. 10. On Sept. 12 American troops reduced a German salient at **St. Mihiel**, taking c.15,000 prisoners.

1918 Aug. 30   Moses Uritsky, head of the Petrograd **Cheka** [Secret Police], was killed. The Cheka began a massive wave of arrests and executions throughout Russia to end the activities of the Social Revolutionaries and other dissenting groups.

1918 Sept. 18   Great Britain's final offensive against the Ottoman Empire (1326–1920) during World War I began with the rout of the Turkish army at Megiddo [Armageddon] in Palestine by **Edmund Henry**

Hynman Allenby, the British commander. Beirut in Lebanon and Damascus in Syria were occupied by Allied troops in October.

1918 Sept. 23 The two largest and strongest anti-Bolshevik **White Russian groups** merged at Omsk in western Siberia and established a government that annulled all Soviet decrees and restored all former land titles. An army was led against the Red army by **Aleksandr Vasilievich Kolchak** (Nov. 16, 1873–Feb. 7, 1920), a former Czarist admiral. Kolchak was unsuccessful, but **Anton Ivanovich Denikin** (Dec. 16, 1872–Aug. 8, 1947), who took over command, was able to set up a South Russian government in southern Russia (1919) until driven out by a Soviet army under **Semën** [Semyon] **Mikhailovich Budënny** (Apr. 25, 1883–Oct. 17, 1973) in 1920.

1918 Sept. 26 The **Allied offensive that ended the war began** with a massive American attack in the **Meuse-Argonne** area. The Hindenburg Line, named for the commanding German general, had been established (1916) after the battle at the Somme as a last line of defense against the Allies. It ran southeasterly from Lens, near Arras, northern France, through St. Quentin to Reims, northeastern France. On Sept. 28 Belgian and British forces went on the offensive in the Armentières region. Both attacks succeeded, and by Nov. 6 the German army was in retreat. French and American troops crossed the Meuse River and moved on Sedan. The advance continued until the armistice on Nov. 11.

1918 Oct. 3 **Prince Max** of Baden [Maximilian Alexander Friedrich Wilhem] (July 10, 1867–Nov. 6, 1929) was named chancellor of Germany. On Nov. 3 the **German fleet** at Kiel, on the Baltic Sea in Germany **mutinied**. Disorder spread as the German people clamored for peace and blamed their leaders for defeat.

1918 Oct. 4 **Austria-Hungary expressed its willingness to accept the Fourteen Points** for peace outlined by **Woodrow Wilson**, president of the U.S., in a letter from **Stephan von Burián von Rajecz** (Jan. 16, 1851–Oct. 20, 1922), the Austrian foreign minister (Apr. 15–Oct. 25). On Oct. 27 **Gyula Andrássy** (June 30, 1860–June 11, 1929), the last foreign minister of Austria-Hungary, agreed to Czech independence and the creation of a South Slav state of the Serbs, Croats, and Slovenes, to which Austria lost Croatia. The Allied armistice with Austria-Hungary took effect on Nov. 4.

1918 Oct. 5 **Cambrai in northern France fell to British and Canadian troops**, who then captured Saint-Quentin on Oct. 1. By Nov. 1 the Germans had been driven east over the Schelde River and were forced from Ghent [Gent] in East Flanders.

1918 Oct. 6 **Poland declared itself an independent republic.** On Nov. 14 **Józef Klemens Piłsudski**, the hero of the Polish struggle for independence, released from prison in Germany, was named Poland's head of state. Piłsudski's first priority was to regain the Polish territories lost in the Partitions of Poland in 1772, 1793, and 1795. As the disarmed German troops evacuated occupied Poland, they were replaced by advancing Russian armies, hoping as an Allied power to be hailed as Poland's liberator.

1918 Oct. 24 In the **battle of Vittorio Veneto**, in northeastern Italy, Italian troops, supported by British and French forces, routed the Austrians, pushing them back into the Trentino region. The advance continued until the armistice of Nov. 3.

1918 Oct. 25 **Mihály Károlyi** (Mar. 4, 1875–Mar. 20, 1955) was appointed head of the state of Hungary by **Charles I** [Karl], emperor of Austria (from 1916) and, as **Charles IV**, king of Hungary (from 1916). Károlyi declared **Hungary an independent republic** on Nov. 16. **Béla Kun**, a Hungarian communist, led a group of communists to Budapest in an effort to overthrow the Károlyi regime. He was arrested (Feb. 19), but Károlyi later handed the government over to Kun, who successfully fought off a Czechoslovakian army and then established a Soviet Republic in Slovakia (June, 1919). In Aug., 1919, the Romanian army overthrew his regime and he fled to Vienna from which he was deported to Russia.

1918 Oct. 28 **Czechoslovakia**, a republic of Czechs and Slovaks, was **declared independent of Austria-Hungary** by the Prague National Council, recognized as the official body representing the Czechoslav nationalist movement, first by France on June 29, Great Britain on Aug. 9, and the U.S. on Sept. 3. On Nov. 13 the new nation of Czechoslovakia established a republic by proclaiming a temporary constitution. **Tomáš Garrigue Masaryk** was elected the first president of the republic of Czechoslovakia on Nov. 14.

1918 Oct. 30 An armistice was signed at Mudros [Moudros], on Lemnos Island in Greece, between the Turks and the Allies, **ending Turkish fighting in**

World War I. The war hero **Mustafa Kemal** had led the Turkish retreat from Palestine to Aleppo, across the Taurus Mountains and into Anatolia. With the armistice the **Young Turks** fled as **Mohammed VI** [Vahid-ed-Din] (Jan. 14, 1861–May 16, 1926) was set up as sultan (to 1922). The Allies occupied İstanbul and the Straits. Italy occupied the southwestern coast of Anatolia on Mar. 29, 1919, and Greece gained parts of Smyrna on May 15.

1918 Nov. 9 **William II**, emperor of Germany, the **last of the ruling Hohenzollern Dynasty** (from 1415), abdicated at the insistence of **Prince Max** of Baden, chancellor of Germany. William fled from Spa, the headquarters of the German high command in Belgium, to the Netherlands. On the same day, Prince Max resigned the chancellorship, turning it over to **Friedrich Ebert** (Feb. 4, 1871–Feb. 28, 1925), who thus became for a day the last chancellor of the German Empire.

1918 Nov. 11 An **armistice**, effective at 11 A.M., **ending the fighting of World War I**, was signed by Allied and German representatives in a railway carriage stationed near **Compiègne** in northern France. German troops west of the Rhine River were to withdraw immediately. Germany was also to give up its war matériel. The armistice was signed for Germany by civilian officials. Both the German war machine and the battered home-front economy were in such a state of exhaustion that had an attempt been made to fight on, the German nation would have faced annihilation. Out of 42,188,810 men mobilized by the Allies, 5,152,115 were killed or died of war-related causes; 12,831,004 were wounded; and 4,121,090 were captured or missing in action—for a total of 22,089,709 casualties, or 52.3 percent of those mobilized. The Central Powers mobilized 22,850,000 men, of whom 3,386,200 died; 8,388,448 were wounded; and 3,629,829 were prisoners or missing, for a total of 15,404,477 or 67.4 percent of those mobilized. Ninety percent of those mobilized by Austria-Hungary became casualties.

1918 Nov. 12 **Charles I** [Karl], the **last ruling Hapsburg** [Habsburg], renounced his title as emperor of Austria and king of Hungary. **Heinrich Lammasch** (May 21, 1853–Jan. 6, 1920) served as prime minister of Austria (Oct.–Nov.), presiding over the dissolution of the empire. **Karl Renner** (Dec. 14, 1870–Dec. 31, 1950) was named the first chancellor of the **Austrian Republic**, which on Oct. 30 had declared itself an independent state under the name Deutschösterreich [German-Austria]. Austria's boundaries were settled by the **Treaty of St. Germain**, signed on Sept. 10, 1919. Former Hapsburg crownlands went to Czechoslovakia—which gained Bohemia and Moravia. Poland, Yugoslavia, Czechoslovakia and Hungary were to be completely independent. Italy gained the southern Tyrol, the province of Friuli with its capital at Trieste on the Istrian Peninsula, and some islands along the Dalmatian coast. Romania gained Bukovina, and Burgenland was ceded by Hungary to Austria. In order to prevent Anschluss, or union with Germany, popular among Austria's large German population, the Treaty of St. Germain included a clause that Austria should never compromise its independence, and Austria was requested to cease calling itself Deutschösterreich (it was then called Österreich).

1918 Nov. 18 The **Latvian Republic** was declared at Riga, its capital. **Karlis Ulmanis** (Sept. 4, 1877–deported to Russia in 1940?, fate unknown) served as Latvia's first prime minister, and presided over its fight for independence from both Germany and Communist Russia.

1918 Nov. 24 The **Kingdom of Serbs, Croats, and Slovenes** was proclaimed by a national council representing the Balkan states of Bosnia, Croatia, Dalmatia, Montenegro, Macedonia, Serbia, and Slovenia. Albania was now under the forced protection of Italy, until Italy recognized its complete independence (Aug. 1920). The remaining area of the kingdom, named **Yugoslavia** in 1931, was carved from the fallen empire of Austria-Hungary, and boundaries with Italy, Austria, Hungary, Romania, and Bulgaria were settled by the **Paris Peace Conference** in June 1920. On Dec. 4 **Prince Alexander**, regent of Serbia since 1914, was named regent until his father **Peter I Karageorgevich**, king of Serbia (from 1903), recovered from an illness to take office as ruler (1918–1921) of the Kingdom of the Serbs, Croats, and Slovenes.

1918 Nov. 26 The Allies began their **occupation of the German Rhineland** by terms of the armistice. The French moved in this day while British and American troops crossed into Germany on Dec. 1. By Dec. 11 the Americans were in Coblenz, and the next day the British took over the Cologne bridgehead.

1918 Nov. 30 The **Act of Union** established **Iceland** as a sovereign state, joined to Denmark under the

Danish crown and sharing with Denmark a joint foreign policy.

1918 Dec. 4 U.S. president **Woodrow Wilson** sailed for France. He took with him a number of high ranking officials and experts in many fields, but no senators, being already at odds with the Republican-controlled Senate. As a result, when it later came to the time when he had to ask that body to ratify the peace treaty, he ran into bitter opposition. Wilson arrived in France on Dec. 13 and was welcomed as a bringer of peace. After spending Christmas Day with some American soldiers, he went to England the next day, where he was also greeted with enthusiasm.

1918 Dec. 14 In Ireland, the Sinn Fein party, founded in 1905, won three-fourths of the Irish seats in the British parliamentary elections. The 73 Irish members of the new Parliament formed their own council, the **Dáil Éireann** [The Assembly of Ireland], in Dublin on Jan. 21, 1919. They elected as president **Eamon de Valera**, in jail at the time and later (1959) president of Ireland. The Dáil Éireann declared an independent Irish republic.

III. ECONOMY AND TRADE

1918 The **Confederácion Regional Obrera Mexicana** [CROM] was formed in Mexico to serve the same functions as the AFL in the U.S. CROM was the largest labor organization in Mexico until the founding in 1936 of the **Confederácion de Trabajadores Mexicanos**.

1918 Feb. 19 **Mexico declared her reserves of oil a national resource**. Mexico was at this time second in world oil production, surpassed only by the U.S.

1918 Apr. 10 The **Webb Export Act** exempted business associations in the U.S. that dealt solely in foreign trade from the provisions of the Sherman Antitrust Act. The Webb Act was an attempt to stimulate foreign commerce.

1918 Apr. 22 The **Soviet government** of Russia instituted government **control over all foreign trade**. Foreigners had to negotiate with government trade representatives rather than private Russian citizens.

IV. RELIGION AND PHILOSOPHY

1918 Feb. 5 The Soviet government declared **separation of church and state in Russia**. The state acquired control of the properties of the Russian Orthodox Church and closed its schools and monasteries. Worship was permitted only in some churches.

V. SCIENCE, EDUCATION, AND TECHNOLOGY

1918 **Harlow Shapley**, an American astronomer, located the center of our galaxy, the **Milky Way System**, and found it to be 30,000 to 40,000 light years from our sun. Shapley did his work at the Mt. Wilson Observatory, near Los Angeles, California, with which he had been associated since 1914.

1918 Mar. 23 The **German bombardment of Paris**, conducted from Coucyle-Chateau-Auffrique, c.26 miles northeast of Paris, began. It lasted intermittently for 140 days and made use of four **Big Bertha** cannons, longer than those used at Liege, Belgium, in 1914. These guns were made at the Krupp works in Germany. Some 367 shells landed in or near Paris and killed 256 people.

VI. ARTS AND LEISURE

1918 Feb. 6 **Gustav Klimt** (b. July 14, 1862), an Austrian painter and a founder of the **Secession group**, died. He and his associates were in revolt against the eclecticism of most art of the late 19th century. Klimt came to the forefront of the **Art Nouveau** world in Vienna. He painted landscapes and portraits with exotic and erotic overtones. Among his paintings were *The Kiss* (1908) and portraits of *Frau Fritza Riedler* (1906) and *Frau Adele Block-Bauer* (1907).

1918 Mar. 9 **Frank Wedekind** (b. July 24, 1864), a German dramatist, died. His plays criticized current sexual attitudes. His works included *Frühlings Ermachen* [*The Awakening of Spring*] (1891); *Der Marquis von Keith* (1901), perhaps Wedekind's most memorable character; and *Totentanz* [*The Dance of Death*] (1906).

1918 Mar. 25 **Claude** [Achille] **Debussy** (b. Aug. 22, 1862), a French composer, died. Debussy's compositions were the musical expression of the impressionist movement in painting. *L'Enfant Prodigue* [*The Prodigal Son*], a cantata, earned for him the

Grand Prix de Rome in 1884. Debussy's works included *Nocturnes* (1899), the opera *Pelléas et Mélisande* (1892–1902), *La Mer* [*The Sea*] (1905), and *Printemps* [*Spring*] (1887).

1918 Mar. 27   Henry Brooks Adams (b. Feb. 16, 1838), an American writer and historian, died. His autobiography and most notable work, *The Education of Henry Adams—A Study of Twentieth Century Multiplicity* (1906), was a third-person account of Adams's life and explained his theory of history. His other works included *Mont-St.-Michel and Chartres* (1904) and a nine-volume *History of the United States of America during the Administrations of Thomas Jefferson and James Madison* (1889–1891).

1918 June 10   Arrigo Boito (b. Feb. 24, 1842), an Italian composer, died. He wrote the opera *Mefistofele* (1868), noted for its musicality and dramatic quality. He also composed *Nerone* (1924) and wrote the libretti for Verdi's *Otello* (1887) and *Falstaff* (1893).

1918 Dec. 2   Edmond [-Eugène-Alexis] **Rostand** (b. Apr. 1, 1868), a popular French playwright, died. His plays for the most part were light and poetic. Among his works were *Cyrano de Bergerac* (1897), a play of dramatic poetry that became his best known; *L'Aiglon* (1900); and *Chantecler* (1910), which was made popular in the U.S. by **Maude Adams**.

1919

I. DISASTERS

1919–1923   A four-year **drought in Siberia** and the Volga district of Russia, and present Ukraine killed c.3 million peasants, despite international aid headed by **Herbert** [Clark] **Hoover** (Aug. 10, 1874–Oct. 20, 1964) of the **American Relief Association** from Sept., 1921, until July, 1923.

1919 May 20   Mt. Kelud, a volcanic mountain on the island of Java, **erupted**, killing c.5,000 persons.

II. POLITICS AND WAR

1919 Jan. 5   The Red army occupied Vilna [Wilno, Wilna, Vilnius], capital of Russian Lithuania, and then entered (Jan. 17) Kaunas [Kovno, Kowno] on the Neman River. They established (Dec. 23) a communist government for Lithuania. **Jozef Piłsudski** led a Polish army against the Soviet troops, capturing Vilna and Kaunas on Apr. 20, 1919. On July 12, 1920, Russia, at war with Poland, signed a peace treaty with Lithuania ceding the disputed city and province of Vilna to Lithuania, and withdrew its forces from the area on Aug. 26. An armistice was signed between Poland and Lithuania on Oct. 7. But two days later Poland again seized Vilna and set up a government, so a new armistice was signed on Nov. 29.

1919 Jan. 6   Theodore Roosevelt (b. Oct. 27, 1858), 26th president of the U.S. (1901–1909), died. An or-

ganizer of the Rough Riders, a volunteer regiment in the Spanish-American War (1898), he achieved renown by leading a charge that was of little importance. Elected vice president on the Republican ticket, he became president upon the assassination of **William McKinley** in Sept. 1901 and won election in his own right in 1904. In office he was known as a trust buster, a conservationist, and an advocate of an active foreign policy. In a three-way contest in 1912, Roosevelt lost the presidential election to **Woodrow Wilson**.

1919 Jan. 11   Gustav Noske (July 9, 1868–Nov. 30, 1946) formed a counterrevolutionary volunteer army in Berlin to defend the government against the **Spartacists** [communists], who had revolted in an attempted coup on Jan. 5 and whose defeat was signalized by the capture and murder (Jan. 15) of the Spartacist leaders **Karl Liebknechkt** (b. Aug. 13, 1871) and **Rosa Luxemburg** (b. Mar. 5, 1870). In elections for the National Assembly on Jan. 19, the Socialists won 163 seats, more than any other organized group, the other 258 seats being divided among a wide variety of political parties.

1919 Jan. 16   The Eighteenth Amendment to the U.S. Constitution was adopted, outlawing the manufacture, sale, transport, importation, or exportation of intoxicating liquors in the U.S. and its territories.

1919 Jan. 18   The **Paris Peace Conference**, called to negotiate treaty settlements following World War I, opened. Present were representatives of the Big Four: **Woodrow Wilson**, president of the U.S.; **Georges Clemenceau**, the premier of France and the president of the Conference; [David] **Lloyd George**, prime minister of Great Britain; and **Vittorio Emanuele Orlando** (May 19, 1860–Dec. 1, 1952), prime minister of Italy.

1919 Feb. 3   In the growing war between the new communist regime and the counter-revolutionary **White Russians** who organized armies to try to restore czarism, the **Bolsheviks** were defeated in a series of **battles in the Caucasus**. The White Russian leaders were **Anton Ivanovich Denikin**, who had recently set up a South Russian government, and **Aleksandr Vasiliyevich Kolchak**, head of the White Army. They had considerable support among the nations of the western Allies, but others did not favor them because the Whites seemed as autocratic, anti-democratic, and anti-Semitic as the overthrown czarist regime. By Oct. 16 one White Russian force was only 25 miles from Petrograd while Denikin was near Tula, west of Moscow. In the meantime, however, **Leon Trotsky's** troops counterattacked and forced the Whites to retreat. Denikin's army was beaten at Orel, south of Moscow, and he fled to Turkey, later going to France to live. On Dec. 24 Kolchak gave up command of the White forces in Siberia. He retreated to Irkutsk, on Lake Baikal, where he was captured on Feb. 7, 1920, and shot. By the end of 1919 the White Russian attempt to regain control of the government was crushed.

1919 Feb. 4   **French citizenship was granted to some Algerians** based on military service during the war, land ownership, and education.

1919 Feb. 6   Meeting at Weimar, Germany, the National Assembly established a republican form of government, often called the **"Weimar Republic"** (to 1933). A federal constitution was adopted on July 31. The assembly elected **Friedrich Ebert** as the first president of Germany.

1919 Mar. 1   Leaders of Buddhist, Christian, and other groups of **Korean patriots declared independence from Japan**. The Japanese used extreme force to crush it, killing several hundred people and wounding thousands. A provisional government in exile was founded later in the year in Shanghai, China.

1919 Mar. 4   The **Comintern** [Communist International] was formed by the Communist party of Soviet Russia and a group of communists from Europe. This **Third International** was the successor to the Second International, which had dissolved during World War I (1914–1918).

1919 Mar. 8   **Saad Zaghlul Pasha** (c.1860–Aug. 23, 1927), head of Egypt's Nationalist party and chief advocate of severing ties with Great Britain to gain complete independence, was deported to Malta by British authorities. Anti-British demonstrations immediately broke out in Cairo. **Egypt** was denied representation at the **Paris Peace Conference**, despite its support of Allied troops against the last Ottoman foothold in the Near East.

1919 Mar. 18   The **Government of India Acts** were passed by the British Parliament. The acts, based on a study and recommendations by **Frederick John Napier** (Aug. 12, 1868–Apr. 1, 1933), Lord Chelmsford, **Edwin Samuel Montagu** (Feb. 6, 1879–Nov. 15, 1924), and **John Morley** (Dec. 24, 1838–Dec. 23, 1923), promoted a slow expansion of democracy in India by increasing the number of Indians in the governmental apparatus and instituting self-governing bodies. The acts were essentially nullified when the Indian government attempted to reinstate the **Defense of India** [called the Rowlatt] **Act** of 1918, a repressive wartime measure. Repassage of the **Rowlatt Act** by the Indian assembly, controlled by British colonial conservatives, undid most of the Government of India Acts and prompted extensive pro-nationalist movements, led principally by **Mohandas** [Mahatma] **Karamchand Gandhi**, as **nonviolent civil disobedience** began on Mar. 30. Violence proved inevitable, and the Amritsar massacre, in the holy city of the Sikhs in the Punjab, northern India, occurred on Apr. 13 when troops under **Reginald Edward Harry Dyer** (Oct. 9, 1864–July 24, 1927) fired on a nationalist meeting, killing c.400 and wounding c.1,200.

1919 Mar. 21   **Béla Kun**, a radical communist leader, allied his party with the Social Democrats to take power in a coup in **Hungary**. Kun brought Hungary into an alliance with Russia. Kun attacked along the borders of Czechoslovakia and Romania in protest against the Allied proposal that Hungary withdraw to purely Magyar lands. But Kun was deposed in a counter-coup and fled to Vienna on Aug. 1. **Romanian forces occupied Budapest**, Hungary's capital, Aug. 3. **Miklós Horthy de Nagybánya** (June 18,

1868–Feb. 9, 1957), a Hungarian aristocrat, led his own monarchical troops into Budapest on Nov. 16 and, with Romanian support, held elections for a new parliament in Jan. 1920. Horthy was declared regent on Mar. 1.

1919 Mar. 23 **Benito Mussolini** founded the fascist organization *Fascio di Combattimento* in Milan. The stagnant economy of Italy and the agitation of the political left bolstered the movement of the **Black Shirts** led by Mussolini.

1919 Apr. 10 **Emiliano Zapata** (b. Aug. 8, 1879), Mexican revolutionary leader and advocate of land reform, was killed by government troops. Zapata, with a slogan "land and liberty," began to seize land in 1910 with the aid of Indian followers. For a while he supported **Francisco Madero** but later turned against him and fought his government as well as those of presidents **Victoriano Huerta** and **Venusitano Carranza**. Between 1911 and his death, Zapata at various times controlled large areas of Mexico, including Mexico City three times.

1919 May 3 The **Third Afghan War** broke out as **Amanullah Khan** (June 1, 1892–Apr. 25, 1960), emir of Afghanistan (1919–1929), invaded British India to free Afghans from British rule. The war ended on May 31, and on Aug. 8 the **Treaty of Rawalpindi**, in present Pakistan, which granted complete **independence to Afghanistan**, was signed.

1919 May 4 The **May Fourth Movement** in China broke out when students at Peking [Beijing] National University protested the cession of Shantung province to Japan. The **Versailles Peace Conference** had confirmed the Japanese acquisition. Chinese students led a boycott of Japanese goods; Shanghai merchants and workers closed the international port for a week. The Chinese government had no choice but to refuse to sign the **Versailles Treaty**, while the May Fourth Movement grew stronger.

1919 June 21 Most of the warships of the **German High Seas Fleet were scuttled** by their crews at Scapa Flow, Britain's main naval base, a body of water in the Orkney Islands off northern Scotland. After Germany's defeat in World War I (1914–1918) the fleet had been ordered there by the Allies for internment. At a prearranged signal, the German sailors opened the seacocks of their ships and before British naval personnel could act, most of the ships were at the bottom.

1919 June 28 The **Treaty of Versailles**, putting an official end to World War I, was signed in the Hall of Mirrors of the Palace of Versailles where in 1871 the Prussians had forced the French to sign a humiliating treaty ending the Franco-Prussian War (1870). This time Germany was the defeated power, and victors who signed were the Allies [except Russia]: France, Great Britain, Italy, Japan, and the U.S. The treaty was effective as of Jan. 10, 1920. Germany was required to admit that it was guilty of having started the war. There were many **changes of territorial rights**, one of them being the return to France of Alsace and Lorraine. Poland received most of West Prussia, including the city of Poznán [Posen] and the Polish Corridor, a strip of land 20 to 70 miles wide, that gave Poland access to the Baltic Sea and divided East Prussia from the rest of Germany. Germany was allowed free passage across the corridor. Danzig [Gdánsk], on the Gulf of Danzig, was made a free city and placed in Poland's customs territory. The Saar, a region in southwest Germany, was put under French administration for 15 years so that France could exploit its rich coal fields to compensate for war losses of such resources. The Rhineland, a region of Germany along the Rhine River, was to be occupied by the Allies for 15 years and was to be permanently demilitarized. In addition to other territorial changes, the German army was to consist of no more than 100,000 men and the navy was also restricted in size. The defeated nation was to have no air force and no weapons that could be used for aggressive purposes. **Germany was to pay massive reparations** to the Allies, both in money and in coal and other products. The official figure was 20,000,000,000 marks, but as Germany's financial situation became chaotic and the mark lost all value for practical purposes, no such sum was ever collected. The terms of the treaty meant that Wilson's Fourteen Points for a generous peace were overridden by the other Allies, especially France and Britain. Wilson did get out of the treaty the realization of his dream of a **League of Nations**, although the U.S. became the one nation of importance that did not join it. The covenant of the League established a system of mandates that stripped Germany of its colonies. The Treaty of Versailles created new problems because of historical enmities and overlapping national groups and, because of its vindictive treatment of Germany, may have helped bring on the worldwide **Great Depression** of the 1930s and the rise of **Adolf Hitler** and Nazism.

1919 July 4 Augusto Bernardino Leguía y Salcedo (Feb. 19, 1863–Feb. 7, 1932) staged a coup to secure the presidency of **Peru** following an election which he had apparently won but in which some of the votes cast for him had been ruled invalid. Leguía served as Peru's president until 1930, during which time he developed the economy, aided by a rubber boom and the opening of the Panama Canal in 1914.

1919 July 27 In a **Chicago race riot** 38 were killed, over 500 injured, and c.1,000 black families made homeless. Rioting had begun shortly after a black man was attacked for swimming into a white beach area.

1919 Sept. 10 The **Treaty of Saint-Germain** was signed by Austria and the Allied powers at Saint-Germain-en-Laye, near Paris. It went into effect on July 16, 1920. The treaty established the boundaries of Austria and forbade its union with Germany, which Austria had hoped to achieve by pleading self-determination, one of the Fourteen Points, for its German-speaking population. Austria was forced to recognize the complete independence of Poland, Hungary, Czechoslovakia, and Yugoslavia. Austria also had to cede Trentino [the southern Tyrol, known as Upper Adige], Gorizia, and Istria [including Trieste] as well as other territories to Italy.

1919 Sept. 12 The Italian writer and war hero **Gabriele D'Annunzio** led an unofficial nationalist force that seized the Dalmatian port of **Fiume** [Rijeka] while Yugoslavia and Italy disputed the region. He set up his own regime and declared Fiume's independence on Dec. 15.

1919 Sept. 25 **Woodrow Wilson**, president of the U.S., collapsed in Pueblo, Colorado, while on a speaking tour to win support for ratification of the **Treaty of Versailles** (1919) by the Senate. Returning at once to Washington, the president suffered a major stroke and until Nov. 1 was totally incapacitated. For the remainder of his term, to Mar. 4, 1921, the business of the chief executive was transacted mainly through his wife. In the meantime, on Nov. 19, by a vote of 55 to 39, the Senate refused to ratify the treaty, which included establishment of the **League of Nations**, anathema to isolationist legislators. **Henry Cabot Lodge** (May 12, 1850–Nov. 9, 1924), chairman of the Senate Foreign Relations Committee, led the successful opposition to the League.

1919 Nov. 28 **Nancy Witcher Langhorne Astor** [Lady Astor] (May 19, 1879–May 2, 1964) became the **first woman elected to the British House of Commons**, in which she served as a member of the Conservative party until 1945. She was the wife of **Waldorf Astor** (May 19, 1879–Sept. 30, 1952) and replaced her husband, who was about to enter the House of Lords as the 2d Viscount Astor. Lady Astor was active on behalf of child welfare, women's rights, temperance, and education.

1919 Nov. 29 The **Treaty of Neuilly** was signed by Bulgaria and the Allied powers at Neuilly-sur-Marne, a suburb of Paris. It went into effect on Aug. 9, 1920. Bulgaria lost territory to Yugoslavia and to Greece, gaining only a small part of Turkey near Edirne. Bulgaria also lost access to the Aegean Sea.

1919 Dec. 8 In an attempt to acquire from Russia territory lost in 1772, **Józef Klemens Piłsudski** led Polish troops in a push eastward to the Berezina River in White Russia [present Belarus] and made advances in Ukraine as well. On Apr. 21, 1920, Piłsudski concluded an alliance with **Simon** [Symon] **Petlyura** (May 17, 1879–May 25, 1926), leader of the Ukrainian independence movement, and together they launched an offensive against the Russians in the Ukraine on Apr. 24. They reached Kiev on May 7, but Russian troops broke through their line on June 8. Poland appealed for aid to the **Conference of Spa** (July 5–16), Belgium. **George Nathaniel Curzon** (Jan. 11, 1859–Mar. 20, 1925), the British foreign secretary, proposed the **Curzon Line** by which Poland would have lost all of White Russia and the Ukraine. Piłsudski made a counterattack which regained earlier Polish advances by the time a truce was signed in October. On Mar. 18, 1921, the **Treaty of Riga** settled the boundary of Russia and Poland east of the Curzon line at the western boundary of the Ukraine and west of Polotsk and Minsk in present Belarus.

III. ECONOMY AND TRADE

1919 The **International Labor Organization** [ILO] was founded in Geneva as an autonomous organization affiliated with the League of Nations (and later with the United Nations). Its chief purpose has been to promote international standards for labor regulation.

1919 Apr. 16   Czechoslovakia enacted land reform aimed at reducing large estates held by Hungarian and German aristocrats under the former Austrian-Hungarian Empire. The maximum amount of land allowed to one owner was 250 hectares (a hectare equals 2.471 acres); of this no more than 150 hectares could be arable. Landowners were reimbursed for their land with Czech currency, which proved stable.

1919 Sept. 22   A long, fruitless **strike against the United States Steel Corporation** began. It lasted until Jan. 8, 1920. The strike turned into a small war between workers and strike breakers in which 18 people were killed.

1919 Oct. 7   The Dutch National Airline, **KLM**, was established.

1919 Nov. 10   The **first international air mail service** was introduced between Paris and London by Aircraft Transport and Travel, Ltd. In the same year, international passenger service began as airlines in Great Britain and France offered flights across the English Channel.

IV. SCIENCE, EDUCATION, AND TECHNOLOGY

1919 June 14   The **first nonstop transatlantic flight** took off from St. John's, Newfoundland, Canada, for Clifden, Ireland. Flying a British-made biplane **John William Alcock** (Nov. 6, 1892–Dec. 18, 1919), an English pilot, and his copilot **Arthur Whitten Brown** (July 23, 1886–Oct. 4, 1948) made the 1,960-mile trip in 16 hours and 12 minutes. The airplane era had begun.

1919 Aug. 8   Ernst Heinrich Haeckel (b. Feb. 16, 1834), a German biologist, died. He extended the **theory of evolution** to the embryo, offering the hypothesis that ontogeny recapitulates phylogeny: Development of a fetus repeats the history of the race.

V. ARTS AND LEISURE

1919   The **Bauhaus School** in Weimar, Germany, was established. Directed by **Walter Gropius** (May 18, 1883–July 5, 1969), a German-born architect, its purpose was to develop master craftsmen as artists. Although its main attention was directed to the construction, interior design, and furnishing of a house, the Bauhaus school impacted all artistic activities, including dance and film. Among the artists assembled by the school were **Paul Klee, Lyonel Feininger, Wassily Kandinsky**, and **László Moholy-Nagy**. The school was relocated to Dessau in 1926 and was closed when **Adolf Hitler** came to power in 1933.

1919 Aug. 9   **Ruggiero Leoncavallo** (b. Mar. 8, 1858), an Italian opera composer, died. His works included **Pagliacci** (1892) and **Zara** (1900).

1919 Aug. 11   **Andrew Carnegie** (b. Nov. 25, 1835), a Scottish-born American philanthropist, died. The wealth he had accumulated in the steel industry was divided among several endowments that promoted education and the arts. The largest, the **Carnegie Corporation of New York**, was established on Nov. 10, 1911.

1919 Aug. 27   The **Soviet film industry was nationalized** and put under the supervision of the **State Commission on Education**. Almost all films of the time concerned the new revolutionary era or depicted historical events from the viewpoint of the revolutionaries. Among the innovative Soviet film producers were **Vsevolod Ularionovich Pudorkin** [Pudovkin] (Feb. 21, 1893–June 30, 1957), whose **Mother** (1926) was based on Maxim Gorky's novel of the same name; **Alexander Dorzhenko** (Sept. 15, 1894–Nov. 26, 1956), whose **Earth** (1930) was a Soviet classic; and **Serge Eisenstein**, whose first major work was the classic **Battleship Potemkin** (1925), a film about the 1905 Potemkin mutiny.

1919 Sept. 12   **Leonid Nikolaevich Andreyev** [Andreev] (b. June 18, 1871), an early symbolist writer in Russia, died. **The Red Laugh** (1904), the allegory **Anathema** (1909); and **He Who Gets Slapped** (1916) were plays. Andreyev's first novel was **In the Fog** (1901), which brought him recognition. In 1909 he published the story **The Seven Who Were Hanged,** an indictment of capital punishment.

1919 Dec. 17   [Pierre] **Auguste Renoir** (b. Feb. 25, 1841), the great French impressionist painter, died. His works included **La Grenouillère** (1869), **Bather** (1870), **La Loge** [The Box at the Theater] (1874), **Portrait of Monet** (1875), **Mme. Charpentier and Her Daughters** (1878), **Boating Party at Chatou** (1879), **Bathers** (1884–1887), **Seated Bather** (1914), **Woman Tying Her Shoe** (c.1918), and **Rest After Bathing** (1919).

VI. SPORTS, GAMES, AND SOCIETY

1919 The **first greyhound race track using a mechanical rabbit** instead of a live one was opened in Emeryville, California, under the name of the Blue Star Amusement Company.

1919 June 11 **Sir Barton** became the **first horse to win the Triple Crown** of U.S. racing when he captured the Belmont Stakes. Sir Barton won the Kentucky Derby on May 10 and the Preakness Stakes on May 14. The jockey in all three races was **Johnny Loftus.**

1919 July 4 In Toledo, Ohio, [William Harrison] **Jack Dempsey** (June 24, 1895–May 31, 1983) won the **heavyweight boxing championship** of the world when he registered a TKO at the end of the third round over **Jess Willard** (Dec. 29, 1881–Dec. 15, 1968), the defending champion.

1920

I. VITAL STATISTICS AND DEMOGRAPHICS

1920 The **population of the world** was c.1,692,520,000. The population, in round figures, of the major regions of the world were: **Africa**, 142,751,000; **Asia**, 872,522,000; **Australasia**, 6,230,000; **Europe**, 464,680,000; **North America**, 150,000,000; and **South and Central America**, 56,338,000. The population of the U.S. was 106,020,000. The world's ten largest cities were: London, 7,476,168; New York, 5,620,048; Paris, 2,888,000; Chicago, 2,701,-705; Tokyo, 2,350,000; Petrograd, 2,318,000; Vienna, 2,150,000; Berlin, 2,071,000; Philadelphia 1,823,779; Moscow, 1,818,000.

II. DISASTERS

1920 Nov.–Dec. **Drought in northern China** resulted in the deaths of c.500,000 people and impoverishing 20 million more. Families were forced to sell children, at prices ranging from about $1.50 to $75.-00, in order to provide food for the rest of the family. At the same time northern China was struck (Dec. 16) by an earthquake with a magnitude of 8.6 on the Richter scale. In Kansu province alone, c.100,000 people died.

III. POLITICS AND WAR

1920 The **Royal Canadian Mounted Police** was formed when the Dominion Police joined with the Royal Northwest Mounted Police.

1920 Jan. 2 A "Red Scare" swept the U.S. when A[lexander] **Mitchell Palmer** (May 4, 1872–May 11, 1936), the attorney general (1919–1921) ordered raids in 33 cities to arrest anyone suspected of being a communist. Palmer's agents arrested c.3,000 persons. In the end only c.300 were deported as illegal aliens or radicals.

1920 Jan. 10 The **Treaty of Versailles** (1919), containing the covenant of The **League of Nations** (to 1946), went into effect. The League's headquarters were to be established at Geneva, Switzerland. Initially, its members included neutral nations and the Allied powers, except the U.S., whose Senate refused to ratify the treaty. The first meeting of the League's Council was held in Paris on Jan. 15 and ratified the selection of [James] **Eric Drummond** (Aug. 17, 1876–Dec. 15, 1951), a private secretary to Lloyd George, prime minister of Great Britain, as its first secretary-general (1919–1933).

1920 Jan. 16 The **Volstead Act** went into effect in the U.S. Designed to enable enforcement of the Eighteenth Amendment, the **Prohibition** Amendment, it defined an intoxicating beverage as containing 0.5 percent alcohol.

1920 Feb. The **Destour** [Constitution] **party**, representing the first modern **Tunisian nationalistic movement**, was founded in Tunisia. At first the party supported the bey and accepted the French Protectorate, but it eventually became committed to national independence and was forced underground.

1920 Feb. 2 Russia and Estonia signed the **Peace of Dorpat** [Tartu, Yurev] in which **Estonian independence** was recognized by the Soviet Union. Finland's border with Estonia was also established by the agreement.

1920 Feb. 10 A plebiscite vote in **North Schleswig**, made under provisions of the **Treaty of Versailles** (1919), favored its return to Denmark. Denmark assumed control on July 5, but Germany refused to recognize its loss of the territory.

1920 Feb. 29 **Czechoslovakia** approved a constitution which established a centralized, but not federal, state with a bicameral legislature, universal suffrage, and a seven-year term for the president. Provisions were made to protect minority rights. **Thomas Masaryk**, leader of the Czech struggle for independence, became the first president of Czechoslovakia in 1918. He was reelected in 1920, 1927, and 1934.

1920 Mar. 13–17 An **uprising in Berlin** by right wing forces attempting to overthrow the **Weimar Republic** and restore the German monarchy was defeated when the Socialist party, the main support of the government, backed by the Communist party, called a general strike. The leaders of the attempted coup felt they could not topple the government even though army troops refused to fire on the supporters of the coup. The uprising became known as the **Kapp Putsch** for its leader **Wolfgang Kapp**, who had the support of most high military officers, including **Erich Ludendorff**, the German war hero. Kapp did succeed in seizing the Berlin government briefly but when his putsch failed he fled to Sweden. Returning to Germany in 1922, Wolfgang Knapp (b. July 24, 1858) died on June 12, 1922, while awaiting trial for treason.

1920 May 20–21 **Venustiano Carranza** (b. Dec. 29, 1859), president of **Mexico** (from 1914), was assassinated after supporters of **Álvaro Obregón**, Carranza's military commander, had forced him to flee Mexico City. **Adolfo de la Huerta** (1881–July 9, 1955) was chosen provisional president until Obregón was elected president (1920–1924).

1920 June 4 The **Treaty of Trianon** was signed by Hungary, now governed by **Miklós Horthy de Nagybánya**, and the Allied powers at Trianon Palace, near Versailles. Although the borders of **Hungary** had already been decided (June 28, 1919), Hungary, then headed by **Béla Kun**, had refused to accept the delimitation, and the Allies had refused to recognize Kun's communist government. With the support of Italy, Hungary now demanded plebiscites for the border areas. The only one actually held was in Sopron [Ödenburg], which Austria consequently returned to Hungary in 1921.

1920 July 12 Lithuania and Russia signed a treaty recognizing **Lithuania's independence** from the Soviet Union. The Soviet Union ceded Vilnia [Vilnius, Vilno, Wilna, Wilno], to Lithuania. On Oct. 9, however, Poland occupied the disputed city. On Feb. 20, 1922, when the Polish assembly voted in favor of incorporating the city and its surrounding province, neither the League of Nations nor the Soviet Union protested.

1920 Aug. The German Workers' party was renamed the **National Socialist German Workers' party**, whose German name Nationalsozialistiche Deutsche Arbeiterpartei [NSDAP] was abbreviated to **Nazi**. In this year **Adolf Hitler** was placed in charge of propaganda for the party, and about this time **Ernst Röhm** organized the **S.A.**, or *Sturmabteilungen*, the "strong-arm" squads Hitler used at first to protect the Nazi party from assaults by communists and socialists, especially at party meetings.

1920 Aug. 10 The **Treaty of Sèvres** was concluded between the Allies and the **Ottoman Empire**, following the Turkish defeat in World War I. Signed by **Sultan Mohammed VI** (ruled July 3, 1918–Nov. 1, 1922), in spite of the opposition of the Turkish Nationalists led by **Kemal Atatürk**, the treaty dispersed the Ottoman territories, bringing to an end the once powerful empire, founded in 1326 by **Osman I**.

1920 Aug. 14 The **Little Entente** was forged by Yugoslavia and Czechoslovakia, and joined (Aug. 17) by Romania, against Hungary, which continued to protest the terms of the **Treaty of Trianon** (1920).

1920 Aug. 26 The **Nineteenth Amendment to the U.S. Constitution** was adopted, declaring that the right to vote, in both federal and state elections, shall not be denied on account of sex.

1920 Oct. 12 **Latvian independence** was recognized by Russia in the preliminary treaty of Riga; it was confirmed Mar. 12, 1921. Latvia had been declared free by the **Treaty of Versailles** (1919). The **Bolsheviks**, not participants in the Treaty of Versailles, had captured Riga on Jan. 3, 1919, but they were driven out by German troops under **Rüdiger von der Goltz** (Dec. 8, 1865–Nov. 4, 1930), with the approval of the Allies, who only withdrew their support when the Germans pushed too far. By Nov. 10, 1919, the Germans had retreated to East Prussia.

1920 Nov. 12 The **Treaty of Rapallo** settled the territory disputed by Italy and Yugoslavia. Trieste went to Italy. **Fiume** [Rijeka] was recognized as an independent state (until 1924), and the occupying forces of **Gabriele d'Annunzio** were ousted by the Italians on Dec. 27 because Annunzio refused to recognize the terms of the treaty.

1920 Dec. 2 **Armenia** and Turkey signed a treaty at Alexandropol [Leninakan], near the present Armenian border with Turkey. On May 26, 1918, the Armenians of Russia had declared their independence and were recognized by the Allies in 1920. After an attack by Turkey from the west and by Russia through Azerbaijan on the east, Armenia was forced to cede Kars to Turkey and to become a Soviet republic on Dec. 3.

1920 Dec. 5 A plebiscite in Greece recalled from exile the former **Constantine I**, king of the Hellenes, who had abdicated in 1917 in favor of his second oldest son **Alexander.**

1920 Dec. 23 The **Government of Ireland Act** was passed by the British Parliament. It established two separate Irish legislatures: one for the 26 Catholic counties comprising four-fifths of Ireland and one for the six counties, most of historic Ulster, predominantly Protestant, forming Northern Ireland.

IV. ECONOMY AND TRADE

1920 Feb. 7 The **Ford assembly line** achieved the production rate of one car per minute.

1920 Feb. 28 The **Esch-Cummins Act** [Transportation Act] provided for the return of U.S. railroads to their private owners on Mar. 1. The Interstate Commerce Commission [ICC] was authorized to regulate them.

V. SCIENCE, EDUCATION, AND TECHNOLOGY

1920 The diameter of a star other than the sun was measured, for the first time, by **Albert A. Michelson,** an American physicist. The star was **Betelgeuse,** a very bright star in the Orion constellation c.500 light-years from Earth. The measurement was made with the use of a stellar interferometer devised by Michelson.

1920 The **Dutch began a vast reclamation project** to block off much of the 2,000-square-mile **Zuider Zee** [Southern Sea], an inlet of the North Sea.

1920 June 11 **Max Weber** (b. Apr. 21, 1864), a German economist and sociologist who attempted to develop a methodology for the social sciences, died. He did not think, as the Marxists did, that economics was the determining factor in society but rather that other aspects of life, such as religion and ideology, played roles. Today his best known work is *Die protestantische Ethik und der Geist des Kapitalismus* [*The Protestant Ethic and the Spirit of Capitalism*] (1920).

1920 Aug. 20 **Radio broadcasting** to the American public began when station 8MK in Detroit, Michigan, aired a program called "Tonight's Dinner." Broadcasting as a commercial venture can be said to have begun on Nov. 2, 1920, when KDKA in Pittsburgh broadcast the results of the presidential election held that day. By 1922 there were 500 radio stations in the U.S.

1920 The **largest known meteorite on Earth** was discovered near Grootfontein, northern South-West Africa [Namibia]. Known as the **Hoba West,** it was estimated to weigh c.60 tons.

VI. ARTS AND LEISURE

1920 Aug. 5 The *Realist Manifesto,* a statement of purpose by the constructivists, was published by the Russian sculptor **Naum Gabo** [Naum Pevsner] (Aug. 5, 1890–Aug. 3, 1977) and his brother **Antoine Pevsner** (Jan. 18, 1886–Apr. 12, 1962), leaders of the movement. It declared that art had a social function as well as an absolute value and that art's basic elements concerned problems of space and time instead of color and line.

1920 Jan. 4 **Benito Pérez Galdós** (b. May 10, 1843), a Spanish novelist, died. His 80 novels included his first *La Fontana de Ora* [*Golden Fountain*] (1868), and his mature *Realidad* [*Reality*] (1890), written mostly in dialogue, with all subjective description and explanation suppressed.

1920 Jan. 16 [Henry Louis] **Reginald De Koven** (b. Apr. 3, 1861), a U.S. composer and conductor, died. He wrote light operas after the style of Gilbert and Sullivan. These included *Robin Hood* (1890), *The*

Three Dragons (1899), and *Rip Van Winkle* (1920). He founded the **Washington Philharmonic Orchestra** in 1902.

1920 Jan. 25 **Amedeo Modigliani** (b. July 12, 1884), an Italian sculptor and painter, died in Paris. Modigliani's unique portraits and female nudes, influenced by African sculpture, were characteristically elongated. Typical examples of his paintings were *Boy in a Blue Jacket* (1918) and *Seated Nude* (c.1919); of his sculpture, *Head* (c.1912).

1920 Mar. 18 **Mrs. Humphrey Ward** [*nee:* Mary Augusta Arnold] (b. June 11, 1851), an English writer, died. Among her best-known books were *Robert Elsmere* (1888), *Marcella* (1894), and *The Marriage of William Ashe* (1905).

1920 May 11 **William Dean Howells** (b. Mar. 1, 1837), an American realistic novelist, died. His best-known work was *The Rise of Silas Lapham* (1884). He was a prolific writer, especially of critical essays. He was also editor of *The Atlantic Monthly* (1871–1881) and one of the most influential literary figures of his generation.

1920 July 4 **Max Klinger** (b. Feb. 18, 1857), a German etcher, painter, and sculptor, died. In his early career he produced rather morbid etchings, such as *Brahms-Fantasie.* Weber then, from 1886 to 1894, did most of his work as a painter. These were usually on a very large scale, as *Christ on Olympus* (1896). Turning to sculpture, his best medium, he did notable work, such as *Salome* and a statue of Beethoven (1902).

1920 Oct. 2 **Max Bruch** (b. Jan. 6, 1838), a German composer, died. His works included *Odysseus* (1872), *Das Lied von der Glocke* (1878), and *Gustav Adolf* (1898), written for chorus and orchestra. His best-known pieces were the *Violin Concerto in G Minor* (1868) and *Kol Nidrei* (1881), for cello and orchestra.

VII. SPORTS, GAMES, AND SOCIETY

1920 Jan. 5 [George Herman] **Babe Ruth** was sold by the Boston Red Sox to the New York Yankees for $125,000. His batting drew great crowds everywhere. After the **Yankee Stadium** in New York City opened on Apr. 18, 1923, it became known as "**the house that Ruth built.**" On opening day he obliged by hitting a three-run homer. On Sept. 30, 1927, Ruth hit the 60th homer of the season, a record for a 154-game season that still stands.

1920 Apr. 15 On May 5 two Italian anarchists, **Nicola Sacco** and **Bartholomeo Vanzetti**, were arrested and charged with the killing of a paymaster and a guard in South Braintree, Massachusetts. On July 14, 1921, both men were convicted and sentenced to death. Despite legal appeals and worldwide demonstrations in their support, Sacco and Vanzetti were executed on Aug. 23, 1927. Their supporters maintained they were convicted simply because they were anarchists. In 1961, with the use of advanced equipment, it seemed certain that a pistol owned by Sacco was used in the murder of one of the victims. It seemed possible that Sacco was guilty and Vanzetti innocent.

1920 Apr. 20–Sept. 12 The sixth Summer **Olympic Games**, originally scheduled for 1916 in Berlin, had been canceled because of World War I. This year, the seventh games were held in Antwerp, Belgium. Austria, Bulgaria, Germany, Hungary, and Turkey were not allowed to take part. Competing were 2,607 athletes from 29 countries. American athletes won 41 gold medals and a total of 96 medals; Sweden 19 and 63; and Great Britain 15 and 43. A lowly regarded American rugby team, almost all California collegians, upset France in the final round, 8 to 0.

1920 May 16 **Joselito** [orig.: José Gomez] (b. May 8, 1895), a noted Spanish matador, was fatally gored as he competed in the arena at Talavera de la Reina with his chief rival, **Jean Belmonte**. Joselito became, in 1912, the **youngest person to receive the title of matador**, and with Belmonte he created the modern style of **bullfighting**, in which the cape is used to elude the charging bull, instead of running away from it.

1920 July 9–16 The **Davis Cup** team of **William T. Tilden** and **William M. Johnston** (Nov. 2, 1894–May 1, 1946) defeated the Australian tennis team in five matches, bringing the Cup to the U.S.

1920 July 15–27 The **America's Cup** was won off New York Bay by the U.S.-manned *Resolute*, which defeated the British challenger *Shamrock IV* three races to two. American yachts had now won all 14 of such races, beginning in 1851.

1920 Sept. 17 Representatives of 12 teams formed the **first professional football league** in the U.S., the **American Professional Football Association**. Meeting in an automobile showroom in Canton, Ohio, each team paid $100 for its franchise. In 1922 the association renamed itself the **National Football League** [NFL].

1920 Oct. 12 **Man o' War** won the Kenilworth Park Gold Cup at Windsor Ontario, Canada, defeating **Sir Barton** in a match race. It was his final race before being retired to stud on a farm in Kentucky. In two years of racing, Man o' War won 20 of 21 races. His single defeat came at Saratoga, New York, in Aug., 1919, at the hands of the appropriately named **Upset**.

1920 Nov. 12 **Kenesaw Mountain Landis** (Nov. 20 1866–Nov. 25, 1944), a judge of the U.S. District Court in Chicago, was elected the **first commissioner of professional baseball**, for a term of seven years, by the club owners. His election reflected the great need the owners felt to restore public confidence in the game following the "**Black Sox**" scandal. On Sept. 28, 1920, eight members of the Chicago White Sox team of 1919 were indicted on charges they conspired to fix the outcome of the 1919 World Series in which they were favored but lost to the Cincinnati Reds. On Aug. 3, 1921, the players were acquitted on a technicality but there was little doubt of their guilt. Landis at once barred the eight from ever playing professional baseball again.

1921

I. DISASTERS

1921 July 13 **Maxim Gorky**, a Russian writer, made an appeal to the world to help Soviet Russia feed its people, who were suffering from widespread **famine**. The **American Relief Association**, under **Herbert Hoover**, established a program that helped save c.11 million lives between Sept., 1921, and July, 1923.

1921 Aug. 24 Near Hull, England, a British dirigible, the **ZR2, broke up** on a trial flight, killing 62 persons.

II. POLITICS AND WAR

1921 The policy of gradual self-government in the **Philippines** faced a setback when the Republicans regained power in the U.S. Filipinos were no longer sought to hold office in the Philippine government. **Leonard Wood** (Oct. 9, 1860–Aug. 7, 1927) was appointed governor general and ruled in a semi-military manner.

1921 Feb. 8 **Pyotr Alekseyevich Kropotkin** (b. Dec. 21, 1842), a member of a princely Russian family, revolutionary, anarchist, and geographer, died. After scientifically valuable explorations in Siberia, Finland and Manchuria, he joined an anarchist group and became a leading theorist of the movement. Kropotkin was arrested and imprisoned in both France and Russia for his activities. After the February Revolution of 1917 in Russia he returned to his native land and fought the Bolshevik influence, but retired from politics when the Bolsheviks took over the government. Kropotkin was steadfastly nonviolent in his beliefs.

1921 Feb. 9 The **first Parliament in India** met in New Delhi. Its members were elected in Oct. 1920, under the Government of India Act (1919), although the **Congress party**, advocates of independence, boycotted the election. This legislature gave India a measure of self-government, but the governor general, representing the British government, was the ultimate authority.

1921 Feb. 9 The **Treaty of Riga** ended the **Russo-Polish War**, which had begun in early 1920.

1921 Mar. 1–18 Sailors at the Soviet naval base in Kronstadt [Kronshlot], on the Gulf of Finland, staged an unsuccessful **mutiny against the Bolshevik government**. They called for greater freedom of expression, free secret elections, and the removal of party members from the military and the government.

1921 Mar. 4 **Warren G**[amaliel] **Harding** of the Republican party was inaugurated as the 29th president of the U.S., having defeated **James M**[iddleton]

Cox (Mar. 31, 1870–July 15, 1957) of the Democratic party. **Calvin Coolidge** (July 4, 1872–Jan. 5, 1933) served as vice president. In the election on Nov. 2, 1920, Harding received 16,152,200 popular votes and 404 in the electoral college. Cox won 9,147,353 and 127 respectively.

1921 Apr. 1   Abdullah ibn-Husein of the **Hashemite Dynasty of Jordan** (to the present) was named emir of **Transjordan**, former Turkish territory mandated to Great Britain following World War I.

1921 Apr. 20   By the **Thomson-Urrutia Treaty**, ratified by the U.S. Senate, Colombia was given $25 million for its loss of Panama in 1903. In return, Colombia granted official recognition to independent Panama when it ratified the treaty on Dec. 22.

1921 May 19   Warren G. Harding, president of the U.S., signed into law the **first generally restrictive immigration law** in the nation's history. Effective on June 3, immigration each year would be restricted to 3 percent of the number of each nationality group that was living in the U.S. in 1910. In 1924 the **Johnson-Reed Act** replaced the 1921 law, establishing a quota of only 2 percent of the nationals of any country residing in the U.S. in 1890. It also prohibited entirely the immigration of Japanese nationals.

1921 July   The **Chinese Communist party** [CCP] was founded. Although small at first it became the chief rival of the Nationalist party [Kuomintang] for control of China.

1921 July 21   Abd-el-Krim [Abdel Krim, 'Abd-al-Karim, Mohammed Abd-al-Karim al-Khattabi] (1885–Feb. 6, 1963), a popular leader of Berber tribes in the mountainous Riff region of northern Morocco, scored a great success against c.20,000 Spanish troops in a **battle at Anual**, near Melilla [Rusaddir], on the northeastern coast of Morocco.

1921 July 6   The **Mongolian Peoples Revolutionary Government**, with support from the Soviet Union, was established after **Roman Nikolaus von Ungern-Sternberg** and his military force of White Russians and allied Mongolians had been driven from Urga [later Ulan Bator] by Soviet troops and their Mongolian allies. **Mongolia** now traces its independence to this day. Ungern-Sternberg (b. 1885) was executed by the Bolsheviks Sept. 18, 1921.

1921 July 16   Greece invaded Turkey from its base at İzmir [Smyrna] on the Gulf of İzmir. At first the Greeks scored some success, capturing Kutahya [Kutalah] in northwestern Turkey. After the nationalist leader **Kemal Ataturk** took command of the Turkish forces the Greek advance was soon halted.

1921 Aug. 16   Peter I Karageorgevich (b. July 11, 1844), king of Serbia (from 1903) and first king of the Serbs, Croats, and Slovenes [later Yugoslavia] (from 1918), died and was succeeded by his son **Alexander I** (to 1934).

1921 Aug. 23   The **Kingdom of Iraq** was created from former Mesopotamia, Turkish territory mandated to the British after World War I. **Faisal** [Faysal, Feisul] of the **Hashimite Dynasty** (in Iraq, to 1958) was named king. He had ruled Syria as king in 1920 before the French overthrew him.

1921 Aug. 25   The **U.S. and Germany signed a peace treaty** putting a formal end to their belligerency in World War I. Since the U.S. did not ratify the **Treaty of Versailles** (1919), it had technically still been at war with Germany until this date. The U.S. had signed (Aug. 23) a peace treaty with Austria and now signed (Aug. 29) one with Hungary.

1921 Nov. 22   Afghanistan was recognized as independent by Great Britain in a treaty resolving the **Third Afghan War** (1919–1921). The unilateral declaration of independence by **Habibullah** [Habib-Allah] **Khan** (ruled from 1901) to the British viceroy of India had led to the outbreak of the Afghan War on May 3, 1919, and had caused his assassination on Feb. 20. Habibullah's third son **Amanullah** [Aman-Allah] **Khan** (June 1, 1892–Apr. 25, 1960) succeeded as king of an independent Afghanistan.

1921 Dec. 6   The **Anglo-Irish Treaty** was signed in London by British and Irish leaders. The treaty, which included terms mandated by the **Government of Ireland Act** (1920), established the **Irish Free State**, with the same constitutional privileges enjoyed by Australia, Canada, New Zealand, and South Africa. Additionally, an oath of allegiance to the British crown was required of the members of the government. In the absence of **Eamon de Valera**, who was in the U.S., the key Irish leaders negotiating this controversial settlement were **Arthur Griffith** and **Michael Collins**. On Dec. 16 it was ratified by the British Parliament, and on Jan. 8, 1922, it was ratified by the **Dáil Éireann** by a margin of only seven votes. A provisional government was established with Michael Collins at its head. Under the treaty the counties of Northern Ireland were permitted to decide whether or not to accept partition. **James Craig** (Jan. 8, 1871–Nov. 24, 1940), long an Ulster Unionist and opponent of Home Rule, became prime minister of **Northern Ireland**, and its Parliament convened there on June 22, 1921. Sectarian riots broke out in Belfast, Northern Ireland's capital. The **Irish Republican Army** [IRA], though officially outlawed, swiftly increased its numbers and virtually ruled in many places in the south and west of Ireland.

1921 Dec. 13 The **Washington Naval Conference**, which opened on Nov. 12, concluded its work with agreement on three treaties that seemed to promise a step toward disarmament and a lessening of international tensions. Represented were Belgium, China, France, Great Britain, Italy, Japan, the Netherlands, and the U.S. Among the achievements were an agreement that some warships would be scrapped and a ratio, based on 1, of capital ship tonnage was agreed on, in order, Great Britain, the U.S., Japan, France, and Italy of 5:5:3:1.67:1.67. The same formula was to apply to aircraft carriers but, as an indication of how unimportant they were considered at this time, the maximum tonnages allowed were much smaller than for capital ships.

1921 Dec. 29 **William Lyon Mackenzie King** became prime minister of **Canada**. He was the leader of the Liberal party which won the most seats, 116, in the House of Commons in the general election of Dec. 6. Thus began the longest prime ministerial career in Canadian history, a total of almost 22 years: Dec. 1921–June 1926; Sept. 1926–Aug. 1930; Oct. 1935–Nov. 1948. King worked hard to preserve the unity of Canada in the face of the problems between the French- and English-speaking sections. He also worked hard for cooperation with the U.S. and Great Britain.

III. ECONOMY AND TRADE

1921 Every nation faced **problems of shifting from production of war to peacetime goods**. Much of Europe was physically devastated and factories, railroads, and other facilities had to be rebuilt. Even the victors were financially exhausted, left with huge debts, most of the money being owed to the U.S. On Mar. 23 Germany announced it would be unable to meet its reparations payments due on May 1, but did

eventually pay. In England, nearly 1,000,000 persons were out of work. Even in the U.S., whose economy had boomed even before it entered the war, the unemployment rate rose to 11.7 percent while the GNP dropped by 24 percent, and large industries made drastic cuts in wages. Germany was in for a long siege of economic troubles but in other countries, especially the U.S., the recession of 1921 soon disappeared.

1921 Feb. 22 The **Gosplan**, or State Planning Commission, was created in the Soviet Union to formulate general plans for economic development. The Gosplan set the goals for the first Five Year Plan (1928).

1921 Mar. 16 The **Anglo-Russian Trade Agreement**, establishing trade between Russia and Great Britain, was concluded, marking the end of the Allied economic blockade of Russia.

1921 Aug. 11 The government of Russia issued a **New Economic Policy** [NEP], which permitted some private enterprise. Peasants could sell their produce in the markets and foreigners could establish business enterprises in the Soviet Union.

IV. RELIGION AND PHILOSOPHY

1921 The **International Missionary Council** was formally organized at Lake Mohonk, New York. The council embraced national conferences of missionary societies and Protestant denominational missionary organizations.

1921 **Abraham Isaac Kook** [Kuk] (1865–Sept. 1, 1935) began a 15-year tenure as chief rabbi of Palestine. A man of wide friendship and considerable powers of persuasion and conciliation, Rabbi Kook prevented serious breaches between religious and secular Jews, Zionists and non-Zionists, during the British mandate over Palestine.

1921 **Rudolf** [Karl] **Bultmann** (Aug. 20, 1884–July 30, 1976) of Marburg University published his controversial *History of the Synoptic Tradition*. This and his later *Jesus* (1926) set forth a literary analysis of the first three Gospels. For Bultmann, the historically valid parts of the Gospels were Jesus's sayings; the accounts of Jesus's actions and the historical framework, except for his crucifixion, were the product of a believing community.

V. SCIENCE, EDUCATION, AND TECHNOLOGY

1921 Daya Ram Sahni (birth and death dates unknown) excavated part of the **ruins of ancient Harappa** (3,000? B.C.) in the Indus River Valley of present Pakistan, revealing one of the earliest civilizations (3200–2400 B.C.). The world was astonished at this discovery of an advanced city of the late Chalcolithic [copper-using] stage in northwestern India. Eventually, artifacts and ruins of towns and cities showed that the civilization covered most of the Indus Valley and extended to the east and west.

1921 The bones of an early type of man, evolutionarily near Neanderthal man [*Homo sapiens neanderthalensis*], were found at Broken Hill, Northern Rhodesia [present Kabwe, Zambia]. Its massive skull, nearly complete, and its pelvic and limb bones were recovered. Called **Rhodesian** [or Kabwe] **man**, it lived c.100,000 B.P.

1921 May **Roy Chapman Andrews**, an American scientist working for the American Museum of Natural History, discovered the fossilized eggs of *Protoceratops*, a small dinosaur of the early Cretaceous Period (135,000,000–115,000,000 years ago), in central Asia.

1921 July 21 The **ability of air power to sink warships** was demonstrated for the first time off Hampton Roads, Virginia, when American army planes bombed and sank a former German battleship, the *Ostfriesland*. The test was carried out at the urging of **William Mitchell** (Dec. 29, 1879–Feb. 19, 1936), an army officer who had commanded the U.S. air force in Europe in World War I. Mitchell continued to criticize American military leaders for what he saw as their neglect of the potentialities of aerial bombardment. As a result, he was court martialed in 1925 and sentenced to five-years suspension from duty with loss of pay. Mitchell resigned from the army the next year.

1921 July 27 The discovery of the hormone **insulin** was announced in Toronto, Canada. The leader of the scientists that made the discovery was **Frederick Grant Banting**, with **Charles H. Best** (Feb. 27, 1899–Mar. 31, 1978) as his chief assistant. The insulin was derived from extracts of pancreas. In 1923 Banting shared with others the **Nobel prize for physiology** or medicine.

1921 Dec. 12 **Henrietta Swan Leavitt** (b. July 4, 1868), an American astronomer, died. After 1895 she was a member of the staff of the Harvard Observatory and became head of its photographic photometry department. Leavitt over the years found four novae and c.2,400 variable stars. In 1912 she determined that the periods of Cepheid variable stars are in close relationship with their true brightness.

VI. ARTS AND LEISURE

1921 Mar. 29 **John Burroughs** (b. Apr. 3, 1837), an American essayist and naturalist, died. Among his friends were Walt Whitman, John Muir, and Theodore Roosevelt. His works included *Birds and Poets* (1877), *Locusts and Wild Honey* (1879), *Signs and Seasons* (1886), *Ways of Nature* (1905), and a volume of poetry.

1921 June 8 **Pavel Orszagh** (b. Feb. 2, 1849), regarded as the most important of all Slovak poets, who wrote under the name of Hvezdoslav, died. His best-known work was the epic narrative poem *The Gamekeeper's Wife* (1886).

1921 Aug. 2 **Enrico Caruso** (b. Feb. 25, 1873), the great operatic tenor, died. He made his debut in his native Naples, Italy, in 1894, triumphed in his London debut in 1902, and achieved even greater instant popularity in 1904 with his debut in *Rigoletto* at the Metropolitan Opera House in New York City. Caruso sang more than 50 operatic roles with a technically perfect but also very warm voice.

1921 Sept. 27 **Engelbert Humperdinck** (b. Sept. 1, 1854), a German composer, died. Humperdinck's best-known work was the opera *Hänsel und Gretel* (1893).

1921 Dec. 16 [Charles] **Camille Saint-Saëns** (b. Oct. 9, 1835), a French composer, died. Saint-Saëns composed operas, symphonies, concertos, chamber music, and works in other forms. His best-known work is the opera *Samson et Dalila* (1877). Also important were his *Rondo Capriccioso* (1863) for piano and orchestra; the symphonic poem *Le Rouet d'Omphale* (1871) and the *Third Symphony* (1886).

VII. SPORTS, GAMES, AND SOCIETY

1921 The **Jazz Age** was getting into full swing, especially in the U.S., where World War I left few marks on the home front. Great Britain had its **Bright**

Young Things, and quite a few Americans spent all or part of the 1920s in Paris, where restraints on lifestyles seemed more relaxed. Women, if they felt like it, now smoked and drank along with the men. They wore skirts to the knee or above, used more cosmetics, and bobbed their hair. In America, under Prohibition, the hip flask and **speakeasy** became a part of life for many. Social dancing, to jazz bands, was frenetic. The growing number of automobiles took courting from parlor sofas to lovers' lanes. Many groups deplored what they saw as the final collapse of civilization, but it was at least in part a reaction to the four years of war.

1921 Mar. 15–Apr. 21   José Raúl Capablanca (Nov. 19, 1888–Mar. 8, 1942), a Cuban chess master, won the **world chess championship** at Havana by defeating **Emanuel Lasker**, the German titleholder (from 1894). He held the title until 1927.

1921 May 1   The United States Golf Association and the Royal and Ancient Golf Club agreed to require play with a **golf ball** weighing no more than 1.62 ounces and measuring not less than 1.62 inches in diameter, later changed to 1.68 inches.

1921 July 2   The **first million-dollar gate** in the history of boxing came with the **Jack Dempsey** vs. **Georges Carpentier** (Jan. 12, 1894–Oct. 27, 1975) heavyweight championship bout in Jersey City, New Jersey. Dempsey knocked out the French champion in the 4th round.

1921 Dec. 1   Henri Désiré Landru, called the **modern French Bluebeard**, was sentenced to death for the murder of ten women and a boy. The evidence was all circumstantial and no bodies were ever found. Landru (b. 1869) was guillotined Feb. 25, 1922.

1922

I. DISASTERS

1922 Sept. 14–15   Fire swept through the ancient city of İzmir [Smyrna] as Turkish troops recaptured it from retreating Greek armies. More than 60 percent of Smyrna burned, with property damage totaling about $100 million and c.100,000 persons left homeless.

II. POLITICS AND WAR

1922 Feb. 9   The U.S. Congress established the **World War Foreign Debt Commission** to negotiate with the 15 European nations that owed the U.S. money as a result of loans made to them during World War I. Great Britain, France, and Italy were the largest debtors. They in turn were owed money by other Allies and were also counting on the reparations required of Germany by the **Treaty of Versailles** (1919) to pay the U.S. After negotiations a figure of about $11,500,000,000 was agreed on, which was to be paid back over a period of 62 years at an interest rate of slightly more than 2 percent. In the end the total would come to more than $22,000,000,000. Payments on this basis were made until 1931, mostly from German reparations, but the world-wide depression of the 1930s put an end to any possibility of payment in full. Finland was the only country to pay every cent of its debt.

1922 Feb. 28   Great Britain ended its protectorate over Egypt, which became a constitutional monarchy under **Ahmad Fuad I** (Mar. 26, 1868–Apr. 28, 1936), son of **Ismail Pasha**, the Khedive of Egypt (1863–1879) and brother of **Tewfik Pasha**, the Khedive (1879–1892) who saw Egypt occupied by the British in 1882. The British retained control of Egypt's foreign policy, and maintained garrisons along the Suez Canal, and in Cairo and the chief Egyptian cities.

1922 Spring   Chang Tso-Lin (1873–June 7, 1928), a Manchurian warlord, invaded Chihli province and captured Peking [Beijing], its capital and the capital of **China**. He was defeated by **Wu P'ei-Fu** (Apr. 22, 1874–Dec. 4, 1939), commander of the Chihli armies. In Oct. 1924, Chang Tso-Lin renewed his drive and defeated Wu P'ei-Fu near Tientsin, southeast of Peking. Chang Tso-Lin and Wu P'ei-Fu then allied against **Feng Yü-Hsiang** (Sept. 26, 1882–Sept., 1948), another Chihli military commander, who had deserted Wu P'ei-Fu to organize the Nationalist Kuominchün [People's army—not communist]. Chang Tso-Lin and Wu P'ei-Fu secured Peking by 1928, in time to meet the challenge of **Chiang Kai-Shek** and his Nationalist army supporters, including Feng Yü-Hsiang and his Kuominchün.

1922 Apr. 3 **Joseph Stalin** [Iosif Vissarionovich Dzhugashvili] was elected **general secretary** of the central committee of the Communist party of Russia. An active Bolshevik since 1903, he was a close associate of Lenin's. As the manager of party affairs, and as one of the five members of the **politburo**, Stalin was in a position to enlarge his power in this new post.

1922 Apr. 16 **Germany was the first nation to recognize officially the U.S.S.R.** when the two nations signed the second **Treaty of Rapallo**. They negated debts owed to one another before the end of World War I, canceled war reparations, and agreed to resume the exchange of diplomats.

1922 June 24 **Walther Rathenau** (b. Sept. 29, 1867), the German foreign minister, was assassinated by two nationalists, who were arrested July 17. By coincidence, on June 24 **Adolf Hitler**, who was soon to become the Nazi leader of such extremists and anti-Semites (Rathenau was Jewish), began serving a **prison term** of a month for inciting a riot. Rathenau was hated by Hitler and his followers because he had signed a treaty with communist Russia and was attempting to make it possible for Germany to pay reparations due the Allies.

1922 July 24 The **League of Nations** approved a **British mandate in Palestine**. By the same order, the League stated that the rights of the other peoples of the region would not be prejudiced in favor of the Jewish national home. The homeland was to include an area on both sides of the Jordan River, conferred (1920) on Great Britain as a protectorate by the Allies. Transjordan, forming four-fifths of the Palestinian mandate, was excluded from the Jewish homeland. The emirate of Transjordan was created in Sept. 1922, with **Abdullah ibn Husain**, of the Hashemite Dynasty in Jordan (1921–to the present), as emir (to 1946, as king 1946–1951).

1922 Aug. **Sun Yat-Sen**, China's Nationalist leader, fled to Shanghai after the warlords in Canton withdrew their support. Sun appealed to the Soviet Union, which officially granted aid in Jan. 1923.

1922 Aug. 12 **Arthur Griffith** (b. Mar. 31, 1872), president of the Dáil in the **Irish Free State**, died

suddenly. Ten days later his successor, **Michael Collins** (b. Oct. 16, 1890), who had been chairman of the provisional government, was ambushed and shot in West Cork while on a military inspection. **William Thomas Cosgrave** (June 6, 1880–Nov. 16, 1965) became president of the provisional government and of the Dáil. That same year he was named president of the executive council of the Irish Free State.

1922 Sept. 9 The **Greek occupation of Anatolia** [central Turkey] ended as the Nationalist Turks rallied to oust the Greeks from the Aegean port city of İzmîr [Smyrna].

1922 Oct. 11 The **Greco-Turkish War** came to an end with the signing of an armistice by the two nations at Mudanya, on the Sea of Marmara in northwestern Turkey.

1922 Oct. 19 The **coalition government of Great Britain**, headed by **David Lloyd George**, the prime minister, was **forced to resign**. Lloyd George, a Liberal, had been prime minister from Dec., 1916, heading a cabinet that saw Britain through the second half of World War I and the Paris Peace Conference [Treaty of Versailles, 1919]. The Liberal government had won a sizable majority in the general election of 1918, but depended much on Conservative party support. The coalition was also being threatened by the growing strength of the Labour party. **Andrew Bonar Law**, leader of the Conservative party, became prime minister but he died the following year.

1922 Oct. 28 Italian fascists, meeting in a party congress at Naples, organized a **March on Rome** to seize power. **Victor Emmanuel III**, king of Italy, bowed to fascist pressure on Oct. 31 and appointed **Benito Mussolini** as prime minister. On Nov. 25 Mussolini won dictatorial powers.

1922 Nov. 1 **Turkey's national assembly abolished the sultanate**. Its decision had been forced by **Mustafa Kemal**, whose armed guards ringed the assembly at Ankara. On Nov. 17 **Mohammed VI** (Jan. 14, 1861–May 16, 1926), the last sultan of Turkey (from 1918), fled to Malta under British protection. There was considerable support for a constitutional monarchy, so **Abdul-Mejid II** (May 30, 1868–Aug. 23, 1944), the sultan's nephew, was retained as caliph, the religious head of Turkey, to whom Turkey's vast majority of Islamic believers looked for spiritual guidance.

1922 Nov. 24 Robert Erskine Childers (b. June 25, 1870), who had long supported the formation of an Irish Republic but opposed the terms of the 1921 Anglo-Irish Treaty, was executed for unlawful possession of a revolver. The Irish government had passed a law stating that the carrying of arms was a capital offense. The author of several books, Childers wrote a popular thriller, *The Riddle of the Sands* (1903), about an imagined German plot to invade England.

1922 Dec. 30 The **Union of Soviet Socialist Republics** [U.S.S.R.] came into being by action of the All-Russian Congress of Soviets, which was dominated by the central committee and the Political Bureau of the Communist party. This action made a federation of Russia, including Siberia, as the Russian Soviet Federated Social Republic (RSFSR), the largest member; Ukraine; White Russia; and Transcaucasia (Georgia, Armenia, and Azerbaijan).

III. ECONOMY AND TRADE

1922 Jan. A **congress of fascist syndicates** held at Bologna, Italy, established a confederation of syndical corporations which for the first time included the middle and intellectual classes among the syndical organizations represented, demonstrating the Italian Fascists' claim to be a party of all classes.

1922 Mar. 10 An **armed rebellion of white mine workers** broke out in the Rand in South Africa. They were protesting against a cut made in their salaries and the dismissal of c.4,000 workers to be replaced by lower-paid black Africans. The revolt led to the **Apprenticeship Act**, which forbade non-whites in semiskilled jobs.

1922 Apr. 7 The **Teapot Dome scandal** began in the U.S. when **Albert Bacon Fall** (Nov. 26, 1861–Nov. 30, 1944), secretary of the interior, without competitive bidding, leased development rights in the federally owned Teapot Dome oil reserve in Wyoming to **Harry Ford Sinclair** (July 6, 1876–Nov. 10, 1956), head of the **Mammoth Oil Company**. A similar lease was granted to the **Pan American Petroleum and Transport Company**, owned by Fall's friend **Edward Lawrence Doheny** (Aug. 10, 1856–Sept. 8, 1935) for the Elk Hill reserve in California. When the Senate investigated these deals it was discovered that Fall had received large "loans" from both Sinclair and Doheny. Fall was later convicted of accepting bribes. Sinclair and Doheny were acquit-

ted, although the former eventually served three months in jail for contempt of the Senate and for hiring detectives to shadow people serving on the jury trying him. In 1927 the Supreme Court restored the oil reserves to the government.

1922 Aug. 14 Alfred Charles William Harmsworth (b. July 15, 1865) [Viscount Northcliffe], a British newspaper publisher and journalist, died. His career as a newspaper publisher began in 1894 when he bought the **London** *Evening News*, in which he pioneered such features as gossip columns, women's news, and serials. Harmsworth founded the *Daily Mail* in 1896 and the *Daily Mirror* in 1903. Five years later he acquired the *Times* of **London** and restored it to financial and editorial health.

1922 Oct. 4 The **Geneva Protocol**, granting a loan of $100 million to Austria through the League of Nations, was issued. The loan was secured by the Social Christian **Ignaz Seipel** (July 19, 1876–Aug. 2, 1932), a conservative Roman Catholic priest and chancellor of Austria (1922–1924), to stabilize the Austrian economy. Austria, in turn, promised to remain independent of Germany for 20 years.

1922 Oct. 24 George Cadbury (b. Sept. 19, 1839), an English candy manufacturer and social reformer, died. He and his brother in 1861 took over management of their father's candy company, which specialized in chocolates and still is in operation today. Both men were concerned with social problems and in 1880 moved the factory to Bournville, where they built housing for the workers that became a model for the "garden city" movement.

1922 Dec. 12 John Wanamaker (b. July 11, 1838), an American pioneer in department store management and merchandising, died. He operated successful stores in Philadelphia and New York City.

IV. RELIGION AND PHILOSOPHY

1922 Jan. 22 Pope Benedict XV (b. Nov. 21, 1854; ruled from 1914), died. His pontificate was concerned almost entirely with the problems brought on by World War I. He remained completely neutral and was respected by all. Benedict's attempts at mediation failed but he provided charitable services on a large scale and assistance to prisoners of war. He was succeeded by **Pius XI**.

1922 May 21 Harry Emerson Fosdick (May 24, 1878–Oct. 5, 1969), perhaps the most influential American preacher of the early 20th century, preached his epoch-marking "**Shall the Fundamentalists Win?**" With it the smoldering Modernist-Fundamentalist controversy resurfaced, especially among the Northern Baptists and the Presbyterians, one of whose pulpits Fosdick, a Baptist but a Modernist, was then occupying.

1922 Sept. 4 Georges Sorel (b. Nov. 2, 1848), a French social philosopher, died. His *Réflexions sur la violence* [*Reflections on Violence*] (1908) was a textbook for syndicalists. At first Sorel hoped labor unions would lead the revolutionary movement, but later he supported the reactionary French Royalists and the Russian Bolsheviks. Sorel believed violence was necessary to release human energy and bring about spiritual revival of society.

V. SCIENCE, EDUCATION, AND TECHNOLOGY

1922 May 30 The **Lincoln Memorial** in Washington, D.C., was officially dedicated. It is a classic Greek temple, 189 feet long and 118 ⅔ feet wide. At the front are 36 Doric columns, one for each of the states of the U.S. in existence when **Abraham Lincoln** was assassinated in 1865. The architect was **Henry Bacon** (Nov. 28, 1866–Feb. 16, 1924). Inside the memorial is a 19-foot statue of Lincoln, seated in a brooding, contemplative pose. It was the work of **Daniel Chester French**, an American sculptor.

1922 Aug. 2 Alexander Graham Bell (b. May 3, 1847), a Scottish-born American inventor, died. For his **invention of the telephone**, he received a patent in the U.S. in 1876. Bell's father had developed a sign language for the deaf and Bell himself devoted much of his experimentation to improving communication by the deaf.

1922 Oct. 16 The 12-mile **Simplon II railroad tunnel** through the Alps was completed, joining Switzerland and Italy. At its greatest depth below the mountain surface, it is 7,005 feet underground.

1922 Nov. 26 The **tomb of Tutankhamen** [Tutankhamon], an Egyptian pharaoh of the 18th Dynasty (c.1580–c.1320 B.C.), found in the Valley of the Kings at Thebes on Nov. 4, was opened by two English archaeologists, **Howard Carter** (May 9, 1873–Mar.

2, 1939) and **George Edward Stanhope Molyneux** (June 26, 1866–Apr. 6, 1923), Lord Carnarvon. It took three years to empty the tomb of its remarkable treasure, now in the Cairo Museum of Antiquities.

1922 Nov. 30 The **Japanese navy** launched the *Hosho,* **the first ship designed as an aircraft carrier,** not simply rebuilt as one. She carried 21 aircraft. The **first aircraft carrier** was a converted U.S. cargo ship (1922), renamed the *Langley.* The first U.S. carrier built as such was the *Saratoga* in 1925.

VI. ARTS AND LEISURE

1922 *Nanook of the North,* a documentary film of Eskimo life, was completed by the U.S. film maker **Robert Joseph Flaherty** (Feb. 16, 1884–July 23, 1951). His other films included *Tabu* (1931), *Man of Aran* (1934), and *Elephant Boy* (1935).

1922 Jan. 27 Nellie Bly [Elizabeth Cochrane Seaman] (b. May 5, 1867), an American journalist whose well-planned feats attracted wide attention, died. She was chiefly known for her trip (1889–1890) around the world.

1922 Feb. 2 *Ulysses* by James Joyce, one of the most notable novels in world literature, was published in Paris on the author's 40th birthday. The publisher was Shakespeare & Company, a bookstore owned by **Sylvia Beach**, an American who had long encouraged Joyce. Although hailed as a work of genius, *Ulysses* was found too difficult to read by many who did not appreciate what Joyce did with the English language. Many others found it pornographic. It was banned from the U.S. until 1933 and did not appear in the United Kingdom until 1936.

1922 July 9 Mori Ogai [real name: Mori Rintaro] (b. Feb. 17, 1862), a Japanese writer, died. His first novel, *Maihime* [*The Dancing Girl*] (1907), was based on his experience as an army doctor studying in Germany, and he translated German classics into Japanese. Ogai's best-known work was *Gan* [*The Wild Goose*] (1911–1913).

1922 Aug. 18 W[illiam] H[enry] Hudson (b. Aug. 4, 1841), author and naturalist, died. Born in Argentina of American parents, he became a British citizen. His best-known work was *Green Mansions* (1904), a tragic romance. Among his other writings were *A Shepherd's Life* (1910) and *Far Away and Long Ago* (1918).

1922 Nov. 18   **Marcel Proust** (b. July 10, 1871), a French writer, died. Proust began his great work `*A la recherche du temps perdu* [*Remembrance of Things Past*] (1922–1932) in July 1909. It was largely autobiographical, mostly an interior monologue, and circular in structure. Proust's hero came to the realization that all he had experienced thus far remained alive in his memory. Time lost became time regained. At the close of the long book the hero is ready to write the tale the reader has just read. The first part *Du Côté de chez Swann* [*Swann's Way*] (1913) received little attention. The second part `*A l'Ombre des Jeunes Filles en Fleurs* [*Within a Budding Grove*] (1919), however, won the Prix Goncourt. *Le Côté de Guermantes* (1920–1921), *Sodome et Gomorrhe I* (1921), and *Sodome et Gomorrhe II* [*Cities of the Plain*] (1922) were published before Proust's death. Though Proust had revised and polished most of them, the last volumes, *La Prisonnière* [*The Captive*] (1923), *Albertine Disparu* [*The* *Sweet Cheat Gone*; orig.:*La Fugitive*] (1925), and *Le Temps Retrouvé* [*Time Regained*] (1927), were published posthumously.

VII. SPORTS, GAMES, AND SOCIETY

1922   *Etiquette in Society, in Business, in Politics, and at Home*, published in the U.S., brought high good manners into the arena of everyday life. Its author, **Emily Post** (Oct. 27, 1872–Sept. 25, 1960), began a syndicated newspaper column after publication of *Etiquette* in order to respond to the immense volume of mail it generated.

1922 Aug. 28   The oldest international team golf match, the **Walker Cup**, was played for the first time between U.S. and British amateur golfers. It was played at Southampton, New York, and the U.S. team won, eight matches to four.

1923

I. DISASTERS

1923 Sept. 1   An **earthquake struck Japan**, particularly in the Tokyo to Yokohama area, virtually destroying the cities. Deaths were estimated at 200,-000; injured 125,000; and homeless 2,000,000. Damage was estimated at $1,000,000,000. At an estimated strength of 8.9 on the Richter scale, this was the **strongest earthquake ever recorded**.

II. POLITICS AND WAR

1923 Jan. 1   **Sun Yat-Sen**, leader of China's Nationalist [**Kuomintang**] party, appointed **Mikhail Borodin,** a Russian communist agent, to reorganize the Nationalist party along the lines of the Soviet Union's Bolshevik party.

1923 Jan. 11   Claiming Germany had defaulted on its reparations payments, **French and Belgian troops marched into the Ruhr**, the heart of German industry, to seize coal and other materials to make up for the default. They were met with strikes and other forms of passive resistance, aggravating the already serious state of the German economy. The German mark began to drop in value. By June an egg cost 800 marks. By November the mark was quoted at about 130 billion to the dollar. With the government paralyzed, **Gustave Stresemann** (May 10, 1878–Oct. 3, 1929), a conservative statesman, became chancellor for a brief period (Aug. 13–Nov. 23) in 1923.

1923 Feb. 3   The **border between Poland and Lithuania was fixed by the League of Nations**. A diet was elected to represent the disputed territory of Vilna [Wilna, Wilno, Vilnius] on Poland's northern border. On Feb. 20, 1922, it voted to join Poland, and on Mar. 15, 1923, the League of Nations ratified the decision.

1923 July 20   [Francisco] **Pancho Villa** [Doroteo Arango] (b. June 5, 1878), a popular Mexican rebel leader, was assassinated in Parral in Chihuahua state, Mexico, by an unknown person.

1923 July 24   The **Treaty of Lausanne**, signed by **Turkey**, the Allies, Greece, Bulgaria, and Yugoslavia, set Turkey's boundaries and recognized its independence. Only ethnic Turkey, or Anatolia proper, and a portion of southeastern Europe, remained Turkish.

1923 Aug. 2 Warren Gamaliel Harding (b. Nov. 2, 1865), president of the U.S., died suddenly in San Francisco while on a tour of the U.S., perhaps from food poisoning. **Calvin Coolidge**, the vice president, was sworn in as president of the U.S. on Aug. 3.

1923 Sept. 13 Charged with keeping order in **Spain** while the Catalans agitated for autonomy, **Miguel Primo de Rivera y Orbaneja** (Jan. 8, 1870– Mar. 16, 1930), military governor of Catalonia, seized Barcelona in a coup d'état and with royal approval issued a *pronunciamento* calling for the suspension of the constitution and the establishment of military rule until an effective government could be formed.

1923 Oct. 29 Turkey was proclaimed a republic, and this day is still celebrated as a national holiday. Ankara had been chosen as the capital on Oct. 13, and on Oct. 30 **Mustafa Kemal** was elected president by Turkey's national assembly.

1923 Nov. 8 An attempt by a group of Nazis, led by **Adolf Hitler** and a top general of World War I, **Erich Ludendorff**, to overthrow the republican government of Germany was put down with some bloodshed. What became known as the **Beer Hall Putsch** began in Munich, Bavaria, when Hitler led his followers from a rally in a beer hall to a confrontation with police. Hitler fled but was arrested two days later and then sentenced to five years imprisonment, of which he served only nine months. During that time he dictated to [Richard] **Rudolph Hess**, a close follower who was imprisoned with him, *Mein Kampf* [*My Struggle*] (1924).

1923 Dec. 6 In the British general election, the protective tariff policy of the Conservative party was rejected. **Stanley Baldwin** (Aug. 3, 1867– Dec. 14, 1947), the prime minister, resigned on Jan. 22, 1924. **Great Britain established its first Labour government** with **James Ramsay Mac-Donald** (Oct. 12, 1866–Nov. 9, 1937) as prime minister.

1923 Dec. 18 The **Tangier Convention** [Statute of Tangier] was signed by Great Britain, France, and Spain. The disputed zone of Tangier, Morocco, at the western end of the Strait of Gibraltar, became a permanently neutral, demilitarized port governed by an international commission.

III. ECONOMICS AND TRADE

1923 Aug. 23 The **United States Steel Corporation instituted the eight-hour work day**. Other steel companies followed suit. For many years steel workers had labored 12 or 14 hours a day, seven days a week.

IV. RELIGION AND PHILOSOPHY

1923 *I and Thou*, a classic of the philosophy of dialogue, was published by **Martin Buber** (Feb. 8, 1878–June 13, 1965), a Viennese-born German Jew. Of modern Jewish thinkers, Buber has been the most influential in the Christian world.

V. SCIENCE, EDUCATION, AND TECHNOLOGY

1923 The **Fifth International Conference of the American States** agreed to begin a road-building project to be known as the **Pan American Highway** that would eventually provide a road for motor vehicles running c.16,000 miles from Alaska to southern Chile, or almost from the Arctic Circle to the Antarctic Circle.

1923 The **Hillel Foundations movement**, created to serve Jewish students on American college and university campuses, was inaugurated by **B'nai B'rith** at the University of Illinois.

1923 Mar. 27 James Dewar (b. Sept. 20, 1842), a Scottish chemist, died. The **Dewar flask** (1892) provided a model for the vacuum thermos bottle. While studying the behavior of gases at low temperatures, he liquefied hydrogen (1898) and was later able to solidify it (1899).

1923 May 3 Two U.S. army lieutenants completed the **first non-stop airplane flight across the continent**. They flew a single engine Fokker T-2 from Hempstead, New York, to San Diego, California, a distance of c.2,800 miles, in 26 hours and 50 minutes.

1923 Oct. 21 The **first modern planetarium** opened at Deutsches Museum in Munich, in southeastern Germany. It was built by the **Carl Zeiss Optical**

Works of Jena, in Germany. It projected images and the motion of the heavenly bodies onto a hemispherical dome simulating the sky.

1923 Oct. 26 Charles Proteus Steinmetz (b. Apr. 9, 1865), an American electrical engineer, died. Born in Germany, he came to the U.S. in 1889. Steinmetz ˮvolutionized electrical engineering when he devis. ˮ a method for making calculations of alternating curreⁱt phenomena. He also discovered the law of hysteresis, showing that the loss of efficiency in electrical apparatus that was caused by alternating magnetism could be reduced.

VI. ARTS AND LEISURE

1923 Jan. 9 Katherine Mansfield [Beauchamp] (b. Oct. 14, 1888), a New Zealand-born English writer, died. Her first collection of short stories was *In a German Pension* (1911), but it was not until publication of *Bliss and Other Stories* (1920) that she received recognition. One more collection, *The Garden Party, and Other Stories* (1922) appeared before her early death from tuberculosis.

1923 Mar. 3 *Time* magazine, the first weekly news magazine, was founded in New York City by **Henry Robinson Luce**, who soon thereafter became its editor-in-chief. *Time* became one of the great successes of American magazine publishing, and Luce went on to found *Fortune* (1930), *Life* (1936–1972), and *Sports Illustrated* (1954).

1923 Mar. 26 Sarah Bernhardt [Henriette Rosine Bernard] (b. Oct. 22, 1844), a French actress called "the divine Sarah" by **Oscar Wilde**, died. From 1866 to 1872 she performed at the Odéon and then returned to the Comédie-Française, where she performed in Racine's *Andromaque* (1873) and *Phèdre* (1874), in the title roles, and as the acclaimed Doña Sol in *Hernani* by **Victor Hugo** in 1877. In 1880 she began world tours that took her to Belgium, Denmark, the U.S. nine times, Canada, Russia, South America, Australia, and Africa. Her touring repertory included *La Dame aux Camélias* by **Alexandre Dumas** fils. A knee injury (1905) led to an amputation (1915), but the actress continued to work with a wooden leg and even made a tour to the U.S. in 1917.

1923 June 10 Pierre Loti [orig.: Louis Marie Julien Viaud] (b. Jan. 14, 1850), a French novelist, died. His best-known works included his first success *Rarahu* (1880), reprinted as *Le Mariage de Loti* [*The Marriage of Loti*] (1882), and *Pêcheur d'Islande* [*An Iceland Fisherman*] (1886).

VII. SPORTS, GAMES, AND SOCIETY

1923 Bobsledding gained international recognition as a sport following the formation of the *Féderation Internationale de Bobsleigh et Tobogganing*.

1923 A craze for playing **Mah Jong**, a game probably of Chinese origin, swept the U.S. It was brought to the U.S. in 1920 by **Joseph Babcock**, an American who had visited China.

1923 Sept. 14 World heavyweight champion **Jack Dempsey** retained his title in a bout in New York City with **Luis Angel Firpo** (Oct. 11, 1896–Aug. 7, 1960) of Argentina, known as "The Wild Bull of the Pampas." Dempsey won by a knockout in the second round, but in the short time the bout lasted, Firpo was knocked down ten times and Dempsey twice.

1924

I. DISASTERS

1924 June 13 The town of Baja, in present southern Hungary, was ravaged by a **tornado**. Property damage was estimated at $3 million.

II. POLITICS AND WAR

1924 Jan. 21 Vladimir I[lyich] **Lenin** [Vladimir Ilyich Ulyanov] (b. Apr. 22, 1870), sometimes known as N. [Nikolai?] Lenin, the leader of Soviet Russia, died. He was succeeded as president of the Soviet of People's Commissars by **Aleksei Ivanovich Rykov** (Feb. 25, 1881–Mar. 14, 1938).

1924 Jan. 27 The **Treaty of Rome** was signed by Italy and Yugoslavia. Italy finally secured the port and district of Fiume, but abandoned, in return, its last claim to the Dalmatian coast of Yugoslavia.

1924 Feb. 3 [Thomas] **Woodrow Wilson** (b. Dec. 28, 1856), former president of the U.S., died in his sleep in Washington, D.C.

1924 Mar. 3 **Turkey abolished the caliphate**, expelling **Abdul-Mejid II**, nephew of the last sultan, who had become caliph in 1922 after the republic was established. Thus, the **Ottoman Dynasty** (from 1299) was effectively ended.

1924 Mar. 25 The **Greek assembly proclaimed a republic** and called for an end to the monarchy. In a plebiscite held on Apr. 13 the people of Greece confirmed the decision. **George II** (July 20, 1890–Apr. 1, 1947), eldest son of **Constantine I**, had been deposed as king in Oct., 1923, after holding the throne for only one year. On Oct. 10, 1935, George was recalled when the assembly voted to restore the monarchy.

1924 May 7 The **Alianza Popular Revolucionaria Americana** [APRA], or the **Aprista party** of Peru, was formed by **Víctor Raúl Haya de la Torre** (Feb. 22, 1895–Aug. 2, 1979) at a student meeting in Mexico City. The Aprista party, hostile to the U.S., influenced political affairs throughout South America.

1924 May 11 **French radicals and socialists won a sweeping victory** by electing 328 members of the National Assembly. **Alexandre Millerand** (Feb. 10, 1859–Apr. 6, 1943), president of France (from 1920) and a strong nationalist, was forced to resign on June 10. He was succeeded (June 13) by **Gaston Doumergue** (Aug. 1, 1863–June 18, 1937), who was in sympathy with the election victors.

1924 June 10 **Giacomo Matteoti** (b. May 22, 1885), socialist deputy of Italy, was assassinated by Italian fascists, whose violent actions he had denounced on May 30. **Benito Mussolini**, Italy's political leader, disavowed the murderers, but liberal and communist agitation spread.

1924 Oct. 29 The **Labour government of Great Britain**, in office only since Jan. 22, was badly beaten in a general election in which it won 151 seats to the 400 of the Conservatives. The election hinged in large part on the public's conception of Labour's attitude toward the communist government of the U.S.S.R. It had recognized that government on Feb. 1. Later the so-called **Zinoviev Letter** was published in England. It purported to be instructions from a high Soviet official on fomenting a communist revolution in Great Britain. **Stanley Baldwin** returned (Nov. 6) to office as a Conservative prime minister (to 1929).

1924 Nov. 26 The **Mongolian People's Republic**, comprising the former Chinese territory of Outer Mongolia, was proclaimed, and its constitution adopted by the **Khural** [Parliament]. The Living Buddha had died; installation of a new one was forbidden. The capital Urga, located in central northern Mongolia, was renamed Ulan Bator [Red Hero].

III. ECONOMY AND TRADE

1924 Sept. 1 The **Dawes Plan**, which established a new and reduced schedule for Germany's reparations payments to the Allies, went into effect. The plan was named for **Charles G**[ates] **Dawes** (Aug. 27, 1865–Apr. 23, 1951), a financier and vice president of the U.S. (1925–1929), who had been appointed in April to be chairman of the Reparations Commission, on which all the Allies were represented. The Dawes Plan reduced the annual payments to the Allies mandated under the Treaty of Versailles. In turn the Allies would remove their occupation troops from the Ruhr. The plan helped stabilize the German economy.

IV. RELIGION AND PHILOSOPHY

1924 The Congregational, Methodist, and some Presbyterian churches of Canada formed the **United Church of Canada**, creating a strong Free Church voice in Canada to compete with the Roman Catholic and Anglican churches.

V. SCIENCE, EDUCATION, AND TECHNOLOGY

1924–1929 **Martin Elmer Johnson** (Oct. 9, 1884–Jan. 13, 1937), an American photographer, and his wife Osa Helen [Leighty] (Mar. 14, 1894–Jan. 7, 1953) **filmed** for the American Museum of Natural History in New York the **vanishing species of wildlife in Africa**. Johnson also produced other documentary wildlife films.

1924 The **wave theory of matter** was formulated by **Louis de Broglie**, a French mathematician, thereby reconciling the two prevailing theories of the nature of light, described as behaving either like waves or like particles. De Broglie held that light can behave like both. De Broglie was awarded the **Nobel prize for physics** in 1929 after the experimental demonstration of his theory in 1927 by **Clinton Joseph Davisson** (Oct. 22, 1881–Feb. 1, 1958) and his colleague **Lester Halbert Germer** (Oct. 10, 1896–Oct. 3, 1971), both of the U.S. Independently, **George Paget Thomson** (May 3, 1892–Sept. 10, 1975), of Aberdeen, Scotland, established the wave properties of moving electrons by studying the diffraction of electrons in crystals. In 1937 Davisson and Thomson were jointly awarded the **Nobel prize for physics**.

1924 The Chinese scholar and former YMCA secretary **James Y.C.** [Jimmy] **Yen** [Yen Yang-Ch'u] (b. Oct. 26, 1893) became chairman of the **Mass Education Movement in China** (1924–1951). He had earlier developed a 1,000-character ideographic system of writing, using the *pai hua* or common spoken language of most Chinese. Within a few years many Chinese could at least read newspapers, leaflets, and revolutionary tracts.

1924 Feb. 12 The sarcophagus of **Tutankhamen** (c.1371–c.1352 B.C.), pharaoh of Egypt from c.1361, was opened for the first time at Luxor, Egypt. The tomb was discovered in 1922. It contained a golden life-size figure clutching a scepter to its breast. The sarcophagus and the mummy are now in Cairo.

1924 Oct. 15 The **longest flight ever made by an airship** ended at Lakehurst, N.J., where the **ZR-3**, a German dirigible, completed a flight of 5,060 miles from Friedrichshafen, Germany, by a roundabout route over the Azores, Newfoundland, and New York City.

VI. ARTS AND LEISURE

1924 **Thomas Mann**, a German writer, published *Der Zauberberg [The Magic Mountain]*, which depicted pre-World War I Europe in terms of life in a Swiss sanitarium for the tubercular.

1924 Jan. 28 [Joaquim] **Teófilo** [Fernandes] **Braga** (b. Feb. 24, 1843), the **first president of Portugal's Republic** (1910), died. A poet, he also wrote on literature and politics, stimulating much interest in Portuguese history and literature. His works included *História da Poesia Popular Portuguesa* (1867), *História do Romantismo em Portugal* (1880), and *A Arcádia Lusitania* (1899).

1924 Feb. 1 **Maurice** [Brazil] **Prendergast** (b. Oct. 10, 1859), a Canadian-born American artist, died. He was one of the so-called Eight, a group of American artists, formed in 1908, whose chief bond was their opposition to the academic school of art. Prendergast exhibited at the controversial Armory Show in New York in 1913. Among his works were *Umbrella in the Rain* (1899) and *Promenade* (1914–1915).

1924 Feb. 12 *Rhapsody in Blue*, by **George Gershwin**, was performed for the first time at Aeolian Hall, New York City, by an orchestra conducted by **Paul Whiteman** (Mar. 28, 1890–Dec. 29, 1967) with Gershwin at the piano.

1924 Apr. 14 **Louis Henri Sullivan** (b. Sept. 3, 1856), a member of the so-called Chicago school of architecture, died. The **development of the skyscraper** to meet spatial and aesthetic needs was attributed to Sullivan, who incorporated in his designs strong and simple vertical lines of steel. His work included the celebrated interior of the **Chicago Auditorium** (1886–1890), the **Schiller Building** (1892), and the **Schlesinger and Meyer Building** (1904), all in Chicago.

1924 Apr. 21 **Eleonora Duse** (b. Oct. 3, 1858), the celebrated Italian actress, died. She appeared in plays by Ibsen, Dumas fils, and others. In 1893 she was acclaimed for her New York and London successes in *La Dame aux Camélias*.

1924 May 26 **Victor Herbert** (b. Feb. 1, 1859), Irish-born American conductor and composer, died. Herbert became known best as the composer of popular operettas, such as *Babes in Toyland* (1903), *The Red Mill* (1906), *Naughty Marietta* (1910), and *Sweethearts* (1913).

1924 June 3 **Franz Kafka** (b. July 30, 1883), an Austrian writer, died. He left instructions for his unpublished manuscripts to be destroyed. Of these, *Der Prozess [The Trial]* (1925), *Das Schloss [The Castle]* (1926), and *Amerika* (1927) were published posthumously.

1924 July 27 Ferruccio Benvenuto Busoni (b. Apr. 1, 1866), an Italian composer and pianist, died. Busoni's works included a long *Concerto*, with an elaborate chorale ending, and *Fantasia Contrappuntistica* (1910), based on one of Bach's unfinished works.

1924 Aug. 3 Joseph Conrad [orig.: Teodor Józef Konrad Korzeniowski] (b. Dec. 3, 1857), a Polish-born English author, died. His novels included *The Nigger of the Narcissus* (1897), *Lord Jim* (1900), and *The Secret Agent* (1907), and he wrote the long short story "Heart of Darkness" (1902).

1924 Oct. 13 Anatole France [nee Jacques Anatole François Thibault] (b. Apr. 11, 1844), a French novelist, poet, and critic, died. He was the leading figure of the French literary world for many years. His first successful novel was *Le Crime de Sylvestre Bonnard* [*The Crime of Sylvester Bonnard*] (1881). Among his other works were *L'Île des pingouins* [*Penguin Island*] (1908), a satire on French history; *Thaïs* (1890); and *La Révolte des anges* [*The Revolt of the Angels*] (1914). France received the **Nobel prize for literature** in 1921.

1924 Nov. 4 Gabriel [Urbain] **Fauré** (b. May 12, 1845), a French composer, died. Fauré's best-known work was his *Requiem Mass* (1888). His other works included the orchestral suite *Pélleas et Mélisande* (1898), the song *Après un rêve* (c.1865), nocturnes and impromptus for the piano, and chamber music.

1924 Nov. 29 Giacomo Puccini (b. Dec. 22, 1858), an Italian opera composer, died. Puccini in his operas gave the orchestra a leading role in the plot's development. This, combined with powerful drama and lyrical melody, brought Puccini success. His operas included *Manon Lescaut* (1893), *La Bohème* (1896), *Tosca* (1900), *Madame Butterfly* (1904), and *Turandot* (1926), the last two scenes of which were completed by **Franco Alfano** (1877–1954). In *La Fanciulla del West* [*The Girl of the Golden West*] (1910) and *Gianni Schicchi* (1918), Puccini departed from his usual tragic plots.

1924 Dec. 29 Carl Friedrich Georg Spitteler [*pseudo.:* Carl Felix Tandem] (b. Apr. 24, 1845), a Swiss poet, died. From 1900 to 1906 he published the poetic epic *Der Olympische Frühling* [*Olympian Spring*]. He received the Nobel prize for literature in 1919.

VII. SPORTS, GAMES, AND SOCIETY

1924 Crossword puzzles were first issued in book form by the American publisher Simon & Schuster.

1924 The first U.S. city to be awarded a National Hockey League franchise was Boston, where the Bruins became an instant success. On Sept. 26, 1925 one of the Canadian franchises, Hamilton, was sold to New York City and renamed the Americans.

1924 Jan. 25–Feb. 4 The first Winter Olympic Games were held at Chamonix, France, with 294 athletes from 16 countries competing. Norwegian athletes won 4 gold medals and 17 medals in all. Finland 4 and 10; and Austria 2 and 3. The U.S. won only 1 gold medal and 4 in all.

1924 May 4–July 27 The eighth Summer **Olympic Games** were held in Paris, France, with 3,092 athletes from 44 countries competing. American athletes won 45 gold medals and 99 medals in all; Finland 14 and 37; and France 13 and 38. The star of the competition was **Paavo Nurmi**, a Finnish track star, who took three gold medals by winning the 1,500- and 5,000-meter races and the cross-country run. In the swimming events, American men and women took 12 gold medals, including three by **Johnny Weismuller** (June 2, 1904–Jan. 20, 1984).

1924 July 31 The two perpetrators of a murder that caused great outrage in the U.S. were sentenced to life imprisonment. They were **Nathan Leopold** (Nov. 19, 1904–Aug. 29, 1971) and **Richard Loeb** (1907–Jan. 28, 1936), bright students at the University of Chicago and members of well-to-do families. On May 21 they kidnapped 13-year-old **Bobby Franks** and murdered him. Leopold and Loeb confessed to the murder on May 31.

1924 Sept. 29 Rogers Hornsby (Apr. 27, 1896–Jan. 5, 1963), second baseman for the St. Louis Cardinals, ended the season with a batting average of .424, finishing with 227 hits in 142 games. Hornsby thus broke the modern mark of .420 set by **Ty Cobb** in 1911 and tied by **George Sisler** (Mar. 24, 1893–Mar. 26, 1973) in 1922.

1925

I. DISASTERS

1925 Mar. 18   In the U.S. a **tornado across Missouri, Illinois, and Indiana** caused enormous destruction. The death toll was 689; 1,980 were injured; and property losses amounted to $16,632,000. The greatest damage occurred in Murphysboro, Illinois, where 60 percent of the city was devastated and 234 people killed.

1925 Sept. 3   The first helium-filled, rigid airship, the U.S. navy's *Shenandoah*, commissioned in 1923, was **destroyed** in a violent storm over Ava, Ohio, killing 14 people.

II. POLITICS AND WAR

1925   A commission appointed in 1921 to decide the **boundary between Northern Ireland and the Irish Free State** based on the preference of the constituency, failed to make conclusive findings. The status quo of the traditional county borders was agreed to be maintained by the two Irelands and Great Britain.

1925 Jan. 5   **Nellie** [nee Tayloe] **Ross** (1876?–Dec. 19, 1977), the **first woman governor in the U.S.**, was inaugurated in Wyoming. Nicknamed the "Equality State," Wyoming had been the first state to grant full woman's suffrage in 1869.

1925 Jan. 22   The National Assembly declared **Albania a republic**. **Ahmed Bey Zogu** [Scanderbeg III, Zog I] (Oct. 8, 1895–Apr. 9, 1961), who had served in several ministerial posts, was elected its first president and was granted dictatorial powers on Mar. 7.

1925 Mar. 4   [John] **Calvin Coolidge** of the Republican party was inaugurated as the 30th president of the U.S., having defeated **John W**[illiam] **Davis** (Apr. 13, 1873–Mar. 24, 1955) of the Democratic party. **Charles G**[ates] **Dawes** served as vice-president. In the election on Nov. 4, 1924, Coolidge received 15,725,016 popular votes and 382 in the electoral college to 8,385,503 and 136 for Davis.

1925 Mar. 12   **Sun Yat-Sen** [Sun Wen, Chung Shan] (b. Nov. 12, 1886), China's revolutionary leader, died. He was one of the founders of the Kuomintang [Nationalist party]. He was provisional president of the republic (Jan., 1912) when he resigned his office to the more powerful Yuan Shih-k'ai. In 1917 he led the **Kuomintang** into establishing the Republic of South China (September). From 1923 Sun Yat-Sen accepted aid from the Soviet Union under the direction of Mikhail Borodin. **Chiang Kai-Shek**, a military aide to Sun, became the leading figure in the Kuomintang upon Sun's death.

1925 Apr. 13   **Abd-el-Krim** [Abdel Krim, Abd-al-Karim'] (1885–Feb. 6, 1963), leader of **Berber resistance** in the Er Rif region of northern Morocco, a Spanish protectorate, attacked French forces in the Wargla [Ouargla] Valley in central northern Algeria, where French intervention threatened his supplies. **Henri Philippe Pétain**, the French marshal who had taken charge (Aug. 26) of the French troops in Morocco, needed as many as 150,000 men to undertake an attack in cooperation with Spanish forces under **Miguel Primo de Rivera**, Spain's dictator. On May 26, 1926, Abd-el-Krim surrendered and was exiled.

1925 Apr. 25   **Paul von Hindenburg**, commander of the German army in World War I (1914–1918) and symbolic hero of that struggle to many Germans, was elected president of Germany.

1925 May 1   **Cyprus became a crown colony of Great Britain**. Cyprus had been annexed by Great Britain on Nov. 5, 1914, at the beginning of World War I following hostile acts by the Ottoman Empire [Turkey].

1925 Oct. 5   The **Locarno Conference** opened as delegates from Germany, France, Great Britain, Italy, Belgium, Poland, and Czechoslovakia met at Locarno, Switzerland, to draw up a plan to establish permanent boundaries and to secure peace and stability in Europe.

1925 Oct. 25   **Adolfo Díaz** (1871?–Jan. 27, 1964) and **Emiliano Chamorro Vargas**, a general and former president of **Nicaragua** (1917–1921), collaborated in a coup against **Carlos Solórzano**, the president of Nicaragua, following the withdrawal earlier this year of the U.S. marines from Nicaragua. Díaz served as president from 1926 to 1928.

1925 Oct. 31 **Riza Shah Pahlevi** [Reza Khan Pah-
lavi] (Mar. 16, 1878–July 26, 1944), in control of the
Persian government since a coup on Feb. 21, 1921,
was elected hereditary shah (to 1941). Pahlevi improved the nation's educational system, built roads
and railroads, and promoted industrialization.
Among his more controversial measures were the
curtailment of many religious customs and laws and
the enforcement of a civil code.

III. ECONOMY AND TRADE

1925 **Clarence Birdseye** (Dec. 9, 1886–Oct. 7,
1956), an American businessman and inventor,
began marketing frozen fish in Gloucester, Massachusetts.

1925 The industrial firm of **I.G. Farben** [*Inter-
essen Gemeinschaft Farbenindustrie Aktiengesell-
schaft*] was formed by the merger of 13 separate
chemical and dye companies. The new firm quickly
made pacts with chemical and related companies on
the continent, in Great Britain, and the U.S. and
became the **largest chemical company in the world**.

1925 The **Brotherhood of Sleeping Car Porters** was
organized in the U.S. by **Asa Philip Randolph** (Apr.
15, 1889–May 16, 1979) in response to a request for
shorter hours and better pay by porters and maids
serving on Pullman trains.

1925 **William Green** (Mar. 3, 1873–Nov. 21, 1952)
succeeded **Samuel Gompers** (d. 1925) as president of
the **American Federation of Labor** [AFL], which
Green headed until his death.

1925 Apr. 28 **Great Britain returned its monetary
system to the gold standard**, which it had abandoned
early in World War I. The value of the British pound
was set at the pre-war rate of approximately $5.00
U.S.

1925 May 30 **A demonstration in support of striking workers** of the British-dominated International
Settlement **in Shanghai turned violent** when police
fired on students and other demonstrators, killing
several.

1925 July 4 The **electric Citroën advertising sign**,
placed near the top of the Eiffel Tower in Paris, was
turned on. Its 250,000 bulbs made the sign visible for
24 miles. Citroën removed the sign 11 years later.

IV. RELIGION AND PHILOSOPHY

1925 Mar. 30 **Rudolph Steiner** (b. Feb. 27, 1861),
an Austrian social philosopher who founded what he
called **anthroposophy**, died. Anthroposophy was a
mystical doctrine that made use of man's spiritual
nature to find an explanation for the world. One of
his works was translated as *Philosophy of Spiritual
Activity* (1922).

V. SCIENCE, EDUCATION, AND TECHNOLOGY

1925 The first direct measure of the **effects of the
ionosphere on long-distance radio waves** was made
by **Edward Victor Appleton** (Sept. 6, 1892–Apr. 21,
1965), an English physicist. He found that short radio
waves were reflected by the ionosphere, called until
this time the Heaviside-Kennelly layer for the effects
described (1902) by **Oliver Heaviside** and **Arthur
Edwin Kennelly**. Appleton's experiments provided
an explanation that held tremendous implications for
the development of radio broadcasting and of radar.
Appleton was awarded the **Nobel prize for physics** in
1947.

1925 **Wolfgang Pauli** (Apr. 25, 1900–Dec. 15,
1958), an Austrian-Swiss physicist, developed the
Pauli Exclusion Principle for which he received the
Nobel prize for physics in 1945. The Exclusion Principle stated that no two electrons could occupy the
same orbit about an atom's nucleus. This concept,
when combined with the theories of quantum mechanics, explained some of the bonding characteristics of different kinds of atoms.

1925 Flint points distinctive of the **Folsom Culture**
were found embedded in the skeletal remains of an
extinct buffalo near Folsom, New Mexico. Carbon 14
tests on the bones proved that Stone Age man lived
here prior to 10,000 B.P.

1925 **Joseph Goldberger** (July 16, 1874–Jan. 17,
1929), an American physician, discovered that **pel-
lagra**, a disease often found in people in the rice-
eating parts of the world and in people with insufficient meat or milk in their diet, was caused by a
deficiency in niacin, one of the B-complex vitamins.

1925 **Otto Struve** (Aug. 12, 1897–Apr. 6, 1963), a
Russian-born astronomer, demonstrated for the first
time, at the Yerkes Observatory of the University of

Chicago at Williams Bay, Wisconsin, that many **stars of high temperatures rotate** on their axes.

1925   Gregory Breit (July 14, 1899–1982 or 1983), a Russian-born American, and **Merle A. Tuve** (June 27, 1901–May 20, 1982), of the Carnegie Institute of Technology, developed radio transmissions of pulses only one millisecond in length in order to explore the ionosphere.

1925 Mar. 13   Tennessee adopted the first American anti-evolution law, making it "unlawful for any teacher in any of the universities, normals, and all public schools of the state, to teach any theory that denies the story of the divine creation of man as taught in the Bible, and to teach instead that man descended from a lower order of animals."

1925 July 7   Afrikaans was recognized as one of the official languages of South Africa and was granted a status equal to that of English and Dutch.

1925   July 10   The controversial **Scopes Trial** ["Monkey Trial"] began as **John Thomas Scopes** (Aug. 3, 1900–Oct. 21, 1970), a biology teacher in a Dayton, Tennessee, high school was accused of teaching the Darwinian theory of evolution in violation of the Tennessee statute enacted on Mar. 13. Despite the defense by attorney **Clarence S**[eward] **Darrow** (Apr. 18, 1857–Mar. 13, 1938), who appealed to academic freedom and constitutional separation of church and state, Scopes lost the trial and was fined $100. The trial, however, clarified the right of instructors to teach information based on scientific findings, which were not directly affected by the Tennessee statute. Furthermore, the trial challenged the adequacy of the Fundamentalist explanation for the origin of species when Darrow examined the theological views of **William Jennings Bryan**, one of the prosecuting attorneys, in a long cross-examination. Bryan (b. Mar. 18, 1860), the "Great Commoner" and a force in American politics since 1895, died on July 26, five days after the end of the trial.

VI. ARTS AND LEISURE

1925   The **Mount Rushmore National Memorial** in South Dakota, U.S., was begun by **Gutzon Borglum** [John Gutzon de la Mothe Borglum]. It was completed in Nov., 1941, by his son **Lincoln Borglum**. The heads of George Washington, Thomas Jefferson, Abraham Lincoln, and Theodore Roosevelt, each 60 to 70 feet tall, were carved in the granite face of Mount Rushmore 500 feet above the ground.

1925   *Der Prozess* [*The Trial*], an unfinished novel by the Austrian writer **Franz Kafka**, was published posthumously by **Max Brod** (May 27, 1884–Dec. 20, 1968), an Israeli writer and close friend of Kafka's. Kafka described people tormented by anxiety and loneliness, continually frustrated by futile attempts to achieve their goals.

1925 Jan. 8   George [Wesley] **Bellows** (b. Aug. 12, 1882), an American artist best known for his realistic portrayals of modern urban life, died. He was a member of "the Eight," a group of fellow artists who came together because of their dislike of academic art. They became known as the **Ashcan School** because of their subject matter. Among his best works were ***Both Members of This Club*** (1909), ***Billy Sunday*** (1923), and ***Dempsey and Firpo*** (1924).

1925 Apr. 15   John Singer Sargent (b. Jan. 12, 1856), a popular American portrait artist, died in London. Among his works were ***Miss Ellen Terry as Lady Macbeth*** (1889), ***Portrait of Graham Robertson*** (1894), ***The Windham Sisters*** (1900), and ***Sir Philip Sassoon*** (1923). He also painted murals and landscapes, such as ***Mountain Fire*** (1895), and executed the decoration of the dome of the Boston Museum of Fine Arts (1916–1925).

1925 May 12   Amy Lowell (b. Feb. 9, 1874), an American imagist poet, died. Her works included ***A Dome of Many-Colored Glass*** (1912), ***Sword Blades and Poppy Seeds*** (1914), ***Patterns*** (1916), a two-volume biography of ***John Keats*** (1925), and ***What's O'Clock?*** *(1925)*.

1925 May 14   Henry Rider Haggard (b. June 22, 1856), an English novelist, died. He was best known for his adventure novels, which included the popular ***King Solomon's Mines*** (1886), ***She*** (1887), and ***Allan Quatermain*** (1887).

1925 May 31   An exhibition labeled "**Arts decoratifs**" opened in Paris, France, and gave its name— as **art deco**—to the most popular style of the 1920s in furniture, dress, architecture, and furnishings in general. An important aspect of art deco was the influence of modern technology, both in the use of new materials and in following what was considered the smooth, sleek temper of 20th-century technology.

1925 July 1 Eric [Alfred Leslie] **Satie** (b. May 17, 1866), a French composer, died. Satie disavowed impressionism along with **Arthur Honegger** (Mar. 10, 1892–Nov. 27, 1955) and other members of a group that called itself *Les six.* His works included *Sarabandes* (1887) and *Gymnopédies* (1988) for the piano; *Three Pieces in the Shape of a Pear* (1903); the ballets *Parade* (1916), *Mercure* (1924), and *Relâche* (1924); and a piece for voice and chamber orchestra, *Socrate* (1918).

1925 Nov. 28 The *Grand Ole Opry,* a country music show, made its debut as a local show over station WSM from Nashville, Tennessee. The Grand Ole Opry became a Nashville tradition.

VII. SPORTS, GAMES, AND SOCIETY

1925 The **Ocean Racing Club** [ORC] [later, the Royal Ocean Racing Club] was founded to stimulate long-distance racing and the design of ocean-going sailboats. The first **Fastnet Race,** from Rydee on the Isle of Wight to Fastnet Rock off the southwestern coast of Ireland and back to Plymouth, Devon, was held later this year. The winner of this first race was *Jolie Brise,* owned by **E.G. Martin** of Great Britain, one of the founders of ORC.

1925 The **Charleston** became the most popular and sensational dance of its day. It apparently originated in Charleston, South Carolina. The dance, performed to the staccato, syncopated 4/4 rhythm, was characterized by criss-crossing the arms repeatedly across the knees, which at the same time were moving rapidly from side to side.

1926

I. DISASTERS

1926 A **troopship** on the Yangtze River [Chang Jiang] in China **exploded** killing c.1,200.

1926 Sept. 18 A **hurricane struck Florida** and the Gulf states, killing 372 people and injuring c.6,000. Some 18,000 families were left homeless and damage was estimated at $80,000,000. The Florida real estate boom had reached its peak in 1925, when prices for property soared. The hurricane put an end to the boom. On Oct. 20 another **hurricane hit Cuba,** leaving c.600 dead.

II. EXPLORATION AND COLONIZATION

1926 May 9 **Richard Evelyn Bird,** an American aviator, and **Floyd Bennett** (Oct. 25, 1890–Apr. 25, 1928) made the **first flight over the North Pole.** They flew non-stop from the Arctic island Spitsbergen [Svalbard], Norway, to the Pole and back in 15 hours and 30 minutes.

1926 May 12 **Roald Amundsen,** a Norwegian explorer, and **Lincoln Ellsworth** (May 12, 1880–May

26, 1951), an American explorer, flew across the North Pole from Spitsbergen to Alaska in the airship *Norge,* designed and piloted by **Umberto Nobile** (Jan. 24, 1885–July 29, 1978), an Italian engineer.

III. POLITICS AND WAR

1926 Jan. 3 **Theodore Pangalos** (Jan. 11, 1878–Feb. 26, 1952), a Greek general and politician who became prime minister of **Greece** in a bloodless coup in June, 1925, now proclaimed himself dictator.

1926 Jan. 8 The **Hejaz** [Al-Hijaz], an Arab principality lying between Nejd and the Red Sea in present Saudi Arabia, surrendered to **Ibn Saud** ['Abd-al-'Aziz ibn-'Abd-al-Raḥman al-Faisal ibn-Su'ud], the sultan of Nejd, who was then proclaimed the first king of the Hejaz in the Mosque of Mecca. Ibn Saud's invasion of the Hejaz began in 1924 after **Husein ibn-Ali** had proclaimed himself caliph. His domain was officially recognized by the major European powers, Great Britain, the U.S.S.R., and the U.S.

1926 May 12 **Józef Klemens Piłsudzki,** marshal of **Poland,** moved troops into Warsaw in a coup against

Stanisław Wójciechowski (Mar. 15, 1869–Apr. 9, 1953), president of Poland, and **Wicenty Witos** (Jan. 22, 1874–Oct. 30, 1945), the prime minister, whose support of parliamentary rule resulted in a lack of authority to deal effectively with the foundering Polish economy. Two days later Wojciechowski willingly stepped down. Piłsudzki refused the title of president, however, even when he was elected by the **Sejm** [National Assembly] on May 31, preferring instead to guide Polish affairs as minister of defense or as prime minister under **Ignacy Mościcki** (Dec. 1, 1867–Oct. 2, 1946), who served as Poland's elected president until Germany's invasion of Poland in 1939.

1926 May 23   Lebanon, administered by France under a mandate from the **League of Nations** as one of the Levant States [Lebanon and Syria], became a republic. **Charles Dabbas**, a Greek lawyer, was elected president, but France continued to control domestic affairs and foreign policy until 1941.

1926 May 28   Bernardino Luiz Machado (Mar. 28, 1851–Apr. 29, 1944), president of **Portugal**, was overthrown by a military coup d'etat led by **Gomes da Costa**. On July 9 a second *coup* marked the end of Portugal's political upheaval as **Antonio Oscar de Fragoso Carmona** (Nov. 24, 1869–Apr. 18, 1951) came to power.

1926 June 15   The French cabinet, of which **Aristide Briand** was premier, resigned in the face of a financial crisis that stemmed from the costs and dislocations of World War I. The French franc was steadily losing value and there was great public complaint about the rapidly increasing price of bread. Briand tried (June 23) to form another government but failed. On July 23 **Raymond Poincaré**, who had previously been premier, formed a government, retaining Briand as foreign minister.

1926 July   Chiang Kai-Shek began the **Northern Expedition** from Canton to increase the sphere of influence held by the **Kuomintang** [Nationalists] party, strong only in Kwangtung [Guangdong] and Kwangsi [Guangxi] provinces in southeastern China, and to unite China by overcoming the factional rule of the warlords. At first Chiang let the CCP [**Chinese Communist party**] precede him into northern China, where its activities helped to break the power of the warlords. China was governed by three major factions: the left-wing Kuomintang in the Wuhan area of southeastern Hubei province under **Wang Ching-Wei** [Wang Chao-Ming] (May 4, 1884–Nov. 10, 1944), an aide earlier to **Sun Yat-Sen**; the warlords who held Peking [Beijing]; and Chiang Kai-Shek, who made his headquarters at Nanking [Nanjing].

1926 Oct. 19   At an **Imperial Conference held in London**, Great Britain and its dominions [Australia, Canada, New Zealand, and South Africa] took an important step toward making the **dominions more independent of the mother country**. The dominions were accepted as autonomous and equal in status with Britain.

1926 Dec. 26   Yoshihito [reign name: Taishō] (b. Aug., 1879), emperor of Japan, died in the 14th year of his reign. He was succeeded by his son **Hirohito**, who had been acting as regent (from 1921) after the emperor was declared mentally incompetent.

IV. ECONOMY AND TRADE

1926   The **International Slavery Convention** suppressing and completely abolishing slavery and all slave trade was signed by 20 members of the **League of Nations**. Both Ethiopia and Portugal, those most affected by the convention, signed, and on Aug. 22, 1931, c.2,000,000 slaves were freed in Ethiopia.

1926   **Japan placed heavy taxes on luxury items**, increasing prices by as much as three and one-half times. Duties on scarce raw materials and necessities were reduced or completely lifted.

1926   The **Model T Ford**, introduced in 1908 at a price of $850, proved such a combination of production efficiency and popularity that by this year it sold for only $310. This price included such design improvements as the **electric self-starter**.

1926 May 3   The national labor unions of Great Britain called a general strike in support of the coal miners' strike and lock-out by the mine operators. For ten days all essential services were almost entirely shut down. Volunteers, mostly from the middle class and upper class, manned buses and other facilities. The coal miners ended their strike (Nov. 19) without having achieved an agreement with the mine owners.

V. RELIGION AND PHILOSOPHY

1926 Oct. 17   Charles Edward Coughlin (Oct. 25, 1891–Oct. 27, 1979), an American Roman Catholic priest, made the first of the radio broadcasts from a local station in Detroit that made him a controversial figure. After 1930 he gained a national audience on the CBS radio network. He supported right-wing causes, spoke in favor of **Huey** [Pierce] **Long** (Aug. 30, 1893–Sept. 10, 1935), a U.S. senator from Louisiana (from 1930) and opponent of the administration of **Franklin Delano Roosevelt.**

VI. SCIENCE, EDUCATION, AND TECHNOLOGY

1926   Erwin Schrödinger (Aug. 12, 1887–Jan. 4, 1961), an Austrian physicist, developed what is known today as the **Schrödinger Equation,** important in the understanding of wave mechanics. Schrödinger, who received the **Nobel prize for physics** in 1933, expanded de Broglie's theory of wave mechanics to postulate that the orbital frequency, or energy level, of an electron in an atom could be represented as the difference of the emission and absorption frequencies of two standing waves.

1926   [Charles] Leonard Woolley, an English archaeologist, uncovered the **ruins of Biblical Ur,** home of Abraham, in southern Iraq and disclosed the royal cemetery. His reports aroused worldwide interest.

1926   **Three American scientists had success in treatment of **pernicious anemia with a diet of raw liver. The scientists were **George** R[ichard] **Minot** (Dec. 2, 1885–Feb. 25, 1950), **William** P[arry] **Murphy** (b. Feb. 6, 1892), and **George** H[oyt] **Whipple** (Aug. 29, 1878–Feb. 1, 1976). Later Minot helped develop a liver extract. For their work the three men shared the **Nobel prize for physiology or medicine** in 1934.

1926   Television was first publicly demonstrated at the Royal Institute in London by **John Logie Baird** (Aug. 13, 1888–June 14, 1946), a Scottish television pioneer. Baird's television operated partly by mechanical means. His system was used in a transmission from England to the *Berengaria* in the mid-Atlantic.

1926 Mar. 16   The **first rocket propelled by liquid fuel,** a mixture of liquid oxygen and gasoline, was launched by **Robert Hutching Goddard** (Oct. 5, 1882–Aug. 10, 1945), an American physicist, in Auburn, Massachusetts. The rocket reached an altitude of 184 feet. Liquid fuel proved more powerful than even the double-base powder [40 percent nitroglycerine, 60 percent nitrocellulose] Goddard had earlier substituted for ordinary black gunpowder.

1926 Apr. 11   Luther Burbank (b. Mar. 7, 1849), an American horticulturist famous for developing new and improved varieties of fruits and vegetables, died. His first success was the **Burbank potato.** One of his most practical experiments developed a spineless cactus that could be fed to cattle. The general public recognized him especially for the Shasta daisy.

1926 July 2   Émile Coué (b. Feb. 26, 1857), a French psychotherapist whose system based on **autosuggestion** caught the fancy of the public, especially in England and the U.S., died. Beginning as a pharmacist, he turned to the study of hypnotism and suggestion. His followers kept repeating his formula: "Every day, in every way, I am getting better and better."

1926 Aug. 22   Charles William Eliot (b. Mar. 20, 1834), a president of Harvard University (1869–1909) and pioneer in higher education, died. During his long regime he turned Harvard into a large university with top level graduate and professional schools. Not neglecting the undergraduate college, he introduced the elective system. Eliot found time to select and edit the *Harvard Classics,* which became known as the "five-foot shelf."

1926 Oct. 20   Eugene V[ictor] **Debs** (b. Nov. 5, 1855), an American socialist and labor leader, died. He became active (from 1875) in labor union affairs when he organized the **Brotherhood of Locomotive Firemen.** He formed (1893) the **American Railway Union,** an industrial type of union, which became involved (1894) in the bitter and violent strike against the Pullman Palace Car Company, Chicago, Illinois. He became a socialist and five times ran (from 1900) for president of the U.S. An outspoken opponent of American participation in World War I (1914–1918), Debs was convicted (1918) of violating the Espionage Act because he criticized the government's treatment of persons prosecuted for sedition. Sentenced to ten years in prison, Debs was released (1921) by **Warren G. Harding,** president of the U.S.

VII. ARTS AND LEISURE

1926 André Gide, a French author, published *Les Faux-Monnayeurs* [*The Counterfeiters*], one of the seminal novels of the 20th century. In it he explored the ways people always try to make themselves seem other than they really are.

1926 Jan. 10 *Metropolis*, a motion picture, had its premiere in Berlin, Germany. It was the work of director **Fritz Lang** (Dec. 5, 1890–Aug. 2, 1976), and in it he created a city of the future where, in the end, the slave masses revolted against the small master class. Another Lang film *M* (1931), about a child molester and murderer, also received international attention.

1926 Apr. 23 Joseph Pennell (b. July 4, 1857), an American etcher and lithographer, died. He illustrated the books his wife, **Elizabeth Robins Pennell** (1855–1936), wrote. Among them were *A Canterbury Pilgrimage* (1885) and *Over the Alps on a Bicycle* (1898).

1926 May 5 Sinclair Lewis, an American novelist, refused the **Pulitzer Prize** which had been awarded him for *Arrowsmith* (1925), a satire on the medical profession. He objected to the terms of this usually highly regarded award because it called for the presentation of "the wholesome atmosphere of American life, and the highest standard of American manner and manhood." The next year the wording was changed: "For distinguished fiction by an American author, preferably dealing with American life."

1926 June 7 Antonio Gaudi y Cornet (b. June 26, 1852), a Spanish architect noted for his unusual forms and his technological innovations, died. Gaudi worked chiefly in Barcelona. His masterpiece was the **church of the Sagrada Familia** which he began in 1883 and which was not completed until 1930, after Gaudi's death. The church is embellished with conical spires and many decorations, both abstract and organic.

1926 June 14 Mary Cassatt (b. May 22, 1845), an American-born painter and printmaker, died. She often used as subject matter groups of friends together or, during her later work, the domestic motif of mothers tending to their children. Among her works were *Lady at the Tea Table* (1885), *La Toilette* (1892), and *Mother and Child* (1905).

1926 Aug. 23 Rudolph Valentino [nee Rodolfo Alfonzo Raffaelo Pierre Filbert Guglielmi di Valentina d'Antonguolla] (b. May 6, 1895), an Italian-born actor, the first great Hollywood screen lover and the idol of women everywhere, died. He achieved instant stardom in *The Four Horsemen of the Apocalypse* (1921). Valentino furthered his matinee idol mystique in *The Sheik* (1921), *Blood and Sand* (1922), and *The Eagle* (1925). His death at 31 was surrounded by mystery, and thousands of women rioted around the funeral parlor in New York City where his body lay.

1926 Oct. 31 Harry Houdini [nee Ehrich Weiss] (b. Mar. 24, 1874), an American magician who thrilled audiences with his escapes from seemingly impossible situations, died. He demonstrated his ability by getting out of sealed containers under water, as well as all kinds of locks and straitjackets. He took his stage name from a French predecessor in magic, **Jean Eugene Robert Houdin**.

1926 Dec. 5 Claude Monet (b. Nov. 14, 1840), a French landscape painter, died. Monet's habit of painting in the open air—introduced by **Eugene Louis Boudin** (July 12, 1824–Aug. 8, 1898)—and of meticulously executing a series of studies of the same subject shown at different hours and seasons won Monet a reputation as the most consistent impressionist. Monet became famous mostly for his series of paintings, first of haystacks (1890), later the Gare Saint-Lazare (1876–1878), the Rouen cathedral (1892–1894) and, most notably, water lilies (1899 and 1904–1925). These last he painted tirelessly from his garden at Giverny, despite increasing blindness, over the last years of his life.

1926 Dec. 29 Rainer Maria Rilke (b. Dec. 4, 1875), a German lyric poet, died. His best works included *Duineser Elegien* [*Elegies from the Castle of Duino*] (1923) and *Sonnets to Orpheus* (1936). The symbolic imagery and emotional content of his work recalled medieval poetry.

VIII. SPORTS, GAMES, AND SOCIETY

1926 Harold S[tirling] **Vanderbilt** (July 6, 1884–July 4, 1970), noted yachtsman and member of a prominent and wealthy American family, **invented contract bridge**. He developed this more challenging game out of auction bridge and within two years it was the form of the game played the most. Vanderbilt won 11 major yacht races, three of them successful defenses of the **America's Cup**.

1926 July The **English Greyhound Racing Association** opened a race track in Manchester, using the American-designed mechanical rabbit. The immediate success at Manchester led to the formation of many companies registered to operate greyhound racing. Sixty-eight such companies were reported in existence by Sept. 30, 1927.

1926 Aug. 6 **Gertrude** [Caroline] **Ederle** (b. Oct. 23, 1906), an American, became the **first woman to swim the English Channel**. Ederle swam from Cape Gris-Nez, France, to Deal, England, in 14 hours and 31 minutes, a new record for either sex. On Ederle's return to America she was given a ticker-tape parade up Broadway by New York City's Mayor **James J.** [Jimmy] **Walker**.

1926 Aug. 30 The **first Hambletonian Stakes**, which became the premier event in harness racing for three-year-old trotters, was run at Syracuse, New York. The winning horse in two straight heats was **Guy McKinney**, and the driver was **Nat Ray**.

1926 Sept. 23 **Gene** [James Joseph] **Tunney** (May 25, 1898–Nov. 7, 1978) beat **Jack Dempsey** to become the **world heavyweight boxing champion** at Philadelphia. A crowd of 118,736 paid $1,895,723 to watch the fight in a rainstorm. In his total of 68 bouts Tunney lost only one.

1927

I. DISASTERS

1927 Apr. Large areas of the Mississippi Valley in the U.S. suffered severe **flooding** over a period of several weeks. At least 4,000,000 acres of land were flooded, making c.600,000 people homeless and drowning several hundred. Property damage was estimated at $300,000,000.

1927 May 22 An **earthquake** registering a 8.3 on the Richter Scale rocked the Nan-Shan area in Qinghai province of northwestern China, killing an estimated 200,000 people.

1927 Oct. 26 An Italian liner *Principessa Mafalda*, carrying immigrants to South America, **sank** off the Brazilian coast after an explosion in the boiler room. All but 68 of the 1,238 passengers and crew were rescued.

1927 Dec. 17 Forty men were killed when the American submarine *S-4*, on a trial run off Provincetown, Massachusetts, **collided with the destroyer** *USS Paulding* and sank. Divers were unable to raise the disabled submarine or to connect air hoses for six men known to be alive inside.

II. POLITICS AND WAR

1927 Feb. 18 The **U.S. and Canada established direct diplomatic relations** for the first time by exchanging ministers. Hitherto such relations had been conducted by way of Great Britain, acting for Canada.

1927 Mar. In Nanking [Nanjing], China, **Kuomintang** [Nationalist] **forces attacked the foreign settlement**. Intervention by British and U.S. gunships, anchored in the Yangtze River [Chang Jiang], drove them out. This attack widened the rift between the Communist and the Kuomintang parties.

1927 Mar. The **Autumn Harvest Insurrection** was led by **Mao Tse-Tung**, supported by the **Chinese Communist party** [CCP], against **Chiang Kai-Shek** and the **Kuomintang** [Nationalists] in Honan [Henan] province in central southeastern China. It failed, and Mao—who advocated revolution in China by the peasants instead of the proletariat as in traditional Marxist doctrine—was dismissed from the CCP politburo. By the winter of 1927-1928 Mao and **Chu Teh** had organized a Red army of c.10,000, which they stationed at the Honan-Kiangsi [Henan-Jiangxi] border.

1927 Apr. 12 **Chiang Kai-Shek**, China's **Kuomintang** [Nationalist] party leader, broke with the **Chinese Communist party** [CCP], maintaining that their activities impeded the political unification and economic growth of China. Chiang launched a bloody purge of communists belonging to the Kuomintang, and he completely alienated not only the CCP but also the rural areas of China, where the

CCP had found support. Chiang established his headquarters at Nanking [Nanjing], in southeastern China, which had fallen to him in March. The left-wing Nationalists at Wuhan allied themselves more strongly with the Kuomintang in July after having **destroyed the CCP at Shanghai**. Chiang then embarked on the **final offensive of the Northern Expedition**, begun in July, 1926, against warlord-held Peking [Beijing], still recognized abroad as China's capital.

1927 May 9 The formal **opening of Parliament House in Canberra**, Australia, marked the transfer of the capital of the dominion from Melbourne to the new Australian Capital Territory.

1927 May 26 **Great Britain broke off diplomatic ties with the U.S.S.R.**, but maintained trade relations. The break had been preceded by the mutual abrogation of the **Anglo-Russian Agreement of 1907**, which had delimited spheres of influence in the Near East.

1927 July 15 **Rioting** that left 89 people dead and more than 600 injured broke out in **Vienna**, Austria. The fighting was between supporters of the socialists, who controlled Vienna, and the monarchists and Pan-Germans who were strong in the rest of the nation. The rioting was triggered by the acquittal of three monarchist followers on charges of attacking two members of the other faction.

1927 July 20 The death of **Ferdinand I** (b. Aug. 24, 1865), king of **Romania** (from 1914), caused confusion as to who was to succeed to the throne. Ferdinand's oldest son Carol (Oct. 15, 1893–Apr. 4, 1953) had renounced his rights to the throne in 1925. The throne was therefore claimed for five-year-old **Michael I** (b. Oct. 25, 1921), son of Carol and grandson of Ferdinand. In 1930, however, Michael's father returned to Romania and took the throne as **Carol II** (ruled 1930–1940).

1927 Aug. **Eamon de Valera** and his **Fianna Fáil** [Republican] party finally took the obligatory oath of allegiance to the British Crown and entered the **Dáil Éireann**, in which they had refused to sit since the adoption of the Anglo-Irish Treaty in 1921. In general elections held Sept. 27, the Republicans won a near majority.

1927 Nov. 14 **Joseph Stalin** expelled **Leon Trotsky** and **Grigori Evseevich Zinoviev** [Gregory Zinovyev, Hirsch Apfelbaum] (Sept. 11, 1883–Aug. 25, 1936)

from Russia's Communist party on the pretext of their ideological differences. On Dec. 18 Trotsky was sent to Alma-Ata in Kazakh SSR, and was permanently exiled from the U.S.S.R. on Jan. 31, 1929. Stalin was free to establish himself without opposition as dictator.

1927 Dec. 14 The **Chinese government** under **Chiang Kai-Shek broke diplomatic relations with the U.S.S.R.**

III. ECONOMY AND TRADE

1927 Two Dutch companies merged to form the **Margarine Union**, which then controlled most of the margarine and soap trade in continental Europe. In 1929 the Margarine Union merged with Great Britain's **Lever Brothers** to form **Unilever**, which ultimately controlled more than 140 individual companies handling much of the food, dairy, and retail store trade in Europe and the U.S.

1927 The **British Broadcasting Corporation** [BBC] began operations with a monopoly of radio broadcasting in Great Britain. It was created by act of Parliament as a public corporation, but by and large was independent of any regulation.

1927 Jan. 7 **Commercial transatlantic radio telephone service** was initiated by the president of the **American Telephone and Telegraph Company** [A.T.& T.] when his voice reached England, saying, "Hello, London."

1927 Apr. 21 The **Charter of Labor** was introduced in Italy, bringing a return of the old concept of the Just Wage. The Charter's provision for a general system of relations between labor and management relied on collective bargaining by syndicates representing both labor and management. Strikes and lockouts were forbidden. **Mussolini** and the fascist regime were establishing a "corporate state" that kept the framework of capitalism but in fact gave the government full control over the economy.

IV. SCIENCE, EDUCATION, AND TECHNOLOGY

1927 **Werner** [Karl] **Heisenberg** (Dec. 5, 1901–Feb. 1, 1976), a German physicist, developed the concept of the **Uncertainty Principle**, which stated that the simultaneous measurement of position and velocity, or energy and duration, cannot be made on extremely small particles without introducing some degree of uncertainty or imprecision into the measurement. Heisenberg, who received the **Nobel prize for physics** in 1932 for his work, thus introduced what became a philosophical principle as well, the principle of indeterminacy, stating that the conventional concept of causality in terms of space and time no longer applied in some circumstances.

1927   Georges Edouard Lemaitre (July 17, 1894–June 20, 1966), a Belgian physicist and astronomer, advanced an **early theory of an expanding universe**. He conceived the beginning of the universe as a condensed primeval atom that exploded, producing the force by which the universe is still expanding.

1927   Hermann Joseph Muller (Feb. 21, 1890–Apr. 5, 1967), an American geneticist, demonstrated for the first time that gene mutations could be artificially induced by the use of X-rays. He used the fruit fly *Drosophila* in his experiments. In 1946 Muller was awarded the **Nobel prize for physiology or medicine**.

1927   Remains of an example of *Homo erectus*, an extinct species of man that lived c.500,000 years ago, were discovered by **Davidson Black** (July 25, 1884–Mar. 15, 1934), a Canadian anthropologist and physician, at Choukoutien [Chowkowtien], 30 miles southwest of Peking [Beijing], China. The remains were named **Peking Man** [*Sinanthropus pekinensis*].

1927 Jan. 9   Houston Stewart Chamberlain (b. Sept. 9, 1855), a leading exponent of the theory of the superiority of the western "Aryan" race, died. English-born, he settled in Germany and became a naturalized citizen in 1916. His theories were set forth in *Foundations of the Nineteenth Century* (1899).

1927 May 20–21   Charles A[ugustus] **Lindbergh**, a 25-year-old American air mail pilot, made the **first transatlantic non-stop solo flight**. Taking off from Roosevelt Field, Long Island, New York, he landed at Orly Field outside Paris, France, after 33½ hours. A crowd of c.100,000 was awaiting him when he landed. On his return from France, he was given a New York City parade watched by an estimated 4,000,000 people. His single-engined plane *Spirit of St. Louis* is now in the Smithsonian Institution in Washington, D.C.

1927 June 4–5   The first non-stop transatlantic airplane flight carrying a passenger was piloted by

Clarence D. Chamberlain (Nov. 11, 1893–Oct. 31, 1976). The flight was made from Roosevelt Field, Long Island, New York, to Eiseleben, Germany, and the passenger was **Charles A. Levine**, a wealthy New Yorker who financed the flight. The trip also set a distance record of 3,911 miles, especially remarkable because it was made in a single-engine plane with no reserve fuel capacity.

1927 Oct. 2   Svante August Arrhenius (b. Feb. 19, 1859), a Swedish chemist and physicist and founder of modern physical chemistry, died. His doctoral thesis *A Theory of Ionic Dissociation* (1884) was so scientifically advanced that it was not generally accepted until the mid-1890s, after the discovery of the electron. He received the **Nobel prize for chemistry** in 1903.

V. ARTS AND LEISURE

1927   The motion picture *Napoleon vu par Abel Gance*, a long historical extravaganza, opened in Paris. The director **Abel Gance** (Oct. 25, 1889–Nov. 10, 1981) began work on the film in 1925. Gance brought to it a number of innovations, such as a **triple screen**, the use of **hand-held cameras**, and a **wide-angle lens**.

1927 Feb. 19   Georg Morris Cohen Brandes (b. Feb. 4, 1842), a Danish critic and writer, died. He was especially noted for his work on Shakespeare (1896) and for a six-volume *Main Currents of Nineteenth-Century Literature* (1872–1876).

1927 May 11   Juan Gris [nee José Victriano González] (b. Mar. 23, 1887), a Spanish painter and leader of cubism, died. His work was primarily still lifes, developed from a simple geometric approach into a more playful, highly colorful style than was typical of cubism. Among his well-known paintings was a *Portrait of Pablo Picasso* (1912), *Guitar and Carafe* (1917), and *The Chessboard* (1917).

1927 June 14   Jerome K[lapka] **Jerome** (b. May 2, 1859), an English humorist, novelist, and playwright, died. His best work was *Three Men in a Boat* (1889). The most successful of his many plays was *The Passing of the Third Floor Back* (1907). In 1902 Jerome and some friends founded *The Idler*, a humorous magazine offering works by a number of well-known authors.

1927 July 9   **John Drew** (b. Nov. 13, 1853), a popular American actor, died. In 1875 he had his first success, playing the young lover opposite **Fanny Davenport** in *The Big Bonanza*. He was also a hit in *Rip Van Winkle,* in which he toured widely with **Joseph Jefferson**. Drew also played opposite **Ada Rehan** and **Maude Adams**.

1927 July 24   **Akutagawa Ryunosuke** [Chokodo Shujin, Gaki] (b. Mar. 1, 1892), who ranked among the world's greatest short-story writers, drank poison in a puzzling suicide. Akutagawa, one of the most widely translated of Japanese authors, wrote many macabre tales, among them *Rashomon* (1915) and *Kappa* (1926–1927).

1927 Sept. 14   **Isadora Duncan** (b. May 27, 1878), an American dancer acclaimed in Europe, strangled as one of her long scarves was caught in the wheel of her open automobile in Nice, France. Duncan was an **originator of modern dance**, borrowing forms from ancient Greece and nature. She sometimes danced barefoot in a costume based on the Greek tunic. Duncan established several schools of dancing, including one for children (1904) near Berlin, Germany.

1927 Oct. 6   The **first commercially successful feature movie** film employing spoken dialogue was *The Jazz Singer,* starring **Al Jolson** [Asa Yoelson] (May 28, 1886–Oct. 23, 1950), in which some songs and a few snatches of dialogue were heard. The first all-talking feature film was *Lights of New York,* which opened on July 6, 1928, in New York City.

VI. SPORTS, GAMES, AND SOCIETY

1927   The **English Women's Cricket Association** was formed, followed shortly by the Australian Women's Cricket Council. Cricket flourished among women in the two countries, especially in the years immediately following World War II.

1927 June 4   The **Ryder Cup** was contested for the first time by American and British professional golfers. At Dorchester, Massachusetts, the Americans won 9½ matches to 2½. The cup was donated by **Samuel Ryder**, a British seed merchant, for match play and was to be contested every other year on sites alternating between Great Britain and the U.S.

1927 Aug. 22   **Nicola Sacco** (b. Apr. 22, 1891) and **Bartolomeo Vanzetti** (b. July 11, 1888) were executed for their implicated role in the 1920 murder of a shoestore paymaster and the theft of $15,000 from him in Braintree, outside of Boston, Massachusetts.

1927 Nov. 19   **Alexander Alekhine** (Nov. 1, 1892–Mar. 24, 1946) won the **world chess championship** at Buenos Aires, Argentina, from **José Raúl Capablanca**. Alekhine was champion until 1935, regained the title in 1937, and retained it until his death. He was Russian-born but became a French citizen after the Russian Revolution of 1917. Alekhine earned the title of chess master by the time he was 16.

1928

I. VITAL STATISTICS AND DEMOGRAPHICS

1928 Dec. 4   Mrs. **Delina Filkins** (b. May 4, 1815) died at the age of 113 years and 214 days; it was considered the **longest fully proven human life span**. **Pierre Joubert** (July 15, 1701–Nov. 16, 1814), who lived 113 years and 124 days, was the former record holder.

II. DISASTERS

1928–1929   About **40,000 people starved in the province of Ruanda** [present Rwanda], then a Belgian trust territory, following a severe drought. Thousands migrated to Uganda to escape the famine.

1928 Mar. 13   The **St. Francis Dam**, c.45 miles north of Los Angeles, California, **burst**, causing c.450 deaths and $15,000,000 in property damage.

1928 Sept. 12–17   **A hurricane swept through the West Indies**, accounting for c.4,000 deaths and great property damage.

1928 Nov. 12   The British steamship *Vestris,* bound for South America, was **sunk** in a gale off the coast of Virginia with the loss of 110 lives.

III. EXPLORATION AND COLONIZATION

1928 May 27 After dropping Italian and Milanese flags at the North Pole, the airship *Italia*, built by **Umberto Nobile** (Jan. 21, 1885–July 29, 1978), an Italian aeronautical engineer and explorer, crashed. **Roald Amundsen**, the Norwegian explorer, who in 1926 had flown over the North Pole in another Nobile airship, the *Norge*, attempted a seaplane flight to rescue Nobile and his crew. After taking off from Tromsoe, Norway, the plane crashed near Spitzbergen, killing Amundsen (b. July 16, 1872). Nobile and his crew were saved by another rescue plane. Nobile was found responsible for the disaster to the *Italia* and resigned (1929) his commission as general in the Italian air force.

IV. POLITICS AND WAR

1928 Chang Tso-Lin (1873–June 4, 1928), the Manchurian warlord, evacuated Peking [Beijing] as the Nationalist armies of **Chiang Kai-Shek** completed their **Northern Expedition** with a march on the capital, aided by the warlord turncoats **Fêng Yü-Hsiang** (Sept. 26, 1882–Sept. 1, 1948), the "Christian General," and **Yen Hsi-Shan** (1883–May 24, 1960) of Shansi [Shanxi] province. **Wu P'ei-Fu** (Apr. 22, 1874–Dec. 4, 1939) had already fled from Peking into retirement earlier in this year. Fêng Yü-Hsiang and Yen Hsi-Shan held Peking until Chiang Kai-Shek entered the city on June 8. The Nationalist victory ended the **Warlord Era** (1916–1928) in China. Chiang established his capital at Nanking [Nanjing] on the Yangtze River [Chang Jiang] in southeastern China.

1928 Feb. 15 Herbert [Henry] **Asquith** (b. Sept. 12, 1852), a British statesman and Liberal party leader who served as prime minister (1908–1916), died. He entered Parliament in 1886 and after becoming prime minister led the government in enacting social welfare legislation providing for old age pensions (1910) and unemployment insurance (1911). In 1911 Asquith also obtained passage of a bill that abolished the veto power of the House of Lords.

1928 Feb. 20 Great Britain signed a treaty with Transjordan [present Jordan] making it a constitutional state ruled by a king. The kingship was to be hereditary in the **Hashimite Dynasty of Jordan** (1921 to the present). Britain saw Transjordan as a buffer between Palestine and the Arabs of the desert regions.

1928 Mar. 25 Antonio Oscar de Fragoso Carmona (Nov. 24, 1869–Apr. 18, 1951) was elected president of Portugal. On Apr. 27 he appointed as minister of finance **Antonio de Oliveira Salazar** (Apr. 28, 1889–July 27, 1970) who, wielding extensive powers, began to restore the country's economy.

1928 Apr. 19 Japanese troops occupied part of Shantung [Shandong] **province** in China, claiming that Japanese lives and property were endangered by the advance of Nationalist troops under Chiang Kai-Shek. On May 11, after heavy fighting, the Japanese captured Tsinan [Chinan], capital of the province. Japan withdrew some of its troops on July 10, but it was not until May 1929 that they were all withdrawn.

1928 May 7 The **British Parliament reduced the voting age for women to 21 from 30**, the same as for men.

1928 June 3 Chang Tso-Lin (b. 1873), the warlord of Manchuria, died as the result of a bomb blast on the train he was riding to Mukden, Manchuria. It was set off by the Japanese who wanted an excuse to invade and claim Manchuria.

1928 July 17 Álvaro Obregón (b. Feb. 19, 1880), the former president and now president-elect of Mexico, was assassinated by José de León Toral, a young fanatic Cristero, in Mexico City. Obregón's supporters were said to have assassinated his opponents, followers of incumbent president Plutarcho Elías Calles. In the worst **church-state conflict** in Mexico's history, the strife had been created by governmental decrees limiting the influence of the Roman Catholic Church, which led to a strike by the clergy on July 31, 1926, who refused to administer sacraments for the next three years. The **Cristeros**, radical Catholic Church Indians operating under the motto "**Cristo Reyes**" [Christ is King], and their supporters opposed the government's measures, which included closing church schools, deporting foreign-born priests and nuns, and prohibiting religious processions. The Cristeros resorted to riots and banditry that came to be known as the **Cristero Rebellion**. The rebellion was harshly suppressed, with the summary hanging of priests and Cristeros and the looting and burning of churches by government troops. Intervention by **Dwight Whitney Morrow**

(Jan. 11, 1873–Oct. 5, 1931), the U.S. ambassador to Mexico, brought a settlement of the church-state issue in June, 1929.

1928 Aug. 8 **Stephan Radic** (b. July 11, 1871), a Croat political leader, died by an assassin's shots (June 20) fired in the Yugoslavian parliament by a Serb, after which the Croats set up a separate parliament at Zagreb.

1928 Aug. 27 The **Kellogg-Briand Peace Pact** was signed by fifteen nations. Designed to prevent wars by arranging for international negotiations, it proved ineffective. It was initiated on Apr. 6, 1927, when **Aristide Briand**, French minister of foreign affairs, suggested France and the U.S. sign such a pact and **Frank Billings Kellogg** (Dec. 22, 1856–Dec. 21, 1937), U.S. secretary of state, agreed but wanted to include all nations.

1928 Sept. 1 **Ahmed Bey Zogu**, president of Albania, was proclaimed King **Zog I** as the republic of **Albania** became a monarchy under a new constitution.

1928 Nov. 15 The **Fascist Grand Council** was made an official state office of Italy and given extensive powers. This followed an electoral law, passed on May 12, that reduced the electorate from c.10,000,000 to 3,000,000 by disenfranchising women and men under 21 and establishing job and property qualifications.

V. ECONOMY AND TRADE

1928 June 24 The **French franc was valued with gold** on a basis of 3.92¢ U.S. as part of an effort by **Raymond Poincaré**, the prime minister and minister of finance, to stabilize the currency and reduce the debt on the part of the French government to its citizens, incurred during World War I. The franc had fallen nearly as low (1926) as 2¢ from a prewar high of 20¢. The stabilization of the franc, even at this low value, was popular because it stimulated foreign trade and provided work.

1928 Oct. 1 The Soviet Union initiated its **first Five Year Plan**, the largest economic development program launched by any modern government up to this time. The Plan had two objectives, rapid industrialization and the bringing of socialism and collectivism to farms and villages.

VI. RELIGION AND PHILOSOPHY

1928 The **Muslim Brotherhood** [Arabic: Al-Ikhwan al-Muslimon] was founded at Ismailia, Egypt. It sought to return the Arabic people of the Near East and North Africa to the basic creed and practices of the Koran. The brotherhood established schools, clinics, and military training camps.

1928 **Yeshiva College** was established in New York City by **Bernard Revel** (Sept. 17, 1885–Dec. 2, 1940), a rabbi and an immigrant (1912) from Lithuania. Organized under Jewish auspices, its program was characterized as "Torah along with secular culture." Yeshiva College was the first Jewish general academic college.

1928 Nov. 12 [William] **Cosmo Gordon Lang** (Oct. 31, 1864–Dec. 5, 1945), archbishop of York (from 1908), was appointed archbishop of Canterbury (to 1942) and therefore head of the Anglican communion. Lang supported the controversial revision of the *Book of Common Prayer*, proposed in 1928.

VII. SCIENCE, EDUCATION, AND TECHNOLOGY

1928 **Arthur Holly Compton** (Sept. 10, 1892–Mar. 15, 1962), an American physicist, noted that X and *gamma* rays exhibited lower frequencies and longer wave lengths due to energy lost when they collided with electrons in matter. The phenomenon is now called the **Compton Effect**. Compton received the **Nobel prize for physics** in 1927.

1928 Archaeologists excavating the ruins of ancient **Anyang** in northern Henan [Honan] province, in central northern China, discovered **writing on bones** that resembled modern Chinese script but was dated as early as 1,500 B.C.

1928 **Vladimir K[osma] Zworykin** (July 30, 1889–July 29, 1982), a Russian-born American scientist, patented an **electronic system for broadcasting and receiving television pictures**. Hitherto the systems being developed used mechanical scanning disks, much less satisfactory in the long run.

1928 The **Iron Lung**, an artificial respiration device for use in the treatment of such maladies as infantile paralysis, where the patient's ability to breathe was impaired, was developed by **Philip Drinker** (Dec. 12, 1894–Oct. 19, 1972). Pumps alternately increased the air pressure inside the device to force air from the lungs then pumped the air out causing the patient to inhale. Only the patient's head was outside the iron lung.

1928 George Nicholas Papanicolaou (May 13, 1883–Feb. 19, 1962), a Greek-born American scientist, developed the Papanicolaou test, commonly known as the **Pap test**, a medical procedure used to detect cancer of the uterine cervix.

1928 *Coming of Age in Samoa* by **Margaret Mead**, a 27-year-old anthropologist, appeared and became a landmark in social anthropology. Mead went to Samoa to study adolescent girls and reported they were well-adjusted and happy in their easy-going, noncompetitive culture.

1928 C[harles] K[ay] **Ogden** (June 1, 1889–Mar. 20, 1957) and I[vor] A[rmstrong] **Richards** (Feb. 26, 1893–Sept. 7, 1979) developed **Basic English**, designed to be an international language. It consisted of 850 words; there were rules for their use and 150 additional words that provided bridges to special fields, such as science. Together, Ogden and Richards had written *The Meaning of Meaning* (1923), a work on semantics.

1928 Feb. 4 Hendrick Antoon Lorentz (b. July 18, 1853), a Dutch physicist, died. He determined the influence of a magnetic field on radiation, which was based on his theory of the electron. He received the **Nobel prize for physics** in 1902 for his work on theories of electricity, magnetism, and light.

1928 Apr. 12–13 Gunther von Huenefeld (1892–Feb. 5, 1929), a German backer/passenger and his crew made the **first successful east-west transatlantic flight**, in the *Breman*, a single engine, all-metal Junkers monoplane, going from Dublin, Ireland, to Greeley Island, an islet in the strait of Belleisle, off Labrador, in 37 hours. They had to be rescued from Greeley Island, where they crash-landed.

1928 May 11 The **first regularly scheduled broadcasts of television programs** began in Schenectady, New York. The pictures were broadcast by the experimental TV station W2XAD and the sound by radio station WGY. There were three transmissions a week, a total of one and a half hours.

1928 May 31–June 8 Charles Edward Kingsford-Smith (Feb. 9, 1897–Nov. 8, 1935) made the **first westward transpacific flight** from Oakland, California, to Brisbane, Australia, more than 8,000 miles in 83 hours, 19 minutes. He flew a tri-engined Fokker by way of Hawaii and Fiji.

1928 June 17–18 Amelia [Mary] **Earhart**, an American aviator, became the **first woman to fly the Atlantic Ocean**. With two male pilots she took off from Boston, Massachusetts, and after a stop in Newfoundland, Canada, flew to Carthmenshire, Wales, Great Britain, in 22 hours. Although an experienced pilot, Earhart said she was never at the controls during the flight. The plane, named *Friendship*, was a twin-engined Fokker.

1928 Sept. 15 Alexander Fleming, a Scottish bacteriologist, discovered by accident that **penicillin**, a mold, had an antibiotic effect. He recognized the potential value of penicillin in the treatment of bacterial organisms but it was not until 1941 that other scientists purified the substance and tested its effectiveness.

1928 Oct. 11–15 The German dirigible *Graf Zeppelin* completed the **longest round-trip ever made by a dirigible**, 6,630 miles between Friedrichshafen, Germany, and Lakehurst, New Jersey. The trip took 4 days, 15 hours, and 46 minutes.

VIII. ARTS AND LEISURE

1928 The first volume of *Tikhii Don* [*The Silent Don*] by **Mikhail Aleksandrovich Sholokhov** (b. May 24, 1905–Feb. 21, 1984) was published in the U.S.S.R. The second volume appeared in 1920; the third in 1933, and the fourth in 1938. It was published in English in two volumes: *And Quiet Flows the Don* (1934) and *The Don Flows Home to the Sea* (1941). Sholokhov was awarded the **Nobel prize for literature** in 1965.

1928 Carl Theodor Dreyer (Feb. 3, 1889–Mar. 20, 1968), a Danish film director, released his most noted film *Le Passion de Jeanne d'Arc* [*The Passion of Joan of Arc*]. While the film was a critical success, it was a financial failure. Other films directed by Dreyer were *Blade af satans bog* [*Leaves from Satan's Book*] (1920); *Ordet* [*The World*] (1955); and his last film *Gertrud* (1964).

1928 Mickey Mouse made his debut in a [Walter Elias] **Walt Disney** (Dec. 5, 1901–Dec. 15, 1966) animated cartoon *Plane Crazy*. The same year Mickey appeared in *Gallopin' Gaucho,* followed by *Steamboat Willie,* which introduced sound to animated cartoons.

1928 Jan. 11   Thomas Hardy (b. June 2, 1840), an English novelist and poet, died. Hardy's greatly successful novels included *Far from the Madding Crowd* (1874), *The Return of the Native* (1878), *Tess of the D'Ubervilles* (1891), and *Jude the Obscure* (1895). His poetical masterpiece was *The Dynasts* (1904–1908), an epic set in the Napoleonic era.

1928 Jan. 28   Vicento Blasco Ibáñez (b. Jan. 29, 1867), a Spanish novelist and socialist, died. He was best known for a romantic novel of World War I, *Los Cuatro Jinetes del Apocalipsis* [*The Four Horsemen of the Apocalypse*] (1916). He described the life of a bullfighter in *Blood and Sand* (1908). Ibáñez, opposed to the Spanish regime, moved to Paris in 1923 and died in exile.

1928 Mar. 31   Medardo Rosso (b. June 20, 1858), a leading Italian impressionist sculptor, died. An important member of the futurists, he influenced such notable sculptors as Rodin and Brancusi. Two of his works were *Sick Child* (1895) and *Impression of an Omnibus* (1883–1884).

1928 Apr. 19   The last volume of *The Oxford English Dictionary* [OED], in 12 volumes the most comprehensive guide to the English language ever published, appeared in Great Britain 71 years after work on it first began. The 12 volumes defined 414,825 words and contained 1,827,306 illustrative quotations. A supplementary volume was published in 1933, and in 1972 this began to be replaced by the first volume of a new four-volume supplement.

1928 July 21   Ellen [Alice] **Terry** (b. Feb. 27, 1847), a noted English stage actress, died. For 24 years she appeared regularly with Henry Irving in productions of Shakespeare. Her last stage appearance was as the nurse in *Romeo and Juliet* (June, 1919).

1928 Aug. 12   Leoš Jánacek (b. July 3, 1854), a Czechoslovakian composer, died. His operas included *Jenufa* (1904), *Katia Kabanova* (1921), *The Matropolos Affair* (1926), and *From the House of the Dead* (1930).

IX. SPORTS, GAMES, AND SOCIETY

1928   Polo became a popular sport in Argentina in the 1920s and resulted in the establishment of the *Copa de las Americas* [*Cup of the Americas*] to be contested for by teams representing Argentina and the U.S. The cup has been played for six times, the U.S. winning in 1928 and 1932, Argentina in 1936, 1950, 1966, and 1969.

1928   The **U.S. Volleyball Association** was formed to take over the governing function that had been shared since 1916 by the Young Men's Christian Association [YMCA] and the National Collegiate Athletic Association [NCAA].

1928 Feb. 11–19   The second Winter **Olympic Games** were held at St. Moritz, Switzerland, with 495 athletes from 25 countries competing. Norwegian athletes won 6 gold medals and 15 medals in all; the U.S. 2 and 6; and Sweden 2 and 5.

1928 May 17–Aug. 12   The ninth Summer **Olympic Games** were held in Amsterdam, the Netherlands, with 3,014 athletes from 46 nations participating. U.S. athletes won 22 gold medals and 56 medals in all; Germany 10 and 31; and Finland 8 and 25. Track and field events for women were included for the first time. Paul Desjardins (1907–May 6, 1985), an American, earned two perfect scores in the springboard diving event, the first time perfect scores were awarded in the Olympics.

1929

I. VITAL STATISTICS AND DEMOGRAPHICS

1929   The **Fifth Aliyah** [*aliyah* = "ascent" in Hebrew], the name applied to the emigration of Jews to Palestine [present Israel], started this year and ended in 1939 when Europe became unsafe for Jews. In all c.250,000 Jews reached Palestine in this decade.

II. DISASTERS

1929 May 15 An **explosion of nitrogen dioxide** and the subsequent fire killed 125 persons at Cleveland [Ohio] Clinic Foundation. The clinic had been founded (1921) by **George Washington Crile** (Nov. 11, 1864–Jan. 7, 1943), an American surgeon who was a pioneer in devising methods to prevent surgical shock.

III. EXPLORATION AND COLONIZATION

1929 Nov. 28–29 The **first flight over the South Pole** was made by **Richard E. Byrd** of the U.S. in a Ford trimotor plane named *Floyd Bennett*. The plane, piloted by **Bernt Balchen** (Oct. 23, 1899–Oct. 17, 1973), took off from Little America, the U.S. base in Antarctica, with a stop at an advance fueling station. The flight took c.18 hours.

IV. POLITICS AND WAR

1929 Jan. 6 **Alexander I**, a Serbian and king of the Serbs, Croats, and Slovenes, suspended the constitution of 1921 and began rule as a dictator. He proclaimed a new constitution on Oct. 3, 1931, which perpetuated his rule, and renamed the nation **Yugoslavia** [Jugoslavia].

1929 Jan. 14 A revolt against **Amnullah Khan**, king of **Afghanistan** (from 1919), forced the monarch to resign. Opposition to him arose because of his attempt to contain the power of religious leaders and to give women more rights. After a few months the rebels were defeated by Amnullah's cousin **Muhammad Nadir Shah**, who ruled (from Oct. 17) as king until he was assassinated in 1933.

1929 Mar. 4 **Herbert Hoover** of the Republican party was inaugurated as the 31st president of the U.S., having defeated **Alfred E. Smith** (Dec. 30, 1873–Oct. 4, 1944) of the Democratic party. **Charles Curtis** (Jan. 25, 1860–Feb. 8, 1936) served as vice-president. Hoover received 21,392,190 popular votes and 444 electoral votes; Smith, 15,016,443 and 87.

1929 Mar. 16 Student protests against the harsh government of **Primo de Rivera**, dictator of **Spain**, caused him to close the University of Madrid. A general uprising of liberal elements did not succeed

in ousting him, but on Jan. 30, 1930, Primo de Rivera resigned and went into exile in Paris.

1929 Mar. 20 **Ferdinand Foch** (b. Apr. 6, 1851), marshal of France and supreme commander of the British, French, and American armies in World War I from Mar. 1918 until victory in November, died. A professional army officer, he played a major role in the **battle at the Marne** (1914), which halted the German advance on Paris.

1929 June 3 The **Tacna-Arica Controversy** between Chile and Peru was finally resolved. The province of Arica was awarded to Chile, Peru acquired Tacna, and landlocked Boliva gained access of the Pacific port of Arica in northern Chile. The dispute originated in the **Treaty of Ancón** (1883), which ended the **War of the Pacific** (1879–1884).

1929 Oct. 3 **Gustav Stresemann** (b. May 10, 1878), a German statesman who did more than any other of his countrymen to reconcile his defeated nation with the victorious Allies of World War I and to mitigate the harsh penalties of the **Treaty of Versailles**, died. He was chancellor in 1923 and foreign minister until his death. Among his peacemaking achievements were: securing evacuation of the Ruhr by the Allies in 1924; acceptance of the **Dawes Plan** (1924) and the **Young Plan** (1929) concerning the payment of reparations; the signing of the **Locarno Pact** (1925); the admission of Germany to the **League of Nations** (1926); and the signing of the **Kellogg-Briand Pact** (1928).

1929 Nov. 17 **Nikolai Bukharin** and other leaders were expelled from the Communist party of the Soviet Union by **Joseph Stalin** and his supporters. Bukharin had led a rightist faction that advocated giving concessions to the peasants instead of forcing their collectivization.

1929 Nov. 23 **Georges Clemenceau** (b. Sept. 28, 1841), a French statesman, known as "the Tiger" for his fierce defense of France in World War I, died. He became premier (1906–1909) and made firm the alliance with Great Britain. A savage opponent of Germany, he was premier again (1917–1920). At the **Versailles Peace Conference** of 1919 he opposed the more lenient terms proposed by Woodrow Wilson, president of the U.S., because he believed the treaty, harsh as it was, did not adequately guarantee the security of France.

V. ECONOMY AND TRADE

1929   From the time of its coming to power in 1917 the **communist regime in Russia** had begun to **collectivize agriculture**. From the beginning the farm people resisted the move and did not produce enough food to feed the population of the urban areas, where nationalization and forced industrialization were the equivalent of the collective farm movement. As a result, by the fall of 1929 force was being used to bring farmers into the collectives. With the government failing to make good on its promise to supply large numbers of tractors to mechanize farming, **Joseph Stalin**, general secretary of the Communist party, in early 1930 felt forced to ease up. Matters became worse in 1932 and 1933, when drought and famine struck. The government took so much of the farm produce for the cities that several million peasants died. Nevertheless, by 1936 almost all Russian farms were collectivized.

1929 June 7   A scaled-down schedule of reparations payments to be made by Germany to the Allies of World War I was agreed to by the nations concerned. It was termed the **Young Plan** in acknowledgment of the man who headed the commission, **Owen D. Young** (Oct. 27, 1874–July 17, 1962), an American corporate executive. The Young Plan put total reparations at $26,350,000,000 to be paid over a period of 58½ years. Annual payments were to be about $473,000,000. No reparation payments were ever made under the Young Plan.

1929 Oct. 29   The **worst collapse of prices to date in the history of the New York Stock Exchange** heralded the start of the **Great Depression**. A record 16,410,030 shares were traded, and the value of all stocks declined by somewhere between 8 and 9 billion dollars. The stock market boom had reached its peak on Sept. 3. From then on the market declined, first going into a state of panic on October 24. It reached its lowest point of the year on Nov. 13. At that time *The New York Times* index of industrial stocks stood at 224, but as the decline persisted, it dropped to 58 by July 1932.

VI. RELIGION AND PHILOSOPHY

1929 Feb. 11   The **Lateran Treaty**, or Concordat, was signed between Italy and the Holy See, granting the **pope full sovereignty over Vatican City** and establishing him as a temporal ruler for the first time since 1870. Vatican City was recognized as forever neutral and inviolable; the Kingdom of Italy and the Savoy Dynasty (1861–1946) were recognized; and Rome was declared the capital. The Italian government agreed that Catholicism was the state religion, and religion was to be taught in the primary and secondary schools.

1929 June 16   [William] **Bramwell Booth** (b. June 16, 1856), eldest son of **William Booth**, the founder of the Salvation Army, and his successor as general (from 1912) of the world-wide movement, died. He was the main organizer and chief of staff of the Army (1880–1912).

VII. SCIENCE, EDUCATION, AND TECHNOLOGY

1929   **Werner Forssman** (Aug. 29, 1904–June 1, 1979), a German doctor, performed the **first cardiac catheterization** in a daring experiment on his own heart. Forssman's work paved the way for great advances in cardiology, most specifically the angiocardiograph. He shared the **Nobel prize for physiology or medicine** in 1956.

1929   The **first subway system built in Asia** opened in Tokyo with 1.5 miles of track. Since then it has been expanded greatly and now operates over 124 route miles.

1929   **Edward A[delbert] Doisy** (b. Nov. 13, 1893–Oct. 23, 1986), an American biochemist, **isolated the female sex hormone estrogen**. In 1936 he succeeded in isolating another such hormone, estradiol. Doisy shared the **Nobel prize for physiology** or medicine in 1943 for the discovery of the chemical nature of vitamin K. With others he synthesized this vitamin in 1939.

1929   **Edwin P[owell] Hubble** (Nov. 20, 1889–Sept. 28, 1953), American astronomer, proposed what became known as **Hubble's Law**: The distance between galaxies increases continuously and so the universe is forever expanding.

1929   **Hans Berger** (May 21, 1873–June 1, 1941), a German psychiatrist, developed the **electroencephalogram [EEG]** for measuring the electrical activity of the brain. Its use enabled physicians to be much more accurate in diagnosing and treating such diseases as epilepsy and stroke.

Feb. 19   Karl Julius Beloch (b. Jan. 21, 1854), the German-born **founding father of historical demography**, died. He produced the first systematic work on ancient populations, *Die Beyolerung der Griechish-Romischen Welt* [*The Population of the Graeco-Roman World*] (1886).

1929 Mar. 15   The **first airplane powered by a rocket motor** was flown in Germany. Its chief inventor was **Fritz von Opel** (May 4, 1899–Apr. 8, 1971), who was also an automobile manufacturer. The second such plane, a Hatry glider with 16 solid fuel rockets, was flown by Opel himself on Sept. 30.

1929 Aug. 3   Thorstein [Bunde] **Veblen** (b. July 30, 1857), an American economist and social critic, died. Veblen took apart the accepted bases of many of society's institutions and gave a new perspective to them. He coined the expression "conspicuous consumption." Veblen's books included *The Theory of the Leisure Class* (1899), *The Theory of Business Enterprise* (1904), and *The Engineers and the Price System* (1921).

1929 Aug. 8–29   The dirigible *Graf Zeppelin* completed a **flight around the world**, the first ever by such an aircraft. The dirigible took off from Lakehurst, N.J., made stops only at Friedrichshafen, Germany; Tokyo; and Los Angeles; before arriving back at Lakehurst in 21 days, 7 hours, and 26 minutes. The ship carried 16 passengers and a crew of 37.

1929 Sept. 25   James H. Doolittle, a lieutenant in the air service of the U.S. army, made the **first blind take-off and landing** in an airplane. He made the flight at Mitchell Field, New York.

VIII. ARTS AND LEISURE

1929   The anti-war novel *Im Westen nichts Neuses* [*All Quiet on the Western Front*], by **Erich Maria Remarque**, was published. In Germany the book soon sold c.1,200,000 copies. In the U.S. in 1929 it was the leading novel of the year with sales of c.300,000. By 1975 the U.S. total reached c.3,425,000 and in 1988, 90 years after Remarque's birth, a new paperback edition was issued.

1929 Feb. 12   Lillie Langtry [nee Emilie Charlotte Le Breton] (b. Oct. 13, 1853), an English actress known as the Jersey Lily because she was born on the Isle of Jersey, died. Her most successful role was Rosalind in *As You Like It*. Langtry was far more noted for her beauty, her role in society, and her affair with Edward VII than as an actress. Oscar Wilde wrote *Lady Windermere's Fan* (1892) for her.

1929 May 16   The **Academy of Motion Picture Arts and Sciences**, in Hollywood, California, presented the first of its annual awards for excellence in movies released the previous year. Among the first winners were: best picture, *Wings,* about World War I aviators; best actor, Emil Jannings in *The Way of All Flesh* and *The Last Command*; best actress, **Janet Gaynor** in *Seventh Heaven, Street Angel,* and *Sunrise;* best director, **Frank Borzage** (Apr. 23, 1893–June 19, 1962) for *Seventh Heaven,* and Lewis Milestone (Sept. 30, 1895–Sept. 25, 1980) for *Two Arabian Nights.*

1929 July 12   Robert Henri [Robert Henry Cozad] (b. June 25, 1865), an American painter and noted art teacher, died. He was the leader of "the Eight," who exhibited in 1908 and greatly influenced the direction of American painting. He taught at the Art Students' League in New York City (1915–1923) and published *The Art Spirit* (1923), a collection of his writings. Among his paintings were *West 57th Street* (1902) and *Himself* (1913).

1929 Aug. 15   Hugo von Hofmannsthal (b. Feb. 1, 1874), an Austrian poet and dramatist, died. His early writings were highly impressionistic, as in his play *The Death of Titian* (1892) and *Poems* (1903). Hofmannsthal wrote a number of librettos, including *Der Rosenkavalier* (1911) and *Ariadne auf Naxos* (1912).

1929 Aug. 19   Sergei [Palovich] **Diaghilev** (b. Mar. 31, 1872), a Russian musical impresario, died. In Paris in 1909 with a troupe of Russian dancers, he founded Diaghilev's *Ballet Russe.* In his ballet productions, scenery and music became as much a part of the performance as dance itself. He employed top dancers, choreographers, composers, and artists, such as **Vaslav Nijinsky**, **Leonide Massine**, **Igor Stravinsky**, and **Pablo Picasso.**

1929 Oct. 1   Antoine Bourdelle (b. Oct. 30, 1861), a major French sculptor and well-known teacher, died. He executed more than 900 pieces of sculpture and thousands of drawings, paintings, frescoes, etc. Among his sculptures are the bas-reliefs of the Théâtre de Champs-Elysées (1910–1912), *Hercules the Archer* (1909), and *The Virgin of Alsace* (1923), which can be seen in the Musée Bourdelle in Paris.

1929 Nov. 8 The **Museum of Modern Art** [MOMA] in New York City opened its doors in rented quarters. Its first exhibit featured the work of the French impressionists.

IX. SPORTS, GAMES, AND SOCIETY

1929 **Women's skirts began to get longer**, falling well below the knees, and dresses once again followed more closely the natural shape of the female body. **Bathing suits** were getting **skimpier**.

1929 Feb. 14 The "**St. Valentine's Day Massacre**," a sensational killing of the gang wars of the Prohibition era, occurred in Chicago, Illinois. Five members of one gang, some dressed as policemen, entered a garage where seven members of the rival **George "Bugs" Moran** (1893–Feb. 25, 1957) gang were preparing for the day's illegal activities. The seven were lined up against a wall and mowed down with submachine guns. No one was ever arrested for the crime.

1930

I. VITAL STATISTICS AND DEMOGRAPHICS

1930 The **population of the world** was c.1,692,520,000. The populations, in round figures, of the major regions of the world were: **Africa**, 125,-000,000; **Asia**, 885,000,000; **Australasia**, 7,000,000; **Europe** [including European Russia], 500,000,000; **North and South America**, 240,000,000. The population of the U.S. was 123,202,624. Osaka, Japan, and Buenos Aires, Argentina, had entered the list of the world's ten largest cities. The world's largest cities were: London, 8,202,818; New York, 6,930,446; Berlin, 4,000,000; Chicago, 3,376,438; Paris, 2,871,-039; Osaka, 2,500,000; Tokyo, 2,300,000; Buenos Aires, 2,100,000; Philadelphia, 1,950,961; Vienna, 1,886,000; Shanghai, 1,000,000; Mexico City, 970,-000.

II. DISASTERS

1930–1938 Terrible **drought in North America** combined with the imprudent cultivation of the Great Plains produced the **Dust Bowl** in the U.S. and Canada. Topsoil turned to dust and was blown in large clouds as far as the Atlantic Ocean and the Gulf of Mexico.

1930 Apr. 21 **Fire** raged through four blocks of the Ohio State Penitentiary at **Columbus**, killing 317 prisoners and injuring 231. Many of the 4,300 convicts in the institution were kept locked up until flames prevented their rescue.

1930 Sept. 3 The death toll was c.2,000 and c.6,000 were injured when **Santo Domingo**, the capital of the

Dominican Republic, in the West Indies, was buffeted by a **hurricane**.

1930 Oct. 5 The **British dirigible R-101 crashed** near Beauvais, **France**, killing 47 of the crew.

III. POLITICS AND WAR

1930 **Mahomed Iqbal** (c.1873–1938), a Pakistani poet and a philosopher, propounded for the **first time the idea of a separate nation for the Muslims of India**, to comprise areas in which they constituted a majority.

1930 In **France** construction began on the **Maginot Line**, fortifications planned to run nearly 200 miles from the Swiss border to the Belgian border. It was intended to prevent Germany from ever again being able to invade France as it had done in 1870 and 1914. The system was named for **André Maginot** (Feb. 17, 1877–Jan. 7, 1932), the French minister of defense (1929–1932).

1930 Feb. 23 **Horacio Vásquez** (1860–1936), president of the **Dominican Republic** (1899–1903, 1903–1907, 1924–1930) was overthrown in a revolt lasting five days. On May 16, after a provisional government, **Rafael Leonidas Trujillo Molina**, an army chief trained during the U.S. occupation (1916–1924) of the Dominican Republic, was named president (1930–1938, 1942–1952), beginning a long, oppressive dictatorship.

1930 Mar. 28 The Turkish government changed the name of its former capital, **Constantinople**, to

İstanbul. The city, in northwestern Turkey on both sides of the Bosporus was originally named Byzantium, but for 1,600 years had been Constantinople.

1930 Apr. 22   The **U.S., Great Britain, and Japan** signed a **naval pact** in London, in which the U.S. was limited to 15 capital ships; Great Britain, 15 capital ships; Japan, 9 capital ships. The three powers agreed to scrap their excess tonnage. **Aircraft carriers** were not yet considered important enough to be included in the treaty. France and Italy, the other major naval powers, did not sign the pact.

1930 May 5   Mohandas K[aramchand] **Gandhi**, a leader since 1915 of resistance to British rule of India, was arrested and imprisoned. On Mar. 12, to protest the government salt tax, he had begun a 200-mile march with his followers to the sea, where they made salt from sea water. Gandhi's arrest caused anti-British demonstrations in many parts of India. Gandhi supported Britain in World War I, hoping to receive support for Indian independence later. When this did not happen he began **civil disobedience campaigns of a nonviolent nature** that included fasting. Besides political freedom, Gandhi sought to spur cottage industries, especially the production of textiles, and he fought the caste system. Gandhi was released from prison on Jan. 26, 1931, to attend the **London Round Table Conference on India**.

1930 May 13   **Fridtjof Nansen** (b. Oct. 10, 1861), a Norwegian explorer, scientist, and statesman, died. In an expedition of 1893, Nansen attempted to reach the **North Pole** by drifting on Arctic ice floes. He failed but reached a latitude of 86° 14′ N, the farthest north anyone had gone up to that time. As a statesman, Nansen played an active role in the **peaceful separation of Norway from Sweden** in 1905. After World War I Nansen did important work in humanitarian affairs, both in repatriating war prisoners and in bringing relief to famine-stricken Russia. In 1922 he received the **Nobel Peace Prize**.

1930 June 6   **Carol II** (Oct. 15, 1893–Apr. 4, 1953), king of Romania (1930–1940) **returned to Romania** after a five-year exile in Paris. He supplanted his son **Michael I** who had become king under a council of regency in 1927. On June 8 Carol was crowned in **Bucharest**. He ruled as a dictator while trying to tread a line between the policies of Germany and Russia.

1930 July 28   The Liberal government of **William Lyon Mackenzie King**, prime minister of **Canada**, lost an election to the Conservative party. Conservatives won 137 seats in the House of Commons, compared with 88 Liberals, and 18 minor party members. **Richard Bedford Bennett** (July 3, 1870–June 16, 1947) became prime minister.

1930 Sept. 6   **Hipólito Irigoyen** (1850–1933) **Argentina's** president, (1919–1922; 1928–1930), was overthrown in a coup headed by **José F. Uriburu** (1868–1932), an army general.

1930 Sept. 14   **Adolf Hitler's Nazi party** in Germany won 107 seats in an election for the Reichstag, compared with 12 the party held previously. They became the second largest party, passing the Communist party in *Reichstag* seats. In the deepening depression, about 3,000,000 people were out of work.

1930 Oct. 22   **Fuad I** [Ahmed Fuad Pasha] (Mar. 26, 1868–Apr. 28, 1936), sultan (1917–1922) and king 1922–1936) of **Egypt**, suspended the constitution he had promulgated in 1923 and dissolved parliament in a struggle with the nationalistic, anti-British **Wafd party**. Until 1935 Fuad was for practical purposes dictator of Egypt.

1930 Nov. 2   **Haile Selassie** [Ras Taffari, Ras Tafari] (July 23, 1892–Aug. 27, 1975) became emperor of **Ethiopia** following the death of the empress **Zauditu** [Zawditu] (b. 1876), his cousin, for whom he had been regent and heir to the throne. He attempted to modernize his nation by replacing the traditional chiefs with young, European-trained administrators and introduced the country's **first constitution** on July 16, 1931.

1930 Nov. 3   **Getúlio Dornelles Vargas** became provisional president of **Brazil** after leading a revolt in October. On July 17, 1934, Vargas was elected president, and on Nov. 10, 1937, he staged a coup that overturned the constitution and established the *Estado Novo* [New State]. Vargas governed Brazil until he was ousted in 1945.

IV. ECONOMY AND TRADE

1930   The **Bank for International Settlements** [BIS] was established with headquarters in **Basel**, Switzerland, as part of the **Young Plan** for **regulating Germany's reparations** payments to the Allies in the aftermath of World War I. Its capital was supplied by Belgium, France, Germany, Great Britain, Italy, and by two banking groups, one American and one Japanese.

1930 Open-pit strip-mining reached unprecedented heights of production at Colstrip, Montana, on the property of the **Northern Pacific Railroad Co.**, when a new electrically driven shovel operated by one man dug 15 tons of material at one scoop. Seventy-five men operating the mine could produce 11 million tons of coal in one season.

1930 The **U.S. Dept. of Commerce promulgated regulations** requiring satisfactory aircraft and equipment, qualified pilots and navigators, maintenance efficiency, excellent navigation facilities, and qualified ground personnel.

1930 Apr. 12 By emergency decree, **Heinrich Brüning** (1885–1970), chancellor of Germany (1930–1932), introduced a series of financial measures that resulted in higher food prices and severe deflation in virtually all other sectors of the economy.

1930 Motor vehicle production in the U.S. fell to c.3.4 million cars amd trucks compared with 5.5 million in 1929. Nevertheless, there were now 26.4 million vehicles registered in the country. Of the 3,016,-281 miles of roads in the U.S., only c.660,000 miles were surfaced. Congress appropriated $125 million to give to the states for highway building and surfacing.

1930 June 17 The **Hawley-Smoot Tariff** was signed into law by **Herbert Hoover**, president of the U.S., despite the protest of more than 1,000 economists. It raised duties on 890 items but lowered them on only 235. The tariff angered many U.S. trading partners and contributed to a **sharp decline in trade**. Other nations reciprocated with higher tariffs of their own, causing further strangulation of international commerce.

1930 July 7 Heinrich Brüning, chancellor of Germany, issued a second **emergency decree, drastically raising taxes**. The decree precipitated the political crisis that culminated in elections in September.

1930 Aug. 30 [Michael] **"King" Cullen** opened the **first supermarket, King Kullen's**, in Jamaica, New York.

1930 Dec. The **protectionist measures the German government** had taken on behalf of its inefficient agriculture succeeded so well that the price of German wheat within Germany was twice what it was outside the country.

1930 Dec. 11 The **Bank of the United States**, in New York City, **failed**. (The depositors accounts were not protected but during the next few years were paid almost in full.) In all, 1,351 American banks closed their doors in 1930 and another 2,294 in 1931. By the end of 1930 unemployment stood at c.4,000,000, double the number of persons out of work at the start of the year.

V. RELIGION AND PHILOSOPHY

1930 Feb. A committee of thirteen Bible translators, Americans and Canadians, was formed under the aegis of the **International Council of Religious Education** for the preparation of another **revision of the Authorized** [King James] **Version** of 1611. The financial depression halted work, and some of the committee members died. But further financing was obtained in 1936, several more scholars joined the project, and the New Testament was published on Feb. 11, 1946. The Old Testament joined the New in a Bible published on Sept. 30, 1952.

VI. SCIENCE, EDUCATION, AND TECHNOLOGY

1930 **William C. Geer** (d. Sept. 9, 1964) and **Merit Scott** developed a **practical wing de-icer for airplanes**. It was a strip of vulcanized rubber backed by strong, flexible fabric along the leading edge of the wing. This invention enabled aircraft to fly under conditions that previously would have grounded them.

1930 **Bernard Lyot** (Feb. 27, 1897–Apr. 2, 1952), the French astronomer, invented the **coronagraph**. This enabled astronomers to study and photograph the sun's corona, which they had only been able to do during a total solar eclipse.

1930 **Peter L. Kaptiza** (June 26, 1894–Apr. 8, 1984), a Russian physicist working at the Cavendish Laboratory, Cambridge University, England, produced unusually powerful magnetic fields in the course of his work in **low temperature physics**. Under the right conditions, alternating magnetization and demagnetization can lower the temperature of an object to very near absolute zero.

1930 The **cyclotron**, popularly called the atom smasher, was invented at the University of California, Berkeley, by **Ernest O[rlando] Lawrence** (Aug. 8, 1901–Aug. 27, 1958), an American physicist. Also known as a **particle accelerator**, the device produces beams of charged particles which are directed at high speed at other objects in the field of study of nuclear physics. With the cyclotron Lawrence produced elements that were artificially radioactive and neutrons that could be used in research in such fields as biology and chemistry. Lawrence received the **Nobel prize for physics** in 1939.

1930 The **American Chemical Society** announced in **Atlanta**, Georgia, that **Thomas Midgley** (May 18, 1889–Nov. 2, 1944) had discovered a new non-inflammable and non-toxic refrigerant: dichlorodifluoromethane [**Freon**].

1930 The **flash bulb for taking photographs** under inadequate lighting conditions, became commercially available. It was developed in the U.S. by the **General Electric Company**. The bulb replaced the powder hitherto used, as well as very bright lights which blinded the subject.

1930 Jan. **Frank Whittle** (b. June 1, 1907), an English engineer, applied for the **first patent on a jet-propelled aircraft**.

1930 Jan. **Brazil**, dependent on imports for almost 100 percent of its petroleum products, developed a **motor fuel using a mixture of sugar cane, alcohol, and ether**. It sells for much less than gasoline.

1930 Jan. 21 **Clyde William Tombaugh** (b. 1906), using the new Lawrence Lowell 40-inch reflector telescope at the Lowell Observatory in Flagstaff, Arizona, was the first to discover the ninth and most distant planet in the solar system. It appeared on a photographic plate in the place predicted from calculations made by **Percival Lowell** (Mar. 13, 1855–Nov. 13, 1916) in 1905. Referred to until this discovery and proof as Planet X, it was soon named **Pluto** and calculated to be 5,900,000,000 kilometers (3,670,000,000 miles) from the sun (average).

1930 Apr. A **wireless telephone link was established between England and Australia**, enabling members of the two Commonwealth governments to talk to each other directly.

1930 Apr. Chemists of the **Eastman Kodak Co.** in Rochester, New York, developed a new dye, **neocyanine**, for photographic films which allowed motion picture companies to photograph night scenes in broad daylight at great savings. The same film unexpectedly became a boon to astronomers photographing solar spectrums and other heavenly phenomena because the plates showed the slower vibrating infra-red light not visible to the naked eye and not captured by ordinary film.

1930 May 15 **Ellen Church** (born c.1905), a U.S. registered nurse, became the **first official airline stewardess**, or flight attendant. She flew on a United Airlines tri-motored Boeing 80A that took off from the Oakland, California, airport and flew to Cheyenne, Wyoming, making five stops on the way.

1930 June 11 [Charles] **William Beebe** (1877–June 4, 1962), of the New York Zoological Society, descended to a depth of 1,426 feet off of Bermuda in a specially built spherical diving chamber four feet nine inches in diameter with walls more than one and one half inches thick. The **bathysphere**, as it was called, carried man to the greatest ocean depth yet penetrated. The purpose was to gather scientific information about the biology and physics of the ocean depths.

1930 July 23 **Glenn H[ammond] Curtiss** (b. May 21, 1878) died at Buffalo, N.Y. He was prominent as a manufacturer of airplanes, including many planes built during World War I. He built a flying boat in 1912 and developed the **Navy-Curtiss flying boat**, which made the first transatlantic crossing on May 31, 1919.

1930 Sept. 1–2 **Dieudonné Costes** (Nov. 4, 1893–May 18, 1973) and copilot **Maurice Bellonte** (b. 1896) were the **first to fly non-stop across the Atlantic Ocean** from east to west in a land plane. They took off from Le Bourget Field near Paris 37 hours and 18½ minutes before landing at Curtiss Field, Valley Stream, Long Island, New York.

VII. ARTS AND LEISURE

1930 **Martha Graham** (May 11, 1894–Apr. 1, 1991), already on her way to becoming America's foremost teacher and choreographer of ballet, founded the **Dance Repertory Theater** in New York

City. In 1989 on her 95th birthday, she was still active in her profession.

1930 The **Whitney Museum of American Art** was founded in New York City by **Gertrude Vanderbilt Whitney** (Sept. 1, 1875–Apr. 18, 1942). The museum grew out of the Whitney Studio (1914–1918), the Whitney Studio Club (1918–1928), and the Whitney Studio Galleries (1928–1930). The new museum opened its doors to the public in 1931 on 8th Street. It grew in reputation and size to the extent that on Sept. 27, 1966, it opened in new quarters at Madison Avenue and 75th Street in a large and much admired building designed by Marcel Breuer, a Hungarian-born American architect.

1930 The **League of Leftist Writers** was founded under the aegis of the Chinese author, **Lu Hsün** [Lusin, Chou Shu-jên] (1881–Oct. 19, 1936), to promote revolutionary literature in China. Lu Hsün modeled his western style of writing after that of Gogol. His short story "A Madman's Diary" (1918) was the first truly westernized story written entirely in Chinese. His short story "The True Story of Ah Q" (1921) has been translated into many languages.

1930 Mar. 2 D[avid] H[erbert] **Lawrence** (b. Sept. 11, 1885), an English novelist, died. His *Sons and Lovers* (1913) was generally considered his best, but *Lady Chatterley's Lover* (1928) was his most popular. Among his other novels was *Women in Love* (1921).

1930 Apr. 14 The Russian futurist poet and playwright **Vladimir Mayakovsky** (b. July 19, 1893) committed suicide. Two satirical plays, Mayakovsky's most important works, *The Bedbug* (1929) and *The Bathhouse* (1930) were produced within his last year. In 1930 his works were banned in Soviet Russia, but unrequited love may have had as much to do with his suicide.

1930 Apr. 21 [Seymour] **Robert Bridges** (b. Oct. 25, 1844), the poet laureate of England since 1913, died. Trained as a physician, he began to devote himself to writing in 1882. He is best remembered for *The Testament of Beauty*, a long poem appearing the year before his death. In it he expressed his spiritual philosophy and reflected on the evolution of the human soul.

1930 July 7 **Arthur Conan Doyle** (b. May 22, 1859), an English author and creator of the most popular character in detective fiction, **Sherlock Holmes**, died. The brilliant detective made his first appearance in 1887 in *A Study in Scarlet*. Doyle, a physician, soon abandoned his medical practice and many more Holmes adventures appeared over the years. Doyle's detective became a cult figure, still celebrated by clubs calling themselves the **Baker Street Irregulars**, after the fictional London home of Sherlock Holmes.

1930 Dec. When the American film version of the German novelist **Erich Maria Remarque's** novel *All Quiet on the Western Front* was shown in Germany, Nazi storm troopers took to the streets in protest, and the film was banned. In the U.S. the Motion Picture Academy of Arts and Sciences gave its annual award to *All Quiet* as the best movie of 1929–1930.

VIII. SPORTS, GAMES, AND SOCIETY

1930 **Donald George Bradman** (b. 1908), an Australian **cricketer**, scored 452 runs, not out, to establish a new single-innings batting record. The dominant player of his era (1927–1949), Bradman averaged 99.94 across 80 innings against test match bowlers, and had a career average, in first class matches only, of 95.14 runs.

1930 June 7 By winning the **Belmont Stakes**, **Gallant Fox**, with jockey **Earl Sande** (1898–Aug. 18, 1968), became the second horse to win the **Triple Crown** of American thoroughbred racing. Gallant Fox won the Preakness Stakes (May 9) and the Kentucky Derby (May 17).

1930 June 12 **Max[imilian] Schmeling** (b. Sept. 28, 1905), a German boxer, won the world **heavyweight boxing championship** in New York City when he was fouled in the fourth round of the bout by **Jack Sharkey** [Joseph Paul Zukauskas] (b. Oct. 6, 1902), an American boxer.

1930 July 30 **Jules Rimet**, French head of the Fédération Internationale de Football Association, donated a trophy, now the **World Cup**, for international soccer [Association Football] competition to be conducted every four years, midway between Olympic years. The first competition in 1930 was won by Uruguay, which defeated Argentina 4–2 in Montevideo.

1930 Sept. 27 [Robert Tyre] **Bobby Jones** (Mar. 17, 1902–Dec. 18, 1971), an American amateur golfer, won the **first and only "grand slam"** of the game when he captured the U.S. Amateur championship at the Merion course in Philadelphia, Pennsylvania. Jones had previously this year won the U.S. Open, the British Open, and the British Amateur titles. In all Jones won 13 of the 27 major tournaments in which he played. On Nov. 17, 1930,

he announced he was retiring from competitive **golf**.

1930 Sept. 13–17 The **America's Cup** was successfully defended by the U.S. yacht *Enterprise* which defeated the British challenger *Shamrock V* in four straight races off Newport, Rhode Island.

1931

I. DISASTERS

1931 June 14 In a **gale off St. Nazaire, France**, an excursion steamer sank with the loss of c.450 lives.

1931 Aug. The flooding **Yellow River** [Huang Ho, Huang He] claimed the lives of 3.7 million Chinese. This is the **largest loss of life ever recorded for any natural disaster in history.**

II. EXPLORATION AND COLONIZATION

1931 Sept. 20 George Hubert Wilkins (Oct. 31, 1888–Dec. 1, 1958), an Australian navigator, and **Lincoln Ellsworth** (May 12, 1880–May 26, 1951), an American explorer, completed a **transarctic survey** in the submarine *Nautilus*, reaching as far north under the ice as 82° 15′. They had hoped to reach the North Pole by sailing under the polar ice cap.

III. POLITICS AND WAR

1931 Prempeh II (b. 1871?), king of the Ashanti (1886–1896; 1926–1935) and thereby occupant of the throne known as the Golden Stool, whose rule name was Kwaka Dua III, died. After British troops occupied the capital of Kumasi on Jan. 17, 1896, he submitted to their control. The British seized Prempeh and exiled him to the Seychelles in the Indian Ocean. In 1924 he was brought back as a private citizen to what was then the British crown colony of Gold Coast [present **Ghana**].

1931 Apr. 14 Alfonso XIII, king of **Spain** (from 1902), fled the country following a sweeping victory by republican forces in the election two days earlier. He refused to abdicate but never resumed his throne. **Niceto Alcalá Zamora**, a leader of the peaceful revolution, became the head of a provisional government.

1931 July Carlos Ibáñez del Campo (1877–Apr. 28, 1960), the president of **Chile** (from 1927), was forced to resign and go into exile after a rash of revolts by students and professionals. In the remaining six months of the year several presidents held brief office. In all, Chile had nine presidents in the next two years.

1931 Aug. 24 James Ramsay MacDonald resigned as Labour prime minister of Great Britain. He was invited to form a **coalition government** [National Government] **of Conservatives, Liberals, and the Labour party**, which had split with MacDonald's resignation, to meet the current economic crisis. The drastic economic measures enacted included heavy taxation to support social services for the unemployed, and pay cuts for the navy. Although the Labour party had opposed protectionist trade measures, MacDonald won a large victory in the general elections of Oct. 27, and his coalition ministry was able to remain in office.

1931 Sept. 3 Alexander III, king of the Serbs, Croats, and Slovenes, ended his dictatorship and promulgated a new constitution that provided for a parliament but with procedures such that the government was certain to be victorious in elections. In 1929 the name of the nation became **Yugoslavia** [literally: southern Slavs], probably aimed at binding the polyglot nation closer together.

1931 Sept. 18 The **Manchurian crisis** began when Japanese troops seized the Chinese city of Mukden [Moukden; Shen-yang; Fengtien], in the present province of Liaoning in northeastern China, on the pretext of an incident during military maneuvers. The **occupation of the whole of Manchuria** followed as a result of ineffective Chinese resistance and despite a grass-roots boycott of Japanese goods.

1931 Nov.   Mao Tse-Tung, leader of the Chinese communists, proclaimed the **Chinese Soviet Republic** at Jui-chin, east of Kanchou in Kiangsi province, near the boundary of Fukien province in southeast China.

1931 Dec.   A dictatorship led by **Maximiliano Hernandez Martinez**, a professional army officer, seized control of the government of **El Salvador** from an oligarchy consisting mainly of the "coffee aristocracy" that depended on the export of coffee for its wealth. The Hernandez rule was harsh, with many murders of persons suspected of being communists, but the nation prospered.

1931 Dec. 11   The **Statute of Westminster**, passed by the British Parliament, declared the dominions of the Commonwealth to be sovereign within their borders, thereby establishing the **British Commonwealth of Nations**, now simply the Commonwealth of Nations. The statute applied to Australia, Canada, the Irish Free State, Newfoundland, New Zealand, and South Africa. The same statute provided that the British Parliament would act as the medium for constitutional change in Canada but only at the request of Canada.

1931 Dec. 19   Public dissatisfaction stemming from depressed economic conditions caused the fall of the government of **Australia**, led by the Labour party. A new government was formed by **Joseph A[loysius] Lyons** (Sept. 15, 1879–Apr. 7, 1939), who organized the United Australia party. Lyons did much to make Australia prosperous again, aided by a gradual increase in the price of wool and gold.

IV. ECONOMY AND TRADE

1931   The **Great Depression** made its appearance in France. By the end of 1932, the index of national production had fallen from 102 to 73; the base of 100 had been set in 1927.

1931 Feb.   **American car manufacturers** were building bigger, more powerful cars, with eight cylinders replacing six in Buicks and Marmons. Cadillac was adding a twelve-cylinder model and already had a sixteen-cylinder model. The V-16 model Cadillac had a 148-inch wheel base.

1931 Mar. 21   The announcement of a plan for a **customs union of Germany and Austria** evoked furi-ous complaints from the nations that had fought against the Central Powers in World War I. Great Britain asked the **League of Nations** to take up the question of allowing this union. Faced with such strong opposition, Germany and Austria withdrew the plan on Sept. 3. Two days later the **World Court** decided that the union would have violated the 1919 peace treaties with the two nations.

1931 May 11   Austria's largest bank, the *Kreditanstalt*, **failed**, triggering a drastic worsening of the **Great Depression** in Central Europe. Austria went off the gold standard. The bank failure caused a government crisis in Austria and, as in Germany, economic distress played into the hands of extremists of both left and right.

1931 July 7   A one-year moratorium on the payment of intergovernmental debts and reparations stemming from World War I went into effect. It was proposed by **Herbert Hoover**, president of the U.S., and so was known as the **Hoover Moratorium**. It provided a temporary stimulus to financial markets, but as a result of the worsening of the Great Depression and the rise of the Nazis in Germany, payments were never resumed.

1931 July 13   The *Danatbank*, a key German financial institution, **failed**. In the wake of its collapse all banks in Germany closed until Aug. 5. By the end of 1931 c.6,000,000 Germans were out of work.

1931 Sept. 10   Mass unemployment, reduced unemployment benefits, and other austerity moves of the British government led to demonstrations in Glasgow, London, and other industrial centers. Most surprising of all, and a shock to Britons who thought of the Royal navy as the bulwark of England's defenses, sailors on Sept. 15 at Invergordon, Scotland, went on strike because their pay had been cut. The strike was shortlived but indicated how deeply the worldwide **Great Depression** was felt by those at the bottom of the economic ladder.

1931 Sept. 21   Great Britain, whose currency, the pound sterling, set monetary standards, went **off the gold standard**. This resulted in the devaluation of the pound from $4.86 in U.S. money to $3.49. Six days later, Egypt, Norway, and Sweden also went off the gold standard, and on Dec. 11 Japan made the same move. France and the U.S. clung to the gold basis for their currencies.

1931 Oct. 2   Thomas [Johnstone] Lipton (b. May 15, 1862), a British merchant and sportsman, died. He built up a chain of stores and became a millionaire by age 30. He became known all over the world for Lipton's tea, harvested at his plantation in Ceylon. As a yachtsman, Lipton raced American boats five times for the America's Cup with his yachts, all named *Shamrock* and all unsuccessful.

V. SCIENCE, EDUCATION, AND TECHNOLOGY

1931   Harold C. Urey (May 29, 1893–Jan. 6, 1981), an American chemist, discovered deuterium, or heavy hydrogen, an isotope of hydrogen. From this discovery came what was more popularly known as heavy water, water in which the hydrogen atoms are deuterium, or D_{20}. During World War II Urey was a leading figure in the development by the U.S. of the atomic bomb. He was awarded the Nobel prize for chemistry in 1934.

1931   Kurt Godel (Apr. 28, 1906–Jan. 14, 1978), an Austrian-born American mathematician, propounded what came to be known as Godel's Proof, a theorem in mathematical logic that some propositions cannot be proved on the basis of the axioms existing within the system itself. Thus an entirely self-consistent mathematical system is not possible, but propositions might be proved by logical systems outside mathematics.

1931 Feb.   Friedrich Bergius (Oct. 11, 1884–Mar. 30, 1949), a German chemist, was co-winner of the Nobel prize for chemistry. He worked on a process for converting coal into gasoline and oils. Co-winner of the Nobel prize for chemistry with Bergius was Karl Bosch (Aug. 27, 1874–Mar. 30, 1949), also of Germany, who synthesized ammonia commercially.

1931 Mar.   Hermann Oberth (b. June 25, 1894), a German astronautical engineer, born in Transylvania [now Romania], suggested that an artificial satellite could be sent into orbit about the earth at an altitude of c.500 miles and remain in such orbit by taking advantage of the forces of gravity and centrifugal force. He said such a satellite could send radio data back to stations on earth concerning weather, communications, and electrical phenomena. Oberth worked at Peenemünde, on the Baltic Sea in Germany, the center from 1937 to 1943 for rocket testing in Nazi Germany. He came to the U.S. in 1955.

1931 May 1   The Empire State Building in New York City opened to the public. With its 102 stories and 1,250 feet height, it surpassed the recently built Chrysler Building, also in New York, which was 1,046 feet high.

1931 May 9   Albert Abraham Michelson (b. Dec. 19, 1852), a Prussian-born American physicist, died. Over a period of time he conducted experiments that determined with great accuracy the speed of light. In 1887 the famous Michelson-Morley experiment provided a starting point for the later development of the theory of relativity. In 1907 Michelson received the Nobel prize for physics, the first American to be given this honor.

1931 May 27   The first ascent by man into the stratosphere was made by Auguste Piccard (Jan. 28, 1884–Mar. 24, 1962), a Swiss physicist, and a companion. They made the ascent in a balloon that included an airtight gondola Piccard invented. The balloonists reached an altitude of 51,793 feet. The next year Piccard made another ascent to an altitude of 53,171 feet.

1931 June 23–July 1   Wiley Post and Harold Gatty (Jan. 5, 1903–Aug. 30, 1957), two American aviators, flew around the world in their monoplane *Winnie Mae* in 8 days, 15 hrs., 13 min. They took off from Roosevelt Field, Long Island, New York, and returned there after flying a distance of 15,475 miles. Between July 15 and 22, 1933, Post made the first solo flight around the world in the same airplane. He flew 15,596 miles, in 7 days, 18 hrs., 49 min.

1931 July   Aircraft capable of flying at more than 30,000 feet of altitude and at higher speeds at those altitudes were being built at the Junkerswerke in Dessau, Germany. They were machines with a single motor, a 60-foot wingspan, and a weight of $2\frac{1}{2}$ tons.

1931 Oct.   The death rate from childbirth was higher in the U.S. than in any other of the 20 nations with available statistics. The lowest figure, Denmark and Italy, was 2.6 per 1,000 births, in the U.S. the rate reached 6.6 per 1,000. Howard Wilcox Haggard (July 9, 1891–Apr. 22, 1959), a physiologist and teacher at Yale University, said medical services were not available, mostly because of distances, to most American mothers.

1931 Oct. 4–5 The **first nonstop flight across the Pacific Ocean** was made by two American pilots, **Hugh Herndon** (Oct. 3, 1904–Apr. 5, 1952) and **Clyde Pangborn** (Oct. 28, 1894–Mar. 29, 1958). They took off from Sabishiro Beach, Japan, and landed at Wenatchee, Washington, after 41 hrs., 13 min. They flew 4,860 miles.

1931 Oct. 18 **Thomas Alva Edison** (b. Feb. 11, 1847), an American inventor, died. Edison amassed more than 1,300 U.S. and foreign patents. He said his favorite was the **phonograph**, patented in 1878. The concept of recording sound and playing it back again had never before been registered with the U.S. Patent Office. Edison's other achievements included the light bulb, an improved telephone (1877), and the kinetoscope motion picture camera and viewer.

1931 Nov. In the first public use of the **Sperry gyropilot**, developed by **Elmer Ambrose Sperry** (Oct. 12, 1860–June 16, 1930), an American electrical engineer, which could do everything but land and take off, the pilot of an **Eastern Air Transport Company** transport plane, carrying 18 passengers, took off from Newark Airport in New Jersey, set a compass course for Washington, D.C., threw a switch, and walked out of the cockpit while the plane remained safely and fully on course. He used the same technique to return to Newark.

1931 Nov. 21 The system of communication called **teletype** [teleprinter, teletypewriter] came into use on a general commercial basis with the establishment of the **Teletypewriter Exchange Service** [TWX]. The use of the telegraph was largely superseded by teletype.

VI. ARTS AND LEISURE

1931 Jan. 23 **Anna** [Matveyevna] **Pavlova** (b. Jan. 31, 1881), an internationally renowned Russian ballerina, died. She made her debut in Russia in 1899 and, after achieving wide acclaim at appearances in several European capitals, she danced in 1909 in Paris with the Ballet Russe. Pavlova made her American debut in 1910, after which she formed her own company, in which she excelled in such ballets as *Giselle* and *The Dying Swan*.

1931 Feb. 23 **Nellie Melba** [orig.: Helen Porter Mitchell] (b. May 19, 1859), an Australian operatic soprano, died. She appeared in many parts of the world but sang chiefly at Covent Garden, London,

from 1888, and the Metropolitan Opera, New York City, from 1893. Melba was best known for her coloratura and lyric roles, as in *Rigoletto* and *Lucia di Lammermoor*.

1931 Mar. 27 **Arnold Bennett** (b. May 27, 1867), an English novelist, died. *The Old Wives' Tales* (1908) and *Clayhanger* (1910) were perhaps his most enduring volumes.

1931 Apr. 10 **Kahlil Gibran** (b. Jan. 6, 1883), an expatriate Lebanese writer, poet, and painter, died in New York City. *The Prophet* (1923) was the most popular of his works.

1931 May 5 The **Sadler's Wells Ballet**, later to become the **Royal Ballet**, gave its first performance at the **Old Vic** Theater in London. The ballet got its start when **Lilian Baylis** (May 9, 1874–Nov. 25, 1937), who operated the Sadler's Wells Theater, asked **Ninnette de Valois** [Edris Stannus] (b. June 6, 1898), an Irish teacher of dance, to organize a dance group.

1931 May 14 **David Belasco** (b. July 25, 1853), an American theatrical producer and playwright, died. Belasco's long career in New York City began in 1882, where he became an independent producer in 1895. He wrote (often with a collaborator) such plays as *The Heart of Maryland* (1895), *Madame Butterfly* (1900), on which Puccini based his opera, and *Laugh, Clown, Laugh* (1923).

1931 Aug. 7 [Leon Bismarck] **Bix Beiderbecke** (b. Mar. 10, 1903), an American jazz musician, died. He was a pianist and composer, but it was his brilliance as a cornetist that won him lasting fame.

1931 Oct. 2 **Carl August Nielsen** (b. June 9, 1865), a leading composer and conductor of Denmark, died. His works included the operas *Saul and David* (1903) and *Maskerade* (1907). He was the conductor of the **Danish Royal Symphony Orchestra** at Copenhagen (1908–1927).

1931 Oct. 7 **Daniel Chester French** (b. Apr. 20, 1850), an American sculptor, died. In 1875 he produced one of his best-known works, *The Minute Man*, at Concord, Massachusetts. French did equestrian statues of Ulysses S. Grant and George Washington, portrait busts of Edgar Allan Poe and Ralph Waldo Emerson, and symbolic works, such as *Alma Mater* (1915) for Columbia University, New York

City. Probably his most admired work today is the large, seated Lincoln (1922) in the **Lincoln Memorial**, Washington, D.C.

1931 Oct. 21 Arthur Schnitzler (b. May 15, 1862), an Austrian playwright and novelist, died. He was an important figure in the Austrian theater of psychological dramas, in which he often explored sexual themes. His best-known dramatic work was **Anatol** (1910).

1931 Dec. 2 [Paul Marie Théodore] **Vincent d'Indy** (b. Mar. 27, 1851), a French romantic composer, died. He wrote much chamber music, several operas, and symphonies. Perhaps d'Indy's most popular work was **Symphonie sur un chant de montagnard français** (1886).

1931 Dec. 5 [Nicholas] **Vachel Lindsay** (b. Nov. 10, 1879), an American poet, died. His works included **General William Booth Enters Into Heaven and Other Poems** (1913) and **The Congo and Other Poems** (1914).

VII. SPORTS, GAMES, AND SOCIETY

1931 The **Fédération Internationale du Tir à l'Arc** was formed to conduct annual **archery competition in Europe**. The founding countries were Great Britain, France, Sweden, Czechoslovakia, and Hungary.

1931 Feb. 4 Malcolm Campbell (Mar. 11, 1885–Jan. 1, 1949) raced his specially built speedster "Bluebird" over the sands of Daytona Beach,

Florida, at 245.733 miles per hour, a world record for land vehicles. The Bluebird's engine was a twelve-cylinder British Napier-Lion aviation engine said to be rated at 1,450 horsepower.

1931 Mar. 25 Nine black youths were arrested in Scottsboro, Alabama, on charges of having raped two white girls while riding a freight train. All were found guilty and were sentenced to death or to prison terms of up to 99 years. The **U.S. Supreme Court** twice reversed their convictions on procedural grounds and at a second trial one of the girls recanted her testimony. Charges against five were dropped and three were later freed. Liberals and radicals seized on the **Scottsboro Case**, which became a **symbol of the bigotry** and injustice to blacks in the American South.

1931 Mar. 31 Knute [Kenneth] **Rockne** (b. Mar. 4, 1888), the Norwegian-born football coach at **Notre Dame University**, died in an airplane crash in Kansas. From 1918, across 13 seasons, Rockne coached the Notre Dame **"Fighting Irish,"** who won 105 games, lost 12, tied five, and won fans across the nation for the hitherto little-known Catholic college.

1931 May 6 The **French Colonial Exposition** opened in Paris. The products and the people of France's far-flung colonies in Africa, Asia, and the Pacific were on view. Represented were the c.100,000,000 inhabitants of the **French Empire**. France, one official said, was expressing its thanks for the several hundred thousand colonial troops who fought for France in World War I.

1932

I. DISASTERS

1932–1933 For the second time within a decade, Russia suffered a devastating **famine caused by drought**, which was worsened by a disrupted agricultural system. **Joseph Stalin**, general secretary of the Communist party, refused to divert export grain to relieve the peasants of the Volga German Autonomous S.S.R. and the Ukrainian S.S.R. because they had resisted Soviet efforts to collectivize their farms. It was estimated that from 3 to 10 million **starved**.

1932 Mar. 21 Twenty-seven **tornadoes struck the American states** of Alabama, Georgia, Mississippi, and Tennessee killing 321 persons and doing about $5,500,000 of property damage.

1932 Nov. 9 About 2,500 of the c.4,000 inhabitants of Santa Cruz del Sur, a town on the southern coast of Cuba, died during a **hurricane** and the resulting tidal waves. The town itself was destroyed.

1932 Dec. 26 An **earthquake** killed 70,000 in Kansu [Gansu] province, in central northern China. It registered 7.5 on the Richter scale.

II. POLITICS AND WAR

1932 **Ibn Saud**, sultan of Nejd and king of Hejaz, a member of the **Wahabi Dynasty** (1735 to the present), established the **Kingdom of Saudi Arabia**, comprised of Nejd and Hejaz, with himself as king.

1932 Jan. 7 In response to **Japan's occupation** (from Sept., 1931) **of Manchuria**, **Henry L**[ewis] **Stimson** (Sept. 21, 1867–Oct. 20, 1950), U.S. secretary of state, informed Japan and China that the U.S. would not recognize Japanese rule over any territory it conquered. Stimson's diplomatic note also reaffirmed the **Open Door policy** enunciated unilaterally in 1899 by the U.S. and confirmed in the Nine-Power Treaty. Nevertheless, the Japanese landed (Jan. 22) a large military force at Shanghai, declared (Feb. 18) Manchuria independent as the **republic of Manchukuo**, and installed (Mar. 9) Henry Pu-Yi, former emperor of China, as regent over Manchukuo, as they renamed Manchuria. Japan proclaimed (Sept. 15) Manchukuo a protectorate and made Pu-Yi emperor of Manchukuo on Feb. 28, 1934.

1932 Jan. 21 A **Finnish-Soviet Non-Aggression Pact** was signed, guaranteeing the borders established by the **Peace of Dorpat** in 1920.

1932 Feb. 16 The **Republican** [Fianna Fáil] **party** was victorious in an election to the **Dáil** [parliament] of the **Irish Free State**. The leader of the victors was **Éamon de Valéra** (Oct. 14, 1882–Aug. 23, 1975), who on Mar. 9 was elected president of the Dáil. He immediately abolished the oath of allegiance to the British crown.

1932 Mar. 13 **Paul von Hindenburg** failed to receive a majority vote in his bid for reelection as German president. **Adolf Hitler** of the National Socialist party was second. In a runoff election on Apr. 10, Hindenburg acquired the majority. On May 31, Heinrich Bruning, the chancellor [prime minister] of Germany, resigned. The new chancellor was **Franz von Papen** (Oct. 29, 1879–May 2, 1969), a soldier and diplomat, who organized a ministry made up mostly of members of the nobility and excluded Nazis. When elections were held for the Reichstag on July 31, Hitler's party won 230 seats, the Socialists 133, the Center 97, and the Communists 89. On Aug. 31, Hindenburg offered Hitler the vice chancellorship but he refused. The **Reichstag was dissolved** on Sept. 12, but another election on Nov. 6 did not break the deadlock and on Nov. 17 von Papen resigned as

chancellor. Hindenburg offered the chancellorship to Hitler, but with conditions of limited power. Hitler refused. On Dec. 2 **Kurt von Schleicher**, a soldier and politician, was named chancellor (to Jan., 1933), the **last chancellor of the Weimer Republic**. The year ended with the Nazis pushing nearer their goal of absolute political power.

1932 May 7 **Paul Doumer** (b. Mar. 22, 1857), president of France (from 1931), was assassinated by a Russian émigré who was apparently mentally unbalanced. Doumer had been in politics since 1888 and was governor general (1896–1902) of French Indochina. Doumer was succeeded (May 10) by **Albert Lebrun** (Aug. 29, 1871–Mar. 6, 1950), who was currently president of the Senate. Lebrun proved to be the **last president of the Third Republic** (1870–1940).

1932 May 16 **Tsuyoshi Inukai** (b. 1885), prime minister of Japan since January, was assassinated by military reactionaries who opposed his policy restricting the army's powers in Manchuria. Inukai's death **ended the government of Japan by political parties** until after World War II. He was succeeded (to 1934) by **Makoto Saito** (Nov. 13, 1859–Feb. 26, 1936), an admiral and a moderate among the militarists.

1932 May 20 **Engelbert Dollfuss** (Oct. 4, 1892–July 25, 1934), leader of the Christian Socialist party, became chancellor of Austria. He was pledged to maintain the independence of Austria and was strongly opposed to *Anschluss* [union] with Germany, partly because he disliked Adolf Hitler's **National Socialism**. But Dollfuss became more authoritarian and sought the support of fascist Italy.

1932 May 29 The first contingent of c.1,000 men of the so-called **Bonus Army**, soon to number c.17,000, arrived in Washington, D.C., demanding immediate full payment of their World War I bonus certificates, not officially due until 1945. Jobless, and practically penniless, they camped in open areas and unused buildings, and they vowed to remain until their demands were met. The House approved payment, but the Senate refused; they did approve funds for the veterans' return trips home. When c.2,000 refused to leave, federal troops under General **Douglas MacArthur** drove them out on July 28.

1932 June 24 In **Siam** [present Thailand] a bloodless military coup d'état led by **Luang Pibul Song-**

gram (July 14, 1897–June 11, 1964) forced the absolute monarch Prajadhipok (Nov. 8, 1893–May 31, 1941), who ruled as Rama VII, king of Siam (1925–1935), to grant a constitution, which was approved on Dec. 10. The first general elections were held in 1934.

1932 July 5 **António de Oliviera Salazar** (Apr. 28, 1889–July 27, 1970) became prime minister of **Portugal**, later assuming virtual dictatorship by promulgating a new constitution which went into effect on Feb. 22, 1933.

1932 Sept. 26 **Per Albin Hansson** (Oct. 29, 1885–Oct. 5, 1946), leader (from 1952) of the Social Democratic party of **Sweden**, became prime minister (to 1946). This marked the beginning of 44 consecutive years of rule by the Social Democrats, although at times, when they did not secure an outright majority in the **Riksdag** [parliament], they formed coalitions with other parties.

1932 Oct. 3 **Iraq**, having gained formal independence from Great Britain, was admitted to the **League of Nations** as an independent kingdom headed by **Faisal I** [Feisul], a member of the **Hashimite Dynasty**, who had been placed on the throne by Great Britain in 1921. On June 30, 1930, a treaty of alliance between Great Britain and Iraq had established a British airbase at Habbaniya [Hawr al-Habbaniyah] on the Euphrates River in central Iraq, and British control over Iraq's foreign policy.

1932 Oct. 4 **Julius Gömbös** (Dec. 26, 1886–Oct. 6, 1936), a soldier and minister of war in the **Hungarian government** since 1921, became premier. He promoted an authoritarian, anti-Semitic policy.

III. ECONOMY AND TRADE

1932 **Oil was found in Bahrain** [Bahrein], an archipelago in the Persian Gulf. The sultanate's production began with the granting (May, 1934) of a concession to **Standard Oil of California**.

1932 Jan. 22 The **Reconstruction Finance Corporation** [RFC] was set up with $2,000,000,000 at its disposal to help finance economic recovery in the U.S. It extended credit to financial institutions, such as banks, insurance companies, building and loan societies, farm mortgage associations, and railroads.

1932 July 8 The **Dow Jones Industrial stock average** in the U.S. **reached its Great Depression low** of 41.22.

1932 Mar. 12 **Ivar Kreuger** (b. Mar. 2, 1880), a leading world financier, committed suicide. Born in Kalmar, Sweden, Kreuger gained a near monopoly in the match industry of Europe, and controlled more than 250 factories in 43 nations. The concern also owned banks, forests, pulp mills, and iron and gold mines. In exchange for grants of monopolies he loaned money to various governments, including $125 million to the German *Reichstag* on Jan. 28, 1930. Defaults on such loans during the **Great Depression** years caused him to resort to many shady deals and fraudulent expedients, which led to the collapse of his financial empire.

1932 Dec. The **Reconstruction Finance Corporation** authorized a loan of $62 million for the construction of a **San Francisco-Oakland bridge** with California providing $70 million and agreeing to operate and maintain the bridge. It was expected to provide employment for 12,000 men.

IV. SCIENCE, EDUCATION, AND TECHNOLOGY

1932 The initial section of the *autobahn*, the **first really modern highway system**, was opened, running from Cologne to Bonn, Germany. The *autobahn* featured four-lane roadways, separated by wide median strips, and with limited access entrances and exits. They were engineered for speeds of more than 100 mph. When the **Nazis** came (1932) to power they recognized the military value of such roads and sped their construction.

1932 **Charles Edward Kenneth Mees** (May 26, 1882–Aug. 15, 1960), research director of the **Eastman Kodak Laboratories** at Rochester, New York, **demonstrated photographic plates** sensitized with a new chemical, **xenocyanine**, which could photograph hitherto invisible heat rays. With such plates, new lines have now been photographed in the spectra of 36 chemical elements, and astronomers hope to gather more information about dark stars.

1932 **Karl Jansky** (Oct. 22, 1905–Feb. 14, 1950), an American physicist, detected **radio waves from outside the solar system** while working for **Bell Telephone** laboratories. This was the beginning of the science of radio astronomy.

1932   The **positron**, the first documented antiparticle, was discovered by **Carl David Anderson** (b. Sept. 3, 1905), an American physicist, for which he shared the **Nobel prize for physics** in 1936. Anderson observed the energy produced when an electron collided with a positron. His work confirmed the version of quantum mechanics proposed by Paul Adrien Maurice Dirac in 1928.

1932   The **neutron** was discovered by **James Chadwick** (Oct. 20, 1891–July 24, 1974), an English physicist. Chadwick received the **Nobel prize for physics** in 1935.

1932 Mar. 14   George Eastman (b. July 12, 1854), the American inventor, committed suicide in Rochester, New York. Eastman had introduced the **first Kodak camera**, and from 1888 was instrumental in developing amateur photography as a popular hobby. In 1884 Eastman established a manufacturing company at Rochester and began producing his camera and processing the transparent, flexible film he also introduced at this time. By 1927, he had a virtual monopoly of the photographic industry. Eastman donated approximately $100 million to both the **University of Rochester** and the **Massachusetts Institute of Technology** [MIT].

1932 Mar. 14   Frederick Jackson Turner (b. Nov. 14, 1861), an American historian, died. In July, 1893, he read before a meeting of the American Historical Association, Chicago, Illinois, a paper entitled "**The Significance of the Frontier in American History**." It stated that the frontier, as it moved steadily east to west from the Atlantic to the Pacific oceans, had been the most important influence in shaping the nation and its history. Turner's thesis gradually became a dominant theme in most writing on American history.

1932 Apr.   Announcement was made of the identification and isolation of **vitamin C** [ascorbic acid]. The discovery was largely the work of **Albert von Szent-Györgyi** [von Nagyrapolt] (b. Sept. 16, 1893), a Hungarian-born American biochemist, and **Charles King** (b. Oct. 22, 1896), an American chemist. Szent-Györgyi received the **Nobel prize for physiology** or medicine in 1937.

1932 Apr. 17   Patrick Geddes (b. Oct. 2, 1854), a Scottish sociologist and biologist, died. He was active in city planning and had designed living arrangements at **Edinburgh University** for sociological studies. The **Hebrew University** in Jerusalem was designed by Geddes.

1932 May 20–21   Amelia Earhart, an American aviator, became the **first woman to make a solo flight across the Atlantic Ocean**. She flew from Harbor Grace, Newfoundland, to near Londonderry, Ireland, a distance of 2,026½ miles in 13 hrs., 30 min.

1932 July   John Douglas Cockcroft (May 27, 1897–Sept. 18, 1967) and **E.T.S. Walton** (b. Oct. 6, 1903) **successfully split the atom** in the Cavendish laboratories at Cambridge, England, opening the way to the release of tremendous forces. This discovery led **Oliver** [Joseph] **Lodge** (June 12, 1851–Aug. 22, 1940), an English physicist and noted researcher of psychic phenomena, to express the opinion that control of the phenomenon might fall into the hands of the military.

1932 Aug. 18   James A. Mollison (Apr. 19, 1905–Oct. 30, 1959), a British pilot, made the **first westbound solo flight of the Atlantic Ocean**, going from Portmarnock, Ireland, to Pennfield, New Brunswick. He flew a de Haviland Puss Moth.

VI. ARTS AND LEISURE

1932   The **Waterton-Glacier International Peace Park** was established. It encompassed the Waterton Lakes National Park in Alberta province and the adjoining Glacier National Park in Montana, a total of 1,013,332 acres.

1932 Jan. 21   [Giles] **Lytton Strachey** (b. Mar. 1, 1880), an English biographer, died. Among his best known works were *Eminent Victorians* (1918), *Queen Victoria* (1921), and *Elizabeth and Essex* (1928).

1932 Mar. 5   John Philip Sousa (b. Nov. 6, 1854), an American bandleader and composer, known as the "March King," died. Sousa composed more than 100 marches, among the best known of which are "**Semper Fidelis**" (1888) and "**The Stars and Stripes Forever**" (1897).

1932 Apr. 13   The central committee of the Communist party of the U.S.S.R. declared that all artists' organizations in the Soviet Union were to join the **Union of Soviet Artists** in order to effect greater ideological control over the expression of socialist realism.

1932 Apr. 27 [Harold] **Hart Crane** (b. July 21, 1899), an American poet, committed suicide by leaping from a ship on which he was returning to the U.S. from Mexico. He published only two volumes of poetry in his short lifetime, but they were enough to bring him substantial recognition: *White Buildings* (1926) and *The Bridge* (1930).

1932 May 22 Isabella Augusta Gregory [Lady Gregory, nee Persse] (b. Mar. 5, 1852), an Irish playwright, died. With **William Butler Yeats** and others she founded the **Irish National Theater Society** in 1899 [Abbey Theater, 1904]. She collaborated with Yeats in writing several prose plays, including *Cathleen ni Houlihan* (1902) and *The Pot of Broth* (1902). She translated from Gaelic and wrote many plays, including *The Gaol Gate* (1906), and *Hanrahan's Oath* (1918).

1932 July 22 Florenz Ziegfeld (b. Mar. 21, 1869), an American theatrical producer, famous for his elaborate staging and the beautiful women appearing in his shows, died. In 1907 he set a new standard for light entertainment with the first of the **Ziegfeld Follies**, produced almost every year thereafter for 24 years. In these shows he introduced such performers as Anna Held, Billie Burke, Eddie Cantor, and W.C. Fields.

1932 Dec. 6 Eugène Brieux (b. Jan. 19, 1858), a French playwright, died. Brieux, one of the most popular playwrights in France, specialized in plays with a social message. His first success was *Blanchette* (1892), which attacked teacher-training schools. *Les avariés* [*Damaged Goods*] (1902) was banned in France, Great Britain, and the U.S. for its realistic discussion on the danger of venereal disease. His other plays included *La Robe Rouge* [*The Red Robe: The Letter of the Law*] (1900), *Simone* (1908), and *La Femme seule* (1912).

V. SPORTS, GAMES, AND SOCIETY

1932 "Brother, Can You Spare a Dime?" composed by **Jay Gorney** (Dec. 12, 1896–June 14, 1990), with lyrics by **E.Y. Harburg** (Apr. 8, 1898–Mar. 5, 1981), was one of the most popular songs of the year.

1932 Feb. 4–15 The third Winter **Olympic Games** were held at Lake Placid, New York, with 17 nations sending 306 athletes. The U.S. won 6 gold medals and 12 medals overall; Norway 3 and 10; and Sweden 1 and 3. The star of the games was **Sonja Henie** (Apr. 8, 1912–Oct. 12, 1969), a Norwegian figure skater, who won the women's figure skating title for a second time.

1932 Mar. 1 Charles A. Lindbergh, Jr., the 20-month-old son of the noted aviator and his wife, was kidnapped from the couple's home in Hopewell, New Jersey. On May 12, after a $50,000 ransom demand had been met, the baby's body was found about five miles from Hopewell. On Sept. 19, 1934, **Bruno Richard Hauptmann** (b. Nov. 26, 1900), a carpenter and an immigrant from Germany, who was found in possession of some of the ransom money, was tried, convicted, and on Apr. 3, 1936, electrocuted as the perpetrator of the crime.

1932 June 21 Jack Sharkey of the U.S. regained the world **heavyweight boxing championship** by defeating the champion **Max Schmeling** of Germany at Long Island City, New York. Sharkey won on an unpopular split decision after 15 rounds.

1932 July 3–Aug. 14 The tenth Summer **Olympic Games** were held in Los Angeles, California, with 37 nations and 1,408 athletes competing. The U.S. won 41 gold medals and 104 medals in all; Italy 12 and 36; France 10 and 19; and Sweden 9 and 23. Because of the **Great Depression** the number of athletes and nations competing was the smallest since 1906.

1933

I. DISASTERS

1933 Mar. 10 An **earthquake centered at Long Beach, California,** left 117 dead and more than 4,000 injured.

1933 Apr. 4 The U.S. navy **dirigible Akron went down** off Barnegat Light, New Jersey, killing 73 men. Only four survived. There was a storm at the time, and the airship may have been hit by lightning.

II. POLITICS AND WAR

1933 Jan. 13 The **Howes-Cutting Act**, passed by the U.S. Congress, provided for complete **independence for the Philippines** in ten years. **Herbert Hoover**, president of the U.S., vetoed the measure, but it was overridden by Congress. The act was **rejected by the Philippine legislature** in October.

1933 Jan. 30 **Adolf Hitler** was appointed chancellor by **Paul von Hindenburg**, president of Germany. In a new election for members of the **Reichstag** on Mar. 5, although the Nazis did not win a clear majority of the seats, they controlled with their Nationalist [Deutschnationale Volkspartei] allies more than half. On Mar. 23 Hitler demanded and received from the Reichstag the right to rule by decree for four years. This gave Hitler the power to change the constitution as he wished, and by various decrees the **Weimar Republic** was brought to an end before the year was out.

1933 Feb. 27–28 During the night a **fire** of still undetermined origin almost totally **destroyed the Reichstag building** in Berlin. The **Nazis** asserted that the communists had set the fire, although there was some reason for suspecting that the Nazis themselves had done it to have an excuse for crushing the communists. They persuaded Paul von Hindenburg, president of Germany, to suspend constitutional guarantees of free speech, free press, and other rights and to outlaw the Communist party. A young, mentally handicapped Dutchman, Marinus van der Lubbe, was charged with the arson. He was convicted and on Jan. 10, 1934, beheaded. On Dec. 15, 1980, a court in West Berlin declared him innocent.

1933 Mar. 4 **Franklin Delano Roosevelt** of the Democratic party was inaugurated as the 32nd president of the U.S. In the election of Nov. 8, 1932, he received 22,821,857 popular votes and 472 electoral votes to 15,761,841 and 59 for his Republican opponent **Herbert Hoover**. **John Nance Garner** was sworn in as vice president. In his much admired inaugural address, Roosevelt said: "Let me assert my firm belief that the only thing we have to fear is fear itself."

1933 Mar. 27 Following a report (Feb. 25) by the **League of Nations** censuring it for its **invasion of Manchuria**, **Japan** announced it was resigning from the League, giving two years' notice. Japan's withdrawal marked the beginning of the collapse of the League as influential in international affairs.

1933 Mar. 31–Nov. 8 The inauguration of **Franklin D. Roosevelt** as president of the U.S. brought to national power the **"New Deal"** he had promised during his campaign for the office. The first three months of his administration came to be called "**The Hundred Days.**" Actually the process of change continued long after that. The Congress passed a variety of laws Roosevelt requested: Mar. 31, the **Civilian Conservation Corps** [CCC], to create jobs for young men and to aid in the conservation of forests; May 12, the **Agricultural Adjustment Act** [AAA], to aid farmers by restricting the production of certain crops and livestock, paying for land left idle; May 12, the **Federal Emergency Relief Act** [FERA], appropriating federal funds for the direct relief of needy individuals; June 16, the **National Industrial Recovery Act** [NIRA], which suspended the anti-trust laws and allowed the setting of wages and standards of fair business practices; the **Public Works Administration**, part of NIRA, to create jobs by constructing public buildings, housing, and other facilities; June 16, The **Banking Act of 1933**, which established the Federal Deposit Insurance Corporation [FDIC]; and, Nov. 8, the **Civil Works Administration** [CWA], to provide jobs, mostly of an unskilled nature, for c.4,000,000 unemployed.

1933 Apr. 1 The **Nazi government of Germany ordered a boycott of Jewish businesses**. Jewish lawyers and physicians were forbidden to practice their professions. On Apr. 7 all Jews were ordered removed from government positions. Leaders of independent trade unions were arrested on May 2 and their headquarters closed.

1933 Apr. 5 **Greenland** was returned to **Denmark** by a World Court decision. On July 10, 1931, Norway had annexed the eastern part of Greenland.

1933 May 10 **Paraguay declared war on Bolivia** over the Gran Chaco [Chaco; Chaco Boreal], an oil-bearing region west of the Paraguay River. In 1932 fighting had again erupted in this area, which had seen sporadic violence and continual dispute for c.85 years.

1933 May 10 The **Nazis staged a massive book burning** in a square opposite the University of Berlin to express their hate for Jews, liberals, and intellectuals in general. Some 20,000 books were thrown into the flames, including works by Thomas Mann, Erich Maria Remarque, Sigmund Freud, and H.G. Wells.

1933 May 28 The **National Socialists of Danzig** [present Gdansk], allies of the German Nazis, won an election in the free city. They took over the government on June 20. On Aug. 5 Poland made an agreement with the city government that presumably would give Poles fair treatment.

1933 July 14 The **National Socialist party was proclaimed the only legal political group in Germany.** The Communists were outlawed after the Reichstag fire in February, the Socialists on May 10, while the Nationalist and Catholic parties dissolved of their own accord. A new press law required that all newspaper editors be Aryan and that they not be married to a Jew. On Nov. 12 the **Nazis**, as the only legal party, won all the seats in the Reichstag in a new election, receiving 92 percent of the vote. The remaining voters cast invalid ballots.

1933 Aug. **Fulgencio Batista y Zaldívar** (Jan. 16, 1901–Aug. 6, 1973) headed a coup that ousted **Gerardo Machado y Morales** (Sept. 29, 1871–Mar. 29, 1939) from office as president (1925–1933) of **Cuba.** As Cuba's strongman Batista was virtually dictator throughout a series of administrations until he was elected president (1940).

1933 Sept. 8 **Faisal I** [Feisal] (b. 1885), king of Iraq (1921–1933), died. Beginning in 1916 he participated actively in the revolt against the **Ottoman Empire** (1326–1920) and cooperated with the British in World War I campaigns that resulted in the capture of Jerusalem (1917) and Damascus (1918). A Syrian national congress had proclaimed (Mar., 1920) him king, but the French, who held the League of Nations mandate for **Syria**, deposed him in July, 1920. The next year the British, who held the mandate for **Iraq**, chose him for the throne of that country. Faisal was succeeded by his son Ghazi I (Mar. 12, 1912– Apr. 4, 1939), king of Iraq (to 1939).

1933 Oct. 10 The **nations of the Western Hemisphere**, at Rio de Janeiro, Brazil, signed a treaty of nonaggression and conciliation. In his inaugural address in March, **Franklin D. Roosevelt**, president of the U.S., dedicated his country to **"the policy of the good neighbor"** in its relations with the other lands of North and South America. For many years most of Latin America had looked upon the U.S. as an imperialistic nation that intervened at will in the affairs of its neighbors. On Dec. 3, 1933, at Montevideo, Uruguay, the U.S. joined in a treaty with other American nations which declared that no state had the right to interfere in the internal affairs of another.

1933 Oct. 14 **Germany withdrew from the League of Nations** and began unrestrained rearmament, both to revive the ailing economy and to give the **Third Reich** (to 1945) a dominant role in European affairs. The act was described by **Adolf Hitler** as a protest against British and French duplicity in dealing with Germany, attempting to keep it a second class nation.

1933 Nov. 8 **Nadir Khan** (b. Apr. 10, 1880), king of **Afghanistan**, was assassinated. He was succeeded by his eldest son **Zahir Khan** (b. Oct. 15, 1914), who was only 19. For some years the country was run by several of his uncles.

1933 Nov. 16 The **U.S. granted formal recognition to the U.S.S.R.** for the first time. There had been much hostility to Soviet propaganda and revolutionary activities, but this feeling had died down by the 1930s, and **Franklin D. Roosevelt**, president of the U.S., favored recognition.

1933 Nov. 19 The **first general election** to the **Cortes** [parliament] since **Spain** became (1931) a republic gave the parties of the right [Conservative Republicans, Clericals, and Monarchists] 44 percent of the vote. Parties of the left received 21 percent. While there was thus a shift to the right, the political situation remained unstable, with unpopular coalitions in office. On July 24 c.500 people had been arrested for taking part in an alleged revolutionary plot. **Manuel Azana y Diaz** (Jan. 10, 1880–Nov. 4, 1940), premier since 1931, resigned on Sept. 8. On Dec. 9, an anarchist uprising was put down with 42 deaths and several hundred persons wounded.

1933 Dec. 5 The **Twenty-First Amendment to the U.S. Constitution** was adopted, repealing Prohibition, the Eighteenth Amendment, passed in 1919.

1933 Dec. 21 **Great Britain took over the government of Newfoundland**, hitherto self-governing, because of the collapse of its economy. Government mismanagement and the general problems of the Great Depression were to blame.

III. ECONOMICS AND TRADE

1933 **Minimum wage legislation was enacted in Costa Rica**, making Costa Rica one of the most socially progressive Central American republics.

1933 Jan. 1 The **Second Five-Year Plan of the U.S.S.R.** for managing every detail of the proposed expansion of the economy, both in industry and agriculture, began. Like the First Five-Year Plan, it emphasized mining, industrial production, and the construction of electric power facilities at the expense of consumer goods. Also within the plans there took place the enforced **collectivization of Russian agriculture**, but the second plan allowed for a somewhat larger proportion of consumer goods, badly needed by the Russian people. Because of the unsettled condition of European affairs in the mid-1930s, changes were made in the second plan to increase the production of military equipment. The Russian authorities claimed great success for these plans, and overall Russia made great strides in catching up with the rest of the industrial world.

1933 Mar. 5 One of **Franklin D. Roosevelt's** first acts as president of the U.S. was to declare a **national bank "holiday,"** a euphemism for shutting down the whole banking system before it was completely ruined by nervous depositors. Depositors were withdrawing large sums, and governors of a number of states had already declared such holidays. Among them on Mar. 4 was New York, the center of finance. Calling Congress into session on Mar. 9, Roosevelt presented the legislators with the **Emergency Banking Act**, which they passed in a matter of hours. The law in effect took the U.S. off the gold standard by forbidding the export of gold and the redemption of currency in gold, and by penalizing the hoarding of gold. By Mar. 15 half the banks, representing c.90 percent of all banking resources, were allowed to reopen. About one in 20 were in such poor condition that they never did reopen. In the first three weeks after reopening, banks received more than $1,000,000,000 that depositors brought back to them. Thus, the feared nationwide panic did not occur.

1933 Apr. 22 **Frederick Henry Royce** (b. Mar. 27, 1863), a British engineer and automobile pioneer, died. Royce in 1906 joined with **Charles Stewart Rolls** (Aug. 28, 1877–July 12, 1910), another pioneer in the automobile field, to form the **Rolls-Royce** company. Rolls was the first person to fly across the English Channel and back nonstop. In that same year he died in a plane crash, becoming the first Englishman to be killed in such an accident.

1933 May 18 The **Tennessee Valley Authority** [TVA] was established in the U.S. to improve conditions along the Tennessee River and its tributaries, a 40,000 square-mile area including parts of seven states. Functioning as an independent public corporation, the TVA initiated a program of dam building in order to prevent floods, open waterways to increased traffic, and supply cheap electricity.

1933 May 29 **Saudi Arabia granted the Standard Oil Company of California a 60-year oil concession**. In the following year the **Arabian-American Oil Company** [ARAMCO] was established by Standard Oil and the **Texas Company** to exploit potential Arabian oil resources.

1933 June 12 The **World Monetary and Economic Conference**, with delegates from 64 nations, convened in London to discuss ways of reviving world trade. On the agenda were the problems of stabilizing currencies and reducing tariff barriers. Countries still on the gold standard, led by France, argued for a return to that standard before any other steps were taken. Great Britain and the U.S. led the opposing view, although Roosevelt, the president of the U.S., was at the start of the conference considered willing to be conciliatory. However, on July 3 he sent a message to the conference that in effect torpedoed it. Roosevelt wanted to keep the U.S. free to alter the gold value of the dollar in order to control its purchasing power. The conference disbanded on July 27. The failure of the conference led to more economic protectionism, thereby extending some of the underlying causes of the **Great Depression**.

1933 Nov. The 70-story **RCA Building**, centerpiece of Rockefeller Center, in the heart of Manhattan, New York City, opened. In all, between 1931 and 1939, 14 structures were put up with an **art deco motif in the architecture**. The Rockefeller family interests were the developers of the 12-acre site, the land then being owned by Columbia University. The National Broadcasting Company moved into the complex, and its area became known as Radio City. Another imposing part of the center was **Radio City Music Hall**, seating 6,000 patrons.

IV. RELIGION AND PHILOSOPHY

1933 Leo Baeck (May 23, 1873–Nov. 2, 1956), a rabbi in Berlin, **organized an association to help Jews emigrate** from Germany. He declared that he would remain as long as there were Jews in Germany. In 1943 he was removed to the Therienstadt concentration camp, where he began ministering to the Jewish inmates. Somehow he survived and spent his last years teaching in London and Cincinnati.

V. SCIENCE, EDUCATION, AND TECHNOLOGY

1933 Paul Ádrien Maurice Dirac (Aug. 8, 1902–Oct. 20, 1984), an English mathematician and theoretical physicist, and **Erwin Schrödinger** (Aug. 12, 1887–Jan. 4, 1961), an Austrian physicist, were jointly awarded the **Nobel prize for physics.** Dirac, working with a mathematical hypothesis of his own, predicted (1928) the existence of positrons, antiprotons, and antineutrons in the atomic nucleus; the existence of the positron was proven (1932) by Carl David Anderson. Schrödinger experimented on the wave theory of matter, developing a system of quantum mechanics allowing him to produce a new model of atomic structure.

1933 Edwin H[oward] Armstrong (Dec., 1890–Feb. 1, 1954), an American engineer, build the **first FM** [frequency modulation] **radio station,** permitting static-free broadcasting. The superheterodyne circuit Armstrong invented in 1918 is now used in c.98 percent of radio, radar, and TV reception.

1933 The Institute for Advanced Study, chartered in 1930, opened in Princeton, New Jersey. The institute continues today to be a place designed for scholars and scientists to write and think. **Abraham Flexner** (Nov. 13, 1866–Sept. 21, 1959) was the first director (to 1939).

1933 The Hoover Dam was completed on the Colorado River in southeastern Nevada. It was 276 feet tall and 1,242 feet long.

1933 Jan. Harold Eugene Edgerton (b. Apr. 6, 1903) and **Kenneth J. Germeshausen** developed a **method of taking photographs** with exposures of 1/100,000–1/500,000 of a second at a rate of 4,000 pictures a second.

1933 Sept. Vladimir K. Zworykin, working for the RCA-Victor Research Laboratories, invented a **method of transmitting TV images** of 250 lines to the inch, enabling production of much finer pictures without the intensive lights formerly needed at the sending center.

VI. ARTS AND LEISURE

1933 Jan. 17 Louis Comfort Tiffany (b. Feb. 18, 1848), an American painter and designer of decorative materials and objects, died. He established his own interior decorating firm and in 1878 developed a process for producing an opalescent glass called *favrile*. With this material he manufactured vases, lamps, and stained glass windows that became widely popular. The forms and colors were in the Art Nouveau style, of which he was a leader. Tiffany designed the chapel for the World's Columbian Exposition in Chicago (1893).

1933 Jan. 21 George Moore (b. Feb. 24, 1852), an Irish novelist, died. His best-known works were *Esther Waters* (1894), *The Brook Kerith* (1915), *Héloise and Abélard* (1921), and his autobiography *Hail and Farewell* (1911, 1912, 1914), an evocation of *fin de siècle* social and literary activities.

1933 Jan. 31 John Galsworthy (b. Aug. 14, 1867), an English novelist, died. His best-known work was *The Forsyte Saga* (1922), which was first published as a series of novels (1906–1921). Galsworthy wrote additional novels concerning the Forsyte family in 1924, 1926, 1928, 1929, and 1930, and a number of short stories and plays. He received the **Nobel prize for literature** in 1932.

1933 Sept. 25 Ring[gold] [Wilmer] Lardner (b. Mar. 3, 1885), an American humorist and short-story writer, died. His first collection of stories was *You Know Me, Al* (1916). Another collection was *What of It?* (1925). In 1929 Lardner collaborated with **George S. Kaufman** on a comedy for the stage, *June Moon.*

1933 Oct. 29 George [Benjamin] Luks (b. Aug. 13, 1867), an American artist who specialized in realistic portraits and genre studies, died. After drawing the comic strip *The Yellow Kid* for newspapers, he turned to painting as one of the Eight, also known as the Ashcan School, artists who depicted urban life as it was on its lower levels. His paintings include *The Wrestlers* and *Little Madonna.*

1933 Dec. 4   **Stefan George** (b. Dec. 12, 1868), a German poet who led a revolt against realism and brought to his work a return to classicism, died. He attacked materialism and tried to inspire a society pledged to humanistic ideals. Among his works of verse were *Algabal* (1892), *Das Jahr der Seele* [*The Soul's Year*] (1897), and *Das neue Reich* [*The New Kingdom*] (1928).

VII. SPORTS, GAMES, AND SOCIETY

1933   **Clarence C. Pell**, the best **racquets** player the U.S. has ever produced, won his 12th national championship. He won the title for the first time in 1915. **Stanley E. Mortimer**, his doubles partner, was his only serious competition during this period, defeating him four times for the championship. They won the doubles title nine times. In 1925 Pell won the British amateur singles championship in London, the only American ever to do so.

1933   The state of Florida legalized **pari-mutuel betting** for horses, dogs, and **jai-alai**. Originally a Spanish sport developed from handball, jai-alai was introduced to Cuba c.1900 and to the U.S. at the World's Fair in St. Louis in 1904. Its popularity in the U.S. has been almost entirely as a spectator sport and as a wagering opportunity.

1933 May 25–Nov. 12   A lavish world's fair, the **Century of Progress Exposition**, was held in Chicago to celebrate the city's centennial. It drew c.22,000,000 visitors, who found in the impressive national pavilions and flashy commercial displays a chance to take their minds off the Great Depression. The most popular attraction on the Midway was the **celebrated fan dancer, Sally Rand**. The exposition had a second season in 1934, from May 26 to Oct. 31.

1933 June 29   **Primo Carnera** (Oct. 26, 1906–June 29, 1967), an Italian-born American boxer, won the **world heavyweight championship** when he knocked out the defending title holder Jack Sharkey in the sixth round of a bout at Long Island City, New York.

1933 July 6   The **first All-Star baseball game** between the leading players of the American and the National leagues was played in Comiskey Park, Chicago. The American League won by a score of 4–2 before 49,200 fans. **Babe Ruth** of the New York Yankees **provided the victory edge** for the American League with a home run and a single.

1934

I. VITAL STATISTICS AND DEMOGRAPHICS

1934 May 28   Elzire Dionne (d. Nov. 21, 1986) of Callander, Ontario, gave birth to **quintuplets, the first recorded case** in which all survived. The five girls were named Yvonne, Cécile, Annette, Émilie (d. Aug. 6, 1954), and Marie (d. Feb. 28, 1970). The Canadian physician Dr. Allan Roy Dafoe (May 29, 1883–June 2, 1943) delivered the quintuplets. The babies became a great tourist attraction, and people came from all over the U.S. and Canada to see them.

II. DISASTERS

1934 Jan. 15   In Bihar, in present northeastern **India**, and Nepal, which lies on the northern border of Bihar, an **earthquake** measuring 8.4 on the Richter scale struck, killing more than 10,000 people.

1934 Sept. 8   En route from Havana, Cuba, to New York City the U.S. luxury liner *Morro Castle* off Asbury Park, New Jersey, was **ravaged by fire** which quickly spread through the ship's ventilation system. The SOS was delayed and the ship was claimed to be a total loss; 134 people died in the blaze. The ship was carrying 318 passengers and a crew of 231.

1934 Sept. 21   A **typhoon struck Honshu, Japan**, killing more than 4,000 persons.

III. POLITICS AND WAR

1934   The **Indian Reorganization Act** of the U.S. Congress, also called the **Wheeler-Howard Act**, granted lands to Indian tribes, reversing the trend of the Dawes Act (1887) to grant land only to individuals. The act allows any tribe voting to accept the act to adopt a constitution governing itself and then to incorporate so as to obtain federal loans and carry on business.

1934 Jan. 26 Germany and Poland signed a treaty in which Germany guaranteed it would not try to take by force the **Polish Corridor** for ten years.

1934 Feb. 6–7 Triggered by dissatisfaction with the French government and its alleged implication in the **Stavisky affair**, riots broke out in Paris, leaving 17 dead and several hundred injured. **Serge Alexandre Stavisky**, a Russian-born French citizen, had **sold large quantities of worthless bonds** to a gullible public. When the fraud was discovered, Stavisky (b. Nov. 10, 1886) fled in Dec., 1933, was traced to Chamonix in eastern France, and there either committed suicide or was killed by the police on Jan. 8, 1934. On Jan. 27, in the face of the scandal, the Radical Socialist government of **Camille Chautemps** (Feb. 1, 1885–July 1, 1963), premier of France, resigned. Chautemps was replaced (Jan. 30) by **Edouard Daladier** (June 18, 1884–Oct. 10, 1970), who suppressed the riots but in turn was soon forced to resign. His successor (Feb. 8) was **Gaston Doumergue** (Aug. 1, 1863–June 18, 1937), who held office until Nov. 8. Right-wing forces charged Stavisky had been murdered to obscure the part played by high-ranking persons. After a long trial (1935–1936), 11 of 20 defendants, including the widow of Stavisky, were acquitted of any crime.

1934 Feb. 9 The **Balkan Entente** brought together Greece, Romania, Turkey, and Yugoslavia in a pact to protect the territories pledged to them by the treaties that ended World War I. It was aimed in particular at Bulgaria, which had lost territory, and it expressed opposition to any restoration of the **Hapsburg-Lorraine Dynasty** (1736–1918). This entente complemented the **Little Entente**, an alliance originally formed (1920–1921) by Czechoslovakia, Romania, and Yugoslavia. At a conference in Geneva, Switzerland, beginning on Feb. 16, 1933, the Little Entente treaties were strengthened and made permanent. The intent was to coordinate their policies and defenses against the rising threat of Nazi Germany.

1934 Feb. 17 **Albert I** (b. Apr. 8, 1875), king of the Belgians (from 1909), died. In 1914 he refused the German request to allow its armies to pass through Belgium to attack France. Thereafter he personally led the Belgian army in sturdy resistance to the German invaders throughout World War I and commanded the Allied offensive (1918) that liberated the Belgian coast. After the war Albert worked actively to improve economic and social conditions not only

in Belgium but also in the Belgian Congo. He was killed in a rock climbing accident and was succeeded (to 1951) by his son Leopold III.

1934 Feb. 21 **Augusto César Sandino** (b.1893), who had continued to fight against the U.S. marines until they left his country Jan. 1933, was assassinated along with his brother and two aides by members of the **Nicaraguan National Guard** in Managua. They were under the control of **Anastasio Somoza García** (Feb. 1, 1896–Sept. 29, 1956).

1934 Mar. 22 The **Tydings-McDuffie Act** granting independence to the **Philippines** by 1946 passed the U.S. Congress and was signed by **Franklin D. Roosevelt**, president of the U.S. The act was accepted by the Philippine legislature on Apr. 30, 1934.

1934 Apr. 1 The *Vossische Zeitung*, probably the most widely respected newspaper in Germany, was closed down as a result of **Nazi government** pressure. It had published since 1704.

1934 May 19 **Boris III**, tsar of **Bulgaria** (1918–1943), who had ruled as a constitutional monarch, now set up a fascist regime with the assistance of the military. In 1935 he dismissed **Kimon Georgiev** (Aug. 11, 1882–Sept. 28, 1969), the premier, and ruled as dictator.

1934 May 29 The **U.S. and Cuba signed a treaty** that ended Cuba's status as a virtual protectorate of the U.S. Under the treaty the U.S. retained its lease on the naval base at **Guantánamo Bay**, in southeastern Cuba.

1934 June 30 **Adolf Hitler**, in a **purge of his followers** suspected of plotting to overthrow him, had perhaps as many as 200 persons executed without trial. The most prominent of the victims was **Ernst Röhm** (b. Aug. 28, 1887), head of the **SA** [Sturmabteilung, Brownshirts, Stormtroopers], the private army of the Nazis; **Gregor Strasser** (b. May 31, 1892), at one time second only to Hitler in authority; and **Kurt von Schleicher** (b. April 4, 1882), a former chancellor, not a Nazi, and his wife. The purge, later called the **night of the long knives**, destroyed the influence of the part of the Nazi movement that thought Hitler should pay more attention to the well-being of the working class.

1934 July 9 **Heinrich Himmler** (Nov. 7, 1900–May 23, 1945), chief of Hitler's **SS** [Schutzstaffel], the elite black-shirted guards of the Nazi regime, took over direction of the **concentration camps**, the first of which had been established in Mar., 1933, at Dachau, Bavaria. At the start the camps were set up chiefly because there was not enough room in the prisons for the persons, mostly communists or alleged communists, seized by the Nazis. By Aug., 1933, Jews were being sent to the camps simply because they were Jews.

1934 July 25 **Engelbert Dollfuss** (b. Oct. 4, 1892), the chancellor of **Austria**, was assassinated in Vienna in an attempted **Nazi coup d'état**. **Adolf Hitler** repudiated the coup when Italy threatened to intervene. On July 30 Kurt von Schuschnigg (Dec. 14, 1897–Nov. 18, 1977) was appointed chancellor and continued the struggle to maintain Austria's independence.

1934 Aug. 1 With Paul von Hindenburg, president of Germany, on his deathbed, **Adolf Hitler** had his cabinet pass a law providing that thereafter the offices of president and chancellor would be combined. The next day (Aug. 2), when Hindenburg (b. Oct. 2, 1847), died, Hitler assumed the presidency. On Aug. 19 a plebiscite was held to ask the German electorate to ratify the combining of the two offices. Of the voters, 90 percent approved, but a brave 10 percent voted no. Hitler began using the title **Der Führer** [The Leader].

1934 Sept. 1 **José María Velasco Ibarra** (Mar. 19, 1893–Mar. 30, 1979) was inaugurated as president of **Ecuador** for the first of five times.

1934 Sept. 18 The **Soviet Union was admitted to the League of Nations** and given one permanent seat on the League's Council. The Soviets wanted to join because of fear of the rising power of Germany.

1934 Oct. 6 **Catalonia**, the northeastern region of Spain with Barcelona as its center, **declared**, through its president, Luis Companys, **complete independence** from the rest of the country. The revolt was quickly crushed and Companys was put in prison. He had been elected president in 1933. When Germany overran France, where Luis Companys (b. 1883) had sought refuge after the fall of Spain, Companys was brought back to Spain and executed on Oct. 16, 1940.

1934 Oct. 9 **Alexander I** (b. Dec. 16, 1888), king of **Yugoslavia** [Jugoslavia], was assassinated at Marseille while on his way to a diplomatic session in Paris. **Jean Louis Barthou** (b. 1862), the French foreign minister, was also slain by "Petrus Kaleman," later identified as Vlada Georgieff, a Hungarian friend of Macedonian rebels and anarchists, and one of a group of five selected to kill the king. Georgieff (b. 1900) was killed by the police, military, and citizens near the place of assassination. Alexander's 11-year-old son Peter II became king (to 1945) on Oct. 11, when the three regents named in the will took their oaths of office.

1934 Oct. 15 **Raymond Poincaré** (b. Aug. 20, 1860), president of France (1913–1920), and premier three times (1912–1913, 1922–1924, 1926–1929), died. He was a conservative nationalist who continually urged military preparedness, and who thought the Treaty of Versailles (1919) did not punish Germany enough. As premier Poincaré sent (1923) French troops into the Ruhr region of Germany to try to force payment of overdue reparations. As premier again he managed (1926–1929) a policy of great financial austerity that in a time of economic crisis balanced the budget and stabilized the value of the franc.

1934 Oct. 16 Badly battered by the Kuomintang army under **Chiang Kai-Shek**, the communist Red army of China, led by **Mao Tse-Tung**, began the **Long March**, c.6,000 miles from Kiangsi [Jiangxi] province [called Kiangsi Soviet Socialist Republic by Mao and the Chinese communists], to Yenan [Yan'an], a town in Shensi [Shanxi] province in the northwest, where they formed a new base on Oct. 20, 1935.

1934 Nov. 30 The **Moroccan nationalist movement** was born when a group of young Moroccans, called the **Committee for National Action**, submitted a plan of reforms to the French government.

1934 Dec. 1 **Sergei Mironovich Kirov** (b. 1888), secretary of the Soviet politburo and secretary of the Communist party in Leningrad, was shot to death there by a young communist assassin, Leonid Vasilievich Nikolayev. Of the 71 suspects arrested, 66 were convicted and executed on Dec. 5. A nationwide investigation exposed much dissatisfaction among the people and many of the communist leaders. Many were imprisoned, removed from their positions, exiled to Siberia, or executed in the course of Joseph **Stalin's treason trials and party purge** of the 1930s.

1934 Dec. 29 Japan announced that, as of Dec., 1936, it was **withdrawing from the Washington Naval Treaty** of 1922 **and the London Naval Treaty** of 1930. Both treaties had pledged Japan to maintain its naval strength somewhat below that of Great Britain and the U.S. Japan was now free to build as large a navy as it wished.

1934 Dec. 30 Lázaro Cárdenas (May 21, 1895–Oct. 19, 1970), formerly secretary of war, was **inaugurated as president** of **Mexico** (to 1940). Cárdenas nationalized the railroads and finally, on Mar. 18, 1938, the oil industry, which involved the assets of 17 foreign-owned companies.

IV. ECONOMY AND TRADE

1934 The **Anglo-American-Kuwait Oil company** was formed to explore for oil in Kuwait. Oil was found in 1938 and production begun in 1946 as a joint venture of the **British Petroleum Company** and **Gulf Oil Company** with 50 percent of the profits going to the sheikdom until Jan. 29, 1974, when Kuwait took more than 60 percent of the ownership.

1934 The **Swiss Bank Code of 1934** made it a criminal offense for any employee or officer of a Swiss bank to divulge any information about a customer's bank account to any unauthorized person or agency, including any agency of the Swiss government, except in cases involving a demonstrable violation of Swiss law.

1934 About 150,000 square miles in parts of Kansas, Colorado, New Mexico, and the Oklahoma and Texas panhandles had been seared by **droughts** beginning in 1933, just after a period when farmers, encouraged by high grain prices, had plowed up their grazing lands to grow winter wheat. Winds blowing over the **Dust Bowl**, parched, unprotected earth formed sand dunes c.30 feet tall or accumulated silt in enormous dust clouds, "**black blizzards**" that blew to the Atlantic Coast, and fell as "**brown snow**" in Canada. On the Great Plains soil drifted like snow, livestock died. Many farmers, in some places 60 percent of the population, abandoned their land, many of them heading for California. They were generally known as "**Okies**" because Oklahoma was especially hard hit. It was estimated that as much as 300,000,000 tons of top soil disappeared in the 1930s.

1934 Jan. 20 In **Germany**, a system was established by law in which labor was responsible to management, and management responsible to the state. On Oct. 24 the **Labor Front**, under Robert Ley (Feb. 15, 1890–Oct. 25, 1945), was given complete control over regulating German labor. Professionals and employers came under Labor Front jurisdiction as well as laborers. The Labor Front was allowed to use police to enforce its policies, and this it did freely in support of the Nazi government.

1934 Jan. 30 The **Gold Reserve Act** became law in the U.S. This law allowed the president to set limits to the gold content of the dollar, within certain specifications. Roosevelt the next day fixed the dollar at 59.06 percent of its former gold value. Gold could therefore be bought at $35 per ounce. This action took pressure off the government from inflationists and helped control credit.

1934 Feb. 2 The U.S. government created an **Export-Import Bank** whose purpose was to facilitate trade with Russia. On Mar. 12 a similar bank was set up to promote trade with Cuba. In both cases the purpose was to increase foreign trade by guaranteeing the credit of the participating parties.

1934 June 6 The **Securities and Exchange Commission** [SEC] was established by act of Congress to regulate trading on the U.S. stock exchanges. It was a reaction to the stock market crash of Oct., 1929, after which many fraudulent and unfair practices had been revealed.

1934 Dec. 8 **Weekly airmail service** between Darwin, Australia, and London, England, was begun by Qantas Airlines of Australia and Imperial Airways of Great Britain.

V. RELIGION AND PHILOSOPHY

1934 **Mordecai Menahem Kaplan** (June 11, 1881–Nov. 8, 1983), a professor at Jewish Theological Seminary in New York City, published *Judaism as a Civilization*, the first of a series of books intended to reconstruct the major articles of Jewish belief in a way that would make them compatible with scientific and rational thought. This marked the beginning of the **Reconstructionist movement within Judaism**. A proclamation of excommunication was issued against Kaplan by the **Union of Orthodox Rabbis**, their first such ban.

VI. SCIENCE, EDUCATION, AND TECHNOLOGY

1934 **Frédéric Joliot-Curie** (Mar. 19, 1900–Aug. 14, 1958) and **Irène Joliot-Curie** (Sept. 12, 1897–Mar. 17, 1956), a husband-and-wife team of French scientists, for the first time demonstrated that radioactive substances could be produced by bombarding certain elements with alpha particles. For their work they were jointly awarded the **Nobel prize for chemistry** in 1935. Mrs. Joliot-Curie was the daughter of Pierre and Marie Curie, pioneer scientists in research on radium and radioactivity.

1934 **Vitamin K**, which consists of substances that are necessary to the clotting of blood, was discovered by [Carl Peter] **Henrik Dam** (Feb. 1, 1895–Apr. 17, 1976), a Danish biochemist. In 1939 **Edward Adelbert Doisy**, an American biochemist, isolated **vitamin K** and **synthesized** it. For their work in this field the two men shared the 1943 **Nobel prize for physiology or medicine**.

1934 **Karl** [Raimund] **Popper** (b. July 28, 1902), an Austrian-born British philosopher, published his first work *Logik der Forschung* [*The Logic of Scientific Discovery*], in which he began to formulate his philosophy. Popper rejected the inductive approach to empirical science. He also argued against historicism, the belief that there were general laws of history.

1934 Feb. 1 **Fritz Haber** (b. 1868), a German chemist, died. He was director of the Kaiser Wilhelm Institute for Physical Chemistry in Berlin (from 1911). With Karl Bosch he developed a way of producing ammonia directly from atmospheric nitrogen (1908–1909). He was awarded the **Nobel prize for chemistry** in 1918.

1934 **Vitamin C** was first **synthesized** by **Walter Norman Haworth**, an English chemist. In 1937, with the Swiss Paul Karrer (Apr. 21, 1889–June 18, 1971), Haworth received the **Nobel prize for chemistry**.

1934 July The **Mersey Tunnel** for motor vehicles, Great Britain's largest and most important tunnel of its kind, was officially opened to traffic. It ran under the Mersey River estuary, connecting Liverpool and Birkenhead, central western England. In all the Mersey Tunnel is almost three miles long and at its deepest is 170 feet below the high water mark.

1934 July 4 **Marie Curie** [nee Manya Sklodowska] (b. Nov. 7, 1867), a Polish-born French scientist, with her husband, Pierre, a pioneer in research in radioactivity, died. For their work in this field the couple was awarded, together with another scientist, the **Nobel prize for physics** in 1903. For her work, also with another scientist, in isolating pure radium, Madame Curie won another Nobel prize, for chemistry, in 1911. She was the **first person to win two Nobel prizes**.

1934 Aug. 16 [Charles] **William Beebe** (July 29, 1877–June 4, 1962), an American scientist and explorer, with a companion set a record for **descent into the ocean** when they went down 3,028 feet off Bermuda. They made the voyage in a bathysphere.

VII. ARTS AND LEISURE

1934 **Henry** [Valentine] **Miller** (Dec. 26, 1891–Jan. 1, 1980), an American writer, published *Tropic of Cancer* while living in Paris. Miller's works include *Tropic of Capricorn* (1938), *Colossus of Maroussi* (1941), and the trilogy *The Rosy Crucifixion* (1949, 1953, and 1960).

1934 The **School of the American Ballet**, which in 1948 became the parent company of the **New York City Ballet**, was founded by **Lincoln** [Edward] **Kirstein** (b. May 4, 1907), an American theater executive and author. **George Balanchine**, a Russian-born choreographer, became director of the school. He had graduated from the Soviet State Ballet School in 1921 and in 1924 joined the Ballet Russe as chief choreographer. In America his work established the first important ballet school and Balanchine developed a number of first-rate talents to stardom.

1934 Feb. 23 **Edward Elgar** (b. June 2, 1857), an English composer of chamber and choral music, piano and vocal pieces, and orchestral music, died. He composed the oratorio *The Dream of Gerontius* (1900), the cantatas *The Black Knight* (1893) and *Cataractus* (1898), the oratorios *The Apostles* (1903) and *The Kingdom* (1906). He composed six separate military marches, all named *Pomp and Circumstance* (1901–1907), his work best known to the general public. He also wrote three symphonies.

1934 June 10 **Frederick Delius** (b. Jan. 29, 1862), an English composer of operas and of chamber, choral, and orchestral music, died. He wrote the operas *Koanga* (1895–1897), *A Village Romeo and Juliet*

(1900–1901), and *Fenimore and Gerda* (1908–1910). His orchestral works included *Appalachia Requiem* (1902) and *Sea Drift* (1903).

1934 Sept. 9   Roger [Eliot] **Fry** (b. Dec. 14, 1866), an English painter and critic, died. He was a forceful champion of the post-impressionists, whom he introduced to England. Fry was in the U.S. from 1905 to 1910 as curator of paintings at the Metropolitan Museum of Art, New York City. It was, though, as editor and art critic that his reputation continues high today. Among his writings were *Vision and Design* (1920) and a posthumous collection *Last Lectures* (1939).

1934 Nov. 23   Arthur Wing Pinero (b. May 25, 1855), a prolific and popular English dramatist, died. His first play, *Two Hundred a Year*, was produced in 1877. In the next dozen years he wrote some of the best farces ever seen on the English stage. They included *The Magistrate* (1885) and *The Amazons* (1893). From 1889 on Pinero wrote dramas touching on social problems that had not hitherto been presented on the stage. Most startling of these was *The Second Mrs. Tanqueray* (1893), a sympathetic portrayal of a woman with a questionable past.

VIII. SPORTS, GAMES, AND SOCIETY

1934   Some of **America's most notorious outlaws met violent deaths** this year at the hands of law enforcement agents. On May 23, near Shreveport, Louisiana, Texas Rangers fired on a speeding car carrying **Clyde Barrow** (b. May 24, 1909) and his partner **Bonnie Parker** (b. Oct. 1, 1910), killing them both. For the past four years they had roamed the Southwest robbing banks and gas stations and had killed a dozen people. On July 22 **John** [Herbert] **Dillinger** (b. June 28, 1902), "Public Enemy Number One," was shot and killed by the FBI outside a movie theater on Lincoln Avenue in Chicago, Illinois. A coroner's jury called the death "justifiable homicide." Dillinger was wanted for bank robbery and for 16 murders. On Oct. 22, near East Liverpool, Ohio, [Charles] **Pretty Boy Floyd** (b. 1904) was shot and killed while fleeing from police and FBI agents.

1934 June 14   Max[imilian Adelbert] **Baer** (Feb. 11, 1909–Nov. 21, 1959), an American boxer, won the **world heavyweight championship** by defeating the titleholder **Primo Carnera** in New York City. Baer was awarded a technical knockout in the 11th round after having floored Carnera 12 times.

1934   The **Spartakiáda Stadium**, the **world's largest modern stadium**, holding 250,000 spectators at once, was opened in Prague, Czechoslovakia. In the stadium field, 40,000 gymnasts can perform at the same time.

1934 June 10   The second **World Cup of soccer** was won at Rome by the Italian team, which defeated Czechoslovakia 2–1.

1934 Sept. 17–25   The **America's Cup** was retained by the U.S. when the yacht *Rainbow* defeated the British challenger *Endeavour* off Newport, Rhode Island, 4 races to 2.

1935

I. DISASTERS

1935 May 31   An **earthquake** with a magnitude of 7.5 on the Richter scale struck Baluchistan, in present **Pakistan**, killing more than 50,000 at the capital of Quetta.

1935 Aug. 15   Will [William Penn Adair] **Rogers** (b. Nov. 4, 1879), an American humorist, and **Wiley Post** (b. Nov. 22, 1898), an American aviator, died when their airplane crashed on takeoff at Walkpi, near Point Barrow, in northern Alaska. Rogers was the foremost comedian of his day and author of several books. With another aviator, **Harold Gatty**, Post had flown around the world in 1931. Post had also made the first solo flight, in the *Winnie Mae*, around the world in 1933.

1935 Sept. 3   A hurricane struck Florida killing 408 persons. It was the **first Category 5 storm to hit the U.S.** since records were kept. This designation refers to storms with winds of more than 155 miles per hour and waves 18 feet above normal.

II. EXPLORATION
AND COLONIZATION

1935 Nov. 23–Dec. 5 **Lincoln Ellsworth** (May 12, 1880–May 26, 1951), an American explorer, made the **first airplane flight across the Antarctic** continent. He started from Dundee Island, just off the end of the Antarctic Peninsula, and flew c.2,300 miles to the Bay of Whales, stopping four times en route.

III. POLITICS AND WAR

1935 Jan. 1 **Women participated for the first time in national elections in Turkey**, where 18 women were elected to the 399-member National Assembly.

1935 Jan. 13 In an election in the **Saar**, a region of southwestern Germany, 90 percent of the voters chose reunion with Germany. Before World War I, the Saar had been part of Germany. By the terms of the **Treaty of Versailles** (1919), it was to be administered by France as an autonomous territory, under the supervision of the **League of Nations** until 1935. The plebiscite gave the Saarlanders a choice of opting for remaining under League supervision, union with France, or reunion with Germany. The Saar was returned to Germany on March 1.

1935 Mar. 16 **Adolf Hitler**, dictator of Nazi Germany, repudiated the **Treaty of Versailles** (1919), which ended World War I. He said Germany would no longer abide by its provisions concerning disarmament.

1935 Mar. 21 **Persia officially changed its name** to **Iran**.

1935 May 1 The **Philippine legislature** ratified U.S. legislation providing for the islands' complete independence on July 4, 1946, and establishing the **Commonwealth of the Philippines** for the interim. On Sept. 17 **Manuel** [Luis] **Quezon** (Aug. 19, 1878–Aug. 1, 1944) was elected the **first president of the Commonwealth**.

1935 May 2 The **U.S.S.R. and France signed a treaty of alliance** for mutual protection. On May 16 the U.S.S.R. and Czechoslovakia signed a mutual assistance treaty. It provided for the Soviets to support Czechoslovakia if that country were invaded, but only if France also came to Czechoslovakia's assistance.

1935 May 12 **Józef** [Klemens] **Piłsudski** (b. Dec. 5, 1867), a Polish patriot, statesman, and soldier, died. In World War I he organized and commanded the Polish Legions, which fought against Russia on the Austrian side for a time. Piłsudski, disillusioned with the parliamentary system, marched (May 12, 1926) on Warsaw at the head of a few regiments of troops and overthrew the government. Acclaimed (May 31) president, he refused the post but remained minister of defense until his death. For practical purposes Piłsudski ruled the nation from this position.

1935 June 18 **Germany and Great Britain signed a treaty** by which Germany agreed to limit its fleet to no more than 35 percent of the British fleet. **Hitler** suggested the figure and said it would be the last demand he would make. The French saw the pact as British acceptance of the fact that Germany was rearming and feared it would encourage Hitler to further violate the Treaty of Versailles (1919).

1935 Aug. 8 **Huey** P[ierce] **Long** (b. Aug. 30, 1893), a U.S. senator known as **"The Kingfish,"** was assassinated in Baton Rouge, Louisiana, by the son-in-law of a man whose career he had destroyed. Long's bodyguards immediately shot and killed the assassin. Long, elected governor of Louisiana in 1928 and U.S. senator in 1930, turned Louisiana into a personal fief, much like that of a Latin American dictator. He did, though, see to the construction of badly needed roads, schools, and other projects.

1935 Aug. 14 The **Social Security Act** became law in the U.S., providing for establishment of a pension system by means of contributions from both employers and employees. The monthly pension was originally set at a minimum of $10 and a maximum of $85 per month at age 65. The law also provided for aid for the blind and the handicapped, and set up a system of unemployment insurance.

1935 Aug. 24 The **Social Credit party** won a sweeping victory in the Alberta, Canada, provincial elections, and 17 seats in the federal Parliament. The party gained wide support from farmers and merchants, and even some support from doctors, lawyers, and teachers. Although the Social Credit concepts developed by **Clifford Hugh Douglas** (Jan. 20, 1879–Sept. 29, 1952), an English social economist and engineer, had adherents in many parts of Canada and even in some areas of the United States, it was a dominant political power only in **Alberta**. Behind the idea of Social Credit was the belief that economic depressions could be ended if purchasing power were more equally distributed.

1935 Aug. 31 The **Neutrality Act of 1935** became law in the U.S. It forbade the shipment of arms to belligerents, barred loans or credits to them, and prohibited American vessels from carrying war materials to nations at war.

1935 Sept. 15 Under the **Nürnburg** [Nuremburg] **Laws** passed by the German Reichstag, **Jews lost equal rights** and the right to appeal to the state. The laws were passed "for the protection and honor of Germans." No mixed marriages were allowed, Jews could not wear the Reich symbol [swastika], and women under 45 were forbidden to work.

1935 Oct. The Chinese communists, led by **Mao Tse-Tung**, completed their famous **Long March** from Kiangsi [Jiangxi] province in southeastern China to Shenshi [Shanxi] province in northwestern China where they made Yenan [Yan'an] their capital. About 20,000 persons completed the c.6000 mi. journey; c.70,000 dropped out en route.

1935 Oct. 3 **Italy invaded Ethiopia**, which had no adequate defenses against the modern Italian army using aircraft, tanks, and poison gas. The capital Addis Ababa was occupied on May 5, 1936, and Ethiopia was annexed to the Italian Empire, with Eritrea and Italian Somalia, as Italian East Africa.

1935 Oct. 7 **Ethiopia** having appealed to the **League of Nations** for protection against the unprovoked attack upon it by Italy, the League declared Italy an aggressor. On Nov. 18 the League voted to place economic sanctions on Italy. The sanctions did not, however, include oil, the most vital commodity. Since many nations ignored the sanctions, they did nothing to halt the Italian invasion.

1935 Nov. 3 A plebiscite in **Greece** resulted in the restoration of the monarchy. The republic, established in 1924, had been beset by many financial difficulties and constitutional quarrels ending in political violence and government by faction. **George II** (July 20, 1890–Apr. 1, 1947), king of Greece (1922–1923, 1935–1947), returned (Nov. 25) from exile in England. He named **Joannis Metaxas** (Apr. 12, 1871–Jan. 29, 1941) premier on Apr. 13, 1936. Metaxas dissolved parliament in Aug., 1936, and with royal approval ruled thereafter as a reactionary dictator.

IV. ECONOMY AND TRADE

1935 The **Irish Hospitals Sweepstakes became the most successful lottery in the world**, raising millions of dollars in support of hospitals in Ireland. Winning was based on the English Derby at Epsom, the English Grand National Steeplechase at Aintree, and two others. Although illegal in the U.S., millions of tickets were sold there annually and in many other nations.

1935 Mar. 11 The **Bank of Canada**, Canada's first central bank, was opened. Formation of the bank had been recommended in a Royal Commission report of Nov., 1933, and it was established in 1934.

1935 Apr. 8 The **Works Progress Administration**, later (July 1, 1939) called the Work Projects Administration [WPA], was established to organize federal employment programs in the U.S. It employed c.8,500,000 people over the next eight years, primarily in manual labor and the arts. The total cost of the program (1935–1942) exceeded $10,000,000,000.

1935 May 27 The Supreme Court of the U.S. declared unconstitutional the **National Industrial Recovery Act of 1933**, one of the cornerstones of the New Deal's attempt to halt the economic depression. The court said the law delegated powers to the president improperly and that the test case it was acting on did not involve interstate commerce.

1935 July 3 **André Gustave Citroën** (b. Feb. 9, 1878), a French automobile manufacturer who brought American methods of mass production to France, died. After producing munitions during World War I, he began manufacturing low priced automobiles, but in 1934 lost control of his business in bankruptcy. Citroën financed an automobile caravan to travel from Beirut, Lebanon, to Peking, China in 1932, and paid for a system for lighting the Arc de Triomphe in Paris.

1935 July 5 In the U.S., the **National Labor Relations Act** was completed. It required employers to bargain with their employees, and it specified a number of "unfair labor practices." The law also established a **National Labor Relations Board** [NLRB] with power to hold elections to determine which union should represent the workers in a plant or industry. In Apr. 1937, the Supreme Court upheld the constitutionality of the new law.

1935 Aug. 31 A Soviet miner named **Aleksei Grigorievich Stakhanov** (1905–1977) **mined 102 tons of coal** in one work shift. The feat exceeded by 1,300 percent the normal output. The Soviet government seized on this example and started the **Stakhanov movement motivating workers** to set record levels of output.

1935 Nov. 9 The **Committee for Industrial Organization**, which was formalized as a federation of American labor unions under the name of **Congress of Industrial Organizations** [CIO] in Nov., 1938, was founded. Its moving spirit was **John L**[lewellyn] **Lewis** (Feb. 12, 1880–June 11, 1969), long-time (1920–1960) president of the **United Mine Workers** [UMW]. The UMW, with the **United Automobile Workers** [UAW], was a leading union in the CIO. The CIO organizers believed industrial unions were superior to craft unions in dealing with large production industries. The CIO took in all the workers in an industry regardless of their crafts. In less than two years, unions were recognized in the steel and auto industries, industries that had sworn never to bargain with organized labor.

V. RELIGION AND PHILOSOPHY

1935 **Haj Amin al-Husanyi** [Husseini] (1897–July 4, 1974), the Grand Mufti of Jerusalem and fierce anti-Zionist, united the quarreling leading Muslim families in Palestine and also brought Christians into a common defense against the tide of Jewish immigrants from Germany—61,541 in 1935. From this year on, Arab volunteer groups began organizing for self-determination and for civil war led by the Grand Mufti.

VI. SCIENCE, EDUCATION, AND TECHNOLOGY

1935 The building of five **radar stations in Great Britain** marked the first use of this invention as a method of air defense. This practical application of the technique of finding the location, motion, and nature of an object by bouncing radio waves off it was the work of **Robert Watson-Watt** (Apr. 13, 1892–Dec. 5, 1973), a Scottish physicist. Activating the system at this time was strongly championed by Henry Thomas Tizard (Aug. 23, 1885–Oct. 9, 1950), a scientific adviser to the British government. England soon had 15 more such radar stations.

1935 **Alexis Carrel** (June 28, 1873–Nov. 5, 1944), a French-American surgeon and biologist, with the assistance of **Charles A. Lindbergh**, the American aviator, perfected the **first mechanical heart**, which they had been working on since 1930. It was a pumping device that could keep alive, outside the body, different types of tissues and organs. Carrel won the **Nobel prize for physiology or medicine** in 1912 for work on the transplantation of organs, and in problems of transfusion.

1935 Mar. 22 The **first television station to broadcast in Europe** began operation in Berlin, Germany, but ceased in August. The transmission was of low definition, having only 180 lines per picture.

1935 Apr. 23 The first section of the **Moscow subway** opened. Work began in 1931 and this section extended only 3.5 miles. Since then the lines have reached a total of 114.1 miles.

1935 May 21 **Hugo** [Marie] **De Vries** (b. Feb. 16, 1848), a Dutch botanist, died. He formulated the hypothesis of **evolution by mutation** based on his research on Evening Primroses [*Oenothera*], which confirmed **Gregor Mendel**'s work. De Vries, **Karl Erich Correns** (Sept. 19, 1864–Feb. 14, 1933), a German botanist, and **Erich Tschermak von Seysenegg** (Nov. 15, 1871–Oct. 11, 1962), an Austrian botanist, working independently had rediscovered Mendel's paper, printed in an obscure journal in 1866 and, after testing the experiments, brought it to the attention of the scientific world.

1935 Oct. 24 **Henri Pirenne** (b. Dec. 23, 1862), a Belgian historian, died. Pirenne's *Histoire de Belgique* [*History of Belgium*] (1899–1932) explained the coming together of the Flemings and the Walloons to form a nation. In *Les Villes du moyen âge* [*Medieval Cities*] (1927) he developed a new theory that the revival of trade caused the rise of cities. In *Mahomet et Charlemagne* [*Muhammad and Charlemagne*] (1939), he traced the decline of western civilization to the rise of Islam.

1935 Nov. 22–28 and Dec. 1–6 **Edwin C. Musick** (1894–1938) flew Pan Am Airways' *China Clipper* from San Francisco to Manila and back again in the **first Pacific airmail delivery** and U.S./Philippines crossing.

VII. ARTS AND LEISURE

1935 Isaac Bashevis Singer (b. July 14, 1904), a Polish-born author who wrote in Yiddish, published his first major work *Satan in Goray*, a novella about the strange aftermath of a pogrom in 17th-century Poland.

1935 The era of the **modern paperback book** began in England when **Penguin Books** issued its first ten titles. They were of a literary nature and were priced at six pence. In the U.S. such "mass market" paperbacks were first issued in 1939 by **Pocket Books**, at 25 cents. These were not the first times works of literary merit were published in paper covers. In Great Britain, between 1886 and 1890, **Cassell's National Library** issued 209 titles at three pence. In Germany the **Tauchnitz Collection** of British and American Authors was published from 1841 until 1939.

1935 Feb. 8 Max Liebermann (b. July 20, 1847), a German painter, died. His importance lay more in the fact that he introduced impressionism to Germany than in his own work, which was mostly of the genre type. In 1899 he founded and became the head of the Berlin Secession. Toward the end of his life he was forbidden by the Nazis to paint.

1935 Apr. 6 Edwin Arlington Robinson (b. Dec. 22, 1869), who introduced naturalism into American poetry in the early 20th century, died. Among his most popular works were *The Man Who Died Twice* (1924), and his Arthurian trilogy, *Merlin* (1917), *Lancelot* (1920), and *Tristram* (1927). His *Collected Poems* (1921) won the first **Pulitzer prize** for poetry (1922).

1935 May 15 Kasimir Malevich (b. Feb. 26, 1878), a Russian painter, died. He was the originator of suprematism in art, in which he reduced his paintings to a few stark geometric shapes. His *White on White* series of 1917 was of particular importance.

1935 May 17 Paul [Abraham] Dukas (b. Oct. 1, 1865), a French composer, died. His best-known works were *L'Apprenti sorcier* [*The Sorcerer's Apprentice*] (1897) and the opera *Ariane et Barbe-Bleue* (1897).

1935 May 19 T[homas] E[dward] Lawrence (b. Aug. 15, 1888), a combination of English adventurer, scholar, and soldier, known as "**Lawrence of Arabia**," died in a motorcycle accident in Dorset, England. With the British army in Egypt in World War I, he joined with the Arabs in their fight to throw off Turkish domination. After the war Lawrence continued his interest in the Near East and his work in aid of the independence of the Arab states. Lawrence wrote *The Seven Pillars of Wisdom*, an account of the war in the desert and his part in it. It was privately printed in a limited edition in 1926 and did not appear commercially until 1935. It fascinates its readers even today.

1935 July 17 AE [pseudonym for **George William Russell**] (b. Apr. 10, 1867), an Irish poet, died. His works included: *The Divine Vision* (1903), *Dierdre* (1907), *Collected Poems* (1913), *Gods of War* (1915), *Vale and Other Poems* (1931), and *House of the Titan and Other Poems* (1934). He was editor of *The Irish Homestead* (1905–1910) and *The Irish Statesman* (1923–1935).

1935 Aug. 27 [Frederick] Childe Hassam (b. Oct. 17, 1859), an American painter and etcher, died. He was equally at home painting New York City scenes and New England seascapes. Among his works were *Washington Square, Spring* (1890), *Street Scene in Winter* (1901), and *Sunny Blue Sea* (1913).

1935 Aug. 30 Henri Barbusse (b. May 17, 1873), an expatriate French writer, died in Russia, where he had immigrated in pursuit of his pacifist ideals. A poet and novelist, his most important work was *Le Feu, journal d'une escouade* [*Under Fire*] (1916), an account of action in World War I, for which he received the Prix Goncourt.

1935 Oct. 1 The **Federal Theater Project** of the Works Progress Administration was established and went on to operate theaters in 40 states, develop a black theater company, run a research bureau, and employ more than 10,000 people. It ran afoul of the **House Committee on Un-American Activities** and despite efforts on its behalf by many prominent institutions, the Federal Theater Project was ended (1939) by Congress.

1935 Oct. 10 George Gershwin's *Porgy and Bess*, based on the play *Porgy* by **Dorothy** and **Dubose Heyward**, opened in New York City. It was the first successful attempt to portray black characters in leading roles on Broadway.

1935 Oct. 18 Gaston Lachaise (b. Mar. 1, 1882), a French sculptor, died. Although Parisian-born, he lived most of his working life in the United States and was widely regarded as the best American sculptor of his time. He was best known for his *Standing Woman* figures, of which he did several.

1935 Dec. 24 **Alban** [Maria Johannis] **Berg** (b. Feb. 9, 1885), an Austrian composer of chamber, opera, vocal, and orchestral music, died. His operas included *Wozzeck* (1925) and *Lulu* (1937) and an orchestral work known as *Five Songs for Voice and Orchestra* (1912).

VIII. SPORTS, GAMES, AND SOCIETY

1935 [Machgielis] **Max Euwe** (May 20, 1901– Nov. 26, 1981), a Dutch master, won the **world chess championship** by defeating the defending titleholder, **Alexander A. Alekhine**, a Russian.

1935 May 24 The **first game of major league baseball played at night** under lights took place in Cincinnati, Ohio, at Crosley Field before 25,000 fans. **Franklin D. Roosevelt** switched on the lights from the White House.

1935 June 8 By winning the Belmont Stakes, **Omaha**, with jockey Willis Saunders up, became the third horse to win the **Triple Crown** of American thoroughbred racing. Omaha won the Kentucky Derby (May 6) and the Preakness Stakes (May 11).

1935 June 13 [James Joseph] **Jim Braddock** (Dec. 6, 1905–Nov. 29, 1974), an American boxer, became the **heavyweight champion of the world** when he won a 15-round decision in New York City over the defending titleholder **Max Baer**. Baer held the championship for a day less than a year.

1935 Aug. 13 The **first roller derby** took place in Chicago, Illinois.

1936

I. DISASTERS

1936 About 5,000,000 Chinese starved to death as **floods and droughts** wiped out crops in Honan [Henan] and Szechwan [Sichuan] provinces. With 30 million more on the edge of starvation, reports of banditry, child-selling, and cannibalism were widespread.

II. POLITICS AND WAR

1936 The **Norwegian government passed laws introducing old-age pensions and unemployment insurance**, financed by taxes.

1936 Jan. 15 **Japanese delegates walked out of the London Naval Conference** when their nation was refused naval parity with the U.S. and Great Britain. Later, Italy also withdrew.

1936 Jan. 20 **George V** (June 3, 1865), king of Great Britain (from 1910), died. He was succeeded by his son Edward VIII, the prince of Wales and the future duke of Windsor. George, in spite of his kinship with German royalty, became a popular and unifying figure. His reign saw many constitutional changes,

including establishment of the Irish Free State (1921) and the British Commonwealth of Nations (1931).

1936 Feb. 26 In **Japan an attempted military coup** by dissatisfied young army officers failed. Several prominent political figures were, however, assassinated. The insurgents, who numbered c.1,000, also seized several government buildings, but after three days abandoned their revolt. On July 6, 17 of the ringleaders were sentenced to death. Nevertheless, when **Koki Hirota** became prime minister (Mar. 9) the cabinet he organized was dominated by the military.

1936 Feb. 29 The U.S. extended the **Neutrality Act** (1935) through May 1, 1937. A prohibition against granting loans or credits to belligerent nations was added.

1936 Mar. 7 **Germany occupied the Rhineland** with a military force, in violation of the **Treaty of Versailles** (1919). The Anglo-French acceptance of this invasion freed **Adolf Hitler** to **further his military preparations**.

1936 Mar. 12 The **Mongolian People's Republic and the U.S.S.R. signed a mutual assistance agreement.** Until 1952 the U.S.S.R. was the only nation with which Mongolia enjoyed diplomatic relations.

1936 May 14 **Kurt von Schuschnigg**, chancellor of Austria, forced **Ernest Rüdiger von Starhemberg** (May 10, 1899–Mar. 15, 1956), vice chancellor, to resign. Starhemberg was also the head of the **Heimwehr**, a fascist-type militia.

1936 June 5 A **Popular Front** [*Front Populaire*] government was formed in **France** with **Léon Blum** as premier. Blum was the first socialist and the first Jew to serve as premier of France. His government was a coalition of moderates and leftists consisting of Socialists, Radical Socialists, and Communists, which had won a majority in the French elections (May 3). On June 30 it suppressed the French Fascist party. Among the many reforms it instituted were the 40-hour work week, collective bargaining, compulsory arbitration, nationalization of the munitions industry, and reorganization and nationalization of the Bank of France.

1936 July 17 **Civil War** (to 1939) **broke out in Spain**, triggered by an **army revolt in Spanish Morocco** against the Republican government [the Loyalists]. The Spanish government had been moving steadily leftward and the monarchists [the Carlists] and a new fascist party, the **Falange**, sought to halt this movement. **Francisco Franco**, an army general, emerged as the leader of the rebels, or **Nationalists**. By early August, Germany and Italy began supplying Franco with troops, planes, tanks, and other war matériel. In turn, the U.S.S.R. assisted the **Loyalists**. Great Britain and France tried to establish an international nonintervention policy by getting 27 nations to sign such an agreement. Among the signers were Germany, Italy, and Russia, who had no intention of abiding by the agreement. On Aug. 7 the U.S. proclaimed its own policy of nonintervention. In the end, this policy of the democracies was seen as simply appeasing the fascist aggressors. Italy and Germany recognized the Franco regime on November 18. Gradually, the military struggle went in favor of the Nationalists. Toledo fell (Sept. 28) and Franco's forces began a siege of Madrid (Nov. 6). The government moved to Valencia, on the Mediterranean coast in eastern Spain. In June, 1937, Bilbao, the last Loyalist stronghold in the north, was taken. Among the Loyalist forces was the **International Brigade**, made up of idealistic volunteers from many countries who saw the war as a cause for which they were willing to lay down their lives.

1936 July 20 The **Montreux Convention** was signed in Montreux, Switzerland, by Bulgaria, France, Germany, Great Britain, Greece, Turkey, the U.S.S.R., and Yugoslavia. It regulated the use of the straits between the Aegean Sea and the Sea of Marmara. By the terms of the agreement, military control of the zone was given to Turkey, which could close the straits to warships of all countries when it was engaged in war or threatened. Merchant ships of all nations were assured unrestricted passage in peacetime. The Black Sea powers, which meant chiefly the U.S.S.R., were allowed to send their warships through the straits into the Mediterranean Sea in times of peace.

1936 Aug. 19 The trial of 16 high-ranking Russian officials marked the beginning of the **Great Purge** (to 1938) carried out by **Joseph Stalin**, general secretary of the Communist party. In all c.8,000,000 people were imprisoned, sent to Siberian labor camps, or executed before the reign of terror was over. The first 16 included **Lev Borisovich Kamenev** (July 22, 1883–Aug. 24, 1936) and **Grigory Yevseyevich Zinoviev** (Sept., 1883–Aug. 25, 1936), who with Stalin had at one time been the ruling triumvirate of the party and the country. They were shot. In Jan., 1937, another 17 important figures faced trial, including **Karl Bernhardovich Radek** (1885–1939), an editor, who escaped with a sentence of ten years in prison. In June, 1937, it was the turn of the Red army including its commander, **Mikhail Ivanovich Tukhachevsky** (Feb. 16, 1893–June 11, 1937). He was convicted of treason. Finally, in Mar., 1938, came the last spectacular trials of leading figures. This time, 21 were tried, including **Nikolay Ivanovich Bukharin** (1888–Mar. 13, 1938), former editor of *Isvestia*.

1936 Aug. 26 The last elements of the **British protectorate over Egypt** ended through a treaty providing for the evacuation of British troops from Egypt, except for the Suez Canal Zone. Egypt was admitted to the **League of Nations** on May 26, 1937. Fouad Faruk [Farouk] (Feb. 11, 1920–Mar. 18, 1965), king of Egypt (to 1952), had succeeded to the throne on Apr. 28 on the death of his father Fuad, king of Egypt (from 1922).

1936 Oct. 8 An **autonomous Basque** [Vascongadas] **state** was established by the Republican government of Spain after the outbreak of the Civil War (1936–1939).

1936 Oct. 12 A six-month **general strike by Arabs in Palestine**, to protest Great Britain's allowing Jews to immigrate and to purchase land, ended. The leader of the strike was **Haj Amin al Husayni** [Husseini], the Grand Mufti of Jerusalem. England sent troops to the troubled land, and one clash in April in the Tel Aviv-Jaffa area between Arabs and Jews resulted in 11 deaths and c.50 wounded. Britain appointed a commission which recommended on July 8, 1937, that **Palestine be partitioned among Arabs and Jews**, with Britain controlling some territory, chiefly the holy places. The **Zionists** accepted this plan but the Arabs rejected it, especially because it proposed forcible transfer of Arabs out of what would be the Jewish state.

1936 Oct. 27 Italy and Germany agreed upon a formal alliance commonly called the **Rome-Berlin Axis**. Japan and nations of Europe [Bulgaria, Romania, Hungary, and Finland], which fought on Germany's side in World War II, were all referred to as the Axis powers.

1936 Nov. 23 **Mexican peasants began receiving land** expropriated from large estate owners under the reform program of **Lázaro Cárdenas**, president of Mexico. He also gave support to the labor movement in the cities, nationalized the railroads, and expropriated, with compensation, the holdings of foreign nationals. Cárdenas also instituted reforms in education and medical care, and developed transportation and energy projects.

1936 Nov. 25 Germany and Japan signed the **Anti-Comintern Pact**, directed against the U.S.S.R. Later, on Nov. 11, 1937, Italy joined, thereby establishing a triple alliance, known as the Axis. The pact was the basis for their World War II alliance.

1936 Dec. 5 **Joseph Stalin**, general secretary of the Communist party, proclaimed a new constitution for the U.S.S.R. and a reorganization of the government. It guaranteed universal suffrage, the secret ballot, direct election of assemblies, and various civil liberties. In practice, the Communist party continued its harsh control of the state.

1936 Dec. 8 **Anastasio Somoza García**, after having seized power with the tacit approval of the U.S. government, won the presidential election unop-

posed in **Nicaragua**. A virtual dictator, Somoza remained the strong man in that country for the next 20 years.

1936 Dec. 11 **Edward VIII** (June 23, 1894–May 11, 1972), king of Great Britain, **abdicated** in order to marry an American divorcee, **Wallis Warfield Simpson** (June 19, 1896–Apr. 24, 1986). When Edward's liaison with Mrs. Simpson became known, it caused great public excitement and differences of opinion. The Conservative government refused to agree to a royal marriage of the couple, and a suggestion of a morganatic marriage was also rejected. In a farewell radio address, Edward said he could not be king "without the help and support of the woman I love." He thus became the **first British monarch to give up the throne voluntarily**. He was succeeded by his younger brother, the Duke of York (Dec. 14, 1895–Feb. 6, 1952) as George VI. Edward was given the title of Duke of Windsor and on June 3, 1937, he and Mrs. Simpson were married in France.

III. ECONOMY AND TRADE

1936 The **U.S. Gold Bullion Depository** was constructed at **Fort Knox**, Kentucky. Concrete and steel reinforced walls protect the bulk of the nation's gold bullion.

1936 *The General Theory of Employment, Interest, and Money* by **John Maynard Keynes** (June 5, 1883–Apr. 21, 1946), an English economist, was published. It focused on the problem of unemployment and what governments could do to cure depressions. In times of depression, Keynes said, governments must spend money, even if it means an unbalanced budget, in order to create jobs and thereby purchasing power. There were other important aspects of Keynes's general theory, but the idea of spending one's way out of depression caught the public fancy. Most countries, the U.S. especially, adopted Keynes's ideas, for the most part without quite realizing it.

1936 Sept. 27 **France, the Netherlands, and Switzerland went off the gold standard**. They were the last countries of importance in world trade and finance to do so under the stress of the **Great Depression**. On Oct. 2 France, faced with runaway inflation, devalued the franc. Financial support from Great Britain and the U.S. prevented the shock of this step from creating panic on world markets.

IV. RELIGION AND PHILOSOPHY

1936   In his encyclical *Vigilanti cura* Pope Pius XI praised the **American Legion of Decency** for improving the morality of motion pictures, and called on the bishops of the world to work to make a "power of such universality" as the motion picture into a force for the "highest ends of individual and social improvement."

1936 May 8   Oswald Spengler (b. May 29, 1880), a German philosopher and historian, died. Although he studied and wrote in a number of fields, his best-known work was *Der Utergang des Abendlandes* [*The Decline of the West*] (1918–1922). Spengler believed all civilizations passed through stages from youth to maturity to decay and death. Western culture, he concluded, was in a serious state of decline.

1936 Dec. 31   Miguel de Unamuno (b. Sept. 29, 1864), a Spanish philosopher, died. His criticism of the monarchy and of the dictator **Primo de Rivera** cost him his position at the **University of Salamanca** and he was exiled (1924–1930). At the outbreak of the Civil War (1936–1939) he sided first with the republic, then with the rebels, turning against the latter shortly before his death. Unamuno's chief work was *Del sentimiento trágico de la vida en los hombres y los pueblos* [*The Tragic Sense of Life in Men and Nations*] (1913).

V. SCIENCE, EDUCATION, AND TECHNOLOGY

1936   The **DC-3 made its debut** in the U.S. It was designed and produced by **Donald** [Wills] **Douglas** (Apr. 6, 1892–Feb. 2, 1981). The DC-3 was powered by two 900-horsepower engines, seated 21 in airline use, flew nearly 160 miles per hour, and could go 1,500 miles nonstop. Besides designing and building such planes for the armed forces as the A-20 bomber (1939) and the B-19 bomber (1941), Douglas turned out bigger versions of the DC-3, his last being the DC-8 in 1959. About 11,000 of the DC-3s were manufactured, and it was the backbone of air passenger service in its day. In 1988 a few airworthy DC-3s were still in service.

1936   The first surgical procedure presaging what became the fairly common **prefrontal lobotomy** was performed by **Antonio Caetano de Abreu Freire**

Egas Moniz (Nov. 29, 1874–Dec. 13, 1955), a Portuguese neurologist. The procedure consisted of drilling holes in the skull and severing certain nerve fibers in the brain. Egas Moniz shared the **Nobel prize for physiology** or medicine in 1949.

1936   The **Hoover Dam**, on the Colorado River between Arizona and Nevada, one of the largest dams in the world, was completed. Until 1947, it was known as **Boulder Dam**, and was renamed in honor of Herbert Hoover, president of the U.S. (1929–1933). The dam created **Lake Mead**, the **world's largest reservoir**. Water from the lake is used to produce electricity in one of the world's largest hydroelectric plants and to irrigate more than 1,000,-000 acres of farmland.

1936 Feb. 16   James Harvey Robinson (b. June 29, 1863), an American historian, died. Robinson's work was very influential on other historians. He was the author, among many other books, of *The New History* [with Charles A. Beard] (1911), *The Mind in the Making* (1921), and *The Ordeal of Civilization* (1926).

1936 Feb. 27   Ivan Petrovich Pavlov (b. Sept. 14, 1849), a Russian physiologist, died. Pavlov's best-known research, begun in 1897, was on digestion in which he proved the process was not a simple chemical reaction but involved both mind and body in reflexes based on sight, smell, and mental attitudes. He was awarded the **Nobel prize for physiology or medicine** in 1904. From his work on digestion he began (1903) his pioneer work on conditioned reflexes. He also did pioneer research on the physiology of the heart.

1936 July 4   The **first successful, maneuverable helicopter**, designed and built by **Heinrich Focke** (1890–Feb. 25, 1979), was flown in Germany. It had a twin motor design to eliminate torque, the force which caused earlier craft to spin into the ground. **Igor Sikorsky** (May 25, 1889–Oct. 26, 1972), a Russian-born American engineer, was another helicopter pioneer. He built his first one in 1909, but it was not until Sept. 14, 1939, that he flew what proved to be the first helicopter worthy of commercial production. He called it the VS300.

1936 Nov.   The **British Broadcasting Corporation** [BBC] began the first regular, high-quality television broadcasting service in Europe.

VI. ARTS AND LEISURE

1936   Gian-Carlo Menotti (b. July 7, 1911), an Italian-American composer, registered his first success with a one-act comic opera *Amelia Goes to the Ball*, a radio opera, which was staged the next year by the Metropolitan Opera of New York City. His successes include *The Medium* (1946), *The Telephone* (1947), *The Consul* (1950), and *The Saint of Bleecker Street* (1954). His greatest success proved to be his opera commissioned for television, *Amahl and the Night Visitors* (1951).

1936   Considered by some to have been the **founder of modern Mongolian literature**, **D. Natsagdorj** (1906–1937) was deported from his native Mongolia to Russia, where he died a year later of a stroke.

1936 Jan. 18   Rudyard Kipling (b. Dec. 30, 1865), dubbed poet laureate of British imperialism, died. He was both a serious and a humorous poet, whose best-known collection of poetry was *Barrack-Room Ballads and Other Verses* (1892). His novels include *Kim* (1910) and *The Light that Failed* (1890). He wrote a number of children's stories, including *The Jungle Book(s)* (1894, 1895). He was awarded the **Nobel prize for literature** in 1906.

1936 Apr. 18   Ottorino Respighi (b. July 9, 1879), an Italian composer and conductor, died. His works included *Le Fontane di Roma* [*The Fountain of Rome*] (1917) and *I Pini di Roma* [*The Pines of Rome*] (1924), a favorite in the U.S.

1936 Apr. 30   A[lfred] **E**[dward] **Housman** (b. Mar. 26, 1859), an English poet, died. His three small volumes of poetry—**A Shropshire Lad** (1895), **Last Poems** (1922), and **More Poems** (1936)—constituted a body of poetry nearly unique in English literature for their bittersweet simplicity.

1936 June 14   Maksim [Maxim] **Gorki** [Gorky] (Aleksei Maksimovich Peshkov) (b. Mar. 14, 1868), a Russian playwright, novelist, and essayist, died. Gorky was the most important writer of the **Socialist Realism school** and remains today an idol of Russians. He is widely known now for his short stories, such as those published in *My Fellow Traveler* and *Twenty-Six Men and a Girl* (both 1901), and for such novels as *Mother* (1907) and *The Specter* (a tetrology appearing from 1927 to 1938). His most famous play *The Lower Depths* was first produced in 1903; others were *Yegor Bulychov* (1932) and *Dos-*

tigaeff and Others (1934). He also wrote biographies as well as an autobiography.

1936 June 14   G[ilbert] **K**[eith] **Chesterton** (b. May 29, 1874), an English author, died. He was perhaps best known for his essays, published in the collections **Heretics** (1905) and **Orthodoxy** (1909); for his curious novel *The Man Who Was Thursday* (1908); and most notably for the priest-detective Father Brown, who first appeared in a collection of stories, *The Innocence of Father Brown* (1911). Further collections appeared in 1914, 1926, and 1927. Chesterton's **Collected Poems** was issued in 1927.

1936 Aug. 16   Grazia Deledda (b. Sept. 27, 1875), generally regarded as the finest Italian novelist of the time, died. *The Mother* (1924), a novel set in a small village in Deledda's native Sardinia, told about a young priest pulled between a woman and his mother. Deledda received the **Nobel prize for literature** in 1926.

1936 Aug. 19?   Federico García Lorca (b. June 15, 1899), a Spanish dramatist and poet, died at the hands of the Nationalist rebels, who shot him dead without a trial soon after the start of the **Spanish Civil War** (1936–1939). He was a strong supporter of the Republican government. García Lorca's work was filled with joy and passion, but also with violence. He won great popularity as a poet with **Romancero gitano** [*Gypsy Ballads*] (1928). His other poetry included **Llanto por Ignacio Sánchez Mejías** [*Lament for the Death of a Bullfighter*] (1935) and **Poeta en Nueva York** [*The Poet in New York*] (1940). His dramatic works included **Bodas de sangre** [*Blood Wedding*] (1933), a searing tragedy that made García Lorca famous; **Doña Rosita la soltera** [*Doña Rosita the Spinster*] (1935); and *La Casa de Bernardo Alba* (1936).

1936 Sept. 16   Vishnu Narayan Bhatkhande (b. Aug. 10, 1860), an Indian musicologist and authority on **raga**, a traditional form of Hindu music, died. Recognized as the most influential theorist of the 20th century in India, he was associated especially with the raga of the northern India oral tradition. Bhatkhande wrote many works in his field, including **Lakshyasangit** (1910), **Hindustani Sangit Paddhati** (1910–1932), and **Kramik Pustak** (1920–1936).

1936 Oct. 19   Chou Shu-Jen [pseudonym Lu Hsun] (b. 1881), a Chinese author who pioneered in writing short stories in the western style, died. Two of his best short stories are "Madman's Diary" (1918) and "True Story of Ah Q" (1921). Two collections are *Naha* (1923) and *P'ang-huang* (1926).

1936 Dec. 10   Luigi Pirandello (b. June 24, 1867), an Italian novelist and dramatist, died. He was awarded the **Nobel prize for literature** in 1934. He wrote poems: *Mal Giocando* (1889); short stories: *Amori Senza Amori* (1894), *Il Carnevale dei Morti* (1919), and *Tu Ridi* (1919); novels, including *Il fu Mattia Pascal* [*The Late Mattia Pascal*] (1904) and *I vecchi e i giovani* [*The Young and the Old*] (1913); plays, including *Così e se vi pare* [*Right You Are if You Think You Are*] (1917) and his best-known *Sei Personaggi in cerca d'autore* [*Six Characters in Search of an Author*] (1921). Pirandello sought to show that it was impossible to distinguish between fiction and reality.

VII. SPORTS, GAMES, AND SOCIETY

1936   A book on **skiing** by **Eugen Matthias**, a University of Munich physiologist, and **Giovanni Testa**, the head of the ski school at St. Moritz, foreshadowed a drastic post-World War II shift in downhill skiing techniques from the Arlberg to what came to be called the "reverse shoulder" or "parallel method," in which turns were made with the knees together. Without loss of safety, the new method offered greater speed and less strain on the joints.

1936 Feb. 2   [Tyrus Raymond] **Ty Cobb** (Dec. 18, 1886–July 17, 1961), [George Herman] **Babe Ruth** (Feb. 6, 1895–Aug. 16, 1948), [John Peter] **Honus Wagner** (Feb. 24, 1874–Dec. 6, 1955), [Christopher] **Christy Mathewson** (July 12, 1880–Oct. 7, 1925), and **Walter Perry Johnson** (Nov. 6, 1887–Dec. 10, 1946), "The Big Train," were the **first players elected to baseball's Hall of Fame** at Cooperstown, New York. These five were the only ones to receive the required 75 percent of the total vote by baseball writers.

1936 Feb. 6–16   At the fourth Winter **Olympic Games** held at Garmisch-Partenkirchen, Germany, Norway won 7 gold medals and 15 overall. Germany was second with 3 and 6, and Sweden third with 2 and 7. Twenty-eight nations were represented and 755 athletes participated. The individual star of the games was **Sonja Henie** of Norway who won an unprecedented third gold medal for figure skating. She also won the world figure skating championship ten years in a row.

1936 Aug. 1–16   At the eleventh Summer **Olympic Games** held in Berlin, black American track and field athletes made a mockery of **Adolf Hitler**'s theory of "Aryan superiority" in the dictator's own stadium. They won 8 gold, 3 silver, and 2 bronze medals. **Jesse Owens** (Sept. 12, 1913–Mar. 31, 1980) won four track and field events, setting two world records in the process. Germany won 33 gold medals and 89 in all; the U.S. was second with 24 and 56; and Hungary was third with 10 and 16. Forty-nine nations sent 4,066 athletes to the games.

1937

I. DISASTERS

1937 Jan. 22   Floods swept through the Ohio and mid-Mississippi river valleys, inundating 20,000 square miles. At least 137 people died and c.700,000 were left homeless. Property damage was set at $418 million.

1937 Mar. 18   Leaking natural gas, accumulating in the hollow tile walls of the New London, Texas, Consolidated School, exploded, killing 294 students and teachers.

1937 July 2   Amelia Earhart (b. July 24, 1898), an American aviator, and Frederick J. Noonan (b.

1894), her navigator, disappeared while on a round-the-world flight. They were last heard from by radio while flying between New Guinea and Howland Island in the Pacific Ocean. The U.S. navy searched for them for two weeks without results. Earhart had a number of aviation firsts to her credit: first woman to cross the Atlantic Ocean by plane (1928); first woman to make a solo flight across the Atlantic (1932); and first person to fly alone from Honolulu to California (1935).

1937 May 6   The **German zeppelin** *Hindenburg*, at the end of a transatlantic crossing, burst into flame and **burned** as it approached a landing at Lakehurst, N.J., killing 36 of its 97 passengers and crew.

II. POLITICS AND WAR

1937 Jan. 20   **Franklin D. Roosevelt** was inaugurated for a second term as president of the U.S., having defeated **Alfred M. Landon** of the Republican party. **John N. Garner** was inaugurated again as vice president. In the election of Nov. 3, 1936, Roosevelt carried all but two states [Maine and Vermont], receiving 27,751,612 popular votes and 523 electoral. Landon received 16,687,913 and 8.

1937 Apr. 26   **German warplanes dropped more than 50 tons of incendiary and explosive bombs on Guernica**, a market town of c.7,000 residents in northern Spain, in the Basque region. By one count, 1,654 people died and 889 were wounded. The **Nazis** were supporting the fascist rebels against the Republican government in the **Spanish Civil War** (1936–1939). In May and June **Pablo Picasso**, a Spanish artist of international renown, painted *Guernica*, a large canvas of intense feeling as a political and artistic statement against the horrors of modern warfare.

1937 May 28   [Arthur] **Neville Chamberlain** (Mar. 18, 1869–Nov. 9, 1940), chancellor of the exchequer in the Conservative government of Great Britain, became prime minister when **Stanley Baldwin** resigned.

1937 June 10   **Robert Laird Borden** (b. June 26, 1854), a Canadian politician, died. He was the leader of the Conservative party (1901–1920) and prime minister of **Canada** from 1911 to 1920. He is best remembered today for his direction of the Canadian war effort in World War I and for advocacy of Canada's right to be regarded as a significant and independent force in the international community.

1937 July 7   The **Japanese army attacked Chinese troops near Peiping** [Peking, Beijing], which they captured on July 19, initiating the **Second Sino-Japanese War** (to 1945). In August the Japanese attacked Shanghai, which fell on Oct. 27, after which Nanking [Nanjing], then the capital of China, fell on Dec. 12 to 13 and Hangchow [Hangzhou] on Dec. 24. The capture of the capital became known as "The Rape of Nanking" after Japanese troops were reported to have killed c.350,000 civilians and nearly destroyed the city.

1937 July 21   A new constitution for the **Irish Free State** took effect. It was the work of **Eamon de Val-**

era, prime minister (1937–1948). The constitution declared the country to be a completely sovereign nation, but within the British Commonwealth.

1937 Sept. 14   **Thomás** [Garrigue] **Masaryk** (b. Mar. 7, 1850), a philosopher and **first president** of **Czechoslovakia** (1918–1935), died. Before World War I he worked within the Austro-Hungarian Empire for more rights for the Czech people. During the war he helped form a provisional government in exile, which was recognized (1918) by the Allies after the war. Masaryk was recognized in all parts of the world as one of the foremost democratic leaders of his era. His writings included *The Making of a State* (1927), *Ideals of Humanity* (1938), and *Modern Man and Religion* (1938).

1937 Oct. 1   To halt the influx of Haitian workers and to force the return home of many of the c.200,000 already there, **Dominican troops began murdering Haitians** in large numbers along the border between the two countries. It was estimated that as many as 10,000 Haitians were killed, most with knives and machetes, by Jan. 1, 1938.

1937 Dec. 12   The **U.S. navy gunboat *Panay* was bombed and sunk by Japanese gunfire** in the Yangtze River [Chang Jiang] near Nanking. Two Standard Oil Company vessels were also sunk. Five persons were killed. Japan claimed the *Panay* was mistaken for a Chinese vessel, but apologized and on Dec. 14 promised to pay an indemnity.

III. ECONOMY AND TRADE

1937–1945   **Wartime inflation hit China**, with prices rising by 1944 to more than 200 times 1937 levels, and then accelerating to 2,000 times the 1937 levels by 1945.

1937 Feb. 11   The **General Motors Corporation** [GM] granted the **United Automobile Workers** [UAW] a contract, including recognition of the union, that was a clear victory for the workers. In the sit-down strike, workers stayed in the plant they worked in but stopped all work. The sit-down strike in the U.S. was first used in the rubber industry in 1936, but it was this strike, at a Flint, Michigan, GM plant, beginning on Dec. 30, 1936, that provided the inspiration for many more. By mid-1937 c.500,000 workers had used this technique in making their demands. The **U.S. Supreme Court declared the sit-down strike illegal** on Feb. 27, 1939.

1937 Mar. 13   The **Bolivian government seized the properties of the Standard Oil Company** in Bolivia, rescinding the company's rights to explore and drill there.

1937 May 23   John D[avidson] **Rockefeller, Sr.** (b. July 8, 1839), American billionaire industrialist and philanthropist, died. Rockefeller saw the possibilities in the new oil industry and, with partners, established (1863) a refinery. Rockefeller ran an efficient business, sought mergers, and used questionable practices to get favorable railroad rates and control pipelines. The **Standard Oil Company**, which was organized in 1870, came to dominate the industry. Rockefeller retired in 1911 and devoted himself to philanthropy. He established the Rockefeller Institute for Medical Research [now **Rockefeller University**], and the **Rockefeller Foundation**, among others. By the time he died Rockefeller had given away about $500,000,000, roughly half his fortune.

IV. RELIGION AND PHILOSOPHY

1937   During the summer, two of the four ecumenical movements, first **Life and Work**, and then **Faith and Order**, held conferences of all participating churches, at Oxford and Edinburgh respectively. The free discussions and reports on often controversial subjects among Christians, lay and clerical, from many nations, advanced ecumenicity significantly.

1937   The **Central Conference of American Rabbis** [Reform], meeting at Columbus, Ohio, adopted a new set of principles to supersede the Pittsburgh Platform of 1885. In the **Columbus Platform**, Reform rabbis now expressed approval of **Zionism** and reaffirmed the centrality of the Torah for Judaism.

1937 Mar. 5   **Pope Pius XI** issued an encyclical *On the Condition of the Catholic Church in the German Reich*. The pope denounced the Nazi government, both as to its theories and its actions. The pope at this time also issued a paper, "On Atheistic Communism," in which he decried persecutions taking place in Mexico, Russia, and Spain.

V. SCIENCE, EDUCATION, AND TECHNOLOGY

1937   **James P. Chapin** (July 9, 1889–Apr. 5, 1969) of the American Museum of Natural History in New York went to Zaire [then Belgian Congo] to collect specimens of a peafowl. He had deduced, on the basis of one feather in a native headdress in the museum's collection, that it was a species unknown to science. The bird is now known as African Peafowl, *Afropava congoensis*.

1937   **Xerography**, a printing process based on the principle of electrostatics, was developed by **Chester F[loyd] Carlson** (Feb. 8, 1906–Sept. 19, 1968), an American physicist.

1937 Mar. 15   The **first modern blood bank** was established at the Cook County Hospital in Chicago. Blood transfusions were first used during World War I, but it was some time before techniques were perfected to keep blood from coagulating, and to keep it refrigerated and sterile for more than short periods of time.

1937 May 27   The **Golden Gate Bridge** over the strait between the Pacific Ocean and San Francisco Bay was opened. Its main span of 4,200 feet is the third longest suspension bridge in the world, and its towers at 746 feet in height are the tallest bridge towers. The bridge connects the city of San Francisco with Marin County, California, to the north.

1937 July 12–14   **M. Gromov, S. Danilin** (d. Dec. 1978), and **A. Yumashev** of Russia flew non-stop 6,262 miles from Moscow **over the Arctic** to San Jacinto, California, in 62 hours, 2 min.

1937 July 19   **Guglielmo Marconi** (b. Apr. 25, 1874), an Italian physicist and inventor, died. He developed wireless telegraphy, sending the first long-wave signals over more than a mile in 1895. Three years later he sent messages across the English Channel and in 1901 the first transatlantic message. In the 1930s Marconi worked in the field of short-wave wireless communications. He shared the 1909 **Nobel prize for physics** for his work.

1937 Oct. 19   New Zealand-born **Ernest Rutherford** (b. Aug. 30, 1871), an English physicist, died. He was the **first person to transmute one element into another** when he produced an elementary form of nuclear reaction in his laboratory. One of the most important pioneers in the study of radioactivity, Rutherford worked with **Hans Geiger** in the **development of the Geiger counter** (1913). In 1896 he determined that radioactive substances gave off separate positively and negatively charged rays, which he called alpha and beta rays. On May 7, 1911,

Rutherford announced that the atom consisted of a positively charged nucleus surrounded by negatively charged electrons. His model was confirmed (1913) in experiments made by reflecting a stream of alpha particles from gold foil. Rutherford was awarded the **Nobel prize for chemistry** in 1908.

1937 Dec. 7 Romansch was **recognized as a fourth national language of Switzerland**. The three main national languages, German, French, and Italian, represented respectively 70.5 percent, 19 percent, and 9.5 percent of the population.

VI. ARTS AND LEISURE

1937 The death of **Abdüllah Taran Hâmit** (b. 1852), a Turkish poet, dramatist and diplomat, was officially mourned by the whole nation. A giant of modern Turkish literature, his many works included the plays, written to be read, *Duhter-i Hindû* [*The Indian Maiden*] (1875) and *Târak* (1879), and the romantic narrative *Garam* [*Desire*] (1877).

1937 The great French director, **Jean Renoir** (Sept. 15, 1894–Feb. 12, 1979), made *La Grande Illusion*, a film about prisoners of war in World War I, on the eve of World War II. It ranks with the finest films of all time. Other films by Renoir included *Diary of a Chambermaid* (in English, 1947) and *Le Déjeuner sur l'herbe* (1959).

1937 June 7 **Jean Harlow** [nee Harlean Carpenter] (b. Mar. 3, 1911), an American film star called the "Blonde Bombshell," died. She had genuine talent as a comedienne, but was also a "sex goddess." Both aspects of her talents were shown in her movies, including *Hell's Angels* (1930), *Platinum Blonde* (1931), *Red-Headed Woman* (1932), and *Saratoga* (1937).

1937 June 19 **James M. Barrie** (b. May 9, 1860), a Scottish novelist and dramatist, died. His novels included *The Little Minister* (1891), *Sentimental Tommy* (1895), and *Tommy and Grizel* (1900). His plays included *Quality Street*, *The Admirable Crichton*, and *Little Mary*, all produced in 1903, and *Peter Pan*, produced in 1904. Other Barrie plays were *What Every Woman Knows* (1908) and *Dear Brutus* (1917).

1937 July 11 **George Gershwin** (b. Sept. 26, 1898), a composer of Broadway musicals and jazz, died. His major works included *Rhapsody in Blue* (1924),

Piano Concerto in F (1925), and *An American in Paris* (1928). His musicals, for which his brother **Ira** (Dec. 6, 1896–Aug. 17, 1983) wrote the lyrics, included *Funny Face* (1927), *Girl Crazy* (1930), and *Of Thee I Sing* (1931). *Porgy and Bess* (1935) was written as an opera but was not acclaimed as such by the critics until recently.

1937 Aug. 12 **Edith Wharton** [nee Edith Newbold Jones] (b. Jan. 24, 1862), an American novelist, died in France. Her first successful novel was *The House of Mirth* (1905). Her other important works included *Ethan Frome* (1911), *The Custom of the Country* (1913), and *The Age of Innocence* (1920). Wharton depicted New York society in the early years of the century.

1937 Sept. 26 **Bessie Smith** (b. Apr. 15, 1898), "Empress of the Blues," died in an automobile accident. Her mentor was **Gertrude "Ma" Rainey** (Apr. 26, 1886–Dec. 22, 1939), **first of the great blues singers**. The blues expressed the frustration of many black Americans. Bessie Smith made her first recording with **Columbia Records** in Feb., 1923.

1937 Oct. 17 The **State Academic Folk Dance Ensemble**, which soon became better known as the **Moiseyev Dance Ensemble**, gave its first performance in Moscow. It took its name from Igor Aleksandrovich Moiseyev (b. Jan. 21, 1906), a Russian choreographer, who organized it. The company featured interpretations of the folk dances of Russia, translating them into theatrical presentations.

1937 Dec. 28 **Maurice Joseph Ravel** (b. Mar. 7, 1875), a French composer, died. His cantata *Myrrha* won the Grand Prix de Rome in 1901. Among his best-known works were *Jeux d'Eau* (1901), *Pavane pour une Infante Défunte* (1899), *Rhapsodie Espagnole* (1907), *Daphnis et Chloe* (1912), *Bolero* (1928), *Piano Trio in A Minor* (1915), and *Piano Concerto for the Left Hand* (1931). Ravel was a leading figure in impressionism, a chiefly French movement of musical composition.

VII. SPORTS, GAMES AND SOCIETY

1937 Apr. 17 A crowd of 149,547 **soccer** fans watched Scotland beat England, 3-1 in an international game played at Hampden Park, Glasgow,

Scotland. It still is the **record attendance for a sporting event held in the British Isles**.

1937 June 5 By winning the Belmont Stakes, **War Admiral**, with jockey **Charles Kurtsinger** (1906–Sept. 24, 1946), became the fourth horse to win the **Triple Crown** of American thoroughbred racing. War Admiral won the Kentucky Derby (May 8) and the Preakness Stakes (May 15).

1937 June 22 **Joe Louis** knocked out **James J. Braddock** in the eighth round, winning the **world heavyweight boxing championship** at Chicago.

1937 July 31–Aug. 5 The American J-boat *Ranger*, designed for a syndicate headed by **Harold S. Vanderbilt**, who skippered her, easily defeated T.O.M. Sopwith's British challenger, *Endeavour II* for the **America's Cup**, in four straight races off Newport, Rhode Island.

1938

I. DISASTERS

1938 Mar. 2 **Floods** and landslides caused 144 deaths in southern **California**. Thousands of homes were destroyed, and property losses mounted to nearly $60,000,000.

1938 Sept. 21 A **hurricane and floods** exploded across **New York and New England**, resulting in 680 lives lost, 1,754 injured, and $400 million total damages. **Providence, Rhode Island**, was hit by a **tidal wave**. Thousands of trees were blown down and communication facilities were put out of service.

1938 Nov. 12–16 **Changsha, capital of the Chinese province of Hunan**, was razed by **fire**; 2,000 died.

1938 Dec. 25 A Christmas Day **collision of two passenger trains** near Kishinev, **Rumania**, killed c.350 people and injured c.350.

II. POLITICS AND WAR

1938 An especially severe **black riot occurred in Jamaica**. **Marcus Garvey**, an **American expatriate**, with theories of black nationalism, influenced the protest against unfair British racial policies and unemployment.

1938 A **unified federal penal code abolished capital punishment in Switzerland**, except under martial law, general mobilization, or war.

1938 Jan. 28 Alarmed by the spread of fascist power in Europe and militarism in Japan, **Franklin D. Roosevelt**, president of the U.S., asked Congress for funds to **expand the American armed forces**, es-

pecially the navy. On May 27 Congress appropriated more than $1,000,000,000 to make the U.S. navy strong in both the Atlantic and the Pacific oceans.

1938 Feb. 4 **Adolf Hitler**, German führer, forced two generals, Werner von Blomberg (Sept. 2, 1878—Mar. 22, 1946), minister of war, and Walter von Brauchitsch (Oct. 4, 1881–Oct. 18, 1942), to retire and **made himself commander in chief** of the German armed forces. He also discharged Konstantin von Neurath (Feb. 2, 1873–Aug. 14, 1956), the foreign minister, and replaced him with Joachim von Ribbentrop (Apr. 30, 1893–Oct. 16, 1946).

1938 Mar. 12 **German troops marched unopposed into Austria** to effect *Anschluss* [Union] of the two German-speaking nations. The next day Austria was declared a province of the German **Third Reich** (1933–1945). On Mar. 14 Hitler, who was born in Austria, made a triumphal entry into Vienna. He was greeted with wild enthusiasm by his Austrian Nazi followers. Once Austria was part of Germany, large-scale persecution of Austrian Jews began. A plebiscite approved (Apr. 10) the union with a favorable vote of 99.75 percent.

1938 Apr. 9 A nationalist **civil disobedience campaign** against France was organized in **Tunisia** by **Habib Bourguiba**, leader of the **Neo-Destour party** (1934). As riots occurred in Tunis, the Neo-Destour was outlawed and several thousand of its members, including its leader, were arrested. A state of emergency was proclaimed and political liberties were restricted.

1938 May 10 All **Jews in Germany were required by law to have the letter J** on their clothing, stamped on their passports and other official documents.

1938 Sept. 29 The democracies, represented by France and Great Britain, agreed in the **Munich Pact** to Adolf Hitler's demands and advised **Czechoslovakia** to surrender part of its territory to Nazi Germany. **Neville Chamberlain**, prime minister of Great Britain, returned home, saying the Munich Pact meant **"peace in our time."** Others saw the agreement as **appeasement**, peace at any price, that would only lead to more demands from Hitler. The events leading to the pact began (Sept. 12) when Hitler demanded the right of self-determination for Germans living in the Sudetenland, the border areas with Germany and Austria in Bavaria and Moravia of western Czechoslovakia. Nazi Germans there had been encouraged to cause trouble. Beginning on Oct. 1, German troops occupied the Sudetenland in accordance with the terms of the Munich Pact. Formal incorporation of the region into Germany occurred on Nov. 21. Edvard Beneš (May 28, 1884–Sept. 3, 1948), president of Czechoslovakia, resigned (Oct. 5) and went into exile.

1938 Oct. **Pedro Aguirre Cerda** (Feb. 6, 1879–Nov. 25, 1941) was elected president (1938–1941) of **Chile**, running on the Popular Front ticket, a coalition of leftists and democrats. On Sept. 5 a rightwing force had tried unsuccessfully to seize power from the outgoing president (1932–1938), Arturo Alessandri Palma.

1938 Oct. 17 **Karl** [Johann] **Kautsky** (b. Oct. 16, 1854), a German-Austrian socialist theorist, died. He was a leader in the effort to disseminate Marxist doctrines in Germany and in preparing the **Erfurt Program** (1891), which kept the German Social Democratic party on a Marxist basis. Kautsky was also a leading figure in international socialism before World War I. Kautsky was active as an editor and author. One of his translated works was *Ethics and the Materialistic Conception of History* (1907).

1938 Oct. 21 **Japanese forces captured Canton** [Guangzhou], the important southern Chinese seaport. Four days later they took Hankow [Hankou], in central eastern China on the Yangtze River [Chang Jiang]. In November Japan announced what it called the **"New Order for East Asia,"** meaning Japan considered itself supreme in that area and was not obliged to grant privileges to other nations.

1938 Oct. 25 **Libya**, much of it **occupied by Italy** since 1914, was made an integral part of that country. Italian pacification was completed this year with the death of al-Mukhtar, leader of the Sanusi, a Muslim brotherhood that was the main nationalistic movement in Libya. Under Italo Balbo (June 6, 1896–June 22, 1940), governor general (1933–1940), c.40,000 colonists were sent from Italy. Civic buildings, schools, and hospitals were constructed, and a limited form of citizenship was granted the Muslim inhabitants.

1938 Nov. 9–10 *Kristallnacht* [*Crystal Night*] was the name given to the 24 hours of terror that marked the beginning of the systematic persecution of the Jews in Germany and Austria by the **Nazis**. Thousands of windows of Jewish homes and businesses were broken by Nazi-encouraged hoodlums. Their excuse was that a German embassy aide in Paris had been shot (Nov. 7) by a teenage Polish Jew. It was estimated that 100 Jews were murdered and 20,000 arrested, while c. 200 synagogues and c.7,500 businesses were destroyed, along with an uncounted number of homes. The government (Nov. 14 and 15) barred Jews from economic life, public transportation, and schools and universities. *Kristallnacht* foreshadowed the **Holocaust**, the mass killings of Jews and others that became Nazi policy in 1941.

1938 Nov. 10 **Kemal Ataturk** [Mustafa Kemal] (b. Mar. 12, 1881), the **founder of modern Turkey**, died. As early as 1908 he participated in the successful **Young Turk revolution**. During World War I he served brilliantly in the army. After the war he was the leader and organizer of the forces that on Nov. 1, 1922, forced the sultan to flee. In Ataturk's 12 years as president he changed Turley from a backward Islamic state into a secular nation with a western outlook and practices. Ataturk was succeeded as president by Ismet Inonu (Sept. 24, 1884–Dec. 25, 1973).

III. TRADE AND ECONOMICS

1938 Mar. 18 The **Mexican government expropriated oil fields** of American and British companies worth $450,000,000 as part of a program to end foreign economic domination.

1938 June 27 The **Fair Labor Standards Act**, also known as the **Wages and Hours Act**, was passed and signed into law in the U.S. It set a minimum wage of 40 cents per hour for workers in the employ of industries or businesses engaged in interstate commerce. The act was estimated to have increased the wages of c.750,000 workers and reduced the working hours of c.1.5 million wage earners, mainly in the southeastern states.

1938 July 16 **Samuel Insull** (b. Nov. 11, 1859), a London-born American financier, died. He became head of two Chicago area utilities, which he merged into the **Commonwealth Edison Company**. Insull also came to control Chicago's transit system. Eventually he controlled c.500 generating plants, which he organized into an intricate system of holding companies. At the height of the speculative frenzy of the 1920s, thousands of people invested in his empire, worth $3,000,000,000. When the pyramid of companies collapsed into bankruptcy in 1932, Insull fled to Europe and was extradited back to the U.S. in 1934. Three times he was tried (1934–1935) for mail fraud and embezzlement but was acquitted each time.

IV. RELIGION AND PHILOSOPHY

1938 Apr. 26 **Edmund Husserl** (b. Apr. 8, 1859), a German philosopher and **founder of phenomenology**, died. The universal philosophical method he sought focused on phenomena only. He excluded anything not visible, and therefore not apparent to the consciousness. As to consciousness, he said it had no existence except in relation to the objects it considered. Husserl's most notable writings were *Logische Untersuchungen* [*Logical Inquiries*] (1900–1901) and *Ideen zu einer reinen Phänomenologie und phänomenologischen Philosophie* [*Thoughts toward a Pure Phenomenology and Phenomenological Philosophy*] (1922).

1938 June **Frank** [Nathan Daniel] **Buchman** (June 4, 1878–Aug. 7, 1961), an American clergyman and organizer of religious groups, founded **Moral Rearmament** [MRA] in London. He wished to stress moral and social regeneration on a national scale, rather than as an individual matter. Buchman's movement attracted a substantial following in the atmosphere of a Europe on the verge of war. In 1921 at Oxford University, what became known as the **Oxford Group**, or sometimes **Buchmanism**, got its start.

V. SCIENCE, EDUCATION, AND TECHNOLOGY

1938 **Otto Hahn**, a German chemist, director of the Kaiser Wilhelm Institute for Physical Chemistry, was the **first to create atomic fission** when a sample of uranium was bombarded with neutrons and produced barium. He was assisted by **Fritz Strassmann** (b. 1902) and **Lise Meitner** (Nov. 7, 1878–Oct. 27, 1968). Hahn did not publish the news of his discovery, which was done early in 1939 by Meitner, an Austrian Jew who had been forced by the Nazis to flee to Stockholm.

1938 The **ball point pen** was patented by **Lazlo Biro**, a Hungarian, who further developed it after he moved to Argentina.

1938 Feb. 21 **George Ellery Hale** (b. June 29, 1868), an American astronomer who founded three important observatories, died. He was the organizer, then served as director (1895–1904), of the Yerkes Observatory at Williams Bay, Wisconsin. Hale played the same role (1904–1923) with the Mount Wilson Observatory, near Pasadena, California, and an observatory on Mount Palomar, northeast of San Diego, California. Hale conducted advanced research in his field and invented the **spectroheliograph** (1891), a device for photographing the surface of the sun.

1938 Feb. 24 The **first commercial product using the synthetic fabric nylon**—toothbrushes with nylon bristles—went on sale. A year after that, on Jan. 15, 1939, the first **nylon stockings** [soon known simply as nylons] were on sale. **Nylon** was invented by **Wallace Hume Carothers** (Apr. 27, 1896–Apr. 29, 1937), a chemist working for **E. I. du Pont de Nemours and Company**, Wilmington, Delaware.

1938 Mar. 28 **Electric shock therapy** for the treatment of certain mental illnesses was demonstrated for the first time by two Italian psychiatrists, **Ugo Cerletti** (1877–July 25, 1963) and **Lucio Bini** (b. 1908). The effect of such treatment is to produce convulsions, much like those of epileptics. The therapy is now used chiefly to treat severe depression and schizophrenia.

1938 July 10–13 **Howard** [Robard] **Hughes** (Dec. 24, 1905–Apr. 5, 1976) with a crew of four technicians **flew** a special cabin model monoplane with twin engines built by **Lockheed** and named *New*

York World's Fair 1939 around the world in 3 days, 19 hours, 8 minutes, 10 seconds at an average speed of 208.1 miles per hour. He left Floyd Bennett airfield on Long Island, flew to Paris, Moscow, Omsk, Yakutsk, Fairbanks, and Minneapolis, and returned.

1938 Aug. 10–14 **The first passenger steamship to cross the Atlantic Ocean in less than four days** was the British luxury liner **Queen Mary**, which made the voyage from the U.S. to England in 3 days, 20 hr., 42 min. The *Queen Mary*, more than 1,000 feet long and with a tonnage rated at 80,750, made her maiden voyage to the U.S. in 1936. Her sister ship the **Queen Elizabeth** made her maiden voyage in 1940. She was 1,041 feet long and 83,650 tons. Both ships were heavily used during World War II as troop ships, carrying as many as 15,000 men at a time. The *Queen Mary* is now at Long Beach, California, as a tourist attraction, while the *Queen Elizabeth* ended up in the same status in Hong Kong and later burned.

1938 Dec. A strange fish, 4½ feet long and weighing 127 pounds, was brought ashore by a trawler captain at East London, South Africa. **J.L.B. Smith** (1897–Jan. 7, 1968), an ichthyologist, identified it as a coelocanth named *Latimeria chalumnae*, a group of fishes known until then only as fossils from the Cretaceous Era c.70 million years ago. A second specimen was found in 1952 and since then a few more have been captured alive.

VI. ARTS AND LEISURE

1938 **Leni** [Helene Bertha Amalie] **Riefenstahl's** (b. Aug. 22, 1902) *Olympia*, a skillful documentary on the Olympic Games of 1936, was completed. It was said to have been the high point of pro-German film propaganda during the **Nazi** period.

1938 *Snow White and the Seven Dwarfs*, the first feature-length animated film, was released in the U.S. It also proved to be one of the most successful movies ever produced. It was a Walt Disney production.

1938 Jan. 21 **Georges Méliès** (b. 1861), a pioneer French movie maker, died. He made c.1,200 films, the exact number unknown because he sold all in his possession in 1923 for the value of the celluloid, to be melted down to make a substance used in manufacturing shoes. Only c.100 survive. His most famous film, *Le Voyage dans la Lune*, was made in 1902.

1938 Mar. 10 **Gabriele d'Annunzio** (b. Mar. 12, 1863), an Italian author, soldier, and politician, died. He wrote a book of poems *Primo Vere* (1879) which was not well received. His novels included **Il Piacere** (1889), **Il Trionfo del la Morte** (1894), and **Il Fuoco** (1900). Two of his plays were **La Figlia di Jorio** (1904) and **La Fiaccola sotto il Moggio** (1905). In World War I he served in the Italian air force with great daring, losing an eye in aerial combat. In Sept., 1919, during the controversy between Italy and Yugoslavia over the status of Fiume, he led an unauthorized Italian force and seized the city. D'Annunzio ruled there as a dictator until ousted by Italian government forces in Dec., 1920. He became a fervid supporter of Mussolini's fascist state.

1938 Apr. 12 **Fyodor Ivanovich Chaliapin** (b. Feb. 13, 1873), a Russian operatic bass, died. He began his career in St. Petersburg and then was with the Bolshoi Opera in Moscow (1899–1914). Chaliapin made his debut at La Scala in Milan (1901) and in New York at the Metropolitan Opera (1907). He left Russia for good after the Russian Revolution (1917) and settled in Paris in 1921. Chaliapin was best known for singing the lead role in **Boris Godunov**. His other triumphs included Ivan the Terrible in **Maid of Pskov**, in the title role of **Mefistofele**, and as Mephistofeles in **Faust**.

1938 Apr. 21 **Muhammad Iqbal** (b. 1877) died. Considered one of the great all-India poets, he wrote in Urdu and Persian. *The Secrets of Self* [*Asrar-e Khudi*] is considered today one of his best poems.

1938 May 22 **William James Glackens** (b. Mar. 13, 1879), an American painter of the Ashcan School, died. Typical of his works were **Hammerstein's Roof Garden** (1901), **Chez Mouquin** (1905), and **Washington Square** (1914).

1938 June 15 **Ernst Ludwig Kirchner** (b. May 5, 1880), a German expressionist artist, died. He was one of the founders in 1905 in Dresden of **Die Brucke** [*The Bridge*], a group of young artists to whom the term meant they were a bridge to the art of the future. Among his works were **Girl Under Japanese Umbrella** (1906), **Bathers at Moritzburg** (1908), and **The Street** (1913). In 1938 the Nazis condemned his work as "degenerate art." Kirchner, in poor health, committed suicide.

1938 July 21 **Owen Wister** (b. July 14, 1860), the novelist chiefly responsible for introducing the cowboy as the American folk hero, died. *The Virginian* (1902) first laid down themes now traditional to the Western, a native American mythology.

1938 Aug. 7 Konstantin Stanislavsky [nee Konstantin Sergeyevich Alekseyev] (b. Jan. 27, 1863), a Russian actor, teacher, and theatrical producer and manager, died. In 1897, with Vladimir Nemirovich-Danchenko, he founded the **Moscow Art Theater**, where he produced many plays, including works by Chekhov and Gorky. Stanislavsky strove to eradicate artificial techniques in acting and stressed the need for actors to identify with the characters they were creating. Stanislavsky's several books were guides to what became known as the **"method" style of acting.**

1938 Sept. 15 Thomas [Clayton] **Wolfe** (b. Oct. 3, 1900), whose novels were largely autobiographical, died. His first novel, *Look Homeward Angel* (1929), was followed by *Of Time and the River* (1935). *The Web and the Rock* (1939) and *You Can't Go Home Again* (1940) were published posthumously. Wolfe's work had strong appeal, particularly to his generation.

1938 Oct. 16 *Billy the Kid*, about the outlaw of the West and perhaps the **first American ballet of nationalistic expression,** had its premiere in Chicago, danced by the Ballet Caravan. The music was by **Aaron Copland** and the choreography by **Eugene Loring** (1914–Aug. 30, 1982).

1938 Dec. 24 Karel Čapek (b. Jan. 29, 1890), a Czechoslovakian playwright and novelist, who gave the world the word **"robot,"** died. His best-known work is ***R.U.R.*** [*Rossum's Universal Robots*] (1921). *The Insect Play* (1921) was written with his brother Josef (1887–1927). These, and other of Čapek's writings, satirized the modern world of science, industrialism, and militarism. *Power and Glory* (1937) and *The Mother* (1938), his last plays, deal harshly with totalitarianism.

VII. SPORTS, GAMES, AND SOCIETY

1938 For the fifth time in eight years, **Arsenal won the English League** first division championship, a record unmatched by any other club in the world's most competitive **soccer** league since **Aston Villa's** teams from 1894 to 1900.

1938 The first major U.S. intercollegiate basketball championship tournament, the **National Invitational** Tournament [NIT], was held at Madison Square Garden in New York City and won by Temple University.

1938 June 19 For the second year in succession Italy won the **World Cup of soccer,** defeating Hungary 4-2 at Paris.

1938 July 2 Helen [Newington] **Wills Moody** (b. Oct. 6, 1905), an American **tennis** player, **won her eighth Wimbledon women's singles** championship, defeating another American, **Helen Hull Jacobs** (b. Aug. 6, 1908). Moody also won the American championship nine times and the French four times. In all, she won more than 30 national and international tournaments, including the singles and doubles at the 1924 Olympics.

1938 July 17–18 Although forbidden to make his proposed transatlantic solo airplane flight, **Douglas G. Corrigan** (b. 1907), an American aviator, took off from Roosevelt Field, Long Island. Twenty-eight hours later he landed in Dublin, Ireland. Corrigan claimed with a straight face that he got lost in clouds and that his compass misbehaved so that he did not reach California as he intended. From then on, he was known as **"Wrong-Way" Corrigan.**

1938 Aug. 17 Henry Armstrong [nee Henry Jackson] (Dec. 12, 1912–Oct. 22, 1988) became the **only American professional boxer ever to hold three world titles at the same time** when he won the lightweight championship from **Lou Ambers** (b. Nov. 8, 1913) in a 15-round decision at Madison Square Garden, New York City. On Oct. 29, 1937, Armstrong won the featherweight crown when he knocked out **Pete Sarron** (b. 1918) in the sixth round. On May 31, 1938, he also became the welterweight champ by taking a 15-round decision from **Barney Ross** (Dec. 23, 1909–Jan. 18, 1967). In all Armstrong won 152 of 181 bouts, 100 by knockouts. His record of three titles at once can never be matched, because it is now forbidden for a fighter to hold more than one championship at a time.

1938 Sept. 24 J[ohn] **Donald Budge** (b. June 13, 1915) of the U.S. completed the **grand slam of tennis** by winning the U.S. championship at Forest Hills, New York. Budge had earlier in 1938 won the national championships of Australia, France, and England. He thus became the **first player to win the big four tennis titles in the same year.**

1938 Oct. 30   A **radio broadcast of** an Americanized version of an **H.G. Wells** science fiction novel *War of the Worlds* (1898) was directed by [George] **Orson Welles** (May 16, 1915–Oct. 10, 1985), an actor and director. In his broadcast, the evil Martians landed in New Jersey and began to devastate the countryside. The show was so realistic that large numbers of people fled their homes in panic. Others got out their rifles and shotguns and went hunting for the Martian invaders.

1938 Nov. 16   **Willie Hall** of the Tottenham Hotspurs set a record for **fastest goals in international soccer competition** when he scored 3 goals in 3½ minutes for England against Ireland at Manchester, England.

1939

I. VITAL STATISTICS AND DEMOGRAPHICS

1939   France established the *"Code de la Famille,"* a system of family allowances and related measures, in which the government subsidized the cost of additional children in numbers of French families. The legislation reflected widespread alarm about falling birthrates in Europe and North America during the 1920s and 1930s.

II. DISASTERS

1939   Nearly 200,000 people died in **floods in northern China**. Millions more were left starving and homeless.

1939 Jan. 24   An **earthquake** ravaged 50,000 square miles in Chile, killing c.30,000 and leaving c.700,000 homeless. The quake measured 8.3 on the Richter Scale.

1939 May 23   The American **submarine** *Squalus* **flooded and sank off Portsmouth**, New Hampshire, when one of its two main air induction valves failed to close on a practice dive; 26 sailors drowned. Thirty-three others were rescued (May 24) through use of the McCann diving bell.

1939 June 1   The British **submarine** *Thetis* **sank in Liverpool Bay** with a loss of 99 lives.

1939 July 10   Peñaranda de Bracamonte, a town west of Madrid, Spain, was destroyed as a **munitions factory exploded**; c.100 people were killed and c.1,500 injured. On Mar. 1, an **explosion of a huge munitions dump near Osaka, Japan**, left c.500 dead or injured, c.800 houses destroyed, and more than 8,000 homeless.

1939 Dec. 22   Two **train wrecks in Germany** killed 224 people. Near Magdeburg 125 perished in a collision while 99 were killed in a wreck near Friedrichshafen.

1939 Dec. 26   A series of **earthquakes** followed by floods and blizzards killed c.45,000 people on Turkey's Anatolian plateau. Erzincan [Erzinjan], a city of central Turkey, was destroyed by the earthquake, which killed c.30,000 there and in nearby towns. The quake measured 7.9 on the Richter Scale.

III. POLITICS AND WAR

1939 Jan. 26   The forces of **Francisco Franco** captured Barcelona, a decisive blow by the Nationalist rebels over the Republican government in the **Spanish Civil War** (1936–1939). Over the ensuing weeks Franco's forces conquered Catalonia, and many Loyalists fled to France.

1939 Mar. 15   The **dismemberment of Czechoslovakia** was completed as Bohemia and Moravia were unilaterally declared a German protectorate and occupied by German troops. Slovakia was annexed the following day, and Hungary occupied Ruthenia [Carpatho-Ukraine].

1939 Mar. 23   Germany demanded that **Lithuania surrender the Memel Territory**, on the Baltic Sea, including the port and city of Memel. Lithuania complied. On Dec. 11, 1938, an election in this ethnically German territory, which once had been part of German East Prussia, resulted in a victory for the Nazis, giving Hitler an excuse to demand its surrender.

1939 Mar. 28   **Madrid surrendered to Francisco Franco**, bringing to an end the **Spanish Civil War** (from 1936). It was estimated that nearly 750,000 persons died in the civil war—in battle, in air raids, or by execution.

1939 Mar. 29   **Neville Chamberlain**, prime minister of Great Britain, offered to support **Poland** in any action by Germany that threatened its independence. France also made this offer, and on Apr. 6 a mutual assistance pact formalized the promise.

1939 Apr. 4   **Ghazi** (b. Mar. 21, 1912), king of **Iraq**, died. He was succeeded by **Faisal II** (to 1958), who was four years old. A regency ruled in his name until he reached his majority on May 2, 1953.

1939 Apr. 7   **Italy invaded Albania**, following the efforts of **Zog I**, king of Albania, to lessen Italian control over his country. **Zog sought refuge in Greece**, and on Apr. 12 the Albanian assembly agreed to unite with Italy and recognize Victor Emmanuel III as king.

1939 May 17   A **British White Paper**, approved by Parliament on May 23, established a **new policy for Palestine**, for which Great Britain held a League of Nations mandate. An earlier plan to partition the land between Arabs and Jews was dropped. Jewish immigration was to be limited to 15,000 a year for the next five years, after which it would be up to the Arabs to say whether immigration should continue. Purchase of land by Jews was restricted. An independent, binational Palestine was to come into being within ten years. In effect this policy did away with the **Balfour Declaration of 1920** which had pledged the Jews a homeland.

1939 May 17   **George VI**, king of Great Britain, and **Queen Elizabeth** became the **first reigning British monarchs to visit Canada**.

1939 May 22   The **Pact of Steel**, a treaty between Germany and Italy, was signed in Berlin by **Hitler** and **Mussolini**. It tied Italy irrevocably to Germany and Hitler's actions. It pledged each party to support the other in case of war, but did not specify that the war be one in which Germany or Italy was attacked by an enemy. When war did begin a few months later, Mussolini did not join in at once.

1939 June 7–11   George VI, king of Great Britain, and Queen Elizabeth visited the U.S., the **first reigning British monarchs to** do so. They were guests at the White House of President and Mrs. Roosevelt,

then traveled to New York, where they were received with enthusiasm, and visited the **World's Fair**.

1939 June 23   The **Sanjak of Alexandretta** [Turkish: Iskenderun], since 1920 a semi-autonomous region on the Mediterranean coast between northwestern Syria and southern Turkey, also known during the period as the **Republic of Hatay**, was officially joined to the Turkish Republic in an agreement made by France and Turkey.

1939 Aug. 23   **Nazi Germany and communist Russia**, supposedly the deadliest of ideological enemies, **signed a non-aggression pact** in Moscow. Most of the terms were kept secret, but in effect they divided up the countries lying between the Soviet Union and Germany. Germany was to control Lithuania and half of Poland, while Russia was to control Finland, Estonia, and Latvia, and in southeastern Europe, Bessarabia. France and Great Britain had been negotiating with Russia for a mutual assistance pact, but **Stalin** had little faith in their ability to deal with Germany.

1939 Sept. 1   **World War II** (to 1945) **began** when, without a declaration of war, the **German army invaded Poland**. Hitler sent 40 or so infantry divisions and 14 mechanized, of which six were armored, in action against a badly outgunned foe. The German air force soon controlled Poland's skies. Polish forces fought stubbornly but were steadily forced to retreat. They were completely doomed when Russian forces invaded (Sept. 17) from the east. Warsaw surrendered on Sept. 28, and the last Polish resistance of importance ended on Oct. 5. A weak French attack on the western German frontier on Sept. 17 was no threat to Hitler's plans.

1939 Sept. 1   **Switzerland declared its neutrality** and successfully preserved it during World War II. On Sept. 2 Mussolini proclaimed Italy's non-belligerence.

1939 Sept. 2   The **Irish Free State declared neutrality** in World War II, stating its intention to fight any nation that attacked it.

1939 Sept. 3   **Great Britain declared war on Germany**, which had ignored its ultimatum to stop the invasion of Poland. France, with some hesitation, also went to war a few hours later. Australia and New Zealand at once joined them, but there was no way aid could be given to Poland, which France and England had guaranteed to protect. British bombers (Sept. 4) attacked German warships in the Heligoland Bight with little success. The first part of a **British Expeditionary Force** landed in France on Sept. 10. Within a month c.160,000 British troops were on the continent, but there was no fighting.

1939 Sept. 3   The **war at sea** began almost as soon as England and France declared war. The British passenger liner *Athenia* was sunk (Sept. 4) west of England by a German submarine, the *U-30*, with a loss of 128 lives. On Sept. 17 the British aircraft carrier *Courageous* was sunk by the *U-29*. Three days earlier another carrier *Ark Royal* had narrowly escaped the same fate. Britain decided submarine hunting was no job for aircraft carriers. In the first month of the war 41 Allied and neutral ships, amounting to 154,000 tons, were sunk by German U-boats. Most embarrassing of all to the Royal navy, in mid-October the *U-47* managed to get into the anchorage at Scapa Flow, Britain's greatest naval base, and sink the battleship *Royal Oak*. On the other hand, by the end of the year nine U-boats, a sixth of Germany's total, had been sunk.

1939 Sept. 3   **Heinrich Himmler** (Nov. 7, 1900–May 23, 1945), as head of the **Gestapo**, the **SS** [Schutzstaffel = elite guard], the **SD** [Sicherheitsdienst = intelligence and counterespionage service], and deputy head of the government, took charge of the handling of all Jews in German-occupied territories.

1939 Sept. 4   **J.B.M. Hertzog**, prime minister of **South Africa**, attempted to declare neutrality in World War II, but he was defeated in the Assembly by 80 votes to 67. **Jan Christian Smuts** (May 24, 1870–Sept. 11, 1950) formed a coalition government which on Sept. 6 declared war on Germany.

1939 Sept. 5   **Franklin D. Roosevelt**, president of the U.S., **declared his country's neutrality** in the European war. On Sept. 8 he declared a limited national emergency, which gave him some additional powers.

1939 Sept. 10   The **Dominion of Canada declared war on Germany**. Although it was considered the first time in history that Canada declared war independently, the written approval of the king of England for the declaration was received before the declaration was issued.

1939 Sept. 30   **Germany and the Soviet Union signed a new Treaty of Friendship** that modified the treaty of Aug. 23. A secret protocol (signed Sept. 28) provided for the division of Poland along the line of the Vistula River. This gave Russia the larger part of Poland, but Germany received the bulk of the population as well as industrial and mining areas. In return Russia received most of Lithuania previously allotted to Germany.

1939 Nov. 4   The already amended **American Neutrality Act** (1935) was further amended to allow nations at war to buy arms and ammunition in the U.S. if they paid cash and transported the material in their own ships. American citizens were forbidden to sail on the ships of belligerents, and American ships were not to sail in combat zones.

1939 Nov. 30   **Russia invaded Finland** after Finland refused Russian demands that it cede several islands and that it lease the port of Hangö on the Baltic Sea for use as a naval base. Also, Russia wanted areas on the Karelian Isthmus near Leningrad, and another area in the far north. In return Russia offered to give Finland land totalling about twice what it was asking. The Soviet forces at first were mostly repulsed by the outnumbered Finns, but Russian superiority in men and matériel began to tell in early 1940.

1939 Dec. 17   The German so-called pocket battleship *Admiral Graf Spee* was finally brought to bay off Montevideo, Uruguay, by three British cruisers, and she was scuttled by her captain to avoid capture. The pocket battleship was the German solution to the restrictions imposed by international treaty that allowed Germany to build ships no larger than cruiser size. The *Graf Spee* would have been more than a match for any single British cruiser, since the range of her heavy batteries was greater than that of cruisers.

IV. ECONOMY AND TRADE

1939   **John R**[ichard] **Hicks** (Apr. 8, 1904–May 20, 1989), an English economist, published *Value and Capital*, which attempted to reconcile the differences between the theory of business cycles and the equilibrium theory, which held that economies are self-adjusting. Hicks shared (1972) the **Nobel prize for economics**.

1939 June 28   The **first regular transatlantic passenger air service** began when the **Pan American Air-**

ways flying boat *Dixie Clipper* flew from Port Washington, Long Island, to Lisbon, Portugal, in 23 hrs. 52 min. The four-engine seaplane carried 22 passengers.

V. RELIGION AND PHILOSOPHY

1939 Japan's imperial government firmly enforced a **Religious Bodies Law**, which gave it control over all religious organizations and their activities.

1939 Feb. 10 **Pope Pius XI** (b. May 31, 1857; ruled from 1922) died. He was succeeded (Mar. 2) by **Pius XII**, who issued (Oct. 20) his first encyclical, *Summi Pontificatus*, in which he expounded Catholic principles concerning secularism and the brotherhood of man, the state and the family, and state worship. Coming in the early days of World War II, it was aimed at all the belligerents, but particularly at Nazi Germany. Throughout the war, however, the Vatican retained formal relations with all the belligerents, believing this was the best way to work for peace.

1939 May 10 In the U.S. the Methodist Episcopal Church and the Methodist Episcopal Church South, split since 1845, reunited to form the **Methodist Church**. Also joining the merger was the Methodist Protestant Church. The reunion brought together c.8,000,000 Methodists.

VI. SCIENCE, EDUCATION, AND TECHNOLOGY

1939 **Basil Brown**, an English archaeologist, discovered the remains of a **royal Anglo-Saxon ship** filled with treasures at Sutton Hoo, Suffolk County, east of Ipswich, England. The ship had been fully equipped for royal afterlife, although there was no body. The find was remarkable because ship burials were rare in England.

1939 At Pylos, in southwestern Greece, archeologists led by the American **Carl William Blegen** (Jan. 27, 1887–Aug. 24, 1971), found the **earliest known examples of written Greek**. The find consisted of c.600 clay tablets with a script that was named **Linear B**. The tablets showed that the art of writing was known in the late Bronze Age in Greece more widely than hitherto suspected. The key to the translation of the tablets was not found until 1952.

1939 **Paul Hermann Müller** [Mueller] (Jan. 12, 1899–Oct. 12, 1965), a Swiss chemist, discovered the insecticide power of **DDT** [dichloro-diphenyl-trichloroethane], which had been first synthesized in 1874. Müller received the **Nobel prize for chemistry** in 1948. DDT came into wide use during World War II (1939–1945).

1939 **Adolf** [Friedrich Johann] **Butenandt** (b. Mar. 24, 1903), a German chemist, was awarded, but could not accept, the 1939 **Nobel prize for chemistry**, because of a Nazi decree forbidding acceptance. The award was for his pioneering work in the isolation and identification of **sex hormones**. He discovered the female hormones estrone [estrin] (1929) and progesterone (1934), and the male hormone androsterone (1931). He shared the award with **Leopold Ružička** of Switzerland, who also worked on sex hormones and was the first to synthesize musk.

1939 Two scientists in New York discovered the **Rh** [rhesus] **factor**, a protein substance in the red blood cells in human blood, and a year later another team, also in New York, made (1940) the same discovery independently. The first two were **Philip Levine** (Aug. 10, 1900–Oct. 18, 1987), a Russian-born American immunologist, and **Rufus Stetson** (d. Nov. 13, 1967), an American hematologist. The other two were **Karl Landsteiner** (June 14, 1868–June 26, 1943), an Austrian physician working at the Rockefeller Institute for Medical Research, and **A.S. Wiener** (Mar. 16, 1907–Nov. 6, 1976), an American serologist.

1939 July 8 [Henry] **Havelock Ellis** (b. Feb. 2, 1859), an English physician and author, whose writings on sex were considered scandalous in his time, died. His chief work was *Studies in the Psychology of Sex* (1897–1928). Among his other works were *The Erotic Rights of Women* (1928) and *The Dance of Life* (1923).

1939 Aug. 2 At the urging of fellow scientists, **Albert Einstein** wrote **Franklin D. Roosevelt**, president of the U.S., a letter in which he revealed that it seemed more and more likely that nuclear energy could be used to produce an **atomic bomb**. He said it was urgent to carry on investigations lest others achieve the goal first. Roosevelt appointed the **Uranium Committee**, but it was not until Aug., 1942, that the Manhattan Engineering District [MED], the so-called **Manhattan Project**, was established and placed under army command.

1939 Aug. 27 The first airplane powered by a turbojet engine, called He-178, was flown in Germany. It was the invention of **Ernst Heinrich Heinkel** (Jan. 24, 1888–Jan. 30, 1958), a German airplane builder.

1939 Sept. 23 **Sigmund Freud** (b. May 6, 1856), an Austrian neurologist and the **founder of psychoanalysis**, died in England, a refugee from the Nazis. His study, with Jean Martin Charcot, of the treatment of hysteria through hypnosis led to development of what Freud named psychoanalysis in the treatment of mental patients. Some of his writings that have been translated into English are: *The Interpretation of Dreams* (1900), *A General Introduction to Psychoanalysis* (1920), *The Ego and the Id* (1927), and *Moses and Monotheism* (1939).

1939 Oct. 7 **Harvey [Williams] Cushing** (b. Apr. 8, 1869), an American neurosurgeon and author who made notable contributions to brain surgery, died. Cushing wrote a number of valuable books in his field, such as *The Pituitary Body and Its Disorders* (1912), and also wrote *The Life of Sir William Osler* (1925).

VII. ARTS AND LEISURE

1939 Jan. 28 **William Butler Yeats** (b. June 14, 1865), a celebrated Irish poet and playwright, died. With Lady Augusta Gregory and George Moore he helped organize the **Irish Literary Theatre**, which later (1902) became the Irish National Theatre Society. His poetry, often based on Irish folktales and legends, included *The Wind Among the Reeds* (1899), *The Wild Swans at Coole* (1917), and *Winding Stair* (1929). His plays included *The Countess Kathleen* (1892), *Deirdre* (1907), and *Cathleen ni Houlihan* (1902). Yeats received the **Nobel prize for literature** in 1923.

1939 Apr. 9 **Marian Anderson** (b. Feb. 17, 1902), a celebrated black concert singer, sang before 85,000 at the Lincoln Memorial in Washington, D.C., on Easter Sunday. Mrs. Franklin D. Roosevelt helped arrange the performance after the Daughters of the American Revolution [DAR] had cancelled Anderson's appearance in February at Constitution Hall in Washington because of **racial prejudice**.

1939 May **Isaac [Emmanuilovich] Babel** (b. July 13, 1894), a Russian short-story writer and playwright, was arrested, disappeared, and died this year (or possibly in 1941), in a prison camp as a victim of **Joseph Stalin's** purges of intellectuals and other dissidents. He was best known for two collections of short stories: *Konarmiya* [*Red Calvary*] (1926) and *Odesskie rasskazy* [*Odessa Tales*] (1927).

1939 May 22 **Ernst Toller** (b. Dec. 1, 1893), a German poet and dramatist, died. Toller's writings strongly reflected his concern with moral, political, and economic issues. His style was expressionist, as in *Masse Mensch* [*Man and the Masses*] (1920). He wrote a historical play about rioting weavers, *Die Maschinensturmer* [*The Machine Wreckers*] (1922). When the **Nazis** came to power they banished him and in 1933 he went to the U.S..

1939 June 26 **Ford Madox Ford** [nee Ford Hermann Hueffer] (b. Dec. 17, 1873), an English author, died. *The Good Soldier* (1915) is generally considered his best work. Also important was *Parade's End*, which consisted of four separate novels published between 1924 and 1928.

1939 July 21 **Ambroise Vollard** (b. 1865), a French art dealer and publisher, died. He organized (1895) the first one-man show by **Paul Cézanne** and became a publisher (1905) by bringing out a collection of colored lithographs by artists **Toulouse-Lautrec**, **Pierre Bonnard**, and others. Such publications helped establish **lithography** as an art medium.

1939 Aug. 18 *The Wizard of Oz*, an American movie of fantasy and music in equal parts, had its premiere. It was based on the children's story *The Wonderful Wizard of Oz* (1900), by L[yman] Frank Baum (May 15, 1846–May 6, 1919). A lavish production, it featured **Judy Garland** (June 10, 1922–June 22, 1969) as Dorothy, the Kansas farm child who is transported by a cyclone to the magical land of Oz.

1939 Sept. 6 **Arthur Rackham** (b. Sept. 19, 1867), an English illustrator of children's books, died. He was the most popular artist in his field and illustrated most of the established children's tales, such as *Fairy Tales of the Brothers Grimm* (1900), *Rip van Winkle* (1905), *Mother Goose* (1913), and *The Pied Piper of Hamelin* (1934).

1939 Dec. 12 **Douglas Fairbanks, Sr.**, [nee Julius Ullman] (b. May 27, 1883), an American hero of the movies in the 1920s, died. He made his first film in 1915 and soon was the epitome of the muscular, swashbuckling leading man who pleased filmgoers of all ages. Among his hit movies were *The Mark of*

Zorro (1920), *The Three Musketeers* (1921), *Robin Hood* (1922), and *The Thief of Bagdad* (1924).

1939 Dec. 15   The film *Gone with the Wind*, made from the 1936 novel by **Margaret Mitchell**, had its world premiere in Atlanta, Georgia, her hometown. A depiction of the American Civil War, it was the model Hollywood epic, starring **Clark Gable** and **Vivien Leigh**. At a cost of $4,200,000, it was the most expensive movie to date; it won ten Academy Awards, including best picture. Near the end was a line that shocked some people at the time when Gable [Rhett Butler] said to Leigh [Scarlett O'-Hara]: "Frankly, my dear, I don't give a damn."

VIII. SPORTS, GAMES, AND SOCIETY

1939 Apr. 30   The **New York World's Fair** opened. Nearly 45 million people came to see the exhibits of 62 nations in celebration of the theme of man's accomplishments in improving world living conditions. The biggest hit of the fair was the General Motors Futurama. By the time the fair closed on Oct. 30, 26 million people had come to the fair. It reopened for another season (May 11 to Oct. 21, 1940). The **Golden Gate International Exposition** was held in San Francisco in the same year. (Feb. 18–Oct. 29).

1939 May 2   [Louis Henry] **Lou Gehrig** (June 19, 1903–June 2, 1941), first baseman for the New York Yankees, ended his **record-setting run of consecutive games played**, at 2,130. Generally unknown at the time was the fact that Gehrig was suffering from a rare and then fatal form of paralysis, **amyotrophic lateral sclerosis**. Two years later, the man known as the "Iron Horse" died from the disease, now called **Lou Gehrig's disease**.

1939 May 17   The **first baseball game to be televised** was played at Columbia University's Baker Field in New York City between Columbia and Princeton. The **National Broadcasting Company** [NBC] used one camera mounted on a 12-foot-high wooden stand. Its signals were transmitted to the Empire State Building and from there broadcast by experimental station W2XBS to the fewer than 400 television sets within range. On Aug. 26 the first major league baseball game was televised from Ebbets Field, Brooklyn, New York, also over W2XBS. This time two cameras were used. The game was between the Brooklyn Dodgers and the Cincinnati Reds of the National League.

1939 June 28–July 15   **Clara Adams** of New York City became the **first woman to fly around the world**. She flew in a Pan American Airways Clipper, a seaplane, from Port Washington, N.Y., returning to Newark, N.J. The total time of her trip was 16 days, 19 hr., 4 min.

1940

I. VITAL STATISTICS AND DEMOGRAPHICS

1940   The **population of the world** was c.1,795,639,000. The populations, in round figures, of the major regions of the world were: **Africa**, 155,063,000; **Asia**, 738,945,000; **Australasia**, 10,-490,000; **Europe**, 408,661,000; **North America**, 174,059,000. **South and Central America**, 115,725,-000; **U.S.S.R.**, 192,696,000. The population of the U.S. was 132,164,569. The world's ten largest cities were: Greater New York, 11,690,520; London, 8,203,942; Tokyo, 6,830,942; Berlin, 4,250,000; Moscow, 4,137,018; Shanghai, 3,418,000; Chicago, 3,384,556; Leningrad, 3,191,304; Osaka, 3,000,000; Paris, 2,793,000.

1940   **Japan's population** was nearly 72,000,000, more than double its 1868 population of 34,000,000. The increase was attributed to urban growth, development of industrial and mining districts, and introduction of commercial agriculture.

II. DISASTERS

1940 Jan. 29   Deaths were estimated at 200, as **two passenger trains collided and caught fire at Osaka**, Japan.

1940 Mar. 4   At Ningpo [Ningbo], in Chekiang [Zhejiang] province in southeastern China, c.250 people drowned when a **boat capsized** and sank in the Yung [Yong] River.

1940 Apr. 23 A disastrous **fire swept the Rhythm Night Club**, a corrugated iron building in Natchez, Mississippi, where c.300 blacks had gathered for a dance. Windows were boarded shut to prevent gate-crashing, and there was only one available exit. Smoke inhalation and trampling caused most of the 198 deaths; 40 people were badly injured.

1940 May 7 A **fire in the municipal building at Sandona**, southwestern Colombia, killed 103 persons of whom 67 were children, and injured 125 others.

1940 May 24 An **earthquake in Callao**, Lima, and other coastal cities in central Peru left c.350 dead and c.1,500 injured.

1940 Nov. 10 About 400 persons were killed and 800 hurt by an **earthquake centered on Focsani**, east central Romania.

III. POLITICS AND WAR

1940 Mar. 13 A **peace treaty between Russia and Finland** signed at Moscow ceded the entire Karelian Isthmus to the U.S.S.R. along with Viipuri, northern Rybachi Peninsula, the port of Hangö and islands in the Gulf of Finland.

1940 Mar. 30 The **Japanese set up a puppet Chinese government** in Nanking [Nanjing], in eastern China on the Yangtze [Chang Jiang], with **Wang Ching-Wei** [Wang Chao-Ming] (May 4, 1883–Nov. 10, 1944) as its head. Wang, once an ardent Nationalist, in 1938 became pro-Japanese, and advocated peace with the invaders.

1940 Apr. 9–June 7 German forces **invaded Denmark and Norway**. Denmark was unable to offer real resistance, and its capital, Copenhagen, fell within 12 hours. In Norway the Germans made five seaborne landings and two by airborne troops. The Allies responded by sending troops to land at three places in Norway between Apr. 14 and 18. Two of them had to be withdrawn by May 2. Only in the far north, at Narvik, did the Allies have any success. They captured the city from the Germans on May 27, but on June 7, with France about to collapse in the face of the German invasion there, the last Allied troops left Norway. With them went **Haakon VII**, king of Norway, the rest of the royal family, and the government. A government in exile was established in London. The **Nazis** put **Vidkun Quisling** in power. He was a Norwegian politician who had turned fas-

cist. After the war Quisling (b. July 18, 1887) was convicted of treason and shot on Oct. 24, 1945. His name is now synonymous with traitor.

1940 May 10–June 5 **German forces invaded Luxembourg, the Netherlands, and Belgium**. They made no assault on France's **Maginot Line** but left a holding force facing it. The German strategy was to overrun the Low Countries, which were unable to offer much opposition, and then to turn south to invade France along its unfortified northern border. The Dutch and Belgian armed forces were put to rout in spite of fierce resistance in places. The Dutch army gave up on May 15 and **Leopold III**, the king of Belgium (1934–1951), surrendered on May 28. The Dutch established a government in exile in London, with Wilhelmina, the queen of the Netherlands, at its head. Leopold was held prisoner by the Germans. By May 20 the Germans reached Abbeville, France, on the English Channel, and turned north to isolate Dunkirk and surround large numbers of British and French troops there. Moving into France, the German forces reached the Somme and Aisne rivers on June 5.

1940 May 10 **Neville Chamberlain**, prime minister of Great Britain, resigned in the face of the disaster in Norway and the invasion of western Europe. He was succeeded by **Winston Churchill**, who had been first lord of the admiralty, and for years a strong advocate of British rearmament in the face of the rise of Naziism. On May 13 he made the first of his inspiring addresses to his nation, declaring: "I have nothing to offer you but blood, toil, tears, and sweat."

1940 May 10 **Great Britain occupied the Faeroe Islands** en route to occupying Iceland (May 10) in order to prevent Germany from seizing havens for U-boats. The Faeroes had been a Danish possession.

1940 May 14 **Emma Goldman** (b. June 27, 1869), a Russian-born American anarchist leader, died. Active in the U.S. movement, she went to prison (1893) for inciting to riot. She was a founder and editor of the anarchist paper *Mother Earth* (1906–1907) and was jailed again (1917) for trying to obstruct the draft. Goldman was deported to Russia (1919) but left (1921) because of a falling out with the communist government. She was allowed to reenter the U.S. in 1924. Goldman wrote *My Disillusionment in Russia* (1923) and *Living My Life* (1931).

1940 May 26–June 4 One of the greatest and most inspiring military operations in history was conducted at **Dunkirk**, France, where several hundred thousand Allied troops were encircled, except for the English Channel side, by the victorious German army. Abandoning tons of equipment, by June 4 c.338,000 troops (c.224,000 of them British) were taken from the beaches and transported to England. Only c.2,000 men were lost on ships sunk on the way to safety. The evacuation was made possible not only by the Royal navy but also by fishermen, lifeboatmen, yachtsmen, and others. In all 860 vessels of all kinds and sizes were utilized. Six destroyers and more than 200 small boats were lost.

1940 June 5–25 The **German advance into France** from the north continued almost unchecked. The French government declared Paris an open city (June 11), and the Germans marched in unopposed (June 14). They continued their advance southward, reaching Lyon on June 20. Cherbourg on the Atlantic coast was taken (June 19), while to the east the French troops in the Maginot Line were bottled up from behind.

1940 June 10 With Germany on the verge of crushing France, **Italy declared war on France and Great Britain**. No offensive was undertaken until June 20, when an attempted invasion of France was checked by a small French force.

1940 June 10 **Marcus [Moziah] Garvey** (b. Aug. 17, 1887), a black nationalist leader in Jamaica and the U.S., died. Garvey had a dream of worldwide unity of the black race, and he opposed efforts at racial integration. He began a "back to Africa" movement and for a time was the foremost spokesman for blacks. However, in raising money for a black steamship line to transport blacks to Africa he was indicted and convicted of mail fraud. After serving two years in prison he was deported (1927) to his native Jamaica, where his influence declined.

1940 June 16–22 When France asked Germany for an armistice, **Paul Reynaud** (Oct. 15, 1878–Sept. 21, 1966), premier of France, expressed disagreement with the request and was replaced by **Philippe Pétain**, a military hero of World War I. On June 22, at Compiègne, in the same railroad car in which German officials formally recognized defeat in the first World War, French officials signed the armistice with Germany. By its terms the French army was to be disarmed and about three-fifths of the country was to be under **Nazi occupation**. The French puppet government was established at Vichy. Later in 1940 Reynaud was imprisoned.

1940 June 28 Great Britain recognized **Charles de Gaulle**, a French military officer, as head of a Free French movement. He escaped to England in June and organized the French who wished to continue to struggle against Germany. Several French colonies gave him their support. In France a military court of the **Vichy government** sentenced him to death in absentia.

1940 June 28 The **Alien Registration Act** became law in the U.S., requiring aliens to register and be fingerprinted. The law also made it a crime to belong to any organization advocating overthrow of the government. About 5,000,000 aliens were registered.

1940 July 3 Three British battleships and other naval vessels entered the harbor at Oran, Algeria, where the greater part of the **French navy** lay and presented an ultimatum to the French commander: join Britain in the war against the Germans, sail to a British port, or sail to the French West Indies, where they would be demilitarized or placed under control of the U.S. The French commander elected to fight. The British sank or damaged three battleships, two destroyers, and other French naval vessels, thus preventing the ships from joining enemy fleets. The British also seized two French battleships, nine destroyers, and some smaller ships that were in the English ports of Plymouth and Portsmouth.

1940 July 10 At Vichy a **French parliament voted the Third Republic out of existence** and adopted a constitution that set up a fascist state. **Pétain** became chief of state. The citizenship of naturalized Jews was revoked (July 16), and they were barred (July 18) from government positions and from management posts in business and industry. Pétain collaborated with the Germans.

1940 July 10–Dec. 29 The **Battle of Britain** was fought in the skies over England as the German **Luftwaffe** sought to destroy the Royal air force so **Hitler** could invade the British Isles. At first the Germans attacked coastal defenses and radar installations. When British air strength proved greater than expected, the German attack shifted to airfields and aircraft factories. Beginning Sept. 7 the Germans turned to night bombing of British cities, especially London, in what became known as the **blitz**. By November the Germans had lost 1,733 aircraft and the British 915 fighters. The night bombings caused much damage and killed large numbers of civilians, but failed to break British morale. Birmingham, Liverpool, and Plymouth were among other cities bombed. On Nov. 14 and 15 an attack over Coventry destroyed the 11th-century Cathedral of Saint Michael. Attacks declined during the winter, were resumed to some extent in the spring of 1941, and ended on May 16. The Battle of Britain was the **first major defeat suffered by the Nazis** and caused Hitler to call off **Operation Sea Lion**, the invasion of England.

1940 July 18 The British government, under pressure from Japan, closed the **Burma Road**, Nationalist China's vital route for war materials. The road ran from Lashio in Burma 700 miles to Kunming, Yunan province, in southwestern China.

1940 Aug. 1–8 **New Soviet Socialist republics were absorbed by Russia**: Lithuania on Aug. 1, Moldavia on Aug. 2, Latvia on Aug. 3, and Estonia on Aug. 8.

1940 Aug. 4 **Italian armies invaded and conquered British Somaliland**. The east coast of Africa was important to the British and their allies since it posed a threat to the approaches to the southern entrance to the Suez Canal and ultimately to Britain's control of the eastern Mediterranean.

1940 Aug. 21 **Leon Trotsky** [Lev Davidovich Bronstein] (b. Nov. 8, 1879), the exiled Russian war minister and Marxist ideologue, died in his home in Coyoacán, Mexico, near Mexico City. He had been wounded by an ax blow to the head the day before by an assassin, **Ramón Mercador del Rio** (1914–Oct. 18, 1978), who was an agent of the Russian N.K.V.D.

1940 Aug. 26 **Chad became the first French territory to declare for the Gaullist Free French cause**, a course followed later by French Equatorial Africa and Cameroon.

1940 Sept. 3 By executive action, **Franklin D. Roosevelt**, president of the U.S., **traded 50 over-age destroyers of the American navy to Great Britain** in return for 99-year leases on areas in the British West Indies and Bermuda for the construction of naval bases. Britain badly needed the ships to keep the sea lanes to Great Britain open.

1940 Sept. 6 **Carol**, king of **Romania**, was forced to abdicate by **Ion Antonescu** (June 15, 1882–June 1, 1946), the prime minister, who was fascist-oriented and a supporter of the **Iron Guard**, an influential nationalistic and anti-Semitic organization. Carol was succeeded by his son **Michael I**. On Nov. 23 **Romania joined the Axis powers**. On Nov. 23 **Hungary also joined the Axis**.

1940 Sept. 16 The **Selective Service Act** was passed by the Congress, providing for the **first American peacetime draft**. It required all men between 21 and 36 to register and 900,000 were to be selected for service each year.

1940 Sept. 22 **Japan began an invasion of northern Indochina**.

1940 Sept. 23–25 **Free French forces**, assisted by the British navy, **attempted to capture Dakar**, French West Africa [present Senegal]. In the battle that followed, the invading forces were driven off.

1940 Sept. 27 **Germany, Italy, and Japan signed the Tripartite Pact**, in which they agreed each of them would declare war on any nation that joined in the war against any one of them.

1940 Oct. 28–Dec. 13 **Italian forces invaded Greece** from their bases in conquered Albania. The ferocious resistance by the Greek army stunned the Italians. During November the Greeks trapped one Italian division, took c.2,000 prisoners in another engagement, and by Nov. 21 drove almost all the invaders back into Albania. Hitler considered the attack by Italy an unnecessary diversion. On Dec. 13 Hitler issued orders to prepare for a German invasion of Greece.

1940 Nov. 11–12 The **British navy attacked the Italian naval and supply base at Taranto** in southern Italy with 21 torpedo-bombers from the deck of the aircraft carrier *Illustrious*. Three Italian battleships, two cruisers, and other vessels were destroyed. This gave the British naval control of the Mediterranean.

1940 Dec. 11 **Sidi Barrani** in northwestern Egypt fell to the counterattacking **British Eighth Army**. The Italians had captured the town on Sept. 17, but their advance then stalled. Its goal had been seizure of the Suez Canal.

IV. ECONOMY AND TRADE

1940 Mar. The **Sun Oil Company became the sponsor** of the televised newscasts of **Lowell Thomas** (Apr. 6, 1892–Aug. 29, 1981). It was the **first time any business sponsored a regularly appearing television program on a continuing basis.**

1940 June 30–1945 Dec. 31 From the start of the United States' defense program gearing up for World War II until the end of the war, the **government raised about $380,000,000,000.** About 40 percent of that came from taxes and other non-borrowing sources, while approximately $228,000,000,000 came from the sale of government securities.

V. RELIGION AND PHILOSOPHY

1940 Abraham Joshua Heschel (1907–Nov. 23, 1972), a Polish-American Jewish theologian and philosopher, emigrated to the U.S. In the U.S. he taught at Hebrew Union College, Cincinnati, Ohio, and from 1945 at the Jewish Theological seminary, New York City. Heschel, an influential philosopher of religion in both Jewish and Christian circles, sought to show the significance of the relationship of man and God, emphasizing the holiness of life. He was also active in the civil rights movement. His writings included *The Earth Is the Lord's* (1950), *God in Search of Man: A Philosophy of Judaism* (1956), and *The Prophets* (1962).

1940 Feb. 22 The 14th **Dalai Lama** (b. July 6, 1935) was installed in Tibet. Although only five years old at the time, he was in theory the spiritual leader of Tibetan Buddhism and the temporal ruler of Tibet.

VI. SCIENCE, EDUCATION, AND TECHNOLOGY

1940 Chester F. Carlson (Feb. 8, 1906–Sept. 19, 1968), an American patent lawyer and inventor, patented the **first xerographic machine**, which produced dry photocopies by the use of electric charges. Carlson sold (1947) the development rights to the Haloid Company, which later became the Xerox Corporation.

1940 Edwin [Mattison] **McMillan** (b. Sept. 18, 1907) discovered neptunium and, with **Glenn** [Theodore] **Seaborg** (b. Apr. 19, 1912) discovered plutonium. McMillan and Seaborg shared the **Nobel prize for chemistry** in 1951.

1940 Apr. 26 Carl Bosch (b. Aug. 27, 1874), a German chemist, died. In 1909 he developed the process invented (1908) by Fritz Haber for obtaining nitrogen from the air to be used in industrial operations. He also invented (1925) a process for manufacturing hydrogen. Bosch shared the **Nobel prize for chemistry** in 1931.

1940 Sept. 12 Five boys stumbled upon the **Lascaux Cave**, near Montignac in southwestern France, and thereby revealed to the world one of the great treasures of the art of the hunter society of the Paleolithic Age.

VII. ARTS AND LEISURE

1940 Graham [Henry] **Greene** (b. Oct. 2, 1904) published *The Power and the Glory*, a novel set in Mexico about a drunken, lecherous priest who in the end was a martyr of sorts and reflected the strength of the Roman Catholic Church.

1940 Jan. 11 The Ballet Theater, which became the **American Ballet Theater** in 1957, gave its first performance, in New York City.

1940 Mar. 4 Hamlin Garland (b. Sept. 14, 1860), an American author, died. Garland's bleak, realistic picture of life in what he called the "middle border"—the midwestern U.S. from Wisconsin to the Dakotas was an important step in American literature's move, early in this century, away from the American myth and toward the American reality. His best-known books were *Main-Travelled Roads* (1891) and the autobiographical *A Son of the Middle Border* (1817) and *A Daughter of the Middle Border* (1921).

1940 Mar. 16 Selma Lagerlöf [Selma Ottiliana Lovisa] (b. Nov. 20, 1858), a Swedish novelist, died. She won the **Nobel prize for literature** in 1909. Her most famous novel was *The Story of Gösta Berling* (1891). She was the first woman to be elected to the Swedish Academy (1914). Two of her other works were *The Miracles of Antichrist* (1897) and *The Girl from the Marsh Croft* (1908).

1940 Apr. 9 Mrs. Patrick Campbell [nee Beatrice Stella Tanner] (b. Feb. 9, 1865), a noted English actress, died. She played the leading role in *The Second Mrs. Tanqueray* in 1893 and became a star. She played a great variety of roles, including Eliza Doolittle in *Pygmalion*, which George Bernard Shaw wrote for her. Shaw described Mrs. Campbell as "perilously bewitching," and she was also known for her wit.

1940 Apr. 28   Luisa Tetrazzini (b. June 29, 1871), an Italian coloratura soprano, died. Tetrazzini was one of the most successful opera singers of her era because of her brilliant high notes, as in *Rigoletto* and *La Traviata.*

1940 June 21   Edouard Vuillard (b. Nov. 11, 1868), a French painter, died. Vuillard became an important member of the **Nabi group** ["The Prophets"], which included Bonnard. After 1900, influenced by Japanese prints, he became, along with Bonnard, an intimist.

1940 June 29   Paul Klee (b. Dec. 14, 1879), a Swiss painter and author, died. He published the first of his influential works on the nature of art, *Padododisches Skizzenbuch* [*Pedagogical Sketchbook*] in Munich in 1925. With *Uber die moderne Kunst* (1945) and *Das bildnerische Denken* (1956), it had great influence on the development of modern art. Among his best-known paintings were *The Twittering Machine* (1922), *Around the Fish* (1926), and *Death and Fire* (1940).

1940 Sept. 2   Giulio Gatti-Casazza (b. Feb. 3, 1869), an Italian opera manager, died. In Milan he directed La Scala Opera Company (1898–1908), then became the long-time director of the Metropolitan Opera, New York City (1908–1935).

1940 Dec. 5   Jan Kubelik (b. July 5, 1880), a Czech violinist and composer, died. He began (1908) his career in Vienna, Austria, and was soon recognized for his skill in other parts of Europe. Kubelik performed in the U.S. many times, beginning in 1902. Kubelik's work included a symphony and six violin concertos.

1940 Dec. 21   F[rancis] **Scott** [Key] **Fitzgerald** (b. Sept. 24, 1896), an American author, died. His best novels were *The Beautiful and the Damned* (1922), *The Great Gatsby* (1925), and *Tender is the Night* (1934).

VIII. SPORTS, GAMES, AND SOCIETY

1940 Apr. 13   The **first 15-foot pole vault** in history was accomplished by **Cornelius A. Warmerdam** (b. June 22, 1915), an American athlete, at Berkeley, California.

1940 Dec. 8   The Washington Redskins, champions of the Eastern Division of the National **Football** League, led by **Samuel Adrian "Sammy" Baugh** (b. Mar. 17, 1914), were stunned by the Western Division champions, led by quarterback **Sid**[ney] **Luckman** (b. Nov. 21, 1916), 73–0. The Redskins could find no defense for the new T-formation attack that the Chicago Bears used.

1941

I. DISASTERS

1941 Feb. 16–18   A **hurricane struck the Atlantic coast of Spain and Portugal** and the Bay of Biscay, leaving 145 dead. In addition the storm started a fire in Santander, northern Spain, that made c.30,000 people homeless.

1941 Apr. 15   A **tidal wave and the eruption of Colima volcano** at Colima, Mexico, following an earthquake, killed c.175 people and injured as many more.

1941 May 25   Storms struck several villages in the Ganges Delta in India, drowning c.5,000 persons.

1941 June 5–6   An **explosion at an ammunition dump at Smederevo**, on the Danube River in eastern Yugoslavia, near Belgrade, killed c.1,500 persons and injured c.2,000.

II. POLITICS AND WAR

1941 Jan. 3–Apr. 11   The **British Eighth Army in North Africa began an advance into Libya.** Two days later Bardia was taken, with c.45,000 Italian prisoners of war; Tobruk, Jan. 22; Benghazi, Feb. 7; El Aghella, Feb. 9. With the Italians routed, the British advance was halted so many of its men and planes could be transferred to Greece, where a German invasion appeared imminent. **Hitler** decided to come to the aid of **Mussolini:** the **Afrika Corps** was organized, its advance detachment reaching North Africa on Feb. 14. Under the command of **Erwin** [Johannes Eugen] **Rommel** (Nov. 25, 1891–July 18, 1944), the

Afrika Corps took the offensive and forced the British to evacuate Benghazi on Apr. 3. By Apr. 11 the British were pushed back across the Egyptian border except for a force under siege in **Tobruk**.

1941 Jan. 6   Franklin D. Roosevelt, in an address to the U.S. Congress, defined the general world aims of American policies known as the **Four Freedoms**: Freedom of Speech, Freedom of Worship, Freedom from Want, and Freedom from Fear.

1941 Jan. 20   Franklin D. Roosevelt was inaugurated president of the U.S. for an unprecedented third term. **Henry A[gard] Wallace** (Oct. 7, 1888–Nov. 18, 1965) was inaugurated as vice president. In the election on Nov. 5, 1940, Roosevelt and Wallace, on the Democratic party ticket, defeated Republicans **Wendell L[ewis] Willkie** (Feb. 18, 1892–Oct. 8, 1944) and **Charles L[inza] McNary** (June 12, 1874–May 9, 1944) by 27,244,160 to 22,305,198 in the popular vote and 449 to 82 in the electoral vote.

1941 Mar. 1   Boris III, king of Bulgaria (1918–1943), signed the Tripartite Pact and allowed German troops to enter his country. On Apr. 6, **Bulgaria joined the Axis forces** in their invasion of Yugoslavia and Greece, and declared war on the Soviet Union on June 22, and on the U.S. and Great Britain on Dec. 13.

1941 Mar. 11   The **Lend-Lease Act** was signed by **Franklin D. Roosevelt**. Under its terms he was empowered to sell or lend, lease or transfer war matériel to those nations considered vital to the defense of the U.S. Repayment, when made, was to be in kind or in any way satisfactory to the president.

1941 Mar. 27   A **coup d'état in Yugoslavia**, in opposition to the country's adherence to the Tripartite Pact (Mar. 25), overthrew the regency of pro-German **Prince Paul**. As **Peter II** took power and announced neutrality, his country was invaded by Germany on Apr. 6 and forced to surrender on Apr. 18.

1941 Apr. 1   Rashid Ali al-Ghailani (1893?–Aug. 28, 1965), a pro-Axis politician, seized power in **Iraq**, ousting the pro-British emir who was regent for **Faisal II**, the child king of Iraq. British troops arrived (Apr. 17) at the port of Basra to reinforce the regular garrison. Al-Ghailani surrendered on May 31. German aircraft and their crews, who had come to Iraq to support al-Ghailani, left.

1941 Apr. 5–Nov. 27   Having invaded Ethiopia from Italian Somaliland, **British forces and Ethiopian patriots captured the capital, Addis Ababa**, from Italian forces. A month later **Haile Selassie**, the emperor, was restored to his throne. Italian resistance continued until Nov. 27 when the last force surrendered at Gonder [Gondar], in northwestern Ethiopia. Meantime, other British troops entered Eritrea, another Italian colony, from the Anglo-Egyptian Sudan and took its capital, Asmara, on Apr. 1. Mussolini's African empire had come to an end.

1941 Apr. 6–17   German troops overran both Greece and Yugoslavia in less than two weeks. Greece was assisted by a hastily assembled British force, but the forces were split by the German tactics. Most British troops got away to safety by sea to Crete. In Yugoslavia Belgrade, the capital, fell on Apr. 12.

1941 Apr. 13   The **Soviet Union and Japan concluded a five-year neutrality pact.**

1941 May 10   Rudolf Hess, a close associate of **Hitler** since 1920, secretly secured an airplane and flew from Augsburg, Germany, to near Glasgow, Scotland, where he landed and was arrested. He claimed he came to propose a plan for peace between Germany and England. Most authorities agree he acted on his own initiative. Hess, sentenced to life imprisonment as a war criminal, served 40 years in Spandau prison in Berlin, where he died at age 93.

1941 May 17   The **Althing [parliament] of Iceland** severed ties with Denmark and established a regency under **Sveinn Björnsson** (1881–1952). The Althing assumed royal power and direction of its foreign affairs.

1941 May 20–31   Germany drove the Greeks and British out of Crete, attacking by parachute, by glider, and by troop carrier plane. In all c.22,000 troops arrived in this manner. The total British and Greek forces numbered more than 50,000, but the Germans speedily overpowered the Allied forces. Only c.16,500 of the Allied troops were evacuated by May 31, all the rest being casualties or prisoners. In addition three British cruisers and six destroyers were sunk by German planes. The Germans suffered c.7,000 casualties, including c.4,000 dead.

1941 May 27 The powerful German battleship *Bismarck* was sunk in the Bay of Biscay, with loss of almost its entire crew of more than 2,000, by torpedo planes from the British carrier *Ark Royal*, and torpedos from the *Dorsetshire* after a chase of 1,750 miles. It had earlier blown up the British heavy battlecruiser *Hood* with a loss of all but 3 of its 1,458 men.

1941 June 8 British and Free French forces entered Syria and Lebanon to prevent their occupation by Axis forces.

1941 June 22–Dec. 5 Despite the non-aggression pact signed with Russia in 1939, **Hitler's armies began an invasion of the Soviet Union** on three fronts. The surprise of the attack and German air and tank superiority carried the three army groups rapidly into Russia. Within a week Minsk fell and by August 5 Smolensk, only 200 miles from Moscow, was taken. Leningrad was completely encircled on Sept. 15 and remained besieged until early 1944. Four days later, Kiev was in German hands. Odessa fell on Oct. 15, Kharkov on Oct. 24. In the middle of November the Germans began a push to take Moscow. On Dec. 2 they reached Moscow's suburbs but there the drive stalled. Three days later the Russians counterattacked and drove the Nazis back in some places in spite of Hitler's order of no retreat. The Russian winter settled the issue. **Operation Barbarossa**, aimed at forcing Russia to sue for peace, had not succeeded, despite the hundreds of thousands of Russians killed or taken prisoner.

1941 July Two guerilla resistance groups were forming in Yugoslavia to fight the Nazi occupiers. One, called the *chetniks*, was headed by **Draza Mihajlovic**, a soldier and royalist. The chief of the other was **Josip Broz**, known simply as **Tito**, an active communist who was imprisoned (1929–1934) as a political agitator. Tito was supported by the Soviet Union, and Mihajlovic had the approval of the Yugoslav royal government in exile in London, and of the British.

1941 July The **Holocaust**, the massacre of Jews by the Nazis, began in earnest. Along with it went the slaughter of many Russians as well. By the end of the year, as many as 500,000 Russian Jews were massacred and as many more Russians. Beginning in late September **Babi Yar**, a large ravine on the northern outskirts of Kiev, became the Nazis' favorite slaughterhouse. About 34,000 Jews were machine-gunned

to death initially. As many as 100,000 probably ended up in the mass grave of Babi Yar before the killings ended. About 30,000 Jews were killed near Riga, Latvia, on Nov. 30 and Dec. 8. As many more died at Vilna, Lithuania, at this time. Vilna's Jewish population decreased from c.80,000 to c.4,000 between 1941 and 1945.

1941 July 23 Japan occupied all of French Indochina, a step begun initially on Sept. 22, 1940. The U.S. reacted to the new expansionist policy by **freezing Japanese assets in the U.S.** on July 26 and by placing an **oil embargo on Japan** on Aug. 1. The Dutch meanwhile froze Japanese assets in the Dutch East Indies. By this time most of Japan's normal sources of oil were cut off.

1941 Aug. 14 The **Atlantic Charter**, declaring the common aims of the U.S. and Britain after the war, was issued by **Winston Churchill** and **Franklin D. Roosevelt** after they conferred (Aug. 9–12) aboard a warship anchored in Placentia Bay, southeastern Newfoundland: Territorial gains by the Allies were renounced; territorial changes should not be made except with the consent of those involved; restoration of self-government and other rights to those deprived of such rights by the war; equal access after the war of all nations to raw materials, and a relaxation of restrictions on commerce; better economic and social conditions were to be secured by international cooperation; the abandonment of the use of force by all nations; the current aggressor nations to be disarmed.

1941 Aug. 25 British forces invaded Iran from the south while the U.S.S.R. entered from the north following the pro-Nazi stand taken by **Riza Shah Pahlevi**, shah of Iran. Riza Shah abdicated (Sept. 16) in favor of his son **Mohammad Riza Pahlevi**, who adopted a pro-Allied policy.

1941 Sept. The United States mission to the Soviet Union headed by **W[illiam] Averell Harriman** (Nov. 15, 1891–June 24, 1986), overseas lend-lease administrator, issued the **Moscow Protocol**, in which the U.S. agreed to send to the Soviets in 1942 $1,015,-000,000 worth of military and civilian supplies.

1941 Sept. 6 The **Nazi authorities ordered that all Jews over the age of six in territory occupied by Germany must wear the Star of David**, as required within Germany. By this time the Vichy French government was cooperating fully with its Nazi conquerors in the treatment of Jews. Between May and August c.22,000 French Jews were rounded up and sent to German labor camps.

1941 Sept. 24–Dec. 19 Britain sent to **Malta** a strong force, including three battleships and an aircraft carrier escorting transports and supply ships. The Italian navy and air force attempted to intercept the convoy but inflicted only minor damage. However, German U-boats slipped past Gibraltar into the Mediterranean, posing a serious danger to Allied ships supplying North African forces. On Nov. 13 the carrier *Ark Royal* was sunk by a U-boat near Gibraltar. She and the *Argus*, another British carrier, had just ferried fighter planes to Malta. The island was regularly and heavily bombed until the war ended. Rations were short, but it never surrendered.

1941 Oct. 9 **Arnulfo Arias** (b. Aug. 15, 1901), elected president of **Panama** in June, 1940, was removed from office after he tried to alter Panama's constitution.

1941 Oct. 16 **Hideki Tojo**, a military leader and advocate of Japanese expansion by force of arms, became prime minister of **Japan**. The war party would control the country until its defeat in 1945. Tojo was tried and convicted as a war criminal and was hanged on Dec. 23, 1948.

1941 Oct. 30 The American destroyer *Reuben James* **was torpedoed by a German U-boat and sank** off the coast of Iceland with the loss of 96 members of its crew. It was the first U.S. warship lost in World War II.

1941 Nov. 17 The **U.S. Neutrality Act** was amended to allow merchant ships to be armed and to sail to the ports of belligerents.

1941 Nov. 18–Dec. 31 The British, reorganized and reinforced, went on the offensive, again moving into Libya from Egypt. Between the border and Tobruk, a fierce engagement (Nov. 23) cost the German **Afrika Corps** heavily. **Rommel** retreated westward, giving up the **siege of Tobruk** (Dec. 4). The Germans retreated westward to the easily defensible position of El Agheila.

1941 Dec. 7 On this Sunday morning at 7:55 a.m., **planes from Japanese carriers struck Pearl Harbor,** Hawaii, the main U.S. naval base in the Pacific area. Of eight American battleships, four were

sunk and four severely damaged. Eleven other vessels were sunk or put out of action. Of American aircraft, 188 were destroyed and 63 damaged. Somewhat more than 3,400 persons were killed or wounded. The Japanese lost only 29 planes and probably suffered fewer than 100 casualties. The Japanese fleet returned home triumphant, and the U.S. was for the time being without naval power in the Pacific.

1941 Dec. 7 **Panama declared war against Japan** immediately after the attack on Pearl Harbor, followed within 48 hours by: Colombia, Costa Rica, Cuba, Dominican Republic, Guatemala, Haiti, Honduras, Nicaragua, and El Salvador. These same nations declared war a few days later against Germany and Italy after those nations declared war against the U.S.

1941 Dec. 8 Calling Dec. 7 "**a day that will live in infamy,**" **Franklin D. Roosevelt** appeared before Congress and asked for **a declaration of war against Japan**. It was promptly given, unanimously in the Senate and with one dissenting vote in the House of Representatives. On Dec. 11, in accordance with the Tripartite Treaty, Germany and Italy declared war on the U.S. Congress then voted that a state of war existed between the U.S. and those nations.

1941 Dec. 9 **China declared war on Germany, Italy, and Japan.** China had actually been at war with Japan since 1931, although there had been no official declaration by either side.

1941 Dec. 10–25 **Japanese troops landed on Luzon.** By the end of the year American and Filipino forces were in full retreat. On Dec. 10 the Japanese also took the island of **Guam**, defended by only c.300 U.S. troops. At sea on Dec. 9 the British battleship *Prince of Wales* and the cruiser *Repulse,* attempting to intercept a landing of Japanese forces on the Malay Peninsula, were easy targets for Japanese torpedo bombers from aircraft carriers. Both ships were sunk on Dec. 10. Escorting destroyers were able to rescue c.2,000 of the 2,800 crew members. An attack on **Wake**, another U.S. island, began on Dec. 7 and on Dec. 23 it surrendered. Finally, on Christmas Day the **British surrendered Hong Kong**.

1941 Dec. 22–Jan. 1, 1942 At a meeting on war strategy in Washington, **Winston Churchill** and **Franklin D. Roosevelt,** together with their top military advisers, **agreed to focus their joint efforts on**

Europe. A **policy of defensive action in the Pacific** was to be in effect until the Allies had the resources to go on the offensive against Japan.

III. ECONOMY AND TRADE

1941   In the U.S. a **"Don't Buy Where You Can't Work"** campaign was organized to protest employment practices discriminatory against blacks. The **Fair Employment Practices Commission** of 1941 grew out of these efforts.

1941 June   The **first license for a commercial television station** in the U.S. was issued by the Federal Communications Commission [FCC] to the National Broadcasting Company [NBC] for station WNBT in New York City. There were c.4,700 set owners in the city.

1941 June 14   The **Treasury Department froze all Swiss assets** in the U.S., including Swiss national gold reserves. This was done even though the U.S. had not yet entered the war and Switzerland was neutral.

IV. RELIGION AND PHILOSOPHY

1941   **Joseph Dov Soloveitchik** (b. 1903), scion of a preeminent Lithuanian rabbinical family, was appointed professor of Jewish philosophy at Yeshiva University. Soloveitchik emigrated to the U.S. in 1932, where his lectures and discourses soon made him the unchallenged leader of enlightened Orthodoxy and the mentor of a generation of American-trained Orthodox rabbis.

1941   A new version of the New Testament for Roman Catholics was published under the title *The New Testament of Our Lord and Savior Jesus Christ*. It was prepared by scholars of the Catholic Biblical Association of America and sponsored by the Episcopal Confraternity of Christian Doctrine. The version was based on the **Vulgate**, the Latin and official version of the Catholic Church, dating back to the late fourth century. A translation of the Old Testament was also made, based on original Hebrew texts. It appeared in four volumes (1952–1969).

1941 Jan. 3   **Henri Bergson** (b. Oct. 18, 1859), a French philosopher, died. Bergson believed in two opposing tendencies, the life force—which he called élan vital—and the material world. Intellect, through which man could know and measure the

world, contrasted with intuition, by which man was aware of the life force. Bergson won the **Nobel prize for literature** in 1927. Among his works translated into English were *Time and Free Will* (1889), *Creative Evolution* (1907), and *The Creative Mind* (1934).

V. SCIENCE, EDUCATION, AND TECHNOLOGY

1941   The **largest cathedral in the world**, the **Cathedral of St. John the Divine**, of the Protestant Episcopal Church, in New York City, was opened for worship. Work began in 1892 on a structure that was to be Romanesque in style. In 1911, however, plans were changed to a Gothic design of the architect **Ralph Adams Cram** (Dec. 16, 1863–Sept. 22, 1942). Because of financial problems, the cathedral was never fully completed.

1941 Jan. 5   **Amy Johnson** (b. 1903), an English aviator, died. She set many records for women pilots, the first being a solo flight from England to Australia in 1930. The next year she set a record for a round trip flight England-Japan, and in 1932 made an England to South Africa and return flight. Johnson continued to make flights of this sort through 1936. In 1939 at the outbreak of war, she enlisted in the auxiliary transport service and was killed in a crash into the Thames estuary while on duty.

1941 Feb. 12   **Penicillin was used for the first time to treat a human patient**, at Oxford, England, by **Howard Florey** (Sept. 24, 1898–Feb. 21, 1968), an Australian-born pathologist, and **Ernest Boris Chain** (June 19, 1906–Sept. 14, 1979), a German-born biochemist. World War II created the demand for large quantities of penicillin, first discovered by **Alexander Fleming**. Fleming, Florey, and Chain were awarded the **Nobel prize for physiology or medicine** in 1945.

1941 Feb. 21   **Frederick Grant Banting** (b. Nov. 14, 1891), a Canadian physiologist, died. In 1921, working with **Charles H. Best** (Feb. 27, 1899–Mar. 31, 1978), he isolated from the pancreas the hormone later called **insulin** in a form suitable for treating diabetes. Banting and Best shared the **Nobel prize for physiology or medicine** in 1923.

1941 Apr. 13   **Annie Jump Cannon** (b. Dec. 11, 1863), an American astronomer, died. Her chief work was a catalogue of c.225,000 stellar spectra.

She also discovered 300 variable stars and five new stars.

1941 July 11   Arthur John Evans (b. July 8, 1851), an English archeologist, died. He spent much of his career, from 1898 to 1935, carrying out **excavations on the island of Crete**. At Cnossus he found the remains of an ancient civilization, which he named Minoan and which had been destroyed c.1400 B.C. Among Evans's most spectacular finds was the royal palace.

1941 Dec. 11   Emile Picard (b. July 24, 1856) died in Paris. One of the continent's leading mathematicians for 60 years, he formulated two important theorems, which are named after him: Picard's First Theorem in 1879 and his Second in 1880.

VI. ARTS AND LEISURE

1941 Jan. 13   James [Augustine Aloysius] **Joyce** (b. Feb. 2, 1882), an Irish novelist, died. His first published fiction was a book of short stories *Dubliners* (1914), followed by a novel *Portrait of the Artist as a Young Man* (1916). It was when *Ulysses* appeared in 1922 that the literary world became aware that the course of the novel in English was forever changed. *Ulysses* dealt with one day's activities of Leopold Bloom. Joyce followed *Ulysses* with *Finnegans Wake* (1939), a difficult work, presumably the musings of a Dublin pub keeper, but also displaying the content of some universal consciousness.

1941 Mar. 6   ** [John] **Gutzon [de la Mothe] **Borglum** (b. Mar. 25, 1867), an American sculptor, died. His first important commission was in 1901 for the **statue of Abraham Lincoln in the Rotunda of the Capitol** in Washington, D.C. Borglum is now best known for the carving of the heads of George Washington, Thomas Jefferson, Abraham Lincoln, and Theodore Roosevelt on the face of **Mount Rushmore** in South Dakota. The heads are 60 ft. high.

1941 Mar. 8   Sherwood Anderson (b. Sept. 13, 1876), an American writer, died. He was known for his portraits of American small town life, especially as depicted in the collection of short stories *Winesburg, Ohio* (1919). His other works included: *Beyond Desire* (1932), *Death in the Woods* (1933), and *Home Town* (1940).

1941 Mar. 17   ** The **National Gallery of Art opened in Washington, D.C. The impressive building, designed by architect **John Russell Pope** (Apr. 24,

1874–Aug. 22, 1937), was made possible by a gift of $15,000,000 from **Andrew W**[illiam] **Mellon** (Mar. 24, 1855–Aug. 26, 1937), financier and former secretary of the treasury. He also gave it his collection of 130 American portraits.

1941 Mar. 28   ** [Adeline] **Virginia Woolf (b. Jan. 25, 1882), an English novelist and critic, died. *Mrs. Dalloway*, her first great novel, was published in 1925. It depicted the complexity of a woman's life by means of her thoughts and actions during a single day in post-World War I London. Her other works included: *To the Lighthouse* (1927), *The Common Reader* (1925), and *Roger Fry* (1940).

1941 Apr. 16   Émile Bernard (b. 1886), a French painter and theorist who developed the style of painting known as **cloisonnism** [French: *cloisonnage*], died. **Paul Gauguin**, a co-developer, received much of the credit for the style, which he named **synthetism**, or **pictorial symbolism**. The style emphasized two-dimensional flat paintings without shadow, working from memory rather than direct from nature, and using unshaded colors, generally bright.

1941 May 7   James George Frazer (b. Jan. 1, 1854), a Scottish anthropologist and author, died. His most famous work, *The Golden Bough*, first published in 1890, was an attempt, through the study of folklore, to gain a coherent picture of primitive societies, but was a work of both anthropology and literature. It is now most highly regarded as literature. By 1915 the work had expanded to twelve volumes; a one-volume version was issued in 1922.

1941 June 1   Hugh [Seymour] **Walpole** (b. Mar. 13, 1884), a New Zealand-born English novelist, died. He is remembered best for his *Herries Chronicle*, four historical novels: *Rogue Herries* (1930), *Judith Paris* (1931), *The Fortress* (1932), and *Vanessa* (1933).

1941 June 29   Ignace Jan Paderewski (b. Nov. 18, 1860), a pianist, composer, and Polish statesman, died in New York City. A great piano virtuoso, he toured the U.S. in 1891 and returned several times to raise money for the support of Polish independence and relief. He wrote symphonies, concertos, and many piano pieces; his most popular piece was *Minuet in G*. After Poland regained its independence at the end of World War I, Paderewski headed the government from Jan. to Nov., 1919. From 1940 to

1941 he was head of the Polish government in exile during World War II.

1941 July 10   Jelly Roll Morton [nee Ferdinand Joseph La Menthe] (b. Sept. 20, 1885), an American jazz musician and composer, died. He began his career in 1902 as pianist in New Orleans. It was a series of recordings made with the **Red Hot Peppers** (1926–1930) that established him as one of the alltime great men of jazz. His compositions included **"King Porter Stomp"** (1924) and **"Jelly Roll Blues"** (1924).

1941 Aug. 7   Rabindranath Tagore [Ravindranatha Thakura] (b. May 6, 1861), an Indian author, philosopher, and guru, died. He was a prolific writer and an impressive personality. He sought to make people aware of their unity rather than their divisions. Tagore wrote c.100 books of verse, 50 dramas, and 40 novels. Among his most notable works were a collection of poetry *Gitanjali* (1912) and his most significant philosophical treatise *Sadhana: The Realization of Life* (1913). He received the **Nobel prize for literature** in 1913.

1941 Oct. 25   Robert Delaunay (b. Apr. 12, 1885), a French artist, died. He was a founder of **orphism**, which sought to introduce a lighter element of lyricism into the rather sober intellectualism of cubism. Among Delaunay's works were *La Tour Rouge* (1911) and *La Ville de Paris* (1912).

VII. SPORTS, GAMES, AND SOCIETY

1941 May 15 [Joseph Paul] **Joe DiMaggio** (b. Nov. 25, 1914), a centerfielder for the New York Yankees of American major league baseball, began a **consecutive-game hitting streak** that lasted for 56 games, ending on July 17. During this period DiMaggio made 91 hits, including 15 home runs, in 223 times at bat.

1941 June 7 The **Triple Crown** of American thoroughbred racing was won for the fifth time when **Whirlaway**, with jockey **Eddie Arcaro** (b. Feb. 19, 1916), captured the Belmont Stakes. Whirlaway had previously won the Kentucky Derby (May 3) and the Preakness Stakes (May 10).

1942

I. DISASTERS

1942 Apr. 26   A mining disaster claimed 1,572 lives in a coal dust explosion at the Honkeiko Colliery, Manchuria, China.

1942 Oct. 2 When the liner *Queen Mary* collided with a British cruiser off Curacao in the West Indies, 338 of the cruiser's crew died.

1942 Oct. 16   A cyclone that struck Bengal, India, left c.40,000 persons dead.

1942 Nov. 28 Only c.100 of the c.800 merrymakers at Boston's **Coconut Grove** nightclub escaped injury as a **fire** sped through the structure. At least 150 shock victims were saved by blood plasma injections, a technique developed just four years earlier.

1942 Dec. 13 Sixty-four Canadian and U.S. servicemen were among the 100 people who perished in a **fire at a servicemen's dance** at St. John's, Newfoundland. At least 100 more people were injured as the Knights of Columbus's hostel burned.

1942 Dec. 19 An **earthquake in the Anatolia region** of Turkey killed c.475 people and injured c.600.

II. POLITICS AND WAR

1942 Jan. 1 Twenty-six nations signed the **Declaration of the United Nations**, pledging to fight to the end against the Axis powers and never to sign a separate peace. **Franklin D. Roosevelt** called them the United Nations.

1942 Jan 1–May 6 Manila, capital of the Philippines, on Jan. 1, was **entered by Japanese troops**. By Jan. 6 many American and Filipino troops were forced to retreat to the **Bataan Peninsula** on the west side of Manila Bay. They held out until Apr. 9, when they were forced to surrender. The remaining Americans and Filipinos were on **Corregidor**, an island in Manila Bay. The Japanese subjected the island to a long and heavy bombardment before invading it. On May 6 the last opposition to the invaders ended. The estimated number of Americans and Filipinos who surrendered on Bataan and Corregidor range from 70,000 to 95,000. They were forced to march to a prison camp c.60 miles north of Manila. On the so-called "**Death March,**" little food or water was given the prisoners, many of whom were already weakened by disease, and Japanese soldiers killed those who could not keep up. Perhaps as many as 10,000 died.

1942 Jan. 11–Mar. 9 On Jan. 11, The **Japanese landed troops on Borneo and Celebes**. On Mar. 1 they continued on to Java, and on Mar. 9 the Dutch surrendered. New Guinea was invaded on Mar. 7.

1942 Jan. 20 The fate of millions of European Jews was sealed at a conference in Berlin. Called the **Wannsee Conference** for the villa in which it was held, it brought together high Nazi officials who were empowered by **Hitler** to work out plans for a "**final solution**" [*Endlosüng*] to the problem of what to do with the very large number of persons, mostly Jews, being held in concentration camps. While mass killings had begun, the methods used were considered slow and inefficient. The conference recommended that a gas—**Zyklon B**—be used. The bodies would then be reduced to ashes in ovens which could dispose of 4,000 in 24 hours. The first gassings took place at Belzec, a village in southeastern Poland, on Mar. 17. The camp had a capacity of 15,000 killings a day.

1942 Jan. 21–Nov. 20 The **German Afrika Corps launched a new offensive** against the British Eighth Army in North Africa. By Feb 4, the British had fallen back to Al-Gazala [El Gazala], on the coast of northeastern Libya. The Germans struck again (May 26), capturing **Tobruk**, also in northeastern Libya, on June 21. By July 1, the British were pushed back into Egypt, at **Al-Alemein** [El Alamein], only c.65 miles west of Alexandria. In a battle fought from July 1 to 3, the German advance was halted. On Sept. 3 the exhausted Afrika Corps began a slow withdrawal to the west. The Eighth Army, now under the command of **Bernard Law Montgomery**, on Oct. 23 took the offensive west from Al-Alemein. On Nov. 7 the Germans retreated from Mersa Matruh to Sidi Barrani, both on the coastal road in northwestern Egypt, and on Nov. 20 the British retook Tobruk. This was the end of the attempt by the Axis powers to seize the Suez Canal.

1942 Jan. 30–Feb. 15 After landing on the Malay Peninsula Dec. 8, 1941, Japanese forces steadily drove the British defenders south. On Jan. 30, 1942, the last defending force withdrew to **Singapore Island**. The Japanese invaded Singapore on Feb. 8 and within a week, although outnumbered by the defenders, forced the surrender of the British colony (Feb. 15). Singapore was supposed to be the impregnable naval bastion protecting the British Empire in all of southeast Asia.

1942 Feb. Canada ordered all ethnic Japanese **within her borders**, of whom around 90 percent were Canadian citizens, **to be sent to various isolated areas** in the interior of the country. Eventually, c.21,000 of them, none of whom had been charged with any criminal or subversive acts, were deported.

1942 Feb. 19 Planes from Japanese carriers bombed Darwin, Australia. Not much damage was done.

1942 Feb. 27–Mar. 1 A naval force of American, Australian, British, and Dutch warships was badly beaten in a **battle on the Java Sea**, between Java and Borneo. The five cruisers and 11 destroyers that were trying to prevent the Japanese from landing on Java were almost wiped out. The Japanese suffered little damage and proceeded with their landings on Java.

1942 Mar. 6–Apr. 30 The **Japanese, having invaded Burma** [Myanmar] in December, forced the British to abandon Rangoon [Yangon], the chief city, and two days later entered it. They pushed steadily north and on Apr. 30 captured Lashio, in eastern Burma, and thus cut the **Burma Road**, the only overland supply route to Nationalist China.

1942 Mar. 23 Acting on a presidential order of Feb. 20, **c.120,000 Japanese-Americans**, most of them citizens, were ordered to be **placed in internment camps** in Colorado, Utah, and elsewhere in the west. None of them had been accused of any disloyalty to the U.S., but many people on the West Coast had visions of Japanese spies everywhere. Young male *Nisei*, who had their own unit in the U.S. army, proved to be among the most daring and courageous of all infantrymen.

1942 Apr. 14 The Germans forced **Philippe Pétain**, nominal head of the **Vichy French government**, to restore **Pierre Laval** to the power he had exercised in the government as vice premier and foreign minister before Pétain dismissed and arrested him on Dec. 16, 1940. By Nov., 1942, Pétain relinquished all important authority to Laval. Laval, eager to cooperate with the Nazis, agreed to supply them with French laborers, and in general did all he could to put down French resistance to the Nazis. After the German defeat (1945), Laval was seized by the Americans and turned over to the newly freed French government. Pierre Laval (b. June 28, 1883) was tried for treason, found guilty, and executed on Oct. 15, 1945.

1942 Apr. 18 Sixteen U.S. army B-25 bombers dropped bombs on Tokyo, Nagoya, and Kobe. The planes took off from the aircraft carrier *Hornet* c.650 miles east of Japan. Since the planes could not carry enough fuel to return to the *Hornet,* they went on to Chinese airfields. Of the 82 men on the mission, 70 eventually returned. Three were executed by the Japanese.

1942 May 4–9 The battle of the Coral Sea, between Australia and the Solomon Islands, began when U.S. observation planes spotted a large concentration of Japanese ships in the area. The Japanese lost the aircraft carrier *Ryukyu,* three destroyers, four cruisers, and others. The U.S. aircraft carrier *Lexington* was lost in this battle. This was the first large naval battle in which neither fleet ever came within sight of the other.

1942 May 17–Dec. 31 German forces on May 17 **started two major attacks aimed at Stalingrad** and at the Caucasus in an attempt to capture the oil fields at Baku on the Caspian Sea. By early October the Germans were at Stalingrad but were unable to take the city in the face of stubborn Russian resistance. The German attack stalled and a large German army was surrounded and trapped (Nov. 24). In the Caucasus the Germans penetrated within 150 miles of Baku, but on Nov. 19 the Russians began driving the Germans back on all fronts in southern Russia. The Germans attempted an offensive starting Dec. 18 to relieve Stalingrad, but it failed in the face of Russian attacks north and south of Stalingrad.

1942 May 22 Mexico entered the war on the side of the Allies. Mexico's action was prompted by the sinking of two Mexican tankers by German submarines.

1942 May 30 The British air force bombed Cologne [Köln], Germany, with 1,046 planes. Six hundred acres of the city were wiped out, and 40 bombers were lost. Two days later 956 planes bombed (June 1) Essen, Germany, but did not do much damage because weather conditions made it difficult to locate assigned targets. Thirty-one aircraft were lost.

1942 June 3–4 The battle of Midway was fought by American and Japanese fleets c.1,100 miles west northwest of Hawaii. The Japanese fleet, which included transports intended to land soldiers on Midway, consisted of c.200 ships. The heart of its strength lay in its 8 carriers, 11 battleships, 22 cruisers, 65 destroyers, and 21 submarines. On the carriers c.600 planes were ready for combat. The American fleet, by contrast, consisted of 76 ships, some of which were never in position to take part in the battle. As a result of the Pearl Harbor disaster, the Americans had no battleships present, and only three carriers with 233 planes. The Japanese lost four carriers and more than half their planes. The U.S. fleet lost one carrier and almost two-thirds of its planes, many of them torpedo bombers. In retrospect, **Midway was the turning point of the war in the Pacific.**

1942 June 5 The U.S. declared war on Bulgaria, Hungary, and Romania.

1942 June 7 A Japanese task force was heading north to invade the **Aleutian Islands** off the coast of Alaska, the only actual U.S. territories taken by the Japanese during World War II. Troops landed unopposed on Attu and Kiska, islands of no military value to Japan.

1942 June 9–10 The Germans wiped out the village of Lidice, near Prague, Czechoslovakia. On May 31 Czech resistance fighters attempted to assassinate **Reinhard Heydrich,** a high official of the Gestapo, Hitler's secret police, and "protector" of Bohemia and Moravia. Heydrich (b. Mar. 9, 1904) was wounded and died on June 4. In retaliation, the Germans executed all male inhabitants of Lidice, c.200, and sent all the women to concentration camps and all the children to German institutions. They also destroyed the village completely.

1942 Aug. 7–Feb. 7, 1943 In the first American land offensive of World War II, U.S. marines landed on **Guadalcanal Island,** one of the Solomon Islands in the western Pacific Ocean. The Japanese at once dispatched ships and troops to prevent the invasion. This activity led to a naval **battle near the Eastern**

Solomons (Aug. 24) in which a Japanese carrier was sunk. Later the Americans lost two carriers to Japanese submarines. Meantime the fighting on land was fierce, especially for control of Henderson Field, the one airfield on the island. The Japanese launched an all-out offensive (Oct. 24) but were beaten back with heavy losses. In November more sea fighting took place when Japan attempted to reinforce land troops. Between Nov. 13 and 15 the U.S. lost two cruisers, a Japanese battleship was so badly damaged it had to be scuttled, and seven Japanese transports were sunk so that only c.4,000 of c.11,000 reinforcements were able to land. By January Japan decided to withdraw gradually from Guadalcanal, the end coming on Feb. 7, 1943.

1942 Aug. 22   A **commando force of c.6,000**, mostly Canadians, but with some British and a few Americans and Free French, **raided Dieppe**, a French seaport on the English Channel. The site was too strongly fortified for the attack to succeed, and the attacking force lost more than 60 percent of its manpower. The only gain for the Allies was as a practice for full-scale invasion.

1942 Aug. 22   **Brazil became one of the Allies** in World War II, enabling the U.S. navy to establish a base at Recife, and providing a small infantry force to fight in Europe (1944). This was the only South American force to fight there.

1942 Nov. 8–Dec. 24   **Operation Torch** began with the landing of Allied troops, mostly American, at Casablanca, French Morocco, and Oran and Algiers, Algeria. In some places the invaders were welcomed by the French officials, but in others there was opposition. On Nov. 13 **Jean François Darlan**, the commander in **French North Africa**, ordered a surrender to the Allies after reaching an agreement with **Dwight D[avid] Eisenhower**, commander of the Torch operation. Meanwhile, on Nov. 11, German troops began to occupy the part of France that they had hitherto left to the Vichy government. The Nazis and the Italians also began to send troops and supplies to Tunis, to the east of the invading Allies. Allied forces began moving toward Tunis and were within 12 miles of the city by Nov. 27, where the advance ended in the face of Axis counterattacks, the raw American troops being poorly commanded in combat. A new Allied offensive was planned for Dec. 24 but had to be abandoned in the face of impossible weather. Also Darlan (b. Aug. 7, 1881) was assassinated on Dec. 24. He was succeeded by **Henri**

Honoré Giraud (Jan. 18, 1879–Mar. 11, 1949), commander of the French troops in North Africa.

1942 Nov. 27   In the harbor of Toulon, a French seaport on the Mediterranean, a large part of the **French fleet**, which had been interned there since the armistice of June 1940, was **scuttled** on orders of its admiral. Three battleships, 7 cruisers, 16 submarines, and other small craft went to the bottom. Thus they were kept out of the hands of the Germans.

III. ECONOMY AND TRADE

1942 Jan. 5   **Wartime rationing began in the U.S.** with automobile tires. On May 15 gasoline began to be rationed in 17 eastern states and soon nationwide, on Dec. 1. Sugar was the first food rationed, on May 5, with coffee following on Nov. 29.

1942 Dec.   A number of workers at the Patiño mines of Cataví, central western **Bolivia**, were shot down by government troops called in to break their strike for higher wages. The so-called "**Cataví Massacre**" was the worst in a series of conflicts between Bolivian miners and their employers, in which the government identified with the employers.

IV. RELIGION AND PHILOSOPHY

V. SCIENCE, EDUCATION, AND TECHNOLOGY

1942   **Long-range navigation [Loran]** was developed and became operational, enabling a ship or aircraft almost anywhere in the world to determine its geographical position. Loran measured the lapse of time between radio pulses from two or more stations located in different places.

1942 Mar. 22   The **Grand Coulee Dam**—550 ft. high and 4,173 ft. long—on the Columbia River in Washington State was completed. Behind it now is one of the largest reservoirs in the world, used to generate enormous amounts of hydroelectric power.

1942 July 28   [William Matthew] **Flinders Petrie** (b. June 3, 1853), an English archeologist, died. He spent 45 years excavating ancient sites in Egypt and wrote 75 books about his work. Petrie made important finds at Memphis, and at Thebes he discovered a stele with the earliest known reference by Egyptians to Israel.

1942 Oct. 28   The **Alcan Highway** was completed. It was built to provide an overland route to Alaska, threatened by Japanese invasion. The highway runs today from Dawson Creek, British Columbia, to Fairbanks, Alaska, a distance of 1,523 miles.

1942 Dec. 2   At the **University of Chicago**, a team of scientists, working under the leadership of **Enrico Fermi**, an Italian-American physicist, achieved the **first nuclear chain reaction in an atomic pile** whose essential elements were graphite blocks and uranium. This year too the **Manhattan Project**—to develop an atomic bomb—selected Los Alamos, New Mexico, as the site for its research laboratory. J[ulius] **Robert Oppenheimer** (Apr. 22, 1904–Feb. 18, 1967), an American physicist, was named director.

1942 Dec. 21   **Franz Boas** (b. July 9, 1858), a German-American pioneer in anthropology, died. Boas became Columbia University's first professor of anthropology in 1899 and held that position for 37 years. He was by far the most influential anthropologist of his time and was the teacher and inspiration of a whole generation of anthropologists. A prolific author, he wrote such books as *The Mind of Primitive Man* (1911), *Race, Language, and Culture* (1940), and *Race and Democratic Society* (1945).

VI. ARTS AND LEISURE

1942   **Richard Lippold** (b. May 3, 1915), an American sculptor, began to make his abstract, geometrical constructions that seemed to owe as much to engineering as to art. Most of Lippold's works were designed to be suspended in large spaces. Typical of these were *Flight* (1963) and *Gemini II* (1968).

1942   **Theip-pan Maung Wa** (b. 1899) was murdered by bandits in his native Burma [Myanmar]. A versatile and prolific prose writer, he was the major advocate of an important experimental style [*Khitsan*] in **Burmese literature**.

1942 Jan. 6   **Emma Calvé** (b. Aug. 15, 1858), a French operatic soprano, died. She made her debut in Brussels in 1882 and in 1893 was first heard at the Metropolitan Opera in New York City where she appeared for the next 13 years.

1942 Feb. 12   **Grant** [De Volsen] **Wood** (b. Feb. 3, 1892), an American artist, died. Grant's subjects for the most part are stern and seem to evoke the feel of the Midwest. Among his best-known paintings are *American Gothic* (1930), *Daughters of Revolution* (1932), and *Dinner for Threshers* (1934).

1942 Feb. 23   The Austrian-born writer **Stefan Zweig** (b. Nov. 28, 1881) killed himself. Zweig was a biographer, poet, critic, and travel writer. His best-known works were his biographies of *Balzac* (1944) and *Marie Antoinette* (1932), his many essays, and *Reminiscences* (1943).

1942 Mar. 27   **Julio Gonzalez** (b. Sept. 21, 1876), a Spanish sculptor, died. He worked in metal, being an expert in welding iron. He often interpreted the human figure, as in *Hombre-Cactus* (1939–1940).

1942 May 11   **Hagiwara Sakutaru** (b. Nov. 1, 1886), who wrote *Isuki ni hoeru* [*Baying at the Moon*], the first volume of which appeared in 1917, died. The work ushered in a new kind of poetry to Japan. Perception of thoughts and ideas were expressed in harsh, often ugly, terms rather than in amorphous descriptions. Other works by Hagiwara were *Atarashiki yokugo* [*New Desires*] (1922) and (posthumously) a collection of his poems entitled *The Face at the Bottom of the World* (1969).

1942 May 29   **John Barrymore** (b. Feb. 15, 1882), an American actor and member of a famous stage family, died. He was the matinee idol of his time, known as "The Great Profile." Early in his career he played roles on the stage, but turned more and more to the movies. Here he played a variety of roles, as in *Moby Dick* (1930), *Grand Hotel* (1932), *Rasputin and the Empress* (1933), and *Dinner at Eight* (1933).

1942 Aug. 22   **Michel Fokine** (b. Apr. 26, 1880), a Russian-born American choreographer, died. As a dancer he made his debut with the Imperial Russian Ballet (1898) but soon became (1900) the chief choreographer for Diaghilev's Ballet Russe. Fokine created c.60 ballets in all, among them *Les Sylphides* (1909), *The Firebird* (1910), and *Petrouchka* (1916).

1942 Nov. 5   **George M**[ichael] **Cohan** (b. July 4, 1878), an American showman, actor, and composer, died. He wrote 20 musicals—words, music, and story. Most of all, though, he was the epitome of the friendly, extrovert, patriotic American. This was reflected in his musicals, such as *Forty-Five Minutes from Broadway* (1906) and *The Song and Dance Man* (1923). Cohan's spirit as "a real live nephew of my Uncle Sam" was particularly seen in his songs: "**You're a Grand Old Flag**" (1906), "**The Yankee Doodle Boy**" (1904), "**Mary's a Grand Old Name**" (1905), and "**Give My Regards to Broadway**" (1904). Cohan's classic was "**Over There**" (1917), written as the U.S. entered the war.

VII. SPORTS, GAMES, AND SOCIETY

1942 Mar. 8 José Raúl Capablanca y Grauperra (b. Nov. 19, 1888), a Cuban champion **chess** player, died. He began to play the game at the age of four and by the time he was 12 he was the champion of Cuba. Capablanca won the world championship in 1921 when he defeated **Emanuel Lasker** of Germany, and held the title until 1927, when he lost it to **Alexander A. Alekhine**. Capablanca did not lose a single game between 1916 and 1924. Besides his chess activities Capablanca served in the Cuban diplomatic service from 1916.

1943

I. DISASTERS

1943 Sept. 6–Dec. 16 On Sept. 6, the Pennsylvania Railroad's **Congressional Limited**, enroute from New York City to Washington, D.C., **derailed** in Philadelphia, killing 79. Seventy-three died on Dec. 16 when the northbound **Atlantic Coast Line Champion** plowed into its derailed southbound sister express near Buies, N.C.

1943 Oct. 30 Off the coast of Florida, **two tankers** loaded with aviation gasoline and blacked out because of wartime conditions, **collided**. In the explosion and fire that followed, 88 crewmen died.

1943 Nov. 26. An **earthquake in northern Turkey** killed c.1,800 people and left about another 2,000 injured.

II. POLITICS AND WAR

1943 A mass grave containing c.9,000 bodies was discovered in Vinnitsa, a Ukrainian city, in southwestern U.S.S.R. All appeared to have died in 1938, the last year of **Stalin's Great Purge**, and had been killed by shots in the back of the neck.

1943 Jan. 12–Mar. 19 The Russians, fighting below Vorenezh, on Feb. 8 retook Kursk, 150 miles to the west, and two days later Belgorod to the south. Meanwhile the **German forces in the Caucasus were retreating** to the northwest, but another German army was attacking south of the Russian offensive. The Germans escaped from the Caucasus and on

Mar. 15 forced the Russians out of Kharkov, in eastern Ukraine, which the Red army had taken only on Feb. 16. On Mar. 19 they retook Belgorod.

1943 Jan. 14–23 Franklin D. Roosevelt and Winston Churchill held a **conference at Casablanca**, Morocco, at which they made plans for an invasion of Sicily and decided to postpone a cross-channel invasion of Europe until 1944.

1943 Jan. 31 Most of the German army surrounded at **Stalingrad** surrendered to the Russians, with a last group holding out until Feb. 2. The German army suffered c.300,000 casualties here in dead, wounded, and prisoners. The Russian army suffered c.50,000 deaths.

1943 Feb. 20–May 13 A German attack westward drove through the **Kasserine [Al-Qasrayn] Pass** in northern Tunisia, but by Feb. 21 it was contained by American troops. To the east, on Mar. 20, the British attacked Axis troops on the Mareth Line in southeastern Tunisia, which they broke (Mar. 28). Bizerte and Tunis on the northern coast of Tunisia fell to the Allies on May 7, and on May 13 the last Axis forces surrendered. The **Germans and the Italians**, at a cost of nearly a million men, **were out of North Africa**.

1943 Mar.–July After a disastrous March in which the Allies lost 120 merchant ships, **U-boats began to suffer such heavy losses** that on May 23 the German navy withdrew them entirely from the North Atlantic. During June, July, and August, the U-boats sank only 58 merchant ships in all parts of the world, while 79 of the U-boats were sunk.

1943 Mar.–Dec.   Bombing raids on Germany, Italy, and German-held France, intensified as the U.S. army Eighth Air Force reached full strength. The B-17 Flying Fortress joined the British Lancaster as the heavy bombers. Between Mar. 3 and July 12 British bombers made 43 raids on the Ruhr. Between July and November British and American bombers made 33 major raids on cities, especially Hamburg. The Ruhr raids cost the Allies 872 planes. In a Flying Fortress raid of Oct. 14, sixty were shot down and 128 damaged out of 291. On July 19, 500 Allied planes raided Rome and its vicinity. On Aug. 1 the Ploesti oil fields in Romania were hit by U.S. planes. During 1943 the Allies poured c.200,000 tons of bombs on Germany. Despite this, Germany's production of armaments was estimated to have increased by half.

1943 Mar. 2–4   In a battle in the Bismarck Archipelago in the western Pacific Ocean, Allied planes sank all eight transports carrying Japanese troops to reinforce New Guinea. Also sunk were four of the eight escorting destroyers. The Allies lost c.20 men; but the Japanese lost c.3,600 men.

1943 Apr. 9–May 16   Of the c.380,000 Jews in the Warsaw ghetto when the war began, only c.70,000 remained. They now took up arms against their Nazi conquerors. The Germans sent in troops and tanks. To their surprise the Jews fought desperately with such arms as they had. It was not until May 16 that resistance ended after the Nazis burned the whole ghetto and, as a last gesture, blew up the Tlomacki Synagogue. They rounded up 56,065 Jews, executed c.7,000 of them at once, and sent the rest to concentration and labor camps. The others died in the revolt.

1943 Apr. 13   A German radio broadcast announced that Nazi forces in Russia had found the mass graves of several thousand Polish army officers in the **Katyn Forest**, ten miles west of Smolensk. The Germans claimed the Russians had carried out the slaughter. An international commission admitted to the site by the Nazis found 4,443 bodies. When the Russians retook (Sept. 1942) Smolensk, they brought in a commission that accused the Nazis of the massacre. A later inquiry (1952) by the Polish communist government agreed that the Nazis were to blame. In 1989, however, Poland reported (Feb. 1989) that a Polish Red Cross commission had exhumed 15,000 bodies from the mass graves and concluded that they had been killed between the end of March and the beginning of May 1940, when the Soviets were in control of the region. Another 10,500 Polish officers disappeared at the same time as the Katyn massacre and have never been heard from. The **U.S.S.R. admitted** (Apr. 13, 1990) that the **Soviet secret police carried out the killings at Katyn** but has not yet informed the world of the fate of the other 10,500 officers.

1943 May 11   Two U.S. forces converged on Attu, in the Aleutians, bypassing Kiska, and landed strong forces which by May 30 wiped out the Japanese defenders. On the last day of the Japanese defense they resorted to a banzai charge on the American lines, and c.2,000 died, 11 were captured, and a few survivors escaped to the hills to become snipers. When the Americans and Canadians landed on Kiska on Aug. 15 they found the Japanese had evacuated their troops.

1943 May 11–27   At the third Washington Conference, Winston Churchill and **Franklin D. Roosevelt** discussed plans to put more pressure on Italy and increase air raids over Germany. Plans for the invasion of France were discussed, and a target date of May 1, 1944, was agreed on.

1943 June 3   Formation of a Committee of National Liberation for France was agreed to by **Charles De Gaulle** and **Henri Giraud**, the two main anti-Vichy French leaders. De Gaulle soon became the dominant figure, and Giraud was relegated to the position of a military adviser.

1943 June 4   The overthrow by a military coup of the regime of **Ramon S. Castillo** (Nov. 20, 1873–Oct. 12, 1944), president of **Argentina**, marked the beginning of the rise to power of **Juan** [Domingo] **Perón**, a colonel who participated in the coup.

1943 June 21   American troops began landing on the New Georgia Islands of the Solomons in the southwestern Pacific Ocean. The Japanese airfield at Munda on New Georgia Island itself, was not taken until Aug. 5.

1943 July 4   Wladyslaw [Eugeniusz] **Sikorski** (b. May 20, 1881), a Polish politician and soldier, died in an airplane crash. A leader in the fight for Poland's independence in World War I, Sikorski served as prime minister of **Poland** (Dec., 1922–May, 1923). Following the German conquest of Poland in 1939, he became prime minister of the Polish government in exile.

1943 July 5–Nov. 6 The **Germans began an offensive against the Russian salient west of Kursk**. On July 12 the Russians struck back north of Kursk. On Aug. 5 they retook both Orel and Belgorod. The Russian advance continued, and the Nazis lost (Sept. 25) Smolensk, 250 miles southwest of Moscow. Kiev, in Ukraine, was in Russian hands on Nov. 6.

1943 July 10 **American and British armies landed on Sicily**. The capital, Palermo, fell on July 22, and on Aug. 18 the capture of Messina at the northeast point of the island ended resistance. About 100,000 German and Italian troops escaped to the mainland.

1943 July 25 **Benito Mussolini**, dictator of Italy for 22 years, was forced to resign by **Victor Emmanuel III**, king of Italy. Mussolini was then arrested, and **Pietro Badoglio** (Sept. 28, 1871–Oct. 31, 1956) was named premier. On Sept. 12, after the Allied invasion of Italy, a bold rescue of Mussolini was accomplished by a Nazi parachute unit. "Il Duce" was taken from a site in the Abruzzi Mountains in central Italy to Salò in northern Italy.

1943 Aug. 17–24 The **Quadrant Conference** was held in Quebec, Canada, by Allied leaders. Besides **Roosevelt** and **Churchill**, the conference included **William Lyon Mackenzie King**, prime minister of Canada, and [Tzu-Wen] **T.V. Soong** (1894–Apr. 25, 1971), foreign minister of China. Plans for the invasion of France were approved.

1943 Sept. 3–Dec. 31 British troops landed at **Reggio**, on the toe of the Italian boot. On Sept. 8 another Allied force went ashore at Taranto, on the inside of the heel. The next day a further force, mostly American, was landed at Salerno, south of Naples. The **German army immediately occupied all of northern and central Italy** north of Naples. Meanwhile, the **post-Mussolini government**, located at Brindisi on Italy's Adriatic coast, **announced** (Sept. 8) **its surrender** to the Allies and declared war (Oct. 13) on Germany and the other Axis powers. On Oct. 1 Naples was taken and on Oct. 12 an Allied drive toward Rome began. Progress was slow, casualties heavy. The Germans established the **Gustav Line** across Italy, c.100 miles south and east of Rome. At year's end, this line was intact, except at its eastern

end, with the Allies bogged down by bad weather and exhaustion.

1943 Nov. 1–23 **American forces landed on Bougainville**, the largest of the Solomon Islands. Not until Mar. 23, 1944, was the island completely in American hands. On Nov. 20 **Tarawa** and **Makin** islands in the Gilbert Islands [present Kiribati] were invaded. Makin was quickly taken, Tawara was defended by more than 5,000 Japanese troops and Korean laborers. By Nov. 23 the last Japanese was dead, except for 17 wounded prisoners and c.100 Koreans. U.S. marines lost nearly 3,400 dead and wounded.

1943 Nov. 9 The **United Nations Relief and Rehabilitation Administration** [UNRRA] was established by agreement among 44 nations, later increased to 52. Its purpose was to provide assistance to lands liberated from the Axis powers. The nations contributed about $4,000,000,000, which was used to supply food and medicine, restore public facilities, and help revive agriculture and industry.

1943 Nov. 22–26 **Roosevelt**, **Churchill**, and **Chiang Kai-Shek**, president of the Chinese Nationalist government, met in Cairo, Egypt, to discuss plans for carrying on the war against Japan. It was agreed that only unconditional surrender would be accepted.

1943 Nov. 28–Dec. 1 **Roosevelt and Churchill met in Teheran**, Iran, with **Joseph Stalin**. They coordinated plans for carrying on the war against Germany. Stalin said Russia would declare war on Japan once the Nazis were defeated.

1943 Dec. By the end of the year **Tito controlled a considerable part of Yugoslavia**. The forces of the other guerilla leader, **Draza Mihajilovic**, were dwindling and he was widely acused of cooperating with the Nazis at times instead of fighting them. Allied support was shifting to Tito but it was not until 1944 that he was fully recognized as the leader-to-be of post-war Yugoslavia. In 1946 Mihajlovic (b. 1893) was seized by Tito's forces, tried for treason, and executed on July 17.

1943 Dec. 20 **Gualberto Villarroel** became president of **Bolivia** (1943–1946) following a coup led by the newly formed **Movimiento Nacionalista Revolucionario** [MNR].

1943 Dec. 24 **Dwight D. Eisenhower** was appointed Supreme Commander of Allied Forces in Europe in charge of **Operation Overlord**, the invasion of Normandy.

1943 Dec. 26 The **German battlecruiser *Scharnhorst*** was sunk in the North Atlantic by the British battleship *Duke of York* and other warships. The **Scharnhorst** at the time of her sinking was attempting to prey on a convoy carrying lend-lease supplies to Russia.

III. ECONOMY AND TRADE

1943 Apr. 7 **Bolivia**, which now **declared war on the Axis powers**, was benefiting from the increased demand for its tin and wolframite.

1943 Apr. 30 **Beatrice** [Potter] **Webb** (b. Jan. 22, 1858), an English economist and socialist activist, died. In 1892 she married **Sidney James Webb** and thereafter they revitalized the **Fabian Society**, a socialist but anti-Marxist group, and through it influenced the Labour party so that it adopted the society's tenets. In 1895 the Webbs founded the **London School of Economics** and in 1913 the **New Statesman**, still an influential journal. The Webbs also wrote a number of books together, including **Industrial Democracy** (1897) and **Consumers' Cooperative Movement** (1921).

1943 June 10 The **Current Tax Payment Act** of 1943 established for the **first time compulsory withholding of federal income taxes** from the wages and salaries of U.S. workers.

1943 June 20 A **race riot broke out in Detroit**, Michigan. Its immediate cause was the influx of 60,000 or more African Americans from the South, seeking jobs in war industries. In two days 35 people, almost all black, were killed and more than 500 were injured. Police arrested c.500 persons, mostly whites. During the summer of 1943 there were similar riots on a smaller scale in other cities: Mobile, Alabama, on May 25; Los Angeles, California, June 4; Beaumont, Texas, June 19; and the Harlem section of New York City on Aug. 1. On June 25, 1941, **Franklin D. Roosevelt**, president of the U.S., had issued an executive order forbidding racial discrimination in plants holding defense contracts. Partly by reason of this order, but also because of serious labor shortages, African Americans' share of such jobs increased from 3 percent to 8 percent. Also, many

more found employment with the federal government.

1943 July The **Congress of Industrial Organization [CIO] formed a Political Action Committee**, looking ahead to the elections of 1944. The CIO-PAC soon became an important factor in American politics.

IV. SCIENCE, EDUCATION, AND TECHNOLOGY

1943 The American fighter plane, the P-47, called the **Thunderbolt** and built by Republic, was able to exceed 420 mph and attain an altitude of 35,000 feet, matching the capabilities of the British Hurricane and Spitfire, the German Messerschmitt 109 and FW-190, and the Japanese AGM Type Zero.

1943 **Streptomycin**, an antibiotic, was isolated by **Selman** [Abraham] **Waksman** (July 2, 1888–Aug. 16, 1973), a Russian-born American biologist. Waksman received the **Nobel prize for physiology** or medicine in 1952.

1943 Jan. 5 **George Washington Carver** (b. Jan. 5, 1864), an American botanist and chemist, died. Born a slave, he earned a college degree after he became free. Carver spent his life upgrading the economy of the South, and especially of its blacks, through improvements in agriculture and agricultural products. He found more than 300 uses for peanuts and more than 100 for sweet potatoes. Carver also devised uses for soybeans and cotton waste.

1943 Jan. 7 **Nikola Tesla** (b. July 10, 1856), a Croatian-born American electrical engineer and inventor, died. He invented a number of machines and processes that contributed to the development of radio and the industrial uses of electricity. Tesla's feats attracting the most public attention were his scheme for lighting electric lamps without wires from 25 miles away, and the creation of artificial lightning (1899–1900).

1943 Feb. 14 **David Hilbert** (b. Jan. 23, 1862), a German mathematician, died. He did work on the theory of numbers and of invariants, investigated multidimensional space, and made contributions to the kinetic theory of gases and of radiation. Among his writings was *Methoden der Mathematischen Physik* (1924).

V. ARTS AND LEISURE

1943 Mar. 13 Stephen Vincent Benét (b. July 22, 1898), an American poet, novelist, and short-story writer, died. Two volumes of his poetry were published while he was an undergraduate at Yale. His first novel was *The Beginning of Wisdom* (1921). Benét's finest achievement was his long narrative poem about the American Civil War, *John Brown's Body* (1928). *Ballads and Poems, 1915–1930* (1931) was a collection of his poetry. Benét wrote the librettos for two one-act operas, *The Headless Horseman* (1937) and *The Devil and Daniel Webster* (1939).

1943 Mar. 28 Sergei Vasilyevich Rachmaninoff (b. Apr. 1, 1873), noted Russian composer, pianist, and conductor, died. He was regarded as one of the best pianists of his time. He wrote operas: *The Niggardly Knight* (1941), and *Francesca da Rimini* (1941), symphonies, songs, and cantatas, including *Isle of the Dead* (1907) and *The Bells* (1913). In 1917, he left the country and never returned, emigrating to the U.S. in 1935 after living in Switzerland.

1943 Mar. 31 *Oklahoma!*, destined to be a landmark in the history of the American musical theater, opened in New York City. The music was composed by **Richard Rodgers** (July 28, 1902–Dec. 30, 1979) and the lyrics were by **Oscar Hammerstein II** (July 12, 1895–Aug. 23, 1960). *Oklahoma!* told a serious story of life and love on the frontier around 1900. The music was of the highest quality, and the dancing was authentic ballet, choreographed by **Agnes De Mille**.

1943 Apr. 3 Conrad Veidt (b. Jan. 23, 1893), a German actor of the stage and movies, died. In Germany his best-known role was as the somnambulist in the film *The Cabinet of Dr. Caligari* (1919). In Hollywood he appeared in *The Man Who Laughs* (1928) and other movies. Returning to Germany, Veidt scored an acting triumph playing the part of Metternich in *Congress Dances* (1931). In the 1930s and early 1940s he appeared in films in England and the U.S., including *Casablanca* (1943).

1943 Apr. 13 Oscar Schlemmer (b. Sept. 4, 1888), a German painter and stage designer, died. He was associated (1920–1929) with the **Bauhaus**, where he taught stage design as well as painting and sculpture.

1943 Apr. 25 Vladimir [Ivanovich] **Nemirovich-Danchenko** (b. Dec 23, 1858), a Russian playwright and theatrical producer, died. In 1897, with **Constantin Stanislavsky**, he founded the **Moscow Art Theater**, which became internationally influential.

1943 June 2 Leslie Howard [nee Leslie Steiner] (b. Apr. 23, 1893), an English actor of Hungarian background, died when the aircraft in which he was flying from Lisbon, Portugal, to England was shot down by enemy action. Howard was popular in both England and the U.S., on the stage and in the movies. He starred in such films as *Of Human Bondage* (1934), *The Petrified Forest* (1936), and *Romeo and Juliet* (1936). He also played the gentle, faithful Ashley Wilkes in *Gone with the Wind* (1939).

1943 Aug. 8 Mei Lan-Fang (b. 1893), a noted Chinese actor, died. Making his debut when 13 years old, he became famous for the female roles he created. In 1930 he toured the U.S. with his company of 22 actors.

1943 Aug. 9 Chaim Soutine (b. 1894), a Lithuanian-born French painter of the expressionist school, died. His style was rough and slashing; his content, often psychologically disturbing. Typical of Soutine's work are *Side of Beef* (c.1925), *Hanging Turkey* (c.1926), and *Page Boy at Maxim's* (1927).

1943 Aug. 22 Shimazaki Toson (b. Mar. 25, 1872), whose first novel *Broken Commandment* was published in Japan in 1908, died. Toson was one of the great figures of modern Japanese literature.

1943 Oct. 7 [Marguerite] **Radclyffe Hall** (b. 1886?), an English author, died. She wrote eight novels and four volumes of poetry, but *The Well of Loneliness* (1928), a novel that spoke openly of lesbianism, attracted far more attention than anything else she did. After a trial for obscenity, the book was banned in England.

1943 Oct. 21 André Antoine (b. Jan. 31, 1857), one of the major figures in both the 19th and 20th century western theater, died. He founded the **Théâtre-Libre** in Paris, which held its first performance on Mar. 30, 1887. The Théâtre helped revolutionize the theater in France and had effects even in Berlin and Moscow by providing a showcase for the new naturalistic staging. After the theater failed financially in 1894, Antoine founded the Théâtre Antoine, which carried on his work.

1943 Oct. 24 **Hector de Saint Denys Garneau** (b. June 13, 1912), a French-Canadian poet, died. His most noted work was *Regards et jeux dans l'espace* [Glances and Games in Space] (1937).

1943 Oct. 31 **Max Reinhardt** (b. Sept. 9, 1873), a German theatrical director, died. He established theaters in Berlin and produced the dramas *Sumurun* (1911), *The Miracle*, *Everyman*, and *Oedipus Rex* (1911–1912). Anti-Jewish attitudes drove him from Berlin in 1933. His film version of *A Midsummer Night's Dream* (1935) was one of his noteworthy accomplishments.

1943 Dec. 22 [Helen] **Beatrix Potter** (b. July 6, 1866), an English author and illustrator of books for children, died. Self-taught as an artist, she began her first book as a letter. It was *The Tale of Peter Rabbit* (1901). She wrote and illustrated more than 20

such books over the next 30 years. Although her animals lived in a fantasy land, they were depicted in a realistic and intelligent manner and became classics.

VI. SPORTS, GAMES, AND SOCIETY

1943 The "zoot suit" appeared in the U.S., worn by young males. It featured high-waisted trousers that ballooned out, then ended in very narrow cuffs. The jacket was extra long, the lapels extra wide, and the shoulders thickly padded.

1943 June 5 The **Triple Crown** of American thoroughbred horse racing was won for the sixth time when **Count Fleet**, with jockey **Johnny Longdon** (b. Feb. 14, 1910) up, captured the Belmont States. Previously Count Fleet won the Kentucky Derby (May 1) and the Preakness Stakes (May 8).

1944

I. DISASTERS

1944 Jan. 3 Between 500 and 800 people died in a **train wreck** in the Torro Tunnel, Léon province, Spain.

1944 Jan. 15 An **earthquake in the Andes Mountains** in western Argentina did great damage to San Juan, killing c.900 people and leaving c.70,000 homeless.

1944 Mar. 2 Fumes from a train stalled in a tunnel near Salerno, Italy, asphyxiated 426, including the crew, and injured another 521 persons.

1944 June 23 **Tornados in the American states** of Indiana, Ohio, Pennsylvania, and West Virginia left 153 persons dead.

1944 July 6 From the high wires, circus star **Herman Wallenda** was first to spot the **fire** that turned the 19-ton Ringling Brothers' big top into a raging inferno at an afternoon performance in Hartford, Connecticut. Many in the audience were trapped as the tent collapsed. The death toll was 168, with 487 injured.

1944 July 17 **Two ammunition ships blew up** at Port Chicago, northeast of San Francisco, California,

killing 322 persons and causing great damage to nearby buildings.

1944 Sept. 12–16 A **hurricane** of great strength swept the eastern coast of the U.S. from North Carolina to New England, killing 389 people.

1944 Oct. 20 **Liquid gas tanks exploded**, setting fire to a 50-block area in Cleveland, Ohio. The death toll was 130; property damage was $10,000,000.

II. POLITICS AND WAR

1944 Great Britain's Parliament granted a new constitution to **Jamaica** providing universal men's suffrage and an elected House of Representatives.

1944 Jan. Representatives of Australia and New Zealand met in Canberra, Australia, to discuss mutual cooperation in matters of defense. The result was the **Canberra Agreement**, "a Pacific charter of permanent collaboration and cooperation."

1944 Jan. 3–May 13 A **Russian winter offensive** captured Novigrad-Volynsk and the next day crossed the border into pre-war Poland. Równe [Rovno] fell on Feb. 5 and the same day Łuck [Lutsk], 100 miles inside Poland, was entered. To the south, Nicopol was given up by the Germans on Feb. 8. The Russians captured Khersen at the mouth of the Dnieper on Mar. 13. A German force, isolated in the Crimea, surrendered Odessa on Apr. 10. Sevastopol fell on May 10, and the last Germans in the Crimea surrendered on May 13.

1944 Jan. 22–May 23 **British and American forces landed at Anzio** on the west coast of Italy, south of Rome. The German response was strong and for a time the beachhead was in danger of disaster. Meanwhile, the American Fifth Army, the British Eighth Army, and Free French, New Zealand, and Polish units were trying without success to break the **Gustav Line**. A key point on it was the Benedictine abbey of Monte Cassino. Believing it was being used by the Germans as an observation post, the Allies bombed and destroyed it (Feb. 15). It was later found that the Germans did not use it until after the bombardment, when its ruins provided an almost insurmountable obstacle to Allied tanks. Assaults between Mar. 15 and 23 failed to pierce the Gustav Line. Finally, the line collapsed in battles fought from May 11 to 18. On May 23 the Allies broke out of the Anzio beachhead, joined the other forces, and pushed on toward Rome.

1944 Jan. 27 The **Russians broke the siege of Leningrad**, and their armies moved toward Estonia, Latvia, and Lithuania.

1944 Feb. 1–Aug. 9 **American forces began a year of Pacific island hopping.** The aim was to move northward toward Japan, taking essential Japanese-held islands but leaving other islands to die of lack of support from home. Americans landed on **Kwajalein**, in the Marshall Islands, on Feb. 1 and took it with little trouble. The same was true of **Eniwetok**, captured from Feb. 17 to 21. In support of this operation, a raid was carried out against the heavily fortified Japanese base at **Truk**, in the Caroline Islands. Carrier-based planes sank two cruisers, four destroyers, and many tankers and freighters. They also shot down c.250 Japanese planes while losing only 25. On Apr. 22 Allied forces landed on **New Guinea**. The next island taken was **Saipan**, in the Mariana Islands. Invaded on June 15, it was secured on July 9 after fighting that caused c.3,400 American casualties and c.27,000 Japanese. **Guam**, largest of the Marianas, returned to U.S. possession when invaded and secured between July 20 and Aug. 10. In this same period, on June 15, the **first air raid by B-29 Superfortresses on a Japanese home island**, Kyushu, was made from bases in China.

1944 Feb. 20–Dec. 31 Between Feb. 20 and 27 large numbers of **Flying Fortresses struck at aircraft manufacturing plants in Germany**, and on Mar. 6 carried out an 800-plane daytime attack on Berlin. The Royal air force made a heavy raid (Feb. 19 and 20) on Leipzig. On Apr. 15 U.S. planes flying from Italy raided the Ploesti oil fields in Romania, suffering serious losses. On May 12 bombers from England hit oil targets in Germany. Meanwhile, the RAF was concentrating on targets in France, such as railroads, to hinder German transportation when D-Day came. When Berlin was attacked on June 17, the American bombers flew on to land in Russia, where they refueled and rearmed, and made another raid on their way back to England.

1944 Mar. 19–Dec. 4 On Mar. 19 **Germany invaded Hungary**, in part because Hungary now wished to get out of the war and in part because Russian forces were drawing near. **Romania announced on Aug. 23 that it was now at peace with the Allies** and declared war on Germany. Nevertheless, Russian forces entered Bucharest, the capital, on Aug. 31. Bulgaria was officially at war with the U.S. and Great Britain but not with Russia. When Germany demanded that Bulgaria declare war on the U.S.S.R., Russia declared war (Sept. 5) on Bulgaria and invaded the country without meeting resistance. **Bulgaria asked for peace** and declared war (Sept. 8) on Germany. Russian armies then moved into Hungary and toward Yugoslavia. By Dec. 4 Budapest, the Hungarian capital, was surrounded while the **Germans were driven out of Belgrade**, the Yugoslav capital, on Nov. 20. The Russians joined with Tito's partisans in this offensive.

1944 Mar. 22–July **Japanese forces invaded India** from Burma [Myanmar], driving toward Imphal, Manipur state, and Kohima, Nagaland state, as their first objectives. By Apr. 6 Kohima was surrounded, but a British counteroffensive drove back the Japanese on Apr. 14. British air superiority contributed a great deal to their advance. During July the **British moved into Burma** to the Chindwin River. The Japanese no longer were a threat to India.

1944 May 8 A student-led general strike caused the downfall of **Maximiliano Hernandez Martinez** (Oct. 29, 1882–May 17, 1966), the president of **El Salvador**. His ouster came shortly after he put down an attempted military coup with considerable bloodshed.

1944 May 26   A plebiscite in Iceland approved the **dissolution of the Icelandic-Danish Act of Union** (1918). Iceland was proclaimed a republic on June 17 with **Sveinn Björnsson** (Feb. 27, 1881–Jan. 25, 1952) as president (to 1952).

1944 June   Russian troops deported the last Crimean Turks from their homeland to distant parts of Asia for alleged collaboration with the Germans. At least 80,000 died as a result, concluding a genocidal program begun (1920) against the Crimean Turks by the Bolsheviks, when from 60,000 to 70,000 had been shot in a reign of terror led by **Béla Kun**, the Hungarian communist leader, and continued (1921–1922) when more than 100,000 were allowed to starve, as the Soviet government continued its **compulsory grain exports from the Crimea** despite known local shortages.

1944 June 4–Dec. 4   The **Allies entered Rome** on June 4 without resistance and immediately moved farther north. By July 15 they reached a new **German defensive line on the Arno River**, from Pisa to Florence and eastward. On Aug. 25 another offensive began. On Dec. 4, Ravenna was captured.

1944 June 6   Today was **D-Day for Operation Overlord**, the **Allied invasion of France**. An armada of c.4,600 warships, transports, supply ships, and landing craft put c.175,000 troops ashore. Shortly before the landings two American and one British airborne divisions were dropped behind the beachheads to destroy communications. The troops landed on five beaches in Normandy: on the west, Utah and Omaha beaches were American objectives; to the east, the British landed on Gold and Sword, while the Canadians hit Juno, between Gold and Sword. The landings were made with rather heavy losses, but the only important setback on the first day was the failure to capture Caen.

1944 June 7–Sept. 12   Break-out from the Normandy beachheads was not as rapid as the Allies hoped. On July 9, however, the British and Canadians took Caen, a transportation hub, and on July 18, St. Lo fell to the Americans. Cherbourg, the largest port at the western end of Normandy, was captured on June 26, but the Germans wrecked its facilities so that it was of no use until August. The Allies launched offensives from Caen and St. Lo on July 25 and also from Avranches on July 31. The Americans were able to push rapidly east while the British and Canadians headed northeast. **Paris was abandoned** by the Germans, and on Aug. 25 the Allies, led by a Free French unit, entered the city. Five days later **Charles De Gaulle** arrived and established a provisional French government. By early September most of France was liberated, as was Luxembourg, and on Sept. 12 **U.S. troops first crossed into German territory**. Meanwhile, to the north Brussels was liberated on Sept. 3 and the next day Antwerp.

1944 June 10–Sept. 14   The **U.S.S.R. invaded Finland**. Fighting both Finnish and German troops, the Russians attacked on the Karelian Isthmus and captured the port of Vyborg June 21. Though **Finland withdrew from the war** Sept. 4, it was not until Sept. 10 that the war ended with the surrender of Finland.

1944 June 19–20   In the **battle of the Philippine Sea**, a naval engagement that grew out of the landing of American forces in the Marianas, the Japanese force of aircraft carriers was crippled. Aircraft from the carriers attempted to prevent the American landing on Saipan but lost 218 planes. The Americans lost 29. Two Japanese carriers were sunk by U.S. submarines. On June 20 the two fleets engaged again. The Japanese lost 65 more planes, a large carrier, a battleship, two light cruisers, and a heavy cruiser. The American fleet lost 100 planes, most of them when attempting to find and land on their carriers in the dark. Many of the crews were rescued.

1944 June 23–Dec. 31   The **Russian summer offensive** struck first north of the Pripet [Pripyat] Marshes, near the Polish border, where the Germans still held some Soviet territory. In capturing Minsk, which fell on July 3, the Russians inflicted c.200,000 German casualties. The **Germans were forced out of Belorussia** by the middle of July, and a good part of northeastern Poland was overrun by the Red army. On July 14 the Russians attacked south of the Pripet Marshes. They captured Lwow on July 27, and that same day the **Germans gave up Brest-Litovsk**. By year's end the Russians were within reach of Warsaw.

1944 July 1   **Jorge Ubico Castateñda** (Nov. 10, 1878–June 14, 1946), president of **Guatemala** since 1931, resigned in the face of a democratic uprising. Ubico had increased school, health, and other public facilities, constructed a road network, and ended government corruption. His methods, however, were oppressive and arbitrary. **Juan José Arévalo** (b. Sept. 10, 1904) was chosen president in an election held from Dec. 17 to 19.

1944 July 9   Raoul [Gustav] Wallenberg (Aug. 5, 1912–?1947), a Swedish businessman and diplomat, was sent to Budapest by the Swedish government, with the encouragement of other nations, to try to protect the **Jews of Hungary** from the Nazis, now in control of the country. Already c.400,000 Hungarian Jews had been sent to concentration camps. Wallenberg set up "protected houses" that flew the Swedish flag or the flags of other neutral nations, and put Jews in them. The estimates of how many he saved in this way run from 4,000 to 35,000. Shortly after the **Russians entered Budapest** on Jan. 17, 1945, Wallenberg was arrested. It was known that he was taken to Russia, but he was not seen at liberty again. The Russians later claimed that he died in prison of a heart attack, but there are reports of his having been seen in a prison hospital as recently as 1980.

1944 July 20   An attempt by German officers to kill Hitler failed. One of them, Count von Stauffenberg, carried a bomb in a briefcase into a conference room at Hitler's headquarters at Rastenberg, East Prussia. Just before it went off, someone moved it slightly so that a thick table support came between it and Hitler. When it exploded four persons were killed and 20 others injured but Hitler escaped with minor injuries. In the Berlin headquarters of the plotters, it was believed for a while that Hitler was dead, and the group began steps to take over the government. It became clear that Hitler was not dead, and the plot collapsed. **Claus Schenk von Stauffenberg** (b. Nov. 5, 1907) and others were put to death before the end of the day (July 20). Arrests and trials went on for some time and in all c.5,000 men and women were executed, many of them not directly involved in the plot.

1944 Aug. 1–Oct. 2   Polish patriots began an uprising to drive the Germans out of Warsaw. At first they took control of most of the city, but the Germans struck back in force. The Poles thought they were coordinating their uprising with the advance of the Russians from the east. The Russians arrived were just across the Vistula River, but made no move to assist the Poles. British and American planes tried unsuccessfully to drop arms and other supplies from the air. By Oct. 2 thousands of Poles were dead, the struggle was over, and the Germans retaliated by destroying most of Warsaw.

1944 Aug. 15   Free French and American troops landed on the Mediterranean coast of southeastern France between Cannes and Toulon. Meeting only slight German resistance, they moved westward to take Marseilles on Aug. 28. The invasion force then advanced up the Rhône River, capturing Lyon on Sept. 3 and later linking up with the American Third Army to swing eastward toward Germany.

1944 Aug. 21–Oct. 7   A conference held at Dumbarton Oaks, then a private estate in Washington, D.C., between delegates of China, the United Kingdom, the U.S., and the U.S.S.R., resulted in an agreement to establish an international organization.

1944 Sept. 11–16   Franklin D. Roosevelt and **Winston Churchill** held a second conference in Quebec, Canada, called the **Octagon Conference.** Besides discussing plans for continuing the war against Germany and Japan the two leaders discussed the postwar status of the Axis nations.

1944 Sept. 17–25   Operation Market Garden began with troops of three Allied airborne divisions dropping in Holland in an attempt to seize five bridges over canals and rivers in order to speed the Allied advance into the northern German plain before winter. The area involved was from Eindhoven in the south to Arnhem in the north, where there was a key bridge over the Rhine River. The airborne troops met more resistance than anticipated, and ground troops were unable to link up and give them support. The operation, mainly British, was called off on Sept. 25 after a heroic stand at Arnhem, and 2,163 men were evacuated. About 6,400 were left behind as prisoners, and casualties amounted to c.1,350. Arnhem was not to be in Allied hands until Apr. 13, 1945.

1944 Oct. 20–26   American forces commanded by Douglas MacArthur invaded Leyte Island in the Philippines. MacArthur was the U.S. commander in the Philippines when war broke out (Dec., 1941) and he was evacuated by submarine. The Japanese assembled three fleets to thwart the invasion. In the ensuing **battle of Leyte Gulf** (Oct. 23–26), one of the Japanese forces was to approach from the southwest and another from the northwest to attack the American transports and guardian warships from two sides. Meanwhile, the third Japanese fleet, to the northeast, was intended to draw the main elements of the American Third Fleet away from Leyte. The deception worked for a time, but in the end all three Japanese task forces suffered heavy damage and had to withdraw. In terms of the number of ships involved, this was the **largest modern naval battle—**

282 ships in all. The Japanese lost four carriers, three battleships, six heavy cruisers, three light cruisers, and eight destroyers. American losses consisted of one light carrier, two escort carriers, and three destroyers. Again the Japanese lost many carrier planes and their pilots. The Japanese navy, which also lost from 7,500 to 10,000 sailors, was never after this a serious threat.

1944 Nov. 12   British Lancaster bombers attacked the last remaining German battleship while it lay an anchor at Sandesund in Tromsö Fjord, northern Norway. The *Tirpitz*, a sister ship of the *Bismarck*, was seriously damaged, and it was towed to Tromsö, where she was at last sunk, thus enabling British warships to enter the Pacific war.

1944 Dec. 16–27   Hitler massed 25 divisions of the Fifth and Sixth Panzer [tank] armies along a sector between Luxembourg and Aachen [Aix-la-Chapelle], to which he also assigned most of his available combat planes. The attack launched (Dec. 16) against the **Allies in the Ardennes Forest** caught them completely by surprise. The Germans pushed a bulge 65 miles deep into the American lines nearly, but not quite, breaking through. The troops in **Bastogne**, in southeastern Belgium, were encircled but held out under the command of **Anthony [Clement] McAuliffe** (July 2, 1898–Aug. 11, 1975). He refused to surrender and replied in an earthy phrase (officially given as "Nuts") to the German request. Bastogne was resupplied by air, and this plus the Allied troops on both sides of the bulge, and great superiority in the air and in tanks, stopped the German advance by Dec. 27. "**The Battle of the Bulge**" was over, with heavy casualties to both sides.

III. ECONOMICS AND TRADE

1944   Friedrich A[ugust von] Hayek (b. May 8, 1899), an Austrian-born British economist, published *The Road to Serfdom*, a book denounced by liberals and social planners. Hayek contended that the welfare state was incompatible with democracy, believing that the more people depended on government, the more likely would be the rise of such dictators as Hitler. He was awarded the **Nobel prize for economics** in 1974.

1944 July 1–15   Delegates of 44 nations met at Breton Woods, New Hampshire, to discuss postwar financial matters. They agreed on the establishment of an **International Monetary Fund** [IMF] and of an **International Bank for Reconstruction and Development**, commonly called the **World Bank**.

IV. RELIGION AND PHILOSOPHY

1944 May 15   Sergius [nee Ivan Nikolayevich Stragorodsky] (b. Nov. 23, 1867), the **patriarch of the Russian Orthodox Church**, died. On July 27, 1927, Sergius issued a declaration asserting that the faithful should openly support the Soviet government. This position produced a split of the Russian Orthodox, especially in the West. In 1943, when the Soviet government allowed the position to be filled, he became the first recognized patriarch since 1925.

1944 Oct. 26   William Temple (b. Oct. 15, 1881), 96th archbishop of Canterbury (1942–1944), therefore primate of the Church of England, died. His father was the 93rd archbishop. Temple was an educator as well as a clergyman before becoming archbishop of York in 1929. Interested in social welfare, he was the first president (1908–1924) of the **Workers' Educational Association**. He was also a leader in the movement to organize a world council of churches.

V. SCIENCE, EDUCATION, AND TECHNOLOGY

1944   The first "blue baby" operation was performed by two American doctors, **Helen [Brooke] Taussig** (May 24, 1898–May 20, 1986) and **Alfred Blalock** (May 5, 1899–Sept. 15, 1964). The operation was performed on babies with congenital heart defects whose skin turned blue because their blood was deprived of oxygen. Taussig was the first in the U.S. to warn (1962–1963) against the drug **thalidomide**, which was causing numerous birth defects in Europe.

1944   The theory of phase stability, which made possible the development of atomic high-energy particle accelerators, was first propounded by the Russian scientist, **Vladimir Iosifovich Veksler** (Mar. 4, 1907–Sept. 22, 1966). Phase stability was discovered independently by the American scientist **Edwin McMillan** in Sept. 1945.

1944   The first electronic digital computer using vacuum tubes was built at Harvard University. It was designed by **Howard [Hathaway] Aiken** (Mar. 8, 1900–Mar. 14, 1973) and a team of engineers. The computer, a bulky apparatus 8 ft. high and 51 ft. long, used punched paper tape for programming. It took 3 seconds to multiply large numbers.

1944 Late in the year the British formed the **first operational squadron of jet fighter planes**. The Germans followed in Jan., 1945. Earlier they had introduced (1944) a rocket-powered plane, the ME163-B-1, but it tended to explode without warning and so was not of much use. Jet fighters were too new and too few to affect World War II.

1944 Feb. 23   Leo Hendrik Baekeland (b. Nov. 14, 1863), a Belgian-American chemist and inventor, died. In 1909 he produced the **first important plastic**, which he named **Bakelite**. Widely used as a substitute for hard rubber and other materials, it became useful in insulating electrical apparatus because it was a nonconductor.

1944 May 14   Eugen Steinach (b. Jan. 27, 1862), an Austrian physiologist and endocrinologist, died. He became famous worldwide because of his experiments in grafting sexual glands of young animals onto rats and men to try to rejuvenate them. The effect lasted for no more than six months.

1944 June 13   Germany introduced the V-1 [*Vergeltenungswaffe*, vengeance weapon], a flying bomb powered by a jet engine and controlled by an autopilot. The Germans aimed them at London from bases in Belgium. The V-1 had a speed of nearly 400 mph, caused property damage, and killed people but had no effect on the outcome of the war. **Hitler** believed the V-1 would make the British sue for peace and so refused his generals' pleas to use it against the Allied forces just then invading Normandy. Because of its engine noise the V-1 was called the "**buzz bomb**" by the British. On Sept. 13 the Germans introduced the **V-2**, propelled by a liquid fuel rocket. It flew higher, farther, and faster [c.3,500 mph] than the V-1 and could not be shot down. The Germans used it against London and also against Antwerp, Belgium, then in the hands of the Allies. The V-2 also had no military effect although it killed c.2,700 people in England and c.5,000 in Antwerp. Both bombs were developed by German scientists working at Peenemünde, an island in the Baltic Sea. The launching sites were bombed after the V-1 and V-2 became operational.

1944 June 22   The Servicemen's Readjustment Act, known as the **G.I. Bill**, was signed into law. It provided for special benefits for U.S. veterans of World War II returning to civilian life. Most significantly, funds were set up for tuition and maintenance costs for students.

1944 Nov. 2   Thomas Midgley, Jr. (b. May 18, 1889), an American chemist, died. He made two useful discoveries: in 1921 he found that **tetraethyl lead** prevents knocks in gasoline engines, and in 1930 he developed **freon**, a gas for use in refrigerators.

1944 Nov. 5   Alexis Carrel (b. June 28, 1873), a French surgeon, died in Paris. Carrel laid the foundation for the transplantation of organs and blood vessels through his investigations of preservation of tissue outside the body. For this work and for his technique of suturing blood vessels, Carrel was awarded the **Nobel Prize for physiology or medicine** in 1912. During World War I, he helped develop the Carrel-Dakin method of treating wounds with antiseptic irrigations. On Apr. 10, 1914, Carrel performed the **first successful heart surgery**—on a dog.

1944 Nov. 22   Arthur Stanley Eddington (b. Dec. 28, 1882), an English astronomer and physicist, died. He formulated the concept that a gaseous star's radiation is dependent not on its diameter but on its mass. He was especially concerned with the study of stars, their evolution, motion, and internal constitution. Eddington was the author of many books, some written for the layman, such as *The Expanding Universe* (1933) and *The Philosophy of Physical Science* (1939).

VI. ARTS AND LEISURE

1944   Robert [Burns] **Motherwell** (b. Jan. 24, 1915), an American painter and a leader of the American expressionist school, was given his first one-man show, at the Century Gallery in New York City. Among his paintings are *Indian Summer #2* (1962–1964), *Africa* (1964–1965), and a series entitled *Open* (1967–1969).

1944   Lawrence Olivier (b. May 22, 1907), an English actor and director, produced, directed, and starred in *Henry V*. He received a special **Academy Award** for his achievement.

1944 Jan. 4   Kaj [Harald Leininger] **Munk** (b. Jan. 13, 1898), a Danish playwright, Catholic priest, and patriot, was killed by the Nazi **Gestapo** for resisting the German occupation of his country. His plays had ethical and religious themes. Among them were *En

Idealist (1928), *Cant* (1931), and *Niels Ebbeson* (1942).

1944 Jan. 23 Edvard Munch (b. Dec. 12, 1863), a Norwegian artist, died. Munch first exhibited in Germany in a controversial show in 1892, after an earlier exhibition in Oslo. His work was later included in the Nazi exhibition of "degenerate" art held in 1935. Munch's paintings were of unpleasant subjects, as in *The Sick Child* (1886), *The Cry* (1893), and *In Hell, Self-Portrait* (1895).

1944 Jan. 31 [Hippolyte] **Jean Giraudoux** (b. Oct. 29, 1882), a French dramatist, novelist, and diplomat, died. Although he served in the French diplomatic corps for 30 years (1910–1940), he is known today for his plays, offering elegant, even extravagant language. His work included *Amphitryon 38* (1929); *Judith* (1931); *Ondine* (1938); *La Guerre de Troie n'aura pas lieu* (1935), translated into English by **Christopher Fry** in 1955 as *Tiger at the Gates*; and *La Folle de Chaillot* [*The Madwoman of Chaillot*] (1945).

1944 Feb. 1 Piet[er Cornelis] **Mondrian** (b. Mar. 7, 1872), a Dutch painter, died. A founder of the magazine *De Stijl* in 1917, he worked in rectangles, and eventually only in straight horizontal and vertical lines, going so far at one point as to resign from *De Stijl* in a dispute over the use of diagonal lines. Among his paintings were *The Red Tree* (1908), *Still Life with Gingerpot* (1911–1912), and *Victory Boogie Woogie* (1943, unfinished).

1944 Mar. 28 Stephen [Butler] **Leacock** (b. Dec. 30., 1869), a Canadian professor of economics but known best for his humorous short stories and essays, died. He wrote many books in his own field, and also history and biography, but the general reading public remembers him for such books as *Literary Lapses* (1910), *Frenzied Fiction* (1917), and *Winnowed Wisdom* (1926), and his autobiography *The Boy I Left Behind Me* (1946).

1944 May 12 Arthur Quiller-Couch [pseud.: Q] (b. Nov. 21, 1863), an English author, anthologist, and professor of English literature, died. He reached his largest public as anthologist, particularly *The Oxford Book of English Verse* (1st ed. 1900). Q was also a poet and novelist, often writing of his native Cornwall and of the sea, as in *Dead Man's Rock* (1887) and *Lady Good-for Nothing* (1910).

1944 May 16 George Ade (b. Feb. 9, 1866), an American author noted for his use of the vernacular, died. His best-known work was *Fables in Slang* (1899). Ade also wrote the books for several musical comedies, among them *The Sultan of Sulu* (1902).

1944 July 31 Antoine de Saint-Exupery (b. June 29, 1900), a French author and aviator, died. His writings were based on his experiences as a pilot who developed a mystical relationship with the heavens. Typical of this spirit was *Terre des hommes* [*Wind, Sand, and Stars*] (1939). Saint-Exupery's most popular work was *Le petit prince* [*The Little Prince*] (1943). He was killed on a military reconnaisance flight during World War II.

1944 Oct. 5 Aristide Maillol (b. Dec. 25, 1861), a French sculptor, died. Maillol was one of the great 20th-century sculptors of the female form, which he portrayed in a formal, almost classical style, returning to classical Greek models. Typical of Maillol's work were *Night* (1902), *Action in Chains* (1906), and *Flora* (1911).

1944 Dec. 2 Josef Lhevinne (b. Dec. 3, 1874), a Russian-born American pianist, died. He made his debut in Moscow in 1889 and his American debut in New York City in 1906. Lhevinne's romantic style was noted for its meticulous musicianship.

1944 Dec. 23 Charles Dana Gibson (b. Sept. 14, 1867), a popular American illustrator, died. His fame rests chiefly on his creation of the "Gibson Girl," an idealized young woman of the Edwardian era, beautiful but a bit aloof, socially elite, and every young man's sweetheart. Gibson illustrated many books, such as *The Prisoner of Zenda*. His drawings were collected in books, including *The Education of Mr. Pipp* (1899), *A Widow and Her Friends* (1902), and *The Social Ladder* (1902).

1944 Dec. 13 Wassily Kandinsky (b. Dec. 4, 1866), a Russian expressionist painter, died. The first exhibition of *Der Blaue Reiter* [The Blue Rider] school was held in Munich on Dec. 18, 1911, a seminal event in the development of expressionism. *Der Blaue Reiter* proved essential to the development of abstract art, and therefore to the development of modern art in general. Kandinsky's *First Abstract Watercolor* (1910) is considered the **first purely abstract painting**. His other works included *With the*

Black Arch (1912), *Autumn* (1914), *Affirmed Pink* (1932), and *Tempered Élan* (1944). He wrote the influential *Concerning the Spiritual in Art* (1912).

1944 Dec. 30   Romain Rolland (b. Jan. 29, 1866), a French writer, died. An idealist and pacifist as well as a great writer, his masterpiece was the immense *Jean Christophe* (20 vols., 1904–1912), one of the longest novels ever written. In the Sept. 15, 1914, edition of the *Journal de Génève*, he wrote an article calling for respect and admiration for German culture despite the military conflict. He also wrote plays, including *Les Loups* (1898) and *Danton* (1900), and biographies of Beethoven (1903) and Mahatma Gandhi (1924). Rolland received the **Nobel prize for literature** in 1915.

VII. SPORTS, GAMES, AND SOCIETY

1944 Apr. 19   [Thomas] **Tommy Hitchcock, Jr.** (b. Feb. 11, 1900), an American **polo** player regarded as the best of all time, died in a crash of his U.S. army air corps plane in England during World War II. From 1922 through 1940, with the exception of 1935, he held a ten-goal rating, the highest in the sport. In World War I (1914–1918), while still in his teens, Hitchcock flew with the Lafayette Escadrille, American pilots fighting for France.

1944 Apr. 30   **Paul Poiret** (b. Apr. 20, 1879), a French fashion designer who **dominated the world of women's clothing styles** from shortly before World War I to shortly after, died. One of his designs was the hobble skirt, long and so tight at the bottom that its wearers were reduced to taking small, mincing steps. Poiret, not a good businessman, went bankrupt in 1929 and later worked as a bartender and a farmer.

1945

I. DISASTERS

1945 Jan. 30   A Soviet submarine in the Baltic **sank the *Wilhelm Gustoff*,** carrying German civilians fleeing Poland ahead of the advancing Russian armies. A total of 7,700 persons went down with the ship, the **greatest toll ever in the sinking of one ship.**

1945 Apr. 9   A U.S. **ship loaded with aerial bombs blew up** in the harbor at Bari, southeastern Italy, killing c.360 persons and injuring c.1,730.

1945 July 18   **Halifax, Nova Scotia, was rocked by a munitions explosion** when a magazine blew up in its inner harbor. Casualties were few, and there was little damage.

1945 July 28   A **B-25 bomber,** flying from New Bedford, Massachusetts, to Newark, New Jersey, **rammed into the fog-shrouded Empire State Building** on Fifth Avenue, New York City, between the 78th and 79th floors, 915 feet above street level. Ten people in the building were killed, in addition to the three airmen aboard the plane.

II. POLITICS AND WAR

1945 Jan. 4   A **British offensive, in Burma** [Myanmar], began to accelerate. The Japanese abandoned Akyab on the northwestern coast; Shwebo in central Burma was occupied on Jan. 10; and Monywa, west of Mandalay in central Burma, on Jan. 22. The Japanese left Mandalay at the southern end of the **Burma Road** on Mar. 20. By May 6 Rangoon [Yangon], in southern Burma, was in British hands and **Burma was liberated.** The Burma Road was now open to carry supplies to the Chinese Nationalists.

1945 Jan. 9–Aug. 15   Escorted by 164 ships, **American forces landed at Lingayen Gulf,** on Luzon, 110 miles north of Manila. American troops entered Manila on Feb. 3 but it was not until Mar. 4 that it was entirely cleared of enemy troops. On Apr. 27 an offensive was begun against Japanese forces in northern Luzon, but the struggle did not end until Japan's surrender in August, when the last 40,000 or so Japanese troops on Luzon gave up.

1945 Jan. 12–May 2   The **Russians took Warsaw** on Jan. 17 and Kraków [Cracow] on the 19th. The next day the Russians crossed into Silesia, and their armies stood on German territory. By the end of the month they were at the Oder River, only 50 miles from Berlin. It was not until Apr. 22, though, that the Russians reached Berlin and May 2 before they took control of the city. Meanwhile other **Russian forces took control of Vienna** on Apr. 13. While the last battles of the war were taking place, **Russian and American troops came together** on Apr. 26 for the first time c.60 miles south of Berlin at Torgau and at Strehla on the Elbe River.

1945 Jan. 20   Franklin D. Roosevelt was inaugurated president of the U.S. for a fourth term. **Harry S. Truman** became vice president. Roosevelt, the Democratic candidate, defeated **Thomas E[dmund] Dewey** (Mar. 24, 1902–Mar. 16, 1971), the Republican candidate, in the election of Nov. 7, 1944. Roosevelt received 25,602,504 popular votes to Dewey's 22,006,285, and 432 electoral votes to 99.

1945 Jan. 20–Nov. 4   With most of **Hungary freed of German troops**, Budapest, the capital, was not relieved until Feb. 13, when a new Hungarian government declared war on Germany. This government had been established Dec. 22, 1944, under Russian auspices. All political factions were represented and **Bela Miklos** [Béla Dáinoki-Miklós] (b. 1891–Nov. 24, 1948) was prime minister. An election was held on Nov. 3, 1945, in which the anti-communist Smallholders party was victorious, with the Russian-backed communists receiving only about a fifth of the vote. **Zoltan Tildy** (b. 1889–Aug. 3, 1961), a clergyman and politician, became premier in a coalition government.

1945 Feb. 2–Mar. 27   With World War II in Europe in its final stages, the **Latin American countries that had not yet done so declared war on the Axis powers**: Ecuador on Feb. 2; Paraguay, Feb. 8; Peru, Feb. 13; Chile, Feb. 14; Venezuela, Feb. 16; Uruguay, Feb. 23; and Argentina on Mar. 27.

1945 Feb. 4–11   **Winston Churchill, Franklin D. Roosevelt**, and **Joseph Stalin** met at **Yalta** in the Crimea. (The full text of the agreements made at Yalta were not revealed until 1947.) The big three decided, for example, to divide Germany into four occupation zones, the fourth to go to the French. In addition, a four-power commission would control Berlin. It was agreed that war crime trials of Germany's leaders would be held. In return for entering the war against Japan within three months of Ger-

many's surrender, Stalin was promised the Kurile Islands, southern Sakhalin, and a zone of influence in Korea. The autonomy of Outer Mongolia was recognized by the U.S. and Great Britain. Besides proposing to sponsor, along with China and France, a conference in April to organize the **United Nations**, the three leaders agreed that the permanent members of the Security Council would have veto power and that Ukraine and Belorussia would be full member nations of the UN. Roosevelt was criticized in some quarters as having given in to Stalin. On the other hand, Stalin did not keep his word about several matters, so there was nothing short of going to war that the U.S. and Great Britain could do by the late 1940s.

1945 Feb. 12   **Civil war in Greece** came to an end. A truce was arranged between the communist-led rebels, the *Ethnikon Apeleth erotikon Metopon* [EAM], and the government of Greece and the British forces that took part in freeing the country. A regency had been established (Dec. 31, 1944) under **Archbishop Damaskinos** [orig.: Dimitrios Papandreou] (Mar. 3, 1891–May 20, 1949). Parliamentary elections were scheduled for 1946.

1945 Feb. 13–14   An air raid wiped out a large part of the city of Dresden, Germany, a city famous for its art and architecture. First the RAF sent c.250 heavy bombers to shower incendiary bombs on the city. The next day c.450 American bombers added to the destruction, followed by c.550 more RAF planes at night. The c.650,000 incendiary bombs dropped caused a firestorm that burned out eight square miles. The number of dead was estimated as high as 135,000. Most of the city's notable landmarks were destroyed. The raids aroused anger and caused heart-searching agony among even Germany's most dedicated enemies. No military advantage was gained. **Kurt Vonnegut, Jr.** (b. Nov. 11, 1922), an American soldier in Dresden at the time as a prisoner of war, wrote about his experience in *Slaughterhouse Five; or, The Children's Crusade* (1969). Vonnegut was working in an underground slaughterhouse at the time of the raids.

1945 Feb. 19–Mar. 26   U.S. marines went ashore on **Iwo Jima** Island, 750 miles south of Tokyo. Air strikes were made daily beginning Dec. 8, 1944, and during the last three days before the invasion included an intense bombardment from the guns of warships. Nevertheless, the Japanese defenses were little affected, and the marines suffered c.2,500 casualties on the first day. The final conquest of Iwo Jima did not take place until Mar. 26. By that time the marines had suffered c.25,000 casualties while the final count of Japanese dead was c.25,000, with only c.1,000 taken prisoner. One of the most striking photographs of the war was that of marines raising a flag raising on Mt. Suribachi, on Iwo Jima.

1945 Feb. 21–Mar. 8 The **Inter-American Conference on War and Peace** was held in Chapultepec Castle in Mexico City. The **Act of Chapultepec** was adopted, in which the signatories agreed that the security of the nations of the Western Hemisphere should be protected by collective action. The act applied to aggression by one American nation against another as well as aggression from outside the hemisphere.

1945 Feb. 23 **Turkey declared war against Germany and Japan** after having been neutral throughout the war. One reason for Turkey's action at this time was to make the nation eligible to take part in the conference that would establish the United Nations.

1945 Feb. 24 **Ahmed Maher Pasha** (b. 1888), premier of **Egypt** (from Oct. 9, 1944), was assassinated as he stood before parliament to read a decree of **Farouk** [Faruq], king of Egypt, declaring war on Germany. His assassin was a young pro-Nazi lawyer who was arrested and executed. The foreign minister, **Mahmoud Fahmy el-Nokrashy Pasha**, became premier.

1945 Mar. 3 Following the surrender of the fascist regime of **Romania** to invading Russian troops, a new government was established. The head of the government, **Peter Groza** (Dec. 6, 1884–Jan. 7, 1958), was not a communist, but communists held the key positions in the cabinet.

1945 Mar. 7–May 7 The **American Third Army broke through German defenses** on Mar. 7 and soon reached the Rhine River near Koblenz [Coblenz], Germany. Farther north on the same day the Americans at **Remagen** found a bridge across the Rhine that the Germans failed to destroy. They established a firm bridgehead across the river. Still farther north, on the Rhine near Wesel, the British forced their way over the river and by the 28th were 20 miles beyond it. By May 7 the Allied line was at Magdeburg on the Elbe River and at Leipzig, both cities less than 100 miles from Berlin.

1945 Mar. 9–10 **American B-29 Superfortresses**, 279 in number, **dropped c.2,000 tons of incendiary bombs on Tokyo**. About a quarter of the city—almost 16 square miles—was burned out. The bombs created a firestorm, and the estimates of the number of persons killed ranged from 100,000 to 185,000. Osaka, Kobe, and Nagoya were devastated by similar raids in the ensuing days.

1945 Mar. 22 The **Arab League** was created and headquartered at Cairo by the states of Egypt, Iraq, Trans-Jordan [present Jordan], Lebanon, Saudi Arabia, Syria, and the Yemen Arab Republic. The League initiated a strong resurgence of Arab nationalism.

1945 Mar. 26 **David Lloyd George** (b. Jan. 17, 1863), a British statesman and prime minister (1916–1922) during most of World War I, died. As wartime prime minister, he rallied the nation to the fight against Germany. Lloyd George remained the leader of the Liberal party (1926–1931) but in that period it was replaced by the Labour party as one of the two main political groups. Before the beginning of World War II, he opposed appeasement of Adolf Hitler.

1945 Apr. 1–June 22 **Three U.S. marine and four army divisions**, totaling c.170,000 combat troops, **began landing on Okinawa**, an island 350 miles south of Japan. The Americans met little resistance at first except from planes attacking from Japan. On Apr. 6 and 7 large numbers of air attacks by Kamikaze pilots on suicide missions sank or damaged 13 American destroyers, but most of the c.700 attacking planes were shot down or were deliberately flown to crash into their targets. On June 22 all resistance was quelled. The Japanese were estimated to have lost 110,000 men. American casualties totaled c.49,000, of which c.12,500 were killed.

1945 Apr. 7 The **Japanese battleship *Yamato*** was sunk by U.S. carrier aircraft off Okinawa. It was on a suicide mission with no air protection. It had a small escort of other warships and only enough fuel for the outward voyage. The *Yamato* and her sister ship ***Musashi***, which was sunk by American carrier aircraft on Oct. 24, 1944, in the **battle of Leyte Gulf**, were the largest battleships ever built. Each had nine 18-inch guns, more than any other battleship ever had. Both went down without ever having fired these guns at the enemy.

1945 Apr. 9–May 2 The **British army in Italy broke through the Argenta Gap** on the east on Apr. 18, and the Americans won a victory that by Apr. 19 put them at the outskirts of Bologna. On Apr. 19 the Germans signed an agreement for unconditional surrender to take effect on May 2.

1945 Apr. 12 **Franklin D. Roosevelt** (b. Jan. 30, 1882), president of the U.S. (from 1933), died suddenly of a massive cerebral hemorrhage. He was succeeded by **Harry S Truman**, vice president (from Jan. 20). Roosevelt was elected president four times (1932, 1936, 1940, and 1944). He was elected to the New York state Senate in 1910, was assistant secretary of the navy (1913–1920), and was the Democratic candidate for vice president in 1920. Badly crippled by polio in 1921, Roosevelt's political career appeared to be over. Yet, in 1928 he was elected governor of New York state. As president in his first term in the midst of the **Great Depression**, he inaugurated the **New Deal**, an unprecedented program of social and economic reform. Later, Roosevelt was a stirring leader of a nation at war. His "fireside chats" made listeners feel they were near him and that he cared about them. Because the policies he put into effect were such a break with the past, he was both the most hated and the most beloved American president of the 20th century.

1945 Apr. 13 The horror of what became known as the **Holocaust** [Hebrew: *Sho'ah* or *Hurban*] began to be revealed when American troops reached the **Buchenwald concentration camp**, near Weimar, Germany. There they found skeleton-like survivors of the millions of Jews and others who had been put to death by the Nazis as part of "the final solution" [*die Endlosung*]. The final solution was a program of genocide to kill all Jews, along with others, especially Slavs, whom the **Nazis** also considered an inferior race, and communists, and homosexuals. On Apr. 14 **Bergen-Belsen** near Celle in Lower Saxony and on Apr. 29 **Dachau** near Munich in Bavaria, both in Germany, were liberated, revealing the same horrors as at Buchenwald. There were other similar extermination camps in Poland, chief among them being **Oświcim** [Auschwitz], in southern Poland, the largest of the camps, where c.2,500,000 persons were killed; **Chełmno** [Culm, Kulm], in central northern Poland; **Majdanek** [Maidanek], near Lubin in southeastern Poland; and **Treblinka**, in central eastern Poland. Some of the camps were nothing but killing grounds. Others sooner or later worked most of the prisoners to death by hard labor combined with a starvation diet. In all c.6,000,000 Jews died in these camps, most of them German and Polish. In addition, perhaps as many as an additional 10,000,000, mostly Slavs, also died in German camps.

1945 Apr. 21 The **U.S.S.R. signed a mutual assistance treaty with the Lublin government of Poland**. The Russians recognized this communist-dominated government after they freed the city of Lublin, southeast of Warsaw, on July 25, 1944.

1945 Apr. 27–28 **Mussolini**, ex-dictator of Italy, and his mistress, **Clara Petacci** (b. 1912), along with a few faithful followers, were seized by partisans at Como in northern Italy as they attempted to flee to Switzerland. Benito Mussolini (b. July 29, 1883), his mistress, and 11 others were shot and hung head down in the main square of Milan on Apr. 28.

1945 Apr. 30 **Adolf Hitler** (b. Apr. 20, 1889), dictator of Nazi Germany (from Jan., 1933), committed suicide in a bunker underneath the Reichstag building in Berlin while the final battle for the city was fought above him. **Hitler shot himself**. Dying with him by poison was his long-time companion **Eva Braun** (b. Feb. 6, 1912). They were married shortly before their joint suicide. In accordance with Hitler's instructions, his body was taken out of the bunker, doused with gasoline, fired, and then buried. His remains were never found. [Paul] **Joseph Goebbels** (b. Oct. 29, 1897), Hitler's propaganda chief, committed suicide in the bunker on May 1, after poisoning his wife and their six children. Before his death Hitler designated **Karl Doenitz** (Sept. 16, 1891–Dec. 24, 1980), a German admiral, as his successor. On May 1 Doenitz in a radio broadcast to the German people announced defeat, saying, "It is my duty to save the German people from destruction by the Bolsheviks." His government was dissolved by the Allies after Germany's formal surrender (May 7). Doenitz was convicted as a war criminal and imprisoned (1946–1956).

1945 May 8 **V-E Day** [Victory in Europe] became official. On the previous day, in a schoolhouse in Reims in northeastern France that was serving as the headquarters of **Dwight D. Eisenhower**, commander of Allied forces in western Europe, German army and navy officers signed a document of unconditional surrender. The same document was signed by the Germans and Russians in Berlin. The European phase of World War II ended three months and 23 days short of six years after it began.

1945 May 8 A **clash between police and Algerian nationalists** in Sétif, east of Algiers, was followed by riots during which c.90 Europeans were killed. The French rulers responded by killing c.1,500, and perhaps as many as 10,000, Muslims. This outbreak was an early manifestation of the restlessness of people under the colonial rule of the European powers.

1945 May 12 **Allied forces occupied Prague**, Czechoslovakia, and a restored government, with **Eduard Beneš** as president, took over the country. Beneš had been president (from 1939) of the Czech government-in-exile in England.

1945 June 5 An **Allied Control Commission**, the interim government of defeated Germany, held its first meeting in Berlin. The commission ordered the release of all political prisoners held by the Nazis and the evacuation of all occupied territories outside the Reich. Nazis suspected of war crimes were to be arrested and all armaments factories dismantled.

1945 June 10 **José Luis Bustamante y Rivero**, a moderate, was elected president of **Peru** with the support of the **Alianza Popular Revolucionaria Americana** [APRA], a political party founded in 1924.

1945 June 18 **William Joyce**, called **Lord Haw Haw** by the British, went on trial in London for treason for broadcasting Nazi propaganda from Germany during World War II. Joyce (b. 1906) was convicted and sentenced to die. He was hanged on Jan. 5, 1946. Joyce was born in Brooklyn, New York, of Irish immigrant parents but lived in England from 1922. There he joined a fascist group, then moved to Germany in 1939.

1945 June 26 The **charter of the United Nations** [UN] was signed at San Francisco, California, by representatives of 50 nations, meeting there since Apr. 25. The **U.N.** came into formal existence on Oct. 24 when the first 29 nations ratified the charter. The purpose of the U.N., its charter said, was "to save succeeding generations from the scourge of war to maintain international peace and security to employ international machinery for the promotion of the economic and social advancement of all people."

1945 July 5 In the first general election in ten years, the **Labour party won an unexpected victory in Great Britain. Winston Churchill**, leader of the na-

tion through the darkest days of World War II, was rejected by the voters. Labour won 393 seats in Parliament to the Conservatives 213, with the Liberals and others winning 33. On July 26 **Clement Attlee**, the leader of the Labour party since 1935 and a member of Churchill's wartime coalition cabinet, became prime minister.

1945 July 11 The **first meeting of the Inter-Allied Council for Berlin** was held. Berlin, captured by the Russians at the end of the war, lay entirely within the occupation zone of eastern Germany allotted to the U.S.S.R. Nevertheless, since Berlin was the capital of Germany and its political heart, the western Allies felt entitled to a share in its control. The Russians agreed to turn over sections of the city to the Americans and the British. They, in turn, allotted some of their sectors to the French. Joint control failed to work from the start.

1945 July 17–Aug. 2 The leaders of the three principal Allied nations held their last conference, this time at **Potsdam**, near Berlin. The U.S. was now represented by **Harry S Truman**. During the conference Winston Churchill was replaced by **Clement Attlee. Stalin** alone remained of the original three. The three reached agreement on the occupation zones of Germany and on steps to end forever Germany's military power. German territory east of the Oder and Neisse rivers, including East Prussia, Pomerania, and Silesia, were put under Polish control, and the Germans there returned to a reduced Germany. Russia kept control of areas in former eastern Poland. The borders of Poland were to remain fixed until the terms of a final peace treaty were agreed on. On July 26 the conference issued the **Potsdam Declaration**, in effect an ultimatum to Japan to surrender or be destroyed. Nevertheless, the final agreement of the Potsdam Conference soon fell apart.

1945 Aug. 6 The **first atomic bomb was dropped on Hiroshima**, Japan, by an American B-29 bomber, the *Enola Gay*. It destroyed most of the city and killed c.80,000 of its c.350,000 inhabitants. Many more died of burns and radiation in the months and years following. The bomb was of the uranium fission type and its strength was the equivalent of 20,000 tons of TNT. On Aug. 9 a **second atomic bomb**, based on plutonium, was **dropped on Nagasaki**, killing c.40,000 Japanese. These were the only two atomic bombs the U.S. had so far manufactured.

1945 Aug. 8   Russia declared war on Japan, three months after the German surrender, as Stalin promised. The next day Soviet troops in Siberia invaded Japanese-held Manchuria, meeting with little opposition.

1945 Aug. 15–Sept. 2   V-J Day [Victory over Japan] arrived on Aug. 15 when **Hirohito**, emperor of Japan, broadcast a message to the Japanese people, telling them the decision to accept unconditional surrender had been made by him the day before. Hirohito was allowed to retain his throne but, beginning Aug. 30, American occupation forces under **Douglas MacArthur**, supreme commander of Allied forces in the Southwest Pacific, landed in Japan and became the effective rulers of the country. **Japan's formal surrender** was signed on Sept. 2 on the deck of the U.S. battleship *Missouri* anchored in Tokyo Bay.

1945 Aug. 17   Indonesian nationalists, led by **Achmed Sukarno, proclaimed a republic** and the end of Dutch rule. The Dutch refused to relinquish control and armed conflict went on for four years.

1945 Aug. 26   Negotiations between **Chiang Kai-Shek**, head of the Nationalist government of China, and **Mao Tse-Tung**, leader of the communists, to reach an agreement for the future of their country broke down. The result was a civil war (to 1949), with both sides trying to take over the territory being evacuated by the Japanese invaders.

1945 Sept. 2   Vietnamese nationalists, led by **Ho Chi Minh** [orig.: Nguyen Thant Thank], a communist, **proclaimed a republic** in French Indo-China, a region that also included Cambodia and Laos.

1945 Sept. 8   The **occupation of Korea** by American and Russian troops began. Before the end of World War II it was agreed by the Allies that Korea would receive its independence from Japan. For the time being the dividing line of occupation was set at the 38th parallel—Russia to the north, the U.S. to the south. Though a free democratic election was to be held in the near future, Russia never allowed it to take place.

1945 Sept. 13   The **shah of Iran asked the Americans, British, and Russians to withdraw their troops**, some of which had been in his country since Aug. 1941. At the **Teheran Conference** (1943) all three countries promised to respect and guarantee the independence and territorial integrity of Iran.

1945 Oct. 18   Isáias Medina Angarita (July 6, 1897–Sept. 15, 1953) president of **Venezuela** (1941–1945), was overthrown by a military coup headed by **Rómulo Betancourt** (Feb. 22, 1908–Sept. 28, 1981). He put into effect a number of social reforms, instituted universal suffrage, and forced foreign oil companies to pay half their profits to Venezuela.

1945 Oct. 21   The French went to the polls, electing to the Assembly 152 communists, 151 socialists, and 138 members of **Charles De Gaulle's** Popular Republican Movement [MRP]. On Nov. 13 De Gaulle was elected president of the provisional government although lacking a majority in the assembly. He included communists and socialists in his cabinet.

1945 Oct. 29   Getúlio Dornelles Vargas, president of **Brazil**, was ousted by a military coup. In an election Dec. 2, 1945, **Eurico Gaspar Dutra** (May 18, 1885–June 11, 1974), a former minister of war, was elected president. Vargas, who remained popular with many Brazilians after his ouster, was reelected president in 1950.

1945 Nov. 20–Oct. 1, 1946   With the approval of the **General Assembly of the U.N.**, an **International Military Tribunal met in Nürnberg** [Nuremberg], Germany, to hear charges of war crimes allegedly committed by German officials, civilian and military. The judges represented France, Great Britain, the U.S.S.R., and the U.S. There were 22 major defendants. The most **prominent of the former Nazi and military figures on trial** were: **Hans Fritzsche** (Apr. 21, 1900–Sept. 29, 1953), an aide to Goebbels; **Herman Göring** (Jan. 12, 1893–Oct. 15, 1946), second in power to Hitler in the Third Reich; **Rudolph Hess**, who had been in British hands since 1941; **Wilhelm Keitel** (Sept. 22, 1882–Oct. 16, 1946), a German general and Nazi supporter; **Franz von Papen** (Oct. 29,1879–May 2, 1969), vice chancellor under Hitler for a time; **Joachim von Ribbentrop** (Apr. 30, 1893–Oct. 16, 1946), minister of foreign affairs (1938–1945); **Hjalmar** [Horace Greeley] **Schacht** (Jan. 22, 1877–June 4, 1970), minister of economics (1934–1937); **Albert Speer** (Mar. 19, 1905–Sept. 2, 1981), minister of armaments and war production (1942–1945); and **Julius Streicher** (Feb. 12, 1885–Oct. 16, 1946), leader of anti-Semitic campaigns. Charges against one or more of these men included conspiracy to wage aggressive war; crimes against humanity, as in the extermination of populations and the use of slave labor; the looting of defeated countries; and the murder of prisoners of war. Judgments were not handed down until Sept. 30 and Oct. 1, 1946. Only three of the 22 were acquitted—Fritzsche, von Papen, and Schacht. Seven received prison sentences of from ten years to life. Hess received a life sentence, which he served; Speer, a 20-year term. The other 12 were sentenced to hang, and the sentences were carried out on Oct. 16, except in the case of Göring, who managed to commit suicide on Oct. 15.

1945 Nov. 25 An election in recently liberated **Austria** reconstituted the republic. The People's and the Socialist parties formed a coalition government, and the pre-Anschluss constitution was restored with some revisions. On Dec. 20 **Karl Renner** (Dec. 14, 1870–Dec. 31, 1950) was elected president. Renner remained president until his death.

1945 Nov. 29 A new constituent assembly proclaimed **Yugoslavia** a Federal People's Republic following an election (Nov. 11) which the communists won, in part because moderate elements boycotted the election.

1945 Nov. 30 The Christian Democrats won a parliamentary election in **Italy**, with **Alcide De Gasperi** (Apr. 3, 1881–Aug. 19, 1954), one of the founders of the party, becoming premier. Between 1945 and 1953 De Gasperi was premier of eight different coalition cabinets led by the Christian Democrats, a center-right party that took its platform from the social teachings of the Roman Catholic Church.

1945 Dec. 2 An election in which only Communist party members were allowed to be candidates established a post-war government in **Albania** with **Enver Hoxha** (Oct. 16, 1908–Apr. 11, 1985) as premier. Hoxha was the leader of the far left-wing partisans who fought the occupying forces of the Axis during World War II. He also led a civil war (1943–1944) against non-communists in Albania. Hoxha remained premier and dictator until his death.

1945 Dec. 21 **George S[mith] Patton, Jr.** (b. Nov. 11, 1885), a brilliant American general, died of injuries suffered in an automotive accident in Germany on Dec. 9. Patton in World War II commanded a corps in the North African campaign and the Seventh Army in Italy. Further advancement in rank was delayed after he was penalized for slapping a soldier suffering from battle fatigue. He also commanded the American Third Army, an armored force, in the invasion of Europe. His ability to exploit

opportunities made his army an irresistible force. On Oct. 2, 1945, however, he was relieved of his command for seeming leniency toward Nazi elements while serving as governor of Bavaria.

III. ECONOMICS AND TRADE

1945 Oct. 16 The **Food and Agricultural Organization [FAO]**, was established as a specialized agency of the **United Nations**. Its objective was to improve the conditions of producers and consumers of agricultural products.

IV. RELIGION AND PHILOSOPHY

1945 Apr. 13 **Ernst Cassirer** (b. July 28, 1874), a German philosopher of the Marburg School, much influenced by **Kant**, died. He was professor of philosophy at Hamburg University from 1919 until he was ousted by the Nazis in 1933. He lectured at Oxford University in England and at Yale and Columbia in the U.S. Cassirer's books included *Freiheit und Form* (1918) and *Determinismus und Indeterminismus in der Modernen Physik* (1937).

V. SCIENCE, EDUCATION, AND TECHNOLOGY

1945 **Canada built a small nuclear reactor** at Chalk River, Ontario, the first such plant outside the U.S. Since then, the Chalk River facility has grown and become important in research into the peaceful uses of nuclear energy. On Dec. 12, 1952, the **first serious accident at a nuclear reactor** occurred here, when four control rods were accidentally removed, causing a partial meltdown of the uranium fuel core. Though millions of gallons of radioactive water accumulated, there were no known injuries.

1945 July 16 A **successful test of the first nuclear device** ever detonated occurred near Alamogordo, New Mexico. Code named **Trinity**, the test was made by exploding the device from the top of a 100-foot tower. The explosive force was the equivalent of 20,000 tons of TNT, which was more than expected.

1945 Aug. 10 **Robert Hutchings Goddard** (b. Oct. 5, 1882), an American physicist and pioneer in rocket technology, died. In 1926 he developed a liquid rocket fuel and in 1935 successfully fired the first rocket using liquid fuel.

1945 Sept. 24 [Johannes] **Hans** [Wilhelm] **Geiger** (b. Sept. 30, 1882), a German physicist, died. Working in England, he and **Ernest Rutherford** advanced research in radioactivity by inventing (1913) an alpha-particle counter. In Germany Geiger led a group of researchers who invented (1928) the **portable radiation counter** carrying his name.

1945 Nov. 20 **Francis William Aston** (b. Sept. 1, 1877), an English physicist and chemist, died. Using a spectograph he invented, Aston discovered 212 of the 287 isotopes of nonradioactive elements. He was awarded the **Nobel prize for chemistry** in 1922.

1945 Dec. 4 **Thomas Hunt Morgan** (b. Sept. 25, 1866), an American geneticist, died. Morgan's work with fruit flies [*Drosophila melanogaster*] demonstrated the physical basis of heredity. He was awarded the **Nobel prize for physiology or medicine** in 1933.

VI. ARTS AND LEISURE

1945 The French film industry, despite restrictions put on it by the German occupation, managed to produce some memorable films: **Marcel Carné's** (b. Aug. 18, 1909) *Les Enfants de paradis* and *Les Visiteurs du soir* (1942); and **Jean Delannoy's** (b. Jan. 12, 1908) *L'Eternel Retour*, with a script by **Jean Cocteau**.

1945 The Italian film industry flowered once the war ended. Its memorable films included **Roberto Rossellini's** (May 8, 1906–June 3, 1977) *Roma, città aperta* (1945) and *Paisan* (1946); **Luchino Visconti's** (Nov. 2, 1906–Mar. 17, 1976) *Ossessione* (1942) and *La terra trema* (1948); and **Vittorio de Sica's** (July 7, 1901–Nov. 13, 1974) *Ladri di biciclette* (1948).

1945 The jazz world of the 1940s was caught up in **bop** and **cool**, or **progressive**, jazz. Bop was complex, filled with asymmetrical phrases, and focused on harmony rather than melody. Among its leading exponents were **Dizzy** [John Birks] **Gillespie** (b. Oct. 21, 1917), **Thelonius** [Sphere] **Monk** (Oct. 10, 1917–Feb. 2, 1982), and [Charles Christopher] **Charlie "Bird" Parker** (Aug. 20, 1920–Mar. 12, 1955). The leading proponents of cool jazz were **Dave Brubeck** (b. Dec. 6, 1920) and **Miles Davis** (b. May 25, 1926). It was lighter and more relaxed than bop.

1945 *Two Solitudes*, a novel by **Hugh MacLennan** (b. Mar. 20, 1907), was published in Canada, depict-

ing the gulf between English and French Canadians. MacLennan's other works include *Barometer Rising* (1941) and *The Watch That Ends the Night* (1959).

1945: Mar. 20 **Alfred** [Bruce] **Douglas** (b. Oct. 22, 1870), an English poet, remembered chiefly for his association with **Oscar Wilde**, died. It was this association that led to Wilde's imprisonment for homosexual practices and Wilde's writing *De Profundis* (1905), his letter of sorrow and confession to Douglas. Douglas's poetry included *The City of the Soul* (1899) and *Sonnets and Lyrics* (1935). He also translated Wilde's play *Salome* from the French.

1945 Apr. 22 **Käthe** [Schmidt] **Kollwitz** (b. July 8, 1867), a German sculptor and graphic artist, died. She first gained favorable attention when she illustrated **Gerhart Hauptmann's** *The Weavers* (1892) and **Émile Zola's** *Germinal* (1885). Kollwitz, a pacifist and socialist, in most of her work as a sculptor showed her bitter feelings about poverty and hunger, as in *Death and the Mother* (1934).

1945 May **Ezra Pound**, an American poet, was arrested in Italy by American officials and charged with treason. A longtime resident of Italy, Pound during World War II made c.300 radio broadcasts full of fascist propaganda and anti-Semitism. In 1946 he was judged mentally incompetent to stand trial and was confined to St. Elizabeth's Hospital in Washington, D.C.

1945 May 9 **René Lalique** (b. Apr. 6, 1860), a French designer of jewelry and glassware, died. He was famous for his designs in the **art nouveau style**. In the 1920s his luxurius articles of molded glass were the height of fashion. Lalique designed a fountain for the Esplanades des Invalides in Paris and salons for the ocean liners *Paris* and *Normandie*.

1945 June 8 **Robert Desnos** (b. July 4, 1900), a French surrealist poet, died. His work included *La Liberté ou l'amour* [*Liberty or Love*] (1927), *Contrée* [*Thwarted*] (1944), and *Choix de poems* [*Choice of Poems*] (1945). Desnos also wrote a novel, *Le Vin est Tiré* [*The Wine is Killed*] (1943). He was arrested by the Nazis for taking part in the French Resistance and sent to a concentration camp. It is not known whether he died there or shortly after being released by Allied troops.

1945 July 13 **Alla Nazimova** [nee Alla Leventon] (b. June 4, 1879), a Russian-born American actress, died. She studied with Stanislavsky and appeared with the Moscow Art Theater. Emigrating to the U.S. in 1905, she made her stage debut in English in 1906 in *Hedda Gabler*. Nazimova was acclaimed for her roles in *The Cherry Orchard* (1928) and *Mourning Becomes Electra* (1931). She also performed in the movies, including *Camille* (1921) and *The Bridge of San Luis Rey* (1944).

1945 July 20 [Ambroise] **Paul** [Toussaint Jules] **Valéry** (b. Oct. 30, 1871), one of the most important French poets of the 20th century, died. A symbolist, his books of poetry included *La Jeune Parque* (1917) and *Charmes* (1922). Valéry's critical and philosophical prose works included *L'Âme et la danse* [*Dance and the Soul*] (1921) and five collections of essays (1942–1944). After his death his extensive notebooks were published in 29 volumes as *Cahiers* (1957–1961). Valéry was elected to the Académie Française in 1925.

1945 Aug. **Yü Ta-Fu** [Yü Wên] (b. 1896), a Chinese short-story writer, was killed by Japanese occupation forces on Sumatra, an island in present Indonesia. While in Japan in 1920 he was a founder of the **Creation Society**. As a writer of Chinese fiction, Yü was a pioneer in the first person confessional short story, as in his collection *Ch'ên-Lun* (1921). He also wrote *Kuo-Ch'ü* (1927) and *Ch'ü Pen* (1935).

1945 Aug. 2 **Pietro Mascagni** (b. Dec. 7, 1863), an Italian composer, died. His most famous work, an opera in one act, was *Cavalleria Rusticana* (1890). Others of his works were *L'Amico Fritz* (1891), *I Rantzau* (1892), *Parisina* (1913), and *Nerone* (1935).

1945 Aug. 26 **Franz Werfel** (b. Sept. 10, 1890), an Austrian author, died. His best-known works were *Die vierzig Tage des Musa Dagh* [*The Forty Days of Musa Dagh*] (1933) and *Das Lied von Bernadette* [*The Song of Bernadette*] (1941). His plays included *Bocksgesang* [*Goat Song*] (1921) and *Jacobowsky und der Oberst* [*Jacobowsky and the Colonel*] (1944). Werfel fled from the Nazi regime in 1938 and emigrated to the U.S. in 1940.

1945 Sept. 16 **John** [Francis] **McCormack** (b. June 14, 1884), an Irish-American tenor, died. He made his operatic debut in London in 1907 but appeared chiefly in the U.S. after 1909. Among his best roles were Rodolpho in *La Bohème* and Pinkerton in *Madame Butterfly*. His recordings of sentimental songs, mostly Irish, made him a popular favorite.

1945 Sept. 24 **Argentinita** [Encarnación Lopez] (b. Mar. 25, 1909), a Spanish dancer, died. She became popular in Spain for both her footwork and her castanet playing. In Spain in 1932 she organized the **Madrid Ballet**, with which she toured the U.S. and Latin America in 1938.

1945 Sept. 26 **Béla Bartók** (b. Mar. 25, 1881), a Hungarian composer, pianist, and folk song collector, died. He wrote concertos, piano pieces, and sonatas. Other Bartók works included a one-act opera, *Bluebeard's Castle* (1918), a ballet, *The Miraculous Mandarin* (1926), and *Sonata for Two Pianos and Percussion* (1937). Bartók's style joined elements of traditional techniques, atonality, and folk music. From 1912 to 1914 he and his countryman **Zoltán Kodály** collected folk songs of eastern Europe. About 6,000 such songs were published eventually. Bartók emigrated to the U.S. in 1940.

1945 Oct. 8 **Felix Salten** [Salzmann] (b. Sept. 6, 1869), an Austrian author and journalist, died. Although he wrote novels and plays, he was best known for his children's books, especially *Bambi* (1923), the story of a deer in the forest, which was made into a Walt Disney animated movie (1943).

1945 Nov. 11 **Jerome** [David] **Kern** (b. Jan. 17, 1885), an American composer, died. He was one of the most successful composers to write for the musical comedy stage. Among Kern's many shows were *Sunny* (1925); *Show Boat* (1927); and *Roberta* (1933). Kern also wrote for the movies, composing such hits as "The Way You Look Tonight" (1936) and "The Last Time I Saw Paris" (1940).

1945 Nov. 21 **Ellen** [Anderson] **Glasgow** (b. Apr. 22, 1864), an American novelist, died. In her works she disavowed the sentimental tradition of the old South. Her many novels included *The Romantic Comedians* (1926), *They Stooped to Folly* (1929), *Vein of Iron* (1935), and *In This Our Life* (1941).

1945 Dec. 27 **Theodore Dreiser** (b. Aug. 27, 1871), an American author, died. His novel *An American Tragedy* (1925) was an outstanding example of American naturalism. In it Dreiser implied that criminals were largely a product of uncontrollable forces, including pure chance. His other works included *Sister Carrie* (1900), *The Financier* (1912), *The Titan* (1914), and *The Bulwark* (1946).

VII. SPORTS, GAMES, AND SOCIETY

1945 Mar. 19   **Torger Tokle** (b. 1920), a Norwegian immigrant to the U.S., was killed in combat in northern Italy, while leading a ski patrol of the U.S. army. Tokle popularized **ski jumping** in the U.S., first in the

East and then in Washington and Michigan. In 1942 he set a new American ski jump record of 289 ft. at Iron Mountain, Michigan. During his career Torkle broke 24 records and won 42 of 48 tournaments he entered.

1946

I. DISASTERS

1946 May 31   An **earthquake** in **Turkey's** eastern provinces of Mus and Erzurum killed at least 1,330 people.

1946 Aug. 2   In the sinking of the steamer *Vitya* in **Lake Nyasa, Tanganyika**, 295 people lost their lives.

1946 Dec. 7   A **fire** in the Winecoff Hotel in **Atlanta, Georgia**, killed 119 persons and injured c.100. Many died when they leaped from the 15-story building to escape the flames.

1946 Dec. 21   An **earthquake and six tsunamis** caused damage in c.60,000 square miles of **Honshu, Japan**. More than 1,000 people died and c.94,000 were left homeless. The quake registered 8.4 on the Richter scale.

II. POLITICS AND WAR

1946 Jan. 1   Hirohito, emperor of Japan, in a New Year's message to the country, said he was not a living god as centuries of tradition held. He wanted his relationship to the Japanese people to be based on "mutual trust and affection."

1946 Jan. 10   The General Assembly of the **United Nations**, with 51 member countries present, held its first session in London. **Trygve** [Halvdan] **Lie** (July 16, 1896–Dec. 30, 1968), a Norwegian statesman, was elected (Feb. 1) the first secretary general of the UN. The Assembly voted (Feb. 14) to establish permanent headquarters in New York City and held its first session there beginning on Dec. 11.

1946 Jan. 11   An army coup resulted in the resignation of **Élie Lescot** (Dec. 9, 1883–Oct. 22, 1974), president of **Haiti** (from 1941). He went into exile in the U.S.

1946 Feb. 6   The first judges were elected to the **International Court of Justice**, established by the **United Nations** to be its judicial arm. The court held its first session on Apr. 18 at The Hague, the Netherlands, its permanent seat.

1946 Feb. 24   In an election called by the military rulers of Argentina, **Juan Perón** was chosen president by a very large majority. Originally an army officer, Perón as a cabinet minister earned the approval of the mass of workers by supporting their demands and granting them many benefits. Perón's regime became dictatorial, censoring the press, jailing political opponents, and disregarding civil liberties. Perón's popularity was enhanced by that of his wife, **Eva María Duarte de Perón** ["Evita"] (May 7, 1919–July 26, 1952), whom he married in 1945. Formerly an actress, Evita was charismatic, and large numbers of Argentinians came to idolize her.

1946 Mar. 5   In a speech at Westminster College, Fulton, Missouri, **Winston Churchill** warned against Soviet aggression, saying: "From Stettin in the Baltic to Trieste in the Adriatic, an **iron curtain** has descended across the Continent." He was warning of the ideological as well as the physical barriers Russia erected after World War II between itself and its eastern European satellites on the one hand and the western, democratic world. The phrase Iron Curtain became a synonym for this division. The term **Cold War** was apparently first used on Apr. 17, 1947, by **Bernard M**[annes] **Baruch** (Aug. 19, 1870–June 20, 1965), an American businessman and adviser to many U.S. presidents and administrations, who said in a speech: "Let us not be deceived. We are today in the midst of a cold war."

1946 Apr. 14   **Civil war** broke out between the Nationalist government of **Chiang Kai-Shek** and the Communists, led by **Mao Tse-Tung**. At first the Nationalists had the edge but at the end of 1946 the outcome remained uncertain.

1946 Apr. 15 Shukri al-Kuwatli (1891–June 30, 1967) was elected the first president of the **Republic of Syria** by an assembly chosen in elections held on July 10 and 26.

1946 Apr. 11 **Forced labor was abolished in French West Africa**, due to the efforts of **Félix Houphouët-Boigny** (b. Oct. 18, 1905), a French deputy (1946–1959) from the Ivory Coast.

1946 May 25 The **Hashemite Kingdom of Transjordan** [present Jordan] was proclaimed on the basis of a treaty with Great Britain, which held the League of Nations mandate for Palestine (from 1924). **Abdullah**, the emir of Transjordan, became king.

1946 May 25 In a national election in **Czechoslovakia**, the Communists won a third of the votes and became the dominant party in a coalition government. The government was headed by **Klement Gottwald** (Nov. 23, 1896–Mar. 4, 1953) as prime minister. **Edward Beneš**, a non-communist, was re-elected president on June 19.

1946 June 2 In a national referendum the Italian people by a small majority voted to abolish the monarchy and establish a republic. **Victor Emmanuel III** had abdicated as king on May 9 in favor of his son **Umberto** (Sept. 15, 1904–Mar. 18, 1983), to whom he had delegated (1944) his powers. On June 13, as a result of the referendum, Umberto went into exile in Portugal. **Enrico de Nicola** (Nov. 9, 1877–Oct. 1, 1959) served as provisional president of the republic until a new constitution went into effect on Jan. 1, 1948.

1946 June 9 **Ananda Mahidol** (b. Sept. 20, 1925), who reigned as **Rama VIII**, king of Thailand (from 1935), was found dead of a bullet wound in his head. A commission of investigation decided it was most likely murder. In May he had proclaimed a new constitution and on June 1 presided at the opening of the first legislative session under the new law. Rama VIII was succeeded by his brother Bhumibol Adulyadej (b. Dec. 5, 1927), who was selected by the legislature and now reigns as **Rama IX**.

1946 June 26 **Juan Antonio Ríos** (b. 1888) president of **Chile** (from 1942), died in office. A moderate, he guided Chile through World War II, maintaining

neutrality in an attempt to satisfy both the pro-western feelings of many Chileans and the ardently pro-Nazi feelings of others. Chile eventually declared war against the Axis powers in 1945. **Gabriel González Videla**, a member of Ríos's Radical party, won the election that was called immediately to fill the presidency (to 1952).

1946 July 4 The **Republic of the Philippines became completely independent** of the U.S. **Manuel Roxas** (Jan. 1, 1892–Apr. 15, 1948) was the first president. Roxas during World War II appeared to assist the Japanese puppet regime but was actually a spy for the Philippine underground movement. Independence was the culmination of gradual steps toward sovereignty which had been promised when the U.S. won the islands from Spain in the Spanish-American War (1898).

1946 July 17 **Draza Mihajlovic** (b. 1893?), the leader in World War II of a Yugoslavian partisan band at odds with **Tito**, was executed for treason along with eight of his followers. They were arrested on Mar. 13, put on trial on June 10, and convicted on July 16.

1946 July 22 Members of the **Irgun** [*Zvail Leumi*, National Fighting Organization], a Jewish guerilla group dedicated to driving the British out of Palestine by force, detonated a bomb in the King David Hotel in Jerusalem. Part of the hotel was being used for British government offices. The bomb killed 91 persons: 41 Arabs, 28 British, 17 Jews, and 5 others. Nearly 50 persons were injured. The British arrested several hundred Jews and instituted a curfew. The leader of the Irgun was **Menachem Begin** (b. Aug. 16, 1913) who eventually became prime minister (1977) of the state of Israel. The incident did much to create a decided anti-Jewish bias in the British army. As Jews, Arabs, and the British became involved in the struggle for the future of Palestine, terrorist acts became widespread.

1946 July 25 In an election to choose a constituent assembly to draft a constitution for India as a self-governing dominion of the Commonwealth of Nations, the Congress party, now dominated by the Hindu majority, won 201 of the 210 seats allotted to Hindus. The Muslim League, which favored dividing India on religious lines, won 73 of the 78 seats available to Muslims. The leader of the Congress party was **Jawaharlal Nehru**, an early advocate of Indian independence who was imprisoned by the

British from Oct., 1941, to June, 1945, for his political activities. The leader of the Muslim League was **Muhammad Ali Jinnah** (Feb. 25, 1876–Sept. 11, 1948), also in the forefront of the struggle for independence. The growing conflict resulted (Aug. 16–18) in serious riots between Hindus and Muslims. About 3,500 people were killed in Calcutta alone.

1946 Sept. 1   In a plebiscite 70 percent of the Greek voters chose to have **George II** return from wartime exile as their monarch. At this time guerilla warfare was carried on in the north by communist bands, and civil war threatened.

1946 Sept. 15   Bulgaria was proclaimed a People's Republic following a vote (Sept. 8) to abolish the monarchy. **Simeon II** (b. June 16, 1937), king of Bulgaria (1943–1946) went into exile in Spain. On Oct. 27 general elections gave an overwhelming victory to the Fatherland Front, the communist-dominated party, whose leader **Georgi Dimitrov** (June 18, 1882–Feb. 7, 1949) became prime minister (Nov. 21) and held the post until his death.

1946 Oct. 9   Following the death of **Per Albin Hansson**, **Tage Fritiof Erlander** (June 13, 1901–June 21, 1985), became prime minister of Sweden (to 1969), continuing the unbroken rule (from 1932) of the Social Democratic party. Sweden, to preserve its neutrality, chose not to join the North Atlantic Treaty Organization [NATO] or the European Community [EC].

1946 Oct. 13   French voters approved a new constitution (to 1958) that established the **Fourth French Republic**, also known as the **French Union** because it incorporated into the nation its colonies. The constitution was drafted by an assembly elected on June 2. On Nov. 10, in an election of a new assembly, the Communist party received the most votes, with the Popular Republicans second, and the Socialists third. The Communists were excluded from the center-left coalition.

1946 Oct. 13   The French colony of **Somaliland**, in eastern Africa at the southern end of the Red Sea, was renamed the **French Territory of the Afars and Issas**, for its two main ethnic groups, and became part of the French Union. The Union made the colonies integral parts of the national state.

1946 Oct. 15   Two hours before he was to be hanged as a convicted war criminal, **Hermann Gör-**

ing (b. Jan. 12, 1893), second highest ranking official in the Third Reich, committed suicide by poison. A hero of the German air force in World War I, Göring was an early member of the Nazi party and participated (1923) in the failed Munich "beer hall putsch." In May, 1945, he surrendered to American troops and, at the Nürnberg [Nuremberg] trials, he was the most outspoken and unrepentant of all the defendants.

1946 Oct. 18   The newly formed *Rassemblement démocratique africain* [RDA, African Democratic Rally] met at Bamako in present Mali. It was attended by representatives from France's African colonies. **Félix Houphouët-Boigny**, then a French deputy (1946–1959) from the Ivory Coast [present *Côte d'Ivoire*], and a founder of the RDA, was elected president.

1946 Nov. 23   The **French Indochina War** (1946–1954) began when Vietnamese nationalists and French troops fought in Haiphong, east of Hanoi. French warships then bombarded the city, killing c.6,000 persons. The Vietnamese were led by **Ho Chi Minh** and the **Viet Nam Doc Lap Dong Minh** [League for the Independence of Vietnam], commonly known as the **Viet Minh**. It was then a communist and non-communist coalition, but by 1951 the communists became dominant.

1946 Dec. 1   **Miguel Alemán Valdés** (Sept. 29, 1902–May 14, 1983), a supporter of the labor movement, was inaugurated president (to 1952) of Mexico. He was the first civilian to reach the post through the electoral process since **Francisco Madero** took office in Nov. 1911. He raised the general standard of living through his educational, reclamation, power, and communication projects.

III. ECONOMY AND TRADE

1946   The **largest steel mill in South America** was completed at Volta Redonda, a city of eastern Brazil. It still produces more than half of Brazil's steel.

1946 Feb. 14   The Labour government of Great Britain **nationalized the Bank of England**, which had been privately owned since its founding (1694). The bank is today the central bank of Great Britain.

1946 Apr. 21   **John Maynard Keynes** (b. June 5, 1883), an English theorist and the most influential economist of the 20th century, died. *The General*

Theory of Employment, Interest, and Money (1936), his most important work, was a guide book for governments for nearly 50 years. Keynes was a member of the British delegation that helped draw up the **Treaty of Versailles** (1919) ending World War I (1914–1918). He wrote at the time that forcing Germany to pay enormous reparation payments would disrupt the international economy.

1946 Dec. 14 The **International Labor Organization** [ILO], established (1919) as part of the Treaty of Versailles ending World War I, became a specialized agency of the **United Nations**. The purpose of the ILO was to improve working conditions and living standards and thereby contribute to a peaceful world. The ILO was awarded the **Nobel Peace Prize** in 1969.

IV. RELIGION AND PHILOSOPHY

1946 The **Revised Standard Version** [RSV] **of the New Testament of the Bible was published.** This new version was a revision of the American Standard Version (1901), which in turn was a revision of the King James Version (1611).

1946 **Geoffrey Francis Fisher** (May 5, 1887–Sept. 14, 1972) was named the 99th archbishop of Canterbury (resigned 1961) and primate of the Anglican Communion. Fisher was president (1946–1954) of the **World Council of Churches**.

1946 July 7 **Mother Frances Xavier Cabrini** [nee Maria Francesca Cabrini] (July 15, 1850–Dec. 22, 1917) became the **first American citizen to be canonized**, in a ceremony conducted by **Pope Pius XII**. She was beatified in 1938 by **Pope Pius XI**. Born in Italy, Mother Cabrini in 1880 founded the Sisters of the Sacred Heart of Jesus, of which she became the superior general for life in 1910. In 1889 **Pope Leo XIII** sent her to the U.S. to aid Italian immigrants. She worked chiefly in New York City and Chicago, establishing schools, hospitals, orphanages, and nurseries. Her work also extended to Latin America. Mother Cabrini became an American citizen in 1909.

V. SCIENCE, EDUCATION, AND TECHNOLOGY

1946 ENIAC [Electronic Numerical Integrator and Calculator], the **first all-electronic, all-purpose computer**, was completed by **John William Mauchly** (Aug. 30, 1907–Jan. 8, 1980) and **John Prosper Eckert, Jr.**, (b. Apr. 6, 1919). ENIAC was a 30-ton construction with its vacuum tubes arranged so as to display decimal numerals. It could not use binary numerals. In Aug. 1949, Mauchly and Eckert put into operation BINAC [Binary Automatic Computer] which was the **first electronic stored-program computer in the U.S.**

1946 The **official language of the Mongolian People's Republic**, Khalkha Mongolian, switched to the use of the Cyrillic alphabet. Until this time it was written in the old Uigur-Turkic script.

1946 *The Common Sense Book of Baby and Child Care*, by **Benjamin** [McLane] **Spock** (b. May 2, 1903), was published. In a remarkably short time it became the most widely used guide by American parents. In all its editions since publication it has sold more than 25,000,000 copies. It advises parents to treat a baby as a human being, and not to worry about keeping to rigid schedules.

1946 **Willard Frank Libby** (Dec. 17, 1908–Sept. 8, 1980), an American chemist, developed the **carbon-14 technique** for dating very old objects. Because the rate of decomposition of carbon-14 was known and since all organic matter contained carbon, the technique could be used to determine the age of archeological and geographical material. Libby was awarded the **Nobel prize for chemistry** in 1960.

1946 Jan. 10 **Radar signals were reflected off the moon** for the first time, by the U.S. Signal Corps. Signals took 2.4 seconds for the round trip.

1946 June 30 An **atomic device was detonated over Bikini atoll** in the Marshall Islands of the western Pacific Ocean. It was dropped from an American B-29 bomber and sank and damaged a number of obsolete warships below it. On July 25 the **first test of an atomic bomb exploded underwater** sank and damaged warships anchored above it. The inhabitants of the atoll were removed to other islands because of the radioactive fallout from the bombs.

1946 Sept. 17 **James** [Hopwood] **Jeans** (b. Sept. 11, 1877), an English astronomer, physicist, and mathematician, died. His work included the mathematical theory of electricity and magnetism, the origins of binary stars, and the kinetic theory of gases. Jeans became a popularizer of science with his writings, including *The Universe Around Us* (1929), *The Mysterious Universe* (1930), and *Through Space and Time* (1934).

1946 Nov. The first synchrocyclotron, built this year at the University of California, Berkeley, was able to produce alpha particles with an energy of 380,000,000 volts. This energy level in turn was high enough to produce pions, lightest of the meson family of elementary particles.

1946 Nov. 4 The **United Nations Educational, Scientific, and Cultural Organization** [UNESCO] was established as a specialized agency of the **United Nations**. Its purpose was to foster international understanding. Its immediate task was to help restore war-damaged facilities, such as libraries and museums.

1946 Dec. 19 Paul Langevin (b. Jan. 23, 1872), a French physicist, died. He did important work in many areas of physics, such as the Brownian movement, the theory of magnetism, and the theory of relativity.

1946 Dec. 24 The first nuclear reactor in the **U.S.S.R.** went into operation. It was built under the direction of **Igor Vasilyevich Kurchatov** (Jan. 12, 1903–Feb. 7, 1960), who then developed (1949) the first Russian atomic bomb.

VI. ARTS AND LEISURE

1946 Ingmar Bergman (July 14, 1918) directed his first Swedish film *Crisis*. Recognized as one of the greatest of all film-makers, his many movies included *Smiles of a Summer Night* (1955), *The Seventh Seal* (1957), *Wild Strawberries* (1957), and *Scenes from a Marriage* (1974).

1946 Jan. 9 Countee Cullen (b. May 30, 1903), an American writer, and a leading figure of the Harlem Renaissance, died. Cullen's first book of verse was *Color* (1925). Others included *The Ballad of the Brown Girl* (1927) and *The Black Christ and Other Poems* (1929). Cullen also wrote a novel, *One Way to Heaven* (1931).

1946 Feb. 5 George Arliss [orig.: Augustus George Andrews] (b. April 10, 1868), an English actor of the stage and the movies, died. He made his debut (1886) in London, then moved (1901) to the U.S.,

where he starred in *The Second Mrs. Tanqueray* (1902), among other productions. After 1920 Arliss appeared in movies. His memorable films included *Alexander Hamilton* (1931) and *Cardinal Richelieu* (1935).

1946 June 6 Gerhart [Johann Robert] Hauptmann (b. Nov. 15, 1862), a German dramatist and novelist, died. Hauptmann's impressive work included *Die Weber* [*The Weavers*] (1892), a portrayal of the 1844 rebellion of Silesian weavers; a romantic play *Die versunkene Glocke* [*The Sunken Bell*] (1897); a novel *Der Narr in Christo Emanuel Quint* [*The Fool in Christ, Emanuel Quint*] (1910); and an epic of post-World War I Germany, *Till Eulenspiegel* (1918). Hauptmann received the **Nobel prize for literature** in 1912.

1946 June 23 William S[urrey] Hart (b. Dec. 6, 1872), an American actor and the first cowboy star of the movies, died. On the stage (1889–1914) he starred in such plays as *Ben Hur* and *The Squaw Man*. Turning to the movies in 1914, he became internationallly popular as the strong, silent hero on a horse, in such movies as *Hell's Hinges* (1916), *Gunfighter* (1917), *Wild Bill Hickock* (1923), and *Tumbleweeds* (1925).

1946 July 13 Alfred Stieglitz (b. Jan. 1, 1864), an American photographer, generally considered the creator of modern photography, died. He did much to make photography an art form. In 1905 he established the gallery called "291" because it was located at 291 Fifth Avenue, New York City. Stieglitz not only exhibited photographs but also introduced to the U.S. the work of French painters of the period. His best work consisted of two series of c.400 prints each. One was of his wife **Georgia O'Keefe**, the painter, and the other of cloud patterns.

1946 July 15 Wên I-Tuo (b. 1889), a Chinese poet and scholar, died. His first book of verse, published while he was in the U.S., was *Red Candle* (1923). After returning to China, Wên was a university professor and an editor of *Crescent Monthly*. He also published a second book of verse, *Dead Water* (1928). Wên created natural rhythms, strong and regular. When he became involved in politics, Wên was murdered by the Nationalists.

1946 July 27 Gertrude Stein (b. Feb. 3, 1874), an American novelist and critic, died. An expatriate in Paris, she was the center of a group of leading artists and writers. Her writing style was unique, her language the equivalent of cubism in art. Though she was highly regarded in literary circles, the general public could not fathom her work. Stein's early fiction included *Three Lives* (1909), and *The Making of Americans*, written between 1906 and 1911 but not published until 1925. She wrote her autobiography under the title *The Autobiography of Alice B. Toklas* (1933). Toklas (Apr. 30, 1877–Mar. 7, 1967) was her longtime companion and secretary. Stein wrote an opera *Four Saints in Three Acts* (1934), with music by **Virgil Thomson**. She did not coin, but did make well-known, the phrase "the **Lost Generation**," referring to post-World War I expatriates in Europe.

1946 Aug. 13 H[erbert] G[eorge] **Wells** (b. Sept. 21, 1866), an English writer, died. His long and versatile career began with such imaginative fiction as *The Time Machine* (1895) and *The War of the Worlds* (1898). He was also the writer of such novels as *Kipps* (1905), *Tono Bungay* (1909), and *The History of Mr. Polly* (1910).

1946 Sept. 20 The first **International Cannes Film Festival** opened in the city of Cannes, France. The event was originally scheduled for 1939 but the start of World War II forced its postponement. The festival is now generally regarded as the most important of several such affairs. A number of awards are made, the chief being the *Palme d'or* [Golden Palm] for the best film shown.

1946 Nov. 5 Joseph [orig.: Giuseppe] **Stella** (b. June 13, 1877), an Italian-born American painter, died. Coming to the U.S. in 1896, he studied in New York City and exhibited at the controversial Armory Show there in 1913. Stella showed in his paintings the excitement of New York City: *Battle of Lights, Coney Island* (1913), *The Gas Tank* (1918), and *Brooklyn Bridge* (1920).

1946 Nov. 14 Manuel de Falla y Matheu (b. Nov. 23, 1876), a Spanish composer, died. One of the first Spanish composers to receive international acclaim, he drew on the musical traditions of his native land in developing his own style. De Falla's first important work was a one-act opera *La vida breve* [*The Short Life*] (1908). He later wrote a piano concerto and two ballets, *El amor brujo* [*Wedded by Witchcraft*] (1915) and *El sombrero de tres picos* [*The Three Cornered Hat*] (1919).

1946 Dec. 25 W.C. Fields [orig.: William Claude Dukenfield] (b. Jan. 29, 1880), an American comedian of the stage and movies, died. He began his career as a comedy juggler, taking his first step toward stardom in the *Ziegfeld Follies* (1915). In the movies, Fields was the cantankerous, bibulous character whose fans loved him even though he professed to hate children and dogs. Among his movies were *You Can't Cheat an Honest Man* (1939), *The Bank Dick* (1940), and *Never Give a Sucker an Even Break* (1941). In contrast to his usual roles, Fields gave a perfect portrayal of Mr. Micawber in *David Copperfield* (1935).

1946 Dec. 30 Charles Wakefield Cadman (b. Dec. 24, 1881), an American composer, died. He was particularly interested in the songs of the American Indians, on which many of his compositions are based. Cadman wrote operas, including *Shanewis* (1918) and *Witch of Salem* (1926). Although Cadman composed nearly 200 songs, his most popular by far was "**From the Land of the Sky Blue Water**" (1908).

VII. SPORTS, GAMES AND SOCIETY

1946 The **ranch house** began to appear in American suburbs, as the veterans of World War II returned home and began to marry and raise families. The rectangular, one-story home, with a low-pitched roof, bore some resemblance to the family living quarters on ranches in the West.

1946 The **bikini**, a woman's two-piece bathing suit covering only a small part of the female anatomy, was seen on beaches. It took its name from the Pacific atoll where U.S. atomic bombs were tested this year.

1946 Mar. 24 Alexander Alekhine [orig.: Aleksandr Aleksandrovich Alyokhin] (b. Nov. 1, 1892), the chess champion of the world, died. Born in Russia, he left after the revolution of 1917 and became a French citizen ten years later. Alekhine won the world championship in 1927 from **José Capablanca** of Cuba and held it until 1935 when he lost it to **Max Euwe** (May 20, 1901–Nov. 26, 1981) of the Netherlands. He regained the title in 1937 and held it until he died.

1946 June 1 The **Triple Crown** of American thoroughbred horse racing was won for the seventh time in its history by **Assault**, which triumphed in the

Belmont Stakes. Assault won the Kentucky Derby on May 4 and the Preakness Stakes on May 11. The winning jockey was **Warren Mehrtens.**

1946 Sept. 1   The **first U.S. Women's Open golf tournament** was won by [Patricia Jane] **Patty Berg** (b. Feb. 13, 1918) at Spokane, Washington. By the time she retired (1962) Berg had won 55 tournaments.

1946 Dec. 26   The U.S. won the **Davis Cup** by defeating Australia 5 matches to 0. It was the first contest for the cup since competition was interrupted in 1939 by World War II.

1947

I. DISASTERS

1947 Jan. 19   The Greek steamship *Himera* struck a mine, presumably left from World War II, in the Gulf of Petalia, c.20 miles offshore from Athens. Of 637 passengers 392 were killed or drowned.

1947 Feb. 15   Near Bogota, Colombia, an **Avianca Airlines plane hit El Tablazo**, a cliff 30 miles northwest of the city, killing all 53 persons aboard. On May 30 near Port Deposit, northeastern Maryland, an **Eastern Air Lines DC-4 crashed**, killing 54 passengers.

1947 Mar. 25   An **explosion and fire** in a bituminous coal mine at Centralia, central southern Illinois, took the lives of 111 miners.

1947 Apr. 10   **Cyclones** that swept through western Texas and Oklahoma killed 134 persons and injured c.1,300.

1947 Apr. 16–17   The French freighter *Grandcamp*, loading ammonium nitrate at Texas City, Texas, **caught fire and exploded.** Two sightseeing planes were knocked out of the air, and a 15-foot tidal wave lifted a loaded 150-foot barge 100 feet onto land. Under a rain of red-hot metal, a Monsanto Chemical Company plant and most of the port area caught fire. Firefighters could not contain the inferno, and on the 17th the burning ship *High Flyer* exploded, tearing another freighter in two. At least 560 people were killed, c.120 missing, c.3,000 injured, and c.2,500 made homeless. With most of Texas City destroyed, property damage exceeded $50 million.

1947 Aug. 3   At least 400 people died in a **train wreck near Pematangsiantar on Sumatra**, in the strife-torn Dutch East Indies.

1947 Aug. 15   **Trapped in the undersea workings of a mine** at Whitehaven, Cumberland, England, on the coast of the Irish sea, 104 miners died.

1947 Sept. 15–19   Homes of c.100,000 people were destroyed and more than 1,000 deaths occurred when **tsunamis scoured Japan's Honshu and Shikoku islands**.

1947 Oct. 5   In East Bengal [present Bangladesh], in northeastern India, **floods** destroyed c.100,000 tons of rice, thousands of cattle, and left c.1,000,000 people homeless. The number of dead was in the thousands.

1947 Dec. 1   A **hurricane in the area of Oporto, Portugal**, wiped out the fishing fleet, killing or drowning c.160 fishermen.

II. POLITICS AND WAR

1947 Jan. 1   The French colonies of **French Guiana, Guadeloupe and Martinique, and Réunion**, in the Indian Ocean, **became overseas departments of France** in accordance with the new constitution of Oct. 13, 1946. Their inhabitants became citizens of the French Union, equal before the law to those in France.

1947 Jan. 19   In an election for the Polish National Assembly the communist dominated Democratic Bloc won 382 of the 444 seats. **Boleslaw Bierut** (Apr. 18, 1892–Mar. 12, 1956), a long-time communist organizer, was elected (Feb. 4) president by the assembly. A provisional constitution went into effect (Feb. 19), which gave the government the right to rule by decree.

1947 Feb. 10 The World War II Allies signed separate **peace treaties** in Paris with the former enemy states of **Bulgaria, Finland, Hungary, Italy, and Romania.**

1947 Mar. 9 **Carrie Chapman Catt** [nee Lane] (b. Jan. 9, 1859), an American reformer, died. Catt, as much as any other one person, was responsible for the adoption in 1920 of the **Nineteenth Amendment to the U.S. Constitution** which gave women the vote. After 1923 she devoted her efforts chiefly to the peace movement.

1947 Mar. 12 In an address before Congress, **Harry S Truman**, president of the U.S., declared that America must aid nations threatened with subversion and revolution by communist forces. Establishing what became known as the **Truman Doctrine**, he said: "I believe it must be the policy of the U.S. to support free peoples who are resisting attempted subjugation by armed minorities or by outside pressure." He asked Congress to appropriate $400,000,-000 to aid Greece, where a communist revolt was already in progress, and Turkey. The aid bill was signed into law on May 22.

1947 Mar. 19–Dec. 31 The balance in the **Chinese civil war** tipped toward the Communists by the end of the year. On Mar. 19 the Nationalists captured Yenan [Fushih, Yanan], in central northern China, the Communist's capital. In October government forces took Weihai and Chefoo [Yantai] in Shantung [Shandong] province, northeastern China. However, before the end of the year the Communists secured complete control of Manchuria and began to move into central China. The Nationalist government of **Chiang Kai-Shek** was losing popularity because of inflation, food shortages, and police brutality.

1947 Mar. 29 A nationalist **rebellion against French rule** broke out in **Madagascar,** [present Malagasy Republic], off the east coast of Africa. White settlers were massacred, plantations sacked, and garrisons attacked. Troops sent by France in August took a year to suppress the uprising. Pacification was considered ended on Dec. 1, 1948, at a cost in lives estimated between 11,000 and 80,000.

1947 Apr. 2 The **Trust Territory of the Pacific Islands**, to be held by the U.S., was established by the **United Nations.** The islands involved were the Caroline Islands, the Marianas Islands, and the Marshall Islands (except for Guam, which was an American possession since 1898).

1947 Apr. 20 **Christian X** (b. Sept. 26, 1870), king of Denmark (from 1912), died. Although he was able to keep his country neutral during World War I, it was invaded (Apr., 1940) by German forces in World War II. Christian steadfastly refused to cooperate with the Nazis and did as much as possible to keep up his people's morale. In Aug. 1943, the Germans placed him under house arrest where he remained until freed by the Allies' victory in 1945. He was succeeded by his son **Frederick IX**, who had also been placed under house arrest during the war.

1947 May 25 The government of **Leonardo Argüello** (1873–Dec. 15, 1947) was overthrown in Nicaragua. He had been inaugurated on May 1, having won the election of Feb. 2 in which he was supported by **Anastasio Somoza García**, the strongman of the country who was not eligible to succeed himself as president. Once in office Argüello attempted to curb the role of the National Guard, control of which was the source of Somoza's power, but Somoza continued to be the real ruler of the country.

1947 May 27 **Tetsu Katayama** (July 28, 1887–May 30, 1978) became the first prime minister of **Japan** under a new constitution written by the American occupying forces. An election (Apr. 25) for the House of Representatives [lower house] of the Diet [parliament] secured for the Social Democratic party a plurality, but not a majority, so Katayama formed a coalition government, which proved unstable.

1947 May 31 While **Ferenc Nagy** (Oct. 8, 1903–June 12, 1973), the anticommunist premier of **Hungary** was out of the country, a Communist coup overthrew his government. He was replaced by **Lajos Dinnyes** (Apr. 16, 1901–May 4, 1961), who was first elected to parliament in 1929 and during World War II was forced to go into hiding when the Germans occupied the country. The leader of the Small Landholders party, which was part of a coalition government with the Communists, Dinnyes remained as premier even though his party was badly defeated in an election on Aug. 31.

1947 June 5 American financial aid to restore the economies of the nations of Europe was proposed by **George C. Marshall**, secretary of state of the U.S. Speaking at Harvard University, he said: "Our policy is not directed against any country or doctrine, but against hunger, poverty, desperation, and chaos. We of the United States are deeply conscious of our responsibilities in the world." The program that came out of this proposal was known as the **Marshall Plan**.

1947 July 6   An election was held to approve a **Law of Succession** proposed on Apr. 1 by **Francisco Franco**, the dictator of Spain. In it he declared that **Spain** was a kingdom (although it had no king at this time) and that he, Franco, was chief of state. He proposed that he be succeeded by "a person of royal blood," who would have to be approved by the *Cortes* [parliament] by a two thirds vote. In the election the Spanish gave their approval to this law, 82 percent favoring it.

1947 July 13–Dec. 26   On July 13, 1,500 **communists invaded** northwestern **Greece** from Albania and attacked Konitsa, but were driven back. The government became more stable when **Themistocles Sophoulis** (Nov. 25, 1861–June 24, 1949), leader of the Liberal party, became premier (Sept. 7) for a few months as head of a Liberal-Populist coalition. A "people's democratic government of Free Greece" was proclaimed (Dec. 24) by radio, the announcement apparently coming from Belgrade, Yugoslavia, with little to support it. Two days later the government outlawed the Communist party.

1947 July 19   **U Aung San** (b. 1914?), known as the father of Burmese independence, was assassinated on orders of his rival **U Saw**. Aung for a while supported the Japanese puppet government after 1941. In 1945, however, he switched his support to the Allies when Japanese defeat was near. Aung was de facto prime minister (1946–1947) as leader of the Anti-Fascist People's Freedom League. He was the chief negotiator (1947) of the independence of Burma [Myanmar] from Great Britain. Saw was also a negotiator, but refused to sign the treaty of Jan. 27, 1947, that granted independence. U Saw (b. 1900) was convicted of conspiracy to murder and was executed on May 8, 1948.

1947 Aug. 15   India became the two independent dominions of India and Pakistan, within the Commonwealth of Nations. **Louis Mountbatten**, a British admiral, had been appointed the last British viceroy of India on Feb. 20, 1947, and presided over the final negotiations, rancorous because of Muslim-Hindu enmity. The Muslims wanted a separate state and got it. Pakistan was in two sections, one on each side of the much larger Indian, and predominantly Hindu, territory. **Mohammad Ali Jinnah**, leader of the Muslims, became governor-general of Pakistan. In India Mountbatten became governor-general, with **Jawaharlal Nehru**, leader of the Hindu Congress party, as prime minister. After partitioning, c.16,000,000 people fled from one division to the other on the basis of their religion. In the process ferocious fighting between Hindus and Muslims left more than half a million dead before the year ended. A struggle over Kashmir, a princely state between northwestern India and northeastern Pakistan, was the cause of more bloodshed. A majority of its inhabitants were Muslims but its ruler was a Hindu. He placed Kashmir under the rule of India, which sent troops to put down a revolt of the Muslims.

1947 Sept. 1   The French National Assembly approved the **Statute of Algeria**, intended to give the Muslim inhabitants of that colony more political power. Most of the statute's provisions were never put into effect and the French colonists in Algeria, together with the government in Paris, continued to control affairs.

1947 Sept. 2   The **Inter-American Treaty of Reciprocal Assistance**, commonly known as the **Rio Treaty**, was signed in Rio de Janeiro, Brazil. It was ratified by all 20 Latin American republics and by the U.S. By the treaty's terms, any attack or act of aggression against any one of the nations, whether by a member country or an outside power, would be considered an attack on all.

1947 Sept. 4   The French territory of **Upper Volta** [present Burkina Faso] was reconstituted as a separate colony, centered around its capital Ouagadougou [Wagadugu], where the Mossi tribe was dominant. Under the new regime Upper Volta was a member of the French Union and had its own assembly.

1947 Oct. 5   The **Cominform** [Communist Information Bureau] (to 1956) was established by the Communist parties of nine European nations: Bulgaria, Czechoslovakia, France, Hungary, Italy, Poland, Romania, the U.S.S.R., and Yugoslavia. The Cominform could not make binding decisions but it was intended to show the unity of its members.

1947 Nov. 9   The government of **Pridi Phanomyang** in Thailand was overthrown by a military coup led by **Pibul Songgram**. Pridi fled the country.

1947 Nov. 29 The General Assembly of the **United Nations** voted to **divide Palestine into two states, Arab and Jewish**. In the UN vote, the British abstained, the U.S. and the U.S.S.R. supported the resolution, and the Arab nations walked out in protest. The UN set boundary lines for the two proposed nations, with Jerusalem to be administered as an international city. The effective date of the partition was to be on May 15, 1948. At this time there were a little more than 1,000,000 Muslim Arabs, c.600,000 Jews, and nearly 150,000 Christians in Palestine.

1947 Dec. 14 **Stanley Baldwin** (b. Aug. 3, 1867), a British politician and statesman, died. His three terms as prime minister were marked by the difficulties of the post-World War I, especially unemployment. In international affairs Baldwin temporized in standing up to Adolf Hitler but finally began a rearmament program.

1947 Dec. 28 **Victor Emmanuel III** (b. Nov. 11, 1869), king of Italy (1900–1946), emperor of Ethiopia (1936–1943), and king of Albania (1939–1943), died in exile in Egypt. As a monarch he was generally ineffectual and unpopular with his subjects. Victor Emmanuel passed (1944) his throne to his son **Umberto II** and abdicated (1945).

1947 Dec. 30 The communist-controlled government of **Romania** forced **Michael I** to abdicate as king, and a people's republic was proclaimed. Michael was the last remaining monarch in communist-dominated East Europe.

III. ECONOMY AND TRADE

1947 **Paul A**[nthony] **Samuelson** (b. May 15, 1915), an American economist, published *Foundations of Economic Analysis,* an early attempt to apply mathematical procedures to economic problems. Since then he has made many other contributions to his field, not the least of which is a college textbook *Economics: An Introductory Analysis* (1948). He won the **Nobel prize for economics** in 1970.

1947 Jan. 1 An unusual **cold spell** in February and March stalled transportation to such an extent that coal deliveries were at a virtual standstill. As a result **Great Britain**, dependent on coal for energy, suf-fered a crippling **shortage of electric power** as well as heating and transportation.

1947 Feb. The **Leduc oil field**, southwest of Edmonton, Canada, began to produce, beginning the trend toward **increased Canadian oil output**–about 23-fold over the next decade.

1947 Apr. 4 **Henry Ford** (b. July 30, 1863), an American automobile manufacturer, died. Ford achieved his success by introducing the assembly line method of producing cars. Ford was extremely conservative on social and political issues. He established the **Ford Foundation** in 1936. When it received several billion dollars from his estate, it became the **largest philanthropy in the world**.

1947 June 23 The **Labor-Management Relations Act**, known as the **Taft-Hartley Act**, was passed by Congress over the veto of **Harry S Truman**. By amending the **National Labor Relations** [Wagner] **Act** of 1935, it curtailed the powers of labor unions.

1947 Oct. 13 **Sidney** [James] **Webb** (b. July 13, 1859), an English economist and civil servant, died. With his wife, **Beatrice Potter Webb**, he was a moving force in the **Fabian Society** (from 1884), in the growth of the **Labour party** (from 1906), and in the founding (1895) of the **London School of Economics**. Webb was elected to Parliament in 1922 and held cabinet positions in the Labour government.

1947 Nov. 27 All the **private banks of Australia were nationalized** by a previously adopted act of Parliament. Provisions were made for the protection of shareholders and employees.

IV. PHILOSOPHY AND RELIGION

1947 Spring The discovery of ancient manuscripts and fragments, on leather and papyrus, known today as the **Dead Sea Scrolls**, was made by a Bedouin in a cave in the Qumran region at the northwestern end of the Dead Sea. Later, thousands of scroll fragments were found in caves nearby. The scrolls were apparently the remains of the library of a sect known as the Essenes, a Jewish communal community, ascetic in its rules and its way of life, that existed from the second century B.C. to sometime in the second century A.D.

1947 Dec. 30 Alfred North Whitehead (b. Feb. 15, 1861), an English philosopher and mathematician, died. He collaborated with **Bertrand Russell** on *Principia Mathematica* (1910–1913), a milestone in the field of logic. He also wrote *Science and the Modern World* (1925), *Process and Reality* (1929), and *Modes of Thought* (1938).

V. SCIENCE, EDUCATION, AND TECHNOLOGY

1947 Dennis Gabor (b. Feb. 9, 1879), a Hungarian-born English physicist, developed the theoretical concept of **holography**, enabling a three-dimensional image of an object to be produced. Gabor received the **Nobel prize for physics** in 1971.

1947 Apr. 28 Thor Heyerdahl (b. Oct. 6, 1914), a Norwegian anthropologist and explorer, drifted from Callao, near Lima, Peru, to Polynesia on a raft of balsa wood in an attempt to prove that natives of South America could have reached and populated the islands of that area of the central and southern Pacific Ocean. He sighted (July 30) Pukapuka, an island on the eastern edge of the Tuamoto Archipelago, 3 months and 1 day after leaving Peru. He described his voyage in *Kon Tiki* (1950), the name he gave the raft.

1947 The first tubeless tires for motor vehicles were introduced in the U.S. by Goodyear.

1947 Feb. 12 A meteorite, appearing to be a great ball of fire with a thick black tail, hit the Sikhote-Alin Mountains in **eastern Siberia**. It made a number of craters, the largest of which was c.130 feet in diameter. Judging from fragments found over a wide area, there was a rain of iron as the meteorite exploded in the atmosphere.

1947 May 16 Frederick Gowland Hopkins (b. June 30, 1861), an English biochemist, died. He devoted himself to establishing that a deficiency in the diet might be responsible for certain diseases, and that such diseases might be cured by correcting the deficiency. In 1929 he shared the **Nobel prize for physiology or medicine** with **Christian Eijkman**, the Dutch medical researcher who studied the causes of beri-beri.

1947 June 17–30 The first round-the-world passenger airline service was inaugurated by Pan American Airways when the four-engine Lockheed Constellation *America* took off from La Guardia Airport, New York City. The 22,219 mile flight took 13 days, 3 hrs., 10 min., of which 101 hrs, 32 min. was actual flying time. Fare for the trip was $1,700.

1947 Oct. 3 Max [Carl Ernst Ludwig] **Planck** (b. Apr. 23, 1858), a German physicist who developed the quantum theory, died. He was professor of physics at the University of Kiel, then at the University of Berlin. He discovered that matter radiates energy in small amounts [quanta], not continuously as formerly thought. He also worked in the fields of thermodynamics, mechanics, electrical and optical problems, and heat radiation. Planck received the **Nobel prize for physics** in 1918.

1947 Oct. 14 The first piloted aircraft to fly faster than sound was flown at Muroc Air Force Base, California, by **Charles E**[lwood] **Yeager** (b. Feb. 13, 1923) of the U.S. air force. He piloted the Bell X-1 at a speed of 967 mph (Mach 1.05) at an altitude of 70,140 feet.

VI. ARTS AND LEISURE

1947 *Het Achterhus,* the diary of **Anne Frank** (June 12, 1929–Mar., 1945), a German-Jewish girl who died of typhus in the notorious Bergen-Belsen Nazi concentration camp, was published. The diary appeared in English as *The Diary of a Young Girl* (1952). As a book, and later as a play and a movie, it brought home to millions the horror of the Nazi regime. At the same time it reaffirmed the strength of the human spirit, even in a young person, to face that horror. Anne and her family, along with a number of others wanted by the Nazis, were hidden from July 9, 1942, until Aug. 4, 1944, in a warehouse in Amsterdam, the Netherlands.

1947 The first annual Edinburgh International Festival of Music and Drama was held in that Scottish city. Among the artists who appeared were: William Primrose, viola; Artur Schnabel, piano; and Joseph Szigeti, violin.

1947 Jan. 11 Eva Tanguay (b. Aug. 1, 1878), a Canadian-born American vaudeville star, died. She had a great success with such numbers as "I Don't Care" (1905) and "It's All Been Done Before, But Not the Way I Do It." Tanguay lost her health and fortune in 1929 and lived the rest of her life in obscurity.

1947 Jan. 23 Pierre Bonnard (b. Oct. 3, 1867), a French artist, died. He was a member of the **Nabis**, a group of painters who admired the work of **Paul Gauguin**. Over the course of his career Bonnard experimented with various styles and subjects. His many attractive works include *Bowl of Fruit* (1933) and *Southern Landscape* (1940).

1947 Mar. 12 Winston Churchill (b. 1871), an American author of popular historical novels, died. Three of his best-remembered novels are *Richard Carvel* (1899), *The Crisis* (1901), and *The Crossing* (1904).

1947 Apr. 7 The first **Antoinette Perry [Tony] Awards** for outstanding contributions to the American theater were awarded for the 1946 to 1947 season. Many awards were given, the main ones being: acting, **Jose Ferrer**, for *Cyrano de Bergerac*; **Frederic March**, for *Years Ago*; **Ingrid Bergman**, for *Joan of Lorraine*; **Helen Hayes**, for *Happy Birthday*; and **Patricia Neal**, for *Another Part of the Forest*. The playwright **Arthur Miller** and the director **Elie Kazan** won for *All My Sons*. The awards were named for **Antoinette Perry** (June 27, 1888–June 28, 1946), a founder of the American Theater Wing and known for assisting young stage performers.

1947 Apr. 24 Willa [Sibert] Cather (b. Dec. 7, 1876), an American novelist, died. She wrote mostly about the people of the American Midwest, where she grew up, and about the Southwest. Cather's works included *O Pioneers* (1913), *My Ántonia* (1918), and *Death Comes for the Archbishop* (1927).

1947 Nov. 30 Ernst Lubitsch (b. Jan. 28, 1892), a German-born American film director, died. In Germany he made a name for himself with the movie *Madame Du Barry* (1919). In the U.S. after 1922, Lubitsch directed a long series of sophisticated films, among them: *Lady Windermere's Fan* (1925), *Ninotchka* (1939), *The Shop Around the Corner* (1940), and *Heaven Can Wait* (1943).

VII. SPORTS, GAMES, AND SOCIETY

1947 Jan. 25 Al[phonse] Capone (b. Jan. 17, 1899), the American gangster who epitomized the crime-ridden prohibition era of the 1920s, died. Beginning his gangland career in Chicago in 1920 he became the boss of bootlegging, prostitution, and gambling by defeating rival gangs in murderous wars. Capone was never convicted of any crime of violence. In 1931, he was sent to prison for income tax evasion and served until 1939.

1947 Feb. 2 Christian Dior (Jan. 21, 1905–Oct. 24, 1957), a French fashion designer, revealed his **"New Look."** It called for narrow shoulders, an emphasized bust, a pinched waist, and a long wide skirt. Dior had salons in 15 countries by 1958.

1947 Apr. 11 [Jack Roosevelt] **Jackie Robinson** (Jan. 31, 1919–Oct. 24, 1972) became the **first black American to play in a major league baseball game** when he appeared in an exhibition contest between his team, the Brooklyn Dodgers, and the New York Yankees. Robinson's presence on the baseball diamond was the result of the determination of **Branch [Wesley] Rickey** (Dec. 20, 1881–Dec. 9, 1965), president of the Brooklyn club, to bring blacks into professional baseball.

1947 July 24 The phenomenon of the **Unidentified Flying Object [UFO]** or "flying saucer" was said to have started when a man reported a group of strange flying objects flying over Mt. Rainier in Washington state. They were said to have moved rapidly and to have glistened in the sun. From then on similar sightings and even radar contacts with UFOs became common.

1947 Aug. 29 Manuel Rodriguez y Sanchez (b. July 5, 1917), a Spanish bullfighter known as **Manolete**, died after being gored by a bull he fought on the previous day. Manolete's style was undramatic, his demeanor always calm.

1947 Nov. 20 The wedding of **Princess Elizabeth** (b. Apr. 21, 1926), heiress presumptive to the throne of Great Britain and Northern Ireland, and **Philip Mountbatten** (b. June 10, 1921), duke of Edinburgh, was celebrated in Westminster Abbey, London. Elizabeth was the elder daughter of **George VI**.

1948

I. VITAL STATISTICS AND DEMOGRAPHICS

1948 Japan initiated the **world's first modern birth control policy**—the Eugenic Protection Act—based on abortion and contraception.

II. DISASTERS

1948 Jan. 26 On **Réunion Island** in the Indian Ocean a **hurricane** killed at least 300 persons and left c.10,000 homeless.

1948 Jan. 28 Off **Okayama, Japan,** in the Inland Sea, the passenger ship *Joo Maru* **struck a mine** and c.250 persons drowned.

1948 June 11 In the **Kattegat**, off the Jutland peninsula, the Danish passenger ship *Kjoebenhavn* **struck a mine and sank** with the loss of 140 lives.

1948 June 28 **Fire in the wake of an earthquake** destroyed 70 percent of Fukui, on the Sea of Japan, with widespread damage on the remainder of Japan's Honshu Island. Deaths numbered c.3,200, with c.7,500 injured. The quake registered 7.3 on the Richter scale.

1948 Aug. 7 **Floods** in the valleys of both the **Yangtze River** [Chang Jiang] and the **Yellow River** [Huang Ho, Huang He] left an estimated 3,000,000 people homeless.

1948 Dec. It was reported that 4,727 people, of whom 3,879 were children, **died of cold and hunger in Shanghai, China**. This disaster was an indirect result of the civil war, now drawing to a close, between the Nationalists and the Communists.

1948 Dec. 3 A passenger ship *Kiangya* struck a mine and sank off Shanghai, China, with a loss of c.3,000 lives.

III. POLITICS AND WAR

1948 Jan. 4 Burma [Myanmar] became an independent republic outside the British Commonwealth. The first prime minister was **U Nu** (b. May 25, 1907), a political leader who was known as Thankin Nu before attaining the honorific U.

1948 Jan. 30 **Mohandas** [Karamchand] **Gandhi** (b. Oct. 2, 1869), known as the Mahatma [Great Soul], was assassinated in New Delhi by a Hindu fanatic who hated Gandhi because he showed compassion for Muslims as well as his fellow Hindus. An advocate of non-violence as a means of achieving political goals, Gandhi led marches, fasted, and otherwise protested against British rule. As a result he was twice imprisoned. In his work in India, Gandhi refused to own property, dressed in a loincloth and shawl, and lived a simple life.

1948 Feb. 4 The British crown colony of Ceylon [Sri Lanka] became a self-governing dominion in the Commonwealth of Nations. **Don Stephen Senanayake**, leader of the United Nation party, became its first prime minister following the 1947 elections.

1948 Feb. 11 The Fianna Fáil lost its majority in the Irish parliament, forcing **Eamon De Valera** to resign as prime minister. All the other parties then combined to elect **John A**[loysius] **Costello** (June 20, 1891–Jan. 5, 1976) prime minister.

1948 Feb. 17 **Yahya al-Mutawakkil** (b. 1869), of the Qasimid Dynasty (c.1592–1962) and imam [ruler and spiritual leader] of Yemen (from 1904), was slain in a coup led by **Sayyid Abdullah ibn-Ahmad el-Wazir**, who was proclaimed the new imam. Supporters of the heir to the throne, **Seif el-Islam Ahmed**, defeated the coup leader. Sayyid Abdullah (birth date unknown) was hanged on Apr. 8.

1948 Feb. 25 The **Communist party in Czechoslovakia** seized control of the government in a bloodless coup headed by **Klement Gottwald**, the communist premier of a government in which power was shared with democratic representatives. A Soviet-style constitution, establishing a one-party state, was adopted on May 9. **Eduard Benés**, president of Czechoslovakia, refused to sign it and resigned on June 6. Gottwald took over the presidency on June 14. Meanwhile **Jan** [Garrigue] **Masaryk** (b. Sept. 14, 1886), the foreign minister and a devoted patriot and democrat, was found dead on Mar. 10 below a third story window. The communists said he committed suicide.

1948 Mar. 1 The Costa Rican Congress overruled the results of the February election, declaring the incumbent, **Teodoro Picado Michalski** (Jan. 10,

1900–June 1, 1960), the winner. Civil war broke out, ending with a ceasefire on Apr. 13. **José Figueres Ferrer** (b. Sept. 25, 1908) assumed power (May 8) with the aid of a junta. Picado went into exile.

1948 Apr. 1 Without warning, the **Soviet Union refused to let Great Britain and the U.S.** send trains or motor vehicles **across the Russian zone of Germany to West Berlin**, the Allies' enclave in that city. The Allies on June 26 began an **airlift** to get food and fuel to the c.2,000,000 inhabitants of West Berlin. During the three-month airlift, the Allies flew more than 275,000 flights into the isolated city. In all British and American aircraft carried 2,325,000 tons of food, fuel, and other supplies into the city.

1948 Apr. 3 The so-called **Marshall Plan** became law. For the first year the act provided $5,300,000,-000 to help war-damaged nations of Europe reestablish their economies. The U.S.S.R. refused to participate, saying it was an American capitalistic scheme to control other nations, and it also did not let its satelite countries in Eastern Europe take part.

1948 Apr. 6 Finland and the Soviet Union signed a **Treaty of Friendship, Cooperation and Mutual Assistance**. By its terms, if Germany or a German ally attacked the Soviet Union through Finnish territory, the Soviet Union would give military assistance to Finland.

1948 Apr. 9 **Jorge Eliécer Gaitan** (b. Jan. 26, 1902), the leftist leader of the Liberal party of **Colombia**, was assassinated in Bogotá on Apr. 9, 1948. His death set off riots and violence that continued for a decade as a **civil war** between conflicting social and political groups.

1948 Apr. 15 **Manuel Roxas y Acuña**, the first president of the Republic of the Philippines, died. He was succeeded in office by the vice president, **Elpidio Quirino** (Nov. 16, 1890–Feb. 8, 1965).

1948 Apr. 18–19 Italy held its first general election under a new constitution. The Christian Democrats won the election over a Popular Front coalition led by the Communists. **Alcide De Gasperi** continued as premier.

1948 Apr. 19 The assembly of the Nationalist government of China reelected **Chiang Kai-Shek** as president. Three days afterward, the Communists captured Yenan [Yanan], capital of Shensi [Shanxi]

province in northern China. On Sept. 1 they proclaimed a People's Republic in the province.

1948 Apr. 30 The **Organization of American States** [OAS] was established by the 21 American republics at a conference in Bogotá, Colombia. It was the successor organization to the **Pan American Union**.

1948 May 1 A **Democratic People's Republic was proclaimed** in Soviet-occupied **North Korea**, with Pyongyang as the capital. An election for a national assembly was held (Aug. 25) with only a single slate of candidates. **Kim Il Sung** (b. Apr 15, 1912) was elected premier.

1948 May 10 United Nations-sponsored elections were held in **South Korea**. The new assembly adopted (July 12) a constitution and elected (July 20) **Syngman Rhee** (Apr. 26, 1875–July 19, 1965) president. The **Republic of Korea**, with Seoul as its capital, was proclaimed on Aug. 15.

1948 May 15 The **state of Israel was proclaimed** by Jewish leaders in Palestine as soon as the British trusteeship ended at midnight (May 14) and the **partition of Palestine** by the **United Nations** became effective. The U.S. recognized the new nation the next day and the U.S.S.R. followed on May 17. On May 16 the armies of **Egypt, Iraq, Lebanon, Syria, and Trans-Jordan** [present Jordan] **attacked Israel**. The Israelis not only held on to their territory but also the New City area of Jerusalem. On May 28, however, they surrendered the Old City of Jerusalem to the Jordanians. The United Nations, with **Folke Bernadotte** as its mediator, arranged a truce effective June 11 and a second truce on July 17. Bernadotte (b. Jan. 1, 1895) was assassinated on Sept. 17 by Jewish extremists of the Stern Gang. He was a Swedish official who was active in the Red Cross and in asssisting prisoners in World War II. He was succeeded by **Ralph** [Johnson] **Bunche** (Aug. 7, 1904–Dec. 9, 1971), an American official of the UN. Previously Bunche had been the first black to head a division of the U.S. department of state. Beginning in mid-October **Israel and Egypt fought for control of the Negev**, a desert region now in southern Israel, with Israel gaining the upper hand. By Dec. 31 Israel was in control of the region. Egypt occupied the Gaza Strip, a coastal area in southwestern Palestine. Trans-Jordan forces held on to territory west of the Jordan River known as the West Bank, and later annexed it. This region was intended to be part of a Palestinian Arab state, according to the UN partition plan. Bunche was finally able on Jan. 7, 1949, to arrange a ceasefire that held. For his efforts Bunche received the **Nobel Peace Prize** in 1950. Israel ended up with more territory than was allotted to it by the UN, and c.700,000 Palestinian Arabs left the area, mostly for refugee camps, including settlements in the Gaza Strip. The Israeli government was headed by **Chaim Weizmann** as president (1948–1952) and **David Ben-Gurion** as prime minister (1948–1953). Weizmann was a chemist of note and president of the **World Zionist Organization** (1920–1931, 1935–1946). Ben-Gurion, born in Poland, settled in Palestine in 1906. He led the political resistance to Great Britain's efforts to discourage Jewish independence and immigration to Palestine.

1948 May 26   The Nationalist party in **South Africa**, favoring segregation, in elections for the national assembly defeated **Jan C. Smuts**'s coalition of the United and Labour parties. **Daniel F. Malan** (May 22, 1874–Feb. 7, 1959) formed a government and remained prime minister until 1954. His government speeded up the trend toward the system that came to be called **apartheid**.

1948 July 15   **John J**[oseph] **Pershing** (b. Sept. 13, 1860), commander of the American Expeditionary Force [AEF] in World War I, died. He also served in the Spanish-American War (1898); in the campaign against the Moros, Filipino Muslim insurgents (1899–1903); and in the pursuit of the Mexican revolutionary, **Francisco Villa**, into Mexico (1916–1917).

1948 Sept. 4   **Wilhelmina**, queen of the Netherlands (from 1890), abdicated and was succeeded (to 1980) by her daughter **Juliana** (b. Apr. 30, 1909). In World War I Wilhelmina's efforts helped protect her nation's neutrality. In World War II she and her government were forced to flee to London in the face of the Nazi invasion (1940). She returned in May, 1945.

1948 Sept. 11   **Mohammed Ali Jinnah** (b. Dec. 25, 1876) died and was succeeded as governor-general of Pakistan by **Khwaja** [Khawaja] **Nazimuddin** (July 19, 1894–Oct. 22, 1964), premier of East Pakistan.

1948 Sept. 12   Indian troops invaded the state of **Hyderabad** in central southern India. The state was ruled by a Muslim prince [nizam] although the population was more than 86 percent Hindu. In a plebiscite the populace approved the takeover by India. Hyderabad was partitioned (1956) among four other Indian states.

1948 Oct. 10   **Carlos Prío Socarrás** (July 14, 1903–Apr. 5, 1977) was inaugurated as president of Cuba. He succeeded **Ramón Grau San Martín** (1889–July 28, 1969), who had been president from 1944.

1948 Nov. 2   Puerto Ricans, in their first election, chose as governor **Luis Muñoz Marín** (Feb. 18, 1898–Apr. 30, 1980) of the Popular Democratic party.

1948 Nov. 12   At the War Crimes Trials in Tokyo, Japan, the Allied tribunal found **Hideki Tojo** (b. 1884), extreme militarist and former prime minister (1941–1944), and six colleagues guilty of wartime crimes, and they were hanged on Dec. 23, 1948.

1948 Nov. 15   **William Lyon Mackenzie King**, Liberal party prime minister of Canada from Oct. 23, 1935, resigned. He had led his party to three consecutive election victories, beginning on Oct. 14, 1935, and ending on June 11, 1945. King was succeeded by **Louis S**[tephen] **St. Laurent** (Feb. 1, 1882–July 24, 1973), a member of Parliament and of the cabinet since 1942. His administration was active in passing legislation concerning social insurance, educational facilities, and cultural affairs.

1948 Nov. 23   **Romulo Gallegos** (Aug. 2, 1884–Apr. 4, 1969), the president of Venezuela, was overthrown by reactionary army officers. He had been inaugurated on Feb. 15, having run in the election as the candidate of the left of center Acción Democrática party. The election was the first in **Venezuela** that allowed a direct popular vote for president as provided in the constitution of 1947.

1948 Dec. 10   The General Assembly of the **United Nations** adopted the **Universal Declaration of Human Rights**. Its basic philosophy was stated in Article I: "All human beings are born free and equal in dignity and rights. They are endowed with reason and conscience and should act toward one another in a spirit of brotherhood."

1948 Dec. 14   The government of **El Salvador** under **Castañeda Castro** (Aug. 6, 1888–Mar. 5, 1965) was overthrown by a military coup. The junta that took control ran the country along moderately liberal lines.

1948 Dec. 28   **Nokrashy Pasha** (b. 1888), the prime minister of Egypt (from Dec. 9, 1946) was assassinated by a member of the Muslim Brotherhood, an outlawed organization of extreme nationalists. The defeat of Egypt by Israel triggered the assassination.

IV. ECONOMY AND TRADE

1948 Jan. 1 The **General Agreement on Tariffs and Trade** [GATT] was established as a specialized agency of the **United Nations**. The original membership consisted of 21 countries, but eventually it was expanded to include most of the countries of the non-communist world that were involved to any important degree in foreign trade. Member nations agreed to try to reduce barriers to international trade, such as import quotas and discriminatory treatment of one nation compared with another.

1948 Jan. 1 A **customs union among Belgium, Luxembourg, and the Netherlands** went into effect.

1948 Apr. 1 The **British Electricity Authority** was established to take over all electricity production in Britain, including that which had previously been private.

1948 May 2 **Wilhelm von Opel** (b. May 5, 1871), a German automobile manufacturer, died. His company produced more than 1,000,000 autos. He remained chairman of his company until 1946 when the victorious Allies of World War II forced him to resign because he was a member of the Nazi party.

1948 May 25 **General Motors Corporation and the United Automobile Workers union** signed a contract that provided for a **sliding wage scale**. Wages were to be adjusted in relation to the cost of living index.

V. RELIGION AND PHILOSOPHY

1948 Aug. 23 The **World Council of Churches**, an international organization of Protestant and Orthodox Eastern churches, was established at a conference in Amsterdam, the Netherlands. Representatives of 147 church groups from 44 countries were present, including such ancient churches as the Coptic Church of Egypt and such new ones as the Church of South India.

1948 Dec. 27 **József Cardinal Mindszenty** [nee József Pehm] (Mar. 29, 1892–June 6, 1975), the Roman Catholic primate of Hungary and a long-time opponent of totalitarian governments, was arrested by the communist government of Hungary because he had refused to accept the nationalization of Roman

Catholic schools. He was charged with treason and black market dealings in currency. At first tried and sentenced to death, he confessed guilt after being tortured and drugged, was retried, found guilty, and sentenced to life imprisonment on Feb. 8, 1949.

VI. SCIENCE, EDUCATION, AND TECHNOLOGY

1948 The **steady state theory of the universe** was proposed by three astronomers: **Hermann Bondi** (b. Nov. 1, 1919) and **Thomas Gold** (b. May 22, 1920) of Austria, and **Fred Hoyle** (b. June 24, 1915) of Great Britain. This theory said that the universe has no beginning and no end. It agreed that the universe is continually expanding but maintained matter is also continually being created so that its density remains the same.

1948 *Cybernetics, or Control and Communication in Man and the Machine* by **Norbert Wiener** (Nov. 26, 1894–Mar. 18, 1964), an American mathematician, was published. It was the first major analysis of the science of **cybernetics**, a term Wiener coined, to describe the problems of control and communication systems in both human beings and machines.

1948 The **transistor**, an electronic device that replaced the vacuum tube in computers and calculators, was invented by three American physicists working at the Bell Telephone Laboratories in New Jersey: **John Bardeen** (b. May 23, 1908), **Walter H**[ouser] **Brattain** (b. Feb. 10, 1902), and **William Bradford Shockley** (Feb. 13, 1910–Aug. 12, 1989). The three scientists received the **Nobel prize for physics** in 1956.

1948 An improved theory of quantum dynamics was developed by **Richard** [Phillips] **Feynman** (May 11, 1918–Feb. 15, 1988), an American physicist. Working independently, two other physicists also developed this theory: **Seymour Schwinger** (b. Feb. 12, 1918), an American, and **Shin'ichiro Tomonaga** (Mar. 31, 1906–July 8, 1979), a Japanese. Feynman's theory aided scientists in predicting the effect of electrically charged particles on one another. For their work the three shared the **Nobel prize for physics** in 1965.

1948 The Polaroid Land Camera, the **first camera to develop and print photos within itself**, went on sale. It was the invention of Edwin H[erbert] Land

(b. May 7, 1909), an American physicist and inventor.

1948 Research begun in 1941 by **Edward Kendall** (Mar. 8, 1886–May 4, 1972), and **Philip Showalter Hench** (Feb. 28, 1896–Mar. 30, 1965) demonstrated the therapeutic value of **cortisone**, a steroid hormone. It has proven an effective treatment for rheumatoid arthritis and other diseases.

1948 Mar. 2 A[braham] A[rden] **Brill** (b. Oct. 12, 1874), an Austrian-born American psychiatrist, died. After studying in Switzerland he moved (1908) to the U.S., where he pioneered in advancing the practice of psychoanalysis. Brill wrote *Fundamental Conceptions of Psychoanalysis* (1921).

1948 Apr. 7 The **World Health Organization** [WHO], a specialized agency of the United Nations, began operations. Its stated purpose was "the attainment by all peoples of the highest possible level of health."

1948 Apr. 15 Merck & Company, an American pharmaceutical concern, announced that a team of scientists headed by **Karl August Folkers** (b. Sept. 1, 1906) had isolated **vitamin B-12**. This vitamin is now a specific for treating anemia.

1948 June 21 The **long playing** [LP] **recording disc** was demonstrated for the first time. It was invented by **Peter C[arl] Goldmark** (Dec. 2, 1906–Dec. 7, 1977), a Hungarian-born American engineer employed by the CBS Laboratories.

1948 July 5 Britain's **National Health Service** began operation. The **National Insurance Act** took effect at the same time, providing insurance against sickness and unemployment and establishing old age pensions.

1948 Sept. **Brandeis University**, a nonsectarian, Jewish-sponsored, liberal arts institution of higher learning in Waltham, Massachusetts, opened its doors to 106 students and a faculty of 13.

1948 Sept. 17 **Ruth** [Fulton] **Benedict** (b. June 5, 1887), an American anthropologist, died. In her fieldwork she studied a number of American Indian tribes. Her broader interest was in the study of the phenomenon of culture, as applied to national and other groups, a concept she did much to develop. Among Benedict's books were *Patterns of Culture*

(1934), *Race: Science and Politics* (rev. ed. 1943), and *The Crysanthemum and the Sword* (1946).

VII. ARTS AND LEISURE

1948 **Willem de Kooning** (b. Apr. 24, 1904), a Dutch-American painter, had his first one-man exhibition at the Charles Egan Gallery in New York City. He became a leading figure in the 1940s among the abstract expressionists. Typical of his paintings were *Black Friday* (1948), *Woman I* (1952), *Two Women in the Country* (1954), and *Untitled III* (1980).

1948 **Norman Mailer** (b. Jan. 31, 1923), an American writer, published *The Naked and the Dead,* quickly hailed as the first outstanding novel of World War II as experienced by U.S. fighting men.

1948 **Giacomo Manzù** (b. Dec. 22, 1908), an Italian sculptor, won the first prize for sculpture at the Venice Biennale.

1948 Jan. 8 **Kurt Schwitters** (b. June 20, 1887), a German artist, died. Influenced first by dadaism, he went further and devised what he called **merz**, in which pictures consisted of materials of all sorts, rather than forms and paint. After 1940 Schwitters lived in England, where he created collages out of odds and ends.

1948 Jan. 21 **Ermanno Wolf-Ferrari** (b. Jan. 12, 1876), a composer of Italian and German parentage, died. He composed 12 operas, most of which were first produced in Germany. Wolf-Ferrari's best-known work was *Il segreto di Susanna* [*The Secret of Suzann*] (1909).

1948 Feb. 11 **Sergei Mikhailovich Eisenstein** (b. Jan. 23, 1898), Russia's famous film director, died. After 1917, Eisenstein entered the theatrical world in Moscow, first as a scene designer and then as a director. He directed his first film in 1925, *Stachka* [*Strike*] and his next *Bronenosets Potemkin* [*The Battleship Potemkin*], also in 1925, about the failed revolution of 1905. Although Eisenstein's work began to be criticized by the communist authorities, he was appointed to direct *Alexander Nevksy* (1938), a patriotic epic about the defeat of Teutonic invaders. His last film was *Ivan Groznyi* [*Ivan the Terrible*], of which the first part, completed in 1944, met with **Joseph Stalin**'s approval. He began work on part II but was accused of distorting history and fell out of favor. As a result this second part was not shown until five years after Stalin died. A planned third part was never filmed.

1948 Apr. 24   Manuel [Maria] **Ponce** (b. Dec. 8, 1882), a Mexican composer, died. He was a teacher at the Mexico City Conservatory (1909–1945) as well as a composer. Ponce's most interesting compositions were his pieces for the guitar, including *Concierto del sur* [*Concerto of the South*] (1941).

1948 May 23   Claude McKay (b. Sept. 15, 1890), an American poet and novelist, born in Jamaica, died. His poetry included *Songs of Jamaica* (1912). His *Home to Harlem* (1928), the story of a black soldier returning from World War I (1914–1918), made McKay the first black author to write a bestseller. McKay was a leader of the Harlem Renaissance and also was involved for a time in radical political agitation.

1948 July 5   Georges Bernanos (b. Feb. 20, 1888), a French novelist and writer on politics and morals, died. From 1926, with the publication of the novel, *Sous le soleil de Satan* [*The Star of Satan*], he was an important figure in the French literary world, noted especially for the novel *Journal d'un curé de campagne* [**The Diary of a Country Priest**] (1936).

1948 July 21   Arshile Gorky [orig.: Vosdanig Adoian] (b. Apr. 15, 1895), an Armenian-born American painter, committed suicide. In the early 1940s, he became a pioneer of abstract expressionism. His paintings include *How My Mother's Embroidered Apron Unfolds in My Life* (1944), *Diary of a Seducer* (1945), and *The Betrothal II* (1947).

1948 July 23   D[avid] **W**[ark] **Griffith** (b. Jan. 23, 1875), a pioneer American movie director, died. The first movie he directed, *The Adventures of Dolly* (1908), was a typical one-reel melodrama of its day. Griffith soon developed new vistas for the movies: the shot as the basic element rather than the scene as in the theater; the close-up; and a more natural style of acting. Griffith produced numerous films but is remembered chiefly for two. *The Birth of a Nation* (1915) remains a landmark of the American cinema although it has rightly been criticized for its racist portrayal of blacks. The other major film was *Intolerance* (1916), which was not a success.

1948 Sept. 1   Charles A[ustin] **Beard** (b. Nov. 27, 1874), an American historian, died. A university pro-

fessor and a prolific writer on American history, he concentrated on what he saw as an all-important connection between economic interests and politics. This was revealed most clearly in *An Economic Interpretation of the Constitution* (1913), with its thesis that the U.S. Constitution reflected chiefly the conservatism and wealth of the men who drafted it. To the general reader Beard was best known for *The Rise of American Civilization* (1927), written in collaboration with his wife, **Mary Ritter Beard** (Aug. 5, 1876–Aug. 14, 1958), also a historian.

1948 Oct. 24   Franz Lehar (b. Apr. 30, 1870), a Hungarian-born Austrian composer, died. His operettas were internationally successful. The first was *Die lustige Witwe* [*The Merry Widow*] (1905), still performed in the late 20th century.

VIII. SPORTS, GAMES, AND SOCIETY

1948 Jan. 30–Feb. 8   The fifth Winter Olympic Games, the first since 1936 because of World War II, were held at St. Moritz, Switzerland. Participating were 713 athletes from 28 countries. Sweden and Norway each won four gold medals and ten medals overall.

1948 June 12   The Triple Crown of American thoroughbred racing was won for the eighth time when **Citation** took the Belmont Stakes. Citation won the Kentucky Derby on May 1 and the Preakness Stakes on May 15. **Eddie Arcaro** was the jockey, becoming the first to ride two Triple Crown winners.

1948 July 29–Aug. 14   The 14th Summer Olympic Games, the first since 1936 because of World War II, were held in London, England, with 4,099 athletes from 59 countries taking part. The U.S. won 38 gold medals and 84 in all. Sweden was second with 16 and 43, and France third with 10 and 29.

1948 Aug. 16   [George Herman] Babe Ruth (b. Feb. 6, 1895), generally considered America's greatest baseball player, died. Ruth began his career in Boston as a pitcher of unusual ability but, because of his talents as a hitter, was made into an outfielder. Sold to the **New York Yankees** in 1920, he played all except his final year, 1934, with them. In 1927 he hit 60 home runs, a record not broken until 1961. His career total of 714 homers was not exceeded until 1974. Ruth in 1936 became the second person elected to the Baseball Hall of Fame.

1948 Dec. 15 **Alger Hiss** (b. Nov. 11, 1904), a former U.S. Department of State official and since 1947 president of the Carnegie Endowment for International Peace, was indicted by a federal grand jury on two counts of perjury. The indictment grew out of charges made in Aug., 1948, by **Whittaker Chambers** (Apr. 1, 1901–June 9, 1961), a magazine editor, that

Hiss helped him transmit confidential government documents to the Soviet Union. His trial began on May 31, 1949, and ended on July 8 with a deadlocked jury. Hiss went on trial again on Nov. 17 and on Jan. 21, 1950, he was found guilty. He was sentenced to five years in prison but was released in Nov., 1954.

1949

I. DISASTERS

1949 Feb. 12 In Quito, Ecuador, a **radio broadcast of** a dramatization of H.G. Wells' *War of the Worlds* frightened people to such an extent that when it was learned the story was fictional a mob stormed the radio station and the offices of the city's leading newspaper. In the melee 20 persons were killed and the damage done to property was estimated at $350,-000.

1949 Aug. 5–7 **Earthquakes in central Ecuador** destroyed four towns and damaged many others over about a 1,500-square-mile area. About 8,000 persons were killed, c.100,000 left homeless, and $86,000,000 of damage done. The quake registered 6.8 on the Richter scale.

1949 Sept. 4 **Chungking** [Chongqing], on the Yangtze [Chang Jiang] in Szechuan [Sichuan] province in southern China, was **swept by fire**, killing c.1,700 persons and leaving c.100,000 homeless.

1949 Sept. 17 The Canadian cruise ship *Noronic* **burned** while docked overnight in Toronto. Of the 512 passenges and 170 crew members, 170 died by the fire or by drowning.

1949 Oct. 22 More than 200 people died as the **Danzig** [Gdansk]-**Warsaw express jumped the tracks** near Nowy Dwor, in northern Poland.

1949 Nov. 1 Over the National Airport in Washington, D.C., a U.S. air force P-38 **fighter plane and an Eastern Airlines passenger plane collided**, killing 55 persons. Only the fighter pilot survived.

II. POLITICS AND WAR

1949 Jan. 1 **Juan Manuel Galvez** was inaugurated as president of Honduras. He succeeded **Tiburcio**

Carías Andino (1876–Dec. 23, 1969), president from 1933.

1949 Jan. 20 **Harry S Truman** was inaugurated as president of the U.S., having won the election of Nov. 2, 1948, in a major upset. His opponent was **Thomas E. Dewey**, Republican. Truman, on the Democratic ticket, received 24,104,836 popular votes and 303 electoral votes. Dewey received 21,969,500 and 189. **Alben W**[illiam] **Barkley** (Nov. 24, 1877–Apr. 30, 1956) was inaugurated as vice president.

1949 Jan. 25 In the **first election for the Israeli Knesset** [parliament] the winner was the Mapai party, moderately socialistic, which won 44 seats of the total of 120. The Mapam party of socialists further to the left, won 18 seats. Joined by some smaller religious parties, the Mapai formed a government with its leader **David Ben-Gurion** continuing as prime minister. **Chaim Weizmann** was reelected president on Feb. 17 by the Knesset. Israel was admitted to the United Nations on May 11. Israel proclaimed (Dec. 14) its capital to be **Jerusalem** [the New City section].

1949 Feb. 17 **Niceto Alcalá Zamora** y Torres (b. July 6, 1877), a Spanish statesman, died. He served in various positions under the monarchy, but in 1930 he became a republican and was put in jail for his political activities. The next year he was a leader of the revolution that ousted **Alfonso XIII** and he was provisional president of the new republic from April until October. Alcalá Zamora then became president (1931–1936) of the constitutional republic.

1949 Mar. 8 An agreement between the French government and **Bao Dai** [orig.: Nguyen Vinh Thuy] (b. Oct. 22, 1913), the former emperor of Annam (1926–1945), **recognized the independence of Vietnam** within the French Union. The new nation, comprising Annam, Cochin China, and Tonkin, was proclaimed on July 1 in Saigon with Bao Dai as chief of state (1949–1955).

1949 Mar. 30–Dec. 28 Shukri al-Kuwatli (1891–June 30, 1967), president of Syria (from 1943), was overthrown in a military coup led by **Husni al-Zayim** (b. 1897), who was elected president (June 25) but was killed in another army coup on Aug. 14, 1949. On Dec. 19 **Adib al-Shiskakli** [Odib Shiehekly] (1909–Sept. 27, 1964) came to power, but on Dec. 28 **Khalid el-Azam** (1903–Feb. 18, 1965) became president.

1949 Mar. 31   Newfoundland joined the Canadian confederation, becoming Canada's tenth province.

1949 Apr. 4   The **North Atlantic Treaty**, which established (Aug. 24) the **North Atlantic Treaty Organization** [NATO], was signed in Washington, D.C., by Belgium, Canada, Denmark, France, Great Britain, Iceland, Italy, Luxembourg, the Netherlands, Norway, Portugal, and the U.S. Greece and Turkey joined in 1952. West Germany signed in 1955, Spain in 1982. France withdrew from NATO in 1966 but remained committed to assist in the defense of Western Europe.

1949 Apr. 18   The **Republic of Ireland** proclaimed its independence and left the Commonwealth of Nations. The **Ireland Act** was recognized on May 17 by Great Britain which, however, reasserted **Northern Ireland**'s status in the United Kingdom.

1949 May 5   The **Council of Europe** was formed, at first, with ten nations and finally with 22. The object of the council is "to achieve a greater unity among its members for the purpose of safeguarding and realizing the ideals and principles which are their common heritage and facilitating their economic and social progress."

1949 May 9   Louis II (b. July 12, 1870), prince and ruler (1922–1949) of the principality of Monaco, died. He was succeeded by his grandson, **Rainier III** (b. May 23, 1923), who became the 30th ruler of this 370-acre principality on the Mediterranean Sea.

1949 May 21   The **Federal Republic of Germany** [West Germany] was established. Representatives of France, Great Britain, and the U.S., and German political leaders signed (Apr. 25) a constitution for the new republic. In an election (Aug. 14) the Chris-

tian Democratic party and its ally, the Christian Social Union, centered in Bavaria, won a plurality in the Bundestag [parliament]. **Konrad Adenauer** was named the first chancellor (1949–1963). **Theodor Heuss** (Jan. 31, 1884–Dec. 12, 1963) was elected the first president (1949–1959).

1949 June 2   Transjordan became the **Hashemite Kingdom of Jordan**, named after the Hashemite [Hashimid] Dynasty (from 1921) of Transjordan. The change in name reflected the acquisition of the West Bank, an area of Palestine west of the Jordan River, in the Arab-Israeli War (1948). This region, c.2,165 square miles in extent, was intended by the United Nations to be part of a new independent state for the Palestinian Arabs. In Dec., 1949, **Jordan reached an armistice agreement with Israel** and formally annexed the West Bank in early 1950.

1949 June 30   American forces left South Korea, except for 500 men of a military advisory group.

1949 July 12   Douglas Hyde (b. Jan. 17, 1880), an Irish politician and author, died. He was the first president (1938–1945) of independent Ireland [then Eire]. The first president of the Gaelic League (1893–1915), Hyde was also a well-known author whose pen name was **An Craiobhin Aoibhinn** [the Fair Branch]. He wrote histories, plays, and verse. Among his works were *Songs of Connacht* (1893), *Literary History of Ireland* (1899), and *Legends of Saints and Sinners*. (1915).

1949 Oct. 1   The **People's Republic of China** was proclaimed in Peking by the victorious Communists who this year completed the defeat of the forces of **Chiang Kai-Shek** and the Nationalist [Kuo-mintang] government. **Mao Tse-Tung**, chairman of the Communist party, became the head of government. **Chou En-Lai** (1898–Jan. 8, 1976) became premier (1949–1976) and foreign minister (1949–1958). On Dec. 8 Chiang, with his followers and the remnants of the Nationalist army, moved to Taiwan [formerly Formosa] where they established the Republic of China.

1949 Oct. 7   The **German Democratic Republic** [East Germany] was established, in the Russian occupation zone of Germany. The government was under the control of the Socialist Unity party [SED], a communist organization. **Wilhelm Pieck** (Jan. 3, 1876–Sept. 7, 1960) was elected president (1949–1960). **Otto Grotewohl** (Mar. 11, 1894–Sept. 21, 1964) became the first prime minister.

1949 Oct. 16   The **Greek civil war**, ongoing sporadically since 1943, **ended** when the communist-led rebels announced they were ending their efforts to overthrow the government.

1949 Nov. 8   An agreement was signed between the French government and Cambodian leaders making **Cambodia an independent nation** within the French Union.

1949 Nov. 26   In India on Jan. 23, 1950, **Rajendra Prasad** (Dec. 3, 1884–Feb. 28, 1963) was elected first president of the federal republic and was inaugurated three days later. Prasad was a follower of **Mahatma Gandhi** and his non-violent resistance movement and later served as president of the Congress party (1934, 1939, 1947).

1949 Dec. 10   In a general election in Australia the Labor party was defeated by the combined Liberal and Country parties. **Robert Gordon Menzies** (Dec. 20, 1894–May 14, 1978), leader of the Liberal party and previously prime minister (1939–1941) assumed that office again (to 1966).

1949 Dec. 27   The **Federal Republic of Indonesia was proclaimed** with **Achmed Sukarno** as the first president. Independence came after four years of warfare with the Dutch, who refused until this year to grant independence in spite of pressure put on them by the United Nations.

III. ECONOMY AND TRADE

1949 Jan. 1   The **Council for Mutual Economic Aid** [COMECON], with headquarters in Moscow, was formed by the U.S.S.R. and five satellite nations in Eastern Europe. Other nations have joined since then, but the membership has fluctuated. COMECON's stated purpose was to encourage trade and research among its members and to coordinate industrial production and economic development.

1949 June   Measures to strengthen **apartheid** were taken in **South Africa**. The **Citizenship Act** made it more difficult for newcomers to achieve citizenship. The **Mixed Marriages Act** made all marriages between whites and others illegal. Race relations and conditions among blacks steadily worsened.

1949 July 20   The **Housing Act** of 1949, signed into law by **Harry S Truman** today, financed slum clear-

ance, the building of publicly owned housing in cities, and similar aid for rural areas.

1949 Sept. 18   **Great Britain devalued the pound sterling** from its official rate of $4.03 to $2.80 in an attempt to increase British exports and reverse the foreign trade deficit. Britain came out of World War II with a run-down industrial establishment and an enormous government debt. Most European nations followed England's example and devalued their currencies also.

IV. RELIGION AND PHILOSOPHY

1949   [William Franklin] **Billy Graham** (b. Nov. 7, 1918), an American Protestant evangelist, first attracted national attention when he staged a revival in Los Angeles for the Youth for Christ International movement. His preaching drew c.2,000 persons on opening night and the nightly number grew steadily, reaching c.6,000. His three-week "crusade" was extended to eight and by the end c.4,000 "decisions for Christ" were reported.

1949 June 19   **Josef Beran** (1888–May 17, 1969), the Roman Catholic archbishop of Prague and primate of Czechoslovakia, was seized by Czech authorities as he preached and was made a prisoner (to 1965) in his own residence. He was guilty of opposing attempts of the communist government to control the church. In February negotiations had broken down when the government tried to destroy the political influence of the formerly strong Catholic Social Democratic party. The government established (June 9) a Catholic Action Committee, to which some priests and lay Catholics adhered, but which Beran at once denounced.

1949 Oct. 1   The **People's Republic of China was proclaimed**, initiating many communist-style reforms. Included among these was the confiscation and nationalization of all schools, colleges, and hospitals operated by western foreign mission societies. A subservient indigenous Christian church was tolerated.

V. SCIENCE, EDUCATION, AND TECHNOLOGY

1949   **Philip** [Cortelyou] **Johnson** (b. July 8, 1906), an American architect, designed and built for himself at New Canaan, Connecticut, a house consisting mostly of glass. The principal section featured all glass walls. It was a unique architectural creation whose effect was one of austerity rather than glitter.

1949 Feb. 27–Mar. 2 The **first non-stop flight around the world** was made by a U.S. air force B-50 Superfortress bomber, carrying a crew of 13. Named *Lucky Lady II*, the plane departed from and returned to Carswell Air Force Base, Texas, in 94 hrs., 1 min. It traveled 23,452 miles and was refueled four times in flight.

1949 Mar. 30 **Friedrich Karl Bergius** (b. Oct. 11, 1884), a German chemist, died. In 1913 he developed a process for producing gasoline from coal. He also found a method for making sugar from wood. In 1931 Bergius shared the **Nobel prize for chemistry** both for his work in general and for inventing high-pressure methods of chemical production.

1949 May 1 **Frederic Stanley Kipping** (b. Aug. 16, 1863), an English chemist, died. His research over a number of years made possible the development of silicones, polymers produced from silicon and oxygen.

1949 July 27 The **first jet-propelled passenger airplane**, the British de Haviland Comet, was rolled out. It could fly at a speed approaching 500 mph at an altitude of 36,000 to 40,000 ft. Commercial airlines ordered 16 of the craft, but the Comet did not go into regular service until 1952.

1949 Sept. 13 **Schack August Steenberg Krogh** (b. Nov. 15, 1874), a Danish physiologist, died. For his discovery of the regulation of the motor mechanism of the capillaries, he received the **Nobel prize for physiology or medicine** in 1920.

1949 Sept. 23 **Harry S Truman** announced that the **U.S.S.R.** was known to have **tested its first nuclear bomb**. It was believed the test occurred about Sept. 1, but it was unclear whether the U.S. learned of it by espionage or by scientific means, such as the use of seismographs or geiger counters. This was the ninth such device to be exploded, the other eight having been American, and it meant that the U.S. monopoly on such weaponry was at an end. A short time later, Truman ordered work to proceed on the **development of a hydrogen** [thermonuclear, or fusion] **bomb** of still greater destructive power than the atomic, or fission, bomb.

VI. ARTS AND LEISURE

1949 A terrifying novel of life under a future totalitarian regime, *1984*, was published by **George Orwell**, an English author. In it the official language was Newspeak, and Doublethink was the way minds were required to work so that the past could be modified at will to reflect what the authorities wished it to and so that slogans such as "Freedom is Slavery" were accepted by the masses. Although never seen, the all-powerful head of the state was known as Big Brother. The hero of the novel was finally broken by the Thought Police.

1949 May 6 **Maurice Maeterlinck** (b. Aug. 29, 1862), a Belgian dramatist and poet, died. Maeterlinck's plays included *Pelléas and Melisande* (1892), *L'Oiseau bleu* [*The Bluebird*] (1909), and *La Mort* (1913). Maeterlinck was awarded the **Nobel prize for literature** in 1911.

1949 June 10 **Sigrid Undset** (b. May 20, 1882), a Norwegian novelist born in Denmark, died. Her trilogy **Kristin Lavransdatter** (1920–1922), a tale of medieval Scandinavia, has been cited as one of the greatest historical novels. Among her novels were *Olaf Audunsson* (1925–1927), *The Axe* (1928), *The Snake Pit* (1929), *In the Wilderness* (1929), and *The Burning Bush* (1932). Undset was awarded the **Nobel prize for literature** in 1928.

1949 July An **All-China Conference** of the representatives of Literary and Art Workers was held at Peking and asserted the need for **art and literature to be used to strengthen socialism**. Under the new communist regime **Marxist ideology was to be taught in all schools**. In December plans were announced for a People's University.

1949 Aug. 17 **Margaret Mitchell** (b. Nov. 4, 1900), an American author, died as a result of injuries received in a traffic accident in her native Atlanta, Georgia. Her novel *Gone with the Wind* (1936), a romantic tale of the South during the American Civil War, almost immediately became one of the bestselling works of fiction of all time and by 1941 was translated into 18 other languages, of which the German edition was the most popular. Altogether it has sold more than 20 million copies in 27 languages. In 1939 the novel, the only one the author ever wrote, was made into a lavish movie that like the book has never lost its popularity.

1949 Sept. 6   Lucien Descaves (b. Mar. 18, 1861), a French novelist and critic, died. His writings were replete with observations on everyday life and his sympathies for people in humble walks of life was clear. His novels and short stories included *Une Vieille Rate* (1883); *Misères du sabre* (1887) and *Sous-Offs* (1889), both of these being rough satires of army life, with which Descaves was familiar; *La Colonne* (1902), set in the time of the Commune; and *Barabbas* (1914).

1949 Sept. 7   José Clemente Orozco (b. Nov. 23, 1883), a Mexican artist known for his murals offering passionate socialistic content, died. In their time he and **Diego Rivera** were the leaders of a renaissance of Mexican art. Orozco's first controversial murals were done in Mexico, including **The Rich Banquet While the Workers Quarrel** (1923–1924). Orozco lived in the U.S. from 1927 to 1934. His work while there included *Prometheus* (1930) at Pomona College, Claremont, California; a series (1931) for the New School for Social Research in New York City; and *Epic of Culture in the New World* (1932–1934) at Dartmouth College, Hanover, New Hampshire. Returning to Mexico, he painted murals for a number of government buildings. One of his most notable works, *Allegory of Mexico*, was begun in 1940 at the Gabino Oritz Library in Jiquilpán, southwestern Mexico.

1949 Sept. 8   Richard [Georg] **Strauss** (b. June 11, 1864), a German composer and conductor, died. Strauss wrote 15 operas as well as symphonies, ballets, and other compositions, including c.200 songs. Among his operas were *Salome* (1905), based on **Oscar Wilde**'s play and controversial as being lewd and blasphemous; *Elektra* (1909), which like *Salome* forced female singers to dramatic extremes; *Der Rosenkavalier* (1911), his most popular work, which combined comedy and Viennese waltzes; and *Ariadne auf Naxos* (1912). Among Strauss's tone poems were *Don Juan* (1889), his first major success; *Till Eulenspiegel* (1895); *Also Spake Zarathustra* (1896); and *Don Quixote* (1898), the masterpiece of his tone poems.

1949 Oct. 20   Jacques Copeau (b. Feb. 4, 1878), a French theatrical producer and actor, died. In 1913 he opened his own theater, the Vieux-Colombier, to offset what he saw as too much realism on the French stage. In his theater he staged both outstanding productions of Shakespeare's plays and the works of young playwrights. From 1936 to 1941 he was a producer for the Comédie Française.

1949 Oct. 31   Édouard Dujardin (b. Nov. 10, 1861), a French author, died. His novel *Les Lauriers son coupés* [*We'll to the Woods No More*] (1888) is now usually considered the first fictional work to employ the stream of consciousness technique. The thoughts and feelings of the protagonist, in this case a young man named Daniel Prince, are given as though at a preverbal level, without intervention by the author. **James Joyce** was said to have been influenced by Dujardin's book in the writing of *Ulysses* (1922). Dujardin, who was associated with the symbolists, wrote plays and poetry as well as novels. Among his works are *Le Délassement du Guerrier* (poetry, 1904), and *Le Mystere du Dieu mort et ressuscité* (drama, 1923).

1949 Dec. 28   [William] **Hervey Allen** (b. Dec. 8, 1889), an American novelist, poet, and biographer, died. He was best known to the general public for his picaresque novel *Anthony Adverse* (1933), with its setting in the Napoleonic era. In the field of literary studies his biography of Edgar Allan Poe, *Israfel* (1926), is still highly regarded.

VII. SPORTS, GAMES, AND SOCIETY

1949   A new card game called **canasta**, based on the older game of rummy, became a craze in the U.S. It was played for the first time the year before in Argentina and Uruguay. By the end of 1949 there were said to be c.10,000,000 players in the U.S., and 24 books were already written about how to play it.

1949 Feb. 17   [Richard Totten] **Dick Button** (b. July 18, 1929), an American figure skater, won the world championship at Paris. During 1948 and 1949, while a student at Harvard, he became the first person to hold at one time the five major figure skating titles: U.S., North American, European, World, and Olympic. Button won the U.S. title from 1946 to 1952, and the Olympic gold medal in both 1948 and 1952. His prowess began a new era of athleticism in the sport. He was, for example, the first person to achieve a real triple loop jump (1952).

1949 Mar. 1   Joe Louis, heavyweight boxing champion of the world since June 22, 1937, announced his retirement. He was undefeated in 25 bouts since winning the title. **Ezzard Charles** (July 7, 1921–May 28, 1975) was declared (June 22) the new champion when he defeated **Jersey Joe Walcott** [Arnold Raymond Creamer] (b. Jan. 31, 1914) in 15 rounds at Chicago, Illinois. Louis attempted a comeback in 1950 but was defeated by Charles in 15 rounds. Again in 1951 Louis returned to the ring, only to be knocked out by **Rocky Marciano** [Rocco Francis Marchegiano] (Sept. 1, 1923–Aug. 31, 1969).

1949 Mar. 25 Mildred E. Gillars [nee Sisk] (1901– June 25, 1988), known as "**Axis Sally,**" an American who during World War II made radio broadcasts from Germany on behalf of the Nazis, was sentenced to 10 to 30 years in prison and fined $10,000 after being convicted of treason in a U.S. federal court. She moved to Germany in the 1930s to be with her lover, a German citizen who formerly taught in America. She was arrested by American authorities in Germany after the war. Gillars was released from prison after serving 12 years.

1949 June 27 Francis Sydney Smythe (b. July 6, 1900), a pioneering English mountaineer, died. In 1931 he led a party to the top of Kamet, a peak in the Himalaya Mountains 25,447 feet high. At that time it was the highest peak ever climbed.

1949 Aug. 3 The **National Basketball Association** [NBA], an American professional sports organization, was formed by the merger of the Basketball Association of America and an older group in the Midwest, the National Basketball League. The first championship of the NBA was won by the Minnesota Lakers, who defeated the Syracuse Nationals 4 games to 2, from Apr. 8 to 27, 1950.

1949 Aug. 28–31 The last meeting [encampment] of the **Grand Army of the Republic** [GAR], the organization of army and navy veterans who fought for the Union in the **American Civil War** (1861–1865), was held at Indianapolis, Indiana. Of the 16 surviving members, 6 attended. It was the 83rd encampment, the first having been held on Nov. 20, 1866, also at Indianapolis. The last member of the GAR died in 1956. In 1889 the veterans of the war on the side of the Confederate States of America formed the United Confederate Veterans. Its membership never quite reached 50,000. The GAR in 1890 had a peak membership of more than 400,000.

1949 Oct. 28 Marcel Cerdan (b. July 22, 1916), a former world champion middleweight boxer and a popular sports hero of France, died in an airplane accident in the Azores while on his way to the U.S. to attempt to regain the title. Cerdan won it on Sept. 21, 1948, but lost it to **Jake La Motta** (b. July 10, 1921), an American fighter, in June, 1949. Cerdan fought 100 bouts, losing only two and being disqualified in two others.

1950

I. VITAL STATISTICS AND DEMOGRAPHICS

1950 The **world population** was c.2,497,000,000 with c.150,000,000 in the U.S., c.325,000,000 in the **Americas**, c.515,000,000 in **Europe**, c.1,150,000,000 in **Asia**, and c.205,000,000 in **Africa**. London was the world's largest city, with 8,346,137 in population. The next nine were New York, 7,835,099; Tokyo, 5,385,000; Moscow, 4,137,018; Chicago, 3,631,835; Shanghai, 3,600,000; Berlin, 3,357,000; Leningrad, 3,191,304; Buenos Aires, 2,982,500; Paris, 2,725,374.

1950 Poland's 1946 population of c.24,100,000 was roughly what it had been just before World War I. That war had claimed the lives of 4 million Poles, and World War II 6 million. A substantial demographic loss occurred between 1944 and 1948, when c.7,300,000 Germans and German-speaking Poles fled or were expelled from Poland's western provinces, under German control since the partition of Poland in the 18th century.

II. DISASTERS

1950 Mar. 12 A British Avro Tudor **plane crashed** on landing at Llandow Field near Cardiff, Wales. All but three of the 80 persons aboard were killed.

1950 Apr. 6 At least 110 persons were killed when several cars of a **train plunged into the Idios River** near Tanguá, Brazil.

1950 July 9–11 In northeastern Colombia c.150 people were killed by a series of **earthquakes** that destroyed a number of villages.

1950 July 21 A **tornado at Cambrai**, in northern France, killed at least six people, injured c.200, and left c.200 homeless. Property damage was estimated at more than $2,850,000.

1950 July 27 In the Inland Sea off Hiroshima prefecture, Japan, a live **torpedo** from World War II naval operations **exploded** when caught in a fish net. Thirty fishermen were killed and ten injured.

1950 Aug. 15 An **earthquake** measuring 8.7 on the Richter scale struck India's Assam state. Whole towns were destroyed, and rivers changed course or vanished. Flooding caused more destruction than the earthquake itself. Estimates of deaths ranged from 20,000 to 30,000.

1950 Aug. 29 Off the northwest coast of Ceylon [present Sri Lanka] c.500 fishermen were drowned or missing when a **storm destroyed a fishing fleet**.

1950 Nov. 22 A **Long Island Railroad commuter train**, bound for Babylon, New York, **crashed** into the rear of a heavily loaded local train at Richmond Hill, killing 78 passengers and injuring 352. Just months before, 31 passengers had died (Feb. 17) when two Long Island trains collided head-on near Rockville Center.

III. POLITICS AND WAR

1950 **Yugoslavia**, under Tito, began receiving U.S. military and economic aid.

1950 The **Pathet Lao** [Lao Country], a new nationalist Laotian movement, was formed in opposition to the French. Its leader was Prince Souphanouvong [Luang Prabang] (b. July 13, 1909), and it was encouraged by the **Viet Minh** [short for Vietnam Independence League], its communist-led counterpart in Vietnam.

1950 The **Hukbalahap guerrillas** [Huks] in the **Philippines**, promising land reform and employing terrorist tactics, won virtual control of some five provinces, principally among peasant folk in central Luzon.

1950 Jan. 26 **India became a sovereign democratic republic** when its new constitution became effective on this date. **Jawaharal Nehru**, prime minister (since 1947) and leader of the **Congress party**, won an over-

whelming victory during the subsequent first general elections (1951–1952).

1950 Feb. 7 Before a Republican women's club in Wheeling, West Virginia, **Joseph R[aymond] McCarthy** (Nov. 14, 1908–May 2, 1957), Republican senator from Wisconsin, declared he had in his hand **a list of "known communists" in the U.S. state department**. No such list was ever revealed by McCarthy, but he continued to make charges of communism against many individuals and groups. As his activities became more and more extreme, they were an embarrassment to his senatorial colleagues. On Dec. 2, 1954, they voted, 67 to 22, to condemn him for contempt of a Senate subcommittee and for insults to the Senate as a body. After this, McCarthy's influence and prestige steadily diminished.

1950 Feb. 14 The **U.S.S.R. and the People's Republic of China signed a 30-year treaty of friendship** to take effect on Apr. 10. By the pact the two countries agreed to unite against an attack by any country, with Japan apparently most in mind. Russia agreed to return to China Port Arthur [Lüshun], a naval base district that had been administered by a Sino-Soviet board since 1945, and the section of the Trans-Siberian Railroad that crossed Manchuria to reach Vladivostok. Both countries agreed to recognize the communist Mongolian People's Republic [Outer Mongolia], which had been established in 1924.

1950 Feb. 23 In a general election the Labour party government of **Great Britain** lost most of its majority in the House of Commons. It won 17 more seats than its main rival, the Conservative party, but had an overall majority of only six. Labour's rule now was unstable and another election was held on Oct. 25, 1951, in which the Conservatives gained a majority of 16 seats. **Winston Churchill** once more became prime minister (to 1955).

1950 Mar. 26 In **El Salvador**'s elections, **Oscar Osorio** (1910–Mar. 6, 1969, leader of the Partido Revolución Ario de Unificación Democrátic [PRUD], was chosen president and a new constitution was adopted. His term of office began on Sept. 14. During his six-year regime the government promoted new industries, public works and housing; it legalized labor unions, developed a social security system, and created an electric power network.

1950 Mar. 30 **Léon Blum** (b. Apr. 9, 1872), a former premier of France (1936–1937), died. Long an active socialist, Blum created (1936) a coalition of the Radical Socialist, Socialist, and Communist parties that won a general election and became known as the **Popular Front**. In 1940, he was arrested by the Vichy government, remaining in prison until the end of World War II. He once again became premier (1946–1947), but for only a little more than a month.

1950 Apr. 1 Great Britain turned over its postwar control of Italian Somaliland to the United Nations, following a U.N. resolution on Nov. 21, 1949. The U.N. then assigned the trusteeship to Italy. By direction of the U.N., the country was renamed **Somalia** and was granted autonomy in internal affairs in 1956 and full independence in 1960.

1950 May 14 Elections in **Turkey** resulted in a victory for the young Democratic party, which favored more liberal measures. Both **Celal Bayar** (May 15, 1882–Aug. 22, 1986), the president, and **Adnan Menderes**, the prime minister, favored aligning the nation more firmly to the West, and they directed the state socialism promulgated by the Republican People's party toward more private enterprise and foreign investment.

1950 June 25 The **Korean War** (to 1953) began when North Korean armed forces, in an unprovoked attack, crossed the 38th parallel into South Korea. They captured Seoul, the capital, on June 29. Meanwhile the **United Nations** condemned (June 25) the invasion and called (June 27) on member nations to assist South Korea. The U.S.S.R., by refusing to participate in the Security Council debate on the matter, lost its opportunity to veto this action. On June 30 **Harry S Truman**, president of the U.S., ordered the use of American armed forces to repel the North Korean invasion. A week later the U.N. placed under U.S. command the forces of the 15 of its members who had responded to the call for assistance. **Douglas MacArthur**, an American general, was appointed commander (July 9) of U.N. forces in Korea.

1950 July 22 **William Lyon Mackenzie King** (b. Dec. 17, 1874), the recent Liberal party prime minister of **Canada** (1921–1930, 1935–1948), died. He had served as prime minister longer than any other in a Commonwealth country when he left office on November 15, 1948. He was especially honored for his stout positioning of Canada beside the United States in World War II and his work with Franklin D. Roosevelt in creating a permanent joint [U.S.-Canadian] board of defense.

1950 July 22 **Leopold III**, king of **Belgium** (1934–1951), returned from exile in Switzerland, following a barely favorable Belgium referendum on March 12. The vigorous opposition of the Socialist party following his return induced Leopold to hand over royal power (Aug. 1) to his eldest son **Baudouin** (b. Sept. 7, 1930), who assumed the royal prerogatives on Aug. 11. Leopold abdicated July 16, 1951, and Baudouin was crowned the next day.

1950 July 25 **Walter Ulbricht** (Jan. 30, 1893–Aug. 1, 1973), became the effective leader of the **German Democratic Republic** [East Germany] when he was elected secretary general of the Socialist Unity party [SED], a staunchly Stalinist group. Ulbricht had been a leading communist in Germany before World War II. In exile in Russia during the war he aided Stalin in the persecution of Trotskyites and others the Russian leader wished to purge. Opposed to reconciliation with West Germany, he made East Germany the most Soviet-like country of all Russia's Eastern European satellites.

1950 Aug. 15 The **United States of Indonesia**, consisting of Java and 15 "territories," was terminated by nationalist forces, and a unitary republic was established with a new constitution. **Sukarno** was reelected president (to 1966).

1950 Sept. 5 The South Korean army, supported by American and other United Nations forces, withdrew from invading North Korean forces to the **Pusan** area of extreme southeastern Korea, where they established a defense perimeter. The **North Koreans now controlled most of the Korean peninsula**.

1950 Sept. 6 The government of **Syria** promulgated a new constitution providing for parliamentary government. **Adib al-Shishakli** (1909–Sept. 27, 1964), who had gained power in a coup (1949), suspended the constitution in late 1951 and ruled as a virtual dictator until 1954.

1950 Sept. 11 **Jan Christian Smuts** (b. Aug. 1, 1870), a South African statesman and military commander, died. In the **Boer War** (1899–1902) he led guerrilla troops against the British but later decided cooperation with Great Britain was South Africa's best course. He was a leading figure in creating the **Union of South Africa** (1910). In World War I Smuts commanded troops in Africa and sat in the highest war councils of the British Empire. He was twice prime minister of South Africa (1919–1924, 1939–1948).

1950 Sept. 15–Dec. 31   U.N. troops executed an amphibious landing behind North Korean lines at Inchon, a seaport in northwestern South Korea, near Seoul. U.N. troops recaptured Seoul (Sept. 26), and within three days the North Koreans were forced back to the 38th parallel, their starting point in June. The U.N. authorized (Oct. 9) MacArthur, commander of the U.N. troops, mostly Americans and South Koreans, to cross the 38th parallel. The rout of the North Koreans continued, and their capital, Pyongyang, was captured (Oct. 19). By Nov. 24 the pursuit took the U.N. troops almost to the **Yalu River**, the boundary between North Korea and China. Two days later, however, **Chinese troops entered the war** on a massive scale. Joining with the North Koreans, they forced the U.N. troops into a desperate retreat in bitter winter weather. MacArthur's forces gave up (Dec. 5) Pyongyang and, by the end of the year, the North Korean forces were again south of the 38th parallel.

1950 Sept. 16   Dong Khe, a French fort guarding the border of French Indochina and communist China, was attacked by a massive force of communist **Viet Minh** under the command of **Vo Nguyen Giap** (b. Sept. 1, 1912). The Vietnamese wiped out the 200 French Foreign Legionnaires defending Dong Khe and within weeks took the other French forts guarding the border.

1950 Sept. 20   The U.S. Congress passed the **McCarran-Wood Act** of 1950 over the veto of **Harry S Truman**, president of the U.S. This legislation, known also as the **Internal Security Act**, required the registration of all communists with the attorney general and made it unlawful for those with communist affiliations to be engaged in defense or government work. The act's chief sponsor was **Patrick Anthony McCarran** (Aug. 8, 1876–Sept. 28, 1954), Democratic senator of Nevada.

1950 Oct. 21   Tibet, which had ousted Chinese representatives at Lhasa following the Chinese communist victory over the Nationalists in 1949, was occupied by forces of the People's Republic of China. After an unsuccessful appeal to the U.N. (Nov. 10), Tibet surrendered its independence to China on May 23, 1951.

1950 Oct. 29   Gustav V [Gustaf, Gustavus] (June 16, 1858), king of **Sweden** (1907–1950), died. A popular monarch, he helped keep his country neutral in both world wars. During his reign a number of reforms were introduced, beginning with universal suffrage in 1907. He was succeeded (to 1973) by his son **Gustav VI Adolf**.

1950 Nov. 1   Two Puerto Rican members of a political group seeking independence for Puerto Rico attempted unsuccessfully to enter Blair House, the temporary presidential residence in Washington, D.C.—the White House was being renovated—to assassinate **Harry S Truman**. One of the Puerto Ricans was captured; the other and a guard were killed. The surviving nationalist, whose death sentence was reduced to life imprisonment by Truman, was granted clemency (Sept. 6, 1979) by President **Jimmy Carter**.

1950 Nov. 7   Tribhuvana [Tribhuvana Bir Bikram Shah Deva], king of **Nepal** (from 1911, 1951–1955), was deposed by his prime minister for favoring the democratic reforms demanded by the newly formed Nepali Congress party. The prime minister was the latest member of the noble **Rana family** to hold power in Nepal. The king was reinstated on Feb. 15, 1951, with the help of **Jawaharal Nehru**, prime minister of India, and introduced further reforms as Rana power waned.

1950 Nov. 10–11   Anastasio Somoza, the strongman of **Nicaragua** was elected president over token opposition. In 1948 the Organization of American States had reprimanded Somoza for aiding rebels attempting to bring down the government of neighboring Costa Rica.

1950 Nov. 13   Carlos Delgado Chalbaud (b. 1909), president of **Venezuela** (from 1948), was assassinated by opponents who apparently meant to kidnap, not kill, him. He was the leader of the military junta that seized power in 1948, and the other two members of the junta continued to rule the country. They were **Luis Llovera Páez** and **Marcos Pérez Jiménez** (b. Apr. 25, 1914). The latter took the post of president in 1952.

IV. ECONOMY AND TRADE

1950 Jan. 8   Joseph A[lois] **Schumpeter** (b. Feb. 8, 1883), an Austrian-American economist, died. After teaching in Europe and serving as Austrian finance minister (1918–1920), he moved to the U.S. in 1932 and taught at Harvard University until his death. Schumpeter said that the acceptance of social welfare legislation, as necessary as it might be, would sap the vitality of capitalism. He was also a foremost student of business cycles. Among Schumpeter's books were *Capitalism, Socialism, and Democracy* (1942), and the posthumous *History of Economic Analysis* (1954).

1950 Mar. 24   Harold [Joseph] **Laski** (b. June 30, 1893), a British political scientist, economist, and politician, died. For most of his life he was at the same time a university teacher, a lecturer, and a political leader. He was a member of the executive committee of the Fabian Society (1922–1936) and chairman of the Labour party (1945–1946). Laski was an advocate of government leadership in bringing about reforms of a socialist nature. He was a prolific author. Among his many books were *Democracy in Crisis* (1933), *The Rise of European Liberalism* (1936), *The American Presidency* (1940), and *Reflections on the Revolution of Our Time* (1943).

1950 Nov. 28   The **Colombo Plan** for Cooperative Economic Development in South and Southeast Asia was launched by seven nations of the Commonwealth at a conference in Colombo, Ceylon [present Sri Lanka]. It was intended to strengthen the economies of the non-communist countries of the area and it worked out development plans for Ceylon, India, Malaya [part of present Malaysia], North Borneo [present state of Sbah, Malaysia], and Pakistan. More nations became members of the plan but, when some of them turned communist, the name of the organization was changed to the Colombo Plan for Cooperative Economic and Social Development in Asia and the Pacific.

1950 Dec. 30   Saudi Arabia and **ARAMCO** [Arabian-American Oil Company] granted the Saudi government half the profits from Saudi Arabian oil production. This was the first application in the Near East of the principle established in the **Venezuelan Petroleum Agreement** (1943). A similar agreement was signed between **Iran** and the **Anglo-Iranian Oil Company** on Aug. 5, 1954. Such agreements signaled a shift in the balance of power between the oil companies and the oil-producing nations.

V. RELIGION AND PHILOSOPHY

1950   Daisetz Teitaro Suzuki (Oct. 18, 1870–July 12, 1966), a Japanese Zen scholar and renowned Buddhologist, began lecturing at major North American universities under the sponsorship of the Rockefeller Foundation. More than anyone else, Suzuki **intro-**

duced Zen to the western world. Among Suzuki's many books were *Essays in Zen Buddhism* (1927–1933), *An Introduction to Zen Buddhism* (1949), and, posthumously, *Outlines of Mahayana Buddhism* (1963).

1950 July 17   Evangeline Cory Booth (b. Dec. 25, 1865), the general (1934–1939) of the worldwide **Salvation Army**, died. She was the seventh child of William Booth, the founder of the Army. Booth commanded the Army in Canada (1895–1904) and in the U.S. (1904–1934). She was the author of *Songs of the Evangel* (1927) and *Woman* (1930).

1950 Nov. 1   Pope Pius XII issued the bull *Muni ficentissimus Deus* [*Most Bountiful God*] to define the dogma of the Assumption of the Virgin Mary. The pope declared she "was assumed body and soul into heavenly glory," but avoided the problem of her physical death. On Aug. 12 Pius issued an encyclical, *Humani Generis* [*Of the Human Race*], warning Roman Catholics against existentialism, evolutionism, and historicism.

VI. SCIENCE, EDUCATION, AND TECHNOLOGY

1950   Laurent Schwartz (b. Mar. 5, 1915), a mathematician at the University of Paris, formulated his theory of statistical distributions in *Théorie des distributions*. It bring the mathematics of classical analysis closer to the mathematics of probability.

1950 Feb. 14   Karl Guthe Jansky (b. Oct. 22, 1905), an American electrical engineer, died. While seeking the reason for interference with radio telephone transmissions for the Bell Telephone Laboratories, he found (1931) some **radio waves that were of extraterrestrial origin**. He determined (1933) that these emissions were coming from the Milky Way. Jansky's work laid the foundations for radio astronomy.

1950 Feb. 25   George Richards Minot (b. Dec. 2, 1885), an American physician and pathologist, died. A specialist in diseases of the blood, he developed in 1926 a raw liver diet as treatment for pernicious anemia. Later he was among those who developed liver extract. For his work Minot shared the **Nobel prize for physiology or medicine** in 1934.

1950 Mar. 18   [Walter] **Norman Haworth** (b. Mar. 19, 1883), an English chemist, died. His research on carbohydrates and vitamin C resulted in the first synthesis of a vitamin (1933). For his work he shared the **Nobel prize for chemistry** in 1937 with **Paul Karrer** (Apr. 21, 1889–June 18, 1971), a Swiss chemist, who determined (1931) the constitution of vitamin A.

1950 June 17   The **first kidney transplant** from a cadaver to a living human being was performed in Chicago by **Richard H[arold] Lawler** (Aug. 12, 1895–July 24, 1982), an American surgeon and educator.

1950 July 1   [Gottlieb] **Eliel Saarinen** (b. Aug. 20, 1873), a Finnish-American architect, died. Before moving (1923) to the U.S., his designs, especially of the Helsinki, Finland, railroad station (1904–1914), made his reputation in Europe. Although Saarinen became a foremost exponent of the bold look of a new generation of skyscrapers, his best work was elsewhere. He designed buildings for the Cranbrook Foundation, Bloomfield, Michigan, and headed its school of art (1932–1948). Among his best works were the Crow Island Elementary School, Winnetka, Illinois (1939) and Christ Lutheran Church, Minneapolis, Minnesota (1949–1950).

VII. ARTS AND LEISURE

1950   *Rashomon*, a film written, directed, and produced by **Akira Kurosawa** (b. Mar. 23, 1910), brought Japanese films into international prominence. Kurosawa's other major films included *Ikuru* (1952), *Seven Samurai* (1954), and *Yojimbo* (1961).

1950 Jan. 2   **Emil Jannings** (b. July 23, 1886), a prominent German actor, died. He won wide acclaim for his role in *Der Latzte Mann* [*The Last Laugh*] (1024). In Hollywood Jannings' most notable performance was in *The Last Command* (1928), playing a former Russian general now a movie extra. Later, back in Germany, he scored another success with *Der Blaue Engel* [*The Blue Angel*] (1930). Because he cooperated with the Nazi propaganda ministry during World War II, he was blacklisted by the Allies.

1950 Jan. 20   **George Orwell** [pen name of Eric Arthur Blair] (b. June 25, 1903), an English author, died. His first novel was *Burmese Days* (1934), based on his experiences with the Indian police. Other of his works, such as *Down and Out in Paris and London* (1933), are autobiographical. Orwell fought on the Republican side in the Spanish Civil War (1936–1939). He wrote *Homage to Catalonia* (1938), revealing his disillusionment with the Republicans. His most effective works were *Animal Farm* (1945) and *1984* (1949), both satires on totalitarianism.

1950 Feb. 25   The American television comedy show *Your Show of Shows* went on the air. Although the live 90-minute show ran only until June 5, 1954, it offered some of the most original comedy available in any medium at that time. The stars were **Sid Caesar** (b. Sept. 8, 1922) and **Imogene Coca** (b. Nov. 19, 1908), and the writers, among others, were **Mel Brooks** (b. June 28, 1928), **Neil Simon** (b. July 4, 1927), and **Woody Allen** (b. Dec. 1, 1935).

1950 Feb. 26   **Harry** [MacLennan] **Lauder** (b. Aug. 4, 1870), a Scottish music hall singer and entertainer, died. After his first appearance in London (1900) he became extremely popular for his style of singing Scottish ballads and songs and for his good-natured comedy. Lauder's fame was worldwide, and he wrote many of his songs himself, such as "I Love a Lassie" (1906) and "Roamin' in the Gloamin'" (1911).

1950 Mar. 1   *The Consul*, an opera by **Gian-Carlo Menotti** (b. July 7, 1911), was given its premier performance at the Shubert Theater in Philadelphia. On Mar. 15 the Broadway run in New York City began at the Ethel Barrymore Theater.

1950 Mar. 12   **Heinrich Mann** (b. Mar. 27, 1871), a German novelist, died. Mann was a leading intellectual of the Weimar Republic (1919–1933) until the Nazi regime forced him into exile, first in France and then in the U.S. Mann's novel *Professor Unrat* (1905) became the noted film *The Blue Angel* (1930). He also wrote *Der Untertan* [*The Patriot*] (1918), and *Ein ernstes Leben* [*The Hill of Lies*] (1932), among many works of fiction and nonfiction. He was the elder brother of the novelist Thomas Mann.

1950 Mar. 19   **Edgar Rice Burroughs** (b. Sept. 1, 1875), an American author, died. He became famous worldwide as the author of the Tarzan books, beginning with *Tarzan of the Apes* (1914), a tale of the son of an English peer brought up in infancy by apes in the African jungle. Millions of copies of the Tarzan books have been sold in nearly 80 languages.

1950 April 3   **Kurt Weill** (b. March 2, 1900), a German-American composer of theater music, died. In

Germany he had, with Bertholt Brecht, created a satirical musical version of *The Beggar's Opera* by **John Gay**. His music proscribed by the Nazi government, Weill fled Germany in 1933. His best-known American compositions were the songs added to **Maxwell Anderson's** *Knickerbocker Holiday* (1938), to *Street Scene* (1947) by **Elmer Rice**, to *Love Life* (1949) by **Alan Jay Lerner**, and the scores for *Lady in the Dark* (1941) and *One Touch of Venus* (1943). A revised, posthumous production (1954) of *The Beggar's Opera*, now called *The Threepenny Opera*, was a smashing Broadway success.

1950 Apr. 7 **Walter Huston** (b. Apr., 6, 1884), an American actor of the stage and the movies, died. He was successful on the Broadway stage before making his first movie, *Gentlemen of the Press* (1929). His most memorable movies were *Abraham Lincoln* (1930) and *The Treasure of the Sierra Madre* (1948), which was directed by his son **John Huston** (Aug. 5, 1906–Aug. 28, 1987). Huston is also remembered for his part in **Kurt Weill's** Broadway production (1944) of *Knickerbocker Holiday* (1938) by **Maxwell Anderson**, in which he sang "September Song."

1950 Apr. 8 **Vaslav Fomich Nijinsky** (b. Feb. 28, 1890), a Russian ballet dancer and choreographer, died. He made his debut in St. Petersburg in 1907 then went to Paris, where he became the premier danseur of Sergey Diaghilev's Ballet Russe. Nijinsky was the first to dance the leading roles in a number of now-famous ballets, including *Petrouchka*, *The Afternoon of a Faun*, and *Till Eulenspiegel*. He choreographed the latter. His career ended in 1919, when he became insane, and he spent most of the rest of his life in mental institutions.

1950 May 4 **William Rose Benét** (b. Feb. 2, 1886), an American poet and editor, died. Among his collections of poetry were *Merchants from Cathay* (1913) and *The Spirit of the Scene* (1951). *The Dust Which Is God* (1941) was his autobiography in verse.

1950 May 5 **Edgar Lee Masters** (b. Aug. 23, 1861), an American poet, died. *Spoon River Anthology* (1915), printed 75 times in its first 35 years, was his only durable book. It revealed, in simple but somber epitaphs, the secret lives of the dead who had lived in a small American town.

1950 May 11 *La cantatrice chauve* [*The Bald Soprano*], a one-act play by **Eugène Ionesco** (b. Nov. 26, 1912) opened in Paris, his first to be produced. One of the leading figures of the so-called *Theater of the Absurd*, Ionesco's work attacked the notion that human life and endeavor was anything but absurd. Among his successful plays in English were *The Lesson* (1955), *Rhinoceros* (1960), and *Exit the King* (1963).

1950 Oct. 19 **Edna St. Vincent Millay** (b. Feb. 22, 1892), a leading American poet of the first half of the 20th century and a symbol of life in the early 1920s in Greenwich Village, New York City, died. She burst upon the literary scene with the remarkable volume *Renascence* (1917), whose title poem she wrote at age 19. Among her later volumes were *A Few Figs from Thistles* (1920), *The Harp Weaver* (1924), *Conversation at Midnight* (1937), and *Make Bright the Arrow* (1940). Her sonnets were recognized as among the best written by an American.

1950 Oct. 23 **Al Jolson** [orig.: Asa Yoelson] (b. May 28, 1883), a Russian-born American vaudeville and movie singer, died. Jolson's initial appearance on Broadway was in 1911. As a star in the movies, he is remembered especially for his performance in *The Jazz Singer* (1927), the first feature film with a complete soundtrack.

1950 Nov. *Short Symphony* by **Howard Swanson** (Aug. 18, 1907–Nov. 12, 1978), a young black composer from Atlanta, Georgia, was given its premier by the New York Philharmonic-Symphony Orchestra, **Dimitri Metropoulos** conducting.

1950 Nov. 2 **George Bernard Shaw** (b. July 26, 1856), an English dramatist and critic, died at age 94. The greatest force in the English theater for over a half a century, Shaw proved that a "play of ideas" could grip and entertain an audience. Among the scores of his plays dealing with social problems or problems of individual development and self-discovery were *Caesar and Cleopatra* (1898), *Major Barbara* (1905), and *Pygmalion* (1912). Under the title *My Fair Lady*, Pygmalion was internationally popular both as a stage musical (1956) and a movie (1964). Shaw's own favorite was *Back to Methuselah* (1921), but his most popular play on the stage was *St. Joan* (1923). *Arms and the Man* (1894) and *Heartbreak House* (1916) are also memorable.

Shaw received the **Nobel prize for literature** in 1925.

1950 Nov. 16   *Clarinet Concerto* by **Aaron Copland** (b. Nov. 14, 1900), commissioned by **Benny Goodman**, was given its first performance by the NBC Symphony Orchestra with Goodman as soloist.

1950 Nov. 25   **Johannes Vilhelm Jensen** (b. Jan. 20, 1873), a Danish author, died. His three-volume work *Himmerlandshistorier* [*Himmerland Stories*] (1898–1910) presents tales of Jutland, Denmark. Among Jensen's many books of fiction, poetry, travel, and essays are *Kongens Fald* [*The Fall of the King*] (1899–1902) and two books of tales based on his experiences in America, *Madame d'Ore* (1904) and *Hjulet* (1905). Jensen was awarded the **Nobel prize for literature** in 1944.

1950 Dec. 20   **Walter** [Johannes] **Damrosch** (b. Jan. 30, 1862), Prussian-born musician and conductor, died. he left for the U.S. in 1871 and devoted his entire life to the world of music. In the 1890s Damrosch popularized the music of Richard Wagner, brought Peter Ilyich Tchaikovsky to the U.S. (1891), and introduced the music of Camille Saint-Saëns and Hector Berlioz to concert audiences. He was the director of the **New York Symphony Orchestra** (1903–1927) and musical director of the **National Broadcasting Company** (1928–1950).

1950 Dec. 27   **Max Beckmann** (b. Feb. 12, 1884), a German painter, died. His early style was impressionistic, but his experiences in World War I pushed him toward the objectivist manner of George Grosz. His paintings became so forceful as to be brutal, with grotesque figures that were his comments on the postwar world. Beckmann's best-known work was a triptych, *Departure* (1932–1935).

VIII. SPORTS, GAMES, AND SOCIETY

1950   **Emilio Pucci** [Marchese Emilio Pucci di Barsento] (b. Nov. 20, 1914), an Italian fashion designer, astounded and delighted seekers of the latest styles with his colorful and elegant sportswear.

1950 Mar. 1   **Klaus** [Emil] **Fuchs** (Dec. 29, 1911–Jan. 28, 1988), a German-born English physicist, pleaded guilty in London to violating the **Official Secrets Act** and was sentenced to 14 years in prison. A long-time communist, he fled Germany in 1933 and became a British citizen. In 1943 he worked in the U.S. on the development of the atomic bomb and later was chief physicist at a British atomic energy development project. During all this time he sent a steady stream of secret information on atomic matters to the U.S.S.R. Fuchs was released from prison in 1959 and went to East Germany, where he became director of the Institute for Nuclear Physics.

1950 June 3   A six-man team of mountaineers, led by **Maurice Herzog** (b. Jan. 5, 1919), a French mountaineer, became the first to reach the top of **Annapurna I**, 26,504 feet high, in central northern Nepal.

1950 July 16   Uruguay defeated Brazil in the **World Soccer Cup Final**, by a score of 2 to 1. About 205,000 soccer fans crowded into Rio de Janeiro's new municipal stadium for the event.

1950 Dec. 25   The **Stone of Scone** [Stone of Destiny; Scots Gaelic, *Lia Fail*] was stolen by Scottish nationalists from Westminster Abbey, London, and taken to Scotland. The stone, weighing 336 pounds, had long been the seat on which the kings of Scotland were crowned. Edward I seized it in 1296 and took it to England. It was later placed under the coronation chair to indicate that Scotland and England were united. On Apr. 11, 1951, the stone was recovered and returned to the Abbey.

1951

I. DISASTERS

1951 Jan. 3   A poorly timed dynamite blast caused an **avalanche** that buried at least 132 railroad workmen near Chimbote, Peru.

1951 Jan. 4   Two days of **tornados** sweeping over Comoro Island, between Madagascar and Africa, killed c.500 people.

1951 Jan. 18–21   The **eruption of Mount Lamington** in the Owen Stanley Range in Papua New Guinea, killed c.3,000 persons.

1951 Feb. 6   A Pennsylvania Railroad commuter train, "The Broker," **derailed** near Woodbridge, New Jersey, killing 85 passengers and injuring 330.

1951 July   **Flooding of the Kansas River** drowned 1 million acres of agricultural lands and destroyed c.2,500 homes. Damage, chiefly along the river in eastern Kansas, totaled $870 million.

1951 Aug. 3   Potosi, northwest of Managua, Nicaragua, was wiped out and most of its c.1,000 inhabitants killed when an **earthquake** split the side of a nearby dormant volcano and released water that had collected in its crater.

1951 Nov. 1–20   Three weeks of **rainstorms** in the Po River Valley of northern Italy left c.150 persons dead and c.150,000 homeless.

II. POLITICS AND WAR

1951   In **Burma** [Myanmar] the **Anti-Fascist People's Freedom League** [AFPFL] triumphed, and **U Nu** became premier of a provisional government, which promoted a program of nationalization. After elections held from June 1951 to Apr. 1952, independent Burma's first permanent cabinet was installed on May 16, 1952.

1951 Jan. 4   In the **Korean War** (1950–1953) a new offensive by the Chinese and North Koreans captured Seoul once more, and Inchon, a seaport c.25 miles southwest of Seoul, fell to the invaders on Jan. 21. However, a U.N. counteroffensive pushed the communists back to the 38th parallel, and Seoul was reoccupied on Mar. 14.

1951 Jan. 27   **Carl Gustav Mannerheim** (b. June 4, 1867), a Finnish statesman and military commander, died. In 1918 he led Finnish forces against the new Soviet Russian regime and helped secure his country's independence. He was named regent in 1919. Mannerheim commanded Finland's army in the **Russo-Finnish War** (1939–1940) and again (1941–1944) when Finland allied itself with the Germans during World War II. He became president of **Finland** on Aug. 1, 1944, but resigned for reasons of health on Mar. 4, 1946.

1951 Mar. 7   **Ali Razmara** (1901–Mar. 7, 1951), prime minister of **Iran**, was assassinated by a militant nationalist. The **National Front** forced the nationalization of the British-owned Anglo-Iranian Oil Company, and the militant Nationalist party leader **Muhammad Mossadegh** [Musaddiq] was appointed (Apr. 28) prime minister by **Muhammad Riza Shah Pahlevi**, shah of Iran.

1951 Mar. 15   **Jacob Arbenz Guzman** (Sept. 14, 1913–Jan. 27, 1971) was inaugurated as president of **Guatemala**. He expropriated large estates, including many of the United Fruit Company, and legalized the Communist party.

1951 Apr. 10   **Harry S Truman** removed **Douglas MacArthur** from command of Allied forces in the Far East and named **Matthew B. Ridgway** (b. Mar. 3, 1895) to succeed him. MacArthur had argued for an all-out offensive against the communists, including the Chinese, and had advocated attacking China, contrary to instructions from Truman, and had even written to Congress urging its support.

1951 May 6   In the **Bolivian** elections, **Victor Paz Estenssoro** (b. Oct. 2, 1907), secretary of the outlawed National Revolutionary Movement [MNR], led all candidates for president with 43 percent of the votes cast, and would clearly be elected in a run-off election. The incumbent president **Mamerto Urriolagoitia** thereupon turned the government over to a military junta to forestall a leftist government.

1951 May 10   **Arnolfo Arias Madrid**, fascistic president of **Panama**, was again ousted from the presidency after organizing a personal secret police force and suspending the constitution.

1951 July 10   Negotiations for a cease fire in the **Korean War** (1950–1953) began at Kaesong, North Korea, near the 38th parallel, separating the U.N. command and the Chinese and North Koreans. Little progress was made and in October the talks were moved to **Panmunjom**, a town on the 38th parallel. The negotiations dragged on for two years. Meanwhile fighting continued, but for the most part the lines remained stalemated near the 38th parallel.

1951 July 20   **Abdullah** [Abdallah] **ibn-Husein** [ibn Husain] (b. 1882), king of **Jordan** (from 1946), was shot and killed in Aksa Mosque in Jerusalem by a Palestinian. Abdullah had annexed (Apr. 24) the West Bank, a part of Palestine that the U.N. had designated Arab territory. But the Palestinians had anticipated creation of a new country to be headed by **Amin el-Husseini** [Adim ibn-Husain] (1871–July 4, 1974), Grand Mufti of Jerusalem under the British regime in Palestine. Abdullah was succeeded (Sept. 26) by his son **Talal** (Feb. 26, 1907–July 9, 1972), but he was deposed by the Jordanian parliament Feb. 11, 1952, for mental illness, in favor of his son **Hussein I** (b. Nov. 14, 1935), king of Jordan.

1951 July 23 The **North Atlantic Treaty Organization** [NATO] established its joint military command headquarters near Paris with **Dwight D. Eisenhower** as commander (1951–1952).

1951 July 23 **Henri Philippe Pétain** (b. Apr. 24, 1856), a former marshal in the French army and "chief of state" of the collaborative Vichy government of France in World War II, died on the island of Yeu, a prisoner since 1945 for the crime of treason. Known as the "**hero of Verdun**," he served as ambassador (1939) to Spain before being brought back to France by premier Paul Reynaud and named vice premier to boost French morale. An early advocate of surrender to Germany, Pétain succeeded Reynaud on June 16, 1940, and signed an armistice with Germany on June 22 and with Italy on June 24. He then led the Vichy government for unoccupied France but, with his popularity gone and age sapping his strength, he was superseded by Paul Laval in Apr., 1942. At Pétain's trial for treason, he was sentenced to death, but Charles de Gaulle commuted the sentence to life imprisonment.

1951 Sept. 1 The **ANZUS** [from Australian, New Zealand, U.S.] **treaty**, also known as the Pacific Security Treaty, was signed by representatives of the three countries. The three signatories pledged to come to the aid of any one of them that was attacked.

1951 Sept. 8 A peace treaty between **Japan and most of its World War II opponents**, 49 nations in all, was signed in San Francisco, California. India and Burma [Myanmar] refused to attend the conference, and the USSR, Poland, and Czechoslovakia refused to sign the treaty. The treaty went into effect April 28, 1952. Japan lost her overseas possessions. Japan and the U.S. also signed a security treaty allowing the U.S. to continue to maintain troops in Japan.

1951 Oct. 16 **Liaquat Ali Khan** (b. 1895), prime minister of **Pakistan**, was assassinated by an Afghan

fanatic. His successor was **Khwaja Nazimuddin** (to 1953).

1951 Dec. 14 The *Organizacion de Estados Centroamericanos* [ODECA] was established and its charter ratified by the last of the five nations to sign it. The charter was essentially a commitment between Guatemala, El Salvador, Honduras, Nicaragua and Costa Rica to work together more closely to achieve common goals.

1951 Dec. 24 The United Kingdom of **Libya** became an independent nation under **Idris I** (Mar. 13, 1890–May 25, 1983), king of Libya (1951–1969), the leader of the nationalistic Sanusi [Senussi] Muslim brotherhood. The brotherhood was founded in 1837 in Mecca and was based on the Muslim literary and philosophical movement known as **Sufism**.

III. ECONOMY AND TRADE

1951 Jan. 26 The **Wage and Price Control Board**, created by the U.S. Congress, announced wage and price freezes, to be effective for two years. In February the labor representatives on the board withdrew, charging it with pro-business bias.

1951 Jan. 30 **Ferdinand Porsche** (b. Sept. 3, 1875), a German auto manufacturer who gave his name to a prestigious luxury car, died. At Adolf Hitler's request he designed (1934) a "people's car," the **Volkswagen**. Porsche was jailed by the French for a short time after the war because of his Nazi connection.

1951 Feb. 8 **Fritz Thyssen** (b. Nov. 9, 1873), a German industrialist who was an early supporter of Adolf Hitler, died. As early as 1923 he began to give money to the Nazi party. With Hitler in power, Thyssen became (1933) dictator of the Ruhr, Germany's chief industrial region. However, he had a falling out with Hitler and fled (1936) to Switzerland but was captured and imprisoned (1941) by the Nazis. In 1948 a German denazification court fined him as a "minor Nazi."

1951 May 2 Under the leadership of **Muhammad Mossadegh**, leader of the National Front party and prime minister of **Iran** (from Apr. 29), **Iran nationalized the oil industry**, seized the property of the British-owned **Anglo-Iranian Oil Company**, and renamed it the **National Iranian Oil Company**.

1951 Aug. 14   William Randolph Hearst (b. Apr. 29, 1863), one of America's most successful publishers of newspapers and magazines, died. In 1887 he took charge of his father's paper, the *San Francisco Examiner*, and in 1895 acquired the *New York Morning Journal*. In competition with Joseph Pulitzer, Hearst ushered in the era of "yellow journalism" with sensational reportage. His empire expanded to 18 newspapers and a number of successful magazines, such as *Good Housekeeping*. Hearst's editorial policies began on the liberal side but he later turned into a bitter conservative.

1951 Oct. 10   The **U.S.S.R.'s fifth Five-Year Plan** was launched. As in earlier plans, its emphasis was on the speedy industrialization of Russia and increased agriculture production on the collectivized farms.

IV. RELIGION AND PHILOSOPHY

1951 Apr. 29   Ludwig [Josef Johann] **Wittgenstein** (b. Apr. 26, 1889), an Austrian-British philosopher, died. His work established a new focus for 20th-century philosophy, especially in the U.S. and Great Britain. The proper use and analysis of language, Wittgenstein contended, should always be the chief concern of philosophy. One of his most important works was *Tractatus Logico-philosophicus* (1921). Others were published posthumously: *Philsophische Untersuchungen* [*Philosophical Investigations*] (1953) and *Bemerkung en über die Grundlagen der Mathematik* [*Remarks on the Foundations of Mathematics*] (1956).

V. SCIENCE, EDUCATION AND TECHNOLOGY

1951   Barbara McClintock (b. June 15, 1902), an American geneticist, announced that her experiments with corn showed that genes of living cells were not stationary. They move and affect other genes, thus causing diversity in the development of organisms. McClintock was awarded the **Nobel prize in physiology or medicine** in 1983.

1951   Nikolaas Tinbergen (b. Apr. 15, 1917), a Dutch-British zoologist and ethologist, published *A Study of Instinct*, a landmark in research on animal behavior. With **Konrad Lorenz**, Tinbergen made ethology an important part of the scientific world. He concluded from his studies that inheritance and learning are both involved in animal behavior. One of his important books was *The Herring Gull's World* (1953). He also wrote *Animal Behavior* (1965) and shared the **Nobel prize for physiology or medicine** in 1973 with Conrad Lorenz and **Karl von Frisch**.

1951   Cortisone and cholesterol, steroids, were synthesized by **Robert Burns Woodward** (Apr. 10, 1917–July 8, 1979), an American chemist. Woodward also synthesized quinine (1944) and chlorophyll (1960). For his work he won the **Nobel prize for chemistry** in 1965.

1951   Fritz Albert Lipmann (June 12, 1899–July 24, 1986), a German-born American biochemist discovered acetylcoenzyme A, which breaks down fats, carbohydrates, and some portion of proteins to obtain energy. Lipmann shared the **Nobel prize for physiology or medicine** in 1953.

1951 June 14   UNIVAC [Universal Automatic Computer], the first electronic computer produced for commercial use, went into operation at the U.S. Census Bureau office in Philadelphia. It was also the first computer to store data on **magnetic tape**.

1951 June 25   The **first commercial television broadcast in color** was presented by the **Columbia Broadcasting System** [CBS] in five American cities. CBS thereafter was on the air with color programs for two and a half hours a day.

VI. ARTS AND LEISURE

1951   The building from scratch of **Chandigarh**, the new capital city of the Punjab state of India, began. A new capital was needed when the old capital, Lahore, was assigned to Pakistan by the partition of 1947. The architect of the main buildings was the noted Swiss-born **Le Corbusier** [Charles Édouard Jeanneret Gris] (1887–Aug. 27, 1965), but many city planners and other architects were also involved.

1951   *The Cisco Kid*, a syndicated Western, became the **first television series to be filmed in color**.

1951 Jan. 10   Sinclair Lewis (b. Feb. 7, 1885), a prolific novelist who satirized middle-class American life, died. His first of 22 novels, *Main Street* (1920), was iconoclastic and sociologically on target. *Babbitt* (1922) provided a name for all small-minded, complacent businessmen. *Arrowsmith* (1928) showed the frustrations within the medical profession. Lewis won the **Nobel prize for literature** in 1930, the first American to be so honored.

1951 Feb. 19 André Gide (b. November 22, 1869), an influential and controversial French author, died. He was controversial because of his defense of homosexuality and his espousal—and later disavowal—of communism. The unconventional novel *The Immoralist* (1902) earned him a small reputation, which was added to by *Strait Is the Gate* (1909), *Lafcadio's Adventures* (1914), and *The Counterfeiters* (1926). Gide was awarded the **Nobel prize for literature** in 1947.

1951 Mar. 6 Ivor Novello [orig.: David Ivor Davies] (b. Jan. 15, 1893), an English actor, playwright, and composer, died. He was the composer of one of the memorable songs of World War I, "**Keep the Home Fires Burning**" (1915). Among Novello's plays and musical comedies were *Symphony in Two Flats* (1929) and *Careless Rapture* (1936).

1951 Mar. 22 Willem [Josef] **Mengelberg** (b. Mar. 28, 1871), a Dutch conductor and composer, died. For 50 years (1895–1945) he was the conductor of the **Amsterdam Concertgebouw** and made it a musical organization of the highest quality. During World War II Mengelberg conducted in Nazi Germany and as a result was banned from his profession. He spent his remaining years in retirement.

1951 Apr. 15 Artur Schnabel (b. Apr. 17, 1882), an Austrian-born American pianist and composer, best known for his vigorous interpretation of Schubert and Beethoven's music, died.

1951 June 4 Serge [Alexandrovich] **Koussevitsky** (b. July 26, 1884), a Russian-born American conductor and composer, died. He moved (1924) to the U.S. where he became conductor of the **Boston Symphony Orchestra** (1924–1949). Koussevitsky was noted for including American music in his programs, such as works by **Aaron Copland** and **Samuel Barber**. Koussevitsky was the **founder** (1940) **of the Berkshire Music Center, Tanglewood**, Massachusetts.

1951 June 28 The *Amos and Andy Show* premiered on American television, the first TV series with a black cast. The series ended on June 11, 1953.

1951 July 13 Arnold Schoenberg [orig.: Schönberg] (b. September 13, 1874), an Austrian composer who

originated (1921) a 12-tone technique of serial music, died. A controversial musician, he was nevertheless regarded by his severest critics as a pioneer in new modes of musical expression and an influential teacher. Some consider his greatest work was his unfinished opera *Moses and Aron* (1930), not produced until 1957.

1951 July 15 *The Catcher in the Rye*, by J[erome] D[avid] **Salinger** (b. Jan. 1, 1919), an American writer, was published. A friendly, humorous, sympathetic book about the painful adolescence of a boy named Holden Caulfield, it quickly became a favorite novel of American teenagers and became popular in Europe as well.

1951 July 23 Robert Joseph Flaherty (b. Feb. 16, 1884), an American explorer and filmmaker, called the father of the documentary film, died. After exploring in northern Canada, he made his first documentary *Nanook of the North* (1920–1922), showing how those who lived there meshed with their environment. He also produced outstanding documentaries in various parts of the world: *Tabu* (1931), set in Tahiti; *Man of Aran* (1934), about the people of that Irish island; *Elephant Boy* (1936), set in India. His last production, which was often considered his best, was *Louisiana Story* (1948).

1951 Aug. 16 Louis Jouvet (b. Dec. 29, 1887), a French actor and theatrical producer, died. He became a leading figure of the French theater in the period preceding World War II. He was the director of the Comédie des Champs-Élysées (1924–1945), and then director of L'Athénée (1934). Among his first-rate productions were *Knock, ou le Triomphe de la médicine* (1923) and *La Folle de Chaillot* (1945).

1951 Aug. 21 [Leonard] **Constant Lambert** (b. Aug. 23, 1905), an English composer, died. Diaghilev commissioned him to write the ballet *Romeo and Juliet* (1925) and five year's later Lambert became director of the Sadler's Wells Ballet (to 1947). Besides ballets, Lambert composed various other works: *The Rio Grande* (1927), for piano, orchestra, and chorus, and *Summer's Last Will and Testament* (1932–1935).

1951 Sept. 8 John [French] **Sloan** (b. Aug. 2, 1871), an American painter, died. Beginning with an exhibition in New York with other artists in 1908, he became well known as a member of the *Ashcan*

School. Among Sloan's paintings were *Wake of the Ferry* (1907), *McSorley's Bar* (1912), and *Backyards, Greenwich Village* (1914).

1951 Oct. 15 The first episode of television's *I Love Lucy* went on the air. Starring **Lucille Ball** (b. Aug. 6, 1911) and her husband **Desi**[derio Alberto] **Arnaz** (Mar. 2, 1917–Dec. 2, 1986), it established the format for the **situation comedy**.

1951 Nov. 9 **Sigmund Romberg** (b. July 29, 1871), a Hungarian-born American composer of popular operettas, died. Moving to the U.S. in 1909, he wrote the scores for c.70 operettas. Among Romberg's most popular were *Blossom Time* (1921), *The Student Prince* (1924), *The Desert Song* (1926), and *The New Moon* (1928).

1951 Dec. 24 *Amahl and the Night Visitors*, the first opera written for television, was given its initial broadcast on Christmas Eve by the National Broadcasting Company. Its composer was **Gian-Carlo Menotti**, and it told the story of a lame shepherd boy who gives his crutch to the Three Wise Men as a gift for the Christ Child.

VII. SPORTS, GAMES AND SOCIETY

1951 [Carey] **Estes Kefauver** (July 26, 1903–Aug. 10, 1963), U.S. senator from Tennessee, as chairman of the Senate Committee to Investigate **Organized Crime** in Interstate Commerce, in televised hearings exposed the operations of organized crime and its connection with politics in some U.S. cities.

1951 The **American Bowling Congress** approved the use of **automatic pin-setting machines**, which solved the problem of the shortage of pin boys for the burgeoning indoor sport.

1951 Feb. 12 **Riza Pahlevi**, shah of **Iran**, married **Soraya Esfandiari**, the 19-year-old daughter of a tribal chief, in a Muslim ceremony.

1951 Feb. 25–Mar. 9 The **first Pan American Games**, open to athletes from all the nations of the Western Hemisphere, were held in Buenos Aires, Argentina. In unofficial team scoring, Argentina was first and the U.S. second.

1951 Mar. 29 **Julius Rosenberg** and his wife **Ethel** were found guilty of conspiracy to commit wartime espionage and were sentenced (Apr. 5) to death. They had obtained classified information concerning the **Manhattan Project** which they allegedly turned over to the Soviet consul in New York City. After many appeals, Julius (b. May 12, 1918) and Ethel (b. Sept. 28, 1915) Rosenberg were executed on June 19, 1953 at Sing Sing Prison, Ossining, New York.

1951 May 25 **Guy Burgess** (1911–Aug. 30, 1963) and **Donald** [Duart] **Maclean** (May 25, 1913–Mar. 11, 1983), British Foreign Office officials, fled the country as they were about to be arrested on charges of spying for the Soviet Union. Recruited to communism when they were undergraduates at Cambridge University, the pair passed many secrets, including information on atomic energy developments, to Russia during and after World War II.

1951 July 18 The **world heavyweight boxing championship** was won by **Jersey Joe Walcott** who knocked out the champion **Ezzard Charles** in the seventh round of their bout at Pittsburgh, Pennsylvania.

1951 Sept. 11 **Florence Chadwick** (b. Nov. 9, 1917), an American swimmer, became the **first woman to swim the English Channel** from England to France, the more difficult crossing. Her time was 16 hrs., 19 min.

1952

I. DISASTERS

1952 Mar. 4 A **railroad accident** at **Rio de Janeiro, Brazil**, took 119 lives, when a train derailed and then was struck by another.

1952 Mar. 4 The discontinuous **eruption** across nine years of the volcano **Parícutin**, Michoacan state, in central western Mexico, ended. Parícutin created a cone 6,265 feet high by its many eruptions, having spewed out more than 1 billion tons of lava.

1952 Mar. 21–22 Tornadoes swept through Alabama, Arkansas, Kentucky, Missouri, and Tennessee, killing c.250 persons. Judsonia, Arkansas, was wiped out and 45 of its inhabitants killed.

1952 Apr. 26 The U.S. minesweeper *Hobson* collided in the Atlantic Ocean off the Azores with the aircraft carrier *Wasp* and sank. Deaths totaled 176.

1952 Sept. 6 Post-monsoon storms in the Himalaya Mountains reportedly killed c.350 religious pilgrims near Chamba, in northern India.

1952 Oct. 21–22 A typhoon in the central Philippines left c.400 persons dead and c.350 missing.

1952 Dec. 20 A U.S. air force C-124 transport plane crashed and burned near Moses Lake, Washington, with a loss of 87 lives.

II. POLITICS AND WAR

1952 Feb. 6 George VI (b. Dec. 14, 1895), king of Great Britain and Northern Ireland (from 1936), died. He was noted for his interest in improving the social and industrial conditions of Great Britain and for his courage and steadfastness during World War II. George was succeeded by his daughter Elizabeth II (b. April 21, 1926).

1952 Feb. 6 The Canadian Parliament, for the first time in Canada's history, formally proclaimed that a British monarch, Elizabeth II, was Canada's monarch.

1952 Feb. 28 Vincent Massey (Feb. 20, 1887–Dec. 30, 1967), a Canadian statesman, was sworn in as governor-general of Canada (to 1959), the first native-born Canadian to hold the post. He had also been the first Canadian minister in Washington, D.C. (1926–1930) and had served as high commissioner in London (1935–1946).

1952 Mar. 10 Fulgencio Batista y Zaldivar, a former president (1940–1944), seized power in Cuba through a military coup. The upcoming elections were aborted.

1952 Mar. 22 Don Stephen Senanayake (b. Oct. 20, 1884), the first prime minister of Ceylon [present Sri Lanka] (1947–1952), died. He was succeeded by his son Dudley S. Senanayake (1911–Apr. 12, 1973), the minister of agriculture and lands.

1952 Apr. 12 In Bolivia the *Movimento Nacional Revolucionario* [MNR], having been deprived of the rightful election of its leader Victor Paz Estenssoro (b. Oct. 2, 1907) in 1951, ousted the military junta after several days of fighting in which nearly 3,000 persons were killed. Paz was inaugurated president on Apr. 15.

1952 May 26 West Germany, Great Britain, France, and the U.S. signed the Bonn Convention. It ended allied military occupation and affirmed the principle of West Germany's sovereignty.

1952 May 27 The European Defense Community [EDC] was formed by Belgium, France, Italy, Luxembourg, the Netherlands, and West Germany with the intent of establishing an integrated army. The army was to be integrated with NATO.

1952 June 15 Norodam Sihanouk (b. Oct. 31, 1922), chief of state and king of Cambodia, took over the government after dissolving the parliament, in the wake of civil disorders caused by extremist parties. Sihanouk began a campaign to gain complete independence from France.

1952 July 22 Muhammad Riza Shah Pahlevi, shah of Iran, was forced to reinstate Muhammad Mossadegh, the prime minister, who had been dismissed (July 17) chiefly for his refusal to negotiate a settlement with foreign oil interests in Iran.

1952 July 22 Poland adopted a new constitution, which established a people's republic. Modeled after that of the U.S.S.R., it replaced the office of president by a council of state, elected by the Sejm [parliament].

1952 July 23 Gamal Abdal Nasser, an Egyptian army officer, headed up a military coup, led nominally by Muhammad Naguib, an Egyptian general, that deposed Fouad Farouk, king of Egypt (from 1936). On June 18, 1953, the monarchy was abolished and Naguib became president and premier of the new republic.

1952 July 25 Puerto Rico became a commonwealth. A new constitution took effect giving somewhat greater autonomy to the island. Muñoz Marin (Feb. 18, 1898–Apr. 30, 1980), first elected governor on Nov. 2, 1948, was reelected this year and again in 1956 and 1960.

1952 Aug. 5   Syngman Rhee, president (1948–1960) of the Republic of Korea [**South Korea**], was reelected. Rhee advocated unification of the two Koreas.

1952 Aug. 12   The campaign of **Joseph Stalin** against **Russian Jewish culture** culminated in the execution of 24 leading Soviet Jewish literary figures. They had been put on trial (July 11-18, 1952) after being held and tortured for nearly four years in Lubyanka Prison in Moscow.

1952 Aug. 14   Mátyás Rákosi (Mar. 14, 1892–Feb. 5, 1971), a Hungarian communist politician, became premier of the country. Rákosi remained premier only until July 4, 1953, when he was replaced by **Imre Nagy**.

1952 Sept. 18   Bishara al-Khuri (Aug. 10, 1890–Jan. 11, 1964), president of **Lebanon**, was forced to resign as a general strike developed in opposition to his regime. **Camille Chamoun**, a Maronite Christian, was elected president on Sept. 23.

1952 Sept. 24   Romania adopted a new constitution that reflected its increasing **Sovietization**. Industry and natural resources had been nationalized (1948) and agriculture had been collectivized, and Romania had joined (1949) the **Council of Mutual Economic Assistance** [COMECOM].

1952 Oct. 20   The **Mau Mau insurrection** in **Kenya** began. A secret organization, chiefly of Kikuyu tribesmen determined to oust white settlers, the Mau Mau would soon step up terrorist activities. The British declared a state of emergency in Kenya and sent in troops.

1952 Oct. 27   Jigme Dorji Wangchuk (1928–July 21, 1972) became king (to 1972) of the Himalayan country of **Bhutan**.

1952 Nov. 9   Chaim [Azriel] **Weizmann** (b. Nov. 27, 1874), the first president of **Israel** (1948–1952), died. Russian-born and trained as a chemist, he became a British subject in 1910 and during World War I aided the war effort by inventing a synthetic used in the manufacture of explosives. He played a leading role in securing the **Balfour Declaration** of 1917, promising the Jews a homeland in Palestine. Weizmann became head of the Zionist movement, serving as president of the **World Zionist Organization** (1920–1931, 1935–1946). In World War II he again did research in aid of the British military.

1952 Dec. 1   Adolfo Ruiz Cortines (Dec. 30, 1891–Dec. 3, 1973) was elected president of **Mexico** (1952–1958). His presidency was a period of reform in such areas as taxes and land distribution to the peasants.

1952 Dec. 3   Rudolf Salzmann Slansky (b. July 31, 1901), the secretary general (1945–1951) of the Communist party, which ruled **Czechoslovakia**, was hanged along with ten others. In an internal purge of the Communist party, they were accused of plotting with Jewish intellectuals to overthrow the government.

III. ECONOMICS AND TRADE

1952   Holiday Inns was incorporated by **Charles Kemmons Wilson** with one hotel, located in Memphis, Tennessee.

1952   Denmark, Iceland, Norway, and Sweden formed the **Nordic Council**, a consultative body instituted to treat all matters of common interest, such as passports, patent rights, and economic development, except foreign policy and defense.

1952   The **Saudi Arabian Monetary Agency** [SAMA] was established, providing that country's first central bank and introducing modern finance.

1952 July 25   The **European Coal and Steel Community** [ECSC], established by Belgium, France, Italy, Luxembourg, the Netherlands, and West Germany, became operative. Members agreed to abolish duties on coal and steel in commerce between the members; to establish rules for the regulation of cartels and mergers; to harmonize transportation rates; and in case of emergency to control prices and production.

IV. RELIGION AND PHILOSOPHY

1952 June 1   John Dewey (b. Oct. 20, 1859), a philosopher and a leader in the progressive movement in American education, died. Dewey advocated abandonment of authoritarian methods in teaching and advocated experimentation and practice as roads to learning. Among Dewey's many books were *The School and Society* (1899), *Human Nature and Conduct* (1922), and *Freedom and Culture* (1939).

1952 Sept. 26   George Santayana (b. Dec. 16, 1863), a Spanish-born American philosopher and man of letters, died. The precision of his thought and the elegance of his style added luster to the literary world. His books included *The Sense of Beauty* (1896), *The Life of Reason* (1905–1906), *Skepticism and Animal Faith* (1923), *The Realm of Being* (1927–1940), and one novel, *The Last Puritan* (1935).

1952 Nov. 20 Benedetto Croce (b. Feb. 25, 1866), an Italian philosopher, historian, and statesman, died. He held public office before the coming of fascism, which he opposed, and after Italy was defeated in World War II he was president (1943–1952) of the reorganized Liberal party. Croce's idealistic philosophy is presented, for example, in a four-part work, *Filosofia della spirito* [*Philosophy of the Spirit*] (1902–1917).

V. SCIENCE, EDUCATION AND TECHNOLOGY

1952 A successful vaccine to prevent **poliomyelitis** was developed by **Jonas** [Edward] **Salk** (b. Oct. 28, 1914), an American physician and microbiologist. It was placed in general use in 1954 when the **National Foundation for Infantile Paralysis** began (Apr. 26) the mass inoculation of school children.

1952 The **first breeder reactor** of the Nuclear Age was built by the **U.S. Atomic Energy Commission** near Idaho Flats, Idaho. It utilized non-fissionable U-238, an isotope of uranium, which was converted by neutron bombardment to fissionable plutonium-239.

1952 R[ichard] **Buckminster Fuller** (July 12, 1895–July 1, 1983), an American engineer and architect, displayed his "**geodesic dome**," a structure shaped like a hemisphere, that could be constructed of various materials and was strong for its weight.

1952 **Linear B**, a hitherto untranslated Mycenaean script, found at the ancient city of Knossos on the island of Crete, was deciphered by **Michael** [George Francis] **Ventris** (July 12, 1922–Sept. 5, 1956), an English cryptologist. The work of Ventris showed that it was the **oldest known form of the Greek language**.

1952 **Kathleen Mary Kenyon** (Jan. 5, 1906–Aug. 24, 1978), an English archeologist, began a six-year excavation and exploration of the site of the prehistoric and Old Testament site of **Jericho** near the modern town of Ariha, c.14 miles from Jerusalem,

that showed it was the **oldest known settlement in the world**, dating to c.11,000 B.P.

1952 The first publicized case of a **sex change through operations** and hormone treatments was that of **George Jorgensen** (May 30, 1926–May 3, 1989), who became **Christine** Jorgensen. The process was carried out at a Copenhagen, Denmark, hospital.

1952 July 7 The turbine-powered *United States*, launched earlier this year, set **steamship speed records** by crossing the Atlantic Ocean in 3 days, 10 hours, 40 minutes at an average speed of 41 miles per hour.

1952 Nov. 1 The **first thermonuclear** [fusion] **bomb**, also called the **H-bomb** [hydrogen bomb], was exploded by the U.S. at Eniwetok, an atoll in the Marshall Islands in the central western Pacific Ocean. The group of scientists who developed the device was led by **Edward Teller** (b. Jan. 15, 1908), a Hungarian-born American physicist, who had also been active in the development of the first atomic bomb during World War II.

1952 Dec. 12 The **first known serious accident at a nuclear reactor** occurred in a government-owned plant at Chalk River, northwest of **Ottawa, Canada**. A technician mistakenly removed four control rods, causing the nuclear core to explode. Millions of gallons of radioactive water accumulated inside the reactor but no injuries were reported.

VI. ARTS AND LEISURE

1952 Dutch-born American painter **William de Kooning** (b. April 24, 1904) showed his *Woman I* for the first time at a one-man show in New York City.

1952 Ralph [Waldo] **Ellison** (b. Mar. 1, 1914), an American author and teacher, published *Invisible Man*, a novel that caused an unusual stir because of its portrayal of a young black man's attempt to find a place in a society that seemed to exclude black people.

1952 Feb. 19 Knut **Hamsun** (b. Aug. 4, 1859), a Norwegian novelist, died. The author of *Hunger* (1890), *Pan* (1894), and his masterpiece *The Growth of the Soil* (1917), he was awarded the **Nobel prize for literature** in 1920. His popularity was spoiled because of his Nazi sympathies in World War II.

1952 Apr. 1 Ferenc Molnar (b. Jan. 12, 1878), a Hungarian playwright, died. In 1909 he wrote his most highly regarded play *Liliom*, which later formed the basis for the Rodgers and Hammerstein musical *Carousel* (1945). Among Molnar's many other plays were *The Guardsmen* (1910), *The Swan* (1920), and *The Play's the Thing* (1926).

1952 May 26 The Supreme Court of the United States for the first time applied **First Amendment guarantees to a motion picture**. The decision came in **Burstyn v. Wilson**, a case involving the Italian film *The Miracle*, which had been declared sacrilegious by the New York Board of Education censors.

1952 Sept. 20 The *Jackie Gleason Show* premiered on the CBS Television Network. For more than a decade, [Herbert John] **Jackie Gleason** (Feb. 26, 1916–June 24, 1987) was one of the most inventive comedians on television.

1952 Nov. 18   Paul Éluard [pen name of Eugene Grindel] (b. Dec. 14, 1895), a French poet who was a leader among the surrealists, died. He became politically active in the Communist party and during World War II was a member of the French Resistance. Éluard wrote, among many other volumes of verse, *Le Devoir et l'inquiétude* (1917), in which he expressed his early pacifistic views, and *Poèmes politiques* (1948).

VII. SPORTS, GAMES AND SOCIETY

1952 Feb. 14–25 The sixth Winter **Olympic Games** were held at Olso, Norway, with 732 athletes from 30 countries participating. Norwegian athletes won 7 gold and 16 medals in all, followed by the U.S. with 4 and 11, and Finland with 3 and 9.

1952 May 3   Eddie Arcaro, riding Hill Gail, became the **first jockey to ride five Kentucky Derby winners**, in 1938, 1941, 1945, 1948, and 1952.

1952 July 19–Aug. 3 The fifteenth Summer **Olympic Games** were held at Helsinki, Finland, with 4,925 athletes from 69 nations competing. American athletes won 40 gold and 76 medals in all, followed by the USSR with 22 and 71, and Hungary with 16 and 42.

1952 Sept. 23 The **world heavyweight boxing championship** was won by **Rocky Marciano**, at Philadelphia, when he knocked out the defending titleholder **Joe Walcott** in the 23rd round. Marciano defended his title six times and retired on Apr. 27, 1956. In his career he won all 49 of his bouts, all but six by knockouts.

1952 Sept. 29   John Cobb (b. Dec. 2, 1899), an Englishman, immediately after achieving a breakthrough of the supposed 200 miles per hour barrier for motorboats with a clocking of 206 miles per hour over a measured mile in his jet-propelled **Crusader** on Loch Ness, Scotland, was killed when his boat disintegrated.

1953

I. DISASTERS

1953 Jan. 9 A South Korean ferry, *Chang Tyong-Ho*, sank off the port of Pusan [Fusan], on the Korea Strait, with the loss of 249 lives.

1953 Jan. 31–Feb. 1 Spring tides lashed by **gale winds devastated coastal areas** of the **Netherlands, Belgium, and England**. About 2,000 people died. There was about $400,000,000 worth of damage. The giant sea dike in Zeeland broke, leaving large areas of the Netherlands under water. More than 1,700 Dutch citizens and c.250,000 farm animals were killed.

1953 Feb. 21 Two **trolley cars collided** in **Mexico City**, killing 79 persons.

1953 Mar. 18 An **earthquake in northwestern Turkey**, left more than 1,200 dead and c.50,000 homeless. The quake registered 7.2 on the Richter scale.

1953 May 11 A **tornado hit downtown Waco**, Texas, during business hours. Deaths numbered 114, with 597 injured and property damage set at $41,-150,000.

1953 June 18 A U.S. air force **C-124 crashed** and burned near Tokyo, killing 129.

1953 Dec. 24 A Wellington-Auckland **express train plunged into the swollen Wanganui River** near Wairouru, in central North Island, New Zealand, killing 155 passengers.

II. POLITICS AND WAR

1953 Jan. 20 **Dwight D. Eisenhower** was inaugurated as the 34th president of the U.S. Running on the Republican party ticket, he defeated **Adlai E[wing] Stevenson** (Feb. 5, 1900–July 14, 1965), the Democratic party candidate, in the election of Nov. 2, 1952. Eisenhower received 33,938,285 popular votes and 442 electoral college votes. Stevenson received 27,312,217 and 89. **Richard M[ilhous] Nixon** was inaugurated as vice president.

1953 Feb. 12 Egypt and Great Britain signed an agreement to end their 54-year-old system of **joint sovereignty** over the Anglo-Egyptian **Sudan**. The Sudanese were to become independent within three years.

1953 Mar. 5 **Joseph Stalin** [Josif Vissarionovich Dzhugashvili] (b. Dec. 21, 1879), head of the Communist party of the U.S.S.R. (since 1922) and virtual dictator of Russia (since 1927), died. He was buried next to Lenin in the Red Square mausoleum, but his body was moved (1961) to a cemetery for heroes near the Kremlin wall, evidence that since his death he had fallen out of favor with the new rulers of Russia. Stalin was succeeded the next day as chairman of the Council of Ministers and as head of the Communist party by **Georgi** [Maximilianovich] **Malenkov**. However, he held this latter post only until Sept. 12, when **Nikita Khrushchev** succeeded him. Malenkov and Khruschev were long-time associates of Stalin, holding high office in the party, but these changes reflected a struggle for power within the party hierarchy. On July 10 **Lavrenti** [Pavlovich] **Beria**, head of the secret police under Stalin, and a deputy premier in the new regime, was arrested on charges of conspiracy. Beria (b. Mar. 29, 1899), and six alleged accomplices in a plot to seize power, were executed on Dec. 23.

1953 Apr. 7 **Dag Hammarskjöld**, a Swedish statesman who had served his country in its cabinet and on diplomatic missions, was elected secretary general of the **United Nations** and served until his death. While Hammarskjöld (b. July 29, 1905) was on a peacekeeping mission to the Congo [present Zaire], his plane crashed in Northern Rhodesia [present Zambia] and he was killed on Sept. 18, 1961. Hammarskjöld was posthumously awarded the **Nobel Peace Prize** in 1961.

1953 Apr. 8 **Jomo Kenyatta**, an African activist, was convicted of being an instigator of the **Mau Mau uprisings** in Kenya. Imprisoned, he was finally exiled (1959) until 1961.

1953 Apr. 18 **Mohammad Ali Bogra** replaced **Khwaza Nazimuddin** as prime minister (to 1955) of **Pakistan**. Dissatisfaction with the central government was increasing, especially in East Bengal.

1953 Apr. 27 In the first election held in **British Guiana** [Guyana] under the new constitution of 1952, the communist-oriented People's Progressive party [PPP] won, and its leader, **Cheddi Jagan** (b. Mar. 22, 1918) formed a government. In October, however, British authorities suspended the constitution because of pro-communist strikes and riots, establishing a caretaker government.

1953 May 2 **Faisal II** succeeded to the throne of **Iraq**, after a long regency following the early death of his father, **Ghazi**. Pro-Western Faisal (b. May 2, 1935) was killed on July 14, 1958, in the revolution led by **Abdul Karim Kassem**.

1953 May 28 **Greenland** was made an integral part of **Denmark**, a constitutional monarchy, by the adoption by plebiscite of a new constitution. Greenland thereafter had its own two representatives in the unicameral **Folketing** [parliament].

1953 June 13 **Gustavo Rojas Pinilla** (Mar. 12, 1900–Jan. 17, 1975), a general in the Colombian army, became the head of a new provisional government in **Colombia**, ousting the archconservative dictator (from 1950) **Laureano Gómez**, whose repressive civilian government had failed to put down the widespread violence.

1953 June 17–18 Crowds of East Berlin workers, protesting economic hardships and communist-imposed work rules, rioted. The protest swelled to a **general strike over most of East Germany**. Soviet military forces suppressed the revolt and 16 people were killed.

1953 June 18 The monarchy of **Egypt** was abolished and a republic proclaimed. **Muhammad Naguib** became president, but the seat of power was in the hands of the **Revolutionary Command Committee** [RCC], whose dominant voice was that of **Gamal Abdal Nasser** .

1953 June 21 **Adib a-Shishakli**, virtual dictator of **Syria** since his coup of Dec., 1949, put forward a new constitution providing a presidential form of government, which was duly approved by voters. Not surprisingly, a-Shishakli was elected president and continued his dictatorial ways until his ouster in early 1954.

1953 July 26 **Fidel Castro** (b. Aug. 13, 1927), Cuban lawyer and critic of the Batista regime, with c.170 followers, led an ill-fated attack on an army post in Santiago de Cuba. Imprisoned (1953) but released (1955), Castro went to Mexico, where he began organizing the "**26th of July Movement**" of guerrillas.

1953 July 27 A truce ending the **Korean War** (from 1950) was signed at **Panmunjom** after three years of fighting between the U.N. and the North Korean and Chinese forces. The boundary between North and South Korea remained the same—the 38th parallel, with a no-man's land 1.24 miles wide on either side of the boundary. U.S. losses were c.54,000 dead, c.103,000 wounded. Korean losses for each side were probably ten times as many. It was estimated that the Chinese suffered 900,000 casualties.

1953 July 30 **Libya** signed a 20-year treaty with Great Britain, conceding military bases in exchange for an annual subsidy. Libya made a similar deal with the U.S. in 1954.

1953 Aug. 2 **Bolivia's** agrarian reform decree was promulgated by the nationalistic, leftist *Movimiento Nacional Revolucionario* [MNR] government. It was a broad and ambitious measure, including the expropriation of large landholdings, extension of civil rights and suffrage, and the initiation of health, education and construction projects.

1953 Aug. 16 **Muhammad Riza Shah Pahlevi**, the shah of **Iran**, and his family fled the country to escape arrest by **Muhammad Mossadegh**, the antiwestern prime minister (from 1951) whom the shah had tried to dismiss on Aug. 13. Very shortly a proroyalist coup (Aug. 18–19) by **Fazlollah Zahedi** (1897–Sept 2, 1963), an army general whom the shah had appointed prime minister (to 1955), supported by the U.S. **Central Intelligence Agency** [CIA], arrested Mossadegh, enabling the royal family to return on Aug. 22. Muhammad Mossadegh (b. 1880) was tried for treason and sentenced to life imprisonment; after serving three years he was placed under house arrest until he died on Mar. 5, 1967.

1953 Aug. 20 The French government deposed and exiled to Corsica **Mohammad V** [Sidi Muhammad ben Youssef], the sultan of **Morocco** (from 1927). He had given his support to the **Istiglal**, a nationalist organization demanding independence for both French and Spanish Morocco. The French replaced Mohammad with pro-French **Mohammad VI** [Sidi Moulay Muhammad ben Arafa] (1890–July 18, 1976) as sultan. Faced with growing restiveness and resistance to colonial rule, the French restored Mohammad V as sultan on Nov. 5, 1955.

1953 Aug. 29 The **U.S.S.R.** exploded its first thermonuclear bomb.

1953 Sept. 26 The U.S. and Spain signed agreements allowing the **U.S. to establish air and naval bases in Spain**. In return economic and military aid was promised by the U.S. On Sept. 6 a similar pact was signed by the U.S. and Portugal.

1953 Oct. 22 France granted independence to **Laos** except in military affairs. However, the **Pathet Lao**, a communist nationalist movement aided by Vietnam communists, gained control of northern Laos and set up a rival government headed by **Prince Souphanouvong**. Civil war ensued.

1953 Oct. 23 Northern Rhodesia and Nyasaland, together with the self-governing colony of Southern Rhodesia, were combined as the **Federation of Rhodesia and Nyasaland** with a governor general appointed by Great Britain.

1953 Nov. 9 **Ibn Saud** [Abd-al-'Aziz ibn-'Abd-al-Rahman al-Faisal ibn-Su'ud] (born c.1888), founder and king of Saudi Arabia (1924), died. He had defeated (1924–1925) **Husayn ibn Ali** of the Hijaz and added this region to his own Najd. In 1932 Ibn Saud had named his kingdom **Saudi Arabia** and ended the tribal vendettas and the extortion practiced on Muslim pilgrims to Mecca. He was succeeded by his eldest son **Saud IV** [Abd al-Azizas Saud] (Jan. 15, 1902–Feb. 23, 1969), who was deposed in 1964.

1953 Nov. 10   Ramón Magsaysay, the Philippine minister of defense, defeated **Elpidio Quirino**, president of **Philippines**, in the national election. His presidency was marked by close relations with the U.S. and the pursuit of land and government reform.

1953 Dec. 8   An "**Atoms for Peace**" proposal was made by **Dwight D. Eisenhower**, president of the U.S. Basic to it was the recommendation that an **International Atomic Energy Agency** be established to encourage international cooperation in building nuclear power plants and developing other possible peacetime uses of atomic energy.

III. ECONOMY AND TRADE

1953   Canada's **Interprovincial Pipeline** was opened. It connected the recently discovered major oil fields in the western province of Alberta with the Great Lakes port city of Sarnia in southern Ontario.

1953   The **mining** of the recently discovered vast resources of lead, zinc, and copper began in the area near Bathurst, New Brunswick, Canada.

1953 Jan. 1   The **People's Republic of China**, assisted by the U.S.S.R., launched its **first Five Year Plan**. Its goals were the nationalization of industry and the collectivization of agriculture.

1953 Feb. 10   The **European Coal and Steel Community** effectively established a single market for coal and, on May 1, a single market for steel.

IV. SCIENCE, EDUCATION AND TECHNOLOGY

1953   **James Dewey Watson** (b. Apr. 6, 1928), an American biologist, and **Francis** [Harry Compton] **Crick** (b. June 18, 1916), an English geneticist, developed a model for the structure of **deoxyribonucleic acid** [DNA]. Called the **double helix** [two spirally wound chains], it described the genetic code of chromosomes and explained how heredity is transmitted in living organisms. Watson and Crick shared the **Nobel prize for physiology or medicine** in 1962.

1953   **Charles Hard Townes** (b. July 28, 1915), an American physicist and discoverer in 1951 of the basic principles that led to the development of the maser, built with others the first such device to amplify radio waves. This led to the development in

1958 by Townes and **Arthur L. Schawlow** (b. May 5, 1921) of the laser, a device for amplifying light waves. Townes was, with two Russian physicists, awarded the **Nobel prize for physics** in 1964 for his microwave research and subsequent applications.

1953 May 18   Jacqueline Cochran (1910?–Aug. 9, 1980), an American pilot, became the **first woman to fly faster than sound**, attaining a speed of 652 miles per hour in an F-83 Sabre jet.

1953 Sept. 28   Edwin Powell Hubble (b. Nov. 20, 1889), an American astronomer, died. His work in the early 1920s established the existence of other galaxies beyond the Milky Way in all directions.

1953 Dec. 19   Robert Andrews Millikan (b. Mar. 22, 1868), an American physicist, died. In 1925 he named cosmic rays and investigated how this radiation from outer space, known since 1911, was absorbed by the atmosphere and by the water in deep lakes. Earlier (1913) Millikan measured the charge electrons carry and confirmed Planck's constant. He received the **Nobel prize for physics** in 1923.

V. ARTS AND LEISURE

1953 Jan. 5   The play *En Attendant Godot* [*Waiting for Godot*], by **Samuel Beckett**, an Irish-French playwright, was given its first performance at the Petit Théâtre de Babylone in Paris. Beckett portrayed trapped individuals, but seen with humanity, poignancy, and kindly humor.

1953 Mar. 4   Sergei [Sergeyevich] **Prokofiev** (b. Apr. 7, 1891), a Russian composer, pianist, and conductor, died. Of his seven symphonies, the First (1917) and the Fifth (1944) have been the most popular. Of five important operas, perhaps *The Love for Three Oranges* (1921) is today the best known. His *Romeo and Juliet* (1940) is a standard ballet, and the fairy tale in music, *Peter and the Wolf* (1936), is popular with generations of adults and children.

1953 Mar. 23   Raoul Dufy (b. June 30, 1877), a French painter, illustrator and decorator, died. An early Fauvist (1905–1908), Dufy later developed his own colorful style, painting landscapes, seascapes, and scenes of social life.

1953 May 14   Yasuo Kuniyoshi (b. Sept. 1, 1893), a Japanese-American artist, died. He moved to the U.S. in 1906 and in 1948 was given the first one-man show ever presented by the Whitney Museum of Art, New York City. Among his paintings were *I'm Tired* (1938), *Desert Woman* (1943), and *Juggler* (1952).

1953 June 9 **Ugo Betti** (b. Feb. 4, 1892), an Italian dramatist but a judge by profession, died. Betti wrote 27 plays of which 24 were produced. His last play, *The Gambler*, was produced in 1951. Betti wrote about life as he saw it from the bench, with guilt and forgiveness the chief concern. His greatest successes included *La padroma* [*The Mistress of the House*] (1927) and *Delitto all'isola della capre* [*Crime in Goat Island*] (1950).

1953 July 16 [Joseph] **Hilaire** [Pierre] **Belloc** (b. July 27, 1870), a French-born English author, died. One of his earliest works was *A Bad Child's Book of Beasts* (1896). For the young he also wrote *Cautionary Tales* (1907) and *Cautionary Verses* (1941). Belloc's more serious works included *The Path to Rome* (1902), *The Servile State* (1912), and the novel *Belinda* (1928).

1953 July 17 **Maude** [Ewing] **Adams** [orig.: Kiskadden] (b. Nov. 11, 1872), an American actress, died. In 1905 she appeared in the title role of *Peter Pan* (1904) and played Peter many times in later years. Adams's other successes included *What Every Woman Knows* (1908) and *The Merchant of Venice*.

1953 Oct. 1 **John** [Cheri] **Marin** (b. Dec. 23, 1870), an early exponent of modern art in the U.S., died. He was best known for his watercolors, such as *Lower Manhattan from the River* (1920), *Maine Islands* (1922), *Tunk Mountains, Maine* (1945) and, especially, for his earlier *Woolworth Building* (1912).

1953 Oct. 3 **Arnold** [Edward Trevor] **Bax** (b. Nov. 8, 1883), an English composer, died. His most important works were his seven symphonies (1922–1939).

1953 Nov. 8 **Ivan Bunin** (Oct. 10, 1870), the **first Russian writer to be awarded (1933) the Nobel prize for literature**, died. Coming to notice first as a poet, Bunin soon produced two novels in the classic Russian style, *The Village* (1910) and *The Dry Valley* (1912), which brought him international fame. *The Gentleman from San Francisco* (1914), the title story in a collection of powerful short stories, represented Bunin at his peak. After leaving Russia (1919) for France, Bunin wrote *The Well of Days* (1930), an autobiographical novel, and *Memories and Portraits* (1950), reminiscences.

1953 Nov. 9 **Dylan** [Marlais] **Thomas** (b. Oct. 14, 1914), a Welsh poet and prose writer, died. His first volume of verse, *Eighteen Poems*, was published in 1934; his *Collected Poems* appeared in 1952. Thomas's prose works included *Portrait of the Artist as a Young Dog* (1940), a collection of autobiographical stories, and *Adventures in the Skin Trade* (1955). His best known work was *Under Milk Wood*, a play written for radio, giving impressions of a spring day in Wales and first broadcast in Jan., 1954, by the BBC.

1953 Nov. 27 **Eugene O'Neill** (b. Oct. 16, 1888), America's leading playwright, died. O'Neill borrowed from German expressionist drama and employed the techniques of stream of consciousness and subtle psychological analysis. His works included: *The Emperor Jones* (1920); *Anna Christie* (1921); *The Hairy Ape* (1922); *Desire Under the Elms* (1924); *Mourning Becomes Electra* (1931); *A Moon for the Misbegotten* (1946); and, posthumously produced, *Long Day's Journey into Night* (1956), and *A Touch of the Poet* (1958).

VI. SPORTS, GAMES, AND SOCIETY

1953 May 29 **Edmund Percival Hillary** (b. July 20, 1919), a New Zealand mountain climber and explorer, and his Sherpa guide **Tenzing Norkay** became the first persons to reach the top of **Mount Everest** (29,028 feet) in the Himalaya Mountains, the highest elevation on earth.

1953 June 5 [William Tatem] **Bill Tilden** (b. Feb. 10, 1893), a great American tennis player, died. During the 1920s he dominated international **tennis**. He won the U.S. championship six years in a row (1920–1925). In 1920 he also took the British title and repeated that feat twice. In Davis Cup play Tilden led the American team to seven straight triumphs (1920–1926).

1953 Sept. 7 **Maureen Catherine "Little Mo" Connolly** (Sept. 17, 1934–June 21, 1969), an American **tennis** star, became the first woman and the second person to achieve the "grand slam" in tennis when she won the U.S. Lawn Tennis Association women's championship. Connolly had earlier this year won the Australian, French, and British championships.

1954

I. DISASTERS

1954 Feb. 13 A **rush of Hindus** attempting to bathe in the Ganges River near Allahabad, northern India, during a religious festival resulted in c.500 deaths and injuries to c.2,000.

1954 May 26 Off Quonset Point, on Narragansett Bay, an explosion and **fire aboard the U.S. aircraft carrier** *Bennington* took the lives of 103 crew members.

1954 Summer In China, continual **monsoon rains** raised the water level of the Yangtze River almost five feet above previous record flood levels. In eastern China, more than 10,000,000 people were evacuated, and c.42,000 square miles were flooded.

1954 Aug. 31 **Hurricane Carol struck the U.S. east coast**, hitting especially hard Long Island, New York; Connecticut; and Rhode Island. Abnormally high sea levels and tidal waves battered the coastline in a 150-mile swath; 68 persons died and damage was estimated at $500 million.

1954 Sept. 9–12 A series of **earthquake** tremors nearly destroyed the Algerian town of Orléansville, west of Algiers, and killed more than 1,600 persons.

1954 Sept. 26 The Japanese ferry *Toya Maru* capsized during a typhoon in Tsugaru Strait near the Japanese island of Honshu; 1,086 persons drowned.

1954 Oct. 12–13 A second **hurricane** of the season, Hazel, struck the east coast of the U.S. and this time also ravaged Haiti and southern Canada. Haiti suffered 410 deaths with c.5,000 persons injured. In the U.S. the death toll was 99 and in Canada 24. Property damage was estimated at $100 million.

II. POLITICS AND WAR

1954 Feb. 25 **Adib al-Shishakli**, president of **Syria** and proponent of union with Egypt, was overthrown in a coup by elements opposing his foreign policy. The 1950 constitution was reinstated and a civilian government formed (Feb. 28) with **Hashim al-Atassi** (1864–Dec. 6, 1960) once again as president.

1954 Mar. 1 Four **Puerto Rican nationalists**, three men and a woman, opened gunfire from the gallery of the U.S. House of Representatives, wounding five Congressmen. The gunmen, later imprisoned, were proponents of independence for Puerto Rico, trying to dramatize their cause.

1954 Apr. 26–July 21 The **Geneva Conference** met to restore peace in Korea and Indochina. Many nations attended, but there was no progress toward permanent peace in Korea even though peace agreements were signed by Vietnam, Cambodia, and Laos.

1954 May 7 Viet Minh forces under **Vo Nguyen Giap** captured the French military base at **Dien Bien Phu** in northern Vietnam. This hard-won victory came after a 55-day siege resulting in c.6,000 French casualties and c.10,000 French prisoners. It was the end of French power in Indochina.

1954 May 17 The leader of the **Huk** [Hukbalahap] **guerrillas** in the Philippines, **Luis Turuk**, surrendered. The campaign of conciliation on land reform, plus the military pressure of **Ramón Magsaysay**, when he was defense minister, had proven effective.

1954 May 17 In a landmark decision, *Brown v. the Board of Education of Topeka, Kan.*, the U.S. Supreme Court held unanimously that all **segregation in public schools** is "inherently unequal," and that black students so segregated are denied equal protection of the law. The "separate but equal" ruling (1896) of the Supreme Court was overturned.

1954 June 18 **Pierre Mendes-France** (Jan. 11, 1907–Oct. 18, 1982), a French politician, became premier. Determined to end French involvement in Indochina, he agreed on July 21 to the terms of the **Geneva Conference** calling for French withdrawal from North Vietnam. In Tunisia on July 31 he issued a declaration that recognized **Tunisia's right to autonomy**.

1954 June 18 In a military coup **Carlos Castillo Armas** and Guatemalan troops took Guatemala City, forcing **Jacobo Arbenz Guzmán**, president of **Guatemala**, to flee the country. On Sept. 1, Castillo Armas was elected president for a six-year term.

1954 July 21 A cease-fire agreement, ending the **Indochina War**, was signed in Geneva. After 7 years and 7 months the French and pro-French forces suffered c.253,000 casualties, of which c.92,000 were killed or missing. More than 200,000 Viet Minh troops, which included forces from Cambodia and Laos as well as Vietnam, were killed. Vietnam was partitioned along the 17th parallel with the Viet Minh government of **Ho Chi Minh** in control of the north and the nationalistic government of **Bao Dai**, chief of state of Vietnam, in the south.

1954 Aug. 24 **Getúlio Vargas** (b. Apr. 19, 1883), president of **Brazil**, who had dominated his country from 1930, shot and killed himself after he was forced to resign. He was succeeded by **Jaōa Café Filho** (Feb. 3, 1899–Feb. 20, 1970), who had been the vice president.

1954 Sept. 8 The **Southeast Asia Treaty Organization** [SEATO] was formed by representatives of Australia, New Zealand, Pakistan, Thailand, the Philippines, Great Britain, France, and the U.S. **John Foster Dulles** (Feb. 25, 1888–May 24, 1959), U.S. secretary of state, promoted SEATO successfully in Indochina; it aimed at thwarting further territorial expansion of communism in Southeast Asia.

1954 Oct. 5 The territorial dispute over the **Free Territory of Trieste** was settled by a compromise agreement negotiated by Western powers. The settlement partitioned the territory, Italian-speaking Trieste and environs to Italy, the rest to Yugoslavia.

1954 Oct. 10 In the **Honduras** election, liberal **Ramón Villeda Morales** (Nov. 26, 1908–Sept. 8, 1971), outpolled other candidates with a 47 percent plurality, insufficient to win election. The National Congress, empowered to choose the winner, named (Dec. 6) the outgoing vice president, **Julio Lozano Díaz** (1895?–Aug. 20, 1957) the winner.

1954 Oct. 11 At a meeting in Peking, the governments of **China and the U.S.S.R.**, pledged political cooperation and Russian economic assistance for China. The USSR also agreed to turn over to China by May 31, 1955, the city of Port Arthur [Lü-shun], which it had occupied jointly with China since 1945.

1954 Oct. 19 Great Britain and Egypt signed an agreement whereby British troops would leave the **Suez Canal Zone** after 72 years of occupation.

1954 Nov. 1 An open revolt against French rule broke out in **Algeria**, led by the newly formed National Liberation Front [Front de Libération Nationale, or FLN]. Police and government offices in northeastern Algeria were attacked. The **FLN** goal was the establishment of an autonomous Algerian state.

1954 Nov. 17 **Gamal Abdal Nasser** assumed the powers of the presidency of **Egypt**. The former president **Mohammad Naguib** had resigned (Feb. 25) as premier and Nasser became (Apr. 18) premier and military governor.

1954 Dec. 9 **Ichiro Hatoyama** (Jan. 1, 1883–Mar. 5, 1959), leader of the Democratic party, became prime minister of **Japan**, succeeding (from 1947) **Shigeru Yoshida**.

III. ECONOMY AND TRADE

1954 **Ecuador** claimed territorial jurisdiction up to 200 miles off its coast. The current international practice recognized only a 12-mile exclusive fisheries zone. Ecuador's claim set the stage for the so-called "tuna war" with the U.S. tuna fishing industry.

1954 Apr. The **United Automobile Workers Union** [UAW] began a strike against the Kohler Company at Sheboygan, Wisconsin, that would last eight years.

1954 Aug. 5 Iran and a consortium of British, American, French, and Dutch oil companies entered into an agreement for the operation of Iran's former **Anglo-Iranian Oil Company**, on the basis of an equal sharing of the profits.

1954 Sept. 9 Libya and the U.S. signed an agreement under which the U.S., in exchange for financial aid of $40 million across 20 years, secured the **military base at Wheelus Field** near Tripoli.

IV. SCIENCE, EDUCATION, AND TECHNOLOGY

1954 The **first successful kidney transplant** operation was performed at Peter Bent Brigham Hospital in Boston by a surgical team headed by **Joseph Edward Murray** (b. Apr. 1, 1919) of the Harvard Medical School.

1954 Jan. 21 The U.S. navy launched the **first nuclear-powered submarine**, the *Nautilus*. The first submarine capable of indefinite submersion, it was 319 feet long, with a displacement of 3,180 tons, and capable of speeds up to 20 knots.

1954 Mar. 25 The **first color television sets** were manufactured by the Radio Corporation of America [RCA]. Designed to be mass-marketed for use in the home, they were 15-inch models, selling for $1000 each.

1954 May 26 Exploring the **tomb of Khufu** [Cheops] (fl. c.2600 B.C.), king of Egypt, archeologists found the remains of a boat made of cedar. It was originally c.142 feet long and apparently was intended to carry the dead pharaoh to the next world in state.

1954 June The **U.S.S.R. put into operation its first nuclear power plant**, at Obninsk, c.55 miles from Moscow. It could produce c.5,000 kilowatts.

1954 June 7 **Alan** [Mathison] **Turing** (b. June 23, 1912), an English mathematician, died. During World War II Turing's theories took practical shape as a machine called **Colossus**, which the British used to decipher the supposedly unbreakable German codes that used the Enigma machine. This was the first all-electronic calculating device.

1954 Nov. 3 **Linus Carl Pauling** (b. Feb. 28, 1901), an American chemist, was awarded the **Nobel prize for chemistry** for his work on chemical bonds and molecular structure. In 1962 Pauling was awarded a second **Nobel prize**, this time the **Peace Prize**.

1954 Nov. 28 **Enrico Fermi** (b. Sept. 29, 1901), an Italian-born American physicist, died of cancer in Chicago, where he was professor of physics. In 1938 he was awarded the **Nobel prize for physics** for his experiments with radioactivity. Fermi led a team at Chicago that created the first self-sustaining chain reaction (Dec. 2, 1942). In 1943 he moved to Los Alamos, New Mexico, to work on the atomic bomb that was successfully tested on July 16, 1945.

V. ARTS AND LEISURE

1954 **William** [Gerald] **Golding** (Sept. 19, 1911–June 19, 1993), an English novelist, published *Lord of the Flies*, a first novel which captured and held readers over the years with its chilling account of a group of boys, marooned on an island, who resort to savagery. Among Golding's other novels were *Pincher Martin* (1956), *The Spire* (1964), *Darkness Visible* (1980), and *Fire Down Below* (1989). Golding was awarded the **Nobel prize for literature** in 1983.

1954 **Françoise Sagan** [pen name of Françoise Quoirez] (b. Nov. 9, 1935), a 19-year old French writer, made a sensational debut with a short novel *Bonjour Tristesse*, the story of a girl's attempt to prevent her father's remarriage. It became an international bestseller.

1954 **Federico Fellini** (b. Jan. 20, 1920), an Italian movie director, scored a solid international hit with his *La Strada* [*The Road*]. His other notable films were *Nights of Cabiria* (1957), *La Dolce Vita* [*The Sweet Life*] (1960), *8½* (1963), and *Amercord* (1973).

1954 Jan. 11 **Oscar Straus** (b. Apr. 6, 1870), an Austrian composer, died. He was best known for his popular and successful operettas, especially *A Waltz Dream* (1907) and *The Chocolate Soldier* (1908).

1954 May 19 **Charles Ives** (b. Oct. 20, 1874), an American composer and organist, died. His works often incorporated musical themes drawn from the American scene. His *Third Symphony* (1947) was praised in particular.

1954 May 29 The **Robert Joffrey Ballet** made its debut with a performance in New York City of *Pas des déesses* and *Le Bal masqué*. The ballet's founder was **Robert Joffrey** [orig.: Abdullah Jaffa Bey Khan] (b. Dec. 24, 1930), a dancer and choreographer.

1954 July **Rock 'n' roll** as a recognized form of popular music was said to have begun with the recording of "That's All Right, Mama" by a young southern-born American entertainer **Elvis** [Aron] **Presley**. Emphasis was placed on rhythm coming from electric guitars and drums, played very loudly.

1954 July 3 **Reginald Marsh** (b. Mar. 14, 1898), an American painter and illustrator, died. He was an illustrator for a number of leading magazines and also was a scene designer for the theater, but he was best remembered for his paintings of New York City street life. Among them were *The Bowery* (1930), *Tattoo and Haircut* (1932), and *Twenty-Cent Movie* (1936).

1954 July 14   Jacinto Benavente [Jacinto Benavente y Martínez] (b. Aug. 12, 1866), the leading Spanish playwright of the first half of the 20th century, died. *Los intereses creados* [*The Bonds of Interes*], first played on December 9, 1907, is now his best-known play in English. Among his other plays were *La noche del sábado* [*Saturday Night*] (1903), *Los malhechores* [*The Evil Doers of Good*] (1905), *Alfilerazos* [*Pinpricks*] (1924), and *La infanzona* [*The Noblewoman*] (1945). He won the **Nobel prize for literature** in 1922.

1954 Aug. 3   Sidonie Gabrielle Colette (b. Jan. 28, 1873), a French novelist, died. Her first books appeared under the pen name of her husband Willy, but she became widely known in France and abroad simply as Colette. Among her very popular books were *Chéri* (1920), *La Fin de Chéri* (1926), and *Gigi* (1945).

1954 Sept. 8   André Derain (b. Jan. 10, 1880), a French painter, died. Among his well-known works were *Collioure, Mountains* (1905), *Cadaqués* (1910), *Forest, Fontainbleau* (1927), *Gravelines* (1934), and *Portrait of Isabel* (1936).

1954 Sept. 27   Television's *The Tonight Show* went on the air for the first time. Its first host was **Steve Allen** (b. Dec. 26, 1921).

1954 Nov. 3   Henri Matisse (b. Dec. 31, 1869), a French painter, sculptor, illustrator, and decorator, died. A giant of 20th century art, Matisse was a master in many fields. *Luxe, calme and volupté* (c. 1905), *The Green Line* (1905), *The Blue Nude* (1907), *The Piano Lesson* (1916), *The Moorish Screen* (1921), and *The Lady in Blue* (1937) were among his best known paintings. He designed for the ballet and produced many sculptures, etchings, and textile designs. At nearly 80 he decorated the chapel of the Dominican nuns at Vence, France.

1954 Nov. 15   Lionel Barrymore (b. Apr. 28, 1878), a member of a family of prominent American actors, died. He was successful on the stage and in the movies. On stage he appeared in *Peter Ibbetson* (1917) and many other plays. Barrymore became much better known to the public in his movies, including *Rasputin and the Empress* (1932), in which he costarred with his sister **Ethel** and his brother **John**.

1954 Nov. 19   The **New York Shakespeare Festival**, founded by **Joseph Papp** (b. June 22, 1921), was chartered as an education project for the production of plays free of admission charges in New York City.

1954 Nov. 30   [Gustav Heinrich Martin] **Wilhelm Furtwängler** (b. Jan. 25, 1886), a German conductor and composer, died. His conducting of orchestras in Lübeck and Mannheim (1911–1920) made him the leading young German orchestra leader of the time. He then became known chiefly as conductor of the Berlin Philharmonic Orchestra, beginning in 1922, but in 1934 he resigned this and other posts as a result of difficulties with the Nazi regime. After 1945 Furtwängler was again active in Germany, and in Italy and England as well.

VI. SPORTS, GAMES, AND SOCIETY

1954   The **World Cup** of international soccer was won by West Germany, defeating Hungary 3–2 at Zurich, Switzerland.

1954 May 6   Roger Gilbert Bannister (b. Mar. 23, 1929) became the **first runner to break the four-minute mile**. Bannister achieved a time of 3 minutes 59.4 seconds at the Iffley Road track in Oxford, England.

1954 Nov. 13   Jacques Fath (b. Sept. 6, 1912), a well-known French **fashion** designer, died. Fath's designs appealed to the sophisticated woman.

1955

I. DISASTERS

1955 Apr. 1   An **earthquake** in the Philippines left 432 persons dead and more than 2,000 injured. The quake was centered on the Mindanao area.

1955 Apr. 3   Deaths estimated at 300 resulted when the Guadalajara-Manzanillo night **express plunged into a canyon** near Guadalajara, Mexico.

1955 June 13   Soon after the start of the annual 24-hour endurance race at **Le Mans**, France, a Mercedes Benz driven by Pierre Levegh slammed into a retaining wall and exploded over a crowd of spectators, killing 77, including Levegh.

1955 Aug. 20   Floods along the Atlantic coastline, caused by **Hurricane Diane**, devastated areas of Connecticut, Massachusetts, Pennsylvania, South Carolina, New Jersey, and Rhode Island. It was estimated that 400 persons died.

1955 Sept. 19   **Hurricane Hilda** struck along the Gulf of Mexico's coast in the Tampico-Vera Cruz region of eastern Mexico, killing c.150 people and injuring c.1,000. On Sept. 28 **Hurricane Janet** ravaged the Yucatan peninsula and left c.500 dead.

II. POLITICS AND WAR

1955–1956   Agitation for freedom for **Cyprus**, a British crown colony (since 1925), and for union [*enosis*] with Greece turned to violence. Anti-Greek riots erupted in İstanbul (Sept. 6, 1955) on behalf of Turkish Cypriots. Tension was further heightened when British authorities deported (Mar. 9, 1956) **Makarios III** (Aug. 13, 1913–Aug. 2, 1977) archbishop of Cyprus and leader of the **enosis movement, charged with abetting terrorism.**

1955 Jan. 2   **José Antonio Remón**, (b. June 1, 1908), president of **Panama**, was assassinated. His vice president and successor, **José Guizado** (1899?–Nov. 3?, 1964), was impeached (Jan. 15) for suspected involvement in the assassination.

1955 Jan. 11   **Costa Rica** was invaded again by Nicaraguan-based guerillas, this time led by the former Costa Rican president, **Cololerión Guardia** (Mar. 10, 1900–June 9, 1970). The **Organization of American States** [OAS] rebuked Nicaragua, and the border war came to an end.

1955 Jan. 25   Panama and the U.S. concluded a new treaty for the **Panama Canal** in the face of rising nationalist agitation. The U.S. agreed to an annuity of $1,930,000, up from $434,000 set in 1939, and to build a new bridge over the Pacific end of the canal.

1955 Jan. 28   The U.S. Congress, at the request of **Dwight D. Eisenhower**, president of the U.S., declared it would protect **Taiwan** [Formosa] and the Nationalist government of **Chiang Kai-Shek** against

any invasion by the communist government of mainland China.

1955 Feb. 8   **Nikolai Bulganin** succeeded **Georgi Malenkov** as premier of the **U.S.S.R.** in a major shake-up. Malenkov was blamed for the failure of the government's agricultural program.

1955 Feb. 24   The **Baghdad Pact** for military defense against growing communist influence in the Near East was signed by Turkey and Iraq, and later this year by Iran, Pakistan, and Great Britain.

1955 Mar 2   **Norodom Sihanouk** abdicated the throne of **Cambodia** in favor of his father, **Norodom Suramarit**, but entered politics, was elected premier, and controlled the Popular Socialist Community party he had founded.

1955 Mar. 13   **Tribhubana** [Tribhubana Bir Bikram Shah Deva] (b. June 30, 1906), king of **Nepal** (from Dec. 11, 1911), died. He was succeeded (to 1972) by his son **Mahendra** [Mahendra Bir Bikram Shah Deva].

1955 Apr. 5   **Winston Churchill** resigned as prime minister of Great Britain because of age (80). He refused a peerage, customarily offered to a retiring prime minister, so that he could remain in the House of Commons. He was succeeded (Apr. 6) by **Anthony Eden**, who had been foreign secretary and who was elected (Apr. 21) head of the Conservative party.

1955 Apr. 18–24   Representatives of 29 so-called **non-aligned nations** held a conference at Bandung, Indonesia. The tone of the final statement of the conference was anti-Western, and especially critical of the U.S.

1955 May 5   **West Germany** was recognized by most nations, including the U.S.S.R., as the Federal Republic, becoming a sovereign state, and thus formally ending its status as an occupied country. West Germany also became (May 9) a member of **NATO**, and provisions for the rebuilding of her armed forces were adopted.

1955 May 11–14   The **Warsaw Treaty of Friendship, Cooperation, and Mutual Assistance** [the **Warsaw Pact**] was created by the communist bloc nations of Eastern Europe in response to the remilitarization of West Germany under the **Paris Pact** of 1954. As a mutual defense organization it was the counterpart of the North Atlantic Treaty Organization [NATO].

1955 May 13   The **last French troops left Haiphong**, a port on the Red River east of Hanoi, capital of present Vietnam, ending the French presence in Indo-China.

1955 May 15   The **Second Austrian Republic** was established with the signing of the **Austrian State Treaty** by the U.S., Great Britain, France, and the U.S.S.R. The treaty provided for withdrawal of occupying forces, prohibited deployment of offensive weapons and union with Germany, and reestablished its borders of 1937.

1955 July 18–25   A so-called **Summit Conference** was held at Geneva, Switzerland, in an effort to ease the tensions of the **Cold War** (c.1945–c.1985). The chief items on the agenda were German reunification, European security, and disarmament. Present were leaders of the U.S., the U.S.S.R., Great Britain, and France. No agreements on substantive matters were reached.

1955 Aug. 20   Rioting broke out in **Morocco**, and in **Algeria** the National Liberation Front [**FLN**] made extensive attacks on French colonists. About 2,500 Europeans were murdered, nearly 1,400 in Algeria, among them women and children. The **French Foreign Legion** responded in kind. In an attempt to conciliate the Berber tribesmen the French agreed to recall **Mohammad V**, who had been exiled.

1955 Sept. 15   In **Indonesia** the first general election for a house of representatives was held. A second election chose (Dec. 29) members of a constituent assembly. Both elections demonstrated the ideological split between **Sukarno**, who represented the forces of nationalism and anti-colonialism, and **Mohammed Hatta** (Aug. 12, 1902–Mar. 14, 1980), who represented close relations with the West and economic stability.

1955 Sept. 16–19   **Juan** [Domingo] **Perón**, president of **Argentina** (from 1946), was ousted in a coup and resigned on Sept. 19. Perón fled to Paraguay, later to Spain. **Pedro Eugenio Aramburu** (May 23, 1903–July 16, 1970) headed an interim military government, which set out to rid the country of Peronism.

1955 Dec. 1   The arrest of **Rosa Parks** (b. Feb. 4, 1913), a black woman, in Montgomery, Alabama, for refusing to give up her seat on a bus to a white man, turned out to be the spark that ignited the **civil rights movement** of the 1950s and 1960s in the U.S. On Dec. 5 a boycott of the bus system began, led by **Martin Luther King, Jr.**, a Baptist clergyman. The boycott spread to other states and to such other facilities as lunch counters. As for Mrs. Parks, she was arrested and fined $14, which she never paid. On Nov. 14, 1956, the U.S. Supreme Court declared the segregation laws of Montgomery unconstitutional.

1955 Dec. 14   The **United Nations** gained 16 more member states, bringing the total to 76.

III. ECONOMY AND TRADE

1955 Apr. 15   **McDonald's**, a fast-food restaurant, opened in Des Plaines, Illinois. It was owned by [Raymond Albert] **Ray Kroc** (Oct. 5, 1902–Jan. 14, 1984), who had bought the idea from the McDonald brothers.

1955 Dec. 5   The **American Federation of Labor** [AFL] and the **Congress of Industrial Organizations** [CIO], the two largest and most influential labor organizations in the U.S., signed a merger agreement, ending 20 years of rivalry. The new **AFL-CIO** elected **George Meany** (Aug. 16, 1894–Jan. 10, 1980), veteran secretary-treasurer of the AFL, as its president.

IV. RELIGION AND PHILOSOPHY

1955 Apr. 10   [Marie Joseph] **Pierre Teilhard de Chardin** (b. May 1, 1881), a French philosopher and paleontologist, died. Trained as a Jesuit, he spent his life concerned with the problem of reconciling the doctrine of original sin with his study of human evolution. As a paleontologist, his field work in China (1926–1946) included participation in the discovery (1927) of the remains of Peking Man. Among Teilhard's writings, published posthumously, were *The Phenomenon of Man* (1955) and *The Future of Man* (1957).

1955 Oct. 18   **José Ortega y Gasset** (b. May 9, 1883), a Spanish philosopher and writer, died. Ortega's *The Revolt of the Masses* (1929) attracted international attention. In it he detailed a crisis in European culture that he attributed to the overwhelming influence of the mass mind. His other notable works included *Toward a Philosophy of History* (1941) and *The Dehumanization of Art* (1948).

V. SCIENCE, EDUCATION, AND TECHNOLOGY

1955 **Owen Chamberlain** (b. July 10, 1920), an American physicist, and **Emilio** [Gino] **Segrè** (Feb. 1, 1905–Apr. 22, 1989), an Italian physicist, with colleagues at the University of California, Berkeley, proved the existence of the antiproton [a subatomic particle] which had been suggested in 1928. For their work Chamberlain and Segrè were awarded the **Nobel prize for physics** in 1959.

1955 The **heart-lung machine** by now was making open-heart surgery feasible. The machine systematically takes the blood from the veins, reoxygenates it, and returns it to the arteries.

1955 The **first microscope able to picture an individual atom** was developed by **Erwin Wilhelm Mueller** (June 13, 1911–May 17, 1977), a German-American physicist.

1955 The **first practical hovercraft** was developed by **Christopher Cockerell** (b. June, 1910), an English engineer. A hovercraft is supported above the surface of the ground or water by air pressure so that its passage creates no friction to slow it.

1955 Mar. 11 **Alexander Fleming** (b. Aug. 16, 1881), a Scottish bacteriologist and discoverer (1928) of **penicillin**, died. For his work on penicillin, he shared (1945) the **Nobel prize for physiology or medicine** with the English pathologist **Howard Walter Florey** (Sept. 24, 1898–Feb. 21, 1968) and a German-born chemist **Ernest Boris Chain**.

1955 Apr. 18 **Albert Einstein** (b. Mar. 14, 1879), the renowned physicist, died at Princeton, New Jersey. He had been awarded the **Nobel prize for physics** in 1921 for his theory of relativity, and his original writings on the equivalence of mass and energy, the Brownian movement, and the photon theory of light. Born in Ulm, Germany, Einstein became a U.S. citizen in 1940.

1955 June 23 **M.D. Lyne** piloted a British air force *Canberra* jet bomber 3,200 miles from Norway to Alaska in 6 hours, 45 minutes, in the **first jet flight over the North Pole** from Europe to America.

VI. ARTS AND LEISURE

1955 **Friedrich Dürrenmatt** (b. Jan. 5, 1921), a Swiss playwright and novelist, published his best-known play *Der Besuch der Alten Dame* [*The Visit*] (1956).

1955 **Allen Ginsberg** (b. June 3, 1926), an American poet, at this time a graduate student at the University of California, Berkeley, read for the first time his long, discursive poem "Howl."

1955 Jan. 7 **Marian Anderson** (b. Feb. 17, 1902), an American contralto, became the **first black singer** to be named a permanent member of the company of the **Metropolitan Opera**, New York City. She made her debut in *Un Balla in Maschera*.

1955 Jan. 15 **Yves Tanguy** (b. Jan. 5, 1900), a French painter who was one of the outstanding artists of the surrealist school, died. He was noted for his odd landscapes, inhabited by strange yet familiar human beings and other forms. Among his works were *Mama, Papa Is Wounded* (1927) and *Rose of the Four Winds* (1950).

1955 Feb. 23 **Paul** [Louis Charles Marie] **Claudel** (b. Aug. 6, 1868), a French playwright, poet, and diplomat (ambassador to the U.S., 1927–1933), died. Claudel's finest play was probably *L'Annonce faite à Marie* [*Tidings Brought to Mary*] (1912). Among his poetic works was *Cinq Grandes Odes* (1910).

1955 Apr. 7 **Theda Bara** [nee Theodosia Goodman] (b. July 20, 1890), an early American screen star and the original vamp, died. In *A Fool There Was* (1915) she first created her image of the *femme fatale* who lured men to their doom with her seductiveness. She played the same role in other movies, for example, *Carmen* (1915), *Cleopatra* (1917), and *Salome* (1918).

1955 July 12 The **American Shakespeare Festival at Stratford**, Connecticut, opened its first season with a performance of *Julius Caesar*. **Lawrence Langner** (May 30, 1890–Dec. 26, 1962) was the primary founder and first president of the Festival.

1955 Aug. 2 **Wallace Stevens** (b. Oct. 2, 1879), an American who combined a career in insurance with the writing of poetry, died. He wrote most of his poetry after he was 50 years old, and it was not until the year before his death that he received general recognition with the publication of his **Collected Poems**. Among his best-known poems were "Thirteen Ways of Looking at a Blackbird" (1917), "The Emperor of Ice Cream" (1923), and "Sunday Morning" (1923).

1955 Aug. 12   Thomas Mann (b. June 6, 1875), the outstanding 20th-century German literary figure, winner (1929) of the **Nobel prize for literature**, died. His first novel **Buddenbrooks** (1901) brought him instant fame. His work included the novella **Der Tod in Venedig** [**Death in Venice**] (1912) and the novel **Der Zauberberg** [**The Magic Mountain**]. The 4-volume **Joseph und seine Brüder** [**Joseph and His Brethren**], published across a decade (1933–1943), had occupied him for 16 years. A self-imposed exile, Mann lived in the U.S. and Switzerland after 1938.

1955 Aug. 17   Fernand Léger (b. Feb. 4, 1881), a French painter, died. He was first influenced by cubism but after World War I he became fascinated by machines and by the abstract shapes they seemed to him to take. Among Léger's paintings were **The City** (1919), **Les Constructeurs** (1950), and **The Great Parade** (1954).

1955 Oct. 7   Symphony Hall in Boston was the scene of two symphonic premiers during the fall season: on this date **Symphony No. 6** by **Darius Milhaud**, a French composer of ballets, operas, and orchestral works; and on November 5 **Symphony No. 5** by **Walter Piston** (Jan. 20, 1894–Nov. 12, 1976), an American composer and Harvard professor of music, who was widely known for his **Symphony No. 3** (1948).

1955 Nov. 5   Maurice Utrillo (b. Dec. 25, 1883), a French painter, died. His paintings of the streets and churches of Montmartre, the area of Paris in which he was born, were among the most familiar in the world. Typical of his work were **L'Impasse Cotin** (c.1910) and **Café on the Rue Muller, Montmartre** (1912).

1955 Nov. 14   Robert E. Sherwood (b. Apr. 4, 1896), a prominent American dramatist, died. His works included: **Waterloo Bridge** (1930), **The Petrified Forest** (1935), **Idiot's Delight** (1936), **There Shall Be No Night** (1940), and **Abe Lincoln in Illinois (1938)**.

1955 Nov. 27   Arthur Honegger (b. March 10, 1892), a French-born Swiss composer, died in Paris. He was a member of the group of Parisian composers called **Les Six**. His works include the operas **Judith** (1926) and **Antigone** (1927).

VII. SPORTS, GAMES, AND SOCIETY

1955 Mar. 12–16   The second **Pan American Games** were held at Mexico City. In the unofficial team standings the U.S. took first place, followed by Argentina and Mexico.

1955 July 17   The **first Ladies Professional Golf Association [LPGA] championship** was won by Beverly Hanson (b. Dec. 5, 1924) at the Orchard Ridge Country Club, Ft. Wayne, Indiana. She defeated Louise Suggs (b. Sept. 7, 1923) in an 18-hole playoff, 4 and 3.

1955 July 18   Disneyland opened in Anaheim, near Los Angeles, California.

1955 Dec. 27   Ely Culbertson (b. July 22, 1891), an American authority on contract bridge, died. He was the first to devise a systematic bidding system for the game. Culbertson founded (1929) and edited **Bridge World** magazine and wrote a number of books about the game.

1956

I. DISASTERS

1956 Feb. 1–29   Extremely cold weather accompanied by **blizzards battered all of western Europe** for four weeks. There were 907 deaths, and damage to crops was estimated at $2,000,000,000.

1956 June 10–17   More than 2,000 persons in Afghanistan died as a result of a series of **earthquakes in the Hindu Kush** mountain range in Afghanistan's northeastern region. The quake registered 7.7 on the Richter scale.

1956 June 30 A **TWA Superconstellation and a United Airlines DC-7 collided** over the Grand Canyon in Arizona. All 128 passengers and crew on both planes were killed.

1956 July 25 The Italian liner *Andrea Doria* collided with the Swedish liner *Stockholm* off Nantucket, Massachusetts, causing 52 deaths. The icebreaker bow of the *Stockholm* rammed so deeply into the *Andrea Doria's* watertight compartments that the *Doria's* heavy list prevented the lowering of life boats. On July 26, after 1,652 persons had been rescued, the *Andrea Doria* sank.

1956 Aug. 7 Seven military trucks loaded with more than 30 tons of **dynamite and gasoline exploded** in the industrial city of Cali, Colombia, razing eight city blocks and causing about $40 million in property damage. Of the official casualty list of 1,290, there were 403 verified dead.

1956 Aug. 8 At Marcinelle, in southwestern Belgium, a **fire in a coal mine** took 262 lives.

1956 Nov. 23 In India, the Madras-Tuticarin **train plunged down an embankment**, killing 143 people. Earlier 121 people died (Sept. 2) when the collapse of a bridge had plummeted two railroad coaches into a river near Secunderabad in central southern India.

II. POLITICS AND WAR

1956 Jan. 1 The Anglo-Egyptian **Sudan** was granted independence as a democratic republic. **Abdullah Khalil** (1891–Aug. 23, 1970), leader of the National Unionists party [NUP] which had favored union with Egypt, became prime minister (July 5).

1956 Feb. 14–25 Nikita Khrushchev, party chairman, denounced Stalinism to the **20th Congress of the Communist party** of the U.S.S.R. Khrushchev decried Stalin's policies, methods, his use of the "cult of personality," and other crimes against his communist associates.

1956 Feb. 29 **Pakistan** adopted a new constitution and formally became a republic. Its first president was **Iskander Mirza** (Nov. 13, 1899–Nov. 13, 1969).

1956 Mar. 2 **Hussein** [Husain] **I**, king of **Jordan**, in the face of anti-Western riots directed especially against the British, dismissed **John Bagot Glubb** ["Glubb Pasha"] (Apr. 16, 1897–Mar. 17, 1986), commander (from 1939) of Jordan's well-trained Arab Legion.

1956 Mar. 2 **Morocco** became independent of France by a protocol signed in Paris by **Christian Pineau** (b. Oct. 14, 1904), prime minister of France, and **M'barek Bekkai** (1907–Apr. 13, 1961), prime minister of Morocco. The new independent state became the Kingdom of Morocco with **Mohammad V** [Sidi Muhammad ben Youssef] of the **Filali** [Alawid, Alaouite, Alawite] **Dynasty** (from 1666) as king on Aug. 11, 1957.

1956 Mar. 4 **José Maria Lemus** (b. July 22, 1911), the candidate of the military junta, was elected president of **El Salvador**, succeeding **Oscar Osorio**. Lemus began by pardoning political prisoners and following the generally progressive program begun by Osorio.

1956 Mar. 20 France and **Tunisia** signed a protocol which gave Tunisia full independence as a monarchy under **Mohammad VIII al-Amin**, bey of Tunis (from 1943). Five days later the more radical Neo-Destour party of **Habib Bourguiba** overwhelmed the Destour [Constitutional] party in open elections for a constituent assembly. Bourguiba was named prime minister on Apr. 10.

1956 Apr. 10 The United National party lost the elections and thus the power in **Ceylon** [Sri Lanka] in favor of the People's United Front, a leftist coalition organized by the Freedom party's leader **Solomon West Ridgeway Dias Bandaranaike** (1899–Sept. 26, 1959). Bandaranaike became prime minister (Apr. 12) and began a non-aligned policy in foreign affairs.

1956 June 17 **Manuel Prado y Ugartiche** (1889–Aug. 14, 1967), who had served as **Peru's** president from 1939 to 1945, was returned to office in the first national election held in Peru in which women were allowed to vote.

1956 June 28 Striking workers and rioting students in Poznán, central western Poland, clashed with the police. Discontent became widespread and mass demonstrations sprang up everywhere. Scores were killed as Soviet armed forces attempted to put down the rebellion. The political situation was settled by the Soviet acceptance of **Wladyslaw Gomulka** (Feb. 6, 1905–Sept. 1, 1982) as first secretary of the Communist party of **Poland** on October 19, 1956.

1956 July 16 The U.S. withdrew the offer it had made to **Egypt** to provide a major portion of the funding of its **Aswan High Dam**. Great Britain followed suit. The project was a key element in the scheme of **Gamal Adbel Nasser**, president of Egypt, to increase Egypt's arable land and hydroelectric power. On July 26 he nationalized the **Suez Canal** and expelled British embassy and oil personnel.

1956 Aug. 6 **Hernán Siles Zuazo** (b. Mar. 19, 1914), **Bolivian** vice president under **Victor Paz Estenssoro** and candidate of the **Movimiento Nacional Revolucionario** [MNR] party, became president following a peaceful election (June 17).

1956 Sept. 29 **Anastasio Somoza** (b. 1896), president-dictator of **Nicaragua** (1937–1947, 1950–1956), died eight days after being shot by an assassin, who was gunned down on the spot. Somoza ruled Nicaragua as if it were his private estate. Anastasio Somoza was succeeded as president (to 1962) by his son **Luis Somoza Debayle** (1922–Apr. 13, 1967).

1956 Oct. 19 **Japan and the U.S.S.R. signed a peace declaration** ending their technical state of war since World War II. Diplomatic and trade relations were reestablished and the U.S.S.R. stopped vetoing Japan's entry to the United Nations, which came about on Dec. 18.

1956 Oct. 21 A military junta ousted **Julio Lozano Díaz**, president of **Honduras**, following a fraudulent election by which Lozano had attempted to legitimize his power.

1956 Oct. 22 Elections in **Jordan** showed a sharp increase in anti-Western and pro-Egyptian influence, which led to a political crisis for **Hussein**, king of Jordan. He ousted the Nabulsi government (Apr. 10, 1957) and proclaimed martial law (Apr. 25).

1956 Oct. 23 An **anti-communist revolution swept across Hungary**. The moderate former premier **Imre Nagy** was recalled to head the new government, which withdrew from the **Warsaw Treaty**, declared Hungary's neutrality, and asked the **U.N.** for aid. On Oct. 30 **Cardinal Mindszenty**, released from prison (from Dec. 27, 1948), took refuge in the American legation. **János Kádár**, one of Nagy's ministers, formed a pro-Soviet counter-government and appealed to the U.S.S.R. **Soviet tanks and troops entered Budapest**, capital of Hungary, on Nov. 4, and after some fighting with ill-equipped revolutionaries,

crushed the rebellion. As many as 30,000 revolutionaries were probably killed; c.190,000 refugees fled the country. Kádár became premier. Imre Nagy (b. 1895?) was tricked into capture and executed on June 16, 1958.

1956 Oct. 29 **Israel**, its patience over Egypt's border raids at an end, and fearful of loss of the **Suez Canal** to its commerce with the West, entered the Gaza Strip and Egypt's Sinai Peninsula in force. Two days later (Oct. 31), British and French planes bombed Egyptian airfields, and their troops made a joint attack on Port Said and occupied the Canal Zone (Nov. 5–6). The **UN** negotiated an Israeli-Egyptian ceasefire on Nov. 6 and a general ceasefire was in place on Nov. 7. On the 7th UN observers entered the Canal Zone. Meanwhile, the canal had been blocked by sunken vessels. Israel withdrew its troops from the Sinai in Jan., 1957, and from the Gaza Strip in March.

1956 Nov. 12 Three Arab nations—Morocco, the Sudan, and Tunisia—were elected to membership in the **UN**. This brought the so-called **Asian-African bloc** in the world body to a total of 26 nations.

1956 Dec. 2 **Fidel Castro**, with his brother **Raul** (b. June 3, 1931), **Ernesto "Che" Guevara**, and 82 rebel followers, returned to **Cuba** after more than a year in exile in Mexico. The invaders, landing in Oriente province, survived an encounter with the military, fleeing into the hills of the Sierra Maestra.

1956 Dec. 6 **Paul E. Magloire** (b. 1907), president of **Haiti** (from 1950), was forced to resign after refusing to leave office at the end of his six-year term. Magloire had become president in a rigged election in 1950. During his tenure money provided by the U.S. to build a river dam for flood prevention, irrigation, and power mysteriously disappeared. The dam had not been started. Opposed by students, young militant workers, and shopkeepers, Magloire left (Dec. 12) for exile. A chaotic nine-month period followed, ending with the election of **François Duvalier** on Sept. 22, 1957.

III. ECONOMY AND TRADE

1956 June 19 **Thomas J[ohn] Watson** (b. Feb. 17, 1874), the longtime head of the **International Business Machines Corporation** [**IBM**] (1914–1949), died. He began a small data processing company in 1914. By the time of his death IBM had c.60,000 employees and was by far the largest computer manufacturing company in the world.

1956 Oct. 17 The **world's first large-scale nuclear plant**, located at Calder Hall near Whitehaven, England, began supplying electricity to the public.

IV. RELIGION AND PHILOSOPHY

1956 French Dominican scholars at the Dominican Biblical School [École biblique] in Jerusalem published in Paris *La Bible de Jérusalem* under the general editorship of **Roland de Vaux** (1903–Sept. 9, 1971), the director of the school. This was the first complete translation of Holy Scriptures by Catholic scholars directly from the original tongues.

1956 Oct. Bhimrao Ramji Ambedkar (Apr. 14, 1893–Dec. 6, 1956), a leader of India's Untouchables, in a protest against Hinduism's caste system, led c.300,000 Hindus into Buddhism on the celebration of the **2,500th anniversary of the birth of the Buddha**.

V. SCIENCE, EDUCATION, AND TECHNOLOGY

1956 In **Ceylon** [Sri Lanka] the government proclaimed **Sinhala** to be the nation's official language. In 1958 the minority **Tamils** (c.24 percent) rioted over their demands for official recognition of the Tamil language and the creation of a separate but federated Tamil state.

1956 An **oral contraceptive** was tested for the first time on a large scale. The test was carried out by the developers, **Gregory Pincus** (Apr. 9, 1903–Aug. 22, 1967) and **John Rock** (Mar. 24, 1890–Dec. 4, 1984) in Puerto Rico with c.1,300 women participating. The test was successful, and **"the Pill"** went on sale commercially in 1960.

1956 Two Chinese-born American physicists, **Chen Ning Yang** (b. Sept. 22, 1922) and **Tsung-Dao Lee** (b. Nov. 24, 1926), carried out an experiment that disproved the long-standing principle of parity. This principle held that a moving particle spinning in a clockwise motion would have a mirror image particle whose only difference would be that it spun in a counterclockwise manner. Yang and Lee showed that this was not true in weak interactions. The concept of parity is still of importance in nuclear physics.

For this discovery Yang and Lee were awarded the **Nobel prize for physics** in 1958.

1956 The building of **Brasilia**, a new capital in the central highlands, was initiated by **Juscelino Kubitschek**, president of Brazil. The master plan was the work of Brazilian architect **Lucio Costa** (b. Feb. 27, 1902), and the city was laid out in 1957. The chief architect was another Brazilian, **Oscar Niemeyer** (b. Dec. 15, 1907), noted for his daring and original conceptions.

1956 May 11 Walter S. Adams (b. Dec. 20, 1876), an American astronomer, died. Adams became noted for his spectroscopic studies of sunspots and the rotation of the sun and for his work in determining the distances and velocities of thousands of stars. Perhaps most notable was his discovery that the "dark" companion of Sirius, known as Sirius B, was a white dwarf star, determined from its so-called "Einstein red-shift."

1956 Sept. 22 Frederick Soddy (b. Sept 2, 1877), an English chemist, died. In 1921 he was awarded the **Nobel prize for chemistry** for his discovery (c.1910) of isotopes.

1956 Sept. 24 The **first transatlantic telephone cable** began operation. Twin cables ran 2,250 miles from Clarenville, Newfoundland, to Oban, Scotland.

VI. ARTS AND LEISURE

1956 The moving picture *The Forty-First* by **Grigori Chukrai** (b. May 23, 1921), a Russian film producer, signaled the release of pent-up creativity among Soviet film-makers that followed the death of Stalin. It won a jury prize at the **Cannes Festival**.

1956 Satyajit Ray (b. May 21, 1921), an Indian motion picture director, script writer, and producer, was awarded a special jury prize at the **Cannes Film Festival** for his simple, humane, and stunningly beautiful *Pather Panchali* (1955), based on an autobiographical novel of Bengali village life.

1956 Jan. 13 Lyonel [Charles Adrian] **Feininger** (b. July 17, 1871), an American artist, died. He taught at the Bauhaus in Weimar (1919–1933). His paintings were included in what the Nazis called an exhibit of degenerate art in 1933. Feininger returned to the U.S. in 1937. Among his works are *The Glorious Victory of the Sloop Maria* (1926) and *Dawn* (1938).

1956 Jan. 23 Alexander Korda [orig.: Sándor Kellner] (b. Sept. 16, 1883), a Hungarian-born film director and producer, died. By the time he was 25 he was the leading director in Hungary. He left there in 1919 and made films in Austria, Germany, and the U.S., but after 1931 worked mostly in England, where he created his own company and large studios. Among Korda's outstanding films were *The Private Life of Henry VIII* (1933), *The Scarlet Pimpernel* (1934), *Things to Come* (1936), and *Elephant Boy* (1936).

1956 Jan. 29 H[enry] **L**[ewis] **Mencken** (b. Sept. 12, 1880), an American journalist and critic, associated (from 1906) with the *Baltimore Sun* or *Evening Sun,* died. The unremitting enemy of sham, complacency, and sacred cows wherever found, Mencken, as editor of *Smart Set* and the *American Mercury,* or in the columns of the *Nation* or the *Sun* papers, was a pungent, colorful, and cynical critic of the American cultural scene. His most enduring work is the landmark *The American Language* (1919; revised 1936, with supplements in 1945 and 1948).

1956 Jan. 31 A[lan] **A**[lexander] **Milne** (b. Jan. 18, 1882), an English author most remembered for the books he wrote for children, died. Chief among these was *Winnie the Pooh* (1926) and its successor *The House at Pooh Corner* (1928), both of which have a toy bear as the central character. *Now We Are Six* (1927) was a popular book of verse for young people. Milne was also a light comic dramatist, novelist, and essayist.

1956 Apr. 13 Emil Nolde (b. Aug. 7, 1867), a German painter and graphic artist, died. Nolde with some of his young associates were refused exhibition of their works by the Berlin Secession, the refuge of anti-establishment artists. In 1911 Nolde formed the New Secession [Neue Sezession]. With the advent of the Nazi regime, Nolde's work was largely confiscated, his expressionist style condemned. Among Nolde's works were his woodcut *The Prophet* (1912), his watercolor *Flowers,* and such religious paintings as *Dance Around the Golden Calf* (1910) and *The Life of Christ* (1911–1912).

1956 May 8 *Look Back in Anger*, a play by **John** [James] **Osborne** (b. Dec. 12, 1929), opened at the Royal Court Theatre in London. The play's main character, Jimmy Porter, was the original "angry young man."

1956 May 20 [Henry] **Max**[imilian] **Beerbohm** (b. Aug. 24, 1872), an English caricaturist, critic, and essayist, died. One of the wittiest men of the English literary world of the turn-of-the-century period, he commented on the world with his drawings as well as his writings. His first book was boldly entitled *The Works of Max Beerbohm* (1896). His only novel, *Zuleika Dobson* (1911) was a satirical portrait of undergraduate life at Oxford University.

1956 June 22 Walter De la Mare (b. Apr. 25, 1873), an English poet and novelist, died. Most of his poetry was presumably for children but was enjoyed by many adults. The title poem of *The Listeners (1912)* was his best-known work. Also successful was *Peacock Pie* (1913). His novels included *Memoirs of a Midget* (1921) and *Early One Morning* (1935).

1956 Aug. 11 Jackson Pollock (b. Jan. 28, 1912), a controversial American abstract expressionist painter, died in an automobile accident on Long Island, New York. From the time (1944) of his first one-man show in New York City, Pollock was in revolt against the realism found in American painting. He first used a distinctive and controversial technique of drip-painting in 1946. Pollock's innovative methods and techniques became known before his death as "action painting." Among Pollock's representative paintings were *Male and Female* (1942), *Gothic* (1946), *Full Fathom Five* (1947), *Number 32* (1950), and *Scent* (1955).

1956 Aug. 14 [Eugen Berthold Friedrich] **Bertolt Brecht** (b. Feb. 10, 1898), a German dramatist, died in East Berlin, to which he had returned in 1948 after a 15-year exile in Denmark and the U.S. A poet and a bold experimenter in stage production, Brecht, in his postwar role as director of the state-supported Berliner Ensemble, was a force in contemporary drama. He was most readily recognized by English-speaking theatergoers as the creator of *The Threepenny Opera* [*Die Dreigroschenoper*] (1928), based on John Gay's *Beggar's Opera* (1728), with music by Kürt Weill. It was his first major success and brought him fame and money. Other major works were *Mother Courage and Her Children* (1941), *The Good Woman of Setzuan* (1943), and *The Caucasian Chalk Circle* (1955).

VII. SPORTS, GAMES, AND SOCIETY

1956 Jan. 26–Feb. 5   The seventh winter **Olympic Games** were held at Cortina D'Ampezzo, Italy, with 818 athletes from 32 nations competing. Soviet athletes won 7 gold medals and 16 medals in all; Austria, 4 and 11; and Finland, 3 and 7.

1956 Apr. 19   **Rainier III**, ruling prince of Monaco, married **Grace [Patricia] Kelly** (Nov. 12, 1929–Sept. 14, 1982), an American movie actress and member of a wealthy Philadelphia family. A civil ceremony was followed by a nuptial mass in St. Nicholas Cathedral in Monaco before 1,200 guests, including dignitaries from various nations.

1956 Aug. 13   The **New Code of Personal Status**, presented by **Habib Bourguiba**, prime minister of **Tunisia**, abolished polygamy, gave wives the right to institute divorce proceedings, and permitted women to vote for the first time.

1956 Sept. 27   **Mildred [Babe] Didrikson Zaharias** (b. June 26, 1914), America's great all-around woman athlete, died of cancer. An all-American basketball player in 1930, she entered eight events at the women's national track championships and won five of them. In the 1932 **Olympic Games** she won the high hurdles and javelin events and finished second in the high jump. Taking up golf in 1935, she won the British women's open championship once and the U.S. open three times, as well as scores of other amateur and professional tournaments.

1956 Nov. 22–Dec. 8   The 16th summer **Olympic Games** were held in Melbourne, Australia, with 3,342 athletes from 67 nations competing. Russian athletes won 37 gold medals and 98 medals in all; the U.S. 32 and 74, and Australia, 13 and 35.

1956 Nov. 30   **Floyd Patterson** (b. Jan. 4, 1935) won the **world's heavyweight boxing championship** title by knocking out [Archibald Lee] **Archie Moore** (b. Dec. 13, 1916?) in the fifth round.

1957

I. DISASTERS

1957   The Soviet Union admitted (June 16, 1989) that a serious **accident occurred this year at a nuclear weapons factory** in the Ural Mountains north of Chelyabinsk. Soviet officials denied the accident even though **Zhores A[leksandrovich] Medvedev** (b. Nov. 14, 1925), a Russian scientist and political dissident, wrote (1980) a book about it. The U.S.S.R. contended there had been no casualties, but Medvedev reported that hundreds of persons were fatally contaminated by debris from the explosion. The government admitted that more than 10,000 people were evacuated from the area. Other investigators found that 30 towns and villages in the region had disappeared from Soviet maps.

1957 June 27–30 Hurricane **Audrey** and tidal waves that followed it struck the coastal areas of Louisiana and Texas, in the southern U.S., leaving 531 persons dead or missing and c.40,000 homeless.

1957 July 2   The first of **Iran's two major earthquakes** this year took place in the northwest, not far from the Caspian Sea. An estimated 1,500 persons were killed. On December 13 and again from December 15 to 17, a series of quakes in western Iran killed about another 1,400 persons. The July quake registered 7.4 on the Richter scale and the December quake 7.1. In 1958, quakes in northeastern Iran destroyed scores of small villages.

1957 Sept. 1   Nine cars of a 12-car excursion **train hurtled into a ravine** near Kendal, central southern Jamaica, in the West Indies, killing 175 persons and injuring c.400. The engineer claimed brake failure.

1957 Sept. 29   An express **train crashed** into a standing oil train at Montgomery, West Pakistan, killing nearly 300 persons.

1957 Dec. 4   Ninety-two people lost their lives and 187 were injured as **two commuter trains crashed** in thick fog near St. John's Station, in the southeastern section of London, England.

II. POLITICS AND WAR

1957 **Souvanna Phouma**, premier of Laos, tried to settle the **Laotian civil war** by inviting his half-brother **Prince Souphanouvong**, head of the pro-communist **Pathet Laos**, into the government. The Laotian right wing, supported by the U.S., rejected his policy. After the rightists failed to establish a stable government, the U.S. and the U.S.S.R. meeting at the 14-nation **Geneva Conference** (1961–1962) accepted a coalition government under the premiership of Souvanna Phouma in an attempt to neutralize Laos.

1957 France employed an estimated half-million troops in a drive to end terrorism in the cities of **Algeria**. Electrified barriers along the Algerian borders with Morocco and Tunisia were emplaced to restrict the infiltration of men and matériel. The **FLN** was now limited to guerrilla actions in rural areas. By August, after 34 months of fighting, it was estimated that 36,000 insurgents had been killed and 20,000 captured by French forces. French losses were much less: c.4,000 members of security forces had been killed, c.10,000 wounded or missing. Among the civilian population c.6,000 Muslims had been killed, and about another 6,000 wounded or missing; among the French, c.1,000 killed and c.3,000 wounded or missing. In France official policy was adamantly opposed to Algerian **independence**; in the U.S. sentiment, led by **John F. Kennedy**, senator from Massachusetts and future president of the U.S., was rising in favor of promoting a ceasefire and independence.

1957 Jan. 1 The **Saar Territory** became a state of West Germany in accordance with a Franco-German agreement signed in 1956. The customs union with France was terminated in July, 1959. This ended 40 years of disputes between France and Germany over the coal-rich, highly industrialized, predominantly German region.

1957 Jan. 5 **Dwight D. Eisenhower**, president of the U.S., announced a new aspect of U.S. foreign policy, soon called the **Eisenhower Doctrine**. Military and economic aid were now made available upon request to any Near East country wishing protection against communist aggression.

1957 Jan. 10 **Harold Macmillan** succeeded (to 1963) **Anthony Eden**, who had resigned the previous day for reasons of health, as prime minister of Great Britain. In his six-year Conservative ministry Macmillan consistently strove, without notable success, to further East-West relations and to take Great Britain into the **European Common Market**. He was more successful in repairing Anglo-American relations, damaged during the Suez Canal crisis.

1957 Jan. 20 **Dwight D. Eisenhower** was inaugurated for a second term as president of the U.S. In the election of Nov. 6, 1956, as the Republican party candidate, he polled 35,387,015 popular votes and 457 electoral votes to 25,875,408 and 74 for **Adlai E. Stevenson**, the Democratic party candidate. **Richard M. Nixon** continued as vice president.

1957 Feb. The Supreme Soviet of the U.S.S.R. provided for the return of the Buddhist **Kalmyks** to their homelands, on the northwestern shore of the Caspian Sea. In 1956 **Nikita Khrushchev**, first secretary of the Communist party, had denounced Stalin's treatment of them: They had resisted Stalin's collectivization of their stock-raising and farming in the 1920s, and c.25,000 of them had been deported to Siberia; some Kalmyks had fought the Russians in World War II (1939–1945) in collaboration with the Germans, and all Kalmyks [1939 census, 134,327 persons] had been deported to labor camps and their autonomous republic had been dissolved. This was now reversed, an estimated 100,000 Kalmyks were repatriated, and their republic, the **Kalmyk Autonomous Soviet Socialist Republic**, was reestablished within the Russian Soviet Federated Socialist Republic [Russian SFSR] in 1958.

1957 Feb. 9 **Miklós Horthy de Nagybanya** (b. June 18, 1868), a Hungarian admiral and regent, died. After commanding the Austro-Hungarian navy in World War I (1914–1918), he was among the leaders of the rightist forces that helped overthrow the communist government that had seized power in Hungary in 1919. Horthy became regent in 1920 of what was officially a kingdom but had no king. After German troops occupied Hungary in Mar., 1944, Horthy was forced to resign and was held prisoner by the Germans until freed by American troops at the end of World War II (1939–1945).

1957 Feb. 25 **Nobosuke Kishi** (b. Nov. 13, 1896) became prime minister of **Japan** succeeding (to 1960) **Tanzan Ishibashi** (from 1956). He had been one of the organizers of the conservative Liberal Democratic party that has ruled Japan ever since. Because of opposition to a new security treaty (1960) with the

U.S., Kishi was forced to resign (July, 1960) to be succeeded (to 1964) by **Hayato Ikeda** (Dec. 3, 1899–Aug. 13, 1965), the new leader of the Liberal Democratic party. An election (Nov. 20, 1960) gave the Liberal Democrats more than twice as many seats in the House of Representative [lower house] of the Diet [parliament] as their nearest rivals, the Socialists. Ikeda's policies encouraged business and industry, laying the basis for the amazing growth in the Japanese economy in the ensuing years.

1957 Feb. 27 On this date and again on Mar. 12, **Mao Tse-Tung**, the leader of the **People's Republic of China**, made speeches that seemed to indicate a relaxation in the totalitarian rule of the Communist party. **"Let a hundred flowers bloom, a hundred schools of thought contend"** (Feb. 27). He said there could be no conflict between the people and the rulers under communism and that persuasion, not repression, should be used. As a result, students, intellectuals, and others were encouraged to attack the government on various grounds. The government reacted by issuing a stern warning at the National People's Congress (June 26–July 15) to the dissenters, who were called "rightist," to cease their agitation.

1957 Mar. 6 British Togoland [West Togoland] and its Gold Coast colony united and were granted independence within the Commonwealth of Nations as the state of **Ghana**. **Kwame Nkrumah**, leader of the Convention People's party, became its first prime minister.

1957 Mar. 14 In general elections the densely populated state of **Kerala** in southwestern India elected **India's first communist state administration**. As a result of communist policies the opposition parties began non-violent demonstrations (June, 1959), which nevertheless resulted in casualties. Fearing collapse of the local government, the federal government dismissed (July 31, 1959) the state's communist government, including the legislature, and a coalition government formed by the opposition parties took over in new elections called in 1960.

1957 Mar. 17 **Ramón Magsaysay** (b. Aug. 31, 1907), a reformist and popular president of the **Philippines**, was killed in an airplane crash soon before the presidential election he was expected to win again. In 1952, as minister of national defense, he had brought to an end the terrorism of the communist-led Hukbalahap guerrillas ["Huks"]. He was

elected president in 1953. His administration was marked by progress in land and governmental reform and good relations with the U.S. Magsaysay was succeeded by **Carlos P. Garcia**, the vice president, who in November was elected to a full term.

1957 April 14 **Hussein I**, king of **Jordan**, weathered a crisis when he crushed a rebellion led by the chief of staff of Jordan's chief defense arm, the Arab Legion. The rebels sought a less-Western, more nationalistic orientation. Hussein's own bravery, supported by ever-loyal Bedouin troops, pulled the king through.

1957 May 10 A military junta in **Colombia**, backed by both liberals and conservatives, terminated the repressive and scandal-ridden dictatorship of **Gustave Rojas Pinilla**, who had just been re-elected (May 8) by his puppet legislature. On July 20 the leaders of the two main parties formed the National Front Coalition to bring stability to the country. They agreed to divide the major offices and to alternate holding of the presidency. The coalition held together until late 1973, despite challenges in the 1960s by Rojas Pinilla and his new party, the popular National Alliance. The decade or so of strife that now ended was known as *La Violenica* and had caused the deaths of about a quarter of a million people. Perhaps three times as many had fled the country. At first the violence was politically motivated, but as time went on a good deal of it was merely criminal activity.

1957 June 10 After 22 years in power in **Canada** the **Liberal party lost a parliamentary election** to the Progressive Conservative party, although neither party won a clear majority of seats in the House of Commons. The Progressive Conservatives won 112 seats; the Liberals, 105; and other parties, 48. As a result Louis St. Laurent was replaced as prime minister on June 21 by **John** [George] **Diefenbaker** (Sept. 18, 1895–Aug. 16, 1975). In another election on Mar. 31, 1958, the Progreessive Conservatives won a sweeping victory, taking 208 seats to the Liberals 48. Diefenbaker held office as prime minister until Apr. 18, 1963.

1957 June 29 **Nikita Khrushchev**, first secretary of the Soviet Communist party, removed from the party's central committee **Georgi Malenkov**, **Vyacheslav Molotov** ["the hammer"; orig.: Scriabin], **Lazar Kaganovich** (Nov. 22, 1893–c. 1963), and **D.T. Shepilov** (b. Nov. 4, 1905). These men were charged with being an "anti-party faction"; they were in fact obstacles to Khrushchev's plan to decentralize the Soviet economy announced in April, and threats to his leadership. **Nicolai Bulganin**, premier of the Soviet Union, was removed in 1958.

1957 July 11   Aga Khan III [orig.: Sultan Sir Mohammed Shah] (b. Nov. 1, 1877), the hereditary imam [ruler] of the Muslim Ismaili sect (from 1885), died. Endowed with both great wealth and great power, he founded the **All-India Muslim League** (1909) to support Muslim interests in India. He was India's representative at the League of Nations (1932, 1934–1937) and president of its assembly (1937). The khan lived mostly in Europe where he devoted much time to horse breeding and racing. He was a generous giver to Muslim causes. His grandson **Prince Karim** (b. Dec. 13, 1936) succeeded him as the Aga Khan IV.

1957 July 25   The constituent assembly (elected Mar. 25, 1956) of newly independent (1956) **Tunisia** abolished the monarchy, desposing **Mohammad VIII al-Amin**, bey of Tunis (from 1943), bringing an end to the **Husain Dynsasty** (from 1705). At the same time the assembly proclaimed Tunisia a republic, adopting (June 1, 1959) a constitution modeled after that of the U.S.

1957 July 26   Carlos Castillo Armas (b. Nov. 4, 1914), a anti-communist president of **Guatemala**, was assassinated. He had been placed in power in 1954 by a military force, aided by the U.S., to replace Jacobo Arbenz Guzman, labor and agrarian reformist. After a disputed election (Oct. 20), a three-man military junta took power (to 1958). In an election (Jan. 19, 1958), **Miguel Ydigoros Fuentes** (b. Oct. 17, 1905), a general, received the most votes but not a majority. Consequently the congress elected (Feb. 13) him president and he took office on Mar. 2.

1957 Aug. 14   Sayyid [Sa'id] bin Taimur (b. Aug., 1910), the sultan of Muscat [Masquat] and **Oman** ['Uman] (1932–1970), of the long-ruling **Al-Busayyid** [Busa'id] **Dynasty** (1741–to the present), with British aid, suppressed a revolt of Arab tribes of the interior desert plateau, led by **Ghalib bin Ali**, iman of Oman, and his brother **Talib ibn Ali**. Talib escaped to Cairo and, with the support of several Arab nations hostile to British-influenced Oman, set up an imanate-in-exile.

1957 Aug. 31   The **Federation of Malaya**, consisting of the nine Malay states plus Penang and Malacca, became an independent state within the Commonwealth of Nations and was admitted into the United Nations. **Tuanku** [Prince] **Abdul Rahman Putra** (b. Feb. 8, 1903) was chosen its first prime minister. **Indonesia** became openly hostile to the reorganized nation, charging a British subterfuge for imperialism. Three additional states, **Singapore**, **Sabah** [British North Borneo, North Borneo] and **Sarawak** bordering Sabah on the northern part of the island of Borneo, joined (Sept. 16, 1963) the federation, now renamed the **Federation of Malaysia**. Singapore, however, became (1965) a separate nation.

1957 Sept. 17   A military coup in **Thailand**, led by **Sarit Thanarat** (1908–Dec. 8, 1963), a field marshal, ousted the veteran militarist **Pibul Songgram**, the premier. **Thanom Kittikachorn** (b. Aug. 11, 1911) was named premier on Oct. 20, but in 1958, Sarit, professing to combat communism, ousted Thanom and declared martial law, setting aside the constitution. On Jan. 28, 1959, **Rama IX** [Bhumibol Adulyadej], king of Thailand (from 1946; crowned 1950), proclaimed an interim constitution and named Sarit premier.

1957 Sept. 21   Haakon VII (b. Aug. 3, 1872), king of Norway (from 1905), died. He was the first king of **Norway**, elected by the Storting (parliament) Nov. 18, 1905, after the separation of Norway and Sweden. During the Nazi occupation of Norway in World War II (1939–1945) he took his government into exile in London. Haakon was very popular with his subjects. He was succeeded by his son as **Olaf V** (b. July 2, 1903).

1957 Sept. 22   Francois Duvalier ["Papa Doc"], a physician and previously Haiti's minister of health and of labor, was easily elected president of **Haiti** with the help of the military. Thus began a 14-year dictatorship, longest in Haiti's history, marked by the unbridled use of power and terror.

1957 Oct. 27   Elections again returned the government of **Adnan Menderes**, premier of **Turkey**, to power, but by a smaller margin. As the tide against it continued to rise, the government tried tighter political controls, jailed offending journalists, and revived some pre-Kemal religious and cultural practices to gain rural support. A coup toppled the Democratic party and Menderes in 1960.

1957 Nov. 2–10 At the observance in Moscow of the 40th anniversasry of the Bolshevik Revolution of 1917, attended by the heads of state of all the major communist nations except **Tito** of Yugoslavia, **Mao Tse-Tung**, chairman of the People's Republic of China, was a star attraction. He vigorously attacked Tito, the U.S., and others of what he termed capitalistic and imperialist nations. Mao emphasized China's solidarity with the U.S.S.R. but in such a way as to indicate that he now considered his country to be an almost equal partner with the Soviet Union. The implication was that China and Russia now shared the leadership of the communist world, hitherto the prerogative of the U.S.S.R.

1957 Nov. 15 The first Liberal president of **Honduras** in 25 years, **Ramón Villeda Morales**, was elected by a constituent assembly, and a new constitution was promulgated. His pro-labor program aroused opposition, symbolized by the United Fruit Company. He was overthrown (1963) by a military coup on the eve of general elections.

1957 Dec. 5 **Sukarno**, president of **Indonesia**, expelled all Dutch nationals, following the denial of his claim to the Dutch-controlled territory of West New Guinea [West Irian]. On Dec. 9 the Indonesian government expropriated all Dutch property and repudiated its debt to the Netherlands.

III. ECONOMY AND TRADE

1957 **Kenneth** [Joseph] **Arrow** (b. Aug. 23, 1921), an American economist, published *Social Choice and Individual Values,* which discussed his work in the field of welfare economics and his concern with the general equilibrium theory. Arrow was a member (1962) of the president's Council of Economic Advisers. He was the author of *General Competitive Analysis* (1972) and *The Limits of Organization* (1974). He shared (1972) the **Nobel prize for economics**.

IV. RELIGION AND PHILOSOPHY

1957 The **Armenian Church in America** developed a schism when a group of its parishes transferred their allegiance from the Catholicos of All the Armenians in Etchmiadzin in the Soviet Socialist Republic of Armenia to the Catholicos of Cicilia in Antelias, Lebanon. Turkish oppressions in 1915 and 1920 had driven **Armenians** from their homeland into Russia or scattered them. Attempts to reunite the c.326,000 American Armenian Christians are still ongoing.

1957 Oct. 2 **Martin Luther King, Jr.**, paster of the Dexter Avenue Baptist Church in Montgomery, Alabama, and president of the **Southern Christian Leadership Conference** [SCLC], which had just been formed in Atlanta, Georgia, announced in Chicago, Illinois, a registration drive among blacks in the South. It was the first of many similar drives the Conference undertook. King had been strongly influenced by the non-violent concept of **Gandhi**. Through the SCLC King broadened his civil-rights activities, blending non-violence with an aggressive policy of confrontation of Southern white institutions, in order to secure implementation of federal equal-rights laws.

V. SCIENCE, EDUCATION, AND TECHNOLOGY

1957 **King Saud University** was founded in Riyadh, the capital city of **Saudi Arabia**. The country's first university, it opened with 21 students. It has today c.34,000 students, including 9,000 women and a campus that cost $3,400,000,000 dollars. It has had a major impact on not only Saudi Arabian society but also on the whole Muslim world of the Near East.

1957 **Jet propulsion** came of age when new high-energy fuels [petroleum derivatives] were put into commercial production. These fuels increased jet ranges nearly 50 percent.

1957 The U.S.S.R. introduced the **MIG-21**, an improved version of the **MIG-15**, which had proved in the **Korean War** (1950–1953) to be the equal of the best U.S. high-altitude interceptor, the **F-86**. Already, in 1955, the Soviets had turned out an intercontinental jet bomber comparable to the U.S. **B-52**.

1957 **Noam** [Avran] **Chomsky** (b. Dec. 7, 1928), an American linguist and educator, began his revolutionary study of language with the publication of *Syntactic Structures*. Chomsky stated that language began with rudimentary sentences, not minimal sounds as the structural linguists held. Language, according to him, was an innate and universal facility. He developed his theory into a complex system of "transformational rules" and in support of his ideas wrote such books as *Aspects of a Theory of Syntax* (1965) and *Language and Mind* (1972).

Chomsky was both influential and controversial. Besides his work in linguistics he was a leader in opposing American involvement in the **Vietnam War** (1961–1975).

1957 At the site of Gordium, an ancient city southwest of Ankara, Turkey, once the center of the Kingdom of Phrygia (c.825–c.680 B.C.), archeologists discovered what was believed to the **tomb of Gordius**, a king who flourished c.700 B.C., according to Greek mythology. In a double walled wooden chamber the skeleton rested on a four poster bed, surrounded by bronze vessels and other implements. It was Gordius who, according to tradition, tied the Gordian knot which defied all attempts to untie it until **Alexander the Great** cut it apart with a blow of his sword.

1957 **Interferon**, a protein produced in the human body in cells infected with a virus and which fights the virus, was discovered by **Alick Isaacs** (July 17, 1921–Jan. 26, 1967), a Scottish bacteriologist, and **Jean Lindenmann** (b. Sept. 18, 1924).

1957 Jan. 15–18 The **first non-stop round-the-world flight by a jet plane** was accomplished by three U.S. air force B-52 bombers. The planes took off from and returned to Castle Air Force Base, Merced, California. The time of the flight was 45 hrs., 19 min. and the distance flown was 24,325 mi. at an average speed of 525 mph.

1957 Feb. 8 **John von Neumann** (. Dec. 3, 1903), a Hungarian-born American mathematician, the propounder of the theory of games, died. In this theory statistical logic was used to decide on strategies. With a collaborator he wrote *Theory of Games and Economic Behavior* (1944). This theory is now also applied to military problems. Von Neumann was a major contributor to the development of the atomic bomb and later of the world's first hydrogen bomb. In addition he was a foremost figure in the theory and practical development of the modern electronic computer. He wrote *Computer and the Brain* (1958).

1957 Mar. 11 **Richard Evelyn Byrd** (b. Oct. 25, 1888), an America aviator and explorer, died. On Mar. 9, 1926, he and a companion were the first persons to fly an airplane over the North Pole. In 1927, a month after **Charles A. Lindbergh** made his historic first flight from New York to Paris, Byrd and a crew of three also flew this route. They carried mail, making it the first such airmail flight, although no regular service was established at this time.

Byrd's most important work was done in Antarctica where his various expeditions and discoveries created most of the Antarctic claims of the U.S. With a crew of three Byrd made (Nov. 28–29, 1929) the first flight over the South Pole. In the winter of 1933 to 1934 he spent several months alone at an advance base near the South Pole. Byrd was put in command of all U.S. activities in Antarctica in 1955.

1957 May 15 **Great Britain tested its first thermonuclear bomb. China** tested its first on June 17, 1967, **France** on Aug. 24, 1968.

1957 July 1 The **International Geophysical Year** [IGY] began, a period [actually to Dec. 31, 1958] for intensive geophysical and astronomical observations at 40 stations around the world, 7 in the U.S. In Antarctica 12 nations cooperated in research and exploration programs. Scientists of 66 nations participated. Discoveries were made in many fields, including cosmic rays, oceanography, and plate tectonics.

1957 Aug. 16 **Irving Langmuir** (b. Jan. 31, 1881), an American chemist, died. He made a varied assortment of contributions to practical problems: a gas-filled tungsten lamp; high vaccum investigation relative to radio tubes; and a process for atomic-hydrogen welding. For his work on surface chemistry, in which he developed a technique for the study of layers of molecules only one molecule thick, he received the **Nobel prize for chemistry** in 1932.

1957 Aug. 26 The U.S.S.R. announced that it had successfully tested an **intercontinental ballistic missile [ICBM]** a few days earlier. On Dec. 17 the U.S. announced that in late November it had successfully launched an Atlas ICBM 6,000 miles to a target area in the South Atlantic Ocean.

1957 Oct. 1 The **Atomic Energy Agency, International**, was created at a conference opening on this day in Vienna, Austria. Under the aegis of the **UN**, the agency was designed to promote the peaceful uses of atomic energy and to establish and administer, from its headquarters in Vienna, safeguards to prevent use of its services for military purposes or to the danger to public health.

1957 Oct. 4 The U.S.S.R. opened the eyes of the world by putting the **first artificial satellite into orbit** around the earth. Known as **Sputnik**, the satellite apparently stayed in orbit until Jan. 4, 1958. The

Space Age had now begun. Over the next decade, more than 300 satellites were sent into orbit, while craft from earth landed on the moon, and other probes reached as far as Mars and Venus.

1957 Oct. 7 A fire in Windscale Pile No. 1, a nuclear reactor near Liverpool, England, spread radioactive matter over a wide area. For three weeks milk from farms within a 200 mile radius of the reactor was not allowed to be distributed. No injuries were reported.

1957 Nov. The **Mackinac Straits Bridge** crossing the straits that connect Lake Huron and Lake Michigan and joining the two parts of Michigan state, was opened. With a main span of 3,800 feet it was the fourth longest suspension bridge in the world. The bridge was especially strengthened to withstand the wind, ice, and snow of northern winters.

1957 Dec. The **first nuclear reactor of practical importance** was completed at Shippingport, western Pennsylvania. A pressurized water reactor, it produced 60,000 kilowatts of electrical energy. Four other small reactors went into operation in the U.S. this year at Chicago, Illinois; Ft. Belvoir, Virginia; Santa Susana, California; and Vallecitos, California.

VI. ARTS AND LEISURE

1957 **Lawrence** [George] **Durrell** (b. Feb. 27, 1912), an English author and foreign service officer, published the first novel, *Justine*, in a tetralogy now known as *The Alexandria Quartet*, named for their setting in the Egyptian city. The others successively were *Balthazar* (1958), *Mountolive* (1958), and *Clea* (1960). His first novel *The Black Book* was published in 1938. His novels, travel books, and poems since *The Quartet* have reflected his years in diplomatic service.

1957 The publication of a novel *On the Road* by **Jack Kerouac** (Mar. 3, 1922–Oct. 21, 1969), an American writer, brought international attention to the **Beat Movement**. The book was more or less autobiographical and told of a young man's unsettled life, traveling here and there, partying, and womanizing. The Beat Generation of the late 1950s and the 1960s derided the values and lifestyle of the American middle class. Later they were seen to have a relationship to nature and the environment and a scepticism about the virtues of technology that became more acceptable in the 1980s. Besides Kerouac, the two most representative figures among the beats were **Allen Ginsberg** and **William S**[eward] **Burroughs** (b. Feb. 15, 1914). Ginsberg published *Howl and Other Poems* (1956). The title poem condemned modern materialism and was Whitmanesque in spirit. Burroughs's contribution at this point was *Naked Lunch* (1959), which dealt realistically with the world of the drug addict. The books of Ginsberg and Burroughs were deemed obscene in some quarters. Kerouac wrote a number of other novels, most notably *The Dharma Bums* (1958) and *The Big Sur* (1962). The former hailed Zen Buddhism as the way to truth while the latter was a sequel to *On the Road*. Ginsberg continued to write prolifically. One of his best works was *Kaddish and Other Poems* (1961). Ginsberg also took up Zen Buddhism and he was the originator of the idea of "flower power," remaking the world by peaceful but somewhat mystical means. Burroughs published such novels as *The Soft Machine* (1961) and *City of the Red Night* (1980). His work tended to be fantastic satires on the world. As a revolt against a society they disliked, the leaders of the Beat Generation were not unusual; but their withdrawal from society, instead of making a positive effort to change it, presented a rather different philosophy.

1957 Jan. 10 **Gabriela Mistral** [pen name of Lucila Godoy Alcayaga] (b. Apr. 7, 1889), a Chilean poet who in 1945 was the **first Latin American and the first woman poet** to win the **Nobel prize for literature**, died. Her first volume of poetry was *Desolacion* (1922). Her writings reflected her concern for and interest in children, love, and those suffering poverty. *Tala* (1938) and *Lager* (1954) were other collections of her verse. Mistral was also a teacher and a diplomat.

1957 Jan. 14 **Humphrey** [De Forest] **Bogart** (b. Dec. 25, 1899), an American actor, died. After 1930 he left the stage for a movie career but did not achieve stardom until he appeared in *The Petrified Forest* (1936). In general he played the part of the hardboiled male, cynical but with a touch of softness underneath. Sometimes he was a gangster, sometimes a private detective. Bogart made films that are now classics: *The Maltese Falcon* (1941), *Casablanca* (1943), *The Treasure of the Sierra Madre* (1948), *The African Queen* (1951), and *The Caine Mutiny* (1954).

1957 Jan. 16 **Arturo Toscanini** (b. Mar. 25, 1867), an Italian-born virtuoso conductor, outstanding especially in performing the works of Verdi, Beethoven, and Wagner, died. When 19 years old, as a cellist at a Rio de Janeiro opera house, he was asked to fill in for the conductor and performed Verdi's *Aïda* from memory. From 1886 to 1907 he was Italy's premier conductor of opera. In 1908 he began a six-year tenure as conductor at the Metropolitan Opera, New York City. After returning to Italy for the war years and then reorganizing the La Scala Orchestra, he returned to New York City as conductor of the New York Philharmonic Orchestra from 1926 to 1936, from which he moved in 1937 to the NBC Symphony Orchestra formed for him. He retired in 1954.

1957 Feb. 4   Miguel Covarrubias (b. Feb. 24, 1904), a Mexican-born American artist and author, died. In New York City after 1923, he quickly won popular attention with his caricatures in chic magazines. He worked also as a muralist and a lithographer. Becoming interested in ethnology, he wrote and illustrated a number of books, including *The Island of Bali* (1937), *Mexico South* (1946), and *The Eagle, the Jaguar, and the Serpent* (1954).

1957 Mar. 7   [Percy] **Wyndham Lewis** (b. Nov. 18, 1882), an English author and painter, died. Lewis was extremely versatile and, while associated with **Ezra Pound** as cofounder and editor of *Blast*, a magazine of the short-lived art movement called **Vorticism**, controversial. Later, as a painter Lewis turned successfully to conventional works. As a critic and quasi-philosopher Lewis wrote *The Art of Being Ruled* (1926) and *The Writer and the Absolute* (1952) among other titles. His novels included *Apes of God* (1930), *The Revenge for Love* (1937), and *Self-Condemned* (1954).

1957 Mar. 16   Constantin Brancusi (b. Feb. 21, 1876), a modernist Romanian sculptor, died. His best known abstract sculptures, *The Kiss* (1908), *Sleeping Muse* (1910), and the *Portrait of Mlle. Pogany* (1923) had aroused much controversy. In 1927 Brancusi had taken the U.S. customs service to court for attempting to value and tax a sculpture of his as raw metal. The decision in Brancusi's favor opened the way for the importation of abstract art free of duty.

1957 Apr. 22   The **United States Supreme Court** handed down the significant **Roth decision**, in which it held that obscenity was not protected by the First Amendment to the Constitution. It did not, however, state what kinds of materials were obscene. Criteria

for judging obscenity were developed by the Court in later decisions.

1957 May 12   Eric von Stroheim (b. Sept. 25, 1885), an Austrian-born American film actor and director, died. His first important work was *Blind Husbands* (1918), which he wrote, designed, and directed. He excelled, both as actor and director, in the realm of sophisticated and decadent settings, as in *Foolish Wives* (1921). His production of the **Frank Norris** novel *Greed* (1923) exemplified both his talent and his inability to work within the constraints of schedules and budgets. Stroheim's most remembered role was as the German prisoner of war camp commandant in *La Grande Illusion* (1937). To many he came to personify the brutal Prussian army officer.

1957 July 10   Sholem Asch (b. Nov. 1, 1880), a Polish author who wrote mainly in Yiddish, died. The best known of his works translated into English were three biblical novels: *The Nazarene* (1939), *The Apostle* (1943), and *Mary* (1949). Asch moved to the U.S. in 1914 and later lived in Europe. His novel *East River* (1946) has a New York setting. He wrote several plays, most notably *The God of Vengeance* (1910).

1957 Sept. 20   Jean [Julius Christian] **Sibelius** (b. Dec. 8, 1865), Finland's greatest composer, died. Best known for his orchestral works, his tone poems and seven symphonies (1899, 1901, 1907, 1911, 1915, 1923, and 1924) were closely tied to his native land, its landscapes, its themes, and its nationalism. In addition to his symphonies his best known works today are his Violin Concerto (1903), and three tone poems, *The Swan of Tuonela* (1893), *Finlandia* (1900), and *Valse Triste* (1903).

1957 Sept. 26   *West Side Story*, a modern musical version of *Romeo and Juliet*, opened in New York City to enthusiastic audiences. It had music by **Leonard Bernstein** (b. Aug. 25, 1918), book by **Arthur Laurents** (b. July 14, 1918), lyrics by **Stephen Sondheim** (b. March 22, 1930), and choreography by **Jerome Robbins** (b. Oct. 11, 1918). Bernstein at the time was assistant conductor of the New York Philharmonic Orchestra and a composer of distinction, but was also well known throughout the entertainment world for his songs written for such musicals as *Wonderful Town* (1953) and *Candide* (1956) and for the score of the movie *On the Waterfront* (1954). In 1958 he was named musical director of the Philharmonic. His *Mass* (1971), which Bernstein described as "a theater piece for dancers, singers, and players," was chosen for performance at the opening of the John F. Kennedy Center for the Performing Arts in Washington, D.C.

1957 Oct. 25   Henry Clemens van de Velde (b. Apr. 3, 1863), a Belgian architect and designer, died. He became noted especially for his furniture and tableware, and was a leader of the **Jugendstil**, the art nouveau movement in Germany. He founded his own school in Weimar, with emphasis on the arts and crafts movement of the time. Among van de Velde's architectural creations was the Werkbund Theater in Cologne (1914) and the university library in Ghent (1935–1940).

1957 Nov. 25   Diego Rivera (b. Dec. 8, 1886), a Mexican mural painter, died. His periods in Europe (1907–1909, 1912–1921) and his association with Cezanne, Picasso, and exiled Russian communists made him enthusiastic about painting for the people in public places, which he then did in Mexico on Mexican themes, becoming a national hero. In the U.S. Rivera did frescoes in San Francisco and murals in the Detroit Institute of Arts. A mural for Rockefeller Center in New York City was removed by his client when he included a portrait of Lenin in it. Rivera reproduced the mural for the Palace of Fine Arts, Mexico City.

1957 Dec. 18   Dorothy L[eigh] Sayers (b. June 13, 1893), an English master writer of the detective story, died. Her witty and sophisticated stories, with clever plots, featured the noble, debonair, man-about-town Lord Peter Wimsey. Typical of her tales were *Strong Poison* (1930), *Murder Must Advertise* (1933), *The Nine Tailors* (1934), and *Busman's Honeymoon* (1937. Sayers was also a scholar of the medieval period with a strong interest in Christianity. She wrote a play *The Man Born to Be King* (1942) and after 1949 worked on a translation of Dante's *Divine Comedy*.

VII. SPORTS, GAMES, AND SOCIETY

1957 Mar. 27–30   The **first annual men's United States Curling Championship** was held in Chicago, Illinois. The Hibbing [Minnesota] Curling Club won the title over the Minot [North Dakota] Curling Club by a score of 12 to 6.

1957 July 19   Don Bowden (b. Aug. 8, 1936) became the **first American to break the four-minute mark** in the mile run. At Stockton, California, he did it in 3:58.7.

1957 Aug. 23   For the first time the **international Little League competition in baseball** was won by a team other than one representing the U.S. The winning nine came from the Monterrey Industrial Little League of Monterrey, Mexico. Their pitcher hurled a perfect game.

1957 Nov. 3   Wilhelm Reich (b. Mar. 24, 1897), an Austrian-born American psychiatrist, whose theory of "orgone energy" excited public interested but was derided by fellow scientists, died. Coming to the U.S. in 1939, he propounded (1942) his belief that "orgones," units of cosmic energy, permeated the earth and all individuals. To enable people to rid themselves of this troublesome energy, Reich devised the "orgone box." He was ordered (1954) by the U.S. government to cease producing these clearly useless boxes and when he persisted he was convicted (1956) of contempt of court and sent to prison where he died. Reich was the author of *The Function of Orgasm* (1927) and *Character Analysis* (1945).

1957 Dec. 27   At Melbourne, Australia, the Australian **Davis Cup** team defeated the U.S. team three matches to two in the competition for this emblem of international tennis supremacy for the third straight year. In 1955 and 1956 Australia won by scores of 5 to 0.

1958

I. EXPLORATION AND COLONIZATION

1958 Mar. 2   Vivian Ernest Fuchs (b. Feb. 11, 1908), an English geologist and explorer leading a five-man group, completed the **first entirely overland crossing of Antarctica**. The party began the 99-day, 2,158-mile trek by dog sleds and snow tractors on Nov. 24, 1957 at Shackleton base near the Weddell Sea, reached the South Pole on Jan. 20, 1958, and ended at Scott base on the Ross Sea.

II. DISASTERS

1958 Jan. 26–27 A **storm** off the southern and eastern coasts of Japan sank seven ships with a loss of 271 lives.

1958 Sept. 27–28 **Typhoon Ida** struck the Tokyo, Japan, area, leaving 579 persons dead, 495 injured, and another c.500 missing and presumed dead.

1958 Dec. 1 A **fire** starting in a stairwell of Our Lady of the Angels elementary school in Chicago took the lives of 92 children and three teacher-nuns. There were c.1,300 students and teachers in the building at the time of the fire.

III. POLITICS AND WAR

1958 Jan. 3 The **West Indies Federation** was established by ten British territories, including most of the British Leeward and Windward islands, the Bahamas and British Virgin Islands being notable exceptions. Jamaica withdrew (1961) following a national referendum. The territory of Trinidad and Tobago followed suit (1962) and the federation was then dissolved.

1958 Jan. 23 A popular revolt in **Venezuela** forced **Marcos Pérez Jiménez** (b. Apr. 25, 1914), the military dictator, to flee the country after six years of police-state rule.

1958 Feb.–Sept. **Indonesia's** army quelled a widespread rebellion that began on Sumatra and spread to other islands, notably Celebes. The revolt stemmed from the desire of native tribes for greater autonomy and the favoritism shown by **Sukarno** to the Javanese military.

1958 Feb. 1 **Gemal Abdal Nasser**, president of Egypt, and **Shukri al-Kuwatly**, president of Syria, meeting in Cairo, agreed to unite their countries to form the **United Arab Republic** [UAR] (to Sept. 28, 1961), with Nasser as president. Their respective nations enthusiastically approved (Feb. 21) in a referendum. Though the union was soon dissolved, Nasser kept the name United Arab Republic for Egypt alone.

1958 Feb. 8 The **French air force bombed** the **Tunisian** border village of **Sagiyat Sidi Yusufwas** on the grounds that Algerian guerrillas were using it as a haven.

1958 Feb. 14 **Hussein I**, king of **Jordan**, and **Faisal II**, king of **Iraq**, meeting at Amman, Jordan, formed an **Arab Federation** of their countries within the Arab Union as a countermeasure to the United Arab Republic [UAR] of Egypt and Syria. Hussein dissolved the union (Aug. 1) after a military coup in Iraq of **Abdul Karim Kassem** [Kassim] (Nov. 21, 1914–Feb. 9, 1963) toppled the monarchy, killing Faisal II (b. May 2, 1935), the crown prince, and members of the royal family on July 14.

1958 Feb. 22 **Arturo Frondizi**, a lawyer, economist, and leader of the Radical party, was elected president of **Argentina** in a landslide. Many Perónists and communists supported him. It was said to have been the first free election since 1928.

1958 Feb. 26–Apr. 28 At Geneva, Switzerland, 86 nations at a U.N. conference wrestled with maritime law in an attempt to codify it and to resolve some currently troublesome issues. The conference was unable to resolve the question as to the breadth of ocean territory to which a nation can claim sovereignty.

1958 Mar. 26 **Nikita Khrushchev** became premier of the Soviet Union after **Nicholoi Bulganin** was forced to resign.

1958 Apr. 15 **Kwame Nkrumah**, prime minister of Ghana, opened the **first conference of independent African states** at Accra, Ghana. It had no practical effect.

1958 May 9 **Camille Chamoun**, president of Lebanon (from 1952), called for U.N. observers and U.S. troops to help stabilize his country. Chamoun, a Maronite Christian, accused the **United Arab Republic** [UAR] of instigation. His regime was attacked by Muslim elements for its pro-Western policies and his acceptance of U.S. financial aid under the Eisenhower doctrine. In the elections of July 31, a nonpolitical figure, **Fouad Chebab** (Mar. 9, 1902–Apr. 25, 1973) was elected president (to 1964).

1958 May 27 A state of emergency was declared in **Ceylon** [present Sri Lanka], as the **Tamils**, a minority Hindu people [23 percent] in a land dominated by the Buddhist **Sinhalese**, erupted in a series of riots, demanding the creation of a separate Tamil state within a federation and official recognition of their language. Some concessions were made on language, but short of the creation of a dual system.

1958 June 1   Charles de Gaulle, head (1944–1946) of France's provisional government after World War II, was recalled by the National Assembly to resolve a crisis in the government that threatened to bring chaos to the country. The trouble stemmed largely from the situation in **Algeria** where on May 13 French colonists, supported by elements of the French military stationed there, demonstrated against the home government. On June 2 the assembly voted de Gaulle full power to rule by decree for six months. On Sept. 28 a new constitution was adopted in a referendum that overwhelmingly supported de Gaulle's demand for a strong executive. On Dec. 21 the electoral college named him president, to take office on Jan. 8, 1959. With new executive power, de Gaulle decided to allow the Algerians self-determination, which resulted in more anger and demonstrations by French colonists. De Gaulle held firm and, in 1962, an agreement was reached that brought **independence to Algeria** on July 3.

1958 July 11   The **Swiss government announced plans to arm the country with nuclear weapons**. In 1962 the people of Switzerland, in a national referendum, defeated the Socialist party's proposal to prohibit nuclear weapons in Switzerland.

1958 July 15   U.S. marines landed in Lebanon in response to the appeal of Camille Chamoun, president of Lebanon, to avert a possible takeover by radical Muslim elements, egged on by Nasser, president of the United Arab Republic. The marines were withdrawn on Oct. 25.

1958 Sept. 1   Iceland, to protect its fishing industry, extended from 4 to 12 miles from the coast the limitation on foreign fishing, which precipitated the "**cod war**" between Iceland and Great Britain. For two years Icelandic coast guard vessels and British destroyers occasionally exchanged fire. On March 10, 1961, Great Britain accepted the Icelandic limits.

1958 Sept. 3   Mao Tse-Tung, head of state and chairman of the Chinese Communist party and the country's most powerful figure, launched his economic program known as the **Great Leap Forward**. Mao was eager to promote a Chinese form of communism and to increase productivity by expanding cooperatives into labor-intensive communes. The program bogged down because of neglect of agricultural production and three consecutive years of bad crop weather, a shortage of industrial equipment,

and the withdrawal in 1960 of Soviet aid and technicians.

1958 Sept. 28   In a referendum seven of France's overseas territories voted to join the **French Community** which, under a new constitution adopted at the same time, established the **Fifth Republic** and ended the **French Union**. The seven were: Dahomey, French Sudan [which became the Sudanese Republic], Ivory Coast, Mauritania, Niger, Senegal, and Upper Volta. They all became autonomous republics within the Community.

1958 Oct. 1   Tunisia was admitted to membership in the **Arab League. Habib Bourguiba**, the president of Tunisia, soon made his presence known by accusing Egypt of complicity in a plot to kill him.

1958 Oct. 7   Iskander Mirza, president of **Pakistan**, dissolved the Assembly in an effort to end the political dissension that plagued the country. On Oct. 27, however, **Muhammad Ayub Khan** (May 14, 1907–Apr. 19, 1974) took over the presidency in a bloodless coup.

1958 Oct. 20   Sarit Thanarat, strong man of **Thailand**, dismissed his own choice as premier, **Thanom Kittikachorn**, suspended the constitution, and established martial law.

1958 Oct. 29   U Nu [Thakin Nu] (b. May 25, 1907), nationalist-socialist premier of **Burma** [Myanmar], turned the government over to army chief **Ne Win** [Shu Maung] (b. May 24, 1911).

1958 Oct. 31   An agreement signed in Geneva between the U.S.S.R. and the U.S. **banned nuclear weapons testing** while arrangements were being made for further talks on arms limitations.

1958 Nov. 17   Ibrahim Abboud, commander in chief of the **Sudanese** army, overthrew the government without bloodshed. Abboud abolished political parties and suspended the constitution.

1958 Nov. 30   Elections in **Uruguay** gave the conservative Blancos [Whites] victory over the Colorados [Reds] and control of the government for the first time in 93 years. **Benito Nardone** (1906–Mar. 25, 1964) assumed leadership of the Blancos and became president (1960–1961) of the National Government Council, a coalition that had replaced the presidency in 1934.

1958 Dec. 31 With the forces of **Fidel Castro** pressing hard on several fronts, **Fulgencio Batista**, president and virtual dictator of **Cuba**, fled the country. Immediately, the last defenders of such cities as Santa Clara and Santiago surrendered.

IV. ECONOMY AND TRADE

1958 British Overseas Airlines Corporation, National Airlines, and Pan American World Airways all began **jet transport** service between the U.S. and Europe. American Airlines began the first American transcontinental jet airliner service, and Air France established the first jet passenger service flying over the North Pole.

1958 Jan. 1 The **European Economic Community** [EEC], called the "**Common Market,**" and the **European Atomic Energy Community** [Euratom] became operative, based on the **Treaties of Rome** (Mar. 25, 1957). The founding members of the two groups were Belgium, France, Belgium, Italy, Luxembourg, the Netherlands, and West Germany. The objective of the EEC was the gradual abolition of customs barriers between the countries, and the development of common economic policies. Euratom was intended to aid in the common development of Europe's nuclear resources.

1958 Feb. 3 A treaty establishing the **Benelux Economic Union** was signed by Belgium, Luxembourg, and the Netherlands. The new economic union was to become effective in 1960 when there would be a full and free flow of people, capital, and goods and services, among the three.

1958 Sept. The revolutionary government of **Iraq** limited the acreage of irrigated land held by any landholder to 600 acres and expropriated and redistributed holdings beyond that limit. More than one million acres were redistributed in the program's first 15 years.

V. RELIGION AND PHILOSOPHY

1958 Oct. 9 **Pope Pius XII** (b. Mar. 2, 1876; ruled from 1939) died. Pius was widely criticized for not protesting the persecution of the Jews during World War II. A staunch anti-communist, he encouraged the formation of national Catholic Action organizations in which the laity participated militantly in the mission of the Church. His bull *Munificentissimus Deus* (1950) defined the dogma of the Assumption of the Virgin Mary. Pius was succeeded (Oct. 28) by **John XXIII.**

1958 Oct. 24 **George Edward Moore** (b. Nov. 4, 1873), an English philosopher, who edited the important journal *Mind* for more than a quarter of a century (1921–1947), died. In *Principia Ethica* (1903) he began considering the problem of distinguishing between the things a person can know and the ways in which he can be said to know them. In general he is now associated with the "New Realism." Moore also wrote *Philosophical Studies* (1922) and *Some Main Problems in Philosophy* (1953).

VI. SCIENCE, EDUCATION AND TECHNOLOGY

1958 **Claude Levi-Strauss** (b. Nov. 28, 1908), the **founder of cultural anthropology**, published *Structural Anthropology*, describing his theories. In considering such social structures as kinship, religion, and art, for example, he believed that relationships among such phenomena were of the first importance. Levi-Strauss also wrote *Race and History* (1952) and *Totemism* (1962).

1958 Jan. 31 The United States launched its first artificial satellite, *Explorer I*, from Cape Canaveral, Florida, at 10:48 a.m. It weighed 30.8 pounds and orbited the earth every 114 minutes at a maximum altitude of 2,000 miles and a minimum of 230. When radiation counters on this satellite failed, **James A[fred] Van Allen** (b. Sept. 7, 1914), an American astrophysicist, suspected that unusually high levels of radiation were the cause. Accordingly he designed a new counter that was carried aloft by Explorer IV on July 26. This device discovered what came to be called the **Van Allen radiation belt**, outside the earth's atmosphere.

1958 Aug. 1 The **first undersea crossing of the North Pole** was made by the U.S. nuclear submarine *Nautilus*. It sailed under the Arctic ice cap for 96 hours, from the Pacific Ocean, a distance of 1,830 miles, without surfacing.

1958 Sept. 25 **John B[roadus] Watson** (b. Jan. 9, 1878), an American psychologist who founded the school called behaviorism, died. Watson held that, except for the emotions of fear, hate, and love, all behavior could be learned or unlearned by conditioning. Among Watson's writings were *Behaviorism*

(1925) and *Psychological Care of Infant and Child* (1928).

1958 Oct. 1 By act of the U.S. Congress, the **National Aeronautics and Space Administration [NASA]** was established. Its purpose was to take over all the nation's activities in the exploration of space.

1958 Nov. 25 Charles F[rancis] **Kettering** (b. Aug. 29, 1876), an American inventor with c.140 patents to his credit, died. He was known chiefly for inventing the self-starter for automobiles (first placed in use in 1912), which made driving possible for women and those with handicaps. Despite his reputation for emphasis on practicality, Kettering advocated basic research as the father of practical developments.

VII. ARTS AND LEISURE

1958 The **first annual Spoleto Festival of Two Worlds** was held in Spoleto, Italy. It was chiefly the idea of **Gian-Carlo Menotti**, the composer, and was intended to display the talents of young artists in music and the theater.

1958 **Jasper Johns** (b. May 15, 1930), an American artist whose work foreshadowed pop art, had his first one-man show in New York City. Johns had become known for his use of everyday objects, especially the American flag, in his paintings. Among his paintings were *Target with Plaster Casts* (1955) and *Field Painting* (1963–1964).

1958 Jan. 15 *Vanessa*, the first opera by **Samuel Barber**, an American composer, was given its first performance in the Metropolitan Opera House in New York City.

1958 Feb. 13 Georges [Henri] **Rouault** (b. May 27, 1871), a French painter, died. Rouault recreated an almost medieval feeling in his work. He worked in media ranging from ballet set designs to stained glass, but was known most notably for his oils and prints. Among Rouault's canvases were *Christ Mocked by Soldiers* (1932), *Head of a Clown* (1948), and *Christian Nocturne* (1952).

1958 Mar. 28 W[illiam] **C**[hristopher] **Handy** (b. Nov. 16, 1873), a black American musician often called the father of the blues, died. He was a songwriter, band leader, and music publisher. Some of his compositions are now classics: "**Memphis Blues**" (1912), "**St. Louis Blues**" (1914), and "**Beale Street Blues**" (1917).

1958 Apr. 13 [Harry Lavan] **Van Cliburn** (b. July 12, 1934) achieved worldwide recognition when he won the prestigious **International Tchaikovsky Competition** in Moscow. The triumph of a young American in such an event won Cliburn a ticker tape parade up Broadway, New York City, an honor usually reserved for aviators and sports heroes.

1958 May 5 James Branch Cabell (b. Apr. 14, 1879), an American novelist, died. He set a long series of novels in an invented medieval kingdom, Poictesme. One of these, *Jurgen* (1919), was perhaps his best and certainly the most famous because it was temporarily suppressed on charges of obscenity. *The Cords of Vanity* (1909) and *The Rivet in Grandfather's Neck* (1915) represent his early fiction; *The Cream of the Jest* (1917) and *The Silver Stallion* (1926) his later.

1958 May 19 *The Birthday Party* by **Harold Pinter** (b. Oct. 10, 1930), an English playwright, opened in London, his first to be performed there. It was not a success.

1958 May 29 Juan Ramón Jiménez (b. Dec. 24, 1881), a Spanish poet, died. With the publication of *Platero y yo* [*Platero and I*] (1017), a work that has been called the best collection of prose poems in Spanish, he became widely known. English translations of Jiménez's poetry have appeared in *Three Hundred Poems: 1903–1953* (1962) and *Forty Poems* (1967). He was awarded the **Nobel prize for literature** in 1956.

1958 Aug. 26 Ralph Vaughan Williams (b. Oct. 12, 1872), an English composer, died. His early orchestral pieces, *The Fen Country* (1904) and *Norfolk Rhapsodies* (1905–1907), set his own individual style and reflected his absorption in English folk idiom. Notable among his full orchestral works were *A London Symphony* (1914), *A Pastoral Symphony* (1921), and *Sixth Symphony* (1947). Shakespeare's *Merry Wives of Windsor* provided him with a story for his opera *Sir John in Love* (1929), as did **John Bunyan's** *The Pilgrim's Progress* (1951), and **J.M. Synge's** *Riders to the Sea* (1937).

1958 Sept. 22 Mary Roberts Rinehart (b. Aug. 12, 1876), an American novelist and playwright, died. It was the publication of her first mystery novel, *The*

Circular Staircase (1908), followed quickly by *The Man in Lower Ten* (1909), that brought her a vast readership that eagerly awaited her next well-plotted puzzler. Rinehart wrote a stream of bestsellers, translating nine of them to the stage, assisted by **Avery Hopwood**. At the time of her death, sales of her books had exceeded 10 million copies.

1958 Oct. 16   The TV quiz show "Twenty-One" was canceled as a result of a growing **scandal over the rigging of the big-money quiz shows** to increase their popularity.

1958 Oct. 23   The **Nobel prize for literature** was awarded to **Boris Pasternak**, a Russian poet, novelist, and translator. He accepted but almost immediately was forced by the communist authorities of the U.S.S.R. to decline. They were displeased with his novel *Doctor Zhivago*, which gave an unfavorable view of communist society and expressed some Christian idealism. Pasternak was expelled from the Soviet Writers Union and lived the rest of his life until his death in 1960 in what amounted to internal exile near Moscow.

1958 Dec. 29   **Doris Humphrey** (b. Oct. 17, 1895), an American dancer, choreographer, and teacher, died. As a featured soloist with the Denishawn Company, later in a performing and teaching partnership with **Charles Weidman**, Humphrey was one of the **American pioneers in modern dance**.

VIII. SPORTS, GAMES, AND SOCIETY

1958 Mar. 1   **Garfield Sobers** (b. July 28, 1936), a **cricketer** for the West Indies, completed his innings of 365 runs, not out, to set the single-innings record for test match competition.

1958 Mar. 25   **Sugar Ray Robinson** [orig.: Walker Smith] (May 3, 1920–Apr. 12, 1989), regained the **world middleweight professional boxing championship** for the fifth time, a record for winning and losing a title never equaled. He defeated **Carmen Basilio** (b. Apr. 2, 1927) in a 15-round decision at Chicago.

1958 Apr. 17–Oct. 19   A **World's Fair** was held in Brussels, Belgium, lasting six months, with 45 nations exhibiting and c.41½ million persons visiting it. The fair was outstanding in exhibiting developments in atomic physics.

1958 June 29   In the finals of the **World Cup** competition in soccer Brazil defeated Sweden 5–2 at Stockholm.

1958 Sept. 20–27   The **America's Cup**, the international yachting trophy, was successfully defended by the U.S. sloop **Columbia**, which defeated the British challenger *Sceptre* in four straight races off Newport, Rhode Island.

1959

I. EXPLORATION AND COLONIZATION

1959 Dec. 1   Twelve nations signed the **Antarctic Treaty**, which reserved this continent for free, cooperative, peaceful, and nonpolitical scientific investigation. Military operations, nuclear explosives, and disposal of radioactive wastes were prohibited.

II. DISASTERS

1959 Jan. 9   The Vega de Tera **dam at Rivadelago, Spain, burst** and 123 people were drowned by the flood waters.

1959 May 8   An excursion **boat floundered** in the Nile River near Cairo. Although it was only six yards from shore the passengers panicked and c.200 lives were lost.

1959 Sept. 26–27   **Typhoon Vera** struck the Japanese island of Honshu, causing 4,466 deaths. From Sept. 15 to 19, 1947, nearly 1,000 people died and 1,616 were injured in a typhoon and flood on Honshu.

1959 Dec. 2   The **collapse of the Malpasset Dam** at Fréjus, in southeastern France, caused a flood that killed 412 people.

III. POLITICS AND WAR

1959 Abdul Karim Kassem, nationalist premier of **Iraq**, renewed relations with the U.S.S.R. (February) and quelled a pro-communist uprising (July). He formally withdrew from the **Baghdad Pact** (Mar. 24) but retained correct relations with Turkey and removed pro-Egyptian officials from positions of influence, so his relations with the **United Arab Republic** [UAR] deteriorated.

1959 *Euskadi Ta Askatasuna* [ETA; Basque Homeland and Liberty] was founded by militant **Basques**, inhabitants from ancient times of the northern region of Spain that borders on the eastern shore of the Bay of Biscay and the western Pyrenées. Its members carried out terrorist acts, particularly against policemen.

1959 Jan. 3 **Alaska** was admitted into the union, the 49th American state.

1959 Jan. 8 **Fidel Castro**, Cuban revolutionary, marched triumphantly into Havana, from which **Fulgencio Batista** had fled in the early hours of Jan. 1. Castro soon declared himself prime minister and put in place his agrarian reform program, which nationalized all large farms and foreign-owned estates.

1959 Jan 17 Senegal and the Sudanese Republic [French Sudan] joined to form the **Federation of Mali** in an attempt to federate the former French territories of West Africa. Political differences soon foreshadowed the end of the federation. On June 20, 1960, the Sudanese Republic became the Republic of Mali, with Modibo Keita (May, 1915–May 16, 1977) as its president. **Senegal** left the federation on Aug. 20.

1959 Feb. 11 The **Federation of the Emirates of the South**, in the southern Arabian Peninsula, was formed by six emirates and sultanates within the British protectorate at Aden. Their capital was al-Ittihad.

1959 Feb. 12 **Nepal** promulgated a democratic constitution. In the first general elections (Apr. 3) the Nepali Congress party won 74 of 109 seats in the parliament. Gurkha Paris became the official opposition party, with 19 seats.

1959 Feb. 19 Great Britain, Greece, and Turkey reached an agreement whereby the island of **Cyprus**, in the eastern Mediterranean Sea, previously a British colony, would become independent in one year. This meant that Cyprus would neither become entirely part of Greece nor divided between Greece and Turkey.

1959 Mar. 13–27 **Tibetans** revolted against their Chinese communist rulers, partly because they thought the **Dalai Lama**, their spiritual leader, was in danger. The Chinese broke the revolt with superior military force, and the Dalai Lama fled (Mar. 31) into exile in India. In July the International Commission of Jurists at Geneva, Switzerland, charged the Chinese communists with systematically destroying traditional Tibetan life and religion. About 65,000 Tibetans were known to have died and c.20,000 were deported.

1959 May 29 A customs union, called the **Council of the Entente**, was created by three former French West African colonies, the Ivory Coast, Nigeria, and Upper Volta [present Burkina Faso].

1959 June 3 **Singapore** became a self-governing state, ending its status as a crown colony of Great Britain but remaining within the Commonwealth of Nations. The socialist People's Action party [PAP], led by **Lee Kuan Yew** (b. Sept. 16, 1923), won 43 of 51 legislative seats in the 1959 election, and Lee became prime minister.

1959 July 25 **Richard M. Nixon**, vice president of the U.S., visited Moscow in connection with the opening of the American National Exposition. There, Nixon and **Nikita Khrushchev**, premier of the U.S.S.R., engaged in the so-called "**kitchen debate**," on the merits of capitalism and communism. The U.S. exhibit showed a house intended to show how comfortably an American steel worker could live under capitalism. Khrushchev claimed that communist Russia also had such appliances as dishwashing machines. At home the American people felt Nixon had won the debate.

1959 Aug. 19 The **Baghdad Pact** (from 1955), or the Middle East Treaty Organization [METO] (from 1959), was reorganized as the **Central Treaty Organization** [CENTO], following the withdrawal of the new Iraqi regime on Mar. 24. The alliance was headquartered in Ankara.

1959 Aug. 21   **Hawaii** was admitted into the union, the 50th American state.

1959 Sept. 15–27   **Nikita Khrushchev**, premier of the U.S.S.R., toured the U.S. in a highly publicized visit to promote peaceful co-existence. He stopped, among many other places, at Hyde Park, New York, to see **Eleanor Roosevelt**, and at the **Roswell Garst** farms in Coon Rapids, Iowa. Returning to Washington, D.C., he visited **Dwight D. Eisenhower**, president of the U.S., at Camp David.

1959 Sept. 26   **S.W.R.D.** [Solomon West Ridgeway Dias] **Bandaranaike** (b. Jan. 8, 1899), prime minister of **Ceylon** [Sri Lanka] since 1956 and founder (1951) of the Sri Lanka Freedom party, died after being shot by a dissident Buddhist monk the day before. He was succeeded as party leader by his wife **Sirimavo Bandaranaika**, who became (1960) prime minister after her party won a general election.

1959 Oct. 8   The Conservative party won a third straight general election in **Great Britain**. The party captured 365 seats to 258 for their main rival the Labour party. **Harold Macmillan** continued as prime minister.

1959 Oct. 12   The U.S. and the **Philippines** signed a memorandum that shortened the length of the lease of U.S. military bases from 99 to 25 years.

1959 Oct. 16   **George C**[atlett] **Marshall** (b. Dec. 31, 1880), an American soldier and diplomat, died. A career army officer, he capped his military life by being chief of staff of the U.S. army (1939–1945) and in this position was one of the major planners of Allied strategy in World War II. While secretary of state (1947–1949) he proposed the European Recovery Program, which soon became known as the **Marshall Plan** and which played a vital role in the economic recovery of Western Europe after the devastation of World War II. Resigning in 1949, Marshall was once more called to duty and served as secretary of defense (1950–1951). For his sponsorship of the recovery program he was awarded the **Nobel Peace Prize** in 1953.

1959 Dec. 22   **Dwight D. Eisenhower**, president of the U.S., and **Muhammad V**, king of **Morocco**, signed

an agreement for the U.S. evacuation of its military bases in Morocco.

IV. ECONOMICS AND TRADE

1959 Jan. 27–Feb. 5   At a meeting of the Congress of the Communist party of the **U.S.S.R.**, a **Seven-Year Plan** for the economy was adopted. It called for raising industrial production by 80 percent by 1965, with emphasis on chemicals and artificial fertilizers.

1959 Mar. 18   **Oil deposits were found in Libya** by American prospectors, at Bir Tlaksin in Tripolitania and at Zelten in Cyrenaica (June 11). Libya overnight became a wealthy state.

1959 June 26   Dwight D. Eisenhower, president of the United States, and Elizabeth II, queen of Great Britain, officially opened the **St. Lawrence Seaway**. It was now possible for vessels 730 feet long, drawing 27 feet of water, to pass through canals and locks to the farthest of the Great Lakes, a distance of 2,342 miles. The cost was $400 million.

1959 July 15   The **longest steel strike in U.S. history** began. It continued for 116 days, ending when the U.S. Supreme Court upheld an injunction against the strike under the **Taft-Hartley Labor Act** (1947). The strike against 12 steel makers idled c.500,000 steel workers and thousands more in industries dependent on steel.

1959 Nov. 20   The **European Free Trade Association** [EFTA] was organized by Great Britain, Austria, Denmark, Norway, Portugal, Sweden, and Switzerland to promote free trade among the members and broader commercial relations with the Common Market nations.

1959 Dec. 14   The **Council for Mutual Economic Aid** [COMECON], first formed in 1949 by the USSR and five of its satellites, adopted a new, formal charter. **COMECON** now took on greater stature as a response to the Common Market and the European Free Trade Association.

1959 Dec. 31   The **Inter-American Development Bank** was established by 19 Latin American republics and the U.S. with an initial capitalization of $1,000,000,000, of which the U.S. contributed $450,000,000.

V. RELIGION AND PHILOSOPHY

1959 Jan. 25 **Pope John XXIII** announced that he intended to convoke a council to consider the position of the Roman Catholic Church in the late 20th century.

VI. SCIENCE, EDUCATION, AND TECHNOLOGY

1959 In the Olduvai Gorge in Tanzania, East Africa, **Mary** [Douglas] **Leakey** (b. Feb. 6, 1913), an English anthropologist and archeologist, discovered a hominid fossil, which she labeled *Zinjanthropus*, thought to be 1.75 million years old.

1959 **C**[harles] **P**[ercy] **Snow** (Oct. 15, 1905–July 1, 1980), an English novelist who had begun his adult career as a scientific researcher at Cambridge University, published *The Two Cultures and the Scientific Revolution*. Snow deplored what he saw as the growing gulf of understanding between scientists, especially those in the physical sciences, and the "literary intellectuals."

1959 Jan. 2 The U.S.S.R. launched **Lunik I** [Luna I] into orbit around the sun. The satellite, the **first craft to escape Earth's gravity**, made a fly-by of the moon.

1959 Feb. 15 **Owen** [Willans] **Richardson** (b. Apr. 26, 1879), an English physicist, died. In 1911 he proved that electrons are emitted from heated metals. From his work he formulated **Richardson's law** relating the rate of emission to temperature. For his work he received the **Nobel prize for physics** in 1928.

1959 Mar. 3 The U.S. launched **Pioneer IV**, its **first lunar probe**. On Aug. 7 the American solar satellite Pioneer V telemetered and transmitted information from 22.5 million miles.

1959 July 31 The **first nuclear-powered merchant ship** ever built was christened at Camden, New Jersey. The nuclear **Savannah** was a ship of 22,000 tons, 595.5 feet long, and it cost $40 million.

1959 Nov. 15 **Charles Thomson Rees Wilson** (b. 1869), a Scottish physicist, died. In 1911 he invented the Wilson cloud chamber, which proved virtually indispensable in the study of subatomic particles, and which contributed, among other things, to the discovery (1932) of the positron. For his invention

Wilson shared the **Nobel prize for physics** in 1927 with **Arthur Holly Compton**.

VII. ARTS AND LEISURE

1959 French films swept the major awards at the **Cannes Festival**. This was the outpouring of French talent known as the *nouvelle vague* [New Wave], notably **Francois Truffaut** (Feb. 6, 1932–Oct. 21, 1984), **Claude Chabrol** (b. June 24, 1930), and **Jean-Luc Godard** (b. Mar. 30, 1930). Two other directors of importance in this period were **Alain Resnais** (b. June 3, 1922) and **Roger Vadim** (b. Jan. 26, 1928).

1959 The release of the British movie *Room at the Top*, directed by **Jack Clayton** (b. Mar. 1, 1921), followed quickly by *Look Back in Anger*, from the play by **John Osborne**, a London stage hit in 1956, directed by **Tony** [Cecil Antonio] **Richardson** (b. June 5, 1928) opened an era of new vitality in British film making.

1959 Jan. 21 **Cecil B**[lount] **DeMille** (b. Aug. 12, 1881), an American movie producer and director, died. His trademark became the mammoth spectacle movie, best exemplified by his production of **The Ten Commandments** (1923).

1959 Feb. 12 **George Antheil** (b. July 8, 1900), a modernist American composer, died. From 1922 to 1936 he lived and worked in Berlin and Paris. Among his works were **Airplane Sonata** (1922) and **Sonata sauvage** (1923). Antheil also composed the **Ballet mécanique** (1925) and an opera **Transatlantic** (1930).

1959 Feb. 28 **Maxwell Anderson** (b. Dec. 15, 1888), an American playwright, died. His first success was *What Price Glory?* (1924), a collaboration with Laurence Stallings (Nov. 25, 1894–Feb. 28, 1968), with a World War I setting. A number of Anderson's plays were historical, including *Elizabeth the Queen* (1930), in blank verse, and *Anne of the Thousand Days* (1948), about Anne Boleyn. He also wrote: *Gods of the Lightning* (1928), about the Sacco-Vanzetti case; *High Tor* (1937), a fantasy; *Knickerbocker Holiday* (1938), a musical set in Peter Stuyvesant's New Netherland; and *The Bad Seed* (1955) a tragic story of a truly evil girl.

1959 Apr. 9 **Frank Lloyd Wright** (b. June 8, 1869), a giant of modern architecture, died. His "prairie style" homes in the Chicago area, characterized by wide overhangs and open interiors, opened the eyes of other architects to new materials and new techniques, as well as challenging their aesthetics. Wright's beautiful **Imperial Hotel** in Tokyo withstood the disastrous earthquake of 1923. Startling and controversial with its spiral ramp for viewers was his **Guggenheim Museum**, New York City. Eye-catching was his Kaufmann house, **Falling Water**, cantilevered over a waterfall at Bear Run, Pennsylvania, and his own homes, **Taliesin** (1911) at Spring Green, Wisconsin, and **Taliesin West** (1936–1959) at Scottsdale, Arizona.

1959 Apr. 16 The **Bolshoi Theater Ballet**, the leading dance group of the Soviet Union, gave its first performance in the U.S. at the Metropolitan Opera, New York City. *Romeo and Juliet* was danced with **Galina Ulanova** (b. Jan. 1, 1910) in the leading role. This eight-week tour of the U.S. and Canada was only the fourth time in nearly 200 years that it had performed outside Russia.

1959 June 8 **Ethel Barrymore** (b. Aug. 15, 1879), a great American actress, died. Daughter of Maurice and Georgiana Drew Barrymore, sister of Lionel and John, Ethel made her debut at age 14, on Jan. 25, 1894, in Sheridan's *The Rivals*. She achieved stardom in Clyde Fitch's *Captain Jinks of the Horse Marines* in 1901. Among her later successes were her roles in *A Doll's House* (1905), *Trelawney of the Wells* (1911), *The Second Mrs. Tanqueray* (1924), *Whiteoaks* (1938), and *The Corn Is Green* (1940–1942). She won an **Oscar** in 1944 as best supporting actress for her role in *None But the Lonely Heart*.

1959 June 11 The **postmaster general of the U.S.** **banned** from the mails the novel *Lady Chatterley's Lover* by **D.H. Lawrence**, first published in 1928. He declared that "taken as a whole" it was "an obscene and filthy work." On July 21, however, a federal judge ruled that the banning was unconstitutional.

1959 July 6 **George Grosz** (b. July 26, 1893), a German-American artist, cartoonist, and caricaturist, died. He worked in Paris and Berlin where he published *la Vie d'un socialiste* (1920) and *Miroir du bourgeois* (1925). He was a leader in the German artistic movement known as *die Neue Sachlichkeit* [The New Objectivity], a revival of realism. On March 8, 1933, he became the first of many German artists and writers to be stripped of citizenship by the new Nazi government. Grosz came to the U.S. in 1933 as an instructor at the Art Students League,

New York City, and he became an influential teacher. He became a U.S. citizen in 1938.

1959 July 15 **Ernest Bloch** (b. July 24, 1880), a Swiss-born composer, an American citizen since 1924, died. Bloch's abiding interest was in the expression in music of the spirit of the Jewish people. He composed such works as *Two Psalms* (1912–1914), *Trois Poèmes Juifs* (1913), the *Israel* symphony (1912–1916), the *Baal Shem Suite* (1923), *Sacred Service* (1933), and *Méditation Hebraïque* (1924). He also composed the tone poem *Hiver-Printemps* (1904–1905), the opera *Macbeth* (1910), and a symphonic rhapsody, *America* (1938).

1959 Aug. 19 **Jacob Epstein** (b. Nov. 10, 1880), an American-born sculptor who worked mostly in England and became a British citizen, died. Much of his sculpture was monumental, for example, *Venus* (1917), *Christ* (1919), *Adam* (1939), and *Social Consciousness* (1957–1958). Epstein also did many portrait busts of well-known persons, including Albert Einstein and Jawaharlal Nehru.

1959 Aug. 29 A major new **Obscene Publications Act** was passed in England, attempting to be both more liberal and more precise than earlier laws had been. In the view of those who supported it, it tried to protect literature while attacking pornography.

1959 Nov. 17 **Heitor Villa-Lobos** (b. Mar. 5, 1887), a Brazilian composer, died. The influence of Brazilian folk and popular music is apparent in his *Choros*, a series of compositions during the 1920s ranging from solo to orchestra works. He eventually composed more than 2,000 works.

VIII. SPORTS, GAMES, AND SOCIETY

1959 A group of sports-minded millionaires created the **American Football League**. Franchises were awarded to New York, Los Angeles (moved to San Diego in 1961), Dallas (moved to Kansas City in 1963), Boston, Buffalo, Denver, Houston, and Oakland.

1959 Feb. 1 [William Frederick] **Willie Hoppe** (b. Oct. 11, 1887), an American **billiard** champion, died. He won his first world title in Paris in 1906. Before he retired in 1952 he had been competing for 46 years and during that span had won 51 world championships.

1959 Apr. 10   Akihito (b. Dec. 23, 1933), crown prince of **Japan**, **married Michiko Shoda**, a commoner. It was the first time an heir to the Japanese throne had wed outside the nobility.

1959 May 16   Sam Snead (b. May 27, 1912), an American **golf**er, scored a 59 at Greenbrier, White Sulphur Springs, West Virginia. The next day Snead scored a 63 for a record low 36-hole tournament score of 122.

1959 June 26   Ingemar Johansson (b. Sept. 22, 1932) of Sweden won the **world heavyweight professional boxing championship** from Floyd Patterson (b. Jan.

4, 1935) of the U.S. At New York he knocked out the titleholder in the third round.

1959 Aug. 27–Sept. 7   The third **Pan-American Games** were held at Chicago. In the unofficial team standings the U.S. was first and Argentina second.

1959 Sept. 3   Gilbert Adrian (b. Mar. 3, 1903), an American **fashion** designer whose reputation and influence stemmed largely from the clothes he designed for movie stars, died. In the 1930s and 1940s he dressed such glamorous stars as Joan Crawford, Greta Garbo, and Norma Shearer.

1960

I. VITAL STATISTICS AND DEMOGRAPHICS

1960   According to the latest available census reports, the **world population** was c.2,915,383,000. The populations of the major regions of the world were: **Africa**, 250,898,000; **Asia**, 1,613,887,000; **Oceania**, 15,413,000; **Europe**, 422,050,000; U.S.S.R., 208,827,-000; **North America**, 264,702,000; **South America**, 139,606,000. The 18th census of the U.S. gave its population as 179,323,175. The ten largest cities of the world were: Tokyo, 10,261,425; London, 8,171,-902; New York City, 7, 781,984; Shanghai, 7,100,-000; Moscow, 5,032,000; Mexico City, 4,829,402; Bombay, 4,152,056; Peking, 4,140,000; São Paulo, 3,850,000; Buenos Aires, 3,799,200.

II. DISASTERS

1960 Jan. 21   The **collapse of a mine** at Coalbrook, in northern Orange Free State, South Africa, killed 417 miners.

1960 Feb. 29–Mar. 1   Two **earthquakes**, a tidal wave, and fire destroyed the city of Agadir, a seaport in southwestern Morocco, killing c.20,000 persons. The quakes registered 5.8 on the Richter scale.

1960 May 21–29   An **earthquake** off Chile's southern coast caused a tidal wave and was accompanied by volcanic eruptions. An estimated 10,000 people were killed. Tidal waves resulting from the earthquake struck (May 24) Hawaii, Okinawa, and Japan,

leaving c.240 dead. The quake registered 8.3 on the Richter scale.

1960 June 9   In Fukien [Fuhkien, Fujian] province, China, **typhoon Mary** caused c.1,600 deaths. In Hong Kong, farther south along the coast of Kwangtung [Guangdong] province, c.90 persons were dead or missing.

1960 July 14   A **fire in a hospital** in Guatemala City, Guatemala, killed 225 and injured c.30 of its c.1,500 patients.

1960 Sept. 9–12   Hurricane Donna, striking the Caribbean Sea area and the eastern coast of the U.S., killed 138 persons. In Puerto Rico 102 died. Damage was estimated at $1,000,000,000.

1960 Oct. 10   Cyclones and tidal waves struck the Bay of Bengal area and East Pakistan [present Bangladesh], killing c.6,000 persons.

1960 Nov. 13   A **fire in a movie theater** in Amude, in northeastern Syria on the border with Turkey, killed 152 children and left c.20 more injured.

1960 Dec. 16   Two **commercial airliners collided** over New York harbor, one falling into a Brooklyn street, the other on Staten Island. All on board and 6 on the ground were killed, a total of 134.

1960 Dec. 19   A **fire on the aircraft carrier Constellation**, under construction in the Brooklyn Navy Yard, New York City, killed 50 workmen and injured c.150 others.

III. POLITICS AND WAR

1960 Jan. 1–Nov. 28 During this period 14 former African **colonies of France became independent** nations: Cameroon, Togo, Madagascar, Dahomey, Niger Upper Volta, Ivory Coast, Chad, Ubangi-Shari, Congo, Gabon, Senegal, Mali, and Mauritania.

1960 Feb. 1 In Greensboro, North Carolina, four black college students were arrested for insisting on service at a lunch counter in a Woolworth store. The action was organized by the **Student Nonviolent Coordinating Committee [SNCC]**.

1960 Mar. 21 A demonstration against the pass law, which limited the movement of blacks, led by the **Pan Africanist Congress** in Sharpeville, near Johannesburg, **South Africa**, ended in bloodshed when police opened fire on the peaceful protesters, killing c.70 and wounding c.190.

1960 Apr. 3 **Norodom Suramarit** (b. Mar. 6, 1896), king of **Cambodia** [Kampuchea] (from 1955), died, and his son **Norodom Sihanouk** declared himself head of state. Sihanouk had been king (from 1941) but abdicated on Mar. 2, 1955, in order to enter the nation's political arena. He organized the **Popular Socialist party**, and held the office of premier at the time of his father's death.

1960 Apr. 27 **Syngman Rhee** (Mar. 26, 1875–July 19, 1965), president of **South Korea** (from 1948), was forced to resign after antigovernment riots that resulted in the police shooting (Apr. 19) of 125 student protesters. It was charged that the March election had been fraudulent.

1960 May 1 A **U-2 plane**, an American high-altitude reconnaisance plane, crashed or was shot down near Sverdlovsk in the Ural Mountains, U.S.S.R., and the pilot, **Francis Gary Powers** (Aug. 17, 1929–Aug. 1, 1977), was captured. On May 16 **Dwight D. Eisenhower**, president of the U.S., announced that no more such spy flights would be made. Powers confessed to charges of collecting military information on a flight that had left Pakistan and was supposed to cross Russia and land in Norway, and a Soviet court sentenced him (Aug. 19) to ten years in prison. On Feb. 10, 1962, the Russians exchanged Powers for one of their spies, **Rudolf** [Ivanovich] **Abel** (1902–Nov. 15, 1971), who had been in American custody.

1960 May 27 The **Turkish** government was overthrown by a military coup headed by **Cemal Gursel** (1895–Sept. 14, 1966). Leaders of the former government were tried for having violated the constitution and several were executed. On July 9 a new constitution was voted and after an election on Oct. 15 Gursel became president.

1960 June 30 The **Republic of the Congo** became independent with **Patrice** [Emergy] **Lumumba** as prime minister and **Joseph Kasavubu** (1910–Mar. 24, 1969) as head of state. Personal and ethnic rivalries soon led to violence and the army mutinied (July 4). On July 11 the province of **Katanga** [present Shaba] was declared independent by **Moise Tshombe** (Nov. 10, 1919–June 29, 1969), its president. The U.N. Security Council decided (July 14) to send troops to restore order. Lumumba, who sought Soviet help, was dismissed (Sept. 5) and Joseph Ileo (b. 1922) replaced him; but the head of the army Joseph Mobutu (b. Oct. 14, 1930) seized power (Sept. 14). On Feb. 13, 1961, it was announced that Lumumba (b. July 2, 1945) had been killed on Jan. 18, allegedly while fleeing from prison.

1960 July 1 The United Republic of **Somalia** [present Somali Democratic Republic, or Somalia] came into being as an independent nation when the former Italian Somaliland and British Somaliland united. The first president was **Aden Abdullah Osman** (b. 1908), leader of the Somalia Youth League.

1960 July 1 **Ghana** was transformed into a republic by **Kwame Nkrumah** (Sept. 29, 1909–Apr. 27, 1972), who made himself president for life. A new constitution had been adopted in April.

1960 July 16 **Albert Kesselring** (b. Nov. 30, 1885), a top commander of German forces in World War II, died. In Mar. 1945, he was named commander of the armies in western Europe and on May 5 surrendered to the U.S. forces. Tried in 1947 as a war criminal for his part in the massacre of Italian hostages, Kesselring was sentenced to death. This was commuted to life imprisonment and he was released in 1952.

1960 July 21 **Sirimavo R. D. Bandaranaike** became prime minister of **Ceylon** [present Sri Lanka], the **first woman prime minister in the world**.

1960 Aug. 5   Arthur Meighen (b. June 16, 1874), twice Conservative prime minister (1920–1921, 1926) of **Canada**, died.

1960 Sept. 30   Sixteen independent African nations were admitted to membership in the **U.N.**: Cameroon, Central African Republic, Chad, Congo, Dahomey [Benim], Gabon, Ivory Coast, Malagasy Republic, Mali, Niger, Nigeria, Senegal, Somalia, Togo, Upper Volta [Burkina Faso], and Zaire. Cyprus, another recently free nation, was also admitted at this time.

1960 Oct. 1   Walter Ulbrichts (June 30, 1893–Aug. 1, 1973) was named chairman (to 1973) of the Council of State of the German Democratic Republic [**East Germany**]. He was already first secretary of the Socialist Unity party and the effective ruler of the state.

1960 Oct. 1   Nigeria became an independent nation and a member of the Commonwealth of Nations. **Abubakar Balewa** became the first prime minister.

1960 Oct. 5   White South African voters in a referendum approved a plan to establish an independent **Republic of South Africa**, severing ties with the British monarchy and the Commonwealth of Nations. Urban English-speaking voters opposed the plan but were outvoted by the Boers, of Dutch descent.

1960 Dec. 9   The government of **Laos**, headed by Souvanna Phouma (Oct. 7, 1901–Jan. 10, 1984) as premier, collapsed in the face of opposition from both rightists and communists. Leftist forces of the **Pathet Lao** were led by **Prince Souphanouvong** (b. July 13, 1909) while the pro-Western rightists were under the command of **Phoumi Novasan**. On Dec. 18 a rightist regime was installed with **Boun Oum** (b. Dec. 12, 1912), a prince, as head of the government.

1960 Dec. 10   Albert John Mvumbi Luthuli (1898–July 21, 1967), a Zulu chief and a leader in opposing the apartheid rule of **South Africa**, became the **first black African to be awarded the Nobel Peace Prize**. He was president of the **African National Congress**, the political arm of the blacks (1952–1960). A strong advocate of non-violence, he was accused nevertheless of treason in 1956 but was released from prison the next year. The government banished him to his village in 1959.

IV. ECONOMY AND TRADE

1960 Jan. 4   Sweden joined **European Free Trade Association** [EFTA].

1960 Feb. 6   El Salvador, Guatemala, and Honduras signed a **Treaty of Economic Association**. The group looked forward to eventual establishment of completely free trade.

1960 Feb. 18   Argentina, Brazil, Chile, Mexico, Paraguay, Peru, and Uruguay established the **Latin American Free Trade Association**, looking toward elimination of tariffs among them.

1960 Nov. 14   The **Organization of Petroleum Exporting Countries** [OPEC] came into being, following a meeting in September of representatives of Iran, Iraq, Kuwait, and Saudi Arabia. Venezuela and many other oil producers joined later. The purpose of OPEC was to maintain high prices by limiting oil production.

1960 Dec. 14   The **Organization for Economic Cooperation and Development** [OECD] was formed by 18 European nations, including the members of the **European Economic Community**, and the United States and Canada. Japan joined later. The OECD was established to promote international trade and encourage economic progress.

V. RELIGION AND PHILOSOPHY

1960 Jan. 4   Albert Camus (b. Nov. 7, 1913), a French philosopher and novelist, died in an auto accident. During World War II he was an intellectual leader of the French Resistance. Beginning in 1942 he wrote the works that brought him international attention. Among them were: *Le Mythe de Sisyphe* [*The Myth of Sisyphus*] (1942); *L'Étranger* [*The Stranger*] (1942); *Caligula* (1944), a play; *La Peste* [*The Plague*] (1947); and *L'Homme révolté* [*The Rebel*] (1951). Although Camus was often identified with the existentialists, he believed man should stand firm against circumstances opposing him. He was awarded the **Nobel prize for literature** in 1957.

1960 Apr. 22   The **American Lutheran Church** was created by the merger of the Evangelical Lutheran Church, the American Lutheran Church, and the United Evangelical Lutheran Church.

1960 June 5 Pope John XXIII created the secretariat for the **Promotion of the Unity of Christians** to provide an office of the Roman Catholic Church to discuss problems of relationship with Protestant churches.

1960 June 26–July 3 The **Baptist World Alliance** held its quinquennial congress in Rio de Janeiro, Brazil, with a record 13,000 delegates from all over the world. **João Soren**, a Rio clergyman, was elected president of the Alliance.

1960 Aug. The **37th international Eucharistic Congress** of Roman Catholics was held in Munich, Germany, and attracted nearly 500,000 participants. Masses were said in the Roman, Byzantine, Armenian, Maronite, and European rites.

1960 Dec. 2 **Pope John XXIII** met in the Vatican with **Geoffrey Fisher, archbishop of Canterbury**, marking the first meeting between a pope and the head of the Anglican church in 400 years.

VI. SCIENCE, EDUCATION, AND TECHNOLOGY

1960 The **first laser** was developed this year by **Theodore H[arold] Maiman** (b. July 11, 1927). It was originally called an optical maser because it evolved from the maser, first operated in 1954 by **Charles H[ard] Townes** (b. July 28, 1915) and others.

1960 **Allan Rex Sandage** (b. June 18, 1926), an American astronomer, discovered the **first quasar**. It is believed that the light coming from quasars seen today was emitted when the universe had barely come into being.

1960 Jan. 23 Manning the U.S. navy **bathyscaphe** *Trieste,* **Jacques Piccard** (b. July 28, 1922), a French scientist, and **Donald Walsh**, an officer in the U.S. navy, reached a depth of 35,800 feet in the Pacific Ocean off Guam, the **deepest descent a human has ever made**.

1960 Feb. 13 **France tested its first nuclear bomb** in the Sahara Desert near the Reggan Oasis, provoking much criticism from Asian and African nations.

1960 Feb. 20 **Charles Leonard Woolley** (b. Apr. 17, 1880), an English archeologist internationally known for his years of excavation at **Ur** of the Chaldees, died. His first archeological work was in 1907; from 1922 to 1934 he labored at Ur. He later excavated several sites in Syria.

1960 Mar. 11 **Roy Chapman Andrews** (b. Jan. 26, 1884), an American naturalist and explorer, died. He did his most important work in Tibet, China, Burma [Myanmar], Mongolia, and the Gobi Desert. In the Gobi he made his most interesting and important discoveries, including dinosaur eggs, remains of *Baluchitherium,* the largest land animal known, and plants never before recorded. Andrews was director (1935–1942) of the American Museum of Natural History, New York City.

1960 Apr. 21 **Brasília**, an entirely new city in central southern Brazil, became the capital of the country. The city plan was laid out (1957) in the shape of an airplane by **Lúcio Costa** (b. Feb. 27, 1902), a Brazilian architect. The architect who supervised the actual construction and designed some of the buildings was **Oscar** [Soares] **Niemeyer** (b. Dec. 5, 1907), also a Brazilian.

1960 May 10 The **Triton**, an American nuclear submarine, completed an 84-day submerged journey of more than 33,000 miles around the world.

1960 May 23 **Georges Claude** (b. Sept. 24, 1870), a French inventor, died. He devised (1896–1910) the principle behind **neon** lighting.

1960 June 22 A Boeing **707 made its maiden flight**, powered by four turbofan jet engines, marking the start of the commercial use of engines that use fans in place of afterburners for added thrust.

1960 June 25 **Walter Baade** (b. Mar. 24, 1893), a German astronomer, died. In 1952 Baade reported that his calculations showed the universe to be twice as old and twice as big as previously thought. This meant that the galaxies were twice as remote as previously thought.

1960 July 20 A Polaris missile, capable of carrying nuclear warheads, was **fired** successfully for the first time from a submerged **submarine**. The *George Washington* discharged a missile from 30 feet below the surface of the water. It traveled more than 1,100 miles.

1960 Dec. 26   Giuseppe [Mario] **Bellanca** (b. Mar. 9, 1886), an Italian-American aircraft designer, died. He designed the first monoplane with an enclosed cabin, and one of his planes was the first to fly (Oct., 1931) nonstop from Japan to the U.S.

VII. ARTS AND LEISURE

1960 Feb. 9   Ernö Dohnányi (b. July 27, 1877), a Hungarian composer and pianist, died. He became conductor of the Budapest Philharmonic in 1919. Dohnányi came to the U.S. in 1949. In addition to composing three operas, a ballet, three symphonies, and other works, he toured internationally as a leading pianist.

1960 May 14   Lucrezia Bori [Lucrezia Borja] (b. Dec. 24, 1888), a Spanish soprano noted for her beauty as well as her voice, died. She made her debut in Rome in 1908 and her debut at the Metropolitan Opera, New York City, on Nov. 11, 1912. In 1935 she became a director of the Metropolitan, the first singer ever to hold such a position.

1960 May 30   Boris [Leonidovich] **Pasternak** (b. Feb. 10, 1890), a Russian poet and novelist, died. He was best known for his novel *Doctor Zhivago* (1958). His poetry made him one of the most important literary figures in the early years of the Russian communist regime, but during the Stalin purges of the 1930s Pasternak was not allowed to publish his own poetry. An autobiographical work *Okhrannaya gramota* appeared in 1930 but was not translated into English until 1945.

1960 Aug. 23   Oscar Hammerstein II (b. July 12, 1895), an American lyricist who collaborated with composers on some of the most successful musicals of his era and who helped point the U.S. musical stage in new directions, died. Hammerstein's successes included *Showboat* (1927) with music by **Jerome Kern**, and *Oklahoma* (1943) with music by **Richard Rodgers**.

1960 Nov. 2   Dimitri Mitropoulos (b. Feb. 18, 1896), a Greek born symphonic and opera conductor, died. After conducting in Europe he came (1936) to the U.S., where he headed the **Minneapolis Symphony** (1937–1949), the **New York Philharmonic** (1949–1958), and the **Metropolitan Opera** (1954–1960).

1960 Nov. 5   Mack Sennett [Michael Sinnott] (b. Jan. 17, 1884), an American movie pioneer, died. His first film was produced in 1910 and he made c.1,000 in all. Most of them were the highly popular slapstick comedies featuring the Keystone Kops and bathing beauties. His *Tillie's Punctured Romance* (1914) was the first American feature-length comedy.

1960 Nov. 16   ** [William] **Clark Gable (b. Feb. 1, 1901), a romantic leading man of American movies, died. Gable made his debut in 1930 and in 1934 won an Academy award for his role in *It Happened One Night*. In his most famous role he played Rhett Butler in *Gone with the Wind* (1939).

1968 Nov. 18   Richard [Nathaniel] **Wright** (b. Sept. 4, 1908), a black American author, died. Especially effective was his novel *Native Son* (1940), sensational but moving in its story of a black youth in a Chicago slum without hope of finding a place in the world. His other novels included *The Outsider* (1953) and *The Long Dream* (1958). His autobiographies, *Black Boy* (1945) and *American Hunger* (1977), reflected the real-life background of his fiction. Wright lived in Paris after 1946.

VIII. SPORTS, GAMES, AND SOCIETY

1960 Feb. 18–28   ** The eighth Winter **Olympic Games were held at Squaw Valley, California, with 665 athletes from 30 nations competing. Soviet Union athletes won 7 gold medals and 21 medals in all; the U.S. 3 and 10; and Norway 3 and 6.

1960 Feb. 19   ** The **first child born to a reigning British monarch since 1857 arrived at Buckingham Palace, London, the son of Queen Elizabeth II and the Duke of Edinburgh, her consort. He was named **Prince Andrew Albert Christian Edward**.

**1960 Aug. 25–Sept. 11   ** The 17th Summer Olympic Games were held in Rome with 5,348 athletes from 83 nations participating. Athletes of the Soviet Union won 43 gold medals and 103 medals in all; the U.S. was second with 34 and 71; Italy third with 13 and 36. In all 54 Olympic records were broken.

1961

I. DISASTERS

1961 Jan. 7 In the Persian Gulf a **motor launch** on its way from Iran to Kuwait **sank** after catching fire. Eighty-eight Iranians died.

1961 Mar. 31 Reports from Kiev, U.S.S.R., indicated that 145 persons had been killed and 143 injured in a **mud slide** at a reclamation project.

1961 Apr. 10 A British passenger ship the *Dara* sank in the Persian Gulf two days after a fire broke out, possibly caused by a bomb. A total of 212 of the 697 persons aboard were lost.

1961 July 7 A **gas explosion** in a coal mine at Colna Suce, Czechoslovakia, killed 108 miners.

1961 July 8 The Portuguese ship *Save* ran aground near Quelimane, Mozambique, then exploded and sank. Of the 549 passengers 259 were killed or missing.

1961 Aug. 29 A French air force **jet training plane severed the cable of an aerial lift** in the Valley of Chamonix, in eastern France. Six persons in cars cut loose were killed on the glacier below.

1961 Oct. 7 In Bihar state, in northeastern India, 25 inches of rain that fell within 48 hours caused **floods** that drowned c.1,000 people.

1961 Dec. 17 A gasoline **fire**, set by an arsonist seeking revenge against his former employers, consumed the main tent at a performance of the Estanovitch Brothers' circus at Niteroi, near **Rio de Janeiro**, Brazil. The death toll was 323 dead and c.800 injured.

II. POLITICS AND WAR

1961 Jan. 6–8 In a referendum held in France and Algeria, voters approved allowing the Algerians to choose between independence and a continued relationship with France. **Charles De Gaulle**, president of France, proposed this referendum as a step toward ending a six-year rebellion.

1961 Jan. 20 **John F**[itzgerald] **Kennedy** (May 29, 1917–Nov. 22, 1963) was inaugurated president of the U.S. **Lyndon B**[aines] **Johnson** became vice president. Running on the Democratic party ticket, Kennedy defeated **Richard M. Nixon**, the Republican candidate, in the Nov. 8, 1960, election with 34,226,731 popular votes to Nixon's 34,108,157, and 303 votes to 219 in the Electoral College.

1961 Feb. 4 A war for independence started in Portuguese West Africa [now **Angola**] as guerrillas of the **Popular Movement for the Liberation of Angola** [MPLA] attacked the São Paulo fortress and police headquarters. Portuguese troops arrived in April and many lives were lost in the fighting to suppress the uprising.

1961 Feb. 26 **Mohammad V** (b. Aug. 10, 1909), king (sultan before 1957) of **Morocco** (1927–1953, 1955–1961), died and was succeeded by his son Moulay Hassan as **Hassan II** (b. July 9, 1929).

1961 Mar. 1 **John F. Kennedy**, president of the U.S., established the **Peace Corps** by executive order and in September Congressional action made it permanent. The corps was to enlist Americans to go to developing countries to assist programs in agriculture, sanitation, education, and other endeavors. On Mar. 13 Kennedy proposed an **Alliance for Progress** [*Alianza para el Progreso*] between the U.S. and the nations of Latin America. The ten-year plan, to operate under the aegis of the **Organization of American States** [OAS], was implemented at an Inter-American Economic and Social Conference which opened (Aug. 5) in Punta del Este, Uruguay.

1961 Apr. 9 **Ahmed Bey Zog** (b. June 10, 1895), president of Albania (1925–1928) and king (1928–1939), died. He took steps to unify and modernize his small nation but was forced (Apr. 1939) to flee into exile when Italy invaded Albania.

1961 Apr. 17 Trained in Guatemala by the U.S. **Central Intelligence Agency** [CIA], c.1,500 Cuban exiles landed on the southern coast of Cuba at the *Bahia de Cochinos* [**Bay of Pigs**] in an attempt to overthrow the government of **Fidel Castro**. The invasion was a complete failure, crushed by Apr. 19 with c.300 invaders killed and c.1,200 captured. The maneuver had been planned during the Eisenhower administration, but **John F. Kennedy**, president of the U.S., who refused to send U.S. air support, took responsibility.

1961 Apr. 27 **Sierra Leone** was granted independence by Great Britain and became a member of the Commonwealth of Nations. **Milton** [Augustus Strieby] **Margai** (Feb. 7, 1895–Apr. 28, 1964), leader of the Sierra Leone People's party, was the first prime minister.

1961 May 1 Great Britain granted **Tanganyika** full internal self-government, with **Julius** [Kambarage] **Nyerere** (b. Mar. 21, 1922), leader of the Tanganyika African National Union, as the premier. On Dec. 9, 1962, the Republic of Tanganyika was established within the Commonwealth of Nations with Nyerere as its president.

1961 May 14 A group of "**Freedom Riders,**" black and white students sent to the South by bus under the auspices of the **Congress of Racial Equality** [**CORE**], was attacked in Anniston and Birmingham, Alabama, when the students attempted to test desegregation at bus depots.

1961 May 16 A 14-nation conference convened in Geneva, Switzerland, to try to bring peace to the warring factions in **Laos** and to establish the neutrality of the country. The conference agreed on neutrality, and a provisional government, with all factions represented and **Souvanna Phouma** as premier, was set up on June 23, 1962. The agreement did not last, and warfare resumed in 1963 with the **Pathet Lao** trying to seize control of the country.

1961 May 16 In a military coup the government of **South Korea** led by **John M. Chang** [Chang Myun] (Apr. 28, 1899–June 4, 1966) was overthrown, largely as a result of unsolved economic problems. On July 3 a coup within the military junta brought **Park Hung Hee** (Sept. 30, 1917–Oct. 26, 1979) to power. He was elected president in 1963 and reelected in 1967.

1961 May 30 **Rafael Leonidas Trujillo Molina** (b. Oct. 24, 1891), dictator of the **Dominican Republic** since 1930, was assassinated by army officers. **Joaquin Balaguer** (b. Sept. 1, 1907), whom Trujillo had made president in 1960, continued in office.

1961 May 31 The Union of **South Africa** officially became a republic and withdrew from the Commonwealth of Nations. It adopted a republican constitution and a parliamentary form of government.

1961 June 3–4 **John F. Kennedy**, president of the U.S., and **Nikita Khrushchev**, premier of the U.S.S.R. and first secretary of the Communist party, met fruitlessly in Vienna to attempt to ease the tensions of the **Cold War** between the two nations.

1961 June 19 **Kuwait** became an independent Islamic emirate headed by **Abdullah III** [al-Salim al-Sabah] (1895–Nov. 24, 1965) emir of the **Sabah Dynasty** (from 1759). On June 25 **Iraq claimed sovereignty over Kuwait** and on June 30 the emir appealed to Great Britain for protection against a threatened invasion. Troops were sent at once and Iraq backed down.

1961 July 13 The **U.S. and South Vietnam signed a treaty** of amity and economic assistance. In May the U.S. had agreed to pay the cost of an increase in the size of the South Vietnam army in view of the continuing success of the **Viet Cong** guerrillas who were supported by communist North Vietnam. On Nov. 13 **John F. Kennedy**, president of the U.S., decided to increase the number of American military advisers in South Vietnam. An additional 200 U.S. air force instructors were sent at once to augment the 700 military advisers already there.

1961 Aug. 3 The New Democratic party was formed at a convention in Ottawa, **Canada**, and elected **Thomas C. Douglas** (Oct. 20, 1904–Feb. 25, 1986), the **Cooperative Commonwealth Federation** [**CCF**] premier of the province of Saskatchewan, as its first leader. It was the most leftist of the major Canadian political parties.

1961 Aug. 13 The **border between communist East and democratic West Germany was closed** by the former, and construction was begun on a 29-mile long barbed wire and concrete **wall to seal off East Berlin from West Berlin**. Fear of such action had increased the influx of refugees from East Germany, the total reaching 13,332 by August.

1961 Aug. 25 Charges of courting the U.S.S.R. and carrying the **Brazilian** economy too far to the left caused the resignation of **Jànio de Silva Quadros** (b. Jan. 25, 1917) as president, a post to which he had been elected the previous Oct. 3. The army was also hostile to the vice president **João Goulart** (Mar. 1, 1918–Dec. 6, 1976), another leftist, but allowed him to be sworn in as president on Sept. 7.

1961 Sept. 17   Adnan Menderes (b. 1899), premier of **Turkey** from 1950 until his overthrow by a military coup in May 1960, was hanged. Accused of corruption and extravagance, he was sentenced to death in Sept. 1960.

1961 Sept. 29   A rightist military coup in **Syria** resulted in the country's withdrawal from the **United Arab Republic**. A conservative, **Nazim al-Qudsi** [Nazen el-Kudsi] (b. 1906), was elected president of Syria on Dec. 14.

1961 Oct. 16–Nov. 11   At the **22nd Congress of the Communist party of the U.S.S.R.**, the party leadership, under **Nikita Khrushchev**, continued the attack begun in 1956 against the late **Joseph Stalin** and his regime. Khrushchev denounced what he termed an "anti-party" group, meaning the remaining officials who had been part of the Stalin era. He read three of them out of the party: **Lazar M. Kaganovich**, who held various high posts under Stalin; **Georgi Malenkov**, Stalin's first successor in 1953; and **Vyacheslav M. Molotov**, a former foreign minister.

1961 Oct. 19   Sergio Osmeña (b. Sept. 9, 1878), the second president of the **Philippines** after independence, died. He was active in the independence movement and founder of the **Nationalist party** in 1907. He held the presidency from Aug. 1944 until Apr. 1946.

1961 Dec. 18   The **Portuguese territories** of Goa, Daman, and Diu, were annexed by India. Indian troops invaded the enclaves after Portugal refused to give them up.

1961 Dec. 30   Diosdado Macapagal (b. Sept. 28, 1910), leader of the Liberal party, was elected president of the **Philippines**, succeeding **Carlos P. Garcia**.

III. ECONOMY AND TRADE

1961 Aug. 10   Great Britain applied for membership in the **European Economic Community** [EEC]. After long debate, France vetoed Britain's entry on Jan. 29, 1963.

1961 Sept. 26   Charles E[rwin] **Wilson** (b. July 18, 1890), head of **General Motors Corporation** (1941–1953), died. Under his leadership during World War II, his company became the largest producer of war materials in the world. Wilson served as U.S. secretary of defense (1953–1957).

1961 Nov. 24   Axel Wenner-Gren (b. June 5, 1881), Swedish financier and philanthropist, died. He made a large fortune manufacturing vacuum cleaners and refrigerators but was alleged to have had dealings with the Nazis in World War II.

IV. RELIGION AND PHILOSOPHY

1961 Jan. 23   The **National Council of the Churches** of Christ in the United States of America, a Protestant group, announced its approval of artificial methods of birth control and family planning.

1961 Apr.   The **Russian Orthodox Church** applied for membership in the **World Council of Churches**, making 12 orthodox bodies in all that were members of the council.

1961 May 4   Maurice Merleau-Ponty (b. Mar. 14, 1908), a French philosopher and one of the leading exponents of phenomenology, died. This philosophy described phenomena and excluded anything that was not evident to the consciousness. Among his works were *La Structure du comportement* [*The Structures of Behavior*] (1942) and *Phénoménologie de la perception* [*The Phenomenology of Perception*] (1945).

1961 May 31   Geoffrey Francis Fisher (May 5, 1887–Sept. 14, 1972), archbishop of Canterbury (1945–1961), and head of the world-wide Anglican communion, retired because of age. Fisher was energetic in revitalizing the **Church of England** after World War II and he established autonomous provinces of the church in Africa and the Near East. He served (1946–1954) as president of the World Council of Churches. He was succeeded (to 1974) as archbishop by [Arthur] **Michael Ramsey** (Nov. 14, 1904–Apr. 23, 1988).

1961 July 4   The union of the Congregational Christian Churches with the Evangelical and Reformed Church was completed in the U.S. with the adoption of a constitution for the new body. To be known as the **United Church of Christ**, it had a membership of more than 2,000,000.

1961 July 14   Pope John XXIII issued the encyclical *Mater et Magistra* concerning social and economic issues. He said the rights of individuals were based on natural law. The pope asked that all workers be given a share in the firms they work for and urged that those with more food than needed share it.

1961 Aug. 7 Frank [Nathan Daniel] **Buchman** (b. June 4, 1878), the founder of the Oxford Group, died. An ordained American Lutheran minister, he formed the group at Oxford University in 1921. In 1938 he renamed his movement **Moral Re-Arma-ment** [MRA]. Buchman's goal was "a God-guided campaign to prevent war by moral and spiritual awakening."

1961 Aug. 26 **Buddhism** was made the state reli-gion of **Burma** [Myanmar] but freedom for others was to be permitted.

V. SCIENCE, EDUCATION, AND TECHNOLOGY

1961 *Webster's Third New International Dictio-nary of the English Language, Unabridged* was pub-lished. It was the largest American dictionary ever issued and the eighth in a series that began in 1828 with Noah Webster's original work. It contained definitions of 450,000 words and the publishers said it cost $3.5 million to produce.

1961 **Thalidomide**, a drug prescribed since 1958 in Europe as a sedative and anti-emetic for pregnant women, had by the end of this year caused between 2,000 and 3,000 birth defects in West Germany and c.500 in England, the two countries where it was used most often. In all c.8,000 fetuses were probably affected. The fetal malfunctions included phocome-lia, eye defects, absence of gastrointestinal tract openings, and other malformations. In the U.S. it had never been approved by the Federal Food and Drug Administration.

1961 Jan. 4 Erwin **Schrödinger** (b. Aug. 12, 1887), an Austrian theoretical physicist, died. The **Schröd-inger equation**, a mathematical formulation of wave mechanics, replaced Newtonian mechanics in de-scribing atomic phenomena. He shared the **Nobel prize in physics** in 1933.

1961 Mar. 8 **Max Conrad** (d. Apr. 5, 1979), an American pioneer aviator, completed a record flight around the world for a light plane. He landed in Miami, Florida, after 8 days, 18 hrs. and 49 min. from the time he took off there. By the time of his death Conrad had logged more than 50,000 hours of flying time, more than any other pilot in the history of aviation.

1961 Apr. 12 **Yuri Gagarin**, a Soviet cosmonaut, became the **first human being to travel in space** when he made one orbit of the earth, lasting 1 hour 48 minutes, in the spacecraft *Vostok I*.

1961 May 4 Two U.S. navy officers, **Malcolm D. Ross** and **Victor G. Prather**, ascended in a research balloon to the record height of 113,740 feet. They took off from the USS *Antietam* in the Gulf of Mex-ico. Prather was killed during the recovery of the balloon.

1961 May 5 **Alan B[artlett] Shepard, Jr.** (b. Nov. 18, 1923) became the **first American in space** when he completed a suborbital flight that reached 116.5 miles above the earth. He flew in the spacecraft *Freedom 7*, traveling for 15 minutes 22 seconds.

1961 May 29 Arnold L[ucius] **Gesell** (b. June 21, 1880), an American psychologist and educator, died. He was noted for his study of children. Among his numerous works were *Foundations of Experimental Psychology* (1929) and *The Child from Five to Ten* (1946).

1961 June 6 **Carl Gustav Jung** (b. July 26, 1875), a Swiss psychiatrist, one of the founders with Sigmund Freud and Alfred Adler of modern psychiatry, died. He was also the founder of analytic psychology. Jung broke with Freud who, he believed, put too much stress on sexuality. His works included *Wandlungen und Symbole der Libido* (1912), translated as *Psy-chology of the Unconscious* (1916), and *Psychologis-che Typen* (1921). An individual, Jung believed, could become whole only by bringing the conscious and the unconscious into harmony.

1961 June 30 **Lee De Forest** (b. Aug. 26, 1873), an American inventor called "the father of radio" be-cause of his invention (1907) of the Audion, or triode, tube, died. De Forest held more than 300 patents and his work made possible television and talking pictures as well as radio. He established a radio sta-tion as early as 1916.

1961 Sept. 1 **Eero Saarinen** (b. Aug. 20, 1910), a Finnish-American architect, died. An innovative de-signer, he made unique architectural statements with such projects as the **General Motors Technical Center**, Warren, Michigan, (1951–1955); a chapel and auditorium at the Massachusetts Institute of Technology (1955); and the **Jefferson National Ex-pansion Memorial Arch** in St. Louis, Mo. (completed

1964). He was the son of Eliel Saarinen, also a noted architect.

VI. ARTS AND LEISURE

1961 The *Beatles*, a music group formed in Liverpool, England, by four working class youths, became the international standard bearers of rock music. The musicians were **John** [Winston] **Lennon** (b. Oct. 9, 1940), **Paul McCartney** (b. June 18, 1942), **George Harrison** (b. Feb. 25, 1943), and **Ringo Starr** [orig.: Richard Starkey] (b. July 7, 1940). Most of the music they played was written by Lennon and McCartney.

1961 Feb. 20 **Percy** [Aldridge] **Grainger** [George Percy Grainger] (b. July 8, 1882), an Australian-born composer and pianist who lived in the U.S. after 1914, died. He made his concert debut in New York City in 1915. Among the most popular of his compositions were *Molly on the Shore* (1907), *Shepherd's Hey* (1908–1909), *Handel in the Strand* (1912), and *Country Gardens* (1919).

1961 Mar. 8 **Thomas Beecham** (b. Apr. 29, 1879), an English opera and orchestra conductor, died. He did much to revive the performance of opera in England. In 1932 Beecham founded the **London Philharmonic Orchestra** and in 1946 the **Royal Philharmonic Orchestra**.

1961 May 13 **Gary Cooper** [Frank James] (b. May 7, 1901), an American actor, died. Famous as the hero of few words and simple honesty, Cooper appeared in such films as *The Winning of Barbara Worth* (1926); *Lives of a Bengal Lancer* (1935), and *High Noon* (1952).

1961 June 16 **Rudolf Nureyev** (b. Mar. 17, 1938), a talented and popular Soviet ballet dancer, defected while in Paris with the **Leningrad Kirov Ballet**. A week later he performed the leading male role in *Sleeping Beauty* with the **Grand Ballet du Marquis de Cuerva**.

1961 July 2 **Ernest** [Miller] **Hemingway** (b. July 21, 1899), an American author who broke new ground in the writing of modern fiction, died, a suicide by gunshot. Hemingway's spare use of the English language, and an emphasis on courage and self-reliance, set a new literary style. His first book, published in Paris, was *Three Stories and Ten Poems* (1923). He initially made a stir with readers and critics when he published *The Sun Also Rises* (1926),

a story of the moral collapse of some members of the "lost generation." *A Farewell to Arms* (1929) was a wartime love story, ending unhappily. Becoming increasingly concerned with the world political situation, he wrote *For Whom the Bell Tolls* (1940), with a setting in the Spanish Civil War (1936–1939). After that Hemingway's most important writing was *The Old Man and the Sea* (1952), an example of his admiration for men who stand up to nature. He was awarded the **Nobel prize for literature** in 1954.

1961 Oct. 31 **Augus.us** [Edwin] **John** (b. Jan. 4, 1878), an English painter, died. John painted such personages as James Joyce, Queen Elizabeth II, George Bernard Shaw, and Dylan Thomas. Typical of his landscapes, of which he also did many, was *Encampment on Dartmoor* (1906).

1961 Nov. 15 At auction in New York City the **Metropolitan Museum of Art** paid $2.3 million for **Rembrandt's** painting *Aristotle Contemplating the Bust of Homer*. When Rembrandt painted it in 1652, he was said to have received the equivalent of about $7,500.

1961 Dec. 13 [Anna Mary Robertson] **Grandma Moses** (b. Sept. 7, 1860), an American modern primitive painter, died. She did not begin painting in earnest until middle age and had her first one-woman show in New York in 1940 when she was 80. Her paintings delighted a large public with their nostalgic and cheerful atmosphere. Typical were *Catching the Turkey* (1940), *Sugaring Off* (1943), and *Out for the Christmas Trees* (1946).

VII. SPORTS, GAMES, AND SOCIETY

1961 **Natalie Wood** [Natasha Gurdin] (July 20, 1938–Nov. 29, 1981) became the **first movie star to appear naked** in a Hollywood feature film when she rose from a bathtub in the movie *Splendor in the Grass* and ran down the hall. Although the scene was not shown in theaters during the movie's general release, it was a sign of things to come.

1961 The **Twist**, a new dance craze struck the U.S. and spread to other countries. It was inspired by a song with that title and was performed in night clubs called discotheques, or discos for short. The music was fast and so loud as to be termed pounding. The dance pairs did not touch each other but performed wild gyrations of the lower part of the body.

1961 Hubert de Givenchy (b. Feb. 21, 1927), a French **fashion** designer, saw the clothes he created for **Audrey Hepburn** (b. May 4, 1929), starring in the movie *Breakfast at Tiffany's*, become widely popular. A high bosomed dress, without sleeves or belt, was the centerpiece of the style.

1961 July 17 Ty[rus Raymond] **Cobb** (b. Dec. 18, 1886), an American baseball legend, died. Perhaps the greatest major league player of all time, Cobb was known as a ferocious offensive player who would do anything to win. Cobb was the first player elected to the **Baseball Hall of Fame** in 1936.

1961 Oct. 1 In the last game of the major league season, **Roger Maris** (Sept. 10, 1934–Dec. 14, 1985), New York Yankee outfielder, hit his 61st home run of the season, thereby exceeding the former record of 60 set by **Babe Ruth**, also of the Yankees, in 1927. The record still stands. Maris accomplished his feat in a season of 162 games; Ruth in a season of 154 games.

1961 Nov. The so-called **instant replay**, permitting immediate playback of live television coverage, and in slow motion, was introduced during this fall's football season by ABC Television Sports.

1962

I. VITAL STATISTICS AND DEMOGRAPHICS

1962 Sept. 1 The U.N. estimated that the **world population** at mid-year was 3,115,000,000 and growing at an annual rate of 1.8 percent.

II. DISASTERS

1962 Jan. 10 An **avalanche down Mt. Huascaran**, a 22,205-foot high extinct volcano in Peru's Andes Mountains, buried 16 villages and killed c.3,000 people.

1962 Feb. 7 A methane **gas mine explosion** in Saarbrücken, West Germany, killed 298 coal miners.

1962 Feb. 17 **Hurricane** winds along the North Sea coast of West Germany, left at least 343 people dead. Damage was estimated at $250 million.

1962 May 3 A commuter **train in Tokyo plowed into the wreckage** of a freight train and another commuter train that had already collided, killing 163 persons and injuring more than 300.

1962 June 3 The **crash of an Air France Boeing 707**, bound for New York, at takeoff from Paris killed 130 of the 132 aboard.

1962 Sept. 1 An **earthquake centered at Danesfahan** in northwestern Iran rocked a 23,000-square-mile area leaving 12,403 dead. In all c.10,000 persons were injured, c.200 towns destroyed, and c.100,000 persons made homeless. The quake registered 7.1 on the Richter scale.

1962 Sept. 24–27 In Barcelona, northeastern Spain, **floods** killed more than 800 persons, injured c.1,000, and did $80 million of damage.

1962 Oct. 27 **Tropical storm Harriet** hit three provinces of southern Thailand, killing 769 people, including c.500 who died when a whole village was swept into the sea. There were also 142 missing and 252 seriously injured.

III. POLITICS AND WAR

1962 Jan. 1 **Western Samoa** became independent of New Zealand, which had held the mandate of the territory since 1920.

1962 Jan. 18 In the **Dominican Republic**, the Trujillo family drove president **Joaquin Balaguer** from office and on Mar. 7 he fled into exile in Europe. In December **Juan Bosch** (b. June 30, 1909) was elected president.

1962 Jan. 22 The **United Nations** asked its members to purchase $200 million worth of bonds, to carry 2 percent interest. By Dec. 5, nearly $118 million of the bonds were subscribed.

1962 Jan. 29 After three years of work, the conference between the U.S., the U.S.S.R., and Great Britain on banning the **testing of nuclear weapons** adjouned, deadlocked over the problem of a central monitoring system.

1962 Jan. 31 At a conference in Punta del Este, Uruguay, the **Organization of American States** [OAS], by a 14 to 1 vote, with 6 nations abstaining, decided to exclude **Cuba** from its activities.

1962 Feb. 14 **John F. Kennedy**, president of the U.S., announced that American troops in **South Vietnam**, sent to help train that country's army, had been told to fire to protect themselves if fired upon. He added that they "are not combat troops in the generally understood sense of that word."

1962 Mar. 1 A new constitution ended four years of martial law under **Mohammad Ayub Khan** (May 14, 1907–Apr. 19, 1974), president of **Pakistan**.

1962 Mar. 2 The government of **Burma** [Myanmar] was overthrown in a bloodless military coup led by **Ne Win** (b. May 24, 1911). He set up a revolutionary council, founded the Burma Socialist Program party, and banned all other political parties. On Mar. 28 banks and major industries were nationalized.

1962 Mar. 29 **Arturo Frondizi** (b. Sept. 28, 1908), president of **Argentina**, was deposed by a military coup. José Maria Guido was installed (Mar. 30) as president and he recessed (May 20) congress and dissolved all political parties pending an election in 1963 in which the Peronistas were prohibited from entering candidates.

1962 Apr. 7 **Milovan Djilas** (b. June 12, 1911), formerly a high ranking official of the Yugoslavian government, was arrested and charged with having divulged secrets of the regime in his latest book, *Conversations with Stalin*. On May 14 he was convicted and sentenced to five years in prison, but was granted amnesty in Dec. 1966.

1962 May 12 **John F. Kennedy**, president of the U.S., ordered **American forces into Thailand** to prevent a possible communist invasion from Laos. In all c.4,000 men were sent, including c.1,800 marines. Except for a token force they were withdrawn on July 27.

1962 May 31 [Karl] **Adolf Eichmann** (b. Mar. 19, 1906) was hanged in Israel, having been found guilty of crimes against humanity and the Jewish people. In World War II Eichmann had been in charge of Nazi Germany's central agency for sending Jews to concentration camps, where c.6 million died in the Holocaust.

1962 July 1 Ruanda-Burundi became independent as two countries: the **Republic of Rwanda**, with **Grégoire Kayi Banda** (b. May 21, 1924) as president; and the **Kingdom of Burundi** under **Mwanbutsa II** [IV] (b.1912) as king.

1962 July 3 **Algeria became independent** of France. A National Constituent Assembly was elected (Sept. 20) and chose (Sept. 26) **Ahmed Ben Bella** as premier.

1962 July 18 The military in **Peru** seized power to prevent the inauguration of **Victor Raul Haya de la Torre**, who had won a small plurality in the June 10 election. He was regarded as leaning too much to the left.

1962 Aug. 5 **Jamaica** became independent within the Commonwealth of Nations. [William] **Alexander Bustamante** (Feb. 24, 1884–Aug. 6, 1977), of the Labor party, became prime minister.

1962 Aug. 15 An agreement was reached by which **The Netherlands** would transfer West Irian [West New Guinea] to **Indonesia** on May 1, 1963.

1962 Aug. 31 **Trinidad and Tobago** became independent of Great Britain but remained within the Commonwealth of Nations. **Eric Eustace Williams** (Sept. 25, 1911–Mar. 29, 1981) was the first prime minister.

1962 Sept. 18 Ahmed bin Yahya Mohammad **Hamid Ud Din** (b. 1891?), iman or king of **Yemen** (from 1946), was assassinated and the next day **Muhammad al-Badhr** (b. 1927), the crown prince, became the iman, or, in fact, king of Yemen, later taking the name **Mansur Billah Muhammad**. Eight days later, he was deposed by an army coup led by **Abdullah al-Salal**, who declared establishment of a republic. War followed between the royalist and republican factions and continued off and on for years.

1962 Oct. 9 **Uganda** became independent of Great Britain, remaining a member of the Commonwealth of Nations. [Apollo] **Milton Obote** (b. Dec. 28, 1924), the leader of the Uganda People's Congress, became the first prime minister.

1962 Oct. 22   The **Cuban missile crisis** came to a head when **John F. Kennedy**, president of the U.S., ordered a **blockade of Cuba** because aerial photographs had discovered that the U.S.S.R. was constructing missile bases in Cuba. Russian ships carrying missiles to Cuba turned back on Oct. 24, and on Oct. 28 **Nikita S. Khrushchev**, premier of the U.S.S.R., agreed to withdraw all missiles and destroy the bases. The U.S. ended its blockade on Nov. 20 and by the end of the year some Russian jet bombers as well as all the missiles had left Cuba.

1962 Nov. 6   The kingdom of **Saudi Arabia officially abolished slavery**.

1962 Nov. 7   [Anna] **Eleanor** [Roosevelt] **Roosevelt** (b. Oct. 11, 1884), widow of Franklin D. Roosevelt and world famous in her own right for her humanitarian endeavors, died. Mrs. Roosevelt was chairman of the U.N. Commission on Human Rights (1945–1951) and a leading figure in securing adoption of the **Universal Declaration of Human Rights** in 1948.

1962 Nov. 14   **Eritrea** became fully integrated as a part of Ethiopia. This gave Ethiopia access to the Red Sea.

1962 Nov. 21   **China** declared a **unilateral ceasefire** in an undeclared war with India over the boundary in Kashmir and other border areas between the two countries.

1962 Nov. 28   **Wilhelmina** [Wilhelmina Helena Pauline Maria] (b. Aug. 31, 1880), former queen of the **Netherlands** (1890–1948) and member of the House of Orange, died. In World War II she was a symbol of resistance for her countrymen after the Nazis overran (1940) the Netherlands. On Sept. 4, 1948, she had abdicated in favor of her daughter Juliana.

1962 Nov. 30   **U Thant** (Jan. 22, 1909–Nov. 25, 1974), a Burmese politician and diplomat, was elected secretary general of the **U.N.** for a term ending on Nov. 3, 1966. He had been acting secretary general since the death in an airplane accident of **Dag Hammarskjold** on Nov. 3, 1961.

IV. ECONOMY AND TRADE

1962 Jan. 16   **R**[ichard] **H**[enry] **Tawney** (b. Nov. 30, 1880), an English economic historian, died. A socialist, he aided the British Labour party in formulating social and economic policies. He is best known now for *Religion and the Rise of Capitalism* (1948), in which he found a close relationship between the Protestant ethic and the work ethic characteristic of capitalism.

1962 July 11   **Owen D. Young** (b. Oct. 27, 1874), an American corporation executive, died. The 1929 program for reducing Germany's payments to the Allies, worked out by a commission he headed, became known as the **Young Plan**. He was chairman of the board of the **General Electric Company** (1922–1939).

1962 Oct. 11   **John F. Kennedy**, president of the U.S., signed the **Trade Expansion Act**, just passed by the U.S. Congress. The act gave the president greater authority to reduce tariffs on a reciprocal basis.

V. RELIGION AND PHILOSOPHY

1962 Feb.   **John Courtney Murray**, S.J. (Sept. 10, 1904–Aug. 16, 1967), in his St. Thomas More Lectures at Yale University, brought to wide attention the effect of contemporary atheism on the problem of the existence and meaning of God. The theological debate became known as "the death of God" controversy.

1962 Feb. 24   **Hu Shih** (b. Dec. 17, 1891), a Chinese philosopher and statesman, died. He taught at Peking National University and wrote **Outline of Chinese Philosophy** (1919). As a statesman he was the Nationalist Chinese ambassador to the U.S. (1938–1942) and followed the Nationalist government of Chiang Kai-Shek to Taiwan after the communist victory.

1962 June 8   **Southern Baptists**, in convention in San Francisco, overwhelmingly passed a resolution reaffirming the faith of the denomination "in the entire Bible as the authoritative, authentic, infallible word of God."

1962 June 25   The **Supreme Court of the U.S.**, 6–1, declared unconstitutional a New York State law that contained a 22-word prayer to be recited in classrooms. Even though recitation of the prayer was not required, the court in effect **forbade public schools from opening sessions with prayer.**

1962 July The **Christian Commercial Men's Association** of America, better known as **Gideons**, International, at its 63rd annual convention in Pittsburgh, Pennsylvania, celebrated the distribution of more than 50,000,000 copies of the King James Bible in hotels and other public places.

1962 Oct. 11 **Vatican Council II** (to Dec. 8, 1965), the 21st General [Ecumenical] Council held by the Roman Catholic Church, was convoked in Vatican City by **Pope John XXIII.** Its stated purpose was to bring about a spiritual renewal of the church and to consider how it should relate to the 20th-century world. Nearly 3,000 members of the Catholic clergy had been invited as well as observers from Protestant and Eastern Orthodox church groups. This first session ended on Dec. 8.

1962 Dec. The **Israeli High Court** ruled against **Daniel Oswald Rufeisen** (b. 1922), a Carmelite friar, on his claim to Israeli citizenship by ethnic origin. Father Daniel had become a Christian in 1942 and a Carmelite in 1945. The court said that apostasy to Christianity removed a person from Jewish nationality.

VI. SCIENCE, EDUCATION, AND TECHNOLOGY

1962 Feb. 20 **John H[erschel] Glenn, Jr.** (b. July 18, 1921) became the **first American to orbit the earth,** making three orbits in the spacecraft **Friendship 7.** His feat was completed in 4 hours, 55 minutes, 23 seconds.

1962 Mar. 5 The last airplane race for the **Bendix Trophy** was won by a U.S. air force B-58 bomber that flew a round trip from Los Angeles to New York and return in 4 hrs., 42 min., 32 sec. The plane's average speed was 1,214.71 mph.

1962 Mar. 15 **Arthur Holly Compton** (b. Sept. 10, 1892), an American physicist, died. He shared the **Nobel prize for physics** in 1927 for his discovery and interpretation of changes in the wavelengths of X-rays when the rays are scattered. Compton was one of the scientists who developed the atomic bomb in 1945. Compton wrote a number of books, includ-

ing *The Human Meaning of Science* (1940) and *Atomic Quest* (1956).

1962 Mar. 24 **Auguste Piccard** (b. Jan. 28, 1884), a Swiss scientist and explorer, died. He long held records for ascents into the stratosphere and descents in his bathyscape into the ocean.

1962 Apr. 23 The U.S. launched the unmanned spacecraft *Ranger IV* to investigate the moon. Onboard equipment malfunctioned, however, so no pictures were received but *Ranger* hit the moon on Apr. 26.

1962 May With the publication of *Silent Spring*, **Rachel [Louise] Carson** (May 27, 1907–Apr. 14, 1964), an American author and marine biologist, warned that overuse of **pesticides** threatened all life on the planet. Manufacturers denied her charges, but environmentalists and governmental bodies acted to ban such chemicals as DDT.

1962 May 15 An entirely new **Cathedral Church of St. Michael**, a stunning piece of 20th-century church **architecture**, was consecrated in Coventry, England, to replace the 11th-century cathedral that was almost completely destroyed by a German air raid on Nov. 14, 1940, during World War II. It was designed by the English architect **Basil Spence** (Aug. 13, 1907–Nov. 19, 1976) to stand next to the ruins of the old cathedral.

1962 June 4 **Charles William Beebe** (b. July 29, 1877), an American naturalist and explorer, died. Beebe led expeditions to such diverse places as Nova Scotia and the Himalaya Mountains, and wrote a number of books about his experiences, including *Jungle Peace* (1918) and *Galápagos, World's End* (1923).

1962 June 8 **Eugène** [Marie-Eugène-Léon] **Freyssinet** (b. July 13, 1878), a French civil engineer, died. He developed **prestressed concrete**, a method of embedding steel wire in concrete, in 1928.

1962 July 11 **Telstar I**, a communications satellite launched from Cape Canaveral, Florida, transmitted the **first live television pictures by satellite** across the Atlantic Ocean from Andover, Maine, to Pleumeur Bodou, France. The Telstar was developed by the Bell Telephone Laboratories.

1962 July 21 George Macaulay Trevelyan (b. Feb. 16, 1876), a popular English historian, died. Trevelyan belonged to the "literary" school that believed history, however factual it ought to be, should be written felicitously. His most popular work was a one-volume *History of England* (1926). More scholarly were such works as *British History in the Nineteenth Century* (1922) and *England Under Queen Anne* (1930–1934).

1962 Aug. 11–15 A Russian cosmonaut, **Adrian G. Nikolayev** (b. Sept. 5, 1929), made 64 orbits of the earth in the spacecraft **Vostok 3**. **Pavel** [Romanovich] **Popovich** (b. Oct. 5, 1930) was launched (Aug. 12) in **Vostok** 4 and made 48 orbits. Thus the Russians had two men in space at the same time. Both landed on Aug. 15.

1962 Aug. 22 The **first nuclear-powered cargo ship**, the *Savannah*, made its maiden voyage from Yorktown, Virginia, to Savannah, Georgia.

1962 Aug. 26 Vilhjalmur Stefansson (b. Nov. 3, 1879), a Canadian-born American explorer and ethnologist, died. Twice he lived (1906–1907, 1908–1909) with Eskimos in the Arctic region, adopting their way of life to show how well suited it was to the conditions under which they existed. Among Stefansson's many books were *My Life with the Eskimo* (1913) and *Unsolved Mysteries of the Arctic* (1939).

1962 Sept. 4 The **Trans-Canada Highway**, running c.4,850 miles from St. John, Newfoundland, to Victoria, British Columbia, was officially opened. The total cost was $1,000,000,000, including c.500 bridges.

1962 Sept. 30 At the **University of Mississippi**, **James Meredith** (b. June 25, 1933), a black student, attempted to register in a school that had never admitted anyone of his race. With federal marshals escorting him, Meredith was duly enrolled. Rioting broke out on the campus and **John F. Kennedy**, president of the U.S., sent troops to end it. At least two persons were killed and c.50 injured.

1962 Nov. The **Robert McMath Solar Telescope** at the Kitt Peak National Observatory near Tucson, Arizona, was dedicated. With an 80-inch heliostat mirror, it is the largest instrument of its kind in the world.

1962 Nov. 6 The **greatest known ocean depth** was located in the **Mindanao Trench** in the western Pacific Ocean by the British ship *Cook*. A depth of 37,783 feet was recorded.

1962 Nov. 18 Niels [Henrik David] **Bohr** (b. Oct. 7, 1885), a Danish physicist, died. He was awarded the **Nobel prize for physics** in 1922 for his work on the theory of atomic structure. In the U.S. during World War II he participated in the **Manhattan Project**, which produced the first atomic bomb in 1945. In 1913 Bohr theorized that in an atom the electrons move around the nucleus and he described the way in which an atom absorbs and emits energy.

1962 Dec. 14 Mariner II, a U.S. spacecraft launched on Aug. 24, **circled Venus** at a distance of 21,648 miles, sending back valuable information on the planet.

VII. ARTS AND LEISURE

1962 Publication of **Yevtushenko: Selected Poems** by **Yevgeny** [Aleksandrovich] **Yevtushenko** (b. July 8, 1933), a Russian poet, caused the Soviet authorities to censure him. The book contained the poem **"Babi Yar"** concerning the massacre, beginning in Sept. 1941, by the Nazis of thousands of Russian Jews at a ravine called Babi Yar, near Kiev in the central northern Ukraine.

1962 Jan. 20 [John] **Robinson Jeffers** (b. Jan. 10, 1887), an American poet, died. Much of his poetry used the Carmel and Big Sur region of California as setting. *Tamar and Other Poems* (1924) treated, in the title poem, the biblical story in a modern setting. *The Women at Point Sur* (1927) concerned a mad clergyman; *Cawdor, and Other Poems* (1928) was also tragic in nature.

1962 Jan. 29 Fritz Kreisler (b. Feb. 2, 1875), an Austrian-born violinist, died. He made his New York debut in 1888. After serving in the Austrian army in World War I, he returned to the U.S. and became a citizen. Kreisler composed many pieces for the violin, such as *Caprice Viennois* and *Liebesfreud*, and a successful operetta, *Apple Blossoms* (1919).

1962 Feb. 17 Bruno Walter [Bruno Walter Schlesinger] (b. Sept. 15, 1876), a German-born conductor, died. He led opera and symphony orchestras in Germany and Austria before moving permanently (1939) to the U.S. as an exile from Nazi Germany.

Walter was first guest conductor of the **NBC Symphony Orchestra** and then conductor of the **New York Philharmonic**.

1962 Apr. 12   Antoine Pevsner (b. Jan. 18, 1886), a Russian-born, naturalized French sculptor and painter, died. With his brother **Naum Gabo Pevsner** (Aug. 15, 1890–Aug. 23, 1977) he issued in 1920 the "**Constructivist Manifesto**." A pioneer of modern sculpture, Pevsner employed glass, metal, and other materials in his work.

1962 May 13   Franz [Joseph] **Kline** (b. May 23, 1919), an American painter of the abstract expressionist school, died. After 1949 he turned to abstract expressionism. Among his works were *Nijinksy* [*Pétrushka*] (c.1950) and *Mahoning* (1956).

1962 June 2 [Victoria Mary] **Vita Sackville-West** (Mar. 9, 1892), an English novelist and a member of the **Bloomsbury Group** of writers and painters, died. She is best remembered today for her novel *The Edwardians* (1930). Among her other works were the novel *All Passion Spent* (1931) and *Collected Poems* (1933).

1962 June 13 [Aynsley] **Eugene Goosens** (b. May 26, 1893), an English conductor and composer, died. He began his career as a violinist in 1915. Goosens was (1923–1946) the conductor of the Rochester and Cincinnati symphony orchestras and then led (1947–1955) the Sydney, Australia, Symphony.

1962 July 6   William Faulkner [orig.: Falkner] (b. Sept. 25, 1887), one of America's most important authors, died. Readers of his many novels were intrigued by the violence in them, but in a deeper way they reflected Faulkner's concern with what he saw as the long tragedy of the South where he was born and lived. Many of his books have settings in an imaginary Mississippi county Yoknapatawpha he created. *Sartoris* (1920) was the first of these. A wider readership began two years later with another novel *Sanctuary*, a story of rape and other violence. His output of significant works continued until his death and included *Absalom, Absalom* (1936), set in the early 19th century; *The Hamlet* (1940), the first volume of a trilogy about the despicable Snopes family; and *The Reivers* (1962), telling of a boy's adventures. Faulkner was awarded the **Nobel prize for literature** in 1949.

1962 Aug. 5   Marilyn Monroe [nee Norma Jean Baker] (b. June 1, 1926), the voluptuous and glamorous American film star, died. Monroe made 22 movies, most notable among them being *The Seven Year Itch* (1955), *Bus Stop* (1956), *Some Like It Hot* (1959), and *The Misfits* (1961). Her life ended tragically in suicide.

1962 Aug. 9   Herman Hesse (b. July 1, 1877), a German novelist and poet, died. His writings were replete with spiritual themes and show the artist isolated and in search of spiritual fulfillment. Among Hesse's major works were *Demian* (1919), *Der Steppenwolf* [*Steppenwolf*] (1927), *Narziss und Goldmund* [*Death and the Lover*] (1930), and *Das Glasperlenspiel* [*Magister Ludi: The Glass-Bead Game*] (1943). Hesse won the **Nobel prize for literature** in 1946.

1962 Sept. 3   E[dward] **E**[stlin] **Cummings** (b. Oct. 14, 1894), who changed his name to e. e. cummings, an important American poet and novelist, died. His writings, both whimsical and bittersweet, employed oddities of typography and punctuation. *The Complete Poems, 1913–1962* was published in two volumes in 1972. Cummings is also remembered for *The Enormous Room* (1922), a novelistic account of imprisonment during World War I.

1962 Sept. 7   Isak Dinesen [Karen Christence Dinesen, Baroness Blixen-Finecke] (b. Oct. 17, 1885), a Danish writer, died. Best known for her tales of the supernatural in *Seven Gothic Tales* (1934), she also wrote a popular account of her life on a coffee plantation, *Out of Africa* (1937).

1962 Oct. 4   Sylvia [Woodbridge] **Beach** (b. 1887), an American publisher and bookseller, who opened (1919) what became the famous **Shakespeare & Company** shop in Paris, died. Most of the expatriate American intellectuals of the 1920s visited her store. On Feb. 2, 1922, Beach became the first publisher in book form of **James Joyce's** *Ulysses* when others would not issue it for fear of charges of obscenity.

1962 Dec. 7   Kirsten [Malfrid] **Flagstad** (b. July 12, 1895), a Norwegian operatic soprano, died. She made her debut in Oslo in 1913 and in New York at the Metropolitan Opera in 1935. Flagstad was best known for her roles in Wagnerian operas.

1961 Dec. 15   Charles Laughton (b. July 1, 1899), an English-born actor of stage and screen who made many Hollywood movies, died. He first earned fame in 1933 with *The Private Life of Henry VIII* and followed with such favorites as *Mutiny on the Bounty (1935) and Ruggles of Red Gap (1936)*.

VIII. SPORTS, GAMES, AND SOCIETY

1962 Yves [Mathieu] **Saint-Laurent** (b. Aug. 1, 1936), a French **fashion** designer, opened his house of haute couture in Paris. Having started as an assistant to another designer, **Christian Dior**, he became the head of that house on the death of Dior in 1957.

1962 Jan. 26 [Salvatore] **Lucky Luciano** (b. Nov. 11, 1896), once the top **Mafia** chief in the U.S., died. Born in Sicily he was brought to America at the age of nine. Between 1919 and 1936 he was arrested 25 times on charges concerning narcotics, gambling, prostitution, and other crimes. Luciano was finally convicted in 1936 as head of a vice ring and sentenced to 30 to 50 years in prison. In 1946 the sentence was commuted on condition that he leave the U.S. and never return, which he did, settling in his native land.

1962 Mar. 2 [Wilton Norman] **Wilt Chamberlain** (b. Aug. 21, 1936) set a record for points scored in one game in a professional **basketball** contest when he registered 100, playing for the Philadelphia 76ers against the New York Knicks in an NBA game.

1962 Apr. 8 **Juan Belmonte y Garcia** (b. Apr. 14, 1892), a popular Spanish **bullfighter**, died. With Joselito, he created the modern 20th-century style of bullfighting. His manner was to stand very close to the bull in an erect and unmoving posture, counting on his agility to evade the bull's charge. Belmonte is considered the **greatest matador ever**.

1962 June 17 Brazil won the **World Cup** of soccer by defeating Czechoslovakia, 3–1, at Santiago, Chile.

1962 Sept. 10 **Rod**[ney George] **Laver** (b. Aug. 8, 1938) of Australia completed the grand slam of the top four **tennis** titles of the world by winning the U.S. Lawn Tennis Association men's singles title. He had previously this year won the Australian, French, and British championships.

1962 Sept. 15–25 For the 18th consecutive time since 1851 the U.S. successfully defended the **America's Cup**, yachting's prime international trophy. The *Weatherly* defeated the challenging Australian 12-meter sloop *Gretel* in four out of five races held off Newport, R.I.

1963

I. DISASTERS

1963 Feb. 1 A Lebanese passenger jet and a Turkish air force **C-47** transport **plane collided** in a dense fog in Ankara, Turkey. Flaming wreckage fell on the city, and 95 persons in the air and on the ground were killed, with at least 153 injured.

1963 Mar. 17–21 **Mt. Agung**, a volcanic mountain, **erupted** on the island of Bali, Indonesia, killing 1,584 persons.

1963 Mar. 21 After a **fire** spread for four hours through a waterfront area of Saigon, South Vietnam, c.300 children were missing and presumed dead. More than 100 were injured and c.40,000 persons made homeless.

1963 Apr. 10 The American nuclear-powered submarine **Thresher sank** c.200 miles east of Boston in the Atlantic Ocean while making deep diving tests. All 129 crew members were lost.

1963 June 3 A U.S. military chartered **DC-7 plunged into the Pacific Ocean** off Queen Charlotte Island, British Columbia. All 101 on board died.

1963 July 26 Most of Skopje, Yugoslavia, was destroyed by an **earthquake**. The death toll was 1,011 with 3,350 injured. The quake registered 6.0 on the Richter scale.

1963 Oct. 4–8 **Hurricane Flora** raged over the West Indies. Haiti, with a death toll of c.5,000, lost more than 66 percent of its coffee crop. Cuba, where c.1,000 died, lost half its sugar crop and had to evacuate more than 150,000 people from Oriente province. Nearly 50 people died on the islands of Tobago, Granada, Trinidad, and Jamaica.

1963 Oct. 9 As the result of an **earthslide** into the reservoir behind northern Italy's Vaiont Dam, a 300-foot high wave swept over the dam, scouring the Piave River Valley and killing c.1,800 people. The town of Longarone and several villages were destroyed.

1963 Nov. 9 A freight **train, derailed near Yokohama**, was hit by two heavily loaded passenger trains, causing at least 162 deaths and injuring 72.

II. POLITICS AND WAR

1963 Jan. 22 **France and West Germany signed a treaty** in Paris pledging amity and cooperation.

1963 Feb. 8 A military coup in **Iraq** led by **Abdul Salam Aref** overthrew the regime of Abdul Karim Kassem (b. Nov. 21, 1914), who was executed on the next day. The **Ba'ath party**, socialist and aiming for Arab unity, dominated the new regime. In November, another coup by Aref expelled the Ba'ath members of the governing council.

1963 Mar. 2 A boundary and **trade agreement** between **Pakistan and China** brought the two nations together. The boundary settlement gave both countries part of what they claimed.

1963 Apr. 8 In **Canada** the Liberal party won the general election, with 129 seats for itself and 136 for all other parties. On Apr. 22 the Liberal leader **Lester B[owles] Pearson** (Apr. 27, 1897–Dec. 27, 1972) succeeded the Conservative **John G. Diefenbaker** as prime minister, who had held the office since 1957.

1963 May 22–26 Thirty of the 32 independent nations of Africa met in Addis Ababa, Ethiopia, and formed the **Organization of African Unity [OAU]**. The purpose of the new group was to eradicate all traces of colonialism, to defend each other, to promote economic, social, and welfare measures, and to promote unity in general.

1963 June 19 **Levi Eshkol** [Levi Shkolnik] (Oct. 25, 1895–Feb. 26, 1969), finance minister and a leader of the **Israeli** Labor party [Mapai], became prime minister after the resignation of **David Ben-Gurion** on June 16.

1963 June 20 The U.S. and the U.S.S.R., after negotiations in Geneva, Switzerland, to agree to establish a **"hot line,"** a direct system of communication by teletype between Washington and Moscow.

1963 July 1 The British government revealed that [Harold Adrian Russell] **Kim Philby** (Jan. 1, 1912–May 11, 1988) had been a spy for the Soviet Union for 30 years. He disappeared in Beirut, Lebanon, after being questioned, and the USSR announced (July 30) that he had been granted asylum in Russia. It was now clear that Philby was the "third man" hinted at in 1951 when two other highly placed British government officials, **Guy Burgess** and **Donald MacLean**, were uncovered as spies.

1963 July 11 **Carlos Arosemena Monroy** (b. 1920), president of **Ecuador**, was ousted in an army coup. He had taken power through a similar coup in Nov. 1961, and was now accused of drunkenness and communist sympathies. **Ramon Castro Jijón** (b. Nov., 1915) became the head of a military junta that held power until 1966.

1963 Aug. 28 A **civil rights demonstration** organized by **Martin Luther King, Jr.** brought c.200,000 persons to Washington, D.C., to demonstrate peacefully. Before the huge assemblage King delivered his now famous **"I Have a Dream"** speech, his vision of the day when equality would exist in the U.S.

1963 Sept. 4 **Robert Schuman** (b. June 29, 1886), a French statesman and leading advocate of European unity, died. In World War II he was active in the Resistance and from Nov., 1947, to July, 1949, he was premier of France. In 1950 Schuman developed plans for European unity which resulted in the creation of the European Coal and Steel Community in 1952.

1963 Sept. 16 The nation of **Malaysia** was formed by the union of Malaya, Sabab [North Borneo], Sarawak, and Singapore, with a federal parliamentary government and its capital at Kuala Lumpur, Malaya. Malaysia's first prime minister was **Tuanku** [prince] **Abdul Rahman Putra**, who retired in 1970.

1963 Oct. 3 With elections scheduled for Oct. 13, when the term of **Ramon Villeda Morales**, president of **Honduras**, was to expire, a military coup with heavy casualties overthrew what had been the most stable and effective government in the country's history. The new head of the state was **Osvaldo Lopez Arellano**, who dissolved Congress and ruled by decree.

1963 Oct. 10 A limited nuclear test ban treaty, signed on Aug. 5 by the U.S. and the U.S.S.R., went into effect, banning testing in the atmosphere, outer space, and under water.

1963 Oct. 15 **Park Chung Hee** (Sept. 30, 1917–Oct. 26, 1979), chairman of the Supreme Council of National Reconstruction of **South Korea**, won a narrow victory in a presidential election and took office as president on Dec. 16.

1963 Oct. 16 **Konrad Adenauer** resigned as chancellor of the **Federal Republic of Germany** [West Germany] and was succeeded by **Ludwig Erhard**. Both were Christian Democrats.

1963 Oct. 19 **Alexander** [Frederick] **Douglas-Home** (b. July 2, 1903) became prime minister of **Great Britain** upon the resignation of **Harold Macmillan**. Macmillan resigned partly for reasons of health and partly because of a recent sex scandal involving a member of the cabinet.

1963 Nov. 1 The government of **South Vietnam** was overthrown in a military coup, and **Ngo Dinh Diem** (b. Jan. 3, 1901), the president, was executed (Nov. 2). On Nov. 4 **Nguyen Ngoc Tho** took office as provisional premier. There had been four chiefs of state, two premiers, and two presidents in the course of a year.

1963 Nov. 12 **Amin al-Hafez** (b. 1911) became premier of **Syria**. On Mar. 8 a bloodless coup had brought to power a group representing both the military and the Ba'ath elements who were socialistic and pan-Arabic. The most powerful official was Hafez, who had put down a coup on July 18 and had 20 of its leaders hanged or shot.

1963 Nov. 22 While riding in a motorcade in Dallas, Texas, **John F. Kennedy**, president of the U.S., was **shot and killed** by an assassin firing from a nearby building. **Lyndon B**[aines] **Johnson**, vice president, was sworn in as president later in the day. The assassin, also captured that day, was **Lee Harvey Oswald** (b. Oct. 18, 1939), who was shot (on Nov. 24) as he was being taken from the basement of the municipal building to the county jail and died soon after. His killer was **Jack Ruby** [Jacob Rubenstein] (b. 1911), a night club operator who died in prison on Jan. 3, 1967, having been convicted of the murder on Mar. 14, 1964. Johnson appointed (Nov. 29, 1963) a seven-member commission to investigate the assassi-

nation. It was headed by **Earl Warren**, chief justice of the U.S. The commission reported on Sept. 27, 1964, that Oswald had acted on his own and not as the agent of any group or nation.

1963 Dec. 10 **Zanzibar** became independent of Great Britain but remained a sultanate within the Commonwealth of Nations. The first head of state was **Jamshi ibn Abdullah** (b. 1930?), sultan of Zanzibar. On Jan. 12, 1964, this government was overthrown in a bloody coup by **John Okello**, an army officer. The sultan was banished, and a people's republic proclaimed. **Abeid Karume** (1905?–Apr. 7, 1972), leader of the Afro-Shirazi party, became president of the new nation.

1963 Dec. 12 **Kenya** was granted independence from Great Britain but remained in the Commonwealth of Nations. The leader of the Kenya National African Union, **Jomo Kenyatta**, became the first prime minister.

III. ECONOMY AND TRADE

1963 Mar. 1 With wages and prices rising rapidly, the government of **Switzerland** announced it would **restrict the admission of foreign workers**. These workers represented about 20 percent of employed persons in the country.

1963 Dec. 9 The **Studebaker Corporation** of South Bend, Indiana, announced that except for a plant in Hamilton, Ontario, Canada, it was going out of the business of manufacturing automobiles.

IV. RELIGION AND PHILOSOPHY

1963 Mar. *Honest to God*, by **John A**[rthur] **T**[homas] **Robinson** (June 15, 1919–Dec. 5, 1983), bishop of Wooolwich, England, became an immediate bestseller in Great Britain and the U.S. and touched off a lively controversy in Protestant circles in general and Anglican in particular. Calling the Virgin birth, biblical creation, and heaven-and-hell concepts religious myths, Robinson urged a demythologizing of religious thinking. The bishop said he wanted to further the cause of vital faith stripped of non-essentials.

1963 Mar. 12 **G**[arfield] **Bromley Oxnam** (b. Aug. 14, 1891), a Methodist bishop and long time religious leader of liberal causes, died. Ordained in 1916, he became a bishop in 1936. Oxnam was president

(1944–1946) of the Federal Council of Churches, an American Protestant organization, and president (1948–1954) of the World Council of Churches.

1963 Apr. 10 Pope John XXIII issued his eighth encyclical, *Pacem in Terris [Peace on Earth]*. The encyclical was addressed to men of good will everywhere, not just Catholics. It outlined the pope's prescription for world peace, beginning with human relations built on individual rights and responsibilities.

1963 June 3 Pope John XXIII (b. Nov. 25, 1881; ruled 1958–1963), died. He was the best loved and most outgoing of all recent popes. His main aims had been to renew the spirit of the Roman Catholic Church and to review its attitude toward other church bodies. He was succeeded by **Pope Paul VI**.

1963 Dec. 4 The second session of **Vatican Council II**, which had convened on Sept. 29, adjourned. The session closed with **Pope Paul VI** issuing two decrees. One allowed English and other languages to be used in the celebration of the mass, the first time any tongue other than Latin had been permitted since Latin replaced Greek in the third century. The second decree concerned mass communication and called for freedom of information.

V. SCIENCE, EDUCATION, AND TECHNOLOGY

1963 An effective **vaccine against measles** was approved for use this year. It was developed by **John Franklin Enders** (Dec. 10, 1897–Sept. 8, 1985), an American bacteriologist. Enders shared the **Nobel prize for physiology or medicine** in 1954 for his work in discovering a method of cultivating viruses in tissue culture.

1963 Jan. 28 Jean [Felix] **Piccard** (b. Jan. 28, 1884), a Swiss born chemical engineer and balloonist, died. On Oct. 23, 1934, with his wife, he made his first successful stratospheric flight, rising to a height of 11 miles.

1963 June 16–19 The **first female space traveler**, Russian cosmonaut **Valentina V. Tereshkova** (b. Mar. 26, 1937), made 48 orbits of the earth in the Soviet spacecraft **Vostok 4**. Her trip took 70 hours 50 minutes.

1963 Aug. 18 James H[oward] **Meredith** became the **first black to graduate from the University of Mississippi**. On June 6, 1966, Meredith was shot and wounded from ambush while participating in a voting rights march from Memphis, Tennessee, to Jackson, Mississippi.

1963 Aug. 27 W[illiam] E[dward] B[urghardt] **Du Bois** (b. Feb. 23, 1868), a black American educator, writer, and radical protagonist for his race, died. He was one of the founders of the **National Association for the Advancement of Colored People [NAACP]** in May, 1910. One of his most provocative books was **The Souls of Black Folk** (1903). An early advocate of Pan-Africanism, he published **The World and Africa** (1947).

1963 Oct. 10 Linus [Carl] **Pauling**, an American scientist, became the first person to win two full Nobel prizes when he was awarded the **Peace Prize**. He had won the **Nobel prize for chemistry** in 1954. The Peace Prize was given to Pauling in acknowledgment of his efforts to secure a nuclear test ban treaty.

1963 Nov. 5 At **L'Anse aux Meadows** on the northern tip of Newfoundland archeologists found remains of a **Viking settlement**, the ruins of nine rectangular sod-walled houses and a smithy. Radiocarbon dating indicated that the smithy dated from c.500 years before Columbus reached the New World in 1492.

VI. ARTS AND LEISURE

1963 [Jorge] **Mario** [Pedro] **Vargas Llosa** (b. Mar. 28, 1936), a Peruvian author, published his first major novel, *La ciudad y los perros [The Time of the Hero]*. It described a Latin American military academy where violence and injustice were the order of the day, a theme typical of Vargas's protests against social wrongs and national degeneration.

1963 Jan. 29 Robert [Lee] **Frost** (b. Mar. 26, 1874), an American poet, died. Frost's unadorned verse and symbols disguised the profound nature of his subject matter, as in the poem "The Road Not Taken" (1916). Among his books were *New Hampshire* (1924), *Collected Poems* (1931), *A Further Range* (1937), and *A Witness Tree* (1943).

1963 Jan. 30 Francis-[Jean Marcel] **Poulenc** (b. Jan. 7, 1899), a French composer and pianist, died. A member of "Les Six," who gave concerts together, he composed chamber and orchestral music, songs, and for the stage. Among Poulenc's many works were *Rapsodie nègre* (1917), the song cycle *Le Bestiaire* (1919), a ballet *Les Biches* (1924), *Oboe Sonata* (1962), as well as operas, piano music, and compositions with a religious background.

1963 Mar.–June   The first large exhibition of **Pop Art** was held at the Guggenheim Museum, New York City. Among the artists whose work was shown were **Jasper Johns**; **Roy Lichtenstein** (b. Oct. 27, 1923); **Claes Oldenburg** (b. Jan. 28, 1939), a sculptor; **Robert Rauschenberg** (b. Oct. 22, 1925), and **Andy Warhol** [Andrew Warhola] (Aug. 6, 1927–Feb. 21, 1987).

1963 Mar. 4   **William Carlos Williams** (b. Sept. 17, 1883), an American poet and physician, died. In 40 years of medical practice he delivered more than 2,000 babies and in the same period wrote 40 books of poetry. Among them was *Paterson* (1946–1958) and his *Autobiography* (1951).

1963 June 25   The **National Association for the Advancement of Colored People** [**NAACP**] launched an attack against **racial bias in the movie industry**. Although the NAACP did not achieve equality for blacks in the industry, it did much to improve the portrayal of black characters in the movies and the economic position of blacks working in Hollywood.

1963 Aug. 14   **Clifford Odets** (b. July 18, 1906), a leading American playwright of the 1930s depression era, died. His plays voiced social protest against what he saw as a number of ills of modern society. Among the plays were *Waiting for Lefty* (1935), *Paradise Lost* (1935), and *Golden Boy* (1937).

1963 Aug. 31   **Georges Braque** (b. May 13, 1882), a French painter who with **Pablo Picasso** helped develop **cubism**, died. Braque was the first living painter to have his work exhibited at the Louvre, Paris. Some of his many paintings are **Piano and Lute** (1910), *The Musician's Table* (1913), *Nude Woman with Basket of Fruit* (1926), *The Bathers* (1931), and *Still Life with a Mandolin* (1935).

1963 Oct. 11   **Jean Cocteau** (b. July 5, 1889), a French poet, playwright, novelist, designer, critic, and filmmaker, died. A sampling of his work in his many fields of endeavor shows: design of a modernistic ballet *Parade* (1917); theatrical production of

plays with classic themes, such as *Orphée* (1926); original dramas, as *The Typewriter* (1947); novels, including *Les Enfants terribles* [*Children of the Game*] (1929), set in a world of fantasy; a number of volumes of verse; and the films he wrote and directed, which included the surrealistic *Le Sang d'un Poète* [*The Blood of a Poet*] (1932) and *La Belle et la bête* [*Beauty and the Beast*] (1945).

1963 Oct. 11   **Edith Piaf** [orig.: Edith Giovanna Gassion] (b. Dec., 1915), an internationally popular French cabaret singer, died. In 1930 she was singing for a living in small cafés and sometimes on the streets of Paris. Her voice was exactly right for the love songs of her repertoire, such as "**La Vie en rose.**"

1963 Nov. 15   **Fritz Reiner** (b. Dec. 19, 1888), a Hungarian-born conductor, died. He came to America in 1922 to be conductor of the **Cincinnati Symphony**. Reiner was musical director (1948–1953) of the **Metropolitan Opera** and as leader (1953–1962) of the **Chicago Symphony** made it one of the best in the world.

1963 Nov. 22   **C**[live] **S**[taples] **Lewis** (b. Nov. 29, 1898), an English scholar and writer of works of fantasy, died. In **The Allegory of Love** (1936) he explored the literary treatment of romantic love in the Middle Ages. Lewis's fantasies, such as *Out of the Silent Planet* (1938) and *That Hideous Strength* (1945), carried a moral message. Lewis wrote a number of religious works, among them *The Screwtape Letters* (1942), in which an older, experienced devil instructs a young, inexperienced one in the weaknesses and temptations to which ordinary Christians succumb.

1963 Nov. 22   **Aldous** [Leonard] **Huxley** (b. July 26, 1894), an English novelist and critic, died. Ironical and sometimes bitter in his writings, he produced such novels as *Antic Hay* (1923), *Point Counter Point* (1928), and *Brave New World* (1932), a pessimistic view of the future.

1963 Nov. 26   **Amelita Galli-Curci** [nee Galli] (b. Nov. 18, 1882), an Italian-born coloratura soprano, died. She made her debut as Gilda in **Rigoletto** in Rome in 1909 and her American debut in the same role in 1916 with the Chicago Opera. Her florid style made her famous in such roles as Lakme in **Lakme** and Lucia in **Lucia de Lammermoor**.

1963 Dec. 25   **Tristan Tzara** [orig.: Samuel Rosenfeld] (b. Apr. 4, 1896), a Rumanian-born French writer and founder (1916) in Zürich of the **dada movement**, died. Dadaism, applied to the literary and art fields, was a protest against what its followers saw as the insanity of World War I.

1963 Dec. 28   **Paul Hindemith** (b. Nov. 16, 1895), a German composer, died. Forced out of Germany by the Nazis, he taught in Europe and the U.S. Hindemith wrote operas such as *Cardillac* (1926) and *Mathis der Maler* (1934). He composed ballets, including *Hérodiade* (1944), and orchestral and chamber music, *Die Harmonie der Welt* (1951) and *Kammermusik no. 1* (1922), among others.

VII. SPORTS, GAMES, AND SOCIETY

1963   The **Women's Liberation Movement** was born in the U.S. this year with the publication of *The Feminine Mystique* by **Betty** [Naomi] **Friedan** [nee Goldstein] (b. Feb. 4, 1921). It was a call to arms to women to make the world understand that they had more of a part to play than simply being mothers and housewives.

1963 Jan. 5   **Rogers Hornsby** (b. Apr. 27, 1896), the greatest righthanded batter in the history of **baseball**, died. He began his career in 1915 with the St. Louis Cardinals, played for a number of other teams, and managed several. In the course of his career Hornsby won seven batting titles, two home run titles, and three runs batted in titles, as well as ending with a lifetime batting average of .358. He was elected to the **Baseball Hall of Fame** in 1942.

1963 Mar.–May   **Mikhail Botvinnik** (b. Apr. 17, 1911), a Russian master, lost the **world chess championship** to **Tigran Petrosian** (June 17, 1929–Aug. 14, 1984), another Russian master, in a championship series held in Moscow. Botvinnik first won the title in 1948.

1963 Mar. 20   **Hope Cooke** (b. June 21, 1940), a young American woman, was married in the royal palace in Gangtok, **Sikkim**, to **Palden Thondup Namgyal** (May 22, 1923–Jan. 29, 1982), the crown prince. Sikkim, on the border of northern India, was a protectorate of that country.

1963 Aug. 8   In a **train robbery** near Cheddington, England, 12 masked men seized 120 mailbags on a train bound from Glasgow to London. The bags contained $7,368,715 of old bank notes that were being sent for pulping. Eventually all the thieves were caught because they left their fingerprints in a farmhouse they used as a hideaway. However, only $961,654 of the loot was ever recovered.

1963 Dec. 28   For the first time since 1958 Australia lost the **Davis Cup**, emblem of international tennis supremacy. The U.S. defeated Australia three matches to two.

1964

I. DISASTERS

1964 Feb. 29   A British Bristol Britannia turboprop passenger **plane with skiers aboard crashed** into Mt. Glungezer near Innsbruck, Austria, and fell into a gorge. All 83 persons aboard died.

1964 Mar. 27   **North America's strongest recorded earthquake**, measuring 8.5 on the Richter scale, shook southern Alaska, killing 117 persons. It destroyed the business section of Anchorage and damaged five other places. Property damage was estimated at $750 million.

1964 May 24   At Lima, Peru, **fans** poured out of the stands of the National Soccer Stadium during a match between Peru and Argentina to protest a referee's decision. In the ensuing panic 318 were killed, most of them **trampled to death**. About 500 others were injured.

1964 July 23   In Bône, Algeria, a **munitions ship exploded** while being unloaded at dockside. The blast left c.100 people missing and c.160 injured.

1964 July 26   A **train** carrying weekend seaside visitors **derailed** at Pôrto [Oporto], northwestern Portugal, killing 94 and injuring c.80.

1964 Sept. 5   **Typhoon Ruby** struck Hong Kong and Kwangtung [Guangdong] province, in southeastern China, killing more than 730 persons.

1964 Nov. 12 Floods following two typhoons caused c.7,000 deaths in northern South Vietnam. The floods spread over 5 million acres and made 1 million people homeless.

II. POLITICS AND WAR

1964–1965 Racial confrontations were widespread in the U.S. On Aug. 4, 1964, three civil rights workers were found dead on a farm near Philadelphia, Mississippi. They were **James Chaney** (b. 1943?), a black of Meridian, Mississippi, and **Andrew Goodman** (b. 1944?) and **Michael Schwerner** (b. 1942?), both whites from New York City. They had disappeared (June 21) after being arrested for speeding. No suspects were ever tried in Mississippi court, but 21 Mississippians were arrested (Dec. 4) on federal charges of violating the civil rights of the three, who had been shot. Seven were convicted and one pleaded guilty. In the North, meanwhile, a **race riot** broke out (July 18) in the Harlem section of New York City after a white policeman shot a black youth who had allegedly attacked him with a knife. A more serious riot occurred (Aug. 28–31) in Philadelphia, Pennsylvania, in which more than 500 people were injured and c.350 arrested. On Feb. 1, 1965, **Martin Luther King, Jr.**, the civil rights leader, and nearly 800 others, both black and white, were arrested in Selma, central Alabama, when they demonstrated against discrimination in voting registration. Then, on Mar. 21, under King's leadership, more than 3,000 persons began a march from Selma to Montgomery, Alabama, the state capital. National guard troops were ordered to protect them. The march, lasting five days, ended (Mar. 25) in a massive demonstration involving c.25,000 people at the capitol. Earlier **James Reeb**, a Unitarian minister, was beaten (Mar. 9) in Selma where he was taking part in a civil rights drive and died two days later on Mar. 11, 1965. Though three men were arrested (Dec. 10), they were found not guilty in state court. Another civil rights worker, **Viola Gregg Liuzzo** (b. 1925), who came from Detroit, Michigan, was killed on Mar. 25, 1965, in Selma. Three men were convicted (Dec. 3) in federal court on charges of conspiracy and were sentenced to ten years in prison. In Watts, a black section of Los Angeles, California, rioting (Aug. 11–16), caused by alledged police brutality, left 35 dead, c.1,000 injured, and nearly 4,000 arrested. Property damaged was estimated at $200 million.

1964 Cyprus, the scene of fighting between Greek and Turkish ethnic groups, accepted (Jan. 2) an invitation from Great Britain, Greece, and Turkey to a conference in London. It failed to settle anything. In April a **U.N.** peacekeeping force was sent. After bloody fighting between the warring groups, the U.N. was able to arrange a ceasefire on Aug. 10.

1964 Jan. 30 The government of **South Vietnam** was overthrown by a military coup led by **Nguyen Khanh** (b. Nov. 8, 1927), who charged that the ruling junta had planned to neutralize the country, thus ending the war with North Vietnam. Khanh held office as president or premier at various times during the year.

1964 Feb. 11 In his effort to keep **Cambodia** neutral in the Indochinese struggle, **Norodom Sihanouk**, chief of state, called for an international conference, but nothing came of it.

1964 Feb. 19 Georgios Papandreou (Feb. 13, 1888–Nov. 1, 1968) became prime minister of **Greece**, his Center Union party having won a majority of the seats in parliament in the Feb. 16 election. **Constantine II** (b. June 2, 1940) became king of the Hellenes, ascending the Greek throne immediately upon the death of his father Paul I (b. Dec. 14, 1901) on Mar. 6, 1964. Papandreou, an opponent of the monarchy, was forced to resign on July 15, 1965.

1964 Mar. 11 In **Venezuelan elections**, the new president (to 1968) was **Raúl Leoni** (Apr. 26, 1905–July 5, 1972). He succeeded **Rómulo Betancourt** (Feb. 22, 1908–Sept. 28, 1982). They were both founders of the Democratic Action party.

1964 Apr. 2 In the face of a military uprising, **João Goulart**, president (from 1961) of **Brazil**, fled into exile in Uruguay. He had faced growing opposition because of serious economic problems and because he appeared to be favoring communism. Congress elected (Apr. 11) **Humberto Castelo Branco** (Sept. 20, 1900–July 18, 1967), an army officer, who took office (Apr. 15) as president (to 1967).

1964 Apr. 5 Douglas MacArthur (b. Jan. 26, 1890), a U.S. military commander in three wars, died. He led the Rainbow Division in World War I. Recalled to duty in 1941, he became the Allied supreme commander in the southwest Pacific theater in 1942. On Sept. 2, 1945, he accepted the Japanese surrender ending World War II. Once again called to duty for the Korean War (1950–1953), he commanded U.N. forces there (1950–1951), at first achieving success, but coming near disaster when China entered the war. On Apr. 11, 1951, he was relieved of his post by Harry S. Truman for refusing to accept the government's policy for fighting the war.

1964 Apr. 26 **Tanganyika and Zanzibar** agreed to become a single nation, the **United Republic of Tanzania**. The union took effect on Oct. 29 with **Julius K. Nyerere** of Tanganyika as president and **Abeid Karume** of Zanzibar as prime minister.

1964 May 2 **Nancy Astor**, [nee Nancy Witcher Langhorne] (b. May 19, 1879), a Virginia-born British politician and social figure who became the **first woman to be elected to Parliament**, died. She married (1906) **Waldorf Astor** (May 19, 1879–Sept. 30, 1952), a British publisher and politician. Nancy Astor was first elected to the House of Commons on Nov. 28, 1919.

1964 May 25 **François Duvalier**, dictator of **Haiti**, promulgated a new constitution under which he was declared president for life. A referendum on June 14 confirmed this action with what was called an almost unanimous vote. His iron grip on the country was the result of his position as a voodoo priest and his brutal security police, the *Tontons Macoutes*.

1964 May 27 **Jawaharlal Nehru** (b. Nov. 11, 1889), prime minister of India since independence, died. Associated with Mahatma Gandhi as early as 1919, Nehru had fought for Indian independence and had been imprisoned several times by the British. He had been president of the Indian National Congress since 1929. Nehru was succeeded (June 9) by Lal Bahadur Shastri (Oct. 2, 1904–Jan. 11, 1966), a cabinet minister and general secretary of the Congress party.

1964 May 28 The **Palestine Liberation Organization** [PLO], formed to fight Israel for a Palestinian homeland, was established when the Palestine National Congress met in the Jordan-held section of Jerusalem. The first head of the PLO was **Ahmed Shukairy** (1908–Feb. 26, 1980).

1964 June 9 **William Maxwell Aitken** [Lord Beaverbrook] (b. May 25, 1879), a British newspaper publisher and politician, died. Canadian-born, he went to England in 1910 and that year was elected to Parliament. Beaverbrook's career as a publisher

began in Dec., 1916, when he bought the *Daily Express*.

1964 June 11 **Nelson Mandela** [Rohihlahla] (b. July, 1918), a deputy president of the **African National Congress** [ANC] and a leader in the fight against apartheid, was sentenced, along with seven others, by a South African court to life imprisonment on charges of treason, sabotage, and violent conspiracy. Mandela was the son of a Tembu tribal chief and a lawyer who had joined the ANC in 1944. At first he advocated non-violent resistance to apartheid, but after the **Sharpeville incident** (1960) in which police fired on and killed a number of blacks, he began to advocate sabotage. He was first tried for treason in 1961 and acquitted, but since 1962 Mandela had been serving a five-year sentence for incitement when he was indicted on charges that led to life imprisonment.

1964 July 1 **Lyndon B. Johnson**, president of the U.S., signed into law the **Civil Rights Act of 1964**, the most far-reaching legislation of its kind since the days of post-Civil War Reconstruction. The act gave legal recognition to equal treatment in voting, education, employment, and the use of public facilities regardless of race.

1964 July 5 **Gustavo Díaz Ordaz** (Mar. 12, 1911–July 15, 1979) was elected president of **Mexico** for a six-year term to succeed **Adolfo López Mateos** (May 26, 1910–Sept. 22, 1969), president from 1958, and took office on Dec. 1.

1964 July 6 The former British protectorate of **Nyasaland** became the independent nation of **Malawi** and a member of the Commonwealth of Nations. The first prime minister was **Hastings Kamuzu Banda** (b. May 14, 1906) of the Malawi Congress party.

1964 Aug. 7 Congress passed a resolution which had been drafted by the administration of **Lyndon B. Johnson**, president of the U.S., authorizing the executive to take any measures it believed necessary to combat attacks on U.S. forces and to protect America's allies in Southeast Asia. The resolution was the result of an alleged attack on Aug. 4, on U.S. navy ships in the **Gulf of Tonkin** by North Vietnamese vessels.

1964 Sept. 4 In the first election in **Chile** in which women were allowed to vote, **Eduardo Frei Mon-**

talva (Jan. 16, 1911–June 22, 1982) was elected president (to 1970), thanks largely to the women's votes.

1964 Sept. 21   Malta was granted independence by Great Britain but remained in the Commonwealth of Nations. **George Borg Olivier** (July 5, 1911–Oct. 29, 1980) of the Nationalist party was the first prime minister.

1964 Oct. 15   The central committee of the Soviet Communist party removed **Nikita S. Khrushchev** from chairmananship of the council of ministers [premier] and first secretary of the party. He was replaced by **Leonid I[lyich] Brezhnev** as first secretary (to 1982) and by **Alexei N[ikolayevich] Kosygin** as premier.

1964 Oct. 16   In **Great Britain** the Labour party defeated the Conservative party, which had been in office for 13 years, in a close vote that gave Labour 317 seats in Parliament to the Conservatives' 303, with 9 held by Liberals. [James] **Harold Wilson** (b. Mar. 11, 1916) leader of the Labour party, became prime minister.

1964 Oct. 20   Herbert Clark Hoover (b. Aug. 10, 1874), 31st president of the U.S., died. A mining engineer, he came to public attention in World War I, when he organized relief efforts in Europe that saved the lives of millions. In the presidential election of 1928 he easily won over the Democratic candidate Alfred E. Smith. However, the Great Depression of the 1930s which began the next year, ruined Hoover's reputation in spite of efforts he thought would bring back prosperity. He was defeated for reelection in 1932 by Franklin D. Roosevelt.

1964 Oct. 24   The British protectorate of **Northern Rhodesia** became the independent republic of **Zambia**, within the Commonwealth of Nations. **Kenneth Kaunda** (b. Apr. 28, 1924), leader of the United National Independence party, became the first president.

1964 Nov. 2   Saud IV, king (from 1953) of **Saudi Arabia**, was deposed and replaced by **Ibn al Saud Faisal**, his half brother, as **Faisal II**.

1964 Nov. 5   René Barrientos Ortuño became **Bolivia's** chief of state when he overthrew the government of **Victor Paz Estenssoro** (b. Oct. 2, 1907). Barrientos had been vice president. There had been violence all year in Bolivia, ending with Paz's civilian

militia being defeated by the armed forces in support of Barrientos.

1964 Nov. 19   Eisaku Sato (Mar. 27, 1901–Jan. 3, 1975) became prime minister (to 1972) of Japan. As prime minister he was active in foreign affairs and helped Japan regain its place in the world following its defeat in World War II. An agreement in 1965 with Korea normalized relations with that country which had once been occupied (1910–1945) by Japan. Sato was awarded the **Nobel Peace Prize** in 1974.

1964 Nov. 25   To end a rebellion against the government of the **Democratic Republic of the Congo** [present Zaire], c.600 Belgian paratroopers were flown in by U.S. air force planes. The rebels held c.2,000 hostages, including c.60 Americans, and threatened to kill them all. The paratroopers captured Stanleyville [present Kisangani] and other towns, freeing most of the hostages, but more than 80 were killed, including two American medical missionaries.

III. ECONOMY AND TRADE

1964 Feb. 26   The **Revenue Act of 1964** was signed by **Lyndon B. Johnson**, providing a massive tax cut that was intended to stimulate the national economy. The total amount involved was about $11,500,000,000. Personal income taxes were lowered by $6,100,000,000 for 1964 and another $3,600,000,000 in 1965. Corporate taxes were also reduced.

1964 Aug. 11   The **Economic Opportunity Act**, a major item in the Johnson administration's "**war on poverty**," became law. Nearly $1,000,000,000 was to be spent on a **Job Corps**; a domestic peace corps known as **Volunteers in Service to America** [VISTA]; and for education and job training, among other purposes. In 1986 c.40,000 young men and women were trained for better jobs.

IV. RELIGION AND PHILOSOPHY

1964 Jan. 5   Pope Paul VI, on a three-day visit to the Holy Land, met with **Athengoras I** [Aristokles Spirou] (Mar. 25, 1886–July 6, 1972), patriarch of the Eastern Orthodox Church. It was the first meeting between a Roman Catholic pope and an Orthodox patriarch since 1439.

1964 May 21 Meeting in Oklahoma City, Oklahoma, representatives of the **United Presbyterian Church** in the U.S.A. elected **Edler G. Hawkins** (b. June 13, 1908) moderator of the 176th General Assembly. He was the first black to hold this position.

1964 Sept. 14 The third session of **Vatican Council II** convened in Vatican City. It was agreed that the bishops of the church should join collectively with the pope in the governance of the church. The Virgin Mary was proclaimed the "Mother of the Church," and the ordination of married deacons of "mature age" was approved. This session adjourned on Nov. 21.

V. SCIENCE, EDUCATION, AND TECHNOLOGY

1964 Work was completed this year to restore **China's Grand Canal**, bringing the world's longest man-made waterway back into use over its full length. The Grand Canal, the oldest section of which is believed to have been built in the fourth century B.C., is now more than 1,000 miles long and connects Hangchow and Peking.

1964 Mar. 18 **Norbert Wiener** (b. Nov. 26, 1894), who studied control and communication mechanisms in people, died. He was known as the **father of automation**. Wiener's books included *Cybernetics* (1948) and *The Human Use of Human Beings* (1950).

1964 Apr. 17 **Jerrie Mock**, an American aviatrix, the **first woman to fly around the world alone**, completed her trip when she landed at Columbus, Ohio, in her single engine plane. She made 21 stops during the trip which began Mar. 19 and she flew 22,858.8 miles.

1964 Apr. 24 **Gerhard** [Johannes Paul] **Domagk** (b. Oct. 30, 1895), a German biochemist, died. His discovery of the bacterial action of sulfanilamide and related sulfa compounds was a major factor in the battle against infectious diseases. Domagk's work won him the **Nobel prize for physiology or medicine** in 1939, but the Nazi government forced him to decline the honor.

1964 May 30 **Leo Szilard** (b. Feb. 11, 1898), an American nuclear physicist born in Hungary, died. With **Enrico Fermi** he helped produce (1942) the first atomic chain reaction. Beginning in 1942 he and

Fermi had been in charge of the scientific work of the **Manhattan Project** that led to the first atomic bomb.

1964 Oct. 12–13 Three Russian cosmonauts became the first men to orbit the earth in a spacecraft carrying more than one person. They were **Vladimir M**[ikhaylovich] **Komarov** (Mar. 16, 1927–Apr. 24, 1967), **Konstantin P**[etrovich] **Feoktistov** (b. Feb. 7, 1926) and **Boris B**[orisovich] **Yegorov** (b. Nov. 26, 1937). They made 16 orbits in 24 hours, 17 minutes in *Voskhod 1*.

1964 Oct. 16 China tested its first nuclear bomb near Lake Lop Nor in Sinkiang province.

1964 Nov. 21 In New York City, the **Verrazano-Narrows Bridge** was opened, spanning the harbor between Staten Island and Brooklyn. It carried the name of **Giovanni da Verrazano**, an Italian explorer who was probably the first European to enter (1524) New York Harbor. The total length of the bridge was 6,690 feet with the main span being 4,260 feet. The bridge cost $325 million.

1964 Dec. 1 **J**[ohn] **B**[urdon] **S**[anderson] **Haldane** (b. Nov. 5, 1892), a Scottish geneticist and author, died. Beside charting the human chromosomes, he developed a simple treatment for tetanus and pioneered in high pressure oxygen surgery and therapy.

1964 Dec. 27 The UN **World Health Organization** [WHO] reported that **tuberculosis**, though it had declined worldwide in the 20th century, continued to be a serious health menace, especially where high population density coincided with poor public health standards and conditions.

VI. ARTS AND LEISURE

1964 Feb. 25 **Alexander P**[orfiryevich] **Archipenko** (b. May 30, 1887), an American sculptor born in Russia, died. He was a pioneer in **cubism** and in his sculptures used such materials as wood, paper, metal, and cement. Among his abstract shapes are *Woman with Child* (1909), *Boxing Match* (1913), and *The Gondoliers* (1914).

1964 Mar. 20 **Brendan Behan** (b. Feb. 9, 1923), an Irish author and playwright, died. Arrested in 1939 for his involvement with the **Irish Republican Army** [IRA], he served time in a reform school and wrote of his experience in *Borstal Boy* (1958). As a play-wright he used this episode and recollections of other jail terms he served to write *The Quare Fellow* (1956). *The Hostage* (1958) was another Behan play that showed his wit in the humorless setting of an Irish prison.

1964 Apr. 23   An exhibit and panorama marked the first celebration of the **400th anniversary of the birth of William Shakespeare**, at Stratford-on-Avon. Representatives of 113 nations took part.

1964 June 24   **Stuart Davis** (b. Dec. 7, 1894), an American artist, died. Although he was to some extent a cubist, he was also a member of the "ashcan" group of New York painters who portrayed lower class scenes. Davis's works included *House and Street* (1931), *Garage Lights* (1931), *Owh! in San Pao* (1951), and *Ready-to-Wear* (1955).

1964 July 1   **Pierre Monteux** (b. Apr. 4, 1875), a French-born conductor, died. During his career of half a century he led many of the world's best orchestras, beginning with the orchestra of the Ballets Russes in Paris (1911–1914). Monteux also conducted the Boston Symphony Orchestra (1919–1924), the San Francisco Symphony Orchestra (1936–1952), and the London Symphony Orchestra (1961–1964).

1964 Aug. 6   **Cedric** [Webster] **Hardwicke** (b. Feb. 19, 1894), a versatile English actor, died. He was especially noted for his roles in the plays of **George Bernard Shaw**. Hardwicke made his Broadway debut in 1936 in *Promises*. He appeared in many movies, such as *The Keys of the Kingdom* (1945).

1964 Sept. 18   **Sean O'Casey** [John Casey] (b. Mar. 30, 1880), an Irish playwright, died. He did much of his writing for the Abbey Theater of Dublin. O'Casey's first play was *The Shadow of a Gunman* (1923). His other works included *Juno and the Paycock* (1924) and *The Plough and the Stars* (1929). His plays usually dealt with Irish patriotism, which he thought had its dangers, and with the life of the lower classes.

1964 Oct. 15   **Cole** [Albert] **Porter** (b. June 9, 1891), a preeminent American composer and lyricist, died. He was noted for the wit of his lyrics and the sophistication of his music. Porter composed for such stage successes as *Fifty Million Frenchmen* (1929) and *Silk Stockings* (1955), as well as writing individual song hits such as "**Night and Day**" (1932) and "**You're the Top**" (1934).

1964 Oct. 25   **Robert Delauney** (b. Apr. 12, 1885), a French painter who founded **Orphism** by producing cubist paintings with brilliant colors, died. His work included *La Tour rouge* (1911) and *Une fenêtre* (1912).

1964 Dec. 9   **Edith** [Louisa] **Sitwell** (b. Sept. 7, 1897), an English poet, died. She was noted for poems that utilized the musical qualities of language often at the expense of meaning. Besides publishing a number of volumes of poetry, she attracted wide attention in 1923 with a public reading of her work *Façade*, composed of a series of her poems and set against a musical background. Her last volume of *Collected Works* appeared in 1957.

VII. SPORTS, GAMES, AND SOCIETY

1964   A new note in **fashion** that was eagerly accepted, especially by younger women, was struck by **Mary Quant** (b. Feb. 11, 1934), an English designer. Quant brought in the **miniskirt, hot pants, and vinyl boots**.

1964 Jan. 29–Feb. 9   The ninth Winter **Olympic Games** were held at Innsbruck, Austria, with 1,186 athletes from 36 nations participating. Soviet athletes won 11 gold medals and 25 in all; Austria 4 and 12; and Norway 3 and 15. The U.S. won only one gold medal.

1964 Feb. 25   The **world heavyweight boxing championship** was won by **Cassius Clay** (b. Jan. 17, 1942), who knocked out the defending titleholder [Charles] **Sonny Liston** (May 8, 1932–Jan. 5, 1971) in the seventh round at Miami, Florida. On the next day Clay announced he was becoming a Black Muslim and would change his name to **Muhammad Ali**, the name he fought under thereafter. Ali proved to be one of the greatest heavyweights of all time, holding the title without difficulty until June, 1967, when, on religious grounds, he refused to be inducted into the U.S. armed forces. He was stripped of his title, but on June 20, 1970, the Supreme Court overturned his conviction on technical grounds. Ali regained his title on Oct. 30, 1974, in Kinshasa, Zaire, when he knocked out **George Foreman** (b. Jan. 10, 1949).

1964 Apr. 22   The **New York World's Fair** opened with attendance for its two seasons projected as 70 million. However, when the fair closed its gates on

Oct. 18, 1965, only 51,607,037 admissions had been sold. The General Motors Futurama and Michelangelo's *Pieta*, loaned by the Vatican, were the most popular exhibits.

1964 July 14 Jacques Anquetil (1934–Nov. 18, 1987), a professional French road-race cyclist, won the **Tour de France** for the fifth time, a record, and the fourth year in succession.

1964 Sept. 2 America's doughboy hero of World War I, Sgt. **Alvin** [Cullum] **York** (b. Dec. 13, 1887), died. On Oct. 18, 1918, during the Meuse-Argonne offensive, he singlehandedly killed 25 German soldiers of a machine gun company, then went forward and captured 132. York was awarded the **Congressional Medal of Honor** and more than 50 other decorations from other nations.

1964 Sept. 15–21 The U.S. won the **America's Cup**, international yachting's prime trophy, the American boat *Constellation* defeating the British challenger *Sovereign* in four straight races off Newport, Rhode Island. This was the 19th consecutive successful defense of the cup by the U.S.

1964 Oct. 10–24 The 18th Summer **Olympic Games** were held in Tokyo, with 93 countries represented by 5,140 athletes. The U.S. won 36 gold medals and 90 in all; the USSR was second with 30 and 86; Japan third with 16 and 29.

1964 Oct. 29 In a daring **jewel robbery**, thieves stole part of a collection of rare gem stones from the American Museum of Natural History, New York City. Among the gems taken were the world's largest sapphire, the 565-carat **Star of India**, and the 100-carat **DeLong ruby**. A tip led to the arrest of three men. Their leader was **Jack R. "Murf the Surf" Murphy** (b. May 26, 1937), a professional swimmer.

1965

I. DISASTERS

1965 Mar. 28 An **earthquake** in central Chile broke a 230-foot dam. The released water rushed onto the village of El Gobre in a valley, killing more than 400 people.

1965 Apr. 11 Illinois, Indiana, Iowa, Michigan, and Ohio were pounded by 37 separate **tornadoes**. About 270 persons were killed and c.5,000 injured. Property damage was estimated at $250 million.

1965 May 11–12 Along the southern coast of East Pakistan [present Bangladesh], a **cyclone** and tidal waves left c.17,000 persons dead, c.600,000 injured, and as many as 5 million homeless. Then a second strong windstorm (June 1–2) killed c.30,000. A third cyclone (Dec. 15) struck much the same region, leaving about another 10,000 dead or missing.

1965 May 20 On its approach to the Cairo airport, a Pakistan Airlines **Boeing 720-B**, flying the Karachi to London route, **crashed** and killed 121 of the 127 persons on board.

1965 May 23 At Zomba, Malawi, a **ferryboat capsized** when a cable guiding it broke. More than 200 people were thrown into the crocodile-infested Shire River, and c.150 persons died.

1965 May 28 An **explosion** in the Dhori Colliery near Dhanbad, in northeastern India, burned out the mine and buildings above ground. At least 400 miners were trapped and killed.

1965 Aug. 9 An **explosion and fire in a Titan II missile silo** in Searcy, Arkansas, trapped and killed 53 civilian workers.

1965 Nov. 9–10 The **most extensive power failure in history** struck much of the northeastern U.S. and Ontario, Canada, over an area of c.80,000 square miles, inhabited by c.30,000,000 people. In **New York City** the **blackout** lasted 13.5 hours. The failure was attributed to a malfunctioning relay device near Niagara Falls.

1965 Nov. 13 A fire on the cruise ship *Yarmouth Castle*, enroute from Miami to Nassau in the Bahamas, caused the ship to sink. Of its 550 passengers, 90 died and many others suffered burns.

1965 Dec. 6 In Togo, in West Africa, **two trucks** went out of control and **crashed** into a crowd during a festival in Sotouboua, killing 125 or more people.

II. POLITICS AND WAR

1965 Jan. 7 **Abubakar Tafawa Balewa** became prime minister of **Nigeria** following an election held on Dec. 30, 1964. Many voters in the south boycotted the election, and there were charges of fraud.

1965 Jan. 20 **Lyndon B. Johnson** was inaugurated as president of the U.S. In the election of Nov. 3, 1964, Johnson, the Democratic party candidate, defeated the Republican party candidate **Barry [Morris] Goldwater** (b. Jan. 1, 1909). Johnson received 43,126,506 popular votes and 486 electoral college votes to 27,176,799 and 52 for Goldwater. **Hubert H[oratio] Humphrey** (May 27, 1911–Jan. 13, 1978) became vice president.

1965 Jan. 21 **Hassan Ali Mansur** (b. 1923), premier of **Iran**, was assassinated by fundamentalist Muslim extremists, and in this same month an unsuccessful attempt was made on the life of the shah. Mansur was succeeded (Jan. 27) by **Amir Abbas Hoveida** (Feb. 18, 1919–Apr. 7, 1979).

1965 Jan. 24 **Winston [Leonard Spencer] Churchill** (b. Nov. 30, 1874), the leader who kept Great Britain fighting against Nazi Germany in the darkest days of World War II, died. A journalist who covered several wars, Churchill was elected to Parliament in 1900 and was first lord of the admiralty during part of World War I and again at the start of the second World War in 1939. He became prime minister in May 1940, when the Nazi invasion of Western Europe caused the Chamberlain government to resign. Churchill was equally noted as an author of historical and biographical works. His major works were *The Second World War* (1948–1953) and *A History of the English-speaking Peoples* (1956–1958). He was without parallel as an orator with a gift for memorable phrases. When invasion by Nazi Germany seemed imminent, he concluded his rallying speech: "We shall fight on the beaches, we shall fight on the landing grounds, we shall fight in the fields and in the streets, we shall fight in the hills, we shall never surrender."

1965 Jan. 28 **Maxime Weygand** (b. Jan. 21, 1867), a French general in both World Wars, died. It was he who accepted the surrender of the Germany army on Nov. 18, 1918, but who, recalled to service in World War II, was forced to surrender the French army to the Germans in June 1940. After the war Weygand was charged (1945) with collaborating with the enemy, but his poor health delayed his trial and he was officially rehabilitated in 1948.

1965 Feb. 7 A step in the escalation of the **Vietnam War** began with the **first major air raid by American bombers** on North Vietnamese targets, among them the Don Hoi base. By early March raids were an almost daily occurrence. In the meantime the **first U.S. combat troops**—c.3,500 marines—arrived (Mar. 8–9), augmenting the 23,500 American advisers already in South Vietnam. **Lyndon B. Johnson,** president of the U.S., announced (July 28) that American troop strength would be increased to 125,-000 and that the draft would be doubled to 35,000 per month. The first major battle involving U.S. forces took place (Aug. 19) when a Viet Cong stronghold in South Vietnam was destroyed.The **first large anti-war demonstration** occurred Nov. 17, when an estimated 15,000 to 25,000 people gathered in Washington, D.C.

1965 Feb. 16 An election in **Honduras** for a constituent assembly resulted in a victory for the National party, which won 55 of the 64 seats at stake. The assembly elected (March) **Osvaldo Lopez Arellano** as president.

1965 Feb. 18 **Gambia**, in West Africa, became independent within the Commonwealth of Nations. It was a parliamentary state with **Dawda Kairaba Jawara** (b. May 16, 1924), leader of the People's Progressive party, as the first prime minister (June 12).

1965 Mar. 19 **Gheorghe Gheorghiu-Dej** (b. Nov. 8, 1901), president of **Romania** (from 1961), died. A communist from youth he was active, with Stalin's help, in establishing a communist government in Romania after World War II (1939–1945). Gheorghiu was prime minister (1952–1955) and became president of the State Council in 1961. He was succeeded as head of the Communist party (Mar. 23) by **Nicolae Ceausescu**.

1965 Apr.–Sept. **India and Pakistan** fought an off-and-on **border war** over territory in dispute between them since independence (1947). Fighting first broke out (April) in the Rann of Kutch, Gujarat in western India. A cease-fire was agreed to (June 30), but Pakistan renewed (Aug. 14) the fighting. Pakistan launched (Sept. 1) a large contingent of armored forces into the Jammu and Kashmir regions in the far north of both countries, and India countered (Sept.

6) with an invasion of Pakistan. The UN arranged (Sept. 22) another ceasefire, and the two nations agreed to meet to try to resolve their territorial differences.

1965 Apr. 24   A revolt against the government of **Donald Reid Cabral** of the **Dominican Republic** was begun by followers of the former president Juan Bosch. The government fell the next day, but civil war broke out between the two factions. On the grounds that American lives were in danger, **Lyndon B. Johnson**, president of the U.S., ordered (Apr. 28) c.400 **marines** to the troubled land. Eventually this force grew to c.20,000. The **Organization of American States** [OAS] called (May 6) for a ceasefire and an inter-American peacekeeping force, which gradually replaced the U.S. troops. On Sept. 3 an uneasy peace was agreed to, and **Hector Gaceres Garcia-Godoy** (Jan. 11, 1921–Apr. 20, 1970) was accepted as provisional president. The OAS supervised a presidential election (June 1, 1966) in which the rightist candidate **Joaquín Balaguer** defeated Bosch.

1965 May 14   **Elizabeth II**, queen of Great Britain, in a ceremony at Runnymede, west of London, where King John signed the Magna Carta in 1215, bequeathed three acres to the people of the U.S. as a **memorial to John F. Kennedy**.

1965 June 10   A bloodless coup overthrew **Ahmed Ben Bella**, president of **Algeria**. The coup was led by the vice president and minister of defense **Houari Boumedienne** (Aug. 23, 1932–Dec. 27, 1978), who disliked the declining influence of the army and was concerned about internal economic problems. Boumedienne suspended the constitution, but said that the former socialist policies would be continued.

1965 June 19   After eight changes of government in **South Vietnam** since the overthrow of Diem (Nov. 1, 1963), a military junta took control of the government with **Nguyen Van Thieu** (b. Apr. 5, 1923), a general, as chief of state, and **Nguyen Cao Ky** (b. Sept. 9, 1930), another general, as prime minister. This regime was able to crush a **Buddhist revolt** that had been battling the government.

1965 June 22   A **peace treaty** signed in Tokyo **between Japan and South Korea** normalized relations between the two countries for the first time since Japan annexed Korea in 1910. Despite much opposition to the treaty in Korea, on Aug. 14 the National Assembly ratified the pact.

1965 July 19   **Syngman Rhee** (b. Apr. 16, 1875), the first president of the **Republic of Korea** (1948–1960), died. He began (1911) his lifelong fight for Korean independence after Korea's annexation (1910) by Japan, and organized (1919) guerrilla operations against the Japanese. As president Rhee assumed dictatorial powers, but strong opposition forced him to flee (May 29, 1960) to Hawaii.

1965 July 26   The **Maldive Islands**, a British protectorate in the Indian Ocean, southwest of Sri Lanka, gained independence as **The Maldives**, a sultanate. The ruler was **Amir Muhammad Farid Didi**, who was elected sultan for life.

1965 Aug. 9   **Singapore** seceded from the **Malaysian federation** and became an independent nation with **Lee Kuan Yew** (b. Sept. 16, 1923) as prime minister. Singapore joined (1965) the Commonwealth of Nations and pressed a policy of industrialization and foreign trade.

1965 Aug. 15   **Pakistani army units invaded part of Kashmir** claimed by India in an escalation of guerrilla fighting in the region. Pakistan launched a major tank attack on Sept. 1 which was countered by India on Sept. 7, resulting in what became the heaviest tank battle since World War II. The **United Nations** secured agreement to a ceasefire on Sept. 22.

1965 Sept. 28   **Fidel Castro**, premier of Cuba, announced that any **Cubans who wished to leave the country could do so**. An exodus began, and **Lyndon B. Johnson** said (Oct. 3) the refugees would be welcome. The U.S. and Cuba agreed (Nov. 6) on an orderly flow of 3,000 to 4,000 persons a month by airlift.

1965 Sept. 30   In **Indonesia** an abortive **coup by communist forces** was easily defeated by the army under **Suharto** (b. June 8, 1921). As a result Suharto gradually assumed power from **Sukarno** (June 1, 1901–June 21, 1970), the president, leaving the latter a figurehead. Masses of people took the law into their own hands against the communists and Chinese residents, and in the last quarter of 1965 as many as 750,000 people were thought to have been killed.

1965 Nov. 11   **Ian Smith**, the prime minister of **Southern Rhodesia** [present Zimbabwe], a British colony, declared that country independent. A referendum in May had supported the dominant white

Rhodesian Front party, whose white supremacist members had forced (Apr. 13, 1964) **Winston Field** (June 6, 1904–Mar. 17, 1969), the previous prime minister from office.

1965 Nov. 25 In the Democratic **Republic of the Congo** [present Zaire], **Seso Seke Mobutu**, head of the army, deposed **Joseph Kasavubu**, president, in a power struggle that had been going on in the country since independence in 1960. Kasavubu fled and Mobutu named himself president.

1965 Dec. 30 Ferdinand E[dralin] **Marcos** was inaugurated as president of the **Philippines**. He was the candidate of the National party and defeated Diosdada Macapagal of the Liberal party for reelection by c.650,000 votes.

III. ECONOMY AND TRADE

1965 Mar. The stock of the **General Aniline and Film Corporation**, 93.5 percent of which had been seized during World War II by the U.S. government as suspected German assets, was sold to the highest bidder among American underwriting houses. The government received $189,200,000 for the **War Claims Fund**, and $17,500,000 as back taxes.

1965 Mar. 4 **Lyndon B. Johnson**, president of the U.S., asked Congress to free the **Federal Reserve** from a requirement that it have 25 percent of gold against its deposit liabilities. Congress complied, and the action freed $5,000,000,000 of gold.

1965 June 20 **Bernard** [Mannes] **Baruch** (b. Aug. 19, 1870), an American statesman and businessman, died. An adviser to presidents, he was chairman of the War Industries Board during World War I and economic adviser to the American delegation to the Paris Peace Conference in 1919. Named as U.S. representative on the United Nations Atomic Energy Commission in 1946, he proposed the Baruch Plan for the international control of nuclear energy, but it was vetoed by the U.S.S.R.

1965 July 29 **France and Algeria reached an agreement concerning oil**. To avoid nationalization of its oil properties, France agreed to a $400 million aid program, mostly in the form of loans. The 15-year agreement would mean higher taxes on the oil and would raise Algeria's oil revenue from $80 million to an expected $240 million by 1970.

IV. RELIGION AND PHILOSOPHY

1965 June 13 **Martin Buber** (b. Feb. 8, 1878), a German Jewish philosopher and writer, died. He had considerable influence on both Christian and Jewish thought. His many books included *Ich und Du* [*I and Thou*] (1923) and *Moses* (1945). He was concerned that man's relation with God, nature, and other men be direct, not impersonal.

1965 Sept. 4 **Albert Schweitzer** (b. Jan. 14, 1875), a French philosopher, musician, theologian, and physician, died. He founded (1913) a mission hospital at Lambaréné, French Equatorial Africa [in present Gabon], where he cared for the impoverished people of the region. Schweitzer published a biography of Johann Sebastian Bach and with a collaborator edited Bach's music for the organ. Among other books, Schweitzer wrote *The Quest of the Historical Jesus* (1906) and his autobiography, *Out of My Life and Thoughts* (1932). He received the **Nobel Peace Prize** in 1952.

1965 Sept. 14 The fourth and final session of **Vatican Council II** convened in Vatican City, where it adopted a number of decrees concerning the governance and organization of the Roman Catholic Church. Racial discrimination, especially anti-Semitism, was condemned, and Jews were relieved of collective responsibility for the death of Christ. The right to religious liberty and freedom of conscience was recognized. Its final adjournment came on Dec. 8.

1965 Oct. 22 **Paul** [Johannes] **Tillich** (b. Aug. 20, 1886), a German-born American theologian, died. After teaching in Germany, he came to the U.S. in 1933, forced out by the Nazis. Tillich taught at Union Theological Seminary, New York City (1933–1955), at Harvard University (1955–1962), and the University of Chicago (1962–1965). In his theology he worked into Christian doctrine elements of depth psychology and existentialism. Tillich's most important writing was *Systemic Theology* (3 vol., 1951–1953). In a more popular vein he wrote *The Courage to Be* (1952) and *The New Being* (1955).

V. SCIENCE, EDUCATION, AND TECHNOLOGY

1965 Feb. 13 The U.S. Congress passed a law requiring that beginning on Jan. 1, 1966, a health **warning be printed on all cigarette packages**. In Jan.,

1964, the surgeon general had issued a report, *Smoking and Health*, which said that cigarettes created "a health hazard of sufficient importance in the U.S. to warrant appropriate remedial action."

1965 Mar. 18　A Russian cosmonaut, **Alexei Arkhipovich Leonov** (b. May 30, 1934), became the **first man to float in space** when he left *Voskhod 2*. Attached to a 16.5-foot lifeline, he floated for ten minutes.

1965 Apr. 6　The world's **first commercial communications satellite** was launched by the U.S. Called **Early Bird**, it was the property of the Communications Satellite Corporation, a government-sponsored operation. It began service on June 28, transmitting telephone messages, television programs, and other communications.

1965 June 3–7　During the flight of the *Gemini-Titan 4* spacecraft, **Edward H[iggins] White, 2nd,** (Nov. 14, 1930–Jan. 27, 1967) became the **first American to walk in space**. He was outside the craft for 20 minutes, attached to a 23.3-foot tether. White propelled himself with a handgun operated by compressed oxygen.

1965 July 14　**Photographs of the planet Mars** were sent back to earth by the U.S. spacecraft *Mariner 4*, which had been launched on Nov. 28, 1964.

1965 July 30　**Lyndon B. Johnson**, president of the U.S., signed into law an act to establish two national health insurance programs, called **Medicare** and **Medicaid**. The former program provided for most people more than 65 years of age hospital care, and, by deductions from Social Security payments, medical care. Medicaid was a program of health care for low income persons, the blind, disabled, pregnant women, and dependent children. It was financed jointly by the federal government and the states.

1965 Aug. 27　**Charles Edouard Jeanneret** (b. Oct. 6, 1887), known as **Le Corbusier**, a Swiss architect and city planner who worked all over the world, died. Among his notable buildings were the **Ministry of Education** (1936) in Rio de Janeiro, and the Visual Arts Center at Harvard University (1963).

1965 Sept. 9　**Herman Staudinger** (b. Mar. 23, 1881), a German chemist, died. His work on theories of molecular organization was the basis for the development of modern synthetic fibers and plastics. Staudinger was awarded the **Nobel prize for chemistry** in 1953.

VI. ARTS AND LEISURE

1965 Jan. 4　T[homas] S[tearns] **Eliot** (b. Sept. 26, 1888), one of the most influential of 20th-century poets writing in English, died. Born in the U.S., he moved (1914) to England and became (1927) a British subject. Eliot was a leader among those who developed a new literature after World War I, epitomized by *The Love Song of J. Alfred Prufrock* (1915), in which the spiritual decay of society was made manifest. *The Waste Land* (1922) was an even stronger expression of Eliot's view of the world as sterile. Eliot also wrote verse dramas, two of them being *Murder in the Cathedral* (1935), about the murder of Thomas à Becket, and *The Cocktail Party* (1949), a drawing room comedy with religious reflections on redemption. Eliot was awarded the **Nobel prize for literature** in 1948.

1965 Feb. 23　**Stan Laurel** [Arthur Stanley Jefferson] (b. June 16, 1890), a movie comedian, died. Teaming (1926) with **Ollie Hardy** [Oliver Newell Hardy] (Jan. 18, 1892–Aug. 7, 1957), he was the well-meaning but bumbling character while Hardy was the pompous know-it-all. Together they appeared in c.200 slapstick movies.

1965 Apr. 27　**Edward R[oscoe] Murrow** (b. Apr. 25, 1908), an American journalist and pioneer in radio and television newscasting, died. He first came (1941) to wide public attention with his live radio broadcasts from London during the blitz of World War II. He developed "See It Now," the first television documentary series of importance, which began on Nov. 18, 1951. Murrow was one of the few media figures who dared attack **Joseph McCarthy**, senator from Wisconsin, during his communist witch hunt in the mid-1950s.

1965 Dec. 16　W[illiam] **Somerset Maugham** (b. Jan. 24, 1874), an English novelist, short-story writer, and playwright, died. His novels included *Of Human Bondage* (1915), *The Moon and Sixpence* (1919), *Cakes and Ale* (1930), and *The Razor's Edge* (1944). Maugham was a master of the short story, his most memorable story being "Rain" (1921), about the downfall of a missionary on a tropical island.

VII. SPORTS, GAMES, AND SOCIETY

1965 Mar. 16 **Amos Alonzo Stagg** (b. Aug. 16, 1862), the "grand old man" of American **football**, died. At Yale he was chosen (1889) for the first All-American college team. Stagg coached successfully at the University of Chicago (1892–1932) and did not give up coaching entirely until he was 98. His final record stood at 309 victories, 200 loses, and 35 ties.

1965 Apr. 1 **Helena Rubinstein** [Princess Gourielli] (b. 1871), the creator of a **cosmetics business empire**, died. She opened (1902) her first salon in France and later (1915) came to New York City.

1965 Apr. 9 The **Astrodome**, the largest indoor arena in the world, opened in Houston, Texas. Costing $20.5 million, it covered nine and a half acres, had an inside diameter of 642 feet, and a height of 208 feet.

1965 Oct. 28 **Gateway Arch**, a stainless steel structure 630 feet high, standing on the banks of the Mississippi River at St. Louis, Missouri, was completed. It was erected to symbolize the city as the gateway to the West in the 19th century. Gateway Arch was designed by the architect **Eero Saarinen**.

1966

I. VITAL STATISTICS AND DEMOGRAPHICS

1966 The **five largest cities** and their estimated populations were **Tokyo**, 8,907,000; **New York City**, 7,960,000; **Shanghai**, 6,977,000; **Moscow**, 6,464,000; and **São Paulo**, 5,000,000.

II. DISASTERS

1966 Jan. 24 An Air India **Boeing 707 jet passenger plane flew into Mont Blanc**, France, killing all 117 persons aboard.

1966 Jan. 29–31 A **blizzard** struck the eastern coast of the U.S. from North Carolina to New England, causing 165 deaths.

1966 Feb. 4 An All-Nippon **Boeing 727**, arriving at Tokyo, **plunged into Tokyo Bay**, killing all 133 aboard.

1966 Mar. 5 Taking off from Tokyo for London, a BOAC **Boeing 707 caught fire and crashed** into **Mt. Fuji**, Honshu Island, Japan, killing 124 persons.

1966 Aug. 19–20 Turkey's eastern provinces were struck by an **earthquake** that destroyed 139 villages. The death toll was 2,394 and 1,494 were injured. The quake registered 6.9 on the Richter scale.

1966 Sept. 24–30 Hurricane **Inez** caused 293 deaths in the Dominican Republic, Haiti, Cuba, the Bahamas, and southern Florida. It hit Cuba twice before it ended with torrents of rain in the Tampico, Mexico, area.

1966 Oct. 21 At **Aberfan, Wales**, an **avalanche of coal, mud, rocks, and waste** from mining operations killed 144 persons, including 116 children in a schoolhouse.

1966 Nov. 4 A 30-hour rainfall in much of northern Italy did great **damage to art treasures in Florence and Venice**. About 113 lives were lost. In Florence the bronze main door of the cathedral was swept away, and thousands of books in the National Library were waterlogged. In the Strozzi Palace antique furniture, along with records 400 years old, was destroyed. More than 100,000 negatives of works of art in the basement of the Uffizi Gallery were lost.

1966 Dec. 8 Heavy seas in the Aegean Sea tore the Greek ferryship **Heraklion** apart after a 16-ton trailer it was carrying broke loose from its fastenings. At least 264 died and c.47 persons survived.

III. POLITICS AND WAR

1966 Jan. 10 Meeting in Tashkent, U.S.S.R., with Soviet officials as mediators, Pakistan and India reached an agreement that improved relations between the two countries following the Sept., 1965, **ceasefire in their border war over the Kashmir**.

1966 Jan. 12   American bombing raids on North Vietnam were resumed (Jan. 31) after a 37-day lull. American air raids grew heavier during the year: on May 30 and 31 as many as 300 planes were in action and on June 29 the U.S. for the first time bombed areas near the two major cities of Hanoi and Haiphong. A new tactic was tried beginning on Sept. 23 when planes dropped defoliating chemicals to attempt to reveal Viet Cong supply trails. This chemical became known as **Agent Orange**.

1966 Jan. 15   A junta of army officers of the Ibo ethnic group overthrew the government in Lagos, the capital of **Nigeria**, killing the federal premier **Abubakar Tafawa Balewa** (b. Dec. 12, 1912) and two regional premiers. The coup was led by **Johnson Aguiyi-Ironsi**. The reaction against the changes made by the junta resulted in another coup on July 29. It was led by army officers of the Hausa group, and Johnson T[homas] U[mananke] Aguiyi-Ironsi (b. Mar. 3, 1924) was killed soon after July 29. **Yakubu Gowon** (b. Oct. 19, 1934) became the head of government.

1966 Jan. 17   Four U.S. hydrogen bombs fell from a B-52 bomber when it collided with a refueling plane over Spain. They did not explode.

1966 Jan. 24   Lal Bahadur Shastri (b. Oct. 2, 1904), prime minister of **India**, having died on Jan. 11, after concluding a treaty with Pakistan. **Indira** [Priyaharshini Nehru] **Gandhi** (Nov. 19, 1917–Oct. 31, 1984) was chosen to succeed him.

1966 Jan. 25   Harold Holt (Aug. 5, 1908–Dec. 17, 1967) succeeded **Robert** [Gordon] **Menzies** (Dec. 20, 1894–May 5, 1978) as prime minister of **Australia**.

1966 Feb. 23   A military coup by the extremist wing of the **Ba'ath party in Syria** toppled the government of Amin al-Hafez. The coup was led by **Salah al-Jadid** and **Nereddin al-Attassi**, with the latter becoming head of state.

1966 Feb. 24   A coup led by **Joseph A**[rthur] **Ankrah** (b. Aug. 18, 1915) overthrew **Kwame Nkrumah**, president of **Ghana**. The coup was welcomed at home and abroad.

1966 Mar. 7   Charles de Gaulle, president of France, announced that his nation would withdraw from the military arrangements of the **North Atlantic Treaty Organization** [NATO]. No NATO bases would be allowed on French territory, the French forces in Germany would no longer be under Allied control, and all foreign military units would have to leave France by Apr. 1, 1967.

1966 Mar. 28   Mortally ill, **Cemal Gursel**, president of **Turkey**, was declared unable to hold office, and the national assembly elected **Cevdet Sunay** (Feb. 10, 1900–May 22, 1980), chief of staff of the armed forces, to succeed him.

1966 Mar. 31   In a general election in **Great Britain**, the Labour party increased its margin of three seats in the House of Commons to 97 in a major defeat for the Conservative party. The government of **Harold Wilson**, who continued as prime minister, had announced its intention to nationalize the steel industry.

1966 May 26   British Guiana became the independent nation of **Guyana** and a member of the Commonwealth of Nations. The first prime minister was [Lindon] **Forbes** [Sampson] **Burnham** of the People's National Congress.

1966 June 6   James [Howard] **Meredith** (b. June 25, 1933), the first black student at the University of Mississippi, at Oxford, was **shot in the back while on a civil rights march** in Mississippi. On June 25, recovered from his wounds, Meredith rejoined the march.

1966 June 13   The U.S. Supreme Court by a 5–4 vote in **Miranda v. Arizona** ruled that under the Fifth Amendment a criminal suspect must be informed of the **right to remain silent and to have counsel** before being questioned by law enforcement officers.

1966 June 28   A bloodless coup military removed **Arturo Illia**, president of **Argentina**, because he was considered too tolerant of the radical Peronist party. On June 30 the presidency was assumed by **Juan Carlos Ongania** (b. Mar. 17, 1914), a right wing enemy of Illia.

1966 July 8   Mwembutsa IV, king of **Burundi**, was deposed by his son **Charles Ndizeye** (b. Dec. 2, 1947) who became **Ntare V**. However, on Nov. 28, Ntare was overthrown by a military coup, which established a republic with **Michel Micombero** (1940–July 16, 1981) as president.

1966 Aug. 5   Mao Tse-Tung announced the beginning of the **Cultural Revolution**, intended, he said, to restore China's revolutionary ardor. The movement was to wipe out all remnants of "capitalism, feudalism, and revisionism." The Revolution was led by the **Red Guards**, mostly teenagers, who attacked anyone or any institution they thought bourgeois.

1966 Aug. 11   Indonesia and Malaysia agreed to end their three-year war and resume diplomatic relations. The war cost Malaysia 295 military and civilian casualties and Indonesia 1,583.

1966 Sept. 6   Hendrik F[rensch] **Verwoerd** (b. Sept. 8, 1901), the prime minister of **South Africa**, was stabbed to death at his desk in parliament by a messenger. He was succeeded by the minister of justice, **Balthazar J**[ohannes] **Vorster** (Dec. 13, 1925–Sept. 10, 1983). Verwoerd's assailant, found mentally deranged, was committed to indefinite detention.

1966 Sept. 21   Paul Reynaud (b. Oct. 15, 1878), a French statesman, died. He was prime minister from March to June, 1940, when the Nazi army was overrunning France. Reynaud was interned by the Vichy government, and the Germans jailed him from 1942 until 1945.

1966 Sept. 30   Botswana, formerly Bechuanaland, became an independent nation, within the Commonwealth of Nations. The first president of the new republic was **Seretse M. Khama** (July 1, 1921–July 13, 1980).

1966 Oct.   The National Organization for Women [NOW] was formed in the U.S. by a group of leaders of the women's liberation movement. Its manifesto declared that it would "confront with concrete action the conditions which now prevent women from enjoying equality of opportunity and freedom of choice which is their right as individual Americans and as human beings."

1966 Oct. 1   Two high-ranking officials of Nazi Germany, who had been convicted (1946) as war criminals, were released from Spandau War Crimes Prison in Berlin after serving their 20-year sentences. **Albert Speer** had been in charge of all war production, and **Baldur von Schirach** (May 9, 1907–Aug. 8, 1974) had been gauleiter of Austria.

1966 Oct. 4   Basutoland became the independent nation of Lesotho and a member of the Common-wealth of Nations. The heads of the government were King **Mosheshoe II** (b. 1933?) and **Leabua Jonathan** (Oct. 30, 1914–Apr. 5, 1987), prime minister.

1966 Oct. 27   In **West Germany** the government of **Ludwig Erhard** fell when the Free Democratic party withdrew from its coalition with the Social Democrats. **Kurt** [Georg] **Kiesinger** (Apr. 6, 1904–Mar. 9, 1988) was elected chancellor by the Bundestag. He formed a coalition (to 1969) of his Christian Democratic party, the Social Democratic party, and the Christian Social Union.

1966 Nov. 30   Barbados became an independent country, within the Commonwealth of Nations, with a parliamentary form of government. The first prime minister was **Errol W**[alton] **Barrow** (Jan. 21, 1920–June 1, 1987), of the Democratic Labour party.

1966 Dec. 13   Stanislaw Mikolajcyk (b. July 18, 1901), a Polish statesman, died. He was prime minister of the Polish government in exile in London (1943–1944). Returning to Poland after the war, he joined the provisional government as a deputy prime minister. Warned that he was to be arrested for spying for America, Mikolajcyk fled to England and then to the U.S., where he remained.

IV. ECONOMY AND TRADE

1966   Wassily Leontief (b. Aug. 5, 1906), a Russian-born American economist, published ***Input-Output Economics***, in which he presented a new method of economic analysis based on preparing a table showing what all companies in a given country buy from and sell to each other. When the equivalent figures for government, consumers, and trade with foreign nations were added, the size and growth of the economy would be revealed. This method is widely used by governments for economic planning. Leontief was awarded the **Nobel prize for economics** in 1973.

V. RELIGION AND PHILOSOPHY

1966   The **International Society for Krishna Consciousness**, organized in Calcutta, India, in 1958 by A[bhay] C[haranaravinda] **Bhaktivedanta Prabhupada** (Sept. 1, 1896–Nov. 14, 1977), was brought to the U.S. and Canada and spread to Europe also. Better known as the Hare Krishna movement, it attracted a large number of young people who wore orange robes, lived communal lives, and marched around the streets chanting a Mantra. They also proselytized and begged.

1966 The **Maharishi Mahesh Yogi** (b. 1911), a Hindu monk, created the **Student's International Meditation Society** and attracted a considerable following, especially in the U.S. He taught **Transcendental Meditation** [TM], a process by which a believer was said to reach a state of pure consciousness, in which the mind would be unaware of anything in particular.

1966 Feb. 8 **Pope Paul VI** reorganized the Holy Office as the Congregation for the Doctrine of the Faith to establish a more open era in doctrinal discipline. In addition, the action marked the end of some inquisitional procedures, called for more consultation of local bishops, and abolished the office that condemned books.

1966 Apr. 6 [Heinrich] **Emil Brunner** (b. Dec. 23, 1889), a Swiss theologian, died. He was a leading figure in the movement toward Neo-Orthodoxy, a revolution in Protestant thought after World War II. Brunner maintained that the basis of faith was the encounter between man and God as revealed in the Bible. Among his important writings was *The Divine Imperative* (1932).

1966 Nov. 11 The Methodist Church and the Evangelical United Brethren Church agreed to merge, effective April 23, 1968, as the **United Methodist Church**. The new organization would the second largest Protestant denomination in the U.S.

VI. SCIENCE, EDUCATION, AND TECHNOLOGY

1966 The year was notable for **five "firsts"** in the exploration of space. On Feb. 3 the U.S.S.R. *Luna 9* made the **first successful soft landing of a manmade craft on the moon.** It sent back to earth photographs of the moon's surface. On June 2 the U.S. *Surveyor 1* landed on the lunar surface. By July 14, when its batteries went dead, it had sent back more than 11,000 photos. On Mar. 1 the U.S.S.R. *Venus 3*, launched on Nov. 16, 1965, crash landed on Venus. As far as was known, it was unable to send back any data. On Mar. 16 **David** [Randolph] **Scott** (b. June 6, 1932) and **Neil** [Alden] **Armstrong** (b. Aug. 5, 1930) guided *Gemini 8* to a connection with an Agena target vehicle after a six-and-a-half-hour chase. When a thrust rocket on the *Gemini* malfunctioned, causing a violent tumbling in space, the mission had to be aborted. On Apr. 3 the U.S.S.R. *Luna 10* became the **first manmade object to orbit the moon.**

1966 Two books published this year increased interest in **ethology. Konrad** [Zacharias] **Lorenz** (Nov. 7, 1903–Feb. 27, 1989), an Austrian zoologist and ethologist, published *On Aggression*, in German *Das sagenannte Böse* (1963). Lorenz asserted that aggressive behavior in man was innate but could be altered by social controls. Lorenz shared the **Nobel prize for physiology or medicine** in 1973. The other book was *The Territorial Imperative* by **Robert Ardrey** (Oct. 16, 1908–Jan. 14, 1980), an American playwright and author. He too contended that man was innately aggressive and that this trait could be suppressed only by society.

1966 Aug. 8 The **first successful artificial heart pump** was installed in a patient at Methodist Hospital in Houston, Texas. The operation was performed by a team headed by heart surgeon **Michael Ellis DeBakey** (b. Sept. 7, 1908). The pump was about the size of a grapefruit and was attached to the patient's chest. The patient was able to return home within a month.

1966 Sept. 6 A pioneer of planned parenthood, **Margaret** [Louise] **Sanger** [nee Higgins] (b. Sept. 14, 1883), died. She first used the term "birth control" in 1914 in a magazine she published. Sanger once served 30 days in jail for distributing literature about birth control. She founded (1921) the **American Birth Control League**, which became (1946) the **Planned Parenthood Federation**.

1966 Nov. 2 **Peter Joseph William Debye** (b. Mar. 24, 1884), a Dutch-American physicist, died. He was awarded the **Nobel prize for chemistry** in 1936 for his work on the structure of molecules. Debye also did important work in the conductivity of electricity in salt solutions.

VII. ARTS AND LEISURE

1966 Jan. 11 **Alberto Giacometti** (b. Oct. 10, 1901), a Swiss sculptor, died. He is known for his elongated human figures. Among Giacometti's well-known works are *City Square* (1948), *The Chariot* (1950), and *Caroline* (1961).

1966 Feb. 1   The comedian [Joseph Francis] **Buster Keaton** (b. Oct. 4, 1895), died. In 1917 he appeared in *The Butcher Boy*, beginning a career from which he never fully retired. He was the perfect deadpan, portraying the little man who battled oppressive odds.

1966 Feb. 17   **Hans Hofmann** (b. Mar. 21, 1880), a German-born painter who emigrated to the U.S. in 1930, died. By his painting and teaching he greatly influenced the development of abstract expressionism. Hofmann's paintings featured strong, sometimes clashing colors. Among them were *Germania* and *Elegy*. *Spring* (1940), one of the earliest paintings to use the dripping technique.

1966 Mar. 5   **Anna Akmatova** [Anna Andreyevna Gorenko] (b. June 23, 1882), a Russian poet, died. Her poetry was personal and emotional, sometimes ironic. Silent a good deal of the time because of government oppression, Akmatova was expelled (1946) from the Union of Soviet Writers for "bourgeois decadence." Poems of Akmatova appeared in English translation in 1973.

1966 Apr. 10   **Evelyn** [Arthur St. John] **Waugh** (b. Oct. 28, 1903), an English satirical novelist, died. His early works satirized the life style of the 1920s, as in *Decline and Fall* (1928) and *Vile Bodies* (1930). Other Waugh novels that combined the comic spirit with social satire were *Black Mischief* (1932) and *A Handful of Dust* (1934). *Brideshead Revisited* (1945) recounted the moral problems of an aristocratic English Roman Catholic family. It was made into a successful television series in 1980.

1966 June 7   **Jean or Hans Arp** (b. Sept. 16, 1887), a French sculptor, died. He was connected with the surrealists and the dadaists. In the 1930s he produced sculptures that hinted at organic forms without quite bringing them into actuality. Among Arp's significant works were a very large wood relief carving at Harvard University, Cambridge, Massachusetts (1950), a monumental sculpture for the University of Caracas, Venezuela, (1953), and a relief for the UNESCO building, Paris (1958).

1966 July 3   [Joseph] **Deems Taylor** (b. Dec. 22, 1885), an American composer and music critic, died. An orchestral suite *Through the Looking Glass* (1919) was his first important composition. Among his 50 or more works were two operas, *The King's Henchman* (1927) and *Peter Ibbetson* (1931). Taylor wrote *The Well-Tempered Listener* (1940) and did radio commentaries on music for the Columbia Broadcasting System (1936–1943).

1966 July 10   **Malvina Hoffman** (b. Jan. 15, 1887), an American sculptor, died. Between 1930 and 1933, she sculpted 110 bronze figures of racial types for the Field Museum, Chicago, Illinois. Hoffman did a number of notable portrait busts and wrote *Sculpture Inside and Out* (1939).

1966 Sept. 16   The new **Metropolitan Opera House** opened at Lincoln Center for the Performing Arts in New York City. The first work presented was commissioned for the occasion, *Antony and Cleopatra* by **Samuel Barber**. It was the beginning of the Met's 84th season.

1966 Sept. 28   **André Breton** (b. Feb. 18, 1896), a French poet and critic, died. First a dadaist, he became (1922) a leader of the surrealists and their chief spokesman. Breton was one of the first French writers to publicize the work of Sigmund Freud. He also helped found several journals and wrote books, among them *Nadja* (1928) and *Fata Morgana* (1942).

1966 Sept. 28   The **Whitney Museum of American Art** opened its new building in New York City. The Whitney was designed by **Marcel Breuer** (May 22, 1902–July 1, 1981) and was a five story granite structure shaped like an inverted ziggurat. Among other museums opened this year were: the **Tapei Museum** on Taiwan; the **Iraq Museum** in Baghdad; one in Ponce, Puerto Rico; and a **Museum of Antiquities** in Basel, Switzerland.

1966 Dec. 15   [Walter Elias] **"Walt" Disney** (b. Dec. 5, 1901), the American film producer who created animated cartoons, died. His most famous cartoon character **Mickey Mouse** first appeared in Oct., 1928. Disney also produced full-length animated films, such as *Snow White and the Seven Dwarfs* (1937). In 1955 he created the enormously successful amusement park, **Disneyland**, in California and followed it with **Walt Disney World** in Florida.

VIII. SPORTS, GAMES, AND SOCIETY

1966 Apr. 28   The Boston Celtics won their eighth consecutive **National Basketball Association championship**, defeating the Los Angeles Lakers four games to three.

1966 May 3 *The Times of London*, founded in 1785, appeared for the first time, except in emergencies, with news stories on its front page instead of advertisements.

1966 June 8 The **National Football League and the American Football League agreed to merge**, ending inter-league warfare over the services of star college players, attendance by fans, and television contracts.

1966 July 30 England defeated West Germany 4–2 in the final game of the **World Cup** soccer competition at Empire Stadium, Wembley, England. It was Britain's first victory in this competition.

1966 Aug. 1 The worst of **three mass murders in the U.S.** this year occurred in Austin, Texas, where

Charles J[oseph] **Whitman** (b. 1941), a student, killed 16 people and wouded 31 others. Having killed his wife and mother, he went to the top of a 27-story tower on the University of Texas campus and fired on people at random for more than an hour and a half before being shot dead by a policeman. No motive was found for the killings. On July 14 in Chicago eight nurses were slain in their home, which served as a dormitory for a nearby hospital. **Richard F. Speck** (b. Dec. 6, 1941) was arrested for the crimes and on Apr. 15, 1967, was found guilty. Again there seemed no motive. On Nov. 12 in Mesa, Arizona, five women and two children were shot in a beauty parlor. Five of them died. The killer, **Robert Smith**, an 18-year-old, said he got the idea from the two earlier shootings.

1967

I. DISASTERS

1967 Jan. 6 A **bus convoy** carrying Catholic pilgrims near Manila, the Philippines, came to a disastrous end when the ninth bus in line went out of control and hit the bus in front. Both **fell into a gorge**, leaving 83 dead and c.60 injured.

1967 Jan. 18–24 As a result of **floods in eastern Brazil**, c.894 persons were killed.

1967 Mar. 18 The **supertanker** *Torrey Canyon*, enroute from Kuwait, **ran aground** off the Isles of Scilly, releasing 860,000 barrels of the oil it was carrying. A slick polluted more than 100 miles of the Cornwall, England, beaches and then hit beaches of northern Brittany, France. To help stop the spread of oil, the ship was set on fire (Mar. 28 and 29) by aerial bombing.

1967 Apr. 20 A Swiss passenger turboprop **plane** homeward bound from a tour of the Orient **crashed** into a small hill at Nicosia, Cyprus, while trying to land in bad weather. Of the 130 aboard only four survived.

1967 Apr. 23 A 100-year-old **rope bridge** near Katmandu, Nepal, **collapsed**, throwing at least 100 persons into the Sun Kosi River, where they drowned.

1967 May 22 *L'Innovation*, the second largest department store in Brussels, Belgium, **caught fire**. The official toll was 322 dead.

1967 July 6 At a grade crossing in Langenweddengen, near Magdeburg, East Germany, a double deck **commuter train collided with a gasoline truck**, killing 83 persons and injuring 50.

1967 July 16 In the wooden barracks of a **state prison road camp** at Jay, Florida, brawling prisoners broke a gas line, causing an **explosion**. As a result 37 of them were killed and 6 injured.

1967 July 29 Off the coast of North Vietnam a **fire aboard the U.S. aircraft carrier Forrestal**, begining with an explosion on the flight deck, killed 134 of the ship's personnel and injured c.100. Sixty planes and helicopters were destroyed or damaged, and total damage was estimated at $135 million.

II. POLITICS AND WAR

1967 By the end of the year, **474,300 American military personnel were in Vietnam**. The government reported (Oct. 5) that the total number of Americans killed or wounded since 1961 had reached 100,000. Battles were fought on an ever larger scale, but there were no decisive victories on either side.

1967 Jan. 21 A revised constitution for **Brazil** was adopted by the national congress. It increased powers for the executive branch and established indirect election of the president. On Mar. 15 **Artur da Costa e Silva** (1902–Dec. 17, 1969), an army general, succeeded **Humberto de Alencar Castelo Branco** (Sept. 20, 1900–July 18, 1967) as president. His military regime brought protests from many quarters, including students and the Catholic Church.

1967 Apr. 15 **Anti-Vietnam War demonstrators** marched on U.N. headquarters in New York City, with the number of paraders estimated as high as 400,000. A similar protest on the same day in San Francisco brought out c.50,000. In Chicago a National Congress for New Politics convened (Aug. 31 to Sept. 4) with 2,100 delegates representing 200 organized anti-war groups. On Oct. 21–22 in Washington, D.C., c.50,000 participants protested outside the Pentagon. More than 600 were arrested in clashes with soldiers. Demonstrations on college campuses were numerous. A parade and demonstration in support of the war had taken place (May 13) in New York City with an estimated 70,000 participants.

1967 Apr. 19 **Konrad Adenauer** (b. Jan. 5, 1876), first chancellor of West Germany (1949–1963) after World War II (1939–1945), died. He was mayor of Cologne in 1933 when the Nazis dismissed him from office. After the war he was a founder of the Christian Democratic party and one of those who wrote the constitution for the Federal Republic of Germany [West Germany]. As first chancellor of the new state (1949–1963), *Der Alte* [The Old One], as he became known, strove to bring Germany back into mainstream European life.

1967 Apr. 21 An army coup in **Greece** following a period of political unrest resulted in **Constantine II**, king of the Hellenes (1964–1967), going into exile (Dec. 14) in Italy, after the failure of a counter coup (Dec. 13). **Georgios Papadopoulos**, a rightist colonel, became prime minister and imposed order by jailing hundreds of communists and royalists alike.

1967 May 30 The eastern region of **Nigeria**, stronghold of the Ibos, was declared the independent **republic of Biafra** by **Chukwuemeka Odumegwu Ojukwo** (b. Nov. 4, 1933), an army officer. Nigerian national forces invaded Biafra on July 6 and after some early Biafran successes gained the upper hand, but the civil war went on.

1967 June 5 The **Six-Day War** broke out with a preemptive strike by Israeli forces against Egypt, Jordan, and Syria after a period of sorties by both sides. By June 10, when a United Nations cease fire was agreed on, **Israeli forces had seized the Gaza Strip and the Sinai** Peninsula from Egypt, the **Golan Heights** from Syria, and the **West Bank**, including the **old section of Jerusalem**, from Jordan. The Israeli victory was overwhelming, with a claim of 374 enemy planes destroyed in one day.

1967 June 8 A communications ship of the U.S. navy, *Liberty*, sailing in international waters in the Mediterranean Sea off the Sinai coast, **was sunk by Israeli gunboats and planes**. In the attack 34 Americans were killed and 64 injured. Israel apologized for its action.

1967 July 23–28 **Racial riots** occurred in cities all over the nation: Detroit, Michigan, July 23–28; Boston, June 2; New York City, July 24–27; Newark, New Jersey, July 12–17; Buffalo, New York; Cincinnati, Ohio; Hartford and New Haven, Connecticut; and Waterloo, Iowa. The riots resulted from dissatisfaction with the progress of the civil rights movement and with poverty and unemployment. During the year Cleveland, Ohio, and Gary, Indiana, elected black mayors.

1967 July 24 **Charles de Gaulle**, president of France, caused a furor on a visit to Montreal, Canada, when he publicly exclaimed: *"Vive le Quebec libre!"* Quebec separatists, led by **René Levesque** (Aug. 24, 1922–Nov. 1, 1987), who agitated for complete independence from the rest of Canada, rejoiced. Other Canadians and many Frenchmen found it an unforgivable interference in domestic affairs.

1967 Aug. 8 Meeting in Bangkok, Thailand, the **Association of Southeast Asian Nations** [ASEAN] was formed by Indonesia, Malaysia, the Philippines, Singapore, and Thailand. The five countries hoped to stabilize the region and to improve economic and social conditions by cooperation.

1967 Oct. 2 **Thurgood Marshall** (b. July 2, 1908) was sworn in as the **first black justice of the U.S. Supreme Court**. Nominated by **Lyndon B. Johnson**, Marshall was the great grandson of a slave. He had headed (1938–1962) the Legal Defense and Education Fund of the NAACP and had successfully argued the landmark case *Brown v. Board of Educa-*

tion of Topeka (1954), which resulted in the Supreme Court ruling that racial segregation in public schools was unconstitutional.

1967 Oct. 8 Clement [Richard] **Attlee** (b. Jan. 3, 1883), a prime minister of Great Britain (1945–1951), died. A leader of the Labour party, he served in the coalition cabinet during World War II (1939–1945). As prime minister he led the government that carried out the nationalization of industry, created the welfare state, and presided over the end of the British Empire as the colonies became independent.

1967 Oct. 9 Ernesto "Che" Guevara (b. June 14, 1928), an Argentinian-born revolutionist, died after apparently having been shot the previous day by Bolivian government forces hunting down guerrilla units. Guevara first came to notice when he was an important aide to **Fidel Castro** in the Cuban revolution (1956–1959). He also fought in the Congo as well as Latin America.

1967 Nov. 30 South Yemen became an independent republic with **Qahtan Muhammad al-Shaabi** (b. 1920), of the Marxist-oriented National Liberation Front, as the first president.

1967 Dec. 17 Harold [Edward] **Holt** (b. Aug. 5, 1908), the prime minister (from 1966) of **Australia**, drowned in a swimming accident in Victoria. He was succeeded by **John Grey Gorton** (b. Sept. 9, 1911), who also became the leader of the Liberal party.

III. ECONOMY AND TRADE

1967 Feb. 28 Henry [Robinson] **Luce** (b. Apr. 3, 1898), an American magazine publisher, died. With a Yale classmate he founded *Time*, the weekly news magazine in Mar. 1923. His other successes included *Fortune* (1930) and *Life* (1936).

1967 May 15 Three years of negotiations within the **General Agreement on Tariffs and Trade** [GATT], an agency of the United Nations, ended with agreement on the largest tariff cuts so far in foreign trade among industrial nations. In general tariff reductions of one-third were to be phased in by 1972.

1967 July 1 The **European Community** [EC] was created by the merger of the governing commissions of the European Coal and Steel Community [ECSC] (1951), the European Economic Community [EEC] (1958), and the European Atomic Energy Community [Euratom] (1958).

1967 July 30 Alfried Krupp von Bohlen und Halbach (b. Aug. 13, 1907), head of the **Krupp industrial empire**, died. He became the sole owner of the industrial complex in 1943. In 1947 Krupp was tried at Nürnberg [Nuremberg] along with other alleged Nazi war criminals and was sentenced to have his property forfeited and to serve 12 years in prison. In 1951, however, he was released and most of his property returned. Economic troubles in early 1967 caused the firm to become a public corporation.

1967 Sept. 29 The **International Monetary Fund** [IMF] and the **International Bank for Reconstruction and Development** [the World Bank], meeting in Brazil, adopted a plan to increase the money supply of the world by creating an international monetary reserve known as **Special Drawing Rights** [SDR], which could be used under certain conditions to settle international accounts.

1967 Nov. 18 With international confidence in the British pound dropping, the government of **Great Britain devalued the pound** from $2.80 to $2.40. Great Britain also raised the bank rate from 6.5 percent to 8 percent and arranged for a loan of $1,400,-000,000 from the International Monetary Fund [IMF].

IV. RELIGION AND PHILOSOPHY

1967 Jan. 10 Rosemary Goldie, an Australian, was named undersecretary in the Council of the Laity, a new administrative body established by **Pope Paul VI**. She was the first woman to be appointed to so high a rank in the Vatican.

1967 Oct. 31 Today marked the **450th anniversary of Martin Luther's nailing of his 95 theses** to the door of the castle church at Wittenberg [present East Germany], thereby launching the Protestant Reformation.

V. SCIENCE, EDUCATION, AND TECHNOLOGY

1967 The **first pulsar was discovered**, thought to be a celestial object that gave out regular, brief pulses of radio waves. Such pulses were first noted by **Jocelyn Bell** (b. July 15, 1943), an assistant to British astronomer **Anthony Hewish** (b. May 11, 1924).

Hewish shared the **Nobel prize for physics** in 1974, but Bell's contribution was not recognized. Pulsars are now thought to be neutron stars, remnants of supernovas.

1967 Jan. 27 Three astronauts, **Roger B. Chaffee** (b. Feb. 15, 1935), **Virgil I. Grissom** (b. Apr. 3, 1926), and **Edward H. White 2nd** (b. Nov. 14, 1930) were killed in a fire that broke out in their *Apollo 1* spacecraft while they were training in it on the ground at Cape Canaveral, Florida. Something had gone wrong with the electrical system.

1967 Feb. 6 The **longest suspension bridge in Latin America** was opened over the Orinoco River in Venezuela. Its main span was 2,336 feet.

1967 Feb. 18 J[ulius] **Robert Oppenheimer** (b. Apr. 22, 1904), an American physicist, died. In 1943 he was named head of the Los Alamos, New Mexico, laboratory of the **Manhattan Project** and he was present at the first explosion (July 15, 1945) of the atomic bomb he helped create. Later Oppenheimer was deprived of his security clearance, partly because he had opposed creation of the hydrogen bomb as morally wrong and partly because of his association with communists many years before. Oppenheimer remained director (1947–1966) of the Institute for Advanced Study at Princeton, New Jersey, and received the **Enrico Fermi Award** in 1963.

1967 Mar. 29 France's first nuclear submarine, *Le Redoutable,* was launched.

1967 Apr. 17 The People's Republic of **China** tested its first hydrogen bomb.

1967 Apr. 19 *Surveyor 3*, an American unmanned space probe, launched on Apr. 17, landed on the moon. It was programmed to dig a small trench and send back photographs of the soil it turned up. It proved that the moon's surface would support humans. On June 12 the Soviets launched *Venera 4* toward Venus where it parachuted (Oct. 17) a capsule of scientific instruments toward the surface. The instruments stopped functioning before they landed, but during the descent they revealed that the atmosphere of Venus was mostly carbon dioxide.

1967 Apr. 24 Russian cosmonaut **Vladimir Mikhaylovich Komarov** (b. Mar. 16, 1927) died when his craft, *Soyuz 1,* crashed in landing. After 18 orbits he started to return to earth, but the craft became entangled in its parachute and fell several miles.

1967 June 11 **Wolfgang Köhler** (b. Jan. 21, 1887), a German psychologist, died. As director (1913–1920) of a research facility at Tenerife in the Canary Islands, he became known for his experiments with apes in problem-solving situations. Köhler moved to the U.S. in 1934 and brought with him the ideas of **Gestalt psychology**, which asserted that in organizing phenomena the whole is greater than the sum of the distinct parts that make up the phenomena. Köhler wrote *Gestalt Psychology* (1929) and *The Mentality of Apes* (1931).

1967 Sept. 18 **John Douglas Cockcroft** (b. May 27, 1897), an English physicist, died. With an associate he shared the **Nobel prize for physics** in 1951 for work that led to the transmuting of atomic nuclei by bombarding them with highly accelerated atomic particles.

1967 Sept. 20 The *Queen Elizabeth II* was launched in England. At 66,851 gross tons and 963 feet in length, it was destined to be the last of the superliners. At about this time, the *Queen Mary* made its last voyage, to Long Beach, California, to become a hotel and exhibition ship.

1967 Nov. 9 A U.S. Saturn V rocket launched *Apollo 4* into orbit in a test that was part of the program planned to put a man on the moon.

1967 Nov. 20 **Casimir Funk** (b. Feb. 23, 1884), a Polish-born American biochemist, died. In July, 1912, he made public his discovery of certain vitamins, coining the name for them. Funk's work led him to believe in the existence of vitamins B-1, B-2, C, and D. He also made contributions to the knowledge of hormones.

1967 Dec. 3 The **first human heart transplant** was performed at Groote Schuur Hospital in Cape Town, South Africa, by **Christiaan** [Neething] **Barnard** (b. Nov. 8, 1922) and a team of 20 specialists. They transplanted into a 55-year-old man the heart of a 24-year-old man. The patient lived until Dec. 21, dying of a lung infection. In the next eight months more than 30 human heart transplants were performed, with varying degrees of success.

1967 Dec. 14 Biochemists at Stanford University in Palo Alto, California, produced the **first synthetic DNA**, the master chemical of life that controls heredity.

VI. ARTS AND LEISURE

1967 Jan. 3   Mary Garden (b. Feb. 20, 1874), a Scottish-born soprano who sang mostly in the U.S., died. She made her debut (1900) in Paris in the title role of *Louise* and her American debut (1907) in *Thaïs*. Beginning in 1910 and until she retired in 1931 Gardner sang with the Chicago Civic Opera and served as general manager for one year (1921–1922).

1967 Feb. 20   The National Gallery of Art, Washington, D.C., bought **Leonardo da Vinci's** painting *Ginevra dei Benci* from **Francis Joseph II**, prince of Lichtenstein, for more than $5 million.

1967 Mar. 6   Zoltán Kodály (b. Dec. 16, 1882), a Hungarian composer whose compositions reflected Hungarian folk music and contemporary French music, died. With **Bela Bartók**, Kodály made an important study of his land's folk music. He also wrote a good deal of choral music, especially for children, such as *Psalmus Hungaricus* (1923) and *The Music Makers* (1964). He wrote three operas, one of them being *Háry János* (1926), and orchestral music, including *Dances of Marosszék* (1930) and *Peacock Variations* (1939).

1967 Mar. 10   Geraldine Farrar (b. Feb. 28, 1882), an American soprano, died. She was a star of the Metropolitan Opera, New York, from 1906 until 1922 when she retired. Farrar sang the title roles in such operas as *Madame Butterfly*, *Carmen*, and *Tosca*.

1967 May 12   John [Edward] **Masefield** (b. June 1, 1878), an English writer and poet laureate (from 1930), died. Masefield's poems of the sea were collected in *Salt Water Ballads* (1902). *The Widow in the Bye Street* (1912) and *Dauber* (1913) were narrative poems. He also wrote plays, autobiographies, and novels.

1967 May 15   Edward Hopper (b. July 22, 1882), an American painter known for his realistic scenes of modern urban life that imparted a sense of loneliness, died. Typical of Hopper's style were *Early Sunday Morning* (1930), *Nighthawks* (1942), and *Second Story Sunlight* (1960).

1967 May 22   [James] **Langston Hughes** (b. Feb. 1, 1902), a leading figure in the **Harlem Renaissance**, died. He was a poet, novelist, and playwright, beginning his career with a book of poems on black themes, *The Weary Blues* (1926). Hughes's poetry was concerned with the problem of race, mostly in urban settings. His two novels were *Not Without Laughter* (1930) and *Tambourines to Glory* (1958).

1967 June 10   Spencer Tracy (b. Apr. 5, 1900), an American actor who starred in more than 60 films, died. Among his notable films were *Captains Courageous* (1938) and several, such as *Pat and Mike* (1952) and *Guess Who's Coming to Dinner* (1967), in which he played opposite **Katherine Hepburn**.

1967 July 7   Vivien Leigh [nee Vivian Mary Hartley] (b. Nov. 5, 1913), an English actress of stage and movies, died. In 1937 she played Ophelia to Lawrence Olivier's Hamlet. They were married that year. Leigh is remembered by most Americans for her role as Scarlett O'Hara in *Gone with the Wind* (1939). In the 1950s and early 1960s she appeared on stage in both England and America is such plays as *Duel of Angels* (1957) and *The Lady of the Camellias* (1961).

1967 July 22   Carl Sandburg (b. Jan. 6, 1878), an American writer, poet, folklorist, and biographer of Abraham Lincoln, died. His poetry, always in down-to-earth language, included *Chicago Poems* (1915), *Cornhuskers* (1918), *Smoke and Steel* (1920), and *The People, Yes* (1936), all of them hymns for America and its people. His biography of Lincoln, a sympathetic portrayal, appeared in two sections: *The Prairie Years* (1926) and *The War Years* (1936–1939), six volumes in all. Sandburg also wrote books for children and a novel *Remembrance Rock* (1938).

1967 Aug. 15   René Magritte (b. Nov. 21, 1898), a Belgian painter, one of the surrealists, died. He combined irony with a strange sort of realism. Among Magritte's works were *Human Condition* (1934), *The Rights of Man* (1945), and *The Tomb of the Wrestlers* (1960).

1967 Aug. 31   Ilya [Grigorevich] **Ehrenburg** [Erenburg] (Jan. 27, 1891), a Soviet writer who fled (1908) tsarist Russia for Paris and did not return until after the Russian Revolution (1917), died. His first novel of importance was *Neobychainye pokhozhdeniya Khulio Khurenit* [*The Extraordinary Adventures of Julio Jurenito*] (1921) which satirized the civilization of modern Europe. *Burya* [*The Storm*] (1948) was a novel of World War II. In *Ottepel* [*The Thaw*] (1954) Ehrenburg wrote, rather critically, about the regime of Joseph Stalin and the title gave its name to the period of easier censorship that followed Stalin's death in 1953.

1967 Sept. 1 Siegfried [Lorraine] **Sassoon**, one of the leading English poets of World War I, died. His poetry included *Counter-Attack* (1918) and *The Path to Peace* (1960).

1967 Oct. 9 André Maurois [Émile Salomon Wilhelm Herzog] (b. July 26, 1885), a French novelist, biographer, and essayist, died. Among his biographies were *Ariel* (1923), about **Percy Bysshe Shelley**; *Disraeli* (1927); *Proust* (1949); *Lélia* (1953), about **George Sand**; and *Olympio* (1954), about **Victor Hugo**. Maurois also wrote a number of novels, including *Bernard Quesnay* (1926) and *Le Cercle de famille* [*The Family Circle*] (1932).

1967 Dec. 29 Paul Whiteman (b. Mar. 28, 1890), an American orchestra conductor who did much to make jazz a respectable musical form, died. He formed (1919) his own band and played in many places for many years, but he was best remembered for the world premiere he gave of **George Gershwin's** *Rhapsody in Blue* on Feb. 12, 1924, in New York's Aeolian Hall.

VII. SPORTS, GAMES, AND SOCIETY

1967 Apr. 21 The **daughter of the late Joseph Stalin**, Svetlana Alliluyeva (b. Feb. 28, 1926) came to the U.S. to live. She was the youngest of Stalin's three children. Alliluyeva married an American.

1967 Apr. 27 Expo 67, Canada's first world's fair, opened in Montreal. When it closed on Oct. 29 it had set a record for a six-month run of 50,306,648 visitors.

1967 May 28 Francis Chichester (Sept. 17, 1901–Aug. 26, 1972), an English yachtsman, arrived in Plymouth, England, completing a solo trip around the world in his 53-foot ketch *Gipsy Moth IV*. He sailed from Plymouth on Aug. 23, 1966, reached Sydney, Australia, on Dec. 12, and sailed on around Cape Horn and home.

1967 June 6 National Hockey League franchises were awarded to teams in Los Angeles, Minnesota, Oakland, Philadelphia, Pittsburgh, and St. Louis, doubling the size of the league.

1967 June 30 *Hustler*, the jet-propelled motorboat of **Lee Taylor**, recorded a speed of 285.213 miles per hour over a measured mile, run twice on a lake at Guntersville, Alabama. This set a world record. At Coniston, England, **Donald Campbell** (b. Mar. 23, 1921) was killed on Jan. 4 when his jet-powered boat went out of control, spun up in the air, then quickly sank. At that time he was traveling at c.300 miles per hour.

1967 July 1 Color television broadcasting began in Great Britain with coverage of the tennis matches at Wimbledon.

1967 July 4 The British Parliament passed the **Sexual Offences Act**, which legalized homosexual acts between consenting adults in private.

1967 July 23–Aug. 6 The fifth **Pan-American Games** were held at Winnipeg, Canada, with the U.S. winning the most gold medals, 120.

1967 Sept. 12–18 The **America's Cup** was successfully defended by the U.S. The yacht *Intrepid* defeated the Australian challenger *Dame Pattie* in four straight races held off Newport, Rhode Island.

1967 Dec. 14 The *Lawn Tennis Association of Great Britain* announced that beginning in 1968 the tournaments played under its auspices would be open to amateurs and professionals. Prize money would go to the winners if they were pros.

1968

I. VITAL STATISTICS AND DEMOGRAPHICS

1968 The **population of the world** was estimated to be 3,500,000,000, an increase of 70 million in a year.

The U.N. calculated that if this growth rate continued the world population would double by the year 2006.

II. DISASTERS

1968 Jan. 15–16 **Earthquakes** on the island of **Sicily** destroyed four towns and many smaller places. In all 235 persons died, c.1,500 were missing, c.1,500 hurt, c.83,000 homeless, and damage of about $320 million done.

1968 Jan. 25 Three **submarine disasters** within four months occurred. The Israeli *Dakar* went down today in the Mediterranean Sea with 69 crew members perishing. On Jan. 27, also in the Mediterranean, the French *Minerve* disappeared with 52 sailors. On May 21 the U.S. nuclear-powered *Scorpion* sank in the Atlantic Ocean near the Azores with 99 men aboard. There were no survivors in any of the accidents.

1968 Apr. 10 A **hurricane** with winds of 123 miles per hour sank the *Wahine*, a large inter-island car ferry, in Wellington Harbor, New Zealand. Of 727 persons aboard, 52 were drowned; the rest were rescued.

1968 Apr. 20 A South African Airways **Boeing 707** taking off from Windhoek, South-West Africa [present Namibia], bound for London, **crashed**, killing 122 passengers and crew. Six survived.

1968 May 11 At Visayawada, India, a gasoline lamp **in a wedding pavilion** started a **fire**. In the ensuing panic 58 people were burned or crushed to death and more than 200 injured.

1968 Aug. 18 Loosened by rains of **Typhoon Polly**, earth slid onto a highway at Gifu, in Honshu, Japan, sweeping two buses into the flooded Hida River. At least 102 women and children died.

1968 July 29–31 At San José, capital of Costa Rica, the 5,249-foot **volcano Mt. Arenal**, which had not **erupted** in 500 years, blew its top, scattering rocks and lava over a 30-mile area, killing 52; 112 were missing.

1968 Aug. 31–Sept. 4 **Earthquakes** in Iran destroyed 11 populated areas in Khurasan province, leaving c.30,000 officially dead, c.17,000 injured, and c.100,000 homeless. The quakes registered 7.4 on the Richter scale.

III. POLITICS AND WAR

1968 Andre [Dmitriyevich] **Sakharov** (b. May 21, 1921), a Russian nuclear physicist, published outside Russia the essay "**Progress, Coexistence, and Intellectual Freedom.**" In it he urged the reduction of armaments by the leading powers, and indicated a belief that eventually communism and capitalism would change and blend into a form of democratic socialism.

1968 Jan. 16 The government of **Great Britain** announced that all British forces east of Suez would be withdrawn by the end of 1971 and that the defense budget would be reduced.

1968 Jan. 23 The *Pueblo*, an American intelligence-gathering ship, and its crew of 83 were **seized** in the Sea of Japan **by North Korean forces**. North Korea claimed the ship was in its territorial waters; the U.S. said it was in international waters. After long negotiations the crew of 83 was released (Dec. 22), but the ship was retained. The U.S. signed a document saying it agreed the ship had been in North Korean waters.

1968 Jan. 31 The **Viet Cong** guerilla forces and the North Vietnamese army launched a surprise major offensive on all 40 of South Vietnam's major urban centers and on the American and South Vietnamese troops defending them. The Viet Cong attack on Saigon, the South Vietnamese capital, penetrated (Jan. 31) into the American embassy compound before being repulsed. The major battle of the **Tet offensive**, so-called because it coincided with the Asian New Year, took place at the ancient capital **Hue**, just south of the 17th parallel that divided Vietnam. On Feb. 24, American and South Vietnamese forces finally retook the city. Although the offensive was defeated on the battlefield, the psychological victory went to the Viet Cong and the North Vietnamese. It had not been believed they could mount this kind of all-out war and in the U.S. anti-war sentiment was greatly increased.

1968 Jan. 31 The United Nations trust territory of **Nauru** in the western Pacific Ocean became an independent nation. With an area of 8½ sq. mi., it was the **world's smallest democratic republic**. Nauru's phosphate exports made it one of the world's richest nations on a per capita basis.

1968 Feb. 19 An arbitration commission handed down its decision on the territory in the **Rann of Kutch**, for three years in dispute between India and Pakistan. Pakistan received 300 square miles and India 3,200. Pakistan welcomed the decision, but there were angry protests in India.

1968 Mar. 1 A law **restricting the immigration of Asians** holding British citizenship into Great Britain went into effect. It was aimed particularly at those persons, mostly Indians and Pakistanis, living in Kenya, who were being deprived of their livelihoods by the government of Kenya. Under the new law only 1,500 heads of families and their dependents were allowed to enter England each year.

1968 Mar. 12 **Mauritius**, an island in the Indian Ocean, became independent and a member of the Commonwealth of Nations. The first prime minister was **Seewoosagur Ramgoolam** (Sept. 18, 1900–Dec. 15, 1985).

1968 Mar. 31 **Lyndon B. Johnson** surprised the nation when, at the end of a television address in which he announced a **partial end of bombing of North Vietnam**, he also said he would not seek another term as president in the November election. His popular support was waning rapidly because of the **war in Vietnam**, as shown by his poor showing (Mar. 12) in the New Hampshire Democratic primary.

1968 Apr. 4 **Martin Luther King**, Jr., an American black civil rights leader, was shot to death at a motel in Memphis, Tennessee. His assassin, identified as **James Earl Ray** (b. Mar. 10, 1928), was arrested (June 8) in London and sentenced (Mar. 10, 1969) to 99 years in prison for murder. The assassination caused outbreaks of **racial violence in many U.S. cities**. A Baptist clergyman, King had first fought segregation in Montgomery, Alabama, and was (1957) a founder and the president of the Southern Christian Leadership Conference. He was awarded the **Nobel Peace Prize** in 1964.

1968 Apr. 6 Upon the resignation of **Lester Pearson**, **Pierre Elliott Trudeau** (b. Oct. 18, 1919) was chosen leader of the **Canadian** Liberal party and on Apr. 20 became prime minister. An election on June 28 resulted in a triumph for the Liberals, as they won 155 seats in the House of Commons to 109 for the other three parties.

1968 Apr. 24 Columbia University in New York City was closed after two days of **student strikes**. The proximate cause of the strikes was a plan to build a gymnasium on land some thought should be used for other community purposes. More profound causes were **resistance to the war in Vietnam**, the demand for black studies, and more participation by students in deciding university policies. On April 30, police entered the campus and used force to remove students from five buildings. Similar strikes, sit-ins, and other protests occurred on campuses around the country.

1968 May 2 **Leftist French students occupied buildings** first at the University of Nanterre and then at the University of Paris, and on May 14 disrupted the Sorbonne. They were opposed to a proposed new system of literary studies, but this was in part an excuse for a general display of dislike for the government. The students were joined by factory workers, who demonstrated on such a scale that by May 20 the country was virtually paralyzed, with 10 million on strike. **Charles de Gaulle**, president of France, called a general election, the second round of which was held on June 30. The Gaullist party won an absolute majority in the assembly, and de Gaulle continued as president.

1968 June 2 **José Maria Velasco Ibarra** (Mar. 19, 1893–Mar. 30, 1979) was elected president of **Ecuador** for the fifth time; he was inaugurated on Sept. 1.

1968 June 6 **Robert F[rancis] Kennedy** (b. Nov. 20, 1925), brother of the assassinated John F. Kennedy and former attorney general of the U.S. and currently senator from New York, died of gunshot wounds inflicted the day before in a Los Angeles hotel where he was campaigning for the Democratic nomination for president. His assailant was **Sirhan B[ishara] Sirhan** (b. Mar. 19, 1944), a Jordanian immigrant. Brought to trial, he was found guilty (Apr. 17, 1969) of first degree murder and sentenced (May 21) to die in the gas chamber. Before Sirhan could be executed, the California Supreme Court declared (on Feb. 18, 1972) the death penalty unconstitutional, and Sirhan remained in jail.

1968 July 12 A bloodless coup in **Iraq** overthrew the government of **Abdul Rahman Arif** (b. 1901), who was accused of leftist tendencies. The leader of the coup was **Ahmad Hassan al-Bakr** (1914–Oct. 4, 1982), an army officer and prominent in the **Ba'ath party**. Bakr became the head of a Revolutionary

Command Council, which promulgated (Sept. 22) a provisional constitution that declared Iraq a democratic nation with Islam as the state religion.

1968 July 20   Student protest movements in Mexico City demanded more say in the running of the nation's universities and the freeing of political prisoners. Eventually they were able to mobilize c.300,000 persons for marches. The unrest came to a head on Oct. 2 in Tlatelolco Plaza, Mexico City, when army and security forces opened fire on the protesters. The official death toll was put at 32 but it may have been as high as 350. More than a thousand were injured and several thousand were arrested. Some received prison terms of as much as 16 years.

1968 Aug. 20   Soviet armed forces, together with troops from Bulgaria, East Germany, Hungary, and Poland, **invaded Czechoslovakia**. The Russians claimed they had been invited in to restore order, but in fact they were there to put an end to the liberal reform government of **Alexander Dubček** (b. Nov. 27, 1921), who had become first secretary of the Communist party on Jan. 5. **Ludvik Svoboda** (Nov. 25, 1895–Sept. 20, 1979) was in power with him from Mar. 10. The Soviets vetoed (Aug. 23) a U.N. Security Council resolution condemning the invasion. Dubček and Svoboda, with other officials, were arrested by the Soviets and taken to Moscow while the invading troops cowed the country. They signed (Aug. 26) an agreement to discontinue the relaxation of political and cultural rules and not to seek economic cooperation with the Western democracies. They were allowed to return to Prague and resume their duties. The Czech National Assembly approved a treaty allowing Russia to continue to station troops in the country. Dubček had striven for what he called "socialism with a human face," and his short time in power was hailed as the "**Prague Spring**."

1968 Aug. 26–28   The **Democratic party convention, in Chicago**, turned into a bitter affair, accompanied by rioting in the streets. Thousands of nondelegates, many of them college students, went to Chicago to express **opposition to the Vietnam War** and to rally support for candidates who agreed with them. On the night of Aug. 28, after **Hubert H. Humphrey** had been nominated and the Democrats had adopted a platform supporting the war, large-scale rioting broke out in the streets. In addition to most of the Chicago police force, c.13,000 National Guardsmen were on hand. Hundreds were injured, including bystanders and representatives of the media. With the convention and the rioting both carried by national television, and with the country's growing distaste for the war, Humphrey's campaign was crippled before it began.

1968 Sept. 6   Swaziland, in southern Africa, was granted independence from Great Britain and became a constitutional monarchy within the Commonwealth of Nations. The king was **Sobhuza II** (July 22, 1899–Aug. 21, 1982) and the prime minister was Prince **Makhosini Dlamini**.

1968 Sept. 26   António Salazar, premier of **Portugal** from 1932, was succeeded by **Marcello José das Neves Alves Caetano** (Aug. 17, 1906–Oct. 26, 1980), a close associate. António [de Oliveira] Salazar (b. Apr. 28, 1889), who had suffered a stroke on Sept. 10, died on July 27, 1970. He had been a virtual dictator for nearly 40 years, running a right wing corporative state.

1968 Oct. 3   A military coup in Peru overthrew the regime of **Fernando Belaunde Terry**, who had attempted reforms but was overwhelmed by government deficits, inflation, and disputes over nationalization of foreign companies. He was succeeded by **Juan Velasco Alvarado** (June 16, 1910–Dec. 24, 1977), who took on dictatorial powers.

1968 Oct. 12   Equatorial Guinea [formerly Spanish Guinea], in western Africa, was granted independence from Spain and became a republic. Its first president was **Francisco Macias Nguema** (1922–Sept. 29, 1979).

1968 Oct. 12   Arnulfo Arias (Aug. 15, 1901–Aug. 10, 1988), president of **Panama**, was ousted after only 11 days in office. Elected president on May 12, almost certainly by fraudulent means, he had been inaugurated on Oct. 1. The coup was led by **Omar Torrijos Herrera**, commander of the National Guard. **José M. Pinilla** (b. Mar. 28, 1919) was made provisional president but real power in the country was in Torrijos's hands.

1968 Dec. 19   Norman [Mattoon] **Thomas** (b. Nov. 20, 1884), six times (1928–1948) the Socialist party candidate for the U.S. presidency, died. A clergyman, Thomas joined (1918) the Socialist party and helped found (1930) the **American Civil Liberties Union**. As a political candidate and reformer he advocated many measures that later became law, such as unemployment insurance and minimum wages.

1968 Dec. 30 **Trygve** [Halvdan] **Lie** (b. July 16, 1896), a Norwegian statesman and **first U.N. secretary general** (Feb. 1, 1946–Apr. 10, 1953), died. At the U.N. he competently faced such issues as the seating of communist China, the Berlin blockade of 1948, and the Korean War in 1950.

IV. ECONOMY AND TRADE

1968 Jan. 1 To reduce the outflow of dollars, Lyndon B. Johnson placed **restrictions on foreign private investments** and asked Americans to reduce travel abroad.

1968 Mar. 13 A serious **outbreak of hoof and mouth disease,** which had struck livestock in Great Britain in Oct. 1967, was declared under control by the Agricultural Ministry. About 2,300 farms were affected and 400,000 head of livestock had to be destroyed.

1968 Mar. 17 Belgium, Great Britain, Italy, the Netherlands, Switzerland, the U.S., and West Germany agreed on a **two-price system for gold.** An upsurge in the demand for gold had threatened to disrupt international markets and currencies. Central banks had already lost $3,000,000,000 of their gold reserves. The seven nations agreed that transactions between governments would remain at the $35 per ounce price but that the private market would be allowed to fluctuate. At the end of the year the free market price in London was $41.90.

1968 July 15 The **first direct commercial air service between the U.S. and the U.S.S.R.** began with planes of the Soviet airline Aeroflot and Pan American World Airways flying the New York-Moscow route.

V. RELIGION AND PHILOSOPHY

1968 July 29 The encyclical *Humanae Vitae* [*Of Human Life*] issued by **Pope Paul VI** reaffirmed the Church's stand against birth control, saying "every marriage act must remain open to the transmission of life."

1968 Nov. 15 **Augustin Cardinal Bea** (b. May 28, 1881), a German-born prince of the Roman Catholic Church, and president of the Vatican Secretariat for Christian Unity, died. He was the main architect of the church's recent ecumenical policy and implemented the actions of Vatican Council II.

1968 Dec. 9 **Karl Barth** (b. May 10, 1886), a Swiss Protestant theologian, died. Barth, who taught in Germany until he was deported (1935) to Switzerland for refusing to take an oath of allegiance to Adolf Hitler, believed that the principles of the Reformation should be the basis of religious belief and practice. Barth's major work was ***Der Kirchliche Dogmatic*** [*Church Dogmatics*] (1932–1962).

1968 Dec. 10 **Thomas Merton** [Father M. Louis] (b. Jan. 31, 1915), an American Trappist monk whose writings on religion and philosophy attracted world attention, died. He entered the Trappist order in 1941. Merton's best-known work, ***The Seven Storey Mountain*** (1948), described his spiritual malaise and his conversion to Catholicism.

VI. SCIENCE, EDUCATION, AND TECHNOLOGY

1968 The **Oroville Dam** on the Feather River in California was completed and at 770 feet became the highest dam in the U.S.

1968 Jan. 6 The **first successful heart transplant operation in the U.S.** was performed at the Stanford University Medical School, Palo Alto, California. The patient was a 54-year-old man, and the chief surgeon was **Norman Edward Shumway.** The patient died on Jan. 21.

1968 Feb. 21 **Howard Walter Florey** (b. Sept. 24, 1898), an Australian-born British scientist, died. He isolated and purified penicillin, making its clinical use possible in 1939. Florey shared the **Nobel Prize for physiology or medicine** in 1945.

1968 Mar. The **Krasnoyarsk hydroelectric power plant** on the Yenisei River in the U.S.S.R. was completed, producing 6,096,000 kilowatts from 12 turbines.

1968 June 1 **Helen** [Adams] **Keller** (b. June 27, 1880) died. Although made blind, deaf, and mute by illness at age 19 months, she learned to read, write, and communicate by means of the manual alphabet and became an effective advocate of education for the blind. Her tutor was **Anne Sullivan Macy** (Apr. 14, 1866–Oct. 20, 1936), who had learned the alphabet at the **Perkins Institute for the Blind** (1829), Boston, Massachusetts. Miss Keller was graduated *cum laude* from **Radcliffe College** in 1904 and devoted her life to lecturing. She wrote *The Story of My Life* (1902) and *Helen Keller's Journal* (1938).

1968 July 28   **Otto Hahn** (b. Mar. 8, 1879), a German chemist, died. He did much of the essential work resulting (1938) in the splitting of the uranium atom and thus making possible nuclear chain reactions. Hahn shared the **Nobel prize for chemistry** in 1944.

1968 Aug. 24   **France tested its first hydrogen bomb** in the South Pacific Ocean.

1968 Sept. 21   The Soviet unmanned spacecraft *Zond 5* made a soft landing on earth, becoming the **first man-made craft to make a trip around the moon and back**. In November *Zond 6* repeated this feat. The flights were used to test new systems and equipment for future space exploration.

1968 Oct. 27   **Lise Meitner** (b. Nov. 7, 1878), an Austrian physicist, died. She was a pioneer in the study of radioactivity and, working with Otto Hahn for 30 years, shared in the discovery of nuclear fission.

1968 Dec. 24   The crew of the spacecraft *Apollo 8* became the **first men to orbit the moon**. The craft went around the moon ten times, taking photographs at an altitude of 69.8 miles. The crewmen were **Frank Borman** (b. Mar. 14, 1928), **James Lovell, Jr.** (b. Mar. 25, 1928), and **William** [Alison] **Anders** (b. Oct. 17, 1933).

VII. ARTS AND LEISURE

1968   *2001: A Space Odyssey*, a movie directed by **Stanley Kubrick** (b. July 26, 1928), was shown. Kubrick, an American who worked (from 1960) chiefly in England, also directed *Paths of Glory* (1957), *Lolita* (1962), *Dr. Strangelove: Or How I learned to Stop Worrying and Love the Bomb* (1963), and *A Clockwork Orange* (1971).

1968 Jan. 1   C[ecil] **Day-Lewis** (Apr. 27, 1904–May 22, 1972) was named poet laureate of Great Britain. His *Collected Poems* appeared in 1954. Day-Lewis translated Virgil and was professor of poetry at Oxford University (1951–1956) and Harvard University (1964–1965). Beginning in 1935 with *A Question of Proof*, he wrote many detective novels under the pen name Nicholas Blake.

1968 June 5   **Dorothy Gish** (b. Mar. 11, 1898), an American actress of the stage and movies, died. With her sister Lillian she first appeared on the screen in 1912. She acted with Lillian in *Hearts of the World* (1918) and *Orphans of the Storm* (1922). She was also brilliant in comedy roles. After 1928 Gish made stage appearances chiefly, as in *Brittle Heaven* (1934) and *The Chalk Garden* (1956).

1968 June 14   **Salvatore Quasimodo** (b. Aug. 20, 1901), an Italian critic and poet, died. His most important work was *Ed è subito sera* (1942). Quasimodo received the **Nobel prize for literature** in 1959.

1968 July 21   **Ruth St. Denis** [Ruth Dennis] (b. Jan. 20, 1879), founder (1915), with her husband **Ted Shawn** (Oct. 21, 1891–Jan. 9, 1972) of the **Denishawn School of Dance**, died. She had great influence on dance in America with the use of philosophical themes and Oriental forms, being the founder (1931) of the Society of Spiritual Arts. Among her choreographed works were *Radha* (1906) and *Tragica* (1925).

1968 Oct. 2   **Marcel Duchamp** (b. July 28, 1887), a French artist who lived mostly in the U.S. after 1942, died. He created a sensation in 1912 with a painting in the Cubist manner *Nude Descending a Staircase*. Duchamp invented the medium he called "ready mades," an example being *Bicycle Wheel* (1913).

1968 Nov. 6   **Charles Munch** (b. Sept. 26, 1891), a French conductor, died. He was a founder and conductor (1935–1938) of the **Paris Philharmonic** and led (1949–1962) the **Boston Symphony**. During much of this period he was also director of the **Berkshire Music Center**.

1968 Nov. 25   **Upton** [Beall] **Sinclair** (b. Sept. 20, 1878), an American writer, died. His novel *The Jungle* (1906) helped reform the unsanitary meat packing industry. Other Sinclair works were also aimed at social ills, such as the novels *The Money Changers* (1908) and *King Coal* (1917). In 1934 he was the Democratic candidate for governor of California, running unsuccessfully on a socialistic platform he called End Poverty in California [EPIC].

1968 Dec. 20   **John** [Ernst] **Steinbeck** (b. Feb. 27, 1902), an American novelist, died. He was noted especially for the novel *The Grapes of Wrath* (1939), but he wrote many other works, including

Tortilla Flat (1935), *Of Mice and Men* (1937), *The Moon Is Down* (1942), and *East of Eden* (1952). Steinbeck was awarded the **Nobel prize for literature** in 1962.

VIII. SPORTS, GAMES, AND SOCIETY

1968 Feb. 6–18   The tenth Winter **Olympic Games** were held at Grenoble, France, with 1,239 athletes from 36 countries competing. Norway won 6 gold medals and 14 medals overall; the U.S.S.R. 5 and 13; and France 4 and 9. The U.S. won only one gold medal when Peggy Fleming (b. June 27, 1948) became the figure skating champion.

1968 May 27   Montreal, Canada, became the first city outside the U.S. to be awarded a franchise in **major league baseball**. The National League, deciding to expand to 12 teams in 1969, chose

Montreal and San Diego from a field of five applicants.

1968 Sept. 9   **Arthur** [Robert] **Ashe, Jr.** (b. July 10, 1943) became the first black to win the men's **U.S. tennis championship**, defeating his opponent in five sets. Ashe was a lieutenant in the U.S. army at the time.

1968 Oct. 12–27   At the 19th Summer **Olympic Games**, held in Mexico City, with c.6,000 athletes from 112 nations participating, the U.S. won 45 gold medals and a total of 107; the USSR, 29 gold medals and a total of 91; Japan 11 and 25.

1968 Oct. 19   **Jacqueline Bouvier Kennedy** (b. July 28, 1929), widow of John F. Kennedy, was married to **Aristotle Socrates Onassis** (Jan. 15, 1906–Mar. 15, 1975), a multimillionaire Greek shipping magnate.

1969

I. DISASTERS

1969 Jan. 31   A blowout of an **offshore oil rig** threw a river of crude petroleum into the Santa Barbara Channel of southern California. It was not capped until Feb. 8 and in the meantime 235,000 gallons of oil covered an 800-square-mile area. Great harm was done to bird and marine life.

1969 Feb. 9–10   A snowstorm of up to 15 inches left 166 persons dead **in New England, New York, New Jersey, and Pennsylvania.**

1969 Mar. 16   At Maracaibo, Venezuela, a Venezuelan **DC-9** enroute from Caracas to Miami **plunged to the ground and exploded** in a residential area on takeoff. The crash left 155 dead—75 passengers, 10 crew, and c.70 on the ground.

1969 Mar. 31   One hundred eighty miners trapped 800 feet underground by **explosions that collapsed two shafts** of a coal mine at Barroterán, Mexico, were given up for dead.

1969 May 17–21   Winds and **tidal waves along the Bay of Bengal** coast struck villages and the city of Vijayawada, leaving 618 dead. Many cattle were killed and serious damage done to ricelands.

1969 June 2   The Australian aircraft carrier *Melbourne* rammed the U.S. destroyer *Evans* in the South China Sea, cutting it in half and killing 74 crewmen.

1969 June 15   Celebrating the opening of a new restaurant in San Rafael, near Madrid, Spain, c.500 patrons were trapped when the **second story sagged and walls collapsed.** At least 57 died and c.140 were injured.

1969 July 5   Near Cuttack, India, when a passenger pulled an emergency brake because he wanted to get off, a train carrying pilgrims to Puri for the "juggernaut" festival was **struck from behind by a fast freight train.** At least 81 were killed and more than 150 injured.

1969 Aug. 17–20   Hurricane Camille ravaged Alabama, Louisiana, Mississippi, and Virginia, leaving c.400 dead or missing and doing $1,000,000,000 of damage.

1969 Sept. 28–Oct. 8   After five years of drought, ten days of **torrential rains** reduced half of Tunisia to mud and water. About 500 persons lost their lives and c.50,000 homes were destroyed.

II. POLITICS AND WAR

1969 U.S. troop strength in Vietnam reached c.550,000. **Richard M. Nixon**, president of the U.S., announced (Nov. 3) plans were being made with the government of South Vietnam for the gradual withdrawal of American forces and the **Vietnamization** of the struggle. About 60,000 Americans were withdrawn by the end of the year. **Ho Chi Minh** (b. May 19, 1890), president of North Vietnam since 1945, died on Sept. 2. He had been a fervid communist since 1920, had led the **Viet Minh** that occupied Hanoi in 1945, and had declared Vietnam's independence. Ho inspired the defeat of the French colonial forces (1946–1954) and then turned to the use of force to unite the south with the north. He was succeeded by Le Duan as party general secretary.

1969 Student unrest in the U.S. continued, with demonstrations at such schools as the University of Wisconsin's Madison campus; the University of North Carolina, Chapel Hill; Harvard University; Cornell University, Ithaca, New York; and the University of California, Berkeley. Although there were demands for black studies, women's studies, and open admissions, in the background at all times was the student **opposition to the war in Vietnam**.

1969 Jan. 8 The government of **Abdullah Yafi** (b. 1901), premier of **Lebanon**, resigned. He had been much criticized for his failure to defend the Beirut airport against an Israeli attack on Dec. 28, 1968. **Rashid Karami** (Dec. 30, 1921–June 1, 1987) became (Jan. 15) premier, but he resigned (Apr. 24) when his government could not control **Palestine guerrilla clashes with the Lebanese army**. However, he remained the head of a caretaker government until Nov. 25, when he was able to establish a more stable regime. An agreement on a ceasefire between the army and the Palestinians had been arranged (Nov. 2), with the latter receiving permission to raid Israeli bases from Lebanon.

1969 Jan. 20 **Richard M. Nixon**, the Republican party candidate in the election of Nov. 5, 1968, was inaugurated president of the U.S. He had defeated Hubert H. Humphrey, the Democratic candidate, with 31,785,480 popular votes and 302 electoral votes to Humphrey's 31,275,166 and 191. **George C[orley] Wallace** (b. Aug. 25, 1919), a former governor of Alabama, running on a third party ticket, won 9,906,403 popular votes and 45 electoral votes. **Spiro** T[heodore] **Agnew** (b. Nov. 9, 1918) became vice president.

1969 Feb. 3 **Yasir Arafat** (b. Feb. 17, 1929), the head of the Palestinian guerrilla group **Al Fatah**, became the leader of the **Palestine Liberation Organization** [PLO], both groups dedicated to the destruction of Israel and the establishment of a Palestinian nation.

1969 Mar. 2 A major clash along the **Ussuri** [Wusuli] **River** in northeastern China, which forms the border with Russia north of Vladivostok, involved c.3,000 troops on each side. The main point at issue was possession of **Domansky** [Chinese: Chenpao] **Island** in the river.

1969 Mar. 17 **Golda Meir** (May 3, 1898–Dec. 8, 1978), became the **first woman prime minister of Israel**. She succeeded Levi Eshkol [orig.: Shkolnik] (Oct. 25, 1895–Feb. 25, 1969), who had been prime minister from 1963. Born in Russia, Meir was taken to the U.S. in 1906 where she later became a school teacher. In 1921 she emigrated to Palestine.

1969 Mar. 25 **Ayub Khan**, president of **Pakistan** since 1960, resigned following rioting that had begun in the fall of 1968. Most of it had been the result of the continuing **tension between East and West Pakistan**. On Mar. 31 he was succeeded by **Yahya Khan** (Feb. 4, 1917–Aug. 8, 1980), head of the army, who established martial law.

1969 Mar. 28 **Dwight D[avid] Eisenhower** (b. Oct. 14, 1890), 34th president of the U.S. and commander of the Allied armies defeated the German forces of Adolf Hitler, died. A West Point graduate, in his career after World War II Eisenhower was president of **Columbia University** (1948–1950) and commander of the NATO forces (1950–1952). As president (1953–1961) he continued the Truman policy of attempting to contain communism, especially in Asia where several treaties were concluded, among them one that established (1954) the Southeast Treaty Organization [SEATO]. At the same time he tried to soften the tensions of the Cold War with the U.S.S.R.

1969 Apr. 19–21 **Violence between Catholics and Protestants** broke out in **Northern Ireland** [Ulster], and **British troops were sent to Belfast** and Londonderry to restore order and protect public facilities. Ever since 1922, when the **Republic of Ireland** was established, the Catholic minority in the northern province of Ulster had been discriminated against economically and politically. As the years passed the illegal **Irish Republican Army** [IRA] became more violent and the Catholic population of Northern Ireland increased. The leader of the dominant Protestant hard-liners was **Ian** [Richard Kyle] **Paisley** (b. Apr. 6, 1926), a clergyman. The worst rioting of the year took place from Aug. 12 to 16. Police fired on Catholic demonstraters, killing ten. Overall 514 civilians and 226 policemen were injured. British troops called in to restore order would stay indefinitely to take over security functions.

1969 May 13   Riots broke out in Kuala Lumpur, Malaysia, between Malays and Chinese. Before the rioting ended 196 were dead and 439 were injured. A National Operations Council directed emergency rule until Dec. 29, when civilian control was resumed.

1969 May 25   A bloodless military **coup in the Sudan**, led by **Gaafur Muhammad al-Nimeiry** (b. Jan. 1, 1930), overthrew **Muhammad Ahmed Mahgoub** (b. 1908), the prime minister, and set up a leftist Revolutionary Council and established al-Nimeiry as president.

1969 June 16   Harold [Rupert Leofric George] **Alexander**, 1st Earl Alexander of Tunis (b. Dec. 10, 1891), a British commander in World War II, died. A combat veteran of World War I, he was put in command (1942) of British forces in the Near East in World War II and led the Allied invasion of Sicily and Italy. After 1944 he was supreme commander of Allied forces in the Mediterranean Theater. Following the war Alexander was governor general of Canada (1946–1952).

1969 June 20   Georges [Jean Raymond] **Pompidou** (July 5, 1911–Apr. 2, 1974) took office as president of **France**, having won election in the second round of voting on June 15 with 58.21 percent of the popular vote. He succeeded **Charles de Gaulle**, who had quit as president (from 1959) on Apr. 28 because he had been rebuffed by the voters in a referendum on his policies.

1969 June 20   A referendum in Rhodesia [present Zimbabwe] in which 88,217 whites and 6,634 blacks were eligible to vote, approved a new constitution that perpetuated white supremacy and declared Rhodesia a republic.

1969 June 23   Warren [Earl] **Burger** (b. Sept. 17, 1907) was sworn in as chief justice of the United States. He had been a judge (from 1956) of the Court of Appeals for the District of Columbia. Appointed by **Richard Nixon**, president of the U.S., Burger was an advocate of judicial restraint.

1969 July 1   Charles (b. Nov. 14, 1948) **was invested as Prince of Wales** by his mother **Elizabeth II**, queen of Great Britain and Northern Ireland, in a ceremony at Caernarvon Castle, Wales.

1969 July 7   The Canadian House of Commons gave final approval to the **Official Language Act**, which went into effect in September. The law made both English and French official languages of the federal government.

1969 July 14   The so-called **Football War** broke out when **El Salvador's troops invaded Honduras**. Honduras had charged foul play in a soccer game in San Salvador on June 22, but the underlying causes were economic and immigration matters in dispute between the two nations. On July 29, prodded by the **Organization of American States** [OAS], El Salvador agreed to withdraw its troops, but tension continued.

1969 July 22   Francisco Franco, fascist dictator of **Spain**, named **Juan Carlos de Borbon y Borbon** (b. Jan. 5, 1938) to be his successor and king of Spain as **Juan Carlos I** when Franco died or retired. Juan Carlos was the grandson of Alfonso XIII, the last king of Spain (from 1902), who was deposed in 1931.

1969 Sept. 1   While in Turkey undergoing medical treatment, **Idris I** (Mar. 13, 1890–May 25, 1983), king of **Libya**, was overthrown in a bloodless coup by a group of young leftist army officers led by **Muammar al-Qaddafi** [Gadaffi] (b. 1942). Qaddafi became in effect head of state.

1969 Oct. 14   [Sven] **Olof** [Joachim] **Palme** (Jan. 30, 1927–Feb. 28, 1986) became prime minister (to 1976) of **Sweden**. He succeeded **Tage Fritiof Erlander** (June 13, 1901–June 21, 1985), who had held the office since 1946. Palme was critical of the U.S. role in the war in Vietnam.

1969 Oct. 15   What organizers termed **Vietnam Moratorium Day** was observed in the U.S. by thousands of people opposed to participation in the conflict in Southeast Asia. Prayer vigils, candlelight processions, mass meetings, and the wearing of black armbands marked the day. Other thousands demonstrated in support of U.S. policy on Nov. 11, Veterans' Day. A second Moratorium Day was observed on Nov. 14 and c.250,000 people paraded on Nov. 15 in the nation's capital against the war. A similar demonstration in San Francisco attracted c.100,000 participants.

1969 Oct. 21   Willy Brandt (b. Dec. 18, 1913), who changed his name from **Herbert Ernst Karl Frahm** when the Nazis forced him to flee to Norway in 1933, became chancellor of **West Germany**, succeeding **Kurt Georg Kiesinger** (from 1966). His party, the Social Democrats won a plurality and formed a coalition government with the Free Democrats, thus ousting the Christian Democrats from power for the first time since the formation (1949) of the West German government. Brandt was awarded the **Nobel Peace Prize** in 1971 for his efforts on behalf of East-West detente.

1969 Nov. 12   Liu Shao-Chi (b. 1898), former chairman [chief of state] of the **People's Republic of China**, died under mysterious circumstances. His death was was not officially confirmed until Jan. 28, 1979. For many years Liu had been the right hand man of **Mao Tse-Tung** and, when Mao resigned (1959) his government position, retaining his power through personal prestige and his leadership of the Communist party, Liu succeeded him. But Liu fell out with Mao by opposing the **Cultural Revolution** (1966–1969). He was termed (Oct., 1968) a "renegade, traitor, and scab," deprived of his office, and expelled from the Communist party. Eventually Liu was officially exonerated (Feb., 1980) of all crimes against the party and the government.

1969 Nov. 17   Strategic arms limitation talks [SALT] opened in Helsinki, Finland, between the U.S. and the U.S.S.R., with the goal of limiting and reducing the number of strategic nuclear weapons and delivery systems. It was agreed to open formal negotiations in Vienna, Austria, on Apr. 16, 1970.

1969 Nov. 24   The U.S. and the U.S.S.R. signed the **Nuclear Non-proliferation Treaty**, which pledged signatories not to spread technological information of materials that would aid in developing nuclear weaponry. The pact was approved by the U.N. General Assembly.

III. ECONOMY AND TRADE

1969 Jan. 10   The publishers of the **Saturday Evening Post**, founded in Philadelphia in 1821, announced it would suspend publication and did so in February. Long one of the nation's favorite weeklies, it was beset by rising costs and loss of advertising revenue.

1969 Sept. 10   Seeking the right to drill for **oil on the Alaskan North Slope**, oil companies bid $900,220,590 for leases on 179 tracts totaling 450,858 acres. Alaska was to receive a royalty of 12.5 percent on the oil produced and other considerations. Oil reserves there were estimated at between 50 and 100 billion barrels.

1969 Sept. 14   The **Northwest Passage**, around the northern end of the North American continent, was **traversed for the first time by a commercial ship**. It was the 115,000 ton tanker **Manhattan**, designed for the purpose. It sailed from the east coast of the U.S. and had to be assisted several times by a Canadian icebreaker. The purpose of the trip was to determine whether it was feasible to ship oil from Alaska's North Slope to America's east coast ports. In the end, the idea was abandoned.

1969 Oct. 20   The **International Labor Organization** [ILO], a specialized agency of the U.N., was awarded the **Nobel Peace Prize** for 1969. The award was made to honor the ILO's endeavors to improve the conditions of labor and to promote social welfare.

IV. RELIGION AND PHILOSOPHY

1969 Feb. 26   Karl [Theodor] **Jaspers** (b. Feb. 23, 1883), a German philosopher and psychiatrist, died. He was a university professor until barred (1939) from teaching and publishing by the Nazis. His philosophy concerned itself with man's existence and the true understanding of it. English translations of Jaspers's works included **Man in the Modern Age** (1933) and **Reason and Existence** (1956).

V. SCIENCE, EDUCATION, AND TECHNOLOGY

1969 Jan. 16   For the **first time men in one spacecraft transferred in orbit** to another. The Russians put **Soyuz 4** with one man aboard in orbit on Jan. 14 and **Soyuz 5** with three men aboard the next day.

After four hours of mingling the crews separated their spacecraft.

1969 Jan. 16 The **first total synthesis of an enzyme** was accomplished by researchers in the U.S. The enzyme was ribonuclease.

1969 Mar. 2 The **first test flight of the Anglo-French** *Concorde,* the supersonic jet transport plane, took place at Toulouse, France. The **first public flight of the Boeing 747**, a jet intended to carry from 350 to 500 passengers, took place on Dec. 2.

1969 Apr. 4 The **first artificial heart implant** took place at St. Luke's Episcopal Hospital in Houston. The operation was performed by a surgical team led by **Denton A. Cooley** (b. Aug. 22, 1920). The recipient, a 47-year-old man, was given a human heart from a donor 65 hours later. On April 8 the patient died of pneumonia and kidney failure.

1969 July 5 **Walter** [Adolph] **Gropius** (b. May 18, 1883), a German-born American architect, died. In 1919 in Weimar, Germany, he founded the *Bauhaus,* which became influential world wide in art and architecture. Gropius remained its director until 1928. In his own work Gropius stressed the use of glass walls. He designed the Harvard Graduate Center (1949–1950) and the U.S. Embassy in Athens, Greece (1960).

1969 July 20 **Neil A. Armstrong**, U.S. astronaut, stepped down from the lunar excursion module [LEM] of Apollo 11 onto the surface of the moon and said, via television to the world: "That's one small step for a man, one giant leap for mankind." He was joined by **Edwin E. "Buzz" Aldrin** (b. Jan. 20, 1930), while **Michael Collins** (b. Oct. 30, 1930) remained in the command ship in lunar orbit. The two astronauts spent 21 hours on the moon and collected samples of moon rock and soil. They returned to the command ship on July 21, and on July 24 Apollo 11 returned safely to earth.

1969 Aug. 17 **Ludwig Mies van der Rohe** (b. Mar. 27, 1886), a German-born architect who came to the U.S. in 1937, died. He was director of the *Bauhaus* (1930–1933). In his architecture he emphasized simple forms and glass curtain walls and became a leader of the **International style** in architecture. Among his buildings were the **Seagram Building** (1956–1958), with Philip Johnson, New York City, and the **New National Gallery** (1968), Berlin.

1969 Nov. 10 **Sesame Street**, the U.S. television program planned to entertain and instruct preschool children, made its first appearance on 170 noncommercial stations. It became and remained enormously popular. On its 20th anniversary (Nov. 1989), Sesame Street was being watched by 11 million American households via the **Public Broadcasting System** [PBS] and by children in more than 80 countries.

1969 Nov. 22 Harvard Medical School scientists announced they had succeeded in **isolating a single gene**, the basic unit of heredity, for the first time.

VI. ARTS AND LEISURE

1969 Jan. 25 **Irene** [Foote] **Castle** (b. 1893), a popular dancer of the World War I era, died. With her husband **Vernon** [Blythe] **Castle** (May 2, 1887–Feb. 15, 1918) she popularized new dance steps, such as the **Castle Walk** and the two step.

1969 Feb. 3 **Boris Karloff** [orig.: William Henry Pratt] (b. Nov. 22, 1887), an English-born American actor, died. Although an actor of all-around ability, he became the monster everyone loved to watch, as in the movie *Frankenstein* (1931), his first of many successes.

1969 Mar. 14 **Ben**[jamin] **Shahn** (b. Sept. 12, 1889), an American artist born in Lithuania, died. He devoted much of his artistic work to social and political causes. Among his works were *The Red Stairway* (1944) and *Death of a Miner* (1947).

1969 Mar. 25 **Max** [Forrester] **Eastman** (b. Jan. 4, 1883), an American social and literary critic, died. A radical for much of his life, he was a founder and editor of the leftist magazine *The Masses* (1913–1918). Later he turned against communism and socialism to write such works as *Reflections on the Failure of Socialism* (1955). He also wrote *The Literary Mind: Its Place in an Age of Science* (1931) and *The Enjoyment of Poetry* (1913). His poetry was collected in *Poems of Five Decades* (1954).

1969 June 22 **Judy Garland** [Frances Gumm] (b. June 10, 1922), an American singer and actress, died. Her many films included *The Wizard of Oz* (1939), *Meet Me in St. Louis* (1944), and *A Star Is Born* (1954). Garland's appearances in concert brought her adulation in many cities of the world.

1969 Aug. 27 Ivy Compton-Burnett (b. June 5, 1884), an English novelist, died. Among her novels were *Pastors and Masters* (1925), *Parents and Children* (1941), and *A Father and His Fate* (1957).

1969 Oct. 5 Monty Python's Flying Circus, a unique television comedy, made its first appearance in England. Written, produced, and acted by a group of young men, it was zany, off-beat, and successful. The show featured such skits as "The Ministry of Silly Walks" and "The Hospital for Overacting." It also became a hit in the U.S.

1969 Dec. 22 Josef von Sternberg [orig.: Jonas Sternberg] (b. May 29, 1894), an Austrian-born American film director, died. One of his great successes was *The Last Command* (1928). Sternberg is now best known for the films he made starring **Marlene Dietrich**, beginning spectacularly with one produced in Berlin, *Der Blaue Engel* [*The Blue Angel*] (1930). His other Dietrich movies, included *Shanghai Express* (1932), *The Scarlet Empress* (1934), and *The Devil Is a Woman* (1935).

VII. SPORTS, GAMES, AND SOCIETY

1969 Jan. 12 The New York Jets beat the favored Baltimore Colts in **Super Bowl** III and won, 16–7, at Miami, Florida.

1969 Apr. 22 Robin Knox-Johnston (b. Mar. 17, 1939) of Great Britain became the **first person to sail singlehandedly and nonstop around the world**. He had had been alone at sea for 312 days.

1969 June 24–25 At **Wimbledon** tennis courts in London [Richard Alonzo] **Pancho Gonzales** (b. May 9, 1928) beat fellow American **Charles Pasarell** (b. Feb. 12, 1944) in a 5 hr., 12 min. match played over two days. Gonzales, 16 years older than his opponent, lost the first two sets before darkness ended play on June 24, but he came back the next day to win three sets and the match.

1969 July 18 **Thor Heyerdahl**, a Norwegian explorer and anthropologist, and his crew abandoned the **Ra**, their boat made of papyrus, c.600 miles from the Western Hemisphere after having sailed from Safi, Morocco, on May 25. Heyerdahl had sought to show that the Inca and Mayan civilizations of the Americas had been influenced by Egyptian culture long before Columbus reached the New World. The expedition traveled 2,600 miles before having to abandon ship.

1969 Aug. 15–17 A rock concert, the **Woodstock Music and Art Fair**, held at Bethel, N.Y., attracted c.400,000 persons who overwhelmed traffic, food, water, and sanitary facilities. About 80 arrests were made for drug use, although marijuana smokers were not bothered.

1969 Sept. 8 **Rod Laver** of Australia became the only person ever to win the grand slam of **tennis** twice when he took the U.S. men's singles championship. Previously in 1969 he had won the Australian, French, and British titles.

1969 Dec. 18 The British House of Lords completed parliamentary action **ending capital punishment in Great Britain**.

1970

I. VITAL STATISTICS AND DEMOGRAPHICS

1970 The **world population** was estimated to be 3,647,739,000: **Africa**, 350,836,000; **Asia**, 2,073,299,-000; **Europe**, 460,352,000; **North America**, 315,871,-000; **Oceania**, 18,939,000; **South America**, 186,694,-000; USSR, 241,748,000. The U.S. census counted 204,765,770 resident Americans, an increase of 13.3 percent over 1960. The ten largest metropolitan areas were: Tokyo, 23,123,358; New York, 11,900,-000; Shanghai, 10,000,000; London, 7,703,410; Moscow, 7,061,000; Peking, 7,060,000; Bombay, 5,700,-358; Cairo, 5,925,400; São Paulo, 5,648,706; Jakarta, 4,349,950.

II. DISASTERS

1970 Jan. 5 An **earthquake in Yunnan province**, China, killed c.10,000 people. There were reports that the provincial capital of Kunming had been destroyed, but the Chinese government did not disclose the earthquake until several years later.

1970 Jan. 27–28 In the Elburz Mountains northeast of Teheran, Iran, **snow avalanches** sweeping over a highway landed c.150 vehicles in a deep ravine. The accident caused 43 deaths; but c.1,000 were rescued.

1970 Feb. 1 A passenger **train crashed** into a stalled commuter train near Buenos Aires, Argentina, killing 141 persons and injuring 170.

1970 Mar. 28–31 An **earthquake in Kutahya province**, Turkey, killed 1,087, injured c.1,500, and left c.90,000 persons homeless.

1970 May 2 By this time c.**50,000 Biafrans had died of starvation** since the surrender of their insurrectionary forces to the Nigerian army on Jan. 15. The International Red Cross was feeding c.2,500,000 persons, most of them children, while c.30,000 hospital patients were suffering from malnutrition.

1970 May 31 An **earthquake** centered 12 miles off the coast of Peru caused 66,794 deaths over a wide area inland. It was estimated that 800,000 were made homeless.

1970 Nov. 1 A **fire swept through a crowded dance hall** at St. Laurent du Pont, near Grenoble, France, causing the deaths of 146 youths between the ages of 17 and 25.

1970 Nov. 12–13 A **cyclone** drove tidal waves from the Bay of Bengal onto the coast and deltas of East Pakistan [present Bangladesh]. The official death toll was 200,000, but the U.N.'s estimate was 1,000,-000, with c.100,000 missing, and damage estimated at $2,000,000,000.

1970 Dec. 15 In the Korea Strait a **ferryboat capsized** because of its unbalanced cargo, throwing 278 passengers and crew members into icy waters. At least 261 died.

III. POLITICS AND WAR

1970 Jan. 15 The 31-month **civil war in Nigeria** ended when the Ibo people of the **Biafra** area surrendered. Their last stronghold Owerri had been captured (Jan. 12), and the surrender was announced by **Yakubu Gowon**, president of Nigeria. The insurrection leader, **Chukwuemeka Odumegwu Ojukwu** (b. 1933), fled the country.

1970 Jan. 26 **Student rioting broke out in Manila**, capital of the **Philippines**, to protest the corruption of the government of **Ferdinand Marcos**, the president. Demonstrators tried (Jan. 30) to break into the grounds of the presidential palace. They were fired on, leaving 5 dead and 157 wounded. Rioting broke out again on Mar. 31 and ended on Apr. 2 after Marcos said he would not run for a third term.

1970 Mar. 2 Under the leadership of **Ian [Douglas] Smith**, **Rhodesia declared itself a republic** and severed all ties with the British crown. The British government called the action illegal and said Rhodesia was still a colony.

1970 Mar. 4 **Students at Kent State University**, Athens, Ohio, during a protest against American military involvement in Southeast Asia, were fired on without warning by Ohio National Guardsmen. Four students were killed and nine wounded. The action led to nation-wide demonstrations on campuses. Criminal charges against eight of the guardsmen were dropped on Nov. 8, 1974.

1970 Mar. 5 The **Treaty on the Non-Proliferation of Nuclear Weapons** went into effect, having been ratified by the U.S., the U.S.S.R., and Great Britain, as well as by 40 other countries.

1970 Mar. 18 The National Assembly of **Cambodia voted to depose Norodom Sihanouk**, a prince and head of state, while he was in Moscow. **Lon Nol** (b. Nov. 13, 1913) remained prime minister and became the most powerful person in the government. Sihanouk took refuge in China. A republic was proclaimed (Oct. 5) in Cambodia with Lon Nol as president.

1970 Apr. 29 **U.S. and South Vietnamese forces invaded** the section of neutral **Cambodia**, known as the Parrot's Beak, to attack supply lines being used by the **Viet Cong** and North Vietnamese troops during the **Vietnam War**. Vowing support for the Cambodian regime of **Lon Nol**, **Richard M. Nixon**, president of the U.S., withdrew (June 29) American forces. Notwithstanding, more than 500,000 tons of bombs were dropped on Cambodian soil by Aug. 1973.

1970 May 9 **Protests against the war in Vietnam** were begun in the U.S. because of the American invasion of neutral Cambodia. Ten days later c.100,000 anti-war demonstrators gathered in Washington, D.C. Nearly 450 colleges and universities were said to be the scene of strikes protesting the war. On May 20 in New York City there was a counter demonstration supporting American policy in Southeast Asia. **Richard M. Nixon**, president of the U.S., established (June 13) a **Commission on Campus Unrest**. It reported that many of America's youth were against the war, concerned about racial injustice, and unhappy with modern American life.

1970 June 8 Amid growing violence by guerrilla groups both left and right, the **Argentine army staged a coup** that forced the resignation of **Juan Carlos Ongania**, president of Argentina (from 1966). He was replaced by **Roberto Marcello Levingston** (b. Jan. 10, 1920), an army general.

1970 June 11 **Alexander Feodorovich Kerensky** [Aleksandr Feodorovich Kerenski, Fyodorovich] (b. Apr. 22, 1881), a one-time head of the Russian government, died. Active in opposition to the czarist regime for many years, he led the revolutionary government from July 1917 until his regime was overthrown by the Bolshevik [Russian] Revolution on Nov. 6. Kerensky fled (1918) to Paris and later moved (1940) to the U.S. He taught, lectured, and wrote several books, among them *The Crucifixion of Liberty* (1934) and *The Kerensky Memoirs* (1966).

1970 June 18 In **British elections**, the Conservative party defeated the Labour party. The Conservatives won 360 seats in Parliament to Labour's 287. **Edward** [Richard George] **Heath** (b. July 9, 1916) replaced [James] **Harold Wilson** as prime minister.

1970 June 21 **Sukarno** (b. June 1, 1901), first president of independent Indonesia, died. Before World War II he had fought Dutch rule and after 1942 he collaborated with the Japanese invaders. In 1945 his group declared Indonesia independent and fought the Dutch until 1949, when independence was granted. Sukarno was deposed on Mar. 12, 1967.

1970 July 5 **Luís Echeverría Álvarez** (b. Jan. 17, 1922) was elected president of **Mexico** for a six-year term. He was the candidate of the **Institutional Revolutionary party**, which had dominated Mexican politics for many years.

1970 July 23 In a palace coup **Qaboos** [Qabus] (b. Nov., 1940), of the **Al-Busayyid** [Busa'id] **Dynasty** (1741–to the present), deposed his father **Sayyid** [Sa'id] **bin Taimur**, sultan of **Oman and Muscat**

(from 1932), a nation on the Arabian Sea. The son charged his father with holding back the progress of the country, especially in light of its growing wealth from oil production. Qaboos lifted the bans on smoking, singing, and wearing western clothes. He allowed foreign journalists into the country and allowed foreign travel. The name of the country was changed from the Sultanate of Muscat and Oman to the **Sultanate of Oman**. Qaboos ruled by decree.

1970 Aug. 28 **Western Somoa** became the first independent non-Commonwealth state to join the Commonwealth.

1970 Sept. 4 **Salvador Allende Gossens**, a lawyer and physician who had been active in politics for many years, became the **first avowed Marxist to be elected president of a nation in the Western Hemisphere**. His leftist coalition had a margin of only about one percent of the popular vote.

1970 Sept. 6–30 Three **passenger jet planes**, one American, one British, and one Swiss, **were hijacked** in Europe en route to New York by **Palestinian terrorists** and forced to fly to Jordan. The passengers were held hostage until the hijackers' demands for the release of certain imprisoned fellow terrorists were met. The last passengers were not set free until Sept. 30 and the hijackers then blew up all three planes. There were numerous other attempts and successful hijackings this year.

1970 Sept. 17 Heavy fighting broke out in Jordan between the army and **Palestine Liberation Organization** [PLO] guerrillas. The PLO was strong in the northern part of the country and for a while held part of the capital, Amman. Syrian forces crossed the border to assist the guerrillas. The Jordanian army gained the upper hand and the guerrillas agreed (Sept. 25) to a ceasefire although they continued to hold two strongholds in the north. Between 1,500 and 5,000 persons, including civilians, were killed in the fighting and more than 10,000 injured.

1970 Sept. 29 **Gamal Abdel Nasser** (b. Jan. 15, 1918), president of the **United Arab Republic** [Egypt] (from 1956), died. An army officer, he led the coup that overthrew Farouk, king of Egypt (from 1936), in July, 1952. In 1956 he nationalized the Suez Canal, thus removing it from British control. Nasser was president of the United Arab Republic (1958–1961), which attempted to join Egypt and Syria. Egypt continued to use the UAR name. During his presidency economic and social reforms were instituted, but Nasser's most notable asset was his ability to make Arabs feel proud of their heritage.

1970 Oct. 6 In **Bolivia** a military junta overthrew the leftist government of **Alfredo Ovando Candia** (Apr. 6, 1918–Jan. 24, 1982). The junta, in power only one day, in turn was ousted by a left-wing group headed by **Juan José Torres Gonzales** (b. Mar. 5, 1921), a general. He strengthened ties with the Soviet Union and pursued an anti-American policy.

1970 Oct. 10 Fiji, in the southwestern Pacific Ocean, became an independent republic. The first prime minister was **Ratu Kamisese Mara** (b. May 13, 1920) of the multiracial Alliance party. Fiji became a member of the Commonwealth of Nations.

1970 Oct. 10 Édouard Daladier (b. June 18, 1884), the premier (1938–1940) of **France** at the time of the Munich crisis in 1938, died. He had also been premier in 1933 and 1934 for brief periods. Daladier followed a policy of appeasing Hitler and Germany after he became premier in Apr. 1938. He resumed his political career after World War II, but never regained prominent office.

1970 Oct. 19 Lázaro Cárdenas (b. May 21, 1895), 45th president of **Mexico** from 1934 to 1940, died. He broke up large estates and distributed more than 40 million acres of land to poor farmers. In 1938 Cardenas nationalized the oil industry.

1970 Nov. 5 Peter II (b. Sept. 6, 1923), of the **House of Karageorgevich** and the **last king of Yugoslavia**, died. He came to the throne on Oct. 9, 1934, after his father was assassinated. In 1941 he was forced by the German invasion to leave the country, and in 1945 the monarchy was abolished.

1970 Nov. 9 Charles [André Joseph Marie] **de Gaulle** (b. Nov. 22, 1890) died. He was three times wounded in World War I and, after France fell (1940) to the Nazi invasion, he made himself head of the Free French forces and carried on the struggle. After France was liberated, he headed (1944–1946) a provisional government of France; then he served as president (1959–1969), having established (1958) a new constitution for the Fifth Republic.

1970 Nov. 13 The moderate wing of the **Ba'ath party**, led by the defense minister **Hafez al-Assad** (b. Oct. 6, 1930), seized power in a bloodless coup in **Syria**, ousting **Nureddin Louai al-Attassi**. Assad assumed the post of president on Feb. 22, 1971, and a national referendum (Mar. 12) confirmed him in the position for a seven-year term.

1970 Dec. 7 The **first direct national election in Pakistan** was won by the Awami League of East Pakistan, led by **Sheik Mujibur Rahman** (Mar. 17, 1920–Aug. 15, 1975), which took 151 seats in the 300-seat national assembly. The leader of the opposition, **Agha Muhammad Yahya Khan** (Feb. 14, 1917–Aug. 8, 1980), president of Pakistan, then postponed the meeting of the assembly scheduled for Mar. 1, 1971.

1970 Dec. 15 Polish workers in Gdansk and other Baltic coast cities **rioted** when increases in food prices were announced. As a result **Wladyslaw Gomulka**, who had headed the Communist party for 14 years, was forced to resign. He was succeeded by **Edward Gierek** (b. Jan. 6, 1913), who had been active in Communist party affairs since World War II.

1970 Dec. 31 The U.S. government reported that since Jan. 1, 1961, 44,241 **Americans** had been **killed in the Vietnam War** and 293,529 wounded. The South Vietnamese army had lost 117,007 killed and 249,540 wounded. American troop strength in Vietnam was down to 343,700 from its peak of more than 500,000.

IV. ECONOMY AND TRADE

1970 Feb. 23 Under [Linden] **Forbes Sampson Burnham** (Feb. 20, 1923–Aug. 6, 1985), prime minister, **Guyana was proclaimed a cooperative republic.** The objectives, Burnham said, were to eradicate the "colonial mentality" and to create a "self-help program based on a national system of cooperative ventures."

1970 Oct. 19 The **British Petroleum Company** announced discovery of a **major oil field in the North Sea** 110 miles northeast of Aberdeen, Scotland.

V. RELIGION AND PHILOSOPHY

1970 Feb. 1 Pope Paul VI said that **priestly celibacy** could not be questioned.

1970 Feb. 2 Bertrand [Arthur William] **Russell**, Third Earl Russell (b. May 18, 1872), an English philosopher and mathematician, died. Among his principal works were *Principia Mathematica* (1910–1913), with **A. N. Whitehead**, and *An Outline of philosophy* (1927). He won the **Nobel prize for literature** in 1950.

1970 Mar. 16 Publication of **The New English Bible** was completed with the appearance of the Old Testament, the New Testament having been issued in 1961. The translation was made directly from ancient texts by a body of English scholars representing the Protestant churches of the British Isles.

1970 Sept. 30 **The New American Bible** appeared under the sponsorship of the Bishops' Committee of the Confraternity of Christian Doctrine. It was the first translation of the whole Bible under Roman Catholic auspices directly from original sources. The work was carried out by 51 scholars, four of them Protestants.

VI. SCIENCE, EDUCATION, AND TECHNOLOGY

1970 The **High Aswan Dam** [Sadd-el-Aali] on the Nile River in Upper Egypt was completed this year. The dam is 364 feet high and 121,565 feet long at the top. It was paid for chiefly by the U.S.S.R. During construction the ancient Egyptian **Temple of Abu Simbel** was cut free from its rock strata, where it would have been submerged by the new Lake Nasser when the dam was finished, and raised to a position where it would be above water and so remain available to visitors.

1970 Apr. 7 The U.S. manned spacecraft **Apollo 13**, which had blasted off on Apr. 11 on a trip to the moon, ended an aborted flight with a successful splashdown.

1970 Apr. 22 The **first Earth Day**, organized to call attention to dangers to the environment posed by pollution, was celebrated in the U.S. Rallies were held in a number of cities, with as many as 25,000 people turning out for those in Chicago, New York, and Philadelphia. The day was said to have been observed on c.2,000 college campuses and by c.10,000 elementary and high schools.

1970 June 3 University of Wisconsin scientists announced **synthesis of a gene from chemical components**. The leader of the group achieving this feat was **Har Gobind Khorana** (b. Jan. 9, 1922).

1970 Sept. 20 An unmanned Russian spacecraft, *Luna 16*, landed on the moon, having been launched on Sept. 12. It landed back on earth on Sept. 24. On Nov. 17, *Luna 17*, launched on Nov. 11, also landed on the moon. It carried with it a self-propelled vehicle called Lunokhod 1 which traveled c.300 feet across the moon's surface, taking pictures that were transmitted back to earth. On Aug. 17 the Russians launched *Venera 7*, which reached the planet Venus on Dec. 15. However, it ceased transmitting signals 35 minutes after it began descending into the atmosphere of thick clouds.

1970 Oct. 21 **Norman Ernest Borlaug** (b. Mar. 25, 1914), an American scientist, was awarded the **Nobel Peace Prize** for his work in plant pathology that had made him the **"father of the Green Revolution"** in agriculture. Working first in Mexico, he developed strains of wheat that by 1949 were producing twice as much as older strains. These new varieties were introduced into India and Pakistan in 1963 and brought greatly increased yields.

VII. ARTS AND LEISURE

1970 Feb. 17 S[hmuel] Y[osef] **Agnon** [orig.: Samuel Josef Czaczkes] (b. July 17, 1888), an Israeli novelist and active Zionist, died. Agnon wrote almost entirely in Hebrew, and his work dealt with the problems of Jews in their relationships with other cultures. Among his works were *Ha-khnasat kallah* [*The Bridal Canopy*] (1930), *Oreah natah lalun* [*A Guest for the Night*] (1939), and *Ad olam* [*Forever More*] (1954). Agnon shared the **Nobel prize for literature** in 1966, the first Hebrew writer to receive this award.

1970 Feb. 25 **Mark Rothko** [orig.: Marcus Rothovich] (b. Sept. 25, 1903), a Russian-born American abstract expressionist painter, committed suicide. Rothko's very large canvases reflected a certain calmness of spirit. Among them were *No. 2, 1948* (1948), *The Black and the Red* (1956), and *Black on Grey* (1970).

1970 Apr. 11 **John** [Henry] **O'Hara** (b. Jan. 31, 1905), an American novelist and short-story writer, died. He published eight collections of short stories in addition to his other works. His first novel was *Appointment in Samarra* (1934), a taut, realistic story set in a Pennsylvania city that was the milieu for much of his work. He followed this with *Butterfield Eight* (1935), *A Rage to Live* (1949), *Ten North*

Frederick (1955), *From the Terrace* (1958), and many other novels.

1970 June 7 E[dward] M[organ] **Forster** (b. Jan. 1, 1879), an English novelist and essayist, died. His novels included *Where Angels Fear to Tread* (1905), *The Longest Journey* (1907), and *A Room With a View* (1908). *Howard's End* (1910) established Forster as a novelist of first rank, but *A Passage to India* (1924) is now judged his most important work.

1970 July 28 John Barbirolli [Giovanni Battista] (b. Dec. 2, 1899), a British conductor, died. He directed a number of orchestras, including the **Scottish Orchestra**, the **Halle Orchestra**, and the **Houston Symphony**. In 1936 he succeeded **Arturo Toscanini** as conductor of the **New York Philharmonic Orchestra** and led it for six years.

1970 July 29 George Szell (b. June 7, 1897), a Hungarian-born American conductor, died. After conducting in several European cities, including Berlin, Prague, and Strasbourg, he made his first appearance in the U.S. in 1931. Eight years later he moved to America and became (1946–1970) conductor of the **Cleveland Symphony**.

1970 Sept. 1 François Mauriac (b. Oct. 11, 1885), a French novelist, playwright, and essayist, died. His writings were permeated by problems of sin and the struggle of human beings to find redemption. Typical are *Le Désert de l'amour* [*The Desert of Love*] (1925), *Thérèse Desqueyroux* (1927), and *Le Noeud de vipères* [*Vipers' Tangle*] (1932). Mauriac's views on religion and philosophy were seen in *La Vie de Jésus* [*The Life of Jesus*] (1936) and *Dieu et Mammon* [*God and Mammon*] (1929). He received the **Nobel prize for literature** in 1952.

1970 Sept. 4 Natalia Makarova (b. Nov. 21, 1940), a leading ballerina of the **Leningrad Kirov Ballet**, defected in London while the troupe was performing there. Going immediately to the U.S., she joined the **American Ballet Theater** and danced (Oct. 11) in *Giselle*.

1970 Sept. 25 Erich Maria Remarque (b. June 22, 1898), a German author who won fame with his world-wide bestseller *Im Westen nichts Neues* [*All Quiet on the Western Front*] (1929), died. He also wrote *Three Comrades* (1937) and *Arch of Triumph* (1946).

1970 Sept. 28 John [Roderigo] **Dos Passos** (b. Jan. 14, 1896), an American novelist, biographer, and essayist, died. *Manhattan Transfer* (1925), although not his first book, set his style and viewpoint. Dos Passos became best known for his trilogy *U.S.A.* which consisted of *The 42nd Parallel* (1930), *1919* (1932), and *The Big Money* (1936). In this account of the first 30 years of the 20th century he pictured America as a decaying civilization.

1970 Oct. 8 Aleksandr [Isayevich] **Solzhenitsyn** (b. Dec. 11, 1918), a Russian author, was awarded the **Nobel prize for literature**. He applied to the Soviet officials for permission to go to Stockholm, Sweden, to receive the award. When it was indicated he might not be allowed to return, he withdrew the request. From 1945 to 1957 he had been in prison camps and suffered internal exile for a slighting remark about Joseph Stalin. In 1962, when anti-Stalinism had become acceptable, he published *One Day in the Life of Ivan Denisovich*, a novel set in a prison camp. *The First Circle* (1964) and *The Cancer Ward* (1966), depressing depictions of life under communism, were published in the West but not in the U.S.S.R.

1970 Nov. 25 Yuko Mishima [Kimitake Hiraoka] (b. Jan. 14, 1925), a Japanese novelist, playwright, and essayist, died by committing ritual suicide [suppuku] to protest what he believed to be the spinelessness of post-World War II Japan. His writings showed regret for the disappearance of the ideals of an older Japan, as well as concern with the place of love, beauty, violence, and death in modern civilization. Among Mishima's works were *Shiosai* (1954); *Gogo no eiko* [*The Sailor Who Fell from Grace With the Sea*] (1965), produced as a movie in 1974; and the tetralogy *Hojo no umi* [*The Sea of Fertility*] (1965–1971).

VIII. SPORTS, GAMES, AND SOCIETY

1970 Feb. 16 After **Muhammad Ali** was stripped (1967) of his **world heavyweight boxing** title for refusing induction into the U.S. armed forces, a new champion was crowned. He was **Joe Frazier** (b. Jan. 17, 1944) who, in a bout in New York City, knocked out **Jimmy Ellis** in the fifth round.

1970 June 21 Brazil defeated Italy in the **World Cup** final of soccer in Mexico City, 4–1.

1970 Aug. 12 Curt[is Charles] **Flood** (b. Jan. 18, 1938) lost his $4.1 million suit against organized baseball. Flood challenged the "reserve clause" in players' contracts, which in effect prevented a player from bargaining with any other club. The court said federal antitrust laws did not apply to **professional baseball**.

1970 Sept. 3 [Vincent Thomas] **Vince Lombardi** (b. June 11, 1913), a celebrated **American football** coach, died. He became (1959) head coach of the Green Bay Packers, leading them to six conference titles and five National Football League [NFL] championships before retiring in 1968. Lombardi is remembered for his words: "Winning isn't everything—it's the only thing."

1970 Sept. 12 Margaret Smith Court (b. July 16, 1942) of Great Britain became the second wo-man to win the grand slam of **tennis** when she took the women's singles championship at the U.S. Open tournament. She had previously this year won the Australian, French, and British titles.

1970 Sept. 13 Expo '70, a world's fair, in Osaka, Japan, closed. Total attendance was 64,218,770, a record.

1970 Sept. 15–28 The **America's Cup** of international yacht racing was successfully defended by the American entry *Intrepid*, which defeated the Australian challenger *Gretel II* in four straight races off Newport, Rhode Island.

1971

I. DISASTERS

1971 Feb. 2 At the end of a **soccer game in Glasgow**, Scotland, a crowd of fans attempted to force its way through a steel barrier, resulting in the **death** of 66 persons.

1971 Feb. 9 An **earthquake struck southern California**, affecting especially the San Fernando Valley. It left 65 people dead and c.1,000 injured. The quake registered 6.5 on the Richter scale.

1971 Mar. 18 An **avalanche of mud, rocks, and water**, triggered by a slight earthquake near Canta, c.40 miles north of Lima, Peru, caused the deaths of about 600 persons.

1971 June 6 A DC-9 commercial **airliner and a U.S. marine Phantom F-4 fighter plane collided** at 12,000 feet over the San Gabriel Mountains near Azusa, California. All 49 passengers and the marine pilot died.

1971 July 30 An All-Nippon Boeing **727 and a Japanese air force F-86 collided** at an altitude of 26,000 feet over Morioka, Honshu, Japan. All 162 passengers were killed. The student pilot of the air force plane parachuted to safety.

1971 Sept. 4 At Juneau, Alaska, an Alaskan Airlines Boeing **727**, approaching the airport, **hit a** mountainside and fell into a deep gorge. All 111 persons aboard died.

1971 Dec. 25 An **explosion and fire in a restaurant in Seoul**, South Korea, killed 162 persons and injured c.100.

II. POLITICS AND WAR

1971 Jan. 25 A **military coup led by Idi Amin** (b. 1925), an army officer, overthrew the regime of [Apollo] **Milton Obote**, president of **Uganda** (from 1966). Obote fled to Tanzania. Amin, a Muslim, began a purge of Christians, whom he considered a threat to the new regime.

1971 Feb. 2 Swiss voters approved giving women the right to vote in federal elections and to hold national office.

1971 Feb. 3–9 Fighting between Protestants and Catholics in **Northern Ireland** broke out again, leaving 11 dead. **James Chichester-Clark** (b. Feb. 12, 1923) resigned (Mar. 20) as prime minister, having been criticized for not being tough enough in suppressing the violence. He was succeeded (Mar. 23) as prime minister (to 1972) by **Brian Faulkner** (b. Feb. 18, 1921) of the Unionist [Protestant] party. The British government announced (Aug. 9) a **policy of preventive arrest** under which it was free to arrest suspected members of the **Irish Republican Army**

[IRA]. This triggered further violence. During the year 47 soldiers and policemen and 76 civilians were killed.

1971 Feb. 8 **South Vietnamese troops**, with U.S. air support, **invaded Laos** in an attempt to cut cupply lines of the North Vietnamese fighting in the south. The incursion ended Mar. 24, when all but c.500 of the c.20,000-man task force left Laos.

1971 Feb. 11 Sixty-three nations in ceremonies in London, Moscow, and Washington signed a **treaty banning installation of nuclear weapons on the seabed** beyond any country's 12-mile coastal limit.

1971 Mar. 12 **Suleiman Demirel**, leader of the **Justice party**, resigned as prime minister of **Turkey**. He was replaced by **Nihat Erim** (1912–July 19, 1980), leader of the **Republican People's party**, who declared limited martial law.

1971 Mar. 18 **Indira Gandhi** was sworn in as prime minister of **India** for the third time. In elections held from Mar. 1 to 10, her Congress party won 349 out of 521 seats in the Indian Parliament.

1971 Mar. 22 A coup by a military junta removed [Roberto] **Marcelo Levingston**, president of **Argentina**. The coup was led by **Alejandro** [Agustin] **Lanusse** (b. Aug. 28, 1918), whose junta had put Levingston in office only the year before. On Mar. 26 Lanusse was sworn in as president.

1971 Mar. 26 **East Pakistan declared its independence** as the nation of **Bangladesh**. It was then occupied by the Pakistan army, all of whose troops were from West Pakistan. Civil war followed, with several hundred thousand civilians killed and as many as 10 million fleeing to India.

1971 Mar. 29 A court martial convicted **William L[aws] Calley, Jr.** (b. 1943), a U.S. army lieutenant, of the murder of 22 South Vietnam civilians at the hamlet of **My Lai** on Mar. 16, 1968. Calley was sentenced to life imprisonment. **Richard M. Nixon**, president of the U.S., ordered Calley freed from the army stockade and placed under house arrest while he appealed. A general who reviewed the case reduced (Aug. 20) his sentence to 20 years and on Sept. 25, 1974, a federal court overturned his conviction.

1971 Apr. 7 **Richard M. Nixon**, president of the U.S., announced that by Dec. 1 there would be a

reduction of 100,000 in the number of U.S. troops in South Vietnam. The next day peace talks in Paris between America and the North Vietnamese, which had been suspended by the North Vietnamese on Mar. 18, resumed. By the end of the year **U.S. troop strength in Vietnam** was down to c.184,000 and the death toll had reached 45,543. About 200,000 turned out for an anti-war march (Apr. 24) on Washington, and there was another demonstration (May 3–5), during which nearly 13,000 people were arrested.

1971 Apr. 21 **François Duvalier** (b. Apr. 14, 1907), the dictator of **Haiti**, died. In 1957 "Papa Doc" had been elected president for life. He ruled through superstition and terror. Before dying he had the constitution amended so that he could be succeeded by his 19-year-old son **Jean-Claude** (b. July 3, 1951), known as **"Baby Doc."**

1971 May 3 **Erich Honecker** (b. Aug. 25, 1912) became first secretary of the Communist party of the **German Democratic Republic** [East Germany], replacing **Walter Ulbricht** (June 30, 1893–Aug. 1, 1973), who said he was old and sick. Honecker had been a communist since the age of 14 and had been held in prison by the Gestapo from 1935 to the end of World War II, after which he helped set up the East German government, a satellite of the USSR.

1971 June 6 **Ramón Ernesto Cruz Uclés** (b. Jan. 4, 1903) became president of **Honduras**, having won the election of Mar. 28. He represented a return to constitutional government, with all political parties supporting national unity. But real power was retained by **Osvaldo Lopez Arellano**, who had headed to military juntas (1956–1957, 1963–1965) and had been elected president (1965–1971).

1971 June 13 *The New York Times* began publication of what became known as the "Pentagon Papers," extracts from a 47-volume report prepared by the U.S. Department of Defense under the title *History of the U.S. Decision-Making Process on Vietnam Policy*. The report covered the subject to 1968 and was classified "top secret-sensitive." The government at once tried to stop publication, but the Supreme Court upheld (June 30) the *Times*'s right to publish by a 6 to 3 vote. The report revealed acts of deception, miscalculation, and arrogance on the part of the U.S. government. When it was revealed that **Daniel Ellsberg** (b. Apr. 7, 1931), a former Defense Department analyst, was the person who gave the material to the *Times*, he was indicted (June 28) on charges of violating the **Espionage Act**. On May 13, 1973, a federal judge dismissed the charges against Ellsberg.

1971 June 14   Carlos [Polestico] **Garcia** (b. Nov. 14, 1896), president of the **Philippines** (1957–1961), died. In a political career of 45 years he lost only one election. In World War II he fought as a guerrilla against the Japanese.

1971 June 30   Ohio became the 38th state to ratify the Twenty-Sixth Amendment to the U.S. Constitution, making it effective. The amendment lowered the voting age to 18.

1971 July 13   The **Jordanian army began a campaign to oust Palestinian guerrillas** from their bases in northern Jordan. After heavy fighting the army succeeded and claimed that 2,300 of 2,500 guerrillas had been taken prisoner.

1971 July 19   A group of leftist army officers led by **Babikr Nur Osman** overthrew **Muhammad Gaafur al-Nimeiry**, president of the **Sudan**. However, on July 22 Libyan army planes forced down a civilian plane carrying the new leaders at Benghazi, Libya, and al-Nimeiry regained power. Four officers who led the coup were executed.

1971 July 23   William V[acanarat] **S**[hadrach] **Tubman** (b. Nov. 29, 1895), president of **Liberia** since 1944, died. The country had prospered under his rule as the result of the discovery of iron ore and aid from developed nations. Tubman was succeeded (to 1980) by **William Richard Tolbert, Jr.**, the vice president (from 1951).

1971 Aug. 14   Bahrain became a fully independent state following the withdrawal of Great Britain from the Persian Gulf area. Sheik **Isa ibn Sulman al-Khalifa** (b. July 3, 1933), head of state (from Dec. 16, 1961), took the title of emir.

1971 Sept. 11   Nikita [Sergeyevich] **Khrushchev** (b. Apr. 17, 1894), first secretary of the Communist party of the U.S.S.R. from 1953 to 1964, died. He also held the title of premier from 1958 to 1964. Khrushchev was buried without public ceremony.

1971 Oct. 15   By a vote of 75 to 35, with 17 abstentions, the **U.N. General Assembly admitted the People's Republic of China** to membership and **expelled the Republic of China** [Taiwan]. The U.S., which had hitherto opposed China's admission, was now prepared to accept what was inevitable.

1971 Nov. 28   Wasfi al-Tal (b. 1920/1921), prime minister of **Jordan**, was assassinated in Cairo by members of the **Black September**, a Palestinian terrorist group, seeking revenge for Jordan's recent destruction of the power of the **Palestinian Liberation Organization** [PLO] in that country. Tal was in Cairo to attend a meeting of the Arab League Defense Council. He was succeeded by **Ahmed Abdel Kareem al-Lawzi** (b. 1925).

1971 Dec. 2   The **Trucial States of the Arabian Peninsula became fully independent**. Abu Dhabi, Dubai, Sharjah, Ajman, Umm al-Qaywayn, and Fujairah federated as the United Arab Emirates. The emirates were ruled by a supreme council of the rulers of the states.

1971 Dec. 18   Richard M. Nixon signed into law the **Alaska Native Claims Settlement Act**. By its terms the government was to pay over 11 years c.70,000 Aleuts, Eskimos, and Indians $462,500,000 to settle their claims to Alaskan land. Also, Alaska native corporations would gain control of 44 million acres of land and over the years were expected to receive another $500 million from revenue earned by the sale of minerals found in Alaska.

1971 Dec. 21   Kurt Waldheim (b. Dec. 21, 1918), an Austrian diplomat, was elected U.N. secretary-general. Waldheim had served as foreign minister of Austria and at the time of his election was Austria's chief representative at the UN.

III. ECONOMY AND TRADE

1971 Jan. 1   A **federal ban on cigarette advertising**, a large source of revenue for the U.S. radio and television networks, became effective.

1971 Feb. 15   Great Britain completed the phasing in of a decimal system of currency. The centuries-old shilling, crown, and half crown disappeared. The British pound now consisted of 100 pence.

1971 Aug. 15   Richard M. Nixon announced a number of steps intended to reduce inflation and stimulate the U.S. economy, in recession. Included were **wage and price controls**. The convertibility of foreign-held dollars into gold was suspended and in

December the dollar was devalued by increasing the official price of gold.

1971 Sept. 28   Salvador Allende, president of **Chile**, drastically reduced the amount that was to have been paid to foreign-owned copper companies whose properties were being nationalized. He said he was deducting "excess profits" from the previous price.

1971 Dec. 12   David Sarnoff (b. Feb. 27, 1891), a Russian-born American pioneer in radio and television, died. As a young telegraph operator in 1912 stationed on top of the John Wanamaker department store in New York City he was the **first to hear distress signals from the sinking passenger liner** *Titanic*. He became general manager of the **Radio Corporation of America** [RCA] (1921), president (1930–1947), and chairman (1947–1970). Sarnoff organized the **National Broadcasting Company** [NBC] in 1926. In the late 1930s he fostered the beginnings of television broadcasting.

IV. RELIGION AND PHILOSOPHY

1971 June 1   Reinhold Niebuhr (b. June 21, 1892), a noted American theologian and social critic, died. Giving up his liberalism and the hope that the churches would reform society in the early 1930s, he became a politically active socialist. After World War II he became more conservative, defending Christianity as the best explanation of the nature of humanity. Niebuhr's books included *Moral Man and Immoral Society* (1932), *The Nature and Destiny of Man* (1941–1943), and *Faith and History* (1949).

V. SCIENCE, EDUCATION, AND TECHNOLOGY

1971 Feb. 5   *Apollo 14* landed two American astronauts on the moon. In their first excursion the astronauts spent 4 hrs., 49 min. on the moon's surface, setting up experiments and collecting 43 pounds of rock and soil. The spacecraft returned to earth on Feb. 9. *Apollo 15* landed two more men on the moon on July 30, found rocks believed to be 4,150,000,000 years old, the oldest yet. It returned to earth on Aug. 7.

1971 Apr. 20   The U.S. Supreme Court, in a unanimous decision, ruled that **busing of students** in order to achieve racial integration was constitutional.

1971 May 25   A Soviet Supersonic Transport [SST], the TU-144, a passenger jet, made its first appearance in the West when it was shown at the Paris air show. The TU-144 made its first flight in 1968. It could fly at a speed of 1,430 mph. On this same date the *Concorde*, the SST developed by France and Great Britain, made its first intercontinental flight, traveling from Toulouse, France, to Dakar, Senegal, at an average speed of 1,130 mph.

1971 May 30–Nov. 13   *Mariner 9*, an unmanned U.S. space probe, became the **first craft to orbit Mars**. It sent back c.7,300 pictures, including views of Martian moons.

1971 June 30   Three Russian cosmonauts who had just completed 23 days in space were found dead in the spacecraft *Soyuz 11* when it landed. An explosive charge used to jettison the instrument section of the craft apparently broke a seal. The atmosphere rushed out into space and the men suffocated. The cosmonauts were **Georgi T**[imofeyevich] **Dobrovolsky** (b. June 1, 1928), **Viktor V**[anoue] **Patsayev** (b. June 19, 1933), and **Vladislav N**[ikolayevich] **Volkov** (b. Nov. 23, 1935).

VI. ARTS AND LEISURE

1971 Mar. 8   Harold [Clayton] **Lloyd** (b. Apr. 20, 1893), an American film comedian, died. He appeared in more than 300 films, mostly short features. In his best feature films Lloyd played the eager youth, seemingly bound to fail, but in the end getting the girl. Some of his silent films are *Grandma's Boy* (1922), *Safety Last* (1923), and *The Freshman* (1925). In *Movie Crazy* (1932) he made a successful transition to the talkies.

1971 Apr. 6   Igor [Fyodorovich] **Stravinsky** (b. June 17, 1882), a Russian composer who spent most of his career in France (after 1910) and the U.S. (after 1939), died. He attracted international attention at an early age with *The Firebird* (1910) for the Ballets Russes. *The Rite of Spring* (1913), with its irregular rhythyms and harsh dissonances, was booed at its premier, but was soon recognized as a landmark in modern music. Stravinsky's other compositions included four operas and 14 ballets.

1971 June 14 Margaret Bourke-White (b. June 14, 1904), an American photographer, died. She joined *Life* magazine in 1936 when it began publication and remained with it and its companion journals until 1969. She made her mark particularly with her photo coverage of World War II in Germany, Italy, and Russia.

1971 July 6 Louis [Daniel] Armstrong (b. July 4, 1900), an American singer and trumpet player, died. Known as "Satchmo" first appeared on the national jazz scene at the age of 22 when he joined King Oliver's Creole Jazz Band in Chicago. Armstrong made the soloist the center of jazz performances. In 1932 he made his first of many trips abroad and became as popular internationally as he was at home.

1971 Sept. 8–9 The John F. Kennedy Center for the Performing Arts, designated by the U.S. Congress as the National Cultural Center and the official memorial to the president who was assassinated in 1963, opened with a varied program. The feature of the opening was the first performance of Leonard Bernstein's *Mass, composed for the occasion.*

VII. SPORTS, GAMES, AND SOCIETY

1971 Jan. 10 Gabrielle [Bonheur] Chanel (b. Aug. 19, 1883), one of France's most successful fashion designers, known familiarly as "Coco," died. She founded her first haute couture salon in Paris in 1914, demonstrating that casual could be elegant. Chanel's perfume Chanel No. 5 was probably the best-known scent in the world.

1971 Apr. 10 An American table tennis team arrived in Peking [Beijing], China, by invitation and played a number of exhibition matches. The event was a surprise since the U.S. and China had had no diplomatic or other official relations since the communists came to power in 1949.

1971 Oct. 1 Walt Disney World [Disneyworld], opened near Orlando, Florida. It covered 100 acres and was to be part of a $400,000,000 development, including hotels.

1971 Oct. 12 An elaborate four-day celebration of the 2,500th anniversary of the Persian Empire began at the famed ruins of Persepolis, the ancient capital. Sponsored by the Shah of Iran, its cost was estimated at $100,000,000.

1972

I. DISASTERS

1972 Feb. 26 At Man, West Virginia, an earthen dam collapsed after torrential rains, the ensuing flood killing more than 118 people.

1972 Apr. 10 An earthquake centered c.600 miles south of Teheran, Iran, killed c.5,000 people. It registered 6.9 on the Richter scale.

1972 May 2 Fire swept through the Sunshine Silver Mine at Kellogg, Idaho, killing 91 miners. Among the 108 who escaped, two were rescued a week after the fire.

1972 May 13 Fire in Play Town, a cabaret on the top floor of a seven-story department store in Osaka, Japan, resulted in the deaths of 117 and injuries to 37.

1972 June 6 An explosion in a mine near Wankie, Rhodesia [present Zimbabwe], killed 427.

1972 June 9–10 A flood washed out an earthen dam, sending flood waters racing into Rapid City, South Dakota. The city suffered 235 casualties and c.500 homes were destroyed.

1972 June 15–25 Hurricane Agnes, first striking Florida and the Carolinas, flooded parts of Virginia, West Virginia, Pennsylvania, Maryland, New Jersey, and New York. The death toll was 134, and c.128,000 homes and businesses were destroyed.

1972 Oct. 5 Near Saltillo, in northeastern Mexico, a speeding train jumped the tracks and caught fire, killing 208 religious pilgrims and injuring almost 700.

1972 Oct. 13 An **Aerflot Ilyushin-62 jet airliner**, attempting to land at the Moscow airport, **crashed** with a death toll of 176.

1972 Nov. 14 The **Afghanistan government began attempting to get food** to remote areas to prevent **starvation** of an estimated 50,000 to 100,000 people.

1972 Dec. 3 During takeoff from the airport at Santa Cruz de Tenerife, Canary Islands, a chartered Spanish **jet carrying West German tourists crashed** and killed all 155 aboard.

1972 Dec. 23 **Managua**, capital of Nicaragua, was **leveled by an earthquake.** An estimated 10,000 to 12,000 people died, and 15,000 were injured. More than 300,000 persons were homeless, and the devastated city had to be evacuated. The quake registered 6.2 on the Richter scale.

1972 Dec. 30 An Eastern Airlines Lockheed 1011 TriStar **jet crashed** on its approach to the Miami, Florida, airport, killing 101 passengers, with 75 surviving.

II. POLITICS AND WAR

1972 The last **U.S. ground combat troops left Vietnam** on Aug. 12. U.S. planes bombed North Vietnam heavily in January, and the mining of ports was begun on May 8. In December **Richard M. Nixon** ordered full-scale bombing resumed to get the North Vietnamese to agree to peace terms. Hanoi said it would not negotiate while bombing went on. American bombing above the 20th parallel was halted on Dec. 20. The North Vietnamese launched (Mar. 14) their biggest ground offensive in four years, across the Demilitarized Zone. They captured (May 1) the capital of Quang Tri province, north of Hue. The South Vietnamese recaptured the city in September. In Paris peace negotiations continued without progress.

1972 **Tribal warfare devastated Burundi**, in central eastern Africa. The ethnic war was between the oppressed **Hutu**, 85 percent of the population, and the **Tutsi**, who dominated the government. Estimates of the number killed during the year ranged from 50,000 to 200,000, with c.500,000 homeless.

1972 Jan. 12 Returning from imprisonment in Pakistan, **Mujibur Rahman** (1920–Aug. 15, 1975), the leader of what had been East Pakistan, became the first prime minister of the newly independent country of **Bangladesh**. He faced a daunting task in trying to rehabilitate his devastated country.

1972 Jan. 13 A group of army officers ousted **Kofi A. Busia** (July 11, 1913–Aug. 28, 1978), prime minister of **Ghana**. His government had become unpopular because of austerity measures he introduced. The new government was led by **Ignatius Kutu Archeampong** (b. Sept. 23, 1931), an army officer.

1972 Jan. 14 **Frederick IX** (b. Mar. 11, 1899), king of **Denmark** (from 1947), died. As crown prince during World War II, he helped lead resistance to the Nazi occupation. Frederick's eldest daughter became **Margrethe II** (b. Apr. 16, 1940), queen of Denmark (to the present). A Margrethe I had ruled (1387–1412) but was never crowned because there was no provision then for a female monarch.

1972 Jan. 31 **Mahendra** [Mahendra Bir Bikram Shah Deva] (b. June 11, 1920), king of **Nepal** (from 1955), died. He had made a strong effort to modernize the country. He was succeeded (to the present) by his son **Birenda** [Birenda Bir Bikram Shah Deva] (b. Dec. 28, 1945), the crown prince.

1972 Feb. 21–18 **Richard M. Nixon visited China**, in a historic change of attitude toward the People's Republic of China. Nixon conferred with the top Chinese leaders, and a joint communique said (Feb. 27) both parties had agreed to work toward normalizing diplomatic relations and to increase other ties.

1972 Feb. 22 In a bloodless coup **Khalifa bin Hamad al-Thani** (b. 1934) deposed his cousin **Ahmed bin Ali al-Thani** (b. 1917) as sheik and ruler of **Qatar**, a nation on the Persian Gulf. Khalifa had been deputy ruler and premier. The deposed ruler had spent much of his time abroad on holidays.

1972 Mar. 30 Because of **violence between Catholics and Protestants**, and the warlike activities of the **Irish Republican Army** [IRA], the **British government assumed direct rule of Northern Ireland. Brian Faulkner**, the prime minister, and his cabinet resigned. **William** [Stephen Ian] **Whitelaw** (b. June 28, 1918), a British government official, was named secretary of state for Northern Ireland with full legislative and executive powers.

1972 Apr. 10 In ceremonies in London, Moscow, and Washington, 70 nations signed a **treaty prohibiting the stockpiling of biological weapons. Sponsored by the U.N. General Assembly, the treaty also pledged the signatory nations to destroy current stocks and to refrain from developing new biological warfare weapons.

1972 Apr. 27 **Kwame Nkrumah** (b. Sept. 21, 1909), president of **Ghana** (1960–1966), died. He led the Gold Coast of Africa to independence in 1957. Nkrumah was also a leader in the pan-African movement, but at home he became more and more dictatorial. A coup overthrew his regime on Feb. 24, 1966, while he was in China.

1972 May 22 What had been Ceylon proclaimed a new constitution and at the same time changed its name to the **Republic of Sri Lanka**, the Sinhalese name for the island. Sri Lanka remained in the Commonwealth of Nations.

1972 May 22–30 **Richard M. Nixon** made an official visit to Moscow, the first time an American president had gone to Russia. While there he and **Leonid I. Brezhnev**, general secretary of the Communist party, signed (May 26) an agreement placing some limits on nuclear weapons. The agreement became known as the **Strategic Arms Limitation Treaty** [SALT I] and was ratified by the U.S. Senate on Aug. 3.

1972 May 30 Three **Japanese terrorists** at the Lod Airport, Tel Aviv, **Israel**, **opened fire** on a crowd of c.300 persons, killing 28 and wounding 76. They had just disembarked from a passenger jet arriving from Rome. Two of the gunmen died, one by suicide and the other apparently from the guns or grenades of fellow terrorists, and the third was captured. That person said the three belonged to the **Army of the Red Star**, a Japanese group, and that they were acting on behalf of Palestinian guerrilla factions.

1972 June 16 At the adjournment of the **Conference on Human Environment** in Stockholm, Sweden, the 114 nations represented adopted 26 environmental guidelines. Among the most important matters on which the conference urged action were a pact to prevent the dumping of harmful materials in the oceans, the exploration of ways to control population growth, and worldwide monitoring of hazards to human health in the atmosphere and on sea and land.

1972 June 17 What would become known as the **Watergate Affair** began when five men, acting for the Republican Committee to Reelect the President [CREEP], attempted to burglarize the headquarters of the Democratic National Committee in Watergate, a luxury housing and office complex in Washington. Caught in the act, the five were indicted on Sept. 15, along with two former aides to **Richard M. Nixon**.

1972 June 29 The **U.S. Supreme Court** found that the **death penalty** as carried out under current state laws was "cruel and unusual punishment" and so violated the **Eighth Amendment** to the Constitution.

1972 July 3 **Indira Gandhi**, prime minister of India and **Zulfikar Ali Bhutto**, president of Pakistan, ended a six-day meeting in which they agreed to renounce the use of force against each other and to improve relations in the economic and cultural spheres.

1972 July 6 **Kakuei Tanaka** (b. May 4, 1918) became prime minister of **Japan**, chosen by Liberal Democrats in the Diet. He succeeded **Eisaku Sato** (Mar. 27, 1901–June 3, 1975), who had held the position for seven years and eight months. Tanaka, a millionaire builder, was expert at political organization.

1972 Sept. 23 **Ferdinand Marcos**, president of the **Phillipines**, proclaimed martial law. Efforts of the army to hunt down communist rebels were unsuccessful.

1972 Nov. 19 **Willy Brandt** [Herbert Ernst Karl Frahm] (b. Dec. 18, 1913) continued in office as chancellor of **West Germany** when the Social Democratic party and its ally the Free Democratic party won a majority of 46 seats in the 496-seat Bundestag.

1972 Nov. 25 The Labour party of **New Zealand** won a general election, taking 56 of the 87 seats in the House of Representatives. The National party, turned out of power, won only 31. **Norman** [Eric] **Kirk** (b. Jan. 6, 1923) became prime minister and almost at once announced that New Zealand would withdraw from the **Southeast Asia Treaty Organization** [SEATO] and recognize communist China.

1972 Dec. 2 For the first time in 23 years the **Australian Labour party** won a general election, defeating the Liberal-Country party and winning 67 of 125 seats in the House of Representatives. **William McMahon** (b. Feb. 23, 1908) resigned as prime minister and was succeeded by [Edward] **Gough Whitlam** (b. July 11, 1916). The new government prepared to recognize communist China and announced (Dec. 11) the withdrawal of its military training team from Vietnam.

1972 Dec. 23   **Park Chung Hee** was elected to a fourth six-year term as president of **South Korea**.

1972 Dec. 26   **Harry S Truman** (b. May 8, 1884), 33rd president of the U.S., died. Truman had been (1935–1945) a U.S. senator from Missouri, had become (1945) vice president and succeeded to the presidency on Apr. 12, 1945, when Franklin D. Roosevelt died suddenly. In Aug. 1945 he authorized dropping of atomic bombs on Hiroshima and Nagasaki, Japan. He sponsored the **Marshall Plan** of 1947 for economic relief of Europe. An underdog in the 1948 presidential election, Truman won a surprising victory. In 1949 he was one of the leaders of the Allied nations who formed the **North Atlantic Treaty Organization** [NATO]. When North Korea invaded South Korea in June, 1950, Truman at once ordered American troops to Korea, as part of a UN force.

1972 Dec. 27   **Lester B**[owles] **Pearson** (b. Apr. 23, 1897), prime minister of **Canada** (Apr. 22, 1963–Apr. 20, 1968), died. Notable also in international affairs, Pearson was president (1952) of the United Nations General Assembly and was awarded (1957) the **Nobel Peace Prize** for his part in defusing tensions in the Near East after the Suez crisis.

III. ECONOMY AND TRADE

1972 Jan. 22   In Brussels, Belgium, a treaty enabled Denmark, Great Britain, Ireland, and Norway to join (effective Jan. 1, 1973) the **European Community** [EC], which also meant joining the **European Economic Community** [EEC]. Norway voted (Sept. 24–25) against joining the EC, the only member of NATO not to do so.

1972 July 8   **Richard M. Nixon** announced that the **U.S.S.R. would purchase** $750 million worth, or more, of **American wheat** in the next three years. In fact much more than that was bought and the result was a rise in price in the U.S. from $1.00 a bushel to more than $5.00 by Aug. 1973.

1972 Dec. 3   A referendum of **Swiss voters endorsed** entry into a **free trade agreement with the European Economic Community**.

IV. RELIGION AND PHILOSOPHY

1972 June   The sixth **International Conference on Charismatic Renewal** attracted c.12,000 neo-Pentecostal Catholics to the University of Notre Dame, South Bend, Indiana. **Pentecostals** believed in the direct witness through them of God's Holy Spirit. Some were said to have the "gift of tongues," and others engaged in prayerful healing.

1972 June 3   **Sally J**[ane] **Priesand** (b. June 27, 1946), a graduate of Hebrew Union College-Jewish Institute of Religion, Cincinnati, Ohio, became the **first female rabbi in the U.S.** She was appointed an assistant rabbi at the Stephen Wise Free Synagogue in New York City.

1972 June 12–17   The **Campus Crusade for Christ**, International, staged "Explo '72" in the Cotton Bowl, Dallas, Texas. About 75,000 young people, mostly white Protestants, attended the week-long meeting designed to call youth to Christ. They heard preaching by **Billy Graham** (b. Nov. 7, 1918), listened to religious rock music, and made plans to evangelize the world.

1972 July 7   **Athenagoras I** (b. Mar. 25, 1886), 268th ecumenical patriarch of the **Eastern Orthodox Church** (1948–1972), died. He was remembered for his three meetings with **Pope Paul VI** to pursue ecumenism. Athenagoras was metropolitan of Corfu (1923–1930) and archbishop of North and South America (1930–1948) before becoming patriarch. He was succeeded on July 17 by **Dimitrios I** [Dimitrios Papadopoulos] (b. 1914).

1972 Aug. 16   The **World Council of Churches** elected its first non-Caucasian secretary-general, **Philip** [Alford] **Potter** (Aug. 19, 1921). Potter was born in Dominica and was a Methodist clergyman. He succeeded **Eugene Carson Blake**.

V. SCIENCE, EDUCATION, AND TECHNOLOGY

1972 Mar. 2   The U.S. launched the unmanned _Pioneer 10_, intended to probe Jupiter, 620 million miles away. On May 25 _Pioneer_ closed on the orbit of

Mars and entered a region of space never before penetrated by an object made by men.

1972 Apr. 27 *Apollo 16*, a U.S. manned spacecraft, was launched to make America's fifth landing on the moon. Two astronauts spent 71 hrs., 2 min. there, before the spacecraft returned to earth on Apr. 27. It brought back c.213 pounds of lunar rocks. On Dec. 7, 1972, *Apollo 17* began a similar journey. This time two astronauts spent 75 hours on the moon, a record, and brought back (Dec. 19) c.250 pounds of rocks. This was the sixth and **last of the moon landings by NASA**.

1972 Oct. 20 **Harlow Shapley** (b. Nov. 2, 1885), an American astronomer, died. His research enabled him to determine the size of the Milky Way and he postulated that the sun was in the outer area of the galaxy. Shapley wrote several books, including **Of Stars and Men** (1958).

1972 Oct. 26 **Igor** [Ivanovich] **Sikorsky** (b. May 25, 1889), a Ukrainian-born aviation pioneer, died. He was the **principal developer of the helicopter**. He developed bombers for the U.S. during World War II.

1972 Dec. 10 **John Bardeen** (b. May 23, 1908), an American scientist, became the **first person ever to win two Nobel prizes for physics**. He shared the 1972 prize with two others for his theoretical work on superconductors. He had previously shared the prize in 1966 for the discovery of the transistor.

1972 Dec. 23 **Andrei** [Nikolaevich] **Tupolev** (b. Nov. 11, 1888), a Russian aircraft designer, died. He developed more than 100 civilian and military planes and was known especially for designing the TU-144, a supersonic commercial jet.

VI. ARTS AND LEISURE

1972 Jan. 1 **Maurice** [Auguste] **Chevalier** (b. Sept. 12, 1888), a popular entertainer in France and the U.S., died. He appeared on the stage often but was best remembered for his films, of which he made 40 in the U.S. and France. His most popular film was *Gigi* (1958).

1972 Jan. 9 **Ted Shawn** [orig.: Edwin Myers] (b. Oct. 21, 1891), an American dancer and choreographer, died. In 1932 he established the **Jacob's Pillow Dance Festival** at Lee, Massachusetts.

1972 Jan. 11 **Padraic Colum** (b. Dec. 8, 1881), an Irish poet and playwright, died. He lived (from 1914) in the U.S. As a young man he was a participant in the Irish literary renaissance and helped found the Abbey Theatre.

1972 Feb. 5 **Marianne** [Craig] **Moore** (b. Nov. 15, 1887), an American poet, died. She was editor of *The Dial* (1925–1929), an avant-garde magazine, and published her own first book *Poems* in 1921. Moore, a woman of wide interests, embraced such diverse fields as zoos and baseball. Among her published volumes of poetry were *Pangolin, and Other Verses* (1936), *Nevertheless* (1944), and *The Complete Poems of Marianne Moore* (1967).

1972 Apr. 16 **Yasunari Kawabata** (b. June 11, 1899), the first Japanese to win the **Nobel prize for literature** (1968), committed suicide. Kawabata's novels included *Yukiguni* [*Snow Country*] 1948, *Sembazuru* [*Thousand Cranes*] (1952), and *Utsuku-shimi to kanashimi* [*Beauty and Sadness*] (1965).

1972 May 21 **Michelangelo's** *Pieta*, in St. Peter's Basilica, Vatican City, **was damaged** by a mentally disturbed Hungarian, **Laszlo Toth** (b. 1939). Using a hammer, he broke off the left arm, shattered the hand, and chipped the nose and one eye.

1972 June 12 **Edmund Wilson** (b. May 8, 1895), an American man of letters, died. Wilson was the most influential critic of his day. Among his literary studies were *Axel's Castle* (1931), concerning symbolism; *The Wound and the Bow* (1941), dealing with neurosis and the creative imagination; and *Patriotic Gore* (1962), a view of the literature of the American Civil War. In *To the Finland Station* (1940) he examined revolutionary ideology. Wilson also wrote *The Scrolls from the Dead Sea* (1955) and *Apologies to the Iroquois* (1960). His works of fiction included *I Thought of Daisy* (1929) and *Memoirs of Hecate County* (1946).

1972 Aug. 14 **Jules Romains** [Louis Farigoule] (b. Aug. 26, 1885), a French novelist, playwright, and philosopher, died. Among his plays were *Knock, ou le Triomphe de la médecine* (1920) and *Donogoo* (1923). His 27-volume novel *Les Hommes de bonne volonté* [*Men of Good Will*] (1932–1947), presented a panoramic view of French life from 1908 to 1933. He was elected to the Académie Française in 1946.

1972 Nov. 1 **Ezra** [Weston Loomis] **Pound** (b. Oct. 30, 1885), a poet and critic, died. Pound was an early advocate of authors as different as T.S. Eliot and James Joyce. Pound wrote numerous prose works, but his best efforts are seen in his poetry. For half a century Pound published *Cantos*, beginning with *Quia Pauper Amavi* (1919) and including *The Pisan Cantos* (1948). These poems covered almost every subject imaginable from Pound's own rather peculiar viewpoint.

1972 Dec. 8 It was announced that *Life* magazine **would cease publication** with the Dec. 29 issue. It failed finally because of television, which was taking from it enormous advertising revenue aimed at the mass market.

VII. SPORTS, GAMES, AND SOCIETY

1972 Feb. 3–13 The 11th Winter **Olympic Games** were held in Sapporo, Japan, with 1,232 athletes from 35 nations entered in the various events. Athletes of the U.S.S.R. won 8 gold medals and 16 overall; East Germany 4 and 14; and Switzerland 4 and 10.

1972 Mar. 23 **Cristóbal Balenciaga** (b. Jan. 21, 1895), a Spanish **fashion** designer, died. Balenciaga was the favorite coutourier of much of Europe's remaining royalty and aristocracy. His designs often featured large coats and long suits.

1972 Aug. 26–Sept. 10 The 20th Summer **Olympic Games** were held in Munich, West Germany, with 7,147 athletes from 122 countries competing. Athletes of the U.S.S.R. won 50 gold medals and 99 in all; the U.S. 33 and 94; and East Germany 20 and 66. The star of the games was **Mark Spitz** (b. Feb. 10, 1950) of the U.S. who won or shared seven gold medals in swimming events.

1972 Sept. 1 [Robert James] **Bobby Fischer** (b. Mar. 9, 1943) became the **first American world chess champion** when he won a match with the defending champion **Boris** [Vasilievich] **Spassky** (b. Jan. 30, 1937) of the U.S.S.R. The match, held in Rejkjavik, Iceland, began on July 11 and ended with Fischer winning by 12½ to 8½ points.

1972 Sept. 5–6 At the 20th Summer **Olympic Games** in Munich, eight **Palestinian terrorists** invaded a dormitory in Olympic Village and **murdered two Israeli athletes**. They seized nine others as hostages. Early the next day, at the Munich airport, as the terrorists were attempting to flee, the Israeli hostages were killed, along with five of the terrorists and a German policeman. The games were postponed for 24 hours. On Sept. 8 Israeli planes bombed bases of the **Palestinian Liberation Organization** [PLO] in Lebanon and Syria in retaliation.

1973

I. DISASTERS

1973 A continuing, seven-year **drought** threatened to cause terrible famine in six countries; Chad, Ethiopia, Mali, Mauritania, Senegal, and Upper Volta [present Burkina Faso]]. Estimates of deaths as a result of the drought ranged from 50,000 to 100,000 persons for this year.

1973 Jan. 22 A Royal Jordanian Airways **Boeing 707** carrying Muslim pilgrims home from Mecca **crashed** in a dense fog at Kano, Nigeria. Of the 205 persons aboard 176 died.

1973 June 3 At the Paris International Air Show a Russian supersonic TU-144 passenger **jet exploded** in midair during a demonstration flight. Wreckage fell on the town of Goussainville, killing seven villagers. All six crewmen also died.

1973 July 11 A Varig [Brazilian] Airlines **Boeing 707 crashed** near Orly Airport, Paris, killing 122 of the 134 people aboard.

1973 Aug. 28 An **earthquake in Mexico** struck the states of Pueblo, Veracruz, and Oaxaca, causing c.600 deaths, injuring c.4,000, and destroying c.10,000 buildings. It registered 6.4 on the Richter scale.

1973 Oct. 24 On the New Jersey Turnpike near Kearny, New Jersey, **65 vehicles piled into each other**, killing 9 persons and injuring c.49. Dense fog and smoke from a nearby garage fire cut visibility to zero.

1973 Sept. 30 The U.N. estimated that more than 100,000 persons were dead of sickness and starvation as a result of **drought in Ethiopia**. No crops had grown for two years and almost all the cattle had died.

1973 Nov. 29 Fire in a department store in Kumamoto, Kyushu, Japan, caused the deaths of 103 persons.

II. POLITICS AND WAR

1973 Jan. 15 Richard M. Nixon ordered military operations against North Vietnam forces halted because progress was being made in the peace talks in Paris. The U.S. and South Vietnam on the one hand and North Vietnam and the Viet Cong on the other signed (Jan. 27) an agreement ending the war.

1973 Jan. 20 Richard M. Nixon was inaugurated for a second term as president of the U.S. In the election of Nov. 7, 1972, Nixon, the Republican party candidate, won 45,767,218 popular votes and 521 electoral votes. His opponent **George** [Stanley] **McGovern** (b. July 19, 1922), the Democratic party candidate, received 28,357,668 popular votes and 17 electoral votes. **Spiro T. Agnew** continued as vice president.

1973 Jan. 22 Lyndon B[aines] **Johnson** (b. Aug. 27, 1908), 36th president of the U.S. (1963–1969), died. Johnson was first elected to the Senate in 1948, won the vice presidency in 1960, succeeded John F. Kennedy as president after his assassination in 1963, and in 1964 won an unprecedented popular majority of 15 million votes in the presidential election. A strong advocate of civil rights and social welfare legislation, he pushed reform measures through Congress. Unfortunately, he got the U.S. deeply involved in the Vietnam War until, perceiving his unpopularity, he chose not to run for a second full term as president.

1973 Jan. 30 The **Watergate affair** became the focus of national attention when **G. Gordon Liddy** (b. Nov. 30, 1930) and **James W. McCord** (b. 1918) were found guilty after five others had pleaded guilty to **burglary at Democratic Party headquarters**. A Senate committee launched an investigation and four presidential aides, **Richard** [Gordon] **Kleindienst** (b. Aug. 5, 1923), **John** [Daniel] **Ehrlichman** (b. Mar. 20, 1925), H[arry] R[obert] **Haldeman** (b. Oct. 27, 1926) and **John** [Wesley] **Dean III** (b. Oct. 14, 1938) resigned on Apr. 30. Nixon denied any personal involvement. Ehrlichman, Haldeman, **John** N[ewton] **Mitchell** (b. Sept. 15, 1913–Nov. 9, 1988),

former attorney general, and four others involved were convicted on Jan. 1, 1975, of conspiracy, obstructing justice, and making false statements. Ehrlichman and Haldeman were sentenced to up to five years in prison; Mitchell was sentenced to up to eight years.

1973 Feb. 12 Although they did not depose him, a military junta in **Uruguay** forced **Juan Maria Bordaberry Aroncea** (b. June 17, 1928), who had been elected president in 1971, to share power with them through a council of state. There was social unrest, and the Tupamaro National Liberation Front, a Marxist guerrilla group, was carrying out terroristic acts.

1973 Feb. 21 The government of **Laos** and the communist-led **Pathet Lao** insurgency, which controlled about two-thirds of the territory of the country, **agreed to a ceasefire**. Fighting had been going on since 1963 with the government receiving large amounts of aid from the U.S. while North Vietnam supported the Pathet Lao.

1973 Feb. 21 Israeli fighter planes shot down over the Sinai a **Libyan civilian Boeing 727** that had strayed off course. Only 5 of the 113 aboard survived. Israel, which said it would pay compensation to families of the victims, claimed the Libyan plane had ignored warnings but admitted its planes had erred.

1973 Feb. 22 A joint **U.S.–China communique** revealed that **Henry** [Alfred] **Kissinger** (b. Mar. 27, 1923), the national security adviser to **Richard M. Nixon**, president of the U.S., had been secretly in China for five days: The two countries agreed to **establish liaison offices** in each other's capitals, representing the first U.S. diplomatic acknowledgement of the Chinese communist regime.

1973 Feb. 28 In Ireland, the **Fianna Fáil lost a parliamentary election**, defeated by a coalition of the Fine Gael and the Labour party, which won 73 seats to the Fianna Fáil's 69. **John Lynch** (b. Mar. 15, 1917), prime minister since 1966, left office. On Mar. 14 he was succeeded as prime minister by **Liam Cosgrave** (b. Apr. 30, 1920), who held office until July, 1977.

1973 Mar. 11 Hector José Campora (Mar. 26, 1909–Dec. 19, 1980), the candidate of the Peronista forces, was chosen president of **Argentina**. **Juan Perón**, unseated by a military coup in 1955 and exiled, had been allowed to return to Argentina in Nov. 1972. Campora took office on May 25, but on July 13 he resigned to make way for Peron who, on Sept. 23, was elected president. He and his third wife **Maria Estela Martinez de Perón** (b. Feb. 6, 1931), who was elected vice president, received 62 percent of the vote.

1973 Apr. 15   Muammer al-Qaddafi [Gadaffi], dictator of **Libya**, announced a reform program that would suspend laws then in force and make new ones; give dominance to Islamic thought; provide all loyal citizens with arms; and put politics in the people's hands. The next day Qaddafi proposed a cultural revolution that would ban all books containing ideas stemming from imperialism, capitalism, communism, and Jews.

1973 Apr. 15   Naim Talu (b. July 22, 1919), by forming a coalition of two political parties, became prime minister of **Turkey**. He succeeded **Ferit Melen**, a former defense minister, who had taken office as prime minister on Apr. 17, 1972, but proved unable to control civil strife. He left office on Apr. 7, 1973.

1973 June 1   Georgios Papadopoulos (b. May 5, 1919), prime minister of **Greece**, declared the monarchy abolished. Constantine XII (b. June 2, 1940) had been in exile since Dec. 14, 1967. A referendum (July 29) approved the end of the monarchy and the establishment of a presidential republic with Papadopoulos as president.

1973 July 10   The Bahamas, c.700 islands and islets southeast of Florida, **became an independent nation** within the Commonwealth of Nations. **Lynden O**[scar] **Pindling** (b. Mar. 22, 1930), leader of the Progressive Liberal party, continued as prime minister.

1973 July 17   **An army coup led by a former premier **Mohammad Daoud Khan deposed **Mohammad Zahir Shah**, the king of **Afghanistan**, who had ruled for 40 years and was Daoud's brother-in-law. A coup committee elected Daoud president and premier of the new republic.

1973 July 25   Louis St. Laurent (b. Feb. 1, 1882), prime minister of **Canada** (1948–1957), died. The leader of the Liberal party, he was the second French-Canadian to become prime minister. He has been credited with the idea that led to the **North Atlantic Treaty Organization** [NATO], and he increased Canada's influence in international affairs.

1973 Aug. 1   Walter Ulbricht (b. June 30, 1893), a leading figure in the founding (1949) of the **German Democratic Republic** [East Germany], died. Early in life a socialist, Ulbricht helped found the German Communist party after World War I. In 1961, after more than 3 million persons had fled East Germany for the West, Ulbricht had the **Berlin Wall** erected to halt the embarrassing flow. As chairman (from 1960) of the Council of State, Ulbricht was in effect the president of East Germany.

1973 Sept. 11   **A military uprising overthrew the regime of Chilean president **Salvador Gossens Allende, a Marxist who had attempted to make **Chile** into a socialist state. Allende (b. July 26, 1908) died during the coup on Sept. 11, presumably a suicide although there were charges that he was murdered. On Sept. 13 **Augusto Pinochet Ugarte** (b. Nov. 25, 1915) became president.

1973 Sept. 15   Gustav VI Adolf [Gustavus] (b. Nov. 11, 1882), king of **Sweden** died. He had succeeded his father in 1950 after 43 years as crown prince. As an archeologist, Gustav took part in expeditions in Sweden, Greece, Italy, and China. He was succeeded (to the present) by his grandson **Karl XVI Gustav** (b. Apr. 30, 1946).

1973 Oct. 6   **The so-called **Yom Kippur War began when Egyptian and Syrian forces suddenly attacked Israel. Initially the attacking forces were successful, advancing into the Golan Heights and crossing the east bank of the Suez Canal. By Oct. 11, however, the Israelis were on the offensive and were advancing on the Syrian capital of Damascus. In the west they defeated the Egyptians and crossed to the west bank of the Suez on Oct. 15. A ceasefire was proposed on Oct. 22 by the U.N. and was effective on both fronts by Oct. 28.

1973 Oct. 10   Spiro T[heodore] **Agnew** resigned as vice president of the U.S. after pleading no contest to a charge of income tax evasion. Other charges against him concerning bribery while involved in politics in Maryland were dropped. Agnew was fined $10,000 and placed on three year's probation. **Gerald R**[udolph] **Ford** [nee Leslie King] (b. July 14, 1913) took office on Dec. 12, the first vice president to be appointed under procedures specified in the Twenty-Fifth Amendment.

1973 Dec. 1   David Ben-Gurion [David Gruen] (b. Oct. 16, 1886), a Polish-born Jew who was a **founder**

of the state of Israel, died. He led the movement for independence that came in 1948 and was Israel's first prime minister (1948–1953), and again (1955–1963). Ben-Gurion emigrated to Palestine in 1906 and was an early Zionist. During both World War I and World War II he cooperated with the British who came to control Palestine. When Britain did not live up to its promise to provide a homeland for Jews, Ben-Gurion took up the fight against them.

1973 Dec. 20 Luis Carrero Blanco (b. Mar. 4, 1903), prime minister of **Spain**, was assassinated in Madrid. His chauffeur and a police bodyguard were also killed. The militant Basque separatist organization *Euskadi Ta Askatasuna* [ETA, Basque Homeland and Liberty] took credit for the deed, saying it was in retaliation for the killing of nine of their number by the government.

1973 Dec. 25 Ismet Inonu (b. Sept. 24, 1884), president of **Turkey** (1936–1950), died. A close associate of **Mustafa Kemal Ataturk**, the founder of modern Turkey after World War I, Inonu served as prime minister (1923–1937) and succeeded to the presidency on Ataturk's death.

III. ECONOMY AND TRADE

1973 The **U.S. devalued the dollar by 10 percent** on Feb. 12, and the next day Japan let the yen float in relation to it. On Feb. 23 six European central banks intervened to support the dollar as gold rose to $95 an ounce. Leading European exchange markets, as well as Japan's, closed on Mar. 2 and did not reopen until Mar. 19 because of the international monetary crisis. At that time six leading EEC nations arranged to float their currencies jointly against the dollar. By the end of the year consumer prices in the industrialized nations had increased 8 percent and **inflation** seemed a greater threat than recession.

1973 Jan. 31 Ragnar [Anton Kittil] **Frisch** (b. Mar. 3, 1895), a Norwegian economist who was a pioneer in econometrics, died. Frisch spent almost his entire career on the faculty of the University of Oslo and was a founder of the journal *Econometrica* (1933–1955). He shared the **Nobel prize in economics** in 1969, the first time it was awarded.

1973 Oct. 16 The **Organization of Petroleum Exporting Countries** [OPEC] **cut oil production**, reduced shipments to Europe and Japan, and cut off supplies entirely to the U.S. and the Netherlands. At the same time the price of crude oil was increased and American oil companies operating in the Near East were forced to grant much better terms. In the U.S. gasoline was hard to find at service stations, and the price rose sharply. Great Britain was hardest hit, the energy shortage becoming so serious that the government put the country on a three-day work week beginning on Jan. 1, 1974. By the end of 1973 several of the Persian Gulf oil producing states had raised the price of a barrel of crude oil from $5.11 to $11.65, and Libya began asking $18.77.

IV. RELIGION AND PHILOSOPHY

1973 Mar. The **Dalai Lama** (b. July 6, 1935) the leader in exile in India of Tibetan **Buddhism**, conducted a mass ceremony in New Delhi for 4,000 Harijans, or **untouchables**, who had converted to Buddhism. It was believed that over the past two decades c.2 million of India's untouchables had become Buddhists.

1973 Apr. 28 Jacques Maritain (b. Nov. 18, 1882) a French Neo-Thomist philosopher, died. A Protestant who converted to Catholicism, Maritain became the leading interpreter of the philosophy of St. Thomas Aquinas to the 20th century. Among his works were *Art and Scholasticism* (1920) and *On the Use of Philosophy* (1961).

1973 June 24 Pope Paul VI signed a declaration prepared by the Sacred Congregation for the Doctrine of the Faith that reaffirmed the dogma of **papal infallibility**.

1973 Oct. 8 Gabriel [Honoré] **Marcel** (b. Dec. 7, 1889), a French existentialist philosopher and playwright, died. Marcel concerned himself with the relation of the individual to his existence and to the human situation. Communion with God became the path to one's acceptance of existence on earth. Among Marcel's books were *Étre et avoir* [*Being and Having*] (1935), **Le Mystère de l'être** [*Mystery of Being*] (1951), and **Philosophy of Existentialism** (1961). He wrote a number of plays, including **Un Homme de Dieu** [*A Man of God*] (1925) and **Le Chemin de Crète** [trans. *Ariadne*] (1953).

V. SCIENCE, EDUCATION, AND TECHNOLOGY

1973 Mar. 18 A new **comet was discovered** by **Lubos Kohoutek** (b. 1935), a Czech astronomer working in Hamburg, West Germany, and was named for him. Astronauts in the U.S. Skylab 3 were able to photograph it. On Dec. 28 Kohoutek rounded the sun, passing within 13 million miles of its surface on a path that would bring it past the earth before it headed for outer space. It turned out not to be as bright or spectacular as anticipated.

1973 May 3 In **Chicago the Sears Tower** was topped out at 1,454 feet, making it the **tallest building in the world.** When a television antenna was added it rose to 1,559 feet.

1973 May 25–June 22 The **first U.S. orbiting space station** *Skylab* was visited by the first of three 3-man teams of American astronauts. They completed assembly of the space station and conducted medical and scientific experiments. From July 28 to Sept. 25 three more astronauts spent 59 days aloft and from Nov. 16 to Feb. 8, 1974, three others spent 84 days in the space station.

1973 Aug. 20 **The New York Times** reported that a **new rabies vaccine** was in the final testing stage. Derived from a virus grown in human tissue, it would require only one injection. The current vaccine currently is derived from virus grown in horse tissue and requires 14 injections, one a day.

1973 Aug. 25 **Computerized Axial Tomography,** called **CAT scan,** was introduced to the medical and scientific world by its inventors, **Allan MacLeod Cormack** (b. Feb. 23, 1924), a South African-born American physicist, and **Godfrey Newbold Hounsfield** (b. Aug. 28, 1919), an English physicist. CAT scan provided a cross-sectional view of the internal structure of the body. The body was swept with x-rays, and the results seen as a pattern of electrical impulses.

1973 Oct. 30 A new **bridge over the Bosporus,** joining the Asian and European sections of İstanbul, Turkey, opened. Its opening marked the first time in nearly 2,500 years, when Darius I the Great, king of Persia, placed galleys together to form a crossing.

VI. ARTS AND LEISURE

1973 Jan. 26 **Edward G. Robinson** [orig.: Emanuel Goldenberg] (b. Dec. 12, 1893), a Romanian-born American actor, died. He made his first stage appearance in New York City in 1915 and he played in his first movie in 1923. After his gangster role in

Little Caesar (1930) he became famous for his tough guy characterizations.

1973 Mar. 6 **Pearl S**[ydenstricker] **Buck** (b. June 26, 1892), an American author and winner of the **Nobel prize for literature** in 1938, died. She was best known for *The Good Earth* (1931), a novel about life in China where she spent most of her life until 1924. It was the first novel of a trilogy, the others being *Sons* (1932) and *A House Divided* (1935). Another popular novel was *Dragon Seed* (1942). Buck produced more than 85 literary works, including an autobiography *My Several Worlds: A Personal Record* (1954).

1973 Mar. 18 **Lauritz** [Lebrecht Hommel] **Melchior** (b. Mar. 20, 1890), a native of Denmark who became the outstanding Wagnerian tenor of his time, died. He first appeared on the international scene in 1924 when he sang at Covent Garden, London. He continued to perform there as well as at the **Metropolitan Opera,** New York City (1926–1950) and at **Bayreuth** (1924–1931).

1973 Mar. 25 **Edward** [Jean] **Steichen** (b. Mar. 27, 1879), one of the great photographers of his time, died. Born in Luxembourg, he was best known for his portraits. He organized the "**Family of Man**" **exhibition** in 1955.

1973 Apr. 8 **Pablo** [Ruiz] **Picasso** (b. Oct. 25, 1881), born in Spain, the most influential artist of the 20th century, died. Picasso's lasting influence on art began in 1910, when he became a prominent figure in the development of **cubism.** Among his almost innumerable paintings, drawings, and sculptures, a few of the most significant were *The Old Guitarist* (1903), *Les Demoiselles d'Avignon* (1907), *Woman's Head* (1909), *Two Seated Women* (1921), and *The Three Musicians* (1921). His best known work was *Guernica* (1937), a painting condemning war and fascism and inspired by the brutal bombing of the Spanish town of Guernica during the Spanish Civil War.

1973 May 28 **Jacques Lipchitz** (b. Aug. 22, 1891), a French sculptor born in Lithuania, died. Among his works were *Prometheus* (1936) and *The Spirit of Enterprise* (1960).

1973 June 10 **William Inge** (b. May 3, 1913), an American playwright, died. Inge's first success was *Come Back, Little Sheba* (1949), followed, among less successful plays, by *Picnic* (1953), which was made into a movie, and *The Dark at the Top of the Stairs* (1957). Inge also wrote two novels.

1973 Aug. 17 Conrad [Potter] **Aiken** (b. Aug. 15, 1889), an American poet and novelist, died. His poetry was very much concerned with the problem of self-knowledge and how to move beyond that to an understanding of the world outside the self. *Earth Triumphant* (1914) contained his early work; his later poetry included such volumes as *A Letter from Li Po* (1955) and *The Morning Song of Lord Zero* (1963). Aiken's novels included *Blue Voyage* (1927), *King Coffin* (1935), *A Heart for the Gods of Mexico* (1939), and *Conversations; or, Pilgrims' Progress* (1940).

1973 Aug. 31 John Ford [Sean Aloyisius O'-Feeney] (b. Feb. 1, 1895), an American who directed c.130 movies and won six Academy Awards, died. Among his successes were *Stagecoach* (1939), *The Grapes of Wrath* (1940), and *How Green Was My Valley* (1941).

1973 Sept. 2 J[ohn] **R**[onald] **R**[euel] **Tolkien** (b. Jan. 3, 1892), an English authority on medieval literature and author of popular books of fantasy, died. As a professor at Oxford University, England, he wrote *A Middle English Vocabulary* (1922) and *Beowulf: The Monster and the Critics* (1937). He was known to the general public for *The Hobbit* (1937) and the trilogy *Lord of the Rings* (1954-1956).

1973 Sept. 23 Pablo Neruda [pen name of Neftali Ricardo Reyes Basoalto] (b. July 12, 1904), a Chilean poet, died. He first attracted praise as a poet with *Veinte poemas de amor y una cancion desesperada* [*Twenty Love Poems and A Song of Despair*] (1924). While serving in the Chilean consular and diplomatic service, Neruda began to write of the decay and anguish of the world he saw around him, culminating in *Estravagario* (1950). Much of his poetry was published in translation in *The Selected Poems of Pablo Neruda* (1970). He was awarded the **Nobel prize for literature** in 1971.

1973 Sept. 26 Noel [Pierce] **Coward** (b. Dec. 15, 1899), an English actor, playwright, and composer who entertained the world for many years, died. In all he wrote c.50 plays, including such hits as *Bitter Sweet* (1929), *Private Lives* (1930), and *Blithe Spirit* (1941). During World War II he wrote *In Which We Serve* (1942) and *This Happy Breed* (1943).

1973 Sept. 29 W[ystan] **H**[ugh] **Auden** (b. Feb. 21, 1907), a poet and major literary figure of the English-speaking world, died. Born in England, he became an American citizen in 1946. Auden's first verse appeared as *Poems* (1930). With Christopher Isherwood he had several plays produced, including *The Dog Beneath the Skin* (1935) and *The Ascent of F6* (1936). Perhaps his most important work was *The Age of Anxiety: A Baroque Eclogue* (1948), a long dramatic poem lamenting man's isolated fate.

1973 Oct. 18 Patrick [Victor Martindale] **White** (b. May 28, 1912) became the first Australian to be awarded the **Nobel prize for literature**. His first novel was *Happy Valley* (1939), an ironic title for a tale of an Australian village. Other novels followed, and White gained an international reputation with *The Tree of Man* (1955) and *Voss* (1957), epics of struggle against nature in the Australian wilderness.

1973 Oct. 20 A new opera house opened in Sydney, Australia. Jutting out into the harbor, it featured sloping, white roofs that looked like billowing sails.

1973 Oct. 22 Pablo Casals [Catalan Pau] (b. Dec. 29, 1876), a composer, conductor, and cellist, died. By 1910 he was considered the finest cellist in the world. In 1950 he founded a music festival at Prades, in southern France, and another in Puerto Rico in 1957. Casals taught many talented pupils and composed instrumental and choral pieces, among them *Le vision de Fray Martiin* (1893), a symphonic poem; *Eucaristica* (1934), sacred choral music; and *Hymn to the United Nations* (1971), secular vocal music.

VII. SPORTS, GAMES, AND SOCIETY

1973 Jan. 11 The American League adopted, on a trial basis, the "**designated hitter**" rule, whereby an additional player was used to bat for the pitcher. The National League refused to follow suit.

1973 June 9 The Triple Crown of American thoroughbred horse racing was won for the ninth time, when **Secretariat** captured the Belmont Stakes. It marked the first time that a horse had won all three races in 25 years. The colt had previously won the Kentucky Derby on May 5 and the Preakness Stakes on May 19. The jockey in all three races was **Ron Turcotte** (b. July 22, 1941). He set stakes records in all three races, although a timer malfunction in Baltimore denied him official recognition in the Preakness. His 31-length win in the Belmont was one of the most magnificient performances by a thoroughbred in history. In the Kentucky Derby, Secretariat raced every quarter mile faster than the previous one.

1973 Oct. 2   Paavo [Johannes] **Nurmi** (b. June 13, 1897), the "Flying Finn," died. Between 1921 and 1923 broke more than two dozen records for foot races from 1,500 to 40,000 meters. He also won seven individual gold medals in Olympic competition.

1973 Nov. 13   Elsa Schiaparelli (b. Sept. 10, 1896), an Italian **fashion** designer of the 1930s, died. Schiaparelli was the first to use rough-textured material for formal fashions.

1974

I. DISASTERS

1974 Feb. 1   Fire in the top 14 floors of a new 25-story office building in São Paulo, Brazil, trapped hundreds of workers. At least 227 died.

1974 Mar. 3   A Turkish Airlines **DC-10 crashed** in a forest c.26 miles northeast of Paris, France, killing all 346 passengers and crew members.

1974 Apr. 25   In the central Andes Mountains of Peru, enormous **landslides** wiped out several villages and killed out c.1,000 persons.

1974 Early June   The worst smallpox epidemic of the 20th century swept India, mainly in the state of Bihar, where c.20,000 were estimated to have died.

1974 Aug. 30   A passenger **train,** approaching the station in Zagreb, Yugoslavia, failed to slow down, struck a curve and **hit live power lines,** killing 124 persons.

1974 Mid-Sept.   News leaking out of the U.S.S.R. revealed that a *Kashinclass* **destroyer,** carrying guided missiles, had **exploded** and sunk in the Black Sea. The entire crew was lost, causing c.225 deaths.

1974 Sept. 19–20   Hurricane Fifi struck Honduras, killing c.5,000 people and leaving c.100,000 homeless. The storm also destroyed half or more of the banana crop.

1974 Dec. 28   An earthquake in northeastern Pakistan destroyed nine villages, killed c.5,200 people and injured c.15,000. The quake registered 6.3 on the Richter scale.

II. POLITICS AND WAR

1974 Jan. 18   Israel and Egypt agreed to separate their forces along the Suez Canal, thus ending the conflict that began on Oct. 6, 1973. On May 31 **Israel and Syria agreed to disengage** their forces in the Golan Heights, and on June 23 Israel completed its pullout from Syrian territory, except for the Golan Heights.

1974 Jan. 25   Bülent Ecevit became prime minister of **Turkey.** He had formed a coalition of his left-of-center party with a right wing group, but after ending this arrangement, he failed in an attempt to form a different coalition and so he resigned (Sept. 18). **Sadi Irmak** (b. May 15, 1904) became (Nov. 17) prime minister, but his government lasted only 12 days. The year ended with Irmak heading a caretaker government.

1974 Feb. 7   Grenada, in the West Indies, **became independent** and a full member of the Commonwealth of Nations. Its first prime minister was **Eric Gairy** (b. Feb. 18, 1922) of the United Labour party.

1974 Feb. 28   In a general election in Great Britain, Labour won 301 seats in the House of Commons, Conservatives 296, Liberals 14, and others 24. **Edward** [Richard George] **Heath,** the Conservative prime minister, resigned and was replaced (Mar. 4) by [James] **Harold Wilson** (b. Mar. 11, 1916), leader of the Labour party, who formed a minority government. Labour settled (Mar. 6) a miners' strike by granting a larger wage increase than Heath had been willing to give. Confident of a clear majority, the Labour party called another election for Oct. 10 and in it won a three-seat majority in Parliament.

1974 Mar. 15 **Ernesto Geisel** (b. Aug. 3, 1908), a general, became president of **Brazil**. Geisel, who had been president of Petrobras, the government oil company, had been chosen by the electoral college on Jan. 15.

1974 Apr. 2 **Georges** [Jean Raymond] **Pompidou** (b. July 5, 1911), president of France, died. When **Charles De Gaulle** came to power in 1958, Pompidou became one of his chief aides. He became premier on Apr. 16, 1962, and was elected president on June 15, 1969. In that office he dealt with the deteriorating economy by devaluing the franc and ordering a price freeze. In foreign affairs, he withdrew France's opposition to Great Britain's entry into the European Common Market.

1974 Apr. 10 **Golda Meir**, prime minister (from 1969) of Israel, announced she would resign, a decision triggered by a report of a judicial commission which blamed her government for military unpreparedness at the start of the **October** (1973) **War**. **Yitzhak Rabin** (b. Mar. 1, 1922), a military leader, diplomat, and leader of the Labor party, was chosen (Apr. 22) to form a new government.

1974 Apr. 25 A group of young army officers ousted the government of **Marcello Caetano** of **Portugal**. **Antonio Spinola**, a popular army general, assumed (May 15) the provisional presidency and formed a cabinet of the center and left. However, with continuing bickering within the government, Spinola resigned (Sept. 30) and was succeeded by **Cosa Gomes**, another general, whose regime soon came to be controlled by leftists.

1974 May 16 **Helmut Schmidt** (b. Dec. 23, 1918), the former finance minister in the Social Democratic government, became the new chancellor (10 1982) of **West Germany**, succeeding **Willy Brandt**, who had resigned (May 6) after it was revealed that one of his aides had been spying for East Germany.

1974 May 20 **Muhammad Ayub Khan** (b. May 14, 1907), president of Pakistan (1958–1969), died. Ayub resigned the presidency in 1969 because of student unrest and loss of confidence in his leadership.

1974 May 28 The **Northern Ireland Executive**, a governing body formed on Jan. 1, 1974, as a Catholic-Protestant regime that would attempt to bring peace to strife-torn **Northern Ireland**, collapsed. The British government again assumed direct rule. On Nov. 29 the **Irish Republican Army** [IRA] was outlawed. The entire year of 1974 would see 90 murders in Northern Ireland and 40 deaths resulting from bombings in England that were blamed on the IRA.

1974 June 18 **Georgy** [Konstantinovich] **Zhukov** (b. Dec. 2, 1896), one of the leading military figures of World War II, died. In Oct. 1941, he took command of an army group that kept the Nazis from capturing Moscow, and in 1942 he commanded the defense of Stalingrad. His post-war attempts to make the Soviet army more independent resulted in his dismissal (Oct. 1957) from all his posts.

1974 June 27 **Valéry Giscard d'Estaing** (b. Feb. 2, 1926), leader of the Conservative party, became president of **France**, having narrowly defeated the Socialist candidate **François** [Maurice] **Mitterand** (b. Oct. 26, 1916) in a runoff election May 19. Giscard received 50.81 percent of the vote, only c.400,000 votes separating the two candidates out of more than 26 million cast.

1974 July 1 **Juan** [Domingo] **Perón** (b. Oct. 8, 1885), president of **Argentina** (1946–1955, from 1973), died in office. He was succeeded by his wife **Mariá Estela Martínez de Perón**, who had been vice president. Juan Perón established a strongly nationalistic policy, aimed at making Argentina self-sufficient. When first elected (1946) he organized the trade unions, made up of the *descamisados* [shirtless ones] into a militant force along fascist lines. He also jailed political opponents, censored the press, and placed controls on education. Unfortunately, the economy rapidly deteriorated, and Perón was toppled (Sept., 1955) by a military coup.

1974 July 1 The legislature of **Guatemala** declared **Kjell Laugerud Garcia** (b. Jan. 24, 1930) to have won the election of Mar. 3 and so he became president. No candidate had secured a majority and it seemed likely that **Efrain Rios Monti** (b. Aug. 16, 1926), an anti-government candidate, had a plurality of the votes cast. Laugerud restricted imports, established certain price controls, and provided government financing for such items as fertilizer.

1974 July 3 In Moscow, **Richard M. Nixon** and **Leonid I. Brezhnev**, agreed to negotiate terms for continuation of **restrictions on nuclear weapons** in effect since 1972. The two leaders also signed an agreement not to conduct underground nuclear tests of a strength of more than 150 kilotons.

1974 July 8 **Canada's** Liberal party won a clear majority of seats, 141, in the House of Commons and returned to power with **Pierre Elliott Trudeau** again prime minister.

1974 July 9 **Earl Warren** (b. Mar. 19, 1891), chief justice of the U.S. (1953–1969), died. The court he led made decisions that broke precedents and charted new constitutional paths. Especially notable was the 1954 decision that racial segregation in schools must end. Warren served as governor of California (1943–1953).

1974 July 15 After Greek officers of the national guard led a coup that overthrew the government of Archbishop **Makarios III**, Eastern Orthodox archbishop and president of the island nation of **Cyprus**, **Turkish forces invaded** (July 20). Turkey acted to protect Turkish inhabitants. Turkey, Greece, and Great Britain agreed (July 30) to a ceasefire and to expand the role of the United Nations peacekeeping force that had been on the island since 1965. Turkish forces resumed (Aug. 14) military operations against the Greek Cypriots, and in December Makarios returned from exile to work for peace between Greeks and Turks.

1974 July 24 The junta that had ruled **Greece** from Nov. 25, 1973, with **Phaedon Gizikis** as president, resigned. It turned power over to a civilian government with **Constantine Karamanlis** as president. Martial law was lifted (Oct. 9) and Karamanlis (Nov. 17) won a legislative election.

1974 Aug. 9 Ending the two-year controversy known as the **Watergate Affair**, Richard **Nixon resigned the U.S. presidency**. **Gerald R. Ford**, the vice president, was sworn in as the new president. Nixon tried desperately to keep tapes of his White House conversations from being made public. When he was finally ordered to do so by the Supreme Court on July 24, the tapes clearly showed his complicity in the coverup of the affair. Meanwhile, the House Judiciary Committee had approved (July 27–30) three articles of impeachment to be presented to the House of Representatives. **Ford granted** (Sept. 8) **Nixon a full pardon** for any crimes he might have committed. Ford nominated (Aug. 20) **Nelson A[ldrich] Rockefeller** (July 8, 1908–Jan. 26, 1979), former governor of New York, to replace him as vice president. Rockefeller was sworn in on Dec. 19.

1974 Sept. 4 The **independence of Sikkim**, a kingdom on the northeastern border of India, **ended** when India forced it to accept the status of an "associated state" of India, rather than letting it continue as a protectorate. In an election (Apr. 15–16), the pro-India party won 31 of 32 seats in the national assembly. On June 20 **Palden Thondup Namgyal**, the maharaja of Sikkim (from 1963), signed a new constitution which reduced his role to titular ruler.

1974 Sept. 10 **Guinea-Bissau**, long the West African colony of Portuguese Guinea, **became an independent republic**. The first president of the new nation was **Luis de Almeida Cabral** (b. 1931), a Marxist labor leader and freedom fighter.

1974 Sept. 12 **Haile Selassie** (July 23, 1892–Aug. 27, 1975), emperor of **Ethiopia** (from 1930), was deposed by the army, which had secured control of the government earlier in the year. A Provisional Military Administrative Council took power, with **Aman Andom** as chairman. Parliament was dissolved and the constitution suspended. About 60 officials of the former government were executed. A struggle within the new ruling junta resulted in the rise to power of **Teferi Benti** on Nov. 23, and Aman Michael Andom (b. 1924) was executed on the next day.

1974 Oct. 14 The **U.N. General Assembly voted to recognize the PLO** as "the representative of the Palestinian people" by a vote of 105 to 4. The assembly further voted (Nov. 22) that the Palestinians had a right to independence and granted the PLO observer status.

1974 Oct. 28 Twenty **Arab heads** of state, meeting in Rabat, Morocco, **called for the creation of an independent Palestinian state** and recognized the PLO as the "sole legitimate representative of the Palestinian people."

1974 Nov. 12 The **U.N.** General Assembly voted 91 to 22 to **suspend the Republic of South Africa** from participation in its current session. South Africa recalled its ambassador.

1974 Nov. 24 **Gerald R. Ford**, president of the U.S., and **Leonid I. Brezhnev**, general secretary of the Russian Communist party, met in Vladivostok, U.S.S.R. The two leaders reached a tentative agreement to put a **limit on offensive strategic nuclear weapons** and delivery systems through 1985. **Strate-**

gic Arms Limitation Talks [SALT] were to resume once more in Jan. 1975.

1974 Nov. 25 U Thant (b. Jan. 22, 1909), a diplomat of Burma [Myanmar] and the third U.N. secretary-general, died. An educator and civil servant, he fought the Japanese invaders of his country in World War II. In 1957 he became Burma's chief delegate to the U.N. Elected twice as secretary-general, he served from 1962 to 1971. In both his terms Thant was faced with mediating quarrels and wars of member states of the U.N. Thant was more successful in guiding the U.N. in measures to aid Third World countries.

1974 Dec. 9 Takeo Miki (Mar. 17, 1907–Nov. 13, 1988), leader of the Liberal Democratic party, was elected prime minister of **Japan** (to Dec., 1976) by the Diet. He succeeded **Kakuei Tanaka** (b. May 4, 1918), who had resigned (Nov. 26) after being accused of using his office to secure a personal fortune.

III. ECONOMY AND TRADE

1974 The **major industrial countries slipped into recession** during the year while inflation increased greatly, a phenomenon called "**stagflation.**"

1974 June 26 Bankhaus I.D. Herstatt K.G., one of West Germany's biggest private banks, was ordered liquidated. The bank had incurred losses in currency trading estimated to be as high as $200 million.

1974 Oct. 8 The **Franklin National Bank**, New York City, was declared insolvent. The bank had suffered losses in currency trading—perhaps as much as $39 million—and since May depositors had withdrawn $1,700,000,000. Nine bank officials were indicted for fraud, and a former employee and a stockbroker pleaded guilty to embezzling nearly $1 million from the bank.

1974 Dec. 31 The **sale of gold bullion**, illegal in the U.S. from 1933, became legal again. In London the price of gold fell from $195.25 an ounce to $186.50.

IV. RELIGION AND PHILOSOPHY

1974 Jan. 20 John H[enry] Tietjen (b. June 18, 1928), president of Concordia Theological Seminary, St. Louis, Missouri, was suspended by the Lutheran Church-Missouri Synod on a charge of advocating false doctrine. Most of the faculty and student body

of c.600 left the seminary in protest and founded the Seminary in Exile in St. Louis.

1974 May 14 [Frederick] **Donald Coggan** (b. Oct. 9, 1909) was appointed the 101st **archbishop of Canterbury**, thus becoming the head of the Church of England and the worldwide Anglican communion. He succeeded [Arthur] **Michael Ramsey** who had announced he would retire from the post on Nov. 15.

1974 July 29 Eleven women deacons of the **Protestant Episcopal Church** were ordained to the priesthood in Philadelphia, Pennsylvania, with four bishops participating. At a special meeting (Aug. 14–15) of the House of Bishops, the ordinations were ruled invalid by a vote of 120 to 9.

1974 Dec. 24 Pope Paul VI, tapping three times on the door of St. Peter's Basilica in Vatican City, signaled the start of a Holy Year in 1975. The door had been walled up since the end of the previous Holy Year of 1950.

V. SCIENCE, EDUCATION, AND TECHNOLOGY

1974 The American *Mariner 10* sent back (Feb. 5) measurements and photos that showed Venus had no close resemblance to Earth as some experts had thought it might. By Mar. 29 *Mariner 10* was within 466 miles of Mercury and sent back close-up photos showing it to be somewhat like the moon. Radio signals from the American **Pioneer 10** showed (Apr. 13) a temperature on Jupiter of 800° F. By Dec. 2 *Pioneer 10* was within 26,000 miles of Jupiter and sent back photos of its biggest moon, Callisto. The Russian *Mars 5* began orbiting (Feb. 13) Mars and photographed it. *Mars 6* landed on Mars but did not function well.

1974 Mar. Chinese peasants digging a well near Sian [Xi'an] on the Wei River [Wei He] came upon some life-size terra cotta figures. Archeologists identified the find as a partly underground mausoleum, the **tomb of Shih Huang-Ti**, emperor of the **Ch'in** [Ts'in] **Dynasty**. The first part of the find uncovered c.6,000 life-size pottery soldiers, plus chariots and horses.

1974 May 18 India for the first time exploded underground a nuclear device at a desert site in Rajasthan. India claimed it was developing nuclear energy for peaceful purposes.

1974 June 28 **Vannevar Bush** (b. Mar. 11, 1890), an American scientist, died. Beginning in 1930 he worked with a team of scientists to develop the **first electronic analog computer**. In 1941 Bush was named director of the Office of Scientific Research and Development, which supervised all U.S. scientific research for the war, including the **Manhattan Project**. He served (1939–1955) as president of the Carnegie Institution of Washington, which supports basic scientific research.

1974 July 13 **Patrick** [Maynard Stuart] **Blackett**, (b. Nov. 18, 1897), a British physicist, died. Using a Wilson cloud chamber, a device for detecting elementary particles, he was the first to photograph (1925) nuclear reactions. During World War II Blackett was a leading figure in scientific research related to the war. He was awarded the **Nobel prize for physics** in 1948, partly for his improvements in the Wilson cloud chamber.

1974 July 18 The **Warszawa Radio Tower**, the **tallest man-built structure in the world**, was completed at Konstantynow, Poland. It was 2,120 feet, 8 inches high and weighed 615 tons.

1974 Aug. 26 **Charles A**[gustus] **Lindbergh** (b. Feb. 4, 1902) died. He became instantly world famous on May 21, 1927, when he landed in France as the first man to fly the Atlantic alone and nonstop. In the late 1930s he became an isolationist, believing that Nazi Germany could not be defeated.

1974 Sept. 26–27 Two separate studies reported that **chlorofluorocarbons** [Freon], used in refrigeration and as propellants in sprays, might be destroying the earth's **ozone layer**, an atmospheric shield protecting the earth against excessive ultraviolet radiation.

1974 Oct. 17–18 In Ethiopia, near the Awash River, anthropologists found the bones of a hominid more than 3 million years old. The hitherto unknown species, given the scientific name *Australopithecus afarensis*, was taken to be about 4 ft. tall, had walked upright, eaten meat, and used tools.

VI. ARTS AND LEISURE

1974 Jan. 31 **Samuel Goldwyn** [orig.: Samuel Goldfish] (b. Aug. 27, 1882), a Polish-born pioneer of movie making in the U.S., died. He was a founder (1910) of the company that produced one of the first full-length feature films, *The Squaw Man* (1913). Goldwyn produced a variety of films, many of them outstanding. Among the 70 or so Goldwyn films of merit were *Dead End* (1937), *Wuthering Heights* (1939), *The Best Years of Our Lives* (1946), and *The Secret Life of Walter Mitty* (1947).

1974 Mar. 17 **Louis** [Isadore] **Kahn** (b. Feb. 20, 1901), a Russian-born architect who practiced mostly in the U.S., died. Notable among his achievements were the Yale University Art Gallery (1951) and the capital buildings in Dacca, Bangladesh, commissioned in 1963.

1974 May 24 [Edward Kennedy] **Duke Ellington** (b. Apr. 29, 1899), an American jazz composer, pianist, and band leader, died. He first attracted notice when he brought his band to the famous **Cotton Club** in Harlem, New York City. In the "**big band**" era he and his musicians were among the most popular both in the U.S. and abroad. He wrote such hit songs as "**Mood Indigo**" (1930), "**It Don't Mean a Thing**" (1932), and "**Solitude**" (1934). His more extended compositions included **Creole Rhapsody** (1931), **Black, Brown and Beige** (1943), and **Liberian Suite** (1947).

1974 June 22 **Darius Milhaud** (b. Sept. 4, 1892), a French composer, died. His more than 400 works were presented in many different forms. In the 1920s he wrote scores for ballets, such as *La Création du monde* (1923). His opera *Christoph Colomb* (1930) was an immediate success. Milhaud also wrote 12 symphonies, 25 film scores, orchestral music, and vocal music.

1974 June 30 **Mikhail Baryshnikov** (b. Jan. 28, 1948), a leading dancer with the **Bolshoi Ballet** of Russia, defected in Toronto, Canada. On July 27 he made his American debut in *Giselle*, with the **American Ballet** Theater in New York City.

1974 July 11 **John Crowe Ransom** (b. Apr. 30, 1888), an American poet and critic, died. He was a leader of the **Agrarians**, a group of writers of the American South. Ransom founded and edited (1939–1959) the **Kenyon Review**, a distinguished quarterly of criticism, poetry, and fiction. His books included *Selected Poems* (1945, 1963, and 1969), and *The World's Body* (1938), a volume of criticism.

1974 Nov. 13 **Vittorio De Sica** (b. July 7, 1901), an Italian film director, died. He became a leader of the neorealist movie makers with *Sciuscia* [*Shoe-shine*] (1946) and *Ladri di Biciclette* [*Bicycle Thief*] (1948). His most important movie with a social and political theme was *Il gardino dei Finzi-contini* [*The Garden of the Finzi-Continis*] (1970), dealing with the treatment of Jews in fascist Italy. De Sica in the 1950s acted in more than 50 movies.

VII. SPORTS, GAMES, AND SOCIETY

1974 April 8 [Henry] **Hank Aaron** (b. Feb. 5, 1934) set a new major league **baseball** record when he hit his 715th home run, surpassing **Babe Ruth**'s total. When he retired in 1976, Aaron had increased his lifetime total to 755.

1974 July 7 West Germany won the **World Cup** of soccer by defeating the Netherlands 2–1 in Olympic Stadium, Munich.

1974 July 21 **Eddy Merckx** (b. June 17, 1945) of Belgium won the **Tour de France** cycling race for the fifth time, by a margin of eight minutes, equaling the record of Jacques Anquetil.

1974 Sept. 10–17 The **America's Cup** was successfully defended by the American yacht *Courageous*, which defeated the Australian challenger *Southern Cross* in four straight races off Newport, Rhode Island.

1974 Oct. 2 **Pelé** [Edson Arantes do Nascimento] (b. Oct. 23, 1940) ended his career as Brazil's greatest **soccer** star with a record of 1,216 goals, scored in 1,254 games. Pelé came out of retirement in 1975 to play for the New York Cosmos of the North American Soccer League. On his final retirement, two years later, his total had reached 1,281 in 1,363 games.

1974 Oct. 30 **Muhammad Ali** regained the **heavyweight boxing championship of the world** when he knocked out the defending titleholder **George Foreman** in the eighth round of a bout at Kinshasha, Zaire.

1975

I. DISASTERS

1975 Jan.–June A **drought in East Africa** affected c.800,000 people in the Ogaden region of Ethiopia and in neighboring Somalia. It was estimated that 40,000 persons died.

1975 Apr. 4 A **C-5A jet**, the largest air force plane at the time, **crashed** after takeoff in Saigon, South Vietnam, killing 150 or more persons, most of them children.

1975 Aug. 3 Two excursion **ferries on the Hsi River collided** and sank in the dark and in heavy fog near Canton, China. About 500 persons were drowned.

1975 Aug. 3 Near Imzizen, Morocco, a **Boeing 707**, in a heavy fog, **hit a mountain** on its approach to the Agidir airport and burned. All 188 aboard perished.

1975 Sept. 6 An **earthquake destroyed Lice**, Turkey, and affected a wide area, killing 2,312 persons and injuring 3,372. The quake reistered 6.8 on the Richter scale.

1975 Dec. 13 A **fire in a tent city at Mina**, Saudi Arabia, caused by an explosion of bottled gas, killed 138 Muslims and injured 151. More than 2 million pilgrims were gathered for the annual feast of Id al-Adha.

1975 Dec. 27 Two **mine explosions near Dhanbad**, Bihar state, India, caused millions of gallons of water from an old shaft to pour into the mine. All 372 miners at work died.

II. POLITICS AND WAR

1975 Jan. 28 **Antonin Novotny** (b. Dec. 10, 1904), a former president (1957–1968) of **Czechoslovakia**, died. After fighting the Nazis occupiers of his country in World War II, he became first secretary of the Czech Communist party in 1953. He was forced to resign from the presidency because of his stand against the liberal and reformist elements in the party and the government, but was reinstated (1971) to party membership after the reform movement was suppressed.

1975 Feb. 24 Nikolay [Aleksandrovich] **Bulganin** (b. June 11, 1895), premier of the U.S.S.R. (1955–1958), died. He had been a member of Stalin's elite State Defense Committee during World War II and held several other important posts. He was put out of office (Mar. 27, 1958) by **Nikita Khrushchev**, chairman of the Communist party, who succeeded him as chairman of the Council of Ministers.

1975 Mar. 17 Kukrit Pramoj (b. Apr. 20, 1911), was installed as premier of **Thailand**, having been elected (Jan. 26) under terms of the constitution promulgated in Oct. 1974.

1975 Mar. 25 Faisal ibn Abd al-Aziz (b. 1905), king of **Saudi Arabia** (from 1964), was assassinated by his nephew **Faisal ibn Musad ibn abd Aziz**. Faisal was succeeded by his half-brother **Khalid ibn abd al-Aziz Al Saud** (1913–June 13, 1982). Prince Faisal (b. 1947) was executed in a public beheading on June 18.

1975 Apr. 5 Chiang Kai-Shek (b. Oct. 31, 1887), president of the Republic of China [Taiwan], died. Chiang's career began when he participated in the revolution (1911) that overthrew the **Ch'ing** [Manchu] **Dynasty** (1644–1911). He grew in importance in the **Kuomintang** [Nationalist] party that was gradually coming into control of the Chinese government. He led its army (1926) in the capture of a number of China's major cities. During World War II he was the symbol of China's fight against the Japanese invaders. After the war Chiang became president of the Nationalist government and fought the communists until forced to flee (Dec., 1949) with his government and followers to Taiwan. There he reestablished the **Republic of China** and was a virtual dictator until his death. Chiang was succeeded by the vice president Yen Chia-Kan (b. Oct. 23, 1905), but real power was in the hands of Chiang's eldest son **Chiang Ching-Kuo**, who had been made president of the Executive Yuan, or premier, on May 17, 1972.

1975 Apr. 13 Civil **war** between Christians and Muslims broke out **in Lebanon**. In Beirut right-wing Christians of the Phalangist party and Palestinian guerrillas were the opponents. By year's end casualties were estimated at 6,500 dead and 13,000 wounded.

1975 Apr. 17 Five years of **civil war in Cambodia** [Kampuchea] ended when the government surrendered to the communist **Khmer Rouge** forces, which entered Phnom Penh, the nation's capital. The Khmer Rouge force was led by **Pol Pot** [known also as Saloth Sar] (b. May 19, 1925), who had been a founder (1960) of the Cambodian Communist party. The Khmer Rouge government adopted a harsh policy of driving people out of the cities and into the countryside. With no means of subsistence, the homeless people soon began starving. The Khmer Rouge policy resulted in deaths estimated at between one and three million people.

1975 Apr. 30 The **war between North and South Vietnam** came to an end after nearly 20 years when North Vietnamese forces, which had been advancing on Saigon, captured the South Vietnamese capital and changed its name to **Ho Chi Minh City**. On Apr. 29 the U.S. presence in Vietnam came to an end after 15 years when the last Americans there were evacuated by air.

1975 May 12 Cambodian forces seized the *Mayaquez*, an American merchant ship, in what the U.S. claimed was international waters in the Gulf of Siam. An American rescue mission recaptured (May 14) the ship but lost 15 killed, 3 missing, and c.50 wounded. In addition 23 servicemen in a helicopter on its way to participate in the rescue were killed in a crash. The *Mayaquez* had a crew of 39, all of whom were released.

1975 June 25 Mozambique, Africa, a Portuguese colony, became the independent People's Republic of Mozambique. A constitution establishing a Marxist state was proclaimed and **Samora Moises Machel** (b. Sept. 29, 1933) became president.

1975 June 26 A nationwide emergency was declared by the government of **Indira Gandhi**, prime minister of **India**. Hundreds of opposition leaders were arrested and the press was censored. Public unrest stemmed from a court's decision (June 12) that Gandhi had won (1971) her Parliament seat by illegal methods, but she refused to give up her post. A constitutional amendment was approved (Aug. 10) that absolved her.

1975 July 2 At the **International Women's Year World Conference** of the United Nations in Mexico City, Mexico, c.1,300 delegates unanimously adopted a ten-year **World Plan of Action** aimed at improving women's status. The conference also adopted a **Declaration of Mexico** which condemned colonialism, Zionism, and apartheid.

1975 July 5 The **Cape Verde Islands** off West Africa in the Atlantic Ocean **became independent** of Portugal. **Aristides Pereira** (b. Nov. 27, 1924) became the first president. Two other Portuguese colonies, in the Gulf of Guinea, became independent as the **Republic of São Tomé and Principe** on July 12, with **Manuel Pinto da Costa** (b. 1910) as head of state.

1975 Aug. 1 Leaders of 33 European nations, plus the U.S. and Canada, signed the **Final Act of the Conference on Security and Cooperation** in Europe after a three-day meeting in Helsinki, Finland. The intent was to provide a basis for peaceful cooperation in many fields. The signers also pledged themselves to respect civil and human rights in their respective countries. The treaty has become known generally as the **Helsinki Convention**.

1975 Aug. 15 **Sheikh Mujibur Rahman** (b. Mar. 17, 1920), leader of the government of **Bangladesh** since independence was won in 1972, was assassinated in a military coup. After an internal struggle, the army won control and **Abu Sadat Mohammed Sayem** (b. Mar. 1, 1916) became (Nov. 6) president.

1975 Aug. 16–20 In Colombo, Sri Lanka, 85 nations held the fifth meeting of their 20-year old **Non-Aligned Movement**. Major attention was concentrated on "**economic imperialism**," and the rich nations were called upon to do more for the developing nations of the Third World.

1975 Aug. 23 The **Pathet Lao** (from 1950), a communist-led, nationalist movement, **took over Vientiane**, capital of **Laos**. The monarchy was abolished (Dec. 3) and the People's Democratic Republic of Laos was established. **Souvanna Phouma** became president.

1975 Aug. 29 **Eamon De Valera** (b. Oct. 14, 1882), a native-born New Yorker who became a **founder of the Republic of Ireland**, died. An influential figure in Irish politics for half a century, De Valera was president of the provisional government (1918–1922), prime minister (1937–1948), and president (1959–1973).

1975 Sept. 4 **Egypt and Israel signed a treaty** easing tensions that remained from the **Six-Day War** (1967) and the **Yom Kippur War** [1973]. Israel agreed to withdraw from c.1,000 sq. mi. of the Sinai Peninsula, leaving 95 percent still in their hands, but returning the Abu Rudaya oil field to Egypt. Egypt agreed to let goods destined for Israel pass through the Suez Canal but continued its ban on Israeli ships.

1975 Sept. 5 [Lynette Alice] **Squeaky Fromme** (b. 1949), a follower of **Charles Manson**, a cult leader whose group killed seven people in 1969, aimed a revolver at **Gerald Ford**, president of the U.S., in Sacramento, California, but was prevented from firing by a Secret Service agent. In San Francisco 17 days later, **Sara Jane Moore** (b. Feb. 15, 1930), a political activist, fired a pistol at the president, but a bystander struck her arm and deflected the shot.

1975 Sept. 16 **Papua New Guinea became an independent nation** and a member of the Commonwealth of Nations. It had been a dependency of Australia. **Michael T. Somare** became the first prime minister.

1975 Nov. 10 The U.N. General Assembly passed an Arab-sponsored **anti-Israel resolution** declaring that "Zionism is a form of racism and racial discrimination." The vote was 75 to 35, with 32 nations abstaining.

1975 Nov. 11 In Angola, Africa, two governments were proclaimed, one the Soviet-backed **Popular Movement for the Liberation of Angola** [MPLA], the other by the **National Front for the Liberation of Angola** [FNLA] and the **National Union for Total Independence of Angola** [UNITA].

1975 Nov. 11 **John Kerr** (b. Sept. 24, 1914), governor general of **Australia**, as representative of the British crown, removed from office the prime minister, **Gough Whitlam** of the Labour party. Whitlam's government had been unable to secure adoption of a budget. **Malcolm Fraser** (b. Mar. 21, 1930) was asked to form a caretaker government. In an election on Dec. 13 Fraser's Liberal-National Country party coalition took 90 of the 137 seats in the House of Representatives.

1975 Nov. 20 **Francisco Franco** (b. Dec. 4, 1892), head of the government of Spain, died. Officially Spain had been a monarchy with Franco as regent and, because Franco was critically ill, **Juan Carlos de Borbón y Borbón** (b. Jan. 5, 1938) had assumed (Oct. 30) the powers of chief of state. On Nov. 22 he was proclaimed king as **Juan Carlos I** (to the present). Although friendly to the Axis powers in World War II, Franco kept Spain neutral.

1975 Nov. 25 **Surinam**, South America, **became an independent republic**. The first head of government was **Henck** [Alphonsus Eugene] **Arron** (b. Apr. 25, 1936).

1975 Dec. 18 **Indonesia seized control of Portuguese Timor**, part of the island of Timor, c.400 miles northwest of Australia. After Portugal announced it would conduct a referendum in 1975 to let the inhabitants choose between Portuguese rule, independence, or Indonesian rule, fighting broke out (June 27) between right- and left-wing forces. The referendum was never held.

III. ECONOMY AND TRADE

1975 Mar. 9 Construction of the 799-mile-long **Alaska Pipe Line** began. Oil from the Prudhoe Bay field would flow to the ice-free port of Valdez on the Gulf of Alaska. The pipeline was estimated to cost $8,000,000,000 and to employ 15,000 workers.

1975 Apr. 22 The government of **Oswaldo Lopez Arellano** (b. Jan. 30, 1924), president of **Honduras**, fell after it was revealed that he had taken a **bribe of $1.25 million from an American company**, United Brands, to reduce the export tax on bananas. Lopez was succeeded by **Juan Alberto Melgar Castro**, head of the armed forces, who canceled a contract with the American company. However, agreements were reached so that the banana exporting business would continue.

1975 June 11 **Oil from Great Britain's North Sea** fields began to flow from the Argyll Field off Scotland. The flow was c.40,000 barrels a day.

1975 July 16 The U.S.S.R. **made heavy purchases of grain** from the U.S. to prevent famine. Within a week 177 million bushels of corn and 51 million of barley were purchased. The U.S. and the Soviets signed (Oct. 20) an agreement for the sale of six to eight million tons of grain a year over a five-year period.

1975 Oct. 4 The **world's largest airport**, Mirabel, opened near Montreal, Canada. It was to cover 17,-000 acres eventually, and an additional 71,000 acres were zoned for environmental and noise protection.

1975 Oct. 15 A **200-mile restricted fishing zone** around its island was put into effect by **Iceland**, to replace the usually accepted 12-mile limit. Iceland had earlier unilaterally established a 50-mile limit, saying it had acted to conserve its fishing supply. Some other nations followed Iceland's example and extended their offshore zones.

1975 Dec. 14 The U.S.S.R. **announced a new five-year plan** in which emphasis was once more put on the development of heavy industries.

IV. RELIGION AND PHILOSOPHY

1975 May 6 **Jozsef Cardinal Mindszenty** [Jozsef Pehm] (b. Mar. 29, 1892), a Hungarian prelate who had fought Hungarian communism for many years, died. Arrested on Dec. 26, 1948, the cardinal was tried for treason and espionage and sentenced to life imprisonment. Freed in the abortive uprising of 1956, he took refuge in the U.S. embassy in Budapest. The Vatican attempted to get him to leave there, but he refused until Sept. 1971. In 1974 Pope Paul VI removed him as primate of Hungary.

1975 July An **International Congress of World Evangelism** met in Lausanne, Switzerland, with c.2,500 evangelical Protestant leaders from 150 countries present. They adopted the **Lausanne Covenant**, which reaffirmed belief in the traditional evangelical views of biblical interpretation.

1975 Sept. 10 **Mother Elizabeth Seton** [nee Elizabeth Ann Bayley] (Aug. 28, 1774–Jan. 4, 1821) was canonized in Rome by Pope Paul VI as the **first American-born saint of the Roman Catholic Church**. Mother Seton founded the Sisters of Charity, the first American Catholic religious society, on July 9, 1813.

1975 Dec. 4 **Hannah Arendt** (b. June 14, 1906), a German-born American political philosopher, died. Forced to flee (1933) Nazi Germany, she emigrated (1941) to the U.S., where she lectured and taught. In 1958 she became the first woman full professor at Princeton University. Arendt established herself as a distinguished thinker with *Origins of Totalitarianism* (1951). In *The Human Condition* (1958) she presented her views on what she saw as a decline of values in the modern world. In *Eichmann in Jerusalem: A Report on the Banality of Evil* (1963) she analyzed the wartime crimes of the Nazis.

V. SCIENCE, EDUCATION, AND TECHNOLOGY

1975 E[dward] O[sborne] **Wilson** (b. June 10, 1929, an American biologist, published *Sociobiology: The New Synthesis* and thereby began a controversy among fellow scientists and others. Wilson seemed to be saying that the principles underlying the structure of the societies animals create apply as well to human beings in their social behavior. Those who disagreed held that free will as well as cultural and environmental factors were far more important in forming human societies.

1975 **Ivermectin**, a semi-synthetic derived from microbiological cultures found in soil samples in Japan, was developed by Merck and Company, an American pharmaceutical concern. It was found to have several uses, but seemed especially promising for treating **onchocerciasis**, commonly known as "**river blindness.**" The disease is widespread in Africa and prevalent in parts of South America, affecting as many as 20 million persons worldwide.

1975 Feb. 14 **Julian** [Sorell] **Huxley** (b. June 22, 1887), an English biologist and philosopher of science, died. He was the first director general of **UNESCO** (1946–1948). Huxley's numerous books included *Religion without Revelation* (1927) and *Towards a New Humanism* (1957).

1975 May At the Western Deep Levels Mine, Carletonville, South Africa, **mining operations** reached a depth of 12,394 feet, the **deepest** ever. The temperature at the bottom was 131° F [55°C].

1975 July 17–19 The Russian *Soyuz 19* and the American *Apollo 18 linked up*, and the crews performed joint and individual experiments in this first international manned space flight.

VI. ARTS AND LEISURE

1975 Jan. 8 **Richard Tucker** [orig.: Reuben Ticker] (b. Aug. 28, 1913), an American operatic tenor, died. He spent most of his career (1945–1975) with the Metropolitan Opera, New York City, appearing in 30 different roles. Tucker began to perform in Europe in 1947.

1975 Jan. 19 **Thomas Hart Benton** (b. Apr. 14, 1889), an American artist, died. His vigorous, realistic style was well-suited to his scenes of life in the American Midwest. Benton also excelled as a muralist. Among his paintings were *Cotton Pickers* (1932), *Homestead* (1934), and *July Hay* (1943).

1975 Feb. 14 P[elham] G[renville] **Wodehouse** (b. Oct. 15, 1881), an English novelist, died. Wodehouse wrote more than 120 books, many of them involving Jeeves, the unflappable butler, and his twitty employer, Bertie Wooster. Typical of these are *The Inimitable Jeeves* (1923), and *Carry On, Jeeves* (1925). Wodehouse was also a success as a writer of musical comedies and plays.

1975 Feb. 17 **Thieves stole 28 paintings** from the Gallery of Modern Art, Milan, Italy, including works by Cezanne, Renoir, Van Gogh, and Gaugin. On Feb. 6 the National Gallery in Urbino had been robbed of three Renaissance paintings, including one by Raphael.

1975 Apr. 12 **Josephine Baker** [Freda Josephine McDonald] (b. June 30, 1906), a black American entertainer who became an international favorite in France, died. She moved to Paris in 1925 and became a star of the Folies-Bergère. In World War II Baker aided the French Resistance. Her flamboyant style on stage and off captivated the French.

1975 July 8 An **earthquake at Pagan**, c.90 miles southwest of Mandalay, Burma [Myanmar], destroyed hundreds of ancient temples, pagodas, and images of Buddha. Pagan was the capital of the Buddhist **Pagan Dynasty** (1044–1287), which established the first unified Burmese state (to 1299). There were c.2,000 structures in all and c.80 percent of them were damaged.

1975 July 15 **Charles** [Edward] **Weidman, Jr.** (b. July 22, 1910), an American choreographer and dancer, died. After performing with the **Denishawn dance group** (1921–1927) he and **Doris Humphrey** (Oct. 17, 1895–Dec. 29, 1958) formed the **Humphrey-Weidman dance group**, which continued until 1945. Among the ballets Weidman choreographed were *Happy Hypocrite* (1931) and *Daddy Was a Fireman* (1943). He also produced the dances for such Broadway hits as *As Thousands Cheer* (1933).

1975 Aug. 9 **Dimitry** [Dimitriyevich] **Shostakovich** (b. Sept. 25, 1906), a Russian composer, died. He wrote 13 symphonies in all. Shostakovich was often in trouble with the Soviet authorities who thought his compositions clashed with "socialist realism."

His opera *Lady Macbeth of the Mtsensk District* (1930–1932) had to be withdrawn from production for this reason. Shostakovich also composed ballet music, including *The Golden Age* (1930); vocal music such as *The Sun Shines on Our Motherland* (1952); and chamber and piano music.

1975 Sept. 20   Saint-John Perse [pen name of Marie René Auguste Alexis Saint-Léger] (b. May 31, 1887), a French poet and diplomat, died. His diplomatic assignments and travels in the Far East greatly influenced his poetry. An early volume was *Éloges* (1911); some had themes, such as *Pluies* [*Rains*] (1943). An English translation of his *Collected Poems* appeared in 1971 and his *Oeuvres complètes* in 1972. Perse won the **Nobel prize for literature** in 1960.

1975 Oct. 22   Arnold [Joseph] **Toynbee** (b. Apr. 14, 1889), an English historian, died. Director of studies of the Royal Institute of International Affairs (1925–1955), he was best known for his monumental 12-volume work *A Study of History* (1934–1961) in which he examined the rise and fall of 21 civilizations.

1975 Dec. 7   Thornton [Niven] **Wilder** (b. Apr. 17, 1897), an American novelist and playwright, died. *The Bridge of San Luis Rey* (1927), a novel of the ironies of fate, brought him sudden success. Other novels included *The Eighth Day* (1967) and *Theophilus North* (1973). Wilder's plays included *Our Town* (1938); *The Matchmaker* (1954), which became the musical comedy *Hello, Dolly* (1963); and *The Skin of Our Teeth* (1942).

1975 Dec. 25   Gaston Gallimard (b. Jan. 18, 1881), an influential French publisher, died. With other writers and intellectuals, he established (1908) what became a leading journal of the arts, *La Nouvelle Revue Française*. In 1911 he formed the publishing house that from 1919 was known as **Librairie Gallimard**. Gallimard's authors included **Georges Simenon**, **Albert Camus**, and **Marcel Proust**.

VII. SPORTS, GAMES, AND SOCIETY

1975 Apr. 3   ** The International Chess Federation stripped [Robert James] **Bobby Fischer (b. Mar. 9, 1943) of his **world chess championship** because he refused to play a match for the title with **Anatoly** [Yevgenyevich] **Karpov** (b. May 23, 1951) of the U.S.S.R. Karpov was declared (1976) world champion by default.

1975 May 16   Junko Tabei (b. 1940) of Japan became the **first woman to reach the summit of Mt. Everest**, the highest mountain in the world. She was accompanied by a male Sherpa guide.

1975 July 5   Arthur Ashe (b. July 10, 1943), an American athlete, became the first black player to win the men's singles tennis championship at **Wimbledon**, England. He defeated [James Scott] **Jimmy Connors** (b. Sept. 2, 1952), another American player, 6–1, 6–1, 5–7, 6–4.

1975 Aug. 3   ** The **Superdome, covering 13 acres and 27 stories high at its peak, was opened at New Orleans, Louisiana, as the largest indoor arena in the world, superseding the Houston Astrodome.

1975 Oct. 10–26   ** The seventh **Pan-American Games were held in Mexico City. The U.S. won 116 gold medals, followed by Cuba and Canada in victories.

1976

I. DISASTERS

1976   ** Among the year's **earthquakes were Feb. 4: *Guatemala City*, with nearly 23,000 deaths, 75,000 injuries, and perhaps a million people made homeless. This quake registered 7.5 on the Richter scale. May 6: *northeastern Italy*, several towns destroyed and nearly 1,000 persons killed by a quake registering 6.5. July 14: *Bali*, 500 plus killed, including many schoolchildren. July 28: *Tangshan*, Hopeh [Hebei] province, China, registering 8.2 on the Richter scale, c.750,000 deaths. Damage was also done to Tientsin [Tianjin] and Peking [Beijing], both c.80–100 miles from Tangshan. The Chinese government did not reveal details of this tragedy for three years. Aug. 17: *Mindanao*, the Philippines, c.8,000 deaths after a tidal wave and an earthquake registering 7.8 on the Richter scale. Nov. 24: *Van province*, eastern Turkey, c.4,000 deaths in an earthquake registering 7.9 on the Richter scale.

1976 Jan. 18 Off Mindanao, the Philippines, a Japanese fishing boat rescued two merchant seamen who had been adrift for 20 days on a life raft. They were the only survivors of an **explosion that sank** (Dec. 30) the 224,000-ton Norwegian freighter *Berge Istra*. Thirty crewmen died.

1976 Jan. 30 A **nursing-home fire in Chicago**, Illinois, killed 23 women, most of them from heavy smoke, in the home's chapel.

1976 June 5 The 307-foot high **Grand Teton Dam** in the Snake River Valley in eastern Idaho **collapsed** as it was being filled with water for the first time. Fourteen persons were killed, and c.14,000 were made homeless. There had been safety warnings before the dam was built.

1976 Sept. 10 At an altitude of 33,000 feet near Zagreb, Yugoslavia, a British Airways **Trident jet and a Yugoslav DC-9 collided**. In all 176 people died.

1976 Dec. 15 A Liberian-registered tanker *Argo Merchant* **ran aground** and broke up near Nantucket Island, Massachusetts. It spilled c.180,000 barrels of fuel oil into a valuable fishing ground. Winds and tides prevented extensive damage to fish.

II. POLITICS AND WAR

1976 This year for the **first time women were admitted to the three U.S. armed forces academies**.

1976 Jan. 8 **Chou En-Lai** (b. 1898), a Chinese statesman, died. Chou was a **founder of the Chinese Communist party** (1922), but for most of the 1920s he worked with the **Kuomintang** [Nationalist] forces of Chiang Kai-Shek. After Chiang broke with the communists (1927), Chou became a fugitive and eventually joined the **Long March** (1934–1935) of the communist army to northwest China. Chou was named premier in Oct. 1949, when the communists gained control of China.

1976 Jan. 11 A bloodless **military coup overthrew the government of Ecuador**. The junta imposed a state of siege and declared martial law.

1976 Feb. 7 **Hua Kuo-Feng** (b. 1920) was named acting premier of the **People's Republic of China** in succession to Chou En-Lai. On Apr. 7 he became premier and vice chairman of the Communist party, moving up to chairman in October after the death of **Mao Tse-Tung**.

1976 Feb. 11 The **Organization of African Unity** [OAU] recognized the **Angolan People's Republic**, which had been established by the **Popular Movement for the Liberation of Angola** [MPLA] as the legitimate government and admitted it to membership in the OAU.

1976 Feb. 23 The **Association of Southeast Asian Nations** [ASEAN] held its first meeting in Bali, Indonesia. Indonesia, Malaysia, the Philippines, Singapore, and Thailand voted to create a High Council to settle disputes through direct negotiations.

1976 Feb. 25 The government of the U.S.S.R. confirmed American charges that the **U.S. embassy in Moscow had been bombarded with microwave radiation** to disrupt U.S. listening devices.

1976 Mar. 16 **Harold Wilson**, leader of the Labour party, resigned as prime minister of **Great Britain** for personal reasons. On Apr. 5, by a vote of the party's members of Parliament, [Leonard] **James Callaghan** (b. Mar. 12, 1912), the foreign secretary, was chosen to succeed Wilson.

1976 Mar. 24 **Mariá Estela Martínez de Péron**, Juan Perón's third wife and the first woman head of state in Latin America, was ousted as president of **Argentina** by a military coup. **Jorge Rafáel Videla** (b. Aug. 2, 1925), an army general, became president (Mar. 29), and the congress was replaced by an advisory commission.

1976 Mar. 24 **Bernard Law Montgomery** (b. Nov. 17, 1887), a British field marshal and one of the foremost Allied generals of World War II, died. In Nov. 1942, his British Eighth Army won the **battle at El-Alamein** in North Africa, resulting eventually in the defeat of the Nazis in Africa. In Europe from 1944 to the end of the war he commanded the 21st Army Group in the Allied drive into Germany.

1976 Apr. 5 **Norodom Sihanouk** resigned as chief of state of **Cambodia** after a new constitution was promulgated and an election for the National Assembly was lost by his supporters. He was replaced (Apr. 11) by **Khieu Samphan** (b. 1932), but **Pol Pot**, as premier and leader of the communist Khmer Rouge, held the real power.

1976 Apr. 14 Morocco and Mauritania signed an agreement to partition the former Spanish overseas province of **Spanish Sahara**, from which Spain had officially withdrawn (Feb. 26). The partition was resisted by the Algerian-based **Polisario Front**, whose goal was to establish the Saharan Arab Democratic Republic. A long struggle began for control of the region.

1976 May 28 The U.S. and the U.S.S.R. signed a five-year treaty limiting the size of **underground nuclear explosions** undertaken for peaceful purposes.

1976 June 16–21 **Rioting in South Africa** took c.128 lives, injured more than 1000, and did property damage estimated at $34.5 million. The riots began after a government order that black students must learn Afrikaans and that it be used in teaching certain subjects.

1976 June 25 After the **Polish government announced price increases** averaging 60 percent on many staple items, demonstrations and strikes broke out. The government withdrew the increases but many protesters were arrested.

1976 July 2 The National Assembly in Hanoi proclaimed the **Socialist Republic of Vietnam** with **Ton Duc Thang** (Aug. 20, 1888–Mar. 30, 1980) as president and **Pham Van Dong** (b. Mar. 1, 1906) as premier. This step marked the official **reunification of North and South Vietnam**, divided since 1954.

1976 July 2 The **U.S. Supreme Court**, by a 7-2 vote, decided that the death penalty of itself did not violate the Constitution's ban on **"cruel and unusual punishment."** It upheld death penalty statutes of Florida, Georgia, and Texas, but struck down laws of Louisiana and North Carolina because they made the death penalty mandatory in certain cases. On Jan. 17, 1977, **Gary Mark Gilmore** (b. 1941), a convicted murderer, became the first person to suffer the death penalty in the U.S. in nearly ten years.

1976 July 3 **Adolfo Suárez González** (b. Sept. 25, 1932) was appointed prime minister of **Spain**. Suarez led the National Movement, a rightist political group. Nevertheless, a reform bill was agreed on and approved (Dec. 15) by 94 percent of the voters in a referendum. The bill provided for a two-house popularly elected legislature and a Court of Constitutional Guarantees.

1976 July 3–4 **Israeli commando forces were flown 2500 miles to Entebbe**, Uganda, to rescue hostages taken by Palestinian hijackers, who were holding an Air France jet. The commandos took the 10 hijackers by surprise, killed 7 of them and 20 Ugandan soldiers who tried to interfere, then returned to Israel with 91 passengers and 12 crew members. Three Israeli hostages were killed.

1976 July 4 **José López Portillo** (b. June 16, 1920) was elected president of **Mexico**, winning almost 95 percent of the vote. A law professor and minister of finance, he was a member of the Institutional Revolutionary party [PRI].

1976 July 23 **Mario** [Alberto Nobre Lopes] **Soares** (b. Dec. 7, 1924) became prime minister of **Portugal**. A constituent assembly had approved (Apr. 2) a new constitution calling for nationalization of certain businesses, central planning, control of management, and more power for labor.

1976 Sept. 9 **Mao Tse-Tung** (b. Dec. 26, 1893), chairman (from 1935) of the Chinese Communist party, and effective head (from 1949) of the government of the **People's Republic of China**, died. An organizer of the **Chinese Communist party** (1922), Mao worked with the **Kuomintang** [Nationalist] forces until the split with the communists (1927). Mao then helped build up the party and the Red army, becoming the leader on the **Long March** (1934–1935) to northwestern China. In 1949 he was elected chairman of the central government council of the new People's Republic of China. In 1958 he launched the **Great Leap Forward**, to establish small industries controlled by peasants, but it failed completely. The **Cultural Revolution** (1966–1969) marked a power struggle within the party, which Mao won but only after oppression of dissidents and disruption of the nation economically and intellectually.

1976 Sept. 23 **Elias Sarkis** (b. July 20, 1924) took office as president of **Lebanon in** the midst of a continuing **civil war** between Christians and Muslims. He had been elected by parliament on May 8, but the incumbent **Suleiman Franjieh** (b. June 14, 1910) refused to give up the office until now. **Syrian troops entered Lebanon** on a large scale beginning on June 1. They occupied the Bekka Valley in the east and fought Palestinian leftists. A ceasefire was arranged (Oct. 21) among Lebanon's warring factions. It was to be supervised by the **Arab League**, whose troops in the country consisted chiefly of the Syrians. Syrian troops entered (Nov. 18) Beirut to attempt to separate the Christian and Muslim groups fighting each other.

1976 Sept. 30   California became the first state in the U.S. to grant to terminally ill persons the **right to have life-sustaining procedures discontinued**.

1976 Oct. 4   Thorbjörn Fälldin (b. Apr. 24, 1926) took office as prime minister of **Sweden**. Fälldin headed a coalition of center and right parties that won 180 seats in the Riksdag [parliament] to the Social Democrats' 169. Fälldin won chiefly on the issue of opposing nuclear power.

1976 Oct. 26   The **Republic of South Africa** declared **Transkei**, in the eastern part of the country and inhabited almost entirely by the Bantu people, an independent republic and sovereign state. The first prime minister was **Kaiser Dadiwonga Matanzima** (b. June 15, 1915), a chief of his people. The UN General Assembly refused to recognize the territory as a sovereign state.

1976 Nov. 15   In the province of Quebec, Canada, the *Parti Québécois*, which stood for the independence of the province and its withdrawal from the Canadian federation, won a victory in an election for seats in the provincial legislature. Led by **René Lévesque**, the party won 71 of the 110 seats.

1976 Dec. 24   Takeo Fukuda (b. Jan. 14, 1905), of the Liberal Democratic party, deputy prime minister of **Japan**, succeeded **Takeo Miki**, who resigned as prime minister. An election (Dec. 5) had resulted in the worst setback for the ruling party in 20 years.

III. ECONOMY AND TRADE

1976 Jan. 8   Finance ministers attending a meeting of the **International Monetary Fund** in Kingston, Jamaica, voted to let **currencies float on the world market** in accordance with supply and demand.

1976 Feb. 4   It was revealed that the **Lockheed Aircraft Corporation** of the U.S. had paid $7.1 million in **bribes to right-wing Japanese** military leaders to help sell aircraft. According to a Senate subcommittee, Lockheed had also paid bribes in Italy, Mexico, the Netherlands, and Turkey. The head of the Turkish air force resigned (Mar. 5) because of these charges and **Kahuei Tanaka**, former prime minister

of Japan, was arrested (July 27) for taking $1.7 million in bribes while in office. Prince Bernhard (b. June 29, 1911) of the Netherlands resigned (Aug. 26) most of the military and business positions he held because of the charge that he had accepted $1.1 million from Lockheed. It was said that Lockheed, between 1968 and 1975, had made such payments amounting to $25 million. Lockheed neither admitted nor denied having made the payments but agreed not to do so in the future.

1976 Apr. 5   Howard [Robard] Hughes, Jr. (b. Dec. 24, 1905), a reclusive American industrialist, died. He made a fortune in the family business of manufacturing oil field drilling equipment, then became even richer from motion pictures, hotels, Las Vegas gambling casinos, and the aviation industry. Hughes became a recluse in the 1950s, moving from country to country and accompanied by a large retinue.

1976 May 24   The supersonic **Concorde** began regular commercial service between London and Paris and Dulles International Airport, Washington, D.C. The Concorde flew from Europe to the U.S. in a little under four hours.

1976 June 6   J[ean] Paul Getty (b. Dec. 15, 1892), a wealthy American oilman, died. His greatest coup came in 1949, when he secured a half interest in a large oil field in Saudi Arabia. Getty lived in England after the early 1950s. He left $1,100,000,000 to establish the **J. Paul Getty Museum** of art in Malibu, California.

1976 Oct. 14   Milton Friedman (b. July 31, 1912), an American economist, was awarded the **Nobel prize for economics**. Friedman, a monetarist, is known for his conservative views. His writings include *A Theory of the Consumption Function* (1957) and *Capitalism and Freedom* (1962).

IV. RELIGION AND PHILOSOPHY

1976   Buddhists celebrated the **26 hundredth anniversary of the birth of Prince Siddhartha** [Buddha Gautama], founder of Buddhism.

1976 Jan. 15   In *Declaration on Certain Questions Concerning Sexual Ethics*, the Vatican strongly condemned sex outside marriage, homosexuality and masturbation.

1976 May 26   Martin Heidegger (b. Sept. 26, 1889), a German philosopher, died. He had enormous influence among existentialists, especially in Germany and France. Man, he thought, was capable of understanding his existence, but must confront nothingness in the process. Heidegger's most important work was *Sein und Zeit* [*Being and Time*] (1927).

1976 Aug. 1–8 The 41st **International Eucharistic Congress** was held in Philadelphia, Pennsylvania, with nearly a million Roman Catholics participating. The Congress celebrated the central position of the Eucharist in the life of the Church.

1976 Aug. 29 About 6,000 Catholics, in Lille, France, attended mass celebrated in the Old Latin style by **Archbishop Marcel LeFebvre** (b. Nov. 29, 1905), who for some time had been **defying the reforms of Vatican Council II**. He had been suspended (July 24) by **Pope Paul VI** for holding such masses and for ordaining 13 priests of the Society of St. Pius X, which was dedicated to maintaining the old mass.

1976 Sept. 16 The **General Convention of the Protestant Episcopal Church** in the U.S. approved the ordination of women. The Anglican Church of Canada had already taken such action, and six women were ordained on Nov. 29, 1976.

1976 Dec. 4 Splitting off from the Lutheran Church-Missouri Synod, a conservative denomination, moderate Lutheran members formed the **Association of Evangelical Lutheran Churches**. The new group began with c.75,000 members in 150 congregations, out of the 2.8 million members of the Synod.

V. SCIENCE, EDUCATION, AND TECHNOLOGY

1976 Feb. 1 **Werner** [Karl] **Heisenberg** (b. Dec. 5, 1901), a German physicist, died. He revolutionized physics when he discovered (1925) a way to formulate quantum mechanics in terms of mathematical matrices. Later he developed (1927) the principle of indeterminacy. He was awarded the **Nobel prize for physics** in 1932.

1976 Feb. 4 **UNESCO** reported that there were now 800 million **illiterates** in the world, c.65 million more than in 1965.

1976 Mar. 8 Near Kirin, China, more than 100 stony **meteorites fell to earth**. The biggest weighed nearly two tons.

1976 July 8 The **first Asian communications satellite,** Indonesia's *Palapa*, was launched from Cape Canaveral, Florida. In stationary orbit over Indonesia, the satellite linked the country's 40 cities with the outside world.

1976 July 20 *Viking I*, an unmanned U.S. spacecraft, **landed on Mars** after an 11-month flight, and was joined on Sept. 3, 1976, by *Viking II*, which landed in a different area. Both collected data on biological activity and photographed the Martian landscape. The north polar cap was found to consist of frozen water, and nitrogen was found in the atmosphere. Samples of soil showed no organic compounds.

1976 July 21–24 At an American Legion convention in a Philadelphia hotel, 180 delegates were stricken with a flu-like ailment. Of those taken ill, 29 died. Outbreaks of the disease began to appear elsewhere, with 11 more deaths within the year. The disease came to be known as **Legionnaires' Disease**.

1976 Nov. 20 **Trofim** [Denisovich] **Lysenko** (b. Sept. 29, 1898), a Soviet biologist, died. He believed that environment could cause hereditary changes in plants, a position that supported Marxist theory. Lysenko so dominated Soviet science that it was handicapped for years.

VI. ARTS AND LEISURE

1976 Jan. 12 **Agatha** [Mary Clarissa] **Christie** [nee Miller] (b. Sept. 15, 1890), a writer of mystery stories, died. Several hundred million copies of her 25-odd books have been sold and they were still selling long after her death. Her first success was *The Murder of Roger Ackroyd* (1926). Christie created two detectives who captured the fancy of readers, Miss Jane Marple, a quiet spinster, and Hercule Poirot, a fussy Belgian private eye. Christie's play *The Mousetrap* opened in London on Nov. 25, 1952, and is still on the boards there.

1976 Jan. 23 **Paul** [Bustill] **Robeson** (b. Apr. 9, 1898), an American actor and singer, who was the son of a former slave and an All-American football player at Rutgers University, died. His first success as an actor was in the title role of **Eugene O'Neill's *Emperor Jones*** (1920) in 1925, and he was acclaimed for his roles in **DuBose Heyward's *Porgy*** (1927) in 1928 and in *Othello* in 1930. Robeson's name is forever connected with the song "Ol' Man River" from

Showboat (1927) in 1928 and the movie in 1936. When Robeson supported communist causes, he became a controversial figure, especially when he accepted the International Stalin Peace Prize (1952).

1976 Feb. 13   Lily Pons [nee Alice Josephine Pons] (b. Apr. 12, 1904), a coloratura soprano, died. Born in France, she first appeared (1931) at the Metropolitan Opera in New York City and was an overnight success. She sang leading roles there for 25 years.

1976 Mar. 17   Luchino Visconti (b. Nov. 2, 1906), a pioneering Italian film director, died. He revolutionized post-World War II movie making with realistic portrayals of people trying to survive in modern society. Among his many films were *The Leopard* (1964) and *Morte a Venezia* [*Death in Venice*] (1971).

1976 Apr. 1   Max Ernst (b. Apr. 2, 1891), a German-born painter and sculptor, died. He was a leader among the surrealists and pioneered **dadaism** in Germany. Ernst lived at times in the U.S. and France as well as Germany. Typical of his works were *Here Everything Is Still Floating* (1920), *The Elephant of the Célebès* (1921), *The Barbarians March Westward* (1935), and *The King Playing with the Queen* (1944).

1976 Aug. 2   Fritz Lang (b. Dec. 12, 1890), an Austrian-born movie director and writer who made films in Europe and America, died. His first film was *Halbblut* [*The Half-Breed*] (1919). He made several Dr. Marbuse films, beginning with *Dr. Marbuse der Spieler* [*Dr. Marbuse the Gambler*] (1922). Lang is now known especially for *M* (1931), based on a series of child killings. His Hollywood movies included *Fury* (1936), *Western Union* (1941), *Rancho Notorious* (1952), and *The Big Heat* (1953).

1976 Aug. 26   Lotte Lehman (b. Feb. 27, 1888), a German-born American soprano, died. She sang in various cities of Europe until she was forced to leave (1938) Austria by the menace of Naziism. Lehman had made her American debut in Chicago in 1930 and sang at the Metropolitan Opera, New York City (1934–1945). She was the best lyric-dramatic soprano of her era.

1976 Oct. 14   Edith [Mary] **Evans** (b. Feb. 8, 1888), a talented English actress, died. Dame Edith played many roles in Shakespearean and Restoration drama, including Portia, Rosalind, and Mrs. Malaprop.

1976 Nov. 11   Alexander [Milne] **Calder** (b. July 22, 1898), an innovator in modern sculpture, died. In 1932 he began to build mobiles, among them *A Universe* (1934) and *Mobile* (1958). Calder also did non-moving sculptures, which he called stabiles.

1976 Nov. 12   Walter [Hamor] **Piston** (b. Jan. 20, 1894), an American composer and teacher, died. He taught at Harvard University from 1926 to 1960). Besides his eight symphonies, Piston composed a ballet, *The Incredible Flutist* (1938); an orchestral suite, *Three New England Sketches* (1959); and chamber music as well as pieces for viola, violin, clarinet, and piano.

1976 Nov. 18   Man Ray [orig.: Emmanuel Radnitsky] (b. Aug. 27, 1890), an American painter, photographer, and film maker, died. He was part of both the dadaist and the surrealist movements, producing objects he called "ready mades." Typical of his works were *Object to Be Destroyed* (1923) and the painting *Observatory Time—The Lovers* (1932–1934).

1976 Nov. 23   André Georges Malraux (b. Nov. 13, 1901), a French author, died. He fought with the Republican forces in the **Spanish Civil War** and in the **French Resistance** during World War II. After the war he served as minister of cultural affairs (1958–1969) under **Charles De Gaulle**, president of France. His novels mirrored his personal adventures as well as his involvement in public affairs. They included *La Condition humaine* [*Man's Fate*] (1933), *L'Éspoir* [*Man's Hope*] (1938), and *Le Temps du mépris* [*Days of Wrath*] (1936).

1976 Dec. 4 [Edward] **Benjamin Britten** (b. Nov. 22, 1913), an English composer noted for his operas, died. His operas included *Peter Grimes* (1945), *The Turn of the Screw* (1954), and *Death in Venice* (1973). Britten also wrote instrumental works and music for church pageants.

VII. SPORTS, GAMES, AND SOCIETY

1976 Feb. 4–15 The 12th Winter **Olympic Games** were held at Innsbruck, Austria, with 1,128 athletes from 37 nations competing. U.S.S.R. athletes won 13 gold medals and 27 in all; East Germany, 7 and 19; and the U.S., 3 and 10.

1976 July 4 The U.S. celebrated the **200th anniversary of the Declaration of Independence**. Leading the observance was the pageantry in New York Harbor, where 53 warships of 22 nations appeared, along with 16 "tall ships," square-rigged sailing vessels. It was estimated that six million people looked on and enjoyed the massive fireworks display that ended the day.

1976 July 16–18 A gang of c.20 **thieves made their way into the vault of a branch bank of the Société Générale in Nice, France**, and proceeded to loot it for 48 hours over a weekend. They took time off to enjoy the food and wine they brought with them. Their loot was estimated at between $8 and $10 million in cash, gold, jewelry, and gems.

1976 July 17–Aug. 1 The 21st Summer **Olympic Games** were held in Montreal, Canada, with 6,085 athletes from 92 countries participating. Athletes of the U.S.S.R. won 49 gold medals and 125 in all; East Germany, 40 and 90; and the U.S., 34 and 94.

1976 Dec. 28 **Mainbocher** [orig.: Main Rousseau Bocher] (b. Oct. 9, 1891), the first American fashion designer to become a success in Paris, died. Mainbocher's clothes were known both for their simplicity and their cost.

1977

I. DISASTERS

1977 Jan. 10 Nyiragongo, in Zaire, at 11,400 feet Africa's second highest active **volcano, erupted**. It dumped lava on the town of Goma, eight miles away, killing c.2,000 people.

1977 Feb. 4 In Chicago, Illinois, two elevated **trains collided**. Two cars fell to the street while two others dangled dangerously. Eleven persons were killed and 189 injured.

1977 Mar. 4 An **earthquake** destroyed most of the heart of Bucharest, Romania, killing 1,541 persons, injuring more than 11,000, and leaving c.80,000 homeless. The quake registered 7.5 on the Richter scale.

1977 Mar. 27 At the airport at Santa Cruz de Tenerife, the Canary Islands, a KLM Royal Dutch Airlines **Boeing 747**, about to take off, **ran into a Pan American World Airways 747** that was taxiing off the runway. In all 582 persons died.

1977 May 28 A fast-spreading **fire at the Beverly Hills Supper Club** in Southgate, Kentucky, killed 164 and injured more than 130.

1977 June 28 Near São Paulo, Brazil, two **trucks collided** in a fog, setting off a chain reaction that eventually involved 46 buses, 12 trucks, and 74 passenger cars. At least 65 persons were killed and 229 injured.

1977 Nov. 19 **Tidal waves swept over Andhra Pradesh state**, India, following a cyclone in the Bay of Bengal, leaving c.20,000 dead and 2 million homeless. In all 21 villages were destroyed and 44 others battered.

1977 Dec. 13 A chartered **DC-3 crashed** while taking off from the Evansville, Indiana, airport, killing 29 persons. The dead included all 14 members of the University of Evansville basketball team and its coach.

II. POLITICS AND WAR

1977 Jan. 6 A manifesto proclaiming the **Charter 77 group** was signed by c.240 prominent intellectuals of **Czechoslovakia**. It demanded respect for the human rights established by the **Helsinki agreement** of 1975.

1977 Jan. 14 [Robert] **Anthony Eden** (b. June 12, 1897, a British statesman, died. He was foreign secretary three times in Conservative governments and prime minister from Apr. 1955, to Jan. 1957. Opposing the government's policy of appeasing Hitler, he resigned as foreign minister in 1938. Eden also resigned as prime minister after the condemnation of Anglo-French intervention in Egypt following nationalization of the Suez Canal in 1956.

1977 Jan. 20 [James Earl] **Jimmy Carter** (b. Oct. 1, 1924) was inaugurated as the 39th president of the U.S. The Democratic party candidate in the election of Nov. 2, 1976, he defeated **Gerald R. Ford**, the incumbent and the candidate of the Republican party. The popular vote was 40,828,929 for Carter and 39,148,940 for Ford. The electoral vote was 297 for Carter and 240 for Ford. **Walter F**[rederick] **Mondale** (b. Jan. 5, 1928) was inaugurated as vice president.

1977 Jan. 21 Nearly 10,000 **young men opposing the war in Vietnam** who evaded the military draft between Aug. 4, 1964, and Mar. 28, 1973, were **pardoned by Jimmy Carter**, president of the U.S. The pardon did not apply to the c.100,000 deserters from the armed forces.

1977 Feb. 3 In a gunfight among members of the Provisional Military Administrative Council [PMAC], the ruling body of **Ethiopia's** government, **Teferi Benti** (b. 1921), the head of the council, died. On Feb. 11 **Mengitsu Haile Mariam** (b.1937), vice chairman of the council, took over the top position.

1977 Feb. 16 The **brutality of the regime of Idi Amin** in **Uganda** was called to the world's attention by the deaths of the Anglican archbishop and two cabinet ministers, reportedly under torture and possibly at the hands of Amin himself. There was also a slaughter of members of the Lango and Acholi tribes, many of whom were Christians.

1977 Feb. 20 **Carlos Humberto Romero** (b. 1924), a general, was elected president of **El Salvador**. The opposition claimed fraud in the election, and riots broke out in which c.100 people were killed. A state of siege was declared (Feb. 26) but was lifted after Romero took office on July 1.

1977 Mar. 7 The first general election under civilian rule since independence in 1947 was held in **Pakistan**. The Pakistan People's party, led by **Zulfikar Bhutto**, president of Pakistan, won 155 of the 200 seats in the National Assembly. Faced with charges of fraud in the elction, Bhutto agreed (June 14) to hold new elections, but he was overthrown (July 5) in a bloodless coup led by **Mohammad Zia Ul-Haq**, the army commander. Bhutto was arrested and on Mar. 18, 1978, was convicted of having ordered the murder of a political opponent. Zulfikar Bhutto (b. Jan. 5, 1928) was sentenced to death and hanged two years later, on Apr. 4, 1979.

1977 Mar. 15 **Anatoly** [Borisovich] **Shcharansky** (b. Jan. 20, 1948), a Russian Jew who had been a leader in the campaign for the right of Jews to emigrate from the Soviet Union, was arrested. He was charged (June 1) with treason, espionage for the U.S., and anti-Soviet agitation. He was sentenced (July 4, 1978) to three years in prison and ten years in a labor camp, but as part of an exchange of prisoners with the U.S. he was allowed to emigrate (Feb. 11, 1986) to Israel.

1977 Mar. 19 **Marien Ngonabi** (b. 1938), president of the **People's Republic of the Congo**, was assassinated. He had made the nation a Marxist-oriented state. An 11-man military committee took over the rule of the country until Apr. 4, when **Joahim Yhombi-Opango** (b. 1940) became head of state.

1977 Mar. 20 The government of **Indira Gandhi**, prime minister of **India** (from 1971), was defeated in a general election. The Janata party, led by **Morarji R**[anchodji] **Desai** (b. Feb. 29, 1896) won 270 seats to the Congress party's 153. Desai became prime minister and ended the emergency rule in effect since 1975. He also restored civil rights.

1977 May 5 **Ludwig Erhard** (b. Feb. 4, 1897), chancellor of the Federal Republic of Germany (1963–1966), died. A Christian Democrat, Erhard as finance minister (1949–1963) did much to bring economic recovery to West Germany after World War II.

1977 May 17 The Labor party of **Israel** lost a general election. Labor lost 19 of its 51 seats in the Knesset (parliament) while the Likud party took 43 seats and with allies was able to form a government. **Menachem Begin** (b. Aug. 16, 1913) became prime minister on June 21, replacing **Yitzhak Rabin**.

1977 June 15 The **first free election in Spain since 1936** was won by the Union of the Democratic Center, a coalition of 12 parties led by **Adolfo Suarez** (b. Sept. 25, 1932), the prime minister. Suarez continued as prime minister, pledging to continue à program of democratic reform.

1977 June 16 In **Ireland** the **Fianna Fáil** won 84 seats in the Dáil [parliament] to 60 for the coalition of Fine Gael and Labour. **Liam Cosgrave** was replaced as prime minister by [John] **Jack Lynch** (b. Aug. 15, 1917).

1977 July 21 The United National party, led by **Junius Richard Jayawardene** (b. Sept. 17, 1906), won the general election in **Sri Lanka**, gaining 139 seats in parliament to only 8 for the supporters of **Sirimavo Bandaranaike**, who had been prime minister since 1960. Jayawardene promised to increase food rations and reduce prices.

1977 June 27 The territory of the Afars and the Issas [French Somaliland] became the **Republic of Djibouti**. **Issa Hassan Gouled Aptidon** (b. 1916) was elected president.

1977 Oct. 10 The **Nobel Peace Prize** was awarded to **Amnesty International** (1961), headquartered in London. In making the award the sponsors said it was for "giving practical, humanitarian and impartial support to people who have been imprisoned because of their race, religion, or political views."

1977 Oct. 18 Flying to Mogadishu, Somalia, West German **commandos attacked a hijacked Lufthansa Boeing 737** that had been forced to land there. Three of the four hijackers were killed and 86 hostages were freed. The pilot had been killed by the hijackers. The **Palestinian terrorists** responsible for the hijacking had demanded release of terrorists in jail in West Germany and Turkey.

1977 Nov. 4 The U.N. Security Council unanimously declared an **embargo on military shipments of any kind to the Republic of South Africa**. The action was aimed at South Africa's **apartheid** policy.

1977 Nov. 18 **Kurt von Schuschnigg** (b. Dec. 4, 1897), the **last chancellor of Austria** before the Nazi takeover (1938), died. He formed a Christian Social government in 1934 and when Hitler's Germany made impossible demands on Austria he called a plebiscite to seek popular support, to be held on Mar. 13, 1938. Schuschnigg was then imprisoned by the Germans and held until the end of World War II.

1977 Nov. 20 To achieve peace in the Near East, **Anwar el-Sadat**, president of Egypt, spoke before the Israeli Knesset. He said he recognized **Israel's right to exist**, but demanded that the occupied Arab territories be given up. A meeting (Dec. 2–4) of Arab nations in Tripoli, Libya, denounced Egypt's action and Sadat in turn announced (Dec. 5) that Egypt was severing diplomatic relations with Syria, Iraq, Libya, South Yemen, and Algeria. Representatives of Israel and Egypt, joined by American officials, met (Dec.

14) in Cairo, Egypt, to attempt to implement the diplomatic breakthrough.

1977 Dec. 4 **Jean-Bedel Bokassa** (b. Feb. 22, 1921), president of the Central African Republic, had himself declared His Imperial Majesty **Bokassa I** and renamed his country the **Central African Empire**. The ceremony was estimated to have cost at least $20 million. The nation was one of the poorest in the world.

1977 Dec. 4 **British troops** numbering c.250 **arrived in Bermuda** to quell rioting and looting in the normally tranquil island. Trouble began after two black political activists were hanged as convicted murderers. During three days of rioting three people died when the Southampton Princess Hotel was set on fire.

1977 Dec. 6 **Bophuthatswana**, in northern South Africa, became the second homeland to be declared independent by the government of the **Republic of South Africa**. **Lucas Mangope** (b. Dec. 27, 1923), whose party held almost all the seats in the legislative assembly, became the first president. Bophuthatswana was not recognized by the rest of the world as a sovereign state.

III. ECONOMY AND TRADE

1977 **Inflation in Latin America** led to strikes and unrest in several countries, including Ecuador, Guyana, Colombia, and Argentina.

1977 Jan. 1 The **Organization of Petroleum Exporting Countries** [OPEC] raised the price of a barrel of oil 10 percent, but Saudi Arabia and the United Arab Emirates held the increase to 5 percent. Thus, on Jan. 5 Aramco, operating the Saudi oil fields, announced an increase from $11.51 to $12.09. On July 1 the basic price went to $12.70, but OPEC said there would be no further increase in 1977.

1977 July 28 The **first oil from the Prudoe Bay** fields on Alaska's North Slope on the Arctic Ocean coast reached the loading port of Valdez in southern Alaska.

1977 Nov. 11 The U.S. formally canceled its membership in the **International Labor Organization** [ILO], a body of the United Nations. The U.S. had been paying $20 million a year to the ILO, c.25 percent of its total budget.

IV. RELIGION AND PHILOSOPHY

1977 July 20–24 A **Conference on the Charismatic Renewal** in the Christian Churches attracted c.45,000 persons to Kansas City, Missouri. About 45 percent of them were Roman Catholics and 30 percent from non-denominational Protestant churches. Pentecostal Protestants were well represented. In June about the same number, all Roman Catholics, attended a charismatic conference in Montreal, Canada.

1977 Sept. 16 About 1,750 **dissident Episcopalians**, including c.350 clergymen, ended a three-day meeting in St. Louis, Missouri, at which they discussed the formation of a new church. They were protesting the action of the church hierarchy, which had voted to permit the ordination of women. They also disagreed with the church in its stand on abortion, divorce, ecumenism, and homosexuality. They voted to found the **Anglican Church in North America**.

V. SCIENCE, EDUCATION, AND TECHNOLOGY

1977 Jan. 19 At the Max Planck Institute in Bonn, West Germany, radio astronomers reported they had found **water molecules existing in a nebula** 2.2 million light years away, suggesting that there might be other solar systems with conditions resembling ours.

1977 Mar. 10 Several groups of astronomers reported at about the same time that they had detected evidence of at least **five rings around the planet Uranus**. Scientists from Cornell University, the Lowell Observatory, and the Perth Observatory in Australia were the discoverers.

1977 June 16 **Wernher von Braun** (b. Mar. 23, 1912), a German-born engineer, died. During World War II he was the technical director of the facility at Peenemünde, a small island of Germany, where the V-1 and V-2 liquid-propelled rockets were developed for Hitler's Germany. U.S. authorities brought von Braun to America after the war and he began to assist in the development of a space exploration program. Von Braun was a leader in devising the first U.S. space probe, fired into orbit on Jan. 31, 1958. Then, as deputy director (1970–1972) of the **National Aeronautics and Space Administration** [NASA] he developed the Saturn 5 rocket that propelled the Apollo flights to the moon.

1977 July 5 Members of the **European Community** [EC], including Belgium, France, Italy, the Netherlands, and West Germany, signed an agreement to cooperate in the development of **fast breeder nuclear reactors**.

1977 Aug. 20 The U.S. *Voyager 2* was launched, and *Voyager 1* followed on Sept. 5. The two space craft were headed for Jupiter and other outer planets.

1977 Aug. 23 The **first successful flight of a man-powered aircraft** took place at Shafter, California, over a three-mile course designed to test the craft's airworthiness. The pedal-powered plane, named the *Gossamer Condor*, weighed 77 pounds. It was invented by **Paul MacCready** (b. Sept. 29, 1925), an aeronautical engineer, and was flown by **Bryan Allen**. The plane won for its inventor $85,000, the Kremer prize offered by the Royal Aeronautic Society of Great Britain.

1977 Oct. 18 The U.S. **aircraft carrier *Dwight D. Eisenhower*** was commissioned. With a load displacement of 91,000 tons, it was one of the largest warships in the world.

1977 Nov. 2 Geneticists at the University of Illinois, headed by **Carle Moese**, announced the identification of **methanogens**, a separate form of life, different genetically from modern bacteria as well as more complex cells. Methanogens could exist only in an oxygen-free environment, used carbon dioxide and gave off methane as a waste product.

1977 Nov. 24 It was announced that the **tomb of Philip II**, king of Macedonia and father of Alexander the Great, had been found at Vergina in northern Greece. Seventeen feet below ground, under a mound 40 feet high, it was identified as Philip's tomb by five carved ivory heads that matched known portraits of the king and his family.

VI. ARTS AND LEISURE

1977 Jan. 12 **Henri Georges Clouzot** (b. Nov. 20, 1907), a French film director, died. His specialty was psychological thrillers. Because he directed a film produced during the World War II occupation of France by the German army, he was not permitted to make any more movies until 1947. His later interesting films included *Le Salaire de la peur* [*The Wages of Fear*] (1952), *Les Diaboliques*

[The Fiends] (1954), and *La Verité* *[The Truth]* (1960).

1977 Jan. 31 The *Centre National d'Art et de Culture Georges Pompidou* [Georges Pompidou National Art and Cultural Center], named for the late president (1969–1974) of France, was officially opened. Known popularly as the *Beaubourg* for its location in Paris, its architecture caused worldwide comment. Its exterior, with exposed pipes and beams, looked more like an oil refinery or a factory than a cultural institution. The completely functional building housed a variety of art exhibits, libraries, and other facilities and functions.

1977 Feb. 9 A miniseries, *Roots*, was reported to have set a record by having been watched, at least in part, by c.130 million Americans. One episode attracted 71 percent of the TV audience. The series was shown for eight (Jan. 23–30) consecutive nights. It was made from the book *Roots* by **Alex** [Palmer] **Haley** (b. Aug. 11, 1921), a black American, who wrote the partly fictionalized account after tracing his ancestry back to a slave brought from Africa in 1767.

1977 Apr. 11 **Jacques Prévert** (b. Feb. 4, 1900), a French poet, playwright, and script writer, died. Among movies for which he wrote the scripts were *Les Enfants du paradis* (1945) and *Les Portes de la nuit* (1946). Prevert's collected poems appeared as *Words for All Seasons* (1979).

1977 May 10 **Joan Crawford** [nee Lucille Lesueur] (b. Mar. 23, 1908), an American movie actress, died. She first attracted attention as the personification of the flapper of the 1920s in such movies as *Our Dancing Daughters* (1928). Thereafter she starred mostly in melodramas, for example *Strange Cargo* (1940) and *Mildred Pierce* (1945). Her last movie was a tale of horror *What Ever Happened to Baby Jane* (1962).

1977 June 3 **Roberto Rossellini** (b. May 8, 1906), an Italian film director, died. His 1945 film *Roma Cita Aperta* [*Open City*] attracted attention world-wide. *Paisan* (1945) also became a classic of its kind and *Il Generale della Rovere* won the grand prize of the Venice Film Festival in 1959.

1977 July 2 **Vladimir** [Vladimirovich] **Nabokov** (b. Apr. 23, 1899), a novelist, died. Russian-born, he lived in the U.S. and several European countries. His works did not attract notable attention until he published *Lolita* (1955), a novel of a middle-aged man's infatuation with a 12-year-old "nymphet." *Pale Fire* (1962) consisted of a 999-line poem and commentary on it by a mad scholar, showing Nabokov's singular skill with satire and humor. *Ada; or Ardor: A Family Chronicle* (1969) was on the surface science fiction but enabled the author to demonstrate his mastery of many subjects. Nabokov wrote movingly of his childhood in *Speak, Memory* (1951).

1977 Aug. 3 **Alfred Lunt** (b. Aug. 19, 1893), an American actor, died. In 1922 he married **Lynn Fontanne** (Dec. 6, 1887–July 30, 1983), an English actress. They appeared together many times after their marriage. Among their successes were *The Guardsman* (1924), *Pygmalion* (1926), *Idiot's Delight* (1936), and *O Mistress Mine* (1945).

1977 Aug. 16 **Elvis** [Aaron] **Presley** (b. Jan. 8, 1935), the king of rock and roll, died. Presley won the adoration of young people. Outstanding among his many hits was "Heartbreak Hotel" (1956), the first of 28 of his recordings to sell a million or more copies. In all, they sold c.600 million copies, and he made 33 movies, of which *Love Me Tender* (1956) was the first. Today his home, Graceland, Memphis, Tennessee, where he is buried, has become a shrine, visited annually by faithful followers, young and old.

1977 Oct. 14 [Harry Lillis] **Bing Crosby** (b. May 2, 1904), an American singer and actor, died. He began his career in 1927 with Paul Whiteman's orchestra and his relaxed manner and soothing voice soon made him popular on the radio and in the movies. Among the films in which he had lead roles and always a chance to sing numbers that became hits were *Holiday Inn* (1942), *Going My Way* (1944), *White Christmas* (1954), and *High Society* (1966).

1977 Dec. 16 **Maria Callas** [nee Maria Anna Sofia Cecilia Kalogeropoulos] (b. Dec. 23, 1923), an American operatic soprano, died. Callas made her debut in 1945 with the Athens Opera, first appeared in 1950 at La Scala in Milan, where she sang often, and in New York in 1956.

1977 Dec. 25 **Charles** [Spencer] **Chaplin** (b. Apr. 16, 1889), an English-born actor who became a star in motion pictures, died. In the U.S. in 1913 he joined Mack Sennett's Keystone film company. His first important movie was *The Tramp* (1915), which also gave him the character of the sad but resourceful little tramp he played many times, with a cane and a waddling walk. Other notable Chaplin movies were *The Kid* (1921), *The Gold Rush* (1925), *City Lights* (1931), *Modern Times* (1936), and *The Great Dictator* (1940). This last was a satire on Hitler's Germany. Chaplin lived his last years in Vevey, Switzerland.

1977 Sept. 13   Leopold [Antony] **Stokowski** (b. Apr. 18, 1882), an English-born conductor, died. He is chiefly known today as the conductor of the **Philadelphia Orchestra** (1912–1938). Stokowski gave early performances of modern composers, such as Igor Stravinsky.

VII. SPORTS, GAMES AND SOCIETY

1977   **Men's fashions showed a trend to conservatism.** Ties were narrow, as were the lapels on jackets. Casual wear favored the traditional country look of tweeds, pullover sweaters, with moccasins or low boots.

1977 May 19   The government of **Kenya banned big-game hunting.** The step was a blow to Kenya's profitable tourist business.

1977 May 22   The *Orient Express* made a final 60-hour trip over the 1,900-mile route from Paris to İstanbul. The luxury train had operated for 94 years.

1977 May 29   **Janet Guthrie** (b. Mar. 7, 1938) became the **first woman to compete in the Indianapolis 500,** the American auto racing classic. Her car developed mechanical problems and she was forced to drop out after 27 laps.

1977 June 11   The **Triple Crown** of American thoroughbred horse racing was won for the tenth time when **Seattle Slew** took the Belmont Stakes. The colt had previously won the Kentucky Derby (May 7) and the Preakness Stakes (May 21). The jockey in all three races was Jean Cruguet.

1977 Sept. 3   A **new world's record for home runs** hit by a professional baseball player was set by **Sadaharu Oh** (b. May 20, 1940) of the Yomiuri Giants of Japan. He hit his 756th homer, one more than the record of the American Henry Aaron when he retired in 1976. When Oh retired at the end of the 1980 season he had reached 868.

1977 Sept. 7–8   A Canadian swimmer, **Cynthia Nicholas** (b. Aug. 20, 1957) completed a **double crossing of the English Channel**, becoming the first woman to do so. Her time of 19 hours, 55 minutes beat the previous record for the round trip by either sex by more than ten hours.

1977 Sept. 13–18   The **America's Cup** was successfully defended by the Americana yacht *Courageous*, which beat the challenger *Australia* in four straight races off Newport, Rhode Island.

1977 Dec. 31   **Steve Cauthen** (b. May 1, 1960), an American jockey, set new records this year. By June when his apprentice year ended, he had ridden 524 winners and won a total of $4,300,000 in purses. For the calendar year his total purses were $6,151,750, also a record.

1978

I. DISASTERS

1978 Jan.–Feb.   A-Victoria and A-Texas **influenza** strains caused c.6,000 deaths in 21 major cities in the U.S.

1978 Jan. 1   An Air India **Boeing 747 exploded** in mid-air after taking off from Bombay and fell into the Arabian Sea, killing 213 people.

1978 Mar. 16   The Liberian-registered supertanker *Amoco Cadiz* **ran aground** two miles off the coast of Brittany, France. The ensuing spill of its 1.62 million barrels of oil created a slick c.10 miles wide and c.80

miles long. The oil greatly damaged fishing and tourism in Brittany.

1978 Apr. 16   A **tornado that struck India's Orissa state** killed nearly 500 persons, injured c.1,000, destroyed c.500 homes, and damaged another c.1,200.

1978 July 11   A tanker **truck** containing c.1,500 cubic feet of propylene **overturned** and went over a stone wall near Tarragona, Spain. The ensuing fire killed c.200 and badly burned c.100.

1978 Sept. 16   In eastern Iran an **earthquake** that registered 7.7 on the Richter scale wiped out the city of Tabas and other villages, killing perhaps as many as 25,000 persons.

1978 Sept. 25   Over San Diego, California, a Pacific Southwest Airlines Boeing **727 collided in the air with a small plane** carrying a student pilot. The planes crashed in a residential area, killing all 137 aboard both planes and c.10 people on the ground.

1978 Nov. 15   In attempting to land at Colombo, Sri Lanka, during a thunderstorm, an Icelandic Airways **DC-8 crashed** with 249 Muslim pilgrims aboard, killing 183.

1978 Nov. 22   A **boat packed with Vietnamese refugees was sunk** off the coast of Malaysia after Malaysian police and villagers refused to let it land. About 200 refugees drowned.

II. POLITICS AND WAR

1978 Jan. 3   **Indira Gandhi**, former prime minister of India, was expelled from the Congress party which she had long dominated. Gandhi at once formed her own party, called the **Congress I party**— the "I" standing for Indira. She was indicted (July 22) on a charge of conspiracy and criminal misconduct in her election campaign in 1977. She was expelled on Dec. 19 from Parliament and ordered to be jailed for the rest of the session, but was released on Dec. 26.

1978 Jan. 6   The **Crown of St. Stephen**, symbol of the Hungarian nation, which had first been used to crown a king in the year 1000, was returned to Hungary by the U.S. The U.S. had secured it toward the end of World War II and kept it from falling into the hands of the Soviets.

1978 Jan. 13   **Hubert** [Horatio] **Humphrey** (b. May 27, 1911), an American politician and statesman, died. In a long career in which he sponsored social legislation, he was senator from Minnesota (1949–1965 and 1970–1977), vice president (1965–1969), and unsuccessful Democratic candidate for president in 1968.

1978 Feb. 19   **Egyptian commandos** at Larnaca airport, Cyprus, **attacked a Cypriot airplane held by two Palestinian terrorists** who had killed a prominent Egyptian in Nicosia, Cyprus. Members of the Cypriot National Guard fought the commandos, killing 15 of them. Another 22 persons were wounded

including seven guardsmen. After the battle the hijackers surrendered, freeing 11 hostages and four crewmen they had been holding. The hijackers were tried and sentenced to death, but their sentences were commuted (Apr. 4) to life imprisonment.

1978 Mar. 3   **Ian Smith**, prime minister of **Rhodesia**, and three black leaders agreed to a transfer of power that would give the black majority control of the nation by the end of the year. The black leaders were **Abel** [Tenbekay] **Muzorewa** (b. Apr. 14, 1925), **Ndabaningi Sithole** (b. July 31, 1920), and **Jeremiah Chirau**.

1978 Mar. 14   A strong **Israeli military force invaded southern Lebanon** with the announced purpose of clearing out bases used by Palestinian guerrillas in raids on Israel. An attack of this kind on Mar. 11 had killed 30 Israelis. Israel announced (Mar. 15) that it had established a "security belt" in Lebanon. Its forces reached the Litani River, six miles north of Tyre, but left that city untouched. The **United Nations** voted (Mar. 19) to send a peacekeeping force to Lebanon, which it did. The Israelis withdrew all their troops by mid-June and by then c.265,000 Lebanese and Palestinians had fled northward to escape the invasion. Lebanon also suffered in 1978 from continued outbreaks of strife between Muslims and Christians. In September and again in October Syrian-backed Muslims fought with rightist Christian forces.

1978 Apr. 20   **Soviet warplanes forced down a Korean Air Lines Boeing 707** that had strayed over Russian Siberia air space. After being fired on, the plane crash-landed on a frozen lake 280 miles from Murmansk. Of the 113 persons on the plane, two were killed and 13 injured.

1978 May 9   The body of **Aldo Moro** (b. Sept. 23, 1916), twice (1963–1968, 1974–1976) Christian Democratic prime minister of **Italy**, was found in a parked car in Rome, the victim of a shooting. He had been kidnapped (Mar. 16) by **Red Brigade terrorists** who had demanded the release from jail of 15 of their fellows, but the Italian government refused to negotiate.

1978 May 18   The **Italian Senate voted** 160 to 148 to **legalize abortion**, which the Chamber of Deputies had already approved (Apr. 14) 308 to 275. Abortion was made available on demand to any woman 18 or older.

1978 June 15 Giovanni Leone (b. Nov. 3, 1908), president of **Italy**, was forced to resign because of his involvement in tax evasion, real estate deals, and improper use of his high office. He was succeeded by **Alessandro Pertini** (b. Sept. 25, 1896).

1978 June 16 The U.S. and Panama exchanged ratifications of two treaties that would give possession of the **Panama Canal** to Panama at the end of 1999.

1978 June 24 Ahmed Hussein Ghashmiles (b. 1941?), president of the Yemen Arab Republic [Yemen], was assassinated by a bomb carried by an envoy from the People's Democratic Republic of Yemen [South Yemen]. On June 26 **Salem Ali Robaye** [Rubayyi] (b. 1935), president of the People's Democratic Republic of Yemen [South Yemen], was deposed and executed by a pro-Russian faction that was implicated in the death of Ghashmi. In Yemen on July 17 **Ali Abdullah Saleh** (born c.1942), an army officer, became president. In South Yemen **Abdul Fattah Ismail** (b. July 28, 1939) became president (to 1980) but was not formally elected until Dec. 27.

1978 July 10 The government of **Moktar Ould Daddah** (b. Dec. 25, 1924) of **Mauritania** was overthrown in a bloodless coup by the military. He was succeeded by **Mustafa Ould Salek** (b. 1936), an army officer. The coup was the result of the continued fighting with the **Polisario front**, a guerrilla group seeking to win independence for the Western Sahara. Mauritania was being drained economically by the warfare with the Polisarios.

1978 July 16 In an election in Ecuador, **Jaime Roldós Aguilera** (b. Nov. 5, 1940), a lawyer and politician, won the most votes but not a majority. The ruling junta postponed a runoff election until Apr. 29, 1979, at which time Roldós, defeating a rightist candidate, was elected to a five-year term.

1978 July 19 The National Election Court of **Bolivia** voided the election (July 1) for president, which had been won by **Juan Pedreda Asbún**, a general, on the grounds of fraud. The incumbent president **Hugo Banzer Suarez** resigned (July 21) in the face of a revolt led by Pereda, who assumed office. Pereda's government was overthrown (Nov. 24) by a military junta headed by **David Padilla Arancibia**.

1978 Aug. 12 Japan and the People's Republic of China signed a ten-year treaty according to which they would respect each other's territory, cooperate economically and culturally, and not interfere in each other's internal affairs. The state of war between the two nations had existed since the 1930s.

1978 Aug. 22 Jomo [Kamau Ngenge] **Kenyatta** (b. Oct. 20, 1891), president of Kenya (from 1964), died. He had been a nationalist leader when Kenya was still a British colony and by the time of his death was the elder statesman of African politics. He was succeeded by **Daniel Arap Moi** (b. Sept., 1924), who had been vice president.

1978 Aug. 22 Sandinista guerrillas opposing the **Nicaraguan** government of **Anastasio Somoza Debayle**, president and dictator, stormed the National Palace in Managua, the capital. The guerrillas seized c.1,500 hostages, including members of the legislature. They freed them only after Somoza agreed to release 59 political prisoners and give the Sandinistas $500,000. On Aug. 27 businessmen, not always in sympathy with the left-leaning rebels, agreed to support a general strike, but Somoza remained in office.

1978 Sept. 17 A summit meeting of **Jimmy Carter**, president of the U.S., **Menachem Begin**, prime minister of Israel, and **Anwar al-Sadat**, president of Egypt, which began on Sept. 6, concluded successfully at Camp David, in Maryland. Begin and Sadat agreed on a basic framework for peace and undertook to achieve a treaty in three months. Matters to be covered were the withdrawal of Israel from the Sinai Peninsula, the status of Israeli settlements on the West Bank, and the establishment of normal diplomatic relations. Some Arab nations (Sept. 21) denounced the agreement and broke relations with Egypt. The **Nobel Peace Prize** for 1978 was awarded to Begin and Sadat on Oct. 27.

1978 Sept. 28 Pieter Willem Botha (b. Jan. 12, 1916) became prime minister of South Africa, succeeding **Balthazar Johannes Vorster**, in office from 1966. Vorster resigned to accept election to the presidency, the incumbent **Nicholaas J. Diederichs** (b. Nov. 17, 1903) having died on Aug. 21, 1978.

1978 Oct. 15 João Batista Figueirdo (b. Jan. 15, 1918), a general, was elected president of Brazil by the electoral college, which consisted of both houses of congress. He was not to take office until Mar. 15, 1979.

1978 Oct. 17 Giovanni Gronchi (b. Sept. 10, 1897), an Italian statesman and president (1955–1962), died. He was a founder of the Christian Democratic party (1944). He opposed Mussolini's fascist rule from 1924 on, and during World War II was active in the underground.

1978 Dec. 3 Luis Herrera Campins (b. May 4, 1925) of the Social Christian party won the presidential election in Venezuela. The winner charged the outgoing administration with corruption and inefficiency in handling the country's large oil revenues.

1978 Dec. 8 Golda Meir [Goldie Mabovitch] (b. May 3, 1898), prime minister of Israel (1969–1974), died. Born in Russia, Meir lived in the U.S. (1906–1921), where she taught school before emigrating to Palestine. She held high government positions after Israel became independent (1948), including minister to Moscow (1948) and foreign minister (1956–1966). After the **Yom Kippur War** (1973) with Egypt and Syria, she was criticized as being unprepared for the surprise onslaught. Unable to form a new coalition government, she resigned in Apr. 1974.

1978 Dec. 27 Houari Boumédienne [orig.: Mohammed Ben Brahim Boukharrouba] (b. Aug. 23, 1927), president of Algeria (from 1965), died. He was a leader in the war against French rule that ended with independence in 1962. Boumédienne was succeeded on an interim basis by **Rabah Bitat** (b. Dec. 19, 1925), speaker of the national assembly.

1978 Dec. 29 Shahpur Bakhtiar (b. 1916) was appointed prime minister of **Iran** by the shah. Demonstrations and rioting began in January, spurred by religious leaders who hated the shah's western ways. In February there was rioting in Teheran. Muslim extremists were thought to be responsible for a fire (Aug. 20) in a movie theater in Abadan that took 430 lives. In what amounted to a massacre, the army fired (Sept. 8) on a crowd in Teheran. Officially, c.100 were killed but the total may have been ten times that. **Martial law** was declared. Oil workers went on strike (Oct. 31), demanding an end to martial law as well as asking for higher wages. By early November oil production had been cut by more than half.

III. ECONOMY AND TRADE

1978 Dec. 5 The **European Economic Community** [EEC] agreed to establish a **European Monetary System** [EMS] as of Jan. 1, 1979. The currencies of Belgium, Denmark, France, Luxembourg, the Netherlands, and West Germany would be allowed to float against each other.

IV. RELIGION AND PHILOSOPHY

1978 June 9 The leaders of the **Church of Jesus Christ of Latter-Day Saints** [Mormons] announced they had received a revelation that permitted worthy males to become members of the church's priesthood regardless of race.

1978 Aug. 6 Pope Paul VI [orig.: Giovanni Battista Montini] (b. Sept. 26, 1897; ruled from 1963), died. On Aug. 25 Albino Cardinal Lucian, the patriarch of Venice, was elected pope and took the name of **John Paul I**. John Paul (b. Oct. 17, 1912) died, apparently of a heart attack, on Sept. 28, his 35 days in office being the shortest papal reign since the 18 days of **Pope Leo XI** in 1605. Karol Cardinal Wojtyla (b. May 18, 1920), archbishop of Kracców [Cracow], Poland, was chosen (Oct. 16) as the 264th head of the Roman Catholic Church and took the name of **John Paul II**.

1978 Aug. 10 A grant of $85,000 by the **World Council of Churches** to the black **Patriotic Front of Rhodesia** aroused considerable controversy. Although the grant was made for humanitarian aid only, some saw it as interfering in the affairs of Rhodesia and encouraging bloodshed.

1978 Sept. 19 Étienne Henry Gilson (b. June 13, 1884), a French philosopher and historian, died. A university professor in France (1921–1951), he was also a **cofounder of the Pontifical Institute of Medieval Studies** (1929) at Toronto, Canada, where he became a full-time professor (1951). Gilson was a leader of the Roman Catholic neo-Thomist movement, exponents of the philosophy of Thomas Aquinas. Among his many writings were *Christianisme et philosophie* [*Christianity and Philosophy*] (1936) and *L'Être et l'essense* (1948, 1962).

1978 Nov. 18 At the headquarters of a religious sect in Guyana, South America, **mass suicide and murder** took the lives of 911 persons, c.200 of them children. [James Warren] **Jim Jones** (b. May 13,

1931), leader of the **People's Temple**, ordered his followers to drink soft drinks laced with cyanide. The action was triggered by the murder (Nov. 18) at the local airport of **Leo Ryan**, a California congressman, who had come to investigate charges of atrocities allegedly perpetrated by the People's Temple when it was located in his district. When Jones heard of the shootings he ordered his followers to kill each other or commit suicide. Jones was among those found dead, apparently a suicide.

V. SCIENCE, EDUCATION, AND TECHNOLOGY

1978 **Smallpox**, common throughout the world for centuries, was believed entirely eradicated, thanks to vaccine and disease prevention programs. The smallpox virus now existed only in four laboratories, kept there in case the vaccine was ever needed again.

1978 Jan. 11 Two Soviet cosmonauts in *Soyuz 27* **linked up with the space lab** *Salyut 6*, which had been in orbit for a month. The feat demonstrated the possibility of multiple linkups in space.

1978 Jan. 14 **Kurt Gödel** (b. Apr. 28, 1906), a Czechoslovakian-born American mathematician and logician, died. He emigrated to the U.S. in 1940. Gödel was known particularly for his theorem (1931) in which he argued that the propositions on which the branches of mathematics are based cannot be proved within the system itself.

1978 Jan. 24 The five-ton Soviet reconnaissance satellite *Cosmos 954* **disintegrated** while entering the earth's atmosphere and its pieces fell in a remote area of Canada's Northwest Territories. Some 100 pounds of uranium-235 aboard powered its reactor. Fragments discovered (Feb. 4) on the ice of Great Slave Lake had a dangerous level of radiation.

1978 Feb. 11 **James Bryant Conant** (b. Mar. 26, 1893), an American educator, chemist, and ambassador, died. As president of Harvard University (1933–1953) he gave much attention to achieving a balanced general curriculum. During World War II Conant helped shape policy on the use of science. He was appointed (1955) U.S. high commissioner to Germany and then became the first ambassador to West Germany (1955–1957).

1978 May 20 The U.S. launched the unmanned space craft *Pioneer Venus 1* toward the planet **Venus**. It began orbiting (Dec. 4) the planet and transmitting photographs of the surface. *Pioneer Venus 2* was launched on Aug. 8 and it sent (Dec. 6) four probes to the planet's surface and began transmitting data about the atmosphere and surface conditions on Venus.

1978 July 25 The **first documented birth of a human being conceived outside its mother's womb** took place in Oldham, Lancashire, England. Doctors had removed an egg from the mother's ovaries and fertilized it in a petri dish with sperm from the husband. The fertilized egg was then implanted in the mother's womb.

1978 Sept. 17 **Willy Messerschmitt** (b. June 26, 1898), a German aeronautical engineer, died. He developed the Me-109, a fighter much feared by Allied pilots in World War II. Near the end of the war he produced the Me-262, the first operational jet fighter.

1978 Nov. 2 Soviet scientists **correctly predicted the time and magnitude of an earthquake** that occurred today but were not precise in locating it. The quake registered 7 on the Richter scale and occurred in the Altai Mountains, near the border between Tadzhikistan and Kirghizia. This was c.90 miles from the predicted location.

1978 Nov. 15 **Margaret Mead** (b. Dec. 16, 1901), an American anthropologist, died. She attracted attention with her book *Coming of Age in Samoa* (1928), which was based on a field trip she made. It contended that the Samoans avoided the stresses of the modern world by a relaxed attitude toward life, including sexual mores. Mead was associated with (1926–1969) the American Museum of Natural History, New York City. Mead also wrote *Male and Female* (1949), *Continuities in Cultural Evolution* (1964), and *Blackberry Winter* (1972).

VI. ARTS AND LEISURE

1978 Apr. 21 Several million dollars worth of **paintings were stolen from the Pitti Palace** in Florence, Italy, including **Peter Paul Rubens'** *The Three Graces*. Italian police recovered them all undamaged two days later.

1978 May 1 **Aram [Ilich] Khachaturian** (b. June 6, 1903), a Russian Armenian composer, died. His

Piano Concerto (1936) made him popular in the U.S.S.R. and abroad. Khachaturian composed ballets such as *Gayane* (1942), symphonies, film scores, and patriotic songs.

1978 June 1 The **East Building of the National Gallery of Art** in Washington, D.C., was opened. It was designed by **I**[eoh] **M**[ing] **Pei** (b. Apr. 26, 1917), a Chinese-born American architect. Although original and striking in design, the East Building did not conflict with the neo-classical style of the original building.

1978 June 20–27 The **art collection of the Baron Robert von Hirsch** (1883–1977), sold at auction in London, brought $37.6 million, the most to date for any art collection.

1978 June 26 The 17th-century royal palace at **Versailles**, France, was **bombed by terrorists**, destroying three ground floor rooms, including valuable works of art. Three groups claimed credit for the attack, but the French police were inclined to blame the **Breton Republican Army**.

1978 Aug. 2 **Carlos** [Antonio de Padua] **Chavez** (b. June 13, 1899), a Mexican composer, died. He made use of Mexican melodic patterns and rhythms in his work. Among his best-known compositions were *Sinfonia Antigona* (1933) and *Concerto for Violin* (1950).

1978 Aug. 6 **Edward Durrell Stone** (b. Mar. 9, 1902), a leading American architect, died. Among his striking works were the designs for the Museum of Modern Art, New York City (1937) and the American embassy in New Delhi, India (1958).

1978 Aug. 21 **Ignazio Silone** [orig.: Secondo Tranquilli] (b. May 1, 1900), an Italian novelist, died. Strongly anti-fascist, he lived in Switzerland until after World War II when, returning to Italy, he became a leader of the Democratic Socialist party. His novels included *Fontamara* (1930) and *Pane e vino* [*Bread and Wine*] (1937).

1978 Aug. 26 **Charles Boyer** (b. Aug. 28, 1899), a French-born actor who played in many Hollywood movies, died. He was cast opposite such glamorous leading ladies as **Greta Garbo** in *Tovarich* (1937), **Hedy Lamar** in *Algiers* (1938), and **Ingrid Bergman** in *Gaslight* (1944).

1978 Sept. 9 **Jack** [Leonard] **Warner** (b. Aug. 2, 1892), a Hollywood film producer and one of the Warner Brothers, died. In 1927 he produced *The Jazz Singer*, the first talking feature-length film.

1978 Oct. 9 **Jacques Brel** (b. Apr. 8, 1929), a French singer and actor, died. An idol of the public in the 1950s, Brel composed c.500 songs in all. After 1967 he appeared in a number of French movies.

1978 Nov. 9 **Norman Rockwell** (b. Feb. 3, 1894), America's best-loved illustrator, died. His scenes of everyday American life appeared on more than 300 covers of the *Saturday Evening Post*, beginning in 1916.

1978 Nov. 20 **Giorgio de Chirico** (b. July 10, 1888), an Italian painter, died. His paintings attempted to get behind ordinary reality and remove the normal emotional meaning of objects. Typical of his work were *Engima of an Autumn Afternoon* (1910), *Mystery and Melancholy of a Street* (1914), and *Grand Metaphysical Interior* (1917).

VII. SPORTS, GAMES, AND SOCIETY

1978 May 1 Traveling by dogsled, **Naomi Uemura** (b. Feb. 12, 1941), a Japanese athlete, reached the **North Pole** from Ellsmere, the first person ever to make such a trip alone.

1978 May 24 **Princess Margaret** (b. Aug. 21, 1930), sister of Elizabeth II, queen of England, **and** her husband of 18 years, **Antony** [Charles Robert] **Armstrong-Jones** (b. Mar. 7, 1930), the earl of Snowden, were granted a divorce.

1978 June 10 The **Triple Crown** of American thoroughbred horse racing was won for the 11th time when **Affirmed** captured the Belmont Stakes. The horse had previously won the Kentucky Derby (May 6) and the Preakness Stakes (May 20). The jockey in all three races was **Steve Cauthen**.

1978 June 15 **Hussein I**, king of Jordan, married **Elizabeth Halaby** (b. Aug. 23, 1951), an American and daughter of a former head of Pan American World Airways. The bride, who had converted to Islam, became queen, taking the name **Noor al-Hussein**.

1978 June 25 Argentina defeated the Netherlands 3 to 1 to win its first **World Cup** of soccer, in Buenos Aires.

1978 Sept. 15 Muhammad Ali won the **world heavyweight boxing championship** for the third time. He defeated **Leon Spinks** (b. July 11, 1953) in a 15-round decision at New Orleans. Ali had lost the championship to Spinks on Feb. 15 at Las Vegas, Nevada, on a decision.

1978 Oct. 17 Anatoly Karpov of the USSR retained the **world championship of chess** by defeating **Victor Korchnoi** (b. 1931), a Russian living in Switzerland. Karpov won the 32nd game, when the players were tied at 5-5.

1978 Nov. 5 Stanley Mark Rifkin (b. 1946), an American computer consultant, was arrested on charges of having **defrauded the Security Pacific National Bank of Los Angeles** of $10.2 million on Oct. 15. Rifkin, not a bank employee, learned a secret **computer code that enabled him to order the transfer of the money** to a New York bank. When arrested, Rifkin pleaded guilty to two charges of wire fraud and on Mar. 26, 1979, was sentenced to eight years in prison. The bank eventually recouped its loss.

1979

I. DISASTERS

1979 Mar. 28 In an **accident in a nuclear power plant** at **Three Mile Island**, near Harrisburg, Pennsylvania, a small amount of radioactive gas was released. Small children and pregnant women within a five-mile radius of the plant were evacuated for a short time. Human error and malfunctioning equipment were found to have allowed the reactor to lose its coolant and cause the radioactive fuel to overheat. The plant could never be put back in operation.

1979 Apr. 10 Severe **tornados struck the Texas-Oklahoma border**, with Wichita Falls, Texas, hardest hit. Deaths totaled 59, injuries c.800.

1979 May 25 A **DC-10 of American Airlines crashed** after takeoff at O'Hare International Airport, Chicago, killing all 272 persons aboard and two on the ground. One of the plane's engines had fallen off in flight.

1979 June 3 An **oil well in the Gulf of Mexico blew out,** spilling perhaps as much as 45,000 barrels a day. It was not fully capped until it had dumped 3.1 million barrels. Much damage was done to wildlife, commercial fishing, and tourism, with more than 100 miles of Texas coastline fouled.

1979 July 19 Two supertankers, the *Atlantic Express* and the *Aegean Captain*, **collided** 18 miles off the coast of the island of Tobago in the Caribbean Sea, spilling 1.02 million barrels of oil. None of the oil reached the coast of Tobago.

1979 Aug. 11 Water from the swollen Machhu River caused an **earthen dam to collapse**, sending a 20-foot wall of water surging over Morvi in Gujarat state, western India. The death toll was c.5,000.

1979 Aug. 11 Two Aeroflot **Tu-134 passenger jets collided** over the Ukraine. According to reports, there were no survivors among the 173 persons on the planes.

1979 Aug. 30–Sept. 14 **Hurricane David** and **Hurricane Frederick** struck within two weeks of each other. From Aug. 30 to Sept. 7 David ravaged Caribbean islands and the eastern seaboard of the U.S., killing more than 1,000 people and doing billions of dollars of damage. Frederick, striking the U.S. eastern seaboard from Sept. 12 to 14, killed only eight, but damage to property reached $2,500,000,000.

1979 Nov. 1 In Galveston Bay, Texas, the tanker *Burmah Agate* **collided with another ship.** As a result c.255,000 barrels of oil were spilled or burned.

1979 Nov. 26 A Pakistan International Airline **Boeing 707 crashed** on takeoff from Jidda, Saudi Arabia. All 256 aboard, pilgrims returning from Mecca, were killed.

1979 Nov. 28 An Air New Zealand **DC-10** on a sightseeing flight over the South Pole **crashed** into Mt. Erebus. All 257 persons aboard were killed.

II. POLITICS AND WAR

1979 Jan. 7 Phnom Penh, the capital of Cambodia, **fell to army forces from Vietnam**, and a dissident group of the **Khmer Rouge** called the National United Front for National Salvation, led by **Heng**

Samrin (b. 1934), established (Jan. 8) a new government. **Pol Pot**, leader of the defeated Khmer Rouge government, appealed to the UN, but a resolution of support in the Security Council was vetoed (Jan. 15) by the U.S.S.R., which supported Vietnam. The Chinese continued their support of the Khmer Rouge.

1979 Jan. 16   Mohammad Riza Pahlevi, shah of **Iran** (from 1941), left for Egypt, ending the **Pahlevi Dynasty** (from 1925). **Ayatollah Ruhollah Moussari Khomeini** returned (Feb. 1) after nearly 15 years in exile. His supporters took over the government and the Ayatollah appointed (Feb. 5) **Medhi Bazargan** (b. Sept., 1907) prime minister. The army leadership announced (Feb. 11) its neutrality, assuring Khomeini of control. Iran thus became a Shiite state with religious rather than political leadership.

1979 Jan. 26   Nelson A[ldrich] **Rockefeller** (b. July 8, 1908), a prominent American political figure, died. He was elected governor (1954–1973) of New York state four times and served as vice president of the U.S. (1974–1977). He left his great collection of paintings, sculpture, and primitive art to the Museum of Modern Art and the Metropolitan Museum of Art in New York.

1979 Feb. 17   Alleging intrusions into its territory, in addition to the **Vietnamese invasion of Cambodia**, **China sent c.100,000 troops into Vietnam**. By Feb. 26 these forces were c.25 miles into that country. The Chinese said (Mar. 25) they had accomplished what they sought and that their troops had been withdrawn.

1979 Mar. 13   The government of **Eric Gairy** (b. Feb. 18, 1922), prime minister of **Grenada**, an island in the Caribbean Sea, since independence in 1974, was overthrown while he was in New York City. The coup was carried out by the New Jewel Movement, led by **Maurice Bishop** (May 29, 1944–Oct. 19, 1983), who became prime minister and established a People's Revolutionary Government.

1979 Mar. 16   Jean [Omer Marie Gabriel] **Monnet** (b. Nov. 9, 1888), a French economist and diplomat, died. More than any other one person he was responsible for bringing together, economically and politically, most of the nations of western Europe in the **European Community** [EC]. Monnet drafted the **Schuman Plan**, which established the **European Coal and Steel Community**, and was its first president (1952–1955). In 1955 he was the moving spirit

in the founding of the Action Committee for a United States of Europe and served as its president. Out of these various endeavors grew the European Community (from 1967).

1979 Mar. 26   In a ceremony at the White House, **Jimmy Carter, Menachem Begin**, and **Anwar al-Sadat** put their signatures to a **peace treaty**. The treaty provided for gradual withdrawal of Israeli forces from the Sinai Peninsula and abandonment of civilian settlements there. Diplomatic relations were to be established and further negotiations held concerning Palestinian self-rule on the West Bank which, with the Gaza Strip, was occupied by Israel.

1979 Mar. 28   The British House of Commons voted no confidence in the government by a vote of 311 to 310. **James Callaghan**, prime minister and head of the Labour party, called an election (May 3) in which the Conservatives won 339 seats, a majority in the 635-seat Parliament. Labour won 268. As a result **Margaret** [Hilda] **Thatcher** (b. Oct. 13, 1925) became **prime minister, the first woman** to hold that position in **Great Britain**.

1979 Apr. 11   Tanzanian forces, aided by Ugandan exiles, entered Kampala, the capital of **Uganda**, and overthrew the regime of **Idi Amin**, who fled to Libya, which had supported him. **Yusufu K. Lule** (b.1911) was sworn in (Apr. 13) as new head of state. When a vote (June 20) of no confidence by the National Consultative Council forced Lule to resign, he was succeeded by **Godfrey L. Binaisa** (b. May 30, 1920), another leader of the anti-Amin forces.

1979 Apr. 17–21   In the **first universal suffrage election in Rhodesia** since its independence, the United African National Council, headed by **Abel** [Tenbekay] **Muzorewa** (b. Apr. 14, 1925), was victorious, winning 51 of the 72 seats allotted to blacks. When there were charges of fraud, the UN Security Council voted (Apr. 30) to condemn the election and continue its boycott. This was intended to get Muzorewa, who became prime minister on May 29, to negotiate with the leaders of the guerrilla Patriotic Front, **Joshua Nkomo** (b. June 19, 1917) and **Robert** [Gabriel] **Mugabe** (b. Feb. 21, 1924). A ceasefire was arranged (Dec. 5) and Rhodesia became (Dec. 7) once again, but temporarily, a British colony with [Arthur] **Christopher** [John] **Soames** (Oct. 12, 1920–Sept. 16, 1987) as governor. The Muzorewa government voted (Dec. 11) itself out of office and preparations were made to hold a new election.

1979 May 22   In a general election in Canada the Liberal party, led by **Pierre Trudeau**, the prime minister, lost its majority. The Progressive Conservatives won 136 seats in the House of Commons to 114 for the Liberals. The New Democratic party took 20 seats and others 6. [Charles] **Joseph Clark** (b. June 5, 1939), the leader of his party, formed a minority government of the Progressive Conservatives. Clark's government was defeated (Dec. 13) in a vote on the budget. A new election was scheduled for Feb. 2, 1980.

1979 June 18   **Jimmy Carter** and **Leonid Brezhnev**, first secretary of the Communist party and chief of state (from 1977) of the U.S.S.R., meeting in Vienna, signed the **Strategic Arms Limitation Treaty II** [SALT II]. The treaty was intended to set limits on weapon launchers, missile silos, and manned bombers, but it was not ratified by the U.S. Senate.

1979 July 5   The people of the **Isle of Man**, in the Irish Sea, observed the **1,000th anniversary of their legislature**, called the, **Tynwald**. The Isle of Man was occupied in the ninth century by Vikings and a century or so later the Tynwald was established.

1979 July 15   **Gustavo Diaz Ordaz** (b. Mar. 12, 1911), president of **Mexico** (1964–1970), died. He was remembered mostly for the tragedy of his regime, the so-called "massacre at Tlatelolco" on Oct. 2, 1968, when troops and police fired on demonstrating students.

1979 July 16   **Saddam Hussein al-Tikriti** (b. Apr. 28, 1937), vice chairman of the Revolutionary Command Council, became president (to the present) of **Iraq** upon the resignation of **Ahmad Hassan al-Bakr** (1914–Oct. 4, 1982), president of Iraq from 1968. Hussein at once began a purge of the council, the military command, labor leaders, and the **Ba'ath party** itself. Hussein thereafter ruled by decree.

1979 July 17   **Anastasio Somoza Debayle**, president of **Nicaragua**, resigned and went into exile. His family had controlled the nation for 46 years and amassed an enormous fortune. In seven weeks of civil war, the victorious opposition was led by the **Sandinistas**, who had been carrying on guerrilla warfare for years. Control of the nation was taken over (July 20) by a five-member Government Junta of National Reconstruction.

1979 Aug. 16   **John G**[eorge] **Diefenbaker** (b. Sept. 18, 1895), a former prime minister of Canada (1957–1963), died. As leader of the Progressive Conservative party, he guided the party to its greatest victory in 1958, when it won 208 of the 265 seats in the House of Commons.

1979 Aug. 27   **Louis** [Francis Albert Victor Nicholas] **Mountbatten** [Earl Mountbatten of Burma] (b. June 25, 1900), a British military commander and statesman, died when the **Irish Republican Army** blew up his fishing boat off the coast of Ireland. He was supreme Allied commander in Southeast Asia (1943–1946) in World War II. As the last viceroy (1947) of India the earl presided with distinction over the coming of independence to India and Pakistan.

1979 Oct. 26   **Park Chung Hee** (b. Nov. 14, 1917), president of **South Korea** (from 1963), was assassinated by one of his closest associates **Kim Jae Kyu**, head of the Korean Central Intelligence Agency [KCIA]. Six others were killed in the shootout by KCIA agents. **Choi Kyu Hah** (b. July 16, 1919) was appointed (Oct. 27) provisional president and elected (December) president by the National Conference for Reunification. Kim and six of his aides were sentenced to death on Dec. 20.

1979 Nov. 4   A mob of students and other **militants stormed the American embassy in Teheran**, Iran, and took c.90 persons hostage. Of them c.60 were American citizens. On Nov. 14 the U.S. froze Iranian assets in the U.S. and halted the purchase of Iranian oil. Iran released some of the hostages, but at year's end 52 Americans remained in captivity.

1979 Dec. 10   **Mother Teresa** [nee Agnes Gonxha Bojaxhiu] (b. Aug. 27, 1910), for devoting most of her life to the care of the ill, the dying, and the abandoned, was awarded the **Nobel Peace Prize**. Born in present-day Czechoslovakia of Albanian parents, she joined an Irish order of nuns as a teenager and later taught school in Calcutta, India. She began ministering to the poor and founded a new order, the **Missionaries of Charity**.

1979 Dec. 27   **Soviet troops with air support poured into Afghanistan**, ousting (Dec. 27) the regime of **Hafizullah Amin** (b. Aug. 1, 1929), who was killed in the process. Amin had been in power only since September, when he led the overthrow of **Nur Mòhammad Taraki** (b. July, 1917). The Russians installed (Dec. 27) as head of state **Babrak Karmal** (b.1929), whom they brought back from exile in Czechoslovakia. Guerrilla resistance forces soon formed and fought fiercely against the invaders, with the aid of supplies from the U.S. by way of Pakistan.

III. ECONOMY AND TRADE

1979 The **Organization of Petroleum Exporting Countries** [OPEC] raised prices as of Apr. 1 to a level that had been promised not to come into effect until October. By July 1 Saudi light crude was $18 a barrel, up from $13.34 as of Jan. 1. By year's end some oil was selling for $24 a barrel, or more. As a result **inflation** increased, and by the end of the year the prime rate in the U.S. was up to 15.75 percent; in Canada, 15 percent; and in Great Britain, 17 percent. The inflation rate in Canada was 9.5 percent; in Great Britain, 17 percent; in the U.S., 13.3 percent for the year. Japan was able to hold its rate to 3 percent.

1979 Jan. 3   Conrad [Nicholson] **Hilton** (b. Dec. 25, 1887), an American hotel operator, died. Beginning with a $5,000 investment in 1931 in a hotel in Cisco, Texas, he forming the **Hilton Hotel Corporation** in 1946. He controlled c.185 hotels before he retired in 1966, including the Palmer House in Chicago and the Waldorf-Astoria in New York City.

1979 Apr. 12   After five and a half years of negotiations, a new international agreement concerning export-import trade was initialed in Geneva, Switzerland, with 99 nations taking part under the **General Agreement on Tariffs and Trade** [GATT] (1947). Most of the less developed nations did not sign, claiming that special concessions promised them in 1973 had not materialized.

1979 May 9   Cyrus [Stephen] **Eaton** (b. Dec. 27, 1883), a Canadian-born businessman who made a fortune in the U.S., died. In July 1959, he held the first of his **Pugwash conferences**, named for his home in Nova Scotia. To these annual sessions he brought scholars in many fields and from many nations, aiming especially at improving relations with Russia in a number of areas.

1979 June 29   In Tokyo the five leading **industrial nations** of Europe and the U.S. and Japan reached an **agreement to limit oil imports** through 1985. The U.S. was to import a maximum of 8.5 million barrels a day. In the course of the year the price of gasoline in the U.S. crossed the $1 a gallon mark for the first time, and shortages developed.

1979 July 11   The **International Whaling Commission** voted to ban for at least ten years all whale hunting in the Red and Arabian seas and most of the Indian Ocean.

1979 Oct. 3   The U.S. announced that the **U.S.S.R.** would be permitted **to buy 25 million metric tons of American wheat and corn** in the next 12 months. In late November the Soviets reported Russian grain production was 179 million metric tons this year, the worst harvest since 1972.

IV. RELIGION AND PHILOSOPHY

1979 July 9   Robert [Alexander Kennedy] **Runcie** (b. Oct. 22, 1921), bishop of the diocese of St. Albans, England, was appointed the 102nd archbishop of Canterbury, becoming head of the Anglican church worldwide. He was to take office on Jan. 26, 1980, upon the retirement of the current archbishop **Donald Coggan**.

1979 July 29   Herbert Marcuse (b. July 19, 1898), a German political philosopher, died. Student radicals and others resonated to his call for a social revolution and echoed his belief that modern society was a "repressive monolith." Among his books were *Eros and Civilization* (1955) and *One Dimensional Man* (1964).

1979 Sept. 12   The triennial **General Convention of the Episcopal Church** of the U.S. gave final approval to a revised *Book of Common Prayer* to replace the 1928 edition. The convention's two houses also voted (Sept. 17–18) to bar practicing homosexuals from ordination.

1979 Nov. 20   About 200 armed **fundamentalist Muslims seized the Great Mosque in Mecca**, Saudi Arabia. Saudi military forces had to battle the invaders until Dec. 4 before they were ousted. More than 150 persons died in the conflict. The fundamentalists were protesting the western customs appearing in Saudi society.

1979 Nov. 21   Scientists who examined the **Shroud of Turin**, kept in the Cathedral of San Giovanni in Turin, Italy, and venerated by some as the burial cloth of Jesus, reported that tests so far conducted neither proved nor disproved this claim.

1979 Dec. 18 The Vatican declared **Hans Küng** (b. Mar. 19, 1928), a Swiss-born theologian and professor at Tübingen University, West Germany, no longer a Roman Catholic theologian and forbade him to teach the subject. Küng had aroused controversy with his book *Infallible? An Inquiry* (1970), which questioned the doctrine of **papal infallibility**.

V. SCIENCE, EDUCATION, AND TECHNOLOGY

1979 Mar. 5 *Voyager 1*, an unmanned U.S. spacecraft flew within 172,000 miles of the planet Jupiter. It sent back photographs of Jupiter's four moons, showing a volcano erupting on one of them. This was the first evidence of such a phenomenon in the solar system outside the earth.

1979 July 11 *Skylab*, a 77-ton unmanned space station launched by the U.S. on May 17, 1973, fell to earth, breaking up in the process after 34,981 orbits. Pieces of it, some weighing nearly two tons, fell harmlessly over a 4,000-mile path from the Indian Ocean to the Great Victoria Desert and the Great Sandy Desert of Western Australia.

1979 Sept. 1 The U.S. *Pioneer 11* passed within 12,500 miles of the planet Saturn, sending back photographs disclosing that the planet had at least one more ring than previously known and an 11th moon. The rings were seen to be composed of water and ice.

VI. ARTS AND LEISURE

1979 Jan. 9 **Pier Luigi Nervi** (b. June 21, 1891), a noted Italian architect, died. His designs were daring and made much use of curves and arches. With others, he designed the **UNESCO headquarters** in Paris (1950). Nervi received the gold medals of both the Royal Institute of British Architects and the Institute of American Architects.

1979 Feb. 12 **Jean Renoir** (b. Sept. 15, 1894), one of France's best film directors, died. Of his 36 films, the best known is *La Grande Illusion* (1937), in which war and nationalism are the illusions.

1979 Feb. 27 The Italian government said it would spend $550,000 to restore **Leonardo da Vinci's** fresco *The Last Supper*, which was painted (1496–1498) by the master on a wall of Milan's Church of Santa Maria delle Grazie. The painting had deteriorated badly as a result of air pollution.

1979 Mar. 15 **Léonide Massine** [orig.: Leonid Feodorovich Miassin] (b. Aug. 9, 1896), a Russian choreographer and dancer, died. Performing first with Diaghilev's Ballets Russes (1914–1921), his long career took him to the very top of his field. He **founded and directed the Ballet Russe de Monte Carlo** (1938–1942) and then directed the National Ballet Theater (1941–1945) in New York City. Massine choreographed c.100 ballets in all.

1979 May 29 **Mary Pickford** [nee Gladys Mary Smith] (b. June 4, 1893), a Canadian-born actress who became the most popular of all stars of the early days of the movies, died. As early as 1914, with *Tess of the Storm Country*, she reached stardom. Such movies as *Rebecca of Sunnybrook Farm* (1917) and *Pollyanna* (1919) made her "America's Sweetheart," the lovable ingénue. In 1919 **Douglas Fairbanks**, **Charlie Chaplin**, Pickford, and **D.W. Griffith** formed **United Artists** .

1979 June 11 **John Wayne** [Marion Michael Morrison] (b. May 26, 1907), a movie actor who typified the rugged American hero of the West and of warfare, died. Among his more than 200 films were *Stagecoach* (1939), *The Sands of Iwo Jima* (1949), and *True Grit* (1969).

1979 Aug. 22 **James T**[homas] **Farrell** (b. Feb. 27, 1904), an American novelist noted for his portrayal of lower middle class life in Chicago, died. In a trilogy he described the life of a youth from this background: *Young Lonigan* (1932), *The Young Manhood of Studs Lonigan* (1934), and *Judgment Day* (1935).

1979 Oct. 1 **Roy** [Ellsworth] **Harris** (b. Feb. 12, 1898), an American composer, died. He wrote 16 symphonies and c.185 other major works. His themes were apparent from the titles of many of his compositions, such as *When Johnny Comes Marching Home* (1935), *Kentucky Spring* (1949), and *Walt Whitman Suite (1944)*.

1979 Oct. 22 **Nadia** [Juliette] **Boulanger** (b. Sept. 16, 1887), a French teacher of music who helped formed the talents of noted conductors and composers, died. She was a conductor of skill herself, but made her mark as a teacher of such musicians as

Virgil Thomson, Aaron Copland, and Leonard Bernstein.

1979 Dec. 30   Richard Rodgers (b. June 28, 1902), one of the most talented composers of popular music in the U.S., died. His music has not lost its freshness and appeal–consider just *Oklahoma* (1943) and *South Pacific* (1959). Among his c.1,500 songs were such classics as "**Oh, What a Beautiful Morning**" and "**People Will Say We're in Love.**"

VII. SPORTS, GAMES, AND SOCIETY

1979 May 24   The six-square-mile **island of Iona**, one of the Inner Hebrides, off Scotland, was bought for $3.09 million by **Hugh Fraser**, a wealthy British merchant. The seller was the 12th **Duke of Argyll** (b. Aug. 28, 1937), whose family had owned Iona for 300 years. He said he needed the money to pay death duties owed by his family.

1979 June 26   Muhammad Ali resigned his world heavyweight championship. He had scored 57 victories, 37 of them by knockouts. He lost only three times.

1979 July 1–15   The eighth **Pan-American games** were held in San Juan, Puerto Rico, with athletes from 20 nations competing. The U.S. finished first in gold medals with 127.

1979 July 24   Gerry Spiess of White Bear Lake, Minnesota, completed a 54-day trans-Atlantic trip alone in a 10-foot boat. He started out from Virginia Beach, Virginia, and came ashore at Falmouth, England.

1979 Aug. 11–14   A gale sank 23 of the 303 craft sailing in the 605-mile **Fastnet Challenge Cup race** from Cowes, Isle of Wight, to Fastnet Rock, Ireland, and back. Eighteen lives were lost, and 85 boats finished the course.

1979 Aug. 20   Diana Nyad (b. Aug. 22, 1949), an American, became the **first person to swim the 89 miles between the Bahamas and the U.S.** when she waded ashore at Juno Beach, Florida. She had been in the water for 27 hours, 38 minutes. She had been escorted by relays of other swimmers to keep jellyfish away from her.

1979 Sept. 9   [Gordon] **Gordie Howe** (b. Mar. 21, 1928), the durable Canadian star in the **National Hockey League**, announced his retirement. Most of his career of 26 seasons was spent with the Detroit Red Wings (1946–1971). In 1973 he moved to the Houston Aeros of the new American Hockey League, taking two hockey-playing sons with him, but in 1979 he went back to the NHL with the Hartford Whalers for a last season. With the NHL he set records for most games played, 1,767; most goals, 801; most assists, 1,049; most points, 1,850.

II. DISASTERS

1980 Mar. 27   Mt. Saint Helens, a volcano in Washington state, dormant since 1857, **erupted** following a series of earthquakes. The eruption threw volcanic ash 14,500 feet in the air over parts of Washington and Oregon. An even more violent eruption (May 18) killed 34 people, with another 53 missing and believed dead.

1980 Mar. 27   A storm in the Eskofisk oilfield in the North Sea off Norway caused the collapse of a platform used to house workers, throwing the 228 men aboard into the sea or trapping them in their quarters as the platform sank. Of those on the rig, 123 died.

1980 Apr. 25   At Santa Cruz de Tenerife, Canary Islands, a chartered **Boeing 707 carrying 138 passengers and 8 crew members **struck a mountain** during its approach to a landing. All aboard were killed.

1980 May 20   A wooden home housing elderly women caught **fire in Kingston, Jamaica, leaving 144 dead and 11 missing.

1980 July–Aug.   In six states of India, **monsoon rains caused floods over an area of c.7,500 square miles, leaving c.600 dead. In August and September, monsoons in West Bengal state brought floods and landslides that killed nearly 1,500 people.

1980 July 7   A Soviet **airliner taking off from Alma-Ata in Kazakh, U.S.S.R. [present Kazakhstan], **crashed** and killed 163 passengers and crew.

1980 Aug. 2   A bomb exploded in the central train station of Bologna, Italy, killing 76 persons and injuring c.200. The explosion was blamed on neofascist terrorists.

1980 Aug. 4–11   Hurricane Allen struck the Caribbean area, Mexico, and the U.S. First to feel its effects were the islands of Barbados and St. Lucia. On Aug. 7 the Yucatán Peninsula of Mexico was ravaged and two days later, having changed course, the hurricane hit the coast of Texas. In the Gulf of Mexico c.4,500 workers were evacuated from oil drilling rigs. In all Hurricane Allen took 272 lives.

1980 Aug. 19   A Lockheed **L-1011 jet of Saudi Arabian Airlines, trying to return to the airport in Riyadh, Saudi Arabia, **crashed** after it caught fire and killed all 301 persons on board.

1980 Oct. 10   Two **earthquakes shook Asnam, Algeria, destroying most of the city. More than 4,000 persons were killed, c.60,000 injured, and c.300,000 made homeless. The quake measured 7.3 on the Richter scale.

1980 Nov. 21   A fire in the MGM Grand Hotel in Las Vegas, Nevada, caused 84 deaths, mostly by carbon monoxide poisoning. About 3,500 people trapped on the upper floors were rescued, although a few jumped to their deaths.

1980 Nov. 24   An **earthquake rocked the southern provinces of Naples, Salerno, Avelino, and Potenza, Italy. The dead were estimated at 3,000 and the homeless at 310,000, with tens of thousands injured. The quake measured 7.2 on the Richter scale.

III. POLITICS AND WAR

1980 Jan. 3 & 6   Elections in **India returned **Indira Gandhi** to office as prime minister, the office she had lost in 1977. Her Congress party won 350 of the 542 seats in the lower house of the legislature while the Janata party, which had ousted her, retained only 31 seats.

1980 Jan. 4   In protest against the **Russian invasion (Dec. 1979) **of Afghanistan**, President **Jimmy Carter** imposed an **embargo on American sales to the Soviet Union** that would **limit grain exports** to 8 million metric tons and declared that 17 million additional tons on order would not be sold. Carter also cut off the shipment of high technology equipment, restricted fishing rights in American waters, postponed the opening of new consulates, and delayed economic and cultural exchanges.

1980 Jan. 19   William O[rville] Douglas (b. Oct. 16, 1898), a retired justice of the U.S. Supreme Court, died. His service (Apr. 17, 1939–Nov. 12, 1975) on the court was the longest in the history of the court. Douglas was a determined defender of civil rights and free speech.

1980 Jan. 22   Andrei [Dmitrievich] Sakharov, a noted Russian physicist and vocal advocate of human rights, was sentenced to internal exile in Gorky for alleged subversive activities against the U.S.S.R. He had urged the UN to exert pressure on the Soviet

Union to remove its troops from Afghanistan. For his promotion of human rights Sakharov had been awarded the **Nobel Peace Prize** in 1975.

1980 Jan. 28 With the aid of Canadian officials, six **American employees of the U.S. embassy in Teheran**, were able to **escape** from Iran by air, using Canadian diplomatic passports. The four men and two women had fled the embassy on Nov. 9, 1979, when an Iranian mob had taken the other Americans there prisoners.

1980 Jan. 30 Juliana, queen (from 1948) of the Netherlands, announced she would abdicate on her 71st birthday, citing age as her reason. Her successor was to be her eldest daughter **Beatrix** (b. Jan. 31, 1938), who succeeded to the throne on May 1. Beatrix, one of four daughters of Juliana, was married (Mar. 10, 1966) to **Claus von Amsberg** (b. Sept. 6, 1926), a West German diplomat.

1980 Feb. 18 Pierre Elliott Trudeau became prime minister of **Canada** for the second time when his Liberal party won 44 percent of the vote and 147 seats in the 282-seat Parliament. He took office on Mar. 3, replacing [Charles Joseph] **Joe Clark** (b. June 5, 1939) of the Progressive Conservative party, who had held office since June 4, 1979.

1980 Feb. 27 In Bogotá, **Colombia**, 16 guerrillas of the leftist April 19th Movement **invaded the Dominican Republic's embassy** during a diplomatic reception and took 44 of those present hostage. They included 16 ambassadors, among them the U.S. ambassador, **Diego C. Asencio** (b. July 15, 1931). The situation remained stalemated for two months until April 27, when the guerrillas were allowed to fly to Havana, taking 12 hostages with them. In Havana these hostages were released, and the guerrillas were welcomed by the Cuban government.

1980 Mar. 21 Civil war broke out in Chad, Africa, between forces under the command of **Goukouni Oueddei** (b. 1944), the president of Chad (from Aug. 21, 1979), and forces led by **Hissène Habré** (b. 1942), the prime minister. More than 500 persons were reported killed in the first few days of fighting in N'Djaména, the capital. In early November **Libyan forces entered Chad** in support of Oueddei and by Dec. 8 were in control of the capital. Habré's forces, on the defensive, kept fighting while c.70,000 Chadians fled to Cameroon.

1980 Mar. 24 Oscar Arnulfo Romero (b. Aug. 15, 1917), the archbishop of **El Salvador**, **was assassinated** in San Salvador as he celebrated mass. The killing was believed to be the work of extreme rightists. On Mar. 30, when a large crowd gathered in front of the cathedral where funeral services for the archbishop were to be held, explosions and gunfire broke out. At least 20 people were killed and 200 or more injured. This terrorist act was believed to be the work of leftists. In the first half of the year c.4,000 civilians were killed in such violence. Later in the year a military coup seized power (Oct. 15) but was unable to stop the violence. **José Napoléon Duarte** (Nov. 23, 1926–Feb. 23, 1990), a member of the ruling junta, was elected (Dec. 13) president of El Salvador.

1980 Mar. 31 Ton Duc Thang (b. Aug. 19, 1888), the president of Vietnam, died. Thang had fled to France (1921) because of his involvement in anticolonial activity. He returned (1927) to Vietnam and later served 16 years in prison, until 1945, for sedition and complicity in murder. He held various official positions after a communist government came to power in North Vietnam in 1954.

1980 Apr. 12 A coup in Liberia, Africa, led by enlisted men of the army, overthrew the government of **William R[ichard] Tolbert, Jr.** (b. May 13, 1913), killing him in the process. Tolbert had been president since July 23, 1971. **Samuel K[anyon] Doe**, an army master sergeant who led the coup, became the head of a government run by a People's Redemption Council. Martial law was declared, the constitution was suspended, and 13 upper level government officials were executed (Apr. 22) by a firing squad.

1980 Apr. 18 Zimbabwe, formerly Rhodesia, Africa, **became an independent nation**. After 15 years of conflict in which a white minority tried to establish its rule, an election (Mar. 4) established the new regime. In the election, the African National Union, led by **Robert Mugabe**, won 57 of the 80 seats reserved for blacks in the new 100-seat parliament. Mugabe, who had been a leader of the Union and active fighter for independence, became the first prime minister.

1980 Apr. 24 A U.S. airborne **military expedition to rescue American embassy personnel held hostage in Teheran**, Iran, ended in disaster. Six C-130 transport planes and eight RH-53 helicopters were to carry 90 commandos to a rendezvous point in the Iranian desert c.300 miles southwest of Teheran. Two of the helicopters were unable to reach this point, and a third was disabled after it arrived. The mission was then aborted by order of **Jimmy Carter**, president of the U.S. In the withdrawal a plane and a helicopter collided, killing eight servicemen and wounding others.

1980 May 3   **Pieter Botha**, prime minister of **South Africa**, announced that coloreds [mixed race], Indians, and Chinese were to be included in a council to advise the president on important issues. While the council was to include whites, it was not to have any black members. When the 60-member council was appointed, 45 were white.

1980 May 4   **Tito** [Josip Broz] (b. May 7, 1892), the long-time president of Yugoslavia, died. He was the first head of a Communist party and state to defy the U.S.S.R. Tito fought in World War I in the Austro-Hungarian army. In World War II he was a leader of partisans in Yugoslavia fighting the German invaders. Tito, the effective head (from 1944) of the state, was the first elected president (1953).

1980 May 5   British commandos and **police stormed the Iranian embassy** in the Kensington section of London, where 5 gunmen had held 19 hostages for five and a half days. The gunmen were apparently Arabs seeking autonomy for an Arabic-speaking region of Iran. Negotiations went on until the gunmen said they would kill a hostage every 30 minutes until their demands were met. In fact they killed two just before the raid started. Three of the gunmen were killed in the raid, the other two were captured, and the rest of the hostages were freed.

1980 May 20   In a referendum held in the province of **Quebec**, Canada, voters rejected independence. The vote was 59.6 percent against the idea, and a majority of the French-speaking citizens voted "no."

1980 May 27   **Milton Obote**, a former prime minister (1962–1966) and president (1966–1971) of **Uganda**, returned from exile in Tanzania and led (Sept. 17) the Uganda People's Congress in a takeover of the government. In an election (Dec. 10–11) the opposition Democratic party appeared to have won, but the electoral committee declared (Dec. 13) that the UPC was the victor. Two days later Obote was inaugurated president for the second time.

1980 June 30   **Iceland** for the first time elected a woman president, **Vigdis Finnbogadóttir** (b. Apr. 15 1930). In the election she ran against three male candidates and received 33.6 percent of the vote, compared with 32.1 percent for her nearest rival. Finnbogadóttir had been a teacher and theater company director.

1980 July 27   **Mohammad Riza Pahlevi** (b. Oct. 26, 1919), the former shah (1941–1979) of Iran, died. The shah built up a powerful army with the strong support of the U.S. and tried to rush the modernization of Iran through central planning and large public works. He initiated land distribution for peasants and emancipation of women, but also countenanced corruption and torture of his opponents. The shah fled Iran in 1979 under pressure from Islamic fundamentalists and the local Communist party.

1980 July 28   **Military rule in Peru** ended with the inauguration of **Fernando Belaúnde Terry** as president for the second time. Belaúnde entered (1945) politics and founded (1956) the Popular Action party. Winning election to the presidency in 1963, he brought about reforms in several fields and encouraged economic development. He was ousted by military leaders in 1968.

1980 July 30   The **New Hebrides**, a group of islands in the southwestern Pacific Ocean, **became independent** as the **Republic of Vanuata**. The first prime minister of the nation of 72 islands and a population of c.112,000 was **Walter Lini** (b. 1942), an Anglican priest.

1980 Aug. 14   A period of **labor unrest and upheaval in Poland** began when c.17,000 workers at the Lenin Shipyard in port of Gdańsk [formerly Danzig] went on strike, demanding better pay and working conditions. An unemployed electrician, **Lech Walesa** (b. Sept. 29, 1943), became the leader of **Solidarity**, the strikers' name for their union. The Polish communist government underwent a sudden shakeup (Aug. 24), and **Edward Babiuch** (b. Dec. 28, 1927), the prime minister of Poland, was replaced by **Jozef Pinkowski**, the secretary of the central committee. The government granted (Aug. 31) many concessions, including the right to form independent unions, to the Gdańsk strikers, who then ended their walkout.

1980 Aug. 27   **Chun Doo Hwan** (b. Jan. 21, 1931), a general, was elected president of **South Korea** by the

Electoral College. He succeeded **Choi Kyu Hah** (b. July 16, 1919,), president of South Korea (from Dec., 1979), who resigned. The military had taken control (May 17) of the country, declaring martial law, closing the universities and colleges, and forbidding political activity. At Kwangju, south of Seoul, violence then broke out (May 27) in which 144 civilians and 26 police and soldiers were killed.

1980 Sept. 12 In a **bloodless coup** the military forces seized power **in Turkey**, ousting the government of **Suleyman Demirel**, the prime minister. The leader of the coup and of the new National Security Council was **Kenan Evren** (b. 1918), commander of the armed forces. The military leaders ordered martial law, dissolved parliament, and abolished the 13-year-old constitution. The council appointed (Sept. 20) as prime minister **Bulent Ulusu** (b. 1923), a retired admiral, who then assumed (Oct. 27) the position of chief of state.

1980 Sept. 17 **Anastasio Somoza Debayle** (b. Dec. 5, 1925), former president and dictator of **Nicaragua**, was assassinated in Asunción, Paraguay, by gunmen. For 13 years he had been president or effective ruler of the country until revolutionary forces, led by the **Sandinista National Liberation Front**, caused him to flee (1979) the country.

1980 Sept. 22 **Iraqi troops crossed** the southern frontier **into Iran**, and Iraqi planes attacked airfields and oil refineries. Naval and air battles followed with attacks on cities and oil installations of both nations. On Dec. 25 Iraq said it had invaded Iran's Kurdistan province on the northern frontier. The war became a stalemate with heavy casualties.

1980 Oct. 5 In a general election in the Federal Republic of Germany [West Germany] the Social Democrats and their coalition associates the Free Democrats increased their majority in the Bundestag from 10 to 45, with 218 and 53 seats, respectively. This victory over the Christian Democrats, a conservative party, assured **Helmut Schmidt** of four more years as chancellor.

1980 Oct. 30 In a general election in **Jamaica**, **Edward P**[hilip] **G**[eorge] **Seaga** (b. May 28, 1930) gained the prime minister's post when his Labour party won 51 of the 60 seats in Parliament.

1980 Nov. 20 The so-called **Gang of Four** went on trial in Peking charged with, among other charges, attempting to overthrow the government of the People's Republic of China after the death (1976) of Mao Tse-Tung. The four were: **Chiang Ching** (Mar. 1914–May 14, 1991), Mao's fourth wife, who tried to take control of the cultural life of the country; **Chang Chun-Chiao** (1937–1991), a member of the politburo since 1969; **Wang Hung-Wen** (b. 1937), a deputy chairman of the Communist party since 1973; and **Yao Wen-Yuan** (1935?–Aug. 3, 1992), also important in the Cultural Revolution and in ruling Shanghai. All four had been held without trial since Oct. 12, 1976. The trial ended on Dec. 29 and guilty verdicts were pronounced on Jan. 25, 1981. Chiang and Chang were sentenced to death, but the sentences were commuted to life imprisonment; Wang received a life sentence and Yao 20 years.

1980 Dec. 12 **Aleksey** [Nikolayevich] **Kosygin** (b. Feb. 20, 1904), the premier of the U.S.S.R. until his retirement on Oct. 23, died. He had been the official head of government since Oct. 15, 1964. Kosygin fought in the Red army during the civil war that followed World War I and joined the Communist party in 1927.

1980 Dec. 31 **Leopold Sedar Senghor**, president of **Senegal** since independence in 1960, resigned. On Jan. 1, 1981, he was succeeded by **Abdou Diouf** (b. Sept. 7, 1935), who had been premier since 1970.

IV. ECONOMY AND TRADE

1980 **Inflation** rates were up, the foreign exchange markets were unstable, and increases in the **Gross National Products** [GNP] were lower compared with 1979. Overall, the developed non-communist nations showed an increase in GNP of only 1.24 percent, compared with 3.4 percent in 1979. Japan led the way with a 4.2 percent gain; Canada and West Germany managed increases of only 1.2 and 1.8, respectively; while Great Britain's GNP declined by 1.8 and the U.S.'s by 0.2 percent. Inflation was especially troublesome in the U.S., where it reached 12.4 percent while the prime rate went to 20 percent, the highest since the 1830s.

V. RELIGION AND PHILOSOPHY

1980 Mar. 25 **Robert** [Alexander Kennedy] **Runcie** (b. Oct. 2, 1921) was enthroned as the 102nd Archbishop of Canterbury, primate of the Anglican communion. Runcie had been a teacher and bishop of St. Albans.

1980 Apr. 6 The **Church of Jesus Christ of Latter-Day Saints** [Mormons] observed the 150th anniversary of its founding with a General Conference in Salt Lake City, Utah, its headquarters.

1980 Apr. 15 **Jean-Paul Sartre** (b. June 21, 1905), a French philosopher and writer, died. He wrote particularly on existentialism, depicting man in a godless universe, totally responsible for himself. The major expression of Sartre's thought was in *L'Être et le néant* [*Being and Nothingness*] (1943). As a novelist Sartre wrote *Les Chemins de la liberté* [*The Roads to Freedom*] (a trilogy, 1945, 1951), set in the pre-war and early days of World War II. In 1964 he refused the **Nobel prize for literature**, saying he did not want to be "transformed into an institution."

1980 July 17 **Marjorie Swank Matthews** (b. July 11, 1916) became the **first woman bishop of a church in the U.S.** Ordained a Methodist minister in 1965, she became (September) the ranking Methodist in Wisconsin.

VI. SCIENCE, EDUCATION, AND TECHNOLOGY

1980 Jan. 1 A group of scientists headed by **Walter** [Clement] **Alvarez** (b. June 13, 1911) offered a theory to explain the **disappearance of dinosaurs** and other species c.65 million years ago. They found in a clay sediment between the Cretaceous period and the Tertiary period some heavy metal iridium in concentration more than 100 times compared with earlier or later times. They believed an asteroid had struck the earth c.65 million years ago and they estimated it had a diameter of c.6 miles and made a crater as much as 90 miles in diameter. The impact created a dust cloud that covered the earth for as much as five years, preventing the sun from getting through normally and therefore diminishing photosynthesis and plant production, on which dinosaurs and other animals ultimately depend. Alvarez's father, **Luis** [Walter] **Alvarez** (July 23, 1884–June 18, 1978), a physicist, participated in the work leading to the **extinction-by-asteroid theory**. He did important work concerning subatomic particles and played a major role in establishing (1947) the first linear accelerator at Berkeley, California. He received the **Nobel prize in physics** in 1968.

1980 Jan. 16 The successful production of human **interferon** in bacteria was announced by Biogen S.A., a pharmaceutical research organization. **Charles Weissmann** of the University of Geneva, Switzerland, was the leading scientist in the research involved. Interferon, a natural substance produced in the human body when attacked by a virus, was discovered in 1957, but there was no practical way to produce it in useful quantities.

1980 Apr. 30 The world's first commercial firm to market the **launching of satellites** was formed in Europe with France and West Germany as the main partners among 11 European countries. Called **Arianespace**, the company first used a launcher to put a TV relay satellite into orbit.

1980 May 17 An **antipollution pact**, sponsored by the UN Environmental Program, was signed by most of the nations bordering on the Mediterranean Sea, and the remaining countries were expected to sign soon. The agreement was endorsed by the **European Economic Community** [EEC].

1980 June 24 **David Burpee** (b. Apr. 5, 1893), an American seedsman, died. Taking over his family's business in 1915, Burpee built a worldwide business that sold seeds by distributing four million catalogs a year. He developed many new strains, such as the first hybrid zinnia and a red-and-gold marigold. Burpee sold the company in 1970 after having headed it for 55 years.

1980 Sept. 16 **Jean Piaget** (b. Aug. 9, 1896), a Swiss psychologist and pioneer in educational theory, died. Piaget made a systematic study of how children acquired understanding. Piaget was the author of *The Language and Thought of the Child* (1926), *The Origin of Intelligence in Children* (1954), and *The Early Growth of Logic in the Child* (1964), among others.

VII. ARTS AND LEISURE

1980 Feb. 22 **Oskar Kokoschka** (b. Mar. 1, 1886), an Austrian painter and dramatist, died. He first came to public attention with his so-called psychological portraits. After World War I he was prominent as an expressionist, specializing in landscapes. Kokoschka emigrated (1938) to Great Britain, where he produced large allegorical paintings. Among his works were *Double Portrait* (1912), *The Power of Music* (1919), *Tomás G. Masaryk* (1936), and *Prometheus Triptych* (1950). As a dramatist Kokoschka wrote *Orpheus and Euridyke* (1923), among other plays.

1980 Mar. 26   Roland [Gerard] **Barthes** (b. Nov. 12, 1915), a semiotician and literary critic, died. In 1976 he was the first person to hold the chair of semiology at the Collège de France. His most controversial work was *Le Degré zero de l'écriture* [*Writing Degree Zero*] (1953), which treated writers of the 17th to 20th centuries. Also important was *Eléments de Sémiologie* [*Elements of Semiology*] (1964).

1980 Apr. 29   Alfred [Joseph] **Hitchcock** (b. Aug. 13, 1899), a popular English movie director, died. He was a master of the suspense film. Hitchcock's early notable film was *The Thirty-Nine Steps* (1935), in which the hero was pursued over a good deal of Scotland. In Hollywood he made *Rebecca* (1940), a film version of **Daphne Du Maurier's** novel. Other noteworthy Hitchcock movies included *The Lady Vanishes* (1938); *Lifeboat* (1944); *To Catch a Thief* (1955); and *Psycho* (1960).

1980 May 22   "Pablo Picasso: A Retrospective" opened at the Museum of Modern Art in New York City. All the galleries of the museum were filled with c.1,000 paintings, drawings, and sculptures. Works in all Picasso's changing styles, from his early to his late years, were shown.

1980 June 7   Henry [Valentine] **Miller** (b. Jan. 20, 1891), an American author, died. With his bawdy humor and his frank treatment of sex, he was a controversial writer. Most of his writings showed an autobiographical tinge. Notable among them were *The Tropic of Cancer* (1934) and *The Tropic of Capricorn* (1939), both of which were banned for a time in the U.S.

1980 June 28   José Iturbi (b. Nov. 28, 1895), a Spanish pianist and conductor, died. As a pianist he began touring Europe and South America in 1923 and made his debut in the U.S. in 1929. From 1936 to 1944 Iturbi led the Rochester [N.Y.] Philharmonic Orchestra.

1980 July 1   C[harles] **P**[ercy] **Snow** (b. Oct. 15, 1905), an English scientist and novelist, died. By training a chemist, he was an adviser to the British government in World War II. Snow established his literary reputation with his series of eleven novels, *Strangers and Brothers* (1940–1970). In his *The Two Cultures and the Scientific Revolution* (1959), he deplored what he saw as a growing gulf between literary intellectuals and physical scientists.

1980 Sept. 18   Katherine Anne Porter (b. May 15, 1890), an American author, died. A collection of short stories, *Flowering Judas* (1930), earned her a reputation as a stylist and was followed by *Pale Horse, Pale Rider* (1939). Porter's novel *Ship of Fools* (1962) used the voyage of a German passenger liner in 1931 as an allegory, representing "the collusion between good and evil."

1980 Dec. 2   Romain Gary [orig.: Romain Kacew] (b. May 8, 1914), a Russian-born French author and diplomat, committed suicide. He was depressed by the suicide of his former wife, actress **Jean Seberg** (Nov. 13, 1938–Aug. 31, 1979). In World War II Gary flew with the British Royal air force and then with the Free French forces. His best-known work was *Les Racines de ciel* [*Roots of Heaven*] (1956).

1980 Dec. 8   John [Winston] **Lennon** (b. Oct. 9, 1940), one of the **Beatles**, was shot fatally at the entrance to his New York apartment house. Lennon composed many of the Beatles' songs and appeared in their movies. His killer was a former mental patient, **Mark David Chapman** (b. May 10, 1955), who pleaded guilty on June 22, 1981, and was sentenced to 20 years to life in prison.

1980 Dec. 27   A Leonardo da Vinci notebook, "Of the Nature, Weight, and Movement of Water," was sold for $5,126,000 in London. The purchaser was **Armand Hammer** (b. May 21, 1898), an American industrialist and collector.

1980 Dec. 31   [Herbert] Marshall McLuhan (b. July 21, 1911), a Canadian critic and theorist in the field of communications, died. He spent his career at the University of Toronto, studying the ways in which modern mass media and technology affect the cultural and psychological lives of people and nations. His two major works were *The Gutenberg Galaxy* (1962) and *The Medium Is the Message* (1967).

VIII. SPORTS, GAMES, AND SOCIETY

1980 Feb. 14–23   The 13th Winter Olympic Games were held at Lake Placid, New York, with 1,067 athletes of 37 countries competing. Athletes of the U.S.S.R. won 10 gold medals and 22 overall; East Germany 9 and 23; the U.S. 6 and 12. **Eric Heiden** (b. June 14, 1958) of the U.S. became the first person in the history of the Olympics to win five gold medals in individual events when he came in first in all five speed skating events from 500 to 10,000 meters.

1980 Apr. 23 **David Scott Cowper**, an English surveyor and yachtsman, set a new **world record for a solo voyage around the world** when he arrived at Plymouth, England. His total time was 249 days, including layovers, and he sailed c.30,000 miles.

1980 July 19 The 22nd Summer **Olympic Games** opened in Moscow with 6,000 athletes from 81 nations participating. On Jan. 20 U.S. President **Jimmy**

Carter had announced that the U.S. would not participate, in protest against the **invasion of Afghanistan** by Russian troops in Dec. 1979. Sixty-five other nations did not participate, more than half of them in support of the American stand. The U.S.S.R. won 80 gold medals, and East Germany 47.

1980 Sept. 16–25 The America's Cup was successfully defended by the U.S. boat *Freedom,* which defeated the Australian challenger *Australia* four races to one off Newport, Rhode Island.

1981

I. DISASTERS

1981 Jan. 6 In Brazil, on a tributary of the Amazon River, a **ferryboat sank**, drowning 230 persons, including 50 children.

1981 Jan. 27 In the Java Sea an Indonesian passenger ship *Tamponas II* **caught fire** and sank with the loss of 580 lives.

1981 June 6 A **train ran off a bridge** near Mansi, India. The death toll was 268, but more than 300 others were reported missing.

1981 June 11 A severe **earthquake in Kerman province**, Iran, left an estimated 1,000 to 3,000 dead.

1981 July 12–16 **Monsoon rains caused severe flooding** of the Yangtze River [Chang Jiang] in China from Szechwan [Sichuan] province toward the East China Sea. It was estimated that c.1,300 were dead or missing, c.28,000 injured, and more than 1,500,-000 made homeless.

1981 July 17 The **collapse of concrete aerial walkways** in the Hyatt Regency Hotel in Kansas City, Missouri, onto people attending a tea dance below, killed 113 people and injured nearly 200.

1981 Late Aug. **Poisonous cooking oil**, illegally sold from door to door in Spain since early May, killed c.600 people and did harm to an estimated 25,000 more.

1981 Nov. 1 A **tropical storm** accompanied by tidal waves and winds of up to 145 miles per hour, caused

the disappearance of more than 500 fishermen and their boats in the Arabian Sea, off the coast of India.

II. POLITICS AND WAR

1981 The **Iran-Iraq War** (1980–1988) went on fitfully this year with neither side showing any signs of winning the conflict. Oil facilities were reciprocally bombed. In January Iraq occupied a large area of Kurdistan in northwestern Iran. Iraq, failing in its attempts to capture Abadan, in western Iran, bombed the city into ruins.

1981 Jan. 17 **Ferdinand Marcos**, president of the **Philippines**, ended the state of martial law in effect for eight years and four months. He also freed 341 political prisoners and returned to the National Assembly the legislative powers he had been exercising. A plebiscite amended (Apr. 17) the constitution to change the form of government from a parliamentary to a presidential system. Marcos was elected (June 16) to a new six-year term.

1981 Jan. 20 **Ronald** [Wilson] **Reagan** (b. Feb. 6, 1911) was inaugurated as president of the U.S. In the Nov. 4, 1980, election, running on the Republican party ticket, he defeated **Jimmy Carter**, the Democratic incumbent. Reagan received 489 electoral votes to Carter's 49, and 42,797,153 popular votes to 34,434,100. **George** [Herbert Walker] **Bush** (b. June 12, 1924) was inaugurated as vice president.

1981 Jan. 20 **Iran released 52 American hostages** it had held (from 1979) in the embassy in Teheran. The release became official minutes after Ronald Reagan had been sworn in to succeed Jimmy Carter as president of the U.S. The hostages had been held for 444 days.

1981 Feb. 4   Gro Harlem Brundtland (b. Apr. 20, 1939) became **Norway's first woman prime minister.** She was the leader of the Labor party and had been active in politics since 1974. Her term proved a short one when her party lost a legislative election on Sept. 13.

1981 Feb. 9   Labor unrest brought about the fall of the Polish government, and **Wojciech** [Witold] **Jaruzelski** (b. July 6, 1923) become the new prime minister. He also took over (Oct. 18) as first secretary of the Communist party. Jaruzelski had been defense minister since 1968. Labor unrest increased with half a million members of the labor union **Solidarity** on strike (Mar. 20) in protest against the beating the previous day of some workers by the police.

1981 Feb. 23   In Madrid a dissident group of Civil Guards entered the lower house of the Spanish Cortes [parliament] and seized nearly 350 of the members as hostages. They were led by **Antonio Tejero Molinas,** a colonel of the guard. Quick action by **Juan Carlos,** king of **Spain,** who organized a governmental and military emergency council, defused the uprising without bloodshed in a few hours by standing firm. Tejero surrendered and was arrested.

1981 Mar. 1   Irish prisoners in Maze Prison, Belfast, **Northern Ireland,** began a hunger strike. The British government had refused their demand that they be considered political prisoners rather than common criminals. One of the prisoners, [Robert Gerard] **Bobby Sands** (b. Mar. 1954), died May 5 after going without food for 66 days. By Oct. 3 nine more hunger strikers had died. The remaining prisoners were persuaded to end their strike.

1981 Mar. 11   Augusto Pinochet Ugarte (b. Nov. 25, 1915) began a new eight-year term as president of Chile. He had become president in a coup (1973).

1981 Mar. 26   The new Social Democratic party was organized in **Great Britain** by dissident members of the Labour party. Its leaders were **Roy** [Harris] **Jenkins** (b. Nov. 11, 1920), a member of Parliament for 28 years; **David** [Anthony Llewellyn] **Owen** (b. July 2, 1938), who had been foreign minis-

ter (1977–1979); and **Shirley** [Vivien Teresa] **Williams** (b. July 27, 1930), a member of Parliament since 1964. They were joined by 24 other Labour party MPs and one Conservative.

1981 Mar. 29   Roberto Eduardo Viola, a general, replaced **Jorge Rafael Videla,** whose term ended, as president of **Argentina.** But the military junta that held the real power in the country removed (Dec. 11) Viola from office, and **Leopoldo Fortunato Galtieri** (b. July 15, 1926), a member of the junta, became president (Dec. 22).

1981 Mar. 30   Ronald Reagan, president of the U.S., was shot and seriously wounded by a would-be assassin as he left a Washington, D.C., hotel. Reagan underwent an operation on his chest and was able to return to the White House on Apr. 11. His assailant was **John W. Hinckley, Jr.** (b. May 29, 1955) of Evergreen, Colorado. Hinckley was found (June 21) not guilty by reason of insanity, a verdict that shocked and angered the public. He was ordered held indefinitely in a Washington hospital for the mentally ill.

1981 Apr. 11–12   In **Great Britain a race riot** broke out in the Brixton section of London, a mostly black area. The mob's fury seemed directed chiefly at the police, 30 of whom were seriously injured. Similar riots occurred in Liverpool (July 3–7), Manchester (July 8), and again in London (July 10–11). While much of the rioting appeared to have a racial basis, chronic unemployment among inner city young people may also have played a part.

1981 May 10   François [Maurice] **Mitterand** (b. Oct. 26, 1916) was elected president of France, defeating the incumbent **Giscard D'Estaing.** Mitterand was the first socialist head of the country since the Fifth Republic was formed in 1958. Mitterand planned to nationalize many French industries and businesses. In elections (June 14 and 20) for the National Assembly the socialists won a sizable majority for Mitterand.

1981 May 13   Pope John Paul II was shot and seriously wounded as he rode in an open car in St. Peter's Square, Vatican City. He underwent an operation and was pronounced out of danger on May 23. His assailant was **Mehmet Ali Agca** (b. 1958), a Turkish terrorist and murderer. He was convicted (July 22) in a trial and sentenced to life imprisonment.

1981 May 29   Madame Sun Yat-Sen [Soong Ch'ing-Ling] (b. Jan. 27, 1893), died. She was of great symbolic importance in China as the widow of the founder of the Chinese republic, whom she married in 1915. She opposed the government of **Chiang Kai-Shek** and in 1949 when the communists won control of China, she remained in China and became an official of the new regime.

1981 May 30   Ziaur Rahman (b. Jan. 19, 1936), president of **Bangladesh**, was assassinated in a military coup. He was succeeded by **Abdus Sattar** (b. Mar. 1, 1906), who had been vice president and who was elected to the presidency on Nov. 15.

1981 June 7   In an airplane bombing raid, **Israeli forces destroyed a nuclear reactor** under construction near Baghdad, Iraq. Israel claimed it feared the plant would produce materials to make atomic bombs to be used against it. The U.N. Security Council unanimously condemned (June 19) Israel's action.

1981 June 28   A bomb planted by anti-government forces exploded while the Iranian Majlis [parliament] was in session, killing 72 members of the government. The chief justice of **Iran** and four members of the cabinet were among those killed.

1981 June 28   Giovanni Spaldini (b. June 21, 1925) became premier of Italy, heading a coalition of five parties. As leader of the Republican party he was the first non-Christian Democratic party member to head the government since World War II. He was also the 41st premier since that time. Spaldini succeeded **Arnoldo Forlani**, the prime minister whose government had resigned (May 26) in the face of a scandal involving a secret and illegal Masonic lodge called P-2.

1981 June 29   Hu Yaobang (b. 1915) was named chairman of the Communist party of the People's Republic of China, replacing **Hua Kuo-Feng**. Hu had held many important positions in the regime and was a member of the politburo. On Sept. 7, 1980, **Zhao Ziyang** (b. Oct. 17, 1919) had been named prime minister, also replacing Hua. Hu and Zhao were in favor with **Deng Xiaoping**, the most powerful person in the government.

1981 July 7   Sandra Day O'Connor (b. Mar. 26, 1930) was appointed by **Ronald Reagan** as the **first woman member of the U.S. Supreme Court.** She came to the high court from the Arizona State Court of Appeals.

1981 July 17   Israeli warplanes bombed Beirut, Lebanon, killing c.300 persons. The Israeli's main target was the offices of **al-Fatah**, a guerrilla unit of the **Palestine Liberation Organization** [PLO]. Israel said the raid was in retaliation for terrorist attacks on Israeli territory.

1981 July 31   Omar Torrijos Herrera (b. Feb. 13, 1929), as commander of the Panamanian National Guard the real ruler of the country, was killed in an airplane crash near Penonomé in central Panama. He had been in power since 1968 when he overthrew the government. Torrijos was succeeded as head of the guard by **Florencio Florez**.

1981 Aug. 10   The **U.S. began producing neutron warheads.** President **Jimmy Carter** had approved (1978) the manufacture of parts, but none were to be assembled. The government said 380 would be produced. The neutron bomb was devised to kill people while doing little damage to physical property.

1981 Sept. 1   Albert Speer (b. Mar. 19, 1905), Adolph Hitler's chief architect (1942 to 1945) and in charge of all of Nazi Germany's armaments and munitions production, died. At the post-World War II trials of Nazi leaders, Speer was the only one to plead guilty to war crimes. He served 20 years in prison and eventually expressed remorse for his part in the Nazi regime.

1981 Sept. 21   Belize [former British Honduras], a small country of Central America, **became independent.** The first prime minister was **George Cadle Price** (b. Jan. 15, 1919), who had been first minister (from 1961) of the colony.

1981 Oct. 6   Muhammad Anwar el-Sadat (b. Dec. 25, 1918), president (from 1970) of **Egypt**, was assassinated by dissident Islamic soldiers as he reviewed a military parade in Cairo. Sadat's military and political career was capped by his successful efforts (1977–1979) to bring about a treaty of peace with Israel. In 1978 he and **Menachem Begin**, prime minister of Israel, shared the **Nobel Peace Prize.** Sadat was succeeded by **Muhammad Hosni Mubarak** (b. May 4, 1928), vice president (from 1975) of Egypt, and a former air force commander.

1981 Oct. 16   Moshe Dayan (b. May 20, 1915), an Israeli military leader and statesman, died. After serving with the British forces in World War II, he was a commander of Israeli troops in the war that secured independence (1948), and later, as chief of staff (1953–1958) and minister of defense (from 1964) Dayan was given credit for Israel's success in the **Sinai Peninsular campaign** (1956) and the **Six-Day War** (1967). But he was blamed for Israel's unpreparedness before the **Yom Kippur War** (1973) and resigned from the cabinet in May, 1974. He was also a notable archaeologist and wrote *Living with the Bible* (1978).

1981 Oct. 18   The Panhellenic Socialist Movement, led by **Andreas Papandreou** (b. Feb. 5, 1919), won 172 seats in the 300-seat Greek parliament. Papandreou became (Oct. 31) prime minister and promised to carry out what he called his "mandate for change." In politics since 1963, he had been jailed in 1967 by the military government then in power.

1981 Nov. 11   **Antigua and Barbuda**, islands in the eastern Caribbean Sea, including the uninhabited island of Redonda, became an independent nation. In all the nation's area was 442 square miles and the population c.76,000. The first prime minister was **Vere Cornwall Bird** (b. Dec. 7, 1910), who had been chief minister (from 1960) of the colony.

1981 Dec. 13   The **Polish government declared martial law.** The headquarters of **Solidarity** in Gdansk were raided, and many persons considered dangerous were arrested for their alleged agitation against the state. On Dec. 14 **Ronald Reagan** said no more **U.S. economic aid** would go **to Poland** until martial law was lifted. Accusing the U.S.S.R. of being responsible for the situation in Poland, Reagan ordered (Dec. 29) **sanctions against the U.S.S.R.,** such as suspension of the export of high technology products and closing of ports and airfields to Russian ships and planes.

1981 Dec. 14   **Israel annexed the Golan Heights**, a strategic region between northeastern Israel and southwestern Syria that had been Syrian territory until occupied by Israel in the **Six-Day War** (1967). The U.S. expressed disapproval of the move.

1981 Dec. 15   The General Assembly of the United Nations elected **Javier Peréz du Cúellar** (b. Jan. 19, 1920), Peru's ambassador to the U.N., as the new secretary general for a term of five years. He succeeded **Kurt Waldheim**, who became (1986) head of state of Austria.

1981 Dec. 31   **Jerry** [John] **Rawlings** (b. June 22, 1947), an army officer, led a coup that overthrew the government of **Ghana**, Africa, headed by **Hilla Limann** (b. Dec. 12, 1934), who had been president from 1979. The constitution of 1979 was suspended and a civilian government backed by Rawlings and the military took power.

III. ECONOMY AND TRADE

1981 Feb. 13   [Keith] **Rupert Murdoch** (b. Mar 11, 1931), an Australian publisher, bought *The Times* of London and *The Sunday Times.* Starting as a publisher in his native Australia, Murdoch spread his empire widely by acquiring in the 1960s and 1970s two other English papers, *The News of the World* and the *Sun.*

IV. RELIGION AND PHILOSOPHY

1981 May 28   Stefan Cardinal Wyszynski (b. Aug. 3, 1901), primate (from 1949) of Poland, died. He was made a cardinal on Jan. 12, 1953. His protests to the government about its policies caused his arrest in 1956, but he was soon released. The cardinal called for domestic peace but defended the interests of the workers and the intellectuals.

V. SCIENCE, EDUCATION, AND TECHNOLOGY

1981   The U.S. Centers for Disease Control identified **Acquired Immune Deficiency Syndrome** [**AIDS**] as a separate disease.

1981 Jan. 4   The **first cloning of mammals** was reported by Swiss scientists at the University of Geneva. Using cells from mouse embryos, they produced three mice that were genetically identical with the original embryos.

1981 Mar. 2   Two American astronomers, **Hyron Spinrad** (b. Feb. 17, 1934) and **John Richard Stauffer** (b. Oct. 27, 1952) announced the discovery of two galaxies 10,000,000,000 light years distant from the earth.

1981 Apr. 12   The **first flight ever of a reusable, manned space shuttle** began when the *Columbia* blasted off from Cape Canaveral, Florida. The craft, which cost $9,900,000,000 and weighed 2,200 tons, orbited the earth 36 times, then landed at an air force base in California after 54 hours, 22 minutes in space. The *Columbia* became (Nov. 12) the first manned spacecraft to be used more than once, in a mission cut short (Nov. 14) because of a malfunctioning fuel cell.

1981 June 17 The **Humber Bridge** over the Humber Estuary on the east coast of England was officially opened. The main span of 4,626 feet makes it today the **longest suspension bridge in the world.**

1981 June 18 The U.S. Department of Agriculture announced development of a safe **vaccine to prevent hoof and mouth disease** in cattle. The department had worked with a genetic engineering firm, Genentech, in developing the vaccine.

1981 Aug. 25 The U.S. *Voyager 2* came within 63,-000 miles of the clouds that cover the planet **Saturn.** For the first time pictures and data revealed thousands of rings but no moonlets around the planet. *Voyager* then headed for Uranus, which it was due to reach in 1986.

1981 Sept. 8 **Hideki Yukawa** (b. Jan. 23, 1907), a Japanese physicist, died. He predicted (1935) the existence (confirmed 1947) of the meson, a small energized particle that bonds protons and neutrons in atomic nuclei. Yukawa was awarded the **Nobel prize for physics** in 1949, the first Japanese to receive a Nobel prize.

1981 Sept. 22 The French government put into operation a high speed train known as the *Train à grande vitesse* **TGV**, running from Paris to Lyon. With new tracks, locomotives, and cars, the train set a record for railroads by traveling at a maximum speed of 162 mph.

1981 Oct. 30 The U.S.S.R. launched *Venera 13* toward Venus, where it landed on Mar. 1, 1982, and sent back the first X-ray fluorescence analysis of the planet's surface. After 127 minutes of transmission *Venera 13* went dead. Before then it reported the temperature on the surface of Venus to be 854.6°F and the atmospheric pressure to be 89 times that of the earth.

VI. ARTS AND LEISURE

1981 Jan. 23 **Samuel Barber** (b. Mar. 9, 1910), an American composer, died. Among his noteworthy works were *Dover Beach* (1931), for baritone and string quartet; *The School for Scandal* (1933), an overture; and *Antony and Cleopatra* (1966), an opera composed for the opening of the new home of the Metropolitan Opera in Lincoln Center, New York City.

1981 Mar. 15 **René Clair** [orig.: René Chomette] (b. Nov. 11, 1898), a French filmmaker, died. In *Sous les toits de Paris* (1930) he was among the first to demonstrate how sound could be combined effectively with the moving picture. Among his other notable films were; *À nous la liberté* (1931), *The Ghost Goes West* (1935), and *Les Grandes Manoeuvres* (1955). In 1960 Clair became the first filmmaker elected to membership in the Académie Française.

1981 Mar. 30 [William Roy] **DeWitt Wallace** (b. Nov. 12, 1889), an American editor and publisher, died. He and his wife **Lila Bell Acheson Wallace** (Dec. 25, 1889–May 8, 1984) founded (1922) *Reader's Digest,* a magazine offering condensations of articles published first in other publications. By the time Wallace died *Reader's Digest* had a circulation of 30.5 million copies in 16 languages.

1981 May 5 **William Saroyan** (b. Aug. 31, 1908), an American writer, died. A prolific author of short stories, novels, and plays, his works included *The Daring Young Man on the Flying Trapeze* (1934), *The Human Comedy* (1943), and *The Time of Your Life* (1939).

1981 May 5 The **Royal Ballet of Great Britain** observed its 50th anniversary with a performance of *The Sleeping Beauty* at Covent Garden, London.

1981 May 25 **Rosa Ponselle** [Rosa Melba Ponzillo] (b. Jan. 22, 1897), a leading dramatic soprano of the Metropolitan Opera of New York City for 19 years (1918–1937), died. She had had little formal training when she made (1918) her debut in *La forza del destino.* Her warmth and rich voice were especially appealing in the operas of Bellini, Mozart, and Verdi.

1981 July 1 **Marcel** [Lajos] **Breuer** (b. May 21, 1902), a Hungarian-born American architect, died. He was associated as student and teacher with the **Bauhaus** in Germany in the 1930s. Breuer emigrated (1937) to the U.S., where he became a leading practitioner of the international style. Among buildings he designed were the **UNESCO headquarters** in Paris (1953–1958), St. John's Abbey, Collegeville, Minnesota (1953–1956), and the **Whitney Museum of American Art**, New York City (1963–1966). Breuer also designed furniture.

1981 Sept. 10   Pablo Picasso's *Guernica* (1937) arrived in Spain after having been in the Museum of Modern Art, New York City, since 1939. Picasso would not allow it to be seen in his native land until the fascist dictatorship of **Francisco Franco** came to an end.

1981 Sept. 12   Eugenio Montale (b. Oct. 12, 1896), an Italian poet, died. In his writing he attempted to clarify philosophically the moral problems of a troubling age. His first collection was *Ossi di seppia* [*Cuttlefish Bones*] (1916). His continuing work brought him further recognition as a poet of world-wide stature. Among his works were *Le occasioni* [*Occasions*] (1939) and *La farfalla di Dinard* [*The Butterfly of Dinard*] (1956). *New Poems* (1976) was a selection of Montale's poetry in English. He was awarded the **Nobel prize for literature** in 1975.

VII. SPORTS, GAMES, AND SOCIETY

1981 Apr. 12   Joe Louis [Joseph Louis Barrow] (b. May 13, 1914), the great heavyweight champion, died. Louis won the title on June 22, 1937, and retained it for 12 years. He defended the title 25 times before retiring. Later he returned to the ring for a few bouts, the last bout of significance taking place in 1951.

1981 May 22   Peter B. Sutcliffe (b. 1945), a truck driver of Bradford, England, known as the **Yorkshire Ripper**, was convicted of murder and sentenced to life imprisonment. He was arrested (Jan. 2) as a serial murderer, suspected of killing and mutilating 13 women and of attacking 4 others. He confessed on Apr. 29.

1981 June 12–July 31   A 49-day strike of all 650 players in **U.S. baseball's two professional major leagues** shortened the season. The strike was caused by a dispute with the owners over terms of compensation of free agents. The players won most of what they sought.

1981 July 29   Charles, Prince of Wales (b. Nov. 14, 1948), heir to the British throne, married **Diana** [Frances] **Spencer** (b. July 1, 1961) in St. Paul's Cathedral, London. The engagement of the couple was announced on Feb. 25.

1981 Aug. 28   For the third time in one year, the **record for the one-mile run** was broken. **Sebastian Coe** (b. Sept. 29, 1956) of England ran the distance in 3:47.33. On Aug. 19 he had set a record at 3:48.53, but a week later **Steve Ovett** (b. Oct. 9, 1955), also of England, registered a time of 3:48.40.

1981 Oct. 24   Edith Head (b. Oct. 28, 1907), an American fashion designer who costumed c.1,000 movies, died. She began her career in the 1930s and often dressed such stars as **Marlene Dietrich, Ingrid Bergman**, and **Elizabeth Taylor**. Head's hallmark was combined simplicity and elegance.

1981 Nov. 9–12   A distance record for balloon flights was set by the helium-filled *Double Eagle V* when it crossed the Pacific from Nagashima, Japan to Covello, California, a distance of 5,208.68 miles. The crew members were **Ben**[jamin] [James] **Abruzzo**, [Hiraoki] **Rocky Aoki, Ron Clark**, and **Larry M. Newman**.

1981 Nov. 20   A match for the **world championship of chess**, which began on Oct. 1 in Merano, Italy, ended with **Anatoly Karpov** (b. May 23, 1951) of the U.S.S.R., retaining his championship, beating **Victor Korchnoi** (b. 1931), a defector from the Soviet Union, six games to two.

1982

I. DISASTERS

1982 Feb. 15   All 84 workmen aboard the *Ocean Ranger,* the largest submersible oil rig in the world, were drowned when it **sank** in heavy seas off the coast of Newfoundland, Canada.

1982 July 9   A Pan American **Boeing 727 airliner crashed** at Kenner, Louisiana, shortly after take-off, killing all 146 persons on board and 8 on the ground.

1982 July 31 In a **ten-vehicle pile-up** near Beaune, France, 44 children and 9 adults died.

1982 Early Sept. Monsoon flooding at Orissan, India, killed c.1,000 people, left c.8,000 homeless, and swept away c.2,000 head of cattle.

1982 Oct. 6 Heavy rain in Liberia caused an **avalanche of iron ore waste** to crush a mining camp on the Mano River. The avalanche left c.45 dead, c.150 missing, and c.29 injured.

1982 Oct. 20 As many as **340 soccer fans were killed** while watching a match in Moscow between a Russian and a Dutch team. The police were trying to send too many fans down one staircase. Many who had begun to leave tried to get back into the stadium when they heard that the Moscow team had scored a goal. A deadly crush ensued.

1982 Nov. 2? An **explosion in a tunnel in northern Afghanistan** was believed to have killed hundreds of Soviet soldiers and Afghan civilians. A fuel truck and the lead truck of a Russian military convoy were said to have collided.

1982 Dec. 13 An **earthquake in Yemen** killed c.2,800 people, and left c.700,000 homeless.

1982 Dec. 19 Near Caracas, Venezuela, an 80,000-gallon **tank of fuel oil in a power plant caught fire** and exploded. At least 129 persons were killed and 500 injured.

II. POLITICS AND WAR

1982 Feb. 18 In a general election in Ireland, neither the Fine Gael nor the Fianna Fáil party won a majority in the Dáil [parliament]. Eventually **Charles [James] Haughey** (b. Sept. 26, 1925), leader of the Fianna Fáil, formed (Mar. 9) a coalition with some small parties and became prime minister, succeeding **Garret Fitzgerald** of the Fine Gael. A dispute within the Fianna Fáil and economic problems combined to bring down (Nov. 4) Haughey's government. In another election (Nov. 24), Fitzgerald was able to combine with the Labour party and become prime minister again (Dec. 14).

1982 Mar. 7 In an election in **Guatemala**, the voters apparently chose **Anibal Guevera** as president, but **Efrain Ríos Montt** (b. June 16, 1926), a general, declared the election void and led a coup (Mar. 23)

that overthrew the government. Montt dismissed (June 9) the other two members of the junta and declared himself head of the government.

1982 Mar. 22–Nov. 1 In the **Iran-Iraq War**, an Iranian offensive that began on Mar. 22 drove the Iraqis out of the province of Khuzestan, in southwestern Iran. Iraq then said it would withdraw from all Iranian territory and suggested that a peaceful solution be sought. In reply, Iran made unacceptable demands and launched (July 14) another offensive, directed at the Iraqi city of Basra, but the attack was repelled. Another Iranian attack (Nov. 1) also bogged down.

1982 Mar. 24 After the government of **Abdu Sattar**, president of **Bangladesh**, was overthrown, **Hossain Mohammed Ershad** (b. Feb. 1, 1930), the commander of the army, emerged as the strong man by virtue of his position as administrator of martial law.

1982 Apr. 2 Argentina seized the Falkland Islands [Islas Malvinas]. These islands, off the coast of South America, were administered by **Great Britain** and populated by c.1,800 persons of English stock. On Apr. 3 the British government announced it would send a task force to reclaim the islands. The Argentine cruiser **General Belgrano was sunk** (May 2) by a British submarine with the loss of 321 lives. In turn the Argentines struck (May 4) the British destroyer **Sheffield** with a plane-launched missile, killing 20 sailors and forcing abandonment of the ship. British forces landed (May 21) on the islands and swiftly defeated the Argentine forces, which surrendered on June 14. British losses were put at 225 dead; Argentina's at 712. On June 17 **Leopoldo Galtieri**, president of Argentina, resigned. He was succeeded (July 1) by another general, **Reynaldo Bignone** (b. Jan. 21, 1928).

1982 Apr. 17 A constitution was formally proclaimed in Ottawa, **Canada**. It included a charter of 34 rights and freedoms that were to be observed.

1982 Apr. 30 The U.N.-sponsored **Conference on the Law of the Sea** voted to adopt the draft of a treaty. One hundred thirty nations voted yes, four no; and 17 abstained. The four negative votes were cast by Israel, Turkey, the U.S., and Venezuela. Western European and Soviet bloc countries made up most of the abstentions. The treaty set boundaries for exclusive offshore rights of nations, and regulated the free passage of ships through various bodies of water. Most controversial were provisions for a global authority to mine minerals found on the sea floor. On Dec. 10, 119 nations officially signed the treaty, ensuring that it would go into effect.

1982 May 16   Salvador Jorge Blanco (b. July 5, 1926), a moderate leftist, was elected president of the Dominican Republic. He took office on Aug. 16. Meanwhile, **Silvestre Antonio Guzmán Fernandez** (b. Feb. 12, 1911), who had been president from Aug. 16, 1978, killed himself on July 4, 1982, after having found corruption among some of his aides.

1982 June 6   Israeli armed forces invaded Lebanon to destroy the strongholds of the **Palestine Liberation Organization** [PLO]. A ceasefire went into effect (June 11), by which time Israel controlled most of Lebanon's west coast south of Beirut. The PLO agreed to terms calling for its withdrawal from Lebanon, the last of its fighters leaving by Sept. 1.

1982 June 13   Khalid [Khalid ibn Abd al-Aziz Saud] (b. 1913), king and prime minister of Saudi Arabia (from 1975), died. Khalid was succeeded immediately by his half-brother **Fahd** [Fahd ibn Abd al-Aziz al-Saud] (b. c.1922), who was crown prince (from 1975). Fahd said he would start the nation on the path to democracy.

1982 June 30   Spain became a member of the **North Atlantic Treaty Organization** [NATO], making 16 nations in all in the alliance.

1982 June 30   The proposed Equal Rights Amendment [ERA] to the U.S. Constitution failed of ratification by the necessary three-fourths of the states by the deadline set by Congress. Thirty-five states had approved the Amendment fairly promptly but the other three necessary approvals were never forthcoming.

1982 July 4   Miguel de la Madrid Hurtado (b. Dec. 12, 1934) was elected president of Mexico with 75 percent of the vote. He was the candidate of the Institutional Revolutionary party [PRI]. Conservatives received 14 percent of the vote.

1982 Aug. 2   About 800 U.S. marines landed in Beirut, Lebanon, to cooperate with French and Italian contingents in the evacuation of Palestinian and Syrian guerrilla fighters. On Sept. 10 the marines were withdrawn, but Lebanon asked (Sept. 20) that they return to help maintain internal order. The marines

landed again on Sept. 29 and a day later suffered their first casualties when one was killed and three wounded while defusing a bomb.

1982 Aug. 7   Belisario Betancur Curatas (b. 1923) was inaugurated president of **Colombia** (to 1986), having been elected (May 30) with 47 percent of the total vote. He attempted to secure a truce with the **M-19 Movement**, a leftist guerrilla group that had been carrying on warfare against the government for a number of years.

1982 Aug. 21   Sobhuza II (b. July 22, 1899), king of Swaziland, Africa, died. His father died the year he was born and he was elected to succeed him by a council of tribal elders. Sobhuza was not formally installed as king of the Swaziland until 1921.

1982 Aug. 29   Nahum Goldmann (b. July 10, 1895), a Lithuanian-born Zionist, died. He was editor and publisher of the *Encyclopedia Judaica* (1st vol, 1922) in Germany, but was forced to flee (1934) because of Nazi persecution. He was a leader in founding the **World Jewish Congress** (1936) and served as its president (1951–1978). Goldmann was also president of the **World Zionist Organization** (1956–1968).

1982 Sept. 14   Bashir Gemayel (b. Nov. 10, 1947), who had been elected president of **Lebanon** on Aug. 23, was assassinated in a bomb explosion. On Sept. 21 the Lebanese parliament elected as his successor his older brother **Amin Gemayel** (b. 1942). Both brothers were Maronite Christians and leaders of the Phalange party.

1982 Sept. 16–18   Christian Phalangist militiamen entered two Palestinian refugee camps, Sabra and Shatila, in West Beirut, Lebanon, and **massacred 1,300** or more men, women, and children. The raid was apparently in retaliation for the assassination (Sept. 14) of **Bashir Gemayel**, the newly elected president of Lebanon. The Israeli army, which had troops in the area, was blamed widely for not having prevented the killings. On Feb. 8, 1983, an official Israeli board of inquiry found **Ariel Sharon** (b. 1928), the defense minister, and three generals guilty of neglect of duty. Sharon resigned (Feb. 11) but remained in the cabinet as a minister without portfolio.

1982 Oct. 1   Helmut [Michael] **Kohl** (b. Apr. 3, 1930), leader of the Christian Democratic Union, replaced **Helmut Schmidt** as chancellor of the Federal Republic of Germany [West Germany] when the Social Democratic party government received a vote of no confidence in the Bundestag. Kohl was the leader of the Christian Democrats when the party lost the 1976 election to the Social Democrats.

1982 Oct. 8 The **Polish parliament voted to outlaw Solidarity**. New unions of limited freedom were to be established. In protest workers at the Gdansk shipyard went on strike (Oct. 10), resulting in the arrest of 148 of their leaders. **Ronald Reagan**, president of the U.S., in protest suspended (Oct. 27) the most-favored-nation status of Poland with the U.S.

1982 Oct. 18 **Pierre Mendès-France** (b. Jan. 11, 1907), a former premier of France, died. A socialist, he began his career in 1932 as the youngest member of the National Assembly. With the Free French forces in World War II, Mendès-France was premier from June 1954 to Feb. 1955, and in that short time brought an honorable end to the colonial war in Indochina.

1982 Oct. 28 In a general election, the Socialist party won a majority of seats in the Spanish Cortes [parliament]. **Felipe González Márquez** (b. Mar. 5, 1942), for some time an active socialist, became prime minister.

1982 Nov. 10 **Leonid** [Ilyich] **Brezhnev** (b. Dec. 19, 1906), the general secretary of the Communist party of the U.S.S.R., died. Brezhnev had served in the army in World War II and had long held high posts in the communist regime. He achieved (Oct. 1964) the top party post when **Nikita S. Khrushchev** was removed from power. On June 16, 1977, he became chief of state, the first person to hold both positions. Brezhnev was succeeded (Nov. 12) by **Yury** [Vladimirovich] **Andropov** (June 15, 1914–Feb. 9, 1984), a member of the politburo who had headed the KGB since May 1967.

1982 Nov. 27 **Yasuhiro Nakasone** (b. May 27, 1918) was elected prime minister of Japan by the members of the Diet [parliament] of his Liberal Democratic party. Nakasone succeeded **Zenko Suzuki** (b. Jan. 11, 1911), who had retired on Oct. 12.

1982 Dec. 31 **Martial law in Poland was suspended**. The government announced that most political prisoners were to be freed, including **Lech Walesa**, a founder of Solidarity and generally acknowledged to be its leader.

III. ECONOMY AND TRADE

1982 Jan. 8 The **American Telephone and Telegraph Company** agreed to divest itself of its 22 operating systems on Jan. 1, 1984, open the way for other companies to compete, especially in the area of long distance phone service.

1982 Aug. 6 **Liquidation of the Banco Ambrosiano of Milan**, the largest private bank in Italy, was ordered by the government. The bank was insolvent. **Robert Calvi** (b. 1920?), president of the bank, had been found dead (June 18), hanging from Blackfriars Bridge in London. The bank had ties to the **"Vatican Bank"** of the Roman Catholic Church, officially known as the **Institute for Religious Works**. The Vatican Bank eventually agreed to pay $250 million toward claims against the failed bank.

IV. RELIGION AND PHILOSOPHY

1982 June 29 Two branches of **Presbyterianism** in the U.S. agreed to merge. They were the United Presbyterian Church and the Presbyterian Church in the United States, with combined membership of 3 million.

1982 July 16 **Sun Myung Moon** (b. Jan. 6, 1920), the founder of the **Unification Church**, was found guilty in New York of income tax fraud and conspiracy to obstruct justice. The Korean clergyman was sentenced to 18 months in jail and fined $25,000.

V. SCIENCE, EDUCATION, AND TECHNOLOGY

1982 Feb. 20 **René Jules Dubos** (b. Feb. 20, 1901), a French-born microbiologist who spent most of his professional career at Rockefeller University in New York City, died. His research led (1939) to the first production of a commercial antibiotic. He was the author of 20 books, many of which went far beyond his specialty. Among them were *Unseen World* (1962), *So Human an Animal* (1968), and *Celebration of Life* (1981).

1982 Oct. 9 **Anna Freud** (b. Dec. 3, 1895), the youngest child of Sigmund Freud and herself a psychoanalyst of note, died. Austrian-born, she went (1938) with her father to England to escape the Nazis. After World War II she established a center for studying child development.

1982 Oct. 11 The remains of an English warship the *Mary Rose,* which had been buried in mud near the entrance to the harbor of Portsmouth, England, for 437 years, was brought to the surface. Less than half of it could be recovered, but it provided a chance to study aspects of the period. The ship was built (1509–1510) when **Henry VIII** was king of England.

1982 Dec. 2 The first successful transplant of an artificial heart into a human being took place at the University of Utah Medical Center, Salt Lake City, Utah. The recipient was **Barney Clark**, a retired dentist who was near death. The device of plastic and aluminum was invented by **Robert K. Jarvik** (b. May 11, 1946). Barney B. Clark (b. Dec. 21, 1921) died on Mar. 23, 1983, after having lived for 112 days with the artificial heart.

VI. ARTS AND LEISURE

1982 Feb. 17 **Lee Strasberg** [Israel Strassberg] (b. Nov. 17, 1901), a drama teacher and director, died. Beginning his career as an actor, Strasberg was successful, but he became much better known for his teaching of the **method technique** of acting, whereby his students were taught to internalize their feelings about their roles. His work was based on the system devised by the Russian actor and teacher **Konstantin Stanislavsky**.

1982 Mar. 1 The J. Paul Getty Museum of Art in Malibu, California, received about $1,100,000,000 from the estate of the late billionaire oilman J[ean] **Paul Getty** (Dec. 15, 1892–June 6, 1976).

1982 Apr. 2 The largest exhibit ever of paintings of **El Greco** opened at the Prado in Madrid, Spain. The exhibit then went to Washington, D.C.; Toledo, Ohio; and Dallas, Texas. A total of 66 paintings were shown.

1982 Apr. 20 **Archibald MacLeish** (b. May 7, 1892), an American poet and dramatist, died. His works included *Conquistador* (1932), *The Fall of the City* (1937), and *J.B.* (1958). *New and Collected Poems* appeared in 1974. MacLeish served (1939–1944) as Librarian of Congress.

1982 May 10 **Peter** [Ulrich] **Weiss** (b. Nov. 8, 1916), a German-born Swedish dramatist, novelist, film director, and painter, died. He was best known for his drama *Die Verfolgung und Ermordung Jean-Paul Marats, dargestellt durch die Schauspielgruppe des Hospizes zu Charenton unter Anleitung des Herrn de Sade* [*The Persecution and Assassination of Jean-Paul Marat as Performed by the Inmates of the Asylum of Charenton under the Direction of the Marquis de Sade*] (1964), known better as *Marat/ Sade.*

1982 June 10 **Rainer Werner Fassbinder** (b. May 31, 1946), an avant garde filmmaker of West Germany, died. Fassbinder, only 37 when he died, made 41 films in 14 years. His films include *Warum läuft Herr R. Amok* [*Why Does Herr R. Run Amok*] (1969) and *Angst essen Seele auf* [*Fear Eats the Soul*] (1974).

1982 June 19 **John Cheever** (b. May 5, 1927), an American writer, died. Most of the stories concerned well-to-do suburbanites whose way of life he found unappealing. They were collected in a number of volumes, beginning with *The Way Some People Live* (1943) and ending with *The Stories of John Cheever* (1978). Two of his novels, *The Wapshot Chronicle* (1957) and *The Wapshot Scandal* (1964), were accounts of a wealthy, eccentric Massachusetts family.

1982 July 10 **Maria Jeritza** [Mitzi Jedlicka] (b. Oct. 6, 1887), an Austrian-born operatic soprano, died. She joined the Vienna Opera (1912) and sang (1921–1932) at the Metropolitan Opera, New York City, singing 20 roles.

Aug. 29 **Ingrid Bergman** (b. Aug. 29, 1915), a world-famous actress, died. Swedish-born, she went (1938) to Hollywood after achieving success in her native land. Among her most popular movies were *Casablanca* (1942) and *Gaslight* (1944). Her last film was *Autumn Sonata* (1978).

1982 Sept. 14 **Grace, princess of Monaco** [nee Grace Patricia Kelly] (b. Nov. 12, 1929), a former American movie actress and wife of the ruler of Monaco, was killed in an auto accident. She made 11 movies in all, one of her most popular being *To Catch a Thief* (1955).

1982 Oct. 4 **Glenn Gould** (b. Sept. 25, 1932), a Canadian pianist, died. He first performed with the Toronto Symphony Orchestra when he was 14. It was his recording of Bach's *Goldberg Variations* (1956) that made him an international star. After 1964 he gave up concert appearances but continued to record. Gould was considered a first-rate interpreter of Bach and Schoenberg [Schönberg].

1982 Oct. 21   The **Nobel prize for literature** was awarded to **Gabriel Garcia Márquez** (b. Mar. 6, 1928), a Colombian author. His first important novel *El coronel no tien quien le escriba* [*Nobody Writes to the Colonel*] (1958) brought him critical attention and translations found him a growing readership. Typical of his works of magic realism are *Cien años de soledad* [*One Hundred Years of Solitude*] (1967), *El otoño del patricara* [*The Autumn of the Patriarch*] (1975), and *Cronica de una muerte anunciade* [*Chronicle of a Death Foretold*] (1982).

1982 Nov. 1   **King** [Wallis] **Vidor** (b. Feb. 8, 1894), an American movie director, died. His first significant film was *The Big Parade* (1925), a treatment of World War I. His first sound film was *Hallelujah* (1929), which was also the first movie with an all-black cast. Two of Vidor's later films were *The Fountainhead* (1949) and *War and Peace* (1956).

1982 Nov. 5   **Jacques Tati** [orig.: Jacques Tatischeff] (b. Oct. 9, 1908), a French actor and film director, died. His first full-length film was *Jour de Fête* (1947), in which a village postman's ineptitude provided an opportunity for zany visual jokes. *Mon Oncle* (1958) was a light comedy about a boy and his uncle.

1982 Dec. 12   **Artur Rubinstein** (b. Jan. 28, 1887), a celebrated Polish-born American pianist, died. He made his debut at the age of six and his U.S. debut in 1906 with the Philadelphia Orchestra. Over the years he became noted especially for his interpretations of Beethoven, Brahms, and Chopin, with magnificent style but also with personal warmth.

1982 Dec. 24   **Louis Aragon** (b. Oct. 3, 1897), a French writer of poetry, novels, and essays, died. He was a **founder of surrealism** and *Le Paysan de Paris* [*Nightwalker*] (1926) was a novel of that genre. He was active in the Resistance in World War II, and his experiences figure in his poetry of the 1940s, including *Le Crève-coeur* (1941). Among Aragon's novels were *La Semaine Sainte* [*Holy Week*] (1958) and *La Mise à mort* (1965).

VII. SPORTS, GAMES, AND SOCIETY

1982 June 29   **Pierre Alexandre Balmain** (b. May 18, 1914), a highly successful fashion designer of the post-World War II era, died. The elegance of his designs attracted many famous and wealthy women.

1982 July 1   In Madison Square Garden, New York City, **2,075 couples were united in marriage** by **Sun Myung Moon**, the Korean founder of the **Unification Church**. The matching of the couples was done by Moon and his wife, and many of those wed hardly knew their partners.

1982 July 11   The **World Cup** of soccer was won by Italy, defeating West Germany, 3 to 1, in the final game in Madrid, Spain.

1982 Sept. 29–Oct. 1   **Cyanide placed in capsules of Extra Strength Tylenol**, the largest selling non-prescription pain reliever in the U.S., caused seven deaths in the Chicago area. Investigation showed that the cyanide must have been inserted in the drug after the bottles were placed on store shelves. Johnson and Johnson, the manufacturers of Tylenol, recalled c.264,000 bottles. On Oct. 22 the Food and Drug Administration cleared the company of any blame.

1983

I. DISASTERS

1983 Feb. 16–20   In Australia **brush fires** fanned by high winds burned more than 6,700 square miles of forest, scrub, and farm land. At least 72 persons lost their lives.

1983 Mar. 7   A **gas explosion** and rock fall in a mine near Eregli, Turkey, killed 98 miners.

1983 Mar. 31   An **earthquake** at Popayan, Colombia, killed 264 persons, destroyed c.3,000 buildings, and left c.150,000 people homeless.

1983 May 25   A passenger **steamer,** *10th of Ramadam,* **caught fire** from a butane gas explosion in Lake Nasser, near Aswan, Egypt, and sank. The dead numbered 272 persons, and c.75 more were missing and presumed dead.

1983 June 5 Reports indicated that c.400 persons died when a cruise **ship on the Volga River ran into a bridge** at Ulyanovsk, c.500 miles from Moscow. The upper deck was severed from the rest of the ship, and a freight train on the bridge fell onto the ship.

1983 Aug. 10 The U.S. government announced that in June a Russian nuclear **submarine had sunk** off the Kamchatka Peninsula, in Siberia. The Soviets said nothing about the disaster.

1983 Oct. 30 An **earthquake in eastern Turkey** destroyed 44 villages. About 1,300 died, c.500 were hurt, and thousands were left homeless. The quake measured 7.1 on the Richter scale.

1983 Nov. 27 Near Madrid, Spain, an Avianca **Boeing 747 crashed** and exploded near the airport. Of the 194 persons on board, 183 died.

II. POLITICS AND WAR

1983 Jan. 3 New **labor unions were sanctioned by the Communist government of Poland**, restricted to one workplace per union.

1983 Jan. 17 The **Nigerian government ordered all illegal aliens to leave the country** by the end of the month. It was estimated that there were 2,000,000 such persons in the country, including thousands of teachers and other skilled workers. Most of the aliens were Ghanaians.

1983 Jan. 18 The government of **South Africa** dissolved the National Assembly of **South-West Africa** [Namibia] and assumed direct control of the territory. The move was seen as a blow to the attempts of the **U.N.** to secure South-West Africa's independence.

1983 Jan. 25 **Klaus Barbie** (b. Oct. 15, 1913), a top German Gestapo official in World War II, was arrested in Bolivia and returned (Feb. 5) to France to stand trial. Known as **"The Butcher of Lyon,"** Barbie was accused of having been directly responsible for the deaths of c.4,000 persons and of having sent about another 7,500 to Nazi concentration camps. He had already been tried (1954) in absentia and sentenced to death.

1983 Jan. 27 **Georges** [Augustin] **Bidault** (b. Oct. 5, 1899), a former premier of France (1946 and 1949–

1950), died. Leader of the Popular Republicans, he strongly opposed the post-war government of **Charles de Gaulle** when it took steps to give Algeria its independence. As a result, Bidault was charged (1962) with plotting against the state. He went into exile and never again participated in French politics.

1983 Feb. 24 More than 1,300 persons were killed in the state of Assam, **India**, during **three weeks of violence** resulting from ethnic and political differences. Hindus protested the government's move to allow voting and other rights to alien Muslims who had settled in Assam.

1983 Mar. 5 In a general election the Australian Labour party defeated the Liberal-National Country party, and **Robert** [James Lee] **Hawke** (b. Dec. 9, 1929) became prime minister, replacing [John] **Malcolm Fraser** (b. May 21, 1930).

1983 Mar. 6 **Helmut Kohl** remained in office as chancellor of the Federal Republic of Germany [West Germany] even though his Christian Democratic Union and its Bavarian allies fell short of achieving a majority of seats in an election for seats in the Bundestag. The Christian Democrats secured a majority by allying with the Free Democrats.

1983 Mar. 23 **Ronald Reagan** proposed building a missile defense shield that would protect the nation from nuclear attack. He called his proposal the **Strategic Defense Initiative**, but it became popularly known as **"Star Wars."** The shield would employ laser beams, particle beams, and other high technology devices to shoot down incoming missiles.

1983 Apr. 18 The **U.S. embassy in Beirut**, Lebanon, was almost totally **destroyed by a bomb** that exploded in a car driven at it by a terrorist. Of the 63 persons killed, 17 were Americans. The **Islamic Jihad**, a pro-Iranian group, claimed responsibility.

1983 Apr. 22 The West German magazine *Stern* claimed it had possession of 60 volumes of **personal diaries of Adolf Hitler**. By May, experts had proved the alleged diaries to be a forgery. *Stern* was said to have paid $3,700,000 for the diaries.

1983 June 9 **Margaret Thatcher** retained office as prime minister of Great Britain when the Conservative party won 397 seats of 650 in Parliament. In the election, the Labour party won 209 seats, its worst showing since World War II. The Alliance party

(1981) received 25 percent of the vote but won only 23 seats.

1983 June 16   Yury Andropov, general secretary of the Communist party of the U.S.S.R., became chairman of the Presidium of the Supreme Soviet as well.

1983 June 24 In the **civil war in Chad**, the rebel forces of **Goukouni Oeueddi**, the former president, again assisted by troops from neighboring Libya, captured Faya-Largeau, a strongpoint in the northern part of the country. Though the U.S. sent military aid to **Hissen Habré**, president of Chad, and France sent (Aug. 9) c.3,000 paratroopers as military instructors, at year's end Habré remained in power.

1983 July 22   Martial law was formally **ended by the Polish government.**

1983 Aug. 4   Bettino Craxi [Benedetto Craxi] (b. Feb. 24, 1934) became the first socialist premier of Italy. He headed a five-party coalition that formed Italy's 44th government since World War II. Craxi was supportive of ties with the U.S. and favored deployment of cruise missiles if arms reduction talks failed.

1983 Aug. 21   Benigno S[imeon] **Aquino, Jr.**, (b. Nov. 27, 1932), the leader of the opposition to **Ferdinand Marcos**, president of the **Philippines**, was shot and killed as he left an airliner at Manila on his return from three years of exile in the U.S. His alleged assassin was immediately slain. Public suspicions that the government had arranged the assassination prompted Marcos to name (Oct. 22) a board of private citizens to investigate. On Oct. 24, 1984, the board said **Fabian C. Ver** (b. Jan. 20, 1920), armed forces chief of staff, was involved, and Ver took a leave of absence from his command. A trial was scheduled for 1985.

1983 Aug. 28   Menachem Begin announced that for personal reasons he would resign as prime minister of Israel and leader of the Herut party. On Oct. 10 **Yitzhak Shamir** [Yitzhak Jazernicki] (b. Nov. 3, 1914), who had been foreign minister, was sworn in as Begin's successor. He at once devalued the shekel and reduced government subsidies on basic goods and services.

1983 Sept. 1   A Soviet military plane shot down a South Korean passenger airliner that had for unknown reasons strayed into Russian air space over Sakhalin Island north of Japan. All 269 persons on board died. A few days later the U.S.S.R. vetoed (Sept. 12) a U.N. Security Council resolution condemning the action.

1983 Sept. 19   St. Kitts-Nevis, in the Leeward Islands of the West Indies, **became an independent nation.** The first prime minister was **Kennedy A. Simmonds** (b. Apr. 12, 1936) whose People's Action Movement, after an election, formed a coalition with a smaller party. Simmonds had been premier of the colony for three and a half years. St. Kitts-Nevis remained a member of the Commonwealth of Nations.

1983 Sept. 25   Leopold III (b. Nov. 3, 1901), a former king of the Belgians, died. Leopold surrendered (1940) the Belgian forces to the German invaders after hard fighting, and he was held by the Nazis for the rest of the war. Even so, he was accused of cooperating with the Germans, and he was not allowed to return (1945) to the throne. He became an exile in Switzerland. On July 15, 1951, Leopold abdicated and his son **Baudoin** became king.

1983 Oct. 23 An **explosive-laden truck blew up in front of a U.S. marine headquarters** and barracks at the Beirut, Lebanon, airport. The driver of the truck died in the blast. The final death toll was 241 marines and navy personnel. The terrorists responsible were not identified. At the same time a similar blast at a building occupied by French peacekeeping forces caused 58 deaths.

1983 Oct. 25   U.S. military forces, with token troops from six Caribbean nations, **invaded the island of Grenada**, north of Trinidad. The only serious opposition came from Cuban soldiers and workers who were building a new airport. The U.S. claimed that Grenada, which had a Marxist government, was about to become a pawn and a base of the U.S.S.R. and Cuba. Almost all American forces were withdrawn by the end of the year, and a new provisional government established. In the fighting 19 Americans, 24 Cubans, and 44 Grenadians were killed.

1983 Oct. 30   Raúl Alfonsin (b. Mar. 13, 1926), leader of the Radical Civic Union, was elected president of Argentina, the first civilian head of state in nearly eight years. He announced he would annul the amnesty the military junta had granted itself in an attempt to prevent prosecution for the kidnapping and torture of its opponents in recent years.

1983 Nov. 16   In a general election in Turkey the Motherland party won a majority of seats in the one-house parliament. As a result, **Bulent Ulusu** resigned (Nov. 24) as prime minister and was succeeded (Dec. 13) by **Turgut Özal** (1927–Apr. 17, 1993).

1983 Dec. 4   Twenty-eight carrier-based **planes of the U.S. navy attacked Syrian anti-aircraft positions** near Hammana, a village east of Beirut, Lebanon. The attack was in retaliation for the Syrians having fired the day before on unarmed American reconnaissance planes. Two U.S. planes were shot down and another damaged. One pilot was killed and one crewman captured. The captured flier was released after a month in a Syrian prison.

1983 Dec. 20   The **Syrian army forced c.4,000 guerrillas** of the **Palestinian Liberation Organization** [PLO] **to evacuate the port of Tripoli**, Lebanon. The U.N., with support from Greece and France, supervised the evacuation to friendly Arab countries. On June 24 Syria had expelled **Yasir Arafat**, head of the PLO, from Syria, where he had found refuge after the Israeli invasion (1982) of Lebanon.

III. ECONOMY AND TRADE

1983   The **economies of the developed, industrialized nations improved** somewhat this year, partly due to lower oil prices and to fiscal and monetary restraint on the part of the larger nations. In the U.S., for example, the Gross National Product [GNP] was up 3.5 percent; in Canada 3.3 percent; and in Japan 3.25 percent.

IV. RELIGION AND PHILOSOPHY

1983 Oct. 14   The **National Council of the Churches of Christ**, an American organization of Protestant denominations, announced a new translation of some Bible passages that eliminated references to God as being male only. The readings were prepared by a committee of 11 biblical scholars.

1983 Oct. 17   **Raymond Aron** [Raymond-Claude-Ferdinand Aron] (b. Mar. 15, 1905), a French philosopher, died. Aron, a rational humanist, was a leader among those who did not accept existentialism. As a teacher in several schools, including the Sorbonne (1955–1968), Aron exerted considerable influence on modern thought. Among his books were *L'Opium des intellectuels* [*The Opium of the Intel-*

lectuals] (1955), *La République impériale: Les États-Unis dans le monde, 1945–1972* [*The Imperial Republic: The United States in the World, 1945–1972* (1973), and *Histoire et dialectique de la violence* (1973).

1983 Dec. 1   A booklet issued by the Vatican, *Educational Guidance in Human Love,* condemned sexual relations by the unmarried, masturbation, and homosexuality.

V. SCIENCE, EDUCATION, AND TECHNOLOGY

1983 June 13   The U.S. unmanned spacecraft *Pioneer 10* left the solar system for outer space, the first ever to do so. Launched in 1972, *Pioneer 10* entered (July 15) the asteroid belt, the first spacecraft to do so. On Dec. 3, 1973, it reached Jupiter, coming within 81,000 miles of the planet. Photographs of Jupiter's "great red spot" indicated it was a towering mass of clouds. With the aid of Jupiter's gravity *Pioneer 10* attained a speed of 82,800 mph.

1983 July 1   **R**[ichard] **Buckminster Fuller** (b. July 12, 1895), an American engineer and architect, died. He devoted his career to inventions that would satisfy his **Dymaxion principle**: to get as much output as possible from as little input of energy and materials as possible. His **geodesic dome** was his most valuable contribution to this cause.

1983 July 21   The **lowest natural temperature ever recorded** on the planet Earth, -128.6°F, was registered at the Russian station Vostok in Antarctica.

1983 Aug. 9   A U.S. satellite orbiting Earth found evidence of **solid objects in orbit around the star Vega**. The Jet Propulsion Laboratory in Pasadena, California, said this was the first direct evidence of such objects of any size outside the solar system and that the objects could be planets at a different stage of development than Earth.

VI. ARTS AND LEISURE

1983 Feb. 25   [Thomas Lanier] **Tennessee Williams** (b. Mar. 26, 1911), an American dramatist, died. His first success was *The Glass Menagerie* (1944). Williams went on to write many other successful and significant plays, among them: *A Streetcar Named Desire* (1947), *Cat on a Hot Tin Roof*

(1955), *Suddenly Last Summer* (1958), and *Sweet Bird of Youth* (1959). Williams wrote one novel, *The Roman Spring of Mrs. Stone* (1950).

1983 Mar. 3   Arthur Koestler (b. Sept. 5, 1905), a Hungarian-born author noted for his pentrating analysis of the communist mentality, died. He left (1938) the Communist party and published *Darkness at Noon* (1941), his best-known novel, which was based on the Moscow trials of the 1930s, in which Stalin purged his enemies. His other books included *The Yogi and the Commissar* (1945), *The Lotus and the Robot* (1961), *The Ghost in the Machine* (1967), and *Janus: A Summing Up* (1978).

1983 Mar. 8   William [Turner] **Walton** (b. Mar. 29, 1902), an English composer, died. His best-known works were *Façade* (1923), *Belshazzar's Feast* (1931), and *Troilus and Cressida* (1954).

1983 Mar. 15   José [Luis] **Sert** (b. July 1, 1902), a Spanish-born architect, died. He specialized in city planning and urban development. Sert came (1941) to the U.S. and was dean of the Graduate School of Design at Harvard University (1953–1969). He designed the Spanish pavilion for the 1937 Paris World's Fair.

1983 Mar. 15   Rebecca West [nee Cicily Fairfield] (b. Dec. 21, 1892), an English author and journalist, died. Among her novels were *The Judge* (1922) and *The Birds Fall Down* (1966). Her reputation, however, rested chiefly on her political journalism, especially *Black Lamb and Gray Falcon* (1942), a study of Yugoslavia, and *The Meaning of Treason* (1947), one of her writings dealing with the trials of Nazi leaders as war criminals after World War II.

1983 Apr. 30   George Balanchine [Georgy Melitonovich Balanchivadze] (b. Jan. 9, 1904), a Russian-born choreographer and founder of 20th-century dance, died. In his long career he was active in Russia, in Paris (1924–1929) with the Ballet Russe, and after 1934 in the U.S. Among his ballets were *Apollo* (1928), *La Concurrence* (1932), and *Serenade* (1935). In 1936, by choreographing *Slaughter on 10th Avenue* for *On Your Toes,* he introduced to Broadway musicals dancing integrated with the story.

1983 July 29   Luis Buñuel (b. Feb. 22, 1900), a Spanish-born filmmaker, died. His work showed contempt for conventional morality and hypocrisy, which he found rampant in the world. His films included *l'Age d'Or* (1930), *El Angel Esterminador* [*The Exterminating Angel*] (1962), *Le Journal d'une Femme de Chambre* [*Diary of a Chambermaid*] (1964), and *le Charme Discret de la bourgeoisie* [*The Discreet Charm of the Bourgeoisie*] (1972).

1983 Oct. 10   Ralph [David] **Richardson** (b. Dec. 19, 1902), an English actor internationally known on the stage and in the movies, died. Richardson became one of a trio of English stage greats with **John Gielgud** and **Lawrence Olivier**. On the stage he won plaudits for his performance as Sir Toby Belch, Peer Gynt, and Sir John Falstaff, among other roles. He appeared in more than 40 movies, including *The Fallen Idol* (1948), *Richard III* (1955), and *Long Day's Journey into Night* (1962).

1983 Dec. 6 A 12th-century illuminated manuscript, *The Gospel of Henry the Lion,* was sold at auction in London for $11.7 million, the highest price to this date ever paid for any kind of work of art.

1983 Dec. 13   Mary Renault [Mary Challans] (b. Sept. 4, 1905), an English author of historical novels, died. Among her best novels were *The King Must Die* (1958) and *The Bull from the Sea* (1962).

1983 Dec. 25   Joan Miró (b. Apr. 20, 1893), a Spanish surrealist painter, died. His style has been called surrealistically decorative but Freudian, as exemplified by *Dutch Interior* (1928). Among his representative works were *Harlequin's Carnival* (1924–1925), *Dog Barking at the Moon* (1926), *The Beautiful Bird Revealing the Unknown to a Pair of Lovers* (1941), and *Blue III* (1961).

VII. SPORTS, GAMES, AND SOCIETY

1983 May 31 [William Harrison] **Jack Dempsey** (b. June 24, 1895), once heavyweight boxing champion, died. One of the best professional fighters ever, he held the title from 1919 to 1926. His bout with **Georges Carpentier** of France was (1921) the first to attract a million dollar gate. Dempsey lost his title on Sept. 23, 1926, to **Gene Tunney**. Of the 69 fights of his career Dempsey lost only 5.

1983 Aug. 14–28 The **Pan American Games** were held in Caracas, Venezuela, with 4,000 athletes from 35 countries competing. The U.S. won 137 gold medals and 281 overall; Cuba 79 and 175; and Canada 18 and 109.

1983 Sept. 12 A **robbery** in the West Hartford, Connecticut, warehouse of the **Wells Fargo** Armored Car Service Corporation netted the thieves $7.1 million. The affair began when a company guard, **Victor Gerena**, subdued two fellow workers. He and his associates then made off with the cash. Only about $80,000 of the loot was ever recovered.

1983 Sept. 26 For the first time since the initial competition in 1851, the U.S. lost the America's Cup. In the 1983 competition the Australian yacht *Australia II* defeated the U.S. *Liberty*, four races to three, off Newport, Rhode Island.

1984

I. DISASTERS

1984 Feb.–June A **dysentery epidemic in India** left c.3,300 people dead, most of them in West Bengal state.

1984 Mid-May An **explosion in an ammunition depot** near Murmansk, U.S.S.R. [present Russia], set off a chain reaction of explosions and fires, leaving from 200 to 300 dead.

1984 Sept. 2–3 A **typhoon** striking seven major islands of the southern Philippines left more than 1,300 dead, many missing, and c.1,120,000 homeless.

1984 Oct. As many as **10,000 to 22,000 caribou** were estimated to have drowned during their annual migration across rivers in northern Quebec, Canada. They were part of the George River herd, the largest in North America. Some blamed Hydro-Quebec, a utility company, for having let too much water flow over a dam intended to regulate the flow in the two rivers.

1984 Nov. 19 A **gas truck explosion** in a liquid gas storage area north of Mexico City set off other explosions and caused fires that wiped out 66 acres of structures. At least 1,000 persons died and thousands were injured.

1984 Nov. 25 Northeast of Ankara, Turkey, a **bus hit a truck** in a heavy fog, killing 31.

1984 Dec. 4 **Methyl isocyanate**, a chemical used in the manufacture of insecticides, **escaped** in gaseous form in large quantities from a Union Carbide Corporation plant in **Bhopal**, India. The gas spread throughout the city, killing c.2,000 people. Over an area of 25 square miles c.200,000 persons were affected.

II. POLITICS AND WAR

1984 Jan. 1 **Mohammed Buhari** (b. Dec. 17, 1942), an army officer, announced he had taken over the government of **Nigeria** from **Alhaj Shehu Shagari** (b. Apr., 1925), the president, in a bloodless coup. Shagari was blamed for the near-collapse of the Nigerian economy.

1984 Jan. 1 **Brunei**, a self-governing sultanate on the island of Borneo, **became independent**. Brunei, with immense oil and gas resources, had the highest per capita income in Asia. The new nation joined the Commonwealth of Nations (Jan. 1) and the Association of South East Asian Nations [ASEAN] (Jan. 7). The nation was ruled (Oct. 5, 1967–to the present) by **Muda Hassanal Bolkiah**, the sultan of Brunei.

1984 Jan. 10 The **U.S. and the Roman Catholic Church**, after a hiatus of 116 years, **resumed full diplomatic relations**. In 1983 Congress had repealed a prohibition against using government funds for this purpose.

1984 Feb. 5 The government of **Lebanon** resigned in the midst of conditions threatening political disintegration of the country. **Amin Gemayel** continued as president of Lebanon (from 1982). Another governmental cabinet was not formed until Apr. 30, when **Rashid** [Abdu Hamil] **Karami** (b. Dec. 30, 1921) was able to organize one. Karami brought into his cabinet representatives of most of the warring factions in the country, yet civil conflict continued, especially in Beirut.

1984 Feb. 7 **Ronald Reagan** ordered the c.1,400 U.S. **marines** in **Lebanon** as part of a peacekeeping force to **withdraw to ships** of the Sixth Fleet lying offshore. On Mar. 24 the French withdrew the last of their c.1,250-man contingent. The task of ending the civil conflict seemed hopeless.

1984 Feb. 9   Yury V. Andropov (b. June 15, 1914), general secretary of the Communist party of the U.S.S.R., died. **Konstantin** [Ustinovich] **Chernenko** was named (Feb. 13) to replace him and on Apr. 14 was made president. Chernenko had been a protégé of the late Leonid Brezhnev.

1984 Feb. 22   In the **Iran-Iraq War**, Iran launched an offensive, termed the "final push," which carried into Iraq and captured part of the Majnoon oilfields north of Basra. The drive then bogged down. Iran had to give up its "human wave" tactics, which sent young, poorly trained Iranians into mass charges that the Iraqis had by now learned to contain. In March Iraq began attacking oil tankers serving Iran in the Persian Gulf, and Iran replied in May by attacking Kuwaiti and Saudi tankers, which supplied Iraq.

1984 Mar. 16   Mozambique and South Africa signed an agreement not to support rebel organizations operating from their countries. Thus Mozambique would not let **African National Congress** [ANC] guerrillas use its territory for operations against South Africa. In turn the latter would not support **Renamo**, a guerrilla group fighting the Mozambique government.

1984 Mar. 27   Ahmed Sékou Touré (b. Jan. 9, 1922), president of Guinea since it became (1958) independent, died. A nonaligned moderate in international affairs, Touré had been a ruthless ruler at home. **Louis Lansana Beavogui**, who had been premier, assumed (Mar. 27) the post of president. However, he was overthrown (Apr. 3) in a military coup led by **Lansana Conté** (b. 1934), a leader of the Military Committee for National Redress, which held supreme power in the country. Conté was declared president Apr. 5.

1984 May 6   José Napoléon Duarte (Nov. 23, 1925–Feb. 23, 1990) was elected president of El Salvador and became the nation's first civilian leader in 49 years. Duarte, of the moderate Social Democratic party, received 54 percent of the vote. His chief opponent was **Roberto d'Aubuisson** (b. 1944), leader of the right-wing Nationalist Republican Alliance. Duarte had been a member of the ruling junta since 1980.

1984 May 6   Nicolas Ardito Barletta Vallarina (b. Aug. 21, 1938) was chosen president of Panama by a narrow margin. He took office (Oct. 11) but re-

signed (Sept. 1985) in favor of **Eric Arturo Devalle** (b. Feb. 2, 1937), vice president of Panama. Real power in Panama remained with **Manuel Noriega** (b. Feb. 11, 1938), commander of the National Guard.

1984 May 10   The **International Court of Justice** ruled that the U.S. should stop blockading or **mining the waters off Nicaragua**. The U.S. refused to participate in the proceedings, claiming the court had no jurisdiction.

1984 June 6   About 300 persons were killed when the **Indian army attacked the Golden Temple**, the holiest shrine of the **Sikh religion**, in Amritsar, India, near the Pakistani border. Hundreds of people had been slain in fighting between Sikhs and Hindus. The Indian government said the Golden Temple was being used as a fort and arms depot.

1984 Aug. 4   The regime of **Thomas Sankara** (1948–Oct. 16, 1987) celebrated the end of its first year in power by changing the name of Upper Volta to **Burkina Faso**.

1984 Sept. 4   The Conservative-Progressive party swept a general election in Canada, winning 211 of 282 seats in the House of Commons. **Brian Mulroney** (b. Mar. 20, 1939), leader of the victors, was sworn in (Sept. 17) as prime minister. He succeeded **John N. Turner** (b. June 7, 1929) of the Liberal party, who had been prime minister since Pierre Elliott Trudeau resigned on June 16. Mulroney, who had not held public office, said his main concerns were "jobs and the economy."

1984 Sept. 13   The Israeli Knesset approved a coalition government formed by the Labor party and the Likud. It was agreed that **Shimon Peres** (b. Aug. 1, 1923) of the Labor party would be prime minister for the first half of a 50-month period. Prime minister for the second half would be **Yitzhak Shamir** of the Likud.

1984 Sept. 17   France and Libya agreed to withdraw their troops from Chad where they had been on opposite sides of a civil war that remained unsettled. All French troops were out (Nov. 9) of Chad, but Libya did not live up to its part of the agreement.

1984 Sept. 20   A **car loaded with bombs** and driven by a suicidal terrorist **exploded at the U.S. embassy**

in Beirut, Lebanon, killing c.23 persons, two of them Americans. About 70 others were injured.

1984 Oct. 31   Indira Gandhi, prime minister of **India**, was slain by two of her Sikh bodyguards, perhaps in retaliation for the Indian army attack on the Golden Temple in Amritsar. As her successor the Indian Parliament chose her son **Rajiv Gandhi** (b. Aug. 20, 1944), who had been an airline pilot before entering politics. Rioting by Hindus after the assassination, by official count, took the lives of 2,733 Sikhs.

1984 Nov. 4   In the first general election since 1979, **Daniel Ortega Saavedra** (b. Nov. 11, 1945) was elected president of Nicaragua, the Frente Sandinista de Liberación Nacional [FSLN] receiving 63 percent of the vote.

1984 Dec. 12   Moaouya Ould Sidi Ahmed Taya (b. 1943), the prime minister (from 1981) and commander of the army of **Mauritania**, Africa, seized power in a bloodless coup. The coup overthrew the government of **Mohammed Khouna Ould Haidalla**, the president (from 1980), who was out of the country at the time. Taya became president and head of the Military Committee for National Salvation [CMRN].

1984 Dec. 19   The **People's Republic of China and Great Britain signed an accord** settling the future of **Hong Kong**. The British 99-year lease on the Hong Kong territory was to expire on July 1, 1997. It was agreed that at that time sovereignty would be returned to China. China in turn guaranteed that Hong Kong's capitalist system would continue for 50 more years.

III. ECONOMY AND TRADE

1984 Mar. 12   A **strike began in Great Britain**, called by the National Union of Mineworkers, to protest the plans of the National Coal Board to close about half of 174 mines. Many miners did not strike because the walkout had been called by the union leadership without a vote of the miners. A court fined (Oct. 10) the union $250,000 for contempt.

1984 June 15   The **Gulf Corporation was bought by Standard Oil of California** [SOCAL] for $13,400,-000,000. The deal made SOCAL the third largest oil concern in the U.S.

IV. RELIGION AND PHILOSOPHY

1984 Feb. 18   The government of **Italy and the Holy See signed an agreement** that ended the status of Roman Catholicism as the state religion of Italy.

1984 Mar. 6   Martin Niemöller (b. Jan. 14, 1892), a German theologian and church leader, died. A submarine commander in World War I, he at first supported **Adolf Hitler** and National Socialism. However, he became the leader of the Protestant opposition when Hitler organized his "German Christian Church." As a result he was imprisoned from 1938 until the Allies released him in 1945. Niemöller was president of the **World Council of Churches** (1961–1968).

1984 July 9   The magnificent **cathedral of York**, England, was **damaged by a fire** believed started by lightning. The medieval roof was heavily damaged and the famous **Rose Window** cracked, but was repairable.

1984 Sept. 3   The Vatican issued a statement critical of "**liberation theology**," which had recently been embraced by many radical priests and nuns, especially in Latin America. The Vatican warned that the Marxist approach, teaching class struggle and violence, could not be condoned.

1984 Oct. 14   The **Nobel Peace Prize** was awarded to **Desmond** [Mpilo] **Tutu** (b. Oct. 7, 1931), a South African bishop, for his efforts to resolve the problem of the system of **apartheid**. Tutu had been ordained (1961) in the Anglican Church and had become (1976) bishop of Lesotho. On Apr. 14, 1986, he was elected archbishop of Cape Town and so became the first black head of the Anglican Church in South Africa. His outspoken tactics made him the intellectual leader of his race in the struggle to end white minority rule.

V. SCIENCE, EDUCATION, AND TECHNOLOGY

1984 Feb. 7   American astronauts **Bruce McCandless** (b. June 8, 1937) and **Robert L. Stewart** (b. Aug. 13, 1942), using powered backpacks to propel them, practiced working in space outside the space shuttle *Challenger*, which had been launched on Feb. 3. They were 170 miles above the earth and traveling at the same speed as the shuttle, 17,500 mph.

1984 **Apr. 21** French scientists reported that they had succeeded in isolating the virus believed to cause **Acquired Immune Deficiency Syndrome** [AIDS]. On Apr. 23 the U.S. Centers for Disease Control reported that the virus had been isolated there also. They termed it **HTLV-3**; the French used LAV to denote it. By the end of the year c.7,000 cases of AIDS had been reported in the U.S., and 3,300 victims had died.

1984 **May 15** At a site called Rio Zaul near Ixcanrio, Guatemala, an untouched **Mayan tomb was discovered**. It contained the skeleton of a male, some pottery and wall paintings, and was believed to be the tomb of an important person. The tomb was believed to date from 420 to 470 a.d.

1984 **June 4** The **reproduction of genes from an extinct animal** was reported by scientists at the University of California, Berkeley. They extracted the genetic material DNA from dried muscle tissue of a quaga, an animal related to the horse and the zebra. The animal had been preserved for 140 years in West Germany.

1984 **Oct. 2** Three Soviet cosmonauts returned to earth after spending 237 days in space aboard *Salyut 7*. They were **Oleg Atkov** (b. May 9, 1949), **Leonid Kizim** (b. Aug. 5, 1941), and **Vladimir Solovyov** (b. Nov. 11, 1946). They had been lifted aloft (Feb. 8) by *Soyuz 10*, which docked with and transferred them to the manned space station *Salyut 7*. The space station had been aloft since 1982 with different crews aboard at different times.

1984 **Oct. 26** At the Loma Linda University Medical Center in California a **baboon's heart was transplanted into a 15-day-old baby** girl who was dying as a result of severe birth defects. The child died on Nov. 15.

1984 **Nov. 30** The first volume of the first dictionary of the **world's first written language, Sumerian**, was published at the University of Pennsylvania, Philadelphia.

1984 **Dec. 4** In the eastern Mediterranean Sea the **earliest shipwreck ever excavated** yielded artifacts of the Bronze Age, such as copper and tin ingots, gold, medallions, beads, and pottery.

1984 **Dec. 10** American astronomers observed a **very large gaseous object** that could be a planet start-ing to form. It was orbiting Van Biesbroeck 8, a faint star 21 light-years from Earth.

VI. ARTS AND LEISURE

1984 **Apr. 26** [William] **Count Basie** (b. Aug. 21, 1904), an American jazz pianist and band leader, died. Many of the best jazz soloists of the period played in his band. Basie's many recordings included such classics as **"One O'Clock Jump"** (1937) and **"Jumpin' at the Woodside"** (1938).

1984 **May 3** The **Mark Rothko Foundation**, disposing of works left by the late American abstract expressionist artist, announced it would give c.1,000 items to 19 museums around the world. The core of the collection was to go to the National Gallery of Art, Washington, D.C.

1984 **May 19** **John Betjeman** (b. Aug. 28, 1906), the poet laureate of Great Britain (from 1972), died. His witty and satiric poetry found wide popularity. Betjeman's **Collected Poems** (1958, 1962) enjoyed success.

1984 **July 27** **James** [Neville] **Mason** (b. May 15, 1900), an English film star, died. His films included **Odd Man Out** (1947), **The Desert Fox** (1951), **Julius Caesar** (1953), and **Lolita** (1962).

1984 **Aug. 5** **Richard Burton** [orig.: Richard Jenkins] (b. Nov. 10, 1925), an English actor of stage and movies, died. His reputation as a magnificent actor with voice and personality to match, was first earned on the London stage, mostly in Shakespearean plays. He became known to a wider audience for his movie roles, in such films as **The Robe** (1953), **Cleopatra** (1962), **The Spy Who Came in from the Cold** (1965), and **Who's Afraid of Virginia Woolf** (1966).

1984 **Aug. 14** J[ohn] B[oynton] **Priestley** (b. Sept. 13, 1894), an author popular in the English-speaking world in the 1930s and 1940s, died. He wrote more than 100 books and plays and had his first success with his second novel, **The Good Companions** (1929). Among his plays was the successful **Dangerous Corner** (1932).

1984 **Sept. 14** **Janet Gaynor** (b. Oct. 6, 1906), an American movie actress, died. Her performance in **Sunrise** (1927) won her (1929) the first **Academy Award** [Oscar] for best actress. Much more popular was **Seventh Heaven** (1927), a romantic drama in which she starred. Her co-star was **Charles Farrell** (Aug. 9, 1901–May 6, 1990) and for seven years they were the most popular romantic couple in the movies. Other notable Gaynor performances were in *Daddy Long-Legs* (1931) and *A Star Is Born* (1937).

1984 Oct. 21 **François Truffaut** (b. Feb. 6, 1932), a French leader of the **nouvelle vague** [new wave] of filmmakers, died. His first success was *Les Quatre cents coups* [*The 400 Blows*] (1959). One of his most noteworthy films was *La nuit américaine* [*Day for Night*] (1972).

VII. SPORTS, GAMES, AND SOCIETY

1984 Jan. 20 [Peter John] **Johnny Weissmuller** (b. June 2, 1904), an American champion swimmer and **movie portrayer of Tarzan** of the Apes, died. He won two gold medals at the 1924 Olympic Games and another in 1928. In all Weissmuller won 52 American championships and set 67 world records. Between 1932 and 1948 he played the title role 19 times in Tarzan movies.

1984 Feb. 7–19 The 14th Winter **Olympic Games** were held at Sarajevo, Yugoslavia, with 1,278 athletes from 49 countries competing. East German athletes won 9 gold medals and 24 overall; the U.S.S.R., 6 and 25; and the U.S., 4 and 8.

1984 May 8 The U.S.S.R. announced it would boycott the Summer **Olympic games** to be held in Los Angeles, California, in August. The Soviets claimed the action was taken because of "gross flouting" of Olympic ideals by the U.S. Other Soviet bloc nations soon followed the Russian example. The American athletes had boycotted the 1980 Olympics in Moscow.

1984 June 27 **Oswald Jacoby** (b. Dec. 8, 1902), one of the best contract **bridge** players ever, died. In 1935, as a member of the U.S. team, he was instrumental in winning the first world championship of contract bridge. By 1967 Jacoby had amassed 10,000 master points.

1984 July 28–Aug. 12 The 23rd Summer **Olympic Games** were held in Los Angeles, California, with 7,708 athletes from 141 nations competing. American athletes won 83 gold medals and 174 overall; Romania 20 and 53; and West Germany 17 and 59.

1984 Sept. 18 The **first solo crossing of the Atlantic Ocean in a helium-filled balloon** was achieved by **Joe W. Kittinger** (b. 1928), a retired U.S. air force colonel. He took off from Caribou, Maine, and landed near Savona on the Italian Riviera in just under 84 hours. The distance he traveled, 3,535 miles, was a record for a solo balloon flight.

1984 Sept. 26 One of Spain's most popular **bullfighters**, [Francisco] **Paquirri Rivera** (b. 1948?), died on the way to a hospital after having been gored by a bull. He was performing near Córdoba, Spain.

1985

I. VITAL STATISTICS AND DEMOGRAPHY

1985 At mid-year the U.N. estimated the **world's population** at 4,842,042,000, an increase of 79,000,000 since the previous year. The U.N. projected world population for the year 2000 at 6,127,000,000.

1985 Jan. 3 About 10,000 **Ethiopian Jews were flown to Israel** in recent years, the government of Israel announced. The airlift probably began in 1977 when it was ruled that these Ethiopians were descendants of the tribe of Dan and so were entitled to Israeli citizenship.

II. DISASTERS

1985 Jan 13 In Ethiopia, c.100 miles east of Addis Ababa, a five-car **passenger train derailed** as it crossed a bridge and fell into a ravine. The casualty toll was c.392 dead and 370 injured.

1985 Feb. 19 A Spanish **jetliner**, after hitting a TV tower, **crashed** into a mountain near Durango, northern Spain, c.18 miles from the Bilbao airport, killing all 148 aboard.

1985 Mar. 3 In Chile an **earthquake** with its epicenter c.40 miles north of Santiago, left c.177 dead, c.2,000 injured and c.150,000 homeless. The quake measured 7.8 on the Richter scale.

1985 Mar.–Apr. A **cholera epidemic**, first discovered in a refugee camp in northwestern Somalia, East Africa, killed more than 1,500 persons.

1985 May 25 A **cyclone** that swept water up to 15 feet high over a region of Bangladesh comprising islands in the Ganges River delta and the Bay of Bengal killed 2,540 people by the official count. Other estimates ranged from 11,000 to 40,000.

1985 June *Listeria monocytogenes* **bacteria** in unpasteurized Mexican-style cheese caused an outbreak of disease that killed c.140 persons, most of them in California, but affecting six other states in all.

1985 June 23 An Air India Boeing 747, enroute from Toronto, Canada, to Bombay, **exploded** off Ireland, killing all 329 persons aboard. An investigation concluded that a bomb was the cause of the tragedy.

1985 July 10 A Russian **passenger jet** flying between Karshi and Leningrad **crashed**, and c.150 persons aboard were believed killed.

1985 July 10 The **collapse of an earthen dam** sent mud and water pouring over Stava, Italy, an Alpine resort. Three hotels were destroyed and c.250 people killed.

1985 Aug. 2 A Delta Air Lines L-1011 jet, attempting to land at the Dallas-Ft. Worth, Texas, airport, nose dived and **crashed** onto a highway. Of the 162 persons aboard, 135 were killed. Wind shear, a sudden, strong shift in wind direction, was blamed.

1985 Aug. 12 A Japan Air Lines **Boeing 747 crashed** into a mountain in central Japan, killing 520 of the 524 persons aboard.

1985 Sept. 19–20 An **earthquake** registering 7.8 on the Richter scale devastated central and southwestern Mexico, including Mexico City, where c.400 buildings were destroyed. At least 4,200 people were killed, c.2,000 missing, c.40,000 injured, and c.31,000 left homeless. The epicenter of the quake was c.250 miles southwest of Mexico City.

1985 Oct. 7 A **landslide** brought on by 15 inches of rain in 36 hours produced by tropical storm Isabel buried a shantytown near Ponce, Puerto Rico. It was believed c.150 people died in the landslide.

1985 Nov. 14 Nevada del Ruiz, a **volcano** 60 miles northwest of Bogota, Colombia, and dormant since 1595, **blew off its ice cap** and sent a **lahar**—a landslide of ice, mud, and rocks—sweeping over a number of towns and devastating the chief coffee growing region of Colombia. The death toll was estimated at 25,000 and the homeless at 19,000.

1985 Dec. 12 An Arrow Air **DC-8 jet** passenger plane, under charter to the U.S. army, **crashed** on takeoff from Gander, Newfoundland. Of the 256 persons aboard, all of whom were killed, 248 were men of the 101st Airborne Division returning for Christmas after six months' duty with the peacekeeping force in the Sinai Peninsula.

III. POLITICS AND WAR

1985 Jan. 10 **Daniel Ortega Saavedra** was sworn in as president of **Nicaragua**. **Fidel Castro** was the only foreign head of state to attend the ceremony. Later the U.S. imposed (May 7) a total **trade embargo on Nicaragua** because of its dislike of Ortega's Marxist government. The American Congress approved (June 12) $12 million in "non-lethal" aid for the **Contras**, an armed group fighting the government.

1985 Jan. 15 By a heavily favorable vote in the electoral college, **Tancredo de Almeida Neves** was elected as the first civilian president of Brazil in 21 years. He promised bold efforts and "irreversible changes" to improve economic conditions. Neves, however, became so seriously ill that **José Sarney** (b. Apr. 30, 1930), the vice president, was sworn in (Mar. 15) as interim president. President-elect Tancredo de Almeida Neves (b. Mar. 4, 1910) died on Apr. 21, and Sarney became (Apr. 22) president.

1985 Jan. 20 **Ronald Reagan** was inaugurated for a second term as president of the U.S. Running on the Republican ticket he defeated **Walter F. Mondale**, the Democratic party candidate, in the election held on Nov. 6, 1984. Reagan received 525 electoral college votes to 13 for Mondale, and 54,455,075 popular votes to 37,577,185. **George Bush** continued as vice president.

1985 Feb. 4 **David** [Russell] **Lange** (b. Aug. 4, 1942), prime minister of **New Zealand**, refused to allow a U.S. navy destroyer to dock in his country unless the U.S. stated that it was not carrying **nuclear weapons**. The U.S. refused to answer and canceled joint naval exercises that were to have been held with New Zealand and Australia.

1985 Feb. 14 The **Vietnamese invaders of Cambodia** surrounded a main base of the **Khmer Rouge** at Phnom Malai in their attempts to fully pacify the country under their control. In addition to the Khmer Rouge, other groups were fighting the invaders: the non-communist **Khmer People's National Liberation Front** and the **Armée Nationale Sihanoukist**, the followers of **Prince Sihanouk**. As the warfare continued, c.250,000 Cambodian civilians fled into neighboring Thailand.

1985 Mar. 1 In Uruguay, **Julio Maria Sanguinetta Cairolo** (b. Jan. 6, 1936) was sworn in as president. He was a member of the Colorado party.

1985 Mar. 6 In Beirut, **Lebanon**, in the continuing **civil war** between Christian and Muslim forces, a bomb exploded near the headquarters of the **Party of God**, an extremist Muslim group. It killed 62 people, wounded c.200, and destroyed a five-story building. Two days earlier, 15 had been killed and 55 injured in a blast near a mosque in Beirut, while on May 22 a **car bomb**, also in Beirut, killed 50 and wounded 172.

1985 Mar. 10 **Konstantin** [Ustinovich] **Chernenko** (b. Sept. 24, 1911), general secretary of the Russian Communist party and president of the U.S.S.R., died. Chernenko was succeeded (Mar. 11) as general secretary by **Mikhail S**[ergeyevich] **Gorbachev** (b. Mar. 2, 1931). Gorbachev, a full member (from 1980) of the politburo, at once said he would seek to improve the economy and bring about a reduction of armaments.

1985 Mar. 11 As the **Iran-Iraq War** neared the end of its fifth year, Iran opened another major offensive on the southern front that managed to cross the Tigris River but was then stopped with heavy losses. Both sides took to bombing each other's cities, and Iraq again bombed Iran oil installations on Kharg Island as well as steel and other manufacturing facilities. Intelligence experts in Europe estimated that Iran had lost between 420,000 and 580,000 soldiers, and Iraq c.300,000.

1985 Mar. 21 **South African police killed 19 blacks** when they fired into a crowd at Uitenhage, a town on the southeastern coast. The policy of **apartheid** and extremely poor economic conditions were making black South Africans more militant.

1985 Apr. 6 A military coup led by **Abdul Rahman Siwar al-Dahab** (b. 1934), the defense minister, ousted **Gaafar al-Nimeiry** as president of the **Sudan**, ending a 15-year rule. Two days earlier, a general strike against a government-decreed increase in the price of food and gasoline, as well as a demonstration against U.S. influence, had taken place.

1985 Apr. 11 **Enver Hoxha** (b. Oct. 16, 1908), the communist leader of Albania, died. After fighting against Germany and Italy as a guerrilla during World War II, Hoxha became the head of a hard-line Stalinist-type regime for 40 years. Hoxha was succeeded (Apr. 13) by **Ramiz Alia** (b. Oct. 18, 1925), who had held the title of president and now became the first secretary of the Communist Party of Labor.

1985 Apr. 15 The **South African** government announced that it was abolishing laws that forbade marriage or sexual relations between whites and non-whites.

1985 Apr. 24–28 Representatives from 82 nations of the **Non-Aligned Movement** met in Bandung, Indonesia, to commemorate the first meeting of the group held here in 1955. The Non-Aligned Movement then held (Sept. 4–9) a regular session in Luanda, Angola, with more than 100 countries represented. They urged economic sanctions against South Africa for its **apartheid** policy and condemned the U.S. for its anti-Sandinista policy in Nicaragua.

1985 May 5 In a brief ceremony that aroused international protests, **Ronald Reagan visited a military cemetery at Bitburg**, a West German town 16 miles north of Trier. The controversy arose after it was revealed that among the 2,000 soldiers buried in Bitburg there were 49 members of the Nazi SS. Jews and World War II veterans led the protest. Reagan, accompanied by **Helmut Kohl**, the West German chancellor, said his presence was meant to symbolize the reconciliation that had taken place since the war ended. Reagan's earlier visit to the site of the Bergen-Belsen concentration camp, near Celle in Lower Saxony, did little to quell the protests.

1985 June 14 The **hijacking of a Trans World Airline Boeing 727** by two Shiite Muslim terrorists resulted in some of the 153 people aboard being held hostage for 17 days. Of the passengers 104 were Americans. The plane was hijacked after taking off from Athens on a flight to Rome and was forced to fly to Beirut, Algiers, Beirut again, Algiers again, and finally on June 16 to Beirut once more. Women, children, and elderly passengers were released, but a U.S. navy diver, **Robert Dean Stethem**, had been shot to death (June 14), and his body thrown onto the airport tarmac. The remaining hostages, except for three crew members, were taken (June 17) from the plane to various locations in the Beirut suburbs. Israel released (June 24) 31 of the Shiite prisoners it held, and U.S. navy ships gathered offshore. Finally, the 39 Americans still held were freed (June 30) by their captors. A trial of one of the hijackers would be held a few years later.

1985 June 21 A grave in Embu, 25 miles south of São Paulo, Brazil, was found to contain the body of **Josef Mengele** (Mar. 16, 1911–Feb. 7, 1979), a physician who had sent thousands to their deaths in the Auschwitz concentration camp during World War II. On many of them he had first performed pseudo-medical experiments. After escaping from Germany at the end of the war, Mengele lived in the São Paulo area for many years. He drowned in 1979 and was buried under another man's name.

1985 July 10 In the harbor of Auckland, New Zealand, two **explosions sank the *Rainbow Warrior***, killing one man, a Dutch citizen. The ship, owned by the **Greenpeace** group, was preparing to depart to protest French nuclear weapons tests in the Pacific Ocean. A man and woman, both French security agents carrying Swiss passports, were arrested (July 23). When the **French government admitted** (Sept. 22) that **the boat had been blown up** on orders from officials in France, the French defense minister resigned and the head of the French intelligence agency was dismissed. A New Zealand court sentenced (Nov. 22) the two saboteurs to ten years in prison.

1985 July 20 Ending a three-day meeting in Addis Ababa, Ethiopia, the **Organization of African Unity** [OAU] asserted that most African nations were near economic collapse. The OAU blamed the situation on the nations of the developed world.

1985 July 24 The government of **India** and leaders of the **Sikhs** reached an agreement intended to end the turmoil of recent years. By the agreement, the Indian government was to change the boundaries of the Punjab, the Sikh area in northern India, to bring more Sikhs within it; to be more lenient in its treatment of the Sikhs who had been jailed during rioting; and to increase the compensation to Sikhs injured in 1984 anti-Sikh rioting. On Aug. 20 **Sant Harchand Singh** (b. 1928), president of Akali Dal (from 1980), the Sikh political party, was killed by extremist fellow Sikhs because he had signed the agreement.

1985 July 27 **Milton Obote** was removed as president of **Uganda** by a military coup. **Tito Okello** (b. 1914), a long-time associate of Obote, became (July 29) interim head of state.

1985 July 28 **Alan García Pérez** (b. May 23, 1949) became president of Peru, succeeding **Fernando Belaúnde Terry**. In an attempt to conserve resources and improve the shattered economy, García promised that no more than 10 percent of the nation's export profits would be used in servicing Peru's $14,-000,000,000 foreign debt.

1985 Aug. 27 The government of **Mohammeed Buhari**, president of **Nigeria** (from Dec. 31, 1983), was overthrown in a coup led by **Ibrahim Babangida** (b. Aug. 17, 1941), an army general, who had also been the prime mover in the coup that brought Buhari to the presidency. Babangida became president and chairman of the Armed Forces Ruling Council.

1985 Oct. 7 Four **Palestinian terrorists**, members of the **Palestine Liberation Front**, **seized** the Italian cruise ship *Achille Lauro*, with 80 passengers and a large crew, while it was at sea between Alexandria and Port Said, Egypt. They demanded the release of 50 Palestinians held by Israel. **Leon Klinghoffer**, a disabled American confined to a wheel chair, was killed on Oct. 8 and his body thrown overboard. The terrorists surrendered (Oct. 9) to Egyptian authorities after being promised safe passage. When the U.S. learned the terrorists were being flown out of Egypt, U.S. fighter planes intercepted (Oct. 10) the aircraft and forced it to land in Sicily where the hijackers were turned over to Italy for trial. The hijackers were found guilty (Nov. 18) on a weapons charge and sentenced from four to nine years in prison. The U.S., believing that **Mohammed Abul Abbas** (b. 1947), a Palestinian terrorist who had been on the intercepted airplane, had masterminded the hijacking of the ship, issued a warrant for his arrest, but Abbas slipped out of Italy bound for Yugoslavia, from where he disappeared.

1985 Oct. 11 The **Nobel Peace Prize** was awarded to a group named the **International Physicians for**

the Prevention of Nuclear War. This organization had been founded (1980) by **Bernard Lown** (b. June 7, 1921) of the U.S. and **Yevgeny I. Chazov** (b. June 10, 1929), of the U.S.S.R., both heart specialists. The prize was given to the organization because of its work in spreading information about the dangers of nuclear warfare.

1985 Oct. 27   **Ali Hassan Mwinyi** (b. May 8, 1925) was elected president of Tanzania and took office on Nov. 5. He succeeded **Julius Nyerere**.

1985 Nov. 6   About 60 members of the rebel **M-19 Movement invaded the Palace of Justice** in Bogotá, Colombia, and held about two dozen justices, among others, hostage. Army commandos stormed (Nov. 8) the building and in the ensuing battle c.100 people were killed, mainly by the guerrillas, including the president of the Supreme Court.

1985 Nov. 15   **Margaret Thatcher**, prime minister of Great Britain, and **Garret Fitzgerald**, prime minister of Ireland, signed an agreement intended to ease the Catholic-Protestant conflict in Northern Ireland. The agreement established an **Anglo-Irish confer-ence** with joint chairmen, and Ireland undertook to be responsible for the Irish Catholic minority in Northern Ireland. The parliaments of both countries approved the agreement.

1985 Nov. 17   **Lon Nol** (b. Nov. 13, 1913), a Cambodian military and political figure, died. Lon Nol served as premier (1970–1972) and president (1972–1975).

1985 Nov. 19–21   **Ronald Reagan and Mikhail Gorbachev met** for the first time in Geneva, Switzerland. No specific results were reported.

1985 Nov. 23   An Egyptian **Boeing 737 airliner was hijacked** on its flight between Cairo and Athens and forced to land on Malta. The next day, after two passengers had been killed, Egyptian commandos stormed the plane. In the fight, 57 of the 98 passengers and crew members were killed. **Palestinian ter-rorists** were blamed for the hijacking.

1985 Dec. 2   A court in Manila, the **Philippines**, acquitted all 26 persons accused of murder in the shooting death (Aug., 1983) of **Benigno S. Aquino, Jr.** Among those acquitted was **Fabian C. Ver**, former head of the armed forces, who later fled the country with Ferdinand Marcos.

1985 Dec. 9   Three former presidents of **Argentina** were convicted of crimes in connection with the sei-zure, torture, and murder of as many as 10,000 persons who had been accused of being subversives or leftists. About that many people, who became known as the *desaparecidos*, had disappeared in the past few years. **Jorge Videla** received a life sentence, and **Roberto Eduardo Viola** and **Leopoldo Galtieri** received lesser sentences.

1985 Dec. 15   **Carlos P[eña] Romulo** (b. Jan. 14, 1899), a Philippine diplomat, died. He was the last of the 51 high government officials who participated in the **founding of the United Nations** in 1945. Romulo was the first Asian president of the U.N. General Assembly (1949–1950).

1985 Dec. 27   In almost simultaneous **terrorist at-tacks at the Rome and Vienna airports**, Palestinian gunmen, using grenades and automatic weapons, killed 18 persons and wounded c.110. The attacks centered on Israel's El Al Airline ticket counters. Of the seven gunmen, four were killed and three were wounded and captured.

IV. ECONOMICS AND TRADE

1985 Feb. 25   **Tjalling Charles Koopmans** (b. Aug. 28, 1910), a Dutch economist, died. He shared the Nobel prize in economics in 1975 for his contributions to the theory of optimum allocation of resources. Koopmans taught at Yale University.

1985 Mar. 3   After almost a year, the **British coal miners' union voted to end its strike**, unsuccessful in the attempt to prevent the National Coal Board from closing unprofitable mines and putting thousands out of work.

1985 Mar. 29   Spain and Portugal were approved to become the 11th and 12th members of the **European Economic Community** [EEC] on Jan. 1, 1986.

1985 June 14   The government of **Argentina** announced "a profound reform of our economic system with the objective of reconstructing and modernizing Argentina." The reforms included the introduction of a new currency, salaries to be frozen as of July 1, and prices to be kept at the June 13 level.

1985 July 8   **Simon Kuznets** (b. Apr. 30, 1901), a Russian-born American economist, died. After emigrating (1922) to the U.S. he developed the concept of the **Gross National Product** [GNP] to measure a nation's economic output. His most important work was contained in *National Income and Its Composition, 1919 to 1938* (1941). Kuznets was awarded the **Nobel prize for economics** in 1971.

1985 Aug. 13 J[ohn] **Willard Marriott** (b. Sept. 17, 1900), an American hotel operator, died. By the time of his death the **Marriott** chain consisted of 143 hotels. In addition he controlled c.1,400 restaurants, including such chains as **Roy Rogers**, and an airline food catering service with 90 kitchens in various countries.

1985 Aug. 21 The **A.H. Robins Company**, makers of the **Dalkon Shield**, an interuterine birth control device, filed for bankruptcy as a result of suits brought against it by women who claimed to have been harmed by its use. Those suing said use of the device had caused pelvic infections, infertility, birth defects, and involuntary abortions. Payments by the manufacturer to settle suits plus establishment of a fund to pay later claims more than wiped out the net worth of the firm.

1985 Sept. 22 **Axel Springer** (b. May 12, 1912), West Germany's leading publisher, died. His company owned 18 newspapers and magazines, the most successful of which was *Bild Zeitung*, with a circulation of 4 million. In building Germany's largest post-World War II press organization, Springer gave voice to his right-wing views.

1985 Nov. 19 A jury in Houston, Texas, ruled that **Texaco, Inc. should pay the Pennzoil Company** $10,-530,000,000, plus interest, for interfering in a takeover deal in 1984. Pennzoil had made an agreement with the Getty Oil Company to buy 43 percent of it for $5,300,000,000. A few days later Texaco offered Getty $10,100,000,000. Pennzoil then sued Texaco, claiming that it had a legally binding contract with Getty. Eventually, the case was settled for far less— only $3,000,000,000.

1985 Dec. 8 Representatives of the 13 member nations of the **Organization of Petroleum Exporting Countries** [OPEC], meeting in Geneva, Switzerland, agreed to try to recapture OPEC's share of world markets by cutting prices.

1985 Dec. 11 The **General Electric Company** agreed to pay $6,280,000,000 for the **RCA Corporation**. The merger created the seventh largest industrial concern in the U.S. RCA was best known as the parent of the National Broadcasting Company [NBC].

V. RELIGION AND PHILOSOPHY

1985 Feb. 14 The **U.S. Assembly of Conservative Judaism** voted to permit women to become rabbis. **Amy Eilberg** (b. 1955) became the first such rabbi when she was ordained (May 12) at Jewish Theological Seminary, in New York City.

1985 Apr. 24 **Pope John Paul II** created 28 new cardinals, representing 19 countries. This action brought the College of Cardinals membership to 152, 60 of whom had been named by John Paul.

1985 July 4 **Willem Adolph Visser't Hooft** (b. Sept. 20, 1900), a Dutch clergyman, died. As a leader of the Protestant ecumenical movement, he was one of the most influential clergymen of his time. He was the general secretary of the **World Council of Churches** from its formation in 1938 until 1966. Ordained in the Dutch Reformed Church (1936), Visser't Hooft wrote c.20 books including *The Kingship of Christ* (1947) and *The Ecumenical Movement and the Racial Problem* (1954).

1985 July 17 **Susanne K. Langer** [nee Susanne Katherina Knauth] (b. Dec. 20, 1895), an American philosopher, died. She devoted much attention to analyzing the sources, forms, and effects of art. Her best-known book was *Philosophy in a New Key; A Study in the Symbolism of Reason, Rite, and Art* (1942), which was widely used as a textbook.

1985 July 31 **Eugene Carson Blake** (b. Nov. 7, 1906), an American Protestant leader and advocate of ecumenism, died. He was president of the National Council of Churches (1954–1957) and general secretary of the **World Council of Churches** (1966–1972).

1985 Dec. 8 An **Extraordinary Synod of Bishops** of the Roman Catholic Church ended two weeks of deliberations at the Vatican. When **Pope John Paul II** summoned the synod, many liberals feared the sessions would set back the accomplishments of **Vatican II**. The final document satisfied church liberals and conservatives. It stated that regional and national bishops' conferences were "useful, even necessary," and expressed agreement that a "universal catechism" for the official theology of the church should be developed.

VI. SCIENCE, EDUCATION, AND TECHNOLOGY

1985 The **United Nations Educational, Scientific and Cultural Organization** [**UNESCO**] estimated that there were **889 million adult illiterates** in the world, more than a quarter of the adult population of the world.

1985 July 22 A 23-week-old **fetus was partly removed from its mother's womb, operated on** to correct a blocked urinary tract, and then returned to the uterus. Nine weeks later the baby boy was born in good condition. **Michael R. Harrison,** a pediatric surgeon associated with the University of California at San Francisco, headed the team that performed the extraordinary operation.

1985 Aug. 31 [Frank] **Macfarlane Burnet** (b. Sept. 3, 1899), an Australian virologist, died. He contributed greatly to knowledge about viruses, including that of influenza, and was co-winner of the **Nobel prize for medicine or physiology** in 1960 for the discovery of acquired immunological tolerance to tissue transplants.

1985 Sept. 1 The wreck of the passenger liner *Titanic,* which sank on Apr. 15, 1912, was located at a depth of 12,100 feet in the Atlantic Ocean c.560 miles south of Newfoundland. The discovery was made by a combined U.S.-French group, headed by **Robert D. Ballard** (b. June 30, 1942) of the Woods Hole Oceanographic Institution of Falmouth, Massachusetts. The investigators concluded that the fatal iceberg had not cut a gash in the *Titanic,* as had long been thought, but had buckled some of the hull's steel plates, enabling water to rush in.

1985 Sept. 2 The **World Health Organization** [WHO] reported that there were 1,284 known cases of **AIDS** in Europe, 727 in Latin America, and 103 in Australia. The U.S. Centers for Disease Control said (Nov. 21) there were 14,739 known American cases and that 7,418 had died of AIDS. New York City led in the number of known cases anywhere in the world.

1985 Sept. 9 **Paul J**[ohn] **Flory** (b. June 19, 1910), a U.S. chemist, died. He won the **Nobel prize for chemistry** in 1974 for his work concerning the synthesis and nature of polymers. Flory's discoveries led to the commercial production of nylon and synthetic rubber.

1985 Sept. 30 **Charles Francis Richter** (b. Apr. 26, 1900), an American seismologist, died. He was the developer (1935) of what became known as the **Richter scale** for measuring the strength of earthquakes. The scale is logarithmic, so that an increase of one unit of magnitude means a tenfold increase in general motion.

1985 Dec. 13 Differences over the rights to tests used for determining whether or not a person has the virus for **AIDS** led to a patent suit by the French government. At stake was the money to be earned by devising and patenting a test to use on humans. A later agreement gave the parties equal shares of the royalties.

VII. ARTS AND LEISURE

1985 Feb. 22 **Efrem** [Alexandrovich] **Zimbalist** (b. Apr. 9, 1890), a Russian-born violin virtuoso, died. He made his debut in Berlin and London in 1907 and his American debut in 1911. Zimbalist composed songs and chamber music and did a great deal to revive interest in early violin music. He also served as head (1941–1968) of the Curtis Institute, in Philadelphia.

1985 Mar. 12 **Eugene Ormandy** (b. Nov. 18, 1899), a Hungarian-born conductor, died. At age five he became the youngest person ever admitted to the **Budapest Royal Academy**. He emigrated (1921) to the U.S. and directed (1931–1936) the Minneapolis Symphony Orchestra. He was most widely known for his term as conductor of the Philadelphia Orchestra (1938–1980).

1985 Mar. 28 **Marc Chagall** (b. July 7, 1887), a Russian-born painter who worked in Russia, France, Israel, and the U.S., died. Besides paintings, he produced ceramics, mosaics, and tapestry. Some of Chagall's art was in the Russian and Jewish traditions, and works dealing with the horrors of war were prominent. Among Chagall's murals are two he did for the Metropolitan Opera House, in New York City. He also illustrated books and designed (1945) costumes for **Igor Stravinsky's** ballet *The Firebird.*

1985 May 12   Jean Dubuffet (b. July 31, 1901), a French artist, died. **Art brut** was a term applied to some of his work which used such materials as sand and glass, as well as oils. His production was naive and humorous by turns, and increasingly took the form of collages. Dubuffet often did his works in series with an overall title, such as *Metro* (1943), which imitated a child's drawings, and *Corps de Dame* (1949–1950).

1985 July 16   Heinrich Böll (b. Dec. 21, 1917), a German writer who projected a pessimistic and strongly pacifistic view of the world, died. Böll's works included *Billiard um halb zehn* [*Billiards at Half-Past Nine*] (1959), *Ansichten eines Clowns* [*The Clown*] (1963), and *Die ver Lorene ohre der Katherina Blum* [*The Lost Honor of Katherina Blum*] (1974). Böll was awarded the **Nobel prize for literature** in 1972.

1985 Sept. 19   Italo Calvino (b. Oct. 15, 1923), an Italian writer of fiction, died. Among his writings were *Fiabe italiane* [*Italian Fables*] (1956), *Le cosmicomiche* [*Cosmocomics*] (1965), and *Se una notte d'inverno un viaggiatore* [*If on a Winter's Night a Traveler*] (1979). *Mr. Palomar*, published shortly after his death, showed his sly humor and originality at their best.

1985 Sept. 30   Simone Signoret [nee Simone Kaminker] (b. Mar. 25, 1921), a French stage and movie actress, died. In her native land she was one of the most popular actresses of the century. Her best performances in the movies were in *Room at the Top* (1958) and *Ship of Fools* (1965). In all Signoret appeared in more than 40 movies.

1985 Oct. 10 [George] **Orson Welles** (b. May 6, 1915), an American film producer, director, and actor, died. Welles is best known for *Citizen Kane* (1941), based on the life of the publisher William Randolph Hearst. Among other notable films he made were *The Magnificent Ambersons* (1942) and *Touch of Evil* (1958).

1985 Nov. 3 At the National Gallery of Art, Washington, "The Treasure Houses of Britain" opened, an exhibition of 750 objects representative of more than 500 years of collecting by British nobility and gentry.

1985 Nov. 15 A young American scholar **Gary Lynn Taylor** (b. Sept. 2, 1953) discovered in the Bod-leian Library at Oxford University, England, what he believed to be a hitherto unknown poem by **William Shakespeare**. He found the work, a nine-stanza love lyric, in a portfolio anthology the library had held since the mid-18th century. A scholarly debate over the poem's authorship has not yet been resolved.

1985 Nov. 28   Fernand [Paul] **Braudel** (b. Aug. 24, 1902), a French historian, died. He was a leader of the *Annales* **school**, which attempted to include in its studies all events, not just political and military ones. Braudel and his school thought it was important to know what people ate, how they went about their work, and how they handled their personal finances. The power of this kind of history was demonstrated with the publication of Braudel's *la Méditerranée et le monde méditerranéen à l'époque de Philip II* [*The Mediterranean and the Mediterranean World in the Age of Philip II*] (1949) followed by his three-volume work *Civilization matérielle, économie et capitalisme, xvième–xviiième siècle* [*Civilization and Capitalism, 15th–18th Century*] (1979).

1985 Dec. 7   Robert [Ranke] **Graves** (b. July 24, 1895), an English poet, novelist, and critic, died. His most popular novel was *I, Claudius* (1934). *The White Goddess* (1948) was a study of the mythological sources of poetry and later he translated, with comments, *The Greek Myths* (1955).

VIII. SPORTS, GAMES, AND SOCIETY

1985 Jan. 24 The **libel suit of Ariel Sharon**, former defense minister of Israel, **against** *Time* **magazine** ended. An article in the magazine of Feb. 21, 1983, had pictured Sharon as indirectly responsible for the massacre (1982) of hundreds of Palestinian refugees by Lebanon Christian Phalangists. The jury found the article was false and defamatory, but that *Time* was innocent of reckless disregard of the truth. No monetary damages were assessed, but the jury reprimanded *Time*.

1985 Feb. 18   William C. Westmoreland (b. Mar. 16, 1914), a former commander of U.S. forces in Vietnam, dropped his **libel suit against the Columbia Broadcasting System**. CBS had asserted in a documentary TV program that Westmoreland had deliberately underestimated the strength of enemy forces before the nearly disastrous North Vietnamese Tet offensive (Jan. 1968). In an out-of-court settlement CBS did not pay any damages but issued a statement that it never meant to denigrate the general's ability or patriotism. Both sides were to pay their own legal fees.

1985 Feb. 20   The Dáil, lower house of the Irish parliament, voted 83 to 80 to **legalize the sale of nonmedical contraceptives** to anyone over 18. The Senate also approved, and the law went into effect in March. Before 1979, when contraceptives were legalized for married couples if bought by prescription, they were illegal in Ireland.

1985 Apr. 21   **Rudi Gernreich** (b. Aug. 8, 1922), an Austrian-born fashion designer who worked in the U.S., died. He first attracted (1964) wide attention with a topless bathing suit for women. Gernreich continued to startle and please customers with psychodelic colors, mini-skirts, and safari suits.

1985 Apr. 23   The **Coca Cola Company** of the U.S. shocked the public by announcing that it was abandoning its 99-year-old recipe for its soft drink in favor of a new formula. Coke drinkers everywhere responded so unfavorably that Coca Cola announced (July 10) it would offer the drink made with the old formula as well as the new.

1985 July 16   Running at Nice, France, **Steve Cram** (b. Oct. 14, 1960) of Great Britain and **Said Aouita** (b. Nov. 2, 1960) of Morocco both **lowered the world 1,500-meter record**. Cram finished in 3 min. 29.67 sec., .04 sec. faster than Aouita. On July 27 at Oslo, Norway, Cram took more than a second off the record for the mile, running it in 3 min. 46.30 sec. Aouita then took the 1,500 meter record on Aug. 23 in West Berlin with a time of 3 min. 29.45 sec. On Aug. 21 at Zurich, Switzerland, **Mary Decker Slaney** (b. Aug. 4, 1958) of the U.S. set a new women's record for the mile with a time of 4 min. 16.71 sec.

1985 July 21   **Bernard Hinault**, a French professional bicycle racer, became the third man to win the **Tour de France** five times. He came in first in the 2,500-mile contest run over three weeks even though he broke his nose in a crash and spill during one day's run.

1985 Sept. 17   **Laura Ashley** (b. Sept. 7, 1925), an English fashion designer popular worldwide, died. Ashley's dresses gave an impression of softness and of flowing freely, pleasing both young and middle-aged women.

1985 Sept. 27   **Richard Ramirez** (b. 1960?), believed to be the serial killer known as the **"Night Stalker,"** was indicted in California on 68 charges, including 14 for murder and 22 for sexual assault. The case had possible elements of Satanism as pentagrams were found painted on the walls of some of his alleged victims' homes. Four years later, he was convicted of 13 murders and 30 other felonies.

1985 Nov. 9   After a 14-month contest, **Gary Kasparov** [orig.: Gary Weinstein] (b. Apr. 13, 1963) defeated the defending champion **Anatoly Karpov** in Moscow for the **world chess championship**. Karpov had held the title since 1975. Both players are Russian, and Kasparov at 22 was the youngest person ever to win the title.

1985 Dec. 5   A **record price for a single bottle of wine** was bid in London when a 1787 bottle of Château Lafitte brought $156,450 at auction. The winning bidder for the bottle, believed to have been set aside for **Thomas Jefferson**, was a representative of *Forbes* magazine. The wine was flown to New York and put on display.

1986

I. VITAL STATISTICS AND DEMOGRAPHICS

1986 July 7   The **World Population** Institute estimated that the world population would reach 5,000,000,000 today. It also said the world's population was growing at the rate of c.85 million a year. The U.S. Census Bureau forecast (Dec. 21) that by the year 2000 the population of the world would be 6,200,000,000. The U.N. 1986 State of the World Population Report estimated (May 9) that the world's urban population would increase from the present 2,000,000,000 to 5,100,000,000 by the year 2025. It further estimated that by the year 2000 there would be five supercities, with populations of 16 million or more: Mexico City, São Paulo, Tokyo-Yokohama, Calcutta, and Greater Bombay.

II. DISASTERS

1986 Mar. 31 A Mexicana Airlines **Boeing 727 crashed** c.100 miles northwest of Mexico City on a flight to Los Angeles. All 166 people aboard were killed. An investigation revealed there had been an explosion aboard the plane, but whether it was caused by a bomb could not be determined.

1986 Apr. 20 A **ferry sank** in a storm on the Dhaleswari River, in Bangladesh. Of the estimated 1,000 passengers aboard, it was feared that as many as 600 died. Later a similar ferry went down (May 25) in a storm on the Meghna River, in Bangladesh. There were c.1,000 passengers on this ship also and c.450 of them died.

1986 Apr. 26 An **accident at the the Chernobyl nuclear power plant** at Pripyat, in the Ukraine, U.S.S.R., shocked the world. One of four units of the facility had been shut down for overhaul when there was a sudden increase of power. A reaction caused the formation of hydrogen, which exploded, releasing large amounts of radioactive gases. Fire raged through the reactor, and part of the structure collapsed. Soviet officials did not seem fully aware of the extent of the danger and did not evacuate people from the area for 36 hours. They then moved out c.25,000 people living within a radius of six miles. A Soviet official said (May 2) reservoirs near the plant were contaminated, and the next day it was reported that 49,000 people in all had been evacuated. On June 5 the Soviets said the death toll had reached 26. Radiation six times the normal level was detected (Apr. 27) in Finland. Sweden (Apr. 28) and Poland (Apr. 29) also recorded unusual radiation levels. The **European Economic Community** [EEC] banned (May 12) the importation of fresh food from several countries within c.600 miles of Chernobyl. A study by the Lawrence Livermore National Laboratory of California found that the Chernobyl reactor gave out as much long-term radiation as the combined nuclear tests and bombs ever exploded. Three years later, tests showed dangerous levels of radiation in villages 200 miles from the explosion, and preparations were being made to evacuate another 100,000 people.

1986 Aug. 21 A **toxic gas that erupted from Lake Nios** in western Cameroon killed between 1,500 and 1,800 people, most of them dying in their sleep. The lake lies in the crater of a volcano that may have erupted, causing carbon dioxide to rise through the waters of the lake.

1986 Aug. 31 A Soviet passenger vessel *Admiral Nakhimov* and a freighter *Pyotr Vasev* collided eight miles outside the Black Sea port of Novorossisk. Of the 888 passengers and 346 crew members aboard the passenger ship, which sank, 398 drowned.

1986 Sept. 16 A **fire that created toxic gas** in the Kinross gold mine 60 miles east of Johannesburg, South Africa, killed 177 miners, all but five of them blacks. The General Mining Union Corporation, owner of the mine, admitted (Sept. 19) to flaws in safety procedures.

1986 Oct. 3 Fire broke out on a Soviet nuclear submarine c.1,200 miles east of New York City in the Atlantic. A Russian merchant ship took the sub in tow, but the sub sank (Oct. 6) after the crew had been evacuated, taking with it to the bottom two nuclear reactors and 32 nuclear warheads.

1986 Oct. 10 An **earthquake** registering 5.4 on the Richter scale did great damage to San Salvador, capital of El Salvador. The government reported 976 dead, 8,176 injured, c.31,000 homeless, and property damage of up to $1,000,000,000.

1986 Dec. 25 An Iraqi Airways **Boeing 737 crashed** and burned on a remote airstrip in Saudi Arabia shortly after being hijacked by several gunmen. Iraqi officials put (Dec. 31) the death toll at 67. The plane was enroute from Baghdad to Aman, Jordan, when the terrorists exploded at least two grenades. Iraq accused Iran of the hijacking.

1986 Dec. 31 A **fire** in the luxury Dupont Plaza Hotel in San Juan, Puerto Rico, killed 97 guests and injured more than 140. On Apr. 24, 1987, three former employees of the hotel pleaded guilty to charges of arson.

III. POLITICS AND WAR

1986 Jan. 13 A coup in the **People's Democratic Republic of Yemen** [South Yemen] turned into a 12-day civil war that resulted in the ouster of **Ali Nasser Mohammed al-Hassani**, the president, and the deaths of perhaps 10,000 people. Hassani fled to neighboring Yemen and his place was taken (Jan. 24) by **Haidar Abu Bakr al-Attas**. Hassani was sentenced (Dec. 12) to death in absentia on charges of treason.

1986 Jan. 20   Justin Metsino Lekhanya (b. Apr. 7, 1938), the army commander of **Lesotho**, led a coup that overthrew [Joseph] **Leabua Jonathan**, the prime minister.

1986 Jan. 29   Yoweri [Kaguta] **Museveni** (b. 1914), leader of the guerrilla group called the National Resistance Army [NRA], became president of **Uganda** when he overthrew the regime of **Tito Okello**. An armed struggle had been going on for several years against Okello and his predecessor **Milton Obote**.

1986 Feb. 1   Alva [Reimer] **Myrdal** (b. Jan. 31, 1900), a Swedish diplomat and government official, died. She devoted a large part of her life's work to the promotion of disarmament. She was director (1951–1955) of the department of social science of **UNESCO** and later represented Sweden at U.N. disarmament talks in Geneva. Her work was recognized when she shared the **Nobel Peace Prize** in 1982.

1986 Feb. 7   In the face of growing anti-government violence, **Jean-Claude Duvalier** (b. July 3, 1951), the president of **Haiti** (from 1971), flew to exile in France. A 19-member provisional government was formed with **Henri Namphy** (b. Nov. 2, 1932), commander of the armed forces, as its head.

1986 Feb. 10   Iran launched an offensive against Iraq in the ongoing war in the area of the confluence of the Tigris and Euphrates rivers. The oil port of Fao was captured. Late in the year Iraq repulsed another Iranian attack in the Fao area. Throughout the year Iraq used its superiority in the air to do considerable damage to Iranian oil installations.

1986 Feb. 16   Mario [Alberto Nobre] **Soares** (b. Dec. 7, 1924) was elected president of Portugal in a runoff election. He had previously been prime minister twice (1976–1978, 1983–1985). A candidate of the Socialist party, Soares became the first civilian president since 1926.

1986 Feb. 25   Ferdinand Marcos, president of the **Philippines** for 20 years, was flown to exile, first to Guam and later to Hawaii. A presidential election had been held (Feb. 7) with Marcos running for reelection against **Corazon C**[ojuangco] **Aquino** (b. Jan. 25, 1933), the widow of **Benigno S. Aquino, Jr.** On Feb. 15 the National Assembly, under Marcos's control, had declared him the winner. The election fraud proved to be the straw that broke his long

dictatorship. Aquino, whose claim to victory in the election was legitimate, was proclaimed the new president.

1986 Feb. 28   Olaf Palme (b. Jan. 30, 1927), prime minister of **Sweden**, was assassinated as he and his wife walked home from a movie in Stockholm. Two bullets were fired, one of them grazing Mrs. Palme. There was no indication of who the assassin might be and no discernible motive. The investigation of the killing was muddled and much criticized. After **Carl Gustav Christer Petterson** (b. 1947?), a convicted killer, was arrested, convicted, and sentenced to life imprisonment, an appeals court overturned the conviction and ordered Petterson released.

1986 Mar. 6   A U.S. demand that the U.S.S.R. reduce the size of the Soviet, Ukrainian, and Byelorussian missions at the UN began a **year of mutual expulsions and spy charges**. During October and November, the U.S.S.R. complied with the demand, but retaliated with comparable requests that the U.S. reduce the number of its representatives in the U.S.S.R. On Aug. 23 **Gennadi F. Zakharov**, a Russian physicist employed at the U.N., was arrested by the U.S. on espionage charges; on Aug. 30 the Russians arrested **Nicholas S. Daniloff** (b. Dec. 30, 1934), an American journalist, on similar charges. On Sept. 29 Daniloff left Russia, and on the next day Zakharov left the U.S.

1986 Mar. 16   Gaullists of the Rassemblement pour la République [RPR] and centrists of the Union de la Démocracie Française [UDF] won a majority of the seats in the National Assembly of France. As a result **Jacques** [René] **Chirac** (b. Nov. 29, 1932), leader of the RPR, became (Mar. 20) prime minister. The Socialist party, which had held a majority, was defeated and so France had a socialist president, **François Mitterand**, and a right-leaning prime minister sharing power.

1988 Apr. 10   A period of unrest and violence began in **Pakistan** with the return from exile in England of **Benazir Bhutto** (b. June 21, 1953), the daughter of Zulfikar Ali Bhutto, former prime minister. As the new leader of the Pakistan Peoples's party, she bitterly opposed **Mohammed Zia ul-Haq**, president of Pakistan. Demonstrations in opposition to the ruling regime culminated (Aug. 14) in a riotous rally at Lahore. Bhutto was arrested (Aug. 24) and sentenced to 30 days in prison, but she was released early.

1986 Apr. 11 The **U.S.S.R. announced it was ending its unilateral moratorium** (from Aug. 5, 1985) **on underground nuclear testing** because continued American testing was a threat to its security. The U.S. had conducted nine underground tests since Russia's moratorium, two of them in 1986.

1986 Apr. 14 **American aircraft hit installations in Libya.** The night attacks were carried out by 18 F-111 air force planes flying from Great Britain, which were refueled in the air enroute because France refused to let them fly over its airspace. Also, 15 navy planes from two aircraft carriers in the Mediterranean Sea took part. In all five bases were bombed, three near Tripoli and two near Benghazi. One F-111 was lost and its crew presumed dead. The U.S. said the attack was retaliation for the bombing (Apr. 5) of a discothèque in West Berlin in which an American soldier and a Turkish woman were killed, and c.200 injured. Libya said the attack killed 15 and wounded 16. Among the dead was said to be a 15-month-old adopted daughter of **Muammar al-Qaddafi**, the Libyan leader.

1986 Apr. 18 The government of **South Africa** announced that the pass laws regulating where blacks could live and work would no longer be enforced. The government further announced (Apr. 23) it would abolish laws prohibiting blacks from moving freely within the country and from moving into to the black sections of cities.

1986 Apr. 25 **Mswati III** (b. 1968) was installed as king of **Swaziland**, Africa. Mswati was one of nearly 70 sons and 20 daughters his father sired with c.50 wives. The new king had studied at an English boarding school.

1986 May 5 The heads of government of Canada, France, Great Britain, Italy, Japan, the U.S., and West Germany, meeting in Tokyo, adopted a strong statement condemning **terrorism**. Among specific steps, the seven agreed to refuse to export arms to nations that support terrorism, to improve extradition procedures, and to institute stricter immigration and visa controls with regard to nationals of countries suspected of supporting terrorism. In the previous three months, there had been five bomb explosions in Paris and one aboard a French train, all blamed on Arab terrorists. There were eight more such bombings in France in the course of the year, killing four and injuring 135. Great Britain broke (Oct. 24) diplomatic relations with Syria because

there was evidence that Syrian diplomats and intelligence agents were connected with an attempt to bomb an Israeli airliner in England.

1986 May 21 The Christian Democratic Appeal party won a plurality of two over the Labor party in parliamentary elections in the Netherlands, enabling **Ruud** [Rudolphus Franciscus Maria] **Lubbers** (b. May 7, 1939) to form a coalition with the People's Party for Freedom and Democracy, a liberal party. Lubbers, who had first been elected prime minister on Nov. 4, 1982, continued in office.

1986 June 8 **Kurt Waldheim** was elected to a six-year term as president of **Austria** in a runoff election in which he won 53.9 percent of the vote. Waldheim's campaign for the largely ceremonial post aroused international controversy because of accusations against him stemming from his service in World War II. It was charged that while a low-ranking German army officer in the Balkans he served with a unit that carried out brutal reprisals against Yugoslavian guerrillas and that sent thousands of Greek Jews to Nazi death camps. Waldheim, a former secretary general of the U.N., denied any wrongdoing. The U.S. justice department in 1987 placed Waldheim on a list of people barred from entering the U.S.

1986 June 27 **Bettino** [Benedetto] **Craxi** (b. Feb. 24, 1934) resigned as prime minister of **Italy** after a secret vote the day before in the Chamber of Deputies went against him, but he remained in the post as caretaker leader. The leaders of the parties that made up the Craxi government agreed (July 29) to reorganize their coalition with Craxi continuing as prime minister but that he, a Socialist, would resign in Mar. 1987 in favor of a Christian Democrat.

1986 July 10 **Le Duan** (b. Apr. 7, 1908), secretary general of the Vietnamese Communist party and a North Vietnamese leader in the war against South Vietnam, died. In recent years Le Duan had urged economic incentives to spur the country's lagging productivity.

1986 July 28 In **Lebanon a bomb planted in an auto exploded** in a Christian suburb of Beirut, killing 31 people and wounding 120. Within two weeks the total of deaths by bombings, carried out by several different factions since the beginning of the year, reached 137. In addition, street fighting in the same period killed more people than the bombings. The

Syrian army, the army of the Lebanese government, the Christian Phalangists, the PLO, and the Shiah's Amal militia were all involved. The fighting between the PLO and Amal by itself accounted for 462 dead and 1,056 wounded in bitter fighting between Nov. 24 and Dec. 10.

1986 Aug. 2–3   Parliamentary elections in **Malaysia** gave the National Front coalition headed by **Mahathir Mohammad** (b. Dec. 20, 1925), the prime minister, 148 of the 177 seats in parliament, and Mahathir's own party, the United Malays National Organization, accounted for 83 of them.

1986 Aug. 7   **Virgilio Barco Vargas** (b. Sept. 17, 1921) was inaugurated president of Colombia, having won election (May 26) by a very large majority. Barco pledged to combat poverty and end the violence that had plagued Colombia for 30 years. He also promised to battle the narcotics traffic.

1986 Aug. 13   The U.S. opposition to the Marxist Sandinista regime in **Nicaragua** was indicated when the American Congress voted to send $100 million worth of military supplies to the **Contras.**

1986 Aug. 16   **Joaquin Balaguer** (b. Sept. 1, 1907) was inaugurated president of the **Dominican Republic** for the fifth time, having won the election of May 16. Balaguer, considered to have close ties to the business interests of the country, pledged to show no favoritism.

1986 Aug. 22   **Celal Bayar** (b. May 15, 1882), a founder of the Turkish Republic and president of Turkey (1950–1960), died. He was the last surviving member of the Grand National Assembly that held its first meeting on Apr. 23, 1920, in Ankara to begin a fight against the Ottoman Empire (1326–1920) for Turkish independence.

1986 Aug. 31   **Urho** [Kaleva] **Kekkonen** (b. Sept. 3, 1900), president of Finland (1956–1981), died. Kekkonen managed to stay on good terms with the nations of Western Europe while preserving Finland's neutrality and refusing to give in to all the demands the Soviets made on his small country.

1986 Sept. 6   Two **Arab terrorists broke into a synagogue** in the Jewish quarter of İstanbul, Turkey, **killing 21 worshippers.** The explosions of their grenades set fire to the synagogue, which had recently been refurbished. Both terrorists were found dead.

Responsibility for the attack was claimed by the Fatah Revolutionary Council.

1986 Sept. 22   The **Conference on Confidence and Security Building Measures and Disarmament in Europe,** which had been meeting in Stockholm, Sweden, since Jan. 1984, ended with an agreement on **arms control.** Attending the conference were 35 countries, including all the NATO and Warsaw Pact nations. Advance notices and annual calendars of planned military movements would hereafter be provided and would cover all troop movements from the Atlantic Ocean to the Ural Mountains.

1986 Oct. 10   **Shimon Peres,** prime minister of Israel, resigned to make way for **Yitzhak Shamir** to replace him in accordance with an agreement made between Peres's Labor party and Shamir's Likud bloc in Sept. 1984.

1986 Oct. 12   **Ronald Reagan** and **Mikhail S. Gorbachev** ended two days of talks in Reykjavik, Iceland, in complete disagreement and on an acrimonious note. They had seemed near agreement on a reduction of nuclear weapons, but Reagan refused to compromise in the least on his proposed **Strategic Defense Initiative** [SDI], and Gorbachev refused to make any agreement without a compromise.

1986 Oct. 14   **Elie Wiesel** (b. Sept. 20, 1938), a Romanian-born American human rights activist, was awarded the **Nobel Peace Prize.** The award cited him as "one of the most important spiritual leaders and guides in an age when violence, repression, and racism continue to characterize the world." Wiesel survived two Nazi concentration camps during World War II and came to the U.S. in 1976. *La Nuit* [*Night*] (1958) told of his wartime experiences.

1986 Oct. 15   **Hossain Mohammed Ershad,** who had first come to power in **Bangladesh** in Mar. 1982, in a coup, was elected president. His opponents boycotted the election and claimed the results were fraudulent. Ershad's party had already won (May 7) a parliamentary election, taking 183 of 330 seats, including all 30 that had been reserved for women.

1988 Oct. 19   **Samora M**[oïsés] **Machel** (b. Sept. 23, 1933), president of **Mozambique** since it won its independence from Portugal in 1975, was killed in an air crash. He was flying home from a meeting in Zambia when his plane went down in South African territory. Machel was succeeded (Nov. 3) by **Joa-**

quim A[lberto] **Chissano** (b. Oct. 22, 1939), who had been foreign minister (from 1975).

1986 Oct. 22 **Ye Jianying** (b. 1897), a veteran of the communist regime in China, died. He participated in the **Long March** (1934–1935) that forged the Red army and the Mao Tse Tung leadership. Ye was defense minister (1975–1978) with the rank of marshal, and chairman of the Standing Committee of the National People's Congress (1978–1983).

1986 Oct. 31 The president of **Laos**, **Prince Souphanouvong**, resigned for reasons of health. He was succeeded by **Phoumi Vongvichit**, who had been deputy premier. The prince had led the communist **Pathet Lao** that came to power in 1975 after 20 years of fighting against the royal government.

1986 Nov. 6 The U.S. government admitted it had been sending **military materiel to Iran** in the hope of influencing moderates in the government there and of securing the release of Americans held hostage in Lebanon. Beginning on Aug. 30, 1985, weapons had been sent indirectly through Israel. **Ronald Reagan** admitted (Nov. 12) the operation had taken place but defended the "secret diplomatic initiative" while ordering (Nov. 19) that there be no further shipments of arms to Iran. **Edwin Meese 3rd** (b. Dec. 2, 1931), the attorney general, revealed (Nov. 25) that up to $30 million of the money received from Iran had been illegally turned over to the Nicaraguan rebels [**Contras**]. The president announced the same day that **John M. Poindexter** (b. Aug. 12, 1936), his national security adviser, had resigned, and that **Oliver L. North** (b. Oct. 7, 1943), a marine officer and assistant to Poindexter, had been dismissed. These two had been the key planners and operators of the secret deals. Reagan announced (Nov. 26) the appointment of a three-man panel headed by John G. Tower (b. Sept. 29, 1925), a former senator, to investigate the National Security Council staff. It was revealed on the following day that North had destroyed a number of documents when the affair was first disclosed. As criticism mounted, Reagan asked (Dec. 2) for the appointment of an independent prosecutor, and **Lawrence E**[dward] **Walsh** (b. Jan. 8, 1912), a former federal judge and Vietnam peace negotiator, was named to be the special prosecutor on Dec. 19.

1986 Nov. 8 **Vyacheslav M**[ikhailovich] **Molotov** (b. Mar. 9, 1890), one of **Joseph Stalin**'s closest aides, died. He took part in the Bolshevik [October] Revolution of 1917. Molotov was best known to the West as the cold, immovable foreign secretary (1939–1949, 1953–1955). However, after the Soviet repudiation of Stalin, Molotov was denounced and expelled (1962–1984) from the Communist party.

1986 Dec. 15 An election in **Trinidad and Tobago** ended 30 continuous years in power of the People's National Movement, which had ruled ever since independence from Great Britain. The victorious party was the National Alliance for Reconstruction, which took all but 3 of the 36 seats in the House of Representatives. The new prime minister was **Arthur N**[apoleon] **R**[aymond] **Robinson** (b. Dec. 16, 1926).

1986 Dec. 17 The three most important political leaders of **Vietnam** resigned: **Pham Van Dong** (b. Mar. 1, 1906), the prime minister; **Truong Chinh**, general secretary of the Communist party and president; and **Le Duc Tho** (Oct. 14, 1911–Oct. 13, 1990), an influential member of the ruling group. **Ngyuen Van Linh** (b. July 1, 1915), long a political administrator, was named (Dec. 18) party secretary. Later **Pham Hung** (June 11, 1912–Mar. 10, 1988) became (June 18, 1987) prime minister. **Vo Chi Cong** (b. 1914) took the title of president which Chinh had held. Le Duc Tho, chiefly responsible for negotiating an armistice (Jan. 27, 1973) that eventually ended the Vietnam War, was awarded the **Nobel Peace Prize** in 1973, which he shared with **Henry A. Kissinger**, who negotiated for the Americans. Le Duc Tho refused the award because the fighting in Vietnam was still continuing between the North and South Vietnamese.

1986 Dec. 20 **Libyan forces invaded northern Chad** and attacked guerrilla forces of **Goukouni Oueddei**, a former president of Chad whom Libya had previously supported against his enemy **Hissène Habré**, the current president. In October, Goukouni and **Muammar el-Qaddafi**, the dictator of Libya, had had a falling out and Goukouni was shot and wounded. He was still being held under house arrest in Tripoli. The invading Libyans were opposed by both the guerrillas and the Chadian government forces.

1986 Dec. 29 [Maurice] **Harold Macmillan** (b. Feb. 10, 1894), former prime minister of Great Britain (1957–1963), died. He was first elected to Parliament in 1924 as a member of the Conservative party. He held cabinet posts and during World War II he was Britain's chief diplomat in the Mediterranean region, where he carried out delicate missions with great skill.

1986 Dec. 30 **Japan** abandoned a ten-year-old policy that held military expenditures to no more than one percent of the Gross National Product [GNP] and announced that the 1987 **arms budget** was $22,000,000,000, or c.1.004 percent of GNP.

IV. ECONOMICS AND TRADE

1986 Mar. 13 **Barber B**[enjamin] **Conable, Jr.** (b. Nov. 2, 1922), a former member of the U.S. House of Representatives (1964–1984), was nominated by **Ronald Reagan** to become president of the **Bank for International Reconstruction and Development** [World Bank]. Conable took office (July 1) for a term of five years.

1986 Apr. 18 **Guiness P.L.C.**, a brewing company, acquired the **Distillers Company**, England's largest Scotch whisky and gin concern. Guiness paid $4,100,000,000, and the combined organization had annual sales of more than $4,500,000,000.

1986 July 15 Great Britain and the Soviet Union reached an agreement settling the matter of **czarist Russia's bonds**, in default ever since the Bolshevik Revolution of 1917. To pay $600 million claimed by c.37,000 British individuals and companies, only about $68 million would be available, and the $1,350,000,000 claimed by the British government would not be paid at all. Russia claimed losses in Britain of $3,500,000,000 but was to receive only about $4 million. The Russian claims stemmed from the British seizure of Russian assets

1986 Sept. 15 The eighth round of negotiations under the **General Agreement on Tariffs and Trade** [GATT] began in Punta del Este, Uruguay. At the top of the list of problems to be addressed was improving "the competitive environment of agriculture" by a gradual reduction of governmental subsidies.

1986 Dec. 18 **Michel Camdessus** (May 1, 1933), a French banking expert, was elected managing director of the **International Monetary Fund** [IMF] by the executive board. Camdessus was a former French finance minister and chief of the Banque de France, the central bank.

1986 Dec. 20 Meeting in Geneva, Switzerland, representatives of the **Organization of Petroleum Exporting Countries** [OPEC] agreed to cut their production enough so that the price of oil would quickly rise to $18 a barrel. Iraq refused because it would be allocated a smaller daily production quota than Iran, with which it was at war. By the end of the year oil was near $18 a barrel.

1986 Dec. 24 For the first time since the establishment (1949) of the communist People's Republic of China, a **stock market** was to open (Jan., 1987) in Peking, the capital.

V. RELIGION AND PHILOSOPHY

1986 Apr. 2 Curators at the New Orleans Museum of Art found inside a Buddhist sculpture **Chinese manuscripts that appeared to date to the 12th century.** The papers, which apparently had not been disturbed for 800 years, included three sutras, or scriptures, printed by woodblocks on paper of high quality. One was inscribed with a Chinese date corresponding to 1155 A.D.

1986 Apr. 5 The **Vatican** issued a document entitled "**Christian Freedom and Liberation**," which defended the right of the poor to struggle against injustice, but it also warned against totalitarianism and revolution that led to "new forms of slavery." It defended the right of the oppressed to revolt, but said some current movements of the left could lead to new tyrannies rather than liberation.

1986 May 20 Geneva, Switzerland, began a celebration of the **450th anniversary of its acceptance of the Protestant Reformation** with an ecumenical mass in Protestant Saint Peter's Cathedral.

1986 May 30 **Pope John Paul II** issued his fifth encyclical, entitled **Dominum et Vivificantem** [*The Lord and Giver of Life*]. It was a reflection of the Pope's thinking about the Holy Spirit, the mysterious third person of the Holy Trinity. John Paul also took the occasion to criticize the modern world for its materialism and ideologies that he saw as inimical to a spiritual vision of humanity.

1986 Aug. 24 Three **Lutheran Churches in the U.S. voted to merge** effective on Jan. 1, 1988: the Lutheran Church in America, the American Lutheran Church, and the Association of Evangelical Lutherans.

1986 Oct. 22 At a synod of 400 delegates the white **Dutch Reformed Church** of South Africa adopted a resolution denouncing **apartheid**. It said, "The church is convinced that forced separation of people cannot be seen as a prescription from the Bible."

1986 Oct. 28 The **Vatican** issued new **guidelines for Catholic priests in their dealings with homosexuals.** It recommended that homosexuals be encouraged to practice the sacraments and, though psychological and medical factors must be taken into account, homosexuals should recognize the sinfulness of their acts as a first step toward reconciliation with the church.

VI. SCIENCE, EDUCATION, AND TECHNOLOGY

1986 Jan. 28 The U.S. space shuttle *Challenger* **blew apart** 74 seconds after blast-off from Cape Kennedy, Florida, killing **Michael J[ohn] Smith** (b. Apr. 30, 1945), **Francis R[ichard] Scobee** (b. May 19, 1939); **Ellison S. Onizuka** (b. June 24, 1946), **Ronald E. McNair** (b. Oct. 12, 1950), **Gregory B. Jarvis** (b. Aug. 24, 1944), and **Judith A. Resnick** (b. Apr. 5, 1949). A special passenger was also killed: [Sharon] **Christa McAuliffe** (b. Sept. 2, 1948), a Concord, New Hampshire, school teacher, who had been chosen to be the first private citizen to fly in a space shuttle. A 13-member commission appointed by President Ronald Reagan said (June 8) the failure of a booster rocket was the specific cause of the explosion. The commission criticized both the National Aeronautics and Space Administration [NASA] and the manufacturer of the rocket, Morton Thiokol, Inc., for managerial mistakes and for failing to do anything about problems that had arisen previously with the solid-fuel booster rocket.

1986 Feb. 20 France and Great Britain agreed to build a **tunnel beneath the English Channel** to connect the two countries. It was to run from Cheriton, near Folkestone, England, to Fréthun, near Calais, France. The tunnel, 31 miles long with one tube in each direction for traffic and a third for service, was to be used by trains only, but the trains will carry autos as well as passengers and freight. The trip was to take about 30 minutes.

1986 Mar. 6 **Halley's Comet** made its first appearance since 1910 and for the first time was subject to close-up viewing by unmanned satellites. First to examine it was a Russian probe *Vega I*, which flew within 5,600 miles of it; on Mar. 14 *Giotto*, a probe of the European Space Agency, came within 335 miles of it; and on Mar. 19 *Vega II*, another Russian spacecraft, passed within 5,126 miles. The comet proved to have a two-lobe nucleus, somewhat like a peanut, and to be covered with dust-coated ice. It was about 9 by 5 miles in size, much larger than had been thought.

1986 Apr. 18 Marcel Dassault [orig.: Marcel Bloch] (b. Jan. 2, 1892), a French aviation pioneer, died. He began his career at the end of World War I and by 1936 was so successful that the Popular Front government nationalized his company. After World War II Dassault created the successful **Mystère** and the delta-winged **Mirage**, which have been sold to air forces around the world.

1986 July 8 Hyman G[eorge] Rickover (b. Jan. 27, 1900), the "father of the nuclear navy," died. Born in Russian-Poland, he was brought to the U.S. in 1904. A graduate of the U.S. Naval Academy, he became interested in the possibilities of nuclear power and proposed that it be used to propel submarines. On Jan. 21, 1954, the submarine *Nautilus* was launched, the world's first undersea ship powered by nuclear energy. Rickover retired as a four-star admiral after 63 years of service, more than any other naval officer in American history.

1986 July 14 Raymond [Fernand] Loewy (b. Nov. 5, 1893), a French-born American designer, died. His first success was (1929) the redesign of an American dictating machine. Eventually he give a sleek, streamlined look to hundreds of machines, creating in the process the profession of **industrial design.** Among his creations were the first all-welded locomotive, a non-metal lipstick tube to save metal during World War II, and the classic glass-and-metal Lever House in New York City.

1986 July 24 Fritz A[lbert] Lipmann (b. June 12, 1899), a German-born American biochemist, died. In 1945 he isolated coenzyme A, a vital substance in converting fatty acids, steroids, amino acids, and hemoglobins into energy. His work provided a basis for understanding how cells convert food into energy. Lipmann was a co-winner of the **Nobel prize in physiology or medicine** in 1953.

1983 Aug. 3 **Beryl Markham** (b. Oct. 26, 1902), an English aviation pioneer, died. She became (Sept. 4–5, 1936) the first woman to fly the Atlantic Ocean solo from east to west. She was slightly injured. Markham spent much of her life in Kenya, where she engaged in big game hunting and bred horses. She published her memoirs as *West With the Night*, (1942) which became a bestseller when it was re-issued in 1983.

1986 Sept. 19 U.S. government officials announced that an experimental drug prolonged the lives of some persons suffering from **AIDS**. The drug, **azidothymidine [AZT]**, had first been synthesized in the 1960s, when it was hoped it could be used against cancer. The World Health Organization [WHO] announced (Nov. 20) it was beginning a worldwide campaign against AIDS, which it called "a health disaster of pandemic proportions."

1986 Oct. 4 The **Netherlands** put into operation a **technologically advanced ocean barrier**: 62 gates, each weighing 500 tons, 17 ft. thick, and 130 ft. wide. The barrier stretched for a mile and a half across the three channels of the Eastern Scheldt River in western Holland. It was estimated that only once in five years was there likely to be a storm fierce enough to require closing the barrier.

1986 Oct. 22 **Albert Szent-Györgyi** (b. Sept. 16, 1893), a Hungarian-born American biologist, died. His work (1928–1932) led to the isolation of vitamin C [ascorbic acid]. He wrote *Bioenergetics* (1957).

1986 Dec. 23 The **first non-stop flight around the world without refueling** was completed at Edwards Air Force Base, California. The 25,012-mile flight of *Voyager* took 9 days, 3 min., and 44 sec. The pilot was **Richard G. Rutan** and the co-pilot **Jeana Yeager** (b. 1952?). The plane, made of stiffened paper and plastic, carried about five times its weight in fuel, and when it landed there were only five gallons of usable fuel left.

1986 Dec. 31 Scientists at the University of Houston and at Bell Laboratories in New Jersey reported significant advances in the attempt to achieve **superconductivity**, a phenomenon at which materials lose all resistance to electricity. The Houston researchers reported that, by using very high pressures and a combination of elements, superconductivity had been achieved at temperatures higher than previously experienced.

VII. ARTS AND LEISURE

1986 Jan. 4 **Christopher** [William Bradshaw] **Isherwood** (b. Aug. 26, 1904), an English novelist and playwright, died. He lived (1929–1933) in Berlin and from his experiences there came *Goodbye to Berlin* (1939). One of the sketches in the book was dramatized by **John Van Druten** as *I Am a Camera* (1951). It was turned into a successful stage musical *Cabaret* (1968), which in turn became (1972) a hit movie. With **W.H. Auden**, a life-long friend, Isherwood wrote a play *Ascent of F6* (1936), with symbolism concerning political leadership.

1986 Feb. 26 **Robert Penn Warren** (Apr. 24, 1905– Sept. 15, 1989), an American novelist, poet, and critic, was appointed the **first official poet laureate of the U.S.** The appointment was made by **Daniel Boorstin** (b. Oct. 1, 1914), Librarian of Congress. Warren was a founder and editor of the *Southern Review* (1935–1942). His best-known novel was *All the King's Men* (1946), with a corrupt southern governor as the major character.

1986 Mar. 6 **Georgia O'Keeffe** (b. Nov. 15, 1887), an American artist, died. She had her first one-woman show in 1916 and continued to paint for another 60 years, in the process becoming an artist of unique accomplishments. She lived during much of her career in New Mexico where her subject matter was mostly bones, rocks, and mountains. She was especially known, however, for her paintings of flowers, large, lush, and often with an atmosphere of sexuality. Among such works were *Black Iris* (1926), *Jack-in-the-Pulpit No. 2* (1930), and *Sunflower, New Mexico II* (1935).

1986 Mar. 18 **Bernard Malamud** (b. Apr. 26, 1914), an American novelist and short-story writer, died. *The Natural* (1952), his first novel, looked at the American hero as baseball player. *A New Life* (1961) was a satirical treatment of a Jewish college professor at a small college. Malamud's collections of short stories included *The Magic Barrel* (1958) and *Rembrandt's Hat* (1973).

1986 Mar. 30 **James** [Francis] **Cagney, Jr.** (b. July 17, 1899), an American movie actor who began his career in vaudeville, died. Cagney became noted for his gangster roles, as in *The Roaring Twenties* (1939), and his vaudeville experience saw brilliant use in *Yankee Doodle Dandy* (1942), a movie about **George M. Cohan.**

1986 Apr. 12   Valentin [Petrovich] **Katayev** (b. Jan. 28, 1897), a Russian novelist, short-story writer, and playwright, died. Although many of his works took a satirical view of Soviet Russia, they were allowed to be published. His major work was a tetralogy *Volny chernogo morya* [*Black Sea Waves*] (1936–1961). His most successful play *Kvadratura kruga* [*Squaring the Circle*] (1928) was a farcical view of the difficulties of two newly married couples trying to cope with housing problems.

1986 Apr. 14   Simone [Lucie Ernestine Marie Bertrand] **de Beauvoir** (b. Jan. 9, 1908), a French novelist, essayist, and radical feminist, died. Among her writings she was best known for *Le Seconde Sexe* [*The Second Sex*] (1949), a protest against the subsidiary status of women, which was translated into more than a dozen languages. Among her novels *Les Mandarins* [*The Mandarins*] (1954) attracted attention for its thinly disguised portrayal of the leading existentialists of her day.

1986 Apr. 15   Jean Genet (b. Dec. 19, 1910), a French novelist, poet, and playwright, died. His first novel of consequence was *Notre-Dame-des-Fleurs* [*Our Lady of the Flowers*] (1948). He was better known for his plays, such as *Les Bonnes* [*The Maids*] (1947), a good example of his view of how moral values can be inverted; and *Le Balcon* [*The Balcony*] (1959), in which characters find real life roles less satisfactory than the same roles as dreams.

1986 Apr. 23   Otto [Ludwig] **Preminger** (b. Dec. 5, 1905), an Austrian-born American stage and film actor, director, and producer, died. After an early career in Austria as a theatrical producer, he emigrated (1935) to the U.S. His films included *Laura* (1944), *Forever Amber* (1947), *Lady Windermere's Fan* (1949), *The Man With the Golden Arm* (1955), *Bonjour Tristesse* (1958), and *Advise and Consent* (1961).

1986 June 13 [Benjamin David] **Benny Goodman** (b. May 30, 1909), an American musician, the **King** of Swing, died. He made his debut as a clarinetist in 1921 and founded his first band in 1934. It was an immediate success. Goodman also organized trios and quartets and was the **first to lead racially mixed jazz groups.** On Jan. 16, 1938, he and his band gave the **first jazz concert ever heard in Carnegie Hall,** New York City. Goodman also played and recorded with classical music groups, such as the Budapest Quartet.

1986 June 14   Jorge Luis Borges (b. Aug. 24, 1899), an Argentinian short-story writer, poet, and essayist, died. Although little known outside his native land before 1961, he achieved international renown as time went on. His best-known collection of stories was *Ficciones* (1944). A collection of his poetry appeared in translation as *Selected Poems: 1923–1967* (1972).

1986 Aug. 6   Emilio Fernández (b. Mar. 26, 1904), a Mexican movie director and actor, died. He made 42 films, many of them dealing with the fate of the Indians of Mexico. Among his films were *Maria Candelaris* (1943) and *Enamorada* (1946). As an actor Fernández appeared in a number of American movies that were filmed in Mexico, such as *The Wild Bunch* (1969).

1986 Aug. 31   Henry [Spencer] **Moore** (b. July 30, 1898), an English sculptor, died. He was famous for his large figures, carved in stone and best suited to an outdoor environment. In the U.S. many public buildings feature a Moore sculpture as part of their setting. Many of Moore's works were of women, such as *Madonna and Child* (1943–1944), *Reclining Figure* (1951), and *Draped Reclining Figure* (1952–1953).

1986 Sept. 12   Jacques-Henri Lartigue (b. June 13, 1894), a French photographer, died. He began using a camera at the age of seven and had taken more than 280,000 photos by 1975. Many of his photographs were playful; all expressed his amusement at the quirks of the human condition. *Diary of a Century* (1970) was a collection of his pictures with comments from his diary.

1986 Oct. 16   Wole Soyinka (b. July 13, 1934), a Nigerian playwright and poet, became the first black African to be awarded the **Nobel prize for literature.** His plays made use of Nigerian folklore, as in *A Dance of the Forests* (1960) and *Madmen and Specialists* (1970). Soyinka published several volumes of poetry, including *Idanre and Other Poems* (1967) and *Poems from Prison* (1969).

1986 Nov. 29   Cary Grant [orig.: Archibald Alexander Leach] (b. Jan. 18, 1904), an English-born American actor, died. Grant had some stage experience in England and the U.S. before making his first Hollywood movie, *Blonde Venus* (1932). *Bringing Up Baby* (1938) was an example of his comedic talent. He also played the reluctant hero in suspense films, such as *Notorious* (1946) and *North by Northwest* (1959).

1986 Dec. 9   The *Musée d'Orsay* opened in Paris. Occupying what was originally a railroad station of 1900 vintage and its accompanying hotel of *belle époque* grandeur, the new museum included collections of painting, sculpture, architecture, photography, and design from the second half of the 19th century and the first few years of the 20th.

1986 Dec. 15   Serge Lifar (b. Apr. 2, 1905), a Russian-born French dancer and choreographer, died. He first appeared with the Ballets Russes (1923–1929), and his first role of note was in Léonide Massine's *Zéphire et Flore* (1925). Lifar was ballet master at the Paris Opera (1929–1945, 1947–1958). Among his ballets were *Phèdre* (1950) and *Daphne and Chloë* (1958).

VIII. SPORTS, GAMES, AND SOCIETY

1986   An explosive **rise in the use of crack**, a new form of cocaine in the U.S., increased the drug abuse problem nationwide. It was a serious threat to the health of addicts, affecting the lungs and circulatory system, and often leading to coronary attacks. By mid-1986 it was easy to buy it in c.17 of the larger cities, and estimates of the number of persons who had tried it varied from one to ten million. The New York City area, Atlanta, Detroit, Houston, and Miami were high on the list of places affected. In hospitals the number of persons needing emergency treatment because of its use grew alarmingly.

1986 May 9   Tenzing Norkay [orig.: Namgyal Wangdi] (b. 1914), the Sherpa guide who with Edmund Hillary of Great Britain on May 29, 1953, became **one of the first two men to reach the top of Mount Everest**, died.

1986 June 26   Irish voters, by almost two to one, voted to **keep the country's ban on divorce**. The vote was a setback for Garrett Fitzgerald, prime minister of Ireland, who had actively campaigned in favor of ending the ban. On Nov. 27 the Supreme Court of Argentina ruled that a 98-year-old law barring divorce was unconstitutional. Only six countries now prohibited **divorce**: Andorra, Ireland, Malta, Paraguay, the Philippines, and San Marino.

1986 June 29   Argentina defeated West Germany 3–2 to win the **World Cup** of soccer. The game, played in Mexico City, was Argentina's second World Cup.

1986 July 3   The U.S. rededicated the renovated **Statue of Liberty** in New York Harbor with entertainment, lights, and fireworks. The cost of the restoration over a three-year period was $66 million.

1986 July 23   By a margin of one vote, the British House of Commons voted to abolish **corporal punishment** in state-supported schools. Punishment by caning could still be administered in privately financed schools, but not to students whose fees were subsidized by the state.

1986 July 23   Prince Andrew (b. Feb. 14, 1960), son of Queen Elizabeth II and fourth in line of succession to the British throne, married **Sarah Ferguson** (b. Oct. 15, 1959), a commoner, in Westminster Abbey, London.

1986 July 27   Greg[ory James] **Lemond** (b. June 26, 1961) became the **first American to win the Tour de France**, the world's most prestigious bicycle race. Lemond's elapsed time was 110 hr., 35, min., 19 sec. for the 2,500-mile race.

1986 Oct. 3   About 180 delegates from 16 countries, including 120 prostitutes, ended a three-day conference at Brussels, Belgium, under the sponsorship of the **International Committee for Prostitutes' Rights**. The delegates drew up a list of human rights abuses affecting prostitutes, including deprivation of civil liberties and harassment by pimps. They also urged the use of condoms to prevent the spread of **AIDS** and other sexually transmitted diseases.

1987

I. VITAL STATISTICS AND DEMOGRAPHICS

1987 Jan. 29 As a result of warfare and economic dislocation, the **highest infant and child mortality rates** in the world were found in Angola and Mozambique, according to the **United Nations Children's Fund** [**UNICEF**]. In the two countries the mortality rate for children less than five years old was 325 per 1,000 children, and for infants less than a year old was 200 for each 1,000 live births.

II. DISASTERS

1987 Jan. 20 A ten-day **cold spell in Europe** caused c.300 deaths, half of them in the U.S.S.R. The temperature fell to minus 35°C, or minus 31°F, in Leningrad. In London the cold froze the works of Big Ben so that it was unable to sound its chimes.

1987 Mar. 5–6 A series of **earthquakes in Napo** province, northern Ecuador, killed c.300 people and left c.4,000 missing. The country's main oil pipeline was ruptured, halting the export of crude oil.

1987 May A **forest fire**, called by the Chinese the **Black Dragon fires**, raged through millions of acres of evergreens in the Greater Hinggan Forest along the Amur River in eastern Siberia and in Manchuria. Estimates of the areas burned ranged from 9 to 15 million acres in the Soviet Union and 1.5 to 3 million in China.

1987 May 9 A Soviet-built **Ilyushin 62M**, operated by LOT, the Polish airline, **crashed** in a wooded area near Warsaw, killing all 183 people aboard.

1987 July 2 A trailer-truck **crashed** into the side of a train at a crossing in southeastern Zaire, Africa, killing c.125 people.

1987 July 18 A **heat wave began in Athens**, Greece, that by July 28 had killed at least 700 people. A temperature of 45° C, or 113° F, was reported on one day of the heat wave.

1987 Aug. 16 A Northwest Airlines **MD-80 jet crashed** in flames shortly after taking off from the Detroit Metropolitan Airport. Of the 157 people on board only one survived, a four-year-old girl whose parents and brother died in the crash. It was later found that the pilots failed to follow proper procedures before takeoff.

1987 Sept. 29 A five-day **rainstorm in Natal** province, eastern South Africa, ended after causing floods that killed c.250 people. The government reported 50,632 people homeless. The floods wrecked the four aqueducts that supply water to Durban and destroyed 14 major highway bridges.

1987 Nov. 25–26 **Typhoon Nina** struck Luzon 150 miles southeast of Manila, causing c.500 deaths. About 450,000 were left homeless.

1987 Nov. 28 A South African Airways **Boeing 747 jet went down** in the Indian Ocean east of Mauritius with 159 persons aboard. The plane was enroute from Taipei to South Africa when a fire apparently broke out in the cockpit.

1987 Nov. 29 A Korea Air **Boeing 707** jet enroute from Baghdad to Seoul **crashed** near the Burma-Thailand border. All 115 persons aboard were killed. A man and woman, who had left the plane at Abu Dhabi, United Arab Emirates, were held for questioning and attempted to commit suicide by biting into cyanide pills. The man died, but the woman survived and confessed that they had placed a time bomb on the plane on orders from North Korea. That government denied the charge.

1987 Dec. 20 At least 1,600 people died in the **collision of the interisland ferry *Dona Paz* and the oil tanker *Victor*** off Mindoro, in the Philippines.

III. POLITICS AND WAR

1987 Jan. 9 In the **Iran-Iraq War** an Iranian offensive was launched east of Basra, in southeastern Iraq. The attack ended in February after 58 sq. mi. had been taken with an estimated loss of 45,000 Iranians killed. Iran began mining the Persian Gulf to impede the oil traffic of Kuwait. As a result the U.S. offered to reflag Kuwaiti tankers with American flags and to escort them. During the first such operation a mine damaged (July 24) the supertanker *Bridgeton*. Later in the year the U.S. navy destroyed (Oct. 19) two Iranian oil platforms in the gulf in retaliation for attacks on shipping.

1987 Jan. 16 **Hu Yaobang**, general secretary of the Communist party of the **People's Republic of China**, was forced to resign. He was accused of "mistakes on major issues of political principles." **Zhao Ziyang**, the prime minister, was appointed acting general secretary of the party and later named (Nov. 2) party general secretary. **Li Peng** (b. Oct. 1928) was appointed (Nov. 24) acting prime minister, being confirmed in the post on Apr. 9, 1988, by the National People's Congress.

1987 Jan. 27 **Mikhail S. Gorbachev** proposed that voters in the U.S.S.R. be given a choice of candidates in party elections and that the voting be secret. He also charged the party with stagnation and failure to prevent an economic crisis. The next day the central committee of the party approved the plan. As evidence of Gorbachev's policies of *glasnost* [openness] and *perestroika* [restructuring], 140 political prisoners were pardoned (Feb. 10), and Gorbachev charged (Nov. 2) Joseph Stalin, the late dictator, with "enormous and unforgivable crimes." In the same speech he praised two other former officials: Nikita Khrushchev, the former leader (1953–1964), and Nikolay I. Bukharin, an early revolutionary, who was executed by Stalin in 1938.

1987 Feb. 2 A new constitution, proposed by **Corazon C. Aquino**, president of the **Philippines**, was approved by c.80 percent of the voters in a plebiscite. A two-house legislature was established.

1987 Feb. 22 **Ethiopia** officially became a Marxist state as the People's Democratic Republic of Ethiopia. The formal change was not expected to affect the status of **Mengistu Haile Mariam**, leader of the communist regime.

1987 Feb. 26 A three-man review board appointed by President **Ronald Reagan** to investigate **secret arms deals with Iran**, issued a detailed report. It said Reagan was a confused and remote figure who did not understand or control what his subordinates were doing. The report further said that the president should take responsibility for a policy that caused "chaos" at home and worldwide embarrassment to the U.S. In a nationwide broadcast the president said (Mar. 4) he took "full responsibility" for the affair which, he admitted, had degenerated into a failed attempt to trade arms for the release of Americans being held hostage in Lebanon. A joint committee of the two houses of Congress issued (Nov. 18) a report of its 11-month investigation into

the **Iran-Contra affair**, blaming Reagan because he did not "take care that the laws be faithfully executed," and said he bore the "ultimate responsibility" for the illegal and bungled operation.

1987 Mar. 23 Communist **China and Portugal reached an agreement** for the return in 1999 to China of **Macao**, a Portuguese colony on the southern China coast. Residents of Macao were guaranteed the right to continue their present way of life for 50 years after 1999.

1987 Mar. 29 Voters in **Haiti** approved a new constitution that ended the term of the current provisional government on Feb. 7, 1988. A nine-member civilian commission was to supervise an election to be held on Nov. 29. However, on that date, officials called off the voting after three hours of violence. Attacks by thugs allied with the ousted Duvalier dictatorship and Haitian soldiers were blamed.

1987 Apr. 17 About 120 miles north of Colombo, Sri Lanka, **Tamil guerrillas ambushed** a convoy of three buses and two trucks. They killed 127 people and wounded c.60, almost all ethnic Sinhalese. The Sinhalese, the majority ethnic group, controlled the government and the army. The ethnic Tamils had been demanding greater autonomy. On July 29, 1987, **Sri Lanka** and India signed an agreement whereby an Indian army peacekeeping force would be sent to the island. About 3,000 troops arrived the next day, to be stationed in the Jaffna Peninsula area in northern Sri Lanka. The main Tamil guerrilla groups agreed (Aug. 5) to surrender their arms, and the government was preparing legislation to give the Tamils greater autonomy. Some guerrilla forces did not surrender, and during October more than 200 Indian troops were killed and about another 700 wounded.

1987 Apr. 26 In a general election, the coalition government of **Steingrimur Hermannsson** (b. June 22, 1928), prime minister of **Iceland** (from May 27, 1983), was defeated. A new government was formed on July 8 when **Thorsteinn Pálsson** (b. Oct. 29, 1947) became prime minister. He formed a coalition of the Independence, Progressive, and Social Democratic Peoples parties.

1987 Apr. 30 A meeting of all ten Canadian provincial premiers and the prime minister reached an agreement that labeled **Quebec** a "distinct society." All the provinces were given broader powers in relation to the federal government, such as no changes of provincial boundaries without their consent. A formal signing of the final agreement took place in Ottawa on June 3, but a vote on ratification was to be held.

1987 May 6 In an election in which only whites could vote, the National party of **Pieter W. Botha**, president of **South Africa**, won a majority of the seats in Parliament, increasing its representation from 127 to 133 seats.

1987 May 12 **Eddie Fenech Adami** (b. Feb. 7, 1934), leader of the conservative Nationalist party, became prime minister of **Malta** as a result of an election held on May 9. His victory ended 16 years of Labor party rule.

1987 May 17 A French-made Exocet **missile**, fired from an Iraqi warplane, **struck** the *Stark,* an American guided missile frigate, in the Persian Gulf. Thirty-seven sailors were killed and the ship badly damaged. Iraq admitted the attack, saying it was a mistake. It later agreed to pay compensation to the families of the sailors.

1987 May 28 A young West German, **Matthias Rust, flew a single-engine Cessna 172** through 400 miles of Soviet air space from Helsinki, Finland, **and landed safely in Red Square** in Moscow. He apparently had no political motive, but he was arrested and sentenced (Sept. 4) to four years in a labor camp but was freed after a year.

1987 June 1 **Rashid** [Abdul Hamid] **Karami** (b. Dec. 30, 1921), the prime minister of **Lebanon** (from Apr. 26, 1984), died when a bomb exploded in a military helicopter in which he was flying from Tripoli to Beirut. A Sunni Muslim, he had held the post of prime minister 10 times in 32 years. The identity of the assassins was unknown. **Selim al-Hoss** (b. 1930), a former prime minister and a member of Karami's cabinet, was named acting prime minister.

1987 June 11 **Margaret Thatcher** retained her position as prime minister when the Conservative party won 376 seats in the House of Commons, a loss of 21 from the previous election, to 229 for the Labour party, which gained 20 seats.

1987 July 28 Ending a five-month political crisis in **Italy**, **Giovanni Goria** (b. July 30, 1943) became prime minister, heading a coalition government of five parties. Goria had been treasury minister for five years.

1987 July 31 The **Organization of African Unity** [**OAU**], with a membership of 50 nations, ended its 23rd annual meeting in Addis Ababa, Ethiopia, with little agreement on major issues.

1987 Aug. 7 **Camille Nimer Chamoun** (b. Apr. 3, 1900), a former president (1952–1958) of Lebanon, died. A prominent Christian leader for many years, he had been in politics since 1929. Chamoun was the head of the main Christian alliance, the Lebanese Front, and founder of the National Liberal party (1958), which he headed until 1986.

1987 Aug. 7 The presidents of five **Central American countries signed an agreement** intended to resolve conflicts in the region and to bring about democracy. Prime developer of the plan was **Oscar Arias Sánchez** (b. Sept. 13, 1941), president of Costa Rica. The other signing nations were El Salvador, Guatemala, Honduras, and Nicaragua. The plan called for talks to begin at once between governments and unarmed oppositions; immediate ceasefires where there was armed conflict; restoration of full democratic rights in the near future; free elections; suspension of military aid to insurgents and irregulars; and refusal to let the territory of one nation be used for attacks on neighbors. On Oct. 13 Arias was awarded the **Nobel Peace Prize** for his leadership in this regional peace effort.

1987 Aug. 8 A surprise **attack by Chadian troops on Libyan forces** occupying the village of Aozou, in northern Chad, routed the invaders. Then Chad raided (Sept. 5) the Matan as Sarra air base 60 miles inside Libya, and claimed it destroyed the base as well as 26 Libyan planes. The base had been used for bombing raids on Chad. In September the **Organization of African Unity** [OAU] brought about a ceasefire.

1987 Aug. 17 **Rudolph Hess** (b. Apr. 26, 1894), at one time second only to Adolf Hitler in the Nazi regime, died. Since 1947, under a sentence of life imprisonment as a war criminal, he had been held by the Allies in **Spandau Prison** in Berlin. Hess on May 10, 1941, commandeered a fighter plane and flew it to Scotland where he landed by parachute. Hess said he came to try to negotiate the end of World War II, but the British did not take him seriously.

1987 Sept. 3 A military coup ousted **Jean-Baptiste Bagaza** (b. Aug. 29, 1946), president of **Burundi**, in central Africa, while he was attending a conference in Canada. Bagaza had seized power 11 years earlier. The leader of the coup was **Pierre Buyoya**, also an army officer, who became head of a Military Committee of National Redemption.

1987 Sept. 13 A referendum in the French-ruled islands of **New Caledonia** in the Pacific Ocean resulted in 93.3 percent voting to remain "within the French Republic," rather than become independent. However, a group favoring independence had urged its followers not to vote.

1987 Oct. 1 The Marxist Sandinista government of **Nicaragua** began to implement the peace accord it had signed on Aug. 7 along with the heads of four other Central American countries. It allowed *La Prensa*, an opposition newspaper, shut down more than a year earlier, to resume publication. The next day a Roman Catholic radio station, closed down 21 months before, was allowed back on the air. The government announced (Nov. 5) it was ready to negotiate indirectly with the **Contra rebels**, whose leaders said they were willing in principle to accept the offer. The government asked (Nov. 6) **Miguel Cardinal Obando y Bravo** (b. Feb. 2, 1926), the Catholic primate of Nicaragua, to mediate the talks. On Nov. 22 the government freed 985 political prisoners, most of them Contras.

1987 Oct. 15 The U.S.S.R., owing the **UN** $225 million, announced it was paying in full. The U.S. remained the U.N.'s largest debtor, owing $414.2 million as of Sept. 30. In all, before the Russian action, the U.N. was owed $877 million by its member nations.

1987 Oct. 15 The regime of **Thomas Sankara**, president of **Burkina Faso**, was overthrown in a coup led by **Blaise Compaoré** (b. Feb. 3, 1951), an army officer and longtime adviser to Sankara. Sankara (b. 1948) and 12 other officials were executed on Oct. 16 without trial.

1987 Nov. 6 **Noboru Takeshita** (b. Feb. 26, 1924) became prime minister of **Japan**. He had been elected (Oct. 31) president of the Liberal Democratic party, which had ruled the country since the establishment of representative government after World War II. Takeshita succeeded **Yasuhiro Nakasone**, whose term expired on Oct. 30.

1987 Nov. 7 Declaring that **Habib Bourguiba**, president of **Tunisia**, was too ill to govern, **Zine al-Abidien** [Abidine] **Ben Ali** (b. Sept. 3, 1936), the prime minister, took power. Ben Ali was a former general who had been named prime minister in October. Ben Ali granted (Dec. 5) amnesty to 2,487 prisoners, including 608 members of the Islamic Tendency Movement, a fundamentalist group that Bourguiba had sought to quash.

1987 Nov. 10 **Seyni Kountché** (b. July 1, 1931), president of **Niger**, in West Africa, since seizing power in a coup in 1974, died of a brain tumor. He was succeeded by **Ali Syebou**, chief of staff of the army and a cousin of Kountché's.

1987 Nov. 25 An election in **Suriname** resulted in a resounding defeat for **Dési Bouterse**, who had headed a military dictatorship for seven years. A three-party opposition coalition won nearly all the seats in the National Assembly. A referendum had approved (Sept. 30) a new constitution, providing for the election of the president by the assembly.

1987 Nov. 29 **Polish voters rejected a government proposal for an economic austerity program**. A majority of those who voted approved the plan, but Polish law required that a majority of all eligible voters approve and this did not occur. It was estimated that the cost of living would have risen 40 percent under the austerity plan. Two weeks later the government announced (Dec. 15) that consumer prices would rise by an average of 27 percent in 1988.

1987 Dec. 8 **Ronald Reagan** and **Mikhail S. Gorbachev** signed in Washington, D.C., the **first treaty to reduce the size of their nations' nuclear arsenals**. All American and Soviet short-range and medium-range missiles were to be destroyed. Provision was made for weapons inspections by each side in the other's territory. The U.S. Senate ratified the treaty in the following year.

1987 Dec. 17 **Roh Tae Woo** (b. Dec. 4, 1932), candidate of the Democratic Justice party, the governing party of **South Korea**, was elected president. He received only 36.2 percent of the popular vote, but two main opposition candidates split most of the rest of the vote.

1987 Dec. 17 **Gustav Husak** (Jan. 10, 1913–Nov. 18, 1991) resigned as head of the **Czechoslovakian** Communist party. Husak may have been too rigid to suit the policies of **Mikhail S. Gorbachev.** He was succeeded by **Milos Jakes** (b. Aug. 12, 1922), a member of the Presidium of the ruling party and responsible for the country's economic sector.

1987 Dec. 21   Thousands of Arabs **in Israel,** the Gaza Strip, and the West Bank took part in a **general strike** to protest Israel's handling of their demonstrations, which had been going on for two weeks. By now c.22 Palestinians had been killed by Israeli soldiers, who were attacked by stone throwing Arabs, mostly young men. The immediate cause of the demonstrations was an auto accident (Dec. 8) in which 4 Arabs were killed and 17 injured and which was alleged to have been arranged by Israelis. The UN Security Council, with the U.S. abstaining, denounced (Dec. 22) the harsh measures adopted by the Israelis to suppress the demonstrators, but the U.S. did criticize the soldiers' use of live ammunition.

1987 Dec. 31   **Bantu Holomisa,** a general, staged a coup in **Transkei.** He took over power from **Stella Sigcau,** daughter of a tribal chief, who had been prime minister since Oct. 5. In early October Homisa had ousted **George Matanzima,** who had been prime minister since 1979. In both cases he charged the government with corruption.

IV. ECONOMICS AND TRADE

1987 Feb. 19   U.S. President **Ronald Reagan lifted the economic sanctions imposed on Poland** in 1981 and 1982. The action reduced tariffs on goods imported from Poland and allowed Poland to seek loans from American banks. Reagan said the action was taken because Poland had released political prisoners and eased its harsh attitude toward the labor union **Solidarity** and the Roman Catholic Church.

1987 Apr. 17   **Cecil King** (b. Feb. 20, 1901), an English publisher, died. Under King's direction the **International Publishing Corporation** grew into a conglomerate that by 1968 controlled more than 250 newspapers and magazines, with interests in printing, newsprint, television, and book publishing.

1987 May 17   [Karl] **Gunnar Myrdal** (b. Dec. 6, 1898), a Swedish economist and sociologist who shared the **Nobel prize for economics** in 1974, died. Although he was a leading pacifist, reformer, and architect of the Swedish welfare state, Myrdal was

best known for his book *An American Dilemma* (1944), a study of the racial problem in the U.S.

1987 June 26   As part of the policy of **perestroika, Mikhail S. Gorbachev** won the approval of the Communist party's central committee for his ambitious plan to restructure the Russian economy. Among the extensive changes called for were an end to fixed, subsidized prices, and to the centralized control exercised over thousands of enterprises. The plan called for "a drastic expansion" in the independence of business enterprises.

1987 June 26   **Arthur F[rank] Burns** (b. Apr. 27, 1904), an Austrian-born American economist, died. Burns was adviser to two presidents, Dwight D. Eisenhower and Richard M. Nixon, but it was as chairman of the **Federal Reserve Board** (1970–1978) that he exercised the most influence. He took strong measures to prevent excessive inflation.

1987 Aug. 22   A leading Japanese newspaper declared that in 1987 **Japan became the richest nation** in the world, with assets amounting to $43,700,000,-000,000. Japan replaced the U.S., whose total 1987 assets were estimated to be $36,200,000,000,000.

1987 Sept. 29   **Henry Ford 2nd** (b. Sept. 4, 1917), an American automobile manufacturer, died. In 1945, with family and other backing, he had seized control of the **Ford Motor Company,** which was losing money. His grandfather, Henry Ford, was senile, and his father, Edsel, had died. It took him ten years to restore what had once been the leading auto manufacturer of the world to meet the competition of its rivals, especially **General Motors.** Ford retired as chief executive in 1979.

1987 Oct. 19   The **Dow Jones industrial average fell 508 points** and a record 604.33 million shares were traded. The fall amounted to a 22.6 percent decline, compared with the 12.82 percent decline on Oct. 28, 1929, which with the further drop of 11.7 percent the next day ushered in the Great Depression of the 1930s. The Dow had reached its highest point, 2,722.42, on Aug. 25, and since then had dropped almost 1,000 points, closing at 1,738.74 on Oct. 19. Reasons given for the stock debacle were rising interest rates, the fall in the value of the dollar, and fear of war with Iran over incidents in the Persian Gulf. Blame was also placed on the so-called program traders, whose computer-driven selling dumped huge blocks of stock on the market without notice. On Oct. 20 the Dow rose 102.27 points, a record, and on Oct. 21 it rose another 186.84 points. Trading on Oct. 20 set a new record for volume with 608.12 million shares traded. Trading continued to be volatile the rest of the year and the Dow ended 1987 at 1,988.83, down 733.59 points from its August high.

1987 Nov.   Kentucky Fried Chicken opened an out-let in Beijing, China. Business prospered and two more restaurants were planned.

1987 Dec. 14   After a six-day session, members of **OPEC** agreed to extend their current production quotas through the first half of 1988. They hoped thereby to hold the price of crude oil at $18 a barrel. Iraq refused to sign the agreement because its quota was not raised to the same level as Iran's.

1987 Dec. 28   The government of **Vietnam** announced a new policy that in effect **abandoned centralized planning**. Effective on Jan. 1, 1988, managerial decisions in state-owned enterprises would be made at the factory level. Incentives for workers to produce more would also be introduced.

V. RELIGION AND PHILOSOPHY

1987 Feb. 27   The Italian government and the Union of Italian Jewish Communities signed an **agreement replacing laws governing Jewish life** that had been enacted by the Fascist regime of Benito Mussolini. It provided, among other things, that Jews in hospitals, homes for the elderly, and in the military be assured of access to religious services and kosher food, and that Jews would be allowed to take days off on Jewish holidays.

1987 Mar. 10   The **Vatican condemned test-tube fertilization** and called for restrictions on medical interference with human procreation. The church also condemned surrogate motherhood, among other practices, but approved artificial insemination within marriage, when the technical means supplement the conjugal act, and the use of fertility drugs.

1987 Apr. 4   The Roman Catholic bishops of the U.S. introduced a **revised text of the New Testament** that avoided the use of the word "man" when both men and women are meant. As an example, Matthew 4:4 "One does not live by bread alone," replaced "Not by bread alone is man to live."

1987 May 1   Pope John Paul II beatified a Jewish-born Carmelite nun, **Edith Stein** (Oct. 12, 1891–Aug. 10?, 1942), who was killed in the Nazi concentration camp at Auschwitz, Poland. She had converted (1922) to Catholicism and become Sister **Teresa Benedicta** of the Cross, and was in a convent in the Netherlands when she was seized by the Gestapo.

1987 June 18   The General Assembly of the **Presbyterian Church** [USA] voted to "identify, expose and counteract the bigotry and prejudice" evident in the U.S. against Muslims and Arabs. A study prepared in advance of the meeting said that Christian attitudes toward Muslims and Arabs were often "distorted by ignorance and prejudice."

1987 July 31   On the eve of the annual Muslim pilgrimage, or *hajj*, **rioting broke out in Mecca**, Saudi Arabia, the holiest place of Islam, between Shiites, mostly from Iran, and Saudi Arabian police. The official count was 402 dead: 275 Iranians, 42 other pilgrims; and 85 policemen. Iran blamed Saudi Arabia for the bloodshed, but the incident was seen as a deliberate Iranian protest against Saudi Arabia's backing of Iraq in the Iran-Iraq War.

VI. SCIENCE, EDUCATION, AND TECHNOLOGY

1987   American astronomers reported (Jan. 5) that for the first time they had observed a **giant galaxy being born**. It had a mass of about 100 billion suns. In an unrelated event astronomers in Chile reported (Feb. 24) that a **massive star had exploded** closer to earth than any observed since 1604. The new supernova was 163,000 light-years from earth. Continuing observation puzzled astronomers: The **supernova** halted its increase in brightness and seemed to be changing color from blue to red. Then further observation showed it had two points of light, close together. Elsewhere Canadian astronomers reported (June 18) they had found evidence of objects outside the solar system, which were thought to be "giant, gaseous bodies, not unlike Jupiter." Strong evidence was reported (Nov. 10) by American astronomers of a sizable object orbiting a star other than the sun. It was deemed likely to be the first known **brown dwarf**, a celestial object previously hypothesized as a body intermediate between a planet and a star. Finally, British and American astronomers reported (Dec. 3) the discovery of two celestial objects farther from earth than any previously known. The bodies, two quasars whose nature was still obscure, were 12 billion light-years away.

1987 Feb. 24 Scientists at Brigham Young University, Provo, Utah, reported that x-ray examination of fossil eggs 150 million years old had revealed the outlines of what was probably the **oldest dinosaur embryo** ever found. The egg was found (Sept. 1986) south of Price, Utah. On June 6 scientists exploring near Milk River, 186 miles southeast of Calgary, Canada, found a nest of dinosaur eggs also containing fertilized embryos. They were probably laid by duck-billed dinosaurs, creatures that grew to 33 feet in length.

1987 Mar 4 Great Britain approved the use of **azidothymidine [AZT]** for the treatment of **AIDS**, a drug that appeared to prolong the lives of patients. The U.S. Food and Drug Administration also approved (Mar. 20) its use. Attempts to find a vaccine were in progress: A French researcher reported (June 2) promising results from small-scale tests on humans of an experimental vaccine. In the meantime the **World Health Organization** [WHO] said (Feb. 13) that AIDS had been found in 91 countries and that c.75,000 persons worldwide had died of AIDS.

1987 Mar. 19 Louis [Victor] **de Broglie** (b. Aug. 15, 1892), a French physicist, died. His work on the development of the quantum theory won him the **Nobel prize for physics** in 1929. In 1924 de Broglie showed mathematically that particles exhibited wavelike properties, a proposition confirmed (1927) by others.

1987 Apr. 16 The U.S. government announced it would allow **patenting of new forms of animal life** created through gene splicing and other new technologies of genetic engineering. The policy statement also said that patenting of new genetic characteristics in human beings would not be permitted. The U.S. had permitted patenting of genetically engineered bacteria since 1980 and of genetically engineered plants since 1986.

1987 May 11 Emanuel Vitria (b. 1920) of France, the longest surviving **heart transplant** patient, died. With the heart of a 20-year-old man he had survived c.18.5 years. Vitria continued to drink, smoke, and eat rich food after his operation. An American, **Willem Van Buren**, who received a heart transplant at Stanford University, California, almost 18 years ago, became the longest living survivor of the procedure.

1987 July 29 As France and Great Britain ratified their agreement to construct a **tunnel under the English Channel**, workers at Sangatte, near Calais, sank a shaft 180 ft. in diameter and 230 ft. deep into the ground to allow boring machines to be lowered to start the tunneling. Before the end of the year, the British began work on their side at Lower Shakespeare Cliff, near Dover, by assembling boring machines underground.

1987 Sept. 16 In Montreal, Canada, at a conference sponsored by the **U.N. Environment Program**, 24 nations and the European Community signed an agreement intended to protect the earth's fragile ozone shield. Forty-nine other countries indicated their approval but for various reasons did not sign the protocol. The agreement called for control of the use of **chlorofluorocarbons** and subsequent reductions in its use. Researchers reported (Sept. 30) that the ozone shield over the Antarctic continent had dwindled to its lowest level since the first measurements ten years earlier.

1987 Oct. 2 Peter [Brian] **Medawar** (b. Feb. 28, 1915), an English zoologist, died. He performed pioneering work in the development of the science of immunity, which helped open the way to transplant surgery. Medawar and an associate proved that an organism can be induced to overcome a normal tendency to reject foreign tissues and organs. For this work he shared the **Nobel prize for physiology or medicine** in 1960.

1987 Oct. 20 Andrei N. Kolmogorov (b. Apr. 25, 1903), a Russian mathematician, died. In the 1930s he made a rigorous mathematical system out of the ideas of chance and probability. In the 1940s Kolmogorov pioneered a technique that enabled probability to be used to make predictions in the face of randomness.

1987 Nov. 7 Federico Mayor Zaragoza (b. Jan. 27, 1934), a Spanish biochemist, was elected director general of **UNESCO**. He succeeded Amadou-Mahtar M'Bow of Senegal, director general for 13 years. M'Bow had been accused of mismanagement and of trying to politicize the organization. As a result the U.S. (1984) and Great Britain (1985) had withdrawn from membership.

VII. ARTS AND LEISURE

1987 Feb. 17   Dmitri [Borisovich] **Kabalevsky** (b. Dec. 30, 1904), a Russian composer, died. He was best known for his suite *Komediantï* [*The Comedians*] (1940) and the opera *Colas Breugnon* (1938).

1987 Feb. 22   Andy Warhol [orig.: Andrew Warhola] (b. Aug. 6, 1928) a founder of pop art, died. He became well known for his enlarged, exact copies of such items as Coca Cola bottles and Campbell Soup cans. He also did portraits of celebrities, such as the **Marilyn Monroe Diptych** (1962). He also produced films such as **The Chelsea Girls** (1966) and **Trash** (1971).

1987 Apr. 1   A new **Turner Building** opened at the Tate Gallery in London. Named for **J.M.W. Turner**, it housed 19,331 works of art Turner bequeathed to his country when he died in 1851. Under the terms of the will, Great Britain was obligated to build a new gallery just for his bequest. It took 136 years to fulfill the obligation.

1987 Apr. 11   Primo Levi (b. July 31, 1919), a Jewish-Italian writer, died. A chemist by training, he survived the Nazi death camp of Auschwitz, Poland, because he was put to work in a synthetic rubber factory. Levi wrote of his experiences in *Se questo è un umo* [*If This Is a Man*] (1947) and *La Tregua* [*The Awakening*] (1958). As a novelist he wrote *Se non ora, quando?* [*If Not Now, When?*] (1982). The last volume of Levi's autobiography *Il sistema periodica* [*The Periodic Table*] (1975) consisted of 21 sections of imaginative writing, each named for a chemical element.

1987 Apr. 11   Erskine [Preston] **Caldwell** (b. Dec. 17, 1903), an American author, died. Although he wrote more than 50 books, he was best known for two novels, *Tobacco Road* (1932) and *God's Little Acre* (1933). They were best sellers and they were also controversial because of their depiction of the passions, anger, brutality, and obscene language of poor southerners.

1987 May 14   Rita Hayworth [nee Margarita Carmen Cansino] (b. Oct. 17, 1918), an American movie actress of great beauty, died. She was the Great American Love Goddess in such movies as *Blood and Sand* (1940), *You'll Never Get Rich* (1941), and *Gilda* (1946). Among her marriages was one to Aly Khan,

prince and spiritual leader of millions of Ismaili Muslims.

1987 June 2   Andrés Segovia (b. Feb. 21, 1893), a Spanish musician who established the guitar as an instrument for serious music, died. During his career, he toured the world repeatedly. Segovia's performance of his transcriptions of the music of J.S. Bach entranced listeners.

1987 June 22   Fred Astaire [orig.: Frederick Austerlitz] (b. May 10, 1899), an American dancer, died. He was the foremost dancer in the history of the movies. His successful movies included *Flying Down to Rio* (1933), *Top Hat* (1935), *Easter Parade* (1948), and *The Band Wagon* (1953). Movie goers thrilled especially to the dance numbers Astaire performed with **Ginger Rogers** (b. July 16, 1911), a glamorous movie star in her own right.

1987 Aug. 28   John Huston (b. Aug. 5, 1906), an American film director, died. He began his career in the movies as a script writer. In his debut as a director he made an instant classic, *The Maltese Falcon* (1941). A superb craftsman, Huston went on to make many other movies, including *The Treasure of the Sierra Madre* (1948), *The African Queen* (1952), *The Misfits* (1961), and *Prizzi's Honor* (1985).

1987 Sept. 5   London's longest-running farce, *No Sex Please, We're British*, which opened on June 3, 1971, ended with its 6,761st performance. When it opened only one London critic thought the play was funny.

1987 Sept. 25   [George] Emlyn Williams (b. Nov. 26, 1905), a Welsh actor, dramatist, and director, died. His first success as a playwright was *A Murder Has Been Arranged* (1930), and his first success as an actor came a year later on Broadway in *The Case of the Frightened Lady* (1931). His best plays were *Night Must Fall* (1935), about a psychopathic murderer; and *The Corn Is Green* (1938), a tribute to the schoolteacher who guided him to a life outside the Welsh mining world.

1987 Oct. 3   Jean [Marie Lucienpierre] **Anouilh** (b. June 23, 1910), a French dramatist, died. Tragedy and comedy were mixed in his work. Among his c.40 plays were *Antigone* (1944), *L'Invitation au Château* [*Ring Around the Moon*] (1947), *La Valse des Toréadors* [*The Waltz of the Toreadors*] (1952), *L'Alouette* [*The Lark*] (1953), and *Becket* (1959).

1987 Oct. 9 [Ann] **Clare Booth Luce** (b. Apr. 10, 1903), an American editor, playwright, Congresswoman, and diplomat, died. She was managing editor of *Vanity Fair* (1933–1934); wrote a successful play and movie, *The Women* (1936); served in the House of Representatives (1943–1947); and was U.S. ambassador to Italy (1953–1956). In 1935 she married **Henry R. Luce**, the founder of *Time*.

1987 Oct. 28 **André Masson** (b. Jan. 4, 1896), a French artist of the surrealist school, died. He espoused automatism, in which he let his hand and brush run free without prior thought or conscious guidance. Among his paintings were *Battle of the Fishes* (1926) and *Iroquois Landscape* (1942). He also illustrated books and designed stage settings.

1987 Nov. 22 **Emmanuel** [Bernard] **Le Roy Ladurie** (b. July 19, 1929), a French historian, was appointed director of the **Bibliothèque Nationale**, Paris. Two of Le Roy Ladurie's notable books were *Les Paysans de Languedoc* [*The Peasants of Languedoc*] (1966), and *Montaillou: Village Occitan de 1294 à 1324* [*Montaillou: The Promised Land of Error*] (1975).

1987 Dec. 10 **Jascha Heifetz** (b. Feb. 2, 1901), a Russian-born American virtuoso violinist, died. He made his debut with the **Berlin Philharmonic** when he was ten. Heifetz moved (1917) to the U.S. and over the following years became regarded by many as the greatest violinist of his generation.

1987 Dec. 17 **Marguerite Yourcenar** [nee Marguerite Crayencour] (b. June 8, 1903), a Belgian-born French writer, died. She had lived in the U.S. since 1940. Among her books were *Denier du rêve* [*A Coin in Nine Hands*] (1934), *Le Coup de grâce* [*Coup de Grâce*] (1939), and *Mémoires d'Hadren* [*Memoirs of Hadrian*] (1951). She was the first (1981) woman ever elected to the **Académie Française**.

VIII. SPORTS, GAMES, AND SOCIETY

1987 Feb. 4 The U.S. won back the **America's Cup** when the yacht *Stars and Stripes* defeated the Australian defender *Kookaburra* in four straight races off Fremantle, Australia.

1987 Apr. 1 **Steven M. Newman**, an American from Bethel, Ohio, completed a **walk around the world** that began four years earlier, on Apr. 1, 1983. He started eastward from his hometown to Boston, through Europe and North Africa, southern Asia, Australia, and the western U.S., ending where he started.

1987 Apr. 3 A two-day auction at Geneva, Switzerland, of the **jewels of the late Duchess of Windsor** (Wallis Simpson) brought a total of $50,281,887.

1987 June 6 **Sachio Kinugasa** (b. Jan. 18, 1947), a third baseman for the Hiroshima Carp professional baseball team, tied the record of the late Lou Gehrig, of the New York Yankees, for playing in the **most consecutive games**, 2,130. Kinugasa had not missed a game since Oct. 18, 1970.

1987 Aug. 8–23 The tenth **Pan-American Games** were held in Indianapolis, Indiana, with the U.S. winning 369 medals, including 168 gold. Cuba was second with 75 gold and 175 in all; Canada third with 30 and 162.

1987 Sept. 4 A rare example of *sati*, immolation of a widow on her husband's funeral pyre, took place at Deorala, India. The widow, **Roop Kunwar** (b. 1969), placed herself, or was placed, on the pyre. In the course of the next month thousands of persons in sympathy with the custom came to Deorala to pay tribute to her. The authorities arrested (Sept. 19) Kunwar's father-in-law **Sumer Singh** but did not at once decide whether to charge him with murder or with abetting a suicide. *Sati* was outlawed (1929) in India but is still practiced once or twice a decade.

1987 Nov. 10 The British House of Commons by a vote of 293 to 87 agreed to allow **pubs to stay open continuously** from 11 A.M. to 11 P.M., Monday through Saturday. For the past 71 years they had been required to close for two and a half hours in the afternoon.

1987 Dec. 16 A **Mafia trial ended in Palermo**, Sicily, with 338 of 452 defendants found guilty on various charges connected with the running of their criminal enterprise. The jury ordered life sentences, the maximum penalty, for 19 of the defendants. The penalties added up to 2,665 years in prison and nearly $10 million in fines. The jury deliberated for 35 days.

1988

I. VITAL STATISTICS AND DEMOGRAPHICS

1988 Apr.   The **Soviet Union allowed 1,086 Jews to emigrate** this month, the largest number since May 1981, when 1,141 departed. The pace of emigration had increased in 1987 for the first time since 1979.

1988 June 1   **India's population** passed the 800 million mark and was increasing at the rate of 16 million a year. China's 1988 population was estimated at nearly 1,100,000,000.

1988 July 14   Because of the **civil war in Mozambique**, an estimated 600,000 persons had fled to neighboring Malawi since Sept. 1986. Most of the refugees were destitute and near starvation. Malawi, a nation of 7.5 million people, was itself suffering from drought and a serious infestation of insects.

1988 Aug. 12   More than 300,000 **Somali refugees fled to Ethiopia** in the last two months in order to escape the civil war in their own country, relief officials reported. The refugees were mostly without shelter and they were in a region where water was scarce. Food was in short supply, as Ethiopia was also suffering a severe food shortage.

II. DISASTERS

1988 Jan. 2   About 18,000 barrels of **diesel fuel** flowed into the **Monongahela River** 25 miles south of Pittsburgh, Pennsylvania, when an oil tank of the Ashland Oil Company ruptured. Thousands of birds and fish were killed.

1988 Mar. 16   A **bus** carrying 105 members of a Muslim wedding party **overturned and caught fire** near Simga, a village in central India, killing c.90 persons. One report said the blaze was started by passengers' firecrackers.

1988 Apr. 6   U.N. officials reported that c.170 **Vietnamese boat people**, fleeing their homeland, had died since the end of January when their boats were rammed or pushed off the coast of Thailand by police, navy, and Thai fishing vessels in an attempt to discourage refugees from entering that country.

1988 June 3   A two-week **heat wave in India**, centered in the state of Rajasthan, killed more than 450 people and left many others ill. In some areas temperatures of about 49° C, or 120° F, were registered.

1988 June 23   A **landslide** that poured half a million tons of mud and rock onto the village of Çatak, Turkey, took c.300 lives. The main road in the village was covered with a 30-foot mound of debris.

1988 July 6   An **explosion on an oil platform** in the North Sea, c.120 miles northeast of Aberdeen, Scotland, took the lives of 167 workers. An accumulation of gas aboard the Piper Alpha platform, owned by Occidental Petroleum, apparently triggered the blast.

1988 July 29–39   Heavy rains followed by flash **flooding in Zhejiang province**, China, took 264 lives with about another 50 missing. Since the beginning of 1988 floods, landslides, drought, and cold weather killed c.11,600 Chinese and left c.470,000 homeless.

1988 Aug. 4–5   A **rainfall** of 8.25 inches, six times as much as in all of 1987, **poured on Khartoum**, capital of the Sudan. It left 1.5 million of the city's 4 million people homeless. The population had increased enormously in recent years because of drought conditions and the civil war in the southern part of the nation. The refugees for the most part had no electricity, sewage system, or water supply.

1988 Aug. 21   An **earthquake** registering 6.5 on the Richter scale struck Nepal and the state of Bihar, India. About 700 persons were killed and as many as 10,000 injured.

1988 Sept. 10   In Bangladesh heavy **monsoon rains**, falling off and on since June, had by now flooded three-fourths of the country and left a fourth of its 110 million inhabitants homeless. One newspaper estimated the death toll at 1,450. Gastrointestinal diseases were widespread: on Sept. 9 alone, 21,412 new cases were reported. Then a cyclone struck (Nov. 29) coastal areas of Bangladesh and eastern India taking a toll of c.2,000 lives, with reports of another c.15,000 missing.

1988 Sept. 12–18   **Hurricane Gilbert** struck (Sept. 12) Jamaica in the West Indies, leaving a quarter of the population homeless, although the death toll was only c.30. Damage was estimated at $300 million. Gilbert became even stronger when it hit (Sept. 14) the Yucatan Peninsula of Mexico. The barometric pressure fell to 26.13 inches, the lowest on record in the Western Hemisphere, and the winds rose to 272 mph. It killed c.29 people and left more than c.300,000 homeless. Continuing on, Gilbert struck the northern coast of Mexico c.120 miles south of Brownsville, Texas. At the inland city of Monterey, Mexico, four buses carrying people fleeing the hurricane overturned in flood waters and only 13 of 160 were rescued. Damage in Mexico was estimated at $880 million.

1988 Oct. 19   Two **airplane crashes** in India within an hour on the same day took 164 lives. An Indian Airlines Boeing 737 with 135 aboard crashed at Ahmadabad, on a flight from Bombay. Five passengers survived. A Fokker Friendship flown by the Vayadoot Airline crashed near Gauhati, in the state of Assam, killing all 34 aboard.

1988 Nov. 6   An **earthquake** registering 7.6 on the Richter scale struck a remote mountainous area of China, claiming c.730 lives. The number injured was put at c.4,000 and the number made homeless at c.200,000.

1988 Dec. 7   An **earthquake** registering 6.9 on the Richter scale, with an aftershock at 5.8, devastated several cities of Armenia, U.S.S.R., near the Turkish border. By the time most of the rescue operation was finished, 24,854 bodies had been recovered from the ruins. The number of homeless was put as high as 500,000.

1988 Dec. 21   A **Boeing 747**, Pan Am flight 103 enroute from London to New York City, **exploded** in midair over the village of Lockerbie, Scotland. All 259 persons on board were killed, as were 11 on the ground. Within a week investigators determined that a powerful explosive device had caused the tragedy.

III. POLITICS AND WAR

1988   In the **Sudan**, civil war, floods, and starvation plagued the nation all year. The government, Muslim dominated, was accused of massacring southerners, who were mostly black Christians and animists. Near the end of the year it was estimated that 200,-000 Sudanese had been killed or starved to death in the past five years. In addition c.1.5 million had left their home areas, many of them moving to overcrowded Khartoum, others to drought-stricken Ethiopia.

1988 Jan.–Dec.   The Palestinian revolt against Israel became known as **Intifada** ["cast off the yoke of the past"]. Those who participated in it were mostly rock-throwing young males in the Gaza Strip and the West Bank. The Israelis began (Jan. 1988) jailing many Palestinians without trial. By the end of January, Israeli troops were beating Palestinians on the grounds that this was more humane than using live ammunition. By year's end the violence had diminished somewhat, but c.285 Palestinians had been killed by Israeli troops.

1988 Jan. 5   **Sean MacBride** (b. Jan. 26, 1904), an Irish revolutionary and diplomat, died. For 20 years (to 1937) he fought the British as a leader of the **Irish Republican Army** [IRA]. He then served as Ireland's foreign minister (1948–1951) and as an assistant secretary general of the U.N. (1973–1976). For his work on behalf of human rights, MacBride in 1974 shared the **Nobel Peace Prize**.

1988 Jan. 13   **Chiang Ching-Kuo** (b. Mar. 18, 1910), prime minister (1972–1978) and president (from 1978) of the **Republic of China** [Taiwan], died. He was the political heir of his late father **Chiang Kai-Shek**. He was succeeded by his designated successor, **Lee Teng-Hui** (b. Jan. 15, 1923), the vice president of Taiwan. Lee, educated in the U.S. as an expert in agricultural planning, was the first native-born Taiwanese to hold the presidency.

1988 Jan. 24   In **Haiti** the electoral council declared that in the election of Jan. 17 the winner was **Leslie F[rançois] Manigat** (b. Aug. 16, 1930), a professor of political science who had spent most of the period of the Duvalier regime in exile. He was inaugurated (Feb. 5), replacing **Henri Namphy** (b. Nov. 2, 1932), a general who had headed a military junta since the overthrow of Jean-Claude Duvalier on Feb. 7, 1986. When Manigat attempted to reorganize the armed forces, Namphy deposed (June 19) him and declared himself president. In early September incidents of violence in Port-au-Prince were blamed on Namphy, and he was ousted (Sept. 17) in a coup led by **Prosper Avril**, another general, who had been associated with the Duvaliers.

1988 Jan. 31   Andreas G. Papandreou, prime minister of **Greece**, and **Turgut Özal**, prime minister of **Turkey**, ended a two-day meeting in Davos, Switzerland, with an announcement that they had agreed on various matters intended to make relations peaceful between their two nations.

1988 Feb. 1   It was reported that **Georgi M**[aximilianovich] [Georgy Maksimilianovich] **Malenkov** (b. Jan. 8, 1902), briefly successor to Joseph Stalin as master of communist Russia, had died, probably in January. Within 24 hours of Stalin's death on Mar. 5, 1953, Malenkov became head of the government and of the party as chairman of the council of ministers, prime minister, and first secretary of the Communist party. Rivals in the ruling circles forced him (Sept. 12) to give up the leadership of the party, and on Feb. 8, 1955, Malenkov resigned as prime minister. After his resignation he disappeared from public view.

1988 Feb. 8   The **Soviet government announced it would begin withdrawing** (May 15) **troops from Afghanistan**, where they had been fighting anti-communist guerrillas (from Dec. 1979). The pullout was to be completed by Feb. 15, 1989. Afghanistan, Pakistan, the U.S.S.R., and the U.S. reached (Apr. 14) an agreement providing for the withdrawal and for the restoration of a non-aligned Afghan nation. The Soviets said their forces had suffered 13,310 deaths and 35,478 wounded.

1988 Feb. 13   The first of a series of strikes and demonstrations, sometimes involving violence, broke out in the **Nagorno-Karabakh Autonomous Region** of the Soviet Socialist Republic of **Azerbaijan**. The population of the region consisted largely of Christian Armenians, but overall in Azerbaijan there was a Muslim majority. There was (Feb. 28) rioting in Sumgait, a city in Azerbaijan, that took the lives of c.32 people. By Mar. 24 Soviet troops were in Yerevan, the Armenian capital, to put down protests. By December more than 100,000 people from Armenia and Azerbaijan had fled their homes to escape the violence.

1988 Feb. 14   Alfredo Stroessner was elected to an eighth consecutive term as president of **Paraguay**. Election officials said he received 89 percent of the ballots, but opponents of the government claimed fraud, and many did not vote.

1988 Feb. 21   George Vassiliou (b. May 21, 1931), a businessman backed by the Communist party, won a runoff election to become president of **Cyprus**. He received 51.6 percent of the votes.

1988 Feb. 25   Eric Arturo Delvalle, president of **Panama**, attempted to dismiss **Manuel Antonio Noriega** (b. Feb. 11, 1938), the commander of the nation's Defense Forces and *de facto* ruler of the country. Noriega refused to accept his dismissal and forced the National Assembly to remove Delvalle from office. In his place the assembly elected as president **Manuel Solis Palma**, an ally of Noriega. Meantime a U.S. **federal grand jury indicted Noriega** (Feb. 4) on drug and racketeering charges.

1988 Mar. 14   The **Nicaraguan government and the Contra rebels signed a ceasefire agreement** to be in effect for 60 days. Negotiations for a permanent peace were to take place during the period but the talks broke down (June 9). Though a timetable for putting an end to the fighting seemed near, the Contras at the last moment insisted on speeding up the process in a way the government would not agree to. **Ronald Reagan** had signed (Apr. 1) a law that provided $47.9 million for the Contras, none of it to go for military matériel.

1988 Mar. 16   After an 11-month inquiry headed by a special prosecutor, a federal grand jury in Washington indicted four key figures in the **Iran-Contra Affair**: **John M. Poindexter**, former national security adviser; **Oliver L. North**, a member of Poindexter's staff; **Richard V. Secord**, a retired air force general engaged by North to direct the arms sales and to handle covert aid to the Contras; and **Albert Hakim**, an Iranian-American business partner of Secord, who acted as financial middleman. In a 23-count indictment, the four were accused of stealing money from the U.S. government, transferring some of it to the **Contras**, and wire fraud.

1988 Mar. 20   In elections in **El Salvador** the right-wing Nationalist Republican Alliance, known as Arena, won a majority of the 60 parliamentary seats. The presidency continued to be held by **José Napoleon Duarte** of the Christian Democratic party. Robert d'Aubuisson, the founder of Arena, along with associates had been accused of operating assassination squads in their campaign against communists.

1988 Apr. 18–Sept. 16   U.S. naval forces fought (Apr. 18) **with Iranian forces** in several incidents in the Persian Gulf. After warning Iranians to leave two oil platforms, the Americans destroyed them in retaliation for damage done (Apr. 14) to a U.S. navy frigate by a mine, presumably laid by Iran in international waters. When Iranian speedboats fired on American ships, the Americans retaliated, probably sinking two and damaging four others. On this same day Iranian gunboats raided the United Arab Emirates' offshore Mubarak oilfield. U.S. carrier planes sank one of them and damaged the other two. The U.S. announced (Apr. 29) that its ships in the Persian Gulf would defend any neutral ship that was under attack. On Sept. 16, the American government said it would halt full-time escorting of oil tankers in the gulf. In the **Iraq-Iran War**, Iraqi planes attacked (Mar. 19) two Iranian supertankers at the Kharg Island oil facility, resulting in the deaths of 54 merchant seamen. Three Iranian gunboats fired (Mar. 30) on a Kuwaiti military outpost on an island in the northern gulf, killing two Kuwaitis. Iran's attack was in retaliation for Kuwait's support of Iraq. Iran fired (Apr. 20) a surface-to-surface missile at Kuwaiti territory. Iraq carried out (May 14) another raid on Iranian supertankers, this time at Larak Island near the mouth of the gulf. Five ships were set on fire, and 22 seamen were killed or missing.

1988 Apr. 27 The ruling Democratic Justice party suffered a major defeat in elections in **South Korea** for seats in the National Assembly. It secured only 124 of the 299, yet remained the largest single seat holder. The Party for Peace and Democracy became the leading opposition party by winning 70 seats, three times as many as it held before the election. The vote also made **Kim Dae Jung** (b. Jan. 6, 1924) the chief political opposition figure in South Korea.

1988 Apr. 29 More than 7 million of **Ethiopia's** 47 million inhabitants were in need of emergency food relief, according to officials of humanitarian aid groups.

1988 May 8 **François Mitterand** of the Socialist party won election to a second seven-year term as president of **France**. With 54.3 percent of the vote, he defeated **Jacques Chirac**, the rightist prime minister who headed the *Rassemblement Pour la République* [RPR], a Gaullist party. After his loss Chirac resigned (May 10) and Mitterand named **Michel Rocard** (b. Aug. 23, 1930), also of the Socialist party, to the post to form a minority government. An election for the National Assembly gave (June 12) the Socialist party 276 seats, more than any other but not a majority of the 577 seats at stake.

1988 May 8 **Rodrigo Borja Cevallos** (b. June 19, 1935) of the Democratic Left party won a runoff election to become president of **Ecuador**. Borja faced serious economic problems because of the decline of oil prices in recent years.

1988 May 18 A ten-day siege by the Indian army of the **Golden Temple**, in Amritsar, the Punjab, ended with the surrender of 48 Sikh militants. At least 36 were killed during the siege and another 146 surrendered earlier. In the first four months of the year c.750 persons had been killed, almost all of them Hindus. The fighting continued after the siege of the temple, with thousands of Hindus fleeing the violence in the region.

1988 May 22 The general secretary of the Communist party of **Hungary**, **Janos Kádár**, was replaced by **Karoly Grosz** (b. Aug. 1, 1930), the prime minister (from June 25, 1987) and a long time communist. The change was a result of a power struggle in which Kádár and other hard-liners of the central committee and the politburo were replaced by men more inclined to liberalization at the expense of state control. Grosz resigned (Nov. 23) as prime minister and was succeeded by **Miklos Nemeth**, a member of the politburo.

1988 May 29 **Siaka P. Stevens** (b. Aug. 24, 1905), a former president of **Sierra Leone**, died. He became (1968) prime minister of the country seven years after Sierra Leone became independent of Great Britain, and assumed the presidency on Apr. 21, 1971, when the nation became a republic.

1988 June 1 **Mikhail S. Gorbachev and Ronald Reagan ended a four-day summit conference** in Moscow with expressions of goodwill but little in the way of accomplishments.

1988 June 9 The leaders of 17 Arab states ended a summit conference at Algiers, Algeria, by adopting a resolution in support of the *Intifada* in Israel. They pledged "all necessary help and assistance in all necessary forms," but did not agree to supply all the funds requested by the **PLO**, which had asked for as much as $400 million.

1988 June 22 The National Assembly of **Vietnam** elected **Do Muoi** (b. 1917) prime minister to succeed **Pham Hung** who died on Mar. 10. Muoi was the third-ranking member of the politburo.

1988 July 1 At a Communist party conference in Moscow drastic **changes in the political system of the U.S.S.R.** proposed by **Mikhail S. Gorbachev** were approved. However, for the first time in c.70 years some delegates voted in opposition to what their leaders wanted. On Dec. 1 the Supreme Soviet, again with some opposition, approved a law to put the changes into effect: creation of the post of president, to replace the general secretary of the Communist party as the top executive; establishment of a new national legislature with broad authority; fixed terms for office-holders; permitting multiple candidates to run for the same office; secret balloting; increased civil liberties; and some decentralization of the economy.

1988 July 3 Mistaking an **Iran Air A300 passenger jet** for a hostile F-14 fighter plane, the U.S. *Vincennes*, on patrol in the Persian Gulf, fired surface-to-air missiles that **downed** the passenger plane. All 290 people aboard were killed. An investigation by the navy concluded that the firing was due to crew error. **Ronald Reagan** said (July 11) compensation would be paid to the families of the passengers.

1988 July 24 A parliamentary election gave victory to the ruling coalition of **Prem Tinsulandond**, prime minister of **Thailand** (from 1980), but the prime minister declined a second term. He was succeeded (Aug. 4) by **Chatichai Choonhavan** (b. 1922), a supporter of Prem Tinsulandond's coalition.

1988 July 27 **U Sein Lwin** (b. Dec. 10, 1912), a former army general, was elected president of **Burma** [Myanmar] by Parliament. The day before he had been named chairman of the Burma Socialist Program party, the most powerful position in the country. He succeeded **U Ne Win**, who resigned as party chairman in the face of student-led demonstrations that had been going on for months. Ne Win's extreme isolationism, combined with a communist economic policy, had turned resources-rich Burma into one of the ten poorest countries in the world. But Sein Lwin's accession to power brought on even worse rioting, forcing his resignation (Aug. 12), and **U Maung Maung** (b. Jan. 11, 1925), the attorney general, was then elected (Aug. 19) president and head of the party. As the demonstrations continued, the military seized (Sept. 18) power and abolished all government bodies. **Saw Maung** (b. 1928), a general and a hardliner, became chairman of a new Organization for Building Law and Order. The army proceeded to deal even more harshly with the demon-

strators, killing by the end of the year c.1,000 and exiling thousands to remote areas of the country.

1988 July 31 **Hussein**, king of **Jordan**, announced that his country was abandoning all claims to the **West Bank**, which had been ruled (1948–1967) by Jordan and was occupied by Israel in the **Six-Day War** (1967). Hussein said he was taking this step to allow the **PLO** to be the sole representative of the Palestinians in the West Bank. The move was seen as a way for the king to consolidate his control over Jordanians of Palestinian descent, who form more than half of the East Bank's population of c.3 million people. The PLO welcomed its new role in West Bank affairs but wondered how to pay for the municipal services Jordan had been supplying.

1988 Aug. 6 The **Iraqi army began a major offensive** (to Aug. 31) against guerrilla rebels among the 3 million **Kurds** who live in northern Iraq. Kurds charged Iraq with using chemical weapons that killed more than 500 persons and injured c.3,000. About 60,000 Kurds fled into southeastern Turkey. The U.S. government said (Sept. 8) it was sure the Iraqis had used poison gas, but other sources could not confirm this. Earlier, Iraq had admitted (July 1) using chemical weapons in its war with Iran but claimed Iran had used them first.

1988 Aug. 8 Angola, Cuba, and South Africa agreed on an immediate **cease-fire in Angola** and in Namibia [South-West Africa], a step marking the beginning of the end of a dispute (from 1966) that concerned the status of **Namibia**. The South-West Africa People's Organization [SWAPO] had begun (1966) a guerrilla war for the independence of Namibia, which South Africa controlled even though it had been stripped (1966) of its trusteeship rights by the U.N. The last large-scale fighting occurred in Sept. 1987, when South Africa repulsed an invasion into Namibia staged by Angolan and Cuban troops. After the cease-fire, negotiations continued and Angola, Cuba, and South Africa signed (Dec. 22, 1988) an accord at Brazzaville, Congo, providing for the independence of Namibia and the withdrawal of the c.50,000 Cuban troops from Angola by July 1991.

1988 Aug. 10 U.S. President **Ronald Reagan** signed into law an act that apologized for the government's **forced relocation of Japanese-Americans** during World War II and established a $1,250,000,000 trust fund to compensate those placed in the camps and their families. The government was to pay $20,000 to each internee or designated beneficiary of the c.112,000 detainees. On Sept. 22, 1988, the Canadian government agreed to pay $17,325 in compensation to each of c.12,000 surviving Japanese-Canadians who had been forcibly interned in British Columbia during the war.

1988 Aug. 10   Arnulfo Arias [Madrid] (b. Aug. 15, 1901), three times president of Panama, died in exile in Miami, Florida, where he had lived since 1968. All three times he was president (1940–1941, 1949–1951, 1968) he was deposed by military coups.

1988 Aug. 16   Mohammed Zia ul-Haq (b. Aug. 12, 1924), president of **Pakistan**, was killed, along with 29 others, when a Pakistan air force plane crashed in eastern Pakistan. Zia had been president for 11 years taking power in a military coup in 1977. **Gulam Ishaq Khan**, leader of the Senate, assumed the duties of the presidency.

1988 Aug. 20   A cease-fire in the Iran-Iraq War (from Sept. 22, 1980) went into effect, having been accepted (Aug. 8) by the two nations under the auspices of the **U.N.** A 350-member U.N. team of observers was in place to monitor compliance. Peace talks between the two countries, with U.N. guidance, opened (Aug. 25) in Geneva, Switzerland, but no progress was made toward signing a permanent peace accord. The eight-year war was estimated to have resulted in 1 million deaths, 1.7 million wounded, and 1.5 million refugees. In addition Iran lost oil revenues of $23,000,000,000 and Iraq $65,-000,000,000.

1988 Aug. 22   Ethnic violence in **Burundi** had within a week taken a toll of c.5,000 lives. The fighting was between the Hutu tribe, almost 85 percent of the population, and the Tutsi, a minority of c.15 percent, who controlled the government and the army. About 40,000 Hutu had already fled to neighboring Rwanda.

1988 Aug. 30   Morocco and the Polisario Front guerrillas agreed, under U.N. auspices, to a peace plan to end the desultory warfare that had been going on in the **Western Sahara**, a former Spanish colony with valuable phosphate deposits. The plan called for a cease-fire in the near future and for the **U.N.** to take over the administration pending a referendum to decide the future of the region.

1988 Sept. 2   A new Brazilian constitution, to take effect on Sept. 23, was adopted by a Constituent Assembly after 19 months of debate. It strengthened civil liberties, labor rights, and social welfare benefits.

1988 Sept. 5   The government of Canada signed an agreement that gave to c.39,000 Indians, **Eskimos**, and people of mixed ancestry title to c.200,000 sq. mi. of the Arctic region of the nation. The agreement also gave non-whites a major role in the development of another 1.1 million sq. mi. in northern Canada. The agreement provided for a cash settlement to non-whites of $400 million over a 20-year period.

1988 Sept. 19   Zbigniew Messner, prime minister of **Poland**, and his cabinet resigned because of national dissatisfaction with his government's management of the economy. On Sept. 25 **Mieczyslaw Rakowski** (b. Dec. 1, 1926) was named prime minister. He was known as a foe of **Solidarity**, the independent labor union.

1988 Sept. 23   Amin Gemayel, president of **Lebanon**, appointed a military government to rule the country. This new cabinet was headed by **Michel Aoun** (b. Sept. 30, 1935), a Christian general. The other four members of the government represented various Christian and Muslim factions. Muslim leaders contended that the existing cabinet of **Selim al-Hoss**, a Sunni Muslim, was the legitimate government. The two rival governments continued to operate into 1989, each controlling certain areas.

1988 Sept. 29   The Nobel Peace Prize for 1988 was awarded to the **United Nations Peacekeeping Forces**. The awarding committee said they "represent the manifest will of the community of nations to achieve peace through negotiations." At the time of the award peacekeeping forces were active along the India-Pakistan border, in the Sinai, Golan Heights, Lebanon, and Cyprus.

1988 Sept. 30   The position of Mikhail S. Gorbachev in the U.S.S.R. was strengthened by the ouster of long-time members of the politburo: **Andrei A. Gromyko**, who had previously been foreign minister for 28 years and had assumed the presidency in 1985; and **Yegor K[uzmich] Ligachev** (b. Nov. 29, 1920), the party ideologist, who was replaced by **Vadim A. Medvedev** (b. Mar. 29, 1929). **Boris N[ikolayevich] Yeltsin** (b. Feb. 2, 1931) had lost (Feb. 18) his post as party chief in Moscow because he criticized as too slow the reforms being instituted.

On Oct. 1 **Gorbachev was elected president**, formally chairman of the Presidium of the Supreme Soviet. He also retained his post as general secretary.

1988 Oct. 5 Chilean voters rejected a bid by **Augusto Pinochet**, president for the past 15 years, to have his term extended for another eight years. In a referendum 54.7 percent voted against the proposal.

1988 Oct. 21 A federal grand jury in New York City indicted **Ferdinand Marcos**, former president of the Philippines, his wife **Imelda** [Romualdez] **Marcos** (b. Feb. 2, 1931), and eight associates on racketeering charges. They were said to have embezzled more than $100 million of Philippine government money and to have taken bribes. The funds were used to buy office buildings in New York as was $165 million in loans obtained fraudulently.

1988 Nov. 3 A band of armed mercenaries invaded the Indian Ocean republic of the **Maldives** at Male, the capital. On Nov. 4 Indian troops quickly overcame the several hundred invaders who had killed c.30 people and wounded the same number. After a two-day chase Indian navy warships caught a vessel on which some of the mercenaries were fleeing with 24 hostages, of whom four were killed and the rest freed. Indian and Sri Lankan officials said (Dec. 17) they had concluded that the mercenaries, who had been hired to overthrow the Maldives regime, were members of an ethnic guerrilla group, the **People's Liberation Organization of Tamil Eelam**, operating in Sri Lanka.

1988 Nov. 3 A referendum approved a number of political changes proposed by **Chadli Bendjedid**, president of **Algeria** (from 1979), to quiet rioting which in recent weeks had taken c.250 lives, mostly in Algiers. The major change would end the role of the National Liberation Front as the sole political party. On Nov. 5 **Kasdi Merbah** (b. 1938), a former cabinet officer and army commander, became prime minister.

1988 Nov. 15 **Yasir Arafat**, chairman of the **PLO** proclaimed the establishment of an **independent Palestinian state**. He did not specify what territory was included in this state. Arafat's public comments for the first time suggested that the PLO recognized the state of Israel, at least implicitly. Therefore, **Ronald Reagan** approved (Dec. 14) the beginning of talks concerning peace in the Near East with the PLO.

1988 Nov. 16 In an election for the National Assembly of **Pakistan**, the People's party, led by **Benazir Bhutto**, won 92 seats, more than any other party, but not a majority. On Dec. 1 she became prime minister of Pakistan, and the **first woman leader of a modern Islamic nation**.

1988 Nov. 16 The government of **Noboru Takeshita**, prime minister of **Japan**, secured approval in parliament of a major revision of the country's tax laws. The main features were a reduction of income tax rates and the imposition of a 3 percent sales tax.

1988 Nov. 21 In **Canadian** elections for the House of Commons, the Progressive Conservative party government of **Brian Mulroney**, prime minister, won 170 of the 295 seats to 82 for the Liberal party and 43 for the New Democrats. In effect the election was a referendum on the proposed **free trade treaty with the U.S.** The Progressive Conservatives were in favor of it, but the other two parties were opposed. The election result ensured the treaty's approval (Dec. 10) by Parliament.

1988 Dec. 1 **Carlos Salinas de Gortari** (b. Apr. 3, 1948) was inaugurated as president of **Mexico**. Salinas was an economist and a former minister of the budget and planning.

1988 Dec. 4 **Carlos Andrés Pérez** (b. Oct. 27, 1922) was elected president of **Venezuela** with 54.9 percent of the vote. Pérez had previously held (1973–1979) the office, but the Venezuelan constitution required the passage of two five-year terms before a person could seek reelection.

1988 Dec. 7 **Mikhail S. Gorbachev** announced that the **U.S.S.R. would make a unilateral cut in its armed forces** by 500,000 men and 10,000 tanks over the next two years. These cuts amounted to about ten percent of the total Soviet troop strength.

1988 Dec. 19 The Labor and Likud parties of **Israel** agreed to form a coalition government with **Yitzhak Shamir** of the Likud bloc continuing as prime minister. **Shimon Peres**, leader of the Labor party, became finance minister.

1988 Dec. 19 **Ranasinghe Premadasa** (June 23, 1924–May 1, 1993) was elected president of **Sri Lanka** with 50.4 percent of the vote. He was to succeed **Junius Jayewardene** on Jan. 2, 1989. Premadasa had been prime minister for the past ten years.

1988 Dec. 30 **Branko Mikulic** (b. June 10, 1928), prime minister of **Yugoslavia**, and his cabinet resigned. Mikulic said he had been frustrated by parliament and criticized for his government's handling of the economy. Yugoslavia was burdened with a $21,000,000,000 foreign debt, an annual inflation rate of c.200 percent, and an unemployment rate of 15 percent.

IV. ECONOMICS AND TRADE

1988 The use of **fax machines** ballooned this year as their cost went down and the speed of their transmission went up. A document could be sent around the world in 20 seconds and machines could be purchased for $800 or even less.

1988 Jan. 2 U.S. President **Ronald Reagan** and **Brian Mulroney**, prime minister of Canada, signed a **trade agreement** that would eliminate tariffs and reduce other barriers to trade and investment by the end of the century. The two countries were already each other's biggest customers, with trade in goods and services totaling $150,000,000,000 a year. The pact was ratified in both countries before the end of the year.

1988 Apr. 25 In **Poland a strike** began in a steel manufacturing plant near Kraków [Cracow] and spread to other mills. Workers in the Gdansk shipyard went (May 1–May 10) on strike, asking for higher pay and legalization of the **Solidarity** labor union. Later, strikes began (Aug. 1) in a number of coal mines and, with bus drivers also on strike, the government took (Aug. 22) emergency measures, such as the use of riot police, to try to end the labor turmoil. By Sept. 3 strikers in various fields began to go back to work.

1988 June 7 **Thirty-three nations agreed to open all of Antarctica to development**, on a regulated basis, of its oil and mineral resources. The agreement was thwarted when Australia and France jointly announced (Aug. 18, 1989) that they could no longer support the pact. They said they were opposed to any development at all of Antarctica's mineral resources.

1988 Oct. 15 The *Banco Español de Crédito* and *Banco Central* merged to create the **largest commercial bank in Spain**. The merged bank had about $59,-000,000,000 in assets and 4,247 branches.

1988 Oct. 27 The Soviet government admitted for the first time that the **U.S.S.R. had been running large budget deficits** for a number of years and that for the current year the deficit would be about $58,-000,000,000, or c.4 percent of Gross National Product [GNP]. The equivalent U.S. deficit at this time was somewhat more than 3 percent of GNP.

1988 Nov. 28 Representatives of **OPEC**, meeting in Vienna, Austria, agreed on a production quota system to which all 13 member nations consented. The accord was to begin on Jan. 1, 1989, and was to last for a six-month period. Production was set at 18.5 million barrels a day, much lower than the 23 million barrels OPEC nations had been pumping in recent weeks. It was hoped that lower production would increase the price to $18 a barrel from the current $12.

1988 Dec. 21 **Drexel Burnham Lambert, Inc.**, a major U.S. investment firm, agreed to plead guilty to six felony charges and to pay a fine of $650 million. The firm faced indictment on charges of mail fraud, wire fraud, and securities fraud. Of the total, $300 million would go to the federal government as a fine and $350 million would be used to pay investors and clients who claimed they lost money as a result of Drexel's illegal activities.

V. RELIGION AND PHILOSOPHY

1988 Feb. 19 **Pope John Paul II** issued an encyclical letter entitled *Sollicitudo Rei Socialis* [*The Social Concerns of the Church*] that condemned both East and West for their ideological rivalry. He wrote that this rivalry was harmful to poor nations by subjecting them to imperialistic "structures of sin" that held back their freedom and development. The encyclical was critical of both capitalism and Marxism. The pope said poor countries "need effective and impartial aid from all the richer and more developed countries" without involving them in ideological struggles.

1988 Mar. 21 The **Templeton prize**, worth $369,-000, was awarded for the first time to a Muslim, **Inamullah Khan**, secretary general of the World Muslim Congress, which was financed by Saudi Arabia. Khan had not only worked for greater unity among Muslims but had also maintained ties between the congress and Jewish groups. The Templeton Prize was established in 1972 to be the equivalent of the Nobel prizes in other fields. It was set up by **John Templeton** (b. Nov. 19, 1912), an American-born investor who was now a British citizen.

1988 Mar. 13   American Conservative Judaism, in its first statement of principles in the 143-year history of the movement, rejected fundamentalism, whether Christian, Jewish, or Muslim. After three years of work a committee issued "**Emet Ve-Emunah** [*Truth and Faith*]: Statement of Principles of Conservative Judaism," which supported loyalty to tradition but "without resigning from the 20th century." Fundamentalism was attacked not especially for its strict interpretation of scripture but for the way its followers tried to impose their beliefs on others.

1988 June 5   A service in the Patriarchal Cathedral of the Epiphany in Moscow began a year-long celebration of the **1,000th anniversary of the Russian Orthodox Church**. Although the church had been persecuted for 70 years by the communist regime, with c.50,000 clerics killed during the period of Stalin's dictatorship, under the leadership of **Mikhail S. Gorbachev**, dozens of churches and monasteries had been restored and reopened.

1988 Aug. 24   The governing council of the **United Church of Canada**, its largest Protestant denomination, voted to admit homosexual men and women to the clergy.

1988 Sept. 24   The **first woman to become a bishop of the Episcopal Church** in the U.S., **Barbara C. Harris** (b. 1903), was elected by the diocesan convention of the Diocese of Massachusetts. Harris, a black who was ordained in 1980, was at the time of her election associate rector of the Church of the Advocate, Philadelphia, Pennsylvania. Upon her consecration Harris became the suffragan, or assistant, bishop of the Diocese of Massachusetts.

1988 Sept. 30   Pope John Paul II issued an apostolic letter "**On the Dignity of Women**" which strongly defended their dignity but reaffirmed opposition to the ordination of women, characterizing female identity in what he termed the "vocations" of motherhood or virginity.

1988 Oct. 13   The Roman Catholic Church announced that the **Shroud of Turin** was not authentic. Tests conducted in three different laboratories showed that the linen dated from the Middle Ages. The shroud had been venerated by many Christians for centuries as the burial cloth of Jesus.

VI. SCIENCE, EDUCATION, AND TECHNOLOGY

1988   The Soviets launched (July 7 and 12) two unmanned spacecraft headed for Mars and intended particularly to examine the Martian moon Phobos. Contact with the first craft was lost in August and with the second in Mar. 1989, after it reached Phobos. Israel launched (Sept. 19) a satellite that was probably a first step toward developing a reconnaissance satellite. Named *Ofek 1* [Horizon], it was to be in space about a month. The American space shuttle program was resumed (Sept. 29) with *Discovery* launched safely into orbit from Cape Canaveral, Florida. It landed four days later at Edwards Air Force Base, California, having deployed a $100 million communications satellite. Russia celebrated (Nov. 15) the success of the flight of its first reusable spacecraft, the 100-ton *Buran*, meaning snow or blizzard, which blasted off from the Baikonur space center in central Asia and completed two orbits of the earth before returning. A new record for time spent in space was set (Dec. 21) by two Soviet cosmonauts who returned to earth after 366 days aboard the space station *Mir*. The record setters were **Vladimir Titov** (b. Jan. 1, 1947) and **Musa Manarov**.

1988 Jan. 11   I[sidor] **I**[saac] **Rabi** (b. July 28, 1898), a great figure in 20th-century physics, died. Rabi's main achievement was to develop a method for measuring the magnetic properties of atoms, molecules, and atomic nuclei. For his work Rabi received the **Nobel prize for physics** in 1944. Rabi was also an influential teacher and a leader in the debate over the moral implications of nuclear power.

1988 Feb. 15   Richard P[hillips] **Feynman** (b. May 11, 1918), an American physicist, one of the most influential of his generation, died. As a young scientist, he worked on the atomic bomb project at Los Alamos, New Mexico. He invented the "**Feynman diagrams**" of particle behavior. In these diagrams, using symbols in an abstract manner, it is possible to understand complicated events that otherwise would take weeks to calculate. They show the track made by a particle in both space and time and thus provide a way to describe interactions of particles. Feynman shared the **Nobel prize for physics** in 1965 for his research into the basic principles of quantum electrodynamics.

1988 Feb. 27   A **Gulfstream Jet IV** set a new east-to-west round-the-world speed record of 36 hr. 8

min. when it landed at Hobby Airport, Houston, Texas. The jet averaged 636 mph and traveled 19,-988 mi., 125 more than the minimum required.

1988 Mar. 3 Sewall Wright (b. Dec. 21, 1889), an American geneticist, died. He was generally considered the leading American evolutionary theorist of this century, helping to establish (from 1915) a mathematical basis for evolution. He was also a leader in experimental genetics.

1988 Mar. 13 The **longest undersea tunnel** in the world, the Seikan Tunnel between Aomori, Honshu, and Hakodate, Hokkaido, Japan, was opened. It was a railroad tunnel, 33.44 miles long, and passed under the Tsugaru Strait. At its deepest the tunnel was 787 feet below the water.

1988 Mar. 21   Patrick Steptoe (b. June 9, 1913), an English obstetrician, died. Steptoe developed a process for removing mature egg cells from a woman's ovary in order to be fertilized by sperms in a glass dish. After a fertilized egg was allowed to develop for a short time, it was returned to the womb. The first child conceived by this process was born on July 25, 1978.

1988 Apr. 12   The U.S. Patent Office issued a patent to Harvard University for a mouse developed by researchers at the Harvard Medical School by means of genetic manipulation. The patent was for "**transgenic nonhuman mammals**." The mouse is expected to provide an effective model for studying the ways genes contribute to the development of cancer, especially breast cancer.

1988 May 30   Ernst August Friedrich Ruska (b. Dec. 25, 1906), a German electrical engineer who invented the **electron microscope**, died. The electron microscope uses an electron beam made up of energy packets that behave in some ways like discrete particles and in other ways like waves. Ruska shared the **Nobel prize for physics** in 1986.

1988 June 5 A new **altitude record for a hot-air balloon** was set by a British balloonist **Per Lindstrand** in an ascent over Laredo, Texas. He reached a height of 58,700 ft.

1988 June 16 An international conference on **AIDS**, in Stockholm, Sweden, attracted c.7,500 scientists concerned with consolidating the vast amount of data collected thus far. On Apr. 27 it had been announced that an experimental **AIDS vaccine HPG-30** would be tested in Great Britain during the summer. In January an official of the **World Health Organization** [WHO] had estimated that there were between 5 and 10 million people worldwide infected with the HIV virus.

1988 June 28 The Canadian Parliament voted to **ban all cigarette advertising**, effective on Jan. 1, 1989. On July 17 **Nigeria** announced that it would ban cigarette advertising by the end of 1988. On Aug. 13 the government of **India**, where c.800,000 deaths a year were attributed to tobacco, said it was preparing to ban such advertising.

1988 Sept. 1   Luis W[alter] **Alvarez** (b. June 13, 1911), an American physicist, died. His use of bubble chambers to detect new subatomic particles won him the **Nobel prize for physics** in 1968. Earlier he had worked on the development of the atomic bomb at Los Alamos, New Mexico. Alvarez also devised a type of radar helpful to landing aircraft.

1988 Sept. 13 Archeologists announced the recent discovery of a rich cache of **pre-Columbian artifacts**, a 1500-year-old tomb located c.420 miles northwest of Lima, Peru. It was believed to be the tomb of a high-ranking warrior-priest of the Mochica [Moche] people (A.D. c.150 to A.D. c.800). The find included a gold face mask, a warrior's gold shield, and two strands of gold and silver beads.

1988 Oct. 9   Felix Wankel (b. Aug. 13, 1902), a German engineer who invented the **rotary automobile engine** that bore his name, died. Though he built the first Wankel engine in 1929, it was not until the late 1960s that it was used in the Japanese-built **Mazda** cars. The Wankel engine, not introduced into the U.S. until 1971, had only two moving parts, a triangular rotor, and a single elliptical chamber. Unlike the conventional combustion engine, it had no piston or cylinders.

1988 Oct. 12   José Sarney, president of Brazil, announced **measures to slow the destruction of the Amazon rain forest**. If they were put into effect and enforced, there would be an end to tax breaks, subsidized loans, and other incentives for development projects that harm the environment.

1988 Oct. 28 The French government ordered a pharmaceutical company to resume distribution of the abortion-inducing drug known as **RU 486**. The company that manufactured it, **Groupe Roussel Uclaf**, had yielded (Oct. 26) to the protests of anti-abortion interests and withdrawn it from the market. The drug was approved (Sept. 18) in China and in all c.10,000 women had already used RU 486.

1988 Nov. 22 **Raymond A[rthur] Dart** (b. Feb. 4, 1893), an Australian-born South African anatomist, died. His discovery (1924) of the skull of a child in a rock at a mine southwest of Johannesburg, South Africa, represented the first early human fossil find in Africa.

1988 Dec. 14 The **first fiber-optic cable** across the Atlantic Ocean went into operation. Using pulses of laser light, the new cable could simultaneously carry 40,000 calls, voice or computer data.

VII. ARTS AND LEISURE

1988 Feb. 14 **Frederick Loewe** (b. June 10, 1901), a German-born American composer, died. Outstanding among his works for the musical comedy stage were *Brigadoon* (1947) and *My Fair Lady* (1956). Loewe's long-time collaborator (from 1942), who wrote the lyrics for his compositions, was **Alan Jay Lerner** (Aug. 31, 1918–June 14, 1986).

1988 Feb. 19 **René Char** (b. June 14, 1907), a French poet, died. Under the *nom de guerre* **Capt. Alexander**, he led a resistance unit against the Nazis during World War II. Among his works were *Le Marteau Sans Maître* [*Hammer Without a Master*] (1934) and *Feuillets d'Hypnos* [*Leaves of Hypnos*] (1946). An English translation of his poetry appeared as *The Poems of René Char* (1976).

1988 Mar. 1 **Jean Le Poulain** (b. Sept. 12, 1924), one of France's most talented actors, died. He was particularly successful in the 1960s, when he had his own company and acted in more than 100 plays. He performed in a wide range of roles, from Shakespeare and Molière to Brecht and Corneille. Le Poulain was named (1986) administrative director of the *Comédie Française*.

1988 Mar. 25 **Robert Joffrey** [orig.: Abdullah Jaffa Bey Khan] (b. Dec. 24, 1930), the founder (1956) and director of the Robert **Joffrey Ballet** in New York City, died. Joffrey established a reputation as a teacher and was also resident choreographer (1957–1962) for the New York City Opera. Among his ballets were *Persephone* (1952) and *Astarte* (1957).

1988 Apr. 11 The **100th anniversary** of the *Concertgebouw*, Amsterdam's famed concert hall, was celebrated with a musical program attended by Beatrix, queen of the Netherlands.

1988 Apr. 12 **Alan Paton** (b. Jan. 11, 1913), a South African author and political leader, died. His novel *Cry, the Beloved Country* (1948) turned much of the world against the apartheid policy of his native land. When the Liberal party was founded (1953) to stand for universal suffrage, he became its president. The party was forced (1968) to disband when interracial parties became illegal. Paton nevertheless remained active politically. Among his writings were the novels *Too Late the Phalarope* (1953) and *Ah, But Your Land Is Beautiful* (1981). *Tales from a Troubled Land* (1961) was a volume of short stories. The first volume of his autobiography *Towards the Mountain* appeared in 1980.

1988 Apr. 17 **Louise Nevelson** [nee Louise Berliawsky] (b. Sept. 23?, 1899), a Russian-born American sculptor, died. Her sculptures mostly took a box or wall form. *Sky Cathedral* (1958) and *Bicentennial Dawn* (1975) were examples.

1988 May 22 The **National Gallery of Canada**, Ottawa, opened its new museum, a three-level building of stainless steel, granite, and glass with 350,000 sq. ft. of space.

1988 Aug. 18 **Frederick Ashton** (b. Sept. 17, 1904), an English choreographer and former director of the Royal Ballet of Great Britain, died. A choreographer in the classical manner, his first ballet was *A Tragedy of Fashion* (1926). Among others were *Facade* (1931), *Dante Sonata* (1940), and *Picnic at Tintagel* (1952).

1988 Oct. 13 **Naguib Mahfouz** (b. Dec. 11, 1911), an Egyptian novelist and playwright, became the first writer of Arabic to be awarded the **Nobel prize for literature**. The author of 40 novels and collections of short stories, he was only now becoming known in the English-speaking world. Mahfouz's trilogy, *Between the Palaces, The Palace of Aspiration,* and *The Sugar Pot* (1945–1957), was generally considered the best epic novel written in Arabic.

1988 Oct. 31 **John Houseman** [orig.: Jacques Haussmann] (b. Sept. 22, 1901), an American actor and producer, died. He directed the opera *Four Saints in Three Acts* (1934) and was associated with **Orson Welles** in various ventures, both on the stage and on radio. Houseman produced 18 movies, among them *The Blue Dahlia* (1946) and *Lust for Life* (1956). He captivated TV audiences as the law school professor in **The Paper Chase** series.

1988 Dec. 30   Isamu Noguchi (b. Nov. 17, 1904), an American-born sculptor who spent his early years in Japan, died. His work drew on the traditions of both East and West: meditative gardens and monumental works in front of office towers. Among his notable works were a sunken garden for the Beinecke Library at Yale University (1960–1964); *Red Cube* (1968), a 24-foot high sculpture for the Marine Midland Bank, New York City; and a basalt sculpture (1979) on Shikoku Island, Japan, where he had a home.

VIII. SPORTS, GAMES, AND SOCIETY

1988 Jan. 26   Australia, now independent, observed the **200th anniversary** of its beginnings as an English colony. Eleven tall sailing ships in Sydney Harbor reenacted the arrival of the first settlers.

1988 Feb. 13–28   The 14th Winter **Olympic Games** were held in Calgary, Canada, with nearly 1,800 athletes from 57 countries taking part. Soviet Union athletes won 11 gold medals and 29 medals overall; East Germany 9 and 25; and Switzerland 5 and 15. The U.S. won only 2 and 6.

1988 Mar. 31   Officials in Italy and the U.S. announced the **indictment of 233 suspected members of a Sicilian Mafia** drug ring as the result of a two-year joint investigation.

1988 Apr. 17   A new **world record for the marathon** was set by **Belaney Densimo** of Ethiopia with a time of 2 hr., 6 min., 50 sec.

1988 May 9   The parliament of Iceland completed action on a bill to **legalize beer**, with an alcohol content of 2.5 percent. Complete prohibition of alcoholic beverages was in effect in Iceland from 1915 to 1933, when alcoholic beverages, except for beer, were legalized.

1988 June 5   Kay Cottee of Australia became the **first woman to sail around the world alone** and nonstop when she arrived back at Sydney after a voyage of 189 days. Her 36-foot sloop *Blackmore's First Lady* sailed 23,000 miles in an easterly voyage.

1988 June 12   Andy Hampsten became the first American cyclist to win the *Giro d'Italia* [*Tour of Italy*] since it was first held in 1909. The race covered a distance of 2,235 miles from Urbino.

1988 Aug. 14   Enzo Ferrari (b. Feb. 20, 1898), an Italian racing car designer and driver, died. His cars, of which he produced only c.1,000 a year, became the epitome of automotive power, acceleration, and perfect handling at high speeds, as well as status symbols that cost more than $100,000. Ferrari won his first race in 1924 but gave up racing in 1932 to supervise the production and racing of his cars.

1988 Sept. 7–9   In two straight races the **America's Cup** was successfully defended off San Diego, California, by the *Stars and Stripes*, which defeated *New Zealand*. The New Zealand challenger won the right to race with a 132-foot monohull. The American defenders replied by constructing a 60-foot multihull catamaran. On Mar. 28, 1989, a New York State judge ordered the San Diego Yacht Club, sponsor of the *Stars and Stripes*, to forfeit the cup on the grounds that it had won unfairly, but on Sept. 19, a New York appeals court overturned this decision.

1988 Sept. 9   An **auction in London** of jewelry, used clothing, and various artifacts belonging to the rock singer **Elton John** (b. Mar. 25, 1947) brought $8,224,637. John said he was selling his possessions to change his image and because he had no more room in his home.

1988 Sept. 10   [Stefanie Maria] **Steffi Graf** (b. June 14, 1969) of West Germany won the grand slam of **tennis** when she took the women's title at the U.S. Open. Earlier in the year she had won the Australian, British, and French championships.

1988 Sept. 17–Oct. 2   The 24th Summer **Olympic Games** were held in Seoul, South Korea, with nearly 10,000 athletes from 160 countries competing. Athletes of the Soviet Union won 55 gold medals and 132 medals overall; East Germany 37 and 102; and the U.S. 46 and 94. **Ben Johnson** (b. Dec. 30, 1961) of Canada set a world record of 9.79 sec. for the 100-meter dash but was disqualified after tests showed he had been using anabolic steroids. Six other athletes tested positive and also were disqualified.

1989

VITAL STATISTICS
AND DEMOGRAPHICS

1989   In mid-year the Population Reference Bureau estimated the **population of the world** at 5,234,000,-000. The populations, in round figures, of the major regions of the world were: **Africa**, 646,000,000; **Asia**, 3,061,000,000, of which 1,103,900,000 were in China; **Europe**, 499,000,000; **Latin America**, 438,-000,000, of which 115,000,000 were in Central America, 33,000,000 in the Caribbean area, and 290,000,000 in South America; **North America**, 275,-000,000; **Oceania**, 26,000,000; and the U.S.S.R., 289,000,000. The estimated population of the ten largest metropolitan areas were [figures in parentheses are for the city proper]: Tokyo, Japan, 1985, 27,824,000 (1988, 8,328,000); New York City, U.S., 1987, 18,053,800 (1986, 7,262,700); Mexico City, Mexico, 1985, 17,321,800 (1985, 9,931,400); Osaka, Japan, 1985, 15,891,000 (1988, 2,647,000); São Paulo, Brazil, 1985, 15,233,500 (1985, 7,032,500); Los Angeles, U.S., 1987, 13,470,900 (1986, 3,259,-300); Shanghai, China, 1986, 12,323,300 (1986, 6,987,200); London, England, 1986, 12,290,500 (1986, 6,775,200); Buenos Aires, Argentina, 1985, 10,750,00 (1986, 2,924,000); Calcutta, India, 1985, 10,462,000 (1981, 3,300,000).

1989   Mostly because of war and drought, but partly because of xenophobic governments, **large migrations of population** from one country or region to another occurred. A border dispute between Senegalese farmers and Mauritanian herders in West Africa ended with the repatriation of c.100,000 Mauritanian nationals living in **Senegal** and 85,000 Senegalese in **Mauritania**. Following this, between May and July, about 40,000 black Mauritanians were forced out of their own country by their Arab or Berber countrymen. Across Africa, **Ethiopia**, already suffering from famine and civil war, had been invaded by more than 500,000 refugees. About 350,-000 moved east from the **Sudan** in an attempt to escape both civil war and famine there. About 150,-000 refugees came west from **Somalia** to escape the civil war there. The Sudan, in turn, not only had absorbed about 20,000 refugees fleeing the civil war of the late 1970s and the 1980s in **Chad** to the west, but also over the past 20 years had absorbed c.625,000 persons escaping the fighting of Eritrean rebels attempting to secure independence from Ethi-

opia. The United Nations estimated that, in spite of its large-scale relief efforts, 250,000 people had died of starvation in the Sudan, mostly in the south, in 1988. In Europe, beginning in May, the Bulgarian government exerted pressure on its c.1.5 million ethnic Turks to leave for Turkey. By mid-August, as many as 310,000 people had left, some of their own free will, for **Turkey**. The Turkish government then announced (Aug. 21) that it would not allow any more Bulgarian Turks in, citing its inability to care for them. In the Near East, since the start (1975) of the civil war in **Lebanon**, residents had been fleeing the country, with **Cyprus** usually their first stop. In all more than 1,000,000 persons had by now fled Lebanon, with **France** absorbing c.120,000, more than any other country. During the year a different kind of movement of people occurred when 62,500 Jews were allowed to leave the **Soviet Union**, a record number, surpassing the 51,320 mark set in 1979, and far more than the slightly fewer than 20,000 allowed to emigrate in 1988. In 1989, c.10,000 emigrated to Israel; most of the others went to the U.S.

1989 Jan. 31   The U.S. Census Bureau projected that the population would peak at c.302,000,000 persons in 2038 and would then gradually decline to c.292,000,000 by 2080. The bureau also estimated that by 2030 there would be 66 million people 65 years of age or older, or 22 percent of the population, compared with 30 million this year. As of July 1989, the bureau estimated the **U.S. population** at 248,-239,000, an increase of 8.7 percent, compared with the 1980 census figure. The U.S. government announced (Oct. 11) that for the first time the Hispanic population of the country had passed the 20 million mark, constituting 8.2 percent of the population, compared with 6.5 percent in 1980. The government also announced (Oct. 30) that the number of babies born this year was nearing the 4 million mark, a figure not reached since 1964. During the baby boom (1945–1964), women had slightly more than three children each. Now they were having somewhat fewer than two, but there were many more of them.

II. EXPLORATION
AND COLONIZATION

1989 Dec. 11   A six-man team of international explorers reached the South Pole, the first expedition to achieve this by dog sled since Roald Amundsen's trek of 1911. The expedition left (July 28) the Antarctic Peninsula on its 4,000-mile journey across the continent, reaching (Mar. 3, 1990) a Soviet base at the opposite end of the continent. It was the **first overland crossing of Antarctica.**

III. DISASTERS

1989 Jan. 23 A mudslide, set off by an **earthquake** that registered 5.5 on the Richter scale, killed c.300 persons in three settlements in Tadzhikistan, in central southern U.S.S.R. A buildup of water from melting snow and work on an irrigation canal were blamed for the severity of the mudslide.

1989 Feb. 1 In the **first environmental disaster in Antarctica,** an Argentinian **supply ship** *Bahia Paraiso*, which had earlier **run aground** off the Antarctic Peninsula about 600 miles south of Cape Horn, began leaking diesel fuel and threatening wildlife in the area. Penguin rookeries were endangered and adult flying birds left their nesting areas. Krill, a main source of food for several species, was reported being killed off.

1989 Feb. 8 A **Boeing 707** jet, operated by Independent Air Holdings, a small American charter service, **crashed** into Pico Alto, the highest mountain in the **Azores**, while trying to land at the Santa Maria airport. All 144 persons aboard, who were Italian vacationers on their way to the Caribbean, were killed. The fault for the crash seemed to lie with the pilots and air controllers, who appeared confused by radio messages.

1989 Mar. 24 The **worst oil spill in U.S. territory** began when the supertanker *Exxon Valdez*, owned by the Exxon Corporation, ran aground in Prince William Sound in southeastern Alaska, dumping 240,000 barrels of oil. By Mar. 27 winds of 70 mph were hampering salvage efforts, and the next day the state and fishermen, whose livelihood was endangered, took over the work of containing the spill. Wind and currents spread the oil more than 50 miles from its source, coating beaches and covering marine and bird life with oil. In all, 730 miles of coastline were eventually affected. By September, it was estimated that as many as 400,000 animals, including birds and fish, had suffered. Tests showed that the captain of the tanker, **Joseph J. Hazelwood,** had been drinking and that an uncertified officer had been at the helm when the ship hit the reef. It was reported (Dec. 4) that Exxon had spent $1 billion in

its cleanup effort, which was thought to have been slow and inefficient. Exxon was indicted (Feb. 27, 1990) by a federal grand jury on five criminal counts and faced fines of up to $600 million if convicted. Hazelwood was acquitted (Mar. 22, 1990) by an Alaskan court of the three serious charges brought against him and was convicted of a single charge of misdemeanor negligence. The next day a judge sentenced him to 1,000 hours of community service cleaning the beaches his ship had fouled. Exxon agreed (Mar. 13, 1991) with Alaska and the federal government to pay a penalty of $100 million and provide $1 billion over a period of ten years to continue the cleanup. Later, both sides changed their minds and rejected the agreement. The matter was finally settled (Oct. 8, 1991) when Exxon agreed to pay an extra $25 million penalty. Hazelwood's conviction was overturned (July 10, 1992) by an Alaskan court, which cited a federal statute that grants immunity to those who report oil spills.

1989 Apr. 7 A **Soviet nuclear-powered submarine,** presumably armed with nuclear weapons, caught fire while submerged, rose to the surface, and then **sank** in the Norwegian Sea, about 270 miles north of **Norway.** The Soviets said (May 8) that 42 crew members had died. A second Russian nuclear-powered submarine, cruising north of Norway, burst a pipeline (June 26) in its reactor but was able to return safely to its home port.

1989 Apr. 15 A **crush of fans in an overcrowded soccer stadium** at Sheffield, **England,** resulted in the deaths of 95 and injuries to 170. The report (Aug. 4) of an investigation into the tragedy largely blamed the police for lack of leadership and experience, but mention was also made of the unruly behavior of fans who had been drinking, and of inadequate ticketing procedures.

1989 Apr. 19 An **explosion and fire** in a 16-inch-gun turret of the U.S. battleship *Iowa*, c.300 miles northeast of Puerto Rico, killed 47 sailors. The other 11 men in the gun crew were six levels deep in the turret and survived the blast. A Navy investigation concluded (Sept. 7) that the explosion was "most probably" sabotage and blamed a gunner's mate, who was termed despondent and suicidal. The investigation also disclosed serious mismanagement aboard the ship and recommended disciplinary action against senior officers. Amid rumors of murder, suicide, and a homosexual relationship, many persons, including members of Congress, cast doubt on the Navy's findings. As a result, and on the basis of tests on powder bags, the Navy announced (May 24, 1990) that it was reopening its investigation. It also ordered all battleships not to fire their 16-inch guns until further orders.

1989 June 3   A **gas pipeline explosion** on the route of the trans-Siberian railway, near Ufa, 250 miles northwest of Kuibyshev, in the Ural Mountains, engulfed two passenger trains in flames and killed c.500 people. Another c.200 were missing and c.720 were injured. The trains, moving in opposite directions, were mainly filled with families on vacation. Negligence by pipeline operators had allowed gas to escape and accumulate in the valley through which the railroad ran. It was believed a spark from one of the trains ignited the explosion.

1989 June 7   A Suriname Airways **DC-8** with 182 people aboard **crashed** in a jungle area near the airport of Paramaribo, **Suriname**, on the northern coast of South America. Of the passengers and crew, 168 were killed and others injured as the plane attempted to land in a dense fog at an airport that had no radar. Three of the passengers were star Dutch soccer players of Suriname origin.

1989 June 23–24   Three **oil spills** within 12 hours fouled American coastlines from New England to Texas. Off Providence, Rhode Island, the tanker *World Prodigy*, Greece-registered and Liberian-owned, spilled c.10,000 barrels of No. 2 fuel oil. Because this oil evaporates quickly, it was soon cleaned up. The shipping company and the captain of the tanker pleaded guilty (Aug. 16) to federal charges of causing the spill and were fined $510,000. At La Porte, Texas, in the Houston Ship Channel, an oil barge collided with a cargo ship and spilled c.6,000 barrels of heavy crude oil, a type fairly easy to clean up. Near Claymont, Delaware, a Uruguyan tanker, *Presidente Rivera*, went out of the shipping lane and hit (June 24) a rock in the Delaware River, spilling c.10,000 barrels of No. 10 fuel oil. The oil came to the surfaced in blobs and floated down the river, ending up at various places along the shore.

1989 July 19   After struggling for 45 minutes to control his disabled plane, the pilot of a United Airlines **DC-10 crashed** it just short of the runway of the Sioux City, Iowa, airport. Of the 296 persons aboard, 185 survived. A study of parts of the plane found over a wide area of farmland indicated that a crack caused an engine disk to break apart.

1989 Sept.   3 A Cuban Airlines **Ilyushin 62-M crashed** into a village shortly after its takeoff from the José Marti airport in Havana, **Cuba**, headed for Milan, Italy. Of the 126 people aboard, only one survived; 14 people were killed on the ground and 23 injured. Of the passengers, 113 were Italian tourists.

1989 Sept. 17–22   **Hurricane Hugo**, one of the most powerful storms of the century, began its northwesterly rampage across the Caribbean Sea and toward the U.S. mainland when it hit Guadeloupe, an island in the West Indies, with winds of up to 150 mph and left c.3,000 people homeless. On the island of Montserrat, nearly all its 12,000 residents were left homeless, without food, water, or electricity. Hugo reached (Sept. 18) Puerto Rico, killing 19 persons and leaving c.50,000 homes destroyed or damaged. American military police were sent (Sept. 20) to the U.S. Virgin Islands to put down two days of looting after those islands were hit. The hurricane struck the U.S. coast (midnight Sept. 21) with winds of 115 mph. Charleston, South Carolina, which bore the brunt of the onslaught, lost many landmark buildings, and the surrounding beach areas were destroyed. In spite of the fury of the hurricane, the tenth most severe to hit the U.S. in the 20th century, it took only 51 lives, 24 of them in the U.S. Estimates of property losses ran as high as $3.7 billion in South Carolina alone and $1 billion in Puerto Rico.

1989 Sept. 19   A Union des Transports Aériens [UTA] **DC-10 jet** with 171 people aboard **disappeared** on a flight from Ndjamena, **Chad**, to Paris, France. It was located the next day in the Niger desert, apparently the victim of a mid-air explosion that killed all on board. Evidence was found that there had been explosives on the plane, but there was no clue as to who was responsible.

1989 Oct. 17   An **earthquake** registering 6.9 on the Richter scale, with its epicenter near Santa Cruz, California, 80 miles southeast of San Francisco, rocked the area with the worst tremor in U.S. history since the San Francisco quake of 1906. Although property damage was estimated at as much as $10 billion, the quake killed only 66 persons, with 2,874 receiving medical treatment. Most of the dead—41—died in the collapse of a section of the double-deck Nimitz Freeway in Oakland, across the bay from San Francisco. The earthquake occurred minutes before the third baseball game of the 1989 World Series in San Francisco's Candlestick Park. The stadium, with over 60,000 people in it, was only slightly damaged, and the spectators were evacuated without incident.

1989 Oct. 21 The **worst airplane crash in Central American** history occurred at Las Tablitas, 25 miles south of Tegucigalpa, capital of **Honduras**, when a Honduran Airline Boeing 727, on a flight from San José, Costa Rica, crashed into Cerro Hules, a 6,500-foot peak. Of the 131 persons aboard, all but 15 were killed.

1989 Nov. 27 An Avianca Airlines **Boeing 727 exploded** and crashed into a hillside on the outskirts of Bogota, **Colombia**, killing all 107 persons on board. It had just taken off on a flight to Cali, Colombia. Some hours later a telephone caller to a radio station claimed a group connected with the Colombian drug trade had caused the disaster. Investigators said (Dec. 5) that they had found evidence that a bomb had been aboard the aircraft. It was widely believed that one of Colombia's powerful drug cartels had planted the bomb, perhaps to kill an informant believed to be aboard.

1989 Dec. 28 The first **earthquake** ever to strike a large urban area of **Australia** was registered at 5.5 on the Richter scale at Newcastle, 75 miles north of Sydney, on the coast of New South Wales. In a population of c.500,000, only 10 people were killed, most of them in the collapse of the Newcastle Workers' Club. About 100 were injured, and damage was estimated at $600 million.

IV. WAR AND POLITICS

1989 Jan. 4 In the Mediterranean Sea **warplanes** from the *John F. Kennedy*, an American aircraft carrier, **shot down two Soviet-built MIG-23** Libyan fighter planes over international waters off the Libyan coast. The American pilots said the Libyan planes trailed them in a hostile manner; **Libya** claimed its planes were unarmed and on a routine patrol. The U.S. said (Jan. 5) that it had visual evidence that the Libyan planes were armed with missiles. The incident came at a time when the U.S. was expressing concern about a chemical plant in Libya that, it claimed, had been built to produce chemical weapons. Libya denied this.

1989 Jan. 7 **Hirohito** (b. Apr. 29, 1901), emperor of **Japan** (from Dec. 25, 1926), the nation's longest reigning monarch, died. Hirohito came to the throne to rule over a nation growing in both industrial

strength and armed might. Whether or not he tried to restrain the militarists, first in the invasion (1931) of Manchuria and then in the moves that took (1941) Japan into World War II (1939–1945), remained unclear. Apparently, however, he did make (1945) the decisive choice in favor of peace, and in a radio broadcast (Aug. 15) he told the nation it had been defeated. Hirohito made (Jan. 1, 1946) another memorable broadcast when he repudiated "the false conception that the emperor was divine." In his private life the emperor was a dedicated marine biologist, who wrote several authoritative books. His state funeral, with all the pomp of ancient tradition, was held Feb. 24. In accordance with Japanese custom, Hirohito's reign was given an honorific name, Showa [= bright peace]. Hirohito was succeeded (to the present) by his eldest son Akihito (b. Dec. 23, 1933).

1989 Jan. 11 Representatives of 140 nations, meeting in Paris, France, **condemned the use of chemical weapons** and urged greater efforts to complete a treaty that would ban the development, production, and possession of them. This declaration in effect affirmed a 1925 convention, drafted as a result of the first use of such weapons in World War I (1914–1918), but which banned only the use of chemical weapons. The U.S. and France, who had convoked the conference, did so partly because of their alarm at the large-scale use of chemical weaponry by Iraq in the **Iraq-Iran War** (1980–1988). The Soviet Union had announced (Jan. 8) that it would begin to destroy its chemical weapons, but gave no timetable.

1989 Jan. 16 In Vienna, Austria, the **Conference on Security and Cooperation in Europe** [CSCE], consisting of all the nations of Europe, except Albania, plus Canada and the U.S., produced a new agreement for the protection of **human rights**. Among those rights were: to distribute and have free access to information; to be protected in the monitoring of such rights; equality of men and women; and freedom from discrimination on grounds of religion. In addition the conference condemned terrorism and agreed to cooperate in opposing it.

1989 Jan. 19 **Ante Marković** (b. Nov. 25, 1924), a member of the collective presidency of Croatia, became prime minister of **Yugoslavia**, succeeding **Branko Mikulic**, who had resigned (Dec. 30, 1988) and was now the caretaker prime minister. He had stepped down because his budget was opposed in parliament and his proposals for drastic economic reforms were not accepted. The new prime minister, who had long been a member of the Communist party and had fought as a guerrilla with Tito during World War II (1939–1945), was expected to support economic change to counter high inflation and unemployment.

1989 Jan. 20   George [Herbert Walker] **Bush** was inaugurated as the 41st president of the U.S. As the Republican party candidate in the election (Nov. 7, 1988), he received 48,881,011 popular votes and 426 electoral votes to 41,828,350 and 112 for the candidate of the Democratic party, **Michael S**[tanley] Dukakis (b. Nov. 3, 1933). J[ames] **Danforth Quayle** (b. Feb. 4, 1947) was inaugurated as vice president.

1989 Jan. 28   At an unusual gathering in Moscow, comprised of American, Cuban, and Soviet officials who had been involved in the superpower showdown (Oct. 1962) over Russian nuclear weapons, the Russians revealed that, unknown to **John F. Kennedy**, the American president, there were 20 **nuclear warheads in Cuba** before he declared (Oct. 23, 1962) a naval blockade of Cuba. The Soviets said the warheads, though not attached to missiles, could have been deployed in a matter of hours.

1989 Feb. 3   A military coup that took c.300 lives resulted in the ouster of **Alfredo Stroessner**, dictator of **Paraguay** (from 1954). The coup was led by **Andrés Pedotti Rodríguez** (b. June 19, 1924), a general long associated with Stroessner, and was essentially not a blow against dictatorship but a blunt struggle for power within the ruling clique. Stroessner went into exile in Brazil, and Rodriguez assumed the presidency. In an election (May 1), Rodriguez became president with 74 percent of the vote.

1989 Feb. 9   In an election in **Jamaica**, the People's National party, led by **Michael N. Manley**, won a majority of the seats in Parliament, thus defeating the Jamaica Labour party of **Edward P. G. Seaga**, the prime minister. Manley became prime minister for a second time, having previously served (1972–1980). In his earlier term, he had not been friendly toward the U.S. and had made much of his friendship with **Fidel Castro**, the Communist leader of Cuba, but in the election campaign he said he would follow a conciliatory course in foreign affairs.

1989 Feb. 14   The presidents of **five Central American nations** [Costa Rica, El Salvador, Guatemala, Honduras, and Nicaragua], meeting in Tesoro Beach, El Salvador, **reached an agreement** whereby the bases in Honduras of the **Contra rebels**, opponents of the Marxist regime in Nicaragua, would be closed; in return **Nicaragua** was to hold a free and open election on Feb. 25, 1990. A plan was to be drawn up within 90 days to arrange for the disarming and relocation of the Contras. Nicaragua agreed to set free most of the 3,300 Contras and former National Guardsmen it held in prison. This plan brought about a new agreement (April) between **George Bush**, president of the U.S., and the Congress, which had been refusing to give more military aid to the Contras, that $4.5 million a month for food, clothing, shelter, and medical supplies would go to the Contras through Feb. 1990. At another meeting (Aug. 7), the five presidents announced an accord for closing the Contra bases in Honduras by December under international supervision, but nothing had been done as of the end of the year.

1989 Feb. 15   The **last Soviet troops** of an invasion force that had occupied **Afghanistan** (from Dec. 27, 1979) left the country as agreed at an international conference (Apr. 1988). It was estimated that at its peak the Soviet force in Afghanistan totaled 115,000 and that c.15,000 of them had been killed in the course of the occupation. But the civil war went on between the Soviet-backed Marxist government and their guerrilla opponents based in Pakistan, who were supplied with arms by the U.S. The rebels proclaimed (Feb. 24) a "free Muslim state" and set about attacking government-held positions. After some initial successes, its military operations bogged down, and by the end of the year, they had made little progress. The Soviet government admitted (Oct. 23) that its invasion and occupation had violated both Russian law and the normal standards of international behavior.

1989 Feb. 16   A parliamentary election returned the United National party, headed by **Ranasinghe Premadasa**, who continued as president of **Sri Lanka**, to power. The party won 125 of 225 seats. The Sri Lanka Freedom party took 67 seats. The campaign had been marred by extreme violence by the People's Liberation Front, a left-wing Sinhalese guerrilla group, and by Tamil separatists. More than 1,000 people were killed by election day. The ethnic and separatist violence continued all year, and in December Amnesty International said more than 1,000 persons a month were dying.

1989 Feb. 17   A third grouping of Arab nations was formed at a meeting in Marrakech, Morocco, consisting of Algeria, Libya, Mauritania, Morocco, and Tunisia. Named the **Maghreb Union**, it was organized primarily to encourage trade among the five and to allow them to present a united front to the **European Community** [EC]. Two days earlier, in Baghdad, Iraq, four other Arab countries [Egypt, Iraq, Jordan, and North Yemen] had established the **Arab Cooperative Council** [ACC], also intended to encourage economic relations. The third group, the **Gulf Cooperation Council** [CCC] (1981), consisted of Bahrain, Kuwait, Oman, Qatar, the United Arab Emirates, and Saudi Arabia, the most powerful of the group, which took the lead but did not dominate the affairs of its neighbors.

1989 Feb. 23 Voters in **Algeria approved a new constitution** by a 70 percent to 30 percent margin. It was intended to institute a multiparty political system for the first time since Algeria won (1962) independence from France. The new document also guaranteed freedom of expression. It was a step in the direction of social and political changes that had been promised by **Chadli Benjedid** (b. Apr. 14, 1929), president of Algeria (from 1979), who had been elected (Dec. 1988) to a third five-year term.

1989 Mar. 8 Showing its growing support for international organizations, the **Soviet Union** announced it **would accept binding arbitration by the International Court of Justice** in disputes arising from five human rights agreements. It was the first time the U.S.S.R. had agreed to allow outside jurisdiction over disputes arising from conventions and treaties which it had signed. The matters in dispute would concern conventions dealing with such matters as genocide, women's rights, and racism.

1989 Mar. 8 Following three days of violent protests against Chinese rule of **Tibet**, the **Chinese Army imposed martial law on Lhasa**, the capital. In the most serious uprising against China since 1959, at least 12 people were killed and more than 100 wounded earlier in the week. The Tibetans were demanding political freedom and the return of their spiritual leader, the **Dalai Lama**, who had fled (1959) into exile in India during previous disturbances.

1989 Mar. 20 **Alfredo Cristiani** (b. Nov. 22, 1947), leader of the rightist National Republican Alliance [Arena], was elected president of **El Salvador**, receiving about 53 percent of the vote against six opponents and replacing the more liberal Christian Democrats not only in the presidency but also in control of the National Assembly. Arena, organized eight years earlier, was associated with death squads that murdered political opponents at will. The election was a disappointment to the U.S. government, which had strongly supported the moderate outgoing president **José Napoléon Duarte**, in his struggle against both Arena and a strong leftist guerrilla movement.

1989 Mar. 26 In the **Soviet Union the first free election** in 70 years resulted in a rebuke to the ruling Communist party. The election was held to establish a new body, the Congress of People's Deputies, consisting of 2,250 persons. Of these half were to be appointed by the Communist party and the other half elected by the voters. The voters had the power to defeat high-ranking party members who chose to run for election. They did so with a vengeace, rejecting such persons as the mayor of Moscow and the party leader in Leningrad. At the same time vocal dissidents of the **Mikhail S. Gorbachev** regime, such as **Boris N**[ikolayevich] **Yeltsin** (b. Feb. 2, 1931), recently deposed as head of the party in Moscow for his dissent, were elected.

1989 Apr. 2 In the first free election since achieving independence from France (1956), **Tunisian voters chose Zine al-Abidine Ben Ali** as president with 99.3 percent of the ballots they cast. Ben Ali had ruled the country since he deposed (Nov. 7, 1987) **Habib Bourguiba**. Although he had urged a more diversified body, his Constitutional Democratic Rally won all 141 seats in parliament.

1989 Apr. 5 **Vietnam** announced that its troops, which had invaded (Dec. 25, 1978) **Cambodia**, would be withdrawn by September. Vietnam reported (Sept. 26) that the last 26,000 of its troops had left the country. Vietnamese strength in Cambodia was believed to have been as high as 200,000. During the year talks were held among the various nations and factions about what sort of government Cambodia should have. The **search for a political solution** was complicated by a great power rivalry: China supported the **Khmer Rouge**; the U.S., **Prince Sihanouk**, a former head of state; and Russia, the Vietnamese-installed government. The General Assembly of the U.N. voted (Nov. 16) in favor of a settlement that would give the Khmer Rouge a role in an interim government led by Sihanouk, while preparations were made for an internationally supervised election. The government of Cambodia accepted (Dec. 11) this arrangement.

1989 Apr. 9–June 19 The **U.S.S.R.**, which encompassed within its sprawling boundaries 104 different nationalities, was faced with **violent unrest** among some of them, which stemmed from many years of dissatisfaction with Russian and Communist rule and was probably triggered by the loosening of governmental reins by the regime of **Mikhail S. Gorbachev**. Within each area where demonstrations occurred there were also ethnic groups at odds with one another. Troops and demonstrators fought (Apr. 9) in Tbilisi, the capital of **Soviet Georgia**, east of the Black Sea. At least 19 persons were killed and hundreds injured. Violence that struck (June 4–11) in **Uzbekistan** S.S.R., in central-southern U.S.S.R., was an ethnic battle between Uzbeks and Meskhetians, a Turkish minority. Troops were required to put down the fighting, which took c.100 lives, and an airlift was used to fly most of the 16,000 Meskhetians to safety. Rioting that broke out (June 19) in **Kazakhstan** S.S.R., also in central southern U.S.S.R., was blamed on poor living conditions.

1989 Apr. 15 **Hu Yaobang** (b. Nov. 1913), a former chairman of the Communist party of the People's Republic of China, died. He began his career at age 14 when he joined the Communist guerrilla forces. Purged twice from positions of growing importance, Hu rebounded both times and became (1981) party chairman, at the top of the ruling hierarchy. However, it was announced (Jan. 16, 1987) that he had resigned. He had obviously fallen out of favor with the rest of the governing clique, but the exact reason for his downfall was never made clear.

1989 Apr. 16 With about 53 percent of the voters approving, a referendum in **Uruguay** upheld a 1986 law that granted **immunity to military personnel for offenses against human rights** committed from 1973 to 1985. During that period of military rule, c.200 Uruguayans were killed or disappeared, c.100 policemen and left-wing Tupamaros guerrillas were killed, and c.5,000 persons were imprisoned, most of them also being tortured.

1989 Apr. 25–Aug. 9 In the face of a growing **scandal over the bribery of high government officials**, **Noboru Takeshita**, prime minister of **Japan**, announced he would resign. The scandal, which first came to public notice in July 1988, concerned the Recruit Company, an information services organization, which sought to influence officials by giving them cash, stock, and other items. By the time of Takeshita's resignation, 42 politicians and officials

had resigned and 14 had been arrested. Takeshita, head of the ruling Liberal Democratic party as well as prime minister, admitted that he and some aides had received $1.1 million. With the party and the government in disarray, it was not until June 2 that a successor to Takeshita in both his posts, was found. He was **Sousuke Uno** (b. Aug. 27, 1922), who had been foreign minister (from 1987). He promised to end the corruption, but was soon beset by troubles of a different sort when a former geisha accused (June 9) him of a relationship four years earlier that involved "immoral" behavior. This charge aroused the usually docile women of Japan who, through the **Housewives Association**, demanded his resignation. Both scandals affected the results of an election (July 23) for 126 of the 512 seats in the upper house of parliament, less powerful than the lower house. The Liberal Democratic party lost 33 of 69 seats, while the Socialist party gained 24 for a total of 46. The next day Uno said he would resign as prime minister and party leader and the Liberal Democrats selected (Aug. 9) **Toshiki Kaifu** (b. Jan. 2, 1931), a former minister of education, for the posts. Kaifu named two women to his cabinet, the first time more than one had served in such a position.

1989 Apr. 25 The Communist party of the U.S.S.R. carried out a **purge of its powerful Central Committee**, apparently as part of the effort of **Mikhail S. Gorbachev** to rid himself of hardliners impeding his policies for change and liberalization. In all 110 inactive party officials were removed and the Central Committee was reduced from 310 to 251 members. Those removed included some long-time Communist officials, among them Andrei A. Gromyko, for many years the foreign minister.

1989 May 4 **Oliver L. North**, a former official of the U.S. National Security Council, was convicted by a federal jury on charges stemming from his part in the **Iran-Contra affair**, in which arms were sold clandestinely to Iran and money from the operation illegally funneled to the Nicaraguan Contra rebels. North was found guilty on three counts concerning the destroying of documents and aiding and abetting the obstruction of Congress. He was acquitted on nine other charges. A federal judge had dismissed (Jan. 13) the main criminal charges against North because the administration of President **Ronald Reagan** had refused to release certain classified documents. The judge fined (July 5) North $150,000, placed him on two years probation, and ordered him to perform 1,200 hours of community service in drug programs.

Richard V. Secord, a former Air Force general, who had organized the operation that shipped arms to Iran, pleaded guilty (Nov. 8) to a charge of making false statements to Congress, and was sentenced (Jan. 24, 1990) to two years probation. **Albert A. Hakim**, an Iranian-born arms dealer, who had been associated with Secord, also pleaded guilty (Nov. 8) to a misdemeanor, and was fined (Feb. 1, 1990) $5,000 and placed on two years probation. The remaining figure in the case, **John M. Poindexter**, national security adviser at the time of the affair, was convicted (Apr. 7, 1990) in a federal court of five criminal charges mostly concerning false statements he made to Congress. On Sept. 16, 1991, all charges against North were dropped by a federal judge because the trial testimony used to convict him had been affected by testimony he had given Congress under immunity.

1989 May 15 The U.S. admitted for the first time that a **hydrogen bomb had been lost** (Dec. 6, 1965) 80 miles off a small Japanese island and still lay on the sea floor. The one-megaton bomb was on a plane that fell into the sea from the carrier *Ticonderoga*. The accident occurred about 200 miles northeast of Okinawa in the Ryukyu Islands, south of the main Japanese islands. In Japan the government was criticized for seeming to be unconcerned about the matter. About three quarters of the tritium in the warhead had decayed by now, but the bomb probably had burst from water pressure, leaking plutonium onto the ocean bed.

1989 May 18 The leaders of the People's Republic of China and of the U.S.S.R., **Deng Xiaoping** and **Mikhail S. Gorbachev**, ended a four-day summit meeting that reconciled the two largest Communist nations after 30 years of estrangement growing out of rivalry and disagreement on matters of Communist policy. The two leaders promised more contacts between the two powers and specifically agreed to reduce military forces and tensions on the long border between the two nations. They failed, however, to agree on a common policy toward Cambodia.

1989 May 25 **Mikhail S. Gorbachev**, head of the Communist party (from 1985) and head of state [president] of the **U.S.S.R.** (from 1988), was elected to a revised and enhanced presidency by the Congress of People's Deputies. This body, meeting for the first time, was the first national assembly in seven decades in which most of the members were chosen in competitive elections. Some of its members

closely questioned Gorbachev before electing him to a post that under a governmental reorganization was to become the chief executive of the nation for a five-year term. The Congress also chose a Supreme Soviet, the main legislative body, which was to meet twice a year. A prime minister and cabinet officers were to take charge of the day-to-day operation of the government.

1989 June 3–4 Ending **student-led protests** that had begun (Apr. 19) on a large scale, **Chinese soldiers invaded the central square Tiananmen**, in Peking [Pinyin: Beijing], and fired on the mass of pro-democracy demonstrators gathered there. No accurate casualty figures became available, but the best evidence indicated that about a dozen policemen and soldiers died and that between 400 and 800 civilians were killed, although the government said only c.300 fatalities occurred. The most reliable figure for those injured was c.5,000. While the **demonstrators occupied Tiananmen Square**, a power struggle within the ruling Politburo erupted over how to handle the uprising. In the end the hardliners won and, after the square was cleared, the government began to arrest protest leaders throughout China, announcing (June 10) that more than 400 had been taken into custody, of whom 24 were executed in Peking and elsewhere by June 22. The behind-the-scenes power struggle involved, on the one hand, **Zhao Ziyang**, general secretary of the Communist party, who favored lenient treatment of the protesters, and, on the other hand, **Li Peng**, the prime minister and a hardliner who had the backing of **Deng Xiaoping**, the most powerful man in the country. With the issue settled, Zhao was dismissed (June 24) and was replaced by **Jiang Zemin** (b. July, 1926), an electrical engineer who had been the head of the Communist party in Shanghai.

1989 June 4–Aug. 19 In the first free election in 44 years, **Polish voters largely endorsed candidates backed by the Solidarity** labor union in opposition to Communist party candidates. In this and a runoff election (June 18), **Solidarity** won all 161 seats allotted to opposition candidates in the Assembly. The Communists and their allies were guaranteed 299 seats of a total of 560. In open balloting, Solidarity won 99 of the 100 seats in the Senate. The new parliament met (July 4) and elected (July 19) **Wojciech Jaruzelski**, the Communist party chief, president of the nation. He resigned (July 29) as party leader and was replaced by **Mieczyslaw** [Franciszek] **Rakowski** (b. Dec. 1, 1926), who had been prime minister. He, in turn, was replaced (Aug. 2) as prime minister by **Czeslaw Kiszczcak** (b. Oct. 19, 1925), who had been interior minister. Under pressure for a further lessening of Communist party control, Kisczcak resigned (Aug. 17) and his place taken (Aug. 24) by **Tadeusz Mazowiecki** (b. Apr. 18, 1927), a senior Solidarity official, who thus became Poland's first non-Communist prime minister since shortly after World War II (1939–1945). To his cabinet of 22 members he appointed nine Solidarity representatives and four members of the Communist party.

1989 June 4 **Ruhollah Khomeini** (b. May 27, 1900), the ayatollah [= religious leader] and de facto ruler of Iran, died. As early as 1941, he had been a stern opponent of the Iranian monarchy. Arrested (1963 and 1964) for his opposition, he was ordered exiled in the latter year, going first to Turkey and later to France. After the overthrow of the shah (Jan. 1979), he returned (Feb. 1, 1979) to Iran and was hailed as a hero. In the ensuing years he turned **Iran into a fundamentalist Islamic nation**. His hatred for the U.S., which he termed the **"Great Satan"** for its support of the deposed shah, found violent form (Nov. 4, 1979) when the American embassy in Teheran was seized and its staff taken hostage. Most of them were not released until Jan. 20, 1981. The ayatollah insisted on fighting the **Iran-Iraq War** (1980–1988) to a bloody stalemate, in which hundreds of thousands of ill-trained young Iranian soldiers were slaughtered. The day Khomeini died an assembly of theological experts selected **Ali Hojatolislam** [Sayed] **Khamenei** (b. 1939), the country's president for the past eight years, as the new religious leader.

1989 June 16 **Imre Nagy**, who was hanged (June 16, 1958) and buried in an unmarked grave for leading an uprising (1956) against Soviet troops and Communist domination of **Hungary**, was **given a hero's funeral** 31 years later in a solemn ceremony in Budapest. As premier Nagy formed (1956) a coalition government, declared Hungary's neutrality, and withdrew from the Warsaw Pact. The Hungarian Supreme Court declared (July 6) Nagy and eight associates innocent and formally rehabilitated them.

1989 June 18 In an election for the **European Parliament**, voters of the 12 nations of the **European Community** [EC] favored the Socialists and environmentalists at the expense of the more conservative parties. Socialists gained 22 seats to secure 188 seats in the 518-member parliament, while the environmentalists [Greens] gained 27 for a total of 37. In

Great Britain the Labour party won 45 seats to 32 for the governing Conservative party. In seven of the other EC nations the party in power also lost seats.

1989 June 22 The government of **Angola**, led by the **Popular Movement for the Liberation of Angola** [**MPLA**], and a rebel guerrilla group, the **National Union for the Total Independence of Angola** [**UNITA**], agreed to a cease-fire to end the fighting that had been going on since Angola achieved (1975) independence from Portugal. The truce never took effect, however, as the two sides disagreed on the interpretation of its terms. Another cease-fire was to be signed (Sept. 18), but **Jonas** [**Malheiro**] **Savimbi** (b. Aug. 3, 1934), leader of UNITA, refused to attend.

1989 June 30 A military coup led by **Omar Hassan Ahmad al-Bashir** (b. 1927) overthrew the civilian government of the **Sudan**, headed by **Sadiq al-Mahdi**, that had been unable to end the six-year civil war between the Islamic government and the southern animist and Christian rebels. Bashir said he would end the war and declared (July 4) a one-month cease-fire. He also promised to hold, if necessary, a referendum on the issue of imposing Islamic law on the south. The new regime was faced with the chronic problems of drought and famine that had ravaged the Sudan for some years.

1989 July 1 An unusual combination of the conservative New Democracy party and The Alliance of the Left and Progress, which included Communists, formed a government in **Greece** with **Tzannis Tzannetakis**, a conservative and a former cabinet minister and member of parliament, as prime minister. In a national election (June 18), **Andreas Papandreou**, the Socialist prime minister (from 1981), had lost his majority in the legislature when the Socialist party received only 45 percent of the vote. The coalition government was made possible by the desire of both the far left and the right to punish Papandreou for alleged misdeeds. Parliament voted (Sept. 20) to make him stand trial on charges of illegally wiretapping telephones of private citizens as well as government officials. In an attempt to break the political deadlock, another election for parliament was held (Nov. 5), but neither the New Democracy party nor the Socialist party was able to win a majority. A coalition government of all parties, led by the New Democratic party and including the Socialist party and a Communist-led left-wing grouping, was formed on Nov. 21. **Xenophon Zolotas** (b. Mar. 26,

1904), a former governor of the Bank of Greece, became prime minister.

1989 July 2   Andrei A[ndreyevich] **Gromyko** (b. July 18, 1909), for 28 years the foreign minister of the U.S.S.R., died. Joining the Communist party in 1931, he was appointed ambassador to the U.S. in 1943. When the UN was formed he became Russia's representative (1946), and by the time he left (July 1948) he had exercised the Soviet veto power 25 times. Gromyko was named foreign minister (Feb. 1957) and achieved (Apr. 27, 1973) full membership in the Politburo. With the coming to power of **Mikhail S. Gorbachev**, Gromyko was elevated (July 1985) to the then-ceremonial post of president. He lost (Oct. 1, 1988) this post and was dropped (Apr. 1989) from the Politburo. Gromyko's always stony visage became a symbol of the Cold War (c.1945–c.1985).

1989 July 3   The U.S. Supreme Court, by a sharply divided 5 to 4 vote, gave the **states the right to impose restrictions on abortions** beyond any hitherto approved. The decision upheld a law of the state of Missouri that in effect prohibited the government from taking any part, financial or otherwise, in performing abortions. The rights of private doctors and clinics were not affected. Many observers saw the ruling as coming near to overturning the *Roe vs. Wade* decision (1973), which seemed to have established a woman's right to abortion.

1989 July 6   János Kádár (b. May 26, 1912), a former head (from June 29, 1957) of the Hungarian Socialist Workers' [Communist] party of Hungary, died. A Communist as a teenager, he was an anti-Nazi guerrilla during World War II (1939–1945). After the war he became a cabinet officer in the ruling Communist regime and became prime minister after the anti-Communist uprising (Oct. 25, 1956) was suppressed (Nov. 4) by Soviet armed forces. Although the Russian government had selected him to govern Hungary, by 1962 he had purged hardline Communists and had begun to introduce changes, both political and economic, that made **Hungary** more tolerant and more prosperous than other Communist regimes. By the 1980s, however, Kádár was seen as not having kept up with the times and was replaced (May 22, 1988) as head of the Hungarian Socialist Workers' party.

1989 July 6   Speaking before the Council of Europe in Strasbourg, France, **Mikhail S. Gorbachev**, president of the U.S.S.R., **renounced** the **use of force** against the **Communist states** of eastern Europe. "Any interference in domestic affairs and any attempts to restrict the sovereignty of states—friends, allies, or any others—are inadmissable," he stated. He thus abandoned the **Brezhnev Doctrine**, named for a former head of the Soviet Union, which held that the use of force was justified to keep a member nation of the Warsaw Pact from leaving it and abandoning communism.

1989 July 8   Carlos Saúl Menem (b. July 2, 1930) was inaugurated as president of **Argentina**, having won the election (May 14) as the political heir of the Peronist movement. The law called for the new president to take office Dec. 10, but faced with runaway inflation and other economic ills, the incumbent president, **Raúl Alfonsin**, agreed to resign at this time. Menem, a lawyer of flamboyant personality from a Syrian immigrant family background, had a strong appeal to the working class of the country. Menem's immediate steps to restore the ruined economy included a devaluation of the currency, a price freeze, and a wage and salary increase to offset inflation, which was running at the rate of more than 100 percent a month.

1989 July 12   Charles J. Haughey, prime minister of **Ireland**, formed a coalition government after a setback in an election (June 15) for seats in parliament. Expecting victory for his Fianna Fáil party, Haughey found instead that it lost three seats, ending up with only 77 in the 166-seat legislature. After long negotiations, he formed his alliance with the small Progressive Democratic party, which held six seats. The Fine Gael party, with 55 seats, refused to join a coalition unless it could share the prime ministership with Haughey.

1989 July 21   The government of **Burma** [Myanmar] placed under house arrest **Daw Aung San Suu Kyi** (b. June 19, 1945), daughter of **Aung San**, a leader of the Burmese fight for independence, and **U Tin Oo**, both prominent opposition leaders. Under intense pressure from strikes, the ruling Burma Socialist Program party officially disbanded, but in reality it merely changed its name to the National Unity party and set about suppressing dissent. Reports from Burma indicated that thousands were arrested and many of them tortured. Earlier the government had announced (June 19) that the name [in English] of the country was changed to the **Union of Myanmar** and its capital Rangoon to Yangon.

1989 July 23 Ending two months of haggling within the Christian Democratic party, **Giulio Andreotti** became prime minister of **Italy**, heading the 49th government of the nation since the end of World War II (1939–1945). The previous prime minister, **Ciriaco De Mita**, also a Christian Democrat, who had held the post for 13 months, had resigned (May 19) after being deliberately undermined politically by Andreotti and by another former prime minister, **Bettino Craxi**, a leader of the Socialist party.

1989 Aug. 3 **Hojatolislam Hashemi Rafsanjani** (b. 1934), speaker of the parliament of **Iran**, was inaugurated as president, having easily won the election (July 28). He succeeded **Ali Khamenei**, who had been named the chief spiritual leader of the nation after the death (June) of Ruhollah Khomeini. Rafsanjani's cabinet appointments, which parliament approved (Aug. 29), indicated some turning away from the recent period of Islamic fundamentalism and hostility toward Western nations, but the opposition to such changes remained strong. The new president said he would put major emphasis on reviving the war-damaged economy.

1989 Aug. 6 **Jaime Paz Zamora** (b. Apr. 15, 1939), a former leftist who now considered himself a Social Democrat, was inaugurated president of **Bolivia**. In an election (May 7) he had finished third in a field of ten, thus making necessary a runoff election (Aug. 5) in the congress. He won this balloting when **Hugo Banzer Suaréz**, a former head of the army who had finished second (May 7), threw his support to Paz Zamora. It was expected that Banzer would be the power behind the throne in the new administration. Paz Zamora succeeded **Victor Paz Estenssoro**.

1989 Aug. 8 **Geoffrey Palmer** (b. Apr. 21, 1942) became prime minister of **New Zealand**, replacing **David Lange**, who had resigned the previous day for reasons of health. Both were members of the governing Labour party and Palmer had been deputy prime minister. Lange had attracted worldwide attention by his **refusal to let nuclear-powered ships**, or ships carrying nuclear weapons, even those of its ally the U.S., **use New Zealand ports**.

1989 Aug. 18 The Soviet Union admitted for the first time that **Joseph Stalin's government** and that of **Adolf Hitler**'s Nazi Germany had signed (Sept. 28, 1939) a **secret agreement giving** them certain **spheres of influence in Eastern Europe**. After the nonaggression pact (Aug. 23, 1939), which made it safe for Hitler to invade (Sept. 1, 1939) Poland and thus start World War II (1939–1945), the two countries signed the additional secret protocol, by the terms of which Russia and Germany divided up Poland, and the Soviet Union was given a free hand in Latvia and Estonia as well as a border area of Romania. They then signed (Jan. 10, 1941) a further secret protocol that transferred predominance in Lithuania to Russia. In the course of the war and its aftermath, the Soviet Union annexed all three Baltic nations and seized much of eastern Poland. The Congress of People's Deputies declared (Dec. 24) that the secret agreements were illegal and violated the sovereignty and independence of other nations. Admitting for the first time that it had found a Russian-language copy of the secret agreement, the Soviet Foreign Ministry printed (Feb. 27, 1990) photographs of the document in an official magazine.

1989 Sept. 4 As a result of a parliamentary election, **George Price**, leader of the People's United party, returned to power in **Belize** as prime minister. He replaced **Manuel Esquival** of the United Democratic party, who had been in office for the past five years. Until that time, Price had been prime minister ever since Belize [formerly British Honduras] won independence from Great Britain (1981).

1989 Sept. 7 A **conference of** so-called **nonaligned nations** meeting in Belgrade, Yugoslavia, issued a final report of its session that omitted the usual harsh words about the U.S., South Africa, and Israel. Urged on by Yugoslavia and in the light of greatly reduced tensions between East and West, the statement upheld human rights and supported women's rights. At the conference were representatives of 100 nations and two nationalist movements, Palestinian and Namibian.

1989 Sept. 10 A mass **exodus of East Germans** seeking to emigrate **to West Germany** began when Hungary, which had recently opened its borders, announced it would allow the East Germans who had flocked there to leave by way of Austria. East Germany demanded to no avail that Hungary disallow this migration, but within two days c.10,000 East Germans were on their way to live in West Germany. East and West Germany agreed (Sept. 30) that thousands of East Germans who had fled to Czechoslovakia would be allowed to cross East Germany by train and enter West Germany as immigrants. By Nov. 1 at least 50,000 East Germans had fled to the West. The majority of them were between

20 and 40 and took with them skills badly needed in their homeland.

1989 Sept. 18   India and Sri Lanka signed an agreement under which India would withdraw its 40,000-man army by December. The Indian troops had been in Sri Lanka (from July 1987) to help put down the ethnic Tamil guerrillas who were fighting the Sri Lankan government controlled by the majority Sinhalese. By now the Indians had suffered casualties of more than 1,000 killed and 3,000 wounded without crushing the **revolt**. At the same time a Sinhalese radical group, the Sinhalese People's Liberation Front, had also been at war with the government. Since 1983, when the fighting began, c.17,000 persons had been killed as a result of the Tamil revolt, while two years of Sinhalese Liberation Front terrorism had taken c.5,000 lives.

1989 Sept. 19   Bowing to pressure from six opposition groups, the Socialist Workers' party, the ruling Communist party of **Hungary**, agreed to begin a transition from a one-party state to a multi-party democratic parliamentary government. The party voted (Oct. 7) to transform itself into a Socialist party that would presumably make it a counterpart of European democratic socialism rather than doctrinaire Marxism. As a further step the New Socialist party elected (Oct. 9) **Rezso Nyers** (b. Mar. 21, 1923), who had been the chief of a four-member presidency (since June), as president of the party. Ending more than 40 years of one-party rule, the **Hungarian parliament voted** (Oct. 19) **to legalize opposition political parties**. The governing Socialist party called an election (Nov. 26) to endorse its plan to hold a presidential election (Jan. 7, 1990) while it still was in power and before a democratically elected parliament was in place, but the voters rejected this proposal.

1989 Sept. 20   F[rederik] W[illem] de Klerk (b. Mar. 18, 1936) was inaugurated as president of **South Africa**. He had been acting president since the resignation (Aug. 15) of **Pieter W. Botha**, who had had a stroke (Jan. 18) and had been forced to step down as head of the governing National party but had refused to leave the presidency. In an election (Sept. 6) the party had retained its domination of South African politics for 41 years, but had lost seats in the all-white parliament to both conservatives and liberals. At his inauguration de Klerk promised to lead the country away from its policy of **apartheid**. Among his first moves were: the opening of residen-

tial areas in four cities to all races; desegregating beaches; and releasing from jail eight prominent black political prisoners, including **Nelson Mandela**, who had been imprisoned for 26 years.

1989 Sept. 20   At a special meeting of the Central Committee of the Communist party of the **U.S.S.R.**, **Mikhail S. Gorbachev**, head of the party and president of the Soviet Union, **purged the Politburo** of 3 of its 12 members. All hardliners, they were: **Valdimir V. Shcherbitsky** (b. Feb. 17, 1918), the party chief in the Ukraine; **Viktor M. Chebrikov** (b. Apr. 27, 1923), a former head of the KGB; and **Viktor P. Nikonov** (b. Feb. 28, 1929), secretary for agriculture. Also ousted were two nonvoting members of the Politburo. Gorbachev apparently considered those removed as out of sympathy with his plans for restructuring the Russian government and economy.

1989 Sept. 28   Ferdinand E[dralin] **Marcos** (b. Sept. 11, 1917), former president of the Philippines (1965–1986), died in exile in Hawaii. He had fought against the Japanese in World War II (1939–1945) and had entered public life in 1949. Becoming more and more autocratic in the presidency, he imposed martial law (1972–1981), and with his wife **Imelda** accumulated vast wealth, estimated as high as $10 billion. Criticized for corruption, violation of human rights, and for fraudulently claiming reelection in voting (Feb. 1986), Marcos came under increasing pressure at home and from the U.S. to resign. He fled the country (Feb. 25, 1986) and went to Hawaii. At his death Marcos was under indictment in the U.S. on criminal charges of having stolen $100 million from his country and used it to buy real estate and art in the U.S. His widow, Imelda, was acquitted (July 2, 1990) in a federal court in New York City of similar charges.

1989 Oct. 2   Three centrist parties agreed to form a coalition government of **Norway** after elections (Sept. 10–11) gave no party a majority in the 165-seat parliament. The outgoing Socialist Labor party, which had established a minority government (from 1986), retained 63 seats, a loss of 7. The coalition parties [Conservative, Center, and Christian People's] together held only 62 seats and would depend on the tolerance of the somewhat right-wing Progress party to stay in power. **Jan P. Syse**, a lawyer and the leader of the Conservative party, was named prime minister. The Socialist Labor party suffered at the polls because of its austerity policies and high unemployment.

1989 Oct. 2   At its annual conference the **British Labour party** voted to abandon its pledge to bring about unilateral **nuclear disarmament in Great Britain**. This stand had been blamed, at least in part, for Labour having been out of power for ten years and for having lost three consecutive general elections, the last one in 1987. The delegates voted to continue working for worldwide nuclear disarmament, to oppose modernization of the short-range nuclear forces of the **North Atlantic Treaty Organization** [NATO], and to ask NATO to adopt a policy banning first use of nuclear weapons.

1989 Oct. 7   **Ruud Lubbers** began his third term as prime minister of the **Netherlands** by forming a coalition of his Christian Democratic Appeal party and the Labor party. His previous government had been forced to resign (May 2) when a dispute over the financing of environmental protection plans broke up the then-existing coalition of the Christian Democrats; the People's Party for Freedom and Democracy, a liberal party; and some smaller groups. Lubbers continued to head a caretaker government until a parliamentary election (Sept. 6), which confirmed the Christian Democrats as the largest single party. The next seven weeks were consumed with negotiations to form a viable coalition. The new government was expected to spend more on social welfare and to continue approving measures to clean up the environment.

1989 Oct. 10   The Communist party of the People's Republic of **China** announced that **Jiang Zemin**, general secretary of the party, had been designated to become the nation's paramount leader when **Deng Xiaoping**, the most powerful member of the ruling party and government, gave up his role or died. Jiang, chosen by Deng, was seen as having, at least for the time being, outmaneuvered **Li Peng**, the prime minister, in any duel for the right to succession to supreme authority. Deng resigned (Nov. 9) his last formal government post, that of chairman of the Central Military Commission, and Jiang was named to replace him. It was assumed, however, that Deng was not giving up his overriding influence on public affairs.

1989 Oct. 18   In the face of **massive demonstrations by the people of East Germany**, **Erich Honecker**, Communist party leader (from May 1971) and head of state (from Oct. 1976), resigned both posts. Beginning in Dresden (Oct. 8) and Leipzig (Oct. 9), hundreds of thousands of protesters had demanded an end to the Communist regime. Honecker was succeeded by **Egon Krenz** (b. Mar. 19, 1937), the youngest member of the governing politburo. Along with other former top officials, Honecker was placed (Dec. 5) under house arrest when corruption and their luxurious life style were discovered. Bowing to continued protests, the cabinet resigned (Nov. 7), and parliament elected (Nov. 20) **Hans Medrow** (b. Jan. 27, 1928), a prominent Communist, as prime minister. He promised to form a coalition cabinet. Parliament amended (Dec. 1) the constitution to eliminate the clause assigning the leading political role to the Communist party. Facing still more popular anger, Krenz resigned (Dec. 3) as head of state and of the party. **Manfred Gerlach** (b. May 8, 1928), chief of the Liberal Democratic party, which, despite its name, had been allied with the Communists, became (Dec. 6) interim president of the country. **Gregor Gysi** (b. Jan 16, 1948), a lawyer and active Communist, was elected (Dec. 9) chairman of the party. Meanwhile, opposition groups and the Communists met and agreed (Dec. 7) to hold elections (May 6, 1990) for parliament and to adopt a new constitution.

1989 Oct. 29   In an election for seats in the Spanish parliament, the Socialist Workers party of **Felipe González**, the prime minister, won a third term for him by the narrowest of margins, taking exactly half the seats in the 350-seat legislature. In previous elections the party had won 202 seats in 1982 and 184 in 1986. Parties on both the left and the right made some gains. With the aid of small party groups and independents, González was expected to continue his efforts to modernize **Spain's** economy as a new member of the European Community [EC].

1989 Oct. 31   On the third ballot the Turkish parliament elected **Turgut Özal**, the prime minister, president of the nation for a seven-year term. The office was chiefly ceremonial, but Özal was expected to try to run the affairs of his Motherland party from his new post. To take office Nov. 9, he was the first civilian president since 1960 and the first prime minister to move to the presidency. Özal named **Yildirim Akbulut** (b. 1935), speaker of the national assembly, to replace him as prime minister.

1989 Nov. 7–11   In an election to choose a constituent assembly that would write a constitution for **Namibia** [South-West Africa] preparatory to its becoming (1990) an independent nation, the South-West Africa People's Organization [SWAPO] won 41 of the 72 seats at stake. The Democratic Turn-halle Alliance, a coalition of several ethnic groups, took 21 seats, the remainder going to fringe organizations. Thus SWAPO gained a majority but not the two-thirds necessary for it to impose its will without compromises. **Sam Nujoma** (b. May 12, 1929), the leader of SWAPO, **promised to practice multi-party democracy**. The new constituent assembly agreed (Dec. 20) in principle on a democratic constitution. The election had been the latest step in a long process during which South Africa had attempted to keep control of Namibia in spite of U.N. rulings against it and in the face of assistance to SWAPO by the Angolan government and the c.50,000 Cuban troops in that country. When it became independent, Namibia would face serious economic problems. The economy was controlled by whites who were expected not to give up their privileges, and c.80,000 Namibian exiles were expected to return to find jobs scarce.

1989 Nov. 8 In the first general election in 22 years, **Jordan's** voters chose an 80-seat parliament. The Moslem Brotherhood, a fundamentalist Islamic group, won 25 seats and 23 went to others who were in opposition to the policies of **Hussein**, the king of Jordan. Earlier demonstrations against price increases and government corruption had led to the resignation (Apr. 24) of **Zaid al-Rifai** (b. Nov. 27, 1936) as prime minister. He had been replaced by **Zeid bin Shaker** (b. Sept. 4, 1934), who in turn resigned (Dec. 4) as a result of the election. The position next went (Dec. 6) to **Mudar Badran** (b. 1934), who had held the office twice before (1976–1979, 1980–1984) and was considered more sympathetic than his predecessors to the Islamic fundamentalists, although he excluded them from his cabinet. Badran announced (Dec. 19) that martial law, which had been in effect for 22 years, was being lifted. Hussein retained the power to dissolve parliament and to veto laws passed by it.

1989 Nov. 9 Abandoning its losing struggle against **emigration to West Germany**, the reconstituted (from Oct. 18) government of East Germany allowed its citizens to cross at will into the west through the **Berlin Wall** (erected 1961) and at other border crossings. Within two days up to one million persons a day were crossing into affluent West Berlin, a sharp contrast to drab East Berlin. The Berlin Wall was partially dismantled. The **Brandenburg Gate**, a landmark on the border between East and West Berlin, was ceremonially opened (Dec. 22) for the first time since 1961. By this time half of the population of East

Germany had spent a day or so in West Germany. By Dec. 31 more than 340,000 East Germans had moved permanently to West Germany in 1989. All of these people received West German citizenship and full social benefits.

1989 Nov. 10 Recognizing the course of events that had recently swept the Communist governments of Poland, Hungary, and East Germany, successively, out of power, **Todor I. Zhivkov**, chairman of the Communist party of **Bulgaria** (from 1954) and prime minister and then president (from 1962), resigned. His place was taken by **Peter T. Mladenov** (b. Aug. 22, 1936), the foreign minister, who called for democratic reforms and purged the politburo of hardliners. Zhivkov was expelled (Dec. 13) from the Communist party and faced charges of corruption. Mladenov said (Dec. 11) that the party should give up its monopoly on power and that free elections would be held in the spring of 1990. To those seeking democracy, the pace of change was too slow, and a large demonstration (Dec. 28) in Sofia, the capital, emphasized this feeling.

1989 Nov. 12 **Dolores Ibarruri** (b. Dec. 1895), a long-time president of the Spanish Communist party, who came to be known as "La Pasionaria" during the Spanish Civil War (1936–1939) because of her rousing oratory on behalf of the Republican government, died. A founder (1921) of the Spanish Communist party, she was elected (1930) to its central committee, and to the Spanish parliament (1934). After the Fascist victory in the civil war, Ibarruri moved to Moscow and did not return to Spain until 1977, when she was again elected to parliament in the post-Fascist era.

1989 Nov. 12–23 The leftist **rebels of El Salvador launched their largest offensive** in almost ten years in various parts of the country, but with their main effort aimed at San Salvador, the capital. They raided heavily the neighborhoods where the wealthy lived, hitherto protected from such violence. The U.S.-supported government claimed (Nov. 23) that the rebel offensive had been defeated but it had taken a toll of c.250 civilian dead and nearly 700 wounded. It was estimated that since the rebel revolt began a decade earlier, c.70,000 Salvadorans had been killed. While the offensive was going on, six Jesuit priests, who had been active in seeking a negotiated end to the civil war, and their housekeeper and her daughter, were murdered (Dec. 16) in San Salvador by men in military uniform. **Alfredo Cris-**

tiani, president of El Salvador, said (Jan. 13, 1990) that three army officers and five enlisted men had been arrested in connection with the killings. An army colonel was convicted (Sept. 28, 1991) of murder and terrorism and was sentenced (Jan. 24, 1992) to 30 years in prison.

1989 Nov. 13   Franz Joseph II (b. Aug. 16, 1906), prince and head of state (from 1938) of the small principality of Liechtenstein in central Europe, died. During his reign he helped his land become industrialized and a tax and banking haven that brought prosperity to the inhabitants. He was the twelfth ruler of the 270-year-old nation, and his family was noted for its art collection. Franz Joseph was succeeded by his son **Hans Adam II** (b. Feb. 14, 1945), the crown prince, who had been exercising his father's executive powers since 1984.

1989 Nov. 20   The General Assembly of the **U.N.**, after ten years of negotiation, adopted an international **Convention on the Rights of the Child**. Containing 54 articles, the convention required that 20 nations ratify it before it became effective. It provided for a child's right to a name, survival, education, and protection against exploitation and abuse.

1989 Nov. 22   The government of the Congress party of **India**, led by **Rajiv Gandhi** as prime minister (from 1984), lost its majority in parliament in a national election (Nov. 22–26). Gandhi's popularity had declined as had confidence in his ability to meet India's many problems. In addition, his administration had been charged with corruption in the taking of kickbacks in connection with military procurement contracts. Gandhi resigned (Nov. 29) and **V**[ishwanath] **P**[ratap] **Singh** (b. Jan. 25, 1931) who had led the opposition National Front in the election campaign, took office (Dec. 2) as the new prime minister. Originally a member of the Congress party, he resigned (1987) in a controversy with Gandhi. The coalition he headed had slightly more than the 263 seats needed to make a majority.

1989 Nov. 22   René Moawad (b. 1925), a Maronite Christian who had been elected (Nov. 5) president of **Lebanon** by its parliament and who favored peaceful coexistence with Muslims, was assassinated in Beirut when a powerful bomb blew up his motorcade, killing 23 other people and injuring hundreds. He had had the support of Syria, whose army occupied much of the country, but he was not recognized by **Michel Aoun**, another Christian leader, who claimed

to be head of the government by virtue of having been appointed (Sept. 22, 1988) to the post of prime minister by **Amin Gemayel**, then president, just before his term expired. Moawad's election had followed a meeting in Taif, Saudi Arabia, under the auspices of the **Moslem League**, of the Lebanese parliament. That meeting agreed on a plan it was hoped would end the 14-year-old civil war by giving the Muslim majority more power at the expense of the Christian minority, and by approving the military presence of Syria in Lebanon. As successor to Moawad, the parliament elected (Nov. 24) **Elias Hrawi** (b. Sept. 4, 1925), also a Maronite Christian, a legislator, and a former cabinet minister. Under the **Taif agreement** the prime minister was to be a Sunni Muslim and the speaker of parliament a Shiite Muslim. Aoun continued to refuse to recognize this government, and the year ended with a standoff between his army and the Syrian forces.

1989 Nov. 24   Yielding to massive protest **demonstrations** (beginning Oct. 28) **in Prague** and other cities, the leadership of the **Czechoslovakian** Communist party resigned with **Milos Jakes**, the general secretary, being replaced by **Karel Urbanek** (b. Mar. 22, 1941), a former head of the party in Bohemia. This reshuffling of a failing government did not satisfy the dissidents, who demanded further reforms and called a one-day general strike. The party removed (Nov. 29) the guarantee in the constitution that gave it a dominant role in the country, and a new cabinet (Dec. 3) contained non-Communists for the first time in 21 years. **Ladislav Adamec** (b. Sept. 10, 1926), prime minister (from Oct. 12, 1988), resigned (Dec. 7), and **Marián Calfa** (b. 1946), a Communist, replaced him. **Gustáv Husák**, a Communist and president (since May 1975) also resigned (Dec. 10). Another cabinet was formed (Dec. 10) with 11 non-Communists and 10 Communists. Opposition groups, organized as the **Civic Forum** and under an agreement with the Communist-controlled parliament, elected (Dec. 28) as speaker **Alexander Dubček**, who had headed the nation in 1968 when his attempt to bring about "socialism with a human face" resulted in his overthrow by force by the Soviet Union. Climaxing the struggle to end Communist rule, **Václav Hável** (b. Oct. 5, 1936), an internationally known playwright who had been the leading Czech dissident since the invasion of 1968, was elected (Dec. 29) president of the country by parliament. As part of the about-face in politics and government, the reorganized politburo of the Communist party acknowledged (Dec. 1) that the Soviet-led invasion of 1968 that ended the "**Prague Spring**" had been wrong. Also condemning (Dec. 4) the invasion were the Soviet Union itself and the four satellites [Bulgaria, East Germany, Hungary, and Poland] which had participated.

1989 Nov. 26   A centrist candidate won the presidency of **Uruguay** with a plurality of 38 percent of the votes cast, but the Broad Front, a leftist group of Communists and former guerrillas, won control of the city council of Montevideo, the nation's capital, where nearly half the population of the country lived. The president-elect was **Luis Alberto Lacalle** (b. 1941) of the National party, who defeated the candidate of the Colorado party, which held the presidency going into the election. Lacalle, a lawyer, was inaugurated on Mar. 1, 1990. He said he would move to cut inflation, then running at 50 percent a year, in half, to balance the nation's budget, and to increase social welfare programs.

1989 Nov. 26   By the narrow margin of just over 50 percent of the vote, **Hondurans elected** as their next president **Rafael Leonardo Callejas** of the National party, who ran against **Carlos Flores** of the governing Liberal party. Callejas, trained in the U.S. as an economist, took office Jan. 27, 1990. This marked the first transfer of power to an opposition party since 1932.

1989 Nov. 27–Dec. 15   Ahmed Abdullah Abderemane, president of the **Comoro Islands**, located in the Mozambique Channel between the African nation of Mozambique and the island nation of Madagascar, was assassinated, either by rebels of the 700-man army or by the presidential guard of mercenaries led by **Bob Denhard**, a Frenchman. The mercenaries took over control of the islands. To restore order **France sent a naval force**, and after negotiations, during which Denhard was said to have demanded a large sum of money to leave, he and 21 other mercenaries flew (Dec. 15) to a temporary haven in South Africa. When the Comoro Islands secured (1975) independence from France, Abderemane became head of state. He was overthrown within a month, but returned to power (1978) with the aid of Denhard and his mercenaries.

1989 Nov. 30   Ahmadou Ahidijo (b. Aug. 1924), **first president of Cameroon**, West Africa, after it won its independence from France (1960), died. He remained president for 22 years and was one of the generation of black leaders who founded the new post–World War II (1939–1945) nations of Africa. He resigned as president (Nov. 1982), and went into exile (Aug. 1983) when he was accused of plotting against the government. He was sentenced to death in absentia (early 1984), a sentence which was later commuted, but Ahidijo never returned to Cameroon.

1989 Dec. 1–9   A rebellion by army troops threatened the government of **Corazan C. Aquino, president of the Philippines**, but was put down with the loss of 79 lives and the wounding of c.500 persons. The rebels attacked the presidential palace and two military bases, and then seized the main business district of Manila before withdrawing on Dec. 7. Beyond toppling the Aquino regime, the aims of the rebels were not clear, except for a statement by one of their leaders that they wished to set up a "nationalist reformist government." A factor in the government victory was the appearance (Dec. 1) **of American fighter planes, authorized** by **George Bush**, president of the U.S., to keep rebel planes on the ground, which they did without firing a shot.

1989 Dec. 2   A 41-year-old **insurgency of Communist guerrillas ended** when an agreement was signed in Hat Yai, **Thailand**, by the Communist party of Malaya [Peninsular Malaysia] and Thailand. The 1,200 guerrillas who had been operating along the frontier between Malaysia and Thailand agreed to lay down their arms and return to civilian life. The revolt, which had taken thousands of lives, began (1948) when Great Britain ruled what was then the colony of Malaya.

1989 Dec. 2   The **first election in Taiwan in 40 years in which opposition parties were legal** resulted in an expected victory for the Nationalist party, which had ruled the island nation from 1949. But the Democratic Progressive party, in its first official appearance, won 21 seats in the Legislative Yuan [parliament]. The Nationalists took 72 of the 101 seats that were at stake in the 283-seat body.

1989 Dec. 3   George Bush, president of the U.S., and **Mikhail S. Gorbachev**, president of the U.S.S.R., **ended their first summit meeting**, which had been held on ships of the two nations in the harbor of Valletta, Malta. The meetings were disrupted by a fierce storm that caused cancellation of some of the visiting back and forth that had been planned. In closing statements, both presidents said in effect that the **Cold War** (c.1945–c.1985) **was over**. The two leaders also discussed nuclear disarmament and the improvement of trade relations between the two countries.

1989 Dec. 7 **Fidel Castro**, president and de facto Communist dictator of Cuba, completely **rejected the political and economic changes** taking place in the hitherto Communist nations of Eastern Europe. He declared that **Mikhail S. Gorbachev**, president of the Soviet Union, was "slandering socialism, destroying its values, discrediting the party, and liquidating its leading role." Castro's defiance of Moscow came despite $5 billion a year in aid Cuba received from the U.S.S.R.

1989 Dec. 8 **Benin** [formerly Dahomey] officially **abandoned the Marxism-Leninism** that had been its guiding ideology for 15 years. It was the first African nation to take such a step. The change in government philosophy did little, however, to end dissatisfaction with the regime of **Mathieu Kérékou** (b. Sept. 2, 1933), president and head of state since a military coup (1972). Large crowds protested the extremely strained economic conditions in demonstrations in Cotonou, the commercial center of the country.

1989 Dec. 14 **Andrei D**[mitrivich] **Sakharov** (b. May 21, 1921), a Russian scientist who was a leader in that country's development of both the fission and the hydrogen bomb, and who at the same time was the leading dissenter and the outspoken conscience of the nation against Communist tyranny, died. His most recent ventures in dissent had been in the new **Congress of People's Deputies**, to which he had been elected this year, and his last such appearance had come only two days before his death. He then demanded that the Congress repeal the Communist party monopoly on political power, but he was cut off by **Mikhail S. Gorbachev**, president of the U.S.S.R., who nevertheless praised him after his death as "a man of conviction and sincerity." A steady critic of Soviet policy, Sakharov was seized (Jan. 22, 1980) and exiled to Gorki, 250 miles east of Moscow, where he was kept in virtual isolation until Dec. 1986, when the more liberal regime instituted (1985) by Gorbachev permitted him to return to Moscow. Sakharov's most notable dissent was an essay he wrote (1968), which appeared in the West but not in Russia. In it he denounced the shortcomings of the Soviet regime, especially in regard to human rights and freedom of speech. He had been awarded the **Nobel Peace Prize** in 1975.

1989 Dec. 14 In the first free election in over 16 years, **Chilean** voters chose **Patricio Aylwin** (b. Nov. 26, 1918), a lawyer, former senator, and leader of the Christian Democratic party, as president, giving him 55.2 percent of the votes cast. In ceremonies (Mar. 11 and 14, 1990), Aylwin took office, replacing **Augusto Pinochet**, a general who had ruled Chile harshly since a coup (Sept. 11, 1973). The new president was considered a moderate who would restore democracy to the country. He had already reached (Jan. 5, 1990) an accord with the military chiefs that would greatly reduce the power they had exercised during the Pinochet regime.

1989 Dec. 17 In a runoff election in **Brazil**, **Fernando Collor de Mello** (b. Aug. 12, 1949), the center-right candidate, defeated his Socialist opponent. It was the first time since 1960 that Brazilians had been able to elect a president by direct balloting. Collor, son of a wealthy businessman, who was to serve a five-year term, promised to promote a free market economy and to end the widespread corruption in government.

1989 Dec. 19 **Herbert A**[lbert] **Blaize**, prime minister (from 1984) of **Grenada**, died. In and out of office as chief minister (1960–1974) under British rule, he regained power after the U.S. invasion (1983) overthrew a Marxist government. Blaize led a center-oriented coalition that won an election (Dec. 3, 1984). He attempted to bring stable government and economic progress to the nation after an era of trouble and violence.

1989 Dec. 20 About 24,000 **American troops**, half of whom were already stationed in **Panama** and half flown in from the U.S., **invaded** that country in an attempt to overthrow and capture **Manuel Antonio Noriega**, the military dictator (from Aug. 1985), who had been indicted in the U.S. on drug trafficking charges. The American forces met with fairly stiff resistance from Noriega's Panama Defense Forces, but by Dec. 25 resistance was nearly at an end. Noriega, however, eluded the Americans and sought refuge (Dec. 24) in the Vatican embassy in Panama City. Negotiations to have him turned over to the U.S. or to allow him to go to some other country ended (Jan. 3, 1990) when he surrendered to the Americans and was at once flown to the U.S. to stand trial. The American forces suffered casualties of 23 killed and 323 wounded; 314 members of the Panama military were killed and 124 wounded. The number of noncombatant Panamanians killed in the fighting and in street disorders was uncertain but appeared to be c.200. Earlier in the year in an election (May 7), **Carlos Duque**, Noriega's handpicked candidate, was declared elected, although impartial sampling of the vote showed that the opposition candidate, **Guillermo Endara** (b. May 12, 1936), had won by a three-to-one margin. Bowing to the charges of fraud, Noriega cancelled the election results and had the Council of State elect (Sept. 1) as president **Francisco Rodriguez**, the comptroller general and an ally of Noriega. The U.S. refused to recognize him. An attempted coup (Oct. 3) by dissident Panamanian officers failed, and Noriega executed ten or more of the rebels. The National Assembly named (Dec. 15) Noriega chief executive with full power to conduct foreign affairs, and he then declared the country in a state of war with the U.S. At the time of the invasion, Endara, with the support of the U.S. government, was sworn in as president.

1989 Dec. 20–28   The **Communist party** of Lithuania voted to **sever its ties with the party leadership in Moscow**, and declared its aim was "an independent, democratic Lithuanian state." Earlier the party had voted (Dec. 7) to abolish its monopoly on political power and to legalize other parties. Neighboring **Latvia** took (Dec. 28) the same step. **Mikhail S. Gorbachev**, president of the U.S.S.R., **expressed** (Dec. 21 and 23) alarm at such actions. He warned that any move by the Baltic states to secede from the Soviet Union would "sow discord, bloodshed, and death." The Soviet legislature had, however, endorsed (July 27) the plans of **Lithuania** and **Estonia** to develop **market-oriented economies** apart from the central-planning officials in Moscow. The Baltic republics, Estonia, Latvia, and Lithuania, had been absorbed into the Soviet Union in Aug. 1940, as Soviet Socialist republics.

1989 Dec. 20–31   The brutal and paranoid dictatorship of **Nicolae Ceausescu**, head of the Communist party of **Romania** (from 1965), was overthrown by massive **demonstrations in Bucharest**, the capital, which followed the bloody crushing (Dec. 16) of an antigovernment demonstration in Timisoara in western Romania. Nicolae Ceausescu (b. Jan. 26, 1918) and his wife **Ilena** (b. Jan. 1, 1919), who had ruled with him, fled, but were captured (Dec. 23), tried, convicted, and executed on Dec. 25 by a military court. Meanwhile, bitter fighting went on in Bucharest and elsewhere with the army siding with the dissidents against the much feared and hated **Securitate**, Ceausescu's security police. A provisional gov-

ernment, the Council of National Salvation, was formed (Dec. 23), consisting of dissident intellectuals and disaffected Communists, with **Ion Iliescu** (b. Mar. 3, 1930), a former member of the Central Committee of the Communist party, as its head. By the end of the year all members of the old politburo were said to be in custody. The best estimate of the number killed as a result of the uprising was 7,000. Of the six nations of Eastern Europe [Bulgaria, Czechoslovakia, East Germany, Hungary, Poland, and Romania] that overthrew Communist governments in 1989, only Romania suffered violence on a large scale.

1989 Dec. 27   **Egypt and Syria agreed to restore diplomatic relations**, which had been broken for 12 years (from Jan. 1977), when **Anwar el-Sadat**, president of Egypt, visited Jerusalem and opened negotiations that two years later resulted in a peace treaty between the two nations, the only one Israel has ever signed with an Arab country. Seventeen Arab nations had cut their ties with Egypt after 1979, but with this move all but Libya had resumed relations with Egypt.

V. ECONOMICS AND TRADE

1989 Feb. 3   With clearance from the U.S. Federal Trade Commission [FTC], **Kohlberg, Kravis, and Roberts & Company**, an American firm that specialized in buyouts and takeovers, **acquired RJR Nabisco, Inc.**, for $25,000,000,000, the **largest takeover in history**. With the Beatrice Companies, which had been acquired (1986) in a leveraged buyout, the two concerns accounted for 13 percent of all U.S. food manufacturing. The FTC required Kohlberg to sell within one year certain operations of Beatrice and RJR Nabisco that would otherwise reduce competition.

1989 Mar. 16   The central committee of the Communist party of the **U.S.S.R.** endorsed a proposal by **Mikhail S. Gorbachev**, president, to **decentralize agriculture** and allow private farmers to operate in what would gradually become a free market. Cooperative banks were to be established and state-owned land would be leased to farmers for life with the right to pass the lease on to their children. The central agricultural bureaucracy was to be dismantled and some state-owned farms sold. The government announced (Aug. 10) that it would pay farmers for part of their crops in much sought after foreign currency instead of Russian rubles.

1989 Apr. 27 Konosuke Matsushita (b. Nov. 27, 1894), whose life as a Japanese industrialist was a rags-to-riches story, died. He established (1918) the **Matsushita Electric Industrial Company** with one product. By the time of his death his company made 14,000 different items, employed 120,000 people, and had annual sales of about $42 billion. Matsushita, by making home appliances easily available, was compared to Henry Ford as a modern industrialist. He typified the post–World War II (1939–1945) industrialized and consumer-oriented Japan.

1989 May 20 John R[ichard] **Hicks** (b. Apr. 8, 1904), an English economist, who had shared the **Nobel prize for economics** in 1972, died. He made substantial contributions to general economic equilibrium theory and also to welfare theory. His work was in the field of concepts concerning large economic systems, which used a mathematical framework. He was the author of a number of books, including *Theory of Wages* (1932), *Capital and Growth* (1965), and *Causality in Economics* (1979).

1989 July 24 Time, Inc., won control of Warner Communications, Inc., merging the two American firms to create the largest media and entertainment conglomerate in the world. As **Time Warner, Inc.**, the new corporation had a stock market value of $15 billion and annual revenues of $10 billion. Time was chiefly a magazine and book publishing company, while Warner was a producer of movies and recordings. Both also had sizable cable television operations.

1989 July 27 The **Squibb Corporation** and the **Bristol-Myers Company** of the U.S. announced they would **merge**, thereby creating the second largest pharmaceutical company in the world. The deal valued the two companies at $12 billion. **Merck & Company** remained the largest drug company. The merger relegated **SmithKline Beecham** of Great Britain to third place, after it had held second place following the merger (Apr. 12) of SmithKline Beckman Corporation with the Beecham Group P.L.C. A major reason for such deals was seen in the need for very large expenditures for research.

1989 Aug. 9 George Bush, president of the U.S., signed into law a measure to rescue and reorganize the **savings and loan institutions** of the country, many of which were failing as a result of ill-considered loans, mismanagement, and corruption. It was expected that the process would cost about $300,000,000,000 over 30 years, and of this $225 billion would come from the nation's taxpayers. By early 1990 the estimated cost of the bailout had risen to at least $500 billion and possibly twice that. In the last quarter of 1989 alone, the institutions already seized by the government had operating losses of $2.6 billion and those on the verge of seizure losses of $2.1 billion. A new government body, the **Resolution Trust Corporation**, was established to merge or liquidate institutions in trouble so as to protect depositors.

1989 Aug. 29 The Mitsui Bank and the Taiyo Kobe Bank, both of Japan, announced they would merge to form the second largest bank in the world, with deposits of $298,000,000,000. The **ten largest banks in the world were now all Japanese**, the largest being **Dai-Ichi Kangyo** with deposits of $312,000,000,000. The latter announced (Sept. 18) that it would buy control of a finance unit of the Manufacturers Hanover Corporation, a New York City bank, for $1,400,-000,000.

1989 Oct. 9 The **Supreme Soviet approved a law granting workers the right to strike**, an unusual step for a Communist nation, but it banned strikes in such areas as public transportation, power, defense industries, and others. This action came after a summer in which the Russian economy had been seriously damaged by strikes of coal miners. In July as many as 250,000 miners were on strike, chiefly in Siberia, but also in the Ukraine. The strikers complained of food shortages and the scarcity of other goods.

1989 Oct. 13 On the New York Stock Exchange the **Dow Jones average of industrial stocks fell 190.58 points**, the **second largest decline** in its history, exceeded only by the 508 point drop on Oct. 19, 1987, but only the 12th worst in terms of percentage. The average closed at 2,569.26. A wave of selling of potential takeover stocks was set off by the failure of one proposed large transaction of this kind to find bank financing. On the next business day (Oct. 16) the Dow Jones rose by 88.12 points to regain about half its loss. The market average had reached (Oct. 9) an all-time high of 2,791.41, breaking the previous record set Aug. 24, 1987. The Dow Jones closed the year at 2,753.20, a gain of 584.63, or 21.23 percent, from Dec. 31, 1988. The Japanese stock market, now at least as important as that of New York, closed the year with the Nikkei 225 index at 38,915.87, an increase of 31 percent for 1989.

1989 Oct. 16   By declaring the **African elephant an endangered species**, the **Convention on International Trade in Endangered Species**, meeting in Lausanne, Switzerland, **banned trade in ivory**. Five member states [Botswana, Burundi, Malawi, Mozambique, and Zimbabwe] said they would not abide by the ban. South Africa had said (June 20) that it opposed the ban. Poaching for the much-desired ivory of elephant tusks had reduced the population of the species from an estimated 1,192,000 (1981) to 622,000 (1989). In the five years (1979–1987) African nations had exported 6,828 tons of ivory. The ban took effect Jan. 18, 1990, although the U.S. government earlier (June 1989) ended the importation of ivory from African elephants and found a year later that the market for ivory artifacts had collapsed. By this same time the price of raw ivory in Africa had declined by up to 90 percent.

1989 Oct. 30   The **Mitsubishi Estate Company** of Tokyo, one of the largest real estate development firms in the world, bought 51 percent of the Rockefeller Group's ownership in several buildings making up the core of the handsome art deco **Rockefeller Center** in midtown Manhattan, New York City. The deal included the central structure, the GE Building [formerly the RCA Building], an outstanding example of skyscraper design.

1989 Nov. 28   The **Organization of Petroleum Exporting Countries** [OPEC] agreed to raise its overall production ceiling to 22 million barrels a day for the first six months of 1990. The current ceiling was 20.5 million barrels, but it was largely ignored, and it was thought that OPEC nations were pumping 23 million barrels at a time of increasing demand. The average price of OPEC oil was $17.16 a barrel, or about $6 more than a year earlier. OPEC's growing domination of the oil world was also seen in the fact that four of its member nations' national oil companies were among the first ten worldwide, with the Saudi Arabian Oil Company at the top.

1989 Dec. 7   The 12 member nations of the **European Community** [EC] and the six countries [Austria, Finland, Iceland, Norway, Sweden, and Switzerland] of the **European Free Trade Association** [EFTA] agreed to a closer linkage between the two groups. Their joint free trade zone would make easier the movement of goods, services, and capital among the 18 countries. The EC's imports and exports with EFTA were higher than the EC's trade with either the U.S. or Japan.

1989 Dec. 13   At the UN an agreement was reached on steps to **end the use of huge fishing nets** that are 30 or more miles in length, and which had been widely condemned because they took in so many fish as to deplete future supplies while also killing many sea birds, seals, dolphins, and porpoises that become trapped in the nets. The agreement called for an end to the use of the nets after June 1992, and for an immediate reduction in their use in the South Pacific, where Japan and Taiwan had been criticized for excessive use. Japan had announced (Sept. 19) that it would cut by two-thirds the number of ships using the nets.

VI. RELIGION AND PHILOSOPHY

1989 Jan. 28   The tenth **Panchen Lama** (b. 1938), the most important spiritual leader of **Tibet** after the **Dalai Lama**, died. Unlike the Dalai Lama, he supported Chinese control of Tibet and tried to act as a mediator between that country and his own. Also unlike the Dalai Lama, he did not leave the country when China invaded (1959), holding several high positions under the Peking [Pinyin: Beijing] regime. He had been chosen (1941) as one of three boys to be candidates for the position, and he was confirmed (1948), under pressure from China, it was said, to become the tenth incarnation of the Panchen Lama.

1989 Feb. 10   In a document titled "**The Church and Racism**," the **Vatican** condemned all forms of racism. It called the South African system of **apartheid** an extreme case, but noted that racism was present on every continent. The statement called anti-Semitism "the most tragic form" of racism. Also attacked was discrimination suffered by migrants, such as foreign workers in western European countries. "Harboring racist thoughts and entertaining racist attitudes is a sin," the document declared.

1989 Apr. 15   Under new policies of the regime of **Mikhail S. Gorbachev**, president of the U.S.S.R., many Russian Orthodox and Roman Catholic **churches were being allowed to reopen**, and for the first time in a half century or more they were permitted to ring their bells. Before World War II (1939–1945), most Russian churches had been closed, but during the war c.50,000 were allowed to reopen as an aid to wartime morale. With the end of the war, religion was again persecuted. **Pope John Paul II** appointed (July 26), with the approval of the government, the first Roman Catholic bishop of the Byelorussian republic since 1926.

1989 June 11   **Moral Majority** (1979), a politically active organization of the right wing of American Protestantism, was to be disbanded, its founder and leader, **Jerry Falwell** (b. Aug. 11, 1933), a Baptist clergyman, announced. He claimed its mission had been accomplished. At its peak Moral Majority had only 6.5 million members, but it raised (1984) $11 million for political lobbying. The organization was a strong supporter of **Ronald Reagan**, president of the U.S. (1981–1989). It was extreme in its opposition to abortion, pornography, homosexuality, and the Equal Rights Amendment to the Constitution. Its influence was on the wane, partly because of recent financial and sexual scandals involving television evangelists who were its symbols in its days of prosperity and power.

1989 June 27   A[lfred] J[ules] **Ayer** (b. Oct. 29, 1910), an English philosopher and professor of logic at Oxford University (1959–1978), died. As a philosopher of logical positivism, he introduced the beliefs of that school to the English-speaking world. Logical positivism sought to apply to philosophy the rigid methods of mathematics and the natural sciences, holding that statements of principle that were unverifiable by experience were of no meaning. Ayer's most influential book was an early one, *Language, Truth, and Logic* (1936). He also wrote *The Foundations of Empirical Knowledge* (1940) and *The Problem of Knowledge* (1956).

1989 July 12   **Sidney Hook** (b. Dec. 20, 1902), an American political philosopher and a founder (1950) of the **Congress for Cultural Freedom**, intended to counter the activities of Communist intellectuals, died. Hook was a pragmatist with a strong belief in secularism and rationalism. He wrote and spoke widely on Marxism, education, and the philosophy of democracy. Among his books were *From Hegel to Marx* (1936), *The Hero in History* (1943), and *Pragmatism and the Tragic Sense of Life* (1974).

1989 July 17   After a hiatus of 44 years, the **Vatican and Poland**, homeland of **Pope John Paul II**, **resumed full diplomatic relations**, marking the first such ties with a Warsaw Pact nation. The move was made possible in part by Poland's action (May) establishing freedom of religion. In Czechoslovakia the government allowed four new Catholic bishops to be appointed for the first time in several decades. Yugoslavia, an unaligned Communist nation, already had ties with the Vatican.

1989 July 22   **Pope John Paul II** accepted from **Félix Houphouët-Boigny**, president of the **Ivory Coast**, the nearly completed basilica, **Our Lady of Peace of Yamoussoukro**, which was to be the **largest Christian church in the world**. The structure was 623 feet long, and its tower, with a 30-foot cross, would rise 489 feet. The air-conditioned interior would seat 18,000, while a square with colonnades would hold 300,000. The basilica's cost was estimated at about $250 million. The **largest cathedral in the world was St. John the Divine**, in New York City.

1989 Sept. 28   The House of Bishops of the **Episcopal Church**, meeting in Philadelphia, Pennsylvania, **adopted a compromise statement** on the ordination of women that appeared to remove the danger of a fundamental split within the church body. The statement noted that opposition to the ordination of women continued to be "a recognized theological position," and that church leaders should be "pastorally sensitive" to those who will not accept women as priests. Of the 27 national and regional churches in the worldwide Anglican communion, five ordained women. The American church was the only one with a female bishop.

1989 Oct. 5   The **Dalai Lama**, the religious and political leader of Tibet, who had been in exile since the Chinese crushed a rebellion in Tibet (1959), was awarded the **Nobel Peace Prize**. The committee bestowing the honor said he had "advocated peaceful solutions based upon tolerance and mutual respect in order to preserve the historical and cultural heritage of his people." Since his exile, the Dalai Lama (enthroned Feb. 22, 1940) had sought by nonviolent means to restore Tibet's freedom.

1989 Nov. 25   **Salo Wittmayer Baron** (b. May 26, 1895), a Polish-born American scholar whose special field, in which he was paramount, was Jewish history, died. His life's work was *A Social and Religious History of the Jews*, which first appeared (1937) as a three-volume work. By the time of his death, this monumental project had grown to 18 volumes and he was working on a 19th. At the trial of **Adolf Eichmann**, accused in Israel as a Nazi war criminal, Baron's testimony (Apr. 24, 1961) established the historical background through his learned but impassioned account of anti-Semitism in Germany.

1989 Dec. 1   In the first meeting between a Communist leader of the Soviet Union and a Roman Catholic pope, **Mikhail S. Gorbachev**, president of the U.S.S.R., and **John Paul II met** at the Vatican. They agreed in principle to establish diplomatic relations and Gorbachev promised to **expand religious freedom in Russia**. The pope, expressing his special interest in the Ukrainian Catholic Church, banned in 1946, insisted it be made legal again.

1989 Dec. 15   For the **first time in Great Britain a movie was banned for blasphemy**. The film was *Visions of Ecstasy* and depicted erotic fantasies of a 16th-century Spanish Carmelite nun, **St. Theresa of Avila**, a mystic, a leading figure in the Catholic Reformation, and one of the principal saints of the Roman Catholic Church. During her lifetime she said she had had "raptures" about Jesus Christ and had experienced a "mystic marriage" with him. In the 18-minute film she was shown caressing and kissing Christ. There was much criticism of the ban.

VII. SCIENCE, EDUCATION, AND TECHNOLOGY

1989 Jan. 27   **Thomas Sopwith** (b. Jan. 18, 1888), an English aviator and aircraft designer, died. As a stunt flier he made enough money to establish (1912) the **Sopwith Aviation Company**. World War I (1914–1918) brought prosperity to the company, which produced c.16,000 warplanes, including the **Sopwith Camel**, a one-engine biplane, one of the most successful fighter planes of its time. One of these, flown by a Canadian air ace, shot down (1918) Germany's best known ace, Manfred von Richthofen (May 2, 1892–Apr. 21, 1918), the Red Baron.

1989 Feb. 27   **Konrad** [Zacharias] **Lorenz** (b. Nov. 7, 1903), an Austrian zoologist and ethologist, died. He used his study of animals to demonstrate that much of human behavior, such as aggression, was inherited. Lorenz also became known for his demonstrations of "imprinting," in which, for example, he showed he could make young geese loyal to him as though he were their parent. His best-known books were *The Study of Instinct* (1951), *King Solomon's Ring* (1952), a popular best-seller, and *On Aggression* (1966). Lorenz shared the **Nobel prize for physiology or medicine** in 1973.

1989 Mar. 22   Meeting in Basel, Switzerland, under the auspices of the U.N. Environmental Program, 117 nations adopted a **treaty to restrict the shipment of hazardous waste** across national boundaries, which was being done more and more in an unautho-

rized and dangerous manner. The treaty would require exporters of waste to notify and secure the consent of receiving countries, and to assure that both exporting and importing nations discarded the waste in an environmentally sound manner. Developing nations said the treaty did not do enough to control hazardous waste disposal. The treaty was to go into effect 90 days after 20 nations formally ratified it.

1989 Mar. 23   Two chemists at the University of Utah, Salt Lake City, Utah, claimed they had achieved **nuclear fusion at room temperature** in a jar of water. They were **B**[obby] **Stanley Pons** (b. Aug. 23, 1943) of the university, and **Martin Fleischmann** (b. Mar. 29, 1927) of the University of Southampton, England. Fusion, occurring when two light nuclei are squeezed into one heavier nucleus, ordinarily takes place at temperatures of several hundred million degrees, so it had not yet become a practical source of energy. Most scientists were skeptical of the results claimed for the **Pons-Fleischmann process**, both as to whether it existed at all or, if it did, whether it produced enough energy to matter. Though other scientists around the world soon claimed they had duplicated the Utah experiment, many others found they could not do so. A conference (May) sponsored by the U.S. government, brought together hundreds of scientists in different fields, who delivered a strong negative verdict.

1989 Mar. 23   An **asteroid** half a mile in diameter and consisting of rocks and dust **came within 500,000 miles of the earth**, the closest approach of such an object in 50 years. The asteroid was traveling at a speed of 46,000 mph, and if it had struck the earth it would have made a crater five to ten miles wide and a mile deep.

1989 Mar. 27   Contact with *Phobos 2*, an unmanned Russian spacecraft launched on July 12, 1988, was lost a few days before it was scheduled to land on Phobos, the moon of Mars. *Phobos 2* had orbited Mars for nearly two months before going out of control. It had sent back data showing that magnetic forces around Mars were controlled by "winds" consisting of electrified gases from the sun, rather than from magnetism generated by the planet. This phenomenon may have caused Mars to lose its atmosphere. The data also indicated that Phobos was a small asteroid captured by the planet's gravity. *Phobos 1*, which had been launched July 7, 1988, was lost a little more than a month later. The failure of these two probes was a serious setback to the Soviet Union's project to land a man on Mars within 25 years.

1989 Apr. 22   Emilio G[ino] **Segrè** (b. Feb. 1, 1905), an Italian-American nuclear scientist, who shared the **Nobel prize in physics** in 1959, died. He and a colleague confirmed (1955) the existence of the anti-proton, or antimatter with a negative charge, that can destroy the positive proton and the neutron. During World War II (1939–1945), Segrè contributed to the discovery of plutonium and to the fact that it was fissionable. Earlier (1937) he produced technetium, the first artificial element.

1989 May 5   Meeting in Helsinki, Finland, representatives of 80 countries agreed that the production of **chemicals that destroy the ozone layer should be banned** by the end of the century. The industrialized nations said they would assist developing nations to reach this goal. It was also the consensus that the agreement reached (Sept. 1987) at Montreal, Canada, was no longer adequate. The 12 nations of the **European Community** [EC] had already (March) agreed to the end of the century target date.

1989 May 22   With the approval of the U.S. government the **first successful transfer of cells containing foreign genes into a human being** was performed at the U.S. National Institutes of Health, Bethesda, Maryland. The altered cancer-fighting cells were placed in the bloodstream of a cancer patient. Although this patient was not expected to benefit, doctors hoped that tracking the cells would eventually help them develop techniques for transplanting foreign genes in such a way as to cure or control genetic diseases.

1989 June   The **World Health Organization** [WHO] estimated that worldwide there had so far been c.600,000 cases of **Acquired Immune Deficiency Syndrome** [AIDS], and that 6 million people carried the virus [HIV]. Nearly 106,000 cases had been reported in the U.S., of whom c.61,000 had died, and it was estimated that by the end of 1992 there would be between 179,000 and 208,000 new cases. Departing from their usual practice, U.S. federal health officials announced (Sept. 28) that they would allow an experimental drug, **dideoxyinosine** [**DDI**], to be prescribed while it was still being tested. Meanwhile, first tests of a drug, **AZT**, approved earlier, showed improvement on the part of patients using it. In the face of protests about the high cost of AZT, its manu-

facturer, the Burroughs Wellcome Company, announced (Sept. 18) that it was cutting the price by 30 percent and said further (Oct. 25) that it would distribute the drug free to children with AIDS, of whom there were c.1,900 in the U.S. 12 years old or younger.

1989 June 9   George W[ells] **Beadle** (b. Oct. 22, 1903), an American geneticist, died. With a colleague he performed (1941) experiments that demonstrated the way in which genes control the basic chemistry of living cells. In his experiments he used bread mold, which was subjected to x-rays and ultraviolet light so as to produce mutations. Beadle shared the **Noble prize for physiology or medicine** in 1958. Among other works he wrote *The Language of Life* (1966).

1989 July 14   The world's largest particle accelerator, the **Large Electron-Positron** [LEP] **collider**, successfully completed its first test run near Geneva, Switzerland, and a month later produced (Aug. 14) its first **Z particle**. A project of the **European Center for Nuclear Research** [CERN], it was intended to enlarge knowledge of nature's basic forces by causing atoms to collide at tremendous speeds. LEP, a circular tunnel 16.6 miles in circumference buried under farms, villages, and the Jura Mountains on the border between France and Switzerland, was supported by the 14-nation group of CERN, took seven years to build, and cost nearly $1 billion. Operating a smaller atom smasher, American scientists at the Stanford Linear Accelerator Center, Palo Alto, California, beat LEP by producing (Apr. 12, 1989) the Z particle. The Stanford machine was a two-mile long tunnel that cost $120 million. The Z particle was discovered (1983) at CERN, and it was hoped that a complete analysis of its behavior would lead to a theory explaining how all the forces of the universe are related.

1989 Aug. 23   R[onald] **D**[avid] **Laing** (b. Oct. 7, 1927), an English psychiatrist and a pioneer in new methods of treating schizophrenia, died. His theories were based on his concern for the rights of mental patients and on a belief that treatments used before the late 1950s, such as insulin-induced convulsions and lobotomies, were morally wrong. Laing experimented with mescaline and LSD in treating patients. Many mental health practicioners did not agree with him. Laing wrote, among other works, *The Divided Self* (1960) and *The Making of a Psychiatrist* (1985).

1989 Sept. 30 **William M**[artin] **Fairbank** (b. Feb. 24, 1917), an American physicist who spent years in pursuit of the elusive **quark**, the building block of particles of nature, died. His work involved the cooling of an experimental device to as near absolute zero as possible. He attempted to verify his report (1978) that individual quarks existed, although conventional physics held they were always inseparably bound to other quarks. Much about the nature of quarks remains today unsolved or in dispute.

1989 Oct. 4 The U.S. National Science Foundation announced that the **oldest known rocks on earth** were found in northern Canada, near the Arctic Circle. They are 3.96 billion years old, which is 100 million years older than any previously discovered, and within about 500 million years of when the earth came into existence.

1989 Oct. 17 With some opposition, the **All-Union Society of Psychiatrists of the U.S.S.R.** was **conditionally readmitted** to the **World Psychiatric Association** at a conference in Athens, Greece. The Soviet group withdrew (1983) from the association as a result of charges that it had abused dissidents committed to psychiatric institutions. A representative of the Soviet delegation admitted that psychiatric abuses had occurred for political reasons.

1989 Oct. 18 The unmanned U.S. spacecraft *Galileo* was launched from the space shuttle *Atlantis* to begin a six-year journey to the planet Jupiter, 2.5 billion miles away. *Galileo* was scheduled to reach Jupiter on Dec. 7, 1995, and would be the first space probe to orbit any of the large outer planets. It was to drop a 745-pound capsule into the dense atmosphere of the planet with the expectation that it would send back hitherto unknown facts about Jupiter for 75 minutes before being crushed by heat and pressure. Galileo took (Oct. 29, 1991) the first photographs of a rocky asteroid, Gaspra, a body about 12 miles long.

1989 Nov. 7 **J**[abez] **C**[urry] **Street** (b. May 5, 1906), an American physicist, who with a colleague **discovered the muon**, a fundamental particle of matter, died. His discovery was made (1937) when it was found that the muon resembling the electron but heavier, appeared to be the main constituent of cosmic rays that rain on the earth. During World War II (1939–1945), Street directed the production of the prototype of the **Loran Navigation System** [LORAN] that became universally used in the navigating of ships and planes.

1989 Nov. 19 American astronomers announced that there had been detected a **source of light coming from near the edge of the universe and the beginning of time**. If the age of the universe was assumed to be c.15 billion years, this quasar would have come into being a little more than 1 billion years after the Big Bang. In the meantime, other astronomers reported (Aug. 28, 1989) that they had discovered what they believed was a **galaxy being born**. It was a giant cloud of hydrogen about 65 million light years from earth. Still other astronomers said (Dec. 14) that they had noted what they believed to be the most distant star in the Milky Way, about 160,000 light years from the earth.

1989 Nov. 27 The **first U.S. liver transplant** using a living donor was successfully completed at the Chicago [Illinois] Medical Center at the University of Chicago. Four other such operations had been performed in other countries. In the operation a mother gave a third of her liver to her 21-month-old daughter. A second such operation took place successfully at the same medical center on Dec. 8.

1989 Nov. 29 Representatives of China's Environmental Protection Agency and of Wildlife Conservation International, a unit of the New York Zoological Society, signed an agreement to establish the **world's largest wildlife preserve**, an area of 100,000 square miles in Chinese-ruled Tibet. The tract, the Qian Tang region of northwestern Tibet, consisted of mountains, plains, and lakes. It was mostly uninhabited except for a wide variety of animal life.

VIII. ARTS AND LEISURE

1989 Jan. 8 After 3,486 performances (from Aug. 25, 1980) in New York City, *42nd Street*, based on a popular 1933 movie, closed as the second longest-running musical in Broadway history. Its run was exceeded only by that of *A Chorus Line*, which was still being performed after having opened May 21, 1975. A London performance closed (Jan. 7) after 1,823 performances.

1989 Jan. 20 **Beatrice** [Gladys] **Lillie** (b. May 29, 1894), a Canadian-born English comedienne, died. She made (1914) a successful debut in London and was a popular performer for many years thereafter. Her success came not just from her clever songs and patter but even more from the captivating way in which she delivered them. One of her typical songs was **"Mad Dogs and Englishmen"**; another was

"There Are Fairies at the Bottom of My Garden." Her autobiography (1972), in keeping with her spirit, was titled *Every Other Inch a Lady*.

1989 Jan. 23   Salvador Dali (b. May 11, 1904), a Spanish artist and a pioneer of surrealism in Europe, died. After his first (1929) one-man show in Paris, he went on to rapid success, based in part on his paintings and in part on his personality. Dali was extravagant in words and action, in keeping with the shock of his brilliantly surfaced paintings. In his heyday Dali painted *The Persistence of Memory* [also known as *Soft Watches*] (1935) and *Soft Constructions with Boiled Beans—Premonition of Civil War* (1936). After he turned to religion in the late 1940s, Dali painted *Sacrament of the Last Supper* (1955).

1989 Feb. 14   Ruhollah Khomeini, the ayatollah [= religious leader] and most powerful person in Iran, declared [Ahmed] **Salman Rushdie** (b. June 19, 1947), author of *The Satanic Verses* (1989), a blasphemer and sentenced him to death because he considered the book insulting to Islam. Khomeini called on all Muslims to execute Rushdie. In the novel a character who could be taken to be Mohammed, the founder of the Islamic religion, was depicted with all too human a nature. Rushdie, born in India but living in Great Britain, expressed (Feb. 18) regret at the distress the novel caused and went into hiding where he remained all year. Some bookstores in England and the U.S. temporarily removed the book from sale, fearing danger to their employees. In Europe some publishers hesitated to print the book. All 12 nations of the **European Community** [EC] **recalled their envoys from Iran** in protest against the death threat. Muslims in other countries demonstrated against the book, but 46 Muslim nations rejected (Mar. 16) the Iranian position, while condemning the novel. Rushdie issued (Dec. 24, 1990) a statement in which he said that any passages in his book that insulted Mohammed did not represent his own views. Nevertheless, Khomeini had declared (Dec. 26) that the death decree was irreversible.

1989 Mar. 12   Maurice Evans (b. June 3, 1901), an English actor noted for his roles in plays of **William Shakespeare**, died. He made his London debut in 1927, scoring there his first major success (1929) in *Journey's End*, an immensely popular, realistic, antiheroic World War I drama by **R**[obert] **C**[edric] **Sherriff** (June 6, 1896–1975). Beginning in 1934 he appeared in a number of Shakespeare plays in both England and the U.S., his *Richard II* (1937) being

greatly admired. Evans was also a success in such modern plays as *Dial M for Murder* (1952) and in the movies.

1989 Mar. 27   Malcom Cowley (b. Aug. 24, 1898), an American critic, editor, and poet, died. He was the foremost chronicler of the post–World War I (1914–1918) "lost generation," writing about them in *Exile's Return* (1934). As an editor he was an early promoter of such writers as **William Faulkner**, **John Cheever**, and **Jack Kerouac**. Among Cowley's many writings were *The Literary Situation* (1954), a volume of poetry *Blue Juanita: Collected Poems* (1968), and *And I Worked at the Writer's Trade* (1978).

1989 Mar. 29   The second edition of *The Oxford English Dictionary* [OED 2], in 20 volumes the most comprehensive dictionary of the English language ever published, was issued. Replacing the first edition (1928), OED 2 consisted of 20,000 pages, more than 500,000 definitions, and c.60 million words. The new work was computerized so that revisions could be made easily.

1989 Mar. 29   A new entrance to the **Louvre Museum** in Paris, striking in its contrast to the longstanding buildings housing many of the great art treasures of the world, was officially opened by **François Mitterand**, president of France. The entrance consisted of a glass pyramid, designed by **I.M. Pei** an American architect, that contrasted sharply but not discordantly with its surroundings. The 71-foot-high structure led to an underground addition to the museum of more than 650,000 square feet, where there were shops, cafeterias, an auditorium, and a depot for tourist buses.

1989 Apr. 19   Daphne du Maurier (b. May 13, 1907), a popular English author of romantic and Gothic novels, died. She was best known for the very readable *Rebecca* (1938), which was made (1940) into an equally successful movie. The novel, set in Cornwall, was the story of a second wife who came to a mansion she found haunted by the image of the first wife. Du Maurier's other novels included *Jamaica Inn* (1936) and *Frenchman's Creek* (1941); a biography of her actor father was *Gerald: A Portrait* (1934).

1989 Apr. 26   Lucille [Desiree] **Ball** (b. Aug. 6, 1911), an American actress, one of the most popular stars of her day in movies, and on radio and television, died. She first appeared (1933) in the movies, making in all about 50 films. She was on radio in the 1930s and 1940s. Fame bordering on adoration came to her after the start (Oct. 14, 1951) of the *I Love Lucy* television series. Appearing with her then-husband **Desi Arnaz**, she played the seemingly scatterbrained but resourceful wife, in a setting in which her ability to pantomime and her perfect sense of timing made the show the most popular on the air until its end in 1957, after 179 episodes.

1989 May 26 The 10,000th episode of "The Archers," Great Britain's longest-running and most popular radio serial, was broadcast, the first episode having been heard on May 29, 1950. The show began with a farm locale and dealt with such problems as increasing pig productivity. In the 1980s, however, more women appeared on the program with their concerns about rights and other public affairs. The serial had five million regular listeners.

1989 May 30 **Zinka Milanov** [née Kunc] (b. May 17, 1906), a Yugoslavian-born dramatic soprano, who starred at the Metropolitan Opera, New York City, for almost 30 years, died. She made her debut (1937) there and soon became noted not only for her voice but also for her acting and her ego. Milanov's specialty was in roles in Verdi operas, singing, for example, *Aida* 75 times. She made her last operatic appearance on Apr. 14, 1966, and after that coached younger singers.

1989 May 31 **C**[yril] **L**[ionel] **R**[obert] **James** (b. Jan. 4, 1901), a Trinidadian-born leader of the pan-African movement, as well as a historian, literary critic, and philosopher, died. As a leader of black nationalism, he influenced a number of the first-generation heads of the African nations that achieved independence in the 1960s. Among his many books that espoused his causes were *Minty Alley* (1927), one of the first novels in English written in the West Indies; *World Revolution* (1937); and *A History of Negro Revolt* (1977).

1989 June 28 [Georg Henri Anton] **Joris Ivens** (b. Nov. 19, (1898), a Dutch producer of documentary films, of which he made more than 50, died. Most of them concerned revolutionary struggles, although an early one, *The Bridge* (1928), had a Rotterdam setting. He was best known for *The Spanish Earth* (1937), made in Spain and sympathetic to the Republican government in its fight against the fascist Falangists in the Spanish Civil War (1936–1939).

1989 July 11 **Laurence** [Kerr] **Olivier** (b. May 22, 1907), an unusually talented English actor and director, died. After making his professional debut (1926), he became known for both his dramatic and his comic roles. He excelled in such diverse parts as Sir Toby Belch in *Twelfth Night* and as *Richard II*. Olivier made his movie debut (1929), and in that medium was best remembered for *Wuthering Heights* (1939) and *Rebecca* (1940). He was the first artistic director (1963–1973) of the British National Theater, where he directed a notable *Hamlet* and appeared as Othello and Shylock.

1989 July 16 **Herbert von Karajan** (b. Apr. 5, 1908), who had resigned (Apr. 24) as conductor of the Berlin Philharmonic Orchestra for reasons of health and because of a dispute with the West Berlin government, died. He had been artistic director of the orchestra for 34 years. Born in Austria, he made his debut in 1929. Joining the Nazi party (1933), he was able to continue his musical career during Hitler's rule; but after World War II (1939–1945), the victorious Allies forbade him to direct for two years.

1989 July 22 **Donald Barthelme** (b. Apr. 7, 1931), an American author known for his minimalist, postmodern writing style, died. The publication of his first novel *Snow White* (1967) brought him attention for what critics called his surrealistic and erotic interpretation of the fairy story. Barthelme concentrated mostly on short stories, and among collections of them were *Come Back, Dr. Caligari* (1964) and *Unspeakable Practices, Unnatural Acts* (1968). Another novel was *The Dead Father* (1975), while *The Slightly Irregular Fire Engine* (1971) was an award-winning children's book.

1989 Sept. 4 **Irving Berlin** [orig.: Israel Baline] (b. May 11, 1888), a Russian-born American composer and lyricist of both spectacular quality and quantity, died. In all he wrote c.1,500 songs, including those for 19 Broadway musicals and 18 movies. Although Berlin never learned to read or write music, he came to be recognized as the heart and soul of American popular music for nearly six decades. His first hit was "Alexander's Ragtime Band" (1911). Others that never lost their popularity included "A Pretty Girl Is Like a Melody" (1919), "Blue Skies" (1927), "Easter Parade" (1933), "God Bless America" (1939), "White Christmas" (1942), and "There's No Business Like Show Business" (1946). In the U.S. Army in World War I (1914–1918), Berlin wrote a musical comedy that included a song, "Oh, How I Hate to

Get Up in the Morning" (1918), his own rendition of which also made him lastingly famous.

1989 Sept. 30   Virgil [Garnett] **Thomson** (b. Nov. 25, 1896), an American composer and critic, died. As a composer he was best known for the opera *Four Saints in Three Acts* (1934), with libretto by Gertrude Stein. He also collaborated with her on *The Mother of Us All* (1947). Thomson composed music for films, one being *Louisiana Story* (1948). He was perhaps even better known as the chief music critic (1940–1954) of the **New York** *Herald Tribune*.

1989 Oct. 6 [Ruth Elizabeth] **Bette Davis** (b. Apr. 5, 1908), for 60 years one of the greatest actresses of American movies, during which time she made c.100 films in all, died. She made her acting debut in 1929 and scored her first film success in *The Man Who Played God* (1932). Of a strong and volatile temperament, she was well suited to her roles in *Of Human Bondage* (1934), *The Old Maid* (1939), *The Little Foxes* (1941), and *All About Eve* (1950). In her later career Davis appeared in a remarkable horror movie *What Ever Happened to Baby Jane?* (1962).

1989 Oct. 10   Helen Hayes [née Brown] (Oct. 10, 1900–Mar. 17, 1993), an American actress, was **hailed on the occasion of her 89th birthday** by colleagues and friends at a reception in New York City. Through the years she took leading roles in a great variety of plays. One of her early successes was in *Dear Brutus* (1918). She starred in *Caesar and Cleopatra* (1925), *Victoria Regina* (1935), and *A Long Day's Journey Into Night* (1971). She also acted on the radio, on TV, and in the movies, being highly praised in the film *The Sin of Madelon Claudet* (1932). In 1955 a theater in New York City was renamed for Hayes to mark the 50th anniversary of her first appearance on the stage as a child actress.

1989 Oct. 19   Camilo José Cela (b. May 11, 1916), a Spanish author of great vigor, both in his writings and his personal life, was awarded the **Nobel prize for literature**. His first novel *La familia de Pascual Duarte* [*The Family of Pascual Duarte*] (1942) was successful and also initiated a style [**tremendismo**] steeped in violence and despair, and in distorted reality. The book was supposedly the autobiography of a murderer. Among Cela's 60-odd books were *La Colmena* [*The Hive*] (1951) and *San Camilo, 36* (1969).

1989 Oct. 20 [John] **Anthony Quayle** (b. Sept. 7, 1913), an English actor who appeared in a variety of roles on the stage, in the movies, and on television, died. He made his stage debut in 1931 and the next year joined the Old Vic Company, where he played a number of different types of roles, including Shakespearean. The first of the more than 30 films he appeared in was *Pygmalion* (1938). Other major movie roles were in *The Guns of Navarone* (1961) and *Lawrence of Arabia* (1963). Quayle's most lasting contribution was as director (1948–1956) of the Shakespeare Memorial Theater at Stratford-on-Avon, which he helped make a major center of theater in Britain.

1989 Oct. 25   Mary [Therese] **McCarthy** (b. June 21, 1912), an American novelist, journalist, and critic, known for her strongly expressed opinions, died. Among her novels, which were outspoken about sexual matters, were *The Man in the Brooks Brothers Shirt* (1941), *The Company She Keeps* (1942), and *The Group* (1963). McCarthy's literary and drama criticism was sometimes harsh but always witty. She wrote autobiographically in *Memories of a Catholic Girlhood* (1957) and *How I Grew* (1987).

1989 Nov. 1   Lincoln Kirstein (b. May 4, 1907), an American dance impressario, writer, and businessman, retired as general director of the New York City Ballet and as president of the School of American Ballet. In 1933 he invited **George Balanchine**, a noted Russian choreographer and teacher, to emigrate to the U.S and the next year they founded what became the ballet company and the school. Kirstein, the chief patron of both institutions until his retirement, had a seminal role in the flowering of classical ballet in the U.S. He wrote a number of books, among them *Blast at Ballet* (1938) and *Movement and Metaphor* (1971).

1989 Nov. 5   Vladimir Horowitz [né Gorowitz] (b. Oct. 1, 1904), a Russian-born American pianist whose talent and personality made him the most popular performer of his generation, died. He appeared in recitals in Russia in the early 1920s, then toured Europe, and first played in the U.S. in New York City in 1928. After an active career (to 1953), Horowitz went into retirement for 12 years before making a triumphal return to the concert stage (May 1965). After an absence of 61 years, he returned (1986) to Russia, where his playing was welcomed with great enthusiasm.

1989 Nov. 30 With the sale in New York of Pablo Picasso's *Pierrette's Wedding* for $51.3 million, six of the **highest prices yet paid at auction for paintings** were registered this year, and this Picasso sale was the second highest ever. Also in 1989, *Yo Picasso*, a self-portrait, went for $47.9 million; a third Picasso, *Au Lapin Agile* for $40.7 million; *Halberdier* by Jacopo Pontormo, $35.2 million; *Rue Mosnier, Paris, Decorated With Flags on June 30, 1878* by Edouard Manet, $26.4 million; and *Mirror*, by Picasso, also $26.4 million. In addition, William de Kooning's *Interchange* was sold (Nov. 8) for $20.7 million, a record at auction for a living artist, while Jackson Pollock's *No. 8, 1950* was sold (May 2) for $11 million, the most ever paid for a work by this artist.

1989 Dec. 1 **Alvin Ailey** (b. Jan. 5, 1931), an American choreographer, dancer, and director, a leader in establishing the popularity of modern dance, died. He made his debut as a dancer in 1950 in Los Angeles and his first appearance on Broadway in 1954. He **founded** (1958) **the Alvin Ailey American Dance Theater** of black dancers. Ailey's choreography and dancers had roots in classical ballet, black culture, and jazz, and the American Dance Theater became the most popular dance group in the U.S. Equally well-received abroad, they performed in 45 countries on six continents. Among Ailey's own works were *Revelations* (1960) and *Masekela Language* (1969).

1989 Dec. 22 **Samuel** [Barclay] **Beckett** (b. Apr. 13, 1906), an Irish-born playwright, novelist, and poet who worked (after 1937) in France, died. As a novelist his best work was the trilogy *Molloy* (1951), *Malone Dies* (1951), and *The Unnameable* (1953), the search of an old, handicapped man for his mother. As a playwright Beckett, with the first performance of *Waiting for Godot* (1953), was recognized as the perfect voice of the theater of the absurd. Throughout his work the meaninglessness of life and the inevitability of death are offset only by the life of the mind. *Endgame* (1957) and *Krapp's Last Tape* (1958) were two more plays that solidified his position as the dramatist who altered the course of modern theater. Beckett also wrote poetry, some of it gathered in *Collected Poems in English and French* (1977). He received the **Nobel prize for literature** in 1969.

IX. SPORTS, GAMES, AND SOCIETY

1989 Feb. 11 **René Jacquot** became the **first Frenchman to win a world boxing championship** in 30 years when he won a 12-round decision in a bout at Grenoble, France, to decide the World Boxing Council's super-welterweight title. **Alphonse Halimi** (b. Feb. 18, 1932), the last Frenchman to win a world championship, held (1957–1959) the bantamweight title.

1989 Mar. 14 **Zita** (b. May 9, 1892), the former empress (1916–1918) of Austria-Hungary, died, in exile in Switzerland. A daughter of the duke of Bourbon-Parma, she was the widow of **Charles I**, the last emperor of Austria-Hungary (1916–1918), who ascended the throne in the midst of World War I (1914–1918). The war ended the Hapsburg-Lorraine Dynasty (1736–1918), and Charles and Zita were forced (1919) into exile. Zita's funeral service (Apr. 1) in Vienna, once the capital of the Austro-Hungarian monarchy, was marked by imperial pomp and circumstance and lasted four and a half hours.

1989 Mar. 29 **Sergei Priakin** became the **first Soviet Union athlete permitted to play for a professional team in North America** when he signed a contract with the Calgary [Canada] Flames of the **National Hockey League** [NHL]. He had played for the Russian national team for four years. Later in the year four more Soviet players joined the NHL.

1989 Apr. 26 The **largest lottery prize in American history**, $115,578,980.14 was shared by 14 winning tickets in the Pennsylvania drawing. One winning ticket was held by a group of 14 factory workers who pooled their ticket purchases. Each of the 14 winning tickets was to receive more than $8.2 million over 26 years.

1989 May 26 A trimaran, *Great American*, broke the **sailing record for the New York–San Francisco run** when it sailed under the Golden Gate Bridge one hour short of 77 days after a 14,500-mile journey. The previous record had been set (Feb. 12) when *Thursday's Child* completed the same voyage in 80 days, 20 hrs. Prior to these two voyages the record was held by the clipper ship *Flying Cloud*, which made (1854) the trip in 89 days, 8 hrs.

1989 July 14 France celebrated the **200th anniversary of the storming of the Bastille**, which marked the beginning of the French Revolution (1789–1799).

Under the direction of François Mitterand, president of France, 32 heads of state and government joined the observance. The day's events ended with "The Festival of the Planet's Tribes," featuring more than 6,000 performers, among whom were 1,600 drummers carrying French flags and wearing helmets with tiny lamps on top.

1989 July 23   **Greg Lemond**, who became (1986) the first American to win the **Tour de France** bicycle race, captured first place for a second time, winning by only eight seconds, the smallest victory margin ever. **Jeannie Longo**, a French cyclist, won the women's Tour de France for the third consecutive year.

1989 July 29   **Javier Sotomayor** (b. Oct. 13, 1967), a Cuban track star, became the **first person to high jump 8 feet** (2.44 meters) in a meet at San Juan, Puerto Rico. The 6-foot mark had been first reached on Mar. 17, 1876, and the 7-foot mark on June 29, 1956.

1989 Aug. 19   One of the **most lavish parties of the century** was given by **Malcolm S. Forbes** (Aug. 19, 1919–Feb. 24, 1990), an American magazine publisher, who hosted it in a palace in Tangier, Morocco, to celebrate his 70th birthday. Invited were 600 or so glamorous, rich, and famous guests, some of them flown in by Forbes on chartered jets. The evening's entertainment included hundreds of belly dancers, a charge by Berber horsemen, and fireworks. The party was estimated to have cost $2 million. Forbes said he would not try to take any of the cost as a tax deductible business expense.

1989 Aug. 20   The **oldest world record in a major running event was broken** by **Said Aouita**, a Moroccan track star, when he ran the 3,000-meter event in a meet at Cologne, West Germany, in 7 min., 29.45 sec. The former mark was 7:32.1 set (June 27, 1978) by Henry Rono (b. Feb. 12, 1952) of Kenya.

1989 Aug. 22   **Diana Vreeland** [née Dalziel] (b. 1903?), for many years the most influential **fashion** editor in the U.S., died. Her career began (1936) with a column in *Harper's Bazaar*, of which she became fashion editor the next year. During the 1960s, as editor of *Vogue*, she was the presiding arbiter of women's fashion. Her hold on the world of style became even firmer beginning (1973) with the costume exhibits she staged annually for the Metropolitan Museum of Art, New York City.

1989 Aug. 24   **Pete Rose**, a longtime star of professional baseball, who held the record for most career hits (4,256) by any player, was **permanently banned from baseball**. The action was taken by **A. Bartlett Giamatti**, the commissioner of baseball, who said he believed Rose had bet on baseball games, including those of his own team, something strictly forbidden. Rose denied this, even though a four-month investigation had turned up evidence to the contrary. It was stipulated that Rose, who had been manager of the Cincinnati Reds, could apply for reinstatement after one year. On July 19, 1990, he was sentenced to five months in prison for filing false income tax returns. He was also fined $50,000 and ordered to serve 1,000 hours of community service.

1989 Sept. 1   A[ngelo] **Bartlett Giamatti** (b. Apr. 4, 1938), commissioner of baseball (since Apr. 1), and president of Yale University (1978–1986), a Renaissance scholar, and an avid baseball fan for many years, died. He left Yale (June 1986) to become president of the National Baseball League. In his short career as a baseball executive he was praised for his view of sports as more than athletics and entertainment but as part of America's cultural life. As an educator he wrote *A Free and Ordered Space: The Real World of the University* (1988).

1989 Sept. 14   **Valentina Nicholaevna Sanina Schlee** (b. May 1, 1904), a Russian-born **fashion** designer, known professionally by her first name, died. She opened (1928) her first shop in New York City, but became best known for dressing stars of the theater and the movies, beginning with **Judith Anderson** (1933). Other Valentina clients included **Lynn Fontane**, **Katherine Hepburn**, and **Gloria Swanson**. With her dashing personality, Valentina was her own best advertisement for the turbans and flowing gowns for which she was noted.

1989 Sept. 29   In the **largest drug raid ever in the U.S.**, federal agents seized 20 tons of cocaine in a warehouse in Sylmar, in the San Fernando Valley of southern California. The wholesale value was estimated at at least $2 billion, and one of the seven suspects arrested said 60 tons had passed through the warehouse during the year. In Texas, near the Mexican border, and also on a Panamanian ship, agents seized (Oct. 4) 14 tons of cocaine; in New York City more than 5 tons of drugs were found (Nov. 10) hidden in drums of toxic chemicals.

1989 Oct. 1   Under a law passed (May) by the Danish parliament, six male **homosexual couples were**

legally joined in a "registered partnership," the first such unions of this kind in the world. The law gave couples of both sexes most of the rights of normally married people, except the right to adopt or obtain custody of children. Lesbians objected to this provision. In general these couples would have most of the advantages and disadvantages of marriage. The Evangelical Lutheran Church, to which almost all Danes belonged, did not recognize such unions.

1989 Oct. 15 **Wayne Gretzky** (b. Jan. 26, 1961), of the Los Angeles Kings of the **National Hockey League** [NHL], became the **highest scorer in NHL history** in a game against the Edmonton Oilers when he registered his 1,850th point. The record broken had been set by **Gordie Howe** in 26 seasons. This was Gretzky's 11th season.

1989 Oct. 22 **Gary Kasparov**, the Russian chess champion of the world, **defeated *Deep Thought***, the computer chess champion, in a two-game match in New York City. Deep Thought can scan 720,000 positions a second, but Kasparov, who had a rating of 2,795 as a chess grandmaster, said *Deep Thought* should be rated at about 2,500. In three to five years time, however, a more powerful computer was expected to be a thousand times faster and then the era of human chess supremacy might end.

1989 Nov. 7 **Richard Ramirez** was sentenced to death in the gas chamber as the **"Night Stalker"** murderer who terrorized southern California in 1985. He had been convicted (Sept. 2) of 13 murders and 30 other crimes, including rape, sodomy, and burglary. Ramirez's method of operation was to enter unlocked houses at night and attack people in their beds.

1989 Nov. 22 **Kirby Puckett** (b. Mar. 4, 1961), a centerfielder for the Minnesota Twins of the **American Baseball League**, became the **first $3 million-dollar-a-year player** when he signed a three-year contract for $9 million. This figure was soon (Dec. 1) exceeded when **Mark Langston** (b. Aug. 20, 1960), a left-handed relief pitcher, agreed to a five-year contract with the California Angels for $16 million, or $3.2 million a year; and **Mark Davis** (b. Oct. 19, 1960), also a left-handed relief pitcher, signed (Dec. 11) with the Kansas City Royals for $13 million for four years, or $3.25 million a year.

1989 Nov. 28 **Nadia Comaneci**, the gymnastic star of the 1976 Olympic Games, fled her native Romania to Hungary and arrived in New York City (Dec. 1).

She traveled on to Florida, where she was welcomed with some reservations when it was revealed that her traveling companion on her journey from Romania was a married man with four small children.

1989 Dec. 6 A gunman who singled out women as his targets killed 14 and wounded 13 other people at the University of Montreal, Canada. Shouting "You're all a bunch of feminists," he separated the men in a classroom from the women before he began firing. The gunman, **Marc Lepine**, then committed suicide. He left a note in which he said women had ruined his life.

1989 Dec. 10 The overthrow of the Communist government of **East Germany** revealed a **program of pampering of world-class athletes** that enabled this small country to trail only the U.S.S.R. and the U.S. in medals won at Olympic Games since 1968. Bonuses of $21,000 were given for winning a gold medal at these events. Such athletes also received automobiles, luxury apartments, and other favors unavailable to the general public. The leaders of the German Sports and Gymnastic Union agreed to resign (Dec. 11) in the face of public protests over the excessive support for athletics for the sake of national prestige.

1989 Dec. 13 **Eleven nations** [Australia, Bulgaria, Czechoslovakia, Great Britain, Italy, Norway, South Korea, Sweden, the U.S.S.R., the U.S., and West Germany] **signed an agreement in Rome for the testing of one another's athletes** for the use of drugs that enhance performance. The agreement was effective Jan. 1, 1990, and was supervised by the **International Olympic Committee's medical commission**.

1989 Dec. 15 In the year's climax to a **war between the government of Colombia and the powerful drug cartels** of the country, one of the largest cocaine traffickers, **José Gonzalo Rodríguez Gacha**, was killed in a shootout with security forces. His son and 15 bodyguards died with the billionaire ruler of the Médellin cocaine cartel. The war began in earnest after the assassination (Aug. 18) by drug dealers of **Luis Carlos Galán**, the candidate for president of the governing Liberal party. The government took into custody c.10,000 persons accused of being connected with the drug traffic and seized 134 airplanes used by the smugglers. Ranches and other properties were confiscated. Unintimidated, the drug cartels began bombings on a large scale, including (Aug. 24) the offices of the two largest political parties and two radio stations. Nine banks were bombed (Aug. 27). Despite the government crackdown and its efforts to seize and extradite drug dealers to the U.S., many top figures remained at large.

1989 Dec. 31 **Lily Daché** (b. 1892?), a French-born American **fashion** designer, whose specialty in hats,

especially turbans, made her world famous, died. Her clients included, among others, such movie stars as **Audrey Hepburn**, **Carole Lombard**, and **Loretta Young**. When she saw that women's hats might go out of fashion, Daché developed snoods as an alternative.

1990

I. VITAL STATISTICS AND DEMOGRAPHICS

1990 According to the United Nations, about 15 million persons were **refugees** outside their homelands. In **Africa** civil strife had made refugees of 4.4 million people. **Western Europe** braced for a surge of refugees from **Eastern Europe**, where the nations newly liberated from communism were suffering economic maladjustments. Perhaps 5 to 20 million people would seek to leave their homes. Within the **U.S.S.R.**, political, economic, and ethnic unrest resulted in floods of people fleeing from one part of the nation to another. One of the largest movements saw nearly 200,000 Russian Jews pour into **Israel**. In **Hong Kong**, 55,000 Vietnamese refugees awaited word on their fate while 62,000 residents left, anticipating the Chinese takeover in 1997. In the Persian Gulf, the Iraqi invasion (Aug. 2) of **Kuwait** caused hundreds of thousands of Indians, Pakistanis, Bangladeshis, Egyptians, Palestinians, Filipinos, and others to flee or be forced out without notice.

1990 The **population of the world** was estimated to be 5.321 billion. By regions the population was: **Africa**, 661 million; **Asia**, 3.116 billion; **Europe**, 501 million; **Latin America**, 447 million; **North America**, 278 million; **Oceania**, 27 million; and the U.S.S.R., 291 million. The United Nations Fund for Population Activities predicted (May 14) that the world's population would reach 6.25 billion by the end of the century. The United Nations Childrens Fund predicted (Dec. 18) that births worldwide would rise to 149 million a year by the year 2000, compared with the present rate of 142 million, but would decline to 144 million by 2020.

1990 As of mid-year, the **population of the ten largest metropolitan areas** was estimated to be: Tokyo-Yokohama, Japan, 26,952,000; Mexico City, Mexico, 20,202,000; São Paulo, Brazil, 18,052,000; Seoul,

South Korea, 16,268,000; New York, U.S., 14,622,-000; Osaka-Kobe-Kyoto, Japan, 13,826,000; Bombay, India, 11,777,000; Calcutta, India, 11,663,000; Buenos Aires, Argentina, 11,518,000; Rio de Janeiro, Brazil, 11,428,000.

1990 Oct. 30 **China**, after the most thorough census in its history, announced that as of July 1 its **population** was 1,133,682,501. It was estimated that since that time the population had increased by another 5.5 million. The annual growth rate was 1.47 percent.

1990 Dec. 27 The **U.S.** Census Bureau reported that the decennial census, taken as of Apr. 1, showed a **population** of 249,632,692, an increase of more than 23 million over the 1980 census. Rural areas lost population while cities gained. The largest relative increases occurred in the southern and sunbelt states, with California, Texas, and Florida leading.

II. DISASTERS

1990 Jan. 2 The first of six **oil spills** during 1990 in the **Arthur Kill** and the **Kill van Kull**, two narrow channels between Staten Island, New York, and New Jersey, occurred when an underwater pipeline burst and allowed more than 200,000 gallons of heating oil to flow into Arthur Kill. A hole in a barge allowed (Feb. 28) more than 24,000 gallons of heating oil to leak into the Kill van Kull. An explosion (Mar. 6) on a barge in the Arthur Kill let more than 100,000 gallons of oil of the nearly 4 million in its cargo to flow into the Arthur Kill. In the same region, a British tanker ran aground (June 7), dumping 260,-000 gallons of fuel oil. When two barges collided (July 18), 37,000 gallons of heating oil flowed into the water. A barge without a valid operating permit sank (Sept. 27) with c.50,000 gallons of some oil product escaping.

1990 Jan. 4 Pakistan's **worst train accident** occurred at the village of Sangi, in Sind province, about 225 miles north of Karachi, when an improperly set switch caused a passenger train to crash into an empty freight train on a siding. At least 307 persons were killed, and authorities feared another 150 might be trapped in coaches that had been driven into waterlogged soil by other coaches piling on top of them.

1990 Jan. 25 A Colombian Avianca **Boeing 707** passenger jet, nearing its New York destination on a flight from Bogota, Colombia, **crashed** near Glen Cove, Long Island, when it ran out of fuel. Of the 161 persons aboard 72 were killed and almost all the others injured. The plane's crew had asked Kennedy International Airport for priority in landing, but apparently did not use the exact language necessary to indicate that its fuel was limited.

1990 Jan. 25 The first of three unusually **severe windstorms** struck the British Isles and Western Europe, the others following on Feb. 3 and Feb. 20, taking in all a toll of more than 140 lives. Winds of more than 140 mph knocked out electrical power, damaged buildings, including the House of Commons in London and Chartres Cathedral in France, and blew down thousands of trees, including rare and exotic species in London's Kew Gardens.

1990 Feb. 7 A tanker, the *American Trader*, struck an underwater object in the Pacific Ocean within two miles of the southern California coast at Huntington Beach and spilled more than 9,500 barrels of crude oil. Much of the oil washed ashore, where 1,300 persons worked to clean it up.

1990 Feb. 14 An Indian Airlines **Airbus 320 crashed** as it was about to land at Bangalore in southern India. Of the 146 passengers and crew aboard, 93 were killed.

1990 Mar. 25 A **fire** in a crowded illegal club, the **Happy Land Social Club**, in the Bronx, New York City, claimed 87 lives, after a man who had been ejected for quarreling with a former girl friend returned, threw gasoline near the door, and set it afire. The club had been ordered closed for various fire and building code violations 16 months earlier. One of the survivors was the arsonist's ex-girl friend.

1990 Apr. 7 Fire aboard a Danish ferry, the *Scandinavian Star*, which was on an overnight trip from Oslo, Norway, to Frederikshavn, on the northern coast of Denmark, took the lives of c.175 passengers and crew of the approximately 500 aboard.

1990 May 9–10 The worst **cyclone** in ten years moved in from the Bay of Bengal, smashed 1,400 villages, and killed at least 210 people along India's southeastern coast, mostly in the state of Andhra Pradesh. Thousands of homes were destroyed and 3 million people left homeless.

1990 June 21 An **earthquake** that registered 7.7 on the Richter scale struck the Iranian provinces of Zanjan and Gilan, northwest of Teheran on the southern shore of the Caspian Sea, destroying more than 100 towns and villages. Besides aftershocks following the first quake, two more rocked (June 24) the area, the largest registering 5.7 on the Richter scale. After a week of international rescue efforts, officials put the toll at c.40,000 dead, c.60,000 injured, and c.105,000 families made homeless.

1990 July 2 At Mecca, Saudi Arabia, 1,426 Muslims making a pilgrimage [**hadj**] to the holiest shrine of the Islamic religion were killed when a **stampede occurred in a 500-yard-long pedestrian tunnel** that linked the city with a tent camp for pilgrims. The failure of an air conditioning and ventilating system in 112°F heat was blamed for the tragedy.

1990 July 16 An **earthquake** registering 7.7 on the Richter scale with its epicenter 55 miles north of Manila, struck Luzon, the main island of the Philippines, killing at least 674 people and injuring more than 2,600. It was feared that hundreds more were buried and dead in the rubble of buildings, including a number of hotels.

1990 Aug. 24 In the worst mining disaster in Yugoslavia's history, an **explosion in a coal mine** at Dobrnja, Yugoslavia, 85 miles southwest of Belgrade, killed c.169 miners, who were buried 1,600 feet underground by the blast.

1990 Oct. 2 A **Boeing 737** jet of China's national airline, hijacked after it left Xiamen [formerly Amoy], an eastern port city, **crash-landed** at Canton in southern China, where it rammed into an empty Boeing 707 and then into a Boeing 757 with passengers aboard. In the fiery collision 128 people died, including 45 in the plane on the ground.

1990 Nov. 13   A **typhoon** with winds of up to 150 miles an hour killed at least 112 persons in the central Philippines. Hardest hit were Cebu City and Negros Occidental province, where the sugar cane crop was damaged. Thirty of the country's 73 provinces were declared disaster areas.

1990 Dec. 31   The Sudan was threatened with its third **famine** in six years, the result of drought, civil war, and the refusal of the fundamentalist Islamic government to allow relief supplies to reach the rebellious southern part of the country, which is Christian and animist. The government of Ethiopia said (Nov. 21) that 4.3 million of its people were in danger of starving in 1991 and asked for 800,000 tons of food. Most of the danger was in the northern provinces of Eritrea and Tigre, where civil war had been going on for several years.

III. WAR AND POLITICS

1990 Jan. 10   The **Chinese government lifted martial law**, which had been declared to put down the student-led pro-democracy movement of 1989. The U.S. government then announced that it was dropping its opposition to loans to China by the World Bank. China released (May 10) 211 of the dissidents it had jailed as a result of the demonstrations, and later (June 6) another 97.

1990 Jan. 15   As a result of **violence in the republic of Azerbaijan**, in southern Russia on the Caspian Sea, the government of the U.S.S.R. declared a state of emergency and sent 11,000 troops and police to the area. The trouble was caused by ethnic violence between Azerbaijanians and Armenians and also from an uprising of the Azerbaijanian Popular Front against the Communist government. The Soviets did not gain control of the situation until Jan. 21, after much fighting in Baku, the capital. In central Asia anti-Armenian rioting occurred (Feb. 12–13) in **Tadzhikistan** and in **Uzbekistan** (Feb. 16). In **Kirghizia**, in the same region, (June 6–10) rioting between Kirghiz and Uzbeks left more than 148 dead.

1990 Jan. 20   **Naruhiko Higashikuni** (b. Dec. 3, 1887), who became prime minister of **Japan** (Aug. 17, 1945) two days after his nation surrendered at the end of World War II (1939–1945), died. A member of the royal family, he became (1937) chief of military aviation and took charge (1941) of home defense. His government lasted only until Oct. 9,

1945. Afterward, Higashikuni was deprived of his princely title and he became a monk.

1990 Jan. 22   The Yugoslav Communist party, which had ruled the country for 45 years, voted to give up its monopoly and declared in favor of a multiparty system. This move came when ethnic rivalries among the inhabitants of the nation's constituent republics threatened to break up the country. In the first free election (Apr. 8), the northernmost republic of Slovenia gave a majority to a center-right coalition that favored independence, and in a referendum (Dec. 23) **Slovenes voted almost unanimously for independence**. An election (May 6, 1990) in **Croatia**, also in northern Yugoslavia, resulted in a sweeping victory for the Croatian Democratic Union, which wanted the nation to become a confederation of sovereign states. In **Serbia**, the nation's largest republic, an election (Dec. 23) was won by the former Communist party, renamed Socialist. Since the winners favored a strong central government, the victory was seen as a further sign of the conflict of interests within **Yugoslavia**.

1990 Feb. 1   A struggle within the Communist party of **Bulgaria**, regarding which changes should be made in its policies, resulted in the resignation of the government. Parliament had taken (Jan. 15) from the Communists their long-time guarantee of political monopoly. However, when parliamentary elections were held (June 10), the Communists, renamed the Bulgarian Socialist party, won 211 of the 400 seats. As a result of demonstrations and strikes, caused largely by dissatisfaction with economic conditions, **Andrei Lukanov** (b. Sept. 26, 1938), a former Politburo member who had been prime minister since February, resigned (Nov. 29). Parliament elected (Dec. 7) a politically independent judge, **Dimitar Popov**, as prime minister and approved (Dec. 20) the first multiparty government in 40 years.

1990 Feb. 2   **South Africa** lifted its 30-year ban on the **African National Congress [ANC]**, the leading and predominantly black anti-apartheid movement, and released (Feb. 11) from prison after 27½ years **Nelson Mandela**, its best-known leader, who had been convicted (1964) of sabotage and treason. Mandela resumed (Mar. 2) active leadership of the ANC. Emergency regulations in three of the four provinces, in effect for four years, were lifted (June 7); racial discrimination in parks, swimming pools, libraries, and other public facilities became (Oct. 15) illegal; and the government agreed (Nov. 2) to a phased release of political prisoners.

1990 Feb. 6 After **Hungary** announced it was removing restrictions on the **Roman Catholic Church**, which had been in effect for 40 years, the Vatican said it was resuming diplomatic relations. The Vatican also restored (Mar. 15) diplomatic ties with Russia for the first time in 67 years; with Czechoslovakia (Apr. 10); with Romania (May 15); and with Bulgaria (Dec. 6).

1990 Feb. 7 The Central Committee of the Russian **Communist party**, acting on a proposal by **Mikhail Gorbachev**, president of the **U.S.S.R., agreed to give up its monopoly of political power**, looking forward to the establishment of a cabinet system of government. The Soviet parliament voted in favor of a strong presidency, as urged by Gorbachev. Elected (Mar. 15) to the post, he promised to act speedily to bring about a market economy. In a Communist party election (July 10), he retained leadership of the party. With emergency powers granted (Sept. 24) as the nation's economy slid toward disaster, Gorbachev used (Nov. 17) those powers to reshuffle the structure of the government, abolishing the post of prime minister and establishing a Federation Council, made up of the presidents of the 15 Soviet republics. As conditions continued to worsen and as **political strife** became more open, the nation was stunned by the sudden resignation (Dec. 20) of **Eduard A. Shevardnadze**, foreign minister and a close associate of Gorbachev. He charged that the country was threatened by a dictatorship of reactionaries because the president was not moving quickly enough toward a more open society. **A. Bessmertnyk** (b. Nov. 10, 1933), ambassador to Washington, was appointed (Jan. 15, 1991) to succeed Shevardnadze.

1990 Feb. 15 **Great Britain and Argentina agreed to resume diplomatic relations** for the first time since the Falkland Islands War (1982). The question of sovereignty over the islands, which Argentina calls the Malvinas, was not raised. **Britain resumed** (Sept. 27) **diplomatic relations with Iran**, which had been broken 16 months earlier when Islamic Iranian leaders condemned the British author **Salman Rushdie** to death, charging he was blasphemous in his novel, *The Satanic Verses*.

1990 Feb. 18 The Liberal Democratic party, in office in **Japan** for 35 years, retained its rule in elections to the lower house of parliament by winning

275 of 512 seats, although it lost 20. The Socialist party was second with 136 seats, a gain of 53.

1990 Mar. 10 Turmoil in **Haiti** continued with the resignation of **Prosper Avril**, a general who had ruled the nation for 18 months, after a week of protests triggered by reports of torture of prisoners and the lack of progress toward holding free elections. With the support of the army, **Ertha Pascal-Trouillot** (b. Aug. 13, 1943), the only woman member of the Supreme Court, was named (Mar. 13) provisional president. When an election was held (Dec. 16), the winner of the office of president, with about 70 percent of the votes, was **Jean-Bertrand Aristide** (b. July 15, 1953), a Roman Catholic priest, an enemy of the military and of the conservative church hierarchy. He was inaugurated Feb. 7, 1991.

1990 Mar. 11 By a vote of 124 to 0, the **Lithuanian parliament declared the nation independent** of the Soviet Union, which had seized it in 1940. **Mikhail Gorbachev**, president of the U.S.S.R., said (Mar. 13) that the action was "illegitimate and invalid," and began putting political and economic pressure on the Lithuanians. Russian armed forces were sent (Mar. 21) into the country and oil and natural gas supplies were cut off (Apr 18–19). Lithuania agreed (June 29) to suspend its declaration of independence, and Russia lifted its economic sanctions.

1990 Mar. 11 A 499-member congress, elected by **Estonians** outside the established political system, called on the United Nations and the Russian parliament to make the country independent and thus free it of its 40-year forced incorporation within the Soviet Union.

1990 Mar. 13 **Israel's fragile coalition government collapsed** when **Yitzhak Shamir**, prime minister and leader of the Likud party, dismissed **Shimon Peres**, finance minister and leader of the Labor party. Two days later parliament formally dissolved the government. Peres tried to form a viable government, but gave up (Apr. 26). Shamir was then able to form a new government, which parliament approved (June 11), 62 to 57, but he had to rely on the support of small religious and far right groups, which made his government the most conservative ever in Israel.

1990 Mar. 13 As the result of a parliamentary election, **Nicholas Braithwaite**, who had headed the government of **Grenada** for 13 months after the U.S. invasion (1983), became prime minister. His National Democratic Congress, a centrist party, won only 7 of the 15 seats, but he was able to win enough other support to take office.

1990 Mar. 14 The **Communist party of Mongolia** voted to abandon its monopoly of political power after four months of demonstrations against its rule. However, when an election was held (July 25), the Communists won more than 70 percent of the seats in the Great People's Hural [parliament].

1990 Mar. 21 **Lee Teng-Hui**, who as vice president of **Taiwan** had succeeded to the presidency on the death (1988) of **Chiang Ching-kuo**, was elected to a six-year term by the nearly unanimous vote of the National Assembly. He was the first native Taiwanese to hold the presidency.

1990 Mar. 21 After having been under the control of South Africa for nearly 70 years, **Namibia** [formerly South-West Africa] **became an independent nation**. Its first parliament had adopted (Feb. 9) a liberal democratic constitution providing for a multiparty system and guarantees of human rights. **Sam Nujoma**, who had led the South-West People's Organization [SWAPO] in the fight (since 1966) for independence, became Namibia's first president.

1990 Apr. 8 The center-right Democratic Forum led six other parties in **Hungary's first free election since 1945**, winning 165 of the 386 seats in parliament. Forming a coalition with two other parties—the Smallholders with 43 seats, and the Christian Democrats with 21—**József Antall** (b. Apr. 8, 1932), a teacher and museum director and leader of the Democratic Forum, became (May 31) prime minister.

1990 Apr. 8 A parliamentary election in **Greece** gave the conservative New Democracy party a one-seat majority, and its leader, **Constantine Mitsotakis** (b. Oct. 18, 1918), became prime minister. His defeated opponent was a former prime minister, **Andreas Papandreou**, leader of the Pan-Hellenic Socialist Movement.

1990 Apr. 10 Three hostages—**Jacqueline Valente** [French], **Fernand Houtekins** [Belgian], and their two-year-old daughter, **Sophie-Liberté**, who had been born in captivity—**were released in Beirut**, Lebanon, by the **Fatah Revolutionary Council**, after having been held since Nov. 1987. **Robert Polhill**, an American held hostage since Jan. 24, 1987, was re-

leased (Apr. 23) in Lebanon by the Islamic Holy War for the Liberation of Palestine. Another American, **Frank Herbert Reed**, who had been kidnapped Sept. 9, 1986, was released (Apr. 30) by the Organization of Islamic Dawn. Other hostages released this year were: (Aug. 9) **Emanuel Christen**, a Swiss Red Cross worker held for ten months; (Aug. 14) another Swiss Red Cross worker, **Elio Erriquez**, also held for ten months; and (Aug. 23) **Brian Keenan**, an Irish teacher who had been seized Apr. 11, 1986. Thirteen hostages, including six Americans, were still being held by Islamic fundamentalists.

1990 Apr. 25 Having won (Feb. 25) election to the presidency of **Nicaragua**, **Violetta Barrios Chamorro** (b. Oct. 18, 1929), the widow of Pedro Joaquim Chamorro, a newspaper editor, slain (Jan. 10, 1978) for his opposition to the then dictator **Anastasio Somoza Debayle**, was inaugurated in the first democratic transfer of power in the country's history. Chamorro's National Opposition Union [UNO] had defeated the leftist **Sandinista National Liberation Front** [FSLN], which had become a Marxist regime in July 1979. The UNO also won 52 seats in the national assembly to 38 for the FSLN.

1990 May 4 The parliament of **Latvia**, one of the former Baltic republics overrun by Soviet Russia in 1940, voted to begin a transition period intended to lead to full **independence**. **Mikhail Gorbachev**, president of the U.S.S.R., **condemned (May 6) Latvia's action** and hinted at economic or political retaliation. On the day (May 7) that **Russian tanks moved through Riga**, the capital, in a show of force, the Latvian parliament chose **Ivars Goodmanis**, an economist, as its leader on the path to independence.

1990 May 8 **Rafael Angel Calderón** (b. Mar. 14, 1949), son of a former president, was inaugurated president of **Costa Rica**, having won election (Feb. 4) with about 51 percent of the vote. It was the tenth successive peaceful transfer of power since a civil war in 1948.

1990 May 16 **Joaquin Balaguer**, president of the **Dominican Republic**, won reelection in a close race with his chief rival, **Juan Bosch**, a former president. The official results gave Balaguer 35.7 percent of the vote to Bosch's 34.4 percent. It was the fifth time Balaguer, 83, and Bosch, 80, had run against each other for the presidency.

1990 May 22 Yemen, a pro-Western nation, **and Southern Yemen**, Marxist and Soviet-oriented, **merged** to form the **Yemeni Republic**. The two small nations, at the southwestern end of the Arabian Peninsula, had been independent for 23 years following Great Britain's withdrawal from the region. **Ali Abdullah Saleh**, president of Yemen, became president of the unified country.

1990 May 27 Voters of **Myanmar** [formerly Burma] repudiated their harsh military rulers in the first multiparty election in 30 years by winning 392 of 483 seats in the National Assembly. The leader of the victorious National League for Democracy, **Daw Aung San Suu Kyi**, had been under house arrest since July 1989, and was forbidden to run for office. The military junta held on to power, refused to let the new assembly meet, and demanded (Nov. 12) the sole right to draft a new constitution.

1990 May 29 Boris N. Yeltsin (b. Feb. 1, 1931), a Russian politician critical of **Mikhail Gorbachev**, president of the U.S.S.R., for his slowness in instituting economic and political reforms, was elected president of the **Russian Republic**, by far the largest both in area and in population of the 15 constituent republics of the Soviet Union.

1990 June 1 George Bush, president of the U.S., and **Mikhail Gorbachev**, president of the U.S.S.R., signed in Washington an **agreement to make large cuts in nuclear weapons**. The U.S. would reduce its arsenal of missiles from c.12,000 to c.9,500; the Soviets would reduce theirs from c.11,300 to c.6,900. To achieve these totals both sides would also scrap missile submarines and bombers. An agreement concerning chemical weapons called for the destruction of at least 50 percent of stocks by 1999.

1990 June 8 José Figueres Ferrer (b. Sept. 25, 1906), three times president of **Costa Rica** (1948–1949, 1953–1958, and 1970–1974), who was the person most responsible for the establishment (1948) of democracy in his country, died. At that time he led an irregular force that defeated both the Communist-led guerrillas and the Costa Rican army, and he became the head of a ruling junta. Figueres disbanded the army and instituted reforms.

1990 June 8–9 In the first free election for parliament since 1946, voters in **Czechoslovakia** firmly repudiated their former rulers, the Communist party, by giving the Civic Forum and its sister

party, Public Against Violence, 87 seats to 24. The Christian Democrats won 20 seats and other parties 17. **Vaclav Havel**, president and leader of the Civic Forum, renamed **Marián Calfa**, who had resigned (Jan. 18) from the Communist party, as prime minister. Parliament reelected (July 5) Havel as president. Ending a dispute between the nation's two regions, parliament voted (Apr. 20) to rename the country the **Czech and Slovak Federative Republic**.

1990 June 12 The **Islamic Salvation Front** [FIS] swept the first free elections in **Algeria** since French rule ended (1962), winning control of 32 of the 48 provinces and 838 of the 1,533 municipal councils. Defeated was the National Liberation Front [FLN], which had controlled the country since independence. The winners began to enforce fundamentalist Islamic codes, though the FLN remained in control of the central government.

1990 June 20 Ion Iliescu (b. Mar. 3, 1930), a former Communist party official who had helped overthrow (Dec. 1989) the **Romanian** regime of **Nicolae Ceausescu** and who had been provisional president since, was inaugurated president. This followed an election (May 20), the first open vote in more than 50 years, in which Iliescu won 85 percent of the vote for president and his National Salvation Front, consisting mainly of former Communists, captured two-thirds of the seats in the national assembly and senate.

1990 June 23 In **Canada**, a three-year effort to satisfy the demands of the French-speaking province of Québec with regard to the new constitution of 1982 collapsed when two provinces—Manitoba and Newfoundland—**refused to ratify an agreement that would have conferred on Québec a special status** within the Canadian confederation.

1990 July 16 Ukraine, in western Russia and the second largest of the 15 constituent republics of the U.S.S.R., **declared its sovereignty**, but stopped short of claiming full independence. The Ukrainians sought more self-determination and more control over its vast natural resources. Another republic, **Byelorussia**, north of the Ukraine, took (July 27) the same step. Still more republics followed: **Tadzhikstan**, in central Asia (Aug. 24); **Georgia**, in southern Russia (Oct. 29); and **Kirghizia**, in central Asia (Dec. 12).

1990 July 28   **Alberto Fujimori** (b. July 28, 1938), an agronomist and the son of Japanese immigrants, was inaugurated president of **Peru**, having won (June 10) a run-off election. In the first round of voting, the leader had been **Mario Vargas Llosa** (b. Mar. 28, 1936), a novelist. Fujimori faced continued insurgency by the vicious Maoist-oriented **Shining Path** guerrillas. About 3,400 people were killed in 1990 as result of their violence.

1990 July 29   **Bruno Kreisky** (b. Jan. 22, 1911), Austria's longest serving chancellor (1970–1983), died. A Socialist, he was first elected to parliament in 1956 and then became foreign minister (1959–1966). Kreisky's policy of "active neutrality" made him popular outside **Austria** as well as within.

1990 Aug. 2   Initiating the **Persian Gulf War** (1990–1991), **armed forces of Iraq**, without warning, invaded **Kuwait**, its small neighbor to the south, and overan it in a matter of hours. Iraq had long laid claim to some Kuwaiti territory and said that Kuwait had been stealing Iraqi petroleum from an oilfield that lay under both nations. The **United Nations** Security Council at once demanded Iraq's withdrawal and ordered (Aug. 6) a trade and financial boycott. The U.S., saying (Aug. 7) that **Saudi Arabia**, Kuwait's neighbor, was also threatened with invasion, ordered troops, armor, aircraft, and ships to the Saudi kingdom. By Aug. 9 a naval blockade was forming and all export of oil from Iraq and Kuwait was cut off. Meeting (Aug. 10) in Cairo, 12 of the 21 member nations of the **Arab League** voted to support the U.N. and U.S. actions. Reacting to these moves, **Saddam Hussein**, president of Iraq, said (Aug. 18) that thousands of foreign nationals in Iraq would be held hostage, but most foreigners were allowed to leave the country by mid-December. About 230,000 American troops were in Saudi Arabia by Nov. 8, and **George Bush**, president of the U.S., announced that 150,000 more would be sent. The U.N. Security Council voted (Nov. 29), 12 to 2 (with 1 abstention), to authorize the U.S. and its allies to use force to expel Iraq from Kuwait if its troops did not leave by Jan. 15, 1991. By the end of 1990, 580,000 Iraqi troops were believed to be in southern Iraq and Kuwait. Facing them were 485,000 troops and navy vessels of the allies, consisting, besides U.S. forces, of units from Bangladesh, Bahrain, Canada, Denmark, Egypt, France, Great Britain, Italy, Kuwait, Morocco, the Netherlands, Oman, Pakistan, Qatar, Saudi Arabia, Senegal, Syria, and the United Arab Emirates.

1990 Aug. 6   Declaring that the government of **Benazir Bhutto**, prime minister of **Pakistan** (since Dec. 1988), had lost the confidence of the National Assembly, **Ghulam Ishaq Khan** (b. 1915), the president, dismissed her from office. A caretaker government headed by **Ghulam Mustafa Jatoi**, once a Bhutto supporter, was sworn in. In a parliamentary election (Oct. 24), Bhutto's opponents won 105 of the 207 seats. Her Pakistan People's party won only 45, a loss of 48. **Nawaz Sharif** (b. Dec. 25, 1948), leader of the right-wing coalition that won the election, was sworn in (Nov. 6) as prime minister.

1990 Aug. 7   Having won (May 27) the presidential election, **César Gaviria Trujillo** (b. Mar 31, 1947) was inaugurated president of **Colombia**. An economist, he had been the candidate of the governing Liberal party. A guerrilla group known as **M-19** took part in elections for the first time, after having agreed two months earlier to lay down its arms. It won 13 percent of the vote. However, fighting between the government and another rebel group, the Revolutionary Armed Forces of Colombia, continued.

1990 Sept. 10   **Samuel K. Doe** (b. May 6, 1951), president (since 1980) of **Liberia**, was captured and killed by rebel forces led by **Prince Johnson**, who had taken part (1985) in an unsuccessful attempt to unseat Doe. His forces controlled Monrovia, the capital, while another rebel group led by **Charles Taylor** (b. 1948?), a former minister in the Doe government, was also in action. These forces had been fighting the government since Dec. 1989, when they invaded Liberia from the Ivory Coast. In an attempt to end the civil war, troops of five West African nations— Gambia, Ghana, Guinea, Nigeria, and Sierra Leone—had entered (Aug. 24) Monrovia and took control (Sept. 2) there, by which time the Johnson and Taylor forces were fighting each other as well as Doe. The peace-keeping force was finally able to establish (Nov. 1990) an interim government.

1990 Sept. 30   The largest gathering ever at the United Nations of heads of state and government, about 70 in all, constituted the first **World Summit for Children** and set goals intended to improve the condition of poor children in all parts of the world. The conference resolved to attempt to save the lives of at least a third of the 14 million infants who die every year before reaching the age of five.

1990 Oct. 3 East Germany [the German Democratic Republic] **became part of West Germany** [the Federal Republic of Germany], ending the separation of the two sections of the country, which had existed since the end of World War II (1939–1945), when the Allies, Russia on the one hand and France, Great Britain, and the U.S. on the other, split on ideological grounds, ushering in the **Cold War** (c. 1945–c.1985). The four former allies had retained occupation rights over both parts of Germany, until formally relinquishing them on Oct. 1. The two parliaments had endorsed union on Sept. 20. An election for the Bundestag [parliament] of the reunited country, the first fully free election since 1932, was held (Dec. 2) and resulted in a victory for the Christian Democratic party, the ruling party in West Germany, and its partner, the Free Democratic party. Together they won 347 seats of 662. The Social Democratic party took 239 and the former Communist party, running as the Party of Democratic Socialism, won 17 seats, most of its votes coming from the former Communist state of East Germany. The environmentalist Greens lost ground, winning only 8 seats, all in former East Germany.

1990 Oct. 7 In a parliamentary election in **Austria**, the governing Socialist party was returned to power when it won 81 seats, a gain of 1, though its mildly conservative partner, the People's party, lost 17 seats while retaining 60. The far-right Freedom party won 33 seats, a gain of 15, while the Greens took 9, gaining 1.

1990 Oct. 8 Twenty-one Palestinians were killed and more than 100 injured when Israeli police fired on thousands of Arabs who were throwing rocks and bottles at Jews praying at the Western Wall in Jerusalem outside the **Al Aksa mosque**. The riot was apparently triggered by a threat from an extremist Jewish group to rebuild on the site of the mosque the temple that **Herod I**, king of Judea (37–4 B.C.), had constructed in 20 B.C. The **U.N. Security Council voted** (Oct. 12) **to condemn Israel**, the resolution being a compromise between the **Palestine Liberation Organization** [PLO] and other Arab sympathizers who wanted stronger terms, and the U.S., usually Israel's defender but now anxious not to offend Arab nations because of its ongoing confrontation with Iraq during the Persian Gulf War (1990–1991). Israel denounced (Oct. 14) the resolution, which called also for a U.N. inquiry group to visit Israel. The Security Council reproved (Oct. 14) Israel for its refusal to cooperate, and after Israel changed its position, the

U.N. decided (Nov. 14) to send an envoy. An Israeli investigation had reported (Oct. 26) that police commanders did not make adequate preparations for possible trouble the day of the riot.

1990 Oct. 13 Le Duc Tho (b. Oct. 10, 1911), a high-ranking official of North Vietnam, who was his country's chief negotiator of the agreement that led to the end of the Vietnam War (1954–1973; U.S., 1962–1972), died. He was a founder (1929) of the Indochinese Communist party and fought against French rule. After France's defeat (1954), Tho was a member of the North Vietnam Comunist party Politburo (1955–1986). He first held negotiating sessions with the U.S. in 1969, and in 1973 he and **Henry Kissinger**, the American negotiator, were jointly awarded the **Nobel Peace Prize**. Tho refused the award because true peace had not yet been attained.

1990 Oct. 15 Mikhail S. Gorbachev, president of the U.S.S.R., was awarded the **Nobel Peace Prize** for his efforts to end the Cold War (c.1945–c.1985) and for helping bring about political changes in Eastern Europe. He was praised for "his leading role in the peace process which today characterizes important parts of the international community."

1990 Oct. 21 Mahathir Mohamad (b. Feb. 20, 1925) was elected to a third term as prime minister of **Malaysia**. His National Front party won 127 of the 180 seats in the National Assembly, giving Mahathir the two-thirds majority necessary to amend the constitution. He had been prime minister since 1981 and won a second term in a 1986 election.

1990 Oct. 27 The National party won 68 of 97 seats in the **New Zealand** parliament in a landslide victory that ended six years of rule by the Labor party. A high unemployment rate of 7.9 percent was a factor. As a result of the election [James B.] **Jim Bolger** (b. 1935) became prime minister. He promised to improve relations with the U.S., which had been damaged in recent years by New Zealand's refusal to allow nuclear-powered ships or ships carrying nuclear weapons to dock in New Zealand's ports.

1990 Oct. 28 In the first free election since 1960, **Ivory Coast** voters returned to office **Félix Houphouët-Boigny** with 81.67 percent of the ballots. He became president of the country in 1960, when it achieved independence from France, and was now both the oldest and the longest-serving head of a black African nation. In a parliamentary election

(Nov. 25) his Democratic party won 163 of the 175 seats, with the main opposition, the Popular Front, taking 9 and independents 2. Demonstrations for political freedom and against deteriorating economic conditions, which had at first been put down by force, eventually led to the elections.

1990 Nov. 1   Forty-three countries, including all the leading industrial nations of the world, meeting in London, agreed to **end all dumping of industrial waste at sea** by 1995. The measure was legally binding on all 64 nations that had signed the 20-year-old treaty known as the **London Dumping Convention**.

1990 Nov. 3   **Gro Harlem Brundtland**, leader of the Labor party, became prime minister of **Norway** for the third time, following the **collapse of the government** of Jan Syse, leader of the Conservative party. Syse resigned when some members of his right of center coalition refused to follow his plans for closer ties with the **European Community** [EC]. The Labor party was the largest in Norway's parliament with 63 of the 165 seats, but like the outgoing government had to rely on a coalition, in this case of left-of-center parties.

1990 Nov. 5   **Meir Kahane** (b. Aug. 1, 1932), founder of the militant anti-Arab **Jewish Defense League**, was shot and killed at a Zionist conference in New York City. The suspected gunman, **El Sayyid A. Nosair**, Egyptian-born and said to be a devout Muslim, was wounded and captured. Nosair was acquitted (Dec. 21, 1991) of murder but convicted on lesser charges. Kahane, a rabbi, founded (1968) the Jewish Defense League in New York City. He moved (1971) to Israel and was elected (1984) to parliament there. An extremist, he advocated expelling all Arabs from Israel. His Kach party, which he founded, was banned (Oct. 1988) in Israel on the ground that it was racist and undemocratic.

1990 Nov. 7   **Mary Robinson** (b. May 21, 1944), a leftist lawyer, was elected the first woman president of **Ireland** when she won 52.8 percent of the votes in a run-off election. She was opposed by both the Fianna Fáil and Fine Gael, the two largest Irish political parties. Robinson had campaigned for legalizing both divorce and contraception.

1990 Nov. 9   **Birenda**, king of **Nepal**, the small mountain kingdom between India and China, **gave final approval to a new constitution** that **ended the absolute monarchy** and established a multiparty constitutional monarchy.

1990 Nov. 10   **Chandra Shekhar** (b. Apr. 27, 1927), leader of a faction of the Janata Dal party, became prime minister of **India**, succeeding **V.P. Singh**, whose minority government resigned (Nov. 7) when Shekhar and others withdrew their support. Singh's fall from power came near the end of a year of violence and unrest in which at least 7,000 persons were killed. There was conflict all year in the states of **Punjab** and of **Jammu and Kashmir**, in northern India. In Punjab, where the **Sikhs** were in the majority and sought independence, the militants among them fought with the Hindu population and the Indian Army. In Jammu and Kashmir, the only Indian state in which Muslims outnumbered Hindus, violence between the two groups and battles with the army resulted in c.1,500 deaths.

1990 Nov. 12   **Akihito**, emperor of **Japan**, was formally enthroned in Tokyo as the 125th ruler of his line. He had succeeded his father, **Hirohito**, at the time of the latter's death (Jan. 7, 1989). The ceremony in the courtyard of the Imperial Palace used ancient rituals, but made clear for the first time that sovereignty rested with the people.

1990 Nov. 19   Meeting in Paris, the leaders of 20 European nations, plus the U.S. and Canada, signed the **most extensive arms control treaty in history**, intended to reduce non-nuclear arms in Europe on a large scale. The **North Atlantic Treaty Organization** [NATO] and the **Warsaw Pact** would each be limited to 20,000 tanks, 20,000 artillery pieces, 30,000 armored vehicles, 6,800 airplanes, and 2,000 helicopters. Current levels of those weapons ranged from about 10 percent higher to more than double. In addition the U.S. and newly unified Germany agreed to a level of no more than 195,000 American forces in Central Europe and no more than 370,000 personnel in the German armed forces. Thirty-two European nations and the U.S. and Canada signed (Nov. 21) the **Charter of Paris**, a general peace treaty intended to formalize the end of the **Cold War** (c.1945–c.1985) between West and East, which had poisoned international relations since shortly after the end of World War II (1939–1945). The pact called for a "steadfast commitment to democracy based on human rights and fundamental freedoms." Other events marking the end of the Cold War included an agreement (Nov. 3) by the six member nations of the Warsaw Pact on the distribution of weapons among them; the signing (Nov. 9) of a treaty between unified Germany and the U.S.S.R. that called for "good-neighborliness, partnership, and cooperation"; and the signing (Nov. 14) by Germany and Poland of a treaty that guaranteed the current boundary between the two nations as marked by the Oder and Neisse rivers.

1990 Nov. 22   Unsuccessful in meeting a challenge to her leadership of the Conservative party of **Great Britain**, **Margaret Thatcher**, who had been prime minister for 11½ years, the longest tenure in the twentieth century, announced she would resign both posts. **John Major** (b. Mar. 29, 1943), chancellor of the exchequer, was elected (Nov. 27) leader of the Conservative party, and the next day became prime minister, the youngest person to hold the office in the twentieth century.

1990 Nov. 28   **Goh Chok Tong** (b. May 20, 1941), first deputy prime minister of **Singapore**, an island nation south of the Malay Peninsula, was sworn in as prime minister, succeeding **Lee Kuan Yew**, who had held the post for 31 years. Yew first assumed the position when Singapore became (1959) part of the newly independent **Malaysian Federation**, and he continued when Singapore was expelled (1965) from the federation for refusing to follow orders of the central government. Since then Singapore had enjoyed an average economic growth rate of 9 percent, giving the small nation of 2.7 million people the **second highest living standard in Asia** after Japan.

1990 Nov. 30   **Mozambique**, in southeastern Africa on the Indian Ocean, **adopted a new constitution** by the terms of which the Mozambique Liberation Front [Frelimo] of **Joaquim A. Chissano**, president, which had ruled the country since independence (1975), gave up its monopoly of political power. It was hoped the move toward democracy and free elections would cause the rebel movement of the Mozambique National Resistance [Renamo] to enter into negotiations to end the 15-year-old civil war.

1990 Dec. 1   Entering **Chad** from the Sudan, **rebel forces captured** (Nov. 10) **Ndjamena**, the capital, and **Hissèn Habré**, president (since 1982), fled. The rebels were led by **Idris Deby**, who had helped Habré secure the presidency. Deby dissolved parliament and suspended (Dec. 3) the constitution, then declared (Dec. 4) himself president.

1990 Dec. 4   **Hussain Mohammad Ershad**, president of **Bangladesh** (from 1982), resigned in the face of seven weeks of **demonstrations by opposition po-**litical parties that claimed security forces had killed 100 people. The government said only six had died. **Shahabuddin Ahmed**, chief justice of the Supreme Court, was chosen (Dec. 5) to be caretaker president pending elections.

1990 Dec. 11   Following three days of **demonstrations** led by students, the Communist party of **Albania**, the only such ruling group left in Europe outside the U.S.S.R., announced it would allow the formation of other political parties. The next day the Democratic party was organized and recognized (Dec. 19) by the government.

1990 Dec. 12   Although the Social Democratic party won 69 of 179 seats, a gain of 14 in **Denmark's** Folketing [parliament], a coalition headed by **Poul Schlüter** (b. Apr. 3, 1929), leader of the Conservative party, remained in office. For eight years he had headed the government of a country where the existence of eight political parties made it difficult for any one to gain a majority in parliament. The election had been called because of a dispute over income tax rates.

1990 Dec. 17   **Kenneth Kaunda**, president of **Zambia** for 26 years, and whose United National party had been the only legal political organization since 1973, approved new laws that would **legalize political opposition.**

1990 Dec. 22   **Lech Walesa**, the Gdansk shipyard electrician whose leadership of a strike there in 1970 led to his becoming one of the founders of **Solidarity**, a trade union that defied the Communist government, was sworn in as president of **Poland** after winning (Dec. 9) the first free direct election in the country's history. He had defeated, with 74.25 percent of the vote, **Stanislaw Tyminski** (b. 1948), a last-minute arrival in the country from Canada and Peru, where he had business interests while continuing to hold Polish citizenship. Walesa named (Dec. 29) **Jan Krzysztof Bielecki** (b. May 3, 1951), an economist and businessman, as prime minister. The country's Communist party had voted (Jan. 29) to disband and become a left-of-center party. Five cabinet members, the most prominent Communists still in government office, had been dismissed (July 6). **Wojciech Jaruzelski**, president (from July 1989) had announced (Sept. 19) he would resign so that an election could be held to replace him.

1990 Dec. 24   The army of **Suriname**, a small country on the northeastern coast of South America, under its acting commander **Ivan Graannoogst**, took control of the government of **Ramsewak Shankar**, president (from 1987). Graanoogst was acting on behalf of **Desi Bouterse**, a general who had been dictator (1980–1988) of the country and who remained the real power in the government, even after his resignation (Dec. 23) as commander of the army. Shankar resigned (Dec. 24) from his powerless presidency, and a puppet of Boterse, **Johan Kraag**, was sworn in as president.

1990 Dec. 29   Military leaders who were responsible for the deaths of at least 9,000 persons during the political repression known as the "**dirty war**," of leftist guerrillas and other political opponents during the 1970s were pardoned by **Carlos Saúl Menem**, president of **Argentina**. Among those freed were two generals who had also been presidents as well as army commanders, **Jorge Vedela** and **Robert Viola**.

IV. ECONOMY AND TRADE

1990 Jan. 31   The **first McDonald's fast-food restaurant in the U.S.S.R.** opened in Moscow and was besieged by so many customers that there was a wait of up to two hours to get into the 700-seat facility, even though a Big Mac with fries and a cola cost half a day's wages for many customers. By the end of February, 30,000 Russians a day were being served.

1990 Feb. 10   **Perrier**, the bottled mineral water from France, was **withdrawn from sale** after the chemical benzene was found in a small sample of bottles. In all 160 million bottles, worth c.$70 million, were removed from American stores and restaurants. The company announced that the benzene had been in a cleanser used by mistake to clean machinery. Perrier was back on the U.S. market in early May, but sales did not recover quickly.

1990 Feb. 24   **Malcolm Forbes, Sr.** (b. Aug. 19, 1919), a multi-millionaire American magazine publisher with a wide range of hobbies, died. As editor (from 1954) of *Forbes*, a family-owned magazine, he had made it one of the most successful business publications. Among his outside interests were contract bridge, motorcycling, ballooning, and collecting Fabergé eggs.

1990 May 6   Subject to approval of its 152 member nations, the **International Monetary Fund** [IMF] **voted to increase its resources** from $120 billion to $180 billion in order to make more money available

to help third world countries handle their foreign debts and to speed up the movement toward free market economies in Eastern Europe.

1990 May 29   Western Europe and other industrial and democratic countries, numbering 40 in all, established a **European Bank for Reconstruction and Development** with capital of $12 billion to aid the nations of Eastern Europe primarily but also the Soviet Union. The **European Community** [EC] agreed (Dec. 14) to provide $2 billion in emergency food, medical, and technical assistance to the faltering Russian economy. George Bush, president of the U.S., approved (Dec. 12) a $1 billion loan for the purchase of food and other agricultural products, thus lifting a 15-year-old ban on such credits to the U.S.S.R.

1990 June 21   The **Budapest** [Hungary] **Stock Exchange** opened for trading for the first time since it was closed 42 years earlier by the Communists then ruling the country. It was the first Western-style securities exchange to open in the Eastern European countries that overthrew communism in 1989.

1990 July 3   Expanding into Europe and becoming the second **largest manufacturer of mainframe computers** after the **International Business Machines Corp.**, Fujitsu, Ltd., of Japan bought 80 percent of ICL, Ltd., the only British mainframe manufacturer, for $1.29 billion. Before the deal, Fujitsu had been third in the field after the Digital Equipment Corp. of the U.S.

1990 July 16   On the **New York Stock Exchange** the **Dow Jones industrial average reached an all-time high** when it closed at 2,999.75. The next day it closed at the same point.

1990 Sept. 2   [Michael] **Robert** [Hamilton] **Holmes à Court** (b. July 27, 1937), South African-born and an Australian entrepreneur and corporate raider who started with a small woolen mill and acquired a fortune estimated at $1 billion, died. His career peaked when he bought large amounts of stock of leading American corporations, but the stock market crash in Oct. 1987 forced him to sell much of his holdings. He later regained a fortune and had far-flung interests in real estate, movies, television, oil, gas, coal, and banking. Holmes à Court was also known as a horse breeder and a collector of art and antique cars.

1900 Oct. 12 The **largest award ever made in a patent infringement case** resulted from an order in a U.S. federal court that the **Eastman Kodak Co.** pay the **Polaroid Corp.** $909 million. Kodak had been found guilty (1985) of infringing seven of Polaroid's instant photography patents. The decision forced Kodak out of the instant photography business.

1990 Oct. 26 **William S. Paley** (b. Sept. 28, 1901), founder of the **Columbia Broadcasting System** [CBS], which he built into the world's foremost communications enterprise, first in radio and then in television, died. With money from his father's cigar manufacturing business, Paley bought (Sept. 26, 1928) a controlling interest in the struggling radio network. In the 1940s CBS pioneered the coverage of World War II (1939–1945). Paley's network was equally successful with entertainment programs, such as *I Love Lucy* and the **Jack Benny** show. CBS also pioneered the **long-playing** [LP] **phonograph record**, introducing it in 1948.

1990 Nov. 1 The **McDonald's Corp**, America's largest fast-food chain, with 8,500 restaurants, yielding to the concerns of consumers and environmentalists, announced it would abandon its well-known plastic "clamshell" hamburger box in favor of **recyclable paper**. The plastic package had been introduced Sept. 22, 1975, and McDonald's was currently using about 75 million pounds of foam packaging a year.

1990 Nov. 21 **Michael R. Milken** (b. July 4, 1946), credited with creating the "junk bond," an investment instrument promising high interest rates but with more than normal risk, was sentenced to ten years in prison for violating federal securities laws and for other crimes. He was also placed on probation for three years and was to perform 5,400 hours of community service during that period. Milken and others had been indicted (Mar. 29, 1989) on 98 criminal charges, including illegal insider trading. He pleaded guilty (Apr. 28, 1990) to six charges of securities fraud and conspiracy and agreed to pay $600 million in fines and other penalties. Milken had been the highest paid financial figure in history, having collected more than $1 billion for his dealings in the junk bond market between 1983 and 1987.

1990 Nov. 26 In a deal valued at $6.13 billion, **MCA, Inc.**, one of America's largest entertainment enterprises, agreed to be acquired by the **Matsushita Electric Industrial Co.** of Japan. It was the largest purchase to date of an American company by a Japa-

nese. MCA had interests in movie production, recordings, cable TV, theme parks, and publishing. Matsushita, best known for its consumer electronic products, controlled 87 companies in Japan and many others abroad.

1990 Dec. 7 After four years of negotiations that began in Uruguay in Sept. 1986, discussions among the 107 participating nations of the **General Agreement on Tariffs and Trade** [GATT], broke down in Brussels, Belgium. The failure came when the **European Community** [EC] **refused to cut its farm subsidies** as much as the U.S. demanded. The negotiators also failed to reach agreements to protect European and American drug and software companies, whose patents were not recognized in the developing countries, and American music and movie companies from copyright pirates.

1990 Dec. 10 **Armand Hammer** (b. May 21, 1898), an American entrepreneur, philanthropist, and art collector, whose business relations with the U.S.S.R. remained steady during the Cold War (c.1945–c.1985), died. His chief business enterprise was the Occidental Petroleum Corp., of which he acquired control in the 1950s, and which he built into one of the largest, though not very profitable, energy concerns. Beginning with **V.I. Lenin** in the 1920s, Hammer, whose family was Russian, knew and had dealings with every Soviet leader through **Mikhail Gorbachev**. Hammer promoted cancer research and established an art museum bearing his name.

1990 Dec. 31 The nations of Eastern Europe—Bulgaria, Czechoslovakia, Hungary, Poland, and Romania—which had ridded themselves (1989) of their Communist governments, made disappointingly slow progress in adjusting to a new economic order. **Poland took the most drastic steps toward a capitalistic economy** by removing (Jan. 1) almost all price controls and subsidies to industry. Though Poland's inflation rate came down, industrial production and wages fell more than 20 percent. Czechoslovakia and Hungary planned to remove most price controls on Jan. 1, 1991. Bulgaria and Romania were slower to move toward economic freedom.

1990 Dec. 31 A general **worldwide slowdown of economic activity** marked 1990, with a decline almost everywhere of financial markets. One index showed a drop of 30.8 percent in 24 markets, not including the U.S., where the Dow Jones industrial average closed at 2,663.66, down 4.3 percent. The

Dating Committee of the National Bureau of Economic Research declared (Dec. 29) that the U.S. had entered a recession. The Canadian government had said (Dec. 2) that Canada's economy was in a recession.

V. RELIGION AND PHILOSOPHY

1990 Feb. 21 **Spain** signed an accord with **Jewish and Protestant** leaders that officially placed them **on a par with Roman Catholics**, thus in effect nullifying the decree (1492) of **Ferdinand** and **Isabella**, king and queen of Spain, which ordered the conversion or expulsion of all Jews. At that time there were 400,-000 Jews; in 1990 there were 15,000 practicing Jews and 60,000 active Protestants.

1990 mid-Apr. Officials of the **Church of Jesus Christ of Latter-Day Saints** [Mormon Church] confirmed that changes had been made in some sacred rituals of the church. It dropped a vow in which women pledged obedience to their husbands and also a requirement that they veil their faces at a point in one ceremony. The changes were in the "endowment" ceremony, which the church considered necessary to assure Mormons of life after death.

1990 Apr. 17 **Ralph David Abernathy** (b. Mar. 11, 1926), a black American clergyman who was a pioneer in the civil rights movement, died. An early associate of **Martin Luther King, Jr.**, the best-known figure in the movement, Abernathy went to jail with King 17 times as a result of demonstrations they led in the South in the 1950s and 1960s. After King's assassination (Apr. 1968), Abernathy took over the presidency of the **Southern Christian Leadership Conference**, but he left (1977) that post in the face of criticism that he was too conservative and had allowed the conference to become disorganized.

1990 May 3 **Sergei M. Izvekov** (b. July 23, 1910), who as Patriarch Pimen was the leader of the **Russian Orthodox Church**, died. He became a monk when he was 17 years old, a bishop in 1957, an archbishop in 1960, and was named patriarch in 1971. Pimen was considered a follower of the official Communist party line, especially in the area of foreign relations.

1990 June 5 The **Presbyterian Church** [U.S.A.] **adopted a new statement of faith**, the first since 1983, when the church was reunited after a split over slavery during the Civil War (1861–1865) era. While reaffirming the basic Christian beliefs of the denomination, the statement declared that everyone was equal "in God's image, male and female, of every race and people, to live as one community."

1990 June 12 For the twelfth year in succession, **conservatives retained control** of the **Southern Baptist Convention**, the largest Protestant denomination in the U.S., by electing a fundamentalist, **Morris Chapman**, a clergyman of Wichita Falls, Texas, as president with 58 percent of the votes of the delegates. Since gaining control in 1979, the conservatives had placed limits on the roles of women and of divorced men and women in the ministry, as well as insisting that all teachers in Baptist seminaries believe in the inerrancy of the Bible.

1990 June 25 The **Central Conference of American Rabbis**, representing Reform Judaism, which with 1.5 million members was the largest branch of American Judaism, voted to admit active homosexuals to the rabbinate. The matter had been at issue before reform rabbis for 15 years.

1990 July 11 Meeting in Indianapolis, Indiana, delegates to the **55th world conference of the Seventh Day Adventist Church** voted, 1,173 to 377, to continue the ban on the ordination of women. Support for women's ordination came from the European and North American delegates, but those representing churches in Africa, Asia, and Latin America voted for the ban, indicating that the sect, which got its start in the U.S. in the nineteenth century, was no longer basically an American church.

1990 July 18 A disciplinary committee of the **Evangelical Lutheran Church** in America **suspended two congregations** for having ordained an openly gay man and two lesbian women. The suspensions were for five years and could lead to expulsion of the two churches if there were no change in policy. The church had previously accepted the ordination of gay men who were silent about their sexual orientation.

1990 July 25 **George** [Leonard] **Carey** (b. Nov. 13, 1935), bishop of Bath and Wells, was appointed to be the 103rd archbishop of Canterbury, head of the Church of England and titular leader of the worldwide Anglican community. He was to succeed the current archbishop, **Robert** [Alexander Kennedy] **Runcie** (b. Oct. 2, 1921), who had held the post since 1980 and had announced his intention to retire on Jan. 31, 1991. Carey, who had been a bishop for only three years, was considered a leader of the evangelical wing of the church, stressing traditional beliefs. He was enthroned Apr. 19, 1991.

1990 Sept. 6   At a meeting in Prague, Czechoslovakia, representatives of the **Vatican Commission on Relations with the Jews**, and the **Jewish Committee on Interreligious Consultations** agreed on a need to combat **anti-Semitism in Eastern Europe**. The delegates from 16 nations stated that they recognized the "special problems" of anti-Semitism in that region. A statement issued at the close of the session said, "One cannot be authentically Christian and engage in anti-Semitism."

1990 Sept. 25   **John Paul II**, pope of the Roman Catholic Church, issued a document titled "**The Apostolic Constitution on Catholic Universities**," that was generally hailed by American Catholic educators as favorable to academic freedom. The document included only a brief set of guidelines concerning homosexuality and abortion. It did, however, call on teachers to adhere to Catholic doctrine and required that a majority of faculty members be Catholics.

1990 Sept. 26   The legislature of the **U.S.S.R.** approved a **law on freedom of conscience**, which ended the long-time Communist opposition to religious practice. The law stated that the government would not "restrict the study, financing, or propagandizing" of religion. The Soviet government had announced (Apr. 23) that it would charter direct flights to Mecca, Islam's holiest place, so that Muslims might make their *hajj* [pilgrimage].

1990 Sept. 30   The **New Revised Standard Version of the Bible**, successor to the Revised Standard Version (1952), the Bible used officially by the major U.S. Protestant denominations, was published. Prepared by a panel that included Protestant, Eastern Orthodox, Catholic, and Jewish scholars, the new edition made several notable changes: although God was still "our Father," elsewhere masculine terms were removed, as "man" to "one"; "dark but comely" became "black and beautiful"; and archaic "thees" were modernized.

1990 Sept. 30   A service of consecration at the **Cathedral Church of St. Peter and St. Paul**, Washington, D.C., marked the completion of its construction. Work on it had begun on Sept. 29, 1907. An Episcopal church and popularly known as the **National Ca-**

thedral, it was Gothic and was built in the medieval fashion, using no steel. In total area it was the sixth largest cathedral in the world.

1990 Oct. 27   In Vatican City a synod of 238 Roman Catholic bishops from around the world ended their sessions by ruling out any change in the requirement that priests be celibate. At the same time the synod recognized the shortage of priests in many countries and urged efforts to recruit and train a better clergy. In the course of the meetings it was revealed (Oct. 17) that the pope had approved of two married men in Brazil becoming priests. They were ordained on condition that they abstain from sex and were described as *viri probati*, a term for men who have proved to be spiritually mature.

1990 Nov. 26   **Feng Youlan** (b. Dec. 4, 1895), the best-known Chinese philosopher of his time, died. He was educated in both China and the U.S. His *History of Chinese Philosophy* (1931) became a standard work. After the Communist party came to power (1949) in China, Feng reinterpreted his thought in terms of Marxism-Leninism, though at times he was out of favor with party authorities.

VI. SCIENCE, EDUCATION, AND TECHNOLOGY

1990 Mar. 10   Chinese workmen building a new road near the ancient capital of Sian, about 500 miles southwest of Peking [Beijing], came upon an extensive **tomb** believed to be that **of Liu Ch'i** (d. 195 B.C.; ruled 206–195 B.C.), an emperor of the Western [Early] Han Dynasty (206 B.C.–A.D. c.9). Though only partly excavated in 1990, the tomb was found to contain thousands of terracotta figures, about two feet tall, of men, boys, and horses. They were naked figures, armless, but with many different facial expressions. This find was considered comparable with the discovery (1974) only 25 miles away of the **tomb of Shih Huang-Ti**, the first emperor of the earlier Ch'in Dynasty.

1990 Mar. 13   **Bruno Bettelheim** (b. Aug. 28, 1903), an Austrian-born psychoanalyst who came to the U.S. after his release in 1939 from a Nazi concentration camp and who became widely known for his studies of and efforts to deal with the emotional problems of children, died. His first important work was *Love Is Not Enough: The Treatment of Emotionally Disturbed Children* (1950), which had considerable influence on workers in the field. Bettelheim was best known for *The Uses of Enchantment* (1976), a profound and entrancing study of the relationship between fairy tales and the development of children.

1990 Apr. 25   Seven years behind schedule, the **Hubble Space Telescope** was launched by the U.S. space shuttle *Discovery* into an orbit 381 miles above the earth. The $1 billion instrument, weighing 12 tons, had been scheduled for launch in 1983, but was delayed by technical problems and by the disruption of the American space program after the shuttle *Challenger* exploded in 1986. The Hubble Telescope was expected to enlarge the vision of astronomers tenfold and to bring into view 5 to 10 trillion objects in the universe. However, when the instrument was opened (Apr. 27) to the heavens after some difficulty, and with more difficulty focused properly, it was discovered (June 27) that there was a serious flaw in its main light-gathering mirrors. Nevertheless, the telescope began to produce some valuable observations: an unexpected concentration of stars around what had thought to be an ordinary galaxy (Aug. 29); new views of Saturn and Pluto (Oct.. 4); the first sighting of a faint quasar billions of light years from earth (Nov. 4); and an unusually clear picture of a storm around Saturn (Nov. 20).

1990 June 3   **Robert N. Noyce** (b. Dec. 12, 1927), an American engineer and inventor who **devised the computer chip** that revolutionized the electronics industry, died. He was awarded (1959) a patent for his invention, a system of interconnecting transistors on a single microchip, known as **integrated circuitry**. This device became the basis of modern computers, and made it possible to handle many times more information and to miniaturize electronic elements. With an associate Noyce founded (1968) the **Intel Corp.**, which developed what became the heart of most personal computers, the microprocessor.

1990 June 26   A "golden calf," dating from the second millennium B.C. and representing the object of worship denounced in the Bible by early Judaism, was found by Harvard University archaeologists on the site of the ancient port city of Ashkelon, on the Mediterranean coast of Israel. Weighing a little less than a pound, the calf was about 4½ inches tall. It was made of several different metals and is the only one of its kind ever found.

1990 July 4   **Nathaniel C[onyers] Wyeth** (b. Mar. 10, 1910), an American engineer who invented the **plastic soda bottle**, died. He developed the product, made of polyethylene terephthalate [PET], in the mid-1970s, and it soon replaced glass.

1990 July 18   **Karl [Augustus] Menninger** (b. July 22, 1893), an American psychiatrist who, with his father and brother, founded (1925) what became the world-famous **Menninger Clinic and Foundation** of Topeka, Kansas, died. Menninger's writings were both popular and professional, as in *The Human Mind* (1930), *Theory of Psychoanalytic Technique* (1959), and *The Crime of Punishment* (1968). His father was **Charles Frederick Menninger** (July 11, 1862–Nov. 28, 1953) and his brother was **William Claire Menninger** (Oct. 15, 1899–Sept. 6, 1966).

1990 July 26   **Albert Rose** (b. Mar. 30, 1910), an American scientist whose research made the **modern television picture tube** possible, died. As a researcher with the Radio Corporation of America [RCA], he invented the image orthicon television camera tube during World War II (1939–1945) for military use. Later Rose headed a group of scientists who developed the first photoconductive sensor, a tube used in studio broadcasting and in high definition television.

1990 July 31   An advisory committee of the U.S. Food and Drug Administration recommended the approval of the drug **Interferon alpha-2**, which showed promise of curing patients with **hepatitis B**, a serious liver disease, the ninth leading cause of death in the world. The drug is a synthetic version of a hormone that occurs naturally in the immune system.

1990 July 31   Experiments to treat illnesses in humans by the insertion of new genes into body cells was approved for the first time by an advisory committee of the U.S. National Institutes of Health. One **gene therapy** procedure would treat children with adenosine deaminase [ADA], an immune disorder in which there is a lack of an enzyme necessary to break down certain dangerous by-products that can destroy immune cells. The second therapy approved would treat melanoma, a deadly skin cancer, by isolating a certain type of blood cell.

1990 July 31   Between 8 and 10 million people worldwide are infected with the **AIDS** virus, the **World Health Organization** [WHO] reported. Large increases in the number of infections in Asia, Latin America, and sub-Sahara Africa were noted and, with the incidence among women and children rising, WHO predicted (July 28) that at least 3 million of them would die during the 1990s. The number of infected persons in Asia had risen to 500,000 from almost none two years earlier.

1990 Aug. 10 The unmanned U.S. spacecraft *Magellan*, launched (May 4, 1989) by the shuttle *Atlantis*, reached its destination, **Venus**. After some difficulty on earth in maintaining radio contact, *Magellan* began mapping the surface of Venus. Active volcanoes, fractured landscapes, and a thin plastic crust were revealed, unlike anything seen before in the solar system. It was announced (May 29, 1991) that *Magellan* had completed a survey of one Venus-year and had mapped 94 percent of the planet's surface.

1990 Aug. 18 B[urrhus] F[rederic] **Skinner** (b. Mar. 20, 1904), a leading American psychologist of the behaviorist school, who believed a better world could be created by the scientific modification of behavior, died. Skinner's best-known work was *Walden Two* (1948), a novel that depicted a community where all of society's ills had been cured by behavioral engineering. The book gradually acquired a cult following. Skinner also wrote *Science and Human Behavior* (1953) and *Beyond Freedom and Dignity* (1973).

1990 Sept. 4 At the National Institutes of Health, Bethesda, Maryland, a 4-year-old girl whose name was withheld, became the **first person ever to receive human gene therapy**, a method of treating disease by placing in the body copies of genes that are lacking. The girl was suffering from an immune deficiency that resulted from the lack of a gene that regulates an enzyme necessary to keep immune cells alive.

1990 Oct. 6 After four delays due to technological problems, the U.S. manned spacecraft *Discovery* was launched and the same day put into orbit the unmanned spacecraft *Ulysses*, which was intended to survey the southern hemisphere of the sun from May to September 1994. Its course was to take it 500 million miles to Jupiter before it used that planet's gravity to head toward a solar orbit where it would take various measurements. *Discovery* returned to earth Oct. 10. The project was a joint venture of the National Aeronautics and Space Administration [NASA] of the U.S. and the European Space Agency.

1990 Oct. 25 Surgeons at the Stanford University Medical School in California performed a historic operation when they **transferred part of a mother's lung into her 12-year-old daughter**, who was dying as a result of severe scarring of her lungs. Hitherto such operations had been performed using organs from persons who had recently died and such transplants were often rejected by the patient's body. If the operation could be performed on very young infants, it would reduce the number of deaths occurring as a result of lung scarring in premature babies.

1990 Nov. 11 **Stormie Jones**, who, when not quite seven years old, became the **first person in the world to receive a heart and liver transplant in the same operation** (Feb. 14, 1983), died in the Pittsburgh, Pennsylvania, hospital where the operation was first performed. She was given a second liver transplant (Feb. 20, 1990) because the first had been damaged by hepatitis.

1990 Nov. 27 Archaeologists investigating the **ruins of La Isabela**, an ill-fated colony founded by **Christopher Columbus** on the northern coast of the present-day **Dominican Republic** in late 1493, turned up artifacts, some of which could have been used by the explorer himself. Finds included fragments of earthenware plates and bowls, roofing tiles, and the rim of what was probably a chamber pot. There were also found the foundations of a building and skeletons in a cemetery.

1990 Dec. 11 The U.S. space shuttle *Columbia* landed one day short of its planned ten-day mission, troubled both by problems in the shuttle itself and with its star-gazing mission. The mysterious appearance of lint fouled the shuttle's cooling system and caused the failure of computers that controlled ultraviolet and X-ray telescopes on board. As a result only 140 of 250 planned targets were observed, although valuable data on stars, galaxies, quasars, supernovas, and a comet were garnered.

1990 Dec. 31 American and British climatologists reported (Jan. 1991) that **1990 had been the warmest year the world had experienced** since comparable records began in 1880. The average was 59.81°F. The seven warmest years since 1880 all occurred in the last 11 years, with the average in 1981 and 1988 ranking second at 59.64°F.

VII. ARTS AND LEISURE

1990 Jan. 4   Vladimir [Alexis] **Ussachevsky** (b. Nov. 3, 1911), a Russian-born American composer who wrote the **first piece of electronic music** heard (1952) in concert in the U.S., died. He pioneered further as one of the founders (1959) of the Columbia-Princeton Electronic Music Center. Ussachevsky began composing directly on magnetic tape in 1951, and an example of his work was *Of Wood and Brass* (1965).

1990 Jan. 20   Barbara Stanwyck [née Ruby Stevens] (b. July 16, 1907), an American actress of the stage, movies, and television, died. A chorus girl at the age of 15, she had a leading role in a Broadway play, *Burlesque* five years later. Among her movies were *Stella Dallas* (1937), *The Lady Eve* (1941), and *Double Indemnity* (1944).

1990 Jan. 25   Ava [Lavinia] **Gardner** (b. Dec. 24, 1922), an American movie actress, everywhere regarded as one of the most seductive stars ever seen on movie screens, died. At the age of 24 she won stardom in *The Killers* (1946). Among her movies were *The Snows of Kilimanjaro* (1952), *The Barefoot Contessa* (1954), and *On the Beach* (1959).

1990 Jan. 25   After a 7-month renovation costing $1.65 million, the **Tate Gallery** in London reopened to the public with each of its 30 rooms given a theme, such as "William Blake and His Followers." Themes were to change within a year to allow more of the Tate's collection to be shown.

1990 Jan. 26   Lewis Mumford (b. Oct. 19, 1895), an American critic whose commentaries covered literature, history, culture, politics, and city planning, died. His intellectual and moral views stemmed from those of such nineteenth-century Americans as **Ralph Waldo Emerson**. Mumford was highly critical of the uses to which modern technology was put, and he was an early and vocal advocate of city planning. His views were expressed in such books as *Technics and Civilization* (1934), *The Culture of Cities* (1938), and *The Transformation of Man* (1956).

1990 Feb. 19   Michael [Latham] **Powell** (b. Sept. 30, 1905), a British movie director and producer, died. His first success was *Rynox* (1931), a thriller. Among his other movies were *The Edge of the World* (1937), made in the Shetland Islands; *The Life and Death of Colonel Blimp* (1943), which made fun of the British military establishment; *The Red Shoes* (1948), which successfully transferred ballet to film; and *The Tales of Hoffmann* (1951).

1990 Mar. 17   The **Bastille Opera**, a new opera house in Paris near the site of the infamous Bastille prison, opened with a performance of *Les Troyens* by **Hector Berlioz**. Work on the ornate building, which had a main auditorium seating 2,700, began in 1982 and replaced the Opera Garnier of 1875 as the home of French Opera.

1990 Mar. 25   An exhibit opened at the Vatican to mark the completion of ten years' labor to clean **Michelangelo's frescoes on the ceiling of the Sistine Chapel**. Created between 1508 and 1512, the paintings had become dirtied and dulled by smoke and other pollutants.

1990 Apr. 3   Sarah [Lois] **Vaughan** (b. Mar. 17, 1924), an American jazz singer with a voice more impressive and of more scope than most performers of popular music, died. She made her debut (1942) with [Earl] Fatha Hines' band and in the 1945–1946 season began her career as a soloist. Vaughan's first hit was her recording (1947) of "**Tenderly**." Known appropriately both as "**Sassy**" and the "**Divine Sarah**," she sang in recital and recorded a variety of music, including "**Make Yourself Comfortable**" (1954) and an album, *Gershwin Live!* (1982).

1990 Apr. 15   Greta Garbo [née Greta Lovisa Gustafson] (b. Sept. 18, 1905), a Swedish-born American movie actress of magnetic and elusive beauty, died. She made (1924) her first important film in Sweden and her first in Hollywood two years later. Garbo's films mostly featured her seductiveness, as in *Flesh and the Devil* (1927). Among her other highly regarded movies were *Anna Christie* (1930), *Mata Hari* (1931), *Anna Karenina* (1935), and *Ninotchka* (1939). After making 27 movies Garbo retired (1941) and thereafter lived a reclusive life.

1990 Apr. 23   Paulette Goddard [née Marion Levy] (b. June 3, 1911), an American film actress able to play both comedy and femme fatale roles, died. She made her first important screen appearance with **Charlie Chaplin**, whom she later married, in *Modern Times* (1936). Goddard's versatile talent was exhibited in such movies as *Nothing But the Truth* (1941) and her most notable film *The Diary of a Chambermaid* (1946). She retired in 1958.

1990 Apr. 28 *A Chorus Line*, the longest-running show in the history of the Broadway theater, closed after 6,237 performances. The musical opened on July 25, 1975, and on Sept. 29, 1983, became the longest-running show, surpassing *Grease* with its 3,389th performance. In the course of its run *A Chorus Line* was seen by c.6,543,000 people and had 510 performers.

1990 May 10 **Walker Percy** (b. May 28, 1916), an American writer whose novels had their settings in the present-day South, died. All of his novels, of which the first was *The Moviegoer* (1961), showed his intellectual resources both as a storyteller and a philosopher. The theme of man's relationship to God and the universe appeared in such works as *Love in the Ruins* (1971) and *The Thanatos Syndrome* (1987).

1990 May 15 In New York the **highest price ever paid for a work of art** at an auction, $82.5 million, was brought by **Vincent Van Gogh's** painting *Portrait of Dr. Gachet*. The second highest price for a painting was registered (May 17) when *At the Moulin de la Galette* by **Pierre Auguste Renoir** went for $78.1 million. The purchaser of both paintings was **Ryoei Saito** (b. Apr. 17, 1916), a Japanese industrialist.

1990 May 16 [James Maury] **"Jim" Henson** (b. Sept. 24, 1936), an American puppeteer whose creation, the **Muppets**, delighted and educated millions of young people, died. His creatures first appeared (1954) on television, but worldwide fame came after *Sesame Street*, a program for preschoolers, began (1969), featuring such characters as Kermit the Frog and the Cookie Monster. *The Muppet Show*, when it began (1976) its telecasts, found millions of adult as well as young viewers. The egotistical Miss Piggy became a cult figure.

1990 May 16 **Sammy Davis, Jr.** (b. Dec. 6, 1925), a black American entertainer who combined singing, dancing, and acting, died. On the vaudeville stage with his family from the time he was three, Davis developed a rakish charm that endeared him to audiences. He was a star of the Broadway musical *Mr. Wonderful* (1956), made hit recordings such as "I've Gotta Be Me," and appeared in movies such as *Porgy and Bess* (1959) and *Tap* (1989).

1990 June 2 **Rex** [Carey] **Harrison** (b. Mar. 5, 1908), a British actor known for the suave elegance he brought to his roles on stage and screen, died. His stage appearances began (1930) in London and did not end until 1989. He also made more than 40 movies. In this long and varied career Harrison was best known for his role of Professor Henry Higgins in *My Fair Lady* (1956, stage; 1964, movie). He appeared in such different plays as *The Cocktail Party* (1950) and *Heartbreak House* (1984); in movies in *The Ghost and Mrs. Muir* (1947) and *Cleopatra* (1963).

1990 June 10 **Medieval art works and illuminated manuscripts**, missing since the end of World War II (1939–1945), were discovered in Whitewright, a small town in north-central Texas. Investigation indicated that the collection belonged to a church in the town of Quedlinburg, Saxony-Anhalt state, in former East Germany. The investigation also indicated that the materials had been shipped (Apr. 1945) to the U.S. by **Joe T. Meador** (d. Feb. 1, 1980), an American army lieutenant, who apparently found them in a mine where they had been placed for safekeeping. An agreement was reached (Feb. 25, 1992) whereby the artworks would be returned to Germany and members of the Meador family would receive $2.75 million.

1990 July 29 The **"Vincent Van Gogh Retrospective,"** an exhibit in two museums in Amsterdam, the Netherlands, which had opened in March, closed on the 100th anniversary of his death, after having been viewed by 1.2 million visitors. In all 75 private and public collections contributed to the exhibits, which included 133 canvases and 248 drawings. The paintings on loan in this largest ever showing of Van Gogh's work were insured for $3 billion.

1990 Aug. 6 **Gordon Bunshaft** (b. May 9, 1909), an American architect whose expressive use of steel and glass made him a leader in the design of International Style skyscrapers, died. He pioneered a trend with his first important work, **Lever House** (1952) in New York City. Other notable Bunshaft structures were the **Pepsi-Cola building** (1952) and the **Manufacturers Hanover Bank** (1954), both in New York City, and the **Beinecke Rare Book Library** (1963) at Yale University, New Haven, Connecticut.

1990 Aug. 17 **Pearl** [Mae] **Bailey** (b. Mar. 29, 1918), an American singer of black and Indian ancestry, whose warm and mischievous style made her extremely popular for many years, died. After appearing in small clubs, she made her New York debut (1941) and thereafter appeared as a soloist or with dance bands. Her first role in a musical was in

St. Louis Woman (1946), but her greatest stage success was in *Hello Dolly* (1967–1969). Among her most popular songs were "Birth of the Blues" and "From Mouton to Muskrat to Mink." Bailey also appeared in a number of movies.

1990 Aug. 25 Morley [Edward] **Callaghan** (b. Sept. 22, 1903), a Canadian writer known for his emphatic realism and hardboiled approach to his subject matter, died. His first participation in the literary life was among the American expatriates in Paris in the 1920s; his first novel, *Strange Fugitive* (1928), had a bootlegger as its principal character. Over a career of 60 years, Callaghan wrote such novels as *The Many Colored Coat* (1960), *A Fine and Private Place* (1975), and *The Wild Old Man of the Road* (1980).

1990 Sept. 4 Irene Dunne (b. Dec. 20, 1898), an American singer and actress whose combination of genteel beauty, sophistication, and humor earned her a faithful following, died. She toured with the **Jerome Kern** musical *Show Boat* (1929), and she also appeared (1936) in its movie version. Dunne reached the height of her popularity in such movie comedies as *The Awful Truth* (1937) and *My Favorite Wife* (1940). Later she played more mature roles, as in *Life With Father* (1947) and *I Remember Mama* (1948).

1990 Sept. 26 Alberto Moravia [orig. Alberto Pincherle] (b. Nov. 28, 1907), an Italian author of wide popularity, died. He published his first novel, *Gli indifferenti* [*The Time of Indifference*] (1920) at his own expense. Moravia's later novels, all of which deprecated what he saw as the low morals of the middle class and its emphasis on money and sex, included *La mascherata* [*The Fancy Dress Party*] (1941), *L'amore coniugale* [*Conjugal Love*] (1951), *L'attenzione* [*The Lie*] (1965), and *La vita interiore* [*Time of Desecration*] (1978).

1990 Sept. 30 Patrick [Victor Martindale] **White** (b. May 28, 1912), an Australian author, most of whose books had an Australian background, died. His works, which did not flatter his country, also contained more general themes stressing emptiness and isolation. White's first novel was *Happy Valley* (1939), an ironic title. *The Tree of Man* (1955) detailed the struggle of an Australian farmer. Other works included *Voss* (1957), *The Vivisector* (1970), and *The Eye of the Storm* (1973). White was awarded the **Nobel prize for literature** (1973).

1990 Oct. 3 Eleanor Steber (b. July 17, 1914), an American soprano who was much praised for her roles in Mozart and Strauss operas, died. She made her debut (1940) at the Metropolitan Opera, New York City, in *Der Rosenkavalier*, and between then and 1966 performed there 404 times in 33 roles. Steber had a strong, warm voice and was popular in recitals as well as operatic roles.

1990 Oct. 11 Octavio Paz (b. Mar. 31, 1914), known for both his poetry and his essays as a social philosopher, became the first Mexican writer to win the **Nobel prize for literature**. Throughout his poetry, which was both erotic and lyrical, there was a sense of the loneliness of man as well as a reverence for Mexico, its past and its physical nature. Among Paz's volumes of poetry were *Piedra de sol* [*Sun Stone*] (1957) and *Selected Poetry* (1963), English translations of various works. His most important prose work was *El laberino de la soledad* [*The Labyrinth of Solitude*] (1950), a search for the soul of Mexico and all of Latin America through an examination of its history. In addition to his literary work, Paz was in the diplomatic service for 25 years, ending in 1968.

1990 Oct. 14 Leonard Bernstein (b. Aug. 25, 1918), an American conductor, composer, and pianist, died. He was best known as a conductor, having been the musical director (1958–1969) of the New York Philharmonic Orchestra. The scope of Bernstein's talents as a composer were shown by the range of his works: orchestra, *Jeremiah Symphony* (1942) and *Kaddish Symphony* (1963); Broadway musicals, *On the Town* (1944) and *West Side Story* (1957); ballet, *Fancy Free* (1944); and film score, *On the Waterfront* (1954).

1990 Nov. 3 Mary [Virginia] **Martin** (b. Dec. 1, 1913), an American star of musical comedy, died. Her first appearance on Broadway in *Leave It to Me* (1938) made her an instant and permanent favorite. Her other successes included *One Touch of Venus* (1943); *South Pacific* (1949); *Peter Pan* (1954), the title role of which was her favorite; and *The Sound of Music* (1959). Martin projected vitality and happiness in songs she was especially associated with, such as "My Heart Belongs to Daddy" and "I'm in Love with a Wonderful Guy."

1990 Nov. 7 Lawrence [George] **Durrell** (b. Feb. 27, 1912), a British novelist and poet known particularly for his exotic fiction, died. Durrell achieved international notice with the Alexandria Quartet, a series of four novels, *Justine* (1957), *Balthazar* (1958), *Mountolive* (1958), and *Clea* (1960). These novels evoke the exotic and seedy elements of both the city of Alexandria, Egypt, and the characters in the books, giving overall a haunted feeing of time and place. Durrell's poetry included *Collected Poems* (1979).

1990 Nov. 7   Hugh MacLennan (b. Mar. 20, 1907), a Canadian novelist, died. His writings were early attempts to express the character of Canadians, as in *Barometer Rising* (1941) and *Two Solitudes* (1945). Other similar works were *The Watch That Ends the Night* (1959) and *Return of the Sphinx* (1967).

1990 Nov. 11   Alexis Minotis [orig. Alexander Minotakis] (b. Aug. 8, 1900), the dean of Greek actors and a prominent figure in the Greek National Theater, died. He was known for his acting in and staging of dramas of various cultures and by many playwrights: ancient Greece, Shakespeare, and Ibsen, for example. Minotis was married to and performed on the stage with **Katina Paxinou**, who became better known internationally than her husband.

1990 Nov. 23   Roald Dahl (b. Sept. 13, 1916), a British writer whose touch of the macabre in his stories entranced both children and adults, died. Among his books for children were *James and the Giant Peach* (1961) and *Charlie and the Chocolate Factory* (1964), for which he also wrote the screenplay as *Willy Wonka and the Chocolate Factory* (1971). Among his collections of short stories for adults were *Someone Like You* (1953), *Kiss Kiss* (1960), and *Switch Bitch* (1974).

1990 Dec. 2   Aaron Copland (b. Nov. 14, 1900), a composer whose works emphasized American themes, died. He composed operas; ballets; film scores; and orchestral, chamber, piano, and choral music and songs, some in a classical style but preeminently in an American vein. Among these were the ballets *Billy the Kid* (1940), *Rodeo* (1942), and *Appalachian Spring* (1944); an orchestral number, *Fanfare for the Common Man* (1942); and songs for 12 poems by **Emily Dickinson** (1950).

1990 Dec. 7   Joan Bennett (b. Feb. 27, 1910), an American stage and movie actress known first as a blond ingénue and later as a dark-haired siren, died. Her first movie was *Bulldog Drummond* (1929). After her performance in *Little Women* (1933), she

took up different roles, as in *Algiers* (1938), a smoldering melodrama. Other successes were *The Woman in the Window* (1944) and *The Woman on the Beach* (1947). After the early 1950s Bennett appeared mainly on the stage.

1990 Dec. 14   Friedrich Dürrenmatt (b. Jan. 5, 1921), a Swiss playwright, novelist, and essayist, noted for his bizarre irony, died. His best-known and most disturbing play was *Der Besuch der alten Dame* [*The Visit of the Old Lady*] (1956), in which greed causes a village's citizens to execute a man. Other Dürrenmatt tragi-comedies were *Die Ehe des Herren Mississippi* [*The Marriage of Mr. Mississippi*] (1952) and *The Physicists* (1962), about three scientists in a madhouse. Other writings included the novel *Justice* (1985).

VIII. SPORTS, GAMES, AND SOCIETY

1990 Mar. 1   The U.S. State Department reported that in spite of the nation's war on drugs, the **worldwide production of opium poppies, coca, marijuana, and hashish had increased greatly** in the past year. It was estimated that opium production had gone up 47 percent and marijuana 21 percent. Of the world cocaine supply, 80 percent came from Colombia, while Myanmar [formerly Burma] was the largest opium producer.

1990 Mar. 9   The **most lucrative television contract ever** negotiated was concluded between the **National Football League** [NFL] and the networks [ABC, CBS, NBC, ESPN, and Turner] and would pay the league more than $3.6 billion over four years. Each of the 28 teams in the NFL would receive about $32 million per year, nearly double the current amount. A maximum of 119 games a season would be on view in any city.

1990 Mar. 26   Roy Halston Frowick (b. Apr. 23, 1932), an American designer known professionally as Halston, whose influence on fashion was greatest in the 1970s, died. His sober, tailored, and more traditional designs were credited with putting an end to the anti-establishment extremes of the 1960s.

1990 Mar. 29   The **Belgian parliament voted to allow abortions** in the first 12 weeks of pregnancy for women "in a state of distress," thus overturning the law, in effect since 1867, that banned all abortions. Ireland was the only other European country with a complete ban. The new law provided that the "state of distress" would be left to the woman and her doctor to decide. Consultation on alternatives and a six-day waiting period were prescribed. When **Baudouin I**, king of Belgium, said he could not in good conscience sign the act, parliament suspended his powers for one day while the cabinet assumed his powers and promulgated the law.

1990 May 20 At a track and field meet in Los Angeles, **Randy Barnes** of the U.S. set a **new world record for the shot put** of 75 ft., 10¼ in., exceeding the previous record by 2¼ in. Barnes was suspended (Nov. 6) from competition for two years on charges that a urine test showed traces of an anabolic steroid. He appealed, but a panel of sports officials ruled (Jan. 4, 1991) that he had not proved the urine sample had been tampered with and so the suspension (through Aug. 7, 1992) stood.

1990 June 27 **José Canseco** (b. July 2, 1964), an outfielder for the Oakland Athletics of the American League, became the highest paid player in professional **baseball** history when he signed a contract that would earn him $23.5 million over a five-year period. By the end of 1990 more than 20 percent of major league players were being paid $1 million or more a year.

1990 July 7 **Martina Navratilova** (b. Oct. 18, 1956), a Czechoslovakian-born American tennis player, **set a record by winning the women's singles championship at** the **Wimbledon**, England, tournament for the ninth time. She had been tied previously with **Helen Wills Moody**, who had won eight times, the last in 1938. Navratilova won her other eight titles in 1978–1979 and 1982–1987.

1990 July 8 West Germany won the **World Cup** of soccer in Rome by defeating Argentina, the defending champion, 1–0 on a penalty kick. It was the lowest scoring title game in 60 years of play for the World Cup. The tournament, which had been going on for a month in Italy, was generally conceded to be the dullest and nastiest played, with so few goals scored that even dedicated fans were bored.

1990 Aug. 1 The **longest and costliest criminal proceedings** in U.S. history ended after more than three and a half years when a judge in Los Angeles dismissed all charges against **Raymond Buckey**. The original trial began (Apr. 20, 1987) with Buckey and his mother, **Peggy McMartin Buckey**, charged with 65 counts of child molestation and conspiracy in con-

nection with a school they ran. After a trial that involved 124 witnesses and 60,000 pages of court records, Mrs. Buckey was acquitted (Jan. 18, 1990) of all molestation charges and the judge dismissed a conspiracy charge. Buckey was acquitted on 40 molestation charges but was retried on 13 counts. After a jury reported (July 27) that it was deadlocked, the judge dismissed (Aug. 1) all charges against Buckey.

1990 Aug. 28 **B'nai B'rith International**, a fraternal order of Jewish men, voted to admit women as full members. An affiliated group, B'nai B'rith Women, was to continue as a self-governing body, and its leaders said there was need for an organization to formulate women's special interests. B'nai B'rith had 500,000 full and affiliated members, of whom 120,000 belonged to B'nai B'rith Women. Founded in 1843 by European Jewish immigrants to the U.S., B'nai B'rith [Sons of the Covenant] had become known as a defender of human rights and a sponsor of interfaith and interracial relations.

1990 Sept. 8 **Ellis Island**, in New York Harbor, through whose facilities 12 million immigrants entered the U.S. between 1892 and 1924, its busiest years, **reopened as a museum of immigration**. Immigration processing had ended in 1954, and the buildings, badly deteriorated, had now been restored at a cost of $156 million through private contributions. The chief feature of the restoration was the 160-foot long, two-story high Registry Room, where began the process that determined whether a would-be immigrant was allowed to enter the U.S.

1990 Oct. 25 In his first defense of the **world heavyweight boxing** title, which he had held only since Feb. 11, [James] **Buster Douglas** (b. Apr. 7, 1960) lost it to **Evander Holyfield** (b. Oct. 19, 1962) when he was knocked out in the third round of a bout at Las Vegas, Nevada. Douglas had won the title in the February match in Tokyo when he knocked out the then-champion **Mike Tyson** (b. June 30, 1966) in the tenth round in a surprising upset. Tyson had held the title since Nov. 23, 1986, when he knocked out Trevor Berbick in the second round of a fight in Las Vegas.

1990 Nov. 6 In defiance of law and tradition, 47 women of prominent families of **Saudi Arabia** drove their cars, mostly Mercedes and Cadillacs, through the streets of Riyadh, the capital. They were stopped by police and the government announced (Nov. 14) that it intended to keep the **ban on women driving**

automobiles. It said Muslim scholars had determined that such action "degrades and harms the sanctity of women." The government further stated (Nov. 16) that all **demands and demonstrations for more rights for** the **women** of the country were **forbidden**.

1990 Dec. 31   Alice Marble (b. Sept. 13, 1913), an American tennis star who was the outstanding player of the late 1930s, died. She also brought about a fundamental change in women's tennis by adopting the serve and volley style instead of the usual baseline game. Marble first won the U.S. champion-

ship in 1936 and then for three consecutive years (1938–1940). She also won once at Wimbledon (1939). With a partner she won the U.S. women's double title four consecutive years (1937–1940).

1990 Dec. 31   In a world championship chess match that began in New York City (Oct. 8) and ended in Lyons, France, **Gary Kasparov** retained his title by defeating the challenger **Anatoly Karpov** 12½ to 11½. The players, both Russian, matched wits in 24 games, most of which ended in draws. For his victory Kasparov earned $1.7 million while Karpov received $1.3 million.

1991

I. VITAL STATISTICS AND DEMOGRAPHICS

1991 Jan.–Mar.   In the first two months of the year c.17,000 **Albanian citizens**, most of them ethnic Greeks, **fled their country** for neighboring Greece because of political and economic conditions in their homeland. In early March, as conditions worsened in Albania, others began fleeing to Italy by ship. During the month c.20,000 Albanians sought asylum, but Italy turned back most of them.

1991 Mar. 25   According to new census figures, the **population of India** had risen to 844 million, an increase of 161 million in ten years. The census also revealed that for every 1,000 men there were only 920 women.

1991 May 25   Israel completed an airlift that in 36 hours brought 14,500 **Ethiopian Jews to Israel**. While civil war raged in Ethiopia, 35 airplanes shuttled the Ethiopians over the route of more than 1,500 miles.

1991 June   American officials estimated that since the Iraqi invasion (Aug. 2, 1990) of Kuwait and the end (Feb. 27) of the **Persian Gulf War** (1990–1991) at least 5 million persons from more than 30 countries had been displaced, either temporarily or permanently. The **forced migrations** affected not only the other nations of the Middle East, but also countries as far away as the Philippines, many of whose nationals had been brought to Kuwait to work in menial jobs. Among the largest groups were the nearly 1.5 million Kurds who fled Iraq to Turkey and Iran.

About 250,000 Jordanians and Palestinians were forced to leave Kuwait.

1991 Oct. 2   The government of **Vietnam**, in a reversal of past policy, agreed to accept the forced **return of Vietnamese refugees**, of whom there were estimated to be more than 100,000 in camps throughout Southeast Asia. Hong Kong, where about half of them had found shelter, began (Nov. 9) forcibly returning them with an initial boatload of 59 people.

1991 Dec.   Starvation continued to threaten the lives of millions of people **in Africa**, partly as a result of drought conditions, but mostly because of civil wars in Ethiopia, Somalia, and the Sudan. Several hundred thousand Ethiopians, who had fled to Somalia, returned home to escape fighting there; meanwhile, several hundred thousand Somalians fled to Ethiopia. The United Nations and other organizations made efforts—though hampered by government inefficiency and corruption and by inadequate communication and transportation systems—to feed the needy.

1991 Dec. 31   About 135,000 **Russian Jews emigrated to Israel** this year. As the emigrants flowed in, it became apparent that the long era of religious repression under communism had left many of them with little knowledge of Judaism or Zionism.

II. DISASTERS

1991 Feb. 1   A USAir **Boeing 737**, landing at the Los Angeles airport, **crashed** head-on into a SkyWest commuter plane about to take off from the same runway. All 12 persons on the smaller plane were killed while 22 of the 89 persons aboard the USAir plane were killed and some 30 injured. An air traffic controller apparently cleared the two planes to use the same runway.

1991 Feb. 1 An **earthquake** registering 6.8 on the Richter scale, and centered in the Hindu Kush mountains, some 200 miles north of Kabul, Afghanistan, killed c.1,200 people in that country and in neighboring Pakistan. The number of injured in remote areas was uncertain.

1991 Feb. 15 After a **tractor-trailer** carrying dynamite to a stone quarry overturned, it **exploded**, killing 100 persons and injuring 86 others in southern Phang Nga province of Thailand. Those killed and injured were in a crowd that gathered to view the original accident.

1991 Mar. 1 More than 150 of some 700 persons crowded into a boat carrying them from the civil war in Somalia to Kenya were drowned when the **ship ran aground** only several hundred yards from the end of its 250-mile journey.

1991 Mar. 21 Ninety-two of 95 Senegalese soldiers and all six crew members were killed when a Saudi Air Force **C-130 plane crashed** while landing at an air base in Saudi Arabia. The Senegalese were part of a 500-man force their country had sent to join the multinational force that had recently driven Iraqi invaders out of Kuwait.

1991 Apr. 29 An **earthquake** registering 7.0 on the Richter scale struck Georgia in the southern Soviet Union, killing c.100 people, injuring at least 500, and leaving 80,000 homeless. One small village was buried so completely that none of its buildings was visible.

1991 Apr. 30 A **cyclone** with winds up to 150 mph, which brought high waves and caused floods, killed c.140,000 people and left c.10 million homeless in southeastern Bangladesh. Many were threatened with starvation and disease in spite of international relief efforts. The U.S. sent 7,500 troops, ships, and aircraft to assist in the rescue work.

1991 May 27 A **Boeing 767-300** passenger jet of Lauda Air, an Austrian charter airline, **exploded** sixteen minutes after taking off from Bangkok, Thailand, on a flight to Vienna. All 223 persons aboard

the plane were killed. The malfunction of a computer that switched one of the jet engines into reverse was blamed for the disaster.

1991 June 9 A series of **eruptions of Mt. Pinatubo**, a volcano in the western part of Luzon Island, the Philippines, began, killing c.435 people and leaving over 300,000 homeless or in lack of food and water. Volcanic ash forced 14,000 persons at or near the American installation of Clark Air Base to leave. Later the U.S. said the base would be permanently abandoned. Subic Naval Station to the south was covered by layers of ash but not abandoned.

1991 July 11 A **DC-8 airliner** carrying Muslim pilgrims home to Nigeria **crashed** shortly after takeoff at an airport near Mecca, Saudi Arabia, killing all 261 persons aboard, including a 14-member crew. The Nigerians had been on a religious pilgrimage to the holy cities of Mecca and Medina. The pilot was said to have reported a fire in the plane's landing gear.

1991 July 17 Severe **flooding in central China** along the Yangtze River system had by now killed at least 1,700 people and affected the lives of 220 million. Eighteen of China's 30 provinces suffered from the floods and damage was estimated at $7 billion.

1991 July 22 The **World Health Organization** [WHO] reported that **cholera** had so far this year killed 3,488 people in Africa and 2,618 in Central and South America, most of the latter in Peru. By the end of the year total deaths in Latin American reached c.4,000; in Africa 45,000 cases had been reported; and in the Americas 250,000.

1991 Oct. 5 A **C-130 Indonesian military transport plane crashed** near Jakarta, on the northwestern coast of Java, shortly after takeoff, killing all 132 airmen aboard. It was reported that one of the plane's engines had caught fire and that another had failed.

1991 Oct. 10 An **earthquake** that registered 6.1 on the Richter scale shook a remote area in the foothills of the Himalayan mountains in northern India. The death toll was estimated to be at least 670, while c.2,000 were injured, and some 500 villages damaged or destroyed.

1991 Nov. 5 **Flash floods** brought by a typhoon hit the island of Leyte in the eastern Philippines, causing an estimated 5,500 deaths and leaving 20,000 people homeless. The city of Ormoc, struck by floodwaters ten feet high, suffered the most damage.

1991 Dec. 14 As many as 471 persons were apparently drowned when the *Salem Express*, carrying about 650 people returning from a religious festival in Saudi Arabia, **sank** after hitting coral reefs in the Red Sea near Safaga, Egypt, about 300 miles southeast of Cairo. Strong winds blew the 1,105-ton ship onto the reefs.

III. WAR AND POLITICS

1991 Jan. 7 **Cancellation of the largest weapons program** ever terminated was announced by the U.S. Defense Department. The project involved was the **A-12 Avenger**, a Navy plane of the radar-evading type. The planes were to have cost $57 billion, but the program was already eighteen months behind schedule and more than $2.7 billion over budget.

1991 Jan. 8 **Four Belgians, held hostage** for three years and two months **in Lebanon** by the Fatah Revolutionary Council, **were released**. They were a man and wife and their two children. It was announced at the same time that Belgium would release a member of the council who was serving a life term in prison for an attack on Jewish children in Antwerp.

1991 Jan. 13 **Mário Soares** was reelected president of **Portugal** for a second 5-year term, winning around 70 percent of the votes. His victory had been widely forecast, though nearly 40 percent of those eligible did not vote. The post of president was largely ceremonial.

1991 Jan. 14 Two of the highest ranking leaders of the **Palestine Liberation Organization** [PLO] were shot and killed in Tunis, Tunisia, by one of their bodyguards. The slain men were **Saleh Khalef** [known as Abu Iyad], who was the acknowledged heir to **Yasir Arafat**, the head of the PLO, and **Hayel Abdel-Hamid** [known as Abu al-Hol].

1991 Jan. 15 A U.N. deadline for Iraq to withdraw its forces from Kuwait, which it had occupied (Aug. 2, 1990), expired without any response from **Saddam Hussein**, president and dictator of Iraq. Accordingly, allied forces, led by the U.S., began (Jan. 17) a new phase of the **Persian Gulf War** (1990–1991) with **air attacks against Iraq**. Besides military targets, allied planes struck power plants, oil refineries, and Iraqi

installations suspected of being sources of chemical or nuclear warfare products. By Jan. 20 more than 20,000 sorties had been flown. Iraq still not having withdrawn its forces from Kuwait, a ground war began (Feb. 24) with **allied troops advancing on a 300-mile front into Kuwait** and Iraq. Resistance was lighter than expected and 50,000 prisoners were taken in three days. Iraq's ground troops were routed and **Kuwait was freed** (Feb. 27), at which time **George Bush**, president of the U.S. and leader of the anti-Iraq coalition, ordered an end to offensive military operations. Iraq said (Mar. 3) it would comply with previous U.N. resolutions which demanded that it void its annexation of Kuwait, pay reparations to that country, free all prisoners of war and Kuwaiti citizens it had detained, reveal the location of all mines it had laid on land or in the sea, and allow the inspection and destruction of any facilities for manufacturing chemical or nuclear weapons. The U.S. Defense Department estimated (June 4) that c.100,000 Iraqi soldiers had been killed, c.300,000 wounded, and that another 150,000 had deserted. There were no reliable figures on civilian casualties, although one estimate said 13,000 had been killed. A report (Mar. 21, 1992) by the U.N. said that c.72,000 persons had been made homeless. Allied casualties were extremely light: U.S. forces suffered 146 combat deaths, of which 35 were by friendly fire, and 467 wounded, 72 of them by friendly fire. British troops suffered 17 combat deaths, 43 wounded, and 8 missing. The **cost of the Persian Gulf War** was estimated at $61 billion, of which c.$50 billion was contributed by Germany, Japan, Kuwait, and Saudi Arabia.

1991 Jan. 17 **Olaf V** (b. July 2, 1903), king of Norway (1957–1991), the oldest monarch in the world, died. When Nazi Germany invaded (1940) his country, Olaf, then crown prince, fought the enemy for two months before joining the Norwegian government in exile in London. As king he was known for his unassuming manner and for mingling with his subjects. Olav was succeeded by his son **Harald V** (b. Feb. 21, 1937).

1991 Jan. 26 **Eight leaders of the pro-democracy demonstrations** (1989) in Tiananmen Square, Beijing [Peking], **China**, were sentenced to prison for their part in the affair. **Ren Wanding**, a leading human rights advocate, received a 7-year sentence, while **Wang Dan**, a student leader, received a 4-year sentence. Six others were to serve terms of two to four years (released Feb., 1993). Two more dissidents received (Feb. 12) the longest sentences in connection with the demonstrations when 13-year terms were meted out to **Wang Juntao** and **Chen Ziming**, both leading advocates of democracy.

1991 Jan. 26 **Mohammed Siad Barre**, president (from 1969) of **Somalia**, was forced out of office by rebel forces representing the United Somali Congress. The congress chose (Jan. 29) **Ali Mahdi Mohammed** as interim president. Another rebel group, however, the Somali Patriotic Movement, refused to recognize the new regime and fighting broke out (Feb. 10) between the rival forces. Later (Nov. 17) warfare began within the ranks of the United Somali Congress between factions representing Ali Mahdi and **Mohammed Farrah Aidid**, chairman of the congress. Both men belonged to the Hawiye ethnic group, but they were members of different subclans. Fighting raged mostly in Mogadishu, the capital, which was largely destroyed. By the end of the year c.30,000 people had been killed or wounded.

1991 Jan. 29 The **African National Congress** and the **Inkatha Freedom Party**, the two largest black political movements of **South Africa**, after a bloody rivalry that since 1984 had taken c.10,000 lives, agreed to end their differences. Inkatha represents the Zulus of South Africa. The two groups pledged to be mutually tolerant and to work together against white minority rule. The congress elected (July 5) as president **Nelson Mandela**, who had been deputy president and who was generally recognized as the country's foremost black spokesman. The Zulu leader was **Mangosutha Gatsha Buthelezi** (b. Aug. 27, 1928), chief of the Zulu homeland of KwaZulu. The two black groups and the South African government agreed (Sept. 14) to plans that it was hoped would end black factional violence. Inflammatory language was to be avoided, new codes of conduct were established for both parties, and security forces and special courts were to deal with political violence.

1991 Feb. 3 **Italy's Communist party**, the second largest political force in the country, but which had seen its strength gradually dwindle for fifteen years, **changed its name** to the Democratic Party of the Left. Its policies would now presumably be more in the tradition of European democratic socialism than those of Marxism.

1991 Feb. 7 **Jorge Serrano Elías** (b. Apr. 26, 1945) was inaugurated president (to 1993) of **Guatemala**, having won a runoff election the day before. He had

led the first balloting (Nov. 11, 1990) but did not receive a majority. Serrano was a right-wing businessman and an evangelical Christian who ran on a law-and-order platform. His inauguration marked the first transfer of power in the country from one civilian to another.

1991 Feb. 9 In a **plebiscite in Lithuania**, 91 percent of the ballots were cast for independence from the Soviet Union. Similar balloting (Mar 3) in the other two Baltic states, **Estonia** and **Latvia**, resulted in a 77 percent vote in both countries in favor of independence.

1991 Feb. 23 A military coup led by **Sunthorn Kongsompong**, chief of the armed forces, overthrew the government of **Thailand**, headed by **Chatichai Choonhavan**, who had been prime minister for two and a half years. Martial law was imposed, the constitution of 1978 abolished, and a National Peacekeeping Council established. The coup leaders named (Mar. 7) **Anand Panyarachun** (b. Aug. 9, 1932), a businessman and diplomat, as interim prime minister. The constitutional monarch, **Bhumibol Adulyadel** [Rama IX; from 1946] approved (Dec. 9) a new constitution, Thailand's fifteenth since 1932. It assured military control of any elected government.

1991 Feb. 25 The **Warsaw Pact**, created (1955) by the U.S.S.R. with its Eastern European satellite nations—Bulgaria, Czechoslovakia, East Germany, Hungary, Poland, and Romania—as a counterforce to the North Atlantic Treaty Organization [NATO], voted to dissolve as of Mar. 31.

1991 Mar. 10 In elections for the National Assembly of the Central American country of **El Salvador**, the right-wing Nationalist Republican Alliance [ARENA] lost its outright majority, winning 39 of 84 seats. ARENA stayed in power with the aid of allies. The Christian Democratic party won 26 seats, while the Democratic Convergence, representing the nonrevolutionary left, took 8 seats. For the first time in more than ten years the Farabundo Marti National Liberation Front [FMLN], which was carrying on an armed struggle against the government, did not try to sabotage the election process.

1991 Mar. 15 **Borisav Jovic**, the leader of **Yugoslavia's** eight-member ruling council, and the Serbian representative on it, resigned when the council refused to grant his request for emergency powers that would have given him control of the armed forces, whose officers were chiefly Serbs. The president of Serbia, Yugoslavia's largest republic, **Slobodan Milosevic** (b. Aug. 29, 1941), resigned from the council (Mar. 16), saying he refused to recognize the authority of the central government. The country was plunged into further constitutional difficulties when Serbia maneuvered to block the installation of **Stipe Mesic**, a Croat, as the federal president, a post that normally was rotated among the six republics. After two months of bickering, Mesic was confirmed, but the presidency split (Oct. 4) in half, basically representing the feud between Serbia and Croatia. Mesic resigned (Dec. 5) as head of the collective presidency, though he had ceased for some time to function in the office.

1991 Mar. 17   In a general election for the Finnish Eduskunta [parliament] the Conservative-Social Democratic coalition, which had governed since 1987, lost ground, with the Centre party winning the most seats of any party. It formed (Apr. 24) a center-right coalition government with **Esko Aho** (b. 1954) as prime minister, the youngest in **Finland**'s history.

1991 Mar. 20   The government of **Kuwait**, widely criticized for its inefficiency in restoring public services after Iraqi invasion forces were driven out (Feb. 27), resigned. The outgoing prime minister was **Saad al-Abdullah al-Sabah**, who was also crown prince, but control of the government remained in the hands of the royal family, headed by **Jaber al-Ahmed al-Sabah**, the emir. A new parliament, replacing one the emir had dissolved in 1986, was elected (June 10). Government supporters won all 50 seats at stake; the other 25 were appointed by the emir, who must approve any laws the parliament might pass. Martial law was ended (June 26), and Saad al-Abdullah al-Sabah resumed the post of prime minister.

1991 Mar. 20   **Khaleda Zia**, widow of **Ziaur Rahman**, the first president of **Bangladesh**, became prime minister. In an election (Feb. 27), her Bangladesh National party won 138 of 300 seats in parliament, and with the backing of a smaller Islamic religious party she was able to form a government.

1991 Mar. 24   In the first free election in nearly thirty years, voters in **Benim**, in northwestern Africa, in a runoff poll, elected **Nicéphore Soglo** (b. Nov. 29, 1934), the prime minister, as president over **Mathieu Kérékou**, who had ruled the country since seizing power (1972) in a coup. Soglo won two-thirds of the votes. Kérékou was a Marxist-Leninist, and the victor was expected to lead a move toward democracy and a free economy.

1991 Mar. 26   A military coup in **Mali**, in northwestern Africa, overthrew the government of **Moussa Traoré**, who had seized power (1968) and had headed a one-party state (from 1979). Looting and violence accompanied the coup, with 59 people killed and c.200 injured. The military leaders named (Apr. 2) a civilian, **Soumana Sacko**, to be interim prime minister, pending elections for which no date was set.

1991 Mar. 28   **Iraqi troops began all-out attacks**, centered on the city of Kirkuk, in the northeastern part of the country, **against Kurdish forces** which had been carrying on a revolt against **Saddam Hussein's** government since the latter's defeat (Feb. 27) in the **Persian Gulf War** (1990–1991). By Apr. 2 Kurds by the thousands were being forced to flee the towns and cities for the mountains and to seek refuge in Turkey and Iran. **George Bush**, president of the U.S., ordered (Apr. 5) air force planes to drop food, blankets, and clothing to the refugees. With the total number of refugee Kurds reaching c.550,000 in the mountainous area between Turkey and Iraq, and more than 1.2 million around the Iraq-Iran border, Bush announced (Apr. 12) plans for a military force to enter the area to build refugee camps. The first contingent arrived on Apr. 20. At the demand of the U.S. and its allies, Iraq began (Apr. 21) to withdraw its troops near the border with Turkey. Allied troops set up a **security zone in northern Iraq**, and some Kurds began (Apr. 26) returning to their home areas. The size of the security zone was doubled (May 2) to c.1,500 sq. mi. The last refugee camp on the Turkish border was closed (June 1) as the Kurds continued to return.

1991 Mar. 29   **Italy's 49th government since World War II** (1939–1945) collapsed when **Giulio Andreotti**, head of the Christian Democratic party, resigned as prime minister after a falling out with a former prime minister, **Bettino Craxi**, head of the Socialist party, one of the five political parties that had formed the coalition government. Andreotti was able (Apr. 11) to put together another coalition of the same parties, and he became prime minister for the seventh time.

1981 Mar. 31   In the first free election in 68 years, the Communist party of **Albania** won 162 seats in the

250-member parliament. The Democratic party, founded only the previous December, won 75 seats. The inaugural session of the first multiparty parliament broke up (Apr. 15) when the Democrats boycotted the legislature to protest the killing (Apr. 2) of four of its members. The parliament reelected (Apr. 30) as president **Ramiz Alia**, who had headed the Communist party (from 1985). He gave up that post (May 4). A general strike and street demonstrations against the all-Communist cabinet resulted in its resignation (June 4). The next day **Ylli Bufi**, a Communist and an economist, was named prime minister, and parliament approved (June 12) a cabinet only half of whose members were Communists. At the same time the Communist party changed its name to the Socialist party. The Democratic party, which held 7 of the 21 cabinet posts, withdrew (Dec. 4), charging that the dominant Socialists were delaying economic reform measures.

1991 Apr. 3   The **U.N. Security Council voted to lift sanctions**, imposed on **Iraq** as a result of its invasion of Kuwait and the subsequent **Persian Gulf War** (1990–1991), provided that country agreed to a number of conditions: pay compensation to Kuwait for the damage its invasion caused; destroy all chemical and biological weapons; and allow inspection of all facilities for manufacturing weapons of mass destruction with a view to destroying them. Iraq agreed (Apr. 6) to these terms. It admitted (July 8) that it had been operating secret programs to produce enriched uranium that could be used in nuclear bombs, and a report (July 30) by U.N. inspectors said they had found four times as many chemical weapons as Iraq had acknowledged. The U.N. reported (Aug. 18) that Iraq had returned to Kuwait c.$700 million of gold bullion it had looted during the invasion. Inspection of suspected weapons sites by U.N. observers continued with Iraq briefly holding (Sept. 23–28) 44 of them in an attempt that failed to make the observers return documents they had seized.

1991 Apr. 9   The parliament of the republic of **Georgia**, in the southern Soviet Union, **declared its independence** from the U.S.S.R. This action followed a referendum (Mar. 31) in which voters approved a move for independence. In Georgia's first direct presidential election (May 26), the victor was **Zviad Gamsakhurdia** (b. 1939), with 87 percent of the vote.

1991 Apr. 30   **Civil strife in Lebanon**, which for fifteen years had pitted government forces against guerrilla groups, and Christian and Muslim militias

against each other, **began to come to an end** when an agreement for disarmament of the various factions went into effect. The Lebanese army began moving into areas it had previously been unable to control. Lebanon and **Syria**, which maintained 40,000 troops in the country, signed (May 22) a treaty establishing a special relationship between the two countries. They were to cooperate in matters of defense, foreign policy, and the economy. As a result of a general amnesty (Aug. 26) for war crimes, **Michel Aoun**, commander of a Christian militia force that had fought the government until he was forced to take refuge (Oct. 1990) in the French embassy in Beirut, was allowed (Aug. 29) to go into exile in France. The Lebanese police estimated (Mar. 9, 1992) that in the 15 years of civil war, more than 144,000 people had been killed and nearly 200,000 wounded.

1991 May 12   In the first free election since June 1959, the voters of the Asian kingdom of **Nepal** gave 106 seats of the 205-member House of Representatives to the Nepali Congress party, which narrowly nosed out the Communist party. **Krishna Prasad Bhattarai**, the prime minister and leader of the victorious party, resigned because he lost his seat in the house. **Girija Prasad Koirala**, of the Congress party, became (May 29) prime minister. He had been a leader of the movement for the return of democracy (from Apr. 1990).

1991 May 15   **Edith** [Campion] **Cresson** (b. Jan. 27, 1934) became the **first woman prime minister of France** when she was appointed by **François Mitterand**, president, to succeed **Michel Rocard**, who resigned. Cresson, a Socialist like the president, had been a cabinet minister most of the time since 1981.

1991 May 21   In the face of advancing rebel forces, **Mengitsu Haile Mariam**, Marxist president and dictator of **Ethiopia** (from 1977), fled to Zimbabwe. The Mengitsu government had been responsible for the deaths of thousands of Ethiopians. The major rebel groups were the Eritrean People's Liberation Front and the Tigre People's Liberation Front. The former fought to make the province of Eritrea an independent nation and it captured (May 24) Asmara, capital of Eritrea. Addis Ababa, capital of Ethiopia, was taken (May 28) by rebel Tigre forces. That same day a temporary government was formed under the name of the Ethiopian People's Revolutionary Democratic Front, with its leader, **Meles Zenawi**, as its head.

1991 May 21 Rajiv Gandhi (b. Aug. 20, 1944), prime minister of **India** (1984–1989), was killed in a mammoth explosion in Madras, on India's southeastern coast, as he campaigned in a general election. The final two phases of the election were postponed until June 12 and 15. The assassination was blamed on **Tamils**, who hated Gandhi for having sent (1987) Indian troops to the island nation of **Sri Lanka** to help put down a revolt by Tamils. The need for a general election had been triggered (May 6) by the resignation of the government of **Chandra Shekhar**. His minority government fell when the Congress party, led by Gandhi, boycotted parliament, thus withdrawing its support. When the election resumed (June 12), the Congress party won the most seats, 236, but fell short of a majority in the 543-seat parliament. P[amulaparti] V[enkata] **Narasimha Rao** (b. June 28, 1921), of the Congress party, became (June 21) prime minister with the support of other parties.

1991 May 31 After sixteen years of civil war a **peace agreement** was signed by the government of **Angola**, led by **José Eduardo dos Santos**, president and leader of the Popular Movement for the Liberation of Angola [**MPLA**], and **Jonas Savimbi**, leader of the rebel National Union for the Total Independence of Angola [**UNITA**]. The government had dropped (March) its Marxist policies and the formation of new political parties was now permitted.

1991 June 3 France announced it would sign the **Nuclear Nonproliferation Treaty**, which had gone into effect in 1970 and had been agreed to by 139 other nations. Tanzania had promised in the previous week to sign, and Zambia in May. South Africa signed (July 8) and China announced (Aug. 10) that it would also. The U.S. said (Oct. 19) that it would withdraw all nuclear arms from South Korea, leading North Korea to agree (Jan. 30, 1992) to the pact.

1991 June 20 By a vote of 337 to 320 the German parliament voted to move the **seat of government from Bonn** in western Germany 350 miles east **to Berlin**. Berlin had become the capital of the German Empire when the country was first unified (1870). After Germany's defeat in World War II (1939–1945), when the country was divided, East Berlin was the capital of East Germany and Bonn became (1949) West Germany's capital. The two Germany's had been reunited in 1990. The resolution allowed 12 years to complete the move.

1991 June 25 The parliaments of the two northernmost republics of federal **Yugoslavia, Slovenia and Croatia, voted for independence**. The Yugoslavian army, controlled by Serbia, began military action. Both Slovenian and Croatian forces resisted the attacks, and the central government ordered (July 19) its troops to withdraw from Slovenia. **Heavy fighting** continued, however, **between the army and Croatian forces**. Several cease-fire agreements did not hold, though both sides finally accepted (Jan. 1, 1992) a proposal of the United Nations to deploy a peacekeeping force. **Macedonia**, a republic in the southern part of Yugoslavia, voted (Sept. 8) for independence in a referendum, in which about 75 percent of the voters favored such a move.

1991 June 27 The Communist party of **Vietnam** elected a new general secretary, **Do Muoi** (b. Feb. 2, 1917), a long-time party official, who succeeded **Nguyen Van Linh**. Named (Aug. 9) to succeed Do Moi as prime minister was **Vo Van Kiet**, who was seen as a reformer inclined to shift the country from a Marxist regime toward a free market system.

1991 June 30 The two warring political factions of **Liberia**, in northwestern Africa, agreed to cooperate to bring peace to the country, where fighting had been going on since the overthrow (Sept. 10, 1990) of the government of **Samuel K. Doe**. The accord was between the National Patriotic Front, headed by **Charles Taylor**, and the interim government, headed by **Amos Sawyer** as president. The two groups agreed (Sept. 17) on procedures for disarming Taylor's forces, which controlled about 95 percent of the country, while the government held Monrovia, the capital. In the course of the civil war, about half of Liberia's population of 2.5 million had become refugees, fleeing to neighboring countries. A five-nation peacekeeping force from other African countries began (Nov. 16) to regain control of rebel-held territory, and thousands of Liberians began returning home. It was estimated that the war had taken more than 13,000 lives.

1991 July 5 In **Colombia**, in northern South America, a new constitution, replacing that of 1886, which had been the oldest in Latin America, went into effect. It opened the previous two-party system to other political groups, reserved seats in congress for Indians, ended privileges allowed the Roman Catholic Church, and permitted divorce. When the first election under this new constitution took place (Oct. 27), the governing Liberal party retained a small majority in the house and senate.

1991 July 10   Boris N. Yeltsin was inaugurated president of the **Russian Republic**, now for practical purposes independent of the **collapsing U.S.S.R.** In the first free election (June 13) in Russian history, he had won the office with about 60 percent of the vote. He had earlier (May 29, 1990) been chosen president of Russia as part of the Soviet Union, by parliament.

1991 July 31   At a summit meeting in Moscow, **George Bush**, president of the U.S., and **Mikhail S. Gorbachev**, president of the U.S.S.R., signed a **treaty calling for a large reduction in the nuclear arms** of their countries. The treaty required that within seven years the Soviet Union cut its nuclear warheads from 10,841 to 8,040, while the U.S. would make a reduction to 10,395 from its current total of 12,081. Various categories of weapons were included in the cuts.

1991 Aug. 8   The **first of nine hostages**, held by Islamic terrorists in Lebanon, **to be released** between now and December, was freed. He was **John McCarthy**, a British citizen and television journalist, who had been seized on Apr. 17, 1986. **Edward Austin Tracy**, an American who had been held since Oct. 21, 1986, was freed Aug. 11. Other releases followed: Sept. 24, **Jack Mann**, a retired British airline pilot, held since May 12, 1989; Oct. 21, **Jesse Turner**, an American science and mathematics teacher, kidnapped Jan. 24, 1987; Nov. 18, **Terry Waite** (b. May 31, 1939), who had once negotiated for the release of hostages on behalf of the archbishop of Canterbury, seized Jan. 20, 1987; and **Thomas M. Sutherland**, an American, dean of agriculture at the American University in Beirut, held since June 9, 1985; Dec. 2, **Joseph J. Cicippio**, an American and acting controller of the American University, taken Sept. 12, 1986; Dec. 3, **Alan Steen**, an American and an instructor in journalism at Beirut University College, missing since Jan. 24, 1987; and, Dec. 4, **Terry Anderson** (b. Oct. 27, 1947), an American and Middle East correspondent for the Associated Press when taken hostage Mar. 16, 1985. Anderson had been the longest held of all. The only remaining hostages were two Germans, **Thomas Kemptner** and **Heinrich Strübig**. A body found (Dec. 22) on a Beirut street was that of **William S. Higgins**, an American army colonel who was commander of a UN observer force when he was seized (Feb. 17, 1988). His abductors had shown (July 31, 1989) a photograph of a hanged man they said was Higgins. The remains of another American, **William Buckley**, who had been the chief Central Intelligence Agency officer in Lebanon, and

kidnapped (Mar. 16, 1984), were identified on Dec. 27. His captors said they had killed him Oct. 4, 1985.

1991 Aug. 18   Unhappy with the steady drift toward the collapse of the **U.S.S.R.** and with proposed reforms, a **coup by hardline Communist leaders** of the military and of the KGB, the secret police and intelligence agency, seized control of the government and put under house arrest **Mikhail S. Gorbachev**, president of the U.S.S.R., at his summer vacation home in the Crimea. The leaders of the coup were **Gennadi Ivanovic Yanayev** (b. 1937), the vice president, who said he was assuming the presidency; **Vladimir A. Kryuchkov** (b. Feb. 29, 1924), chairman of the KGB; **Dmitri T. Yazov** (b. 1923), minister of defense; and **Boris Karlovich Pugo**, minister of internal affairs. They announced they were forming a State Committee for the State of Emergency and banned protest meetings, closed independent newspapers, and moved troops and tanks into Moscow. Thousands of people defied the ban on meetings, while soldiers seemed reluctant to support the coup. Most of all, **Boris N. Yeltsin**, president of the Russian republic, openly defied the coup with his own forces. In the face of almost total resistance, the coup leaders lost their nerve and the **revolt collapsed** abruptly (Aug. 21) as Gorbachev returned to Moscow. One of the coup leaders, Pugo, committed suicide, and the others were arrested. Gorbachev resigned (Aug. 24) as head of the Communist party and banned the party from any further role in the rule of the nation. Yeltsin had now surpassed Gorbachev in authority, and the liberal forces which had defied the coup held the upper hand. For practical purposes the Communist party, which had ruled with an iron hand for seventy years, ceased to exist. Gorbachev tried, without success, to reach agreements with the breakaway republics that would salvage some sort of Soviet Union. The Russian republic took over (Dec. 24) the permanent seat on the U.N. Security Council. **Gorbachev resigned** (Dec. 25) **as president of the U.S.S.R.**, in effect putting an **end to the Soviet Union**.

1991 Aug. 25   The collapse of a coup attempt (Aug. 19–21) by Communist hardliners to overthrow **Mikhail S. Gorbachev**, president of the U.S.S.R., and the subsequent disruption of the central government of the Soviet Union, led to further and final **secessionist action by some of the constituent republics**: Ukraine (Aug. 24), **Byelorussia** (Aug. 25), **Moldavia** (Aug. 27), **Azerbaijan** (Aug. 30), **Uzbekistan** and **Kirghizia** (Aug. 31), and **Turkmenia** (Oct. 27).

1991 Aug. 28 **Gnassingbé Eyadéma**, president and dictator (from 1967) of the western African nation of **Togo**, agreed to surrender power to **Joseph Koffigoh** (b. 1948) as prime minister after the latter was selected by a national conference of political leaders. Violence broke out (Nov. 28) when troops loyal to Eyadéma laid siege of the palace of the prime minister. Koffigoh was seized (Dec. 3) by the military and agreed (Dec. 31) to expand the cabinet to include three members of Eyadéma's party.

1991 Aug. 31 In a general election in the city-state of **Singapore**, in southeast Asia, the People's Action party [PAP], led by **Goh Chok Tong**, the prime minister (from Nov. 28, 1990), won 77 of the 81 seats in parliament. Nevertheless, Goh was disappointed because his party's share of the vote was down slightly from the 1988 election. He had relaxed some rules, such as those concerning censorship, but now indicated he might become more paternalistic and authoritarian.

1991 Sept. 15 The Social Democratic party of **Sweden**, which had ruled the country for all but 6 of the last 59 years, was defeated in a general election for the **Riksdag** [parliament]. The party won 138 seats, a loss of 18, in the 349-seat legislature. With their allies they won 154 seats to 195 for the five non-Socialist parties. **Ingvar Carlsson**, prime minister (from 1986), resigned and was succeeded (Oct. 3) by **Carl Bildt** (b. July 15, 1949) of the Moderate party, which formed a four-party coalition. Sweden was noted as the original welfare state, but voters came to look with disfavor on high taxes and bureaucratic inefficiency.

1991 Sept. 15 The first direct legislative election ever held in **Hong Kong**, the British colony in Asia that was to revert (1997) to Chinese control, resulted in an almost complete victory for the United Democrats, who won 16 of the 18 seats at stake. The party stood for more democracy in the colony. Those elected became part of a 60-seat Legislative Council, of which all the other members were appointed by the governor or elected indirectly. It was expected they would represent mostly conservative business interests.

1991 Sept. 17 Seven nations were elected to membership in the **United Nations**, making a total of 166. The new members were: Estonia, Latvia, Lithuania, the Marshall Islands, Micronesia, North Korea, and South Korea.

1991 Sept. 19 The **U.N. Security Council agreed to ease the complete trade embargo on Iraq**, in effect since the **Persian Gulf War** (1990–1991), to the extent of allowing the sale during the next six months of $1.6 billion worth of oil. The money received would be paid to the U.N., which would use a third of it to compensate victims of Iraq's invasion (Aug. 2, 1990) of Kuwait. The remainder would be used to purchase food and other essential supplies for Iraq's civilian population. Iraq refused to accept the terms imposed, and later (Jan. 5, 1992) said acceptance would "severely undermine Iraq's sovereignty as a free country."

1991 Sept. 27 **George Bush**, president of the U.S., announced the **elimination of all tactical nuclear weapons** on land and on navy ships in Europe and Asia. In addition, long-range bombers would no longer be on twenty-four-hour alert status. Pending negotiations with the U.S.S.R., long-range nuclear weapons on land, submarines, and bombers would be retained, but intercontinental ballistic missiles [ICBMs] would be taken off alert status at once. **Mikhail S. Gorbachev**, president of the U.S.S.R., announced (Oct. 5) much the same reduction of nuclear weaponry. In addition, he said, the number of Soviet strategic warheads would be reduced to 5,000 within seven years, rather than the 8,000 called for by the recent (July 31) treaty.

1991 Sept. 29 **Mobutu Sese Seko**, president and dictator (from Nov. 24, 1965) of **Zaire**, following a week of rioting and looting by unpaid soldiers that left more than 100 persons dead, agreed to share power with a new prime minister. In the next two months he named four prime ministers, but rioting continued. Mobutu proclaimed (Dec. 5) that, although his seven-year term as president had just ended, he would remain in office until new elections were held. No date for them was set.

1991 Sept. 30 A military mutiny in **Haiti** ousted **Jean-Bertrand Aristide** (b. July 15, 1953), president (from Feb. 7) and forced him to go to Venezuela. The U.S. suspended (Oct. 1) economic assistance to Haiti and refused to recognize the military junta. The Organization of American States [OAS] agreed (Oct. 2) to begin a diplomatic campaign to restore Aristide to office. The Haitian National Assembly named (Oct. 8) **Joseph Nerette**, a justice of the supreme court, to be provisional president. With negotiations for Aristide's return stalled, the U.S. imposed (Oct. 29) a ban on all trade with Haiti. After further negotiations,

Aristide accepted (Dec. 22) as a condition of his return the appointment of **Rene Theodore**, a Communist of moderate political views, as prime minister. It was expected that this step would eventually enable Aristide to return from exile. A Roman Catholic priest with leftist ideological leanings, Aristide had been elected (Dec. 6, 1990) president in the first fully free election since the overthrow (1986) of the longtime (1957–1986) dictator François Duvalier.

1991 Oct. 4 Meeting in Madrid, Spain, 24 countries, including the U.S., signed an **agreement banning mineral and oil exploration in Antarctica** for 50 years. The agreement constituted an addition to the Antarctic Treaty (drafted 1959; in effect 1961), which had 26 full member nation signatories, two-thirds of whom would have to agree to an end to the ban.

1991 Oct. 6 A parliamentary election in **Portugal** gave the government of **Anibal Cavaco Silva**, prime minister (from 1985), 50.4 percent of the vote, assuring his right-of-center Social Democrats a 20-seat majority in the 230-seat Legislative Assembly. The Socialist party ran second with 29.3 percent of the ballots.

1991 Oct. 13 Bulgaria's 1 million **Muslim Turks** played a key role in an election for seats in the 240-seat parliament when their party, the Movement for Rights and Freedom, won 24 seats. The Union of Democratic Forces [UDF], in opposition to the Bulgarian Socialist party, formerly the Communist party, took 110 seats to the latter's 106. The UDF thus had to depend unwillingly on the support of the ethnic Turks, whose relationship with the majority Bulgarians was one of mutual suspicion.

1991 Oct. 14 **Daw Aung San Suu Kyi**, leader of the opposition to the right-wing military government of **Myanmar** [formerly Burma] and who had been under house arrest (from July 1989), was awarded the **Nobel Peace Prize** for 1991. The daughter of **U Aung San**, regarded as the founder of independent Burma and who was assassinated (1947), Daw had led the National League of Democracy (from 1988). Although her party won 392 of 485 seats in parliament in an election (May 1990), the military, ruling as the State Law and Order Restoration Council [Slorc], refused to surrender power.

1991 Oct. 20 The True Path party of **Turkey** upset the ruling Motherland party in a parliamentary election, winning 180 seats in the 450-seat legislature. The Motherland party took 113 and the Social Democratic Populist party 88. As a result **Suleyman Demirel**, leader of the True Path party, became prime minister for the seventh time by arranging a coalition with the Social Democrats.

1991 Oct. 23 Under the auspices of China, the U.S.S.R., and the U.S., the **Cambodian government**, controlled by Vietnam, and three rebel factions **signed an agreement** in Paris **aimed at ending the wars** and factional fighting that had devastated the Southeast Asian country for twenty-three years. The three rebel factions were the **Khmer Rouge**, which had seized power (1975) and had caused 1 million deaths before being ousted (1978) by the Vietnam army; the **Khmer People's National Liberation Front**, a conservative group; and a faction headed by **Norodom Sihanouk**, king (1941–1955) and prime minister (1955–1970). Under the agreement a cease-fire was to become effective at once. The U.N. would take over the administrative work of the government and arrange for free elections by early 1993.

1991 Oct. 27 With about 100 different political parties contesting for seats in the 460-seat **Polish parliament**, no party received more than 12.2 percent of the vote in the first completely free election since World War II (1939–1945). The result was taken to indicate that many voters wanted the pace of economic reform slowed. The Democratic Union, organized by some who had taken part in the defeat (1989) of communism, won 51 seats, and coming in second, with 50 seats, was the ex-Communist party, renamed the Democratic Left Alliance. **Lech Walesa**, president, appointed (Dec. 6) as prime minister **Jan Olszewski** (b. Aug. 20, 1930), who succeeded **Jan Krzysztof Bielecki**. Olszewski came from the center-right group of parties and was a critic of the current free market program. By a narrow margin his cabinet was accepted (Dec. 23) by parliament.

1991 Oct. 30 Israel and the Arab nations that border it met face to face for the first time to attempt to reach an overall peace settlement for the Middle East. The meeting was held in Madrid, Spain, with **Mikhail S. Gorbachev**, president of the U.S.S.R., and **George Bush**, president of the U.S., as co-sponsors. The Arab nations present were Jordan, Lebanon, and Syria, together with a delegation representing the Palestinians. The first direct talks between Israel and individual Arab nations took place on Nov. 3.

Further sessions in Washington, D.C., ended (Dec. 18) after ten days of futile discussions of agendas and procedures.

1991 Nov. 2 **Frederick** [Jacob Titus] **Chiluba** (b. Apr. 30, 1943), a labor leader, was inaugurated president of **Zambia** in south-central Africa, having won (Oct. 31) the first free presidential election in twenty-seven years with c.85 percent of the vote. He had defeated **Kenneth D. Kaunda**, who had been president since Zambia achieved (1964) independence from Great Britain and had ruled (from 1972) a one-party state.

1991 Nov. 6 **Kiichi Miyazawa** (b. Oct. 8, 1919), who had at various times held all the most important cabinet posts, became prime minister of **Japan**, succeeding **Toshiki Kaifu**, who had sought a second term but had been turned down by the leadership of the Liberal Democratic party, the conservative political organization that had ruled Japan for 36 years.

1991 Nov. 24 Though the governing coalition of Christian Democrats and Socialists retained a majority in an election for the lower house of the legislature in **Belgium**, it lost 14 of its 134 seats. The election results showed that voters were much concerned about the environment, immigration, and law and order, as the Greens, environmentalists, and libertarians gained 16 seats. After protracted negotiations the same coalition agreed (Mar. 7, 1992) on **Jean-Luc Dehaene** (b. Aug. 7, 1940), a Flemish Christian Democrat, as prime minister.

1991 Nov. 27 **Great Britain and the U.S. demanded of Libya** that it turn over to them two intelligence agents they said were responsible for the bombing (Dec. 21, 1988) of **Pan Am flight 103** over Scotland that killed 270 people. The U.S. had indicted (Nov. 14) the pair, **Lamen Khalifa Fhimah** and **Abdel Basset Ali al-Megrahi**. Libya refused to give up the men, but a judge there said (Dec. 8) that he had ordered them put under house arrest.

1991 Dec. The **Canadian government agreed to grant political rule over 770,000 sq. mi.**, about one-fifth of its total territory, **to the** 17,500 **Inuit** [Eskimos] who inhabit the region to be carved out of the Northwest Territories, which extends north beyond the Arctic Circle. In addition the government would pay to the Inuit more than $1 billion over 14 years. The new political subdivision was to be called **Nunavut**, "our land" in Inuit. The inhabitants of the area

by a 54 percent majority approved (May 4, 1992) the plan. It was expected that by 1997 Nunavut would be officially a territory and would have its own elected government.

1991 Dec. 3 After having been unanimously recommended by the **U.N.** Security Council, **Boutros Boutros-Ghali** (b. Nov. 14, 1922), deputy prime minister of Egypt for foreign affairs, was elected by the General Assembly to be the sixth secretary general of the world organization for a five-year term beginning Jan. 1, 1992. He succeeded **Javier Peréz de Cuéllar** and would be the first Arab and the first person from Africa to hold the post.

1991 Dec. 5 Having won (Dec. 1) 61.5 percent of the vote in an election, **Leonid N. Kravchuk** (b. Jan. 10, 1934) was sworn in as president of **Ukraine**. A former Communist party official, he had recently changed his politics and now promised to carry out radical economic reform. In the election the voters had also by a large margin approved independence for this large and basically wealthy section of the western Soviet Union.

1991 Dec. 11 Meeting in Maastricht, the Netherlands, the 12-member **European Community** [EC] agreed on a treaty to bring about closer political and economic unity, including common foreign and defense policies, and a common currency and central bank by 1999. The only dissent came from Great Britain, which insisted and was granted the right to decide which measures it would adopt.

1991 Dec. 13 **North and South Korea** signed in Seoul, South Korea, a **treaty of reconciliation and nonaggression**, renouncing the use of armed force against each other and promising to bring a **formal end to the Korean War** (1950–1953).

1991 Dec. 16 The General Assembly of the **U.N. voted to revoke a resolution** of Nov. 10, 1975, which stated that **"Zionism is a form of racism and racial discrimination."** The vote was 111 nations in favor of revoking, 25 opposed, with 30 countries not voting. The original resolution, coming during the Cold War (c.1945–c.1985), had pitted the U.S.S.R. and Arab nations against the U.S., Israel, and their allies.

1991 Dec. 17 **Patrick Manning** (b. Aug. 17, 1946), a geologist and former cabinet minister, was elected prime minister of **Trinidad and Tobago**, an island nation in the Caribbean Sea, when his People's National Movement won 21 of 36 seats in a parliamentary election. Defeated was the government of **A.N.R. Robinson** and his National Alliance for Reconstruction, which had ruled (from 1986), but in this election lost all except two of its 33 seats. The outgoing government had aroused voter hostility by its program of economic austerity that followed rules laid down by the **International Monetary Fund** [IMF].

1991 Dec. 19 **Robert Hawke**, prime minister (from 1983) of **Australia**, was removed from his post by a 56–51 vote of the Labor party members of Parliament. It was the first time in Australia's history that a prime minister had been forced from office by his own party. He was succeeded (Dec. 20) as prime minister and leader of the party by **Paul Keating** (b. Jan. 18, 1944), who had been treasury minister (from 1983) until he resigned (June) when a first attempt to oust Hawke failed.

1991 Dec. 21 Eleven of the 15 republics of the fast disappearing U.S.S.R., meeting in Alma-Ata, Kazakhstan, constituted themselves the **Commonwealth of Independent States** [CIS] in a move intended to bring political and economic order out of the confusion resulting from the **continuing breaking up of the Soviet Union**. The 11 states were: Armenia, Azerbaijan, Belarus [former Byelorussia] Kazakhstan, Kyrgyzstan [formerly Kirghizia], Moldova [formerly Moldavia], Russia, Tajikistan [formerly Tadzhikistan], Turkmenistan [formerly Turkmenia], Ukraine, and Uzbekistan. Of the other four former Soviet republics, the three Baltic states [Estonia, Latvia, and Lithuania] were already separately independent, and Georgia did not choose to join the CIS.

1991 Dec. 21 In the first full election since the government of **Taiwan** was established (1949) by the Kuomintang [Nationalists] fleeing from China after their defeat by the Communists, the ruling Nationalist party won 254 seats in the 325-seat National Assembly to 66 for the main opposition group, the Democratic Progressive party. The path to more democracy was further eased when an end to 43 years of emergency rule was declared on Apr. 30

1991 Dec. 25 The **Union of Soviet Socialist Republics** [U.S.S.R.] (from 1922) **formally ceased to exist** when **Mikhail Gorbachev**, president of U.S.S.R. (from Oct. 1, 1988), resigned and the flag of Russia was raised over the Kremlin.

1991 Dec. 26 The Islamic Front, a party of Muslim fundamentalists, won the first round of a parliamentary election in **Algeria**, earning 189 seats in the 430-member legislature to only 16 for the ruling National Liberation Front. The Front for Socialist Forces, a secularist party, took 20 seats. There were to be runoff elections (Jan. 15, 1992) for those seats in which no candidate had won a majority of the votes, and it seemed certain that the Islamic Front would easily win enough more seats to reach a majority. Alarmed by this turn of events, army commanders forced **Chadli Benjedid** (b. Apr. 14, 1929), president (from 1978), to resign on Jan. 11, 1992. A Constitutional Council named **Sid Ahmed Ghozali** (b. Mar. 31, 1937), prime minister (from June 1991), to administer the country's affairs. The **government nullified the results of the Dec. 26 election** and cancelled (Jan. 12, 1992) any further balloting.

1991 Dec. 27 The **Philippine government ordered the U.S. to withdraw from its Subic Bay** naval base, 50 miles west of Manila, by the end of 1992, thus ending an American military presence that began when the U.S. took the islands from Spain in the Spanish-American War (1898).

IV. ECONOMY AND TRADE

1991 Jan. 1 The nations of **Eastern Europe**, freed from Communist control, **took steps toward free market economies**. Among such moves, Czechoslovakia lifted (Jan. 1) price controls on most goods in retail stores and within a month they had almost doubled. In Romania, when government control and subsidization of food prices ended (Apr. 1) after 40 years, staples doubled in price. Poland received (Mar. 15) much needed relief when Western governments agreed to forgive half the $33 billion owed them. The Polish government announced (June 27) that it would transfer 25 percent of all state-owned industry to private ownership and that every adult citizen would receive some of the proceeds. In the Russian republic, land reform began (Dec. 28) with the issuance of an order that would give collective farm workers the right to buy and sell plots of land. Prices of most goods were to be freed (Jan. 1, 1992), but bread and other staples remained under control (to Mar. 7).

1991 Mar. 26 The presidents of four South American nations—Argentina, Brazil, Paraguay, and Uruguay—meeting in Asunción, Paraguay, signed an agreement establishing the **Southern Cone Common**

Market, stating that by Dec. 31, 1994, they would have a common tariff and free movement of goods among themselves. If successful the result would be a unified market of 190 million people.

1991 Apr. 16 For the first time since the outbreak of World War II (1939–1945), a **stock market opened in Warsaw**, Poland. Shares in only five concerns, recently privatized after having been run by the previous Communist government, were available for trading.

1991 May 6 In a deal valued at $7.4 billion, the **American Telephone and Telegraph Co. [AT&T]**, the largest telephone operation in the U.S., **acquired the NCR Corp.**, the fifth largest computer manufacturer in the country. AT&T, which had been losing money on its own computer operations, hoped the merger would enable it to counter its competition.

1991 June 20 **Isaac Wolfson** (b. Sept. 17, 1897), a British businessman and philanthropist, who controlled **Great Universal Stores**, the largest retail mail order house in Europe, and operator of 2,200 shops in Great Britain, died. He first went to work in the early 1930s for the company he later acquired and built up. He established (1955) the Wolfson Foundation, which was active in aiding young people and in health education, as well as establishing new colleges at both Oxford and Cambridge universities.

1991 June 28 The **Council for Mutual Economic Assistance [Comecon]**, established (1949) on the initiative of the U.S.S.R. to bind its satellite nations closer to it, **went out of business** when its member nations signed an agreement to take effect on Sept. 26. The nations besides the Soviet Union were Bulgaria, Cuba, Czechoslovakia, Hungary, Mongolia, Poland, Romania, and Vietnam. The end of Comecon was the result of the fall (1989) of the Communist governments of Eastern Europe and the continuing disintegration of the Soviet Union.

1991 July 5 Banking regulators in Great Britain, the U.S., and five other nations seized control of the **Bank of Credit and Commerce International**, which had been founded (1972) by a Pakistani financier, **Aga Hassan Abedi**, but was controlled by the emir of the Middle Eastern emirate of Abu Dhabi and other officials there. The bank, which operated in 69 countries, supposedly had assets of $20 billion, but investigation revealed it was bankrupt as a result of false accounting and fictitious loans. The bank had also

been involved in handling funds for drug dealers and in laundering drug money. The bank pleaded guilty (Dec. 19) to criminal charges in the U.S. and was ordered to pay a $550 million penalty, half of which would go to aid the financial situation of two American banks, the ownership of which it had acquired secretly. The government of Abu Dhabi agreed (Feb. 21, 1992) to pay up to $2 billion to creditors of the bank, but this meant they would receive only 30 to 40 cents on the dollar.

1991 July 15 The first of three **mergers** that **created the second, third, and fourth largest banks in the U.S.** took place when **Chemical Bank and Manufacturers Hanover Trust**, both of New York City, said they would combine to form the third largest banking institution with assets of $139,000,000,000. The second largest was created (Aug. 15) by the merger of **Bank America Corp. and Security Pacific Corp.**, both of California, with assets of $190,000,000,000. The fourth largest stemmed from approval given (Nov. 20) to the merger of **NCNB Corp.** of North Carolina and **C&S/Sovran Corp.** of Georgia with assets of $115,000,000,000. Citicorp remained the largest U.S. bank with assets of $216,000,000,000.

1991 Aug. 5 **Soichiro Honda** (b. Nov. 17, 1906), a pioneer Japanese auto manufacturer, whose products bearing his name became very popular in the U.S., died. The son of a blacksmith, Honda began a motorcycle manufacturing company after World War II (1939–1945) and added (1957) auto making, becoming a strong competitor of the **Toyota** and **Nissan** auto enterprises. **Honda** was the first Japanese auto maker to build factories in the U.S.

1991 Sept. 25 The **Organization of Petroleum Exporting Countries [OPEC]** agreed to raise its total daily output by somewhat more than 1 million barrels a day to a total of 23.6 million barrels. It was hoped this move would hold oil prices at the present level of about $19 a barrel. In this matter Saudi Arabia, by far the largest producer, had its way, saying it wanted to encourage the recovery of the world economy by keeping oil prices moderate. Earlier (Mar. 12) in the year, when the price of oil had fallen to below $18 a barrel, OPEC cut production by about a million barrels a day.

1991 Oct. 22 The **largest trading bloc in the world** was created by an agreement signed in Paris between the twelve-member **European Community [EC]** and the seven-member **European Free Trade**

Association [EFTA]. At this time, the members of the latter group were Austria, Finland, Iceland, Liechtenstein, Norway, Sweden, and Switzerland, Great Britain, Denmark, and Portugal having left earlier to join the EC. The new common market would be known as the **European Economic Area [EEA]** and would have a population of 380 million, accounting for 46 percent of the world's trade. Sweden and Austria had already applied for membership in the EC and others were expected to follow.

1991 Nov. 5   Robert Maxwell [orig. Ludvik Hoch] (b. June 10, 1923), head of a British communications conglomerate with worldwide interests, died when he fell, jumped, or was pushed from his yacht as it cruised off the Canary Islands. An autopsy report (Dec. 11) indicated he had died of a heart attack rather than drowning, but did not say how he got into the water. Lloyd's of London, a British insurer that had a $36 million accident insurance policy on Maxwell, said (Feb. 21, 1992) that it would not pay because its investigators believed he had killed himself. Maxwell's death revealed that his multibillion dollar publishing empire was bankrupt. Maxwell's two sons and heirs filed (Dec. 5) for bankruptcy for two of the family's private companies, and the flagship company, **Maxwell Communications Corporation**, followed suit (Dec. 16). The bankruptcy filings indicated that creditors might lose as much as $1.6 billion.

1991 Dec. 18   The General Motors Corp. [GM], the largest automobile manufacturer in the U.S., announced that over the next few years it would close 21 of its 125 assembly and parts-making plants in North America and eliminate 70,000 jobs, representing nearly 18 percent of its employees in the U.S. and Canada. GM said these steps would save it $2 billion in 1992 and $5 billion a year by 1995. **International Business Machines** [IBM], the world's largest maker of computers, announced (Nov. 26) that it was reorganizing as a federation of smaller units that would make it quicker in reacting to its competition. In the process IBM would reduce its work force by 20,000.

1991 Dec. 31   In spite of a **continuing recession in the U.S.**, the **Dow Jones industrial average** ended the year on the New York Stock Exchange by setting a new all-time high, 3,168.83, 20 percent above the Jan. 1 average. The need for economic stimulation was indicated when the U.S. Federal Reserve cut (Dec. 20) its discount rate to banks to 3.5 percent, the

lowest in twenty-seven years, and the Bank of Japan followed by cutting its rate to 4.5 percent. Showing that poor economic conditions were worldwide was the sluggish growth of only 1.4 percent in the economies of the ten most highly developed industrial nations. The developing countries did better, averaging growth of 3.5 percent, with China leading the way at 5.5 percent. In Eastern Europe and the Soviet Union, however, output declined sharply by 9.5 percent.

V. RELIGION AND PHILOSOPHY

1991 Jan. 22   In the first papal encyclical concerning missionary activity since 1959, **Pope John Paul II** urged all of his faith to evangelize around the world, even in Islamic countries, where such activity is against the law. The encyclical was entitled *Redemptoris Missio* [*The Church's Missionary Mandate*]. The pope noted that the number of non-Christians in the world was increasing, and Vatican officials said the pope was responding to the growth of Islam and the spread of Protestant fundamentalism.

1991 Feb. 5   Pedro Arrupe (b. Nov. 14, 1907), a Basque-born Roman Catholic clergyman, who was the superior general (1965–1983) of the Society of Jesus [Jesuits], died. Arrupe was often at odds with the popes who found his leadership too independent of the Vatican and too liberal. He was rebuked by both **Paul VI** and **John Paul II**. When he resigned (1983) he was the first superior general not to die in office.

1991 Feb. 17   The **World Council of Churches**, meeting in Canberra, Australia, admitted the **China Christian Council**, bringing to 317 the number of member churches from more than 100 countries, and representing nearly all the Protestant and Orthodox denominations, except the Adventists and the Salvation Army.

1991 Mar. 25   Marcel [François] **LeFebvre** (b. Nov. 29, 1905), a French archbishop of the Roman Catholic Church, who was excommunicated (June 1988) in the first schism in the church (since 1870), died. He had defied the pope by consecrating four bishops to aid him in his struggle to force a return to the Latin mass and other practices that had been rejected or modified by the ecumenical conference, **Vatican II** (1962–1965). At his death there were about 300 priests who had been ordained in his order, the Fraternity of St. Pius X.

1991 May 2 Although praising capitalism in an encyclical, *Centesimus Annus* [*The Hundredth Year*], **Pope John Paul II** warned that it needed to cure injustices in the system. The pope used the fall (1989–1990) of communism in Eastern Europe as a background for stating that if a market economy was to replace communism, it must be based on an "ethical and religious" approach to human freedom. The encyclical marked the 100th anniversary of one issued by **Leo XIII** concerning economic conditions.

1991 May 29 **Pope John Paul II announced the appointment of 23 cardinals of the Roman Catholic Church**, including a Chinese archbishop who had spent 30 years in prison and who had been named (1979) secretly. Fifteen countries were represented, with eight Italians and two Americans among the appointees.

1991 Oct. 2 **Dimitrios I** (b. Sept. 8, 1914), the ecumenical patriarch (from 1972) of the Eastern Orthodox Church, died. Somewhat more liberal than the church he headed, he was the 269th successor to St. Andrew, the apostle to whom Orthodox Christians trace their roots. Metropolitan Dimitrios Archontonis (b. 1940) of Chalcedon was elected (Oct. 22) to succeed him as Patriarch **Bartholomew I**.

1991 Dec. 21 **Changes in the Mexican constitution** were adopted that for the first time since the constitution of 1917, drawn up after the Mexican Revolution (1910–1915), would grant legal recognition to religious institutions and allow parochial education. The change applied to all faiths and denominations, but it was intended mostly to end the conflict between the state and the Roman Catholic Church, to which an estimated 91 percent of the population belonged in spite of the ban. Clergymen could now vote, but they would also pay income tax, while convents and monasteries, already existing in defiance of the law, were formally recognized.

VI. SCIENCE, EDUCATION, AND TECHNOLOGY

1991 Jan. 11 **Carl D**[avid] **Anderson** (b. Sept. 3, 1905), an American physicist who discovered (1932) the positron, also known as the positive electron, a tiny part of the atom, died. The discovery grew out of his studies of cosmic rays, using apparatus he designed and constructed. Anderson was co-winner (1936) of the **Nobel prize for physics** for his work.

1991 Jan. 30 **John Bardeen** (b. May 23, 1908), an American physicist, co-inventor (1947) of the transistor that made modern electronics possible, died. The transistor, on a silicon chip, was first used (1952) in telephone switching equipment. Because it eliminated the need for vacuum tubes, the miniaturization of electronic elements became possible. Bardeen later developed a theory of low-temperature superconductivity. As a result he became the first person to receive (1956, 1972) the **Nobel prize twice in the same field**, in this case **physics**.

1991 Feb. 16 Researchers in London reported they had found a tiny mutation in a single gene that can cause **Alzheimer's disease**, a progressive neurological illness. The discovery ended a debate as to whether a substance that accumulates in the brains of those with Alzheimer's is a cause or a byproduct. It now appeared that the defect found in the gene caused cells to produce the substance, amyloid protein. The finding left unresolved the question of whether the disease is always inherited and whether there are other genes that can cause Alzheimer's.

1991 Feb. 21 The **U.S. Food and Drug Administration** [FDA] **approved** for use the **first of a new type of genetically engineered drugs** for fighting infections that often affect cancer patients undergoing chemotherapy. It was hoped the drug, **granulocyte colony stimulating factor** [G-CSF], might later be an effective treatment for various infections.

1991 Mar. 11 **Edwin H**[erbert] **Land** (b. May 7, 1909), an American inventor who was the first to devise **instant photography**, died. His original **Polaroid** Land Camera appeared in 1948, developing black and white photos as soon as they were taken. An instant color photography system went on sale in 1963.

1991 Apr. 7 The 17-ton, $600 million **Gamma Ray Observatory** was launched into orbit from the U.S. space shuttle *Atlantis* to begin studying emissions that result from violent explosions in outer space when stars collapse and matter and antimatter collide. In some cases these gamma rays are the only source of information about such events. When the observatory was first launched, an antenna did not extend itself properly and two astronauts had to take a spacewalk to free it.

1991 May 14 The **United Nations Educational, Scientific, and Cultural Organization** [UNESCO] reported that for the first time in recent years the number of **illiterate people** in the world declined. In 1990 there were 948 million illiterates compared with a 1985 estimate of 950 million. Illiterate people make up 26.6 percent of the world's population.

1991 May 14   Archaeologists reported the discovery of the **tomb** and remains **of an eighth-century Mayan ruler** who, they believed, began a policy of militarism and territorial expansion that eventually doomed **Mayan civilization**. The elaborate tomb was found deep within a pyramid at Dos Pilas, the capital of the ancient Petexbatun area of northern Guatemala. Known so far only as Ruler 2, this monarch reigned between 698 and 725. The discovery and other finds, such as fortifications, led some scholars to believe the Mayans to have been more warlike than hitherto pictured.

1991 May 18   **Helen Sharman** became the first Briton in space when she was launched into orbit for an eight-day mission with two Russian cosmonauts aboard a *Soyuz TM-12.* The craft was to rendezvous with the orbiting space station *Mir.* After having won a contest in Great Britain, Sharman had spent two years in training in Russia.

1991 May 25   **Larry Heinsohn**, the first person to receive (May 9) a transplant of a **fully portable heart pump**, died in a Houston, Texas, hospital. The heart pump, connected to a battery pack that could be slung over the shoulder, was not intended to be permanent. Though the device worked well, death was caused by the failure of several organs, including the liver and kidneys.

1991 May 31   The French Supreme Court, saying that **surrogate motherhood** violated a woman's body and undermined the process of adoption, outlawed the practice. The case involved a woman who had agreed to be artificially inseminated and to turn the baby over to the biological father and his wife, who was infertile. She carried out the agreement, and the court did not order the couple to return the baby to her.

1991 June 17   With the rate of **AIDS** infection slowing in the industrialized countries, but growing in developing nations, the **World Health Organization** [WHO] predicted that by the year 2000 40 million people would be carrying the HIV virus that causes AIDS. Of the 8 to 10 million people currently infected, WHO said, most live in third world countries,

and by 2000 90 percent will be found there. About half a million children already have AIDS by transmission from their mothers during pregnancy, and by 2000 c.10 million children would be orphaned.

1991 July 3   Great Britain became the third country to approve the sale of the **abortion pill known as RU 486**, which had been devised (1988) and used in France. China was the other country to permit its use. In Britain it was to be available only in state-run hospitals that perform abortions under controlled circumstances, and would be used to abort fetuses up to the ninth week of pregnancy.

1991 Sept. 19   Mountain climbers in the Austrian Alps, near the Italian border, found in a glacier the **frozen corpse of a man that** scientists established (Feb. 21, 1992) had lived 5,000 to **5,500 years ago**. This meant the body dated from the late Stone Age. He wore clothing of fur and leather and had a kind of wooden backpack. His possessions included a fire flint, a stone necklace, and an axe made of copper, which helped confirm the dating, because if the body had been more recent, as was first thought, the axe would have been made of bronze.

1991 Nov. 1   Archaeologists and explorers, aided by ancient maps and aerial surveys by satellites in space, discovered in southern Oman on the Arabian Peninsula what they believed to be the **long-lost city of Ubar**, which had been the center of trade in frankincense, the highly valued gum resin used chiefly as incense. Early excavations at the site uncovered eight towers and deposits of artifacts dating as far back as 2,000 B.C. and perhaps earlier. In its day Ubar was noted for its architecture, its fruit trees, and its great wealth. Its destruction and disappearance from history resulted apparently from its location: It was built over a very large limestone cavern which collapsed, carrying down many of the buildings, and the site was eventually covered with drifting sand.

1991 Nov. 9   Scientists for the first time produced a significant amount of power from **controlled nuclear fusion** in an experiment at the Joint European Torus [JET] reactor in Oxfordshire, England. The reactor produced between 1.5 million and 2 million watts in a pulse lasting two seconds.

1991 Dec. 12   An international team of archaeologists announced the discovery in the lower Amazon River basin of northwestern Brazil of the **oldest pot-**

tery yet found in the **Western Hemisphere**. The fragments, some of them decorated with painted patterns, were probably 7,000 to 8,000 years old, which made this pottery c.1,000 years older than any previously discovered in the Americas.

VII. ARTS AND LEISURE

1991 Jan. 17 Giacomo Manzù (b. Dec. 22, 1908), a leading Italian sculptor, died. His work, which ranged from portrait busts to monumental bronze doors, often reflected religious, allegorical, or sexual themes. Most notable were the doors (commissioned 1950) he designed for **St. Peter's Basilica** in Vatican City. In the U.S. he later did two reliefs for the **Palazzo d'Italia** in Rockefeller Center, and a statue of a woman holding a child at the United Nations, also in New York City.

1991 Feb. 21 Margot Fonteyn [née Margaret Hookham] (b. May 18, 1919), a British dancer generally considered the prima ballerina of the century, died. Making her debut in 1934, she became the leading dancer of the Royal Ballet. Fonteyn was especially noted for her performances in ballets created for her by **Frederick Ashton** and by her partnership with the dancer **Rudolph Nureyev** in the 1960s and 1970s.

1991 Feb. 24   An exhibit that recreated in large part the show (1937) in Munich, Germany, which its Nazi sponsors termed "Entartete Kunst," or "Degenerate Art," opened at the Los Angeles County Museum of Art. It included 175 of the works that had been in the Munich show. Among the artists considered degenerate were **Marc Chagall**, **Oskar Kokoschka**, and **Wassily Kandinsky**. The intent of the Nazis was to flaunt their belief that modernism was pornographic and subversive.

1991 Mar. 11 Elie Siegmeister (b. Jan. 15, 1909), an American composer, died. *American Holiday* (1933) was an early example of his use of American songs in symphonic form. Major influences on Siegmeister were jazz, blues, and the composers **Aaron Copland** and **Charles Ives**. He wrote a number of operas, including *The Mermaid in Lock No. 7* (1958) and six symphonies (1947–1983).

1991 Apr. 1 Martha Graham (b. May 11, 1894), an American dancer and choreographer who revolutionized dance and invented for it a new and codified language, died. In her career Graham choreo-

graphed more than 180 works, the first being *Heretic* (1926) and the last *Maple Leaf Rag* (1991). Several of her ballets explored themes from mythology, as *Clytemnestra* (1958), while a number were based on American themes, as *Appalachian Spring* (1944).

1991 Apr. 3 Graham Greene (b. Oct. 2, 1904), an English writer, noted both for his novels of moral inquiry and those of crime and intrigue, died. His travels throughout the world gave him subject matter for his books, which included essays, children's stories, and autobiography. Among Greene's serious novels were *The Power and the Glory* (1940), about a drunken Mexican priest who in the end dies for his religion; *The Heart of the Matter* (1948), in which an Englishman in the Congo is torn between his religion and his lust; and *The Quiet American* (1955), the story of a well-meaning but bumbling American in Vietnam. Greene's lighter works, which he called "entertainments," were very popular and included *The Ministry of Fear* (1950), set in London during World War II, and *Our Man in Havana* (1959), an amusing and ironical spy story set in Cuba.

1991 Apr. 4 Max Frisch (b. May 15, 1911), a Swiss novelist, playwright, and essayist, died. His writings were marked by his concern for the individual's effort to retain his identity in a changing and disruptive world. Among his novels were *Stiller* [*I'm Not Stiller*] (1954) and *Mein Name sei Gan Gantenbein* [*A Wilderness of Mirrors*] (1964). The destruction of war was the theme of his first major play, *Nun singen sie wieder* [*Now They're Singing Again*] (1945). Frisch was praised by critics for the clarity of his prose and for the universal appeal of his themes.

1991 Apr. 16 David Lean (b. Mar. 25, 1908), a British film director whose movies won 28 **Academy Awards**, died. An early success was *In Which We Serve* (1942), a tribute to the Royal Navy. Also notable in the 1940s were two films of novels by Charles Dickens, *Great Expectations* (1946) and *Oliver Twist* (1948). Lean's later films were often on a large scale, including *The Bridge on the River Kwai* (1957) and *Lawrence of Arabia* (1962), which ran for nearly four hours. His last triumph was *A Passage to India* (1984), which combined the lushness of its background with an intimate story about problems of class and race.

1991 Apr. 23 Sean O'Faolain [orig. John Francis Whelan] (b. Feb. 22, 1900), an Irish novelist, playwright, and biographer but noted especially for his mastery of the short story, died. His first novel was *A Nest of Simple Folk* (1933), and in this as in all his books he wrote with humor and sympathy of the people of his native land. Among more than 20 books was *The Collected Stories of Sean O'Faolain* (1983).

1991 Apr. 26 A[lfred] B[ertram] **Guthrie, Jr.** (b. Jan. 13, 1901), an American author of authentic novels of the West in the 19th century, died. Taken together, three of his novels—*The Big Sky* (1947), *The Way West* (1949), and *These Thousand Hills* (1956)—constitute a history of the first settling of the West. Guthrie also wrote one children's book, one volume of poetry, and five mystery novels.

1991 May 8 **Rudolph Serkin** (b. Mar. 28, 1903), an Austrian-born American pianist, one of the most successful and highly regarded of the century, died. He made his concert debut (1915) in Vienna and first played in the U.S. in 1933. Serkin was a master technician and a representative of the Viennese tradition, combining classical and romantic styles. He was director (1968–1975) of the **Curtis Institute** in Philadelphia, and one of the founders (1949) of the **Marlboro Festival** in Vermont.

1991 May 31 **Angus** [Frank Johnstone] **Wilson** (b. Aug. 11, 1913), a South African-born British writer, noted for his novels with a satirical view of the middle class, died. He wrote some 50 books in all, the best among them being the novels *Anglo-Saxon Attitudes* (1956) and *The Middle Age of Mrs. Eliot* (1958), both of which describe the complicated relationships of their protagonists. *No Laughing Matter* (1967) was a family saga covering three generations. Wilson also wrote biographies of **Charles Dickens**, **Rudyard Kipling**, and **Émile Zola**.

1991 June 3 **Eva Le Gallienne** (b. Jan. 11, 1899), an English-born American actress, director, and producer, a leading figure in the theater for more than half a century, died. One of her earliest starring successes was as Julie in *Liliom* (1921). She was known as a leading interpreter of Ibsen. Le Gallienne founded (1926) the **Civic Repertory Theater** in New York to stage classics at popular prices.

1991 June 6 **Stan Getz** (b. 1927), an American jazz musician, known both for his influence on his fellow musicians and for his skill as a tenor saxophonist, died. He began performing professionally when he

was fifteen. He became noted for his improvisations. Getz had considerable influence on both cool jazz and bossa nova.

1991 June 8 **Claudio Arrau** (b. Feb. 6, 1903), a Chilean and one of the greatest pianists of the 20th century, died. A prodigy, he made his concert debut in Santiago, Chile, when he was five years old. He began (1914) recital appearances in Europe, made his London debut (1922), and in the U.S. the following year. The power of Arrau's playing was best shown in his interpretation of Beethoven, but he was also noted for his performances of such romantic composers as Liszt.

1991 June 10 **Jean** [Marcel] **Bruller** (b. Feb. 26, 1902), a French author who wrote under the name Vercors, after a mountain region at the foot of the French Alps, died. He was chiefly noted for the novel *Le Silence de la mer* (1942), an indictment of the Nazi occupation of defeated France during World War II. The book sold more than a million copies in seventeen languages. Other novels by Vercors included *Sylva* (1961) and *Le Redeau de la Meduse* (1969).

1991 June 14 **Peggy** [Edith Margaret Emily] **Ashcroft** (b. Dec. 22, 1907), a British actress internationally known for her stage, movie, and television performances, died. She achieved (1935) her first triumph as Juliet in *Romeo and Juliet*. Over the years she played a great variety of roles, but she is best remembered for her acting in a movie and a television series, both set in India. The film was *A Passage to India* (1984) and the mini-series was *The Jewel in the Crown* (1984), in which she played the part of an elderly, somewhat eccentric, retired missionary.

1991 June 19 **Jean Arthur** [née Gladys Georgianna Greene] (b. Oct. 17, 1900), an American movie star of great charm, who often portrayed the softhearted woman beneath a hardboiled surface, died. She made her film debut in 1923. With her husky voice Arthur soon became a distinctive personality, with leading roles in such movies as *The Whole Town's Talking* (1935), *Mr. Deeds Goes to Town* (1936), and *Mr. Smith Goes to Washington* (1939). Arthur was the star of a television series, *The Jean Arthur Show* (1966).

1991 June 24 **Rufino Tamayo** (b. Aug. 26, 1899), for more than sixty years one of the leading artists of the

Mexican Renaissance, died. His work was rooted in his Indian origins and was expressed in color and subject matter that stemmed from Mexican folk art. Tamayo spent part of his career in the U.S., where he painted *Nature and the Artist* (1943), a mural for Smith College, Northampton, Massachusetts.

1991 July 5   Howard Nemerov (b. Mar. 1, 1920), an American novelist, critic, and poet, died. He was best known for his poetry, much of it brought together in *The Collected Poems of Howard Nemerov* (1977). His novels, which were both satirical and comic, included *The Melodramatists* (1949). He was the third **U.S. poet laureate** (1988–1990).

1991 July 16   Robert Motherwell (b. Jan 24, 1915), an American artist who was a major figure of the Abstract Expressionist school, died. He was known for his cheerful collages and for his moody abstract paintings. An example of his early style was *Pancho Villa: Dead and Alive* (1943). His later style was seen in *Indian Summer: #2* (1962–1964), but especially in a series he called "Elegies to the Spanish Republic." The most recent painting in this series was titled *Elegy to the Spanish Republic No. 172 (With Blood)* (1989–1990).

1991 July 24   Isaac Bashevis Singer (b. July 14, 1904), a Polish-born American author of novels, short stories, and books for children, died. He wrote in Yiddish, but his more than 30 books were translated into many languages. Singer's subject matter was Jewish life in Poland and the U.S. He combined a realistic style with a wide variety of atmospheres. Singer's first novel was *Satan in Goray* (1935); others of note included *The Family Moskat* (1950) and *The Magician of Lublin* (1960). Among several works of memoirs was *In My Father's Court* (1966), and his books for children included *Mazel and Schlimazel* (1966). Singer was awarded (1978) the **Nobel prize for literature**.

1991 Aug. 22   Colleen Dewhurst (b. June 3, 1924), a Canadian-born American actress, equally talented and popular on stage, the screen, and television, died. Over a career of 40 years she was particularly effective in *Mourning Becomes Electra* (1973), while on the movie screen she appeared as recently as 1991 in *Dying Young*. Dewhurst had also been seen that year on television as the domineering mother in the comedy series *Murphy Brown*.

1991 Sept. 3   Frank Capra (b. May 18, 1897), an Italian-born American film director, noted for his loving treatment of the common man, died. His comedies, such as *It Happened One Night* (1934), were offbeat and set new standards for freedom from convention. In *Mr. Deeds Goes to Town* (1926) and *Mr. Smith Goes to Washington* (1939), he portrayed honest unknowns fighting corruption. Capra's ultimate expression of his view of the world was contained in *It's a Wonderful Life* (1946), in which the embattled hero is saved by a guardian angel.

1991 Sept. 14   Michelangelo's *David*, one of the most famous sculptures in the world, was damaged by a deranged man who used a hammer in the Galleria dell'Academia, Florence, Italy, to break off the second toe of the left foot. The statue could be repaired as all the fragments were found. The perpetrator said a 16th-century Venetian artist's model had told him to attack the statue.

1991 Sept. 17   Zino Francescati (b. Aug. 9, 1902), a French violinist known for his championship of 20th-century music, died. He gave his first public recital when he was five years old, and made his professional debut in 1918. Francescati toured Europe and South America but did not appear in the U.S. until 1939. He was noted for his relaxed lyrical style.

1991 Sept. 24   Theodor Seuss Geisel (b. Mar. 4, 1904), an American author of children's books, who wrote under the name of Dr. Seuss and who entertained millions of readers all over the world, died. His great gift of humor and imagination was shown delightfully in the odd animals he created. Seuss's first book was *And to Think That I Saw It on Mulberry Street* (1937). Featured in some of his books were Norton, an elephant, and Yertle the Turtle. *How the Grinch Stole Christmas* (1957) was especially popular. Seuss's last book, as much for adults as for children, was *Oh, the Places You'll Go* (1990).

1991 Sept. 28   Miles [Dewey] Davis [3d] (b. May 25, 1926), an American jazz trumpeter and composer, who pioneered several styles of jazz, died. He made his first recording in 1945, and in 1964 formed his most admired ensemble, a quintet. Starting in the bebop era, Davis initiated or played a leading role in other styles, such as hard-bop and jazz-funk, but he was at his best in establishing cool jazz, an elaborately orchestrated style.

1991 Oct. 3 Nadine Gordimer (b. Nov. 2, 1923) became only the seventh woman in ninety years to win the **Nobel Prize for literature**. A native of South Africa, she regularly expressed strong opposition to the policy of apartheid. Gordimer's first novel was *The Living Days* (1954). *July's People* (1981) and *My Son's Story* (1990) are novels dealing with the harsh realities of black-white relations in South Africa. Her most recent novel was *Safe Houses* (1991), about an affair between a socialite and a revolutionary.

1991 Oct. 24 Gene [Eugene Wesley] **Roddenberry** (b. Aug. 19, 1921), an American writer and producer for television and the movies, who created the internationally successful *Star Trek*, died. The much-praised science fiction series first appeared on television in 1966 and was seen in 48 countries. Beginning in 1979, a dozen full-length movies were made. *Star Trek*, with a large and fanatical cult following, took viewers into the 23rd century aboard the starship *Enterprise*.

1991 Oct. 31 Joseph Papp [orig. Yosl Papirofsky] (b. June 22, 1921), an American theatrical producer and director, who staged more than 350 plays in his career, died. He first attracted wide attention with his staging (1956) of free Shakespearean productions outdoors, including shows in Central Park, New York City. Papp's two most successful long-running productions were *Hair* (1967) and *A Chorus Line* (1975).

1991 Nov. 9 Yves Montand [orig. Ivo Livi] (b. Oct. 13, 1921) an Italian-born French actor and singer, died. He became a popular singer in Paris in the 1940s and made his first movie, *Star Without Light*, in 1946. In all Montand acted in more than 50 films, notable among them being *Z* (1969) and *Jean de Florette* (1986). He made his first singing tour of the U.S. in 1959.

1991 Dec. 5 *The Oxford Dictionary of New Words*, containing more than 2,000 words and phrases that had come into use (from 1980), was published. More than half were American, and the subjects ranged among business, drugs, health, music, and many others. Among the entries were "dink," meaning "double income, no kids"; "dweeb," a boring unfashionable person; and

"gobsmacked," a British term meaning astounded or flabbergasted. It was expected that about half the words in this volume would be lasting enough to appear in the next edition of the stately *Oxford English Dictionary*.

VIII. SPORTS, GAMES, AND SOCIETY

1991 Jan. 17 The **first successful crossing of the Pacific Ocean by hot-air balloon** ended when **Richard Branson** (b. July 18, 1950) and **Per Lindstrand** landed their craft 150 miles west of Yellowknife in the Northwest Territories of Canada. They had left Miyakonojo in southeastern Kyushu, Japan, 46 hrs., 6 min. before coming down. They also set a new distance record of 6,761 miles for a hot-air balloon, and for balloon size, 196 feet high.

1991 Feb. 14 A **law allowing the formal registration of domestic partnerships** by homosexuals and unmarried heterosexual couples went into effect in San Francisco, California. Although the law conferred no legal rights, about 200 couples registered on the first day.

1991 Mar. 3 Arthur Murray [orig. Arthur Murray Teichman] (b. Apr. 4, 1895), an American who became a millionaire by teaching ballroom dancing, died. Starting as a dance instructor, he opened (c. 1917) his own studio, and by its peak his organization operated more than 300 franchised studios in the U.S. and other countries. Murray also sold mail order dance lessons. Many rich and famous people were among his clients.

1991 Mar. 26 Ending an accepted practice of long standing, the Supreme Court of Brazil ruled that a man could no longer be acquitted of a charge of murder when he killed his wife on the grounds that it was a **"defense of honor."** The excuse had been used in thousands of cases in which men had killed women they accused of adultery. In the case that set this new precedent, a husband had stabbed to death both his wife and her lover.

1991 Mar. 27 Four female nurse's aides were given sentences ranging from 15 years to life in prison by a court in Vienna, Austria, after they had been convicted of having **murdered scores of elderly** and infirm patients by lethal injections or by forcing water into their lungs. The four had confessed (April 1989) to having killed in Lainz Hospital 49 patients who they thought were bothersome or too demanding.

1991 Apr. 3   Charles H[enry] **Goren** (b. Mar. 4, 1901), an American champion contract bridge player and the inventor of the most popular bidding system, died. In *Contract Bridge Complete* (1942) and *Point-Count Bidding* (1949), he developed his system for counting the value of face cards and other factors to constitute a simple but effective system. Goren won (1950) a world championship and held (1944–1962) the career master-point top ranking.

1991 Apr. 23   Christophe Auguin of France won a **27,000-mile solo boat race** around the world when he arrived in Newport, Rhode Island, where the race had begun (Sept. 15, 1990). There had been three lengthy stopovers and Auguin's total sailing time was 120 days, 22 hrs., 36 min., 35 sec., in a 60-foot sailboat, *Groupe Sceta*. The $100,000 prize came from the sponsor of the race, the BOC Group, a London-based company.

1991 June 9   The London Monarchs won the first championship of the **World League of American Football** by defeating the Barcelona Dragons, 21–0. The league had played its first games on Mar. 23. It consisted of ten teams, three representing European cities (Barcelona, Frankfurt, and London) and seven North American localities (Birmingham, Montreal, New York–New Jersey, Orlando, Raleigh-Durham, Sacramento, and San Antonio). In effect it was a minor league operation of the National Football League [NFL].

1991 July 9   Lifting of the ban on South African participation in the Olympic Games was announced by the International Olympic Committee [IOC]. The ban, a protest against apartheid, had been in effect since 1970. The IOC decided South Africa had made enough progress toward ending **apartheid** to warrant this step. South African athletes could now compete in the 1992 Olympic Games.

1991 Aug. 5   Sergei Bubka (b. 1963) of the Soviet Union became the first **pole vaulter to clear 20 feet** outdoors when he reached 20 ft., ¼ in. in a meet at Malmö, Sweden. He had (Mar. 23) previously at Grenoble, France, established a new indoor record of 20 ft., ½ in. Bubka was the first and so far only person to pole vault 20 feet.

1991 Aug. 25   Carl Lewis (b. July 1, 1961) of the U.S. set a **new world record of 9.86 sec. for the 100-meter dash** at the world championships in Tokyo. Lewis's feat took 4 one hundredths of a second off the old record.

1991 Aug. 30   Mike [Michael Anthony] **Powell** (b. Nov. 10, 1963) of the U.S. set a **new record for the long jump** when he leaped 29 ft., 4 ½ in. at the world championships in Tokyo. This leap was two inches more than the former record, which was the oldest track and field record, having been set in 1968.

1991 Oct. 10   The Canadian government announced it was about to end its policy of **banning homosexuals from joining the armed forces**. Hitherto if people were identified as homosexual after joining, they were not discharged but were ineligible for promotion or reenlistment.

1991 Nov. 30   The **first world championship in women's soccer** was won by the U.S., which defeated Norway, 2–1, at Gangzhou, China.

1991 Dec.   Judit Polgar (b. July 23, 1976) of Hungary became the **youngest chess player ever to achieve the rank of grandmaster** when she defeated a field of ten grandmasters this month at the Super Championship of Hungary, held in Budapest. Heretofore the youngest person to achieve the rating was the former world champion, **Bobby Fischer**, when he was one month older than Polgar. She was the youngest of three expert chess playing sisters and only the fourth woman ever to become a grandmaster.

1991 Dec. 1   France won the **Davis Cup**, emblematic of world team tennis, for the first time since 1932 by defeating the U.S., the defending champion, 3 matches to 1. In 1932 France had won its sixth Davis Cup in succession, also defeating the U.S.

1991 Dec. 2   Bobby Bonilla, an outfielder, became the **highest paid player in professional team sports** when he signed a contract with the New York Mets of the National League for $29 million over a five-year period. Jack Morris of the Toronto Blue Jays became (Dec. 12) the highest paid pitcher by signing a two-year contract for $10.85 million.

1992

VITAL STATISTICS AND DEMOGRAPHICS

1992 Mar. 19 The **Nigerian** government released the results of a census taken (Nov. 1991) that counted the **population** at 88 million. This figure was lower than expected, some estimates having placed the population count as high as 110 million.

1992 Apr. 25 The **World Health Organization** [WHO] reported that **Japanese live longer** than other people, the average **life expectancy** for men being 76.2 years and for women 82.5. French women have the second longest life expectancy at 81.5 years. American males average 71.8 years and females 78.6 years.

1992 Apr. 28 The United Nations Population Fund predicted that the **population of the world** would increase from 5.48 billion in mid-1992 to 10 billion in 2050. It was also estimated that the world would add 97 million people a year until the year 2000, and then 90 million a year until 2025. The fund called for a sustained and concerted program to curb this expansion.

1992 Dec. 3 Revising its 1988 forecast of the growth of the **American population**, the U.S. Census Bureau estimated that the population, now c.225 million, would reach 275 million by the year 2000 and 383 million in 2050. The previous estimates had been 268 million and 300 million. The increases in the estimates were the result of anticipated rises in the birth rate and immigration. The report also said the Hispanic population would pass the black population in 2013, by which time there would be 42.1 million of the former compared with 42 million blacks.

1992 Dec. 15 For the first time in more than two decades, **Saudi Arabia** completed a census and announced that its **population** was 16.9 million, of which 4.6 million were foreigners. The report also said that, with a birth rate between 3.5 and 3.8 percent, Saudi Arabia had one of the highest growth rates in the world.

1992 Dec. 31 Throughout the year **drought and civil war**, mostly **in Africa and Asia**, but with a particularly appalling situation in the Balkans, brought death and dislocation to several million people. The worst devastation struck **Somalia**, a poor nation on the Horn of Africa, where civil war between clans and terrorism by roving unaffiliated bands claimed many lives. Most deaths, however, as many as 300,-000, resulted from starvation. Although a long drought began to end, many Somalis had been driven off their land by armed gangs. In the **Sudan** the government appeared on the verge of subduing the rebels of the southern part of the country and this resulted in thousands of people fleeing to Kenya, where c.300,000 had already sought refuge. With the 14-year war ended in **Afghanistan**, as many as 600,-000 Afghanis who had been refugees in Pakistan began returning to their homeland. In eastern Asia the flight of Vietnamese from their country appeared to have ended after 17 years, during which more than 1.5 million had fled. With **Yugoslavia** having fallen apart, a no-holds-barred war, mainly between Serbia and Bosnia and Herzegovina, sent about 210,-000 refugees to seek asylum in Western Europe, bringing the total number of refugees since trouble began to more than 600,000. On the brighter side, c.100,000 Russian Jews emigrated to **Israel** by choice. A portent of future difficulties in feeding and finding useful employment for millions of people could be seen in **Latin America**, now the most urbanized part of the developing world with 73 percent of its population city dwellers, compared with 34 percent in Africa and 33 percent in Asia. It was estimated that, for example, the population of Lima, Peru, was increasing by 400,000 people a year and São Paulo, Brazil, by 450,000.

II. DISASTERS

1992 Jan. 20 On its way from Lyon, in central France, to Strasbourg, in northeastern France, an Air Inter Airbus **A-320 jet crashed** into a ridge, killing 87 of 96 persons aboard. All the survivors were injured except for a 20-month-old-girl.

1992 Feb. 1–Mar. 13 During this period of 41 days, three types of disaster struck Turkey, taking a total of more than 1,000 lives. **Blizzards** (Feb. 1) caused avalanches in southeastern Turkey that killed c.217 persons and buried one whole village. About 300 lives were lost (Feb. 21) when an **explosion** occurred **in a coal mine** at Kozlo on the Black Sea. An **earthquake** that registered 6.8 on the Richter scale struck

(Mar. 12) three provinces in eastern Turkey, killing c.500 persons and injuring at least 600.

1992 Apr. 22 At least 180 people were killed when **explosions** destroyed c.1,400 homes and tore up five miles of streets in a working-class neighborhood of Guadalajara in central western Mexico. About 1,000 others were injured. An investigation showed that the explosions were caused by a buildup **of gasoline fumes** from a leaking pipe, the property of Pemex, the government-owned oil company. Nine persons, officials of the company and government employees, were held (May 1) and charged with negligent homicide.

1992 May 10 Authorities reported that more than 200 people had died in Orisa, a state in eastern India, as the result of **drinking illegally brewed liquor.** More than 684 others had been admitted to hospitals after imbibing the drink containing poisonous methyl alcohol. To date 35 persons had been arrested for selling an estimated 5,000 gallons of the liquor.

1992 June 28 The most powerful **earthquake to strike California** in 40 years, registering 7.4 on the Richter scale, hit a desert area of southern California, east of Los Angeles, and was followed in three hours by another whose center was 19 miles away from the first. Only one person, a child, was killed. Homes and businesses throughout the area were damaged. The quake was felt as far north as Washington state and Idaho. Earlier (Apr. 25) northern California had been rocked by a quake that registered 6.9 and which caused $3.5 million worth of damage.

1992 July 31 A Thai Airways **A310-300 Airbus jet,** flying from Bangkok, Thailand, to Katmandu, Nepal, **crashed** into a Himalayan mountain near its destination, killing all 113 persons aboard. The wreckage was found in a wooded area 8,500 ft. high. A similar accident occurred (Sept. 28) when a Pakistani International Airlines **Airbus 300 jet crashed** into a hillside as it approached the airport. All 167 persons aboard were killed.

1992 July 31 A **Chinese jet airliner**, a Soviet-built Yakovlev-42, **crashed** as it was taking off from Nanjing in east central China. Only 17 of the 126 persons aboard survived and all of them were injured.

1992 Aug. 24 The most powerful **hurricane** ever to strike the U.S. mainland roared across southern Florida with winds of up to 150 mph. The hurricane, named **Andrew,** killed only 38 people, either directly or in the storm's aftermath, but 85,000 homes were destroyed, and 250,000 persons made homeless. Damage was estimated as high as $30 billion, including the destruction of Homestead Air Force Base. Andrew then (Aug. 26) struck southern Louisiana, leaving 25,000 people homeless.

1992 Sept. 4 Raging **floods** from unusually heavy rains began sweeping through northern Pakistan, destroying homes and bridges. The death toll reached at least 2,000, with hundreds of thousands homeless. It was estimated that 20 percent of the nation's cotton crop was destroyed. The same floods also did heavy damage in the northwestern Indian state of Jammu and Kashmir.

1992 Sept. 11 **Hurricane Iniki,** the most powerful storm to strike Hawaii in this century, blasted the island of Kauai. With gusts up to 160 mph, Iniki killed two people and injured 98, while destroying or damaging 10,000 homes on the island which had a population of c.55,000.

1992 Sept. 26 Taking off from Lagos in southwestern Nigeria, a military transport plane, a **Hercules C-130, crashed**, killing all 163 persons aboard. Most of the dead were believed to be officers of the armed forces.

1992 Oct. 5 An El Al **Boeing 747-200 cargo jet crashed** into a ten-story apartment building in Amsterdam, the Netherlands, shortly after takeoff. Three days after the crash 40 bodies had been recovered but c.250 others were unaccounted for as authorities had difficulty in determining how many people had been in the building at the time. The crash was the first in the 40-year history of El Al, the Israeli airline, and was the Netherlands worst air disaster.

1992 Oct. 12 An **earthquake** centered about twenty miles southwest of Cairo, Egypt, and registering 5.9 on the Richter scale, killed 552 people, injured nearly 10,000, and left 3,000 families homeless, mostly in a poor quarter of Cairo where buildings were old and badly constructed.

1992 Nov. 20 A **fire in Windsor Castle,** 30 miles west of London, for more than 850 years one of the homes of British monarchs, did extensive damage to the northeastern corner of the rambling structure, particularly in the large, ornate banquet area known as St. George's Hall. Some valuable works of art were damaged but most were carried out to safety. It was estimated that it would cost c.$90 million, to be paid by the British government, to repair the damage.

1992 Nov. 24   On a flight from Canton [Guangzhou], a city in southern China, to Guilin, a popular tourist area in southern China, a **Boeing 737-300 jet** of China Southern Airlines, **crashed** into a mountain about 15 miles from its destination, killing all 141 people on board. It was China's worst reported air disaster.

1992 Dec. 3   A **Greek tanker**, *Aegean Sea*, carrying 23.8 million gallons of crude oil, **ran aground** while attempting to enter the harbor of La Coruna, in northern Spain, during a storm. An explosion and fire occurred and an estimated 21.5 million gallons of its cargo was spilled into the water. As a result 60 miles of coast line was inundated, killing much wildlife and ruining the area's shellfish industry.

1992 Dec. 8   An **avalanche of mud**, the result of torrential rains, buried the mining camp of Llipi, in western Bolivia, c.90 miles north of La Paz. Hundreds were feared dead, but there was no way of telling how many bodies were buried under the 35-foot high wall of mud or had been swept away by the Tipuani River.

1992 Dec. 11   An unusual and unusually fierce **nor'easter struck** the tri-state area of Connecticut, New Jersey, and New York, centered on New York City. Though only six persons were killed and about a score injured, the combination of wind, with gusts of 90 mph, snow, rain, and record high tides, brought the region to an almost complete standstill. More than 12,000 homes were damaged or destroyed; almost 1 million homes and businesses lost power, some for several days; most public transportation ceased to function; and damage to private property and public facilities was estimated at more than $500 million. Damage that could not be estimated in dollars was done to miles of beaches.

1992 Dec. 12   An **earthquake** variously registered at 6.8 or 7.5 on the Richter scale shook the Indonesian island of Flores and two other islands c.1,000 miles east of the capital, Djakarta, on the island of

Java, killing nearly 2,500 persons. Tidal waves of up to 80 feet swept away complete villages.

1992 Dec. 22   On a flight from Benghazi to Tripoli, both on the Mediterranean shore of northern Libya, a Libyan **Boeing 727 passenger jet crashed**, killing all 157 persons aboard. The official press agency announced the accident but gave no details as to the cause or exactly where it took place.

1992 Dec. 31   The worst **drought** in 40 years had by the end of the year affected 110 million people **in African countries south of the Sahara**, and the UN estimated that 18 million of them were in danger of dying of starvation if more relief was not provided. The countries affected, some of which were also torn by civil wars, were Angola, Botswana, Kenya, Lesotho, Malawi, Mozambique, Namibia, Somalia, South Africa, Swaziland, Tanzania, Zaire, Zambia, and Zimbabwe. About 2 million people had become refugees in their search for food. Kenya, for example, which normally exported food, had to import 500,000 tons. The worst situation existed in Somalia where the combination of drought and an especially brutal civil war had already caused an estimated 300,000 deaths from starvation with another 1.5 million endangered out of a population of c.4.5 million.

III. WAR AND POLITICS

1992 Jan. 1   Having voted (Sept. 8, 1991) for independence, **Macedonia**, previously one of the republics of the federation of **Yugoslavia**, officially detached itself from that crumbling nation. Macedonia, however, ran into problems in securing recognition of its independence by other nations. Greece, whose province of Macedonia abutted the new nation, complained that using this name implied claims to its province. As a result the **European Community** [EC], whose twelve members included Greece, refused recognition, as did the U.S. Though two-thirds of its population was Slavic, Macedonia refused the suggestion that it call itself Slavic Macedonia.

1992 Jan. 3   A cease-fire arranged by the U.N. stopped fighting that had been going on between the Yugoslav army and Serbian militia on the one hand and Croatian forces on the other for control of that part of newly independent **Croatia** populated by Serbs. The U.N. voted (Feb. 21) to send a peacekeeping force to the region. By Apr. 3 fighting had spread to **Bosnia and Herzegovina** where Serbian irregulars, supported by the Yugoslav army, clashed with Muslims and Croatians. Bosnia's population was 44 percent Muslim Slavs, 31 percent Eastern Orthodox Serbs, and 18 percent Roman Catholic Croats. The civil war thus became an ethnic and religious war. Serbian forces shelled **Sarajevo**, Bosnia's capital, day after day, causing many casualties. The Serbs also rounded up Muslims and began so-called **ethnic cleansing** to drive them out of the country. The **U.N. Security Council imposed** (May 30) **economic sanctions on Yugoslavia**, which now consisted of Serbia and Montenegro only, and banned (Oct. 9) all military flights over Bosnia. But no steps were taken to enforce the ban. Further moves to isolate Yugoslavia came (Sept. 22, Nov. 16) when the U.N. **General Assembly voted to expel Yugoslavia from membership** and to impose a naval blockade. Meanwhile, Croatian forces had occupied some of northern and western Bosnia, so that by December the Bosnian government controlled no more than a third of Bosnia and Herzegovina.

1992 Jan. 6 After two weeks of rebellion against his nine-month regime, **Zviad K. Gamsakhurdia** (b. 1939), president of **Georgia**, fled Tbilisi, the capital. A ruling military council selected (Mar. 10) **Eduard A. Shevardnadze**, a former foreign minister of the U.S.S.R., and a native Georgian, to be chairman of a State Council that wielded both legislative and executive power. An election (Oct. 11) gave Shevardnadze a large majority and he became speaker of the parliament, the equivalent of the presidency.

1992 Jan. 11 A military coup forced **Chadli Benjedid**, president (from Feb. 7, 1979) of **Algeria**, to resign in order to form a regime that would deal more forcefully with the rising fundamentalist movement known as the **Islamic Salvation Front**. The military council named (Jan. 16) **Mohammad Boudiaf** (b. June 23, 1919), a political leader who had been in exile for 27 years, as head of a presidential council. Violence between government forces and fundamentalists resulted in many arrests and the Front was banned on Mar. 4. Boudiaf was assassinated (June 29), but the motive of the assassin was unclear. He was succeeded (July 2) by **Ali Kafi**, the leader of the Veterans Organization. By the end of the year continuing armed attacks by Islamic militants threatened the existence of the government.

1992 Jan. 13 The **Vatican**, ahead of all European countries, **recognized the independence of Croatia and Slovenia**, breakaway republics of Yugoslavia. **Pope John Paul II** apparently wanted to show his

support for these two areas that are mostly Roman Catholic.

1992 Jan. 15 The 12 member nations of the **European Community [EC]** formally **recognized the independence of Croatia and Slovenia**, former republics of the now dismembered Yugoslavia. The independence of a third republic, **Bosnia and Herzegovina**, was recognized on Apr. 5. On the same day the U.S. gave its recognition to all three. Other nations around the world followed suit. Slovenia, the northernmost of the three, seemed viable and secure, but more than a quarter of Croatia was controlled by the Yugoslav national army. It had agreed to remove its troops, but other irregular Serbian forces carried on armed resistance.

1992 Jan. 16 The government of **El Salvador** and a **guerrilla movement** that had carried on a civil war (from Oct. 1979) **signed a treaty intended to bring peace** by the end of the year. The struggle had cost c.75,000 lives. A cease-fire was to take effect (Feb. 11) and within nine months the rebel military force was to disarm under international supervision. Meanwhile, the government was to reduce the size and political influence of the armed forces. Though the end of the war was officially proclaimed (Dec. 15), the government had failed to keep its promise to purge the ranks of the armed forces.

1992 Jan. 19 In **Bulgaria's** first direct presidential election since the overthrow (1989) of communism, **Zhelyu Zhelev** (b. Mar. 3, 1935), a philosopher and long-time dissident, who had been serving by appointment (Aug. 1990) of parliament, was elected to a five-year term, receiving 53.5 percent of the vote. He represented the Union of Democratic Forces, now in control of the government. The Socialist party, the former Communist party, was defeated.

1992 Jan. 30 The **Conference on Security and Cooperation** in Europe, based on the **Helsinki Final Act** (1975) that established human rights principles for Europe and North America, **admitted ten former Soviet republics** to membership. They were Armenia, Azerbaijan, Belarus, Kazakhstan, Kyrgyzstan, Moldova, Tajikistan, Turkmenistan, Uzbekistan, and Ukraine. Russia had already taken the place of the U.S.S.R., and Estonia, Latvia, and Lithuania had been admitted in 1991.

1992 Jan. 30 A year of change and controversy in **Ireland's** politics began with the announced resignation and retirement (Feb. 10) of **Charles J. Haughey**, prime minister for eight of the previous twelve years. He was succeeded by **Albert Reynolds** (b. Nov. 3, 1935), a former cabinet minister, who was endorsed (Feb. 6) for the post by his Fianna Fáil party, and formed a coalition cabinet with the Progressive Democrats. This government collapsed (Nov. 5) when the Progressive Democrats abandoned the coalition and Reynolds lost a vote of confidence in parliament. An election (Nov. 25) resulted in a stalemate because it would take some combination of three parties to achieve a majority in parliament. Inconclusive negotiations continued to the end of the year.

1992 Jan. 31 The annual report on **human rights** of the U.S. State Department was especially critical of **China** and **Syria**, even though the latter had supported America in the **Persian Gulf War** (1990–1991). **Israel** was criticized for torturing Palestinian detainees; **India** for the unsettled situation in Jammu and Kashmir; and **Myanmar** [formerly Burma] for holding 2,000 political prisoners.

1992 Feb. 1 **George Bush**, president of the U.S., and **Boris Yeltsin**, president of Russia, signed a declaration proclaiming an **official end to the Cold War** (c.1945–c.1985) and ushering in a new era of friendship and partnership. Other events attested to the changes brought by the fall (Dec. 25, 1991) of the U.S.S.R.: 24 nations agreed (Mar. 24) on an **Open Skies Treaty** to allow a number of reconnaissance flights a year over each other's territories; twenty-seven nations signed (Apr. 3) an agreement intended to help stop the **spread of nuclear arms** by controlling exports; the U.S. and four of the nations formed from the Soviet Union [Belarus, Kazakhstan, Russia, and Ukraine] agreed to comply with the **arms reduction treaty** negotiated (1991) with the U.S.S.R; and NATO and the countries of the defunct Warsaw Pact agreed (July 6) on limits on the number of troops each would maintain.

1992 Feb. 25 **Jean-Bertrand Aristide**, ousted (Sept. 1991) and exiled president of **Haiti**, signed an agreement with the prime minister designate of the interim government that pledged both sides to form a government of national unity. The Haitian **parliament**, however, **refused** (Mar. 18) **to ratify the pact**. A new regime took office (June 19) when **Marc L. Bazin** (b. Mar. 6, 1932), a lawyer and a former World Bank official, was sworn in as prime minister. Aristide remained in exile.

1992 Feb. 28 The **U.N.** Security Council voted to send a **peacekeeping force** of 22,000 to **Cambodia** in an effort to end a civil war that had been going on for over 20 years. The U.N. was to take over the administration of the country for as long as 18 months while working out a peace plan with the four warring factions. These groups signed (Apr. 20) an agreement to respect civil, political, economic, and social rights. The U.N. set a deadline of June 15 for all sides to put down their arms, but the **Khmer Rouge**, a guerrilla faction that had ruled and terrorized (1975–1978) the country, refused to do so. A ten-nation conference was held (Nov. 8) in Beijing, China, but the Khmer Rouge rejected a new appeal to disarm and said it would not take part in an election originally planned for May 1993. The U.N. then imposed (Nov. 30) a trade embargo on the part of Cambodia controlled by the Khmer Rouge.

1992 Mar. 1 **Ibn al-Saud Fahd**, king of **Saudi Arabia** (from 1982), announced a **new constitution** for his country, and **issued** a number of **decrees intended to speed modernization**. A Consultative Council, whose 60 members were to be appointed by the king, was created. Governors and assemblies in the 14 provinces were given considerable autonomy, while a new bill of rights protected privacy and arrest without cause. Fahd said (Mar. 29) that free elections would not be held as they were not suitable for a traditional Arab society. On the other hand, he expressed (Dec. 21) opposition to Muslim fundamentalists.

1992 Mar. 2 **Nine nations were admitted to the United Nations**, eight of them formerly part of the U.S.S.R.: Armenia, Azerbaijan, Kazakhstan, Kyrgystan, Moldova, Tajikistan, Turkmenistan, and Uzbekistan. San Marino, the world's oldest (from 1631) independent republic, was also admitted. Three former Yugoslav republics [Bosnia and Herzegovina, Croatia, and Slovenia] were admitted (May 22), bringing the total membership to 178 nations.

1992 Mar. 5 Twenty-two nations, a record number, were criticized for **human rights abuses** during the previous year in a report of the U.N. Human Rights Commission. Particularly criticized and slated for stricter supervision were **Cuba**, **Equatorial Guinea**, **Haiti**, **Myanmar** [formerly Burma], **Sudan**, and **Indonesia**.

1992 Mar. 6 In the face of a popular uprising, **Ayaz Mutalibov** (b. May 12, 1938), president (from Sept.

1991) of **Azerbaijan**, resigned. His downfall was the result of his failure to defeat the warring Armenian dissidents who made up most of the population of the enclave of **Nagorno-Karabakh**. Parliament voted (May 19) to transfer power temporarily to a National Council. An election (June 7) was won by **Adulfaz Eichibey**, an anti-Communist dissident (from the 1970s), and with the support of the Popular Front he became president. Fighting in the disputed area continued.

1992 Mar. 9 Menachem [Wolfovich] **Begin** (b. Aug. 30, 1913), Russian-born prime minister (1977–1983) of Israel, and a leader of the revolt that established (1948) the independence of the nation, died. Imprisoned by Russia, but released (1941), he made his way to Palestine and joined the British army. After 1943 he became the leader of the Irgun, an underground terrorist movement that used weapons and explosives to end British rule in Palestine. Begin joined with **Anwar el-Sadat**, president of Egypt, and **Jimmy Carter**, president of the U.S., to sign (Mar. 26, 1979) an **Israeli-Egyptian peace treaty**, the first between the Jewish state and an Arab nation. He and Sadat shared the **Nobel Peace Prize** in 1978.

1992 Mar. 17 Eligible voters, all white, approved by a 68.7 percent majority a proposal by **F. W. de Klerk**, president of **South Africa**, to negotiate an **end to white minority rule** in the country, long noted for its policy of **apartheid**. Preliminary talks had begun (Jan. 20) between the government and black groups, of which the **African National Congress** [ANC] was the most important. At odds over various issues, the most important of which was de Klerk's insistence that a majority of 75 percent be required to change the constitution, the talks broke down (mid-May). Negotiations were further threatened by a **massacre** (June 17) in which at least 40 persons were killed in the black township of **Boipatong**. The ANC charged that the attackers, also black, had been aided by white police. Further talks resulted in de Klerk agreeing to a 70 percent majority for change, while the ANC offered an arrangement whereby the white minority would be assured of a share of power indefinitely. No final agreement was achieved.

1992 Mar. 22 Political parties associated with the military government that took over (1991) the rule of **Thailand** in a coup, won 53 percent of the seats in the lower house of parliament in a general election. As a result **Suchinda Kraprayoon**, a general and leader of the coup, was named (Apr. 7) prime minister.

Protests against his rule **broke out**, and after violent confrontations the government declared (May 17) a state of emergency. With scores killed and 400 reported missing, Krapayoon resigned on May 25. The five-party coalition that had brought him to power turned against him and amended (May 25) the constitution to require that the prime minister be a member of parliament, which he was not. A former prime minister, **Anand Panyarachun**, took office (June 10) and dismissed (Aug. 1) the top military commanders. Another election (Sept. 13) made it possible for a four-party coalition of democratic tendencies to form a government, and **Chuan Leekpai** (b. July 28, 1938), the leader of the Democratic party, became (Sept. 23) the newest prime minister.

1992 Mar. 23 The Democratic party came to power in **Albania** when a parliamentary election gave it 92 seats to 38 for the Socialist party, formerly the Communist party, which had won (1991) the previous election. **Ramiz Alia**, a former Communist, resigned (Apr. 3) as president. He was succeeded (Apr. 9) by vote of parliament by **Sali Berisha**, a cardiologist and the leader of the Democratic party.

1992 Mar. 25 Percival J. Patterson became prime minister of the Caribbean island nation of **Jamaica**, succeeding **Michael N. Manley**, who had held (from 1989) the office and who resigned because of ill health. Patterson reached his new position by being elected head of the governing People's National party, of which Manley had been the leader.

1992 Mar. 31 The U.N. Security Council voted to impose, beginning Apr. 14, **sanctions on Libya** for its refusal to surrender two agents suspected of being implicated in the bombing (Dec. 1988) of an American airliner over Scotland, and of a French airliner over Niger (1989). The two bombings took 400 lives. By the terms of the sanctions all international flights into Libya were forbidden as were sales of arms to the country.

1992 Apr. 3 Pierre Bérégovoy (Dec. 23, 1925–May 1, 1993), the finance minister, was appointed prime minister (to Mar. 29, 1993) by **François Mitterand**, president of **France**. He succeeded **Edith Cresson**, who had (May 15, 1991) been named France's first female prime minister. She had become widely unpopular in part because of the poor showing of Mitterand's Socialist party in regional elections on Mar. 22 and 29.

1992 Apr. 6   A parliamentary election in **Italy** gave the ruling coalition of the Christian Democratic, Socialist, Social Democratic, and Liberal parties only 48.8 percent of the vote and a reduced margin of 16 seats in the lower house. **Guilio Andreotti**, the prime minister, resigned (Apr. 24), but wrangling over seats in the cabinet and other matters delayed the formation of a new government of the same four parties until **Guiliano Amato** of the Socialist party was named (June 18) prime minister. **Oscar Luigi Scalfaro** (b. Sept. 9, 1918) had been chosen president on May 25, 1992.

1992 Apr. 9   In a close parliamentary election in **Great Britain**, the Conservative party won an unexpected victory, keeping the government of **John Major**, prime minister (from Nov. 1990), in office. The Conservatives lost 32 seats in the House of Commons, but retained 336 to 271 for the Labour party, and 44 for smaller groups.

1992 Apr. 16   As rebel factions neared the capital, Kabul, **Najibullah** (b. 1947), president of **Afghanistan** (from May 1986), was ousted from power. The rebel groups, often at war with each other, had agreed (Apr. 10) on a temporary ruling council, and by Apr. 24 six factions were in control of Kabul. Fighting, however, soon broke out among the warring factions and continued all year.

1992 Apr. 23   **Saw Maung**, head (from Sept. 1988) of the military government of **Myanmar** [formerly Burma], was replaced because of ill health, according to an official announcement. His duties were taken over by **Than Shwe**, who had been vice chairman of the ruling council. In the course of the year several hundred political prisoners were released and martial law, imposed (1989), was lifted on Sept. 26.

1992 Apr. 27   Recognizing that the former Communist federation of **Yugoslavia** was irretrievably broken up by the **secession of four of its constituent republics** (Bosnia and Herzegovina, Croatia, Macedonia, and Slovenia], the two remaining republics, **Montenegro and Serbia**, proclaimed themselves the **Yugoslav Republic**.

1992 Apr. 29   After four white, **Los Angeles**, California, policemen were acquitted of beating a black man—a beating that was recorded on video tape—**rioting** broke out in the largely black and Hispanic central southern section of the city. Before order was restored two days later by a police force that had been poorly prepared and by National Guard troops, 51 persons were dead, 2,116 injured, 6,345 arrested, and 3,767 buildings burned. Many stores were looted.

1992 Apr. 30   **Joseph Momoh**, president (from 1985) of **Sierra Leone** in northwestern Africa, was overthrown by a military coup. The junta chose (May 2) as it leader **Valentine Strasser**, a military officer.

1992 May 6   The worst **economic crisis in Lebanon's** 49 years of independence brought about **riots** and the resignation of the government, headed by **Omar Karami**, prime minister. **Rashid Solh**, a lawyer and a member of parliament, was named (May 13) to replace him. Elections for a new parliament, in which by agreement (1990) the 128 seats were shared equally by Christians and Muslims, were held (Aug. 21, 30, and Sept. 6) and resulted in gains by Islamic fundamentalists. To head a new government in association with the new parliament, **Rafik al-Hariri** (b. 1944), a Muslim billionaire, was named (Oct. 12) prime minister.

1992 June 17   The last two **hostages** held by Lebanese Islamic terrorist groups were freed and flown to Germany. They were **Thomas Kemptner** and **Heinrich Strubig**, who had been working for a German organization aiding Palestinian refugees when they were seized on May 16, 1989.

1992 June 21   **Li Xiannian** (b. June 23, 1909), president of **China** (1983–1988), a long-time official of the Communist government, died. He led troops in the Communist takeover (1949) of the government and had become (1945) a member of the party's central committee. Li's most important post was as a member of the politburo (1956–1987). After his retirement he remained influential and was known as an advocate of old-fashioned, hard-line Communist policies.

1992 June 23   In a general election in **Israel** the Labor party defeated the incumbent conservative Likud party, winning 45 parliamentary seats to 32. With a total of 120 seats at stake, Labor, led by **Yitzhak Rabin**, a former prime minister (1974–1977), formed a coalition with minor parties and again became the governing party. As prime minister (from July 13), Rabin was expected to be more conciliatory in peace neogtiations with the Arab nations than his predecessor, **Yitzhak Shamir**.

1992 June 28   The **Mongolian People's Revolutionary party**, formerly the Communist party that had ruled Mongolia until it gave up (1990) power, won 72 of the 76 parliamentary seats in an election. The opposition, called the Democratic Coalition, was poorly organized, and many voters were dissatisfied with the economic problems that had arisen since the overthrow of communism.

1992 June 30   **Fidel V. Ramos** (b. 1928), the former top military commander of the **Philippines**, was inaugurated president, succeeding Corazon C. Aquino. He had won the election (May 11) with 5.29 million votes to 4.45 million for his closest rival. Ramos had led the mutiny that forced the deposition (1986) of Ferdinand Marcos as president, and he had defended Aquino against several coup attempts.

1992 July 5   **Sixto Durán Bellén** (b. 1922) was elected president of **Ecuador** with 57 percent of the votes cast. Educated in the U.S., he was a supporter of economic change through a free market system.

1992 July 8   Having won (May 24) a runoff election with 57 percent of the vote, **Thomas Klestil** (b. Nov. 4, 1932), candidate of the People's party, was sworn in as president of **Austria**. A rightist, Klestil was a diplomat and an economist. He succeeded **Kurt Waldheim**, who throughout his term (from 1986) had been boycotted by most nations because of the revelation during his election campaign of his alleged connection with Nazi brutality during World War II (1939–1945).

1992 July 8   **Hanna Suchocka**, a law professor, was nominated **Poland**'s first female prime minister, succeeding **Waldemar Pawlak**, a farmer who had resigned after holding office only since June 5. He, in turn, had succeeded **Jan Olszewski** (b. Aug. 20, 1930), who was dismissed (June 5) by parliament after having served for five months. Suchocka's government consisted of a coalition of seven parties based on the Solidarity movement.

1992 July 10   After a trial in a federal court in Miami, Florida, **Manuel Noriega**, former military dictator (Aug. 1985–Dec. 1989) of Panama, was sentenced to 40 years in prison on eight counts of drug trafficking, money laundering, and racketeering. Noriega had been seized (Dec. 1989) by American troops who had invaded his country primarily to capture the dictator.

1992 Aug. 21   **Hubert A. Ingraham** (b. 1947), leader of the Free National Movement, was sworn in as prime minister of the **Bahamas**, an island nation north of Cuba. His party had defeated the Progressive Liberal party of **Lynden O. Pindling**, prime minister (from 1973), in an election (Aug. 19) in which Ingraham's party won 32 of the 49 seats in the House of Assembly.

1992 Aug. 24   **China and South Korea formally established diplomatic relations** for the first time. China had supported North Korea in the Korean War (1950–1953) and had officially considered North Korea to be the only Korean government. It was thought that China might now play a part in negotiations to unite the two Koreas. South Korea for its part agreed to break off diplomatic relations with the Chinese Nationalist government of Taiwan.

1992 Sept. 7   After months of armed clashes between supporters and opponents, **Rakhman Nabiyev**, president of **Tajikistan**, a republic of Central Asia formed when the Soviet Union broke up (Dec. 1991), resigned. He was a hard-line Communist who had headed (1982–1985) the party. **Akbarsho Iskandarov** became acting president. Fighting continued all year, involving Communists, clans, regional factions, and Islamic fundamentalists.

1992 Sept. 12   **Abimael Guzmán**, leader of the **Shining Path** [*Sendero Luminoso*], a Peruvian guerrilla group professing the most hard-line type of communism, was captured by police in Lima. He was convicted (Oct. 7) of treason and sentenced to life in prison. Guzmán had been a professor of philosophy when he founded (1970) Shining Path and the movement began (May 18, 1980) armed insurgency aimed at overthrowing the government by killing public officials and bombing public buildings.

1992 Sept. 29–30   The first free election since independence (1975) in **Angola**, in southwestern Africa, resulted in a victory for **José Eduardo dos Santos**, president (from 1979) and leader of the Popular Movement for the Liberation of Angola [MPLA], over **Jonas Savimbi**, leader of the National Union for the Total Independence of Angola [UNITA], who had carried on (from 1976) a war against the government. MPLA also won a majority in the 223-seat legislature. Savimbi refused to accept the result, claiming fraud, and **fighting broke out** anew (Oct. 11). Though a cease-fire was signed (Nov. 26), fighting soon erupted again.

1992 Oct. 1 The parliament of **Ukraine** voted to dismiss the government of the former Soviet republic a day after **Vitold Fokin**, the prime minister (from Nov. 1990), resigned in the face of a worsening economic situation. Living standards had plunged as inflation soared by 2,200 percent during the year. **Leonid Kuchma**, director of a plant that produced military rockets, was appointed (Oct. 13) prime minister.

1992 Oct. 4 The government of **Mozambique**, in southeastern Africa, headed (from 1986) by **Jaoquin A. Chissano**, and Renamo, a rebel group led by **Alfonso Dhlakama**, signed a treaty ending hostilities. A U.N. peacekeeping force began (Dec. 16) to monitor the agreement. The civil war (from 1976) had devastated the nation, making refugees of a fourth of the population.

1992 Oct. 5 **Chadi Jagan**, who had been prime minister (1957–1964) when **Guyana**, on the northeastern coast of South America, was still British Guiana, was elected president with 54 percent of the vote in the first free election since 1964. He defeated **Desmond Hoyte**, the incumbent president (from 1985).

1992 Oct. 5 A slighting blow against the government and ruling royal family of **Kuwait** was struck in a parliamentary election in which opposition groups, consisting both of advocates of more democracy and conservative Muslims, won 31 of the 50 seats in the national assembly. Nevertheless, the emir renamed (Oct. 12) **Saad al-Abdulla al-Sabah** (b. 1930), the crown prince, as prime minister.

1992 Oct. 8 **Willy Brandt** [orig. Herbert Ernst Karl Frahm] (b. Dec. 18, 1913), chancellor of West Germany (1969–1974), who sought peaceful relations between his country and the Communist nations of Eastern Europe, died. Hounded by the Nazis, he escaped (Apr. 1933) to Norway. After World War II (1939–1945), Brandt became active in politics and was elected (Sept. 1957) mayor of West Berlin. While chancellor he negotiated (1970) treaties with the U.S.S.R. and Poland that normalized relations for the first time since the war. He was awarded the **Nobel Peace Prize** in 1971.

1992 Oct. 16 **Rigoberta Menchú**, a Quiché Indian of **Guatemala**, was awarded the **Nobel Peace Prize** "in recognition," the Nobel Committee said, "of her work for social justice and ethno-cultural reconciliation based on respect for the rights of indigenous peoples." Menchú had been forced to flee her native land to escape the violence of the government in its treatment of those native Indians who opposed it.

1992 Oct. 26 **Canadian** voters rejected a package of constitutional changes intended to keep Québec in the federation and to satisfy demands of various other parts of the country. Approval was required by all ten provinces and the two territories, but six provinces and the Yukon Territory registered "no" votes, Québec and the four western provinces among them. The agreement voted on had been worked out (Aug. 22) at a conference in Charlottetown, Prince Edward Island, by Canada's prime minister, the ten provincial premiers, and territorial and native leaders. French-speaking Québec was to be termed a "distinct society," an elected instead of an appointed senate would have given greater power to the western region, and the native peoples were recognized to have an inherent right to self-government.

1992 Nov. 3 **William J[efferson] Clinton** (b. Aug. 18, 1946), the candidate of the Democratic party, was elected president of the U.S. Bill Clinton defeated the incumbent president **George Bush** of the Republican party by 370 to 168 votes in the Electoral College. Sen. **Albert Gore, Jr.**, was elected vice president. The Democrats retained control of both the Senate and the House of Representatives.

1992 Nov. 3 In the first presidential election since he seized power (1981), **Jerry J. Rawlings** was elected president of **Ghana** with 58.7 percent of the vote to 30 percent for his nearest rival. A former air force pilot, Rawlings had ruled Ghana with left-wing policies.

1992 Nov. 7 **Alexander Dubcek** (b. Nov. 27, 1921), first secretary of the **Czechoslovak** Communist party (from Jan. 1968) until his regime was overthrown by the invasion (Aug. 20, 1968) of his country by the combined forces of Bulgaria, East Germany, Hungary, Poland, and the U.S.S.R., died. A long-time member of the Communist party, Dubcek during World War II (1939–1945) fought as a partisan against the Nazi invaders. When named head of the regime he promised "a free, modern, and profoundly humane society," and his efforts to soften the workings of the totalitarian regime brought a brief period known as the **Prague Spring**. After the invasion Dubcek was expelled from the party and lived in obscurity until welcomed back (Nov. 1989) to public life when Communist rule ended.

1992 Nov. 21   **Kaysone Phomvihan** (b. Dec. 13, 1920), president (from Aug. 1991) of **Laos**, a onetime guerrilla leader who accomplished the Communist takeover (1975) of the country and who had been its effective leader ever since, died. Until the late 1980s he had kept Laos isolated, but he then eased up on control of the economy to privatize farming and commerce. The Laos parliament elected (Nov. 25) another hard-line Communist, **Nouhak Phoumsavan**, to succeed him.

1992 Nov. 24   By a vote of 59 to 3, with 79 nations abstaining, the U.N. General Assembly approved a resolution calling for an end to the U.S. thirty-year **embargo of trade with Communist Cuba**. The resolution was not binding on the U.S. The vote was prompted by a law, the **Cuban Democracy Act**, that was signed (Oct. 23) by **George Bush**, president of the U.S. The law made the embargo applicable to foreign subsidiaries of American companies, and many nations considered this an infringement of their sovereignty.

1992 Nov. 25   The parliament of **Czechoslovakia** voted approval of the **separation of the nation into the Czech Republic and Slovakia** as of midnight Dec. 31. Czechoslovakia had been formed (1918) at the end of World War I (1914–1918).

1992 Dec. 6   Reacting to increasingly **vicious attacks on refugees** who had sought asylum in **Germany**, the main political parties agreed on a law that would make it more difficult for refugees to gain asylum. Neo-Nazi groups, mostly "skinhead" youths, had carried out attacks in several cities and had killed (Nov. 23) three female Turks. The government banned (Nov. 27) one neo-Nazi group and later three others. **Germans rallied to protest the neo-Nazi violence**, a half million parading (Dec. 20) in a dozen cities. Asylum seekers had been entering Germany at the rate of 60,000 a month; rightists had carried out c.2,000 attacks, killing at least 17 persons.

1992 Dec. 8   In the first election since **Slovenia** separated (1991) from Yugoslavia, **Milan Kucan** (b. Jan. 14, 1941), a former Communist who had been serving as president, was elected to the post with 61

percent of the vote. He ran as a moderate independent.

1992 Dec. 9   **Charles**, Prince of Wales, heir to the British throne, and **Diana**, Princess of Wales, **agreed to a separation**, according to an announcement from Buckingham Palace, residence of **Elizabeth II**, queen and mother of Charles. It was also announced that there would be no divorce, that the couple would share in raising their two sons, that they would continue to perform public duties, and that their positions as future king and queen were not affected.

1992 Dec. 9   A contingent of **U.S. Marines**, the first of a large force, **went ashore in Mogadishu**, the capital of **Somalia**, on the northeastern coast of Africa, to begin a relief operation to distribute food in a land wracked by starvation, civil war, and drought. The U.N. Security Council had approved (Dec. 3) such a move by U.S.-led forces that would include troops from a number of other nations.

1992 Dec. 14   Surrendering to the opposition of the Congress of People's Deputies, **Boris Yeltsin**, president of **Russia**, abandoned attempts to have **Yegor T. Gaidar** confirmed as prime minister. Gaidar had been the leader of Yeltsin's program of rapid economic change. In his place **Viktor S. Chernomyrdin** (b. 1938), who had been in charge of the nation's fuel and energy complex, was named prime minister. He was expected to slow the pace of economic reform.

1992 Dec. 17   **Israel expelled 415 men** who had been identified as members of **Hamas** [Islamic Resistance Movement] in retaliation for the murder (Dec. 13) of an Israeli border policeman Hamas had kidnapped, demanding for his return the release from jail of their founder. Israeli troops took the 415 over the border into its security zone in southern Lebanon. The Lebanese, however, refused to allow the men into territory it controlled. Israel agreed to take back ten men who had mistakenly been arrested, but the rest remained in a no man's land, suffering from winter weather. The U.N. Security Council voted (Dec. 18) to condemn Israel for the expulsion.

1992 Dec. 18   The **treaty for European political and economic union**, worked out (Dec. 1991) by the 12-member **European Community** [EC] was approved by the German parliament. This action brought to ten the number of EC members approving, but in a referendum (June 2) Danish voters had rejected the pact, while Great Britain had put off action until May 1993. France had approved (Sept. 20), but by a narrow 51–49 percent vote. Thus the treaty could not go into effect (Jan. 1, 1993) as originally envisaged.

1992 Dec. 18   Kim Young Sam (b. Dec. 20, 1927), a former dissident who once had been under house arrest for opposing the authoritarian government of **South Korea**, was elected president with 42 percent of the vote. He would be the first non-military president in three decades. Kim had given up (1990) his opposition and joined the ruling Democratic Liberal party.

1992 Dec. 20   Slobodan Milosevic was reelected president of **Serbia**, defeating **Milan Panic** (b. Dec. 20, 1929), prime minister of Yugoslavia, which now consisted of Serbia and Montenegro only. Milosevic, the former Communist party chief of Serbia, was elected (1990) president in Serbia's first post-Communist election. He was the driving force in the current Serbian armed attempt to force other ethnic groups out of Bosnia and Herzegovina. Panic, a Serbian-born American millionare from California, had returned to his native land to become (July 14) prime minister.

1992 Dec. 24   George Bush, president of the U.S., granted full **pardons to six former federal officials** of the administration (1981–1989) of **Ronald Reagan**. All were involved in the **arms-for-hostages scandal** in which they were accused of playing some part in illegal deals to supply arms to Iran in return for that country's aid in securing the release of Americans held hostage in Lebanon by militant Arab groups. The pardons removed three guilty pleas, one conviction, and two cases yet to go to trial. Most prominent among those pardoned were **Caspar W. Weinberger** (b. Aug. 18, 1917), former secretary of defense, and **Robert C. McFarlane** (b. July 12, 1937), former national security adviser.

1992 Dec. 27   A U.S. F-16 warplane shot down an Iraqi warplane after it violated the no-flight zone of southern Iraq below the 32nd parallel. The U.S. and its allies had warned (Aug. 26) against such flights to prevent armed attacks by Iraqi forces on the Shiite Muslim population of the region.

1992 Dec. 29   The first multiparty election in **Kenya** in 16 years resulted in the reelection of **Daniel Arap Moi**, president (from 1978). He received 36 percent of the vote with his three main rivals splitting the rest. Moi's ruling Kenya African National Union party did not fare well, as the opposition won 88 of the 188 seats at stake in the parliament. Violence and protests against governmental corruption earlier in the year had forced Moi to schedule the election.

1992 Dec. 29   As an impeachment trial in the senate was beginning, **Fernando Collor de Mello**, president (from Mar. 1990) of **Brazil**, resigned. He had been accused of various forms of corruption, and the lower house of congress had voted (Sept. 29) to impeach him, making him liable to trial by the senate. Collor was succeeded by **Itamar Fancco**, the vice president of Brazil and a little-known politician with a reputation for honesty and caution.

IV. ECONOMY AND TRADE

1992 Jan. 1   A year of **economic turmoil in Russia** and the other republics that had become independent after the breakup (Dec. 1991) of the U.S.S.R. was ushered in when Belarus, Moldova, and Ukraine followed Russia's example and freed the prices of most consumer goods, except for some food items. There were protests in a number of cities as the cost of living increased. Russia's overall economic reform plan, aimed at achieving a free market system, was endorsed (Mar. 31) by the **International Monetary Fund** [IMF], which meant that it might soon be eligible to receive up to $4 billion in aid and to become a member of the Fund. The seven leading industrial nations, led by Germany and the U.S., announced (Apr. 1) a $24 billion aid program for Russia. As the Russian economy deteriorated, the government deficit grew, the IMF increased its demands regarding fiscal stability and internal political opposition to the government's plans mounted, the various aid packages were delayed indefinitely.

1992 Jan. 27   One of the largest department store operators in the U.S., **R.H. Macy & Co., filed for bankruptcy.** The company's troubles stemmed from a management buyout (1986) that saddled the firm with $3.5 billion of debt. Macy operated 251 stories nationwide and had 69,500 employees.

1992 Jan. 28   The **Association of Southeast Asian Nations** [ASEAN], meeting in Singapore, agreed to create a six-nation common market, similar to those being formed in Europe and North America. The **ASEAN Free Trade Area** would include Brunei, Indonesia, Malaysia, the Philippines, Singapore, and Thailand.

1992 Feb. 24   The largest U.S. auto manufacturer, **General Motors Corp., announced it would close 21 plants** in the U.S. and Canada over several years. The first 12 plants to be closed would put 16,300 workers out of their jobs. At the same time GM reported a loss in 1991 of $4.45 billion, the largest in American corporate history.

1992 Mar. 6   In a major merger in the music recording business, the British conglomerate, **Thorn EMI, bought the Virgin Music Group.** The acquisition put Thorn EMI, which paid c.$960 million for Virgin, among the top three such companies in terms of market share.

1992 Mar. 23   **Friedrich von Hayek** (b. May 8, 1899), an Austrian-born British economist, and a strong advocate of free market economic systems, died. He taught in Austria, Great Britain, and the U.S., and gradually developed a following of other economists who agreed with his views that government intervention in the economy was almost always a bad idea and that socialism was bound to fail. He expressed these views in his most notable book, *The Road to Serfdom* (1944). Hayek shared the **Nobel prize for economics** in 1974.

1992 Apr. 5   **Samuel Moore Walton** (b. Mar. 29, 1918), founder of **Wal-Mart Stores, Inc.**, one of the most successful enterprises in the U.S., died. Walton, after opening his first store in 1962, depended on large stores in small towns, offering a wide variety of merchandise and sizable discounts. At the time of his death the chain had 1,735 outlets and the Walton family wealth was estimated at $23 billion in Wal-Mart stock alone.

1992 Apr. 16   In Milan, Italy, a court convicted **Carlo de Benedetti** (b. Nov. 14, 1934), one of the most powerful business figures in the country, and 32 co-defendants, on charges of fraud stemming from the **collapse** (1982) **of Italy's largest private bank, Banco Ambrosiano.** Benedetti was sentenced to six years and four months in prison, but appeals were expected to keep him out of jail for several years. He was the chairman of Olivetti, a large computer firm.

1992 Apr. 27   Membership in the **International Monetary Fund** [IMF] and the **World Bank** [International Bank for Reconstruction and Development] was offered to **Russia, Ukraine**, and most of the other former U.S.S.R. republics. Such membership would be a major step in fitting these formerly Communist nations into the world economy.

1992 May 14   **Olympia and York Developments Ltd.**, the largest real estate developer in the world, **filed for bankruptcy** in Toronto, Canada. At the center of its troubles, at a time of recession and weakness in the real estate market, was the vast, uncompleted office development, Canary Wharf, in London. Owned by the Reichmann family, and with interests in Canada, Great Britain, and the U.S., the company had debts of more than $18 billion and had lost $1.76 billion in its 1991 fiscal year.

1992 May 17   Swiss voters approved, 55.8 to 44.2 percent, **Switzerland joining the International Monetary Fund** and the **World Bank**. This broke a long tradition of neutrality and isolation, even from such organizations as these, and there were indications that Switzerland would apply for membership in the European Community [EC].

1992 May 18   **Czechoslovakia began the largest sale of companies** ever undertaken when it offered shares in 1,446 state-owned businesses to the public, marking an end to Communist economics and a move to a free market system. Of the nation's 11 million adults, 8.6 million elected to take part in this sale of assets valued at $9.3 billion. Those involved had purchased vouchers for $37 each, which allowed them to bid a total of 1,000 points for shares.

1992 June 1   On the New York Stock Exchange the **Dow Jones industrial average** closed above 3,400 for the first time, ending the day at 3,413.21.

1992 July 3   In **Kenya**, eastern Africa, **privatization of government-owned businesses** began when 207 companies were put up for sale, including the state airline and a mountain inn. The sale was the result of pressure brought upon the one-party government by Western nations and international aid agencies, which had suspended c.$600 million of aid to force the government to reform both economically and politically.

1992 Aug. 12   An agreement for **free trade for all of North America** was announced by Canada, Mexico, and the U.S. Key elements of the pact included: the elimination of tariff barriers on thousands of items;

the setting up of obstacles to prevent Asian and European nations from avoiding U.S. tariffs by shipping goods through Mexico; and the opening of the Mexican banking, insurance, and securities businesses to others. The agreement would create a trading bloc of 370 million people. Formal signing of the pact took place (Dec. 17) in Washington. In the U.S., approval by Congress was required and, in Canada, by its parliament.

1992 Aug. 20 *Fortune* magazine's ranking of the world's billionaires placed the **Sultan of Brunei** (b. July 15, 1946), ruler of that Pacific island nation, at the top with a worth of $37 billion. In all, 223 persons were listed with an average wealth of $2.7 billion.

1992 Aug. 28 In the face of a falling stock market and weaknesses in the banking system, resulting in part from a rapid decline in real estate prices, the **Japanese government announced the largest program of economic stimulus** in the nation's history. Government spending for the year was to be increased by c.$86 billion, more than doubling the spending on public works and offering incentives to business. The Tokyo stock market had fallen (Aug. 10) to its lowest level in six years.

1992 Sept. 16 The **European Monetary System** [EMS], intended to keep the currencies of eleven of the twelve member nations of the European Community [EC] stable in value in relation to each other, came near collapse when the British pound fell sharply in value and Great Britain dropped out, at least temporarily, of the EMS. Italy withdrew the next day and Spain devalued its currency. The French franc fell but was somewhat stabilized (Sept. 24) by a joint effort of France and Germany. The EMS remained in difficulty the rest of the year as the German mark continued to be much stronger than the other currencies. On Nov. 22, Portugal also devalued its currency.

1992 Oct. 1 The **Russian government began issuing** to some 148 million eligible citizens one **voucher** each, valued at 10,000 rubles [c.$40], to be used, beginning Dec. 1, **for buying state-owned industries** and businesses. The vouchers could also be sold and individuals could pool vouchers to undertake joint ventures. Between 5,000 and 7,000 large- and medium-sized factories would be reorganized as joint stock companies, while smaller shops and businesses would also be available. The total value of the vouchers was placed at $4.5 billion. When the pro-

cess actually began (Dec. 9), the first business offered for privatization was a pastry-making factory, followed by a refrigerated warehouse.

1992 Oct. 13 **British Coal**, the government body operating the coal mines of Great Britain, announced it **would close 31** of its remaining 50 **mines**, laying off 30,000 miners and other employees. The announcement caused so much public protest that the government hastily said (Oct. 19) that only ten mines would be shut down with a loss of 7,500 jobs. Since 1947, when the coal mining industry was nationalized, the demand for coal had fallen steadily, dropping, for example, from 80 million tons in 1990 to an expected 40 million tons in 1993.

1992 Nov. 20 The European Community [EC] and the U.S., after six years of often acrimonious negotiations, reached agreement on a method for reducing **government subsidies of farm products**. The U.S. had long contended that such subsidies created unfair conditions in international trade. France, the largest agricultural producer and exporter in the EC, said (Nov. 21) that the terms of the agreement were unacceptable but admitted (Nov. 22) that under EC rules it had no legal right to veto it. The agreement called for a 21 percent reduction in tonnage of subsidized grain exports. If this arrangement held, the way would then be opened for broader negotiations as part of the **General Agreement on Tariffs and Trade** [GATT].

1992 Nov. 27 The **Organization of Petroleum Exporting Countries** [OPEC], meeting in Vienna, Austria, agreed to **cut daily oil production** by c.400,000 barrels to a total of 24.58 million. OPEC hoped thereby to hold the price of crude oil at c.$20 a barrel.

1992 Dec. 15 The world's largest computer maker, **International Business Machines Corp.** [IBM], though in recent years unable to match its competitors' offerings, said it would **cut 25,000 jobs** in 1993, bringing the total number of employees to 275,000 from a peak (1986) of 400,000. IBM also announced it expected to show a loss for 1992 of $4.75 billion, which would be the **largest in U.S. corporate history**.

1992 Dec. 20 **Stephen** [Jay] **Ross** [orig. Stephen Jay Rechnitz] (b. Apr. 5, 1927), an American entrepreneur, head of **Time Warner**, Inc., the world's largest media and entertainment company, died. From operating a funeral home, to a car rental business, to the entertainment world, the flamboyant Ross masterminded (1989) the merger that brought his Warner Communications and Time, Inc., together. The result was a company strong in publishing, films, music recordings, and cable systems and programming.

V. RELIGION AND PHILOSOPHY

1992 Apr. 12 About **300 men who had been secretly ordained as Roman Catholic priests in Czechoslovakia** during the Communist regime (1948–1989) were ordered by the Vatican to report to their local bishops. The unmarried ones among them could apply for formal ordination after being tested about their knowledge of the church's liturgy and teachings. Those who were married were informed they must give up performing the duties of the priesthood. The Vatican said this action was based on doubt about the validity of the secret ordinations, but some saw the move as triggered by the church's rule against married clergy.

1992 May 11 How to deal with the problems of **homosexuality and abortion continued to concern Protestant denominations in the U.S.**, as indicated by the action of the General Conference of the United Methodist Church, the second largest such denomination, when it reaffirmed its position that homosexuality was in conflict with Christian teaching. The Southern Baptist Convention, the largest Protestant body, banished (May 19) two congregations for accepting homosexuals. The Presbyterian Church (U.S.A.) backed away (June 8) from a previous strong stand in support of abortion rights by adopting a statement that discouraged abortion, although continuing to endorse a woman's right to secure one.

1992 July 23 For the first time a **woman, Naamah Kelman, was ordained** in Jerusalem, Israel, **as a rabbi** of Reform Judaism.

1992 Aug. 24 A German theologian, **Konrad Raiser**, was elected the new secretary general of the **World Council of Churches**, which represents Protestant and Orthodox denominations. An ordained minister of the Evangelical Church in Germany, Raiser was a professor of theology at Ruhr University. He was to succeed (Jan. 1, 1993) the Rev. **Emilio Castro** (b. May 2, 1927) of Uruguay, who was retiring.

1992 Sept. 21 After 136 years **Mexico and the Vatican reestablished full diplomatic relations**. Viewing the Roman Catholic Church as too influential and liberal, Mexico restricted its rights in the 19th century and again after the Mexican Revolution (1910–1915). For a long time, however, the restrictions on clerical garb, parochial schools, and religious observances had been largely ignored in a nation where 90 percent of the population considers itself Catholic.

1992 Oct. 31 In a speech in Rome, Italy, **Pope John Paul II** acknowledged that the church had erred in 1633 when it condemned the astronomer **Galileo** for maintaining that the earth moves around the sun, instead of vice versa. Galileo had been forced to recant, and had been kept under house arrest for eight years.

1992 Nov. 11 The **Church of England**, after a bitter debate, **voted to allow women to be ordained as priests**. Voting separately at the church's General Synod, the bishops approved by a wide margin, as did the clergy, but the laity's vote was barely over the two-thirds required. Parliament and **Elizabeth II** still had to give their approval. Many of those opposed threatened to leave the church. Of the 28 self-governing provinces of the worldwide Anglican Communion, 12 had already ordained women as priests.

1992 Nov. 16 In preparation since 1985, a **new catechism**, the first since 1555, was **issued by the Roman Catholic Church**, reaffirming many traditional tenets of the faith, but also covering problems of modern society. The catechism restated the church's historic opposition to abortion, divorce, homosexuality, artificial birth control, the ordination of women as priests, and other matters. It also newly defined as sins such activities as drug abuse, genetic engineering, drunken driving, tax evasion, artificial insemination, and abuse of the environment.

1992 Nov. 18 After nine years of drafting and debating, the **U.S. National Conference of Catholic Bishops** refused to adopt a proposed pastoral letter on the **place of women in the church** and in society. The vote was 137 to 110 in favor of the final text, but this did not reach the necessary two-thirds majority. The final draft had affirmed the equality of men and women, and opposed discrimination in business. However, it opposed ordaining women into the priesthood, and in general supported the conservative positions of the Vatican.

1992 Dec. 6   A mob of thousands of **Hindu militants attacked a Muslim mosque** in Ayodhya, in northern India, and destroyed it, using only hand tools and bare hands. The mosque had been erected (1528) by **Baber** [Babur], emperor (1526–1530) of the Mogul [Mughal] Empire of Hindustan (1526–1857), but the Hindus claimed it stood on the spot where their god **Rama** [Ram] was born, and they proposed to build a Hindu temple in place of the mosque. As a result of the destruction, **Hindu-Muslim riots** broke out all over India.

VI. SCIENCE, EDUCATION, AND TECHNOLOGY

1992 Feb. 12   Ten to 12 million people worldwide have contracted **HIV** [human immunodeficiency virus], which causes **AIDS**, the **World Health Organization** [WHO] reported. It also said that since the early 1980s, when the disease first became known, there had been 2 million cases of AIDS. Another report (June 3), from a group at the Harvard School of Public Health, predicted that by the year 2000 from 40 to 110 million people would be infected with the virus. HIV was spreading rapidly in Southeast Asia, and by 2000 the largest proportion of infected persons would be Asians rather than Africans. More women, in proportion, were becoming infected and accounted for 40 percent of HIV cases, compared with 25 percent in 1990.

1992 Feb. 20   Scientists reported they had identified what they believed to be the **earliest known fossil of a member of the Homo line** of human ancestors. They dated it as being 2.4 million years old, about 500,000 years earlier than previous findings. The discovery was based on a new dating technique used on a three-inch long skull fragment that had been found more than a quarter-century ago near Lake Baringo in Kenya, eastern Africa.

1992 Mar. 30   **Manolis Andronicos** (b. Oct. 23, 1919), a Greek archaeologist who discovered (1977) what was probably the tomb of Philip II, king of Macedon (359–336 B.C.), and father of **Alexander the Great**, died. Andronicos had been carrying on excavations at Vergina, a village in northern Greece, for 40 years and had found a number of tombs and artifacts of ancient times when he made his most important find. The tomb was 17 feet underground and in it were ivory heads that resembled portraits of Philip and Alexander. There were also paintings,

weapons, and silver and gold ornaments. A gold casket held what may be Philip's bones.

1992 Apr. 8   **Daniele Bovet** (b. Mar. 23, 1907), a Swiss-born biochemist who worked in both France and Italy in his successful search for the **first antihistamine**, died. His experiments (1937–1941) resulted in the chemical formulas upon which most antihistamines, used principally to treat allergies, are based. Earlier (1929–1935) he and other scientists discovered **sulfanilamide**, the first of the so-called "**wonder drugs.**" Bovet was awarded the **Nobel Prize for physiology or medicine** in 1957.

1992 Apr. 16   The U.S. Food and Drug Administration ordered **restrictions on the use of silicone breast implants** until more study was undertaken as to their safety. Dow Corning Corp., the largest manufacturer of the implants, had decided (Mar. 18) to stop making them, though it declared they were safe. It had been revealed (Jan. 12), however, that the company had not made safety studies as recommended by its own scientists.

1992 Apr. 23   Significant support for the **Big Bang theory** of the creation of the universe was seen in a report by scientists that, looking back toward the beginning of time, they had been able to detect wrinkles in the fabric of space. This constituted the first evidence as to how the cosmos, that was at first smooth, had evolved into the stars and galaxies existing today.

1992 May 13   For the first time, **three astronauts ventured into space together**, and with their gloved hands held onto a wayward satellite. The astronauts were part of the crew of the U.S. space shuttle *Endeavor*. They wrestled the 4.5-ton, 17-foot satellite into the cargo bay of the *Endeavor*.

1992 June 14   The **Earth Summit**, attended by most of the countries of the world, including many heads of state and of government, **ended in Rio de Janeiro**, Brazil, with agreements on a number of treaties intended to aid the environment. Among the pacts was one aimed at protecting the world's plant, animal, and microbial species, which, however, the U.S. refused to sign; another was intended to curb the emission of gases thought to warm the climate; while a nonbinding statement encouraged nations to minimize damage to their forests.

1992 June 11 Four teams of scientists, working independently, reported they had found **evidence that planetary systems resembling our solar system** when it was young may exist in comparatively nearby parts of the galaxy that earth is in. The evidence consisted of chemical substances that astronomers found in a disk around a star that were similar to substances that once encircled the sun.

1992 June 28 In an operation in a Pittsburgh, Pennsylvania, hospital, a **baboon's liver was transplanted into a human** for the first time. The 11½-hour operation was performed on a 35-year-old man who was dying of hepatitis B. He died on Sept. 6 after suffering a massive stroke that doctors said was not related to any rejection of the implant.

1992 June 29 The universe may be older and larger than many scientists had thought, according to astronomers who reported on the results of observations made by the **Hubble Space Telescope.** They now estimated the age of the universe as being at least 15 billion years. Earlier (Jan.) astronomers using the telescope were surprised to see dense clusters of young blue stars in globular clusters that had been assumed previously to be among the oldest structures in the universe.

1992 July 9 The U.S. space shuttle *Columbia* landed at Cape Canaveral, Florida, after a flight of two weeks, the longest for such a craft. The shuttle traveled 5,760,000 miles and circled the globe 221 times.

1992 Aug. 5 Astronauts aboard the U.S. space shuttle *Atlantis* were forced to abandon attempts to place an Italian satellite in orbit at the end of a 12-mile tether. After several efforts the cable became stuck when only 845 feet of it was extended. The shuttle and the satellite were to have flown together to test the dynamics of tethered vehicles.

1992 Aug. 14 Israeli archaeologists reported the discovery earlier of a family **tomb,** buried in a cave on the outskirts of Jerusalem, that may contain the bones of [Joseph] **Caiaphas,** the Jewish high priest (c.18–36) who presided at the trial of Jesus. These bones, if those of Caiaphas, would be the remains of the only major figure in the New Testament for which such evidence exists.

1992 Sept. 2 Barbara McClintock (b. June 16, 1902), an American geneticist who was one of the most influential figures in her field for fifty years, died. Working alone and not publishing some of her findings for many years, she was one of the first to understand the nature of genes and how they interact. McClintock used corn to explore the manner in which genes and chromosomes operate. She was awarded the **Nobel prize for physiology or medicine** in 1983. She was the first woman to win an unshared Nobel Prize in that category, and the third woman to win an unshared Nobel Prize in any of the sciences.

1992 Sept. 15 Astronomers reported that, using a telescope in Hawaii, they had detected beyond Neptune and Pluto a small object that could be evidence of a **belt of icy minor planets.** They could be the source of comets that come from the fringes of the solar system. The objects sighted were c.120 miles in diameter.

1992 Sept. 20 The first shuttle flight devoted to Japanese research ended when the U.S. craft *Endeavor* landed at Cape Canaveral, Florida. Among the experiments carried out was the fertilization and hatching of frog eggs. The result was the birth of 155 tadpoles, the first creatures other than insects to be brought to life in a weightless situation. The flight was also notable for carrying in space the first married couple, the first black woman, and the first Japanese astronaut.

1992 Sept. 25 The U.S. launched an unmanned spacecraft bound for Mars, the first such flight in 17 years. The 5,700-pound *Mars Observer* was to make the 11-month, 450 million-mile journey so as to rendezvous with the planet on Aug. 24, 1993. It would then spend a Martian year of 687 earth days photographing Mars to record its geological and climatological features.

1992 Oct. 8 A study made in Edinburgh, Scotland, found that the French abortion pill, **RU 486,** was also **effective as a morning-after pill to prevent pregnancy.** Family planning experts welcomed this finding and hoped it would make the drug more acceptable to those who oppose abortion. Pro-life groups, however, contended that morning-after pills were the moral equivalent of abortion. The argument rested in part on when pregnancy occurs, which many medical experts hold is not until about a week after an egg is fertilized. RU 486 was sold only in China, France, Great Britain, and Sweden.

1992 Oct. 9 *Pioneer 12*, an unmanned U.S. spacecraft that was launched May 20, 1978, to study Venus, plummeted through the atmosphere of the planet and thus ended its career. Originally expected to perform its tasks for only a year, *Pioneer 12* worked for 14 years and sent back more than 400 billion bits of data.

1992 Oct. 12 Using the **world's largest radio telescopes**, one located in Puerto Rico and another in California, astronomers began the **most comprehensive search for evidence of extraterrestrial life**. The ten-year project was to use signal processing systems able to search more than 10 million channels simultaneously over a wide range of the microwave radio spectrum.

1992 Nov. 25 Faced with new evidence that the earth's **ozone layer** is being depleted more widely than feared, representatives of 87 nations, meeting in Copenhagen, Denmark, agreed to move forward from the year 2000 to Jan. 1, 1996, the **deadline for ending the production of chemicals**, especially **chlorofluorocarbons** [CFCs], which destroy the ozone.

1992 Dec. 1 Of the world's megacities, **London**, **New York**, and **Tokyo** have the **cleanest air**, according to a study by the **World Health Organization** [WHO], while **Mexico City**'s air is the dirtiest and **Los Angeles** among the worst in ozone pollution.

1992 Dec. 30 A report of an investigation by the U.S. Federal Office of Research Integrity said that **Robert C. Gallo** (b. Mar. 23, 1937), a research scientist, had falsely reported (1984) a critical fact in a paper in which he claimed he had isolated the virus that causes **AIDS**. He was said to have misled colleagues to take credit for himself and to lessen credit that had accrued to French scientists for work that they had already done in this field. Gallo denied the charges.

VII. ARTS AND LEISURE

1992 Jan. 3 **Judith Anderson** [née Frances Margaret Anderson] (b. Feb. 10, 1899), an Australian-born, internationally known star of the stage, movies, and television, died. She made her stage debut (1915) in Sydney, Australia. Her most dazzling success (1947) on the New York stage was in the title role of *Medea*. In the movies Anderson made (1940) notable a supporting role in *Rebecca*. On television she was acclaimed for her portrayal of Lady Macbeth.

1992 Jan. 26 **José** [Vincente] **Ferrer** [y Cintrón] (b. Jan. 8, 1912), a Puerto Rican-born American actor, producer, director, and writer for over half a century, died. His first leading stage role (1940) was in *Charley's Aunt*. He made his movie debut (1948) in *Joan of Arc*. Ferrer was best known for playing the title role in *Cyrano de Bergerac* on the stage (1947), on television (1949), and on film (1950). He was noted for his restrained approach to acting, combined with intelligence and versatility.

1992 Feb. 10 **Alex Haley** (b. Aug. 11, 1921), an American author whose best-selling book *Roots* (1976) traced his ancestry from a young black man living in Africa in 1750 before being seized as a slave to the present day, died. A television miniseries based on the book was one of the most popular programs, being viewed by as many as 36.3 million households. The book had sold c.5.5 million copies.

1992 Feb. 15 **William** [Howard] **Schuman** (b. Aug. 4, 1910), an American composer and educator who used jazz and folk music in his work, died. He first came to notice with his Third Symphony (1941). In all Schuman created ten symphonies, five ballets, and other instrumental and vocal works. As an educator, Schuman was president (1945–1962) of the **Juilliard School of Music**, New York City, and the first president (1962–1969) of the **Lincoln Center for the Performing Arts**, New York City.

1992 Mar. 14 **Jean Poiret** (b. Aug. 17, 1926), a French dramatist and director, best known for the stage and movie success *La Cage aux Folles*, died. He acted in the original Paris production of the play, about an aging homosexual couple. It became a movie (1979) that developed a cult following, and finally was turned into a musical which, beginning in 1983, ran for more than four years in New York City. Poiret appeared in some 40 movies, including *Chicken in Vinegar* (1985) and *Inspector Lavardin* (1986).

1992 Mar. 29 **Paul Henreid** (b. Jan 10, 1908), an Austrian-born American actor who on stage, screen, and television was impressive as a suave leading man, died. He first won wide recognition in *Victoria Regina* (1937), but it was as an anti-Nazi leader in the movie *Casablanca* (1942) that he was best remembered. In all Henreid acted in or directed more than 300 films and television dramas.

1992 Apr. 5 Vakhtang Mikhailovich Chabukiani (b. Mar. 12, 1910), a Soviet ballet master and choreographer, known as one of the most accomplished dancers of his time, died. With a very athletic style of dancing, he was well suited to roles as the hero in Soviet ballets. An early example was his dancing of the lead role in *Flames of Paris* (1932). The best-known ballets choreographed by Chabukiani were *The Heart of the Hills* (1938) and *Laurencia* (1939). Both, in keeping with the times, concerned lower-class persons involved in political revolt.

1992 Apr. 6 Isaac Asimov (b. Jan. 2, 1920), an American author, noted both for the quality and the quantity of his science fiction novels and short stories, died. He wrote c.500 books in all, dealing with history, science, and literature, as well as science fiction. His major work of science fiction was *Foundation Trilogy* (1951–1953). Asimov sold his first short story when he was 18 years old, then became a college teacher of biochemistry, and published his first science fiction novel, *Pebble in the Sky*, in 1950. In *I, Robot* (1950) Asimov set a standard for the use of such machines in fiction with his Three Laws of Robotics to govern the relation of robots to humans.

1992 Apr. 6 Molly Picon (b. June 1, 1898), an American actress known for her performances in English and Yiddish, died. Her talent for comedy first appeared when she was 15 years old. She reached stardom with *Yankele* (1923), a kind of Yiddish Peter Pan story. Picon said she had performed in it 3,000 times. Another hit was the musical *The Kosher Widow* (1959), but her greatest success on Broadway was another musical, *Milk and Honey* (1961).

1992 Apr. 8 *Punch*, Great Britain's old and famous satirical magazine, suspended publication after 150 years because of financial difficulties. Founded in 1841, it came to represent everyone's idea of British humor.

1992 Apr. 20 [Alfred Hawthorn] Benny Hill (b. Jan. 21, 1925), a popular British television comedian whose shows amused viewers around the world, died. A master of the double-entendre, his typically British style of bawdy humor sometimes caused him to be accused of sexism. Hill's seemingly innocent choir boy's grin made him a television star in the 1950s, and he was especially successful with a series of half-hour programs that began in 1979.

1992 Apr. 23 Satyajit Ray (b. May 2, 1921), an Indian film maker, died. Though his films were seldom popular successes, Ray's work won many prizes. His first movie was *Pather Panchali* [*Song of the Road*] (1955). His Calcutta trilogy consisted of *Days and Nights in the Forest* (1969), *The Adversary* (1971), and *The Target* (1972). *Branches of the Tree* (1990) was Ray's commentary on what he saw as the loss of ethical standards in India. His last movie, *Agantuk* [*The Stranger*] (1991), concerned a mysterious visitor to a Calcutta family.

1992 Apr. 27 Olivier [Eugene Prosper Charles] Messiaen (b. Dec. 10, 1908), a French composer whose work reflected an especially wide variety of sources, from bird songs to religious mysticism and Balinese rhythmic modes, died. His works included orchestral and chamber music as well as choral, piano, and organ pieces. Messiaen's first published compositions were eight Preludes for piano (1929). Among his notable works were an orchestral piece, *L'ascension* (1933) and *Sept. Haikai* (1962), which was influenced by a trip to Japan.

1992 Apr. 28 Francis Bacon (b. Oct. 28, 1909), an Irish-born British painter, whose blunt, satirical style of portraiture made him a controversial figure, died. The first of his paintings to bring him wide attention, *Three Studies for Figures at the Base of the Crucifixion* (1944), set an example for characters that seemed drawn from anger. In such exhibits as those of 1962 and 1985 in London, Bacon shocked many with his gallows humor of howling figures and twisted human beings.

1992 May 6 [Marie Magdalene] Marlene Dietrich (b. Dec. 27, 1901), a German-born actress and the most glamorously sensual star of her time, died. She became an international sensation with the movie *Blue Angel* (1930), in which she portrayed a seductive night club singer. Among Dietrich's other films of particular note were *Morocco* (1930), *Shanghai Express* (1932), *Destry Rides Again* (1939), and *Touch of Evil* (1958). Her elegant legs and cool, dreamy face, which exuded a world-weary sophistication, made Dietrich a compelling figure in any role.

1992 June 3 Robert Morley (b. May 26, 1908), an English actor, director, and playwright, noted especially for his portly figure and his roles as a jolly, humorously pompous figure, died. Making his London stage debut in 1928, he achieved stardom (1936) in the title role of *Oscar Wilde*. Other stage successes were leading parts in *Major Barbara* (1939) and *Edward My Son* (1947), of which he was co-author. In the movies, Morley was much appreciated in *Topkapi* (1964) and *Who Is Killing the Great Chefs of Europe?* (1978).

1992 June 22   M[ary] F[rances] K[ennedy] **Fisher** (b. July 3, 1908), an American author of fiction and essays, who was best known for her writings about food, died. Her first book, *Serve It Forth* (1937), was an example of her attitude that eating should be a pleasure. One of Fisher's best-known books was *How to Cook a Wolf* (1942). As a novelist she wrote *Not Now But Now* (1947). Later books included the autobiographical *Sister Age* (1983) and a volume for children, *The Boss Dog* (1991).

1992 July 21   The 60 million words of the second edition of the *Oxford English Dictionary*, in 20 volumes, were made available on a single computer disk. In reply to a query, the disk in a computer searches all 20 volumes in a matter of seconds. The disk was priced at $875, compared with $2,750 for the printed version.

1992 July 24   **Arletty** [née Arlette-Léonie Bathiat] (b. May 15, 1898), a French actress who was noted for her beauty and who achieved instant stardom with her role in the movie *Hotel dú Nord* (1938), died. After working as a model and chorus girl, she made her first movie in 1930. Among her more than 50 films were *Le Jour Se Lève* (1939) and *Les Enfants du Paradis* (1945). Arletty made few movies outside of France, but one of her last roles was in the American film *The Longest Day* (1962).

1992 Aug. 12   **John** [Milton] **Cage** [Jr.] (b. Sept. 5, 1912), an American avant-garde composer, died. He made formal classification difficult by using his own atonal system and electronic devices to write such compositions as *Imaginary Landscape, No. 1* (1939) and *Hpschd* (1969) for 7 harpsichords, 51 tapes, films, slides, and colored lights. Cage also on occasion tossed coins to determine what elements were to go into a composition, as with *Music of Changes* (1951). He was both much admired and much criticized, and had considerable influence on the minimalist movement in ballet and art as well as in musical composition.

1992 Oct. 8   **Derek Walcott** (b. Jan. 23, 1930) of Santa Lucia became the first writer from the West

Indies to be awarded the **Nobel prize for literature**. A poet and a playwright, Walcott was cited for his historical vision, the outcome of a multicultural commitment. An early volume of Walcott's poetry appeared in 1964 and his latest, *Omeros*, in 1990. His newest play was *The Odyssey* (1992).

1992 Oct. 29   **Kenneth MacMillan** (b. Dec. 11, 1929), a British choreographer and director of the Royal Ballet (1970–1977), died. He began (1946) his career as a dancer, and then created (1953) his first ballet, *Sonambulism*. MacMillan was director (1966–1970) of the Deutsche Opera of West Berlin, and an artistic associate (1984–1990) of the American Ballet Theater. Among his other ballets were *The Burrow* (1958) and *The Invitation* (1960).

1992 Nov. 2   [Harold Eugene] **Hal Roach** (b. Jan. 14, 1892), a pioneer American movie writer, producer, and director, died. He was particularly noted for his achievements in comedy. Roach helped make stars of such actors as **Harold Lloyd**, **Harry Langdon**, **Will Rogers**, the comedy team of **Laurel and Hardy**, and the kids who played in the numerous **Our Gang films**. Typical of his popular movies was *Safety Last* (1923), starring Lloyd.

1992 Nov. 18   **Dorothy Kirsten** (b. July 6, 1910), an American lyric soprano who sang leading roles at the Metropolitan Opera, New York City, for 30 years, died. She was particularly noted for her performances of the leading roles in Puccini operas, such as Mimi in *La Bohème*. Kirsten made her professional debut in 1939 and her operatic debut the following year in Chicago. She also sang in Europe and appeared (1962) in the Soviet Union with the Bolshoi Opera.

1992 Nov. 25   The 40th anniversary of the opening of *The Mousetrap*, a murder mystery by **Agatha Christie**, which was by far the **longest-running play in the history of the London theater**, was observed at a luncheon. The play had been seen by 9 million people, had earned $32 million, had involved 259 actors and actresses, had been performed in 44 countries, and had been translated into 24 languages.

1992 Dec. 8   **William Shawn** [orig. William Chon] (b. Aug. 31, 1907), an American editor noted for his quiet but firm direction (1952–1987) of *The New Yorker*, died. He began (1935) his career as an editor and soon made his mark as one who insisted on the best and who could bring out excellence in the magazine's contributors. One of Shawn's special coups was to devote an entire issue to *Hiroshima* (1946), an account of the atomic bombing of the city and its aftermath, by **John Hersey** (June 17, 1914–Mar. 24, 1993) .

1992 Dec. 21   Stella Adler (b. Feb. 10, 1901), an American actress and an admired teacher of the craft of acting, died. She made her debut when she was only four years old, and became popular in the Yiddish theater. She also starred on Broadway and opened (1949) the Stella Adler Conservatory of Acting. Here she was an exponent of the Method school and stressed the importance of imagination over memory. Her theories were set forth in *Stella Adler on Acting* (1988).

1992 Dec. 21   Nathan [Mironovich] **Milstein** (b. Dec. 31 1904), a Russian-born American violinist, much praised for his mastery of the 19th-century Romantic repertory, died. He made (1920) his debut in Odessa, left (1926) Russia, and made (1929) his American debut. Although Milstein was the complete technician, he was popular for the warm, silvery tone of his playing. His autobiography was *From Russia to the West: The Musical Memoirs of Nathan Milstein* (1990).

VIII. SPORTS, GAMES, AND SOCIETY

1992 Jan. 13   For the first time **Canada granted refugee status to a homosexual** because of persecution in his homeland, Argentina, where the law allowed the arrest of homosexuals. Similar rulings had previously been made in Germany and the Netherlands, but this was the first case of its kind in North America.

1992 Feb. 8–23   The XVI Winter **Olympic Games** were held in Albertville, France, with 2,174 athletes, a record, from 64 countries taking part. Germany won 10 gold medals and 26 overall; the Unified Team, representing the lands that formerly made up the Soviet Union, 9 and 23; and Austria 6 and 21. Of the 11 medals won by U.S. athletes, 8 went to women, including all 5 gold medals. Stars of the games were: **Raisa Smetanina** (b. Feb. 29, 1952) of the Unified Team, a skier who in five Olympics had now won 10 medals; **Toni Nieminen** of Finland, who at 16 years old became the youngest gold medalist; and **Kim Yoon Man** of South Korea, who became that country's first Olympic medalist when he finished second in a speed-skating event.

1992 Feb. 10   Mike Tyson, former world heavyweight boxing champion (1986–1990), was convicted of rape in Indianapolis, Indiana, and was sentenced (Mar. 26) to six years in prison. Tyson had been charged (July 19, 1991) with raping an 18-year-old beauty pageant contestant.

1992 Feb. 17   Martina Navratilova, a Czech-born American **tennis** star, in Chicago, Illinois, **won her 158th tournament title**, a record for the women's tour. She broke the mark held until then by **Chris Evert**. Navratilova won (1973) her first tournament in Czechoslovakia. She also held the **record for career earnings by women tennis players** at $17.7 million.

1992 Feb. 27   The **Supreme Court of Canada**, in a unanimous decision, ruled that it was legitimate to **outlaw pornography that was harmful to women**. The ruling came even though, the court said, the nation's law on obscenity infringed on freedom of expression. In effect, the court redefined obscenity as consisting of sexually explicit material that involved degradation or violence. The court also set a precedent by agreeing that pornography can harm women.

1992 Mar. 2   Ryne Sandberg of the Chicago Cubs became the **highest paid player in the history of American major league baseball** when he signed a four-year contract worth $28.4 million.

1992 Mar. 27   Easley Blackwood (b. June 25, 1903), an American contract **bridge** expert who devised (1933) the widely used Blackwood convention, died. His method called for the partner of a four no-trump bidder to show by his bidding the number of aces he held. Blackwood was also a teacher of bridge and author of a number of books on the subject, including *The Complete Book of Opening Leads* (1983).

1992 Apr. 4   Samuel [Herman] **Reshevsky** [orig. Rzeszewski] (b. Nov. 26, 1991), a Polish-born American **chess** expert, who defeated three world champions, though never when the title was at stake, died. Learning to play when he was five years old, he toured Europe three years later as a child prodigy. Moving to the U.S. in 1920, Reshevsky won the national championship seven times (1936, 1938, 1940, 1942, 1946, 1969, and 1971).

1992 Apr. 8   Arthur Ashe (b. July 10, 1943), the first and only black player to win (1968) the men's U.S.

Open and the British [Wimbledon] (1975) tennis championships, revealed that he had contracted **AIDS**, apparently as the result of a blood transfusion during an operation (1988). Ashe died on Feb. 6, 1993.

1992 Apr. 9　**Manuel Antonio Noriega**, former dictator (Aug. 1985–Jan. 1990) of Panama, was convicted in a U.S. federal court in Miami, Florida, on eight counts of cocaine trafficking, racketeering, and money laundering, in the **first case in American history in which the head of a foreign country was found guilty on criminal charges**. On July 10 he was sentenced to 40 years in prison. Noriega had surrendered (Jan. 3, 1990) in Panama City, Panama, to U.S. forces that had invaded (Dec. 20, 1989) the country. He was accused of allowing the Medellin drug cartel of Colombia to ship large quantities of cocaine to the U.S. via Panama in return for millions of dollars in bribes. Noriega had originally been indicted in the U.S. on Feb. 5, 1988.

1992 Apr. 12　**Euro-Disneyland**, an enormous entertainment complex, built by the American Walt Disney Co., **opened** at Marne-La-Vallée, 20 miles east of Paris. The first Disney theme park in Europe, it was built at a cost of $4 billion and covered 4,800 acres. The park included 29 rides and other attractions, 6 hotels, artificial lakes, and an entertainment area. Some French intellectuals sneered at what they considered a boorish American display of poor taste, but the builders aimed at attracting 11 million visitors the first year. This goal was not attained.

1992 Apr. 20　**Expo '92**, the largest world's fair ever, covering 540 acres, opened (to Oct. 12) in Seville, Spain, with its theme "The Age of Discoveries," a celebration of the 500th anniversary of the first voyage of Christopher Columbus to the Western Hemisphere. Costing $2 billion, the exposition offered displays housed in more than 100 national, regional, and theme pavilions. Musicians, dancers, and other entertainers from 111 countries were to be seen at 21 theaters during the course of Expo '92.

1992 June 26　The German parliament adopted a new **law allowing abortion on demand** in the first three months of pregnancy if the woman said she was in distress and if she first underwent counseling. The law made consistent the rules governing abortion in what had been East and West Germany before unification in Oct. 1990. East Germany's law had allowed women to decide the matter for them-

selves during the first 12 weeks of pregnancy, but in West Germany the decision had been made by the woman's doctor.

1992 July 6　Members of one of London's most prestigious men's clubs, the 161-year-old **Garrick**, voted 363 to 94 not to admit women. One member commented: "I don't think women are clubbable . . . the only case for joining is to get away from women." However, the 156-year-old **Reform Club**, founded by radicals of the day who wished to broaden the right to vote, had begun to admit women in 1981.

1992 July 11　**Tracy Austin** (b. Dec. 12, 1962) of the U.S. became the youngest person ever inducted into the **International Tennis Hall of Fame**, Newport, Rhode Island. She had become (1979) the youngest U.S. Open champion and was rated (1980) No. 1 among women players. Austin's career came to an early end (Aug. 3, 1989) when she broke a leg in an auto accident.

1992 July 22　**Pablo Escobar Gaviria** (b. 1949), the top drug baron of Colombia, **escaped from a prison** in Envigado, in northwestern Colombia, near Medellin, the drug capital of the country and the center of Escobars's activities. He had surrendered (June 19, 1991) to authorities. Investigation showed that his prison, paid for by the government, was actually a luxurious private home from which he continued to manage the shipment of cocaine to the U.S. and elsewhere. He had a gymnasium, a bar, television, and other luxuries, while the guards acted as servants to him.

1992 July 25–Aug. 9　The XXV Summer **Olympic Games** were held in Barcelona, Spain, with more than 10,700 athletes from 172 countries competing. Athletes of the Unified Team, representing 12 of the now independent, former republics of the U.S.S.R., won 45 gold medals and 112 medals overall; the U.S. 37 and 108; and Germany, competing as one nation for the first time since before World War II (1939–1945) 33 and 82. Notable for its proportionate gain was China, which took 54 medals compared with 28 in 1988. An Israeli athlete won a medal for his country, the first since its founding in 1948; a Spanish swimmer won a gold medal in that sport for the first time; Croatian and South African athletes won medals, the first time for the former and the first since 1932 for the latter because his country had been banned after the 1960 games for its policy of apartheid. In the closest marathon in Olympic history, **Valentina Yegorova**, of the Unified Team, won by eight seconds. **Vitaly Scherbo**, also of the Unified Team, won 6 gold medals in gymnastics. **Kevin Young** of the U.S. set a world's record of 46.78 sec. in the 400-meter hurdles, being the first ever to break the 47 sec. mark. Attracting the most attention at the games was the U.S. basketball squad, composed for the first time almost entirely of professional players from the National Basketball Association [NBA], and known as the **Dream Team**. They flew on chartered jets, stayed at a luxury hotel instead of the Olympic Village, and won the gold medal by defeating their opponents by an average of almost 44 points. They were widely criticized for their arrogance.

1992 Sept. 2–Nov. 5   By winning ten games to his opponent's five, **Bobby Fischer**, an American and a former world **chess** champion, won $3.35 million. His opponent, who received $1.65 million, was **Boris Spassky**, a Russian and also a former world champion. The match, in which 15 games were drawn, was held in Yugoslavia.

1992 Sept. 5   At a track and field meet in Talence, France, **Dan O'Brien** of the U.S. set a new **world record for the decathlon** by scoring 8,891 points. The former record was 8,847 points.

1992 Sept. 19   **Sergei Bubka** of Ukraine, at a meet in Tokyo, Japan, set a new **world record for the pole vault** when he cleared 20 ft., 1 $\frac{1}{2}$ in. This bettered his own previous record by half an inch.

1992 Nov. 1   An extensive **no-smoking law** went into effect in France, banning the use of tobacco in restaurants, airports, subway stations, hotels, government buildings, and open spaces in offices and factories. A ban on all tobacco advertising was to go into effect Jan. 1, 1993. In the nation, 40 percent of adults and 65 percent of those between 18 and 24 smoked. The government reported that c.54,000 French citizens died each year from tobacco-related ailments.

1992 Nov. 13   The professional **world heavyweight boxing championship** was won at Las Vegas, Nevada, by **Riddick Bowe**, who earned a unanimous 12-round decision over the defending champion, **Evander Holyfield**. Bowe, who had his first pro fight on Mar. 6, 1989, was now undefeated in 32 matches, 27 of which he had won by knockouts.

1992 Nov. 29   **Emilio Pucci** (b. Nov., 20, 1914), an Italian fashion designer, noted for brilliant colors and geometric patterns, died. An all-around sportsman, he became a designer somewhat accidentally when a tight-fitting ski suit he had produced for himself attracted attention. He first designed sportswear, but in the 1960s his silk scarves, blouses, and dresses, using as many as sixteen colors, were widely popular.

How to Use This Index

The index lists, in alphabetical order, the names of people, places, and other items that one might find in the index of any book. There are, however, also smaller subject category indexes within the main index. Each of the topics listed below is a main entry in the index, with an alphabetical listing following the heading.

Agriculture and Agricultural Products
Architecture
Arts
Assassinations
Aviation Accidents
Aviation
Battles
Bible
Books
Bridges and Tunnels
Business
Calendar
Catastrophes and Natural Disasters
Cities
Clothing
Crime
Dance
Economics
Education
Exploration and Discovery
Film
Fishing
Fruits and Vegetables
Furniture
Games, Sports, and Recreation
Government
Hunting
Indians, Native Americans
Labor
Language
Laws
Maps

Medicine
Money, Monetary Systems
Music
Newspapers and Publications
New Technology
Nobel Prizes
Nuclear Energy
Nuclear Weapons
Opera
Organizations
Paintings
Poetry
Population
Postal Systems
Prison
Religion
Religious Meetings
Religious Statements
Riots
Roads
Sculpture
Ships
Slavery
Space and Space Exploration
Steel
Taxes
Theater
Transit Systems
Treaties
United Nations
Wars

If, for example, one wanted to find out about Elvis Presley, two listings for him could be found under his name, as follows:

The passages appear in the body of the book as follows:

1954 July Rock 'n' roll as a recognized form of popular music was said to have begun with the recording of "**That's All Right, Mama**" by a young southern-born American entertainer **Elvis** [Aron] **Presley**. Emphasis was placed on rhythm coming from electric guitars and drums, played very loudly.

1977 Aug. 16 Elvis [Aron] **Presley** (b. Jan. 8, 1935), the king of rock and roll, died.

Presley won the adoration of young people. Outstanding among his many hits was "**Heartbreak Hotel**" (1956), the first of 28 of his recordings to sell a million or more copies. In all, they sold c.600 million copies, and he made 33 movies, of which *Love Me Tender* (1956) was the first. Today his home, Graceland, Memphis, Tennessee, where he is buried, has become a shrine, visited annually by faithful followers, young and old.

In addition, all of the information that appears in bold-face type appears in the index. Therefore, one could also find the information shown above by looking for "Heartbreak Hotel" under the Music entry in the index, as well as by looking for *Love Me Tender* under the Film entry in the index.

Many of the entries about people in this book are listed in an obituary-type format. Therefore, be sure to look up the entry because the date that is listed in the index may be the date on which the person in question died, rather than the date on which a particular event occurred.

All death dates for people in the twentieth century appear.

The designation of B.C. and A.D. were only used when a date was near the year 0. Any date listed that is higher than the current date (2050, for example) is understood to be B.C..

Index

A. afarensis, 3,800,000
Aaron, Hank, 1974 Nov. 13, VII
Aaron's rod, 997, III
Abbas, Mohammed Abul, 1985 Oct.
    7, III
Abbaside
    Caliphate, 749 Nov. 28, II; 754
      June 5, II; 756, II; 786, II;
      936, III; 1256, III
    caliphs, last, 1258 Jan. 17, III
    Dynasty, 809 Mar., III; c.833, III
Abbas I the Great, 1587, II; 1603
    Oct. 21, IV
Abbas II, 1914 Dec. 18, III
Abbas III, 1730, III
Abbevillian, 1,000,000
Abboud, Ibrahim, 1958 Nov. 17, III
Abd-al-Hafiz, 1912 Mar. 30, II
Abdallah, 1040, III
Abd-al-Mumin, 1130, V; 1147, III;
    1159, I
Abd al-Yusuf, 1912 Mar. 30, II
Abdel-Hamid, Hayel, 1991 Jan. 14,
    III
Abd-el-Kader, 1837 May 30, IV;
    1844 Aug. 6, III
Abd-el-Krim, 1921 July 21, II; 1925
    Apr. 13, II
Abd-er-Rahman I, 756, II
Abd-er-Rahman II, 1844 Aug. 6, III
Abd er-Rahman III, 929, III
Abdul-Hamid II, 1876 Aug. 31, IV;
    1908 July 24, IV
Abdullah, 1946 May 25, II
Abdullah, Jamshi ibn, 1963 Dec. 10,
    II
Abdullah III, 1961 June 19, II
Abdul-Mejid II, 1922 Nov. 1, II;
    1924 Mar. 3, II
Abedi, Aga Hassan, 1991 July 5, IV
Abel, Niels Henrik, 1829 Apr. 6, VI
Abel, Rudolf, 1960 May 1, III
Abélard, Pierre, 1115, V; 1140, V
Abercromby, Ralph, 1801 Mar. 21,
    III
Abernathy, Ralph David:
    died, 1990 Apr. 17, V
Abomey, kingdom of, c.1625, III
aborigines, 25,000

Abovian, Khachatur, 1848, VIII
Abraham, 1900–1700, II
Abruzzo, Ben, 1981 Nov. 9–12, VII
Abu-al-Abbas, 749 Nov. 28, II
Abu-al-Atahiyah, 826, VII
Abu-Bakr, 632, II; 632 June 8, III
abu-Hanifah, 820 Jan. 20, V
Abu-Nuwas, 813, VII
Abydos, 780–560, I
Abyssinia, 1492, III
Academy, 385, III
Acadians, 1755 Mar., II
Achaea, 780–560, I
Achaean League, 146, III
Achaemenid Dynasty, 331 Oct. 1, III
Achaia, 146, III
Achard, Franz Karl, 1797, V
Acheulean, 2,000,000
    Acheulian culture, 1,000,000
A.D. began, 0 B.C., V
Adadnirari II, 934–783, I
Adadnirari III, 934–783, I
Adamec, Ladislav, 1989 Nov. 24, IV
Adami, Eddie Fenech, 1987 May 12,
    III
Adams, Clara, 1939 June 28–July 15,
    VIII
Adams, Henry Brooks:
    died, 1918 Mar. 27, VI
Adams, John, 1770 Mar. 5, IV; 1776
    June 10, IV; 1776 July 4, IV;
    1782 Nov. 30, IV; 1798 Apr. 3,
    IV
    died, 1826 July 4, III
    elected president, 1797 Mar. 4, IV
    second term as vice president,
      1793 Mar. 4, IV
    vice president of U.S., first, 1789
      Feb. 4, IV
Adams, John Quincy, 1814 Dec. 24,
    IV; 1819 Feb. 22, III
    elected president, 1825 Mar. 4,
      III
    lost election, 1821 Mar. 5, IV
Adams, Maude, 1918 Dec. 2, VI;
    1927 July 9, V
    died, 1953 July 17, V
Adams, Samuel, 1772 Nov. 2, IV;
    1773 Dec. 16, IV

Adams, Walter S.:
    died, 1956 May 11, V
Adams, Will, 1600 May 16, III
Addams, Jane, 1889 Sept., VI
Addison, Joseph, 1709 Apr. 12, V;
    1807, VI
Addison, Thomas, 1860 June 29, VII
Ade, George:
    died, 1944 May 16, VI
Adenauer, Konrad, 1949 May 21, II
    died, 1967 Apr. 19, II
    resigned, 1963 Oct. 16, II
Adi-Buddha, c.1000, V
Adler, Felix, 1876, VI
Adler, Stella:
    died, 1992 Dec. 21, VII
Adolf, Gustav II, 1611 Oct. 30, III
Adolf, Gustav VI, 1950 Oct. 29, III
    died, 1973 Sept. 15, II
Adrian, Gilbert:
    died, 1959 Sept. 3, VIII
Adulyadel, Bhumibol, 1991 Feb. 23,
    III
Aegean Civilization, 3000, I
Aegospotami, 405, III
Aehrenthal, Alois Lexa von, 1908
    Oct. 6, IV
Aelian, c.220, VI
Aemilianus, P. Cornelius Scipio, 133,
    III; 146, III
Aeschylus, c.484–c.468, V; c.468, V
Aesop:
    died, c.560, VIII
Aëtius, 437, II; 451 June 20, I
Afghan, 1730, III; 1761 Jan. 14,
    III
Afghanistan:
    Amnullah Khan resigned, 1929
      Jan. 14, IV
    Anglo-Indians massacred, 1842
      Jan. 6, III
    coup, 1973 July 17, II
    Durrani emir, 1747 July?, II
    fighting broke out, 1992 Apr. 16,
      III
    Great Britain, recognized
      independence, 1921 Nov. 22,
      II
    independence, 1919 May 3, II